# Grammar codes used in the Dictionary

Letters show the type of verb:

[D] a transitive verb that is followed by a direct object and an indirect objec[illegible]
[I] an intransitive verb with no [illegible]
[L] a linking verb [illegible] the subject. [L] v[illegible]
[T] a transitive ve[illegible] t
[V] a transitive ve[illegible] is followed by a direct [illegible] and a verb form
[X] a transitive ver[illegible] is followed by a direct object and a complement that represents the direct object



Numbers show what follows the verb:
[Ø] not followed by anything
[1] a noun or pronoun
[3] a verb in the *to*-form (infinitive)
[4] a verb in the *-ing* form
[5] a clause beginning with *that*
[6] a clause beginning with *who, what, where, why, when, how,* or *as if*
[7] an adjective
[9] an adverbial

Small letters show the position of the adverb or preposition:
[a] the adverb or preposition comes just after the verb
[b] the adverb or preposition is separated from the verb

# Short forms used in the grammar codes

| | |
|---|---|
| OFF | = an adverb |
| *off* | = a preposition |
| off | = an adjective or pronoun or noun |
| (OFF/*off*) | = an adverb or preposition that can be used |
| obj | = object (can be the object of a transitive verb or of a preposition) |
| *to-v* | = the *to*- form of a verb, for example **to go**, **to think** |
| *v-ing* | = the *-ing* form of a verb, for example **going**, **thinking** |
| *that*-clause | = a clause beginning with *that*, as in: *He denied to the police* **that he had stolen the car**. |
| *wh*-clause | = a clause beginning with *who, what, where, why, when, how,* or *as if*; for example: *You must bring home to John* **where the problem lies**. |

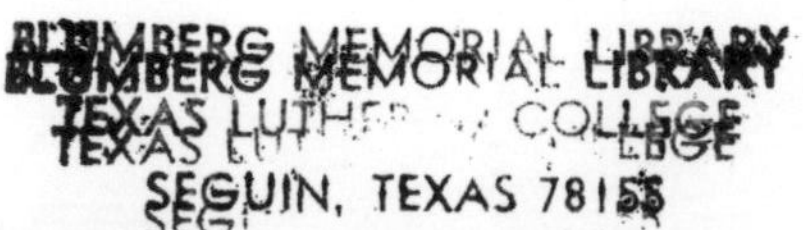
BLUMBERG MEMORIAL LIBRARY
TEXAS LUTHERAN COLLEGE
SEGUIN, TEXAS 78155

# Longman Dictionary of **Phrasal Verbs**

# Longman Dictionary of **Phrasal Verbs**

Rosemary Courtney

**Longman Group UK Limited,**
*Longman House, Burnt Mill, Harlow,*
*Essex CM20 2JE, England*
*and Associated Companies throughout the world.*



First published by Longman Group Limited 1983
Thirteenth impression 1990

ISBN 0-582-55530-2 CSD

Set in 8/8½ pt Linotron 202 Times New Roman

Produced by Longman Singapore Publishers (Pte) Ltd.
Printed in Singapore

**British Library Cataloguing in Publication Data**

Courtney, Rosemary
Longman dictionary of phrasal verbs.
1. English language – Phrasal verbs – Dictionaries
I. Title
428.2 PE1698

**Library of Congress Cataloging in Publication Data**

Courtney, Rosemary, 1933–
Longman dictionary of phrasal verbs.
1. English language – Verb phrase – Dictionaries.
I. Title.
PE1319.C68 1983 423'.1 82-20800

## Acknowledgements

I am deeply grateful to the following people for helping to make this book possible:

Paul Procter, Della Summers, John Ayto, Adrian Stenton, Michael Upshall, Sue Lambert, Martin Manser, and Jenny Potts for their patience, kindness, and good advice;

Professor Randolph Quirk, of University College. London, for his firm advice, and for permission to use the Survey of English Usage; Perry Lee for computer programs for the cross-references; my brother, J. Michael Gale, for advice on verbs to do with boats and ships;

my friends and family, especially my husband Richard and my children Anne (Chung) and John, for their helpful suggestions, and for their patience over so many years;
and my mother, Nellie Gale, for giving me from birth a love of words.

*star shows idiomatic phrasal verb

definition, written from a list of 2,000 words

***call by**[1] *v adv*
*not fml* to visit when passing a place: [IØ (*often simple tenses*)] *When you're next in town, do call by.*

example of how the expression is used

literal verb combination

**call by**[2] *v prep*
to address (usu. someone) using (a name): [T1 + *by*] *If you call him just by his last name he won't answer you.*

verb + preposition

another phrasal verb with the same meaning

**clean out** *v adv*
**1** also **clear out** to empty, tidy, or clean (something): [X9 + OUT] *I've asked the children to clean out their drawers. I need some help in cleaning out the animal shelter.* **—cleaning-out, clean-out** *n* → **do out** (1), **muck out**

verb + adverb

words formed from phrasal verbs are shown at the end of the entry

arrow (→) shows other phrasal verbs with related meanings. (**1**) means "see meaning **1**"

numbers (1, 2) show different meaning. Here only meaning 2 is an idiomatic phrasal verb and so has a star

**come unstuck** *v adj*
**1** to fail to remain stuck to something: [L7 + unstuck] *I didn't open your letter, the envelope came unstuck.*
***2** *not fml* to meet difficulties or failure: [IØ] *All his grand plans for the future of the firm came unstuck when the price of oil went up so much.*

shows that the expression is only used in certain situations

shows an expression used mostly in American English

**flunk out** *v adv*
*AmE infml* to fail, or state that (someone) has failed, as in an examination: [IØ + OUT (*simple tenses*)] *How many students have flunked out this year?* [T1 + OUT (*usu. pass.*)] *Twenty students have been flunked out and had to leave the college.*

**kick round** *v adv* → **KICK ABOUT** (6)

shows that **kick round** is defined at **kick about** because it has the same meaning

idiomatic meaning contrasted with normal meaning

**rub in**[1] *v adv*
**1** to cause (something such as a liquid) to enter a surface by rubbing: [T1 + IN] *Leave the mud to dry; if you try to clean it now, you'll only rub it in.*
***2** *not fml* to teach (something) by forceful repetition: [T1 (*often simple tenses*)] *A skilled teacher can make any class learn any set of facts by simply rubbing the information in. The lesson of this sad story should be well rubbed in.* → **hammer in** (3), etc.
**3 rub it in** *not fml* to keep reminding someone of a fault, failure, etc.: *I know I ruined the performance, there's no need to rub it in.*

numbers ([1,2]) show when a verbal combination is used both as a verb + adverb and verb + preposition

**rub in**[2] *v prep*
**1** to force (something such as a liquid) to enter (usu. a surface) by rubbing: [T1 + *in*] *Rub this oil in the wood to protect it. "Rubbing salt in a wound" is a way of expressing the idea of making something bad even worse.* → **rub into** (1)
**2 rub someone's nose in it** *not fml* to keep on reminding someone, esp. in an unkind manner, about something he has done wrong: *Don't keep talking about that letter. I know I shouldn't have written it, but there's no need to rub my nose in it.*

shows a fixed idiom in which the phrasal verb is used

grammar codes show how to use the expressions

# What are phrasal verbs?

Phrasal verbs are idiomatic combinations of a verb and adverb, or a verb and preposition (or verb with both adverb and preposition). They cause difficulties for students of English because of their meaning and grammar.

Many verbs in English can be used together with an adverb or preposition, and are straightforward for the student to use and understand, as in, for example:

*The girl walked along the road.* (verb + preposition)

You could just as easily say:

*The girl walked down the road.* (verb + preposition)

Combinations of verb and adverb can also be easily understood:

*He opened the door and looked inside.* (verb + adverb)
*He entered the room and sat down.* (verb + adverb)

Often, however, a verbal combination (verb + adverb or verb + preposition) can have not only its normal meaning but can also mean something different. The combination of **hold** and **up**, for example, can be used with a normal meaning:

*Hold up your right hand and repeat these words after me.*

But it can also have a completely different meaning, 'to stop by force in order to rob', as in:

*The criminals held up the train and stole all the passengers' money.*

Here the meaning of the expression cannot be guessed from the verb alone; it is an example of a phrasal verb. In the dictionary, phrasal verbs (idiomatic combinations) are marked with a * sign. **Hold up**, then, has both a normal and an idiomatic meaning, and is shown in the dictionary like this:

**hold up** *v adv*
**1** to raise (something): *Hold up your right hand and repeat these words after me.*
***2** to stop (a vehicle) by force in order to rob it: *The criminals held up the train and stole all the passengers' money.*

There are three types of phrasal verb:

**(a) verb + adverb** (marked *v adv*), as in:
*The old lady was taken in (= deceived) by the salesman.*

**(b) verb + preposition** (marked *v prep*), as in:
*She set about (= started) making a new dress.*

**(c) verb + adverb + preposition** (marked *v adv prep*), as in:
*I can't put up with (= bear or suffer) him – he's always complaining.*

# What this dictionary contains

This book includes entries for:

1. Phrasal verbs, that is, idiomatic combinations of verb + adverb, verb + preposition or verb + adverb + preposition. If the verbal combination has a normal meaning as well as an idiomatic meaning, then both are listed, but only the idiomatic meaning has an * sign.
2. Phrasal verbs such as ***depend on** or ***despair of** where the verb, although it always has the same meaning, can only be used with a certain preposition when used in combination. We cannot say *depend from*, or *depend with*.
3. Idioms which are formed from phrasal verbs, such as **let the cat out of the bag**. These idioms are printed in **heavy type**. Idioms have a meaning which is different to the meaning of the single words, and usually have a fixed word order.

The dictionary also includes combinations of verb + adjective and verb + pronoun which, like phrasal verbs, have a different meaning when used together. Examples are **lie low** (*v adj*), which is a verb + adjective, and **kid oneself** (*v pron*) which is a verb + pronoun.

The dictionary does not include simple verbal combinations such as *walk along* and *sit down* where the meanings are easily guessed from the parts. Of course, if the verbal combination also has an idiomatic meaning, then both senses are included.

# How to use the Dictionary

## Order of headwords

Phrasal verbs in this dictionary are listed in alphabetical order under the main verb. Thus, at **see** all the different combinations of **see** + adverb or **see** + preposition that can be used with it are listed alphabetically before the next main verb, **seek.** In this way **see through** comes in the dictionary before **seek after**.

Phrasal verbs that can be used both as verb + adverb (*v adv*) and verb + preposition (*v prep*) have a separate numbered entry for each grammatical use; the entries are marked by small numbers ([1,2]). For example, **see through** is listed as **see through**[1] *v adv* and then **see through**[2] *v prep*. Here is an example of the order of headwords in the dictionary:

**see round**[1] *v adv*
**see round**[2] *v prep*
**see through**[1] *v adv*
**see through**[2] *v prep*
**see to**
**see up**
**see with**
**seek after**
**seek for**

## Order of definitions

If a verbal combination has more than one meaning, then each meaning is given a separate numbered sense. The senses are shown by large numbers, in this order:

1. Ordinary meanings
2. Idiomatic meanings, marked with a star *
3. Fixed idioms in which the phrasal verb is used.

For example, the entry for **get down to** is listed:

> **get down to** *v adv prep*
> **1** to (cause to) descend to (a lower level): *The cat has climbed the tree, and can't get down to the ground.*
> (ordinary meaning)
> ***2** to begin to give serious attention to (something such as work): *I really must get down to my studies.*
> (idiomatic meaning)
> **3 get down to brass tacks** to talk about facts or practical matters: *All this talk is interesting, but let's get down to brass tacks and see if the plan will really work.*
> (idiom formed from phrasal verb)

So, to find the meaning of a phrasal verb, look first for the main verb, and when you have found the main verb look down the page until you come to the expression you are looking for. If the phrasal verb is listed more than once, decide if the expression you want is *v adv* or *v prep*. Look through the different numbered meanings to see which is the right one.

## Defining vocabulary

All the definitions are written using a defining vocabulary of 2,000 words. The list of words can be found in the Longman Dictionary of Contemporary English.

## Examples

The definition is followed by one or more examples, many of which are taken from newspapers and books. The examples help you to understand the meaning of the expression; they are also important because they can give information on how the expression is used. For example, **abstain from** is defined as "to keep oneself from (doing something)", and has the example:

> *The leaders asked their workers to abstain from voting.*

From this we learn that a typical use of **abstain from** is when we are talking about elections and voting. If you are not sure how to use the expression you have found, it is a good idea to follow the example as much as possible.

## Related words

There is often a noun or adjective which is formed from the phrasal verb. These related forms are listed at the end of the entry. Usually, the related form is not difficult to understand because it looks very similar to the phrasal verb. **Make up**, for example, has the related noun **make-up**; and from the expression **wash up** we can talk about the **washing-up**. The related form is shown like this:

> ***wash up** *v adv*
> **1** to clean (dishes etc) with water: *How many plates are there to wash up?* — **washing-up** *n*

Note, however, that sometimes the related noun or adjective cannot be used for all the meanings of the expression. An example is at **break out**:

> **break out** *v adv*
> **1** . . .
> ***2** to begin, usually suddenly: *War broke out in 1939.* — **outbreak** *n*
> ***3** to escape from: *Three men broke out of prison yesterday.* — **breakout** *n*

This means that for sense (2) we can use the noun **outbreak**:

> *The outbreak of the war was in 1939.*

But for sense (3), we must use **breakout**:

> *Three men escaped from the prison in a breakout yesterday.*

## When and where the phrasal verbs are used

When an expression is not in general use, a note is included before the definition. Thus, **go below** is shown like this:

> ***go below** *v adv*
> *naut* to go downstairs on a ship or a boat

Here *naut* means "nautical; used about ships and sailors". A list of these notes ("Short forms used in this dictionary") can be found at the front of the book. There are four main types of these notes:

(a) notes that tell you where an expression is used. They are shown like this:

> ***goof off** *v adv*
> *AmE* to spend time lazily . . .

This means that ***goof off** is used mostly in American English and may not always be understood by people in Britain.

(b) notes that tell you that an expression is only used in certain professions. Examples of these include *naut* (nautical) and *mil* (military).

(c) notes that tell you the attitude of the speaker, such as *humor* (humorous, making people laugh) and *derog* (derogatory, showing dislike or lack of respect).

(d) notes on the level of use of the expression.

Most of the entries in the dictionary are unmarked, that is, they can be used in any situation. If there is a note such as *fml* (formal) or *infml* (informal) before the definition, then the expression should not be used generally. For example, the entry for **lam into** reads:

> ***lam into** *v prep*
> *sl* to attack violently, with blows or words

Here *sl* tells you that the expression is "slang; thought to be incorrect by many people", and you should not use it at an interview, or when writing a formal letter.

## Alternatives

Where different forms can be used without changing the meaning of the expression, they are listed like this:

> **sit on/upon** *v prep*

These alternative forms are also found with some idioms. For example, the entry at **make for** includes:

> **make a bolt/dash for** to try to escape towards (something)

Thus, we can say either "The prisoner made a bolt for the open door", or "The prisoner made a dash for the open door"; the meaning is the same.

## Cross-references

The dictionary also shows where there are other expressions with related or opposite meanings. For example:

> ***book in** *v adv*
> **1** to (cause to) report one's arrival, as at a hotel, airport, etc.— **book out** (1), **check in** (2), **check out** (2)

**Check in** can be used with the same meaning as **book in**; **check out** and **book out** are used when talking about somebody leaving a hotel or airport. Cross-references can be used to help you find a word you are not sure of. For example, if you know the expression **come in** but you do not know how to say "to make somebody come in", then you will find at the entry for **come in** an expression you can use: **bring in**, **take in**, or **wheel in**.

# How phrasal verbs are used

Phrasal verbs cause problems for the student not only because of their meaning, which cannot always be guessed from the meaning of the verb, but also because of their grammar. Sometimes the parts of the phrasal verbs can be separated. We can say, for example,

> *The soldiers blew up the bridge.* (a)
> *The soldiers blew the bridge up.* (b)

Some phrasal verbs are always used as in (a), such as **leave off** in "He left off working". Others must always be used as in (b) as with **keep open** in: "She kept the door open". **Blow up** is an example of a phrasal verb where you can use either (a) or (b). Information about word order is given by the grammar code.

## Grammatical Information

Every entry includes a grammar code before the examples. The codes are taken from the Longman Dictionary of Contemporary English, and consist of a letter (D, I, L, T, V, or X) followed by a number (Ø to 9). The letters show the type of verb, and the numbers show what comes after the verb. Phrasal verbs (those with a *sign) are single units of meaning, and the grammar code explains the grammar of the complete expression. Verbal combinations (which are not idiomatic) have a grammar code for the main verb alone. The entry for **hold up**, then, is:

> **hold up** *v adv*
> **1** to raise (something): [X9 + UP] *Hold up your right hand and repeat these words after me.*
> **2** . . .
> ***3** to stop (a vehicle) by force in order to rob it: [T1] *The criminals held up the train and took all the passengers' money.*

Thus, **hold up(1)** is a verbal combination. "X" means it is transitive, and "9" means it is followed by an object and a complement. **Hold up(3)** is a phrasal verb; "T" means it is transitive, and "1" means it is followed by a noun or pronoun. The grammar codes are shown in full at the front of the dictionary.

Many expressions can be used either with or without an object. They have a definition like this:

> ***blow up** *v adv*
> **6** to (cause to) explode; destroy

and an example is given for both the transitive and intransitive use:

> [T1] *The soldiers blew up the enemy bridge.* (transitive)
> [IØ] *A chemical factory blew up in the North of England.* (intransitive)

When these expressions have a pronoun object, the pronoun comes directly after the verb, as in "The soldiers reached the bridge and blew it up."

# Grammar codes for the phrasal verbs

[D1] a transitive verb with two objects: a direct noun object and a noun indirect object:

***help to** *v prep*
to serve (someone or oneself) with (something such as food): [D1]

| *Can I* | *help* | *you* | *to* | *some more potatoes?* |
|---|---|---|---|---|
| | *v* | obj | *prep* | obj |

***put down to** *v adv prep*
to consider (something) to be the result of (something else): [D1]

| *I* | *put* | *his bad temper* | *down* | *to* | *his recent illness.* |
|---|---|---|---|---|---|
| | *v* | obj | *adv* | *prep* | obj |

[D5] a transitive verb with two objects: a direct object and a noun indirect object. The direct object is a clause beginning with *that*:

**represent to** *v prep*
***3** to express (an idea) to (someone): [D5]

| *I* | *represented* | *to* | *him* | *that it would be dangerous to do what he suggested.* |
|---|---|---|---|---|
| | *v* | *prep* | obj | *that*-clause |

NOTE: [D5] verbs are not used in the passive.

[D6] a transitive verb with two objects: a direct object and a noun indirect object. The direct object is a clause beginning with a *wh*- word, *how*, or *as if*:

**dictate to** *v prep*
***3** to enforce (something over which one has power) on (someone): [D6]

| *The government tries to* | *dictate* | *to* | *people* | *how they should spend their money.* |
|---|---|---|---|---|
| | *v* | *prep* | obj | *wh*-clause |

***bring home to** *v adv prep*
**2** to persuade (someone) to believe (something): [D6]

| *You must* | *bring* | *home* | *to* | *John* | *where the difficulty lies.* |
|---|---|---|---|---|---|
| | *v* | *adv* | *prep* | obj | *wh*-clause |

NOTE: [D6] verbs are not common in the passive.

## [I∅]

an intransitive verb. It need not be followed by anything:

**break down** *v adv*
*__3__ (of machinery) to stop working; fail to work: [I∅]

| The car | broke | down | on the way to the airport, and I had to get a taxi. |
|---|---|---|---|
| | v | adv | |

**lie low** *v adj*
***3** *infml* to hide, esp. to escape from the police: [I∅]

| You'd better | lie | low | here for a few days until the police have stopped looking for you. |
|---|---|---|---|
| | v | adj | |

## [I3]

an intransitive verb followed by a verb in the *to*-form (infinitive):

***set out** *v adv*
**3** to intend (to do something): [I3]

| I | set | out | to make | the dress by myself. |
|---|---|---|---|---|
| | v | adv | to-v | |

***lower oneself** *v pron*
to behave unworthily: [I3]

| I hope you wouldn't | lower | yourself | to cheat | in the examination. |
|---|---|---|---|---|
| | v | pron | to-v | |

## [I4]

an intransitive verb, followed by the *-ing* form of a verb:

**go on** *v adv*
***5** to continue (doing something) esp. after interruption: [I4]

| He | went | on | hitting | the boy although I told him to stop. |
|---|---|---|---|---|
| | v | adv | v-ing | |

## [I5]

an intransitive verb, followed by a clause beginning with *that*:

**look out** *v adv*
***2** *infml* to take care; be watchful: [I5]

| Look | out | that you don't catch cold. |
|---|---|---|
| v | adv | *that*-clause |

**[I6]** an intransitive verb, followed by a clause beginning with a *wh*-word, *how*, or *as if*:

*__mind out__ *v adv*

**1** *not fml* to take care; be watchful; move out of the way: [I6]

| *Mind* | *out* | *where you're walking,* | *the ground is muddy.* |
|---|---|---|---|
| *v* | *adv* | *wh-clause* | |

**[L1]** a linking verb with a noun complement that refers to the subject:

*__act as__ *v prep*

to fulfil the purpose of (something): [L1]

| *A trained dog can* | *act* | *as* | *a guide* | *to a blind person.* |
|---|---|---|---|---|
| | *v* | *prep* | *n* | |

NOTE: [L1] verbs are not used in the passive.

**[L4]** a linking verb with a complement that refers to the subject. The complement is a verb in the *-ing* form:

*__end up__ *v adv*

**2** to finish by (doing something): [L4]

| *Be careful, you could* | *end* | *up* | *hurting* | *yourself.* |
|---|---|---|---|---|
| | *v* | *adv* | *v-ing* | |

*__come across as__ *v adv prep*

to seem to be (judging by behaviour): [L4]

| *He* | *comes* | *across* | *as* | *being* | *very sincere.* |
|---|---|---|---|---|---|
| | *v* | *adv* | *prep* | *v-ing* | |

NOTE: [L4] verbs are not used in the passive.

**[L7]** a linking verb with a complement that refers to the subject. The complement is an adjective:

**come in** *v adv*

*__11__ to serve a purpose: [L7]

| *That empty box will* | *come* | *in* | *very* | *handy.* |
|---|---|---|---|---|
| | *v* | *adv* | | *adj* |

NOTE: [L7] verbs are not used in the passive.

**[L9]** a linking verb with a complement that refers to the subject. The complement is an adverbial:

*__end up__ *v adv*

**3** *not fml* to arrive at or in (a place), esp. after time or events: [L9]

| *He'll* | *end* | *up* | *in prison* | *if he goes on behaving like that.* |
|---|---|---|---|---|
| | *v* | *adv* | *adverbial* | |

NOTE: [L9] verbs are not used in the passive.

## [T1]

a transitive verb with a noun direct object:

***blow up** *v adv*

**6** to destroy (something or someone) by or as if by explosion: [T1]

| *They* | *blew* | *up* | *the bridge.* |
|---|---|---|---|
| | *v* | *adv* | obj |

or

| *They* | *blew* | *the bridge* | *up.* |
|---|---|---|---|
| | *v* | obj | *adv* |

| *They* | *blew* | *it* | *up.* |
|---|---|---|---|
| | *v* | *pron* | *adv* |

***depend on** *v prep*

to trust; be sure of (someone or something): [T1]

| *I* | *depended* | *on* | *the map.* |
|---|---|---|---|
| *I* | *depended* | *on* | *it.* |
| | *v* | *prep* | obj |

***get round to** *v adv prep*

to find time for (something), esp. after delay: [T1]

| *The committee will* | *get* | *round* | *to* | *your suggestion* | *after they've dealt* |
|---|---|---|---|---|---|
| | *v* | *adv* | *prep* | obj | |

*with urgent business.*

| *They'll soon* | *get* | *round* | *to* | *it.* |
|---|---|---|---|---|
| | *v* | *adv* | *prep* | obj |

## [T1a]

a transitive verb with a noun direct object. The adverb always comes just after the verb:

***give off** *v adv*

to send out (something, esp. a liquid, gas, or smell): [T1a]

| *Boiling water* | *gives* | *off* | *steam.* |
|---|---|---|---|
| | *v* | *adv* | obj |

## [T1b]

a transitive verb with a noun direct object. The adverb or adjective is always separated from the verb:

***let through** *v adv*

to allow (something or someone) to pass: [T1b]

| *Although not completely satisfied the committee* | *let* | *the report* | *through.* |
|---|---|---|---|
| | *v* | obj | *adv* |

| *They* | *let* | *it* | *through.* |
|---|---|---|---|
| | *v* | obj | *adv* |

**keep open** *v adj*
***3** to save (a job) for someone, esp. during a time away: [T1b]

| *If you take this six-month overseas contract, will your firm* | *keep* | *your job* |
|---|---|---|
| | *v* | obj |

| *open* | *for you?* |
|---|---|
| *adj* | |

| *Yes, they'll* | *keep* | *it* | *open.* |
|---|---|---|---|
| | *v* | obj | *adj* |

---

**[T4]** a transitive verb with a direct object. The object is a verb in the *-ing* form:

***give up** *v adv*
**1** to stop doing or having (something): [T4]

| *The doctor told Jim to* | *give* | *up* | *smoking.* |
|---|---|---|---|
| | *v* | *adv* | *v-ing* |

or

| *I* | *gave* | *smoking* | *up* | *years ago.* |
|---|---|---|---|---|
| | *v* | *v-ing* | *adv* | |

**lead to** *v prep*
***4** to be the cause of (something or doing something): [T4]

| *It's sleeping late in the morning that* | *leads* | *to* | *missing* | *the bus.* |
|---|---|---|---|---|
| | *v* | *prep* | *v-ing* | |

***get round to** *v adv prep*
to find time for (doing something), esp. after delay: [T4]

| *After a long delay, he* | *got* | *round* | *to* | *writing* | *the letter.* |
|---|---|---|---|---|---|
| | *v* | *adv* | *prep* | *v-ing* | |

---

**[T4a]** a transitive verb with a direct object. The object is a verb in the *-ing* form. The adverb always comes just after the verb:

**leave off** *v adv*
***2** to stop (doing something); cease: [T4a]

| *Do you think it will* | *leave* | *off* | *raining* | *soon?* |
|---|---|---|---|---|
| | *v* | *adv* | *v-ing* | |

---

**[T5]** a transitive verb with a direct object. The object is a clause beginning with *that*:

***point out** *v adv*
to show; explain; draw attention to (something or someone): [T5]

| I would like to | point | out | that it is getting very late. |
|---|---|---|---|
| | v | adv | *that*-clause |

NOTE: [T5] verbs are not common in the passive.

## [T6]

a transitive verb with a direct object. The object is a clause beginning with a *wh*-word, *how*, or *as if*:

***figure out** *v adv*

**2** to understand (something or someone) with difficulty: [T6]

| No one can | figure | out | how the fire started. |
|---|---|---|---|
| | v | adv | *wh*-clause |

NOTE: [T6] verbs are not common in the passive.

## [V3]

a transitive verb with a noun direct object and verb in the *to*-form (infinitive):

**lead on** *v adv*

***3** to influence (someone) (to do something bad): [V3]

| The boy claimed that his criminal companions had | led | him | on | to steal | the jewels. |
|---|---|---|---|---|---|
| | v | obj | adv | to-v | |

***pick on** *v prep*

**2** to choose (someone) for a purpose, often unpleasant: [V3]

| The examiners can | pick | on | any student | to answer | questions. |
|---|---|---|---|---|---|
| | v | prep | obj | to-v | |

***keep on at** *v adv prep*

to repeatedly ask (someone) (to do something): [V3]

| She | kept | on | at | me | to buy | her a new coat, until in the end I agreed. |
|---|---|---|---|---|---|---|
| | v | adv | prep | obj | to-v | |

## [V4a]

a transitive verb with a noun direct object and a verb in the *-ing* form. The preposition comes just after the verb:

***result in** *v prep*

to have (something) as a result; end in (something): [V4a]

| The quarrel | resulted | in | his mother | leaving | the house. |
|---|---|---|---|---|---|
| | v | prep | obj | v-ing | |

**[V4b]** a transitive verb with a noun direct object and a verb in the *-ing* form. The preposition or adverb is always separated from the verb:

**keep from** *v prep*
***2** to prevent or delay (someone or something) from (something or doing something): [V4b]

| *Don't let me* | *keep* | *you* | *from* | *going* | *out.* |
|---|---|---|---|---|---|
| | v | obj | prep | v-ing | |

***put up to** *v adv prep*
**1** to encourage; give (someone) the idea of (doing something, usu. wrong): [V4b]

| *I think I know who* | *put* | *him* | *up* | *to* | *cheating.* |
|---|---|---|---|---|---|
| | v | obj | adv | prep | v-ing |

**[X1]** a transitive verb with a noun direct object and a noun complement that refers to the object:

***regard as** *v prep*
to consider (someone or something) to be (something): [X1]

| *They* | *regard* | *him* | *as* | *their* | *enemy.* |
|---|---|---|---|---|---|
| | v | obj | prep | | n |

**[X7]** a transitive verb with a noun direct object and a complement that refers to the object. The complement is an adjective:

***regard as** *v prep*
to consider (someone or something) to be (something): [X7]

| *Why do you* | *regard* | *him* | *as* | *foolish?* |
|---|---|---|---|---|
| | v | obj | prep | adj |

**[X9]** a transitive verb with a noun direct object and a complement that refers to the object. The complement is an adverbial:

***fit up** *v adv*
**1** to supply (something or someone) with necessary things: [X9]

| *The bedroom can be* | *fitted* | *up* | *as an office.* |
|---|---|---|---|
| | v | adv | adverbial |

# A

**abandon to** *v prep*
to give (something, someone, or oneself) completely to (something, such as a feeling or condition, or someone), often with a loss of effort or hope: [T1 + *to*] *After her mother died, she abandoned herself to grief. The affairs of the nation have been abandoned to dishonest politicians.*

**abase oneself** *v pron*
**1** *fml* to make oneself humble: [T1 + oneself] *In former times, priests used to abase themselves before the gods.*
**2** to lower oneself morally: [T1 + oneself] *You have abased yourself by stealing from a poor old man.*

**abbreviate to** *v prep*
to shorten (usu. a word) to (a shorter form): [T1 + *to* (*often pass.*)] *December is usually abbreviated to Dec.*

**abet in** *v prep*
to help (someone) in (usu. wrongdoing): [T1 + *in*] *The jewel thieves were abetted in the robbery by some of the servants at the great house.*

**abide at** *v prep* → **ABIDE IN**

***abide by** *v prep*
**1** to be faithful to; obey (laws, agreements, etc.): [T1] *If you join the club, you must abide by its rules.* → **comply with, conform to**
**2** to accept (something): [T1 (*no pass.*)] *You must abide by the results of your mistakes.*

**abide in** *v prep* also **abide at**
*old use* to live or stay in (a place): [L9 + *in/at*] *The king went to visit his daughter and abode in her palace for ten days.*

**abide with** *v prep*
*old use* to stay with (usu. someone): [L9 + *with*] *"Abide with me; fast falls the eventide; The darkness deepens; Lord, with me abide."* (Henry Francis Lyte, religious song)

**abound in** *v prep*
**1** to exist in quantity in (somewhere): [L9 + *in* (*simple tenses*)] *Good fish abound in the North Sea.* → **teem in**
***2** to be full of (something): [T1 (*no pass., simple tenses*)] *The book abounds in printing mistakes. The North Sea abounds in good fish.* → **abound with, swarm with, teem with** (1)

***abound with** *v prep* → **abound in** (2), **swarm with, teem with** (1)
to be full of (something): [T1 (*no pass.*)] *The book abounds with printing mistakes.*

**abscond from** *v prep*
**1** *fml* to go away from (a place) suddenly and secretly, esp. because one has done something wrong: [I∅ + *from*] *The boy had absconded from his school.*
***2** to avoid (a duty) by leaving: [T1] *You cannot abscond from your responsibilities.*

**abscond with** *v prep* → **elope with, go away** (4), **go away with** (2), **go off**[1](10), **go off with** (2), **run away with** (5), **waltz off with** (2)
*fml* to go away secretly taking (something or someone) without permission; steal (something): [I∅ + *with*] *The thief absconded with all the jewellery.*

**absent from** *v prep*
*fml* to keep (oneself) away from (something) on purpose: [T1 + *from* (*no pass.*)] *If you absent yourself from more than two practices, you will be asked to leave.*

**absolve from/of** *v prep*
*fml* to declare (someone) free from (guilt, blame, a duty, etc.): [T1 + *from/of* (*usu. simple tenses*)] *State education does not absolve a parent from his responsibilities to his child. The teacher absolved the child of any blame.*

**absorb in** *v prep* → **drown in** (3), **engross in, immerse in** (2), **immure in** (2), **soak in**[2] (2), **steep in** (2), **submerge in** (2), **wrap up in** (3)
**be absorbed in** to give all one's attention to (something or doing something): *The writer was so absorbed in her work that she did not hear her visitor enter the room. Time passes quickly when you are absorbed in reading a good book.*

**absorb into** *v prep*
**1** to make (a substance) melt into or become part of (something such as (part of) the body): [T1 + *into* (*often pass.*)] *Certain chemicals are easily absorbed into the bloodstream, while others are not.*
**2** to make (someone or something) gradually become part of (a larger group): [T1 + *into* (*usu. pass.*)] *People of many different nationalities have, over the years, been absorbed into the population of the city. Most little shops have been absorbed into big businesses.* → **assimilate into** (1)

**abstain from** *v prep* → **forbear from** (2), **refrain from** (2)
to prevent oneself from (doing something); avoid (something or doing something) by choice, but often with an effort: [I∅ + *from*] *His family have always abstained from drink. The leaders asked their workers to abstain from voting.*

**abstract from** *v prep*
**1** to take (something) out of (something); separate; reduce: [T1 + *from* (*often pass.*)] *The article was abstracted from a longer book. Scientists can abstract precious medicines from ordinary substances.*

**2** *euph.* to steal (something) from (something or someone): [T1 + *from*] *The thieves abstracted the jewellery from her drawer.*

**abut against** *v prep*
to come to an end at (somewhere such as a point): [L9 + *against* (*usu. simple tenses*)] *The wall abuts against the corner of the field which is the other farmer's property.*

**abut on** *v prep* → **border on** (1), **verge on** (1)
*fml* (of land or a building) to lie next to; touch (something): [L9 + *on* (*no pass., usu. simple tenses*)] *The newly independent republic abuts on the lake.*

***accede to** *v prep*
**1** *fml* to follow someone and take (a position, etc): [T1 (*pass. rare*)] *When his father died, the prince acceded to the position of head of state.* → **succeed to**
**2** *fml* to give approval to (a request, agreement, etc.): [T1 (*pass. rare*)] *The directors have agreed to accede to the workers' demands. By signing the papers, all the parties acceded to the contract.* → **agree to**, etc.

**accept as** *v prep* → **acknowledge as**
to believe that (something or someone) is (what he/she/it is claimed to be): [T1 + *as*] *The crowd accepted his statement as truth. The king accepted the girl as his daughter.*

**acclimatize to** *v prep* → **adapt to**, etc.
to accustom (someone or oneself) to (different weather, ideas, etc.): [T1 + *to* (*often pass.*)] *It takes mountain climbers several days to acclimatize themselves to the thinner air at great heights.*

**accommodate to** *v prep* → **adapt to**, etc.
*fml* to change (something) to suit (something else): [T1 + *to*] *When someone stops working, they have to accommodate their desires to a new standard of living. This chair accommodates its shape to a person's position.*

**accommodate with** *v prep*
*fml* to provide (someone) with (something), often as a favour: [T1 + *with*] *It was very good of you to accommodate me with the ticket for my journey.*

**accompany with** *v prep*
to add to (something) (something done or happening at the same time): [T1 + *with* (*usu. simple tenses*)] *The speaker accompanied his angry words with forceful movements of the hands.*

***accord with** *v prep*
*fml* to match or suit (something): [T1 (*no pass., simple tenses*)] *Unfortunately, the young man's political principles do not accord with those of his father. The government's recent statement of the unemployment figures does not accord with the facts.*

***account for** *v prep*
**1** to be or give a reason for (something or doing something); explain: [T1 (*often simple tenses*)] *He could not account for his foolish mistake. Melting snow accounts for the regular spring floods in the valley.* [T4 (*often simple tenses*)] *How do you account for losing such a large sum of money?* [T6a (*often simple tenses*)] *Can you account for why our team lost?*
**2** also **answer for** to give a statement about (something), esp. one showing how money or goods left in one's care have been dealt with: [T1 (*to*) (*often simple tenses*)] *You have to account to Head Office for any stamps that you use. All the men are present or accounted for, sir.* [T6a (*often simple tenses*)] *You'll have to account for where every penny goes.* —**unaccounted for** *adj*
**3** *infml* to kill, shoot, or catch (aeroplanes, people, animals): [T1 (*usu. simple tenses*)] *The gunmen accounted for five terrorists at the airport. After a long hunt, the fox was at last accounted for.*
**4** to give back money or suffer punishment for (a wrongdoing): [T1 (*usu. simple tenses*)] *It will take him twenty years in prison to account for such a terrible crime.*
**5 account for preferences/tastes** to be able to explain people's likes and dislikes: [(*usu. neg.*)] *Have you seen the man she married? It shows that there's no accounting for tastes!*

***account to** *v prep* → ANSWER TO (4)

***accredit to** *v prep*
*fml* to state that (something) belongs to, was done by, or is connected with (someone): [D1 (*often pass.*)] *The soldier was respected for the brave deed which had been accredited to him.*

***accredit with** *v prep* → CREDIT WITH (2)

**accrue to** *v prep*
(esp. of money) to come to (someone), by right, etc.: [IØ + *to*] *Money kept in a savings bank will accrue to you with interest.*

**accuse of** *v prep*
to say that (someone) is guilty of (something wrong): [T1 + *of*] *She accused her brother of the crime. She accused her brother of stealing the jewels.*

***accustom to** *v prep* → **habituate to, use to**
to make (someone, oneself, or something) used to (something or someone): [D1 (*often pass.*)] *I am not accustomed to your laws. Let the child get accustomed to her new teacher. It is difficult to accustom oneself to the new ideas of younger people.* [V4b (*often pass.*)] *I am not accustomed to public speaking. You have to accustom yourself gradually to using metric measurements.*

**ache for** *v prep*
**1** to feel pity for (someone): [IØ + *for*] *My heart aches for you.* → **feel for** (4)
***2** to have a great desire for (something or someone): [T1 (*pass. rare*)] *All winter I have been aching for sunshine.*

**acknowledge as** *v prep* → **accept as**
to recognize formally (someone or something) as (what he/she/it is claimed to be): [T1 + *as*] *The people acknowledged the victo-*

*rious enemy as their new rulers. You have to acknowledge your defeat as complete.*

***acquaint with** *v prep*

**1** to make (someone or oneself) familiar with (something): [D1] *You should acquaint yourself with the facts before making a decision.*

**2 be acquainted with** to know (someone or something): *I am not acquainted with your aunt. I'm not acquainted with this piece of music.*

***acquiesce in/to** *v prep* → **agree to**, etc.

*fml* to accept or give no opposition to (something such as a plan): [T1 (*usu. simple tenses*)] *He acquiesced in the new arrangements his parents had made for him. The late delivery of letters by the Post Office is mostly acquiesced to without complaint.*

**acquit of** *v prep*

*law* to declare that (someone) is not guilty of (blame, a crime, etc.): [T1 + *of* (*often pass.*)] *The young man was acquitted of the murder.*

***act as** *v prep*

to fulfil the purpose of (something): [L1] *A trained dog can act as a guide to a blind person.*

***act for** *v prep* → **appear for, plead for** (2)

to represent (someone); perform duties as a lawyer, etc., in the place of: [T1 (*pass. rare*)] *Mr Jones will act for you on this case. As the chairman is ill, I am asking Mr Sharp to act for him.*

**act on/upon** v prep

**1** to perform on (something): [IØ + *on/upon*] *"It's a long time since I acted on this stage," said the actor.* → **appear on** (2)

**2** to have an effect on (something): [IØ + *on/upon*] *The medicine acted on his fever at once.*

***3** to behave according to; follow (something); take action as a result of (something): [T1] *The police are acting on information received.*

**act out** *v adv*

**1** to play (a part), esp. in actions and behaviour rather than in words: [T1 + OUT] *Let's act out the story of the three bears once more.*

***2** to give expression to (thoughts, unconscious fears, etc.) in actions and behaviour rather than in words; perform (one's feelings): [T1] *Children often act out their troubled feelings in their games.* [IØ] *Don't take her seriously, she's just acting out.* → **play out** (6)

***act up** *v adv*

**1** → **PLAY UP** (4)

**2** *infml* (of part of the body) to become painful: [IØ] *Mother's leg seemed quite better after her operation, but recently it's been acting up again.* → **play up** (5)

***act up to** *v adv prep* → **LIVE UP TO** (1)

**act upon** *v prep* → **ACT ON**

**adapt as** *v prep*

to change (something) to become (something else): [T1 + *as* (*often pass.*)] *Many of Dickens' books have been adapted as films.*

**adapt for** *v prep*

to change (something) to suit (something else): [T1 + *for* (*often pass.*)] *Several of D.H. Lawrence's books have been adapted for the cinema. Many city vehicles have been adapted for use as school buses.*

**adapt from** *v prep*

to change (something) from (its former state): [T1 + *from* (*often pass.*)] *The film "A Clockwork Orange" was adapted from the book of the same name.*

**adapt to** *v prep* → **acclimatize to, accommodate to**

to become used to; change (something, someone, or oneself) to suit or be able to deal with (usu. something): [IØ + *to*] *Many British people have had difficulty in adapting to metric measurements.* [T1 + *to*] *It is difficult to adapt oneself to sudden changes of temperature. We must adapt our needs to our income. The hospital was quickly adapted to the special needs of the sick children.*

**add in** *v adv*

to add (something), usu. in the middle of a mixture or calculation; include: [T1 + IN] *Add in the flour a little at a time. Before you finish the totals, please add in these new figures.*

**add on** *v adv*

to add (something), usu. at the end of a calculation or list: [T1 + ON] *Please add these names on at the end. The price does not include tax added on.*

**add to** *v prep*

**1** to make a sum of (one figure and another or others); put (something) with (something) so as to increase it: [T1 + *to*] *Add the first total to the second (and third). Can we afford to add another room to the house?*

***2** to increase (something): [T1] *The bad weather added to the helplessness of the shipwrecked sailors.*

**3 add fuel to the flames** *not fml* to make someone feel even more strongly about something: *Nothing would help her when she became angry and trying to calm her down just added fuel to the flames.*

**4 add insult to injury** *not fml* to make matters even worse, esp. by causing someone sorrow as well as harm: *Expecting him to pay for the damage which they had caused was simply adding insult to injury.*

**add together** *v adv*

to make a total or whole: [T1 + TOGETHER] *When you add all the figures together, the sum is 728.* [IØ + TOGETHER (*simple tenses*)] *The facts add together to give a hopeless picture of the firm's future.*

**add up** *v adv*

**1** to (cause to) make a total of (numbers): [T1 + UP] *Add these figures up and see what*

*the total is.* [IØ + UP (*simple tenses*)] *These figures don't add up correctly.* → **figure up**
*2 *infml* to make sense: [IØ (*simple tenses*)] *I can't understand this case; the facts just don't add up.*

**add up to** *v adv prep*
1 to make a total of (a figure): [IØ + UP + *to* (*simple tenses*)] *The separate numbers add up to 472.* [T1 + UP + *to*] *How quickly can you add the figures up to their total?* → **amount to** (1), **come to**² (14)
* 2 *not fml* to seem to be (something) in fact; be equal to; mean: [T1 (*no pass., simple tenses, often present*)] *This conversation adds up to a difference of opinion between us.* → **amount to** (2)

**addict to** *v prep*
**be addicted to**
1 to be dependent on; have increasing need of (a habit-forming drug); *She became addicted to a painkilling medicine which she had been given in hospital.* → **hook on** (2)
2 *not fml* to like (something or doing something) very much: *Sarah is addicted to music. Jim's addicted to collecting coins.* → **hook on** (3)

**address to** *v prep*
1 to send (a letter, etc.) to (someone) by putting his name and address on the outside: [T1 + *to*] *Don't open letters that are not addressed to you.* → **direct to** (1)
*2 to send; aim (speech or writing) to (usu. someone): [D1] *You must address your complaints to Head Office. My speech is addressed to the boys and girls of this school, rather than to the parents.* → **direct to** (2)
3 **address oneself to** *fml* to speak to (someone): *Kindly address yourself to the chairman, not directly to other representatives at this meeting.*
4 **address oneself to** *fml* to make (oneself) busy with; turn the attention of (oneself) to (something): *Let us address ourselves to the matter in hand. Let us address ourselves to completing the business of the meeting.*

***adhere to** *v prep*
1 to stick to (something): [T1] *Wet clothes adhere to the skin.* → **cleave to** (1), **cling to** (1), **stick to** (1)
2 *fml* to steadily follow or be faithful to (an idea, opinion, belief, etc.): [T1 (*usu. simple tenses*)] *They adhered to their original plan of climbing the mountain in spite of the bad weather.* → **cleave to** (2), **cling onto** (3), **cling to** (4), **depart from** (2), **deviate from** (2), **diverge from, hold by** (1), **hold to** (3), **keep to** (3), **stand by**² (3), **stay with** (3), **stick by** (2), **stick to** (6), **stick with** (4)

**adjourn for** *v prep*
to delay the completion of (something already started) for (a purpose or length of time): [T1 + *for*] *Let us adjourn the committee meeting for lunch.* [IØ + *for*] *The court will adjourn for the night, and meet again tomorrow.*

**adjourn to** *v prep*
to leave (what one is doing) and go to (another place) or wait until (another time): [IØ + *to*] *The meeting adjourned to the nearest public house.* [T1 + *to*] *Let us adjourn the meeting to next Monday.*

**adjudicate in** *v prep* → **arbitrate in**
*fml* to act as a judge in (a disagreement): [IØ + *in*] *A leading citizen has been asked to adjudicate in the disagreement between the city council and the workers.*

**adjudicate on** *v prep* → **arbitrate on**
*fml* to act as a judge on (a matter causing disagreement): [IØ + *on*] *It is the chairman's right to adjudicate on any question on which the committee members cannot agree.*

**adjust to** *v prep*
1 to become used to (something or someone): [IØ + *to*] *I cannot adjust easily to metric measurements. Jim found it difficult to adjust to his wife's mother.*
2 to change (something) to fit (something or someone): [T1 + *to*] *You can adjust the belt to the size that you want. It is difficult to adjust one's habits to someone else.*

**administer to** *v prep*
1 *fml* to give; serve (something) to (someone): [T1 + *to*] *For twenty years the judge administered justice to all who came into his court.*
*2 → MINISTER TO

***admit of** *v prep* → ALLOW OF

**admit to** *v prep*
1 to allow (someone) to enter (a place, event, membership, profession etc.): [T1 + *to*] *We admit students to these concerts at half price. You have to pass the professional examinations to be admitted to the society.*
2 to tell the truth about (one's guilt) to (someone): [T1 + *to*] *The prisoner admitted his guilt to the police.*
*3 to tell the truth about (something such as one's guilt or an opinion): [T1] *The young man admitted to his part in the crime. I have to admit to a dislike for modern music.* [T4] *The young man admitted to stealing the jewels. I have to admit to liking modern art.* → **confess to** (2)
*4 **admit to the bar** *fml* to make (someone) a lawyer.

**adopt as** *v prep*
1 to take (someone, esp. a child) into one's family as a relation for ever and to have the full responsibilities in law of the parent: [T1 + *as*] *The family have adopted three children as their own.*
2 to accept (someone else's child) at (a certain time in its life): [T1 + *as*] *I was adopted as a baby, and never knew my real parents.*
3 to choose (someone) as (a representative): [T1 + *as*] *The local party workers have adopted Julia Green as their representative for the coming election.*

**adorn with** *v prep* → **decorate with** (1), etc.

*fml* to ornament (oneself, someone, or something) with (something attractive or valuable) to make finer or more beautiful: [T1 + *with*] *He likes to show his wealth by adorning his wife with jewels. The temple was adorned with valuable paintings, gold statues, and other precious objects. He adorned his story with all sorts of interesting details.*

**advance on/upon** *v prep*
to threaten by moving towards (usu. a place): [IØ + *on/upon*] *The enemy advanced on Rome, and at last conquered it.*

**advance to** *v prep*
to reach: come as far as (usu. a place): [IØ + *to*] *The enemy have advanced to the edge of the forest.*

**advance towards** *v prep*
**1** to come nearer (something, someone, or a place): [IØ + *towards*] *The storm is advancing towards the city.*
* **2** to begin to become or reach (something such as a state): [T1 (*no pass.*)] *The world political system is advancing towards disorder.*

**advance upon** *v prep* → **ADVANCE ON**

* **advert to** *v prep* → **talk about** (1), etc.
*fml* to mention (something or someone): [T1 (*usu. simple tenses*)] *The chairman of the committee adverted to a recent decision, and stated that no change could be made.*

**advertise for** *v prep*
to try to obtain (something or someone) by means of notices in newspapers, etc.: [IØ + *for*] *Mother has been advertising for a cleaner for weeks without success. The council are advertising for a teacher in this week's newspaper.*

**advise about/on** *v prep*
to give (someone) advice about (something or doing something): [T1 + *about/on*] *Priests advise their churchgoers about many personal troubles. Experienced seamen will advise you about sailing in this weather. Experienced seamen will advise you about whether you should sail the boat in this weather/whether to sail the boat in this weather.* [IØ + *about/on*] *Doctors advise about many things other than medicine. Experienced seamen will advise about sailing the boat in this weather. Experienced seamen will advise about whether you should sail the boat in this weather/whether to sail the boat in this weather.*

**advise of** *v prep*
to give information or warning (to someone) about (something): [T1 + *of*] *The motoring organizations have advised motorists of thick mists on the mountains.* [IØ + *of*] *The motoring organizations have advised of thick mist on the mountains.*

**advise on** *v prep* → **ADVISE ABOUT**

* **advise with** *v prep* → **consult with** (2)
*old use* or *AmE fml* to meet and talk with; get advice from (someone): [T1] *Before making any decision, the President usually advises with leading members of his special information committee.*

* **affiliate to/with** *v prep*
to join; have a special connection with (usu. a larger group): [D1 (*often pass.*)] *The cricket club is affiliated to/with the national organization. The local committee wants to affiliate the club to the national body.* [T1 (*no pass.*)] *Do you think our group should affiliate with the national organization?*

**affix to** *v prep* → **attach to** (1)
*fml* to fasten or add (something) to (something such as a paper): [T1 + *to* (*usu. simple tenses*)] *Affix an airmail stamp to each envelope that is going abroad. As soon as the director's signature is affixed to the contract, we can order the supplies needed for the work.*

* **afflict with** *v prep*
to cause (someone) to suffer from (something); trouble (someone) with (something): [D1 (*usu. pass.*)] *Aunt Kate has been afflicted with a serious illness.*

**agitate for** *v prep* → **campaign for** (2), etc.
to argue strongly in favour of; demand (something), esp. publicly: [IØ + *for*] *More people are agitating for improvements in prison conditions.*

**agree about** *v prep* → **agree on** (1), **disagree about**
to have the same opinion about (usu. something): [IØ + *about*] *Musicians rarely agree about the way a piece of music should be played.*

**agree on/upon** *v prep*
**1** to have the same opinion about (usu. something): [IØ + *on/upon*] *Musicians rarely agree on the way a piece of music should be played.* → **agree about, disagree about**
* **2** to decide on (something or doing something): [T1] *We've agreed on Spain for our holiday next year.* [T4] *We've agreed on fighting the evil in society, now let's do something about it.* → **decide on**, etc. — **agreed-on** *adj.*

**agree to** *v prep* → **accede to** (2), **acquiesce in, assent to, consent to, dissent from, fall in with** (4)
to accept; approve; promise to follow (something): [IØ + *to* (*usu. simple tenses*)] *Do you agree to my plan? The committee has agreed to your request.*

**agree upon** *v prep* → **AGREE ON**

**agree with** *v prep*
**1** to have the same opinion as (someone): [IØ + *with* (*usu. simple tenses*)] *I agree with your father; it's a foolish risk.* → **disagree with** (1)
**2** to accept (something): [IØ + *with* (*usu. simple tenses*)] *I agree with your last remark.*
* **3** to be in accordance with; be the same as (something): [T1 (*no pass., simple tenses*)] *Your story agrees with his in everything except small details.* → **correspond to**, etc.
* **4** (in language) to have a form matching (another word): [T1 (*no pass., simple tenses*)] *A verb must agree with its subject in number.*

***5** to suit the health of (someone): [T1 (*no pass., simple tenses*)] *The onions did not agree with me, and have given me a pain. Does the thin mountain air agree with you?* → **disagree with** (4)

**aim at/for** *v prep* → **take at** (2)
**1** to point or direct (a gun, etc.) towards (someone or something): [IØ + *at/for*] *I didn't mean to hit the cat, I was aiming at/for the tree.* [T1 + *at/for*] *You will have to aim your gun more carefully at the chosen object.* → **shoot at** (1)
***2** to make an effort towards (something or doing something); try to gain (something): [T1] *The factory must aim at/for increased production this year.* [T4] *You should always aim at doing your job well.* → **drive at** (2) **drive for** (2), **go after** (2), **go for** (6), **shoot at** (2)

**alert to** *v prep* → **awaken to,** etc.
to warn (someone) about (something such as a threat); make (someone) watchful about: [T1 + *to*] *We must alert the people to the dangers facing our country.*

**alienate from** *v prep*
to cause (someone) to feel unfriendly or unsympathetic towards (usu. someone else): [T1 + *from* (*often pass.*)] *By her unkind actions, Christine alienated her husband from his brother. Young people are often alienated from the ideas of their parents.*

**alight from** *v prep* → **get off** (3), **get on**[2] (2), **get onto** (2), **get out of** (1), **let off**[2] (1), **put off**[2] (1), **take on** (1)
*fml* to descend from (usu. a vehicle): [IØ + *from*] *The Queen alighted gracefully from her carriage at the entrance to the Houses of Parliament before the opening ceremony.*

**alight on/upon** *v prep*
**1** to come down from the air onto (something): [IØ + *on/upon*] *The bird alighted on the branch.* → **light on** (1)
* **2** *old use fml* to find (something) by chance: [T1 (*simple tenses*)] *How did you alight on the old photograph?* → **happen on**, etc.

**align with** *v prep*
**1** to bring (something) into a straight line with (something else): [T1 + *with* (*often pass.*)] *You have to align the bricks with the rest of the wall. When you put the picture up, make sure it's aligned with the others.*
* **2** to bring (usu. someone or oneself) into agreement with (someone): [D1 (*usu. pass.*)] *Most of the members were aligned with the chairman; only a few disagreed. We must align ourselves with the workers in the struggle for better conditions.*

**allocate to** *v prep* also **allot to**
to give a share of (something) officially to (someone): [T1 + *to* (*often pass.*)] *The committee has allocated some of the club's money to the young people. Certain duties have been allocated to each member.*

**allow for** *v prep*
**1** to give (usu. money) for (a certain purpose), often by law; provide (something such as a time or place) for (something): [T1 + *for* (*usu. simple tenses*)] *The court allowed a sum of money for clothing. We must allow an hour for the meeting. Buy the children's shoes big enough to allow room for growth.*
***2** to take (something) into consideration: [T1] *You have to allow for the boy's age. Allowing for the bad weather, we should set off soon.* [T4] *We must allow for losing our way in the dark.* [V4a] *You'd better allow for the members voting against you. Allowing for the train being late, we should be back by 10.30.* → **make for** (6)

**allow in** *v adv; prep* → **permit in**
to permit (usu. someone) to enter (a place): [X9 + IN/*in* (*often simple tenses*)] *The children are not allowed in (the school) until the school bell rings, whatever the weather. I don't allow cats in my kitchen! Most modern hospitals allow the mother in when a baby is ill.*

**allow into** *v prep* → **permit into**
to permit (usu. someone) to enter (a place): [X9 + *into* (*often simple tenses*)] *Children are not allowed into this cinema without their parents.*

***allow of** *v prep* also **admit of, permit of**
*fml* to give the possibility of (something): [T1 (*no pass., simple tenses, usu. neg.*)] *The law is worded so as not to allow of any misunderstanding. The facts allow of no other explanation.*

**allow out** *v adv* → **permit out**
to permit (someone) to go out of doors, leave a room or building, etc.: [X9 + OUT] *The prisoners are allowed out for half an hour's exercise each day. I've sent the boy to his room and will not allow him out until he says that he's sorry.*

**allow through** *v adv; prep* → **permit through**
to permit (someone) to pass through (something): [X9 + THROUGH/*through*] *The soldiers had orders to allow no stranger through (the gates).*

**allow to** *v prep*
to give (usu. money) by law to (someone): [T1 + *to* (*usu. simple tenses*)] *The court allowed a sum of money to each child for clothing.*

**allow up** *v adv* → **permit up**
to permit (someone who has been ill) to get out of bed: [X9 + UP (*often simple tenses*)] *The doctor will not allow Mother up until her leg is better.*

***allude to** *v prep*
*fml* to mention (something or someone) indirectly: [T1] *It was kind of you not to allude to his prison record.*

***ally to** *v prep*
**1** to add (something) to (something): [T1 (*usu.*

*pass.)] Allied to the musician's gift for making tunes is a strong sense of timing.*

**2 be allied to** to be related to (something): *French is allied to Spanish and other Latin languages.*

**ally with** *v prep*

**1** to unite (oneself) with (someone or something else); join forces with (usu. a nation): [T1 + *with* (*usu. pass.*)] *Britain was allied with the United States many times in history. The smaller country allied itself with the stronger power.*

* **2** to make oneself a partner with or supporter of (someone or something): [T1] *Will the workers in the steel factories ally with those in the coalmines against the government?*

**alternate between** *v prep*

to change from (one thing, esp. a state) to (another thing): [L9 + *between*] *Mary's spirits alternated between hope and sorrow.*

**alternate with** *v prep* → **interchange with**

to change (one person or thing) for (another) and then change back again: [L9 + *with*] *The weather will consist of sunshine alternating with periods of light rain.* [X9] *I am only taking two dresses on holiday with me, so I will have to alternate the green dress with the blue one.*

**amalgamate with** *v prep* → **combine with** (1), **merge together, merge with**

to unite (one thing) with (another, formerly separate): [T1 + *with*] *The members decided to amalgamate the tennis club with the cricket club, forming one combined sports club.* [IØ + *with*] *The company has decided to amalgamate with the parent firm.*

***amount to** *v prep*

**1** to make a total of (a figure): [T1 (*no pass., simple tenses*)] *The separate numbers amount to 472.* → **add up to** (1), **come to²** (14)

**2** to seem to be in fact; be equal to (something): [T1 (*no pass simple tenses, often present*)] *This conversation amounts to a difference of opinion between us.* → **add up to** (2)

**3** to reach success in (anything, little, much): [T1 (*no pass., usu. simple tenses, usu. neg.*)] *Jim moves from job to job so often that I don't see how he can ever amount to much.* → **come to²** (10)

**amuse with** *v prep*

to give (someone or oneself) pleasure by playing with (someone, something, or doing something): [T1 + *with*] *He could amuse us for hours with his stories of the theatre. There are plenty of toys to amuse the children with while we're out.*

* **angle for** *v prep* → FISH FOR (3)

* **angle towards** *v prep* → SLANT TOWARDS (2)

* **animadvert on/upon** *v prep*

*pomp* to express an opinion about (a subject), often at length and in a way that finds fault: [T1] *The old politician can be depended upon to animadvert upon his party's principles and intentions whenever the chance arises, even on unsuitable occasions.*

**annex to** *v prep*

to take (usu. a place) often by force, and add it to (existing property) by declaring it to belong by law: [T1 + *to*] *The conquering enemy annexed the formerly free island to their nation.*

**announce to** *v prep*

to make (news) known to (someone or a group), esp. publicly: [T1 + *to*] *The date of the examination will be announced to all schools later in the year. In a solemn voice, the councillor announced the names of the winners to the crowd.* [T5 + *to*] *It was such a surprise when Mary announced to the family that she was getting married.*

**anoint with** *v prep*

*fml* to bless (a person, his head, or his body) with (oil), esp. in a formal royal or religious ceremony: [T1 + *with*] *The priest anointed the new king with oil.*

***answer back** *v adv*

to reply to (someone) rudely or in defence of oneself: [IØ (*to*)] *Don't answer back (to your grandmother), it's not polite. Tom was angry that people could attack his book when he could not answer back.* [T1] *When your Dad punishes you, you shouldn't answer him back.*

**answer for** *v prep*

**1** to give a reply in the name of (someone else): [IØ + *for*] *I will answer for my wife as well as myself.* → **speak for** (3)

***2** → ACCOUNT FOR (2)

***3** to act, pay, or suffer as a result of (something): [T1 (*often simple tenses*)] *You will have to answer for your violent behaviour in court.*

***4** to take the responsibility or blame for (someone or something): [T1 (*usu. simple tenses*)] *I will answer for the boy's behaviour in future. The parents of that badly behaved child have a lot to answer for.*

**5 be answered for** to be promised to someone: *Are all these seats answered for?* → **speak for** (5)

**answer to** *v prep*

**1** to obey (something): [IØ + *to* (*often simple tenses*)] *The children answered to their father's call by running home.*

***2** to behave as if knowing (a name); be called by (a name): [T1 (*no pass., usu. present simple tense*)] *The lost dog answers to the name of Lucky. No one in this office answers to the name you have given us.*

***3** to match (something, usu. a description): [T1 (*no pass., usu. simple tenses*)] *The man at the police station answers to the description of the wanted murderer.* → **correspond to**, etc.

* **4** also **account to** to be responsible to (someone) for an explanation: [T1 (*for*) (*no pass., often simple tenses*)] *You will have to answer to Head Office for any stamps that you use. If anything is missing when I get back, you'll have to answer to me!*

* **5** to obey (a control): [T1] *The sails are not answering to our pull on the ropes; the fastening must have got twisted somehow.* → **respond to** (4)

**answer up** *v adv* → **speak out, speak up, talk up** (1, 2)
to answer clearly; not be afraid to reply: [IØ + UP] *Answer up when the judge asks you a question.*

***ante up** *v adv*
esp. *AmE infml* to pay (an amount): [IØ] *The money has been owing for months; when will your brother ante up?* [T1a] *The government anted up $10,000 to send the children's theatre company on tour.*

**apologize for** *v prep*
to say that one is sorry about (something or doing something): [IØ + *for*] *I must apologize for my carelessness. I must apologize for breaking the window.*

**apologize to** *v prep*
to say that one is sorry to (someone): [IØ + *to*] *Apologize to your grandmother for that rude remark.*

**appeal against** *v prep*
**1** to ask a higher court of law to reconsider (a judgment made by a lower court): [IØ + *against*] *In the High Court, the man appealed successfully against the judgment that he was guilty, and was freed from prison.*
**2 appeal against the light** (in cricket, tennis, etc.) to ask for play to stop because the light is too faint for the player(s) to see the ball clearly: *Our team would have lost if our captain had not successfully appealed against the light.*

**appeal for** *v prep* → **beg for** (2)
to make a special request for (usu. money or behaviour): [L9 + *for*] *The international organization is appealing for more money to help people suffering from the floods in the East. The two drivers whose cars had crashed appealed for help from passing motorists. The government is appealing for calm in the face of increasing money troubles.*

**appeal to** *v prep*
**1** to ask for a reconsidered judgment in (a higher court of law): [IØ + *to*] *The man refused to admit that he was guilty as the court had judged, and appealed to the High Court.*
**2** to ask (someone): [L9 + *to* ] *The universities are having to appeal to the government for more money. The government is appealing to everyone to save power.*
* **3** to attract; seem good to (someone): [Tl (*no pass., simple tenses*)] *Does this piece of music appeal to you?*
* **4** to look for support in (something): [T1] *By appealing to his better nature, we persuaded the boy to change his behaviour. The chairman appealed to reason to win his argument.*

**appear at** *v prep*
**1** to arrive at (a time or place): [IØ + *at*] *The chief guest appeared at 11 o'clock, when the party was over. Suddenly a face appeared at the window.*
**2** to perform at (a theatre, etc.): [L9 + *at*] *The famous actor is now appearing at the Grand Theatre.*
**3** to have to face (a court of law): [L9 + *at*] *The two thieves will appear at New Street Court tomorrow morning.* → **appear before** (2)

**appear before** *v prep*
**1** to arrive before (a time): [IØ + *before*] *Jim appeared a few minutes before the end of the party.*
**2** to have to face (someone in a court of law): [L9 + *before*] *The man appeared before the judge on a charge of murder.* → **appear at** (3)

* **appear for** *v prep* → **act for, plead for** (2)
to perform duties as a lawyer for (someone) in court: [T1 (*no pass.*)] *Mr Jones will appear for you in court tomorrow.*

**appear in** *v prep*
**1** to be seen in (a place or clothes): [IØ + *in*] *Mary suddenly appeared in the doorway. Mary appeared in her best dress. You must appear in court tomorrow.*
**2** to perform in (usu. a play): [L9 + *in*] *She is now appearing in "Long Day's Journey into Night" at the Grand Theatre.*
**3 appear in print** to be printed and made public: *When does Tom's new book appear in print?*

**appear on** *v prep*
**1** to be able to be seen on (something such as a place): [L9 + *on*] *The writer's full name appears on the title page of the book.*
**2** to perform on (something such as a stage or television programme): [L9 + *on*] *"It's a long time since I appeared on this stage," said the actor.* → **act on** (1)

**appear under** *v prep* → **go by**[2] (7), etc.
to perform using (a name): [L9 + *under*] *The famous actor appeared under a false name.*

**append to** *v prep*
*fml* to add (something) to (a formal paper or book): [T1 + *to* (*usu. pass.*)] *A list of figures is appended to the statement.*

* **appertain to** *v prep*
*fml* to belong to (something) by right: [T1 (*no pass., usu. simple tenses*)] *Does Mr Jones fully understand the responsibilities appertaining to his chairmanship?*

**apply for** *v prep*
to make a formal request for (something such as a job): [IØ + *for* (*to*)] *Father is thinking of applying (to Mr White) for the directorship.*

**apply to** *v prep*
**1** to spread (something such as a thick liquid) on (a surface): [T1 + *to*] *Apply the paint to the prepared wood and allow it to dry. This cream is best applied to the face at night.* → **spread on² (1), spread over² (1), spread with (1)**
**2** to make a formal request to (someone or something such as a school): [IØ + *to* (*for*)] *You must apply to the directors for an increase in pay. How many universities have you applied to?* → **make to** (3)
**3** to (cause to) concern or affect (something or someone): [IØ + *to* (*simple tenses*)] *This part of the new law does not apply to Scotland.* [T1 + *to*] *We have to apply the same rules to everyone, showing no favour.* → **refer to** (3), **relate to** (3)
***4** to make (oneself) work hard at (something): [D1 (*no pass.*)] *You must apply yourself to the job you have to do.*
***5** to use (something such as ability) to help, answer, or work at (something or doing something): [D1] *Scientific discoveries are often applied to industrial production methods.* [V4b] *The driver had to apply all his strength and skill to keeping the car on the road after the wheel fell off.*

**apply within** *v adv* → **enquire within**
to ask inside the building where a notice is shown: [L9 + WITHIN] *Experienced salesman wanted; apply within.*

**appoint for** *v prep*
to fix (a time) for (a purpose): [T1 + *for*] *I'll be there at the time which was appointed for our meeting. We shall have to appoint another day for the rest of our business.*

**appoint to** *v prep*
to choose (someone) for (a position, job, etc.): [T1 + *to*] *Who will be appointed to the chairmanship when Mr Bell leaves?*

***apportion among** *v prep*
*fml* to share (something such as money) among (three or more people or groups): [D1 (*often pass.*)] *When Aunt Elizabeth died, her money was apportioned among her eight grandchildren.*

***apportion between** *v prep*
*fml* to share (something such as money) between (two people or groups): [D1 (*often pass.*)] *The money was apportioned equally between the tennis club and the cricket club.*

**apprentice to** *v prep*
to send (someone, usu. a boy) to (a skilled workman) to learn his trade, for little pay, over a number of years: [T1 + *to* (*usu. pass.*)] *The boy was apprenticed to a bricklayer.*

***apprise of** *v prep*
*fml* to inform (someone) about (something): [D1 (*usu. pass.*)] *We had not been apprised of the chairman's decision.*

**approach about** *v prep*
to make a request to (someone) about (a matter): [T1 + *about*] *Few of the office workers dared to approach the director about their working conditions.*

**appropriate for** *v prep* → **earmark for**
*fml* to take or save (something such as buildings or money) officially for (a special purpose): [T1 + *for* (*usu. pass.*)] *£7,283 has been appropriated for pay increases.*

**appropriate to** *v prep*
*fml* to take (something) by or as if by right for (oneself or one's own use): [T1 + *to*] *I see that the director has appropriated the best office to his own use. That selfish teacher always appropriates the biggest bookcase to himself.*

**approve of** *v prep* → **disapprove of**
to agree to; like; be in favour of (something or someone): [IØ + *of* (*usu. simple tenses*)] *My father did not approve of my marriage to Mary. My father did not approve of Mary.*

***approximate to** *v prep*
*fml* to be like; come very near to (something): [T1 (*no pass., simple tenses*)] *The politician's statement approximated to the government's intentions but was not exactly correct.*

**arbitrate between** *v prep*
*law* to try to form an agreement between (two opposing parties): [IØ + *between* (*in*)] *An experienced lawyer has been appointed to arbitrate between the government and the trade union in their disagreement over permitted wage increases.*

**arbitrate for** *v prep* → **sue for** (2)
*fml* to attempt to gain (a result, esp. peace) by talking (with opposing parties) trying to reach an agreement: [IØ + *for* (*with*)] *A representative of the United Nations was sent to the Middle East to arbitrate for peace with the two nations at war.*

**arbitrate in** *v prep* → **adjudicate in**
*law* to act as a judge in (a disagreement) in order to end it: [IØ + *in*] *A leading judge will arbitrate in the disagreement between the trade union and the employers.*

**arbitrate on** *v prep* → **adjudicate on**
*fml* to give or offer a judgment on (a matter which has not yet reached disagreement but is likely to): [IØ + *on*] *Before you start to argue over your opposing views, I should like to arbitrate on this matter and state that there is a great deal to be said in support of both opinions.*

***arch over¹** *v adv*
to cover; make a curved roof over (a space): [T1 (*often pass.*)] *The passage between the two buildings was arched over to provide shelter from the rain.*

**arch over²** *v prep*
to lean over (something) in a curved shape: [IØ + *over*] *The climbers will have difficulty on this part of the slope, where the overhanging rock arches over their upward track.*

**argue about/over** *v prep* → **quarrel about**, etc.
to disagree or quarrel about (something or doing something): [IØ + *about/over*] *They're always arguing about unimportant matters. Let us not argue about going out tonight. Let us not argue about whether (it is safe) to sail in this weather.*

**argue against** *v prep*
**1** to express an opinion opposing (someone, something, or doing something): [IØ + *against*] *The next speaker will argue against the plan. Why do you always argue against your father? Several members argued against voting so soon.* → **quarrel with** (1), etc.
**2* to disprove; suggest or prove the opposite of (something); suggest that one should avoid (doing something): [T1 (*no pass., simple tenses*)] *Most of the facts you have provided seem to argue against the ideas generally held by the members.* [T4 (*simple tenses*)] *All my experience argues against accepting his offer.*

**argue back** *v adv*
to disagree in return, often unpleasantly or rudely: [IØ + BACK] *Every time I express an opinion, you argue back!*

***argue down** *v adv*
esp. *AmE* to defeat (an opponent) in a speaking competition: [T1] *The speakers were well-informed, but I was able to argue them down.*

**argue for** *v prep*
to express an opinion in favour of (something or doing something): [IØ + *for*] *The Opposition has long argued for changes in parliamentary rules. Many members argued for changing the rules.*

**argue into** *v prep* → **coax into, persuade into, reason into, talk into** (2)
to persuade (someone) by showing reasons for (doing something): [X9 + *into*] *I think I can argue Father into increasing my weekly money.*

**argue out** *v adv*
to talk about (a point of disagreement) thoroughly until a decision is reached: [T1 + OUT] *The teacher and his class argued the whole matter out, and at last agreed to take no action.*

**argue out of** *v adv prep* → **coax out of, dissuade from, persuade out of, reason out of, talk out of**
to persuade (someone) against (doing something) by showing reasons: [X9 + OUT + *of*] *His parents had to argue Jim out of leaving his job.*

**argue over** *v prep* → ARGUE ABOUT

**argue with** *v prep*
**1** to quarrel with (someone): [IØ + *with*] *Father always argues with your brother* → **quarrel with** (1), etc.
**2* to disagree with (an idea); not accept the truth of (something): [T1 (*usu. simple tenses*)] *I do not argue with the facts, only with the meaning you give them.* → **disagree with** (2), **quarrel with** (2)

**arise from/out of** *v prep/v adv prep* → **come from** (2), **come of** (3), **flow from** (2), **grow from** (2), **grow out of** (2), **result from, rise from** (2), **spring from** (2)
to result from (something): [IØ + *from*/ OUT + *of* (*usu. simple tenses*)] *The country's present difficulties arise from the reduced value of its money.*

**arm against** *v prep*
**1** to provide defence for (oneself or someone) with weapons, etc., against (something): [T1 + *against*] *We must arm ourselves against the enemy. We must arm the people against the lowering of our morals.*
**2* to guard against: [T1 (*no pass.*)] *We bought the house to arm against big price rises.*

**arm for** *v prep*
to supply (someone) with weapons for (usu. a battle); prepare for (usu. a battle): [T1 + *for*] *The nation must arm its soldiers for battle.* [IØ + *for* (*no pass.*)] *The two opponents are arming for the fight.*

**arm with** *v prep*
**1** to provide (someone) with (weapons): [T1 + *with* (*usu. pass.*)] *Armed only with a short sword, he drove off five of his attackers.*
**2** to provide (someone) with (the means to gain something): [T1 + *with* (*usu. pass.*)] *Armed with facts like these, I can soon persuade the government to act.*

**arouse from** *v prep*
**1** *fml* to wake (someone) from (sleep): [T1 + *from*] *It proved impossible to arouse the man from his drugged sleep, so he was taken to hospital* → **wake from**, etc.
**2** *fml* to excite (someone) from (a dull state of feeling, inactivity, etc.): [T1 + *from* ] *The nation must be aroused from its unwillingness to work.* → **awaken from (2), waken from (2)**

**arrange about** *v prep*
to make a plan concerning; organize about (something or doing something): [L9 + *about*] *Have you arranged about the music for the wedding? Who arranged about buying the tickets?*

**arrange for** *v prep*
**1** to make a plan about (something); organize for (something to be done): [L9 + *for*] *I have arranged for our guests to be driven to the church. I have arranged for the photographer to take pictures after the ceremony. Who has arranged for the music at the party?*
**2** to make a plan about (something) for (someone): [T1 + *for*] *I have arranged an additional class for you on Tuesday mornings.*
**3** to rewrite the parts of (a piece of music) so as to suit (a certain instrument or instruments): [T1 + *for* (*often pass.*)] *Mussorgsky's "Night on a Bare Mountain" has been arranged for two pianos.*

**arrange with** *v prep*
to make a plan with (someone) (usu. to do something): [L9 + *with*] *I have arranged with*

*the restaurant to expect us at 5.30.* [T1 + *with*] *Can you arrange a meeting with the President?*

**arrive at** *v prep*
**1** to reach (a place): [IØ + *at* (*no pass.*)] *We arrived at the airport two hours late.*
*__2__ to reach (something such as a decision): [T1 (*usu. simple tenses*)] *After many hours' talk, the committee arrived at their decision. How did your calculations arrive at this figure?*

**arrive in** *v prep*
**1** to reach (a place): [IØ + *in*] *He arrived in this country six years ago without a penny, and now he is one of the biggest property owners in the city.*
**2** to reach a place in (a vehicle): [IØ + *in*] *The Queen arrived in a horse-drawn carriage.*

**arrive on** *v prep*
**arrive on the scene** to make an appearance, esp. for the first time: *When did the new teacher arrive on the scene?*

**arrogate to** *v prep*
**1** *fml* to claim (a title, etc.) for (oneself), usu. falsely: [T1 + *to*] *Having seized power in the country, he arrogated to himself the right to change the law.*
**2** *fml* to state unfairly that (something) is had or used by (someone): [T1 + *to*] *Do not arrogate wrong intentions to your friends.*

*__arse about/around__ *v adv* → **mess about** (1), etc.
*taboo sl* to spend time lazily or foolishly: [IØ] *No wonder you never get any work done when you spend half the day arsing around!*

*__ascribe to__ *v prep* → **ATTRIBUTE TO**

**ask about** *v prep* → **enquire about**
to request information concerning (something or someone): [IØ + *about*] *The director is asking about those papers that you promised to have ready. Newspaper reporters have been asking about the missing child all day.*

*__ask after__ *v prep* → **enquire after** (2)
to enquire about the health of (someone): [T1 (*no pass.*)] *"My mother asked after you." "Oh, how kind of her."*

*__ask back__ *v adv* → **have back** (3)
to invite (someone) in return: [T1] *We owe the Millers a dinner invitation; when are we going to ask them back?*

**ask for** *v prep*
**1** to request (something): [IØ + *for*] *The miners are asking for another increase in pay. I asked for the taxi to come at 8 o'clock.*
**2** to look for; try to find (someone), esp. to speak to him: [IØ + *for*] *There's a woman at the door, asking for Mr Sharp.* → **enquire for**
*__3__ *infml* to invite; behave so as to cause (usu. trouble), esp. in the phrs. **ask for it/trouble**: [T1 (*no pass., continuous or perfect tenses*)] *If you climb mountains in fog, you're asking for trouble. I warned you that you would be punished; now you've asked for it.* [V3] *If you go on like that, you're asking for me to punish you.* → **head for** (3), **look for** (4)

**ask in** *v adv* → **invite in**
to invite (someone) to enter: [X9 + IN] *Don't keep Mrs Bell standing at the door, ask her in.*

**ask of** *v prep* → **demand of, expect from, request from, require of**
to request (something) from (someone): [T1 + *of*] *I would like to ask a favour of you. It's not too much to ask of you, to clean your own shoes.*

**ask out** *v adv* → **go about'** (4), **go out** (3), **go out with** (2), **go round'** (3), **have out** (2), **invite out, knock about** (6), **take out** (9), **take round'** (3)
to invite (someone) to a show, meal, etc.: [X9 + OUT] *This is the third time he's asked me out! I've been asked out to a dance on Saturday.*

**ask over** *v adv* → **invite over**, etc.
to invite (someone) to one's home, usu. for a short time: [X9 + OVER] *I would ask you over for coffee, but the children are ill.*

**ask round** *v adv; prep*
**1** to invite (someone) to one's home, usu. for a short time: [X9 + ROUND] *I've asked him round for coffee later.* → **invite over**, etc.
**2** to make enquiries from (many people): [L9 + ROUND] *If you're looking for a good doctor, you'd better ask round.* [L9 + *round*] *If you're looking for a good doctor, you'd better ask round the neighbourhood.*

**ask to** *v prep* → **invite to**
to invite (someone) to be one's guest at (an event or occasion): [X9 + *to*] *Do I have to ask all my relatives to the wedding?*

**ask up** *v adv*
to invite (someone) to come upstairs: [X9 + UP] *When the doctor arrives, ask him up.*

*__aspire to/after__ *v prep*
to want; aim for (something): [T1 (*no pass., often simple tenses*)] *Many unknown writers aspire to fame. A truly religious person aspires after perfection.*

**assail with** *v prep*
*fml* to attack (someone) with (something, often unpleasant and repeated): [T1 + *with* (*often pass.*)] *The crowd assailed the speaker with questions. Mary was assailed with doubts on the day before her wedding.*

**assent to** *v prep* → **agree to**, etc.
*fml* to agree to (a formal suggestion): [IØ + *to* (*usu. simple tenses*)] *The Queen has assented to the new law.*

**assess at** *v prep*
to judge the value of (something) as (usu. an amount): [T1 + *at*] *The lawyers assessed the property at £90,500.*

**assign to** *v prep*
**1** to give (someone) duties concerning (something): [T1 + *to* (*usu. pass.*)] *A different policeman has been assigned to the case.*
**2** to provide; set aside (something such as time or space) for (something or someone): [T1 + *to*] *Which room has been assigned to the committee meeting? It's wise to assign*

*special exercises to the weaker students.*

*__3__ to believe (something) to be the result of (something): [D1 (*usu. pass.*)] *The accident has been assigned to a faulty part in the engine of the bus.* → **attribute to** (1), etc.

*__4__ to declare (something, esp. something written) to belong to (a particular time or a particular writer): [D1 (*usu. pass.*)] *The date of this piece of music is uncertain, but because of its style, it is generally assigned to the early 16th century.*

**assimilate into** *v prep*

**1** to make (someone or something) gradually become part of (a larger group): [T1 + *into* (*usu. pass.*)] *People of different nationalities often take some time to be assimilated into a country.* → **absorb into**(2)

**2** to become part of (a larger group): [IØ + *into*] *Some foreigners assimilate easily into our way of life.*

***assimilate to** *v prep*

*fml* to make (something) like (something else): [D1 (*usu. pass.*)] *The laws of the defeated country were assimilated to those of the stronger country.*

**assimilate with** *v prep*

*fml* to gradually take to oneself the language, customs, and way of life of (another people), so as to become accepted as belonging: [IØ + *with*] *Language is the chief difficulty that faces many newcomers from foreign countries, in trying to assimilate with the existing population.*

**assist at** *v prep* → **assist in, assist with**

to be present at and give help with (something), esp. as part of one's job: [IØ + *at*] *The young nurse was very nervous when she assisted at her first operation.*

**assist in** *v prep* → **assist at, assist with**

to help with (something or doing something): [T1 + *in*] *I am most grateful to my husband, who assisted me in preparing this book. He assisted me in the preparation of this book.* [IØ + *in*] *I am most grateful to my husband, who assisted in preparing this book. I am most grateful to my husband, who assisted in the preparation of this book.*

**assist with** *v prep* → **assist at, assist in**

to help (someone) with (something, someone, or doing something): [T1 + *with*] *Local villagers assisted the doctors with the people wounded in the bus crash.* [IØ + *with*] *The nurse assisted with the preparation of the medicine. She assisted with preparing the medicine.*

***associate with** *v prep*

**1** to be seen in public often with (someone): [T1 (*pass. rare*)] *I won't have my son associating with known criminals.* → **assort with** (2)

**2** to find a connection between (something or someone) and (something or someone else): [D1 (*usu. simple tenses*)] *I always associate the smell of those flowers with my childhood.* → **couple with** (2)

***assort with** *v prep*

**1** *fml* to match or suit (something): [T1 (*simple tenses*)] *The new leader's statement does not assort with some of his party's principles.* → **blend with**, etc.

**2** *fml* to be seen in public often with (someone): [T1 (*no pass.*)] *My daughter will not assort with people of her own age.* → **associate with** (1)

**assure of** *v prep*

to make (someone) certain about (something he is unsure about): [T1 + *of*] *The doctor assured the young father of his baby's safety.*

**atone for** *v prep*

*fml* to make repayment for (something or doing something wrong): [IØ + *for*] *I cannot hope to atone for all my misdeeds. You must atone for lying to your mother.*

**attach to** *v prep*

**1** to fix (something) to (something else): [T1 + *to*] *Attach the handle to the box.* → **affix to**

*__2__ to join (something or oneself) to (something or someone): [D1 (*often pass.*)] *The talkative woman attached herself to me throughout the journey. The youth division is attached to the main club.*

*__3__ to believe that (something such as importance) belongs to (something); connect with: [D1 (*simple tenses*)] *I don't attach much importance to his speech. People in other areas attach a different meaning to that word.*

*__4__ *fml* to (cause to) be part of or connected with (someone): [T1 (*no pass., simple tenses*)] *A great deal of blame attaches to the government for their recent action.* [D1 (*usu. pass.*)] *No fault is attached to the bus driver for the terrible accident at the railway crossing.*

**5 be attached to** to love; be fond of (someone or an animal): *Mary is very (much) attached to the little girl.*

**6 be attached to** to be part of (a military group): *Jim's father was attached to the Home Guard during World War II.*

**7 attach credence to** *fml* to believe (something such as an idea): *The public have heard so many false promises from politicians that they no longer attach much credence to government statements.*

***attain to** *v prep*

*fml* to reach (something desirable): [T1 (*pass. rare, simple tenses*)] *How can we attain to such wealth?*

**attend on/upon** *v prep*

**1** to act as a servant for (someone important): [IØ + *on/upon*] *In former times, a king would have as many as 100 people attending on him.*

**2** to give personal help to (someone) esp. as a nurse, etc.: [IØ + *on* ] *Jane has been attending on her sick mother for years.*

*__3__ *fml* to happen together with (something): [T1 (*simple tenses*)] *Too many dangers* *attended upon the climbers' attempt to reach the top of the mountain, and they had to come down.*

**attend to** *v prep*

**1** to listen carefully to (someone or someone's words); take notice of: [IØ + *to*] *Attend to me, children, I shan't repeat these instructions. I wish now that I'd attended to his advice.* → **pay to** (2)

***2** to give one's attention to (someone, something, or doing something): [T1] *Let's attend to our work instead of talking. "Can I help you sir?" "No, thanks, I'm already being attended to."* [T4] *Let's attend to finishing our work early for a change.* → **pay to** (2)

***3** to give help, esp. medical help, to (someone); take care of (someone or something), often in someone's absence: [T1] *You'd better attend to that thin dark girl, I think she's going to faint. Mother will attend to the baby while I go to the dance. Will you attend to the shop for a few minutes while I go to the bank?*

**attend upon** *v prep* → ATTEND ON

***attest to** *v prep*

*fml* to prove (something): [T1 (*simple tenses*)] *The fingerprints on the gun attested to his guilt.*

***attire in** *v prep*

*fml* to dress (oneself) in special garments): [D1 (*usu. pass.*)] *The Queen was attired in a splendid blue dress with many jewels, made specially for the ceremony.*

**attract to** *v prep*

**1** to cause (something) to come towards (something else): [T1 + *to* (*usu. pass.*)] *In this substance, the atoms are attracted to one another. Certain metals are attracted to a magnet.*

**2** to cause (someone) to like or feel drawn towards (someone or something): [T1 + *to*] *I don't know what attracts me to him, but I keep wanting to see him. All his life, Jim has been attracted to success.*

***attribute to** *v prep* also **ascribe to**

**1** to believe (something) to be the result of (something): [D1 (*usu. simple tenses*)] *Jim attributes his success to hard work.* → **assign to** (3), **impute to** (1), **owe to** (3), **put down to** (2), **refer to** (7), **set down to**

**2** *fml* to believe (something) to have been written by (someone): [D1 (*usu. pass.*)] *The play has been attributed to Shakespeare.* → **impute to** (2)

***attune to** *v prep*

to make (something or someone) suit (something) or become used to (usu. something): [D1 (*often pass.*)] *You have to attune your ears to modern music. Are you attuned to new ways of thinking?*

**auction off** *v adv*

to get rid of (goods) by selling at an auction: [T1 + OFF (*usu. pass.*)] *It was sad to see all grandmother's lovely things being auctioned off.*

***augur ill/well** *v adv* → BODE ILL/WELL

**avail against** *v prep* → **prevail against, triumph over** (2)

*fml* to be successful in opposing (something): [IØ + *against* (*simple tenses*)] *The eagerness of our team didn't avail against the fitness and skill of our opponents.*

***avail of** *v prep*

to give (oneself) the use or advantage of (something): [D1 (*no pass., often simple tenses*)] *You should avail yourself of every chance to improve your English.*

***avenge of** *v prep*

to repay (oneself) for (a wrong done to oneself): [D1 (*usu. pass.*)] *Hamlet was avenged of his father's murder.*

**avenge on** *v prep*

**1** to repay (a crime) by punishing (the criminal): [T1 + *on*] *Hamlet avenged his father's death on his uncle.* → **revenge on** (1)

***2** to repay (oneself) by punishing (someone) for pain or loss one has suffered: [D1 (*for*)] *She avenged herself on her uncle (for his misdeeds). Hamlet was avenged on his uncle.*

***average out** *v adv*

to reach an average: [IØ (*at*)] *How does your pay for the last year average out? The profit averages out at £100 a week.*

**avert from** *v prep*

to turn (usu. one's eyes) away from (something bad): [T1 + *from*] *Mary averted her eyes from the sight of the accident.*

**avouch for** *v prep rare* → VOUCH FOR

**awake from** *v prep* → **wake from**, etc.

to (cause to) become conscious again after (sleep): [IØ + *from*] *I was glad to awake from such an unpleasant dream.* [T1 + *from*] *His servant awoke the king from a restless sleep.*

**awake to** *v prep*

**1** to become conscious again after sleep, hearing or seeing (something): [IØ + *to*] *I awoke to bright sunlight filling my room; it was already midday. Do you like to awake to the sound of a radio?* → **wake to** (1)

***2** to begin to understand; become watchful about (something such as a threat): [T1 (*no pass.*)] *We must awake to the dangers facing our country.* → **awaken to**, etc.

**awaken from** *v prep*

**1** to cause (someone) to become conscious again after (sleep): [T1 + *from*] *I hate being awakened from a deep sleep by a loud bell.* → **wake from**, etc.

***2** to make (someone) conscious of reality instead of (a false idea): [D1] *John was painfully awakened from his dream of owning a large country house when he saw how much they cost.* → **arouse from** (2), **waken from** (2)

**awaken to** *v prep* → **alert to, awake to** (2), **wake to** (2), **waken to**

to warn (someone) about; make (someone) watchful about (something such as a threat): [D1] *We must awaken the people to the dangers facing our country.*

**award to** *v prep*

**1** to give (something such as a prize or money) officially to (someone): [T1 + *to*] *The Councillor has been invited here today to award the school prizes to our successful boys and girls. $50,000 has been awarded to the university for a study of the effect of art on the ways in which children learn.*

**2** to give (something) by a decision in a court of law to (usu. someone): [T1 + *to*] *The judge awarded a large sum of money to those hurt by the explosion.*

**awe into** *v prep*

*fml* to force (someone) into (a state) through fear and respect: [T1 + *into*] *The king's commanding presence awed the citizens into obedience. They were awed into silence by the great man.*

# B

**babble out** *v adv* → **blab out**

to say (something) quickly, often not very clearly; tell (secrets): [T1 + OUT] *In his fear of the police, the prisoner babbled out his guilt. He babbled the secret out to his friends.*

**back away** *v adv* → **back off** (1), **retreat from** (2)

**1** to move backwards to allow space, in fear, etc.: [L9 + AWAY (*from*)] *The crowd backed away to let the wounded man pass through. The child backed away from the fierce dog.*

***2** to be unwilling to consider an idea: [I∅ (*from*)] *I could see she was backing away from the idea.*

**back down** *v adv*

**1** to go down backwards: [L9 + DOWN] *You'll have to back down carefully, the ladder is not steady.*

***2** also esp. *AmE* **back off** to yield in argument, point of view, or claim: [I∅] *The speaker's forceful words persuaded his opponent to back down.* —**backdown** *n* → **climb down** (2)

**back into** *v prep*

**1** to (cause to) enter (a place) facing backwards, esp. when driving a vehicle: [L9 + *into*] *Be careful how you back into the garage, the doorway is very narrow.* [T1 + *into*] *Next you must learn how to back a car into a parking space.*

**2** to (cause to) hit (something) when driving backwards, esp. because the driver is inexperienced or careless: [I∅ + *into*] *I backed into another car as I was coming out of the car park.* [T1 + *into*] *Harry had just bought a new car, and his son went and backed it into a lamppost!*

**back off** *v adv*

**1** to move backwards to allow space, in fear, etc.: [L9 + OFF] *The crowd backed off in terror as the soldiers charged.* → **back away** (1), **retreat from** (2)

***2** esp. *AmE* → BACK DOWN (2)

**back onto** *v prep* → **face onto**

(of a building) to have the back lying opposite to (a place): [L9 + *onto* (*usu. simple tenses*)] *We chose this house because the garden backs onto the tennis courts.*

**back out** *v adv*

**1** to (cause to) move out backwards, esp. when driving a vehicle: [L9 + OUT (*of*)] *The opening is too narrow to turn round, you'll have to back out.* [T1 + OUT (*of*)] *In her first driving lesson, Jane backed the car safely out of the garage.*

***2** *not fml* to fail to fulfil something such as a promise: [I∅ (*of, from*)] *I hope I can depend on you to continue your support, and not back out at the last moment. If you back out of/from your contract, you will have to pay money to the firm.*

**back up** *v adv*

**1** to (cause to) go up backwards: [L9 + UP] *If you can't go up the hill forwards, you'll have to back up.* [T1 + UP] *If you can't drive up the hill forwards, you'll have to back the car up.*

***2** to support (someone or something): [T1] *We need further facts to back up our statements. Most members were against Mr Jones, who would have lost his position if you hadn't backed him up.* [I∅] *Back up, men, we need all the help we can get.* —**back-up** *n, adj*

***3** *naut* to pull tight on the free end of a rope tied round a fixed object: [I∅] *The boat is pulling away, back up there!*

***4** *AmE* (usu. of liquid) to block (a narrow place): [T1a] *The flood water from the storm backed up the pipes for the dirty water.*

***5** (in cricket) to prepare or begin to run to support one's partner: [I∅] *Before you back up, make sure that you are in no danger of being dismissed.*

***6** to (cause to) form a mass through delay: [T1 (*usu. pass.*)] *Many ships are still backed up at the entrance to the harbour. Lines of vehicles were backed up for several kilometres because of the accident.* [I∅] *Mail is backing up at the main post office because of the strike of sorters.* —**back-up** *n*

**badger into** *v prep*

*not fml* to persuade (someone) by repeated and annoying questioning into (doing something): [T1 + *into*] *Can you badger your father into letting us have the car tonight?*

*__bail out__ *v adv*

**1** to obtain (someone's) freedom by paying money (bail) to ensure his appearance in court: [T1] *Clark was to be charged next month with robbing the bank, so his family paid £500 to bail him out.* → **go for** (13)

**2** *not fml* to pay money, or help in some other way, to save (usu. someone) from failure or trouble: [T1] *The government cannot bail out every unprofitable company.*

**3** to remove water from (a boat), so as to prevent it sinking: [T1; IØ] *When the storm rose on the lake, we had to bail out (the boat) to reach the shore safely.* → **bale out** (1)

**4** *AmE spelling* to escape from a plane, by parachute: [IØ (*of*)] *The pilot was able to bail out (of the burning plane).* → **bale out** (2)

*__balance against/with__ *v prep*

to weigh (something) against (something else); consider (something) in relation to (usu. something opposite): [D1 + *against/with*] *We must balance his good qualities against his faults.*

*__balance out__ *v adv*

to (cause to) be of equal weight, importance, or influence to (something or each other): [IØ (*usu. simple tenses*)] *I hope that the figures for income and costs balance out.* [T1 (*usu. simple tenses*)] *The advantages of having a car and the money it costs balance each other out.*

**balance with** *v prep* → BALANCE AGAINST

*__bale out__ *v adv*

**1** to remove water from (a boat), so as to prevent it sinking: [T1; IØ] *When the storm rose on the lake, we had to bale out (the boat) to reach the shore safely.* → **bail out** (3)

**2** *BrE spelling* to escape from a plane, by parachute: [IØ (*of*)] *The pilot was able to bale out (of the burning plane).* → **bail out** (4)

*__balk at__ *v prep* also **baulk at, burke at** → **jib at**

to be unwilling to face or agree to (something or doing something difficult or unpleasant): [T1 (*usu. simple tenses*)] *The horse balked at the high fence. The committee were willing to listen to your ideas before, but have balked at your latest suggestion.* [T4 (*usu. simple tenses*)] *Jim balked at paying such a lot of money to join the club.*

**ball up** *v adv*

**1** to make a ball of (a substance): [T1 + UP] *Children like to ball mud up in their hands.*

***2** *AmE taboo sl* to spoil (something): [T1] *Now you've opened your big mouth, you've balled up the whole plan.* —**ball-up** *n* → **mess up** (2), etc.

**ballot for** *v prep*

to vote for (usu. a decision): [IØ + *for*] *Most of the workers balloted for the new plan. Most of the workers ballotted for shortening the working hours.*

*__balls up__ *v adv*

*BrE taboo sl* to spoil (something): [T1] *Now you've opened your big mouth, you've ballsed up the whole plan.* —**balls-up** *n* → **mess up** (2), etc.

*__band against__ *v prep*

to unite to oppose (something or someone): [T1 (*no pass.*)] *We must band against the common enemy.*

*__band together__ *v adv*

to (cause to) unite, usu. with some special purpose: [IØ (*against*)] *We must band together to fight the common enemy.* [T1 (*against*)] *The workers banded (themselves) together against the employers' position on their pay.*

**bandage up** *v adv*

to wrap (something such as a wound) with a long piece of cloth (a bandage): [T1 + UP] *The nurse bandaged up the nasty cut.*

*__bandy about/around/round__ *v adv*

**1** to spread (esp. unfavourable ideas) about (something) by talking: [T1 (*usu. pass.*)] *I hear that my good name has been bandied about behind my back. When the Websters' marriage failed, the news was quickly bandied about.*

**2** to talk about (something), often disrespectfully, not seriously, or without regard for truth: [T1 (*usu. pass.*)] *Several different figures have been bandied about, but these are the only correct ones.*

**bandy with** *v prep*

**bandy (words) with** to quarrel with (someone), esp. when exchanging angry words quickly: *I heard our neighbours bandying words with each other in the middle of the night.*

**bang about/around[1]** *v adv*

**1** to make a noise: [IØ + ABOUT/AROUND] *Stop banging about, children, Father is trying to sleep.*

***2** to damage (something): [T1b] *This car looks as if it's been banged about.* → **bash about**, etc.

**bang about/around[2]** *v prep*

**1** to make a noise in (a place): [IØ + *about/around*] *The children banged around the house all afternoon and I couldn't rest at all.*

***2** *infml* to travel in different parts of (a place): [T1] *My uncle has been banging about Africa for years.* → **hang about** (2) **kick about** (3), **knock about** (3)

**bang against** *v prep*

**1** to (cause to) strike against (something, usu. a hard object): [T1 + *against*] *I banged my head against the doorpost and hurt it.* [L9 + *against*] *The car banged against the garage door and damaged it.* → **knock against** (1), etc.

**2 bang one's head against a brick wall** also **beat one's head against a brick wall, knock one's head against a brick wall** *not fml* to keep doing something even when it has been proved hopeless: *Grace went on writing to her red-haired boy even though he didn't reply to a single letter for a year; she was banging her head against a brick wall.* → **run against** (4), **run into** (12)

**bang around[1]** *v adv* → BANG ABOUT

**bang around[2]** *v prep* → BANG ABOUT

* **bang away** *v adv*
**1** *infml* to work very hard or with determined effort: [IØ (*at*)] *I haven't finished this work yet: I'll have to keep banging away at it until this evening.*
**2** *taboo sl* to have sex continuously: [IØ] *They've been banging away all night.*

**bang into** *v prep*
**1** to knock (something or oneself) against (usu. a hard object): [L9 + *into*] *I've banged into the doorpost and hurt my arm.* [T1 + *into*] *Tom banged the car into a street light and damaged it.*
* **2** *infml* to meet (someone) by chance: [T1 (*no pass., usu. simple tenses*)] *I banged into an old friend in town today.* → **bump into** (2), etc.

**bang on/upon** *v prep*
to knock heavily on (something hard): [IØ + *on/upon*] *I banged on the door until she let me in.*

* **bang out** *v adv*
**1** to perform (something such as music) loudly: [T1] *Bob is at the piano again, banging out the latest popular tunes.*
**2** *not fml* to write (something) in haste, esp. on a typewriter: [T1] *Tom has been hard at work in his study all day, banging out a new story.*

* **bang up** *v adv*
**1** *AmE infml* to damage: ruin (something): [T1] *He banged up his car in the race.* → **smash up**, etc.
**2** *infml* to wound (a part of the body): [T1] *John banged up his knee playing cricket.*
**3** *AmE sl* to make (a woman) pregnant: [T1 (*usu. simple tenses*)] *Some people think it's OK to sleep with a girl so long as you don't bang her up.* → **knock up** (10), **prang up** (3)
**4** *sl* to put (a prisoner) in a room in a prison, and lock the entrance, esp. for the night: [T1] *When they bang you up, you don't speak to anyone for hours.* → **lock up** (2)

**bang upon** *v prep* → BANG ON

**banish from** *v prep*
**1** to force (someone) to leave (a place such as his country) and not return, as a punishment: [T1 + *from*] *A common punishment in Roman times was to banish a criminal from Rome.*
**2 banish from one's mind** to stop having (thoughts) about (something): *You can banish from your mind any idea of a holiday: we can't afford it.*

* **bank on** *v prep* → **depend on** (1), etc.
to depend on; trust in (someone, something, or doing something): [T1] *I'd like to come with you but that's not a promise; don't bank on it.* [T4] *Don't bank on going abroad this summer, we may not have enough money.* [V3] *Don't bank on your relatives to help you out of trouble.* [V4a] *Don't bank on the weather being fine for your garden party.* —**banked-on** *adj*

**bank up** *v adv*
**1** to (cause to) form into a mass: [IØ + UP] *The morning began fine, but now clouds are banking up.* [T1 + UP] *The wind had banked the snow up against the wall.* —**banked-up** *adj*
**2** to heap something solid around (something), so as to control it: [T1 + UP] *Every spring we have to bank up the river to prevent flooding. At night we bank the fire up so that it is still burning in the morning.* —**banked-up** *adj*

**bank with** *v prep*
to entrust (one's money) to (a certain banking firm): [IØ + *with*] *I have always banked with the Royal Bank.* [T1 + *with*] *I have always banked my money with the Royal Bank.*

**bar from** *v prep*
to forbid (someone) from (something or doing something): [T1 + *from* (*usu. pass.*)] *After the member was caught cheating, he was barred from the club. The doctor was barred from practising after he was proved guilty of improper behaviour.*

**bar in** *v adv; prep*
to prevent (someone or an animal) from leaving (usu. a building), by fastening a bar in the way: [X9 + IN/*in*] *The horses died in the fire because they were barred in (the hut).*

**bar out** *v adv*
to prevent (someone or an animal) from entering (usu. a building), by fastening a bar in the way: [X9 + OUT (*of*)] *The children cried when they couldn't get into the house; their mother had barred them out.*

**bar up** *v adv*
to close (an opening) with a bar or bars: [T1 + UP] *When the family left the house for the winter, they barred the windows up.*

**bargain about/over** *v prep* also **dicker over, haggle over**
to try to reach agreement on the price of (something): [IØ + *about/over*] *The women spend hours in the market, bargaining about the goods.*

**bargain away** *v adv*
**1** to continue talking about a price: [IØ + AWAY] *The women in the market often bargain away for hours.*
* **2** also **barter away** to allow (something) to be sold at a low price or exchanged for something of little value: [T1] *What a fool I was to bargain away my best dishes for this worthless furniture.*
* **3** also **barter away** to allow (something such as an advantage) to be lost in return for something of little value: [T1] *The rights that took years to win were bargained away in a few minutes' talks.*

**bargain for** *v prep*
**1** to try to obtain (goods) at a cheap price: [IØ + *for*] *The dealer spent hours bargaining for the valuable painting.* also **dicker for, haggle over**
* **2** also esp. *AmE* **bargain on** to expect; take

into account; consider (something): [T1 (*usu. neg.*)] *I had not bargained for such heavy rain, and got very wet without a coat.* → **calculate for** (2), **reckon for**

* **bargain on** *v prep*
**1** to depend on; trust in (someone, something, or doing something): [T1] *I'm bargaining on your help to drive us to the airport.* [T4] *Don't bargain on getting any support from her: she's very selfish.* [V4a] *I wouldn't bargain on the speaker arriving soon, as he's got a long way to come.* → **depend on** (1), etc.
**2** esp. *AmE* → **BARGAIN FOR** (2)

**bargain over** *v prep* → **BARGAIN ABOUT**

**bargain with** *v prep* also *not fml* **dicker with, haggle with**
to attempt to agree a price with (someone): [IØ + *with*] *The women are bargaining with their neighbours.*

**barge about/around** *v adv; prep*
*infml* to move awkwardly around (a place): [L9 + ABOUT/AROUND/*about*/*around*] *Please stop the children barging about (the house), they make so much noise.*

**barge against** *v prep*
*infml* to move awkwardly so as to hit (usu. something): [L9 + *against*] *The boy rushed in, barging against the door.*

**barge around** *v adv; prep* → **BARGE ABOUT**

**barge in** *v adv*
**1** *infml* to rush in rudely: [L9 + IN (*to*)] *The door burst open and the children barged in (to the room).*
***2** *infml* to interrupt rudely: [IØ (*to*)] *There was no need for you to barge in (to our conversation) with your remarks.*

**barge into** *v prep*
**1** *infml* to enter (a room, etc.) rudely: [L9 + *into*] *The children barged into the room, shouting.*
**2** *infml* to knock against (someone), usu. by accident: [L9 + *into*] *That rude man barged into me in the shop.*
* **3** *infml* to interrupt (usu. talk) rudely: [T1] *How rude of her to barge into the conversation.*
* **4** *infml* to meet (someone) by chance: [T1 (*no pass.*)] *I barged into an old friend in town today.* → **bump into** (2), etc.

**bark at** *v prep*
**1** (of a dog) to make a noise at (usu. someone): [IØ + *at*] *Our dog always barks at the postman.*
**2** to speak loudly and suddenly to (someone): [IØ + *at*] *I don't like the way that the teacher barks at the children so unkindly.*

**bark out** *v adv*
to shout (words, etc.) suddenly: [T1 + OUT] *The policeman barked out a warning as the gunmen appeared.*

**bark up** *v prep*
**bark up the wrong tree** to have a completely wrong idea about something: [*usu. continuous tenses*] *If you think I wrote that letter, you're barking up the wrong tree.*

* **barrel in** *v adv*
esp. *AmE not fml* (usu. of a storm) to arrive with force: [IØ (*often continuous tenses*)] *Another storm system is barrelling in and should reach eastern areas by tomorrow.*

* **barter away** *v adv* → **BARGAIN AWAY** (2,3)

**barter for** *v prep*
**1** to exchange (something) for (something else): [T1 + *for*] *The women in the market are bartering hens for milk.*
**2** to try to reach agreement about (something one wants): [IØ + *for*] *The captain went to the enemy camp to barter for the prisoner's life.*

**barter with** *v prep*
to try to agree with (someone) to exchange goods, etc.: [IØ + *with*] *The women are bartering with their neighbours.*

* **base on/upon** *v prep* → **found on, ground on**
to give (something) a reason or starting point in (something): [D1] *One should always base one's opinion on facts.*

**bash about/around** *v adv* → **bang about'** (2), **batter about, kick about** (4), **knock about** (4)
*infml* to treat (someone or something) roughly: [T1 + ABOUT/AROUND] *The man was put in prison for bashing his wife about. This old car looks as if it's been bashed about.*

**bash in** *v adv* → **beat in** (2)
**1** *not fml* to beat (something) inwards: [T1 + IN] *The firemen had to bash the door in.* → **crush in** (1), **stave in**
***2** *infml* to wound (usu. part of someone's body) by flattening it: [T1] *The boys robbed the old man and bashed his face in.*

**bash up** *v adv*
**1** *not fml* to damage or ruin (something): [T1 + UP] *He bashed up his car in the race.* → **smash up,** etc.
***2** *infml* to wound (someone) severely by hitting: [T1] *The boys robbed the old woman and bashed her up.* → **beat up** (2), etc. —**bashing-up** *n* —**bashed-up** *adj*

**bask in** *v prep*
**1** to sit or lie enjoying (usu. sunshine) falling on one: [L9 + *in* (*no pass., often continuous tenses*)] *I like to lie on the sand, basking in the sunshine.*
* **2** to enjoy (someone's favour, approval, etc.): [T1 (*no pass., often continuous tenses*)] *He wanted to bask in his employer's approval.*

* **bat around** *v adv*
**1** *infml* to hurry from place to place in a tiring manner: [IØ (*often continuous tenses*)] *The director has been batting around all day as usual, giving everybody orders.*
**2** *AmE sl* to talk about (an idea, etc.) in a free and informal way: [T1] *We batted the plan around for a while, but in the end decided against it as we hadn't enough money.*

**bathe in** *v prep*
**1** to wash oneself or swim in (water): [IØ + *in*] *Is it safe to bathe in this river?*

*__2__ to cover or fill (something) with (something such as light/water): [D1 (*usu. pass.*)] *His face was bathed in tears. The shores of Italy were bathed in sunshine.*

***batten down** *v adv*

**1** to fasten (something) as with boards of wood, usu. on a ship before a storm: [T1a] *Batten down the hatches!*

**2** to take firm action, preparing for trouble: [IØ] *Smith battens down.* (headline about Rhodesia, *The Guardian*, 8 August 1975).

***batten on/upon** *v prep* → **fatten on**

to live well by using (someone) for one's own purposes: [T1] *It's not fair to batten on your relatives.*

**batter about** *v adv* → **bash about**, etc.

to treat (someone or something) roughly: [T1 + ABOUT] *The man was put in prison for battering his wife about. The old car had been battered about by all its drivers.*

**batter down** *v adv*

to destroy (something) by beating continuously with a heavy object: [T1 + DOWN] *In the old days, the enemy would use a whole tree to batter down the door of a castle.*

**batter up** *v adv* → **smash up**, etc.

esp. *AmE* to damage; ruin (something): [T1 + UP] *He battered up his car in the race.* —**battered-up** *adj*

**battle against** *v prep*

**1** to fight (an enemy): [L9 + *against*] *The soldiers battled against the opposing army all day.*

**2** to oppose; try to defeat (something): [L9 + *against*] *The mountain climbers had to battle against great difficulties.*

**battle for** *v prep*

to fight for or struggle to gain or win (something): [L9 + *for*] *Our team and their opponents battled for the prize in the football match. Some rare wild animals are battling for their existence.*

**battle on** *v adv*

to continue to fight or struggle: [L9 + ON] *The opposing armies battled on until night. Women must battle on until they have gained equality.*

**battle out** *v adv*

**battle it out** to fight to a finish: *When I left, the two brothers were still battling it out behind the garage. Political enemies have to battle it out in public.*

**battle over** *v prep*

to fight about (something or someone): [IØ + *over*] *People whose marriage has ended often battle over the children.*

**battle with** *v prep*

**1** to struggle against (an enemy): [L9 + *with*] *Tomorrow we shall battle with our old enemies and defeat them.* → **do with** (12), **join with** (2)

*__2__ to struggle against (something or someone): [T1] *Scientists are still battling with many diseases. I've been battling with my conscience for several days, and now I know I have to write to you.* → **struggle with** (2), etc.

***baulk at** *v prep* → BALK AT

**bawl out** *v adv*

**1** to shout (something) in a loud, rough, ugly voice: [IØ + OUT] *Don't bawl out like that: I can hear you.* [T1 + OUT] *The captain bawled out his orders to the men.*

*__2__ *AmE infml* to scold (someone): [T1] *The director bawled Jim out for being late again.* —**bawling-out** *n* → **tell off** (1), etc.

**be about**[1] *v adv*

**1** to be nearby: [L9 + ABOUT] *There's nobody about, you'd better come back later. Jim is about somewhere, if you'd like to wait.* → **be around** (1).

*__2__ (of a disease, condition, etc.) to be present in quantity: [*There* + IØ] *Do dress warmly, there are a lot of colds about just now. Be careful how you drive, there are small rocks about in this area. Are there many gold coins about now?* → **go about**[1] (3), etc.

**be about**[2] *v prep*

**1** to concern (a subject): [L9 + *about*] *What is your new book about?*

**2** also **be around** to visit; move or travel round (a place): [L9 + *about*] *Where have you been? I've just been about the town.* → **get about**[2], etc.

**3** to do; perform: [L9 + *about*] *What are you about? I'm about my business.* → **send about**, etc.

**be above** *v prep*

**1** to be in a position higher than (something or someone): [L9 + *above*] *There's a branch above you—can you reach it?* → **be over**[2] (1)

**2** to be more than: [L9 + *above*] *The number of students in each class must not be above twenty.* → **be over**[2] (2)

**3** to have a higher rank than (someone or another rank): [L9 + *above*] *The captain of a ship is above a seaman.*

*__4__ to have a better standard of behaviour than (something or doing something): [T1 (*no pass.*)] *Aren't you above such childish behaviour?* [T4] *I would have thought that you were above talking behind someone's back.*

**5 be above oneself** *not fml* to be excited, often in a rude way: [*no pass.*] *The children have been above themselves ever since the rain stopped.*

**6 be above criticism/reproach/reproof/suspicion** to be praiseworthy, free of blame, of high moral standard, etc.: *Her action during the fire was above reproach. The chairman's decision is not above criticism.*

**7 be above one/one's head** to be too difficult for one to understand: *I wanted to hear the speaker, but most of what he said was above my head, so I fell asleep.* → **be over** (8)

**be abreast of** *v adv prep*

**1** to be level with (someone or something ahead): [L9 + ABREAST + *of*] *Jim was* *abreast of the leading runner for a few minutes but then fell behind.* → **keep abreast of** (1), etc.

*__2__ to know all the time the most recent facts about (something non-material): [T1 (*no pass.*)] *Scientists have to be abreast of the latest discoveries and developments if they want to advance in their profession.* → **keep abreast of** (2), etc.

**be after** *v prep*

**1** to be later than (a time): [L9 + *after*] *It's quite dark, it must be after 10 o'clock.*

*__2__ to chase (someone or an animal): [T1 (*no pass.*)] *"Why is the dog running so fast?" "He's after rabbits." Quick, hide me, the police are after me!* → **come after** (2), etc.

*__3__ to want; try to gain (something): [T1 (*no pass.*)] *Jim is after another job. Don't marry him, he's only after your money.* [T4] (*Irish infml*) *The old man is always after borrowing money.* → **go after** (3)

*__4__ *not fml* to scold; find fault with (someone); to keep asking (someone) to do (something): [T1 (*no pass.*)] *She's always after the children for one thing or another.* [V3] *She's been after me for a year to buy her a new coat.* → **go on at** (2), etc.

**be against** *v prep* → **go against** (1,2)

**1** to oppose (someone or something): [T1 (*no pass.*)] *Driving without seat belts may soon be against the law.* [T4; V4a] *Father was against (his daughter) marrying young.* → **go against** (1)

**2** to be opposite to (something): [T1] *Lying is against my principles.* [V3] *It's against nature to wear high shoes.* → **go against** (2)

**be ahead** *v adv* → **move ahead**, etc.

**1** to be in front, esp. in a competition: [L9 + AHEAD (*of*)] *And now Oxford are ahead; they're leading by three lengths.*

*__2__ to be in advance: [IØ (*of*)] *Jane used to have difficulty with her school work, but she's been ahead for several months now. That boy is always ahead of his fellows.*

**be ahead of** *v adv prep* → **keep ahead of**, etc.

**1** to be in a position in front of, beyond, or past (someone or something), as in a race: [L9 + AHEAD + *of*] *For a few minutes Jim was ahead of all the other runners, until his greatest competitor passed him.*

*__2__ to be more advanced than (someone or something): [IØ] *A great painter is usually ahead of his time.*

**be along** *v adv* → **come along** (2), etc.

to arrive: [L9 + ALONG (*to*) (*future tenses*)] *Jim will be along (to the meeting) in a minute.*

**be amiss** *v adj* → **come amiss, go amiss**

*fml* (usu. of an event) to be wrong, unexpected, out of order, etc.: [IØ] *The doctor said there was nothing amiss with her.*

**be around**[1] *v adv*

**1** to be alive, in the same place, or in a place nearby: [L9 + AROUND] *Jim is around somewhere, if you'd like to wait. Will you be around this time next year?* → **be about** (1), etc.

*__2__ (of a disease, condition, etc.) to be present in quantity: [*There* + IØ] *Do dress warmly, there are a lot of colds around just now. Motorists are being warned that there is thick mist around in the hills.* → **go about**[1] (3), etc.

*__3__ *not fml* (esp. of a performer or song, etc.) to be professionally active or popular: [IØ] *The singer you mentioned is still around, though not so well-known now. That song has been around for many years.*

*__4__ *infml usu. derog* to be socially and esp. sexually experienced: [IØ (*perfect tenses only*)] *You can see that she's a woman of the world—she's been around!*

**be around**[2] *v prep* → **BE ABOUT**[2] (2)

***be at** *v prep*

**1** *infml* to aim at; have (something) as a purpose: [T1 (*no pass.*)] *I don't understand what he's at in his new book.* → **drive at** (3), **get at** (4)

**2** *not fml* to scold; repeatedly ask or find fault with (someone): [T1 (*no pass.*)] *She's always at the children for one thing or another.* [V3] *She's been at me for the past year to buy her a new coat.* → **go on at** (2), etc.

**3** to perform (something) actively: [T1 (*no pass.*)] *Jim has been at his work for hours.* → **keep at** (3), etc.

**4** *infml* to be popular or fashionable: [T1 (*no pass.*)] *You must get your clothes in the King's Road; that's where it's at.*

**5** *infml* to touch (something that does not belong to one): [T1 (*no pass.*)] *Who's been at my things again?* → **meddle with** (1), etc.

**6** to attack (someone): [T1 (*no pass.*)] *Our men are ready, sir, all armed and eager to be at the enemy.*

**7** **be at attention** *mil* to be standing in a formal position, stiffly upright: *Do you call that being at attention? Stand up straight, man!* → **stand at** (3), etc.

**8** **be at a dead end** to be hopeless, unable to advance, etc.: *After days of arguing, the peace talks are now at a dead end.* → **bring to**[2] (7), **come to**[2] (19)

**9** **be at each other's throats** to be fierce enemies; attack each other with actions or words: *Don't let those dogs off their chains or they'll be at each other's throats in minutes! It wasn't long before the two leading politicians were at each other's throats as usual.*

**10** **be at ease** *mil* to stand in a comfortable position, with the feet apart and the hands behind the back: *Tell the men to be at ease, captain.* → **stand at** (4), **stand easy**

**11** **be at ease** to feel comfortable, esp. in the mind: *I never liked visiting her house, I was never at ease there in those formal rooms. I do like to be at ease in my mind about the children, so it helps when they telephone.*

**12** **be at an end** to have ceased: *My patience is*

*at an end, I can listen to her complaints no longer.* → **bring to** (8), **put to**[2] (12)

**13 be at a halt/standstill** to have ceased: *Work has been at a halt in the factory since the fire destroyed some of the machinery. The peace talks are at a standstill again*

**14 be hard at it/work** to be working hard: *I see the men are still hard at it—when do you think the digging will be finished? I like the classroom best when all the children are hard at work on ideas that they have chosen themselves.* → **keep at** (3), etc.

**15 be at home: a** to be in the house: *I'm sorry, Mr Baker is not at home; can I take a message?* **b** to be prepared to receive visitors: *If the minister calls, tell him I'm not at home. I'm not at home to any travelling salesmen. Mr and Mrs Fox will be At Home to their friends on Thursday evening from 7.30.*

**16 be at it** *not fml* to misbehave: *Those children are at it again, I'll have to stop them!*

**17 be at loggerheads** to have a severe disagreement: *The chairman and his committee are still at loggerheads, and it seems impossible for them to reach an agreement.*

**18 be at a loss** to be unable to think what to do or say: *The shock was so great that for a moment I was at a loss for words. We were at a loss to know what to do when the jewels were stolen.*

**19 be at odds** to disagree with someone over something: *The union is still at odds with the employers over the matter of working hours.*

**20 be at one** to be united with someone: *It's good to be at one with my husband after that terrible quarrel. We're so pleased that Jim and Mary are at one again.*

**21 be at pains to do something** to take great trouble: *I could hardly refuse the gift after she had been at such pains to make it.*

**be away** *v adv*

**1** to be stored in a container or place: [L9 + AWAY] *When all your toys are away, I will read you a story.*

**2** to leave: [L9 + AWAY] *We must try to be away by 8 o'clock.*

**3** to be absent: [L9 + AWAY] *So many children are away this week with colds.* → **keep away**, etc.

***4** *not fml* to be filled with one's own thoughts: [IØ] *Jim is away in a world of his own these days.*

***5** *not fml* to have a good chance of success: [IØ] *If the directors agree to a meeting, we're away!*

**6 be well away** *not fml* to have good luck; be in a good position: *Since he won all that money at the races, he's been well away!*

**be back** *v adv*

**1** to return: [L9 + BACK] *I'll be back when you least expect me.* → **go back** (2), etc.

**2** to return to fashion: [L9 + BACK] *Long skirts will be back next year.* → **come back** (3)

**3** to be put in its usual place again: [L9 + BACK] *When I returned from the police station, the jewels were back in their box; the thieves must have got frightened and replaced them.* → **put back** (2), etc.

**be before** *v prep*

**1** to be earlier than (someone or something): [L9 + *before*] *King Henry VII was before Queen Elizabeth I.* → **come before** (1)

***2** to appear before (a court of law) on a charge: [T1 (*no pass.*)] *Peter has been before the court again on a charge of driving while drunk.* → **bring before** (1), etc.

**3 be before one's time: a** to have taken place before one was born; belong to an earlier time: *No, I don't remember that film, it was before my time. During the war—but that was before your time, of course—it was difficult to get enough eggs.* **b** to be too advanced to be accepted by the people among whom one lives: *Turner was before his time with many of his paintings.*

**be behind**[1] *v adv*

**1** to be later than others: [L9 + BEHIND] *All the children came running in together, except Dick, who was behind as usual.* → **lag behind**[1] (1), etc.

***2** also **be behindhand** to be late, esp. concerning regular payments of money: [IØ (*in/with*)] *If your payments are behind, the court may take back the goods. If you are behind in/with your payments, the court may take back the goods.* → **get behind**[1] (2), etc.

***3** to be slow in learning: [IØ] *Jane is always top of her class, but Dick is often behind.*

**be behind**[2] *v prep*

**1** to be placed at the back of (something or someone): [L9 + *behind*] *Your letters are behind the clock, where I always put them.* → **keep behind** (1), **place behind** (1), **put behind**[2] (1)

***2** to cause; provide a reason for (something): [T1 (*no pass.*)] *What's behind his offer?* → **lie behind**[2] (3)

***3** to be less advanced than (something or someone): [T1 (*no pass.*)] *Your grandfather's ideas are a long way behind those of today. Why is Jane so often behind the rest of her class? Our production is now behind that of our competitors.* → **fall behind**[2] (3), etc.

**4 be behind bars** to be in prison: *How can he get a job after being behind bars for so long?* → **place behind** (3), **put behind**[2] (2)

**5 be behind the times** to be old-fashioned in one's ideas, not modern or advanced: *She really cares for the children, but some of her teaching methods are badly behind the times. You're behind the times, my dear, everyone talks like that nowadays!*

***be behindhand** *v adv* → BE BEHIND (2)

**be below**[1] *v adv*

**1** to be on a lower level: [L9 + BELOW] *The hotel is on the upper floors, and the shops are below.*

*2 to be under the floor of a ship: [IØ] *The captain was out in the bad weather but we were below where it was dry and warm.* → **go below, send below, take below**

**be below**[2] *v prep*

1 to be on a lower level than (something): [L9 + *below*] *The room where the wine is kept is below ground level.*

2 to be less than (usu. a number): [L9 + *below*] *The coat was below fifty dollars! My class was below ten students this year.* → **drop below** (1), etc.

*3 to be less good than (a standard): [T1 (*no pass.*)] *I'm disappointed in your work; it is below your usual standard.* → **drop below** (2), **fall below** (2), **get below** (2)

*4 to have lower rank than (someone or another rank): [T1 (*no pass.*)] *A captain is below a major. By joining the army late, he found that he was below many men much younger than himself.*

**be beneath** *v prep*

1 to be placed underneath (something or someone): [L9 + *beneath*] *The home of a rabbit is usually beneath the ground.* → **be under** (1)

*2 to be dishonourable for (someone) (to do something): [T1 (*no pass.*)] *Cheating at cards is beneath me.* [V3] *I should have thought it was beneath you to consider such an offer.*

3 **be beneath contempt** to be very low morally: *There is no excuse for him—his cruel treatment of his family is beneath contempt.*

4 **be beneath someone's dignity** to be dishonourable for someone (to do something): *Asking Jim to marry her was beneath Mary's dignity. It was beneath Mary's dignity to ask Jim to marry her.* → **fall beneath** (3)

5 **be beneath someone's notice** to be unworthy of attention: *Don't let what Jack said worry you; that man's opinion of your performance is beneath your notice.*

**be beside** *v prep*

1 to be placed next to (something or someone): [L9 + *beside*] *Your shoes are beside the chair. You shall be beside me in the church.*

2 **be beside oneself** to be very excited, as with happiness or anger: *Mary was beside herself with joy when she heard the good news. When Peter lost the race, he was beside himself with anger.*

3 **be beside the point** to be unconnected, unimportant: *You decided to come home for your own reasons; the fact that it rained is beside the point.*

**be between** *v prep*

1 to be in a position with one of (two things or people) on either side: [L9 + *between*] *The bank is between the shoe shop and the post office. In this photograph, I'm between Fred and my mother.*

2 **be between ourselves/you and me/you, me, and the gatepost** *not fml* to be a secret: *Remember that everything I've told you of the firm's plans is between ourselves. There is news that the Minister is to leave, but that's between you, me, and the gatepost.*

**be beyond** *v prep*

1 to be in a position behind or further than (something such as a place): [L9 + *beyond*] *The deer is beyond the trees; I can't shoot it from this distance. The valley where we live is beyond the mountains.* → **go past**[2] (1), etc.

*2 to go further than is allowed or expected by (something such as a duty): [T1 (*no pass.*)] *The soldier's brave deed was beyond the call of duty. Calling spirits from the dead proved to be beyond the magician's powers. The hospital says that the general is beyond medical help and will soon die. I'm afraid this old piano is now beyond repair so we'd better get rid of it.* → **go beyond** (2)

*3 to be greater than (something, such as an idea): [T1 (*no pass.*)] *The amount of money that I won was beyond all my hopes.* → **go beyond** (3)

*4 to be too difficult for (usu. someone) to do or understand: [T1 (*no pass.*)] *I'm afraid this book's beyond me; have you an easier one? The children tried to build a hut in the garden, but the work was beyond them and they had to ask their mother to help. It's beyond me which house to choose, they're both so nice!* [T4] *Now that he's older, Jim's father feels that he is beyond running the business on his own, and wants to employ someone to help him on busy days.* → **get past**[2] (5), etc.

5 **be beyond caring** → BE PAST (4)

6 **be beyond endurance** also **be past endurance** to be worse than someone can reasonably be expected to bear: *Your rudeness is beyond endurance—kindly leave my house!* → **get beyond** (5), etc.

7 **be beyond a joke** also **be past a joke** to cease being funny; become too serious: *Your continual lateness is now beyond a joke; if you're not on time tomorrow, you will be dismissed.* → **go beyond** (8), etc.

8 **be beyond one's ken** to be too difficult for one to understand or have knowledge of: *The details of different kinds of life insurance are quite beyond my ken, so I have to take the advice of professionals.*

9 **be beyond question** to exist or be true without doubt: *You can't possibly think Sheila took your watch; her honesty is beyond question.*

10 **be beyond redemption** also **be past redemption** to have got so bad as to have no hope of improvement: *In spite of all their efforts to put things right, it looks as if their relationship is beyond redemption. Is the state of the nation truly beyond redemption?*

**be by** *v adv*

1 to be near: [L9 + BY] *I looked round for help, but no one was by.*

* **2** to come near; visit; arrive: [IØ] *I'll be by in the morning and see what I can do.*

**be down** *v adv*

**1** to come downstairs in the morning: [L9 + DOWN] *Is Mary down yet? Her eggs are getting cold.*

* **2** (of a price, number, etc.) to be reduced, as by a certain amount: [IØ] *The price of milk should be down next week. Unemployment figures are down from last year. Bank rates will be down another point by next month.* → **go down¹** (6), etc.

* **3** to be less: [IØ] *Student numbers are down this year compared with last year.*

***4** to be recorded in writing: [IØ] *Make sure everything you've agreed is down on paper before you leave the meeting. Your contract says you must work at least 40 hours a week; it's down here in black and white.* → **write down** (1), etc.

**5 be down in the dumps/mouth** to be unhappy or unwell: *Mother was beginning to feel better, but she's down in the dumps again.*

***be down as** *v adv prep* → **put down as** (2), etc.
to be recorded as (being or doing something): [T1] *I see you're down as a singer, is that right?* [T4] *Why am I down as belonging to the other group?*

***be down for** *v adv prep*

**1** to have one's name entered for (usu. a competition): [T1] *Both the girls are down for the third race.* → **enter for**, etc.

**2 be down for the count/for a count of** (in boxing) to be knocked down while a judge counts ten or (the stated number of seconds): *I think the young fighter is down for the count, yes, it's all over! Last time he was only down for a count of three.*

* **be down on** *v adv prep*

**1** to find fault with (someone): [T1 (*no pass.*)] *The teacher is always down on the slower students. The director was down on Jim this morning for being late again.* → **tell off** (1), etc.

**2** to be quick to find (a mistake): [T1 (*no pass.*)] *Be careful with the report you send to the director, as he'll be down on any little mistake in a moment!*

**3 be down on one's luck** to have a period of bad luck, esp. concerning money: *What are friends for, except to help you when you're down on your luck for a short time?* → **be in¹** (12)

***be down to** *v adv prep*
to have left only (a little money or goods): [T1 (*no pass.*)] *I was down to my last penny when at last I found a job. Thanks so much, I was down to my last cigarette.*

***be down with** *v adv prep* → **come down with** (2), **go down with** (3)
to be ill with (a disease): [T1 (*no pass.*)] *Jane was down with a cold last week, so she didn't come to work.*

**be for** *v prep*

**1** to have (something) as a purpose: [L9 + *for*] *What's this wooden thing for? It's for beating the eggs.*

**2** to be intended as a gift for, or for the use of (someone): [L9 + *for*] *This money behind the clock is for Mary to pay the milkman.*

***3** to support; favour (something, doing something, or someone): [T1 (*no pass.*)] *I'm for the chairman's plan, aren't you?* [T1] *Yes, I'm all for it.* [T4] *No, I'm for keeping the old methods.*

**4 be for it** *infml* to be about to receive punishment: *You'll be for it when they find out who broke the window.* → **be in for** (4)

**5 be for the high jump** *infml* to be about to receive severe punishment: *You'll be for the high jump when they find out who stole that money.*

**be from** *v prep*
to have one's origins in (a place): [L9 + *from*] *Where are you from? I'm from South America.*

***be hip to** *v adj prep* → **get hip to**
*AmE infml* to be knowledgeable about (a subject): [T1 (*no pass.*)] *He likes to be hip to the latest styles in popular music.*

**be in¹** *v adv*

**1** to be in place: [L9 + IN] *Is the nail in?* → **take out** (2), etc.

**2** to be at home or in one's place of work: [L9 + IN] *Phone him at the office, he should be in now.* → **go out** (1), etc.

**3** to arrive: [L9 + IN] *The train will be in a little late tonight.* → **get in¹** (4). etc.

* **4** (of a message, etc.) to be received: [IØ] *As soon as the total figures are in, we can make our calculations.*

***5** to be elected: [IØ] *Let me know who's in as soon as the results arrive.* → **get in¹** (13), etc.

***6** to be fashionable: [IØ] *Long skirts will be in again next year.* → **come in** (10), etc.

***7** (esp. in cricket) to have one's turn on the field of play: [IØ] *If three of our team are out, who's in now?* → **be out** (7), etc. **go in** (5), etc.

***8** (of a fire) to burn: [IØ] *I hope the fire's still in when we get home.* → **keep in¹** (6), etc.

***9** (of a crop) to be gathered, esp. ready for sale: [IØ] *Luckily all the wheat was in before the rain began. The first apples should be in next week.* → **take in¹** (7)

***10** (of the tide) to have reached its position nearest to land; be at high watermark: [IØ] *When the tide is in, it covers most of the sand, and sometimes reaches the seawall.* → **be out** (11), **come in** (7), **go out** (11)

**11 be all in** *infml* to be very tired: *Let us rest here for a while, I'm all in.*

**12 one's luck be in** to have a period of good luck: *I think I'll put some money on the next race, while my luck is in.* → **be down on** (3)

**be in²** *v prep*

**1** to exist in (a place or time): [L9 + *in*] *The*

*photographs are in the bottom drawer. There are cows in that field, let's go another way. That was in the last century, when life was much slower.* → **be out of** (1), etc., **come into** (1), **get into** (1), **go into** (1), **keep in** (1), **remain in²** (1), **stay in²** (1), **stick in²** (6), **stop in²** (1)
**2** to work or be concerned in (a business): [L9 + *in*] *Mary's father did not want her to marry Jim because he was in trade. Two of his brothers are in printing, the other in law.* → **go into** (8)
**3** to exist in (a state or condition): [L9 + *in*] *The price was reasonable, and the house was in good condition. You must understand that you are in a greatly weakened condition after your attack of fever, and must take things easy for a time. How long has this system been in existence? Our plan has been in action for two months now. I've never been in debt before. How can you tell when you're in love? You're lucky to be in work when so many people are unemployed. This government has been in power long enough. Are the new apples in season yet? This train will no longer be in service after next week.* → **get into** (11), etc.
**4 be in abeyance** (usu. of a law, plan, etc.) to be put on one side for the time being; not be enforced yet: *The usual rules of the game are in abeyance during informal practices.* → **go into** (13)
**5 be in someone's bad books/black books/good graces** *infml* to be regarded with disapproval/approval by someone at the present time: *It's no good asking for favours while you're in the teacher's bad books. I think he was given the job because his father was in the director's good graces for some favour he'd done him in the past.* → **get into** (15)
**6 be in bad/good odour (with)** to feel the effect of the low or high opinion of oneself held by (someone): *I won't come to the house while I'm still in bad odour with your mother, though I don't know what I've done to offend her.*
**7 be in cahoots/league (with)** *infml* to have a relationship (with someone) in which secret plans are formed: *Don't trust him with the workers' plans, he's in cahoots with the directors.*
**8 be in the dark (about)** *not fml* to fail to understand (something) or to share a secret or information: *I'm still in the dark as to what the secretaries intend to do to amuse us at the office party.* → **keep in** (7)
**9 be in deep water (over)** *not fml* to be in difficulty (with something): *I seem to be in deep water over this calculation; can you help me?* → **get into** (16)
**10 be in the doghouse** *infml* to be in trouble from someone, often within a family; win disapproval by one's behaviour: *I forgot my wife's birthday, so I'm in the doghouse again!*
**11 be in evidence** to be noticeable: *Young people were much in evidence at the concert.*
**12 be in focus** to be clearly understood or known: *Now that all sides of the question are in focus, can we please reach a decision?* → **bring into** (4), **come into** (6)
**13 be in force** (of a law, rule, etc.) to have power; become law; have to be obeyed: *The new law will be in force as soon as it has been signed by the Queen. Military rule is once more in force on the island.* → **bring into** (5), **come into** (7), **put into** (14)
**14 be in the forefront** to be in an advanced or leading position: *Even while he was in the forefront of the battle, the young soldier kept a cool head and acted bravely. Only a few scientists are in the forefront of knowledge, making new discoveries.*
**15 be in the front rank** to be of the best quality; be ahead of one's opponents: *It won't be long before our company is in the front rank of banking firms, if we go on doing so well.*
**16 be in hand** (usu. of work) to have been started: *The printers say that Tom's book is now in hand and will be ready by the beginning of next month.* → **have in²** (5), **take in²** (10)
**17 be in someone's hands** to be the responsibility of someone: *Trust in God, we're all in his hands. I'm glad that the arrangements are in such safe hands.* → **be out of** (11)
**18 be in hot water/the soup** *infml* to be in trouble: *You'll be in hot water when the director finds out what you've been doing with the supplies.* → **get into** (22)
**19 be in a jam** *not fml* to be in a severe difficulty: *You've got to help me, I'm really in a jam this time; I took some money, intending to put it back, but they've discovered the loss—what can I do?* → **get into** (22)
**20 be in keeping (with)** to be suitable (to something): *Be sure to choose pictures which are in keeping with your style of furniture.* → **be out of** (15)
**21 be in luck** to be lucky on this one occasion: *You're in luck—the very car you want has just come in.* → **be out of** (17)
**22 be in the mire** to have trouble, esp. concerning money: *We've been in the mire for some time, but the firm's future is now looking brighter.*
**23 be in the money** *infml* to be newly rich: *"We're in the money, we're in the money."* (song)
**24 be in the open** to be publicly known, not hidden: *This government's intentions will always be in the open. I'm glad that the affair is in the open at last, and we no longer have the shame of trying to keep it secret.* → **bring into** (7), **come into** (10)
**25 be in order: a** to be neatly or properly arranged: *I want to make sure that all my affairs are in order before I die, so as to save my relatives trouble. Is your desk in order? The director is coming to examine it.* → **be out of** (19a), **keep in** (11), **put in²** (21), **set in²** (11): **b** to

be working properly: *It will be a great help when the telephone is in order again.* → **be out of** (19b): **c** to be correct according to the rules, esp. for speaking formally: *Is it in order for me to ask a question before making my speech?* → **be out of** (19c)

**26 be in the picture** *not fml* to be included in matters; understand what is happening: *Please tell me what this is all about, I'm not in the picture yet.* → **be out of** (20), **put in²** (22)

**27 be in play: a** (of a ball) to have not yet come to rest; be within the limits of space or time in a game: *While the ball is in play, no player may leave the field.* → **be out of** (21), **go out of** (12): **b** to have an effect, influence or force: *Many considerations are in play in this set of peace talks.* → **bring into** (8), **call into** (4), **come into** (12)

**28 be in the public eye** to be well-known through frequent public appearances: *You have to be careful what you say when you're always in the public eye.*

**29 be in one's right mind** to be able to think clearly and use one's reason to make judgments: *The murderer was judged not guilty, as he had not been in his right mind at the time of the murder.* → **be out of** (18), **go out of** (10)

**30 be in the right/wrong: a** to be correct/incorrect in one's judgment: *When we are trying to reach agreement, why do you always act as if you're the only one who's in the right? Why are you always trying to prove that I'm in the wrong?* **b** to behave well/badly: *I'm sorry, I was in the wrong; I shouldn't have spoken so unkindly without thinking.* → **put in² (31)**

**31 be in the running (for)** *not fml* to be regarded as worthy of consideration (for a reward, prize, etc.): *Have you heard that Tom's book is in the running for the Book of the Year prize?* → **be out of** (27)

**32 be in sight/view** to be able to be seen: *Is land in sight yet? Although the town had been in view for an hour, we seemed to be getting no nearer.* → **keep in** (16), etc.

**33 be in step** (of a group, usu. of soldiers) to be marching with the feet moving in the same time together: *The men should not be in step when they cross the bridge.* → **be out of** (30), **keep in** (18)

**34 be well in hand** to be under control: *The fire is well in hand and we are now sure that the building will be saved. Rising prices should be well in hand before the end of the year.* → **have in²** (16)

* **be in at** *v adv prep*

**1** *infml* to be present at (the end or completion of something): [T1] *Having put all this work into the plan, I want to be in at the finish.*

**2 be in at the death/kill: a** to be present when the fox is killed at the end of a hunt: *Is it really a good idea for the children to be in at the kill?* **b** to witness the completion of something: *I hope to be in at the death when the firm at last signs that big contract.*

* **be in for** *v adv prep*

**1** to be able to expect (something, often bad): [T1 (*no pass.*)] *It looks as if we're in for some bad weather.*

**2** to have entered one's name for (a competition): [T1 (*no pass.*)] *Are you in for the running race?* → **enter for**, etc.

**3** to have asked for (a position): [T1 (*no pass.*)] *How many people are in for the director's job now?* → **pony up for, put in for** (4)

**4 be in for it/trouble** to be about to receive punishment: *You'll be in for it/trouble when they find out who broke the window.* → **be for** (4)

* **be in on** *v adv prep*

**1** *infml* to share; take a leading part in (some activity): [T1] *Alice is always wanting to be in on the act. Jane was annoyed because the boys didn't want her to be in on their plans.* → **get in on** (1), etc.

**2 be in on the ground floor** *infml* to start in business at the beginning or lowest level: *The best way to ensure your success is to make sure to be in on the ground floor.* → **get in on** (2), etc.

* **be in with** *v adv prep*

**1** *infml* to be in favour with; share secrets with (someone): [T1 (WELL)] *I think the local police are in with the criminals. I could get you a better price on that, I'm well in with their chief buyer.* → **get in with** (2), etc.

**2 be in accord/harmony with** to have a good relationship with (someone); have the same opinion and tastes as (someone else); match or agree with (something): *Luckily, the chairman's views are in accord with those of his committee. Being in harmony with one's fellow workers is an important part of any job.*

**3 be in bad with** esp. *AmE infml* to have a bad relationship with; have (someone, often in a position of power) as an enemy: *It's no good you expecting me to get favours from the director, I've been in bad with him since my first day, when I broke the machine.* → **get in with** (3)

**4 be in collision with** to crash into (another vehicle or ship): *The car was totally destroyed after being in collision with a bus.* → **collide with** (1)

**5 be in collusion with** to agree secretly with (someone), often to do something unlawful or immoral: *Who would ever have thought that the police themselves were in collusion with the criminals?*

**6 be in line with** to follow (an idea, etc., as a principle or rule) exactly: *His suggestion was refused by the committee because it was not in line with the party's way of thinking.* → **be out of** (16), etc.

**be inside** *v adv*

**1** to be placed in a space or container; be indoors: [L9 + INSIDE] *The key must be inside; how can we reach it? She decided that it was best to be inside in such nasty weather.*

*__2__ *infml* to be in prison: [IØ] *It can't have been Baker who stole the jewels, he's still inside.* → **be out** (16), **come out** (4)

***be into** *v prep*

*infml* to take a (new) interest in (something): [T1 (*no pass.*)] *She doesn't eat meat now, she's really into health food.*

**be of** *v prep*

**1** to have (a quality, feeling, etc.): [L9 + *of*] *Mary is of such a gentle nature.*

**2 be of age** to have reached the age when one is considered by law able to take responsibility for oneself: *I don't get the fortune until I'm of age, so we'll have to wait.* → **come of** (4)

**3 be of one mind** to agree completely: *Luckily, my husband and I are of one mind on such matters.*

**4 be rid of** to be able to lose or be free of (something or someone unwanted): *I'm glad to be rid of that complaining woman at last. Shall we ever be rid of this cold weather?* → **get of** (10), **rid of**

**5 be of sound/unsound mind** *law* to be able/unable to make reasonable judgments; be sane/mad: *The judge ruled that the man had killed himself while he was of unsound mind. I, being of sound mind, wish my wife to have all my property after my death.*

**be off**[1] *v adv*

**1** to be disconnected; not be working: [L9 + OFF] *Make sure the water is off before you leave. Are you sure the lights are off?* → **put off**[1] (3), etc.

*__2__ to go; leave: [IØ] *I must be off now, I've a train to catch.* → **go away** (1), etc.

*__3__ *infml* to go away: [IØ (*usu. imper.*)] *Be off! Get out of my garden! Be off with you!* → **push off** (3), etc.

*__4__ to start moving, esp. in a race: [IØ] *They're off!* (shout at the beginning of a horse race) → **get away** (3), **get off**[2] (6)

*__5__ (of an event) to fail to take place as arranged: [IØ] *Mary has changed her mind again, the wedding is off.*

*__6__ (of food in a restaurant) to be no longer offered: [IØ] *I'm sorry, the lamb is off, may I suggest some chicken?* → **take off**[1] (11)

*__7__ (of food) to have gone bad: [IØ] *This fish is off, I won't buy it.* → **go bad, go off**[1] (8)

*__8__ to be free from duty or hours of work: [IØ] *I'm off at 6.00; let's meet then.* → **get off**[1] (4)

*__9__ *not fml* to begin speaking at length (about a subject): [IØ (*on*)] *Oh dear, Father's off again on his favourite subject—himself!* → **be on about, go on**[1] (7), **keep on** (8), **run on**[1] (1)

*__10__ *not fml* to be provided (with something): [L9 (*for*)] *How are you off for clothes?*

**11 be badly/well off (for)** to have (not) a lot of money or supplies (of something): *Jim is not rich, but he's not badly off. You must be badly off for books if you're reading that silly story. It doesn't matter if your husband isn't well off, if he can make you happy. You seem to be well off for shoes, I've never seen so many!*

**12 be better off** to be in a better position; be wise to choose (doing something): *You'd be better off leaving the country.*

**13 be better off without** to be in a worse position with (something or doing something): *I'd be better off without your everlasting complaints.*

**14 be way off: a** to be distant: *This is the wrong road, we must be way off by now.* **b** to be greatly mistaken: *Your guess was way off, it's nothing like that at all.*

**be off**[2] *v prep*

**1** to have come loose from (something): [L9 + *off*] *There's a button off my coat — would you sew it on for me?*

*__2__ to stay away from (work); finish (work, duty, etc.): [T1 (*no pass.*)] *Jane was off school all last week with her cold. What time are you off work tonight?* → **stay off** (3), etc.

*__3__ to stop taking (medicine): [T1 (*no pass.*)] *How soon can mother be off her medicine?*

*__4__ to cease to want or be interested in (something): [T1 (*no pass.*)] *Jane has been off her food since she caught a cold. I've been off that kind of music for some time now.* → **go off**[2] (2), **put off**[2] (2), **turn off**[2] (3)

**5 be off one's chump/head/nut/rocker** *infml* to have lost one's senses; be unable to make judgments based on reason; be mad: *You must be off your chump, going out in weather like this! Is he off his head? Everyone knows his partner can't be trusted.* → **go off**[2] (7)

**6 be off one's game** (in sport) to be not playing very well at the moment: *I'm sorry, I seem to be off my game today; let's play again tomorrow.*

**7 be off one's hands** *not fml* to cease to be one's responsibility: *I'm so glad to have that troublesome boy off my hands now that his parents have returned from abroad.*

**8 be off the hook** *infml* to be no longer in a position of having to make a decision: *When Jim was called into the director's office, he expected to have to answer some questions, but the conversation was purely social so he was off the hook.* → **be on** (17)

**9 be off limits (to)** *AmE often mil* (of a place) to be forbidden (to certain people) to enter: *Don't let the captain catch you in this cafe; it's off limits to ordinary soldiers.*

**10 be (quick) off the mark** *not fml* to waste no time in taking advantage: *The company was very quick off the mark in printing that book about the capture of the plane, only weeks after the event. You have to be off the mark at once if you're to act on his advice, it always concerns matters of the moment.*

***be off to** *v adv prep*

to begin with (something): [T1] *If Jim and*

*Mary are quarrelling already, it looks as if their marriage is off to a bad start.*

***be off with** *v adv prep* → **be on with**
*not fml* to get rid of (something): [T1] *Be off with the old love before you are on with the new.*

**be on¹** *v adv*
**1** to be fixed or balanced on top: [L9 + ON] *When you've been on for a minute, you will find it easier to keep your balance on the horse. Is the lid on tightly?*
**2** to be connected; be working: [L9 + ON] *I thought you were in when I saw that the light was on.* → **put on¹** (3), etc.
***3** (of an event, performance, court case, etc.) to be arranged; take place: [IØ] *This magazine tells us what's on in town this week. Is the wedding still on? Is there a case on in the Central Criminal Court?* → **have on¹** (3), **put on¹** (9)
***4** to be on duty: [IØ] *Two firemen must be on from midnight to 6 o'clock.* → **come on¹** (13)
***5** to take one's turn on the stage or sports field: [IØ] *Who's on next? After Botham had been on for several minutes, the other team's defeat became certain.* → **come on¹** (4), etc.
***6** *infml* to agree to take part in a plan, etc.: [IØ] *When Father suggested a visit to the island, Jane said, "I'm on!"*
**7 it's not on** *infml* it is impossible or cannot be considered: *Two of the men refused to take the money, saying, "It's not on."*
**8 be well on (into)** (of time) to be getting late towards (part of the day, week, etc.): *It was well on into the evening before the expected telephone call came.*

**be on/upon²** *v prep*
**1** to be fixed, placed, or balanced on top of (usu. something): [L9 + *on/upon*] *There's a big bird on our chimney! Make sure that the lid is firmly on the box. Your meal is already on the table. How long have you been on that bicycle?* → **keep on** (1), **stay on²** (1)
**2** to travel in (a certain direction): [L9 + *on/upon*] *We had been on our way for an hour when the rain started. Are you sure the ship is on the correct course?* → **keep on** (2), **remain on²** (1), **stay on²** (2)
***3** to take one's part or position in (something): [T1 (*no pass.*)] *Two firemen must be on duty from midnight to 6 o'clock. Who's on first base?* → **come on²** (6)
***4** to take (medicine) regularly: [T1 (*no pass.*)] *Mother has been on that medicine for months, and it doesn't seem to do her any good. I've been on this treatment for some weeks and I must say I do feel better.* → **keep on** (3), **stay on²** (3)
***5** (of money) to have been placed as a risk supporting (a competitor): [T1 (*no pass.*)] *My money's on Jim, is yours?* [V3] *Our money's on Northern Dancer to win the third race.* → **bet on** (1), etc.
***6** *not fml* to be paid for by (someone): [T1 (*no pass.*)] *Put your money away, this meal is on me.*
**7 be on the ball** *not fml* to be ready to take opportunities; be quick to see a chance: *If you're to make any money in business, you've got to be on the ball all the time.*
**8 be on the blink** *infml* to fail to work: *The washing machine is on the blink again; we'd better send for the electrician.* → **go on** (12)
**9 be on the boil: a** (of a liquid) to have reached the boiling point: *As soon as the water is on the boil, put the vegetables in.* **b** *not fml* to be ready, as for talk, action, etc.: *If you can catch him while he's still on the boil, you could get him to sign the contract straight away.* → **go off²** (5), **keep on** (4)
**10 be on edge** to be nervous: *I've been on edge all day, waiting for that telephone call.*
**11 be on one's feet: a** to stand, esp. for a long time: *I've been on my feet all day, it's time you did some work.* → **get to** (11), etc. **b** to be well again after illness: *It's good to see that you are on your feet again.* → **get on²** (5), etc. **c** to stand to speak in public: *The speaker has been on his feet for four hours; he must be trying to defeat the time allowance for this new law.* → **get on²** (4)
**12 be on guard: a** to fulfil a military duty: *Two soldiers must be on guard all night.* **b** to be careful: *You must be on guard against making more careless mistakes.* → **put on²** (18)
**13 be hard on** to treat (someone) severely: *Don't be too hard on the boy for what he did, he's only young.*
**14 be on someone's head** to be the responsibility of someone: *If you insist on marrying that man, be it on your own head!*
**15 be hell-bent on** *infml* to desire and attempt to gain (something or doing something) with unceasing effort: *Why is that boy so hell-bent on a job in the theatre? Jim seems hell-bent on winning the race since he lost it last year.*
**16 be on one's honour** to be trusted to keep one's promise, not to cheat, etc.: *You children are on your honour not to look at each other's papers while I'm out of the room.* → **put on²** (21), etc.
**17 be on the hook** *infml* to be forced into a position of having to make a decision: *Faced with the committee's request for urgent action, the director was on the hook.* → **be off²** (8), **get off²** (12), **let off²** (3)
**18 be on the house** (of a drink, meal, etc.) to be free, paid for by the owner of the pub, hotel, restaurant, etc.: *Drinks are on the house tonight!*
**19 be on ice** *not fml* (of a decision) to be delayed till a later time: *All our plans are on ice till we know whether we are leaving the city or not.* → **put on²** (23)
**20 be on the map** (esp. of a place) to be well-known: *This little village has only been on the map since it produced the famous cricketer.* → **put on²** (25)

**21 be on oath** also **be under oath** to have sworn a solemn promise, as to tell the truth in court: *Be careful how you answer, remember you're on oath.* → **put on²** (21), etc.

**22 pressure be on** efforts are being made to force (someone or a group) to do something: *The pressure has been on the firm for some time to move out of the capital city.*

**23 be on the safe side** *not fml* to take no risk: *Let's take more money than we think we'll need, just to be on the safe side.*

**24 be on the scene** to have arrived, as to witness or take part in something: *How long have the police been on the scene? It was not long before a large crowd was on the scene.*

**25 be on top of** → **STAY ON** (8)

**26 be on trial** to face a court of law on a charge: *The prisoner is on trial for murder.*

**27 be on/upon us** to be about to happen: *It won't be long before Christmas is upon us again!*

* **be on about** *v adv prep*

to talk at length about (a subject): [T1 (*no pass.*)] *Is she still talking? What's she on about this time?* → **be off¹** (9), **go on¹** (7), **keep on** (8), **run on¹** (1)

* **be on at** *v adv prep* → **go on at** (2), etc.

*not fml* to scold; repeatedly ask or find fault with (someone): [T1] *She's always on at the children for one thing or another.* [V3] *Mother's always on at me to keep my room tidy.*

* **be on with** *v adv prep* → **be off with**

*not fml* to begin with (something): [T1] *Be off with the old love before you are on with the new.*

* **be onto** *v prep*

**1** to get in touch with (someone), esp. by telephone: [T1 (*no pass.*)] *I've been onto the director, but he says he can't help.* → **get onto** (6), **put onto** (2)

**2** *not fml* to keep asking (someone) (to do something): [V3] *She's been onto me to buy her a new coat for a year.* → **go on at** (2), etc.

**3** *not fml* to discover (a secret or someone doing something wrong): [T1 (*no pass.*)] *Don't think I haven't been onto your little plan for some time. The police are onto us, we'd better hide.* → **get onto** (9), **put onto** (3)

**4 be onto a good thing** *not fml* to understand and seize a lucky chance: *The secret of his success as a businessman is that he always knows when he's onto a good thing.* → **put onto** (4)

**be open** *v adj* → **keep open** (2), **remain open** (2), **stay open** (2), **stop open** (2)

(of a shop, etc.) to do business: [L9 + open] *Are the shops open late on Thursdays?*

**be out** *v adv*

**1** to be removed: [L9 + OUT] *There, the tooth is out now! The mark will be out very soon.* → **take out** (2), etc.

**2** to be not at home or work: [L9 + OUT (*at*)] *I'm sorry, Mr Sharp is out, can I take a message? Mother was out at the shops when they called.* → **go out** (1), etc.

**3** (of a light or fire) to have stopped burning: [L9 + OUT] *The fire was out before the firemen arrived.* → **put out** (13), etc.

* **4** to be on duty in public, esp. out of doors: [IØ (*in*)] *Why are there so many police out today? There are so many soldiers out in the little town today.* → **be out in** (2)

* **5** to appear in flower: [IØ] *The roses should be out next week.* → **bring out** (3), **come out** (5), **fetch out** (2)

* **6** to be unfashionable: [IØ] *Long skirts are out one year and in the next.* → **come in** (10), etc.

* **7** to be forced to stop playing by the rules of a game, as cricket: [IØ] *When Jim was out there were only three men left in the team.* → **be in¹** (7), **bowl out** (1), **catch out** (2), **get out** (16), **give out** (7), **go in** (5), etc., **put out** (21), **run out** (9), **throw out** (13)

* **8** to end: [IØ] *The sun will shine before the day is out.*

* **9** to make mistakes (in something): [IØ (*in*)] *I was out in my calculations. No, I'm sorry, you're a long way out if you think that.* → **throw out** (9), etc.

* **10** to be printed or otherwise made known: [IØ] *It's no use trying to keep it a secret, the story is out now. When will the next magazine be out?* → **let out** (5), etc.

* **11** (of the sea) to be far from the shore: [IØ] *When the tide is out, the sand stretches for a long way.* → **be in¹** (10), **come in** (7), **go out** (11)

* **12** (of the sun, moon, or stars) to appear: [IØ] *Look, the moon is out, isn't it beautiful!*

* **13** to stop working because of disagreement [IØ] *The miners will be out until their demands are met.* → **bring out** (7), etc.

* **14** to be asked to leave a group: [IØ] *If they find out what you did with the club money, you'll be out on your ear! Anyone who refuses to accept the new committee is out at once.* → **throw out** (4), etc.

* **15** *not fml* to be impossible to be considered: [IØ] *In view of the increased cost, I'm afraid a new car is out this year.* → **be out of** (24)

* **16** to be released from prison: [IØ] *When will you be out? I shan't be out for another year yet. You could be out sooner if you behave yourself.* → **be inside** (2), **come out** (4)

* **17** to be unconscious: [IØ] *When he was out for more than ten minutes, we got worried. At the first blow, he was out for the count. He could be hurt, he's out like a light.* → **knock out** (3), etc.

* **18** (of an official paper, as a warrant) to be given as a written order to seize (someone): [IØ (*against*)] *There's a warrant out for your brother—are you hiding him from the police?*

* **19** esp. *AmE not fml* to be not working, usu. through damage: [IØ] *The telephones are out along most of the coast since the storm.*

**20 be out to do something** *not fml* to intend

to do something: *I don't think she was out to cause trouble, she just didn't think. The government is out to prevent people from cheating on unemployment money.*

***be out for** *v adv prep* → **go out** (15)
*not fml* to aim to get: [T1] *Jane was always out for a good time.*

***be out from** *v adv prep*
to have left (a place) by a certain time or distance: [T1 (*no pass.*)] *The boat was two kilometres out from the harbour when the storm struck. Don't give the pilot the letter of instructions until you are at least two hours out from home.*

* **be out in** *v adv prep*
**1** to make mistakes in (something): [T1] *I think that the directors were out in their judgment. I was out in my calculations.* → **throw out** (9), etc.
**2 be out in force/large numbers/strength** to be on public outdoor duty as a considerable number: *Police had to be out in strength in case the crowd caused any trouble.* → **be out** (4)

**be out of** *v adv prep*
**1** to be not in (a place): [L9 + OUT + *of*] *I hadn't heard the news, I've been out of the country. Mr Sharp is out of town until next week. Those rabbits are out of their cages again!* → **be in²** (1), etc., **come out from** (1), **come out of** (1), **get out of** (1), **go out of** (1), **take out of** (1)
**2** to be removed from (something): [L9 + OUT + *of*] *I think that piece of dirt is out of your eye now. Is that dirty mark out of the tablecloth yet?* → **take out** (2), etc.
***3** to lack a supply of (something): [T1 (*no pass.*)] *I'm sorry, we're out of coffee.* (*AmE*) *I'm sorry, we're all out of coffee. Have you any suggestions to make? I'm out of ideas. I'm quite out of patience with this class. No singer should ever be out of breath.* → **give out** (5), **run out** (8), **run out of** (4)
***4** to cease or fail to exist in (a state or condition); be free of (something): [T1 (*no pass.*)] *At last the firm is out of debt. The boy is never out of trouble. Young girls are rarely out of love. This train will be out of service after next Monday. No, we've no local apples, they're out of season. It was good to hear that your mother is out of danger after her operation. How many people in this country are now out of work? We've been out of contact for many years. I can't get this right, I've been out of practice for so long. Yes, the table is out of my way now that you've moved it. I've been out of the habit of locking the door, I must try to remember to do this regularly here in the city.* → **get into** (11), etc.
**5 be out of action** esp. *mil* to be no longer working: *The enemy guns are out of action, so the army can advance.* → **put out** (23), etc.
**6 be out of the blue** to be completely unexpected: *This offer of yours is out of the blue; I must have time to think about it.* → **come out of** (3)
**7 be out of date** to be not considered modern: *Your ideas are all out of date, they're stuck in the last century.* —**outdated** *adj* → **be up to** (7), etc.
**8 be out of one's depth: a** to be in water that is deeper than one's height: *Jim nearly drowned, he was out of his depth.* **b** *not fml* to find something too difficult to do or understand: *I'm out of my depth when it comes to natural sciences.* → **get out of** (20), **go out of** (6)
**9 be out of earshot (of)** to be too far away to hear or be heard (by someone or from a place): *As soon as she was out of earshot of the children, she burst into loud laughter. Make sure you are out of earshot of the others before you tell me the secret.* → **come within** (3), etc.
**10 be out of hand** to be out of control: *That class is out of hand; I should have put a more experienced teacher in charge.* → **get out of** (24)
**11 be out of one's hands** to be no longer under one's control: *The case is out of my hands now that the police have taken charge.* → **be in²** (17)
**12 be out of harm's way** to be in a safe place; do a safe activity, etc.: *The children don't do very much at their youth club, but at least they're out of harm's way.* → **keep out of** (3), **stay out of** (3)
**13 be out of humour** to be in a bad temper: *Why are you so out of humour today? Is it because of the weather?*
**14 be out of it** *infml* to feel strange, unwanted, or not part of a group: *Whenever I'm the only older person among all these young people, I feel that I am out of it.* → **feel out of** (1), **leave out¹** (5), **miss out** (2)
**15 be out of keeping (with)/place** to be unsuitable (to something): *This old style of furniture is out of keeping with the modern appearance of the house. Among the group of polite people, his rough manners were out of place.* → **be in²** (20)
**16 be out of line** *not fml* to be against expected behaviour; be wrong: *Wasn't that remark rather out of line? Your sudden offer to help him was out of line; I think he was offended.* → **be in with** (6), **bring into** (6), **come into** (9), **fall into** (11), **get out of** (29), **keep in** (9)
**17 be out of luck** to be unlucky: *You're out of luck, I just sold the last paper.* → **be in²** (20)
**18 be out of one's mind** to be mad; behave in a foolish way: *Are you out of your mind, giving the baby matches to play with? Poor man, his wife is out of her mind and has to be locked up in a special hospital.* → **be in²** (29), **go out of** (10)
**19 be out of order: a** to be disarranged: *Why are all my papers out of order? I left them in the right places.* → **be in²** (25a), etc.: **b** to be broken, no longer working: *The telephone is*

*out of order, you'll have to make your call from a public phone.* → **be in²** (25b): **c** to be against the rules, esp. for speaking formally: *The chairman ruled that the committee member was out of order and could not be allowed to speak until the first speaker had finished.* → **be in²** (25c)

**20 be out of the picture** *not fml* to have no knowledge of what is happening: *Please tell me what you're doing, I seem to be out of the picture.* → **be in²** (26), **put in²** (22)

**21 be out of play** (of a ball) to be in the wrong part of the court, field of play, etc.: *The judge ruled that the ball was out of play and so the point did not count.* → **be in²** (27a), **go out of** (12)

**22 be out of pocket** to have spent (an amount of) one's own money, as on a business trip: *Claim all your travel costs so that you're not out of pocket on your journey. When I got back to the office, I was £5:50 out of pocket.*

**23 be out of (all) proportion (to): a** to be an unsuitable size or shape to match the rest of something, making it look ugly: *I like the general style of the building, but the chimneys are out of proportion, they're too big.* **b** to be usu. greater or less than is justified by the facts: *His anger is out of all proportion to the size of their quarrel; something must be wrong with him.* → **get out of** (30)

**24 be out of the question** to be impossible to be considered: *In view of the increased cost, I'm afraid a new car is out of the question this year.* → **be out** (15)

**25 be out of range (of)** to be beyond the reach (of a gun): *Run to the far side of the wood, where we shall be out of range of their guns.* → **come within** (4), etc.

**26 be out of (someone's) reach** to be impossible to seize or gain: *The boy climbed the tree, but the apples were still out of (his) reach. You might be employed as a salesman, but the director's job is out of your reach. A beautiful girl like that is sure to be out of reach.*

**27 be out of the running** to fail to deserve consideration or success; not be considered worthy of competition: *The standard is higher this year; your usual effort will be out of the running.* → **be in²** (31)

**28 be out of sight/view** to be unable to be seen: *I waved my handkerchief until the train was out of sight.* → **keep in** (16), etc.

**29 be out of sorts** to be in a not very good temper; be restless, etc.: *The children have been out of sorts all morning, I think this endless wet weather is having a bad effect on their nerves.*

**30 be out of step: a** to step with the left and right leg at a different time (from others): *Make sure the soldiers are out of step when they cross the bridge.* **b** *not fml* to act in a different way (from the rest of the group): *He is out of step with modern life.* → **be in²** (33), **keep in** (18)

**31 be out of true** to be not straight: *This box is out of true, its corners are not right angles. Every time he passes a picture, he puts it straight if it's out of true.*

**32 be out of the way: a** to be in a position so as not to cause annoyance: *This may not be the best place for the old chair, but at least it's out of the way, and we shan't fall over it.* → **get out of** (37), **keep out of** (5), **stay out of** (4): **b** to be in a lonely place: *I'd better show you how to get to the house, as it's rather out of the way and you might get lost.* —**out-of-the-way** *adj*

**33 be well out of it/that** *not fml* to be lucky to escape something: *Let the other firm take the risks, you're well out of it.*

**be outside** *v prep*

**1** to have a position outside (something such as a place): [L9 + *outside*] *There's a strange car outside the house, whose is it?*

*__2__ → FALL OUTSIDE

***be over¹** *v adv*

**1** *not fml* to arrive at someone's home: [IØ] *I'll be over later this evening.* → **be round**

**2** to end: [IØ] *We all thought that the war would be over by Christmas. The rain will soon be over.* → **get over¹** (4), **get through¹** (8), **have over** (2)

**3** to be left, esp. after something is finished: [IØ] *Is there any cake over from the party? There might be a few pieces of cloth over when I've finished making the dress; you can have them.* → **leave over** (2)

**4 be (all) over and done with** *not fml* to be completely finished: *You've come too late for the game, it's all over and done with.* → **finish with** (4), etc.

**5 it's all over with someone** *not fml* the person named is dead: *It's all over with Mother, I'm afraid she died this morning.*

**be over²** *v prep*

**1** to have a position above (something or someone): [L9 + *over*] *That nameplate has been over the school door for fifty years.* → **be above** (1)

**2** to be more than (an amount): [L9 + *over*] *The number of students in each class must not be over twenty.* → **be above** (2)

*__3__ to take usu. a long time doing (something): [T1 (*no pass.*)] *Will you be long over that report?* [T4] *Don't be all night over finishing your book.* → **take over²**

**4 be all over** *not fml* to be spread around (a place or group): *The news of their marriage was soon all over the college.*

**5 be all over** *not fml* to welcome (someone) too warmly: *As soon as she opened the door, the children were all over her.*

**6 be all over** *not fml* to defeat (an opponent) soundly: *The home team were all over the newcomers in the first few minutes.*

**7 be all over the place** to be untidy, scattered: *Someone must have been in, my papers are all over the place!*

**8 be over one's head** to be too difficult to understand: *Most of what the speaker said was over my head, so I fell asleep.* → **be above** (7)
**9 be over the hill** *not fml* to be too old to be useful: *Don't ask the young people if you can help, they think you're over the hill if you're past thirty!*
**10 be over the moon** *infml* to be wild with joy: *When Jim asked her to marry him, Mary was over the moon.*

**be past** *v prep*
**1** to be in a position behind or further than (something such as a place); pass (something or somewhere): [L9 + *past*] *And now the Queen's horse is safely past the winning post! The house is past the church, on your right.* → **go past²** (1), etc.
**2** to be later than (a time): [L9 + *past*] *Surely it's past 10 o'clock? My watch must have stopped again!* → **get past²** (2)
*3 to be too difficult for (usu. someone) to do or understand: [T1 (*no pass.*)] *It's past me what he means! I'll save this book till the children are older; it's a little past them at the moment.* [T4] *The old man felt that he was now past going out every day, so he asked some young people to do his shopping.* → **get past²** (5), etc.
**4 be past caring** also **be beyond caring** to cease to care (about something): *Don't ask me how we're to pay the bills; I'm past caring!* → **go past²** (4), etc.
**5 be past endurance** → BE BEYOND (6)
**6 be past it** *infml* to be no longer able to do the things one could formerly do: *We shall have to dismiss Mr Walker; he has worked here for a long time but has been making a lot of mistakes recently, and it's clear that he's past it. That young fellow was once popular with the girls, but he's a bit past it now.* → **get past²** (8)
**7 be past a joke** → BE BEYOND (7)
**8 be past redemption** → BE BEYOND (10)

***be round** *v adv* → **be over¹** (1)
*not fml* to arrive at someone's house: [IØ] *I'll be round later this evening.*

***be through** *v adv*
**1** *not fml* to have finished (with someone, something, or doing something): [IØ (*with*)] *I don't want anything more to do with you, we're through. When you're through with that book, will you lend it to me? I'm through with living in this cold place!*
**2** to be connected by telephone (with someone or a place): [IØ (*to*)] *You're through (to London) now, caller.* → **come through¹** (6), **get through¹** (6), **get through to** (1), **put through¹** (2)

**be through** *v prep* → GO THROUGH

**be under** *v prep*
**1** to be placed beneath (something or someone): [L9 + *under*] *The home of a rabbit is usually under the ground.* → **be beneath** (1)
**2** to be less than (usu. a number): [L9 + *under*] *The coat was under fifty dollars! My class was under ten students this year.* → **drop below** (1), etc.
*3 to be forced to obey (someone's power): [T1 (*no pass.*)] *The whole army is under the general's command.* → **come under** (3), **fall beneath** (2), **fall under** (2)
*4 → COME UNDER (2)
*5 to be receiving treatment from (usu. a doctor): [T1 (*no pass.*)] *Jane has been under that doctor for three years.*
*6 to feel the effect of (something): [T1 (*no pass.*)] *When Jim came home singing and shouting, we knew that he was under the influence of drink.*
**7 be under (someone's) control** to be controlled by someone: *It took the teacher several minutes before the class was under (his) control again. The fire which threatened to destroy the hospital is now under control.* → **bring under** (2), **get under²** (2), **keep under** (2)
**8 be under the hammer** to be offered for sale at an auction: *One of the world's most famous paintings is now under the hammer.* → **go under²** (4)
**9 be under an illusion** to think (usu. that something is true which is not): *You're under an illusion if you think there will be another train after midnight.* → **labour under** (3)
**10 be under the impression** to think (usu. that something is true which may not be true): *I was under the impression that you hadn't visited the city before, was I right?*
**11 be under oath** → BE ON (21)
**12 be under orders** to be about to act according to orders received, esp. military orders: *I haven't long to spend with the family, we are under orders to sail for the island next week.*
**13 be under starter's orders** (of riders in a horserace) to await the signal to start the race, after receiving the signal to be ready: *They're under starter's orders, but the horses are restless.* → **come under** (9)
**14 be under the weather** *not fml* to be slightly unwell: *You've been under the weather for some days now, why don't you see a doctor?*

**be up** *v adv*
**1** to be raised or high: [L9 + UP] *Why is that ladder still up? Haven't you finished picking the apples? Your hand has been up for some minutes; what do you want?* → **hold up** (1), etc.
**2** (of the sun or moon) to rise: [L9 + UP] *Once the sun is up, we'll be on our way.*
**3** to come up from a lower level: [L9 + UP] *Jim is downstairs; he'll be up in a minute.*
*4 to awake and get out of bed: [IØ] *What time do you have to be up tomorrow?* → **get up** (5)
*5 to stay out of bed at night: [IØ] *Don't worry about ringing the bell, we're often up late.* → **stay up** (3), etc.
*6 to be increased; rise: [IØ] *Production is up this quarter. Jane's temperature is up again.* → **keep up** (2), **remain up** (2)
*7 to rise in price: [IØ] *Eggs are up again this*

*month.* → **go down**[1] (6), etc., **be down** (2)

***8** *infml* to be wrong or unusual; be the matter: [IØ (*with*)] *Something must be up, the children are not usually as quiet as that. What's up? You look pale. I think I know what's up with the washing machine.*

***9** (of a limited time) to have come to its end: [IØ] *Bring the boat in now, your time is up.*

***10** to have arrived at a university or important city: [IØ (*at, in*)] *Are the students up at the university yet? My family are up in London for a few days.* → **go down**[1] (14), etc.

***11** *not fml* to be made to face a court of law: [IØ (*in*) *I'm sorry to hear that the boys are up in court again; what's the charge this time?* → **have up** (2), etc.

**12 be up and about** *not fml* to be out of bed again and able to walk after an illness: *Mother's leg is so much better that she will be up and about soon.*

**13 be all up with (someone)** *infml* to be hopeless for (someone): *You others go ahead and find shelter; it's all up with me.*

**14 one's blood be up** to be angry, as ready for a fight: *I could see that his blood was up, so I avoided a quarrel* → **get up** (18)

**15 the game is up** *infml* one's guilt is known: *"The game is up!" said the policeman. "Come along to the police station with me." At last he knew that the game was up, and let himself be taken by the police.*

**16 be hard up** *not fml* to be poor: *I remember the time when we were so hard up that I only had one pair of shoes.*

**17 the hunt is up!** the chase is about to start: *The hunt is up! The hunt is up! Forward, everybody!*

***be up against** *v adv prep*

**1** *not fml* to be opposed by; have trouble dealing with (a difficulty): [T1] *The firm is up against serious competition from the other company, and will have to double our efforts to succeed.* → **bring up against** (1), **come up against**

**2 be up against it** *not fml* to be having unusual and great difficulties; be in a very bad or dangerous position: *Our firm is really up against it now that our competitors have produced the perfect machine for the job, and cut all our sales.*

***be up for** *v adv prep*

**1** to be being considered for (something such as advancement): [T1 (*no pass.*)] *How many committee members are up for re-election this time? I've heard that your name is up for the chairmanship.* → **come up for** (3), **put up**[1] (12)

**2** to be offered for (sale): [T1 (*no pass.*)] *How long has that house been up for sale?*

**3** to face a court of law charged with (a crime): [T1 (*no pass.*)] *I hear the gardener is up for the robbery at the big house.*

**4 be up for grabs** *infml* to be free for anyone to try and gain: *Since the minister died suddenly, his seat in Parliament is up for grabs.*

**5 be hard up for** *not fml* to be short of (something): *You must be hard up for ideas if you're using that old joke in the show!*

**be up in** *v adv prep*

**1 be up in arms** *infml* to be very angry, usu. about a wrong action by someone else: *The mothers were up in arms when they heard that there was to be no school crossing across the busy road.*

**2 be well up in** to be well-informed about (a subject): *Ask Dr White, he's well up in children's diseases.*

**be up to** *v adv prep*

**1** to reach as far as (something): [L9 + UP + *to*] *Before long, the water was up to their knees, and they began to get worried.*

***2** to be able to do (something, or be doing something): [T1 (*no pass.*)] *I'm not up to such hard work in this hot weather. Mother hasn't been up to much recently, while her leg was bad.* [T4] *I'm not up to going out tonight, I have a headache.* → **feel equal to, feel up to**

***3** *not fml* to do (usu. something wrong): [T1] *I'd better go into the children's room and see what they're up to. That boy's been up to no good, I can tell from the look on his face.*

***4** to equal (something) in standard: [T1 (*often neg.*)] *Your latest effort isn't up to much. Your recent work has not been up to your usual standard. The new film is not up to his last one. Was the book up to your expectations?* → **bring up to** (4), **come up to** (4, 5), **get up to** (4)

***5** to depend on (someone): [*It* + V3] *It's up to you to keep the boy out of trouble.*

***6** *not fml* to have knowledge of (something kept secret): [T] (*no pass*)] *Don't worry, I'm up to all his little tricks.*

**7 be up to date/the minute** to be modern: *This book is excellent, it's (right) up to date.* → **be out of** (7), **bring up to** (3), **get out of** (19), **get up to** (6), **go out of** (5)

**8 be up to one's ears/eyes in** to be very busy with (work): *I can't possibly come out tonight, I'm up to my eyes in work.*

**9 be up to mischief** to behave badly: *I can see from the state of the room that those children have been up to mischief again. Why is the dog always up to mischief? Whenever he sees a sheep he has to chase it.* → **get up to** (7)

**be upon** *v prep* → BE ON

**be with** *v prep*

**1** to be in company with (someone): [L9 + *with*] *You'll find Mr Sharp at the table, he's with two other men. I enjoy being with you at concerts.*

**2** to work for (a company): [L9 + *with*] *I've been with the firm for nearly six months now.*

***3** *not fml* to support (someone): [T1 (*no pass.*)] *We're with you all the way in your fight for equal rights.*

***4** *infml* to understand and like (usu. something modern): [T1 (*no pass.*)] *I'm not with these new fashions, I find them ugly.*

*5 to understand what (someone) is explaining: [T1 (*no pass.*)] *"Are you still with me?" asked the chairman, halfway through his speech. I was with you as far as your last point, then I got confused.*

6 **be with it** *infml* to be modern or up to date: *That teacher will never be popular with the students, he's just not with it.* → **get with** (3)

7 **be quits with** *infml* to make matters even between oneself and (someone else): *Let me hit him just once more and then I'll be quits with him!*

**be within** *v prep*

1 to be inside (a limited area): [L9 + *within*] *The houses of the ancient city were all within the city walls.* → **lie within** (1)

*2 to be part of (a stated limit): [T1 (*no pass.*)] *I can answer your question if it's within my experience.* → **fall within** (2), etc.

3 **be within earshot (of)** to be able to hear or be heard (by someone or from a place): *Don't talk so loud, we're within earshot of the camp.* → **come within** (3), etc.

4 **be within someone's grasp** to be able to be understood or done by someone: *I don't think the students can do that, it's not within their grasp.*

5 **be within range (of)** to be able to be shot (by certain guns): *Don't shoot until the enemy is well within range.* → **come within** (4), etc.

6 **be within one's rights** to have the right (usu. to do something): *You can take the boy away, it's within your rights. Is it within my rights to complain to the director in person?*

7 **be within sight/view** to be able to be seen: *Make sure that the children are within view all the time you're on the shore.* → **keep in** (16), etc.

8 **be within sight/striking distance of** *not fml* to be very near (something such as an aim, or doing something): *Another few dollars, and we would have been within sight of the amount we needed for the children's hospital. We were within striking distance of winning the contract, when our competitors beat us.* → **come within** (6), **get within** (6)

* **be without** *v prep*

to lack (something): [T1 (*no pass.*)] *Many homes in Britain were without electricity during parts of the winter.*

**beam to** *v prep*

to broadcast (a radio or television message) to (a certain place): [T1 + *to*] *The radio station agreed to beam the Minister's speech to the whole of Europe.*

**bear against** *v prep*

**bear a grudge against** → HAVE AGAINST (3)

**bear away** *v adv*

1 also **bear off** *fml* to carry (something or someone) away: [T1 + AWAY] *It took ten cars to bear the wedding guests away. A horse-drawn carriage was coming along the road to bear away the royal party.* → **carry away**[1] (1)

*2 also **bear off** *fml* to win (something): [T1] *Tim bore away most of the prizes at the races.* → **carry off** (3)

*3 (of a boat) to move away: [IØ] *When all the people were on board, the boat bore away.*

*4 *fml* → CARRY OFF (4)

5 **be borne away** to be seized (by a feeling): *Lady Alice was borne away with joy when her child was given back to her.* → **carry away** (5)

**bear down** *v adv*

1 *fml* to carry (usu. something) downwards: [X9 + DOWN] *The boys climbed the ladder to pick the apples off the tree and then bore them down.*

*2 to defeat (something such as opposition or someone): [T1] *His determined efforts at last bore down all opposition.*

*3 to use effort: [IØ] *The driver bore down with all his strength to control the car when the wheel stuck.*

*4 (of a woman) to use effort to give birth to a child: [IØ] *The nurse will tell you when to bear down.*

***bear down on/upon** *v adv prep*

1 *naut* to move directly towards (something): [T1] *With the wind blowing strongly behind, the little boat bore down on the harbour.*

2 to come near (something or someone) threateningly: [T1] *The packed ice bore down on the ship. I could see my aunt bearing down on me from across the room.*

3 to weigh heavily upon (someone): [T1 (*often simple tenses*)] *The responsibility for his family bears down on a young man.*

4 to punish (someone) severely: [T1] *The courts must bear down on young criminals.*

**bear in** *v prep* → **keep in** (10)

**bear in mind** to remember; consider (something or someone): [*often simple tenses*] *You must bear your parents' needs in mind when you make your decision. There are so many questions to be borne in mind. We must bear in mind that the younger people might not like the idea.*

**bear in on/upon** *v adv prep*

**be borne in on/upon** to be brought firmly to the consciousness of (someone): *Slowly it was borne in on the citizens that the enemy had surrounded them.*

***bear left/right** *v adv* → **keep left, turn left**

esp. *BrE* to keep to the left/right on a road, esp. where the road divides: [IØ (*usu. imper.*)] *Bear left when you reach the church, and follow the road round till you come to the village centre.*

**bear off** *v adv*

*1 → BEAR AWAY (1)

*2 → BEAR AWAY (2)

*3 to push a boat away from the shore: [IØ] *Is everyone on board? Let's bear off, we've no time to waste.*

4 *fml* → CARRY OFF (4)

***bear on/upon** *v prep*

1 to show some connection with (something): [T1 (*no pass., simple tenses*)] *How does your*

*story bear on this case?* → **have on²** (4), **touch on** (3)

**2** to affect (someone) in the stated usu. bad way: [T1 (*usu. simple tenses*)] *The rise in the cost of living bears hard on old people living on fixed incomes.*

**3 bring something to bear on** to make something influence (something or someone): [*usu. pass.*] *The combined efforts of all the trade unions will be brought to bear on the government to persuade it to change its mind. A strong influence must be brought to bear on the government to reduce taxes.*

**bear out** *v adv*

**1** *fml* to carry (something or someone) out: [X9 + OUT] *The fireman bore the fainting girl out of the burning house.*

*__2__ to support (someone or the truth of what someone says): [T1 (*usu. simple tenses*)] *The prisoner's story was borne out by his wife. If I tell the judge that I wasn't there, will you bear me out?*

***bear right** *v adv* → BEAR LEFT

**bear to** *v prep*

**1** *fml* to carry (something or someone) in the direction of (something or someone): [X9 + *to*] *Sadly, the men bore the dead child to his mother. A line of servants entered, bearing food to the guests.*

**2 bear a resemblance to** to look like (something or someone else): [*simple tenses*] *What a remarkable resemblance she bears to the famous actress! The finished book bears no resemblance to the material I sent.*

**3 bear witness to** → WITNESS TO (2)

**bear up** *v adv*

**1** *fml* to carry or lift (something or someone) high: [X9 + UP] *The man's body was borne up as he was brought to be buried.*

*__2__ to remain strong, without becoming broken: [IØ (*under*)] *Do you think that the floor will bear up under the weight of the new machinery?*

*__3__ to remain strong or brave: [IØ (*under*)] *Alice bore up well under the news of her husband's death.*

*__4__ to help (someone) to continue living in a time of trouble: [T1b] *How could I have lived through Mother's illness without you to bear me up?*

*__5__ *BrE not fml* to become more cheerful: [IØ] *Bear up, your troubles will soon be over.* → **cheer up**, etc.

*__6__ *naut* to direct a boat away from the wind: [IØ] *We'll have to bear up, the wind is too strong.*

**bear upon** *v prep* → BEAR ON

**bear with** *v prep*

**1** to suffer (something) with (a quality): [T1 + *with*] *You must bear your troubles with patience.*

*__2__ to show patience towards (someone or someone's behaviour): [T1 (*usu. simple tenses*)] *You must bear with his bad temper; he has recently been ill. Bear with me while I try to remember exactly what he said.* → **contend with** (2), **put up with** (3), **stand for** (5)

***beat about¹** *v adv*

**1** to make quick movements in many directions: [IØ] *The swimmer beat about in the water, trying not to drown.*

**2** (of a ship) to change direction: [IØ] *After being in the water for six hours, the ship beat about and sailed for home.*

**3** to search anxiously: [IØ (*for*) (*usu. simple tenses*)] *The prisoner beat about for a way of escape.* → **cast about**

**beat about²** *v prep*

**beat about the bush** *not fml* to refuse or fail to come to the point when speaking about a subject: [*no pass.*] *Don't beat about the bush, come straight to the point!*

**beat against** *v prep*

**1** to beat (something) by hitting it on (something hard); hit (something) repeatedly: [T1 + *against*] *My grandmother used to clean her mats by beating them against the wall of the house.* [IØ + *against*] *The rain was beating against the windows.* → **knock against** (1), etc.

**2 beat one's head against a brick wall** → BANG AGAINST (2)

**beat at** *v prep*

**1** also **beat on** to knock loudly on (a door, etc.): [IØ + *at*] *The visitors beat at the door until he answered.* → **knock at**, etc.

**2** to defeat (someone) at (a game): [T1 + *at*] *The other village always beats our team at cricket.*

**3 beat someone at his own game** *not fml* to do better than someone in his own field of activity: *By winning a prize for writing, Tom beat his teacher at his own game.*

**beat back** *v adv*

**1** to force (someone or something) to go back: [T1 + BACK] *The flames beat the firemen back.*

*__2__ *naut* to sail with difficulty: [IØ] *The boat had to beat back against a strong wind.*

**beat down** *v adv*

**1** to descend fiercely: [IØ + DOWN (*on*)] *The sun beat down mercilessly on the dry earth.*

**2** to flatten (something) by descending heavily: [T1 + DOWN] *The crops were beaten down by heavy rain.*

*__3__ to reduce (a price) by argument or other influence: [T1] *Competition should beat the price down.* → **knock down** (7), **knock off** (3)

*__4__ to persuade (someone) to reduce a price: [T1 (*to*) (*usu. simple tenses*)] *The man was asking £35 for the dress, but I beat him down to £25.* → **knock down** (8)

**beat hollow** *v adv*

*infml* to defeat (an opponent) completely: [T1 + HOLLOW] *Three fast runners entered the race, but Jim beat them all hollow.*

**beat in** *v adv*

**1** to mix (something) by beating: [T1 + IN]

*First put the flour in the bowl, and then beat the eggs in.*

*2 to wound or damage (someone or something) by hitting: [T1] *The boys robbed the old man and beat his head in. The firemen had to beat the door in.* → **bash in** (1, 2), **crush in** (1), **stave in**

*3 to teach (something) by force: [T1] *With children as lazy as these, you have to beat the facts in.* → **hammer in** (3), etc.

**beat into** *v prep*

1 to mix (something) with (something) by beating: [T1 + *into*] *Beat the eggs into the flour.*

2 to reduce (someone or something) to (something smaller) by beating: [T1 + *into*] *You can beat the meat into a flatter piece.* → **hammer into** (2), **pound into** (1)

*3 to force (someone) into (something or doing something): [D1] *You will have to beat the old man into obedience.* [V4b] *You will have to beat the old man into giving you the money.*

*4 to teach (something) to (someone) by force: [D1] *You have to beat the facts into these lazy children.* → **hammer into** (3), etc.

***beat it** v pron

run away: [I∅] *Beat it,here come the police!*

**beat off** *v adv*

to be able to drive (an enemy, etc.) back: [T1 + OFF] *The citizens beat off the first attack but later were defeated.*

**beat on/upon** *v prep* → BEAT AT (1)

**beat out** *v adv*

1 to flatten (something) by beating: [T1 + OUT] *The dish was made of silver, beaten out by hand. The local people had beaten out a path through the forest.*

2 to play (something) by hitting usu. a drum repeatedly: [T1 + OUT ] *The natives send news over long distances by beating out a message on a hollow log.*

3 to stop (a fire) burning by beating it: [T1 + OUT] *All the people from the village gathered branches and beat the fire out.*

*4 *naut* to sail into the wind: [I∅] *The boat beat out when the storm had passed.*

5 **beat one's brains out** *infml* to work very hard at thinking: [*usu. continuous tenses*] *I've been beating my brains out all day over that report, and I still can't find a way to make my suggestions politely.*

6 **beat someone's brains out** *not fml* to hit someone very violently, esp. on the head: *Give it to me, or I'll beat your brains out!*

**beat to** *v prep*

1 to reduce (something or someone) to (a smaller size or weaker condition) by beating: [T1 + *to*] *The old man was beaten to a wreck by the young criminals.*

2 to defeat (someone) by reaching (an aim) first: [T1 + *to*] *I'll beat you to the winning post!*

3 **beat someone to it** *not fml* to win a competition, esp. of time: *We got our product onto the market as fast as we could, but the other firm still beat us to it!*

4 **beat someone to his knees** *not fml* to defeat someone severely, esp. in spirit: [*usu. simple tenses*] *Since her husband died, the effort of working to support the children and running the home at the same time had beaten her to her knees, and she became ill.*

**beat up** *v adv*

1 to mix (something) by beating: [T1 + UP] *Beat up the eggs before you add the flour.*

*2 *not fml* to wound (someone) severely by hitting: [T1] *The boys robbed the old man and beat him up.* → **bash up** (2), **do over** (3), **work over** (2)

*3 → DRUM UP

*4 *naut* to sail before the wind: [I∅] *When a favourable wind came, we were able to beat up.*

5 **be (all) beat up** to be very tired, worn out: *You go ahead and leave me here, I'm all beat up.* —**beat-up** *adj*

**beat upon** *v prep* → BEAT ON

***become of** *v prep* → **come of** (1), **disappear to, get to** (2), **go to** (5)

to happen to (someone or something) often in a bad way: [*What*(*ever*) + T1 (*no pass.*)] *I don't know what will become of the boy if he keeps failing his examinations. Whatever became of that large suitcase we had? Did we give it to a friend?*

***bed down** *v adv* → **bunk down**

to (cause to) become comfortable for the night: [T1] *Would you bed the horses down for me? We'll bed the children down now.* [I∅ (*with*) (*often simple tenses*)] *I'll bed down on the chairs. Can Jane bed down with her sister?*

***bed in** *v adv*

*mil* to fix (a gun) firmly into the ground: [T1 (*often pass.*)] *The big guns all have to be bedded in properly if they're to shoot straight and safely.*

***bed out** *v adv*

to place (young plants) in enough room for growth: [T1] *Will you help me bed out the plants?* —**bedding-out** *adj*

***bed with** *v prep sl* → SLEEP WITH (2)

**bedaub with** *v prep* → **besmear with, smear with**

to cover (something or someone) with (something sticky): [T1 + *with* (*usu. pass.*)] *The walls were bedaubed with sticky black paint.*

**bedeck with** *v prep* → DECK WITH

**bedew with** *v prep*

*old use* to make (something) wet with (a liquid): [T1 + *with* (*usu. pass.*)] *His face was bedewed with tears.*

**bedim with** *v prep*

*old use* to make (something) less bright or cheerful: [T1 + *with* (*usu. pass.*)] *His eyes were bedimmed with sorrow.*

***beef up** *v adv*

esp. *AmE infml* to strengthen or improve (something): [T1 (*usu. simple tenses*)] *We need new young soldiers to beef up the army. We can't print your article as it is; could you try to beef it up a bit?*

***beetle off** *v adv*
*BrE infml* to leave quickly: [IØ (*usu. simple tenses*)] *I turned to answer him and found he had beetled off without waiting for an answer.*

**beg for** *v prep*
**1** to ask (someone) humbly for a gift of (something such as money or food): [IØ + *for*] *The old woman went from house to house, begging for bread.* [T1 + *for*] *They went from house to house, begging the people for bread.*
**2** to make an urgent request for (action): [L9 + *for* (*no pass.*)] *The wounded soldier begged for mercy.* [X9 + *for*] *The wounded soldier begged his enemy for mercy.* → **appeal for** (1)
**3 beg for the moon** to ask the impossible: [*usu. continuous tenses*] *If a poor man asked to marry a princess, that would be like begging for the moon.* → **cry for** (4)

**beg from** *v prep*
to ask humbly (for a gift) from (someone): [IØ + *from*] *I would be ashamed to beg from my neighbours.* [T1 + *from*] *I would be ashamed to beg money from my neighbours.*

**beg of** *v prep*
*fml* to ask (someone) politely: [IØ + *of* (*no pass., usu. present, first person*)] *I beg of you, don't mention her name again.*

***beg off** *v adv* → **cry off**
to (cause to) be excused: [IØ] *Jane has just begged off, can you take her place in the team?* [T1b] *I'll have to beg Jane off, she's sick again.*

**begin as** *v prep* also *fml* **commence as** → **start as**
to start one's life's work by being (a workman in a certain trade, etc.): [L1 + *as*] *Many important businessmen began as factory workers.*

**begin on** *v prep* also *fml* **commence on** → **start on** (1)
to start work on; start dealing with (something): [IØ + *on* (*no pass.*)] *He's a very busy lawyer and has already begun on another case. Tom and his drinking companions began on their third bottle in an hour.*

**begin with** *v prep* also *fml* **commence with**
**1** to start (something) with (something): [IØ + *with* (*no pass., usu. simple tenses*)] *The day began with bad news, and looks like getting worse.* [T1 + *with* (*usu. simple tenses*)] *It is very worrying to begin the day with bad news.* → **start with** (2)
**2 beginning with** continuing from (a starting point): *We need the figures for the twelve months beginning with April. We will now hear the students read their poems, beginning with Tom.* → **start with** (3)
**3 to begin with: a** at first: *It was fine to begin with and then it started to rain.* **b** as a first consideration or statement: *Our difficulties are many; to begin with, we can't get the workers.* → **start with** (4)

**beguile into** *v prep* → **trick into**, etc.
to deceive (someone) into (something or doing something): [X9 + *into*] *Their leaders beguiled the men into a false sense of their own power. Their leaders beguiled the men into making impossible demands.*

**beguile out of** *v adv prep* → **cheat out of**, etc.
to deceive (someone) in order to gain (something he possesses): [X9 + OUT + *of*] *The clever salesman beguiled the old lady out of her money.*

**beguile with** *v prep*
**1** to amuse (someone such as a child) with (a pleasant activity such as stories): [T1 + *with*] *When Jane was sick, her favourite uncle beguiled her with funny stories.*
***2** to pass (time) pleasantly with (an activity): [D1] *We beguiled the warm afternoon with lazy talk.* [V4b] *We beguiled the warm afternoon with swimming and reading.*

**belch out** *v adv*
(usu. of smoke) to (cause to) be sent out in large quantities: [T1 + OUT] *The car belched out clouds of smoke.* [IØ + OUT (*from*)] *Black smoke belched out from the forest fire.*

***believe in** *v prep*
**1** to consider the existence of (something) to be a fact: [T1 (*simple tenses*)] *Do you believe in fairies?* → **disbelieve in** (2)
**2** to have faith or trust in (someone, a god, or religion): [T1 (*simple tenses*)] *Christians believe in God and Jesus.* → **disbelieve in** (1), **have in**[2] (2)
**3** to consider (something) to be true: [T1 (*pass. rare, simple tenses*)] *Do you believe in everything the Bible says?*
**4** to consider (something) to be of worth: [T1 (*simple tenses*)] *Jim believes in fresh air and exercise for his health.* [T4 (*simple tenses*)] *Jane believes in eating carefully to control her weight.*

**believe of** *v prep*
to think that (something such as behaviour, usu. bad) could be done by (someone): [T1 + *of* (*simple tenses, usu.* + *would, could*)] *You mean he hit the child? I would never have believed it of him! I'd believe anything of that woman!*

**bellow out** *v adv*
**1** (of an animal) to make a loud deep noise: [IØ + OUT] *The bull has been bellowing out all morning.*
**2** to shout (words) loudly: [T1 + OUT] *The fireman bellowed out a warning as the burning roof fell.* [IØ + OUT] *The children bellowed out with excitement as their father came home in a new car.*

**belly out** *v adv* → **BILLOW OUT**

***belong to** *v prep*
**1** to be the property of (someone): [T1 (*no pass., simple tenses*)] *The blue coat belongs to Mary.*

**2** to be a member of (a group, nation, etc.): [T1 (*no pass., simple tenses*)] *People of many different political views belong to the club.*
**3** to be connected with (something, such as a period of time): [T1 (*no pass., simple tenses*)] *As a writer, he really belongs to the 18th century.*

***belong under** *v prep* → **come under** (2), etc.
to be classed as or with (a larger group): [T1 (*no pass., simple tenses*)] *Your suggestion belongs under the general heading of employment reorganization.*

**belt along** *v adv; prep*
esp. *BrE infml* to move quickly and easily along (a road): [L9 + ALONG/*along*] *"You got here fast!" "Yes, the new car belted along (the road)."*

**belt down/up** *v prep*
esp. *BrE infml* to hurry in a certain direction along (a road): [L9 + *down/up*] *If you belt down the road, you'll get to the shop before it closes. He belted up the path in the rain.*

**belt out** *v adv*
**1** *infml* to hurry outside: [L9 + OUT (*usu. simple tenses*)] *When I opened the door, the cat belted out.*
***2** *infml* to sing (a song) loudly: [T1] *The singer belted out the song so loud that we could hardly hear ourselves think.*

**belt up** *v adv*
**1** to put on belts: [IØ + UP] *The soldiers belted up and went out to fight.*
**2** *infml* to arrive in a hurry: [L9 + UP (*usu. simple tenses*)] *The criminals had just disappeared round the corner when three policemen belted up.*
***3** *infml* to be quiet: [IØ (*usu. imper.*)] *Belt up, you boys, Father's asleep.* → **shut up** (4), etc.
***4** *not fml* to fasten a seat belt in a car: [IØ] *Many people think it is important to belt up before you start to drive.* → **buckle up** (3), **strap in**

**bend back** *v adv* → **fold back**, etc.
to (cause to) turn, twist, or curve in a backward direction: [L9 + BACK (*usu. simple tenses*)] *The collar bends back in the latest fashion. The top of the box bends back to show the goods. I bent back too far and hurt my neck.* [T1 + BACK ] *Don't bend the book back, you'll damage it.*

**bend before** *v prep*
**1** to lean when facing (usu. a wind): [IØ + *before*] *Trees that don't bend before the wind will break.*
***2** to yield to (something): [T1 (*no pass.*)] *I'd advise you to bend before the old lady's wishes.* → **bow before** (3)

**bend down** *v adv* → **fold down, lean down, stoop down, turn down** (1), **turn in** (1)
to (cause to) fold or lean downwards: [T1 + DOWN] *Don't bend the corners of the pages down, it damages them.* [IØ + DOWN] *Tony was so tall that he had to bend down to get through the doorway.*

**bend forward** *v adv* → **incline forward, lean forward**
to hold oneself or (something) at an angle towards something or someone: [IØ + FORWARD] *Don't bend too far forward, you might fall over.* [T1 + FORWARD ] *I bent my head forward to hear what they were saying.*

**bend in** *v adv*
to (cause to) curve inwards: [X9 + IN] *Don't bend the corners of the pages in, it damages them.* [L9 + IN (*usu. simple tenses*)] *The doctor said that Bob's legs would always bend in as a result of so much horseriding.*

**bend on/upon** *v prep*
**be bent on** to set one's mind on (something or doing something); have (something or doing something) as a fixed purpose: *George used to be bent on law as a profession. Jim seems bent on becoming a musician. He has been bent on becoming one for a long time now.*

**bend over** *v adv*
**1** to (cause to) be turned over, lean to the ground, etc.: [T1 + OVER] *Don't bend the corners of the pages over, it damages them.* [IØ + OVER] *As Jim bent over to pick up the pen, he felt a sharp pain in his back.* → **lean over**[1] (1)
**2 bend over backwards** *infml* also *infml* **lean over backwards** to make every possible effort (to do something): *You mustn't be unkind to your mother when she has bent over backwards to please you.* → **fall over** (2)

**bend to** *v prep*
**1** to lean down towards (something): [IØ + *to*] *Jim bent to the ground to pick up the pen.* → **lean to** (1)
**2** to curve towards (a direction): [IØ + *to* (*usu. simple tenses*)] *Before it reaches the church, the road bends to the left.*
***3** to force (someone) to obey (something): [D1] *Grandfather was a very powerful man, and used to bend us to his wishes.*
***4** → **BOW BEFORE** (3)

**bend upon** *v prep* → **BEND ON**

**benefit by/from** *v prep*
to gain advantages, pleasure, or profit from (something): [IØ + *by/from*] *Did you benefit from your holiday? I think the boy would benefit by further study.*

**bequeath to** *v prep*
to leave (something such as money or property) to (someone) after one's death: [T1 + *to* (*often pass.*)] *This ring was bequeathed to me by my grandmother. I bequeath to my children the rest of my property, to be divided equally.*

**bereave of** *v prep*
**1** (with past participle *bereaved*) to leave (someone) without (someone dear to him) by death: [T1 + *of*] *The plane crash bereaved him of his wife and two children. He was bereaved of his wife and two children by the plane crash.*
**2 be bereft of** to be robbed of (something usu.

good): *When his last plan failed, he was bereft of hope.*

**beset with** *v prep*
**be beset with** to be attacked by (usu. a bad feeling) from all directions: *When John thought about leaving his job, he was beset with doubts about the right thing to do.*

***besiege with** *v prep*
to press or worry (someone) with a lot of (usu. requests): [D1 (*usu. pass.*)] *After her sudden success, the singer was besieged with offers to appear at many concert halls.*

**besmear with** *v prep* → **bedaub with, smear with**
to cover (something or someone) with (something sticky): [T1 + *with* (*usu. pass.*)] *The walls were besmeared with sticky black paint.*

**bespangle with** *v prep*
to ornament (someone or something) with (small shiny things): [T1 + *with* (*usu. pass.*)] *The cover of the film magazine was bespangled with stars showing actresses' photographs.*

**bespatter with** *v prep* → SPATTER WITH

***bestow on/upon** *v prep*
*fml* to give (a reward, title, etc.) to (someone): [D1 (*usu. simple tenses*)] *The Queen bestowed the title of Master of the Queen's Music upon the young musician.*

**bestrew with** *v prep*
*lit* to spread (an area) with (separate things): [T1 + *with* (*usu. pass.*)] *The whole floor was bestrewn with bits of paper.*

**bet on** *v prep*
**1** to risk (money) on the result of (something such as a horse race) or the performance of (a competitor): [IØ + *on*] *Are you going to bet on the white horse?* [T1 + *on*] *I've bet all my money on Apollo in the third race.* → **be on**[2] (5), **gamble on** (1), **put on**[2] (5), **stake on** (1), **wager on** (1)
***2** to take a chance on or be too sure of (something, or something or someone doing something): [T1] *You can't bet on the weather in England. I think it's safe, but don't bet on it.* [T4] *Don't bet on getting the job.* [V4a] *We daren't bet on the train arriving on time.* → **depend on** (1), etc.

**bet with** *v prep*
**1** to risk one's money in competition with (someone): [IØ + *with*] *I won't bet with that man, he's dishonest.*
**2** to place one's money with (someone) on the chance of winning more: [IØ + *with*] *Bet with Honest Joe.*

**betroth to** *v prep* → **engage to, promise to** (2)
*fml* to cause (someone) to promise to marry (someone): [T1 + *to* (*usu. pass.*)] *In some countries, a girl is betrothed to her future husband while she is still a child.*

***beware of** *v prep*
to guard against (something or someone): [T1 (*no pass., simple tenses, usu. imper.*)] *Beware of the dog.* [T4 (*simple tenses, usu. imper.*)] *You should beware of repeating the same mistakes.* [T6 (*simple tenses, usu. imper.*)] *Beware of how you walk on this rocky path.*

**bias against** *v prep*
**be biased against** to have already formed an unfair judgment to the disadvantage of (someone or something): *Many parents are biased against popular music before they even hear it.*

**bicker about/over** *v prep* → **quarrel about**, etc.
to quarrel, esp. on the subject of (something unimportant or small): [IØ + *about/over*] *The two children were always bickering about who should ride the bicycle.*

***bid fair** *v adv*
*fml* to seem likely (to do something): [I3 (*simple tenses, usu. present*)] *The government's action bids fair to anger the voters.*

**bid for** *v prep*
**1** to offer (a price) for (something) at an auction: [T1 + *for*] *The dealers were bidding high prices for the valuable paintings.* [IØ + *for*] *A surprising number of people were bidding for those rather worthless things at the sale.*
**2** to offer (someone) (a price) for (something) at an auction: [D1 + *for* (*usu. pass.*)] *What am I bid for this collection of fine silver dishes?*
***3** to make an attempt to gain or reach (an aim): [T1] *The English climbers are determined to bid for the highest mountain in the world.*
***4** to try to get (approval, support, etc.) by making an offer or promise: [T1] *The politicians are bidding for our favour by making wild promises that they can't keep.*

***bid in** *v adv* → **buy in** (2)
to offer a price for (one's own goods) at an auction: [T1 (*often pass.*)] *The painting failed to reach its agreed price, and was bid in at £68,000.*

**bid on** *v prep*
*AmE* to offer to do (a piece of work) at a certain price: [IØ + *on*] *How many firms bid on the contract to build the bridge?*

***bid up** *v adv*
to raise the price of (goods) at an auction: [T1] *The dealers bid up all the good pieces, to keep out private buyers.*

***bilk out of** *v adv prep*
*infml* to cheat (someone) out of (something such as money): [D1] *The criminals bilked the old man out of all his money.*

**billet on** *v prep*
to provide (someone, esp. a soldier) with lodgings in the home of (someone): [T1 + *on* (*usu. pass.*)] *The villagers did not like having the soldiers billeted on them.*

**billow out** *v adv* also **belly out**
to swell with wind: [IØ + OUT] *The sails billowed out in the strong wind.*

**bind down** *v adv*
**1** to fasten (someone or something) with rope or string, etc.: [T1 + DOWN] *The traveller woke to find himself bound down to the ground with long ropes.* → **tie down** (1)
***2** to limit (someone): [T1 (*often pass., usu. simple tenses*)] *The young scientist felt bound down by a lot of useless and confusing rules. I don't want to bind you down; feel free to use your own ideas.* → **chain down** (2), **tie down** (2)

**bind fast** *v adv*
**1** to fasten (something) tightly: [T1 + FAST] *Bind the rope fast, we don't want it to come loose.*
**2 fast bind, fast find** keep things safe so as not to lose them.

***bind off** *v adv* → **cast off**' (7), **cast on**
*AmE* (in knitting) to remove (a number of stitches) from the needle: [T1a] *At the end of the row, bind off seven stitches.* [IØ] *Be careful not to bind off too tightly, or the work will lose its shape.*

***bind out** *v adv*
esp. *AmE* to arrange for (usu. a boy) to learn a trade from a master: [T1 (*usu. simple tenses*)] *It used to be usual to bind out promising boys for many years.*

***bind over** *v adv*
*BrE law* to make (someone) promise in court to behave well in future: [V3 (*usu. pass.*)] *The two men were bound over to keep the peace for a year.* [T1 (*usu. pass.*)] *This is the third time that they've been bound over.*

**bind to** *v prep*
**1** to fasten (someone or something) to (something): [T1 + *to*] *The prisoner was bound to a post and shot.* → **tie to** (1)
***2** to arrange for (usu. a boy) to learn a trade from (a master): [D1 (*usu. pass.*)] *The youngest son was bound to a master builder for seven years.*
***3** to force (someone) to keep or obey (something): [D1 (*simple tenses*)] *We must bind all the members of the committee to secrecy.*

**bind together** *v adv*
**1** to fasten (two or more things) together: [T1 + TOGETHER] *The sticks of wood were bound together in bunches.* → **tie together** (1)
***2** to (cause to) join: [T1 (*simple tenses*)] *We must bind the members of the club together in loyalty.* [IØ (*simple tenses*)] *The members of the club must bind together in loyalty.*

**bind up** *v adv*
**1** to tie or wrap (a parcel, etc.): [T1 + UP] *Parcels must be properly bound up for posting to other countries.* → **tie up** (1)
**2** to tie (something); wrap something round (something): [T1 + UP] *Mary asked me to help her to bind up her long hair. Do you know how to bind up a broken arm?* → **tie up** (2)
***3** to fix (parts) together into one book: [T1] *The firm has agreed to bind up the six articles into one book.*

**bind up in** *v adv prep* → **tie up** (6)
**be bound up in** to be very busy with (something); be deeply concerned with (someone): *I'm sorry I couldn't meet you, I was bound up in committee meetings. His interests are completely bound up in his wife and family.*

**bind up with** *v adv prep* → **tie in with, tie up with**
**be bound up with** to have a very close connection with (something): *The future of the island is bound up with the fortunes of the ruling power.*

**bitch about** *v prep* → **complain about**
*sl* to complain about (something): [IØ + *about*] *Don't bitch all day long about the heat: do some work!*

***bitch up** *v adv* → **mess up** (2) etc.
*sl* to spoil (something) carelessly: [T1] *Why did you have to bitch everything up by telling John about the arrangements I made for his leaving party?*

**bite back** *v adv*
**1** to return a bite to (a person or animal): [IØ + BACK (*usu. simple tenses*)] *When the dog bit the little girl, she bit back.* [T1 + BACK (*usu. simple tenses*)] *When the dog bit the little girl, she bit him back.*
***2** to control; prevent (something) from being expressed: [T1 (*simple tenses*)] *Peter was about to tell the secret but he bit his words back.*

**bite into** *v prep*
**1** to put one's teeth into (something): [IØ + *into*] *People with false teeth find it difficult to bite into apples.*
***2** to damage (something), esp. on the surface: [T1] *Acid bites into metals.* → **eat into** (1)

**bite off** *v adv*
**1** to take off (part of something) by biting: [T1 + OFF] *The dog seized the meat and bit a piece off.*
**2 bite someone's head off** *infml* also **snap someone's head off** *infml* to be very angry with someone: *I've said I'm sorry, there's no need to bite my head off.*
**3 bite off more than one can chew** *infml* to try to do too much or something that is too difficult: *Jim may be a good runner, but when he entered for the top international competitions, he found he had bitten off more than he could chew.*
**4 bite one's tongue off** to feel immediately sorry for what one has said: *As soon as I made the remark, I could have bitten my tongue off.*

**bite on** *v prep*
**1** to seize (something) with the teeth: [IØ + *on*] *Babies who are getting new teeth like something hard to bite on.* → **chew on** (1).
***2** *infml* to consider; work at (something): [T1] *Jim likes to have some difficult question*

*to bite on.* → **chew on** (2), **chew over**

**blab out** *v adv* → **babble out**
*infml* to tell (a secret) carelessly: [T1 + OUT] *Don't tell Mary our secret, she's sure to blab it out when she gets drunk!*

***black out** *v adv* also **blacken out**
**1** to cover (something such as writing) so that it cannot be seen: [T1] *The advertisement for the concert tells where it will take place, but the date has been blacked out.*
**2** to darken (somewhere) so that no light is seen: [T1] *During the war we had to black out all our windows. The stage was blacked out to hide a change of scenery* —**blackout** *n* —**blacked-out** *adj* → **dim out** (2)
**3** to stop (a television broadcast) by refusing to work: [T1] *Television shows were blacked out as the union trouble spread.* —**blackout** *n*
**4** to prevent (news) from being spread, as for political reasons: [T1] *Reports of the peace talks have been blacked out for twenty-four hours so as to allow freer argument.* —**blackout** *n*
**5** *not fml* to faint: [IØ (*usu. simple tenses*)] *After the accident he blacked out and couldn't remember what happened.* —**blackout** *n* → **pass out** (2)

***black up** *v adv*
to darken one's face and hands: [IØ] *The soldiers were ordered to black up for the night attack.*

**blacken out** *v adv* → **BLACK OUT**

**blame for** *v prep*
to consider (someone) responsible for (something bad): [T1 + *for*] *They blamed George for the failure of the talks. Don't keep blaming your little sister for your bad behaviour. Don't blame me for falling into the water; you pushed me in!*

**blame on** *v prep*
to place the guilt for (something wrong) on (someone): [T1 + on] *They blamed the failure on George. You can't blame the rise in prices on the government. "If you can keep your head when all about you are losing theirs and blaming it on you."* (Rudyard Kipling, *If*)

***blank out** *v adv*
**1** to remove (something), leaving an empty space: [T1] *Part of the newspaper was blanked out by the government, who wanted their guilt kept hidden.*
**2** to suffer a short loss of memory: [IØ (*usu. simple tenses*)] *I blanked out this morning and couldn't remember where I was.*

***blanket with** *v prep*
to cover (something) completely with (something): [D1 (*usu. pass.*)] *The whole garden was blanketed with snow.*

**blast off** *v adv*
**1** to raise or remove (something) by an explosion: [T1 + OFF] *The bomb blasted the roof off.*
***2** (of a space vehicle) to rise into space: [IØ] *The space ship blasted off at 15.30, according to plan.* —**blast-off** *n* → **lift off** (2)

***blaze abroad** *v adv* → **bruit abroad, noise abroad, rumour abroad, spread abroad**
to spread (esp. good news): [T1 (*usu. pass.*)] *His fame was blazed abroad by the country's newspapers and television.*

**blaze away** *v adv*
**1** to continue burning: [IØ + AWAY] *The fire blazed away and destroyed the whole hotel.*
***2** to shoot rapidly and continuously (at someone or something): [IØ (*at*)] *The captain ordered the men to blaze away (at the enemy).*

**blaze down** *v adv*
**1** to burn fiercely down: [IØ + DOWN (*on*)] *The sun blazed down (on the dry earth).*
***2** to come down in flames: [IØ] *The plane was seen blazing down behind the hill, where it crashed.*

**blaze up** *v adv*
**1** to burn again: [IØ + UP] *The fire blazed up when we thought it was out.* → **burn up** (1), **flame out** (1), **flame up** (1), **flare up** (1)
***2** to increase in heat, anger, or violence: [IØ] *Mary's temper blazed up. Mary blazed up when Jim angered her.* → **fire up** (3), **flame out** (3), **flame up** (2), **flare out** (2), **flare up** (2),

***blaze with** *v prep* → **flame with**
to turn red in the face because of (a strong feeling such as anger): [T1 (*no pass.*)] *Mary blazed with anger when she heard how her mother had been treated.*

***bleach out** *v adv*
to (cause to) be removed by whitening with a chemical substance (bleach): [T1] *Do you think that I shall be able to bleach the old colour out?* [IØ] *The tablecloth has a nasty mark on it; do you think it will bleach out?*

***bleed for** *v prep*
**1** to suffer in sympathy with (usu. someone): [T1 (*no pass., simple tenses, usu. present*)] *Our hearts bleed for you in your sorrow.*
**2** *infml* to feel very sorry for (someone); but used when the speaker does not actually have any sympathy for the other person: [T1 (*no pass., simple tenses, usu. present*)] *"I'll have to get up early to catch the train tomorrow." "My heart bleeds for you. I have to do that every morning!"*
**3** *infml* to make (someone) pay (money) unfairly or by a trick: [D1] *The men who took his son bled the father for £20,000.*

**bleed to** *v prep*
**bleed to death** to lose so much blood that one dies: *The young soldier could have been saved if he had not been left to bleed to death on the battlefield.*

***bleed white** *v adj*
*infml* to rob or cheat (someone) of all his money: [T1b] *That moneylender has been bleeding me white with his high rate of interest.*

**blend in** *v adv*
**1** → **MIX IN** (1)

**2** to (cause to) combine pleasantly (with something): [T1 + IN (*with*)] *The builder is trying to blend the style of the house in with the others in the same road.* [IØ + IN (*with*) (*usu. simple tenses*)] *The colour of the paint will blend in (with the curtains) very nicely.*

**blend into** *v prep*
(of two or more things) to become combined into (a single whole): [IØ + *into*] *These houses seem to blend into the surrounding scenery. The houses and the surrounding scenery seem to blend into each other.*

**blend together** *v adv* → **blend with**, etc.
to combine pleasantly: [IØ + TOGETHER (*usu. simple tenses*)] *Do you think these two colours will blend together?*

**blend with** *v prep* → **assort with** (1), **blend together, go together** (4), **go with** (4), **harmonize with**
to combine pleasantly with (something else): [IØ + *with* (*usu. simple tenses*)] *These houses seem to blend well with the trees and the surrounding land. Their voices blend with each other.* [T1 + *with*] *I like to blend the colour of the curtains with the carpet.*

**bless with** *v prep* → **curse with**
**1** to give (someone or oneself) a special gift of (something, often a quality): [T1 + *with* (*simple tenses*)] *May God bless you with a long life!*
**2 be blessed with** to be favoured with (someone or something); be fortunate enough to possess (something): *I have never been a rich man, but I have always been blessed with good health. In his old age, the king was blessed with three fine daughters.*

***blind to** *v prep*
**1** to refuse to allow (someone, esp. oneself) to know (something): [D1] *You cannot blind yourself to the true facts; the position is hopeless. The desire to climb the mountain blinded Jim to all the difficulties.*
**2 be blinded to** to be unable to know (something): *For the first three years of their marriage, Mary was blinded to Jim's faults.*

***blink at** *v prep*
*infml* to show surprise at (something or doing something): [T1 (*often neg.*)] *He didn't blink at the idea of leaving his home and going far away.* [T4 (*often neg.*)] *Jim had such a high opinion of his own abilities that he hardly blinked at winning first prize.*

***blink away/back** *v adv* → **wink away** (2), **wink back** (2)
to try to remove (usu. tears) by opening and shutting the eyes quickly: [T1] *Mary tried hard to blink back her tears, but Jim could see that she had been crying.*

**block in** *v adv*
**1** to fill (a space), esp. with blocks: [T1 + IN] *Now that the well has run dry, we must block it in with bricks.*
**2** to trap (something) and prevent it moving: [X9 + IN] *The traffic was so thick that a whole row of cars got blocked in.*
***3** also **block out** to make a quick drawing or plan showing the general idea of (something): [T1 (*for*)] *Mr Brown has blocked in the plans for the house but has given no details.*

**block off** *v adv* → **seal off**
to prevent (something) from its usual use by closing it: [T1 + OFF] *The gas pipe has been blocked off to prevent escapes. The police blocked off the street where the gunman was hiding.*

**block out** *v adv*
**1** to cover; get in the way of (something): [T1 + OUT] *The clouds have blocked out the sun.*
***2** → BLOCK IN (3)
***3** (in photography or printing) to cover (part of a picture or page) so that it will not show on a copy: [T1] *Block out the bottom of this picture when it is printed; the balance of the page will be better.*

**block up** *v adv*
**1** to close (something); prevent movement through (something): [T1 + UP] *The pipe is blocked up again and there's water all over the floor. You'd better block up that hole in the wall; it's letting the cold in.* → **bring up** (1), **seal up, stop up** (1), **stuff up** (1)
***2** to fix (something) with blocks: [T1] *You will have to block up the wheel of the car to change the tyre.*

**blossom forth** *v adv* → BLOSSOM OUT

***blossom into** *v prep*
to develop into (something or someone good): [T1 (*no pass.*)] *Jane is blossoming into a beautiful girl.*

**blossom out** *v adv* also **blossom forth**
**1** to come into flower: [IØ + OUT] *The roses are blossoming out early this year.*
***2** to develop: [IØ (*often continuous tenses*)] *Jane is blossoming out into a beautiful girl. Our plans are beginning to blossom out at last.*
***3** to become active and cheerful: [IØ] *He used to be very quiet, but he has really blossomed out since he came to live here.*

***blot out** *v adv*
**1** to cover (writing, etc.) with ink, usu. by accident: [T1 (*often simple tenses*)] *I can't read this letter, the ink has run and blotted out half the words.*
**2** to cover; hide (something): [T1] *The mist has blotted out the view.*
**3** to destroy (something such as an idea): [T1 (*often simple tenses*)] *We must blot out the memory of wartime troubles.*

**blow about/around** *v adv*
**1** to (cause to) be blown without direction: [L9 + ABOUT/AROUND] *The leaves are blowing about in the strong wind.* [X9 + ABOUT/AROUND] *The violent wind was blowing broken glass about in the city streets.*
***2** *infml* to talk about (an idea, etc.) with

other people: [T1b] *Let's blow Jim's suggestion around and see if we all agree with it.* → **toss about** (3)

**blow away** *v adv*

**1** to (cause to) go away with or as with the force of wind: [L9 + AWAY] *Quick, catch my hat before it blows away!* [X9 + AWAY (often simple tenses)] *The wind was so strong that people were nearly blown away as they waited for buses.*

**2 blow the cobwebs away** *not fml* to refresh oneself with fresh air and often exercise: *I've been sitting at this desk all morning, I need a walk to blow the cobwebs away.*

**blow back** *v adv*

**1** to (cause to) return with or as with the force of wind: [L9 + BACK (often simple tenses)] *Just when I thought I had lost the letter forever, it blew right back into my hand!* [X9 + BACK (often simple tenses)] *You throw something into the air on a windy day, and the wind blows it back again.*

*__2__ (of gas) to blow in the wrong direction: [IØ] *If the gas blows back you must turn off the supply, as it is dangerous.* → **flare back**

**blow down**[1] *v adv*

**1** to (cause to) fall, by blowing: [X9 + DOWN (often simple tenses)] *The storm blew several trees down in the park.* [L9 + DOWN (often simple tenses)] *When did that old tree blow down?*

**2 blow me down** *BrE infml* (an expression of surprise): *Well, blow me down, if it isn't Jack Roberts: I've not seen you for years!*

**blow down**[2] *v prep*

(of air or breath) to direct (something) or be directed down (something, usu. hollow): [L9 + *down*] *Listen to the wind blowing down the chimney!* [X9 + *down* (often simple tenses)] *Many leaves have been blown down the pipe, and have blocked it.*

**blow in** *v adv*

**1** to (cause to) be blown inwards or indoors by wind: [X9 + IN (*to*) (often simple tenses)] *When the door was opened the wind blew the leaves in.* [L9 + IN (*to*)] *I opened the door and a pile of leaves blew in.*

*__2__ *infml* to (cause to) arrive unexpectedly: [IØ (*to*) (simple tenses)] *Jim just blew in; we weren't expecting him till Tuesday.* [T1 (simple tenses)] *See what the wind blew in!* → **breeze in**

*__3__ (of an oil well) to start producing: [IØ] *Number Three well blew in last night, and is producing 3,000 barrels an hour.*

*__4__ *AmE infml* to spend (money): [T1a] *The theatre company blew in $52,000.*

**blow into** *v prep*

**1** to (cause to) enter (a place) with or as with the force of wind: [X9 + *into*] *When the door was opened the wind blew the leaves into the house.* [L9 + *into*] *I opened the door and a pile of leaves blew into the house.*

*__2__ *infml* to arrive unexpectedly in (a place); esp. in the phr. **blow into town**: [T1 (no pass.)] *The director has just blown into town.*

**blow off**[1] *v adv*

**1** to (cause to) be removed by explosion or force of wind: [X9 + OFF (often simple tenses)] *The bomb blew the soldier's hands off. The wind blew roofs off in several cities.* [L9 + OFF] *When the water boiled, the lid of the pan blew off.*

**2 blow off steam** *infml* to give expression to anger, excitement, etc.: *Let the children blow off steam outside while the weather's fine, they get so restless indoors when it's raining.* → **let off**[1] (6)

**blow off**[2] *v prep*

to make (something) leave (something) by blowing: [X9 + *off* (usu. simple tenses)] *The storm blew the ship off its course. Don't blow the dust off the table, use a cloth.*

**blow on/upon** *v prep*

**1** (of wind or breath) to be directed onto (something or someone): [L9 + *on/upon*] *If you blow on a piece of paper, it moves.*

*__2__ to spoil (something): [T1 (often pass.)] *He used to have a good name but it has been blown upon recently.*

**3 blow the whistle on** *not fml* to put an end to (something that one disapproves of). *It's about time someone blew the whistle on his dishonest practices.*

**blow open** *v adj*

**1** to (cause to) be forced open by blowing: [X9 + **open** (often simple tenses)] *The explosion blew the door open.* [L9 + **open**] *The door blew open in the strong wind.*

*__2__ *infml* to spoil (something that one is trying to prove): [T1b (often simple tenses)] *The story given by the last witness has blown the case wide open.*

**blow out** *v adv*

**1** to (cause to) be sent out by blowing: [X9 + OUT] *The wind blew the seeds out of the plant. The chimney blew out a cloud of black smoke.* [L9 + OUT] *As I was cleaning the cupboard, a lot of feathers blew out.*

*__2__ to clean (something) by blowing: [T1] *We shall have to blow the pipe out, it seems to be blocked.*

*__3__ to fill (something or someone) with air, food, etc.: [T1 (usu. simple tenses)] *The child blew the paper bag out and then burst it. I feel blown out after that heavy meal. Horses are blown out after a race.* → **blowout** *n*

*__4__ to (cause to) stop burning by blowing: [T1] *Jane blew the flame out.* [IØ] *The flame blew out.* → **put out** (13) etc.

*__5__ to (cause to) stop blowing: [T1] *The storm blew itself out after three days.* [IØ] *The storm blew out after three days.* → **rage out**

*__6__ to (cause to) burst: [T1 (usu. simple tenses)] *The heat blew out the tire* [IØ (usu.

*simple tenses*)] *The tyre blew out as I was driving to work.* —**blowout** *n*

*7 to destroy (something) by the force of air or other gas: [T1 (*usu. simple tenses*)] *The bomb blew the windows out.*

*8 (of electrical machinery) to (cause to) stop working: [T1 (*simple tenses*)] *The damaged wire blew out the cooker.* [IØ (*simple tenses*)] *The cooker has blown out.* —**blowout** *n*

*9 (of an oil well) to produce oil uncontrollably: [IØ] *An oil well blew out in the North Sea, causing a very big floating mass of oil.* —**blowout** *n*

**10 blow one's brains out** to kill oneself by shooting oneself in the head: [*usu. simple tenses*] *When his plans all failed, the chairman blew his brains out.* → **dash out** (2)

***blow over** *v adv*

**1** to stop blowing: [IØ] *The storm has lasted a long time, it should soon blow over.*

**2** *not fml* to cease: [IØ] *I hope your troubles will soon blow over.*

***blow round** *v adv*

esp. *BrE infml* to pay a visit informally: [IØ (*usu. simple tenses*)] *Why don't you blow round one evening next week?*

**blow to** *v prep*

**1 blow something to atoms/bits/pieces/smithereens** *not fml* to destroy something by explosion, into many small parts: [(*often pass.*)] *That was a good aim; the target has been blown to pieces.*

**2 blow someone to blazes/glory/kingdom come** *not fml* to kill someone violently as by explosion: [*often pass.*] *Then the bomb went off, and two of our officers were blown to glory.*

***blow up** *v adv*

**1** (of wind) to begin blowing: [IØ (*for*) (*usu. continuous tenses*)] *It looks as if it's blowing up for severe weather.*

**2** (of weather) to arise with the wind: [IØ] *There was a storm blowing up while we were out at sea.*

**3** to arise: [IØ] *Trouble is blowing up again in the Middle East.*

**4** to (cause to) fill with air: [T1] *Help me to blow up these tyres, will you?* [IØ (*simple tenses*)] *These plastic balls don't blow up easily.* → **pump up** (2)

**5** to increase (something such as fire) by blowing: [T1] *You'll have to blow up the fire to make it burn.*

**6** to (cause to) explode; destroy (something or someone) by or as if by explosion: [T1] *The soldiers blew up the enemy bridge.* [IØ (*usu. simple tenses*)] *A chemical factory blew up in the North of England.* → **go up**[1] (7), **send up**[1] (4)

**7** to (cause to) fail, esp. publicly: [IØ (*simple tenses*)] *The lawyer's case blew up because he had no proof. The plan blew up in his face.* [T1] *We'll soon blow up his plan.*

**8** to enlarge (a photograph): [T1] *The photographer blew the picture of the child up and entered it for a national competition.* —**blow-up** *n* —**blown-up** *adj*

**9** to make (something or someone) seem greater than in fact: [T1] *He always blows up his adventures to make them seem better than they were. The crowd blew him up with their praise.*

**10** *infml* to be angry (with someone): [T1 esp. *BrE*] *Mother will blow you up when she finds her best dishes broken.* [IØ (*at*) esp. *AmE*] *Mother will blow up at you when she finds her best dishes broken.* —**blow-up** *n* → **tell off** (1), etc.

**blow upon** *v prep* → BLOW ON

**blubber out** *v adv*

*not fml* to tell (a story) while weeping: [T1 + OUT] *The prisoner at last blubbered out his guilt.*

***bluff into** *v prep*

to persuade (someone) into (doing something) by pretending: [V4b] *Do you think you can bluff the police into believing that you were not at the scene of the crime?*

**bluff out** *v adv*

**1 bluff it out** *not fml* to escape trouble by continuing to pretend: *Although his mother had caught him telling a lie, he tried to bluff it out.* → **brave out, brazen out**

**2 bluff one's way out (of something)** *not fml* to escape (trouble) by pretending not to be guilty: *Now you've been caught actually stealing the goods, you won't be able to bluff your way out of this one.*

***blunder away** *v adv*

to waste (something) by mistaken action: [T1] *The new director blundered away most of the firm's profits.*

***blunder on/upon** *v prep* → HAPPEN ON

***blunder out** *v adv* → **blurt out**

to tell (something such as a secret) without thinking: [T1a (*often simple tenses*)] *The Minister has been blundering out government secrets again.*

***blunder upon** *v prep* → BLUNDER ON

***blurt out** *v adv* → **blunder out**

to tell (something such as a secret) without thinking: [T1 (*usu. simple tenses*)] *Peter blurted out the news before he considered its effect.*

**blush for** *v prep*

**1** to show signs of shame such as a red face, for (a reason): [IØ + *for*] *I blush for shame when I remember how I treated you.*

***2** to be ashamed of (something): [T1 (*no pass., simple tenses, usu. present*)] *When I see the prices that tourists are charged, I blush for my country.*

**bluster out** *v adv*

**bluster it out** to try to defend one's wrong action with forceful words: *When Tom was caught cheating, he tried to bluster it out but he couldn't deceive us.*

**board in** *v adv*

**1** to close (a space) with boards of wood:

[X9 + IN (*often pass.*)] *There used to be a hole in the fence that we could creep through, but it's been boarded in.* → **board up**

*__2__ to take meals at one's lodging or place of work: [IØ] *The fruit pickers can board in or make their own arrangements for food.*

***board out** *v adv*
to (cause to) receive food and lodgings away from home: [T1] *We'll have to board the cat out while we're away on holiday.* [IØ] *Your family is so large that three of the children will have to board out.*

**board up** *v adv* → **board in** (1)
to close (a space) with boards of wood: [X9 + UP (*often pass.*)] *The windows were boarded up when the owner died and the shop was closed.*

**board with** *v prep*
to take meals with (someone): [IØ + *with*] *Jim is boarding with Mrs King while he's in town.*

**boast about/of** *v prep* → **brag about**
to speak too proudly of (one's abilities, successes, or possessions): [IØ + *about/of*] *I do hate the way Bill boasts about his new car. Bill boasts of owning the biggest car in the neighbourhood.*

**bob down** *v adv*
*not fml* to make a quick bending movement downwards: [IØ + DOWN] *Bob down behind the wall, there's a policeman coming.*

**bob to** *v prep*
(of a woman) to bend one's knees to (someone) as a sign of respect: [IØ + *to*] *Don't forget to bob to the princess when she enters the room.*

**bob up** *v adv*
**1** *not fml* to float quickly to the surface: [IØ + UP] *If you try to sink an apple in water, it will keep bobbing up.*

*__2__ *infml* to reappear unexpectedly: [IØ (*usu. simple tenses*)] *Jim bobbed up just when we were sure that he had left.*

**bode ill/well** *v adv* also **augur ill/well**
*fml* to be a bad/good sign for the future: [L9 + ILL/WELL (*for*) (*simple tenses, usu, present*)] *Those dark clouds bode ill for this afternoon's garden party. The sunshine bodes well for this afternoon's garden party.*

**bog down** *v adv*
**1** to (cause to) stick in mud: [T1 (*usu. pass.*)] *The car got bogged down and wouldn't move.* [IØ] *The car has bogged down and won't move.*

**2** *not fml* to (cause to) meet difficulties: [T1 (*usu. pass.*)] *The talks with the men got bogged down on the question of working hours.* [IØ] *The talks with the men bogged down on the question of working hours.*

**bog off** *v adv* → **push off** (3), etc.
*sl* to go away: [IØ (*simple tenses, usu. imper.*)] *Bog off! Get out of here!*

**boggle at** *v prep*
to be very surprised by, and unwilling to believe (something strange), esp. in the phr. **the mind boggles:** [IØ + *at*] *The mind boggles at the idea of life on distant stars.*

**boil away** *v adv*
**1** to continue boiling: [IØ + AWAY] *The water has been boiling away for ten minutes.*

*__2__ to be reduced to little or nothing by boiling: [IØ (*usu. simple tenses*)] *The water had all boiled away and the pan was burnt.*

*__3__ *not fml* to be reduced to nothing: [IØ] *His excitement soon boiled away when the work actually started.*

**boil down** *v adv*
**1** to (cause to) be reduced by boiling: [T1 + DOWN (*to*)] *Use plenty of vegetables because the cooking boils them all down to a small quantity.* [IØ + DOWN (*to*)] *Put a lot of the vegetable in the pan, it all boils down (to a small quantity).*

*__2__ to reduce (something): [T1 (*to*) (*usu. simple tenses*)] *You can boil the long story down to a few sentences and it still has the same meaning.*

***boil down to** *v adv prep*
*not fml* to be reduced to its real meaning (as something): [T1 (*simple tenses*)] *The whole matter boils down to a power struggle between the trade union and the directors.* → **come down** (9), **come down to** (5)

***boil out** *v adv*
to (cause to) be removed by boiling: [T1] *You may want to boil out some of the stiffness.* [IØ (*simple tenses*)] *Some of the stiffness will boil out when you first wash the cloth.*

***boil over** *v adv*
**1** to overflow by boiling: [IØ] *Turn off the gas, the milk is boiling over.*

**2** *not fml* to become out of control (and develop into something): [IØ (*into*)] *The small argument boiled over into a serious quarrel.*

**3** *infml* to become angry: [IØ] *The trade union chief boiled over when the men voted against him.*

**boil up** *v adv*
**1** to heat (food) by boiling: [T1 + UP] *The soup is nearly cold, I'll boil it up again for you.* → **heat up** (1), **hot up** (1), **warm up** (1)

*__2__ *infml* to increase, esp. to a dangerous level: [IØ] *Jim's anger boiled up when he heard how Mary had been treated. Trouble was boiling up in the Middle East.*

**bolster up** *v adv*
*not fml* to give strong moral support to (someone or something): [T1 + UP] *The election results bolstered up the spirits of the newly formed party.*

**bolt down** *v adv*
**1** to fasten (something) with bolts: [T1 + DOWN] *The lid of the box was bolted down.*

**2** to eat (food) hastily: [T1 + DOWN] *Don't bolt your food down like that, it's rude.*

**bolt out** *v adv*
**1** to leave in a hurry: [L9 + OUT (*usu. simple*

*tenses*)] *When I opened the door, the cat bolted out.*

*2 to prevent (someone or an animal) from entering by locking a door: [T1] *When the man tried to get into his own house, he found he had been bolted out.*

***bomb out** *v adv*
to make (someone) homeless by bombing: [T1 (*usu. pass.*)] *My aunt was bombed out during the war, and had to live with my mother.* —**bombed-out** *adj*

***bomb up** *v adv*
to load (a plane) with bombs: [IØ] *The pilot gave the order to bomb up.* [T1 (*usu. pass.*)] *Have all the planes been bombed up?*

**bombard with** *v prep*
**1** to attack (something such as a place) with repeated blows from (something destructive): [T1 + *with*] *For a whole week, the little town was bombarded with enemy shells until the citizens were forced to yield. The machine was made so that the army could bombard the enemy castle with bits of broken rock.*
*__2__ to worry (someone) with (repeated questions, etc.): [D1 (*often pass.*)] *The speaker was bombarded with questions.*

***bone up on** *v adv prep* → **mug up, swot up**
*not fml* to learn (a subject) by hard studying: [T1] *I must bone up on Shakespeare's language if I am to take the test next week.*

***book in** *v adv*
**1** esp. *BrE* to (cause to) report one's arrival, as at a hotel desk, airport, etc.: [IØ (*at, to*)] *It is always advisable to book in early when you want a hotel room in the tourist season.* [T1 (*at, to*)] *I'll just book you in and then you can have a rest.* → **book out** (1), **check in** (2), **check out** (2)
**2** esp. *BrE* to cause to have a place kept for (one) at a hotel: [T1 (*at, to*)] *I've booked you in at the Grand Hotel, I hope you approve.*

***book off** *v adv*
**1** esp. *AmE* to declare that one has finished a period of work: [IØ] *When I was working on the railway, I had to book off after eight hours' work.*
**2** *AmE not fml* to declare one's intention not to work on a particular day, esp. because of a disagreement with one's employer esp. in the phr. **book off sick:** [IØ] *300 men have booked off sick at the car factory where there is still trouble with the unions.*

**book out** *v adv*
*__1__ esp. *BrE* to (cause to) take formal leave of a hotel, etc.; pay one's bill: [T1] *I'll book you out at the same time as myself, shall I?* [IØ] *I'd like to book out early in the morning, please.* → **book in** (1), **check in** (2), **check out** (2)
**2 be booked out** to have all one's space filled: *I'm sorry, the hotel/theatre is booked out.* → **book up** (2)

***book through** *v adv*
*BrE* to buy a ticket for the whole of a divided journey: [IØ (*to*)] *If you have to change trains in London, you may be able to book through* (*to your last station*)*; ask the ticket collector.*

***book up** *v adv*
**1** to arrange for a place to be kept for one, as at a performance: [IØ] *The play has been very popular, you have to book up well ahead.*
**2 be booked up** to have all one's space or time filled: *I'm sorry, the hotel/theatre is booked up. The singer is always booked up for a year ahead.* → **book out** (2)

**boom out** *v adv*
**1** to make a loud hollow noise: [IØ + OUT] *The horn boomed out all night to warn the ships of the dangerous mist.*
*__2__ to say or sing (something) in a loud hollow voice: [T1] *The policeman boomed out a warning.* [IØ] *The singer's voice boomed out, reaching to the back of the hall.*

***boost up** *v adv*
**1** to help (someone) by pushing upwards: [T1] *The small girl had to be boosted up onto the large horse.* —**boost-up** *n*
**2** to support; strengthen (someone): [T1] *The company needs boosting up, if it is not to be defeated by its competitors. Jim is not very cheerful; he needs a holiday to boost him up.*

***boot out** *v adv* → **throw out** (4), etc.
*infml* to make (someone) leave because of a fault: [T1 (*usu. pass.*)] *Two members were booted out* (*of the club*) *for failing to pay the money they owed.*

***booze up** *v adv*
esp. *BrE infml* to drink a large quantity of alcohol: [IØ (*usu. continuous tenses*)] *The men spent the whole evening in the pub boozing up.* —**booze-up** *n*

**border on** *v prep*
**1** to touch; be next to (something): [L9 + *on* (*simple tenses*)] *The bottom of our garden borders on the park.* → **abut on, verge on** (1)
*__2__ to be very much like (something): [T1 (*no pass., simple tenses*)] *Your remarks border on rudeness.* → **touch on** (4), **verge on** (2)

**bore to** *v prep*
to make (someone) lose interest to the point of (something), esp. in the phrs. **bore to death/sleep/tears**: [D1] *The politician's speech bored the crowd to death.*

**borne in on** → BEAR IN ON

**borrow from** *v prep*
**1** to receive (something) from (someone) for a certain time, intending to give it back: [T1 + *from*] *You could borrow some money from your uncle without paying interest. Can I borrow some sugar from you?* [IØ + *from*] *Never borrow from your mother.*
*__2__ to copy (an idea, style, etc.) from (another writer): [D1] *His poetry borrows words from Shakespeare.* [T1] *His poetry borrows from Shakespeare.*

***boss about/around** *v adv*
*not fml* to treat (someone) unpleasantly by

giving unnecessary orders: [T1b] *The new director will not be successful if he goes on bossing the workers about.*

**botch up** *v adv* → **mess up** (2), etc.
*BrE infml* to spoil (something) carelessly: [T1 + UP] *If John botches up his driving test again, I doubt if he'll ever pass it. The last electrician botched up this job; I hope you can mend the wires.* —**botch-up** *n* —**botched-up** *adj*

**bother about** *v prep*
**1** to take trouble concerning (something or someone): [IØ + *about*] *Don't bother about the letters, they're not urgent. Don't bother about seeing me off.* [T1 + *about*] *Don't bother yourself about the arrangements for our holiday; I'm organizing it all.* → **bother with** (1)
**2 be bothered about** to worry about (something or someone): *I'm bothered about those spots that Jane has. I'm bothered about Freda, she's out so late again.*
**3 bother one's head about** to worry about or concern oneself with (a matter): [*usu. neg.*] *The affair is unimportant, and certainly not worth bothering your pretty little head about! I don't bother my head about office politics, they have no interest for me.*

**bother with** *v prep*
**1** to take trouble concerning (something or someone): [IØ + *with*] *Don't bother with the letters, they're not urgent. Don't bother with seeing me off.* [T1 + *with*] *Don't bother yourself with the arrangements for the holiday.* → **bother about** (1)
**2 not be bothered with** *not fml* to not care about (something or someone); dislike (doing something): *I can't be bothered with all her little problems. I can't be bothered with waiting for a bus, let's walk.*

**bottle up** *v adv*
**1** to put (something) in bottles: [T1 + UP] *Father is in the garage, bottling up his home-made beer.*
*__2__ also **cork up, dam up** to control (something such as feelings) in an unhealthy way: [T1] *Bottling up your anger leads to trouble.*

***bottom out** *v adv*
**1** to be at its lowest position: [IØ (*simple tenses*)] *The valley bottoms out at the river.*
**2** to reach the lowest point before rising again: [IØ] *House prices bottomed out in 1989. Peter's feeling of sadness bottomed out and then he began to feel cheerful again.*

**bounce along** *v adv*
**1** to move in a springing manner: [IØ + ALONG] *The rubber ball bounced along.*
*__2__ to move fast: [IØ] *This new car bounces along, doesn't it?*
*__3__ *not fml* to advance well: [IØ (*often continuous tenses*)] *My work is just bouncing along now, thanks.*

**bounce back** *v adv*
**1** to return in a springing manner: [IØ + BACK] *When I threw the ball against the wall, it bounced back.*
*__2__ to return to a more usual and healthy state of feeling or activity: [IØ] *Small children often catch diseases, but they soon bounce back.*
*__3__ *not fml* to have a result or effect: [IØ + ON] *Whatever decision the directors take, it will bounce back on the future of the firm.* —**bounce-back** *n*

**bounce from/off** *v prep*
to return in a springing manner from (usu. a surface): [T1 + *from/off*] *As a child, I used to enjoy bouncing rubber balls from one wall to another.* [IØ + *from/off*] *This hall sounds hollow because the music bounces off the walls.*

**bounce out** *v adv*
**1** to move out in a springing manner: [IØ + OUT (*of*)] *When I opened the cupboard door, an apple bounced out. As soon as Jill woke, she bounced out of bed.*
*__2__ *infml* to make (someone) leave because of a fault: [T1 (*of*)] *Two members were bounced out (of the club) for failing to pay the money they owed.* → **throw out** (4), etc.

**bound up in** → BIND UP IN

**bound up with** → BIND UP WITH

**bow before/to** *v prep*
**1** to bend at the waist in a humble manner, in the presence of (someone important) or as a sign of worship of (a god): [IØ + *before/to*] *All the men in the court bowed (down) before the king as he entered.* → **prostrate before**
*__2__ to yield to (something): [T1 (*no pass.*)] *I bow before your opinion, and will take your advice. I bow to your better judgment, and will take your advice.*
*__3__ also **bend to** to obey (something): [T1] (*no pass.*)] *I will bow before your wishes, and will not follow my original plans. I'd advise you to bow to the old lady's wishes.* → **bend before** (2)
**4 bow before/to the inevitable** to accept that which cannot be avoided: *Since there is no way to escape the winter in this place, I suppose we have to bow to the inevitable and get out our heavy coats and boots, and face increased heating bills.*

***bow down** *v adv*
**1** to weigh down; cause (something) to bend: [T1 (*usu. pass.*)] *The apple tree was bowed down with the weight of its fruit.* → **load down** (1), etc.
**2** to cause (someone) to suffer: [T1 (*with*) (*usu. pass.*)] *Aunt Helen spent years bowed down with grief after the death of her husband.* → **lade with** (2), **load down** (2), **weigh down** (2)
**3** to limit the freedom of (someone) by severe political control: [T1 (*usu. pass.*)] *The people of Russia before 1917 were bowed down by the cruelty of the ruling powers.*
**4** to admit defeat and agree to serve someone: [IØ (*to*)] *We shall never bow down to our enemies.*

***bow in** *v adv* → **bow out** (1)
to bend politely to (someone) as he enters: [T1b (*to*)] *The owner of the restaurant bowed us in when we arrived.*

***bow out** *v adv*
**1** to bend politely to (someone) as he leaves, or as one leaves: [T1] *The servant bowed the guests out as they left.* [T1b (*of*)] *When leaving the presence of the princess, you have to bow yourself out as you go.* → **bow in**
**2** to leave (a competition, etc.) or stop doing (something), esp. in a pleasant manner: [IØ (*of*)] *Jim bowed out of the competition when he learned who his opponent was. The old leader decided to bow out instead of fighting to keep his position.* [T1 (*of*)] *Jim bowed himself out of the competition when he learned who his opponent was.*

**bow to** *v prep* → **BOW BEFORE**

***bowl along** *v adv*
**1** *infml* to move quickly and pleasantly, as in a car: [IØ] *There we were, bowling along nicely, when suddenly the tire burst.* → **spin along**
**2** *infml* to make reasonable advance: [IØ (*usu. continuous tenses*)] *Work is bowling along nicely now, thank you.*

***bowl out** *v adv*
**1** (in cricket) to bring a player's turn to an end by striking his wicket with the ball: [T1 (*usu. simple tenses*)] *The first two men were caught out, and the next player was bowled out.* → **be out** (7), etc.
**2** to surprise or shock (someone) very much: [T1b (*usu. simple tenses*)] *Your sudden news has quite bowled me out.* → **bowl over** (2), etc.

***bowl over** *v adv*
**1** to knock (someone or an animal) down, esp. by running; fall or roll over: [T1 (*simple tenses*)] *Someone ran round the corner and nearly bowled me over.* [IØ (*simple tenses*)] *In the accident, the car bowled over three times but the driver escaped unhurt.*
**2** to surprise or shock (someone) very much: [T1b] *Your sudden news has quite bowled me over.* → **bowl out** (2), **knock back** (5), **knock down** (11), **knock out** (9), **knock over** (3)

***bowse down** *v adv*
*naut* to tighten (a rope): [T1] *Bowse the ropes down; there's a storm coming!*

***box in** *v adv* → **hedge in, hem in**
to surround; enclose (someone or something) tightly: [T1 (*often pass.*)] *The whole army was boxed in by the enemy and had no hope of escape.*

***box off** *v adv*
to separate (something): [T1 (*from*) (*often pass.*)] *The police boxed off the area into smaller parts for better control. He keeps those two ideas boxed off from each other in his mind.*

***box up** *v adv*
**1** to put (something) in boxes, for packing or storing: [T1 (*usu. pass.*)] *When Harry went to sea, his things were boxed up and put in the storeroom. Your books have to be boxed up to send to university.*
**2** esp. *AmE* to close (a space) with boards of wood: [T1] *You'd better box up the doorway until we can get a new door.*
**3** *AustrE* to confuse (usu. an animal): [T1 (*usu. pass.*)] *The sheep were all boxed up, running round in circles.*
**4** to shut (someone) in a small building: [T1 (*usu. pass.*)] *It's good to get outside in the fresh air again, after being boxed up in the house all winter.*

**brace up** *v adv*
**1** to strengthen; support (something) with something strong: [T1 + UP] *The old house was leaning at a dangerous angle and had to be braced up with heavy pieces of wood.*
***2** to (cause to) become stronger, more cheerful, etc.: [T1] *A walk in this good mountain air will brace you up.* [IØ (*simple tenses, often imper.*)] *Brace up! Your troubles will soon be over.* → **cheer up**, etc.

***brace up to** *v adv prep*
to be prepared to face (trouble, etc.): [T1 (*no pass., often simple tenses*)] *You'll have to brace up to your misfortune and get on with your work.*

**brag about/of** *v prep* → **boast about**
*not fml* to speak too proudly of (one's abilities, successes, possessions, etc.): [IØ + *about/of*] *I do hate the way Bill brags about his new car. Bill brags of owning the biggest car in the neighbourhood.*

***branch off** *v adv* → **turn off**[1] (2)
to divide; separate from the main direction: [IØ] *Take the little path which branches off to the left.*

***branch out** *v adv*
**1** (of a tree) to divide into branches: [IØ] *The young tree is beginning to branch out.*
**2** to start something new by dividing one's activities: [IØ (*into*)] *The bookshop has decided to branch out into selling music and records. I'm glad to see that Jim has branched out into more varied sports these days.*

***brass off** *v adv*
esp. *mil infml* to (cause to) complain: [IØ] *The young soldiers are all brassing off again, they're never satisfied.* [T1 (*usu. pass.*)] *We're all brassed off with this terrible food.*

***brass up** *v adv*
**1** to put leather belts and esp. metal ornaments on (a horse): [T1] *The boys are in the yard, brassing up the horses for the show.* [IØ] *Come on boys, let's get brassing up, we must be ready to leave for the horse show in an hour.*
**2** *N. Eng. infml* to pay (an amount of money) as one's share: [IØ] *If everyone brasses up, we'll soon have enough.* [T1] *Each*

*member is asked to brass up his share of the cost.*

**brave out** *v adv* → **bluff out** (1), **brazen out**
**brave it out** to face trouble or blame with courage: *The director has called me into his office to give an explanation of my behaviour; I'd better go and brave it out.*

**brazen out** *v adv* → **bluff out** (1), **brave out**
**brazen it out** to face trouble or blame with shameless daring: *When the police caught the thief in the act, he tried to brazen it out.*

**break away** *v adv*
**1** to (cause to) come apart (from something): [IØ + AWAY (*from*)] *The wing of the plane broke away in mid-air and the plane crashed.* [T1 + AWAY (*from*)] *You'll have to break the branches away to get through the thick forest.* → **break off** (1)
*__2__ to escape (from someone): [IØ (*from*)] *The criminal broke away from the policemen who were holding him.*
*__3__ to end one's connection with or loyalty to (a group): [IØ (*from*)] *Part of the country broke away (from the State) to form a new nation. Modern music has broken away from 18th century rules.* —**breakaway** *adj*

**break back** *v adv*
**1** (of a cricket ball) to twist and rise unexpectedly after hitting the ground: [IØ (*simple tenses*)] *The next ball broke back; the player missed it and was out.* —**break-back** *n*
**2** (in rugby football) to change one's direction without warning: [IØ] *By breaking back, the player was able to confuse the opposing players and run twenty yards with the ball.* —**break-back** *n*
**3** (in tennis) to win a game from an opponent who began it, immediately after losing a game one began oneself: [IØ] *Becker lost the first game on his service, but broke back and won the second game.*

**break down** *v adv*
**1** to destroy (something); reduce (something) to pieces: [T1 + DOWN] *The police broke the door down. The old cars were broken down for their metal and parts.* —**broken-down** *adj*
*__2__ to (cause to) be defeated: [T1] *The police tried to break down the prisoner's opposition.* [IØ] *The prisoner's opposition broke down under repeated questioning.* —**breaking-down** *n*
*__3__ (of machinery) to fail to work; stop working: [IØ (*usu. simple tenses*)] *The washing machine seems to have broken down again. The car broke down on the way to the airport, and I had to get a taxi.* —**breakdown** *n* → **conk out** (1), **cut out** (8), **give out** (6), **kick off** (6), **pack up** (3)
*__4__ to fail: [IØ] *Peace talks have broken down in the Middle East. Your health will break down if you work too hard.* —**breakdown** *n*
*__5__ to suffer poor health; suffer a nervous illness for some time: [IØ (*usu. simple tenses*)] *You will break down if you work too hard. Peter broke down and was unable to work for a year.* —**breakdown** *n* → **break up** (7), **crack up** (3), **crock up**
*__6__ to lose control of one's feelings: [IØ] *Peter broke down and wept when he saw the deer that he had shot.*
*__7__ to (cause to) have a chemical change: [T1 (*into*) (*simple tenses*)] *Chemicals in the body break down our food into useful substances.* [IØ (*into*) (*simple tenses*)] *Our food breaks down in the body into useful substances.*
*__8__ to (cause to) separate into different kinds: [T1 (*into*) (*usu. simple tenses*)] *The figures must be broken down into several lists.* [IØ (*into*) (*simple tenses*)] *The figures break down into several kinds, showing us different ways of looking at the firm's activities.* —**breakdown** *n*

***break even** *v adv*
*not fml* to show neither profit nor loss: [IØ (*often simple tenses*)] *We need to take £5,200 each performance just to break even.* —**break-even** *adj*

**break in** *v adv*
**1** to break (something) inwards: [T1 + IN] *The firemen could enter the burning house only by breaking in the door.* → **burst in** (1)
*__2__ to enter (a building) by force, usu. unlawfully: [IØ (*to*)] *The thieves waited until it was dark enough to break in.*
*__3__ to interrupt: [IØ (*simple tenses*)] *"But I was there!" Jane broke in.* → **burst in** (3), **cut in**' (3)
*__4__ to control; train (a horse) to obey; help (someone) to become accustomed (to work, etc.): [T1] *When horses are about six months old, they have to be broken in. Two weeks in the new office should be enough to break you in.*
*__5__ to wear or use (shoes, an apparatus, etc.) until comfortable or working fully: [T1] *I'm wearing my new boots around the house to break them in. Don't drive the new car too fast, I'm still breaking it in.* → **run in**' (7)

***break in on/upon** *v adv prep* → **burst in on**
to interrupt (someone or something): [T1 (*usu. simple tenses*)] *The loud bell on the clock broke in upon his dreams. I'm sorry to break in on your private thoughts, but I think we should get on with some work.*

**break into** *v prep*
**1** to divide (something) into (smaller parts): [T1 + *into*] *Mary broke the chocolate into pieces, one for each person.*
*__2__ also **burst into** to enter (a building, etc.) by force: [T1] *The thieves waited until it was dark enough to break into the house. This box looks as if it's been broken into.*
*__3__ to interrupt (something): [T1 (*simple tenses*)] *The children broke into the conversation with demands for attention. My aunt's*

*regular visits break into my weekend.* → **cut into** (3)

*__4__ to begin suddenly to give voice to (a sound): [T1 (*no pass., simple tenses*)] *The singers broke into song. Mary broke (forth) into laughter.* → **break out in** (2), **burst into** (3), **burst out** (1), **bust out** (3), **crack out**

*__5__ to begin (something such as a movement) suddenly: [T1 (*no pass., simple tenses*)] *The men broke into a run. As I grew more afraid, I broke into a cold sweat.*

*__6__ to use part of (something such as money) unwillingly: [T1 (*simple tenses*)] *I shall have to break into my savings to pay for the holiday. I don't want to break into a £10 note unless I really have to.* → **cut into** (4)

*__7__ to start; usu. with difficulty, working in (a kind of work): [T1 (*no pass.*)] *Mary is wondering how she can break into show business.*

***break loose** *v adj*

**1** to escape: [IØ (*usu. simple tenses*)] *Three prisoners broke loose as they were being taken to another prison this morning.* → **get free** (1), etc.

**2** to become active, out of control: [IØ (*usu. simple tenses*)] *Violence broke loose in the city last night.*

***break of** *v prep*

to cure (someone) of (a bad habit, etc.): [D1 (*usu. simple tenses*)] *Doctors keep trying to break him of his dependence on the drug.*

**break off** *v adv*

**1** to (cause to) come apart (from something): [IØ + OFF] *The wing of the plane broke off in mid-air and the plane crashed.* [T1 + OFF] *Mary broke off some of the chocolate to give to the children.* → **break away** (1)

*__2__ (usu. of a relationship, agreement, etc.) to (cause to) end: [T1a (*usu. simple tenses*)] *Iran broke off relations with Britain.* [IØ] *Relations between Iran and Britain have broken off.* → **declare off, declare on**[1]

*__3__ to stop speaking: [IØ (*simple tenses*)] *Jim was in the middle of a funny story when he broke off to answer the telephone.* [T4 (*simple tenses*)] *Jim broke off telling the story to answer the telephone.*

*__4__ to stop working for a short time: [IØ (*simple tenses*)] *Let's break off and have a cup of tea.* [T1a (*simple tenses*)] *Let's break off work and have a cup of tea.*

***break open** *v adj*

to open (something) by force: [T1b] *The lock is broken; you'll have to break the case open.*

**break out** *v adv*

**1** to break (something) in an outward direction: [T1 + OUT] *We had to break the door out to escape from the fire.*

*__2__ to begin, usu. suddenly: [IØ (*simple tenses*)] *War broke out in 1939. Fire broke out in the hospital last night.* —**outbreak** *n* → **flare up** (2), etc.

*__3__ to escape (from): [IØ (*of*) (*usu. simple tenses*)] *Three men broke out of prison yesterday. I should like to break out of this meaningless way of life.* —**breakout** *n* → **burst out** (2), **bust out** (2), **crash out**

*__4__ to open (something); unfold: [T1a (*usu. simple tenses*)] *As the Queen stepped on the shore, the ship broke out the royal flag. We must break out a new case of wine for the young man's 18th birthday.*

***break out in** *v adv prep*

**1** to begin to show (something): [T1 (*no pass.*)] *Jane broke out in spots this morning.* —**outbreak** *n* → **bring out in, come out in** (2)

**2** to give voice to (a sound) suddenly: [T1 (*no pass.*)] *Mary broke out in loud laughter.* → **break into** (4), **burst into** (3), **burst out** (1), **bust out** (3), **crack out**

**3 break out in a cold sweat** to show signs of great fear: [*simple tenses*] *When I thought that no one was coming back to save me, I broke out in a cold sweat.*

**break over** *v prep*

**1** (usu. of water) to flow with force across (something): [IØ + *over*] *As a child, I used to enjoy watching the stormy waves breaking over the harbour wall.*

*__2__ (of a sound) to begin forcefully near (someone): [T1 (*no pass., usu. simple tenses*)] *The young singer was pleasantly surprised when waves of cheering broke over her at the end of her first performance.*

***break short** *v adj* → **cut short** (2)

to end (something) suddenly: [T1 (*usu. simple tenses*)] *I'm afraid I must break this conversation short, I have to go now.*

***break through**[1] *v adv*

**1** (of the sun or moon) to appear: [IØ (*often simple tenses*)] *The sun broke through after days of rain.* → **come through**[1] (3)

**2** to advance in spite of opposition: [IØ (*often simple tenses*)] *Foreign forces have broken through on the coast.* —**breakthrough** *n*

**3** to make advances in discovery or any other aim: [IØ (*in*) (*often simple tenses*)] *Scientists think they have broken through in their attempt to find the causes of many major diseases. Now that women have broken through in the field of medicine, we can expect more women doctors.* —**breakthrough** *n*

***break through**[2] *v prep*

**1** to break a way through (something solid): [T1] *We had to break through the solid wall to reach the prisoners.*

**2** to force an advance through (something in the way): [T1 (*often simple tenses*)] *Have our soldiers broken through the enemy's defences yet? The sun broke through the clouds.* —**breakthrough** *n*

**3** to conquer (something in the way): [T1 (*often simple tenses*)] *It was difficult at first to break through her quiet manner. We are now flying faster than the speed of sound; we've* *broken through the sound barrier.* —**breakthrough** *n*

**break to** *v prep*
to tell (usu. bad news) to (someone), in a kind way: [T1 + *to* ] *Will you break the news of Henry's death to his wife, or shall I?*

*****break up** *v adv*
**1** to (cause to) divide into smaller pieces: [T1] *Soon the freezing weather will break up the soil* (into smaller pieces). [IØ] *In the spring the ice on the Great Lakes breaks up.* —**breakup** *n*
**2** to (cause to) be destroyed: [T1 (into)] *The men in the garage will break up the old cars and use their parts.* [IØ (*into*)] *The ship was last seen breaking up in the storm.* → **crack up** (2)
**3** to (cause to) come to an end: [T1 (*usu. simple tenses*)] *The police broke up the fight. "Break it up!" shouted the policeman.* [IØ] *The party broke up when the police arrived.*
**4** (of a group) to divide; cease to be together: [IØ (*often simple tenses*)] *The crowd broke up.*
**5** *BrE* (of school) to end for a holiday: [IØ (*often simple tenses*)] *When does your school break up? We break up next week.*
**6** to (cause to) separate or cease: [IØ] *Their marriage broke up. I hear that Jim and Mary are breaking up.* [T1] *It was money trouble that broke up their marriage.* —**breakup** *n* → **bust up** (3), **split up** (4)
**7** to (cause to) suffer severe anxiety and pain; make (someone) grieve: [T1 (*usu. simple tenses*)] *The terrible news will break him up. The death of his pet cat broke him up.* [IØ (*usu. simple tenses*)] *He may break up under this trouble.* → **break down** (5), **crack up** (3), **crock up**
**8** *AmE infml* to amuse (someone) greatly: [T1b (*simple tenses*)] *His story broke me up, I couldn't stop laughing.* [IØ] *Peter just broke up when we told him what had happened.*
**9** to divide (something) (into smaller parts): [T1 (*into*) (*often pass.*)] *The job can be broken up into several activities, which provides some variety. After his death, his land was broken up into areas suitable for building houses.*

**break with** *v prep*
to cease one's connection with (someone or something): [T1 (*no pass., usu. simple tenses*)] *When he became rich, he broke with his former friends. As you grow wiser, you should break with your old ideas.*

**breathe again** *v adv*
*not fml* to feel safe: [IØ] *I shan't be able to breathe again until the examination results are received.*

**breathe down** *v prep*
**breathe down someone's neck** *infml* to follow or watch someone closely: [*no pass.*] *Stop breathing down my neck, I make mistakes when I'm being watched.*

**breathe in** *v adv*
**1** to take in air through the nose or mouth: [IØ + IN] *In the morning I open the window wide and breathe in deeply.*
***2** to take in (something such as gas) by breathing: [T1] *In large cities people breathe in dangerous gases from cars and chimneys.*

**breathe into** *v prep*
**1** to send out one's breath into (something): [IØ + *into*] *The police asked us to breathe into the chemical to see if we were drunk. You can often save a person's life by breathing into his mouth.*
**2 breathe new life into** to make (something) active again: *The firm was about to fail when a new director was appointed; he breathed new life into the company and soon it was successful.*

*****breathe of** *v prep*
to speak (something) when one should not: [D1 (*simple tenses, usu. neg.*)] *Don't worry, I wouldn't breathe a word of your secret.*

**breathe on/upon** *v prep*
**1** to allow one's breath to fall on (something): [IØ + *on/upon*] *If you breathe on the window you can write your name in the mist.*
***2** *fml* to cause a poor opinion of (something): [T1] *He used to have a good name, but it has been breathed upon recently.*

**breathe out** *v adv*
**1** to let out air through the nose or mouth: [IØ + OUT] *The doctor asked me to breathe in, then to breathe out fully.*
***2** to let (gas) out by breathing: [T1] *At parties, I don't like to be with people who breathe out smoke all over me.*
***3** to express (something): [T1a] *He stood with his arms raised to the sky, breathing out curses.*

**breathe upon** *v prep* → **BREATHE ON**

*****breeze in** *v adv* → **blow in** (2)
*infml* to enter in high spirits: [IØ (*simple tenses*)] *Jim just breezed in, full of the good news.*

**breeze through** *v prep* → **romp through, sail through** (2), **sweep through**[2] (3), **walk through** (3), **waltz through**
*infml* to pass (a test) easily: [T1 (*simple tenses*)] *To his own surprise, John breezed through his driving test this time.*

**brew up** *v adv*
**1** to make (alcohol): [T1 + UP] *I've been brewing up some beer, would you like to try some?*
**2** *BrE not fml* to make (tea), often in large quantities: [T1 + UP] *Let's brew up some more tea.* *[IØ] *The workers are still spending too much time brewing up, this practice will have to stop!* —**brew-up** *n*
**3** to arise gradually: [IØ + UP (*continuous tenses*)] *I think there's a storm brewing up. There's trouble brewing up at the meeting.*

***brick in/up** *v adv*
to close or block (something) with bricks: [T1] *The old well was bricked up when it ran dry.*

***bridge over** *v adv*
**1** to make a way to cross (something): [T1 + OVER] *We shall have to bridge over the stream with these boards of wood.*
***2** to find a way to help (someone) or deal with (something), at least for a short time: [T1a,b] *We must find a way to bridge over the difficulties. This money should bridge you over till next month.* → **tide over**

**bridle at** *v prep*
to be offended by (something): [IØ + *at* (*simple tenses*)] *Mary bridled at her mother's unkind remark about Jim.*

**bridle up** *v adv* → **bristle up** (2)
to be offended: [IØ + UP] *Mary bridled up when someone said unkind things about Jim.*

**brighten up** *v adv*
**1** to (cause to) become brighter: [T1 + UP] *The new paint will brighten up the house.* [IØ + UP] *The day brightened up after the storm passed.*
**2** to (cause to) become more cheerful: [T1 + UP] *Let's brighten up the party with some loud music.* [IØ + UP] *Mary brightened up when she was told that Jim was coming after all.*

***brim over** *v adv* → **bubble over**
to overflow: [IØ (*usu. continuous tenses*)] *You've filled the glass too full, it's brimming over.*

***brim over with** *v adv prep* → **bubble over with**
to be filled (with a feeling, usu. a good feeling): [T1 (*no pass., usu. continuous tenses*)] *Mary was brimming over with joy.*

***bring about** *v adv*
**1** to cause (something): [T1a] *By his own efforts, Charles Fox brought about the fall of the government. Major changes will have to be brought about in British industry.* → **come about** (1)
**2** to make (a boat or ship) change course in the opposite direction: [T1b] *If the wind changes you'll have to bring her about.* → **bring around** (3), **bring round** (5), **come about** (3), **go about**[1] (6), **pull round** (1), **put about** (1)

**bring against** *v prep* → **lay against** (2), **level against, prefer against**
**bring a charge against** to cause (someone) to appear in a court of law, charged with an offence: *The police are going to bring a charge of murder against him.*

**bring along** *v adv*
**1** to bring (someone or something) with one: [T1 + ALONG] *Bring your running shoes along, and we'll get some exercise. Why don't you bring your brother along?* → **come along** (2), etc.
***2** to cause (something or someone) to advance: [T1] *This warm weather should bring the crops along. More study should bring along your English.* → **bring on**[1] (3), etc.

**bring around** *v adv*
**1** to bring (someone or something) to an agreed place: [T1 + AROUND] *Bring the new members around to the meeting tonight.* → **bring over** (1), etc.
***2** to persuade (someone) to change his opinion: [T1 (*to*) (*simple tenses*)] *We must bring the rest of the committee around to our point of view.* → **bring round** (3), etc.
***3** to make (a boat or ship) change course in the opposite direction: [T1b] *If the wind changes you'll have to bring her around.* → **bring about** (2), etc.

***bring away** *v adv* → **come away with** (2), **go away with** (4), **send away with** (1)
to return, usu. from a place, with (something or an idea): [T1a] *Yes, we enjoyed our holiday and brought away happy memories of the island.*

**bring back** *v adv*
**1** to take (usu. something) back; bring (someone or something) with one as one returns: [T1 + BACK] *You must bring these library books back next week. On your way home from your aunt's will you bring back some coffee? Bring me back some coffee.* → **put back** (2), etc.
***2** to recall; bring to mind (things of the past): [T1a (*simple tenses*)] *The smell of these flowers brings back memories.* → **call up** (5), **come back** (4), **come back to** (2), **summon up** (2)
***3** to help (someone) to gain (something): [T1 (*to*)] *We must bring him back to health.* → **pull back** (7)
***4** to cause (an idea or practice) to return or exist again; use (a former method) again: [T1a] *Few people these days are in favour of bringing back the old punishment by death.* → **come back** (7)

***bring before** *v prep*
**1** to force (someone) to appear before (a court of law): [D1 (*often pass.*)] *Peter has been brought before the court on a charge of drunken driving.* → **be before** (2), **come before** (2), **go before**[2] (3), **haul before, send before** (1), **take before** (1)
**2** to send (something such as an idea) for consideration or approval by (someone or a group in power): [D1 (*often pass.*)] *Your suggestion will be brought before the committee at a suitable date.* → **put before** (2), etc.

**bring down** *v adv*
**1** to carry or move (something or someone) down stairs, a hill, etc.: [X9 + DOWN] *You'll need help to bring the piano down. Send one of the boys to bring the car down. Mother wants to come downstairs, but is too weak to walk; it'll take both of you to bring her down.* → **get down** (1), **send down** (1), **take down** (1)
***2** to cause (something or someone) to fall or come down: [T1 (*usu. simple tenses*)] *The gunners brought down three planes. The hunter brought down a deer. In American football, you have to try to bring down your oppo-*

*nent.* → **come down** (2, 3), **get down** (4, 5), **go down** (5), **send down** (4), **shoot down** (1)

*3 to defeat (someone such as an enemy or a political opponent): [T1 (*usu. simple tenses*)] *At the next vote, we must try to bring down the government.*

*4 to reduce (a price): [T1] *Shopkeepers have been asked to bring down their prices.* → **go down¹** (6), etc., **send up¹** (2)

*5 to make (someone) reduce a price: [T1 (*to*) (*usu. simple tenses*)] *We brought the dealer down to a much lower figure.*

*6 to move (a figure) from one list to another, when dividing: [T1 (*usu. simple tenses*)] *When you divide 216 by 4, divide 4 into 21, giving 5 with 1 remaining; then bring down the next figure, 6, and divide this 16 by 4; the answer is 54.*

*7 to bring (something) up to date: [T1] *We have been asked to rewrite the history book, bringing it down to 1990.*

*8 to cause (someone) to meet or suffer (something bad); trouble (something or someone): [T1 (*on*)] *The youngest son has only brought down trouble on the family.*

*9 *AmE* to give or leave (something) to people who are younger or come later: [T1 (*often pass.*)] *This ring has been brought down in my family.* → **hand down** (3), etc.

*10 to reduce (someone) (to a state): [T1 (*to*)] *We are afraid that Helen will bring Simon down to her own level.*

*11 esp. *AmE* to make a public statement about; make (something) known officially: [T1] *The city council will bring down the new spending plans on Monday.* → **hand down** (5)

**12 bring someone down to earth (with a bang/bump)** *not fml* to make someone face reality, unpleasant truth, etc.: *He had no idea how food prices had risen, so a day's shopping soon brought him down to earth with a bump!* → **come down to** (8)

**13 bring the house down** *infml* to be received successfully in a theatre: [*no pass.*] *His amusing performance brought the house down.*

**14 bring someone down a peg or two** to make someone seem more humble: *Frederick has too high an opinion of himself; it's time we brought him down a peg or two.* → **take down** (5)

**bring forth** *v adv*

**1** *old use or fml* to produce (something): [X9 + FORTH] *"Bring forth the horse!"* (Lord Byron, *Mazeppa*) → **come forth, go forth** (1), **send forth** (2), **send out** (4)

*2 to produce (a child); yield (a crop): [T1a] *"Bring forth men children only."* (Shakespeare, *Macbeth*) *"And the earth brought forth grass."* (The Bible)

**bring forward** *v adv*

**1** to carry (something) or lead (someone) to a position nearer the front: [X9 + FORWARD] *If you bring another chair forward, there'll be room for everyone.*

*2 (in business) to move to the top of a list of figures (the total at the bottom of an earlier page), before adding in the figures on the new page: [T1 (*usu. pass., usu. simple tenses*)] *Mark the total at the top of the page "brought forward".* → **carry forward** (1), **carry over** (1)

*3 (in business) to produce or save (work) to be dealt with on a certain date: [T1 (*often simple tenses*)] *We'll bring that matter forward in three weeks' time. I thought we had agreed to bring the new contract forward today?*

*4 to arrange for (something) to take place earlier: [T1] *The election will be brought forward to June as so many people are on holiday in July.* → **put off¹** (4), etc.

*5 to cause (something) to advance: [T1b] *This warm weather should bring the crops forward.* → **bring on¹** (3), etc.

*6 to introduce; suggest (an idea): [T1 (*often pass.*)] *A plan was brought forward to allow workers to share in the profits.* → **come forward** (5)

*7 to produce (something not material): [T1 (*often simple tenses*)] *Can the prisoner bring forward some proof of his story?*

**bring home** *v adv*

**1** to bring (someone or something) to one's home: [T1 + HOME] *I don't like to bring my work home. I'd rather stay late at the office.* → **get back** (2), **get home** (1), **go home** (1), **take home** (1)

**2 bring home the bacon** esp. *BrE infml* to be successful, esp. in providing food and other necessary things for one's family: [*usu. simple tenses*] *Since I'm the one who brings home the bacon, I should help to decide how the money is spent. Our team went to the games without much hope, but they surprised us and brought home the bacon—three first prizes and two second!*

**bring home to** *v adv prep*

**1** to invite (someone) as one's guest, so as to meet (something or someone): [T1 + HOME + *to*] *I like to bring my friends home to a warm welcome from my family.* → **come home to** (1), **get home to** (1)

*2 to persuade (someone) to believe (something): [D1 (*simple tenses*)] *You must bring the difficulty home to John. You must bring home to John what the difficulty is.* [D5 (*simple tenses*)] *You must bring home to John that we don't have enough money.* [D6 (*simple tenses*)] *You must bring home to John where the difficulty lies.* → **come home to** (2), **drive home to, get home to** (2)

*3 to put the blame for (something wrong) on (someone): [D1 (*usu. simple tenses*)] *The courts are making efforts to bring their crimes home to the young people.*

**bring in** *v adv*

**1** to bring (something or someone) indoors, etc.: [X9 + IN] *Bring the washing in, it's raining.* → **come in** (1), **get in¹** (2), **go in¹** (1), **send in** (1), **take in¹** (1), **wheel in** (1)

*2 to gather (a crop): [T1] *The farmers are bringing the apples in early this year because of the warm weather.* → **be in** (9), **get in¹** (5), **take in¹** (7)

*3 to yield (money), as profit or earnings: [T1a] *The sale brought in over £250. The boys are bringing in good wages every week.* → **come in** (17), **go out** (6), **knock down** (9), **knock up** (6), **pull down** (6), **pull in** (10), **take in¹** (7)

*4 to introduce (an idea): [T1] *The government intends to bring in a new law about wearing safety belts in cars. The influence of the Far East has brought in many new fashions.*

*5 to ask (someone) to come to one's help: [T1 (*on*)] *The council are pleased with the results of bringing ordinary citizens in on local library planning.* [V3] *We may have to bring extra workers in to help us with this big job.* → **call in¹** (4), **come in** (14), **get in¹** (8), **have in¹** (2)

*6 to take (someone) to a police station: [T1] *The policeman brought in two boys whom he had caught stealing.* → **pull in** (9), **take in¹** (17), **yank in**

7 **bring in the new year** to hold special ceremonies to mark a new year: *Will you help us to bring in the new year?* → **ring in¹** (2), etc.

8 **bring in a verdict** (in a court of law) to give a judgment on someone being tried: [*simple tenses*] *They have brought in a verdict of "not guilty".*

***bring in on** *v adv prep*

1 to cause (someone) to join or share in (something such as a discussion or agreement): [D1 (*usu. simple tenses*)] *Are you going to bring any of the other board members in on your plan for the election?* → **get in on** (1), etc.

2 **bring someone in on the ground floor** *infml* to begin employing someone in a low or humble position: [*usu. simple tenses*] *It's a good idea to bring students in on the ground floor, so that they can learn on the job.* → **get in on** (2), etc.

**bring into** *v prep*

1 to carry (something) or lead (someone) into (a place): [T1 + *into*] *Will you bring the tea things into the garden? Who brought that unpleasant woman into my home?*

2 to cause (something or someone) to reach (a state or condition): [X9 + *into*] *Another new nation has been brought into being. This sudden warmth is bringing all the trees into leaf. It's a good idea to bring those old mats into use again. Who is responsible for bringing that stupid style into fashion? The telephone brings distant people into contact with each other.* → **get into** (11), etc.

3 **bring something into action** to cause something to start working: *If necessary, the heavy machinery can be brought into action.* → **put out** (23), etc.

4 **bring something into focus** to make something clearly understood or known: *Thank you, your view has helped to bring the historical side of the matter into focus.* → **be in²** (12), **come into** (6)

5 **bring something into force** to cause something such as a law to begin to operate: *The new law will be brought into force by midnight tomorrow.* → **be in** (13), **come into** (7), **put into** (14)

6 **bring someone/something into line (with)** to make someone or something follow the principles (of a group): *Any member who offends against the club rules will have to be brought into line. You must bring your actions into line with party beliefs if you are to remain a member.* → **be out of** (16), etc.

7 **bring something into the open** to cause something to be publicly known, not hidden: *The government must bring this shameful affair into the open if it is to be trusted by the voters.* → **be in²** (24), **come into** (10)

8 **bring something into play** to cause something to have an effect, influence, or force: *Who knows what details may be brought into play when the talks begin?* → **be in** (27b), **call into** (4), **come into** (12)

9 **bring something into sight/view** to cause something to be seen: *The clouds suddenly divided, bringing the sun into view at last. A change of wind brought the little boat into sight.* → **keep in** (16), etc.

10 **bring someone into the world** to give birth to a human being: *Many people are refusing to bring children into the world as it is so full of trouble and violence.* → **come into** (14)

***bring low** *v adj*

to force (someone) into a humble position: [T1 (*usu. pass.*)] *The cruel rulers of old Russia were brought low by the determined action of the people.*

**bring off** *v adv*

1 to take (usu. someone) from a dangerous place: [X9 + OFF] *The lifeboat brought off most of the shipwrecked sailors.* → **take off** (4)

*2 to succeed in (something difficult): [T1 (*usu. simple tenses*)] *Jim's plan seemed hopeless, but he brought it off. Jim was pleased when he brought off a seemingly hopeless attempt.* → **carry off¹** (6), **come off¹** (6), **go off¹** (6), **pass off** (2), **pull off¹** (4)

***bring on¹** *v adv*

1 to cause (someone or something) to appear: [T1] *The waiter brought the next dish on. Bring on the dancing girls! The next player was brought on just before play ended for the day.* → **come on¹** (4), etc.

2 to cause (something such as an illness) [T1] *The sudden cold weather brought on his fever again.* → **come on¹** (5), **draw on¹** (2)

3 to cause (something, or someone) to advance or improve: [T1] *This warm weather should bring on the crops. More study should bring on your English.* [T1 (*in*)] *More study should bring you on in your English.* → **bring along** (2), **bring forward** (5), **come along** (4), **ge**

**along** (6), **get along with** (3), **get on**[1] (5), **get on with** (2), **go along** (4), **go along with** (2), **go on**[1] (11), **go on with** (3), **put ahead** (1), **put back** (6), **put behind**[1], **put forward** (4), **set ahead** (1), **set back** (3), **throw back** (4)

***bring on/upon**[2] *v prep*
to cause (something, usu. unpleasant) to happen to (someone): [D1 (*usu. simple tenses*)] *You've brought the trouble on yourself.*

**bring out** *v adv*
**1** to produce (something), as from a container: [X9 + OUT (*often simple tenses*)] *Suddenly the man brought out a gun and threatened the driver with it. As I brought the handkerchief out of my pocket, several other objects fell out with it.* → **pull out** (1)
**2** to move (something or someone) out of a building or room: [T1 + OUT] *It's warm enough to bring out the garden chairs. Why don't you bring the children out here in the sun?* → **fetch out** (1)
***3** to cause (something) to be seen: [T1] *Jane never brings out her best dishes even when guests arrive. The warm sun brought the flowers out.* → **be out** (5), **come out** (5), **fetch out** (2)
***4** also **show up** to develop: cause (something) to be seen or known: [T1 (*often simple tenses*)] *Difficulties can bring out a person's best qualities. The new dress brought out her hidden beauty. The teacher helped to bring out the meaning of the poem. Plenty of money often brings out the worst in someone.* —**well-brought-out** *adj* → **call forth, call out** (3), **come out** (7), **draw forth, draw out** (8), **fetch out** (3)
***5** to produce (something): [T1] *Tom has brought out another new book. The makers are bringing out a new kind of soap.* → **be out** (21), **come out** (8), **fetch out** (4), **get out** (13)
***6** to encourage (someone) to be bolder, talk more freely, etc., esp. in the phr. **bring someone out of his shell**: [T1 (*of*)] *Mary is very quiet, try to bring her out (of her shell) at the party.* → **come out of** (4), **draw out** (9), **fetch out** (5), **lead out** (2)
***7** to cause (someone) to stop working because of disagreement: [T1] *We'll bring the workers out for more pay.* → **be out** (13), **call out** (4), **come out** (15), **fetch out** (6), **get out** (17), **go back** (8), **go out** (13), **lay down** (13), **put down** (18), **stay out** (3), **stop out** (2), **walk out** (3)
***8** *BrE becoming rare* to officially introduce (someone, usu. a young lady) into upper-class society: [T1] *Is Mrs King-Brown bringing her daughter out this year?* → **come out** (16)
***9** to cause (someone) to move or travel to a new country in which one is now living: [T1 (*to*)] *I had been living here for a year before I had saved enough money to bring the family out.* → **come over**[1] (3), etc.
***10** to express (something spoken such as a word or statement): [T1 (*usu. simple tenses*)] *She was so shocked that she could hardly bring out a word.*
***11** to obtain (something secret): [T1] *It did not take the police long to bring out the truth.* → **let out** (5), etc.

***bring out in** *v adv prep* → **break out in** (1), **come out in** (2)
to cause (someone) to have (a condition of the body or mind): [D1] *Eating all that rich food has brought Jane out in spots as usual. Don't mention what happened last week, it could bring him out in a temper.*

**bring over** *v adv*
**1** to bring (someone) usu. to someone's home: [T1 + OVER ] *Why don't you bring your new boyfriend over one evening? We'd like to meet him.* → **bring around** (1), **bring round** (1), **call by**[1], **call in** (1), **come around** (2), **come over**[1] (2), **drop around, drop by, drop in** (2), **drop over, fetch over** (1), **fetch round** (1), **get over**[1] (2), **get round**[1] (4), **go over** (3), **go round**[1] (1), **take round**[1] (2)
***2** to cause (someone) to move or travel, as to a new country: [T1] *When are you going to bring the rest of your family over?* → **come over** (3), etc.
***3** to persuade (someone) to change his opinion: [T1 (*to*) (*simple tenses*)] *We must bring the rest of the committee over to our point of view.* → **bring round** (3), etc.
***4** *naut* to bring (something) to the other side of the boat: [T1b (*often simple tenses*)] *Bring the sails over, the wind has changed.*

**bring round** *v adv*
**1** to bring (someone) to someone's home or an agreed place: [T1 + ROUND] *Bring the new members round to the meeting tonight.* → **bring over** (1), etc.
***2** to cause (someone) to regain consciousness: [T1b] *Peter has fainted, try to bring him round.* → **bring to**[1] (1), etc.
***3** to persuade (someone) to change his opinion: [T1 (*to*) (*simple tenses*)] *We must bring the rest of the committee round to our point of view.* → **bring around**[1] (2), **bring over** (3), **come around** (6), **come over** (5), **fetch over** (2), **fetch round** (3), **get round**[1] (5), **go over to** (5), **pull round** (4)
***4** to change the direction of (something): [T1] *Father always brings the conversation round to his favourite subject.* → **fetch round** (4)
***5** *naut* to make (a boat or ship) change course in the opposite direction: [T1b (*often simple tenses*)] *If the wind changes you'll have to bring her round.* → **bring about** (2), etc.

***bring through**[1] *v adv* → **carry through**[1] (3), **come through**[1] (7), **pull round** (2), **pull through**[1] (2)
to save the life of (someone very ill): [T1b (*usu. simple tenses*)] *Can the doctor bring Mother through?*

***bring through**[2] *v prep* → **carry through**[2] (2), **come through**[2] (3), **pull through**[2] (2, 3)
to save (someone) from (danger or trouble): [D1 (*usu. simple tenses*)] *The doctor brought Mother through a serious illness. Their courage brought the people through the war.*

*__bring to__[1] *v adv*
**1** to cause (someone) to regain consciousness: [T1b] *Peter has fainted, try to bring him to.* → **bring round** (2), **come around** (5), **come to**[1] (1), **fetch round** (2), **fetch to, pull round** (2)
**2** *naut* to (cause to) stop: [T1b (*usu. simple tenses*)] *The captain was able to bring the ship to just before it hit the little boat.* [IØ] *As the wind dropped, the boat brought to.* → **bring up** (6), **come to**[1] (4), **heave to**

**bring to**[2] *v prep*
**1** to carry or move (something) or lead (someone) in the direction of (someone or something): [T1 + *to*] *Bring your paper to me when you've finished it.* [X9 + *to*] *Last night's storm brought several trees to the ground.*
**2** to cause (something or someone) to reach or be added to (usu. something): [X9 + *to*] *How much experience does he bring to this specialized work? We must bring the rest of the villagers to our help in finding the missing child.* → **come to**[2] (5)
**3** to cause (something or someone) to reach (a total, state, or condition): [X9 + *to*] *This last thing will bring the bill to over £500 First bring the milk to the boil, and then add the powder. At last the criminals are being brought to justice.* → **get into** (11), etc.
**4 bring to attention: a** *mil* to cause (a soldier) to stand stiffly upright: *The captain brought the men to attention as the general arrived.* → **stand at** (3), etc.: **b** to cause (something) to be noticed (by someone): *Thank you for bringing the matter to my attention.* → **come to**[2] (16b)
**5 bring something to the boil** *not fml* to cause something such as a problem to reach an urgent state: *The university's money troubles have been brought to the boil by the recent government cuts.* → **come to**[2] (17)
**6 bring someone to book** to force someone to give a formal explanation of his behaviour: *Any worker who is regularly late will soon be brought to book.*
**7 bring something to a dead end** to prevent the further advance of something: [*often simple tenses*] *Our enquiry was brought to a dead end when we learned that the woman had left the country.* → **be at** (8), **come to**[2] (19)
**8 bring an end to** to end or stop (something): *We must bring an end to suffering and hunger in the world.* → **be at** (12), **put to**[2] (12)
**9 bring someone to his feet** to make someone stand, as to show approval: [*often simple tenses*] *The politician's closing words brought the whole crowd to their feet, cheering wildly.* → **get to** (11), etc.
**10 bring someone to the fore** to cause someone to become noticed as a leader or person of influence or importance: [*often simple tenses*] *He had never been anything more than a good official, but wartime conditions brought him quickly to the fore because of the special qualities of his character.* → **come to**[2] (22)
**11 bring someone to grips with something** to cause someone to deal with a difficulty: *There was no escape from the facts; we were brought to grips with the hard reality of our position.* → **come to**[2] (24), **get to** (13)
**12 bring something to the ground** to destroy something: *This nation will not be brought to the ground by enemy action! It's the members' lack of interest which is bringing the party to the ground.*
**13 bring matters/things to a head** to cause affairs to reach a state where something must be done or decided: [*often simple tenses*] *Matters have been brought to a head in the peace talks; tomorrow they will either succeed or fail.* → **come to**[2] (26)
**14 bring someone to heel** *not fml* to make someone obey one, as a dog is made to follow its master: [*often simple tenses*] *Someone who refuses to follow the party line must be brought to heel before he does lasting damage.* → **come to**[2] (27)
**15 bring someone to himself** to cause someone to regain consciousness or remember his surroundings: [*usu. simple tenses*] *Some cold water on her face might bring her to herself. The sudden sound of the train whistle brought me to myself; I had not known how far I had been walking, deep in thought.* → **come to**[2] (32)
**16 bring someone to his knees** to defeat someone completely: *What can the opposition party do to bring this government to its knees?*
**17 bring something to life** to make something interesting and active: *The performances of these young people succeeded in bringing a dull play to life.* → **come to**[2] (28)
**18 bring something to light** to cause something to be discovered: *We thank the committee for bringing to light some facts which will influence the board's decision.* → **come to**[2] (29)
**19 bring something/someone to mind** to remember something or someone: *I can't seem to bring to mind the name of the place where we last met.* → **call to** (5), **come to**[2] (30), **recall to** (3)
**20 bring something to naught** *fml* to cause the failure of something: [*often pass.*] *All his best efforts were brought to naught by his early death.* → **come to**[2] (31)
**21 bring something to pass** *fml* to cause something to happen: [*often simple tenses*] *The government has promised to improve prison conditions, but I doubt if they will ever bring their promises to pass.* → **come to**[2] (33)
**22 bring something to such a pass/a pretty pass** *not fml* to reduce something to a poor state: *But what has brought the company to such a pretty pass since I last worked for it?* → **come to**[2] (34)
**23 bring something to rest** to cause something such as a machine, to stop: [*often simple tenses*] *After a struggle with the controls, the driver was able to bring the car to rest in a field.* → **come to**[2] (37)

**24 bring someone to his senses: a** to cause someone to regain consciousness: *Some cold water on her face should bring her to her senses.* **b** to make someone become sensible again and think or behave reasonably: *She has been in love with that worthless boy for so long that it will take a real shock to bring her to her senses.* → **come to² (39)**

**bring together** *v adv*

**1** to cause (things) to meet or join: [X9 + TOGETHER] *Bring the broken edges of the plate together exactly where they were and then glue them carefully.*

***2** to cause (two people or groups, as a man and woman, or former enemies) to meet: [T1b] *I'm so glad to have been the means of bringing you two young people together The opposing forces on the island have been brought together for peace talks.* → **chuck together** (3), **come together** (1), **fling together** (2), **hurl together, throw together** (3), **toss together** (3)

***3** to cause (two or more parties) to end a disagreement: [T1b] *I'm glad that the brothers have been brought together after all their quarrels.* → **come together** (3)

***bring under¹** *v adv* → **keep down** (6), etc.

to control and defeat (usu. someone), as by political force: [T1b (*usu. pass.*)] *Those who oppose our wishes will be brought under.*

***bring under²** *v prep*

**1** to include (something) in (a particular class or type): [D1 (*often simple tenses*)] *We can bring your suggestions under several headings.* → **come under** (2), etc.

**2 bring under control** to gain control of (something or someone): [*often simple tenses*] *It was several hours before the fire was brought under control. I shall put an experienced teacher in charge of that class, to bring the children under control.* → **be under** (7), **get under²** (2), **keep under** (2)

**bring up** *v adv*

**1** to bring (something or someone) upstairs or to a higher level: [T1 + UP (*to*)] *When the doctor arrives, bring him up. Mother says would you please bring up the tea things. The road will bring you up to the top of the cliff.* → **come up** (2), **go up¹** (1), **send up¹** (1), **take up** (3)

***2** esp. *BrE* to educate; raise (a child): [T1] *My aunt brought up four children. Your children have been well brought up. I don't want your advice, I'm bringing them up the hard way so that they won't be helpless in later years.* [V3] *I was brought up to respect the law.* → **drag up** (3), **fetch up** (3)

***3** to mention or introduce (a subject): [T1 (*often simple tenses*)] *Mr Chairman, I should like to bring up the question of the reorganization of the committees. Your suggestion will be brought up at the next meeting. There's no need to bring up his past when we are considering him for employment.* → **come up** (8), **fling up** (6), **raise with, sling up** (2), **throw up** (7)

***4** *BrE* to be sick: vomit (one's food): [IØ] *Jane can't come, she's been bringing up all morning.* [T1] *The child has brought up her dinner again.* → **cast up** (5), **chuck up** (2), **come up** (17), **fetch up** (2), **heave up** (2), **sick up, spew up** (1), **spit up** (2), **throw up** (4)

***5** to stop (a horse) suddenly: [T1 (*often simple tenses*)] *The horse is running away, can't you bring him up? The boy was praised for bringing up the runaway horse.*

***6** *naut* to (cause to) stop: [T1b (*usu. simple tenses*)] *The captain was able to bring the ship up just before it hit the little boat.* [IØ (*simple tenses*)] *The ship brought up just before it hit the little boat.* → **bring to² (2), come to (4), heave to**

***7** to cause (someone) to stop suddenly: [T1 (*usu. pass.*)] *John was about to enter the room when he was brought up (short) by a note on the door.*

***8** to cause (someone) to arrive: [T1] *"We shall have to bring up some more soldiers", said the captain.* → **come up** (5)

***9** to scold (someone): [T1b] *The director brought Jim up for being late again.* → **tell off** (1), etc.

***10** to take (someone) to court: [T1 (*usu. pass.*)] *This is the third time that Peter has been brought up before the court for drunken driving.* → **have up** (2), etc.

**11 bring up the rear** to be the last in a line or in a group of soldiers: *The men on horseback brought up the rear in the procession.*

***bring up against** *v adv prep*

**1** to cause (usu. someone) to meet (a difficulty): [D1 (*usu. pass.*)] *Things were working well, when we were brought up against unexpected delays.* → **be up against** (1), **come up against**

**2** to take account of or raise (something) to the disadvantage of (someone): [D1 (*often pass.*)] *Your prison record may be brought up against you.*

**bring up to** *v adv prep*

**1** to pull or drive (something or someone) near to (usu. something): [T1 + UP + *to*] *Bring the car (right) up to the door, it'll be easier to load.* → **come up to** (1)

***2** to cause (something) to reach (something such as a total): [D1 (*often simple tenses*)] *This sum will bring the total up to £200 exactly.*

**3 bring up to date: a** to advance the knowledge of (someone): *We must try to bring Mother more up to date with modern styles, and persuade her not to wear such old-fashioned clothes.* **b** *to bring (something) level, esp. in time: I want to spend this weekend bringing my letter writing up to date.* → **be up to** (7), etc.

**4 bring up to scratch/standard/the mark:** to make (something or someone) reach an expected standard: *The government is making car makers bring their cars up to standard for* *safety reasons. You'd better bring your English up to scratch before you take the examination. How can we bring the boy's behaviour up to the mark?* → **be up to** (4), **come up to** (4, 5), **get up to** (4)

***bring upon** *v prep* → BRING ON

***bring within** *v prep* → **fall within** (2), etc.
to cause (something or someone) to fall within (a stated limit): [D1] *The shops will have to bring the clothes within our price range, or they won't sell them.*

**bristle up** *v adv*
**1** (of hair) to stand stiffly on end: [IØ + UP] *The dog's hair bristled up when it saw the cat.*
**2** to become annoyed: [IØ + UP] *Mary bristled up when she heard how her mother had been treated.* → **bridle up**

***bristle with** *v prep*
**1** to be full of (a strong feeling such as anger): [IØ + *with* (*no pass. simple tenses*)] *Mary bristled with anger when she heard how her mother had been treated.*
***2** to have plenty of (usu. something unpleasant): [T1 (*no pass., simple tenses, often present*)] *This job bristles with difficulties.*

***broach to**[1] *v adv*
*naut* (of a ship) to (cause to) turn sideways to the waves, esp. in rough sea: [IØ] *The captain had to hold the wheel firmly to prevent the ship from broaching to.*

***broach to/with**[2] *v prep*
to suggest (something) for consideration by (someone): [D1 (*usu. simple tenses*)] *I will broach your idea to the committee. We shall have to broach the idea of your marrying Jim with your father.*

**broaden out** *v adv*
**1** to become wider: [IØ + OUT] *The path broadened out as it left the forest.*
**2** to (cause to) become wider or more general: [IØ + OUT] *I'm glad to see that your ideas are broadening out.* [T1 + OUT] *You will have to broaden out your skills.*

**brood about/on/over/upon** *v prep* → **think about** (1), etc.
to worry about (something or someone) for a long time, often unnecessarily: [IØ + *about/on/over/upon*] *It's no good brooding about your troubles. Sandra has been brooding over that boy for too long. Why brood on how it happened? The thing to do is put it right.*

***browbeat into** *v prep*
to force (someone) into (doing something) by threats: [V4b] *We shall never allow our police to browbeat prisoners into admitting their guilt.*

***brown off** *v adv* → **cheese off, feed up** (2), **tire of** (2)
*infml* to make (someone) feel tired and in low spirits, uninterested in anything: [T1 (*usu. pass.*)] *Why should you feel browned off? You're supposed to be on holiday. All this endless bad news browns me off.*

***browse among** *v prep* → BROWSE THROUGH

***browse on** *v prep*
(of an animal) to feed, usu. slowly, on (something): [T1 (*no pass.*)] *Many animals like to browse on leaves.*

**browse through/among** *v prep*
to read here and there in (books or other printed matter), esp. for enjoyment: [IØ + *through/among* (*no pass.*)] *I can spend hours just browsing through books in the library.*

***bruit abroad/about** *v adv* → **blaze abroad, noise abroad, rumour abroad, spread abroad**
*fml or pomp* to make widely known: [T1] *The representative's job is to bruit the company's products abroad.*

**brush aside/away** *v adv*
**1** to sweep (something) away with a brush or one's hand: [X9 + ASIDE/AWAY] *Mother was in the garage, brushing the dirt aside. Brushing away her tears she promised to return.* → **sweep aside** (1)
***2** to deal easily and successfully with (an enemy): [T1] *Brushing the enemy aside, we swept into the next town.*
***3** to refuse to pay attention to (something): [T1] *Brushing away all opposition, he put the matter to a vote. You can't brush your difficulties aside in that easy manner.* → **sweep aside** (2)

**brush down** *v adv*
**1** to remove dust and dirt from (someone or oneself), with hands or brush: [T1 + DOWN] *Come and help me to brush the horses down. She picked herself up, brushed herself down, and started walking again.* —**brush-down** *n* → **dust down** (1)
***2** to scold (someone) for a fault: [T1 (*for*)] *I could hear the director brushing Jim down for being late again.* —**brushing-down** *n* → **tell off** (1), etc.

**brush off** *v adv*
**1** to (cause to) be removed or cleaned with a brush: [L9 + OFF] *Don't worry about that mark, it will brush off.* [X9 + OFF] *Please brush this insect off.*
***2** *infml* to refuse to listen to (something) or have a relationship with (someone): [T1 (*simple tenses*)] *The committee brushed off his enquiries with meaningless promises. Jim's girlfriend brushed him off before he met Mary.* —**brush-off** *n*

**brush over** *v adv*
**1** to sweep (a place): [T1 + OVER] *Please brush the floor over when you have finished.*
***2** to speak about (something), paying little attention to it: [T1a (*usu. simple tenses*)] *The chairman brushed over the question of your appointment.*

**brush past** *v adv; prep*
to pass (something or someone), touching lightly: [L9 + PAST/*past*] *There was only*

*just room to brush past (the pillar) in the crowd.*

**brush up** *v adv*
**1** to raise (something) by brushing: [T1 + UP] *Don't brush my hair up the wrong way, it hurts.*
*__2__ *not fml* to improve (something) by study: [T1a] *I must brush up my French before I go to Paris.* → **polish up** (2), **rub up** (2)

**brush up against** *v adv prep*
**1** to knock lightly against (something): [L9 + UP + *against*] *I brushed up against the door, and some of the wet paint came off onto my coat.* → **rub against, rub up against** (1)
*__2__ to meet (usu. trouble) unexpectedly: [T1 (*usu. simple tenses*)] *I hadn't thought that we would brush up against so much opposition in this town.* → **rub up against** (2)

***bubble over** *v adv* → **brim over**
**1** to overflow: [IØ] *Look out! The pan of milk is bubbling over!*
**2** (of a feeling) to be expressed through difficulty in containing it: [IØ (*into*)] *Her nervousness bubbled over into foolish laughter.*

***bubble over with** *v adv prep* → **brim over with**
to be filled with a need to express (a feeling): [T1 (*no pass., usu. continuous tenses*)] *Mary was bubbling over with joy.*

***buck off** *v adv*
(of a horse) to cause (a rider) to fall by violent movement: [T1] *Some horses are specially trained to buck their riders off, to amuse the crowd at an outdoor performance.*

***buck up** *v adv*
**1** *BrE infml* to hurry: [IØ (*usu. simple tenses*)] *Buck up, we're all waiting.* → **bustle up, hurry up** (1)
**2** *infml* to pay attention to improving (something): [T1 (*often simple tenses*)] *You'd better buck up your ideas.*
**3** *infml* to (cause to) become more cheerful: [T1 (*usu. simple tenses*)] *A good holiday will buck you up.* [IØ (*usu. simple tenses*)] *Buck up, your troubles will soon be over.* → **cheer up**, etc.

***buckle down** *v adv* → **buckle to, knuckle down** (2)
*not fml* to begin seriously to work (at something): [IØ (*to*) (*usu. simple tenses*)] *It's time you buckled down and got some work done. It's time you buckled down to some work.*

***buckle to** *v adv* → **buckle down, knuckle down** (2)
*not fml* to put effort into work, esp. together: [IØ (*often simple tenses*)] *If we all buckle to, we'll soon get the job done.*

***buckle under** *v adv* → **knuckle under**
to admit defeat; yield: [IØ (*to*) (*usu. simple tenses*)] *In the end he had to buckle under and admit that he was wrong. We all had to buckle under to the director's orders.*

**buckle up** *v adv*
**1** to fasten (something) with a buckle: [T1 + UP] *Wendy can already buckle up her shoes although she's only six.*
**2** to twist: [IØ + UP] *Because it was so hot, the metal bridge buckled up, and the cars which were crossing it fell into the river.*
*__3__ *not fml* to fasten a seat belt in a car: [IØ] *According to the new law, all drivers and passengers must buckle up.* → **belt up** (4), **strap in**

***budget for** *v prep*
to calculate enough money for (usu. something): [T1] *The university had to budget for an increase in the number of students.* [D1] *We shall have to budget an additional amount for the new baby's needs.*

***bug out** *v adv*
*AmE mil infml* to pack and move to another place, often in a hurry: [IØ] *Is it true the whole camp is going to bug out in the morning, captain?* —**bug-out** *n*

***bugger about/around** *v adv*
**1** *taboo sl* to spend time lazily: [IØ (*often continuous tenses*)] *Stop buggering about and get on with some work.* → **mess about** (1), etc.
**2** *taboo sl* to cause difficulties for (someone): [T1b] *Leave me alone and stop buggering me about.* → **mess about** (4), etc.
**3** *taboo sl* to cause disorder to (something): [T1b] *Who's been buggering my papers about? I left them all tidy, and now here they are all over the floor.* → **mess about** (3), etc.

***bugger about/around with** *v adv prep* → **mess about with** (1), etc.
*taboo sl* to cause disorder to (something): [T1 (*often continuous tenses*)] I'm sure somebody's been buggering about with my record player.

***bugger around** *v adv* → BUGGER ABOUT

***bugger around with** *v adv prep* → BUGGER ABOUT WITH

***bugger off** *v adv* → **push off** (3), etc.
*taboo sl* to leave: [IØ (*simple tenses, usu. imper.*)] *Bugger off, will you? I don't want you here.*

***bugger up** *v adv* → **mess up** (2), etc.
*taboo sl* to spoil (something) carelessly: [T1] *If John buggers up his driving test again, I doubt if he'll ever pass it.*

***build in** *v adv*
**1** to make (something) a fixed part of usu. a room: [T1 (*usu. pass.*)] *These cupboards have been built in.* —**built-in** *adj*
**2** to make (something) a part of something else: [T1 (*usu. pass.*)] *The difficulties seem to be built in.* —**built-in** *adj*

**build into** *v prep*
**1** to make (something) into (something else), as by adding: [T1 + *into*] *He took some nails and bits of wood, and built them into a rough cupboard.* [IØ + *into*] *These native pots are slowly building into a fine collection.*
*__2__ to fix (something) so as to make it a part of (something else): [D1 (*often pass.*)] *These cupboards are built into the walls.*

*__3__ to cause (something) to be a part of (something else) that cannot be separated: [D1 (*usu. pass.*)] *The difficulties are built into the work. The rate of pay was built into her contract.*

***build on¹** *v adv*
to make (something) as an additional building: [T1 (*often pass.*)] *This part of the hospital was built on later.*

**build on/upon²** *v prep*
**1** to build (something) on top of (something): [T1 + *on/upon*] *We built the house on our own land.* —**unbuilt-on** *adj*
*__2__ to depend on; trust in (someone, something, or doing something): [T1] *I'd like to come with you but that's not a promise, don't build on it.* [T4] *Don't build on going abroad this summer, we may not have enough money.* → **depend on** (1), etc.
*__3__ to base (something) on (something else): [D1] *Don't build your hopes on the chairman's promises. The insurance business is built on trust.*
*__4__ to use (something) as a base for further development: [T1] *In her new job she'll be able to build on her previous experience in marketing.*

**build (out) of** *v (adv) prep*
to make (something) from (a certain material): [T1 (+ OUT) + *of*] *Before bricks were invented, people built their houses out of wood.*

***build over** *v adv* → **build up** (5)
to cover (a place) with buildings: [T1 (*usu. pass.*)] *The fields where I played as a child have been built over.* —**built-over** *adj*

**build up** *v adv*
**1** to make (something) bigger by building: [T1 + UP] *Use more bricks to build the wall up.*
*__2__ to (cause to) increase, develop, or form steadily: [IØ (*into, to*)] *The clouds are building up. Enemy forces have now built up to a dangerous strength. Our hopes for peace are building up.* [T1 (*from, into, to*)] *You must build up your strength after your illness. He has built up a good business over the years from a small beginning.* —**buildup** *n*
*__3__ (of money) to (cause to) increase with interest and additions: [IØ] *My savings are building up nicely.* [T1] *You can build up a fortune by regularly saving money.*
*__4__ (of traffic) to form a mass: [IØ] *A long line of vehicles has built up by the narrow bridge.* —**buildup** *n*
*__5__ to fill (a place) with buildings: [T1 (*usu. pass.*)] *The area has been built up since I lived here.* —**built-up** *adj* → **build over**
*__6__ *not fml* to praise (someone or something) so as to influence the opinion of others, sometimes falsely: [T1] *The singer has been built up into a great success.* —**buildup** *n*

**build upon** *v prep* → BUILD ON

**bulge out** *v adv*
to swell outwards: [IØ + OUT] *The boy put so many things into his pocket that it bulged out.*

***bulk large** *v adj* → **loom large**
*not fml* to seem important or play an important part: [IØ (*simple tenses*)] *The question of replacing the director bulks large with the committee.*

***bulk up** *v adv*
*not fml* to increase; amount (to something): [IØ (*to*)] *Your money could bulk up to a fortune if you save everything you can.*

***bully into** *v prep*
to force (someone) into (something or doing something) by threats or violence: [D1] *Those boys will have to be bullied into action.* [V4b] *The boys bullied the small girl into giving them all her money.*

***bully off** *v adv* → **face off**
to start a game of field hockey: [IØ] *Are you ready to bully off?* —**bully-off** *n*

***bum about/around** *v adv*
*sl* to spend time lazily: [IØ (*often continous tenses*)] *I've been bumming around for the last year without a job.*

***bum along¹** *v adv*
**1** *sl* to move steadily, as in a car: [IØ (*often continuous tenses*)] *We were just bumming along nicely when the tyre burst.*
**2** *sl* to advance steadily: [IØ (*usu. continuous tenses*)] *How's your work going? Oh, just bumming along, thanks.*

***bum along²** *v prep*
*sl* to move steadily, as in a car, along (a road): [T1] *We were just bumming along the road when the tire burst.*

***bum around** *v adv* → BUM ABOUT

***bumble through** *v prep*
to go through (something such as life) in a disorganized manner: [T1] *Mr Green just bumbles through life, I don't know how he ever gets anything done.*

***bump into** *v prep*
**1** to knock oneself into (an object): [T1] *I've bumped into the door again and hurt my knee.*
**2** *infml* to meet (someone) by chance: [T1 (*no pass.*)] *I bumped into an old friend in town today.* → **bang into** (2), **barge into** (4), **knock into** (2), **knock up against** (2), **run into** (7)

***bump off** *v adv* → **do away with** (2), **do for** (7), **do in** (1), **finish off** (4), **knock off** (5), **look after** (3), **make away with** (2), **polish off** (3), **rub out** (2)
*sl* to kill; murder (someone): [T1 (*often pass.*)] *The old man who owned the jewels was bumped off by the thieves.*

***bump up** *v adv*
**1** *infml* to increase; raise (something): [T1] *Two more good results will bump up your average.*
**2 be bumped up** *infml* to be newly or falsely raised in rank: *I don't like the new director much, he seems to have been bumped up from some more humble position.* —**bumped-up** *adj* → **jump up** (3)

**bunch up** *v adv*
to (cause to) form a tight group or fold: [T1 + UP] *Don't bunch the flowers up so tightly, you'll spoil them.* [IØ + UP (*usu. simple tenses*)] *The singers bunched up to make room for one more.*

***bundle away** *v adv* → **bundle off** (2), **pack off** (2)
to (cause to) leave hurriedly: [T1 (*usu. pass.*)] *The children were bundled away when the guests arrived.* [IØ (*usu. simple tenses*)] *The women bundled away when their husbands returned.*

***bundle into** *v prep*
**1** to put (someone) hurriedly into (usu. a vehicle): [D1 (*usu. simple tenses*)] *The guest got very drunk so they bundled him into a taxi and sent him home.*
**2** to put (something) carelessly into (a container): [D1 (*usu. simple tenses*)] *Don't bundle all the clothes into that bag so carelessly.*

**bundle off** *v adv*
**1** to send (something such as a parcel): [T1 + OFF] *Could you bundle these clothes off to my sister?* → **pack off** (1)
***2** to (cause to) leave hurriedly: [IØ (*usu. simple tenses*)] *The women bundled off when their husbands arrived.* [T1 (*usu. pass.*)] *The children were bundled off to bed as soon as the guests arrived.* → **bundle away, pack off** (2)
***3** to send (someone) away hurriedly, usu. after trouble: [T1 (*to*) (*usu. simple tenses*)] *The family were so ashamed of the youngest son that they bundled him off to Canada.* → **pack off** (3)

***bundle out** *v adv*
to (cause to) leave (usu. a vehicle) hurriedly: [IØ (*usu. simple tenses*)] *The taxi door burst open and all the children bundled out.* [T1 (*usu. simple tenses*)] *I shall bundle you out of here very fast if you don't leave by yourself.*

**bundle up** *v adv*
**1** to wrap (a parcel, etc.): [T1 + UP] *Could you bundle up these clothes and I'll take them to the post?* → **parcel up, wrap up** (1)
***2** to (cause to) be well wrapped in clothes: [T1 (*usu. simple tenses*)] *The mother bundled the children up against the cold wind.* [IØ (*usu. simple tenses*)] *In this cold wind you'd be wise to bundle up well.* → **muffle up** (4), **wrap up** (2)

***bung in** *v adv*
**1** *infml* to put (something) in, often rudely: [T1] *Just bung in some old bricks to fill up the hole.*
**2** *infml* to interrupt with (something spoken): [T1] *Can I bung in a word yet?*

***bung up** *v adv*
**1** *not fml* to block or close (something): [T1] *The leaves bunged up the hole.* → **block up** (1), **seal up, stop up** (1), **stuff up** (1)
**2** *not fml* to block (a nose): [T1 (*usu. pass.*)] *My nose is bunged up with cold.* → **stuff up** (2)

***bunk down** *v adv* → **bed down**
to (cause to) become comfortable for the night, in a bed or bunkbed: [T1] *Would you bunk the children down for me?* [IØ] *Two of the boys bunked down together.*

***bunk off** *v adv*
*infml* to run away from school, family, or other responsibilities: [IØ (*usu. simple tenses*)] *More than half the class bunked off last week when there was a test. "The reason he lived with his grandparents was that his father had bunked off and left his mother when he was a baby, and shortly afterwards his mother had got ill and died."* (John Wain, *The Contenders*)

***bunk up** *v adv*
**1** to share a bed or bunkbed (with someone): [IØ] *Two of the boys bunked up together.*
**2** *sl* to have sex (with someone): [IØ (*with*) (*usu. simple tenses*)] *I'd like to bunk up with you.*
**3** *infml* to help (someone) to reach a higher level: [T1] *Bunk me up, over this wall.* —**bunk-up** *n*

***buoy up**
**1** to help (something or someone) to float: [T1 (*often simple tenses*)] *You can use empty oil barrels to buoy up the boards so that you can get across the river.*
**2** to support (something); keep (something) high: [T1 (*often simple tenses*)] *When there was no letter from Mary, Jim buoyed his spirits up by blaming the post. For years, the government has been buoying up wheat prices to keep the wheat farmers in business.*
**3** to keep (someone) in good spirits: [T1 (*often pass.*)] *Doesn't this sunshine buoy you up? What buoyed me up was the thought of a holiday soon.*

***burden with** *v prep*
to load (someone or oneself) with (something or someone unwanted): [D1] *Why do you burden yourself with your sister's children? I don't want to burden you with my troubles.*

***burgeon out** *v adv*
to spread: [IØ + OUT] *In the past 20 years, the city has burgeoned out into the surrounding countryside.*

**buried in** → **BURY IN** (7)

**buried under** → **BURY UNDER** (2)

***burke at** *v prep* → **BALK AT**

**burn away** *v adv*
**1** to continue burning: [IØ + AWAY] *The fire burned away for five days.*
***2** to destroy (something) by burning: [T1] *The skin on his foot was burnt away.* → **burn off** (1)

**burn down** *v adv*
**1** also **burn low** (of a fire) to burn lower, less strongly: [IØ + DOWN] *Let's leave the fire to burn down and go into our tents.*
***2** to (cause to) be destroyed by fire: [IØ] *The old house burned down last night in the big fire.* [T1 (*usu. pass.*)] *The old house was burned down and only ashes were left.* → **burn out** (1)

**burn for** *v prep*

**1** (of a fire or light) to continue burning during (a period of time): [I∅ + *for*] *The fire in the factory has been burning for three days now.*

***2** *not fml* to desire (something such as success) greatly: [T1 (*continuous tenses*)] *The young singer has been burning for a chance to hear the cheers of the crowd.*

***burn into** *v prep*

**1** to fix (a mark, etc.) by burning so that it cannot be removed: [D1] *The owner's mark was burned into the animal's skin.*

**2** to fix (an idea, etc.) so that it cannot be removed: [D1 (*usu. pass.*)] *The habit of obedience was burned into me as a child.*

***burn low** *v adv* → **BURN DOWN** (1)

***burn off** *v adv*

**1** to destroy (something) by burning: [T1 (*often pass.*)] *His hair was burnt off. Now that they have gathered in the crops, the farmers are burning off the stubble in the fields.* → **burn away** (2)

**2** to remove the remains of grain crops from (a field): [T1a] *The farmers are burning off the fields.*

***burn out** *v adv*

**1** to make (usu. a building or vehicle) hollow by fire: [T1 (*usu. pass.*)] *The building was burned out and only the walls remained. The plane was completely burned out after the crash.* —**burned-out** *adj* → **burn down** (2)

**2** to make (someone) homeless by fire: [T1 (*usu. pass.*)] *The family were burnt out of their home twice last year.*

**3** to (cause to) stop burning: [T1b] *The small fire can safely be left to burn itself out.* [I∅] *The small fire can safely be left to burn out.*

**4** to stop working through the action of heat: [I∅ (*usu. simple tenses*)] *The engine has burned out.* [T1 (*usu. pass.*)] *The engine is burned out.* — **burned-out** *adj*

**5** to (cause to) stop being active: [T1] *The poet's ability burned itself out before he was thirty. You'll burn yourself out if you work too hard.* [I∅ (*simple tenses*)] *The poet's ability burned out before he was thirty.* —**burned-out adj**, **burnout** *n*

**burn to** *v prep*

**1** **burn something to ashes/a cinder/a crisp** to burn something, such as food, till it is hard and dry: *Whatever's happened to the meat? It's burnt to a crisp!*

**2** **burn someone to death** to kill someone with fire: [*usu. pass.*] *Twenty-three people were burnt to death in the hotel fire.*

***burn up** *v adv*

**1** to burst into flames again: [I∅] *Put some more wood on the fire to make it burn up.* → **blaze up** (1), **flame out** (1), **flame up** (1), **flare up** (1)

**2** to destroy (something) completely by fire: [T1 (*usu. pass.*)] *All the wood has been burned up.*

**3** to be destroyed by great heat: [I∅] *The spacecraft burned up when it re-entered the earth's atmosphere.*

**4** *AmE infml* to scold (someone): [T1b] *The director burned Jim up for being late again.* → **tell off** (1), etc.

**5** *AmE infml* to cause (someone) to be very angry: [T1b (*simple tenses*)] *I get all burned up when I hear how animals are badly treated.*

**6** *infml* to travel at high speed along (a road): [T1b] *This fast car really burns up the road.* —**burn-up** *n*

**burn with** *v prep*

**1** to be on fire with (something): [I∅ + *with*] *The flames burned with increasing force.*

***2** to feel (something) strongly: [T1 (*no pass.*)] *Jim burned with anger when he heard how Mary had been treated.*

***burst forth** *v adv*

*old use* to suddenly begin: [I∅ (*usu. simple tenses*)] *The trees burst forth in spring. Mary burst forth into song.*

***burst in** *v adv*

**1** to break (something) inwards with force: [T1] *The firemen could enter the burning house only by bursting the door in.* → **break in** (1)

**2** to enter in haste: [I∅ (*usu. simple tenses*)] *Suddenly the door opened and the children burst in.*

**3** to speak suddenly: [I∅ (*simple tenses*)] *"But I was there!" Jane burst in.* → **break in** (3), **cut in**[1] (3)

***burst in on** *v adv prep* → **break in on**

to interrupt (someone) in haste, often noisily: [T1 (*usu. simple tenses*)] *I'm sorry to burst in on you like this, but I have an urgent message.*

***burst into** *v prep*

**1** to enter (somewhere) hastily: [T1 (*no pass., usu. simple tenses*)] *The children burst into the room.*

**2** → **BREAK INTO** (2)

**3** to start (something) suddenly; enter (a state) suddenly: [T1 (*no pass., usu. simple tenses*)] *Mary burst into song/laughter/tears. The paper burst into flames. The weather turned warm unexpectedly, making the trees burst into leaf. Suddenly the leading car in the race burst into sight.* → **break into** (4), **break out in** (2), **burst out** (1), **bust out** (3), **crack out**

***burst on/upon** *v prep*

**1** to interrupt (something) with haste and noise: [T1 (*no pass., simple tenses*)] *We were having a nice quiet meal outdoors when the boys burst upon the scene, shouting and fooling about.*

**2** to discover (something) suddenly: [T1 (*no pass., simple tenses*)] *In the middle of his tests, the scientist burst on the truth.*

**3** to become suddenly known by (someone): [T1 (*no pass., simple tenses*)] *Just then the meaning of what had been said burst upon him, and he knew that he had been right.* → **dawn on** (2)

**burst out** *v adv*
**1** to start (something or doing something) suddenly: [IØ (*in*)] *Everyone suddenly burst out in laughter.* [I4] *Everyone suddenly burst out laughing.* —**outburst** *n* → **break into** (4), **break out in** (2), **burst into** (3), **bust out** (3), **crack out**
**2** to escape (from): [IØ (*of*)] *Three men burst out of prison yesterday.* → **break out** (3), **bust out** (2), **crash out**
**3** to speak suddenly: [IØ (*simple tenses*)] *"Don't hit me!" she burst out.*
**4** to grow too big (for clothes): [IØ (*of*)] *The children are bursting out of their clothes so quickly now.*

*__burst through__ *v adv; prep*
to appear through (something), possibly by force: [IØ (*usu. simple tenses*)] *The clouds rolled away and the sun burst through.* [T1] *The enemy are already bursting through our weakened defences.*

*__burst upon__ *v prep* → BURST ON

*__burst with__ *v prep*
to feel full of (a feeling); have a lot of (health): [T1 (*no pass., continuous tenses*)] *Mary was bursting with joy over the good news. The children are simply bursting with good health.*

**bury in** *v prep*
**1** to put (something) into (a grave, earth, etc.): [T1 + *in*] *The relatives buried the body in the churchyard.*
**2** to cover (something or someone) with a lot of (something or things): [T1 + *in*] *The little children lost in the wood were buried in leaves. I found that envelope, it was buried in some papers on my desk.* → **bury under** (1)
***3** to hide (something or oneself) in (a place): [D1 (*usu. simple tenses*)] *Bob likes to bury himself in the countryside, away from the city. The castle was buried deep in the forest.*
***4** to push (something) deep into (something): [D1] *He buried his hands in his pockets.*
***5** to cover (one's face or head) with (one's hands), so as to hide a feeling: [D1] *Burying his face in his hands, he tried to control his weeping.*
***6** to give all one's attention to (something): [D1 (*usu. simple tenses*)] *I shall have to bury myself in my studies if I am to pass the exam.*
**7 be buried in** to be lost in (something such as thought) so as not to notice anything else: *It's no good talking to Tom, he's buried in his book again.*

**bury under** *v prep*
**1** to cover (something or someone) with (something): [T1 + *under*] *The animals' homes are buried under the leaves. I found that envelope, it was buried under all those papers.* → **bury in** (2)
**2 be buried under** to be very busy with (work): *I'm sorry, I can't join you this weekend, I'm buried under a mountain of work.*

*__bush out__ *v adv*
**1** *AmE* (of a plant) to grow in a spreading manner, like a bush: [IØ] *If you don't cut off some of the branches, that tree will bush out sideways.*
**2** *AmE* to mark (a path across ice) with small evergreen trees: [T1] *The men have gone ahead to bush out a safe way across the frozen lake.*

*__bust out__ *v adv*
**1** *AmE infml* to suddenly show flowers and leaves: [IØ (*continuous tenses*)] *"June is busting out all over."* (song)
**2** *AmE infml* to escape (from): [IØ (*of*)] *"Tom, have you bust out?"* (John Steinbeck, *The Grapes of Wrath*) → **break out** (3), **burst out** (2), **crash out**
**3** *AmE infml* to start (doing something) suddenly: [I4 (*simple tenses*)] *The whole crowd bust out laughing.* → **break into** (4), **break out in** (2), **burst into** (3), **burst out** (1), **crack out**

**bust to** *v prep*
*esp. AmE mil infml* to reduce (someone) in rank to (a lower rank): [T1 + *to*] *The captain has been busted to private.*

*__bust up__ *v adv*
**1** *infml* to damage; destroy; spoil (something): [T1] *Those children have bust up the chairs. The travel company's failure bust up our holiday.*
**2** *infml* to have a quarrel: [IØ] *Jim and Mary were busting up again last night.* —**bust-up** *n*
**3** *AmE infml* to separate or cause (a marriage or friendship) to end: [IØ] *I hear that Jim and Mary are busting up. Their marriage bust up.* [T1] *It was money troubles that bust up their marriage.* —**bust-up** *n* → **break up** (6), **split up** (4)

*__bustle about/around__ *v adv*
to move busily: [IØ] *I remember my grandmother always bustling about in the kitchen.*

*__bustle up__ *v adv* → **buck up** (1), **hurry up** (1)
*not fml* to (cause to) move or do something faster: [IØ (*simple tenses*)] *Bustle up, you children, we must be leaving!* [T1 (*simple tenses*)] *Can't you bustle those children up?*

*__busy with__ *v prep*
to make (oneself) active with (something); fill one's time with (something): [D1 (*often simple tenses*)] *Mother has busied herself with our affairs for too long.*

*__butt in__ *v adv*
**1** to interrupt, usu. by speaking: [IØ (*on, to*)] *When someone else is talking, don't butt in (to their conversation), it's rude.*
**2** *not fml* to cause confusion by trying to help: [IØ (*on*)] *I'd have got the job finished in time if he hadn't come butting in on my work with his unwanted advice.*

*__butter up (to)__ *v adv (prep)*
*not fml* to pay (someone) false respect for one's own gain: [T1] *If you butter Father up, do you think he'll lend us the car? He was just*

*buttering up to the director to try to get a favour from him.*

***button through** *v adv*
(of a garment such as a coat) to fasten with buttons from the top to the bottom: [IØ (*simple tenses*)] *This coat is easy to take off as it buttons through.* —**button-through** *adj*

**button up** *v adv*
**1** to fasten ( a garment) with buttons: [T1 + UP ] *You've buttoned up your coat the wrong way.*
***2** *sl* to keep quiet: [IØ (*usu. imper.*)] *Button up, will you? I'm trying to listen.*
***3** *infml* to complete (something): [T1 (*usu. pass.*)] *Let's button up this job.* —**buttoned-up** *adj*

**buttress up** *v adv*
**1** to strengthen (a building) with strong supports: [T1 + UP] *We shall have to buttress up the old church as it is beginning to lean at a dangerous angle.*
**2** to strengthen (something): [T1 + UP] *The government intends to buttress up its power to control rents by new laws.*

**buy back** *v adv*
to buy (something that one has owned) from the person to whom it was sold: [T1 + BACK] *He changed his mind about moving, but was unable to buy the house back.*

**buy in** *v adv*
**1** to buy a supply of (something): [T1 + IN] *We must make sure to buy in sugar before the price rises again.*
***2** to pay a price for (one's own goods) at an auction: [T1 (*often pass.*)] *The painting failed to reach its agreed price, and was bought in at £68,000.* → **bid in**
***3** to pay for (one's entry) to something; buy shares for (oneself): [T1 (*to*)] *If you want to become a partner in the firm, you will have to buy your way in. Buying yourself in is the only way to get a vote in the company's future.* [IØ] *The company seems to be doing so well that I would like to buy in.*

***buy off** *v adv* also **buy over**
*not fml* to pay (someone) money to persuade him to do or say something, or not to do something: [T1 (*usu. simple tenses*)] *His sister threatened to tell the police, so he had to buy her off.*

***buy out** *v adv*
**1** to gain control of (something) by buying the whole of it: [T1] *Mr Sharp has enough money to buy out the town.* → **buy up** (1)
**2** to gain the freedom of (someone) (usu. from the armed forces) by paying money: [T1 (*of*)] *Bill's parents paid a lot of money to buy him out of the army.*

***buy over** *v adv* → **BUY OFF**

***buy up** *v adv*
**1** to gain control of (something) by buying the whole of it: [T1] *The company bought up all the other cinemas and so became free of competition.* → **buy out** (1)
**2** to buy all the supplies of (something): [T1] *Housewives, afraid of running short, have bought up all the sugar in the shops.*

***buzz off** *v adv* → **push off** (3), etc.
esp. *BrE infml* to go away: [IØ (*usu. imper.*)] *Buzz off, you children, I don't want you in my garden.*

# C

**cadge from/off** *v prep* → **cop from**
*BrE infml* to beg (something) from (someone): [T1 + *from/off* ] *Can I cadge a cigarette from you?*

**cage in/up** *v adv*
**1** to put (usu. an animal) in a cage: [T1 + IN/UP] *You needn't worry about the tigers; they are safely caged in.*
**2 be caged in/up** to feel that one's freedom is limited: *Mothers of young children often feel caged up.* —**caged-in/up** *adj*

**cajole into** *v prep*
to persuade (someone), often by clever means, into (doing something): [X9 + *into*] *Be nice to your father and see if you can cajole him into lending us the car tonight.*

**cajole out of** *v adv prep*
**1** to persuade (someone), often by clever means, away from (doing something): [X9 + OUT + *of*] *I'm sure the boy is not guilty; how can we cajole your grandfather out of punishing him?*
**2** to beg (something such as money) from (someone): [X9 + OUT + *of*] *Do you think you can cajole some more money out of your father?*

**cake (in/up) with** *v (adv) prep*
**be caked (in/up) with** to be thickly covered with (something such as mud): *After the long ride, the horse was caked with mud.*

**calculate for** *v prep*
**1** to make arrangements for (something): [L9 + *for*] *We'd better calculate for a large crowd and provide plenty of food.* → **calculate on** (1)
***2** esp. *AmE* to expect or plan for (something, often unpleasant): [T1 (*usu. simple tenses*)] *We didn't calculate for such bad weather.* [T4 (*usu. simple tenses*)] *We didn't calculate for having such bad weather.* [V4a (*usu. simple tenses*)] *We didn't calculate for the weather turning so bad.* → **bargain for** (2), **reckon for**

**calculate on/upon** *v prep*
**1** to make arrangements for (something):

[L9 + *on/upon*] *We'd better calculate on a large crowd and provide plenty of food.* → **calculate for** (1)

*__2__ esp. *AmE* to depend on; trust in (something or doing something): [T1 (*usu. simple tenses*)] *I'd like to come with you but that's not a promise, don't calculate on it.* [T4 (*usu. simple tenses*)] *Don't calculate on going abroad this summer, we may not have enough money.* [V4a (*usu. simple tenses*)] *Don't calculate on the weather being fine for your garden party.* → **depend on** (1), etc.

**call about** *v prep*

**1** *BrE* to arrive at (someone's) home, office, etc., in connection with (a matter): [IØ + *about*] *There's a man at the door who says he's calling about your insurance.*

**2** *AmE* to telephone (someone) in connection with (a matter): [IØ + *about*] *I tried to call about our meeting, but you weren't in.* [T1 + *about*] *I tried to call you about our meeting.*

**call at** *v prep* → **call in²** (1), **call into** (1), **touch at**

to arrive at (a place), usu. for a short time and with a special purpose: [L9 + *at*] *I called at the office as I was passing, but you were out. The ship calls at several ports to pick up passengers before crossing the ocean.*

***call away** *v adv*

to cause (someone) to leave, usu. on business: [T1 (*usu. pass.*)] *I'm sorry, Mr Sharp is not in the office at the moment, he's been called away to attend a meeting.*

**call back** *v adv*

**1** to shout in return: [IØ + BACK] *The man called from the other side of the river, and his friend called back.*

*__2__ to ask or cause (someone) to return: [T1 (*often pass.*)] *Our representative in Paris must be called back.*

*__3__ to cause (something) to return: [T1] *This medicine should call your strength back.*

*__4__ to pay another visit (to a place): [IØ (*at*)] *The salesman will call back at any house he missed.* —**call-back** *n, adj*

*__5__ to return a telephone call to (someone): [T1] *Would you ask her to call me back?* [IØ] *I'll call back after dinner.* → **ring back**

*__6__ to remember (something): [T1 (*often simple tenses*)] *I cannot call his face back.*

*__7__ to ask (someone) to work again: [T1] *The director was called back to the office. Most of the strikers were called back to work after the strike was over.* —**call-back** *n*

*__8__ to try to prevent the damage caused by (words): [T1] *She wished she could call back her unfortunate remark.*

***call by¹** *v adv* → **bring over** (1), etc.

*not fml* to visit when passing a place: [IØ (*often simple tenses*)] *When you're next in town, do call by.*

**call by²** *v prep* → **go by²**, (7), etc.

to address (usu. someone) using (a name): [X9 + *by*] *If you call him just by his family name he won't answer you.*

**call down** *v adv*

**1** to shout in order to be heard by people on a lower level: [IØ + DOWN] *"Please come upstairs", she called down.*

**2** to ask (someone) to come downstairs: [X9 + DOWN] *Call Jane down again, she'll be late for work.*

*__3__ *AmE not fml* to express a poor opinion of (something): [T1a] *The newspapers called down Tom's latest book.*

*__4__ *AmE infml* to scold (someone): [T1] *The director called Jim down for being late again.* → **tell off** (1), etc.

*__5__ *AmE* to invite (someone) to fight: [T1 (*often simple tenses*)] *A gentleman should call down any man who is rude to his wife.* → **call out** (5)

*__6__ *mil* to order (an attack) to begin, esp. from the air: [T1] *As a last effort, the general called down heavy bombing on the enemy positions.*

***call down on** *v adv prep* → **invoke on**

to ask (something) to descend, as from heaven, on (usu. someone): [T1 (*no pass.*)] *The priests called down punishment on the people for their evil ways.*

**call for** *v prep*

**1** to arrive to collect (something or someone): [L9 + *for*] *I'll call for you at 8 o'clock. The parcel was left at the post office to be called for.* → **pick up** (2)

*__2__ to demand (something or someone); ask for: [T1] *Henry called for the waiter in a loud voice. The opposition are calling for a general election.*

*__3__ to need or deserve (usu. something): [T1 (*simple tenses*)] *This trouble calls for quick action by the government. Your remark was not called for.* —**uncalled-for** *adj*

***call forth** *v adv* → **bring out** (4), etc.

*fml* to cause (something) to be seen or used: [T1 (*usu. simple tenses*)] *Trouble can call forth a person's best qualities.*

**call forward** *v adv*

to ask (someone) to step forward: [X9 + FORWARD] *All the prizewinners were called forward to receive their prizes.*

**call in¹** *v adv*

**1** to pay a short visit: [L9 + IN (*at*) (*often simple tenses*)] *Please call in any time you're in town, I shall be glad to see you. The ship calls in at every port along this coast.* → **call at, call into** (1)

**2** to call (someone) to come indoors: [X9 + IN] *Call the children in now, it's getting cold.*

**3** to invite (someone) to one's home: [X9 + IN] *She called all her friends in for a party.*

*__4__ to ask (someone) to attend, as to give professional advice: [T1] *Mother was so ill last night that we had to call the doctor in.* → **bring in** (5), **come in** (14), **get in¹** (8), **have in¹** (2)

*__5__ to request the return of (something): [T1] *The makers have called in some cars with dangerous faults.*

*6 to demand payment of (a debt): [T1] *The bank has threatened to call in all money lent more than twenty years ago.*

*7 to remove (coins or banknotes) from general use: [T1] *The government called in all old £5 notes.*

*8 *AmE* to telephone (a message) to a certain place, such as an office: [IØ] *The director has just called in to say that she'll be late.* [T1] *All the reporters rushed to the telephone to call in their stories when the game was over.* → **phone in**

**call in²** *v prep*

**1** to visit (a place) for a short time: [L9 + *in*] *Will you call in the bank on your way home?* → **call at, call into** (1)

**2 call in question** to doubt (something): [*often pass.*] *The boy's honesty was never called in question.* —**call into** (5)

**call into** *v prep*

**1** to visit (a place) for a short time: [L9 + *into*] *Will you call into the bank on your way home?* → **call at, call in²** (1), **touch at**

**2 call something into action** to request that something start working or be active: *They called all possible forces into action to defeat the enemy.* → **put out** (23), etc.

**3 call something/someone into being** to make; create something or someone: [*often pass.*] *The committee was called into being to discover the causes of the accident.*

**4 call something into play** to cause something to be active: *Jim had to call all his skill into play to defeat his tennis opponent.* → **be in** (27b), **bring into** (8), **come into** (12)

**5 call into question** to doubt (something): [*often pass*]. *The girl's honesty was never called into question.* —**call in²** (2)

***call off** *v adv*

**1** *AmE* to speak a list of (names, words, etc.): [T1] *The teacher began to call off the names on his list.* → **call over¹** (2)

**2** to cause (something such as an event) not to take place: [T1 (*often simple tenses*)] *The cricket team had to call off the game because of rain.* → **put off¹** (4), **scrub out** (3), **scrub round** (1)

**3** to cause (someone or an animal) to keep away: [T1 (*often simple tenses*)] *Call off your dog, he's biting my leg!*

**4** to stop (something) happening: [T1 (*often simple tenses*)] *It was decided to call off the search when there was no hope of finding the missing child alive.*

***call on/upon** *v prep*

**1** to visit (someone) formally, either socially or on business: [T1] *Permit me to call on you next Tuesday afternoon. The salesman calls on the firm twice a month.* → **wait on²** (3)

**2** to choose; make a demand on (someone); invite (someone), as to do something: [T1 (*for*)] *I will now call on Jean* (*for an answer*). [V3 (*often simple tenses*)] *I will now call on Mr Webster to drink the health of the happy pair. I feel called upon to reply to the speech. Many people call on God to help them.*

**3** to use (something or someone): [T1 (*usu. simple tenses*)] *The cricket team were so short of players that they had to call on the second team.*

**call out** *v adv*

**1** to shout (something) loudly: [IØ] *Jane called out when she saw her friend across the street.* [T1] *Jane called out her friend's name when she saw her across the street.* → **cry out** (1), **roar out, shout out, thunder out, yell out**

***2** to order (someone) to come to one's help: [T1 (*often pass.*)] *The doctor has been called out every night this week. All the firemen in the city were called out to fight the big fire.* → **get out** (18)

***3** to cause (something) to be seen or used: [T1 (*usu. simple tenses*)] *Trouble can call out a person's best qualities.* → **bring out** (4), etc.

***4** *not fml* to cause (workers) to refuse to work (strike): [T1] *The workers' leader has called all the men out for more pay.* → **bring out** (7), etc.

***5** *BrE fml* to invite (someone) to fight: [T1] *A gentleman should call out any man who is rude to his wife.* → **call down** (5)

**call over¹** *v adv*

**1** to ask (someone) to come from a distance: [X9 + OVER] *The man in the restaurant called the head waiter over to complain about the food.*

***2** to speak a list of (names, words, etc.): [T1] *The teacher began to call over the names on his list.* —**call-over** *n* → **call off** (1)

**call over²** *v prep* → **haul over, rake over²** (2)

**call someone over the coals** *not fml* to scold someone for a fault: *The director brought Jim into his office to call him over the coals for being late so often.*

**call round** *v adv*

*not fml* to visit informally: [L9 + ROUND (*at*)] *Why don't you call round one evening? I'm sorry I'm late, I called round at my sister's to see how she was.*

**call to** *v prep*

**1 call someone to account** to ask someone to give reasons or explanations: [*usu. simple tenses*] *The teacher has been called to account for the disorder in his classroom.*

**2 call someone to arms** to order someone to serve in the armed forces: [*usu. pass.*] *All the young men have been called to arms.*

**3 call attention to** to make (someone or something) noticed: *Jane was too proud of her appearance, always calling attention to herself.*

**4 call a halt to** to stop (something): [*often simple tenses*] *We must call a halt to this senseless waste of life on the roads.*

**5 call something/someone to mind** to remember something or someone: [*usu. simple tenses*] *I just can't call his face to mind at the moment.* → **bring to** (19), **come to²** (30), **recall to** (3)

**6 call to order** to ask (someone or a meeting) to behave in an orderly way or keep the rules: *The chairman called the committee to order and the meeting began.*

**call together** *v adv*
to cause (people or things) to gather: [X9 + TOGETHER (*often simple tenses*)] *Call all the members together and we'll take a vote. When I am unwell I find it difficult to call my thoughts together.*

**call up** *v adv*
**1** to shout so as to be heard by people on a higher level: [IØ + UP] *From the bottom of the stairs Jane called up "Have you seen my blue bag?"*
***2** esp. *BrE* to waken (someone): [T1 (*often simple tenses*)] *Please call me up at 7 o'clock tomorrow.*
***3** esp. *AmE* to telephone (someone): [T1 (*often simple tenses*)] *Please call me up tomorrow morning.* → **ring up** (1)
***4** esp. *BrE* to order (someone) to join the armed forces: [T1 (*usu. pass.*)] *During the war, all younger men were called up to fight in the army, the navy, or the air force.* —**call-up** *n, adj*
***5** to bring (something such as a memory) to one's mind: [T1 (*usu. simple tenses*)] *The smell of those flowers calls up my childhood. Can you call up any of your thoughts on the subject?* → **bring back** (2), **come back** (4), **come back to** (2), **summon up** (2)
***6** to cause (someone or something) to arrive: [T1 (*often simple tenses*)] *The strange old lady claims to be able to call up spirits from the dead.* → **raise from** (2), **raise up** (2), **rise from** (4), **summon up** (4)

***call upon** *v prep* → CALL ON

***calm down** *v adv*
***1** to make (someone) calmer: [T1 + DOWN] *Try to calm the children down, will you, they're too excited.*
***2** *to* become calmer: [IØ] *Calm down, there's nothing to worry about. The wind seems to be calming down at last.*

**camp out** *v adv*
**1** to live, usu. for a holiday, in a tent or tents: [IØ + OUT] *The children love camping out when we go on holiday.*
***2** to live for a short time (with someone): [IØ (*with*)] *When they were first married, Jim and Mary had no home of their own, so they had to camp out with Mary's parents.*

**camp up** *v adv* → **ham up**
**camp it up** *infml* to overact, esp. with intentional bad taste, in order to amuse: *You might offend your hosts if you camp it up at the party in your usual way.*

**campaign against** *v prep* → **campaign for** (2), etc.
to attempt to stop or prevent (something) by public means, such as advertising, writing letters, and holding meetings, so as to make people conscious of the need for change, decision, or action: [L9 + *against*] *Smith's family and friends are campaigning against his imprisonment as they believe him to be not guilty.*

**campaign for** *v prep*
**1** to try to win votes for (a political party or a person who wishes to be elected): [IØ + *for*] *I wish to thank all my helpers who have campaigned for me/for our party during the past few months.*
**2** to attempt to gain (an aim) by public means, such as advertising, writing letters, and holding meetings, so as to make people conscious of the need for change, decision, or action: [L9 + *for*] *Many women are campaigning for improvements in the sexual equality laws.* → **agitate for, campaign against, crusade against, crusade for**

***cancel out** *v adv*
**1** (of figures) to (cause to) balance or be equal: [IØ (*simple tenses*)] *The £1 I owed him and the £1 he owes me cancel out.* [T1 (*usu. simple tenses*)] *The £1 I owed him and £1 he owes me cancel each other out.*
**2** to remove the effect of (something); be made ineffective by balancing: [T1 (*usu. simple tenses*)] *The poor quality of his work this year cancels out his former improvement.* [IØ (*simple tenses*)] *His good qualities and his faults cancel out.*

***cant over** *v adv* → KEEL OVER

**canvass for** *v prep*
to try to gain votes for (someone or a party) before an election, as by visiting homes, etc.: [IØ + *for*] *I have to thank all my helpers who canvassed for me and helped me to win this election.*

***capitalize on** *v prep*
to profit by; make full use of (something): [T1] *You should capitalize on every chance you get to improve your English. The firm was able to capitalize on the mistakes made by its competitors.*

**care about** *v prep*
**1** to like (someone or something); be fond of (someone): [IØ + *about* (*simple tenses*)] *I really care about the students in my class.* → **care for** (1)
**2** to be interested in (something such as an idea): [IØ + *about* (*simple tenses*)] *I don't care about what you think. I don't care about your opinion.*
**3** to be worried by; mind (something): [IØ + *about* (*no pass., simple tenses*)] *This writer, unlike most others, does not care about death.* [IØ + *about* (*simple tenses*)] *Don't you care about losing your job?*

**care for** *v prep*
**1** to like (someone or something); be fond of (*someone*): [IØ + *for* (*simple tenses*)] *I really care for the students in my class. I don't care for that colour.* → **care about** (1)
**2** to trouble about; have regard for (someone or something): [IØ + *for* (*simple tenses*)] *He cares only for himself.*

*3 to like to have (usu. something); like (something to happen): [T1 (*simple tenses*)] *Would the children care for some more cake?* [V3 (*simple tenses*)] *That ladder looks unsafe; I would not care for it to fall while you were at the top.*

*4 to nurse; attend (someone): [T1] *Jane spent years caring for her sick aunt. Do you enjoy caring for small children while their mothers are at work?* → **look after** (2), **see after, take of** (3)

*5 to take good care of (something): [T1] *Mary cares for her clothes, to make them last.* —**uncared-for, well-cared-for** *adj* → **look after** (2), **take of** (3)

**carp at** *v prep* → **cavil at**

to complain about (something or someone) in an unpleasant manner: [L9 + *at* (*about*)] *It's no good carping at the boy's behaviour, he'll only get worse. It's no good carping at the boy about his behaviour.*

**carry about/around** *v adv* → **carry along** (1)

to carry (something) with one: [T1 + ABOUT/AROUND] *Why does she always carry that little dog about? I carry memories of my homeland around with me.*

**carry along** *v adv*

**1** to carry (something) with one: [T1 + ALONG] *The director came to the meeting, carrying a big parcel along (with him). The flooded river carried trees along.* → **carry about**

*2 to cause (someone) to share one's feelings, opinions, etc.: [T1] *The politician carried his hearers along with his speech.* → **carry away** (2)

*3 to encourage (someone), as to keep trying: [T1 (*often pass.*)] *The young swimmer got so tired that she wanted to stop but she was carried along by the cheers of her supporters.*

**carry around** *v adv* → CARRY ABOUT

**carry away** *v adv*

**1** also **carry off** to take (something) or someone) away; remove (usu. something): [T1 + AWAY] *The men came and carried the table away.* → **bear away** (1)

*2 to excite or persuade (someone): [T1 (*often pass.*)] *The crowd were carried away by his fine words. The politician carried his hearers away with his speech.* → **carry along** (2)

*3 → CARRY OFF¹ (3)

*4 → CARRY OFF¹ (4)

*5 to excite (someone) esp. so that he is no longer capable of sensible thought or behaviour: [T1 (*often pass.*)] *The whole crowd were quite carried away by the young singer's performance. I didn't intend to buy so many things, but once I started, I just seemed to get carried away.* → **bear away** (5)

**carry back** *v adv*

**1** to return (something or someone): [T1 + BACK] *Would you carry the chairs back into the house for me?*

*2 to make (someone) return in thought or memory: [T1 (*to*) (*simple tenses*)] *This poem always carries me back to my childhood. That smell of freshly baked bread carries me back!* → **go back** (5), **go back to** (4), **take back** (7)

**carry before** *v prep*

**carry all/everything before one** to be completely successful, impossible to defeat: *The army carried everything before them and gained control of all the important towns in a few weeks. "I was never more confident of anything than that I could carry everything before me in that House."* (Benjamin Disraeli, *Letters*, 7 February 1833)

**carry down** *v adv*

**1** to lift (something) to a lower level: [T1 + DOWN] *The tea things are upstairs, could you carry them down for me?*

*2 to give or leave (something such as an idea) to people who are younger or come later: [T1 (*usu. pass.*)] *This custom has been carried down from the 18th century.* → **hand down** (3), etc.

***carry forward** *v adv*

**1** (in business) to move (a total on one page) to the next page; leave (a sum) till a later time: [T1 (*often pass.*)] *When you add up the money at the bottom of the page, write "carried forward" after the total; the same total is then written at the top of the next page, marked "brought forward". This debt has been carried forward from year to year; when will it be paid?* → **bring forward** (2), **carry over** (1)

**2** to cause (something or someone) to advance: [T1] *The politician's successful speech carried him forward.*

**carry into** *v prep*

**1** to lift (usu. something) into (usu. a building): [T1 + *into*] *Please carry the chairs into the house for me.*

**2 carry into action/execution/practice** to perform (something) planned or threatened: *It's time I carried my intentions of hard work into practice.* → **put into** (11), etc.

**carry off¹** *v adv*

**1** → CARRY AWAY (1)

*2 to take (something or someone) by force: [T1] *Thieves carried off the farmer's sheep during the night.*

*3 also **carry away** to win (something): [T1] *Jim carried off most of the prizes at the races* → **bear away** (2)

*4 also *fml* **bear away**, *fml* **bear off, carry away** *not fml* to kill (someone): [T1 (*simple tenses*)] *An attack of fever carried him off.*

*5 to succeed, as in not showing (something): [T1 (*simple tenses*)] *She carries off her age well.*

*6 *not fml* to succeed in doing (something difficult): [T1 (*usu. simple tenses*)] *It was a daring attempt but he carried it off. This piano piece is difficult to carry off.* → **bring off** (2), **come off¹** (6), **go off¹** (6), **pass off** (2), **pull off¹** (4)

*7 to excuse (something): [T1 (*usu. simple*

*tenses)] Quick thinking and ready speech may carry off a little daring.*

**carry off²** *v prep*

**1** to take (someone or something) away from (a place): [T1 + *off*] *She picked up the actor's sword and carried it off the stage.*

**2 carry someone off his feet** *not fml* to fill someone with keenness, excitement, or other strong favourable feeling: [*usu. simple tenses*] *Mary agreed to marry Jim when he carried her off her feet at their first meeting.* → **sweep off** (3)

**carry on** *v adv*

**1** to take (something) on: [T1 + ON] *When you travel by plane, you are allowed to carry on a handbag.*

***2** (often of writing) to (cause to) follow: [T1 (*usu. simple tenses*)] *You'll have to carry that long word on to the next line.* [IØ] *Don't stop reading there, the poem carries on over the page.*

***3** to continue to have or organize (something): [T1] *The baker has carried on business here for years. The men were carrying on a conversation.*

***4** *not fml* to (cause to) continue, sometimes after interruption: [IØ] *Don't let me interrupt you, just carry on. We must try to carry on as if nothing had happened. Carry on, men!* [T1] *Carry on the good work! I shall try to carry on the work in spite of difficulties.* [T4 (*often simple tenses*)] *We must carry on hoping for the best.* → **carry on with** (1), **continue with, get on¹** (8), **get on with** (4), **go on¹** (5), **go on with** (4), **keep on** (5)

***5** *not fml* to behave wildly: [IØ] *If you carry on like this, you'll find yourself in prison. The way he carries on, his doctor won't be responsible for him.*

***6** to behave in an excited or anxious manner, esp. talking or weeping: [IØ] *The children have been carrying on all morning. Mother did carry on so when she heard the bad news!* —**carry-on** *n* → **take on¹** (10)

***7** *not fml* to be angry (with someone): [IØ (*at*) (*usu. continuous tenses*)] *The people upstairs were carrying on again last night, they had me quite worried. Our neighbour is always carrying on at her children.*

***8** *infml* to have a love affair (with someone): [IØ (*usu. continuous tenses*)] *The director and his secretary have been carrying on.* —**carryings-on** *n* → **carry on with** (2)

**carry on with** *v adv prep*

**1** to continue with (something): [IØ + ON + *with*] *Carry on with your work while I'm out.* → **carry on** (4), etc.

***2** *infml* to have a love affair with (someone): [T1 (*usu. continuous tenses*)] *The director has been carrying on with his secretary.* → **carry on** (8)

**3 to carry/be carrying on with** to have for the present time, for now, or for the time being: [*no pass.*] *Here's a few dollars to be carrying on with. This broken knife will do to carry on with till I get a new one.* → **go on with** (5)

**carry out** *v adv*

**1** to lift (something or someone) and take it out: [T1 + OUT] *She fainted in the restaurant and had to be carried out. Can you carry the tea things out into the garden?* —**carry-out** *adj* → **take out** (1)

***2** to fulfil or perform (something): [T1 (*often simple tenses*)] *We all have certain duties and jobs to carry out. The gunmen carried out their threat and shot the man. Every possible test was carried out to decide the nature of her illness.*

***carry over** *v adv*

**1** (in business) to move (a total on one page) to the next page: [T1] *When you add up the money at the bottom of the page, carry the total over onto the next page.* → **bring forward** (2), **carry forward** (1)

**2** to move (something) to a later date: [T1 (*often pass.*)] *The concert will have to be carried over till next week because the singer is ill.* → **put off¹** (4), etc.

**3** to last; be left (from another time): [IØ (*from, to*) (*simple tenses*)] *The habit carries over from my childhood. His influence carried over to the musicians who copied him.* —**carry-over** *n*

**4** to be left (to someone): [IØ (*to*) (*simple tenses*)] *The money will carry over to his children. The rights to the property carry over to the buyer.*

**carry through¹** *v adv*

**1** to lift (something or someone) into another space: [T1 + THROUGH] *The waiter collected the dishes from the kitchen and carried them through into the restaurant.*

***2** to complete (something) in spite of difficulties: [T1] *He was determined to carry through all his suggestions. We must all help to carry the plan through.*

***3** to save by supporting (someone) during troubled times: [T1b] *Only his courage carried Jim through.* → **bring through¹, come through¹** (7), **pull round** (2), **pull through¹** (2)

**carry through²** *v prep*

**1** to lift (usu. something) through (a space): [T1 + *through*] *The table is too wide, we can't carry it through the doorway.*

***2** to help (someone) to live through (danger or trouble): [D1] *Their courage carried the people through the war.* → **bring through, come through²** (3), **pull through²** (3)

**carry with** *v prep*

**1** to take (something) with (one): [T1 + *with*] *If I take only a small bag, I can carry it with me on the plane.*

**2 carry someone with one** to persuade someone to share one's opinion, support one, etc.: *The politician hoped to carry the voters with him by his speech.*

**3 carry something with one** to remember something well: *I shall carry that memory with me for the rest of my life.*

**carve out** *v adv* → **hack out, hew out**

**1** to cut (something such as a pattern) clearly

out of a material, as with a knife: [T1 + OUT] *She bought a wooden dish with a pretty pattern carved out.*

*__2__ to make (something) by hard work: [T1] *He carved out a name for himself in the engineering business. The early settlers carved out a new nation from the wild uncultivated country.*

**carve up** *v adv*

**1** to divide (something) into pieces with a knife: [T1 + UP] *Ask the man in the shop to carve the meat up for you.*

*__2__ *infml derog* to divide (something): [T1 (*usu. pass.*)] *Europe was carved up after World War I.* —**carve-up** *n*

*__3__ *infml* to share (something such as money): [T1] *The thieves carved up the profit from the robbery.* —**carve-up** *n*

*__4__ *sl* to wound (someone) intentionally: [T1] *Threaten to carve him up if he won't give the money, that should make him do it!* → **cut up** (7), **slit up** (2)

*__5__ *not fml* to overtake (someone) fast and dangerously in a car: [T1] *Yes, he does get there sooner, but only by carving up the rest of the traffic on the way—one day he'll have a nasty accident.*

***cash in** *v adv*

**1** to exchange (something) for money: [T1] *I'd like to cash this cheque in, please. You may cash in the shares at the end of five years.*

**2** *not fml* to take advantage or profit (from something): [IØ (*on*)] *You'd better cash in while you can. Let's cash in on this unexpected fine weather and go into the country for the day.*

**3 cash in one's chips** esp. *AmE infml* to die: [*simple tenses*] *I'm afraid old Charlie has cashed in his chips.*

***cash up** *v adv*

**1** (in a shop) to add all the money taken in the day: [IØ] *I'm not ready to go home for a few minutes, I'm still cashing up.*

**2** *infml* to produce (money) required for something: [T1 (*usu. simple tenses*)] *Can the club cash up the money needed to train young players?* [IØ (*often simple tenses*)] *We need money to train young players: will the club cash up?*

***cast about/around/round** *v adv; prep* → **beat about** (3)

to search anxiously about (one) (for something): [IØ (*for*)] *The prisoner cast about for a way of escape. I've been casting around in my mind, but I can't find an easy answer.* [T1 (*for*) (*no pass.*)] *The prisoner cast about him for a way of escape.*

**cast aside** *v adv*

**1** to put (something) out of use for the time being: [X9 + ASIDE (*often simple tenses*)] *It's good to be able to cast aside winter clothes.* → **cast off** (1), etc.

*__2__ to end one's connection with (someone or something): [T1 (*often simple tenses*)] *Henry joined the opposing political party, casting aside his former loyalties.* → **cast away** (2), **cast off** (3), **fling aside** (3), **throw aside** (2), **toss aside** (2)

**cast away** *v adv*

**1** to throw away; get rid of (something): [X9 + AWAY] *"Cast care away!"* (song) *It's time you cast away those dull old clothes and bought some cheerful new ones.* → **throw out** (2), etc.

*__2__ to end one's connection with (someone or something): [T1 (*often simple tenses*)] *When he grew rich, he cast away his old friends.* → **cast aside** (2), etc.

**3 be cast away** to be shipwrecked: *The sailors were cast away on a desert island.* —**castaway** *n*

***cast back** *v adv*

**1** to (cause to) remember: [T1 (*often simple tenses*)] *Let us cast back our minds to the first meeting.* [IØ (*in*) (*often simple tenses*)] *Let us cast back in our minds to the first meeting.* →**throw back** (6)

**2** *AmE* to behave or look like a relative in the distant past: [IØ (*simple tenses*)] *The boy casts back to his great-great-grandfather.* → **throw back** (5)

***cast before** *v prep*

**cast pearls before swine** to waste something good on someone unworthy of it: *He tried to explain the beauty of the music to his pupils but it was just casting pearls before swine.*

**cast down** *v adv*

**1** to point (something) downwards: [X9 + DOWN (*often simple tenses*)] *The girl cast her eyes down modestly.* —**downcast** *adj*

**2** to destroy (something) or defeat (someone): [T1 + DOWN] *True believers must cast down the temples of the false gods.* → **throw down**[1] (3)

*__3__ to lower (someone) in spirit: [T1 (*usu. pass.*)] *Mary was cast down by the bad news about her mother.* —**downcast** *adj*

**cast in** *v prep*

**1** to put (someone) in (the part of a character, or a play): [T1 + *in*] *The director has cast you and Mary in the parts of the sisters.*

*__2__ to express (a meaning) by using (a certain form of words): [D1] *He tends to cast his ideas in long sentences.* → **recast in**

**3 be cast in the same/a different mould** *not fml* to have the same/a different character: *You can't expect the same behaviour from John as from his sister; he's cast in a different mould. The brothers think exactly alike, as if they were cast in the same mould.*

**4 cast in someone's face/teeth** *not fml* to blame someone for (something): *There's no need to cast his recent failure in his teeth in that unkind way.* → **fling in**[2] (2), **throw in**[2] (3)

**cast in with** *v adv prep* → **fling in with, throw in with**

**cast in one's lot with** to decide to join (someone, a political party, etc.): *I'm sorry that the* *boy has cast in his lot with such undesirable people.*

**cast off** *v adv*

**1** to put (something) out of use: [X9 + OFF] *As the sun grew warmer, he cast off his heavy winter clothes.* → **cast aside** (1), **fling aside** (1), **fling off** (1), **lay off** (8), **leave off** (1), **shake off**[1] (1), **throw aside** (1), **throw off**[1] (1, 2), **toss aside** (1), **toss off** (1)

***2** to remove; no longer wear (clothes) and get rid of them: [T1 (*often simple tenses*)] *When you grow too big for your clothes, cast them off and I'll give them away.* —**castoff** *n* —**cast-off** *adj* —**offcast** *n, adj AmE*

***3** to stop having anything to do with (someone or something): [T1 (*often simple tenses*)] *When he grew rich, he cast off his old friends.* —**cast-off** *adj* → **cast aside** (2), etc.

***4** to free oneself from (something unwanted): [T1] *He was pleased to be able to cast off such an unwelcome responsibility. The Russian people rose, casting off the chains of unjust rule.* —**offcast** *adj* → **fling off** (3), etc.

***5** to lose; get rid of (something such as a skin): [T1] *The snake cast off its old skin.* → **shuffle off** (2), **slough off** (1)

***6** to set (a boat or ship) free by untying a rope: [T1] *Don't cast off the boat till everyone is on board. Cast off all ropes!* [IØ] *Are you ready to cast off?*

***7** esp. *BrE* (in knitting) to remove (a number of stitches) from the needle: [T1a] *At the end of the row, cast off seven stitches.* [IØ] *Be careful not to cast off too tightly, or the work will lose its shape.* → **bind off, cast on**[1]

***8** (in printing) to guess the printed length of written material: [T1] *I've cast off your book and think it should come to about 400 pages when it's printed.* —**cast-off** *n*

***9** (in country dancing) to separate from one's partner and pass around the outside of the set: [IØ] *After the next figure, you cast off and meet your partner again at the other end.*

***cast on**[1] *v adv* → **bind off, cast off** (7)

(in knitting) to start making something by putting (the first stitches) onto a needle: [T1] *Cast on seventy-six stitches and work two inches of plain stitch.* [IØ] *I'll start cooking the dinner as soon as I've finished casting on.*

**cast on/upon**[2] *v prep*

**1** to throw (something) on (something): [X9 + *on/upon* (*often simple tenses*)] *The storm cast the little boat on the rocks. The traveller cast his money on the table and left.* → **fling on**[2] (1), **throw on**[2] (1)

**2 cast one's bread on the waters** to perform a good act which may be returned by someone else: "*Cast thy bread upon the waters: for thou shalt find it after many days.*" (The Bible)

**3 cast doubt on** to make people wonder about the truth of (something): *Everyone was prepared to accept the prisoner's story until the opposing lawyer cast doubt on it.* → **throw on**[2] (6)

**4 cast oneself on someone's mercy** to declare that one is dependent on someone's mercy: [*often simple tenses*] *If the judge finds you guilty, you can only cast yourself on his mercy.* → **fling on**[2] (2), **throw on**[2] (8)

**5 cast one's/a shadow on** to cause (something or someone) to be in the shade: *After dinner, the office block to the west casts its shadow on our windows, so we don't see the setting sun.* → **cast over** (3), **throw on**[2] (2), **throw over**[2] (3)

***cast out** *v adv*

**1** to drive (something) out; throw something away: [T1 + OUT (*usu. simple tenses*)] *I really must cast out all these old papers. Perfect love casts out fear. The magician claims to be able to cast out devils.*

***2** make (someone) leave society: [T1 (*often pass.*)] *In former times, criminals were often cast out and had to live in the wild.* —**outcast** *n* → **throw out** (4), etc.

***cast over**[1] *v adv*

to cover (something): [T1 (*usu. pass.*)] *Her eyes were cast over with sorrow.* — **overcast** *adj*

**cast over**[2] *v prep*

**1 cast a damper over** *not fml* to make (something) seem less enjoyable: *Mary's absence cast a damper over the party.*

**2 cast an/one's eye over** to look at (something such as writing) quickly; make a quick examination of (something): *I'd like you to cast your eyes over this letter before I send it to the school, to see if it's satisfactory.* → **pass over**[2] (4)

**3 cast a/one's shadow over** to cause (something or someone) to be in the shade: *Please stand to one side, you're casting your shadow over my work.* → **cast on**[2] (5), **throw on**[2] (2), **throw over**[2] (3)

***cast round** *v adv* → CAST ABOUT

**cast up** *v adv*

**1** to throw (something) upwards: [T1 + UP] *The machine cast up great heaps of earth.* → **chuck up** (1), **fling up** (1), **throw up** (1), **toss up** (1)

***2** to wash (something) onto the shore: [T1 (*on*) (*usu. pass.*)] *Pieces of wood are cast up all along this coast. A body was cast up last night.* → **wash up** (3)

***3** to calculate; make a total of (figures): [T1] *Please cast up this list of figures for me.*

***4** to remind (someone) of (something unpleasant): [T1 (*at*)] *He is always casting up my old failures (at me).* → **fling up** (6), **sling up** (2), **throw up** (7)

***5** esp. *AmE not fml* to be sick; bring up (food): [T1] *Jane has cast up her dinner again.* [IØ] *Jane has been casting up all morning.* → **bring up** (4), etc.

**cast upon** *v prep* → CAST ON

**catch alight** *v adj*

**1** to start burning; take fire: [L9 + **alight** (*often simple tenses*)] *Some dry leaves caught alight and soon the whole forest was on fire.*

→ **place to** (3), **put to²** (17), **set alight** (1), **set on²** (10), **set to²** (5)

*__2__ to become very keen or popular: [IØ (*usu. simple tenses*)] *At the end of his speech, the crowd caught alight and began cheering wildly.* → **set alight** (2)

**catch at** *v prep*

**1** to discover (someone) in the act of (something wrong): [T1 + *at* (*usu. simple tenses*)] *I've caught you at your tricks again!* → **grab at** (1), etc.

*__2__ to try to hold or use (something): [T1 (*usu. simple tenses*)] *A businessman will catch at any chance of making a profit.* → **clutch at** (2), **grab at** (2), **snap at** (3), **snatch at** (2)

**3 catch at a straw** to try to seize any chance, esp. to be saved: [*usu. simple tenses*] *"A drowning man will catch at a straw."* (saying) → **grab at**(3), etc.

**catch behind** *v adv*

**be caught behind** (in cricket) to be dismissed because the wicket keeper has caught the ball off the bat

***catch flat-footed** *v adj*

*infml* to catch (someone) by surprise, as in doing something wrong: [T1b (*usu. pass.*)] *The prisoners were trying to escape but were caught flat-footed in the attempt.*

**catch in** *v adv*

**1** to find (someone) by chance at home, in the office, etc.: [X9 + IN (*usu. simple tenses*)] *You might catch him in about 11 o'clock.* →**catch out** (1)

*__2__ to fasten (something) with a few stitches, as to make it smaller: [T1] *Catch in the waistline very lightly so that it doesn't show.* → **catch up** (6)

**catch in** *v prep*

**1** to trap (usu. part of the body or clothing) in (something): [T1 + *in* (*often simple tenses*)] *"I left the room . . . but caught my foot in the mat."* (George and Weedon Grossmith, *The Diary of a Nobody*) [IØ + *in* (*often simple tenses*)] *My foot caught in the mat and I fell heavily.*

**2 catch someone in the act** to discover someone actually performing a wrong act: [*usu. simple tenses*] *The policeman followed the thieves until they actually picked up the jewels, when he caught them in the act.* → **catch red-handed**

***catch it** *v pron*

*infml* to be in trouble from someone: [IØ] *You'll catch it when your mother learns who broke the dishes.*

**catch napping** *v adj*

**1** to find (someone) asleep: [X9 + **napping**] *Father was supposed to be working, but when I went in I caught him napping.*

*__2__ *infml* to catch (someone) making a mistake, forgetting to be careful: [T1b] *There's another mistake on page thirty-two, I'm afraid I've caught you napping again!*

**catch of** *v prep*

**1 catch hold of: a** to seize (something or someone): *Catching hold of the rope, the climber was able to swing to safety.*→ **get of** (7). **b** to begin to know (an idea): *Are you beginning to catch hold of our methods now?* → **get of** (5)

**2 catch sight of** to see or notice (someone or something) for a moment: *I caught sight of the thieves' car and phoned the police.*

**catch off** *v prep* → **throw off²** (3)

**catch someone off guard** to surprise someone in an undefended moment, when he is weaker: [*usu. simple tenses*] *If you want to persuade the chairman to agree, you'll have to catch him off (his) guard.*

***catch on¹** *v adv*

**1** *not fml* to become popular: [IØ] *I don't think this strange new fashion will catch on.* → **take on¹** (9)

**2** *not fml* to understand what someone has said, esp. a joke: [IØ] *Would you mind repeating that, I didn't quite catch on.* → **latch on** (1)

**3** *not fml* to understand and make use of something: [IØ (*to*) (*often simple tenses*)] *An enquiring mind quickly catches on to a new idea. The best thing about this new worker is that he catches on very fast.*

**catch on²** *v prep*

**1** to (cause to) fasten accidentally on (something): [IØ + *on* (*often simple tenses*)] *My coat caught on a nail and tore.* [T1 + *on*] *I would have been early enough, but I caught my coat on a nail just as I was leaving.*

**2 catch someone on the hop** *infml* to catch someone unexpectedly, often doing something surprising: [*usu. simple tenses*] *I went in without knocking and there was his secretary sitting on his knee; I'd caught him on the hop.*

**3 catch someone on the raw** *not fml* to mention a sensitive matter in a way that hurts someone: [*usu. simple tenses*] *You'll have to be more careful what you say; you really caught him on the raw when you mentioned his first wife.*

**4 catch someone on the wrong foot** *not fml* to find someone unprepared as by doing something unexpected: *Joe came to the party too early and caught us on the wrong foot.*

**catch out** *v adv*

**1** to find (someone) not at home or in the office, etc.: [X9 + OUT (*usu. simple tenses*)] *He was here all morning, but you've just caught him out.* → **catch in** (1)

**2** (in cricket and other ball games) to dismiss (a player), ending his turn by catching the ball directly off his bat: [T1 + OUT (*often pass.*)] *Three of the team were caught out just before tea.* → **be out** (7), etc.

*__3__ *not fml* to discover (someone) doing something wrong such as lying, or being unable to answer a question, often by means of a trick: [T1 (*usu. simple tenses*)] *I'm sure the prisoner* *is not telling the truth; talk to him and see if you can catch him out. The examiners will try to catch you out, so have all your answers well prepared.*

*__catch red-handed__ *v adj* → **catch in$^2$** (2)
*not fml* to catch (someone) actually performing a wrong act: [T1b (*usu. simple tenses*)] *The policeman followed the thieves until they actually picked up the jewellery, when he caught them red-handed.*

**catch short** *v adj* → **take short**
**be caught short** to lack a supply of something suddenly needed: *Have our meat delivered to your freezer, so that you're never caught short when unexpected guests arrive.*

**catch up** *v adv*
**1** to seize (something) quickly: [X9 + UP] *The thieves caught up the money and ran.*
**2** to trap or fasten (something) in a high position: [T1 + UP (*usu. pass.*)] *My coat was caught up on the hook. The big red curtain was caught up with a golden rope.*
*__3__ to make (someone) helpless; fix (someone) in a time or place: [T1] *I was caught up in the busy traffic again this evening.*
*__4__ to reach (someone who is ahead): [T1] *I had to run to catch her up.* [IØ (*with*)] *I had to run to catch up with her.* → **come up with** (1), **get up with** (2), **keep up** (7), **keep up with** (1)
*__5__ to come level with (someone or something): [T1] *We shall have to work hard to catch the other firm up.* [IØ (*on, with*)] *He spent six months catching up with his studies. When you've been away, it takes a long time to catch up on the local news. The tax people will catch up with you in the end.* → **come up with** (2), **keep up** (8), **keep up with** (2)
*__6__ to fasten (something) with a few stitches, as to make a garment shorter: [T1] *Catch up the lower edge with light sewing so that it doesn't show.* → **catch in** (2)
*__7__ *AmE not fml* to show that (someone) is wrong; find fault with (someone): [T1] *The examiners caught him up on the third question. Several people in the crowd caught the politician up during his speech.*
**8 be caught up in** to be deeply interested in and busy with (an activity or group): *Both my children are caught up in the present fashion for rock music. Most citizens do not get caught up in local events. Many politicians started by being caught up in the party when they were very young.*

**cater for** *v prep*
**1** to provide food for (people or an event, etc.): [IØ + *for*] *The bakers specialize in catering for large parties.* "*Weddings catered for.*" (notice)
*__2__ esp. *BrE* to provide what is needed for (people): [T1 (*simple tenses*)] *Politicians should learn to cater for the man in the street.* → **cater to** (1), **provide for** (3)
*__3__ to take (something) into account; consider (something): [T1] *When the differences among the separate parts of the country have been catered for, the general picture remains the same.*
*__4__ *not fml* to provide what is needed to fulfil (a demand): [T1 (*simple tenses*)] *The record company caters for all tastes in music.* → **cater to** (2), **provide for** (3)

*__cater to__ *v prep* → **provide for** (3)
**1** to provide what is needed for; try to satisfy (people): [T1 (*simple tenses*)] *Politicians should learn to cater to the man in the street.* → **cater for** (2)
**2** to provide what is needed to fulfil (a demand): [T1 (*simple tenses*)] *The record company caters to all tastes in music.* → **cater for** (4)

**caution about/against** *v prep*
to warn (someone) officially about (something) or against (doing something): [T1 + *about/against*] *The policeman cautioned the motorist about his speed. The policeman cautioned the motorist against speeding on any future occasion.*

*__cave in__ *v adv*
**1** (of something hollow or covering something hollow) to (cause to) fall inwards: [IØ] *The roof caved in, trapping the miners.* [T1] *The weight of the snow caved in the roof.* —**cave-in** *n*—**caved-in** *adj* → **fall in$^1$** (2)
**2** *not fml* (of a business, etc.) to fail: [IØ] *Why do you want to appoint this man as director? The last firm he worked for caved in.*
**3** *not fml* to yield: [IØ] *I thought he could face his opponent and not cave in so easily, but I was disappointed.* —**cave-in** *n*

**cavil at** *v prep* → **carp at**
to complain about (something) in a way that is unpleasant or unnecessary: [L9 + *at*] *While the teacher liked the way he wrote, she was always cavilling at his spelling and handwriting.*

**cease from** *v prep*
*fml* to stop doing (something): [L9 + *from*] *When can the people cease from their labours? "I will not cease from mental fight, nor shall my sword sleep in my hand."* (William Blake, *Milton*)

*__cede to__ *v prep*
*fml* to give (usu. land) to (usu. another nation): [D1 + *to* (*often pass.*)] *The island was ceded to the mainland nation by its former owners.*

**celebrate for** *v prep*
**be celebrated for** to be famous for (something or doing something): *The city is celebrated for its yearly horse show. The actor was celebrated for drinking too much.*

**censure for** *v prep*
to blame (someone) officially for (something or doing something): [T1 + *for*] *The House censured the Member of Parliament for his*

*rude remark to the Minister. He was censured for making such a rude remark.*

***center in** *v prep* → CENTRE IN

***center on/round/upon** *v prep* → CENTRE ON

***center out** *v adv* → **single out, centre out**
*AmE infml* to choose (someone) from among others, usu. for punishment or special treatment: [T1] *The teacher scolded the child for bad behaviour, but the child then complained that she had been centered out.*

***center round** *v prep* → CENTER ON

***center upon** *v prep* → CENTER ON

***centre in** *BrE*, **center in** *AmE v prep*
to have (something) as its main point of interest and concern: [T1 (*no pass., usu. simple tenses*)] *His life's work centred in the search for a cure for the terrible disease. All our interest centres in our family.* [T4 (*usu. simple tenses*)] *Her chief joy centred in caring for the children.*

***centre on/round/upon** *BrE*, **center on/round/upon** *AmE v prep*
**1** to have (something) as its middle or most important point; surround (something or someone): [T1 (*no pass., usu. simple tenses*)] *The village centred on its market square. The children always centre round the teacher at story time.*
**2** to be concerned with (something): [T1 (*no pass., usu. simple tenses*)] *The conversation centred on the election. The action of the play centres on the struggle between the two women.* [D1 (*usu. pass.*)] *The conversation was centred on the election. The action of the play is centred on the struggle between the two women.* → **focus on** (4), **revolve about** (2)

***centre out** *v adv* → CENTER OUT

***centre round** *v prep* → CENTRE ON

***centre upon** *v prep* → CENTRE ON

***chafe at/under** *v prep*
to be annoyed and impatient with (something): [T1] *People in London are chafing at the continuing delays on the buses. People in prison for the first time chafe under the limitation of their freedom.*

**chain down** *v adv*
**1** to fasten (something) down with chains: [T1 + DOWN] *Don't worry about the heavy load, it's chained down.*
***2** *not fml* to limit (someone): [T1] *I don't want to chain you down; feel free to use your own ideas. My mother always complained of being chained down to housework.* → **bind down** (2), **tie down** (2)

**chain to** *v prep*
**1** to fasten (something or someone) with chains to (something or someone): [T1 + *to*] *In former times, prisoners were chained to the wall or to one another.*
***2** *not fml* to limit (someone) to (something): [D1 (*usu. pass.*)] *My mother always complained of being chained to the house.*

**chain up** *v adv*
to fasten (usu. an animal) in place with a chain or rope: [T1 + UP] *Of course the dog makes such a noise, the poor creature is chained up all day.*

**chalk out** *v adv*
**1** to draw (something) with chalk: [T1 + OUT] *I've chalked out a map on the floor.*
***2** to make a plan of (something): [T1] *The general chalked out his plan for defeating the enemy.*

**chalk up** *v adv*
**1** to write (something) with chalk: [T1 + UP] *The results were chalked up on the blackboard as soon as they came in.*
***2** *not fml* to record (something) to one's success: [T1] *Now we can chalk up another victory for our team.* → **charge against** (1), **charge down** (2), **charge to, mark up** (3), **put down** (8)
***3** *infml* to charge (something such as drink) to someone's account: [T1 (*to*)] *I've no money to pay for the beer, will you chalk it up (to me)?* → **clock up** (2), **log up** (2), **notch up, score up**

***chance it** *v pron*
*infml* to take a risk: [IØ] *I know the police might come, but let's chance it.*

***chance on/upon** *v prep* → **happen on**, etc.
to find (something) by chance: [T1 (*simple tenses*)] *I chanced on this old photograph in the back of the drawer.*

**change back** *v adv*
to (cause to) return from a changed form to (one's former state): [T1 + BACK (*from, into, to*)] *If you're not careful, the evil magician will change you back into the ugly creature that you used to be.* [IØ + BACK (*from, into, to*)] *I hope you'll never change back from the person you have recently become.*

***change down** *v adv* → **change up, gear down** (1), **gear up** (1), **kick down** (2)
(in a car or other vehicle) to change to a lower gear: [IØ] *You have to change down when you drive uphill.* —**change-down** *n*

**change for** *v prep*
**1** to exchange (something) for (something else): [T1 + for] *I'd like to change this dress for one in a larger size.* → **exchange for, swap for, trade for**
**2 change for the better/the worse** to improve or worsen: *I hope the weather will soon change for the better.*

**change from** *v prep*
**1** to take off (clothes one is wearing) in order to put on others: [IØ + *from*] *I shall have to change from these wet clothes.* → **change into** (1), **change out of**
**2** to change (something or someone) from (a state) to another: [X9 + *from*] *The beggar was changed from a prince.* → **change into** (2), etc.

**change into** *v prep*
**1** to change clothes and put on (something else): [IØ + *into*] *I'd better change into some dry clothes.* → **change from** (1), **change out of**

**2** to cause (something or someone) to become (something or someone else): [X9 + *into*] *The prince was changed into a beggar.* [T1 + *into*] *I should like to change these pounds into dollars.* → **change from** (2), **change to, convert into, make into** (2), **metamorphose into, transform into, turn into** (2), **turn to**[2] (6)

**change off.** *v adv*
*to take turns in work such as bell ringing:* [IØ (*usu. simple tenses*)] *It's time for the ringers to change off.*

**change out of** *v adv prep* → **change from** (1), **change into** (1)
to take off (clothes one is wearing) in order to put on others: [IØ + OUT + *of*] *I shall have to change out of these wet clothes.*

**change over** *v adv*
**1** to (cause to) exchange places: [IØ] *Can we change over? I'd like to sit in the sun, too.* [T1] *If you change the words over, the sentence sounds better.* → **change round** (1), **switch over** (2), **switch round**
**2** to (cause to) make a complete change (to something else): [IØ (*from, to*)] *In 1971 Britain changed over to decimal money.* [T1 (*from, to*)] *The chairman decided to change the factory over to bicycle production.* —**change-over** n → **switch over** (3)

**change round** *v adv*
**1** to (cause to) exchange places: [IØ] *Can we change round? I'd like to sit in the sun, too.* [T1] *If you change the words round, the sentence sounds better.* → **change over** (1), **switch over** (2), **switch round**
**2** to change direction: [IØ (*from, to*)] *The wind is changing round, so the storm won't last long.*

**change to** *v prep* → **change into** (2), etc.
to (cause to) become (something different) or make a change to (something or someone different): [IØ + *to*] *The weather looks like changing to rain. I think you should change to a new doctor.* [T1 + *to*] *When they were married, Mary changed her name to his. I should like to change these pounds to dollars.*

**change up** *v adv* → **change down, gear down** (1), **gear up** (1), **kick down** (2)
(in a car or other vehicle) to change to a higher gear: [IØ] *You can't change up yet, you're not going fast enough.*

***change with** *v prep*
**1** to exchange (one's whole life) with (someone else): [T1 (*no pass., usu. simple tenses*)] *I wouldn't change with him for anything.* [D1] *I wouldn't change my life with the life of a king; I'm happy as I am.*
**2 change places with: a** to exchange a position with (someone else): *Will you change places with me? I find it too hot here in the sun.* **b** to exchange one's whole life with (someone else): [*usu. simple tenses*] *I wouldn't change places with him for anything, I'm happier the way I am.* → **exchange with** (1)

**channel off** *v adv*
**1** to direct (usu. water) in a different direction: [T1 + OFF] *The engineers channelled off the rising water of the river to avoid flooding.*
***2** to direct (something) to a different purpose: [T1 (*often pass.*)] *A certain amount of the firm's money was channelled off for training purposes.*

***charge against** *v prep*
**1** to record (something) to (someone's debt): [D1] *Charge the goods against my account.* → **chalk up** (2), etc.
**2** to blame (something) on (someone): [D1 (*usu. pass.*)] *Every mistake you make will be charged against you.* → **hold against**, etc.

**charge at** *v prep*
to rush towards (someone or something), as to attack: [IØ + *at*] *You should have seen me run when that goat charged at me!*

**charge down** *v adv*
**1** to rush forward or down: [IØ + DOWN] *When Mother returned from the hospital, the children charged down to meet her.*
***2** esp. *AmE* to record (something) (to someone's debt): [T1 (*to*)] *Charge the goods down to my account.* → **chalk up** (2), etc.
***3** (in rugby football) to stop (a kicked ball) with one's body: [T1] *Edwards charged down Duckham's kick.*

**charge for** *v prep*
to ask (someone) (a price) for (something): [T1 + *for*] *How much does the hotel charge for a room?* [D1 + *for*] *I've been charged too much for these vegetables.*

**charge into** *v prep*
to rush into (a room, object, etc.); hit (an object) by running: [IØ + *into*] *The children charged into the house to greet their mother. I charged into a doorpost and hurt my arm.*

***charge off** *v adv*
**1** *AmE* to accept (something) as a total loss: [T1 (*often simple tenses*)] *The firm had to charge off the debt as hopeless.* → **write off** (5)
**2** *AmE not fml* to consider (something) to be the result (of something): [T1 (*often simple tenses*)] *The director thinks that the firm can charge off its success to his leadership.*

**charge on** *v prep*
to take (a sum) from (an amount of money): [T1 + *on* (*usu. pass.*)] *30% is charged on the first part of your taxable income.* [D1 + *on*] *Buyers are charged 8% sales tax on all goods.*

**charge to** *v prep* → **chalk up** (2), etc.
to record (something) to (someone's debt): [T1 + *to* (*often simple tenses*)] *Charge the goods to my account/to my husband.*

***charge up** *v adv*
**1** *AmE infml* to excite (someone): [T1] *The speaker charged up her audience with angry words.*
**2** *AmE infml* to (cause to) be under the influence of a drug: [IØ] *Don't take any notice of what he says when he's charged up like this.* [T1] *Take this, this should charge you up all right.*

**charge with** *v prep*

**1** to fill (something) with (electric or explosive power): [X9 + *with* (*usu. simple tenses*)] *The terrorists charged the bomb with an explosive substance.*
**2** to bring (someone) to trial, declaring that he is guilty of (something or doing something wrong); declare that someone is guilty of (something or doing something wrong): [T1 + *with* (*often simple tenses*)] *The prisoner is charged with attempted robbery.* [V4b] *The police charged the prisoner with stealing the jewels.*
*__3__ to place upon (someone) as (a duty); entrust (someone) with (a responsibility); give (someone) the job of (something or doing something): [D1 (*often pass.*)] *Isn't she rather young to be charged with the care of small children?* [V4b (*often pass.*)] *How do you choose the officials who will be charged with fulfilling these duties?*
**4 be charged with** to be full of (a quality): *His poetry is charged with strength and feeling.*

**charm with** *v prep*
**1** to control (usu. someone) with (magic means): [T1 + *with* (*often simple tenses*)] *The wicked old woman charmed the princess with magic words.* → **enchant by** (1)
**2** to delight (someone) with (something pleasant): [T1 + *with*] *The singer charmed her listeners with her sweet voice.* → **enchant by** (2)

**chart out** *v adv*
to make a clear plan of (something): [X9 + OUT] *The committee is charting out the future of the organization.*

***chase about/around** *v adv; prep*
to be active in (a place), esp. (of males) following women with sexual intentions: [IØ (*often continuous tenses*)] *Those children are always chasing about, making a terrible noise.* [T1 (*after*) (*no pass., often continuous tenses*)] *I wish he would stop chasing around the town after young women, and spend his time more sensibly.*

***chase after** *v prep*
**1** to follow (someone or an animal) in order to catch them: [T1] *The huntsmen rode fast, chasing after the fox.*
**2** *infml* to try to draw level with (someone) by running: [T1] *Chase after Anne and ask her to get some eggs while she's at the shops.*
**3** *not fml* to attempt to win the love of (someone): [T1] *She's been chasing after that man for years.*

**chase around** *v adv; prep* → CHASE ABOUT

**chase down** *v adv*
*not fml* to follow (a drink) (with another drink): [T1 + DOWN] *Jim's father likes to drink wine chased down with water.*

***chase up** *v adv*
**1** *infml* to repeatedly ask for (someone's attention or service): [T1] *I've had to chase the Gas Board up again about the cooker.*
**2** *not fml* to try to make sure of the truth or existence of (something): [T1] *I'll have to chase up the actual words of the speech that I was reporting.*

***chat up** *v adv*
*BrE infml* (esp. of men) to try to make friends with (someone such as a young woman) by talking to her: [T1] *Peter is at his usual tricks again, chatting up the girls.*

***chaw up** *v adv*
*AmE infml* to defeat (opposition) completely: [T1] *The speaker chawed up his opponent with some well-chosen words.*

**cheat at** *v prep*
to play (a game) unfairly: [IØ + *at*] *Jim said that his brother had cheated at cards.*

**cheat into** *v prep* → **trick into**, etc.
to persuade (someone) by a trick into (something or doing something): [X9 + *into*] *The clever salesman cheated the old lady into giving him all her money.*

***cheat of** *v prep* → CHEAT (OUT) OF

***cheat on** *v prep* → **step out on**
*not fml* to deceive (usu. one's wife or husband) by having a secret and usu. sexual relationship with someone else: [T1] *Have you been cheating on me while I've been away?*

**cheat (out) of** *v (adv) prep* → **beguile out of, chisel out of, con out of, cozen out of, defraud of, diddle out of, do out of, gull out of, swindle out of, trick out of**
**1** to deceive (someone) in order to gain (something he possesses): [X9 (+ OUT) + *of*] *The clever salesman cheated the old lady (out) of all her money.*
**2** to prevent (someone) unfairly from having or using (something such as a right): [X9 (+ OUT) + *of*] *Many children are cheated (out) of their chance for a good education, simply by living in the wrong place.*

***check back** *v adv*
**1** to search among old records: [IØ] *We checked back in the library among the old books, but could find nothing of this date.*
**2** to see someone again, as for talk and decision: [IØ] *I'll check back tomorrow about that question.*

***check in** *v adv*
**1** to leave (one's bags) in someone else's care: [T1 (*at, to*)] *You can check your suitcases in at the desk.*
**2** to report one's arrival, as at a hotel desk, airport, etc.: [IØ (*at*)] *It is always advisable to check in early to get a good seat on your flight. Has Mr Light checked in at the hotel yet?* — **check in** *n* → **book in** (1), **book out** (1), **check out** (2)
**3** to report one's arrival at work: [IØ] *What time do you have to check in?* → **clock in**, etc.
**4** esp. *AmE* to have the return of (an article) recorded: [T1] *I'm just going to check in these books at the library.* → **check out** (4)

***check off** *v adv*
**1** to mark (something) on a list: [T1] *The*

*teacher checked the children's names off as they entered.* → **tick off** (1)

**2** *not fml* to finish work, esp. at a regular time: [IØ (*often simple tenses*)] *The workers in this factory check off at 5.00.* → **clock out**, etc.

**3** *tech* to pay (trade union membership money) directly to the union before giving the worker his pay: [T1] *This firm has arranged to check off your union membership money from your pay before you get it.* —**check-off** *n*

***check on**[1] *v adv* → **clock in**, etc.
*not fml* to start work, esp. at a regular time: [IØ] *Most of the workers checked on before 8.30 this morning.*

**check on**[2] *v prep*
to find out or consider (something), as by examination: [IØ + *on*] *Wouldn't it be wise to check on the possibility of rain before planning the garden party? How can you check on whether it will rain that day?*

**check out** *v adv*

**1** esp. *AmE* to examine (usu. something in a list) to see if it is correct: [T1 + OUT] *Have you checked out each room to see if it is fit for a guest?*

*__2__ to pay one's bill before leaving, as at a hotel, food shop, etc.: [IØ (*of*)] *"Has Mr Light checked out yet?" "Yes, he left this morning."* —**checkout** *n, adj* → **book in** (1), **book out** (1), **check in** (2)

*__3__ *not fml* to finish work, esp. at a regular time: [IØ (*often simple tenses*)] *The workers in this factory check out at 5.00.* → **clock out**, etc.

*__4__ esp. *AmE* to have the removal of (a thing) recorded: [T1 (*of*)] *I'm just going to check this book out of the library.* → **check in** (4)

*__5__ to be equal or the same: [IØ (*simple tenses*)] *Look at the other list and see if the names check out.*

*__6__ *infml* to be found to be true after enquiries have been made: [IØ (*simple tenses*)] *Does his story check out?*

*__7__ *infml* to die: [IØ (*simple tenses*)] *I'm afraid old Charlie has checked out.*

**check over** *v adv*

**1** to look at (usu. something written) to see if it is correct: [T1 + OVER] *We must check the book over before sending it to the printer.*

*__2__ to examine the general health of (someone): [T1] *I asked the doctor to check me over.* → **check up** (1)

**check through** *v adv; prep*
to look through (usu. something written) to see if it is correct: [L9 + THROUGH/*through*] *We must check through the pages to see if any are missing. I can't send my tax return till it's been checked through by my professional adviser.*

***check up** *v adv*

**1** to examine the general health of (someone): [T1] *I asked the doctor to check me up.* —**check-up** *n* → **check over** (2)

**2** to make enquiries about (something or someone): [IØ (*on*)] *The police are checking up on him.* [T1] *Check the facts up before you write your report.*

**cheek up** *v adv*
*infml* to be impolite to (someone): [T1 + UP] *The teacher will not allow the children to cheek her up.*

**cheer for** *v prep* → **cheer on, pull for** (2), **root for**
to support (a competitor) with cheers, shouting, etc.: [IØ + *for*] *Let's go to the football game and cheer for our favourite team.*

**cheer on** *v adv* → **cheer for, pull for** (2), **root for**
to encourage (someone, a team, etc.): [T1 + ON] *Please come to the sports meeting to cheer our team on.*

***cheer up** *v adv* → **bear up** (5), **brace up** (2), **buck up** (3), **chirk up, keep up** (10), **perk up** (2), **spunk up**
to (cause to) feel happier: [T1] *You need a holiday to cheer you up.* [IØ] *Cheer up! Your troubles will soon be over.* "*Cheer up, the worst is yet to come.*" (Philander Chase Johnson, *Shooting Stars*: in *Everybody's Magazine*, May 1920)

***cheese it** *v pron*

**1** *infml* to stop doing something: [IØ (*simple tenses, usu. imper.*)] *Cheese it! The police are coming!*

**2** *AmE infml* to run away: [IØ (*simple tenses, usu. imper.*)] *Let's cheese it, I can hear the police coming.*

***cheese off** *v adv* → **brown off, feed up** (2), **tire of** (2)
*BrE infml* to cause (someone) to feel tired and in low spirits, uninterested in anything: [T1 (*with*) (*often pass., simple tenses*)] *I'm cheesed off with this endless waiting for buses. It's the way winter goes on and on that cheeses me off about this place.*

**chew away** *v adv*

**1** to continue eating: [IØ + AWAY] *You've been chewing away all afternoon, you can't still be hungry.*

**2** to destroy (something) with the teeth: [X9 + AWAY] *The rats have chewed away some of the woodwork.*

**chew on/upon** *v prep*

**1** to bite repeatedly on (something hard): [IØ + *on/upon*] *Babies who are getting new teeth like to have something hard to chew on.* → **bite on** (1)

*__2__ *not fml* to consider (something such as a question) at length or repeatedly; work at (something difficult): [T1] *Jim likes to have some difficult matter to chew on. The committee want time to chew on the question of the new appointment.* → **bite on** (2), **chew over**

***chew out** *v prep* → **tell off** (1), etc.
*AmE infml* to scold (someone): [T1b] *The director chewed Jim out for being late again.* —**chewing-out** *n*

***chew over** *v prep* → **bite on** (2), **chew on** (2)
*not fml* to consider (something such as a question) at length or repeatedly: [T1] *The committee want time to chew over the question of the new appointments.*

**chew up** *v adv*
**1** to bite (food) into small pieces: [T1 + UP] *Children are always told to chew their meat up well.*
**2** to destroy (something) with the teeth: [X9 + UP] *The dog has chewed up my new shoes!*
***3** *infml* to scold (someone): [T1] *The director chewed Jim up for being late again.* → **tell off** (1), etc.
***4** **be/get chewed up** *AmE infml* to be or become worried, anxious, etc.: *Don't get chewed up about the new law; it won't affect you.*

**chew upon** *v prep* → CHEW ON

***chicken out** *v adv*
*derog sl* to be afraid to continue (with something dangerous or daring): [IØ (*of*)] *He chickened out of climbing up the tree. The boy was afraid that if he did not join the others in the crime, they would say he had chickened out.*

**chime in** *v adv*
**1** (of a bell) to begin to sound along with others: [L9 + IN] *The first bell started to ring, and then the others chimed in.*
***2** *not fml* to interrupt by speaking, esp. to agree with someone: [IØ (*with*)] *The conversation was becoming heated, until Mary chimed in with her opinion, to agree with Jim.*

***chime in with** *v adv prep*
**1** to suit; match (something): [T1 (*no pass., simple tenses*)] *My opinion chimes in with yours. The blue dress chimes in with the colour of her eyes.*
**2** to agree (with something): [T1 (*no pass., simple tenses*)] *The chairman chimed in with the decision of the committee.*

**chip away** *v adv*
**1** to hit something gently but repeatedly, to make a mark or hole: [L9 + AWAY (*at*)] *The boy has been chipping away at that hard rock for hours.*
**2** to (cause to) come away in pieces, a small bit at a time: [L9 + AWAY] *The edge of the stone has chipped away.* [X9 + AWAY] *You'll never be able to chip the paint away.*

***chip away at** *v adv prep*
*not fml* to destroy (something) a little at a time: [T1 (*no pass.*)] *The new director learned to chip away at the firm's methods, rather than try to change everything at once.*

***chip in** *v adv*
**1** *not fml* to interrupt: [IØ (*with*)] *The conversation was very pleasant until our talkative neighbour chipped in.*
**2** *infml* to add (one's share of money or activity): [T1a (*usu. simple tenses*)] *If everyone chips in a few pounds, there'll be enough to help the homeless family. Members of the youth club were asked to chip in a few hours' work each week to help people in the neighbourhood.* [IØ (*towards, with*) (*usu. simple tenses*)] *Everyone chipped in with as much as they could afford, so we soon had enough. Would you care to chip in towards the secretary's leaving present?* → **kick in** (3)

***chirk up** *v adv* → **cheer up**, etc.
*AmE not fml* to (cause to) become more cheerful: [T1] *You need a good holiday to chirk you up.* [IØ] *Chirk up, your troubles will soon be over.*

***chisel in** *v adv*
esp. *AmE infml* to join other people without being invited: [IØ] *He became a member only by chiselling in.* [T1] *The group did not welcome the manner in which he chiselled his way in.*

***chisel out of** *v adv prep* → **cheat out of**, etc.
*not fml* to rob (someone) of (something such as a right) by deceit or improper methods: [D1] *You mean the firm found a way to chisel you out of your overtime pay? There'll be trouble with the union now!*

**chivvy along** *v adv* → CHIVY ALONG
**chivvy into** *v prep* → CHIVY INTO
**chivvy up** *v adv* → CHIVY UP

**chivy along** *v adv* also **chivvy along** → **jolly along**
*infml* to urge (someone or something) to hurry or move forward; encourage (someone) to advance or complete something, often in an annoying manner: [X9 + ALONG] *Stop chivying me along, I'll walk at my own speed! If you chivy the workers along a bit I'm sure they could do the work faster.*

**chivy into** *v prep* also **chivvy into**
*infml* to urge (someone) into (something or doing something): [X9 + *into*] *Members of Parliament must chivy the government into action. People often have to be chivied into finding a job.*

**chivy up** *v adv* also **chivvy up**
*infml* to give (someone) repeated suggestions or orders: [X9 + UP] *You'll have to chivy the children up about their schoolwork.*

**chock up** *v adv*
**1** to fill; overcrowd (something): [X9 + UP (*usu. pass.*)] *The room was chocked up with furniture.* → **choke up** (1), **clog up**
***2** to fix (something) in position, with specially shaped pieces of wood (chocks): [T1] *The driver chocked up the wheels so that the car could not run accidentally down the hill.*

***choke back** *v adv* → **choke down** (2)
to control (something such as a violent feeling): [T1 (*often simple tenses*)] *Jim had to choke back his anger or he would have hit the man.*

***choke down** *v adv*
**1** to swallow (something) with difficulty: [T1] *He hated the meal but choked it down out of politeness.*
**2** to accept (something) with difficulty: [T1 (*often simple tenses*)] *Jim choked down the director's rudeness because otherwise he might*

*have lost his job.* → **choke back**

**choke off** *v adv*

**1** to prevent or stop (something): [X9 + OFF (*often simple tenses*)] *The murderer choked off the woman's cries for help.*

***2** *not fml* to discourage (someone), as from speaking: [T1 (*often simple tenses*)] *He began to tell about his adventures all over again, but I choked him off. Jane wants an invitation to the party; how can we choke her off?*

***3** *infml* to scold (someone): [T1 (*for*)] *The director choked Jim off for being late again.* → **tell off** (1), etc.

**choke out of** *v adv prep*

**choke the life out of: a** to kill (someone) by holding or wrapping his throat tightly to prevent him breathing: *The murderer killed the woman by choking the life out of her.* **b** *not fml* to stop or destroy (something) by controlling it tightly: *By reducing the money which is usually given, the government is choking the life out of our universities.*

**choke up** *v adv*

**1** to fill; overcrowd; block (something): [X9 + UP (*with*) (*often pass.*)] *The room was choked up with furniture. The well was choked up with leaves.* → **chock up** (1), **clog up**

**2 be (all) choked up (about)** *not fml* **a** to be very angry (about something or someone), often without enough cause: *What are you all choked up about? The idea isn't so very terrible, if you think about it.* **b** to lose one's speech because of strong feeling: *The speaker became all choked up and could not continue.* **c** (of a performer or sportsman) to become too nervous to perform well: *Our team were so choked up that they lost the first round.*

**choke with** *v prep*

**1** to fill; overcrowd: [X9 + *with* (*often pass.*)] *The room was choked with people.*

**2** to find difficulty in breathing or speaking because of (something): [IØ + *with* (*usu. continuous tenses*)] *Jim was choking with anger.*

**choose among**

to make a choice from among (usu. three or more things or people): [IØ + *among* (*simple tenses*)] *It is difficult to choose among so many nice houses.* [T1 + *among* (*simple tenses*)] *It is difficult to choose one house among so many nice ones.*

**choose as** *v prep* → **choose for, select as, select for**

to choose (someone or something) to be (someone or something): [X9 + *as* (*simple tenses*)] *We chose this house as our home as soon as we saw it. The teacher chose the cleverest child as the leader of the class.*

**choose between** *v prep*

to make a choice between (usu. two things or people): [IØ + *between* (*simple tenses*)] *It is difficult to choose between two such nice houses.*

**choose for** *v prep* → **choose as, select as, select for**

to choose (someone or something) to be (something): [T1 + *for* (*simple tenses*)] *Jim chose Mary for his wife. We chose this house for our home as soon as we saw it.*

**choose from** *v prep* → **select from**

to elect; choose (someone or something) from among (a large number): [T1 + *from* (*simple tenses*)] *Jane was chosen from the whole class to go on the trip.* [IØ + *from* (*simple tenses*)] *This paint shop offers a wide range of colours to choose from.*

**chop about** *v adv*

**1** to divide (something), usu. carelessly; damage (something): [X9 + ABOUT] *The book has been badly chopped about at the printer's.*

***2** to keep changing direction or action: [IØ] *When the storm arose, the wind chopped about and the little boat nearly sank. Make up your mind, will you? Stop chopping about!* → **chop around**

***chop around/round** *v adv* → **chop about** (2)

to change direction: [IØ] *When the storm arose, the wind chopped around and the little boat nearly sank.*

**chop back** *v adv*

**1** to reduce (something) by cutting: [X9 + BACK] *The tree is too big, you'll have to chop back some of the branches.*

***2** *not fml* to reduce (something) rather severely: [T1 (*usu. simple tenses*)] *The government has promised to chop back its own spending in an effort to encourage the nation to do the same.*

**chop down** *v adv*

**1** to make (something such as a tree) fall, usu. with an axe: [X9 + DOWN] *The whole forest was chopped down to make room for the new airport.* → **hack down** (1), **hew down**

***2** *not fml* to destroy (something): [T1 (*usu. simple tenses*)] *The committee members chopped down the chairman's opinion.*

**chop into** *v prep*

**1** to cut (something) into (smaller pieces): [T1 + *into*] *Ask the man in the shop to chop the meat into little bits.*

***2** to divide (something) into (parts) in order to destroy it: [D1 (*usu. simple tenses*)] *The opposing speakers chopped the politician's argument into pieces.*

**chop off** *v adv*

**1** to cut (something) off, as with an axe: [X9 + OFF] *The king's head was chopped off. You could improve the tree by chopping off some of the upper branches.*

***2** to stop (someone) from speaking: [T1 (*usu. simple tenses*)] *The chairman chopped the speaker off in mid-sentence.*

***chop round** *v adv* → **CHOP AROUND**

**chop up** *v adv*

**1** to cut (something) into smaller pieces: [T1 + UP] *Ask the man in the shop to chop the meat up for you.* —**chopped-up** *adj* → **hash up** (1)

***2** to divide (something) (into smaller parts):

[T1 (*into*) (*usu. simple tenses*)] *After the war, the country was chopped up into several smaller nations.*

**chuck about/around** *v adv*

**1** *infml* to scatter (something or things) in several directions: [X9 + ABOUT/AROUND] *Stop chucking pieces of paper about, you make the street look untidy.* → **fling about** (1), **hurl about** (1), **throw about'** (1), **toss about** (1)

**2** *infml* to wave (one's arms and/or legs) without direction: [X9 + ABOUT/AROUND] *If you just chuck your arms and legs about like that, you'll drown—make the proper swimming strokes!* → **fling about** (2), **hurl about** (2), **throw about'** (2)

**3 chuck one's money about/around** *infml* to spend money foolishly, often so as to show one's wealth: [*usu. continuous tenses*] *Our new neighbour is always chucking his money about, with his colour television and his new car every year.* → **fling about** (3), **hurl about** (3), **throw about'** (3), **toss about** (4)

**4 chuck one's weight about/around** *infml* to give unnecessary orders; try to use one's power over other people: *The youth club leader was dismissed for trying to chuck his weight about, which the young people didn't like.* → **fling about** (4), **hurl about** (4), **throw about'** (4), **toss about** (5)

**chuck at** *v prep*

**1** *infml* to throw (something) at (something or someone): [X9 + *at*] *The boys were chucking snowballs at passing cars.* → **throw at** (1), etc.

**2 chuck oneself at** *infml* to try to win the love of (someone): [*often continuous tenses*] *Did you see the shameless way she was chucking herself at him?* → **fling at** (4), **hurl at** (2), **throw at** (5)

**chuck away** *v adv*

**1** *infml* to throw (something) away; get rid of (something): [X9 + AWAY] *How dare you chuck away my old pipes without asking me?* → **throw out** (2), etc.

*__2__ *infml* to waste (something): [T1] *Never chuck away a chance to improve your English.* → **throw away** (2), etc.

*__3__ *infml* to speak (words) carelessly, often lowering the voice: [T1 (*often simple tenses*)] *You chucked away that last line.* → **fling away** (3), **throw away** (3)

***chuck away on** *v adv prep*

**1** *infml* to waste (something) by using it for (something) or giving it to (someone): [D1 (*often pass.*)] *Why did you chuck your money away on such a worthless plan? Your advice is chucked away on that boy.* → **fling away on** (1), **hurl away on** (1), **throw away on** (1)

**2** *infml* to waste the worth of (someone or oneself) in a bad relationship such as marriage, with (someone considered unworthy): [D1] *Mary's father disapproved of Jim and said that he had no wish to chuck his daughter away on such a person. Why are you chucking yourself away on a woman like that?* → **fling away on** (2), **hurl away on** (2), **throw away on** (2)

**chuck down** *v adv*

**1** *infml* to throw (something) down: [X9 + DOWN] *Climb to the top of the ladder and chuck the apples down to me.* → **fling down** (1), **hurl down** (1), **throw down'**, **toss down**

*__2__ *infml* to place (oneself) quickly at full length on the ground or floor: [T1 (*often simple tenses*)] *When he heard the bomb whistling down, Jim chucked himself down on the floor with his hands over his head.* → **fling down** (2), **fling to** (3), **hurl down** (2), **throw down'** (2), **throw to** (4)

**3 chuck down one's tools** *infml* to go on strike: *The trade union leader suggested to the workers that they should chuck down their tools.* → **fling down** (4), **throw down'** (6)

**chuck in** *v adv*

**1** *infml* to throw (something) in: [X9 + IN] *If the ball goes out of the tennis court, ask one of the boys to chuck it in.* → **fling in'** (1), **pitch in** (1), **throw in'** (1), **toss in'** (1)

*__2__ *infml* to stop doing or attempting (something): [T1 (*usu. simple tenses*)] *Jim has chucked in his studies.* → **give up** (2), etc.

*__3__ *infml* to add (something), often as a gift: [T1 (*usu. simple tenses*)] *If you buy the furniture, the shop will chuck in a television set.* → **fling in'** (3), **throw in'** (3), **toss in'** (2)

*__4__ *infml* to add (words), often as an interruption: [T1 (*usu. simple tenses*)] *There was no need for you to chuck in that remark.* → **put in'** (4), etc.

**5 chuck in one's cards/hand: a** *infml* to stop playing cards: [*usu. simple tenses*] *I've had enough of this game; I'll chuck my cards in and go to bed.* **b** *infml* to give up any attempt; admit defeat: [*usu. simple tenses*] *Jim had no sooner begun the competition than he chucked in his hand.* → **fling in'** (5), **throw in'** (7)

**6 chuck in the towel: a** *infml* (in boxing) to admit defeat in a fight: [*usu. simple tenses*] *After a brave fight, he finally had to chuck in the towel.* **b** *infml* to give up any attempt; admit defeat: [*usu. simple tenses*] *I'm ashamed of you, chucking in the towel so soon after starting the competition.* → **chuck up** (6), **fling in'** (6), **fling up** (10), **throw in'** (8), **throw up** (10)

**7 chuck it in!** *infml* stop that! → **cut out** (14), **pack in** (4), **pack up** (4)

***chuck it** *v pron*

*infml* stop it: [I∅ (*usu. imper.*)] *Chuck it or I'll hit you! "Chuck it, Smith!"* (G.K. Chesterton, *Antichrist*)

**chuck off** *v adv*

**1** *infml* to push or throw (something) off: [X9 + OFF] *The boy ran up to the man and chucked his hat off.* → **cast off** (1), **fling off** (1), **shake off'** (1), **throw off'** (1), **toss off** (1)

*__2__ *infml* to escape from (someone chasing

one): [T1 (*usu. simple tenses*)] *If we run fast we'll be able to chuck the police off.* → **fling off** (2), **shake off**[1] (2), **throw off**[1] (3)
*3 *infml* to get free from (something bad): [T1 (*usu. simple tenses*)] *I don't seem to be able to chuck off this cold.* → **fling off** (3), etc.

**chuck out** *v adv*
**1** *infml* to throw (something) out: [X9 + OUT] *Climb into the hole in the sand and chuck the ball out, will you?* → **fling out** (1), **pitch out** (1), **throw out** (1), **toss out** (1)
***2** *infml* to get rid of (something): [T1] *I really must chuck out all those old newspapers.* → **throw out** (2), etc.
***3** *infml* to make (someone) leave because of a fault: [T1 (*of*) (*usu. simple tenses*)] *Two members were chucked out (of the club) for failing to pay the money they owed. A man was employed to chuck out any troublemakers.* —**chucker-out** *n* → **throw out** (4), etc.
***4** *infml* to make (someone) leave a home: [T1 (*of*) (*usu. pass.*)] *The old lady was chucked out of the house because the owner wanted to pull it down.* → **throw out** (5), etc.
***5** *infml* to refuse to accept (a suggestion, law, etc.): [T1 (*usu. simple tenses*)] *The committee considered your suggestions but chucked them out because they would cost too much.* → **fling out** (6), **hurl out** (2), **throw out** (6), **toss out** (5), **turn down** (4)
***6** *infml* to say (something) suddenly, often carelessly: [T1a (*usu. simple tenses*)] *It was unfortunate that you chucked out that remark.* → **put in**[1] (4), etc.
***7** *infml* to spoil (something): [T1 (*usu. pass.*)] *Our plans were chucked out by bad weather.* → **throw out** (10)

**chuck together** *v adv*
**1** *infml* to gather (things) in a hurry: [X9 + TOGETHER] *I haven't time to pack properly—I'll just chuck a few things together and set off straight away.* → **fling together** (1), **throw together** (1), **toss together** (1)
***2** *infml* to build or write (something) hastily: [T1b (*often pass.*)] *This book looks as if it's just been chucked together.* → **throw together** (2), etc.
***3** *infml* to cause (two people or groups, esp. a man and woman) to meet: [T1b (*usu. pass.*)] *Jim and Mary were chucked together by the war.* → **bring together** (2), etc.

**chuck under** *v prep*
**chuck someone under the chin** to touch someone under the chin, lifting the head with one's finger, usu. to show fondness: *Don't chuck me under the chin like that, I'm not a child any more!*

**chuck up** *v adv*
**1** *infml* to throw (something) up: [X9 + UP] *Come to the bottom of the ladder and chuck up the other brush, will you?* → **cast up** (1), **fling up** (1), **throw up** (1), **toss up** (1)
***2** *infml* to be sick; vomit (food): [IØ (*usu. continuous tenses*)] *Jane can't come, she's been chucking up all morning.* [T1] *The child has chucked up her dinner again.* → **bring up** (4), etc.
***3** *infml* to stop working at or trying to do (something): [T1 (*usu. simple tenses*)] *Jim has chucked up his studies.* → **give up** (2), etc.
***4** *infml* to build (usu. a building) hastily: [T1 (*usu. pass.*)] *The office block looks as if it's just been chucked up.* → **throw together** (2), etc.
***5** *infml* to waste (something): [T1] *Never chuck up a chance to improve your English.* → **throw away** (2), etc.
**6 chuck up the sponge** *infml* to admit defeat: [*usu. simple tenses*] *Why did you chuck up the sponge when you were so near to winning?* → **chuck in** (6), **fling in**[1] (6), **fling up** (10), **throw in**[1] (8), **throw up** (10)

***chum up** *v adv* → **pal up**
*infml* to make friends (with someone): [IØ (*with*)] *It's good to see your children and mine chumming up so well. It's good to see your children chumming up with mine so well.*

**churn into** *v prep* → CHURN TO

**churn out** *v adv*
**1** to produce (butter): [X9 + OUT] *The farmer has churned out more butter this week than last.*
***2** *not fml* to produce a large quantity of (something), by or as if by machinery: [T1] *This factory churns out lots of cars every day. Tom has been churning out crime stories for twenty years.*

**churn to/into** *v prep*
to move (something) round until it becomes (something else): [T1 + *to/into*] *The farmer churned the cream to butter. The heavy wheels churned the earth into mud.*

***churn up** *v adv*
**1** to move (something) violently: [T1] *The heavy wheels churned up the earth.*
**2** *not fml* to sicken (someone); cause to feel strong dislike: [T1 (*usu. simple tenses*)] *Your story quite churned me up.* —**churned-up** *adj*

**circle about/around/round**[1] *v adv*
to move in circles for some time: [L9 + ABOUT/AROUND/ROUND] *The plane was kept circling about, waiting for a turn to land.*

**circle about/around/round**[2] *v prep*
**1** to move in circles round (a place): [L9 + *about/around/round*] *The lion circled about the family of deer, waiting to attack.*
***2** to treat (someone) carefully: [T1] *John circled round the girl at the party, waiting for a chance to talk to her.*
***3** to treat (a subject) carefully: [T1] *The committee have been circling round the main question throughout the meeting.*

**circle around**[1] *v adv* → CIRCLE ABOUT[1]

**circle around**[2] *v prep* → CIRCLE ABOUT[2]

**circle over** *v prep*
(of a plane) to fly in circles over (a landing place): [L9 + *over*] *The plane was kept cir-*

*cling over the airport, waiting for a turn to land.*

**circle round**¹ *v adv* → **CIRCLE ABOUT**¹

**circle round**² *v prep* → **CIRCLE ABOUT**²

***cite for** *v prep*
to praise (someone) officially for (bravery): [D1 (*usu. pass.*)] *After his death, the soldier was cited for bravery.*

**claim against** *v prep*
to ask for (a sum of) money by right according to (a contract): [L9 + *against*] *You should be able to claim against the car insurance.* [X9 + *against*] *You should be able to claim the cost against the car insurance.*

**claim back** *v adv*
to demand the return of (a cost) after it has been paid: [T1 + BACK (*from*)] *Buy the special supplies for the company, and claim back their cost (from the firm's account).*

**claim for** *v prep*
**1** to ask someone to pay (a certain amount of) the cost of (something): [L9 + *for*] *Can I claim for yesterday's journey?* [X9 + *for*] *You can only claim £30 a day for your travel.*
**2** to declare that (something) is possessed by (something or someone): [X9 + *for* (*usu. simple tenses*)] *Magical properties are sometimes claimed for certain medicines. The explorer claimed the island he had discovered for the nation.*

**claim from** *v prep*
to demand (a sum of money) as a right from (usu. someone or a group): [X9 + *from*] *The motorist successfully claimed damages from the other driver, who had caused the accident.* [L9 + *from*] *I don't think you can claim from your own wife.*

***clam up** *v adv* → **shut up** (4), etc.
*sl* to become or remain silent, esp. to keep a secret: [I∅ (*simple tenses, usu. imper.*)] *I told you to clam up, we don't want the whole world knowing our plans. She clammed up whenever I mentioned her father.*

**clamour against** *v prep*
to express loud opposition to (something): [L9 + *against*] *His family and friends clamoured against the man's wrongful imprisonment.*

***clamour down** *v adv*
to make (someone) silent by making too much noise: [T1] *The politician tried to make himself heard, but the crowd clamoured him down.*

**clamour for** *v prep* → **yammer for**
to demand (something) loudly: [L9 + *for* (*often continuous tenses*)] *The people are clamouring for bread. Women are clamouring for improvements in the sexual equality laws.*

***clamp down (on)** *v adv (prep)* → **crack down on**
to control, esp. to limit (something bad); deal firmly with (something or someone bad): [T1] *The government has promised to clamp down on criminal activity. The government has promised to clamp down on young criminals.* [I∅] *We must clamp down now, before it's too late to stop the trouble.* —**clamp-down** *n*

***clap in/into** *v prep*
*infml* to put (someone) by force into (prison): [D1 (*usu. pass.*)] *The two thieves were clapped into prison.*

***clap on**¹ *v adv*
**1** *not fml* to put (something) on hurriedly: [T1 (*usu. simple tenses*)] *He clapped on his hat and ran out of the house.* → **jam on** (1), **slam on** (1), **slap on**¹ (1)
**2** *not fml* to put (something) into use hurriedly, as by pressing: [T1 (*usu. simple tenses*)] *The driver clapped on the brakes but failed to stop in time.* → **jam on** (2), **slam on** (2)
**3** *naut* to bring (something) into use: [T1a (*usu. simple tenses*)] *The captain ordered his men to clap on more sail.* → **crowd on**

***clap on**² *v prep*
**1** *not fml* to put (something) on (someone or something) hurriedly: [D1 (*usu. simple tenses*)] *He clapped his hat on his head and ran out of the house.* → **slap on**² (1)
**2** to hit (someone) gently, usu. with the open hand, on (part of the body): [D1 (*usu. simple tenses*)] *He clapped his old friend on the shoulder in greeting. His boss clapped him on the back approvingly.* → **slap on**² (2)
**3** *not fml* to add (an amount or rate) to increase the cost of (something): [D1 (*usu. simple tenses*)] *When the new tax laws were passed, the taxpayers found that the government had clapped another 5% on cigarettes.* → **slap on**² (3)
**4 clap eyes on** *not fml* to see; catch sight of (usu. someone): [*usu. neg., perfect tenses*] *I haven't clapped eyes on my brother for years.* → **lay on**² (7), **set on**² (7)

**clap out** *v adv*
**1** to beat (a regular time) by hitting the hands together: [T1 + OUT] *The children clapped out a regular time while the teacher played the tune.*
**2 be clapped out** *infml* to be very tired or ruined: *I feel clapped out after that long climb. This old car is clapped out.* —**clapped-out** *adj*

***clap to** *v adv*
to (cause to) close noisily: [I∅ (*simple tenses*)] *The door clapped to.* [T1 (*usu. simple tenses*)] *The girl clapped the door to as she left.*

***clap together** *v adv* → **fit up** (3)
*not fml* to make (something) hastily: [T1 (*often simple tenses*)] *The actors clapped together a stage so that they could have somewhere to perform.*

***clap up** *v adv*
*infml* to make or reach (an agreement): [T1 (*often simple tenses*)] *The two men clapped up a contract.*

**clash against** *v prep*
**1** to hit (something) hard: [L9 + *against*] *I*

*clashed against the streetlight and hurt my head.*
**2** not to match (something): [L9 + *against* (*simple tenses*)] *The orange curtains clash against the red furniture.* → **clash with** (1), **jar with** (1)
*__3__ to disagree with (someone or an opinion): [T1 (*no pass., simple tenses*)] *My opinions clash against yours.* → **conflict with** (2), etc.
*__4__ to meet and fight (someone): [T1 (*no pass.*)] *Greek forces clashed against Turks in the hills.* → **clash with** (4)

**clash on/over** *v prep*
to disagree about (something): [IØ + *on/over*] *Mary and her husband clashed over the question of where they should live.*

**clash with** *v prep*
**1** not to match (something): [L9 + *with* (*simple tenses*)] *The orange curtains clash with the red furniture.* → **clash against** (2), **jar with** (1)
**2** to take place at the same time as (something else): [L9 + *with* (*simple tenses*)] *I was unable to study music at school because it clashed with history. Make sure that your garden party doesn't clash with the football match or nobody will come.* → **coincide with, conflict with** (1)
*__3__ to disagree violently with (someone or something): [T1 (*simple tenses*)] *The chairman's opinion clashed with that of the rest of the committee.* → **conflict with** (2), etc.
*__4__ to meet and fight (someone): [T1] *Greek forces clashed with Turks in the hills.* → **clash against** (4)

**class with** *v prep*
to consider (something or someone) to belong to the same type as (something or someone else) or be equal with (something or someone else): [X9 + *with*] *I would class Tom's latest book with the best crime stories ever written.*

**clatter about** *v adv*
to (cause to) be noisy: [IØ + ABOUT] *Ask the children to stop clattering about, Father's asleep.* [T1 + ABOUT] *Don't clatter those dishes about, you'll break them.*

**claw back** *v adv*
to take back (part of the money one has given) in an indirect way: [T1] *The government claws back some of the money which it gives to arts organizations, in the form of tax.* —**clawback** *n*

**claw off** *v adv*
*naut* to move towards the wind from a sheltered shore: [IØ (*usu. simple tenses*)] *The boat clawed off slowly until it reached the wind, when the sails filled and the boat gathered speed.*

**clean down** *v adv*
to wash (something) thoroughly: [T1] *We were asked to clean down the walls when we left the house that we had been renting.*

**clean of** *v prep*
to wash (something) clean of (marks, dirt, etc.): [T1 + *of* (*often simple tenses*)] *Can you clean the coat of these dirty marks? Lady Macbeth felt that it was hopeless to try to clean her hands of the blood.*

**clean off** *v adv*
(of dirt) to (cause to) be removed: [X9 + OFF] *I hope I shall be able to clean off these black marks.* [L9 + OFF (*simple tenses*)] *I hope these black marks will clean off.*

**clean out** *v adv*
**1** also **clear out** to empty, tidy, or clean (something): [X9 + OUT] *I've asked the children to clean out their drawers. I need some help in cleaning out the animal shelter.* —**cleaning-out, clean-out** *n* → **do out** (1), **muck out**
**2** to remove (something unwanted such as dirt) from something: [X9 + OUT] *I hope you've cleaned out all those sticky old sweet papers and empty envelopes from your drawer this time.* → **clear out** (2)
*__3__ also **clear out** *infml* to empty (a place) by robbing it, esp. of money: [T1 (usu. simple tenses)] *The thieves cleaned out the store.*
*__4__ also **clear out** *infml* to leave (someone) without money: [T1 (*of*) (*simple tenses*)] *The boys have cleaned me out. I'm cleaned out after last night's heavy spending.*
*__5__ *infml* to leave, usu. in a hurry: [IØ (*simple tenses*)] *The thieves took the jewels and then cleaned out.* → **push off** (3), etc.

**clean up** *v adv*
**1** to clean (something such as a room) thoroughly: [X9 + UP] *This room needs cleaning up.* → **clear up** (1), **mop up** (1)
**2** to remove (something unwanted such as dirt) and leave the place clean: [X9 + UP] *Let me clean up the broken glass before someone walks on it.* —**clean-up** *n* → **clear up** (2)
*__3__ esp. *AmE* to wash (oneself): [IØ] *"Wait for me, I have to clean up", said the painter.* [T1] *It won't take me long to clean myself up, and then I'll be ready.* —**clean-up** *n*
*__4__ *not fml* to improve; remove wrong or dishonest activity from (something): [T1] *The newly elected leader has declared his intention of cleaning up the city council.* —**clean-up** *n*
*__5__ *infml* to gain (usu. money), possibly unfairly or unlawfully: [T1 (*usu. simple tenses*)] *The brothers cleaned up a profit in the property market.* [IØ (*usu. simple tenses*)] *It was annoying to lose money on the deal when others cleaned up.* —**clean-up** *n*
*__6__ *mil* to finish destroying or defeating (an enemy): [T1] *Leave a few men behind to clean up the last of the enemy positions.* → **mop up** (2), **wipe up** (3)

***clean up on** *v adv prep*
**1** *AmE infml* to make a profit on (something): [T1 (*usu. simple tenses*)] *The company cleaned up on their recent business arrangement.*
**2** *AmE infml* to defeat (someone): [T1 (*usu.*

*simple tenses)] The fighter cleaned up on his opponent.*

**clear away** *v adv*

**1** to disappear: [L9 + AWAY] *In the afternoon, the clouds cleared away and the rest of the day was fine. When he read the letter, his doubts cleared away.* → **clear off** (1)

**2** to remove (something or someone): [X9 + AWAY] *Please clear your papers away so that I can serve dinner. Does the letter clear away your difficulty? The police cleared the crowd away.* → **clear off** (2)

*__3__ to completely remove (the plates, knives, etc.) from a table after a meal: [IØ] *Please help your mother to clear away.* [T1] *Please clear away the dinner things and then you can watch television.* → **clear off** (3)

**clear of** *v prep*

**1** to free (usu. a place) by removing (unwanted things or people): [T1 + *of*] *Will you help me clear the garden of these stones? We must clear the area of enemy soldiers as soon as possible.*

**2** to prove that (someone) is not guilty of (something): [T1 + *of* (*often pass., simple tenses*)] *The boy was cleared of the charge of stealing. The boy was cleared of taking part in the crime.*

**3 clear one's mind of** to try to forget (something): *I want you to clear your mind of everything that happened before the fire.*

**clear off** *v adv*

**1** to disappear: [L9 + OFF] *In the afternoon, the mist cleared off and the rest of the day was fine.* → **clear away** (1)

**2** to remove (something or someone): [X9 + OFF] *Please clear your papers off so that I can serve dinner.* → **clear away** (2)

*__3__ *AmE* to clear plates, knives, etc. from (a table): [IØ] *Please help your mother to clear off.* [T1a] *Please help your mother to clear off the table.* → **clear away** (3)

*__4__ *infml* to (cause to) leave: [IØ (*simple tenses, usu. imper.*)] *"Clear off!" shouted the angry farmer to the boys in his field.* [T1 (*usu. simple tenses*)] *Go into the field and clear those boys off.* → **push off** (3), etc.

*__5__ to pay (a debt) completely: [T1] *I'm glad I've cleared off the money I owed my mother.*

*__6__ *not fml* to sell (goods) cheaply: [T1] *The shop decided to clear off the summer clothes when the new winter fashions arrived.*

*__7__ to finish (something): [T1] *I'd like to clear off the rest of the work which was waiting for me after my holiday.* → **clear up** (3)

**clear out** *v adv*

**1** → CLEAN OUT (1)

**2** to remove; get rid of (something unwanted) from something: [X9 + OUT] *I hope you've cleared out all those sticky old sweet papers and empty envelopes from your drawer this time.* —**clear-out, clearing-out** *n* → **clean out** (2)

*__3__ → CLEAN OUT (3)

*__4__ → CLEAN OUT (4)

*__5__ *infml* to (cause to) leave: [IØ (*of*)] *"Clear out!" shouted the angry farmer to the boys in his field. The thieves took the jewels and then cleared out.* [T1 (*of*)] *The police cleared all the people out of the hotel after the bomb threat.* → **push off** (3), etc.

*__6__ *infml* to leave home: [IØ] *When I was eighteen, I decided that it was time I cleared out.* → **cut out** (11), **dig out** (6), **light out**

**clear up** *v adv*

**1** to tidy and clean (a place): [X9 + UP] *When you've finished your meal, please clear up the kitchen.* → **clean up** (1), **mop up**

**2** to remove (something unwanted such as dirt) and leave the place clean: [X9 + UP] *Let me clear up the broken glass before someone walks on it.* —**clear-up** *n* → **clean up** (2)

*__3__ to finish (something): [T1] *I'd like to clear up the rest of the work which was waiting for me after my holiday.* → **clear off** (7)

*__4__ to (cause to) improve or brighten: [IØ] *The weather should clear up tomorrow and we should have sunshine at last. Her face cleared up when she read the letter.* [T1] *This medicine should clear up your cold.*

*__5__ to find an answer to (something): [T1] *The police have been trying to clear up the mystery of the man's death.*

**clear with** *v prep*

to obtain official approval of (something or someone) from (someone in power): [T1 + *with*] *Has the parcel been cleared with the border police yet?*

***cleave to** *v prep*

**1** *fml* to stick fast to (something): [T1 (*no pass.*)] *This material cleaves to the skin.* → **adhere to** (1), **cling to** (1), **stick to** (1)

**2** *fml* to be faithful to (someone or an idea): [T1 (*simple tenses*)] *A good wife cleaves to her husband. Loyal party members cleave to their party's political principles.* → **adhere to** (2), etc.

***clew down** *v adv* also **clue down** → **clew up**

*naut* to lower (a sail): [T1 (*usu. simple tenses*)] *Clew the mainsail down, the wind is too strong.* [IØ (*usu. simple tenses*)] *The captain asked the sailors to clew down.*

***clew up** *v adv* also **clue up** → **clew down**

*naut* to raise (a sail): [T1 (*usu. simple tenses*)] *Clew the two small sails up, we need to go faster.* [IØ (*usu. simple tenses*)] *The captain asked the sailors to clew up.*

***click for** *v prep*

*BrE infml* to gain (something) by lucky chance: [T1 (*simple tenses*)] *At last I've clicked for a good job in the right city.*

***click with** *v prep*

**1** *infml* to fall into place; be understood by (someone): [T1] *Her joke clicked with us and we all laughed.*

**2** *infml* to be a success or popular with (someone or a group): [T1] *That film has real-*

*ly clicked with the young people — they're all going to see it.*
**3** *infml* to be a quick success with, or be quickly liked by (someone); (of two people) to quickly like (each other): [T1] *Jim and Mary clicked with each other as soon as they met.*

**climb down** *v adv*
**1** to descend: [IØ + DOWN] *When you reach the top of a mountain, the worst part is climbing down.*
*__2__ *not fml* to yield, in argument, point of view, or claim: [IØ (*often simple tenses*)] *The speaker's forceful words persuaded his opponent to climb down.* —**climbdown** *n* → **back down** (2), etc.

**climb on** *v prep*
**1** to move onto (something higher) by climbing: [IØ + *on*] *I can give you a ride if you don't mind climbing on this load of boxes.*
**2 climb on the bandwagon** *not fml* to copy other people's successful actions: *While prices are rising so fast, many shops think they can climb on the bandwagon and raise their prices, too.* → **jump on** (3)

**climb out of** *v adv prep*
**1** to lift oneself out of (a place) by climbing: [IØ + OUT + *of*] *The cat fell into the hole and couldn't climb out of it.*
*__2__ *infml* to try to clear oneself of blame for (something, often something that one has actually done): [T1 (*often simple tenses*)] *But you were seen taking the book; now try to climb out of that one.*

**cling onto** *v prep*
**1** to hold tight to (someone or something): [L9 + *onto*] *The child clung onto its mother. The climber had to cling onto the cliff.* → **cling to** (2), **keep by** (2), **stay by, stick to** (2), **stick with** (2)
*__2__ to try to keep (something): [T1] *The old lady tried to cling onto her old home, but the builders forced her out. Whenever we move to a new house, we always cling onto far too many possessions.* → **cling to** (3), **hang onto** (3), **hold onto** (2), **stick to** (4)
*__3__ to keep; remain loyal to (something): [T1] *The chairman has always clung onto old-fashioned ideas.* → **adhere to** (2), etc.

**cling to** *v prep*
**1** to stay near or touching (something): [L9 + *to*] *This material clings to the skin. The ship clung to the shore.* → **adhere to** (1), **cleave to** (1), **stick to** (1)
**2** to hold tight to (someone or something): [L9 + *to*] *The child clung to its mother. The climber had to cling to the cliff.* → **cling onto** (1), **keep by** (2), **stay by, stick to** (2), **stick with** (2)
*__3__ to try to keep (something): [T1] *The old lady tried to cling to her old home, but the builders forced her out. Whenever we move to a new house, we always cling to far too many possessions.* → **cling onto** (2), **hang onto** (3), **hold onto** (2), **stick to** (4)
*__4__ to keep; remain loyal to (something) or faithful to (someone): [T1] *She clung to the hope that her son was not dead.* → **adhere to** (2), etc.

**cling together** *v adv*
**1** to stay fixed together: [L9 + TOGETHER] *The pages of this book have clung together.* → **stick together** (1)
*__2__ *not fml* (of two or more people) to be loyal to one another: [IØ] *Members of a family should cling together in times of trouble.* → **stick together** (2), etc.

**clip on** *v adv*
to fasten (something) on one's clothes or person with a special fastener: [L9 + ON (*to*) (*simple tenses*)] *This hairpiece clips on.* [X9 + ON (*to*)] *Please help me to clip this tie on, it's rather awkward.* —**clip-on** *n, adj*

**clip out** *v adv* → **cut out** (1)
to cut (something such as an article) out (of a newspaper, etc.): [T1 + OUT ] *May I clip out the report on my performance?*

**cloak in** *v prep*
**1** to cover (someone) with a loose, outer garment (cloak) made of (something): [T1 + *in*] *She was cloaked in red wool.*
*__2__ to hide (something) in (something): [D1 (*usu. pass.*)] *The actress's life was cloaked in mystery.*

***clock in** *v adv* → **check in** (3), **check off** (2), **check on**[1], **check out** (3), **clock off, clock on, clock out, punch in**[1], **punch out, ring in**[1] (1), **ring out** (4)
*not fml* to start work, esp. at a regular time: [IØ] *Most of the workers clocked in before 8.30 this morning.* —**clocking-in** *n, adj*

***clock off** *v adv* → **clock out,** etc.
*not fml* to finish work, esp. at a regular time: [IØ] *The workers in this factory clock off at 5.00.* —**clocking-off** *n, adj*

***clock on** *v adv* → **clock in,** etc.
*not fml* to start work, esp. at a regular time: [IØ] *Most of the workers clocked on before 8.30 this morning.* —**clocking-on** *n, adj*

***clock out** *v adv* → **check in (3), check off, check on, check out** (3), **clock in, clock off, clock on, punch in** (2), **punch out** (3), **ring in** (1), **ring out** (4)
*not fml* to finish work, esp. at a regular time: [IØ] *The workers in this factory clock out at 5.00.* —**clocking-out** *n, adj*

***clock up** *v adv*
**1** to record (a distance travelled): [T1] *The old car has just clocked up another 50,000 kilometres.* → **log up** (1)
**2** *not fml* to record (something) to one's success: [T1] *Now we can clock up another victory for our team.* → **chalk up** (3), **log up** (2), **notch up, score up**

**clog up** *v adv* → **chock up** (1), **choke up** (1)
to block (something): [T1 + UP (*usu. pass.*)]

*The well was clogged up with leaves. The water won't go down, I think the pipe must be clogged up.*

**clog with** *v prep*
to block (something) with (something): [T1 + *with*] *The water won't go down, I think the pipe must be clogged with dirt.*

**close about/around/round** *v prep*
to surround (something or someone) gradually: [L9 + *about/around/round*] *As darkness closed about them, they decided to return home.*

***close down** *v adv*
**1** (of a shop, factory, etc.) to (cause to) cease doing business: [IØ] *The shop will be closing down for good on Saturday, so everything is half price.* [T1] *The owner is having to close the shop down.* —**closing-down** *adj* → **close up** (4), **shut down** (2), **shut up** (3)
**2** (of a radio or television station) to stop broadcasting for the day: [IØ] *This station is now closing down and we wish you all goodnight.* —**closedown** *n*
**3** *AmE* to get closer; settle: [IØ (*on*)] *Darkness closed down on the city.* → **close in** (3)

**close in** *v adv*
**1** to cause (something) to be shut: [X9 + IN] *The workmen are closing the doorway in.*
*__2__ to have fewer hours of daylight: [IØ] *The days are closing in now that it is September.* → **draw in** (2), **draw out** (4)
*__3__ to get closer (to someone or something), esp. intending to surround and attack it/him; gather nearer: [IØ (*on/upon*)] *Darkness closed in (on the city).* → **close down** (3), **close in on**
*__4__ *infml* to wound (part of the body): [T1] *The youth threatened to close the old man's face in.*

***close in on** *v adv prep* → **close in** (3), **move in on** (3)
to get closer to (someone or something) intending to surround and attack it/him: [T1] *The enemy is closing in on the city. The police are closing in on the criminals. The lion closed in on the family of deer.*

**close off** *v adv*
to block (something such as an entry or road): [T1 + OFF] *The police have closed off the streets so that the President can drive through the city free of traffic.*

**close on/upon** *v prep*
**1** to threaten; enclose as if to imprison (someone): [L9 + *on/upon*] *Last year's tax demands are closing on me.*
**2** to surround (something or someone) gradually: [L9 + *on/upon*] *As darkness closed on them, they decided to return home.*
**3** to close (something such as a door) so as to trap (someone): [T1 + *on/upon*] *I closed the window on my finger and made it bleed.* → **shut in**[2] (2), **shut on** (1)
**4** **close the door on** to declare that there is no hope for (someone or something): *The country's military leaders have closed the door on any further peace talks. I tried to get any kind of job but it seemed that the whole city had closed the door on me.* → **shut on** (2)

***close out** *v adv*
*AmE not fml* to reduce prices of (goods): [IØ] *The store is closing out on Saturday.* [T1] *The store is closing out its goods on Saturday.* —**closing-out** *adj*

**close round** *v prep* → CLOSE ABOUT

**close up** *v adv*
**1** to block or shut (something): [X9 + UP] *We must close up the old well, it's dangerous. The road has been closed up for repairs.*
**2** to (cause to) close completely: [L9 + UP] *I'm glad to see that the wound is closing up nicely.* [X9 + UP] *"Close up his eyes, and draw the curtains close."* (Shakespeare, *King Henry VI, Part II*) → **join up** (1)
*__3__ to (cause to) come nearer to each other; join together: [IØ] *The captain ordered his men to close up.* [T1] *Children have to learn to close up their letters when writing.* —**close-up** *n* → **join up** (1)
*__4__ to (cause to) close for the night or a short time: [IØ] *The shop is closing up, I must ask you to leave.* [T1] *We are closing up the house for the summer.* → **close down** (1), **shut down** (2), **shut up** (3)
*__5__ *not fml* to become silent or secretive: [IØ (*usu. simple tenses*)] *As soon as I mentioned the new appointment, the chairman closed up and refused to talk about the matter.*

**close upon** *v prep* → CLOSE ON

**close with** *v prep*
**1** to bring (something such as an event) to an end with (something): [T1 + *with*] *The priest closed the meeting with a prayer.*
*__2__ *lit* to begin to fight with (someone); come within striking distance of (someone): [T1] *The two men closed with their attackers.*
*__3__ to agree with (someone) about an offer or price: agree to (an offer): [T1] *After hours of talking about the price, the shopkeeper at last closed with the salesman's offer. The two ministers didn't close with each other until near the end of the meeting.*
**4** **be closed with** to be having a private meeting with (someone): *I'm sorry, you can't go in that room, the chairman is closed with the director for an urgent meeting.* → **closet with**

**closet with** *v prep* → **close with** (4)
**be closeted with** to be having a private meeting with (someone): *The king is closeted with his ministers to talk about the government's difficulties.*

**clothe in/with** *v prep*
**1** to dress (someone) in (certain clothes): [T1 + *in/with*] *I like to clothe the children in pure cotton; it's so healthy. The girl was clothed in strange garments.*
*__2__ to cover or hide (something) in (some-

thing): [D1 (*usu. pass.*)] *The hills were clothed in mist. His thoughts were clothed in poetic words.*

**cloud over** *v adv*
**1** (of the sky) to become cloudy: [IØ] *The sky has clouded over; we shan't see the sun again today.*
**2** to (cause to) become less transparent: [IØ] *The windows have clouded over in the steam.* [T1] *The mist has clouded the windows over.* → **cloud up, mist over, steam over, steam up** (1)
**3** (of someone's face) to become less cheerful: [IØ] *Mary's face clouded over when she heard the bad news about her mother's operation.*

**cloud up** *v adv* → **cloud over** (2), **mist over, steam over, steam up** (1)
to (cause to) become less transparent: [IØ] *The windows have clouded up in the steam.* [T1] *The mist has clouded the windows up.*

**club together** *v adv*
**1** to form a group: [IØ] *Why don't the boys club together and join each other's activities?*
**2** also **club up** *not fml* to share the cost of something with others: [IØ] *The family clubbed together to buy the car.*

**clue down** *v adv* → CLEW DOWN

**clue in** *v adv*
*infml* to give (someone) necessary information for understanding something or finding an answer: [T1b (*usu. simple tenses*)] *I can't imagine where you have hidden it, please clue me in.*

**clue up** *v adv*
**1** → CLEW UP
**2** *infml* to inform (someone) thoroughly (about something): [T1 (*about/on*) (*usu. simple tenses*)] *Can you clue me up on the club's activities? Michael is all clued up about radio.* → **gen up**

**cluster around/round** *v prep*
to surround (someone or something) in a tight group: [L9 + *around/round*] *The children clustered round the teacher to hear the story.*

**cluster together** *v adv*
to (cause to) join in a close group; gather: [L9 + TOGETHER] *The deer clustered together near the water.* [X9 + TOGETHER (*usu. pass.*)] *The cars were clustered together near the bridge.*

**clutch at** *v prep*
**1** to try to seize (something or someone) suddenly: [IØ + *at*] *The climber clutched at the swinging rope, but missed. The child clutched at his mother in fear.* → **grab at** (1), etc.
*2 to try to make use of (something): [T1 (*usu. simple tenses*)] *A businessman will clutch at any chance of making a profit.* → **catch at** (2), **grab at** (2), **snap at** (3), **snap up, snatch at** (2)
**3 clutch at straws/a straw** to try to seize any chance, esp. to be saved: [*usu. simple tenses*] *The poor man was just clutching at straws when he took his dying wife to another doctor. "A drowning man will clutch at a straw."* (saying) → **grab at** (3), etc.

**clutch to** *v prep*
**1** to hold (something or someone) tightly to (oneself): [T1 + *to*] *The child clutched the doll to her and would not show it to anyone.*
**2 clutch something/someone to one's bosom** to be very keen on something or someone; accept something or someone eagerly: *When he heard of the plan, the chairman clutched it to his bosom and would not hear of any other suggestion. Although the boy was a stranger, the farmer's family took him in and clutched him to their bosom.*

**clutter up** *v adv*
*not fml* to make (a place) untidy; fill (someone's or one's mind) with confused information: [T1 + UP] *I wish you'd stop cluttering the table up with your books. She's quite clever, but her head is cluttered up with unimportant details, so that she often misses the point.*

**coach for** *v prep*
to train (someone) specially for (an examination, competition, etc.): [T1 + *for*] *Who will coach our team for the games? The boy needs to be specially coached for the examination.*

**coast along** *v adv*
**1** to keep moving without using any power, as on a bicycle without moving the feet, or in a car without using the engine: [IØ + ALONG] *The road was slightly downhill, so we just coasted along enjoying ourselves.*
*2 to advance without effort or speed: [IØ] *Work is just coasting along, thank you.*

**coat with** *v prep*
to cover (something) with a layer of (something): [T1 + *with*] *The car was coated with mud. Thicken the soup until you can coat a spoon with it.*

**coax into** *v prep* → **argue into,** etc.
to persuade (someone) gently into (something or doing something): [X9 + *into*] *Can you coax the boys into greater effort? I think I can coax Father into increasing my spending money.*

**coax out of** *v adv prep* → **argue out of,** etc.
to persuade (someone) gently against (something or doing something): [X9 + OUT + *of*] *Can you coax the boys out of their unreasonable behaviour? His parents had to coax Jim out of leaving his job.*

**cobble up** *v adv*
*not fml* to make (something) roughly: [X9 + UP] *If you give me only a few days, I can only cobble up a table for you; with more time I can make one properly.*

**cock up** *v adv*
**1** to raise (something such as ears): [X9 + UP] *The dog cocked up its ears when it heard its master's voice. The edge of the hat was cocked up.*
*2 *sl* to spoil (something) carelessly: [T1] *He*

*really cocked it up that time.* —**cock-up** *n* → **mess up** (2), etc.

**cocker up** *v adv* → **cosher up**
*old use* to treat (someone) with too much kindness, care, etc.: [X9 + UP] *Cocker up your child, and you will come to fear him.*

**coerce into** *v prep* → **railroad into**
to force (someone) into (something or doing something): [X9 + *into*] *The children have to be coerced into obedience. The committee must coerce its members into attending regularly.*

**coexist with** *v prep*
to live together with (usu. another nation, esp. one with an opposed political system) peacefully: [L9 + *with*] *Each nation must learn to coexist with neighbouring countries.*

**coil around/round** *v prep* → **twist around** (1), **wind around** (1), **wreathe around**
to (cause to) twist around (something) by turning several times: [X9 + *around/round*] *Coil the end of the string round your finger, so that the toy plane can't get loose. The belt had coiled itself round the wheel, stopping the motor.* [L9 + *around/round*] *Keep the plants well separated, or that green climbing plant might coil round the roses.*

**coil down** *v adv*
*naut* to form (a rope) into a curled shape on the ground: [T1 + DOWN] *The sailor coiled the rope down on the ground.*

**coil round** *v prep* → COIL AROUND

**coil up** *v adv*
**1** (of an animal) to (cause to) lie in a curled shape: [L9 + UP] *The dog coiled up in the corner by the fire.* [T1 + UP] *The snake was coiled up on the ground outside the hut.*
**2** *naut* to form (a rope) into a curled shape in one's hand: [T1 + UP] *The sailor coiled the rope up, ready to throw it.*

**coin in** *v adv*
**coin it in** *infml* to earn a lot of money: [*usu. continuous tenses*] *Jim's working in the North Sea oil business, and he's coining it in.*

**coincide with** *v prep* → **clash with** (2), **conflict with** (1)
to happen at the same time as (something else) by chance: [L9 + *with* (*simple tenses*)] *The opening ceremony coincided with the worst storm this century.*

**collaborate with** *v prep*
**1** to work with (someone) as a partner: [L9 + *with*] *One of my students collaborated with me on this book.*
**2** to work with (the enemy) against one's country: [L9 + *with*] *People who collaborated with the enemy during the war were punished afterwards.*

**collect for** *v prep*
to ask people to give (something such as money) to (someone or an organization which helps people in need): [L9 + *for*] *I'm collecting for the Red Cross, please give generously.* [T1 + *for*] *I'm collecting old clothes for poc children, do you have any?*

**collect from** *v prep*
**1** to arrive to take (someone or something from (a place): [X9 + *from*] *Will you colle my dress from the cleaner's? I'll collect yo from the airport.*
**2** to take money owed or promised fro (someone): [L9 + *from*] *When business bad, some companies have difficulty collectin from people who owe them money.*

**collect up** *v adv*
to gather (things) together: [T1 + UP] *Collecting up her belongings, she ran out of th house.*

**collide with** *v prep*
**1** to crash into (something): [L9 + *with* (*usu simple tenses*)] *The car collided with a bu.* → **be in with** (4)
*__2__ to disagree violently with (something): [T (*no pass., simple tenses*)] *The chairman opinion collided with that of the rest of th committee.* → **conflict with** (2), etc.

***collocate with** *v prep* → **construe with**
(of a word) to be regularly used togeth with (another word): [T1 (*no pass., simp tenses*)] *"Depend" collocates with "on".*

**colour in** *v adv*
to fill (something such as a drawing) with co our: [T1 + IN] *The child coloured in the pi ture.*

**colour up** *v adv*
**1** to turn red in the face with strong feelin such as shame or modesty: [L9 + UP] *Ma coloured up when Jim praised her cookin* → **flame up** (3), **flush up**
*__2__ to make (something such as a story) see more exciting: [T1] *The sailor always colou up his adventures to please his hearers.*

**comb for** *v prep*
to search (a place) looking for (something someone): [T1 + *for*] *The police are combir the woods for the missing boy. I've combe the house for your bag, but it's not here.*

**comb out** *v adv*
**1** to comb (hair) thoroughly: [X9 + OU *She spent hours in front of the mirror, com ing out her long hair.* → **comb through** (1)
**2** to remove (something unwanted) fro hair: [X9 + OUT] *She had to spend hou combing out the knots every time she wash her hair. When the weather turns hot we he the dog to keep cool by combing out his loo hairs.*
**3** to search (a place) thoroughly for (some thing or someone): [X9 + OUT] *The village combed out the woods, looking for the missi boy.*
*__4__ to search among other things for (som thing): [T1] *The student spent many hours the library, combing out the facts she want in the old books.* → **comb through** (2)
*__5__ *not fml* to remove (unwanted parts or pe

ple) from a whole or group: [T1] *The committee's job is to comb out those students who are not likely to succeed.* → **weed out** (2)

**comb through** *v prep*

**1** to comb (hair) thoroughly: [IØ + *through*] *She spent hours in front of the mirror, combing through her long hair.* → **comb out** (1)

***2** to search with much effort in (something): [T1] *The student spent many hours in the library combing through old books looking for the facts that she wanted.* → **comb out** (4)

**combine against** *v prep*

to join forces to oppose (something or someone): [L9 + *against*] *Small nations often have to combine against the power of a large one.* [T1 + *against*] *Let us combine our two firms against our competitors.*

**combine with** *v prep*

**1** to (cause to) join with (something else, formerly separate): [X9 + *with*] *The members decided to combine the tennis club with the cricket club, forming one sports club.* [L9 + *with* (*simple tenses*)] *This chemical combines with air to form a liquid.* → **amalgamate with, merge together, merge with**

***2** to add (something) to (something else): [D1 (*often pass.*)] *When rising prices are combined with a lack of jobs, many people suffer and the nation becomes poorer. If he can combine his natural ability with hard work, he should be very successful.*

**come aboard** *v adv* → **go aboard, go ashore, take aboard, take ashore, take on** (1)

to enter or take a place on a ship or plane: [L9 + ABOARD] *"When does the pilot come aboard?" "Just before we enter the harbour." Come aboard! You're all welcome here!*

**come about** *v adv*

**1** to happen; arise: [IØ (*simple tenses*)] *Peace can only come about if each side agrees to yield to the other.* [*It* + L9] "*It all came about in a way which is worth recalling, if only for the light it throws on our Captain's character.*" (Laurens van der Post, *The Hunter and the Whale*) [*It* + I5 (*simple tenses*)] *How did it come about that the man was dismissed?* → **bring about** (1)

**2** (of a ship or wind) to change direction to face the opposite way: [IØ (*usu. simple tenses*)] *It was too stormy to continue the voyage, so the ship came about and headed for the safety of the shore.* → **bring about** (2), etc.

**come across**[1] *v adv*

**1** to travel a short distance; cross a road, water, etc.: [IØ + ACROSS] *When the traffic has all passed, it's safe to come across. Why don't you come across to our house this evening? Many more people have come across to the island since the new bridge was built.* → **come over**[1] (3), etc.

***2** to be understood and received well by someone: [IØ (*usu. simple tenses*)] *Did his speech come across?* → **come over**[1] (4), **get across**[1] (2), **get over**[1] (3), **get through**[1] (7), **get through to** (2), **go across**[1] (2), **go down** (15), **go down with** (2), **go over**[1] (4), **put across**[1] (2), **put over**[2] (2)

**come across**[1] *v prep*

**1** to move across (a place): [IØ + *across*] *The host came across the room to greet his guests.* → **go across**[2], etc.

***2** to find (something) or meet (someone) by chance: [T1 (*no pass. simple tenses*)] *I came across this old photograph in the back of the drawer. Outside the restaurant, we came across a man doing a fire-eating performance.* → **happen on**, etc.

***3** to arise in (someone's mind): [T1 (*no pass., simple tenses*)] *The thought came across my mind that I had met him before.* [*It* + T5 (*simple tenses*)] *It came across my mind that I had met him before.*

***come across as** *v adv prep*

*infml* to seem to be (judging from behaviour): [L1] *He comes across as someone who means what he says.* [L4] *He comes across as being very sincere.*

**come across with** *v adv prep*

**1** to move across water or a distance together with (someone): [IØ + ACROSS + *with*] *My grandfather came across with the first party of settlers.*

***2** → COME THROUGH WITH

**come after** *v prep*

**1** to follow (something or someone) in time: [IØ + *after* (*often simple tenses*)] *I can never remember which king came after which.*

***2** to chase in order to attack (usu. someone): [T1 (*no pass.*)] *I saw the big dog coming after me.* → **be after** (2), **come at** (3), **come for** (2), **get after** (1), **go after** (1), **go at** (3), **go for** (4), **keep after** (1), **make after, make at** (2), **make for** (3)

**come again** *v adv*

**1** to come or visit for a second time; return: [IØ + AGAIN] *I'm so glad you enjoyed your visit; do come again.* → **go back** (2), etc.

***2** *BrE infml* to repeat one's words: [IØ (*simple tenses, usu. imper.*)] *Come again? I didn't hear what you said.* → **come back** (6)

**come along** *v adv*

**1** to pass; arrive: [IØ + ALONG (*often simple tenses*)] *Just then a bus came along so we got on and rode home. My teacher came along just as we were talking about him.* → **come by**[1] (1), **get by**[1] (1), **get past**[1] (1), **go by**[1] (1), **go past**[1] (1)

**2** to arrive together with someone else: [IØ + ALONG (*to*)] *Only Jane was invited to the party, but both her sisters came along too.* → **be along, bring along** (1), **get along** (2), **go along** (2), **send along, take along**

***3** to arrive by chance: [IØ (*usu. simple tenses*)] *Trouble comes along when you least expect it. Take every chance that comes along.* → **turn up** (10)

***4** also **come on** to advance; improve: [IØ (*often continuous tenses*)] *How is your work* *coming along? It's coming along nicely, thank you.* → **bring on** (3), etc.

*5 also **come on** to improve in health: [IØ (*often continuous tenses*)] *The doctor says Mother is coming along nicely now, thank you.*

*6 to hurry: [IØ (*with*) (*usu. imper.*)] *Come along, children, or we'll be late!* → **come on¹** (8)

*7 *also* **come on** to make more effort; work harder: [IØ (*usu. imper.*)] *Come along, Jane, you can do better than that.*

*8 *infml* I don't believe you! [IØ (*imper.*)] *Oh, come along! I know better than that!* → **come on¹** (10), etc.

***come amiss** *v adv* → **be amiss, go amiss**
to happen in a wrong way: [IØ (*simple tenses*)] *I hope nothing comes amiss when we move into our new house.*

***come apart** *v adv*
**1** to break in pieces without force being used: [IØ (*often simple tenses*)] *It just came apart in my hands.* → **fall apart** (1), **fall to²** (3)
**2 come apart at the seams** *not fml* to become ruined or fall into a bad mental state: [*often continuous tenses*] *Their clever plan came apart at the seams when the government changed the tax laws. I'm rather worried about my secretary, he's been coming apart at the seams recently.*

**come around/round** *v adv*
**1** to travel a long way round: [IØ + AROUND/ROUND] *The road was flooded, so we had to come round by the bridge.*
*2 to pay a visit: [IØ (*to*)] *Why don't you come around and see us one evening?* → **bring over** (1), etc.
*3 (of a ship or wind) to change direction: [IØ] *Just then the wind came round so we had to reset the sails. Take the wheel, see if you can stop her from coming around.* → **bring about** (2), etc.
*4 to happen regularly: [IØ (*often simple tenses*)] *Birthdays come around too quickly when one is older.* → **roll around** (3)
*5 to regain consciousness: [IØ] *The girl fainted, but she came round when we threw drops of water on her face.* → **bring to** (1), etc.
*6 to change one's opinion (to another point of view): [IØ (*to*)] *Don't worry about the chairman, he'll soon come around (to our opinion).* → **bring round** (3), etc.
*7 to settle a quarrel; feel friendly or happy again: [IØ] *Jim and Mary often argue, but it doesn't take them long to come around. Father was in a very bad temper this morning, but he had come around by evening.* → **come to¹** (2)

***come around/round to** *v adv prep* → **GET ROUND TO**

**come at** *v prep*
**1** to arrive at (a certain time): [IØ + *at*] *Some of the guests came at 7 o'clock, others at 7.30.* → **go at** (1)
*2 to reach or find (something): [T1 (*usu. simple tenses*)] *Put the food where the cat can't come at it. I wanted to reply to your letter in detail, but I can't come at it anywhere.* → **get at** (1)
*3 to chase in order to attack (usu. someone): [T1] *I saw the big dog coming at me.* → **come after** (2), etc.
*4 to reach and discover (something): [T1 (*usu. simple tenses*)] *It is always difficult to come at the truth.* → **get at** (2)

**come away** *v adv*
**1** to cease touching something: [IØ + AWAY (*usu. simple tenses*)] *When my hand came away, blood poured from the wound.*
**2** to cease being joined to something: [IØ + AWAY (*from*) (*often simple tenses*)] *I tried to pick up the bucket, but the handle came away in my hand.* → **take off¹** (1), etc.
**3** to leave a place or person: [IØ + AWAY (*with*) (*often simple tenses*)] *Come away with me on my next holiday. I had to come away before the end of the party. The young writer asked his teacher's wife to come away with him.* → **go away** (1), etc.
*4 *ScotE not fml* to enter a room: [IØ (*imper.*)] *Come away! The door's open!*

**come away with** *v adv prep*
**1** to leave a place together with (someone) or carrying (something): [IØ + AWAY + *with* (*often simple tenses*)] *Come away with me on my next holiday.* → **go away** (1)
*2 to leave a place or event with (feelings, memories, etc.): [T1 (*no pass., simple tenses*)] *We came away with such happy memories of the town that we are sure to go back.* → **bring away, go away with** (4), **send away with** (1)

**come back** *v adv*
**1** to return: [IØ + BACK (*to*)] *We'd like to come back next year. When Jane comes back, will you give her a message?* → **go back** (2), etc
*2 to begin performing again after inactivity [IØ] *Is the singer expected to come back?* —**come-back** *n*
*3 to become fashionable or popular again [IØ] *Long skirts are expected to come back next year.* → **be back** (2)
*4 to return to one's memory: [IØ (*to*)] *Her name will come back (to me) soon.* [*It* + I (*to*)] *It came back to me where I had seen her before.* → **bring back** (2), **call up** (5), **come back to** (2), **summon up** (2)
*5 to reply, usu. forcefully: [IØ (*at, with*) (*simple tenses*)] *"But you're just as guilty!" Jan came back. She always comes back at anyone who tries to be polite to her. I shall speak for twenty minutes and then you can come back at me with your questions.* —**come-back** *n*
*6 *infml* to repeat one's words; speak again [IØ (*simple tenses*)] *I didn't hear you, could you come back? I will now ask the first speaker to come back.* → **come again** (2)
*7 (of a former method) to be used again

[IØ] *Some people are hoping that the old system of punishment by death will come back.* → **bring back** (4)

**come back to** *v adv prep*

**1** to return to (a place or someone): [IØ + BACK + *to*] *I always come back to the same town for a holiday as it's so nice.* → **go back** (2), etc.

***2** to return to the memory of (someone): [T1] *The details of the story are coming back to me now, although it happened a long time ago.* [*It* + T1] *It suddenly came back to me where we met.* → **bring back** (2), **call up** (5), **come back** (4), **summon up** (2)

***3** to return, in talking, to (a subject): [T1] *I think it's time to come back to the most important question: who is to pay for the new building?* → **get back** (3), **get back to** (2), **go back** (4), **go back to** (3)

**come before** *v prep*

**1** to happen earlier than (something or someone): [IØ + *before* (*simple tenses*)] *Did the invention of the telephone come before the end of the last century?* → **be before** (1)

***2** to appear to face (a court of law or other powerful group): [T1 (*no pass., usu. simple tenses*)] *When you come before the judge, you must speak the exact truth.* → **bring before** (1), etc.

***3** to be sent for consideration or approval by (someone or a group in power): [T1 (*no pass., usu. simple tenses*)] *Your suggestion came before the board of directors yesterday, but I haven't heard the result of their meeting.* → **put before** (2), etc.

***4** to have a higher rank than (someone else); take first place in front of (someone else): [T1 (*no pass., simple tenses*)] *Members of the Royal Family come before lords and ladies.*

***5** to be more important than (something): [T1 (*no pass., simple tenses*)] *Consideration of a fellow worker's health must come before my own professional pride.* → **put before** (4), etc.

**come between** *v prep*

**1** to happen between (two events): [IØ + *between* (*simple tenses*)] *The third race comes between the high jump and the throwing competition.*

***2** to try to separate (two people or animals): [T1 (*no pass, usu. simple tenses*)] *Never come between husband and wife. It is dangerous to come between two fighting dogs.* → **get between** (2)

***3** to try to prevent (someone) from having or doing something: [T1 (*no pass., usu. simple tenses*)] *The true artist lets nothing come between himself and his work.* → **get between** (3), **stand between** (3)

**come by[1]** *v adv*

**1** to pass; arrive: [IØ + BY (*usu. simple tenses*)] *Just then a bus came by so we got on and rode home. My teacher came by just as we were talking about him. Move aside, please, the firemen want to come by.* → **come along, fly by[1], get by[1]** (1), **get past[1]** (1), **go by[1]** (1), **go past[1]** (1)

***2** esp. *AmE* to pay an informal visit: [IØ (*usu. simple tenses*)] *Why don't you come by some afternoon and have coffee with me?*

***come by[2]** *v prep*

**1** to obtain (something): [T1 (*simple tenses*)] *How did you come by that beautiful picture? A good job that you enjoy doing is hard to come by.*

**2** to receive (something), usu. accidentally: [T1 (*simple tenses*)] *How did you come by that wound on your arm?*

***come clean** *v adj*

*infml* to admit everything: [IØ (*simple tenses*)] *After hours of stating firmly that he was not guilty, the prisoner came clean and admitted to stealing the jewels.*

**come close to** *v adv prep* → **come near, get near, go near**

**1** to move near (something or someone): [IØ + CLOSE + *to* (*often simple tenses*)] *Come close to each other so that I can get you all in the photograph.*

***2** to be very near or like (something or doing something): [T1 (*no pass., simple tenses*)] *Your suggestion comes close to what we were looking for. The book comes close to perfection.* [T4] *The boy came close to falling off the high wall.*

**come down** *v adv*

**1** to move to a lower level: [IØ + DOWN] *Come down, Jane, your breakfast's ready!* → **go down[1]** (1), **go down to** (1), **go down with** (1), **go up[1]** (1)

**2** to fall, drop, or descend: [IØ + DOWN] *Several trees came down in last night's storm. The child, running too fast, came down and hurt his knee. When the hunters fired, three of the deer came down.* → **bring down** (2), **get down** (5), **go down[1]** (5), **send down** (4), **shoot down** (1)

**3** to be destroyed: [IØ + DOWN] *Three of the enemy planes came down in the battle. The old hotel is coming down and a new one is to be built.* → **bring down** (2), **go down[1]** (5), **pull down** (3), **send down** (4), **shoot down** (1), **take down** (3)

**4** (of a plane) to land: [IØ + DOWN] *The plane came down safely in spite of the mist.*

***5** to lessen; be reduced: [IØ] *The price came down. My weight has come down again.* → **go down[1]** (6), etc., **go up** (3)

***6** to be given or left to people who are younger or come later: [IØ (*simple tenses, often perfect*)] *This ring has come down in my family for two centuries. This ring has come down from my great-grandmother.* → **hand down** (3), etc.

***7** to travel south or away from an important place such as a capital city or (*BrE*) university: [IØ (*from*)] *I can't come down till I've* *finished my last examinations. When is your aunt coming down from London? The whole family are coming down to stay for Christmas.* → **go down¹** (14), etc.

**8 to be considered less worthy: [IØ] *He has come down in my opinion.* → **come up** (12), **go down¹** (16), **go up¹** (12)

**9 to be reduced to its real meaning (as something): [IØ (*to*) (*simple tenses*)] *When it all comes down, there isn't much in his story. The whole matter comes down to a power struggle between the trade union and the directors.* → **boil down to, come down to** (5)

**10 to provide money, often as a gift: [IØ (*usu. simple tenses*)] *Do you think your uncle will come down when we need more money?* → **come through with**

**11 come down in the world** to be reduced to a humbler standard of living or social level: *When their business failed, the family came down in the world.* —**come-down** *n* → **come up** (19), **go down¹** (19), **go up¹** (15)

****come down on** *v adv prep*

**1** *not fml* to demand firmly from (someone): [T1] *The debt collector came down on us for payment.* [V3] *Mother came down on me to clean my room.*

**2** to punish (someone): [T1 (*often simple tenses*)] *The courts will come down (heavily) on young criminals.*

**3** *infml* to scold (someone): [T1 (*often simple tenses*)] *The director came down on Jim for being late again.* → **tell off** (1), etc.

**4** *not fml* to attack (something): [T1] *The enemy came down on the town during the night.*

**5** to decide in favour of (an opinion): [T1 (*no pass., usu. simple tenses*)] *The chairman will have to come down on one side or the other soon.*

**come down to** *v adv prep*

**1** to move towards (something or someone) from a higher level: [IØ + DOWN + *to*] *Come down to the ground, I can't hear you at the top of the ladder.*

**2** to reach (a point): [IØ + DOWN + *to*] *His hair comes down to his shoulders. Our land comes down to the water's edge.*

**3 to reach the matter of (something such as a subject or quality): [T1] *When we come down to details, the plan seems possible. When it comes down to a matter of principle, it seems we have no choice.* → **get down to** (2)

**4 to be passed to (someone): [T1 (*no pass.*)] *This ring has come down to me from my grandmother.* → **hand down** (3), etc.

**5 to be reduced to its real meaning as (something): [T1 (*no pass., simple tenses*)] *The whole matter comes down to a power struggle between the trade union and the directors.* → **boil down to, come down** (9)

**6 to be reduced to (something or doing something humble): [T1 (*no pass.*)] *Has he come down to this?* [T4] *He came down to selling matches on street corners.* → **come to²** (11) **reduce to** (12)

**7 come down to brass tacks** *infml* to talk about facts or practical matters: *All this talk about ideas is getting us nowhere, let's come down to brass tacks and arrange about moving the machinery.* → **get down to** (3)

**8 come down to earth (with a bang/bump)** *not fml* to return to reality, suddenly or with a shock: *I'm glad Mary has come down to earth and stopped dreaming of being rich. If he thinks prices have stayed the same, send him shopping—he'll soon come down to earth with a bump!* → **bring down** (12)

****come down with** *v adv prep*

**1** → COME THROUGH WITH

**2** to be taken ill with (a disease): [T1 (*no pass.*)] *Jane has come down with a bad cold* → **be down with, go down with** (3)

**come first** *v adj*

**1** to win a competition: [L7 + first (*usu. simple tenses*)] *Jim came first in the race, and the two younger boys came next.*

**2 to be more important to oneself: [IØ (*simple tenses*)] *My family comes first, my work second.* → **come next** (4)

**3 first come, first served** people will be served in order of arrival

**come for** *v prep*

**1** to arrive to collect (something or someone): [IØ + *for* (*usu. simple tenses*)] *I've come for my parcel. I'll come for you at * o'clock.* → **go for** (2)

**2 to advance towards (usu. someone) in a threatening manner: [T1 (*no pass., often continuous tenses*)] *I saw the big dog coming for me.* → **come after** (2), etc.

**come forth** *v adv* → **bring forth** (1), **go forth** (1), **send forth** (2), **send out** (4)

*old use* to come out: [IØ + FORTH] *The castle gate was opened and the king and all his servants came forth.*

**come forward** *v adv*

**1** to step forward; move to the front: [IØ + FORWARD] *Just then, the crowd divided and three men came forward to hand the citizens' request to the king.* → **go forward** (1), **step forward** (1)

**2 to stand out; be on a different level: [IØ] *The great door was ornamented with figures, some coming forward so that they looked real.*

**3 to offer oneself, as to help: [IØ] *The police have asked for witnesses of the accident to come forward. Only two people have come forward for election to the committee.* → **step forward** (2)

**4 to become ready to be used or sold: [IØ] *Few chances like this come forward. There are not many new houses coming forward for sale.*

**5 to be introduced for consideration, as at a meeting: [IØ (*usu. simple tenses*)] *Your sug* *gestion will come forward at the next committee meeting.* → **bring forward** (6)

**come from** *v prep*
**1** to arrive from (somewhere); have one's origins in (something or somewhere): [IØ + *from* (*simple tenses*)] *Eggs come from chickens. What country do you come from? Danger comes from unexpected places.*
***2** to result from (something or doing something): [T1 (*no pass., simple tenses*)] *What results do you expect to come from all this activity?* [T4 (*no pass., simple tenses*)] *That's what comes from sleeping late, you have a headache all morning.* → **arise from,** etc.
***3** to be descended from (people): [T1 (*no pass., simple tenses*)] *She comes from a long line of singers.* → **come of** (2), **descend from** (3)

**come home** *v adv*
**1** to travel, esp. return to one's home, country, etc.: [IØ + HOME] *When are you coming home tonight? "Leave them alone and they'll come home, bringing their tails behind them."* (children's poem)
***2** *naut* (of an anchor) to fail to take a firm hold in the seabed: [IØ (*usu. simple tenses*)] *Why is the ship moving? The anchor must have come home; we shall have to lower it again in a different place to see if it holds there.*

**come home to** *v adv prep*
**1** to return to one's home to find (something or someone): [IØ + HOME + *to*] *I like to come home to a nice warm fire. It's good to come home to a loving family.* → **bring home to** (1), **get home to** (1)
***2** to become fully known by (someone): [T1 (*no pass., usu. simple tenses*)] *At last the real difficulty has come home to John.* [*It* + T1 (*usu. simple tenses*)] *It has come home to John that we haven't enough money.* → **bring home to** (2), **drive home to, get home to** (2)

**come in** *v adv*
**1** to enter: [IØ + IN] *"Come in!" called the director when he heard the knock at his door. The door opened and the man came in.* → **bring in** (1), **get in¹** (2), **go in¹** (1), **send in** (1), **take in¹** (1), **wheel in** (1)
**2** (of something unwanted) to come inside: [IØ + IN] *Quick, get a bucket, the water's coming in!* → **get in¹** (3), **get into** (4)
**3** to arrive; be received: [IØ + IN] *As soon as the fresh vegetables come in, we put them on sale. Some more letters of complaint have just come in. News of the death of the famous actress began coming in just as we were starting the broadcast.* → **take in¹** (7)
***4** (of weather or time) to start: [IØ] *March comes in like a lion.* [L7] *This week came in very windy. It's coming in very cold for September.* → **go out** (8)
***5** to join a business as a partner: [IØ] *My father started the insurance firm, and I came in when I was 18.*
***6** to take one's position in a game or at work: [IØ] *Has Mr Sharp come in yet? The next player was very nervous as he came in.* → **go in¹** (5), etc.
***7** to arrive as expected: [IØ] *The tide is coming in. Did your plane come in on time? When will the sales figures come in?* → **be in¹** (10), **get in¹** (4), etc., **go out** (11)
***8** to take a place in a competition: [L9] *Where did Jim come in?* [L7] *Jim came in third in the running race.* → **come out** (14)
***9** to be elected: [IØ] *If your party comes in at the next election, what will you do about taxes?* → **get in¹** (13), etc.
***10** to become fashionable, seasonable, etc.: [IØ] *Long skirts are coming in again. The new crop of tobacco will be coming in soon.* → **be in¹** (6), **be out** (6), **go out** (7)
***11** to serve a purpose, esp. in the phrs. **come in handy/useful:** [L7] *Don't throw it away, it might come in useful another time. That empty box will come in very handy.*
***12** to appear; happen: [IØ] *This is where the mistakes come in.*
***13** to take part; gain advantage: [IØ] *This is where you come in: we want you to help us rob the bank. I heard you talking about sharing out the money but where do I come in?*
***14** to join an activity: [IØ] *We can run our own affairs without all the lawyers coming in.* → **bring in** (5), **call in¹** (4), **get in¹** (8), **have in¹** (2)
***15** to begin singing, playing, speaking, etc.: [IØ] *When the singer comes in, don't play so loudly. The main character in this play does not come in until the second act. I'd like to come in here to tell of my own experiences in this area. "Please let me tell you", she came in. And now, our musical adviser will add his remarks. Come in, Mr Parker.*
***16** (in radio) to answer a message; begin speaking: [IØ] *Calling all stations, come in please.*
***17** (of money) to be received or earned: [IØ] *I haven't a lot of money coming in just now.* —**income** *n* → **bring in** (3), etc.
***18** (of an oil well) to start producing oil: [IØ] *Number three well came in last night.*
**19 when one's ship comes in** *not fml* when one becomes rich: *When my ship comes in, my dear, you'll have everything you could desire!*
**20 this is where we came in** *infml* we are back to the beginning again.

**come in for** *v adv prep*
**1** to enter in order to get (something or someone): [IØ + IN + *for*] *I've come in for my other coat. Do come in for dinner.* → **go in for** (1)
***2** to gain (something such as money) after someone's death: [T1 (*no pass., usu. simple tenses*)] *Henry came in for a large share of his father's fortune.* → **come into** (3)
***3** to receive (something such as blame or praise): [T1 (*no pass., usu. simple tenses*)]

*The eldest sister always came in for much of the blame.*

**come in on** *v adv prep*

**1** to come inside on top of (someone or something): [IØ + IN + *on*] *The rain is coming in on my head.*

***2** to surround (someone) uncomfortably: [T1 (*no pass.*)] *I don't like big rooms with crowds of people coming in on me.*

***3** to join (something): [T1 (*no pass., usu. simple tenses*)] *Can I come in on your plan?* → **get in on** (1), etc.

***4** to cause (someone) to remember (something): [*It* + T1 (*simple tenses*)] *Suddenly it came in on me that I had left the key behind. Just then it came in on me where I had seen her before.*

**5 come in on the ground floor** *not fml* to start in business at the beginning or lowest level: [*usu. simple tenses*] *I can only offer you a humble position, but it's often to your advantage to come in on the ground floor.* → **get in on** (2), etc.

**come into** *v prep*

**1** to enter (a space such as a room or building): [IØ + *into*] *The door opened and the children came into the room. Come into the house and see my pictures. "Come into the garden, Maud."* (Alfred, Lord Tennyson, *Maud*) → **be in²** (1), etc.

***2** to join (a group or activity): [T1 (*no pass.*)] *Several new members have come into the club since Christmas. We can run our own business without all the lawyers coming into it.*

***3** to gain (something such as money) after someone's death: [T1 (*no pass., often simple tenses*)] *Charles came into a fortune when his father died.* → **come in for** (2)

***4** to begin to be in (a state or activity): [T1 (*no pass.*)] *High shoes came into fashion a few years ago. The trees should come into leaf soon. New companies come into existence every year. Your suggestions will come into consideration. New ways of thinking have come into being. The new machinery will come into use next week. You must have come into contact with someone suffering from an infectious disease. A new political party has come into power.* → **get into** (11), etc.

**5 come into action** to begin being used: *When the big guns came into action, we knew the battle would soon be over.* → **put out** (23), etc.

**6 come into focus** to become clearly understood or known: *The picture of industrial development is coming into focus now, thanks to your work on the enquiry board.* → **be in** (12), **bring into** (4)

**7 come into force** (of something such as a law) to start operation; have to be obeyed: *New laws to control rising prices have recently come into force.* → **be in²** (13), **bring into** (5), **put into** (14)

**8 come into someone's head** to be thought of by someone: *A lovely tune just came into my head; I'll sing it and you see if you recognize it.*

**9 come into line (with)** to start to obey the same rules (as others); follow (a principle): [*no pass.*] *The government has asked all the trade unions to come into line and keep the price and wage agreement.* → **be out of** (16), etc.

**10 come into the open** to become publicly known, not hidden: *It's a good thing that this shameful affair has at last come into the open* → **be in²** (24), **bring into** (7)

**11 come into one's own** to gain independence or recognition; show one's true worth: [*no pass.*] *Mother has come into her own since the children left home, and is making a new life for herself. The scientific study of dreams has not yet come into its own.*

**12 come into play** to begin to have an effect, influence, or force: *Who knows what forces come into play when these decisions are made?* → **be in** (27b), **bring into** (8), **call into** (4)

**13 come into sight/view** to begin to be able to be seen: *At last the shore came into view. By the time the town came into sight, we were too tired to go on.* → **keep in** (16), etc.

**14 come into the world** (of a human being) to be born: *Is there ever a good time to come into the world? We all come into the world without possessions.* → **bring into** (10)

***come it** *v pron* → **come up** (16)

*infml* to pretend that one is more important than one is (or than someone else): [IØ (*over*) (*usu. neg. imper.*)] *Don't try to come it! Don't you come it over me!*

**come loose** *v adj*

to stop being fixed to something else: [L7 + *loose*] *Can you fix this handle? It's coming loose.*

**come near/near to** *v prep; adv prep* → **come close to, get near, go near**

**1** to move towards (something or someone): [IØ + *near*/NEAR + *to*] *Come near (to) me, child, I can't hear you. The bus comes near (to) the station.*

***2** to be very near or like (something or doing something): [T1 (*no pass., simple tenses*)] *Your suggestion comes near (to) what we were looking for. The book comes near (to) perfection.* [T4 (*simple tenses*)] *The boy came near (to) falling off the high wall.*

**come next** *v adv*

**1** to follow in time: [L9 + NEXT (*usu. simple tenses*)] *Who came next after that king? Mrs Brown was the first to arrive, and her daughter came next.*

***2** to result: [IØ (*usu. simple tenses*)] *Everyone moved to the cities looking for work, and the severe lack of housing came next. The military government refused to allow the people their right to vote; what came next was violence and lawlessness.*

***3** to be the next thing to do: [IØ (*usu. simple tenses*)] *I've finished that little job; what comes next?*

***4** to be of less importance to oneself: [IØ (*simple tenses*)] *My family come first, and my work comes next.* → **come first** (2)

**come of** *v prep*

**1** to happen to (someone or something), often in a bad way: [T1 (*no pass., simple tenses*)] *I don't know what will come of the boy if he keeps failing his examinations. What has come of my blue bag?* → **become of, disappear to, get to** (2), **go to** (5)

**2** to be descended from (people): [T1 (*no pass., simple tenses*)] *She comes of a good family.* → **come from** (3), **descend from** (3)

**3** to result from (something or doing something): [T1 (*no pass., simple tenses*)] *I don't know what will come of your actions.* [T4 (*simple tenses*)] *That's what comes of sleeping late, you have a headache all morning.* → **arise from**, etc.

**4 come of age** to reach an age (usu. 18, 19, or 21) when one is considered by law to be responsible for oneself: [(*no pass., usu. simple tenses*)] *We'll have a splendid party when Jane comes of age. In Britain a young person comes of age on his or her 18th birthday.* —**coming-of-age** *n* → **be of** (2)

**come off¹** *v adv*

**1** to cease being joined to something: [L9 + OFF] *I tried to pick up the bucket, but the handle came off in my hand.* → **take off¹** (1), etc.

**2** to fall from something high such as a horse: [L9 + OFF] *You have to come off seven times before you can call yourself a rider.*

**3** to be able to be removed: [L9 + OFF (*usu. simple tenses*)] *Do you think that dirty mark will come off? The top part of the machine comes off for cleaning.* → **wash off¹**, etc.

***4** to leave, usu. a place: [IØ] *Come off with me and have some coffee, I'm tired of listening to this speech.* → **go away¹** (1), etc.

***5** *not fml* to take place as planned: [IØ (*simple tenses*)] *The wedding came off in spite of Jim and Mary's last-minute quarrel.* → **go off¹** (6)

***6** *not fml* to succeed: [IØ (*simple tenses*)] *It was a bold idea, but it came off.* [L9 (*simple tenses*)] *The attempt did not come off as well as we had hoped.* → **bring off¹** (2), **carry off¹** (6), **go off¹** (6), **pass off¹** (2), **pull off¹** (4)

***7** to have or suffer a result: [L9 (*simple tenses*)] *Jim came off best. The boys came off with only slight wounds.*

***8** to cease public performance: [IØ] *The play is a failure and will come off next week.* —**come-off** *n* → **take off¹** (10)

**come off²** *v prep*

**1** to cease being joined to (something): [L9 + *off*] *This button has come off my coat.* → **pull off²** (1), **take off²** (1)

**2** to fall from (something): [L9 + *off*] *The rider came off the horse. The branch has come off the tree.*

***3** to be removed from (something such as a price): [T1 (*no pass.*)] *If the tax is reduced, that 5% will come off the price of the goods.*

***4** to leave (something): [T1 (*no pass.*)] *Many people think that Britain's money troubles began when she came off the gold standard before World War II. I shan't be seeing you any more, I'm coming off your case.* → **go off²** (1), **take off²** (4)

**5 come off it** *infml* stop lying or joking!: [*no pass., imper.*] *Come off it: tell the truth!*

**come on¹** *v adv*

**1** to advance in order to attack: [IØ + ON] *The general ordered the soldiers to come on.*

**2** to follow; travel later: [IØ + ON] *I'll go ahead, and you come on later. The teacher went by train to his new job, and the family came on by bus.*

***3** (of a light or other electrical machine) to start working: [IØ] *Just as I entered the house, all the lights came on.* → **put on¹** (3), etc.

***4** to appear in turn, as on the stage or sports field: [IØ] *The next player came on. When does the great actor come on?* → **be on¹** (5), **bring on¹** (1), **go on¹** (16), **go on at¹** (1), **send on¹** (3), **take off¹** (16)

***5** to begin: [IØ] *I can feel a cold coming on. Night came on.* [*It* + I3] *It came on to snow.* → **bring on¹** (2), **draw on¹** (2)

***6** → COME ALONG (4)

***7** → COME ALONG (5)

***8** to hurry: [IØ (*usu. imper.*)] *Come on, children, or we'll be late!* → **come along¹** (6)

***9** → COME ALONG (7)

***10** *infml* I don't believe you!: [IØ (*imper.*)] *Oh, come on! I know better than that!* → **come along¹** (8), **get along¹** (8), **get along with¹** (6), **get away¹** (6), **get away with¹** (8), **get off¹** (18), **get off with¹** (6), **get on¹** (10), **get on with¹** (5), **go along¹** (6), **go along with¹** (6), **go on¹** (18), **go on with¹** (6)

***11** to take place, esp. in turn: [IØ] *When does his case come on? The new film comes on next week.* → **have up¹** (2), etc.

***12** *infml* to visit; join someone: [IØ + BY/IN/OVER/ROUND/UP] *Come on over next time you're in town. Ask the doctor to come on up. Come on in, the water's fine.*

***13** to appear on duty: [IØ] *The new man doesn't come on till midnight.* → **be on¹** (4)

**come on/upon²** *v prep*

**1** to arrive seated on (something such as a horse): [IØ + *on/upon*] *Most of the guests arrived by car, but Jane came on her horse!*

***2** to discover (something) by chance: [T1 (*simple tenses*)] *I came (up)on this old photograph in the back of the drawer.* → **happen on²**, etc.

***3** to happen to, seize, or have an effect on (someone): [T1 (*no pass., usu. simple tenses*)] *Fear came upon him as he stood in the empty house. Bad luck has come on us ever since we bought that old bed.* → **come over²** (2)

***4** to attack (usu. something): [T1 (*no pass.*)] *The enemy came upon the town by night.*

***5** to return to the memory of (someone): [*It* + T1 (*simple tenses*)] *Suddenly it came on me where I had seen her before.* → **come to²** (6, 30)

*6 to take one's part in (something): [T1 (*no pass.*)] *What time do you come on duty?* → **be on² (3)**
**7 come on the scene** *not fml* to arrive, esp. to take part in something; be born: [*simple tenses*] *Things haven't been the same since the new director came on the scene. That was long before you came on the scene.*
**8 come on top of** to follow (something usu. bad) to add to its effect: [*usu. present participle*] *This bad cold, coming on top of the severe winter, is enough to kill the old lady.*

**come onto** *v prep*
**come onto the market** to begin to be offered for sale: *When did the house come onto the market?* → **put on²** (26)

**come out** *v adv*
**1** to move outside a room or building, etc.: [IØ + OUT (*of*)] *Ask the whole family to come out so that I can take their photograph. We met each other coming out of the concert hall.* → **go out** (1), etc.
**2** to fall out: [L9 + OUT] *My tooth has just come out.* → **take out** (2), etc.
**3** to be able to be removed: [L9 + OUT] *Do you think that dirty mark will come out?* → **wash off**, etc.
*4 to be freed, as from a prison: [IØ (*of*)] *It's been a long year, but he comes out next Friday.* → **be inside** (2), **be out** (16)
*5 to appear; be seen or heard: [IØ] *The flowers are coming out in everyone's gardens. The sun came out as soon as the rain stopped.* → **be out** (5), **bring out** (3), **fetch out** (2)
*6 to be expressed in speech: [IØ (*usu. simple tenses*)] *I intended to make a joke, but my remark came out as unintentionally rude.*
*7 to become clear or known: [IØ (*usu. simple tenses*)] *The truth came out at the enquiry. The meaning comes out as you read further. When do the examination results come out? Her gentle nature comes out when she is helping children. He came out as a surprisingly good father.* [*It* + I5] *It came out that he had been in prison before.* → **bring out** (4), etc.
*8 to be published: [IØ] *When does Tom's new book come out? The writer's opinion comes out in the newspaper every morning.* → **be out** (21), **bring out** (5), **fetch out** (4), **get out** (13)
*9 to be seen, as in a photograph; be developed: [IØ (*usu. simple tenses*)] *Mary always comes out well in her pictures. How did the photographs come out? I'm afraid our holiday photos didn't come out.*
*10 to reach an answer: [IØ (*usu. simple tenses*)] *This sum won't come out.* → **get out** (15), **work out** (4)
*11 to reach a result: [L9 (*simple tenses*)] *Let me know how the voting comes out.*
*12 (of information) to be discovered: [IØ (*simple tenses*)] *His secret came out when a missing year was noticed in his record. I don't want the news about our wedding to come out yet.* [*It* + I5] *It came out at the enquiry that he had been trying to avoid paying his income tax.* → **let out** (5), etc.
*13 to reach a total; amount (to a sum): [L9 (*at, to*) (*usu. simple tenses*)] *The figures come out at 47,598. The total comes out to 8,076.* [L7] *The two lists come out equal.* → **come out at, run out at, work out at**
*14 to result, esp. in a competition: [L9 (*simple tenses*)] *Everything will come out all right. Mrs Brown came out well after her suffering. Jim came out third in the examination.* → **come in** (8)
*15 to refuse to work; start a strike: [IØ] *The Post Office workers have come out.* → **bring out** (7), etc.
*16 esp. *BrE fml, becoming rare* (of a young lady) to be officially introduced in upper-class society, usu. at a formal, showy, and costly dance: [IØ] *Is Mrs King-Brown's daughter coming out this year?* —**coming-out** *n, adj* → **bring out** (8)
*17 to move to a distant country, esp. across water: [IØ (*to*)] *When are your family coming out to join you?* → **come over¹** (3), etc.
*18 to develop; appear: [IØ] *We shan't know which disease it is until the spots come out.*
*19 esp. *AmE* to be offered for public viewing or sale: [IØ] *The famous collection of rare old furniture is coming out next week.*
*20 to declare one's opinion: [L9 + *against/for*] *The politician came out against the government. The speaker came out for improved rights for all women everywhere.* → **come out against** (20), **come out for** (3), **come out in** (4)
*21 to be regarded, as in trouble or competition: [L9] *Although the more experienced speaker won the argument, our representative came out well, we thought. The President did not come out well in the enquiry.*

***come out against** *v adv prep* → **come out** (20), **come out for** (3), **come out in** (4)
to oppose (something); declare one's opposition to (something or someone): [T1 (*no pass., usu. simple tenses*)] *The politician took a risk by coming out against the government's action.*

***come out at** *v adv prep* → **come out** (13), **run out at, work out at**
to amount to (a total): [T1 (*no pass., simple tenses*)] *The figures come out at 47,598.*

**come out for** *v adv prep*
**1** to leave a room or building with the purpose of (something): [IØ + OUT + *for*] *Will you come out for a walk after tea?*
*2 (of workers) to go on strike in order to gain (something such as money): [IØ + *for* (*no pass.*)] *The Post Office workers have come out for more pay.*
*3 to support; declare one's support for (something or someone): [T1 (*no pass., usu. simple tenses*)] *The speaker came out for all women*

*everywhere.* → **come out** (20), **come out against, come out in** (4)

**come out from** *v adv prep*

**1** to leave (a place): [IØ + OUT + *from*] *The hungry criminals came out from their hiding place.* → **be out of** (1), etc.

***2** to result from (something): [T1 (*no pass., simple tenses*)] *What came out from your long talks with the director?* → **come out of** (2)

**come out in** *v adv prep*

**1** to come outdoors wearing (a garment or colour): [IØ + OUT + *in*] *Mary came out in her best blue dress.*

***2** to begin to show (something): [T1 (*no pass.*)] *Jane came out in spots this morning.* → **break out in** (1), **bring out in**

**3 come out in the open** to be honest about one's opinions: [*no pass.*] *I wish politicians had the courage to come out in the open and say what they really think.*

**4 come out in support/favour of** to declare one's support for (something or someone): [*no pass.*] *The speaker came out in support of all women everywhere.* → **come out** (20), **come out against, come out for** (3)

**5 come out in the wash** *infml* to be all right in the end: [*simple tenses, usu. future*] *Don't worry about the details of the sale, it'll all come out in the wash.*

**come out of** *v adv prep*

**1** to leave (a place): [IØ + OUT + *of*] *The hungry criminals came out of their hiding place.* → **be out of** (1), etc.

***2** to result from (something): [T1 (*no pass., simple tenses*)] *What came out of your long talks with the director?* → **come out from** (2)

**3 come out of the blue** *not fml* to arrive or happen unexpectedly: [*usu. simple tenses*] *The news of the firm's failure came out of the blue—everyone thought the company was very successful.* → **be out of** (6)

**4 come out of one's shell** *not fml* to become bolder and less nervous in the company of others: *Mary has really come out of her shell since she went to university.* → **bring out** (6), **draw out** (9), **fetch out** (5), **lead out** (2)

**come out on** *v prep*

**1 come out on the right/wrong side** *not fml* to make a good/bad deal; make a profit/loss: [*simple tenses*] *Even with the taxes and other costs, we should come out on the right side. Because of increased costs, the company has come out on the wrong side this year.*

**2 come out on top** *not fml* to win; be successful: [*simple tenses*] *That boy has the most wonderful ability to come out on top even when everything seems to be going against him!*

**come out with** *v adv prep*

**1** to come outdoors together with (someone or something): [IØ + OUT + *with*] *The children came out with a strange dog.*

***2** to say (something), often unexpectedly: [T1 (*usu. simple tenses*)] *Jim came out with a strange remark.*

**come over**[1] *v adv*

**1** to pass overhead or above: [IØ + OVER] *It's terribly noisy living near the airport, planes are coming over all the time.* → **go over**[1] (1)

***2** to travel a short distance, as across water or a road, or to pay a visit: [IØ (*to*)] *Why don't you come over to our place one evening?* → **bring over**[1] (1), etc.

***3** to travel, esp. from a distance or over water: [IØ (*often simple tenses*)] *I came over to North America in 1967. My husband's family came over with William the Conqueror.* → **bring out**[1] (9), **bring over**[1] (2), **come across**[1] (1), **come out**[1] (17), **get across**[1] (1), **get over**[1] (1), **go across**[1] (1), **go out**[1] (2), **go out to**[1] (2), **send across**[1], **send forth**[1] (1), **send out**[1] (2), **send over**[1], **take across, take out**[1] (6), **take over**[1] (1)

***4** to be understood and well received: [IØ (*simple tenses*)] *Did his speech come over?* → **come across**[1] (2), etc

***5** to change one's opinion, political position, etc. [IØ (*to*) (*usu. simple tenses*)] *Don't worry about the chairman, he'll soon come over (to our opinion). Many members of the opposition are coming over to our party.* → **bring round**[1] (3), etc.

***6** (of weather, sky, etc.) to become, gradually: [L7] *The sky came over dark while I was working.*

***7** *BrE* (of people) to become, often suddenly: [L7] *He came over faint.*

***8** to be heard on radio or stage: [L9 (*simple tenses*)] *Let me know how I come over. Your voice comes over rather well.*

**come over**[2] *v prep*

**1** to pass over (someone or something): [IØ + *over*] *It's terribly noisy living near the airport, with planes coming over the house all the time.* → **go over**[1] (1)

***2** to happen to; have a result or effect on (someone): [T1 (*no pass.*)] *An attack of faintness came over him. What has come over you?* → **come on**[2] (3)

***3** *infml* to pretend that one is (a kind of person) for effect on (someone): [D1] *He's been coming the great political leader over us all since he won the election.*

**4 come it over** *infml* to pretend that one is more important than (someone): *Don't try to come it over me!*

**come round** *v adv* → COME AROUND

***come round to** *v adv prep* → COME AROUND TO

***come short of** *v adj prep* → **fall short of**

to be less or lower than (something): [T1 (*no pass., simple tenses*)] *The supply has come short of our needs. Your work comes short of the expected standard.*

**come through**[1] *v adv*

**1** to pass through something: [IØ + THROUGH (*often simple tenses*)] *Just then the branches divided and a small head came* *through. The leather has worn, and the point of the knife comes through.* → **get through**[1] (1), **go through**[1] (1)

*****2** to arrive as expected: [IØ] *Has the train come through? My examination results will come through by post. Your permission to take a week's holiday with pay has just come through.*

*****3** to appear: [IØ] *The sun came through after days of rain.* → **break through**[1] (1)

*****4** to show clearly: [IØ (*simple tenses*)] *His ability did not come through when we examined his papers.* → **show through**[1] (2)

*****5** (of a cricket ball) to rise to a low height, as off soft ground: [L9 (*usu. simple tenses*)] *The ball came through at a surprisingly low height.* → **get up**[1] (13)

*****6** to be received, as by radio or telephone: [IØ (*on*)] *The message has just come through on the radio that the general is dying.* → **be through**[1] (2), **get through**[2] (6), **get through to**[1] (1), **put through**[1] (2)

*****7** to live in spite of danger or difficulty: [IØ (*usu. simple tenses*)] *Most of our men came through unharmed.* → **bring through**[1], **carry through**[1] (3), **pull round**[1] (2), **pull through**[1] (2)

*****8** to do what is needed or expected; be dependable (for something): [IØ (*with*)] *I knew that in the end John would come through* (*with the answer to our difficulty*). *Whatever the trouble, he always comes through.*

**come through**[2] *v prep*

**1** to pass through (something): [IØ + *through* (*often simple tenses*)] *Just then the branches divided and a small head came through the leaves. The rain is coming through the roof.*

*****2** to be seen or known in (something): [T1 (*no pass., simple tenses*)] *His opinion came through all that he was saying. A feeling of sadness comes through his music.*

*****3** to continue to live after (something such as a danger): [T1 (*no pass., usu. simple tenses*)] *Bill came through his operation as cheerful as ever. All my family came through the war.* → **bring through**[2], **carry through**[2] (2), **pull through**[2] (3)

*****come through with** *v adv prep* also **come across with, come down with** → **come down** (10)
*not fml* to provide (usu. money or information) when needed: [T1 (*no pass., usu. simple tenses*)] *Good old Arthur came through with a cheque to cover the last payment.*

*****come to**[1] *v adv*

**1** to regain consciousness: [IØ] *The girl fainted, but she came to when we threw drops of water on her face.* → **bring to**[1] (1), etc.

**2** to feel friendly or happy again: [IØ] *Father was in a very bad temper this morning, but he had come to by dinner time.* → **come around** (7)

**3** (of a ship, etc.) to come nearer to the wind: [IØ (*usu. simple tenses*)] *Take the wheel, see if you can make her come to.*

**4** (of a ship, etc.) to stop moving: [IØ (*usu. simple tenses*)] *As the wind dropped, the boat came to.* → **bring to**[1] (2), **bring up** (6), **heave to**

**come to**[2] *v prep*

**1** to move near (something or someone); arrive at (a place); attend (an event): [IØ + *to*] *When did you come to London? All the children came to the teacher as soon as she called them. Please come to the concert with me on Saturday. Several trees came to the ground in last night's storm.* → **go to** (1), **take to** (1)

**2** to reach or happen to (someone): [IØ + *to*] *Fame came to him while he was still young. I don't want any harm to come to the children. At this point, the water only comes to your knees.*

*****3** to become (something); turn into: [T1 (*no pass.*)] *What is the world coming to? It is to be hoped that the quarrel between the two nations will not come to war.*

*****4** to reach (a total, condition, or time): [T1 (*no pass, simple tenses*)] *The bill comes to £5.50. When the milk comes to the boil, add the powder. This happy state of affairs must not be allowed to come to an end. The two brothers quickly came to blows during their quarrel. Those criminals will come to justice in the end. Will the children come to any harm there? The committee have not yet come to a decision. When it comes to 5 o'clock, I must turn the meat over. We should be able to come to a special arrangement with our bank.* → **get into** (11), etc.

*****5** to begin (something such as work) bringing a quality, esp. of mind: [X9 + *with*] *It's lucky that you came to your marriage with an open mind. It's no use coming to this kind of work with already formed ideas.* → **bring to**[2] (2)

*****6** to return to the memory of (someone): [*It* + T1 (*no pass., simple tenses*)] *Suddenly it came to me where I had seen her before.* [T1 (*no pass.*)] *At last the name of the book came to mind.* → **come on**[2] (5)

*****7** (of money, property, etc.) to be received by (someone) after someone's death or as a debt: [T1 (*no pass.*)] *The house came to me after my father's death. You will have some money coming to you next month.*

*****8** *infml* (of trouble, punishment, etc.) to be about to be received by (someone): [T1 (*no pass., continuous tenses*)] *You've got it coming to you. I hope he gets what's coming to him.*

*****9** to result in (something): [T1 (*no pass.*)] *I'm disappointed that my efforts have come to so little. All his plans came to nothing.*

*****10** to succeed in becoming (something): [T1 (*no pass.*)] *The boy has no character, he will never come to much.* → **amount to** (3)

*****11** to be reduced to (something or doing something humble): [T1 (*no pass., usu. simple tenses*)] *Has he come to this?* [T4 (*no pass., usu. simple tenses*)] *He came to selling matches.* → **come down to** (6), **reduce to** (12)

*****12** to concern (something): [T1 (*no pass.,*

*simple tenses*)] *When it comes to politics, I know nothing.*
*****13** to mean (something): [T1 (*no pass., simple tenses*)] *His speech comes to this; the country is deeply in debt.*
*****14** to amount to (a total): [T1 (*no pass., simple tenses*)] *The bill came to £19.* → **add up to** (1), **amount to** (1)
**15 come to someone's aid/assistance/help** to help someone: *All the villagers came to our assistance in searching for the missing child.*
**16 come to attention: a** *mil* to stand stiffly upright: *All the soldiers came to attention as the general arrived.* → **stand at** (3), etc.: **b** also **come to (someone's) knowledge/notice** to be learned by (someone): *Why hasn't this come to my attention sooner? It has come to my attention that you have been cheating.* → **bring to²** (4b)
**17 come to the boil** *not fml* to reach an urgent state: *The university's money troubles have come to the boil because of the recent government cuts.* → **bring to²** (5)
**18 if/when it comes to the crunch/push** *not fml* if/when matters become really urgent; in a time of difficulty: *If it should come to the crunch, we can always sell the house to get some money.*
**19 come to a dead end** to stop advancing: [*often simple tenses*] *Our enquiry came to a dead end when we learned that the woman had left the country.* → **be at** (8), **bring to²** (7)
**20 come to one's ears** to be heard or learned: *It came to my ears that he had lost his job.*
**21 come to one's feet** to stand, as politely or to show approval, etc.: [*often simple tenses*] *When I was at school, all the pupils had to come to their feet whenever a teacher entered the classroom. The whole crowd came to their feet to cheer the young singer.* → **get to** (11), etc.
**22 come to the fore** to become noticeable as a leader or person of influence or importance: [*no pass., often simple tenses*] *A worker with ability and character will always come to the fore.* → **bring to²** (10)
**23 come to grief** *not fml* to meet with accident or failure: *When money became scarce, the firm came to grief. I'd rather you didn't have a motorcycle, you might come to grief on the road.*
**24 come to grips with** to struggle with (something): *I have to come to grips with this difficult question.* → **bring to²** (11), **get to** (13)
**25 come to hand** to be nearby or received: *Your letter of the 16th has come to hand, and I am passing your request to the chairman. I would use a pencil if one came to hand readily.*
**26 come to a head** to reach a state where urgent decision is necessary: [*often simple tenses*] *Matters have come to a head in the peace talks; tomorrow they will either succeed or cease.* → **bring to²** (13)
**27 come to heel** *not fml* to obey, as a dog follows its master closely: [*often simple tenses*] *All those lazy workers must come to heel, or they will lose their jobs.* → **bring to²** (14)
**28 come to life** to become interesting and active: *The dull play really came to life in the performance by these young people.* → **bring to²** (17)
**29 come to light** to be discovered: *The family were so pleased when the long-lost jewels came to light.* → **bring to²** (18)
**30 come to mind** to be remembered: *Although I know it well, the name just won't come to mind.* → **bring to²** (19), **call to** (5), **come on²** (5), **recall to** (3)
**31 come to naught/nought** to fail; be useless: *All his efforts came to naught since he died before completing the job.* → **bring to²** (20)
**32 come to oneself** to regain consciousness or remember one's surrounding: [*usu. simple tenses*] *She came to herself when we threw cold water on her face. I had been lost in thought for so long that it was only when the train whistle blew that I came to myself.* → **bring to²** (15)
**33 come to pass** *fml* to happen; become real: [*often simple tenses*] *I doubt if the government's promises will ever come to pass.* → **bring to²** (21)
**34 come to such a pass/a pretty pass** *not fml* to be ruined; fall into a bad condition; be a poor state of affairs: [*often simple tenses*] *I know you two have never agreed, but how did your relationship come to such a pass? It's come to a pretty pass when people can earn more from unemployment pay than from work.* → **bring to²** (22)
**35 come to the point: a** to talk about the subject directly; make one's meaning clear: *Please come to the point, I want to know what you're trying to say.* **b** to reach a certain stage: *It has come to the point where I must speak to the boy severely. I hope it never comes to the point that we have to dismiss workers.*
**36 come to someone's/the rescue** to save someone or something: *If that woman keeps me talking, will you please come to my rescue and take me away from her on some urgent business? The government may have to come to the rescue of the mine in order to save the workers' jobs.*
**37 come to rest** to stop: [*often simple tenses*] *The car at last came to rest in a field after the driver had struggled with the controls.* → **bring to²** (23)
**38 come to the same thing** to be equal or the same: "*It all comes to the same thing at the end.*" (Robert Browning, *Any Wife to Any Husband*)
**39 come to one's senses: a** to regain consciousness: *She came to her senses when we threw cold water on her face.* **b** to behave sensibly and reasonably again: *After being in love with that worthless boy for so long, she at last came to her senses and knew he would*

*never be a good husband.* → **bring to**[2] (24)

**40 come to something** *not fml* to reach a shocking state of affairs: [*often perfect or continuous tenses*] *It's coming to something when workers can earn more from unemployment pay than from their jobs.*

**41 come to terms** to make an agreement (with someone): [*no pass.*] *The two fighting nations must come to terms (with each other).*

**42 come to terms with** to learn to accept (a difficulty, etc.): [*no pass.*] *After years in a hospital bed, you come to terms with your illness.*

**43 if it comes to that** if necessary; for that matter: [*no pass.*] *Let me drive you home, or if it comes to that, you could spend the night here.*

**44 come to this** to reach a condition, usu. bad: *Have we really come to this, that we can't speak without quarrelling? So this is what the city has come to since the developers bought all the land!*

**45 if the worst comes to the worst** if the very worst state of affairs actually happens; if things get really bad: *If the worst comes to the worst, we can always sell the house and live on that money.*

**come together** *v adv*

**1** to gather; meet: [L9 + TOGETHER] *The family must come together for the parents' silver wedding. Jim and Mary first came together during the war.* → **bring together** (2), etc.

**2** *infml* to unite in a high point of sexual activity: [L9 + TOGETHER] *The lovers came together.*

***3** to end a disagreement: [IØ] *I'm so glad that you two have decided to come together at last. The different parties in the peace talks came together last week to give a statement.* → **bring together** (3)

***come true** *v adj*

(of a wish, fear, or plan for the future) to end by being real: [IØ] *May all your dreams come true.*

**come under** *v prep*

**1** to move so as to be beneath (something): [IØ + *under*] *Come under this tree with me and we'll both keep dry.*

***2** also **be under** to be placed in a list or class with (a heading): [T1 (*no pass., simple tenses*)] *Your suggestion comes under (the general heading of) reorganization.* → **belong under, bring under** (1), **come within (1), fall into** (3), **fall under** (3), **go under**[2] (2)

***3** to be controlled by or feel the power of (something or someone): [T1 (*no pass., usu. simple tenses*)] *This area comes under the powers of the local court. In his youth he came under the influence of Beethoven.* → **be under** (3), **fall beneath** (2), **fall under** (2)

***4** to suffer; receive (something, usu. bad): [T1 (*no pass., usu. simple tenses*)] *The town came under attack again last night.*

**5 come under fire** *not fml* to be attacked with words: [*no pass., often simple tenses*] *The Minister's speech against the government came under fire from other Members of Parliament. The Minister came under fire when he opposed the government.*

**6 come under the hammer** → **GO UNDER**[2] (4)

**7 come under observation** to be watched: [*no pass., usu. simple tenses*] *The brothers came under observation as soon as they left the prison.*

**8 come under review** to be reconsidered: [*no pass., usu. simple tenses*] *Your pay comes under review every year.*

**9 come under starter's orders** (of riders in a horse race; to receive the signal to be ready to start the race: *The riders have come under starter's orders, but there may be delay before the start, as the horses are restless.* → **be under** (13)

**come unstuck** *v adj*

**1** to fail to remain stuck to something: [L7 + unstuck] *I didn't open your letter, the envelope came unstuck.*

***2** *not fml* to meet difficulties or failure: [IØ] *All his grand plans for the future of the firm came unstuck when the price of oil went up so much.*

**come up** *v adv*

**1** to rise; grow: [L9 + UP] *I like to get up early and watch the sun come up. The flowers should be coming up now it is spring.*

**2** to move to a higher level, as upstairs or above the surface of water: [IØ + UP] *Ask the doctor to come up. His head came up for the third time; it was our last chance to save him from drowning.* → **bring up** (1), **go up**[1] (1), **send up**[1] (1), **take up** (3)

***3** to pay a visit: [IØ] "*Come up and see me some time.*" (Mae West in *Diamond Lil*)

***4** to happen; arise: [IØ (*simple tenses*)] *I'll let you know if anything comes up. A chance may come up soon. A light wind came up.*

***5** to move near: [IØ] *While I was waiting for the bus, a man came up and started asking questions. I could hear footsteps coming up behind me. More soldiers are coming up soon to help in the battle.* → **bring up** (8)

***6** to be about to happen: [IØ (*continuous tenses*)] *A new type of young parent is coming up. There's a new film coming up next week. What's coming up on the television?*

***7** to appear or take place, esp. in turn: [IØ] *His case comes up next week. The furniture we want to buy is coming up next week at the auction.* → **have up** (2), etc.

***8** to be mentioned: [IØ (*often simple tenses*)] *Your question came up at the meeting. His name never comes up in our conversation these days.* → **bring up** (3), **raise with**

***9** *infml* to be chosen: [IØ] *My number will never come up.*

***10** *not fml* to win: [IØ] *Did your horse come up?*

***11** to rise in society or rank: [IØ] *He was*

*born poor, and came up the hard way. This officer came up from the lowest rank through his own ability.*

*12 to be considered more worthy: [IØ] *That politician has come up in my opinion since I heard his last speech.* → **come down** (8), **go down** (16), **go up¹** (12)

*13 to arrive: [IØ] *Did you come up just for the meeting?*

*14 to arrive at a more important place, as a capital city or university; enter the armed forces: [IØ] *When do the students come up? Do come up to London and see us. When do the next lot of young soldiers come up?* → **be up** (10), **come down** (7), **go down** (14), **go up¹** (10), **go up to** (4), **send down** (3)

*15 *not fml* to become clean or shiny: [L9] *The paintwork came up beautifully.*

*16 *infml* to pretend that one is more important than one is: [IØ (*neg. imper.*)] *Don't you try to come up, young man!* → **come it**

*17 to be brought up from the stomach; be vomited: [IØ] *Poor Jane is being sick again this morning, that light meal I gave her came up in a few minutes.* → **bring up** (4), etc.

**18 come up the hard way** to learn from experience, esp. by being poor: *Someone like Jim, who has come up the hard way, understands reality better than a person who always had money.*

**19 come up in the world** to rise to a better standard of living or social level: *Hasn't your brother come up in the world! He used to have such a humble position, and now he's advising government officials and leading society.* → **come down** (11), **go down** (19), **go up¹** (15)

**20 come up smiling** to remain cheerful in defeat: *The young man lost all his money at the horse races, but still came up smiling.*

**21 come up trumps** to surprise people by one's good qualities, as generosity: *Father came up trumps and paid for the meal after all!* → **turn up** (13)

**22 come up!** an encouragement to horses. → **gee up, get up** (14), **giddy up**

**come up against** *v adv prep* → **be up against** (1), **bring up against** (1)

to meet (something such as difficulty or opposition): [T1 (*no pass.*)] *We are sorry to be late with the goods, but we came up against some unexpected delays.*

**come up for** *v adv prep*

**1** to rise or arrive, esp. at a higher level, in order to obtain (something): [IØ + UP + *for*] *I've come up for my glasses, I left them in the drawer. This machine enables you to stay underwater longer without needing to come up for air.*

*2 to be offered on sale by (auction or sale): [IØ + *for*] *It was sad to see grandmother's lovely old things coming up for auction. The house comes up for sale next month.*

*3 to offer oneself for (election): [T1 (*no pass.*)] *One third of the committee comes up for election every year.* → **be up for** (1), **put up¹** (12)

**4 come up for air** *not fml* to take a rest: *I can't work at this kind of material for very long without coming up for air.*

**come up to** *v adv prep*

**1** to reach (something): [L9 + UP + *to* (*often simple tenses*)] *The little boy has grown; he comes up to my waist now! The path comes up to the top of the cliff. The car can come right up to the door to unload.* → **bring up to** (1)

**2** to move near to (someone): [IØ + UP + *to*] *A man came up to me and asked for a match.* → **go up to** (6)

*3 to get near to (something): [T1 (*no pass., often continuous tenses*)] *The time is coming up to 10 o'clock.*

*4 to reach; equal (something): [T1 (*no pass., usu. simple tenses*)] *Your behaviour does not come up to the expected standard. The play came up to all our expectations. As a poet, she comes up to any in this century.* → **be up to** (4), **bring up to** (4), **get up to** (4)

**5 come up to scratch** *not fml* to be as good as expected or needed: [*no pass., usu. simple tenses*] *Your work does not come up to scratch.* → **be up to** (4), **bring up to** (4), **get up to** (4)

**6 come up to someone's shoulder** *not fml* to be of equal quality with someone: *As a musician, he doesn't come up to his father's shoulder.*

***come up with** *v adv prep*

**1** to reach (someone who is ahead): [T1 (*no pass.*)] *I had to run to come up with her.* → **catch up** (4), **get up with** (2), **keep up** (7), **keep up with** (1)

**2** to come level with (someone or something): [T1 (*no pass.*)] *We shall have to work hard to come up with the other firm.* → **catch up** (5), **keep up** (8), **keep up with** (2)

**3** to think of; have an idea about (something): [T1 (*no pass., usu. simple tenses*)] *I hope you can come up with a better plan than this.*

**come upon** *v prep* → COME ON

**come within** *v prep*

*1 to be placed in a list or class with (a heading): [T1 (*no pass., simple tenses*)] *Your suggestion comes within the general heading of reorganization.* → **come under** (2), etc.

*2 to become part of (a stated limit): [T1 (*no pass.*)] *We will not buy the house unless it comes within our price range. Such behaviour has never come within my experience.* → **fall within** (2), etc.

**3 come within earshot (of)** to begin to be able to hear or be heard (by a person or from a place): *When we come within earshot of the camp, we had better lower our voices.* → **be out of** (9), **be within** (3), **get out of** (21), **get within** (3), **go out of** (7)

**4 come within range (of)** to begin to be able to be shot (by certain guns): *Don't shoot until* *the enemy come within range* (*of our guns*). → **be out of** (25), **be within** (5), **get out of** (31), **get within** (4)

**5 come within sight/view (of)** to begin to be able to be seen (by a person or from a place): *At last the little town came within sight; our journey was nearly over*. → **keep in** (16), etc.

**6 come within sight/striking distance of** *not fml* to reach very near (something such as an aim, or doing something): *Another few dollars, and we shall come within sight of the amount we need for the children's hospital. We came within striking distance of winning the contract, when our competitors beat us*. → **be within** (8), **get within** (6)

**commence as** *v prep fml* → **BEGIN AS**

**commence on** *v prep fml* → **BEGIN ON**

**commence with** *v prep fml* → **BEGIN WITH**

**commend for** *v prep* → **recommend for** (1)

*fml* to praise (someone or something) on account of (a good quality or action): [T1 + *for* (*often simple tenses*)] *The girl should be commended for her bravery in saving the drowning child. The reporters have commended Tom's book for its interesting story, but expressed dissatisfaction with the development of the characters.*

***commend to** *v prep*

**1** *fml* to trust or give the care of (something or someone) to (someone): [D1 (*often simple tenses*)] *The dying man commended his soul to God*. → **recommend to** (3)

**2** *fml* to praise (something or someone) to (someone): [D1 (*often simple tenses*)] *I can commend this book to you*. → **recommend to** (1)

**3** to give (itself) a favourable appearance to (someone): [D1 (*no pass., simple tenses*)] *His ideas do not commend themselves to me.*

**comment on/upon** *v prep*

to express one's opinion about (something or someone): [I∅ + *on/upon*] *I will now ask a leading politician to comment on the government's latest action. Would you care to comment on any troublesome students in your class?*

**commentate on** *v prep*

(esp. in broadcasting) to report on (an activity), usu. while it is taking place: [L9 + *on*] *A well-known sports broadcaster has been asked to commentate on the horse race.*

**commingle with** *v prep fml* → **MINGLE WITH** (1)

***commiserate with** *v prep* → **condole with, sympathize with**

to express sympathy for (someone): [T1 (*on*)] *The whole village commiserated with the farmer's family in their sorrow. The teacher commiserated with the student on his failure.*

**commit for** *v prep*

to send or hold (someone) for (a purpose): [X9 + *for* (*usu. pass.*)] *The prisoner was committed for trial.*

***commit on** *v prep*

**commit oneself on** to make one's opinions known about (something or someone): [T1 + *on*] *You can't change your mind now, you've already committed yourself on that question.*

***commit to** *v prep*

**1** to send; give; entrust; leave (something or someone) in the care or power of (something): [D1 (*usu. simple tenses*)] *I commit this evil book to the flames. The boy was committed to the care of his aunt. The criminals were committed to prison. The old man was committed to a hospital for mad people.* → **confide to** (1), **consign to** (2)

**2** to hold (someone or oneself) to a promise or duty to (someone, something, or doing something): [D1 (*often pass.*)] *He was a good worker who was committed to his family as well as to his work. I must go, I have committed myself to the club tonight and the members are expecting me. The doctor was committed to practical medicine. I should not like to commit myself to an opinion at this stage.* [V4b (*usu. simple tenses*)] *A thinking person must commit himself to working for peace.*

**3** to fix (something) in or on (something): [D1 (*usu. simple tenses*)] *Don't commit your promises to paper. The actor committed the part to memory.*

***commune together** *v adv*

*fml or lit* (of two or more people) to talk or think in a close relationship: [I∅] *It is pleasant for a family to commune together in their living room.*

**commune with** *v prep*

***1** *fml or lit* to talk or think in a close relationship with (someone or something): [T1] *Sometimes I like to sit by the fire and commune with my family, even in silence. At other times I walk in the woods, communing with nature.*

**2 commune with oneself/one's thoughts** *fml or lit* to think deeply; consider matters: [*no pass.*] *Very often I sit comfortably in my room, communing with my thoughts.*

**communicate about/on** *v prep*

to talk about; send effective messages to one other about (a subject): [L9 + *about/on*] *The two nations' leaders were unable to communicate on methods of limiting atomic explosions.*

**communicate to** *v prep*

to tell (news) to (someone or a group of people): [X9 + *to*] *You have a duty as a scientist to communicate your discovery to the world.*

**communicate with** *v prep*

to speak to; send a message to; be understood by (someone): [L9 + *with*] *It is always difficult to communicate with someone who speaks a foreign language. The girl claims to be able to communicate with the dead. Politicians are often unable to communicate with ordinary people.*

**commute between** *v prep*

to travel daily between (two places, as home and work): [L9 + *between*] *My father used to commute between his home in the country and his office in the city.* [X9 + *between*] *My father used to commute the ten miles between his home in the country and his office in the city.*

**commute for** *v prep*
*fml* to exchange (something such as a kind of payment) for (something else such as another kind of payment): [X9 + *for*] *Regular train travellers may commute a single monthly payment for daily tickets.*

**commute from** *v prep* → **commute into**
**1** to travel daily from (a place such as home): [L9 + *from*] *My father used to commute from his home in the country.* [X9 + *from*] *My father used to commute ten miles from his home in the country.*
**2** to reduce (a punishment) from (a severe level): [X9 + *from* (*usu. pass.*)] *The punishment was commuted from death.*

**commute into/to** *v prep* → **commute from**
**1** to travel daily to or into (a place such as a city at a distance from one's home): [L9 + *into/to*] *My father used to commute into the city.* [X9 + *into/to*] *My father used to commute ten miles to the city.*
**2** to reduce (a severe punishment) to (a less severe punishment): [X9 + *into/to* (*usu. pass.*)] *His punishment of death was commuted to life imprisonment.*

**compare to** *v prep* → **compare with, equate to, liken to**
to (cause to) be regarded as being like or equal to (something or someone, often important): [X9 + *to* (*often simple tenses*)] *The writer was compared to Shakespeare. I can compare her poetry to the greatest poems of the present century. "Shall I compare thee to a summer's day?"* (Shakespeare, *Sonnet 18*) [L9 + *to* (*simple tenses*)] *Social life in a village cannot compare to that of a large city.*

**compare with** *v prep* → **compare to, equate to, liken to**
**1** to examine (one thing, person, or group) together with (another) to find things that are the same or different: [X9 + *with*] *We can start by comparing the work of the historian with the work of the politician. It is unfair of a man to compare his wife with his mother.*
***2** to be regarded as being like or equal to (something or someone): [T1 (*no pass., simple tenses*)] *Social life in a village cannot compare with that of a large city.* [T4] *But for peace and quiet, city life can't compare with life in the country.*

**compel from** *v prep*
to obtain (something) by force from (someone): [T1 + *from*] *You cannot compel good work from unwilling students.*

**compensate for** *v prep*
**1** to pay (someone) back for (money spent or lost): [D1] *The firm must compensate you for your travelling costs. The city compensates owners for land taken from them for public building.* → **repay for** (1), etc.
**2** to provide a balance for (something wrong): [T1] *A beautiful autumn day like this compensates for the wet summer we have had. The loss of money is more than compensated for by the joy of having free time.* [T4] *Meeting you unexpectedly certainly compensates for missing the train!* [V4b] *Nothing could ever compensate me for losing my husband.* → **repay for** (2)

**compete against** *v prep* → **compete with, contend against, contend with, contest against**.
**1** to try to win something such as a prize or trade, in competition with (others); try to defeat (someone or something): [L9 + *against*] *Jim competed against the world's best runners in the Games, and did well to come third. The firm is too small to compete against large international companies.*
***2** to struggle against (something) with hope of success: [T1] *We try to make the trains run on time, but we can't compete against the weather.*

**compete for** *v prep* also *fml* **contend for**
to try to win (something such as a prize or trade) in competition with others: [L9 + *for*] *Runners from many countries are competing for the international prize. Firms from across the country may compete for the contract.*

**compete in** *v prep*
to take part in (a competition): [L9 + *in*] *Runners from many countries are competing in the Games.*

**compete with** *v prep* → **compete against, contend against, contend with, contest against**
**1** to try to win something such as a prize or trade, in competition with (others); try to defeat (someone or something): [L9 + *with*] *Jim competed with the world's best runners in the Games, and did well to come third. The firm is too small to compete with large international companies.*
***2** to struggle against (something) with hope of success: [T1 (*usu. simple tenses*)] *We try to make the trains run on time, but we can't compete with the weather.*

**complain about** *v prep* → **bitch about, complain of** (1), **gripe about, grouse about, grumble about, grumble at**
to find fault with (something or someone); express difficulty with (doing something): [IØ + *about*] *I wish to complain about the washing machine that I bought last month, it's stopped working again. Go to the teacher and complain about that boy who sits behind you. Go to the teacher and complain about needing more time to do the work. Go to the teacher and complain about that boy kicking you. You've got nothing to complain about, so be quiet.*

**complain of** *v prep*
**1** to find fault with (something or someone); express difficulty with (doing something): [IØ + *of*] *I wish to complain of your son's be-*

*haviour. Go to the teacher and complain of that boy who sits behind you. Go to the teacher and complain of needing more time to do the work. Go to the teacher and complain of that boy kicking you. You've got nothing to complain of.* → **complain about,** etc.

*2 to suffer from; state that one is suffering from (something such as a pain): [T1 (*pass. rare*)] *Jane is complaining of a headache again. Your mother tells me that she complained of continuing pain in her legs for a year, and then the pain stopped, is that right?* → **suffer from** (1)

**complain to** *v prep*

**1** to express to (someone) one's dissatisfaction with something or someone: [IØ + *to*] *You'll have to complain to Head Office if the washing machine stops working again. Complain to the boy's mother, not to me!*

**2** to make a formal report (as, to the police) (about someone or something causing annoyance): [IØ + *to* (*about*)] *If you can't stop your dog barking all night, I shall have no choice but to complain to the police (about it).*

**compliment on** *v prep* → CONGRATULATE ON (1)

**comply with** *v prep* → **abide by** (1), **conform to**

to be faithful to; obey (something): [L9 + *with*] *If you join the club, you must comply with its rules. He promised to comply fully with my requests.*

***comport with** *v prep*

*fml* to suit (something): [T1 (*no pass., often neg.*)] *His decisions do not always comport with his responsible position.*

**compose of** *v prep* → **comprise of, consist in, consist of**

**be composed of** to be made up of (something, things, or people): *A cricket team is composed of eleven players. The cake was composed of flour, butter, eggs, and sugar.*

**compound with** *v prep*

**1** to mix (something) with (something else): [X9 + *with*] *The substance was compounded with certain chemicals to make an explosive material.*

**2** *fml* to come to an agreement with (someone) about (something such as a debt or quarrel): [L9 + *with*] *The farmer compounded with the bank for a reduction in the interest rate on the money he owed.*

**compress into** *v prep*

**1** to make (something) take up less space in (a smaller form): [T1 + *into*] *This machine can compress the paper into thick cardboard.*

**2** to express (thoughts, ideas) in (fewer words): [T1 + *into*] *It is going to be very difficult to compress this mass of material into a book of ordinary length.*

**comprise of** *v prep* → **compose of, consist in, consist of**

**be comprised of** to be made up of (things or people): *A cricket team is comprised of eleven players. A storm is comprised of heavy rain and high winds.*

**compromise with** *v prep*

to make an agreement with (someone) by allowing him part of his demands: [L9 + *with* (*over*)] *Is the government prepared to compromise with the workers over their pay demand?*

**con into** *v prep* → **trick into,** etc.

*sl* to trick (someone) into (doing something), esp. by clever talk: [X9 + *into*] *The man in the train conned me into lending him some money to put into his business.*

**con out of** *v adv prep* → **cheat out of,** etc.

*sl* to cheat (someone) out of (something such as money), esp. by clever talk: [X9 + OUT + *of*] *The salesman tried to con the old lady out of her money, but she was too clever for him.*

**conceal from** *v prep* → **hide from**

to hide (something, someone, or oneself) from (someone or something): [T1 + *from*] *You cannot conceal your guilt from the police. The child tried to conceal himself from the teacher. The thieves thought that they had concealed the jewels from discovery.*

**concede to** *v prep*

to give (something) to (someone); admit that a victory or right in (something) belongs to (someone else): [T1 + *to* (*often simple tenses*)] *The former leader conceded the election to the opposing party. The defeated nation conceded some of their land to the enemy.*

***conceive as** *v prep*

*fml* to have the original idea of (something) as being (something): [X1 (*usu. pass.*)] *Local government is conceived as a single means of sending messages between the elected councillors and the citizens.*

***conceive of** *v prep*

to form the idea of (something or doing something): [T1 (*simple tenses*)] *I cannot conceive of such cruelty as to take a child away from its mother.* [T4] *It's difficult to conceive of travelling to the moon.* [V4a (*simple tenses*)] *Can you conceive of her doing such a stupid thing?*

**concentrate at** *v prep*

*mil* to (cause to) gather in force at (a certain place: [X9 + *at* (*often pass.*)] *When the enemy's ships are all concentrated at the entrance to the harbour, it must mean trouble.* [L9 + *at*] *Most of our forces have concentrated at the bridge.*

**concentrate on/upon** *v prep*

**1** to direct (something such as one's thoughts) firmly on (a subject): [X9 + *on*] *We must concentrate our efforts on finding ways to reduce costs.* → **focus on** (2), **keep on** (13)

**2** to fix one's attention on (something, someone or doing something): [L9 + *on*] *Please be quiet, I'm trying to concentrate on my work. If the teacher can organize some of the* *children into groups to work together, he will have more time to concentrate on those who need most help. Many firms are concentrating on increasing their markets overseas.* → **focus on** (3)

**concern about/over** *v prep*
to give one's attention to or worry (oneself) about (something or someone): [X9 + *about/over* (*often pass.*)] *Why are you so concerned about the boy's safety? It's a waste of time to concern yourself over other people's troubles.*

**concern in/with** *v prep*
to busy (oneself) with; take for (oneself) an interest or active part in (something): [X9 + *in/with*] *The law firm was concerned in the building contract. Don't concern yourself with matters that are not your business.*

**concern over** *v prep* → **CONCERN ABOUT**

**concern with** *v prep* → **CONCERN IN**

**conclude with** *v prep fml* → **END WITH** (1)

**concur in** *v prep* → **concur with**
*fml* to agree about (an opinion or doing something): [L9 + *in* (*usu. simple tenses*)] *All the members of the committee concurred in the chairman's decision. Did all the members of the Board concur in dividing the money in that way?*

**concur with** *v prep* → **concur in**
*fml* to agree with (someone or something): [L9 + *with* (*usu. simple tenses*)] *All the members of the committee concurred with the chairman when he made his decision.*

**condemn as** *v prep*
to declare that (something) is (something bad): [X9 + *as* (*often pass.*)] *The house was condemned as unfit for people to live in.* [T1 + *as*] *Most people are willing to condemn violence of any sort as evil.*

**condemn for** *v prep*
to have a poor opinion of (someone or something) because of (something bad): [X9 + *for* (*often simple tenses*)] *The whole town condemned the girl for her wild behaviour. The city was condemned for its high crime rate.*

***condemn to** *v prep*
**1** to punish (someone) with (something): [X9 + *to* (*often pass.*)] *In former times a murderer who was found guilty would be condemned to death.*
**2** to force (someone) into (an unfortunate state or position): [X9 + *to*] *His bad leg condemns him to a wheelchair.*

***condescend to** *v prep*
**1** to treat (someone) as if he was lower or less important: [T1] *A teacher should never make the mistake of condescending to children.*
**2** to lower oneself to (wrong behaviour): [T1 (*no pass.*)] *I'm surprised at you, condescending to such tricks!* [T4] *I never thought he would condescend to cheating.* → **descend to** (3), etc.

***condition to** *v prep*
to make (someone) used to (something, often difficult): [D1 (*often pass.*)] *A child born in the far north is soon conditioned to the long cold dark winters.*

***condole with** *v prep* → **commiserate with, sympathize with**
*fml* to sympathize with (someone), esp. in grief: [T1 (*on, over*)] *The priest visited the family to condole with them on the loss of their son.*

***conduce to/towards** *v prep* → **contribute to** (2)
*fml* to lead towards; help to cause (something): [T1 (*no pass., simple tenses*)] *Fresh air and exercise conduce to good health.*

**conduct away/out** *v adv*
to lead (someone), often by force, away from a group; make (someone) leave a meeting, etc.: [X9 + AWAY (*from*)/OUT (*of*)] *Any person who refuses to keep silent will be conducted out of the room.*

***cone off** *v adv*
esp. *BrE* to mark (part of a road) with cones, to prevent its use by traffic: [T1 (*usu. pass.*)] *Part of the main road was coned off after the accident.*

**confederate with** *v prep*
*fml* to (cause to) unite with (another nation or part of a nation) in a political sense: [L9 + *with*] *The small state decided to confederate with the island kingdom in order to form a more powerful nation together.* [X9 + *with*] *The government decided to confederate the small state with the island kingdom so that they would form a more powerful nation together.*

**confer on/upon** *v prep*
**1** *fml* to talk together, esp. to try to reach agreement (about a matter): [IØ + *on*] *The ministers are still conferring on the question of labour relations.*
***2** *fml* to give (an honour) to (someone) formally: [D1 (*usu. simple tenses*)] *The Queen conferred a title on the brave sailor.*

**confer with** *v prep*
*fml* to consider something at length with (someone): [L9 + *with*] *The prisoner asked permission to confer with his lawyer.*

**confess to** *v prep*
**1** *tech* to tell one's guilt to (a priest or God): [IØ + *to*] *Many Christians regularly confess to a priest.* [T1 + *to*] *Many Christians regularly confess their guilty actions and thoughts to a priest.*
**2** to admit (something such as guilt or an opinion): [T1 (*often simple tenses*)] *The prisoner confessed to his part in the crime. I have to confess to a hatred of modern music.* [T4 (*often simple tenses*)] *The prisoner confessed to stealing the jewels. I have to confess to hating modern music.* → **admit to** (3)

***confide in** *v prep* → **take into** (6)
to trust (someone) with a secret: [T1] *You*

*can confide in me, my dear, your affairs will be kept private.*

* **confide to** *v prep*

**1** to give (something or someone) into the care of (someone or something): [D1 (*often pass.*)] *You had better confide your jewels to the bank in future. The boy was confided to the care of his aunt.* → **commit to** (1), **consign to** (2)

**2** to entrust (something secret) to (someone) by telling it: [D1 (*often simple tenses*)] *She confided her secret to her best friend. The firm's plans were confided only to the chairman and the directors.*

**confine to** *v prep*

to limit (something, someone, or oneself) to (something such as a place or subject): [X9 + *to*] *Confine your remarks to the subject of the meeting. Mother was confined to bed with her bad leg.*

**confine within** *v prep*

to limit (someone or something) within (something such as an area): [X9 + *within*] *Doctors are trying to confine the disease within the city. I have been confined within these four walls for a week.*

**confirm in** *v prep*

**1** to make (someone) sure of belonging to (something); declare the firm position of (someone) in (something): [T1 + *in* (*usu. pass.*)] *The director was confirmed in his position as chairman. Twenty boys and girls were confirmed in the Christian Church.*

***2** to strengthen (someone) in (something such as a belief or habit): [D1 (*usu. simple tenses*)] *Your behaviour has only confirmed me in my opinion of you.*

**confiscate from** *v prep*

to seize and keep (something) by law or other power from (someone): [T1 + *from*] *The state used to confiscate land from those who opposed the king. The teacher had to confiscate a dangerous weapon from the child.*

**conflict with** *v prep*

**1** to take place at the same time as (something else): [L9 + *with*] *Make sure that your garden party doesn't conflict with the Minister's speech, or you'll lose your crowd. I was unable to study music at school because it conflicted with history.* → **clash with** (2), **coincide with**

**2** to disagree violently with; be opposite to (something): [L9 + *with* (*simple tenses*)] *My opinions conflict with yours. The chairman's opinion conflicted with that of the rest of the committee. Doesn't the prisoner's story conflict with the known facts?* → **clash against** (3), **clash with** (3), **collide with** (2), **jar with** (2), **run counter to**

**conform to/with** *v prep* → **abide by** (1), **comply with**

to (cause to) agree or be in accordance with (something): [L9 + *to/with*] *The boy's behaviour conforms to the expected pattern.* [X9 + *to/with*] *We have to conform our ideas to those of the society in which we live.*

**confront with** *v prep*

**1** to face (someone or something) with (a quality such as courage): [T1 + *with*] *The writer confronted his pile of work with determination. Fearless hunters confront wild animals with bravery.*

**2** to make (someone) face (something, usu. bad): [T1 + *with*] *The police confronted the prisoner with proof of his crime.*

**confuse about** *v prep*

**be confused about** to be not clear in one's mind about (something): *Many people are confused about the new ways of measuring temperature.*

**confuse with** *v prep*

**1** to make (someone) not clear in the mind by giving him (something): [T1 + *with*] *The teacher confused the student with too many questions. My mind is made up; don't confuse me with facts.*

***2** to mistake (someone or something) for (someone or something else): [D1] *It's impossible to confuse Mary with her sister, they're not at all alike.* → **mistake for, take for** (3)

**congratulate on/upon** *v prep*

**1** to express one's pleasure to (someone) about (something or doing something good): [X9 + *on/upon*] *The whole family congratulated Jim on his new appointment. The whole family congratulated Jim on getting the job.* also **compliment on,** *fml* **felicitate on**

***2** to feel pleased with (oneself) about (something): [D1] *We can congratulate ourselves on our good luck in finding the right house so quickly.*

**conjure away** *v adv*

to make (something) disappear as if by magic: [X9 + AWAY] *A walk in the fresh air soon conjured her headache away.*

* **conjure up** *v adv*

**1** to cause (something or someone) to appear by or as if by magic: [T1a (*usu. simple tenses*)] *Jim's sister conjured up a meal in minutes.*

**2** to bring (something) to mind: [T1a (*simple tenses*)] *This music conjures up a picture of flowing water.* —**conjured-up** *adj*

* **conjure with** *v prep*

**1** to perform stage tricks as if by magic using (something or someone) to help: [IØ + *with*] *She's been conjuring with rabbits for several years now. I can only conjure with the aid of my young brother.*

***2** **a name to conjure with** a powerful and influential name, one that commands respect

* **conk out** *v adv*

**1** *infml* (of machinery) to fail to work; stop working: [IØ] *The car conked out on the way to work, and I had to telephone for a repair vehicle.* —**conked-out** *adj* → **break down** (3), **cut out** (8), **give out** (6), **kick off** (6), **pack up** (3)

**2** *infml* to become very tired; fall asleep or

become unconscious: [IØ] *The climbers were halfway up the mountain when two of them conked out and had to turn back.*
**3** *infml* to die: [IØ (*simple tenses*)] *I'm afraid old Charlie has conked out.* → **pass away** (3), etc.

**connect to** *v prep*
**1** to join (something) to (something else): [T1 + *to*] *Is the house connected (up) to the electricity supply?*
**2** to join (usu. someone) to (someone else) by telephone: [T1 + *to*] *Would you try that call again, please, I've been connected to the wrong person.*

**connect up** *v adv*
to join (two or more things) together; join (something) to a supply: [T1 + UP (*to*)] *First you connect up the two wires. Is your telephone connected up yet?*

**connect with** *v prep*
**1** to see a relationship between (something or someone) and (something or someone else): [X9 + *with* (*simple tenses*)] *Small children do not connect thunder with lightning. The police did not connect her with the crime.*
**2** to (cause to) join (something): [L9 + *with* (*simple tenses*)] *This river connects (directly) with the sea.* [X9 + *with* (*often pass., simple tenses*)] *The hotel is connected with the station by a covered walkway.*
**3** to enable (someone) to speak on the telephone with (someone or a place): [X9 + *with*] *Can you connect me with London, please?*
**4** (of a train, plane, etc.) to arrive at a suitable time for people to travel further by (another train, plane, etc.): [L9 + *with* (*simple tenses, often present*)] *This train connects with the one leaving for London half an hour later.*
**5 be connected with** to be related to (a family) or work for (a business, firm, etc.); have something to do with (something): *Her family is connected with the King-Browns. Our chief salesman has been connected with the shoe trade for twenty years. The less severe winters are connected with the presence of a large body of water, which cools slower than land.*

***connive at** *v prep* → **wink at** (2)
to pretend not to know about (something wrong) in order to allow it to take place; give one's silent approval to (something wrong), perhaps giving some help: [T1 (*often simple tenses*)] *The thieves paid the servants to connive at the robbery. "Then do you connive at her escape."* (R.B. Sheridan, *The Rivals*) [T4] *Who connived at letting the prisoner escape?* [V4a] *How many of you connived at the prisoner escaping?*

***connive with** *v prep* → **conspire with, intrigue with** (1), **plot with**
to plan secretly with (someone) to do something wrong: [T1 (*usu. simple tenses*)] *The thieves connived with the servants in the big house to steal the jewels.*

**conscript into** *v prep*
to force (someone) by law to join (the armed forces): [X9 + *into*] *In the last war, all healthy young men were conscripted into the army, navy, or air force.*

**consecrate to** *v prep*
**1** to declare (usu. something) as being holy to (God): [X9 + *to* (*often simple tenses*)] *The priest consecrated the church to God.* → **dedicate to** (1)
***2** to give (something) completely to (someone, something, or doing something): [D1 (*often simple tenses*)] *The doctor consecrated his life to the sick people in the hot country. The doctor consecrated his life to the service of mankind.* [V4b (*often simple tenses*)] *The doctor consecrated his life to curing the sick.* → **dedicate to** (2), **devote to** (2)

**consent to** *v prep* → **agree to,** etc.
to give one's permission, when requested, for (something): [L9 + *to*] *Will your father consent to the marriage? Mary's father unwillingly consented to her marrying Jim.*

**consider as** *v prep*
to regard (someone or something) as (being or doing something): [X9 + *as* (*simple tenses*)] *I considered him as a fool. I considered him as foolish. I considered him as belonging to a group of misguided thinkers.*

**consign to** *v prep*
**1** to send (something) to (a place): [T1 + *to* (*often pass.*)] *The shipment of apples was consigned to London.*
***2** *fml* to send; give; entrust; leave (something or someone) in the care or power of (something or someone): [D1 (*simple tenses*)] *I consign this evil book to the flames. His family consigned his body to the grave. The boy was consigned to the care of his aunt. She tried to make sure that her terrible experience was consigned to forgetfulness.* → **commit to** (1), **confide to** (1)

***consist in** *v prep* → **compose of, comprise of, consist of, inhere in, subsist in**
*fml* to be found in (something); have (something) as its main part: [T1 (*no pass., simple tenses*)] *The beauty of this picture consists in its balance of colours.* [T4 (*simple tenses*)] *Education does not consist in forcing students to learn lists of uninteresting facts. "Love consists in this, that two solitudes protect and touch and greet each other."* (Rainer Maria Rilke)

***consist of** *v prep* → **compose of, comprise of, consist in, inhere in, subsist in**
to be made up of (something or someone): [T1 (*no pass., simple tenses*)] *A cricket team consists of eleven players. The cake consisted of flour, butter, eggs and sugar.*

***consist with** *v prep* → **consort with** (2)
*fml* to suit; match; be equal to or the same as (something): [T1 (*no pass., simple tenses*)] *The politician's actions do not consist with the*

*promises in his speeches.*

***console with** *v prep*
to give (oneself) the comfort of (something such as knowledge): [D1] *At least we can console ourselves with the fact that even this winter cannot last for ever.*

***consort with** *v prep*
**1** *fml* to have a relationship with; be seen in public with (someone): [T1 (*no pass.*)] *No son of mine shall consort with common criminals.*
**2** *fml* to suit; match; be equal to or the same as (something): [T1 (*no pass., simple tenses*)] *The politician's actions do not consort with the promises in his speeches.* → **consist with**

**conspire against** *v prep* → **intrigue against, plot against**
to make a secret plan with others to take action against (usu. someone or the state): [L9 + *against*] *The men who tried to destroy Parliament with explosives were punished with death for conspiring against the King. The government speaker said that trade union leaders were conspiring against the good of the country.*

**conspire with** *v prep* → **connive with, intrigue with** (1), **plot with**
to make a secret plan with (other people), usu. to do something wrong: [L9 + *with*] *The thieves conspired with the servants to steal the jewels.*

**constrain from** *v prep*
*fml* to prevent (someone) by force or law from (something or doing something): [X9 + *from*] *The police used horses to constrain the crowd from violence. The police used horses to constrain the crowd from breaking the shop windows.*

**construct from** *v prep*
to make (something) from (something already existing): [T1 + *from*] *The hut was constructed from trees that grew in the nearby forest. The writer constructed the story from memories of her childhood.*

**construct of/out of** *v prep; adv prep*
to make (something) from (original material): [T1 + *of*/OUT + *of*] *The hut was constructed (out) of wood.*

***construe as** *v prep*
*fml* to understand (something) as being (something): [D1 (*often pass.*)] *His action was construed as a threat. I shall construe your remark as offensive. Any mention of this part of the agreement shall be construed as including a mention of the following parts.*

**construe with** *v prep* → **collocate with**
to use a word together with (a certain grammatical form): [X9 + *with* (*usu. pass.*)] *The word "without" can be construed with a noun or a participle, as in "He left without a word" or "He left without saying goodbye."*

**consult about** *v prep*
to ask the advice of (someone) about (something or someone): [T1 + *about*] *We consult a doctor about our health, and a banker about our money. Parents can consult the teachers about their children.*

***consult with** *v prep*
**1** esp., *AmE* to ask the advice of (someone): [T1 (*pass. rare*)] *I intend to consult with my tax lawyer before sending in my tax return.*
**2** *fml* to have a formal meeting with (someone) in order to reach a decision: [T1 (*no pass.*)] *The Queen consults with her advisers before making a speech to Parliament.* → **advise with**

**consume away** *v adv*
to waste (something): [X9 + AWAY] *The fire had consumed half the forest away before it was stopped.*

**consume with** *v prep*
**be consumed with** to be overcome by (a very strong feeling): *When he read the letters, he was consumed with jealousy. Shirley was consumed with love for John during their days at university.*

**contain for** *v prep*
to control (oneself) because of (a good feeling such as joy): [T1 + *for* (*often neg., usu.* + *can*)] *She could scarcely contain herself for delight when she opened the parcel.*

**contend about/over** *v prep*
*fml* to quarrel about (usu. something) which both parties wish to possess: [L9 + *about*/*over*] *The two nations have been contending about the rights to deep-sea fishing in their waters. The fairy king and queen were contending over possession of the beautiful boy. When a marriage ends, the former husband and wife often contend over the children.*

**contend against** *v prep* → **compete against, compete with, contend with, contest against**
**1** *fml* to try to win something such as a prize or trade, in competition with (someone or something): [L9 + *against*] *Jim had to contend against the world's best runners in the Games, and did well to come third. The firm is too small to contend against large international companies.*
***2** to struggle against (something) with hope of success: [T1 (*usu. simple tenses*)] *We try to make the trains run on time, but we can't contend against the weather.*

**contend for** *v prep fml* → COMPETE FOR

**contend over** *v prep* → CONTEND ABOUT

**contend with** *v prep* → **compete against, compete with, contend against, contest against**
**1** *fml* to compete with (someone): [L9 + *with*] *Jim had to contend with the world's best runners in the Games, and did well to come third. The firm is too small to contend with large international companies.*
***2** to struggle against (something); suffer from dealing with (something): [T1 (*usu. simple tenses*)] *It's difficult enough trying to make the trains run on time without having to contend with bad weather. Many students leave the university because there are too many difficulties*

*to contend with.* → **bear with** (2), **put up with** (3), **stand for** (5)

**content with** *v prep*
to satisfy (oneself) with (something less than one had hoped): [X9 + *with*] *There was no fresh meat in the market today, so you'll have to content yourselves with something out of a tin. It was too wet to go outside, so the children had to be contented with playing indoors.*

**contest against/with** *v prep* → **compete against, compete with, contend against, contend with**
**1** to compete against (others): [L9 + *against/with*] *Jim had to contest against the world's best runners in the Games, and did well to come third. The firm is too small to contest with large international companies.*
*__2__ to struggle against (something) with hope of success: [T1 (*usu. simple tenses*)] *We try to make the trains run on time, but we can't contest with bad weather.*

**continue with** *v prep* → **carry on** (4), etc.
to go on or advance with (something): [IØ + *with*] *Is it worth continuing with our holiday plans when we don't know where we shall be living afterwards?*

**contract for** *v prep*
*fml* to offer one's price for making or supplying (something): [L9 + *for*] *The builders have contracted for three new bridges this year.*

***contract in** *v adv*
to promise officially to take part (in an activity): [IØ (*to*)] *How many of the companies have contracted in so far?*

***contract out** *v adv*
**1** to give (a job) by contract: [T1a] *The city council has already contracted out the work on the new road.*
**2** esp. *BrE* to refuse to join (in an agreement, etc.): [IØ (*of*)] *Workers are permitted to contract out of the latest old-age insurance plan.*

**contract with** *v prep*
**1** *fml* to make (an arrangement) or form (a relationship) with (someone): [X9 + *with*] *The woman claims that she contracted a form of marriage with the prisoner, who already has a wife.*
**2** to make an agreement in law with (someone or a firm): [L9 + *with* (*for*)] *The city council has contracted with White and Company for the new road.*

***contrast with** *v prep*
**1** to compare (something or someone) with (something or someone completely different or opposite): [D1 (*usu. simple tenses*)] *We can contrast this story, set in a large modern city, with this other one that tells of life on a lonely farm.*
**2** to be completely different or opposite to (something or someone else): [T1 (*no pass., simple tenses*)] *The yellow curtains contrast with the blue bedcover. The poet's rough life contrasts with his sensitive poetry. His stated principles contrast with his behaviour.*

**contribute to/towards** *v prep*
**1** to give (something such as money or time) to (something): [L9 + *to*] *Please contribute to this collection of money for homeless families.* [X9 + *to*] *The firm contributed £10,000 to the collection. All the children contributed their free time to the concert. Each prisoner is expected to contribute half an hour a day to sweeping the paths.*
**2** to supply (written material) to (a book, magazine, etc.): [L9 + *to*] *It is an honour to be invited to contribute to your magazine.* [X9 + *to*] *I've been asked to contribute an article to the language magazine.*
*__3__ to help to cause; be partly responsible for (something): [T1 (*no pass., simple tenses*)] *Fresh air and exercise contribute to good health. Public opinion can contribute to government decisions.* → **conduce to**

**convalesce from** *v prep*
to finish regaining one's health after (an illness, accident, etc.): [L9 + *from*] *Mother enjoyed convalescing from her operation in the small hospital by the sea.*

***converge on** *v prep*
to gather and move towards (something or someone) from different directions: [T1] *Angry crowds converged on the speaker. People converged on the political meeting from all parts of the city.*

***converse about/on** *v prep*
to have a conversation about (a subject): [IØ + *about*] *Old men were sitting in the park, conversing about the weather.*

**converse with** *v prep*
to have a conversation with (someone): [IØ + *with*] *I wasted half an hour this morning conversing with my neighbour in the garden.*

**convert from** *v prep* → **convert to**
**1** to (cause to) change one's religion from (a former religion): [T1 + *from*] *Priests converted many people from the worship of the spirits of trees and rivers.*
**2** to (cause to) change from (something else): [X9 + *from*] *Britain converted her money from the old system to a decimal one.* [L9 + *from*] *Many difficulties were caused by converting from the old money system.*

**convert into** *v prep* → **change into** (2), etc.
to change (something) into (something else): [X9 + *into*] *A poet is one who can convert ordinary words into a meaningful and effective piece of writing. How much does it cost today to convert pounds into dollars? If two chemicals are put together and heated, they can be converted into a completely different substance.* [L9 + *to*] *This seat converts into a bed.*

**convert to** *v prep* → **convert from**
**1** to (cause to) change one's religion to (another religion): [T1 + *to*] *Priests converted many people to Christianity.* [IØ + *to*] *Many people willingly converted to Christianity.*

**2** to (cause to) change to (something else) or to use (something else): [X9 + *to*] *Coal can be converted to gas by burning. We have converted our house to North Sea gas. Britain converted her money to a decimal system.* [L9 + *to*] *People as they grow older often convert to new ways of thinking. Does electricity convert easily to other forms of power? Difficulties were caused when Britain converted to a decimal money system.*

**convey to** *v prep*

**1** to send or carry (something or someone) to (a place): [X9 + *to*] *This train conveys passengers to London. The firm conveys goods to all parts of the country.*

***2** to make (something) known to (someone): [D1] *How can I convey these ideas to the children?*

***3** *law* to pass possession to (property such as a house) to (the new owner): [D1] *The house will not be conveyed to you until after the agreement has been signed.*

**convict of** *v prep*

**1** to declare (someone) to be guilty of (a crime): [T1 + *of* (*usu. pass.*)] *The prisoner was convicted of robbery. The prisoner was convicted of stealing the jewels.*

***2** *fml* to persuade (someone) to believe the truth of (something he has done wrong): [D1 (*usu. simple tenses*)] *It was difficult to convict him of the falsity of his beliefs.* [V4a (*usu. simple tenses*)] *At last the chairman was convicted of having made a wrong decision.* → **convince of**

**convince of** *v prep* → **convict of** (2)

to persuade (someone) to believe the truth of (something): [X9 + *of* (*usu. simple tenses*)] *We were able to convince the students of the need for wider reading. Were you able to convince the government of the reality of the danger?*

***convulse with** *v prep*

to make (someone) shake helplessly with (usu. a feeling): [D1 (*usu. pass.*)] *Mary was convulsed with laughter, as she found the man's jokes so funny.*

***cook out** *v adv*

*AmE not fml* to cook food out of doors: [IØ] *We're cooking out tonight, it's too hot indoors.* —**cook-out** *n*

**cook up** *v adv*

**1** to cook (food) quickly: [X9 + UP] *Can you cook up a simple egg dish for us right away?*

***2** *infml* to invent; think of (usu. something wrong): [T1] *Some of the younger workers cooked up a plan for cheating the firm. If the police catch us, shall we be able to cook up a story? You children will cook up any excuse not to do your work.* —**cooked-up** *adj*

**cool down** *v adv*

**1** to (cause to) become less hot: [X9 + DOWN] *A rest in the shade will cool you down.* [L9 + DOWN] *We had to stop at the top of the hill and wait for the engine to cool down.* → **cool off**[1] (1)

***2** (of an excited person or a violent feeling) to (cause to) become calmer or less excited: [IØ] *Don't try to argue with your father till he's cooled down.* [T1] *A small payment now will cool his anger down.* → **cool off**[1] (2), **simmer down** (2)

***3** to become less attracted to someone or an idea: [IØ] *He used to say he loved me, but recently he seems to have cooled down. I liked your offer at first but now I have cooled down.* → **cool off**[1] (3)

**cool off**[1] *v adv*

**1** to (cause to) become less hot: [X9 + OFF] *A rest in the shade will cool you off.* [L9 + OFF] *We had to stop at the top of the hill and wait for the engine to cool off.* → **cool down** (1)

***2** (of an excited person or a violent feeling) to (cause to) become calmer or less excited: [IØ] *She didn't cool off for hours after that argument.* [T1] *I tried to cool her off but she was still very angry when she left.* → **cool down** (2), **simmer down** (2)

***3** to become less attracted to someone or an idea: [IØ] *He used to say he loved me, but recently he seems to have cooled off. I liked your offer at first, but now I have cooled off.* —**cooling-off** *adj* → **cool off**[2] (3)

***4** to (cause to) become less keen: [IØ] *He used to be our keenest player, but he's cooled off since he lost so many games.* [T1] *His recent run of bad luck has cooled him off.*

***cool off**[2] *v prep*

to become less attracted to (someone or an idea): [T1 (*no pass.*)] *He used to say he loved me, but recently he seems to have cooled off me. I liked your offer at first, but now I have cooled off it.*

***cool out** *v adv*

*AmE not fml* to discourage (a business opponent) by competition and other means: [T1] *Do you think you'll be able to cool the other firm out?* —**cooling-out** *adj*

***coop up** *v adv* also *AmE not fml* **coop in**

*not fml* to enclose; limit the freedom of (someone or an animal): [T1 (*usu. pass.*)] *All last week we were cooped up in the house by bad weather. Kept at home with a bad cold, I began to feel cooped up. It's unkind to coop the dog up all day.*

**cooperate on** *v prep* → **cooperate with** (1)

to be helpful with (something such as a plan): [L9 + *on*] *I should like you to cooperate on the writing of my next book.*

**cooperate with** *v prep*

**1** to be helpful with (something such as a plan): [L9 + *with*] *I should like you to cooperate with the writing of my next book.* → **cooperate on**

**2** to be helpful towards (someone): [L9 + *with*] *All citizens are asked to cooperate with the council in keeping crime off the streets.*

**coopt onto** *v prep*
to give (an additional person) a place on (usu. a committee): [X9 + *onto*] *Since the lawyer has offered his help without payment, can we coopt him onto the committee?*

**coordinate with** *v prep*
to make (something) match (something else), often in time: [X9 + *with*] *The sound has to be coordinated with the picture.*

**cop from** *v prep* → **cadge from**
*AmE infml* to beg (something) from (someone): [T1 + *from*] *Can I cop a cigarette from you?*

**cop out** *v adv*
**1** *AmE infml* to admit one's guilt to the police: [IØ] *The younger of the thieves copped out and so they were all caught.*
**2** *infml often derog.* to avoid one's responsibilities (to someone or something) often by leaving or refusing to keep a promise, etc.: [IØ (*of*)] *He said he would help us and then he copped out. You can't cop out of your responsibility to your children. You can't cop out of raising your children.* —**cop-out** *n* → **opt in' opt out**

**cope with** *v prep*
*not fml* to find a way to deal with (something or someone, often troublesome or difficult): [L9 + *with*] *I can't cope with such a pile of work this weekend. How is Mary coping with Jim's mother? I don't know how she copes with looking after her family and doing a full-time job.*

**copulate with** *v prep*
*fml* to have sex with (someone): [L9 + *with*] *Boys are not allowed to copulate with girls under sixteen.*

**copy down** *v adv*
to copy (something) from something, as a notice on a wall: [X9 + DOWN] *While you're in the hall, copy down the dates of the concert practices.*

**copy out** *v adv*
to copy (something) carefully or in full, usu. at a desk: [X9 + OUT] *Copy out the article in your best handwriting, including all the corrections I have made.*

**cordon off** *v adv*
to close (something such as an area or street), by means of a line of men on guard, a fence, etc.: [T1] *The police have cordoned off the area where the gunman was last seen.*

**cork up** *v adv*
**1** to fasten (something such as a bottle) with a cork: [X9 + UP] *Help me to cork up this bottle, it's so tight.*
*__2__ *infml* → **BOTTLE UP** (2)

**correlate with** *v prep*
*fml* to (cause to) be like or close to (something else): [L9 + *with* (*simple tenses*)] *His story does not correlate with the facts.* [X9 + *with* (*usu. simple tenses*)] *The committee found it impossible to correlate the facts supplied by the directors with their knowledge of the firm. Anyone in the production market tries to correlate demand with supply.*

**correspond about** *v prep*
(of two people) to write letters to each other about (a subject): [L9 + *about*] *The governor wishes to know what you and the prisoner have been corresponding about.*

***correspond to** *v prep* → **agree with** (3), **answer to** (3), **correspond with** (2), **disagree with, tally with**
to match; be nearly equal to; fulfil the same purpose as (someone or something): [T1 (*no pass., simple tenses*)] *Find a word in your own language which corresponds to 'beautiful.' The working of this machine corresponds to that of the human brain. In our firm, the director corresponds to the general of an army. The prisoner's appearance corresponds to the description of the wanted criminal.*

**correspond with** *v prep*
**1** to write letters to and receive letters from (someone): [L9 + *with*] *Are you still corresponding with your former boyfriend?*
*__2__ to match (usu. something): [T1 (*no pass., simple tenses*)] *Her photograph corresponds with the description that he gave us.* → **correspond to**, etc.

**cosher up** *v adv* → **cocker up**
esp. *AmE* to treat (someone) with too much kindness, care, etc.: [X9 + UP] *Cosher up your child, and you will come to fear him.*

**cost out** *v adv*
esp. *AmE* (in business) to guess the cost of fulfilling a contract: [X9 + OUT] *We shall have to bring in professional advisers to help us to cost out this job.*

**cosy up to** *v adv prep* → **cozy up to**

***cotton on** *v adv*
*infml* to understand (something): [IØ (*to*) (*often simple tenses*)] *He had been speaking for half an hour before I cottoned on. Did you cotton on to what the politician was saying?*

***cotton to** *v prep*
esp. *AmE infml* to be attracted to; like (someone or an idea) at once: [T1 (*no pass., usu. simple tenses*)] *The children cottoned to each other as soon as they met. The chairman didn't cotton to your suggestion; you'd better try your idea elsewhere.*

***cotton up to** *v adv prep* → **cozy up to**
esp. *AmE infml* to try to start a friendship with (someone): [T1 (*pass. rare*)] *I saw you cottoning up to the new student; was he friendly?*

***couch in** *v prep*
to express (something) in (a form of words): [D1 (*usu. simple tenses*)] *Kindly couch your request in more polite words. The government's refusal was couched in unfriendly language.*

***cough down** *v adv*
to drown the sound of (someone speaking)

with coughing: [T1] *The speaker was coughed down by the unfriendly crowd of students.*

**cough off** *v adv*

**cough one's head off** to cough and continue coughing violently: *Jane has been coughing her head off all morning, perhaps we should send for the doctor.*

**cough out** *v adv*

**1** to send (something) out of the mouth by coughing: [X9 + OUT] *Mother made the jelly with salt instead of sugar, so the children coughed it out.* → **cough up** (1), **spit up** (1)

*__2__ *infml* to tell (something) unwillingly or with difficulty, often after persuasion: [T1] *The police may be able to make him cough out his story.* → **cough up** (2), **pay up, stump up**

**cough up** *v adv*

**1** to send (something) out of the throat by coughing: [X9 + UP] *Jane has just coughed up a fishbone.* → **cough out** (1), **spit up** (1)

*__2__ *infml* to produce (something such as money or information) unwillingly: [T1] *See if you can make the prisoner cough up the names of his companions. Will Father cough up the money we need for the new car?* [IØ] *I suppose I shall have to cough up as usual!* → **cough out** (2), **pay up, stump up**

*__3__ *infml* to admit one's guilt: [IØ (*usu. simple tenses*)] *After hours of questioning, the prisoner coughed up and admitted that he had stolen the jewels.* [T1 (*usu. simple tenses*)] *Come on, cough it up, we know you're guilty.*

**count against** *v prep* → **hold against,** etc.

to be recorded as unfavourable to (someone): [L9 + *against* (*simple tenses*)] *You will find that your prison record counts against you when you are trying to get a job.*

*__count among__ *v prep* → **reckon among**

to regard (something or someone) as belonging to (a group): [D1 (*simple tenses*)] *I am proud to count you among my friends. Her poetry is counted among the best-known this century.*

*__count as__ *v prep* → **reckon as, regard as**

to regard (something or someone) as being (something): [L1 (*simple tenses*)] *In cricket, a no ball counts as one run.* [L4 (*simple tenses*)] *Any unemployed person counts as deserving government help.* [L7 (*simple tenses*)] *A person's birth in a country which was formerly part of the British Empire counts as equal to British citizenship.* [X1 (*simple tenses*)] *The city council counts its library as an important part of public service.* [X4 (*simple tenses*)] *A member of the tennis club is counted as belonging to the whole sports club.* [X7 (*simple tenses*)] *Any member of the committee is counted as fit to take the chairmanship.*

*__count down__ *v adv*

to count backwards in seconds to zero, esp. before sending a space vehicle into the sky: [IØ] *The people at Control have already begun to count down.* [T1] *The spaceship is already being counted down.* —**count-down** *n*

*__count for__ v prep → **go for** (16)

to be worth (usu. much, little, or nothing) [L9 + *for* (*simple tenses usu. present*)] *Mone counts for too much in our society. His past suc cesses count for nothing. Attending regularly an taking an active part in class argument counts fo 20% of your mark for the year.*

**count from** *v prep* → **count to** (1), **reckon to**

to start telling the number (of things or peo ple) beginning at (a given point such as number): [L9 + *from*] *I'll count from page 3 if you've counted up to there.* [X9 + *from No, count the pages from number 1.*

*__count in__ *v adv*

**1** to count (people or things) as part of group: [T1] *When the city declares its popula tion numbers, does it count in farmers in oute areas? My job at the beginning of the year wa to count the students in. Have you counted i the members who were absent?* → **count out** (2) **reckon in**

**2** *infml* to include (usu. someone) by choice [T1b (*simple tenses*)] *If you're having a party count me in. I'm trying to make a list of peopl who support the students' demands; can count you in?* → **count out** (4)

**count off** *v adv* → **count out** (3)

*AmE* to count (things or people), esp. to se if the number is the same as expected: [X9 OFF] *At the beginning of each class, I count o the students to see if the number present agre with the attendance lists. Count off the playin cards to see if you have a full set.*

*__count on/upon__ *v prep* → **depend on** (1), etc.

to depend on; trust in (someone, somethin or doing something): [T1] *You can alwa count on Jim, he'll never fail you. I'd like t come with you but that's not a promise, don count on it.* [T4] *Don't count on going abroa this summer, we may not have enough mone* [V3] *Don't count on your relatives to he you out of trouble.* [V4a] *Don't count on th weather being fine for your garden party.*

**count out** *v adv*

**1** to count aloud: [IØ + OUT] *The little gi could only remember her numbers by countin out.*

**2** to count (usu. people) as they leave: [X + OUT] *The secretary counted the members o as they passed his desk.* → **count in** (1), **reck in**

*__3__ to count (things or people) one by one unt none are left, to find how many there ar [T1a] *The king was in his counting hous counting out his money. It's difficult to put price on insuring the books until you ha counted them out.* → **count off**

*__4__ *infml* to not include (usu. someone) b choice: [T1b (*simple tenses*)] *If you're goi for a walk in the rain, you can count me o* → **count in** (2)

*__5__ *infml* to regard (someone) as unworthy c consideration: [T1b (*simple tenses*)] *Two c the men who want the job are unsuitable, s* *you can count them out.*

**6** to declare (a boxer) as losing a fight after he has been knocked down for a count of ten seconds: [T1] *The old fighter was counted out at the end of the third round.*

**7** *BrE* to declare that there are not enough members present in (Parliament) and so to close its meeting: [T1 (*usu. pass.*)] *The House was counted out.*

**8** esp. *AmE* to prevent (someone) from being elected by counting the votes incorrectly: [T1 (*usu. pass.*)] *He wasn't voted out, he was counted out.*

**ount to** *v prep*

**1** to count, usu. from zero, as far as (a number): [L(UP)9 + *to*] *You count to 100 while we hide.* → **count from, reckon to**

**2 count something to someone's credit** to give someone approval for something he has done; raise one's opinion of someone: [*usu. pass.*] *His kind action in saving the child from drowning will be counted to his credit.*

**ount up** *v adv* → **reckon up** (1)

to find the total of (something, things or people): [T1 + UP] *Count up all your money and see if you have enough. Count up the books and see if we have enough for each child to have one. You can count up the great poets still alive, on the fingers of one hand.*

**ount upon** *v prep* → **COUNT ON**

**ount with** *v prep*

to be valued by (someone): [L9 + *with*] *"If neither foes nor loving friends can hurt you, And all men count with you, but none too much."* (Rudyard Kipling, *If*)

**ounter with** *v prep*

**1** (in boxing) to reply (to a blow) with (an attack, of either hand): [L9 + *with*] *And now the old fighter counters with a blow to the body. His young opponent counters with his left.*

**2** to oppose (something such as an attack) with (a strong return): [X9 + *with*] *Always counter your opponent's attack with a strong return. The chairman countered the committee member's suggestion with another question. The trade union leaders countered the government's offer with further demands.* [L9 + *with* (*usu. simple tenses*)] *If you say anything to Jane, she's likely to counter with a bitter remark.*

**ouple on** *v adv* → **join on²**

to fasten (something usu. to be pulled) onto (a train, car, etc.): [T1] *Additional carriages can be coupled on (to the train) as needed.*

**ouple together/up** *v adv*

to join (usu. two things): [X9 + TOGETHER/UP] *The two main parts of the train remained coupled up after the crash. Couple the two pipes together so that the water can flow freely.*

**ouple with** *v prep*

**1** *old use* to have sex with (someone): [L9 + *with*] *Sir, I will not have you coupling with my wife!* → **lie with** (2), **sleep together** (2), **sleep with** (2)

***2** to connect (something or someone) with (something or someone else): [D1 (*usu. pass.*)] *The fall in the number of empty jobs is coupled with the rise in the cost of living. His name has been coupled with hers in the society page of the newspaper.* [V4a] *Working too hard, coupled with not getting enough sleep, made her ill.* → **associate with** (2)

**course through** *v prep*

to flow freely through (something such as a blood vessel or one's mind): [L9 + *through*] *I could feel the warm blood coursing through my veins as the ice melted. Wild ideas came coursing through my brain as I read the letter.*

**covenant for** *v prep* → **covenant with**

*fml* to make a formal agreement in law for (something): [L9 + *for*] *My uncle has covenanted for the property with the farmer.*

**covenant with** *v prep* → **covenant for**

*fml* to make a formal agreement in law with (someone): [L9 + *with*] *My uncle has covenanted with the farmer for the property.*

**cover against** *v prep* → **INSURE AGAINST** (1)

***cover for** *v prep*

**1** to guard (someone) from failure or discovery, as by taking his place; provide an excuse for (someone): [T(UP)1 (*no pass.*)] *Will you cover for me at the telephone switchboard while I run out to post a letter? The actor forgot his words, so the other people on stage covered for him by inventing the next few lines.* also **cover up for** → **stand in for**, etc.

**2** → **INSURE FOR**

**cover in¹** *v adv* → **cover over, fill in** (1), **fill up** (1), **roof in**

to cover (a space) completely; put a roof over (something): [T1 + IN] *The workmen covered in the hole in the road. The car park is covered in, to keep your car dry.* —**covered-in** *adj*

**cover in/with²** *v prep*

**1** to cause (someone or something) to have a lot of (something or things) on top: [T1 + *in/with*] *Last night's storm covered the ground in snow. I'd better cover the child with more bedclothes. Nature has covered the bear with a warm coat of thick fur. The trees are covered in new leaves now that Spring is here.*

***2** to cause (oneself) to receive (something such as honour or dishonour): [D1] *The brave soldier covered himself in glory.*

**3 be covered in/with** to be overcome by (a strong feeling): *Mary was covered with shame when she learned how unkind she had been to Jim.*

**cover over** *v adv* → **cover in¹, fill in** (1), **roof in**

to cover (a surface) completely: [T1 + OVER] *The policeman covered the dead body over. You'll have to cover over the hole in the broken window until you can get the new glass. The ground was covered over with snow.*

**cover up** *v adv*
**1** to put a cover such as clothing over (something or someone): [T1 + UP] *The child kept kicking the bedclothes off, so his mother had to keep covering him up. Cover yourself up, it's cold. Cover up the soup to keep it hot.*
*__2__ *not fml* to hide (something bad such as a wrong action or one's real intentions) usu. by deceit: [T1a] *He tried to cover up his guilt by lying.* —**cover-up** *n* → **hush up** (2), **smother up**

***cover up for** *v adv prep not fml* → COVER FOR (1)

**cover with** *v prep* → COVER IN

**cow down** *v adv*
to make (someone) feel frightened, defeated, or lower in spirits: [X9 + DOWN (*usu. pass.*)] *Don't let yourself be cowed down by the director's heavy scolding.*

**cow into** *v prep*
**cow someone into submission** to force someone to obey or agree through fear: *Don't worry about opposition from the younger members, we can soon cow them into submission.*

**cower away/back/down/forward** *v adv*
to move in a frightened manner, as bending away/back/down/forward: [L9 + AWAY/BACK/DOWN/FORWARD] *The woman cowered away/back when the jewel thief pointed a gun at her. The dog cowered down when the man threatened him with a whip. The servant cowered forward when the cruel king ordered him to come near.*

***cozen into** *v prep* → **trick into,** etc.
*old use esp. lit* to trick (someone) into (something or doing something): [D1] *A clever lawyer can cozen the judge into agreement.* [V4b] *A clever lawyer can cozen the judge into freeing the prisoner.*

***cozen (out) of** *v (adv) prep* → **cheat out of**, etc.
*old use esp. lit* to cheat (someone) out of (something that he possesses): [D1] *A clever lawyer can cozen your neighbour out of his rights*

***cozy up to** *v adv prep* also **cosy up to** → **cotton up to**
*AmE infml* to try to start a friendship with (someone): [T1 (*pass. rare*)] *I saw you cozying up to the new student; is he friendly?*

***crack down on** *v adv prep* → **clamp down on**
*not fml* to control, esp. to limit (something bad); deal firmly with (something or someone bad): [T1] *The government has promised to crack down on criminal activity. The government has promised to crack down on young criminals.* —**crack-down** *n*

**crack open** *v adj*
**1** to break (something) open by force: [L7 + open] *You have to crack the shell open to get at the nut.*
*__2__ *not fml* to destroy (someone's argument): [T(WIDE)1b] *A clever lawyer will be able to crack your case wide open.*

***crack out** *v adv* → **break into** (4), **break out in** (2), **burst into** (3), **burst out** (1), **bust out** (3)
*infml* to start (doing something such as laughing) suddenly: [I4 (*usu. simple tenses*)] *Everyone at the party cracked out laughing when Jim walked in wearing his funny clothes.*

**crack up** *v adv*
**1** (of earth) to become dry and cracked: [L9 + UP] *After the hot dry summer, the soil is cracking up.*
*__2__ (esp. of a plane, car, etc.) to (cause to) suffer damage or crash; *not fml* (of a business) to fail: [T1 (*simple tenses*)] *Sudden engine failure cracked the plane up. Joe cracked up the car for good in the accident.* [I∅ (*simple tenses*)] *The plane cracked up in the sudden storm. It surely can't be that the old firm is cracking up after all these years!* —**crack-up** *n* → **break up** (2)
*__3__ *infml* to suffer a nervous illness for some time: [I∅] *Peter cracked up and was unable to work for a year.* —**crack-up** *n* → **break down** (5), **break up** (7), **crock up**
*__4__ *infml* to praise (someone or something) often rather too highly: [T1] *He's always cracking up the town as very good.* [V3 (*often pass.*)] *His abilities are not what they were cracked up to be.* → **cry down, cry up, run down'** (7)
*__5__ *infml* to become helpless with laughter: [I∅] *Mary cracked up when Jim walked in wearing his funny clothes.* → **double up** (2), etc

**cram for** *v prep* → **swot for**
to study hurriedly and in detail, in preparation for (an examination): [I∅ + *for*] *Although there are no lessons this week, the students are all cramming for next week's tests*

**cram in** *v adv* → **crowd in** (1), etc.
to force or pack (things or people) tightly in a space: [X9 + IN] *You'll have to catch the next bus, we can't cram any more passengers in.*

***cram into** *v prep* → **crowd into** (1), etc.
to (cause to) be tightly packed into (a small space): [T1 (*no pass.*)] *Seven people crammed into the small car.* [D1] *I shall have to cram all my clothes into this small case.*

**cram up** *v adv*
to study (something) very hard, usu. for an examination: [I∅ + UP] *You'd better start cramming up if you want to pass the examination.* [X9 + UP] *I have to cram up three subjects for my examinations.*

**cram with** *v prep* → **jam with**
to fill (something or someone) tightly with (something, things, or people): [X9 + *with* (*often pass.*)] *The room was crammed with people wanting to buy the furniture. It's unhealthy to cram the children with so much food. All the shops are crammed with goods for the Christmas trade.*

***crane forward** *v adv*
to lean forward, esp. by stretching the neck as to see better: [I∅] *Only by craning forwa*

*out of the window could we get a view of the sea from our hotel room.*

**crank up** *v adv*
to start (usu. a car engine) with a handle: [X9 + UP] *I hated that old car, I had to crank it up every morning to get it started.*

**crap out** *v adv*
*AmE infml* to lose a game of craps by throwing a certain combination of numbers with dice: [IØ (*simple tenses*)] *I'm not lucky at this game, it's the third time I've crapped out tonight.*

**crash about/around**[1] *v adv*
to make a lot of noise by moving awkwardly: [L9 + ABOUT/AROUND] *Now, I don't want any of you children crashing about upstairs while your father's asleep.*

**crash about/around**[2] *v prep*
**1** to make a lot of noise in (a place) by moving awkwardly: [L9 + *about/around*] *Please don't crash about the living room while I have visitors in there.*
**2 crash about/around one's ears** *not fml* to fail suddenly: *All our careful plans crashed about our ears when the government changed the tax laws.* → **fall about**[2]

**crash around**[1] *v adv* → **CRASH ABOUT**[1]

**crash around**[2] *v prep* → **CRASH ABOUT**[2]

**crash down** *v adv*
to fall heavily, with a loud noise: [L9 + DOWN] *Did you hear the big tree come crashing down in last night's storm?*

**crash into** *v prep*
to (cause to) hit (something or someone) with force, usu. accidentally: [L9 + *into*] *I crashed into a street light and hurt my knee. The car crashed into a bus on the bridge.* [T1 + *into*] *John has crashed the car into the gate again.*

**crash out** *v adv*
**1** *infml* to escape (usu. from prison): [IØ (*of*) (*often simple tenses*)] *Three men crashed out of the prison yesterday. Are you one of the prisoners who crashed out?* → **break out** (3), **burst out** (2), **bust out** (2)
**2** *sl* to go to sleep quickly: [IØ] *He crashed out after a hard day's work.*

**crash with** *v prep*
*AmE infml* (esp. among young people) to sleep or lodge in the home of (someone) informally, usu. without payment and often with little comfort: [T1 (*no pass.*)] *My parents have thrown me out, can I crash with you for tonight?*

**crave for** *v prep*
**1** to have an uncontrollable desire for (usu. something): [T1 (*no pass., usu. simple tenses*)] *A woman who is soon to have a child often craves for strange foods. I can't seem to stop craving for cigarettes.*
**2** *fml* to ask forcefully for (something): [T1 (*no pass., usu. simple tenses*)] *Kneeling before the king, the prisoner craved for mercy.*

***crawl to** *v prep*
*not fml* to behave very humbly towards (someone, usu. in power) in order to win favour, etc.: [T1 (*pass. rare, usu. continuous tenses*)] *You should be ashamed of yourself, crawling to the director like that.*

***crawl with** *v prep*
*not fml* to be covered with or full of (small nasty creatures, such as insects); (of a place) to be filled with (people): [T1 (*no pass., continuous tenses*)] *The cheap room was dark, dirty, and crawling with spiders. Don't buy that meat, it's crawling with flies. After the explosion, the town was crawling with soldiers.*

**cream off** *v adv*
**1** to remove (cream) from milk: [T1 + OFF] *When we have creamed off the top of the milk, we can make butter with this cream.* → **skim off** (1)
***2** *not fml* to remove (the best) by choosing: [T1] *The school gained an advantage by creaming off the cleverest students from other schools.* → **skim off** (2)

**crease up** *v adv*
**1** to cause (a material such as paper or cloth) to fold untidily: [T1 + UP] *You've creased up my good shirt. Be careful not to crease up the pages.*
***2** (of a face) to become lined, as with sadness, age, etc.: [IØ] *The child's face creased up and soon he started crying.* [T1 (*usu. pass.*)] *The old woman's face was creased up with age.*
***3** to become helpless with laughter: [IØ (*usu. simple tenses*)] *Mary creased up when Jim walked in wearing his funny clothes.* → **double up** (2), etc.

**credit for** *v prep*
to praise or value (someone) for (something such as a quality, or doing something good): [X9 + *for*] *Even if you don't agree with the member's opinion, you must credit him for his loyalty. Whatever the quality of the student's work, he must be credited for having tried hard.*

**credit to** *v prep*
**1** (in banking) to show a payment of (a sum of money) to (someone or an account): [X9 + *to*] *I have today credited $300 to your account.* → **credit with** (1), **debit against, debit to, debit with**
***2** to believe (something good) to be possessed by (something or someone): [D1 (*usu. pass.*)] *Magical powers are credited to this medicine. Deeds of courage have been credited to him.*

**credit with** *v prep*
**1** (in banking) to show a payment to (someone or an account) of (a sum of money): [X9 + *with*] *The bank has credited you/your account with the amount of the cheque.* → **credit to** (1), **debit against, debit to, debit with**

*__2__ to believe; regard (someone) as (doing or having something good such as a quality): [D1 (*often pass.*)] *He arrived at the school already credited with many honours.* [V4b (*simple tenses*)] *I credited you with having better sense than that.* also **accredit with** → **give for** (5), **give to** (8), **take for** (5)

**creep in/into** *v adv; prep*
**1** to enter (somewhere) rather slowly and quietly, secretively, or with the body close to the ground: [L9 + IN/*into*] *I opened the door and the cat crept in. There was a movement outside the tent, and then a snake crept into the tent.*
*__2__ to happen gradually in (something): [IØ (*to*)] *After I've been writing for two hours, mistakes start creeping into my work. Doubt began to creep in as the man kept me talking at the door.*

***creep on** *v adv*
to advance gradually, esp. in time: [IØ] *Old age creeps on without being noticed. Time is creeping on and we have done so little!*

**creep over** *v prep*
**1** to move rather slowly and quietly, secretively, or with the body close to the ground, over (a surface): [L9 + *over*] *The snake crept over the ground towards the tent. Mist is creeping over the lake.*
*__2__ to have a gradual effect on (usu. someone): [T1 (*no pass.*)] *Fear crept over me as I stood in the empty house. Sleepiness crept over the children as night came.*

**creep up** *v adv*
**1** to come near gradually and secretively: [L9 + UP] *The thief crept up while no one was looking, and stole the jewels.*
*__2__ to advance gradually: [IØ] *Darkness was creeping up as the travellers left the forest.*

***creep up on** *v adv prep* → **sneak up on, steal up on**
**1** to reach (something, someone, or an animal) gradually and usu. silently: [T1 (*no pass.*)] *The thief crept up on the jewels. The cat crept up on the mouse.*
**2** to begin to surround (something) or have an effect on (someone): [T1 (*no pass.*)] *Darkness was creeping up on the house. Doubt crept up on me about his truthfulness.*

**crib from** *v prep*
*infml* to copy (something) dishonestly from (something written or someone): [IØ + *from*] *There will be no cribbing from anyone else's work!* [T1 + *from*] *The boy cribbed the answer from a book that he was hiding. These answers have been cribbed from another student!*

***cringe before** *v prep*
to behave very humbly towards (someone), from fear or the desire to gain something: [T1 (*no pass.*)] *Why are you cringing before that man? He doesn't have any real power.*

***crisp up** *v adv*
to make (something such as food or leaves) dry and breakable, as by drying or heating; become dry: [T1a] *The autumn air has crisped up the leaves ready to fall.* [IØ] *If you leave the bread out without wrapping it, it will crisp up.*

***crock up** *v adv* → **break down** (5), **break up** (7), **crack up** (3)
*infml* to (cause to) become ill in body or mind: [IØ] *I think the director is crocking up, he's had a lot of worries this year.* [T1] *This latest heart attack has really crocked him up. My broken leg prevents me from leaving the house; I'm really crocked up.*

***crop out** *v adv* → **crop up** (1)
(esp. of rocks) to show here and there above the surface of the land: [IØ] *Be careful how you walk in this field, there are lots of rocks cropping out.* —**outcrop** *n*

***crop up** *v adv*
**1** (esp. of rocks) to show here and there above the surface of the land: [IØ] *Be careful how you walk in this field, there are lots of rocks cropping up.* → **crop out**
**2** *not fml* to arise; happen unexpectedly: [IØ] *Some difficulties have cropped up, so we must work late to deal with them.* → **pop up** (2)
**3** *infml* to make a mistake: [IØ] *You seem to have cropped up badly on page 34, your facts are wrong.*
**4** *sl* to provide sex: [IØ (*simple tenses*)] *That's a pretty girl with a nice figure; do you think she'll crop up?*

**cross in** *v prep*
**1** **be crossed in love** to love someone without that love being returned by the loved one: *The boy looks thoughtful and unhappy; perhaps he's been crossed in love.*
**2** **cross in the post** (of a letter or letters) to pass in the post, both letters being delivered at the same time, each having been posted before the other is received: [*no pass.*] *I got your letter this morning asking for the information, but in fact I had just sent it; our letters must have crossed in the post. Your letter asking for the information must have crossed mine in the post, as I had just sent it.*

***cross off** *v adv; prep* → **cross out,** etc.
to remove (something such as words) from (something usu. written) by drawing a line through it: [T1] *I'll cross your name off.* [D1] *I'll cross your name off the list.*

***cross oneself** *v pron*
(of some Christians) to make the sign of the cross over one's body with one's hand, as a prayer, etc.: [IØ] *The worshipper crossed himself as he entered the church.*

***cross out** *v adv* → **cross off, score out, scratch out** (1), **scrub out** (4), **strike off** (3), **strike out** (2), **strike through**
to draw a line through (writing) to remove it: [T1] *Cross out the last two names, they're not members any more.* —**crossing-out** *n*

**cross over** *v adv*
**1** to move across a road, room, sea, etc.: [L9

+ OVER (*to*)] *Cross over at the traffic lights, where the road is safe. He crossed over to the window to see if it was still misty. If we had a boat we could cross over to the island.*

*2 esp. *BrE* to change one's loyalty, esp. political: [IØ (*to*)] *The Minister has threatened to cross over to the other side if the government refuses to accept his decision. The politician crossed over and joined the Opposition.*

**cross with** *v prep*

**1** to move across (usu. a road) with (someone or something): [T1 + *with*] *The children must cross the road only with a teacher or parent.* [IØ + *with*] *Cross with care at all traffic lights.*

*2 to unite (an animal or plant) with (a different kind of animal or plant) to produce a mixed kind of young or new plant: [D1] *If you cross soft wheat with hard wheat you can produce flour suitable for making bread. You can't cross a dog with a cat, but you can cross a tiger with a lion and get a different kind of big cat.*

**3 cross someone's hand/palm with silver** to pay someone to tell one's fortune: [*usu. imper.*] *Cross my palm with silver, kind sir, and I will tell you all your future.*

**4 cross swords with** to start a difference of opinion, often friendly, with (someone): *A Minister in the new government crossed swords with a member of the Opposition on the first day after Parliament opened.*

**crouch down** *v adv*

to bend one's knees and body so as to take up less space: [IØ + DOWN] *The tall policeman crouched down to talk to the lost child. The cat crouched down, ready to spring on the mouse.*

**crow off** *v adv*

**crow one's head off** *not fml* to express loud pride in a victory: *After the game, the winning team could be heard crowing their heads off in the changing room.*

**crow over** *v prep*

**1** to delight in (one's success): [L9 + *over*] *Our team are crowing over their victory.* → **exult at**

*2 to express delight in the defeat or misfortune of (someone): [T1] *It's unkind to crow over a fellow student who has failed his examination. The nasty boy crowed over his enemy's failure.* → **exult over**

**crowd in** *v adv*

**1** to (cause to) enter a building or enclosed space in large numbers: [L9 + IN] *When the gates of the ground were opened, all the football supporters crowded in.* [X9 + IN] *It's impossible to crowd any more football supporters in.* → **cram in, crush in** (2), **fit in**[1] (2), **jam in**[1], **pack in** (1), **pile in** (1), **throng in**

*2 to fill one's timetable with difficulty with (things, something, or someone): [T1] *Mr Sharp is seeing people all morning, but if the matter is urgent I'll see if I can crowd you in. The trouble with your day is that you have too many activities crowded in.* → **fit in**[1] (3), **squeeze in** (2)

***crowd in on/upon** *v adv prep*

**1** to surround (someone): [T1] *Don't all crowd in on me, I will see your books one at a time.*

**2** (usu. of memory) to fill the mind of (someone): [T1] *Happy memories crowded in on me as I looked at the photographs.*

**crowd into** *v prep*

**1** to (cause to) fill a space: [L9 + *into*] *The buyers crowded into the sale room.* [X9 + *into*] *Too much furniture had been crowded into the sale room.* → **cram into, crush into** (2), **jam into**[2], **pack into** (1), **pile into** (1), **throng into**

*2 to fit (someone or something) into (a time), with difficulty: [D1] *You have crowded too many activities into your day. If the matter is urgent, I'll see if I can crowd you into Mr Sharp's timetable today.* → **pack into** (2)

***crowd on** *v adv* → **clap on**[1] (3)

**crowd on sail** *naut* to spread more sails to make a ship go faster: [T1] *The captain ordered his men to crowd on more sail.*

**crowd out** *v adv*

**1** to leave in large numbers: [L9 + OUT (*of*)] *When the performance was over, the people crowded out (of the theatre).* → **throng out**

*2 to refuse entry or space for (someone or something), for lack of room: [T1 (*usu. pass.*) (*of*)] *The additional supporters were crowded out (of the football ground). We would have liked to print your letter in the newspaper, but it was crowded out by important news.* → **crush out** (2), **squeeze out** (3)

*3 to fill (a space) completely: [T1 (*often pass.*)] *The sale room was crowded out with people wanting to buy the furniture.*

**crowd round** *v adv; prep*

to gather in large numbers closely round (something or someone): [L9 + ROUND/*round*] *The children crowded round (the teacher) to hear the story.*

**crowd with** *v prep*

to fill (space or time) too full with (something, things or people): [X9 + *with* (*often pass.*)] *The office was crowded with people complaining about the washing machines. You have crowded your day with too many activities.*

**crown with** *v prep*

**1** to place on the head of (someone) a crown of (something) as a mark of royalty, honour, or respect: [T1 + *with* (*often pass.*)] *The Queen was crowned with a crown formerly worn by an ancient king. The victorious leader was crowned with an ornament of leaves.*

**2** to cover the edge of (a tooth) with (a substance such as metal or cement): [T1 + *with*] *His teeth had to be crowned with special cement.*

*3 to cover (something) with (something on top): [D1 (*usu. pass.*)] *These mountains are crowned with everlasting snow.*

**4 be crowned with** to reward (something such as activity) with (something good): [*usu. pass.*] *All his attempts were crowned with glory. The chairman's year in office has been crowned with success. "The head that once was crowned with thorns. Is crowned with glory now."* (Thomas Kelly, religious song) *"And crown thy good with brotherhood from sea to shining sea."* (Katherine Lee Bates, *America the Beautiful*)

**crumble away** *v adv*

**1** (of a hard material such as stone) to break off in small pieces; be gradually destroyed: [L9 + AWAY] *The government closed the cave to protect the ancient paintings, which were beginning to crumble away when open to the air. It is not safe to visit the stone temples of the ancient civilization; after 3,000 years they are crumbling away.*

*__2__ to cease gradually: [IØ] *The former leader's influence over his party members has been crumbling away for several months. The British Empire has been crumbling away for half a century.*

**crumble up** *v adv*

to reduce (something) to very small pieces: [T1 + UP] *Crumble up these pieces of bread and give them to the ducks.*

**crumple up** *v adv*

**1** to (cause to) become crushed or twisted: [IØ + UP] *The railway bridge crumpled up in the high wind.* [T1 + UP] *Don't crumple up the newspaper! The car was crumpled up in the crash.*

*__2__ to fall helplessly: [IØ (*usu. simple tenses*)] *A shot was fired; the man crumpled up and fell dead.*

*__3__ to become twisted and lined: [IØ (*usu. simple tenses*)] *The child's face crumpled up and he began to cry.*

*__4__ *infml* to (cause to) be defeated or lowered in health or spirits: [T1 (*often simple tenses*)] *The politician's speech crumpled up the opposition.* [IØ (*often simple tenses*)] *When the business failed, the owner just crumpled up. He crumpled up under the shocking news. The enemy will crumple up under an attack of this force.* → **curl up** (3)

*__5__ to become helpless with laughter or pain: [IØ (*usu. simple tenses*)] *Mary crumpled up when Jim walked in wearing his funny clothes. The fighter crumpled up under the sudden heavy blow.* → **double up** (2), etc.

**crunch down/up** *v adv*

to reduce (something) to very fine pieces or powder: [T1 + DOWN/UP] *This machine crunches the rock up so that it can be used for road building.*

**crusade against** *v prep* → **campaign for** (2), etc.

to attempt, from a deep belief, to stop or prevent (something) by public means such as advertising or writing letters, so as to make people conscious of the need for change, decision, or action: [L9 + *against*] *His family and friends are crusading against the imprisonment of a man whom they believe to be not guilty.*

**crusade for** *v prep* → **campaign for** (2), etc.

to attempt, from a deep belief, to gain (an aim) by public means such as advertising or holding meetings, so as to make people conscious of the need for change, decision, or action: [L9 + *for*] *Many women are crusading for improvements in the sexual equality laws.*

**crush down** *v adv*

**1** to flatten (something) with weight or force: [X9 + DOWN] *If you walk in the farmer's field, be careful not to crush down any growing crops.*

**2** to press (something hard such as rock) to very fine pieces or powder: [X9 + DOWN] *This machine crushes the rock down so that it can be used for road building.* → **crush up**

*__3__ to stop (something such as action) by force: [T1] *The cruel king crushed down any sign of opposition from the people. The council has promised to crush down criminal activity in the city.*

**crush in** *v adv*

**1** to wound (part of the body) or damage (something), esp. by flattening it with weight or force: [X9 + IN] *The heavy steel beam fell, crushing the workman's head in. The car door was crushed in during the accident.* → **bash in** (1), **beat in** (2), **stave in**

**2** to (cause to) enter a building or enclosed space in a tightly packed mass: [L9 + IN] *When the gates of the ground were opened, crowds of football supporters crushed in.* [X9 + IN] *It's impossible to crush in any more football supporters, the ground is already full.* → **crowd in** (1), etc.

**crush into** *v prep*

**1** to press (something) into (smaller pieces): [T1 + *into*] *This machine is made to crush the rock into powder.* → **crush to** (1)

**2** to (cause to) enter (a building or enclosed space) in a tightly packed mass: [L9 + *into*] *When the gates were opened, crowds of football supporters crushed into the ground.* [X9 + *into*] *It's impossible to crush any more football supporters into the ground, it's already full.* → **crowd into** (1), etc.

**3 crush someone into submission** to make someone or a group obey, by using force or cruelty: *The conquerors believed in crushing the defeated people into submission, knowing that they could not win their loyalty by the victory.*

**crush out** *v adv*

**1** to obtain (something) by pressing: [X9 + OUT (*of*)] *Use this kitchen machine to crush the juice out (of the oranges) instead of pressing the fruit by hand.*

*__2__ to refuse entry or space for (someone or something), for lack of room: [T1 (*of*) (*usu.*

*pass.*)] *The additional supporters were crushed out* (*of the football ground*). → **crowd out** (2), **squeeze out** (3)

***3** to take (a quality) from (someone), as by force, hardship, etc.: [T1 (*of*) (*often pass.*)] *Much of her youthful spirit had been crushed out of her by the terrible conditions which she had had to suffer.*

**crush to** *v prep*

**1** to reduce (something solid) to (smaller pieces) by pressing: [T1 + *to*] *This machine crushes the rock to powder.* → **crush into** (1)

**2 crush someone to death** to kill someone by pressing: [(*usu. pass.*)] *When the fire started, so many people rushed to the doors that three people were crushed to death in the crowd.*

**crush up** *v adv* → **crush down** (2)

to press (something) into very fine pieces or powder: [T1 + UP] *This machine crushes the rock up so that it can be used for road building.*

**crust over** *v adv*

to (cause to) form a hard surface on top: [X9 + OVER (*usu. pass.*)] *The ground was crusted over with snow.* [L9 + OVER] *The night grew very cold, and by morning the snow had crusted over.*

**cry down** *v adv*

**1** to silence (a speaker) by shouting: [T1] *Before the politician was halfway through his speech, the crowd cried him down.*

**2** *not fml* to refuse to accept (an idea): [T1] *I'm afraid the committee has cried down your suggestion.*

**3** *not fml* to express a poor opinion of (something or someone): [T1] *That man who writes for the newspaper is always crying down her performances, although many people enjoy them. His family are most unkind to Harry, always crying him down. Never cry down a child's small success or he can feel defeated for life.* → **crack up** (4), **cry up, do down** (2), **run down**' (7)

**cry for** *v prep*

**1** to weep because of (something): [I∅ + *for*] *That child is always crying for no good reason.*

**2** to express a desire for (something or someone) by weeping: [L9 + *for*] *The child is crying for his lost ball.* → **cry over** (1)

**3** to need (something) very much: [T1 (*no pass., continuous tenses*)] *The garden is crying for rain.* → **cry out** (2), **cry out for**

**4 cry for the moon** to want the impossible: [*no pass.*] *If a person of humble origins wished to marry a princess, we could say that he was crying for the moon.* → **beg for** (3)

**cry off** *v adv; prep* → **beg off**

*not fml* to fail to fulfil (a promise or arrangement); excuse oneself: [I∅] *Jim had arranged to play in the game, but he cried off at the last minute, so we had to find another player.* [T1 (*no pass.*)] *Why did Mary cry off the party?* [T4] *Why did she cry off joining your birthday party?*

**cry out** *v adv*

**1** to shout (something) loudly; express pain, surprise, etc.: [L9 + OUT] *'Be careful!' she cried out. The wounded soldier cried out in pain.* [X9 + OUT] *The dying man cried out his mother's name. The people cried out their complaints until the government took action.* —**outcry** *n* → **call out** (1), **roar out, shout out, thunder out, yell out**

***2** to be in great need (to have something done): [I3] *The garden is crying out to be watered.* → **cry for** (3), **cry out for**

**3 cry one's eyes/heart out** to weep long and bitterly: *The child was crying his eyes out in a corner of the classroom.*

**4 for crying out loud** *sl esp. BrE* (used to give strength to a demand, request, etc.): *For crying out loud shut that door!*

***cry out against** *v adv prep*

to complain strongly about; express one's disapproval of (something such as action): [T1 (*pass. rare*)] *The people cried out against the unjust imprisonment of the honest doctor.*

***cry out for** *v adv prep* → **cry for** (3), **cry out** (2)

to need (something) very much: [T1 (*no pass., continuous tenses*)] *The garden is crying out for rain. The organization is crying out for more people.*

**cry over** *v prep*

**1** to weep because of (something or someone): [L9 + *over*] *The boy was crying over his dead dog. The student is crying over his disappointment.* → **cry for** (2)

**2 cry over spilt milk** to waste one's sorrow over something that cannot be undone: [*no pass.*] *When his money was stolen he quickly realized there was no point in crying over spilt milk.*

**cry to** *v prep*

**1** to direct one's request or complaint to (someone): [I∅ + *to*] *The people cried to the king to be saved from the unjust enemies.*

**2 cry oneself to sleep** to fall asleep with the effort of weeping: *Can't you hear Mary crying herself to sleep? Go and see if you can comfort her.*

***cry up** *v adv* → **crack up** (4), **cry down** (3), **do down** (2), **run down**' (7)

*not fml* to praise (someone or something) often rather too highly: [T1a] *He's always crying up the town where he lives.* [V3] *His abilities are not what they were cried up to be.*

**cuddle up** *v adv*

to sit or lie close (to someone), touching or holding tightly, for warmth, comfort, or love: [L9 + UP (*to*)] *Stop crying, child, and come and cuddle up to me. The boy lay curled in the big soft armchair, cuddled up with his dog. The lovers cuddled up in bed.*

***cue in** *v adv*

**1** *not fml* (esp. in theatre, music, etc.) to give

(someone) a sign to be ready (to do something): [T1 (*usu. simple tenses*)] *The director will cue you in when it's your turn to sing.*
**2** esp. *AmE not fml* to add (words or music) at a certain point in a play: [T1 (*usu. pass.*)] *The new song is cued in here.*

**cull from** *v prep*
to choose and take (something) from (something): [X9 + *from* (*usu. pass.*)] *All his ideas are culled from books that he has read.*

* **cull out** *v adv* → **cut out** (6)
to choose to remove (usu. an animal) from among others: [T1] *The leader asked his best rider to cull out the sick cow from the group.*

* **culminate in** *v prep*
to reach (a result) at last: [T1 (*no pass., usu. simple tenses*)] *All his efforts culminated in failure.* [T4] *Will all our efforts culminate in selling the house?* [V4a] *At last our work culminated in our firm winning the contract.*

**cup together** *v adv*
to place (one's hands) together in a hollow shape, for holding something: [X9 + TOGETHER] *She cupped her hands together and drank from the river.*

**cure of** *v prep*
**1** to make (someone) completely better in health or spirits after an attack of (an illness): [X9 + *of*] *Doctors are now able to cure people of many diseases which in former times would have killed them.* also *fml* **heal of**
**2** to stop (someone) from (doing something bad) habitually: [X9 + *of*] *Will kindness cure him of stealing?*
**3** to cause (someone) to stop being in love with (someone, usu. of the opposite sex): [X9 + *of*] *I don't know what can be done to cure you of that boy.*

**curl up** *v adv*
**1** to (cause to) form into a curved shape: [L9 + UP] *The snake curled up in the long grass. The leaves are curling up in the cold autumn air. "And he smiled a kind of sickly smile, and curled up on the floor."* (Bret Harte, *The Society upon the Stanislaus*) [X9 + UP] *The snake was curled up in the long grass. The boy curled himself up in the big soft armchair with a book. Jim's aunt curled up her lip with disapproval.* → **shrivel up** (1)
**2** to rise in a curled shape: [L9 + UP] *In the still air, smoke could be seen curling up from the chimney.*
* **3** *infml* to (cause to) become helpless in body or mind: [T1] *The fighter's well-aimed blow curled his opponent up. The loss of his business just curled him up.* [IØ] *When the blow hit the fighter, he curled up on the floor. When his business failed, the owner just curled up and died.* → **crumple up** (4)
* **4** *not fml* to become helpless with laughter: [IØ (*usu. simple tenses*)] *Mary just curled up when Jim walked in wearing his funny clothes.* → **double up** (2), etc.
* **5** *not fml* to (cause to) feel an unpleasant dislike: [IØ (*simple tenses*)] *I just curled up when I saw the colours he had chosen.* [T1 (*simple tenses*)] *His choice of colours really curls me up.*

**curry with** *v prep*
**curry favour with** to behave with insincere goodwill towards (someone) for one's own advantage: *I hear that new student has been currying favour with the teacher, but that won't get him better marks.*

**curse with** *v prep* → **bless with**
**be cursed with** to be unlucky to have (something or someone): *Poor Mother is cursed with bad health. The old king was cursed with two ungrateful daughters.*

**curtain off** *v adv*
to separate (something such as a space) with a curtain: [X9 + OFF] *I have curtained off this part of the room, where the bed is.* —**curtained-off** *adj*

**cut about** *v adv* → **cut up** (2), etc.
to wound (part of the body) in several places: [X9 + ABOUT (*usu. pass.*)] *Her face was badly cut about in the car crash.*

**cut across** *v prep*
**1** to shorten a journey by travelling across (a corner): [L9 + *across*] *I got here early by cutting across the field.*
* **2** to divide; be opposite to (something): [T1 (*no pass., simple tenses*)] *The voting cut across the usual political divisions. The chairman's decision cuts across the opinion of the whole committee.*
* **3** to interrupt (something): [T1 (*no pass., usu. simple tenses*)] *The new building cuts across our view. Her loud voice cut across the conversation.*

**cut ahead of** *v adv prep* → **cut in**[1] (4)
(of a vehicle) to move directly and usu. suddenly in front of (another vehicle): [L9 + AHEAD + *of* (*usu. simple tenses*)] *We were driving peacefully along the road when this red car cut ahead of us, forcing us to slow down.*

**cut ahead to** *v adv prep* → **cut to** (2), **jump to** (1)
to reach (something) by leaving out part: [L9 + AHEAD + *to*] *Cut ahead to page 31, we'll miss the middle scene at this first reading.*

* **cut along** *v adv* → **cut off** (9)
*infml* to go quickly: [IØ (*usu. imper.*)] *Cut along to your grandmother's, will you, and take her this basket of food; and be careful in the forest.*

**cut at** *v prep*
to aim a blow at (something or someone) with a weapon; use a sharp instrument on (something): [L9 + *at*] *The farmer cut at the snake with a stick. Only after cutting at the rope for an hour was he able to get free.*

**cut away** *v adv*
**1** to remove usu. a bad part of (something) by cutting: [X9 + AWAY] *If you cut away some of the dead wood, you will have a healthier tree. The doctor had to cut away some*

*flesh from the wounded leg.*
**2** to remove (part of something); shape (something) so as to show something different underneath or behind: [X9 + AWAY (*usu. pass.*)] *The front of the coat was cut away to show the colours underneath. The collar was cut away according to the fashion. The working model was cut away to show the inside of the building.* —**cutaway** *adj*

**cut back** *v adv*
**1** to shorten (something such as a plant): [X9 + BACK] *Gardeners argue about whether one should cut roses back in the spring or autumn.*
**2** to return in time: [L9 + BACK (*to*)] *The film cut back to the earlier scene so that we understood her reasons.* —**cut-back** *n* → **flash back, flash forward**
**3** to change direction suddenly when running: [L9 + BACK (*usu. simple tenses*)] *The footballer pretended to run forward, then cut back and took the ball the other way.*
***4** *not fml* to reduce (something), esp. to save money: [T1] *The factory's production has been cut back.* [IØ (*on*)] *We shall have to cut back on our spending.* —**cut-back** *n* → **cut down** (3), **cut down on**
***5** to shorten (a word): [T1 (*usu. pass.*)] *This word has been cut back to save space.* —**cut-back** *n*, **cutback** *adj*

**cut dead** *v adj*
to refuse to notice; pretend not to know (someone). [X7 + dead] *I passed Mrs King-Brown in the street today but she cut me dead; I wonder what I've done to offend her.*

**cut down** *v adv*
**1** to make (something such as a tree) fall by cutting: [X9 + DOWN] *Half the forest was cut down to make room for the new road.* → **get down** (3)
**2** to reduce the size of (something such as clothing, writing, etc.): [X9 + DOWN] *I could cut your father's trousers down for the boy. Your article will have to be cut down to fit into the book.* —**cut-down** *adj* → **make down**
**3** *not fml* to reduce (something), esp. to save money: [T1] *The factory's production has been cut down.* → **cut back** (4), **cut down on**
**4** to kill (someone): [T1 (*usu. pass.*)] *The soldier was cut down in his youth.* → **cut off** (8)
**5** *not fml* to destroy (an argument): [T1] *Your arguments are too easy to cut down.*
**6** *not fml* to defeat (someone); make (someone) feel less important: [T1] *Jim was beginning to argue wildly again, getting his facts wrong, so his father cut him down.* → **cut down to** (2)
**7** to persuade (someone) to reduce a price: [T1 (*by, to*)] *He's asking too much for the chairs, can't you cut him down? In the end I cut the dealer down by another £3.00.*

**cut down on** *v adv prep* → **cut back** (4), **cut down** (3)
*not fml* to reduce (something), usu. out of necessity, as to save money: [T1 (*no pass.*)] *The factory cannot afford to employ any more workers, so it will have to cut down on production.* [T4] *In these times of rising prices, we must all cut down on our spending. The doctor advised Father to cut down on smoking.*

**cut down to** *v adv prep* → **cut down** (6)
***1** to cause (someone) to reduce a price to (a lower price): [T1 + *to*] *We were able to cut the dealer down to £3.25.*
**2 cut someone down to size** to show that someone is less important than he pretended: *The director is too proud, he needs to be cut down to size.* → **cut down** (6)

**cut fine** *v adj*
**cut it fine**
**1** to leave something till it is almost too late; do something only just in time: *You've cut it fine, haven't you? The train's just leaving.* → **cut short** (4)
**2** *AmE* to calculate something exactly: *This answer is correct to the last cent; you've cut it (very) fine.*
***3** to see small differences between things that are much alike: *But the two meanings are almost exactly the same; aren't you cutting it rather fine, saying they should be separated?*
**4** to leave oneself only just enough money: *By the time we've paid the bill we have $42 left, which I call cutting it a bit fine.*

**cut for** *v prep*
to choose from a pack of playing cards to see who shall be or have (something): [IØ + *for*] *First, we cut for dealer, then begin the game. Aren't we going to cut for who has the first turn?*

**cut free** *v adj*
**1** to free (something, someone, or an animal) by cutting something binding: [X7 + free (*from*)] *Cut the boat free, we're ready to sail. Firemen were called to the scene of the accident to cut the driver free from the wreck of his car. Cut the poor dog free quickly, his neck is caught in the rope!* → **cut loose** (1)
***2** to free (oneself) by force or effort (from something or someone): [T1b (*from*)] *The painter cut himself free from family responsibilities and went to live on a tropical island.* → **cut loose** (2)

**cut from** *v prep*
**1** to remove (part) of (something such as a plant) by cutting: [T1 + *from*] *If you cut a branch from this tree, it can grow into a new tree.*
**2** to remove (part) from (something, as material): [T1 + *from*] *You will have to cut about twenty pages from your book, it's too long.*
***3 cut the ground from under someone's feet** *not fml* to remove the cause of someone's argument, complaint, etc.: *The Opposition had been telling the voters about the government's inaction, but the government then cut*

*the ground from under their feet by doing the right things just before the election.*

**cut in**[1] *v adv*

**1** to mix (something) gently by cutting with a metal edge: [X9 + IN] *Mix the sugar and butter, then cut the flour in with a knife or spoon.*
**2** to add (something) by cutting and fastening: [X9 + IN] *We'll cut in the piece of film that we have already made. Here is where you cut this new wire in.*
***3** *not fml* to interrupt someone speaking, dancing, etc.: [IØ (*on*) (*usu. simple tenses*)] *"May I join you?" a loud voice cut in. I was enjoying the dance until that rude man cut in. Don't cut in on other people's conversations.* → **break in** (3), **burst in** (3)
***4** to move suddenly in front of someone or a vehicle: [IØ (*on*) (*usu. simple tenses*)] *We were driving peacefully along the road when this red car cut in (on us), forcing us to slow down. I had been waiting behind six other people for the bus, when this fat woman cut in (in front of me).* → **cut ahead of**
***5** *infml* to allow (someone) to join (a game of cards, a business deal, etc.): [T1 (*on*) (*usu. simple tenses*)] *Would you like to join our card game? I can cut you in. The chief buyer says he can cut you in (on the deal).*

**cut in**[2] *v prep* → **cut into** (1), **divide in**

to divide (something) by (a part): [T1 + *in*] *Cut the cake in four and share it equally. The car was cut in half in the crash.*

**cut into** *v prep*

**1** to divide (something) into (parts): [T1 + *into*] *Cut the cake into quarters and share it equally. The ship was cut into several pieces in the accident.* → **cut in**[2], **divide into, separate into**
**2** to start cutting (something): [L9 + *into*] *Mother said we could cut into the new cake.* → **slice into**
***3** to interrupt (something): [T1 (*usu. simple tenses*)] *The children cut into the conversation with demands for attention. My aunt's regular visits cut into my weekends.* → **break into** (3)
***4** to use part of (something such as money) unwillingly: [T1 (*no pass., usu. simple tenses*)] *I shall have to cut into my savings to pay for the holiday. I don't want to cut into a £10 note if I can help it.* → **break into** (6)

**cut loose** *v adj*

**1** to free (something, someone, or an animal) from something binding: [X7 + loose] *Cut the boat loose, we're ready to sail. Firemen were called to the scene of the accident to cut the driver loose from the wreck of his car. Cut the poor dog loose quickly, his neck is caught in the rope!* → **cut free** (1)
***2** to free (oneself) by force or effort (from something or someone): [T1b] *The painter cut himself loose from family responsibilities, and went to live on a tropical island.* → **cut free** (2)
***3** *infml* to behave wildly: [IØ (*simple tenses*)] *When Jim gets drunk, he always cuts loose.*

**cut off** *v adv*

**1** to remove (part of something) by cutting: [X9 + OFF] *King Charles had his head cut off. Show the child how to cut the top off before he eats his egg.* → **slice off, snip off, strike off** (1), **swish off**
***2** to interrupt (someone or something): [T1 (*usu. simple tenses*)] *The chairman will cut a speaker off if he talks too long. Our telephone conversation was cut off.* → **cut short** (3)
***3** to prevent or stop (something): [T1] *"I wil give them an everlasting name, that shall not be cut off."* (The Bible) *"He that cuts off 2C years of life, cuts off so many years of fearing death."* (Shakespeare, *Julius Caesar*) —**cut-off** *n, adj*
***4** to stop (something such as a supply): [T1 (*usu. simple tenses*)] *The electricity supply will be cut off if we don't pay our bill.*
***5** to separate (someone or something) (from something): [T1 (*from*) (*often pass.*)] *We were cut off by the incoming sea and nearly drowned. The army was cut off from its supplies. Last night's severe snowstorm cut off three villages.*
***6** to make (someone or oneself) lonely: [T1 (*from*) (*usu. simple tenses*)] *Why did the old woman cut herself off from society like that? Was there an unhappy story in her youth?*
***7** to stop a supply of money to (someone) esp. after one's death, esp. in the phrs. **cut someone off without a penny**: [T1 (*usu. simple tenses*)] *I'll cut you off without a penny.* → **cut out** (5)
***8** to kill (someone): [T1 (*usu. pass.*)] *The soldier was cut off in his youth.* → **cut down** (4
***9** *infml* to go quickly: [IØ (*imper.*)] *Cut off now before the shop closes.* → **cut along**
**10 cut off someone's escape/retreat** to prevent someone from getting away by blocking the way: *Don't let those enemy soldiers get free cut off their escape by sending some of your men into the woods behind them.*
**11 cut off one's nose to spite one's face** to punish oneself unnecessarily: [(*usu. simple tenses*)] *He seems to enjoy making things difficult for himself, in fact he would cut off his nose to spite his face.*

**cut on** *v prep*

**cut one's teeth on** *not fml* to learn to know or do (something) when very young; to have known or done (something) for a long time *Does she know anything about modern music Why, she cut her teeth on it.*

**cut open** *v adj*

to wound (part of the body) with a deep cut [X7 + open] *The child fell in the playground and cut her head open.*

**cut out** *v adv*

**1** to cut (something such as paper) from ( larger paper): [X9 + OUT (*of*)] *May I cut out the article about my performance? The child likes to play with figures cut out of paper* —**cut-out** *n, adj* → **clip out**

**2** to shape (something) by cutting: [X9 + OUT (*of*)] *Would you help me cut out this dress? The natives have cut out a path through the forest.*

***3** to miss out; remove (something): [T1] *I think you'd better cut out that last sentence.*

***4** *infml* to stop (something or doing something): [T1] *The doctor told my husband to cut out meat from his food. I wish she would cut out that stupid behaviour.* [T4] *The doctor told my husband to cut out smoking.*

***5** to remove (someone) from one's will: [T1 (*of*)] *He cut his brother out* (*of his will*) *after their quarrel.* → **cut off** (7)

***6** to choose to remove (usu. an animal) from among others: [T1] *The leader asked his best rider to cut out the sick cow from the group.* → **cull out**

***7** *not fml* to replace (a competitor) in love or business: [T1 (*often simple tenses*)] *Mary was going to marry Charles but Jim cut him out. The big new store is going to cut all the small shops out.*

***8** (of an engine or machine) to stop working: [IØ (*simple tenses*)] *We were halfway up the hill when the engine cut out. The heating cuts out when the room reaches a certain temperature.* —**cutout** *n* → **break down** (3), **conk out** (1), **give out** (6), **kick off** (6), **pack up** (3)

***9** *AmE infml* to go faster: [IØ (*simple tenses*)] *When we reached the main road we really cut out.*

***10** (of a vehicle) to move suddenly out of a line of traffic: [IØ] *It's dangerous to cut out when all the cars are moving fast.*

***11** esp. *AmE infml* to leave: [IØ] *It's time I left home; I'll cut out next week.* → **clear out** (6), **dig out** (6), **light out**

**12 cut out the dead wood** *not fml* to remove useless parts, people, or methods: *If you cut out some of the dead wood, the firm might begin to show a profit.*

**13 be cut out for/to be** *not fml* to be suited for (a profession): *I don't think you're cut out for teaching, you haven't the necessary patience. I don't think you're cut out to be a teacher, you haven't the necessary patience.*

**14 cut it out!/cut that out!** *infml* stop that! → **chuck in** (7), **pack in** (4), **pack up** (4)

**15 have one's work cut out** *infml* to have a lot of work to do: *You'll have your work cut out to finish before Christmas.*

**cut short** *v adj*

**1** to make (something) shorter by cutting: [X7 + short] *Ask the man to cut the boy's hair short.*

***2** to make (something) shorter in time: [T1] *I'm afraid we must cut our visit short, as we want to get home before dark.* → **break short**

***3** to stop (someone) talking: [T1 (*usu. simple tenses*)] *The chairman will cut a speaker short if he talks too long.* → **cut off** (2)

**4 cut it short** to take a risk of missing something, as by being late: *You've cut it short, haven't you, the train's just leaving.* → **cut fine** (1)

**5 cut a long story short** to tell something with little detail: [(*often inf.*)] *And then he said—well, to cut a long story short, he refused to give us permission.*

**cut through** *v prep*

**1** to cut (something) with sharp metal through (something): [X9 + *through*] *They had to cut their way through the forest with axes.* [L9 + *through*] *I cut through two pieces of cloth by mistake.*

***2** to shorten (something); work faster with (something): [T1] *Let's cut through the usual committee stage and get the plan approved faster. Can't we cut through some of these formalities and get on with the real business of the meeting?*

**3 cut through the red tape** to refuse to use official methods which waste time and effort: *We haven't time to go through the proper means of asking a favour; let's cut through the red tape and take your request straight to the director.*

**cut to** *v prep*

**1** to reduce (something) to (something less): [T1 + *to*] *Hospital waiting time must be cut to the least possible. The universities are having to cut student numbers to 75% of last year.*

**2** to reach (something) by leaving out part: [L9 + *to*] *Cut to page 31, we'll miss the middle scene at this first reading. Stop the film here and cut to the next scene.* → **cut ahead to, jump to** (1)

**3 cut (prices) to the bone** *not fml* to reduce prices as much as possible without making a loss: *We've cut our prices to the bone, and still the public aren't buying.*

**4 cut someone to the quick/heart** *not fml* to hurt the feelings of someone deeply: [(*usu. pass.*)] *I was cut to the quick not to be invited to my own daughter's wedding.*

**5 cut to pieces/shreds** *not fml* to destroy (someone or something): [(*often pass.*)] *The enemy have been cut to pieces; victory is ours! The speaker cut his opponent's argument to pieces.*

***cut under** *v adv*

**1** to make (prices) lower than those of one's competitors: [T1b] *He cut his prices under to try to win their customers.* —**undercut** *v*

**2** to compete with (another firm) by lowering one's prices: [T1b] *We must try to cut the other shop under.*

**cut up** *v adv*

**1** to cut (something) in small pieces: [X9 + UP] *Please cut up the meat for the dog as his teeth are bad now.* → **slice up**

**2** to wound (someone or part of the body) in several places: [X9 + UP (*usu. pass.*)] *Her face was badly cut up in the car crash. There were no deaths in the crash, but several passengers were cut up.* → **cut about**

**3** to provide enough of something such as

material or food: [L9 + UP (*into*) (*simple tenses*)] *The chicken cut up well, there was enough for everyone. That cloth should cut up into three dresses.*

*__4__ *not fml* to destroy or severely damage (usu. something): [T1 (*usu. pass.*)] *The town was (badly) cut up in last night's bombing. The enemy are being cut up in the battle.*

*__5__ *infml* to express a poor opinion of something or someone): [T1 (*usu. pass.*)] *Her performance was (badly) cut up in the next day's newspapers.*

*__6__ *infml* to cause suffering to (someone): [T1 (*usu. pass.*)] *She was cut up about her failure in the concert. The bad report in the newspapers cut her up terribly.*

**7** *sl* to wound (someone) intentionally: [T1] *Threaten to cut him up if he won't give the money, that should make him do it!* → **carve up** (4), **slit up** (2)

**8** *infml* to behave widly: [IØ] *It's been raining for a week and the children are really cutting up.*

*__9__ *AmE infml* to play the fool: [IØ] *Jim like[s] to cut up at parties.* —**cut-up** *n*

*__10__ *infml* to leave money after one's death [IØ (*for*) (*simple tenses*)] *How much do yo[u] think he'll cut up for?*

**11 cut up rough** to act in a violent manner lose one's temper: *Father will cut up roug[h] when he hears you've lost money at cards.*

**cut with** *v prep*

**1** to divide (something) or wound (someone by using (a sharp tool): [T1 + *with*] *Don't tr[y] to cut your meat with a fork! I've cut mysel[f] with the axe.*

**2 cut the air with a knife** *not fml* to sense [a] heavy feeling in a group: [(*simple tenses*)] *When the two brothers were in a roo[m] together, you could cut the air with a knife.*

**3 cut no ice with** to have no effect on (someone): [(*simple tenses*)] *Her air of great wealt[h] cuts no ice with me.*

# D

**dab at** *v prep*

to touch (something, esp. a surface) lightly or gently, usu. several times, without rubbing: [X9 + AT] *She dabbed at the stain on her dress with a wet cloth.*

**dab off** *v adv*

to remove (something such as dirt) with light quick strokes: [X9 + OFF] *Dab the mud off carefully, don't rub too hard or you'll make it worse.*

**dab on** *v adv*

to put (something liquid or nearly liquid) on something with light quick strokes: [X9 + ON (*to*)] *Don't dab the paint on, brush it on smoothly.*

***dab out** *v adv*

*not fml* to wash (a few garments) by hand: [T1] *I would rather dab out my stockings and underclothes every morning than save them for a large wash.*

***dabble at/in/with** *v prep*

to perform (an activity); take an interest in (a subject), for enjoyment, but without serious intentions: [T1] *Every time an election takes place, Jim dabbles in politics until it is over.* [T4] *Mary has been dabbling at painting this winter.*

**dally over** *v prep*

**1** *not fml* to waste time over (something): [L9 + *over*] *Don't dally over your meal, we don't want to be late for the performance.* → **dawdle over**

**2** *not fml* to be slow to make a decision about (something): [L9 + *over*] *We dallied so long over whether to buy the house that it was sol[d] to someone else.*

***dally with** *v prep*

**1** *not fml* to consider (an idea) not very seriously: [T1 (*pass. rare*)] *Father often dallies with the thought of going to live on a tropica[l] island.* → **play with** (3), **toy with** (2), **trifle with** (1)

**2** *not fml* to play at a love relationship with (someone, usu. of the opposite sex): [T1 (*pass. rare*)] *Never dally with a woman whom you don't intend to marry.* → **flirt with** (1), etc.

**dam up** *v adv*

**1** to keep back (water) by building a wall o[r] bank in its way: [T1 + UP] *The local peopl[e] dammed up the river to make a lake for thei[r] water supply.*

*__2__ → **BOTTLE UP** (2)

**damn with** *v prep*

**damn something/someone with faint praise** t[o] show one's disapproval of something or someone by giving only a few favourable words: *To say that her performance was quite nice is damning it with faint praise, as all the othe[r] reporters went wild with joy over her singing.*

**damp down** *v adv* also **dampen down**

**1** to make (a surface) slightly wet all over: [T1 + DOWN] *The best way to lay the dust is to damp the floor down, and then rub it al[l] over with a cloth.* → **wet down**

*__2__ to make (a fire) burn more slowly, often by covering with ash or by controlling the flow o[f] air: [T1] *Don't forget to damp down the campfire before going to bed.*

*3 to control so as to reduce (something): [T1] *A few weeks' hard work should damp down his keenness.*

*4 to lessen: [IØ] *My hopes of a better job damped down after six years' waiting.*

**damp off** *v adv*
(of plants) to die because of too much water: [IØ] *It rained so much last winter that half the vegetable crops damped off.*

**dampen down** *v adv* → DAMP DOWN

**dance on/upon** *v prep*
**dance attendance on/upon** *fml* to give much attention to (a person), esp. in order to get something in return: *The young man danced attendance on his rich aunt, but got nothing from her when she died.*

**dance to** *v prep*
1 to move one's feet and body in a way that matches the speed and movements of (music): [IØ + *to*] *I like dancing to quiet music.*
2 **dance to someone's tune** *not fml* to obey someone's orders: *When the new director arrives, we shall all have to dance to his tune.*
3 **dance to another tune** *not fml* to change one's behaviour according to different conditions: *If the teacher sees you climbing up the wall, you'll dance to another tune.*

**dance upon** *v prep* → DANCE ON

**dangle about/around/round¹** *v adv*
1 to hang or swing loosely: [L9 + ABOUT/AROUND/ROUND] *I don't like the look of all those ropes dangling around.*
*2 to stay close to someone to whom one is attracted: [IØ] *She always has lots of men dangling round.*

**dangle about/around/round²** *v prep*
1 to (cause to) hang or swing loosely in or near (something): [L9 + *about/around/round*] *She wears too much jewellery, like shiny earrings that dangle about her head.* [X9 + *about/around/round*] *At Christmas, we dangle pretty lights around the room.*
*2 to (cause to) stay close to (someone to whom one is attracted): [T1 (*no pass.*)] *Pretty girls always seem to have lots of men dangling round them.* [D1] *She likes to dangle her men around her.*

**dangle around¹** *v adv* → DANGLE ABOUT¹

**dangle around²** *v prep* → DANGLE ABOUT²

**dangle before** *v prep*
1 to (cause to) hang or swing loosely in front of (someone): [X9 + *before*] *Dangle the ball on a string before the cat.* [L9 + *before*] *The toys were dangling before the boys in the shop.*
*2 to offer (something attractive) to someone, so as to persuade him to do something: [D1] *A pay increase was dangled before him when he threatened to leave the company.*

**dangle from** *v prep*
to hang or swing loosely from (something such as a fastening): [L9 + *from*] *Dangling from the end of my fishing line was an old boot.*

**dangle round¹** *v adv* → DANGLE ABOUT¹

**dangle round²** *v prep* → DANGLE ABOUT²

**dart at** *v prep* → **flash at, shoot at** (3), **throw at** (2)
**dart a glance/look at** to look at (something or someone) very quickly for a moment: *Jane darted an anxious look at the clock as she tried to finish her examination question. While the others were talking, Jim darted a glance at Mary to see whether she agreed.*

**dash against** *v prep* → **dash over, dash to**
to (cause to) hit (something) quickly and violently: [L9 + *against*] *The sea has been dashing against this cliff for centuries.* [X9 + *against*] *Heavy waves dashed the boat against the rocks, where it broke to pieces.*

**dash away** *v adv*
1 *not fml* to leave in a hurry: [IØ + AWAY (*usu. simple tenses*)] *I'm sorry, I must dash away now, I'm already late for the concert.* → **dash off** (1), **tear away** (2), **tear off¹** (2)
2 to remove (usu. tears) hastily: [X9 + AWAY] *She turned round, and dashed away the tears with a corner of her handkerchief.*

**dash off** *v adv*
1 *not fml* to hurry away: [IØ + OFF (*usu. simple tenses*)] *Excuse me, please, if I dash off now, I have a class in five minutes.* → **dash away** (1), **tear away** (2), **tear off¹** (2), **tear out** (2)
*2 *not fml* to write or draw (something) very quickly: [T1] *I must dash off this letter before the post is collected.* → **fling off** (6), **knock off** (4), **knock out** (7), **tear off¹** (4), **throw off¹** (7), **toss off** (3), **write off** (2)

**dash out** *v adv*
1 *not fml* to hurry outside: [IØ + OUT (*usu. simple tenses*)] *The door opened and the children dashed out.* → **tear away** (2), **tear off¹** (2), **tear out** (2)
2 **dash one's/someone's brains out** to kill oneself or someone by breaking the head open: *The climber fell from the cliff and dashed his brains out on the rocks below.* → **blow out** (10)

**dash over** *v prep* → **dash against, dash to**
to (cause to) cover (something) quickly and violently, as with liquid: [L9 + *over*] *Very big waves dashed over the sea wall at the height of the storm.* [X9 + *over*] *She's fainted, quick, dash some cold water over her face.*

**dash to** *v prep* → **dash against, dash over**
**dash something/someone to pieces** to destroy something or someone violently: *The boat was dashed to pieces against the rocks.*

***date back to/from** *v adv prep; prep* → **go back** (6), **go back to** (5), **reckon from**
to have existed since (the date of building or origin): [T1 (*no pass., simple tenses*)] *The church dates back to 1173. The custom dates from the time when men wore swords.*

**daub on** *v adv*
to spread (a thick liquid) onto something such as a surface: [X9 + ON] *Don't daub your paint on like that, spread it with your brush.*

**daub onto/over** *v prep*
to spread (a thick liquid) so as to cover (a surface): [X9 + *onto/over*] *The children love daubing mud all over themselves when they play on the shore. Why are you daubing that ugly colour onto your nails?*

**daub up** *v adv*
*AmE not fml* to paint (something) in spots: [X9 + UP] *The children have daubed up the walls with uneven drops of paint.*

**daub with** *v prep*
to cover (something such as a surface) with (a thick liquid): [X9 + *with*] *Some children have been going round the neighbourhood, daubing the house doors with black oil.*

**dawdle along** *v prep*
to move lazily along (a road): [IØ + *along*] *The donkey dawdled along the sandy path.*

*__dawdle away__ *v adv*
to waste (something such as time): [T1] *I've dawdled the whole afternoon away, talking to you!*

**dawdle over** *v prep* → **dally over** (1)
to waste time over (something): [IØ + *over*] *Don't dawdle over your meal, we don't want to be late for the performance.*

**dawn on/upon** *v prep*
**1** (of a day) to begin in (a place); give light to (darkness): [IØ + *on/upon*] *A grey day dawned upon the sleeping city.*
***2** to become gradually known by (someone): [T1 (*no pass., simple tenses*)] *The answer dawned on me when I wasn't thinking about the work.* [*It* + D5 (*simple tenses*)] *It dawned on me that I was lost.* [*It* + D6 (*simple tenses*)] *It dawned on me where I had seen him before.* → **burst on** (3)

**deaden with** *v prep*
**1** to cause (part of the body) to have no feeling because of (something): [X9 + *with* (*usu. pass.*)] *My fingers are deadened with cold.*
**2** to make (a sound) less with (something): [X9 + *with*] *You can deaden the noise of the machines with rubber mats.*

*__deal at__ *v prep* → **deal with** (1), **do with** (13), **trade at, trade with**
to be a customer of (a business such as a shop): [T1 (*no pass.*)] *I've been dealing at Brown's for twenty years.*

*__deal by__ *v prep*
to treat (someone) in a certain manner, as well or badly: [T1 (*often pass.*)] *Mr Sharp has always dealt fairly by me.*

*__deal in[1]__ *v adv*
to include (someone) in a game of cards, by giving him his share of the cards: [T1b] *You're not too late to join the game, shall I deal you in?*

*__deal in[2]__ *v prep* → **trade in[2]**
to buy and sell; trade in (something such as goods): [T1 (*no pass., usu. simple tenses*)] *This shop deals in woollen goods.*

**deal out** *v adv*
**1** to give (things) to several people: [X9 + OUT] *Please deal out the cards and then we can start to play.*
***2** to give (something), esp. to several people: [T1] *The children felt that the teacher had been unfair in dealing out the punishment to the whole class.* → **mete out**

*__deal with__ *v prep*
**1** to be a customer of (someone or a business): [T1 (*no pass., usu. simple tenses*)] *I've dealt with this shop for twenty years. I've always dealt with Mrs Brown the dressmaker.* → **do with** (13), **trade at, trade with**
**2** to take action about (something or someone, usu. troublesome): [T1 (*often simple tenses*)] *Head Office deals with all complaints. How do you deal with noisy children? There are many difficulties to be dealt with when starting a new business.*
**3** to be concerned with; treat (a subject): [T1 (*simple tenses*)] *Tom's latest book deals with police methods.* → **treat of**
**4** to have a relationship with (someone); have talks with (someone): [T1 (*no pass.*)] *Why is she refusing to deal with our new neighbour?*
**5** to punish (someone): [T1 (*usu. simple tenses*)] *I'll deal with that boy when he comes home! All those who opposed us have now been dealt with.* → **reckon with** (6)

*__debar from__ *v prep* → **disbar from**
*fml* to prevent (someone) from (something or doing something) by a rule: [T1 (*no pass.*)] *The doctor was debarred from his practice after he was found guilty.* [V4b] *The judge debarred the drunken man from driving for a year.*

**debate about** *v prep*
**1** to speak or argue at length, often formally, about (a subject): [L9 + *about*] *The class have decided to debate about the housing question. The family is still debating about where to go for their holiday.* → **debate on**
**2** to think; have doubts about; try to decide about (something): [L9 + *about*] *I'm still debating about whether to let you go to camp.* → **debate in, debate with** (2)

**debate in** *v prep* → **debate about** (2), **debate with** (2)
**debate in one's mind** to think; have doubts about; try to decide (something): *I'm still debating in my mind whether to let you go to camp.*

**debate on/upon** *v prep* → **debate about** (1)
to speak or argue at length, often formally, on (a subject): [L9 + *on/upon*] *The class have decided to debate on the housing question.*

**debate with** *v prep*
**1** to argue formally with (an opposing speaker or speakers): [L9 + *with*] *We had to debate with two speakers expressing the opposing view.* [X9 + *with*] *We had to debate the housing question with two speakers expressing the opposing view.*
**2 debate with oneself** to think; have doubts

about; try to decide about (something): *I'm still debating with myself whether to let you go on holiday alone.* → **debate about** (2), **debate in**

**debit against** *v prep* → **credit to** (1), **credit with** (1), **debit to, debit with**
(in banking) to take (a sum of money) from (an account): [X9 + *against*] *I have today debited £300 against your account.*

**debit to** *v prep* → **credit to** (1), **credit with** (1), **debit against**
(in banking) to take (a sum of money) from (someone or an account): [X9 + *to* (*usu. pass.*)] *The amount of the cheque has been debited to your account.*

**debit with** *v prep* → **credit to** (1), **credit with** (1), **debit against**
(in banking) to show a debt against (someone or an account) of (a sum of money): [X9 + *with*] *The bank has debited your account with the amount of the cheque which you wrote.*

**decamp with** *v prep*
*not fml* to leave, often suddenly and secretly with (someone or something); take (someone or something) away without permission: [L9 + *with*] *Your uninvited guest has just decamped with the silver. The young writer decamped with his teacher's wife.*

**deceive in** *v prep*
**be deceived in** to discover that (someone) is not worthy or as one thought; be disappointed in (someone): *We've been deceived in that boy; we thought his behaviour was improving, but now it's worse than ever.*

**deceive into** *v prep* → **trick into,** etc.
to trick (someone) into (doing something) by lying: [X9 + *into*] *The clever salesman deceived the old lady into lending him all her money for his business, by telling her that she would get rich.*

**deceive with** *v prep*
**1** to trick (someone) by means of (something): [X9 + *with*] *Advertisers are now forbidden to deceive the public with false claims.* → **delude with** (1)
**2** to be unfaithful to (someone, esp. one's wife or husband) by having a love affair with (someone else): [X9 + *with*] *I think you've been deceiving me with your secretary.*
**3 deceive oneself with** to believe (something) falsely: *Janet deceived herself with dreams of success but they never came true.* → **delude with** (2)

**decide against** *v prep*
**1** to make a decision not in favour of (something or doing something): [L9 + *against* (*usu. simple tenses*)] *The committee decided against the plan. The family have decided against camping in the mountains. The government has decided against increasing taxes.* → **decide on,** etc.
**2** (in law) to give judgment against (someone making a request in court): [L9 + *against* (*usu. simple tenses*)] *The judge decided against the man who had made the claim.* → **decide for, find against, find for** (2)

**decide between** *v prep*
to choose between (two things or people or doing different things): [L9 + *between* (*usu. simple tenses*)] *It's difficult to decide between these two clever students for the prize. I can't decide between these two attractive houses. It's often difficult to decide between going for a walk and having a swim.*

**decide for** *v prep* → **decide against** (2), **find against, find for** (2)
(in law) to give judgment in favour of (someone making a request in court): [L9 + *for* (*usu. simple tenses*)] *The judge decided for the man who had made the claim.*

***decide on/upon** *v prep* → **agree on** (2), **decide against** (1), **determine on, settle on** (2)
to choose (someone, something, or doing something): [T1 (*usu. simple tenses*)] *Have the committee decided on the prize-winning student? We decided on blue paint for the bedroom.* [T4 (*usu. simple tenses*)] *Have you decided on spending your holiday at home?* [T6 (*usu. simple tenses*)] *Have you decided on where to camp?*

***deck out/up** *v adv* → **dress up** (2), etc.
to make (someone or something) more beautiful or cheerful: [D1 (*in*) (*often pass.*)] *Mary decked herself up for the party. The street was decked out in flags when the victory was won.*

***deck with** *v prep* also **bedeck with** → **decorate with** (1), etc.
to ornament (someone or something) with (pretty things): [D1 (OUT) (*often pass.*)] *The Christmas tree was decked with gifts. Deck the halls with green branches.*

***declaim against** *v prep*
*fml* to attack (usu. an idea) in words: [T1] *The speaker declaimed against the government's new law.*

**declare against** *v prep*
***1** to state one's opposition to (someone, something, or doing something): [T1 (*usu. simple tenses*)] *The electors declared against their former Member of Parliament. The workers declared against the new rules.* [T4 (*usu. simple tenses*)] *The city council has declared against building the new road.* → **declare for**
**2 declare war against** to state that one's nation is now at war with (another nation): *To declare war against the small island state looks like the action of a cowardly nation.* → **declare on**[2] **(1), make on** (9a), **wage against** (1)
**3 declare war against** to state that one will make every effort to stop or destroy (something, usu. bad): *The police chief has again declared war against violent crime.* → **declare on**[2] **(2), make on** (9b)

***declare for** *v prep*
to state one's support of (someone, something, or doing something): [T1 (*usu. simple*

*tenses*)] *The electors declared for their present Member of Parliament. The workers declared for the offer of increased pay and holidays.* [T4 (*usu. simple tenses*)] *The city council has declared for improving the public bus system.* → **declare against** (1)

**declare off** *v adv* → **break off** (2), **declare on¹**
to state that (something) will not take place: [X9 + OFF] *The public meeting has been declared off. The two sides declared the agreement off.*

**declare on¹** *v adv* → **break off** (2), **declare off**
to state that (something) will take place: [X9 + ON (*usu. pass.*)] *The public meeting has been declared on.*

**declare on²** *v prep*
**declare war on**
**1** to state that one's nation is now at war with (another nation): *To declare war on the small island state looks like the action of a cowardly nation.* → **declare against** (2), **make on** (9a), **wage against** (1)
**2** to state that one will make every effort to stop or destroy (something, usu. bad): *The police chief has again declared war on violent crime.* → **declare against** (3), **make on** (9b)

***declare oneself** *v pron*
to make one's views public: [IØ (*usu. simple tenses*)] *When are you going to declare yourself? The people are anxious to know which side you will take.*

**declare to** *v prep*
**1** to make a public or firm statement (about something) to (someone): [X9 + *to*] *The politician declared his views to a group of reporters from radio, television, and the newspapers.* [T5 + *to* (*usu. simple tenses*)] *I declare to you that I have never lied about the affair.*
**2** to admit possession of (goods) to (a customs officer): [T1 + *to*] *You'd better declare the diamonds to the official.*

**decorate for** *v prep*
to honour (someone) with a medal for (a good or brave deed or doing something good or brave): [X9 + *for* (*often simple tenses*)] *The Queen decorated the young soldier for courage in the face of the enemy. The girl was decorated for saving the child from drowning.*

**decorate with** *v prep*
**1** to ornament (something) with (pretty things): [T1 + *with*] *At Christmas we decorate the living rooms with coloured paper and lights.* → **adorn with, deck with, festoon with, ornament with**
**2** to improve the appearance of (a house, room, etc.) with (materials such as paint or paper): [T1 + *with*] *We decided to decorate the bedroom with blue paint and a gold paper.*
**3** to honour (someone) with (a medal) for a good or brave deed: [X9 + *with*] *The young soldier was decorated with the Military Cross.*

**decrease from** *v prep*
to become less than (an amount) or since (a time): [IØ + *from*] *The new unemployment figures have decreased from last month's. The average house price has not decreased from the high level of a few years ago.*

**decrease in** *v prep*
to become less as regards (a part): [IØ + *in*] *The newspaper has decreased in size, but not in quality.*

***dedicate to** *v prep*
**1** to declare (something) as being holy to (God): [D1] *The priests dedicated the church to God.* → **consecrate to** (1)
**2** to give (oneself or something) completely to (someone, something, or doing something): [D1] *The doctor dedicated his life to the sick people in the hot country. The doctor dedicated himself to the service of mankind.* [V4b] *The doctor dedicated his time to curing the sick.* → **consecrate to** (2), **devote to** (2)
**3** to write (something) in honour of (someone): [D1] *The writer dedicated her first book to her husband.*

**deduce from** *v prep* → **infer from**
to reach (an answer) by reasoning from (given facts): [X9 + *from* (*simple tenses*)] *What do you deduce from the voting figures? I deduce from the small crowd that the speaker is not very popular.*

**deduct from** *v prep*
to take (something such as a part) from (a total): [X9 + *from* (*usu. simple tenses*)] *Certain allowances are deducted from your income before tax is calculated.*

***deed over** *v adv*
*AmE fml* to make a formal gift of (something): [T1 (*to*) (*usu. simple tenses*)] *Father decided to deed the house over to his eldest son before he died, to avoid paying tax.*

**deface with** *v prep*
to spoil the appearance of (something) by marking it with (something): [T1 + *with*] *Someone has defaced the wall with rude messages in red paint.*

**default on** *v prep*
to fail to pay (a debt): [L9 + *on* (*usu. simple tenses*)] *The firm has defaulted on its payments for the goods.*

**defect from** *v prep*
to desert (a group to which one was formerly loyal): [L9 + *from* (*often simple tenses*)] *The politician defected from his own party and joined the Opposition.*

**defect to** *v prep*
to desert usu. a nation and offer one's loyalty to (another nation or group): [L9 + *to* (*often simple tenses*)] *Many writers, threatened with imprisonment, have defected to the West.*

**defend against** *v prep* → **defend from**
to take action to guard (oneself or someone) against (someone or something bad): [X9 + *against*] *The army prepared to defend the nation against attack by the enemy. What can we do to defend ourselves against continuously rising prices?*

**defend from** *v prep* → **defend against**
to protect (someone or something) from (someone or something bad): [X9 + *from* (*usu. simple tenses*)] *Lord, defend us from the terrors and dangers of this night. The wall was built to defend the road from being washed away by the sea.*

**defend with** *v prep*
to protect (oneself, someone, or something) with (a means of defence): [X9 + *with*] *If you go alone into the forest, you'd better defend yourself with a knife. The fighter defended his body with some clever blows to his opponent. A thinking father defends his family with insurance. The country is defended with a strong navy.*

***defer to** *v prep* → **submit to** (2)
*fml* to yield to (someone or something); show respect towards (someone): [T1 (*usu. simple tenses*)] *I will defer to your advice, which has always been helpful. New workers soon learn to defer to more experienced people.*

**define as** *v prep*
to state the meaning of (something such as a word) as being (something): [T1 + *as*] *You can define the word 'difficult' as 'not easy.' In the contract agreed between the union and the employers, overtime is defined as work after 6 p.m. on weekdays, and anytime on Saturdays, Sundays, and public holidays.*

**deflect from** *v prep*
**1** to turn (something such as a bullet) aside from (a direction): [X9 + *from*] *This special metal shield will deflect a bullet from its course.*
***2** to cause (someone) to leave (something such as work): [D1] *Concern for his family deflected him from his studies.* → **distract from, divert from**

**defraud of** *v prep* → **cheat out of,** etc.
**1** to deceive (someone) in order to gain (something he possesses): [X9 + *of*] *The clever salesman defrauded the old lady of all her money.*
**2** to prevent (someone) from having (something such as a right): [X9 + *of*] *Many children are defrauded of a chance for a good education, simply because they live in the wrong place.*

**degenerate into** *v prep*
to become lowered, morally or in quality to (something less good): [L9 + *into*] *The workers' demands for their rights have degenerated into troublemaking. Everyone needs time to play, but some let it degenerate into laziness. The children in your class need gentle treatment, but don't let your kindness degenerate into weakness.*

**delegate to** *v prep* → **depute to**
to pass (one's own duties, responsibility, etc.) to (someone else) in one's place: [T1 + *to*] *The chairman is unable to attend the meeting, so he has delegated his voting powers to the secretary.*

**delete from** *v prep* → **erase from** (1), **leave out**[1] (3), **miss out** (1), **omit from**
to take (something such as words) out of (usu. something written or printed): [T1 + *from*] *Why have the names of the performers been deleted from the advertisements for the concert? The offending passage has been deleted from the new printing of the book.*

**deliberate about/on/over/upon** *v prep*
*fml* to consider (something) at length and with care: [L9 + *about/on/over/upon*] *The committee have been deliberating all afternoon over the question of the new appointments.*

**delight at/by** *v prep*
**be delighted at/by** to be very pleased about (something): *We are all delighted at your success.*

***delight in** *v prep* → **glory in** (1), **rejoice at, rejoice in** (1), **rejoice over, take in**[2] (7)
to take great pleasure in (someone, something, or doing something): [T1 (*no pass., usu. simple tenses*)] *Mary delights in the new house.* [T4] *Jim delights in driving his new car.*

**delight with** *v prep*
**be delighted with** to be very pleased with (something or someone): *The whole family is delighted with the new house. When the baby was born, his elder sister was delighted with him.*

**deliver from** *v prep*
**1** to take (something) usu. to a building, from (a place which sold, supplied, or sent it): [T1 + *from*] *Has the furniture been delivered from the factory yet?*
***2** to save (someone or something) from (something bad, as a threat): [D1] *"And lead us not into temptation, but deliver us from evil."* (The Lord's Prayer) *We need a strong leader to deliver the country from the dangers of falling money values.*

**deliver of** *v prep*
***1** *old use* to rob (someone) of (something such as money): [D1] *The thieves delivered the passengers of their money.* → **ease of** (2), **relieve of**
**2 be delivered of** *fml* to give birth to (a child): *Mrs Brown was safely delivered of a fine boy in the early hours of this morning.*
**3 deliver oneself of** to express (something such as an opinion): *It's so uninteresting to listen to a politician delivering himself of his views.*

**deliver over/up** *v adv* → **give up** (7), etc., (8), etc.
*fml* to yield (someone or something) (usu. to someone): [X9 + OVER/UP (*to*)] *We delivered the thief over to the police. When the sale is complete, you must deliver the house over (to the new owner). The citizens were forced to deliver up the town to the enemy.*

**deliver to** *v prep*
**1** to take (something such as post) to (someone): [T1 + *to*] *The postman delivered this*

*parcel to our address, but it's for you.*

**2** to cause (something) to reach (someone): [X9 + *to*] *You will be able to deliver your speech to the crowd after the Minister has spoken. The new wage demands have delivered another blow to the government's plan for price controls.*

**deliver under** *v prep* → **give under** (2)

**deliver under hand and seal** *law* to make (an agreement) lawful by formally giving it to the other party: [(*usu. pass.*)] *This agreement is delivered under my hand and seal this day . . .*

**deliver up** *v adv* → DELIVER OVER

**delude into** *v prep*

**1** to mislead (someone) intentionally into (something or doing or believing something): [T1 + *into*] *We have been deluded into false hopes by the government's meaningless promises. The clever salesman deluded the old lady into thinking that she would get rich if she lent him her money for his business.* → **trick into,** etc.

**2 delude oneself into** to be falsely hopeful about (doing or believing something): *Don't delude yourself into thinking that prices will ever fall.*

**delude with** *v prep*

**1** to mislead (someone) intentionally with (something false): [T1 + *with*] *Any clever politician can delude the voters with election promises.* → **deceive with** (1)

**2 delude oneself with** to believe (something) falsely: *That dull child's mother is deluding herself with dreams of his future success.* → **deceive with** (3)

**deluge with** *v prep* → **flood with,** etc.

**1** to flood (an area) with (water): [X9 + *with* (*usu. pass.*)] *The fields were deluged with rain.*

***2** to crowd: overwhelm (someone or something) with (a lot of things): [D1 (*often pass.*)] *The crowd deluged the speaker with questions. The office was deluged with complaints.*

**delve into** *v prep*

to search in (something) for information: [L9 + *into*] *I like to delve into old books looking for forgotten history. Before he was appointed, the committee delved into his past record.*

**demand from** *v prep*

to ask firmly; command (something) from (someone or something): [T1 + *from*] *The thieves demanded money from the passengers. The captain demanded obedience from his men.*

***demand of** *v prep* → **ask of,** etc.

to expect (something) from (someone or something): [D1] *Hard work will be demanded of students in this course. The increased population is demanding too much of the electricity supply. Is it wrong for the police to demand help of the public in fighting violent crime?*

***demean oneself** *v pron*

**1** *old use* to behave: [IØ (*simple tenses*)] *How did my son demean himself in the presence of the king?*

**2** *fml* to behave in an unworthy way; lower oneself socially or morally: [IØ (*simple tenses*)] *I wouldn't demean myself by living in such a dirty place. Never demean yourself by taking money as a reward for doing something wrong.* → **descend to** (3), etc.

**demonstrate against** *v prep*

to show publicly one's disapproval of (something), usu. in a crowd: [L9 + *against*] *The workers are holding a mass meeting with speeches and songs to demonstrate against the government's new law.*

**demonstrate to** *v prep*

**1** to show the practical working of (something) to (someone): [T1 + *to*] *Let me demonstrate this machine to you.* [T6 + *to*] *Let me demonstrate to you how this machine works.*

**2** to show (something) clearly to (someone); prove (something) to (someone): [X9 + *to* (*usu. simple tenses*)] *I hope this message demonstrates my feelings to the students. I hope this demonstrates to you how I feel. How can I demonstrate to you that my story is true?*

**demote from** *v prep*

to lower (someone) from (a higher rank or position): [X9 + *from*] *You shall be demoted from the rank of general as a punishment.*

**demote to** *v prep*

to lower (someone) to (a less important rank or position): [X9 + *to*] *The general was demoted to captain as a severe punishment.*

**demur at/to** *v prep* → **object to, protest against, raise to** (6), **take to** (13)

*fml* to oppose (something) slightly; express objection to (an idea): [X9 + *at/to* (*usu. simple tenses*)] *The committee demurred at the suggestion that they should meet again the next day. Even the government's own party demurred to the new election rules.*

**denounce for** *v prep*

to express great disapproval of (someone) because of (something or doing something); complain about (someone), often to the police: [T1 + *for*] *The woman denounced her neighbour for helping the enemy.*

**dent up** *v adv*

esp. *AmE not fml* to damage (something) by hitting: [T1 + UP] *John dented up the car in the accident.*

**denude of** *v prep*

to make (something) bare of (something it usually has); take all from (someone): [X9 + *of*] *The country was denuded of trees. The thieves denuded him of money.*

***deny oneself** *v pron*

to be unselfish, esp. in not having something: [IØ] *By denying herself, Mother gave the children a good education.* [D1] *By denying her-*

*self her own needs, Mother gave the children a good education.*

**deny to** *v prep*

**1** to state that (something) is not true to (someone): [T1 + *to*] *The prisoner denied the charge to the police.* [T5 + *to*] *The prisoner denied to the police that he had taken part in the robbery.*

***2** to refuse to allow (something) to be given to (someone): [D1 (*usu. simple tenses*)] *The university rules deny entry to large numbers of clever students. A fair chance in life is denied to many children.* → **refuse to**

**depart from** *v prep*

**1** to leave (a place): [IØ + *from*] *This train departs from London at 10.00.*

***2** to leave; act in a different way from (something usual or good): [T1] *The club chairman suggested that they should depart from their usual custom and finish the season with a concert instead of a dance. Tell your story without departing from the truth. "Train up a child in the way he should go: and when he is old, he will not depart from it."* (The Bible) → **adhere to** (2), etc.

**depend on/upon** *v prep*

***1** to trust; be sure of (someone or something): [T1] *You can always depend on Jim, he won't fail you. I depended on the map but it was wrong.* [V3] *I depend on you to do it.* [V4a] *You can't depend on the weather being fine for anything you plan in England.* → **bank on, bet on** (2), **build on** (2), **calculate on** (2), **count on, figure on** (1), **gamble on** (2), **reckon on, rely on** (1), **trust in, trust to** (1), **wager on** (2)

***2** to be dependent on or supported by (someone or something): [T1 (*simple tenses*)] *My wife and children depend on me. The people depend on his leadership.*

***3** to vary according to; be influenced or decided by (something): [T1 (*no pass., simple tenses*)] *Whether the game will be played depends on the weather.* [T6 (*simple tenses*)] *His decision will depend on how soon he meets the committee. The success of the sports day depends on whether it rains or not.* → **hang on** (2), **hinge on, pivot on** (2), **rely on** (2), **ride on²** (4), **turn on²** (3)

**4 depend on/upon it** to be quite sure; (at the beginning or end of a sentence): [(*imper. or with can, may*)] *I'll be there, (you can) depend on it!*

**deplete of** *v prep*

to empty or almost empty (something) of (something it contained): [X9 + *of*] *I have had to deplete my bank account of most of my money, to pay for the holiday. After the thieves had left, the room was depleted of its furniture and valuables. Mankind must take care not to deplete the earth of its valuable minerals.*

***depose to** *v prep*

*fml* to make a formal sworn statement in court about (having done something): [T4] *The witness deposed to having seen the two men steal the jewels.*

***deprive of** *v prep*

to cause (someone or something) to be without (something needed): [D1] *The hot sun deprived the flowers of water. You cannot deprive me of my rights. Many children are deprived of a good education, simply because they live in the wrong place.*

***depute to** *v prep* → **delegate to**

*fml* to pass (one's own duties, responsibility, etc.) to (someone else) in one's place: [D1] *The chairman is unable to attend the meeting, so he has deputed his voting power to the secretary. I have deputed the keeping of the accounts to John while I am in hospital.*

**deputize for** *v prep* → **stand in for,** etc.

to take the place of (someone): [L9 + *for*] *I would like you to deputize for me as chairman while I am on holiday.*

**derive from** *v prep*

***1** to get (something) from (something or someone): [D1] *She derives great pleasure from her grandchildren. His income is derived from several different businesses.* → **draw from** (4)

***2** (of a word) to (cause to) have its origin in (another word or language): [T1 (*no pass.*)] *The word 'warmth' derives from 'warm.'* [D1 (*usu. pass.*)] *The word 'grammar' is derived from Greek.*

**3 be derived from** to be made from (something); have its origin in (something): *This oil is derived from minerals found deep in the earth. The custom of raising one's hat to a lady is derived from the old practice of covering one's face with a metal guard which one would lift on greeting a friend or lady.*

***derogate from** *v prep*

*fml* to lessen (something good): [T1 (*no pass.*)] *Recent action by the Minister has derogated from the respect usually given him by the electors.*

***descant on/upon** *v prep*

**1** (in music) to sing another tune above (a main tune): [T1 (*no pass.*)] *The boy singers were asked to descant on the tune.*

**2** *fml* to say something further or at length about (a subject): [T1 (*pass. rare*)] *Would the speaker care to descant upon the subject raised by the questioner?*

**descend from** *v prep*

**1** *often fml* to come down from (something higher): [IØ + *from*] *The Queen descended from her carriage when it arrived at the palace.*

***2** to be passed down from (someone living in an earlier time): [T1 (*no pass.*)] *This ring has descended from my great-grandmother.* → **hand down** (3), etc.

**3 be descended from** to have one's family origins in (usu. someone): *He claims to be de-*

*scended from kings.* also **be descended of** → **come from** (3), **come of** (2)

**descend into** *v prep*
*often fml* to go down into (something beneath one): [IØ + *into*] *The miners descended into the cave to search for the missing climbers.*

***descend on/upon** *v prep* → **swoop on**
**1** to arrive suddenly to stay with (someone): [T1] *The whole family descends on us every Christmas.*
**2** to attack (someone) suddenly: [T1 (*usu. simple tenses*)] *Thieves descended on the travellers while they slept.*

**descend to** *v prep*
**1** *often fml* to come or go down to (something lower): [IØ + *to*] *The actress descended to the stage on the end of a strong wire.*
***2** to pass to (someone) after someone's death: [T1 (*no pass.*)] *The property descended to the man's eldest son.*
***3** to lower oneself morally to (something or doing something wrong): [T1 (*no pass.*)] *If a prisoner is badly treated he may descend to violence.* [T4] *I'm surprised that you would descend to lying.* → **condescend to** (2), **demean oneself** (2), **lower oneself, sink to** (5), **stoop to** (2)
**4 descend to particulars** to start talking about details: *If we want to reach an agreement before midnight, we must now descend to particulars; we've dealt with all the general points.*

***descend upon** *v prep* → DESCEND ON

**describe as** *v prep*
to say that (someone, oneself or something) is (something): [X9 + *as* (*not continuous tenses*)] *I would describe him as an excellent teacher. Would you describe this piece of music as well written? The prisoner described himself as an unemployed painter.*

**describe to** *v prep*
to tell about the nature, appearance, etc., of (something or someone) to (someone or a group): [T1 + *to*] *Can you describe your attacker to the court? You will have to describe the stolen articles to the police.* [T6 + *to*] *It is impossible to describe to you how I feel.*

**deserve of** *v prep*
**deserve better/ill/well of** *fml* to be worthy of better treatment, punishment, or reward from (someone or a group): [*simple tenses, often perfect*] *The student has deserved ill of this school, and must be asked to leave. This man has deserved well of his countrymen, and shall be honoured by them. I thought I had deserved better of the firm than to be dismissed with so little reason.*

**design for** *v prep*
**1** to plan the shape and style of (something) for (someone or a purpose): [X9 + *for*] *This man designs dresses for the Queen. The mat has been designed specially for the children's room. The family designed the house for their own needs.* [IØ + *for*] *She designs for a famous shop.*
***2** to intend (something) specially for (something or someone): [D1 (*usu. pass.*)] *This dictionary is designed for foreign students. The meal was designed for a large party of children, but only a few arrived.*

***designate as** *v prep*
*fml* to appoint (someone or something) to be (something): [X1] *The hospital has been designated as a university hospital. I designate Mr Sharp as the next chairman of this committee.*

**desist from** *v prep*
*fml* to cease (doing something): [IØ + *from* (*simple tenses*)] *Kindly desist from treating the furniture so badly.*

***despair of** *v prep*
**1** to be without hope of (something or doing something): [T1 (*simple tenses*)] *The general's life was despaired of, but he refused to die.* [T4 (*simple tenses*)] *Do not despair of seeing your father again.*
**2** to feel very anxious about (someone), esp. as regards his behaviour: [T1 (*no pass., simple tenses*)] *I despair of those children.*

**despatch to** *v prep* → DISPATCH TO

**despoil of** *v prep*
*fml* to rob (something) of (something): [X9 + *of*] *The enemy have despoiled the whole valley of its crops. The trees were despoiled of their leaves in the high wind.*

**destine for** *v prep*
**be destined for**
**1** to be intended to be sent to (a place): *This load of fruit is destined for the city.*
**2** *fml* to be intended, by or as if by fate, for (something): *Born in the theatre, he seemed to be destined for the stage.*

**detach from** *v prep*
**1** to unfasten or unfix (something) from (something): [T1 + *from*] *It was difficult to detach the tyre from the wheel.*
***2** to separate (someone or oneself), as in thought, from (someone or something): [D1] *The woman had no wish to detach herself from her lover. I have to detach myself from the activity round me in order to work. "Remember Jesus said he came bringing a sword. But he was so detached from the goods of this world that he left it behind him."* (Michael Arlen, *Man's Mortality*)

***detail off** *v adv* → **tell off** (3)
*mil* to order (a group usu. of soldiers) (for a special duty, or to do a special job): [T1 (*for*) (*often pass.*)] *A small group of men were detailed off for burial duty. The officer detailed a small party off and put them to clearing the road.* [V3] *The soldiers were detailed off to dig ditches.*

**detect in** *v prep*
**1** to notice (something) in (something): [T1 + *in* (*usu. simple tenses*)] *I can detect signs of improvement in your thinking. Only a trained eye could detect such small faults in the lettering.*

**2** to catch (someone) doing (something wrong): [X9 + *in* (*usu. simple tenses*)] *The policeman waited to detect the prisoner in a lie.*

**deter from** *v prep* → **discourage from**
to prevent (someone) by discouragement from (something or doing something): [X9 + *from* (*simple tenses*)] *Nothing will deter him from success. Will atomic weapons deter powerful nations from war? Bad weather did not deter us from going out.*

**determine on/upon** *v prep* → **decide on**, etc.
to choose (someone, something, or doing something) firmly: [T1 (*simple tenses*)] *Have the committee determined on the prize-winning student? We determined on blue paint for the bedroom.* [T4 (*simple tenses*)] *Have you determined on spending your holiday at home?* [T6 (*simple tenses*)] *Have you determined on where to camp?*

**detract from** *v prep* → **take away from** (5), **take from** (10)
*fml* to make (something) seem less valuable or important; lessen the effect of (something): [T1 (*no pass., simple tenses*)] *The fact that you had some help does not detract from your success.*

**develop from** *v prep*
to (cause to) grow from; arise out of (something): [L9 + *from*] *This tall tree developed from a small seed. Who knows what results will develop from your first success? A reduced standard of living will develop from increased taxation and rising unemployment.* [X9 + *from*] *Jim's father developed the business from small beginnings. The book has been developed from a short story.*

**develop into** *v prep*
to (cause to) grow into; become (something or someone): [L9 + *into*] *Jane is developing into a fine figure of a young woman. A small seed can develop into a tall tree. Unhappy experiences in childhood often develop into violent and criminal tendencies in a man.*

**deviate from** *v prep*
**1** *fml* to be different from (something): [T1 (*pass. rare*)] *The boy's behaviour deviates from the usual pattern.*
**2** *fml* to act in a different way from (something usual or good): [T1 (*pass. rare*)] *Let us not deviate from our plan. Tell your story without deviating from the truth.* → **adhere to** (2), etc.

**devil for** *v prep*
to work for (a lawyer): [T1 (*no pass.*)] *The judge began his working life as a young man by devilling for a clever lawyer.*

**devolve on/upon** *v prep*
*fml* (of duties, responsibility, power, etc.) to go to (another person or group); be passed to (someone): [T1 (*no pass., usu. simple tenses*)] *In many countries the government devolves some power on towns and cities to control their own affairs. When the girl fell ill, the care of her baby devolved on her mother.*

**devote to** *v prep*
***1** to give (something) completely to (something or doing something): [D1 (*usu. simple tenses*)] *This department of the store is devoted to machine tools and engineering needs.* [V4b (*usu. simple tenses*)] *I have to devote part of my income to repaying my debts.*
***2** to give (oneself, one's time, etc.) freely and with care to (something): [D1 (*usu. simple tenses*)] *He devotes his time to the garden. He has always devoted himself to his music.* [V4b (*usu. simple tenses*)] *He devoted every Saturday afternoon to fishing.* → **consecrate to** (2), **dedicate to** (2)
**3 be devoted to** to care very much about (someone or something): *Jim is devoted to his wife and family. A true artist is devoted to his work. All the soldiers were devoted to their leader.*

**devour with** *v prep*
**be devoured with** to be filled with; give all one's attention to (a strong feeling): *Mother was devoured with worry when the children did not come home at the usual time.*

***dice away** *v adv*
to waste (money) by gambling: [T1] *He had a lot of money, but was foolish enough to dice most of it away.*

**dice with** *v prep*
**dice with death** to take unnecessary risks: *If those climbers go up the mountain in this bad weather they will be dicing with death.*

**dicker for** *v prep not fml* → **BARGAIN FOR** (1)

**dicker over** *v prep not fml* → **BARGAIN ABOUT**

**dicker with** *v prep not fml* → **BARGAIN WITH**

**dictate to** *v prep*
**1** to read (words) aloud to (someone such as a secretary), who writes them down: [L9 + *to*] *How fast do you dictate to your secretary?* [X9 + *to*] *Don't go home yet, I have three letters to dictate to you.*
***2** to give orders to (someone): [T1 (*usu. simple tenses*)] *Don't try to dictate to children, they will obey you better if you ask them politely. No person of a strong character likes to be dictated to.*
***3** to enforce (something over which one has power) on (someone): [D1 (*usu. simple tenses*)] *You should be able to dictate the terms of the agreement to the firm which you are buying.* [D6 (*usu. simple tenses*)] *The government tries to dictate to people how they should spend their money. No one is going to dictate to me where to live!*

**diddle out of** *v adv prep* → **cheat out of**, etc.
**1** *infml* to deceive (someone) in order to gain (something he possesses): [X9 + OUT + *of*] *The clever salesman diddled the old lady out of all her money.*
**2** *infml* to prevent (someone) from having (something such as a right): [X9 + OUT + *of*] *Many children are diddled out of a chance for a good education, simply because they live in the wrong place.*

***die away** *v adv* → **fade away** (1), **fade out** (1)
(esp. of a sound, wind, light) to become weaker or fainter until it ceases: [IØ] *The sound of the music died away.*

***die back** *v adv* → **die down** (1)
(of plants) to die but remain alive at the roots: [IØ (*often simple tenses*)] *The bushes may have died back in this cold autumn but they will grow again next spring.* —**dieback** *n*

**die by** *v prep*
**1** to die by means of (something): [IØ + *by*] *They that deny the power of the king shall die by the sword. Many people died by drowning in the great floods.* → **die from, die of** (1)
**2 die by one's own hand** to kill oneself: *The family are refusing to say, but many people think their son may have died by his own hand.*

***die down** *v adv*
**1** (of plants) to die but remain alive at the roots: [IØ] *The bushes may have died down in this cold autumn but they will grow again next spring.* → **die back**
**2** to become gradually less strong until it ceases: [IØ] *The fire is dying down, put some more wood on! The wind died down at last and all was quiet. When the hunt has died down we shall be able to leave our hiding place.* → **settle down** (8)

**die for** *v prep*
**1** to be prepared to die to support (an idea) or save (someone): [L9 + *for*] *Many religious people would die for their beliefs. It used to be considered part of a young man's duty to die for his country. Christians believe that Christ died for them.*
**2 be dying for** to want (something) very much: *It's so hot today, I'm dying for a drink.*

**die from** *v prep* → **die by, die of** (1)
to die following (something, except illness or feeling): [L9 + *from*] *In a severe winter, wild animals can die from lack of food. The young driver died from the wounds that he received in the road accident. The child died from her fall out of the high window.*

**die game** *v adj*
to die bravely: [L9 + **game**] *The old general died game, fighting death to the last.*

**die hard** *v adj*
**1** to die painfully or slowly: [L9 + **hard**] *My grandmother died hard, suffering through a long illness.*
***2** to be slow to cease: [IØ (*simple tenses*)] *Old customs die hard.* —**diehard** *n, adj*

**die in** *v prep*
**1** to die during (an event) or in (a place): [IØ + *in*] *The young driver died in the car crash. Fewer people die in hospital than at home.*
**2 die in one's bed** to die peacefully and naturally: *I was glad that my uncle died in his bed.*
**3 die in harness** to die while still working at one's usual job: *It was typical of the great actor to die in harness, actually during a performance.*

**die of** *v prep*
**1** to die because of (something such as an illness or feeling): [L9 + *of*] *In a severe winter, many wild animals can die of hunger. My grandmother died of grief soon after her husband's death. "She died of a fever, and no one could save her."* (song) → **die by, die from**
**2 be dying of** to feel (something) very strongly: *The children are dying of curiosity to see what's in the parcel.*

***die off** *v adv*
(of a group of living things) to die one by one: [IØ (*often continuous tenses*)] *The trees have been dying off during the severe winter, and there are few left. The deer in the forest are all dying off from disease.*

***die out** *v adv*
(of families, types, practices, and ideas) to cease to exist; disappear: [IØ] *If too many of these rare animals are killed, their kind will die out. It's time this selfish habit died out. That style of music died out ten years ago.*

**die with** *v prep*
**1** to die having (something or someone): [IØ + *with*] *He died with his family all around him, and with his soul at peace.*
**2** to be lost at the death of (someone): [L9 + *with*] *His secret died with him, and now we shall never know the truth.*
**3 die with one's boots on** to die while still active: *Please don't send Grandfather to a rest home for old people, I know he would rather die with his boots on.*
**4 die with dignity** to die as nature intended, without false means of being kept alive, such as machines: *Does everyone have the right to choose between being kept alive by heart and breathing machines, and being allowed to die with dignity?*

**differ about** *v prep* → **DIFFER ON**

**differ from** *v prep*
**1** to be different from (someone or something): [L9 + *from* (*no pass., simple tenses*)] *She differs from her sister in the colour of her eyes. I think that the desk in the shop differs from the one I have at home.*
***2** to disagree with (an opinion, or someone): [T1 (*no pass., simple tenses*)] *I must differ from your opinion on the matter. I have to differ from you on the question of cost.* → **differ with**

**differ in** *v prep*
to be different with regard to (a part): [L9 + *in* (*simple tenses*)] *Materials differ in the way the threads are woven together. She and her sister differ in eye colour. The two brothers differ in their judgment of this piece of music.*

**differ on/about** *v prep*
to have different opinions concerning (a subject): [L9 + *on/about* (*simple tenses*)] *The committee differed on the question of appointing the next chairman. The two brothers differed about politics.*

***differ with** *v prep* → **differ from** (2)
to disagree with (someone or an opinion): [T1 (*no pass., simple tenses*)] *I have to differ with you on the question of cost. I must differ with your opinion on the matter.*

***differentiate between** *v prep*
**1** to make or tell the difference between (two people or things): [T1 (*no pass.*)] *You can differentiate between the houses by the shape of their chimneys.* → **distinguish between,** etc.
**2** to treat (different people) unfairly, showing favour to one group: [T1 (*no pass.*)] *Women complain that many employers differentiate between male and female workers when calculating their rank and pay.* → **discriminate between** (2)

***differentiate from** *v prep*
**1** to see (one thing or person) as different from (another): [D1] *The house is differentiated from its neighbour by the shape of its chimney.* → **discern from, discriminate from** (1), **distinguish from** (1)
**2** to show the difference between (someone or something) and (someone or something else); set (someone or something) apart from (someone or something else): [D1] *It is the power of speech which most clearly differentiates man from the animals.* → **tell from** (2), etc.

***dig at** *v prep*
*not fml* to speak to (someone) in an unpleasant way: [T1] *The children don't like that teacher, she's always digging at them.*

**dig down** *v adv*
**1** to dig below the surface of the earth: [IØ + DOWN] *If you dig down far enough, you may find some valuable old coins.*
***2** *AmE infml* to pay with an effort: [IØ] *Come on, you can afford to give us something, just dig down a little.*

**dig for** *v prep*
**1** to dig in order to find (something): [IØ + *for*] *Please stop the dog digging in my garden for his bones.* [T1] *People are still digging for gold in these hills.*
***2** to try to find (information) with effort: [T1 (*no pass.*)] *I've been digging for the figures in the library, but without much success.*
**3 dig for victory** *BrE* to grow food as part of a war effort: *We grew vegetables in the garden during the war; like all our neighbours, we were digging for victory.*

**dig in[1]** *v adv*
**1** to mix (something) with the soil by digging: [X9 + IN] *Dig this chemical in thoroughly and your crops will grow faster.*
**2** to push (something sharp) inwards: [X9 + IN] *This meat is so hard, you have to dig the knife in before you can cut it.*
***3** to dig a protective place (for oneself, a gun, etc.): [IØ] *The soldiers were ordered to dig in.* [T1] *The soldiers were ordered to dig themselves in.*
***4** *not fml* to make certain of the position of (oneself), as at work: [T1] *I had plenty of time to dig myself in when I started the new job. Get dug in as quickly as you can, then the work won't worry you.*
***5** *infml* to start eating: [IØ (*usu. imper.*)] *Dinner's ready, dig in, everybody!* → **tuck in** (4), etc.
**6 dig one's heels/toes in** *not fml* to act firmly; refuse to change one's mind: *The committee tried to persuade the chairman to give them more time for a decision, but he dug his heels in and refused to listen.* → **stick in[1]** (4)

**dig in[2]** *v prep*
**1** to push (something sharp) into (something): [X9 + *in*] *You have to dig a fork in the fruit to hold it steady.*
**2 dig someone in the ribs** to touch someone with one's elbow, in sharing a joke, esp. secretly: *Hiding his laughter, he dug me in the ribs, but I didn't see what was so funny.*

**dig into** *v prep*
**1** to mix (something) with (soil, etc.) by digging: [X9 + *into*] *Farmers dig all kinds of chemicals into the soil to help the crops to grow.*
**2** to (cause to) be pushed into (something or someone): [L9 + *into*] *Please move away a little, your books are digging into me.* [X9 + *into*] *When I dug the spade into the ground I felt something hard.*
***3** *infml* to start eating (food) hungrily: [T1] *He sat down and at once dug into his meal.* → **tuck into** (3), etc.
***4** *not fml* to examine (something) thoroughly: [T1] *The police are digging into this case.*
***5** *not fml* to make certain of the position of (oneself) at (work): [D1] *I had plenty of time to dig myself into the new job. Get dug into your new duties as soon as you can, it saves worry.*
***6** to (cause to) work hard at (something): [T1 (*no pass.*)] *I'd better dig into my studies, the examinations start next week.* [D1 (*usu. pass.*)] *I'd better get dug into my studies, the examinations start next week.*

**dig out** *v adv*
**1** to find and take out (something) by digging: [X9 + OUT] *The hunters dug out the fox. The doctor had to dig the bullet out. Copper is dug out of the earth.*
**2** to make (a hollow space) by digging: [X9 + OUT (*of*)] *The climbers dug out a cave in the side of the mountain, for shelter that night. They travelled in a boat dug out of a log.* —**dug out** *n, adj*
***3** to free (someone, something, or oneself) from being buried in earth or esp. snow: [T1 (*of*)] *After the snowstorm we had to dig ourselves out. We had to dig the car out of a bank of snow. How long did it take to dig out the buried miners?* [IØ (*AmE*)] *Three towns in the North are digging out this morning.*
***4** *not fml* to obtain (information or money) by searching: [T1 (*of*)] *The police should be able to dig the truth out of him. It must have*

*taken a long time to dig the facts out of all these old books.*

*__5__ *infml* to find (something) by searching: [T1] *I dug out these old trousers to give to the boy.*

*__6__ esp. *AmE not fml* to leave; move quickly away: [IØ (*for*)] *The fox dug out for the forest where he would be safe.* → **clear out** (6), **cut out** (11), **light out**

**dig over** *v adv*

**1** to dig (a surface of earth) thoroughly: [X9 + OVER] *Be sure to dig the whole garden over before winter.*

*__2__ *not fml* to reconsider (something): [T1a] *I'd like some time to dig over the questions raised in today's meeting.*

**dig up** *v adv*

**1** to destroy (something) by digging: [X9 + UP] *During the war people dug up their flower gardens to grow vegetables.*

*__2__ to remove (something) by digging: [T1] *The old rose bush has died and ought to be dug up.*

*__3__ to find (something buried) by digging: [T1] *A rare find of valuable ancient Christian silver has been dug up in a field near us.*

*__4__ *infml* to find (something, as an idea) by searching: [T1] *Where did you dig that idea up? How he always manages to dig up a fresh excuse for being late, I'll never know.*

*__5__ *infml* to collect (something) by searching: [T1] *Between us we should be able to dig up enough money for your ticket.*

**digress from** *v prep*

to wander in one's speaking or thinking, away from (the subject): [L9 + *from*] *Mr Chairman, you're digressing from the purpose of this meeting.*

***dilate on/upon** *v prep* → **expatiate upon**

*fml* to speak or write at length about (a subject): [T1] *She kept dilating on her son's cleverness.*

**dilute with** *v prep*

**1** to make (a liquid) thinner by adding (more liquid): [T1 + *with*] *If you dilute the soup with hot water it will feed more people.*

*__2__ to weaken (something such as an idea) with (something): [D1] *The government's new law on wage and price control is diluted with exceptions.*

**dim down** *v adv* → **dim up**

(in theatre, etc.) to reduce the brightness of (lighting) gradually: [T1 + DOWN] *Dim the stage lights down during scene three, when evening is supposed to be falling.*

**dim out** *v adv*

**1** to make (light) fainter: [T1 + OUT] *The lights were dimmed out when the electricity supply was reduced.*

*__2__ to partly darken (a place) by fading the lights: [T1] *The whole city was dimmed out when the electricity supply was reduced.* —**dim-out** *n* → **black out** (2)

**dim up** *v adv* → **dim down**

(in theatre, etc.) to increase the brightness of (lighting) gradually: [T1 + UP] *During the first scene, which begins early in the morning, we'll dim the lights up to give the effect of growing daylight.*

***din in/into**[1] *v adv; prep* → **hammer in** (3), etc. **hammer into** (3), etc.

*not fml* to teach (something) with force and repetition: [T1] *The speaker tried to din in his point, but the crowd were not interested.* [D1] *Can't you din some manners into that boy?*

***din in**[2] *v prep*

(of a noise) to sound loudly in (someone's ears): [T1 (*no pass., usu. continuous tenses*)] *The noise of the party was still dinning in my ears as I drove away.*

***din into** *v prep* → DIN IN[2]

**dine at** *v prep*

to eat dinner at (a certain place): [L9 + *at*] *We usually dine at a nice little restaurant in town when we have visitors.*

**dine in** *v adv* → **dine out, eat in, eat out** (1)

to eat dinner at home: [L9 + IN] *Are we dining in tonight?*

**dine off** *v prep*

**1** to eat one's food from (certain dishes): [L9 + *off*] *Does the Queen really dine off gold plates?* → **eat off**[2] (1), **eat out of** (1), **feed off** (1)

**2** to eat (certain food), esp. for dinner: [L9 + *off*] *I wish I could afford to dine off fresh meat every day.* → **eat off**[2] (2), **feed off** (2), **feed on** (1), **live off** (1), **live on**[2] (2)

*__3__ to eat at the cost of (someone else): [T1 (*no pass.*)] *He's been dining off his brother for weeks.* → **eat off**[2] (3), **live off** (2), **live on**[2] (3)

*__4__ to gain social success with (often a story or news): [T1 (*pass. rare*)] *Ever since his adventure in the mountains, he has been dining off the story. How long can she dine off her former success?* → **dine out on**

**dine on** *v prep*

to eat (certain food): [L9 + *on*] *How pleasant it is to dine on fine well-cooked fish and fresh vegetables, in such charming surroundings!*

**dine out** *v adv* → **dine in, eat in, eat out** (1)

to eat dinner in a restaurant or at someone else's home: [L9 + OUT] *Let's dine out tonight, I'm too tired to cook. Haven't you remembered that we're dining out at the Millers' tonight?*

***dine out on** *v adv prep* → **dine off** (4)

to gain social success and often a free meal with (often a story or news): [T1 (*pass. rare*)] *Ever since his adventure in the mountains, he has been dining out on the story. How long can she dine out on her former success?*

**dip in** *v adv*

**1** to put (something) into liquid for a short time: [X9 + IN] *I think the water's too cold to swim, so I'll just dip a toe in.*

*__2__ *not fml* to share: [IØ] *Put the presents in the*

*middle of the room so that everyone can dip in.*

**dip into** *v prep*

**1** to put (something) quickly into (liquid): [X9 + *into*] *I'll allow the children to dip their bread into the soup.* → **dunk in**

**2** to (cause to) reach into (a container): [L9 + *into*] *The children were invited to dip into the barrel for a present.* [X9 + *into*] *The children were invited to dip their hands into the barrel for a present.*

**3** to swim for a short time in (water): [L9 + *into*] *The swimmer dipped into the river but it was too cold.*

*__4__ to seem to sink suddenly into (water): [T1 (*no pass.*)] *The sun dips into the sea each evening.*

*__5__ *not fml* to examine (something) quickly or not deeply: [T1 (*no pass.*)] *I usually dip into a book before deciding whether to read it. If you dip into the future you can see fearful dangers ahead.* → **look into** (3)

*__6__ to use part of (one's money): [T1 (*no pass.*)] *I had to dip into the money I had saved to pay for the holiday.*

**7 dip into one's pocket/purse** to provide money: *I had to dip deep into my pocket to pay for the holiday.*

**8 dip into the till** to steal money, usu. from the firm where one works: *The secretary was dismissed when it was discovered that she had been dipping into the till for several years.*

**dip to** *v prep*

to be lowered to (something): [IØ + *to*] *The international exchange rate dipped to a low point yesterday.*

**direct to** *v prep*

**1** to address (something such as a letter) to (someone or a place): [X9 + *to*] *The parcel was directed to the wrong address.* → **address to** (1)

**2** to speak; intend (something) for (usu. someone): [X9 + *to*] *My next remarks are directed to the boys and girls of this school. Please direct all complaints to Head Office.* → **address to** (2)

**3** to explain the correct way to (someone) to reach (a place): [X9 + *to*] *Could you please direct me to the Post Office?*

**4** to aim (something) towards (a purpose): [X9 + *to*] *The system is directed to providing help for old people. The government will direct the additional taxes to industries in greatest need.* also **direct towards**

**5 direct one's/someone's attention to** to (cause to) notice, think, or take action about (something or doing something): *The government has promised to direct its attention to the needs of children with special learning difficulties. Isn't it time we directed our attention to packing the books? Thank you for directing my attention to this excellent magazine.* → **draw to**[2] (2)

**dirty up** *v adv* → **foul up** (1), **mess up** (1), **muck up** (1)

*AmE not fml* to make (something) very dirty: [T1 + UP] *You've dirtied up your dress in that mud!*

***disabuse of** *v prep*

*fml* to free the mind of (someone or oneself) from (something such as a wrong idea): [D1] *What can we do to disabuse the chairman of his false views?*

**disagree about/on/over** *v prep* → **agree about, agree on** (1)

to have a different opinion about (something or someone): [L9 + *about/on/over* (*often simple tenses*)] *Musicians usually disagree on the way a piece of music should be played. I must disagree about the singer's performance. The teachers disagree over the boy; some think he cannot be blamed, others want him to be punished.*

**disagree with** *v prep*

**1** to have a different opinion from (someone): [L9 + *with* (*often simple tenses*)] *I disagree with your father; I think it would be quite safe to do as you plan.* → **agree with** (1)

**2** to refuse to accept (something): [L9 + *with* (*simple tenses*)] *I have to disagree with your last remark.* → **argue with** (2), **quarrel with** (2)

*__3__ to fail to match; be completely different from (something): [T1 (*no pass., simple tenses*)] *Your story disagrees with his in every detail.* → **correspond to,** etc.

*__4__ (of food, air, or weather) to harm the health of (someone): [T1 (*no pass., usu. simple tenses*)] *The onion disagreed with me and has given me a pain. City air disagrees with me.* → **agree with** (5)

**disappear from** *v prep*

**1** to be no longer seen in (usu. a place): [IØ + *from*] *My blue bag has disappeared from the shelf where I left it.*

**2 disappear from sight/view** to be no longer able to be seen: *The car gathered speed and soon disappeared from view.*

**disappear to** *v prep* → **become of, come of** (1), **get to** (2), **go to** (5)

to leave suddenly for (a place); be taken away to (somewhere): [IØ + *to*] *If the police are chasing us, we'd better disappear to London. Where can my blue bag have disappeared to?*

**disappoint at** *v prep* → **dissatisfy at**

**be disappointed at** to fail to be pleased at (doing something): *I was disappointed at missing your visit because I was out of town. The secretary was disappointed at not getting the increased pay that he had hoped for.*

**disappoint in/with** *v prep* → **dissatisfy with**

**be disappointed in/with** to fail to be pleased with or approve of; feel unhappy about (something or someone): *I'm disappointed in your work this year. Why were you so disappointed with the new house? I'm dis-*

*appointed in you; I thought you had a stronger character than that.*

**disapprove of** *v prep* → **approve of**
to refuse to agree to; have a poor opinion of (something); dislike (someone), usu. for a fault: [L9 + *of*] *Jim's father disapproved of his marriage to Mary. Jim's father disapproved of Mary.*

**disbar from** *v prep* → **debar from**
to prevent (a lawyer) from (practice or practising) for a fault: [T1 + *from* (*usu. pass.*)] *The young lawyer was disbarred from practice after he had been found guilty of unlawful acts.*

**disbelieve in** *v prep*
**1** to refuse to have faith in (someone or something): [L9 + *in* (*simple tenses*)] *Mary's mother used to be religious, but now she disbelieves in God.* → **believe in** (1)
**2** to consider (something) to be false: [L9 + *in* (*simple tenses*)] *Since she lost her religious faith, Mary's mother disbelieves in the Bible.* → **believe in** (2), **have in**[2] (2)

***disburden of** *v prep*
*fml* to set (someone) free from (a duty): [D1 (*often pass.*)] *The chairman has been disburdened of his responsibility as head of the committee.*

**discern between** *v prep*
**1** to see or know (a difference, sameness, or connection, etc.) between (two things or people): [X9 + *between*] *How can we discern the difference between two books in a dark room? It is easy to discern a connection between high rents and the lack of housing.*
***2** to tell the difference between (two things), esp. by eye or mind: [T1 (*no pass., simple tenses*)] *Some people find it difficult to discern between blue and green. Even lawyers cannot always discern between fine points of the law.* → **distinguish between**, etc.

**discern from** *v prep* → **differentiate from** (1), **discriminate from** (1), **distinguish from** (1)
to see or know the difference between (one thing) and (another): [X9 + *from*] *Some people find it difficult to discern blue from green. Even the police cannot always discern truth from lies.*

**discharge from** *v prep*
**1** to send (someone) away from or allow (someone) to leave (something such as a place or work): [T1 + *from*] *Mother was discharged from the hospital only two weeks after her operation. Since you were caught helping the jewel thieves, I have no choice but to discharge you from my service. He was honourably discharged from the army with a severe leg wound.*
**2** to empty (something) from (something such as a container or vehicle): [T1 + *from*] *The big ship has been discharging oil from its broken containers into the water.*

**discharge into** *v prep*
to send or empty (something or itself) into (something such as air or sea): [X9 + *into*] *The river Thames discharges itself into the sea some miles east of London. The hunter discharged his gun into the air.*

**disconnect from** *v prep*
to remove (something) from being joined by or as by a wire to (something such as electricity): [T1 + *from*] *For your safety, always disconnect an electric motor from the electricity supply before you try to mend it.*

**disconnect with** *v prep*
**be disconnected with** to have no connection or relationship with (usu. something): *The accident rate seems to be disconnected with the road conditions and weather.*

***discord from/with** *v prep*
*fml* to disagree with (something); not suit or match (something): [T1 (*no pass., simple tenses*)] *The opinion that the speaker has just expressed discords with the principles of this society.*

**discourage from** *v prep* → **deter from**
to try to prevent (someone) from (doing something) by persuading him that it is not a good idea, or by making it seem difficult, etc.: [X9 + *from*] *What can we do or say to discourage our daughter from taking dangerous drugs? Only the worst weather will discourage Jim from taking his daily outdoor exercise.*

***discourse upon/on** *v prep*
*fml* to write or speak at length about (something): [T1 (*no pass.*)] *The minister discoursed upon the effectiveness of religious belief for over two hours. His latest book discourses upon the evils of violence.*

***discriminate against** *v prep*
*derog* to treat (usu. someone) unfairly, as less important or worthy: [T1] *It is unjust and unlawful to discriminate against people of other races. Women complain that employers discriminate against female workers when calculating their rank and pay.*

***discriminate between** *v prep*
**1** to tell small differences between (two people or things that are much alike); judge between (two things): [T1 (*usu. simple tenses*)] *The two brothers are so much alike, it is difficult to discriminate between them. Only a trained eye can discriminate between the two paintings.* → **distinguish between**, etc.
**2** to treat (different people) unfairly, showing favour to one group: [T1] *The new law discriminates between people employed in the same firm.*

***discriminate from** *v prep*
**1** to make or tell small differences between (one thing or person) and (another very much like it/him): [D1 (*usu. simple tenses*)] *The two brothers are so much alike, it is difficult to discriminate one from the other. How can he discriminate the real painting from the false one?* → **differentiate from** (1), **discern from, distinguish from**
**2** to show the difference between (someone

or something) and (someone or something else); set (someone or something) apart from (someone or something else): [D1] *It is the power of speech which most clearly discriminates man from the animals.* → **tell from** (2), etc

**discuss with** *v prep*
to have usu. long talks about (a subject) with (someone), usu. trying to reach agreement: [T1 + *with*] *I've discussed the matter with my lawyer, and we have decided to settle the case out of court. Have you been discussing me with your friends?*

**disembark from** *v prep*
to (cause to) leave (a ship or plane): [L9 + *from*] *It was good to disembark from the ship after such a long voyage.* [X9 + *from*] *The sailors disembarked the passengers from the ship.*

***disembarrass of** *v prep*
*fml or pomp* to rid (someone or oneself) of (something or someone unwanted): [D1] *The school wishes to be disembarrassed of the troublesome boy. It is impossible to disembarrass his parents of their responsibility for his behaviour. The islanders' representative offered to disembarrass the government of its protection of the small dependent state. Let me disembarrass you of that heavy bag, sir.*

**disengage from** *v prep*
*fml* to free or separate (something, someone, or oneself) from (something such as a duty): [X9 + *from*] *The naval commander disengaged the two largest ships from the sea battle. The judge asked to be disengaged from the next case on the grounds of* (= because of) *conscience.* [L9 + *from*] *The country should disengage from any international agreement which is not to its advantage.*

**disentangle from** *v prep*
to separate (something, someone, or oneself) with difficulty from (something or someone): [X9 + *from*] *Can you disentangle the loose threads from this wool? I don't know how I'm going to disentangle my work from this pile of papers. It is difficult to disentangle your children from unsuitable companions. The police tried to disentangle the hidden truth from the lies which the prisoner told them. With a guilty conscience, the man's wife tried to disentangle herself from her lover.*

**disguise as** *v prep*
to hide (someone, oneself, or something) by pretending that he/one/it is (someone or something else), often by changing the appearance, clothes, etc.: [X9 + *as*] *Jim went to the party disguised as a princess. The prisoners made their escape by disguising themselves as guards. The government is trying to disguise its tax increases as protection of the nation's income, in order to help the people.*

**disguise in** *v prep*
to hide the real appearance of (someone, oneself, or something) by covering with (something): [X9 + *in*] *The prisoners made their escape by disguising themselves in guards' clothing. The student tried to disguise her disappointment in cheerfulness. The firm tried to disguise its failure in false statements.*

**disguise with** *v prep*
to hide (something) by means of (something): [X9 + *with*] *The boys disguised their laziness with a show of hard work whenever the teacher looked their way. The cook disguised the flavour with onions.*

***dish out** *v adv*
**1** *not fml* to serve (food): [T1] *Please help me to dish out the vegetables.* → **dish up** (1)
**2** *AmE* to shape (a hole) like a dish: [T1] *This small desert animal dishes out a shelter for itself in the sand.*
**3** *infml* to give (things) to several people: [T1] *Stand at the door and dish out the papers as the students come in. The government dishes out payments to people without jobs.* → **give out** (2, 3), **hand out** (2, 3)
**4** *infml derog* to give (something) too freely: [T1] *Aunt Mabel likes to dish out advice to young people, whether they want it or not. This young teacher dishes out rewards to his students to try to win their favour.* → **hand out** (4), **ladle out** (2)
**5 dish it out** *infml* to punish or scold someone freely: *Try to keep away from the teacher, she's really dishing it out this morning.* → **hand out** (5)

***dish up** *v adv*
**1** *not fml* to prepare or serve (food): [T1] *Could you help me dish up the dinner?* [IØ] *I shall be ready to dish up in a few minutes; are the family all at table?* → **dish out** (1)
**2** *infml* to produce; give (something such as information): [T1] *Our history teacher has been dishing up the same old lessons for twenty years. I hope the next speaker dishes up his arguments in a more interesting manner.*

**disincline for/towards** *v prep*
**be disinclined for/towards** not to wish for (something); be unwilling to do or have (something): *I'm disinclined towards yet another move. Many workers feel disinclined for a long journey from home to work. The government is disinclined for another election so soon.*

**dislodge from** *v prep*
to move (something or someone) usu. by force from (the place where it/he was): [T1 + *from*] *The boy's ball accidentally dislodged the top brick from the wall. Shall we be able to dislodge the other team from their position at the top of the averages?*

**dismiss as** *v prep*
to put the idea of (someone or something) aside as being (unworthy): [X9 + *as*] *The chairman dismissed the question as unimportant. How can you dismiss his suggestion as stupid?*

**dismiss for** *v prep*
**1** to make (someone) leave his job or place

of work for (a reason or doing something wrong): [T1 + *for*] *The worker was dismissed for laziness/for stealing bicycle parts.*

**2** (in cricket) to put an end to the turn of (a batsman) after he has made (a number of runs): [T1 + *for*] *To the shock of the team, Underhill was dismissed for only twelve runs.*

**dismiss from** *v prep*

**1** to make (someone) leave (his job or place of work): [T1 + *from*] *The worker was dismissed from the factory when he was caught stealing bicycle parts. Have you ever been dismissed from any job?*

**2 dismiss something/someone from one's mind/thoughts** to try to forget something or someone: *The judge asked the whole group to dismiss the lawyer's remark from their minds.*

**dismount from** *v prep*

to get down from (something or an animal that one is riding): [L9 + *from*] *The rider dismounted from his horse and came towards me on foot. I had to dismount from my bicycle halfway up the hill.*

**dispatch to** *v prep* also **despatch to**

to send (someone or something) to (a place): [X9 + *to*] *The young soldier was dispatched to a distant island to help govern the natives. The firm will dispatch the goods to London.*

***dispense from** *v prep*

*fml* to excuse (someone) from (something or doing something, as a duty): [D1 (*often pass.*)] *Since you feel ill, I will dispense you from your duties for the rest of the week.* [V4a (*often pass.*)] *May I be dispensed from attending the meeting?*

***dispense to** *v prep*

to give (something) to (several people): [D1] *For twenty years the judge had dispensed justice to all kinds of offenders.*

***dispense with** *v prep* → **do without**[2](1), **go without**[2] (2), **live without, manage without**[2]

to choose to do without; get rid of (something or someone): [T1] *The firm will have to dispense with your services. Let us dispense with the usual formalities and open the meeting at once. Since we have been ordered to spend less money in the office, we shall have to dispense with one of the secretaries.*

***disport oneself** *v pron*

*pomp* to play, esp. outdoors: [I∅] *When the weather turned warm, hundreds of people could be seen disporting themselves by the lake.*

***dispose of** *v prep*

**1** to get rid of (something) by selling it or giving or throwing it away: [T1] *We have too much furniture; let's dispose of these old chairs. While you're cleaning out the garage, please dispose of those piles of old newspapers. We shall have to dispose of all Mother's property to pay the death duties.*

**2** to destroy (an argument or opponent): [T1 (*simple tenses*)] *The next speaker quickly disposed of his weak argument. The experienced politician disposed of the attack in a few minutes. It did not take long for the old fighter to dispose of his young but inexperienced opponent.*

**3** to find an answer to (a difficulty, doubt, etc.): [T1 (*simple tenses*)] *Well, that disposes of the difficulty of choosing a holiday place.*

**4** to eat or drink (something) until it is finished: [T1] *Those children certainly disposed of all the food that I prepared for the party!*

**5** *mil* to have a supply of (men or materials): [T1 (*simple tenses*)] *We should be able to dispose of 450 big guns placed around the area.*

**dispose towards** *v prep*

**be disposed towards** *fml* to give a feeling of the stated type towards (something or someone): *The taxpayers are unfavourably disposed towards the recent tax increases. Students are usually well disposed towards this informal method of teaching.*

***dispossess of** *v prep*

*fml* to take away from (someone), by force of law, (his possessions): [D1 (*usu. pass.*)] *Anyone who offends the king will be dispossessed of all his lands.*

**dispute about/over** *v prep*

to argue about (something): [L9 + *about/over*] *The government and the farmers are disputing about/over the land for the airport.*

**dispute against/with** *v prep*

to argue with (someone or something): [L9 + *against/with*] *The farmers are disputing with the government about where the airport should be built. How dare you dispute against my orders?*

**dispute over** *v prep* → **DISPUTE ABOUT**

**dispute with** *v prep* → **DISPUTE AGAINST**

**disqualify for** *v prep*

**1** to state that (someone) is not suitable, because of (a reason): [T1 + *for*] *The player was disqualified for breaking the rules.*

**2** to state that (someone) is not suitable for (something): [X9 + *for*] *He was disqualified for army service because of his weak eyesight.* → **disqualify from**

**disqualify from** *v prep* → **disqualify for** (2)

to state that (someone) is not suitable for (something or doing something): [X9 + *from*] *He was disqualified from army service because of his weak eyesight. Jim was disqualified from entering the race because he was over the age limit.*

**dissatisfy at** *v prep* → **disappoint at**

**be dissatisfied at** to be displeased with; feel rather angry about (doing something): *Many people are dissatisfied at not finding suitable jobs.*

**dissatisfy with** *v prep* → **disappoint in**

**be dissatisfied with** to fail to approve of or be pleased with; feel rather angry about (usu. something): *The teacher said that he was dis-*

*satisfied with the student's work, and she would have to do better. Why are you dissatisfied with the new house?*

* **dissent from** *v prep* → **agree to,** etc.
*fml* to refuse to agree with (something): [T1 (*no pass.*)] *Many good men have dissented from the opinion of the Church.*

* **dissociate from** *v prep*
*fml* to separate (someone or something) in one's mind from (someone or something): [D1] *The chairman stated that he dissociated himself and his committee from the views expressed by the director. It is difficult to dissociate the writer's work from the facts known about his life. Many mothers working at home feel dissociated from real life.*

**dissolve in** *v prep*
**1** to (cause to) melt in (usu. a liquid): [L9 + *in*] *Salt dissolves in water.* [X9 + *in*] *Dissolve the chemical in this special liquid. Dissolve the washing powder in hot water before adding the clothes.* → **dissolve into** (1), **melt in** (1), **melt into** (1)
**2** to fade under (something not transparent) when hidden by it: [L9 + *in*] *The open road dissolved in a blinding snowstorm.* → **dissolve into** (2), **melt into** (2)
**3 dissolve in tears** to (cause to) weep freely: *Mary (was) dissolved in tears when she heard the sad news.* → **dissolve into** (3), **melt into** (3)

**dissolve into** *v prep*
**1** to become (something) by melting: [L9 + *into*] *Left out in the sun, the jelly dissolved into a pool of melted fruit juice.* → **dissolve in** (1), **melt in** (1), **melt into** (1)
**2** (in film and television) to (cause to) fade into (the next scene): [L9 + *into*] *The picture then dissolved into a view of the house from the outside.* [X9 + *into*] *We'll dissolve this scene into the one where the murderer enters the house.* → **dissolve in** (2), **melt into** (2)
**3 dissolve into tears** to start weeping freely: *Mary dissolved into tears when she heard the sad news.* → **dissolve in** (3), **melt into** (3)

**dissuade from** *v prep* → **argue out of,** etc.
to persuade (someone) against (something or doing something): [T1 + *from*] *How can I dissuade the director from this foolish course of action? Jim's father tried to dissuade him from marrying Mary.*

* **distinguish between** *v prep* → **differentiate between** (1), **discern between** (2), **discriminate between** (1), **tell between**
to recognize the difference between (two things or people): [T1 (*usu. simple tenses*)] *Some people find it difficult to distinguish between right and wrong. When you are lost in a dark forest, you cannot distinguish between day and night.*

* **distinguish from** *v prep*
**1** to recognize (someone or something) apart from (someone or something else) by special qualities: [D1 (*usu. simple tenses*)] *Some people find it difficult to distinguish right from wrong. When you are lost in a dark forest, you cannot distinguish day from night.* → **differentiate from** (1), **discern from, discriminate from** (1)
**2** to show the difference between (someone or something) and (someone or something else); set (someone or something) apart from (someone or something else): [D1 (*simple tenses*)] *Elephants are distinguished from other animals by their long noses.* → **tell from** (2), etc.

* **distinguish oneself** *v pron*
**1** to act in such a way as to earn praise: [IØ] *Jim distinguished himself in the examinations, reaching the top place in all his subjects.*
**2** to make oneself noticeable by one's behaviour: [IØ] *I see you've been distinguishing yourself at school again, I've had a lot of complaints about your behaviour.*

**distract from** *v prep* → **deflect from** (2), **divert from**
to turn the attention of (usu. someone or his mind or thoughts) away from (usu. something or doing something). [T1 + *from*] *A woman whose husband has just died needs activity to distract her from her grief. Stop making so much noise, you're distracting me from my work!* [T4] *If you can distract the policeman from watching the shop door for a moment, I shall be able to get in. King Alfred burned the cakes while his mind was distracted from watching them.*

* **distrain upon** *v prep*
*law* to take (someone's goods) in place of a debt, as for rent: [T1] *The owner may ask the court for an order to distrain upon the furniture of any person who fails to pay his rent.*

**distribute among** *v prep*
to give (something or things) to (several people or places); share (something or things) among (several people or places): [X9 + *among*] *The money that has been collected will be distributed among all the children's hospitals in the area. When someone has died without leaving instructions, it is difficult to distribute his property fairly among his relatives.*

**distribute over** *v prep*
to scatter (something or things) over (an area): [X9 + *over*] *The wreck of the crashed plane was distributed over a wide area.*

**distribute round** *v prep*
to give (something or things) to (a group of people severally): [X9 + *round*] *Please distribute the examination papers round the class.*

**distribute to** *v prep*
to give or send (something or things) to (people, a group, or places): [X9 + *to*] *The printers will arrange to distribute the books to every important city in the country. Please distribute the examination papers to all the students.*

* **divagate from** *v prep*
*fml* to wander away from (a subject): [T1 (*no pass., simple tenses*)] *The book divagates from*

*its main point in Part 2, but returns at the end to prove the writer's opinion.*

**dive in** *v adv*

**1** to enter water headfirst: [L9 + IN] *The water's quite deep enough to dive in. He dived in cleanly, entering the water in a straight line.*

***2** *infml* to start eating or other activity keenly: [IØ (*usu. simple tenses*)] *Dinner's ready, dive in, everybody! When the argument started I wanted to dive in.* → **tuck in** (4), etc.

**dive into** *v prep*

**1** to enter (water) headfirst; dive: [L9 + *into*] *The swimmer dived into the river to save the drowning child.*

***2** *infml* to start eating (food) or joining (any activity) keenly: [T1 (*no pass., usu. simple tenses*)] *He sat down and at once dived into a pile of potatoes. Jim dived into the argument as usual without thinking.* → **tuck into** (3), etc.

***3** *infml* to enter (a place) suddenly and often secretively: [T1 (*no pass., usu. simple tenses*)] *I was following the man when he dived into a small restaurant and I lost track of him.*

***4** *not fml* to (cause to) search inside (a container) quickly: [T1] *Diving into her bag, she found a handkerchief just in time.* [D1] *He dived his hand into his pocket in an attempt to find the key.*

**dive off** *v prep*

**1** to enter water headfirst from (something high): [L9 + *off*] *The competitors will dive off the highest board. How many of our girls dived off the top board?*

**2 dive off the deep end** to become suddenly and unreasonably angry: *There she goes, diving off the deep end again!* → **go off** (6), **jump off** (2)

**diverge from** *v prep* → **adhere to** (2), etc.

to take a different direction from (something): [L9 + *from*] *Don't diverge from the main path, but go straight through the wood. Tell your story without diverging from the truth.*

**diverge to** *v prep*

to turn towards (a direction): [L9 + *to*] *At the end of the wood, the path diverges to the left.*

**divert from** *v prep* → **deflect from** (2), **distract from, divert onto**

to turn (something) in a different direction from (something): [X9 + *from*] *To prevent flooding, we shall have to divert the river from its course. If you can divert the policeman's attention from the shop door for a moment, I shall be able to get in. Using a mirror, you can divert light from its path. Money collected through taxes is often diverted from the purposes for which it was intended. Traffic is being diverted from the main road because of the accident.*

**divert onto** *v prep* → **divert from, divert to**

to turn (traffic) onto (another way): [X9 + *onto*] *Traffic is being diverted onto a side road because of the accident.*

**divert to** *v prep* → **divert from, divert onto**

to turn (something) aside, towards (something): [X9 + *to*] *Competition can divert your trade to other markets. The train was diverted to Cambridge because of engineering works on the main line.*

**divert with** *v prep*

to amuse (someone) with (something): [T1 + *with*] *The little girl diverted the people at her mother's party with her funny sayings. The crowd was greatly diverted with the performance.*

***divest of** *v prep*

**1** *fml* to remove (clothing) from (someone): [D1] *The servants helped to divest the king of his royal garments.*

**2** *fml* to cause (someone or oneself) to be without (an official position or special rights): [D1] *It might become necessary to divest the chairman of his power.*

**3** *fml* to rid (someone or oneself) of (something unwanted): [D1] *I shall be pleased to divest myself of the responsibility of such important work.*

**divide against** *v prep*

**be divided against** *old use* to quarrel with (oneself): *"If a house be divided against itself, that house cannot stand."* (The Bible)

**divide among** *v prep* → **share among**

to share (something or things) among (several people): [X9 + *among*] *Divide the cake equally among all the children. The different responsibilities are divided among the committee members.*

**divide between** *v prep*

**1** to share (something or things), as between (people or activities): [X9 + *between*] *Divide the money equally between your two brothers. I like to divide my time between work and pleasure.* → **share between**

**2 be divided between** to be uncertain which to choose of (one person, thing, or doing something) and (another): *I can't make up my mind where to go for my holiday; I'm divided between the sea and the mountains. The boy was divided between going to university and taking a job. Many women's loyalty is divided between home and work.*

**divide by** *v prep*

to separate (something, as a figure) into (a number of parts): [X9 + *by*] *If you divide 24 by 6, the answer is 4.* [L9 + *by*] *Will 28 divide by 3?*

**divide from** *v prep* → **separate from** (1)

to separate (something or someone) from (something or someone else): [X9 + *from*] *I want to build a fence to divide the flower garden from the vegetable garden. Separating the students into good and bad is like dividing the sheep from the goats.*

**divide in** *v prep* → **cut in²**, **cut into** (1), **divide into, separate into**

to (cause to) be separated by (a part): [X9 +

*in*] *Divide the cake in four and share it equally. The road is divided in half, for safety.* [L9 + *in* (*simple tenses*)] *The river divides in two at this point.*

**divide into** *v prep* → **cut into** (1), **divide in, separate into**
to (cause to) be separated into (parts): [X9 + *into*] *Divide the cake into quarters and share it equally.* [L9 + *into* (*simple tenses*)] *The class divided into several smaller groups to talk about different parts of the subject. The river divides into two streams at this point.*

**divide off** *v adv* → **fence off** (1), **rail off, separate off, wall off**
to separate (something): [X9 + OFF] *This part of the field has been divided off with a fence, to keep the cows in.*

**divide on** *v prep*
**be divided on** to have different opinions about (something): *The committee are divided on the choice of a new chairman. The students are divided on the quality of teaching in the university.*

**divide out** *v adv* → **share out**
to share (something or things) among a number not stated: [X9 + OUT] *How shall we divide out the money that we have collected?*

**divide with** *v prep* → **share with** (1)
to share (something), usu. equally, with (someone): [X9 + *with*] *I'll divide my apple with you, if you give me half of your cake. It was generous of the eldest son to divide the property with his younger brothers.*

**divorce from** *v prep*
**be divorced from**
**1** to end a marriage with (a wife or husband): *This famous actress has been divorced from three husbands.*
*__2__ to be completely different or separate from (something): *His hopes for the future are often divorced from reality.*

**divulge to** *v prep*
to tell (a secret) to (someone): [X9 + *to*] *The soldier was shot for divulging the plans to the enemy.*

**divvy up** *v adv*
*infml* to share (something such as money): [T1] *The thieves agreed to divvy up the profit when the jewels were sold.*

**do about** *v prep*
to take action about (something or doing something): [X9 + *about*] *We shall have to do something about our methods if we are to get any results. What can the public do about improving prison conditions? "The best thing to do, when you've got a dead body and it's your husband's on the kitchen floor and you don't know what to do about it, is to make yourself a good strong cup of tea."* (Anthony Burgess, *One Hand Clapping*)

**do as** *v prep* → DO FOR (1)

**do away with** *v adv prep*
**1** to get rid of (something): [T1] *The firm decided to do away with the old machinery. It is time to do away with some of the old laws.*
**2** *infml* to murder; kill (someone or oneself): [T1] *The criminals did away with the old man. My neighbour tried to do away with herself by taking poison.* → **bump off**, etc.

**do badly** *v adv*
**1** to be unsuccessful: [L9 + BADLY] *The firm has done badly for five years and may have to close. The roses did so badly last year with all that rain and cold weather.* → **do well** (1)
**2** to fail in health: [L9 + BADLY ] *Mother has been doing badly ever since her operation.* → **do well** (2)

**do by** *v prep*
**1** to perform (something) before a certain time: [T1 + *by* (*simple tenses*)] *I have to do the work by next week.*
*__2__ to treat (someone), usu. well or badly: [T1 (*simple tenses*)] *He does well by his family. The firm that does badly by its workers will not succeed.*
**3** **be hard done by** to be treated unfairly: *Why do you feel hard done by? The firm kept you in your job although they dismissed many other workers.*
**4** **do by halves** *not fml* to do (something) in an unfinished way, not thoroughly: [(*simple tenses, usu. neg.*)] *Jim never does anything by halves; if he starts something you can be sure that he will finish it and produce excellent results.*
**5** **do as you would be done by** to treat others as you would like them to treat you: *I respect other people's property and expect them to respect mine: I believe you should do as you would be done by.*

***do down** *v adv*
**1** *BrE not fml* to defeat (someone), often by unfair means: [T1] *The firm is always trying to do its competitors down.*
**2** *BrE not fml* to speak ill of (someone): [T1] *It has become fashionable these days to do down one's own class. The student will be unpopular if he goes on doing down his fellow students.* → **cry down** (3), **cry up, run down**[1] (7)
**3** *BrE not fml* to make (oneself) feel ashamed or less proud of oneself: [T1] *There's no need to do yourself down; you weren't to blame.*

**do for** *v prep*
**1** to serve the purpose of (something): [L9 + *for* (*simple tenses*)] *This box will have to do for a table until the furniture arrives. A bicycle will do for getting around until we can afford a car.* also **do as** → **serve as, serve for, use for, utilize for**
**2** to be suitable for (someone or something): [L9 + *for* (*simple tenses*)] *This dress will do for Mary. This lid will do for carrying the pots.*
**3** to work at (something) to gain (something,

esp. a living): [I∅ + *for*] *What does he do for a living? He does practically nothing for his living.*

**4** to perform (a purpose); give or add (something) to (something or someone); give (help) to (someone): [X9 + *for*] *That dress doesn't do much for your figure. I'm grateful to you for doing so much for the village. What has the government ever done for me? Singing does something for me, it makes me more cheerful. What can I do for you?*

***5** to have; be provided with (something such as supplies): [T1 (*no pass.*)] *How will you do for food when you are camping? We've been doing quite well for new contracts recently. The children have never done badly for gifts of money.*

***6** esp. *BrE not fml* to keep house or do cleaning for (someone): [T1 (*no pass.*)] *Mrs Whitehead has been doing for the local doctor ever since his wife died.*

***7** *infml* to kill; murder (someone): [T1 (*usu. simple tenses*)] *I'll do for that policeman when I get out of prison.* → **bump off**, etc.

***8** *not fml* to ruin; destroy (something); defeat (someone): [T1 (*simple tenses*)] *The severe storm did for most of the farm buildings. It was the other player's ability to move quickly that did for me.*

**9 be done for** *not fml* to be finished; ruined; worn out; very tired; about to die, etc.: *I'm done for. This coat is done for. The nation is done for now that this party is in power. If the government increases our taxes any further, the business is done for.*

**10 do well for oneself** to become rich and/or socially important: *I can see from the size of your house that you've been doing very well for yourself.*

***do good** *v adj*

**1** to make (someone) more healthy or feel better: [T1b] *A breath of fresh air will do you good.*

**2** to improve (something): [T1b] *All this rain will do the crops good.*

**3** to attempt to help people's lives, often in an unpractical or unwelcome way: [I∅] *The doctor's wife has been doing good in the village all her life.* —**do-gooder** *n*

***do in** *v adv*

**1** *infml* to murder; kill (someone or oneself): [T1] *The criminals have done in the old man. My neighbour tried to do herself in by taking poison.* → **bump off**, etc.

**2** *not fml* to ruin (someone): [T1] *I've been done in by a clever trick! A dishonest firm can easily do in its competitors.* → **do up** (8)

**3 be done in** esp. *AmE infml* to be very tired: *You'd better go ahead; I'm done in and must rest here.* → **tire out**, etc.

***do into** *v prep* → **render into, translate from, translate into, turn into** (3), **turn to** (7)

*fml* to translate (something) into (another language): [D1 (*usu. pass.*)] *This collection of the ancient poems newly done into English is a fine translation.*

***do out** *v adv*

**1** *not fml* to clean and tidy (a room, etc.) [T1] *The only way to keep the garage clean and tidy is to do it out thoroughly once a year.* —**doing-out** *n* → **clean out** (1), **muck out**

**2** *not fml* to ornament (a room), as with paint, paper, etc.: [T1] *The bedroom has been beautifully done out in blue and gold.*

***do out of** *v adv prep* → **cheat out of**, etc.

**1** *not fml* to deceive (someone) in order to gain (something he possesses): [D1] *The clever salesman did the old lady out of all her money.*

**2** *not fml* to prevent (someone) from (doing or having something such as a right): [D1] *Many children are done out of a chance for a good education, simply because they live in the wrong place.* [V4b] *You can't do the children out of going to the theatre, that would be too unkind.*

***do over** *v adv*

**1** esp. *BrE not fml* to paint or otherwise improve the appearance of (usu. a room): [T1] *Doesn't the bedroom look nice now that we've done it over!*

**2** esp. *AmE* to do (something) again; repeat or remake (something): [T1] *If you don't like the colour of the paint, we'd better do the room over. You'd better do over the stitching in the dress to make sure that it lasts. Let's do the concert over, it was such a success!*

**3** *infml* to attack and wound (someone) [T1b] *The thieves did the old man over before they robbed him.* → **beat up** (2), etc.

***do proud** *v adv*

**1** *not fml* to work hard for; put effort into pleasing; be generous to (someone): [T1 (*usu. simple tenses*)] *Mother, what a wonderful meal! You've done us proud. When 30 members arrived for the yearly meeting, the hotel did them proud.*

**2** *not fml* to give (someone or oneself) cause for pride: [T1b (*usu. simple tenses*)] *Jim's success in the examinations did his family proud. You've done yourself proud, getting such a good job!*

**do to** *v prep*

**1** to cause (something such as harm, good, or change) to happen to (someone or something): [X9 + *to*] *What have you done to the poor boy? Look what the thieves did to the furniture! What harm have I ever done to you? Look what the rain has done to the flowers. All this rain will do good to the crops.*

**2** to wound (part of the body): [X9 + *to*] *What have you done to your hand? It's bleeding.*

**3** to finish (something) as far as (something) [T1 + *to* (*usu. simple tenses*)] *The meat is done to perfection. The actors did the play to a very high standard.*

**4 do credit to** to show (something or some

one) to be good: *This piece of work does credit to you. The success of the business does credit to the firm's organization.*

**5 do someone to death** to kill someone: *The guards had no right to do the prisoners to death.*

**6 do something to death** to destroy the effect of (something) by doing it too often: *This play has been done to death in all the theatres.*

**7 do homage to** to show one's respect for (someone), often in a formal manner: *Crowds of people gathered to do homage to the king when he visited their city.* → **pay to** (5)

**8 do justice to** to treat (someone or something) fairly: *I don't think the newspaper reporters have done justice to a fine performance.*

**9 do justice to** *not fml* to show that one has enjoyed (something such as a meal) properly: *That was a wonderful meal; you can see that we've all done justice to it by eating it all.*

**10 do something to** to have an effect on (someone): *That music does something to me; do you feel it, too?*

**o up** *v adv*

**1** to (cause to) fasten: [T1] *You've done your buttons up the wrong way. Please help me to do up this knot.* [IØ (*simple tenses*)] *These old-fashioned trousers do up with buttons.* → **fasten up, hook up** (1)

**2** to wrap (something or things): [T1] *Do up these papers and send them to Head Office. The presents were all done up in shiny paper and put under the Christmas tree.*

**3** to tie (something) in an arrangement: [T1] *Will you help me to do up my hair?*

**4** *infml* to repair; improve (something): [T1] *We shall have to do up the house next spring. Do you think I could do up my old skirt and go on wearing it?*

**5** *infml* to make (oneself) more beautiful: [T1] *Mary has done herself up for the party. Mary came to the party all done up in her best dress.* → **dress up** (2), etc.

**6** *AmE* to preserve (food such as fruit): [T1] *Mother is doing up some blackberries, so that we can eat them during the winter.* → **put up**[1] (14)

**7** *AmE* to wash and press (clothes): [T1] *Can you do up my best shirt before tomorrow?*

**8** *infml* to ruin (someone): [T1] *I've been done up by that old trick! A dishonest firm can easily do up its competitors.* → **do in** (2)

**9 be done up** esp. *BrE not fml* to be very tired: *You go on ahead, I'm done up and must rest here.* → **tire out,** etc.

**o well** *v adv*

**1** to be successful; act in a worthy manner: [IØ] *Jim did well in the examinations, reaching the top place in most subjects. Well done, Jim! How well did he do? The roses are doing so well this year, with all this sunshine.* → **do badly** (1)

**2** to improve in health: [IØ] *Mother is doing well after her operation, thank you.* → **do badly** (2)

**3** to make (someone or oneself) comfortable, as at a hotel; provide good food and/or other comforts for (someone or oneself): [T1b (*usu. simple tenses*)] *You've done yourself well, haven't you, staying in the best hotel. They do you very well at this restaurant.*

**4** to be well advised; be wise; gain advantage: [I3 (*simple tenses*)] *You would do well to take the offer. I did well to listen to my father's advice.*

**do with** *v prep*

**1** to find a use for (something): [*what* + L9 + *with* (*simple tenses*)] *He gave me this strange object for my birthday, and I don't know what to do with it. The play was terrible; half the actors didn't know what to do with their hands.*

***2** to treat; deal with (someone): [*what* + T1 (*no pass., simple tenses*)] *The teacher didn't know what to do with the class. 'What shall we do with the drunken sailor?'* (song)

***3** to take; hide; steal (something): [*what* + T1 (*no pass., simple tenses*)] *What has that girl done with the urgent papers? What have you done with my blue bag?*

***4** to have a reason for having (something): [*what* + T1 (*no pass., continuous tenses*)] *What are you doing with my fur coat? I don't know what such a young boy is doing with a gun. I wonder what they're doing with such a big house.*

***5** to be satisfied with (something or someone less than one hoped): [T1 (*no pass., inf.*)] *If we can't afford meat we shall have to do with fish. If the usual team is unable to come, we shall have to do with other players.*

***6** to need to use or have (something or someone): [*can* + T1 (*no pass.*)] *I could do with a cup of tea. We can do with an additional secretary.* [*can* + T4] *This house could do with painting.*

***7** to be unable to bear; suffer (something or doing something): [*can not* + T1 (*no pass.*)] *I can't do with loud music.* [*can not* + T4] *He couldn't do with waiting any longer, and left.* [*can not* + V4a] *Mother can't do with the children making so much noise.*

***8** to spend time; busy (oneself): [*what* + T1 (*no pass., simple tenses*)] *The boys didn't know what to do with themselves when school ended.*

***9** to control (oneself): [*what* + T1 (*no pass., simple tenses*)] *The children didn't know what to do with themselves as Christmas drew near. The nervous girl didn t know what to do with herself when the man kissed her, she was so excited and fearful.*

**10 be/have done with** to be finished with (something or someone): *Are you done with the newspaper? Your operation will soon be over and done with. Tom keeps asking me for an opinion on his book so I'd better read it* *and have done with it/have it done with.* → **finish with** (4), etc.

**11 be/have to do with** to have a connection with; concern (something or someone): *The rise in prices all has to do with the increased cost of oil. His job has to do with telephones. I'm interested in anything to do with music. I had nothing to do with the committee's decision. I'll have nothing to do with your plans to rob the bank. What's this bill? If it's to do with the arrangements for the wedding, give it to father.*

**12 do battle with: a** to fight (an enemy): *Tomorrow we shall do battle with our old enemy.* **b** to struggle against (something or someone): *I had to do battle with my conscience before I wrote to you. We've been doing battle with City Council for months now over the street crossing that we are demanding.* → **battle with** (1, 2), **struggle with** (2), etc.

**13 do business with** to have business dealings with (someone), concerning goods or service: *I refuse to do business with that garage again after they tried to cheat me.* → **deal at, deal with** (1), **trade at, trade with**

*__do without__[1] *v adv* → **go without**[1], **manage without**[1]
to live or continue in spite of lacking something: [IØ] *If there's no sugar you will have to do without.*

*__do without__[2] *v prep*
**1** to live or continue in spite of lacking (something, someone, or doing something): [T1] *It is unhealthy and dangerous to do without sleep. The director cannot do without a secretary.* [T4] *Mr Sharp is not here, you will have to do without speaking to him.* → **dispense with, go without**[2](2), **live without, manage without**[2]

**2** *not fml* to wish not to have (something, or someone doing something): [*can* + T1 (*no pass.*)] *I can do without any more silly suggestions from you, thank you. I could do without that loud music, can you turn it off?* [*can* + T4] *We could have done without missing the train.* [*can* + V4a] *Mother says she could do without the children making so much noise.*

**dock off** *v adv*
*not fml* to take part of (one's pay) before paying it: [X9 + OFF (*usu. pass.*)] *My pay isn't much to take home once it has had tax and insurance payments docked off.*

**doctor up** *v adv*
*not fml* to change; spoil; add to (something such as a liquid): [T1 + UP] *This wine tastes as if it's been doctored up.*

**dodder along** *v adv*
to walk or act in a weak manner, like an old person: [L9 + ALONG] *Learning to walk again after her operation, Mother could only dodder along at first, but now she's walking well. The government seems to be doddering along until the next election.*

*__dole out__ *v adv*
*not fml* to give to several people in need (usu. money or food in small quantities): [T1 (*to*)] *The Red Cross flew to the area of the floods, ready to dole out supplies of food, medicine, bedding, and tents. The State has to dole out money in troubled times to those in greatest need.*

*__doll up__ *v adv* → **dress up** (2), etc.
*infml* to dress (someone or oneself) prettily, as for a special event: [T1] *Mary dolled herself up for the party. Why are the children all dolled up? Is somebody important coming?*

*__dolly in__ *v adv* → **dolly out**
esp. *AmE tech* (in film and television) to move the camera forwards on wheels, towards the scene being filmed: [IØ] *I want a picture just of the girl's face, dolly in after she's made her big speech.*

*__dolly out__ *v adv* → **dolly in**
esp. *AmE tech* (in film and television) to move the camera backwards on wheels, away from the scene being filmed: [IØ] *When the two men have finished talking, dolly out so that we get a view of the whole house.*

**dominate over** *v prep* → **domineer over**
*not fml* to have power, control, or influence over (usu. someone), often in an unhealthy way: [L9 + *over*] *Powerful nations usually dominate over small weak countries. The teacher must learn not to dominate over her class.*

*__domineer over__ *v prep* → **dominate over**
to use the force of power to control (usu. someone) unpleasantly: [T1] *A mother who domineers over her family is likely to lose her children's love.*

**doom to** *v prep* also **foredoom to** → **sentence to** (2)
**be doomed to** to be fated to meet (something bad): *Why are my hopes always doomed to disappointment? Many fine old houses in the city are doomed to destruction.*

*__dope out__ *v adv*
**1** *AmE infml* to find an answer to (something): [T1] *Let me see if I can dope out a way out of your difficulty.*

**2** *AmE infml* (in horseracing) to make (a horse) unfit for a race by giving it a drug: [T1] *Half the runners have been doped out.*

**dope up** *v adv*
*AmE not fml* to cause (someone) to feel the full effect of (a drug): [T1 + UP] *The doctor has doped me up with all sorts of medicine to try to control the fever. I wish she hadn't come to the party doped up like that.*

**dose with** *v prep*
to give (someone or oneself) a measured amount of (medicine): [X9 + *with*] *When you have a bad cold, it is best to dose yourself with aspirin. Doctors dose only people who are dying or in great pain with these powerful dangerous drugs.*

**doss down** *v adv*
esp. *BrE sl* to find a place, usu. humble, to sleep: [IØ] *Don't worry about me, I'll doss down on these chairs. Poor people are not allowed to doss down in the park.*

**dot about/around** *v adv; prep* → **scatter about**
**be dotted about/around** to be scattered (in an area): *Be careful as you cross the field, there are rocks dotted about. There were a few sheep dotted around in the fields, but no other signs of life. There are several good painters dotted around this city. Potted plants were dotted about the room in various corners.*

**dot with** *v prep*
**be dotted with** to have (things) scattered on it: *I could see from the boat that the lake was dotted with flowers. The mountainside was dotted with goats.*

**dote on/upon** *v prep*
to have or show too much fondness for (someone): [T1 (*simple tenses*)] *This foolish woman dotes on the young artist. "Not so young, sir, to love a woman for singing, nor so old to dote on her for any thing."* (Shakespeare, *King Lear*)

**double as** *v prep*
(usu. of an actor) to play the part of (a character) in addition to his/her own part: [L1] *In the play, Mary is playing the part of the dancer, but agreed to double as the mother.*

**double back** *v adv*
**1** to return along the same path: [IØ] *If you get lost in a forest, it is best to double back the way you came.*
**2** to fold (something), as in half: [T1] *Double the map back so that we can read it more easily. We double the top of the sheet back over the covers, for comfortable sleep.* → **fold back**, etc.

**double for** *v prep* → **stand in for**, etc.
to act as a replacement for (someone): [T1] *Who will double for the secretary while he is on holiday? I'll double for you in the committee meeting.*

**double in** *v prep*
**double in brass**
**1** *AmE* to be able to play another musical instrument, as brass or wind, as well as one's usual one: *Can any of the players double in brass?*
**2** *AmE infml* to be able to do something else as well as the work in which one specializes: *I think we should appoint the younger man, because he can double in brass by writing as well as printing the magazine.*

**double over** *v adv*
**1** to fold (something), as in half: [T1] *Double the map over so that we can read it more easily.* → **fold back**, etc.
**2** to (cause to) bend, as with pain, laughter, etc.: [IØ] *Mary doubled over when Jim walked in wearing his funny clothes. The fighter doubled over at the sudden heavy blow.* [T1] *We found grandfather in his chair, doubled over with pain. The blow doubled the fighter over.* → **double up** (2), etc.

***double up** *v adv*
**1** to fold (something), as in half: [T1] *We shall have to double up the sheets to get them in the drawer.* [IØ] *This mat is too thick to double up.* → **fold back**, etc.
**2** to (cause to) bend, as with pain, laughter, etc.: [IØ] *Mary doubled up when Jim walked in wearing his funny clothes. The fighter doubled up at the sudden heavy blow.* [T1] *We found grandfather in his chair, doubled up with pain. The blow doubled the fighter up. The joke doubled the crowd up.* → **crack up** (5), **crease up** (3), **crumple up** (5), **curl up** (4), **double over** (2), **fold up** (3)
**3** *not fml* to increase one's numbers, esp. in a room or bed; share something such as space: [IØ (*with*)] *When all the family are here for Christmas, the children will have to double up in one room. Do you mind doubling up with Jane tonight?*

**double with** *v prep* → **double as**
to act (one part) in the same performance as (another part): [X9 + *with*] *In the play 'Hamlet,' it is usual for an actor to double the first gravedigger with the spirit of Hamlet's father.*

**doubt of** *v prep*
*fml* to be uncertain of (something): [T1 + *of*] *How can you doubt of the firm's future?*

**dovetail into** *v prep*
**1** (usu. of objects made of wood) to (cause to) fit exactly into (something such as another part): [T1 + *into* (*usu. simple tenses*)] *The sides of the drawer should be dovetailed into each other to join well.* [L9 + *into* (*simple tenses*)] *See how the blade dovetails into the handle.*
***2** to fit well with (something such as an idea): [T1 (*no pass., simple tenses*)] *How well do these new ideas dovetail into the existing system?*

***doze off** *v adv* → **drop off** (6), **get off**[1] (11), **go off**[1] (9), **nod off, put off**[1] (10), **send off** (5)
to fall asleep or partly asleep unintentionally: [IØ] *Did the Minister notice that I dozed off in the middle of his speech?*

**draft out** *v adv*
to make rough notes for (a piece of writing); give a general idea of (something): [X9 + OUT] *I wonder who helped that politician to draft out his speech. The government has drafted out its plans for future laws.*

**drag at** *v prep* → **drag on, draw at** (1), **puff at, pull at** (2), **pull on**[2] (2)
to suck on (a pipe, cigarette, etc.) deeply: [L9 + *at*] *It's so annoying, the way he keeps dragging at his pipe.*

**drag away** *v adv*
**1** to remove (something or someone) by pulling: [X9 + AWAY (*from*)] *It will take two elephants to drag all this wood away. His*

*mother dragged the child away from the fire just in time.* → **drag off, jerk away, pull away** (1), **take away** (1), **yank away**

*2 to cause (someone) to leave (something or someone) with difficulty: [T1b (*from*)] *Have you ever tried dragging a child away from a television set? How can I drag myself away from your arms?* → **pull away** (4), **tear away** (3)

**drag behind** *v adv; prep*

1 to move more slowly than (usu. someone): [L9 + BEHIND/*behind*] *Don't drag behind (the others), you'll make us all late.* → **lag behind** (1), etc.

2 to fail to remain level with (the quality of something): [L9 + BEHIND/*behind*] *Your work has been dragging behind (the general standard) recently, you'll have to do better.* → **fall behind²** (3), etc.

**drag down** *v adv*

1 to pull (something) downwards: [T1 + DOWN] *The box is too heavy to carry down the slope, we'll have to drag it down.* → **pull down** (2)

*2 to make (someone) feel weak, as after an illness: [T1] *It's the fever that's been dragging him down.* → **pull down** (4)

*3 to reduce (someone) to a lower level, socially or morally; ruin (someone): [T1] *If you marry that man, he'll drag you down.* → **pull down** (5)

**drag in** *v adv*

1 to pull or force (someone or something) indoors: [X9 + IN] *The children are so busy playing that they don't want their dinner, you'll have to drag them in. You look like something the cat dragged in.*

*2 *not fml* to introduce (mention of something unconnected) with difficulty or unnecessarily: [T1] *There's no need to keep dragging in my father's opinion, it has nothing to do with your argument.* → **drag up** (2)

**drag into** *v prep*

1 to pull or force (someone or something) into (something such as a space): [X9 + *into*] *You'll have to drag the children into the house, they're too busy playing to want their dinner. The farmer had to drag the unwilling cow into the field.*

*2 *not fml* to persuade (someone) with difficulty to help with (an activity or doing something): [D1] *Don't try to drag me into your plans.* [V4b] *I was dragged into helping with the concert.*

*3 to introduce (a subject) unnecessarily into (talk): [D1] *Why does he have to drag politics into every conversation?*

**drag off** *v adv* → **drag away** (1), **pull away** (1), **take away** (1)

to pull (someone or something) away: [X9 + OFF] *I wanted to stay, but she dragged me off to help her shop.*

**drag on¹** *v adv*

1 to pull or force (someone or something) onto an area: [X9 + ON] *The actors dragged on a boat with wheels. The writer of the play was dragged on at the end, to receive the cheers of the crowd.*

*2 *not fml* to last an unnecessarily long time, usu. unpleasantly: [IØ] *The meeting dragged on all morning. My debt to the bank is still dragging on.* → **drag out** (2)

*3 to live (one's life) unhappily: [T1a] *The writer dragged on an unhappy existence for many years until in the end she killed herself.* → **drag out** (3)

**drag on²** *v prep* → **drag at, pull on²** (2)

to suck at (a pipe, cigarette, etc.) deeply: [L9 + *on*] *It's so annoying, the way he keeps dragging on his pipe.*

**drag out** *v adv*

1 to pull (usu. something) out: [T1 + OUT] *It's so annoying having to drag out the sewing machine every time I want to make a dress.* → **fetch out** (1), **get out** (5), **lay out** (2), **put out** (3), **set forth** (3), **set out** (5)

*2 *not fml* to (cause to) last an unnecessarily long time, usu. unpleasantly: [IØ] *The meeting dragged out all morning.* [T1] *The politician dragged his speech out for over two hours.* → **drag on¹** (2)

*3 to live (one's life) unhappily: [T1a]. *The writer dragged out an unhappy existence for many years until in the end she killed herself.* → **drag on¹** (3)

*4 to force (information) from someone: [T1 (*of*)] *At last the police were able to drag the truth out of the prisoner.*

**drag through** *v prep*

1 to (cause to) move slowly through (something which prevents it from advancing): [X9 + *through*] *The natives have to drag the wood for their huts through the forest, as they do not have the wheel.* [L9 + *through*] *The sail was dragging through the water.*

2 **drag someone/someone's name through the mire/mud** *not fml* to bring shame on a person by making public something bad, unpleasant etc.: *See if you can settle the case out of court I don't want my son's good name dragged through the mud.*

**drag up** *v adv*

1 to pull (usu. something) upward or forward: [X9 + UP] *All the supplies for the attempt on the next part of the mountain have to be dragged up by the climbers. Drag up a chair and join the conversation.* → **draw up** (1), **pull up** (2)

*2 *not fml* to raise (a subject, esp. from the past) unnecessarily: [T1] *There was no need to drag up the time he spent in prison.* → **drag in** (2)

*3 *not fml* to educate (a child) in a poor way esp. without good manners: [T1 (*usu. pass.*)] *The way that child behaves, you'd think she's been dragged up, not brought up.* also **fetch up** → **bring up** (2)

***dragoon into** *v prep*

to force or threaten (someone) into (doing

something): [V4b] *It was easy in those days to dragoon the younger children into helping with the farm work.*

**drain away** *v adv*

**1** to (cause to) flow away: [L9 + AWAY] *We shall have to put in another pipe to let the water drain away.* [X9 + AWAY] *Doctors used to cut people open to drain the diseased blood away.* → **drain off** (1)

*__2__ to (cause to) attract away: [IØ; T1 (*to*)] *Some of the cleverest men in Britain (were) drained away to the United States after the war.*

*__3__ to (cause to) weaken: [T1] *This hard work has drained away my keenness.* [IØ] *My strength is draining away.*

*__4__ to (cause to) be used or spent: [T1] *The rise in costs has drained all our profit away.* [IØ] *Now that prices are rising so fast, all my money is draining away.*

**drain from** *v prep*

**1** to (cause to) flow away from (something): [L9 + *from*] *The blood drained from her face as she learned what had happened.* [X9 + *from*] *Drain the liquid from the tin before you serve the vegetables.*

*__2__ to leave; be attracted away from (a place): [T1 (*no pass.*)] *Thousands of clever men drained from Britain in the years just after the war.* [D1] *The chance of better pay and advantages has drained many good men away from Britain.*

**drain into** *v prep* → **empty into** (2), **flow into**

(of a river or land) to allow its waters to flow into (a body of water): [L9 + *into* (*simple tenses*)] *The whole island drains into the one river. All the rivers on the east side of England drain into the North Sea.*

**drain of** *v prep*

**1** to empty (something) of (its contents): [X9 + *of*] *First, you have to drain the container of all the old oil.*

*__2__ to empty (someone or something) of (something or people): [D1 (*often pass.*)] *The country has been drained of its best men. I felt as if I had been drained of all my strength.*

**drain off** *v adv*

**1** to (cause to) flow away: [L9 + OFF] *Open the pipe to let the water drain off.* [X9 + OFF] *Drain off the rest of the wine from this barrel.* → **drain away** (1)

**2** to drink (a quantity of liquid) completely: [X9 + OFF] *With an effort, he drained off the whole bottle.*

**drain out** *v adv*

**1** to (cause to) flow freely outwards: [IØ + OUT] *When the pipe was unblocked, the water drained out.* [T1 + OUT] *First you must drain the dirty water out and then clean the pipe.*

*__2__ to be lost; cease: [IØ] *All his strength drained out when he was discouraged in what he was doing.*

**drape in** *v prep*

to wrap; cover (someone or something) with (a large piece of cloth): [X9 + *in*] *The actress stood at the back of the stage, draped in the flag. Drape the furniture in sheets before you leave the house for the summer.*

**drape over** *v prep*

**1** to hang (cloth) loosely across (something such as furniture): [X9 + *over*] *The bed was not made, and the bedclothes were draped over a chair.*

**2** to place (oneself or part of the body) in a loose position across (something): [X9 + *over*] *The singer draped herself over the piano. The children draped their arms over the side of the boat and let their hands hang in the water.*

**drape round** *v prep*

**1** to place (something such as cloth) loosely round (something such as someone's shoulders): [X9 + *round*] *I'll drape this coat round your shoulders to keep you warm.*

**2** to cause (something) to rest in a position all round (something): [X9 + *round*] *She draped her arms round his neck.* (*not fml*) *The car was draped round the street light after the accident.*

**drape with** *v prep*

to cover (something) loosely with (something such as cloth): [X9 + *with*] *The plain wooden box containing the soldier's body was draped with the flag.*

*__draw ahead__ *v adv* → **move ahead,** etc.

**1** to lead; go in front: [IØ (*of*)] *The horse that we had chosen began to draw ahead halfway through the race.*

**2** to advance; go in front, esp. in a competition: [IØ (*of*)] *Our team were at the bottom of the local competition, but now they are drawing ahead.*

*__draw alongside__ *v adv; prep* → **lay alongside, lie alongside, pull alongside**

to come to rest next to (something such as a ship): [IØ] *A police car drew alongside and signalled to me to stop.* [T1 (*no pass.*)] *Draw alongside the ship and we will help you aboard.*

**draw apart** *v adv*

**1** to open (curtains): [X9 + APART] *Draw the curtains apart, and let in the sunlight.*

*__2__ to move, think, or live in separate ways: [IØ (*from*)] *After twelve years of marriage, their lives began to draw apart. The lovers drew apart from each other as other people came into the room.* → **drift apart** (2)

**draw aside** *v adv*

**1** to (cause to) move to one side: [X9 + ASIDE] *Drawing the curtain aside, he looked down into the street.* [L9 + ASIDE] *The crowd drew aside to let the prisoner pass.* → **pull aside** (1)

*__2__ to take (someone) on one side for private conversation: [T1] *Try to draw the chairman aside after the meeting, and let him know our views.* → **go aside, pull aside** (2), **take apart** (1), **take aside, take on**[2] (11), **take to** (20)

**draw at** *v prep*

*1 to suck at or draw smoke through (usu. a pipe): [T1] *Harold drew at his pipe while he considered what decision to make.* → **drag at, drag on, puff at, pull at** (2), **pull on**[2] (2)

**2 draw the line at** to regard (something or doing something) as beyond the limit to which one is prepared to go: *I don't mind being polite to that woman, but I draw the line at inviting her into my home.*

***draw away** *v adv*

**1** to (cause to) move away: [IØ] *The crowd cheered as the ship drew slowly away.* [T1 (*from*)] *She put her hand on his shoulder and then drew it away.*

**2** to move ahead of someone, as a competitor: [IØ (*from*)] *And now the leading horse is drawing away from the rest, putting a greater distance between himself and the nearest runner.*

**draw back** *v adv*

**1** to pull (something) back: [X9 + BACK] *He drew the curtain back and looked down into the street. Drawing the sheet back, he could see that the man was dead.* → **pull back** (1)

***2** to move backwards or away: [IØ] *The crowd drew back to let the firemen through. The mouse drew back in terror as the cat sprang.* → **pull back** (2)

***3** to hold oneself at a distance: [IØ (*from*)] *Mary drew back from other people at the party.*

***4** to be unwilling to fulfil (a promise): [IØ (*from*)] *The firm drew back from its agreement and wanted to talk about a new contract. It may already be too late to draw back.* → **pull back** (3)

**draw down** *v adv*

**1** to pull (something) downwards: [X9 + DOWN] *Draw down the window coverings, the sunlight is too bright. He drew his hat down firmly over his eyes.* → **pull down** (1)

***2** to attract; invite (something bad): [T1] *If you go on behaving like that, you'll draw down blame on our heads. Don't risk drawing down his anger.*

**draw for** *v prep*

to decide who gets (something or someone) by chance, as by choosing a card unseen or pulling pieces of paper out of a box: [L9 + *for*] *Now it's time to draw for the big prize! Before we start the card game, let's draw for partners.*

**draw forth** *v adv*

**1** *old use* to pull (something) out: [X9 + FORTH] *He drew forth his sword and ran towards the attacker.*

***2** *fml* to cause (something) to be seen or used: [T1] *Trouble can draw forth a person's best qualities. Her appearance drew forth admiration from every man in the room.* → **bring out** (4), etc.

**draw from** *v prep*

**1** to make a drawing from (an idea): [T1 + *from*] *The artist drew the scene from memory.*

**2** to take (something) out of (a supply or place): [X9 + *from*] *He drew a gun from his pocket and pointed it at me. How much water can you draw from the well in one bucket? I need to draw some more money from the bank. I would like to draw £20 from my account. Her performance as the dying dancer drew tears from the crowd.*

**3** to obtain (something) from (someone): [X9 + *from*] *The police are trying to draw the truth from the prisoner.*

***4** to obtain (something) from (something): [D1 (*usu. simple tenses*)] *What answer can you draw from the proofs that are offered? The moral to be drawn from this story is that honesty is best. His income is drawn from several different businesses.* → **derive from** (1)

***5** to copy (something or someone invented) from (something): [D1 (*usu. simple tenses*)] *All the characters in the story are drawn from life. The writer drew the stories from her own experience.*

***6** to gather or choose (people) from (somewhere or a group): [D1 (*usu. simple tenses*)] *Members of Parliament are drawn from all classes of society. The children chosen to perform in the city concert have been drawn from schools all over the city. Farmers have to draw seasonal helpers from the unemployed.*

**draw in** *v adv*

**1** to pull (something) in: [X9 + IN] *The fishermen drew in their nets full of fish. Draw in a deep breath and let it out slowly.* → **haul in** (1), **pull in** (1)

***2** (of days that follow each other) to have fewer hours of daylight: [IØ] *The days are drawing in now that it is autumn.* → **close in** (2), **draw out** (4)

***3** (of a single day) to become dark: [IØ] *Close the curtains, the evening is drawing in.*

***4** (usu. of a train or bus) to arrive (in a station), slowing down to a stop: [IØ (*to*)] *The train drew in (to the station) and all the passengers got off.* → **get in**[1] (4), etc.

***5** to move to one side of the road: [IØ (*usu. simple tenses*)] *The bus drew in to let the car pass.* → **pull in** (4), **pull off**[1] (3), **pull over**

***6** to attract (people): [T1] *The play drew large crowds.* → **pull in**[1] (7)

***7** to persuade (someone) to join: [T1 (*to*)] *It's your private quarrel, don't try to draw me in. Gradually the other performers were drawn in.*

***8** to collect (money owed): [T1] *Next year the bank will draw in some of the money it has lent.*

***9** to be careful about (spending money): [T1 (*usu. simple tenses*)] *If prices continue to rise we shall have to draw in our spending even further.* [IØ (*usu. simple tenses*)] *I've spent all my income for the month and will have to draw in.*

**10 draw in one's claws** to stop attacking som

one: *Why did the politician suddenly draw in his claws after opposing the government fiercely for months?*
**11 draw in one's horns** *not fml* to be less keen or active, and more careful: *You've been using up your strength too much recently; hadn't you better draw in your horns a little? You'd better draw your horns in or you'll have no money left.* → **haul in** (2), **pull in** (13)

**draw into** *v prep*
**1** (usu. of a train or bus) to arrive in a station, slowing down to a stop: [T1 (*no pass.*)] *The train is just drawing into the station; if we hurry we can catch it.*
**2** to encourage (someone) to join (something); attract (someone or something) into (something): [D1 (*usu. pass.*)] *My brother was drawn into a fight outside the hotel. Many other areas are being drawn into the government's plans for rehousing the population.*

**draw mild** *v adj*
**draw it mild** *not fml* to tell a story plainly, without stretching the truth: *We expected to hear exciting things about his adventures, but he drew it mild and we were disappointed.*

**draw near** *v adv*
**1** to come closer: [IØ] *The car drew near so that I could see the people sitting inside.*
**2** to be about to happen soon: [IØ] *As your birthday is drawing near, what would you like for a present?*

**draw off** *v adv*
**1** to pull (something such as tight clothing) off: [X9 + OFF] *Help me to draw off these muddy boots.* → **take off¹** (1), etc., (2), etc.
*__2__ to remove (something or someone): [T1] *Quickly, draw off some hot water before the pipes burst.* → **take off¹** (2)
*__3__ *mil* to (cause to) move away; go back a little space: [IØ] *The soldiers drew off and waited for the next attack.* [T1] *We have orders to draw off our forces.*
*__4__ to turn (something) aside: [T1 (*usu. simple tenses*)] *A sudden shout drew the policeman's attention off, and the prisoner escaped.*

**draw on¹** *v adv*
**1** to pull (something such as tight clothing) on: [X9 + ON] *Help me to draw on these boots, they're very tight.* → **put on¹** (2), etc.
**2** to come near in time, gradually: [IØ] *Winter is drawing on.* → **bring on¹** (2), **come on¹** (5)
**3** to encourage (someone), as to talk, move, act, etc.: [T1] *Her refusal only drew her lover on. They drew the poor child on with false promises. Try to draw the animals on so that they fall into the trap.* [V3] *He drew the prisoner on to tell his guilt.*

**draw on/upon²** *v prep*
**1** to make a drawing on (material): [IØ + *on*] *Children like drawing on large sheets of paper.* [T1 + *on*] *The plans were drawn on the back of an envelope.*
**2** to make use of (something such as money or thoughts): [T1] *I shall have to draw on the money I have saved to pay for the holiday. A writer has to draw on his imagination and experience.*
*__3__ to take (money) from (someone or an account): [D1 (*usu. simple tenses*)] *This cheque has been drawn on the wrong account. Feel free to draw on me for anything you need.*
*__4__ (esp. in horseracing) to reach; begin to come level with (another competitor): [T1 (*no pass.*)] *Black Prince is beginning to draw on the leading horse.*
**5 draw a gun on** to threaten (someone) with a gun: [*often simple tenses*] *I wasn't going to give him the money, but he drew a gun on me so I had no choice.*

**draw out** *v adv*
**1** to take (something) out: [X9 + OUT (*of*)] *He put his hand in the drawer, and drew out a gun.* → **get out** (5), **pull out** (1), **take out** (3), **take out of** (3)
*__2__ to stretch (something): [T1] *Draw out the wire until it is very thin.* → **pull out** (4)
*__3__ to lengthen (something): [T1] *The politician drew out his speech to almost two hours.* —**long-drawn-out** *adj*
*__4__ (of days that follow each other) to have more hours of daylight: [IØ] *The days are drawing out now that it is spring.* → **close in** (2), **draw in** (2)
*__5__ to (cause to) leave: [IØ (*of*)] *When all the passengers were on board, the train drew out of the station.* [T1] *British forces will be drawn out of the troubled area.* → **pull out** (5)
*__6__ to move across traffic: [IØ] *Suddenly the car in front of us drew out and nearly caused an accident.* → **pull out** (5)
*__7__ to show the general idea of (something): [T1] *The committee drew out a plan for the reorganization, without showing any details.*
*__8__ to develop; cause (something) to be seen or known: [T1] *The teacher helped to draw out the meaning of the poem. Plenty of money often draws out the worst in people.* → **bring out** (4), etc.
*__9__ to encourage (someone), esp. to talk: [T1] *Mary is very quiet; try to draw her out at the party.* → **bring out** (6), **come out of** (4), **fetch out** (5), **lead out** (2)
*__10__ to get (something) by talking: [T1 (*of*)] *I was able to draw his story out of him by patient questioning.*
*__11__ to take (money) from a bank account: [T1] *I shall have to draw out some more money to pay all these people.* → **get out** (6), **get out of** (4), **take out** (4), **take out of** (4)
*__12__ to remove (a tooth): [T1] *This tooth really hurts; I may have to have it drawn out.* → **take out** (2), etc.

**draw over** *v prep*
**1** to pull (something) over (something or someone): [X9 + *over*] *Draw a sheet over the dead body.* → **pull over²** (1), etc.
**2 draw a veil over** to refuse to talk about (something wrong) in the hope of causing it to

be forgotten: *We will draw a veil over your behaviour at the party when you were drunk.*

**draw to¹** *v adv* →**pull to¹**, etc.
to close (curtains): [X9 + TO] *Will you draw the curtains to, the light is hurting my eyes.*

**draw to²** *v prep*
**1* to attract (someone) towards (someone or something): [D1] *He has something in his character that draws people to him. I was drawn to music from my earliest years. "They could never see the two of us in conversation without being drawn to us . . . to demand what we were discussing."* (Laurens van der Post, *The Hunter and the Whale*)
**2 draw (someone's) attention to** to make someone notice (something, someone, or oneself): [*often simple tenses*] *Thank you for drawing my attention to this excellent magazine. Her loud voice only draws attention to her bad manners.* → **direct to** (5)
**3 draw to a close** to come to an end, often gradually: *The King's life is drawing peacefully to a close.*

***draw together** *v adv*
to (cause to) meet or come closer: [T1] *The man and woman were drawn together by an interest in poetry.* [IØ] *The two cars drew too near together, and crashed.*

**draw up** *v adv*
**1** to pull (something) forward: [X9 + UP] *Draw up a chair, and join the conversation. The boat was drawn up on the shore.* → **drag up** (1), **pull up** (2)
**2** to fold (something); put (something) out of the way: [X9 + UP] *The bridge is drawn up, we cannot cross the river. She sat on the floor with her legs drawn up under her.*
***3** to place (someone or something) in prepared order: [T1] *The soldiers were drawn up in battle lines. The royal carriage was drawn up outside the palace, ready for the Queen's journey.*
***4** (of a vehicle) to (cause to) stop: [IØ] *A police car drew up just as the robbers left the bank.* [T1] *The driver drew the horses up only just in time to avoid hitting the child.* → **pull in** (5), **pull up** (3)
***5** to make (oneself) stand straight, often proudly: [T1] *He drew himself up to his full height.* → **pull up** (6)
***6** to form; prepare; write (something): [T1] *The general has drawn up a plan to defeat the enemy. Has your lawyer drawn up the contract yet? Draw up a list of the guests for the dinner.*
**7 draw someone up sharp(ly)** to make someone stop speaking, as with a shock: *A sudden noise from the back of the room drew the speaker up sharp in the middle of his speech.*

**draw upon** *v prep* → **DRAW ON**

**dream about** *v prep*
**1** to have a dream about (something or someone): [IØ + *about*] *I dreamed about my old home last night. Do you ever dream about me?* → **dream of** (1)
**2** to have hopes for (something or doing something): [L9 + *about* (*simple tenses*)] *I often dream about the time when my work will be finished. Many people dream about living on an island in the South Seas.* → **dream of** (2)

**dream away** *v adv*
**1** to continue dreaming for some time: [L9 + AWAY] *I found him in the garden, dreaming away as usual.*
***2** to spend (time) in dreaming or lazy thoughts: [T1] *It's too easy to dream away the best years of your life. What I like best is dreaming away an afternoon in the sun.*

**dream of** *v prep*
**1** to have a dream about (something or someone): [IØ + *of*] *I dreamed of my old home last night. Do you ever dream of me?* → **dream about** (1)
**2** to have hopes for (something or doing something): [L9 + *of* (*simple tenses*)] *I often dream of the time when my work will be finished. Many people dream of living on an island in the South Seas. "For one person who dreams of making 50,000 pounds, 100 people dream of being left 50,000 pounds."* (A.A. Milne, *If I May: The Future*) → **dream about** (2)
***3** *infml* to consider; be capable of (something or doing something): [T1 (*no pass., neg., simple tenses, + would*)] *You needn't tell me not to sell the house, I wouldn't dream of it.* [T4 (*neg., simple tenses, + would*)] *I wouldn't dream of hurting a child.* —**undreamed-of** *adj* → **think of** (9)
***4** to imagine (something): [T1] *Scientists now have wonderful drugs of which no one could have dreamed years ago.* —**undreamed-of** *adj*

***dream up** *v adv* → **make up** (3), **think of** (5), **think up**
*not fml* to think of; invent; find (something unusual) in one's imagination: [T1] *Where did you dream up that idea?*

**dredge up** *v adv*
**1** to bring (something) to the surface of water: [X9 + UP] *The police dredged up the body from the muddy river.*
***2** *infml* to produce (usu. something unpleasant, or someone not very good): [T1] *Please don't dredge up the sad facts of his past. Let's not dredge up that old quarrel. Can you dredge up another player? We're one short.* → **rake out** (3), **rake up** (3), **root out** (3), **rout out** (1), **rout up** (1)

**drench in/with** *v prep* → **saturate with** (1), **soak with**
to cover (someone or something) with a lot of (usu. liquid or light): [T1 + *in/with* (*often pass.*)] *The whole city was drenched in spring sunshine. I left the garden chairs out all night and they got drenched with rain.*

***dress down** *v adv*
**1** to dress in a suitably humble fashion for some occasion or company: [IØ] *She dress-*

*down to visit her poor relatives, so as not to offend them by a show of her wealth.*

**2** *infml* to scold (someone): [T1] *The director dressed Jim down for being late again.* —**dressing-down** *n* → **tell off** (1), etc.

**3** to make (leather or a horse's skin) soft or clear by brushing, cleaning, or rubbing: [T1] *Help me to dress the horses down so that they will look nice for the show.*

**dress for** *v prep*

**1** to wear suitable clothes for (an occasion or activity): [L9 + *for* (*simple tenses*)] *If you're going to climb mountains, you'd better take advice on how to dress for it. How should we dress for the party?*

**2** to put on formal clothing for (an occasion): [L9 + *for*] *Tell the guests not to dress for dinner.*

**dress out** *v adv* → **dress up** (2), etc.

to ornament (something); make (something) more beautiful and cheerful: [T1 (*usu. pass.*)] *The street was dressed out in flags when the victory was won.*

**dress up** *v adv*

**1** to dress formally: [IØ] *Are we going to dress up for the wedding, or is it informal? "When you're all dressed up and nowhere to go."* (Benjamin H. Burt, *Title of Song*)

**2** to make (something or oneself) more attractive, as with clothing: [IØ] *Mary dressed up for the party.* [T1] *Mary was dressed up for the party. We shall dress the room up for Christmas.* → **deck out, do up (5), doll up, dress out, fig out, get up (12), rig out (2), tog up, trick out.**

**3** to make (something or someone) seem different: [T1 (*as, in*)] *The prisoners escaped by dressing up as guards. She was dressed up as a lady of high society. The teacher dressed the facts up in amusing details.* → **get up** (12)

**4** (usu. of children) to wear someone else's clothes, for fun and pretence: [IØ] *The children enjoy dressing up in Mother's old clothes.* —**dressing-up** *n, adj*

**5** *mil* to arrange (soldiers) in a straight line: [T1] *Dress up the men so that the general can see them.*

**drift along** *v adv*

**1** to move slowly forward in no particular direction, as in a boat: [L9 + ALONG] *The boat drifted along, with the child asleep inside it and no one guiding its direction.*

***2** to act aimlessly in life: [IØ] *He's still drifting along, without a proper job or any sense of purpose.*

**drift apart** *v adv*

**1** to become separated, as by water: [L9 + APART] *The two small boats drifted apart in the storm, and lost each other.*

***2** to become separate in thought, feeling, etc.: [IØ] *After twelve years of marriage, the two people began to drift apart.* → **draw apart** (2)

**drift away** *v adv*

**1** to be carried away slowly, as by wind or water; leave gradually: [L9 + AWAY] *The piece of paper fell onto the surface of the river and drifted away out of sight. People could be seen drifting away before the end of the concert.* also **drift off**

***2** to begin to think and feel in a different way (from someone or something): [IØ (*from*)] *As children grow up, they drift away from their parents' views.*

**drift in** *v adv*

**1** to be carried in, as by water or wind: [L9 + IN] *Some leaves have drifted in, we'd better sweep them out. A small boat drifted in during the night, with no one on board.*

***2** to arrive, informally: [IØ] *Two of Jane's friends drifted in last night, and are staying here.*

**drift off** *v adv* → **DRIFT AWAY** (1)

**drift out** *v adv*

**1** to be carried out, as by water: [L9 + OUT (*to*)] *In the storm the boat drifted out to sea.*

***2** to spread; move slowly or informally: [IØ] *When the lid came off the box, loose papers drifted out. The crowd drifted out after the performance.*

**drift towards** *v prep*

**1** to be carried by water or wind towards (usu. something): [L9 + *towards*] *With any luck, this boat will drift towards the shore.*

***2** to gradually reach (something such as a state) without making any effort to prevent it: [T1 (*no pass., often continuous tenses*)] *Is the world drifting towards war? The business seems to be drifting towards failure.*

**drill down** *v adv*

to make a deep hole in the ground: [L9 + DOWN] *We had to drill down 200 feet to find water.*

***drill in** *v adv* → **hammer in** (3), etc.

*not fml* to teach (something) with force and repetition: [T1 (*to*)] *The speaker tried to drill in his point but the crowd were not interested.*

**drill into** *v prep*

**1** to make a hole in (something) with a machine or tool: [L9 + *into*] *You'll have to drill into the wood before you can fix the shelf.*

***2** *not fml* to teach (something) by force and repetition to (someone): [D1] *Can't you drill some manners into the boy?* [D5] *How often have I tried to drill into you that you must ask permission first?* [D6] *Parents often try to drill into their children how much they owe them.* → **hammer into** (3), etc.

**drink away** *v adv*

**1** to drink continuously: [IØ + AWAY] *In the hotel, the old men were drinking away as usual.*

***2** to get rid of; waste (something such as money, time, or a feeling) by drinking alcohol: [T1] *Tom drank the whole of his father's fortune away. Some people try to drink their* *sorrows away. It is easy to drink away a whole night.*

**drink deep of** *v adv prep*
**1** to swallow a large quantity of (liquid): [L9 + DEEP + *of*] *After such a long thirsty journey, the travellers drank deep of the fresh spring water.*
***2** to take in a lot of (something): [T1 (*no pass.*)] *Drink deep of the wisdom of experienced people.*

**drink down** *v adv* → **drink up**
to swallow (the whole of a quantity of liquid) by drinking: [T1 + DOWN] *Drink your medicine down, it's good for you.*

**drink in** *v adv*
**1** to take in (liquid), as by drinking: [T1 + IN] *The thirsty plants drank in the welcome rain.*
***2** to listen with attention to; be eager to accept (words or ideas): [T1] *How many of the voters drank in his lies? The students sat round their teacher, drinking in his words of wisdom.*
***3** to take pleasure in giving one's attention to (something such as a sight): [T1] *We stood on top of the hill, drinking in the beautiful view.*

**drink off** *v adv*
to drink a large quantity of (liquid): [T1 + OFF] *Peter drank off a whole litre of beer all at once.*

***drink to** *v prep*
**1** to honour (someone) with a drink; wish (someone or something) good health or success with a ceremonial drink: [T1 (*usu. simple tenses*)] *Let us drink to the happy pair. I drink to the future; may it bring us all happiness. "Drink to me only with thine eyes."* (Ben Jonson, *The Forest:* 9, *To Celia*) → **propose to** (2), **raise to** (3)
**2 drink oneself to death** to ruin one's health; cause one's own death by drinking too much alcohol: *It's a sad story; after many failures, he started drinking and in the end he drank himself to death.*

**drink under** *v prep*
**drink someone under the table** *not fml* to be able to drink more alcohol than someone else without getting drunk: *Jim can take his beer; he can drink any man under the table.*

**drink up** *v adv* → **drink down**
to finish (one's drink): [I∅ + UP] *Drink up, then I'll refill your glass.* [T1 + UP] *Drink your medicine up, it's good for you.*

**drive at** *v prep*
**1** to make (a vehicle) move at (speed): [I∅ + *at*] *Peter was taken to court for driving at an unlawful speed.* [T1 + *at*] *Peter was taken to court for driving his car at an unlawful speed.*
***2** to make an effort towards (something or doing something): [T1 (*no pass.*)] *The factory must drive at increased production this year.* [T4] *The factory must drive at increasing production this year.* → **aim at** (2), etc.
**3 what be driving at** *not fml* to mean; suggest something: [(*no pass., continuous tenses*)] *What on earth are you driving at? You know what I'm driving at, so what are you waiting for?* → **be at** (1), **get at** (4)

**drive away** *v adv*
**1** to (cause to) leave in a vehicle; move (a vehicle) away: [L9 + AWAY] *The guests got into their cars and drove away.* [X9 + AWAY] *The Minister drove his important visitor away. The boy was taken to the police station for driving the car away without the owner's permission.* → **drive off** (1)
***2** to make (someone or something) go away: [T1] *What can I do to drive away these feelings of sadness? Don't drive people away who want to help you. "So I'll not pull her tail, nor drive her away."* (*Only True Mother Goose Melodies: I Love Little Pussy*) → **drive off** (3)

**drive away at** *v adv prep*
**1** to leave in a vehicle at (speed): [L9 + AWAY + *at*] *After the robbery, the thieves drove away at high speed.*
***2** to work very hard at (something): [T1 (*no pass.*)] *She sits at her desk for hours, driving away at her work.*

**drive back** *v adv*
**1** to (cause to) return in a vehicle; cause (a vehicle) to return: [L9 + BACK] *Let's drive back the other way, along the sea road.* [X9 + BACK] *Don't worry about getting home after the party, Jim will drive you back. If I lend you the car to get to the coast, who will drive it back?*
***2** to force (someone such as an enemy) to go back: [T1 (*usu. pass.*)] *The enemy have been driven back in all parts of the battle.*

***drive back on** *v adv prep* → **fall back on** (3)
to force (someone) to use (something) again that he had stopped using: [D1] *This trouble has driven me back on my old habit of biting my nails. Many families have been driven back on cheaper food by the rises in prices.*

**drive between** *v prep*
**1** to (cause to) be directed, or drive a vehicle, between (two things): [I∅ + *between*] *Make sure you drive between the gateposts.* [T1 + *between*] *Can you drive the car between those narrow walls?*
**2 drive a wedge between** to cause (two people or groups) to disagree: *Having different interests drove a wedge between the husband and his wife and they separated.*

**drive crazy** *v adj*
**1** to cause (someone) to become mad: [X9 + **crazy**] *Terrible experiences in childhood at last drove her crazy, and she had to be kept in a special hospital.* → **drive mad** (1)
***2** *infml* to annoy (someone) very much: [T1b] *This endless loud music is driving me crazy.* → **drive mad** (2), **drive out** (3), **go berserk run amok, send berserk**

**drive for** *v prep*
**1** to drive (a vehicle) to help (someone or an organization): [T1 + *for*] *Jim spends much of*

*his free time driving the bus for the blind children.*

*2 to make an effort towards (something): [T1 (*no pass.*)] *The factory must drive for increased production this year.* → **aim at** (2), etc.

**drive home** *v adv*

**1** to (cause to) travel to one's home in a vehicle: [IØ + HOME] *He's had a lot to drink, do you think he ought to drive home?* [T1 + HOME] *No, I think it would be safer if someone else drove him home.*

**2** to force (a nail) tightly into position with a hammer: [X9 + HOME] *When you are sure that the shelf is in the right position, drive the nails home.* → **ram home** (1)

*3 to make (something) clearly understood: [T1] *The person who wins an argument is the one who drives home his point. Advertisers keep repeating the name of the product in order to drive the message home.* → **ram home** (2)

**drive home to** *v adv prep* → **bring home to** (2), **come home to** (2), **get home to** (2)

to force (someone) to believe (something or that something . . .): [D1 (*usu. simple tenses*)] *You must drive the difficulty home to John. You must drive home to John what the difficulty is. You must drive it home to John that we don't have enough money.* [D6 (*usu. simple tenses*)] *You must drive home to John where the difficulty lies.*

**drive in** *v adv*

**1** to (cause to) move indoors or into a space: [IØ + IN (*to*)] *We built the garage joining the house so that you can drive straight in.* [T1 + IN (*to*)] *I'll open the doors and you can drive the car straight in.* [X9 + IN] *When winter comes, the farmers drive the cows in, so that they can be sheltered indoors.* —**drive-in** *n, adj*

**2** to force (a nail) into position with a hammer: [X9 + IN (*to*)] *You have to use strength and skill to drive these long nails in.* → **hammer in** (1), **pound in** (1)

*3 *not fml* to teach (something) with force and repetition: [T1 (*to*)] *The speaker tried to drive in his point, but the crowd were not interested.* → **hammer in** (3), etc.

*4 *mil* to force (enemy soldiers on the edge of the main force) to join the larger group: [T1] *First, drive in the outlying men and then attack the whole enemy force.*

**drive into** *v prep*

**1** to move (a vehicle or animal) into (something such as a space or object): [L9 + *into*] *If I have to have an accident, it would be my bad luck to drive into a police car. I'll open the door, and you can drive straight into the garage.* [X9 + *into*] *He drove the car into a street light and damaged the wheels. In the spring, the farmers drive the cows into the fields again.*

**2** to force (a nail) to pass into (material or an object) with a hammer: [X9 + *into*] *With a cry of joy he drove the last nail into the wood.*

*3 *not fml* to teach (something) by force and repetition to (someone): [D1] *Can't you drive some manners into the boy?* [D5] *I tried to drive into him that his drinking was harmful to himself and others.* [D6] *How can I drive into him why he shouldn't drink so much?* → **hammer into** (3), etc.

*4 to force (someone) into (something such as a state or doing something): [D1 (*usu. continuous tenses*)] *Your behaviour is driving me into a nervous breakdown.* [V4b (*usu. continuous tenses*)] *You are driving me into making a lot of mistakes.* → **drive to** (2)

**5 drive someone into a corner** to put someone in a difficult position, as in an argument: *He soon drove me into a corner with his powerful arguments, and I could find no forceful reply.*

**drive mad** *v adj*

**1** to cause (someone) to become mad; make (someone) lose his senses: [X9 + **mad**] *Terrible experiences in childhood at last drove her mad, and she had to be kept in a special hospital.* → **drive crazy** (1)

*2 *infml* to annoy (someone) very much: [T1b (*usu. continuous tenses*)] *This endless loud music is driving me mad.* → **drive crazy** (2), **drive out** (3), **go berserk, run amok, send berserk**

**drive off** *v adv*

**1** to (cause to) leave, as in a vehicle: [X9 + OFF] *He's driven your sister off in a fast car.* [L9 + OFF] *Without a word, she closed the door and drove off.* → **drive away** (1)

*2 to cause (an attacker) to go back: [T1] *The army drove off the enemy with much effort and loss of life.* → **fight off** (1)

*3 to make (someone or something) go away: [T1] *Sing a song to drive off those feelings of sadness. This medicine will help to drive the disease off. The police used horses to drive the crowds off.* → **drive away** (2)

*4 (in golf) to make the first stroke: [IØ] *How do we decide who is to drive off first?*

**drive on** *v adv*

**1** to drive a vehicle further: [L9 + ON] *There's no one in here; drive on, we'll try the next house.*

*2 to make (someone) use effort (to do something): [T1 (*to*)] *His father's example drove Jim on to success.* [V3] *His father's example drove Jim on to enter the competition.*

**drive out** *v adv*

**1** to drive a vehicle a long way: [L9 + OUT] *Let's drive out into the country, it's such a nice day.* [X9 + OUT] *Don't try to drive the car out until the garage door is open.*

*2 to make (something or someone) move away: [T1] *We had to use cats to drive the rats out. The defending army drove the enemy out. The cows are in the vegetable field, we shall have to drive them out.*

**3 drive someone out of his mind** to confuse someone; make someone anxious, worried, or annoyed; cause someone to become mad:

*Lady Macbeth's feelings of guilt about the murder of the king drove her out of her mind towards the end of the play. That loud music is driving me out of my mind! Please don't be late again without telephoning, I was nearly driven out of my mind with worry.* also *not fml* **drive someone round the bend** → **drive crazy** (2), **drive mad** (2)

**drive over** *v adv*
to (cause to) travel usu. in a car to someone's home: [L9 + OVER] *Why don't you drive over this afternoon?* [X9 + OVER] *I'll drive Grandmother over tomorrow.*

**drive round** *v prep*
**1** to (cause to) go in a vehicle round (an area): [X9 + *round*] *Do let me drive you round the park, it's so pretty.* [L9 + *round*] *I've been driving round and round this city for hours trying to find the right street.*
**2 drive someone round the bend** *not fml* → **DRIVE OUT** (3)

**drive through** *v prep*
to cause (a vehicle) to pass through (something): [T1 + *through*] *He drove the car straight through the shop window.* [L9 + *through*] *He drove straight through the shop window.*

**drive to** *v prep*
**1** to (cause to) travel in a vehicle to (a place): [T1 + *to*] *Can you drive me to the station?* [L9 + *to*] *I want to drive to London before dark.*
***2** to cause (someone) to take up (a habit) or reach (a state): [D1] *I wonder what drives someone to drink? I didn't choose to enter a life of crime, I was driven to it. The children's behaviour is driving me to despair.* → **drive into** (4)

**drive up[1]** *v adv*
to arrive in a vehicle: [L9 + UP] *Just then a friend drove up and gave me a ride. A police car drove up and stopped outside the shop.*

**drive up[2]** *v prep*
**1** to (cause to) move in a vehicle higher or further up (something): [L9 + *up*] *Let's drive up this road and see where it leads.* [X9 + *up*] *It's too hot to walk, let me drive you up the hill.*
**2 drive someone up the wall** *not fml* to annoy someone very much: *That continuous loud music is driving me up the wall, can't you put a stop to it.* → **go up[2]** (2), **send up[2]** (2)

**drivel about** *v prep*
*not fml* to talk foolishly about (a subject): [IØ + *about*] *What's the chairman drivelling about now?*

**drivel on** *v adv*
*not fml* to talk foolishly and at length (about a subject): [IØ + ON (*about*)] *That stupid television speaker is drivelling on again! Why do politicians always drivel on about promises that they can't possibly fulfil?*

**drizzle down** *v adv*
(of rain) to fall in continuous light drops: [L9 + DOWN] *The rain has been drizzling down all afternoon.*

**drone on** *v adv*
to talk at length and in a dull manner (about something): [L9 + ON (*about*)] *As the teacher droned on, one by one the class fell asleep. Whatever is the speaker droning on about now?*

**drone out** *v adv*
to speak (something) in a dull voice: [X9 + OUT] *The politician will never win votes if he drones out all his speeches like that.*

**drool over** *v prep*
**1** (usu. of an animal) to allow drops of liquid to fall from the lips at the sight or smell of (something): [IØ + *over*] *The dogs are drooling over that new dog meat.* → **slobber over** (1)
***2** *not fml* to express one's attraction to (someone); show too much love for (someone such as a child or an animal): [T1] *All the young girls are drooling over the good-looking actor. Every time a new baby arrives in the neighbourhood, she has to go and drool over it.* → **slobber over** (2), **slop over[2]** (2)

**droop down** *v adv*
to hang in a weak or tired manner: [IØ + DOWN] *His head drooped down and a few moments later he fell asleep.*

***drop across** *v prep* → **happen on,** etc.
*not fml* to find (something) or meet (someone) by chance: [T1 (*no pass., simple tenses*)] *I dropped across this old photograph in the back of the drawer. I dropped across an old friend in town today.*

***drop around/round** *v adv* → **bring over** (1) etc.
*not fml* to pay a short informal visit: [IØ] *Why don't you drop around some time?*

***drop astern** *v adv* → **fall astern**
*naut* to take a position behind another ship: [IØ] *When the engine failed, we had to drop astern.*

**drop away** *v adv*
**1** to be suddenly much lower: [L9 + AWAY (*simple tenses*)] *The cliff dropped away at his feet.* → **drop off** (2), **fall away** (2), **fall off[1]** (2)
***2** to become fewer or less: [IØ] *Student numbers have been dropping away recently. Interest in the game has dropped away.* → **drop off** (4), **fall away** (3), **fall off[1]** (3)
***3** to become worse: [IØ] *The quality of performance has dropped away since last year.* → **drop off** (5), **fall away** (4), **fall behind[1]** (3), **fall off** (4), **go off[1]** (7)

**drop back** *v adv*
**1** to (cause to) fall back: [IØ + BACK] *The ball landed on the roof and then dropped back to the ground.* [T1 + BACK] *Drop the egg carefully back into the nest, you had no right to take it.*
***2** to fail to remain level: [IØ] *We thought the horse would win, but he dropped back halfway through the race. This record has dropped back to third place in the popularity list.*

*Don't drop back now, just when you're doing so well. Production has dropped back in the last few months. Prices will never drop back.* → **lag behind** (1), etc.

**drop behind**[1] *v adv*
**1** to fail to remain level: [IØ] *We thought the horse would win, but he dropped behind half-way through the race. Don't drop behind now, just when you're doing so well. Production has dropped behind in the last few months.* → **lag behind** (1), etc.
**2** to be late, as with paying money: [IØ (*with*)] *If your payments of rent drop behind, you will be asked to leave. If you drop behind with your rent, you will be asked to leave.* → **get behind** (2), etc.
**3** to be of a lower standard: [IØ] *The work of this class has been dropping behind recently.*

**drop behind**[2] *v prep*
**1** to (cause to) fall at the back of (something), usu. accidentally: [L9 + *behind*] *The photograph has dropped behind the piano, and I can't get it out.* [X9 + *behind*] *I've dropped my glove behind the chest of drawers—have you another pair you could lend me?*
*__2__ to fail to remain level with (someone or something such as a standard): [T1 (*no pass.*)] *Your work has been dropping behind that of the other students recently. After her illness, she dropped behind the rest of the class for a short time.* → **fall behind**[2] (3), etc.

**drop below** *v prep*
**1** to be reduced to a point less than (a certain amount): [L9 + *below* (*usu. simple tenses*)] *The class has dropped below ten students this year. Why did the exchange rate drop below eighty-eight cents?* → **be below**[2] (2), **be under** (2), **fall below** (1), **get below** (1)
*__2__ to become less good than (a standard): [T1 (*no pass., often simple tenses*)] *I'm disappointed in your work; it has dropped below its usual high standard.* → **be below**[2] (3), **fall below** (2), **get below** (2)

**drop by** *v adv* → **bring over** (1), etc.
*not fml* to pay a short informal visit, often without warning: [IØ] *Drop by any time you're in town.*

**drop dead** *v adj*
**1** to die very suddenly: [IØ (*usu. simple tenses*)] *Poor Mrs Whitehead dropped dead in the street yesterday.*
**2** *not fml* to give up (someone or an activity) suddenly; cease to be connected with (someone or an activity): [T1b (*simple tenses*)] *The government dropped the plan dead when they learned how much it would cost. When he learned that his companions were secret criminals, he dropped them dead.*
**3** *sl* to stop annoying someone; go away: [IØ (*imper.*)] *Drop dead!* → **get lost** (2)

**drop down** *v adv*
**1** to (cause to) descend or fall quickly: [L9 + DOWN] *I heard a noise from the well and saw that the cat had dropped down.* [X9 + DOWN] *Fetch a rope, and drop it down to see if it is safe.*
**2** to lower oneself quickly: [L9 + DOWN] *All the people dropped down on their knees as the king passed by.* → **drop to** (2)
*__3__ *not fml* to pay an unexpected visit: [IØ] *Let's drop down to his summer home and see if he's there.*

**drop in** *v adv*
**1** to (cause to) fall in: [X9 + IN] *When the library is closed, you can drop books in through the special hole in the door.* [L9 + IN (*on*)] *The roof of the cave dropped in on the miners, trapping them.*
*__2__ *not fml* to arrive to pay a short informal visit, often without warning: [IØ (*on*)] *Drop in to see us any time you're in town. Look who's just dropped in! Let's drop in on Jim and Mary while we're in the neighbourhood.* → **bring over** (1), etc.
*__3__ *not fml* to choose to attend or join a social or educational system, a helping organization, etc.: [IØ] *Since they have been allowed to choose their own courses, many more students have been dropping in to classes. The organization has asked the city council for more money for the drug treatment centre, where so many young people are dropping in.* —**drop-in** *adj* → **drop out** (2), **fall out** (4)
*__4__ (in theatre) to lower (scenery) which has been held above the stage: [T1] *While they're playing scene two in front of the curtain, we can drop in the scenery for the next act.*

**drop into** *v prep*
**1** to throw (something); let (something) fall into (somewhere): [T1 + *into*] *The criminals stopped the car just long enough to drop a bomb into the restaurant.*
**2** to let oneself fall on (a piece of furniture), to rest: [L9 + *into*] *Tired after a heavy day's work, she dropped into a chair. I don't feel too well, I think I'll drop into bed for an hour.*
*__3__ *not fml* to visit (a place) informally: [T1 (*no pass.*)] *Let's drop into the hotel for a quick drink.*
*__4__ to let oneself use (language): [T1 (*no pass., usu. simple tenses*)] *He dropped into a country form of speech when talking to his mother on the telephone. Try not to drop into your native language outside class.* → **fall into** (4), **lapse into** (3)

***drop it** *v pron*
**1** *infml* to stop talking about a subject: [IØ] *Let's drop it, shall we?*
**2** *infml* to stop doing something: [IØ] *I think the boy has been concerned in criminal activity, so I've asked him to drop it.*

**drop off** *v adv*
**1** to fall off: [L9 + OFF] *My top button has dropped off and I can't find it.* → **fall off**[1] (1), **tumble off** (1)
**2** to be suddenly much lower: [L9 + OFF (*simple tenses*)] *The cliff drops off suddenly*

*here, be careful.* —**drop-off** *n* → **drop away** (1), **fall away** (2), **fall off**[1] (2)

*3 *not fml* to leave (something or someone) somewhere; leave a vehicle: [T1] *Drop me off at the corner, and I'll walk from there. I just want to drop this letter off. I'll drop my coat off at the cleaner's on my way to the office.* [IØ] *Thanks for the ride, I'll drop off here.* —**drop-off** *n, adj*

*4 to become fewer or less: [IØ] *Student numbers have been dropping off recently. Interest in the game has dropped off.* —**drop-off, dropping-off** *n* → **drop away** (2), **fall away** (3), **fall off**[1] (3)

*5 to become worse: [IØ] *The quality of performance has dropped off since last year.* —**dropping-off** *n* → **drop away** (3), **fall away** (4), **fall behind**[1] (3), **fall off**[1] (4), **go off**[1] (7)

*6 *not fml* to fall asleep: [IØ (*usu. simple tenses*)] *I was sitting in the armchair reading the newspaper when I dropped off. I had a bad night; I went to bed early enough but for some reason I couldn't drop off.* → **doze off**, etc.

**drop on** *v prep*

1 to cause (something) to fall on (someone or a place): [T1 + *on*] *Bombs were dropped on the city last night.*

*2 *not fml* to find (something) by lucky chance: [T1 (*simple tenses*)] *We dropped on the perfect house after searching for weeks.* → **fasten on** (3), **pick on** (1), **pitch on** (1)

*3 *not fml* to choose (someone) for a purpose, often unpleasant: [T1 (*for*) (*often simple tenses*)] *Why does he always drop on me for the worst jobs?* [V3 (*often simple tenses*)] *The examiners can drop on any student to answer questions.* → **fasten on** (4), **pick on** (2), **pitch on** (2)

*4 *not fml* to choose (someone) for punishment, blame, etc.: [T1 (*simple tenses*)] *Why drop on me? It's not my fault.* → **pick on** (3), etc.

*5 *not fml* to visit (someone) by surprise: [T1 (*no pass., usu. simple tenses*)] *Let's drop on Jim and Mary and surprise them.*

**drop out** *v adv*

1 to fall out: [L9 + OUT] *As she picked up the envelope, a key dropped out.* → **fall out** (1), **fall out off** (1), **tumble out**

*2 to choose to leave something such as a competition or a social or educational system: [IØ (*of*)] *One of the runners has dropped out, so you'll be able to compete after all. Two of the team have dropped out, and I don't know where we'll find replacements.* (*not fml*) *He dropped out of high school at the age of sixteen.* (*infml*) *Many young people are dropping out and trying to find new ways of living.* —**drop-out** *n infml*, **drop-out** *adj not fml* → **drop in** (3), **fall out** (4)

3 **the bottom drop out of the market** to have very low prices: *He thought he would make a fortune in property, but just after he had bought several buildings, the bottom dropped out of the market and he lost a lot of money.*

***drop over** *v adv* → **bring over** (1), etc.

*not fml* to pay a short informal visit, often without warning: [IØ] *Do drop over next week.*

***drop round** *v adv* → DROP AROUND

***drop through** *v adv* → **fall down** (3), **fall flat** (2), **fall through**[1] (2), **fall to**[2] (8), **topple down** (2), **tumble down** (2)

*not fml* to fail to be completed: [IØ (*simple tenses*)] *The plan dropped through when it proved too costly.*

**drop to** *v prep*

1 to fall suddenly to (something): [L9 + *to*] *The fruit dropped to the ground right at my feet. The temperature dropped to freezing point last night.*

2 to lower oneself quickly to (usu. one's knees): [L9 + *to*] *All the people dropped to their knees as the king passed by.* → **drop down** (2)

***drop up** *v adv*

esp. *AmE infml* to arrive unexpectedly: [IØ] *She said she'd drop up to tea one afternoon.*

**drown in** *v prep*

1 to (cause to) die in (liquid or a container): [T1 + *in*] *It is cruel to drown the cat in the river. The pilot was drowned in his plane when it crashed into the North Sea.* [IØ + *in*] *It is quite possible to drown in one's bath. Many people drowned in the great floods.*

*2 to cover (a sound) with (noise): [D1] *The crowd drowned his last few words in cheers.*

*3 to keep (oneself) very busy with (something), esp. in learning: [D1] *For years he has drowned himself in the study of English literature.* → **absorb in**, etc.

4 **be drowned in** to be full of; overcome by; lost in (something): *His face was drowned in tears. Worn out by their adventures, the climbers are now drowned in sleep.*

***drown out** *v adv*

1 to make (something or someone) impossible to hear because of other noise: [T1] *Both the speaker and his speech were drowned out by the disapproval of the crowd.*

2 to make (someone) homeless by flooding: [T1 (*usu. pass.*)] *Many families were drowned out when the river burst its banks.* → **flood out** (2)

***drum in/into** *v adv; prep* → **hammer in** (3), etc., **hammer into** (3), etc.

*not fml* to teach (something) with force and repetition (to someone): [T1] *The speaker tried to drum in his point, but the crowd were not listening.* [D1] "*No part of the walls is left undecorated. From everywhere the praise of the Lord is drummed into you.*" (Nikolaus Pevsner, *London, except the Cities of London and Westminster*) [D5] *I tried, but failed, to drum into him that he shouldn't drink so much.* [D6] *I tried, but failed, to drum into him where his drinking was leading.*

**drum on/upon** *v prep* → **knock at,** etc.
to beat quickly and repeatedly on (a surface), often loudly: [X9 + *on/upon*] *He had an annoying habit of drumming his fingers on the table while he listened.* [L9 + *on/upon*] *Rain has been drumming on the windows all night.*

**drum out of** *v adv prep*
*mil* to make (someone) leave (the army) in shame: [D1 (*usu. pass.*)] *The officer was drummed out of the force for refusing to obey orders.*

**drum up** *v adv* also **beat up**
*infml* to try to obtain (something) by advertising, formerly with a drum: [T1a] *While you're in the town, see what you can do to drum up some trade/some support/some new recruits.*

**drum upon** *v prep* → **DRUM ON**

**dry off** *v adv* → **dry out** (1), **dry up** (1)
to (cause to) become dry: [L9 + OFF] *Come and dry off in front of this fire.* [X9 + OFF] *Dry yourself off thoroughly after your swim, or you might catch cold. This high wind will dry the ground off.*

**dry out** *v adv*
**1** to (cause to) become very dry: [IØ] *Will this flooded ground ever dry out?* [T1] *A good hot summer could dry the ground out.* → **dry off, dry up** (1)
**2** *not fml* to (cause to) stop being dependent on alcohol or drugs: [IØ] *If he goes on drinking like that, he will have to spend months in a special hospital, drying out.* [T1] *Will the doctors be able to dry the actor out in time for his next film?*

**dry up** *v adv*
**1** to (cause to) become completely dry: [IØ] *The rivers are all drying up in the hot summer. We have no milk to sell; the cows have dried up.* [T1] *The hot sun is drying the ground up, and the crops can't grow.* —**dried-up** *adj* → **dry off, dry out** (1)
**2** to cease: [IØ] *Will his powers of invention ever dry up?* —**drying-up** *n*
**3** *BrE* to dry dishes: [IØ] *I'll wash the dishes if you'll dry up for me.* —**drying-up** *n, adj*
**4** *infml* to (cause to) be silent: [IØ (*simple tenses*)] *Dry up! I've had enough of your complaining talk. The actor dried up in the middle of his speech.* [T1 (*simple tenses*)] *A funny answer might dry her up for a short time.* → **shut up** (4), etc.

**dub in** *v adv*
(in film, television, and radio) to add (sound): [T1] *The music was dubbed in afterwards. If you make a film in one language and want people in other countries to understand it, you can dub in the voices of other actors speaking the other language, matching the words as nearly as possible to the movements of the original actors' mouths.*

**duck down** *v adv*
*not fml* to bend down quickly, as to avoid a danger: [L9 + DOWN] *Duck down behind this wall and then the policeman won't see you. He's got a gun, duck down!*

**duck into** *v prep*
*not fml* to hide oneself quickly in (a place): [L9 + *into*] *Duck into this doorway and hope he doesn't see us.*

***duck out** *v adv*
*infml* to escape one's responsibility (for something or doing something): [IØ (*of*)] *You can't duck out now, you made a solemn promise.* [T1] *No parent can duck out of his duty to his children.* [T4] *It's unlawful to try to duck out of paying taxes.*

***dull over** *v adv*
to become dull: [IØ] *It was sunny this morning, but now the sky has dulled over.*

**dull up** *v adv*
*AmE* to make (something) dull: [T1 + UP] *This hard meat has dulled up all the knife blades. Hard wear and dirt will dull up the shiny surface of the new paint.*

***dump on** *v prep*
*infml* to deceive or take advantage of (someone): [T1 (*usu. pass.*)] *I've been dumped on too often, I don't make the mistake of trusting people too far. I've had all this work dumped on me.*

**dun for** *v prep*
*becoming rare* to keep making demands on (someone) for (money owed): [X9 + *for*] *The debt-collector keeps dunning me for the rent.*

**dunk in** *v prep* → **dip into** (1)
*not fml* to dip (something) in liquid for a short time: [X9 + *in*] *The children are allowed to dunk their bread in the soup.*

**dust down** *v adv*
**1** to remove dust and dirt from (someone or oneself) usu. with the hands: [X9 + DOWN] *She picked herself up, dusted herself down, and started walking again.* → **brush down** (1)
***2** *infml* to scold (someone): [T1] *The director dusted Jim down for being late again.* —**dusting-down** *n* → **tell off** (1), etc.

**dust off** *v adv*
**1** to remove dust from (something): [X9 + OFF] *He dusted off the old book and handed it to me.*
***2** *not fml* to prepare to use or practise (something) again, after a period of not doing so: [T1] *If the family are all coming for Christmas, I'd better dust off the large meat tin. Dust off your old skills and prepare for new responsibilities.*
***3** *AmE not fml* (in baseball) to throw the ball very close to (the batter): [T1] *Watch me dust him off with this next ball.*

**dust out** *v adv*
to clean (a space) by dusting it thoroughly: [X9 + OUT] *Where has that mark come from? I dusted out the whole room this morning. I found this letter while I was dusting out your drawer.*

**dwell at** *v prep*
*old use* to live at (a place): *The family dwelt at Bath after the London season was over.*

**dwell in** *v prep*
**1** *old use* to live in (a place or building): [L9 + *in*] *"And Cain went out from the presence of the Lord, and dwelt in the land of Nod, on the east of Eden ... He was the father of such as dwell in tents, and of such as have cattle."* (The Bible)
*__2__ *fml* (of a feeling, quality, etc.) to be possessed by (someone): [T1 (*no pass.*)] *There dwells in me a strange feeling that all is not right.*

**dwell on/upon** *v prep*
**1** *old use* to live on (somewhere, as the earth): [L9 + *on/upon*] *In former times there were far fewer people dwelling on earth than there are now.*
*__2__ to think, often too much, about (something, esp. troublesome); worry over (something): [T1] *He sat for a moment in thought, dwelling on the matters that had been raised in the committee meeting. It's no use dwelling on the past. "Our minds tend to dwell on what has been happening to us."* (James Britton, *Language and Learning*) [T6] *Why dwell on how it happened? The thing to do is put it right.* → **think about** (1), etc.
*__3__ to speak or write at length about (usu. something unpleasant): [T1] *The teacher was always dwelling on the boy's failure. "Let other pens dwell on guilt."* (Jane Austen, *Mansfield Park*)

**dwindle away/down** *v adv*
to become smaller little by little: [L9 + AWAY/DOWN] *My savings have dwindled away over the years till there is hardly any money left. Membership has been dwindling down in the last few years.*

**dwindle to** *v prep*
to reach (something such as a quantity, much smaller) little by little: [L9 + *to*] *My savings have dwindled to nothing over the years.*

# E

*__earmark for__ *v prep* → **appropriate for**
to regard (something) as being saved for (a special purpose): [D1] *We have earmarked a quarter of the money for the children's hospital.*

*__earth up__ *v adv*
**1** to block (the course of water) with mud; fill up with earth: [I∅] *The mouth of the river has earthed up again this year.* [T1] *The landslide earthed up the pool where the animals usually drank.* → **land up** (2)
**2** to cover (the roots of a plant) with earth: [T1] *Don't forget to earth up the roots firmly when you plant the tree.* → **land up** (1)

*__ease down__ *v adv*
esp. *naut* to reduce (speed): [T1] *Loosen some sails to ease down the speed of the boat, the wind is dangerously strong.* [I∅] *Ease down, will you, you're going dangerously fast.*

**ease of** *v prep* → **relieve of**
**1** to free (someone) from (something unpleasant): [T1 + *of*] *This medicine will ease you of your pain. Do write to your mother to ease her of her worry.* → **relieve from** (1), **relieve of** (1)
*__2__ *humor* to rob (someone) of (something): [D1] *It won't take a moment to ease the ladies of their jewellery.* → **deliver of** (1), **relieve of** (3)

**ease off** *v adv*
**1** to remove (something) gently: [X9 + OFF] *Use a knife to ease the lid off, so that the contents of the box don't break.*
*__2__ to become less severe: [I∅] *The rain should ease off before midday. The danger of war has eased off. When will this pain ease off?* also **slacken off** → **ease up** (1)
*__3__ *not fml* to become less tight in feelings or actions; lessen effort or speed, etc.: [I∅ (*often simple tenses*)] *Now that the children are back at school, I can ease off. Ease off, we don't need to go so fast now.* → **ease up** (2), **slacken off** (2)
*__4__ *naut* to (cause to) move gently away from the shore: [T1] *Ease her off gently now!* [I∅] *It should be possible to ease off in this light wind.*

*__ease out__ *v adv*
*naut* to loosen (a sail): [T1] *Ease out the large sail or we shall be blown over!*

**ease round** *v adv; prep*
to turn (something such as a car or boat) gently in a circle (round something such as a corner): [X9 + ROUND/*round*] *Turn the wheel slightly so that we can ease the car round (the gateway). This is a tricky corner; we must ease the piano round (it), not push it. Ease the boat round carefully, there's a strong wind.*

*__ease to__ *v adv*
*naut* to turn a boat towards the direction of the wind, so as to reduce the force of the wind on the sails: [I∅] *The wind is too strong, we had better ease to.*

*__ease up__ *v adv*
**1** to become less severe: [I∅] *The rain should ease up before midday. The danger of war has eased up. When will this pain ease up?* → **ease off** (2)
**2** *not fml* to become less tight in feelings or actions; lessen effort or speed, etc.: [I∅ (*on*)

(*often simple tenses*)] *I wish you would ease up on the children; their behaviour gets worse when you make them nervous. Ease up, won't you? We shall get killed at this speed.* → **ease off** (3), **slacken off** (2)

**3** *not fml* to move further along a seat so as to allow room for another or others: [IØ] *Ask the children on the end to ease up, some more people want to sit down.* → **move over** (2), **move up** (2)

**eat away** *v adv*

**1** to eat continuously: [IØ + AWAY] *The children are in the kitchen, eating away as usual.*

**2** to destroy (something) by eating: [X9 + AWAY] *The rats have eaten away most of the woodwork.*

*__3__ to destroy (something) by chemical action: [T1] *The acid has eaten away the metal.*

***eat away at** *v adv prep*

to destroy (something) gradually: [T1 (*usu. continuous tenses*)] *The sea has been eating away at this cliff for centuries.*

**eat in** *v adv* → **dine in, dine out, eat out** (1)

to eat at home: [L9 + IN] *Are we eating in tonight?* —**eat-in** *adj*

***eat into** *v prep*

**1** to damage the surface of (something) by chemical action: [T1] *Acids eat into metals.* → **bite into** (2)

**2** to use part of (a supply of something such as money): [T1] *Our holiday has eaten into our savings.*

**3** to harm; have a bad effect on (something): [T1] *Guilt had been eating into his conscience for some months.*

**eat off**[1] *v adv*

**eat one's head off** to eat a lot, often at great cost: *Those children eat their heads off, it costs a fortune to feed them. The horse that eats its head off is not worth keeping.*

**eat off**[2] *v prep*

**1** to eat (one's food) from (certain dishes): [IØ + *off*] *Does the Queen really eat off gold plates?* [T1 + *off*] *Does the Queen really eat her meals off gold plates?* → **dine off** (1), **eat out of** (1), **feed off** (1)

**2** to eat part of, or have one's meals from (a piece of food): [L9 + *off*] *We can all eat off this large chicken for three days.* → **dine off** (2), **feed off** (2), **feed on** (1), **live off** (1), **live on** (2)

*__3__ to eat at the cost of (someone else): [T1 (*no pass.*)] *He's been eating off his brother for weeks.* → **dine off** (3), **live off** (2), **live on** (3)

**eat out** *v adv*

**1** to eat in a restaurant instead of at home: [L9 + OUT] *Let's eat out tonight, I'm too tired to cook.* → **eat in, dine in, dine out**

**2 eat one's heart out (for)** to be very unhappy; have a purposeless desire (for something or someone): *Jane has been eating her heart out for a new bicycle. She was eating her heart out for a soldier who was away at the war. You can eat your heart out if you like, but I will not give you any more money.*

**3 eat your heart out** *AmE sl humor* I can do better than this famous person in his own field: *Read this great play I've written—William Shakespeare, eat your heart out!*

**eat out of** *v adv prep*

**1** to eat (one's food) from (certain dishes): [IØ + OUT + *of*] *Make sure that the dog always eats out of his own dish.* → [T1 + OUT + *of*] *Make sure that the dog always eats his dinner out of his own dish.* → **dine off** (1), **eat off**[2] (1), **feed off** (1)

**2 eat out of (someone's) hand** *not fml* to be very willing to obey or agree with (someone): *The children in that class were very troublesome before the new teacher arrived, but he soon had them eating out of his hand.*

**3 eat (someone) out of house and home** *not fml* to eat a lot of food at the cost of (someone): *I'm not having that boy to stay again, he's been eating us out of house and home.*

**eat through** *v prep*

**1** to eat most of (food): [L9 + *through*] *That boy has eaten through a week's supply in a day!*

*__2__ to make a hole through (material or an object) by chemical action: [T1] *The acid has eaten through the metal.*

**eat up** *v adv*

**1** to finish eating (something): [T1 + UP] *Eat up your vegetables, there's a good girl!* [L9 + UP] *Eat up, children!*

*__2__ to use a lot of (something): [T1] *This new heating system eats up electricity. The big car ate up the miles.*

*__3__ *not fml* to defeat (an opponent); ruin (someone): [T1] *He was such a clever speaker that he always ate up the opposition. You shouldn't have put the new teacher in charge of that troublesome class, they'll eat him up.*

*__4__ *naut* to cover (a distance) quickly: [T1] *The boat was eating her way up towards the wind.*

*__5__ *not fml* to hurt (someone) in feeling: [T1 (*often pass.*)] *He was eaten up with jealousy. Is something eating her up? She seems worried.*

**eavesdrop on** *v prep*

to overhear the conversation of (someone or a group) by listening on purpose to private talk: [IØ + *on*] *Have you been eavesdropping on your neighbour again?*

**ebb away** *v adv*

**1** (of the tide) to flow back in gradual stages: [L9 + AWAY] *When the tide had ebbed away, the shells of many sea creatures were left on the sand.*

*__2__ to become less strong; fade; gradually go away: [IØ] *The king's life is slowly ebbing away. His keenness soon ebbed away when he learned how much work was needed.*

**echo back** *v adv*

to return the sound or idea of (something):

[T1 + BACK] *This cave echoes back every word you speak. Why do you always have to echo back my opinions like this?*

**echo with** *v prep* → **resound with, reverberate with, ring with** (1)
(of a space) to be filled with the repeating effect of (a sound): [IØ + *with*] *The whole room echoed with his ringing voice.*

**economize on** *v prep*
to save money by spending less on (something): [IØ + *on*] *I'd rather economize on holidays than food.*

***edge away** *v adv*
**1** to move away, esp. sideways, without being noticed: [IØ] *I tried to edge away until I was clear of the crowd.*
**2** to sail slowly away: [IØ] *The little boat edged away quietly, while no one was looking.*

***edge in** *v adv*
**1** to be able to speak (words) in the middle of other loud or continuous talking: [T1] *The noise at the party was so loud that I was hardly able to edge in a remark at all.*
**2** to move gradually (towards someone): [IØ (*on*)] *I tried to edge in on the chairman to speak to him, but he was surrounded by other questioners.* [T1] *There's a small crowd round the speaker, but try to edge your way in.*

***edge out** *v adv*
to put (someone) out of place: [T1] *Jim was winning the race until the thin boy edged him out. You might be able to edge your opponent out of the election.*

**edge with** *v prep*
to finish (an object) with a border of (something): [X9 + *with*] *The tablecloth was edged with a hand-woven pattern.*

***edit out** *v adv*
to remove (unwanted words) when preparing something for printing: [T1 (*of*)] *As his last sentence is rather rude, we'd better edit it out.*

**educate in** *v prep* → **instruct in**
to make sure that (someone) learns (something not a subject): [T1 + *in*] *The government often needs educating in the actual wishes of the people. Young men were once educated in good manners, and how to treat a lady.*

***educe from** *v prep*
*fml* to develop (something) from (something incomplete): [D1 (*usu. pass.*)] *The laws of the island society were educed from native customs.*

***eff off** *v adv infml euph* → **FUCK OFF** (2)

***efface oneself** *v pron*
to behave humbly; make oneself unnoticeable: [IØ] *Women often do not obtain positions of power because they tend to efface themselves.*

***egg on** *v adv*
*not fml* to encourage; urge (someone), usu. to do something: [V3] *His family egged Jim on to enter the race.* [T1] *Jim would not have entered the race if his family had not egged him on.*

**eject from** *v prep*
**1** to throw (someone or something) with force, out of (something): [X9 + *from*] *This safety invention will eject the pilot from a burning plane.*
**2** to make (someone) leave a place or group, as for a fault: [X9 + *from*] *Two members were ejected from the club for failing to pay the money that they owed.* → **throw out** (4, etc., 5, etc.,)

***eke out** *v adv* → **scratch out** (2)
to make (a supply of something) last, as by adding to it; have to live on (a poor income): [T1] *We'll have to eke out the milk till Monday. She ekes out her income by writing.*

***elaborate on** *v prep* → **enlarge on**
to speak or write more about (something such as a subject): [T1] *Please elaborate on this question, we need to know more.*

**elbow aside** *v adv* → **push aside, shoulder aside, thrust aside**
**1** to push (someone) roughly to one side, esp. by using the elbows: [X9 + ASIDE] *That rude man elbowed me aside and got on the bus ahead of me!*
***2** to make (someone) yield place to someone else: [T1b (*usu. pass.*)] *When jobs are scarce, young people entering the work force tend to be elbowed aside in favour of experienced workers with more to offer companies.*

**elbow forward** *v adv* → **push forward** (5), **shoulder forward, thrust forward** (4)
**elbow one's way forward** to force one's way ahead, esp. by using the elbows, as in a crowd: *It's not fair, he got to the front by elbowing his way forward; make him move to the back where he started!*

**elbow through** *v adv; prep* → **push through** (3), **shoulder through, thrust through**
**elbow one's way through** to force one's way through (something such as a crowd), esp. by using the elbows: *That man got to the front by elbowing his way through (the crowd) in a most rude manner.*

**elect as** *v prep*
to vote for (someone) to be (something such as a representative or ruler): [X9 + *as*] *Only someone born in the United States can be elected as President.*

**elect to** *v prep*
to vote for a position for (someone) in (a chosen group): [X9 + *to*] *After only a year in the sports club, the youngest player was elected to the committee.*

**elect with** *v prep* → **return with** (2)
to vote for (someone) with (a number of votes): [T1 + *with*] *The Member of Parliament was elected with an increased number of votes.*

***elevate to** *v prep*
to raise (someone) to (a higher social rank): [D1] *The Queen rewarded the Minister for years of faithful service by elevating him to the House of Lords.*

**eliminate from** *v prep*
**1** to send (something unwanted) out of (something): [X9 + *from*] *Eating the right food helps to eliminate waste matter from the body.*
**2** to cause (someone) to take no or no further part in (a competition): [X9 + *from*] *Jim was eliminated from the tennis competition in the first match.*

**elope with** *v prep* → **abscond with,** etc.
to run away with (someone), usu. to get married secretly: [L9 + *with*] *Mary's father would not give her permission to marry Jim as she was under age, so Jim eloped with her and they were married in Scotland, where the age limit is lower.*

***emanate from** *v prep* → **stem from**
**1** *fml* to flow or come from; originate in (something): [T1 (*no pass., simple tenses*)] *Great sadness emanates from his music. Dependence on alcohol often emanates from unhappiness in the home.*
**2** (of gas, light, etc.) to come out from (something): [T1 (*no pass.*)] *A bad smell emanated from the dead dog on the road.*

**emancipate from** *v prep*
to free (someone) from (a condition): [T1 + *from* (*often pass.*)] *How many black people were emancipated from slavery in the last century? Women still complain that they have not yet been emancipated from all the inequalities of the past.*

**embark for** *v prep*
to start a voyage to (a place): [L9 + *for*] *I shall stay in the seaport overnight before embarking for the United States.*

***embark on/upon** *v prep*
to start (something new or difficult): [T1] *Tom has already embarked on his new book. Mary embarked on her marriage with many hopes and fears.*

***embed in** *v prep*
to fix (something) firmly in (something): [D1 (*often pass.*)] *The magic sword was embedded in the stone. I had such strange ideas about you embedded in my mind. A piece of broken metal had embedded itself in his leg when he was wounded in the war.*

***embellish with** *v prep*
**1** *fml* to make (something) more attractive with (something or things): [D1 (*often pass.*)] *The leather cover of the old book was embellished with gold letters.* → **decorate with** (1, 2)
**2** to add details, often untrue, to (a story): [T1] *The prisoner embellished his story with lies.*

***emblazon with** *v prep*
*fml* to ornament (a shield or flag) with (a special pattern): [D1 (*usu. pass.*)] *The shield that the king carried into battle was emblazoned with his family coat of arms.*

***embody in** *v prep* → **lie in**[2] (3), **repose in** (2), **reside in** (2), **rest in** (2)
to give (something) existence, form, or expression in (something): [D1 (*often pass.*)] *She embodies her principles in her behaviour. The people's rights are embodied in the laws. Real power should be embodied in Parliament.*

**embosom in/with** *v prep*
*poet* to enclose; surround (something) with (usu. things): [X9 + *in/with* (*usu. pass.*)] *The poet's home was in a northern city embosomed in mountains.*

***embroil in** *v prep*
*fml* to cause (someone or oneself) to be part of (usu. something unpleasant): [D1 (*often pass.*)] *Don't embroil me in your quarrel. Why did he get embroiled in that political struggle?*

**emerge from** *v prep*
**1** to come out of (something such as water or a building): [L9 + *from*] *A hand holding the magic sword emerged from the lake.*
***2** *fml* to appear from; leave; result from (something): [T1 (*no pass.*)] *When did Britain emerge from the Dark Ages? What results emerged from your talks? It was not until three years after her husband's death that the woman emerged from her grief.* [*It* + T5] *It emerged from the message that all was well.*

**emigrate from** *v prep*
to leave (one's country) in order to settle in another country: [L9 + *from*] *In the present difficult conditions, many people are emigrating from Britain.*

**emigrate to** *v prep* → **immigrate into**
(from the point of view of the home country) to move oneself, one's family, and possessions to (another country) to start a new life: [L9 + *to*] *With the present difficulties in the National Health Service, many British doctors are emigrating to the United States.*

**emit from** *v prep*
to send (something such as heat, light, smell, sound) out from (something): [T1 + *from*] *The factory has been emitting black smoke from its chimneys, which is against the law.*

**emit into** *v prep*
to send (something such as heat, light, smell, sound) out into (usu. the air): [T1 + *into*] *It is now unlawful for factories to emit black smoke into the air.*

**employ at** *v prep*
**1** to pay (someone) to work at (a particular place, or rate of pay): [T1 + *at*] *Large numbers of female workers are employed at the lowest rates of pay. The company employs thousands of men at their car factory.*
**2** to pay (someone) to work at (something or doing something): [X9 + *at*] *How long have you been employed at this job? Two girls were employed at filling envelopes.* → **employ in** (1)

**employ for** *v prep*
**1** to pay (someone) to work because of (a reason): [T1 + *for*] *Women who help passengers on planes should be employed for their ability, not for their looks.*
**2** to pay (someone) to work for (a particular

time): [T1 + *for*] *The new bus driver has been employed for three months.*
**3** to pay (someone) to work at (a particular job): [X9 + *for*] *The shop usually employs additional sales people for the Christmas toy trade.*

**employ in** *v prep*
**1** to pay (someone) to work in (a place or trade): [T1 + *in*] *The salesman has been employed in the shoe business for twenty years.* → **employ at** (2)
**2** to use (something) for (a purpose): [X9 + *in*] *He employed his great gifts in the service of crime.*
**3 be employed in** to be busy with (something or doing something): *Mother has been employed in preparations for the party all morning. We were employed in separating the papers into different piles. More scientists are being employed in studies to discover new medicines.* → **engage in** (3)

**empty into** *v prep*
**1** to pour (something or the contents of something) into (another container): [X9 + *into*] *Empty your bag into your hand to see if you can find the key. Empty the dirty water into the bowl.*
**2** (of a river) to flow into (usu. the sea): [T1 + *into* (*no pass., simple tenses*)] *All the rivers on the east side of England empty into the North Sea.* [D1 + *into* (*no pass.*)] *This river empties itself into the ocean many miles away.* → **drain into, flow into**

**empty out** *v adv*
to (cause to) be emptied completely; throw away the contents (of a container): [X9 + OUT] *Empty your pockets out, we'll see if you have any money. I've asked the children to empty out their drawers this weekend. When you've emptied the water out, please clean the bucket.* [L9 + OUT] *Open the pipe so that the water can empty out.*

**enamour of** *v prep*
**be enamoured of** *fml* to be in love with (someone); be very fond of (something): *The humble fisherman was enamoured of the princess. The speaker seems to be enamoured of the sound of his own voice.*

**encase in** *v prep*
to cover; enclose; surround (something) with (a covering or material): [X9 + *in* (*often pass.*)] *The witness box was encased in strong glass. The precious gold figure was encased in plastic to protect it.*

**enchant by/with** *v prep*
**1** to charm; control (usu. someone) by (someone with magic powers) or with (magic means): [T1 + *by/with* (*usu. simple tenses*)] *The princess had been enchanted by a magician to sleep for a hundred years. The wicked old woman enchanted the princess with magic words.* → **charm with** (1)
**2** to delight (someone) with (something pleasant): [X9 + *by/with* (*often pass.*)] *The family were enchanted with the new house. The teacher was enchanted by the little girl's sweet voice. The speaker enchanted his listeners with amusing stories.* → **charm with** (2)

**enclose in/within** *v prep*
**1** to shut; imprison (someone or something) in (a space): [X9 + *in/within* (*usu. pass.*)] *All the people who are suffering from the fever must be enclosed within the town. The poor cat has been enclosed in the garage all night.*
**2** to include (something) in (an envelope, parcel, etc.): [X9 + *in/within*] *A key was enclosed in the envelope.*

**enclose with** *v prep*
**1** to surround (usu. a place) with (something): [T1 + *with* (*usu. pass.*)] *The ancient city was enclosed with a wall.*
**2** to include (something else) in the same envelope or parcel as (usu. a letter): [X9 + *with*] *I am enclosing my cheque with this order for the goods.*

**enclose within** *v prep* → ENCLOSE IN

***encompass with** *v prep*
*fml* to surround (something) with (something): [D1 (*often pass.*)] *He is encompassed with doubts. The enemy encompassed the city with their soldiers.*

**encourage in** *v prep*
to add to or strengthen the hopes of (someone) about (something): [T1 + *in*] *Is it kind to encourage the singer in her hopes?*

***encroach on/upon** *v prep*
**1** to advance upon (something): [T1] *The sea has been encroaching on the land for years.*
**2** to make unreasonable demands on (something such as someone's time): [T1] *He has no right to encroach on my time by staying all morning.* → **impinge on** (2), **infringe on, trench on**

***encumber with** *v prep*
**1** to load (something, someone, or oneself) with (something heavy or troublesome): [D1 (*usu. pass.*)] *At a young age, the girl was encumbered with the care of her many brothers and sisters. The business is encumbered with debts.*
**2** to fill (a space) inconveniently full with (something or things): [D1 (*usu. pass.*)] *The stage was encumbered with musical instruments.*

**end in** *v prep* → **finish in**
**1** to have (something) at its end: [L9 + *in*] *The cat's tail ends in white. The rope ended in a knot.*
***2** to finish in (a state): [T1 (*no pass.*)] *The meeting ended in disorder. The chairman's plan ended in failure. The two brothers' quarrel ended in personal hatred.* → **end up** (4)

***end off** *v adv* → **finish off** (1), **finish up** (1), **polish off** (1)
to bring (something) to an end: [T1] *The chairman ended off his speech with a reminde*

*of the main points.*

***end up** *v adv*

**1** *not fml* to finish by becoming (something): [L1 (*as*) (*simple tenses*)] *In spite of the people's opinions, she ended up the winner. The general began his army life as a private soldier and ended up as ruler of his country.* [L7 (*simple tenses*)] *After gaining two fortunes, he ended up poor when he died.* → **fetch up** (4), **finish up** (2), **land up** (3), **wind up** (6)

**2** *not fml* to finish (by doing something): [L4 (*by*) (*simple tenses*)] *I never dreamed that I would end up owning such a lot of property! Be careful, you could end up by getting hurt.* → **fetch up** (5), **finish up** (3), **land up** (4), **wind up** (7)

**3** *not fml* to arrive at or in (a place), usu. accidentally, esp. after time or events: [L9 (*at, in, on*) (*simple tenses*)] *With Jim driving, you never know where you're going to end up. The traveller took the wrong train and ended up at a country village. He'll end up in prison if he goes on behaving like that. The boy's ball ended up on the garage roof.* → **fetch up** (6), **finish up** (4), **land up** (5), **wind up** (8)

**4** *not fml* to (cause to) reach (an unfavourable end): [L9 (*in*) (*simple tenses*)] *The business might end up in failure unless more care is taken with the accounts.* [X9 (*in*) (*simple tenses*)] *Stop spending so fast, or you'll end us up in debt.* → **end in** (2), **fetch up** (7), **finish up** (5), **land in** (3), **land up** (6), **wind up** (9)

**5** *not fml* to receive (something) in the end: [L9 (*with*) (*simple tenses*)] *After much effort, the writer ended up with a contract. Jim entered the competition without much hope, not thinking he would end up with first prize!* → **fetch up** (8), **finish up** (6), **land up** (7), **wind up** (10)

**6 end up nowhere** *not fml* to gain no success: *If you don't work hard, you'll end up nowhere. What's the use of taking exams? So many people with higher degrees end up nowhere in the employment market.* → **fetch up** (9), **finish up** (7), **wind up** (13)

**end with** *v prep*

**1** to bring (something) to an end with (something or doing something): [T1 + *with*] *What shall we have to end the meal with?* [L9 + *with*] *We'll have some nice cheese to end with. I should like to end with reminding members of the purpose of this club.* also *fml* **conclude with** → **finish with** (1)

**2** (esp. of time) to come to an end on (a certain date): [L9 + *with*] *Please send your accounts for the period ending with the last day of March.* → **finish with** (2)

***3** to have nothing more to do with (someone): [T1 (*no pass.*)] *I'm glad that Alice has ended with that worthless young man.* → **finish with** (3)

**endear to** *v prep*

to make (someone or oneself) dear or precious to (usu. someone): [D1 (*often simple tenses*)] *Her smile endeared her to all the people.*

***endow with** *v prep*

**1** to give (someone or usu. something) a lasting gift of (usu. money): [T1] *The rich businessman endowed the hospital with half his fortune.*

**2** *apprec* to give (someone or something) a gift or quality of (something such as an ability or power): [D1 (*often pass.*)] *The writer endows his characters with qualities possessed by his friends. At the princess's birth, the fairies endowed her with beauty, cleverness, and luck. Most children are endowed with natural artistic ability. The cross is endowed with a special meaning for Christians.*

***endue with** *v prep*

*fml* to provide (someone) with (something good): [D1] *Endue her with blessings, and send her your peace. "I thank God I am endued with such qualities that . . . I were able to live in any place."* (Queen Elizabeth I)

**enfold in** *v prep*

*fml* to hold (usu. someone) tightly in (one's arms): [X9 + *in*] *With tears of joy, he enfolded his long-lost daughter in his arms.*

**enforce on** *v prep* → **force on**

to force (something unwanted) onto (someone): [X9 + *on*] *The teacher has no right to enforce his own views on the children.*

***engage in** *v prep*

**1** to cause (someone or something) to be concerned in (something); make (someone) join with one in (something): [D1] *Whichever nation explodes an atomic bomb will engage the whole world in war. Be good enough to engage my aunt in conversation so that I can escape from this dull family party.*

**2** to (cause to) take part in or work at (something); make (oneself) busy in (something or doing something): [D1 (*usu. pass.*)] *The Minister has been engaged in politics all his life.* [T1 (*no pass.*)] *Is it wise to engage in active sports at your age?* [V4b] *The old lady engaged herself in making clothes for her neighbours' children.*

**3 be engaged in** to be busy with (something): *The government and the trade unions are engaged in a war of words. Tom is engaged in planning his next book.* → **employ in** (3)

**engage to** *v prep* → **betroth to, promise to** (2)

**be engaged to** to be promised in marriage to (someone): *Mary was engaged to Jim for three months before their wedding. "I can honestly say that I always look on Pauline as one of the nicest girls I was ever engaged to."* (P.G. Wodehouse, *Thank You Jeeves*)

***engage with** *v prep*

**1** *mil* to attack (the enemy): [T1] *Our army engaged with the enemy at the first light of day.* → **join with** (2)

**2** to connect with (something) as in machinery: [T1 (*no pass.*)] *The engine has stopped because the different parts of the motor are not engaging with each other properly.*

**engorge with** *v prep*
to make (something) swell with (liquid): [X9 + *with* (*usu. pass.*)] *The mouth of the wound was engorged with blood.*

**engraft in** *v prep* also **graft in, ingraft in**
*fml* to place or fix (principles) in (someone's mind): [X9 + *in*] *The school attempts to engraft principles of honour and courage in the minds of the students.*

**engraft into/onto/upon** *v prep* also **graft into, ingraft into**
to place (part of one plant) into a position to grow as part of (another plant): [X9 + *into/onto/upon*] *Good eating apples are grown by engrafting the shoot of a cultivated apple tree into the trunk of a wild apple tree.*

**engrave on/upon** *v prep*
**1** to cut (a mark or pattern) into (a hard material), often for a special purpose: [X9 + *on/upon*] *The jeweller will engrave both your names on the inside of the ring. The names of the dead soldiers were engraved on stone.*
***2** to mark; fix; impress (something) on (someone's mind): [D1 (*usu. pass.*)] *The terrible sight is engraved on my mind.*

**engrave with** *v prep*
to mark (a hard material) with (something cut into it such as words or a pattern), often for a special purpose: [X9 + *with*] *The jeweller will engrave the inside of the ring with both your names. The stone was engraved with the names of the dead soldiers.*

**engross in** *v prep* → **absorb in,** etc.
**be engrossed in** to give all one's attention to (something): *The writer was so engrossed in her work that she did not hear the visitor enter the room.*

**engulf in** *v prep*
**be engulfed in**
**1** to be covered with (usu. liquid): *The whole village was engulfed in the flood.*
**2** to be overcome by (a condition): *It's natural for him to be engulfed in grief on the death of his father. The country's work force is engulfed in a wave of bitterness against the government.*

***enjoin on** *v prep*
*fml* to place (a duty) on (someone); force the idea of (something important) on (someone): [D1] *The teacher enjoined silence on the children. The commander has just enjoined on me the responsibility for the safety of this ship. The government is trying to enjoin on the people the need to save electricity.*

***enlarge on/upon** *v prep* → **elaborate on**
to speak or write more about (something such as a subject): [T1] *Please enlarge on this question, we need to know more.*

**enlighten about/on** *v prep*
*fml* to make (someone) understand more, or be clearer about (something): [T1 + *about/on*] *Would you enlighten me on your plans for the future?*

**enlist in** *v prep*
**1** to join (the armed forces) from choice: [L9 + *in*] *Two boys from our village have enlisted in the navy.*
**2** to obtain (someone or someone's support) to help in (something or doing something): [X9 + *in*] *I have come to enlist your help in the school concert. Can I enlist your support in raising the money? We could enlist half the population of the town in our fight against the council.*

**enmesh in** *v prep*
**1** to fasten (something) unintentionally in (something that catches hold of it such as threads): [X9 + *in*] *The fisherman's line became enmeshed in roots under the water.* → **entangle in, entangle with** (1)
***2** to confuse (someone) with or trap (someone) in (something difficult to understand or oppose): [D1 (*usu. pass.*)] *A committee member has been complaining that he was unable to make a decision because he was enmeshed in the system.*

**enquire about** *v prep* also **inquire about** → **ask about**
to try to get information about (something or someone), as by asking questions: [L9 + *about*] *The director is in the office, enquiring about those papers that you promised to have ready for him today. Newspaper reporters have been enquiring about the missing child.*

**enquire after** *v prep* also **inquire after**
**1** to search for (information) by asking people: [L9 + *after*] *I'm enquiring after any information the library might have on future city planning.*
***2** to ask politely about the health of (someone): [T1] *'My mother enquired after you.' 'Oh, how kind of her.'* → **ask after**

***enquire for** *v prep* also **inquire for** → **ask for** (2)
to look for; try to find (someone), esp. to speak to him: [T1] *There's a woman at the door, enquiring for Mr Sharp.*

***enquire into** *v prep* also **inquire into** → **look into** (4), **see into** (4)
to search for information about; examine (something): [T1] *The police are enquiring into the disappearance of the jewellery.*

**enquire of** *v prep* also **inquire of**
*fml* to ask a question of (someone): [L9 + *of*] *I have enquired of the city planners, but they will give me no information about future plans for the area. You can enquire of your new neighbours where the post office is.*

**enquire within** *v adv* also **inquire within** → **apply within**
*BrE* to ask inside the building where a notice is shown: [L9 + WITHIN] *For sale: small black armchair. Enquire within.*

**enrich with** *v prep*
to make (something or someone) richer, but not with money; improve (something) with

the addition of (something): [X9 + *with*] *Farmers have to enrich the soil with chemicals. His character was enriched with his experiences. A good mind can be enriched with the study of literature.*

**enrol for** *v prep*
to (cause to) have one's name recorded to start (something such as a course of lessons): [L9 + *for*] *How many students have enrolled for this course?* [X9 + *for*] *I must enrol the children for piano lessons before next week.*

**enrol in** *v prep*
to (cause to) join (an organization or group): [L9 + *in*] *The small boy wanted to enrol in the youth club, but he was too young.* [X9 + *in*] *I should like to enrol all my children in the swimming class.*

*** ensconce in** *v prep*
*fml or humor* to fix (oneself) firmly in a comfortable position in (a place): [D1] *Father has ensconced himself in his favourite corner as usual.*

**enshrine in** *v prep*
**be enshrined in** *fml* to be kept as precious or holy in (something): *The rights of the people are enshrined in the laws. The memory of her dead husband is enshrined in her heart.*

**ensue from/on** *v prep*
*fml* to follow; result from (something such as action): [L9 + *from* (*usu. simple tenses*)] *Who knows what troubles may ensue from overpopulation?*

*** ensure against** *v prep* → **insure against** (2)
to (cause to) be protected against (something bad): [T1] *The directors must take steps to ensure against possible failure.* [D1] *The engineers have used special methods to ensure the bridge against danger from high winds.*

**entangle in** *v prep* → **enmesh in** (1), **entangle with** (1)
to fasten (something) unintentionally in (something that catches it): [X9 + *in*] *The fisherman's line became entangled in roots under the water. My hair is entangled in the fastener. Take care not to entangle your long clothes in the wheels.*

**entangle with** *v prep*
**1** to catch (something) unintentionally among (something else): [X9 + *with* (*usu. pass.*)] *The fisherman's line became entangled with roots under the water. The blue wool gets entangled with the gold wool when I am working this pattern.* → **enmesh in** (1), **entangle in**
**2 be entangled with** to keep company with; become influenced by (someone unfavourable): *It looks as if my son has been entangled with criminals. I'm sorry that she was entangled with that worthless young man.*

**enter by** *v prep*
to come into (a place) through (a certain entrance): [L9 + *by*] *Holders of green tickets should enter by the main doors.*

*** enter for** *v prep* → **be down for** (1), **be in for** (2), **go in for** (2), **put down for** (3), **put in**[1] (11), **put in for** (3), **send in for**
to give the name (of oneself or someone) as a competitor in (a competition): [T1 (*pass. rare*)] *Has Jim entered for the competition?* [D1] *The teacher enters all her students for the examination. The Queen has entered two horses for the famous race.*

**enter in** *v prep* → **enter into** (1), **enter up**
to write (something) in (a record): [X9 + *in*] *If you are found guilty, the police will enter your name in the records. At the end of each day, enter the accounts in the book.*

**enter into** *v prep*
**1** to write (something) in (a record): [X9 + *into*] *I shall enter your name into my black book for bad behaviour.* → **enter in, enter up**
*** 2** to begin (something): [T1 (*usu. simple tenses*)] *Our chief competitor wishes to enter into dealings with the firm. Once you have reached informal agreement, you should enter into a contract with the other party. Try to enter into a conversation with the chairman, he might give you his views.*
*** 3** to begin to examine or work with (something such as details): [T1] *Without entering into all the advantages and disadvantages, we can see that the plan is possible.*
*** 4** to share (something); sympathize with (someone or something); become part of (something); act according to (something), esp. in the phr. **enter into the spirit of**: [T1 (*usu. simple tenses*)] *When you read the book, you really enter into the characters' feelings. Every cricket player must enter into the spirit of the game.*
*** 5** to be part of (something): [T1 (*no pass., simple tenses*)] *Cost must enter into consideration. All the matters enter into our plans. The possibility of failure must not be allowed to enter into our calculations.*
*** 6** *fml* to join; take one's place in (something): [T1] *Only good souls shall enter into the kingdom of God.*

*** enter on** *v prep* → ENTER UPON

**enter up** *v adv* → **enter in, enter into** (1)
to record (something): [T1 + UP] *Enter up the day's accounts in the black book.*

*** enter upon/on** *v prep*
**1** *old use* to begin to have or enjoy; take possession of (something): [T1 (*simple tenses*)] *You will be allowed to enter upon your fortune when you are 21.*
**2** *fml* to begin (something): [T1 (*simple tenses*)] *I feel pride mixed with humble gratitude as I enter upon the responsibilities of this office. The scientific world entered on a new age with the splitting of the atom.*

**enthrall with** *v prep*
**be enthralled with** to be charmed, excited, and very pleased with (usu. something): *The music teacher was enthralled with the child's singing. I am not exactly enthralled with your work so far this year.*

***enthrone in** *v prep*
to set (usu. someone) high in the opinion and feeling of (others): [D1 (*usu. pass.*)] *The singer was enthroned in the hearts of her public.*

***enthuse about/over** *v prep*
*not fml* to express great keenness for (something or someone): [T1] *The public are enthusing over the new play. Jane has been enthusing over the boy next door recently.*

**entice away** *v adv*
to persuade (someone) to leave his home or job, by offering an attraction: [X9 + AWAY] *Can I take him to court for enticing my wife away? The other firm has enticed away our best secretary.*

**entice from** *v prep* → **seduce from, tempt from**
to persuade (someone), as with promises, away from (something or someone, usu. that he should stay with): [X9 + *from*] *It is wicked to entice a man from his family. The enemy tried to entice the soldiers from their duty. Nothing will entice the children from television.*

**entice into** *v prep* → **seduce into, tempt into**
to persuade (someone), as with promises, into (something or doing something, often wrong): [X9 + *into*] *Young boys are easily enticed into a life of crime. Nothing will entice Father into breaking the law.*

**entice to** *v prep* → **tempt to**
to persuade (someone) to have (something offered): [X9 + *to*] *Can I entice you to a piece of cake?*

***entitle to** *v prep*
to give (someone) the right to (something): [D1 (*often pass., simple tenses*)] *This ticket entitles you to a free seat at the concert. I am entitled to a repayment for the damaged goods.*

**entomb in** *v prep*
to bury (someone) in (usu. the ground): [X9 + *in* (*often pass.*)] *The miners were entombed in the cave when the roof fell in.*

***entrap into** *v prep* → TRAP INTO

**entreat of** *v prep*
*fml* to request (something) anxiously from (someone): [X9 + *of*] *The people gathered outside the palace to entreat favours of the king.*

***entrench oneself** *v pron*
**1** *mil* to dig a shelter in the ground: [L9] *The army has entrenched itself behind the battle lines.*
**2** to settle into a relationship with others; be regarded as belonging to a group: [L9] *Alice has quickly entrenched herself in the new office, and is liked by everyone.*

***entrust to** *v prep* also **intrust to** → **trust to** (2)
to give the charge of (something or someone) to (someone), with complete faith: [D1] *I entrusted the child to your care. He entrusted the job to me.*

***entrust with** *v prep* also **intrust with** → **trust with**
to give (someone) the charge of (something or someone), with complete faith: [D1] *I entrusted you with the care of the child. I have been entrusted with the job.*

**entwine about/around/round/with** *v prep*
to wind, twist, or curl (something) round (something else): [L9 + *about/around/round/with*] *The plant will entwine round the stick as it grows.* [X9 + *about/around/round/with*] *She entwined her fingers with his and looked into his eyes.*

***enure to** *v prep* → INURE TO

**envelop in** *v prep*
**1** to cover (someone or something) all round in (something): [X9 + *in*] *If you envelop the baby in too many wool covers, he will get overheated.* → **swathe in** (1), **wrap in** (1)
**2** to surround (usu. something) with (something which hides it): [X9 + *in* (*often pass.*)] *The scenery was enveloped in a snowstorm. The sudden change of temperature has enveloped the city in mist.* → **swathe in** (3), **wrap in** (2)
**3** to hide (something such as information) by means of (something): [X9 + *in* (*usu. pass.*)] *Relations between governments are often enveloped in secrecy.* → **swathe in** (2), **wrap in** (3)

**equal in** *v prep*
to be the same or as good as (something or someone) with regard to (a part): [T1 + *in* (*simple tenses*)] *My car equals yours in speed.*

***equate to** *v prep* → **compare to, compare with, liken to**
to consider (something) as being like or as good as (something else): [D1] *You cannot equate life in the city to life in the country.*

***equate with** *v prep*
to consider (something) as being equal to (something else): [D1 (*often pass.*)] *His poems cannot be equated with his plays. The government's activities are rarely equated with its stated intentions or election promises. It is foolish and unrealistic to equate money with happiness.*

**equip for** *v prep*
**1** to provide (someone or something) with necessary things for (something such as an activity): [X9 + *for*] *This hotel room is not equipped for cooking. What does it cost to equip a young man for the navy? The workers are expected to equip themselves for the job.*
**2 be equipped for** to have the necessary ability or quality for (something): *I always felt that Mary was not equipped for motherhood. Many politicians are not equipped for public speaking.*

**equip with** *v prep*
**1** to provide (usu. someone) with (necessary things): [X9 + *with*] *Did she equip the boy with the correct boots?* → **fit out, fit up** (1)
**2 be equipped with** to have (an ability or quality): *He was not equipped with enough ability for the job.*

**erase from** *v prep*
**1** to remove (words) from (something written

or printed): [T1 + *from*] *Why have our names been erased from the list?* → **delete from, leave out**[1] (3), **miss out** (1), **omit from**

*__2__ to remove (something, usu. bad) from (one's thoughts): [D1] *Try as I might, I cannot erase such a terrible experience from my memory. Try to erase all thoughts from your mind, so that you will feel at peace.*

**erupt into** *v prep*
to change violently or develop suddenly into (something worse): [L9 + *into*] *The government is trying to stop local violence from erupting into civil war.*

**escape from** *v prep*
to get free from (someone or something): [L9 + *from*] *Two criminals escaped from prison last night. Explosive gas is escaping from the pipes. Young people often desire to escape from their parents. There is no escaping from history.*

**escape to** *v prep*
to get free and go to (someone or a place): [L9 + *to*] *The criminals escaped to London. I hear that our married neighbour has escaped to her lover.*

**escort from** *v prep*
to guard or protect (someone) when leaving (a place): [X9 + *from*] *The teacher was able to escort all the children from the burning school. Anyone who interrupts again will be escorted from the meeting.*

**escort to** *v prep*
to guard or protect (someone) on his way to (a place): [X9 + *to*] *The teacher escorted the children to safety. Armed guards escorted the criminals to prison.*

**establish in** *v prep*
to place or cause (someone) to settle firmly in (usu. work): [X9 + *in* (*usu. pass.*)] *How long did it take you to become established in the office? The director tends to establish his relatives in the best jobs.*

**estimate at** *v prep*
to guess (usu. a cost or size) to be (a stated amount): [X9 + *at* (*simple tenses*)] *The builder estimates the cost of repairing the roof at £600. I would estimate the size of the garden at 1,000 square metres.*

**estrange from** *v prep*
**be estranged from** to become separated from; cease to love (someone, usu. a wife or husband): *Don't ask him about his wife, he's been estranged from her for over a year now.*

***etch in** *v adv* → **SKETCH IN**

**evacuate from** *v prep*
to remove (someone) from (a dangerous place), esp. in large numbers: [X9 + *from*] *All the children were evacuated from London during the war, to avoid the bombing.*

**evacuate to** *v prep*
to remove (someone) to (a safe place), esp. in large numbers: [X9 + *to*] *All the London children were evacuated to the country, where they would be safe from the bombing.*

***even off/out** *v adv*
**1** to become level: [IØ] *The ground evens out on the other side of the mountain.*
**2** to (cause to) become level or equal: [IØ] *Prices should even off when the crops are gathered.* [T1] *We must even out the differences between social classes.*

***even up** *v adv*
to make (something, or two things) more equal: [T1] *This payment should even up our account. If you two sit at the other table, that should even up the groups. A little more weight on this side will even up the balance.*

***even up on** *v adv prep*
*AmE not fml* to return a favour to (someone): [T1 (*no pass.*)] *We can even up on Bill and Alice by looking after their children next week.*

**evict from** *v prep*
to force (someone) to leave (a place such as one's home) by law: [T1 + *from*] *The family were evicted from their house for failing to pay the rent. The government evicted many farmers from their land, where the airport was planned.*

**evolve from/out of** *v prep; adv prep*
to (cause to) develop in gradual stages from (something different): [L9 + *from*/OUT + *of*] *Some people still do not believe that man evolved from monkeys. The painter's ideas about form and colour evolved out of the work of an earlier artist.* [X9 + *from*/OUT + *of*] *The painter evolved his ideas about form and colour out of the work of an earlier artist.*

**exact from** *v prep* also *old use* **exact of**
to demand and obtain (something) by force or law from (someone): [X9 + *from* (*usu. simple tenses*)] *The government exacts taxes from every wage earner above a certain level of income. The teacher exacts obedience from the class.*

**examine for** *v prep*
to look at (someone or something) carefully, searching for (something such as a fault): [T1 + *for*] *The builder has been examining the wall for cracks. This doctor examines everyone for possible heart disease.*

**examine in** *v prep*
to ask (someone) questions to test his knowledge of (a subject): [T1 + *in*] *The great pianist will examine the students in music.*

**examine on** *v prep*
to ask (someone) questions to test his knowledge of (part of a subject): [T1 + *on*] *Students may be examined on any period of English literature.*

**exceed by** *v prep*
to go beyond (something such as a limit) by (an amount): [T1 + *by*] *My spending has exceeded my income this month by £50. The motorist was charged with exceeding the speed limit by 20 kilometres an hour.*

**exceed in** *v prep*
to do better than (someone) with regard to (something such as a quality): [T1 + *in*] *The*

*worker was rewarded for exceeding his fellow workers in production.*

**excel at** *v prep*
to be very good at (something active such as a sport): [L9 + *at* (*simple tenses*)] *John has always excelled at cricket, even as a young boy.*

**excel in** *v prep*
to be very good at (a subject): [L9 + *in* (*simple tenses*)] *David excels in history.*

**excerpt from** *v prep*
to take out (a part) from (something written such as a book or play): [X9 + *from* (*often pass.*)] *Today's reading is excerpted from the Bible. The theatre company have excerpted scenes from the famous play, to perform in the schools.* → **extract from**

**exchange for** *v prep* → **change for** (1), **swap for, trade for**
to give (something) in return for (something else): [X9 + *for*] *I'd like to exchange this dress for one in a larger size. I'll exchange my apple for your cake. "My early . . . love of reading, which I would not exchange for the treasures of India."* (Edward Gibbon, *Autobiography*)

**exchange with** *v prep*
**1** to take (something) in return for something else, with (someone): [X9 + *with*] *I wouldn't exchange places with him for anything. For our holiday, we exchanged houses with a friend who lives in another part of the country.* [L9 + *with* (*no pass.*)] *I wouldn't exchange with him for anything.* → **change with** (2)
*__2__ to share (words, ideas, etc.) with (someone), as in conversation: [D1] *I've lived here five years and still haven't exchanged more than a few words with my neighbours. The best part of university life is exchanging ideas with other students.*
**3 exchange blows with** to fight (someone): *The motorist exchanged blows with the garage owner after the unsatisfactory repair to his car.*
**4 exchange words with** to quarrel with (someone): *Have you been exchanging words with our neighbour again? We really should try to be friends with her.*

**excite in** *v prep*
to cause (a strong feeling) to arise in (someone): [X9 + *in*] *Unfortunately, Jim's success excited jealousy in his fellow workers. The speaker has been warned not to excite violence in the crowd.*

**exclude from** *v prep*
to keep (something or someone) out of (something); prevent (someone) from entering (something he wishes to enter): [X9 + *from*] *We can exclude the possibility of total loss from our calculations. The university had no right to exclude the student from the examination. Women are still excluded from the priesthood. Nobody can be excluded from blame.*

**excuse for** *v prep*
**1** to forgive (someone) for (a reason or a length of time): [T1 + *for*] *You cannot be excused for such a silly reason. I will excuse you for this once.*
**2** to accept the explanation offered by (someone) for (a fault): [X9 + *for*] *You cannot be excused for rudeness. I cannot keep excusing you for being late.*

**excuse from** *v prep*
**1** to allow (someone) not to complete (something that he was expected to do such as a duty): [X9 + *from*] *Please would you excuse me from my singing lesson as I have a cold? The student asked to be excused from finishing his writing.*
*__2__ *fml* to free (someone) from (blame): [D1] *The fireman was excused from all blame when the woman was burned to death.* → **exonerate from**

***excuse oneself** *v pron*
**1** to politely ask permission to leave: [IØ] *The chairman had another meeting to attend, so he excused himself and left.*
**2** to ask forgiveness for a fault: [IØ] *The foreign visitor excused himself for having offended his host, on the grounds that he had used the wrong word unintentionally.*

**execute in** *v prep*
*fml* to produce (something) in (a material): [X9 + *in*] *The artist executed his imaginative ideas in stone.*

**exemplify in** *v prep*
*fml* to show an example of (something) in the form of (something): [X9 + *in* (*usu. pass.*)] *Our ideas about right and wrong are exemplified in the laws.*

**exempt from** *v prep*
to free (someone) from (a duty or doing something): [T1 + *from* (*usu. simple tenses*)] *Being very small can exempt a man from military service. His record of success exempted the student from taking the first set of examinations.*

***exercise in** *v prep*
to make (someone or an animal) practise (something or doing something) regularly: [D1 (*often pass.*)] *All student teachers should be exercised in the new methods of reading instruction.* [V4a (*usu. pass.*)] *If the horses are exercised in jumping the fences every day, they will give no trouble in the actual race.*

***exercise over** *v prep*
to use (influence or power) to control (someone or something): [D1] *Can't you exercise your influence over the boy to get him to behave better? Many people think that the government exercises too much power over people's ordinary activities.*

**exile from** *v prep*
to make (someone) leave (his native land), usu. as a punishment: [T1 + *from* (*usu. pass.*)] *It is a severe punishment to be exiled from one's native land.*

**exist by** *v prep*
**1** to live or have one's being by means of (something): [IØ + *by*] *"I exist by what I*

*think . . . and I can't stop myself from thinking.*" (Jean-Paul Sartre, *Nausea*) → **live by** (2), **live off** (3), **live on²** (4)

**2** to find a reason or means for living in (something such as a quality): [IØ + *by*] *You can't exist by hope alone, you have to have some properly thought-out plan.* → **live by** (3)

**exonerate from** *v prep* → **excuse from** (2)
*fml* to declare (someone) to be free from (blame): [T1 + *from* (*usu. pass.*)] *The fireman was exonerated from blame when the woman was burned to death.*

**exorcise from/out of** *v prep; adv prep*
to drive (an evil spirit) out of (someone) by magic or prayer: [X9 + *from*/OUT + *of*] *The priests had to exorcise the devil from the body of the young girl, with bell, book, and candle.*

**expand into** *v prep*
to (cause to) be enlarged so as to become (something bigger) or reach (something further): [T1 + *into*] *The director plans to expand the firm into an international company.* [IØ + *into*] *The company intends to expand into a wider market.*

**expand on** *v prep*
to make (a story, argument, etc.) more detailed by addition: [T1] *I'm quite satisfied with your explanation, so there's no need to expand on it.*

**expatiate upon** *v prep* → **dilate on**
*fml* to speak or write at length about (a subject): [T1 (*usu. simple tenses*)] *Our next speaker will expatiate upon the question which was raised at the beginning of this meeting.*

**expect for** *v prep*
to hope and believe that (someoone) will visit to share (a meal): [T1 + *for*] *We'll expect you for dinner on Thursday, then.*

**expect from/of** *v prep* → **ask of**, etc.
to hope and believe that (something usu. good) will be done by (someone): [X9 + *from*/*of*] *Don't expect sudden improvements from this class. The whole family expects great things of him. Aren't you expecting too much of your mother, leaving all your children with her while you go on holiday?*

**expel from** *v prep*
**1** to push (something) out of (something): [T1 + *from*] *These large sea creatures make noises by expelling air from their lungs through a hole in the top of their bodies.*

**2** to make (someone) leave (a place), usu. with dishonour: [T1 + *from* (*usu. pass.*)] *The family were so ashamed when the youngest son was expelled from his school.*

**expend in** *v prep* → **spend in**
*fml* to spend (something such as time or effort) in (doing something): [X9 + *in*] *You may have to expend a further year in completing your book.*

**expend on** *v prep* → **spend for, spend on**
*fml* to spend (something such as money, time, or effort) on (something, someone, or doing something): [X9 + *on*] *The city council has been charged with expending too much of the taxpayers' money on sports buildings. You may have to expend more than a year on your book. The student seems to have expended too much care on this short piece of writing. The enemy expended all their bullets on trying to win the battle.*

**experiment in** *v prep*
to try to make discoveries in (a subject): [L9 + *in*] *You can get into danger by experimenting in magic.*

**experiment on/upon** *v prep*
to make tests on (someone or something) in order to make discoveries: [L9 + *on*] *Many people disapprove of scientists who experiment on animals. Why are you experimenting on the students in this particular class?*

**experiment with** *v prep*
to use (usu. something) in a test; try different methods and ideas with (something or doing something): [L9 + *with*] *Scientists experiment with rats in order to discover facts about human behaviour. Many writers are now experimenting with new forms of music. We are experimenting with living in a high building.*

***explain away** *v adv*
to account for (something wrong, a difficulty, etc.); give an excuse for (something), esp. in order to avoid blame: [T1 (*usu. simple tenses*)] *The criminal tried to explain away the false signature, but it was clear that he was guilty.*

***explain oneself** *v pron*
**1** to make one's meaning clear: [IØ (*simple tenses*)] *Let me explain myself: my plan concerns only those parts of the country with a small population.*

**2** to give an excuse for one's behaviour: [IØ (*simple tenses*)] *This is the third time you've been late this week; can you explain yourself?*

**explain to** *v prep*
to make (something) clear to (someone): [X9 + *to*] *The speaker tried to explain his meaning to the crowd.* [T6 + *to*] *You'll have to explain to me why you haven't finished your work.* [L9 + *to*] *You'd better go and explain to the teacher.*

**explode with** *v prep*
to express one's feelings noisily and often suddenly, because of (a strong feeling such as anger): [L9 + *with*] *Jim exploded with anger when he heard how Mary had been treated.*

**export to** *v prep* → **import from, import into**
to sell (goods) to (another country): [IØ + *to*] *They sell to their own country but they don't yet export to other countries.* [T1 + *to*] *We must try to export more goods to other countries.*

***expose oneself** *v pron*
**1** to leave oneself open to danger: [IØ] *The politician exposed himself by attacking the government's plan. It is unwise to expose yourself by trying to perform music that is too difficult for you.*

**2** (usu. of a man) to show one's sex organs in public: [IØ] *The man had been exposing himself in the park, and was taken to the police station.*

**expose to** *v prep*
**1** to leave (something or someone) open to the effect of (something): [X9 + *to*] *The best way to cure a burn is to expose it to the air. Unfortunately, the film has been exposed to light, and so the photograph cannot develop. What politician dare expose himself to public opinion?*
**2** to make (something wrong) known to (someone), usu. publicly: [X9 + *to*] *His companions have threatened to expose his crimes to the police. We must expose this shameful activity to the newspapers.*

**expostulate about/on** *v prep*
*fml* to argue fiercely about (something): [L9 + *about/on*] *One of the parents came to the school to expostulate about the child's examination results with the teacher.*

**expostulate with** *v prep*
*fml* to argue fiercely with (someone): [L9 + *with*] *One of the parents came to the school to expostulate with the teacher about his child's examination results.*

**expound to** *v prep*
*fml* to explain (something) in detail to (someone): [X9 + *to*] *The society has printed a paper expounding the advantages of the plan to its members. The speaker has an hour to expound his views to the public.*

**express as** *v prep*
to give (something) a form as (something): [X9 + *as*] *Anger is often expressed as violence.*

**express in** *v prep*
to give (something) a form in (something): [X9 + *in*] *The writer expresses his sorrow in his music. Children like to express their difficulties in play. Express the answer in decimal figures. Express your thoughts in good English.*

***express oneself** *v pron*
**1** to speak or write one's thoughts or feelings: [IØ] *The writer expresses himself in moving language. You express yourself well.*
**2** to show one's feelings in any way: [IØ] *The children are expressing themselves in play. Swearing is a way of expressing oneself.*

**express to** *v prep*
to say (something) to (someone): [X9 + *to*] *I should like to express our thanks to the speaker. Any member of the club may express his views to the committee. Let me express my sympathy to you and your family in your great loss.* [T6 + *to*] *I cannot express to you how grateful we are.*

**expropriate from** *v prep*
*fml* to take (something such as land) from (someone) by force of law: [X9 + *from* (*often pass.*)] *Much of the land for the airport was expropriated from local farmers.*

**expunge from** *v prep*
*fml* to remove (something wrong) from (something such as a book): [X9 + *from*] *False statements about events in our history must be expunged from classroom books.*

**expurgate from** *v prep*
*fml* to remove (something nasty) from (something such as a book): [X9 + *from*] *Rude language should be expurgated from classroom books.*

**extend across/over** *v prep*
**1** to cover (an area): [L9 + *across/over* (*simple tenses*)] *High unemployment extends over the whole of Britain. A belt of rain extends across the mountains.*
**2** to (cause to) fill (time): [L9 + *across/over* (*simple tenses*)] *The examinations extend over two weeks.* [X9 + *across/over*] *We shall have to extend the payments over an additional period.*

**extend to** *v prep*
**1** to (cause to) reach (something): [L9 + *to* (*simple tenses*)] *The judge's power extends to all parts of the area.* [X9 + *to*] *The city council has decided to extend the road to the new town. The underground railway is being extended to the airport. The protection of the law is extended to more kinds of animals.*
***2** *fml* to offer (something favourable) to (someone): [D1 (*usu. simple tenses*)] *Let us extend a welcome to our new neighbours. It was kind of you to extend an invitation to us.*

***extort from** *v prep*
to get (something such as money) from (someone) by unlawful force or violence: [D1] *The criminals extorted protection money from the shopkeepers by threatening them with violence.*

**extract from** *v prep* → **excerpt from**
to get or take (something) out of (something or someone): [T1 + *from*] *Many valuable medicines are extracted from humble plants. The doctor had to extract pieces of broken glass from the boy's eye. The police worked hard to extract the truth from the prisoner. I had to extract a promise from the children to be good while I was out. Surely the government dare not extract any more taxes from the voters! Today's reading is extracted from the Bible.*

**extradite from** *v prep*
*fml* to bring (someone who may be a criminal) back from (a country to which he escaped) to face the law in his own country: [X9 + *from*] *The police arranged to extradite the jewel thief from the island state where he had been hiding.*

***extricate from** *v prep*
*fml* to set (oneself, someone, or something) free from (something, usu. bad): [D1] *How can he extricate himself from this trouble? The prisoner cannot extricate himself from the charge.*

**exult at/in** *v prep* → **crow over** (1)
*fml* to be delighted about (something): [L9 + *at/in*] *The whole family exulted at Jim's success. Our team are exulting in their victory.*

**exult over** *v prep* → **crow over** (2)
*fml* to express delight in (the defeat or misfortune of someone): [L9 + *over*] *It's unkind to exult over a fellow student's failure.*

**eye with** *v prep*
to look at (someone or something) closely with (a feeling): [T1 + *with*] *The shopkeeper eyed the cheque with doubt. All the men eyed the beautiful girl with interest.*

# F

***face about** *v adv*
**1** *AmE mil* to (cause to) turn in the opposite direction: [IØ (*usu. simple tenses*)] *About face! shouted the officer.* [T1 (*usu. simple tenses*)] *The officer faced his men about.* → **turn about** (1), **turn around** (1)
**2** to change one's opinion completely, often suddenly: [IØ (*usu. simple tenses*)] *The middle of an election is no time to face about.* —**about-face** *n*

**face away** *v adv*
to take or have a position looking in the other direction (from something or someone): [L9 + AWAY (*from*) (*usu. simple tenses*)] *I could tell that he was lying because he faced away (from me) while he was speaking. The school faces away from the river.*

**face down** *v adv*
**1** to lie with one's face to the ground: [L9 + DOWN (*usu. simple tenses*)] *Everybody face down, there are bombs coming over!*
***2** to defeat (something or an opponent) with boldness: [T1 (*usu. simple tenses*)] *Can you face down such severe questioning? The speaker faced his opponent down.*

**face forward** *v adv*
to (cause to) face towards the front: [L9 + FORWARD (*usu. simple tenses*)] *Face forward, children, and attend to me!* [X9 + FORWARD (*usu. simple tenses*)] *All the pictures should be faced forward.*

***face off** *v adv* → **bully off**
(in hockey) to start a game or part of a game: [IØ (*usu. simple tenses*)] *The two teams are in position, ready to face off.* [T1 (*usu. simple tenses*)] *"John Stolberg faced off the ball."* (*Vancouver Province* 12.5.58) —**face-off** *n*

**face onto** *v prep* → **back onto**
(of a building) to have the front lying opposite to (a place): [L9 + *onto* (*usu. simple tenses*)] *Our new house faces onto the park.*

**face out** *v adv*
to oppose or deal with (someone or something) bravely: [T1 (*usu. simple tenses*)] *He faced the matter out in spite of severe questioning. You will have to face the committee out and explain your actions.* —**outface** *v*

**face round** *v adv* → **turn around**
to turn round, esp. with the head: [L9 + ROUND (*usu. simple tenses*)] *Face round, please, so that I can cut your hair at the back.*

***face up to** *v adv prep* → **shape up to, square up to**
to show courage in accepting, bearing, or dealing with (something difficult or painful): [T1] *Every young father has to face up to his responsibilities. She is too young to face up to the truth about her father.*

**face with** *v prep*
**1** to cover (a surface) with (usu. another material): [T1 + *with* (*often pass.*)] *The house has a wooden frame faced with brick. The dressmaker faced the inside of the woollen suit with silk.*
***2** to make (someone) meet (something bad or difficult): [D1 (*usu. simple tenses*)] *The police faced the prisoner with a simple choice: he could either give the names of his companions, or go to prison. Faced with the threat of losing their jobs, the workers decided to go back to work.*

**fade away** *v adv*
**1** to become gradually fainter: [IØ + AWAY] *The music faded away. This custom is slowly fading away. Memories of the homeland faded away after many years.* → **die away, fade out** (1)
***2** *not fml* to disappear slowly or secretly; leave quietly: [IØ] *When the police arrived, the crowd faded away. Having done my job in starting the club, I decided that it was time that I faded away and left the work to younger members.* → **fade out** (3)
***3** to lose one's strength, health, etc.: [IØ] *During his illness he faded away to nothing. "Old soldiers never die, they only fade away."* (song)

***fade back** *v adv*
(in American football) to move back, clear of a group of players, in order to pass the ball forward: [IØ] *The player had to fade back so as to have room to pass the ball.*

**fade down** *v adv* → **fade up**
to reduce (something such as sound) gradually: [X9 + DOWN] *The radio station faded the music down to give a special news broadcast.*

**fade from** *v prep*
**1** to become paler because of (something or doing something): [IØ + *from*] *The colours of the photograph have faded from being kept in bright light. Your shirts have faded from frequent washing.*

**2** to become gradually less strong or easily seen in (something): [L9 + *from*] *As the mist descended, the hills faded from view. My childhood home will never fade from my memory.*

**3 fade from the picture/scene** *not fml* to cease to be active or have a relationship with someone or a group of people: *When Mary married Jim, Charles faded from the picture. Don't fade from the scene just because you're no longer a member of the club committee.*

***fade in** *v adv* → **fade out** (2)
(in film, radio, and television) to mix (sound and/or picture) slowly by increasing its loudness, brightness, etc.: [T1] *After the introduction, we'll fade in the first scene.* [IØ (*to*)] *A view of the forest faded in. We'll fade in to an outdoor scene.*

**fade into** *v prep*
**1** to (cause to) mix gradually with (something such as another colour or sound): [X9 + *into*] *It will look nice if you can fade the blue into the pink.* [L9 + *into*] *The sky slowly faded into a deep gold. "And fade into the light of common day."* (William Wordsworth, *Ode. Intimations of Immortality*)
***2** to hide among (something): [T1 (*no pass.*)] *We train our soldiers to fade into the woods when the enemy are coming.*

**fade out** *v adv*
**1** to (cause to) become gradually weaker until it ceases: [L9 + OUT] *The music faded out. This custom is slowly fading out. Memories of the homeland faded out after many years. Call the television repair people, the picture has faded out completely. The idea seemed to fade out and the club was never formed.* [X9 + OUT] *Clouds spread across the moon, fading it out.* → **die away, fade away** (1)
***2** (in film, radio, and television) to cause (sound and/or picture) to disappear slowly by gradually reducing its loudness, brightness, etc.; become fainter: [T1] *Fade out the last scene at the end.* [IØ] *We'll fade out to the closing list of names. What's wrong with the radio? The sound keeps fading out.* → **fade in**
***3** *not fml* to disappear slowly or secretly; leave quietly: [IØ] *Having done my job in starting the club, I decided that it was time I faded out and left the work to younger members.* → **fade away** (2)

**fade up** *v adv* → **fade down**
to increase (something such as sound) gradually: [X9 + UP] *The radio station faded the music up again after the special news broadcast.*

***fag away** *v adv*
*infml* to work very hard (at something): [IØ (*at*)] *You've been fagging away (at your writing) all morning, it's time you took a rest.*

***fag out** *v adv* → **tire out,** etc.
esp. *BrE sl* to tire (someone) very much: [T1 (*often pass.*)] *I'm fagged out, let me rest a minute.*

**fail in** *v prep*
**1** to be unsuccessful in (something or doing something): [IØ + *in*] *How could you fail in such an easy test? The chairman failed in trying to persuade the committee to share his opinion. "You know who the critics are? The men who have failed in literature and art."* (Benjamin Disraeli, *Lothair*)
**2** to lack (something): [L9 + *in*] *She writes well, but fails in imagination.*

***fail of** *v prep*
*fml* to be unsuccessful in reaching (a successful end); miss (doing something): [T1 (*no pass.*)] *Your plan seems to have failed of its purpose.* [T4] *It was disappointing to fail of winning the contract.*

**faint away** *v adv*
to lose consciousness completely: [L9 + AWAY] *Peter fainted (clean) away with the shock of the news.*

**faint from** *v prep*
to lose consciousness because of (something): [IØ + *from* (*usu. simple tenses*)] *This poor old man has fainted from hunger; pick him up and when he wakes, feed him.*

**faint with** *v prep*
to become weak or unconscious because of (something): [L9 + *with* (*usu. continuous tenses*)] *This poor old man is fainting with hunger; let him sit down and eat. You have to act this part as though you were fainting with desire.*

***fair up** *v adv*
*N EngE infml* (of weather) to become brighter: [IØ] *It's been raining since early morning, so it should fair up later this afternoon.*

***fake out** *v adv*
*AmE infml* to deceive (someone), as by a trick: [T1] *You could try to fake out the teacher by handing in your book as though you'd done the work; he may not mark the books anyway.*

**fake up** *v adv*
*not fml* to invent (something false); pretend that (something) is real: [T1 + UP] *Do you really think that you can deceive experienced art dealers with an oil painting that you have faked up? You can easily fake up an excuse to avoid going out with him.*

**fall about**[1] *v adv*
**1** to move awkwardly, as when ill or drunk: [L9 + ABOUT] *There's a man falling about in the street; he seems to be suffering from shock.*
***2** *not fml* to be helpless with laughter: [IØ] *All the guests fell about (laughing) when Jim walked in wearing his funny clothes.*

**fall about/around**[2] *v prep* → **crash about**[2] (2)
**fall about/around one's ears** to fail suddenly: *All our careful plans fell about our ears when the government changed the tax laws.*

***fall afoul of** *v adv prep* → **FALL FOUL OF**

***fall among** *v prep*
*old use* to happen to meet (usu. someone bad): [T1 (*no pass., usu. simple tenses*)] *By*

*going to the club, Patrick fell among a bad group of people and started stealing people's money. "A certain man went down from Jerusalem to Jericho, and fell among thieves."* (The Bible)

**fall apart** *v adv*
**1** to break in pieces without force being used: [IØ (*usu. simple tenses*)] *This cup just fell apart in my hands.* → **come apart** (1), **fall to**[2] (3)
**2** *not fml* to end in failure: [IØ] *With all these increasing costs, the business could fall apart. Their marriage seems to be falling apart.*
**3** to separate in a relationship: [IØ] *We used to be good friends, but fell apart about a year ago.*

**fall around** *v prep* → FALL ABOUT

**fall astern** *v adv* → **drop astern**
*naut* to take a position behind another ship: [IØ (*usu. simple tenses*)] *When the engine failed, we had to fall astern.*

**fall at** *v prep* → **fall down** (4)
**fall at someone's feet** to kneel or lie down quickly in front of someone, as with respect or worship: "*And I fell at his feet to worship him*". (The Bible)

**fall away** *v adv*
**1** to come away from something by falling; break off: [L9 + AWAY] *Be careful on this part of the slope, bits of rock have fallen away.*
**2** to be suddenly much lower; take a downward direction: [L9 + AWAY (*to*) (*simple tenses*)] *The cliff fell away at his feet.* → **drop away** (1), **drop off** (2), **fall off**[1] (2)
***3** to become fewer or less: [IØ (*to*)] *Student numbers have been falling away recently. Interest in the game has fallen away (almost to nothing).* → **drop away** (2), **drop off** (4), **fall off**[1] (3)
***4** to become worse: [IØ] *The standard of your work has been falling away recently.* → **drop away** (3), **drop off** (5), **fall behind**[1] (3), **fall off**[1] (4), **go off**[1] (7)
***5** to (seem to) disappear: [IØ (*usu. simple tenses*)] *The wind fell away and all was calm. His smile fell away when he saw who his visitor was. When the brother and sister met again at last, the years of absence fell away and soon they were talking as if they had never been apart. All doubt fell away and we knew we would be victorious.*
***6** to take away one's support: [IØ] *Some of our formerly loyal members have fallen away.* → **fall off** (5)
***7** to grow thin: [IØ] *Her face has fallen away since she lost weight.* → **fall in**[1] (3)
***8** *naut* to allow a ship to swing away from the wind: [IØ (*usu. simple tenses*)] *The leading boat fell away when the wind grew too strong. "Fall away!" ordered the captain.* → **fall off**[1] (6), **pay off** (6), **sag away**
***9** to direct a plane away from others forming a group, line or pattern: [IØ (*usu. simple tenses*)] *The planes rose into the sky in a V-shape; then the leaders fell away and the others followed.*

**fall back** *v adv*
**1** to move backwards by falling, often accidentally: [L9 + BACK (*usu. simple tenses*)] *I fell back and hurt my head. The traveller fell back into the comfortable chair, tired out.*
**2** to take a position or direction further back: [L9 + BACK (*simple tenses*)] *Beyond the mouth of the river, the shore line falls back.*
***3** to move back or away, as in defeat: [IØ] *Our army forced the enemy to fall back. The crowd fell back to let the fire engine through.*
***4** to move to a position behind others; fail to remain level; be reduced: [IØ] *We thought the horse would win, but he fell back halfway through the race. This record has fallen back to third place in the popularity lists. Don't fall back now, just when you're doing so well. Production has fallen back in the last few months. Prices will never fall back.* → **lag behind** (1), etc.

**fall back on** *v adv prep*
**1** to move backwards, falling onto (usu. something): [L9 + BACK + *on* (*usu. simple tenses*)] *Luckily she fell back on grass or she might have hurt her head. The tired traveller fell back on the bed and at once fell asleep.*
***2** *mil* to go back in defeat as far as (a place): [T1 (*no pass.*)] *The battle is going badly for us, we'd better fall back on the town in the hills.*
***3** to need or be able to use (something); turn to (someone) for help, usu. when all else has failed: [T1 (*pass. rare, usu. simple tenses*)] *Doctors sometimes fall back on old cures when modern medicine does not work. If we spend all our holiday money, we can fall back on the traveller's cheques. The band were so short of musicians that they had to fall back on students. I'm glad we kept some money in the bank so that we always have something to fall back on.* → **drive back on**

***fall behind**[1] *v adv*
**1** to fail to remain level; move to a position lower down or behind others: [IØ] *We thought the horse would win, but he fell behind halfway through the race. Don't fall behind now, just when you're doing so well. Production has fallen behind in the last few months.* → **lag behind** (1), etc.
**2** to be late, as with paying money: [IØ (*with*)] *If your payments of rent fall behind, you will be asked to leave. If you fall behind with the rent, you will be asked to leave.* → **get behind** (2), etc.
**3** to be of a lower standard: [IØ] *The work of this class has been falling behind recently.* → **drop away** (3), **drop off** (5), **fall away** (4), **fall off**[1] (4), **go off**[1] (7)

**fall behind**[2] *v prep*
**1** to be dropped behind (something), usu. accidentally: [IØ + *behind* (*usu. simple*

*tenses)] The photograph has fallen behind the piano, and I can't get it out.*
**2** to sink behind (something): [IØ + *behind*] *As the sun fell behind the mountains, the air grew colder.*
***3** to fail to remain level with (something or someone): [T1 (*no pass.*)] *Your work has fallen behind that of the other students. The horse that we were hoping would win gradually fell behind the other runners.* → **be behind[2]** (3), **drag behind, drop behind[2]** (2), **lag behind** (2), **trail behind** (2)

***fall below** *v prep*
**1** to lessen to a point less than (a certain amount): [T1 (*usu. simple tenses*)] *The class has fallen below ten students this year. The exchange rate of the dollar fell below eighty-eight cents today.* → **drop below** (1), etc.
**2** to become less good than (a standard): [T1 (*often simple tenses*)] *I'm disappointed in your work; it has fallen below your usual standard.* → **be below[2]** (3), **drop below** (2), **get below** (2)

**fall beneath** *v prep*
**1** to fall underneath (usu. something): [IØ + *beneath* (*usu. simple tenses*)] *The man fell beneath a train and was killed.* → **fall under** (1)
***2** to feel the effect of (something): [T1 (*no pass., often simple tenses*)] *The students fell beneath the influence of the free-thinking teacher.* → **be under** (3), **come under** (3), **fall under** (2)
**3 fall beneath one's dignity** to be dishonourable for someone (to do something): [*simple tenses*] *Asking her mother for money fell beneath Mary's dignity. It fell beneath Mary's dignity to ask Jim to marry her.* → **be beneath** (3)

**fall between** *v prep*
**1** to drop accidentally between (two things): [IØ + *between* (*usu. simple tenses*)] *The poor dog has fallen between the tree and the cliff face; can we pull him up from there?*
**2** to take a middle position between (two opposite things): [L9 + *between* (*simple tenses*)] *The average temperature falls between the highest and lowest points of heat and cold.*
**3 fall between two stools** *not fml* to be neither one thing nor the other, and lose the advantage of either: [*simple tenses*] *Your plan for the building falls between the two stools of appearance and cost, and so is a failure from either point of view. The writer wanted to write a funny book that was also a serious study of modern life. Unfortunately he has fallen between two stools: the book is not funny and it isn't a serious study of modern life either.*

**fall by** *v prep*
**1** to be lowered by (an amount): [IØ + *by* (*usu. simple tenses*)] *The international exchange rate fell by two cents today.*
**2 fall by the way(side)** to fail to complete something, as a course; become less moral: *We started the year with 200 members, but we always expect a few to fall by the way(side) and have 195 now. Some of the people who used to come to our church have fallen by the wayside recently and are doing bad things in town.*

**fall down** *v adv*
**1** to fall accidentally: [IØ + DOWN (*usu. simple tenses*)] *The child has fallen down and hurt his knee. I tried to build a house of cards but it soon fell down. The hunter fired and the deer fell down dead. "When the people heard the sound of the trumpet, and the people shouted with a great shout, that the wall fell down flat, so that the people went up into the city."* (The Bible) → **fall down on** (1), **fall on** (1), **fall over[1]** (1), **fall to[2]** (1), **tip over, topple down** (1), **topple over, tumble down** (1), **tumble over**
***2** (of a building) to be in a poor state of repair; be about to become a ruin: [IØ (*usu. continuous tenses*)] *We got the house at a cheap price because it was almost falling down.* → **tumble down** (1)
***3** *not fml* to fail (in something): [IØ (*on*)] *His plan fell down when it proved too costly. Don't fall down on this easy test. Jane did quite well in her piano examination; it was on music history that she fell down.* —**downfall** *n* → **drop through, fall down on** (2), **fall flat** (2), **fall through[1]** (2), **fall to[2]** (8), **topple down** (2), **tumble down** (2)
***4** to kneel so as to worship a god or show respect (to someone in power): [IØ (*before*)] *The people fell down and worshipped the god. The worshippers fell down before the god. "All kings shall fall down before him: all nations shall serve him."* (The Bible) → **fall at**

**fall down on** *v adv prep*
**1** to fall accidentally on (a surface, part of the body, etc.): [L9 + DOWN + *on* (*usu. simple tenses*)] *The child fell down on his knee and hurt it. The horse fell down on the hard ground and broke its leg.* → **fall down** (1), **fall on** (1), **fall over[1]** (1), **fall to[2]** (1), **topple down** (1), **tumble down** (1)
***2** *not fml* to fail with regard to (something such as a part): [T1 (*no. pass., simple tenses*)] *Your suggested plan falls down on the question of cost. Jane did quite well in her piano examination, but fell down on music history. We thought he would be a good salesman, but in the end he fell down on the job.* → **fall down** (3), **fall flat** (2), **fall through[1]** (2), **topple down** (2) **tumble down** (2)
**3 fall down on one's knees** to kneel humbly: [*usu. simple tenses*] *He fell down on his knees and thanked God for His mercy.* → **fall on** (14), **fall to[2]** (9)

***fall due** *v adj* → **fall in[1]** (7)
(of a debt) to become payable: [IØ (*simple tenses*)] *The rent falls due tomorrow, don't forget to pay it.*

**fall flat** *v adj*
**1** to lie down quickly with one's face to the

ground: [L9 + **flat** (*usu. simple tenses*)] *When you see the enemy plane, fall flat (on your faces).*

*__2__ *not fml* to be unsuccessful: [IØ (*simple tenses*)] *Trade has fallen flat since the snow began. The chairman's suggestion fell flat at the meeting; no one thought it a good idea. The boys' joke fell flat; their parents did not think it funny.* → **drop through, fall down** (3), **fall down on** (2), **fall through**¹ (2), **fall to**² (8), **topple down** (2), **tumble down** (2)

**fall for** *v prep*

**1** to fall in love with (someone); like (something) very much: [T1] *Jim fell for Mary in a big way when they first met. The whole family fell for the new house as soon as they saw it.* → **fall in**² (3), **fall out of** (4), **tumble for** (1)

**2** *not fml* to be attracted to, tricked by, or believe (something, usu. something deceitful), esp. in the phr. **fall for something hook, line, and sinker**: [T1] *Don't fall for that old trick, he's trying to persuade you to buy his goods. "Did the committee fall for the chairman's plan?" "Yes, they fell for it hook, line, and sinker."* → **tumble for** (2)

***fall foul of** *v adv prep* also **fall afoul of**

**1** *naut* to hit (another ship): [T1 (*no pass., often simple tenses*)] *The sailing boat fell foul of a motor speedboat in mid-river.* → **run foul of** (1)

**2** to become caught in (something) in a disorderly way: [T1 (*no pass., often simple tenses*)] *The chain has fallen foul of plants in the water.* → **run foul of** (2)

**3** to have trouble with (something or someone): [T1 (*no pass., usu. simple tenses*)] *The chairman's plans have fallen foul of opposition. Take care not to fall foul of the director. By parking your car here, you could fall foul of the law.* → **run foul of** (3)

**fall from** *v prep*

**1** to fall down or descend from (something higher): [IØ + *from* (*usu. simple tenses*)] *The painter broke his leg when he fell from the ladder.* → **topple from** (1)

**2** to fail to remain level with (something): [L9 + *from* (*often simple tenses*)] *The standard of your work has fallen from the level we expect from you.* → **lapse from** (1)

**3** *fml* to be expressed by (usu. one's lips): [L9 + *from* (*often simple tenses*)] *Words of praise do not often fall from his lips.*

*__4__ to lose (something good): [T1 (*no pass., usu. simple tenses*)] *The Minister fell from favour and was dismissed from the government. Even the director can fall from his position. Why did the government fall from power?* → **fall out of** (2), **topple from** (2)

**5** **fall from grace: a** to become less moral: *The Church may forgive people who fall from grace.* **b** to lose favour with someone, esp. because of a bad or foolish action: *The Minister fell from grace and was dismissed from the government.* → **lapse from** (2)

***fall ill** *v adj* → **fall sick, go sick, report sick, take ill**¹, **take sick**

to become unwell: [IØ (*usu. simple tenses*)] *The director fell ill in the middle of the meeting, and had to be taken to hospital.*

**fall in**¹ *v adv*

**1** to fall accidentally into something, usu. dangerous or unpleasant: [L9 + IN (*usu. simple tenses*)] *The water's deep here, mind you don't fall in.*

**2** to give way; break inwards: [L9 + IN] *The roof of the mine fell in, trapping the miners. Part of the cliff has fallen in and is dangerous.* → **cave in** (1)

*__3__ to sink inwards; become hollow or thin: [IØ (*usu. simple tenses*)] *His cheeks had fallen in, making him look old and ill.* → **fall away** (7)

*__4__ *not fml* to be ruined: [IØ (*simple tenses*)] *His world fell in when he lost his job.*

*__5__ *mil* to (cause to) form proper lines or order: [IØ (*simple tenses*)] *Fall in, you lot!* [T1 (*simple tenses*)] *The officer fell the men in.* (*infml*) *Get fell in, that man at the back there!* → **fall out** (3)

*__6__ (of an agreement, as to rent a building or land) to come to an end: [IØ (*simple tenses*)] *Our rental agreement falls in at the end of the month; shall we ask for a new one?*

*__7__ (of a debt) to become payable: [IØ (*simple tenses*)] *The city's debts fall in at the end of this year, and the council are worried about paying them.* → **fall due**

*__8__ to agree: [IØ (*usu. simple tenses*)] *Once the chairman had stated his decision, the rest of the committee fell in.*

**fall in**² *v prep*

**1** to be lowered in (something, esp. the opinion of others): [IØ + *in*] *The chairman fell in my opinion after he refused to take a vote.*

**2** to fall accidentally into (something, usu. dangerous): [L9 + *in* (*usu. simple tenses*)] *The child fell in the lake and had to be pulled out.* → **fall into** (1)

**3** **fall in love (with)** to begin to love (someone) or like (something) very much: *Can anyone help falling in love? Jim fell in love with Mary at first sight. The whole family fell in love with the new house as soon as they saw it.* → **fall for** (1), **fall out of** (4)

**4** **fall in place** to become clear: *The whole mystery falls in place when you remember who was in power at the time.* → **fall into** (12)

***fall in alongside/beside** *v adv prep*

to start walking next to (someone who is already walking): [T1 (*no pass., usu. simple tenses*)] *As I was going to the shops, this man fell in beside me, trying to make conversation.*

**fall in with** *v adv prep*

**1** to fall into water or a hole, having, doing, or wearing (something): [L9 + IN + *with* (*usu.*

*simple tenses*)] *The boat sank, and the man fell in with all his clothes on. The child fell in with a cry of surprise and fear. The fish pulled so hard on the line that the fisherman fell in with it.*

*__2__ to meet (someone) by chance: [T1 (*usu. simple tenses*)] *The man who was enjoying a lonely walk in the hills fell in with a party of climbers.*

*__3__ to meet and join (someone); have a relationship with (someone, often bad): [T1 (*no pass., usu. simple tenses*)] *I'm afraid that the boy has fallen in with criminals.*

*__4__ to agree to (someone's ideas) or with (someone): [T1 (*usu. simple tenses*)] *The whole committee at once fell in with the chairman's suggestion. I'm glad to see that you all fall in with me on this question.* → **agree to,** etc.

*__5__ to suit or match (something): [T1 (*no pass.*)] *Will the new chair fall in with the rest of the furniture?*

**fall into** *v prep*

**1** to move down into (something) by falling or being dropped: [L9 + *into* (*usu. simple tenses*)] *The child fell into the lake and had to be pulled out.* → **fall in² (2), tumble into** (1)

*__2__ to begin (something); enter (a state): [T1 (*no pass.*)] *You have fallen into a bad habit of repeating yourself. All the soldiers must fall into step. I fell into conversation with an interesting man at the meeting. It's sad to see one's own son falling into evil ways. After all that wine, Father fell into a deep sleep. The sister and brother, who had not seen each other for four years, fell into eager talk. The old house is falling into decay. Many of our leading politicians have fallen into disfavour with the voters.* → **get into** (11), etc.

*__3__ to be divided into (kinds); belong to (a class): [T1 (*no pass., simple tenses*)] *These books fall into three classes. This book falls into the class of children's stories.* → **come under** (2), etc.

*__4__ to begin to use (a particular kind of language), esp. unintentionally: [T1 (*no pass., usu. simple tenses*)] *He fell into a country form of speech when talking to his mother on the telephone. Try not to fall into your native language outside class.* → **drop into** (4), **lapse into** (3)

**5 fall into someone's arms** to be held lovingly and kissed, etc.: [*usu. simple tenses*] *With a cry of joy, she fell into his arms. The two lovers fell into each other's arms and soon were kissing lovingly.* → **fall on** (15)

**6 fall into arrears** to fail to be paid in time; fail to pay what is owing: *If you let the rent fall into arrears, you will be asked to leave. If you fall into arrears with the rent, you will be asked to leave.*

**7 fall into a decline** to become weak, as through illness or failure: *I'm afraid your grandfather has fallen into a decline, and may not live long. The trade figures have fallen into a decline again.* → **go into** (17)

**8 fall into disrepute** to lose people's good opinion: *The government's election promises have long ago fallen into disrepute.*

**9 fall into disuse** to be no longer needed or used: *The old castle fell into disuse after the ancient wars, and became a ruin. The custom of giving up one's seat on a bus to a lady seems to be falling into disuse.*

**10 fall into someone's/the right/the wrong hands** to be gained by someone; come under someone's control: *The stolen jewels fell into the hands of a dishonest shopkeeper. We don't want your secret papers to fall into the wrong hands. "Fall into the hands of God, not into the hands of Spain!"* (Alfred, Lord Tennyson, *The Revenge*)

**11 fall into line/step (with)** to follow the same course of thought or action (as someone); accept a way of behaving: *The chairman makes sure that all the members fall into line (with the rest of the committee). The leaders of any political party want all the members to fall into line.* → **be out of** (16), etc.

**12 fall into place** to become clear: *The whole mystery falls into place when you remember who was in power at the time.* → **fall in²** (4)

**13 fall into a trap** to be tricked: *Don't fall into the trap of signing something without reading it first.*

**fall off¹** *v adv*

**1** to come off something by falling: [L9 + OFF (*usu. simple tenses*)] *When you are learning to ride a bicycle, you often fall off. My top button has fallen off.* → **drop off** (1), **tumble off** (1)

**2** to become suddenly lower; take a downward direction: [L9 + OFF (*simple tenses*)] *The land falls off here towards the river.* → **drop away** (1), **drop off** (2), **fall away** (2)

*__3__ to become fewer or less: [IØ] *Student numbers have been falling off recently. Interest in the game has fallen off.* —**falling-off, fall-off** *n* → **drop away** (2), **drop off** (4), **fall away** (3)

*__4__ to become worse: [IØ] *The quality of performance has fallen off since last year.* —**falling-off** *n* → **drop away** (3), **drop off** (5), **fall away** (4), **fall behind¹** (3), **go off¹** (7)

*__5__ to take away one's support: [IØ] *Some of our most loyal members have now fallen off.* → **fall away** (6)

*__6__ *naut* to allow a ship to swing away from the wind: [IØ (*usu. simple tenses*)] *The leading boat fell off when the wind grew too strong. "Fall off!" ordered the captain.* → **fall away** (8), **pay off** (6), **sag away**

**fall off²** *v prep*

**1** to come off (something) by falling: [L9 + *off*] *A button has fallen off my coat. Has that child fallen off the bicycle again?*

**2 fall off one's chair** *infml* to be very surprised or amused: *I could have fallen off my chair*

*when Jim walked in after all those years! I laughed so hard I nearly fell off my chair.*
**3 as easy as falling off a log** *infml* very easy: *Of course I can jump that height—why, it's as easy as falling off a log!*
**4 fall off (the back of) a lorry** *BrE infml euph* to be stolen: *"Where did Peter get that paint?" "I don't know, I think it must have fallen off the back of a lorry."*

**fall on/upon** *v prep*
**1** to fall accidentally on (a surface or part of the body, etc.): [IØ + *on/upon* (*usu. simple tenses*)] *The child fell on his knee and hurt it. The horse fell on hard ground and broke its leg. The children laughed to see their teacher fall on his face on the ice.* → **fall down on** (1), **fall to²** (1)
**2** to descend on (usu. a place): [L9 + *on/upon* (*often simple tenses*)] *Snow has fallen on the mountains overnight. Silence fell on the camp. Darkness fell on the little town.*
*__3__ to reach; be directed towards (something): [T1 (*no pass., often simple tenses*)] *Sunlight fell on the water, making it shine. As he was passing, his eye fell on a ring lying in the grass. Suddenly a strange sound fell on our ears.*
*__4__ to take place on (usu. a day): [T1 (*no pass., simple tenses*)] *Christmas Day falls on a Thursday this year. My birthday falls on a Sunday.*
*__5__ to happen on (a particular point): [T1 (*no pass., simple tenses*)] *The strong beat falls on the second note of the tune.*
*__6__ to attack (something or someone) eagerly: [T1 (*no pass., usu. simple tenses*)] *The hungry children fell on the food. The soldiers fell on the enemy.*
*__7__ to work at; think hard about (an idea): [T1 (*no pass., simple tenses*)] *He fell on the new idea and in the course of time wrote an important book about it.*
*__8__ to reach; come to; be the responsibility of (someone): [T1 (*no pass., simple tenses*)] *The cost of the wedding fell on Mary's father. The blame fell on me as usual.*
*__9__ *fml* to be the duty of (someone) (to do something): [*It* + V3 (*simple tenses*)] *It falls on me to thank our chairman for his speech.* → **fall to²** (5)
**10 fall on deaf ears** (usu. of a request) to meet lack of attention or refusal: *All our attempts to change the rules fell on deaf ears and we were powerless to do anything.*
**11 fall flat on one's face** *not fml* to fail in a way that makes one look silly: *I would have made that suggestion, but I was afraid of falling flat on my face.*
**12 fall on one's feet** esp. *BrE* to have good luck in the end, in spite of taking risks, being in difficulties, etc.: *Whatever risks Jim takes, he always seems to fall on his feet.* → **land on** (6)
**13 fall on hard times/evil days** to be unlucky or unsuccessful; meet difficulties, opposition, or lack of money: *I'm sorry to hear that my relative has fallen on hard times; what can I do to help?*
**14 fall on one's knees** to kneel humbly: *He fell on his knees and thanked God for His mercy.* → **fall down on** (3), **fall to²** (9)
**15 fall on someone's neck** to meet someone joyfully: [*usu. simple tenses*] *Scarcely able to control his feeling of joy, he fell on her neck when they met again after a long absence.* → **fall into** (5)

**fall out** *v adv*
**1** to leave something in a downward direction, by falling accidentally: [L9 + OUT (*of*) (*usu. simple tenses*)] *The wind blew so strongly that the nest turned upside down and three baby birds fell out. Three baby birds fell out of the nest. As she picked up the envelope, a key fell out. Your hair is beginning to fall out.* → **drop out** (1), **fall out of** (1), **tumble out**
*__2__ to be carried away as waste: [IØ (*usu. simple tenses*)] *The dirty water falls out through a pipe a long way out to sea. There is a danger of atomic dust falling out over cities.* —**fallout** *n* —**outfall** *n AmE*
*__3__ *mil* to (cause to) leave proper lines or order: [IØ (*simple tenses*)] *Fall out, men!* [T1 (*simple tenses*)] *The officer will fall the soldiers out when he has finished speaking to them.* → **fall in¹** (5)
*__4__ to leave; fail to fulfil a duty: [IØ (*usu. simple tenses*)] *Two of the team have fallen out, and I don't know where we shall find replacements.* —**fall-out** *adj* → **drop in** (3), **drop out** (2)
*__5__ *fml* to happen; result: [*It* + I5 (*simple tenses*)] *It so fell out that the two were not to meet again until after the war.* [L9 (*simple tenses*)] *What makes you think that everything will fall out as you planned?* → **turn out** (1)
*__6__ *not fml* to quarrel (with someone): [IØ (*over, with*)] *Jim and Mary fall out every few weeks, but their quarrels never last. Most married people fall out over money. When did you last fall out with your husband?* —**falling-out** *n*

**fall out of** *v adv prep*
**1** to fall from (something): [L9 + OUT + *of* (*usu. simple tenses*)] *Three baby birds fell out of the nest. A key fell out of the envelope.* → **drop out** (1), **fall out** (1), **tumble out**
*__2__ to cease to feel or enjoy (something): [T1 (*no pass., often simple tenses*)] *The young prince soon fell out of favour with the people when he became king.* → **fall from** (4), **topple from** (2)
*__3__ *becoming rare* to stop (something): [T1 (*no pass., usu. simple tenses*)] *Bad habits are easy to fall into but not so easy to fall out of.* → **get into** (11), etc.
**4 fall out of love (with)** to stop loving (someone): *How can you make yourself fall out of love with someone who you know is unworthy*

*of you?* → **fall for** (1), **fall in**[2] (3)

***fall outside** *v prep* also **be outside, stand outside** → **fall within** (2), etc.
to be beyond (something that one is prepared to consider); not be part of (something): [T1 (*no pass., simple tenses*)] *The question that you have just asked falls outside the agreed subject of our talks, so I will not answer it on this occasion. I can't speak about this matter as it falls outside my field of interest.*

**fall over**[1] *v adv*
**1** to fall accidentally: [L9 + OVER (*usu. simple tenses*)] *I saw the little girl fall over and hit her head. The child tried to build a house of cards but it soon fell over. Don't walk too near the edge of the cliff, you might fall over. The hunter fired and the deer fell over dead.* → **fall down** (1), **fall down on** (1), **fall to**[2] (1), **tip over, topple down** (1), **topple over, tumble down** (1), **tumble over**
**2 fall over backwards** *not fml* to be very eager and willing (to do something): *The students fell over backwards to finish their work on time. All the girls fell over backwards to get the party ready.* → **bend over** (2)

**fall over**[2] *v prep*
**1** to be dropped or fall accidentally over (something steep): [L9 + *over* (*usu. simple tenses*)] *The car fell over a cliff and the driver was drowned.*
**2** to fall by moving awkwardly on (something such as a surface or part of the body): [L9 + *over* (*usu. simple tenses*)] *He fell over a rock in his path. When a man is drunk, he often falls over his own feet.* → **stumble over** (1), **trip over**
**3 fall over oneself/each other** *not fml* to be very eager and willing (to do something): *Mother fell over herself to get the party ready. The children fell over each other to take the parcel from the postman.* → **stumble over** (2), **trip over** (2)

**fall overboard** *v adv* → **go overboard** (1)
to fall into the water from a ship or boat: [L9 + OVERBOARD (*usu. simple tenses*)] *Stop the ship! Someone has fallen overboard!*

***fall short** *v adj*
to be less in amount, distance, etc. than expected: [IØ] *The supply is falling short. He took careful aim, but his arrow fell short.* —**shortfall** *n*

***fall short of** *v adj prep* → **come short of**
to be less, usu. in quality, than expected: [T1 (*no pass., simple tenses*)] *Your work falls short of the expected standard. The pay they offered fell short of my hopes. Supply often falls short of demand.*

***fall sick** *v adj* → **fall ill, go sick, report sick, take ill**[1]**, take sick**
esp. *AmE* to become ill: [IØ (*simple tenses*)] *The director fell sick last week, and had to be taken to hospital.*

**fall through**[1] *v adv*
**1** to descend accidentally through something such as a surface: [L9 + THROUGH (*usu. simple tenses*)] *When you are walking on thin ice, be careful not to fall through.*
***2** to fail to be completed: [IØ (*simple tenses*)] *The plan fell through when it proved too costly.* → **drop through, fall down** (3), **fall down on** (2), **fall flat** (2), **fall to** (8), **topple down** (2), **tumble down** (2)

**fall through**[2] *v prep*
**1** to descend accidentally through (something): [L9 + *through* (*usu. simple tenses*)] *The boy fell through the ice and was drowned.*
**2 fall through the floor** *not fml* to be very surprised: [*simple tenses*] *I nearly fell through the floor when Jim first told me that he was getting married.*

**fall to**[1] *v adv*
**1** to drop so as to close: [L9 + TO (*usu. simple tenses*)] *Let go of the curtains and they will fall to.*
***2** to begin, esp. to eat, attack, or do anything active: [IØ (*simple tenses*)] *When the children saw the food on the table, they fell to eagerly and soon ate everything. The two brothers fell to and fought bitterly. Find a spade and fall to, there's a lot of the garden to be dug.* → **set to**[1]

**fall to**[2] *v prep*
**1** to descend as far as (usu. a place): [L9 + *to* (*usu. simple tenses*)] *The scientist watched an apple fall to the ground, and learned an important law of nature. "I shot an arrow into the air. It fell to earth, I knew not where."* (Longfellow, *The Arrow and the Song*) → **fall down** (1), **fall down on** (1), **fall on** (1), **fall over**[1] (1), **topple down** (1), **tumble down** (1)
**2** to be lowered to (something): [IØ + *to*] *The pound fell to an even lower exchange rate today. The temperature has fallen to its lowest point this winter.*
**3** to break into (pieces or bits): [L9 + *to*] *When I picked up the cake, it fell to pieces.* → **come apart** (1), **fall apart** (1)
***4** to be defeated or killed by (something or someone): [T1 (*no pass.*)] *250 men fell to the enemy gunfire. All through the competition, good players were falling to the new young tennis star.*
***5** *fml* to be the duty of (someone) (to do something): [*It* + V3 (*simple tenses*)] *It falls to me to thank our chairman for his speech.* → **fall on** (9)
***6** to belong by right to (someone), usu. after someone's death: [T1 (*no pass., simple tenses*)] *The property will fall to the eldest son.*
***7** to begin (doing something): [T4 (*simple tenses*)] *I fell to thinking about the happy days of the past.*
**8 fall to the ground** to fail: [*simple tenses*] *The business has fallen to the ground since last year. Your argument falls to the ground when we consider the facts.* → **drop through, fall down** (3), **fall flat** (2), **fall through**[1] (2), **topple down** (2), **tumble down** (2)

**9 fall to one's knees** to kneel humbly: *He fell to his knees and thanked God for His mercy.* → **fall down on** (3), **fall on** (14)

**10 fall to someone's lot/share** to become someone's share of responsibility (to do something): [*usu. simple tenses*] *The care of the children fell to my share when their parents died. It fell to my lot to sell the tickets for the school concert.*

**fall towards** *v prep*

**1** (usu. of land) to slope towards (something lower): [L9 + *towards* (*simple tenses*)] *The cliff falls towards the sea.*

**2** to descend in the direction of (something): [L9 + *towards*] *The returning spaceship fell towards the earth at high speed.*

**fall under** *v prep*

**1** to fall accidentally underneath (something): [L9 + *under* (*usu. simple tenses*)] *The man fell under a train and was killed.* → **fall beneath** (1)

***2** to be controlled by or feel the power of (something): [T1 (*no pass., simple tenses*)] *In his youth he fell under the influence of Beethoven. This area falls under the powers of the local court. Three ships fall under his command.* → **be under** (3), **come under** (3), **fall beneath** (2)

***3** to be placed in a list or class with (a heading): [T1 (*no pass., simple tenses*)] *Your suggestion falls under the general heading of reorganization. "The amount falls under 2 heads—first material damage, total of claim £577,938."* (Paul Kruger, *Communicated to the House of Commons by Joseph Chamberlain*, 18 February 1897) → **come under** (2), etc.

**fall upon** *v prep* → FALL ON

**fall within** *v prep*

**1** to be placed in a list or class with (a heading): [T1 (*no pass., simple tenses*)] *Your suggestion falls within the general area of reorganization.* → **come under** (2), etc.

**2** to be part of (a limited area, as of knowledge): [T1 (*no pass., simple tenses*)] *If the answer to your difficulty falls within my experience, I'll give you all the help I can.* → **be within** (2), **bring within, come within** (2), **fall outside, get within** (2), **lie in**² (5), **lie within** (2)

**falter out** *v adv*

to speak (something) in an uncertain manner: [T1] *At last the prisoner faltered out his story.*

**familiarize with** *v prep*

to make (someone or oneself) familiar with or knowledgeable about (something): [D1] *Give me time to familiarize myself with the details, before making a decision. Let me familiarize you with the facts.*

**fan out** *v adv* → **space out** (1), **spread out** (3)

to (cause to) scatter or spread: [IØ] *The searchers fanned out to look for the missing boy.* [T1] *Fan out the search party, to cover the area better. Fan the cards out, holding them together at the bottom, so that you can see each one.*

***fancy oneself** *v pron*

*not fml* to have too high an opinion of one's appearance, abilities (as something), etc.: [IØ (*as*) (*simple tenses*)] *You can tell that she fancies herself from the way she dresses. She fancies herself as a singer but she doesn't have a very good voice. He fancies himself, doesn't he, hoping to get that job?*

***fare forth** *v adv*

*old use fml* to start a journey: [IØ (*usu. simple tenses*)] *The king fared forth, attended by all his servants and many carriages.*

***farm out** *v adv*

**1** to allow (usu. land) to be used by someone else in return for rent: [T1] *We can get more money by farming out the other fields.*

**2** to send (someone) to work in return for payment: [T1] *The prisoners of war are farmed out to work on the land.*

**3** to send (work) for other people to do: [T1] *The sewing was farmed out among the women of the village. Insurance companies often farm out the risks to several firms.*

**4** to send (usu. children) to be looked after by others: [T1] *Some people farm their children out while they go to work.*

**5** to use up (land) completely, esp. by failing to change the crops regularly: [T1 (*usu. pass.*)] *This whole area has been farmed out, and no crops will grow there now.* → **fish out** (3), **lay in**¹ (4), **mine out, work out** (8)

***fashion after/on/upon** *v prep* → **model after, pattern after**

**1** to form (something) as a copy of (something): [D1 (*usu. simple tenses*)] *The railway system was fashioned after the successful method used in other countries.*

**2** to make (oneself) like (someone whom one admires): [D1 (*often simple tenses*)] *Mary has always fashioned herself on her mother.*

**fashion from/out of** *v prep; adv prep* → **form from, make from, make of** (1), **make out of** (1)

to make (something) from (material): [X9 + *from*/OUT + *of* (*usu. pass.*)] *This evening dress was fashioned out of silk.*

***fashion on** *v prep* → FASHION AFTER

**fashion out of** *v adv prep* → FASHION FROM

**fashion to** *v prep*

to shape or fit (something) to match (something): [X9 + *to* (*usu. simple tenses*)] *We can fashion the dress to your figure. This music is not fashioned to my taste.*

***fashion upon** *v prep* → FASHION AFTER

**fasten down** *v adv*

**1** to fix (something) firmly in place: [T1 + DOWN] *You will have to fasten the lid down with nails.* → **tie down** (1)

***2** *not fml* to make (someone) give a decision: [T1 (*to*) (*usu. simple tenses*)] *Can you fasten him down to a firm date?* → **tie down to** (2)

**fasten off** *v adv*

to finish fastening (something): [X9 + OFF] *Fasten the thread off with a knot.*

**fasten on**[1] *v adv*
to fix (something) on firmly: [X9 + ON] *The lid won't come off accidentally, it's been fastened on.*

**fasten on/upon**[2] *v prep*
**1** to fix (something) on top of (something): [X9 + *on/upon*] *I can't fasten the lid on this box.* → **fasten onto** (1)
***2** to fix or place (something) on (someone): [D1 (*usu. simple tenses*)] *You won't fasten the blame on me. He fastened his eyes on the girl.* → **lay on**[2] (2), **pin on**[2] (2), **place on** (2), **put on**[2] (2), **throw on** (4)
***3** to choose (something): [T1 (*usu. simple tenses*)] *We have fastened on a perfect place for our holiday.* → **drop on** (2), **pick on** (1), **pitch on** (1)
***4** to choose (someone) for a purpose, often unpleasant: [T1 (*for*) (*usu. simple tenses*)] *Why does he always fasten on me for the worst jobs?* [V3 (*usu. simple tenses*)] *The examiners can fasten on any student to answer questions.* → **drop on** (3), **pick on** (2), **pitch on** (2)
***5** to choose (someone) for blame: [T1 (*usu. simple tenses*)] *Why fasten on me? It's not my fault.* → **drop on** (4), **land on** (3), **pick on** (3), **pitch on** (3)
***6** to take and use (something) eagerly: [T1 (*usu. simple tenses*)] *The children have fastened on the idea of camping in the mountains. She fastened mercilessly on the one weak point in her opponent's argument.* → **fasten onto** (2), **hook onto** (2), **latch onto** (3), **seize on**
***7** to force the attention of (oneself) on (someone); keep (oneself) close to (someone): [D1] *Our unpleasant neighbour fastened herself on me throughout the party.* → **fasten onto** (3)

**fasten onto** *v prep*
**1** to fix (something) firmly onto the surface of (something): [X9 + *onto*] *How shall I fasten this notice onto the door?* → **fasten on** (1)
***2** to take and use (something) eagerly: [T1 (*usu. simple tenses*)] *The children have fastened onto the idea of camping in the mountains. At least you have your youth and health; why don't you fasten onto that thought?* → **fasten on** (6), **hook onto** (2), **latch onto** (3), **seize on**
***3** to hold (someone); force one's attention on (someone); stay close to (someone) in body or mind: [T1 (*no pass.*)] *Fasten onto me and you'll be safe crossing the traffic. She fastened onto my arm and wouldn't let go. Our unpleasant neighbour fastened onto me throughout the party. The leader's influence was so strong that many people fastened onto him and became his followers.* → **fasten on** (7)

**fasten to** *v prep*
to fix (something) firmly to (something): [X9 + *to*] *We had to fasten the notice to the door with a nail. Fasten your cheque to the letter so that it won't get lost.*

**fasten up** *v adv* → **do up** (1), **hook up** (1)
to (cause to) close: [T1 + UP] *You've fastened your buttons up the wrong way.* [IØ + UP (*simple tenses*)] *This dress fastens up at the back.*

**fasten upon** *v prep* → **FASTEN ON**

***father on/upon** *v prep*
*old use* to fix (the responsibility for something such as writing, or someone such as a child) on (someone): [D1 (*often pass.*)] *These well-known words have been fathered on many writers, but no one knows who really said them. This mistake has been fathered on me, but I am not to blame. Don't try to father your child on me, he's not my son.*

***fathom out** *v adv*
esp. *BrE not fml* to try to guess or discover (something): [T1a (*usu. simple tenses*)] *Can you fathom out his intentions? They're a mystery to me.* [T6 (*usu. simple tenses*)] *I can't fathom out how to get to the place, as the map isn't clear.*

***fatten on** *v prep* → **batten on**
*not fml* to live well by gaining advantage from (the work of others): [T1 (*no pass.*)] *For years the directors have been fattening on the efforts of the workers.*

***fatten out** *v adv*
**1** to become fatter: [IØ] *You've fattened out during the winter, you should take some exercise to lose weight.* → **fill out** (4), **flesh out** (1), **plump out**
**2** *not fml* to make (writing) seem longer or fuller: [T1] *Your article seems rather thin in places; can you fatten it out a little?* → **fill out** (6), **flesh out** (2), **pad out** (2)

**fatten up** *v adv* → **feed up** (1)
to make (someone or an animal) fatter with food: [T1 + UP] *The farmer is fattening up the chickens for Christmas.*

***favour with** *v prep* → **oblige with**
*fml* to please (someone) with (something); do (someone) a kindness by providing (something): [D1 (*usu. simple tenses*)] *Please favour me with a reply as soon as possible. M... Green will now favour us with a song.*

***fawn on/upon** *v prep* → **toady to**
to try to gain the favour of (someone) by over-praising and being insincerely attentive: [T1] *He fawns on his rich uncle, hoping to gain some of his money. It's no good fawning on the teacher, you have to earn good marks. The former servant gained power by fawning on the king.*

***fear for** *v prep*
to worry about (someone or something): [T1 (*no pass., simple tenses*)] *I fear for the safety of those mountain climbers in this sudden bad weather. All mothers fear for their children when they first leave home.*

**feature in** *v prep*
to (cause to) take an important part in (something): [L9 + *in* (*simple tenses*)] *How far does cost feature in your plan?* [X9 + *in* (*usu. pass.*)] *The latest popular actress is featured in this new film.*

**feed back** *v adv*
to return (something such as information) to someone or something where it started: [T1 (*into, to*)] *The salesmen feed back information to the firm about its sales. If the results are fed back into the computer, this causes a change in its calculations.* [IØ (*into, to*)] *Very little information has been feeding back to the production department about the success of the product.* —**feedback** *n*

**feed in** *v adv*
to introduce (something) into something such as a machine or system: [T1] *You feed the wire in here and it comes out at the other end.*

**feed into** *v prep*
to introduce (something or someone) into (something such as a machine or system): [D1] *You feed the wire into the machine here, and it comes out at the other end. The information and questions are fed into the computer, which then supplies the answers. Feed the cloth gently into the sewing machine. Students are fed into the school from a wide area. How many schools feed their students into this university?*

**feed off** *v prep*
**1** to eat one's food from (a place, a dish, etc.): [L9 + *off*] *The animals can easily feed off the floor.* → **dine off** (1), **eat off**[2] (1), **eat out of** (1)
**2** to use (something) as food: [L9 + *off*] *These little bears feed off the leaves of this special tree. A whole family can feed off a chicken as big as this! You lose weight by feeding off your own fat.* → **dine off** (2), **eat off**[2] (2), **feed on** (1), **live off** (1)
**3** to take something from (a part, esp. a supply): [T1 (*no pass.*)] *The bigger newspapers feed off reports in the smaller papers.*

**feed on/upon** *v prep*
**1** to (cause to) eat (certain food): [L9 + *on/upon*] *These bears feed on the leaves of this special tree.* [X9 + *on/upon*] *We feed our dogs on fresh meat.* → **dine off** (2), **eat off**[2] (2), **feed off** (2), **live off** (1)
**2** to be eager to accept; gain satisfaction from (something): [T1 (*no pass.*)] *The singer feeds on admiration from the public.* → **lap up** (3)

**feed to** *v prep*
**1** to supply (something such as food) to (someone or an animal): [X9 + *to*] *Farmers feed kitchen waste to the pigs. Some of the first Christians were fed to the lions.*
**2** to supply (something such as information) to (usu. someone): [D1 (*usu. simple tenses*)] *Reporters all over the world feed the news to the radio stations. Education does not mean merely feeding facts to students. When you are in danger of losing it, feed the ball to another player.*

**feed up** *v adv*
**1** to feed (someone or an animal) fully: [X9 + UP] *The farmer is feeding up the chickens for Christmas. These hungry children need a lot of feeding up.* → **fatten up**
**2 be fed up (with)** *infml* to be in low spirits; tired of or no longer interested (in something or someone): *I don't know why I feel so fed up this morning. I'm fed up with the children's behaviour. I'm fed up with you, go away.* → **brown off, cheese off, piss off** (2), **tire of** (2)

**feed upon** *v prep* → **FEED ON**

**feed with** *v prep*
to fill, supply, or satisfy (something or someone) with (something): [X9 + *with* (*usu. simple tenses*)] *You feed the machine with this special paper on a roll. The market has to be fed with an endless supply of goods. Education does not mean merely feeding the students with facts. Her job is to stand at the side of the stage and feed the actors with their lines when they forget them. "And feed my brain with better things."* (G.K. Chesterton, *A Ballade of a Book Reviewer*)

**feel about**[1] *v adv*
to search, or examine something, without being able to see what one is doing: [L9 + ABOUT] *I'm feeling about for an answer to our difficulties.*

**feel about**[2] *v prep*
**1** to have an opinion about (someone, something, or doing something): [IØ + *about* (*simple tenses*)] *How do you feel about the new law? How would you feel about moving house again? Do you feel strongly about atomic weapons?*
**2** to use one's hands to find something by touch near (one): [L9 + *about* (*for*)] *Father felt about him for his pipe without looking.* → **feel for** (3), **fish for** (2), **fumble for**

*__feel after__ *v prep* → **fish for** (3)
to try to get (something), usu. with words: [T1 (*no pass.*)] *The singer is always feeling after words of praise.*

*__feel blue__ *v adj* → **look blue** (2)
*infml* to feel sad: [IØ] *There's often no reason for feeling blue, so we sometimes blame it on the weather.*

*__feel cheap__ *v adj*
*infml* to feel ashamed or morally low: [IØ (*often simple tenses*)] *I would feel cheap if I wore my dresses as short as that! I feel cheap not being able to return their invitation.*

*__feel equal to__ *v adj prep* → **be up to** (2), **feel up to**
to feel able or fit for (something or doing something): [T1 (*no pass., simple tenses*)] *Are you sure you feel equal to the job? I don't feel equal to any more work today.* [T4 (*simple tenses*)] *Sometimes I don't feel equal to finishing this book.*

**feel for** *v prep*
**1** to have (a feeling) because of (something): [T1 + *for*] *I don't feel any anger for the way I've been treated.*
**2** to have (a feeling) towards (someone): [X9 + *for*] *How is it possible to feel love for two men at the same time?* → **feel towards**

**3** to try to find (something) by touch: [L9 + *for*] *Blinded by the soap, he had to feel for his glasses. I had to feel about for the light switch in the dark.* → **feel about**[2] (2), **fish for** (2), **fumble for**

*__4__ to sympathize with (someone): [T1 (*no pass., simple tenses*)] *I truly feel for you in your terrible loss. We all feel for the family of the murdered man. "He watched and wept, he prayed and felt, for all."* (Oliver Goldsmith, *The Deserted Village*) → **ache for** (1), **feel with** (2)

**feel free** *v adj*

**1** to feel the lack of control or limitation: [L9 + free] *I feel so free without those tight clothes. Who feels free to choose his own life?*

*__2__ to regard oneself as welcome (to do something): [IØ (*simple tenses, usu. imper.*)] *Treat this house as your own; feel free.* [L3 (*simple tenses, usu. imper.*)] *Feel free to go where you like.*

**feel like** *v prep*

**1** to seem like (something) to the touch: [L9 + *like* (*simple tenses*)] *This new man-made material feels like real leather.*

**2** to feel as if one is (something or someone): [L9 + *like*] *I feel like a criminal, moving round with the lights off. You'll feel like a new woman after your operation.*

*__3__ to want (something or doing something): [T1 (*no pass., simple tenses*)] *Do you feel like a swim? We all feel like a cup of tea.* [T4 (*simple tenses*)] *Do you feel like walking to the corner with me?*

***feel oneself*** *v pron* → **look oneself**

to feel cheerful, well, and in one's usual state of mind: [IØ (*often neg.*)] *Mother isn't feeling herself today, she had a bad night. You'll soon feel yourself again when you've got over the shock.*

***feel out*** *v adv* → **sound out**

to try to discover the opinion of (someone): [T1 (*no pass.*)] *Could you feel the director out on the question of the new appointments?*

**feel out of** *v adv prep*

**1 feel out of it/things** *not fml* to feel strange, unwanted, and not part of a group; feel as if one is not included in an activity: *Whenever I'm the only young person among all these older people, I feel out of it. Since being away for so long, I've been feeling out of things.* → **be out of** (14), **leave out**[1] (5), **miss out** (2)

**2 feel out of place (in)** to feel as if one does not belong (in a certain place, group, or activity): *As the only older person in a group of young people, I felt rather out of place. She has the ability never to feel out of place, either in a palace or in a hut.*

***feel small*** *v adj* → **look small**

to feel humble, ashamed, or wounded in one's self-respect: [IØ (*often simple tenses*)] *I felt small when I learned how badly I had misjudged him. The teacher made the girl feel small by making her stand in front of the class.*

**feel towards** *v prep* → **feel for** (2)

to have (a feeling) with regard to (usu. someone): [X9 + *towards*] *I don't feel any hatred towards the man who robbed me.* [L9 + *towards* (*simple tenses*)] *How do you feel towards the new teacher?*

***feel up*** *v adv* → **touch up** (3)

*sl* to touch (usu. a girl or woman) as if making sexual advances: [T1] *The girl complained to the police that the man had been feeling her up on the train.*

***feel up to*** *v adv prep* → **be up to** (2), **feel equal to**

*not fml* to feel able or fit for (something or doing something): [T1 (*no pass., simple tenses*)] *Do you feel up to a short walk? I'd like to go, but I just don't feel up to it.* [T (*simple tenses*)] *I don't feel up to going out tonight.*

**feel with** *v prep*

**1** to be conscious of the touch of (something) by using (something such as part of the body): [T1 + *with* (*usu. simple tenses*)] *I can feel the hole in my tooth with my tongue. The gardener felt something hard with his spade.*

*__2__ to sympathize with (someone): [T1 (*no pass., simple tenses*)] *The whole nation feels with the families of those who were drowned in the great floods.* → **feel for** (4)

**felicitate on/upon** *v prep fml* → **CONGRATULATE ON** (1)

***fence about/around/round with*** *v adv prep* → **hedge about with**

to surround or limit (something) with (control or protection): [T1 (*usu. pass.*)] *Starting a business of one's own is fenced about with laws and difficulties.*

**fence in** *v adv* → **hedge in, hem in**

**1** to enclose or surround (an area, person, animal) with a fence: [X9 + IN] *Farmers have to fence in their fields to keep the cattle from getting loose. The lions in the park are safely fenced in. All these prisoners-of-war have to be fenced in.* → **rail in, wall in** (1)

*__2__ to surround or limit (someone or something): [T1 (*with*) (*often simple tenses*)] *The small house was fenced in by high office buildings. Almost anything you want to do seems to be fenced in with silly laws. I have feeling fenced in by lack of money. "Don't fence me in."* (song) → **hem about**

**fence off** *v adv*

**1** to separate (usu. land) with a fence: [X9 + OFF] *This part of the field has been fenced off to keep the cattle out. The pool is dangerous and should be fenced off.* → **divide off, rail off, separate off, wall off**

*__2__ to fight against; deal with (something bad or unwanted): [T1 (*usu. simple tenses*)] *The fighter neatly fenced off a dangerous blow. The Minister skilfully fenced off the Opposition's attack with some searching questions of his own.* → **fend off** (1)

**ence out** *v adv*
**1** to keep (usu. animals) out with a fence: [X9 + OUT] *The sheep keep wandering into the vegetable field so we shall have to fence them out.*
*2 to prevent (someone) from entering a group or activity: [T1] *We don't want that awkward man on the committee; do what you can to fence him out.*
**ence round with** *v adv prep* → **FENCE ABOUT WITH**
**ence with** *v prep*
**1** to surround or separate (something such as an area) with a fence made of (a material): [T1 + *with*] *The farmer fenced his land with wire.*
**2** to fight with swords, usu. as a sport, against (someone) or using (a particular weapon): [T1 + *with*] *I should like the chance to fence with a worthier opponent. Shall we fence with long or short swords?*
**3** to argue skilfully with (someone): [T1] *Members of Parliament enjoy fencing with each other on questions on which they disagree.*
**end for** *v prep* → **shift for**
to provide for; look after (someone, esp. oneself): [T1 (*no pass.*)] *Don't worry about me, I'm quite used to fending for myself.*
**end off** *v adv*
**1** to push (something or someone) away: [T1] *Can you fend off the other boat with your pole? It was brave of you to fend off the attackers. The fighter had to fend off a dangerous blow.* → **fence off** (2)
**2** to stop; prevent; deal with (something usu. bad): [T1 (*usu. simple tenses*)] *This soup will help you to fend off hunger for a time. The speaker fended off the difficult questions skilfully.* → **stave off** (1), **ward off** (1)
**3** to prevent (someone) (from doing something): [T1 (*from*)] *It is our duty to fend off a thief from obtaining his gains.* → **stave off** (2), **ward off** (2)
**rret about/around** *v adv*
to search busily, by pushing things about: [I∅ (*for*)] *Why are you ferreting about in my drawer? She was ferreting around in her handbag for her keys.*
**rret out** *v adv*
*not fml* to discover (something such as information) by searching: [T1] *The police had to ferret out the truth. I've been trying to ferret out what really happened.* [T6a] *It wasn't hard to ferret out where they'd gone.* [T6b] *Can you ferret out how to mend the thing?*
**stoon with** *v prep* → **decorate with** (1), etc.
to ornament (usu. a room) with (chains of flowers, paper, etc., hanging in curves): [D1 (*usu. pass.*)] *The room was festooned with gay paper chains.*
**tch in** *v adv*
**1** to bring (something or someone) indoors: [X9 + IN] *I must fetch the washing in, it's raining. Please fetch the children in for their dinner.*
*__2__ to produce as profit; attract (something such as money, or someone): [T1] *The sale of the house should fetch in enough to pay our debts. The advertisements for the concert fetched in large crowds.*
**fetch out** *v adv*
**1** to bring (something or someone) out of doors, out of storage, etc.: [X9 + OUT] *It's warm enough to fetch out the garden chairs. I hate having to fetch out the sewing machine every time I want to do some sewing.*
→ **bring out** (2), **drag out** (1)
*__2__ to cause (something) to be seen: [T1] *Jane never fetches out her best dishes even when guests arrive. The warm sun fetched the flowers out.* → **be out** (5), **bring out** (3), **come out** (5)
*__3__ to develop; cause (something not material) to be seen or known: [T1 (*often simple tenses*)] *The teacher helped to fetch out the meaning of the poem. The struggle fetched out his true character. Plenty of money often fetches out a person's worst qualities.* → **bring out** (4), etc.
*__4__ to produce (something): [T1] *Tom has fetched out another new book. The makers are fetching out a new kind of soap.* → **be out** (21), **bring out** (5), **come out** (8), **get out** (13)
*__5__ to encourage (someone), esp. to talk: [T1] *Mary is very quiet, try to fetch her out at the party.* → **bring out** (6), **come out of** (4), **draw out** (9), **lead out** (2)
*__6__ to cause (someone) to stop working because of disagreement (strike): [T1] *We'll fetch the workers out for more pay.* → **bring out** (7), etc.
***fetch over** *v adv*
**1** to bring (someone), usu. to someone's home: [T1] *Why don't you fetch your new boyfriend over one evening? We'd like to meet him.* → **bring over** (1), etc.
**2** to persuade (someone) to change his opinion: [T1 (*to*) (*usu. simple tenses*)] *We must fetch the rest of the committee over to our point of view.* → **bring round** (3), etc.
***fetch round** *v adv*
**1** to bring (someone) to someone's home or an agreed place: [T1] *Why don't you fetch your new boy friend round one evening? We'd like to meet him.* → **bring over** (1), etc.
**2** *not fml* to cause (someone) to regain consciousness, often rather suddenly: [T1 (*usu. simple tenses*)] *Peter has fainted; this bucket of water should fetch him round.* → **bring to** (1), etc.
**3** to persuade (someone) to change his opinion: [T1 (*to*) (*usu. simple tenses*)] *We must fetch the rest of the committee round to our point of view.* → **bring round** (3), etc.
**4** to change the direction of (something): [T1 (*to*)] *Father always fetches the conversation round to his favourite subject.* → **bring round** (4)

*__fetch to__ *v adv* → **bring to** (1), etc.
*not fml* to cause (someone) to regain consciousness, often rather suddenly: [T1 (*usu. simple tenses*)] *Peter has fainted; this bucket of water should fetch him to.*

**fetch up** *v adv*
**1** to bring (something or someone) upstairs: [X9 + UP] *Please fetch up the tea things. Fetch the doctor up, I'm anxious to see him.*
*__2__ *infml* to be sick; vomit (one's food): [IØ] *Jane can't come, she's been fetching up all morning.* [T1] *The child has fetched up her dinner again.* → **bring up** (4), etc.
*__3__ → **DRAG UP** (3)
*__4__ esp. *BrE infml* to finish by becoming (something): [L1 (*simple tenses*)] *In spite of her family's opinion, she fetched up the winner. Who would have guessed that he would fetch up as director of the firm?* [L7 (*simple tenses*)] *After making his fortune, he fetched up poor when he died.* → **end up** (1), **finish up** (2), **land up** (3), **wind up** (6)
*__5__ esp. *BrE infml* to finish by doing (something): [L4 (*simple tenses*)] *I never dreamed that I would fetch up owning such a lot of property! Be careful, you could fetch up by getting hurt.* → **end up** (2), **finish up** (3), **land up** (4), **wind up** (7)
*__6__ esp. *BrE infml* to arrive at or in (a place), esp. without planning: [L9 (*at, in, on*) (*simple tenses*)] *When Jim's driving, we never know where we'll fetch up. He'll fetch up in prison if he goes on taking risks like that. The boy's ball fetched up on the garage roof.* → **end up** (3), **finish up** (4), **land up** (5), **wind up** (8)
*__7__ esp. *BrE infml* to (cause to) reach (an unfavourable end): [L9 (*in*) (*simple tenses*)] *We shall fetch up in trouble if he goes on spending the firm's money like that.* [X9 (*in*) (*no pass., simple tenses*)] *Stop spending so fast, or you'll fetch us up in debt.* → **end up** (4), **finish up** (5), **land in** (3), **land up** (6), **wind up** (9).
*__8__ esp. *BrE infml* to receive (something) in the end: [L9 + *with* (*simple tenses*)] *After trying so hard, the writer fetched up with a contract. Jim entered the competition, not hoping for much, but fetched up with first prize!* → **end up** (5), **finish up** (6), **land up** (7), **wind up** (10).
**9 fetch up nowhere** esp. *BrE infml* to gain no success: *If you don't work hard, you'll fetch up nowhere.* → **end up** (6), **finish up** (7), **wind up** (13)

**feud with** *v prep*
to quarrel bitterly and often violently for a long time with (someone such as another family): [L9 + *with*] *The farmer and his family have been feuding with their neighbours on the other side of the valley for thirty years, shooting each other and burning the crops; there seems no end to it.*

**fiddle away** *v adv*
**1** *infml* to play a violin continuously: [L9 + AWAY] *We need an experienced player who can fiddle away for hours for the country dancing.*
*__2__ *infml* to waste (time or money): [T1] *You've fiddled away the whole afternoon! It's easy to fiddle away a fortune.* → **idle away** (2), etc.

**fiddle with** *v prep*
**1** *not fml* to play aimlessly with (something): [L9 + *with*] *It's so annoying, the way she keeps fiddling (about) with her hair.* → **fidget with**, **play with** (1), **toy with** (1), **twiddle with**
*__2__ to move the parts of (a machine) in an undirected way, so as to discover a fault: [T1] *Sometimes when the television set doesn' work, you can fiddle with the wires inside an it comes right!* → **tinker with**
*__3__ *infml* to deal with (something) dishonestly: [T1] *Someone's been fiddling with th accounts, there's some money missing.*

**fidget about** *v adv*
to move restlessly: [L9 + ABOUT] *Childre can't help fidgeting about if they're made to s still for too long.*

**fidget with** *v prep* → **fiddle with** (1), etc.
to play nervously with (something): [L9 + *with*] *All through our meeting, the doctor wa fidgeting with his pen.*

**fig out/up** *v adv* → **dress up** (2), etc.
**be all figged out/up** *AmE infml* to be dresse gaily, as for a party: *Where are you going, a figged out like that?*

**fight about** *v prep* → **fight over**
to quarrel or fight with someone about (usu something): [L9 + *about*] *What are tho children fighting about now? Lawyers figl about such small details.*

**fight against** *v prep*
**1** to oppose (someone or a nation) in a battl or quarrel: [L9 + *against*] *Try to stop th children from fighting against each other. I World War II, Britain fought against Ge many.* → **fight with** (3)
**2** to oppose (something or doing something [L9 + *against*] *We must all fight against ur fairness and cruelty. All good Christians mu fight against the forces of evil. I tried to fig against sleep, but couldn't. The worker tried fight against being moved to another city, but was no use. "You cannot fight against the fu ture. Time is on our side."* (W.E. Gladston *Speech on the Reform Bill*, 1866)

**fight among/amongst** *v prep*
to quarrel or fight within (a group): [L9 + *among/amongst*] *Why do the children alwa fight among themselves?*

**fight back** *v adv*
**1** to return an attack; defend oneself: [L9 + BACK] *If he hit you, why didn't you fig back?*
**2** to defend one's views or actions; oppo action taken against one: [L9 + BACK] *If th try to make us leave the house, we will fig back with all the powers at our command.*
*__3__ to struggle to control (usu. tears or laug

ter): [T1] *She fought back her tears as she said goodbye. I had to fight back a desire to laugh at the small child's remark.* → **fight down**

*__4__ to struggle to return (to a former condition): [IØ (*to*)] *Everything seemed to be against me, but I fought back to my old position of strength.* [T1b (*to*)] *She fought her way back to health so quickly after the accident that she was soon back at school.* —**fightback** *n*

**fight down** *v adv* → **fight back** (3)
to struggle to control (usu. a feeling): [T1] *He fought down his terror as darkness descended, and walked on through the wood. Fighting down his doubts, he agreed to give the man the job. It is difficult to fight down a desire to sleep.*

**fight for** *v prep*
**1** to fight to defend (something or someone): [L9 + *for*] *He was away for three years, fighting for his country. Everyone has someone worth fighting for. "The world is a fine place and worth fighting for."* (Ernest Hemingway, *For Whom the Bell Tolls*)
**2** to compete or struggle with (someone or something) to get (something or someone): [X9 + *for*] *We had to fight the other firm for the contract. The student had to fight the rules for his rights. Jim fought his brother for the girl.* [L9 +*for*] *Every year I have to fight for an increase in pay.*
**3 fight for one's life** to be dangerously ill: *The old general fought for his life for a month before he died.*

**fight off** *v adv*
**1** to defeat (someone) in a fight; make (someone) go away by defending oneself: [X9 + OFF] *He fought off three men who attacked him.* → **drive off** (2)
*__2__ to keep (something) away with an effort; struggle to prevent (something unwanted); avoid (someone unwanted): [T1] *I must wear warm clothes, as I am fighting off this cold. The firm had to fight off a lot of competition to win the contract. She was always having to fight off men who wanted to marry her.*

**fight on**[1] *v adv*
to continue fighting: [L9 + ON] *We must fight on until the end.*

**fight on**[2] *v prep*
**1** *mil* to fight in (a place): [L9 + *on*] *At one time our armies were fighting on three fronts.* [X9 + *on*] *We had to fight the enemy on three fronts at once. "We shall fight on the seas and oceans . . . we shall fight on the beaches, we shall fight on the landing grounds."* (Winston Churchill, *Speech, House of Commons,* 4 June 1940)
**2** to oppose (someone) about (a matter): [X9 + *on*] *I'll fight you on that question.*

**fight out** *v adv*
**1** to fight to a finish; fight until there is a result, esp. in the phr. **fight it out**: [T1] *The ancient way to settle a quarrel was to choose a leader from each side and let them fight it out.* → **fight through**[1] **(1)**, **slug out**
**2** to try to settle (a disagreement): [T1] *The committee fought the matter out for hours, and still could not agree.* → **slug out**
**3 fight one's way out** to struggle to leave: *The crowd was so thick that I had to fight my way out (of the theatre).*

**fight over** *v prep* → **fight about**
to quarrel over; compete for (usu. something): [L9 + *over*] *The birds in the garden are fighting over a piece of bread. It's quite an honour to have two men fighting over me.* [X9 + *over*] *The children always fight each other over the best seat. The children always fight each other over who should have the best seat.*

***fight shy of** *v adj prep*
*not fml* to avoid (someone, something, or doing something): [T1] *You can't fight shy of your responsibility for your children. Live an honest life, and fight shy of evil companions.* [T4] *I always fight shy of swimming in cold water.*

**fight through**[1] *v adv*
**1** to (cause to) fight until a result is reached: [L9 + THROUGH] *The two opposing armies fought through to the end.* [X9 + THROUGH] *We must fight this battle through to victory.* → **fight out** (1), **slug out**
*__2__ to struggle to gain approval of (something such as an idea): [T1b] *The committee member had difficulty in fighting his suggestion through.*

**fight through**[2] *v prep*
**1** to struggle through or make (one's way) through (something or someone in the way): [X9 + *through*] *The traveller had to fight his way through the tropical forest with an axe.* [L9 + *through*] *I could only get out by fighting through the crowd.*
**2** to oppose (something) throughout (its advance): [T1 + *through*] *Opposing members of the committee fought the suggested changes through every stage.*
**3** to (cause to) pass with a struggle through (something): [L9 + *through*] *You'll have to fight through a lot of opposition to get the rules changed.* [X9 + *through*] *The committee member successfully fought his suggested changes through the necessary stages.*

**fight to** *v prep*
**fight to a finish** to fight until one party is dead or a result is otherwise clear: *This battle is our last chance; we must fight to a finish.*

**fight together** *v adv*
**1** to fight with someone's help, as friends: [L9 + TOGETHER] *The two brothers fought together against their attackers. We must all fight together to prevent further evil.*
**2** to fight against someone, as enemies: [L9 + TOGETHER] *Two dogs were fighting together in the street.*

**fight with** *v prep*
**1** to fight or oppose (someone or something) using (weapons or other means): [IØ + *with*] *In former times, people used to fight with swords. Now we fight with guns, dangerous chemicals, and atomic bombs.* [T1 + *with*] *The man fought his attacker with a stick. We can only fight evil with good. We will fight the city council with every power we have.*
**2** to fight with the help of (a friend or supporter): [L9 + *with*] *In World War II, the Americans fought with the British and French against the Germans.*
**3** to fight against (an enemy): [L9 + *with*] *In World War II, Britain fought with Germany. Try to stop the children from fighting with each other.* → **fight against** (1)

***figure in**[1] *v adv*
*AmE not fml* to include (something or someone): [T1 (*usu. simple tenses*)] *Have you figured in the cost of the hotel?*

**figure in**[2] *v prep* → **have in**[2] (12)
to have a part in (something, esp. in the mind); appear in (something): [L9 + *in* (*simple tenses*)] *Does the question of cost figure in your plans? Do I often figure in your dreams?*

***figure on** *v prep*
**1** *AmE not fml* to depend on; be sure of (something or doing something): [T1] *You can't figure on the results of the election.* [T4] *Don't figure on going abroad this summer, we may not be able to afford it.* [V4a] *Don't figure on the weather being fine for your garden party.* → **depend on** (1), etc.
**2** esp. *AmE not fml* to intend (doing something): [T4] *Do you figure on staying long in this city?*
**3** esp. *AmE not fml* to expect (something or doing something): [T1] *If you figure on success, you stand a better chance of winning.* [T4] *I always figure on succeeding.*

***figure out** *v adv*
**1** esp. *AmE not fml* to calculate (something): [T1] *Father is trying to figure out his tax.* → **work out** (2)
**2** esp. *AmE not fml* to understand (something or someone) with difficulty: [T1] *Can you figure out this word? I can't figure out what he's trying to say. I can't figure her out, she's a mystery to me.* [T6] *No one can figure out how the fire started.* → **make out** (3), **puzzle out, work out** (5)

**figure to** *v prep*
to imagine; cause (oneself) to imagine (something): [X9 + *to*] *I try to figure to myself what would have happened if I hadn't seen the other car coming on the wrong side of the road. Figure the result to yourself, and you'll see what I mean.*

***figure up** *v adv* → **add up** (1)
*AmE not fml* to reach or make a total (of an amount): [IØ (*to*) (*simple tenses*)] *The bill figures up to $34.78.* [T1] *Can you figure up this bill?*

**filch from** *v prep*
to steal (something) from (someone): [T1 + *from*] *Jack filched a pen from his friend'. pocket.*

**file away**[1] *v adv*
**1** to smooth (something) continuously with a tool having a rough surface: [L9 + AWAY] *You have to file away for hours to get this metal smooth.*
**2** to destroy (something) by rubbing with a rough surface: [X9 + AWAY] *The owner' name marked on this cigarette lighter has bee filed away by the thief.*

**file away**[2] *v adv*
**1** to put (information) away in correct order [X9 + AWAY] *I'll ask the secretary to file thes letters away.*
***2** to make a note of (something) in one' memory: [T1] *I'll file his name away for future use.*

**file down** *v adv*
to reduce or smooth the surface of (something) by rubbing it with a tool having a roug surface: [X9 + DOWN] *The door won't fi you'll have to file it down. File down th woodwork before you paint it. My nails ar too long, I must file them down.*

**file for** *v prep*
**1** to start action in law towards (somethin such as a legal end to one's marriage): [L9 + *for*] *The actor's wife has filed for divorc again.*
**2** *AmE* to offer oneself formally for (a poli ical position): [L9 + *for*] *How many peop have filed for this office?*

**file out** *v adv*
(of more than one person) to leave, movin in a line: [L9 + OUT (*of*)] *When there is fire, it is important that people file out of th building in an orderly way.*

**file past** *v prep*
(of more than one person) to move slowly i a line, past (something to be seen, such as respected dead person): [L9 + *past*] *Hundreds of people filed past the body of the dea leader, to pay their last respects.*

***fill away** *v adv*
*naut* to move with the wind: [IØ] *Then a wir arose, and the little sailing boat filled away.*

***fill in** *v adv*
**1** to fill (something) completely: [T1] *Th workmen dug a hole, mended the pipe, ar then filled the hole in again.* → **cover in**[1], **cov over, fill up** (1), **roof in**
**2** to write what is necessary on (somethin such as a paper): [T1] *You got the date wror when you were filling in the cheque. Son people find it difficult to fill in a form.* → **f out** (1), **fill up** (2), **make out** (1), **write out** (2)
**3** to add (usu. words) to complete somethin [T1] *Fill in your name on the paper. I'll fill the other details for you.*
**4** to pass (time): [T1] *How am I going to f in this afternoon now that he's not coming?*

**5** *not fml* to supply information to (someone): [T1 (*on*)] *Please fill me in on what happened at the meeting that I couldn't attend.*
**6** to act as a replacement (for someone): [IØ (*for*)] *I can't go to the meeting—will you fill in for me? I don't know what to do, I'm just filling in while the regular girl is away.* → **stand in for**, etc.
**7 fill in time** to work in a not very serious way, usu. between real jobs or while waiting for something: [*often continuous tenses*] *I'm not one of the regular people here, I'm just filling in time before I go to college.*

**ill in for** *v adv prep* → **stand in for**, etc.
to act as a replacement for (someone): [T1 (*no pass.*)] *Can you fill in for me at the meeting? I can't go, and someone must take my place.*

**ll out** *v adv*
**1** esp. *AmE* to complete (something such as a paper): [T1] *Some people find it difficult to fill out a form.* → **fill in** (2), **fill up** (2), **make out** (1), **write out** (2)
**2** *AmE* to follow (the doctor's instructions) in mixing a medicine: [T1] *"Have this prescription filled out at the drugstore," said the doctor.*
**3** to swell, usu. with air: [IØ] *The sails filled out and the boat floated away.*
**4** to (cause to) grow fatter: [IØ] *John finished growing taller last year, and now he's filling out.* [T1] *Better health has filled her face out a little.* → **fatten out** (2), **flesh out** (1), **plump out**
**5** esp. *AmE* to complete (something) in time: [T1] *Mrs Young offered to fill out her late husband's last few months as chairman.*
**6** to enlarge (written material): [T1] *Tom has been asked to fill out the last part of his book to balance the first part.* → **fatten out** (2), **flesh out** (2), **pad out** (2)

**l up** *v adv*
to (cause to) become completely full: [L9 + UP] *The lake is filling up after this heavy rain. The theatre began to fill up just before the performance. I'd better call at the garage to fill up, we're nearly out of petrol.* [X9 + UP] *The swimming pool is filled up with mud. We'll have to fill up the page with photographs. I can't see you till tomorrow, the rest of the day is filled up. The driver asked the garage man to fill up his car. "Fill her up," said the driver.* —**fill-up** *n* → **cover in**[1], **fill in** (1)

**l with** *v prep*
**1** to (cause to) become full with (something, things, or people): [L9 + *with*] *The lake is filling with the heavy rain. His eyes filled with tears as he looked lovingly at her. The sails filled with wind.* [T1 + *with*] *Fill the bucket with water. The hall was filled with angry people. The box was filled with gifts. Fill the tyres with air. The secret of happiness is to fill one's life with activity.*
**2** to fill (someone) with (something such as a feeling): [D1 (*usu. simple tenses*)] *The sound of that music fills me with memories. He was filled with pity for the poor girl. The birth of my grandchild filled me with joy.*

***film over** *v adv* → **glaze over, haze over**
to (cause to) become covered with something thin and partly transparent: [IØ] *Her eyes filmed over with tears.* [T1] *A mist filmed over the stars.*

**filter out** *v adv*
**1** to remove (something such as solids or dirt) from something such as liquid or air, by passing it through a material that separates it: [X9 + OUT (*often simple tenses*)] *The solids were filtered out and only the liquid passed into the container. This metal net filters out the dirty air.*
**2** to remove (part of something such as light) by covering it: [X9 + OUT (*often simple tenses*)] *These window coverings filter out the strong sunlight. At this time of day you need to filter out the red light to take a good photo.* → **screen out** (1)
***3** to choose to take no notice of; be unconscious of (something): [T1 (*often simple tenses*)] *The child was able to filter out the noises surrounding him, as he was so busy in his play.* → **screen out** (2)
***4** to become known gradually or unintentionally: [IØ] *The news of his appointment filtered out before it was officially advertised.* → **let out** (5), etc.
***5** (of a group of people) to move slowly out of a building or area: [IØ] *People are filtering out of the cinema; the film must be over.*

**filter through**[1] *v adv* → **percolate through**[1]
**1** to pass slowly through something which removes unwanted parts: [L9 + THROUGH] *The liquid filtered through, and the solids were left behind.*
***2** to become gradually known: [IØ] *Slowly the idea filtered through, and at last he understood.*

**filter through**[2] *v prep* → **percolate through**[2]
**1** to (cause to) pass through (a material which removes part): [X9 + *through* (*often simple tenses*)] *You filter the coffee through this special paper, and it takes out the bitterness.* [L9 + *through* (*often simple tenses*)] *The coffee filters through this special paper.*
**2** to pass in a reduced form through (something): [L9 + *through (often simple tenses*)] *Sunlight filtered through the thick leaves.*
***3** to become gradually known in ( a place): [T1 (*no pass.*)] *The news filtered through the village.*

***find against** *v prep* → **decide against** (2), **decide for, find for** (2)
(in a court of law) to give judgment against (someone): [T1 (*no pass., usu. simple tenses*)] *I'm afraid you were unlucky, the judge found against you.*

**find for** *v prep*
**1** to obtain (something or someone) for (someone or something): [T1 + *for*] *I think I*

*can find the right size for you. You must find the right man for the job.*

*2 (in a court of law) to give judgment in favour of (someone): [T1 (*no pass., usu. simple tenses*)] *The judge found for the defendant, and also said that he should be given the costs of his case.* → **decide against** (2), **decide for, find against**

**find in**[1] *v adv* → **find out** (1)

to find (someone) at home or work: [X9 + IN (*usu. simple tenses*)] *You're lucky to find him in, he's often out of town.*

**find in**[2] *v prep*

**1** to discover (someone or something) in (a certain place): [T1 + *in*] *I found this coin in the garden, is it valuable? I thought I'd find you in here.*

***2** to provide (someone or oneself) with (money or other needs): [D1 (*usu. simple tenses*)] *His uncle found the boy in food and clothing. She doesn't earn enough to find herself in shoes.* → **keep in** (4)

**3 find it in one's heart/oneself** to be cruel enough (to do something): [*simple tenses, nonassertive*] *How could you find it in your heart to refuse the child's pitiful request?*

***find oneself** *v pron*

**1** to become conscious of being (something or somewhere); end by being (in a certain state): [L1 (*simple tenses*)] *He woke one morning to find himself the owner of the firm.* [L7 (*simple tenses*)] *Put your money in my business, and you could find yourself rich.* [L9 (*simple tenses*)] *When he regained consciousness, he found himself in the middle of the forest. You'll find yourself in trouble if you're not careful.*

**2** to discover one's own abilities, wishes, and character: [IØ (*usu. simple tenses*)] *The student left the university to go out into the world and find himself.*

**find out** *v adv*

**1** to find (someone) not at home or work: [X9 + OUT] *I called three times this morning, but found you out every time.* → **find in**[1]

***2** to discover (something); obtain information (about something): [T1] *I'll find out your secret. Find out the islanders' views before making a decision.* [T5] *The teacher was very angry when he found out that the students had been cheating.* [T6a] *Find out where he is going.* [T6b] *How do we find out where to catch the right bus?* [IØ (*about*)] *I won't tell you, you'll have to find out (for yourself). I'll find out about planes to New York. Did you find out about the photographs?*

***3** to discover (someone) in a deceitful act: [T1] *The businessman cheated the tax collectors for several years, but then they found him out and he was punished. Criminals take great care not to get found out. "Be sure your sin will find you out."* (The Bible) [IØ] *I'll put the money back before anyone finds out. I hope nobody finds out.*

***4** to reach; have an effect on (a weakness): [T1a] *This cold weather finds out my old wound.*

**find wanting** *v adj*

**1** to regard (something or someone) as lacking (in something): [X7 + **wanting** (*in*) (*simple tenses*)] *The newspapers found Tom's new book wanting in excitement. We find many of the younger workers wanting in skill.*

**2 be found wanting** to be disappointing; fail to reach a desired standard: *After three months, the new chairman was found wanting and had to be replaced. This machine is found wanting.*

***fine down** *v adv*

**1** to (cause to) become thinner: [T1] *The worker fined the metal down.* [IØ] *Alice has fined down a lot since last year.*

**2** to make (something) better, finer, or more exact: [T1] *As the writer gained experience, she fined down her choice of words.*

**fine for** *v prep*

(in a court of law) to make (someone) pay money as a punishment for (doing something wrong): [T1 + *for*] *The motorist was fined for dangerous driving.* [D1 + *for*] *The motorist was fined £100 for speeding.*

**finish in** *v prep* → **end in**

**1** to have (something) at its end: [L9 + *in* (*usu. simple tenses*)] *The cat's tail finishes in white. The road finished in a narrow path.*

***2** to come to an end in (a state): [T1 (*no pass.*)] *The meeting finished in disorder. The marriage finished in failure.*

**finish off** *v adv*

**1** to finish (something) completely: [T1 + OFF] *I must finish off this sewing while the light is good. Those children have finished off all the fruit.* [L9 + OFF (*with*)] *Let's finish off with some of that excellent cheese.* → **end off, finish up** (1), **mop up** (3), **polish off** (1)

***2** *not fml* to destroy (something): [T1 (*often simple tenses*)] *This last bombing should finish off the town. A long drive like that could finish the car off.*

***3** *not fml* to defeat (a competitor) thoroughly: [T1 (*often simple tenses*)] *You have to finish off three experienced players before you can win the prize.* → **polish off** (2)

***4** *infml* to kill (a person or animal); murder (someone): [T1 (*often simple tenses*)] *The old man who owned the jewels was finished off by the thieves. It was not the operation, but the fever that followed, which finished him off. The tiger's wounded—shall I finish him off?* → **bump off**, etc.

**finish up** *v adv*

**1** to finish (something such as food) completely: [T1 + UP] *I want all you children to finish up your dinners.* → **end off, finish off** (1), **mop up** (3), **polish off** (1)

***2** *not fml* to finish by becoming (something) [L1 (*simple tenses*)] *In spite of her poor hopes, she finished up the winner. The general began his army life as a private soldier and* *finished up as ruler of his country.* [L7 (*simple tenses*)] *After making a fortune in business, he finished up poor at his death.* → **end up** (1), **fetch up** (4), **land up** (3), **wind up** (6)

*__3__ *not fml* to finish by (doing something): [L4 (*simple tenses*)] *I never dreamed that I would finish up owning such a lot of property! Be careful, you could finish up by getting hurt.* → **end up** (2), **fetch up** (5), **land up** (4), **wind up** (7)

*__4__ *not fml* to arrive at or in (a place) accidentally, esp. after time or events: [L9 (*at, in, on*) (*simple tenses*)] *With Jim driving, you're never sure where you might finish up. The traveller took the wrong train and finished up at a country village after many hours. He'll finish up in prison if he goes on taking risks like that. The boy's ball finished up on the garage roof.* → **end up** (3), **fetch up** (6), **land up** (5), **wind up** (8)

*__5__ *not fml* to reach (an unfavourable end): [L9 (*in*) (*simple tenses*)] *The business will finish up in failure if sales don't improve soon.* → **end up** (4), **fetch up** (7), **land in** (3), **land up** (6), **wind up** (9)

*__6__ *not fml* to receive (something) in the end: [L9 (*with*) (*simple tenses*)] *After all the argument, the writer finished up with a contract. We thought Jim had no hope of winning, but he finished up with first prize!* → **end up** (5), **fetch up** (8), **land up** (7), **wind up** (10)

**7 finish up nowhere** *not fml* to gain no success: *If you don't work hard, you'll finish up nowhere. What's the use of taking exams? So many people with higher degrees finish up nowhere when they try to get a job.* → **end up** (6), **fetch up** (9), **wind up** (13)

**inish with** *v prep*

**1** to bring (something) to an end with (something or doing something): [T1 + *with*] *What shall we have to finish the meal with?* [L9 + *with*] *We have some nice cheese to finish with. I should like to finish with reminding members of the purpose of this club.* → **end with** (1)

**2** (esp. of time) to come to an end on (a certain date): [L9 + *with*] *Please send your accounts for the period finishing with 31 March.* → **end with** (2)

*__3__ to have no further relationship with (someone): [T1] *I'm glad that Alice has finished with that worthless young man.* → **end with** (3)

*__4__ to have no further use for (something or someone): [T1 (*usu. perfect tenses*)] *Have you finished with the newspaper? When you've finished with me, sir, I'll leave.* → **be over**[1] (4), **do with** (10, **get over**[2] (5)

*__5__ *not fml* to stop punishing (someone): [T1 (*no pass., usu. simple tenses*)] *You'll be sorry by the time I've finished with you!*

**ire ahead** *v adv* → **fire away** (4), **go ahead** (3)
*infml* to begin, esp. to speak; talk actively or ask questions: [IØ (*simple tenses, often imper.*)] *Fire ahead, we're all listening.*

**fire at** *v prep*

**1** to aim; shoot (bullets) at (someone or something): [L9 + *at*] *The soldiers fired at the house until the enemy came out.* [T1 + *at*] *Fire most of your shots at the middle of the ship. The gunman fired three bullets at the police.*

*__2__ to direct (something spoken such as questions) to (someone): [D1] *The crowd fired questions at the speaker for over an hour.*

**fire away** *v adv*

**1** to begin to shoot: [IØ + AWAY] *The soldiers fired away at the enemy.*

**2** to shoot continuously: [IØ + AWAY] *The soldiers fired away until the enemy yielded.*

**3** to use or waste (bullets): [T1 + AWAY] *We have fired away all our bullets and have none left.*

*__4__ *infml* to begin, esp. to speak; talk actively or ask questions: [IØ (*simple tenses, often imper.*)] *Fire away, we're all listening. The crowd fired away at the speaker.* → **fire ahead, go ahead** (3)

*__5__ to use (all one's arguments): [T1] *Having fired away all his best points, the speaker had no argument left.*

**fire back** *v adv*

**1** to return gunfire: [IØ + BACK] *When the enemy start shooting, you may fire back.*

*__2__ to explode the wrong way with a loud noise: [IØ] *The engine has been firing back (on itself).* —**backfire** *v, n*

**fire into** *v prep*

**1** to (cause to) shoot into (something such as the air or a group): [IØ + *into*] *The men were ordered to fire into the air to make the crowd afraid.* [T1 + *into*] *Fire a few bullets into the house and the enemy will soon come out as prisoners.*

*__2__ to excite (someone) into (doing something): [V4b] *The speaker fired the crowd into marching to Parliament with their demands.*

**fire off** *v adv*

**1** to begin shooting with (usu. a large gun); shoot (bullets): [T1 + OFF] *The enemy are firing off their big guns; now we should attack. This was the first gun that was made to fire off six bullets, one after the other.*

*__2__ to speak (something such as questions) quickly and in quantity: [T1] *The crowd fired off questions at the speakers. The teacher fired off the names on his list. The officer fired off his orders.*

**fire on/upon** *v prep*
to shoot at (someone or something): [L9 + *on/upon*] *The soldiers were charged with firing on women and children. The big guns on the shore fired on the attacking ships.*

**fire over** *v prep*
to shoot in a direction above (something): [IØ + *over*] *The men were ordered to fire over the heads of the crowd.*

**fire up** *v adv*

**1** to start (an engine): [T1 + UP] *We are hav-*

*ing difficulty in firing up the ship's engines.*

*2 to supply (something that gives heat) with material to burn; start producing heat: [T1] *The ship's boilers need firing up.* [IØ] *The factories are firing up after the holidays.*

*3 to (cause to) increase in heat, anger, or violence: [IØ] *Mary's temper fired up. Mary fired up when Jim angered her.* [T1] *She has a quick temper; such little things will fire her up. The speaker fired the crowd up to march to Parliament.* → **blaze up** (2), **flame out** (3), **flame up** (2), **flare out** (2), **flare up** (2)

**fire upon** *v prep* → FIRE ON

***fire with** *v prep*

to fill (someone) with (an excited feeling): [D1] *Your speech fired the crowd with keenness for the plan.*

**firm up** *v adv*

**1** to (cause to) become harder: [L9 + UP] *The soil is firming up now that the weather is drier.* [X9 + UP] *The machine helps to firm the ground up for the game.*

***2** to arrange (something) more firmly; cause to become firm: [T1] *Let's firm up the details of the contract at our next meeting. The government must act to firm prices up.*

**fish for** *v prep*

**1** to try to catch (certain fish), as with a line or net, etc.: [IØ + *for*] *It's no use fishing for trout in this river, there are none left.*

***2** to search for (something) by touch: [T1 (*no pass.*)] *He fished for a coin in his pocket. Blinded by the steam, he had to fish around for the soap in his bath.* → **feel about**[2] (2), **feel for** (3), **fumble for**

***3** also **angle for** to try to get (something) indirectly, as with words: [T1 (*no pass., usu. continuous tenses*)] *The young lady was always fishing for compliments—and they came! I think he must be a policeman, he keeps fishing for information. Are you fishing for a job?* → **feel after**

***4** to try to find (something such as an idea) in one's mind: [T1 (*no pass.*)] *After fishing (around) for the right word, I decided to look in the dictionary.*

**fish in** *v prep*

**1** to try to catch fish in (a body of water): [IØ + *in*] *You're not allowed to fish in this part of the river without special permission.*

**2 fish in troubled waters** to try to succeed in difficult times; try to gain advantage out of other people's difficulties: *He's always been good at fishing in troubled waters; he made a lot of money by buying houses that were bombed in the war.*

**fish out** *v adv*

**1** to bring (something or someone) up from water: [X9 + OUT (*of*)] *Instead of catching fish, all that he fished out was an old boot. The boy fell into the lake and had to be fished out of the water.* → **fish up** (1)

***2** *not fml* to bring (something) up from somewhere: [T1 (*from, of*)] *He fished out a coin from his pocket. She fished the keys out of her bag.* → **fish up** (2)

***3** to empty (a body of water) of all its fish: [T1 (*usu. pass.*)] *This lake has been fished out, let's try the river.* → **farm out** (5), **lay in**[1] (4), **mine out, work out** (8)

**fish up** *v adv*

**1** to bring (something or someone) up from water: [X9 + UP (*from*)] *Instead of catching fish, all that he fished up was an old boot. The boy nearly drowned in the lake; we had to fish him up from the bottom.* → **fish out** (1)

***2** *not fml* to bring (something) up from somewhere: [T1] *He fished up a coin from his pocket.* → **fish out** (2)

***3** *infml* to find (something), usu. as a result of searching: [T1] *The proof was fished up from some old papers. Where did you fish that idea up?*

**fit for** *v prep*

**1** to measure (usu. someone) for (something that must be the right size and shape): [X9 + *for*] *The military hospital will fit any wounded soldier for a false leg.*

***2** to make (someone or oneself) suitable for (something): [D1 (*usu. simple tenses*)] *His great height fitted him for team games. You can best fit yourself for your new responsibility by studying all these papers left by the former chairman.*

**fit in**[1] *v adv*

**1** to be able to be contained in something: [L9 + IN (*usu. simple tenses*)] *I don't think this is the box that this toy came in, it won't fit in.* → **get in**[1] (1), **go in**[1] (2), **put in**[1] (1), **stick in**[1] (1)

**2** to find space for (something): [X9 + IN] *I think we can fit in an additional room behind the kitchen. There was so much furniture in the sale room that it became impossible to fit any more in.* → **cram in, crowd in** (1), **jam in, pack in** (1), **pile in** (1), **throng in**

**3** to find a time for (someone or something): [T1] *Mr Sharp is seeing people all morning, but if the matter is urgent, I'll see if I can fit you in. Although I'm very busy, I'll try to fit in a game of tennis at the weekend.* → **crowd in** (2), **squeeze in** (2)

***4** to behave or feel as if belonging (to a group) or suiting (something): [IØ (*with*)] *Mary joined a painting group but didn't seem to fit in, so she left. Most people who come from other countries seem to fit in with the way of life here.* → **fit into** (2), **fit in with**

**fit in**[2] *v prep* → FIT INTO

***fit in with** *v adv prep* → **fit in**[1] (4), **fit into** (2)

to agree with; match; suit (something or someone): [T1 (*pass. rare, often simple tenses*)] *His ideas did not quite fit in with our aims. I'll change my timetable to fit in with yours. New members must fit in with the rest of the committee.* [D1 (*often simple tenses*)] *I'll try to fit my arrangements in with yours.*

**fit into/in** *v prep*

**1** to (cause to) take the right space or time in

(something): [X9 + *into/in*] *I can't fit this toy in the box, are you sure it's the right one? We have to fit the special train into the timetable.* [L9 + *into/in* (*usu. simple tenses*)] *This toy doesn't fit in the box, are you sure it's the right one? If I gain any more weight, I shan't be able to fit into my clothes.* → **get in**[2] (1), **get into** (1), **go in** (3), **go into** (4), **lay in**[2] (1), **place in** (1), **press in**[2], **push in**[2], **push into** (1), **put in** (1), **put into** (1), **set in**[2] (1), **stick in** (2), **stick into** (1), **thrust in**[2]

*__2__ to (cause to) be suitable for (something): [T1 (*no pass., usu. simple tenses*)] *I don't think she'll fit in the organization. The house fits into the scenery so well that you can hardly see it.* [D1 (*usu. simple tenses*)] *Any new buildings must be fitted into the existing appearance of the city.* → **fit in**[1] (4), **fit in with**

**fit on**[1] *v adv*

**1** to place (something) exactly on something: [X9 + ON] *I don't think this is the right lid for this box, I can't fit it on.* → **get on**[1] (1), **go on**[1] (3), **put on**[1] (1)

*__2__ to try (clothing) to see if it is the right size and shape: [T1] *My dressmaker has asked me to fit on the new suit tomorrow.* → **put on**[1] (2), etc.

**fit on**[2] *v prep*

**1** to place (something) exactly on (something): [T1 + *on*] *I can't fit the lid on this box.*

**2** to fix (something) in place on (something): [X9 + *on*] *Please fit a new handle on my case.*

***fit out** *v adv* → **equip with** (1), **fit up** (1)

to supply (esp. a person or ship) with necessary things: [T1] *The ship has been newly fitted out. We must fit the boy out for school.* —**outfit** *n, v* —**outfitter** *n*

**fit round** *v prep*

**1** to hold or be able to hold (something) tightly: [L9 + *round* (*simple tenses*)] *This boat has a special instrument fitting round the pole. The baby's hands are too small to fit round the ball.*

**2** to make (something) change to suit (something): [X9 + *round*] *I don't mind fitting my timetable round yours.*

**fit to** *v prep*

**1** to be the right size for (something); make sure that (something) is the right size for (something): [L9 + *to* (*simple tenses*)] *See if the frame fits to the door, and if it does, then finish making it.* [X9 + *to* (*simple tenses*)] *See if you can fit any of these odd lids to this set of containers.*

*__2__ to match; suit (something) to (something): [D1] *We all have to fit our spending to your income. We should fit the punishment to the crime.* → **match with** (1), **pair with** (1), **suit to** (1)

**fit together** *v adv* → **piece together**

**1** to join; make (something whole) from separate parts: [T1 + TOGETHER (*from*)] *The shipwrecked sailors were able to fit a rough shelter together from building materials that they found on the island. The police had to fit the story together from details given by different witnesses.*

**2** to form a whole or unity: [IØ + TOGETHER (*simple tenses*)] *These broken pieces of plates don't fit together, they must be parts of different ones. The movements of this piece of music somehow don't fit together.*

***fit up** *v adv*

**1** to supply (something or someone) with necessary things: [T1 (*with*)] *It costs a lot of money to fit up a new office.* [X9 (*as, with*)] *The royal train was fitted up with costly furniture. The room was fitted up with bookshelves. Your uncle should be able to fit you up with a job in his firm. The bedroom can be fitted up as an office.* → **equip with** (1), **fit out, fix up** (3)

**2** to make (something such as a machine) ready; fix (something) in place: [T1] *Please fit the machine up for this afternoon's class. New blackboards have been fitted up in all the classrooms.*

**3** to make or build (something that can be used for a short time): [T1] *Please stay here, we can fit up a bed for the night. The actors had to fit up a stage because there was no theatre in the town.* —**fit-up** *n, adj* → **clap together**

**4** to find (someone) a place to stay: [T1 (*with*)] *I'll fit you up with a bed at my house. Can you fit me up in a good hotel?* → **fix up** (4)

**5** *sl* to make (someone) seem guilty of a crime when in fact he is not: [T1] *I didn't take the jewels—the police have fitted me up.* → **frame up** (2)

**fit with** *v prep*

to supply (someone or something) with (something exactly the right size and shape): [X9 + *with*] *Each office is fitted with bookshelves. I must ask the dentist to fit me with some new teeth.*

**fix for** *v prep*

**1** to arrange (something or someone) for (a date, time, etc.): [X9 + *for*] *Try to fix the football game for Tuesday. The committee meeting is fixed for 3 o'clock. I'm not fixed for Saturday; let's meet then.*

**2** esp. *AmE* to prepare (a meal) for (someone): [T1 + *for*] *Father is fixing breakfast for the whole family.*

**3 be fixed for** *infml* to have a supply of (something): *Are you fixed for money all right? How are the climbers fixed for food?*

**fix on**[1] *v adv*

to make (something) stay firmly in place: [X9 + ON] *The tail won't come off the toy plane, it's fixed on with nails.*

**fix on/upon**[2] *v prep*

**1** to make (something) stay firmly in place on (something): [X9 + *on/upon*] *The tail is fixed on the model plane with nails, it can't come off.*

*__2__ to keep (something) steady with regard to

(something): [D1] *Fix your eyes on the road and we'll be much safer. It's difficult to fix my mind on what I'm doing.* [D6] *Please fix your thoughts on where we're going, or we shall get lost.*
*__3__ *not fml* to decide about; choose (usu. something or doing something): [T1] *Have you two fixed on a date for the wedding yet? We should fix on a place to stay before we leave home.* [T4] *We've fixed on starting tomorrow.* [T6] *Have you fixed on where to go yet?*
**4** **be fixed on** *not fml* to be determined about (something or doing something): *Jim seems fixed on the idea. Jim seems fixed on going abroad for his holiday.*
**5** **fix the blame/crime on** *not fml* to decide that (someone) is guilty: *You can't fix the robbery on me, I can prove I was somewhere else.*

*__fix over__ *v adv*
*AmE not fml* to repair or remake (something): [T1] *Can the garage man fix over the engine? I think I can fix the dress over so that the hole doesn't show.*

*__fix up__ *v adv*
**1** *not fml* to repair or improve (something): [T1] *The garage man fixed up the old car and sold it at a profit. We shall have to fix the house up before we can sell it.*
**2** *not fml* to make arrangements for (something): [T1] *Can you fix up a meeting with the director? We must meet again to fix up the details of the contract.* [IØ + *about*] *Have you fixed up about the photographs for the wedding?*
**3** *not fml* to provide (someone) (with something or someone): [T1 (*with*)] *I can fix you up with a good used car. I know someone who should be able to fix you up. Ask your brother to fix you up with a nice girl. You seem to be fixed up nicely here.*
**4** *not fml* to find (someone) a place to stay: [T1] *He fixed us up in a good hotel. I have a friend who can fix me up for the weekend.* → **fit up** (4)
**5** *AmE not fml* to dress carefully or rather formally: [IØ] *Do I have to fix up to go to the Websters'?*
**6** **fix it/things up (with)** *infml* to make a special arrangement (with someone), sometimes in a dishonest way: *Yes, you can have that other week's holiday, I've fixed it up with the director. Don't worry about the police, Fred is fixing things up. There'll be no difficulty getting tickets, I've fixed it up with my friend in the show.*

**fix upon** *v prep* → FIX ON

**fix with** *v prep*
**1** to mend or fasten (something) by means of (something): [T1 + *with*] *You can fix the toy plane's tail with this glue.*
*__2__ *not fml* to arrange (something) with (someone): [D1] *We've fixed the deal with the builders, they'll start tomorrow. Can you fix it with the Minister so that the meeting will be delayed?*
*__3__ to look at (someone) with (a kind of look): [D1] *Fixing the boy with a steady look, the teacher forced him to tell the truth.*

**fizz up** *v adv* → **foam up, froth up**
*not fml* (of liquid) to rise with noisy bubbles: [IØ + UP] *The drink fizzes up when you first pour it.*

*__fizzle out__ *v adv*
**1** *infml* (of something explosive) to end weakly; not explode as planned: [IØ] *The bomb fizzled out, and no one was hurt.*
**2** *infml* to come to nothing after a good start; end disappointingly: [IØ] *The plan fizzled out for lack of money.*

*__flag down__ *v adv*
to signal to (a driver or vehicle) to stop, by waving one's arm or a flag at the driver: [T1] *After the accident, the passenger flagged down the nearest passing car and asked to be taken to a telephone.*

**flake away/off** *v adv*
to fall off in small, usu. flat pieces: [L9 + AWAY/OFF] *The paint is flaking off in this dry weather.*

*__flake out__ *v adv*
**1** *infml* to faint: [IØ] *I think I'm going to flake out, I'd better sit down.*
**2** *infml* to fall asleep: [IØ] *Tired out by their journey, the travellers flaked out as soon as they reached their hotel room.*
**3** *infml* to feel weak, as from lack of food: [IØ] *When you start flaking out, have something to eat.*

**flame out** *v adv*
**1** to burn again: [L9 + OUT] *The fire flamed out when the wind blew again.* → **blaze up** (1), **burn up** (1), **flame up** (1), **flare up** (1)
**2** to burn brightly so as to show: [L9 + OUT] *The signal flamed out on the hilltop.*
*__3__ to increase in heat, anger, or violence: [IØ] *Mary's temper flamed out. Mary flamed out when Jim angered her.* → **blaze up** (2), **fire up** (3), **flame up** (2), **flare out** (2), **flare up** (2)

**flame up** *v adv*
**1** to burn again: [L9 + UP] *The fire flamed up when we thought it was out.* → **blaze up** (1), **burn up** (1), **flame out** (1), **flare up** (1)
*__2__ to increase in heat, anger, or violence: [IØ] *Mary's temper flamed up. Mary flamed up when Jim angered her.* → **blaze up** (2), **fire up** (3), **flame out** (3), **flare out** (2), **flare up** (2)
*__3__ to turn red in the face with strong feeling as shame, modesty, etc.: [IØ] *The quiet girl flamed up when the man asked her to dance.* → **colour up** (1), **flush up**

*__flame with__ *v prep* → **blaze with**
to turn red in the face because of (a strong

feeling such as anger): [T1 (*no pass.*)] *Mary flamed with anger when she heard how her mother had been treated.*

**flank on/upon** *v prep*
to be placed at the side of (an army): [L9 + *on/upon*] *The second division flanks on the main body of soldiers.*

**flap about/around** *v adv*
**1** to move loosely or aimlessly, without direction: [L9 + ABOUT/AROUND] *The flag was flapping about in the light wind.*
**2** *infml* to worry needlessly: [IØ + ABOUT/AROUND (*often continuous tenses*)] *Do stop flapping about, we'll get the job done in time.*

***flare back** *v adv* → **blow back** (2)
to burn or fire in the wrong direction: [IØ] *Mind that gun, it's flaring back.* —**flare-back** *n*

**flare out** *v adv*
**1** to become wider in one direction: [L9 + OUT] *Her dress flared out towards the bottom.* [X9 + OUT] *The sides of the ship were flared out to allow more room on the top floors.*
***2** to speak angrily: [IØ] *"And don't speak to me like that!" she flared out.* → **flare up** (3), **flash out** (2), etc.

***flare up** *v adv*
**1** to burn again: [IØ] *The fire flared up when we thought it was out.* → **blaze up** (1), **burn up** (1), **flame out** (1), **flame up** (1)
**2** to increase in heat, anger, or violence: [IØ] *Mary's temper flared up. Mary flared up when Jim angered her. Trouble may flare up in the big cities. The disease has flared up again.* —**flare-up** *n* → **blaze up** (2), **break out** (2), **fire up** (3), **flame out** (3), **flame up** (2), **flare out** (2)
**3** to speak angrily: [IØ] *"And don't speak to me like that!" she flared up.* → **flare out** (2), **flash out** (2)

**flash about/around** *v adv*
**1** to move (a light) in several directions: [X9 + ABOUT/AROUND] *Flash your light around and see if anyone is hiding in here.*
***2** *not fml* to show (usu. wealth), so as to win admiration or jealousy: [T1 (*usu. continuous tenses*)] *She keeps flashing that diamond around to show everyone that she is going to be married. I do wish he would stop flashing his money about.*

***flash at** *v prep* → DART AT

***flash back** *v adv* → **cut back** (2), **flash forward**
(esp. in films) to return suddenly to an earlier time: [IØ (*to*)] *The film flashed back to the earlier scene, so that we understood her reasons. My mind flashed back to last Christmas.* —**flashback** *n*

***flash forward** *v adv* → **cut back** (2), **flash back**
(in films) to move suddenly to a later time: [IØ] *The film flashed forward to show us the result of her decision.* —**flash-forward** *n*

***flash on/upon** *v prep*
to become suddenly known by (someone): [T1 (*no pass., simple tenses*)] *The reason for his strange behaviour flashed on me when I met his mother.*

**flash out** *v adv*
**1** to shine in frequent short bursts: [L9 + OUT] *The light flashed out from the little lighthouse by the rocks.*
***2** to speak angrily: [IØ] *"And don't speak to me like that!" she flashed out.* → **flare out** (2), **flare up** (3)

**flash through** *v prep*
**1** to move quickly through (something such as a place): [L9 + *through*] *Lightning flashed through the air.*
**2** to pass quickly through (one's mind): [L9 + *through*] *The thought flashed through my mind that he could be lying.*

**flash up** *v adv*
to hold (something) up and allow it to be seen for a moment: [X9 + UP] *The traveller flashed up a sign to show passing motorists where he wanted to go. The teacher flashed up each word to see if the children would recognize it.*

***flash upon** *v prep* → FLASH ON

***flatten in** *v adv* → **harden in, round in**
*naut* to pull in (ropes controlling certain sails): [T1] *You'd better flatten in the main ropes.*

**flatten out** *v adv*
to (cause to) become flat: [T1 + OUT] *Help me to flatten out the sheets. The garage man had to flatten out the car door, which was twisted by damage in the accident. Flatten the pastry out with your hands before putting it into the dish.* [L9 + OUT (*simple tenses*)] *The hills flatten out here, and the ground is almost level.*

***flatter oneself** *v pron*
to have a high opinion of oneself; have the pleasant though perhaps mistaken opinion (that): [IØ (*on*) (*simple tenses*)] *Don't flatter yourself, you could be wrong next time. The chairman flatters himself on his judgment of people.* [I5 (*simple tenses*)] *I flatter myself that my judgment is usually correct. The government is flattering itself that it can win the next election.*

**flavour with** *v prep*
**1** to give (food) the taste of (something): [X9 + *with*] *This soup is flavoured with onions.*
***2** to make (something such as writing) more interesting by adding (something exciting): [D1 (*often pass.*)] *Newspaper reports are often flavoured with sex and violence.*

**flee from** *v prep*
to run away from; escape from; avoid (something or someone): [L9 + *from*] *All the animals fled from the fire. The prisoners escaped by fleeing from their guards while they were on an outside work party.*

**flee to** *v prep*
to escape to (someone or a place): [L9 + *to*] *When the bombing started, the population fled to places of safety. The child fled to his mother, looking for comfort and safety.*

***flesh out/up** *v adv*
**1** to (cause to) grow fatter: [IØ] *John finished growing taller last year, and now he's fleshing out.* [T1] *Better health has fleshed her face out a little.* → **fatten out** (1), **fill out** (4), **plump out**
**2** *not fml* to make (writing) longer or fuller, esp. to make (characters) seem more real: [T1] *The action in the story is good but the characters aren't very lifelike; see if you can flesh them out a little.* → **fatten out** (2), **fill out** (6), **pad out** (2)

**flick away/off** *v adv*
to remove (something unwanted) with quick light movements: [X9 + AWAY/OFF] *Flick the dust off and we will use this table. The horse flicked the flies away with its tail.*

**flick over** *v adv*
to turn (pages) quickly: [X9 + OVER] *You're not really reading, you're just flicking the pages over.*

***flick through** *v prep* → **flip through, glance over**
to read (a book, magazine, etc.) quickly and carelessly: [T1 (*no pass.*)] *I've just flicked through your article; I'll read it again properly when I've got more time.* —**flick-through** *n*

***flicker out** *v adv*
**1** to stop burning little by little, unevenly: [IØ] *When the candle was only half an inch high it flickered out and the room became dark.* → **putter out**
**2** to cease little by little: [IØ] *The hatred between these two families never quite flickered out.*

**flinch from** *v prep*
**1** to make a quick movement to avoid (something such as a blow or pain): [L9 + *from*] *The fighter could not help flinching from the blow aimed by his opponent, but it saved him from being hurt.*
**2** to avoid (something difficult, dangerous, or uncomfortable), usu. from fear: [L9 + *from*] *A wise man flinches from danger. Many people flinch from speaking in public.*

**fling about/around** *v adv*
**1** to scatter (something or things) in several directions: [X9 + ABOUT/AROUND] *I wish the children would stop flinging their clothes about, but put them away tidily.* → **chuck about** (1), **hurl about** (1), **throw about**[1] (1), **toss about** (1)
**2** to wave (one's arms and/or legs) aimlessly: [X9 + ABOUT/AROUND] *Don't fling your arms and legs about like that, make the proper swimming strokes.* → **chuck about** (2), **hurl about** (2), **throw about**[1] (2)
**3 fling one's money about/around** *not fml* to spend money foolishly, often so as to show one's wealth: *Our new neighbour is always flinging his money about, with his colour television and his new car every year.* → **chuck about** (3), **hurl about** (3), **throw about**[1] (3), **toss about** (4)
**4 fling one's weight about/around** *not fml* to give unnecessary orders; try to use one's power over other people: *The youth club leader was unpopular with the young people because he was always flinging his weight around.* → **chuck about** (4), **hurl about** (4), **throw about**[1] (4), **toss about** (5)

**fling aside** *v adv*
**1** to throw (something) to one side: [X9 + ASIDE] *Flinging aside his coat, he chased after his attacker.* → **cast off** (1), etc.
***2** to disregard; pay no attention to (something such as an opinion): [T1] *Flinging aside the wishes of his parents, the student went abroad for a year before returning to his university. These rules are not made to be flung aside lightly.*
***3** to give up; have nothing more to do with (someone or something): [T1] *Once he got rich, he flung aside his old friends. Henry joined the opposing political party, flinging aside his former loyalties.* → **cast aside** (2), etc.

**fling at** *v prep*
**1** to throw (something) at (something or someone): [X9 + *at*] *Those boys have been flinging stones at passing cars.* → **throw at** (1), etc.
***2** to express (a bad opinion) violently to (someone): [D1] *Why has she been flinging charges of rudeness at me?*
**3 fling mud at** to speak rudely or offensively in public about (someone): *No politician will win the votes of serious-minded people if all he does is fling mud at his opponent.* → **sling at** (2), **throw at** (4)
**4 fling oneself at someone** to force one's attention on someone so as to win his or her love: *If you fling yourself at that boy, he's likely to run away.* → **chuck at** (2), **hurl at** (2) **throw at** (5)

**fling away** *v adv*
**1** to throw (something) away; get rid of (something): [X9 + AWAY] *Let's fling that old furniture away and buy some new.* → **throw out** (2), etc.
***2** to waste (something): [T1] *You shouldn't fling away a chance like that. Don't fling away your education by leaving now. I hope you won't fling away this money that you've won* → **throw away** (2), etc.
***3** to speak (words) carelessly, as by lowering the voice: [T1] *You flung away that last line we couldn't hear you.* → **chuck away** (3), **throw away** (3)
***4** to go away in a bad temper: [IØ] *She turned and flung away without a word.* → **fling off** (8), **fling out** (3)

***fling away on** *v adv prep*
**1** to waste (something) by using it for (something) or giving it to (someone): [D1 (*often pass.*)] *Why did you fling your money away*

*on such a high risk? Your advice is flung away on that boy!* → **chuck away on** (1), **hurl away on** (1), **throw away on** (1)

**2** *not fml* to waste the worth of (someone or oneself) in a bad relationship, as marriage, with (someone considered unworthy): [D1] *Disapproving of Jim, Mary's father said that he had no wish to fling his daughter away on such a person. Why are you flinging yourself away on a woman like that?* → **chuck away on** (2), **hurl away on** (2), **throw away on** (2)

**fling back** *v adv*

**1** to move (part of the body) suddenly in a backward direction: [X9 + BACK] *Flinging back her head, she laughed and laughed.* → **throw back** (2), **toss back** (1)

**2** to return (something) by throwing: [X9 + BACK (*to*)] *Fling me back the ball, will you?* → **throw back** (1)

**fling down** *v adv*

**1** to throw (usu. something) down: [X9 + DOWN] *He flung his books down on the ground and ran after the other children.* → **chuck down** (1), **hurl down** (1), **throw down**[1] (1), **toss down**

*__2__ to place (oneself) quickly at full length on the ground or floor: [T1b] *The soldiers flung themselves down when they heard the bombs falling.* → **chuck down** (2), **fling to** (3), **hurl down** (2), **throw down**[1] (2), **throw to** (4)

*__3__ **fling down the gauntlet** to call someone to fight; offer a challenge: *By calling the election at this time, the government has flung down the gauntlet to the opposing parties.* → **pick up** (23), **take up** (23), **throw down**[1] (5)

**4 fling down one's tools** *not fml* to strike; stop working because of disagreement: *The workers in all the clothing factories flung down their tools, demanding more pay.* → **chuck down** (3), **throw down**[1] (6)

**fling in**[1] *v adv*

**1** to throw (something) in: [X9 + IN] *He opened the door and flung the parcel in.* → **chuck in** (1), **pitch in** (1), **throw in**[1] (1), **toss in**[1] (1)

*__2__ *not fml* to stop attempting; give up (something): [T1] *Jim has flung in his studies. Why did you fling in your job?* → **give up** (2), etc.

*__3__ *not fml* to add (something), often as a gift: [T1] *If you buy the furniture, the store will fling in a television set.* → **chuck in** (3), **throw in** (3), **toss in**[1] (2)

*__4__ *not fml* to add (words), often as an interruption: [T1] *There was no need to fling in that rude remark.* → **put in**[1] (4), etc.

**5 fling in one's cards/hand: a** *infml* to stop playing cards: *I've had enough of this game, I'll fling my cards in and go to bed.* **b** *infml* to give up any attempt: *I'm tired of trying to write a successful book, I think I'll fling my hand in.* → **chuck in** (5), **throw in**[1] (7)

**6 fling in the towel: a** *not fml* (in boxing) to admit defeat in a fight: *After fighting for half an hour, he flung in the towel.* **b** *not fml* to give up any attempt; admit defeat: *If you leave the competition now, everyone will think you've flung in the towel.* → **chuck in** (6), **chuck up** (6), **fling up** (10), **throw in**[1] (8), **throw up** (10)

**fling in**[2] *v prep*

**1** to throw (something) carelessly into (something): [X9 + *in*] *Don't fling your shoes in the cupboard, put them in neatly.* → **throw in**[2] (1), **toss in**

**2 fling something in someone's face/teeth** *not fml* to blame someone for something: *There's no need to fling his recent failure in his teeth in that unkind way.* → **cast in** (4), **throw in**[2] (3)

**fling in with** *v adv prep* → **cast in with, throw in with**

**fling in one's lot with** *not fml* to join someone in a plan or attempt: *It's sad to see that he's flung in his lot with criminals.*

**fling into** *v prep*

**1** to throw (something) carelessly into (something): [X9 + *into*] *Don't fling your clothes into the drawer, put them in neatly.* → **hurl into** (1), **pitch into** (1), **throw into** (1), **toss into** (1)

**2** to cause (someone) to fall into (something such as water or a hole): [X9 + *into*] *The explosion flung him into the sea.* → **hurl into** (1), **pitch into** (1), **throw into** (1), **toss into** (1)

*__3__ to force (someone) to go to (prison): [D1] *The criminal was flung into prison as soon as he was found guilty.* → **hurl into** (2), **throw into** (2), **toss into** (2)

*__4__ to add (words) to (something such as a conversation): [D1] *I wasn't able to fling a word into the argument the whole time. She sat silently, flinging the odd word into the conversation from time to time.* → **throw into** (4), **toss into** (3)

*__5__ to cause (someone or something) to reach (a state): [D1] *Your remarks have flung her into a temper. His speech flung the meeting into confusion.* → **get into** (11), etc.

*__6__ to add (something such as help) towards (a purpose or event, or doing something): [D1] *We flung all the men we had into the battle.* [V4b] *The villagers flung all possible effort into rebuilding the bombed houses.* → **hurl into** (3), **throw into** (5)

**7 fling oneself into** to put much effort, time, and keenness into (usu. an activity): *The best cure for unhappiness is to fling yourself into your work.* → **hurl into** (4), **throw into** (7)

**8 fling one's hat into the ring** *not fml* to declare one's intention of taking part in a competition, esp. an election: *Now that the election of the President is about to take place, how many people have flung their hats into the ring?* → **throw into** (6), **toss into** (4)

**fling off** *v adv*

**1** to throw (something) off: [X9 + OFF] *It's good to fling off heavy clothing now that spring is here.* → **cast off** (1), etc., **chuck off** (1)

*__2__ to escape from (someone chasing one): [T1] *The criminals tried to fling off the police,* *but failed and were caught.* → **chuck off** (2), **shake off**[1] (2), **throw off**[1] (3)

*__3__ to get free from (something unwanted): [T1] *In a new job, one should fling off old habits of thought. He was pleased to be able to fling off such an unwelcome responsibility. I can't seem to fling off this cold, it's been troubling me for a month now.* → **cast off** (4), **chuck off** (3), **shake off**[1] (3), **shuffle off** (3), **slough off, throw off**[1] (4)

*__4__ to defeat (an opponent): [T1] *The young tennis player will never be able to fling off the experienced competitors.* → **throw off**[1] (5)

*__5__ to give out (heat, smell, etc.): [T1 (*usu. simple tenses*)] *When this material burns, it flings off a nasty smell.* → **give forth, give off, give out** (1), **throw off**[1] (6), **throw out** (12)

*__6__ to write (something) easily: [T1] *I can fling off a poem in half an hour.* → **dash off** (2), etc.

*__7__ to speak (something) carelessly: [T1] *Before you fling off a remark like that, think what you're saying.* → **put in**[1] (4), etc.

*__8__ to go away in a bad temper: [IØ (*usu. simple tenses*)] *She turned and flung off without a word.* → **fling away** (4), **fling out** (3)

**fling on**[1] *v adv* → **throw on**[1] (2)

to put (clothes) on hurriedly: [X9 + ON] *We haven't time to change, just fling a coat on over what you're wearing now. Fling a dress on and let's go to the party at once.*

**fling on**[2] *v prep*

**1** to throw (something or oneself) on (something), often carelessly: [X9 + *on*] *The traveller flung his money on the table and left. They flung themselves on the ground as the plane went over.* → **cast on**[2] (1), **fling to** (3), **throw on**[2] (1)

**2 fling oneself on someone's mercy** to place one's trust in someone's kindness: *If the judge finds you guilty, you can only fling yourself on his mercy.* → **cast on**[2] (4), **throw on**[2] (8)

**fling open** *v adj* → **throw open**

**1** to open (something) violently: [X7 + **open**] *The angry father flung the door open and marched into his daughter's room.*

*__2__ to declare (something such as a place or competition) free for anyone to enter: [T1 (*to*) (*usu. pass.*)] *The gardens of the great house are being flung open to the public. Since the tennis competition was flung open to professionals, the standard has improved.*

**fling out** *v adv*

**1** to throw (something) in an outward direction, often violently: [X9 + OUT] *When the train crashed, many passengers were flung out onto the lines. The explosion flung out bits of metal in all directions. He flung out his arms to welcome her.* → **chuck out** (1), **pitch out** (1), **throw out** (1), **toss out** (1)

**2** to throw (something) away: [X9 + OUT] *I really must fling out all these old newspapers.* → **throw out** (2), etc.

*__3__ to leave (a place) in a bad temper: [IØ (*of*) (*usu. simple tenses*)] *She turned and flung out (of the room) without another word.* → **fling away** (4), **fling off** (8)

*__4__ to make (someone) leave because of a fault: [T1 (*of*)] *Two members were flung out of the club for failing to pay the money they owed.* → **throw out** (4), etc.

*__5__ to make (someone) leave a home: [T1 (*of*) (*often pass.*)] *The old lady was flung out of the house because the owner wanted to pull it down.* → **throw out** (5), etc.

*__6__ *not fml* to refuse to accept (a suggestion, law, etc.): [T1 (*often pass.*)] *The new law was flung out when it reached the last stage in Parliament.* → **chuck out** (5), **hurl out** (2), **throw out** (6), **toss out** (5), **turn down** (4)

*__7__ to say (something) carelessly: [T1 (*usu. simple tenses*)] *Why did you fling out that remark?* → **put in**[1] (4), etc.

*__8__ to offer (something such as a suggestion): [T1] *At last the chairman flung out his own suggestion, which the committee were eager to accept.* → **throw out** (8), **toss out** (7)

*__9__ to kick violently: [IØ] *Suddenly the horse flung out and the rider was thrown to the ground.*

**fling to** *v prep*

**1** to throw (something) to (someone, an animal, or a place): [X9 + *to*] *Here, fling this meat to the dogs in the yard. The animal was up the tree, flinging nuts to the ground.* → **throw to** (1)

**2 fling caution/discretion to the winds** to be bold; take risks: *The only thing to do is to fling caution to the winds and make a decision, right or wrong; anything is better than uncertainty.* → **throw to** (2)

**3 fling someone/oneself to the floor/ground** to cause someone or oneself to lie down quickly: *He flung himself to the ground as the bullets flew past overhead. She saved the children's lives by flinging them to the floor.* → **chuck down** (2), **fling down** (2), **fling on**[2] (2), **hurl down** (2), **throw down** (2), **throw to** (4)

**fling together** *v adv*

**1** to gather (things) in a hurry: [X9 + TOGETHER] *At the last minute I decided to go, so I flung a few clothes together and left.* → **chuck together** (1), **throw together** (1), **toss together** (1)

*__2__ to cause (usu. two people) to meet: [T1b (*usu. pass.*)] *Jim and Mary were flung together by the war.* → **bring together** (2), etc.

*__3__ to build or write (something) hastily: [T1] *This poem sounds as if it was flung together in half an hour. The hut isn't safe; it was just flung together.* → **throw together** (2), etc.

**fling up** *v adv*

**1** to throw (something) upwards: [X9 + UP] *The machine flung up great heaps of earth.* → **cast up** (1), **chuck up** (1), **throw up** (1), **toss up** (1)

*__2__ to waste (something): [T1] *You shouldn't*

*fling up a chance like that. Don't fling up your education by leaving now.* → **throw away** (2), etc.

****3** to stop attempting; give up (something): [T1] *Jim has flung up his studies. Why did you fling up your job?* → **give up** (2), etc.

****4** to produce (something): [T1a] *His long search flung up one old letter.* → **throw up** (5)

****5** to build (something) hastily: [T1] *Let's use this wood to fling up a shelter for the night.* → **throw together** (2), etc.

****6** to bring (something) to people's attention; mention (something harmful to someone): [T1] *I don't want his past record flung up in court. Why are you always flinging up my past mistakes?* → **bring up** (3), **cast up** (4), **sling up** (2), **throw up** (7)

**7 fling up one's arms/hands in horror** to express violent fear: *She entered the room, then flung up her hands in horror at the terrible sight that met her eyes.* → **throw up** (8)

**8 fling up one's hands in despair** to lose all hope: *His mother flung up her hands in despair when the boy failed yet another examination.* → **throw up** (9)

**9 fling up one's heels: a** to move quickly: *The horses are flinging up their heels in the warm spring air.* **b** to enjoy oneself: *The children flung up their heels as soon as they were let out of school.* → **kick up** (3)

**10 fling up the sponge** *not fml* to admit defeat: *If you leave the competition now, people will think you're flinging up the sponge.* → **chuck in** (6), **chuck up** (6), **fling in**[1] (6), **throw in**[1] (8), **throw up** (10)

***flip over** *v adv*
to turn (something) upside down suddenly: [IØ] *When the great fish flipped over on its back, we knew it was almost dead.* [T1] *He flipped the envelope over to see who it had come from.*

***flip through** *v prep* → **flick through, glance over**
*not fml* to read (a book, etc.) quickly and carelessly: [T1] *I haven't read the book properly, I just flipped through it to see what it was like.* —**flip-through** *n*

**flirt with** *v prep*
**1** to play at a love relationship with (someone, usu. of the opposite sex), in a harmless way: [L9 + *with*] *I wasn't serious about that girl, I was only flirting with her; we both enjoyed it.* → **dally with** (2), **play with** (2), **sport with** (2), **toy with** (3), **trifle with** (2)

***2** to treat (something) not very seriously: [T1 (*no pass.*)] *You're flirting with danger, taking risks like that. I've been flirting with the idea of leaving my job.*

**flit about** *v adv*
to move quickly and lightly in no special direction: [L9 + ABOUT] *These brightly coloured insects flit about above the surface of the water.*

**flit through** *v prep*
**1** to fly lightly through (something): [L9 + *through*] *The small birds flitted through the branches.*

**2 flit through one's mind** to be remembered for a short time: *His name flitted through my mind, only to be forgotten again. A picture of my daughter in her childhood flitted through my mind when we met again.*

**float about/around/round** *v adv*
**1** to float without direction on the surface of water: [L9 + ABOUT/AROUND/ROUND] *Some leaves were floating about on the still lake.*

***2** *not fml* to be in existence: [IØ (*usu. continuous tenses*)] *There should be some envelopes floating around somewhere.*

***3** *not fml* to move frequently from job to job: [IØ (*usu. continuous tenses*)] *My son hasn't been able to find a steady job; he's been floating round for the past year.*

**float into/through** *v prep*
to pass lazily into or through (one's mind): [L9 + *into/through*] *Strange thoughts float into/through my mind when I am nearly asleep.*

**float on/upon** *v prep*
**1** to rest on (usu. water) without sinking: [IØ + *on/upon*] *The piece of wood is floating on the river.*

***2** to offer (something such as an idea or company) within (a group or system): [T1] *When will it be time to float the new firm on the open market?*

**float round** *v adv* → **FLOAT ABOUT**

**float through** *v prep* → **FLOAT INTO**

**float upon** *v prep* → **FLOAT ON**

**flock after** *v prep*
to follow (someone) in large numbers, as with admiration; try to gain (something): [L9 + *after*] *Crowds flocked after the popular singer as he left the theatre. Firms are flocking after the government's offer of money to help them move to areas needing industry.*

**flock in/into** *v adv; prep*
to arrive in large numbers (in a place): [L9 + IN/*into*] *When the sale was advertised, hundreds of customers flocked in/flocked into the sale room.*

**flock round** *v prep*
to gather round (someone or something) in large numbers: [L9 + *round*] *Angry questioners flocked round the speaker after the meeting.*

**flock to** *v prep*
to go in large numbers to (something); attend (an event): [L9 + *to*] *Large crowds flocked to the performance.*

**flock together** *v adv*
(esp. of those having something in common) to gather in large numbers: [L9 + TOGETHER] *All the young people are flocking together to hear the latest popular group. Birds of a feather flock together.* (saying)

**flog to** *v prep*
**1 flog someone to death** to kill someone with a whip: *Punishment on the old sailing ships was so severe that it was possible for a sailor to be flogged to death for quite a small fault.*
**2 flog something to death** *not fml* to repeat something until people are tired of hearing about it: *That idea of improving our system of voting has been flogged to death; no one is interested any more. When you're selling the product, be careful not to flog it to death, or your customers will lose interest.*

***flood in/into** *v adv; prep*
to come in or arrive in a large quantity (in a place): [IØ] *When I drew the curtains back, the sunlight flooded in. Letters of complaint are still flooding in.* [T1 (*no pass.*)] *Sunlight flooded into the room. Letters of complaint are still flooding into the office.*

**flood out** *v adv*
**1** to cover (usu. an area) completely with unwanted water: [X9 + OUT] *The heavy spring rain has flooded out the ground floor of the hotel.*
***2** to make (someone) homeless by flooding: [T1 (*usu. pass.*)] *Many families were flooded out when the river burst its banks.* → **drown out** (2)
***3** to fill (something) with a lot of (something or things): [T1 (*usu. pass.*)] *The office was flooded out with complaints.*

**flood with** *v prep* → **deluge with, inundate with, swamp with**
**1** to cover (usu. an area) with (water): [X9 + *with*] *The fields were flooded with the heavy rain.*
***2** to crowd; fill (usu. something) with (a lot of things or something): [D1 (*usu. pass.*)] *The office was flooded with complaints about the washing machines. The room was suddenly flooded with light.*

***flop about/around** *v adv*
*not fml* to move in a loose way, often rather noisily: [IØ] *If you wear those shoes that are too big, you'll just flop around in them. Dying fish were flopping about on the wooden boards.*

**flop down** *v adv*
*not fml* to (cause to) fall or drop suddenly: [L9 + DOWN] *The travellers were so tired that they just flopped down in the nearest chairs.* [X9 + DOWN] *The postman flopped his heavy bag down for a short rest.*

**flop into** *v prep*
*not fml* to let oneself fall into (something such as a bed or chair), as when very tired: [L9 + *into*] *The travellers were so tired that they flopped into bed and fell asleep at once.*

***flossy up** *v adv* → **gussy up**
*BrE sl* to ornament (something or oneself) in the hope of improvement: [T1] "*Pinn, who worked afternoons, was usually home by 5, and would then spend a long time flossying herself up.*" (Iris Murdoch, *The Sacred and Profane Love Machine*)

**flounce in** *v adv*
to enter in an awkward or violent manner, as if bad-tempered: [L9 + IN] *That stupid woman has just flounced in here, expecting everyone to pay her attention.*

**flounce out** *v adv*
to go out in an awkward or violent manner, as if bad-tempered: [L9 + OUT] *Mary was so angry that she flounced out of the room.*

**flounder about/around** *v adv*
**1** to struggle to move, in an awkward manner, as in water: [L9 + ABOUT/AROUND] *We found him at last, lost in the forest, floundering about in deep snow.*
***2** to have difficulty in expressing oneself: [IØ] *Your question seems to have unnerved the speaker; he's been floundering around ever since you spoke.*

**flounder through** *v prep*
**1** to struggle to move through (something stopping one's advance): [L9 + *through*] *The horses were still floundering through the mud an hour later.*
***2** to speak (words) awkwardly, as in a foreign language: [T1] *The politician floundered through his speech, making mistakes, as if he were nervous or had not had time to practise it.*

**flow from** *v prep*
**1** (of liquid) to come; pass; run from (something): [L9 + *from*] *There were tears flowing from the eyes of every person in the crowd.*
***2** to result from (something): [T1 (*no pass., simple tenses*)] *Crime flows from many causes, among them unhappy experiences and poor education.* → **arise from,** etc.

**flow in** *v adv*
**1** (of liquid) to move in: [L9 + IN] *When the end of the pipe was opened, the water flowed in.*
***2** (esp. of money) to be received in quantity: [IØ] *Your income from the book should start flowing in next year.*

**flow into** *v prep* → **drain into, empty into** (2)
(of a river, etc.) to allow its water to pass into (usu. a larger body of water): [L9 + *into* (*simple tenses*)] *All the rivers on the east side of England flow into the North Sea.*

**flow out** *v adv*
**1** (of liquid) to move out: [L9 + OUT] *If you unblock the pipe, the water can flow out.* —**outflow** *n*
***2** (esp. of money) to be spent or sent out in quantity: [IØ] *The taxpayers are complaining that their money is flowing out through government spending.* —**outflow** *n*

***flow over** *v prep* also **wash over**
to have no effect on (someone): [T1 (*no pass., usu. simple tenses*)] *All her complaints just flowed over him, leaving him quite unconcerned.*

**flow to** *v prep*
**1** (of liquid) to move to (a place or direction): [L9 + *to*] *All rivers in the end flow to the sea.*
*__2__ (esp. of money) to be received by (someone or something): [T1 (*no pass.*)] *Money tends to flow to businesses that are already succeeding.*

***flow with** *v prep*
to be covered with (liquid): [T1 (*no pass., often continuous tenses*)] *All the city streets were flowing with water after the night's rain. "A land flowing with milk and honey."* (The Bible)

***fluff out** *v adv*
to make (something) swell with air: [T1] *When the weather is cold, birds fluff out their feathers so as to keep warm.*

***fluff up** *v adv* → **plump up, shake up** (2)
to make (a cushion or pillow) fat and comfortable by beating it: [T1] *Fluff up the cushions to make the room look nice for our visitors.*

**flunk out** *v adv*
*AmE infml* to fail, or state that (someone) has failed, as in an examination: [IØ + OUT (*simple tenses*)] *How many students have flunked out this year?* [T1 + OUT (*usu. pass.*)] *Twenty students have been flunked out and had to leave the college.*

**flush away** *v adv*
to get rid of (something unwanted) by a flow of water: [X9 + AWAY] *The criminal put the torn papers in the lavatory and tried to flush them away.*

**flush from** *v prep*
**1** to turn red in the face because of (a feeling such as shame): [IØ + *from*] *The girl flushed from modesty when the man praised her appearance.*
*__2__ to make (someone or an animal) leave (a hiding place): [D1] *The police succeeded in flushing the criminals from their secret meeting place. You have to flush the birds from their hiding place before you shoot them.*

***flush off** *v adv* → **swill down** (2)
*AmE* to wash (a surface) with a lot of water: [T1] *Father asked me to flush off the garage floor.*

**flush out** *v adv*
**1** to clean (something) by pouring a lot of liquid through it: [X9 + OUT] *Flush out the pipes with cold water after adding the cleaning powder. This medicine will help to flush out your body.*
*__2__ to make (someone or an animal) leave a hiding place: [T1] *Use the dogs to flush the rabbits out. The police are hoping to flush out the criminals without any shooting.*

**flush up** *v adv* → **colour up** (1), **flame up** (3)
to turn red in the face with a strong feeling such as shame or modesty: [IØ + UP] *Mary flushed up when Jim praised her cooking.*

**flush with** *v prep*
**1** to turn red in the face with (a strong feeling, usu. pride): [IØ + *with*] *Mary flushed with pride when Jim went to receive his prize.*
**2 be flushed with** to be proud of (something): *Flushed with their victory, the team came home to the cheers of the crowd.*

**fluster up** *v adv*
**be flustered up** to be in a nervous or confused state: *Mary was all flustered up just before the wedding.*

**flutter about** *v adv*
**1** to fly with quick light movements of the wings: [L9 + ABOUT] *There is a bird fluttering about inside the chimney, how can we get it out?*
*__2__ to move with quick nervous movements: [IØ] *The women were all fluttering about finishing their preparations for the wedding.*

**flutter down** *v adv*
to descend in light twisting movements: [L9 + DOWN] *It was autumn, and leaves were fluttering down in the light wind.*

**fly about** *v adv*
**1** to fly without particular direction: [L9 + ABOUT] *There were a lot of birds flying about in the air.*
*__2__ (of news, ideas, etc.) to spread actively: [IØ] *Ideas were flying about in the meeting. News is flying about concerning a royal wedding.*

***fly apart** *v adv*
to break violently: [IØ (*usu. simple tenses*)] *The gun flew apart when I fired it, and wounded my hand.* → **fly to** (4)

**fly at** *v prep*
**1** to (cause to) travel by air at (a certain height, cost, etc.): [IØ + *at*] *We are now flying at 10,000 metres.* [T1 + *at*] *The firm will fly your family here at their own cost.*
*__2__ to attack (someone or an animal) with blows or words: [T1 (*no pass., usu. simple tenses*)] *Mary flew at Jim when she thought that he had been deceiving her. The cat flew at the dog which threatened it.*

**fly away** *v adv*
**1** to leave by flying: [L9 + AWAY] *Every time the little girl nearly caught the bird, it flew away.* → **fly off**[1] (1)
*__2__ (of hair) to be difficult to control: [IØ] *My hair keeps flying away since I washed it this morning.* —**flyaway** *adj*

**fly by**[1] *v adv*
**1** to fly or move quickly past someone or something: [L9 + BY] *A bullet just flew by, but missed me. A rare bird has just flown by.* → **come by**[1] (1), **get by**[1] (1), **get past**[1] (1), **go by**[1] (1), **go past**[1] (1)
*__2__ *not fml* (of time) to pass quickly: [IØ] *Don't you find that Saturday afternoons just fly by?* → **go by**[1] (2), **go on**[1] (8), **go past**[1] (2), **pass by**[1] (2), **run on**[1] (2), **wear on**[1], **wear out** (4)
*__3__ (of planes) to fly ceremonially overhead:

[IØ] *To complete the military ceremony, 100 planes will fly by.* —**flyby** *n* → **fly over[1]** (3), **fly past**

**fly by[2]** *v prep*

**1** to fly at (a certain time): [IØ + *by*] *I have never liked flying by night.*

**2** to travel by air guided by (machinery): [IØ + *by*] *In misty weather, the pilots have to fly by instruments.*

**3** to fly past (usu. something): [L9 + *by*] *100 planes will fly by the castle as a mark of respect.*

**fly from** *v prep*

**1** to leave by air from (a place): [IØ + *from*] *Which airport are you flying from? The bird flew from its nesting place in the branches.*

**2** to escape from (someone or something): [L9 + *from*] *You must fly from the danger!* → **flee from**

**fly high** *v adv*

**1** to fly at a great or certain height: [L9 + HIGH] *How high do these birds fly? We can avoid the storm by flying high.*

*__2__ *not fml* to aim hopefully for success: [IØ (*usu. continuous tenses*)] *Aren't you flying high, hoping for a place in the first team?*

**fly in[1]** *v adv*

to (cause to) arrive by plane: [L9 + IN] *When are the theatre company flying in?* [X9 + IN] *Fresh fish are flown in daily.*

**fly in[2]** *v prep*

**1** to move or travel by air in (something such as a plane or pattern): [IØ + *in*] *I haven't yet flown in one of those very big planes. Wild ducks fly in a V-shape when they are going south for the winter.*

**2 fly in the face/teeth of** to act completely against (something): [*usu. simple tenses*] *Your story flies in the face of the truth.*

**fly into** *v prep*

**1** to move into or hit (something) by flying: [L9 + *into*] *Birds cause damage when they fly into plane engines. You can catch these insects by encouraging them to fly into a trap.*

**2** to (cause to) arrive at (a place) by plane: [L9 + *into*] *When are the theatre company flying into town?* [X9 + *into*] *Only light planes can fly passengers into this heavily forested area.*

*__3__ to suddenly reach (a state or feeling, usu. anger): [T1 (*no pass., usu. simple tenses*)] *Mary flew into a temper when Jim angered her.*

**fly off[1]** *v adv*

**1** to leave by flying: [L9 + OFF] *Every time the little girl nearly caught the bird, it flew off.* → **fly away** (1)

**2** to come off violently: [L9 + OFF] *The car crashed when the wheel flew off.*

*__3__ to hurry away: [IØ (*usu. simple tenses*)] *Mary flew off home as soon as she heard about the accident.*

**4 fly off at a tangent** *not fml* to change the subject suddenly: *Don't fly off at a tangent, stick to the subject.*

**fly off[2]** *v prep*

**1** to (cause to) leave (something such as a place) by flying: [X9 + *off*] *Three wounded sailors were flown off the ship.* [L9 + *off*] *A plane this size can't fly off such a short runway.*

**2 fly off the handle** *not fml* to lose one's temper: *There's no need to fly off the handle, I didn't mean to offend you.*

**fly off with** *v adv prep*

**1** to leave together with (someone or something) by flying: [L9 + OFF + *with*] *The family flew off with all their possessions. Can't you fly off with the rest of the team?* → **make off with** (1)

*__2__ to take (usu. something) away without permission: [T1 (*usu. simple tenses*)] *Someone has flown off with my blue bag.* → **make off with** (1), etc.

***fly open** *v adj*

to come open suddenly: [IØ (*usu. simple tenses*)] *The door flew open and the children rushed in. I was trying to open the box when the lid flew open, hitting me in the face.*

**fly out** *v adv*

**1** to move quickly out of somewhere: [L9 + OUT] *As soon as the school doors were opened, the children flew out to play.*

**2** to (cause to) move by air to a distant place: [X9 + OUT] *The army arranged to fly the men out to the troubled island. No crops can grow here in the frozen North, so all the vegetables have to be flown out.* [L9 + OUT] *My father flew out to see me in hospital.* → **fly over[1]** (2)

**fly over[1]** *v adv*

**1** to fly or pass above a place: [L9 + OVER] *Planes fly over all day, making a terrible noise.*

**2** to (cause to) move by air to another place, often not far: [L9 + OVER] *I think I'll fly over and see my relatives in the next State.* [X9 + OVER] *We'll fly the director over for a meeting with our leading businessmen.* → **fly out** (2)

*__3__ (of planes) to fly ceremonially overhead: [IØ] *To complete the military ceremony, 100 planes will fly over.* → **fly by[1]** (3), **fly past**

**fly over[2]** *v prep* → **pass over[2]** (2)

to move over or cross (something or someone) by or as by flying: [L9 + *over*] *Planes fly over the house all day, making a terrible noise. As part of the military ceremony, planes will fly over the castle. The bridge flies over a whole corner of the lake.* —**flyover** *n* —**overfly** *v*

***fly past** *v adv* → **fly by[1]** (3), **fly over[1]** (3)

(of planes) to fly ceremonially overhead: [IØ] *To complete the military ceremony, 100 planes will fly past.* — **fly-past** *n*

***fly right** *v adv*

*AmE infml* to behave correctly: [IØ] *Make*

*sure you all fly right when you get to the party.*

**fly to** *v prep*

**1** to (cause to) travel by air to (somewhere): [L9 + *to*] *How much does it cost to fly to the United States?* [X9 + *to*] *We'll arrange to fly your director to the meeting.*

**2** to move quickly and eagerly to (a place or person): [L9 + *to*] *As soon as her train arrived, he flew to her arms.*

**3 fly to arms** *fml* to be eager to use weapons: [*usu. simple tenses*] *The people of the island state flew to arms when it was threatened by the powerful nation.*

**4 fly to bits/pieces** to come suddenly, often violently, apart: [*usu. simple tenses*] *The gun flew to bits when I fired it, and wounded my hand.* → **fly apart**

**fly up** *v adv*

**1** to (cause to) move by flying in an upward or northerly direction: [L9 + UP] *The bird flew up from the grass when we walked too near its nest. The general flew up to see his soldiers.* [X9 + UP] *We'll have to fly the electricians up here specially.*

*__2__ to rise or seem to rise: [IØ (*usu. simple tenses*)] *My heart flew up into my mouth when I saw the risk that the child was taking.*

*__3__ *BrE* (in the girl Guide organization) to move formally to the part of the organization for older girls: [IØ] *We should like to welcome three Brownies who are flying up to Guides this week, and we will hold the ceremony at the end of the meeting.*

**foam at** *v prep*

**foam at the mouth: a** to have bubbles forming at the lips, as in certain diseases: [*usu. continuous tenses*] *Avoid any dog that is foaming at the mouth, it has a dangerous disease.* **b** *infml* to be very angry: [*usu. continuous tenses*] *You'd better be careful with the director this morning, he's foaming at the mouth about the committee's decision.*

**foam up** *v adv* → **fizz up, froth up**

(of a liquid) to rise in bubbles: [IØ + UP] *The beer foamed up and overflowed the glass.*

**foam with** *v prep* → **froth with**

**foam with rage** to be very angry: [*usu. continuous tenses*] *I should avoid the director this morning, he's foaming with rage over some decision that's been made.*

***fob off** *v adv*

to wave aside; take no notice of (someone or something): [T1] *He just fobbed off our suggestion. The committee just fobbed us off.*

***fob off on/onto** *v adv prep* → **foist off on, palm off on**

*not fml* to force acceptance of (something such as worthless goods) on (someone) by deceit: [D1] *The salesman fobbed off the faulty machine on the lady.*

***fob off with** *v adv prep* → **palm off with**

*not fml* to deceive (someone) into accepting (something such as worthless goods or an excuse): [D1] *The salesman fobbed the lady off with a faulty machine. I don't believe he means to do the job, he keeps fobbing us off with promises.*

**focus on** *v prep*

**1** to aim (something such as light) directly onto (something): [X9 + *on*] *If you focus bright sunlight on dry wood with a glass, it will start burning.*

*__2__ to direct (something such as one's thoughts) firmly on (a subject): [D1] *We must focus our attention on the question of reducing costs.* → **concentrate on** (1), **keep on** (13)

*__3__ to pay attention to (something or doing something): [T1] *We must focus on our sales force as the chief means of improving trade.* [T4] *Many firms are focusing on increasing their markets overseas.* → **concentrate on** (2)

*__4__ to have (something) as its main point of interest: [T1 (*no pass., simple tenses*)] *This year our meeting focuses on the question of children's rights.* [T4 (*simple tenses*)] *The show focuses on making fun of politicians.* → **centre on** (2), **revolve about** (2)

**foist (off) on** *v (adv) prep* → **fob off on, palm off on**

to force acceptance of (something such as worthless goods) on (someone): [X9 (+ OFF) + *on*] *The salesman foisted the faulty machine (off) on the lady.*

**fold away** *v adv*

to (cause to) bend so as to take up less space and be easily stored: [X9 + AWAY] *These camping chairs can be folded away and put in the car.* [L9 + AWAY (*simple tenses*)] *These camping chairs fold away inside the car.* —**foldaway** *adj*

**fold back** *v adv* → **bend back, double back** (2), **double over** (1), **double up** (1), **turn back** (1)

to (cause to) bend backwards: [L9 + BACK (*simple tenses*)] *The collar folds back in the latest fashion. The top of the box folds back to show the goods.* [X9 + BACK] *Fold the piece of paper back so that we can all see it.* —**foldback** *adj*

**fold down** *v adv* → **bend down**, etc.

to turn part or half of (something) in the opposite direction: [X9 + DOWN] *Help me to fold down the sheets ready for the guests. Don't fold down the corners of the page, it damages the book.*

**fold in[1]** *v adv*

(in cooking) to add (materials) carefully to a mixture, usu. with a spoon: [X9 + IN] *Next, fold in the beaten egg.*

**fold in[2]** *v prep*

**1** to bend (something) in (a part, as half): [X9 + *in*] *If you fold the letter in two, it will fit into the envelope.*

**2** to hold (usu. someone) in (one's arms): [X9 + *in* (*usu. simple tenses*)] *The mother folded the child in her arms to keep him safe.*

**3** (in cooking) to add (materials) carefully to (other materials), usu. with a spoon: [X9 + *in* (*to*)] *Fold the beaten egg in*(*to*) *the flour.*

**fold up** *v adv*

**1** to (cause to) bend, esp. so as to take a smaller space: [X9 + UP] *Help me to fold up the sheets after washing them. You have to fold the letter up to fit it into the envelope.* [L9 + UP (*usu. simple tenses*)] *The corner of the carpet has folded up and won't lie flat.* → **double back** (2), **double over** (1), **double up** (1)

**2** to wrap (something, as in folded paper): [X9 + UP] *I like to fold presents up in pretty paper.*

***3** to (cause to) bend, as with pain, laughter, etc.: [IØ (*usu. simple tenses*)] *Mary folded up when Jim walked in wearing his funny clothes. The fighter folded up at the sudden heavy blow.* [T1 (*usu. simple tenses*)] *We found Grandfather in his chair, folded up with pain. The blow folded the fighter up. The joke folded the crowd up.* → **double up** (2), etc.

***4** *not fml* to fail or break down: [IØ] *The company is in no danger of folding up just yet. When his wife left him, he simply folded up.*

**follow about** *v adv*

to follow (someone) everywhere: [T1 + ABOUT] *The child follows her mother about all day long.*

**follow in** *v prep*

**follow in someone's footsteps** to copy someone's way of life: *"I'm following in father's footsteps."* (song)

**follow on**[1] *v adv*

**1** to come later: [IØ + ON (*often simple tenses*)] *You go ahead, and we'll follow on. The next part of the play follows on from the discovery of the murder in the first act. In this scene, I go on first, and you follow on a few lines later.*

**2** to result: [IØ + ON (*usu. simple tenses*)] *If you don't keep your accounts straight, serious debt could follow on.*

***3** (of a cricket team) to have a second turn of batting immediately after the first when their total is much lower than that of the opposing team: [IØ (*simple tenses*)] *England were forced to follow on when their total was 59 runs in reply to Australia's total of 349.* — **follow-on** *n*

**follow on/upon**[2] *v prep*

to result from (something): [IØ + *on/upon* (*simple tenses*)] *Her illness followed on her mother's death.*

**follow out** *v adv*

**1** to move after (usu. someone) when leaving: [T1 + OUT] *The dog got lost because the children left the door open, and he followed them out.*

**2** to complete (a line of enquiry); carry out (an arrangement) exactly to the end: [T1 + OUT] *We have followed out your instructions down to the last detail. It is important to follow out the exact words of the agreement. The police examination was thoroughly followed out.* → **follow through** (1)

**follow through** *v adv*

**1** to complete (a line of enquiry); obey (an order or arrangement): [X9 + THROUGH] *We have followed your instructions through to the last detail. It is important to follow through the exact words of the agreement. The police examination was thoroughly followed through.* → **follow out** (2)

***2** to continue an effort: [IØ (*with*) (*usu. simple tenses*)] *The fighter followed through with a blow to the body. After the first victory, our army followed through to win every battle.* —**follow-through** *n*

***3** (in tennis and other games) to complete a stroke by continuing to move the arm after hitting the ball: [IØ (*simple tenses*)] *If you learn to follow through when you first start to play, you will increase your skill and style.* —**follow-through** *n*

***follow through with** *v adv prep*

to complete (something such as a plan): [T1] *Does the firm intend to follow through with this idea?*

***follow up** *v adv*

to act further on (something): [T1 (*with*)] *The director will follow up the committee's suggestions. We should follow up this advantage while we can. The salesmen usually follow up a letter with a visit.* [IØ (*with*)] *You start the work, and I'll follow up. The chairman followed up with yet another question.* —**follow-up** *n*

**follow upon** *v prep* → **FOLLOW ON**

**fool about/around** *v adv* → **footle about, mess about** (1,2), etc.

*not fml* to play; behave foolishly; waste time: [L9 + ABOUT/AROUND] *Stop fooling about, we have serious work to do.*

**fool about/around with** *v adv prep*

**1** *not fml* to play with; not treat (something, esp. something dangerous) seriously: [L9 + ABOUT/AROUND + *with*] *Children should not be allowed to fool around with matches.* → **mess about with** (1), etc.

***2** *infml* to have an unwise sexual relationship with (someone): [T1] *Don't fool around with another man's wife.* → **mess about with** (2), etc.

**fool around** *v adv* → **FOOL ABOUT**

**fool around with** *v adv prep* → **FOOL ABOUT WITH**

***fool away** *v adv* → **idle away** (2), etc.

*not fml* to waste (time): [T1] *You can fool away half your life waiting for good luck, or you can work hard and earn success.*

***fool with** *v prep* → **mess about with** (1), etc.

*not fml* to not treat (something, esp. something dangerous or someone) seriously: [T1] *Don't fool with fire or you'll get burned. Guns are not to be fooled with. Don't try any of your tricks with me; you'll find that I'm not to be fooled with.*

***foot it** *v pron* → **hoof it**
*infml* to walk instead of riding: [IØ] *That was the last bus disappearing round the corner, we shall have to foot it.*

***foot up to** *v adv prep*
*not fml* to make a total: [T1 (*no pass., simple tenses*)] *The bill will foot up to $2,000.*

**footle about** *v adv* → **fool about, mess about** (1, 2), etc.
*infml* to play; behave foolishly; waste time: [IØ] *Stop footling about, we have serious work to do.*

***footle away** *v adv* → **idle away** (2), etc.
*infml* to waste (time) foolishly: [T1] *You can footle away half your life playing with such grand ideas; why don't you do some serious work for a change?*

**forbear from** *v prep*
**1** *fml* to prevent oneself from (something or doing something), as with patience; avoid (doing something) by controlling oneself: [L9 + *from* (*simple tenses*)] *How shall I forbear from tears when we part? It is often difficult to forbear from expressing one's opinion.* → **refrain from** (1), **withhold from** (2)
**2** *fml* to avoid (something) with effort: [L9 + *from* (*simple tenses*)] *Jim's doctor advised him to forbear from alcohol.* → **abstain from, refrain from** (2)

**force down** *v prep*
**1** to push (something) forcefully down (a space): [X9 + *down*] *We had to force the pipe down a narrow hole to get it through.* → **push down²** (1), **ram down²** (1), **stuff down** (1), **thrust down** (1)
**2 force something down someone's throat** *not fml* to make someone remember, believe, or accept something unpleasant: *Some students are bitter about the way unpopular subjects are being forced down their throats.* → **push down²** (2), **ram down** (2), **stuff down** (2), **thrust down** (2)

***force from** *v prep* also **force out of**
to get (something) from (an unwilling person): [D1] *She pretended that she couldn't hear, so that they would not force an answer from her.*

**force into** *v prep*
**1** to push (something) with effort into (something): [X9 + *into*] *I can't force the key into this lock, it won't fit.*
**2** to push (someone) by force into (something or doing something): [X9 + *into*] *Public opinion can force the government into action. She was forced into leaving the country.*

***force on/onto/upon** *v prep* → **enforce on**
to push (something unwanted) by force on (someone): [D1] *This painful duty has been forced upon me. You shouldn't force food on children. She has been forcing her unwelcome attentions on me for weeks. The teacher has no right to force his own views onto the children.*

***force out** *v adv*
to make (someone) leave, yield, etc.: [T1 (*of*)] *The owner forced the poor family out of the house when they could not pay the rent. Competition has forced out many small firms.*

**force out of** *v adv prep* → **FORCE FROM**

***force up** *v adv*
to make (something such as a price) rise: [T1] *Prices have been forced up by the poor crop.*

***force upon** *v prep* → **FORCE ON**

***foreclose on** *v prep*
to repossess property because of someone's failure to repay (money that had been borrowed to buy the property): [T1] *The building society will be forced to foreclose on this mortgage because regular payments have not been made.*

**foredoom to** *v prep* → **DOOM TO**

***forge ahead** *v adv*
**1** to go steadily or quickly forward: [IØ] *The ship forged ahead through the waves.*
**2** to advance steadily and purposefully: [IØ (*usu. continuous tenses*)] *My work has been forging ahead recently.*

**forget about** *v prep*
to fail to remember (someone, something, or doing something): [IØ + *about* (*usu. simple tenses*)] *How could you forget about such a large debt. Did you forget about going to the bank? I wish I could forget about your mother coming to stay.*

***forget it** *v pron*
it is no trouble; don't mention it; you're welcome: [IØ (*imper.*)] *"I'm most grateful to you for your help." "Oh, it's nothing, forget it."*

***forget oneself** *v pron*
**1** to behave unselfishly: [IØ (*simple tenses*)] *When you are poor, you have to forget yourself and attend only to the children's needs.*
**2** to behave improperly; lose one's self control: [IØ (*simple tenses*)] *When a man is drunk, he often forgets himself and does and says things that he wouldn't usually dare.*

**forgive for** *v prep*
to show mercy to (someone) for (a fault); cease punishing (someone) for (doing something wrong); excuse (someone) for (a wrong action): [T1 + *for* (*usu. simple tenses*)] *It is difficult to forgive anyone for cruelty. Can you ever forgive me for forgetting your birthday?*

**fork out/over/up** *v adv*
**1** to dig (soil, etc.) or remove (unwanted matter) with a garden fork: [X9 + OUT/OVER/UP] *Fork out the dead plants and put in the new ones. I must be sure to fork over the whole garden before winter. You have to dig down deeply to fork up the roots.*
***2** *infml* to pay (money) unwillingly: [T1] *Father is complaining that he has to fork out more money to the children every week. Every year I have to fork over more taxes to the gov-*

*ernment.* [IØ] *Every year the tax man expects us to fork up.*

**form from** *v prep* → **fashion from, make from, make of** (1), **make out of** (1), **produce from** (1)
to make (something) from (existing parts): [X9 + *from* (*often pass.*)] *Clouds are formed from drops of liquid hanging in the air.*

**form into** *v prep*
**1** to make (something) into (a shape); make (people) into (a group): [X9 + *into*] *Form the pastry into a ball with your hands and then roll it flat. Do you think that this mixed group of young cricketers could be formed into a team?*
*__2__ to make (something) part of (something): [D1 (*usu. pass.*)] *The new train will be formed into the regular timetable from next Monday.*
*__3__ *mil* to (cause to) move into (a particular order): [D1] *Form the men into lines three deep.* [T1 (*no pass.*)] *The soldiers formed into battle order.*

***form up** *v adv*
to make regular lines: [IØ] *The children had to form up (into lines) before being allowed into school.*

***forswear oneself** *v pron* → **perjure oneself**
*fml* to tell a lie in court in spite of a solemn promise and the threat of severe punishment: [IØ (*simple tenses*)] *You must tell the truth to the judge, because if you forswear yourself you could go to prison.*

**fortify against** *v prep*
to strengthen (something or oneself) so as to be able to deal with (something such as an attack): [T1 + *against*] *Walls of earth will fortify the building against enemy bombing. Have some hot soup to fortify you against the cold.*

**fortify with** *v prep*
to strengthen (something or oneself) by adding or using (something): [T1 + *with* (*often pass.*)] *This breakfast food has been fortified with minerals. Fortified with the knowledge of her rights, she was able to deal with the trouble.*

**forward to** *v prep*
to send (letters or parcels ahead to (someone or another address): [T1 + *to*] *Please forward any letters to me while I'm on holiday. I have asked the post office to forward my post to my mother's address.*

***foul out** *v adv*
*AmE not fml* (in certain ball games) to take no further part in play because of an action against the rules: [IØ (*usu. simple tenses*)] *Two of our players have fouled out; we shall have a struggle to win without them.*

**foul up** *v adv*
**1** to dirty (something); ruin (something) with dirt: [T1 + UP] *The seashore is fouled up with oil from the wrecked ship.* → **dirty up** (1), **mess up** (1), **muck up** (1)
*__2__ *infml* to spoil (something): [T1] *Don't foul up this chance. I hope the chairman won't foul things up, we have everything arranged nicely. The post is fouled up by Christmas delays.* —**foul-up** *n* → **mess up** (2), etc.

***found on/upon** *v prep* → **base on, ground on**
to give (something) a reason or starting point in (something): [D1 (*usu. simple tenses*)] *One should always found one's opinion on facts.*

**frame in** *v prep*
to surround (something or someone) with a border of (something): [X9 + *in* (*often pass.*)] *The photographs will look nice framed in black. Her face was framed in a mass of red hair. He stood, a threatening figure, framed in the doorway.*

**frame up** *v adv*
**1** to prepare (writing): [T1 + UP] *It took me all morning to frame up the poem.*
**2** *infml* to make (someone) seem guilty when he is not: [T1 + UP] *I didn't do the job, I've been framed up.* —**frame-up** *n* → **fit up** (5)

***fraternize with** *v prep*
to be friendly with (someone such as an enemy or a person of lower rank): [T1 (*no pass.*)] *The soldiers are not allowed to fraternize with the women of the conquered town.*

***freak out** *v adv*
**1** *infml* to (cause to) become greatly excited or anxious, as because of drugs: [IØ] *Lots of people were at the party, drinking and smoking and generally freaking out. I nearly freaked out when she told me who he was.* [T1] *Don't get freaked out just because your parents are coming. You'd better sit down, this news will freak you out.* —**freak-out** *n*
**2** *infml* to join or copy people opposing ordinary behaviour: [IØ] *She used to be the most correct person, but then suddenly last year she decided to freak out.*

**free from** *v prep* → **free of**
to set (something or someone) free from (something dangerous, difficult, etc.): [T1 + *from*] *Someone has freed the rats from their cages. The United Nations are trying to free the world from the threat of war.*

**free of** *v prep* → **free from**
to empty (one's or someone's mind) of (something such as thoughts): [T1 + *of* (*usu. simple tenses*)] *This letter should free your mind of worry. I am trying to free my mind of any ideas I may have formed about him.*

***freeze in** *v adv*
to hold (something) firmly in ice: [T1 (*usu. pass.*)] *The ship was frozen in for the winter.*

***freeze off** *v adv*
*not fml* to discourage (someone); refuse to accept (something): [T1] *The girls froze him off when he wanted to join the party. We froze off their offer of help.* —**freeze-off** *n*

**freeze onto** *v prep*
**1** to become fixed to (something) because of

severe cold: [L9 + *onto*] *In severe cold, your fingers can freeze onto metal handles, so be sure to cover your hands.*

*2 to attach oneself to (someone or an idea): [T1 (*no pass., usu. simple tenses*)] *The club members froze onto his suggestion for reorganizing the money. His influence is so strong that crowds of followers freeze onto him wherever he goes.*

***freeze out** *v adv*

**1** to make (someone) homeless or uncomfortable with cold: [T1] *The heating went off and we were frozen out! Many families were frozen out in the severe snowstorm.*

**2** *not fml* to discourage; prevent (someone or something) from being included: [T1] *Many big firms freeze out the competition by unfair means. Members who are no longer welcome can easily be frozen out.*

**3** esp. *AmE* to prevent (something) because of great cold: [T1 (*usu. pass.*)] *The game was frozen out.*

**4** (esp. of a plant) to die of cold: [IØ] *Half the fruit crop froze out in the sudden severe autumn.*

**freeze over** *v adv*

**1** (of a body of water) to freeze completely; be covered with ice: [L9 + OVER] *The lake usually freezes over by mid-January.* [X9 + OVER (*usu. pass.*)] *When the lake is frozen over, you can walk across it.* → **ice over**

**2 when hell freezes over** *infml* never: *I'll believe that story when hell freezes over.*

**freeze to** *v prep*

**freeze to death** to be very cold; die of cold: *Put another coat on, you'll freeze to death out there. The bodies of the adventurers were found frozen to death in their tents.*

**freeze up** *v adv*

**1** to freeze completely; become stiff with cold: [X9 + UP (*usu. pass.*)] *The windows are frozen up and I can't open them.* [L9 + UP] *The stream has frozen up; you can see the fish trapped in the ice.* —**freeze-up** *n* → **ice up**

*2 (of an actor) to become too nervous on stage to speak or move: [IØ] *The first time I ever performed on stage, I was so afraid that I froze up completely and the other actors had to invent the rest of the scene.*

**freshen up** *v adv*

**1** (of wind, weather, etc.) to become fresher or colder: [[IØ + UP] *I wish I'd brought my thick coat, this wind has freshened up since we left the house.*

*2 to (cause to) feel more comfortable by washing, changing clothes, etc.: [IØ (*usu. simple tenses*)] *Would you like to freshen up? The bathroom is upstairs.* [T1 (*usu. simple tenses*)] *A hot bath and a change of clothes always freshens me up.*

*3 to make (an idea, writing, etc.) fresher or more attractive: [T1] *That regular television play needs freshening up with some new faces.*

**fret about/over** *v prep*

to worry; become concerned, impatient, or anxious; suffer because of (someone, something, or doing something): [IØ + *about/over*] *For days the boy fretted about his lost dog. Is Alice still fretting over her former boyfriend? It's no use fretting over missing the train, we can always catch the next one.*

**fret into/on/upon** *v prep*

to make marks on (a surface) by a cutting or eating action: [L9 + *into/on/upon*] *The chain has fretted into the wood and damaged it.*

**fret over** *v prep* → **FRET ABOUT**

**fret upon** *v prep* → **FRET INTO**

***frig around** *v adv*

*BrE infml euph* to waste one's time doing aimless, silly, or annoying things: [IØ] *Why don't you do some work instead of just frigging around all day?*

**frighten away/off** *v adv* → **scare away**

to make (someone or an animal) leave through fear: [X9 + AWAY/OFF] *Keep still, or you'll frighten the rabbit away. Don't put your prices too high or you'll frighten the customers off.*

**frighten from** *v prep* → **frighten out of** (1)

to prevent (someone) from (doing something), through fear: [X9 + *from*] *The presence of the police has frightened many criminals from attempting further violence.*

**frighten into** *v prep* → **intimidate into, scare into, terrify into**

to persuade (someone) through fear into (doing something): [X9 + *into*] *The salesman frightened the old lady into signing the paper, by threatening to take away the goods.*

**frighten off** *v adv* → **FRIGHTEN AWAY**

**frighten out of** *v adv prep*

**1** to prevent (someone) from (doing something), through fear: [X9 + OUT + *of*] *The presence of the police has frightened many criminals out of attempting further violence.* → **frighten from**

**2 frighten someone out of his wits** *not fml* to make someone greatly afraid: *You frightened me out of my wits, saying that you wanted to kill yourself.* → **frighten to, scare out of, terrify out of**

**frighten to** *v prep*

**frighten someone to death** *not fml* to make someone greatly afraid or worried: *You frightened me to death, staying out all night! I was frightened to death that I would be dismissed. Flying frightens some people to death.* → **frighten out of** (2)

***fritter away** *v adv* → **idle away** (2), etc.

*not fml* to waste (time or money): [T1] *You've been frittering away the whole afternoon instead of working. It's easy to fritter away a fortune if you're not careful.*

***frivol away** *v adv* → **idle away** (2), etc.

to waste (time or money) foolishly: [T1] *You've been frivolling away the whole after-*

*noon instead of working. It's easy to frivol away a fortune if you're not careful.*

**frizzle up** *v adv*
*not fml* to (cause to) become dry and curled with heat: [L9 + UP] *I don't like to heat my hair with electric curlers as they make it frizzle up and I would rather have it shiny and smooth.* [X9 + UP] *The meat got frizzled up because I forgot to turn the cooker off before we went out.*

***frost over/up** *v adv*
to (cause to) become covered with ice or frozen mist: [IØ] *The windows have frosted over and we can't see out.* [T1] *The cold night has frosted over the trees.*

**froth up** *v adv* → **fizz up, foam up**
to (cause to) rise in bubbles: [IØ + UP] *The beer frothed up and overflowed the glass.* [X9 + UP] *Before washing the clothes, froth up the soap mixture.*

**froth with** *v prep* → **foam with**
**froth with rage** to be very angry: [*usu. continuous tenses*] *I think you should avoid the director this morning, he's frothing with rage over some decision that's been made.*

**frown at** *v prep*
**1** to have a displeased, disapproving, or serious expression on one's face when looking at (something or someone): [IØ + *at*] *Why are you frowning at me? I've done nothing. He frowned at the letter of complaint that he had just received. You must need glasses if you keep frowning at your reading like that.* → **glower at, scowl at**
***2** to disapprove of (usu. something): [T1] *The government frowns at any waste of taxpayers' money.* → **frown on**

***frown down** *v adv*
esp. *AmE* to make (someone) silent with a disapproving look: [T1] *The teacher frowned the child down when he kept repeating his request.*

***frown on/upon** *v prep* → **frown at** (2)
to disapprove of (usu. something): [T1 (*simple tenses*)] *The government frowns on any waste of taxpayers' money.* [T4] *My grandmother has always frowned on spending money needlessly.*

**fry up** *v adv*
**1** to dry or destroy (something) with heat: [X9 + UP] *The unusually hot sun has fried up the crops.*
***2** to reheat (food) by cooking it in hot fat: [T1] *We can fry up some of these pieces of cold meat for our lunch.* —**fry-up** *n*

***fuck about/around** *v adv*
**1** esp. *BrE taboo sl* to spend time lazily: [IØ] *What have you been doing today? Oh, nothing, just fucking around.* → **fuck off** (1), **mess about** (1), etc.
**2** *taboo sl* to treat (someone) without consideration: [T1] *I can't forgive him for fucking me about like that.* → **mess about** (4), etc.

***fuck about with** *v adv prep* → **mess about with** (1), etc.
*taboo sl* to cause disorder to (something): [T1] *Who's been fucking about with these papers? They're all out of order!*

***fuck around** *v adv* → FUCK ABOUT

***fuck off** *v adv*
**1** *AmE taboo sl* to spend time lazily: [IØ] *What have you been doing today? Oh, nothing, just fucking off.* → **fuck about** (1), **mess about** (1), etc.
**2** also *euph* **eff off**, *euph* **naff off** *taboo sl* go away; stop being annoying or troublesome: [IØ (*imper.*)] *Oh, fuck off! I'm tired of your complaints.* → **push off** (3), etc.

***fuck up** *v adv* → **mess up** (2), etc.
*taboo sl* to spoil (something) carelessly; make a mess of things: [T1] *If John fucks up his driving test again, I doubt if he'll ever pass it.* [IØ] *We had great hopes of our team, but they fucked up again today.* —**fuck-up** *n*

**fudge on** *v prep*
*not fml* to refuse to give a direct answer about (a subject): [L9 + *on*] *The board of directors has been fudging on the question of pay increases for the workers.*

***fuel up** *v adv*
(of a plane or other vehicle) to take in more petrol: [IØ] *The long-distance plane has to stop at London Airport to fuel up.*

**fulminate against** *v prep*
*fml* to express opposition to (something such as action) often with bitter anger: [IØ + *against*] *Many people are fulminating against the cruelty of blood sports.*

**fumble for** *v prep* → **feel about**[2] (2), **feel for** (3), **fish for** (2)
to try to get or reach (something) in an awkward manner: [L9 + *for*] *Blinded by the soap, he had to fumble about for his glasses. The climber fumbled for a foothold on the difficult slope. The speaker fumbled for the right word to answer the question.*

**fumble with** *v prep*
to handle (something) awkwardly: [L9 + *with*] *I was fumbling with the key as I couldn't see where the lock was in the dark.*

**fume at** *v prep*
to express great anger because of (something or doing something): [IØ + *at*] *All the passengers were fuming at the delay. He's fuming at not being given the pay rise he asked for.*

***fur up** *v adv*
*not fml* (of a metal container) to develop an inside coating of hard chemical from boiling water: [IØ] *The water here is so hard that all the pans fur up after a single use.*

**furbish up** *v adv*
**1** to polish or make (something) more attractive: [X9 + UP] *If you furbish up these old chairs, you'll have a better chance of selling them.*
***2** to renew (something): [T1] *A marrie*

*woman returning to teaching needs to furbish up her old skills.*

**urnish to** *v prep*
*fml* to provide (something such as an opportunity) to (someone): [D1] *Be careful how you answer, or you might furnish an advantage to your opponent.*

**urnish with** *v prep*
**1** to supply (a building, room, etc.) with (furniture): [X9 + *with*] *The room was furnished with carpets and chairs, but no table.*
**2** *fml* to supply (usu. someone) with (something required, as information): [D1] *Can you furnish the committee with statements of the costs?*

**use with** *v prep*
to (cause to) combine with (something), as by melting under heat: [X9 + *with* (*usu. pass.*)] *The end of the wire had become accidentally fused with the switch, and was dangerous. The bottom of the candle is fused with its holder.* [L9 + *with* (*simple tenses*)] *The end of the wire had fused accidentally with the switch, and become dangerous. The broken part must fuse with the rest of the bone before you can walk again.*

**fuss about/around**[1] *v adv*
**1** to behave in an unnecessarily anxious manner: [IØ + ABOUT/AROUND] *She must be very nervous, she fusses about all the time.*
**2** to annoy (someone) by treating him with anxious attention: [T1 + ABOUT/AROUND] *I wish you would stop fussing me about, I'm quite able to look after myself.*

**fuss about/over**[2] *v prep*
**1** to show care and worry; treat (someone or something) with anxious attention: [IØ + *about/over*] *Mother, please don't fuss about an ordinary cold. The teacher always fusses over the slower children.*
**2 not be fussed about** *BrE infml* not to care greatly about (something): *I'm not fussed about the colour; you choose.*

**fuss around** *v adv* → **FUSS ABOUT**[1]

**fuss over** *v prep* → **FUSS ABOUT**[2]

***fuss up** *v adv*
esp. *AmE not fml* to make too much effort to dress with care or make (something) more attractive: [T1] *The director fussed up the stage with too many people.* [IØ] *Don't fuss up for the party, it's very informal.*

# G

**abble away/on** *v adv*
to talk quickly, continuously, and meaninglessly: [IØ + AWAY/ON] *I expect you spent half the day gabbling away with your neighbours.*

**abble off** *v adv*
to speak (something) quickly and carelessly: [T1 + OFF] *The child gabbled off the poem as though he neither understood nor enjoyed it.*

**abble on** *v adv* → **GABBLE AWAY**

**abble out** *v adv*
to tell (something) hurriedly and not clearly: [T1 + OUT] *Don't gabble out your story, man, tell it calmly and clearly.*

**ad about/around** *v adv; prep* → **gallivant about**
*not fml* to travel round (somewhere) purely to enjoy oneself, esp. in an aimless manner: [IØ] *She gads about a lot.* [T1 (*no pass.*)] *She gads about Europe a lot.* —**gadabout** *n*

**ain by/from** *v prep* → **lose by**
to win advantage from; be improved by (something): [L9 + *by/from*] *Many voters feel that the country would gain from a change of leadership. You can only gain by further study.* [T1 + *by/from*] *What do you hope to gain from this delay that you have caused? There is nothing to be gained by waiting any longer.*

**ain in** *v prep* → **grow in**[2] (2)
to increase or advance with regard to (a certain part or quality): [T1 + *in*] *What you lose in income you will gain in experience.* [IØ + *in*] *The government has gained in numbers but not in wisdom.*

**gain on/upon** *v prep*
**1** (of the sea) to advance on and wash away more of (the land): [L9 + *on/upon*] *The sea has been gaining on the east coast of England for many years.*
***2** to go faster than (someone or something in front of one): [T1 (*pass. rare*)] *The second horse is gaining on the leader, and may pass it and win! The police started chasing the criminals and soon gained on them in their faster car.*
***3** (in business, etc.) to advance ahead of (one's competitors): [T1 (*pass. rare*)] *It is impossible for a small company to gain on the big firms while business is so inactive.*

***gain over** *v adv* → **win over**
to win the loyalty of (someone): [T1] *The new leader's popularity gained over many members of the opposing party.*

**gain upon** *v prep* → **GAIN ON**

**gallivant about/around** *v adv; prep* → **gad about**
*not fml* to behave or move in a not very serious manner, enjoying oneself: [L9 + ABOUT/AROUND] *He just gallivants about instead of working.* [L9 + *about/around*] *She gallivants around Europe a lot.*

**gallivant off** *v adv*
*not fml* to go away in a not very serious man-

ner, enjoying oneself: [L9 + OFF] *The mother has shown a poor sense of responsibility, often gallivanting off somewhere and leaving the children on their own.*

**gallop through** *v prep*
**1** (of a horse or rider) to move at the fastest speed of a horse through (a place): [IØ + *through*] *The rider galloped through the town, warning the people of the enemy's advance.*
***2** *not fml* to hurry through (something such as an activity): [T1] *I'm sure it's not good for the children to gallop through their meals the way they do. If you gallop through your work, you are more likely to make mistakes.*

***galvanize into** *v prep*
to shock (someone) into (action or doing something): [D1] *This surprise vote should galvanize the government into action.* [V4b] *How can we galvanize the students into taking the responsibility for their own work?*

**gamble away** *v adv* also **game away**
**1** to play cards or other games for money, continuously: [IØ + AWAY] *The men have been gambling away all night.*
***2** to lose (money) by playing cards or other games for money: [T1] *It is too easy to gamble away a fortune.*

**gamble on** *v prep* → **bet on, wager on**
**1** to risk (money) on the result of (something such as a horse race) or the performance of (a competitor): [IØ + *on*] *Are you going to gamble on the result of the fight?* [T1 + *on*] *He gambles most of his income on the horses.*
***2** to take a chance on; be too sure of (something, or someone/something doing something): [T1] *You can't gamble on the weather in England. I'm prepared to gamble on the possibility of finding empty seats at the theatre.* [T4] *Don't gamble on getting the job.* [V4a] *It's not safe to gamble on the train arriving late.* → **depend on** (1), etc.

**game away** *v adv* → GAMBLE AWAY

***gang up** *v adv*
*not fml* to work together as a close group, (with or against someone), often in a bad sense: [IØ (*against/on/with*)] *When those big boys start ganging up, you can expect trouble. You've all ganged up against me, it's not fair. You boys should be ashamed of yourselves, ganging up on one helpless child. I'm a little worried about my son ganging up with those rough boys.*

**gape at** *v prep* → **gawk at, gaze at, goggle at, stare at**
to look at (someone or something) with the mouth open, as with surprise or wonder: [IØ + *at*] *She just gaped at me when I told her the news. When the climbers reached the top of the mountain, they gaped at the splendid view.*

**garner in/up** *v adv* → **gather in** (1)
*lit* to gather and store (usu. a crop): [T1 + IN/UP] *When all the fruit is garnered in, the farmers can rest.*

**garnish with** *v prep*
**1** to improve the appearance of (food) by decorating with small pieces of (other food): [T1 + *with*] *Serve the duck garnished with pieces of orange.*
***2** to ornament (something such as writing) with (additions): [D1] *I feel that the writer has garnished the story of his life with a few inventions.*

***gas up** *v adv* → **tank up** (1)
*AmE infml* to supply a vehicle with a full load of petrol: [IØ] *Stop here to gas up before crossing the desert.*

**gasp at** *v prep*
to express surprise, shock, or other strong feeling about (something or someone), esp by taking a sudden breath through the open mouth: [IØ + *at*] *When the young man walked across the high wire fixed between the two tall buildings without a safety net, the crowd gasped at his bravery and skill. My daughter, visiting the city for the first time gasped at the prices of houses here.*

**gasp for** *v prep*
**1** to struggle to get (air), as from tiredness surprise, etc.; breathe quickly with a need for (water, etc.): [IØ + *for* (*often continuous tenses*)] *After running such a long way, the messenger was gasping for breath. Gasping for air, the firemen fought their way through clouds of smoke. Her unexpected rudeness made me gasp for breath. What a hot day! I'm gasping for a cold drink, aren't you?* → **pant for** (1)
***2** to desire (something) strongly: [T1 (*not pass., usu. continuous tenses*)] *Give me a cigarette, will you? I'm gasping for a smoke. For a long time, she's been gasping for a chance to show her acting ability, and now her chance has come!* → **pant for** (2)

**gasp out** *v adv*
**1** to let out one's breath suddenly, as with surprise: [IØ + OUT (*usu. simple tenses*)] *He gasped out when he read the letter.*
***2** to tell (something) with difficulty in breathing: [T1] *The messenger gasped out his story after running all the way from the battle.* → **pant out**

**gather from** *v prep*
**1** to collect (something such as a crop) from (somewhere): [T1 + *from*] *These little animals gather nuts from the ground in the autumn and store them for the winter.*
**2** to arrive in large numbers from (somewhere): [IØ + *from*] *Every time there is an accident, a crowd seems to gather from nowhere.*
**3** to understand (something or that something) because of (something that someone says, or other signs): [T1 + *from*] *What do you gather from his letter?* [T5 + *from*] *Do I gather from the look on your face that you're not pleased with the result? He did not make his intentions clear, but I gathered from wh*

*little he did say that he did not want to employ me.* → **understand by**

**gather in** *v adv*

**1** to collect and store (ripe crops): [T1 + IN] *When all the crops are safely gathered in, the farmers can rest.* → **garner in**

**2** to draw (material) together into small folds, as by sewing: [T1 + IN] *Gather the waist in a little more, with fine stitches.*

*__3__ to receive; collect (something such as money): [T1] *Some of the workers think that big business directors don't do any work, but just sit in their offices gathering in the profits.*

**gather round** *v adv; prep*

**1** to form a crowd near (someone); come closer to (someone); bring (things) closer to (something or someone): [IØ + ROUND] *Gather round, ladies and gentlemen, and see this wonderful new invention.* [IØ + *round*] *A small crowd gathered round the speaker to hear what he had to say.* [T1 + *round*] *The speaker gathered a small crowd round him, eager to listen to what he had to say. The boy gathered his toys round him selfishly.*

*__2__ to come to the support of (someone): [IØ] *The party members gathered round when their leader was attacked.* [T1 (*no pass.*)] *The whole class gathered round the student who had been unfairly failed, and demanded a re-examination.*

**gather to** *v prep*

**1** to collect (someone, people, something, or things) towards (something): [T1 + *to*] *We must gather the people to our side. The dress-maker gathered the cloth to the narrowest part of the waist.*

**2 be gathered to one's fathers** *fml euph* to die: [*usu. perfect tenses*] *We must not be too sad that our much-loved king has been gathered to his fathers.*

**gather together** *v adv*

**1** to (cause to) come closer; form a crowd, group or bunch; collect: [IØ + TOGETHER] *Cows tend to gather together at one end of a field when it is going to rain.* [T1 + TOGETHER] *Gather the ends of the wool together and tie them in a knot. Give me a few minutes to gather my thoughts together. We must gather the people together to demand our rights.* → **get together** (1)

**2 gather oneself together** to control oneself; be in command of one's feelings, etc.: *I shall have to gather myself together to face the whole board of directors.* → **get together** (8), **pull together** (4)

**gather up** *v adv*

**1** to collect; seize and lift; pick up and put in one place (usu. things): [T1 + UP] *Gathering up his scattered papers, he pushed them into his case.* → **pick up** (1)

*__2__ to draw together; tighten (one's body): [T1] *Gather up your muscles and jump.*

*__3__ to collect; prepare (one's feelings): [T1] *Gathering up all his courage, he turned to face the enemy.*

**4 gather up the threads** *not fml* to continue the development (of a piece of work, one's life, etc.) after a period of absence, inactivity, forgetfulness, etc.: *Several books that were very important for my work were lost in the fire, and it's going to be hard to gather up the threads.* → **pick up** (26)

*__gawk at__ *v prep* also **gawp at** → **gape at, gaze at, goggle at, stare at**

*not fml* to look at (someone or something) in a foolish manner, esp. with the mouth open, as in wonder: [T1] *In the summer, crowds of tourists come to gawk at our famous old buildings. I expect that the Queen does not enjoy being gawked at.*

**gaze around/round** *v adv; prep*

to look round (oneself), as in surprise or wonder: [L9 + AROUND/ROUND/*around/round*] *When the climbers reached the top of the mountain, they gazed around (them) in delight at the unexpected beauty of the view.*

**gaze at** *v prep* → **gape at, gawk at, goggle at, stare at**

to look steadily at (someone or something): [L9 + *at*] *The climbers stood on top of the mountain, gazing at the splendid view.*

**gaze on/upon** *v prep*

*fml* to look at (someone or something), as for the first time: [L9 + *on/upon*] *The traveller had never before gazed on such beautiful scenery.*

**gaze out** *v adv*

to look (at something) steadily, from a distance: [L9 + OUT (*over*)] *He stood at the window of the great house, gazing out over the lake.*

**gaze round** *v adv; prep* → **GAZE AROUND**

**gaze upon** *v prep* → **GAZE ON**

*__gear down__ *v adv*

**1** (in a car or other vehicle) to change to a lower gear: [IØ] *You have to gear down when you drive uphill.* → **change down, change up, gear up** (1), **kick down** (2)

**2** to reduce the force or level of (something): [T1 (*usu. pass.*)] *The courses have been geared down to the lower ability of students in these special classes.*

*__gear to__ *v prep*

to arrange (something) so as to make it suitable for (something or someone): [D1 (*often pass.*)] *Education should be geared to the children's needs and abilities.*

*__gear up__ *v adv*

**1** (in a car or other vehicle) to change to a higher gear: [IØ] *When you are going fast enough, you'll be able to gear up.* → **change down, change up, gear down** (1), **kick down** (2)

**2** to prepare (something such as machinery) for increased or improved performance: [T1] *The directors decided to gear the factory up for increased production, by bringing in new machines.* [IØ] *The factory is gearing up for increased production with new machines.*

**3** to prepare (something or someone) for action: [T1 (*often pass.*)] *Are the players geared up for the game? I only feel geared up for work in the mornings.*

***gee up** *v adv* → **come up** (22), **get up** (14), **giddy up**
(command to a horse) to move ahead; go faster: [IØ (*imper.*)] *"Gee up!" he shouted as the horse came near the winning post.*

***gen up** *v adv* → **clue up** (2)
*BrE infml* to (cause to) be knowledgeable (about a subject): [IØ (*about, on*)] *How long will it take me to gen up on this material for my speech?* [T1 (*about, on*) (*often pass.*)] *Make sure that you gen the men up on what they're supposed to do. Michael is all genned up about computers.* —**genned-up** *adj*

**generalize about** *v prep*
to make a general statement concerning (a subject): [IØ + *about*] *It's impossible to generalize about children's books, as they are all different.*

**generalize from** *v prep* → **deduce from, infer from**
to form (a general principle) from (a limited number of examples): [T1 + *from*] *This rule can be generalized from the facts which we have collected.* [IØ + *from*] *Darwin generalized from many facts to reach his idea about the origin of man.*

**get about**[1] *v adv*
**1** to move freely; travel: [L9 + ABOUT] *It's easy in this city to get about by bus. People are getting about much more than they used to.* → **get round**[1] (1), **go about**[1] (1), **go round**[1] (1), **take about**[1] (1), **take round**[1] (1)
**2** to be able to move again after illness: [L9 + ABOUT] *Mother is much better now, thank you, she's able to get about a bit more.* → **get round**[1] (2), **go about**[1] (2)
***3** (of news, etc.) to spread: [IØ] *Stories have been getting about concerning the government's secret intentions. News of the trouble soon got about.* → **go about**[1] (3), etc.

**get about**[2] *v prep* → **be about**[2] (2), **get round**[2] (1), **go about**[2] (1), **go round**[2] (2), **send round**[2], **take round**[2] (1)
to (cause to) be able to move or travel around (a place): [L9 + *about*] *The quickest way to get about the city is by underground train.* [X9 + *about*] *No, a taxi will get you about the city faster.*

**get above** *v prep*
**get above oneself** to think too highly of oneself: [*usu. continuous tenses*] *She's been getting above herself since she won the singing competition.*

**get abreast of** *v adv prep*
**1** to come level with (something or someone in front): [L9 + ABREAST + *of*] *And now one of the other runners has got abreast of the leading horse.* → **keep abreast of** (1), etc.
***2** to reach a position of being well-informed about (something in advance): [T1 (*no pass.*)] *Scientists have to work hard to get abreast of the latest discoveries and developments in their field.* → **keep abreast of** (2), etc.

**get abroad** *v adv*
**1** to be able to travel to a foreign country or countries: [L9 + ABROAD] *We didn't get abroad for our holiday as usual, we couldn't afford it this year.* → **go abroad, take abroad**
***2** (of news, etc.) to spread; become widely known: [IØ] *How did the news of his appointment get abroad before it was made official?* → **go about** (3), etc.

**get across**[1] *v adv*
**1** to (cause to) cross a road, water, etc.: [L9 + ACROSS (*to*)] *Using the new bridge to get across will save people a lot of time.* [X9 + ACROSS (*to*)] *The new boats get people across to the island in half the time.* → **come over**[1] (3), etc.
***2** to (cause to) become understood or accepted: [IØ (*to*) (*usu. simple tenses*)] *Did your speech get across (to the crowd)?* [T1 (*to*) (*usu. simple tenses*)] *I can't seem to get my message across.* → **come across**[1] (2), etc.

**get across**[2] *v prep*
**1** to (cause to) cross (a road, water, etc.): [L9 + *across*] *It's so much safer to get across the road at the traffic lights.* [X9 + *across*] *The new boats get people across the river in half the time.* → **go across**[2], etc.
***2** esp. *BrE infml* to annoy or offend (someone): [T1 (*no pass.*)] *His mother at last got across me, making rude remarks in my own home. Take care not to get across the director: he could have you dismissed.*

**get after** *v prep*
**1** to chase (someone or an animal): [L9 + *after*] *Get after that dog, it's stolen the meat! The police can get after criminals much more easily in their new fast cars.* → **come after** (2), etc.
***2** *not fml* to scold; find fault with (someone); keep asking (someone) (to do something): [T1 (*no pass., often continuous tenses*)] *She's always getting after the children for one thing or another.* [V3 (*often continuous tenses*)] *She's been getting after me for a year to buy her a new coat.* → **go on at** (2), etc.

**get ahead** *v adv* → **move ahead,** etc.
**1** to (cause to) lead or be in front: [L9 + AHEAD] *The horse that we were hoping would win began to get ahead halfway through the race.* [X9 + AHEAD] *An early start will get us well ahead before the crowds.*
***2** to advance; be in front, esp. in a competition; succeed: [IØ (*of*)] *Jane used to be slow in class, but now she is getting ahead. If you want to get ahead in your job, you must listen to advice from more experienced workers. If you want to get ahead, get a hat.* (maker's advertisement) [T1b] *Hard work will get you ahead.*

**get ahead of** *v adv prep* → **keep ahead of**, etc.
**1** to obtain a position in front of, beyond,

past (someone or something), as in a race: [L9 + AHEAD + *of*] *If only our horse can get ahead of the leading runner, it can win the race!*
*__2__ to gain a position in advance of or become more advanced than (something or someone, as a competitor): [T1] *You'll soon get ahead of the rest of the class if you really make up your mind to do so. Our scientists are trying hard to get ahead of those working in enemy countries.* [D1] *Only hard work can get you ahead of your competitors.*
**3 get one step ahead of** *not fml* to advance a little way beyond (someone such as a competitor): *The secret of success in business is to get one step ahead of the other firms, and then stay there.*

**get along** *v adv*
**1** to (cause to) go forward: [L9 + ALONG] *The car could hardly get along on the icy surface.* [X9 + ALONG] *A hot drink will help to get you along on this cold night.* → **get along with** (1), **get on with** (1), **go along with** (1)
**2** to send or take (something or someone): [X9 + ALONG (*often simple tenses*)] *I'll get your clothes along to you as soon as you have a fixed address. You'd better get the boy along to a hospital, that wound looks bad.* → **come along** (2), etc.
*__3__ *not fml* to leave; go away: [I∅] *I think I'll be getting along now, I want to be home quite early. Get along, you boys! I don't want you here!* → **get along with** (5), **go along with** (5)
*__4__ (of time) to become late; (of people) grow older: [I∅ (*for*) (*usu. continuous tenses*)] *Well, well, look how time's getting along! We really must be going! Grandfather is getting along and doesn't see too well any more. It's getting along for midnight, let's go to bed.* → **get on¹** (4), **get on for, go on¹** (14), **go on for**
*__5__ to continue to live, often in spite of difficulties: [L9 (*with, without*)] *We'll get along somehow, don't worry. We can get along without your advice, thank you! We can't get along without more money. I'll get along with a bicycle until we can afford a car.* → **get by¹** (2), etc.
*__6__ to advance; go well: [L9 (*with*)] *How is your work getting along? It's getting along nicely, thank you. How is Tom getting along with his new book?* → **bring on** (3), etc.
**7** to form or have a friendly relationship (with someone): [I∅ (WELL) (*with*)] *How are you and your new neighbour getting along? Does she get along well with your aunt? The two children are getting along very well.* → **get along with** (4), **get on¹** (7), **get on with** (3), **go on¹** (17)
**8 get along (with you)** *infml* I don't believe you!: [*imper.*] *Oh, get along with you! Do you think I'd believe a story like that? Get along! Don't be silly!* → **come on¹** (10), etc.

**et along with** *v adv prep*
**1** to go forward with (someone or something): [L9 + ALONG + *with*] *The drunk man got along with the help of his two companions.* → **get along** (1), **get on with** (1), **go along with** (1)
*__2__ to continue to live, work, etc., often in spite of difficulties, by using (something): [T1] *I'll get along with a bicycle until we can afford a car.* → **get by¹** (2), etc.
*__3__ to advance with (something such as a job): [T1] *How is Tom getting along with his new book?* → **bring on** (3), etc.
*__4__ to form or have a friendly relationship with (someone): [T1] *Does she get along with your aunt all right?* → **get along** (7), **get on with** (3), **go on¹** (17)
**5 get along with you** *infml* go away! [*imper.*] *You boys are not wanted here, get along with you!* → **get along** (3), **go along with** (5)
**6 get along with you** *infml* I don't believe you!: [*imper.*] *Get along with you! Do you think I'd believe a story like that?* → **come on¹** (10), etc.

**get anywhere** *v adv* also *AmE* **get anyplace** → **get nowhere, get somewhere, get there, lead nowhere**
**1** to (cause to) reach some place: [L9 + ANYWHERE (*usu. simple tenses*)] *You can get almost anywhere in this city by bus or train.* [X9 + ANYWHERE (*usu. simple tenses*)] *These buses and trains will get you anywhere.*
*__2__ *not fml* to (cause to) gain or reach some result or success: [I∅] *We shan't get anywhere unless we take direct action ourselves. Are your talks with the union getting anywhere?* [T1b] *Waiting for his reply won't get us anywhere.*

**get around¹** *v adv* → GET ROUND¹

**get around²** *v prep* → GET ROUND²

***get around to** *v adv prep* → GET ROUND TO

***get at** *v prep*
**1** to be able to reach (something or someone): [T1 (*pass. rare*)] *I can't get at the top branches, can you bring the ladder? Put the food where the cat can't get at it. The climbers could not get at the hut because of the deep snow. Don't let the enemy get at our women.* —**get-at-able, unget-at-able** *adj infml* → **come at** (2)
**2** to reach and discover (something): [T1 (*pass. rare*)] *It is always difficult to get at the truth. What I'm trying to get at is how serious your intentions are.* → **come at** (4)
**3** to be able to work at (something or doing something), as after delay, difficulty, etc.: [T1] *I'll go into the office early tomorrow so as to have time to get at that pile of work that's been waiting for me.* [T4] *I'd like to get at repainting the house as soon as the weather is suitable.*
**4** *not fml* to mean; suggest (something): [*What* + T1 (*no pass., continuous tenses*)] *What are you getting at?* → **be at** (1), **drive at** (3)
**5** *not fml* to attempt to influence (someone) wrongly, as by paying money or performing

favours so as to persuade him to do, or not to do, something: [V3] *The prisoners escaped after getting at the guards to leave the gate open.* [T1 (*often pass.*)] *Policemen in this country cannot be got at.* → **get to** (8)

**6** *not fml* to scold; repeatedly ask, annoy, or find fault with (someone): [T1 (*usu. continuous tenses*)] *She's always getting at the children for one thing or another. I feel I'm being got at.* [V3 (*usu. continuous tenses*)] *Stop getting at me to clean my shoes, I'll do them tonight.* → **go on at** (2), etc.

**7** to do something wrong to (something): [T1] *Someone's been getting at my drink, it tastes strange. The thieves tried to get at the lock, but it was too strongly made.* → **meddle with** (1), etc.

**get away** *v adv*

**1** to leave, often with some difficulty: [L9 + AWAY (*usu. simple tenses*)] *I'm sorry I'm late but the telephone rang just as I was about to leave, and I couldn't get away.*

**2** to have a holiday: [L9 + AWAY (*often simple tenses*)] *I couldn't get away at all last year, I was too busy.*

**3** to start, and move away, as in a race: [L9 + AWAY (*often simple tenses*)] *This new car gets away faster than any of our former models. The runners have got away and the long race has begun.* → **be off** (4), **get off**[1] (6)

**4** to take (something or someone) away: [X9 + AWAY (*from*) (*often simple tenses*)] *I couldn't get the children away fast enough; that school was a terrible place. The axe was stuck in the tree, but I pulled hard and got it away.* → **send away** (1), **take away** (2)

*__5__ to escape, esp. from the scene of a crime, or from being caught: [IØ (*often simple tenses*)] *You should have seen the size of the fish that got away! Two thieves got away.* —**getaway** *n, adj*

**6** **get away (with you)** *infml* I don't believe you!: [*imper.*] *Oh, get away (with you)! I know better than that! Get away! I would never have thought it!* → **come on**[1] (10), etc.

**get away from** *v adv prep*

**1** to (cause to) leave or escape from (something or someone): [L9 + AWAY + *from* (*often simple tenses*)] *The prisoners got away from their guards after a struggle. I couldn't get away from her at the party; she just kept talking!* [X9 + AWAY + *from* (*often simple tenses*)] *Can't you get your child away from that terrible school? Get those matches away from the baby!* → **take away from** (1, 2), **take from** (1)

*__2__ to avoid; pay no attention to (something unpleasant): [T1 (*pass. rare, usu. neg.*)] *You can't get away from the fact that the cost of living is always rising. There's no getting away from increasing unemployment.*

**3** **get away from it all** *infml* to escape from city rush, crowds, the worry of modern life, etc.: *We bought a little house in the country to get away from it all.*

**get away with** *v adv prep*

**1** to leave with (someone or something): [L9 + AWAY + *with* (*often simple tenses*)] *I'd like to get away with my wife for a week or two.* → **go away** (1), etc.

*__2__ to succeed in stealing (something): [T1 (*no pass., often simple tenses*)] *The thieves got away with the best of the jewels.* → **make off with** (1), etc.

*__3__ *not fml* to form (an idea or belief): [T1 (*often simple tenses*)] *We mustn't let him get away with the idea that he won't have to pay for it.* → **go away with** (3), **run away with** (8)

*__4__ to succeed in (a deception or doing something deceitful): [T1 (*often simple tenses*)] *Don't try to cheat on your income tax, you'll never get away with it.* [T4 (*often simple tenses*)] *How did he get away with fooling his wife?* → **get by**[1] (5), **get by with** (2)

*__5__ to go unpunished for (something or doing something wrong): [T1 (*often simple tenses*)] *That student never completes his work on time; I don't know how he gets away with it.* [T4 (*often simple tenses*)] *You can't get away with being late every morning.* → **get by with** (3)

*__6__ to escape deserved punishment by receiving (a reduced form): [T1 (*no pass., often simple tenses*)] *The men went to prison but the two boys got away with a warning.* → **get off with** (2), **let off**[1] (3)

**7** **get away with murder** to go unpunished even for some serious fault or wrongdoing: [*often simple tenses*] *That teacher is most unfair: some students are punished for the least little thing, while others who are her favourites can get away with murder.*

**8** **get away with you** *infml* I don't believe you: [*imper.*] *Oh, get away with you! Do you think I'd believe a story like that?* → **come on**[1] (10), etc.

**get back** *v adv*

**1** to move backwards or away: [L9 + BACK (*usu. simple tenses*)] *Get back! The roof is falling!* → **move back** (1), etc.

**2** to (cause to) return, esp. home: [L9 + BACK (*often simple tenses*)] *When did your neighbours get back from their holiday? When Jane gets back, will you give her a message? Get back into bed, you're too ill to be up.* [X9 + BACK (*often simple tenses*)] *Don't worry, I'll get you back safely.* → **bring home** (1), **get home** (1), **go back** (2), etc., **go home** (1), **take home** (1)

**3** to return to a former condition or to a point formerly reached: [L9 + BACK (*to*) (*often simple tenses*)] *Let's get back to what we were saying before we were interrupted. I woke early, but couldn't get back to sleep.* → **come back to** (3), **get back to** (2), **go back** (4), **go back to** (3)

**4** to receive (something) in return; regain (something): [X9 + BACK (*often simple tenses*)] *I lent him £5, but I never got it back. This medicine will help to get your strength back.* → **give back** (1), **hand back** (1), **have back** (1)

**5** to return; replace (something): [X9 + BACK (*often simple tenses*)] *I have to get these books back to the library before it closes. The thieves got the jewels back in their box before the police arrived.* → **put back** (2), etc.

*__6__ esp. *BrE* to return to power, esp. after being without it: [IØ (*often simple tenses*)] *Will the Labour Party get back at the next election?*

**7 get back into circulation** to return to one's usual life, job, etc., esp. to mix with people again: *It's good to get back into circulation after spending so many weeks in hospital.*

**8 get back into harness** to start work again, esp. after illness: *I used to complain about my job, but I was actually glad to get back into harness after so many weeks in hospital.* → **get back to** (5)

**9 get one's own back on someone** esp. *BrE not fml* to return punishment to someone for a wrong done to oneself; gain revenge: *I'd like to get my own back on the man who attacked my daughter.* → **get even,** etc.

**get back at** *v adv prep* → **get even,** etc.
*not fml* to punish (someone) in return for a wrong done to oneself: [T1 (*pass. rare*)] *Students have no way of getting back at a teacher who marks their work unfairly. We can get back at the government for their unfulfilled promises by voting against them at the next election.*

**get back to** *v adv prep*

**1** to return to; reach (a place) again: [L9 + BACK + *to* (*often simple tenses*)] *I'd like to get back to the house before dark. Could you get back to the place where you witnessed the crime?* → **go back** (2), etc.

**2** to return to (a former condition or a point formerly reached): [L9 + BACK + *to* (*often simple tenses*)] *Let's get back to what we were saying before we were interrupted. Grandfather often says that he would like to get back to the good old days. The country may have to get back to a slower rate of growth.* → **come back to** (3), **get back** (3), **go back** (4), **go back to** (3)

**3** to (cause to) return to (something or doing something such as an activity): [L9 + BACK + *to* (*often simple tenses*)] *I'd like to get back to work as soon as I am strong again. When can you get back to digging the garden?* [X9 + BACK + *to* (*usu. simple tenses*)] *My mother always tries to get me back to work as soon as I'm better.*

*__4__ to speak to (someone) again, esp. by telephone: [T1 (*no pass., usu. simple tenses*)] *I'll take advice on this matter and get back to you this afternoon.*

**5 get back to the grindstone** *infml* to return to work, usu. unwillingly: *That was a wonderful holiday; it's a pity I have to get back to the grindstone.* → **get back** (8), **keep to** (7)

***get behind** *v adv* also **get behindhand**

**1** to fail to remain level: [IØ] *Don't get behind now, just when you're doing so well. Production has got behind in the last few months.* → **lag behind** (1), etc.

**2** to fail to produce something such as money on time: [IØ (*with*)] *If your payments of rent get behind, you will be asked to leave. If you get behind with the rent, you will be asked to leave.* → **be behind**[1] (2), **drop behind**[1] (2), **fall behind**[1] (2), **lag behind** (2)

**get below** *v prep*

**1** (of a measurement) to become less than (an amount): [L9 + *below* (*usu. simple tenses*)] *If the temperature gets below freezing point, we should take the plants indoors.* → **drop below** (1), etc.

*__2__ to become worse than (a standard): [T1 (*no pass.*)] *Your work has been getting below its usual standard recently, you must improve it.* → **be below**[2] (3), **drop below** (2), **fall below** (2)

**get between** *v prep*

**1** to (cause to) take a position between (two things or people): [L9 + *between* (*often simple tenses*)] *The cat tried to get between the chair and the wall.* [X9 + *between* (*often simple tenses*)] *The baby has got the ball between his legs.*

*__2__ to try to separate (people or animals): [T1 (*no pass., usu. simple tenses*)] *Never get between husband and wife. It is dangerous to get between fighting dogs.* → **come between** (2)

*__3__ to prevent (someone) from having or doing (something): [T1 (*no pass., usu. simple tenses*)] *The true artist lets nothing get between himself and his work.* → **come between, stand between** (3)

**4 get the bit between one's teeth** *not fml* to be eager and active about something such as one's work or an opinion: *Once the chairman gets the bit between his teeth, it's impossible to stop him talking.* → **take between** (2)

**get beyond** *v prep*

**1** to take a position behind or further than (something such as a place); pass (something or somewhere): [L9 + *beyond* (*often simple tenses*)] *On a clear day, you can see the ships far out to sea, until they get beyond the horizon.* → **go past**[2] (1), etc.

*__2__ to (cause to) advance further than (a stage): [T1 (*usu. simple tenses*)] *Hasn't this class got beyond lesson three?* [D1 (*usu. simple tenses*)] *Even the best teacher cannot get an unmusical student beyond simple piano exercises.* → **get past**[2] (3), **go beyond** (4), **go past**[2] (2)

*__3__ to be too difficult for (usu. someone) to do or understand; find (doing something) too difficult: [T1 (*no pass., usu. simple tenses*)] *I en-*

*joyed the book as far as Part Two; after that, it got a bit beyond me. The children tried to build a hut in the garden, but the work got beyond them and they had to ask their mother to help them.* [T4] *Jim's father got beyond running the business on his own, and employed someone to help him at busy times.* → **get past[2]** (5), etc.

**4 get beyond caring** *not fml* to cease to care (about something): *I've got beyond caring how to pay the bills; people will just have to wait, that's all.* → **go past[2]** (4), etc.

**5 get beyond endurance** esp. *BrE* to become worse than someone can reasonably be expected to bear: *Your rudeness has got beyond endurance—kindly leave my house!* → **be beyond** (6), **get past[2]** (7), **go beyond** (7), **go past[2]** (5)

**6 get beyond a joke** *not fml* to become too serious to be laughed at: *Your continual lateness has got beyond a joke; if you're not on time tomorrow, you will be dismissed.* → **be beyond** (7), **get past[2]** (9), **go beyond** (8), **go past[2]** (6)

**get by[1]** *v adv*

**1** to pass: [L9 + BY (*usu. simple tenses*)] *The crowd moved aside to let the firemen get by.* → **come along** (1), **come by[1]** (1), **fly by[1]** (1), **get past[1]** (1), **go by[1]** (1), **go past[1]** (1)

***2** to continue to live, often in spite of difficulties: [IØ (*on, with*) (*usu. simple tenses*)] *We'll get by somehow, don't worry. We can get by without your help, thank you. She can't get by on such a small income. On such a small income it is impossible to get by. I'll get by with a bicycle until we can afford a car. "I'll get by, as long as I have you."* (song) → **get along** (5), **get along with** (2), **get by with** (1), **rub along** (1), **rub through, scrape along, squeak by, squeeze by** (2), **worry along**

***3** to reach a standard that is acceptable but not very good: [IØ (*usu. simple tenses*)] *Your work will get by, but try to improve it.*

***4** to be accepted: [IØ (*usu. simple tenses*)] *Do you think this dress will get by? It's not exactly suitable.* → **get by with** (4), **get past[1]** (2)

***5** to succeed in a deception: [IØ (*usu. simple tenses*)] *It's a clever plan, but will it get by?* → **get away with** (4), **get by with** (2)

**get by[2]** *v prep*

**1** to be able to move past (someone or something): [L9 + *by* (*usu. simple tenses*)] *She couldn't get by all the people, and so lost him in the crowd. I don't think that the ship will get by the enemy guns.* → **get past[2]** (1)

***2** to be passed or accepted by (someone or something): [T1 (*no pass., usu. simple tenses*)] *What makes you think that such careless work will get by me? Your suggestion has got by the first stage and will now be examined by the committee.* → **get past[2]** (4)

***get by with** *v adv prep*

**1** to continue to live, often in spite of difficulties, by using (something): [T1 (*no pass., usu. simple tenses*)] *I'll get by with a bicycle until we can afford a car.* → **get by[1]** (2), etc.

**2** to succeed in (a deception or doing something deceitful): [T1 (*no pass., usu. simple tenses*)] *Don't try to cheat on your income tax, you'll never get by with it.* [T4 (*usu. simple tenses*)] *How did he get by with fooling his wife?* → **get away with** (4), **get by[1]** (5)

**3** to go unpunished for (something or doing something wrong): [T1 (*usu. simple tenses*)] *That student never completes his work on time; I don't know how he gets by with it.* [T4 (*usu. simple tenses*)] *You can't get by with being late every morning.* → **get away with** (5)

**4** to have (something) accepted: [T1] *Do you think I can get by with this dress, or is it too unsuitable for the party?* → **get by[1]** (4), **get past[1]** (2)

***get cracking** *v adj* → **get going, get moving, get started, get weaving**

*BrE infml* to (cause to) begin to be active: [IØ (*often imper.*)] *We've only just enough time if we start now, so let's get cracking.* [T1b (*usu. simple tenses*)] *The new director will soon get the firm cracking.*

**get down** *v adv*

**1** to descend or bring (someone or something) down to a lower level: [L9 + DOWN (*from*)] *Get down from that horse at once! The cat climbed the tree, and then couldn't get down. You've been up there long enough—down you get!* [X9 + DOWN (*from*)] *The stairs were so steep that it was difficult to get the furniture down. Please get the big dish down from the high shelf for me.* → **bring down** (1), **send down** (1), **take down** (1)

**2** to (cause to) lower one's body, esp. to one's hands and knees: [L9 + DOWN (*on*)] *I had to get down on my knees to clean the floor. You'll have to get down to look for the ring under the piano. Yet again the baby dropped his toy, so down I got for the tenth time to pick it up!* [X9 + DOWN (*on*)] *The baby got me down on the floor to play with him.* → **go down[1]** (2)

**3** to remove or destroy (something), as by cutting: [X9 + DOWN (*usu. simple tenses*)] *We'd better get that tree down, it's dangerous.* → **cut down** (1)

***4** to make (someone) fall: [T1 (*often simple tenses*)] *You get the biggest man down, and I'll fight the other two.* → **bring down** (2), **come down** (3), **go down[1]** (5), **send down** (4), **shoot down** (1)

***5** to kill or destroy (something) by shooting: [T1 (*usu. simple tenses*)] *Did you get down the enemy plane? The hunters got down three deer.* → **bring down** (2), **come down** (2), **go down[1]** (5), **send down** (4), **shoot down** (1)

***6** esp. *BrE* (of children) to leave the table after a meal: [IØ] *"Please may I get down?" "All right, down you get, then, all of you!"*

*7 to swallow (something) with difficulty: [T1] *Try to get the medicine down, it's good for you.* → **go down** (3)

*8 to record (something) in writing: [T1] *Get down every word she says.* → **write down** (1), etc.

*9 *not fml* to make (someone) feel nervous, ill, or sad: [T1b] *This continuous wet weather is getting me down.*

**10 get down in the dumps/mouth** to become very unhappy: *She gets down in the dumps over the least little thing.* → **be down** (5)

**11 get down on one's knees** to pray: [*usu. simple tenses*] *Get down on your knees and give thanks for your safety.* → **go down** (20)

**get down to** *v adv prep*

**1** to (cause to) descend to (a lower level): [L9 + DOWN + *to*] *The cat has climbed the tree, and can't get down to the ground.* [X9 + DOWN + *to*] *We can't get the piano down to the bottom of the stairs, it's stuck halfway.*

*2 to begin to give serious attention to (something such as work, or doing something): [T1] *It's time we got down to work. I really must get down to my studies, I've been lazy too long. When we get down to details, the plan seems possible. The committee got down to business after coffee.* [T4] *While the weather's fine, I must get down to repainting the house.* → **come down to** (3)

**3 get down to brass tacks** *BrE infml* to talk about facts or practical matters: *All this talk about ideas is interesting, but let's get down to brass tacks and see if the plan will really work.* → **come down to** (7)

**4 get something down to a fine art** *not fml* to learn how to do something perfectly: [*perfect tenses*] *Jim always used to miss his train, but now he's got it down to a fine art and knows exactly what time to leave the house.*

**get drunk** *v adj*

to (cause to) come under the influence of alcohol: [IØ] *Father claims that he's not responsible for what he says when he gets drunk.* [T1] *It's not kind to get young girls drunk.*

**get even (with)** *v adv (prep)* → **get back** (9), **get back at, have back** (4), **have on²** (15), **pay back** (2), **pay off** (2), **pay out** (3), **revenge on** (2), **serve out** (2), **take for** (7), **take on²** (10), **wreak on**

to punish (someone) for a wrong done to oneself; have revenge on (someone): [T1 (*often simple tenses*)] *I'd like to get even with the man who attacked my daughter.* [IØ] *How long will it be before I have a chance to get even?*

**get for** *v prep*

**1** to obtain (usu. something) for (someone, a purpose, or price): [T1 + *for* (*usu. simple tenses*)] *I think I can get that special model for you. Can you get tickets for the concert? You can't get this style for less than £30.* → **obtain for, procure for** (1)

**2** to receive (a price) for (goods): [X9 + *for* (*usu. simple tenses*)] *How much did you get for the old radio?* → **pay for** (1), etc.

**get free** *v adj*

**1** to escape: [L9 + **free** (*often simple tenses*)] *Two of the lions have got free and are frightening all the people in the streets. While they were on their way to prison, two of the criminals got free.* → **break loose** (1), **get loose, let loose** (1), **set at** (8), **set free, set loose, slough off** (2), **turn loose** (1)

*2 to become free (from something or someone unwanted): [IØ (*of*) (*usu. simple tenses*)] *I shall be glad to get free of the chairmanship next year. The school was glad to get free of the troublesome boy.*

**get from** *v prep* → **obtain from,** etc.

**1** to obtain or receive (usu. something) from (someone or something): [T1 + *from* (*usu. simple tenses*)] *You can't get hard work from unwilling students. I got this car from the garage down the road. We get milk from cows, and eggs from chickens. Who did you get the present from? It's a long time since I got a letter from you. His story isn't original, he got it from a book. When shall we get a statement from the government?*

**2 get blood from a stone** *not fml* to try to obtain something such as money from someone unwilling to give it: *Asking the director for more time to complete the work was like getting blood from a stone.*

***get going** *v adj* → **get cracking, get moving, get started, get weaving**

*not fml* to (cause to) begin to be active, working, etc.: [IØ (*usu. simple tenses*)] *After I've been ill, I find it hard to get going again. Let's get going, or we'll be late.* [T1b (*usu. simple tenses*)] *It's difficult to get the car going on cold mornings. Getting a business going in these hard times is almost impossible.*

***get hip to** *v adj prep* → **be hip to**

*AmE infml* to become knowledgeable about (a subject): [T1 (*no pass.*)] *I want to get hip to the latest styles in popular music.*

**get home** *v adv*

**1** to (cause to) reach home: [L9 + HOME (*often simple tenses*)] *Did you get home all right?* [X9 + HOME (*usu. simple tenses*)] *Don't worry, I'll get you home safely.* → **bring home** (1), **get back** (2), **go home** (1), **take home** (1)

*2 *not fml* to win: [IØ (*usu. simple tenses*)] *Did your horse get home?*

*3 to (cause to) be understood and accepted (by someone): [IØ (*to*) (*simple tenses*)] *Her remark about people who forget birthdays got home to her husband at last. The President's speech about the need for saving power got home, and everyone started turning off lights.* [T1 (*usu. simple tenses*)] *The speaker got his point home, and many of his listeners were ashamed.* → **go home** (3)

**get home to** *v adv prep*

**1** to (cause to) reach home to meet (something or someone): [L9 + HOME + *to* (*often simple tenses*)] *I always look forward to getting home to my wife and children.* [X9 + HOME + *to* (*usu. simple tenses*)] *You're not well; we must get you home to a warm bed.* → **bring home to** (1), **come home to** (1)

**2* to make (something) understood by (someone): [D1 (*simple tenses*)] *You must get the difficulty home to John. You must get home to John what the difficulty is. You must get it home to John that we don't have enough money.* [D6 (*simple tenses*)] *You must get home to John where the difficulty lies.* → **bring home to** (2), **come home to** (2), **drive home to**

**get hot** *v adj*

**1** to become warmer, heated, etc.: [L9 + **hot**] *This old iron doesn't get hot very quickly. If you get (too) hot, why not have a swim?*

**2* *AmE infml* (esp. of a musician) to perform in an excited lively manner: [IØ] *He's a good horn player, but it takes him half the evening to get hot.*

**get in[1]** *v adv*

**1** to (cause to) enter a space: [L9 + IN] *I'll hold the car door open for you while you get in. In you get—there's plenty of room!* [X9 + IN (*often simple tenses*)] *I knew this case would be too small; I can't get all my clothes in. Can you get this nail in? It's too stiff for me.* → **fit in[1]** (1), **get on[1]** (3), **get out** (3), **go in[1]** (2), **put in[1]** (1), **stick in[1]** (1)

**2** to come indoors or bring (something or someone) indoors: [X9 + IN] *Help me to get the washing in, it's raining. Please get the children in, their dinner's ready. The children like helping the farmer to get the cows in.* [L9 + IN] *I shall be glad to get in, out of this rain.* → **bring in** (1), etc.

**3** (of something unwanted) to enter into all parts of something: [L9 + IN] *We must mend the roof, the rain is getting in!* → **come in** (2), **get into** (4)

**4* to arrive [L9] *The plane got in early for a change. I'm sorry I got in so late last night.* → **be in[1]** (3), **come in** (7), **draw in** (4), **get into** (5)

**5* to collect (something or things): [T1] *The government will have to get in more tax money. The farmers are getting the crops in now they are ripe.* → **be in[1]** (9), **bring in** (2), **take in[1]** (7)

**6* to buy a supply of (something): [T1] *We should get some wine in for the party.* → **have in[1]** (1), **keep in** (7)

**7* to plant (seeds or young plants): [T1] *We must get next year's potatoes in soon while the soil is ready.*

**8* to call (someone) to one's help, esp. in the house: [T1] *Get the doctor in, I don't like the sound of the child's breathing.* → **bring in** (5), **call in[1]** (4), **come in** (14), **have in[1]** (2)

**9* to be able to deliver (something): [T1 (*often simple tenses*)] *Did you get the papers in by the right date? Be sure to get your offer in first.*

**10* to introduce; say (something), esp. by interrupting someone else: [T1 (*usu. simple tenses*)] *May I get a word in? He always gets his favourite story in when he makes a speech. She spoke so fast that I couldn't get a word in.*

**11* *not fml* to take part (in something): [IØ (*at, on*) (*often simple tenses*)] *Alice is always wanting to get in on the act. It's a good idea to get in at the start, whatever you're doing.* → **get in on** (1)

**12* to (cause to) be admitted to a place of education or a competitive group, as after an examination or test: [IØ (*usu. simple tenses*)] *Did your son get in? Mine did.* [T1 (*usu. simple tenses*)] *I couldn't get my best pupil in, the competition was so fierce.*

**13* to (cause to) be elected: [IØ (*usu. simple tenses*)] *He was surprised to get in at his first election.* [T1 (*usu. simple tenses*)] *Only votes, not influence, can get your man in.* → **be in[1]** (5), **come in** (9), **put in[1]** (12), **put into** (21)

**14* to be able to include (something such as an activity): [T1] *I'd like to get in some further reading while we're on holiday. Can you get in another year's study at the university?*

**15 get a blow in** to aim successfully at hitting someone or making a point in an argument: [*often simple tenses*] *The fighter who gets a blow in first is likely to win. Whenever they quarrel, Jim always likes to get a blow in first.*

**16 get one's eye in** to become used to judging with the eye, as in sport, shooting, etc.: *This young cricketer takes a little time to get his eye in, but after that he can't be beaten by any ball.* → **keep in** (8)

**17 get in first** to be the first to do something: *The contract was offered for open competition and our firm got in first. I didn't start the quarrel, she got in first.*

**18 get one's hand in** to become used to performing an action or job skilfully: *Separating an egg is quite easy once you've got your hand in.* → **keep in** (9)

**get in[2]** *v prep*

**1** to (cause to) enter (a space): [L9 + *in*] *Get in the car, and we'll go for a drive.* [X9 + *in* (*often simple tenses*)] *I can't get all my clothes in this case. Can you get the nail in the wall* → **fit into** (1), **go in[2]** (3), **go into** (4), **place in** (1), **put in[2]** (1), **stick in[2]** (2)

**2** to receive (something unwanted) in (part of the body): [X9 + *in* (*often simple tenses*)] *Looking up, she got a drop of rain in her eye. I got a pain in my right leg from sitting on it.*

**3 get in contact/touch (with)** to meet or send messages (to someone): *I'm so glad we got in touch (with each other) again after all these years.* → **keep in** (6), **lose with** (1), **put in[2]** (12), **remain in[2]** (3), **stay in[2]** (3)

**4 get it in the neck** *infml* to receive a sever

scolding or punishment: [*often simple tenses*] *You'll get it in the neck when they find those parts missing.*

**get in on** *v adv prep*

*1 *infml* to share; take a leading part in (some activity): [T1] *Alice is always wanting to get in on the act. Jane was annoyed because the boys didn't want her to get in on their plans.* → **be in on** (1), **bring in on** (1), **come in on** (3), **get in**[1] (11), **get into** (14), **let in on** (1), **let into** (4)

**2 get in on the ground floor** to start a job at the lowest level: [*usu. simple tenses*] *The best way to become director is to get in on the ground floor and work your way up.* → **be in on** (2), **bring in on** (2), **come in on** (5), **let in on** (2)

**get in with** *v adv prep*

**1** to enter by means of (something) or with (someone): [L9 + IN + *with*] *You can get in with this set of keys.*

*2 *not fml* to become familiar or friendly with (someone often in a position of power), usu. for one's own advantage: [T1 (*no pass.*)] *She's been trying to get in with the social leaders of the town for some time. It will be to your advantage to get well in with the leaders of the city council.* → **be in with** (1), **keep in with, keep on** (15), **remain on**[2] (4), **stay on** (6)

**3 get in bad with** esp. *AmE infml* to offend; make an enemy of; earn the dislike or disapproval of (someone, often someone in a position of power): *If you don't want to get in bad with the director, just agree with everything he says, however silly it is.* → **be in with** (3)

**get inside** *v prep*

**1** to (cause to) enter (an enclosed space): [L9 + *inside* (*often simple tenses*)] *A bird has got inside the chimney, and can't get out!* [X9 + *inside* (*usu. simple tenses*)] *Get your hand inside the bag and feel down to the bottom.*

*2 to share the spirit of; know; understand and be able to work with (something): [T1 (*pass. rare*)] *Only the students and teachers can get inside the feeling of what a school is really like. Every actor has to get inside the character that he is playing. Our men are trained to get inside the enemy's information system and learn their secrets.*

**get into** *v prep*

**1** to (cause to) enter (a space): [L9 + *into*] *Get into bed, and I'll bring you a cup of tea. How did the thieves get into the house?* [X9 + *into*] *We can't get any more people into the train. I can't get all my clothes into this small case.* → **be in**[2] (1), **fit into** (1), etc.

**2** to (cause to) stand in or take (a position): [L9 + *into*] *The cricket team got into position, and play started.* [X9 + *into*] *How do you get the pieces of this machine into place?*

**3** to (cause to) fit (clothes): [L9 + *into* (*usu. simple tenses*)] *Since I gained weight, I can't get into my best suit.* [X9 + *into* (*usu. simple tenses*)] *I can't get my head into this hat.*

**4** (of something unwanted) to enter into all parts of (something): [L9 + *into*] *The soap has got into my eyes. Those mice are getting into all the food.* → **come in** (2), **get in**[1] (3)

*5 to (cause to) arrive at (a place): [T1 (*no pass., usu. simple tenses*)] *What time does the train get into London?* [D1 (*usu. simple tenses*)] *The captain got his ship into the harbour safely in spite of rough seas.* → **get in**[1] (4), etc.

*6 to (cause to) be admitted to (a competitive place such as a school or elected body): [T1 (*simple tenses*)] *Did your boy get into the first three places? Is it difficult to get into Parliament? "The world is made of people who never quite get into the first team and who just miss the prizes at the flower show."* (J. Bronowski, *The Face of Violence*) [D1] *I can get you into the accounts department if you want a job.*

*7 to (cause to) be allowed to enter (a performance or building): [T1] *Students get into the concert for half-price.* [D1 (*usu. simple tenses*)] *This ticket will get you into the theatre but not into any special seat.*

*8 to (cause to) start (a habit): [T1] *You'll get into bad habits if you keep borrowing money.* [D1] *His influence got me into bad habits.* → **get out of** (10)

*9 to (cause to) reach (a state or feeling such as anger): [T1 (*no pass.*)] *Try not to get into a temper.* [D1] *Don't get your father into a temper by telling him your results.*

*10 to have an effect on the behaviour of (someone or an animal): [T1 (*no pass., usu. simple tenses*)] *Whatever has got into the children? They're so excitable! The devil has got into this class today.*

*11 to put (oneself or someone else) into (a state): [T1] *Try not to get into trouble while I'm away. I'm sorry to hear that your son got into bad company. I promise never to get into debt again. Do you think our party will get into power at the next election?* [D1] *You got yourself into this; now get yourself out of it.* → **be in** (3), **be out of** (4), **bring into** (2), **bring to** (3), **come into** (4), **come to**[2] (4), **fall into** (2), **fall out of** (3), **fling into** (5), **get out of** (11), **keep out of** (2), **pass into** (5), **remain in**[2] (2), **slide into** (4), **slip into** (4), **stay in**[2] (2), **stay out of** (2), **throw into** (3)

*12 to learn or start (something): [T1 (*no pass.*)] *Are you getting into the new job all right? I must get into training soon; the cricket season starts next month.* → **be in** (3), **keep in** (20), **get out of** (12)

*13 to become interested in or concerned with (something): [T1 (*no pass.*)] *Do you seriously want to get into the book trade? If I'd known what I was getting into, I'd never have offered. Michael got into radio when he was only fourteen.* [D1] *If I'd known what I was getting myself into, I'd never have started.*

**14 get into the act** *not fml* to take part in

something: *Whatever we're doing, Alice always wants to get into the act.* → **get in on** (1), etc.

**15 get into someone's bad/black books** *not fml* to behave in such a way as to earn someone's dislike, disapproval, etc.: *Joe Redhead is the leader of the union; I'd advise you not to get into his black books or he could give you a lot of trouble.* → **be in² (5)**

**16 get into deep water** *not fml* to start something that is too difficult or dangerous: *Don't try to answer examination questions that you haven't studied for, or you'll be getting into deep water.* → **be in² (9)**

**17 get into a fix** *infml* to (cause to) find oneself in difficulties which could have been avoided: *I got into a fix with my income tax return last year, so this year I intend to get professional help. Don't take such a risk, it might get you into a fix.*

**18 get into a flap/panic** *not fml* to become unnecessarily worried or nervous; lose one's self-control: *Don't get into a flap, there's no need to worry. Mother gets into a terrible panic every time she has important guests.*

**19 get into the hang of** to become used to (doing something): *You'll soon get into the hang of driving on the other side of the road if you practise a little.* → **get of** (4), **get out of** (25)

**20 get into one's/someone's head** *not fml* to (cause to) start to believe something, or that something...: *Somehow he got it into his head that everyone was blaming him. Get this into your head; you can succeed if you really try. Why can't I get it into your head that we must save money?* → **take into** (7)

**21 get one's hooks/claws into** *infml* to win the attention of (someone), usu. for one's own advantage: *That woman tries to get her hooks into any man, even if he is someone else's husband.* → **get on² (11)**

**22 get into hot water/a jam** *infml* to get into trouble: *Don't try to cheat on your income tax, or you could get into hot water.* → **be in² (18, 19)**

**23 get into a huff** *infml* to become angry or annoyed: *There's no need to get into a huff just because of one harmless little remark; it was intended as a joke.*

**24 get one's knife into** *infml* to try to cause trouble for (someone); act as an enemy towards (someone): *Don't let that teacher get her knife into you, or your life in this class won't be worth living.*

**25 get into a rut** *not fml* to become fixed in a regular but dull way of life: *I found that I was getting into a rut, so I decided to change my job.* → **get out of** (23)

**26 get into shape** *not fml* to (cause to) become stronger, more healthy, or better organized: *I've got to get back into shape after all that eating and drinking at Christmas. The new director will soon get the firm into shape.*

**27 get into one's stride** *not fml* to begin to perform to the best of one's ability: *The speaker was rather nervous to begin with, but soon he got into his stride and made a forceful speech.*

**28 get one's teeth into** *infml* to deal with (something such as a difficulty) firmly; enjoy working at (something hard): *I like a demanding job, something to get my teeth into.* → **sink into** (6)

**29 get someone into trouble** *euph* to cause an unmarried woman to become pregnant: *If you get your girl into trouble, you should offer to marry her.*

**30 get into the way of** to become used to (something or doing something): *This job seems strange when you start, but you'll soon get into the way of it. Some people get into the way of driving sooner than others.* → **get out of** (39)

***get it** *v pron*

**1** *not fml* to answer the door, telephone, etc.: [IØ (*often simple tenses*)] *There's that bell again; will you get it, or shall I?*

**2** *infml* to understand something, as a joke: [IØ (*simple tenses*)] *I don't get it; please explain.*

**3** *infml* to be punished: [IØ (*simple tenses*)] *You'll get it when your father comes home and sees what you've done!*

**get left** *v adj*

**1** to be left behind: [L9 + left (*simple tenses*)] *I got left when all the others ran ahead, as I could not run so fast.*

***2** to lose a competition; be defeated: [IØ (*simple tenses*)] *When the examination results came out, Jane had got left as usual.*

**get loose** *v adj* → **break loose** (1), **get free** (1), **let loose** (1), **set at** (8), **set free, set loose, slough off** (2), **turn loose** (1)

to escape: [L9 + loose] *Two of the lions have got loose from their cages and are frightening all the people in the streets.*

**get lost** *v adj*

**1** to lose one's way: [L9 + lost] *I'm sorry we're late, we got lost in this unfamiliar city.*

***2** *infml* to stop annoying someone; go away: [IØ (*imper.*)] *I don't want to hear any more, get lost!* → **drop dead** (3)

**get mad** *v adj*

*infml* to (cause to) become angry: [L9 + mad] *Don't get mad if I find I can't come with you after all.* [X9 + mad] *Don't show your father your school report before he has his dinner, as it's sure to get him mad.*

***get moving** *v adj* → **get cracking, get going, get started, get weaving**

*not fml* to (cause to) begin to be active, working, etc.: [IØ (*usu. simple tenses*)] *It's hard to get moving after such a pleasant holiday.* [T1b (*usu. simple tenses*)] *I can't get the car moving, will you telephone the garage? How can we get the government moving on this urgent matter?*

**get near/near to** *v prep; adv prep* → **come close to, come near, go near**

**1** to move closer to (something or someone): [L9 + *near*/NEAR + *to* (*often simple tenses*)] *I want to get near (to) the speaker, I shan't hear what he's saying from the back.*

*__2__ to be very near or like; reach (something or doing something): [T1 (*no pass., simple tenses*)] *This film doesn't get near (to) the quality of his last one.* [T4 (*simple tenses*)] *I never seem to get near (to) winning.*

**get nowhere** *v adv* also *AmE* **get no place** → **get anywhere, get somewhere, get there, lead nowhere**

**1** to (cause to) reach no place: [L9 + NOWHERE] *People who are lost in deserts often walk round in circles, getting nowhere.* [X9 + NOWHERE] *The train stopped in the middle of the country, getting us nowhere.*

*__2__ *not fml* to (cause to) gain no result or success: [IØ] *If we go on talking all round the subject, we shall get nowhere.* [T1b] *Unreasonable treatment of the workers will get the firm nowhere.*

**get of** *v prep*

**1 get the best of both worlds** to combine the advantages of two systems, ideas, etc.: *This house combines country surroundings with city convenience, so getting the best of both worlds.* → **make of** (6)

**2 get the better/best of** to defeat (usu. someone) or deal with (a difficulty): *Don't think that you can get the better of the director, he always wins an argument. Who got the best of the fight?*

**3 get a glimpse/sight of** to be able to see or know (something or someone) for a short time: *Do you think we shall get a sight of the Queen on her way to the Palace? When she won all that money, she got a glimpse of what it is like to be rich.*

**4 get the hang of** *infml* to learn how to do (something or doing something): *Many foreigners can't get the hang of cricket. I never quite got the hang of baking bread.* → **get into** (19), **get out of** (25)

**5 get hold of** to seize (something or someone): [*usu. simple tenses*] *Get hold of this rope, and we'll pull you up.* → **catch of** (1a), **keep of** (3a), **lay of** (1), **lay on²** (12), **lose of** (3) **take of** (10)

**6 get hold of** *not fml* to obtain (something) or find (someone): [*usu. simple tenses*] *I'll try to get hold of the director as he comes out of the meeting. Where can you get hold of this special tool?* → **lay of** (2), **lay on** (12)

**7 get hold of** *not fml* to begin to understand (an idea): [*usu. simple tenses*] *Now that you seem to have got hold of the general idea, let's try a few exercises to test your understanding.* → **catch of (1b)**

**8 get hold of the wrong end of the stick** *infml* to misunderstand; form a wrong idea: *You've got hold of the wrong end of the stick; she wasn't blaming you, but herself.*

**9 get the measure of** to judge the character and ability of (someone): *It should only take a few meetings for the committee to get the measure of the new chairman, and then they will know how to deal with him.*

**10 get rid of** to be able to lose; send or throw away; become free of (something or someone unwanted): *It's time we got rid of that old furniture. The new secretary is useless and must be got rid of.* → **be of** (4), **rid of**

**11 get shot of** *infml* to escape from (someone or something unpleasant): *Now that I'm old enough to leave, I'm glad to get shot of that school.*

**12 get wind of** *not-fml* to hear about (news) unofficially: *I don't know how the other prisoners got wind of the escape. Can you get wind of the examination results before they're made official?*

**13 get the worst of** to suffer from (something such as an event) or lose (a fight): *Whenever they have an argument, Mary gets the worst of it. It was the bigger boy who got the worst of the fight.* → **have of** (5), **make of** (56)

**14 get the worst of both worlds** to combine the disadvantages of two systems, ideas, etc.: *This city has severe winters and uncomfortably hot summers, so we get the worst of both worlds.* → **make of** (57)

**get off¹** *v adv*

**1** to remove (usu. something): [X9 + OFF (*often simple tenses*)] *Get your hands off! I can't get my boots off, my feet must be swollen.* → **take off¹** (1), etc., (2), etc.

**2** to (cause to) descend from a higher level or leave a place: [L9 + OFF] *That branch is dangerous, do get off! That grass is newly seeded, please get off!* → **keep off (1)**

**3** to (cause to) leave a vehicle: [L9 + OFF] *Excuse me, I have to get off at the next stop. That's my bicycle—off you get!* [X9 + OFF (*often simple tenses*)] *The bus driver tried to get the passengers off in time, but they were hit by the train.* → **get on¹** (3), etc., **get out** (3), etc., **put off¹** (2)

*__4__ to clean or remove (a mark, dirt etc.): [T1] *There's a dirty mark on the wall that I can't get off.* → **come off¹** (3), **come out** (3), **get out** (4), **take out** (5), **take out of** (5), **wash off, wash out** (1)

**__5__ to (cause to) leave; start a journey: [IØ (*on, to*)] *We must be getting off now. We have to get off early tomorrow. The plane got off safely in spite of the fog. We have to get off on our journey tomorrow.* [T1] *Getting the children off to school is tiring work.* → **go away** (1), etc.

*__6__ to start, and move away, as in a race: [IØ (*usu. simple tenses*)] *The runners have got off and the long race has begun.* → **be off¹** (4), **get away¹** (3)

*__7__ to save (someone), as from a sinking

ship: [T1] *The last three sailors were got off just before the ship sank.*

*__8__ to (cause to) be posted: [T1] *I'd like to get this letter off by the first post.* [IØ] *Please see that this urgent parcel gets off this morning.* → **send off** (1)

*__9__ *not fml* to (cause to) escape punishment: [IØ (*with*) (*usu. simple tenses*)] *The man went to prison but the two boys got off (with a warning). The thieves got off lightly, as the judge was not severe with them.* [T1 (*usu. simple tenses*)] *His father got him off by promising to control him in future.* → **get away with** (6), **get off with** (2), **let off**[1] (3)

*__10__ to escape harm: [L9 (*with*) (*usu. simple tenses*)] *Seven people in the bus were killed but the train passengers got off lightly.* → **get off with** (3)

*__11__ *not fml* to (cause to) fall asleep: [IØ (*simple tenses*)] *I had a bad night; I went to bed early enough, but for some reason I couldn't get off (to sleep).* [T1 (*simple tenses*)] *Try this sleeping medicine, it should get you off to sleep.* → **doze off**, etc.

*__12__ to learn (something): [T1b] *I've got this poem off by heart already.* → **have off** (3)

*__13__ to stop work, as for the day: [L9 (*simple tenses*)] *I'll meet you after work—what time do you get off? I get off at 5.30.* → **be off**[1] (8)

*__14__ to have (time) as a holiday: [T1b (*simple tenses*)] *I get every Saturday off, so the job's not too bad.* → **have off** (4), **take off**[1] (14)

*__15__ to (cause to) get married or otherwise find a partner in life: [IØ (*simple tenses*)] *I hope my children will get off before too long.* [T1 (*usu. simple tenses*)] *Most parents want to get their children off before they grow old.*

*__16__ *AmE infml* to make (a joke): [T1 (*usu. simple tenses*)] *I got a good one off today!*

*__17__ esp. *AmE infml* to feel the effect (of a drug), or be excited (by something): [IØ (*on*) (*often simple tenses*)] *Why didn't you get off? You can't have taken enough of the drug. He gets off on loud music, but I don't.* → **take off**[1] (18)

**18 get off (with you)!** *infml* I don't believe you; leave me alone!: [*imper.*] *Oh, get off! I know better than that!* → **come on**[1] (10), etc.

**19 get off with you!** *not fml* go away!: [*imper.*] *Get off with you—I'm trying to work.* → **push off** (3), etc.

**20 get off on the right/wrong foot** *infml* to start (something) well/badly: [*usu. simple tenses*] *I like starting a new job, it gives me another chance to get off on the right foot. Her very first day at work, the new girl got off on the wrong foot by making a mistake in the director's accounts. The chairman got the meeting off on the right foot by starting exactly on time. I'm glad that business has been got off on the right foot!* → **start off** (6), **step off**[1] (4)

**21 get off to a good/bad start** *not fml* to start (something) well/badly: [*usu. simple tenses*] *The best way to win a race is to get off to a good start. Her very first day at work, the new girl got off to a bad start by making a mistake in the director's accounts. The chairman got the meeting off to a good start.*

**22 tell someone where he can get off/where he gets off/where to get off** *infml* to scold someone; make someone do something or stop doing something: *If she tries telling me what to do again, I'll tell her where she gets off.*

**get off**[2] *v prep*

**1** to (cause to) be removed from or rise from (something or someone): [X9 + *off* (*usu. simple tenses*)] *Get your hand off my knee! I can't get my boots off my swollen feet. Can you get that dirty mark off the wall?* [L9 + *off* (*usu. simple tenses*)] *How does such a heavy plane get off the ground?* → **pull off**[2] (1), **take off**[2] (1)

**2** to (cause to) descend from (a place or higher level): [L9 + *off*] *Do please get off that dangerous branch.* [X9 + *off* (*usu. simple tenses*)] *Please get those tins off the high shelf for me.* → **keep off** (1), **stay off** (1)

**3** to (cause to) leave (a vehicle): [L9 + *off*] *Did you see a lady in a green coat get off the plane?* [X9 + *off* (*usu. simple tenses*)] *The driver tried to get his passengers off the bus before it was hit by the train.* → **alight from**, etc.

*__4__ to leave (work), as for the day: [T1 (*no pass., simple tenses*)] *What time do you get off work?* → **be off**[1] (8)

*__5__ *not fml* to escape (something or doing something unpleasant): [T4 (*usu. simple tenses*)] *Why should he get off doing the dishes just because he's a boy?* [T1 (*usu. simple tenses*)] *Well, you get off the heavy work just because you're a girl! How did he get off the punishment that he deserved?* → **get out of** (13), etc.

**6 get off one's arse/behind** *infml* to begin to work or be active: [*usu. simple tenses*] *We'll never get this done unless you people get off your arses and start helping.*

**7 get off my back!** *not fml* stop annoying me!: [*imper.*] *I'll finish the job quicker if you stop interrupting—so get off my back!* → **get on**[2] (3)

**8 get something off one's chest** *not fml* to admit or tell something that one has kept secret or controlled: *If you have any complaints about the way I'm running this office, you'd better get them off your chest now. I'm glad that's been got off my chest.*

**9 get off the ground** *not fml* to (cause to) come into existence; make a start: [*usu. simple tenses*] *I doubt if an idea like yours will ever get off the ground. Next month we should be able to get the plan off the ground.*

**10 get something/someone off one's hands** *not fml* to get rid of the responsibility for something or someone: [*usu. simple tenses*] *The school must be glad to get that troublesome boy off their hands. The thieves tried to get the* *jewels off their hands as soon as they had stolen them.*

**11 get off one's high horse** *infml* to stop being too proud: [*simple tenses*] *I wish she'd get off her high horse and stop giving us orders.* → **get on² (10)**

**12 get off the hook** *infml* to (cause to) escape from a difficulty, danger, or blame: [*usu. simple tenses*] *The thieves could have been sent to prison, but their lawyer got them off the hook. I went to see the director, and got off the hook by explaining to him that the accident wasn't my fault.* → **be off²** (8), **be on²** (17), **let off²** (3)

**13 get something/someone off one's mind** *not fml* to be able to forget something or someone: [*usu. simple tenses*] *It was a long time before I got her hurtful remarks off my mind. Poor Grace can't seem to get that red-haired boy off her mind.*

**14 get the weight off one's feet/legs** *not fml* to rest after being active: [*often simple tenses*] *I've been standing at work all day; I'll be glad to get the weight off my legs.* → **take off²** (14)

**get off with** *v adv prep*

**1** to descend, esp. from a vehicle, together with (someone or something): [L9 + OFF + *with*] *Didn't I see you get off with a tall man wearing glasses?* → **alight from**, etc.

*2 to (cause to) escape deserved punishment by receiving (something less severe): [T1 (*usu. simple tenses*)] *The man went to prison, but the two boys got off with a warning.* [D1 (*usu. simple tenses*)] *Your lawyer might be able to get you off with a short imprisonment if you're lucky.* → **get away with** (6), **get off¹** (9), **let off¹** (3)

*3 to escape serious harm and receive (only slight losses or wounds): [T1 (*usu. simple tenses*)] *Seven people in the bus were killed but the train passengers got off with slight cuts.* → **get off¹** (10)

*4 *infml* to (cause to) form a friendly or sexual relationship with (someone, usu. of the opposite sex): [T1 (*no pass., usu. simple tenses*)] *I saw you trying to get off with the new secretary.* [D1 (*no pass., usu. simple tenses*)] *Why don't you stop trying to get me off with your sister?*

**5 get off with you!** *infml* go away!: [*imper.*] *Get off with you! I'm trying to work.* → **push off** (3), etc.

**6 get off with you!** *infml* I don't believe you!: [*imper.*] *Get off with you! Do you think I'd believe a story like that?* → **come on¹** (10), etc.

**et on¹** *v adv*

**1** to put (something such as clothes) on: [X9 + ON] *Get your coat on quickly, the taxi's waiting. I can't get the lid on, the box is too full.* → **fit on¹** (1), **put on¹** (1), **put on¹** (2), etc.

**2** to start or prepare (something such as a fire): [X9 + ON (*usu. simple tenses*)] *Get some more wood on, the fire is dying. Get the light on and let's have a look. You run ahead and get the kettle on, I'm dying for a cup of tea. It won't take me long to get a meal on.* → **put on¹** (3), etc.

**3** to (cause to) take a place on a horse or in a vehicle: [L9 + ON] *Don't be afraid of the horse, get on! Don't be afraid of the horse—on you get! Did a lady in a green coat get on at the last stop?* [X9 + ON (*usu. simple tenses*)] *We can't get any more people on, you'll have to wait for the next bus.* → **get in¹** (1), **get off¹** (3), **get out** (3)

*4 (of time) to become late; (of people) grow older; (of anything else) get nearer: [IØ (*for*) (*often continuous tenses*)] *As one gets on in years, one gets wiser but not stronger. It's getting on for midnight, let's go to bed. Grandfather is getting on and doesn't see too well any more. This house must cost you half your monthly income! Not quite, but getting on that way.* → **get along** (4), **get on for, go on¹** (14), **go on for**

*5 to advance; go well: [L9 (*with*) (*often continuous tenses*)] *How is your work getting on? It's getting on nicely, thank you. How is Tom getting on with his new book?* → **bring on¹** (3), etc.

*6 to obtain a result; succeed in an attempt: [L9] *How did you get on in this morning's meeting? My students didn't get on too well in the early examination, but by the end of the year, all except three had passed.* → **go on¹** (12), **make out** (5)

*7 to form a friendly relationship (with someone): [IØ (WELL) (*with*)] *How are you and your new neighbour getting on? Does she get on well with your aunt? The two children are getting on like a house on fire.* → **get along** (7), **get along with** (4), **get on with** (3), **go on¹** (17)

*8 to continue (with something such as work), often after interruption: [IØ (*with*)] *Don't let me stop you, do get on! Get on with your work, class, while I go to speak to the other teacher.* → **carry on** (4), etc.

*9 *not fml* to hurry (with something): [IØ (*with*)] *Get on, we shall miss the train at this rate. Get on with it, we've a train to catch!* → **go on¹** (6)

**10 get on (with you)!** *infml* I don't believe you!: [*imper.*] *Oh, get on (with you)! I know better than that! Get on! He never said that!* → **come on¹** (10), etc.

**11 get a move on** *infml* to hurry or act urgently: [*usu. simple tenses*] *Get a move on, we've a train to catch! The firm will have to get a move on if it wants to avoid losing business to another company.*

**12 get one's skates on** *infml* to act quickly: [*usu. simple tenses*] *I shall have to get my skates on if I'm to get all this packing done tonight.*

**get on²** *v prep*

**1** to (cause to) move or be placed on top of (something or someone): [L9 + *on*] *Get on my shoulders and have a look over the fence.*

[X9 + *on* (*usu. simple tenses*)] *I can't get the lid on this box, come and help me!* → **get onto** (1)

**2** to (cause to) take a place on (a horse, bicycle, etc.) or in (a vehicle): [L9 + *on*] *Only one person at a time is allowed to get on the horse.* [X9 + *on* (*usu. simple tenses*)] *We can only get two more people on the bus.* → **get off**² (3), **get onto** (2), **take on** (1)

**3 get on someone's back** *not fml* to annoy someone very much: *Ever since she came to stay, your mother has been getting on my back, telling me how to do things and making unkind remarks.* → **get off**² (7)

**4 get on one's feet** to (cause to) stand up or speak in public: *Get on your feet and show respect for your visitor. He never much liked getting on his feet and making speeches, but he got used to it and made a good politician. That should get the crowd on their feet!* → **be on**² (11c), **get to** (11), etc.

**5 get on one's feet (again)** *not fml* to (cause to) become stronger after illness; (cause to) reach a point of reasonable success: *Only a few weeks after leaving the hospital, Mother was able to get on her feet again and start living her usual life. This medicine will help to get you on your feet. You may need to borrow money to get the business on its feet.* → **be on**² (11b)

**6 get a grip on** *not fml* to understand and deal with (something difficult): *It didn't take the new director long to get a grip on things in the office.*

**7 get a grip/hold on oneself** *not fml* to control oneself, esp. the expression of one's feelings such as sadness: [*often simple tenses*] *You can't keep on crying like this, you'll have to get a grip on yourself before you can face the class.* → **take on**² (7)

**8 get one's hands on** *not fml* to obtain (something), often with difficulty: [*usu. simple tenses*] *I think I know where I can get my hands on a piece of property that will yield a nice profit in a year or two.* → **lay on**² (11), **put on**² (19b), **set on**² (13a)

**9 get one's hands on** *infml* to attack (someone), esp. by seizing him: [*usu. simple tenses*] *I'd like to get my hands on the man who treated my daughter so cruelly.* → **lay on**² (11), **put on**² (19c), **set on**² (13b)

**10 get on one's high horse** *infml* to speak proudly and in anger; take offence: *There's no need to get on your high horse just because she didn't like your performance.* → **get off**² (11)

**11 get one's hooks on** *infml* to win the attention of (someone), usu. for one's own advantage: [*often simple tenses*] *That woman tries to get her hooks on any man, even if he is someone else's husband.* → **get into** (21)

**12 get a line on** *infml* to obtain information about (someone or something): *The police were helpless until at last they got a line on the criminal's movements.*

**13 get on the move** to (cause to) travel; move somewhere else: [*often simple tenses*] *In the autumn many wild birds get on the move and fly south for the winter. It takes a lot of organization to get a whole army on the move.*

**14 get on someone's nerves** to annoy someone; make someone nervous or unhappy: *The baby's endless crying gets on my nerves. Continuous wet weather gets on my nerves.* → **grate on** (2), **jangle on, jar on**

**15 get on someone's wick** *infml* to annoy someone very much: *Your mother gets on my wick with her endless complaints.*

**16 get on the wrong side of** *not fml* to annoy (someone); make oneself unpopular with (someone); make an enemy of (someone): [*often simple tenses*] *The director is an awkward man and difficult to deal with, so be careful not to get on the wrong side of him.*

***get on for** *v adv prep* → **get along** (4), **get on**¹ (4), **go on for**

to get nearer (a time or number): [T1 (*no pass., continuous tenses*)] *It's getting on for midnight, let's go to bed. Grandfather is getting on for 80. The population of the city is getting on for 500,000.*

**get on with** *v adv prep*

**1** to move forward or enter a vehicle together with (someone or something): [L9 + ON + *with*] *I know he's on the train, I saw him get on with you! The passenger got on with a large brown case.* → **get along with (1), go along with** (1)

***2** to advance with (something such as a job): [T1 (*continuous tenses*)] *How is Tom getting on with his new book?* → **bring along** (2), **bring forward** (5), **bring on** (3), **come along** (4), **come on** (6), **get along** (6), **get along with** (3), **get on** (5), **go along** (4), **go along with** (2), **go on** (11), **go on with** (3), **put ahead** (1), **put back** (6), **put behind, put forward** (4), **set ahead** (1), **set back** (3), **throw back** (4)

***3** to form a friendly relationship with (someone): [T1] *Does she get on with your aunt? How well do the children get on with each other?* → **get along with** (4), **get on**¹ (7), **go on**¹ (17)

***4** to continue with (something such as work), often after interruption or in spite of difficulties: [T1] *Have you got enough work to be getting on with while I'm away? The government is trying to get on with the job of running the country in spite of impossible difficulties. Stop talking, children, get on with your work. I shan't come out tonight, I want to get on with this very exciting book that I'm reading. Let's get on with it! We can't waste any more time.* → **carry on** (4), etc.

**5 get on with you!** *infml* I don't believe you! [*imper.*] *Oh, get on with you! Do you think I'd believe a story like that?* → **come on**¹ (10) etc.

**6 let someone get on with it** *infml* it doesn't matter to me what someone does: *If she wants* *to think that I stole her ring, let her get on with it. I know I'm not guilty, and that's all that counts. I think the director is making a terrible mistake, but let him get on with it, it's not my business.*

**get onto** *v prep*

**1** to (cause to) move or be placed on top of (something): [L9 + *onto*] *Get onto my shoulders and have a look over the fence.* [X9 + *onto* (*usu. simple tenses*)] *I can't get the lid onto this box, come and help me!* → **get on² (1)**

**2** to (cause to) take a place on (a horse, bicycle, etc.) or in (a vehicle): [L9 + *onto*] *It takes skill to get onto a nervous horse.* [X9 + *onto* (*usu. simple tenses*)] *We can't get any more people onto this train!* → **alight from**, etc.

*__3__ to (cause to) move towards (something that comes next); begin (another action): [T1 (*no pass., usu. simple tenses*)] *Let's get onto the next scene now. When can we get onto the next piece of business?* [D1 (*usu. simple tenses*)] *When the class have finished their study of ancient history, we can get them onto modern times.* → **go on to** (3)

*__4__ to begin to talk about or work at (something): [T1 (*often simple tenses*)] *How did we get onto this subject? It has no connection with what we were talking about.*

*__5__ to (cause to) be elected or appointed to (a group): [T1 (*no pass., usu. simple tenses*)] *My neighbour got onto the city council.* [D1 (*usu. simple tenses*)] *The director's influence gets him onto the boards of many companies.*

*__6__ to get in touch with (usu. someone), esp. by telephone: [T1 (*usu. simple tenses*)] *I'll get onto the director and see if he can help. I must get onto the shop about the order that we've been waiting for.* → **be onto** (1), **put onto** (2)

*__7__ to start (someone) working at (something): [D1 (*usu. simple tenses*)] *I'll get the boys onto the garden this weekend. The main wire has burnt out; we must get the electricians onto it at once.* [V4b (*usu. simple tenses*)] *Can you get the boys onto clearing the snow?*

*__8__ *not fml* to scold (someone); keep asking (someone) (to do something): [T1] *She's always getting onto the children for one thing or another.* [V3] *She's been getting onto me for a year to buy her a new coat.* → **go on at** (2), etc.

*__9__ *not fml* to discover (a secret, or someone doing something wrong): [T1 (*no pass., usu. simple tenses*)] *He tricked people for years until the police got onto him. I got onto his little plan some time ago.* → **be onto** (3), **put onto** (3)

*__10__ to think of or learn about (something): [T1 (*no pass., usu. simple tenses*)] *I've got onto a good idea for improving production.*

*__11__ *AmE* to succeed in understanding (usu. something): [T1 (*no pass., usu. simple tenses*)] *The children didn't quite get onto what the teacher was saying.*

**12 get onto a basis/footing** to (cause to) reach a level, start, or type of relationship: [*usu. simple tenses*] *Since we've got onto this basis, we can talk freely. I'm glad we've got our relationship onto this footing.*

**get out** *v adv*

**1** to (cause to) move out of a space, building, etc.: [L9 + OUT] *One of the climbers has fallen into a deep hole in the snow, and can't get out! The door's locked and I can't get out! No cats in here—out you get!* [X9 + OUT] *Get the horses out first and then try to control the flames.* → **go out** (1), etc.

**2** to remove (something): [X9 + OUT (*often simple tenses*)] *I can't get this nail out, it's too tight.* → **take out** (2), etc.

**3** to (cause to) descend from a vehicle: [L9 + OUT (*at, of*)] *How many passengers got out at the last stop? If you haven't paid for your ride, out you get!* [X9 + OUT (*at, of*)] *The driver tried to get the passengers out (of the bus) before it was hit by the train, but there wasn't time.* → **alight from,** etc., **get in** (1), **get off¹** (3), **get on¹** (3), **get out of** (3)

**4** to clean or remove (a mark, dirt, etc.): [T1 + OUT (*of*)] *This special cleaning liquid should get that spot of oil out (of the cloth).* → **wash off**, etc.

**5** to bring (something) out from a place where it is stored or hidden: [T1 + OUT] *I'll get some clean sheets out for you. I do hate having to get the sewing machine out every time I want to make a dress. Will you get the car out while I get the children ready? The thief got out a gun and forced the owner to give him the jewels.* → **drag out** (1), **draw out** (1), **lay out** (2), **pull out** (1), **put out** (3), **set forth** (3), **set out** (5), **take out** (3), **take out of** (3)

**6** to take (something such as money or a book) from a place where it is officially kept: [X9 + OUT] *The library will only allow you to get six books out at a time. I shall have to go to the bank again and get some more money out.* → **draw out** (11), **get out of** (4), **take out** (4), **take out of** (4)

*__7__ to (cause to) leave; move out or away; escape: [IØ (*of*)] *The meeting went on late, so I got out as soon as I could. This country is not fit to live in, I'm getting out! After raising a family, many women feel the need to get out into the world of work. We shall need a stronger wind than this if we're to get out to sea today. When I knew that they were planning something criminal, I got out fast. Why don't you sell your share in the business now, and get out while the going's good? I don't want you in my garden, get out! Get out of my sight!* [T1 (*of*)] *Get those dirty boots out of my kitchen. If the school really treats the children like that, I shall get them out (of there).* → **push off** (3), etc.

*__8__ to (cause to) escape: [IØ (*from, of*)] *Two prisoners got out (of prison) yesterday. The rabbits have got out from their cages again, and are eating all the vegetables in the garden. The main pipe burst in the severe cold, and the gas has been getting out. Can our man be got* *out safely?* [T1] *How did their friends get them out? I think they must have given the guards money.* → **get out of** (7), **worm out of** (1), **wriggle out of** (1)

*9 (of a secret, news, etc.) to become known unintentionally: [I∅] *How did the news of his appointment get out before it was officially made known?* → **let out** (5), etc.

*10 to discover (something), esp. by using force or effort: [T1b (*of*) (*usu. simple tenses*)] *I'll get the truth out if it takes all night.* → **get out of** (8), **worm out of** (2)

*11 to receive; gain (something) from something else such as an activity or doing something: [T1 (*of*) (*usu. simple tenses*)] *When you take part in any performance, you get out as much as you put in. I get such a lot out of watching my grandson play.* → **get out of** (9)

*12 to speak (words) with difficulty: [T1 (*usu. simple tenses*)] *The prisoner got out a few words in spite of his fear. The speaker was so nervous that he could hardly get out more than a sentence.*

*13 to print or publish (something such as a book): [T1 (*often simple tenses*)] *How long does it take each day to get the newspaper out? Tom hopes to get his new book out before the end of the year. We try to get the magazine out as often as possible.* → **be out** (21), **bring out** (5), **come out** (8), **fetch out** (4)

*14 to prepare and deliver (something written or spoken): [T1 (*often simple tenses*)] *We should be able to get out our plans in another week. I have to go and work, I must get out my next speech. We get the magazine out to our customers by post.*

*15 to calculate; find the answer to (something such as a sum): [T1 (*usu. simple tenses*)] *These days, scientists use computers to help them to get out the difficult calculations concerned with space travel.* → **come out** (10), **work out** (4)

*16 (in cricket) to dismiss (a player who is batting): [T1 (*usu. simple tenses*)] *If we don't get the next two players out before tea, there won't be time to finish the game, and so we can't win. How was Botham got out? Oh, he was caught out at last after a very fine performance.* [I∅ (*simple tenses*)] *How did Botham get out?* → **be out** (7), etc.

*17 to make (someone) stop working because of disagreement: [T1b (*usu. simple tenses*)] *If we get all the workers out, we may be able to force the government to act.* → **bring out** (7), etc.

*18 to cause (someone) to be on duty: [T1 (*usu. simple tenses*)] *We've got police out all over the area, looking for the missing girl. Sorry to get you out at this late hour, doctor, but Mother became suddenly ill in the middle of the night.* → **call out** (2)

**19 get one's rag out** *infml* to become angry: [*often simple tenses*] *There's no need to get your rag out just because of one unfortunate remark.*

**get out of** *v adv prep*

**1** to (cause to) move out of (a space, building, etc.): [L9 + OUT + *of*] *The climber couldn't get out of the deep hole in the snow until his companions brought more rope. The door locked accidentally, and I couldn't get out of the bathroom.* [X9 + OUT + *of* (*usu. simple tenses*)] *Get the horses out of the burning building first before you attend to the fire.* → **alight from** (1), etc., **be out of** (1), etc.

**2** to remove (something) from (something or somewhere): [X9 + OUT + *of* (*usu. simple tenses*)] *Can you get this nail out of the wall? I can't.* → **take out** (2), etc.

**3** to (cause to) descend from (a vehicle): [L9 + OUT + *of*] *Two men with guns got out of the car and threatened the shopkeeper.* [X9 + OUT + *of* (*usu. simple tenses*)] *Why can't they get the cases and bags out of the plane faster?* → **alight from** (1), **get out** (3), etc.

**4** to take (something such as money or a book) from (a place where it is officially kept): [X9 + OUT + *of* (*usu. simple tenses*)] *You can only get six books out of the library at any one time. I shall have to get some more money out of the bank.* → **draw out** (11), **get out** (6), **take out of** (4)

**5** to copy (something) from (something else): [X9 + OUT + *of* (*usu. simple tenses*)] *His story isn't original; he got it out of a book.* → **obtain from**, etc.

*6 to (cause to) leave; escape from (a place or activity): [T1 (*pass. rare*)] *I got out of the meeting as soon as I could, but it went on very late. After raising a family, many women feel the need to get out of the house and be recognized for their own abilities. Once you're in it, you can't easily get out of the race for trade. Why don't you get out of the country if you don't like it? We'll give you till midday to get out of town. Get out of my garden! Get out of my sight!* [D1 (*usu. simple tenses*)] *Get those dirty boots out of my kitchen. I shall get the children out of that school if what they say about their teachers is true.* → **push off** (3), etc.

*7 to (cause to) escape from (something holding one in place): [T1] *Two prisoners got out of prison yesterday. The rabbits have got out of their cages again, and are eating all the vegetables in the garden. Gas has been getting out of the main pipe, which burst in the severe cold.* → **get out** (8), **worm out of** (1), **wriggle out of** (1)

*8 to discover (something) from (someone), esp. with force or effort; hear (something): [D1 (*usu. simple tenses*)] *I'll get the truth out of the prisoner if it takes all night. When shall we get a statement out of the government? Not a word could be got out of the child.* → **get out** (10), **worm out of** (2)

*9 to receive; gain (something) from (some

thing such as an activity or doing something): [D1 (*usu. simple tenses*)] *You get out of any performance only as much as you put in. What does he get out of life, for all his money? You won't get much income out of your book for the first year. The children are always trying to get more money out of their father.* [V4b (*usu. simple tenses*)] *I get such a lot out of watching my grandson play.* → **get out** (11)

*__10__ to (cause to) forget or lose (something such as a habit) [T1 (*often simple tenses*)] How can I get out of the habit of smoking? [D1] *Joining a group will help to get you out of the habit.* → **get into** (8)

*__11__ to (cause to) become free of; escape from (something bad): [T1 (*often simple tenses*)] *Trouble with the director is not easy to get out of. I don't suppose I shall ever be able to get out of debt.* [D1 (*usu. simple tenses*)] *A word from the teacher in your favour could get you out of trouble. You got yourself into this; now get yourself out of it.* → **get into** (11), etc.

*__12__ to (cause to) leave; forget; stop being in a state of (something): [T1 (*no pass., usu. simple tenses*)] *How did my papers get out of order? I had them all carefully arranged. You can soon get out of practice unless you play the piano regularly. No singer should ever get out of breath.* [D1 (*often simple tenses*)] *Who's been getting my papers out of order? I had them all carefully arranged.* → **be in** (3), **get into** (12)

*__13__ to (cause to) escape (something such as a responsibility for something or duty to do something): [T1 (*usu. simple tenses*)] *You can't get out of your share of the blame so easily. Why should you get out of the heavy work just because you're a girl? There are always some unpleasant jobs that can't be got out of.* [T4 (*usu. simple tenses*)] *Well, you get out of doing the dishes just because you're a boy!* [D1 (*usu. simple tenses*)] *Crying won't get you out of your punishment.* → **get off** (5), **let off**[2] (2), **shuffle out of** (3), **slide out of** (2), **slip out of** (4), **sneak out of** (2), **squirm out of, worm out of** (3), **wriggle out of** (2)

**14 get out of bed on the wrong side** *infml* to be bad-tempered, esp. early in the morning, for no real reason: [*often simple tenses*] *What's the matter with you today? Did you get out of bed on the wrong side? You've been doing nothing but complain.*

**15 get the best/most out of** to use (something or someone) to full advantage; try to gain as much as possible from (something or someone): [*usu. simple tenses*] *You will get the best out of your washing machine by never filling it too full. You get the most out of students by respecting their views.*

**16 get blood out of a stone** *infml* to obtain something such as money, with great difficulty: [*often simple tenses*] *Getting a pay rise from the director is like trying to get blood out of a stone.*

**17 get change out of** *infml* to obtain a satisfactory answer or result from (something or someone): [*simple tenses, + any, much, no, some*] *If he tries to make me join the Party, he'll get no change out of me! Did you get much change out of the director? No, he never gives a straight answer, so I don't know what his opinion is.*

**18 get a charge/kick out of** *infml* to find excitement in (someone, something, or doing something): [*usu. simple tenses*] *"I get a kick out of you."* (song) *Jim gets a kick out of beating his director at tennis. I can't see what kicks he gets out of such loud music.*

**19 get out of date** to become considered no longer modern: [*usu. simple tenses*] *The trouble with interesting clothes is that they get out of date so quickly.* → **be up to** (7), etc.

**20 get out of one's depth: a** to try to swim in water too deep to allow one to stand on the bottom: *I'm not a strong swimmer, so I shall be careful not to get out of my depth.* **b** *not fml* to attempt something too difficult: *The pianist began well, but when he reached the difficult parts of the piece, he got out of his depth and made a lot of mistakes.* → **be out of** (8), **go out of** (6)

**21 get out of earshot** to move too far away to hear or be heard: [*usu. simple tenses*] *Don't let the baby get out of earshot, I want to hear what he's doing.* → **come within** (3), etc.

**22 get out of focus** to (cause to) seem unclear: [*usu. simple tenses*] *The film got out of focus when the camera broke. I think you've got the picture out of focus, I can't see the faces clearly. Because of her great love for him, she got his character out of focus.* → **go out of** (9)

**23 get out of the groove/rut** *infml* to be able to free oneself from a fixed and uninteresting way of life: [*usu. simple tenses*] *I had to get out of the rut, so I changed my job.* → **get into** (25)

**24 get out of hand** to get out of control: *The difficult class got out of hand when an inexperienced teacher was put in charge.* → **be out of** (10)

**25 get out of the hang of doing something** *not fml* to forget how to do something that one formerly did without difficulty or as a habit: [*usu. simple tenses*] *You soon get out of the hang of playing the piano unless you practise regularly.* → **get into** (19), **get of** (4)

**26 get someone out of someone's hair** *infml* to take someone away so as not to annoy or be in the way of someone else: [*usu. simple tenses*] *I'll take the children to the park for the afternoon, that'll get them out of your hair for a few hours.*

**27 get someone/something out of one's head/mind** to be able to forget someone or

something: [*usu. simple tenses*] *I can't get this tune out of my head. Jane found it difficult to get her former boyfriend out of her mind.*
**28 get out of it!** *sl* don't talk nonsense!: [*imper.*] *Get out of it! You can't expect me to believe that!*
**29 get out of line** to behave or think wrongly: *The teacher had to watch the children all the time, to see that none of them got out of line.* → **be out of** (16), etc.
**30 get something out of (all) proportion: a** to make something the wrong size or shape in relation to the rest of something: *Your drawing of the head and body is good, but you've got the arms and legs out of proportion, they're too long.* **b** to (cause to) be less or usu. greater than is justified by the facts: *I think your fear has got out of proportion; these little insects can't hurt you! Pride can make you get your sense of your own importance out of proportion.* → **be out of** (23)
**31 get out of range** to move beyond the reach of a gun: *If we had bigger guns, we could get out of range of enemy firing.* → **come within** (4), etc.
**32 get out of reach** to move or change so as to be impossible to seize or obtain: *The fish swam away from the bank and got out of reach. Prices are rising so fast that the kind of house we want to buy keeps getting out of our reach.*
**33 get a rise out of** *not fml* to make fun of (someone) by pretending: *This new teacher is easy to get a rise out of, he'll believe anything we tell him.* → **take out of** (16)
**34 get out of sight/view** to be no longer able to be seen: *I waved my handkerchief until the train got out of sight, and then went sadly home.* → **keep in** (16), etc.
**35 get out of someone's sight** to go away, esp. to stop annoying someone: [*usu. simple tenses, often imper.*] *Get out of my sight! I don't want to see you again! The boys tried to get out of the teacher's sight, but they were too late, and they were caught and punished.*
**36 get something/someone out of one's system** *infml* to drive someone or something such as a worry out of one's mind; stop something from causing one continuous worry, anxiety, or anger, as by expressing one's feelings openly: *The doctor's remark had worried me greatly, so I went for a long walk by myself to get it out of my system. It takes years for Alice to get a man she has loved out of her system.*
**37 get out of one's/the way** to (cause to) move aside so as to make room for someone or something: [*usu. simple tenses*] *When the fire engine came down the street, all the traffic got out of the/its way. Can't you get your car out of the way. Get out of my way! Can't you see I can't get past?* → **be out of** (32a), **keep out of** (5), **stay out of** (4)
**38 get something/someone out of the way** to deal with or finish with something such as work; get rid of someone: [*usu. simple tenses*] *Let me get these letters out of the way before dinner. Get your father out of the way for a few minutes while I wrap his present. You'll find that I can't be got out of the way quite so easily.*
**39 get out of the way of doing something** to forget how to do something: [*usu. simple tenses*] *You soon get out of the way of driving when you haven't had a car for some time.* → **get into** (30)

**get over**[1] *v adv*
**1** to (cause to) to cross a road, water, wall, etc.: [L9 + OVER (*often simple tenses*)] *How can we get over? The traffic's so busy.* [X9 + OVER (*usu. simple tenses*)] *The new boats get people over to the island in half the time. Give me a push up, will you, I can't get my leg over.* → **come over**[1] (3), etc.
**2** to travel or visit someone, usu. from a distance: [L9 + OVER] *When the weather's better, do get over to see us. Get over here as fast as you can, there's been an accident.* → **bring over** (1), etc.
***3** to (cause to) become understood or accepted: [T1 (*to*) (*usu. simple tenses*)] *It takes an experienced politician to get such an unpopular message over.* [IØ (*to*) (*simple tenses*)] *Did your speech get over (to the crowd)?* → **come across**[1] (2), etc.
***4** to reach the end of (usu. something unpleasant): [T1 (*usu. simple tenses*)] *You'll be glad to get your operation over.* → **be over**[1] (2), **get through**[1] (8), **have over**[1] (2)
**5 get something over (and done) with** *not fml* to reach the end of (something unpleasant): *You'll be able to enjoy your holiday now that you've got the examinations over and done with.* → **finish with** (4), etc.

**get over**[2] *v prep*
**1** to (cause to) pass, move, or climb over (something) or cross (a road, water, etc.) [L9 + *over*] *The smallest boy was unable to get over the wall as fast as the others. You can get over the road more safely at the traffic lights.* [X9 + *over* (*usu. simple tenses*)] *How do you get a horse over a high fence? The teacher got the children safely over the busy road.* → **go across**[2], etc.
**2** to (cause to) travel (a distance): [L9 + *over* (*usu. simple tenses*)] *These new cars get over the miles so smoothly. All the horses got over the course, but two of them were badly hurt.* [X9 + *over* (*usu. simple tenses*)] *A lighter bicycle will get you over the distance so much more easily.*
***3** to control; deal with (a feeling, difficulty, etc.): [T1 (*usu. simple tenses*)] *The committee will have to find means to get over the difficulty. I see no way of getting over the lack of paper. The singer had to learn to get over her fear of the public.*
***4** to regain health or success after (illness, failure, etc.): [T1 (*often simple tenses*)] *It a*

*ways takes some time to get over the shock of someone's death. I hope you soon get over your troubles. A shock like that isn't easily got over.* → **recover from** (2), **recuperate from**

*5 to regain happiness after losing the love of (someone): [T1 (*often simple tenses*) *Jim would never get over Mary if they separated. Has Alice got over her former boyfriend yet?*

*6 *not fml* to believe; learn to live with the shock of (something very surprising or shocking): [T1 (*no pass., usu. neg., simple tenses*)] *I can't get over your news, I would never have thought it possible! Tell me again, I can't get over it! We can't get over his sudden decision to leave the country!*

*7 to disprove, deny, or account for (something): [T1 (*usu. neg., simple tenses*)] *Even their lawyer can't get over the fact that they knew they were stealing.*

**get past[1]** *v adv*

**1** to pass: [L9 + PAST (*usu. simple tenses*)] *The crowd moved aside to let the firemen get past.* → **come along** (1), **come by[1]** (1), **fly by[1]** (1), **get by[1]** (1), **go by[1]** (1), **go past[1]** (1)

*2 to be accepted: [IØ (*usu. simple tenses*)] *This dress is rather old but I'd like to wear it to visit these people; do you think it will get past?* → **get by[1]** (4), **get by with** (4)

**get past[2]** *v prep*

**1** to (cause to) be able to pass (someone or something); take a position behind or further ahead of (something or somewhere): [L9 + *past* (*often simple tenses*)] *She couldn't get past all the people, and so lost him in the crowd. I don't think that the ship will get past the enemy guns. Can you get past the open door without being seen?* [X9 + *past* (*usu. simple tenses*)] *The horse that gets its nose past the winning post first is the winner. How did the captain get the ship past the enemy guns?* → **go past[2]** (1), etc.

**2** to be later than (a time): [L9 + *past*] *If it gets past midnight and they haven't returned, I shall telephone the police.* → **be past** (2)

*3 to (cause to) advance further than (a stage): [T1 (*usu. simple tenses*)] *Hasn't this class got past lesson three?* [D1] *Even the best teacher cannot get an unmusical student past simple piano exercises.* → **get beyond** (2), **go beyond** (4), **go past[2]** (2)

*4 to be accepted by (someone or something); advance beyond (someone or something) without meeting any difficulties: [T1 (*no pass., usu. simple tenses*)] *How did the escaping prisoners get past the guards? What makes you think that such careless work will get past me? Your suggestion has got past the first stage and will now be examined by the committee.* → **get by[2]** (2)

*5 to be too difficult for (someone) to do or understand; find (doing something) too difficult: [T1 (*no pass., often simple tenses*)] *I enjoyed the book as far as Part Two; after that, it got a bit past me. It gets past me how he does it! The children tried to build a hut in the garden, but the work got past them and they had to ask their mother to help.* [T4] *Jim's father felt that he had got past running the business on his own, and advertised for help.* → **be beyond** (4), **be past** (3), **get beyond** (3), **go beyond** (5), **go past[2]** (3)

**6 get past caring** to cease to care (about something): [*often simple tenses*] *I've got past caring how to pay the bills; people will just have to wait, that's all.* → **go past[2]** (4), etc.

**7 get past endurance** to become worse than someone can reasonably be expected to bear: *Your rudeness has got past endurance—kindly leave my house!* → **get beyond** (5), etc.

**8 get past it** to be too old for use or work: *This firm keeps an eye on its older workers, and dismisses them the minute they get past it. I'm sorry to tell you that your piano is getting past it; the wood has dried out, loosening the strings, so it will never be in tune again.* → **be past** (6)

**9 get past a joke** to cease being funny; become too serious: *Your continual lateness has got past a joke; be on time tomorrow, or you will be dismissed.* → **be beyond** (7), **get beyond** (6), **go beyond** (8), **go past[2]** (6)

**get right** *v adj*

**1** to make no mistakes in (something such as a calculation or performance): [X9 + **right**] *Start that scene again and get it right this time! If I do the sum three times I'm more likely to get it right.* → **get wrong** (1)

**2** to be correctly informed about (something): [X9 + **right**] *Did I get that right—did you actually say that our best worker should be dismissed? Newspaper reports rarely get anyone's name right.* → **get wrong** (2)

**get round[1]** *v adv* also **get around**

**1** to move freely; travel: [L9 + ROUND] *It's easy in this city to get round by bus.* → **get about[1]** (1), **go about[1]** (1), **take about[1]** (1), **take around[1]** (1)

*2 to be able to move again after illness: [IØ] *Mother is much better now, thank you, she's able to get round a bit more.* → **get about[1]** (2), **go about[1]** (2)

*3 (of news, etc.) to spread: [IØ (*often continuous tenses*)] *Stories have been getting round concerning the government's secret intentions.* → **go about[1]** (3), etc.

*4 to (cause to) visit someone: [IØ (*to*) (*usu. simple tenses*)] *When are you going to get round to our house?* [T1 (*to*) (*usu. simple tenses*)] *Do get your new boyfriend round to see us.* → **bring over** (1), etc.

*5 to persuade (someone) to change his/her opinion: [T1 (*to*) (*usu. simple tenses*)] *We'll soon get him round (to our point of view).* → **bring around** (2), **bring over** (3), **bring round** (3), **come around** (6), **come over[1]** (5), **fetch over** (2), **fetch round** (3), **go over to** (5), **pull round** (4)

**get round[2]** *v prep* also **get around**

**1** to (cause to) move or travel round (a

place or course): [L9 + *round*] *The quickest way to get round the city is by underground train. How many horses got round the course?* [X9 + *round* (*usu. simple tenses*)] *A taxi will get you round the city faster.* → **get about²**, etc.

*****2** to avoid or find a satisfactory way of dealing with (something such as a difficulty): [T1 (*often simple tenses*)] *If you are clever, you can sometimes get round the tax laws. Don't try to get round the question by changing the subject. We could get round the lack of players by removing the last piece of music from the concert programme.* → **scrub round** (2), **skate round** (3), **slide over** (2), **slide round** (2)

*****3** to persuade (someone) (to do something): [T1 (*usu. simple tenses*)] *We shall need to borrow more money to keep up the payments on the house; can you get round your parents again?* [V3 (*usu. simple tenses*)] *I think I can get round my father to lend us the car.*

**4 get round the table** to (cause to) be willing to have talks to try to reach agreement: *When government and unions get round the table, you can expect a long argument. The United Nations can often get two fighting nations round the table to try to agree on a peace settlement.*

**5 get one's tongue round** to be able to speak (usu. the sounds of another language): [*usu. simple tenses*] *I feel sorry for students who cannot get their tongues round some of our English consonant combinations, like "strengths".*

*****get round to** *v adv prep* also **come around to, get around to**

to find time for (something or doing something), esp. after delay: [T1 (*usu. simple tenses*)] *I should be able to get round to that job next week. The committee will get round to your suggestion after they've dealt with urgent business.* [T4 (*usu. simple tenses*)] *After a long delay he got round to writing the letter.*

**get somewhere** *v adv* → **get anywhere, get nowhere, get there, lead nowhere**

**1** to (cause to) reach some place: [L9 + SOMEWHERE] *If you get lost in the desert, calculate your direction by the sun and keep moving, then you're sure to get somewhere.*

*****2** *not fml* to (cause or help to) be successful; [IØ] *That young man shows promise, I'm sure he'll get somewhere in the end.* [T1] *Your degree should really get you somewhere in the chemical industry.*

*****get started** *v adj* → **get cracking, get going, get moving, get weaving**

to (cause to) begin to be active, working, etc.: [IØ (*usu. simple tenses*)] *After I've been on holiday, I find it hard to get started again.* [T1 (*usu. simple tenses*)] *I couldn't get the car started this morning, it was so cold. Getting a business started in these hard times is almost impossible. My uncle gave me a small sum of money to get me started and then I built up the business myself.*

**get there** *v adv* → **get anywhere, get nowhere, get somewhere, lead nowhere**

**1** to (cause to) reach a particular place: [L9 + THERE (*often simple tenses*)] *"What time does the train get there?" "About half-past three."* [X9 + THERE (*usu. simple tenses*)] *The bus gets me there nicely in time for work.*

*****2** *not fml* to (cause to) succeed: [IØ (*usu. simple tenses*)] *It was risky starting the business, but we were sure that it could get there, and we were proved right.* [T1b (*usu. simple tenses*)] *You need influence to get you there, especially if you're not a businessman.*

**get through¹** *v adv*

**1** to (cause to) pass or move through something: [L9 + THROUGH] *The snow was so deep that the climbers could not get through to the hut. Can you get through into the cave?* [X9 + THROUGH (*often simple tenses*)] *No, but we were able to get this pipe through and talk to the trapped miners.* → **come through¹** (1), **go through¹** (1)

**2** (of something unwanted) to enter through something intended to prevent it: [L9 + THROUGH] *You didn't mend the roof very well, the rain is still getting through.*

*****3** to (cause to) pass an examination or reach a standard: [IØ (*to*) (*usu. simple tenses*)] *How many of your students got through? I'm pleased to report that all of you have got through to second year.* [T1b (*usu. simple tenses*)] *With additional classes, I got all my students through except three whose English was the weakest.* → **put through¹** (3)

*****4** to (cause to) pass through Parliament or other law-making body: [IØ (*simple tenses*)] *Buy now before the tax increase gets through next week!* [T1b (*usu. simple tenses*)] *We should have no difficulty getting the new law through, it has been demanded by the public for some time.* → **go through¹** (2), **put through¹** (4)

*****5** to (cause to) reach someone: [IØ (*to*)] *The news of the successful climbing of the highest mountain got through on the very day of the Queen's crowning. As long as the letters get through, I shan't mind the snowstorm.* [T1b] *Whatever happens, we must get these supplies through to our men on the other side of the battle.*

*****6** to reach someone, esp. by telephone, radio, etc.: [IØ (*to*) (*usu. simple tenses*)] *I tried to telephone you but I couldn't get through, the wires were down in the snowstorm. I can't get through to London, the operator keeps giving me the wrong number.* → **be through** (2), **come through¹** (6), **get through to** (1), **put through¹** (2)

*****7** to (cause to) be understood or accepted (by someone): [T1b (*usu. simple tenses*)] *The politician had difficulty getting his message through (to the crowd). I can't seem to get it through to Grandfather that he must rest.* [T5] *I can't get through to Grandfather that he must* *rest.* [I∅ (*to*) (*usu. simple tenses*)] *It's difficult to get through to students who don't want to learn.* → **come across**[1] (2), etc.

*8 to finish something such as work: [I∅ (*simple tenses*)] *Telephone me when you get through, and we'll have dinner together.* [T1b (*simple tenses*)] *I shall be glad to get this job through.* → **be over**[1] (2), **get over**[1] (4), **have over**[1] (2)

**9 get soaked/wet through** to (cause to) get very wet, esp. because of rain: *Goodness me, you've got wet through! Take your things off at once and come and sit by the fire. Trying to cross the river, the soldier got his gun wet through and was unable to fire it.*

**get through**[2] *v prep*

**1** to (cause to) pass through (something such as a space): [L9 + *through* (*often simple tenses*)] *The man was so fat that he couldn't get through the doorway.* [X9 + *through* (*usu. simple tenses*)] *We can't get the piano through this narrow entrance, it'll have to come through the window.* → **go through**[2] (1), **take through**[2] (1)

*2 to (cause to) pass (an examination) or succeed in (a competition): [T1 (*usu. simple tenses*)] *Do you think that John will ever get through his driving test? Of the world's best tennis players, only three got through the first part of the competition.* [D1 (*usu. simple tenses*)] *It was quite an effort to get my weakest students through the difficult English examination.* → **put through**[2] (2)

*3 to cause (something such as a law) to be passed or approved by (Parliament or other law-making body): [D1 (*usu. simple tenses*)] *We should have no difficulty getting the new law through Parliament, it has been demanded by the public for some time.* → **go through**[2] (2), **put through**[2] (3), **take through**[2] (3)

*4 to continue to live through (difficult times): [T1] *I don't know how poor people get through these cold winters. If we can get through the next year on your income, things should be easier after that.* → **go through**[2] (13)

*5 to finish or deal with (something such as work): [T1] *I've a pile of papers to get through before the meeting.*

*6 to spend or use (a quantity of something such as money, food, or supplies): [T1 (*usu. simple tenses*)] *Jim gets through a lot of beer while watching football on television every Saturday. How did you get through all that money in such a short time?* → **go through**[2] (10)

**7 get it through one's (thick) head/skull** *not fml* to learn; begin to understand [*usu. simple tenses*] *I never could get it through my thick head how a car engine works.*

**get through to** *v adv prep*

**1** to reach (someone) by telephone, radio, etc.: [T1 (*usu. simple tenses*)] *I can't get through to London, the lines are all busy.* → **be through** (2), **come through**[1] (6), **get through**[1] (5, 6), **put through**[1] (2)

**2** to (cause to) be understood or accepted by (someone): [T1 (*often simple tenses*)] *Few teachers can get through to students who don't want to learn.* [D1 (*usu. simple tenses*)] *I can't seem to get it through to Grandfather that he must rest.* → **come across** (2), etc.

**3** (esp. in sport) to reach (the next stage of a competition): [T1 (*no pass., usu. simple tenses*)] *We were so pleased when our team got through to the last part of the competition.*

***get through with** *v adv prep*

**1** to finish with (something or doing something): [T1 (*usu. simple tenses*)] *I'll telephone you when I get through with this pile of papers.* [T4 (*simple tenses*)] *When will you get through with painting the house?*

**2** *infml* to finish punishing or scolding (someone): [T1 (*no pass., simple tenses*)] *Wait till I get through with you, your own mother won't recognize you! When the teacher had got through with the class, they felt very ashamed.*

**get to** *v prep*

**1** to (cause to) arrive at (a place): [L9 + *to* (*often simple tenses*)] *What time does this train get to London? What time do you usually get to bed?* [X9 + *to* (*usu. simple tenses*)] *The boat will only get you to the nearest island, you have to make your own way from there. This old car may not run very well, but it gets me to work.* → **go to** (1), **send to** (1), **take to** (1)

**2** to disappear to (somewhere): [L9 + *to* (*usu. simple tenses*)] *Where did you get to? I've been looking for you everywhere. I don't know where my ring has got to, and I think it must have been stolen.* → **become of, come of** (1), **disappear to, go to** (5)

**3** to reach (a part or stage): [L9 + *to* (*simple tenses*)] *Where have you got to in the book? I've got to the middle bit where the murderer is threatening the husband. The talks had to stop when they got to the point where we were all wasting our time and effort. Their argument got to the stage of pointless bad temper.* → **get up to** (2), **go up to** (7), **take up to**

**4** to send or take (something or someone) to (someone or somewhere): [X9 + *to* (*usu. simple tenses*)] *We have to get the book to the printer's this week. Getting the children to school in winter is much more worrying. I must rush and get this letter to the post before it's collected.* → **send to** (2), **take to** (1)

*5 to start (something or doing something): [T1 (*no pass., often simple tenses*)] *We must get to work at once (on the new building plans).* [T4 (*simple tenses*)] *Recently I've got to wondering why I am in this job.*

*6 *not fml* to be understood by (someone): [T1 (*usu. simple tenses*)] *I've tried to help the troublesome boy, but I can't seem to get to him.*

*7 *not fml* to have an effect on the feelings of (someone): [T1 (*no pass., usu. simple tenses*)] *His sad story really got to me, and I was moved to help him.*

*8 *AmE not fml* to attempt to influence (someone) wrongly, as by paying money or performing favours so as to persuade him to do or not do something: [T1] *Somebody must have been getting to the guards; the doors were all unlocked.* [V3] *The prisoners escaped after getting to the guards to leave the gate open.* → **get at** (5)

**9 get access to** to be able to reach (something or someone): *Two newspapermen got access to the politician's private papers and showed the public that he had acted criminally. The directors of the television stations decided that the public must be allowed to get access to television time and produce their own broadcasts.* → **have to** (1)

**10 get to the bottom of** to examine and find an answer to (something mysterious): *The owner of the jewels called in the police to get to the bottom of the mystery of the robbery.*

**11 get to one's feet** to stand up: *At the end of the game, the whole crowd got to their feet and cheered wildly.* → **be on** (11a), **bring to** (9), **come to** (21), **get on**² (4), **keep on** (8), **remain on**² (3), **rise to** (5), **stay on** (4)

**12 get to first base (with)** esp. *AmE not fml* to make a start on something: [*usu. neg.*] *Anybody trying to start a new business in these hard times probably won't even get to first base. We never even got to first base with our plans for improving the conditions in the factory.*

**13 get to grips with** to begin to fight (someone) or deal firmly with (something): *Our soldiers are anxious to get to grips with the enemy. The government has promised to get to grips with the question of rising prices.* → **bring to**² (11), **come to**² (24)

**14 get to the point** to reach the important part of a matter when talking or writing: *The speaker has been talking in generalizations for an hour; I wish he'd hurry up and get to the point. Get to the point—what do you want from me?*

**15 get to the top (of the ladder/tree)** to (cause to) reach the highest possible point of success, esp. in one's profession: *The director got to the top (of the ladder) by hard work. Only hard work and ability will get you to the top of the tree; there's no easy way.*

**16 get to work on** to start actively dealing with (something): *As soon as one performance is over, we get to work on the next concert. It didn't take the children long to get to work on all that food at the party!* → **go to** (41), **set to**² (13)

**17 get to work on** *infml* to try to persuade (someone); treat (someone) violently: [*usu. simple tenses*] *I'll get to work on the director and see if I can make him change his mind. You get to work on the guard while we break the locks.* → **go to** (42)

**get together** *v adv*

**1** to collect (usu. things or people): [X9 + TOGETHER] *It'll take me a week to get together all the materials I need for my talk. Get the children together in the school yard and count them to make sure that none are missing in the fire. Give me a minute to get my thoughts together.* → **gather together** (1)

*2 to (cause to) meet, esp. so as to talk: [IØ (*on*) (*often simple tenses*)] *The unions and the employers get together to talk about common difficulties. If heads of state will get together more frequently, there is a better chance of preventing war. The directors of both firms must get together on the question of fixing prices.* [T1b (*usu. simple tenses*)] *The United Nations should get Foreign Ministers together more often, to settle international disagreements by peaceful talks.*

*3 to combine, esp. to pay for something: [IØ] *All the villagers got together and soon raised enough money for a swimming pool.* [V3] *The shopkeepers got together to put up Christmas lights so as to attract trade.*

*4 *infml* to reach an agreement: [IØ] *I'm glad to see that the two firms have got together at last. Whether the two great powers will ever get together, is impossible to say.*

*5 *not fml* to (cause to) meet together socially: [IØ] *Several members of the club got together for a small party.* [T1b] *It's good to get the family together for Christmas.* —**get-together** *n*

*6 to organize (something) into some form of order: [T1b] *I shall spend most of the day getting the place together for my parents' visit.*

**7 get it together** *BrE infml*, **get one's shit together** *AmE sl* to do something well; get oneself organized: *If I can get it together, I should have this done by next week. Come on, we're tired of waiting, get your shit together and let's go.*

**8 get oneself together** to control oneself: *You have to get yourself together, no one else can do it for you.* → **gather together** (2), **pull together** (4)

**get under**¹ *v adv*

**1** to (cause to) pass or move underneath something: [L9 + UNDER (*often simple tenses*)] *Put the fence deep into the earth so that the rabbits can't get under.* [X9 + UNDER (*usu. simple tenses*)] *The coin has rolled beneath the piano, and I can't get my hand under, so we'll have to leave it there.*

*2 to start to control (something or someone): [T1b (*usu. simple tenses*)] *The firemen got the fire under in only half an hour. The king got the villagers under by threatening them with his army.* → **keep down** (6), etc.

**get under**² *v prep*

**1** to (cause to) pass or move underneath (usu. something): [L9 + *under* (*often simple tenses*)] *The rabbits have got under the fence again, and are eating all the crops!* [X9 + *under* (*usu. simple tenses*)] *I can't get the cleaner under these chairs, so will you help me move them?*

**2 get under control** to begin to be able to control (something or someone): [*often simple tenses*] *It was several hours before the fire was got under control. I shall put an experienced teacher in charge of that class, to get the children under control.* → **be under** (7), **bring under²** (2), **keep under** (2)

**3 get under one's skin** *infml* to (cause to) fill the attention of (someone), esp. by annoying him/her: *His endless complaints really get under my skin. "I've got you under my skin."* (song) = I can't forget you.

**4 get under way** to (cause to) start, esp. a voyage, often after some delay: *After many delays, the ship at last got under way. Let's get under way, we're already late. It took a lot of hard work to get the business under way.*

**get up** *v adv*

**1** to (cause to) move to a higher level, as on a hill or horse: [L9 + UP (*on*) (*often simple tenses*)] *The hill was so steep that the old car had difficulty getting up. She doesn't know how to ride a horse; in fact, she can't even get up on one without falling off. You'll have to get up on the table to change the light.* [X9 + UP (*usu. simple tenses*)] *Since you can't walk up stairs after your operation, I've fixed a machine on the stairs to get you up. If everybody pushes, we'll get the car up.* → **go down¹** (1), **go up¹** (1), **go up to** (1), **send up¹** (1), **take up** (3)

**2** to stand; rise from one's seat, the floor, etc.: [L9 + UP] *When he didn't get up, I knew that he was dead. Get up when the king enters the room. Few men these days get up to give a lady a seat on a bus. Then up got Jim, all ready to attack the speaker.*

**3** to pull (something) up: [X9 + UP (*usu. simple tenses*)] *We shall have to get the tree up by its roots so that it can't grow again.* → **pull up** (1), etc.

**4** to build (something); put (something) up: [X9 + UP (*often simple tenses*)] *Help me to get the Christmas lights up before the family come. Even the fastest builders can't get a new house up in less than a year.*

**5** to (cause to) rise from bed, esp. in the morning: [IØ] *John hates getting up early. Up you get—you'll be late for work!* [T1b (*often simple tenses*)] *Please get me up at 7.30 tomorrow.* → **be up** (4), **get up to** (3), **get up with** (1)

**6** to (cause to) leave one's bed after an illness: [IØ] *Mother is much better but the doctor says she's not to get up yet.* [T1b (*often simple tenses*)] *This letter will get him up faster than any medicine.*

**7** to arise and increase: [IØ] *There's a wind getting up. I hope the boats are safe.* → **go down¹** (7)

**8** to cause (a feeling) to arise: [T1a] *I can't get up any pity for the difficulties of such people, it's their own fault. I doubt if I shall ever get up any keenness for the game again. Don't mention the letter to her, I don't want her to get up any false hopes.* → **work up** (3)

***9** *not fml* to study; prepare (something): [T1a] *How quickly can you get up this piece for the concert? I have to get up a talk for the club's next meeting. I must go and get up my notes ready for the test.* → **work up** (5)

***10** *not fml* to organize (something): [T1a] *The children are getting up a play for next week. The church is getting up a sale to collect money for the homeless children.*

***11** to prepare the appearance of (something): [T1 (*often simple tenses*)] *The printers have got the book up very nicely. I can get up this dress so that it's fit for the party.* —**get-up** *n*

***12** to dress (oneself or someone else) so as to improve or change one's appearance: [T1 (*often simple tenses*)] *Mary got herself up in a nice new dress. The children are got up as ghosts.* [IØ (*simple tenses*)] *I shan't get up too much, the party is very informal.* —**get-up** *n* —**got-up** *adj* → **dress up** (2), etc., (3)

***13** (of a cricket ball) to rise quickly from hard ground: [IØ] *The ball is getting up and is difficult to hit.* → **come through¹** (5)

***14** (command to a horse) to move ahead; go faster: [IØ (*imper.*)] → **come up** (22), **gee up, giddy up**

**15 get up a/one's appetite/thirst** to act so as to make oneself feel hungry/thirsty: *I've got up such a thirst playing tennis. Swimming gets up your appetite, so you eat more and don't lose weight.* → **work up** (7)

**16 get up an appetite for** *not fml* to begin to enjoy or want (something or doing something): [*often simple tenses*] *Early in the morning I find it difficult to get up an appetite for the day's activities. I have to make an effort to get up an appetite for teaching every day.* → **work up** (8)

**17 get someone's back/hackles up** *infml* to annoy or offend someone: *Your mother gets my back up with her endless complaints. It gets my hackles up, the way she is so unfair to the girls who work for her.* → **put up¹** (20)

**18 get someone's blood up** *infml* to make someone very angry: [*often simple tenses*] *His rudeness got my blood up and I hit him in the face.* → **be up** (14)

**19 get one's dander/monkey up** *infml* to become angry: [*often simple tenses*] *Don't get your dander up over one little remark, she didn't mean what she said.* → **have up** (3), **put up¹** (25)

**20 get up on one's hind legs** *infml* to rise to one's feet in order to speak in public: *I'm tired of waiting for the Minister to get up on his hind legs, the newspaper will have to go without his report.*

**21 get up steam: a** (of a steam engine) to raise steam; produce power: *One of the best sounds, to a train-lover, is that of a railway engine getting up steam.* **b** *infml* to become more active; make an effort: [*often simple tenses*] *If we want the meal on time, we'd bet-*

*ter get up steam with the cooking. Can't you get up enough steam to get out of bed in the morning?* → **work up** (9)

**22 get the wind up** esp. *BrE infml* to become afraid: *Don't get the wind up, it's only me. I'm sorry if I gave you a shock! Facing his first battle, the young soldier got the wind up and wanted to run away; but didn't want to be thought a coward, so he pretended to be brave.* → **have up** (5), **put up²** (3)

**get up against** *v adv prep*

**1** to (cause to) stand or move next to (usu. something): [L9 + UP + *against* (*often simple tenses*)] *I got up against the window to try to see out.* [X9 + UP + *against* (*usu. simple tenses*)] *Get the prisoners up against the wall.*

***2** *not fml* to offend; annoy; make an enemy of (someone, usu. in a position of power): [T1 (*no pass., usu. simple tenses*)] *I hope you don't get up against the director in one of his bad tempers.*

**get up to** *v adv prep*

**1** to reach; come level with (someone or something higher or in front): [L9 + UP + *to* (*usu. simple tenses*)] *The boy was too small to get up to the top branches. When I got up to her, I could see that she was a stranger after all.*

***2** to reach as far as (usu. a place in a book or piece of work, etc.): [T1 (*no pass., usu. simple tenses*)] *What page have you got up to? I've got up to Part Three. The history lessons get up to the year 1642 and then stop. The temperature got up to 32° by 9 o'clock.* → **get to** (3), **go up to** (7), **take up to**

***3** to rise from bed, as in the morning, to the sound of (something): [T1] *I like to get up to soft music, not shouting voices.* → **get up** (5), **get up with** (1)

***4** to (cause to) rise or improve so as to reach (a standard): [T1 (*usu. simple tenses*)] *You need more practice to get up to performance.* [D1 (*usu. simple tenses*)] *Some additional lessons might get you up to the standard demanded by the examiners.* → **be up to** (4), **bring up to** (4), **come up to** (4, 5)

***5** to do (usu. something bad or amusing): [T1 (*no pass.*)] *Whatever will the students get up to next? Has that cat been getting up to its silly tricks again?*

**6 get up to date (with)** to modernize one's knowledge (of something); bring (something) level, esp. in time: *Mother, you must get more up to date with modern styles! You can't wear that thing! I want to spend this weekend getting my letter writing up to date.* → **be out of** (7), etc.

**7 get up to mischief** *not fml* to behave badly: *Children get up to mischief if left alone for very long. That dog has been up to mischief again, jumping the fence and chasing the sheep.* → **be up to** (9)

***get up with** *v adv prep*

**1** to rise from bed, as in the morning, with (usu. something): [T1] *I got up with such a terrible headache this morning; I must have drunk too much last night.* → **get up** (5), **get up to** (3)

**2** to reach; come level with (something or someone): [T1 (*usu. simple tenses*)] *We had to run fast to get up with her. Just as I got up with the bus, it drove away.* → **catch up** (4), **come up with** (1), **keep up** (7), **keep up with** (1)

***get weaving** *v adj* → **get cracking, get going, get moving, get started**

*BrE infml* to begin to be active: [IØ (*usu. simple tenses*)] *Let's get weaving, we've a lot to do before tonight.*

**get well** *v adj* → **look well** (1)

to (cause to) become healthy again after illness: [L9 + **well**] *Doctor, tell me truly, do you think she will ever get well?* [X9 + **well** (*usu. simple tenses*)] *Drink your medicine, it's supposed to get you well if you take it regularly.* —**get-well** *adj*

***get wise to** *v adj prep*

*infml* to learn about; come to know (someone or something, esp. bad or deceitful): [T1 (*no pass.*)] *At first I thought he was wonderful, but then I got wise to him and saw that he was just fooling everybody. I've got wise to your tricks, you won't cheat me any more!*

**get with** *v prep*

**1** to obtain (something) by using (something): [T1 + *with*] *You can't get happiness with money. Quick! Get that floating paper with your stick!*

**2 get with child** *old use* to make (a woman) pregnant: [*usu. simple tenses*] *If you get a girl with child, then you must marry her.* → **get into** (29)

**3 get with it** *infml* to become up-to-date, modern, etc.: [*simple tenses, often imper.*] *Come on, do the latest dance, get with it!* → **be with** (6)

**get within** *v prep*

**1** *old use* to (cause to) move inside (something enclosing): [L9 + *within* (*often simple tenses*)] *Get within the walls of the town, the enemy are coming!* [X9 + *within* (*usu. simple tenses*)] *Get the women and children within the city.*

**2** to cause (something) to be correct according to (a limit or law): [L9 + *within* (*usu simple tenses*)] *You'll get within the law if you move your car back two yards.* [X9 + *within* (*often simple tenses*)] *Shops have been ordered to get their price increases within the limits set by the new law.* → **fall within** (2), etc.

**3 get within earshot (of)** to be able to hear or be heard: *If you can get within earshot of the enemy, you might hear some of his secret plans.* → **come within** (3), etc.

**4 get within range (of)** to (cause to) be near enough to be fired at; (cause to) be in reach of enemy guns; move near enough to fire at someone: *Don't get within range of their big guns; surround the camp from a distance. I've* *got the enemy ship within range, shall I fire?* → **come within** (4), etc.

**5 get within sight (of)** to (cause to) be able to see or be seen: *Get the criminal within sight and keep him within sight! As the climbers got to the top of the mountain, they got within sight of the villages on the other side of the valley.* → **keep in** (16), etc.

**6 get within striking distance (of)** to (cause to) be near enough to attack: *Move carefully until you get within striking distance of the enemy, then hold your fire till I give the order. After marching for miles, the army was got within striking distance of the enemy.* → **be within** (8), **come within** (6)

**get wrong** *v adj*

**1** to make a mistake in (something such as a calculation or performance): [X9 + wrong] *I shall have to do this sum again, I think I've got the answer wrong. Many actors have difficulty in learning their lines, and get them wrong even after a lot of practice.* → **get right** (1)

**2** to be incorrectly informed, or give incorrect information, about (something): [X9 + wrong] *No, no, you've got it all wrong, it wasn't my fault! I'm sorry I got your name wrong in my article.* → **get right** (2)

**3 don't get me wrong** *infml* don't misunderstand me: *Now don't get me wrong, I wasn't blaming you!*

**gibe at** *v prep* also **jibe at** → **laugh at** (2), etc.

to make fun of (someone or something) unkindly; make cruel remarks about (someone or something): [L9 + *at*] *It's unkind to gibe at a foreign student's English, even though it may sound amusing.*

**giddy up** *v adv* → **come up** (22), **gee up, get up** (14)

(command to a horse) to move forward: [IØ (*imper.*)]

**giggle at/over** *v prep*

to laugh in a silly way at (something or someone): [IØ + *at/over*] *Two schoolgirls were giggling at/over a letter which one of them had received from a boy.*

**ginger up** *v adv*

*infml* to make (usu. something) more lively, effective, or active: [T1] *More men are needed to ginger up the police force. His speech needed gingering up, it was not very interesting.*

**gird for** *v prep*

**be girded/girt for** *old use* to be supplied with weapon and shield ready for (battle): *When all the soldiers are girded for battle, we will march against the enemy.*

**gird on** *v adv*

*old use fml* to fasten (something such as a weapon or armour) on oneself, as with a belt: [T1] *He girded his father's sword on.*

**gird up** *v adv*

**1** *old use fml* to fasten (something such as clothing), usu. with a belt: [T1 + UP] *The priest girded up his clothing and stepped into the river, to show the people that he had no fear.*

**2 gird up one's loins** *bibl or pomp* to get ready for action: *The nation must gird up its loins to face these difficult times.*

**girdle about/around/round** *v adv*

*fml* to surround; encircle (something) (with usu. pleasant scenery): [T1 + ABOUT/AROUND/ROUND (*with*) (*often pass.*)] *Gentle rolling hills girdled the city about. The palace was girdled around with tall trees.*

**give away** *v adv*

**1** to give someone a present or prize of (something); give (something) free of charge: [T1 + AWAY] *I think I'll give this old furniture away, it's worthless. We have invited a famous former student to give away the school prizes.* —**give-away** *n, adj*

***2** to tell (a secret) intentionally or unintentionally: [T1 (*to*)] *Don't give away the ending of the story, it'll spoil it.* [T6 (*to*)] *The thieves promised each other not to give away (to the police) where the jewels were hidden.* —**give-away** *n*

***3** to inform against (someone): [T1 (*to*) (*usu. simple tenses*)] *The thief gave his companions away (to the police), hoping to escape punishment. One of the worst crimes in war is to give one of your own people away to the enemy.*

***4** *not fml* to show where (someone) comes from, who he/she is, etc.: [T1b (*usu. simple tenses*)] *You won't deceive possible employers by dressing in the right style if your manner of speech gives you away.* —**give-away** *n*

***5** to show an easy answer to (a question): [T1 (*usu. simple tenses*)] *If you read carefully, you will see that the examiners have given question three away; all the facts that you need are hidden in the wording of the question.* —**give-away** *n*

***6** to lose or waste (something) carelessly: [T1] *The politician gave away his best chance to win the election when he foolishly said the wrong thing.* → **throw away** (2), etc.

***7** to deliver (a woman) to her husband at the wedding: [T1 (*usu. pass.*)] *Mary was given away by her father.*

***8** (esp. in boxing and horseracing) to give an advantage of (an amount such as weight) to one's opponent: [T1 (*often continuous tenses*)] *I don't think the experienced fighter will win this fight, he's lost weight and is giving away more than ten pounds. The favourite may not win this race, as he has a heavy rider and is giving away five pounds.*

**9 give the game/show away** *infml* to tell a secret intentionally or unintentionally: *We tried to keep the party a surprise, but Jane gave the game/show away by bringing the wine into the kitchen.*

**give back** *v adv*

**1** to return or repay (something) to its owner or someone who formerly had it: [T1 + BACK (*to*) (*often simple tenses*)] *Give the book back to Penny when you've finished reading it. When can you give back the money that you owe?* → **get back** (4), **hand back** (1), **have back** (1)

**2** to give (something) again (to someone): [T1 + BACK (*to*) (*usu. simple tenses*)] *I hope that the holiday will give me back my good spirits. Even if you punish the murderer, that can't give me back my dead son.*

***3** to throw back (sound or light): [T1 (*to*) (*simple tenses*)] *This cave gives (you) back the sound of your voice.*

**4 give back insult for insult/tit for tat** to repay (someone who is rude or offensive) with equal measure: *Determined not to let Jim get the best of their quarrel, Mary gave (him) back insult for insult.*

***give best** *v adj*

*infml* to admit that (someone) has won: [T1b (*usu. simple tenses*)] *At the end of the tennis game with Jim, although the score was even, I had to give him best as he was clearly the better player.*

**give for** *v prep*

**1** to pay (a sum of money) to obtain (something): [T1 + *for* (*usu. simple tenses*)] *To think that I gave £25 for that coat when I could have got the same one for £18! What would you give for this used car?* [D1 + *for*] *What would you give me for this painting?* → **pay for** (1), etc.

**2** to offer or give (something) in exchange for (something): [T1 + *for* (*usu. simple tenses*)] *The natives give these valuable furs for trade goods such as guns and radios. What wouldn't I give for a cool drink!*

**3** to lose or yield (something such as one's life) for (something or someone): [T1 + *for* (*usu. simple tenses*)] *Many Christians have given their lives for their faith. The brave soldier gave his life for his friend.*

**4 give cause for** to provide (to someone) a reason for (something or doing something): *The state of the nation, especially the rate of unemployment, is giving (the government) cause for concern. What has given you cause for looking so cheerful?*

**5 give credit for** to believe; regard (someone) as (doing or having something good, as a quality); give (someone) the honour of (something or doing something): [*often simple tenses*] *I would never have given that boy credit for such good sense. The swimmer was given credit for saving the child from drowning.* → **credit with** (2), **give to** (8), **take for** (5)

**6 give scope for** to allow (someone) room and possibility for (something): [*often simple tenses*] *We moved to this country because it gave my husband so much more scope for his specialized work. This style of performance gives scope for originality. Students on this course are given no scope for original thought.*

***give forth** *v adv* → **fling off** (5), **give off, give out** (1), **throw off**[1] (6), **throw out** (12)

*old use fml* to produce and send out (a sound, smell, etc.): [T1a (*usu. simple tenses*)] *19th-century factories used to give forth black smoke, spoiling town and countryside alike. This special whistle gives forth a sound that only dogs can hear, as it is too high for human hearing.*

***give in** *v adv*

**1** to deliver (something) (to someone, often who may demand it): [T1 (*to*)] *Give your examination papers in (to the teacher) when you have finished.* → **give in to** (1), **hand in** (2), **pass in**[1] (2)

**2** to offer (a name): [T1 (*to*)] *Give in your name if you are willing to help. Names of all students entering for the examination must be given in by 1 March.* → **give in to** (2)

**3** to yield: [IØ (*to*) (*often simple tenses*)] *The two boys fought until one gave in. The argument went on for hours as neither side would give in. After refusing for months, at last Mary gave in and agreed to marry Jim. Don't give in without a fight.* → **give in to** (5), **give over to** (1), **yield to** (1)

**4** to offer; give (something) to someone in charge; return (something) no longer wanted: [T1 (*to*)] *The director has threatened to give in his resignation unless his demands are accepted. Visitors to the camp must give in any weapons at the main gate. Unwanted tickets can be given in at the theatre office window up to half an hour before the performance.* → **give in to** (4), **deliver over, hand in** (3), **turn in** (4)

***give in to** *v adv prep*

**1** to deliver (something) to (someone, often who may demand it): [T1 + *to*] *Give your examination papers in to the teacher when you have finished.* → **give in** (1), **hand in** (2), **pass in**[1] (2)

**2** to offer (a name) to (someone): [T1 + *to*] *Give your name in to the director if you are willing to help with the school play.* → **give in** (2)

**3** to yield to (someone or something): [IØ + *to* (*often simple tenses*)] *The chairman spoke so forcefully that the rest of the committee gave in to his opinion. After months of refusing Mary gave in to Jim and agreed to marry him. Jane must stop giving in to her desire fo chocolate. It's her mother's fault for giving i to her too often. Only a coward gives in to hi fate.* → **give over to** (4), **give to** (23), **give up t** (4), **surrender to** (2), **yield to** (3)

**4** to offer or give (something) to (someone i charge); return (something no longer wanted to (someone): [T1 + *to*] *The director ha threatened to give his resignation in to th Board. Unwanted tickets can be given in to th theatre before the performance.* → **deliver over give in** (4), **hand in** (3), **turn in** (4)

**give it hot** *v pron prep*
*infml* to punish or scold (someone) severely: [IØ (*to*) (*usu. simple tenses*)] *That officer gives it hot to any man who disobeys orders.*

**give of** *v prep*
**1 give of one's best** to work as well as one can: [*usu. simple tenses*] *He wasn't the cleverest member of the committee, but he always gave of his best—a hard worker with sincere intentions.*
**2 give evidence of** to show signs of (something or doing something): [*simple tenses*] *His wounds gave evidence of a violent attack. This envelope gives evidence of having been opened.*
**3 give evidence/proof of** to produce something or someone to prove (something): [*usu. simple tenses*] *The lawyer called witnesses to give evidence of the prisoner's good character.*

**give off** *v adv* → **fling off** (5), **give forth, give out** (1), **throw off**[1] (6), **throw out** (12)
to send out (something, esp. a liquid, gas, or smell): [T1a] *Boiling water gives off steam. This milk must be bad, it's giving off a nasty smell. These plants need more room in the earth than you would judge from the size of the flowers, because the roots give off branches for a long way.*

**give on/onto/upon** *v prep*
(usu. of part of a building) to have a view of or lead straight to (something): [T1 (*no pass., simple tenses*)] *The library windows give onto the garden, leading down to the lake.*

**give out** *v adv*
**1** to send out (something such as sound or light): [T1] *The sun gives out light and heat to the earth. The ship gave out radio signals for help until she sank.* → **fling off** (5), **give forth, give off, throw off**[1] (6), **throw out** (12)
**2** to give (something or things) to each of several people: [T1] *Give out the question papers ten minutes before the examination. I give more money out to the children every week! The government gives out payments to people out of work.* → **dish out** (3), **hand out** (2), **pass out** (1)
**3** to make (something) known publicly: [T1 (*usu. simple tenses*)] *The news was given out that the political leader had died. The date of the election will be given out soon. It was given out that the government and the union had reached agreement.* → **dish out** (3), **hand out** (3), **pass out** (1)
**4** to declare or claim (something or oneself) (to be something, or that something . . .): [I5 (*usu. simple tenses*)] *He gave out that the President was dead, but it was not true.* [T1 (*as*) (*usu. simple tenses*)] *He gave himself out as a doctor.* [V3 (*usu. simple tenses*)] *He gave himself out to be the real ruler.* → **make out** (8)
**5** to come to an end: [IØ] *His strength gave out after running that long distance. A good teacher's patience never gives out. Our supply of sugar has given out.* → **be out of** (3), **run out** (8), **run out of** (4)
**6** *not fml* to stop working: [IØ] *Halfway up the hill, the engine gave out and we had to push the car the rest of the way. Mother can't walk very far now, her legs quickly give out.* → **break down** (3), **conk out** (1), **cut out** (8), **kick off** (6), **pack up** (3)
**7** (in cricket and other ball games) to declare that (a player) is defeated according to the rules and must leave the field of play: [T1 (*usu. pass., usu. simple tenses*)] *May was given out at last after making 200 runs. How many different ways may a batsman be given out?* → **be out** (7), etc.
**8** to send (work) to be done elsewhere: [T1] *Our factory can't deal with the whole order, we shall have to give some of the smaller jobs out to other firms.*

***give over** *v adv*
**1** *BrE infml* to stop (something or doing something): [IØ] *Do give over! You keep knocking my arm!* [T1a] *It's time you gave over such childish behaviour.* [T4a] *Give over hitting your little brother!*
**2** to yield (someone or something) (usu. to someone): [T1 (*to*)] *When you yield your weapons to the enemy, you will have to give over all your prisoners. Will you give the escaped prisoner over (to the police)?* → **give up** (7), (8), etc.

**give over to** *v adv prep*
**1** to yield (someone or something) to (someone); deliver (someone or something) to (someone): [T1 + OVER + *to* (*usu. simple tenses*)] *Will you give the escaped prisoner over to the police? The keys were given over to a neighbour in their absence.* → **give up** (7), etc., (8), etc., **give up to** (1)
***2** to set (a time or place) aside for special use for (someone, something, or doing something): [D1 (*usu. pass.*)] *The house was given over to the children for their parties during the season. The building was formally given over to the youth club.* [V4b (*usu. pass.*)] *The rest of the evening was given over to singing and dancing.* → **give up to** (2)
***3** to give (oneself or one's time or life) completely to (something or doing something): [D1 (*often pass., usu. simple tenses*)] *When you are starting a business, you have to give yourself over to your work. I'm sorry to say that the young man is given over to evil ways.* [V4b (*usu. simple tenses*)] *The doctor gave his life over to helping the poor natives.* → **give up to** (3)
***4** to yield (oneself) to (a feeling): [D1 (*often simple tenses*)] *Don't give yourself over to sadness, there's still hope!* → **give in to** (3), **give to** (23), **give up to** (4), **surrender to** (2), **yield to** (3)

**give round** *v adv*
to pass (something) round to be shared: [T1 + ROUND] *Give the food round to everyone at the table.*

**give to** *v prep*

**1** to make a present of (something) to (someone or something); hand (something) to (someone or something): [T1 + *to*] *The rich businessman gave his whole fortune to the hospital. Give the book to Jane, you know it's hers. The city gave the park to the people.*
**2** to supply, provide, or pass (something) to (someone); spend (time) on (something): [T1 + *to*] *You ought to give a better example to the children. I think you must have given your cold to the whole family. She has given the best part of her life to her art.*
**3 be given to** to be in the habit of (something or doing something): *The writer was much given to quiet walks in the country. The writer was given to walking in the country to refresh his mind.*
**4 be given to** *fml* to be allowed to (someone); be the fate of (someone): *It is not given to many of us to be born into a wealthy family. Musical ability has to be given to you, it is not something that can be learned.*
**5 give birth to: a** to produce (a child): *My wife has just given birth to a boy!* **b** to produce (an idea): [*usu. simple tenses*] *What can have given birth to the story that we were to separate?*
**6 give colour to** to make (something) seem more likely: [*usu. simple tenses*] *The soldier's wounds gave colour to his story that he had been attacked by a wandering enemy band.* → **lend to** (4)
**7 give credence to** *fml* to make (something) seem true: [*usu. simple tenses*] *The proof that you have offered gives credence to your story.* → **lend to** (5)
**8 give credit to** to believe; regard (someone) (as doing or having something good such as a quality); give the honour to (someone) (for something): [*often simple tenses*] *I would never have given credit to the boy for so much good sense. Did the committee ever give credit to the chairman for inventing the plan? We must all give credit to the citizens for their hard work.* → **credit with** (2), **give for** (5), **take for** (5)
**9 give currency to** to help to spread (something such as bad reports): [*often simple tenses*] *The politician's guilty behaviour gives currency to the story that he had been taking money for political favours. Newspapers should not give currency to frightening news without making sure of their facts.*
**10 give (an) ear/eye to** to listen to or watch (something) carefully: [*usu. simple tenses*] *The citizens should give ear to these warnings. I would advise you to give an eye to the dangers which you might meet. Give an eye to the children while I'm out, will you? It's difficult to give an ear to the doorbell while the radio's playing.*
**11 give effect to** to make (something) begin an action or result: [*usu. simple tenses*] *The new law should give effect to the government's intentions to save power.*
**12 give heed to** to pay attention to; take notice of (something): [*usu. simple tenses*] *Give no heed to her rudeness—she wants to hurt you, so pretend it doesn't matter, and then she'll have failed. Many more people are giving heed to the government's warnings about the dangers of cigarette smoking.* → **pay to** (4), **take of** (9)
**13 give hostages to fortune** *rather lit* to accep responsibilities that may make it hard to ac freely in the future: *Francis Bacon believed that a married man had given hostages to fortune because he had to consider his wife and children before taking any risks.*
**14 give it to** *infml* to scold or punish (someone, esp. a child): [*usu. simple tenses*] *Your father will give it to you when he comes home!*
**15 give the lie to** to show that (something such as a story) is not true: [*usu. simple tenses*] *This student's improvement gives the lie to al his bad reports.*
**16 give pause to** to make (someone) stop to consider (something): [*usu. simple tenses*] *The surprise election results should give pause to the politicians. He accepted the offer of a job in America with great eagerness, but think the cost of living there will give him pause.*
**17 give place to** to be followed or replaced b (someone or something): *The long cruel winter at last came to an end, giving place to gentle warm spring. I am leaving the firm afte all these years as I feel that I should give plac to a younger man.* → **yield to** (4)
**18 give rise to** to cause (something): *The appearance of the enemy so close to the cit has given rise to fears that we shall be conquered.*
**19 give thought to** to think carefully about consider (someone, something, or doin something): *Many young men starting wor give no thought to the future. Giving n thought to her family's feelings, Jane spent th night at a friend's house without informin them. It's time the firm gave serious thought t developing our international trade. Have yo given much thought to the question of ne Christmas? We've given some thought to th difficulty, but haven't found an answer ye Some thought must be given to the question c cost.*
**20 give tongue to** *fml* to express (something aloud: [*often simple tenses*] *I was ver doubtful about the cost, but dared not giv tongue to my fears.*
**21 give vent to** to express (a feeling): *It much healthier to give vent to your anger tha to try to control it.*
**22 give voice to** to express (something such a an opinion): *The people gave voice to the distrust of the government by voting again them at the election.*

**23 give way to** to yield to (someone or something): *The chairman spoke so forcefully that the rest of the committee gave way to his opinion. Jane must stop giving way to her desire for chocolate. It's her mother's fault for giving way to her too often.* → **give in to** (3), **give over to** (4), **give up to** (4), **surrender to** (2), **yield to** (3)
**24 give way to** to yield the right of way to (other traffic): [*simple tenses*] *Give way to traffic on the right.* → **yield to** (1)
**25 give way to** to be replaced by (someone or something): [*often simple tenses*] *Steam trains gave way to electric trains soon after the war. Ice and snow should give way to warmer weather when the wind changes.*
**26 give way to** to allow oneself to feel or express (sorrow, anger, etc.): *Don't give way to your fears, I'm sure he will come home safely. At last I was able to give way to the annoyance which I had felt for many years.*
**27 give weight to** to strengthen (something such as a claim): [*usu. simple tenses*] *A sudden drop in temperature gave weight to the weatherman's warning of a cold weekend. You must produce more papers to give weight to your request to join your family in this country.*

**give under** *v prep*
**1** to offer (something such as a promise) because of (something): [T1 + *under* (*usu. pass.*)] *A promise given under a threat is worthless.*
**2 give under hand and seal** *law* to make (an agreement) lawful by formally giving it to the other party: [*usu. pass.*] *This agreement is given under my hand and seal this day...* → **deliver under**

**give up** *v adv*
**1** to stop doing or having (something); willingly or unwillingly lose (something or someone); get rid of (something); do without (something): [T1] *The doctor told Jim to give up sweets to lose weight. I did want a holiday abroad, but we've had to give up the idea. The Church will give up all claim to the property if the government will pay for necessary repairs and keep it for the nation. The singer was advised to give up all thought/hope of becoming a professional. One of the advantages of living in the city centre is that we have been able to give up a car, as the trains and buses run so frequently. Grace chose to marry a Muslim and give up her Christian faith. It's hard to give up the drinking habit without help. The king was forced to give up his crown and hold elections for a people's government. No mother wants to give up her children to someone else's care.* [T4] *The doctor told Jim to give up smoking, which made him gain weight! I shall have to give up singing when I get too old. Being able to give up driving to work is a real pleasure.*
**2** to stop attempting or working at (something such as a job): [T1] *When you get married, will you give up your job? Why did Jim give up his college course? I thought he liked it. Now why would any respectable man give up a perfectly good job and disappear to a tropical island to paint pictures of native women?* → **chuck in** (2), **chuck up** (3), **fling in**[1] (2), **fling up** (3), **pack in** (3), **resign from, throw in**[1] (5), **throw up** (3), **turn in** (7)
**3** to stop attempting (something): [IØ] *All the girls swam across the lake, except two who gave up only a few yards from the shore. Don't give up without even trying!* [T1] *Sometimes I feel like giving up the struggle to live on my income. Some people in hospital refuse to give up their fight for life.* [T4] *I gave up trying to understand the income tax laws, and let professionals deal with my accounts. The child gave up learning the piano when he learned how long it would take to become a professional musician.*
**4** *not fml* to stop trying to guess a joke or mystery: [IØ (*simple tenses*)] *I give up, tell me the end of the story.*
**5** to stop trying to cure or find (someone): [T1 (*for*) (*usu. simple tenses*)] *The doctors gave my uncle up ten years ago, but he's still alive! The school seems to have given the boy up; he will never learn to behave better. The missing child was given up for dead/lost when she was found by a dog, hidden in some bushes.*
**6** to stop having a relationship with (someone): [T1 (*often simple tenses*)] *The woman gave up her lover to save her marriage. I hope you won't give up your old friends now that you're in such an important position.*
**7** to yield (something, someone, or oneself) (usu. to someone): [T1 (*no pass., often simple tenses*)] *After hiding in the woods for weeks, the criminal gave himself up. If you catch the escaped prisoner, will you give him up (to the police)? When the town was conquered, the councillors refused to give up the records. The sea will never give up its dead. When will the desert give up its secrets?* → **deliver over, give over** (2), **give over to** (1), **hand over** (3), **render up, turn in** (4), **yield to** (1), **yield up** (1)
**8** to yield (usu. something) to someone else: [T1 (*often simple tenses*)] *We had to give up the castle (to the enemy). It's still polite to give up your seat on the bus to an old lady.* → **deliver over, give over** (2), **give over to** (1), **hand over** (3), **turn in** (5), **yield to** (1), **yield up** (2)
**9** *not fml* to stop waiting for (someone): [T1 (*often simple tenses*)] *Where have you been? We'd almost given you up, and were about to start dinner without you!*
**10** *infml* to (pretend to) stop believing in (someone); declare (someone) to be silly, worthless, etc.: [T1 (*simple tenses*)] *You're still not serious; I give you up, you're hopeless!* also **give up on**
**11** to offer to do without (something such as

time or money), usu. for a good purpose: [T1] *Father gave up his holiday to paint the house. All the workers gave up an hour's pay to send money to the family of their fellow worker who was killed in an accident.*

**12 give up the ghost: a** *old use* to die: [*simple tenses*] *The old king gave up the ghost during the night.* **b** *infml* to stop putting any effort into doing something: *What's the use of giving up the ghost halfway through writing your book? You'll have wasted all that time!* → **yield up** (3)

*__give up to__ *v adv prep*

**1** to offer (someone or oneself) as a prisoner; yield (something) to (someone): [T1 + *to* (*often simple tenses*)] *The gunman gave himself up to the police. The councillors refused to give up the town records to the enemy. When will the desert give up its secrets to mankind? It's still polite to give up your seat to an old lady.* → **give over to** (1), **yield to** (1)

**2** to set (a time or place) aside for special use for (someone, something, or doing something): [D1 (*usu. pass.*)] *The house was given up to the children for their parties during the season. The building was given up to the youth club by the church.* [V4b] *The rest of the evening will be given up to singing and dancing.* → **give over to** (2)

**3** to give (oneself or one's time, life, etc.) completely to (something or doing something): [D1 (*often simple tenses*)] *He has given himself up to a life of crime. The scientist gave himself up to a study of the life history of flies.* [V4b (*often simple tenses*)] *The doctor gave his life up to helping the poor natives.* → **give over to** (3)

**4** to yield (oneself) to (a feeling): [D1] *Don't give yourself up to sadness, there's still hope!* → **give in to** (3), **give over to** (4), **give to** (23), **surrender to** (2), **yield to** (3)

*__give upon__ *v prep* → GIVE ON

*__glam up__ *v adv*

*infml* to make (something or someone) seem more attractive, esp. by false means: [IØ] *"Do you think I need to glam up to see the man about this job?" "No, I wouldn't, it's your brains that you're offering him."* [T1] *The shopkeepers put their money together to glam up the street for Christmas.*

**glance at** *v prep*

to look quickly or carelessly, often in passing, at (something or someone): [L9 + *at* (*often simple tenses*)] *Glancing at the clock she saw that she was late. I glanced at the title of the book and saw that it was one that I had just read.*

**glance back** *v adv*

to look quickly behind one: [L9 + BACK (*often simple tenses*)] *A runner can lose a lot of advantage by even glancing back to see how far behind the others are.*

**glance down** *v prep*

to read (something such as a page) quickly: [L9 + *down* (*usu. simple tenses*)] *As she glanced down the list, she saw that she had left out a name.*

*__glance off__ *v adv; prep*

**1** to touch (something) with a light blow, without causing much harm: [IØ (*often simple tenses*)] *He moved his shield quickly, and the sword glanced off.* [T1 (*often simple tenses*)] *The sword glanced off the shield and did not damage it.*

**2** to fail to have an effect on (someone): [T1 (*usu. simple tenses*)] *Every scolding that boy gets just seems to glance off him and not change his behaviour at all.*

**glance over/through** *v prep* → **flick through, flip through**

to read (something) quickly or carelessly: [L9 + *over/through* (*usu. simple tenses*)] *I've only had time to glance over your work, but I can already see how much it has improved. I've glanced through your play and would like a longer time to read it, as it might possibly be worth acting. Will you be able to glance over my report before I send it to the committee?*

**glance round** *v adv; prep*

to look quickly round (something or oneself): [L9 + ROUND/*round* (*often simple tenses*)] *I thought I heard someone following me, and glancing round (me), I caught sight of a dark figure in the shadows.*

**glance through** *v prep* → GLANCE OVER

**glare at** *v prep*

**1** to look at (usu. someone) with anger, hate, etc.: [IØ + *at*] *Don't glare at me like that, you deserved the scolding. The whole class glared at the teacher when he told them their punishment. The two bears glared at each other, then sprang at each other's throats.*

**2 glare defiance at** to look at (someone) with pride and hate but without fear or respect: *The prisoner glared defiançe at the soldiers as they prepared to shoot him.*

**glare down** *v adv*

(of the sun or other bright hot light) to shine pitilessly and continuously (on someone or something): [IØ + DOWN (*on*)] *A surprising number of people live in the desert, where the hot sun glares down all day and little rain falls. Hot stage lights glared down on the singer, making her feel faint.*

*__glass in/glaze in__ *v adv* → **glass over**

to surround; enclose (a space such as part of a building) with glass: [T1 (*usu. simple tenses*)] *The builders glassed in the outside entrance, giving the pleasing effect of an added room.* —**glassed-in** *adj*

*__glass over__ *v adv* → **glass in**

to cover (a hollow space such as part of a building) with glass: [T1 (*often pass.*)] *The archway between the two buildings will be glassed over, so that people crossing from one building to the other can keep dry when it rains.* —**glassed-over** *adj*

*__glaze in__ *v adv* → GLASS IN

**laze over** *v adv* → **film over, haze over**
(of eyes) to (cause to) become almost sightless, covered or as if covered by a nontransparent film: [IØ (*usu. simple tenses*)] *The singer's eyes glazed over and she sank down and fainted.* [T1 (*usu. pass.*)] *His eyes are glazed over; I think he must be dead.*

**leam with** *v prep*
**1** to shine with (something such as polish): [IØ + *with*] *All her furniture gleams with polish and loving care; she makes me ashamed.* → **glisten with** (1), **glitter with** (1)
**2** (of eyes) to shine fiercely with the expression of (a feeling): [IØ + *with*] *The king's eyes gleamed with anger as he listened to the farmer's complaint.* → **glisten with** (2), **glitter with** (2)

**lean from** *v prep*
to obtain (something such as information) indirectly or in small quantity from (something or someone): [T1 + *from*] *Bit by bit the police gleaned the story behind the robbery from a few chance remarks by the prisoner.*

**listen with** *v prep*
**1** to shine with (something such as a liquid or ice): [IØ + *with*] *In the winter sunshine, the lake glistened with its covering of ice. Jane's eyes glistened with tears when she learned that she had not been invited.* → **gleam with** (1), **glitter with** (1)
**2** (of eyes) to shine with the expression of (a feeling): [IØ + *with*] *The king's eyes glistened with sorrow as he heard the farmer's sad story.* → **gleam with** (2), **glitter with** (2)

**litter over** *v adv*
*CanE* to (cause to) become covered with ice after freezing rain: [T1 (*usu. pass.*)] *The road, which was glittered over early this morning, was reported safe for traffic at about 10.30.* [IØ (*usu. simple tenses*)] *I'd like to get home before the roads glitter over.*

**litter with** *v prep*
**1** to shine with (something having a bright but unsteady light such as jewels): [IØ + *with*] *It's such a clear night that the sky is glittering with stars, do come and look.* → **gleam with** (1), **glisten with** (1)
**2** (of eyes) to shine unsteadily with the expression of (a very strong and often bad feeling): [IØ + *with*] *The murderer's eyes glittered with hate as he drew out his knife ready to strike.* → **gleam with** (2), **glisten with** (2)
**3** to be made important or noticeable because of (something special): [T1 (*no pass., often simple tenses*)] *The guest list glittered with famous names.*

**loat over** *v prep*
**1** to enjoy seeing or thinking about (one's possessions, money, or success) etc., in a proud, selfish, and unpleasant way: [L9 + *over*] *Jim likes to gloat over all the sports prizes he has won, which he keeps in a glass case. Our team are gloating over their victory.*
**2** to enjoy (someone else's misfortune or defeat) unpleasantly: [L9 + *over*] *Don't you think it's a little unkind to gloat over your competitor's failure? Why are you gloating over Jane's not being invited? What's it to you?*

***glom onto** *v prep*
*AmE infml* to obtain (something): [T1 (*usu. simple tenses*)] *Where did you glom onto this book? I've been hunting for a copy everywhere!*

***glory in** *v prep*
**1** to take delight in; be very happy about (something or doing something): [T1 (*often simple tenses*)] *The young singer gloried in her unexpected success.* [T4 (*often simple tenses*)] *That teacher glories in making the students feel uncomfortable.* → **delight in, rejoice at, rejoice in** (1), **rejoice over, take in** (7)
**2** to enjoy; cause amusement with (something such as a name): [T1 (*simple tenses*)] *There is an English village which glories in the name of Cold Christmas.* → **rejoice in** (3)

***gloss over** *v prep* → **slough over, slur over, smooth over²**
to speak kindly of or refuse to mention (something bad) so as to hide or excuse its wrongness: [T1 (*often simple tenses*)] *The school can hardly gloss over its failure to control these troublesome boys, now that the report is in all the papers. The prisoner's lawyer tried to gloss over his criminal past by drawing the judge's attention to his recent good behaviour.*

**glow with** *v prep*
**1** to shine at a low level of light, often red, because of (heat, light, etc.): [IØ + *with*] *The whole horizon glowed with the light of the great fire. The city streets glow with advertisements all night.*
**2** to appear bright; shine because of (something such as a feeling, health, etc.): [IØ + *with*] *Mary glowed with pride when Jim received his prize. The children's faces glowed with health after they had been playing in the snow. Jim's eyes glowed with anger when he learned how Mary had been treated at the hospital.* → **kindle with** (3), **shine with**

**glower at** *v prep* → **frown at** (1), **scowl at**
to look at (someone) threateningly: [L9 + *at*] *Stop glowering at me, I've done nothing wrong!*

**glue down** *v adv* → **gum down, stick down** (1), **stick on¹** (1)
to fix (something) firmly down, as to a surface with a sticky substance: [X9 + DOWN] *We must glue the mat down at the edges to stop it curling.*

**glue on** *v adv*
to fix (something) firmly in place with a sticky substance: [X9 + ON] *I can't get the cover off this box, it's been glued on.*

**glue to** *v prep*
**1** to join (something), usu. with a sticky substance to (something else): [X9 + *to*] *Make*

*sure the stamp is properly glued to the envelope.*

*2 to fix (oneself, one's eyes, or attention) on (something), often for a long time: [D1 (*often pass., often simple tenses*)] *I don't like to see children glueing their eyes to the television set for hours on end. You'll never get Mary out tonight, she's glued to a book. While the policeman's attention was glued to the window, the thief escaped through the back door. Why have you got your eyes glued to the keyhole? There's nothing to see in there!*

**glue together** *v adv*
to join (usu. two things) with a sticky substance: [X9 + TOGETHER] *The pages have got glued together—the book is ruined!*

**glut with** *v prep*
**1** to fill (oneself) too full with (food or drink): [X9 + *with*] *Children at any party will glut themselves with cake and ice cream, and not touch healthier foods.*
**2** to supply (a market, trade, etc.) with a quantity of (goods) that is greater than the demand: [X9 + *with* (*usu. pass.*)] *The shops are glutted with fruit from abroad, because nobody will pay the high prices.* → **saturate with** (3)

**gnaw at/on** *v prep*
**1** (of certain animals) to bite with the teeth repeatedly on (something), little by little: [IØ (AWAY) + *at/on*] *The rabbits escaped by gnawing (away) at the fence until they had made a hole big enough to get through. Dogs like to gnaw on a bone.*
*2 to cause suffering to (someone or someone's mind): [T1] *Sorrow is gnawing at my heart. Guilt gnawed away on the prisoner's conscience until he admitted his crime. Doubt gnawed at me so that I felt I had to telephone him.*

**gnaw away** *v adv*
**1** (of certain animals) to bite continuously or repeatedly at something: [IØ + AWAY (*at, on*)] *Lions like to gnaw away at a piece of meat. That dog has been gnawing away on his bone all afternoon.*
*2 (of certain animals) to destroy (something such as wood) with the teeth: [T1 (*often pass.*)] *Some of the woodwork in this old house has been gnawed away by rats.*

**gnaw on** *v prep* → GNAW AT

**go aboard** *v adv* → **come aboard, go ashore, take aboard, take ashore, take on,** *v prep* (1).
to take a place on a ship, or sometimes a plane or train: [L9 + ABOARD] *The man says that we have to go aboard half an hour before the ship sails.*

**go about**[1] *v adv*
**1** to move freely; travel: [L9 + ABOUT] *It's easy in this city to go about by bus. People are going about more now that the weather's better.* → **get about**[1] (1), **get round**[1] (1), **take about**[1] (1), **take round**[1] (1)
**2** to be able to move and see people again after illness: [L9 + ABOUT] *Mother is much better, thank you, she's able to go about a bi[t] more.* → **get about**[1] (2), **get round**[1] (2)
*3 (of news, disease, etc.) to spread: [IØ (*continuous tenses*)] *Stories have been going abou[t] concerning the government's secret intentions. There are a lot of colds going about just now.* → **be about**[1] (2), **be around** (2), **get about**[1] (3), **ge[t] abroad** (2), **get round**[1] (3), **go round**[1] (2), **put abou[t]** (2), **set about**[1]
*4 to be seen together in public (with some one): [IØ (*with*) (*often continuous tenses*)] *Jim had been going about with Mary for tw[o] years before they married. I don't like the ide[a] of my son going about with those rough boys How long have those two been going abou[t] together?* → **ask out**, etc.
*5 *not fml* to move around in the course o[f] one's life (doing something); be publicl[y] noticed (doing something): [I4] *You can't g[o] about saying nasty things like that about hin[m] in public.* → **go round**[1] (10)
*6 *naut* (of a ship) to turn round to face th[e] opposite direction; sail against the wind b[y] moving first to one side and then to th[e] other: [IØ] *The sailors have the hardest tim[e] when going about. To sail forward against th[e] wind, we had to go about.* → **bring about** (2) etc.

**go about**[2] *v prep*
**1** to be able to move or travel around ([a] place): [L9 + *about*] *The quickest way to g[o] about the city is by underground train.* → **ge[t] about**[2], etc.
*2 to start (something or doing something) [T1 (*usu. simple tenses*)] *I wanted to make [a] dress, but I didn't know how to go about i[t]* [T4 (*usu. simple tenses*)] *How do you g[o] about building a boat?* → **set about**[2] (1)
*3 to do; perform (something such as work) [T1 (*no pass.*)] *The best cure for grief is to g[o] about your usual work.* → **be about**[2] (3)
*4 (of news, disease, etc.) to spread round ([a] place or group): [T1 (*no pass., continuou[s] tenses*)] *There are whispers going about th[e] city that the Bank is to raise its interest ra[tes] again. There are a lot of colds going about th[e] school.* → **go round**[2] (3)
**5 go about one's business** *not fml* to be bus[y] with one's own affairs; do only what concer[ns] oneself: *If that reporter comes here askin[g] more questions, tell him to go about his bus[i]ness!* → **send about**, etc.

**go above** *v prep*
**1** to move higher than (something): [L9 *above*] *The plane has gone above the clouds, [I] can't see it any more.* → **go over**[2] (1)
**2 go above someone's head** to be too difficu[lt] for someone to understand: [*simp[le] tenses*] *Some of the jokes were rather rud[e] but luckily they went above the children[']s heads.* → **go over**[2] (9)
**3 go above someone's head** to ask for advi[ce] or judgment from a person in a higher po[s]

tion or rank than someone: *If you think that your captain is giving the wrong orders, you may have to go above his head to his commanding officer, to ask what should be done.* → **go over²** (10)

**go abroad** *v adv* → **get abroad** (1), **take abroad**
to travel to a foreign country or countries: [L9 + ABROAD] *Can we afford to go abroad for our holiday as we used to? The family's youngest son went abroad and has not been seen since.*

**go across¹** *v adv*
**1** to move across a road, water, space, etc.: [L9 + ACROSS (*to*)] *People have been using the new bridge to go across (to the island), as it saves them a lot of time. I'll just go across and get a loaf of bread.* → **come over¹** (3), etc.
*__2__ to become understood or accepted: [IØ (*to*) (*usu. simple tenses*)] *Did your speech go across to the crowd all right?* → **come across** (2), etc.

**go across²** v prep → **come across²** (1), **get across²** (1), **get over²** (1), **put across²** (1), **send across²**, **set across, take across, take over²** (1)
to move across (a road, water, space, etc.): [L9 + *across*] *It's so much safer to go across the road at the traffic lights.*

**go across to** *v adv prep*
**1** to cross a road, water, space, etc., to reach (another place): [L9 + ACROSS + *to*] *I'll just go across to the shop and buy a loaf of bread; I shan't be a minute. We go across to the island every summer, it's so peaceful there.* → **go over to** (1)
*__2__ to change sides or opinion to (another side): [T1 (*no pass.*)] *A leading politician went across to the other party, and is now trying to be elected as its leader.* → **go over to** (5)
*__3__ to move towards (someone), as to speak to him/her: [IØ + *to*] *I went across to the little boy and asked him if he was lost.* → **go over to** (2)

**go adrift** *v adj*
**1** (usu. of a boat) to become free of its fastenings and float away without control: [L9 + adrift] *The boat has gone adrift and there's no one on board!*
*__2__ *infml* (of a navy seaman) to leave without permission: [IØ] *Three of the ship's officers went adrift after the last voyage.*

**go after** *v prep*
**1** to chase (someone): [T1 (*no pass.*)] *Half the guards went after the escaped prisoners, but they got away free.* → **come after** (2), etc.
**2** to aim for (something): [T1 (*no pass.*)] *I think we should go after increased production this year.* → **aim at** (2), etc.
**3** *not fml* to try to win (something or someone): [T1 (*no pass.*)] *I shall have to spend every morning going after a job. You can't go after somebody else's girl! Jim intends to go after the big prize.* → **be after** (3)

**go against** *v prep*
**1** to oppose (someone or something): [T1 (*no pass., often simple tenses*)] *I wouldn't advise you to go against the director. If you go against your father's wishes, you will have to leave home. It's no use going against the customs of a country that you are visiting.* → **be against** (1)
**2** to be opposite to (something): [T1 (*no pass., simple tenses*)] *It goes against my nature to get up early in the morning. Lying goes against my principles.* → **be against** (2)
**3** to be not in favour of (usu. someone); be lost by (someone); act against (someone): [T1 (*no pass.*)] *If the election goes against the government, who will lead the country? I should warn you that if the case goes against you, you may find yourself in prison. Your unfortunate report might go against your chances of winning the contract.*
**4 go against the grain** to be completely opposite to one's wishes: [*simple tenses*] *It goes against the grain that I should have to pay taxes towards military costs that I don't approve of.*

**go aground** *v adv* → **run aground** (1)
(of a ship or boat) to become trapped in water not deep enough: [L9 + AGROUND (*on*)] *We were winning the boat race until our boat went aground (on a sand bank).*

**go ahead** *v adv*
**1** to move in front (of something or someone): [L9 + AHEAD (*of*)] *I'll go ahead and warn the others to expect you later. A man with a red flag had to go ahead of the first railway trains. Go ahead, what are you waiting for? The advance party has gone ahead to see if the mountain is safe for the other climbers. The police examined the cars and then allowed them to go ahead.* → **go forward** (1), **go on¹** (2)
*__2__ to be allowed to continue (with something); take place, as after a difficulty: [IØ (*with*)] *The council gave us permission to go ahead with our building plans. In spite of the chairman's illness, the meeting will go ahead as planned.* —**go-ahead** *n not fml* → **go forward** (4)
*__3__ to begin, esp. to speak: [IØ (*usu. imper.*)] *Go ahead, we're all listening.* → **fire ahead, fire away** (4)
*__4__ to improve; advance: [IØ (*often continuous tenses*)] *Is your work going ahead now that the materials have arrived?* → **go forward** (3)
*__5__ *infml* to take action on one's own: [IØ] *You can't just go ahead and sell the car, it's partly mine.*

**go ahead with** *v adv prep*
**1** to move forward or in front together with (someone or something): [L9 + AHEAD + *with*] *Do you want to go ahead with the advance party, or would you rather be in the second group of climbers? When the first trains ran, a law was passed stating that a man had to go ahead with a red flag to warn people that the train was coming.*
*__2__ to be allowed to continue with (something):

[IØ] *The council at last gave us permission to go ahead with our building plans.*

*3 to continue to speak (something): [IØ (*usu. imper.*)] *Please go ahead with your story, there won't be any more interruptions.*

**go along** *v adv*

**1** to move forward, esp. on a road: [L9 + ALONG] *The roads were so muddy that we had to go along on horseback. As the roads were so icy, the cars were going along very slowly and carefully. As they went along, the roads became more lonely.*

***2** to go somewhere together with someone: [IØ (*to, with*)] *At the last minute, the two youngest children decided to go along.* → **come along** (2), etc.

***3** to advance; move further with something: [IØ (*simple tenses*)] *I like to add up my bank account as I go along, instead of waiting for the statement at the end of the month. Work like this becomes less interesting as you go along.*

***4** to advance; go well: [IØ (*with*) (*often continuous tenses*)] *How is your work going along? It's going along nicely, thank you, if rather slowly. How is Tom going along with his new book?* → **bring on** (3), etc.

***5** *infml* to go away: [IØ (*usu. imper.*)] *Will you children go along, I can't do with you in here!*

**6 go along (with you)!** *infml* I don't believe you!: [*imper.*] *Oh, go along with you! I know better than that! Go along! Don't be silly!* → **come on**¹ (10), etc.

**go along with** *v adv prep*

**1** to move forward with (something or someone): [L9 + ALONG + *with*] *The cars went along with great care on the icy roads. Can I go along with you? I won't get in the way.* → **get along with** (1), **get on with** (1), **take along**

***2** to advance with (something such as work): [T1 (*continuous tenses*)] *How is Tom going along with his new book?* → **bring on** (3), etc.

***3** to accept; agree with (someone or something): [T1 (*often simple tenses*)] *We'll go along with your suggestion, although it's not exactly what we wanted. I go along with you as far as the principles are concerned, but I disagree with the practical side of your decision.* → **play along**¹ (2)

***4** to be found together with (something): [T1 (*no pass., simple tenses*)] *Failing health too often goes along with old age. Increased unemployment has gone along with rising prices all over the world in recent years.* → **go together** (2), **go with** (2)

**5 go along with you** *infml* to go away: [*usu. imper.*] *Go along with you now! You're in my way!* → **get along with** (5)

**6 go along with you!** *infml* I don't believe you!: [*imper.*] *Go along with you! I know better than that!* → **come on**¹ (10), etc.

***go amiss** *v adv* → **be amiss, come amiss**

to happen in a wrong way: [IØ] *Something's gone amiss, he's not here to meet us.*

***go amok/amuck** *v adj* → **RUN AMOK**

***go ape** *v adj*

*AmE infml* to become mad or very keen: [IØ] *Have you heard about Bill? He's gone ape over that new girl in the office!*

**go around**¹ *v adv* → **GO ROUND**¹

**go around**² *v prep* → **GO ROUND**²

**go as** *v prep*

to attend an event dressed to look like (usu. someone): [L9 + *as*] *I'm going to the fancy dress party as King Henry; who are you going as?*

**go ashore** *v adv* → **come aboard, go aboard, take aboard, take ashore**

to leave a ship: [L9 + ASHORE] *We'd better go ashore before the ship sails and takes us with it by mistake! "All ashore that's going ashore!" came the last shout to the passengers' visitors.*

**go aside** *v adv* → **draw aside** (2), **pull aside** (2), **take apart** (1), **take aside, take on**² (11), **take to** *v prep* (20)

to move to one side, away from others: [L9 + ASIDE] *The two men went aside to have a private conversation.*

**go astray** *v adv*

**1** (usu. of animals) to wander: [L9 + ASTRAY] *The farmer spent all night looking for three of his sheep that had gone astray.* → **lead astray** (1)

***2** to be lost: [IØ] *Some of my most important papers have gone astray; I wish you people would keep out of my things.*

***3** to live immorally: [IØ] *Many young girls, living alone in London, go astray for lack of parental control.* → **lead astray** (2)

**go at** *v prep*

**1** to leave at (a certain time): [IØ + *at*] *I have to go at 3.30, my father's meeting me. Go at once!* → **come at** (1)

**2** *not fml* to be sold for (a price, usu. surprising): [L9 + *at*] *There were perfectly good coats going at £23!* → **go for** (3)

***3** *not fml* to attack (usu. someone): [T1 (*no pass.*)] *Our dog went at the postman again this morning, he'll get us into trouble. The newspapers are really going at the government, aren't they!* → **come after** (2), etc.

***4** also **go full tilt at** *not fml* to work hard at (something): [T1 (*no pass.*)] *The students are really going at their studies now that the examinations are near.*

**go away** *v adv*

**1** to leave: [L9 + AWAY] *There was no answer to my knock, so I went away. Go away! I don't want to see you! Away you go now!* → **be off** (2), **come away** (3), **come away with** (1), **come off**¹ (4), **get away with** (1), **get off**¹ (5), **go away with** (1), **go off**¹ (1), **go off with** (1), **send away** (1), **send off** (2), **set forth** (1), **set forward** (2), **set off** (1), **set out** (1), **start off** (2), **start out** (2), **take away** (2), **take off**¹ (5)

***2** (of newly married people, esp. the wife) t

leave after a wedding: [IØ] *Mary wore such a pretty blue suit to go away in.* —**going-away** *adj*

*__3__ to cease: [IØ] *If this pain doesn't go away soon, I shall go mad! "Rain, rain, go away, come again another day."* (song) → **go off'** (3) **pass away** (2), **pass off** (1), **take away** (3), **wear off** (3)

*__4__ to run away (taking someone or something): [IØ (*with*)] *The farmer's daughter and the lawyer's son have gone away together! Let's hope they've gone away to get married. The last time this happened, the young man went away with his best friend's wife! She's gone away with my clock, the thief!* → **abscond with**, etc.

*__5__ (of a horse or runner) to lead a race: [IØ (*continuous tenses*)] *The favourite is going away nicely now, and is sure to win.* → **pull away** (3)

**6 gone away!** (in foxhunting) the fox has been seen and we will chase it: *"Gone away!" cried the huntsman, blowing his horn.*

**go away with** *v adv prep*

**1** to leave with (something or someone): [L9 + AWAY + *with*] *I saw her going away with her mother for a holiday.* → **go away** (1), etc.

*__2__ to take (someone or something) without permission: [T1] *The lawyer's son has gone away with the farmer's daughter! She's gone away with my clock, the thief!* → **abscond with,** etc.

*__3__ *not fml* to believe (an idea): [T1 (*no pass.*)] *Don't go away with the idea that you won't have to pay for it.* → **get away with** (3), **run away with** (8)

*__4__ to leave a place or event with (feelings, memories, etc.): [T1 (*no pass.*)] *After the meeting, everyone went away with something to think about.* → **bring away, come away with** (2), **send away with** (1)

**go back** *v adv*

**1** to move backwards or away: [L9 + BACK (*usu. simple tenses*)] *Go back! The roof is falling! Our army had to go back a few miles when the enemy won an advantage. Go back a step or two, you're too near.* → **move back** (1), etc.

**2** to return: [L9 + BACK (*to*)] *Shall we go back there for our holiday next year? Go back to bed, you're too ill to be up. When do the children go back to school? We'll take this load, and then go back for another load. So back they went again, and still there was nobody there.* → **be back** (1), **come again** (1), **come back** (1), **come back to** (1), **get back** (2), **get back to** (1), **go back to** (1), **send back, take back** (2)

*__3__ to take space: [L9 (*to*) (*simple tenses*)] *Our land goes back all the way to the sea. How far does your property go back? How far back does your property go?* → **go back to** (2), **go down'** (11), **go down to** (2)

*__4__ to return, as in conversation (to something): [L9 (*to*) (*usu. simple tenses*)] *Let us go back to what the chairman was saying. He wants us to go back to the old and tried methods. Don't go back to your old eating habits or you'll gain all that weight again. I woke early, but couldn't go back to sleep. While my typewriter is being repaired, I shall have to go back to writing letters by hand.* → **come back to** (3), **get back** (3), **get back to** (2), **go back to** (3)

*__5__ to return in time, in one's thoughts: [L9 (*to*) (*usu. simple tenses*)] *I'm sorry, my memory doesn't go back that far, but perhaps Grandmother's does. Yes, whenever she talks, she always likes to go back to her younger days.* → **carry back** (2), **go back to** (4), **take back** (7)

*__6__ to have lasted or been recorded (since an earlier time): [L9 (*to*) (*simple tenses*)] *My family goes back 500 years. My family goes back to the 15th century.* → **date back to, go back to** (4), **take back** (7)

*__7__ (of a clock or watch) to be set to an earlier time, usu. one hour, in the autumn: [IØ (*often simple tenses*)] *The clocks go back next week, so it will seem dark sooner.* → **go forward** (6), **put ahead** (3), **put back** (8), **put forward** (6), **put on'** (8), **set ahead** (3), **set back** (5), **set forward** (6)

*__8__ to end a strike; go back to work: [IØ] *I shall be glad when the post office workers go back, it's very difficult not getting any letters.* → **bring out** (7), etc.

**go back on** *v adv prep*

**1** to return on (something such as a vehicle): [L9 + BACK + *on*] *I missed the train, and had to go back on the bus.*

*__2__ to fail to fulfil (a promise, agreement, etc.): [T1 (*pass. rare, often simple tenses*)] *You should never go back on your promise to a child.*

*__3__ to fail to be loyal to (someone): [T1 (*no pass., usu. simple tenses*)] *I was depending on him but he went back on me. Never go back on your friends.* → **let down** (6)

**go back to** *v adv prep*

**1** to return to (someone or a place): [L9 + BACK + *to*] *Will you go back to the same hotel next year? I'm glad she's decided to go back to her husband.* → **go back** (2), etc.

*__2__ to take space as far as (something): [L9 + *to* (*simple tenses*)] *Our land goes back to the sea.* → **go back** (3), **go down to**

*__3__ to return, as in conversation to (something): [L9 + *to* (*usu. simple tenses*)] *Let's go back to what the chairman was saying. He wants us to go back to the old and tried methods. Don't go back to your old eating habits or you'll gain all that weight again. I woke early, but couldn't go back to sleep. When my typewriter is being repaired, I shall have to go back to writing letters by hand. Were you glad to go back to work?* → **come back to** (3), **get back to** (2), **go back** (4)

*__4__ to return in time, in one's thoughts: [L9 +

to (*simple tenses*)] *Whenever Grandmother talks, she always likes to go back to her younger days. Her memory goes back to the last century. We must go back to the Middle Ages to discover the origins of English plays.* → **carry back** (2), **go back** (5), **take back** (7)

*__5__ to have lasted or been recorded since (an earlier time): [L9 + *to* (*simple tenses*)] *My family goes back to the 15th century. This church goes back to 1173.* → **date back to, go back** (6), **reckon from**

**6 go back to square one** *infml* to begin again at the beginning: *Jane lost so much work at school when she was ill that she's had to go back to square one and start all over again.*

**go bad** *v adj* → **be off** (7), **go off**[1] (8)
to turn sour or start to decay: [L9 + **bad**] *Don't drink this milk, it's gone bad. I shall complain to the shop, their meat started going bad the same day I bought it!*

**go badly** *v adv* → **go well**
to happen in an unfavourable way; be unsuccessful: [L9 + BADLY] *My work always goes badly when I'm tired. That business deal is going badly for the firm; perhaps we should not complete it.*

***go bankrupt** *v adj* → **go broke** (1), **go bust**
to declare oneself or one's business to be unable to pay debts: [IØ] *If trade does not improve soon, the firm may go bankrupt, and then all the workers will be out of a job.*

**go before**[1] *v adv*
**1** to be earlier in time: [L9 + BEFORE (*often perfect tenses*)] *We must make more effort than all the governments that have gone before.*

*__2__ *fml* to have lived and esp. died in earlier times: [IØ (*perfect tenses*)] *Let us remember all those who have gone before, and have left us their example of Christian living.*

**go before**[2] *v prep*
**1** to move in front or ahead of (something or someone): [L9 + *before* (*usu. simple tenses*)] *When the first railway trains ran, a man had to go before each train carrying a red flag. The advance party went before the main group of climbers, to see if the mountain was safe.*

*__2__ *fml* to live and esp. die earlier in time than (someone): [T1 (*no pass., perfect tenses*)] *Let us remember all those who have gone before us, and have left us their example of Christian living.*

*__3__ to appear to face (a court of law or someone else in power): [T1 (*no pass.*)] *When you go before the judge, you must speak the exact truth.* → **bring before** (1), etc.

*__4__ to be sent for consideration or approval by (someone or a group in power): [T1 (*no pass., often simple tenses*)] *Your suggestion goes before the board of directors next week.* → **put before** (2), etc.

**5 pride goes before a fall** a person who behaves in a proud and impatient manner is likely to suffer an early misfortune: [*no pass., simple tenses*] *Your failure in the examination will teach you not to be so lazy next time because you were so sure you would pass: pride goes before a fall.*

***go begging** *v adj*
*not fml* to be unwanted: [IØ (*usu. continuous tenses*)] *If those two cakes are going begging, I'll have them!*

**go behind** *v prep*
**1** to move to a position at the back of (someone or something): [L9 + *behind* (*usu. simple tenses*)] *The baby went behind his mother to play a hiding game. The knife has gone behind the cooker, and I can't get it out.*

*__2__ to examine a deeper level of (something): [T1 (*no pass., often simple tenses*)] *You have to go behind the poet's words to see what she really means.*

**3 go behind someone's back** to act secretly, often deceitfully: *Don't let her catch you breaking the rules; she's likely to go behind your back and complain to the committee about your actions.*

***go below** *v adv* → **be below**[1] (2), **send below, take below**
*naut* to go downstairs on a ship or boat: [IØ] *When the weather grew stormy, we went below to keep dry, but the poor captain had to be out in all the rain.*

***go berserk** *v adj* → **drive crazy** (2), **drive mad** (2), **drive out** (3), **run amok, send berserk**
to become wild or out of control: [IØ] *The goats have gone berserk; they broke down the fence and now they're eating all the washing on the line in the garden next door! There's trouble at the prison; some of the prisoners went berserk when they were refused certain rights, and have seized some of the guards and their guns; you'd better send help.*

**go between** *v prep*
**1** to travel between (two places): [L9 + *between* (*usu. simple tenses*)] *The ship 'Queen Elizabeth' went between England and the United States.*

**2** to fit or take a place between (two other things or people): [L9 + *between* (*simple tenses, usu. present*)] *The scene goes between the entrance of the murderer and the discovery of the body. I keep the plays in alphabetical order: for example, Shaw goes between Shakespeare and Sheridan.*

*__3__ to act as a messenger between (two people): [T1 (*no pass.*)] *The little girl was given a bar of chocolate as her payment for going between her sister and her sister's boyfriend.*
—**go-between** *n*

**go beyond** *v prep*
**1** to take a position behind or further than (something such as a place); pass (something or somewhere): [L9 + *beyond* (*usu. simple tenses*)] *As the ship went beyond the horizon it appeared to sink until it could be seen no*

*longer. The deer has gone beyond the trees; I can't shoot at it from this distance.* → **go past²** (1), etc.

* **2** to take further action than is allowed or expected by (something): [T1 (*no pass., usu. simple tenses*)] *Be careful not to go beyond your rights in your quarrel with your neighbour. The policeman was charged with going beyond the law in his treatment of the prisoners. The court has gone beyond its powers in declaring the doctor guilty in spite of an earlier judgment in his favour. The soldier was honoured for performing brave deeds that went beyond the call of duty.* → **be beyond** (2)

* **3** to be greater than (something): [T1 (*no pass., simple tenses*)] *The money that I won went beyond my fondest hopes.* → **be beyond** (3)

* **4** to advance further than (a stage): [T1 (*simple tenses*)] *I don't think this class will be able to go beyond lesson six.* → **get beyond** (2), **get past²** (3), **go past²** (2)

* **5** to be too difficult for (someone) to do or understand; find (doing something) too difficult: [T1 (*no pass., simple tenses*)] *I was interested to hear the speaker, but his speech went beyond me when he had finished introducing his subject. I think this work goes beyond his abilities. This job has gone beyond us; we should have started something easier.* [T4] *I've gone beyond running the business on my own now; I really must get someone in to help.* → **get past²** (5), etc.

**6 go beyond caring** *not fml* to cease to care (about something): [*usu. perfect tenses*] *Don't ask me how we're to pay the bills; I've gone beyond caring!* → **go past²** (4), etc.

**7 go beyond endurance** to be worse than someone can reasonably be expected to bear: [*usu. perfect tenses*] *Your rudeness has gone beyond endurance—kindly leave my house!* → **get beyond** (5), etc.

**8 go beyond a joke** *not fml* to cease being funny; become too serious: [*usu. perfect tenses*] *Your continual lateness has now gone beyond a joke; if you're not on time tomorrow, you will be dismissed.* → **be beyond** (7), **get beyond** (6), **get past²** (9), **go past²** (6)

**go blank** *v adj*

(of one's mind) to be emptied of thoughts: [L9 + blank (*usu. simple tenses*)] *Try to let your mind go blank, then you will feel calmer. I looked at the examination paper and my mind went completely blank—I couldn't answer a single question!*

**go broke** *v adj*

**1** *infml* to declare oneself or one's business to be unable to pay debts: [I∅] *If trade's no better next month, we shall go broke and then what will you people do for jobs?* → **go bankrupt, go bust**

**2 go for broke** *infml* to use every possible effort, esp. to win: *Jim intends to go for broke in the next race, even though the effort may kill him. We must really go for broke in our attempt to win trade from our competitors.* → **go for** (14)

* **go bust** *v adj* → **go bankrupt, go broke** (1)

*infml* to declare oneself or one's business to be unable to pay debts: [I∅] *The firm had only been running for a year when it went bust, and a lot of people lost their money.*

**go by¹** *v adv*

**1** to pass; move past something or someone: [L9 + BY (*often simple tenses*)] *You've missed the bus, it just went by. Guess who went by as I was waiting at the corner? Please drop this parcel at the Post Office as you go by.* → **come along** (1), **come by¹** (1), **fly by¹** (1), **get by¹** (1), **get past¹** (1), **go past¹** (1)

* **2** (of time) to pass: [I∅] *Saturday afternoons go by like lightning! When the days seem to go by slowly, you can tell that you're not enjoying yourself. As the weeks went by, still no letter arrived. The speed of living was much slower in days gone by.* —**bygone** *adj* → **fly by¹** (2), **go on¹** (8), **go past¹** (2), **pass by¹** (2), **run on¹** (2), **wear away** (5), **wear on¹, wear out** (4)

* **3** (of a chance, etc.) to pass without being taken: [I∅ (*simple tenses*)] *You can't afford to let any job go by when you've been out of work for so long.*

* **4** *not fml* (esp. of a fault) to pass without being noticed: [I∅ (*simple tenses*)] *I know you were late again this morning, but we'll let that go by; I wanted to speak to you about something else.*

**go by²** *v prep*

**1** to pass (something or someone): [L9 + *by* (*usu. simple tenses*)] *An arrow went by his ear, narrowly missing his head. I shall complain to the bus company, my bus just went by the stop empty!* → **go past²** (1), etc.

**2** to work by means of (a power or force): [L9 + *by* (*simple tenses*)] *The child thought that the toy car went by magic, but in fact it went by electricity.* → **run on²** (2), **work by**

* **3** to travel using (a means, as a vehicle, road, etc.): [L9] *I think we should go by train, it's safer. Letters with enough stamps can go by air. It'll be quicker if we go by the main roads rather than through the country.*

* **4** to be guided by (something giving directions): [T1 (*no pass.*)] *Having no map to go by, we soon lost our way. Sailors can find their way around the world, going by the stars.*

* **5** to base one's judgment on (something): [T1 (*no pass., often simple tenses*)] *You can't go by what he says, he's very untrustworthy. You make a mistake if you go by appearances. Don't go by that clock, it's been slow for years. This small piece of information is not much to go by.* → **go on²** (7)

* **6** to act according to (something): [T1 (*no pass.*)] *Our chairman always goes by the rules.*

* **7** to be known by (a name): [T1 (*no pass.,*

*often simple tenses*)] *He went by the name of Baker, to avoid discovery by the police.* → **appear under, call by[2]** (3), **pass by[2]** (2), **pass under[2]** (2)

**8 go by the book** *not fml* to obey the rules exactly: *You know what punishment to expect, this judge always goes by the book.*

**go down[1]** *v adv*

**1** to descend: [L9 + DOWN (*often simple tenses*)] *Once we get to the top of the hill, the road starts to go down. The miners go down in a sort of cage. Go down and see what the children are doing downstairs, will you?* → **come down** (1), **get up** (1), **go down to** (1), **go down with** (1), **go up[1]** (1), **go up to** (1), **send up[1]** (1), **take up** (3)

**2** to lower one's body, esp. to one's hands and/or knees: [L9 + DOWN (*usu. simple tenses*)] *I had to go down on the floor to play with the baby. Go down behind the wall, then he won't see us.* → **get down** (2)

*__3__ to be swallowed: [IØ] *The child coughed and coughed because a piece of bread had gone down the wrong way. "A spoonful of sugar helps the medicine go down."* (song) → **get down** (7)

*__4__ (of the sun or moon) to set: [IØ] *As the sun went down below the horizon, the sky became pink and gold.*

*__5__ to fall: [IØ] *The man slipped on the ice and went down heavily. The whole house went down in flames. Down they went with a crash!* → **bring down** (2), **come down** (2, 3), **get down** (4, 5), **send down** (4), **shoot down** (1)

*__6__ to become lower, as in level: [IØ] *The floods are going down now that it's stopped raining. The standard of performance has gone down since last year. I wish my weight would go down. Egg prices usually go down in the spring, when they are more plentiful. If his temperature doesn't go down, I shall call the doctor. The world's total supply of oil is going down all the time, as more and more gets used up. The lights went down in the theatre just before the play began.* → **be down** (2), **be up** (7), **bring down** (4), **come down** (5), **go down to** (3), **go up[1]** (3), **go up to** (2), **keep up** (2), **put up[1]** (4), **remain up** (2), **send down** (2), **send up[1]** (2)

*__7__ to lessen; be reduced: [IØ] *If this wind goes down, we may be able to sail tomorrow. Put some more wood on the fire, it's going down.* → **get up** (7)

*__8__ (in music) to move to a lower note: [IØ (*usu. simple tenses*)] *No no, you go down a 5th here, not a 4th, remember?* → **go down to** (4), **go up[1]** (4), **go up to** (3)

*__9__ to sink; drown: [IØ] *Three ships went down in last night's storm off the coast. "The ship went down like lead."* (S.T. Coleridge, *The Ancient Mariner*) → **go down to** (5), **go down with** (4), **go under[1]** (2)

*__10__ to become less swollen: [IØ] *My ankle is going down nicely, I should be able to walk soon. This tyre keeps going down, I'd better pump it up.* → **go up[1]** (5)

*__11__ to reach; take space: [L9 (*simple tenses*)] *How far does your land go down?* → **go back** (3), **go back to** (2), **go down to** (2)

*__12__ to become less valuable; reach a lower social level: [IØ (*in*)] *The neighbourhood has gone down since those rough people moved in. A new car goes down in value the minute you buy it.*

*__13__ to be recorded, esp. in writing: [L9 (*in*)] *Everything you say will go down in our records. This day will go down in history. Our secret plans must not go down on paper.* → **write down** (1), etc.

*__14__ to leave a university after a period of study, or a city for a less important place: [IØ (*to*)] *It must seem very quiet in the university town when the students have gone down for the summer. I have to go down to the country to see my aunt.* → **be up** (10), **come down** (7), **come up** (14), **go down to** (6), **go up[1]** (10), **go up to** (4), **send down** (3)

*__15__ to be received, esp. with approval; be liked (by someone): [L9 (WELL, *with*) (*usu. simple tenses*)] *How did your speech go down (with the public)? Jim went down well with Mary's parents on his first visit. Tom's new book has gone down better with the newspapers than his last one, I see. The thought of work didn't go down too well as I came to the end of my holiday. The new director's appointment did not go down very well.* → **come across** (2), etc.

*__16__ to be considered less worthy: [IØ (*usu. simple tenses*)] *He went down in my opinion as soon as he mentioned sex.* → **come down** (8), **come up** (12), **go up[1]** (12)

*__17__ to fail: [IØ] *The business has been going down all winter; perhaps trade will be better in the spring. One of my best students went down in the examination!*

*__18__ to be defeated or destroyed: [IØ (*before to*) (*often simple tenses*)] *After so many victories, our team went down in the last game! The city went down before the enemy.* → **go down to** (7)

**19 go down in the world** to be reduced to a humbler standard of living or social level: *It's sad to see such fine old houses going down in the world. I met an old friend who used to be successful, but in the past few years he's gone down in the world.* → **come down** (11), **come up** (19), **go up[1]** (15)

**20 go down on one's knees** to pray: *Go down on your knees and give thanks for your safety.* → **get down** (11)

**go down[2]** *v prep*

**1** to descend (something): [L9 + *down*] *Be careful as you go down the stairs, they're not safe.*

**2** to travel along (a road): [L9 + *down*] *Guess who I met going down the road?*

**3 go down the drain** *infml* to be wasted: *If you leave college, all that money has gone down the drain! All my attempts to help him went down the drain.*

**go down to** *v adv prep*

**1** to descend to (usu. a place): [L9 + DOWN + *to*] *Go down to the bottom of the garden and see if the children are there. The native women go down to the river to wash the clothes. "I must go down to the seas again, to the lonely sea and the sky."* (John Masefield, *Sea Fever*) → **come down** (1), **go down¹** (1), **go down with** (1), **go up to** (1)

*__2__ to reach as far as (somewhere or something): [L9 + *to* (*simple tenses*)] *Our property goes down to the sea. The road goes down to the bottom of the valley. The class history book only goes down to 1960.* → **go back to** (2), **go down¹** (11)

*__3__ to be reduced to (a level): [IØ] *The river has gone down to its usual level now that the floods are over. My weight went down to a satisfactory level and then it went up again! The prices should go down to something more reasonable if they expect people to buy.* → **go down¹** (6), etc.

*__4__ (in music) to move to (a certain lower note): [IØ + *to* (*usu. simple tenses*)] *Can you go down to a low D?* → **go down¹** (8), **go up to** (3)

*__5__ to sink to (somewhere): [IØ + *to*] *Three ships went down to the bottom in last night's storm.* → **go down¹** (9), **go down with** (4)

*__6__ to leave a university or city to go to (a less important place): [IØ + *to*] *I have to go down to the country to see my aunt.* → **go down¹** (14), etc., **go up to** (4)

*__7__ to be defeated or destroyed by (something or someone): [IØ + *to* (*often simple tenses*)] *The famous tennis player went down to an unknown young woman. The old fighter went down to a well-aimed blow.* → **go down¹** (18)

**go down with** *v adv prep*

**1** to descend with (someone or something): [L9 + DOWN + *with* (*often simple tenses*)] *We had to go down with great care, as the hill was so steep. You go down with Mary, and we'll come later.* → **come down** (1), **go down** (1), **go down to** (1), **go up¹** (1)

*__2__ to be accepted or approved by (someone): [L9 + *with* (*usu. simple tenses*)] *Jim went down well with Mary's parents on his first visit. How did your speech go down with the crowd? Tom's new book has gone down better with the newspapers than his last one.* → **come across** (2), etc.

*__3__ to become ill with (usu. a disease): [T1 (*no pass., often simple tenses*)] *Our holiday was fine until Jim went down with a bad cold; after that, it all got rather dull.* → **be down with, come down with** (2)

*__4__ to sink or drown together with (something such as a ship): [L9] *A captain is supposed to go down with his ship, which seems rather pointless.* → **go down¹** (9), **go down to** (5)

***go dry** *v adj*

**1** (of cows) to be unable to give milk: [IØ] *The farmers think that their cattle have a disease, because the cows have gone dry.*

**2** *not fml* to forbid the sale of alcohol: [IØ (*often simple tenses*)] *During the years before the war, many states in the USA went dry, but found that it only caused more crime.*

***go Dutch** *v adj*

*infml* to share the cost, as of a meal: [IØ (*with*)] *Many women these days would rather go Dutch to show their independence, than be paid for by a man.*

***go easy** *v adv*

**1** *infml* to behave calmly: [IØ (*usu. imper.*)] *Go easy, dear, there's nothing to get excited about.* → **go slow** (2), **slow down** (2), **take easy**

**2** *not fml* to treat (someone) kindly, not severely: [IØ (*on, with*)] *Go easy on the child, will you, she's too young to understand what she did.*

**3** *not fml* to use (something) carefully, often to make a supply last: [IØ (*on, with*)] *We'd better go easy on the milk, there isn't a lot left.*

**go far** *v adv*

**1** to travel a long way: [L9 + FAR (*usu. simple tenses*)] *Do you have to go far to your work? This car can go far on very little petrol.*

*__2__ *not fml* to be successful: [IØ (*simple tenses, usu. future*)] *That young man will go far, see if I'm not right!*

*__3__ (of a supply) to last; (of money) to buy plenty of goods: [IØ (*usu. simple tenses*)] *That small loaf won't go far among this large family! Even a reasonable income doesn't go very far these days, with the prices rising all the time.*

*__4__ to help a lot (towards something, as a collection of money): [L9 (*towards*) (*simple tenses, usu. future*)] *Thank you, your gift will go far towards helping to build the children's hospital.* → **go towards** (4)

**5 as far as it goes** *not fml* within limits: *My job is all right as far as it goes, but I don't like fixed working hours.*

**6 go as/so far as** *not fml* to be bold or direct enough (to do something); declare the truth: [*usu. simple tenses*] *I wouldn't go so far as to say that she is a liar, simply that she doesn't always tell the truth.*

**7 go too far** to behave or speak unreasonably: *This time you've gone too far! I will not listen to your rude remarks any longer—kindly leave my house!*

**go farther/further** *v adv*

**1** to travel a greater distance: [L9 + FARTHER/FURTHER (*often simple tenses*)] *Our latest model car can go farther than any earlier model on the same quantity of petrol!*

**2 go farther and fare worse** to be no better off in another space or time, so it is best to be content with what one has: [*usu.* + *could*] *The city is not too bad; my job's all right, and the house is a bit small, but you could go farther and fare worse, I always say.*

**go for** *v prep*

**1** to leave a place to perform (an activity): [L9 + *for*] *I'd like to go for a walk, will you come with me? Let's go for a drive in the country. No, I'd rather go for a swim.* → **take for** (1)

**2** to go somewhere to bring (someone or something): [L9 + *for*] *Would you go for some milk for me? We haven't enough till tomorrow. If the child gets any worse I shall have to go for the doctor.* → **come for** (1), **send for** (1)

**3** to be sold for (a price, usu. surprising): [L9 + *for*] *There were perfectly good coats going for $20!* → **pay for** (1), etc., **go for** (18)

*__4__ *not fml* to attack (usu. someone): [T1 (*no pass.*)] *Our dog went for the postman again this morning, he'll get us into trouble.* → **come after** (2), etc.

*__5__ *not fml* to attack (someone or something) in words: [T1] *The newspapers have really gone for Tom's new book in a big way!*

*__6__ to aim for (something): [T1] *I think we should go for increased production this year. Jim intends to go for the big prize.* → **aim at** (2), etc.

*__7__ to attempt; choose (something): [T1 (*no pass.*)] *I thought I'd go for question three, it looks easy. Shall we go for the second run? I'd rather go for a safe savings plan than one with a high rate of interest but a lot of risk.*

*__8__ to approve of; support (something or someone); enjoy (something): [T1 (*no pass., often neg., simple tenses*)] *I don't go for loud popular music. Will the voters go for him, that's the point? I don't go for his idea, I think it's dangerous. Mary goes for blue rather a lot, don't you think?* → **go in for** (5), **go on** (10)

*__9__ to like; admire; be attracted to (someone, esp. a certain kind of person): [T1 (*no. pass., simple tenses*)] *Do you go for tall men? I go for clever men, whatever they look like. Why are you interested in her? I thought you only went for dark girls.*

*__10__ to concern; be true for (someone): [*this/that* + T1 (*no pass., simple tenses, usu. present*)] *That goes for me, too, I completely agree. You must arrive on time or be dismissed—that goes for all workers, not only those who've been late in the past.*

*__11__ to be regarded as being (a certain kind of person): [T1 (*no pass., usu. simple tenses*)] *He goes for a lawyer, but I don't think he ever studied or practised law.*

*__12__ to intend to become (a certain kind of person): [T1 (*no pass.*)] *Her son is going for a doctor! Isn't that splendid!*

**13 go bail for** to obtain the freedom of (someone) by paying money (bail) to ensure his appearance in court: *I shall have to put you in prison until your case can be heard, unless you can find anyone to go bail for you.* → **bail out** (1)

**14 go for broke** *infml* to use every possible effort, esp. to win: *Jim intends to go for broke in the next race, even though the effort may kill him. We must really go for broke in our attempt to win trade from our competitors.* → **go broke** (2)

**15 go for a burton** *BrE infml* to be killed, destroyed, or ruined: [(*usu. perfect tenses*)] *Two of our planes and one of our best pilots have gone for a burton over enemy country. Our plans to build a new school have gone for a burton because the government can't give us any money.*

**16 go for little/nothing** to be wasted: [(*usu. simple tenses*)] *All our efforts went for nothing, the girl returned to crime as soon as she left the home. All my arguments go for very little, you never take any notice of what I say!* → **count for**

**17 have (got) (something) going for one** *infml* to possess a quality or advantage: *With his character, courage, and charm, he has plenty going for him. This film actor has little ability; all he has going for him are his good looks.*

**18 go for a song** *infml* to be sold at a very low price: *This is a very fashionable area of town now, but when we first came the houses were going for a song.* → **go for** (3)

**go forth** *v adv*

**1** *bibl or fml* to start a journey, esp. for a special purpose: [L9 + FORTH (*usu. simple tenses*)] *Go forth on your journey and take the true faith to the people.* → **bring forth** (1), **come forth, send forth** (2), **send out** (4)

**2** *old use* to be sent out: [L9 + FORTH (*usu. simple tenses*)] *An order went forth that all prisoners should be killed.* → **send forth** (3)

**go forward** *v adv*

**1** to move further in front: [L9 + FORWARD (*often simple tenses*)] *Let's go forward to the front of the hall so that we can hear the speaker more clearly. The advance party have gone forward to see if the mountain is safe for the main group of climbers. In this game, if you throw a six, you can go forward three squares.* → **come forward** (1), **go ahead** (1), **go on**[1] (2), **step forward** (2)

2 *naut* to move to the front of a boat or ship: [L9 + FORWARD] *The captain has asked all the sailors to go forward so that he can speak to them in a group.*

*__3__ to improve; advance: [IØ] *Is your work going forward now that the materials have arrived?* → **go ahead** (4)

*__4__ to continue (with something planned): [IØ (*with*)] *The council gave us permission to go forward with our building plans.* → **go ahead** (2)

*__5__ to be sent further for approval (by someone): [IØ] *Your name will go forward to the committee when they are considering the new* *appointments.* → **put forward** (3), **send forward** (2)

*__6__ (of the hands of a clock or watch) to be moved to a later time: [IØ (*usu. simple tenses*)] *Do the clocks go forward in the spring?* → **go back** (7)

**go from** *v prep*

**1** to start a journey from (a place): [L9 + *from* (*simple tenses*)] *Which station does the train go from?*

**2** to leave (something or someone): [L9 + *from* (*usu. simple tenses*)] *Something has gone from English life. Go from me; we must not meet again.*

**3** to start from; advance from (somewhere): [L9 + *from* (*usu. simple tenses*)] *Let's go from the top of the page. Where do we go from here?* (= What do we do next?) → **take from** (6)

**4 go from bad to worse** *not fml* to get worse and worse: *The weather has gone from bad to worse this winter; first the storms, then the snow, and now this severe cold.*

**5 go from strength to strength** to increase one's power, success or fame rapidly: *The firm has been going from strength to strength since Mr. Brown became director.*

**go further** *v adv* → GO FARTHER

**go haywire** *v adj*

*infml* to go wildly wrong: [IØ] *I had arranged to do the shopping when we got back from our holiday, but my plans went haywire when the train was three hours late.*

**go home** *v adv*

**1** to return to one's home or country: [L9 + HOME] *I must be going home, it's getting very late. "British soldiers go home."* (sign on wall) → **bring home** (1), **get back** (2), **get home** (1), **take home** (1)

*__2__ *infml* to die or be destroyed: [IØ] *I'm afraid old Charlie's gone home; he'd been ill for years. This washing machine's going home already, and we haven't had it long; I shall complain to the makers.*

*__3__ to have an effect, usu. on someone: [IØ (*usu. simple tenses*)] *The chairman's pointed remark went home, and the committee members fell silent.* → **get home** (3)

**go ill with** *v adv prep* → **go well with**

to be unlucky or unfavourable for (someone): [T1 (*no pass.*)] *I'm sorry to hear that the examination went ill with you; will you try again?*

**go in**[1] *v adv*

**1** to move indoors: [L9 + IN] *I have to go in now, my mother's calling me for tea.* → **bring in** (1), **come in** (1), **get in**[1] (2), **send in** (1), **take in**[1] (1), **wheel in** (1)

**2** to fit inside something: [L9 + IN] *This nail won't go in, I think I must have hit a brick. That space is too small, the bookcase won't go in.* → **fit in**[1] (1), **get in**[1] (1), **put in**[1] (1), **stick in**[1] (1)

*__3__ (of the sun, moon, or stars) to disappear behind clouds: [IØ] *At this time of year, when the sun goes in, it is suddenly much colder.*

*__4__ to start work as usual: [IØ] *What time do you have to go in tomorrow?*

*__5__ (esp. in cricket) to take one's turn on the field of play; enter a competition: [IØ] *After three men were out, the captain went in next to try to save the game. Go in and win!* → **be in**[1] (7), **be out** (7) etc., **come in** (6), **put in**[1] (15), **send in** (2), **stay in**[1] (4)

*__6__ *mil* to start an attack: [IØ] *All the soldiers were ordered to go in and seize the enemy position.* → **send in** (5)

*__7__ *not fml* to be understood: [IØ] *I keep trying to understand how a car engine works, but it doesn't seem to go in; am I stupid or something?* → **take in**[1] (10)

**8 go in (at) one ear and out (at) the other** *infml* (of a warning, news, etc.) to be disregarded by a person; make no impression on someone: *I've tried again and again to make the boy listen and obey, but everything I say just goes in at one ear and out at the other!*

**go in**[2] *v prep*

**1** to travel in (a vehicle, clothing, etc.): [L9 + *in*] *You're not going in that old suit, are you? Whose car shall we go in? Please don't go in such a bad temper, you'll only feel worse.* → **take in**[2] (2)

**2** to enter (a building, space, etc.): [L9 + *in* (*usu. simple tenses*)] *I leave the lights on all evening, because I dare not go in the house when it's all dark. Please go in the side door, this one is locked.* → **take in**[2] (1)

**3** to fit in (a space): [L9 + *in* (*usu. simple tenses*)] *The Christmas tree can go in this corner. If your ball goes in the right hole, you win the game. An ordinary nail won't go in a brick wall.* → **fit into** (1), etc.

*__4__ (of money) to be spent on (something or doing something): [T1 (*no pass., simple tenses*)] *Not more than a quarter of your income should go in rent. He used to be rich, but a lot of his fortune went in paying his father's debts.* → **go on**[2] (8)

**5 go in one ear and out the other** *infml* (of a warning, news, etc.) to be disregarded by a person; make no impression on someone: *Didn't you hear me ask you to get ready? Everything I say goes in one ear and out the other.*

**6 go in someone's favour** to be judged in someone's favour; happen so as to suit or support someone: [*usu. simple tenses*] *To his lawyer's surprise, the judge's decision went in the prisoner's favour.*

**7 go in fear of one's life** to be very greatly afraid, esp. for one's own safety: [*usu. simple tenses*] *In many cities in the United States, people go in fear of their lives every time they leave their own homes.*

**8 go in peace!** an expression of a wish for someone's happiness and calmness of mind: [*imper.*] *The war is over so the prisoners can now go in peace.*

**go in for** *v adv prep*
**1** to go indoors for (something, a reason, a length of time, etc.): [L9 + IN + *for*] *I have to go in for my tea now, see you tomorrow. Having already left the house, she went in for her umbrella, as it had begin to rain. I must go in for a rest now. I think I'll go in for an hour or so, it's very hot out here.* → **come in for** (1)
*****2** to try to pass or win (something such as a competition): [T1] *Are all you children going in for the flower-arranging competition? I'd like to go in for a more advanced examination if I can.* → **enter for,** etc.
*****3** to take an interest in (a subject or doing something): [T1] *How long has Jim gone in for stamp collecting? I thought he only went in for music and tennis.* [T4] *How long has Jim gone in for collecting stamps?* → **take up** (9)
*****4** to aim towards (a profession): [T1] *Our son decided to go in for law, much to our surprise. He may end up by going in for politics, he's always liked arguing.*
*****5** to choose; enjoy (something or doing something): [T1 (*usu. simple tenses*)] *I don't go in for loud popular music. Not many people go in for big families these days. Mary goes in for blue rather a lot, don't you think?* → **go for** (8), **go on**[2] **(10)**

**go in with** *v adv prep*
**1** to enter with (something or someone): [L9 + IN + *with*] *Will you go in with me? I'm afraid to go in by myself. Many hospitals allow mothers to go in with their children when they need hospital treatment.*
*****2** to join (someone or a firm), usu. in business: [T1 (*no pass.*)] *I wonder if you would consider going in with me as a partner? There would be a certain amount of risk.*

**go into** *v prep*
**1** to enter (a building, space, etc.): [L9 + *into*] *I have to go into town tomorrow to buy presents, do you want to come? Go into the garden and pick some apples, will you? Two men were seen going into the house after dark. "I was glad when they said unto me. Let us go into the house of the Lord."* (The Bible) → **be in**[2] (1), etc.
**2** to enter; travel to (a place) for a special purpose; take a place in (somewhere): [L9 + *into*] *What time do you have to go into work tomorrow? Mother had to go into hospital for her leg operation. Many university students have to go into lodgings as there is no room for them in a college or hall.* → **go to** (3)
**3** to hit (something) with force: [L9 + *into*] *The car went into a tree and was severely damaged.*
**4** to be able to fit inside (something): [L9 + *into* (*simple tenses*)] *My foot won't go into this boot. Will the radio go into this box? No more clothes will go into this suitcase.* → **fit into** (1), etc.
*****5** to search in; examine (a container) with one's hands, usu. with wrong intentions: [T1] *Who's been going into my drawers? There are some important papers missing. All the cupboards in the house had been carefully gone into by thieves, looking for the jewels.* → **rifle through**
*****6** to examine (something such as a story): [T1] *The police went into the man's story to see if he was telling the truth. The statement that you have made will have to be thoroughly gone into.*
*****7** to mention, examine, or talk about (something): [T1] *There's no need to go into details yet; just give me the general idea. Then he went into a long explanation of why he had come to see me. You will have to go into all your reasons for choosing this college. Let's not go into our argument in front of the neighbours.*
*****8** to join (a group); start in (a business or profession): [T1 (*no pass.*)] *I hear their son has gone into the army. I'd rather mine went into business of some kind.* → **be in** (2)
*****9** to divide (a number) exactly by two or more: [T1 (*simple tenses*)] *2 goes into 6, 3 times, but 2 won't go into 7. 3 into 10 won't go.*
*****10** to begin (an activity): [T1 (*no pass.*)] *This car won't go into reverse.*
*****11** to begin to be in (a condition of mind or body): [T1 (*no pass.*)] *He'll go into a temper at the very mention of that man's name. Mary went* (*off*) *into fits of laughter when Jim walked in wearing his funny clothes. When she saw the body of her son, the mother went* (*off*) *into a dead faint.* → **go off into**
*****12** to wear (different clothing): [T1 (*no pass.*)] *You'll have to go into white if you want to play tennis. It's so nice to go into summer dresses again! Now that it's really cold, I must go into my warm boots. Not many families these days go into mourning after a member of the family has died.*
**13 go into abeyance** *fml* (usu. of a law, plan, etc.) to be placed on one side for a certain time: (*usu. simple tenses*) *The new law will go into abeyance until it has received royal approval. Because of the increased cost, the city's plan to enlarge the underground train service has had to go into abeyance until at least next year.* → **be in**[2] (4)
**14 go into one's act** *not fml* to behave in one's usual manner, often deceitful, to gain an effect or aim: *Watch our best salesman going into his act, you can learn a lot from him.*
**15 go into action** to start something planned, esp. a military attack; become active: *Are you men ready? We go into action at midnight. As soon as the guards left, the prisoners went into action according to their escape plan.* → **put out** (23), etc.
**16 go (off) into a coma** to become uncon-

scious, as in illness: *The girl went into a coma after the car accident three months ago, and has not woken up yet.*

**17 go into a decline** to become very weak, as through illness, grief, etc.: *I'm afraid your grandmother has gone into a decline and may not live long. Business in the area went into a decline, as not many people could afford to buy goods.* → **fall into** (7)

**18 go into hiding** to enter a hiding place and stay there, esp. to hide from the police or an enemy: *If you don't catch the thieves at once after the robbery, you'll never find them, as they will have gone into hiding.*

**19 go into a huddle** *infml* to consider a matter together: *The committee went into a huddle and later declared their decision.*

**20 go (off) into hysterics** to start laughing uncontrollably, usu. as a result of shock: *When she read the letter, she went into hysterics and the family had to hit her in the face to make her stop.*

**21 go into particulars** to explain details (about something): *I don't want to go into particulars (about the meeting) now, I'll tell you all the details later.*

**22 go (off) into a trance** to become as if unconscious, with the mind empty or under someone's power: *The woman claimed to be able to speak with the dead, and would go (off) into a trance and make strange noises.*

**go it** *v pron*

**1** *infml* to act with too much effort, excitement, etc.; travel fast: [IØ (*often continuous tenses*)] *Three concerts in a week is going it rather, isn't it? Driving 800 miles in three days is going it some!* → **go some**

**2 go it alone** *not fml* to act independently: *My father worked for an insurance firm for many years, until he decided to go it alone and start his own insurance business. Although they would be worse off than under the rule of the powerful country, the whole population of the island voted to go it alone and demand their freedom.*

**go mad** *v adj*

to lose one's senses or one's mind: [L9 + mad] *Have you gone mad? Of course you need boots in this weather! It's very sad, his wife went mad and had to be locked up in the special hospital.*

**go native** *v adj*

esp. *BrE not fml* to live by choice in the manner of the (often conquered) people of a place far from civilization: [IØ] *Officers in charge of lonely islands vary in their acceptance of tropical life: some continue to dress for dinner as if they were still in England; others go native, wear the local clothes and eat the native foods, and generally behave like uncivilized men.*

**go near/near to** *v prep; adv prep* → **come close to, come near, get near**

**1** to move closer to (someone or something): [L9 + *near*/NEAR + *to*] *How soon can you teach a baby not to go near (to) the fire? Let's go near (to) the front so that we can hear the speaker more clearly.*

***2** to be very near or like; reach (something or doing something): [T1 (*simple tenses*)] *This film goes near (to) the quality of good old films.* [T4 (*simple tenses*)] *I never seem to go near (to) winning any money on these games.*

**go off¹** *v adv*

**1** to leave, esp. suddenly: [L9 + OFF (*usu. simple tenses*)] *She went off in a bad temper. Why did the painter leave his family and go off to live on a tropical island? That dog's gone off again! Don't go off without saying goodbye, will you? Are you ready, children? Off we go, then!* → **go away** (1), etc.

**2** (of an actor) to leave the stage: [L9 + OFF (*usu. simple tenses*)] *At the end of this scene, the murderer goes off, hearing the police arrive.*

***3** to cease: [IØ] *The pain went off after three treatments. The effect of the drug will go off after two hours.* → **go away** (3), **pass away** (2), **pass off** (1), **take away** (3), **wear off** (3)

***4** to be switched off; not be supplied: [IØ (*often simple tenses*)] *The power went off in several parts of the country during the high wind. You can't light the gas, it's gone off again. The light went off as the policemen entered the room.* → **put off¹** (3), etc.

***5** to explode; make a sudden noise: [IØ (*often simple tenses*)] *A gun goes off every day to mark exactly one o'clock. I'm sorry I'm late; I overslept because my alarm clock didn't go off.* → **let off¹** (2), **set off** (3), **spark off** (1), **touch off** (1), **trigger off** (1)

***6** to take place; succeed: [L9 (*simple tenses*)] *How did your play go off? It went off very well, thank you. The wedding went off as planned.* → **bring off** (2), **carry off¹** (6), **come off¹** (5, 6), **pass off** (2), **pull off¹** (4)

***7** to become worse: [IØ] *The quality of performance has gone off since last year. The book goes off after the first 50 pages.* → **drop away** (3), drop off (5), **fall away** (4), **fall behind¹** (3), **fall off¹** (4)

***8** *not fml* to turn sour or start to decay: [IØ] *Don't drink the milk, it's gone off. I shall complain to the shop; this meat started going off the same day that I bought it.* → **be off¹** (7), **go bad**

***9** *not fml* to fall asleep: [IØ] *I had a bad night; I went to bed early enough, but for some reason I couldn't go off. Have the children gone off yet?* → **doze off**, etc.

***10** to run away (taking someone or something): [L9 (*with*) (*usu. simple tenses*)] *The farmer's daughter and the lawyer's son have gone off together. Let's hope they've gone off to get married. The last time this happened, the young man went off with his best friend's wife.*

*She's gone off with my clock, the thief!* → **abscond with**, etc.

**11 go off at half-cock** *infml* to be only partly successful: [(*often simple tenses*)] *The government's plan to control rising prices and wages went off at half-cock when the trade unions refused to agree to the new laws.*

**12 go off at a tangent** *infml* to change the subject suddenly: *The teacher was telling us about the poet's life, when he went off at a tangent and started talking about his own war experiences.*

**go off² *v prep***

**1** to leave (something): [L9 + *off*] *Many people think that Britain's money troubles started when she went off the gold standard. The train went off the rails and fell into the valley, killing everyone on board. The road goes off the map here. Let's go off the main road and see something of the country. His writing is so large that it looks as if it's going off the edge of the page.* → **come off² (4), take off² (4)**

***2** to cease to like or enjoy (something or someone): [T1] *Has Grace gone off that red-haired boy yet? I went off coffee when I was expecting a baby.* → **be off² (4), put off² (2), turn off² (3)**

**3 go off the air** (of a radio station) to cease broadcasting: *This station is now going off the air until tomorrow.*

**4 go off the beaten track** *infml* to do something unusual: *When Jim's father had been in business for ten years, he decided to go off the beaten track and make all his workers partners in the profits; as a result, he was very successful.*

**5 go off the boil** *infml* to stop being so keen or active: *Keep the public interested, don't let them go off the boil! After their quarrel, Jim and Mary found that their relationship had gone off the boil, and they were never again as loving as they had been.* → **be on² (9)**

**6 go off the deep end** *infml* to speak very angrily, often without cause: *What's she going off the deep end for now? Has somebody said something wrong?* → **dive off** (2), **jump off** (2)

**7 go off one's head/nut/rocker** *infml* to become mad: *The poet went off his head and started wandering around his house with no clothes on, in bitter cold.* → **be off² (5)**

**8 go off the rails** *infml* to begin to behave strangely, as in being unfaithful in marriage, disordered in mind, or in performing a crime: *I would never have guessed that Mary of all people would go off the rails, and here she is seeing another man behind Jim's back. Young people easily go off the rails without people they respect to guide them in their behaviour.* → **keep on** (14), **run off² (6), stay on² (5)**

***go off into** *v adv prep* → **go into** (11)

to start (a state or activity): [T1 (*no pass.*)] *Hearing the story, the old man went off into loud laughter. When she saw the body of her son, the mother went off into a dead faint.*

**go off with** *v adv prep*

**1** to leave with (something or someone): [L9 + OFF + *with* (*usu. simple tenses*)] *I saw her going off with her mother for a holiday.* → **go away** (1), etc.

***2** *not fml* to take (someone or something) without permission: [T1 (*usu. simple tenses*)] *She's gone off with my book! The milkman's gone off with my wife.* → **abscond with**, etc.

**go on¹ *v adv***

**1** to continue travelling; (of a road, river, etc.) continue; stretch into the distance: [L9 + ON (*often simple tenses*)] *The police examined the cars and then allowed them to go on. Do you want to stop in this town, or shall we go on? We can't go on any further, the fall of snow has blocked the road. This range of mountains seems to go on for ever.* → **keep on** (3)

**2** to travel in front: [L9 + ON] *You go on, and I'll follow in a few minutes. The advance party has gone on to see if the mountain is safe for the other climbers.* → **go ahead** (1), **go forward** (1)

**3** to be able to fit on something (such as a part of the body): [L9 + ON (*simple tenses*)] *No wonder this boot won t go on, I've been trying to put it on the wrong foot. If you fill the box too full, the lid won't go on.* → **fit on¹ (1), put on¹ (2)**, etc.

***4** to behave; live: [L9 (*usu. simple tenses*)] *Now that our quarrel is over, can we go on as we did before? I can't go on like this, I've got to get help.*

***5** to continue (doing something) esp. after interruption: [IØ (*to, with*) (*often simple tenses*)] *Do go on, I am listening. When you've finished those questions, go on to page 41. Why have you stopped? Go on with your work! I'd like to go on to the next piece of business.* [I3] *After introducing the speaker, the chairman went on to give details of the meeting.* [I4] *Do go on telling me your adventures. He just went on hitting the boy although I told him to stop! How long can anyone go on being happy?* → **carry on** (4), etc.

***6** to hurry, esp. forward: [IØ (*often simple tenses*)] *Go on! There isn't a moment to lose!* → **get on¹ (9)**

***7** *not fml* to keep talking: [IØ (*about, at*)] *How she does go on! Don't keep going on so, we've all heard your story before. The teacher went on and on about good behaviour, as usual.* → **be off¹ (9), be on about, keep on (8), run on¹ (1)**

***8** to pass; last: [IØ] *As the weeks went on, still no letter arrived. It will get colder as the day goes on. How long did the war go on? As our marriage has gone on, we have grown closer to each other.* → **fly by¹ (2), go by¹ (2), go past (2), pass by¹ (2), run on¹ (2), wear away (5), wear on¹, wear out (4)**

***9** to take place; happen: [IØ (*usu. continuous*

*tenses)*] *There's a wedding going on at the church. A crowd gathered to see what was going on. Now then, what's going on here?* —**goings-on** *n*

*__10__ (usu. of something electrical) to be turned on: [IØ] *The street lights go on when it gets dark, and go off at midnight.* → **put on¹** (3), etc.

*__11__ esp. *NEngE* to advance; go well: [IØ (*with*) (*usu. continuous tenses*)] *How is your work going on? It's going on nicely, thank you. How is Tom going on with his new book?* → **bring on¹** (3), etc.

*__12__ esp. *NEngE* to obtain a result; succeed in an attempt: [L9] *How did you go on in this morning's meeting? My students didn't go on too well in the early examination, but by the end of the year, all except three had passed.* → **get on¹** (6), **make out** (5)

*__13__ to find a way to live; have a supply (of something): [L9 (*for*)] *I don't know how I'd have gone on without his support. How did you go on for money while you were out of work?*

*__14__ (of time) to become late; (of people) grow older; (of anything else) get nearer: [L9 (*for*) (*continuous tenses*)] *Grandfather is going on in years. Grandmother is going on for 80. It's going on for midnight, let's go to bed. I don't know her exact age, but she may be 41 going on 42. "This house must cost you half your monthly income!" Not quite, but going on that way."* → **get along** (4), **get on¹** (4), **get on for, go on for**

*__15__ *not fml* to behave oddly: [IØ] *Does he often go on like that? If you go on this way, I shall have to report you.*

*__16__ to take one's place on the stage or sports field: [IØ (*often simple tenses*)] *I was so nervous when I went on.* → **come on¹** (4), etc.

*__17__ to have a friendly relationship (with someone): [L9 (*with*)] *We all go on well with each other here in the school. "Were all brave, they would lead a very uneasy life; all would be continually fighting; but being all cowards, we go on very well."* (James Boswell's *Life of Johnson*) → **get along** (7), **get along with** (4), **get on¹** (7), **get on with** (3)

**18 go on (with you)!** *infml* I don't believe you!: *Go on with you! I know better than that! Go on! He never said that, did he?* → **come on¹** (10), etc.

**go on²** *v prep*

**1** to travel for (a purpose such as a journey): [L9 + *on*] *When do you go on holiday? The theatre company have gone on tour. The students are going on a special course in the mountains. I'd like to go on a long, long trip away from these troubles.* → **send on², take on²** (2)

**2** to ride on (an animal, boat, or machine, esp. for fun): [L9 + *on*] *The children want to go on the wooden horses. Going on the donkeys at the seaside is one of my best childhood memories.* → **take on²** (1)

**3** to have a usual place on top of (something): [L9 + *on* (*simple tenses*)] *The big meat dish goes on the highest shelf.*

*__4__ to start (something such as an activity): [T1 (*no pass.*)] *I go on duty in half an hour.*

*__5__ to work on (a place which is also a profession): [T1 (*no pass.*)] *He had wanted to go on the stage since being a child.*

*__6__ to begin taking (usu. medicine): [T1 (*no pass.*)] *The doctor says that Mother has to go on this special new drug for her heart.*

*__7__ to judge by (something): [T1 (*no pass., usu. simple tenses*)] *You can't go on what he says, he's very untrustworthy. You make a mistake if you go on appearances. This small piece of information is not much to go on. How can we make a decision? We've nothing to go on.* also **go upon** → **go by²** (5)

*__8__ (of money or time) to be spent on (someone, something or doing something): [T1 (*no pass., usu. simple tenses*)] *Half his fortune went on her, but still she refused to marry him. At least a quarter of the average income goes on housing. Three hours a day goes on mealtimes.* → **go in²** (4)

*__9__ to become part of or listed among (a group): [T1 (*no pass.*)] *You get regular notices from the theatre if you go on their mailing list. I'd like to go on the board of directors and show them how to run the business from experience.*

*__10__ *AmE infml* to like (usu. something): [T1 (*no pass., simple tenses*)] *I don't go on his idea, I think it's dangerous.* → **go in for** (5)

**11 be gone on** *infml* to be hopelessly in love with (someone); be very keen on (something): *Is Grace still gone on that red-haired boy? I thought she'd finished with him. Why are young people so gone on that loud tuneless popular music?*

**12 go on the blink** *infml* (of a machine) to fail to work: *The washing machine has gone on the blink again; I shall complain to the makers.* → **be on** (8)

**13 go on the dole** *BrE infml*, **go on unemployment/welfare** *AmE infml* to be paid by the government when unable to work, etc.: *The numbers of people who have had to go on the dole/unemployment/welfare have risen since jobs became harder to find.*

**14 go on the parish** *BrE old use* to be supported by the local church when without money: *It used to be considered a great shame for a family to be forced to go on the parish.*

**15 go on the streets** *not fml* to earn money by having sex with anyone who will pay for it: *What terrible conditions force these young girls to go on the streets?*

**16 go on the wagon** *not fml* to stop drinking alcohol for a period of time: *My doctor tells me I should go on the wagon until I've got the alcohol out of my blood, before it ruins my health.*

*__go on at__ *v adv prep*

**1** to appear on stage or a sports field at (a certain time): [T1 + *at*] *You go on at about 9.30, at the end of the second act. Shall I go on at the end of the afternoon?* → **come on**' (4), etc.

**2** *not fml* to scold; keep asking (someone) (to do something): [T1 (*no pass.*)] *She's always going on at the children for one thing or another. She's been going on at me for a year to buy her a new coat.* → **be after** (4), **be at** (2), **be on at, be onto** (2), **get after** (2), **get at** (6), **get onto** (8), **keep after** (2), **keep at** (4), **keep on at**

*__go on for__ *v adv prep* → **get along** (4), **get on**' (4), **get on for, go on**' (14)

to get nearer (a time or number): [T1 (*no pass., continuous tenses*)] *It's going on for midnight, let's go to bed. Grandmother is going on for 80. The population of the city is going on for 500,000.*

**go on to** *v adv prep*

**1** to travel further to (a place): [L9 + ON + *to*] *Shall we stop here, or do you want to go on to the next town? The plane stops in London before going on to the Far East.* →**take on**' (2)

**2** to move in front to (a place): [L9 + ON + *to*] *I'll go on to the hotel and leave the cases, and meet you here afterwards.*

*__3__ to move towards; begin (another action): [IØ + *to*] *Let's go on to the next scene now. When can we go on to the next piece of business?* → **get onto** (3)

*__4__ to begin (a different length of work time): [T1 (*no pass.*)] *Many factories have had to go on to short time because trade is so bad. The unions would like workers to go on to a 3-day week provided that they were still paid the same.*

**go on with** *v adv prep*

**1** to travel in front with (someone or something): [L9 + ON + *with*] *Would you like to go on with the advance party, or wait here with the main group? I'll go on with the cases, and you follow in your own time.*

*__2__ to appear on stage with (something): [IØ (*often simple tenses*)] *Don't forget to go on with the letter in your hand.*

*__3__ esp *NEngE* to advance with (something): [IØ (*usu. continuous tenses*)] *How is Tom going on with his new book?* → **bring on** (3), etc.

*__4__ to continue with (something): [IØ] *Go on with your work, children!* → **carry on** (4), etc.

*__5__ to have (something) to last usu. a short time; be able to continue with (something): [T1 (*no pass., infinitive*)] *Here's a few dollars to be going on with. Have you got enough work to go on with?* → **carry on with** (3)

**6 go on with you!** *infml* I don't believe you!: [(*imper.*)] *Go on with you! I know better than that!* → **come on**' (10), etc.

**go out** *v adv*

**1** to go outside; leave: [L9 + OUT (*of, to*)] *I don't think you should go out with that bad cold. The telephone rang just as I was going out (of the house). I must just go out shopping for half an hour. It's their own fault that they got lost on the mountain; they shouldn't have gone out climbing without telling somebody where they intended to go. Are you going out to the post? Take my letter, will you? You children are making too much noise in here —out you go!* → **be in**' (2), **be out** (2), **come out** (1), **get out** (1), **go out of** (1), **go out to** (1), **go out with** (1), **take out** (1)

*__2__ to travel to a distant place: [IØ (*to*)] *If I want that new job overseas, I shall have to go out on my own and bring the family out later. The youngest son went out to Canada and made a fortune. Young men want to go out into the world to find fame and riches.* → **come over**' (3), etc.

*__3__ to go outside socially, as to a theatre, concert, etc.; be seen together in public: [IØ (*with*)] *Let's go out tonight; there's a good film showing at the local cinema. Jim and Mary went out (together) for two years before they were married. Is Grace still going out with that red-haired boy? I thought that was all over.* → **ask out**, etc.

*__4__ (of news, orders, etc.) to be sent or passed to several places or people; (of a radio or television presentation) be broadcast: [IØ] *I thought the wedding invitations had all gone out, but my sister says she hasn't received hers. The special programme on the new Prime Minister goes out tonight at 9 o'clock.*

*__5__ (of a fire, light, etc.) to stop burning: [IØ] *Have you a match? My cigarette has gone out. Don't let the fire go out; there's plenty of wood. "The lamps are going out all over Europe; we shall not see them lit again in our lifetime."* (Lord Grey, *3 August 1914*) → **put out** (13), etc.

*__6__ (of money) to be spent in an attempt to earn more, or on costs: [IØ] *There's more money going out than coming in, and I'm worried about the business.* —**outgo, outgoings** *n* —**outgoing** *adj* → **bring in** (3), etc.

*__7__ to stop being popular; become less fashionable: [IØ] *I thought those ancient machines went out years ago! Formal methods of teaching are going out fast, and new ones are coming in all the time. Long skirts went out after a short season of popularity.* → **come in** (10)

*__8__ (of a period of time) to end: [IØ (*often simple tenses*)] *March comes in like a lion and goes out like a lamb. The year went out with a terrible snowstorm.* → **come in** (4)

*__9__ *infml euph* to die: [IØ (*usu. simple tenses*)] *I hope that when I go out I shall leave a better world behind me.*

*__10__ to cease to be in power or competition: [IØ (*often simple tenses*)] *If the government goes out at the next election, who will lead the country? After many victories, our team went out in the last part of the competition.* —**outgoing** *adj*

*__11__ (of the sea) to flow away from the shore: [IØ] *When the sea goes out, the sand stretches for a long way.* → **be in[1] (10), be out (11), come in (7)**

*__12__ *infml* to lose consciousness, esp. in the phr. **go out like a light**: [IØ (*usu. simple tenses*)] *The robber hit him on the head with an iron bar, and he went out like a light. The old fighter went out for the count in the third round.* → **knock out** (3), etc.

*__13__ to stop working because of disagreement: [IØ] *The Post Office workers went out before Christmas, now the electricians are out; I wonder who'll come out next?* → **bring out** (7), etc.

*__14__ (in golf) to play half the number of holes in a course: [IØ] *Mr Black and his partner are still going out; I don't know what time they'll finish.*

**15 go (all) out (for)** *infml* to use every possible effort (to gain something): *The leading horse is going all out, and is sure to win! The young politician is going out for all the votes he can get. The factory will have to go all out for trade if it is not to fail in these hard times.* → **be out for**

**go out of** *v adv prep*

**1** to leave (a place): [L9 + OUT + *of*] *Just as I was going out of the door, the telephone rang. You will have to go out of the country to find better weather.* → **be out of** (1), etc., **go out** (1), etc.

*__2__ to leave; be reduced in (something): [T1 (*no pass., often simple tenses*)] *The anger went out of her voice when the child began to cry. All the force has gone out of his speeches recently. Most of the fun seems to have gone out of life since the children left home. When she read the letter, the colour went out of her face.*

**3 go out of action** to stop working: *Three trains went out of action yesterday when the severe cold ruined the engines.* → **put out** (23), etc.

**4 go out of business** to stop trading; fail: *Jim's father's firm will never go out of business, as trade is good and he treats his workers so well. In these hard times, even some small banks have gone out of business.* → **put out** (24), **put out of** (3)

**5 go out of date** to be no longer considered modern: *Your methods have long gone out of date; you will have to modernize or risk failure. The worst of interesting clothes is that they go out of date so quickly.* → **be up to** (7), etc.

**6 go out of one's depth: a** to try to swim in water too deep to stand on the bottom: *The sea is quite safe to swim in as long as you don't go out of your depth.* **b** *not fml* to find something too difficult to do or understand: *You'll be going out of your depth if you apply for the director's job; try a lower position.* → **be out of** (8), **get out of** (20)

**7 go out of earshot** to move too far away to hear or be heard: *I want to tell you something privately; let's go out of earshot of all these people at the party.* → **come within** (3), etc.

**8 go out of fashion** to be no longer fashionable or popular: *Formal teaching methods went out of fashion some time ago, and new ideas are coming in all the time. When did long skirts go out of fashion? Loud music with a strong beat is going out of fashion, and sweeter, softer, music is becoming popular.* → **come in** (10), etc.

**9 go out of focus** (of eyes or a camera or other such machine) to stop giving a clear picture: *I don't like taking those drugs, they make my eyes go out of focus and I can't see clearly. If you move too far away, the camera will go out of focus and the photograph will be spoilt.* → **get out of** (22)

**10 go out of one's mind** *not fml* to go mad or be very anxious: *I'm so glad you've come; I was going out of my mind with worry. I shall go out of my mind if I teach that class for another day! It's very sad; his wife went out of her mind and had to be locked up in a special hospital. Have you gone out of your mind, letting the baby play with matches?* → **be in[2] (29), be out of (18)**

**11 go out of someone's mind** *not fml* to be forgotten: *I don't remember his name—it's gone clean out of my mind.*

**12 go out of play** (of a ball) to be put in the wrong part of the field of play: *If the ball goes out of play, the other team wins a point.* → **be in** (27a), **be out of** (21)

**13 go out of sight/view** to be longer able to be seen: *I waved my handkerchief until the train went out of sight, and then went sadly home.* → **keep in** (16), etc.

**14 go out of one's way** to take trouble (to do something): [(*often simple tenses*)] *She always goes out of her way to please her guests. It was good of you to go out of your way to meet us at the station. Please don't go out of your way for us.*

**go out on** *v adv prep*

**1 go out on a limb** *not fml* to take a risk: *I don't mind asking the director in person, but I'm not going out on a limb to get a rise in pay.*

**2 go out on a spree/the town** *not fml* to get drunk and have a good time: *When we won the prize the whole football team went out on a spree and didn't get home till the morning.*

**go out to** *v adv prep*

**1** to go outside to (somewhere): [L9 + OUT + *to*] *Are you going out to the post? Take my letters, will you?* → **go out** (1), etc.

*__2__ to travel to (a distant place): [IØ] *The youngest son went out to Canada and made a fortune.* → **come over[1] (3)**, etc.

*__3__ *fml* (of one's heart, sympathy, thoughts) to feel with (someone); be offered to (someone): [T1 (*no pass., simple tenses*)] *Our hearts go out to you in your sorrow. Our thoughts go out to all those who are less fortunate than ourselves.*

**4 go out to work** to start a paid job; be employed: *More women are going out to work than ever before.*

**go out with** *v adv prep*

**1** to go outside with (something or someone): [L9 + OUT + *with*] *I saw him going out with a policeman. She went out with a suitcase and a large dog.* → **go out** (1), etc.

*__2__ to be seen in public with (someone); go to theatres, concerts, etc. with (someone); begin or have a relationship with (someone, usu. of the opposite sex): [T1 + *with*] *Mary went out with Jim for two years before they were married. Did that red-haired boy ask you to go out with him?* → **ask out,** etc.

**go over[1]** *v adv*

**1** to pass or move over something or someone: [L9 + OVER] *Keep your head down, there are bullets going over. The crowd cheered as the horse went over safely.* → **come over[1]** (1)

**2** to fall; turn over: [L9 + OVER] *Look out, the wall's going over! After the crash, the car went over three times before landing upside down with the wheels spinning. Keep still or the boat will go over!*

*__3__ to move a short way, as to visit or speak to someone: [IØ (*to*)] *When she saw her sister in the station, she went over to talk to her. When are we going over to your mother's again? Shall we go over and join Jim and Mary? They seem to be having an interesting conversation with their former teacher.* → **bring over** (3), etc.

*__4__ to be received, esp. with approval: [L9 (WELL, *with*) (*usu. simple tenses*)] *How did your speech go over (with the crowd)? Jim went over well with Mary's parents on his first visit. This sort of music goes over well with younger people.* → **come across[1]** (2), etc.

**go over[2]** *v prep*

**1** to pass or move over (something): [L9 + *over*] *The crowd cheered as the horse went safely over the last fence. It's dangerous here, with bullets going over our heads all the time.* → **go above** (1), **come over[2]** (1)

*__2__ to look at; examine (something) to see that it is good; search (something) for faults or (someone) for something wrong: [T1 (*often simple tenses*)] *We went over the house thoroughly before buying it. Go over all the prisoners to see that they're not hiding any weapons. The doctor went over the girl carefully but could find no broken bones. You can't have the car back until it's been gone over by the police.* **—going-over** *n* → **go through[2]** (7), **look over[2]** (5), **run over[2]** (5), **run through[2]** (7), **take over[2]** (3), **take through[2]** (2)

*__3__ to examine (usu. something written or spoken) to see that it is correct: [T1] *The police went over his story in detail, but he seemed to have been telling the truth. We must go over the account books together; there's still some money missing.* **—going over** *n* → **go through[2]** (9), **look over[2]** (3)

*__4__ to clean or repair (something): [T1] *I've asked the garage people to go over my car thoroughly before I start my long journey.* **—going-over** *n*

*__5__ to do (something) again; work on top of (something): [T1] *Go over the stitches to make sure that they're firm. When you're satisfied that the spacing is correct, go over the letters in ink. This paint should be gone over with a new brush in the other direction.*

*__6__ to repeat; practise (something), esp. in order to teach or learn it: [T1] *He keeps going over the same story although no one believes him. This teacher goes over the same lesson time and time again. Let's go over that scene again until you're sure you know it. Shall we go over your English exercises together? I want to go over the arrangements for the wedding to make sure that everything will be ready on time.*

*__7__ to consider (something): [T1] *I've gone over your suggestion, and have decided not to accept it.* **—going over** *n* → **look over[2]** (6)

*__8__ to pass; be more than (something): [T1 (*no pass.*)] *Your spending should not go over your income. Don't go over the limit of your allowance.*

**9 go over someone's head** to be too difficult for someone to understand: [(*usu. simple tenses*)] *Some of the jokes were rather rude, but luckily they went over the children's heads.* → **go above** (2)

**10 go over someone's head** to ask for advice or judgment from a person in a higher position or rank than someone: *If you think that your captain is giving wrong orders, you may have to go over his head to his commanding officer, to ask what should be done.* → **go above** (3)

**11 go over the top** *infml* to do something that is foolishly bold or risky; behave in an unrestrained manner: *I was told that he'd gone over the top and accepted the offer of a job in Australia.*

**12 go over the wall** *infml* to escape from prison: *Three prisoners went over the wall last night; I don't know how they got out.*

**go over to** *v adv prep*

**1** to move across a distance or water to (a place): [L9 + OVER + *to*] *More people go over to the island every summer. Why don't we go over to Jim's place and see how he is?* → **go across to** (1)

*__2__ to move towards (someone), as to speak to him: [IØ + *to*] *The policeman went over to the driver and asked him to come to the police station. Why don't you go over to your neighbour and encourage her to join in the party fun?* → **go across to** (3)

*__3__ (in radio) to switch a broadcast to (another place or person): [T1 (*no pass.*)] *We will now go over to Richard Baker at the concert hall, where he is ready to introduce tonight's con-*

*cert. We are now going over to Lord's to hear the latest cricket results.*

*4 to change one's choice to (something else): [T1 (*no pass.*)] *I think you ought to go over to another instrument, you are clearly not suited to the piano. Many young people went over to a freer lifestyle during the 1960s.*

*5 to change one's loyalty to (another group, belief, etc.): [T1 (*no pass.*)] *I hear that a leading politician is thinking of going over to the other party. The minister left the Church of England and went over to Rome.* [T4] *Many people have gone over to believing in world government.* → **bring round** (3), etc., **go across to** (2)

**go overboard** *v adv*

**1** to fall into the water from a ship or boat: [L9 + OVERBOARD] *Stop the ship! Someone's gone overboard!* → **fall overboard**

*2 *infml* to lose one's senses; behave in an odd manner; go mad: [IØ] *My uncle has been acting very strangely recently; the family think he may have gone overboard.*

***go overboard for/about** *v adv prep*

*not fml* to show great keenness for (something or someone): [T1 (*no pass.*)] *Many teachers have gone overboard for the new methods without considering their worth. Grace has really gone overboard for that red-haired boy!*

**go past¹** *v adv*

**1** to pass; move past something or someone: [L9 + PAST] *You've missed the bus, it just went past without stopping, although it wasn't full.* → **come along** (1), **come by¹** (1), **fly by¹** (1), **get by¹** (1), **get past¹** (1), **go by¹** (1)

*2 (of time) to pass: [IØ] *This afternoon has gone past so quickly! The days of cheap food have long gone past.* → **fly by¹** (2), **go by¹** (2), **go on¹** (8), **pass by¹** (2), **run on¹** (2), **wear away** (5), **wear on¹**, **wear out** (4)

**go past²** *v prep*

**1** to pass (something or someone): [L9 + *past*] *An arrow went past his ear, narrowly missing his head. I shall complain to the bus company, my bus just went past the stop empty! The deer has gone past the trees; I can't shoot at it from this distance.* → **be beyond** (1), **be past** (1), **get beyond** (1), **get past²** (1), **go beyond** (1), **go by²** (1)

*2 to advance further than (a stage): [T1 (*usu. simple tenses*)] *I don't think this class will be able to go past lesson six.* → **get beyond** (2), **get past** (3), **go beyond** (4)

*3 to be too difficult for (someone) to do or understand; find (doing something) too difficult: [T1 (*no pass., usu. simple tenses*)] *I was interested to hear the speaker at first, but he went past me after the first half-hour. This job has gone past us; we should have started something easier.* [T4 (*usu. simple tenses*)] *I've gone past running the business on my own now; I must get help.* → **get past²** (5), etc.

**4 go past caring** *not fml* to cease to care (about something): [(*usu. perfect tenses*)] *I've gone past caring how we're to pay the bills; people will just have to wait, that's all.* → **be past** (4), **get beyond** (4), **get past²** (6), **go beyond** (6)

**5 go past endurance** to be worse than someone can reasonably be expected to bear: [(*usu. perfect tenses*)] *Your rudeness has gone past endurance—kindly leave my house!* → **get beyond** (5), etc. **get past²** (7).

**6 go past a joke** *not fml* to cease being funny; become too serious: *Your continual lateness has gone past a joke; be on time tomorrow or you will be dismissed.* → **be beyond** (7), **get beyond** (6), **get past²** (9), **go beyond** (8)

***go phut** *v adv*

**1** *infml* (of machinery) to stop working, often suddenly: [IØ (*usu. simple tenses*)] *In the middle of doing the sheets, the washing machine went phut again; I shall complain to the makers.*

**2** *infml* to fail: [IØ (*usu. simple tenses*)] *Our holiday plans went phut when the cost of living rose again.*

***go public** *v adj*

(of a business) to offer shares in itself for sale to the public on the stock exchange: [IØ] *Jim's father's firm is doing so well that he thinks he may go public next year, if his advisers agree.*

**go right** *v adj* → **go wrong** (1)

to work correctly; result as one planned or wished, etc.: [L9 + **right**] *That washing machine hasn't gone right since I bought it; I shall complain to the makers. I have a nasty feeling that nothing's going to go right today!*

**go round¹** *v adv* also **go around¹**

**1** to move round; travel; make a short journey, as on a visit: [L9 + ROUND (*to*)] *We had to go round the long way because the bridge was destroyed. There's plenty of room for people to go round. Go round to Mrs Page next door and borrow some tea.* → **bring over** (1), etc., **get about¹** (1)

*2 (of news, disease, etc.) to spread: [IØ (*usu. continuous tenses*)] *Stories have been going round concerning the government's secret intentions. There are a lot of colds going round just now.* → **go about¹** (3), etc.

*3 to be seen together in public (with someone): [IØ (*with*)] *How long have those two been going round together? Jim had been going round with Mary for two years before they married. I don't like the idea of my son going round with those rough boys.* → **ask out**, etc.

*4 to be shared: [IØ (*simple tenses*)] *There should be enough soup to go round.*

*5 to visit; be shown round a place: [IØ] *You've expressed a great deal of interest in the new buildings; would you like to go round?* → **show around**, etc.

*6 to be repeated: [IØ] *I have this tune going round in my head, driving me mad!*

*7 to be sent out: [IØ] *A notice of the general*

*meeting is going round; please sign and return it to the main office.* → **send round¹** (1), etc.

***8** to spin or seem to spin: [IØ] *The room's going round; my drink must have been drugged! My head is going round and round this morning; I had a terrible night. "It's love that makes the world go round."* (W.S. Gilbert, *Iolanthe*)

***9** to have a turn, esp. on a mechanical ride: [IØ] *Let me go round just once more before we leave the playground!* —**go-round** *n AmE*

***10** to move around in the course of one's life (doing something); be publicly noticed (doing something): [I4] *You can't go round saying nasty things like that about him in public.* → **go about¹** (5)

***11** **go round in circles** *not fml* to be very active with little result: *No I haven't finished that job yet—I seem to have spent the whole morning going round in circles, getting nowhere!*

**go round²** *v prep* also **go around²**

**1** to reach round (something): [L9 + *round* (*simple tenses*)] *She is so thin that my two hands go round her waist! The fence goes round the whole of our property.*

**2** to move or travel round (a place): [L9 + *round*] *Going round the corner, we were met by a cruelly cold wind. The quickest way to go round the city is by underground train. How does the train go round the mountain? The earth goes round the sun.* → **get about²**, etc.

***3** (of news, disease, etc.) to spread round (a place or group): [T1 (*no pass., usu. simple tenses*)] *There are stories going round the village about the teacher's wife. There are a lot of colds going round the school.* → **go about²** (4)

***4** to be shared among (usu. people): [T1 (*no pass., simple tenses*)] *There should be enough soup to go round the whole family.*

***5** to visit; be shown round (a place): [T1 (*no pass.*)] *You've expressed a great deal of interest in the new buildings; would you like to go round the whole school?* → **look round²** (2), etc.

***6** to be repeated in (one's head): [T1 (*no pass.*)] *I have this tune going round my head, driving me mad!*

***7** to be sent out among (a group): [T1] *A notice of the general meeting is going round the school teachers; please sign and return it to the main office.* → **send around, send round, take round²** (1)

***8** to have a turn on (usu. a mechanical ride): [T1] *Let me go round the roundabout just once more!*

**9** **go round the bend** *BrE infml* to go mad or become very annoyed: *I've been going round the bend with those children today! I shall go round the bend if I see another one of those letters.*

***go scot-free** *v adj*

*not fml* to escape punishment: [IØ (*usu. simple tenses*)] *Both the men went to prison, but the boys went scot-free on account of their age.*

***go short** *v adj*

to lack (something); not have enough: [IØ (*of*)] *If there isn't enough milk for everyone, someone will just have to go short. No old person should have to go short of coal to heat their home in the winter.*

***go sick** *v adj* → **fall ill, fall sick, report sick, take ill¹, take sick**

*not fml* to declare oneself unfit for work or duties, not necessarily through illness: [IØ] *300 railwaymen have refused to work, and 150 others have gone sick; many trains will not run today.*

**go slow** *v adv*

**1** (esp. of a vehicle) to move slowly: [L9 + SLOW] *The city council agreed to put up a sign at the dangerous corner, with a warning saying "GO SLOW."*

***2** to live in a quieter, less active manner: [IØ] *The doctor has advised Jim to go slow for a time, to give his heart a rest.* → **go easy** (1), **slow down** (2), **take easy**

***3** *BrE* to refuse to put more than the least effort into work, as a form of strike: [IØ] *Half the union members will stay away from work tomorrow, and the rest will go slow in sympathy.* —**go-slow** *n, adj* → **work to** (6)

***go some** *v adv* → **go it** (1)

esp. *AmE infml* to be very active, successful, busy, quick, etc.: [IØ (*continuous tenses*)] *Your sister has had three babies in two years? That's going some, isn't it!*

***go steady** *v adj*

(usu. of a man and woman) to have a regular social or sexual relationship, often with an intent to marry: [IØ] *Jim and Mary have been going steady for a year now; are they going to get married?*

***go straight¹** *v adj*

*infml* to live honestly after one has been a criminal: [IØ] *After three years in prison, the former jewel thief decided to go straight, and took a job with a building firm.*

**go straight²** *v adv*

to travel forward without turning: [L9 + STRAIGHT (*usu. simple tenses*)] *When you've passed the church, go straight for three miles and then turn left where the road divides.*

**go strong** *v adj*

**be going strong** to continue to be active healthy, successful, etc.: [IØ] *Grandfather may be nearly 80, but he's still going strong. The government has been in power for twenty years, and is still going strong. "Born 1800 and still going strong."* (advertisement for alcohol)

**go through¹** *v adv*

**1** to pass through something: [L9 + THROUGH] *This material is so stiff that even my thickest needle won't go through.* → **come through¹** (1), **get through¹** (1)

***2** (of a law, etc.) to be passed or approved by

Parliament or other law-making body: [IØ (*often simple tenses*)] *Buy now before the tax increase goes through next week!* → **get through¹ (4), put through¹ (4)**

*__3__ (of an arrangement, etc.) to be approved, agreed, completed, etc.: [IØ (*usu. simple tenses*)] *Has the sale of the house gone through yet? Did your business deal go through?* → **put across¹ (3), put through¹ (1), railroad through, ram through, take through¹ (2)**

*__4__ to wear into a hole: [IØ] *The bottom of the bucket has gone through. The seat of the boy's trousers has gone through again!* → **wear through**

### go through² *v prep*

**1** to pass through (something): [L9 + through (*often simple tenses*)] *The piano won't go through this narrow entrance, it will have to come in through the window. We've been through banks of snow three metres high!* → **get through² (1), take through (1)**

*__2__ (of a law, etc.) to be passed or approved by (Parliament or other law-making body): [T1 (*no pass.*)] *The new law should go through Parliament quite easily, as it has been demanded by the public for some time.* → **get through² (3), put through² (3), take through (3)**

*__3__ to pass or complete (a stage): [T1] *Your suggestion has to go through several stages. Tom's book has gone through three printings. Has the new law gone through all its stages yet?*

*__4__ to be passed among (a group): [T1 (*no pass.*)] *A wild story has been going through the office, that the director's wife has left him. The disease went through the school like a wind.*

*__5__ to ask for the approval of (someone); be dealt with by (someone): [T1] *If you want a special favour, you have to go through the director. All complaints have to go through Head Office.*

*__6__ to suffer (something): [T1] *He has gone through such a lot since his wife died. After all he's been through, he still keeps so cheerful!* → **pass through² (4)**

*__7__ to repeat; practise (something), esp. to teach or learn it: [T1] *Go through your story again from the beginning. Let's go through that scene again until you're sure you know it. I want to go through the wedding arrangements to make sure that nothing's been missed.* → **go over² (2), look over² (5), run over² (5), run through² (7), take over² (3), take through² (2)**

*__8__ to examine (something): [T1] *We must go through the account books together; there's still some money missing. I've been through your report, and it looks quite satisfactory.*

*__9__ to search (something): [T1] *She used to go through her husband's pockets while he was asleep, looking for letters from other women. All the rooms have been gone through by the police, but the jewels are still missing.* → **go over² (3), look over² (3)**

*__10__ to spend or use (a quantity of something such as money or food): [T1] *Gordon goes through a lot of beer while watching football on television every Saturday afternoon. Have you already gone through all the money I gave you?* → **get through² (6)**

*__11__ to wear a hole in (something): [T1 (*no pass.*)] *That boy goes through two pairs of shoes a year!*

*__12__ to perform or take part in (an activity): [T1 (*often simple tenses*)] *The prisoner went through a ceremony of marriage with this young lady, but in fact he already had a wife.* → **go through with**

*__13__ to live or last through (time): [T1] *All winter we just go through the weeks waiting for the spring. This car has been through three severe winters in this city, and is still running well.* → **get through² (4)**

**14 go through fire and water for someone** *not fml* to be prepared to do anything to show one's love or loyalty for someone: [*usu. simple tenses*] *Jim worships Mary; he would go through fire and water for her.*

**15 go through someone's hands** to be part of someone's work; be dealt with by someone in the course of his duties: [*often simple tenses*] *'I've seen so many sad cases go through my hands in these courts,' said the old judge. Large sums of other people's money go through a banker's hands in any one day, but none of it is his.*

**16 go through a hoop** *infml* to be made to suffer or have trouble in order to gain something: [*often simple tenses*] *The salesman really had to go through a hoop to get that contract.* → **put through² (6)**

**17 go through the mill** *not fml* to have to perform all the usual humble jobs in order to advance: *Every reporter who wants to run the whole newspaper has to go through the mill first so that he can learn the job the hard way. Even the director has been through the mill, you know.* → **put through² (8)**

**18 go through the motions** *not fml* to appear to be doing something; pretend to work but without sincere intentions: [*often continuous tenses*] *He's not acting, he's just going through the motions.. Life became unbearable for my aunt after her husband died; she stayed at her usual job, but for some months was only going through the motions.*

**19 go through the proper channels** to take the correct steps to do something; use the usual methods of making a request, etc.: [*often simple tenses*] *Don't come to me with your complaints; you have to go through the proper channels, which means a letter to Head Office and a copy to the director and to myself; then you might be listened to. I intend to go straight to the commanding officer with my request for special permission; going through the proper channels takes far too long.*

**20 go through the roof** *not fml* **a** (of prices) to

rise suddenly and unreasonably: *House prices have gone through the roof this year.* **b** to be very angry: *Don't tell the director how you ruined the job, or he'll go through the roof!*

*__go through with__ *v adv prep* → **go through² (12)** to complete; carry out; refuse to be prevented from (something): [T1 (*usu. simple tenses*)] *Do you intend to go through with this wedding? I can't go through with this performance, I'm so nervous. I will go through with my plan whatever the opposition!*

**go to** *v prep*

**1** to move or travel to (someone or a place): [L9 + *to*] *When I went to the door, there was no one there. Does this train go to London? I'm going to the hospital to see my mother. I went to the school to talk to the teacher.* → **come to² (1), get to (1), send to (1), take to (1)**

**2** to lead or reach as far as (somewhere): [L9 + *to*] *Does this road go to the airport? This chain won't go to the other end.* → **lead to (2), reach to (1)**

**3** to attend (a place, organization, etc.): [L9 + *to*] *My son goes to university. I would like all my children to go to college. How long do children have to go to school in this country? Mother had to go to hospital for her operation. Most young people go to work as soon as they leave school.* → **go into (2)**

**4** to ask (someone) for help, goods, or professional services: [L9 + *to*] *Which hairdresser do you go to? I think you should go to another doctor and get a second opinion. I was lucky in that I went to a good piano teacher when I was young.*

**5** to disappear to (somewhere): [L9 + *to* (*usu. simple tenses*)] *Where's my blue bag gone to? I can't see it anywhere.* → **become of, come of (1), disappear to, get to (2)**

*__6__ to ask (someone) for something; try to gain information, help, a favour, etc. from (someone): [T1 (*no pass.*)] *You have to go to the commanding officer for special permission to leave the camp. If you're so afraid of him, why don't you go to the police?*

*__7__ (of a prize, money, etc.) to be given to (someone): [T1 (*no pass., usu. simple tenses*)] *The house went to his wife after his death. The prize for growing the biggest potato goes to Mr and Mrs Brown, of the village of Little Digging.*

*__8__ to take (trouble, etc.), esp. in the phrs. **go to a lot of/great trouble, go to great pains**: [T1 (*often simple tenses*)] *Please don't go to any trouble to give us special meals or anything. Mother went to great pains to make her guests feel comfortable.* → **put to² (3)**

*__9__ to be placed at (the top or bottom of a competition): [T1 (*no pass., usu. simple tenses*)] *Your work is terrible; go to the bottom of the class! The student worked especially hard and soon went to the top of the honours list.*

*__10__ to enter a state of (something): [T1 (*no pass.*)] *Be quiet, Father has just gone to sleep. The nation seems ready to go to war with its old-time enemy. While we were away on holiday and no one was looking after the garden, all the flowers went to seed.* → **put to² (3)**

*__11__ to add to; give something in the direction of (something): [T1 (*no pass., simple tenses*)] *Many different qualities go to the making of a President.* → **go towards (3)**

*__12__ to add together to make (a total): [T1 (*no pass., simple tenses*)] *In former times, 12 pence went to a shilling and 20 shillings to the pound, but since Britain changed to decimal money, 100 new pence go to the pound.*

*__13__ (usu. of words) to fit (usu. a tune): [T1 (*no pass., simple tenses*)] *This poem goes to the tune of "This Old Man."*

**14 go to the bad** *not fml* to be ruined, esp. morally: *I'm sorry to hear that the boy has gone to the bad, turning criminal so young.*

**15 go to bed: a** to lie down on one's bed, as at night or when tired or ill: *You don't seem well, I think you ought to go to bed.* → **put to² (7), retire to (4), send to (2)** **b** (of a newspaper) to be fully prepared for printing: *Some special news has just come in—has the paper gone to bed yet, or can we include it?*

**16 go to the block: a** *old use* to be killed with an axe as punishment: *A large crowd watched as the queen went to the block.* **b** → **GO UNDER (4)**

**17 go to the country** *BrE* to hold a general election: *If the members of Parliament vote against the government, they will have to go to the country.*

**18 go to the dogs** *BrE infml* to be ruined: *Many old military men think that England has gone to the dogs since she lost her Empire.*

**19 go to earth/ground** (esp. of animals) to hide, in or as in the earth: [*usu. perfect tenses*] *The huntsmen said that the fox had gone to earth and could not be caught. The criminals have gone to ground somewhere, waiting until it is safe to complete their escape.* → **run to (12)**

**20 go to (the) expense (of)** to spend a lot of money on (doing something): *You really shouldn't have gone to the expense of renting the car specially for us. Why did you go to such expense?*

**21 go to extremes** to do anything too much: [*often simple tenses*] *Why does she always go to extremes? She's either gloriously happy or hopelessly sad, never in between.*

**22 go to the other extreme** to do the opposite of one's former action or opinion: *Just because I asked you not to talk so loud, there's no need to go to the other extreme and remain completely silent!*

**23 go to glory/kingdom come** *not fml euph* to die: [*usu. simple tenses*] *When I go to glory I hope to meet my loved ones who have gone before. The old man has gone to kingdom come at last.*

**24 go to someone's head** to excite someone; make someone feel of greater worth than he is: *I think the drink must have gone to her head, she doesn't usually sing in public. Be careful not to let your first success go to your head, you might not be so lucky next time.*
**25 go to the heart of** to reach the most important part of (the matter or question): *The minister did not waste time talking about unimportant details, but went straight to the heart of the matter.*
**26 go to hell/the devil/blazes/Hades/Jericho!** *sl* curse you!: [*usu. imper.*] *I didn't like him so I told him to go to hell!*
**27 go to it!** *infml* put effort into what you are doing!: [*imper.*] *You've done no work all morning. Now go to it!*
**28 go to law** to take someone to court about a disagreement: *If you can't settle your argument with your neighbour over the limits of your property, you may have to go to law.*
**29 go to great lengths** to take much trouble; work hard (to do something): *The chairman went to great lengths to explain to the committee exactly what their duties were.*
**30 go to pieces/bits** *not fml* to fail to control oneself; be disorganized: *Mary almost went to pieces when she heard the bad news, and had to be helped from the room, crying. The government of this country has gone to pieces; what we need is a strong new leader!*
**31 go to the polls** to vote: *Over half the electors have already gone to the polls; voting seems to be heavy this time.*
**32 go to pot** *infml* to be ruined or wasted: [*usu. perfect tenses*] *If nobody takes any notice of my suggestion, all that effort will have gone to pot. My sense of direction seems to have gone to pot; where on earth are we?*
**33 go to press** to be printed or about to be printed: *It's too late to correct those mistakes, the book has already gone to press.*
**34 go to (rack and) ruin** to be spoilt; decay: *Don't let all your good work go to ruin by giving up now! My clothes have gone to rack and ruin since I've been in hospital. The country is going to rack and ruin—what we need is a strong new leader!*
**35 go to sea** to become a sailor: *Many British boys want to go to sea when they are old enough.*
**36 go to seed: a** (of a plant) to pass the time of flowering; become overgrown: *While we were away on holiday and no one looked after the garden; all the vegetables went to seed and were unfit to eat.* **b** *not fml* to become old, useless, unhealthy, etc.: *Grandfather has gone to seed since he finished working; he needs to have something meaningful to do.* → **run to** (15)
**37 go to town** *infml* to act or behave freely or wildly, esp. by spending a great deal of money: *The director is really going to town on this production, renting costly dresses and building lots of scenery, sparing no cost. When you make a complaint you don't spare their feelings, do you? You really go to town!*
**38 go to trial** to have to face a court or law on a charge: *The jewel thieves go to trial next week.*
**39 go to the wall** *not fml* to be defeated in competition; be considered worthless; fail: [*often simple tenses*] *In these hard times, many small firms have gone to the wall because they could not compete with big businesses.*
**40 go to waste** to be wasted: *Let me take these unwanted bits of food home for the dog; I can't bear to see food going to waste. Many women feel that they are going to waste looking after their homes instead of taking jobs.*
**41 go to work (on)** to put effort into (something); work hard: [*often simple tenses*] *We must all go to work if we're to get this concert ready in time! It didn't take the children long to go to work on all that party food!* → **get to** (16), **set to²** (13)
**42 go to work on** to try to persuade (someone); treat (someone) violently: [*often simple tenses*] *I'll go to work on the director and see if I can make him change his mind. You go to work on the guard while we break the locks.* → **get to** (17)

**go together** *v adv*
**1** to go with someone as a companion; be companions: [L9 + TOGETHER] *I don't want to go to the film on my own; shall we go together?* → **go with** (1), **take with** (1)
***2** to be regular companions or lovers, esp. in public: [IØ] *Jim and Mary had been going together for two years before they were married.* → **go along with** (4), **go with** (2)
***3** to happen together; have a common cause or surrounding, etc.: [IØ (*simple tenses*)] *Strength and sensitivity do not often go together. Dirt and disease usually go together.* → **go with** (3)
***4** to match; suit each other: [IØ (*simple tenses*)] *I like the way the blue carpet and the gold curtains go together. Although duck and oranges sound—an unlikely combination, they do in fact go very well together.* → **blend with,** etc.

**go towards** *v prep*
**1** to move in the direction of (something or someone): [L9 + *towards*] *As I went towards her, she began to run away. Go towards the church, then turn right just before you get there.*
***2** (usu. of money) to give or form some part of (an aim): [T1 (*no pass., often simple tenses*)] *Your few pence will go towards a new radio for the hospital.*
***3** to add to; give something in the direction of (something): [T1 (*no pass., simple tenses*)] *Many different qualities go towards the making of a President.* → **go to** (11)
**4 go far/a long way towards** to help a lot with (something or doing something): *Thank you,*

*your generous gift will go a long way towards helping to build the children's hospital.* → **go far** (4)

**go under¹** *v adv*

**1** to be able to pass beneath something: [L9 + UNDER (*usu. simple tenses*)] *The rabbit tried to get beneath the fence but it was too fat to go under.*

***2** (of a ship or anything or anyone floating) to sink: [IØ] *After the explosion, it only took half an hour for the ship to go under. They say that when you go under for the third time, you are going to drown.* → **go down¹** (9)

***3** (of a business, etc.) to fail: [IØ (*to*)] *At first Jim's father thought his firm would go under, but after a short struggle he made a success of the business. Many small firms go under to strong competition from big business.* → **send under**

***4** to lose consciousness by the action of a drug, gas, etc.: [IØ] *Don't start the operation till you're sure she's gone under.*

**go under²** *v prep*

**1** to be able to pass beneath (something or someone): [L9 + *under*] *Those rabbits have gone under the fence again! The coin has gone under the piano and I can't reach it. The rope goes under your arm like this.*

***2** to be placed in the class or group of (something): [T1 (*no pass.*)] *This word goes under G.* → **come under** (2), etc.

***3** to be known by (a name): [T1 (*no pass., often simple tenses*)] *He went under the name of Baker, to avoid discovery by the police.* → **go by²** (7), etc.

**4 go under the hammer** to be sold at an auction: *It was sad to see all Grandmother's lovely things go under the hammer.* also **come under, go to the block** → **be under** (8)

**go unheard** *v adj*

**1** to fail to be heard: [L9 + **unheard**] *From the bottom of the well, the cat's faint cries for help went unheard.*

***2** to be paid no attention: [IØ] *The man's request for correct medical treatment went unheard by the people in charge.*

**go up¹** *v adv*

**1** to move in an upward direction; climb; rise: [L9 + UP (*to*)] *Smoke was going up in a straight line, showing that there was no wind. Who'll be the next climber to go up? Go up to the top of the stairs and turn right, that's my room. Have the children gone up yet? I promised to tell them a story. This hill is too steep, the old car won't go up.* → **bring up** (1), **come down** (1), **come up** (2), **get up** (1), **go down¹** (1) **go down to** (1), **go down with** (1), **go up to** (1), **send up¹** (1), **take up** (3)

**2** to move forward, esp. in public: [L9 + UP] *The crowd cheered as Jim went up to receive his prize.*

***3** to rise; be increased; become higher, as in level: [IØ] *The temperature is going up; will the snow melt? The standard of performance has gone up since last year, as the players have gained more experience. My weight keeps going up although I try not to eat too much. Egg prices have gone up again this month. At the end of the play, the lights went up again.* → **go down¹** (6)

***4** (in music) to move to a higher note: [IØ (*usu. simple tenses*)] *It's easy to go up a 3rd, but difficult to go up a 7th.* → **go down¹** (8), **go up to** (3)

***5** to swell with air: [IØ] *This tyre won't go up however hard I pump; there must be a hole in it.* → **go down¹** (10)

***6** to be built: [IØ] *How many new houses have gone up this year?* → **put up¹** (2), **set up** (1)

***7** to be destroyed by explosion: [IØ (*usu. simple tenses*)] *A chemical factory went up in the North of England, killing many people. The oil tanks went up in flames on the night of the heavy bombing, making a fire bright enough to read a newspaper by.* → **blow up** (6), **send up¹** (4)

***8** (of a loud noise) to arise; be expressed: [IØ (*usu. simple tenses*)] *A cheer went up from the crowd as the Queen stepped onto the shore.*

***9** (of the curtain on stage) to open or rise so as to start the performance: [IØ (*often simple tenses*)] *What time does the curtain go up?*

***10** to travel to a university or important place: [IØ (*to*)] *"When do you go up to your university?" "Next week: all the students go up then." I want to go up to London next week.* → **be up** (10), **come down** (7), **come up** (14), **go down¹** (14), **go up to** (4), **send down** (3)

***11** *BrE* to be allowed to move to the next higher class: [IØ] *"Did all the children go up at the end of the year?" "All except one, who had to stay down in the lower class."* → **go up to** (5), **keep down** (7), **stay down** (5)

***12** to be considered more worthy: [IØ (*often simple tenses*)] *That politician has gone up in my opinion since I heard his latest speech.* → **come down** (8), **come up** (12), **go down¹** (16)

**13 the balloon go up** *infml* to begin something terrible or important; cause great trouble: [*usu. simple tenses*] *The jewel thieves escaped from the house and were safely in hiding before the balloon went up.*

**14 go up in the air** *infml* to become angry: [*usu. simple tenses*] *Mary went up in the air when Jim annoyed her by disliking the meal.*

**15 go up in the world** to rise to a better standard of living or social level: *Hasn't your brother gone up in the world! He used to have such a low position, and now he's advising government officials and leading society.* → **come down** (11), **come up** (19), **go down¹** (19)

**go up²** *v prep*

**1** to climb (something that gets higher): [L9 + *up*] *"Jack and Jill went up the hill."* (children's poem) *Can you go up the stairs two steps at a time?*

**2 go up the wall** *infml* to be very angry: *Th*

*director will go up the wall when he hears that you've been late again; he warned you last week.* → **drive up² (2), send up² (2)**

**go up to** *v adv prep*

**1** to move upward to; climb to (somewhere): [L9 + UP + *to*] *Go up to the top of the stairs and turn right, that's my room. Have the children gone up to bed yet? I promised to read them a story.* → **get up (1), go down to (1), go up¹ (1), send up¹ (1), take up (3)**

***2** to rise to (a level): [IØ + *to*] *When the temperature goes up to 3° Centigrade, the snow will melt. Prices keep going up to ever more impossible levels.* → **go down¹ (6),** etc., **go up (3)**

***3** (in music) to move to (a certain higher note): [IØ + *to* (*usu. simple tenses*)] *Can you go up to a high C?* → **go down to (4), go up¹ (4)**

***4** to travel to (a university or more important place): [IØ + *to*] *"When do you go up to your university?" "Next week." I want to go up to London next week.* → **go down¹ (14),** etc., **go down to (6)**

***5** *BrE* to be allowed to move to the next higher class: [IØ + *to*] *"Did all the children go up to the next class?" "All except one, who had to stay down."* → **go up¹ (11), keep down (7), stay down (5)**

***6** to move closer to (someone), as to ask a question: [T1 (*no pass.*)] *I went up to the man and asked directions, but he was a total stranger.* → **come up to (2)**

***7** to reach as far as (something such as a date): [T1 (*no pass., usu. simple tenses*)] *Our history books only go up to the World War I. Let's go up to the end of Act One and see how it goes.* → **get to (3), get up to (2), take up to**

**go upon** *v prep* → **GO ON (7)**

**go well** *v adv* → **go badly**

to happen in a favourable way; be successful: [L9 + WELL] *My work is going very well at the moment, thank you.*

**go well with** *v adv prep* → **go ill with**

to be lucky or favourable for (usu. someone): [T1 (*no pass.*)] *If all goes well with our plans, we should make a lot of money. I hope all is going well with the young people.*

**go west** *v adv*

**1** to travel in a westward direction or towards the western part of a country: [L9 + WEST] *"Go west, young man."* (J.B.L. Soule, *Terre Haute Express*, Indiana, 1851)

***2** *BrE infml* (of people) to die; (of things) cease to operate or exist: [IØ] *I'm afraid that three of the pilots and their planes have gone west. My new camera has gone west after only three months.*

**go with** *v prep*

**1** to travel with (someone): [L9 + *with*] *Don't leave me alone, let me go with you! We enjoyed our holiday, although we went with our neighbours.* → **go together (1), take with (1)**

**2** to spend time as a regular companion or lover with (someone of the other sex): [T1 (*no pass.*)] *Mary went with Jim for two years before they were married.* → **go along with (4), go together (2)**

***3** to be the result of; be usu. found together with (something else): [T1 (*no pass., simple tenses*)] *Disease often goes with dirt. Money does not always go with happiness.* [T4 (*simple tenses*)] *Responsibility goes with becoming a father.* → **go together (3)**

***4** to match or suit (something): [T1 (*no pass., simple tenses*)] *I like the way the blue carpet goes with the gold curtains. Oranges go surprisingly well with duck.* → **blend with,** etc.

***5** to be sold or rented together with; be part of (something): [T1 (*no pass., simple tenses*)] *The furniture goes with the house. The house goes with the job.*

***6** to agree with (someone): [T1 (*no pass., usu. simple tenses*)] *Do you always go with the chairman?*

**7 go with a bang/swing** *infml* to be very active, busy, and successful: *Come and join the party, it's going with a swing!*

**8 go with the crowd/stream** *infml* to behave or think in the same way as most people: [*often simple tenses*] *He never thinks for himself, but always goes with the crowd.*

**9 go with the tide/times** *infml* to act in a modern way; keep up to date; follow fashion: [*usu. simple tenses*] *Why care about old-fashioned values? You have to go with the times!*

***go without¹** *v adv* → **do without¹, manage without¹**

to live or continue in spite of lacking something: [IØ] *If there's no sugar you will have to go without; it won't do you any harm anyway.*

**go without²** *v prep*

**1** to travel without taking (something or someone): [L9 + *without*] *Run after your father, he's gone without the letters!*

***2** to live or continue in spite of lacking (something): [T1] *It's unhealthy and dangerous to go without sleep.* [T4 (*usu. simple tenses*)] *Mr Sharp is not here, you will have to go without speaking to him.* → **dispense with, do without² (1), live without, manage without²**

**3 it/that goes without saying** *not fml* it is clear without needing to be stated: *It goes without saying that we shall all be glad when spring is here.*

**go wrong** *v adj*

**1** to fail to work correctly or as one had planned or wished: [L9 + wrong] *If that washing machine goes wrong again, I shall complain to the makers. Today is going to be one of those days when everything goes wrong.* → **go right**

**2** to take the wrong road when travelling: [L9 + wrong (*usu. simple tenses*)] *We must have gone wrong somewhere, we should have reached the village by now.*

***3** to live immorally: [IØ] *She used to be such a nice girl until she went wrong; now there's little hope for her.*

***goad into** *v prep* → **provoke into, sting into**
to urge, annoy, or drive (someone) into (something such as a state or doing something): [D1] *The children's bad behaviour at last goaded their mother into anger. What can we do to goad this lazy boy into action?* [V4b] *The Opposition is trying to goad the government into calling an election. The students did their best to goad the teacher into getting angry.*

**goad on** *v adv*
**1** to force (an animal) to move forward, using a pointed stick: [T1 + ON] *The oxen moved slowly in the heat, and had to be goaded on by their drivers.*
***2** to urge, annoy, or drive (someone) (to do something wrong): [T1a] *The boys claimed that they had been goaded on by their criminal companions.* [V3] *Hunger had goaded the woman on to steal the food.*

**gobble down** *v adv* → **gobble up** (1)
to eat (food) quickly: [T1 + DOWN] *The pigs gobbled down the waste food as if they had not been fed for days.*

**gobble up** *v adv*
**1** to eat (food) quickly: [T1 + UP] *The pigs gobbled up the waste food as if they had not been fed for days.* → **gobble down**
***2** to use or take in (something) quickly or in large quantities: [T1] *The big old car gobbles up petrol. Some students gobble up information as fast as they receive it. The train hurried along, gobbling up the miles. The government seems to gobble up the taxpayers' money.*
***3** to overpower; defeat (weaker competitors); be too strong for (someone): [T1] *It's difficult for a small firm not to be gobbled up by big business concerns. Those two are really not suited to marry; she'll gobble him up! The United Nations does its best to prevent the powerful nations from gobbling up small helpless countries.*

***goggle at** *v prep* → **gape at, gawk at, gaze at, stare at**
*not fml* to look at (someone or something) with wide eyes, as in wonder or surprise: [T1] *When the farm boy first came to the city, he goggled at the size of the buildings. The public came in crowds to goggle at the strange new paintings.*

**gone on** → **GO ON** *v prep* (11)

***goof off/around** *v adv* → **mess about** (1), etc.
*AmE infml* to spend time lazily, esp. avoiding work, responsibility, etc.: [IØ] *We didn't go to school today, we goofed off downtown instead. You'll never get your studying done if you spend half your time goofing around.* —**goof-off** *n*

***goof up** *v adv* → **mess up** (2), etc.
*AmE infml* to spoil (something) carelessly: [T1] *If John goofs up his driving test again, I doubt if he'll ever pass it.*

***goose up** *v adv*
**1** *infml* to make (something such as writing) more exciting, esp. sexually: [T1] *Your book's rather dull for today's market; can't you goose it up with some sexy stories?*
**2** *sl* to deceive (someone) into a sexual relationship: [T1] *See that girl? That's one I'd like to goose up!*

**gore to** *v prep*
**gore to death** (of an animal with horns) to kill (someone or an animal) with its horns: *The bullfighter was gored to death before a large crowd.*

**gorge on/with** *v prep*
to fill (oneself) with (food): [X9 + *on* ; L9 + *on*] *Every Christmas, people gorge (themselves) on rich food that they can't afford, and then complain about large bills and stomach troubles!* [X9 + *with* (*usu. pass.*)] *The lion was asleep, gorged with the animal he had killed.*

**gossip about/of** *v prep*
to talk about (someone or something), often spreading stories which may not be true: [IØ + *about/of*] *Who's been gossiping about me? I've been hearing terrible stories about myself. The women stood in the market-place, gossiping of this and that.*

***gouge out** *v adv*
to dig out (something) by force: [T1] *In the Middle Ages, a favourite punishment was to gouge out a prisoner's eyes. The lovers gouged out their names on the tree. Less and less mining is done by hand in Britain; large machines are now used to gouge out most of the coal from the earth.*

**grab at/for/onto** *v prep* also **grasp at**
**1** to try to seize (something): [L9 + *at/for/onto*] *The climber grabbed for the rope, but missed and fell to his death. Grab onto this board, we'll save you from falling through the ice!* → **catch at** (1), **clutch at** (1), **snatch at** (1)
***2** *not fml* to try to make use of (something): [T1a (*usu. simple tenses*)] *A businessman will grab at any chance to make a profit.* → **catch at** (2), **clutch at** (2), **snap at** (3), **snap up**, **snatch at** (2)
**3 grab at a straw** to try to seize any faint chance, as to be saved: [(*usu. simple tenses*)] *"A drowning man will grab at a straw."* (saying) → **catch at** (3), **clutch at** (3), **snatch at** (3)

**grab away** *v adv*
to remove (something) by seizing it suddenly: [T1 + AWAY (*usu. simple tenses*)] *The thief grabbed the bag away from the woman, and disappeared round the corner.*

**grab for** *v prep* → **GRAB AT**

**grab onto** *v prep* → **GRAB AT**

***grace with** *v prep* → **honour with** (2)
to give honour to (an event) with (usu. one's presence); give (someone) the pleasant abilit

or addition of (something): [D1] *We thank the governor for gracing this formal dinner with her presence.*

**grade down** *v adv* → **grade up** (1)
to reduce (someone or something) in rank, level, classification, etc.: [X9 + DOWN (*usu. pass.*)] *Your marks are so poor that you will have to be graded down. The officer was graded down to the ranks after his dishonourable action. The road is no longer fit for heavy traffic, and will be officially graded down.* —**downgrade** *n, v*

**grade up** *v adv*
**1** to raise (someone or something) to a higher rank, level, classification, etc.: [X9 + UP (*usu. pass.*)] *Students who show a great improvement in their marks will be graded up. The improved road has been graded up so as to allow for heavier traffic.* —**upgrade** *n, v* → **grade down**
***2** esp. *AmE* to improve the quality of (a product such as cattle or fruit): [T1] *Scientists have been trying to find methods of grading up cattle to provide better meat with less fat.* —**upgrade** *v*

**graduate from** *v prep*
to complete a course of study in *AmE* school, college, or university, *BrE* university: [IØ + *from* (*usu. simple tenses*)] *My daughter did so well in her studies that she graduated from high school at the age of 16. The famous scientist graduated from London University in 1950 with an honours degree in chemistry.* [*AmE* T1 + *from* (*usu. pass.*)] *She was graduated from this college 20 years ago.*

**graduate in** *v prep*
**1** to obtain a university degree in (a subject): [IØ + *in* (*usu. simple tenses*)] *My son hopes to graduate in law, so as to become a lawyer.*
**2** to mark (a measure) with (units of measurement): [T1 + *in* (*usu. pass.*)] *Is this ruler graduated in centimetres?*

**graduate with** *v prep*
**1** to obtain a university degree with (honours, marks, etc.): [IØ + *with* (*usu. simple tenses*)] *If you graduate with first class honours, you will be able to go on to higher degrees.* [T1 + with (*usu. pass.*)] (*AmE*) *She was graduated with high honours.*
**2** to obtain one's university degree or *AmE* completion of high school, at the same time as (someone else): [IØ + *with* (*simple tenses*)] *The Minister graduated with some of the cleverest students of his day.*

**graft in/on¹** *v adv*
to make (something living) grow as part of a plant or animal: [X9 + IN/ON] *Burns can often be cured by grafting on skin from another part of the same body. Cultivated plants are grown by grafting in part of another tree onto a wild root.*

**graft in²** *v prep* → **ENGRAFT IN**

**graft into** *v prep* → **ENGRAFT INTO**

**graft on** *v adv* → **GRAFT IN**

**graft onto** *v prep* → **ENGRAFT INTO**

**graft upon** *v prep* → **ENGRAFT INTO**

**grant to** *v prep*
**1** *fml* to give (something such as money or a right) to (usu. someone): [T1 + *to*] *The government has been granting money to this group for too long.*
**2** to admit that (a quality) is possessed by (someone): [T1 + *to*] *I grant to him a certain social success, but I still don't approve of him.*

**graph out** *v adv*
to show (information) by means of lines drawn on squared paper: [T1 + OUT] *The movements of trade can be graphed out, enabling the firm to plan their future markets and advertising.*

***grapple with** *v prep*
**1** to fight or struggle with (someone), usu. with one's hands: [T1] *The loyal servant grappled with the thief, but he got away. After grappling with the enemy for three days, our soldiers had to admit defeat.*
**2** to struggle with; deal with (a difficulty): [T1] *It will take a brave politician to grapple with the inequalities in the tax laws.*

**grasp at** *v prep* → **GRAB AT**

***grass on** *v prep* → **inform against,** etc.
*sl* (esp. of a criminal) to inform the police about the action of (other criminals): [T1 (*usu. simple tenses*)] *The police would never have caught the jewel robbers if the prisoner had not grassed on them and told them where they were hiding.*

**grate on** *v prep*
**1** to produce a rough or sharp sound by moving on (something): [X9 + *on*] *Please don't grate your nails on the glass, I don't like the sound it makes.* [L9 + *on*] *These country-style plates may look very nice, but the surface is so rough that the knives and forks grate on it all the time we are eating; it makes mealtimes quite painful!*
**2 grate on someone/someone's ears/nerves** to annoy someone; offend one's sensitivity; cause severe suffering, almost unbearable, to the nervous system: *The baby's endless crying grates on my nerves. Hearing the same complaints over and over again grates on my nerves. The boy's manner of speech grated on the teacher, who came from a different part of the country. The singer's high notes grated on the ears of her listeners.* → **get on² (14), jangle on, jar on**

***gravitate to/towards** *v prep*
**1** to be pulled by a natural force towards (a mass): [T1 (*no pass., usu. simple tenses*)] *The moon gravitates to the earth, but is held in its path by opposing forces from other bodies in space.*
**2** to be attracted to and move in the direction

of (someone or something): [T1 (*no pass.*)] *Students are gravitating towards practical subjects which will help them to get a job. Voters will gravitate to any politician who is a naturally good speaker.*

**graze on** *v prep*
(of certain animals) to (cause to) feed on (grass): [IØ + *on*] *There is good grassland here for your cattle and horses to graze on.* [T1 + *on*] *You can graze your sheep on the field on the other side of the stream.*

**greet with** *v prep*
**1** to meet and/or welcome (something or someone) with (something such as a smile or shout): [T1 + *with*] *The child greeted her mother's return with a cry of delight. The citizens greeted the conquering army with complete silence. She greeted him with a loving kiss.*
*__2__ to face (someone or something) with (something): [D1] *The trade unions are greeting the government's latest move with strong opposition. I hate to greet the committee with bad news, but it can't be helped.*

**grieve for** *v prep* → **lament for, mourn for**
to express grief about (someone dead): [IØ + *for*] *The mother grieved for her dead son for many years.*

**grieve over** *v prep* → **lament over, sorrow over**
to feel sorrow about (something bad or lost or someone dead): [IØ + *over*] *Grieving over his failure, the businessman shot himself. You can't go on grieving over your lost youth as you can never get it back; it's better to accept the joys of middle age.*

**grin at** *v prep*
to smile broadly at (someone or something amusing): [IØ + *at*] *I can't help grinning at the funny things the child says. How can I teach a child who just grins stupidly at me all day?*

**grin from** *v prep*
**grin from ear to ear** *not fml* to smile very broadly and often continuously: *Something must have amused Jim at work today; he came home grinning from ear to ear.*

**grind away** *v adv*
**1** to keep on crushing something into powder: [IØ + AWAY] *This old mill has been grinding away for over 100 years.*
**2** to destroy (something) by endless wear: [X9 + AWAY] *The steps have been ground away by the passing feet of many visitors over the centuries.*

***grind away at** *v adv prep*
to work continuously at (something repeated and uninteresting): [T1 (*no pass.*)] *Yes, I'm still grinding away at the same old job. A law student has to grind away at dull old case books to make a success of his studies.*

**grind down** *v adv*
**1** to crush (something) to a powder: [T1 + DOWN] *Mills used to use heavy stones to grind down the wheat into flour; now they use more modern machinery. This rock can be ground down for road-building material.*
**2** to reduce the size of (something) by hard rubbing with a rough surface: [X9 + DOWN] *A new knife needs to be ground down to get it really sharp.*
*__3__ to treat (someone) cruelly so as to control him: [T1 (*often pass.*)] *The villagers of the Middle Ages were often ground down by their lords and masters. Don't let the army grind you down!*

**grind in** *v adv*
**1** to force (something) in, so that it is difficult to remove: [X9 + IN (*usu. pass.*)] *I can't get the dirt out of this carpet; it's been ground in.* —**ground-in** *adj*
*__2__ *not fml* to force (knowledge) in, so that it is difficult to forget: [T1 (*to*)] *Your only hope of passing the examination is to have these facts ground in by endless repetition.* → **hammer in** (3), etc.

**grind into** *v prep*
**1** to crush (something) into small pieces or powder: [T1 + *into*] *Next, the wheat is ground into flour at the mill.* → **grind to** (1)
*__2__ to press (something) into or onto (a surface): [D1] *He ground his enemy's face into the dirt.*
*__3__ *not fml* to force (knowledge) into (someone): [D1] *That teacher works too hard trying to grind useless facts into the children.* → **hammer into** (3), etc.

***grind on** *v adv*
to move slowly but surely forward; advance little by little: [IØ (*often simple tenses*)] *The slow methods of the police ground on until the thieves were caught.*

***grind out** *v adv*
**1** to speak (something) in a rough voice: [T1 (*usu. simple tenses*)] *Dying of thirst, the desert traveller ground out a request for water.*
**2** to produce (crushed material): [T1] *This machine grinds out the crushed rock ready for road building.*
**3** *derog* to produce (something) with much effort but little pleasure or interest: [T1] *The writer kept on grinding out more stories until the magazine agreed to accept three of the best ones.*
**4** *derog* to keep on playing (music): [T1] *When will the pianist stop grinding out the same old tunes?*

**grind to** *v prep*
**1** to crush (something) to small pieces or powder: [T1 + *to*] *Next, the wheat is ground to flour at the mill.* → **grind into** (1)
**2 grind to a halt** to come slowly but surely to stop, often noisily: *The train ground to a halt only inches from the damaged bus. If trade doesn't improve soon, the industry will grind to a halt.*

**grind together** *v adv*
to rub (things) roughly together: [T1

TOGETHER] *All night he grinds his teeth together, keeping me awake.*

**grind under** *v prep*
**1** to press (something) beneath (something): [X9 + *under* (*usu. simple tenses*)] *He threw the cigarette down and ground it under his heel.*
*__2__ to control (someone) cruelly with the power of (something): [D1] *The powerful lords were guilty of grinding the villagers under their heels.*

**grind up** *v adv*
to crush (something) into small pieces or powder: [T1 + UP] *This rock can be ground up and used for road building.*

**gripe about/at** *v prep* → **complain about,** etc.
*not fml* to complain about (something) in an unpleasant manner; find fault with (someone): [L9 + *about/at*] *What an unpleasant woman your neighbour is, always griping about one thing or another, never satisfied. Any government will always have some people griping at it, whatever it does.*

**groan out** *v adv*
to express (something) in a painful voice: [T1 + OUT (*usu. simple tenses*)] *The dying woman groaned out her last words.* [IØ + OUT (*usu. simple tenses*)] *The dying soldier groaned out in his suffering.*

**groan with** *v prep*
**1** to make a loud complaining noise because of (something such as pain or a sad feeling): [IØ + *with*] *The dying soldier groaned with pain.*
*__2__ to be very heavy with (food): [T1 (*no pass., often continuous tenses*)] *The table was groaning with good things for the many guests to eat.*

**groom for** *v prep*
**1** to brush and otherwise prepare (a horse) for (a show): [T1 + *for*] *Help me to groom the horses for the show this afternoon.*
**2** to prepare (someone) for (usu. an important position): [D1] *He is grooming his son for the directorship of the firm. The new young actor is being groomed for fame and success.*

**grope about/around** *v adv*
**1** to feel one's way by touch, with difficulty: [L9 + ABOUT/AROUND] *Why are you groping about in the dark? Here's the light!*
**2** to try to find (something) with difficulty: [L9 + ABOUT/AROUND (*for*)] *He seemed to be groping around for an excuse to leave.*

**grope after/for** *v prep*
**1** to try to reach (something) by touch, as in the dark: [L9 + *after/for*] *Entering the room, I groped for the light switch.*
**2** to try to find (something in one's mind): [T1 (*no pass.*)] *Why grope after the meaning of a word? Look it up in the dictionary! For centuries thinkers have been groping for the truth, but are no nearer finding it.*

**grope around** *v adv* → GROPE ABOUT

**grope for** *v prep* → GROPE AFTER

*__gross up__ *v adv*
*BrE tax law* to increase the formal value of (a gift or income, as from interest) for tax purposes: [T1 (*usu. pass.*)] *"If the donor bears the tax the value of the gift has to be grossed up to include the tax."* (*The Times*, 12 July 1975)

**ground in** *v prep*
**be (well) grounded in** to be well trained in; know (a subject) thoroughly: *I don't know how well this young lawyer performs in court, but at least he's well grounded in the principles of such cases.*

*__ground on__ *v prep* → **base on, found on**
to have (something) as its starting point: [D1 (*often pass.*)] *The insurance business is grounded on trust. Always ground your opinion on facts.*

**group about/around/round** *v prep*
to (cause to) gather round (something or someone): [L9 + *about/around/round* (*often simple tenses*)] *The children grouped around their teacher whenever she took them out on a trip.* [X9 + *about/around/round* (*often simple tenses*)] *The photograph will look nice if we group the family around the piano.*

**group together** *v adv*
**1** to (cause to) gather in a group: [L9 + TOGETHER (*often simple tenses*)] *The family grouped together for the photograph.* [X9 + TOGETHER (*often simple tenses*)] *The photographer grouped the family together so that he could get them all in the same picture.*
*__2__ to place (things or people) in the same class or division: [T1 (*often pass.*)] *The guards tend to group all the prisoners together although they are all in prison for widely differing crimes. Insects, animals, and birds are all grouped together in the animal kingdom. The paintings have been grouped together according to the style of the different periods of the artist's life.* → **lump together**

*__group under__ *v prep* → **come under** (2), etc.
to place (something or someone) in (a class): [X9 + *under* (*often pass.*)] *All these books should be grouped under Theatre.*

**grouse about/at** *v prep* → **complain about,** etc.
*not fml* to complain about (something) in an unpleasant manner: [L9 + *about/at*] *What's the old man grousing about now? We try to see that he has everything he needs.*

*__grovel before/to__ *v prep*
*derog* to behave too humbly towards (someone), usu. in the hope of gaining an advantage: [L9 + *before*] *If you expect to gain favours from the king, you will have to grovel before him to show your respect and obedience.*

**grovel in** *v prep*
**1** to go or be down on one's hands and knees among (something such as dirt): [L9 + *in* (*often continuous tenses*)] *Why are you grovelling in the dirt? Have you lost something?* → **wallow in** (1), **welter in** (1)

*2 to be concerned in; work among (unpleasant matters): [T1 (*usu. continuous tenses*)] *Can a policeman possibly enjoy grovelling in the dirty side of human behaviour?* → **wallow in** (2), **welter in** (2)

**grow apace** *v adv*
*old use* to spread or increase quickly: [IØ + APACE] *The business has been growing apace for the last year, a wonderful success in these hard times. Ill weeds grow apace.* (= Evil succeeds.)

***grow apart** *v adv*
**1** to grow in different directions: [L9 + APART] *The two halves of the main branch have grown apart, forming separate trees.* → **grow together** (2)
*2 to become separate in thought, feeling or way of life: [IØ] *After only a few years of marriage, Jim and Mary began to grow apart, and their friends feared they might separate.* → **grow together** (3)

**grow away from** *v adv prep*
**1** to grow in a direction leading away from (something such as the parent plant): [IØ + AWAY + *from*] *The biggest branch has grown away from the trunk in a strange twisted shape.*
*2 to become independent of; cease to have a close relationship with (someone such as one's parents): [T1 (*no pass.*)] *It's natural for children to grow away from their family, and a great pity that this often means bitter fights. When I went back to the town, I found that I had grown away from all my old friends and had become a completely different person.*

**grow back** *v adv* → **grow in¹** (2)
to grow again to the length or height that it formerly was: [IØ + BACK] *All her hair was burned off in the fire, but the doctors have promised that it will soon grow back. Don't worry about cutting the rose bushes severely, they always grow back, stronger and healthier than ever.*

**grow down** *v adv*
**1** to become bigger or longer in a downward direction: [IØ + DOWN] *Even if you plant the seed upside down, the roots will still grow down.* → **grow up** (1)
**2** to become shorter: [L9 + DOWN] *The candle grew down until only an inch was left.*

**grow from** *v prep*
**1** to (cause to) become bigger, starting from (something smaller): [IØ + *from* (*usu. simple tenses*)] *This strange little tree grew from a nut that I planted in the garden. There is a new trunk growing from the fallen dead tree.* [T1 + *from*] *Children enjoy growing flowers from seed.* → **grow into** (3), **grow out of** (1)
*2 to develop; result from (a beginning): [T1 (*no pass., usu. simple tenses*)] *Most international firms have grown from small family businesses. The idea grew from a remark made unthinkingly by the chairman.* [T4 (*usu. simple tenses*)] *The singer's interest in music grew from listening to the radio, long before she ever went to a concert.* → **arise from**, etc.

**grow in¹** *v adv*
**1** to become bigger or longer in an inward direction: [IØ + IN] *Your toenails are very long; you ought to cut them before they start growing in, or you could be in a lot of pain.* —**ingrowing, ingrown** *adj* → **grow out**
**2** to begin to grow again where it was before: [L9 + IN] *All her hair was burned off in the fire, but the doctors have promised that it will soon grow in again.* → **grow back**

**grow in²** *v prep*
**1** to (cause to) become bigger in (a container, building, etc.): [IØ + *in*] *I don't think that such a large plant will grow in such a small pot.* [T1 + *in*] *You can't grow these tropical flowers out of doors; you have to grow them in a heated glasshouse.*
**2** to develop with regard to (a quality): [L9 + *in*] *As people get older, they hope to grow in wisdom. We are pleased to report that the club membership is growing in numbers, if not in quality!* → **gain in**

**grow into** *v prep*
**1** to become bigger and push into (something): [IØ + *into*] *The fence posts took root and grew into the earth! The old tree has grown into the wall of the building.*
**2** to grow larger so as to fit (clothing): [IØ + *into*] *Always buy children's clothes a little too big, so that there is room for the children to grow into them.*
**3** to become (someone or something) as one gets older or bigger: [L9 + *into*] *Steve has grown into a fine young man. Lisa is growing into a good artist. Jim's father's firm has slowly grown into a profitable business.* → **grow from** (1), **grow out of** (1)
*4 to become accustomed to (work, etc.) [T1 (*pass. rare*)] *You need time to grow into a new job.*

**grow on/upon** *v prep*
**1** (of a fruit, vegetable, etc.) to have (something natural) as its place for growth: [IØ + *on/upon* (*usu. simple tenses*)] *I used to think that this sweet tropical fruit grew on a bush, but later learned that in fact it grows on the ground. Money doesn't grow on trees!* (= Money is not easy to obtain.)
*2 to gradually give more pleasure to (someone); begin to be liked by (someone): [T1 (*no pass.*)] *I didn't like this painting at first but it's beginning to grow on me. She grows on you when you get used to her.*
*3 to become habitual to (someone): [T1 (*no pass.*)] *Saving regularly soon grows on you. Be careful, a bad habit like that can grow on a person.*

**grow out** *v adv* → **grow in¹** (1)
to become bigger in an outward direction: [IØ + OUT] *The plant is alive after all! There are new leaves growing out. He looks very odd with funny little bunches of hair growing out*

*above his ears.* —**outgrowing** *n, adj*

**grow out of** *v adv prep*

**1** to become longer starting from (a position): [IØ + OUT + *of*] *There is a new trunk growing out of the fallen dead tree. What's this strange green thing growing out of the ground? It offends me to see hairs growing out of someone's nose.* → **grow from** (1), **grow into** (3)

*__2__ to develop; result from (a beginning): [T1 (*no pass., usu. simple tenses*)] *Most international firms have grown out of small family businesses. The idea grew out of a remark made unthinkingly by the chairman.* [T4 (*usu. simple tenses*)] *The singer's interest in music grew out of listening to the radio, long before she ever went to a concert.* → **arise from,** etc.

*__3__ to grow too large to fit (clothes): [T1] *My daughter has grown out of all her old clothes.* —**outgrow** *v* —**outgrown** *adj*

*__4__ to become too old or sensible to like (someone, something, or doing something): [T1] *Isn't it time you grew out of such childish practices? I thought Grace had grown out of that red-haired boy, but it seems I was wrong.* [T4] *Don't worry, he'll soon grow out of wanting to be a fireman.* —**outgrow** *v*

**grow over**[1] *v adv*

to cover (a place) with plants: [T1a (*usu. pass.*)] *When we returned from our holidays after only three weeks, the whole garden was grown over with strange plants with wide leaves and long roots.* —**overgrown** *adj*

**grow over**[2] *v prep*

to (cause to) cover (something) with something growing: [IØ + *over*] *Pretty little spring flowers grow all over these hillsides in March. Climbing plants had grown over the walls, giving the building an appearance much more ancient that it was.* [T1 + *over*] *The wound left a nasty mark on his face, so he grew a beard over it to hide it.*

**grow together** *v adv*

**1** to (cause to) grow in places very near to one another: [T1 + TOGETHER] *Farmers don't usually grow crops and flowers together. These two bushes can grow together, they like the same kind of soil.*

**2** to become larger in such a way as to become joined: [L9 + TOGETHER] *The two trees have grown together to form a double trunk. As the population spread, the two towns grew together, making one large place.* → **grow apart** (1)

**3** to develop a closer relationship: [IØ] *Married people often grow (closer) together over the years. The brother and sister used to quarrel a lot in their childhood, but grew together more as they got older.* → **grow apart** (2)

**grow up** *v adv*

**1** to become bigger in an upward direction: [IØ + UP] *All plants like to grow up towards the sunlight.* → **grow down** (1)

**2** (of children or young animals) to become older and bigger; develop towards manhood, womanhood, full size, etc.: [IØ (*into*)] *Jane is growing up so fast, I think she's going to be a tall woman. Susan wants to be a doctor when she grows up. What made him grow up into a criminal?* —**grown-up** *n, adj*

*__3__ (of people of any age) to develop beyond childish thoughts and ways: [IØ] *Stop acting like a child with your bad temper! Do grow up! David may be thirty but he hasn't grown up yet; he still lives at home and does what his mother tells him to. Isn't she rather young to be a mother? She's hardly had time to grow up herself.*

*__4__ to arise: [IØ (*usu. simple tenses*)] *A custom grew up of dividing the father's land between the sons.*

**grow upon** *v prep* → GROW ON

**growl out** *v adv*

to speak (something) in a deep, often angry, voice: [T1 + OUT (*often simple tenses*)] *The guard growled out a warning, threatening the prisoners with his gun.*

***grub about/around** *v adv*

*not fml* to work or search, usu. among dirty material: [IØ] *Mary got very dirty grubbing about in the mud, looking for the ring that she had dropped.*

***grub up** *v adv*

**1** *not fml* to pull up (something) out of the ground: [T1a] *Wear your old clothes as you will get very dirty grubbing up the roots of the dead plants. The anteater is so called because it feeds on ants which it grubs up with its long nose from their hills.*

**2** *infml* to find (something or someone unpleasant): [T1a] *Where did the leader grub up that nasty bunch of soldiers? You can't call that object 'art'—it looks like some waste material that he's grubbed up from somewhere!*

**grumble about/over** *v prep* → **complain about,** etc.

to complain bitterly and often unreasonably about (something): [IØ + *about/over*] *There's no pleasing our teacher; he always grumbles about our work even when we've done our best. Taxpayers are grumbling about the waste of government money, as usual.*

**grumble at** *v prep* → **complain about,** etc.

to complain bitterly and often unreasonably about (someone); find fault with (someone or something): [IØ + *at*] *There's no pleasing our teacher; he always grumbles at us even when we've done our best. It's no use grumbling at the weather.*

**grumble over** *v prep* → GRUMBLE ABOUT

**guarantee against** *v prep*

to promise to replace (goods) that suffer damage from (a certain risk): [T1 + *against* (*usu. pass.*)] *This washing machine was guaranteed against mechanical failure—I demand a new one! The swimmer bought a special watch guaranteed against water damage. The makers guarantee this special glass against breakage!*

**guarantee for** *v prep*
to promise to replace (goods) in the event of damage or failure, until (a certain length of time) has passed: [T1 + *for* (*usu. pass.*)] *All our electric motors are guaranteed for one year; in the event of mechanical failure, the makers will replace any faulty part free.*

***guard against** *v prep* → **protect against,** etc.
to protect (someone) from (something or doing something bad); take care to prevent or avoid (something): [T1 (*often simple tenses*)] *Take care in your writing to guard against typical mistakes. If you are conscious of your own weaknesses of character, you have a better chance of guarding against them.* [T4 (*often simple tenses*)] *Warm clothing helps to guard against catching cold.* [D1 (*usu. simple tenses*)] *Take this medicine regularly; it will guard you against a return of the illness.*

**guard from** *v prep* → **protect against,** etc.
to protect (someone or something) from (something or doing something bad): [T1 + *from* (*usu. simple tenses*)] *May God guard you from harm this night. The fence along the middle of the road is intended to guard vehicles from crashing into each other. Parents are demanding that the school put a gate at the entrance to the playground, to guard the children from running into the road.*

**guess at** *v prep*
to try to find the answer to (something) without knowing: [I∅ + *at*] *I wouldn't dare to guess at her age. The government can only guess at the causes of the sharp rise in the cost of living.* —**unguessed-at** *adj*

**gull into** *v prep* → **trick into,** etc.
to deceive (someone) into (doing something), often by gaining his trust: [X9 + *into*] *The government tries to gull the taxpayers into believing that their money is being properly spent.*

**gull out of** *v adv prep* → **cheat out of,** etc.
to cheat (someone) out of (something), usu. money, often by gaining his trust: [X9 + OUT + *of*] *The salesman tried to gull the old lady out of her money, but she didn't trust him and would not give him anything.*

**gulp back** *v adv*
**1** to swallow (liquid) quickly and in quantity, rather rudely: [T1 + BACK] *The soldier took pride in being able to gulp back a whole pint of beer at once, by pouring it down his throat.* → **gulp down**
***2** to hold back; control (tears): [T1] *Mary was still crying when unexpected visitors arrived; gulping back her tears, she made an effort to greet them cheerfully.*

**gulp down** *v adv* → **gulp back** (1)
to swallow (food or liquid) quickly and in quantity, rather rudely: [T1 + DOWN] *Don't gulp your food down, it's both rude and bad for your stomach. Late for work again, Jim gulped down a cup of coffee, with no time for anything to eat.*

**gum down/on** *v adv* → **glue down, stick down** (1), **stick on'** (1)
to fasten (paper) down with a sticky substance: [X9 + DOWN/ON] *This old stamp isn't sticky any more; I shall have to gum it down onto the envelope. If you haven't got the special fasteners to fix your photographs into the book, you'll have to gum them on.*

**gum up** *v adv*
**1** to make (something) sticky: [X9 + UP (*usu. pass.*)] *I spent hours sticking the photographs into the family book, and my fingers got all gummed up.*
***2** *infml* to cause trouble in; spoil (something): [T1a] *Our holiday plans have been gummed up by bad weather. The committee was doing well until the chairman's independent action gummed up the works.* → **jam up, mess up** (2), etc.

***gun down** *v adv*
*not fml* to murder (someone helpless or undefended) by shooting: [T1 (*usu. pass.*)] *One of the brothers who wrote the well-known book of records was gunned down outside his home in London.*

***gun for** *v prep*
**1** to hunt for (someone) so as to kill or harm them, esp. with a gun: [T1(*continuous tenses*)] *We know you told the police about our hiding place, so we'll be gunning for you when we get out of prison.*
**2** to intend to attack or punish (someone): [T1 (*continuous tenses*)] *There is one member of the committee who failed to keep the agreement secret, and the chairman is gunning for him.*

**gush forth/out** *v adv*
(of liquid) to flow out quickly and in quantity: [L9 + FORTH/OUT] *Blood gushed forth from the terrible wound, and no one could stop the flow.*

**gush from** *v prep*
**1** (of liquid) to flow quickly and in quantity from (something): [L9 + *from*] *The workmen cheered when oil at last gushed from the pipe.*
**2** to pour from (something): [L9 + *from*] *Tears gushed from her eyes.*

**gush over** *v prep*
to express unpleasantly foolish and insincere admiration for (someone or something): [I∅ + *over*] *That silly woman gushes over every new actress that she meets, telling each one how wonderful she is; I don't know what she hopes to gain by it, except perhaps some rather false gratitude.*

**gush with** *v prep*
to pour freely with (a liquid): [L9 + *with*] *The terrible wound gushed with blood and no one could stop the flow.*

***gussy up** *v adv* → **flossy up**
*AmE sl* to ornament (something) in the hope of improving it: [T1] *Do you think I could gussy up this old dress so that it's suitable for the party? This writer is guilty of trying*

*to gussy up a plain statement to make it fit the rules.*

**guzzle down** *v adv*
*not fml* to drink (liquid) in large quantities, often selfishly: [T1 + DOWN] *You men should be ashamed of yourselves, guzzling down pints of beer just to compete with each other; have you no self-respect?*

# H

**habituate to** *v prep* → **accustom to, use to**
*fml* to accustom (oneself) to (something or doing something): [D1 (*often pass.*)] *The shock of the singer's failure was worse because she had become habituated a success.* [V4b (*simple tenses*)] *One can habituate oneself to living alone, though rarely with any pleasure.*

**hack around** *v adv* → **mess about** (1), etc.
*AmE infml* to spend time lazily: [IØ] *'What have you been doing today?' 'Oh, nothing, just hacking around.'*

**hack at** *v prep*
to cut repeatedly and roughly at (something), usu. with a knife or axe: [L9 (AWAY) + *at*] *After hacking (away) at the tree for hours, the man still could not cut through the trunk; the wood was too hard and his axe needed sharpening.*

**hack down** *v adv*
**1** to make (something such as a tree) fall by cutting it roughly and repeatedly, usu. with an axe: [X9 + DOWN] *I want the boys to hack down that old apple tree, it's unsafe.* → **chop down** (1), **hew down**
*__2__ (in football) to attack (a player on the opposing team) roughly and unfairly, so as to make him fall: [T1] *I think I saw Brown hacking down their centre forward.*

**hack off** *v adv*
to remove (usu. part of something) by cutting it roughly: [X9 + OFF] *You'd better hack off that branch that's hanging over the neighbour's garden.*

**hack out** *v adv* → **carve out, hew out**
**1** to shape or cut (usu. a space) roughly, usu. with an axe: [X9 + OUT] *Early settlers had to hack out a clearing in the forest where they could grow crops.*
*__2__ *not fml* to form (something such as a plan) with difficulty: [T1] *The committee had instructions to hack out a new method of organizing the firm's accounts, even if it took all night.*

**hack up** *v adv*
to cut; destroy (something) roughly, usu. with a knife or other sharp instrument: [X9 + UP] *Not content with stealing the jewels, the thieves hacked up some valuable furniture and left the pieces all over the room. The sailors had to hack up the ice to free the ship.*

**haggle about** *v prep* → **BARGAIN ABOUT**

**haggle for** *v prep* → **BARGAIN FOR** (1)

**haggle over/about** *v prep* → **BARGAIN ABOUT**

**haggle with** *v prep* → **BARGAIN WITH**

***hail down on** *v adv prep* → **rain down on** (2)
to (cause to) descend quickly or in quantity on (someone or something): [D1 (*usu. simple tenses*)] *The old woman hailed down curses on our heads.* [T1] (*no pass., simple tenses*)] *Troubles hailed down on the city in the war.*

***hail from** *v prep*
to come from (somewhere); have (a place) as one's home: [T1 (*no pass., simple tenses*)] *That big ship in the harbour hails from a port in the South Seas. You have a strange manner of speaking—where do you hail from?*

***hail up** *v adv*
*AustrE infml* to stay for a night or nights at an inn: [IØ] *I enjoy travelling through the country hailing up at the nearest inn.*

***ham up** *v adv* → **camp up**
*infml* to overact (something) on purpose or through lack of ability: [T1] *Your story is very funny, but there's no need to ham it up. She would be a better performer if she didn't ham up every song!* —**hammed-up** *adj*

**hammer at** *v prep* → **knock at,** etc.
**1** to work on (material, usu. wood) with a hammer: [IØ + *at*] *As the curtain rises, one of the scene-builders is kneeling on the stage, hammering at a piece of wood.*
*__2__ to give loud and repeated blows on (something hard or noisy): [T1 (*no pass., often continuous tenses*)] *Who's that hammering at the door in the middle of the night? Jane takes her music practice seriously; she's been hammering at the piano all morning. I can hear you hammering at the typewriter from halfway down the street!* → **knock at**, etc.

***hammer away at** *v adv prep*
**1** *not fml* to work hard at (something or doing something): [T1 (*no pass.*)] *Father is in his study, hammering away at a pile of work which he has to finish before morning.* [T4] *If I hammer away at finishing these letters. I can just get them ready in time for the post.*
**2** to shoot continuously at (someone): [T1 (*often continuous tenses*)] *If we can go on hammering away at the enemy for another day, I think we can defeat them.*
**3** *not fml* to repeat (something such as an argument) forcefully: [T1 (*no pass.*)] *The speaker hammered away at his point but the crowd did not believe him.*

**hammer down** *v adv*
to fasten (something) down by hammering nails into it or beating it with a hammer: [X9

+ DOWN] *This mat has to be hammered down at the edges to stop it curling.*

***hammer home** *v adv*
*not fml* to make (something such as a fact or argument) accepted, as by repetition or other forceful methods: [T1] *The speaker hammered his point home with examples that the listeners could not deny.*

**hammer in** *v adv*
**1** to drive (usu. a nail) in with a hammer: [T1 + IN] *Help me to hammer in these last few nails, I'm tired!* → **drive in** (2), **pound in** (1)
**2** to break (something) down or inwards by force: [X9 + IN] *The firemen had to hammer in the door to save the children in the burning room.*
***3** *not fml* to teach (something) by forceful repetition: [T1 (*to*)] *The teacher has been trying to hammer in the danger of failing the examinations.* → **beat in** (3), **din in¹**, **drill in**, **drive in** (3), **drum in**, **grind in** (2), **knock in** (2), **pound in** (2), **pump in** (3), **rub in¹** (2)

**hammer into** *v prep*
**1** to drive (a nail) with a hammer into (material such as wood or something made of such material): [T1 + *into*] *I can't hammer this nail into the wall; either it's bent or I must have struck a brick.*
**2** to beat (something) with a hammer so that it becomes (an object or shape): [X9 + *into*] *The natives used to hammer the metal into arrowheads, using heavy stones. It took all afternoon to hammer the bent wheel (back) into shape.* → **beat into** (2), **pound into** (1)
***3** *not fml* to teach (something) to (someone) by forceful repetition: [D1] *That teacher is wasting his effort trying to hammer useless facts into such children.* [D5] *How often have I hammered into you that you must ask permission first?* [D6] *Parents often try to hammer into their children how much they owe them.* → **beat into** (4), **din in¹**, **drill into** (2), **drive into** (3), **drum in**, **grind into** (3), **knock into** (3), **pound into** (3), **pump into** (3), **rub into** (2)

***hammer on** *v prep* → **knock at**, etc.
to beat or knock loudly on (a door, wall, etc.): [T1 (*no pass., often continuous tenses*)] *Who's that hammering on the door in the middle of the night? Those people next door have been hammering on the walls again.*

**hammer out** *v adv*
**1** to shape (something) by beating with a hammer: [X9 + OUT] *At this college some of the students learn to hammer out beautiful dishes in silver and other precious metals.*
**2** to flatten (metal) by beating with a hammer: [X9 + OUT] *The car door was so damaged in the crash that the garage men had to hammer it out.*
**3** to remove (something) with a hammer: [T1 + OUT] *Can you hammer out these nails for me? I want the wood smooth to handle.*
***4** *not fml* to produce (something) with heavy blows on something noisy: [T1 (*often continuous tenses*)] *I can hear Jane from here, hammering out a tune on the piano; I do wish she would learn to play the instrument gently. Tom is back at work, hammering out anothe story on his old typewriter.*
***5** *not fml* to talk about (something) in detai and come to a decision about it; reach (an answer) after much talk: [T1] *The government must hammer out the difficult question of how to prevent further wars. If we keep talking all night, we should be able to hammer out an agreement.*

**hand back** *v adv*
**1** to return (something) to someone by hand: [X9 + BACK (*to*) (*often simple tenses*)] *Examination papers will be handed back after the marks have been officially recorded. Hand the book back to Penny, she asked for it nicely.* → **get back** (4), **get back** (1), **have back** (1)
***2** to enable someone to have (something again: [T1 (*to*) (*often simple tenses*)] *Having gained power by force and ended the rule of the cruel king, the military leaders then handed back the government to the people.*

**hand down** *v adv*
**1** to pass (something) to someone on a lowe level: [X9 + DOWN (*to*)] *Please hand down the large dish from the top shelf, I can't reac it. When I've finished this part of the wall, I' hand the brushes and paint pots down to yo before I come down the ladder.* → **hand up** (1 **pass down¹** (2), **pass up** (1)
**2** to help (someone) to descend, as from vehicle: [X9 + DOWN] *The loyal servar handed the lady down from her carriage* → **hand in** (1), **hand out** (1), **hand up** (2)
***3** to give or leave (something) to people wh are younger or come later: [T1 (*to*) (*usu pass.*)] *This custom has been handed dow since the 18th century. This ring has bee handed down in my family.* → **bring down** (9 **carry down** (2), **come down** (6), **come down** (4), **descend from** (2), **hand on** (3), **pass down¹** (4 **pass on** (5)
***4** to give (usu. clothes) to a younger or smal er member of the family: [T1 (*to*) (*usu. simple tenses*)] *We hoped that the next child woul be a boy so that we could hand down h brother's clothes. The girl was ashamed wearing clothes that had been handed dow from her sister.* —**hand-me-down** *n, adj* → **pa down¹** (5), **pass on¹** (6), **reach down**
***5** esp. *AmE* to give; make a public stateme about; make (something) known officiall [T1 (*often simple tenses*)] *The city council w hand down the budget on Monday. The jud handed down his decision, which shocked t court into silence. The government thinks can hand down a cure for every difficulty local affairs.* → **bring down** (11)

**hand in** *v adv*
**1** to help (someone) into a vehicle: [X9 + (*to*)] *Part of a gentleman's duty in form times was to hand a lady in when she enter*

*her carriage.* → **hand down** (2), **hand out** (1), **hand up** (2)

**2** to give (something) to someone in charge, by hand: [X9 + IN (*usu. simple tenses*)] *Your test papers must be handed in by Monday. Hand this letter in to the office as you pass, will you?* → **give in** (1), **give into** (1), **pass in**[1] (2)

***3** to offer; give (something) to someone in charge; return (something) no longer wanted: [T1 (*usu. simple tenses*)] *The director has threatened to hand in his resignation unless his demands are accepted. Visitors to the camp must hand in any weapons at the main gate. Unwanted tickets can be handed in at the theatre office window up to half an hour before the performance. If you find some money in the street, you should hand it in to the nearest police station.* → **deliver over, give in** (4), **give into** (4), **turn in** (4)

**hand off** *v adv*

(in rugby football) to push (someone) away with the hand: [T1] *The player caught the ball and ran down the field, handing off any player from the other team who tried to stop him.* —**hand-off** *n*

**hand on** *v adv*

**1** to pass (something) to someone by hand: [X9 + ON (*often pass.*)] *The precious flame representing the spirit of the Games is handed on from runner to runner all the way from the original fire on the ancient mountain to the place where the Games are being held on this occasion.*

***2** to pass (information) to someone else: [T1 (*usu. simple tenses*)] *The secret word is 'forever'—hand it on to everyone on our side. I have some good news to hand on, don't you want to hear it?* → **pass along** (1), **pass down**[1] (1), **pass on**[1] (2)

***3** to give or leave (something such as knowledge) to people who are younger or come later: [T1 (*to*) (*usu. simple tenses*)] *Their custom has been handed on to us by our great-grandfathers. The possession of language enables man to hand on his wisdom and experience to his children and grandchildren.* → **hand down** (3), etc., **pass down**[1] (5), **pass on**[1] (6)

**4** to give control of (something) to someone else: [T1 (*to*) (*usu. simple tenses*)] *The time has come for me to hand on the chairmanship to a younger person.* → **hand over** (2)

**hand out** *v adv*

**1** to help (someone) or lift (something) out of something, as a vehicle: [X9 + OUT] *As the lady tried to step down from the carriage, the gentleman politely handed her out. I'll stay by the car and hand the boxes out to you, so that you can carry them into the house.* —**hand-out** *n* → **hand down** (2), **hand in** (1), **hand up** (2)

**2** to hand (something or things) to each of several people: [X9 + OUT (*usu. simple tenses*)] *Hand out the question papers as the students enter the examination room. The firm paid a man to stand on the street corner handing out advertisements. I hand more money out to the children every week!* —**handout** *n* → **dish out** (3), **give out** (2), **pass out** (1)

***3** to offer; give (something) freely: [T1] *The government hands out payments to people out of work. The Red Cross went at once to the scene of the great floods, to hand out medicine and tents to the homeless people.* —**hand-out** *n* → **dish out** (3), **give out** (3), **pass out** (1)

***4** to give freely (usu. something unwanted): [T1] *Aunt Mabel likes to hand out advice to the young people, whether they want it or not. A government representative has been sent to hand out copies of the prepared statement on their future plans.* —**hand-out** *n* → **dish out** (4), **ladle out** (2)

**5 hand it out** *infml* to punish or scold someone freely: *Try to keep away from the teacher, she's really handing it out this morning.* → **dish out** (5)

**hand over** *v adv*

**1** to give (something) to someone else by hand: [X9 + OVER (*often simple tenses*)] *Hand your cases over to the doorman, he will see that they are delivered to your room. Hand over that bag at once, it's mine!*

***2** to give control of (something) to someone else: [T1 (*to*) (*usu. simple tenses*)] *The command of the ship was handed over to her new captain at a small ceremony this morning.* [IØ (*to*) (*simple tenses*)] *The general handed over to the conqueror. I should like to get rid of the responsibility for this job, but there doesn't seem to be anyone fit to hand over to.* —**handover** *n* → **hand on** (4)

***3** to deliver (someone or something) to people in charge: [T1 (*to*) (*usu. simple tenses*)] *The escaped criminal was handed over to the police. Six leading citizens refused to hand the city over to the enemy, and offered themselves as prisoners instead.* → **give up** (7), etc., (8), etc.

**hand round** *v adv* → **pass round**[1] (1)

to pass (things) by hand among a group of people: [X9 + ROUND] *It was such a wealthy party that special servants were employed to hand the drinks around.*

**hand to** *v prep*

**1** to give or pass (something) by hand to (someone): [X9 + *to* (*usu. simple tenses*)] *Hand the salt to your father, would you?*

**2 hand it to** *not fml* to admire (someone): [(*simple tenses*)] *I have to hand it to you for the way you treated that nasty old man at dinner.*

**hand up** *v adv*

**1** to pass (something) by hand to someone on a higher level: [X9 + UP (*to*)] *Hand the paintbrush up to Father on the ladder.* → **hand down** (1), **pass down**[1] (2), **pass up** (1)

**2** to help (someone) to climb, as into a vehicle: [X9 + UP (*usu. simple tenses*)] *I shall need you to hand me up on this difficult slope.* → **hand down** (2), **hand in** (1), **hand out** (1)

*3 to deliver (something) to someone higher in command: [T1 (*usu. simple tenses*)] *Your request will be handed up to the board of directors.*

***hang about/around/round**¹ *v adv*

**1** *infml* to wait without purpose or activity: [IØ] *Don't hang about, we have a train to catch. I hung around for an hour but he didn't come.*

**2** *infml* to be slow to develop: [IØ] *This cough has been hanging about for two weeks now. The storm hung around for hours without breaking, making me nervous and bad-tempered.*

**hang about/around/round**² *v prep*

**1** to (cause to) swing from or round (a part of the body): [L9 + *about/around/round*] *She had a strange object hanging round her waist.* [X9 + *about/around/round*] *He was so rich that he liked to hang half his fortune about his wife's neck.*

*2 to wait or be present near (a place): [T1 (*no pass., often continuous tenses*)] *There are some people hanging around the door demanding to speak to you, will you see them? Young people today seem to have no work to do, they're always hanging about the house.* → **bang around² (2), kick about (3), knock about (3)**

*3 to stay near; be friendly with (someone): [T1 (*no pass., usu. continuous tenses*)] *The children are always hanging round me, getting in my way! I won't have my son hanging around criminal companions.*

*4 to be near; wait for; threaten (someone): [T1 (*no pass., usu. continuous tenses*)] *There seems to be danger hanging round those who deal in diamonds.*

***hand around**¹ *v adv* → HANG ABOUT

**hang around**² *v prep* → HANG ABOUT

***hang back/off** *v adv* → **hold aloof, hold back** (6), **hold off** (1), **keep aloof, keep at** (5), **keep off** (1), **stand aloof, stand apart, stand off**¹ (2)

to be slow or unwilling to act; keep oneself in the background: [IØ (*usu. simple tenses*)] *Jane is afraid of people, she always hangs back when we take her to a party. He hung back before replying. The bridge looked so unsafe that we all hung back in fear.*

***hang behind** *v adv*

to remain somewhere when others have left; be slow to join: [IØ] *Jane is so annoying whenever we go on a trip, always hanging behind. A few students hung behind after class to speak to the teacher.*

**hang by** *v prep*

**1** to swing from (something such as a rope); be held by (part of the body): [IØ + *by*] *When we drew the bucket up from the well, we saw that most of the rope had worn away, and the bucket was left hanging by a very thin thread. The climber hung by his fingers for over an hour until his companions could bring a rope. For the murder of that helpless woman, you shall hang by the neck until you are dead.* → **hang from**

**2 hang by a hair/thread** (of someone's life, fate, etc.) to be delicately balanced: *At one time Mother's life hung by a hair, but with strength of will she gradually grew stronger and is now out of hospital.*

**hang down** *v adv*

to (cause to) bend downwards); become lower: [L9 + DOWN (*usu. simple tenses*)] *I like the way her hair hangs down so straight and shiny. The branches hung down to the ground with the weight of the apples.* [X9 + DOWN (*usu. simple tenses*)] *The boy hung down his head in shame when he was caught cheating.*

**hang from** *v prep* → **hang by** (1)

to swing from (something such as a rope); be held by (part of the body): [IØ + *from*] *The key was kept hanging from a string round his neck. The climber hung from his fingers until his friends brought help.*

***hang heavy** *v adv*

*not fml* (of time) to seem to pass slowly because of lack of interest, joy, etc.: [IØ (*often simple tenses*)] *Time hangs so heavy when you're away; all I do is wait impatiently.*

***hang in**¹ *v adv*

*AmE infml* to keep going in spite of difficulties: [IØ (THERE) (*imper.*)] *Hang in there! It'll soon be over!*

**hang in**² *v prep*

**hang in the balance** to be in an uncertain position where things may end well or badly: *The votes counted so far have been very even for both parties, and the result of the election will hang in the balance until the last vote is counted.*

***hang it** *v pron*

*infml* an expression of anger, surprise, shock, etc.: [*imper.*] *"Hang it!" he shouted, when he saw his train had already gone.*

***hang off** *v adv* → HANG BACK

**hang on**¹ *v adv*

**1** to continue holding: [L9 + ON] *The climber had to hang on while his companions went to find a rope.* → **hold on** (1)

*2 *not fml* to wait, esp. on the telephone: [IØ] *Hang on, I shan't be a minute. You go ahead, I'll hang on here until the others come. I'm afraid the line is busy, would you like to hang on?* → **hold on** (4)

*3 *not fml* to continue in spite of difficulties: [IØ] *Painting the house is tiring, but if you hang on, the results are worth the effort. The town was surrounded by the enemy and the citizens did not know if they could hang on until help arrived.* → **hang out** (4), **hold on** (5), **hold out** (4), **last out** (3), **stick out** (7)

*4 to last when not wanted: [IØ] *Given proper treatment, a cold can be cured in seven days, but left to itself, it will hang on for a week.*

**5 hang one on** *AmE infml* to go out in order to get drunk: [*simple tenses*] *You rea* *hung one on last night, didn't you!*

**hang on/upon²** *v prep*

**1** to pull on (something); press one's weight on (something): [L9 + *on/upon*)] *You hang on this end until I tell you to let go. You have to hang on the rope for a surprisingly long time before the bell rings. Please don't hang on my arm so heavily.* → **hang onto** (1)

***2** to depend on (something); change according to (something): [T1 (*no pass., simple tenses*)] *The story hangs on the relationship between the two sisters. The case hangs upon the judge's opinion of the prisoner's character.* [T6] *The result will hang on whether the secret is discovered.* → **hinge on, pivot on** (2), **ride on²** (2), **turn on²** (3)

***3** *not fml* to depend on; stick closely to; force one's company on (someone): [T1] *You really shouldn't hang on your elder sister all day, she may not want you with her. Some of the students are always hanging on that particular teacher.* —**hanger-on** *n infml* → **hang onto** (2)

***4** to pay close attention to; wait eagerly for (something): [T1 (*no pass., usu. simple tenses*)] *The boy admires his teacher, he hangs on his every word.*

**5 hang on someone's lips** to listen eagerly to what someone says: *When the owner visited the factory, even the board of directors hung on his lips to hear his opinion. A politician or anyone in public life can hardly hope to express an opinion on anything without having reporters hanging on his lips.*

**6 hang one on** *AmE infml* to strike (someone) with a blow: [*simple tenses*] *He hit me first, but then I hung one on him and down he went like a stone.*

**hang onto** *v prep*

**1** to hold (something or someone) tightly: [L9 + *onto*] *Hang onto my arm on this icy surface. How long can the climber hang onto the cliff? It was so windy that I had to hang onto my hat all the way along the street.* → **hang on²** (1), **hold onto** (1)

***2** *not fml* to stick closely to; force one's company on (someone): [T1] *My little brother is always hanging onto me whether I want him or not.* → **hang on²** (3)

**3** *not fml* to try to keep (something): [T1] *We should hung onto the house and sell it later when prices are higher.* → **cling onto** (2), **cling to** (3), **hold onto** (2), **stick to** (4)

**4** *not fml* to find support or help in (something): [T1 (*usu. simple tenses*)] *The old lady had only her religion to hang onto when all her family had gone. The police have only one fingerprint to hang onto. Hang onto this comforting thought: it'll all be over soon.* → **hold onto** (3)

**hang out** *v adv*

**1** to lean out; stick out: [L9 + OUT (*of*)] *Don't hang out of the window, it's dangerous. The dog lay in the shade with his tongue hanging out, it was so hot.*

**2** to fasten, spread, or show (something) out of doors: [X9 + OUT] *Hang out the flag, the victory is ours! It's such a fine day that I want to hang the washing out to get it dry in this warm wind. The young lawyer rented an office, hung out a sign, and waited for cases to arrive.* → **peg out** (1)

***3** *not fml* to last: [IØ (*usu. simple tenses*)] *Can you make the food hang out till next payday?* → **hold out** (3), **hold up** (6), **keep up** (5), **last out** (1)

***4** *not fml* to last in spite of difficulties; keep going: [IØ] *The town was surrounded by the enemy but the people hung out until help came.* → **hang on¹** (3), etc.

***5** *infml* to live or spend much time: [IØ (*simple tenses*)] *Can you tell me where Jim hangs out?* —**hang-out** *n sl*

**6 let it all hang out** *sl* to tell everything; have no secrets; feel free to do one's own activity: *Tell me the whole story—let it all hang out!*

***hang out for** *v adv prep* → **hold out for, stand out for, stick out for, strike against** (1), **strike for** to demand (something such as money) firmly and wait in order to get it: [T1] *The workers are still hanging out for more pay. Be careful, the dealers may hang out for a higher price.*

**hang over¹** *v adv*

**1** to lean over: [L9 + OVER] *There's a branch hanging over, can you reach it and pull yourself out of the water?*

***2** to continue; remain; result (from something or a time): [IØ (*from*) (*often simple tenses*)] *This custom hangs over from the old days.* —**hangover** *n*

**3 be hung over** to suffer the next morning from having drunk too much alcohol the night before: *Don't try to talk to Jim this morning, he's (badly) hung over and in a very bad temper.* —**hangover** *n*

**hang over²** *v prep*

**1** to (cause to) lean over; cover; be placed above or on top of (something or someone): [L9 + *over*] *There's a branch hanging over the water, can you reach it and pull yourself out? I know she's here, her coat is hanging over the back of the chair! Pupils at this school are not allowed to wear their hair hanging over their shoulders. Please don't hang over me while I'm working, it makes me nervous.* [X9 + *over*] *You can hang your washing over this line to dry. Whenever there's a thunderstorm, Mother hangs a cloth over the mirror, as she thinks that it will prevent the lightning from striking!*

***2** to threaten or be the fate of (something or someone); be likely soon to have an effect on (someone); surround (something), as with fear, doubt, etc.: [T1 (*no pass.*)] *The uncertainty of war hung over Europe for twenty-one years. I hate to have unfinished work hanging over me. There is always doubt hanging over the possibility of changes in the law.* → **hover over** (2)

***hang round**[1] *v adv* → HANG ABOUT

**hang round**[2] *v prep* → HANG ABOUT

**hang together** *v adv*

**1** (of pictures, etc.) to (cause to) be shown or placed on a wall near to one another: [IØ + TOGETHER] *Hanging together above the fireplace were the Queen, Jesus Christ, and the old lord who had owned the house.* [T1 + TOGETHER] *These pictures were painted as a pair and were intended to be hung together.*

**2** (of criminals) to (cause to) be killed by being dropped with a rope round the neck, at the same time or place: [IØ + TOGETHER] *Take care we're not caught for this murder, or we'll hang together.* [T1 + TOGETHER] *The two murderers were hanged together.*

***3** to (cause to) remain in one piece: [IØ (*simple tenses*)] *I don't know how that old car hangs together!* [T1 (*usu. pass.*)] *I do—it's hung together with bits of string!*

***4** to remain united: [IØ (*usu. simple tenses*)] *The team must hang together in spite of their many losses.*

***5** *not fml* to suit each other; seem true or in agreement; support the same idea in each separate part: [IØ (*simple tenses*)] *Your ideas and mine don't quite hang together. A story is good only if the characters hang together. This plan doesn't hang together, and I don't see how it can work.*

**hang up** *v adv*

**1** to place (something such as an ornament or clothing) on a wall or hook: [T1 + UP] *Hang up your hat and coat and come and sit down. My daughter made a strange wall hanging for me in bright pink wool, which I have hung up proudly in the hall for everyone to see.*

***2** to put a telephone receiver down: [IØ (*on*) (*usu. simple tenses*)] *Don't hang up (on me), I haven't finished talking to you!* → **ring off**

***3** *not fml* to delay (something): [T1 (*usu. pass.*)] *The peace talks were hung up while the representatives spoke to their governments* —**hang-up** *n* → **hold back** (4), **hold off** (2), **hold up** (2), **keep back** (5), **keep off** (2)

***4** *infml* to cause (someone) to be busy, anxious, or have a fixed idea (about something or someone): [T1 (*often pass.*)] *The boy is badly hung up on the way his mother treated him. Try not to get hung up in too many activities. The girl is really hung up on that musician.* —**hang-up** *n*

***5** *AustrE infml* to tie (a horse) to a post: [T1] *Hang up your horse and come in for a drink.*

**hang upon** *v prep* → HANG ON

**hang with** *v prep*

to ornament (someone or something such as a wall) with (objects): [X9 + *with* (*usu. pass.*)] *The walls of the restaurant were hung with paintings done by the owner's daughter.*

***hanker after/for** *v prep*

to desire (something) very much: [T1] *This wet summer makes me hanker after a holiday in the sun. Sometimes I can't help hankering for some fattening food.*

***happen along** *v adv*

to arrive by chance: [IØ (*simple tenses*)] *Guess who happened along while I was waiting for the bus? My old neighbour from the other city!*

***happen on/upon** *v prep* also **blunder on** → **alight on** (2), **chance on, come across**[2] (2), **come on**[2] (2), **drop across, light on** (3), **meet with** (1), **run across**[2] (4), **run into** (7), **run up against** (2), **stumble across, tumble on**

to find (something); meet (someone) by chance: [T1 (*simple tenses*)] *I happened on this old photograph in the back of the drawer. Guess who I happened on while I was in the other city? My old neighbour!*

**happen to** *v prep*

**1** to be the fate of (usu. someone): [IØ + *to* (*often simple tenses*)] *Accidents happen most often to those who are careless. "Everything is funny, as long as it's happening to somebody else."* (Will Rogers, *The Illiterate Digest*)

**2** to change; cause wounding or damage to, or loss of (something): [L9 + *to*] *What's happened to my blue bag? I can't find it anywhere. Do you know what happened to the car in the crash? Something strange seems to be happening to me since I've been taking this drug. Whatever has happened to your arm? It's all swollen!*

***happen upon** *v prep* → HAPPEN ON

***harden in/up** *v adv* → **flatten in, round in**

*naut* to pull in (ropes controlling certain sails): [T1] *You'd better harden in the main ropes, the sail's not tight enough!* [IØ] *Harden up a little, we need more speed.*

**harden off** *v adv*

(of a young plant) to (cause to) become strong enough to be planted out of doors: [IØ + OFF] *When the onion plants have hardened off, we can plant them in the garden; they should be ready soon.* [T1 + OFF] *What is the best way to harden off new rose bushes only a few inches high?*

**harden to** *v prep*

**be hardened to** to be made less sensitive to (something or doing something painful) through use: *Poor people often become hardened to suffering. Do you think that John is becoming hardened to failing his driving test? I don't think Mrs Page will ever be hardened to the loss of her son.*

***harden up** *v adv* → HARDEN IN

***hark at** *v prep*

*infml* to listen to (someone) with disbelief or disapproval: [T1 (*no pass., usu. simple tenses*)] *Hark at her! The stories she tells!*

***hark back** *v adv*

**1** (of a hunting dog) to return to the scene where a smell was first learned: [IØ (*to*)] *The dogs have lost the smell of the fox; they will have to hark back to the point where they first picked it up.*

**2** *infml* to talk about happy memories of (the past): [IØ (*to*)] *In any troubled times, the British tend to hark back to wartime days, when people helped each other in a friendly spirit. Aunt Mabel is always harking back to her childhood in the country.*

**hark to** *v prep*
*old use or lit* to listen to (a sound): [IØ + *to*] *"Oh, hark to the big drum calling, Follow me, follow me home!"* (Rudyard Kipling, *Follow Me 'Ome*)

**harmonize with** *v prep* → **blend with,** etc.
(esp. in music) to match or suit; combine pleasantly with (something else such as a sound): [L9 + *with*] *One of the pleasures of singing is to harmonize with the other voices. I like the way the blue carpet harmonizes with the gold curtains.*

**harness to** *v prep*
**1** to fasten (an animal or animals) to (a vehicle) with leather bands: [T1 + *to*] *Oxen are harnessed to the villagers' carts to pull them through the muddy streets.*
*__2__ to make use of (power or something that produces power) to serve (a need): [D1 (*often simple tenses*)] *New ways are always being discovered of harnessing oil and other minerals to the production of electricity. Children put such a lot of strength, effort, and keenness into their play, and so little into their schoolwork; as teachers, we must find a way to harness this energy to classroom work.*

**harness up** *v adv*
to put leather bands on (an animal such as a horse) for riding or pulling a vehicle: [T1 + UP] *As soon as the horses are harnessed up, the group will be ready to leave.*

**harp on/about** *v prep* also **harp on about**
to talk a lot about (something, usu. sad): [T1] *My grandfather still harps on the death of his eldest son, all those years ago.*

**hash out** *v adv* → **thrash out** (2)
*infml* to settle (a difficulty) by long talk: [T1] *We must hash out the question of Mr Brown's appointment, which many of the directors are opposing.*

**hash over** *v adv*
esp. *AmE infml* to talk about (something such as a difficulty) in detail and at length: [T1] *Hasn't the committee finished hashing over the question yet?*

**hash up** *v adv*
**1** to cut (meat) into very small pieces: [T1 + UP] *You'll need a sharp knife and a wooden board for hashing up that meat.* → **chop up** (1)
**2** *infml* to spoil (something) carelessly: [T1] *Don't hash up your driving test like you did last year.* → **mess up** (2), etc.

**hatch out** *v adv*
**1** to (cause to) come out from an egg: [IØ + OUT] *When will the baby chickens hatch out?* [T1 + OUT] *Most birds have to sit on their eggs, keeping them warm, for a certain length of time in order to hatch out their young.*
*__2__ *infml* to (cause to) reach a result; consider and decide about (something): [T1] *The government are hatching out a new plan to deal with rising prices.* [IØ] *No one knows how the new plan will hatch out.* also **hatch up**

***haul before** *v prep* → **bring before** (1), etc.
*not fml* to force (someone) to appear before (a court of law or judge) on trial: [D1 (*often pass.*)] *Peter has been hauled before the court on a charge of drunken driving.*

**haul down** *v adv*
**1** to lower (something such as a flag): [X9 + DOWN] *The first thing that the enemy did when they conquered the town was to haul down the citizens' flag and raise their own. And then the woman tried to haul my trousers down!*
**2** to lift (something heavy) down from a higher level: [X9 + DOWN] *All the farm workers had to help to haul the bags of cattle food down from the cart.* → **haul up** (1)
**3 haul down the flag/colours** *not fml* to yield; admit defeat: *After several weeks of argument; the trade union leaders had to haul down the flag and accept the government's earlier offer.*

**haul in** *v adv*
**1** to pull (something) towards one: [T1 + IN] *We went down to the shore to watch the fishermen hauling in their nets.* → **draw in** (1), **pull in** (1)
**2 haul in one's horns** *not fml* to be less keen or active, and more careful: *You've been using up your strength too much recently; hadn't you better haul in your horns a little? You'd better haul in your horns or the voters will know what you're trying to do.* → **draw in** (11), **pull in** (13)

**haul on/onto** *v prep*
**haul on/onto the wind** *naut* to pull in sails so that they lie near or in the same direction as the desired course, so as to sail closer to the wind: *'Haul onto the wind!' shouted the captain, as the ship tried to leave her course.*

**haul over** *v prep* → **call over, rake over²** (2)
**haul someone over the coals** *not fml* to scold someone for a fault: *The director called Jim into his office to haul him over the coals for being late so often.*

***haul taut** *v adj*
*naut* to pull (a rope) tight: [T1b] *Haul the ropes taut, there's a strong wind coming!* [IØ] *'Haul taut!' ordered the captain.*

**haul up** *v adv*
**1** to lift; pull (something) up with effort: [X9 + UP] *If we can get some strong ropes or wires around the sunken boat, we might be able to haul her up.* → **haul down** (2)
*__2__ *infml* to force (someone) to appear on trial: [T1 (*before*) (*often pass.*)] *If we get caught with the jewels, I hope we're not hauled up before the same judge who dealt with us last time.* → **have up** (2), etc.
*__3__ *naut* to sail closer to the wind: [IØ] *The boat's going off course, we'll have to haul up.*

*4 *naut* to stop: [IØ] *The ship was able to haul up just before it hit the little boat.*

**have about/around**[1] *v adv* → **keep about**
to have (something or someone) near one, as in one's home as an ornament or companion: [X9 + ABOUT/AROUND (*simple tenses*)] *It's a pleasant piece of furniture to have about. Don't go away, I like having you around!*

**have about**[2] *v prep* → also **have around**
1 to have (something or someone) near one, as ornament or companion, in (a place such as home): [X9 + *about* (*simple tenses*)] *It's a nice picture to have about the room. Don't go away, I like having you about the house!* → **keep about**
2 to carry (something) with (one), on one's person: [X9 + *about* (*simple tenses*)] *I should have a pencil about me somewhere, I usually do.* → **have on**[2] **(1)**
3 to possess (thoughts or feelings) towards (someone, something, or doing something): [X9 + *about* (*usu. simple tenses*)] *Don't lend him any money, I have my doubts about his honesty. I have an uneasy feeling about the way the bank is handling my money. Have you any thoughts about how we're to persuade the director? I've no ideas about the best plan for the future. What opinion do you have about this matter?* → **have for** (1), **have on**[2] (2)
4 **have no hesitation about** to be eager to approve of (doing something) at once: [*usu. simple tenses*] *We have no hesitation about accepting your most generous offer.* → **have in**[2] **(8)**
5 **have an inkling/inclination about** to have a suggestion of an idea about (something in the future); be able to make a good guess about (something): [*simple tenses*] *I have no inkling about the examination results, we shall all have to wait and see.*
6 **have misgivings/reservations about** to be unwilling to approve of; be doubtful about (someone, something, or doing something): [*usu. simple tenses*] *His work is quite reasonable, but I have misgivings about his future performance. Does any member of the committee have any reservations about appointing Mr Brown?*
7 **have qualms/scruples about** to feel prevented or discouraged by one's conscience from (doing something): [*often simple tenses*] *Have you any qualms about cheating on your income tax? The thieves had no scruples about taking the jewels.*
8 **have a/this thing about** *infml* to feel strongly about (someone, something, or doing something), either favourably or unfavourably: [*simple tenses*] *Mother has always had a thing about baking her own bread—she refuses to buy any from a shop. Does Grace still have a thing about that red-haired boy? Many people have this thing about walking under a ladder, which they think is unlucky, though it makes better sense to regard it as dangerous. Aunt Mabel really has a thing about horses, she's terribly afraid of them. Jane has this thing about her new bicycle, and won't let anyone borrow it.*
9 **have one's wits about one** to be clever; be conscious of chances, dangers, etc.: [*simple tenses*] *You have to have your wits about you when you're trying to make a new business succeed in these hard times.*

**have against** *v prep*
*1 to consider (something) as a means or reason to oppose or dislike (someone): [D1 (*simple tenses*)] *What do you have against Mr Brown? Don't you think he'll make a good director? I've nothing against Jim as a person, but I just don't think that he's suitable as a husband for Mary.*
*2 to be (a disadvantage) to (someone): [D1 (*simple tenses*)] *It's not easy to give a man a job when he has his time in prison against him.*
3 **have a grudge against** to dislike; feel unfavourably towards (someone), either unfairly or because of a fault or misdeed: [*usu. simple tenses*] *Some employers seem to have a grudge against women; even when they give them work, they pay them less* also **bear against**

**have around**[1] *v adv* → HAVE ABOUT[1], HAVE ROUND

**have around**[2] *v prep* → HAVE ABOUT[2]

***have at** *v prep*
1 *old use* to attack (someone): [T1 (*no pass. usu. imper.*)] *'Have at you!' shouted the swordsman, striking his opponent.*
2 **have a bash/crack/go/shot/stab/try at** *infml* to attempt (something usu. competitive, or doing something difficult): [*often simple tenses*] *Is Jim going to have a bash at the 500 metre race? See if you can have a crack at getting this nail out, I can't move it.*
3 **have something at one's fingertips** to be easily able to do something; have information in one's head: [*simple tenses*] *As a chairman he's remarkable; he always has the necessary facts at his fingertips.*
4 **have something at heart** to be deeply concerned about something: [*simple tenses*] *In offering these suggestions for improvement, I must explain that I only have your interests at heart, believe me.*

**have away** *v adv* → **have off** (6)
**have it away** *sl* to have secret or unlawful sexual relations (with someone): [*often continuous tenses*] *Their marriage broke up when Elizabeth discovered her husband and his secretary having it away behind her back. I suppose you've been having it away with your 'friend' while I've been out of town!*

**have back** *v adv*
1 to regain possession of (something): [X9 + BACK (*simple tenses*)] *Please can we have our ball back?* → **get back** (4), **give back** (1), **hand back** (1)
2 to allow (usu. a wife or husband) to return: [X9 + BACK (*simple tenses*)] *It was very sa*

*Elizabeth, after a year's separation, decided to return to her husband, but he refused to have her back.* → **send back, take back** (4)

*3 to invite (someone) in return: [T1] *We owe the Millers a dinner invitation; when are we going to have them back?* → **ask back**

**4 have one's own back** to be able to return punishment for a wrong done to oneself: *He pushed me into the water, but later I had my own back when I stole his boots.* → **get even,** etc.

**have by** *v prep*

to bear (a child) whose father is (someone): [T1 + *by* (*usu. simple tenses*)] *How many children did Elizabeth have by her second husband?*

**have down** *v adv*

**1** to invite (someone) to stay at one's home, usu. in the country: [T1] *We must have Lord and Lady Redcliff down for our next house party.* → **have up** (1)

**2 have one's tail down** *infml* to be in low spirits: [*simple tenses*] *Our team really have their tails down since they lost so many games, and without the spirit to win, look like being defeated for the whole season.* → **have up** (4)

**have for** *v prep*

**1** to feel or show (something) towards (something or someone): [T1 + *for* (*usu. simple tenses*] *I think you should have more consideration for your family's feelings. Have you no regard for your own honour? Every mother has great fears for her children.* → **have about**[2] (3), **have on**[2] (2)

**2** to eat (food) for (a meal): [T1 + *for*] *We're having fish for dinner tonight.*

**3** to invite (someone) to share (a meal): [X9 + *for*] *When shall we have the Millers for dinner?*

**4 be had for** to be able to be obtained for (something such as a price): *Good jobs like this one can't be had for the asking. Anything in the market can he had for the right price. Some good things in life can be had for nothing.*

**5 have an appeal/attraction/fascination for** to attract (someone); cause (someone) to like it or him: [*simple tenses*] *Rare books have a great fascination for librarians. I can't imagine what appeal that boy has for Grace, but she can't leave him alone.*

**6 have a distaste for** to be unable to like or accept (something): [*simple tenses*] *Well-educated women often have a distaste for housework.*

**7 have an ear/eye/nose for** to be able to tell the qualities, usu. good, of (something): [*simple tenses*] *Any singer needs to have an ear for music. Your uncle has always had an eye for a pretty girl. As a writer, Tom has a good nose for an interesting story with a surprising ending.*

**8 have no fears/terrors for** to be easy for (someone) to do, deal with, etc.: [*simple tenses*] *Languages have no terrors for me, I can speak six and learn others easily. The dark has no fears for a blind person.* → **have of** (4), **hold for** (3)

**9 have a flair/gift for** to have the natural ability for (something or doing something well): [*simple tenses*] *Jim's father declared that the secret of his success was simply having a flair for business. Any successful hostess needs to have a gift for making people feel comfortable.*

**10 have a liking/taste for** to like (something or someone) all the time: [*simple tenses*] *Our dog had a liking for cheese. Mary has a taste for old-fashioned furniture.*

**11 have a soft/weak spot for** *not fml* to be specially fond of (someone): [*simple tenses*] *Although they separated years ago, Grace still has a soft spot for that red-haired boy. Many mothers have a weak spot for their youngest child.*

**12 have no time/use for** *not fml* to have a low opinion of (something or usu. someone): [*simple tenses*] *I've no time for that student, he's a lazy worker and holds worthless views. This firm has no use for workers who are regularly late! I've no time for such old-fashioned methods, we must modernize at once!*

**13 have a weakness for** to like (something) very much, often without good reason: [*simple tenses*] *I have such a weakness for houses with towers on the roof, I would buy one even if it were not in good condition. Peter has a weakness for fast sports cars, although he can't afford them.*

***have in**[1] *v adv*

**1** to keep a supply of (something): [T1 (*simple tenses*)] *Do we have enough wine in for the party?* → **get in**[1] (6), **keep in** (7)

**2** to call (someone) to the house to do some work: [T1] *We are having the builders in next month to improve the kitchen.* → **bring in** (5), **call in** (4), **come in** (14), **get in**[1] (8)

**3** to invite (someone) into one's home: [T1] *Would you like to have your friends in for a few drinks?*

**have in**[2] *v prep*

**1 have all one's eggs in one basket** *not fml* to place all one's money on the same risk; risk everything on one chance: [*simple tenses*] *Insurance firms generally spread the risk among several companies so that they don't have all their eggs in one basket.* → **place in** (8), **put in**[2] (13)

**2 have faith in** to believe in; trust (someone or something): [*usu. simple tenses*] *The voters have just shown that they have no faith in the government. You must learn to have faith in your own abilities. People are leaving the Church when they find that they no longer have any faith in God.* → **believe in** (2), etc.

**3 have a/one's finger in every pie** *infml* to be concerned in many different affairs: *John seems to have a finger in every pie: he owns a business in the town, he's a member of the lo-*

*cal council, and he belongs to several societies and clubs. A clever businessman is one who spreads his interests; Mr Sharp, for example, has his finger in every pie in the city.*

**4 have a hand/part in** to share the responsibility for (something or doing something): [*usu. simple tenses*] *Some of the servants also had a hand in the robbery. The chairman claimed that he had no part in the agreement. The radio had a hand in forming my interest in music.* → **play in² (4), take in² (9)**

**5 have something in hand** to be already doing something; have made a start on something: [*simple tenses*] *Your complaint about the washing machine is being attended to; Head Office have the matter in hand. The builders have the kitchen improvements in hand and hope to be finished by next month.* → **be in² (16), take in² (10)**

**6 have one's heart in** to be really keen on (something or doing something): [*simple tenses*] *It's no good learning the piano if you don't have your heart in it.*

**7 have one's heart in one's boots** to be fearful, nervous, etc.: [*simple tenses*] *As I went into the examination room, I had my heart in my boots.*

**8 have no hesitation in** to be eager to approve of (doing something) at once: [*simple tenses*] *We have no hesitation in accepting your most generous offer.* → **have about² (4)**

**9 have many irons in the fire** *not fml* to be busy with many plans at the same time: [*simple tenses*] *I've asked my uncle if he can help me get a job, but I've got many other irons in the fire as well, so it won't really matter if he can't find anything. Jim's father was not worried about the loss of that contract, as he had many other irons in the fire and would not lose too much business by it.*

**10 have it in one** to possess the ability (to do something): [*simple tenses*] *No one was surprised when Jim passed the examination; we always knew he had it in him. Do you think that Mary has it in her to be a good mother?*

**11 have something in mind** to be thinking about something; intend something or to do something: [*simple tenses*] *What plans for your future do you have in mind? At one time I had it in mind to study law.*

**12 have a place in** to be given an important part in; appear in; matter to (something): [*simple tenses*] *Our first home will always have a special place in our hearts. Training for a job has little place in general education.* → **figure in²**

**13 have someone in one's power/spell** to have a special control over someone, as if by magic: [*simple tenses*] *Soon the speaker had the whole crowd in his spell. Their leader has the whole trade union movement in his power.*

**14 have a say/voice in** to be able to take part in a decision concerning (something or doing something): [*usu. simple tenses*] *Jim felt that he was old enough to have a say in his father's business. By giving their votes at elections, the taxpayers think that they actually have a voice in running the country.*

**15 have a stake in** to have put something of one's own, as money, effort, etc., into (something) which one may therefore lose; value (something) because of one's own part in it: [*simple tenses*] *Jim has a small stake in his father's firm, so it is in his own interests to help it to be successful. Most parents feel that they have a stake in their children's future, and so will use every effort to help them.*

**16 have something well in hand** to be easily able to deal with or control (something such as a difficulty): [*simple tenses*] *The government claims that it will soon have rising prices well in hand.* → **be in² (34)**

**17 have one's tongue in one's cheek** *not fml* to pretend to mean something, often as a joke: [*simple tenses*] *Don't be offended by what he said; can't you tell when he has his tongue in his cheek?*

***have it** *v pron*

**1** *infml* to have reached a hopeless state; be finished, worn out: [IØ (*perfect tenses only*)] *This old chair has had it, we might as well throw it out. Let me rest here, I've had it.*

**2** to accept; allow something: [IØ (*simple tenses, usu. + will*)] *The men were prepared to come to an agreement on working hours, but the directors wouldn't have it.*

**3** to declare or claim (that something): [I5 (*simple tenses*)] *The report has it that no one was to blame for the crash. The directors will have it that the meeting was friendly.*

**4 have it both ways** *not fml* to gain advantage from opposing opinions or actions: [*usu. simple tenses*] *You have to choose one or the other—you can't have it both ways!*

**5 have it coming** *infml* to deserve something, often bad: [*usu. simple tenses*] *I'm sorry he got caught by the police, but after all, he had it coming (to him), didn't he?*

**6 have it good** *AmE infml* to have enough money; be comfortably rich: *Jim has had it good ever since his father died and left him all those shares in the company.*

**7 have it said** to allow a statement (that something): [*usu. neg.*] *I won't have it said that my son is a thief!*

**8 let someone have it** *infml* to scold, punish or shoot (someone): *If Abe comes back without the jewels, I'm going to let him have it!*

**9 you've had it!** *infml* it is no use hoping: *No, I won't lend you the car, you've had it!*

**have of** *v prep*

**1 have the best of** to win (something such as a fight); gain most advantage from (something): *The two dogs fought for hours, but in the end it was the smaller one that had the best of it.*

**2 have control of/over** to be able to control (someone or something): [*simple tenses*] *At last the day came when he had complete con*

*trol of the company, by buying all the shares. That young teacher does not have control of his class; I should have put a more experienced teacher in charge.* → **have over² (1), take of (6)**
**3 have the courage of one's convictions** to be brave enough to act according to one's beliefs: [*usu. simple tenses*] *If you had the courage of your convictions you would go ahead and tell the chairman your opinion of his plans.*
**4 have a fear/horror/terror of** to be greatly afraid of (usu. something or doing something): [*usu. simple tenses*] *Aunt Mabel has a terror of mice. Have no fear of failure, the business is on very sure ground. Most babies have a horror of falling.* → **have for (8), hold for (3)**
**5 have the worst of** to suffer most as a result of (something such as a fight): *Whenever they have an argument, Mary has the worst of it. It was the bigger boy who had the worst of the fight.* → **get of (13), make of (56)**

**have off** *v adv*
**1** to take (something) off; remove (something), usu. by accident: [X9 + OFF (*simple tenses*)] *Mind that sharp knife, it could have your fingers off! If the wind blows any harder, it'll have the roof off!* → **take off¹ (1), etc.**
**2** to be not wearing (an article of clothing): [X9 + OFF (*simple tenses*)] *It is customary in this country for men to have their hats off at a funeral. It was so hot that the road workers had their shirts off.*
***3** to learn (something) ready to speak it from memory: [T1 (*simple tenses*)] *I have the whole poem off (by heart) already.* → **get off¹ (12)**
***4** to have (time) as a holiday, rest, etc.: [T1b] *Can I have Monday morning off to see my doctor?* → **get off¹ (14), take off¹ (14)**
***5** to act or draw a good likeness of (someone): [T1b (*simple tenses*)] *The boy had the teacher off to perfection.* → **hit off (1), take off¹ (15)**
**6 have it off** *sl* to have secret or unlawful sexual relations (with someone): [(*usu. continuous tenses*)] *Jim and Mary were having it off long before they were married, I'm sure! I suppose you've been having it off with your 'friend' while I've been out of town! People are whispering that the director has been having it off with his secretary.* → **have away**

**have on¹** *v adv*
**1** to be wearing (certain clothes): [X9 + ON (*simple tenses*)] *Mary had on her best blue dress. Can you tell us what the missing woman had on? Don't come in! I've nothing on!* → **put on¹ (2), etc.**
**2** to have (something electrical) switched on and working: [X9 + ON (*simple tenses*)] *While I have the iron on, I'll just finish those handkerchieves.* → **put on¹ (3), etc.**
***3** to have (something) arranged to do; be busy with (something such as work): [T1 (*simple tenses*)] *I've nothing on tonight, shall we go to a cinema? I have two concerts on next week. I'm sorry, I can't come, I have too much on.* → **be on¹ (3), put on¹ (9)**
***4** *BrE infml* to deceive (someone) into believing something, for fun: [T1b (*usu. continuous tenses*)] *I know you're only joking, you're having me on again!* → **put on¹ (12)**

**have on/upon²** *v prep*
**1** to carry with (one), on one's person: [X9 + *on/upon* (*simple tenses*)] *I don't think I have that much money on me just now. He had all kinds of strange objects on his person.* → **have about² (2)**
**2** to possess (thoughts or feelings) about (something): [X9 + *on/upon* (*usu. simple tenses*)] *Do you have any feelings on the matter? I have no opinion on your suggestions. Have you any thoughts on the best method of dealing with these people?* → **have about² (3), have for (1)**
***3** *not fml* to have (something) recorded against (someone): [D1 (*simple tenses*)] *You can't take me to the police station, you have nothing on me!*
**4 have a bearing on/upon** to have a connection with (something); have an effect on (something): [*simple tenses*] *What bearing does your story have on this case? The examination results have no bearing on your ability.* → **bear on (1), touch on (3)**
**5 have something/someone on the brain** *not fml* to be continually thinking about something or someone; be unable to forget something or someone: [*usu. simple tenses*] *Have you ever had a tune on your brain, going round and round and you couldn't stop it? Peter has cars on the brain, he never talks about anything else. Grace says that she can't forget her red-haired boy and will probably have him on the brain for the rest of her life.*
**6 have a crush/pash on** *infml* to be foolishly in love with (someone), usu. when one is young: [*often simple tenses*] *Some of the girls have a crush on one of the teachers.*
**7 have designs on/against/upon** *infml* to intend to get (something) or win (someone), often by unfair means: *I think that man has designs on my daughter. One of the committee members has designs on the chairmanship.*
**8 have the edge on/over** *not fml* to have an advantage over (someone) in a competition: [*simple tenses*] *Two men were after the director's job, but the younger man had the edge on the older one. Big firms have the edge on small businesses in world trade, as their prices are often cheaper.* → **have over (2)**
**9 have an effect/impact on/upon** to cause a change in; influence (something or someone): *The government's new laws have had little effect on rising prices. What is likely to have an impact on our sales? Wet weather has an effect on most people.*
**10 have one's eyes on: a** to watch or guard

(someone) in order to prevent trouble: [*often simple tenses*] *Remember, the police will have their eye on you the moment you come out of prison.* **b** to want (something): [*often simple tenses*] *I've had my eye on that dress in the window for weeks.* → **keep on** (5), **watch over**

**11 have one eye on** to be watching or paying attention to (something or someone) while doing something else: [*simple tenses*] *Whatever Jim did, he always had one eye on his own interests. When planning anything, you have to have one eye on the future.* → **keep on** (6)

**12 have something on one's hands** to be left with goods that one cannot sell, a responsibility that cannot be got rid of, etc.: [*simple tenses*] *I don't want to have the house on my hands all the winter, we'd better lower the price a bit. How long am I going to have these children on my hands?* → **take off² (10)**

**13 have something on one's mind** to worry about something: [*simple tenses*] *What's the matter? You look as though you have something on your mind. I'm sorry I forgot to write, I had so much else on my mind.* → **take off² (12)**

**14 have pity/compassion on** to feel sorry for (someone): [*usu. simple tenses*] *I don't want you to give me money just because you have pity on me. God has compassion on those who ask for forgiveness.*

**15 have revenge on/upon** to punish (someone) in return for a wrong done to oneself: *I'd like to have (my) revenge on the man who attacked my daughter.* → **get even,** etc.

**16 have someone on a string** *infml* to deceive someone successfully, esp. as a joke: *Mary had her father on a string for days, thinking she had forgotten his birthday, so that she could surprise him.*

**17 have time on one's hands** to have plenty of time with not much to do: [*usu. simple tenses*] *Once the children had left home, I found that I had time on my hands, so I got a job.*

**have out** *v adv*

**1** to cause (something such as a tooth) to be removed, esp. from one's body: [X9 + OUT (*simple tenses*)] *I shall have to have this tooth out, it's aching unbearably. We'll have the bullet out in a few minutes.* → **take out** (2), etc.

***2** to invite (someone) to a social event or meal, etc.: [T1b] *I'd like to have you out for dinner next week.* → **ask out,** etc.

***3** to settle (a difficulty) by talking freely or angrily, esp. in the phr. **have it out**: [T1b (*with*)] *After yesterday's argument, I called to see her brother to have it out with him. It's no use keeping your anger to yourself; let's have the whole matter out now.*

***4** to be allowed to finish (something): [T1b] *Let Father have his sleep out, he's very tired.*

***have over¹** *v adv*

**1** to invite (someone) to one's home: [T1b] *When are we going to have the Millers over?* → **invite over,** etc.

**2** to come to the end of (something unpleasant): [T1b (*simple tenses*)] *Don't worry, you'll soon have your operation over (and done with).* → **be over¹** (4), etc., **get over¹** (4), **get through¹** (8)

**have over²** *v prep*

**1 have control over** to be able to control (something or someone): [(*simple tenses*)] *What control does the government have over rising prices? First, you have to have control over your horse.* → **have of** (2), **take of** (6)

**2 have the edge over** *not fml* to have an advantage over (someone) in a competition: [*simple tenses*] *Of the two men for the job, I think the younger man has the edge over the older one. Big companies always have the edge over small firms in international trade.* → **have on²** (8)

**3 have a hold over** to have some influence or power, often bad, over (someone): [*simple tenses*] *While I owe him money, he has a hold over me.*

**4 have it over** *not fml* to be better than (something or someone): [*simple tenses*] *I'm certain that our team has it over theirs, we're sure to win! He has it over me that he's been to Egypt and I haven't.*

***have pat** *v adv*

*not fml* to know (something such as words) thoroughly from memory: [T1b (*simple tenses*)] *Only when the actors have their lines (down) pat can we practise the play effectively.*

***have round/around** *v adv* → **invite over,** etc.

to invite (someone) to one's home: [T1b] *When are we going to have the Millers round?*

**have to** *v prep*

**1 have access to** to be able to reach or use (something): [*usu. simple tenses*] *Only two men in the company have access to the secret records. The public must be allowed to have access to television time.* → **get to** (9)

**2 have recourse to** to use (something) as a means for some purpose: [*usu. simple tenses*] *You should be able to pass your examinations without having recourse to cheating.*

**3 have a right to** to be allowed by law or nature to possess (something): [*simple tenses*] *Every prisoner has a right to a fair trial. We should pass laws to make sure that everyone has a right to equal treatment.*

**have up** *v adv*

***1** to invite (someone) upstairs or to an important place, as a city: [T1b] *I'd like to have the workers' leaders up to my office to express their complaints. We had the whole family up to our home in London to see the Queen's crowning.* → **have down** (1)

***2** *not fml* to take (someone) to court: [T

(*for*) (*usu. pass.*)] *This is the third time that Peter has been had up this year!* —**had-up** *n infml* → **be up** (11), **bring up** (10), **come up**[1] (7), **haul up** (2)

**3 have one's hackles up** *infml* to be annoyed: [*simple tenses*] *It's safer to avoid the director when he has his hackles up.* → **get up** (19), **put up**[1] (25)

**4 have one's tail up** to be in high spirits: [*simple tenses*] *The party really have their tails up since their surprising election victory.* → **have down** (2)

**5 have the wind up** *infml* to be afraid, esp. in a cowardly sense: [*usu. simple tenses*] *Don't let the other soldiers see that you have the wind up.* → **get up** (22), **put up**[2] (3)

**have upon** *v prep* → HAVE ON

**have with** *v prep*

**1 have an affair with** to have a love relationship that is usu. sexual, though not lasting, with (someone, usu. of the opposite sex): *Elizabeth left her husband when she discovered that he had been having an affair with his secretary.*

**2 have no truck with** *not fml* to refuse to accept or have any connection with (something or someone of which one disapproves): [*simple tenses, usu. + will*] *Remember, I'll have no truck with such behaviour! Workers will have no truck with people who take their jobs while they are refusing to work.*

**3 have a way with** to be able to relate to (people or animals) by natural ability: [*simple tenses*] *She'd make a good teacher, she has a way with children. The old farmer had a way with horses, they would come whenever he whistled.*

**4 have a way with one** to have a lot of natural charm or a persuasive manner: [*simple tenses*] *Jim has such a way with him, he'll get on in life whoever he has to deal with.*

**5 have a word with** *not fml* to speak to (someone) for a short time, esp. to give or receive advice: *Mr Good, can I have a word with you for a minute in my office? I'd like to ask your advice. You ought to have a word with the boy and try to get him to go to bed earlier.*

**6 have words with** *not fml* to quarrel with (someone); scold (someone): *Since my wife had words with our neighbour, they haven't been speaking. I want to have words with those two boys at the back of the class.*

**hawk around/round** *v adv*
to carry (an idea, goods, etc.) from place to place trying to sell it: [X9 + AROUND/ROUND] *At first Tom had difficulty in getting his books accepted, and had to hawk them around from firm to firm until one agreed that they were worth printing.*

**haze over** *v adv* → **film over, glaze over**
to become misty, covered, or as if covered by a thin nontransparent film: [IØ] *The singer's eyes hazed over and she sank down in a dead faint. The stars hazed over as a large cloud covered the night sky.*

**head after** *v prep*
to begin to chase (usu. someone): [L9 + *after*] *If you head after the robbers now, you might catch them before they leave the town limits.*

**head away from** *v adv prep*
to move in the opposite direction to (something such as a place): [L9 + AWAY + *from*] *Heading away from the mountains, I soon found an easier path leading downhill towards the village.*

**head back** *v adv*
to turn round; begin to return: [L9 + BACK] *We ought to be heading back if we want to reach home before dark.*

**head for/towards** *v prep*

**1** to aim to travel in the direction of (usu. a place): [L9 + *for/towards*] *'Where are you heading for?' 'I'm heading for London.'*

*__2__ to be likely to reach (something often good): [T1 (*no pass., continuous tenses*)] *It looks as if the firm is heading for another record year!*

*__3__ *not fml* to act in such a manner as to cause or fail to avoid (something, usu. bad): [T1 (*no pass., continuous tenses*)] *You're heading for an accident if you drive after drinking alcohol.* → **ask for** (3), **look for** (4)

**head in** *v adv*
(in football) to send (the ball) into the goal with one's head: [X9 + IN] *Wells scored by heading the ball/the pass in during the last two minutes of play.*

**head into** *v prep*
to take a course facing the direction of (usu. the wind): [L9 + *into* (*usu. continuous tenses*)] *Planes, like birds, take off heading into the wind. It looks as though we're heading into a storm; let's stop here in this town overnight and wait till it has passed.*

*__head off__ *v adv*

**1** to cause to move in a different direction; travel in front of (someone), cutting across his course, usu. so as to stop him: [T1] *They were running towards the house, but we headed them off by calling from the field. If you take a short cut through the other valley, you should be in time to head the cattle thieves off where the valleys meet.*

**2** to prevent (something unpleasant, or someone from reaching an unpleasant subject): [T1] *You will have to speak to both groups of men quickly if you want to head off a nasty disagreement. Whenever Mother starts to talk about something that Jane is sensitive about, we try to head her off onto another subject.*

*__head out__ *v adv*

**1** (of a plant) to form a complete part, as of head or ears: [IØ] *The wheat should head out next week if the weather remains sunny.* → **head up** (2)

**2** *AmE not fml* to reach an important or turning point: [IØ (*often simple tenses*)] *After all those hours of arguing, the talks began to head out and it was not long before we were able to reach an agreement.*

**head towards** *v prep* → HEAD FOR

**head up** *v adv*

**1** to lead (a group): [T1 + UP (*often simple tenses*)] *Who is the best person to head up the special committee?*

*__2__ (of a plant) to form a complete part, as of head or ears: [IØ] *When the green vegetables head up, we'll pick what we need and give the rest to our neighbours.* → **head out** (1)

*__3__ (in a newspaper office) to supply a headline for (a page): [T1] *One of my jobs at the newspaper office was to head up the page before it was printed.*

*__4__ *naut* to (cause to) sail nearer the wind: [IØ] *I think we should head up a bit now.* [T1b] *Head her up more, will you?*

**heal of** *v prep fml* → CURE OF (1)

**heal over** *v adv*

**1** (of a wound) to close with the growth of new healthy skin; be cured: [IØ + OVER] *How long will it take for the bullet wound to heal over? When it heals over, will there be a mark to show where it was?* → **heal up**

*__2__ (of a quarrel) to cease; be mended: [IØ] *It was a long time before the bitter quarrel between the two families healed over, with the marriage between two of their children, one from each family.*

**heal up** *v adv* → **heal over** (1)

(of a wound, broken bone, etc.) to get well again: [T1 + UP] *Leaving the burn open to the air is the quickest way to heal it up.* [IØ + UP] *How long will it take for the broken bone to heal up?*

**heap on[1]** *v adv*

to pile (a lot of something or things) on top: [T1 + ON] "*Heap on more wood.*" (Sir Walter Scott, *Marmion*)

**heap on/upon[2]** *v prep*

**1** to pile (a lot of something or things) on (something): [X9+ *on/upon*] *Our host was very generous, heaping food on our plates.* → **heap with** (1), **pile on[2]** (1), **pile onto** (1), **pile with** (1)

*__2__ to give a lot of (something such as honour) to (someone): [D1] *Praises were heaped on him after the game. The crowd heaped curses on the unpopular speaker.* → **heap with** (2), **pile on** (2), **pile onto** (2), **pile with** (2)

**3 heap insult on/upon insult** to continue to be rude to someone: *I was prepared to forgive one thoughtless remark, but she kept heaping insult on insult, so I asked her to leave my house.* → **pile on[2] (3)**

**heap up** *v adv*

**1** to make a pile or large quantity of (something or things): [X9 + UP] *Look how that boy has heaped up the food on his plate! The child heaped up the sand into blocks to build a castle. He was lucky to heap up his fortune before taxes got so high.* → **pile up** (1)

*__2__ *not fml* to cause to encourage (something bad) to happen: [T1 (*often continuous tenses*)] *If you always give the children everything they want, you will be heaping up trouble for yourself.* → **pile up** (3)

**heap upon** *v prep* → HEAP ON

**heap with** *v prep*

**1** to load (a container) with a pile of (something or things): [X9 + *with*] *Our very generous host heaped our plates with food.* → **heap on[2]** (1), **pile on[2]** (1), **pile onto** (1), **pile with** (1)

*__2__ to give (someone) a lot of (something such as honour): [D1 (*often simple tenses*)] *The crowd heaped the singer with praise.* → **heap on** (2), **pile on** (2), **pile onto** (2), **pile with** (2)

**hear about** *v prep* → **hear of** (1), **learn about** (2), **learn of** (1)

to learn about; gain information about (something); listen to people talking about (something or someone): [L9 + *about*] *How did you hear about our product? Was it through our advertisements? Your own parents should not have to hear about your wedding from a newspaper report!*

**hear from** *v prep*

**1** to receive a letter or telephone call from (someone): [L9 + *from* (*often simple tenses*)] *We were so worried when we didn't hear from you for three weeks. Let me hear from you now and again, will you?*

**2** to receive a scolding, warning, or official notice from (someone): [L9 + *from*] *You will be hearing from my lawyer shortly. Do not pay the increased tax until you hear from the government. You'll hear from your father when he gets home!*

**hear of** *v prep*

**1** to learn about; gain information about (someone): [L9 + *of* (*simple tenses*)] *How did you hear of our product? Was it through our advertisements? We like to hear of your activities from time to time. We only heard of your intended visit yesterday!* → **hear about, learn about** (2), **learn of** (1)

*__2__ to come to know; have knowledge of the existence of (something or someone): [T1 (*often neg., simple tenses, often perfect*)] *Where's Newmarket? I've never heard of it. She described herself as a famous singer, but no one in the town had heard of her.* —**unheard-of** *adj*

*__3__ to consider the idea of; allow (something or doing something): [T1 (*neg., simple tenses + will*)] *The firm will not hear of such a suggestion from the workers.* [V4a (*neg., simple tenses + will*)] *I wouldn't hear of you paying for the meal.* —**unheard-of** *adj*

**4 hear tell of** *not fml* to hear about (usu something) from other people: [*simple tenses, often perfect*] *I've heard tell of stranger sights than that! I've heard tell of people* *paying £10,000 for a single picture!*

***hear out** *v adv*
to listen to (someone or a story) to the end: [T1 (*often simple tenses*)] *Don't judge the man guilty without at least hearing his story out. Hear me out, please, I've still a lot to say.*

**hear through** *v adv* → **see through**[1] **(2), sit out (3), sit through (2)**
to hear the whole of (something such as a record or performance): [T1 + THROUGH (*usu. simple tenses*)] *When I go to a concert I like to hear the whole thing through, and not go home halfway.*

***hearken after/to** *v prep*
*old use* to desire to follow or reach (something); listen to (something): [T1] *To hearken to the voice of conscience is a good rule.*

**heat up** *v adv*
**1** to (cause to) become hot again after it has cooled: [T1 + UP] *I can heat up some soup in two minutes, it's all ready.* [IØ + UP] *The hall will soon heat up once the crowd arrives.* —**heated-up** *adj* → **boil up** (1), **hot up** (1), **warm over** (1), **warm up** (1)
***2** to become more lively: [IØ] *The game did not heat up until the second half.* → **hot up** (2), **warm up** (5)

**heave at /on** *v prep*
to pull hard on (something such as a rope): [L9 + *at/on*] *The sailors heaved at the rope to tighten the sail.*

**heave in** *v prep*
**heave in sight**
**1** (of a ship) to appear above the horizon: *We had already floated in our open boat for three weeks since our ship was sunk, and had almost given up hope of being saved; imagine our joy when a ship hove in sight just above the distant horizon!*
**2** *humor* to begin to be seen: *Who's that heaving in sight at the far end of the room? I'm sure I know her.*

**heave on** *v prep* → HEAVE AT

**heave short** *v adj*
*naut* to pull in the anchor chain until it is upright, ready to sail: [T1; IØ] *Heave (the chain) short, we shall be ready to sail in half an hour.*

**heave to** *v adv* → **bring to** (2), **bring up** (6), **come to**[1] **(4)**
*naut* (of a ship or boat) to pull in all sail and face directly into the wind; stop moving: [IØ (*usu. simple tense*)] *When the ship received the signal, she hove to.* —**hove-to** *adj*

**heave up** *v adv*
**1** (usu. of something heavy) to (cause to) be lifted with effort: [IØ + UP] *During the storm, the waves heaved up over the sea wall.* [T1 + UP] *We shall need some machinery to heave the sunken boat up from the bottom of the river. The elephant heaved itself up from its resting position when its master commanded it to stand.*
***2** *infml* to be sick; vomit (something such as food): [IØ] *I shan't send Jane to school today, she's been heaving up half the night. A performance like that makes me want to heave up.* [T1] *The poor child has heaved up her dinner again. I can hear her in the bathroom, heaving her guts up.* (= being very sick.) → **bring up** (4), etc.

**hedge about/around/round with** *v adv prep* → **fence about with**
to surround or limit (something) with (control or protection): [T1 (*often pass.*)] *Starting a business of one's own is hedged about with laws and difficulties. To hedge round a partnership of love with control by law would be to destroy its base of trust in one another.*

***hedge against** *v prep*
to protect; guard against (something such as trouble): [T1] *This money must be saved for the purpose of hedging against changes in the exchange rate.*

***hedge around with** *v adv prep* → HEDGE ABOUT WITH

**hedge in** *v adv* → **box in, fence in, hem about, hem in, rail in, wall in** (1)
to enclose (usu. land) with a hedge: [X9 + IN (*often pass.*)] *These fields, which used to be common land, were hedged in by law during the 18th century, and have been privately owned since that time.* —**hedged-in** *adj*

***hedge round with** *v adv prep* → HEDGE ABOUT WITH

***heel back** *v adv*
(in rugby football) to kick (the ball) backwards with one's heel: [T1] *The player tried to heel the ball back but was stopped by an opponent.*

***heel over** *v adv* → KEEL OVER

***hell around** *v adv* → **mess about** (1), etc.
*AmE infml* to live or act in a careless, irresponsible, often immoral, way: [IØ] *My uncle was known for helling around during his youth, but he settled down when he got to middle age.*

**help along/forward** *v adv*
**1** to help (someone) to move forward: [X9 + ALONG/FORWARD] *Help the old lady along, she can hardly walk.*
***2** to help (something) to advance: [T1b] *Some public support might help the movement along. Our plan would be helped forward by a promise of money from the board of directors.*

**help back** *v adv*
to help (someone) to move back or return: [X9 + BACK] *The sick old lady has fallen on the floor; we must help her back into bed.*

**help down** *v adv; prep*
to help (someone) to carry something down (something): [X9 + DOWN/*down*] *Help me down (the stairs) with this heavy case, will you?*

**help forward** *v adv* → HELP ALONG

**help in** *v adv*
to help (someone) to enter something: [X9 +

IN] *It's still polite to hold a car door open and help a lady in.*

**help into** *v prep*
to help (someone) to enter (something such as a place): [X9 + *into*] *The nurses helped the wounded soldiers into the hospital.*

**help off** *v adv; prep*
to help (someone) to leave (something): [X9 + OFF/*off*] *This wall's too high for me to jump from, will you help me off (it)?*

***help off with** *v adv prep* → **help on with**
to help (someone) to remove (clothing): [D1] *Please help me off with my boots, they're so tight!*

***help on** *v adv*
to encourage (someone or something): [T1] *Your support helped the team on to victory. A few drinks should help the conversation on.*

***help on with** *v adv prep* → **help off with**
to help (someone) to put on (clothing): [D1] *Let me help you on with your coat.*

***help oneself** *v pron*
**1** to take; serve oneself with (something); take (something) without permission: [IØ (*to*) (*often simple tenses*)] *Don't wait to be served, just help yourselves! Do help yourself to some more cake. Those thieves have helped themselves to my jewels!* → **help to**
**2** to be responsible for oneself; control oneself: [IØ (*simple tenses*)] *I couldn't help myself, I burst out laughing.*
**3** to be independent: [IØ (*usu. simple tenses*)] *God helps those who help themselves.*

**help out** *v adv*
**1** to help (someone) to get out of something: [X9 + OUT] *One of the climbers has fallen into deep snow, and needs helping out as he can't move by himself.*
***2** to help (someone) with a need or difficulty, esp. for a short time: [T1] *Can you help me out with my English homework?* [IØ] *Mary helped out at the church sale. I'm not really employed here; I'm just helping out until the new secretary arrives.*

**help over** *v prep*
**1** to help (someone or an animal) to climb (something): [X9 + *over*] *Help me over the wall, will you? It's too high.*
***2** to help (someone) to deal with (a difficulty): [D1] *Thank you for helping over that difficult matter.*
***3** (of money) to last (someone) for (a certain time): [D1 (*simple tenses*)] *Here's a £10 note; that should help you over the next few days.*
**4 help a lame dog over a stile** to help someone in difficulty: *If you're in debt, perhaps Jim's father will lend you a little money; he was always known for helping a lame dog over a stile whenever he could.*

***help to** *v prep* → **help oneself** (1)
to serve (someone or oneself) with (something such as food); give (oneself) something without permission: [D1 (*usu. simple tenses*)] *Can I help you to some more potatoes? Do help yourself to anything you fancy. Those thieves have helped themselves to my jewels!*

**help up** *v adv*
**1** to help (someone) to stand up: [X9 + UP] *People rushed to help the old man up when he slipped on the ice.*
**2** to help (someone) to carry something to a higher level: [X9 + UP] *Help me up with this heavy case, would you?*

***hem about/around/round** *v adv* → **fence in** (2), **hedge in, hem in**
to surround (something or someone): [T1b (*often pass., simple tenses*)] *There's no escaping from the forces of evil that hem us about. The town is hemmed around by mountains.*

***hem in** *v adv* → **box in, fence in, hedge in, hem about, rail in, wall in** (1)
to surround; tightly enclose (something or someone) so as to limit its/his freedom, esp. of movement: [T1 (*usu. pass.*)] *The whole army was hemmed in by the enemy with no hope of escape. I saw him on the other side of the crowd, but couldn't get across to him as I was hemmed in by a fat woman on one side and two policemen on the other. We were hemmed in against the wall and couldn't move.*

***hem round** *v adv* → HEM ABOUT

***herd together** *v adv*
to (cause to) gather in one place in a tight group: [IØ] *The cattle herded together to try to find some protection against the rain.* [T1] *It's terrible, the way people are herded together in rush hour trains, in conditions that wouldn't be allowed for animals!*

**hew down** *v adv* → **chop down** (1), **hack down** (1)
to make (usu. a tree) fall by cutting it, usu. with an axe: [X9 + DOWN (*usu. pass.*)] *The villagers are trying to prevent the ancient tree in the marketplace from being hewn down for safety reasons.*

**hew out** *v adv* → **carve out, hack out**
**1** to shape or cut (something such as space), usu. with an axe: [X9 + OUT] *A path had been hewn out in the forest by natives using only the simplest of tools.*
***2** *not fml* to form (something such as a plan) with difficulty: [T1] *The committee had instructions to hew out a new method of organising the firm's accounts, even if it took them all night.*

***hew to** *v prep*
*AmE* to follow (a rule, principle, etc.): [T1] *I have never been disloyal to the Party; I have always hewed to its political principles.*

**hide away** *v adv* → **hide out**
to (cause to) be hidden completely from sight or knowledge: [T1 + AWAY] *Hide Father's present away until his birthday. Why do you hide your thoughts away from me?* [IØ + AWAY] *The thieves hid away in a friend's house for several weeks after the robbery.* —**hideaway** *n infml*

**hide from** *v prep* → **conceal from**
to (cause to) be covered from the sight or knowledge of (usu. someone): [T1 + *from*] *Hide the present from your father until his birthday. Why do you hide your thoughts from me?* [IØ + *from*] *I know you children are hiding from me in there—come out now and have your dinner!*

**hide in** *v prep*
to (cause to) be covered or kept secret in (usu. a place): [IØ + *in*] *The children enjoyed hiding in the bushes.* [T1 + *in*] *Father's birthday present is hidden in the kitchen cupboard.*

**hide out** *v adv* → **hide away**
to hide oneself, as from the police: [IØ] *You'd better hide out here until the police have stopped trying to catch you.* —**hide-out** *n*

**hide with** *v prep*
to cover or keep (something) secret by means of (something): [T1 + *with*] *The game was to guess the object which was hidden with a cloth.*

**hike up** *v adv*
esp. *AmE not fml* to pull (something) up sharply: [T1 + UP] *Hike up your socks, you look untidy.*

**hinder from** *v prep* → **prevent from**, etc.
to try to prevent or delay (someone or something) from (something or doing something): [T1 + *from*] *Your endless talking hinders me from my work; please be quiet! The fence along the middle of the road is intended to hinder the traffic from crashing.*

**hinge on/upon** *v prep* → **depend on** (3), **hang on²** (2), **pivot on** (2), **rely on** (2), **ride on²** (4), **turn on²** (3)
to depend on; change according to (something such as a fact): [T1 (*no pass., simple tenses*)] *The story hinges on the relationship between the two sisters. The case hinges upon the judge's opinion of the prisoner's character. All our hopes hinged on the firm's success.* [T6] *The result will hinge upon whether the secret is discovered.*

**hint at** *v prep* → **point at** (3), **point to** (4)
to speak about; suggest (something) in an indirect way: [L9 + *at*] *The government minister hinted at an early election, but refused to give an exact date.*

**hint to** *v prep* → **intimate to**
to suggest something in an indirect way, to (someone): [IØ + *to*] *Why don't you hint to the director that it's time you had a rise in pay?*

**hire out** *v adv* → **let out** (10), **rent out**
to allow someone to use (something usu. movable, as a vehicle, or oneself) in return for payment: [T1 + OUT] *I'm thinking of hiring out my boat for the summer, while I'm away. You could always hire yourself out as a tourist guide, seeing that you know the city so well.*

**hiss at** *v prep*
to make a hissing noise to show disapproval of (someone, a performance, etc.): [IØ + *at*] *The singer's performance was so terrible that the crowd hissed at her. Have you ever been hissed at in the middle of a speech?*

***hiss off** *v adv; prep*
to drive (a performer) off (the stage) by making a disapproving hissing noise: [T1; D1] *After only five minutes, the actor was hissed off (the stage) by an angry crowd who demanded their money back.*

**hit against** *v prep* → **knock against** (1), etc.
to (cause to) knock against (something such as a hard object): [T1 + *against*] *Don't hit your hand too hard against the window when you try to open it, you might break the glass. The car hit against the garage door.*

**hit at** *v prep*
**1** to try to hit; aim a blow at (someone or something): [L9 + *at*] *The fighter hit at his opponent but missed. Our cat enjoys hitting at balls of wool.* → **strike at** (1)
***2** to attack (someone or something) with words: [T1] *Many of the newspapers are hitting at the government's latest move.* → **strike at** (2)

**hit back** *v adv* → **strike back**
**1** to return a blow (to someone): [T1 + BACK] *If he hits you first, I suppose it's all right to hit him back.* [L9 + BACK (*at*)] *In reply to last night's bombing attack, our planes this morning hit back at the enemy port.*
***2** to return an attack (to someone): [IØ (*at*)] *In a letter to the newspaper, Tom hit back at those who had found fault with his latest book. A teacher may say unfair things when finding fault with a student, who then has no means of hitting back. The only way the taxpayers can hit back at an unjust government is to vote against them at the next election.*

**hit hard** *v adv*
**1** to give (someone) a severe blow; fight with strength: [T1 + HARD] *You have to hit the window hard to make it open. Don't hit him (too) hard, he's only little.* [L9 + HARD] *The old fighter was known in his youth for hitting hard.* —**hard-hitter** *n* —**hard-hitting** *adj*
***2** to cause (usu. someone) to suffer severely: [T1b (*simple tenses*)] *The death of her son has hit Mrs Page hard; she has been sunk in grief for months. The business was hard hit by the loss of that important contract.*

**hit in** *v adv* → **kick in** (1), **knock in** (1)
to make (something such as a ball) enter by hitting it: [T1 + IN] *At the last moment, the player was able to hit the ball in and so ensure his team's victory.*

***hit it** *v pron* → **hit on** (4), **strike on** (3)
*infml* to be exactly right in what one says: [IØ (*usu. perfect tenses*)] *Yes, that's just what I mean—you've hit it (on the nose)!*

**hit off** *v adv*
***1** *BrE not fml* to copy (someone or something); act a good likeness of (someone) or write exactly like (something): [T1 (*usu. simple tenses*)] *The boy's performance of the teacher hit her off to perfection. Good, you've*

*exactly hit off the writer's style!* → **have off** (5), **take off**[1] (15)

**2 hit it off** *infml* to have or form a good relationship (with someone): *How nice that the two girls hit it off so well. Do you hit it off with your husband's mother?*

**hit on/upon** *v prep*

**1** to knock (something such as part of the body) against (a hard object): [T1 + *on/upon*] *The child was crying because he had hit his head on the doorpost.* → **knock against** (1), etc.

**2** to give a blow to (someone) on (a part of the body): [T1 + *on/upon*] *He hit me on the face!* → **strike on** (2)

***3** to discover (something) by lucky chance; have a good idea about (something): [T1 (*simple tenses*)] *I hope that after all these talks someone will hit on a way out of our difficulty. How did you hit on the right answer so quickly?* [T4] *At last someone hit upon taking the other road through the mountains.* → **strike on** (3).

**4 hit the nail on the head** *not fml* to be exactly right: [(*usu. simple tenses*)] *You seem to have a gift for asking the right awkward question; this time you really have hit the nail on the head.* → **hit it**

**hit out** *v adv*

**1** to deal strong blows, often without direction: [L9 + OUT] *Surrounded by three men who were threatening him, Jim hit out in all directions and soon had them all lying unconscious on the ground.* → **kick out** (2), **lash out** (1), **ram out, strike out** (1)

**2** (in cricket and other ball games) to hit the ball strongly: [L9 + OUT] *You'll never make runs today unless you hit out a bit more, the opposition is too fierce.*

***3** to attack (someone) in words: [IØ (*against, at*)] *A late speech gives a politician a good chance to hit out. The labour unions have hit out against wage controls. The voters are hitting out at the government's latest decision.* → **lash out** (1)

**hit up** *v adv*

**1** to cause (something such as a ball) to rise by hitting it: [T1 + UP] *Try not to hit the ball up as it will easily be caught and then you'll be out.* → **knock up** (1)

**2 hit it up** esp. *AmE infml* to work or esp. play hard: *The band was already hitting it up as the train arrived.*

**hit upon** *v prep* → HIT ON

**hitch to** *v prep*

**1** to fasten (esp. a horse or vehicle to a vehicle or horse) by hooking a rope or metal part over another object: [T1 + *to*] *The farmer hitched the cart to his best horse to pull the heavy load.*

**2 hitch one's wagon to a star** *lit* to have noble or morally improving aims or desires; follow someone's success, hoping to share it: *He was a boy from a poor family who had hitched his wagon to a star and was determined to get a good education for himself. Mr Jones has stopped trying to win the party leadership and has asked his supporters to vote for the likely winner, hitching his wagon to a star.*

**hitch up** *v adv*

**1** to pull (clothing) up, out of the way: [T1 + UP] *Hitching up his trousers, Jim sat down in the chair that his host offered. The woman hitched up her dress and walked into the water to save the child's boat.*

***2** to fasten (a vehicle) to horses, with wood and leather bands: [T1] *The farmer hitched up the cart and the children went for a ride in the fields to help gather the crops.*

***hive off** *v adv*

**1** *not fml* to disappear; go away without warning: [IØ] *Where's Jim? I suppose he has hived off again.*

**2** *not fml* to separate one's activities; start a new line of business: [IØ (*from, into*] *The salesman was so successful that in the end he hived off from the firm into his own business.*

**3** to separate (something): [T1] *The business was becoming so large that the directors decided to hive off some parts of the work and start new firms.*

**hoard up** *v adv*

to save quantities of (something such as money or food), often in a selfish way: [T1 + UP] *During the war it was unlawful in Britain to hoard up tins of food. Many people got rich by hoarding up gold until the price had risen more than ten times.*

**hobnob with** *v prep*

*not fml* to be seen to be very friendly with (someone, often of a higher rank or social level): [L9 + *with*] *Jane's mother likes to hobnob with the leading women of the city, to go forward socially.*

***hoke up** *v adv*

*AmE infml* to treat (something or someone in a silly or false manner, or one foolishly concerned with love: [T1] *The crowd likes something that makes them laugh or cry, so it's worth hoking up the play to give them what they want.*

***hold against** *v prep* → **charge against** (2), **count against, tell against, weigh against** (2)

to blame (something) on (someone); take (something) into account when judging (someone), esp. in the phr. **hold it against** [D1] *I don't hold it against Jim that he has won every year, but some of the other competitors might. You're late again, but I shan't hold it against you as it's not your fault. Your time in prison will not be held against you.*

***hold aloof** *v adv* → **hang back,** etc.

to keep (oneself) at a distance (usu. from people): [T1b] *Mary does not enjoy parties and usually holds herself aloof from the other guests, not joining in conversation.*

**hold at** *v prep* → **hold off** (1), **keep at** (6)
**hold someone/something at bay** to make (an animal or enemy) remain at a distance, esp. for a short time: *The fox turned, and, fighting fiercely, held the dogs at bay for two hours. If we fire all our bullets tonight, we should at least hold the enemy at bay until tomorrow morning.*

**hold back** *v adv*
**1** to keep (something or someone) in place; prevent (something or someone) from coming forward: [X9 + BACK] *The men built banks of earth to hold back the rising flood waters. Police horses were used to hold back the crowd. These leather bands are for holding the horses back.* —**holdback** *n* → **keep back** (2)
***2** to control (something such as a feeling): [T1] *Jim was able to hold back his anger and avoid a fight.* → **hold in**[1] (3), **keep back** (3), **keep down** (4), **keep in** (4)
***3** to prevent the development of (usu. someone): [T1b] *You show promise as a musician but your lack of practice is holding you back.* → **keep back** (4)
***4** to delay (something or someone): [T1] *I can't hold the meal back for more than half an hour to wait for our guest. The workers' promised wage increase is being held back while it is examined by the government to see if it is greater than the law allows. I'm sorry we're late; we started in good time but heavy rain on the road held us back.* → **hang up** (3), **hold off** (2), **hold up** (2), **keep back** (5), **keep off** (2)
***5** to keep (something) secret: [T1] *We must hear the whole story, don't hold anything back.* → **keep back** (6), **keep from** (1)
***6** to be slow or unwilling to act; stay in the background; prevent (someone or oneself) from being active: [IØ (*usu. simple tenses*)] *Mary is afraid of people, she always holds back when we take her to parties. I held back from jumping into the icy water. We must not hold back when other nations are advancing.* → **hang back,** etc.
***7** to prevent (someone or oneself) (from doing something): [T1b] *The fighter accepted money to hold himself back from winning the fight. You have a good chance of winning, so why not try—what's holding you back?* → **keep back** (7)

***hold by** *v prep*
**1** to behave in accordance with (something): [T1 (*usu. simple tenses*)] *Throughout the struggle he held by his principles.* → **adhere to** (2), etc.
**2** to approve of (something): [T1 (*no pass., usu. neg., simple tenses*)] *I don't hold by some of the strange ideas that you believe in.* → **hold with** (1)

**hold captive** *v adj*
**1** to keep (someone) prisoner: [X9 + captive] *Some of our men have been held captive in foreign prisons for years.*
***2** to make (someone) stay, as if fixed in one place with enjoyment, excitement, interest, etc.: [T1a] *The crowd in the concert hall were held captive by the singer's beautiful performance.*

***hold cheap** *v adj* → **hold dear**
to value (something) little: [T1b (*simple tenses*)] *The brave soldier held his life cheap.*

***hold dear** *v adj* → **hold cheap**
to value (something or someone) highly: [T1a (*simple tenses*)] *These are the principles which I have held dear all my life. My family are the people whom I hold most dear.*

**hold down** *v adv*
**1** to make (something or someone) move or stay down; bend (something) downwards; fasten (something) down: [X9 + DOWN] *You should hold your head down with shame. The fighter held his opponent down until the bell rang. The tent was about to blow away in the wind and we had to hold it down until we could get the ropes fixed. The lid is held down with nails.*
***2** to make (something) stay at a lower level: [T1] *Most of the leading food shops have promised to hold prices down until after the new year.* → **keep down** (2), **remain down** (2), **stay down** (2), **stop down** (2)
***3** to keep (food) in place in the stomach: [T1] *Jane is sick again today, she hasn't been able to hold her food down.* → **keep down** (3), **stay down** (3), **stop down** (3)
***4** *not fml* to keep (a job) for a reasonable length of time: [T1] *Jim has never been able to hold down a job for more than a year, usually because he is dismissed for being late.*
***5** to control; limit the freedom of (someone): [T1] *The whole nation was held down by the cruel rule of the former king. You can't hold a good man down.* → **keep down** (6), etc.

***hold firm** *v adj* → **stand fast, stand firm, stand pat** (2), **stick fast** (2)
to keep one's position, in place or argument, in spite of attack or disagreement: [IØ] *The enemy attacked fiercely, but the line held firm. In spite of the unions' efforts to defeat the new wage controls, the government is holding firm.*

**hold for** *v prep*
**1** to keep (something) in safety until someone can have, collect or use it: [T1 + *for*] *Hold my bag for me while I put my coat on. Run ahead and hold the bus for us, will you? I asked my partner to hold the money for me until I got back, but he spent it! The library will hold the book for you till the weekend.* → **keep for, reserve for** (1, 2), **save for** (1)
**2 hold no brief for** to oppose; refuse to support (something) or sympathize with (someone): [*simple tenses*] *Many teachers hold no brief for the present school system. I hold no brief for professional soldiers who fight other people's wars for money.*
**3 hold no fears/terrors for** to be easy for

(someone) to do, deal with, etc.: [(*simple tenses*)] *Languages hold no terrors for me, I can speak six and learn others easily. The dark holds no fears for a blind person.* → **have for** (8), **have of** (4)

**4 hold good/true for** to be equally true in the case of (someone or something else): [(*simple tenses*)] *The firm's promise holds good for all its products. This safety warning holds true for any factory.*

***hold forth** *v adv*

**1** to speak at length, often with false pride and as if to a crowd: [IØ (*often continuous tenses*)] *Father is holding forth on his favourite subject again; let's not stay to listen, he's never very interesting.*

**2** *fml* to offer (something usu. good): [T1a (*often simple tenses*)] *This company holds forth a promise of advancement to its more successful salesmen.* → **hold out** (2)

**3** *old use fml* to stretch (something such as a hand) forward: [T1a (*often simple tenses*)] *The stranger held forth his hand in greeting, but no one in the hall was willing to accept it.* → **put out** (1), etc.

**hold high** *v adj*

**hold one's head high** to be proud: *You students who are leaving this school can go out into the world with your heads held high, unafraid of any difficulties that may face you in your future life.*

**hold in[1]** *v adv*

**1** to pull and keep (something) in an inward direction: [X9 + IN] *Stand straight and hold your stomach muscles in.* → **keep in** (1), **pull in** (2), **tuck in** (2)

**2** to control (an animal): [X9 + IN] *Your horse is trying to go too fast; you must hold him in.* → **pull in** (6)

***3** to control (something such as feelings or oneself): [T1] *Jim was able to hold in his anger and avoid a fight. Jim was angry but held himself in. It was impossible for the children to hold in their laughter any longer.* → **hold back** (2), **keep back** (3), **keep down** (4), **keep in** (4)

**hold in[2]** *v prep*

**1 hold something in one's head** to be able to remember (something such as facts): [*often simple tenses*] *I don't know how the chairman holds all those figures in his head.* → **keep in** (8)

**2 hold something/someone in high/low esteem/regard** to have a high/low opinion of something or someone: [*simple tenses*] *I have always held cheats and liars in low regard. This school is held in the highest esteem in the neighbourhood.*

**3 hold oneself in readiness** to be always fully prepared (for something or to do something): [*often simple tenses*] *A doctor must hold himself in readiness for a sudden call in the middle of the night. I held myself in readiness to run as soon as the man moved towards me.* → **keep in** (14)

**4 hold something in reserve** to save something for a time of need: [*often simple tenses*] *A certain quantity of gold is always held in reserve at the Bank of England. Hold some wine in reserve in case more guests arrive late. Part of the army must be held in reserve at all times.* → **keep in** (15)

***hold off** *v adv*

**1** to (cause to) remain at a distance: [IØ (*usu. simple tenses*)] *The ship will have to hold off from the shore until this storm passes. Mary tends to hold off from people who try to be friendly too suddenly. Buyers have been holding off until the price falls.* [T1] *We must hold off the enemy's attack until after dark. Elizabeth pretended to hold off her lover's advances.* → **hang back,** etc., **hold at, keep at** (6)

**2** to (cause to) be delayed: [IØ] *Will the rain hold off until after the game?* [T1] *The directors will hold off their decision until Monday.* → **hang up** (3), **hold back** (4), **hold up** (2), **keep back** (5), **keep off** (2)

***hold on** *v adv*

**1** to continue holding something; fasten (something) in place: [IØ (*often simple tenses*)] *If a branch is near you, hold on until we can get a rope.* [T1] *Women used to hold their wide hats on with long sharp pins. The car door was held on with string!* → **hang on[1]** (1)

**2** to continue; last: [IØ (*often simple tenses*)] *Rain held on steadily all afternoon.*

**3** to continue travelling: [IØ (*often simple tenses*)] *Hold on down the road until you come to the railway crossing. The ship held on in spite of the storm.*

**4** *not fml* to wait, esp. on the telephone: [IØ (*often simple tenses*)] *Hold on, I shan't be a minute. You go ahead, I'll hold on here until the others come. I'm afraid the line is busy, would you like to hold on?* → **hang on[1]** (2)

**5** *not fml* to continue in spite of difficulties; refuse to yield: [IØ (*often simple tenses*)] *Painting the house is tiring, but if you hold on, the results are worth the effort. The town was surrounded by the enemy and the citizens did not know if they could hold on until help arrived.* → **hang on[1]** (3), etc.

**hold onto** *v prep*

**1** to seize; hold (something or someone) tightly: [L9 + *onto*] *Hold onto my arm on this icy surface. How long can the climber hold onto the cliff? It was so windy that I had to hold onto my hat all the way along the street.* → **hang onto** (1)

***2** to try to keep (something): [T1] *We should hold onto the house and sell it later when prices are higher.* → **cling onto** (2), **cling to** (3) **hang onto** (3), **stick to** (4)

***3** to find support or help in (something): [T1] (*usu. simple tenses*)] *The old lady had only her religion to hold onto when all her family had gone. The police have only one fingerprint to hold onto. Hold onto this comforting thought, it'll all be over soon.* → **hang onto** (4)

**4 hold onto your hat** *infml* expect a surprise or shock: [*imper.*] *Hold onto your hat, I've some real news for you!*

**hold open** *v adj*

**1** to make (something) remain wide open, apart, etc.: [X9 + open] *Use this block to hold the door open, so as to let some air into the house.* → **leave open** (1), etc.

***2** to save (a job) for someone, as after a time away: [T1b] *If you take this six-month overseas contract, will your firm hold your job open for you when you get back?* → **keep open** (3)

**hold out** *v adv*

**1** to stretch (something such as a hand) forward: [X9 + OUT] *Hold out your hand, you bad boy! The thief held out a gun and everyone raised their hands.* → **put out** (1), etc.

***2** to offer (something): [T1a (*often simple tenses*)] *I don't hold out much hope that our traffic troubles will improve.* → **hold forth** (2)

***3** to last: [IØ (*usu. simple tenses*)] *I think the car will just about hold out till we get to London. Will the water supply hold out through the summer?* → **hang out** (3), **hold up** (6), **keep up** (5), **last out** (1)

***4** to continue in spite of difficulties; refuse to yield: [IØ (*often simple tenses*)] *The town was surrounded, but the citizens held out until help at last came.* —**hold-out** *n* → **hang on**[1] (3), etc.

***hold out for** *v adv prep* → **hang out for, stand out for, stick out for, strike against** (1), **strike for**
to demand firmly and wait in order to get (something): [T1] *The men are still holding out for higher pay. Be careful, the dealers may hold out for a higher price.*

**hold out of** *v adv prep*
to keep (part of something) back from (something): [D1] *The company holds some money out of each man's pay to cover future tax demands.*

***hold out on** *v adv prep*

**1** *infml* to keep a secret from (someone): [T1] *Why didn't you tell me at once, instead of holding out on me?*

**2** *infml* to refuse to support or reply to (someone): [T1] *Jim sent his request to Head Office some weeks ago, but they are still holding out on him.*

***hold over**[1] *v adv* → **put off**[1] (4), etc.
to move (an event) to a later date; ask (someone) to wait until another time: [T1 (*usu. pass.*)] *The concert was held over till the next week because of the singer's illness. The actors cannot be held over without additional pay.* —**holdover** *n* esp. *AmE*

***hold over**[2] *v prep*
to use (something such as knowledge) as a threat to (someone): [D1] *He knows I have been to prison and is holding it over me.*

**hold to** *v prep*

**1** to seize (something); fasten (something) to (something): [L9 + *to*] *The storm was so severe that even the sailors had to hold to the ropes.* [X9 + *to*] *These are very poor fasteners holding the pipes to the wall, and they will soon break.*

***2** (esp. of a ship) to (cause to) keep to (a course): [T1] *The ship held to her course in spite of the storm.* [D1] *It will not be easy holding her to her course in this wind.* → **keep to** (1), **stick to** (2)

***3** to (cause to) follow exactly; keep to (something such as a promise): [T1] *Whatever your argument, I shall hold to my decision. The priest held to his beliefs in spite of cruel treatment. Is the prisoner still holding to his original story?* [D1] *If he tries to leave early, we shall hold him to his contract. You should keep a promise without having to have someone or a law to hold you to your word. I'll hold you to that offer.* → **adhere to** (2), etc.

**4 not hold a candle to** to compare unfavourably with (someone or something): [*usu. simple tenses + can*] *That team can't hold a candle to our players, we beat them every time we play. No other product can hold a candle to ours for quality.*

**hold together** *v adv*

**1** to fasten (things or something) together; remain in one piece: [X9 + TOGETHER] *This special chemical can hold broken dishes together. Hold the two wires together while I fix them.* [L9 + TOGETHER] *I don't know how this old car holds together.*

***2** to (cause to) remain united: [T1b] *The party was held together by personal loyalty to the leader. The needs of the children often hold a marriage together.* [IØ (*usu. simple tenses*)] *A good marriage should hold together without considering the children.* → **stick together** (2), etc.

**hold under** *v adv*

**1** to make (something or someone) stay beneath something: [X9 + UNDER] *He tried to swim, but a strong current held him under and he drowned.* → **keep under** (1), **remain under**[1], **stay under, stop under**

***2** to keep (someone) under control by force: [T1b] *Some ancient kings used terribly cruel means to hold their people under.* → **keep down** (6), etc.

**hold up** *v adv*

**1** to raise (something); keep (something) raised: [X9 + UP] *My husband has lost so much weight that he has to wear a belt to hold his trousers up. Hold up your right hand and repeat these words after me. What holds the roof up?* → **be up** (1), **keep up** (1), **remain up** (1), **stay up** (1), **stop up** (2)

***2** to delay (something or someone): [T1 (*often pass.*)] *The building of the new road has been held up by bad weather. We were held up on the road by a nasty traffic accident.* —**holdup** *n* → **hang up** (3), **hold back** (4), **hold off** (2), **keep back** (5), **keep off** (2)

***3** to stop (a vehicle) by force in order to rob it; rob (someone or a place), esp. with a gun:

[T1] *The criminals held up the train and took all the passengers' money. The only way you'll get rich quickly is by holding up a bank! The shopkeeper was held up inside his own shop, and all the day's money was stolen.* —**holdup** *n* → **stick up** (3)

*__4__ *AmE infml* to charge (someone) too much: [T1] *Don't go to that shop, they hold you up. Look at these bills! I've been held up again!* → **pay through, rip off** (3)

*__5__ to show or offer (someone or something) as an example: [T1 (*as*)] *Grandfather always held up his youngest son as a model of hard work. This school is being held up as an example of successful teacher-student relations.*

*__6__ to last: [IØ (*usu. simple tenses*)] *I think the car will just about hold up till we reach London. Will the water supply hold up through the summer? Will the fine weather hold up?* → **hang out** (3), **hold out** (3), **keep up** (5), **last out** (1)

*__7__ to remain in control of oneself: [IØ (*often simple tenses*)] *How does he hold up under such a responsibility?*

**8 hold one's head up** to have or show pride in oneself: [*often simple tenses*] *After the way you've behaved, I can never hold my head up in this town again.*

**9 hold someone/something up to ransom** to take someone away by force, demanding money for his/her return; threaten someone or something: *Three men took away the rich man's son and held him up for ransom. What right do the trade unions have to hold the country up to ransom in this way?*

**10 hold someone/something up to ridicule/scorn** to make unkind fun of; cause someone or something to be the object of laughter, or not to be treated seriously: *People who are different from the rest of society are often held up to ridicule by others who are afraid of them.*

**hold with** *v prep*

*__1__ to approve of (something): [T1 (*no pass., usu. neg., simple tenses*)] *I don't hold with some of the strange ideas that you believe in.* → **hold by** (2)

**2 hold one's own with** to be of good enough quality to be compared equally with (a competitor): *Our country's runners can hold their own with any in the world, as we intend to prove at the Games.*

**hole in** *v prep*

**hole in one** (in golf) to drive the ball into the hole with only one stroke: [*usu. simple tenses*] *How often have you been lucky or skilful enough to hole in one?*

***hole out** *v adv*

**1** (in golf) to drive the ball into the hole: [IØ (*in*) (*usu. simple tenses*)] *I holed out in 4, but my partner holed out in 3, so he won that hole. The idea of the game is to hole out in as few strokes as possible.*

**2** (in cricket) to get out by giving an easy, usu. high curving, catch: [IØ (*usu. simple tenses*)] *He holed out at mid-off.*

***hole up** *v adv* → **lie doggo, lie low** (3), **lie up** (3)
esp. *AmE infml* to hide as a means of escape: [IØ (*often simple tenses*)] *After the jewel robbery, the thieves holed up in the basement of a friend's house until the police stopped looking for them.*

***hollow out** *v adv*
to make a space in (something solid): [T1] *You can make a good if rough boat by hollowing out the trunk of a tree.* —**hollowed-out** *adj*

***home in** *v adv*
to (cause to) find one's way home, usu. with a machine: [IØ (*on*) (*often simple tenses*)] *In thick mist, the captain had to home in by using radar.* [T1 (*often simple tenses*)] *The bomber homed in the airforce boat to a meeting place.*

***home in on/onto** *v adv prep; prep* → **range in, zero in on**
to aim exactly towards (a place): [T1 (*usu. simple tenses*)] *The enemy plane homed in on the arms factory and destroyed it with one bomb.*

**honour for** *v prep*
to praise or reward (someone) officially for (something or doing something good): [T1 + *for* (*often pass.*)] *The old doctor deserves to be honoured for a lifetime of unselfish work among the sick natives. Have you heard? The director is to be honoured for earning so much money for Britain in international trade.*

**honour with** *v prep*

**1** to reward (someone) with (something such as a prize): [T1 + *with* (*often pass.*)] *Famous people can be honoured with a special degree from this university.*

**2** to give or bring honour, pleasure, respect, etc., to (someone or a place) because of (something): [X9 + *with*] *We are most grateful to the Minister for honouring this hospital with a visit.* → **grace with**

***hoof it** *v pron* → **foot it**
*infml* to walk, esp. instead of riding: [IØ] *That was the last bus disappearing round the corner—we shall have to hoof it if we want to get home tonight.*

***hook it** *v pron*
*infml* to run away: [IØ] *I'm tired of school, let's hook it for the day!*

**hook on** *v prep*

**1** to (cause to) fasten on (something) with or as with a hook or hooks: [X9 + *on*] *See if you can hook the end of the rope on that branch that sticks up at the top.* [L9 + *on*] *The house has storm windows which hook on the outside of the window frames.* → **hook onto** (1)

**2 be hooked on** *infml* to be dependent on; have increasing need of (a habit-forming drug): *The actor's mother got hooked on a pain-killing drug that she had been given in hospital.* → **addict to** (1)

**3 be hooked on** *infml* to be very much in love

with (someone); be very keen on (something or doing something): *I'm afraid Grace is really hooked on that red-haired boy. You can easily get hooked on this kind of music. How can a grown man be hooked on collecting stamps?* → **addict to** (2)

**hook onto** *v prep*
**1** to (cause to) fasten onto (something) with or as with a hook or hooks: [X9 + *onto*] *See if you can hook the end of the rope onto that branch that sticks up at the top.* [L9 + *onto*] *The house has storm windows that hook onto the outside of the window frames.* → **hook on** (1)
*__2__ esp. *AmE not fml* to understand and usu. like (an idea): [T1 (*usu. simple tenses*)] *The children quickly hooked onto the suggestion and were eager to go for a swim.* → **fasten on** (6), **fasten onto** (2), **latch onto** (3), **seize on**

**hook up** *v adv*
**1** to (cause to) fasten with hooks; help (someone) to dress in clothing that fastens with hooks: [X9 + UP] *Please hook my dress up at the back, I can't reach. Hook me up, would you, I'm in a hurry.* [L9 + UP] *Why do so many dresses hook up at the back, so that you have to have help in dressing? It's silly!* → **do up** (1), **fasten up**
*__2__ to connect (something) to a supply of gas, electricity, telephone, etc.; connect (places) by radio or telephone: [T1] *The cooker has arrived but it hasn't been hooked up to the gas supply yet. The engineers are preparing to hook up the capitals of many friendly countries so that they can all receive the Queen's Christmas broadcast at the same time.* —**hookup** *n* → **link up**

**hoot down/off** *v adv* → **howl down**
to show disapproval of (someone on public show) by making a loud hollow noise to drown his speaking: [T1] *The politician had not been speaking for more than ten minutes before he was hooted down. This crowd will hoot any bad actor off.*

**hop in** *v adv*
*not fml* to enter something such as a car: [I∅ (*usu. simple tenses, often imper.*)] *Hop in, I'll give you a ride home.*

**hop off** *v adv*
**1** *not fml* to descend from a vehicle: [I∅ (*usu. simple tenses*)] *At the end of the ride, all the children hopped off and ran into the house for their dinner.*
**2** *infml* to go away: [I∅ (*usu. imper.*)] *Hop off, you boys, you have no right to be in my garden!* → **push off** (3), etc.

**hop on** *v prep*
**1** *not fml* to jump onto (a vehicle) as it is passing, or without too much preparation: [T1 (*usu. simple tenses*)] *Hop on a red bus and see London as Londoners see it!*
**2** *AmE infml* to scold (someone): [T1] *The director hopped on Jim for being late again.* also **hop all over** → **tell off** (1), etc.

**hop to** *v prep* → **jump to** (4)
**hop to it** *AmE infml* to act quickly; make haste: [*usu. simple tenses*] *We shall have to hop to it if we're to catch that plane; it leaves in an hour and it's ten miles to the airport!*

***hop up** *v adv*
**1** *not fml* to climb, often quickly, to a higher level, as on a horse or vehicle: [I∅ (*usu. simple tenses*)] *There's room for all of you on top of the cart—hop up!*
**2** *AmE infml* to excite (someone) by means of a drug: [T1 (*usu. pass.*)] *Some of the greatest drummers could only give their best performances when they were hopped up.* → **hype up, psych up**
**3** *AmE infml* to change (a car engine) to make it perform better, go faster, etc.: [T1] *Some drivers cheat in the race by hopping up their engines.* —**hopped-up** *adj* → **soup up**

**hope against** *v prep*
**hope against hope** to continue to hope when there is little chance of success: [*often continuous tenses*] *Although he had said that he refused to see her again, Grace kept on hoping against hope that the red-haired boy would once again become her lover.*

**hope for** *v prep*
**1** to think and believe that (something good) will happen, be given, etc.; hope to gain (something): [I∅ + *for*] *The men have been hoping for a rise; are you going to disappoint them? I don't mind what sex the baby is, but I have to admit we're hoping for a girl. We can always hope for better weather.* —**hoped-for, unhoped-for** *adj*
**2** to be hopeful with regard to (someone); wish (someone) well: [I∅ + *for*] *Good luck in the examination—we'll all be hoping for you!*
**3 hope for the best** to be hopeful of success, a good result, a happy ending; believe in victory: *It's certainly a difficult examination; all we can do is hope for the best. You don't need to make the soup carefully: just mix everything together and hope for the best.*

***horn in** *v adv* → **muscle in**
*not fml* to interrupt; force one's way in; join (something) without being invited: [I∅ (*on*)] *Nobody asked you to horn in on our conversation. That businessman became successful by horning in on any profitable trade that he saw, even if it was someone else's. Who asked you to horn in?*

***horse about/around** *v adv* → **lark about, ramp about, romp about**
*not fml* to play roughly: [I∅ (*often continuous tenses*)] *You boys have been horsing around again, getting yourselves dirty.*

***hose down** *v adv*
to wash (something) thoroughly with a lot of water through a pipe: [T1] *My children hose down the car every week for me. The police hosed down the road after the accident, to get rid of the blood and bits of broken glass.* —**hose down** *n*

*__hot up__ *v adv*
**1** *infml* to heat or reheat (something, as food): [T1] *I can hot up the soup for you in two minutes.* → **boil up** (1), **heat up** (1), **warm over** (1), **warm up** (1)
**2** *not fml* to (cause to) increase in activity, violence, etc., often becoming more exciting or dangerous: [T1 (*usu. continuous tenses*)] *The police are hotting up their inquiry into the bomb threat.* [IØ (*usu. continuous tenses*)] *Industrial troubles are hotting up in the North. The speed of change is hotting up all over the world.* → **heat up** (2), **warm up** (5)

*__hound down__ *v adv* → **hunt down** (4)
*not fml* to hunt (usu. someone) with effort, until found, often for punishment: [T1] *The police have promised to hound down those responsible for the explosion.*

*__hound out__ *v adv*
*not fml* to make (someone) leave (often a position) because of shame: [T1 (*of*)] *When his employers discovered his shameful past, they hounded him out (of the company).*

*__house up__ *v adv*
*AmE not fml* to make (someone) stay in the house, usu. because of illness: [T1 (*usu. pass.*)] *I've been housed up for a week with a bad cold.*

**hover between** *v prep* → **vacillate between, waver between**
to be undecided between; remain uncertain between (one thing such as a course of action) and (another course of action), or between (doing something) and (doing something else): [L9 + *between*] *I'm hovering between the concert and the play tonight, they're both very attractive events. After years of hovering between buying and renting a house, we at last decided that it was better to own property. For a week after her operation, Mother hovered between life and death.*

**hover over** *v prep*
**1** to remain still or nearly still in the air above (something or someone): [IØ + *over*] *The big bird, high in the sky, is hovering over a mouse.*
***2** to threaten (someone): [T1 (*often continuous tenses*)] *The fear of dismissal has been hovering over me ever since the director's warning.* → **hang over**[2] **(2)**

**hover round** *v prep*
to wait near (someone), as if expecting something: [IØ + *round*] *The students hovered round their teacher, hoping to hear the examination results.*

*__howl down__ *v adv* → **hoot down**
to make a loud disapproving or angry sound to prevent (someone) from being heard: [T1] *The students disagreed with the speaker's opinion and howled him down.*

*__huddle together/up__ *v adv*
to (cause to) stay close to one another's bodies for warmth, comfort, etc.: [IØ] *The cattle huddled together in a corner of the field, trying to keep dry.* [T1] *The lost children were huddled up under some fallen leaves, keeping warm.*

*__hug oneself__ *v pron*
*not fml* to be very pleased with oneself: [IØ (*with*) (*often continuous tenses*)] *I'm hugging myself (with delight) at the thought of seeing him again so soon.*

*__hulk up__ *v adv*
(of something very large) to rise, esp. into view: [IØ (*often simple tenses*)] *Suddenly a big ship hulked up out of the mist.*

**hum with** *v prep*
**1** to be filled with (a low continuous noise): [IØ + *with* (*often continuous tenses*)] *The room was humming with the voices of a large number of guests.*
***2** to be very busy with (any kind of activity): [T1 (*no pass., often continuous tenses*)] *The office has been humming with activity ever since the firm won the big contract.*

**hump over** *v prep*
to make (someone) bend awkwardly over (something such as furniture): [X9 + *over* (*usu. pass.*)] *No wonder your back aches when you've been humped over your desk all day!*

**hunch up** *v adv*
to raise (shoulders) awkwardly; place (someone) in a bent position: [T1 + UP (*usu. pass.*)] *Try not to sit with your shoulders hunched up like that, it's bad for your neck muscles. She sat by the grave, hunched up with grief.*

**hunger for/after** *v prep*
**1** to need (food) very much: [IØ + *for/after*] *The poor children hungered for bread.* → **starve for** (1), **thirst for** (1)
***2** to want (something) very much: [T1 (*often simple tenses*)] *The traveller hungered for his native land. It's terrible to hunger for news when the family's letters don't arrive.* → **starve for** (2), **thirst for** (2)

*__hunker down__ *v adv*
esp. *AmE* to sit down on one's heels: [IØ] *The children hunkered down in the yard, playing a game with five stones.*

**hunt after** *v prep*
to try to gain (something); chase and try to catch (something): [IØ + *after*] *Many people hunt after fame in their lives but never find it. Do you approve of hunting after foxes?*

**hunt down** *v adv*
**1** to chase and usu. kill (an animal) for food, sport, etc.: [T1 + DOWN] *Farmers will not be satisfied till all the local foxes that have been killing their chickens have been hunted down.*
***2** to search for (something) until it is found: [T1] *We've been hunting down a good cheap house all over the city.*
***3** to chase (an animal) until it is caught: [T1] *The escaped tigers must be hunted down and shot.*
***4** to succeed in finding (someone), as for punishment, usu. after much effort: [T1] *Th*

*police have promised to hunt down those responsible for the bomb threat.* → **hound down**

**hunt for** *v prep*

**1** to try to obtain (usu. food or skins) by hunting, usu. with a gun: [IØ + *for*] *He's on holiday in Africa, hunting for animals. The natives live by hunting for their food.*

**2** to search for (something or someone): [L9 + *for* (*often continuous tenses*)] *The whole neighbourhood have been hunting for the missing child. I've been hunting for my watch everywhere, and you had it all the time?*

**hunt out** *v adv*

to search for and find (something which one knows or thinks that one has): [T1] *I shall have to hunt out her address; I've got it somewhere—she keeps moving and I can never remember where she lives.*

**hunt over** *v prep*

to ride on horseback chasing something such as a fox, with dogs, across (land): [IØ + *over*] *In some parts of the country, riders have the lawful right to hunt over anyone's fields. This part of the country has been hunted over for 300 years.*

**hunt through** *v prep*

to search through (something): [IØ + *through*] *I had to hunt through all my drawers looking for the old photograph.*

**hunt up** *v adv*

to search for and usu. find (something such as information) often in books, papers, etc.: [T1] *I've never heard of that village where you say you were born; let me see if I can hunt it up in those old maps at the library.*

**hurl about/around** *v adv*

**1** to scatter (something or things) violently in several directions: [T1 + ABOUT/AROUND] *The strong wind was hurling bits of wood about as though they were toys.* → **chuck about** (1), **fling about** (1), **throw about¹** (1), **toss about** (1)

**2** to wave (one's arms and legs) without direction: [X9 + ABOUT/AROUND] *Hurling his arms and legs about wildly, he kept afloat but wasted much effort.* → **chuck about** (2), **fling about** (2), **throw about¹** (2)

**3 hurl one's money about/around** *infml* to spend money wildly, often to show one's wealth: *As soon as he won all that money, he started hurling it about and soon there was none left.* → **chuck about** (3), **fling about** (3), **throw about¹** (3), **toss about** (4)

**4 hurl one's weight about/around** *infml* to give unnecessary orders; try to use one's power over other people: *The youth club leader was dismissed for trying to hurl his weight about, which the young people refused to accept.* → **chuck about** (4), **fling about** (4), **throw about¹** (4), **toss about** (5)

**hurl at** *v prep*

**1** to throw (something) violently at (something or someone): [T1 + *at*] *The men hurled a bomb at the restaurant from their car.* → **throw at** (1), etc.

**2 hurl oneself at** *infml* to try to win the love of (someone) in a wild manner: *Grace ought to be ashamed of herself, hurling herself at that boy so openly.* → **chuck at** (2), **fling at** (4), **throw at** (3)

**hurl away** *v adv*

**1** to throw (something) away with force: [T1 + AWAY] *The soldier picked up the unexploded bomb and hurled it away into the safety of the forest.* → **throw out** (2), etc.

*2 *infml* to waste (something) wildly: [T1] *Fancy hurling away a good chance like that, the silly girl!* → **throw away** (2), etc.

***hurl away on** *v adv prep*

**1** *not fml* to waste (something) by using it for (something) or giving it to (someone): [D1 (*often pass.*)] *I'm afraid your advice has been hurled away on that boy.* → **chuck away on** (1), **fling away on** (1), **throw away on** (1)

**2** *not fml* to waste the worth of (someone or oneself) in a bad relationship, as marriage, with (someone considered unworthy): [D1] *Disapproving of Jim, Mary's father declared his unwillingness to hurl his daughter away on such a useless fellow. Why are you hurling yourself away on a woman like that? You can wreck your whole life!* → **chuck away on** (2), **fling away on** (2), **throw away on** (2)

**hurl down** *v adv*

**1** to throw (something) down; cause (something) to fall: [T1 + DOWN] *The strong wind hurled down bits of the roof. When you get to the top, hurl the rope down, will you?* → **chuck down** (1), **fling down** (1), **throw down¹** (1), **toss down**

***2** to place (oneself) quickly at full length on the ground or floor: [T1] *When he heard the bomb whistling down, Jim hurled himself down on the floor with his hands over his head.* → **chuck down** (2), **fling down** (2), **fling to** (3), **throw down¹** (2), **throw to** (4)

**hurl into** *v prep*

**1** to throw (something) violently into (a space or container); cause (someone) to fall into (something): [X9 + *into*] *The soldier hurled the bomb into the enemy gun post. The boat rocked wildly, hurling him into the water. The explosion hurled bits of broken glass into the street.* → **fling into** (1, 2), **pitch into** (1), **throw into** (1), **toss into** (1)

***2** to force (someone) to go to (prison): [D1 (*often pass.*)] *The criminal was hurled into prison for his terrible crimes.* → **fling into** (3), **throw down¹** (2), **throw to** (4)

***3** to add or give (something such as help) urgently towards (a purpose or event, or doing something): [D1] *We hurled all the men we had into the battle.* [V4b] *The villagers hurled all possible effort into rebuilding the bombed houses.* → **fling into** (6), **throw into** (5)

**4 hurl oneself into** to put much effort, time, and keenness into (something such as an activity or doing something): *The best cure for* *unhappiness is to hurl yourself into your work. Jane really hurls herself into learning any new song, doesn't she?* → **fling into** (7), **throw into** (7)

*__hurl out__ *v adv*

**1** *not fml* to make (someone) leave because of a bad fault: [T1] *I'll hurl you out of the club if you dare tell the secret!* → **throw out** (4), etc.

**2** *not fml* to refuse to accept (a suggestion, etc.): [T1] *The committee hurled out the request as being completely unsuitable.* → **chuck out** (5), **fling out** (6), **throw out** (6), **toss out** (5), **turn down** (4)

*__hurl together__ *v adv* → **bring together** (2), etc.
to cause (two people or groups such as a man and woman) to meet: [T1 (*usu. pass.*)] *Many unlikely combinations of people get hurled together by the false conditions of wartime.*

**hurry along/forward/on** *v adv*

**1** to (cause to) move quickly ahead or to another place: [L9 + ALONG/FORWARD/ON] *Hurry along there, please, there are people waiting behind you.* [X9 + ALONG/FORWARD/ON] *The policeman hurried the crowd on because they were blocking the scene of the accident.*

*__2__ to make (something) advance more quickly: [T1] *Is there any way we can hurry the decision along?*

**hurry away/off** *v adv*
to (cause to) move quickly away: [L9 + AWAY/OFF] *The white rabbit hurried away, looking at his watch.* [X9 + AWAY/OFF] *The prisoners were hurried off before the reporters could have a chance to speak to them.*

**hurry back** *v adv*
to be quick to return: [L9 + BACK] *Hurry back, won't you, we're waiting for the result.*

**hurry down** *v adv*
to descend quickly: [L9 + DOWN] *Hurry down, Jane, your egg's ready!*

**hurry forward** *v adv* → HURRY ALONG

**hurry in** *v adv*
to enter in haste: [L9 + IN] *Hurry in, children, it's raining!*

**hurry into** *v prep*

**1** to (cause to) enter (usu. a building) in a rush: [L9 + *into*] *I hurried into the room, but the telephone stopped ringing as I picked up the receiver.* [X9 + *into*] *Can you hurry the rest of the crowd into the theatre? The performance is about to start!*

*__2__ to (cause to) start (something or doing something) quickly, often too quickly: [T1] *Too many young people hurry into marriage without considering the responsibilities.* [T4] *It's no good hurrying into learning the piano, it's a long slow job.* [D1] *I won't be hurried into a decision, you'll just have to wait!* [V4b] *Don't try to hurry me into writing that letter, it's not so urgent.*

**hurry off** *v adv* → HURRY AWAY

**hurry on** *v adv* → HURRY ALONG

**hurry out** *v adv*
to (cause to) leave a place quickly: [L9 + OUT (*of*)] *Watching the door, the policeman saw one of the thieves hurrying out.* [X9 + OUT (*of*)] *The prisoners were hurried out of the car before reporters could speak to them.*

**hurry up** *v adv*

**1** to (cause to) move or do something faster: [IØ + UP] *Hurry up, children, the taxi's waiting!* [T1 + UP] *I'm sorry to hurry you up like this but the director has been demanding your report for a week. Production can be hurried up but we shall lose quality.* → **buck up** (1) **bustle up**

**2** to arrive; come nearer (someone) in haste: [IØ + UP (*to*)] *A man hurried up to me and asked what the time was.*

**hush up** *v adv*

**1** to (cause to) be quiet: [IØ + UP] *Hush up, children, can't you see Father's asleep?* [T1 + UP] *See if you can hush the dogs up, they're making a terrible noise in the yard.* → **shut up** (4), etc.

*__2__ to keep (information) secret by enforcing silence about it: [T1] *The President tried to hush up the fact that his advisers had lied.* —**hush-up** *n* → **cover up** (2), **smother up**

*__hype up__ *v adv* → **hop up** (2), **psych up**
*sl* to make (someone) excited or eager, with or as with a drug: [T1 (*usu. pass.*)] *If you can get the committee members (all) hyped up before the meeting, we might get some lively action and some meaningful voting.*

# I

**ice over** *v adv* → **freeze over** (1)
(of a body of water) to (cause to) become frozen, covered with ice: [IØ] *The lake usually ices over by mid-January.* [T1 (*usu. pass.*)] *When the lake gets iced over, you can walk right across it to the islands.*

**ice up** *v adv* → **freeze up** (1)
to (cause to) become covered with ice so as to prevent from working, being useful, etc.: [IØ] *The wings of the plane have iced up and it is too dangerous to fly.* [T1 (*usu. pass.*)] *This recent severe cold has iced up all the farm machinery left in the fields; I hope it isn't ruined.*

**identify by** *v prep*
to discover who (someone) or what (something) is, by means of (something): [T1 + *by* (*usu. simple tenses*)] *The police are hoping to identify the body by the gold fillings in the teeth. The stolen car was identified by a special number marked on it in a secret place.*

**identify oneself** *v pron*
to give or prove one's name, as to the police: [IØ (*usu. simple tenses*)] *The man who appeared at the police station identified himself as the wanted criminal. The bank will not change the cheque unless you are able to identify yourself.*

**identify with** *v prep*
**1** to consider (something) to be equal to or the same as (something else): [D1 (*usu. simple tenses*)] *Never identify opinions with facts.*
**2** to cause (oneself, someone, or something) to seem connected with or share in (usu. something): [D1 (*usu. simple tenses*)] *Mrs Bright did not wish to be identified with the committee's statement. Voters tend to identify the Party with unfair treatment of poorer and weaker members of society, which is unfortunate.*
**3** to feel sympathy for (someone); feel that one shares (something): [T1 (*no pass., usu. simple tenses*)] *Reading this book, we can identify with the main character's struggle.*

**idle about/around** *v adv* → **mess about** (1), etc.
to spend time lazily: [IØ + ABOUT/AROUND] *There was no work in the office this afternoon so everyone idled about.*

**idle away** *v adv*
**1** (of a car engine) to run very slowly without being connected to the wheels, continuously or for some time: [IØ + AWAY] *If you leave your car idling away outside the house for an hour or more, you will burn more petrol than you think.*
**2** to waste (time) lazily: [T1] *When you're older you'll be sorry that you idled away your youth instead of preparing for a profession.* → **fiddle away** (2), **fool away, footle away, fritter away, frivol away, laze away** (2), **loaf away, loiter away, lounge away, piddle away, potter away, trifle away**

**illuminate with** *v prep* → **light with**
to brighten; give light to (something such as a place) with (a kind or power supply of light): [T1 + *with*] *The first London theatre to be illuminated with electricity was the Savoy, in 1870.*

**illustrate with** *v prep*
**1** to ornament (something such as a book) with (usu. pictures): [T1 + *with*] *Tom's latest book is illustrated with photographs of the real family upon whom his story is based.*
**2** to help to explain (something) by means of (something such as an example): [X9 + *with*] *Each verb in this dictionary is illustrated with a sentence. The speaker illustrated his talk with readings from the books that he had mentioned.*

***imbue with** *v prep* → **penetrate with, permeate with**
*fml* to fill (usu. someone) with (something such as a quality, feeling, or opinion): [D1 (*usu. pass., usu. simple tenses*)] *A President should be imbued with a sense of responsibility for the nation. A good politician is one who can imbue his listeners with a desire to vote for him. The director said that what he was really dreaming of was a company of actors all imbued with the same spirit.*

**immerse in** *v prep*
**1** to place (something, someone, or oneself) in water deep enough to cover it/him, usu. for a long time: [T1 + *in*] *If the clothes are very dirty, immerse them in soapy water overnight.* → **soak in**[2] (1), **steep in** (1), **submerge in** (1)
***2** to make (oneself) give all one's attention to (something such as study): [D1] *I have a talk to give next month on the famous writer, so first I must immerse myself in his books. The best way to learn a language is to immerse yourself in it totally, speaking nothing else, for a period of at least a month. Father never hears what anyone says when he's immersed in is own thoughts.* → **absorb in,** etc.

**immigrate into** *v prep* → **emigrate to**
(from the point of view of the host country) to come into (a country) to start a new life: [IØ + *into*] *Attracted by its safety and comfort, people from all parts of the world have immigrated into this country in large numbers since the war.*

**immunize against** *v prep* → **inoculate against, vaccinate against**
to give (someone) a small amount of something causing (a certain disease) so as to pre-

vent him from catching it: [T1 + *against*] *Scientists have not yet discovered a trustworthy method of immunizing people against the common cold, although they have been working on it for many years.*

***immure in** *v prep*
**1** *fml* to imprison (someone) in (a place): [D1 (*usu. pass.*)] *The defeated ruler was immured in a dark prison for many years.*
**2 be immured in** *fml* to give all one's attention to (something): *Immured in her work, the writer did not even hear her visitor enter the room.* → **absorb in,** etc.

**impale on** *v prep*
to fix (something or someone) on the end of (a sharp point): [T1 + *on*] *The cruel king used to impale his prisoners on sharp sticks and place them in public view to die. You might get a job as a park keeper, and be given a long stick to impale the pieces of paper on so that you keep the park clean.*

**impart to** *v prep*
**1** *fml* to tell (information) to (someone): [T1 + *to*] *The prisoner hoped, by imparting his companions' hiding place to the police, to escape punishment on his own account.*
***2** *fml* to give or lend (a quality) to (something): [D1] *Only the chairman's strong control was able to impart some sense of seriousness to the meeting.*

**impeach for** *v prep*
to charge (someone in high office) with (something or doing something wrong): [T1 + *for* (*usu. simple tenses*)] *Some people felt that the President should have been impeached for his irresponsible actions/for lying to the public.*

**impel to** *v prep*
to push or force (someone) into (a course of action): [T1 + *to*] *The success of our public request for money impels us to even greater efforts to save the hospital. The prisoner claims that he was impelled to crime by the influence of his more strong-minded companions.*

***impinge on/upon** *v prep*
**1** *fml* to hit or touch (something): [T1] *The machinery will be impossible to repair, as its casing is bent and is impinging on the main wires.*
**2** *fml* to use part of (something belonging to someone else): [T1] *By using the path to the shore, tourists are actually impinging on the owner's property rights.* → **encroach on** (2), **infringe on, trench on**
**3** *fml* to have an important effect on (something): [T1] *The need to see that justice is done impinges upon every decision made in the courts.*

***implant in/into** *v prep* → **inculcate in, instil in**
*fml* to fix (an idea) by teaching (someone), often at an early age: [D1] *How do you implant good manners in young children? Fear of sex was implanted in the minds of most young women of good family in the last century.*

***implicate in** *v prep*
*fml* to make (someone) share the blame for (something such as a crime): [D1 (*often pass.*)] *Did you know that our very respectable neighbour has been implicated in the jewel robbery?*

**import from** *v prep* → **export to, import into**
to buy (goods) and bring them from (another country): [T1 + *from*] *Britain must try to import fewer goods from overseas, so as to help her own industries.*

**import into** *v prep* → **export to, import from**
to buy (goods) from abroad and bring them into (one's own country): [T1 + *into*] *A special tax is placed on goods imported into Britain from any country outside the common market.*

**impose on/upon** *v prep*
**1** to place (something such as a tax or responsibility) on (someone or something): [X9 + *on/upon*] *A special tax is imposed on very high incomes. The university is unwilling to impose upon students the heavy responsibility of choosing their own courses.* → **place on** (2), **put on²** (2)
***2** to force (oneself or one's company) on (someone): [D1] *By imposing his presence on the meeting, the director prevented free expression of opinion. My son's friend imposed himself on us for two weeks as an uninvited guest.*
***3** to cause work and trouble for (someone) take unfair advantage of (someone or something): [T1] *I will only stay till Saturday as I have no wish to impose on you. Mother's good nature is too easily imposed on by unthinking people.* → **put out** (15), etc.

***imprecate on/upon** *v prep*
*fml* to invite; wish (something such as evil) on (someone): [D1] *The wicked magician imprecated a curse on the young princess, that her future would end in sorrow.*

**impregnate with** *v prep*
**1** (in an animal, including man) to cause (an egg) to combine with (a seed) in order to start forming a baby: [T1 + *with*] *In every female animal, an egg has to be impregnated with male seed before the young creature can start to form.*
***2** to fill (something) completely with (a substance): [D1 (*usu. pass.*)] *This cloth has been impregnated with a special chemical which protects it against rain.*
***3** to fill (someone) with (something such as a feeling or quality): [D1 (*usu. pass.*)] *As a result of their training in a highly moral family the children became impregnated with a strong sense of responsibility.*

**impress by** *v prep* → **IMPRESS WITH** (2)

**impress on/upon** *v prep*
**1** to make a mark by pressing (something) on (a surface): [X9 + *on/upon*] *After years of*

*gardening, the marks of the spade were impressed on the skin of the old gardener's hands.* → **impress with** (1)

**2** to fix (something such as an idea) into (someone): [D1] *You must impress on the children the need to be careful when crossing the road. Her performance will be impressed upon my memory for a long time.* → **impress with** (3)

**npress with** *v prep*

**1** to mark (a surface) with the shape of (something): [X9 + *with*] *By impressing a piece of soap with the borrowed key, the thief was able to have an exact copy made.* → **impress on** (1)

**2** to influence (someone) to have a high opinion of (someone or something): [T1 + *with*] *At their first meeting, Jim impressed Mary's parents with his sense of responsibility towards her. I'm impressed with her ability as a singer, but doubt if she will be able to deal with the difficulties of professional musicianship.* also **impress by**

**3** to cause (someone) to believe (something): [D1] *You must impress the children with the need to be careful when crossing the road.* → **impress on** (2)

**nprint on** *v prep* → **imprint with**

**1** to print or fix (a mark) on (a surface): [T1 + *on*] *The firm has a special machine for imprinting the right postage on their envelopes. The footsteps of countless tourists are imprinted on the stone floor of the great church.*

**2** to fix (something such as an idea) firmly in (someone's mind): [D1 (*usu. pass.*)] *Mother's idea of the perfect house was already imprinted on her mind by a picture that she had seen in the newspaper, before we ever started looking at property for sale.*

**nprint with** *v prep* → **imprint on**

**1** to mark (a surface) with (something such as printing): [T1 + *with*] *Our envelopes are imprinted with a return address. The stone floor of the great church is imprinted with the footsteps of countless tourists over the centuries.*

**2** to influence (someone's mind) with (something such as an idea): [D1] *Some of these books are harmful in that they may imprint parent's minds with false hopes of perfectly behaved children.*

**nprison in** *v prep*

to keep (someone) against his will inside (a place such as a prison): [T1 + *in* (*often pass.*)] *It will be good to get out after being imprisoned in my room with the fever.*

**nprove in** *v prep*

to (cause to) become better with regard to (a part or quality): [I∅ + *in*] *The boy seems to have improved in his behaviour since he had that last warning.* [T1 + *in*] *The city has been considerably improved in cleanliness since the new council took charge. The engineers are trying to improve the standard racing car in speed; it is already satisfactory in safety and price.*

***improve on/upon** *v prep*

to produce something better than (something): [T1] *Tom has never improved on his first book, which had a wild success; none of the others are as good. This singer will have to improve on the performance we have just heard if she is to be accepted by the company. It's no use telling gardeners that nature can't be improved upon.*

***impute to** *v prep*

**1** *fml* to consider (something, often unfavourable) to be the result of (something); blame (something) on (something): [D1] *Some politicians impute the rise in crime to the greater freedom being enjoyed by young people.* → **attribute to** (1), etc.

**2** *fml* to give the responsibility for (a saying, opinion, feeling, etc.) to (someone), often in an attempt to blame him: [D1] *His enemies tried to impute some unfortunate remarks to the politician, who denied having said them.* → **attribute to** (2)

**incapacitate for/from** *v prep*

*fml* to make (someone) unfit for (certain work); prevent (someone) from (working), through illness: [T1 + *for* (*usu. simple tenses*)] *Poor eyesight will incapacitate you for a job in the library.* [T1 + *from* (*usu. simple tenses*)] *Mother's operation has incapacitated her from looking after herself, and she has to have both a nurse and a daily woman in to help.*

**incarcerate in** *v prep*

*fml* to imprison (someone) in (a building): [T1 + *in*] *Many people think that the old enemy leader has been incarcerated in his castle prison for too many years.*

***incite to** *v prep* also **instigate to**

to actively encourage; urge (someone) towards (a course of action): [D1] *The leader was charged with inciting the men to violence.*

**incline forward** *v adv* → **bend forward, lean forward**

to bend or lean in a forward direction, esp. in order to see or hear: [I∅ + FORWARD (*usu. simple tenses*)] *The mirror is so badly placed that the driver has to incline forward to see anything in it.*

**incline to** *v prep* → **incline towards**

**1** to bend, lean, or slope towards (something): [I∅ + *to* (*usu. simple tenses*)] *Be careful round the corner, the road inclines steeply to the left.*

***2** to (cause to) be likely to have, do, or think (something): [T1 (*no pass., simple tenses*)] *His family have always inclined to overweight.* [D1 (*simple tenses*)] *My experience inclines me to the view that he is not to be trusted.* → **lean to** (2), **tend to**

**incline towards** *v prep* → **incline to**

**1** to bend, lean, or slope in the direction of (something or someone): [I∅ + *towards* (*usu.*

*simple tenses*)] *The hill inclines towards the sea. I had to incline towards the secretary to hear what she was whispering.* → **slope towards,** etc.

*__2__ to (cause to) move one's opinion more in favour of (something such as an opinion or belief): [T1 (*no pass., usu. simple tenses*)] *More and more countries in Europe are beginning to incline towards some form of socialism.* [D1 (*usu. pass.*)] *The United States is becoming more inclined towards the belief that black people should be fairly treated.* → **lean towards** (2), etc.

**include among** *v prep*
to treat (someone or something) as one of (a number of people or things): [T1 + *among*] *Included among the guests were a number of famous musicians. Do you include walking among your amusements?*

**include in** *v prep*
to regard or count (someone or something) as part of (something such as a group): [T1 + *in*] *Have you included the chairman in your list of committee members? I suppose I shall have to include my insufferable relatives in the wedding party. Electricity and gas bills are not included in the rent.*

**include out** *v adv*
**include me out** *humor* don't ask me to take part: [(*usu. imper.*)] *If you want more work done, you can include me out!*

*__incorporate in/into__ *v prep*
to make (something) a part of (something): [D1] *We shall try to incorporate some of your ideas in/into our future plans.*

**incorporate with** *v prep*
(in business law) to join (a firm) with (another firm): [T1 + *with*] *The firm will be incorporated with the parent company.* [IØ + *with*] *Wells and Company are about to incorporate with National Steel.*

**increase from** *v prep*
to (cause to) become larger from (something smaller): [T1 + *from*] *When is my pay going to be increased from its present rate?* [IØ + *from*] *My pay has not increased from the rate fixed two years ago.*

**increase in** *v prep*
to (cause to) become larger with regard to (a part or quality): [IØ + *in*] *The library has increased in the total number of books, but not in space to hold them. The service must be increased in the frequency of trains.*

**increase to** *v prep*
to (cause to) become larger to (something bigger): [IØ + *to*] *The population of the city has increased to 500,000 this year.* [T1 + *to*] *The directors hope to be able to increase your pay to £6,000.*

*__inculcate in__ *v prep* → **implant in, instil in**
*fml* to fix (an idea) by forceful teaching, in (someone): [D1] *How do you inculcate good manners in young children? Fear of sex was inculcated in the minds of most young women of good families in the last century.*

**indemnify against** *v prep* → **insure against** (1)
*fml* to insure (someone or something) against (a risk): [X9 + *against* (*usu. simple tenses*)] *How much does it cost to indemnify oneself against accidental death?*

**indemnify for** *v prep*
*fml* to repay (someone) for (a loss of money): [X9 + *for* (*usu. simple tenses*)] *The insurance company will indemnify you for the cost of living elsewhere while the fire damage is repaired.*

*__indent for__ *v prep*
*fml* (in business) to make a formal request for (supplies): [T1] *Remember to indent for a fresh supply of order cards at the beginning of every month.*

**indoctrinate with** *v prep*
to teach (someone) to hold (certain fixed beliefs), often by force or cleverness: [T1 + *with*] *It is too easy for any State or Church to indoctrinate young children with the views that it considers correct.*

**induce in** *v prep*
**1** to produce (a change or effect, as electrical or chemical) in (a substance or part of the body): [T1 + *in*] *It is possible to induce magnetism in a piece of iron by placing it near a field of force. Certain chemicals can induce undesirable changes in the nervous system.*
**2** to make (a feeling, behaviour, etc.) arise in (someone): [T1 + *in*] *The coming of spring often induces light-hearted foolishness in many people. Lack of proper care and love in early childhood can induce criminal behaviour in young people.*

*__indulge in__ *v prep*
to allow oneself to enjoy (something), often with a sense of guilt: [T1] *I occasionally indulge in a cigarette, but I am not a serious smoker.*

**infatuate with** *v prep*
**be infatuated with** to be madly in love with (someone) or foolishly proud of (oneself, one's abilities, etc.): *Grace has been infatuated with that red-haired boy for over two years; it's time she found someone else more suitable. Infatuated with his own success, he grew careless and failed in his next attempt.*

**infect with** *v prep*
**1** to cause (someone) to catch (a disease) from oneself: [T1 + *with*] *Go away, I don't want to infect you with my cold.*
*__2__ to fill (someone) with (a feeling): [D1] *The children are infected with a mad desire to swim in the lake in midwinter. A good teacher should be able to infect his students with his own keenness for his subject.*

**infer from** *v prep* → **deduce from, generalize from**
*fml* to reach (an answer) by reasoning from (given facts): [T1 + *from*] *What do you infer from the voting figures? No one can infer such an opinion from his statement. From what you*

*have said, it can only be inferred that you are unwilling to accept the suggestion.*

**infest with** *v prep*
to cause (something such as a place) to have too much of (something) or too many (things) usu. bad: [D1 (*usu. pass.*)] *Be careful, that muddy water is infested with disease-bearing insects. "England is, and always has been, a country infested with people who love to tell us what to do, but who very rarely seem to know what's going on."* (Colin MacInnes, *Absolute Beginners*)

**infiltrate into** *v prep*
to (cause to) pass, in spite of difficulties, into (something), usu. a little or one at a time: [L9 + *into*] *The soldiers infiltrated into the enemy defences.* [X9 + *into*] *The teacher tried to infiltrate her ideas into the children's minds.*

**infiltrate through** *v prep*
to pass, in spite of difficulties, through (something), a little or one at a time: [L9 + *through*] *Our soldiers have infiltrated through the enemy lines, trapping the enemy between our two forces.*

**inflate with** *v prep*
**1** to cause (a hollow object) to swell with (a gas): [T1 + *with*] *The front tyres should be inflated with thirty pounds of air to the square inch.*
**2 be inflated with** to be filled with (a strong feeling): *Receiving his prize, Jim was inflated with pride. I don't like that woman, she's inflated with a sense of her own importance.*

**inflict on** *v prep*
to force (something or someone unwanted) on (someone): [D1] *Don't inflict your ideas on me. Mary inflicted the children on her mother for the weekend. I'm sorry to inflict myself on you so late, but my car has gone into the fence and I must telephone the garage.*

**inform about/of** *v prep*
to tell (someone) about (someone or something): [T1 + *about/of*] *The director complained that he had not been informed of the committee's decision. Why wasn't I informed of her arrival? You ought to inform the police about that man who's been hiding in the bushes outside your gate.*

**inform against/on** *v prep* → **grass on, peach on, rat on** (1), **shit on, shop on, sneak on, snitch on, split on, tell of** (2), **tell on** (2)
to tell the police, or someone in charge, about (someone who has done something wrong): [T1] *The prisoner hoped to gain his own freedom by informing on his companions in the jewel robbery.*

**inform of** *v prep* → INFORM ABOUT

**inform on** *v prep* → INFORM AGAINST

**infringe on/upon** *v prep* → **encroach on** (2), **impinge on** (2), **trench on**
to advance on; act in such a way as to show no respect for; spoil or offend (someone's rights): [T1 + *on/upon*] *In a recent magazine article, the writer complained that his right to remain private had been infringed upon by government inquirers demanding personal information.*

**infuse into** *v prep* → **inspire in**
*fml* to drive (something such as a quality) into (someone): [X9 + *into*] *The general's speech infused keenness into the men.*

**infuse with** *v prep* → **inspire with**
*fml* to fill (someone) with (something such as a quality): [X9 + *with*] *The general's speech infused the men with keenness.*

**ingraft in** *v prep* → ENGRAFT IN

**ingraft into/onto/upon** *v prep* → ENGRAFT INTO

***ingratiate with** *v prep*
to make (oneself) very pleasant to (someone) in order to gain favour: [D1] *I could see the new student trying to ingratiate himself with the teacher, in hopes of better marks.*

***inhere in** *v prep* → **consist in, consist of, subsist in**
*fml* to be found existing in (something), esp. as a right, quality, etc.: [T1 (*no pass., simple tenses*)] *Beauty inheres in art. "The truth... may in the end be found, unexpectedly, inhering in the whole pattern of the life as we now see it."* (*Times Literary Supplement*, 31 October 1975)

**inherit from** *v prep*
to gain (something such as property or characteristics) from (someone who has lived earlier): [T1 + *from* (*usu. simple tenses*)] *I inherited this ring from my grandmother. We think that Mary inherits her blue eyes from her father.*

**inhibit from** *v prep*
to prevent (someone) from (doing something) by a feeling of fear or guilt: [T1 + *from* (*usu. simple tenses*)] *The singer's natural fear of shame tended to inhibit her from singing in public.* [V4a] *Women used to be inhibited from enjoying their sex life.*

**initiate into** *v prep*
**1** to introduce (someone) into (membership of an association or group): [T1 + *into* (*often simple tenses*)] *The organization is known for its strange ceremony of initiating new members into the society.*
***2** to allow (someone) to share (a secret or private knowledge): [D1 (*often simple tenses*)] *Who was the first man to initiate you into the mysteries of sex?*

**inject into** *v prep* → **inject with**
**1** to make (usu. a liquid) enter (someone or a part of the body) by means of a special medical needle: [X9 + *into*] *This drug works best if it is injected directly into the bloodstream.*
***2** to add (something needed) to (something): [D1] *Such a cheerful and active member will inject new life into the club. The government must inject money into our older industries so that they will survive.*

**inject with** *v prep* → **inject into**
**1** to give (someone or a part of the body) (usu. a liquid) by means of a special medical

needle: [X9 + *with*] *Few areas of his arm were left that had not already been injected with hard drugs. This child must not be injected with either of these two drugs, as he is specially sensitive to their effects, and might die.*

*2 to give (something) an addition of (something): [D1] *The club needs injecting with new ideas.*

***ink in** *v adv*
to complete with ink (something drawn in pencil or left unfilled): [T1] *When you're satisfied that the pencil drawing is complete, you may ink it in to make solid blocks of colour.*

***ink over** *v adv*
to cover (usu. a line of writing or drawing) with the same line in ink: [T1] *This list is too faint to read in pencil, please ink the words over so that they can be clearly read.*

**inoculate against** *v prep* → **immunize against, vaccinate against**
to protect (someone) against catching (a certain disease) by giving him a little of the substance which causes it: [T1 + *against*] *If you are travelling to a tropical country, you ought to be inoculated against yellow fever.*

**inoculate with** *v prep* → **vaccinate with**
to give (someone) a small amount of (something causing a certain disease) so as to prevent him from catching it: [T1 + *with*] *All the men in the camp have been inoculated with the yellow fever virus.*

**inquire about** *v prep* → ENQUIRE ABOUT

**inquire after** *v prep* → ENQUIRE AFTER

***inquire for** *v prep* → ENQUIRE FOR

***inquire into** *v prep* → ENQUIRE INTO

**inquire of** *v prep* → ENQUIRE OF

**inquire within** *v adv* → ENQUIRE WITHIN

**inscribe in/on** *v prep*
to mark (usu. words) formally in or on (a surface or object), often to record a gift, honour, etc.: [X9 + *in/on* (*usu. pass.*)] *The names of all my husband's relatives were inscribed in the family Bible when they were born, married, or died. The winning cricket team's name will be inscribed on the silver cup and given to them in a ceremony at the end of the season.*

**inscribe with** *v prep*
to mark (an object) with (usu. words): [X9 + *with*] *The jeweller will inscribe the ring with both your names. The gravestone was inscribed with the name and dates of the dead youth.*

**insert between** *v prep*
to place or add (usu. something) between (two things): [T1 + *between* (*usu. simple tenses*)] *Insert the special cleaning thread between your teeth and pull it gently up and down. If you can insert your hand between the back of the chair and the wall, you may be able to reach the letter that fell down there. 'You've missed the 't' out of 'whistle'; you have to insert a 't' between the 's' and the 'l'.*

**insert in** *v prep*
to place (something such as words) in (something such as a newspaper): [T1 + *in* (*often simple tenses*)] *I wish to insert an advertisement in your newspaper.*

**insert into** *v prep*
to push (something) into (something); add (something) to (usu. something written): [T1 + *into* (*often simple tensess*)] *Inserting the key into the lock, he turned it and pulled the door open. Is it too late to insert a new page into my magazine article?*

**inset in/into** *v prep*
to place or set (something, often smaller) within (usu. something larger): [T1 + *in/into* (*usu. simple tenses*)] *A detailed street plan of the city is inset in a corner of the area map. You will have to inset an additional piece of material into the waistline of the dress to make it large enough for her.*

***insinuate into** *v prep*
to cause (oneself or something) to become part of (something) little by little; introduce (oneself) cleverly and indirectly into (something such as someone's favour): [D1] *That new student has no business trying to insinuate himself into the teacher's favour; it won't make any difference to his marks.*

***insist on/upon** *v prep*
**1** to declare (something) firmly: [T1] *Throughout the trial, the prisoner insisted on his lack of guilt.*
**2** to urge; strongly demand (something or doing something): [T1] *I'm afraid I have to insist on the return of my book at once. Don't let them tell you what they want, insist on your rights.* [T4 (*often simple tenses*)] *I must insist on paying for my share of the meal.*

**inspire in** *v prep* → **infuse into**
to excite (something such as a feeling) in (someone): [T1 + *in*] *The general's speech inspired keenness in the men.*

**inspire with** *v prep* → **infuse with**
to fill (someone) with (something such as a feeling) by excitement: [T1 + *with*] *The general's speech inspired the men with keenness. The sudden reappearance of the murderer inspired the whole village with fear.*

**install in** *v prep* also *AmE* **instal in**
**1** to fix (an object) in (a place): [T1 + *in*] *When are the men coming to install the new cooker in the kitchen?*
***2** to place (someone or oneself) in (a place such as a room or a piece of furniture): [D1 (*usu. simple tenses*)] *Our unwanted visitor seems to have installed himself in the guest room. Once I've installed myself in my favourite comfortable chair, I don't like to get up.*
***3** to place (someone) formally in (a position or rank): [D1 (*usu. pass.*)] *No, he's been installed in the chairmanship for too long to be dismissed now.*

**instigate to** *v prep* → INCITE TO

**instil in/into** *v prep* also **instill in/into → implant in, inculcate in**
to teach (something) patiently and with care to (someone); enforce (something) gradually on (someone or something): [X9 + *in/into*] *Parents try to instil in(to) their children the best of moral principles. We must try to instil some order into the organization.*

**instil with** *v prep*
to fill the mind of (someone) gradually with (an idea): [X9 + *with*] *It is easy to instil the minds of young children with fixed ideas, whether right or wrong.*

**instill in/into** *v prep* → INSTIL IN

**instill with** *v prep* → INSTIL WITH

**institute against** *v prep*
*fml* to start (something such as a trial) against (someone): [T1 + *against*] *The government intends to institute court action against the firm which has disobeyed the wage controls and paid its workers more than is allowed under the new law.*

**institute into/to** *v prep*
*fml* to place (someone) formally in (a church living): [T1 + *into/to* (*usu. simple tenses*)] *Tuesday has been fixed as the date for instituting the minister into his new living.*

**instruct in** *v prep* → **educate in**
to teach; give (someone) formal knowledge of (a subject): [T1 + *in*] *The college will need an additional teacher to instruct the boys in cooking. The soldiers have been thoroughly instructed in the care of their weapons.*

**insulate from** *v prep*
**1** to separate (something) from (something or doing something that may cause damage or difficulty) so as to protect it: [IØ + *from* (*with*)] *The house can be insulated from cold with about four inches of this special plastic. The wires must be insulated from touching each other, with a rubber covering.*
**2** to protect (someone or oneself) from (something usu. harmful): [D1] *It is neither possible nor desirable to insulate young children from the dangers of adventurous play. Living in a high building tends to insulate us from the real life of the city.*

**insure against** *v prep*
**1** to pay money to make (something) safe against loss of money caused by (a danger): [T1 + *against* (*usu. simple tenses*)] *How much will it cost to insure the building against fire?* [IØ + *against* (*usu. simple tenses*)] *It is possible to insure against almost any loss.* also **cover against → indemnify against**
**2** to (cause to) be protected against (something bad): [T1 (*often simple tenses*)] *The directors will take steps to insure against possible failure.* [D1 (*often simple tenses*)] *The engineers used special methods to insure the bridge against damage from high winds.* → **ensure against**

**insure for** *v prep* also **cover for**
to make a contract with an insurance company to protect (something or someone's life) against loss, up to a limit of (a certain sum of money): [T1 + *for* (*usu. simple tenses*)] *The robbery, while worrying, does not mean a total loss, as the jewels were insured for £20,000.*

**insure with** *v prep*
to make an insurance contract regarding (something or someone's life) with (a certain firm): [IØ + *with*] *Which firm do you usually insure with?* [T1 + *with*] *The jewels were insured with Hill and Company, who have always proved very trustworthy.*

**integrate into** *v prep*
to make (someone or something) part of (something, usu. from which he/it was formerly separate): [X9 + *into*] *Most State governments in the United States have promised to integrate black children into their school systems. I integrated your suggestion into my plans and it has improved them.*

**integrate with** *v prep*
to combine (something) with (something else): [X9 + *with* (*usu. simple tenses*)] *The city council tries to ensure that any new buildings are integrated with the existing appearance of the city. Writers of history books often attempt to integrate the past with the present.*

**intend as** *v prep*
to mean or wish that (usu. something) should be, become, or be regarded as (something): [X9 + *as* (*simple tenses*)] *Jim's gift of flowers was intended as a way of saying that he was sorry that he had quarrelled with Mary. My remark was not intended as a joke!*

**intend for** *v prep*
**1** to wish that (someone) would join (a group); direct (someone) towards (usu. a profession): [X9 + *for* (*usu. pass.*)] *Having always been musical from an early age, the singer seems to have been intended for the concert stage.*
**2** to wish to give (something) to or save (something) for (someone): [X9 + *for* (*often pass.*)] *All my property is intended for my grandchildren. The shot which was intended for the President killed one of his soldiers.*

**inter in** *v prep* → **intern in**
*fml* to bury (someone) in (a place): [T1 + *in* (*usu. pass., usu. simple tenses*)] *Sir Winston Churchill had expressed a wish to be interred in the graveyard of a small church in the village which had been his family home, and it is there that he is buried.*

**interact with** *v prep*
to act together with; have an effect on (something else or one another): [IØ + *with*] *These two chemicals interact with each other at a certain temperature to produce a substance which could cause an explosion.*

**intercede for** *v prep* → **intercede with**
*fml* to speak with someone in charge, asking for a favour for (someone): [IØ + *for* (*with*)] *The lawyer has promised to intercede for the prisoner, hoping to free him from prison.*

**intercede with** *v prep* → **intercede for**
*fml* to speak to (someone in charge), asking for a favour for someone: [IØ + *with*] *The lawyer is hoping to be able to intercede with the prison governor, asking that the prisoner should be set free.*

**interchange with** *v prep* → **alternate with**
(of two things) to be put in the place of each other; put (two things) in the place of each other: [L9 + *with*] *The weather will consist of sunshine interchanging with periods of light rain.* [X9 + *with* (*usu. simple tenses*)] *I am only taking two dresses on holiday, so I will have to interchange the green dress with the blue one.*

**interest in** *v prep*
to attract the attention or concern of (someone) to (something); cause (someone) to desire or care about (someone, something, or doing something): [T1 + in (*often pass., simple. tenses*)] *Few teachers are able to interest their students in dull subjects that mean a lot of hard work. I am not interested in your affairs. The singer has always been interested in music. Can I interest you in our latest model car? When did Grace first get interested in that red-haired boy? I don't think Father is seriously interested in the house. Are any members of this family really interested in buying the house? I am interested in joining your company and wonder if you have a suitable position for me.*

**interfere in** *v prep* → **meddle in**
to concern oneself with and usu. take unwanted action about (someone else's business): [IØ + *in*] *Don't interfere in matters that don't concern you.*

**interfere with** *v prep*
**1** to touch or cause damage to (something which is not one's concern): [IØ + *with*] *Somebody's been interfering with my papers again; I do wish everyone would leave them alone, I have them carefully organized.* → **meddle with** (1), etc.
**2* to interrupt or delay (something such as action): [T1] *Nothing must be allowed to interfere with our plans for the weekend. You musn't allow your family duties to interfere with your work.*
***3** *euph* to attack (a woman) sexually: [T1 (*usu. pass.*)] *The police doctor says that the dead girl had been interfered with before her death.*

**interlace with** *v prep*
to cause (something) to be joined, as if by weaving, with (something else), often loosely: [T1 + *with* (*usu. pass.*)] *The thin branches were interlaced with one another, making a beautiful pattern against the night sky.*

***interlard with** *v prep* → **lard with**
*fml* to mix (something, usu. written or spoken) with (something, usu. other kinds of words): [D1 (*usu. pass.*)] *The politician's speech was interlarded with informal expressions that he hoped would attract the ordinary voter.*

**interleave with** *v prep*
to separate the leaves of (a book) by adding (usu. other pages) between them: [T1 + *with* (*usu. pass.*)] *The book of flower drawings was interleaved with transparent paper to protect the pictures.*

**intermarry with** *v prep*
**1** (of a group of people) to become related by marriage to (another group): [IØ + *with*] *The shipwrecked sailors intermarried with the natives living on the island, forming a healthy mixed group which is still strong today.*
**2** to marry each other or someone else (within the same group, family, etc.): [IØ + *with*] *Members of some ancient races intermarried with their own sisters.*

**intermingle with** *v prep*
to mix, often secretly, with (usu. other people): [IØ + *with*] *Policemen in plain clothes intermingled with the crowd to prevent trouble during the foreign ruler's state visit.*

**intern in** *v prep* → **inter in**
to imprison (someone), usu. without trial, in (a place), often in wartime or to prevent trouble; keep (a ship) in (a port): [T1 + *in* (*usu. pass.*)] *Prisoners of war were interned in specially built camps in different parts of the country. The ship has been interned in the harbour until the police are satisfied that the goods that she carries are lawful.*

**interpose between** *v prep* → **intervene between**
*fml* to place (oneself) between (two people or parties), as in an argument: [X9 + *between* (*usu. simple tenses*)] *The chairman interposed himself between the two committee members and settled their disagreement.*

**interpose in** *v prep* → **intervene in**
*fml* to help in (a quarrel): [L9 + *in* (*usu. simple tenses*)] *The chairman interposed in the disagreement between the two committee members, and prevented them from losing their tempers.*

**interpret as** *v prep*
to regard (something) as meaning (something): [T1 + *as* (*usu. simple tenses*)] *Be careful, your silence could be interpreted as an admission of guilt.*

**intersperse among/between** *v prep*
*fml* to place (different things) between or among (something or two or more other things): [X9 + *among/between* (*usu. pass.*)] *Small dots were interspersed among the pattern.*

**intersperse with** *v prep*
*fml* to vary or interrupt (something) with (something or things different): [X9 + *with* (*usu. pass.*)] *The pattern was interspersed with small dots.*

**intervene between** *v prep* → **interpose between**
to come between (two people or parties) t

try to influence or settle a disagreement: [IØ + *between* (*usu. simple tenses*)] *The government asked a leading lawyer to intervene between the workers and the employers in the argument over pay. Do you think that someone should intervene between Jim and Mary when they are quarrelling so bitterly?*

**intervene in** *v prep* → **interpose in**
to enter (a quarrel) so as to try to influence or settle it: [IØ + *in* (*usu. simple tenses*)] *The chairman felt that it was his place to intervene in the disagreement between two of his committee members.*

**interweave with** *v prep*
to weave (something) together with (something else): [T1 + *with* (*usu. pass.*)] *Some wool has been interwoven with the silk, to make the cloth heavier and stronger.*

**intimate to** *v prep* → **hint to**
*fml* to suggest (something) to (someone): [T5 + *to*] *The director intimated to the chairman that a decision was expected from the committee very soon. A government speaker intimated to the reporters that they could expect a statement shortly.*

**intimidate into** *v prep* → **frighten into, scare into, terrify into**
*fml* to persuade (someone) through fear into (doing something): [T1 + *into*] *The salesman intimidated the old lady into signing the paper, by threatening to take away the goods.*

**intoxicate with** *v prep*
**be intoxicated with**
**1** to be drunk because of the effect of (alcohol): *How can Mary be intoxicated with the small amount of wine that she has drunk?*
**2** to be excited by (something): *Intoxicated with her unexpected success, the singer burst into tears of joy.* also **intoxicate by**

**intrigue against** *v prep* → **conspire against, plot against**
to make secret plans, usu. with other people, against (someone or something): [IØ + *against*] *The men were imprisoned for intriguing against the government.*

**intrigue with** *v prep*
**1** to make secret plans together with (someone): [IØ + *with*] *Politicians intrigue with each other all the time to get what they want.* → **connive with, conspire with, plot with**
**2 be intrigued with** to be very interested in (something mysterious): *The natives were intrigued with the colour of our skin.*

**introduce into** *v prep*
**1** to put; push (something) inside (something): [T1 + *into*] *You need a special tool to introduce the pipe into the hole.*
*2 to bring (usu. something) into (a place such as a country) for the first time: [D1] *Horses are not, as is commonly thought, native to North America, but were introduced into the country in the 17th century by conquerors from Spain.*
*3 to add (something new) to (something): [D1] *I introduced a new idea into the conversation. The very end of his speech was the wrong place for the speaker to introduce new points into his argument. Modern scientific inventions have introduced many words into the language.*

**introduce to** *v prep*
**1** to make (someone) known to (someone else): [T1 + *to* (*usu. simple tenses*)] *Allow me to introduce you to my aunt. I would like to introduce my former teacher to you. I introduced Jim to Mary two years before they were married.*
*2 to make (someone) familiar with (something such as an idea); make (something) known to (someone): [D1 (*usu. simple tenses*)] *Mr Bush will introduce you to the details of your work. I was first introduced to university politics on a most unfortunate occasion. A pleasant young woman has been appointed by the city council to introduce official visitors to the city. I shall always be grateful to my former teacher for introducing me to the study of language. At this point in the concert, the singer introduced a new song to the crowd. Tom's latest book may introduce some new ideas to the public.*

**intrude into** *v prep* → **intrude on, obtrude on**
*fml* to interrupt; place (oneself) without invitation in (something such as a place or meeting): [IØ + *into*] *It is dangerous to intrude into the king's presence without permission, even to make an urgent request.* [T1 + *into*] *The angry visitor tried to intrude himself into the council meeting.*

**intrude on/upon** *v prep* → **intrude into, obtrude on**
*fml* to interrupt; place (oneself) without invitation in (something such as a conversation) or with (someone): [IØ + *on/upon*] *I hope I'm not intruding on your time too much by asking you to read this paper. Forgive me for intruding on your private sorrow, I had not heard the sad news.* [T1 + *on/upon*] *You have no right to intrude yourself on me/on my thoughts like this, I am busy working.*

***intrust to** *v prep* → ENTRUST TO

***intrust with** *v prep* → ENTRUST WITH

**inundate with** *v prep* → **flood with,** etc.
**1** to cover (usu. an area) with (water): [T1 + *with* (*usu. pass.*)] *The fields were inundated with the heavy rain.*
**2** to crowd; flood (usu. something) with (a lot of things or something): [D1 (*usu. pass.*)] *The office was inundated with complaints about the washing machines.*

***inure from** *v prep*
*fml* to take effect from (a date): [T1 (*no pass., simple tenses*)] *Your unemployment insurance will inure from the third week of your being out of work.*

***inure to** *v prep* also **enure to**
to make (someone) accustomed to (something difficult or painful, etc.) by experience: [D1

(*usu. pass.*)] *Bears are inured to the cold. Farmers are inured to hard work. The old soldier was so inured to danger that he became careless.*

***invalid home** *v adv*
esp. *BrE* to send (usu. a soldier or government official working abroad) back to his own country because of ill-health: [T1 (*usu. pass.*)] *It's worth getting a small wound to be invalided home.*

***invalid out** *v adv*
esp. *BrE* to allow (someone) to leave (a military force or government service) because of ill-health: [T1 (*of*) (*usu. pass.*)] *Captain Miller was disappointed when he was invalided out (of the army) after a nasty attack of lung disease, as he had intended to become a professional soldier.*

***inveigh against** *v prep*
*fml* to attack (someone or something) bitterly in words: [T1] *Letters appear regularly in the newspaper inveighing against the misuse of the English language.*

***inveigle into** *v prep*
to persuade (someone), often by deceit, into (doing something): [V4b] *The salesman tried to inveigle the old lady into giving him her money, but she was too clever for him.*

**invest in** *v prep*
**1** to place (one's money) in (something) in hope of a profit: [IØ + *in* (*usu. simple tenses*)] *Many people think it safest to invest in property.* [T1 + *in* (*usu. simple tenses*)] *Jim's father invested his own father's fortune in the business, which luckily was successful.*
***2** *not fml* to buy (something): [T1 (*usu. simple tenses*)] *I think it's time I invested in a new pair of shoes.*
***3** to place one's hopes in (something): [T1] *Education is the best way for a nation to invest in the future.*

**invest with** *v prep*
**1** *fml* to clothe (someone) formally in (special clothes): [T1 + *with*] *During the service, a ceremony was held to invest the new priest with the garments of his office.*
***2** *fml* to honour (someone) with (a reward, title, etc.): [D1] *The Queen invested the brave soldier with the Military Cross.*
***3** *fml* to give (someone) (special powers): [D1 (*usu. pass.*)] *The general was invested with the command of the whole army.*
***4** *fml* to give (something) (a quality): [D1 (*often pass.*)] *History books often seem to be invested with an air of unreality.*

**invite in** *v adv* → **ask in**
to ask (someone) politely to enter: [X9 + IN] *Don't keep your aunt standing on the doorstep, invite her in!*

**invite out** *v adv* → **ask out,** etc.
to ask (someone) to share a meal or other social occasion: [X9 + OUT] *This is the second time that nice young man has invited me out!*

**invite over/round** *v adv* → **ask over, ask round, have over' (1), have round**
to ask (someone) to be one's guests, usu. from a short distance: [X9 + OVER/ROUND] *When are we going to invite the Millers over? We owe them a dinner invitation.*

**invite to** *v prep* → **ask to**
to ask (someone) to be one's guest at (an event, occasion, etc.): [X9 + *to*] *Do we really have to invite all my insufferable relatives to the wedding?*

**invoke from** *v prep*
*fml* to call (something) out from (someone): [T1 + *from* (*usu. simple tenses*)] *Careful nursing may gradually invoke life from a dying person.*

**invoke on/upon** *v prep* → **call down on**
*fml* to request that (something) descend, as from heaven, on (someone): [T1 + *on/upon* (*usu. simple tenses*)] *The priest invoked punishment on the people for their evil ways.*

**involve in** *v prep*
to cause (someone or something) to be part of, included in, mixed with, or deeply concerned in (something or doing something): [T1 + *in* (*often simple tenses*)] *Try to involve your mother in the general activity of the house, it'll be good for her. A city bus and a train were involved in a terrible crash at the railway crossing, in which nine people were killed. Don't involve me in your crime—I had nothing to do with it! How many of the children are involved in preparing for the concert?*

**involve with** *v prep*
**be involved with** to have a close relationship with (usu. someone): *How long has Grace been involved with that red-haired boy? I don't want my son to be involved with criminals.*

**iron out** *v adv* → **smooth out**
**1** to flatten (cloth or folds in cloth) with a hot iron: [T1 + OUT] *I always iron out the folds in new sheets, so that they are more comfortable to sleep in.*
***2** to remove or find an answer to (something such as a difficulty): [T1a] *The board of directors are trying to iron out the difficulties connected with the new contract.*

**isolate from** *v prep*
to separate; set apart (something or someone) from (something or someone), as for protection; regard (something) as separate from (something): [T1 + *from*] *Scientists are working to isolate certain chemicals important to medicine, from the natural substances in which they are found. A child with a catching disease should be isolated from other children in the family. Many hospitals still isolate new-born babies from their mothers, in spite of modern medical opinion that this practice is harmful to both mother and child. Alcoholism cannot be isolated from other difficulties caused by crowded city living and the worries of modern life.*

**issue as** *v prep*
to produce (something) in (a certain form): [T1 + *as*] *Tom hopes that his next book will be issued as a paperback, as this will increase the sales. It was clever of the writer to issue this idea as an invention.*

* **issue forth** *v adv*
*old use fml* to come out in a formal manner: [IØ] *The king issued forth from his castle, attended by all his servants and making a show of his wealth and power, to pay a formal visit to a neighbouring ruler.*

**issue from/out of** *v prep; adv prep*
**1** to come out from (something) in quantity: [L9 + *from*/OUT + *of*] *Blood issued from the wound in a flow which could not be stopped.*
* **2** to come or result from (something): [T1 (*no pass., simple tenses*)] *His difficulties issue from his lack of knowledge.*

**issue to** *v prep*
to supply (something needed) to (someone): [T1 + *to*] *The end hut is to be used for issuing guns to the new soldiers.*

* **issue with** *v prep*
to supply (someone) with (something needed): [D1] *Have all the students been issued with books for the new course?*

* **itch for** *v prep* → **long for, sigh for** (2), **yearn for**
*infml* to want to have (something) soon; desire (something) urgently: [T1 (*no pass., usu. continuous tenses*)] *Those two boys are itching for a fight, they've been on the edge of a quarrel all day.* [V3] *I'm itching for them to go.*

# J

**jab at** *v prep* → **poke at** (1), **prod at**
to give a quick sharp push or blow to (something or someone): [L9 + *at*] *He jabbed at the meat with his knife, but it was too hard to cut. The fighter won not by a single blow, but by jabbing at his opponent so often that he weakened him.*

**jab into** *v prep* → **poke into** (1), **stick into** (2)
to push (something) sharply into (something): [X9 + *into*] *Don't jab your finger into my stomach like that—it's rude as well as painful!*

**jab out** *v adv* → **poke out** (2)
to push (something) out with a quick sharp blow: [X9 + OUT] *Mind where you put your elbow, you nearly jabbed my eye out!*

**jack in** *v adv* esp. *BrE* → **pack in** (3)

**jack up** *v adv*
**1** to lift (something such as a vehicle) with a special tool: [T1] *You have to jack up the car in order to change a wheel.* —**jacked-up** *adj*
**2** *infml* to raise (something such as prices or wages): [T1] *Everyone is afraid that taxes will be jacked up again soon.*
**3** *infml* to add strength to; increase (something): [T1] *He needed a small drink to jack up his failing courage.*
**4** *infml* to make arrangements for (something): [T1] *The theatre company are going on tour and want you to jack everything up for them.*
**5** *AmE infml* to scold; find fault with (someone): [T1] *The director jacked Jim up for being late again.* → **tell off** (1), etc.
**6** *AmE infml* to encourage (someone) to fulfil his responsibilities: [T1] *One of the committee members is not doing his fair share of the work; see what you can do to jack him up.*

**jam in**[1] *v adv* → **crowd in**[1] (1), etc.
*not fml* to push, press, or pack (things or people) tightly in a space: [X9 + IN] *You'll have to catch the next bus, we can't possibly jam any more passengers in.*

**jam into/in**[2] *v prep* → **crowd into**[2] (1), etc.
to push, press, or pack (things or people) tightly into (a space): [X9 + *into*/*in*] *How are you going to jam all those clothes in(to) that small case?* [L9 + *into*/*in*] *Far too many football supporters tried to jam into the small ground.*

**jam on** *v adv*
**1** to put (something) on hurriedly and hard: [X9 + ON (*usu. simple tenses*)] *He jammed on his hat and rushed out of the house.* → **clap on**[1] (1), **slam on** (1), **slap on**[1] (1)
* **2** to use (something) hurriedly, as by pressing: [T1 (*usu. simple tenses*)] *The driver jammed on the brakes but failed to stop in time.* → **clap on**[1] (2), **slam on** (2)

**jam together** *v adv*
to (cause to) be packed tightly together: [L9 + TOGETHER] *The crowd jammed together to get a good view of the famous visitor.* [X9 + TOGETHER (*usu. pass.*)] *All the cars were jammed together at one end of the bridge.*

**jam up** *v adv* → **gum up** (2)
**jam up the works** *infml* to spoil; cause difficulty in something: *The committee was doing well until the chairman's independent action jammed up the works.*

**jam with** *v prep* → **cram with**
to fill (a space) tightly with (something, things, or people): [X9 + *with* (*usu. pass.*)] *The roads are jammed with cars taking people to the horse show. The room was jammed with people wanting to buy the furniture.*

**jangle on/upon** *v prep* → **get on**[2] (14), **grate on** (2), **jar on**
**jangle on someone's ears/nerves** (of a noise) to annoy someone; offend someone's sensibili-

ties; be painful or unpleasant to hear: *The baby's endless crying jangles on my nerves. The piano is badly out of tune and jangles on my ears.*

**jar against** *v prep*
to touch (something) with a sharp unpleasant noise: [L9 + *against*] *The boat, coming in too close, jarred against the protective edging of the harbour wall.*

**jar on** *v prep* → **get on²** (14), **grate on** (2), **jangle on**
**jar on someone/someone's ears/nerves** to annoy someone; offend someone's sensitivity; be painful to hear: *The baby's endless crying jars on my nerves. The boy's manner of speech jarred on the teacher, who came from a different part of the country. The singer's high notes jarred on the ears of her listeners.*

**jar with** *v prep*
**1** to not match (something): [L9 + *with* (*usu. simple tenses*)] *The orange curtains jar with the red furniture.* → **clash against** (2), **clash with** (1)
***2** to disagree with; be opposite to (usu. an opinion): [T1 (*no pass.*)] *The chairman's opinion jarred with that of the rest of the committee.* → **conflict with** (2), etc.

***jaw at** *v prep*
*infml* to scold; talk to (someone) at length, esp. to teach (someone) how to behave, work, etc.: [T1] *The head teacher has been jawing at us all morning about the importance of the examinations, as if we didn't know!*

***jazz up** *v adv* → **juice up**
*infml* to make (something) more active, interesting, or enjoyable: [T1] *Let's jazz this party up, it's very dull.*

**jeer at** *v prep* → **laugh at** (2), etc.
to make fun of (someone or something) unkindly; make cruel remarks about (someone or something); make disapproving noises at (someone such as a speaker): [IØ + *at*] *The crowd jeered at the politician when he promised full employment and lower prices, as they knew that he could not possibly fulfil this. At first the public jeered at the modern painter's works, but later they proved to be highly regarded and very valuable.*

**jerk away** *v adv* → **drag away** (1), **pull away** (1), **take away** (1), **yank away**
to pull (something) away sharply: [X9 + AWAY (*usu. simple tenses*)] *Mary put her hand on Jim's, but he was still angry with her and jerked his hand away.*

***jerk off** *v adv* → **play with** (9), **pull at** (4), **toss off** (5)
esp. *AmE taboo sl* (of males) to (cause to) give pleasure by touching the sexual organ; masturbate: [IØ] *A few of the boys who had escaped from the school were found jerking off in the bushes.* [T1b] *They had been taking turns to jerk each other off.*

**jerk out** *v adv*
to speak (something) with difficulty, in quick bursts: [X9 + OUT (*usu. simple tenses*)] *In spite of his fear, he jerked out his request.*

**jerk up** *v adv* → **pull up** (1), etc.
to pull; raise (something or someone) up, sharply and roughly: [X9 + UP (*usu. simple tenses*)] *Suddenly one of the boys jerked his hand up; he was daring to offer an answer! Don't jerk the box up, pull it up smoothly.*

**jest at** *v prep* → **laugh at** (2), etc.
*old use* to make fun of (someone or something) unkindly; not treat (something or someone) seriously: [IØ + *at*] *Why do you jest at my honesty? "He jests at scars, that never felt a wound."* (Shakespeare, *Romeo and Juliet*)

***jib at** *v prep* → **balk at**
*not fml* to be unwilling to face or agree to (something or doing something): [T1 (*often simple tenses*)] *The horse jibbed at the high fence and the rider fell off. The committee were willing to listen to your ideas, but have jibbed at your latest suggestion.* [T4 (*often simple tenses*)] *Jim jibbed at paying such a lot of money to join the club.*

**jibe at** *v prep* → GIBE AT

**jibe with** *v prep*
esp. *AmE* to be the same as; match; agree with (something, often written or spoken): [L9 + *with* (*simple tenses*)] *The prisoner's story jibes with his companion's account of the robbery; it seems that he has been telling the truth.*

***jockey for** *v prep*
**1** (esp. in a horse race) to push others aside in order to gain (a position favourable to winning): [T1 (*often continuous tenses*)] *After jockeying for position, the favourite has now taken the lead.*
**2** to compete for (something), often by pushing others aside, taking unfair advantage, etc.: [T1 (*often continuous tenses*)] *More than ten politicians are now jockeying for the leadership of the Party.*

**jog along/on** *v adv*
**1** to move steadily forward with a half-running step: [IØ + ALONG/ON] *You can see several businessmen jogging along in the park every morning for their health.*
***2** *not fml* to advance steadily, often in a dull manner: [IØ (*usu. continuous tenses*)] *How's work? Oh, jogging along all right, but it isn't exactly exciting.*

***jog in** *v adv* → **set in** (5)
(in theatre) to add (an additional piece of scenery) at an angle to other pieces: [T1] *The scenery does not fill the space properly; we shall have to jog in another piece here.*

**jog on** *v adv* → JOG ALONG

**join in¹** *v adv* → **join in with**
to take part: [L9 + IN (*often simple tenses*)] *Sarah never joins in; she always plays on her own. The sports day is an occasion which we can all join in. At the end of the concert, a lonely listener began to cheer, and soon the whole crowd joined in.*

**join in²** *v prep*
to take part in (something or doing something): share with (someone) in (something such as an activity or meal, or doing something): [L9 + *in* (*often simple tenses*))] *May I join in your conversation? The whole crowd joined in singing the popular song.* [X9 + *in* (*often simple tenses*)] *Do join me in a swim. Will you join me in a drink? Jim joined his father in helping to make the business a success. All the family join me in wishing you a happy future.*

**join in with** *v adv prep*
**1** to take part with (someone): [L9 + IN + *with* (*often simple tenses*)] *My aunt and uncle have asked me to join in with them on their holiday abroad, as I speak the language.* → **join in**
*__2__ to share a cost with (someone): [T1] *We joined in with another family to buy the boat and share it for our holidays. We may have to join in with the other college in building the library.*

**join on¹** *v adv*
to (cause to) be added to something or someone, often by fixing: [L9 + ON (*often simple tenses*)] *When the climbers looked back, they saw that two uninvited visitors had joined on. How do the legs of this toy animal join on?* [X9 + ON (*often simple tenses*)] *The train will stop at the next station to join two more carriages on for the football supporters.*

**join on/onto/to²** *v prep* → **couple on**
to fix; add (something) to (something): [L9 + *on/onto/to* (*often simple tenses*)] *Halfway through the climb, two uninvited visitors joined onto the party of climbers. The head joins on the rest of the toy with wire.* [X9 + *on/onto/to* (*often simple tenses*)] *The house is joined (on)to the one next door by a wall which the two properties share. Join the blue wool onto the end of the gold pattern and work the same stitches into the back.*

**join together** *v adv*
to fix (things) into one whole: [X9 + TOGETHER] *How are the two halves of the machine joined together? Can you join the broken pieces together?*

**join up** *v adv*
**1** to (cause to) come nearer to each other: [L9 + UP] *I'm glad to see that the edges of the wound are joining up nicely.* [X9 + UP] *Children have to learn to join up their letters.* → **close up** (2, 3)
**2** to (cause to) meet and form a group or single thing: [L9 + UP (*with*) (*often simple tenses*)] *The railway tracks join up into a single line on the other side of the town. We plan to join up with the other party of climbers on the other side of the mountain.* [T1 + UP] *Arrangements are being made to join up the two firms, so as to reduce the competition. Engineers can join up distant countries by radio or telephone.* → **link up, marry up**
*__3__ esp. *BrE* to offer oneself for military service: [I0̸] *Did you join up or were you forced into the army?* → **sign off** (1), **sign on¹** (1), **sign up** (1)

**join with** *v prep*
*__1__ to show sympathy for (someone); share the feelings of (someone): [T1 (*in*) (*no pass., simple tenses*)] *We all join with Mr and Mrs Page in their sorrow. We must join with the Party in its struggle for freedom.*
**2 join batttle with** to fight or oppose (usu. someone): *Get a good night's rest, men; we join battle with the enemy at first light. One of the citizens was brave enough to join battle with the government about his right to see what films he chose.* → **battle with** (1), **engage with** (1)
**3 join forces with** to add one's strength or support to that of (someone else). *You will have more effect on the government's plans if you join forces with other groups of citizens sharing the same aims.*
**4 join hands with** to make a show of friendship with (someone such as another nation): *Let us join hands with our friends across the sea who are also working for freedom.*
**5 join issue with** to begin a disagreement with (usu. someone): *I try to change my friends' opinions on politics but they very soon join issue with me.* → **take with** (7)

**joke about** *v prep*
to treat (something) not seriously: [I0̸ + *about*] *Please don't joke about such a delicate subject. Jane's stomach trouble is nothing to joke about.*

**joke with** *v prep*
to share a joke with (someone); have fun with (someone); make a joke about (someone): [I0̸ + *with*] *I'm not serious, I was only joking with you.*

***jolly along** *v adv* → **chivy along**
*BrE not fml* to encourage (someone) through enjoyment; cheer (someone) along: [T1b] *Here comes the sports teacher to jolly us along just when we're tired out! Jane is looking so sad; see if you can jolly her along a bit.*

**jostle for** *v prep*
to push each other aside trying to gain (a position): [L9 + *for*] *A whole group of runners are jostling for first place.*

**jostle with** *v prep*
to be in a group with (others) pushing each other aside: [L9 + *with*] *Look at all those stupid men jostling with each other on the running track, as if the result was so important!*

***jot down** *v adv*
to make a quick note of (something): [T1] *I must jot down that telephone number before I forget it. If you get a good idea, jot it down at once while you remember it.*

**judge between** *v prep*
to decide which is the better of (two things or people): [I0̸ + *between* (*usu. simple tenses*)] *It's impossible to judge between the two paint-*

*ings, they're both charming. It's so hard to judge between two such nice houses.*

**judge by/from** *v prep*

**1** to base one's opinion of (something) on (something): [T1 + *by/from* (*usu. simple tenses*)] *You can't judge a man's character by his looks. The age of a good wine can be judged from its colour, smell, and taste.*

**2** to form an opinion based on (something): [IØ + *by/from* (*simple tenses*)] *To judge by the address, the house is a long way from the town centre. Judging from her letters, Mother seems to be feeling a lot better.*

**juggle about/around** *v adv*

to move (things) in different directions or into different positions: [T1 + ABOUT/AROUND] *Why is Mary always juggling the furniture around? It's in a different arrangement every time we visit the house!*

**juggle with** *v prep*

**1** to throw (objects) from hand to hand, always keeping one or more in the air, as in a performance: [IØ + *with*] *The magician amused the crowd before his main trick, by juggling with some coloured balls and plates.*

***2** to deal with (facts) cleverly, often so as to cheat: [T1] *I don't think I shall be able to juggle with my tax return this year. The directors always spend the last few days of the year juggling with the figures so as to show a profit.*

***juice up** *v adv* → **jazz up**

*AmE infml* to make (something) more lively, interesting, exciting, etc.: [T1] *The writer has thought it necessary to juice up his stories with accounts of his sexual adventures.*

**jumble together** *v adv*

to mix; put (things) together in a disordered pile: [T1 + TOGETHER (*usu. pass.*)] *I left my papers separated neatly in order, and when I got back they had all been jumbled together, and it took me an hour to sort them out.*

**jumble up** *v adv* → **mix up** (2), **muddle up** (1)

*not fml* to confuse; mix; mistake; disorder (things or ideas): [T1 + UP (*usu. pass.*)] *My papers are all jumbled up, and I was trying to keep them in alphabetical order. I'm sorry I got your names jumbled up, they're so much alike. I have a terrible headache and my thoughts are all jumbled up. I got him jumbled up with his brother!*

**jump at** *v prep* → **leap at**

**1** to spring at (usu. someone): [IØ + *at*] *Please stop your dog jumping at me, he'll get my coat dirty.*

***2** *not fml* to be eager to accept (a chance or offer): [T1 (*often simple tenses*)] *We ought to jump at the chance to buy the house at that price, but Mother isn't sure whether she likes it. Everyone was surprised when Jim didn't jump at his father's offer of a partnership.*

**jump down** *v prep*

**1** to spring down (something descending such as stairs): [IØ + *down*] *Try to stop the children from jumping down the stairs, one da[y] they'll get hurt.*

**2 jump down someone's throat** to be (too) quick to be angry with someone: *I daren't te[ll] Mother I broke the dinner plates, she'll jum[p] down my throat. There's no need to jum[p] down my throat, it wasn't my fault!*

**jump in** *v adv* → **leap in**

**1** to enter something with a springing move[-]ment: [IØ + IN] *The water's lovely and war[m] in the pool, jump in!*

***2** *not fml* to be eager to do something; ac[t] urgently: [IØ (*often simple tenses*)] *Don't tak[e] too long deciding, or the other firm may jum[p] in with their offer. As soon as permission t[o] attack arrived, the company jumped in wi[th] both feet.*

**jump off** *v adv*

**1** to leave a place with a springing mov[e]ment: [IØ + OFF] *The boys had a game [of] climbing the wall and then jumping off.*

***2** *mil* to start; advance: [IØ (*usu. simp[le] tenses*)] *The attack will jump off at first ligh[t].* —**jump-off** *n* —**jumping-off** *adj*

***3** (in a horse-jumping competition) to ri[de] the whole course again after several ride[rs] have jumped faultlessly: [IØ + *off*] *The fi[ve] successful riders will now jump off.* —**jump-o[ff]** *n*

**jump off** *v prep*

**1** to leave (something) with a springi[ng] movement: [IØ + *off*] *The boys had a gam[e] of climbing the wall and then jumping o[ff] it.*

**2 jump off the deep end** *infml* to speak ve[ry] angrily, often without cause: *What's she jum[p]ing off the deep end for now? Has somebo[dy] said something wrong?* → **dive off** (2), **go off** [...]

**jump on** *v prep*

**1** to stand on top of (something or someon[e]) quickly: [IØ + *on*] *The paper caught fire, b[ut] Jim put it out by jumping on it.*

***2** *not fml* to scold; find fault with (someon[e]) suddenly: [T1] *The captain was well-kno[wn] for jumping on men whom he disliked, for t[he] least little fault. I don't enjoy this class, I'[m] always afraid of being jumped on.* also **jump over** → **pick on** (3), etc., **tell off** (1), etc.

**3 jump on the bandwagon** *not fml* to co[py] other people's successful actions: *While pric[es] are rising so fast, many shops think they c[an] jump on the bandwagon and raise their pric[es] too.* → **climb on** (2)

**jump out of** *v adv prep* → **leap out of**

**1** to leave (a place) suddenly, with a sprin[g]ing movement: [IØ + OUT + *of* (*often sim[ple] tenses*)] *I was walking up the garden p[ath] when one of the children jumped out of [the] bushes and surprised me.*

**2 jump out of one's skin** *not fml* to receive t[he] shock of a surprise: [(*usu. simple tenses*)] *O[h,] you gave me such a shock, coming up behi[nd] me so quietly, you made me jump out of [my] skin.*

**jump over** *v prep*
**1** to (cause to) pass over (something) by jumping: [IØ + *over*] *Can you jump over this rope?* [T1 + *over*] *And now the leading rider has jumped her horse safely over the last fence.*
**2 jump all over** → **JUMP ON** (2)

**jump to** *v prep*
**1** to go quickly to (another point or scene) by leaving something out: [T1 (*no pass., usu. simple tenses*)] *Let's jump to the next scene and try that next. Suddenly the film jumped to Rose's marriage.* → **cut ahead to, cut to** (2)
**2 jump to attention** *mil* to be quick to stand in a formal position: [(*usu. simple tenses, usu. imper.*)] *Jump to attention when the captain enters.* → **stand at** (3), etc.
**3 jump to conclusions** to be too quick to make a judgment based on too few facts: *Wait until you have all the proofs, don't jump to conclusions.* → **rush to**
**4 jump to it!** *infml* to be quick: [(*usu. imper.*)] *Jump to it, men, we must get all the tents packed in an hour!* → **hop to**

**jump up** *v adv*
**1** to spring upwards: [IØ + UP] *The child was crying because the big dog had jumped up at him. The step isn't high—jump up!* → **leap up** (1)
**2** to rise from one's seat suddenly: [IØ + UP (*from*) (*usu. simple tenses*)] *He jumped up (from his chair) when the doorbell rang, hoping that it was Rose.* → **leap up** (2), **shoot up** (2), **spring up** (1), **start up** (2)
**3 be jumped-up** *infml derog* to have too great an idea of one's own importance, esp. because of having just risen high socially. *Don't take any notice of her false air of importance, She's just jumped-up.* → **bump up** (2)

**justify by** *v prep*
to make (something) seem right because of or by means of (something or doing something): [T1 + *by* (*usu. simple tenses*)] *The prisoner has certainly justified his claims by his actions. The criminal attempted to justify his crime by claiming that he had not been responsible for his actions at the time of the murder.*

**justify to** *v prep*
to make (something) seem right to (someone): [T1 + *to* (*usu. simple tenses*)] *Can you justify your rude behaviour to me? "And justify the ways of God to men."* (Milton, *Paradise Lost*)

***jut out** *v adv* → **poke out** (1), **project from, protrude from, stand out** (2), **stick out** (1)
to be in a position further forward than its surroundings: [IØ (*usu. simple tenses*)] *The wall juts out here to allow room for the chimney. I don't like the way his ears jut out.*

# K

**keel over** *v adv* also **cant over, heel over**
**1** (of a ship or boat) to turn completely over, usu. before sinking: [IØ] *The ship keeled over when it hit the rocks, and sank to the bottom with all its passengers and sailors.*
**2** to fall over, losing control of one's balance: [IØ] *He keeled over with laughter when I told him the joke. "Dorina fainted, keeling over from her chair onto the floor."* (Iris Murdoch, *An Accidental Man*)

**keep about/around**[1] *v adv* → **have about**[1]
to have (something) always present, near one: [T1 + ABOUT/AROUND (*usu. simple tenses*)] *I like to keep a few envelopes about in case I need them.*

**keep about/around**[2] *v prep* → **have about**[2] (1)
to have (something or someone) always present in (somewhere, usu. the house, a place, etc.): [T1 + *about/around* (*usu. simple tenses*)] *People who live in the country often keep two or three dogs around the place for their own protection. Not many people nowadays keep servants about the house.*

**keep above** *v prep*
**keep one's head above water**
**1** to prevent oneself from sinking: *If you can keep your head above water, you won't drown.*
**2** *not fml* to prevent failure; have enough money to live on; be able to deal with work, life, etc.: *The cost of living is now so high that you need to earn a good income just to keep your head above water. I've so much work to do this month that I don't know how I'm going to keep my head above water.*

***keep abreast of** *v adv prep*
**1** to remain level with (someone or something ahead): [T1 (*no pass.*)] *You will have to run fast to keep abreast of our best runner and prevent him from winning.* → **be abreast of** (1), **get abreast of** (1), **remain abreast of** (1), **stay abreast of** (1)
**2** to remain fully informed about (something in advance); stay level with something: [T1 (*pass. rare, often simple tenses*)] *Scientists have to work hard to keep abreast of new discoveries and developments.* → **be abreast of** (2), **get abreast of** (2), **remain abreast of** (2), **stay abreast of** (2)

***keep after** *v prep*
**1** to continue chasing (someone or an animal): [T1 (*no pass., often simple tenses*)] *The police kept after the criminals until at last they caught them.* → **come after** (2), etc.
**2** *not fml* to scold; find fault with (someone); repeatedly ask (someone) (to do something): [T1 (*no pass., often simple tenses*)] *She keeps after the children the whole time, never lets*

*them have a minute's peace.* [V3] *She kept after me for a year to buy her a new coat, till in the end I agreed, to have some peace from her.* → **go on at** (2), etc.

**keep ahead** *v adv* → **move ahead,** etc.

**1** to remain in a forward or leading position, in front of others: [L9 + AHEAD (*often simple tenses*)] *If I can only keep ahead for a few more yards, I can win this race.*

*__2__ to remain in advance, as in a competition: [IØ (*of*)] *Jane used to have difficulty with her school work, but she has been keeping ahead for the past year. If you want to keep ahead in your job, you should ensure that your good work is noticed by those in power.*

**keep ahead of** *v adv prep* → **be ahead of, get ahead of, remain ahead of, stay ahead of**

**1** to remain in a position in front of, beyond, or past (someone or something), esp. in a competition, race, etc.: [L9 + AHEAD + *of*] *If I can only keep ahead of the other runners for a few more yards, I think I can win this race.*

*__2__ to remain in advance of (something or someone such as a competitor): [IØ + *of*] *Unfortunately, my spending always seems to keep ahead of my income. You have to keep ahead of your competitors in business or you will fail. Jane has kept ahead of the rest of the class recently.*

**3 keep one step ahead of** *not fml* to remain only a little way in advance of (someone or something): *Jim's father often said that one secret of his success in business was that he always kept one step ahead of public demand.*

*__keep aloof__ *v adv* → **hang back,** etc.

to remain; keep (oneself) at a distance, (usu. from people): [IØ; T1 (*from*) (*often simple tenses*)] *Mary does not enjoy parties, and usually keeps (herself) aloof from the other guests, not joining in conversation.*

**keep apart** *v adv*

to (cause to) remain separate: [L9 + APART (*from*) (*simple tenses*)] *He's a strange boy, he keeps apart from all the activities in the school.* [X9 + APART (*from*) (*usu. simple tenses*)] *I like to keep my work apart from my family. I don't like to mix business with pleasure, but try to keep the two things firmly apart. We don't want those dogs fighting—keep them apart can't you?*

**keep around**[1] *v adv* → **KEEP ABOUT**[1]

**keep around**[2] *v prep* → **KEEP ABOUT**[2]

**keep at** *v prep*

**1** to have (something) present in (a place): [T1 + *at* (*usu. simple tenses*)] *I keep a warm coat at work in case it suddenly turns cold.*

**2** to delay (someone) at (a place): [X9 + *at* (*usu. simple tenses*)] *I'm sorry I'm late, I was kept at the office.*

*__3__ to (cause to) continue working at (something): [T1 (*often simple tenses*)] *If you keep (hard) at your work, you'll soon have the job finished.* [D1 (*often simple tenses*)] *This new teacher certainly keeps his students hard at their work.* → **be at** (3,14), **stick at** (1), **stick to** (5), **stick with** (3)

*__4__ *not fml* to repeatedly ask (someone) (to do something): [V3 (*often simple tenses*)] *She kept at me for a year to buy her a new coat, until in the end I agreed, just so as to have some peace from her.* → **go on at** (2), etc.

**5 keep someone at arm's length/at a distance** to refuse to have a relationship with someone or allow someone to come near: [(*usu. simple tenses*)] *The director keeps all the office workers at a distance, and does not encourage anyone to be friendly. I have been kept at arm's length from all the committee's decisions.* → **hang back,** etc.

**6 keep someone/something at bay** to make (an animal, enemy, or trouble) remain at a distance, at least for a time: [(*often simple tenses*)] *The fox turned, and, fighting fiercely, kept the dogs at bay for two hours. If we fire all our bullets tonight, we should at least keep the enemy at bay until tomorrow morning. Have some hot soup before you go out, to keep the cold at bay. A piece of cheese will keep hunger at bay for an hour or more.* → **hold at, hold off** (1)

**keep away** *v adv* → **be away** (2), **remain away, stay away, stop away**

to (cause to) remain at a distance, be absent, etc.: [X9 + AWAY (*from*) (*often simple tenses*)] *Nothing will keep me away from an exciting play. We missed you at the party—what kept you away? An apple a day keeps the doctor away. The fence is intended to keep traffic away from the lake shore. I shall keep Jane away from school until her stomach trouble is better. We haven't seen you in ages—what's been keeping you away?* [L9 + AWAY (*from*) (*simple tenses*)] *Keep away, or I'll call the police! Danger: thin ice. Keep away. Keep away from the edge of the water.*

**keep away from** *v adv prep*

**1** to (cause to) remain at a distance from (someone or something): [L9 + AWAY + *from* (*simple tenses*)] *Keep away from me, I've got a bad cold.* [X9 + AWAY + *from* (*usu. simple tenses*)] *The climber used his feet to keep his body away from the cliff face.*

*__2__ to avoid (something harmful): [T1 (*pass. rare, usu. simple tenses*)] *The doctor advised Jim to keep away from fattening foods.* → **keep off**[2] (2), **stay away from, stay off** (2)

**keep back** *v adv*

**1** to remain in a position away from something; move backwards: [L9 + BACK (*from*) (*simple tenses*)] *Keep back! The roof is falling!* → **move back** (1), etc.

**2** to keep (something or someone) in place; prevent (something or someone) from coming forward: [X9 + BACK (*usu. simple tenses*)] *The men built banks of earth to keep back the rising flood waters. Police horses were used to keep back the crowd. These leather bands are*

*for keeping the horse back.* → **hold back** (1)
*3 to control (something such as a feeling): [T1 (*usu. simple tenses*)] *Jim was able to keep back his anger and avoid a fight. She was unable to keep back her tears, and wept freely.* → **hold back** (2), **hold in**[1] (3), **keep down** (4), **keep in**[1] (4)
*4 to prevent the development of (someone): [T1b] *You show promise as a musician but your lack of practice is keeping you back.* → **hold back** (3)
*5 to delay (something or someone): [T1] *I can't keep the meal back for more than half an hour to wait for our guest. I'm sorry we're late; we started in good time, but heavy rain on the roads kept us back.* → **hang up** (3), **hold back** (4), **hold off** (2), **hold up** (2), **keep off**[1] (2)
*6 to keep (something) secret: [T1 (*from*)] *We must hear the whole story, don't keep anything back (from us).* → **hold back** (5), **keep from** (1)
*7 to prevent (someone or oneself) from being active: [T1b] *The fighter accepted money to keep himself back from winning the fight. You have a good chance to win, so why not try—what's keeping you back?* → **hold back** (7)

**keep behind**[1] *v adv*
**1** to remain at a distance behind usu. something: [L9 + BEHIND (*often simple tenses*)] *It's safest to keep a good distance behind in case the car in front suddenly stops.* → **remain behind**[1] (1), **stay behind**[1] (1)
*2 to make (someone) remain after others have gone: [T1b (*often simple tenses*)] *Jane was late home because she was kept behind at school to finish some work.* → **keep in**[1] (5), etc.

**keep behind**[2] *v prep*
**1** to have (something) placed or present at the back of (something): [T1 + *behind*] *You've got a present for me, I know you have, you're keeping your hand behind your back to hide it! I keep urgent letters behind the clock so that I will be reminded to reply to them.* → **be behind**[2] (1), **place behind** (1), **put behind**[2] (1)
**2** to remain at a distance behind (something or someone): [L9 + *behind* (*often simple tenses*)] *It's safest to keep well behind the car in front in case it suddenly stops. Keep behind the leading runner until the last few yards, then pass him.* → **stay behind**[2]

**keep by**[1] *v adv*
to have (something) at hand: [T1 + BY (*usu. simple tenses*)] *I always keep a new tin of coffee by in case we suddenly need some more.*

**keep by**[2] *v prep*
**1** to have (something) at hand near (one or something): [T1 + *by* (*usu. simple tenses*)] *I find it helpful to keep several dictionaries by me so as to compare their wording. I always keep a drink of water by my bedside in case I am thirsty in the middle of the night.*
**2** to remain close to (something or someone): [L9 + *by* (*often simple tenses*)] *Keep close by the leader and then you won't lose your way* → **cling onto** (1), **cling to** (2), **stay by stick to** (2), **stick with** (2)

***keep clear of** *v adv prep* → **remain clear of, stay clear of, steer clear of** (2)
*not fml* to (cause to) avoid (something or someone): [T1 (*usu. simple tenses*)] *When you're in a tropical country, keep clear of insects which may be carrying dangerous diseases.* [D1 (*usu. simple tenses*)] *The police were out on the road with signals to keep the traffic clear of the accident.*

**keep cool** *v adj* → **remain cool, stay cool**
**1** to remain cold; prevent (something or someone) from becoming too warm: [L9 + cool (*usu. simple tenses*)] *How do you keep so cool in such hot weather? I keep cool by staying in the shade and not moving much.* [X9 + cool (*usu. simple tenses*)] *Like clothing also helps to keep you cool. Housewives used to keep milk cool by covering the bottle with a stone pot.*
*2 *not fml* to remain calm; refuse to become excited, afraid, etc.: [I∅ (*usu. simple tenses*)] *The soldier's courage was partly caused by his ability to keep cool in the face of danger.*

**keep dark** *v adj*
**1** to prevent (something) from becoming light or bright: [X9 + dark (*often simple tenses*)] *Keep the background colours dark so that the main figure will show more clearly. A photographer develops his photographs in a small room which has to be kept almost completely dark, lit only by a faint red light.*
**2 keep it dark** *not fml* to keep a secret: [(*usu. simple tenses*)] *If I tell you the secret will you promise to keep it dark?* → **keep mum, keep quiet** (2)

**keep down** *v adv*
**1** to (cause to) remain in a lower position: [L9 + DOWN (*simple tenses*)] *If there's shooting going on, keep down.* [X9 + DOWN (*usu. simple tenses*)] *If there's shooting going on, keep your head down. Keep your heels down when you are riding a horse or bicycle.* → **remain down** (1), **stay down** (1), **stop down** (1)
*2 to (cause to) remain at a lower level; remain less; prevent (something) from increasing: [I∅ (*simple tenses*)] *I hope the wind keeps down, or the sea will be too rough for sailing.* [T1] *Most of the leading food shops have promised to keep prices down until after the new year. Keep your voice down, someone might hear! Some people have more difficulty than others in keeping their weight down.* → **hold down** (2), **remain down** (2), **stay down** (2), **stop down** (2)
*3 to keep (food) in place in the stomach: [T1 (*usu. simple tenses*)] *Jane is sick again today, she hasn't been able to keep her food down.* → **hold down** (3), **stay down** (3), **stop down** (3)
*4 to control (a feeling such as anger): [T1 (*usu. simple tenses*)] *It was all I could do to keep my temper down when I saw the boys*

*treating the dog badly.* → **hold back** (2), **hold in**' (3), **keep back** (3), **keep in**' (4)

***5** to control; reduce (something), esp. by killing: [T1 (*often simple tenses*)] *Chemicals are used to keep the insects down. My mother has such trouble keeping the grass down in her flower garden.*

***6** to limit the freedom of (someone); oppress (someone): [T1b (*often simple tenses*)] *Conquering soldiers used to keep the natives down by force. You can't keep a good man down.* → **bring under**', **get under**' (2), **hold down** (5), **hold under** (2), **keep under**' (3)

***7** *BrE* to make (a child) remain in the same class for a second year, instead of moving to a higher class, as is usual: [T1b] *Jane was afraid that if she failed her examinations again, she would be kept down next year.* → **go up**' (11), **go up to** (5), **stay down** (5)

**keep fit** *v adj*

to (cause to) become or remain healthy, as through exercise: [L9 + fit] *What do you do to keep fit? I play tennis and swim.* [X9 + fit] *More exercise would keep you fit.* —**keep-fit** *adj*

**keep for** *v prep*

**1** to save (something or oneself) for (someone): [T1 + *for*] *The library will keep the book for you till the weekend. Will you keep the money for me till I get back?* → **hold for** (1), **reserve for** (1), **save for** (1)

**2** to (cause to) last or remain unused until (a time): [T1 + *for*] *I want to keep the best dishes for the party. Let's keep the new play for the opening of the theatre.* [IØ + *for* (*simple tenses*)] *Will your story keep for another time?* → **hold for** (1), **reserve for** (2), **save for** (2)

**keep from** *v prep*

**1** to keep (information) secret from (someone): [X9 + *from*] *You'd better keep the bad news from Mother until her operation is over. Can you keep a secret from your wife?* → **hold back** (5), **keep back** (6)

***2** to prevent or delay (someone or something) from (something or doing something): [D1] *I don't want to keep you from your work. Some paint will keep the wood from damage by water.* [V4b] *Don't let me keep you from going out. The government is considering further action to keep the pound from falling in value.* → **prevent from,** etc.

***3** to avoid; prevent oneself from (doing something): [T4 (*simple tenses*)] *He was so pompous, I'm afraid I could hardly keep from laughing when he slipped and fell.*

**4 keep the wolf from the door** *infml* to (allow one to) continue to be able to feed oneself and one's family: *With prices rising so fast, it's hard to keep the wolf from the door.*

***keep going** *v adj*

to (cause to) continue living or in an activity: [T1b] *This meal will keep you going for several hours. We need a new contract to keep the firm going for the rest of the year.* [IØ] *How does the old man keep going? I don't know how the firm will keep going unless we can win another contract.*

**keep in**' *v adv*

**1** to pull and make (something) stay in an inward direction: [X9 + IN] *Stand straight and keep your stomach muscles in.* → **hold in**' (1), **pull in** (2), **tuck in** (2)

**2** to cause (something such as words or actions) to remain as part of (writing, a performance, etc.): [X9 + IN] *But that's the best joke in the play we must keep it in!* → **leave in** (3)

**3 to remain at one side, esp.** while moving, as on a road: [L(WELL)9 + IN (*usu. simple tenses*)] *Keep (well) in, children, there's a lot of traffic coming!*

***4** to control (something such as a feeling or oneself): [T1 (*usu. simple tenses*)] *Jim was able to keep his anger in and avoid a fight. Jim was angry but kept himself in. It was impossible for the children to keep in their laughter any longer. I was very angry but was able to keep it in and speak to him pleasantly.* → **hold back** (2), **hold in**' (3), **keep back** (3), **keep down** (4)

***5** to (cause to) stay indoors, esp. after school as a punishment: [IØ (*usu. simple tenses*)] *If your cold's no better, you should keep in tomorrow.* [T1a (*often simple tenses*)] *Jane was late home from school because the whole class had been kept in for bad behaviour. Bad weather has kept the children in for a week and they're getting impatient.* → **keep behind**' (2), **keep indoors, remain behind**' (2), **remain in**' (1), **remain indoor, stay behind**' (2), **stay in**' (2), **stay indoors, stick in**' (2), **stick indoors, stop behind**, **stop in**' (3), **stop indoors, wait behind**

***6** (of a fire) to (cause to) continue burning [IØ (*simple tenses*)] *Will the fire keep in till we get back?* [T1b (*usu. simple tenses*)] *This new type of air control will keep the fire in all night.* → **be in**' (8), **leave in**' (2), **put out** (13), etc **remain in**' (2), **stay in** (3), **stop in**' (4)

***7** to keep a supply of (something): [T1 (*usu. simple tenses*)] *I always keep some good wine in for unexpected guests.* → **get in**' (6), **have in** (1)

**8 keep one's eye in** to remain used to judging with the eye, as in sport or shooting, usu with practice: *A promising young cricketer should practise frequently to keep his eye in* → **get in**' (16)

**9 keep one's hand in** *not fml* to practise something so as not to lose one's skill: *As a married woman with a family, I made sure to do occasional teaching to keep my hand in.* → **get in**' (18)

**keep in**² *v prep*

**1** to place; have or hold (something or someone) present in (a place): [T1 + *in*] *Why do you keep your hands in your pockets all the time? If you keep the cake in a tin, it won't get dry so quickly. The farmer kept his cows in* *field that was resting between crops. How long should a murderer be kept in prison? I shall have to keep you in hospital for another week. Do you keep the bread in this cupboard?* → **be in² (1)**, etc.

**2** to make (something, someone, or oneself) continue to be in (a state, usu. good): [X9 + *in*] *It's endless work keeping the house in good repair. How do you keep yourself in good condition during the winter?* → **maintain in** (1)

**3** to support (someone such as a wife) in (a certain style): [X9 + *in*] *If you are going to marry my daughter, I must ask you if you are prepared to keep her in the manner to which she has been accustomed. One's children should keep one in comfort in one's old age.* → **maintain in** (2)

**4** to provide (someone or oneself) with (needs): [X9 + *in*] *She doesn't earn enough to keep herself in shoe leather.* → **find in² (2)**

**5 keep something in check** to control the growth or spread of something: [(*often simple tenses*)] *We must keep our spending in check this month. All the villagers helped with the work to keep the floods in check.*

**6 keep in contact/touch (with)** to continue to meet or send messages (to someone): [(*often simple tenses*)] *Now that we've met again after all these years, let's keep in touch (with each other).* → **get in²** (3), **lose with** (1), **put in²** (12), **remain in²** (3), **stay in²** (3)

**7 keep someone in the dark (about)/in ignorance (of)** to refuse to tell someone a secret, information, etc.: *Taxpayers do not like being kept in the dark about/in ignorance of the government's intentions.* → **be in²** (8)

**8 keep something in one's head** to be able to remember something such as facts: [(*usu. simple tenses*)] *I don't know how the chairman keeps all those figures in his head.* → **hold in²** (1)

**9 keep (someone) in line: a** to (cause to) remain in one's proper place, as waiting in order: [(*usu. simple tenses*)] *Teachers of small children often give a class a long rope to hold to keep them in line when crossing the street. Keep in line there—no pushing!* **b** to (cause to) remain obedient to control: [(*usu. simple tenses*)] *All the party's supporters have to keep in line. The government uses various means to keep its own members in line.* → **be out of** (16), etc.,

**10 keep something/someone in mind** to remember; consider something or someone: *You must keep your parents' needs in mind when you make your decision. We must keep in mind that the younger people might not like the idea.* → **bear in**

**11 keep something in order** to have something neatly arranged: *I have to keep my papers in order or I would never find anything. The books are kept in alphabetical order.* → **be in²** (25a), **be out of** (19a), **put in²** (21), **set in²** (11)

**12 keep someone/an animal in order** to control the behaviour of someone or an animal: *Can't you keep those children in order? They're making a terrible noise!*

**13 keep someone in his place** to force someone to remember and behave according to his humble position: [(*often simple tenses*)] *The factory owner did not think that the time had passed when he could keep his workers in their place. Can't you keep your servant in his place? He's been very rude to me, as if he was my equal!* → **put in²** (23)

**14 keep oneself in readiness** to be always fully prepared (for something or to do something): [(*often simple tenses*)] *A doctor must keep himself in readiness for a sudden call in the middle of the night. I kept myself in readiness to run as soon as the man moved towards me.* → **hold in²** (3)

**15 keep something in reserve** to save something for a time of need: *A certain quantity of gold is always kept in reserve at the Bank of England. Keep some wine in reserve in case guests arrive late. Part of the army must be kept in reserve at all times.* → **hold in²** (4)

**16 keep in sight** to (cause to) remain in a position able to be seen: [(*often simple tenses*)] *The watchers kept the ship in sight until it disappeared over the horizon. The children were told to keep in sight (of the house) when they went out to play.* → **be in²** (32), **be out of** (28), **be within** (7), **bring into** (9), **come into** (13), **come within** (5), **get out of** (34), **get within** (5), **go out of** (13), **keep of** (4a), **lose of** (4), **remain in²** (5), **stay in²** (5)

**17 keep something in sight** to remember an aim at all times: [(*usu. simple tenses*)] *It will help you to work at your studies if you keep your examination in sight.* → **keep of** (4b)

**18 keep in step: a** (of more than one person) to march with one's feet moving in the same time together: *The soldiers kept in step until they came to the bridge.* **b** to move at the same rate (as something): *Teachers' pay has not kept in step with the cost of living.* → **be in²** (33), **be out of** (30)

**19 keep someone in suspense** to make someone wait before knowing something: *Tell me the end of the story, don't keep me in suspense!*

**20 keep in training** to (cause to) practise so as to keep one's skill or fitness, esp. for sport or competition: *It's difficult to keep in training for cricket matches during the winter. Running keeps you in training for almost any activity.* → **get into** (12)

***keep in with** *v adv prep* → **get in with** (2), etc.

to remain familiar or friendly with (someone), usu. for one's own advantage: [T1 (*usu. simple tenses*)] *It will pay you to keep in with the director, as his influence could get you a better position in the firm.*

**keep indoors** *v adv* → **keep in¹** (5), etc.

to (cause to) remain inside the house or other building: [L9 + INDOORS (*usu. simple tenses*)]

*Mother was advised to keep indoors for a week after her cough seemed better.* [X9 + INDOORS (*often simple tenses*)] *We keep the dog indoors on cold nights.*

**keep left/right** *v adv* → **bear left, turn left**
to drive or move on the left-hand/right-hand side of the road, etc.: [L9 + LEFT/RIGHT (*simple tenses*)] *Traffic in Britain keeps left.*

***keep mum** *v adj* → **keep dark** (2), **keep quiet** (2)
*infml* to remain silent (about something): [IØ] *The director has been keeping mum about the firm's future plans.* [T1b] *The committee members were told the date but were asked to keep it mum.*

**keep of** *v prep*
**1 keep control of** to remain in control of (something or someone): [*usu. simple tenses*] *The director kept control of most of the shares, but another man was appointed to run the business. The driver had to use all his strength and skill to keep control of the wheel when the tyre burst. The teacher could not keep control of the class any longer.* → **lose of** (1)
**2 keep count of** to be able to know the number or amount of (something, things, or people) without forgetting: *How do libraries keep count of all the books that pass in and out? We need a better system for keeping count of the people who attend our concerts.* → **lose of** (2)
**3 keep hold of: a** to continue to be able to seize or hold (something or someone): [*usu. simple tenses*] *Keep hold of the rope, and we'll pull you up.* → **get of** (5), **keep on²** (10), **lay of** (1), **lose of** (3), **take of** (10) **b** to not lose (an ability, idea, etc.): [(*usu. simple tenses*)] *In a fierce argument, it is often difficult to keep hold of one's main point.* → **lose of** (3)
**4 keep sight of: a** to be able to go on watching (something or someone): [*usu. simple tenses*] *I like to keep sight of the children while they are playing.* → **keep in²** (16), etc. **b** to remember (an aim) at all times: [*usu. simple tenses*] *Always keep sight of your main purpose in life, it gives you something to aim for.* → **keep in²** (17)
**5 keep track of** *not fml* to watch; follow; know where or how (someone or something) is: *How do you keep track of such a large family? The library has a new system for keeping track of its books.* → **keep on²** (17), **lose of** (6)

***keep off¹** *v adv*
**1** to (cause to) remain at a distance; (cause to) not come or happen: [IØ] *Mary tends to keep off from people who try to be friendly too suddenly. A notice was placed on the dangerously thin ice, warning people to keep off.* [T1] *We must keep the enemy's attack off until after dark. Keep your hands off! The natives wear shells to keep off evil spirits. Draw the curtain to keep the sun off.* (= to stop it shining on you.) → **get off¹** (2), **hang back**, etc.
**2** to (cause to) be delayed: [IØ] *Will the rain keep off until after the game?* [T1] *A piece of cheese will keep off hunger for a time. The secretary kept the danger off as long as possible. How long can you keep the angry workers off?* → **hang up** (3), **hold back** (4), **hold off** (2), **hold up** (2), **keep back** (5)

**keep off²** *v prep*
**1** to (cause to) stay away from (something): [L9 + *off*] *Keep off the grass.* [X9 + *off*] *Can't you keep your dog off the road? Keep your dirty fingers off the wet paint. At least the club keeps the young people off the streets.* → **get off²** (2), **stay off** (1)
***2** to (cause to) avoid; cease having (food, a habit, etc.): [T1] *The doctor advised Jim to keep off fattening foods.* [D1] *How did you keep your husband off alcohol all last year?* → **keep away from** (2), **stay away from, stay off** (2)
***3** to avoid mentioning (a subject): [T1] *I suggest that you keep off religion while the priest is here. Remember to keep off the delicate subject of Jane's stomach trouble in her hearing.*
***4** to make (someone) stay away from (a place such as school): [D1] *I shall keep Jane off school until her stomach trouble is better.* → **stay off** (3), etc.
**5 keep one's eyes off** to be able to control one's desire to look at or have (something or someone): [*usu. neg., usu. simple tenses*] *The crowd could not keep their eyes off the beautiful young singer. The thief found it difficult to keep his eyes off the jewels round Miss Rose's neck, as he planned to steal them later that night.*
**6 keep one's fingers/hands off** to not touch or try to possess (someone or something): [*usu. simple tenses*] *Keep your hands off my precious paintings while I'm away. He learned the hard way to keep his hands off other men's wives. Big business organizations cannot keep their hands off successful small firms.* → **lay off²** (4)

**keep on¹** *v adv*
**1** to continue wearing (clothes): [X9 + ON] *I'll keep my coat on, thank you, I can't stay long. It's rude for a man to keep his hat on indoors.* → **leave on¹** (2)
**2** to keep (something such as electricity) switched on: [X9 + ON] *There is no need for tall office buildings to keep their lights on all night, when the government has asked everyone to save power.* → **put on¹** (3), etc.
**3** to continue travelling: [L9 + ON (*usu. simple tenses*)] *Turn left at the corner and keep on as far as the church. "Keep right on to the end of the road."* (song) → **go on¹** (1)
***4** to continue, often in spite of difficulties: [IØ (*with*) (*usu. simple tenses*)] *Even if you fail the examination again, you must try to keep on until you pass. Keep on with your studies, however hard it sometimes seems. I've never won anything yet, but I intend to keep on until I do.*

*5 to continue (doing something): [T4a (*usu. simple tenses*)] *A string broke, but the pianist kept on playing. He just kept on hitting the boy although I told him to stop.* → **carry on** (4), etc.

*6 to continue to employ (someone) or send (someone) to a place: [T1 (*at, in*)] *Were you able to keep both the gardeners on? How long will you keep the children on at that school after all that you've heard about it?* → **stay on**[1] (3), **stick on**[1] (4), **stop on** (3)

*7 to continue to have, esp. to rent (something): [T1] *I'll keep the flat on through the summer, so as to have it ready when we come back. I'd like to keep this car on for another week, if that's possible.*

*8 *not fml* to talk at length (about a subject): [IØ (*about*) (*usu. simple tenses*)] *Don't keep on so, it'll only make you worry more. The teacher kept on and on about good behaviour, as usual.* → **be off**[1] (9), **be on about, go on**[1] (7), **run on**[1] (1)

9 **keep your hair/shirt on** *infml* don't lose your temper: [*usu. imper.*] *All right, keep your hair on! Nobody's blaming you!*

**keep on**[2] *v prep*

1 to (cause to) remain in position on top of (something or someone): [L9 + *on* (*usu. simple tenses*)] *How do you keep on a horse?* [X9 + *on*] *She kept her hat on her head with a long pin.* → **be on**[2] (1), **stay on**[2] (1)

2 to (cause to) continue travelling in (a certain direction): [L9 + *on* (*simple tenses*)] *If we keep on our way for another hour we should reach the village.* [X9 + *on*] *The captain was able to keep the ship on (her) course in spite of the storm.* → **be on**[2] (2), **remain on**[2] (1), **stay on**[2] (2)

3 to (cause to) continue taking (medicine) or following (a course): [X9 + *on*] *The doctor wants to keep Mother on the medicine for another month.* [L9 + *on*] *Will you keep on the course of exercises until you are thinner?* → **be on**[2] (4), **stay on**[2] (3)

4 **keep someone on the boil** *infml* to keep someone interested, esp. in possible future action: *With violent words and fierce expressions, the speaker kept the angry crowd of workers on the boil long enough to persuade the directors to give them their demands.* → **be on**[2] (9), **go off**[2] (5)

5 **keep an/one's eye on** to watch or guard (someone); follow the development of (something): *The police have been keeping an eye on the thief ever since he came out of prison. Property owners try to keep their eyes on future developments in house prices.* → **have on**[2] (10), **watch over**

6 **keep one eye on** to be watching or paying attention to (something or someone) while doing something else: *It's wise to keep one eye on the clock when doing the examination. Whatever Jim was doing, he always kept one eye on his own interests. When planning anything, you have to keep one eye on the future.* → **have on**[2] (11)

7 **keep something on its feet** *not fml* to save something from failure: [*simple tenses*] *This new contract should keep the business on its feet for another six months, but after that the future is uncertain.*

8 **keep on one's feet** to (cause to) remain standing: *The old fighter kept on his feet in spite of punishing blows from his strong young opponent. How do you keep on your feet so long? I would have needed a rest hours ago. It's unlawful to keep workers on their feet for too long at a time.* → **get to** (11), etc.

9 **keep one's finger on the pulse of** *not fml* to be conscious of or fully informed about (something): *A successful politician is one who is able to keep his finger on the country's pulse and knows what to offer the voters.*

10 **keep a firm/tight grip/hold on: a** to continue to be able to seize or hold (something or someone): *Keep a firm hold on the rope and we'll pull you up.* **b** to continue to control (something): *Jim's father kept a tight hold on the business during its difficult early period, and claims that this was partly responsible for its later success.* → **keep of** (3a), **lose of** (3), **take of** (10)

11 **keep someone on the hop** *infml* to keep someone active, interested, waiting, etc.: [*often simple tenses*] *That salesman deserves to be kept on the hop for another week, he annoyed me the last time he called, and he can wait for his sale.*

12 **keep something/someone on ice** *infml* to save something/someone for a later time: *We may have to keep the contract on ice until we have the supplies to fulfil it. So many people wanted the job; I'd like to keep some of the better ones on ice to see if we can find jobs for them later.*

13 **keep one's mind on** to continue paying attention to (something): *It's hard to keep your mind on your work with all this noise going on.* → **concentrate on** (1), **focus on** (2)

14 **keep on the rails** *not fml* to (cause to) behave correctly and lawfully: *It's hard for a former prisoner to keep on the rails. Having the responsibility for a family helps to keep a young man on the rails.* → **go off**[2] (8), **run off**[2] (6), **stay on**[2] (5)

15 **keep on the right side of** *not fml* to remain friendly with; not annoy (someone): *It will pay you to keep on the right side of the director, as if you annoy him he could have you dismissed.* → **get in with** (2). etc.

16 **keep on the right side of the law** to behave lawfully: *The courts will punish less severely, for a first offence, someone who has formerly kept on the right side of the law.* → **remain on**[2] (5), **stay on**[2] (7)

17 **keep tabs on** *infml* to repeatedly or continuously watch or guard; follow; know where or how (someone or something) is: *How do*

*you keep tabs on the accounts of all these different firms? The police keep tabs on all habitual criminals.* → **keep of** (5), **lose of** (6)

**18 keep on top (of)** → **STAY ON**² (8)

***keep on at/onto** *v adv prep; prep* → **go on at** (2), etc.

*not fml* to scold; worry; find fault with (someone); repeatedly ask (someone) (to do something): [T1 (*no pass.*)] *She keeps on at the children all day about one thing or another.* [V3] *She kept on at/onto me for a year to buy her a new coat, until in the end I agreed, if only to get some peace from her.*

**keep open** *v adj*

**1** to make (something) remain wide open, apart, etc.: [X9 + open] *Don't keep your mouth open all the time, it looks ugly. Use this block to keep the door open, so as to let some air into the house.* → **leave open** (1), etc.

**2** to remain open for business: [L9 + open (*usu. simple tenses*)] *The shops in central London keep open late on Thursday evenings.* → **stay open** (2), etc.

***3** to save (a job) for someone, during a time away: [T1b (*for*)] *If you take this six-month overseas contract, will your firm keep your job open for you until you get back?* → **hold open** (2)

**4 keep one's eyes open** to be able to remain awake: [(*usu. neg.*)] *The speaker was so uninteresting that I could hardly keep my eyes open.*

**5 keep one's eyes (and ears) open** *not fml* to be watchful, as for a chance: *Keep your eyes open for a jewel thief in the neighbourhood. Any businessman has to keep his eyes and ears open for a chance of making a profit.*

**6 keep one's options open** *not fml* to make sure that one has a choice; not choose too soon: *Don't leave your present job until you have actually accepted the one that you've been offered, just in case you decide not to take it; that way you will be keeping your options open.*

**keep out** *v adv* → **stay out** (1), **stop out** (1)

to (cause to) stay outside; not enter: [X9 + OUT (*of*)] *This notice should keep unwanted visitors out. Don't keep your aunt out in the cold, ask her to come in! Warm clothing helps to keep out the cold.* [L9 + OUT (*of*) (*usu. simple tenses*)] *The children have been warned to keep out of the fields while the crops are growing. Private property—keep out.*

**keep out of** *v adv prep*

**1** to (cause to) stay outside; not enter (something): [X9 + OUT + *of*] *This notice should keep unwanted visitors out of the building.* [L9 + OUT + *of* (*usu. simple tenses*)] *The children have been warned to keep out of the fields while the crops are growing.* → **stay out of** (1), **stop out of** (2)

***2** to (cause to) stay away from (something such as trouble): [T1 (*no pass.*)] *I always try to keep out of other people's affairs when they don't concern me. I hope you'll keep out of trouble while I'm away. It's not easy to keep out of debt when prices are rising so fast.* [D1] *I hope you'll keep him out of trouble while I'm away. This recent pay rise will help to keep us out of debt a little longer.* → **get into** (11), etc.

**3 keep (someone) out of harm's way** to (cause to) stay in a safe place or activity: *The children don't do much at their youth club, but at least it keeps them out of harm's way.* → **be out of** (12), **stay out of** (3)

**4 keep one's nose out of** *not fml* to avoid entering (something that is not one's concern): *Keep your nose out of my affairs!*

**5 keep out of one's/the way** to remain in or move to a position not annoying someone: [(*usu. simple tenses*)] *Keep out of my way, can't you—I need room to get past!* → **be out of** (32a), **get out of** (37), **stay out of** (4)

**keep quiet** *v adj*

**1** to (cause to) remain silent or satisfied; not make much noise or complaint: [L9 + quiet (*usu. simple tenses*)] *Keep quiet, please, children, Father's asleep.* [X9 + quiet (*often simple tenses*)] *Give the dog a bone, that should keep him quiet. Some small tax cuts might keep the voters quiet.*

***2** to keep (something such as information) secret: [IØ (*about*)] *All the children kept quiet about the trouble they had got into at school.* [T1b] *If I tell you the story, will you promise to keep it quiet?* → **keep dark** (2), **keep mum**

**keep right** *v adv* → **KEEP LEFT**

**keep till/until** *v prep*

**1** to save (something) until (a point in time): [T1 + *till/until*] *The library will let you keep the book till next week. Keep this ring until my return. The teacher kept the whole class till 4.30.* → **save till**

**2** to remain in good condition until (a point in time): [IØ + *till/until* (*simple tenses*)] *The milk won't keep till tomorrow, we'd better drink it now.* → **last for, last till**

***3** to wait until (a time): [T1 (*no pass., simple tenses*)] *Writing that letter will have to keep until tomorrow. Can't your story keep until another time?*

**keep to** *v prep*

**1** to move in or towards (a certain position or place): [L9 + *to* (*simple tenses*)] *Traffic in England keeps to the left. If you keep to the main road you won't get lost. Ask the crowd to keep to one side, to let the firemen get through.* → **hold to** (2), **stick to** (2)

***2** to (cause to) limit oneself to; talk about (something) without letting one's attention wander: [T1 (*no pass.*)] *Do let's keep to the subject; we're trying to reach an agreement, not have a conversation.* [D1 (*usu. simple tenses*)] *It is part of the chairman's duty to keep each speaker to the point, to save wasting time.* → **stick to** (3)

***3** to (cause to) follow; behave exactly according to (something such as a promise or plan):

[T1] *I'd rather keep to the original arrangement. Whatever your argument, I shall keep to my decision. The priest kept to his beliefs in spite of cruel treatment. You must keep to the rules even if you think they're unfair.* [D1] *I shall keep you to your promise to come and see us next year. There's nothing to keep me to such an arrangement.* → **adhere to** (2), etc.

*__4__ to stay in (a place such as a bed or house): [T1] *Mother had to keep to her bed for two weeks after her operation. When Jane is in a, bad temper, she keeps to her room all day.*

**5 keep one's ear (close) to the ground** *not fml* to be conscious of tendencies and future possibilities: *By keeping his ear close to the ground, the young politician learned the best ways to win votes.*

**6 keep something to a/the minimum** to make sure that something is as little as possible: *This new protection on the car is intended to keep damage to a minimum.*

**7 keep one's nose to the grindstone** *infml* to (cause to) work hard and continuously: *Jim's father succeeded in business by keeping his nose to the grindstone, and never taking a holiday. Jane is lazy at school and never does any work unless the teacher keeps her nose to the grindstone.* → **get back to** (5)

**8 keep (oneself) to oneself** to remain private; avoid meeting other people: [(*often simple tenses*)] *Nobody really knows what Mary thinks about anything, she keeps (herself) to herself most of the time, and rarely expresses an opinion.*

**9 keep something to oneself** to keep (something) private; not tell or express (something): *I kept the letter to myself, for fear of offending my friends. Don't keep the news to yourself, let's all share it. I'll thank you to keep your opinion to yourself.*

**10 keep to/on the straight and narrow (path)** to (cause to) behave morally: *Every Sunday, the priest tries to persuade the worshippers to keep to the straight and narrow path. It's no use trying to keep one's children to the straight and narrow path, they will do what they like with their own lives.*

**keep together** *v adv*

**1** (of two or more things or people) to (cause to) remain in the same place or time; [L9 + TOGETHER (*usu. simple tenses*)] *The horses kept together for most of the race, until a leader at last came to the front. When the mist comes down, we must keep together or we'll be lost. You singers must keep together or you will spoil the music.* [X9 + TOGETHER (*often simple tenses*)] *I'd like to keep the children together in school. A library usually keeps books of the same kind together. How do you keep such a large number of musicians together, playing so many different instruments?* → **remain together, stay together** (1)

*__2__ to (cause to) remain united: [IØ (*usu. simple tenses*)] *We try to keep together as a family.* [T1 (*often simple tenses*)] *The party was kept together by personal loyalty to the leader. Facing a common enemy keeps the nation together.* → **stick together** (2), etc.

**keep under¹** *v adv*

**1** to (cause to) remain beneath something: [X9 + UNDER (*often simple tenses*)] *He tried to swim, but a strong current kept him under and he drowned.* → **hold under** (1), **remain under¹, stay under, stop under**

*__2__ to control (something): [T1b] *Jim kept his feelings under with an effort. We tried to keep the fire under, but it spread to the other buildings near it.*

*__3__ to control; limit the freedom of (someone): [T1b] *Former rulers kept the people under, but recently they have been allowed to hold elections and have much more freedom.* → **keep down** (6), etc.

**keep under²** *v prep*

**1** to have a place for (something) beneath (something): [T1 + *under* (*often simple tenses*)] *There is no room for my shoes in the cupboard, so I have to keep them under the bed.*

**2 keep something/someone under control** to continue to be able to control something or someone: *If that fire is not kept under control, it could spread to other buildings in the street. How long can an inexperienced teacher keep a class like that under control?* → **be under** (7), **bring under²** (2), **get under²** (2)

**3 keep something under one's hat** *infml* to keep (information) secret: *If I tell you the date of the election, can you keep it under your hat?*

**4 keep someone under observation: a** to watch what someone does, as in case he does something wrong: *The police keep all habitual criminals under observation from the day they leave the prison.* **b** to keep someone in hospital to discover what he is suffering from: *The doctors cannot understand Jane's stomach trouble, and they want to keep her under observation for a few days.*

**5 keep someone under one's thumb** *not fml* to control someone firmly, often wrongly: [(*often simple tenses*)] *If their mother tries to keep the children under her thumb, they will leave home as soon as they can.*

**keep until** *v prep* → **KEEP TILL**

**keep up** *v adv*

**1** to (cause to) be or remain raised: [X9 + UP (*often simple tenses*)] *My husband lost so much weight that he has to wear a belt to keep his trousers up. What keeps the roof up?* [L9 + UP (*usu. simple tenses*)] *How does that pile of hair keep up, I wonder?* → **hold up** (1), etc.

*__2__ to (cause to) remain high: [T1] *The farmers are keeping the prices up. She kept up her spirits by singing. The shops are trying to keep quality up but prices steady.* [IØ (*usu. simple tenses*)] *Prices have kept up all the year. His* *courage kept up in the face of danger.* → **be up** (6, 7), **go down**[1] (6), etc.

*__3__ to keep (something) in good condition: [T1 (*often simple tenses*)] *How do you keep up a house as large as this without help?* —**upkeep** *n*

*__4__ to continue (something): [T1] *I'm glad that you are keeping up your studies. Jane will have to keep up her piano practice if she wants to be a professional concert performer. The enemy kept up the attack all night, until help arrived in the morning. When people move to another country, they often try to keep up the customs of their native land. How long is the director going to keep up the pretence that business is still good? You'll be able to pay all your debts if you can keep up regular payments. I've kept up a friendship with a girl I was at school with twenty years ago. Well done! Keep up the good work! You boys have done some very good work; I hope you can keep it up.*

*__5__ (usu. of weather) to remain the same; last: [IØ (*usu. simple tenses*)] *Will the fine weather keep up?* → **hang out** (3), **hold out** (3), **hold up** (6), **last out** (1)

*__6__ to (cause to) remain out of bed, as at night: [T1b] *I hope I'm not keeping you up.* [IØ (*usu. simple tenses*)] *No, we often keep up late.* → **stay up** (3), etc.

*__7__ to remain level (with someone): [IØ (*to, with*)] *I had to run to keep up (with the girls).* → **catch up** (4), **come up with** (1), **get up with** (2), **keep up with** (1)

*__8__ to remain level (with a competitor): [IØ] *The other firms are selling so well that we have to work very hard to keep up.* → **catch up** (5), **come up with** (2), **keep up with** (2)

**9 keep up appearances** to make people think, by one's actions, that one has more money than is true; pretend that all is well: *When Father lost all his money, all that Mother could think of was keeping up appearances in the town so that people should not know of the family's shame.*

**10 keep one's chin/pecker up** *BrE infml* to remain cheerful in the face of trouble: *Keep your chin up! Things could be worse!* → **cheer up,** etc.

**11 keep one's end up** to be able to perform or defend oneself well, as in an argument or difficult situation: *The opposition offered some strong speakers, but our man kept his end up all right. I tried to keep my end up in the discussion but everyone else seemed much cleverer than I was.*

***keep up to** *v adv prep*

**1** to (cause to) remain as high as (something such as a level): [T1] *The shops are keeping meat prices up to last month's level, although they are paying the farmers less for producing the meat.*

**2** to remain level with (something or someone): [T1] *I had to run to keep up to the girls. I had to work hard to keep up to the other students.*

**3 keep (someone/something) up to date** to (cause to) remain level with expectations, fashion, time, or modern thinking: *It's always a struggle to keep up to date with the news. How do you keep your letter writing up to date? Throw away your old clothes, keep up to date!*

**4 keep (someone) up to the mark/up to scratch** to (cause to) reach and stay at a high standard: *A pianist has to practise every day to keep up to scratch. This teacher demands hard work from his students, to keep them up to the mark.*

***keep up with** *v adv prep*

**1** to remain level with (someone): [IØ] *I had to run to keep up with the girls. I had to work hard to keep up with the other students.* → **catch up** (4), **come up with** (1), **get up with** (2), **keep up**[1] (7), **keep up**[2] (2)

**2** to remain level with; keep in advance of (an idea, fashion, etc.): [T1] *How do you keep up with the latest styles in popular music? They change so quickly! Everyone has to keep up with the news. Even professional politicians have a struggle to keep up with the changes in public opinion.* → **catch up** (5), **come up with** (2), **keep up**[1] (8)

**3 keep up with the Joneses** *not fml* to stay level with social changes; compete with one's neighbours, as in owning property: *One of the problems of modern city life is that people spend half their effort and income in just keeping up with the Joneses, instead of developing an independent lifestyle and spending their money only on things they need and really want.*

**4 keep up with the times** to follow fashion; be fully informed: *Keeping up with the times can be almost a full-time job!*

**keep with** *v prep*

**1** to have a place for (something) together with (something): [T1 + *with* (*usu. simple tenses*)] *Why do you keep the knives with the forks? I separate mine.*

**2 keep company with** to be seen in public with (someone): *Is Grace still keeping company with that red-haired boy?*

**3 keep faith with** *fml* to be faithful or loyal to (someone or something such as a promise) [(*usu. simple tenses*)] *When Ulysses returned from the war, he found that his wife had kept faith with him for ten long years. She had kept faith with the promise that she had made to him on their marriage.*

**4 in keeping with** suitable to (something): *In keeping with the spirit of the occasion, let us close the meeting with a prayer. The employment exchange tries to find people jobs in keeping with their abilities and experience.*

**5 keep pace/step with: a** to walk at the same speed as (someone): [(*usu. simple tenses*)] *The tall girl took such long steps that I had* *struggle to keep pace with her.* **b** to remain level with (someone or something that is changing or developing quickly): *Scientists have to work hard to keep pace with modern discoveries and developments.*

**keep within** *v prep*

**1** to be limited by (something): [L9 + *within* (*usu. simple tenses*)] *Make sure you keep within the new lower speed limit.* → **remain within** (1), **stay within** (1), **stick within, stop within**

**2 keep (something) within bounds** to (cause to) stay within limits: [(*usu. simple tenses*)] *Make sure that your spending keeps within bounds, or we could be in trouble. The firm's costs must be kept within bounds on this new contract.*

**key up** *v adv*

**1** *now rare* to make (the strings of a musical instrument) be in tune, usu. by tightening them: [T1 + UP (*usu. simple tenses*)] *Are all the strings properly keyed up?*

**2 be keyed up** *not fml* to be excited or nervous (about something): *I was keyed up about the examination.*

**kick about/around**[1] *v adv*

**1** to kick (something) in an aimless manner, without direction: [T1 + ABOUT/AROUND] *Those boys aren't playing football properly, they're just kicking the ball about. Children enjoy kicking piles of dead leaves about.* → **knock about**[1] (1)

*__2__ *infml* to exist; be living: [IØ (*often continuous tenses*)] *Is the same chairman still kicking around? I thought he had left years ago. The idea of world government has been kicking around for a long time, but no one seems to take it seriously.* → **knock about**[1] (2)

*__3__ *infml* to be left unattended or unnoticed: [IØ (*often continuous tenses*)] *I found this book kicking about upstairs; is it yours?* → **knock about**[1] (3), **leave about, lie about**[1] (2)

*__4__ to treat (someone or something) as by kicking or hitting: [T1b] *The mother was taken to court for kicking the children about. There must be something wrong with a child who kicks his toys around. The boy was in such a temper that he started kicking his little brother about. This old suitcase looks as though it has been kicked about a lot.* → **bash about,** etc.

*__5__ *not fml* to give (someone) unnecessary orders; try to control (someone): [T1b] *The directors will find that times have changed; they can no longer kick the workers around and make them do whatever they want.* → **order about, push about**

*__6__ *infml* to talk about (a subject), trying to reach a decision: [T1b] *The committee kicked your suggestion around for over an hour before deciding that they could not accept it.* also **kick round**

**kick about/around**[2] *v prep*

**1** to kick (something or someone) in or on (a place): [T1 + *about/around*] *The boys enjoy kicking a football about a field. The horse kicked its fallen rider about the head.* → **knock about**[2] (1)

*__2__ *infml* to lie unnoticed in (a place): [T1 (*no pass.*)] *No, it's not mine; that old book has been kicking about the house for years.* → **knock about**[2] (2), **lie about**[3] (2)

*__3__ *infml* to travel in different parts of (a place): [T1 (*no pass.*)] *My uncle has been kicking about Africa for years.* → **bang about**[2] (2), **hang about** (2), **knock about**[2] (3)

***kick against** *v prep*

**1** *not fml* to oppose; dislike; express annoyance at (something or doing something): [T1 (*pass. rare*)] *You'll only make yourself feel worse if you kick against your bad luck—you just have to learn to accept it.* [T4] *The customers are kicking against paying such high prices.* → **kick at** (2)

**2 kick against the pricks** *infml* to oppose something without success, harming oneself by doing so: *He spent most of his time at school kicking against the pricks but now he seems to be more settled and willing to accept that rules are necessary.*

**kick around**[1] *v adv* → **KICK ABOUT**[1]

**kick around**[2] *v prep* → **KICK ABOUT**[2]

**kick at** *v prep*

**1** to aim one's foot at (something or someone): [IØ + *at*] *I saw you kicking at my dog! Well, he was trying to bite me! The footballer kicked at the ball but missed and fell flat on his face.*

*__2__ *not fml* to oppose; dislike; express annoyance at (something or doing something): [T1 (*pass. rare*)] *You'll only make yourself feel worse if you kick at your bad luck—you just have to learn to accept it.* [T4] *The customers are kicking at paying such high prices, and they can hardly be blamed.* → **kick against** (1)

**kick away** *v adv*

**1** to kick a ball continuously: [IØ + AWAY] *The famous footballer said that the secret of his success was the time he spent in his youth practising, just kicking away at a ball for hours on end, in an empty field with a few friends.*

**2** to move (something) away with the foot: [T1 + AWAY] *Kicking away the blocks holding the wheels, the pilot jumped into the light plane and flew off.* → **knock away** (2)

**kick back** *v adv*

**1** to kick (someone, or something such as a ball) in return: [T1 + BACK (*usu. simple tenses*)] *Don't blame me for the fight—he kicked me first, and I only kicked him back. The centre forward kicked the ball to the quarterback, who kicked it back to him.*

*__2__ (of a motorcycle engine) to fire in a backward or wrong direction: [IØ (*often simple tenses*)] *Be careful how you start the motor, it sometimes kicks back.* —**kickback** *n*

*__3__ *not fml* (of a disease) to be repeated within a short time: [IØ (*often simple tenses*)] *This*

*kind of feverish cold is slow to cure; it often kicks back just when you think you're better.*
***4** *infml* to return (part of money received as pay, etc.) as a reward, often secretly or unlawfully: [T1 (*usu. simple tenses*)] *We only won the contract because we agreed to kick back 5% of the profit to the man who got us the job.* —**kickback** *n* → **pay off** (4), **rake off**

***kick back at** *v adv prep*
*not fml* to attack (someone or something) in return: [T1 (*pass. rare*)] *Tom wanted to kick back at the people who had written so unfavourably about his new book in the newspapers. Voters at the next election may decide to kick back at the unfair tax laws by voting against the government.*

**kick down** *v adv*
**1** to make (someone or something) fall by kicking: [T1 + DOWN (*usu. simple tenses*)] *That player doesn't play fairly; did you see him kick his opponent down?*
***2** to change a motorcycle engine to a lower gear: [IØ (*usu. simple tenses*)] *When you're going up a steep hill and losing speed, you have to kick down.* → **change down, change up, gear down** (1), **gear up** (1)

**kick downstairs** *v adv*
**1** to push (someone or something) downstairs with the foot or feet: [T1 + DOWNSTAIRS (*usu. simple tenses*)] *The poor cat was kicked downstairs by the children. "Be off, or I'll kick you downstairs!"* (Lewis Carroll, *Alice in Wonderland*)
***2** *infml* to move (someone) to a humbler position: [T1a (*usu. pass.*)] *After the cook had spoilt the meal, he was kicked downstairs and given a job sweeping the floors.* → **kick upstairs**

**kick in**[1] *v adv*
**1** to make (something or someone) enter by kicking: [T1 + IN (*usu. simple tenses*)] *Did you see how he treated the cat? He just opened the door and kicked the poor animal in! In the last minute, the player kicked the ball in and so ensured his team's victory.* → **chip in** (2), **hit in, knock in**[1] (1)
***2** to damage or destroy (something) by kicking: [T1] *The firemen had to kick the door in to get inside the burning building. 'Go on, hit him! Kick his teeth in!' shouted the angry crowd.*
***3** *not fml* to add (one's share of money): [T1a] *We all agreed to kick in 10% of the cost.* → **chip in** (2), **hit in, knock in**[1] (1)

**kick in**[2] *v prep*
**1** to hurt (someone) by pushing one's foot or feet into (a certain part of the body): [T1 + *in*] *While the man was lying on the ground, his attacker kicked him in the face.*
**2 kick someone in the teeth** *infml* to hurt someone's feelings; harm someone on purpose; oppose someone rudely; treat someone inconsiderately: *Mr Wall has been the Member of Parliament for this area for ten years, but at the last election, the voters kicked him in the teeth by electing his opponent.*

**kick off** *v adv*
**1** to remove (something) by shaking the foot: [T1 + OFF (*usu. simple tenses*)] *Take your shoes off and leave them neatly, don't kick them off into a corner the way you usually do. The dog attacked me, biting my ankle, but I kicked him off.*
***2** to start a game of football: [IØ (*simple tenses*)] *What time does this afternoon's game kick off? The teams kick off at 3 o'clock.* —**kickoff** *n*
***3** *infml* to start (something): [IØ (*with*) (*usu. simple tenses*)] *Who will kick off with the first question for our speaker? The cost is too high, to kick off with.* [T1] *The theatre company will kick off the season with a production of 'The Playboy of the Western World.'* —**kickoff** *n* → **lead off**[1] (2)
***4** *AmE not fml* to leave; go away: [IØ (*usu. simple tenses*)] *Well, I really must kick off now, I've stayed long enough.*
***5** *AmE infml* to die: [IØ (*simple tenses*)] *I hear poor old Charlie has kicked off!* → **pass away** (3), etc.
***6** *AmE infml* (of a machine) to stop working; fail: [IØ] *That old washing machine has kicked off again!* → **break down** (3), **conk out** (1), **cut out** (8), **give out** (6), **pack up** (3)

***kick on** *v adv*
(of something electrical, machinery, etc.) to (cause to) begin working, usu. suddenly: [IØ (*usu. simple tenses*)] *Suddenly the motor kicked on, when I had almost given up hope.* [T1 (*usu. simple tenses*)] *The policeman kicked the switch on, and light flooded the room.*

**kick out** *v adv*
**1** to push (something or someone) outside with the foot or feet: [T1 + OUT (*usu. simple tenses*)] *Don't kick the cat out like that, it's cruel; lift him out gently.*
**2** to kick the foot in an outward direction or suddenly: [IØ + OUT (*at*)] *Never walk behind a horse in case it kicks out (at you).* → **hit out** (1), etc.
**3** (in football) to kick (the ball) off the field of play: [T1 + OUT (*usu. simple tenses*)] *If a player on your own team kicks the ball out the other side gets a free turn at the ball.*
***4** *not fml* to make (someone) leave a place, organization, or activity, often for a fault: [T1 (*of*)] *The captain was kicked out of the army for immoral behaviour. If the new actor is no good, kick him out (of the play).* → **throw out** (4), etc.
***5** *not fml* to make (someone) leave a home: [T1 (*of*)] *The old lady was kicked out (of the house) because the owner wanted to pull it down.* → **throw out** (5), etc.

**kick over** *v adv*
**1** to make (something or someone) fall by pushing it with the foot: [T1 + OVER] *Th*

*cow has kicked the milk bucket over again.* → **knock down** (1), **knock over** (1)

**2 kick over the traces** *not fml* to demand one's freedom; behave disobediently: *I had such a formal, moral upbringing that as soon as I grew up, I was glad to kick over the traces and do as I chose, whether my family would approve or not.*

**kick round** *v adv* → KICK ABOUT[1] (6)

**kick up** *v adv*

**1** to raise (something such as dust) with the feet: [T1 + UP] *The children enjoyed playing by the sea, kicking up the sand into each other's faces.*

**2 kick up a dust/fuss/noise/row/shindy/stink** *infml* to make noise and/or trouble: *The director will kick up a fuss if you don't do your work properly. He kicks up a stink as it is, every time I'm late. Why are those dogs kicking up such a row? Can't somebody keep them quiet? The class got out of control, and the shindy they kicked up could be heard at the other end of the school. The tax people will kick up a dust if your return is incorrect.* —**kickup** *n AmE*

**3 kick up one's heels: a** to move quickly: *The horses are kicking up their heels in the warm spring air.* **b** *not fml* to enjoy oneself actively: *The children kicked up their heels as soon as they were let out of school.* → **fling up** (9)

**kick upstairs** *v adv* → **kick downstairs** (2)

*BrE not fml* to get rid of (someone) by giving him a more honourable but less powerful position, as in the House of Lords, usu. for a fault: [T1a (*usu. pass.*)] *The Minister can't be allowed to ruin any more of our plans; I'll have to arrange for him to be kicked upstairs, and then we can appoint someone else who will do the job properly.*

**kid around** *v adv*

esp. *AmE infm* to deceive in a playful manner; play the fool: [IØ + AROUND (*usu. continuous tenses*)] *Don't take any notice of him, he's just kidding around.*

**kid on/up** *v adv*

*infml* to deceive (someone) as a joke: [T1 + ON/UP] *I don't believe you—you're just trying to kid me on/up!*

**kill off** *v adv*

to kill (things or people) one at a time: [T1] *The trees were killed off by the severe winter. This fever has been killing off many of the older people in the city. In this play, all the characters except one get killed off by the last act, so that we know which one is the murderer.*

**kill with** *v prep*

**1** to kill (someone or something) by means of (something): [T1 + *with* (*usu. simple tenses*)] *The jewel thief killed one of the policemen with a knife. You will have to kill these unwanted plants with poison.*

**2 kill oneself (with laughter/mirth)** to find something very funny: [(*continuous tenses*)] *The children are killing themselves with laughter—Father hasn't yet discovered the joke that they've played on him.*

**3 kill someone with kindness** to be too kind to someone, so doing them harm unintentionally: *If you help your students with their work too much, you will be killing them with kindness, as they will not be able to pass the examination.*

**4 kill two birds with one stone** *not fml* to gain two advantages with one action: *If you walk to work, you will get some exercise as well as saving money, so you'll be killing two birds with one stone!*

**kindle with** *v prep*

**1** to light (a fire) by using (small pieces of dry burnable material): [T1 + *with*] *When camping, you can kindle a fire with dry leaves and small pieces of wood.*

**2** to cause (a feeling) to arise in someone by means of (something): [T1 + *with*] *The speaker tried to kindle the crowd's interest with a lively speech.*

***3** to become bright with (usu. a feeling): [T1 (*no pass.*)] *His eyes kindled with desire when he first saw the beautiful woman. Jim's eyes kindled with anger when he learned how Mary had been treated at the hospital.* → **glow with** (2), **shine with**

**kink up** *v adv*

(of hair) to (cause to) become tightly curled: [IØ + UP; T1 + UP (*usu. pass.*)] *My hair kinked up in the salt water.*

**kip down** *v adv*

*infml* to go to sleep: [L9 + DOWN (*often simple tenses*)] *Don't worry about a bed for me, I can kip down on the floor.* —**kip-down** *n*

**kip out** *v adv*

*infml* to sleep out of doors: [L9 + OUT (*often simple tenses*)] *When we go camping, the children sometimes leave their tent and kip out in the open field; they claim that they enjoy sleeping under the stars.*

**kiss away** *v adv*

**1** to kiss continuously: [IØ + AWAY (*continuous tenses*)] *Those two have been kissing away in that room for hours!*

***2** to remove; get rid of (something) by kissing: [T1] *Let me kiss away your tears. The child's mother kissed his fears away. "We have kissed away Kingdoms."* (Shakespeare, *Antony and Cleopatra*)

**kiss goodbye** *v adv*

**1** to say goodbye to (someone) with a kiss: [T1 + GOODBYE] *Don't forget to kiss me goodbye as you leave!*

***2** *infml* to be forced to forget; lose hope of, or lose sight of (something): [T1b (*usu. simple tenses*)] *Well, you can kiss that contract goodbye, there's no hope that we shall get it now!*

**kiss off** *v adv*

**1** to remove (something) by kissing: [T1 + OFF (*often simple tenses*)] *Mind you don't kiss all my face powder off!*

***2** *AmE not fml* to dismiss; regard (something) as lost or gone: [T1 (*usu. simple tenses*)] *"It means yet another delay on any meaningful action while another team studies the matter. Mr Wells says he hopes to have the report in eight months, which means we can kiss off the coming school year and probably the following one too."* (*Toronto Globe and Mail*, 16 April 1976) —**kiss-off** *n infml*

***kit out** *v adv*
to supply (someone or something) with necessary things, as clothing: [T1 (*often pass.*)] *Make sure that your boy is properly kitted out for the tropics. The army must be kitted out with proper clothing, weapons, medical supplies, and tents.*

***kit up** *v adv*
*not fml* to dress (someone or oneself): [T1] *The passengers had kitted themselves up in funny clothes for the dance on the last night of the voyage.*

**kneel down** *v adv*
to (cause to) move or stay down on one's knees: [IØ + DOWN] *Christians often kneel down to say their prayers. I knelt down to play with the baby on the floor.*

**knit together** *v adv*
**1** to knit (two or more threads, stitches, or parts of a garment) at the same time or in the same place: [T1 + TOGETHER] *Knit the next two stitches together to make the garment narrower. If you knit two thicknesses of the wool together, the garment will be very warm and you will finish it quickly.*
***2** (esp. of something broken) to join firmly together: [IØ] *The doctor says that Mother won't be able to walk until the bones of her leg have knitted together.*
***3** to unite (people or things): [T1b (*usu. pass.*)] *Our two nations are knit together by common concerns.*

**knit up** *v adv*
**1** to complete (something) by knitting: [T1 + UP] *How long will it take you to knit up this pattern? I can knit up a baby's coat in a week.*
**2** to be suitable for knitting: [IØ + UP (*simple tenses*)] *This wool knits up well.*
***3** to repair or make (something) good again; mend: [T1a (*usu. simple tenses*)] *Our letters enabled us to knit up our old friendship.* [IØ (*simple tenses*)] *A broken bone soon knits up again.*

**knock about/around[1]** *v adv*
**1** to push (something) from place to place in an aimless manner, without direction: [T1 + ABOUT/AROUND] *There's nothing to do here; let's go into that field and knock a ball about for half an hour or so.* → **kick about[1]** (1)
***2** *infml* to exist; be living: [IØ (*continuous tenses*)] *Is the same chairman still knocking about? I thought he had left years ago. The idea of world government has been knocking about for some time, but no one seems to take it seriously. There's plenty of money knocking about if you know where to look.* → **kick about[1]** (2)
***3** *infml* to be left unattended or unnoticed: [L9 (*continuous tenses*)] *I found this book knocking about upstairs; is it yours?* → **kick about[1]** (3), **leave about, lie about[3]** (2)
***4** to treat (someone or something) roughly; damage (something): [T1] *If that man knocks his wife about any more he'll be sent to prison. That poor old piano has been considerably knocked about in its travels. "I'm one of the ruins that Cromwell knocked about a bit."* (Marie Lloyd, song title) —**knockabout** *adj* → **bash about,** etc., **kick about[1]** (4)
***5** *infml* to travel in various places: [L9 (*often simple tenses*)] *I've knocked about in most parts of the world in my time. Someone who's knocked around a lot is more interesting to listen to than someone who has never travelled.*
***6** *infml* to be seen in public (with someone): [L9 (TOGETHER, *with*)] *How long was Grace knocking about with that red-haired boy before he left her? They knocked about together for a year, I think.* → **ask out,** etc.
***7** *infml* to play; use something such as a vehicle for pleasure: [L9] *Jim bought Mary an old car, just for knocking about in.* —**knockabout** *n, adj* → **run about** (2), **run around[1]** (2)

**knock about/around[2]** *v prep*
**1** to hit (something or someone) in or on (a place): [T1 + *about/around*] *You can get some exercise by knocking a ball about a field with a friend.* → **kick about[2]** (1)
***2** *infml* to lie unnoticed in (a place): [T1 (*no pass., often continuous tenses*)] *No, it's not mine, it's been knocking about the house for years.* → **kick about[2]** (2), **lie about[3]** (2)
***3** *infml* to travel in different parts of (a place): [T1 (*no pass., often continuous tenses*)] *My uncle has been knocking about Africa most of his life. He knocked around India when he was young.* → **bang around[2]** (2), **hang about[2]** (2), **kick about[2]** (3)
***4** *infml* to work roughly in (a place): [T1 (*no pass.*)] *I wear these old trousers for knocking about the garden.* —**knock-about** *adj*

**knock against** *v prep*
**1** to (cause to) strike against (something, usu. a hard object): [T1 + *against*] *I knocked my head against the doorpost and hurt it.* [IØ + *against*] *The car knocked against the garage door and damaged it.* → **bang against** (1), **beat against** (1), **hit against, hit on** (1), **knock on[2]** (2) **knock up against** (1), **run against** (1), **run into** (5), **run up against** (1), **strike against** (2), **strike on** (1)
**2 knock one's head against a brick wall** → **BANG AGAINST** (2)

**knock around[1]** *v adv* → **KNOCK ABOUT[1]**

**knock around[2]** *v prep* → **KNOCK ABOUT[2]**

**knock at** *v prep* → **beat at** (1), **drum on, hammer at** (2), **hammer on, knock on[2]** (1), **pound at** (1) **pound on, rap at, rap on** (1), **smite on** (2), **tap at tap on** (1), **thump on**
to beat on; give blows on; make a noise or

(something such as a door) usu. with one's hand: [IØ + *at*] *Who's that knocking at my door?*

**knock away** *v adv*

**1** to knock continuously or repeatedly, as at a door: [IØ + AWAY (*continuous tenses*)] *I've been knocking away for ages, but nobody has answered the door.*

**2** to push (usu. something) away with a sharp blow: [T1 + AWAY (*usu. simple tenses*)] *Moving quickly from behind the criminal, the policeman was able to knock his gun away.* → **kick away** (2)

**knock back** *v adv*

**1** to knock in reply: [IØ + BACK (*usu. simple tenses*)] *If you knock on the prison wall, another prisoner may knock back.*

**2** to push (something) back with sharp blows: [T1 + BACK] *I had to knock the branches back to reach the hut.*

***3** *infml* to drink (usu. large quantities of liquid): [T1] *How can Gordon knock back eight pints of beer every Saturday afternoon while he watches the football game on television?* → **toss back** (2), **toss off** (4)

***4** *infml* to cost (someone) (usu. a lot): [D1 (*simple tenses*)] *That car must have knocked her back a few pounds!* → **put back** (5), **set back** (6)

***5** *infml* to surprise (someone): [T1b (*usu. simple tenses*)] *The unexpected news fairly knocked me back!* → **bowl over** (2), etc.

**knock dead** *v adj*

**knock them dead** *AmE infml* (of a performer in the theatre) to be very successful with people watching: *Go out there and knock them dead!*

**knock down** *v adv*

**1** to make (something) fall by pushing or hitting it: [T1 + DOWN (*usu. simple tenses*)] *Just when the horse looked like winning, it knocked the last fence down. I'm sorry, dear, I've knocked the gate down with the car.* → **kick over** (1), **knock over** (1)

***2** to make (someone) fall by hitting him, as with a blow or vehicle: [T1 (*usu. simple tenses*)] *Jim was knocked down by a bus, and seriously hurt. This old fighter has never been knocked down by an opponent. "If a madman were to come into this room with a stick in his hand, no doubt we should pity the state of his mind; but . . . we should knock him down first and pity him afterwards."* (James Boswell's *Life of Johnson*) —**knock-down** *n, adj* → **knock over** (2), **run down**[1] (4), **run over**[1] (4, 5), **strike down** (1)

**3** to destroy (a building): [T1] *It was a pity that the old theatre had to be knocked down to make way for the widening of the road.*

**4** to take (something) to pieces so as to move it: [T1] *The furniture has been knocked down ready for the buyer to put it together himself. London Bridge was knocked down stone by stone and rebuilt in the middle of a desert in the United States.* —**knockdown, knocked-down** *adj*

***5** *not fml* to destroy or defeat (someone's argument): [T1] *His speech was poorly prepared, and I soon knocked down his argument.* —**knockdown** *adj*

***6** to sell (goods) at an auction, esp. at a low price: [T1 (*to*)] *The best furniture was knocked down for a low price to the dealer in the second line of seats.* —**knockdown** *adj*

***7** *not fml* to reduce (a price): [T1 (*to*) (*usu. simple tenses*)] *The price was knocked down to £3. Perhaps he'll knock the price down a little if the glass is broken.* —**knockdown** *adj* → **beat down** (3), **knock off**[1] (3)

***8** *not fml* to persuade (a seller) to reduce a price: [T1 (*to*)] *The man was asking £5 for the dress, but I knocked him down to £4.50.* → **beat down** (4)

***9** *AmE infml* to earn (money): [T1 (*simple tenses*)] *A clever lawyer can knock down $40,000 in a good year.* → **bring in** (3), etc.

***10** *not fml* (esp. as in old-style popular theatre) to choose; make a demand on (someone): [T1 (*for*) (*simple tenses*)] *The chairman knocked the next artist down for a song.* → **call on** (2), **prick down**

***11** *not fml* to surprise (someone): [T1b (*simple tenses*)] *The unexpected news fairly knocked him down.* → **bowl over** (2), etc.

**12 you could have knocked me/him/etc., down with a feather** *infml* I/he/etc., was very surprised: *We all thought that my uncle was dead, so when he walked into the room you could have knocked me down with a feather!*

**knock for** *v prep*

**1 knock someone/something for six: a** (in cricket) to hit the ball with one stroke so far that it is worth six runs: [*usu. simple tenses*] *If he gives me one of his tricky slow balls, I'll knock it for six.* **b** *infml* to defeat; destroy; ruin; have a severe effect on (something or someone): [(*usu. simple tenses*)] *In the last battle our army knocked the enemy for six! Once our product reaches the market, it will knock the competition for six!*

**2 knock someone for a loop: a** esp. *AmE infml* to defeat someone in a fight: [(*usu. simple tenses*)] *The young man was proud of his strength and ability to fight, but the old experienced fighter soon knocked him for a loop.* **b** esp. *AmE infml* to confuse someone; make someone helpless in argument: [(*usu. simple tenses*)] *The listener's next question knocked the speaker for a loop; he had not expected such informed opinion.* → **throw for**

**knock in**[1] *v adv*

**1** to make (something) enter by hitting it; drive (something) inwards: [T1 + IN (*often simple tenses*)] *With a sense of great pride I knocked the last nail in. At the last moment, the player was able to knock the ball in and ensure his team's victory.* → **hit in, kick in**[1] (1)

***2** *not fml* to try to teach (something) by

force: [T1 (*to*) (*usu. simple tenses*)] *Why waste valuable teaching time trying to knock in a list of facts, if the children aren't interested.* → **hammer in** (3), etc.

**knock in²** *v prep* → **roll in** (2)

**knock them in the aisles** *infml* (of a performer in the theatre) to amuse the public greatly: *'Is this new man funny, then?' 'Funny! The way he tells these jokes will knock them in the aisles!'*

**knock into** *v prep*

**1** to drive (something) into (something) by hitting it: [T1 + *into* (*often simple tenses*)] *Can you knock this nail into the wood? It takes more skill than it looks, to knock the ball into the hole.*

*__2__ *not fml* to meet (someone) by chance: [T1 (*no pass., simple tenses*)] *I knocked into my old teacher in the town this morning.* → **bump into** (2), etc.

*__3__ *not fml* to teach (something) by force to (someone): [D1 (*usu. simple tenses*)] *Can't you knock some sense into that stupid boy's head?* → **hammer into** (3), etc.

**4 knock something/someone into a cocked hat** *infml* to defeat something or someone completely: [*often simple tenses*] *At the last election, the Government won easily, knocking the Opposition into a cocked hat.*

**5 knock someone into the middle of next week** *infml* to hit someone, esp. as a punishment; usu. as a threat: [*usu. simple tenses*] *If I find you've stolen those things, I'll knock you into the middle of next week!*

**6 knock something into shape** *not fml* to make something more perfect or acceptable: *It'll take the theatre company another week to knock the play into shape.*

**knock off¹** *v adv*

**1** to make (something or someone) fall with a push: [T1 + OFF (*often simple tenses*)] *Just when I had put the glass safely down on the table, the cat jumped up and knocked it off. Your cigarette ash is very long; please knock it off before it falls on the carpet. You're not safe on that ladder; a branch could knock you off. A snowball knocked his hat off.*

*__2__ *infml* to stop work: [IØ] *Let's knock off early and go to the football game. When the whistle goes, all the workers knock off for a cup of tea.* → **knock on¹** (3)

*__3__ *not fml* to reduce; take (part) from a price: [T1 (*usu. simple tenses*)] *If you take both dresses, I'll knock £2 off.* → **beat down** (3), **knock down** (7)

*__4__ *not fml* to write (words or music) quickly, often carelessly: [T1 (*often simple tenses*)] *I can knock off a poem in half an hour.* → **dash off** (2), etc.

*__5__ *infml* to kill; murder (someone): [T1 (*often pass., usu. simple tenses*)] *I don't want to knock the old man off; can't we just tie him up to keep him quiet? The old man who owned the jewels was knocked off by the thieves.* → **bump off**, etc.

*__6__ *BrE infml* to steal (something); rob (a place): [T1 (*often simple tenses*)] *Where did you get all those watches? Did you knock them off? Yes, we knocked off a jeweller's shop last night.* → **knock over** (5), **rip off** (2)

*__7__ *infml* to take (someone) to a police station on a charge: [T1 (*usu. simple tenses*)] *You can't knock me off, I've done nothing!*

*__8__ *infml* to defeat or destroy (someone): [T1] *If he can knock off the next two opponents, he could get into the last part of the competition.*

*__9__ *infml* to finish (something): [T1] *I've a pile of work to knock off before I can take my holiday.*

*__10__ *infml* to eat the whole of (something): [T1] *Those boys have knocked off the whole cake!*

*__11__ *sl* to have sex with (a woman): [T1 (*usu. simple tenses*)] *What a beauty! I'd like to knock her off!* → **knock off with, knock up** (10)

**12 knock someone's block off** *infml* to hit someone, esp. as a punishment; usu. as a threat: [(*usu. simple tenses*)] *Tell me where you've been out so late, or I'll knock your block off!*

**13 knock it off!** *infml* stop that!: [*imper.*] *They were making so much noise that I couldn't sleep, so I told them to knock it off!* → **pack in** (4), **pack up** (4), **turn in¹** (9), **turn up** (11)

**knock off²** *v prep*

**1** to push (something), usu. by accident, off (something): [T1 + *off* (*usu. simple tenses*)] *I'm sorry, I've knocked my glass off the table and broken it.*

*__2__ *infml* to stop (work): [T1 (*no pass.*)] *Let's knock off work early and go to the football game.*

*__3__ *not fml* to reduce; take (part) from (a price): [D1 (*usu. simple tenses*)] *I'll knock £2 off the price of the dress if you'll take both dresses.*

**4 knock someone off his pedestal** *not fml* to cause someone to cease to be admired: *He's no longer the greatest actor we have and one of the most promising young actors is about to knock him off his pedestal.* → **put on²** (34), **set on** (18)

**5 knock spots off** *infml* to be much better than (something or someone): [(*usu. simple tenses*)] *Tom's books knock spots off most writers of crime stories. The singer's performance knocked spots of that of any other competitor.*

***knock off/on with** *v adv prep* → **knock off¹** (11), **knock up** (10)

*sl* to have sex with (a woman): [T1 (*no pass.*)] *She's a real beauty, I'd knock off with her any day! He didn't seem to know that his friend had been knocking on with his wife.*

***knock on¹** *v adv*

**1** (in the theatre) to give (an actor) a signal

as a knock to go on stage: [T1b (*usu. pass.*)] *Hurry up, you're late for your call, you've been knocked on!*
**2** (in rugby football) to move (the ball) forward by knocking in with the hand(s): [T1b] *Don't try to knock the ball on, it's against the rules.* —**knock-on** *n*
**3** *infml* to continue working: [IØ (*often simple tenses*)] *Let's knock on for another half hour. I'd better knock on with the gardening while it's still daylight.* → **knock off**[1] (2)
**4** *not fml* to increase (something): [T1a (*usu. simple tenses*)] *It's the interest payments that knock on the price of a house over the years.* —**knock-on** *adj*

**knock on**[2] *v prep*
**1** to beat on; give blows on; make a noise on (something such as a door), usu. with one's hand: [IØ + *on*] *Someone knocked on the door so I went to answer it. "'Is there anybody there?' said the traveller, Knocking on the moonlit door."* (Walter de la Mare, *The Listeners*) → **knock at**, etc.
**2** to strike (something such as part of the body) on (something such as a hard object): [T1 + *on* (*usu. simple tenses*)] *I knocked my head on the doorpost and hurt it.* → **knock against** (1), etc.
**3 knock on wood** to put one's hand on something wooden in the belief that this will prevent bad luck: *You'd better knock on wood before you go on a long journey in that old car.* → **touch wood**

**knock on with** *v adv prep* → KNOCK OFF WITH

**knock out** *v adv*
**1** to remove (something) with a sharp blow: [T1 + OUT (*usu. simple tenses*)] *The stone which the girl threw knocked the boy's eye out. There was a diamond in my ring, but it must have got knocked out when I dropped it. Knock the ash out before you refill your pipe.*
*__2__ to empty (a pipe) by knocking it against something: [T1] *Knock out your pipe and then refill it.* → **tap out** (2)
*__3__ to make (someone) lose consciousness; make (a boxer) unable to rise before a count of ten seconds: [T1 (*usu. simple tenses*)] *This experienced old fighter has never yet been knocked out. The metal bar swung, hitting the driver on the chin and knocking him out.* —**knockout** *n, adj* → **be out** (17), **go out** (12), **lay out** (5), **put out** (17), **put under**[1]
*__4__ (of a drug, etc.) to make (someone) go to sleep: [T1 (*usu. simple tenses*)] *Many people would rather have gas to knock them out before they have their teeth removed.* —**knockout** *adj* → **put out** (17)
*__5__ to defeat (someone) or destroy (something) completely; make (someone or something) helpless or useless: [T1 (*often simple tenses*)] *Our soldiers had orders to knock out the enemy guns/guards.*
*__6__ *not fml* to tire (someone) very much; make (someone or oneself) ill, as through overwork: [T1 (*usu. simple tenses*)] *Hours of gardening in the sun have quite knocked me out. Don't knock yourself out trying to get the job finished.* → **tire out**, etc.
*__7__ *not fml* to play (music) roughly or unskilfully: [T1] *He can't read music but he can knock out a tune on the piano.* → **dash off** (2), etc.
*__8__ to cause (an opponent) to leave a competition: [T1 (*often pass.*)] *Our team got through to the second part of the competition before they were knocked out.* —**knockout** *n, adj* → **knock over** (4), **walk over**[1] (2)
*__9__ *infml* to surprise (someone); have a strong effect on (someone): [T1 (*usu. simple tenses*)] *Your unexpected news has quite knocked me out! Her beauty knocked out every man in the room.* —**knockout** *n* → **bowl over** (2), etc.

**knock out of** *v adv prep*
**1** to remove (something) from (something else): [T1 + OUT + *of* (*usu. simple tenses*)] *The sudden blow knocked two teeth out of his mouth. The diamond must have got knocked out of my ring when I dropped it. Knock the ash out of your pipe before you refill it. The policeman knocked the gun out of the criminal's hand.*
*__2__ to cause (an opponent) to leave (a competition): [T1 (*often pass.*)] *Our team were knocked out of thhe competition in the second game.*
**3 knock the bottom out of: a** *not fml* to destroy the sense of; prove (an argument) to have no value: [*usu. simple tenses*] *When the next speaker produced all those facts, he knocked the bottom out of my argument.* **b** *not fml* to take away the necessary support of (something): [*often simple tenses*] *The lack of spending money has knocked the bottom out of the toy trade.*
**4 knock someone out of the box** (in baseball) to cause (a pitcher) to be removed by hitting successfully against him: *Our best man was knocked out of the box by their new player.*
**5 knock the hell/the living daylights out of** *infml* to beat (someone) thoroughly, often as a punishment; often as a threat: *If you don't tell me where you got that money, I'll knock the living daylights out of you!*
**6 knock the spirit/stuffing out of** *not fml* to make (someone) feel less keen, proud, etc., often by means of a blow or shock: *The way to deal with a young fighter is to hit him hard in the first few minutes, so as to knock the stuffing out of him. The news that she had lost the competition knocked the spirit out of the young singer.*

**knock over** *v adv*
**1** to make (something) fall by pushing or hitting it, often accidentally: [T1 + OVER (*usu. simple tenses*)] *The cow knocked the milk bucket over. Carelessly, I knocked my teacup over and the tea went all over the tablecloth. Just when the horse looked like winning, it*

*knocked the last fence over.* → **kick over** (1), **knock down** (1)

*__2__ to make (someone) fall by hitting him, as with a blow or vehicle: [T1 (*usu. simple tenses*)] *Jim was knocked over by a bus, but not seriously hurt. Coming too fast down the road, I knocked over a child on a bicycle. Running round the corner, the boys nearly knocked an old lady over.* → **knock down** (2), **run down¹** (4), **run over¹** (4, 5), **strike down** (1)

*__3__ *not fml* to surprise (someone): [T1 (*usu. simple tenses*)] *The unexpected news fairly knocked me over.* → **bowl over** (2), etc.

*__4__ *not fml* to defeat (an opponent) easily: [T1 (*usu. simple tenses*)] *We should be able to knock the other team over without any trouble.* —**knockover** *n* → **knock out** (8), **walk over¹** (2)

*__5__ *AmE infml* to steal (something); rob (a place): [T1 (*usu. simple tenses*)] *Where did you get all those watches? Did you knock them over? Yes, we knocked over a jeweller's shop last night.* → **knock off¹** (6), **rip off** (2)

***knock through** *v adv*

to join (usu. two rooms) by removing the wall; remove (a wall) between usu. two rooms or to make a space: [IØ (*usu. simple tenses*)] *The builders can knock through to make one large room upstairs.* [T1] *What will it cost to knock these two bedrooms through into one? We can knock the wall through to make a new entrance.*

**knock together** *v adv*

**1** (of two things) to (cause to) hit against each other: [IØ + TOGETHER] *My knees were knocking together with fear.* [T1 + TOGETHER] *These two pieces of wood make a funny noise when you knock them together.*

*__2__ to make; build (something) roughly: [T1 (*often simple tenses*)] *I'm no woodworker, but I can knock a bookshelf together when necessary.* → **throw together** (2), etc.

**3 knock their heads together** *infml* to make people see sense by pushing the head of one against the other, or other such means, whether or not violent: [(*usu. pass.*)] *Those stupid boys should have their heads knocked together, then they might have some sense. People who treat animals badly should have their heads knocked together.*

**knock up** *v adv*

**1** to cause (something) to rise by hitting it: [T1 + UP (*often simple tenses*)] *Try not to knock the ball up as it will easily be caught and then you'll be out. A man in the crowd knocked my arm up and I dropped my bag.* → **hit up** (1)

*__2__ *BrE not fml* to wake (someone) by knocking: [T1] *A man used to go around my northern village in the early morning, knocking people up by beating gently on the bedroom windows with a long pole.* —**knocker-up** *n*

*__3__ *not fml* to make; build (something) roughly or in a hurry: [T1 (*often simple tenses*)] *I'm no woodworker, but I can knock up a bookshelf when necessary. The hut looks as if it was knocked up by some children in half an hour's play.* → **throw together** (2), etc.

*__4__ *not fml* to make (something) in a hurry: [T1 (*often simple tenses*)] *What sort of a meal do you expect me to knock up in ten minutes?*

*__5__ (esp. in cricket) to add (something, as runs) to a total: [T1] *The cricket team needs to knock up forty-five more runs before tea, if they're to have a hope of winning.*

*__6__ *BrE not fml* to earn (money): [T1] *Jim's father knocked up over £10,000 last year.* → **bring in** (3), etc.

*__7__ *BrE infml* to tire (someone) very much: make (someone or oneself) ill, as by overwork: [T1 (*usu. simple tenses*)] *Hours of gardening in the sun have quite knocked me up. Don't knock yourself up trying to finish the job.* → **tire out**, etc.

*__8__ to practise before beginning a real game, esp. of tennis: [IØ] *The players are allowed to knock up for four minutes before starting the game.* —**knock-up** *n*

*__9__ *BrE not fml* to try to gain votes by visiting homes before an election: [IØ] *How many helpers can you send knocking up before Tuesday's election?* [T1a] *Our helpers have knocked up the whole of this street. How many votes do you think they knocked up* —**knocker-up** *n*

*__10__ esp. *AmE sl* to make (a woman) pregnant: [T1] *If you knock your girlfriend up, you'll be in trouble with her family.* → **bang up** (3), **knock off¹** (11), **knock off with, prang up** (3)

**11 knock up copy** *not fml* to get written material ready for printing, as in a newspaper: *We'd like to employ you on this newspaper but the person we appoint must be able to knock up copy—can you do that?*

**knock up against** *v adv prep*

**1** to hit (something) by running into it: [IØ + UP + *against* (*usu. simple tenses*)] *Running down the street, I knocked up against the lamppost.* → **knock against** (1), etc.

*__2__ to meet (someone) by chance: [T1 (*no pass., simple tenses*)] *I knocked up against my old teacher in the town this morning.* → **bump into** (2), etc.

**knot together** *v adv*

to fasten (things) together with a knot or knots: [T1 + TOGETHER] *The prisoner escaped from the prison by knotting the sheets together and climbing down them out of the window.*

**know about** *v prep*

**1** to have (information) about (something or someone); be informed about (something or someone): [T1 + *about* (*simple tenses*)] *Tell us everything that you know about the enemy's activities. He knows some damaging facts about the firm's dealings. "You mentioned your name as if I should recognize it, but . . . I know nothing whatever about you."* (A. Con

Doyle, *The Memoirs of Sherlock Holmes*) [I∅ + *about* (*simple tenses*)] *You can't fool me, I know about your secret plan!* → **know of**

**2 I don't know about** *not fml* I doubt (something); I am not too sure of (something): *As for your hope of winning the first prize, I don't know about that. I don't know about famous, but she's certainly very well-known.*

**know apart** *v adv* → **tell from** (2), etc.
to be able to recognize the difference between (two or more things or people): [T1b (*simple tenses*)] *The two brothers are so much alike that even their own mother hardly knows them apart.*

**know as** *v prep*
**1** to call (someone or something) by (a name): [T1 + *as* (*often pass.*)] *You may know this film as 'Never Give an Inch,' its British title. The actress likes to be known as May Diamond, although it is not her real name.*

**2 be known as** to have people think that one is (something or someone): *Dr White is known in the town as a good family doctor.*

**know backwards** *v adv*
to have learned (something such as words) very thoroughly: [T1b (*simple tenses*)] *Every actor ought to know his lines backwards before he goes on stage, as nervousness may make him forgetful. Anybody who writes a dictionary has to know his alphabet backwards.*

**know best** *v adv*
*not fml* to have the best informed opinion; be the best judge (of something or someone): [I∅ (*simple tenses*)] *No, you really ought to stay in bed; remember, Mother knows best!* [T1 (*simple tenses*)] *Doctors should ask nurses their opinion; after all, they know the patients best.*

**know better** *v adv*
**1** to be more well-informed about (something or someone): [T1 + BETTER (*than*) (*simple tenses*)] *You know him better than I do; do you think he'll agree? We need a guide who knows the city better* (*than this man*).

**2** to have more sense (than); not be so silly as (to do something): [I∅ (*simple tenses*)] *You ought to know better than to go out in this cold weather in those thin summer shoes; no wonder your feet got cold!*

**know by** *v prep*
to recognize (something or someone) because of (sight or a sign): [T1 + *by* (*simple tenses*)] *You will know the house by its tall chimneys. I know the singer by sight, but I haven't spoken to her yet.*

**know fine** *v adv*
*ScotE not fml* to know well (usu. that . . .): [T5 + FINE (*simple tenses*)] *. I know fine that he's not to be trusted.*

**know for** *v prep*
**1** to have information about (someone or something) for (a length of time): [T1 + *for* (*simple tenses, often perfect*)] *I have known this city for twenty years, and am saddened to see crime increase in the way it has done recently. I have known Mr Sharp for most of my life, and I can't believe that he has behaved like this!* [I∅ + *for* (*simple tenses, often perfect*)] *There's no need to break the news gently; I've known for some weeks.*

**2** to recognize (someone) as being (a certain kind of person): [T1 + *for* (*simple tenses*)] *I know you for a thief and a liar!*

**know from** *v prep*
**1** to be able to tell the difference between (something or someone) and (something or someone else): [T1 + *from* (*simple tenses*)] *The two brothers are so much alike that it is almost impossible to know one from the other. The child has no table manners; why, he doesn't know a knife from a fork!* → **tell from** (2), etc.

**2 not know someone from Adam** *not fml* not to know who someone (esp. a man) is: [(*simple tenses*)] *Who's this speaker you've invited? I don't know him from Adam!*

**3 not know one's arse from one's elbow** *taboo* to have no ability or sense: [(*simple tenses*)] *This new secretary is useless and must be dismissed at once—he doesn't know his arse from his elbow.*

**4 know from nothing about** *AmE infml* to have no information concerning (usu. a subject): *Why have you asked him to speak? He knows from nothing about music history.*

**know of** *v prep* → **know about** (1)
to have knowledge of; have heard of; be conscious of the existence of (someone or something); possess (information) concerning (something or someone): [I∅ + *of* (*simple tenses*)] *The police know of his activities, and are watching him. I know of his books, but I haven't read any of them. Do you know of a really good hotel in this city?* [T1 + *of*] *What do you know of this theatre company? "As I know more of mankind I expect less of them, and am now ready to call a man a good man . . . more easily than formerly."* (James Boswell's *Life of Johnson*)

**know through** *v adv*
**know through and through** to know (someone) very well: [*simple tenses*] *He thought he knew his wife through and through, until she deceived him.*

**know to** *v prep*
**1 be known to** to be known well by (someone): *Mrs Hall is well known to all the family, and I am certain that she will make a good servant in your house.*

**2 be known to** to have one's name recorded by (officials): *Your new neighbour is known to the police, so you'd better lock your door.*

**3 make oneself known to** to introduce oneself to (someone): *There's a man waiting outside the theatre, who wishes to make himself known to you.*

***knuckle down** *v adv*
**1** *AmE not fml* (in marbles) to place one's hand on the ground with the knuckles touching the ground, in order to shoot: [IØ] *You'll shoot in a truer straight line if you knuckle down.*
**2** *not fml* to begin to work hard (at something or doing something): [IØ (*to*)] *If we all knuckle down, we'll soon get the job done. Every worker should knuckle down to the job of getting the country on its feet again. I really must knuckle down to finding the answer tonight.* → **buckle down, buckle to**

***knuckle under** *v adv* → **buckle under**
*not fml* to admit defeat; yield: [IØ (*to*)] *Should the employers knuckle under to the workers' demands? Women have knuckled under for centuries, and only now are they beginning to demand independence and recognition.*

**kowtow to** *v prep*
**1** to kneel and bow to (someone in power): [IØ + *to*] *All the servants had to kowtow to the king when he entered the room.*
*__2__ to act humbly towards (someone): [T1] *The natives keep in favour by kowtowing to the governing officials. Should a politician kowtow to the voters in order to win their votes?*

# L

**label as** *v prep*
to describe (someone or something) as (someone or something), esp. without much thought or judgment: [T1 + *as* (*often pass.*)] *The new leader was quickly labelled as hot-tempered, at least by his enemies. The council has labelled the house as unfit for people to live in. Women are tired of being labelled as unskilled workers.*

**label with** *v prep* → **mark with** (3)
to mark (something) with (something such as a description): [T1 + *with* (*often pass.*)] *All cases should be clearly labelled with the owner's name. Are all the goods labelled with the correct price? These dangerous tins should be labelled with a warning.*

**labor under** *AmE* *v prep* → LABOUR UNDER

**labour at/over** *v prep* → **toil at, work at** (2), **work on²** (2)
to work hard at; make a lot of effort about (something or doing something): [IØ + *at/over*] *Don't labour at/over your writing, try to make it seem easy and natural. If you labour at perfecting your style, make sure that it doesn't sound false and stiff.*

**labour for** *v prep*
**1** to work hard in the employment of (someone): [IØ + *for*] *Why should we labour for the lord of the village when he gives us no reward?* → **work for** (1)
**2** to work hard so as to gain (money, a purpose, etc.): [IØ + *for*] *The girls in the match factories used to labour for a few pennies a day. The politician declared his willingness to labour for the good of the people. Leaders of many nations are still labouring for peace.* → **work for** (2)

**labour over** *v prep* → LABOUR AT

**labour under** *v prep*
**1** to work underneath (something): [IØ + *under*] *Miners deserve all the pay we can afford to give them, for labouring under the ground in uncomfortable conditions.* → **work under** (1)
*__2__ to be limited by; struggle against; suffer from; have the disadvantage of (something bad): [T1 (*no pass.*)] *For centuries, women have laboured under a misuse of their abilities and a misunderstanding of their needs as people. The firm has been labouring under difficulties for the past year.*
**3 labour under a delusion/misapprehension/misunderstanding** to be greatly mistaken: [(*often continuous tenses*)] *If you think that you can win the next election, when all the voters have declared their support for the other party you are labouring under a delusion. "She probably laboured under the common delusion that you made things better by talking about them."* (Rose Macauley, *Crewe Train*) → **be under** (9)

***lace in** *v adv*
**1** *old use* to make the waist of (someone, esp. a woman) narrow, with tight binding: [T1] *Modern fashions, fortunately, do not demand that women should be laced in.*
**2** (in bookbinding) to fix (the boards) to the pages by fastening bands through holes in them: [T1] *Make sure that the boards are firmly laced in before going on to the next step.*

***lace into** *v prep* → **lay into**, etc.
*infml* to attack (someone) violently, with blows or words: [T1] *Fearlessly, Jim laced into his attackers, and soon they all lay unconscious on the ground. The opposition speaker made a lively speech, lacing into the government for its recent inaction.*

**lace up** *v adv*
(of clothing, esp. shoes) to (cause to) fasten by drawing its edges together with a special string: [T1 + UP] *Most children learn to lace up their shoes by the time they are old enough to start school. At the turn of the century women had to have help in lacing up their tig*

*undergarments.* [IØ + UP (*simple tenses*)] *I like boots that lace up all the way to the top.*

**lace with** *v prep*

**1** to ornament (something such as cloth) with (fine additions such as cloth made of fine thread, or gold): [T1 + *with* (*usu. pass.*)] *The prince's coat was of black silk laced with gold thread. "Here lay Duncan, His silver skin laced with his golden blood."* (Shakespeare, *Macbeth*) → **lay with** (2)

**2** to add taste or strength to (a drink) with (alcohol): [T1 + *with* (*often pass.*)] *Young people often like a lemon drink laced with beer.*

***lack for** *v prep* → **want for** (3)

*fml* to have need of (soomething): [T1 (*no pass., often neg., simple tenses*)] *You shall never lack for money while I am alive. She had a wealthy childhood, never lacking for toys or books. Fish is so plentiful on this coast that the natives never lack for food. I'll see that you lack for nothing while you attend college.*

**lack in** *v prep*

**be lacking in** to fail to have any or enough of (something such as a quality): *This car is lacking in speed. Never lacking in daring, though rather lacking in politeness, the student wrote a letter to the newspaper, attacking the university officials. No one who is lacking in musical ability will ever become a professional singer.*

**lade with** *v prep*

**be laden with**

**1** to be loaded with (something heavy); filled with (something such as water): *The farmer's cart was laden with the vegetable crop. The Christmas tree was laden with gifts. The summer has been good, and the trees are laden with fruit. The sky was laden with the dark clouds of a coming storm. The air was laden with the sweet smell of freshly cut grass. I could see that her eyes were laden with tears.* → **load down** (1), etc.

**2** *fml* to suffer from; feel heavy with; be troubled by (a sad feeling): *My heart is laden with sorrow at the thought of your continued absence.* → **bow down** (2), **load down** (2), **weigh down** (2)

**ladle from** *v prep* → LADLE OUT OF

**ladle into** *v prep*

to serve (liquid or nearly liquid food) with a large deep spoon, into (a dish): [T1 + *into*] *How much soup should I ladle into each person's dish?*

**ladle out** *v adv*

**1** to serve (liquid or nearly liquid food) with a large deep spoon: [T1 + OUT] *I need a bigger spoon to ladle out the soup.*

***2** *not fml* to give (something or things) freely: [T1] *Aunt Mabel likes to ladle out advice to the young people, whether they want it or not. The music competition has so many classes that prizes are being ladled out like sweets.* → **dish out** (4), **hand out** (4)

**ladle out of/from** *v adv prep; prep*

to lift (liquid or nearly liquid food) with a large deep spoon out of (a container, usu. in which it has been cooked): [T1 + OUT + *of/from*] *It's not easy to ladle the soup out of this deep pan without dropping some.*

**lag behind[1]** *v adv*

**1** to fail to remain level: [IØ + BEHIND] *Don't lag behind now, just when you're doing so well. Production has been lagging behind recently. The rest of the family had nearly reached the river, but Jane was lagging behind as usual.* → **be behind[1]** (1), **drag behind** (1), **drop back** (2), **drop behind[1]** (1), **fall back** (4), **fall behind[1]** (1), **get behind** (1), **trail behind** (1)

***2** to be late, as with the payment of money: [IØ (*with*) (*usu. simple tenses*)] *If your payments of rent lag behind, you will be asked to leave. If you lag behind with the rent, you will be asked to leave.* → **get behind** (2), etc.

**lag behind[2]** *v prep*

**1** to be slower than (someone or an animal): [IØ + *behind*] *Why does Jane always lag behind the rest of the family when we're out for a walk? The horse that we choose as the winner is usually the one that lags behind all the other runners.* → **trail behind** (1)

***2** to fail to remain level with (something or someone): [T1 (*no pass.*)] *We must not lag behind other nations in our efforts to help those people made homeless by the great floods. Production is lagging behind last year's total.* → **fall behind[2]** (3), etc.

**lag with** *v prep*

to wrap (something such as a pipe) with (cloth or other thick material) to keep warmth in and cold out: [T1 + *with*] *If you lag the water pipes with pieces of old woollen garments before the winter starts, you can prevent the water from freezing and bursting the pipes.*

***lam into** *v prep* → **lay into**, etc.

*sl* to attack (someone) violently, with blows or words: [T1] *Fearlessly, Jim lammed into his attackers, and soon they all lay unconscious on the ground. The opposition speaker made a lively speech, lamming into the government for its recent inaction.*

***lam out** *v adv* → **hit out** (1), **kick out** (2), **lash out** (1), **strike out** (1)

*sl* to strike violently, usu. without direction: [IØ] *"Lam out with your whip as hard as you can."* (Sir A. Conan Doyle, *The Round Red Lamp*)

**lament for** *v prep* → **grieve for, mourn for**

to grieve, esp. aloud, on account of (someone or something): [IØ + *for*] *Mrs Page is still lamenting for her son, a year after his death. Are the newcomers still lamenting for their homeland?*

**lament over** *v prep* → **grieve over, sorrow over**

to grieve about (a cause of sorrow); feel sorry about (something): [IØ + *over*] *It's no good lamenting over your past mistakes.*

**land at** *v prep*

**1** to (cause to) come to rest on the ground at (a place such as an airport): [IØ + *at*] *The airport was closed because of the snow, so we had to land at the neighbouring one.* [T1 + *at*] *The pilot landed the plane safely at its home airport. The ship will stop to land passengers at the next port.* → **land in** (1), **land on** (1)

**2** *not fml* to (cause to) arrive at (a place, usu. small): [IØ + *at* (*simple tenses*)] *We took the wrong turning and landed at a small village in the middle of nowhere.* [T1 + *at* (*simple tenses*)] *This bus will land you at the church in half an hour.* → **land in** (2), **land on** (1), **land up** (5)

**land in** *v prep*

**1** to (cause to) come to rest on the ground in (a place): [IØ + *in*] *Pilots in training have to learn to land in a field.* [T1 + *in*] *The pilot landed the plane safely in the field. He was able to land the flying boat in comparatively calm water.* → **land at** (1), **land on** (1)

**2** *not fml* to (cause to) arrive in (a place): [IØ + *in* (*simple tenses*)] *We took the wrong turning and landed in this strange town by mistake. The train will land you in Bath before midday* → **land at** (2), **land on** (1), **land up** (5)

***3** *not fml* to (cause to) reach; get into (trouble or something else unpleasant): [T1 (*no pass., simple tenses*)] *If you're not careful you'll land in trouble.* [D1 (*simple tenses*)] *Do stop spending so fast or you'll land us in debt. If you're not careful you'll land us in prison.* → **end up** (4), **fetch up** (7), **finish up** (5), **land up** (6), **wind up** (9)

**land on/upon** *v prep*

**1** to (cause to) come to rest on (a surface), esp. after flying or sailing; fall on (something): [IØ + *on/upon*] *We never imagined that men would land on the moon. The bird landed safely on the branch. A drop of rain just landed on my nose, so it must be starting to rain.* [T1 + *on/upon*] *The captain landed the little boat safely on the shore. In spite of the mist, the pilot landed the plane safely on the ground. He landed the flying boat on the still lake. With an effort, the fisherman landed the fish on the river bank.* → **land at, land in** (1, 2), **land up** (5)

**2** *not fml* to make (a blow) hit (part of the body): [T1 + *on/upon*] *After a few minutes, the young fighter landed one on his opponent's nose which seemed to hurt him.* → **plant on** (2)

***3** *not fml* to choose (someone) for punishment or blame; fix (blame) on (someone): [T1] *I'm not guilty of the crime, so there's no point in landing on me.* [D1] *The police tried to land the blame on me, but it was useless as I was not guilty.* → **pick on** (3), etc.

***4** esp. *AmE infml* to scold; find fault with (someone): [T1] *The director landed on Jim as soon as he came in, for being late again. The newspapers have landed on Tom's latest book as the worst crime story of the year.* → **tell off** (1), etc.

***5** *not fml* to force acceptance of (something or someone unwanted) on (someone): [D1 (*often pass.*)] *Don't try to land your dirty work on me! I had three of our neighbours' children landed on me for the whole afternoon.* → **land with**, etc.

**6 land on one's feet** *not fml* to be lucky, esp. in the end: *Whatever risks Jim takes, he always seems to land on his feet.* → **fall on** (12)

***land up** *v adv*

**1** to block (the course of water) with mud: [T1 (*usu. pass.*)] *The pool has got landed up and the fish are dying.* → **earth up** (2)

**2** to cover the roots or lower parts of (a plant) with soil: [T1 (*usu. pass.*)] *"Repeat this . . . till by degrees they are landed up from 12 inches to 2 feet."* (John Abercrombie, *Gardening*) → **earth up** (1)

**3** *not fml* to finish by becoming (something): [L1 (*simple tenses*)] *In spite of the people's opinions, she landed up* (*as*) *the winner. The general began his army life as a private soldier and landed up as ruler of his country.* [L7 (*simple tenses*)] *After gaining two fortunes, he landed up poorer when he died.* → **end up** (1), **fetch up** (4), **finish up** (2), **wind up** (6)

**4** *not fml* to finish (by doing something): [L4 (*simple tenses*)] *I never dreamed that I would land up* (*by*) *owning such a lot of property! Be careful, you could land up* (*by*) *getting hurt.* → **end up** (2), **fetch up** (5), **finish up** (3), **wind up** (7)

**5** *not fml* to arrive at or in (place), esp. after time or events: [L9 (*at, in, on*) (*simple tenses*)] *With Jim driving, you never know where you're going to land up. The traveller took the wrong train and landed up at a country village. He'll land up in prison if he goes on taking risks like that. The boy's ball landed up on the garage roof.* → **end up** (3), **fetch up** (6), **finish up** (4), **land at** (2), **land in** (2), **land on** (1), **wind up** (8)

**6** *not fml* to (cause to) reach (an unfavourable end): [L9 (*in*) (*simple tenses*)] *The business might land up in failure unless more care is taken with the accounts.* [X9 (*in*)] *Stop spending so fast, or you'll land us up in debt* → **end up** (4), **fetch up** (7), **finish up** (5), **land in** (3), **wind up** (9)

**7** *not fml* to receive (something) in the end: [L9 (*with*) (*simple tenses*)] *After much effort the writer landed up with a contract. Jim entered the competition without much hope, not thinking he would land up with first prize* → **end up** (5), **fetch up** (8), **finish up** (6), **wind up** (10)

**land upon** *v prep* → LAND ON

***land with** *v prep* → **land on** (5), **lumber with** (2), **saddle on, saddle with, thrust on**

esp. *BrE not fml* to force (someone) to accept (someone or something unwanted): [D1 (*often pass.*)] *Don't try to land me with you dirty work! I got landed with three of the neighbours' children for the whole afternoon.*

**languish for** *v prep* → **languish over, pine for, pine over**
to grow weak and unhappy with desire for (something or someone): [IØ + *for*] *How long will Grace go on languishing for her red-haired boy? The struggling young singer is languishing for praise.*

**languish in** *v prep*
to suffer; grow weak and unhappy by living or continuing for a long time in (a poor state or bad place): [IØ + *in*] *The old enemy has been languishing in his castle prison for over twenty-five years; isn't it time we forgave him? In the Tower of London, prisoners used to languish in chains, cold, and darkness.* [L9 + *in*] *How long will she go on languishing in her grief?*

**languish of** *v prep*
*old use fml* to suffer from; be sick with (a disease, wound, etc.): [L9 + *of*] *"He lies languishing of wounds."* (Charles Kingsley, *Hereward the Wake*)

**languish over** *v prep* → **languish for, pine for, pine over**
to suffer; grow weak and unhappy on account of (usu. something): [IØ + *over*] *Grace has been languishing over her unreturned love for that red-haired boy for more than a year.*

**lap about/around/round** *v adv; prep*
esp. *old use* to (cause to) be folded or wrapped round (something): [IØ + *about/around/round* (*simple tenses*)] *The ends of the cloth lap around the pole.* [T1 + ABOUT/AROUND/ROUND] *"And now peace laps her round."* (Matthew Arnold, *Requiescat*)

**lap against/on** *v prep*
(of water) to keep touching (something) gently, with a liquid sound: [L9 + *against*] *The river lapped gently against the sides of the small boat as it floated slowly downstream.* [L9 + *on*] *On a calm day, the sea laps on the rocks like a smooth tongue.*

**lap around** *v adv; prep* → **LAP ABOUT**

**lap in** *v prep*
**1** *old use* to wrap; enfold; surround (something or someone) with (something such as a covering, protection, or state): [X9 + *in* (*usu. simple tenses*)] *He lapped me in his arms. "Beautiful blue world of hills . . . fruitful valleys lapped in them."* (Thomas Carlyle, *History of Friedrich II, called the Great*)
**2 be lapped in luxury** to have every comfort that anyone could want: *Jim's father worked hard in the early days of the business so that he and his family might spend later years lapped in luxury.*

**lap on** *v prep* → **LAP AGAINST**

**lap over¹** *v adv*
**1** to (cause to) fold: [X9 + OVER (*usu. pass.*)] *The edges of the paper have been lapped over. The ends are lapped over to prevent them rubbing.* [L9 + OVER (*simple tenses*)] *This dog's ears are so long that they lap over. The upper wings lap over.*
**2** to lie further than something, in space or time; go beyond a limit: [L9 + OVER (*simple tenses*)] *This mat is too big for the room, it laps over at the edges. Don't forget that we have to see the director at midday; we must make sure that this meeting doesn't lap over.*
—**overlap** *n, v*

**lap over²** *v prep*
to place (something) partly on top of (something else): [X9 + *over*] *The boat is built by lapping the edge of one board over the board underneath.* [L9 + *over* (*simple tenses*)] *The two pictures are made to lap over each other.*
—**overlap** *v*

**lap round** *v adv; prep* → **LAP ABOUT**

**lap under** *v adv*
to fold under: [L9 + UNDER (*simple tenses*)] *Any ends that are not smooth must lap under.*

**lap up** *v adv*
**1** *old use* to fold (something) together: [T1 + UP] *In lapping up a fur, they always put the inner side outwards. I wrote this after I had lapped up my letter.*
***2** (usu. of an animal) to drink (liquid) with the tongue: [T1] *The cat eagerly lapped up the milk that we offered it. Don't lap up your soup, children, it's not polite.*
***3** to be eager to accept or believe (something such as words): [T1] *The singer laps up admiration from her public. These clever students lap up all the information that I can give them. How long will the public go on lapping up the lies of politicians?* → **feed on** (2)

**lapse from** *v prep*
**1** to fail to remain level with; weaken or fall from (a good action, high standard, etc.): [L9 + *from* (*often simple tenses*)] *The singer has recently lapsed from her formerly high standard of performance.* → **fall from** (2)
**2 lapse from grace** to lose favour with someone: [*usu. simple tenses*] *The Minister lapsed from grace after his unfortunate remarks, and was dismissed from the government.* → **fall from** (5)

**lapse into** *v prep*
**1** to sink or pass gradually into (a state), often through lack of effort: [L9 + *into* (*often simple tenses*)] *The conversation lapsed into silence. When I stopped worrying about staying awake all night, I lapsed into sleep. Now that the farmers have left, the countryside seems to be lapsing into uncultivated forest.* → **relapse into**
**2** to fall; weaken into (often a bad action or state), esp. through carelessness: [L9 + *into* (*often simple tenses*)] *In the end she got careless, and lapsed into rudeness. It is easy to lapse into lazy habits when you live on your own.*
***3** to let oneself use (language): [T1 (*no pass.*)] *He lapsed into a country form of speech whenever he talked to his mother on*

*the telephone. Try not to lapse into your native language outside class.* → **drop into** (4), **fall into** (4)

**lard with** *v prep*

**1** to enrich (food, esp. meat) with (fat): [T1 + *with*] *Lard the chicken with pig fat to make it tasty.*

***2** *fml* to ornament (something such as speech or writing) with (additions), often unnecessarily: [D1 (*often pass.*)] *His speech was larded with words of praise calculated to win the crowd's support.* → **interlard with**

***lark about/around** *v adv* → **horse about, ramp about, romp about**

*infml* to play, often noisily; have fun; behave improperly: [IØ (*often continuous tenses*)] *No larking about, now, behave yourselves in church.*

**lash about/around** *v adv*

to (cause to) move restlessly, without direction: [X9 + ABOUT/AROUND] *The tiger lashed its tail about whenever anyone came near its cage.* [L9 + ABOUT/AROUND] *The wounded soldier lashed about in great pain.*

**lash against** *v prep*

to beat hard on (a surface or object): [L9 + *against*] *Heavy rain lashed against the sides of the tent, making a terrible noise. A strong wind lashed against the sails, forcing the boat to change course.*

**lash around** *v adv* → LASH ABOUT

***lash at** *v prep* → **lay into**, etc.

*infml* to attack (someone) violently, with blows or words: [T1] *Fearlessly, Jim lashed at his attackers, and soon they all lay unconscious on the ground. The opposition speaker made a lively speech, lashing at the government for its recent inaction.*

**lash down** *v adv*

**1** to beat down heavily: [L9 + DOWN] *Heavy rain lashed down on the roof, making a terrible noise.*

**2** to fasten (something) down with ropes: [X9 + DOWN (*usu pass.*)] *Heavy goods vehicles have to have their loads firmly lashed down, to meet the safety laws.*

**lash into** *v prep*

**1** to beat (something) into (something such as a form): [T1 + *into*] *A strong head wind lashed the river into waves.*

***2** *not fml* to drive; excite (someone) into (a state, feeling, etc.): [D1] *It's too easy to lash a crowd into anger with violent words.*

***3** *infml* to attack (someone) violently, with blows or words: [T1] *Fearlessly, Jim lashed into his attackers, who soon lay unconscious on the ground. The opposition speaker made a lively speech, lashing into the government for its recent inaction.* → **lay into,** etc.

***lash out** *v adv*

**1** *not fml* to make an attack (on something or someone), with blows or words, often suddenly: [IØ (*against, at*)] *Never walk behind a horse in case it lashes out (at you). He doesn't know how to fight; he just lashes out in al[l] directions. Jim lashed out at his attackers an[d] beat them thoroughly. Be careful of the direc[tor's] tongue; he often lashes out in sudden an[ger] (at anyone who annoys him). The opposi[tion] speaker lashed out against the govern[ment's] new tax laws.* —**lash-out** *n* → **hit out** (1, 3), **kick out** (2), **lam out, strike out** (1)

**2** *infml* to spend freely (on something); give [a] lot of (something): [IØ (*on*)] *He's not ver[y] generous with his money; he'll pay for neces[sary] things, but rarely lashes out. Can w[e] afford to lash out on a colour television?* [T1 (*on*)] *Mother always lashes out food for th[e] children's party. He lashed out half his fortun[e] on his daughter's wedding.* → **launch out** (4)

**lash to** *v prep*

to fasten (something or someone) to (some[thing] or someone) with rope: [X9 + *to*] *Las[h] the piece of wood to the pole, to make it long[er]. The only way to keep the children safe o[n] board in a storm was to lash them to the cen[tral] pole.*

**lash together** *v adv* → **rope together**

to fasten (things or people) together wi[th] rope: [X9 + TOGETHER] *Lash the two piec[es] of wood together, to make them stronger. It['s] not safe to climb without being lash[ed] together.*

**lash up** *v adv*

**1** to tie (something) with rope: [X9 + U[P]] *The door of the hut was lashed up with piec[es] of old rope. Are all the boxes safely lashed u[p]*

***2** (in the theatre) to fix (pieces of scener[y]) firmly in place with ropes: [IØ] *Lash the sce[n]ery up ready for the next act. When the scene is in place, lash up.* —**lash-up** *n*

**last for** *v prep* → **keep till** (2), **last till**

to go on; remain; be enough; wear; contin[ue] for (a length of time): [IØ + *for* (*often simp[le] tenses*)] *This winter seems to last for ev[er]. Those shoes didn't last for a month, and I['m] going to take them back to the shop. I doub[t] this wine will last for the whole party.* [T1 *for* (*often simple tenses*)] *This money has [to] last you for the rest of the month.*

**last out** *v adv*

**1** to remain; be enough; not be used up; li[ve]: [IØ + OUT (*often simple tenses*)] *I think [the] car will just about last out till we get to L[on]don. Will the water supply last out through [the] summer? Who would have thought that [he] would last out to over ninety?* → **hang out**, **hold out** (3), **hold up** (6), **keep up** (5)

***2** to remain living or in existence for [a] period of time): [T1a (*often simple tense[s]*)] *Will the wine we bought last out the party? [The] government may not be able to last out [the] year. I don't think Grandfather will last out [the] winter.* → **see out** (4)

***3** to continue in spite of difficulties; ke[ep] going: [IØ (*often simple tenses*)] *Can [the] townspeople last out until help arrives? I d[on't] think our team can last out till the end of* *competition. Mother wondered if she could last out through another operation.* → **hang on**' (3), etc.

**ast till/until** *v prep* → **keep till** (2), **last for**
to go on; wear; be enough; remain; continue until (a point in time, as a date): [IØ + *till/until* (*often simple tenses*)] *Will the fine weather last until the weekend? This coffee won't last till tomorrow, I shall have to buy some more today.* [T1 + *till/until* (*often simple tenses*)] *This money has to last you till next month.*

**atch on** *v adv*
**1** *not fml* to understand what someone has said, esp. a joke: [IØ (*to*) (*usu. simple tenses*)] *Would you mind repeating that, I didn't quite latch on. The teacher makes a lot of jokes to amuse his students, but they rarely latch on* (*to them*). → **catch on** (2)
**2** *not fml* to join someone or a group of people without invitation: [IØ (*to*) (*usu. simple tenses*)] *The party of climbers was all organized when this other man latched on and demanded to come with us.*

**tch onto** *v prep*
**1** to seize (something or someone) tightly; refuse to let go of (something or someone): [T1 (*usu. simple tenses*)] *The dog latched onto the stick and would not drop it. My host latched onto me at the door, saying that I must not go yet.*
**2** *not fml* to gain; obtain (something): [T1 (*usu. simple tenses*)] *We were lucky enough to latch onto a valuable piece of land at a low price.*
**3** esp. *BrE not fml* to understand and usu. accept (something such as an idea): [T1 (*usu. simple tenses*)] *The children quickly latched onto the suggestion and were eager to go for a swim. It wasn't long before everyone latched onto what was happening.* → **fasten on** (6), **fasten onto** (2), **hook onto** (2), **seize on**
**4** *not fml* to join (someone or a group of people) without invitation; refuse to leave (someone or a group): [T1 (*usu. simple tenses*)] *My talkative neighbour latched onto me throughout the party—I couldn't get away! Once he latches onto our organization we'll never get rid of him. "I met her at some meeting or other last year and she sort of latched onto me."* (Margaret Drabble, *The Needle's Eye*)

**ther up** *v adv*
**1** (of soap) to form a mass of bubbles when mixed with hot water: [IØ + UP (*simple tenses*)] *This cheap soap doesn't lather up very well.*
**2** to cover (usu. part of the body) with soap: [T1 + UP (*usu. simple tenses*)] *Lather your face up thoroughly before you try to remove those hairs from your beard.*

**ugh about** *v prep* → **LAUGH OVER**

**ugh at** *v prep*
**1** to be amused by (something or someone funny): [IØ + *at*] *It's not polite to laugh at your own jokes.* → **laugh over**
*__2__ to refuse to treat (someone or something) seriously; make fun of (someone or something): [T1] *It's not kind to laugh at a child's mistakes. His idea is not to be laughed at. "Though Pope laughed at the advice, we might fancy that he took it to heart."* (Sir Leslie Stephens, *Alexander Pope*) → **gibe at, jeer at, jest at, laugh with, make of** (18), **mock at, poke at** (2), **scoff at** (1)
*__3__ to refuse to take notice of, be afraid of, or worried by (something such as trouble); be careless of: [T1 (*often simple tenses*)] *The daring climbers laugh at danger. I advise you not to laugh at the official warnings.*

**laugh away** *v adv*
**1** to continue laughing: [IØ + AWAY (*continuous tenses*)] *The crowd were still laughing away as they left the theatre.*
*__2__ to stop; get rid of (something) by treating it with humour: [T1 (*often simple tenses*)] *She laughed away her foolish fears. "Pompey doth this day laugh away his fortune."* (Shakespeare, *Anthony and Cleopatra*) → **laugh off**' (1)

**laugh down** *v adv*
to make (someone) silent by laughing loudly: [X9 + DOWN (*often simple tenses*)] *The crowd laughed the speaker down.*

**laugh in** *v prep*
**1 laugh in someone's face** *not fml* to refuse to listen to; show clear disrespect or disobedience to; treat (someone) not seriously: *When the new member made his suggestion, the rest of the committee laughed in his face.*
**2 laugh in one's sleeve** *AmE not fml* to enjoy a secret joke, esp. to someone's disadvantage: *The director listened to my complaints with a straight face, but I felt that all the time he was laughing in his sleeve. "The Gods laugh in their sleeve, To watch men doubt and fear."* (Matthew Arnold, *Empedocles on Etna*) → **laugh up**

**laugh into** *v prep*
to cause (oneself) to reach (a state) by laughing: [X9 + *into* (*usu. simple tenses*)] *When I told Mother what the boys had done, she laughed herself into a state of helplessness.*

*__laugh last__ *v adv*
to be the person who wins in the end: [IØ (*simple tenses*)] *He who laughs last laughs longest. He laughs best who laughs last.* (= Don't be too sure that you have won until all is over.)

**laugh off**' *v adv*
*__1__ to get rid of (a bad feeling) by laughing: [T1 (*often simple tenses*)] *Come to the theatre with me and laugh off your worries.* → **laugh away** (2)
*__2__ *infml* to find a way to escape from (something unpleasant such as trouble) by making a joke of it; refuse to accept blame, etc.: [T1 (*usu. simple tenses*)] *He was caught cheating, but tried to laugh it off. Now we know your secret—laugh that off if you can!*

3 **laugh one's head off** *not fml* to laugh loudly and at length: [*often continuous tenses*] *The crowd must be enjoying the performance, they're laughing their heads off.*

**laugh off**[2] *v prep*

**laugh someone/something off the stage** to remove (something or someone) from (usu. a place) with laughter: [*usu. simple tenses*] *The play was so bad that it was laughed off the stage. He was supposed to be a serious performer, but the crowd laughed him off the stage.*

**laugh on** *v prep* → **laugh out of** (4)

**laugh on the other/wrong side of one's face/mouth** *infml* to get the worst of something that had seemed to be an advantage; have a joke turned against one; change from joy to sorrow; be severely disappointed in one's hopes: [*often continuous tenses*] *Once he hears the results and finds that he hasn't won as he expected, he'll be laughing on the other side of his face.*

**laugh out of** *v adv prep*

**1** to cause (someone) to cease; persuade (someone) not to feel (a sad feeling) by laughing: [X9 + OUT + *of* (*often simple tenses*)] *The doctors tried to laugh Mother out of her fears about her coming operation.*

**2** to drive (someone or something) from (a place) by laughing: [X9 + OUT + *of* (*usu. simple tenses*)] *He was supposed to be a serious performer, but the crowd laughed him out of the theatre. When the young politician made a silly mistake, his fellow Members of Parliament laughed him out of the House.*

**3 laugh someone/something out of court** *not fml* to regard or treat someone or something as completely false, untrue, or deceitful: [*usu. pass.*] *The two men claimed that they had seen travellers from outer space, but they were/their story was laughed out of court.*

**4 laugh out of the other/wrong side of one's face/mouth** *infml* to get the worst of something that had seemed to be an advantage; have a joke turned against one; change from joy to sorrow; be severely disappointed in one's hopes: [*often continuous tenses*] *Once he hears the results and finds that he hasn't won as he expected, he'll be laughing out of the wrong side of his mouth.* → **laugh on**

**laugh over/about** *v prep* → **laugh at** (1)

to be amused by remembering, seeing, or talking about (something): [IØ + *over/about*] *How we laughed over Jim's postcard from his seaside holiday! In years to come we'll laugh about this, though it doesn't seem funny at the moment.*

**laugh to** *v prep*

**laugh someone/something to scorn** to refuse to treat someone or something seriously or with respect: [*often simple tenses*] *Years ago, anyone who saw our future dependence on electricity would have been laughed to scorn.*

**laugh up** *v adv*

**laugh up one's sleeve** *not fml* to enjoy a secret joke, esp. to someone's disadvantage: *The director listened to my complaints with a straight face, but I felt that all the time he was laughing up his sleeve.* → **laugh in** (2)

**laugh with** *v prep* → **laugh at** (2), etc.

to share the laughter of (someone): [IØ + *with*] *"Laugh and the world laughs with you; weep and you weep alone."* (Ella Wheeler Wilcox, *Solitude*) *Please don't be offended, we were laughing with you, not at you.*

**launch against/at** *v prep* → **launch on** (1)

to send; aim (something such as an attack or threat) towards (usu. someone): [T1 + *against/at*] *When is the best time to launch our next attack against the enemy? The politician launched a warning at the government that they were in danger of losing the next election.*

**launch forth** *v adv* → LAUNCH OUT

**launch into** *v prep*

**1** to push or send (something such as a ship) on its first voyage in (something); start to float in (a body of water): [T1 + *into*] *The big ship had to be launched into the river sideways because of her great length. It takes a great deal of power to launch a spaceship into space.* [L9 + *into*] *Would it be wise to launch into this rough sea?*

***2** to begin (something new); esp. with eagerness, strength of will, force, etc.: [T1 (*no pass.*)] *It takes courage to launch (out) into new business in these difficult times. The speaker launched (forth) into a new line of argument.* → **launch on** (3)

***3** to start saying (something), usu. at length: [T1 (*often simple tenses*)] *The politician launched (forth/off/out) into a long uninteresting speech about the government's mishandling of national affairs.*

***4** to give (someone) a start in (something): [D1 (*often simple tenses*)] *Jim's father offered to launch him into business.*

**launch on/upon** *v prep*

**1** to begin; give (something such as an attack) concerning (something): [T1 + *on/upon*] *The opposition speaker launched a bitter attack on the government's mishandling of the taxpayer's money.* → **launch against**

***2** to give (someone or something) for the first time to (usu. someone): [D1] *The music theatre company is about to launch a new performer on the musical world. The firm is almost ready to launch its new product on the market.*

***3** to start (something new), esp. with eagerness, strength of will, force, etc.: [T1] *The director has launched (out) on yet another plan for cutting costs. This is not a suitable time for launching forth on a new business undertaking.* → **launch into** (2)

**launch out/forth** *v adv*

**1** to begin a voyage: [L9 + OUT/FORTH

*Those who dared to launch out beyond the unknown waters became the discoverers of new lands.*
**2** to produce (something): [T1 + OUT/FORTH] *The makers are about to launch out a new product.*
***3** to start something new, such as a large plan, action, or way of life: [IØ (*as, into*) (*usu. simple tenses*)] *Next year you may be ready to launch out as a concert pianist.*
***4** to spend freely (on something): [IØ (*on*)] *Can we afford to launch out on a colour television?* → **lash out** (2)

**launch upon** *v prep* → LAUNCH ON

**lavish on** *v prep*
to spend (something such as time, money, or care) generously on (something or someone): [D1] *If she lavished as much care on the children as she does on the dog, the family would be better off. Why do you lavish so much time on your garden, and at the same time, claim to hate the work? The public lavish their admiration on some completely unworthy singers. The government has no right to lavish public money on worthless ideas.*

**lay aback** *v adv*
*naut* to fasten (a sail) in such a position that the wind blows against its forward edge: [T1] *We must lay the sails aback to stay on course in this wind.*

**lay about¹** *v adv* → LIE ABOUT¹ (1)

**lay about²** *v prep*
**1** *not fml* to hit out around (one) (with a weapon): [T1 (*no pass.*)] *He laid about him with a stick, to defend himself from three men who attacked him.* [D1] *He laid his stick about him, trying to beat off his attackers.* → **set about²** (2)
**2** *not fml* to attack (someone): [T1 (*no pass.*)] *The three men laid about him with their hands and boots.* → **set about²** (3)

**lay against** *v prep*
**1** to place (something or someone) next to (something or someone): [X9 + *against*] *The mother laid the toy against the sleeping child's arm, so that she should find it when she woke. If you lay the blue cloth against the green, both colours seem to change.* → **set against** (1)
**2** to make (a charge) against (someone), in a serious, official, or public way: [T1 + *against*] *Will the police lay charges against the boys, or just give them a warning?* → **bring against, level against, prefer against**

**lay along** *v adv*
**1** to stretch (something or someone) at full length, usu. on the ground: [X9 + ALONG] *Lay the rope along so that we can measure it.*
**2** (of a ship) to lean over with a side wind: [IØ] *A strong crosswind caused the ship to lay along.*

**lay alongside** *v adv; prep* → **draw alongside, lie alongside, pull alongside**
to bring (a ship) near (something): [X9 + ALONGSIDE/*alongside* (*usu. pass.*)] *The king ordered his ship to be laid alongside (the enemy ship).*

**lay aside** *v adv*
**1** to put (something) on one side, esp. for a short time: [X9 + ASIDE] *She laid her sewing aside when the telephone rang.* → **lay away** (1), **lay by¹** (1), **place aside** (1), **place on** (7a), **put aside** (1), **put by** (1), **put on²** (32), **set aside** (1), **set by¹** (1), **set on²** (17a), **throw aside** (1)
***2** to discontinue (something such as work), esp. for a short time: [T1] *Tom laid aside his new book for a year while he wrote some magazine articles and informative material.* → **lay by¹** (2), **place aside** (2), **place on** (7b), **put aside** (2), **put by** (2), **put on²** (32), **set aside** (2), **set by¹** (2), **set on²** (17b)
***3** to cease (something such as a habit): [T1] *It's good to lay aside responsibility for the children now that they are grown up. It's time to lay aside our differences and work together for a shared purpose.* → **lay by¹** (3), **place aside** (3), **place on** (7c), **put aside** (3), **put by** (3), **put on²** (32), **set aside** (3), **set by¹** (3), **set on²** (17c)
***4** to save (money) for future use; keep (time or money) for a special purpose: [T1 (*for*)] *I have a little money laid aside for a rainy day* (= a time when money may be needed). *I've laid aside the whole weekend for house-hunting.* → **lay away** (2), **lay by¹** (4), **place aside** (4), **put apart** (2), **put aside** (4), **put away** (3), **put by** (4), **set apart** (2), **set aside** (4), **set by¹** (4)
***5** to save (a supply of goods) for a customer: [T1] *Would you like us to lay aside the rest of the wool?* → **lay away** (3), **lay by¹** (5), **place aside** (5), **place on** (7d), **put aside** (5), **put away** (4), **put by** (5), **put on²** (32), **set aside** (5), **set on²** (17)

**lay at** *v prep*
**1** to place (something) in front of (a place): [X9 + *at* (*often simple tenses*)] *The worshippers laid their gifts at the feet of the god. The red carpet was laid at the bottom of the steps, to honour the royal visitor. The natives laid the food at the entrance to the cave.* → **put at** (1), etc.
**2 lay the blame/guilt/responsibility/something at someone's door** to blame someone; state that someone is responsible for something: *With the cost of living rising so fast, everyone tries to lay the responsibility at someone else's door; the government blames the unions, the unions blame the big businessmen, the big businessmen blame the oil companies, and so on.* → **lie at** (5)

**lay away** *v adv*
**1** to put (something) on one side, as for a short time, or when no longer in use: [X9 + AWAY (*often simple tenses*)] *"The book is completed, And closed, Like the day; And the hand that has written it Lays it away."* (H.W. Longfellow, *The Belfry of Bruges*) → **lay aside** (1), etc.
***2** to save (usu. money): [T1] *I have a little*

*money laid away for a rainy day* (= a time when money may be needed). → **lay aside** (4), etc.

****3** esp. *AmE* to save (a supply of goods) for a customer: [T1] *I asked the lady in the wool shop to lay away the rest of the red wool, so that I would be certain to get the right colour match when I bought the balls a few at a time, as I could afford them.* —**lay-away** *adj* → **lay aside** (5), etc.

**lay back** *v adv* → **put back** (1), **put forward** (1), **set back** (1), **set forward** (1)
(of an animal) to hold (the ears) in a backward position: [X9 + BACK (*often simple tenses*)] *Don't go near that dog when he shows his teeth and lays his ears back, it's a sign that he's angry and dangerous.*

**lay bare** *v adj*
**1** to take the clothes or covers off (something such as part of the body), to show it: [X9 + bare (*usu. simple tenses*)] *The doctor laid Mother's leg bare, ready for the operation. Pulling back the mat, he laid the floorboards bare to show the cracks between the boards.*
****2** *not fml* to show clearly; make known (something formerly hidden): [T1 (*usu. simple tenses*)] *The speaker accidentally laid bare the government's intention to raise taxes. The director was careful not to lay the firm's plans bare. Mary never lays her private thoughts bare.* → **lay open** (2)

**lay before** *v prep*
**1** to place (something) in front of (something or someone): [X9 + *before*] *Entering the temple, the worshippers laid their gifts before the god.* → **put at** (1), etc.
****2** to offer (something such as a plan) to (an official body such as Parliament) for consideration; bring (something) to the notice or attention of (someone): [D1 (*often pass.*)] *Your suggestion will be laid before the committee at a suitable date.* → **put before** (2), etc.

**lay by**[1] *v adv*
**1** to put something on one side, esp. for a short time: [X9 + BY (*usu. simple tenses*)] *She was reading a book, but laid it by when the telephone rang.* → **lay aside** (1), etc.
****2** to discontinue (something such as work) for a time: [T1b] *Tom laid his new book by for a year while he wrote some magazine articles and informative material.* → **lay aside** (2), etc.
****3** to cease (something such as a habit): [T1b] *It's time to lay our differences by and work together for a shared purpose.* → **lay aside** (3), etc.
****4** to save (usu. money): [T1b] *I have a little money laid by for a rainy day* (= a time when money may be needed). → **lay aside** (4), etc.
****5** to save (a supply of goods) for a customer: [T1b] *The shop will lay the wool by for you; you can buy it a little at a time, to be sure to match the colour.* → **lay aside** (5), etc.
****6** *AmE not fml* to cultivate (a crop) for the last time: [T1] *We're laying by the corn in this field.*
****7** *AmE not fml* to gather (a crop): [T1] *If this fine weather stays, we shall be able to lay the wheat by next week.*
****8** *old use* to make (someone) stay in bed through illness: [T1 (*usu. pass.*)] *"Father is often laid by, and unable to go round the farm."* (Comyns Carr, *Margaret Maliphant*) → **lay up** (4), **lie up** (1)
****9** (of a ship) to (cause to) come to rest: [IØ (*often simple tenses*)] *We shall have to lay by because of the storm.* [T1b (*often simple tenses*)] *Lay the ship by outside the harbour.* → **lay to**[1], **lie by**[1], **lie to**[1]

**lay by**[2] *v prep*
**1** to place (something) beside (something or someone): [X9 + *by* (*often simple tenses*)] *The mother laid the toy gently by the side of the sleeping child.* → **set by**[2] (1)
**2 lay great/little store by** to value (something) very much/little: [(*simple tenses*)] *My grandfather laid great store by his moral principles.* → **lay on**[2] (10). **set by**[2] (2), **set on**[2] (23)
**3 lay someone by the heels** *not fml* to catch someone: *Never fear, the police will soon lay the criminals by the heels.*

**lay down** *v adv*
**1** to place (something, someone, or oneself) down, as on the ground, furniture, etc.: [X9 + DOWN (*often simple tenses*)] *The dinner guest laid down his knife and fork with a look of complete satisfaction. Lay the wounded soldier down carefully so as not to hurt him. She laid herself down in the long grass and fell fast asleep.* → **lie down** (1), **place down, put down** (1), **set down** (1)
****2** to set; make; state or declare firmly; fi[x] (something such as an arrangement): [T (*often pass.*)] *We had to lay down rules for the behaviour of the members. Both firms may lay down conditions for the contract. These price limits are laid down by the government. The law lays it down that speed limits must be obeyed.* [T5 (*simple tenses*)] *The law lays down that speed limits must be obeyed.* → **se[t] down** (2)
****3** to pay or risk (money): [T1 (*often simple tenses*)] *How much are you prepared to la[y] down that our team will win? I'll lay down £ on that horse.*
****4** to build; start to build (something such as [a] ship, railway, etc.): [T1] *We shall have to la[y] down a new floor in the upstairs rooms. The track was laid down in the 19th century and [is] in need of repair. The main body of the sh[ip] was laid down in 1932 but she did not sail un[til] 1936.*
****5** to store (usu. wine) for the future: [T (*often simple tenses*)] *When his grandson w[as] born, the old lord laid down a case of be[st] wine for the boy's 21st birthday.* → **put do[wn]** (10)

*6 to change the use of (land formerly used for growing crops) (usu. to grass or other animal food): [T1 (*in, to, under, with*)] *This year we must lay the big field down to grass.* → **lay off**[1] (10), **put down** (15)

*7 to produce and fix firmly (a substance): [T1 (*usu. pass.*)] *Certain chemicals are made and laid down in the living cells.*

*8 to set down; mark (something) on a plan, map, etc.: [T1] *"He now laid down clearly the island groups of the North Pacific."* (T.F. Tout, *History of England*) → **map out** (1), **set down** (6)

**9 lay down one's arms** to stop fighting; yield to the enemy: *The generals have agreed that we should lay down our arms at midnight.*

**10 lay down the law** to speak with force, expecting obedience: *Father is laying down the law to the children again; I wonder what they've done now.*

**11 lay down one's life** to be killed, esp. in war: [(*simple tenses*)] *This stone is marked with the names of all our brave boys who laid down their lives in the Great War. "Greater love has no man than this, that a man lay down his life for his friends."* (The Bible)

**12 lay down (one's office)** to stop working, esp. after having had power: [(*often simple tenses*)] *I should imagine that the President was glad to lay down his office.*

**13 lay down one's tools** to stop working because of disagreement: *The union leaders have asked workers in all the car factories to lay down their tools, starting tomorrow.* → **bring out** (7), etc.

**lay down to** *v adv prep*

*not fml* to make (oneself) work seriously at (something): [D1 (*usu. simple tenses*)] *He never laid himself down to his job, and the other man won easily.*

**lay flat** *v adj*

**1** to flatten; destroy (something) by flattening: [X9 + **flat**] *The heavy rain has laid the wheat flat in the fields. The whole street was laid flat by the heavy bombing.*

**2** to place (oneself) flat on the ground: [X9 + **flat** (*usu. simple tenses*)] *The soldiers laid themselves flat when they heard the bullets whistling overhead.*

*3 *not fml* to tire (someone) greatly: [T1 (*simple tenses*)] *I'm out of breath—all this running lays me flat.* → **tire out**, etc.

**lay for** *v prep*

**1** to place (something) in position; produce (an egg); prepare (a table), for (someone, a length of time, or a purpose): [T1 + *for*] *'Chicken, lay a little egg for me.'* (song) *The children usually lay the table for me while I cook the meal. After he had been laying bricks for several weeks, he became quite skilled at the job.* → **set for** (3)

*2 to fix (blame) for (a fault): [D1 (*usu. simple tenses*)] *Where can we lay the blame for the increasing cost of living?*

*3 *AmE infml* to wait in hiding to attack (someone): [T1] *Three men were laying for us as we rode through the valley.*

**4 lay an ambush/a snare/trap for: a** to try to catch (someone or an animal, by hiding in wait or fixing an object): *We laid an ambush for the enemy and caught three of their men. Help me to lay these snares for the rabbits. You have to lay a special kind of trap for an elephant.* **b** to try to catch (someone) in a deceit: *The speaker did not know that a trap had been laid for him in the seemingly simple question.* → **set for** (7)

***lay in**[1] *v adv*

**1** to obtain a supply of (something): [T1] *We must lay in a store of coffee as it is soon going to be in short supply.*

**2** to paint (light and shade, or blocks of colour) when beginning a painting: *I use this special brush for laying in the light and shade.* —**laying-in** *n, adj*

**3** *naut* to place (oars) inside a boat, removed from their fastenings: [T1] *When the sail is up, lay in your oars.*

**4** to stop working (a coal mine): [T1 (*usu. pass.*)] *This mine is now laid in.* → **farm out** (5), **fish out** (3), **mine out, work out** (8)

**lay in**[2] *v prep*

**1** to place (something or someone); bury (a body) in (a space): [X9 + *in*] *When the baby was laid in the mother's arms for the first time, she felt a rush of joy. The hens lay their eggs in all sorts of unlikely places.* → **fit into** (1), etc.

**2** to set (a scene) in (a place): [X9 + *in* (*usu. pass.*)] *The scene is laid in a forest surrounding a mysterious castle.* → **set in**[2] (5)

***lay into** *v prep* → **lace into, lam into, lash at, lash into** (3), **let into** (6), **let out** (11), **light into, pitch into** (2), **rip into** (2), **set about**[2] (3), **tear into** (4)

*infml* to attack (someone), with blows or words: [T1] *Fearlessly, Jim laid into his attackers, who soon lay unconscious on the ground. The opposition speaker made a lively speech, laying into the government for its recent inaction.*

**lay low** *v adj*

**1** to defeat (someone) in a fight; knock (someone) to the ground: [X9 + **low** (*usu. simple tenses*)] *With one blow, the experienced fighter laid his young opponent low.*

*2 to make (someone) ill: [T1b (*often pass.*)] *I've been laid low with this terrible cough most of the winter.* → **strike down** (2)

*3 to destroy (something): [T1b (*often pass.*)] *The firm's plans for future development have been laid low by rising costs.*

**lay of** *v prep*

**lay hold of**

**1** to seize (something or someone): [(*often simple tenses*)] *Lay hold of this rope and we'll* *pull you up.* → **catch of, get of** (5), **keep of** (3a), **lay on**[2] (12), **lose of** (3), **take of** (10)

**2** to obtain (something) or find (someone): [(*usu. simple tenses*)] *I'll try to lay hold of the director as he comes out of the meeting. Where can you lay hold of this special tobacco?* → **get of** (6), **lay on**[2] (12)

***lay off**[2] *v adv*

**1** *not fml* to rest: [IØ (*usu. simple tenses*)] *Let's lay off for a few minutes, this work is tiring. The doctor said that Jim ought to lay off more.*

**2** *infml* to stop doing something such as annoying someone: [IØ (*simple tenses, often imper.*)] *Lay off, can't you! Can't you see he's had enough?*

**3** *not fml* to stop employing (someone), often for a short time because of a lack of work: [T1 (*often pass.*)] *500 workers were laid off when the factory was closed after the fire.* **—lay-off** *n* → **lie off** (2), **stand off**[1] (4)

**4** to spread (risks): [T1 (*often pass.*)] *The large insurance contract was laid off among many firms.*

**5** *naut* to anchor (a ship or boat) near a certain position; be at anchor: [T1] *The ship was laid off outside the harbour while the storm lasted.* [IØ] *Some ships reached the harbour but many others were laying off.*

**6** *not fml* to paint over the first brush strokes, in a downward direction: [IØ] *Make your first brush strokes, then lay off to get the surface smooth.* → **lay on**[1] (6)

**7** *not fml* to make allowance for the wind or the animal's movement when aiming a shot: [IØ] *You have to lay off a little to one side when the wind is blowing across the animal's course.* **—lay-off** *n*

**8** esp. *AmE not fml* to stop wearing; put aside (certain clothes): [T1] *It's time we were able to lay off these heavy winter clothes.* → **cast aside** (1), etc.

**9** *AmE not fml* to mark or measure off the edges of (an area): [T1] *First, lay off the size of the picture. Care must be taken to lay off the land in broad divisions.*

**10** to change the use of (land) (into a different crop): [T1 (*into*)] *Some of the farmers are laying off their fields, after a very few crops of corn, into grass.* → **lay down** (6), **put down** (15)

**11** (in football) to pass (the ball) carefully into position, esp. sideways or backwards for a short distance: [T1] *Keegan laid the ball off for Channon to shoot.*

***lay off**[2] *v prep*

**1** *not fml* to stop (something or doing something): [T1 (*no pass., usu. simple tenses*)] *The doctor advised Jim to lay off alcohol.* [T4 (*simple tenses*)] *He also said that he should lay off smoking.*

**2** to dismiss (someone) from (work), esp. for a short time: [D1 (*usu. pass.*)] *500 men were laid off work when the factory closed after the fire.*

**3** *infml* to stop annoying (someone): [T1 (*no pass., simple tenses, often imper.*)] *Lay off me, can't you? I've had enough of your unkind jokes!*

**4 lay one's fingers/hands off** *not fml* to not touch (something or someone); not try to gain possession of (something or someone): [(*usu. simple tenses*)] *Lay your fingers off that cake. I'm saving it for Jane's birthday. He'll learn the hard way to lay his hands off other men's wives.* → **keep off** (6)

***lay on**[1] *v adv*

**1** to supply; connect to a supply of (water, gas, electricity): [T1 (*often pass.*)] *The house has water and electricity laid on.*

**2** *not fml* to provide (something): [T1] *The club laid on a special meal for the visitors. The government laid on a plane for the important visitor.*

**3** to demand; place (something such as a tax or duty): [T1] *Further taxes may be laid on this spring.*

**4** to give; deliver (blows) freely: [T1 (*to*)] *As he laid on blows to the boy's back, a man came up and took the whip out of his hand.*

**5** *old use* to begin to fight: [IØ (*simple tenses*)] *"Lay on, Macduff."* (Shakespeare, *Macbeth*)

**6** to spread (paint), esp. with horizontal brush strokes: [T1] *Don't lay the colour on too thickly or the surface will not be smooth.* → **lay off**[1] (6)

**7 lay it on (thick/with a trowel)** *infml* to stretch the truth; tell an unlikely story; overpraise; make a point firmly: *Aren't you laying it on a bit thick? I'm sure the figures weren't quite as high as you say! "Well said: that was laid on with a trowel."* (Shakespeare, *As You Like It*) → **spread on**[1] (2)

**lay on**[2] *v prep*

**1** to place (something or someone) down on (a surface, furniture, etc.); spread (something) on (something): [X9 + *on*] *She lai her heavy case on the ground and took a res Three nurses helped to lay the unconsciou boy on the operating table. She laid her han comfortingly on mine. She laid a finger on he lips to signal silence. Help me to lay the ne mat on the floor. The painter used a wid brush to lay his colours on the surface that h had prepared.* → **lay with** (1), **place on** (1), **pu on**[2] (1), **set on**[2] (1)

***2** to force; place (something) on (someone): [D1] *The government has to lay heavy taxe on the people. When parents grow older, the lay a special duty on their children. Why ar you trying to lay the blame on me?* → **faste on**[2] (2), **pin on**[2] (2), **place on** (2), **put on**[2] (2), **thro on**[2] (4)

***3** to risk (money) on (something uncertain): [D1 (*often simple tenses*)] *I'm willing to la*

*good money on our team's victory.* → **place on** (3), **put on²** (7), **set on²** (6)
**4 lay a burden on** to cause (someone) to suffer from something such as a responsibility: *The President has expressed his willingness to accept the solemn burden of office that the voters have laid on him.*
**5 lay one's cards on the table** *not fml* to tell the truth, esp. one's own side of a matter; show or make known one's intentions, plans, etc.: *I see that it's time to lay my cards on the table; I am interested in this affair because the woman in the case is my sister.* → **place on** (3), **put on²** (11), **set on²** (6)
**6 lay emphasis/stress/weight on** to regard (something such as a fact) as important; make others know the importance of (something or doing something): *When giving the orders, the captain laid stress on the urgency of the work. The examination instructions lay emphasis on completing the correct number of questions in the limited time.* → **put on²** (13)
**7 lay eyes on** *not fml* to see (something or someone): [*simple tenses*] *Don't ask me where Jim is, I haven't laid eyes on him for weeks.* → **clap on²** (4), **set on²** (7)
**8 lay a finger/hand on** *not fml* to touch; harm (someone): [*usu. simple tenses, neg. or in questions or conditional statements*] *Don't you dare lay a finger on my son! If you lay a hand on me I shall send for the police!* → **set on²** (9)
**9 lay one's finger on** *not fml* to show that (something) is the cause, fault, etc.: [*simple tenses, usu. neg.*] *I can't lay my finger on the reason for the students' sudden lack of interest.* → **put on²** (16)
**10 lay great/little store on** to value (something) very much/little: [*simple tenses*] *My grandfather laid great store on his moral principles.* → **lay by²** (2), **set by²** (2), **set on²** (23)
**11 lay one's hands on: a** *not fml* to find (something): [*simple tenses*] *I can't lay my hands on the account book—have you seen it?* → **put on²** (19a) **b** *not fml* to gain possession of (something): [*simple tenses*] *I'd like to know where I can lay my hands on that special tobacco.* → **get on²** (8), **put on²** (19b), **set on²** (13) **c** *not fml* to seize (something or someone), exp. violently; harm (someone or oneself): [*simple tenses*] *The police will soon lay their hands on the jewel thieves. I'd like to lay my hands on the man who attacked my daughter.* → **get on²** (9), **put on²** (19c), **set on²** (13) **d** *fml* to bless (a person), as in church: *The bishop made a special visit to lay hands on a group of young people, so admitting them to membership of the Church.*—**laying-on of hands** *n*
**12 lay hold on: a** *not fml* to seize (something): [*often simple tenses*] *Lay hold on this rope and we'll pull you up.* → **get of** (5), **lay of** (1), **take of** (10) **b** to obtain (something) or find (someone): [*usu. simple tenses*] *Where can I lay hold on this special tobacco?* → **get of** (6), **lay of** (2)
**13 lay one's hopes on** to have one's hopes depend on (usu. something or doing something): *Jim has laid all his hopes on winning this race. Don't lay your hopes on this job, you may not get it.* → **pin on²** (4), etc.
**14 lay violent hands on oneself** *old use* to kill oneself: [*usu. simple tenses*] *"Or have laid violent hands upon themselves."* (Book of Common Prayer)

**lay open** *v adj*
**1** to cut (part of the body): [X9 + open (*usu. simple tenses*)] *The child fell off his bicycle and laid his face open.*
***2** to make (something) clear or known, esp. no longer secret: [T1a (*usu. simple tenses*)] *The firm's intentions were laid open by the director's accidental remark.* → **lay bare** (2)
**3 lay oneself open to** to put oneself in a position to receive (punishment, trouble, etc.): *By admitting that he had copied part of his article, the student laid himself open to a charge of cheating.*

***lay out** *v adv*
**1** to spread (something), as to view: [T1 (*usu. pass.*)] *The scenery was laid out before the travellers when they reached the top of the hill. All the family's pitiful possessions were laid out in the yard. The goods for sale were laid out attractively.* —**layout** *n* → **set out** (4)
**2** to spread (clothes, food, etc.) for use: [T1] *Please lay out my best suit for the governors' meeting. I'll leave a meal laid out in the kitchen.* → **drag out** (1), **get out** (5), **put out** (3), **set forth** (3), **set out** (5)
**3** to arrange the plan or appearance of (something such as a building): [T1] *Laying out the page well makes all the difference to the ease of reading the book. "The garden... was well laid out."* (Jane Austen, *Pride and Prejudice*) —**layout** *n* → **set out** (6).
**4** *not fml* to spend or risk (usu. a lot of money, strength, etc.): [T1 (*usu. simple tenses*)] *Having laid out his father's fortune into shares, he was able to live on the interest. I had to lay out all my strength to move the rock.* —**outlay** *n* → **put out** (19)
**5** to make (someone) unconscious or dead: [T1 (*usu. simple tenses*)] *With one blow he laid his attacker out. Three of the enemy were laid out at once. I shall be laid out dead long before that happens!* → **knock out** (3), etc.
**6** to tire (someone) very much: [T1 (*usu. simple tenses*)] *This heat has quite laid me out.* → **tire out,** etc.
**7** to prepare (a dead body) for burial: [T1] *Two of the women came to lay out the body.*
**8** to put (oneself) to some trouble (to do something): [V3] *Mother was always willing to lay herself out to help people.* → **put out** (15), etc.
**9** *AmE infml* to scold; find fault with (some-

one): [T1] *The director laid Jim out for being late again.* → **tell off** (1), etc.

*__lay over__[1] *v adv*

**1** *AmE* to make an overnight stop on a journey, esp. by plane: [IØ (*usu. simple tenses*)] *You can lay over without additional charge. This flight lays over at Great Falls before completing the journey to New York.* —**lay-over** *n* → **stop over** (2)

**2** to leave (something) to a later time: [T1 (*usu. pass.*)] *The concert had to be laid over for several days because one of the singers had hurt her throat.* → **put off**[1] (4), etc.

**3** to ornament (something): [T1 (*usu. pass.*)] *The cover of the book was laid over with gold and silver.* —**overlay** *n*

**4** *not fml* to perform better than (usu. someone): [T1a (*usu. simple tenses*)] *"In scolding, a blue jay can lay over anything."* (Mark Twain, *A Tramp Abroad*)

**lay over**[2] *v prep* → **pull over**[2] (1), etc.

to place or spread (something) on top of (something or someone): [X9 + *over*] *He laid his legs carelessly over the arm of the chair. Lay another cover over the sleeping child, it's cold. He tried to hide the stolen painting by laying a coat of paint over the original picture.* —**lay-over** *n* —**overlay** *n, v*

*__lay to__[1] *v adv* → **lay by**[1] (9), **lie by**[1], **lie to**[1]

(of a ship) to (cause to) come to rest: [IØ (*usu. simple tenses*)] *We shall have to lay to because of the storm.* [T1b (*usu. simple tenses*)] *Lay the ship to outside the harbour.*

**lay to**[2] *v prep*

**1 lay something to someone's charge** to blame someone for something; make him responsible: [(*often pass.*)] *You don't want a terrible crime like that laid to your charge; tell the police that your companion did it!*

**2 lay claim to** to claim; demand (someone, something, or doing something): *Both parents are trying to lay claim to the child. Several people have laid claim to the money that was found. The girl is laying claim to having swum across the lake.*

**3 lay someone to rest/sleep** *euph* to bury someone: *She was laid to rest in the family grave.*

**4 lay something to rest** to put an end to something such as a feeling or story: [(*often pass.*)] *Her doubts were quickly laid to rest when he arrived as he had promised.*

**5 lay siege to: a** to surround (a town) until its people yield: *The army laid siege to the town until the hungry citizens were forced to yield.* **b** to attempt to persuade (someone such as a government): *The only way to have the new law stopped is to lay siege to all the members of Parliament and persuade them to vote against it.* **c** to offer love to (someone of the opposite sex); try to win (someone) in love: *Jim laid siege to Mary for a year before she agreed to marry him.*

**lay together** *v adv*

**1** to place (things) side by side: [X9 + TOGETHER] *Don't lay the sticks too close together, or the fire will not burn well.* → **put together** (1)

**2 lay our/your/their heads together** *not fml* to make a plan by considering it with someone else; have discussions together: *Let's lay our heads together and see if we can invent a cheaper and better system.* → **put together** (5)

**lay under** *v prep*

**1** to place (something) underneath (something else): [T1 + *under*] *It saves wear on the mat if you lay a piece of rubber the same size under it.* —**underlay** *n*

**2 lay someone under contribution** *fml* to make someone give money to a collection: [(*usu pass.*)] *All the workers in this firm are laid under contribution to the pension fund.*

**3 lay someone under a/the necessity/obligation** to force someone (to do something): [(*usu simple tenses*)] *Every taxpayer is laid under the necessity of declaring his whole income. The court laid the young thief under an obligation to report to the police station once a week.*

**lay up** *v adv*

**1** to save or store (something) for future use: *These little tree animals lay up nuts for the winter. The power stations are laying up their usual supplies of coal against the rising need for electricity. "Lay up for yourselves treasure in heaven."* (The Bible) → **store up** (1)

**2** to cause (something bad) in the future: [T1 (*often continuous tenses*)] *You're only laying up trouble for yourself if you don't take care of your heart.*

**3** to take (something such as a car or ship) out of use, as for repairs or a winter period: [T1 (*usu. pass.*)] *The car has been laid up for a week for urgent repairs. After the ceremony the new flag will be laid up in the church. At the end of the season, all the boats are formally laid up in the harbour.* —**laying-up** *adj* —**lay-up** *n* → **lie up** (2), **put up**[1] (19)

**4** to (cause to) stay in bed, usu. with an illness): [T1 (*usu. pass.*)] *I've been laid up since Christmas with a bad cough.* → **lay by**[1] (8), **lie up** (1)

**5** (in hand printing) to wash the ink from a bank of type) so as to separate the letters: [T1] *You need plenty of water for laying up the form.*

**lay waste** *v adj*

**1** to waste (something): [X9 + waste] *"The world is too much with us; late and soon, Getting and spending, we lay waste our powers"* (William Wordsworth, *The World is Too Much with Us.*)

*__2__ to destroy (usu. a place), as in war, by killing all plants, burning buildings, etc.: [T1 (*often pass.*)] *The whole area was laid waste by the advancing army, villages destroyed* *crops ruined, forests burnt; the whole place was left bare and spoilt.*

**lay with** *v prep*

**1** to cover (a surface) with (something): [X9 + *with*] *Help me to lay the floor with the new mat. The bottom of the nest is laid with feathers and hair.* → **lay on² (1), place on (1), put on (1), set on² (1)**

*__2__ to ornament (something such as clothes) with (something else): [D1 (*often pass.*)] *The back of the coat was laid with gold threads.* → **lace with** (1)

**laze about/around** *v adv* → **mess about** (1), etc.

to waste time enjoyably, with little effort: [IØ + ABOUT/AROUND] *It's so nice just to laze about in the sun, doing no work for a change.*

**laze away** *v adv*

**1** to be lazy continuously: [IØ + AWAY (*continuous tenses*)] *It's nice for you, lazing away in the sun while I do all the work!*

*__2__ to pass (time) lazily: [T1] *It's so nice to laze away a whole afternoon doing nothing.* → **idle away** (2), etc.

**leach away** *v adv* → LEACH OUT

**leach from/away from/out of** *v (adv) prep*

(of a substance) to (cause to) leave (a material such as soil) through the action of water: [T1 + (AWAY) *from*/OUT + *of* (*often pass.*)] *Much of the goodness has been leached from the soil by the action of continuous heavy rain.* [IØ + (AWAY) *from*/OUT + *of*] *During the recent wet weather, radioactive chemicals have been leaching out of the waste products of the atomic power station.*

**leach out/away** *v adv*

**1** to escape from a material through the action of liquid: [IØ + OUT/AWAY] *The goodness has been leaching out/away during the recent heavy rain.*

**2** to lose (a substance) by the action of a liquid: [T1 + OUT/AWAY] *The makers have recalled lids which leached out dangerous chemicals.*

**leach out of** *v adv prep* → LEACH FROM

**lead against** *v prep*

to direct (someone or something such as an attack) against (someone): [T1 + *against*] *The plane that he was flying was leading a bombing attack against an enemy port at the time that it crashed. The captain led his small band of men against the powerful forces of the enemy.*

**lead astray** *v adv*

**1** to guide (someone or an animal) in the wrong direction: [X9 + ASTRAY] *My trained dog has never been known to lead the sheep astray.* → **go astray** (1)

*__2__ to influence (someone) to behave wrongly or immorally: [T1] *Young girls are easily led astray.* → **go astray** (3)

*__3__ to mislead (someone): [T1 (*often pass.*)] *The unthinking public are easily led astray by the false picture of reality given in television shows.*

**lead away** *v adv*

**1** to guide or take (usu. someone) away from somewhere: [X9 + AWAY (*from*)] *The police at last caught the young jewel thief and led him away. The weeping mother was led away from the graveside by her family.* → **lead off¹** (1)

*__2__ to influence (someone), esp. to leave: [T1 (*from*)] *Some of the most loyal voters may be led away by the young politician's winning manner. A school should not try to lead a child away from his family. The boy claimed that he had been led away by criminal companions.*

*__3__ to take (someone's attention) away: [T1 (*often pass.*)] *My attention was led away by the sudden appearance of a familiar face at the window.*

**lead back** *v adv*

**1** to guide (someone or an animal) in a return direction: [X9 + BACK (*to*)] *Ride your horse as far as the gate, then lead him back (to the yard).*

**2** (of a road, etc.) to provide a way (for someone) in the return direction: [L9 + BACK (*to*) (*simple tenses*)] *Which of these paths leads back (to the village)?*

**lead back to** *v adv prep*

**1** to guide (someone or an animal) back to (a place): [X9 + BACK + *to*] *The boy will lead you back to your home.*

**2** (of a road, etc.) to provide a way (for someone) to return to (a place): [L9/X9 + BACK + *to* (*simple tenses*)] *This path leads (you) back to the village.*

*__3__ to (cause to) return to (something such as a subject or loyalty): [D1] *Father always tried to lead the conversation back to the family quarrel. What can priests do to lead former Christians back to the Church?* [T1 (*no pass.*)] *The talk always leads back to the mysterious affair of the stolen jewels.*

**lead by** *v prep*

**1** (of a road, etc.) to pass beside (something): [L9 + *by* (*simple tenses*)] *You can't miss the post office, the road leads right by it.*

**2** to guide or bring (someone or an animal) by holding (something, esp. a hand): [T1 + *by*] *Parents are arriving at the school gates, leading their children by the hand. This fierce animal can be led by a rope threaded through a ring in its nose.*

**3 lead by the nose** *infml* to control someone completely, often by deceit: *When the taxpayers discovered how they had been led by the nose all these years, they used their voting power to destroy the government.*

**lead down¹** *v adv*

**1** to guide (someone or an animal) to a lower level: [X9 + DOWN] *In spite of the thick mist, the guide led the party of climbers down safely.*

**2** (of a road, etc.) to provide a way (for someone) down a slope, etc.: [L9 + DOWN (*simple tenses*)] *Where do these stairs lead down?* [X9 + DOWN (*simple tenses*)] *How far will the road lead us down?*

**lead down²** *v prep*

**1** to guide (something or someone) down to (a lower level): [X9 + *down*] *It was kind of you to lead the blind girl down the steps. Road signs are intended to lead the traffic down the right road. When you are trying to read quickly, lead your finger down the middle of the page.*

**2** (of a road, etc.) to provide for (someone) a way down (a hill, etc.): [L9 + *down*] *Take the road that leads down the slope.* [X9 + *down*] *Which path will lead us down (to the village)?*

**3 lead down the garden path** *infml* to deceive (someone): *The politicians have been leading us down the garden path all these years: they promised us tax cuts to get our votes, but they've never done anything.* → **lead up** (3)

**lead down to** *v adv prep*

**1** to guide (someone or something) in a downward direction as far as (something such as a place): [X9 + DOWN + *to*] *In spite of the thick mist, the guide led the party of climbers down to safety. This metal bar leads the arm down to the bell, so that the clock strikes at the correct time.*

**2** (of a road, etc.) to provide a way (for someone) down a hill or as far as (a place): [L9 + DOWN + *to* (*simple tenses*)] *The path leads down to the sea.* [X9 + DOWN + *to* (*simple tenses*)] *The road will lead you down to the church.*

**lead forth** *v adv* → **lead out** (1)

*old use* to guide (usu. someone) at the beginning of a journey: [X9 + FORTH] *"He led them forth by the right way; that they might go to the city."* (The Bible)

**lead in** *v adv*

**1** to guide or bring (someone or an animal) indoors or into a space: [X9 + IN] *The owner led in the winning horse. The teacher led the children in when they visited the courthouse.*

**2** to cause (something) to pass inside: [X9 + IN] *Lead the wire in from the roof, through these holes in the back of the radio set.* —**lead-in** *n, adj*

*__3__ to begin (music); introduce (words): [T1] *The brass instruments led in the main tune. And now here is our old friend Victor to lead in the next part of the show.* —**lead-in** *n, adj*

*__4__ *naut* to mark the correct course for entering a harbour: [I∅] *Lights are provided for leading in.*

**lead into** *v prep*

**1** to guide (someone or something) into (a place): [X9 + *into*] *The teacher led the children into the school.*

**2** (of a road, etc.) to provide a way (for someone) to enter (a place): [L9 + *into* (*simple tenses*)] *This path leads halfway into the forest and then stops.* [X9 + *into* (*simple tenses*)] *This road leads traffic into the busiest part of the city.*

**3** to cause (something) to pass into (a space): [X9 + *into*] *Lead these two wires into the holes provided.*

*__4__ to introduce (words, music, etc.): [T1] *The pianist led into the next piece of music. This movement leads straight into the next one, without a break. Quickly the speaker led into his main argument.*

*__5__ to encourage or force (someone) to reach (a bad state): [D1] *Behaviour like this will lead you into trouble. You'll lead us into debt if you go on spending so freely. By clever argument, he led his opponent into a trap. "Lead us not into temptation, but deliver us from evil."* (The Lord's Prayer)

**lead nowhere** *v adv* → **get anywhere, get nowhere, get somewhere, get there**

**1** to go or take someone to no particular place: [L9 + NOWHERE (*simple tenses*)] *This road leads nowhere; it stops in the middle of a field.* [X9 + NOWHERE (*simple tenses*)] *Don't take that road, it'll lead you nowhere.*

*__2__ *not fml* to reach no result: [I∅] *All this talk is leading nowhere.*

**lead off¹** *v adv*

**1** to guide or take (someone or an animal) away from a place: [X9 + OFF] *The captain led his victorious team off, to the cheers of the crowd.* → **lead away** (1)

*__2__ to start (something): [I∅ (*usu. simple tenses*)] *Who will lead off by asking the first question? The next artist is going to lead off with a song.* [T1 (*usu. simple tenses*)] *Which pair will lead off the dance?* —**lead-off** *n* → **kick off** (3)

**lead off²** *v prep*

to guide (someone) away from (a place): [X9 + *off*] *The captain led his victorious team off the field, to the cheers of the crowd.*

**lead on** *v adv*

**1** to show the way (to someone): [L9 + ON] *You lead on, and I'll follow.* [X9 + ON] *The guide led the tourists on, into the great hall.*

*__2__ *not fml* to deceive (someone), often with false hopes: [T1] *Advertisements for houses for sale often lead buyers on with misleading descriptions.* [V3] *I had been led on to believe that I would be given a better position after three months in the office, but this did not happen.*

*__3__ *not fml* to influence (someone) (to do something bad): [T1] *The boy claimed that he had been led on by his criminal companions.* [V3] *The boy claimed that his criminal companions had led him on to steal the jewels.*

**lead out** *v adv*

**1** to guide or bring (something, someone, or an animal) on a journey or out of a place; go in front: [X9 + OUT (*of*)] *The brave girl ran into the burning building and led the horse* *out* (*to safety*). *Road signs lead the traffic out of the city.* [L9 + OUT] *The oldest children will please lead out.* → **lead forth**

*2 to encourage someone to talk: [T1 (*usu. simple tenses*)] *Mary's very quiet; will you look after her at the party and try to lead her out a little?* → **bring out** (6), **come out of** (4), **draw out** (9), **fetch out** (5)

**lead to** *v prep*

1 to guide (something, someone, or an animal) to (a place): [X9 + *to*] *The girl led her little brother to school. You can lead a horse to water, but you can't make him drink.* (saying)

2 (of a road, etc.) to provide a way (for someone) to reach a place: [L9 + *to* (*simple tenses*)] *The road led to a sleepy village.* [X9 + *to* (*simple tenses*)] *Take the left path; it will lead you to the house.* → **go to** (2), **reach to** (1)

*3 to end in (a result): [T1 (*no pass., usu. simple tenses*)] *The students in this college are all taking courses leading to a degree.*

*4 to be (partly) the cause of (something or doing something): [T1 (*simple tenses*)] *Social drinking may lead to alcoholism. Disobeying the law can lead to trouble. An ordinary cold can soon lead to a fever. One thing can lead to another.* [T4 (*simple tenses*)] *It's sleeping late in the morning that leads to being late for work.*

5 **all roads lead to Rome** the result is the same whatever you do; there is more than one way of reaching a result. *Although their methods were different, the results were the same; at this point all roads lead to Rome.*

6 **lead a woman to the altar** *old use* to marry a woman: *"Walter, Walter, lead me to the altar."* (song)

**lead up** *v prep*

1 to guide (someone) up (a hill, slope, stairs, etc.): [X9 + *up*] *The most experienced climber was chosen to lead the others up the mountain.*

2 (of a road, etc.) to go; take (someone) up (a hill, slope, etc.): [L9 + *up* (*simple tenses*)] *Take the path that leads up the side of the hill.* [X9 + *up* (*simple tenses*)] *This road leads you up the hill.*

3 **lead someone up the garden path** esp. *BrE infml* to deceive someone: *The politicians have been leading us up the garden path all these years; they've promised us tax cuts to get our votes but they've never done anything.* → **lead down²** (3)

**lead up to** *v adv prep*

1 to guide or bring (usu. someone) as far or high as (a place): [X9 + UP + *to* (*often simple tenses*)] *A row of lights leads visitors up to the front door.*

2 (of a road, etc.) to go; take (someone) as far or high as (a place): [L9 + UP + *to* (*simple tenses*)] *The stairs lead up to the top floor. A little path led up to the garden gate.* [X9 + UP + *to* (*simple tenses*)] *Which path will lead us up to the top of the hill?*

*3 to prepare to play (a card): [T1] *I could see that my partner was leading up to the king of diamonds.*

*4 to come before (an event); cause (something): [T1] *In the months leading up to the great ceremony, many people took part in the preparations. The newspapers faithfully reported the events that led up to the Minister's dismissal.*

*5 to introduce; prepare to say; suggest (something), esp. indirectly; gradually get near (saying something): [T1] *The speaker took far too long leading up to his main point. What do you suppose he's leading up to? My kind words led up to a request for money.* [T4] *Be careful how you lead up to mentioning a possible pay rise with your employer.* → **work round to** (2), **work up to** (3)

**lead with** *v prep*

1 to start or open a fight, card game, sport, etc., with (something): [IØ + *with*] *The experienced fighter was known for leading with his right* (*hand*). *My partner surprised me by leading with a diamond. From the moment that our team led with a strong attack, I knew that we were sure of victory.*

2 to give (an item of news) as the main story in a newspaper: [IØ + *with*] *Only one of the papers led with the Minister's dismissal.*

3 **lead with one's chin** *not fml* to behave so as to invite trouble: *The Minister deserved to be dismissed for making such unfortunate remarks; he had always been headstrong, tending to lead with his chin.*

***leaf out** *v adv* also *AmE* **leave out**

(of a plant) to come into leaf in the early stages: [IØ] *"There it stood, leafing out hopefully in April."* (Oliver Wendell Holmes, *The Poet at the Breakfast Table*) *The plant you gave me leafed out, just when I thought it was dead* [T1 (*pass.*)] (*AmE*) *The trees in the park are now all leaved out.*

***leaf through** *v adv; prep*

to read a little of; turn pages over inattentively or so as to get a quick idea of (a book, magazine, etc.): [T1] *Waiting to see the doctor, Jim was too nervous to read properly, so he just leafed through some old magazines that were kept in the waiting room.*

**league against** *v prep*

*old use* to join forces in opposition to (a shared enemy): [L9 + *against*] *The neighbouring states leagued against the powerful nation that threatened their independence.*

**league together** *v adv*

to (cause to) unite in a group, esp. with shared interests: [L9 + TOGETHER] *The oil-producing countries have leagued together to fix the price of oil at a high rate.* [X9 + TOGETHER (*often pass.*)] *Criminal groups in general are leagued together against the forces of law and order.*

**league with** *v prep*

*old use* to join forces together with (someone

else): [L9 + *with*] *Some of his countrymen had leagued with the enemy to destroy the power of the king.*

**leak away** *v adv*

**1** (of liquid, gas etc.) to escape gradually through an accidental hole: [IØ + AWAY] *No wonder the engine got overheated, the oil has been leaking away during the whole journey.*

***2** to be gradually lost: [IØ] *With the continued loss of blood, his life was steadily leaking away. "A democracy that has allowed its chief political interests to leak away."* (*The Spectator*, 23 August 1890)

**leak in** *v adv*

(of liquid, gas etc.) to enter through an accidental hole: [IØ + IN] *You didn't mend the boat properly, the water is still leaking in.*

**leak out** *v adv*

**1** (of liquid, gas etc.) to (cause to) escape through an accidental hole: [IØ + OUT] *There's a hole in the bucket and the water is leaking out.* [T1 + OUT] *This pipe seems to be leaking out gas.*

***2** (of a secret) to (cause to) become known unintentionally: [IØ] *The news of his appointment leaked out before it was officially made known.* [T1] *Who is responsible for leaking out the news?* → **let out** (5), etc.

**leak to** *v prep*

to tell (a secret) to (someone): [T1 + *to*] *Who is responsible for leaking the news of the Minister's dismissal to the newspapers?*

**lean against** *v prep*

**1** to (cause to) rest, usu. at an angle, touching (something or someone); slope (something) against (something): [L9 + *against*] *The man leaned against the wall and began to smoke his pipe. We had to lean against the strong wind in order to move forward at all.* [X9 + *against*] *When you lean a ladder against a wall, make sure that its feet are dug firmly into the ground, for safety.* → **lean on** (1)

***2** *law* to regard (someone or an opinion) with disfavour: [T1] *The courts tend to be influenced by a man's past, and lean against such a prisoner, so it is no longer permitted in court to mention a man's earlier crimes.*

**lean back/backwards** *v adv*

to hold oneself or (something) at an angle in a backward direction: [L9 + BACK/BACKWARDS] *I leaned back to get a better view, and fell off the chair.* [X9 + BACK/BACKWARDS] *Please don't lean your chair back, you'll break it.*

**lean down** *v adv* → **bend down,** etc.

to hold oneself or (something) at an angle in a downward direction; bend at the waist: [L9 + DOWN (*to*)] *The branches leaned down to the ground, heavy with the weight of the fruit. Tony was too tall that he had to lean down to get through the doorway.* [X9 + DOWN] *She leaned her face down to be kissed by the child.*

**lean forward** *v prep* → **bend forward, incline forward**

to hold oneself or (something) at an angle towards something or someone: [L9 + FORWARD] *Don't lean too far forward, you might fall overboard.* [X9 + FORWARD] *I leaned my head forward to hear what they were saying.*

**lean on** *v prep*

**1** to place one's weight or the weight of (something), often at an angle, on (something or someone): [L9 + *on*] *She sang the song leaning on the piano. Lean on my arm, I will help you to walk. Don't lean so heavily on me.* [X9 + *on*] *Leaning her head on my shoulder, she began to cry. Don't lean your elbows on the table, it's not polite.* → **lean against** (1)

***2** to depend on (someone or someone's help) for support: [T1] *You have to make your own way in the world, and not lean on your father for the rest of your life. A young politician needs to lean on the experience of older members of his party for several years. "Laws, like houses, lean on one another."* (Edmund Burke, *Tracts on the Property Laws*)

***3** *infml* (usu. among criminals) to threaten or force (someone) to act: [T1] *We were supposed to share the profit from the jewel robbery, but now he's hidden them—we migh[t] have to lean on him a little to make him tell u[s] where the jewels are hidden.*

**lean out** *v adv*

to hold oneself or (something) at an angl[e] outside somewhere, as a window: [L9 + OU[T] (*of*)] *One day you'll lean out too far and fa[ll] to the ground. It is dangerous and unlawful fo[r] passengers to lean out of the windows of rai[l]way carriages.* [X9 + OUT (*of*)] *Lean you[r] head out for a moment and see if it's raining.*

**lean over**[1] *v adv*

**1** to hold oneself or itself at an angle; bend a[t] the waist: [L9 + OVER] *As Jim leaned over t[o] pick up the pen, he felt a sharp pain in hi[s] back.* [IØ + OVER] *The old building is leanin[g] over at a dangerous angle and may fall at an[y] moment.* → **bend over** (1)

**2 lean over backwards** → BEND OVER (2)

**lean over**[2] *v prep*

to bend over (something or someone): [L9 + *over*] *Please don't lean over me while I'[m] working, it annoys me. The pair of lovers wer[e] leaning over the bridge, looking into the water.*

**lean to** *v prep*

**1** to slope; direct oneself or itself in the direc[tion] of (something): [L9 + *to*] *The apple tre[e] leaned to the field, dropping its flowers on th[e] grass. As Jim leaned to the ground to pick u[p] the pen, he felt a sharp pain in his back.* [IØ + *to*] *The old house leans to the right at [a] dangerous angle.* → **bend to** (1), **lean toward[s]** (1)

***2** to be likely to have, do, or think (some[thing]): [T1 (*no pass., usu. simple tenses*)] *His family have always leaned to overweigh[t].* → **incline to** (2), **tend to**

*3 to move one's opinion more in favour of (a different opinion or belief): [T1 (*no pass.*)] *The young politician is beginning to lean to the opinions of the workers.* → **lean towards** (2), etc.

**lean towards** *v prep*
**1** to slope; hold oneself or itself at an angle in the direction of (something): [L9 + *towards*] *I had to lean towards the secretary to hear what she was saying. If you lean too far towards the water, you might fall in.* [IØ + *towards*] *The old house is leaning towards the street, its beams cracked with age.* → **lean to** (1), **slope towards,** etc.
*2 to (cause to) move one's opinion more in favour of a different opinion or belief: [T1 (*no pass.*)] *The young politician is beginning to lean towards the opinion of the workers.* [V4b] *Recent events lean me more towards favouring longer years of imprisonment.* → **incline towards** (2), **lean to** (3), **tend towards, trend towards**

**leap at** *v prep* → **jump at**
**1** to spring at (usu. someone); try to reach (something or someone) with a jump: [IØ + *at*] *Please stop your dog leaping at me, he'll get my coat dirty. The climber leaped at the rope, but missed and fell to his death.*
*2 *not fml* to be eager to accept (a chance or offer): [T1] *We ought to leap at the chance to buy the house at that price, but Mother isn't sure whether she likes it. Everyone was surprised when Jim didn't leap at his father's offer of a partnership.*

**leap forward** *v adv*
**1** to move suddenly ahead: [IØ + FORWARD] *The horse leaped forward, and I got out of the way only just in time. I don't like the way the car leaps forward whenever John drives it.*
*2 *not fml* to develop very fast: [IØ] *Scientific discoveries have leapt forward in recent years.* —**leap forward** *n*

**leap in** *v adv* → **jump in**
**1** to enter something with a springing movement: [IØ + IN (*to*)] *People were standing around Ophelia's grave when Hamlet leaped in.*
*2 *not fml* to be eager to do something; act urgently: [IØ (*usu. simple tenses*)] *Don't take too long deciding, or the other firm may leap in with their offer.*

**leap into** *v prep*
**1** to jump into (a space or body of water): [IØ + *into*] *Suddenly, without warning, he leaped into the river.*
*2 *not fml* to suddenly enter (one's mind); eagerly begin (an activity or doing something): [T1 (*no pass., usu. simple tenses*)] *A great idea just leaped into my mind; let me tell you it. The children leaped into the work of building a sandcastle.* [T4 (*usu. simple tenses*)] *Will he leap into writing the article?*

**leap out** *v adv*
**1** to jump or spring out from somewhere: [IØ + OUT (*of, from*)] *A lion leaped out from behind the bush and killed a deer.*
*2 to be noticeable: [IØ (*at*) (*often simple tenses*)] *His name leaped out at me from the newspaper.*

**leap out of** *v adv prep* → **jump out of**
**1** to leave (a place) with a sudden movement: [IØ + OUT + *of*]. *I was walking up the garden path when one of the children leaped out of the bushes and surprised me.*
**2 leap out of oneself/one's skin** *not fml* to receive the shock of a surprise, sometimes with joy: [(*often simple tenses*)] *Oh, you gave me such a shock, coming up behind me so quietly, you made me leap out of my skin. "Our King being ready to leap out of himself, for joy of his found daughter."* (Shakespeare, *A Winter's Tale*)

**leap up** *v adv*
**1** to spring upwards: [IØ + UP] *The child was crying because the big dog had leapt up at him.* → **jump up** (1)
**2** to rise from one's seat suddenly: [IØ + UP (*from*) (*often simple tenses*)] *He leaped up (from his chair) when the door bell rang, hoping that it was Rose.* → **jump up** (2), **shoot up** (2), **spring up** (1), **start up** (2)
*3 to (cause to) become quick by feeling: [IØ (*usu. simple tenses*)] *"My heart leaps up when I behold a rainbow in the sky."* (Wordsworth, *My Heart Leaps Up*)

**learn about** *v prep*
**1** to gain knowledge about; begin to know (information) about (a subject): [IØ + *about*] *I like reading historical stories because I learn about the lives that people led long ago.* [T1 + *about*] *It's no use learning facts about a subject if you don't understand it.*
**2** to come to hear about; gain information about (something or someone): [IØ + *about* (*usu. simple tenses*)] *How did you learn about our product? Was it through our advertisements? Your own parents should not have to learn about your wedding from a newspaper report! We only learned about your intended visit yesterday.* → **hear about, hear of** (1), **learn of** (1)

**learn by** *v prep*
**1** to learn (something) or become wiser because of (something): [IØ + *by*] *We are all learning by our mistakes.* [T1 + *by*] *Moral principles are best learned by example.* → **learn from** (2)
**2 learn words by heart/rote** to learn words, esp. by repetition, so as to be able to repeat them exactly: *Actors have to learn their lines by heart; they mustn't get a single word wrong.* → **learn off**

**learn from** *v prep*
**1** to gain knowledge; come to know (something) from (someone): [IØ + *from*] *He's the best teacher that I ever learned from.* [T1 + *from*] *You were lucky to learn English from such a good teacher.* → **learn of** (2)

2 to become wiser because of (something such as experience): [I∅ + *from*] *We all learn from our mistakes. "If men could learn from history, what lessons it might teach us!"* (S.T. Coleridge, *T. Allsop's Recollections*) [T5 + *from*] *I have learned from bitter experience that it does not pay to be too hopeful.* [T1 + *from*] *There are many hard lessons to be learned from life.* → **learn by** (1)

**learn of** *v prep*

**1** to come to hear about; gain information about (something or someone): [I∅ + *of* (*usu. simple tenses*)] *How did you learn of our product? Was it through our advertisements? Your parents should not have to learn of your wedding from a newspaper report! We only learned of your intended visit yesterday. I learned of your new address from your parents.* → **hear about, hear of** (1), **learn about**

**2** *old use* to come to know (something) from (someone): [T3 + *of* (*usu. simple tenses*)] *"Teach me at once, and learn of me to die."* (Alexander Pope, *Eloisa to Abelard*) → **learn from** (1)

***learn off** *v adv* → **learn by** (2)

to learn (usu. words) from memory, so as to be able to repeat them exactly: [T1] *Actors have to learn their words off in a very short time.*

**learn up** *v adv*

*not fml* to study; learn (something such as information) thoroughly: [T1 + UP] *I'd better learn up some facts for next week's examination.*

***lease back** *v adv*

(in business) to sell (something such as property) and then rent it from the new owner: [T1] *Many more firms are selling the buildings in which their offices and factories are, and leasing them back, so as to free large sums of money for development.* —**leaseback** *n, adj*

**lease out** *v adv*

to allow the use of (usu. a place) for rent: [T1 + OUT] *Do you lease out land? The land was leased out to a rich farmer.*

**leave about/around** *v adv; prep* → **kick about** (3), **knock about** (3), **lie about**[1] (2)

to let (usu. things) lie untidily in various places around (a place): [X9 + ABOUT/AROUND/*about/around*] *I wish you wouldn't leave your clothes around (the house), I have to pick them up before I can do the cleaning. Don't leave money about, it might get stolen.*

**leave alone** *v adj*

**1** to let (someone or something) remain on his/its own: [T1 + **alone**] *They left the poor child alone in the house all night.*

***2** to not touch or have to do with (something or someone) not trouble (someone): [T1b (*often simple tenses*)] *Leave that bag alone, it's not yours! I leave alone things that I don't understand. Provided that they have water and light, most plants are best left alone to grow in a natural way. Leave her alone! She didn't pick a quarrel with you!* → **let alone** (1)

**3 leave alone** *not fml* not counting (something or someone): *We shall never get six of us in the car, leave alone the bags and boxes.* → **let alone** (2)

**4 leave well alone** *not fml* to be satisfied with existing conditions for fear of making matters worse: [(*often simple tenses*)] *If you're in doubt about whether to try to improve matters, it's usually best to leave well alone.* also *AmE* **leave well enough alone** → **let alone** (3)

**leave around** *v adv; prep* → LEAVE ABOUT

***leave aside** *v adv*

to fail or refuse to take (something) into consideration: [T1] *Even leaving aside the question of the new appointments, it will be impossible for the committee to fulfil all their duties in the next few weeks.*

**leave at** *v prep*

**1** to let (something) remain at (a place); take (someone) to (a place) go away from (someone) at (a place): [T1 + *at*] *I've left the other bag at the station, to be collected later. This message was left at the desk. I haven't seen Jim since I left him at the office. Leave me at the church, please, and collect me after the service.*

**2 leave it at that** *not fml* to say nothing more about a matter: *I don't want to argue any further about the performance; we disagree, so let's leave it at that.*

**3 leave word at** to leave a message at (a place): *I'll leave word at the hotel desk where you can find me.* → **leave for** (6), **leave with** (3)

**leave behind**[1] *v adv*

**1** to forget to take; go away without (usu. something); go away from (a place): [X9 + BEHIND] *Can you tell me the time? I've left my watch behind. The plane is about to leave, and I've left my ticket behind! "Leave your home behind."* (A.E. Housman, *A Shropshire Lad*)

**2** to choose not to take (something or someone): [X9 + BEHIND] *I think I'll leave my heavy coat behind, I shan't need it on holiday —I hope! The wounded had to be left behind when the defeated army left the battlefield.*

***3** to produce (something) afterwards: [T1 (*usu. simple tenses*)] *The last government has left behind a terrible debt. The storm left many damaged buildings and sunken ships behind.*

**leave behind**[2] *v prep*

**1** to place and allow (something) to remain at the back of (something): [T1 + *behind*] *I've left the money behind the clock.*

**2** to go away with (something or someone) remaining behind (one): [X9 + *behind*] *I've gone and left the keys behind me at home. 'The girl I left behind me.'* (song)

***3** to produce (something) after (something or someone): [D1 (*usu. simple tenses*)] *The storm left a heap of destruction behind it. I should like to leave a name behind me when I die.*

***leave cold** *v adj*

*not fml* to fail to move or excite the interest of (someone): [T1 (*simple tenses*)] *Tom's new book is quite well written, but the characters leave me cold. A lot of new music is concerned with thinking rather than feeling, and tends to leave me cold.*

**leave down** *v adv*

**1** to let (something) remain in a low position: [X9 + DOWN] *Leave the handle down so that the children can open it.*

**2** to keep (sound or light) low: [X9 + DOWN] *No, don't turn the lights up, leave them down, it's so pleasant to sit here in the soft light. Leave the radio down or it might wake your father.*

**leave for** *v prep*

**1** to go away in the direction of (a place): [IØ + *for*] *I'm sorry, he's just left for London; can I take a message?*

**2** to cause (something) to remain or wait for (someone): [T1 + *for*] *Has anyone left a message for me? A parcel has been left for you at the desk.*

**3** to go away from (someone, a job, a way of life, etc.) to have or live with (something or someone different): [T1 + *for*] *He left his wife for a worthless actress. The director is thinking of leaving the firm for a better position elsewhere.*

***4** to let (something such as work) remain, waiting for (someone) (to do it) or (another time): [D1] *He leaves all the worst jobs for me. We shall have to leave that decision for another time.* [V3] *We can leave the difficult jobs for the chairman to do.*

**5 leave someone for dead** to regard and treat someone as dead: [(*often pass.*)] *The wounded soldier was left for dead on the battlefield.*

**6 leave word for** to leave a message for (someone): *I'll make sure to leave word for you as to where you can find me.* → **leave at** (3), **leave with** (3)

**leave in[1]** *v adv*

**1** to allow (something) to remain inside a building, hole, etc.: [X9 + IN] *Leave the key in while you turn the handle. If you leave the meat in for three hours, it will be thoroughly cooked. It isn't kind to leave the dog in all day.*

**2** to allow (something, usu. a fire) to remain burning, alight, etc.: [X9 + IN] *Shall we leave the fire in or put it out?* → **keep in** (6), etc.

**3** to allow (words or actions) to remain as part of (writing, a performance, etc.): [X9 + IN] *But that's the best joke in the play, let's leave it in!* → **keep in** (2)

**leave in[2]** *v prep*

**1** to allow (something or someone) to remain in (a place): [T1 + *in*] *I've had to leave my car in the garage for urgent repairs. If you leave your money in the bank in a savings account, it can earn quite a high rate of interest. Don't leave the children in the house without someone looking after them. I left the key in the lock by mistake. "I left my heart in San Francisco."* (song)

**2 leave someone/something in someone's care/charge** to allow someone to look after someone or something: *Make sure that you leave the children in the care of a very responsible person. We left the house in my mother's charge while we were away.*

**3 leave someone in the lurch** to fail to help someone who is in need or trouble: *How could a respectable man leave his family in the lurch and go to paint native women on a tropical island in the South Seas?*

**leave of** *v prep* → **let of**

**leave go/hold of** *not fml* to stop holding (something or someone): [(*usu. simple tenses*)] *Leave go of my arm! If he leaves hold of the rope, he'll fall to his death.*

**leave off** *v adv*

**1** to not wear (clothes): [X9 + OFF] *The day was so warm that I left off my heavy coat.* —**left-off** *n, adj AmE* → **cast off** (1), etc.

***2** to stop (something or doing something); cease: [IØ] *When will the rain leave off? Let's begin the music at the place where we left off last time.* [T1a] *It's time you left off that childish habit of thought.* [T4a (*no pass.*)] *Do you think it will soon leave off raining? He didn't leave off talking for an hour.*

**leave on[1]** *v adv*

**1** to allow (something) to remain in place: [X9 + ON] *We all know that's a new coat, but did you think it necessary to leave the price ticket on?*

**2** to continue wearing (clothes): [X9 + ON] *I feel a bit cold so I'll leave my coat on. It's rude for a man to leave his hat on indoors.* → **keep on** (1)

**3** to allow (something, usu. electrical) to continue burning or working: [X9 + ON] *There is no need for tall office buildings to leave the lights on all night, when the government has asked everyone to save power. I want to leave the soup on all morning, to thicken it.* → **put on[1]** (3), etc.

**leave on[2]** *v prep*

**1** to place (something) on (something) before going away: [T1 + *on*] *I left my visiting card on the table, and went away. Leave a message on the door if I'm out.*

**2** to travel, passing (something) to (one side): [X9 + *on* (*usu. simple tenses*)] *We left the river on our left and followed the road through the valley.*

**leave open** *v adj*

**1** to let (something) remain wide open, apart, etc.: [X9 + **open**] *Leave the window open, we need some air in the house.* → **hold open** (1), **keep open** (1), **remain open** (1), **stay open** (1), **stop open** (1)

**2 leave one's options open** to make sure that one has a choice: *Don't leave your present job until you have actually accepted the one that you've been offered, just in case you decide not to take it; that way you will be leaving your options open.* → **keep open** (6)

**leave out¹** *v adv*
**1** to allow (usu. something) to remain outside: [X9 + OUT] *I left the washing out in the rain all night!*
**2** to place (something) ready for someone: [X9 + OUT] *I'll leave some cold meat out for you when you come in late.*
*__3__ to fail to include (something or someone), as in a list: [T1 (*of*)] *Please complete this cheque properly; the date has been left out. When you were planning the meal, you left out the cheese. The organizer has left Jim out (of the team). I notice that the advertisement leaves out the price of the product.* → **delete from, erase from** (1), **miss out** (1), **omit from**
*__4__ to fail to consider (something): [T1] *No possibility must be left out.*
*__5__ to pay no attention to (someone): [T1 (*usu. pass.*)] *It's Mary's own fault if she feels left out at the party; she makes no effort to be friendly to people. Why am I always left out in the cold?* → **be out of** (14), **feel out of** (1), **miss out** (2)
**6 leave it out** *BrE infml* to stop being troublesome, scolding, etc.: [(*usu. imper.*)] *I've had enough of your complaining for one day—leave it out, will you?*

**leave out²** *v adv AmE* → LEAF OUT

*__leave out of__ *v adv prep*
**1** to fail to include (something or someone) in (something such as a list): [T1] *The organizer has left Jim out of the team. The price of the product has been left out of the advertisement. You can't leave cheese out of your shopping list.*
**2 leave out of account/consideration/reckoning** to fail to consider (something): *No possibility must be left out of account. Don't leave the cost out of consideration.*

**leave over** *v adv*
*__1__ to delay (something): [T1] *We'll leave the consideration of the new appointments over until the next meeting, then.* → **put off¹** (4), etc.
**2 be left over** to remain after the rest has been used or divided: *If you divide 7 by 3, you have 1 left over. After sharing out the apples, there were two left over. It's shameful to see so much food left over in restaurants. When I had finished making the dress, I had only a few square inches of material left over. What little time I have left over from work, I give to reading.* —**leftover** *adj* —**leftovers** *n* → **be over** (3)

**leave to** *v prep*
**1** to give (something such as property) to (someone) in a request (will) after the death of the giver: [T1 + *to*] *Your mother has left most of her property to you. How much was left to the other children?*
*__2__ to allow (someone, something, or doing something) to remain to be dealt with by (someone): [D1] *Leave it (up) to me, I'll see to it. Leave him to his father, he'll deal with him! Why do you leave all the hard work (up) to your mother? I don't like leaving important decisions to inexperienced people. Leave making the arrangements to the chairman.* [V3] *Leave it (up) to the chairman to make the arrangements. Why is it always left (up) to me to pick up the pieces?*
**3 leave something to chance** to trust to luck, not thinking too much about how something will happen: *You can't leave your whole future to chance, but must work hard in order to succeed.*
**4 leave someone to himself/his own devices/resources** to leave someone to look after himself, often after unsuccessfully trying to help him; not to control the activities of someone: *I decided to leave Jim to his own devices after he had refused to accept any of my suggestions. Some teachers believe that students work better if they are left to their own resources.*
**5 leave it/the initiative (up) to** to allow an action, decision, etc., to be made by (someone) according to his own plan and without the help of others: *As for what courses you study, that is left (up) to you. The captain likes to leave the initiative to his men.*
**6 leave someone to it** *infml* to allow someone to continue to do something alone: *You can get on with this job by yourselves—I'll leave you to it. Mary didn't like the way Jim was behaving at the party, so she went home by herself and left him to it.*

**leave up** *v adv*
to allow (something) to remain raised or on show: [X9 + UP] *After Christmas we leave the cards up till the 6 January, which is called Twelfth Night.*

**leave up to** *v adv prep* → LEAVE TO (2, 5)

**leave with** *v prep*
**1** to allow (someone or something) to remain in the care of (someone): [T1 + *with*] *Mary left the children with her mother while she went on holiday. You can leave a message with his secretary. Leave the parcel with me, I'll see that it gets delivered.*
*__2__ to cause (someone) to have (something such as a responsibility): [D1] *The director leaves the chairman with the most difficult decisions. Why should these decisions be left with him?*
**3 leave word with** to leave a message with (someone): *I left word with your mother that I couldn't return as planned. Word can be left with the police where to find you.* → **leave at** (3), **leave for** (6)

*__lech after/for__ *v prep* → **lust after**
*sl* to desire (someone, usu. a woman) sexually, usu. in an unhealthy and unpleasant way: [T1] *Well, you know William, always leching after some woman or other.*

**lecture about/on** *v prep*
to give a serious and often long talk about (a subject), as when teaching in a college or university: [IØ + *about/on*] *Tom has been invited to lecture about his method of writing to a class of English students.*

**lecture at** *v prep*
to scold or warn (someone), often at length: [IØ + *at*] *Don't you lecture at me, I don't have to do what you say! Older children don't like being lectured at.*

**lecture for** *v prep*
**1** to deliver a talk for (a length of time): [IØ + *for*] *After you have been lecturing for an hour, you get thirsty and tired.*
**2** to scold (someone) at length, for (a fault or doing something wrong): [T1 + *for*] *The new secretary was being lectured for the poor quality of her work. The director is always lecturing Jim for being late.*

**lecture on** *v prep* → LECTURE ABOUT

**lecture to** *v prep*
to give a long talk to (people), as when teaching in a college or university: [IØ + *to*] *Tom has been invited to lecture to a class of English students about his method of writing.*

***leech onto** *v prep*
*not fml* to (cause to) follow or admire (someone) without invitation and refusing to be stopped: [T1 (*usu. simple tenses*)] *A group of silly young girls leeched onto the popular singer.* [D1 (*usu. pass.*)] *The old man in hospital has really leeched onto that one particular doctor.*

**leer at** *v prep*
to smile unpleasantly at (someone, often a woman), esp. in a manner suggesting sexual desire: [IØ + *at*] *I want to leave this restaurant, there's a man at the next table who's been leering at me throughout the meal.*

***leg it** *v pron*
*infml* to run fast, esp. to escape: [IØ] *Leg it, the police are coming!*

**legislate against** *v prep*
to make a law or laws to stop (something): [IØ + *against*] *It has been proved necessary to legislate against unequal treatment of women in employment. It should have been legislated against a long time ago.*

***legislate for** *v prep*
*fml* to make plans with; make allowances for (something): [T1] *If you're thinking of travelling on a public holiday, you'll have to legislate for delays in the traffic.*

**lend out** *v adv*
to let people borrow (something or things) freely or in quantity: [T1 + OUT] *Banks will only lend out money at a high rate of interest. Libraries lend out books without charge unless they are returned too late.*

**lend to** *v prep*
**1** to allow the use of (something) to (someone), usu. for a short time, on condition that it is returned: [T1 + *to*] *Just when I needed the ladder, I found that you had lent it to our neighbour; please ask him for it back.* → **loan to**
***2** to give (oneself or something such as one's name or support) to (something such as a plan or activity): [D1 (*usu. simple tenses*)] *We were lucky to persuade a famous judge to lend his name to the movement for improving prison conditions. No son of mine will lend himself to criminal activities. The government has lent its support to the development of new industries in areas of high unemployment. I'm sorry I ever lent my name to your mad plan. The famous singer will lend her voice to the music being performed tonight.*
***3** to give (a quality) to (something): [D1 (*simple tenses*)] *This colour lends warmth to the room, as it gets no natural sunlight. The dark trees lent an air of mystery to the scene.*
**4 lend colour to** to make (something) seem more likely: [(*simple tenses*)] *The wounds on the prisoner's arm lend colour to his story that he was beaten by his fellow criminals.* → **give to** (6)
**5 lend credence to** to make (something) seem true: [(*simple tenses*)] *This sudden storm lends credence to the weathermen's warning.* → **give to** (7)
**6 lend an ear to** to listen to (usu. something): [(*usu. simple tenses*)] *The judge lent a sympathetic ear to the prisoner's story. This teacher lends a deaf ear to his students' requests for help. Lend an ear to those in need.*
**7 lend itself to: a** to be suitable for (something or doing something): [(*simple tenses*)] *The poem lends itself to a musical setting. The room should lend itself to the colour treatment that you have in mind. A wound like this does not usually lend itself to a quick cure.* **b** to be open to or likely to receive (bad treatment): [(*simple tenses*)] *Any system of government by free election naturally lends itself to misuse.*

**lend with** *v prep*
**lend a hand with** to help someone with (something or doing something): *All the teachers were asked to lend a hand with the school concert. Ask the boys to lend a hand with moving the piano.*

**lengthen out** *v adv*
**1** to (cause to) become longer: [IØ + OUT] *Now that it is spring, the days are beginning to lengthen out.* [T1 + OUT] *Could you lengthen your article out a little, by adding some examples?*
***2** *mil* to stretch one's step: [IØ (*usu. simple tenses*)] *Lengthen out there, men, take longer steps!*

**let alone** *v adj*
***1** to not touch or have to do with (something or someone); not trouble (someone): [T1b (*often simple tenses*)] *Let that bag alone, it's not yours! Let her alone! She didn't pick a quarrel with you!* → **leave alone** (2)
**2 let alone** not counting; not to mention (something or someone): *We can't afford a bicycle, let alone a car.* → **leave alone** (3)
**3 let well alone** to be satisfied with existing conditions for fear of making matters worse: [(*often simple tenses*)] *If you're in doubt about whether to try to improve matters, it's*

*usually best to let well alone. You can avoid all kinds of trouble by letting well alone.* also *AmE* **let well enough alone** → **leave alone** (4)

**let at** *v prep*

**let drive/fly at** to aim a blow or attack at (someone): *Jim let drive at one of his attackers, but the blow missed. In his speech, the politician let fly at the government for what he considered misuse of power.*

**let by/past** *v adv*

**1** to allow (someone or something) to pass: [X9 + BY/PAST] *The cars all stopped to let the fire engine by. Let me past, I'm a doctor.*

***2** to take no notice of (usu. something): [T1b] *I shall let that remark by. The teacher woula not let the least little mistake past.*

**let down** *v adv*

**1** to lower; allow (something or someone) to fall or drop: [X9 + DOWN] *The climber is stuck in a deep hole in the snow; we must let a rope down to him. The prisoner let himself down from his window with a rope made of knotted sheets.*

***2** to make (clothes) longer: [T1] *Jane is growing so fast that I have had to let all her skirts down again.* → **take up** (6), **turn up** (3)

***3** to empty (something filled with air): [T1] *Some of the students, angry at their marks, went into the college car park and let down the teachers' tyres.*

***4** (of a plane) to (cause to) descend, as before landing: [T1] *The pilot let the plane down gently once they had crossed the mountains.* [IØ (*usu. simple tenses*)] *The plane let down over the sea before landing at the island airport.* —**letdown** *n*

***5** to lower (a standard, quality, etc.): [T1] *Every time I write an examination I seem to let my own standards down.*

***6** to cause (someone) to be disappointed in one's loyalty; fail to keep a promise to (someone); be disloyal to (something); disappoint (oneself): [T1] *I was depending on him but he let me down. Never let your friends down. Your behaviour has let down the good name of the school. The song sounds fine when you are practising, but I hope you won't let yourself down on the performance.* —**letdown** *n* → **go back on** (3)

***7** *AmE not fml* to work less hard; make less effort: [IØ] *Don't let down now, just when the job's nearly finished.* —**letdown** *n* → **let up** (3)

**8 be let down** to feel disappointed or disheartened: *I've never felt so let down as when I was refused entry to the group that I wished to join.* —**letdown** *n*

**9 let someone down gently** *not fml* to treat someone kindly, considering his feelings and his need for self-respect; reduce the harmful effect on (someone), as when giving bad news: *I won't break the bad news all at once, I'll let her down gently. Grace's red-haired boy didn't even try to let her down gently, but just left her a note and disappeared.*

**10 let one's (back) hair down** *infml* to behave informally; enjoy oneself freely: [*usu. simple tenses*] *Parties are good places for letting your hair down and forgetting the rules.*

**let in** *v adv*

**1** to allow or enable (oneself, someone, or an animal) to enter a place: [X9 + IN] *Open the door and let me in. I'll give you a key so that you can let yourself in. Don't let that cat in here! The public are usually let in half an hour before the performance begins.*

**2** to allow (something such as water or air) to enter: [X9 + IN] *These cheap boots let the rain in. The boat is still letting water in. If you put the insect in a matchbox, you must make holes in the lid to let some air in, or it will die.*

***3** to admit (something): [T1 (*usu. simple tenses*)] *The chairman refused to let in the possibility of doubt.*

***4** (in the theatre) to lower (the roofing part of a piece of scenery) from its folded position above the stage: [T1] *Once the walls of the room are up, let in the ceiling.*

***5** to add (more cloth); sink (something) into a surface; place (something) in a hollow space: [T1] *She had gained so much weight that she had to let in an additional three inches of material at the waist of the dress. The teacher showed us how to cut out part of the surface of the wood and let a pattern in. The doctors decided that a rubber pipe would have to be let in, to enable him to breathe.*

**6 let in the clutch** (in a motor vehicle) to move one's foot to work a pedal which connects the engine with the gearbox: *When John was learning to drive, he used to let in the clutch too quickly, and the car would jump forward sharply.*

***let in for** *v adv prep* → **run in for**

*not fml* to cause (someone or oneself) to have (something such as trouble): [D1] *You're letting yourself in for trouble if you buy that old house. The committee have been let in for a lot of hard work this year. The boy's careless treatment of the car has let me in for a large repair bill. If I'd known what I was letting myself in for, I would never have started the book.*

**let in on** *v adv prep*

***1** *infml* to allow (someone) to share (a plan, activity, etc.): [D1] *Whatever you do, don't let Alice in on the act or she'll want to run the whole show! Jane was annoyed because the boys refused to let her in on their plans.* → **get in on** (1), etc.

**2 let in on the ground floor** *infml* to begin employing someone in a low or humble position: [*usu. simple tenses*] *It's a good idea to let students in on the ground floor, so that they are keen to learn on the job.* → **get in on** (2), etc.

**let into** *v prep*

**1** to allow or enable (oneself, someone, or an animal) to enter (a place): [X9 + *into*] *There's the doorbell; go down and let the doc-*

*tor into the house, will you? I'll give you a key so that you can let yourself into the car. Don't let that cat into my kitchen! We don't let young children into this cinema alone.*

**2** to allow (something such as water or air) to enter (something): [X9 + *into*] *The roof lets water into the bedrooms. This cheap leather lets the rain into my boots. Let some air into the matchbox or your insect will die.*

***3** to allow (someone) to join (a group) or attend (an event): [D1] *Shall we let her into the club? This promising young cricketer should be let into the team, at least for this year, to give him a chance to prove himself. Students are let into most concerts for half price. No visitors are let into the committee meetings.*

***4** to allow (someone) to share (usu. a secret): [D1] *Shall we let the children into the arrangements for Father's birthday? I'll let you into a secret—I don't know the answer!* → **get in on** (1), etc.

***5** to cause (something) to be sunk into the surface of (something) or placed in (a hollow space); add (cloth) to (a garment): [D1 (*often pass.*)] *A pattern was let into the wood. A rubber pipe had been let into his throat to enable him to breathe. She had gained so much weight that she had to let an additional piece of material into the waistline of the dress.*

***6** *BrE infml* to attack (someone), with blows or words: [T1] *Jim let into his attackers, who soon lay unconscious. The politician let into the government for its recent inaction.* → **lay into,** etc.

**let loose** *v adj*

**1** to free (someone, an animal, etc.): [X9 + loose] *Someone has let the tigers loose from their cages and they are terrorizing the whole town. When we escape, shall we let the other prisoners loose?* → **get free** (1), etc.

***2** to give (someone) freedom or the chance to cause trouble, make changes, be in charge, etc.: [T1b (*on*)] *No one should let a young child loose on a car with the engine running. An inexperienced politician should not be let loose on running the party. Who let this teacher loose on that class? Let me loose for a week to reorganize the office and I'll show you that mine is the better system.* → **turn loose** (2)

**let of** *v prep* → **leave of**

**let go/hold of**

**1** to stop holding (something or someone): *Let go of my arm! If he lets go of the rope, he'll fall to his death.*

**2** to lose (something) willingly: [*usu. simple tenses*] *No politician likes to let go of power once he has tasted it.*

**let off**[1] *v adv*

**1** to allow (someone) to leave a vehicle, ship, etc.: [X9 + OFF] *Let me off at the corner, please. The ship stops at the next port to let passengers off.* → **get off**[1] (3), **get off with** (1), **get on** (3), **get out of** (3), **put down** (4), **put off** (2), **set down** (4)

***2** to cause (something) to explode or be fired: [T1] *The gun is let off every day at 1 o'clock. Terrorists have been letting off bombs in Underground trains. The children are gathering in the garden to let off the fireworks.* → **go off**[1] (5), etc.

***3** *not fml* to excuse (someone) from punishment, duty, etc.: [T1 (*with*)] *The judge sent the man to prison but let the two boys off (with a warning). With your record, you can hardly expect to be let off lightly. You should really do the next three exercises, but I'm going to let you off as you've worked so hard.* → **get away with** (6), **get off**[1] (9), **get off with** (2)

***4** to permit the renting of (a building) in separate parts: [T1] *Most of these fine old houses are being let off as flats.*

***5** *taboo* to break wind: [IØ] *It's very rude to let off in a public place.* [T1] *Just as we were being introduced, he let off a really loud one!*

**6 let off steam: a** (of a steam engine) to allow steam to escape, so as to prevent danger: *That's the big boiler letting off steam; it must be getting dangerously hot in there.* **b** *infml* to behave actively, using up strength or a strong feeling: *I'm glad the weather is fine so that the children can play outside and let off steam. When men let off steam, they tend to shout; women, on the other hand, express their feelings by weeping.* → **blow off**[1] (2)

**let off**[2] *v prep*

**1** to allow (someone) to leave (a vehicle, ship, etc.): [X9 + *off*] *Would you let me off the bus at the next stop, please? Will we be let off the ship at the next port?* → **alight from**, etc.

***2** to excuse (someone) from (something such as punishment or duty, or doing something): [D1] *The judge decided to let the boys off the punishment that they deserved, to give them a chance. Girls always get let off the heavy work because they're weaker.* [V4b] *I'll let you off doing the dishes, as you helped with the shopping.* → **get out of** (13), etc.

**3 let someone off the hook** *infml* to free someone from a difficulty, blame, responsibility for decisions, etc.: *The director accepted my explanation that the accident was not my fault, so I got let off the hook. When the judge let the boys off the hook, they were suitably grateful. Those three children were driving me mad until their mother came home and let me off the hook.* → **be off**[2] (8), **be on**[2] (17), **get off**[2] (12)

***let on** *v adv*

**1** *infml* to tell a secret: [IØ (*about*) (*usu. simple tenses*)] *You mean you knew all the time and never let on? Don't let on about the meeting, I want it kept private.* [I5 (*usu. simple tenses*)] *Don't let on that I told you, will you?* [I6 (*usu. simple tenses*)] *You mustn't let on where the jewels are hidden.*

**2** *infml* to pretend: [IØ (*usu. simple tenses*)] *He's not as rich as he lets on.* [I5 (*usu. simple* *tenses*)] *He got the job by letting on that he had a lot of experience.*

**let out** *v adv*

**1** to allow or enable (oneself, someone, or an animal) to leave: [X9 + OUT] *Open the door, and let the cat out. Let me out! I'm locked in! I'd rather not let the children out in this wet weather. Don't trouble to see me to the door, I'll let myself out.*

**2** to set (usu. someone) free (from somewhere): [X9 + OUT (*of*)] *If he was given five years' imprisonment, he could be let out after three years. The doctors are letting Mother out of hospital next week.*

**3** to allow (something such as water or air) to escape: [X9 + OUT (*of*)] *It's a cruel joke to let the air out of somebody's car tyres. She let her breath out with a loud noise. There's a hole in the bottom of the bucket that lets the water out. It's good to let out your feelings in a shout.* **—outlet** *n*

***4** to express (a sound): [T1a (*often simple tenses*)] *He let out a cry of pain as the nail went into his foot.*

***5** to tell (a secret), often unintentionally: [T1 (*usu. simple tenses*)] *The foolish young politician let out the date of the election in an unguarded moment.* [T5 (*usu. simple tenses*)] *Mary accidentally let out that her mother had telephoned.* [T6 (*usu. simple tenses*)] *Jane let out where she had hidden her father's birthday present.* → **be out** (10), **bring out** (11), **come out** (12), **filter out** (4), **get out** (9), **leak out** (2)

***6** to allow (a fire) to stop burning: [T1] *Don't let the fire out, will you?* → **put out** (13), etc.

***7** *not fml* to excuse (someone); enable (someone) to escape blame or unwanted responsibility: [T1 (*of*) (*usu. simple tenses*)] *The regular teacher is back, is he? Good, that lets me out! I was glad to be let out of that nasty affair, and have someone more experienced handle the trouble.* **—let-out** *n*

***8** to make (clothing) wider: [T1] *Jane is growing so fast that I've had to let out all her dresses, especially at the waist!* → **take in**[1] **(13)**

***9** *naut* to unfold; spread (a sail): [T1] *Let out the main sail, let's make use of this wind!*

***10** esp. *BrE* to allow the use of (something) for rent: [T1] *These boats are let out by the hour.* → **hire out, rent out**

***11** *not fml* to attack (someone), with blows or words: [IØ (*at*)] *Jim let out in all directions but his attackers were too strong for him. Once he gets angry, he lets out at anyone who opposes him.* → **lay into,** etc.

***12** *AmE not fml* to finish a meeting, day of work, performance, etc.; empty: [IØ (*usu. simple tenses*)] *School lets out at 3 o'clock. Let's try to get to the cinema just before it lets out.*

**13 let the cat out of the bag** *infml* to tell a secret: *Father wasn't supposed to know about his birthday surprise—now you've let the cat out of the bag!*

**let past** *v adv* → LET BY

**let through**[1] *v adv*

**1** to allow (something or someone) to pass through: [X9 + THROUGH] *We need some partly transparent window shades to let the light through but not the heat. This thin coat lets the cold wind through. Open the gates and let the crowd through.*

***2** to allow (something or someone) to pass; accept (something or someone): [T1b] *Although not completely satisfied, the committee let the report through. The examiners let the weak student through, but warned him that he must improve his work.*

**let through**[2] *v prep*

**1** to allow (something or someone) to pass through (something): [X9 + *through*] *Open the curtains, to let some light through the window. Let the crowd through the gates now, the game will start soon.*

***2** to accept (someone or something) in (something); allow (something or someone) to pass (a stage): [D1] *Although not completely satisfied, the committee let the report through the first stage. The weak student was let through the examination, but warned to improve his work.*

**let up** *v adv*

**1** to allow (someone) to come upstairs or to a higher level: [X9 + UP (*usu. simple tenses*)] *The doctor's here; shall I let him up?*

***2** to lessen; gradually cease: [IØ] *When will this rain let up? Mother thought the pain would never let up.* **—letup** *n*

***3** to work less hard; make less effort: [IØ (*often simple tenses*)] *The doctor has been working for fifty hours without letting up. Don't let up now, just when the job is nearly finished.* **—letup** *n* → **let down** (7)

***let up on** *v adv prep*

**1** to treat (someone) less severely: [T1 (*no pass., often simple tenses*)] *It's unwise to let up on your students just before the examination. I wish their mother would let up on the children: her endless shouting is bad for their nerves.*

**2** to work less hard at (something): [T1 (*no pass., often simple tenses*)] *We cannot let up on our efforts to compete with other more successful firms.*

**level against** *v prep* → **bring against, lay against** (2), **prefer against**

to state (a charge) against (someone): [X9 + *against* (*usu. pass.*)] *The jewel thief was taken to the police station, where a charge of robbery was levelled against him.*

**level at** *v prep*

**1** to aim (something such as a weapon or look) directly towards (someone): [X9 + *at*] *I woke to find a shotgun levelled at my eyes.*

***2** to direct (something such as opposition) towards (someone): [D1 (*usu. simple tenses*)]

*The speaker levelled his remarks at the government's chief Minister.*

**level down** *v adv* → **level up**
to lower (something such as incomes) to an equal level: [X9 + DOWN] *The high rate of income tax has only succeeded in levelling down the incomes of the rich to those of the poor, with no advantage to the latter.*

**level off** *v adv*
**1** to make (a surface) flat, smooth, even, or level: [T1 + OFF] *When the house was built, the garden had to be levelled off with a big earth-moving machine. Level off the shelves with a spirit level.*
**2** to become level, flat, or at a steady rate, usu. after rising: [L9 + OFF] *The plane's flight path climbed to 10,000 metres and then levelled off. The worst of this job is that it levels off after only a few years, and you can get no further in it. On their eastern side, the Rocky Mountains level off quite suddenly into flat land that stretches for 2,000 miles.* → **level out** (1)

**level out** *v adv*
**1** to become level, flat, or at a steady rate, usu. after rising: [L9 + OUT] *The plane's flight path climbed to 10,000 metres and then levelled out. The rise in the unemployment figures should level out soon. The worst of this job is that it levels out after only a few years, and you can get no further in it.* → **level off** (2)
**2** to make (something such as differences) more equal: [X9 + OUT] *The tax system is intended to level out the big differences between rich and poor.*

**level up** *v adv* → **level down**
to raise (something such as incomes) to an equal level: [X9 + UP] *The idea of equal education was to level up the general standard; unfortunately, it sometimes seems to have had the opposite effect.*

**level with** *v prep*
*infml* to speak the truth to (someone) honestly: [T1] *At last the prisoner decided to level with the police and tell them the truth instead of all those lies. Come on, you can trust me —level with me, what's the truth?*

**lever out** *v adv*
**1** to remove (something) with a bar or other strong tool: [X9 + OUT] *We cut the tree down successfully, but had a lot of trouble levering the roots out as they were fixed firmly in the earth.*
**2** to remove (someone), as by a trick: [T1 (*of*)] *Whatever mistakes he makes, it is difficult to lever the chairman out of his powerful position until his appointment comes to an end.*
**3** to make (oneself) rise with difficulty, effort, etc.: [T1 (*of*)] *Breathing heavily, the fat man levered himself out of the deep armchair. Once you're stuck in deep snow, it's difficult to lever yourself out.*

**lever up** *v adv*
**1** to raise (something) with a bar or other strong tool: [X9 + UP] *If you lever up the stone with a stick, you will find lots of insects living beneath it.*
***2** to lift (oneself) up with difficulty, effort, etc.: [T1 (*from*)] *The wounded soldier levered himself up on his elbow and shouted for help.*

**levy on/upon** *v prep*
**1** to demand and collect (something such as a tax) from (someone): [T1 + *on/upon*] *Taxes should be levied more on the rich than on the poor.*
***2** *fml* to take (something such as goods) by law in payment of a debt: [T1 (*usu. simple tenses*)] *The court may have to levy on your property to pay your debts.*
**3 levy war on/upon** *fml* to declare war on (an enemy) after collecting an army and all its supplies: [*usu. simple tenses*] *The king was prepared to levy war on his neighbour after their quarrel over the land.* also **levy war against**

***liaise between/with** *v prep* → **mediate between**
*not fml* to act as a connection between (two people or groups) or with (someone else): [T1 (*often simple tenses*)] *A well-known local lawyer has been appointed to liaise between the employers and the union leaders, since they cannot reach agreement in direct talks. The officer's special job was to liaise with other groups that might prove helpful in friendly countries.*

**liberate from** *v prep*
to set (something or someone) free from (someone, something, or doing something): [T1 + *from*] *A war was fought in the United States in the 19th century to liberate black people from slavery. In recent years, women have been trying to liberate themselves from being regarded as second-class citizens.*

**license for** *v prep*
to give (someone or a place) official permission to do, have, or offer (something): [T1 + *for* (*usu. pass.*)] *The restaurant is licensed for the sale of beer, but not wine. I must ask you to stop singing as the inn is not licensed for music. In England you can get married in a church, or in a special office that is licensed for marriages, but nowhere else.*

**lick into** *v prep* → **whip into** (3)
**lick someone/something into shape** *not fml* to make someone or something reach a fit condition, for whatever purpose: *With a lot of training, we might be able to lick the team into shape in time for next year's games. With some more practice, we'll soon lick this piece of music into shape ready for the performance.*

**lick off** *v adv; prep*
to remove (something such a covering) with the tongue (from something): [T1 + OFF/*off*] *The children have just licked the cream off (the top) and left the jelly!*

**lick up** *v adv*
to take up (usu. a liquid) with the tongue: [T1 + UP] *The cat licked up all the milk which had overflowed onto the floor.*

***lie about/around**[1] *v adv*
**1** to be lazy or do nothing: [IØ] *It's so nice to have the time to lie around in the sun. He lay about all day instead of working.* also **lay about**
**2** to be left unattended, scattered, or untidy: [IØ (*usu. continuous tenses*)] *I found this book lying about upstairs; is it yours? He always leaves his papers lying about so that it is difficult to clean the room.* → **kick about** (3), **knock about** (3), **leave about**

**lie about**[2] *v prep*
to not tell the truth about (something or someone): [IØ + *about*] *Many women lie about their age. The prisoner lied about where he had been at the time of the jewel robbery.*

**lie about**[3] *v prep* also **lie around**
**1** to surround (something or someone): [L9 + *about* (*usu. simple tenses*)] *The hills lie about the valley like a protective wall.* → **kick about** (2), **knock about** (2)
**2** to be left unattended, scattered, or untidy in (a place): [L9 + *about* (*usu. continuous tenses*)] *Please don't leave your clothes lying about the room, it makes it difficult to clean.*

**lie ahead** *v adv*
**1** to be placed in front (of something or someone): [L9 + AHEAD (*of*) (*simple tenses*)] *The driver turned the wheel to avoid a large rock that lay ahead.* → **lie before** (1)
***2** to exist in the future: [IØ (*of*) (*simple tenses*)] *Difficult times lie ahead. Death lies ahead of us all.* → **lie before** (2), **lie beyond**[1] (2)

***lie along** *v adv*
(of a ship) to lean over with a side wind: [IØ (*usu. simple tenses*)] *A strong crosswind caused the ship to lie along.*

**lie alongside** *v adv; prep* → **draw alongside, lay alongside, pull alongside**
(of a ship) to come to rest near (something such as another ship): [L9 + ALONGSIDE/*alongside* (*usu. simple tenses*)] *If the ship that has come to save us can lie alongside the sinking ship, we can move the passengers there from this ship before she sinks.*

***lie around**[1] *v adv* → LIE ABOUT[1]

**lie around**[2] *v prep* → LIE ABOUT[3]

**lie at** *v prep*
**1** *old use* to sleep at (a place): [L9 + *at*] *The traveller decided to lie at an inn that night.*
**2** to take a position or rest next to (something): [L9 + *at*] *The dog liked to lie at his master's feet.*
**3 lie at anchor/its moorings** (of a ship) to be still; stop moving; be anchored, usu. out of a harbour: *Will the ship be safe lying at anchor in this storm?* → **ride at**
**4 lie at death's door** *not fml* to be dying or almost dead: *For a week after the operation, Mother lay at death's door, but then she began to get better.*
**5 lie at someone's door** (of blame, guilt, etc.); to be someone's responsibility: [*simple tenses*] *The fault lies at their own doors.* → **lay at** (2)

**lie back** *v adv*
**1** to take a position with one's head resting, as on a chair, bed, etc.: [L9 + BACK (*often simple tenses*)] *Lie back, dear, you'll be more comfortable.*
**2** (esp. in sport) to move or bend backwards: [L9 + BACK (*usu. simple tenses*)] *He lay back and hit the ball for four.*

**lie before** *v prep*
**1** to be placed in front of (usu. someone): [L9 + *before* (*simple tenses*)] *A wonderful view of the lake lay before us.* → **lie ahead** (1)
***2** to be in the future for (someone): [T1 (*no pass., simple tenses*)] *Difficult times lie before us. Death lies before us all.* → **lie ahead** (2), **lie beyond**[1] (2)
***3** to be more important than (something): [T1 (*no pass., simple tenses*)] *My duty to my family lies before my own interests.* → **put before** (4), etc.

***lie behind**[1] *v adv*
to exist earlier; be past: [IØ (*simple tenses*)] *Memories lie behind of all that has happened. Behind lay a terrible winter; ahead was promised spring.*

**lie behind**[2] *v prep*
**1** to be placed at the back of (something): [L9 + *behind* (*simple tenses*)] *The valley that we are trying to reach lies behind the next hill.*
***2** to exist earlier than; be past (one): [T1 (*no pass., simple tenses*)] *I shall be glad when this year lies behind me. Some difficulties lie behind us, but greater ones lie ahead.*
***3** to be the reason for (something): [T1 (*no pass., simple tenses*)] *I wonder what lies behind his offer?* → **be behind**[2] (2)

**lie beside** *v prep* → LIE BY

**lie beyond**[1] *v adv*
**1** to be in a position further away: [L9 + BEYOND (*simple tenses*)] *I have only ever been as far as the next valley, and have no idea what lies beyond.*
***2** to exist in the future: [IØ (*simple tenses*)] *We can make plans for the next year, but who can tell what lies beyond?* → **lie ahead** (2), **lie before** (2)

**lie beyond**[2] *v prep*
**1** to be in a position further than (something): [L9 + *beyond* (*simple tenses*)] *I have no idea what lies beyond the next valley.*
***2** to exist in the future further than (a time): [T1 (*no pass., simple tenses*)] *We can make plans for the next year, but who can tell what lies beyond that?*
***3** to be greater than or too much for (something such as a quality): [T1 (*no pass., simple tenses*)] *The singer was unwise to choose songs which lay beyond her ability.*

***lie by**[1] *v adv* → **lay by**[1] (9), **lay to**[1], **lie to**[1]
(of a ship) to stop; come to rest: [IØ (*usu.*

*simple tenses*)] *We shall have to lie by because of the storm.*

**lie by/beside**[1] *v prep*
to take a position next to (something): [L9 + *by/beside*] *It's so pleasant to lie by a warm fire.*

***lie doggo** *v adv* → **hole up, lie low** (3), **lie up** (3)
*infml* to lie in hiding, still and silent: [IØ] *Get into this hole and lie doggo until the police have gone past.*

**lie down** *v adv*
**1** to lie at full length, as when resting or sleeping: [L9 + DOWN] *Mother isn't feeling too well and has gone to lie down.* —**lie-down** *n infml* → **lay down** (1)
**2 take something lying down** *not fml* to suffer something bad without complaint or attempt at opposition: [*usu. neg.*] *The unions are not going to take the government's threats lying down: they will even stop working to get more money. The men will not take such treatment lying down. Why do you take her rude remarks lying down?* → **lie down under, sit down under**

**lie down on** *v adv prep*
**1** to lie at full length on (a surface): [L9 + DOWN + *on*] *Would you like to lie down on the bed for a few minutes? You look rather tired.*
**2 lie down on the job** *infml* to refuse to work hard; put no effort into one's work: *Why are the workers lying down on the job? Has there been another disagreement with the employers?*

**lie down under** *v adv prep* → **lie down** (2), **sit down under**
*not fml* to suffer (something bad) without complaint or attempt at opposition: [T1 (*no pass., usu. neg., often simple tenses*)] *No self-respecting fighter will lie down under such a small defeat. The men will not lie down under such treatment.*

**lie fallow** *v adj*
**1** (of a field) to be rested from producing crops: [L9 + fallow] *We produce wheat and other crops on this field for a few years and then we let it lie fallow. You can put your tents in the big field that's lying fallow this year.*
***2** (of someone's mind) to rest; be unproductive: [IØ] *When Tom had finished his last book, he found that no new ideas would come; his brain seemed to be lying fallow.*

**lie in**[1] *v adv*
**1** to remain in bed late in the morning: [IØ] *It's so nice at the weekends to have a chance to lie in.* —**lie-in** *n* → **sleep in** (1)
**2** *old use* (of a woman) to remain in bed for the birth of her child: [IØ] *"You must go visit the good lady that lies in."* (Shakespeare, *Coriolanus*) —**lying-in** *n, adj*

**lie in**[2] *v prep*
**lie in one's teeth/throat** → LIE THROUGH

**lie in**[3] *v prep*
**1** to take a horizontal position in (something): [L9 + *in*] *Have you been lying in bed all morning? It's so pleasant to lie in the warm sun.*
**2** to be placed in (somewhere); (of a dead body) to be buried in (a place): [L9 + *in* (*usu. simple tenses*)] *The house lies in a little valley behind the trees. Don't keep your money lying in the bank; use it to earn interest. I cannot bear to see the suffering that lies in her face. How long will he have to lie in prison? "Two of us in the churchyard lie, My sister and my brother."* (William Wordsworth, *We are Seven*)
**3** to exist in the form of (someone, something, or doing something): [L9 + *in* (*simple tenses*)] *All our hopes lay in him, but he disappointed us. As a singer, her strengths lie in her firm command of musical knowledge, and ability to express songs with feeling; her weakness lies, unfortunately, in the quality of her voice, which is beyond her control. His chief attraction lies in his character, not his looks. His worst mistake lay in thinking that all his workers were trustworthy. Perhaps the answer lies in trying another system.* → **embody in, repose in** (2), **reside in** (2), **rest in** (2)
**4 lie in ambush/wait for** to wait for (someone) hidden, so as to attack him by surprise: *All the passengers' money was taken by three robbers who had lain in ambush for them in a lonely spot.*
**5 lie in someone's power** to be something that someone can do: [*simple tenses*] *I have done everything that lies in my power; the decision now rests with the committee.* → **fall within** (2), etc.
**6 lie in ruins: a** (of a building or buildings) to be destroyed: *After the explosion, half the city lay in ruins.* **b** (of a plan, etc.) to be spoilt: *When the other firm won the contract, all our hopes for the future lay in ruins.*
**7 lie in state** (of the body of an important person) to be shown to the public before burial: *The dead general's body will lie in state for three days before the funeral, to give the people a chance to pay their last respects.* —**lying-in-state** *n*
**8 lie in store (for)** to be about to happen in the future (to someone): [*usu. simple tenses*] *Who knows what troubles lie in store for us? A surprise lay in store for them when they entered the house.*
**9 as far as in me lies** to the best of my ability: *I've done my best to find the information, as far as in me lies.*

**lie low** *v adj*
**1** to be placed in a low position: [L9 + low (*usu. simple tenses*)] *The village lies low in a hidden valley.*
***2** to be humbled: [IØ] *"O mighty Caesar, dost thou lie so low?"* (Shakespeare, *Julius Caesar*)
***3** *infml* to hide, as to escape from police: [IØ] *You'd better lie low here for a few weeks*

*until the police have stopped looking for you.* → **hole up, lie doggo, lie up** (3)

***lie off** *v adv*

**1** (of a ship) to keep a short way from the shore or another ship: [IØ (*usu. simple tenses*)] *We'll have to lie off until the storm is over.*

**2** to stop working: [IØ (*usu. simple tenses*)] *"As soon as he makes a little money, he lies off and spends it."* (Rudyard Kipling, *City of Dreadful Night*) → **lay off**[1] (3), **stand off**[1] (4)

**lie on** *v prep*

**1** to take a horizontal position on (a surface or part of the body): [L9 + *on*] *The only way to test a bed that you are thinking of buying is to lie on it. I love to lie on the sand, getting brown in the sun. You'll be more comfortable if you lie on your back.*

**2** to be placed or left on (something): [L9 + *on*] *A goodbye note lay on the kitchen table. There's a parcel lying on the front step. The remains of Jane's dinner lay on her plate untouched.*

**3 lie heavy on** to cause discomfort, unpleasant feelings to (someone or part of someone): *That cheesecake has been lying heavy on my stomach all night. The old man's death lay heavy on the murderer's conscience. His conscience lay heavy on him, so he went to the police and admitted his part in the crime.*

**lie open** *v adj*

**1** to be in an opened position: [L9 + **open**] *The Bible lay open at a suitable place. The door lay open, inviting us to enter.*

***2** to be in a likely position; be possible (to receive something): [IØ (*for, to*) (*simple tenses*)] *In this position, our ships lie open to attack. The way lies open for a re-examination of the facts.*

**lie out** *v adv*

**1** to stretch oneself at full length, as out of doors: [L9 + OUT (*in*)] *You'll find her in the garden, lying out in the sun.*

**2** to be far away: [L9 + OUT (*simple tenses*)] *The borders of his hand lie out far beyond one's line of sight.* —**outlying** *adj*

***3** (of money) to be placed so as to earn interest: [IØ (*often continuous tenses*)] *Half the money that he won is already lying out at interest.*

***lie over** *v adv* → **put off**[1] (4), etc.

to wait or be delayed until another time: [IØ] *We'll have to leave the question lying over till next week.*

**lie through** *v prep*

**lie through one's teeth/throat** *not fml* to tell a very big lie: *Don't trust him when he tells you that he's very rich, so as to persuade you to lend him money for his business; he's lying through his teeth, he hasn't a penny and is trying to rob you.* also **lie in one's teeth/throat**

***lie to**[1] *v adv* → **lay by**[1] (9), **lay to**[1], **lie by**[1]

(of a ship) to be still or almost still when facing the wind: [IØ (*usu. simple tenses*)] *The captain gave the order to lie to.*

**lie to**[2] *v prep*

to not tell the truth to (someone): [IØ + *to*] *The prisoner was severely punished for lying to the court.*

**lie to**[3] *v prep*

to be placed in (a certain direction): [L9 + *to* (*simple tenses*)] *The town lies* (*some distance*) *to the south of here.*

***lie up** *v adv*

**1** to stay in bed, esp. for a long period: [IØ] *Mother was so ill after her operation that she had to lie up for a month.* → **lay by**[1] (8), **lay up** (4)

**2** (of a boat or ship) to go into or remain in a harbour, esp. for repairs or out of season: [IØ] *My boat has been lying up in the harbour all winter.* → **lay up** (3), **put up**[1] (19)

**3** to hide as a means of escape: [IØ] *You'd better lie up here for a few weeks until the police have stopped looking for you.* → **hole up, lie doggo, lie low** (3)

***lie with** *v prep*

**1** to be the responsibility of (someone): [T1 (*no pass., simple tenses*)] *The job of ensuring an equal sharing of national wealth lies with the government.* [*It* + V3] *It lies with the police to prove that the prisoner actually stole the jewels.* → **rest with**

**2** *old use* to have sex with (someone): [T1] *The innkeeper found the traveller lying with his daughter.* → **couple with** (1), **sleep together** (2), **sleep with** (2)

**lie within** *v prep*

**1** to be placed inside (an area or surrounding): [L9 + *within* (*simple tenses*)] *The temple lies within the city walls. The castle lay deep within the forest.* → **be within** (1)

***2** to belong to; be part of; be able to be influenced by (something such as someone's power): [T1 (*no pass., simple tenses*)] *If it lies within my power to do it, I will. The whole area lies within his control.* → **fall within** (2), etc.

**lift down** *v adv*

to lower (something or someone): [T1 + DOWN (*from*)] *The fireman lifted the child down to safety from the burning room. Please lift the box down from the shelf for me, I can't reach.* [D1 + DOWN] *Life me down those two boxes, will you?*

**lift from** *v prep*

**1** to move or usu. raise (something) from (a position): [T1 + *from*] *The climber had to be lifted from the deep hole with a strong rope. This stone is too heavy to lift from the ground.*

***2** *not fml* to copy (something) from (someone else's writing): [D1] *Parts of your article have been lifted bodily from a well-known magazine; this is a form of cheating and you will be severely punished for it.*

**lift off** *v adv*

**1** to remove (something) by raising it: [T1 +

OFF] *When he lifted off his hat, I saw that he was wearing false hair. Steam power was discovered when its inventor watched the steam lifting off the lid of a pan.*

*2 (of a space vehicle) to rise from the earth: [IØ] *What time does the spaceship lift off?* —**lift-off** *n* → **blast off** (2)

**lift up** *v adv*

**1** to raise (something or someone): [T1 + UP] *The stone is too heavy to lift up. The mountains lift up their snowy heads to the sky. Lift me up over this wall, will you?* —**lift-up** *n* → **pull up** (1), etc.

*2 to encourage; raise; make (something such as a feeling) more cheerful: [T1] *This sunshine should lift up your spirits a little. "Lift up your hearts."* (title of religious broadcast) —**uplift** *n*

**3 lift up one's eyes** to look upwards: *"I will lift up mine eyes unto the hills, from whence cometh my help."* (The Bible)

**4 lift up one's voice** to express a sound or opinion loudly: *"Lift up your hearts, lift up your voice."* (Charles Wesley, *Rejoice, the Lord is King*)

***light into** *v prep* → **lay into,** etc.

esp. *AmE infml* to attack (someone) violently, with blows or words: [T1] *Fearlessly, Jim lit into his attackers, who soon lay unconscious on the ground. The opposition speaker made a lively speech, and lit into the government for its recent inaction.*

**light on/upon** *v prep*

**1** to land on (something): [IØ + *on/upon*] *The bird lighted on the branch. A drop of rain just lighted on my hand. The blow lighted exactly on the point of his chin and he fell unconscious.* → **alight on** (1)

*2 (of one's eyes, look, etc.) to be directed towards (something or someone): [T1 (*no pass., usu. simple tenses*)] *"It was said of... Henry VIII that his eye lighted upon few women whom he did not desire, and he desired few whom he did not enjoy."* (Robertson Davies, *Tempest-Tost*)

*3 to discover (something, usu. good) by chance: [T1 (*simple tenses*)] *If you look hard enough in this field, you could light on some valuable ancient coins.* → **happen on,** etc.

**light out** *v adv* → **clear out** (6), **cut out** (11), **dig out** (6)

esp. *AmE infml* to leave, often in a hurry: [IØ (*for, of*) (*simple tenses*)] *The fox lit out for the forest. It's time I left home; I shall light out next week. The criminals lit out of the bank as soon as they had seized the money.*

**light to** *v adv*

*naut* to give enough rope to be fastened: [IØ (*simple tenses*)] *We need more rope there, light to!*

**light up** *v adv*

**1** to make (a place such as a room or city) brighter: [T1 + UP] *These new lamps light up the room much better, don't they?*

*2 to light (a cigar or pipe); start smoking: [IØ] *I had difficulty lighting up my cigar in the strong wind. You must not light up after the formal dinner until the Queen's health has been drunk.*

*3 *BrE* to switch on lights in a street or car: [IØ] *Be sure to light up as soon as the sun sets, or the police may stop your car.* —**lighting-up** *adj*

*4 to (cause to) become more cheerful: [IØ (*usu. simple tenses*)] *Her face lit up with joy when she heard the good news.* [T1 (*usu. simple tenses*)] *A smile lit up his face.*

**5 be lit up** *infml* to be drunk: *Jim only shouts when he gets lit up.* → **load up** (3), **tank up** (2)

**light upon** *v prep* → LIGHT ON

**light with** *v prep* → **illuminate with**

to brighten; give light to (something such as a place) with (a kind or power supply of light): [T1 + *with*] *The first London theatre to be lit with electricity was the Savoy, in 1870.*

***liken to** *v prep* → **compare to, compare with, equate to**

to show that (something or someone) is like (something or someone else): [D1 (*often pass.*)] *This calculating machine can be likened to a human brain. Someone has likened this flower to an elephant's ear.*

***limber up** *v adv* → **loosen up** (2)

to exercise (oneself), esp. to be ready for action: [IØ] *The team spends half an hour limbering up before each game.* [T1] *It's dangerous to run a fast race without limbering yourself up first.* —**limbering-up, limber-up** *n*

**limit to** *v prep* → **restrict to**

to reduce; control; keep (something or someone) down to (something such as a certain amount or level); save (something) for (a certain group): [T1 + *to* (*often pass.*)] *Payments are limited to 10% each month. The height of new buildings in this city is now limited by law to forty-five feet. The noise of your radio must be limited to a level that we can all bear. The printing of this fine book has been limited to 500 copies. Invitations to the wedding must be limited to the family. I intend to limit my remarks to a general view of the subject. Eact speaker is limited to five minutes.*

**line out** *v adv*

to mark (something such as a plan) with lines: [X9 + OUT] *Let me line out the plan of the house on this piece of paper.* —**outline** *n, v*

***line up** *v adv*

**1** to (cause to) wait in order: [IØ] *I hate lining up in the cold to go to a cinema.* [T1] *The children were lined up ready to go into school. The funeral cars are lined up, ready to leave.* —**line-up** *n* → **queue up**

**2** to place (usu. people) in a row: [T1] *The prisoners were lined up against a wall and shot. Line up these men and see if the witness can recognize the criminal.* —**line-up** *n*

**3** to arrange (people) in a special order: [T1]

*Line up the team in order of play.* —**line-up** *n*
**4** to organize; get (things or people) together; arrange for a supply of (usu. something): [T1 (*often pass.*)] *Have you got the seating arrangements lined up? Who have you lined up to speak at the meeting? What shows are lined up for tonight's broadcast?* —**line-up** *n*
**5** to provide or obtain (something): [T1] *Will you be able to line up much support for your idea?*
**6** to combine, as in political matters: [IØ] *Many of the smaller nations are lining up so as to deal more effectively with the more powerful countries.* —**line-up** *n*
**7** to make (something, esp. written or printed) level with other lines: [T1] *Line up these two words with the rest of the page.*
**8** (esp. in sport) to prepare (something such as an aim): [T1] *We didn't line the shot up properly, and the ball went wide of the mark.*

*__line up against__ *v adv prep*
**1** to (cause to) stand in a row next to or touching (something): [IØ + *against*] *Line up against the window so that you can be seen.* [T1 + *against*] *The prisoners were lined up against the wall and shot.*
**2** to (cause to) oppose (something or someone): [T1 (*no pass.*)] *How many voters have lined up against the politician?* [D1] *We must line more people up against the government.*

**line up alongside/with** *v adv prep*
**1** to stand in a waiting line together with (someone): [IØ + UP + *alongside/with*] *Please line up alongside the guide if you want to visit the great hall.*
**2** to make (something) level with (something): [T1 + UP + *alongside/with*] *The child enjoyed lining up his bricks alongside the others. Line up these two words with the rest of the page.*
*__3__ to support (someone) in an opinion: [T1 (*no pass.*)] *I'm surprised to hear that he has lined up alongside the workers in their opinions.*

*__line up behind__ *v adv prep*
to follow; support (someone) as a leader: [T1 (*no pass.*)] *All the members of the party have lined up behind the newly elected leader, even those who voted against him.*

**line up in** *v adv prep*
*__1__ to (cause to) form a waiting line in (a place or condition): [IØ + *in*] *I do hate lining up in the cold to go into a cinema.*
**2 have something lined up in one's sights** to have a good view of something in the sights of one's gun: *With the deer lined up in his sights, the hunter fired and the animal fell dead.*

**line up with** *v adv prep* → LINE UP ALONGSIDE

**line with¹** *v prep*
to provide (something) with a covering or inner side of (something such as material): [T1 + *with*] *Please line the drawers with clean paper after you have emptied them. The coat is lined with silk.*

**line with²** *v prep*
**1** to provide (a place) with a row of (things or people): [T1 + *with* (*usu. pass.*)] *The river banks were lined with people watching the boat race. The path to the house is lined with bushes.*
**2 be lined with** (usu. of the skin) to have lines caused by (something such as a feeling or age): *Her face is lined with suffering. His skin was lined with age.*

**linger about/around** *v adv* → **linger on¹** (1)
to stay, as when others have left; remain for a long time: [IØ + ABOUT/AROUND] *All the other guests had gone home, but my friend lingered about as though she wanted to talk to me. Even when the flowers were taken away, the smell lingered about most pleasantly.*

**linger on¹** *v adv*
**1** to stay, as when others have left; remain for a long time: [IØ + ON] *All the other guests had gone home, but my friend lingered on as though she wanted to talk to me. Even when the flowers were taken away, the smell lingered on in the room. "The song is ended; but the melody lingers on."* (song) → **linger about**
**2** to continue to live in spite of illness: [IØ + ON] *The sick girl lingered on in great pain for many months until at last she died. It's not kind to keep the wounded animal lingering on.*

*__linger on²__ *v prep* → **think about** (1), etc.
to think, often for some time, about (something, often pleasant): [T1] *He lingered on the thought of his loved ones.*

**linger over** *v prep* → **loiter over**
to take a long time about; give a lot of attention to (something or doing something): [IØ + *over*] *Don't linger over the meal, we have a train to catch. Why are you lingering over writing that letter? The book has been read, reread and lovingly lingered over. This report tends to linger over the more unpleasant facts of the murder.*

**link to** *v prep*
to join (something or someone) to (something or someone) with or as with a chain: [T1 + *to* (*usu. simple tenses*)] *The prisoners were linked to each other by irons around their legs. The new bridge will link the island to the mainland. A common wall links the house to its neighbour.*

**link together** *v adv* → **link with**
**1** to join (usu. things): [T1 + TOGETHER (*usu. simple tenses*)] *The railway line links the two towns together.*
**2** to connect the ideas of (two or more things or people): [T1 + TOGETHER (*often pass.*)] *Their names have been linked together in newspaper reports.*

**link up** *v adv*
**1** to (cause to) join or combine: [T1 + UP (*usu. simple tenses*)] *Arrangements are being made to link up the two firms, so as to reduce*

*the competition. Engineers can link up distant countries by radio or telephone.* —**linkup** *n*

*__2__ to join or combine: [IØ (*with*)] *The scattered groups of soldiers have been trying to link up with each other since the army's defeat.* —**linkup** *n*

**link with** *v prep* → **link together**

**1** to join (one thing or group of things) to (another): [T1 + *with* (*usu. simple tenses*)] *Railway lines link country towns with the capital.*

**2** to connect the idea of (one person or thing) with (someone or something else): [T1 + *with* (*often pass.*)] *High unemployment is not necessarily linked with the rise in prices. The Minister's name will always be linked with the disgraceful matter of the harbour payments. The film actress has been linked with one man after another in the newspaper reports.*

**lisp out** *v adv*

to speak (words) in a childish manner or one with faulty 's' sounds: [T1 + OUT] *The little girl lisped out her story. With difficulty, the gardener lisped out the names of the plants.*

**listen for** *v prep*

to try or wait to hear (a sound): [IØ + *for*] *Even though the mother was asleep, she was unconsciously listening for her baby's cry. For over an hour, his arrival had been listened for.*

**listen in** *v adv*

**1** to listen on purpose to a radio broadcast: [IØ (*to*)] *I missed the broadcast, I forgot to listen in. Listen in to this station next week for the continuation of the story.* —**listen-in** *n* → **look in**[1] (2), **tune in** (1)

**2** to listen on purpose to someone else's conversation: [IØ (*on*)] *You shouldn't listen in when other people are talking privately. How dare you listen in on my telephone conversation!*

**listen out** *v adv*

(in two-way radio) to finish listening: [IØ (*continuous tenses*)] *Listening out now, I'll talk to you again tomorrow.*

**listen out for** *v adv prep*

to wait expectantly for (something): [T1] *Always listen out for new ideas in your subject.*

**listen to** *v prep*

**1** to hear (something or someone) intentionally: [IØ + *to*] *Listen to the birds, what a noise they're making now it's spring! Will you listen to me when I'm talking to you! "Oh, listen to the band."* (song) *"I was never tired of listening to his wisdom."* (Sir Winston Churchill, *My Early Life*) *"One can either go on listening to the news—and of course the news is always bad, even when it sounds good. Or . . . one can make up one's mind to listen to something else."* (Aldous Huxley, *Time Must Have a Stop*)

*__2__ to pay attention to; obey (someone or something): [T1] *If you'd listened to me, you wouldn't be in trouble now. Don't listen to such foolish advice. "The man who listens to Reason is lost; Reason enslaves all whose minds are not strong enough to master her."* (G.B. Shaw, *Man and Superman. Maxims for Revolutionists*)

**litter about/around** *v adv; prep*

to scatter (things) untidily (about a place): [T1 + ABOUT/AROUND/*about*/*around*] *I can't possibly clean this room with all your clothes littered about (it)!*

* **litter down** *v adv*

to make a bed for (an animal): [T1 (*usu. pass.*)] *Are the horses littered down for the night?*

**litter up** *v adv*

to make (a place) untidy: [T1 + UP] *Why do you always litter up the table with all these newspapers?*

**live above** *v prep*

**1** to make one's home on top of or at a higher level than (something such as a place): [IØ + *above*] *The owners live above the shop.* → **live over**[2]

**2 live above one's income/means** → LIVE BEYOND (2)

**live after** *v prep*

to continue or last after the end or death of (something or someone): [IØ + *after* (*simple tenses*)] *The acts of good men live after them in our memories.*

**live among** *v prep*

to make one's home in an area populated by (a certain kind of people): [IØ + *among*] *After living among the natives for twenty years, the painter forgot his own language and civilized ways of life.*

**live apart** *v adv*

(of a married person or pair) to live separately although remaining married: [L9 + APART (*from*)] *After Mary had been living apart from Jim for six months, she decided to return to him. After their worst quarrel, Jim and Mary wondered if they should live apart for a time to try to improve their relationship.*

**live at** *v prep* → **live in**[2] (1), **live on**[2] (1), **reside in** (1)

to have one's home at (an address, home, or small place): [IØ + *at*] *When the house was damaged by fire, we had to live at a hotel for several weeks. No one lives at the corner of the street now, it's all shops and offices. Jim and Mary live at 33 Wells Road.*

**live beyond** *v prep*

**1** to have one's home in a place further distant than (somewhere): [L9 + *beyond*] *The farmer's family live beyond the next valley.*

**2 live beyond one's income/means** to spend money too freely: *When you first start working, it is difficult to organize your spending so that you don't live beyond your means.* also **lie above** → **live within** (2)

**live by** *v prep*

**1** to have one's home next to (something): [IØ + *by*] *Isn't it dangerous living by the river? You must get flooded every spring!*

2 to make a living from (something or doing something): [I∅ + *by*] *He lived by buying and selling houses. She tried to live by her writing, but it did not provide a good enough income.* → **exist by** (1), **live off** (3), **live on**² (4)

*3 to find a reason or means for living in (something): [T1] *"Man does not live by bread alone, but by faith, by admiration, by sympathy."* (R.W. Emerson, *Lectures and Biographical Sketches: The Sovereignty of Ethics*) → **exist by** (2)

*4 to live according to (something such as a principle): [T1] *I have always tried to live by the moral laws which my parents taught me. It is difficult always to live by your principles.*

5 **live by oneself** to live alone: *How can you bear living by yourself? Don't you get lonely?* → **live on**² (7)

6 **live by one's wits** to have no proper profession but use any means to gain an income, including dishonest means: *Unable to get a job when he left school, the boy lived by his wits and in the end turned to crime.* → **live on**² (8)

***live down** *v adv*

to cause people to forget or forgive (something bad or foolish in one's past) by improved behaviour, directing their attention elsewhere, etc.: [T1] *You shouldn't have to spend the rest of your life living down one silly mistake in your youth. If the family hear what you did, you'll never live it down!*

**live for** *v prep*

1 to remain alive for (a length of time): [I∅ + *for*] *It is possible to live for several weeks without food, but only for a short time without water.*

*2 to have as a reason for living; give too much attention to; take great interest in (something or someone): [T1 (*pass. rare, often simple tenses*)] *He lives only for his music, and does not care about his family's needs. "She's the sort of woman who lives for others—you can always tell the others by their hunted expressions."* (C.S. Lewis, *The Screwtape Letters*)

*3 to wish for (something in the future) very much, esp. in the phr. **live for the day when**: [T1 (*no pass., often simple tenses*)] *Father lives for the day when he will be able to stop work.*

**live from** *v prep*

1 **live from day to day** to be concerned only with the present: *A sick man faced with certain death learns to live from day to day in the short future that is left to him.*

2 **live from hand to mouth** *not fml* to have to use one's money only to support oneself, without being able to save any; live poorly: *The unemployed worker tried hard to get a job, as he was worried about his family living from hand to mouth, borrowing money and never being sure where their next meal was coming from.*

***live high** *v adv* → **live well** (1)

esp. *AmE not fml* to live in a wealthy manner, in a state of unusual comfort: [I∅] *Can you afford to live so high?*

***live in**¹ *v adv* → **live out** (1), **sleep in** (2), **sleep out** (2)

to live in the same place as where one works or studies: [I∅] *Servants used to live in, and have their own rooms in their master's house. Will you live in when you go to college or will you get a room in town?* —**live-in, living-in** *adj*

**live in**² *v prep*

1 to make one's home in (a place or building): [I∅ + *in*] *How long have you lived in this country? This old house smells as if it hasn't been lived in for years.* —**lived-in** *adj* → **live at, live on** (1), **reside in** (1)

2 to be able to exist in (something) or because of (someone): [I∅ + *in*] *I couldn't live in such conditions. How long can the ship live in this wild sea? "For in him we live, and move, and have our being."* (The Bible)

3 **live in a fool's paradise** *not fml* to be unconscious of faults or dangers; have too unrealistic hopes: *If you think you can make an income from writing stories, you must be living in a fool's paradise.*

4 **live in hope(s) (of)** to have good hope or expectation (of something); be hopeful (about something): *I haven't found a suitable job yet, but I live in hope. All through the winter we live in hopes of warmer weather.*

5 **live in the past** to have old-fashioned ideas and values; not think in a modern way; be unconscious of changing times: *Parents who think that they can control their children's choice of friends are living in the past.*

6 **live in the present** to have realistic ideas of modern times; accept new ideas; behave in a way suited to what is happening now: *Grandmother seems quite unable to live in the present; her mind is buried in her memories, and she has no idea how much things have changed.*

7 **live in sin** to live with a person with whom one has a sexual relationship, without being married to him or her: *The Church still regards their relationship as living in sin, but many people nowadays use the phrase as a joke.*

**live off** *v prep*

1 to eat (certain food): [L9 + *off*] *These animals with long necks live off the leaves of tall trees.* → **dine off** (2), **eat off**² (2), **feed off** (2), **feed on** (1), **live on**² (2)

*2 to live at the cost of (someone else): [T1] *He's been living off his brother for nearly a year.* → **dine off** (3), **eat off**², **live on**² (3)

*3 to find enough food or income in (something): [T1] *How can you live off the land without experience in farming? I'm afraid that she will not be able to live off her writing as much as she hopes that she will.* → **exist by** (1), **live by** (2), **live on**² (4)

**4 live off the fat of the land** *not fml* to live well; have plenty of money, food, amusement, etc.: *In spite of the government's attempts to share the nation's wealth more equally, some businessmen still make big profits and live off the fat of the land, while some unskilled workers earn hardly enough to feed their families.* → **live on² (5)**

***live on¹** *v adv*
**1** to continue to live: [IØ (*often simple tenses*)] *The baby lived on for a week after its mother died.*
**2** to continue to exist, often for a long time: [IØ (*usu. simple tenses*)] *This custom will live on for centuries. Long after he was dead, his name lived on because of his good deeds.*

**live on²** *v prep*
**1** to have one's home on (something, often in water): [L9 + *on*] *Do sailors enjoy living on boats? I have always wanted to live on an island in the middle of a lake.* → **live at, live in² (1), reside in (1)**
**2** to eat (certain food): [L9 + *on*] *These animals with long necks live on the leaves of tall trees.* → **dine off (2), eat off² (2), live off (1)**
***3** to live at the cost of (someone else): [T1] *He's been living on his brother for nearly a year; it hardly seems fair when he is able to work.* → **dine off (3), eat off² (3), live off (2)**
***4** to find enough income in (something); support oneself with (money): [T1] *I'm afraid that she will not be able to live on her writing, much as she hopes that she will. Many more people are now living on unemployment insurance.* → **exist by (1), live by (2), live off (3)**
**5 live on the fat of the land** *not fml* to live well; have plenty of money, food, amusement, etc.: *In spite of the government's attempts to share the nation's wealth more equally, some businessmen still make big profits and live on the fat of the land, while some unskilled workers earn hardly enough to feed their families.* → **live off (4)**
**6 live on one's name/reputation** to use one's past success to provide an income or social position: *Tom has only written one best-selling book; he can't live on his reputation for ever.*
**7 live on one's own** to live alone: *How can you bear living on your own? Don't you get lonely?* → **live by (5)**
**8 live on one's wits** to have no proper profession but use any means to gain an income, including dishonest means: *Unable to get a job when he left school, the boy lived on his wits and in the end turned to crime.* → **live by (6)**

**live out** *v adv*
**1** to live in a place away from one's work: [IØ] *Some of the students have rooms in their college, but most have to live out as there isn't room for them all.* → **live in², sleep in (2), sleep out (2)**
**2** to live to the end of (a period of time): [T1a (*usu. simple tenses*)] *Will the old man live out the year? She lived out the rest of her life quietly in a country village. I should like to live out my days in peace and comfort.*
**3** to live (a certain sort of life): [T1a (*usu. simple tenses*)] *Christians try to live out their lives following the Bible.*

**live out of** *v adv prep*
**1** to live away from (a place): [L9 + OUT + *of*] *We chose to live out of town and travel in to work every day, to get some fresh air and avoid high property prices.*
***2** to keep all one's necessary possessions in (a container): [T1] *I'm so tired of all this travelling, living out of suitcases. I carry so many things in my handbag that the family all joke that I could live out of it for a week!*
***3** to take one's food from (a container such as a tin): [T1] *Many men on their own will live out of tins rather than cook meals for themselves.*

***live over¹** *v adv*
**1** to repeat (something), usu. in the mind: [T1a] *The old man keeps living over his memories.*
**2** to relive (something): [T1] *If I had my life to live over (again), I would make many different decisions.*

**live over²** *v prep* → **live above (1)**
to make one's home on top of or at a higher level than (something such as a place): [L9 + *over*] *The owners live over the shop.*

***live rough** *v adv* → **rough it, sleep rough**
to live without the usual comforts: [IØ] *The children enjoy camping and living rough but I'm getting a little too old for such a hard life. When he lost his job, he wandered from place to place, living rough, too proud to ask his parents for money.*

**live through** *v prep*
**1** to remain alive during (a time): [IØ + *through* (*usu. simple tenses*)] *I doubt if Grandfather will live through the night. I don't know how I lived through the next week, waiting for the result.*
***2** to experience; remain alive in spite of or through the time of (something): [T1 (*usu. simple tenses*)] *My aunt has lived through three wars. She has lived through some terrible experiences.*

**live to** *v prep*
**1** to live as long as (a certain age): [IØ + *to* (*usu. simple tenses*)] *If you live to 100 you get a message from the Queen. Many people have no wish to live to old age.*
**2 live to oneself** to live alone without the desire for company; not try to be friendly: [*usu. simple tenses*] *He always had a lonely nature and chose to live to himself.*

**live together** *v adv*
**1** to exist at the same time or in the same place; share the same home; have a working relationship: [IØ + TOGETHER] *Powerful nations must learn to live together in peace. Why can't dogs and cats live together? Few mothers*

*and daughters can live together, they nearly always quarrel.* → **live with** (1)

***2** (of two people, usu. of opposite sexes) to live as if married: [IØ] *Did Jim and Mary live together before they were married?* → **live with** (2)

**live under** *v prep*

**1** to make one's home beneath (something): [L9 + *under*] *Rabbits live under the ground.*

**2** to be controlled by (a power): [L9 + *under*] *For years the people lived under the rule of cruel princes.*

**3 live under someone's roof** to make one's home in someone's house; be a guest or member of the family: *While the children are living under my roof they will obey my orders!*

**4 live under the same roof (as)** to share a house or other living space (with someone): *I cannot live under the same roof as a person whose principles are so opposed to mine.*

**live up** *v adv*

**live it up** *infml* to enjoy life; have fun; have a good time or enjoy unusual pleasures: *If we win all that money, first we'll pay off our debts, then live it up for a time before making sensible decisions about how to spend the rest.*

***live up to** *v adv prep*

**1** to behave according to; fulfil (an expectation): [T1] *Children will always live up to your expectations of them. High River has been living up to its name in the recent floods!* also **act up to**

**2** to behave in a manner worthy of (something such as a high standard): [T1 (*usu. simple tenses*)] *Do you always live up to your principles?*

**3** to copy; try to be worthy of (someone whom one admires): [T1 (*usu. simple tenses*)] *His wife was so clever that he felt that he could never live up to her.*

**live well** *v adv*

**1** to live in a wealthy manner: [IØ + WELL] *He must be making a good income, he seems to be living (very) well.* → **live high**

***2** to live in a moral manner: [IØ (*often simple tenses*)] *He lived well, helping the poor, and considering all other people; he died penniless and unknown.*

**live with** *v prep*

**1** to share a living place with; exist at the same time or in the same place as; make one's home with; spend one's life with (someone or something): [L9 + *with*] *Powerful nations must learn to live with each other in peace. Dogs and cats cannot live with each other in the same house.* → **live together** (1)

***2** to live with (someone, usu. of the opposite sex) as if married: [T1] *Did Jim live with Mary before they were married?* → **live together** (2)

***3** to learn to accept (something unpleasant): [T1] *I don't like the winter, but we all have to live with it, don't we? It's hard to live with the knowledge that you are a failure.*

**live within** *v prep*

**1** to live inside (the limit of an area): [IØ + *within*] *If you live within the city border, you pay higher taxes.*

**2 live within one's income/means** to spend only what one can afford: *When prices rise so fast and pay remains the same, it gets increasingly difficult to live within one's means.* → **live beyond** (2)

**live without** *v prep* → **dispense with, do without**[2] **(1), go without**[2] **(2), manage without**[2]

to find it possible to go on existing in spite of lacking (something or someone): [IØ + *without* (*often simple tenses*)] *She tried for a little while to live without him but couldn't. We may live without books, music, and art, but our lives would be poorer.*

***liven up** *v adv*

*not fml* to (cause to) become more interesting, active, or cheerful: [IØ] *When is this party going to liven up? It's very dull.* [T1] *At least his silly remarks livened the meeting up a bit.*

**load against** *v prep*

**load the dice against** to put (someone) at a disadvantage: [*usu. pass.*] *She has been looking for a suitable job for over a year, but so far has had no luck; the dice seem to be loaded against her.*

**load down** *v adv*

**1** to give (something or someone) a heavy load (of something): [T1 + DOWN (*with*) (*usu. pass.*)] *The farmer's cart was loaded down with the vegetable crop. The trees are loaded down with the weight of the fruit. The postman is loaded down with all those parcels.* → **bow down** (1), **lade with** (1), **load with** (1), **weigh down** (1), **weight down**

**2 be loaded down (with)** to suffer from; feel heavy with or troubled by (something such as a responsibility): *The young man seemed to be loaded down with the worries of fatherhood.* → **bow down** (2), **lade with** (2), **weigh down** (2)

**load into/onto** *v prep*

to put a load of (something, things, or people) into (a space) or onto (something that will carry it): [T1 + *into/onto*] *Help me to load the goods into the back of the car. We can't load any more people onto this bus. The climbers loaded the supplies onto their backs.*

**load up** *v adv*

**1** to fill, cover, or weigh (something or someone) down with a load or heavy weight: [T1 + UP] *Don't load the car up too much when you are going on a long journey. When all the climbers were loaded up with ropes and supplies, they began the long climb.* [IØ + UP] *Start loading up when all the passengers are on board.*

***2** esp. *AmE not fml* to fill (someone or oneself) with information, sometimes imaginary: [T1] *There is no need to load yourself up with unnecessary facts for the examination. The man on the train tried to load me up with stories of his wealth.*

**3 be loaded up** *AmE infml* to be drunk: *He tried to drown his sorrows by getting loaded up.* → **light up** (5), **tank up** (2)

**load with** *v prep*

**1** to make (something) full or heavy with (a weight): [T1 + *with* (*often pass.*)] *The farmer's cart was loaded with the vegetable crop. I was so loaded with heavy shopping that my back was aching. The air is loaded with smoke and dirt.* → **load down** (1), etc.

**2** to fill; supply (a gun) with (something such as a kind of bullet): [T1 + *with*] *This gun must be loaded with .22 bullets.*

***3** to give (someone or something) a lot of (something or things): [D1 (*usu. simple tenses*)] *The nation loaded the general with honours after his famous victory. This play is loaded with action, but lacks interesting character development.*

**4 be loaded with** *infml* to have plenty of (usu. money): *Her father can afford a splendid wedding ceremony, as he is loaded with money.*

**loaf about/around** *v adv; prep*

to spend time lazily, often wandering around without purpose or activity (in a place): [IØ + ABOUT/AROUND/*about*/*around*] *One of the pleasures of being on holiday is the freedom to loaf around without feeling guilty. I don't like to see young people loafing about the town with nothing to do. "He allowed me to waste those two precious years in loafing about at home."* (Mark Pattison, *Memoirs*)

**loaf away** *v adv* → **idle away** (2), etc.

to waste (time) lazily: [T1] *Have you been loafing away the whole afternoon instead of getting on with your work?*

**loan to** *v prep* → **lend to** (1)

to lend (something or someone) to (someone or a group): [T1 + *to*] *Money which has been loaned to city councils by the central government can be repaid at a low rate of interest. We are grateful to all the parents who have loaned some of their precious possessions to the school for use in the play. Our most able worker has been loaned to the delivery department to help them find the answer to their difficulties.*

**lob along** *v adv*

to move forward in an awkward uneven manner: [L9 + ALONG] *The wounded horse lobbed along, trying to reach the farm where it knew it could get help.*

**lob at** *v prep*

(esp. in tennis) to send (a ball) to (an opposing player) in a high curve: [T1 + *at*] *Every time she lobs the ball at me, I find it more difficult to return.*

**lobby against** *v prep*

to try to persuade people in power, not to approve (something such as a law); try to prevent (something) by political action, writing letters, etc.: [IØ + *against*] *Hunters and other sportsmen have been lobbying against intended changes in the gun laws.*

**lobby for** *v prep*

to try to persuade people in power, to approve (something such as a law) or take (action); try to obtain (something) by political action, writing letters, etc.: [IØ + *for*] *Concerned groups have recently been lobbying for increased government support for the arts.*

***lobby through** *v adv*

to reach or obtain (something such as a law) by political action: [T1 (*usu. pass.*)] *In spite of opposition from the other parties, the changes in the law have been lobbied through.*

**lock away** *v adv*

**1** to keep (something) safe under lock and key: [X9 + AWAY (*in*)] *Although the jewels were locked away (in a strongbox), the thieves stole them without any difficulty.* → **lock up** (1), **shut up** (3)

**2** to put (someone) in prison or a hospital for mad people and keep him there by force: [X9 + AWAY] *Don't worry, the dangerous criminals have all been locked away. He ought to be locked away for behaving like that!* → **lock up** (2), **put away** (6), **shut away, shut up** (2)

***3** to keep (something) secret: [T1 (*in*) (*usu. simple tenses*)] *She locked her memories of him away in her heart.* → **lock up** (4)

**lock in**[1] *v adv*

**1** to keep (something, someone, or oneself) inside a building or container, with or as with a lock and key: [X9 + IN] *Send someone over with another key, I've locked myself in by mistake. The poor dog has been locked in all day.* → **lock out** (1)

***2** to surround (something): [T1 (*usu. pass.*)] *The small country has no seacoast, but is locked in by other nations.*

***3** to fix (something) so that it will not wander: [T1 (*usu. pass.*)] *On the newer television sets, the colour is locked in so that you don't need to keep changing the controls.*

**4 be locked in** (of money) to be placed where it cannot be taken out until a certain time or other condition: *Money paid into this insurance contract is locked in until you die or stop working.* —**locked-in** *adj* → **lock up** (5)

**lock in**[2] *v prep*

**1** to keep (something, someone, or oneself) inside (a place or container) with a lock and key: [X9 + *in*] *You can't keep the poor dog locked in the garage all day, it's cruel. Jane has locked herself in her room and refuses to speak to any member of the family. Although the jewels were locked in a strongbox, the thieves stole them without any difficulty.*

**2** to fasten (something or someone) in a position where he/it is unable to move, in (something): [X9 + *in* (*usu. pass.*)] *The lovers were locked in each others' arms. The horns of the two animals were locked in a death struggle. The ship was locked in the ice all winter.*

**lock into** *v prep*

to become fixed inside or closely together with (something): [L9 + *into* (*simple tenses*)]

*This part of the machine locks into the special wheel here, to connect the driving belt.*

**lock on¹** *v adv*

**1** (usu. of machinery) to (cause to) join: [L9 + ON (*to*) (*simple tenses*)] *Does this part of the train lock on here?* [X9 + ON (*to*)] *Lock the carriages on (to the engine) with this hook.*

*__2__ *mil* (of a tracking machine or weapon, esp. moving) to (cause to) find and follow an object which it is intended to attack: [IØ (*simple tenses*)] *When I give the order, lock on!* [T1 (*to*) (*usu. pass.*)] *This new invention can be locked on (to an enemy plane) and will destroy it without human help.*

**lock on²** *v prep* → **lock onto** (1)

to (cause to) fasten onto (something): [L9 + *on* (*simple tenses*)] *The carriages of the toy train lock on the engine.* [X9 + *on*] *Lock the carriages on the engine with this special hook.*

**lock onto** *v prep*

**1** to (cause to) connect tightly to (something): [L9 + *onto* (*simple tenses*)] *The carriages of the toy train lock onto the engine with a special hook.* [X9 + *onto* (*often simple tenses*)] *During this exercise, the spaceship will be locked onto the other side of the space station, so that the men can move from one vehicle to the other.* → **lock on²**

*__2__ *mil* (of a tracking machine or weapon, esp. moving) to find and follow (the object that it will attack): [T1 (*simple tenses*)] *This latest invention consists of a moving weapon which takes aim by itself and locks onto its target until the right time for destroying it.*

*__3__ to fix one's attention or part of the body on (someone): [T1 (*no pass., usu. simple tenses*)] *Taking hold of me, she locked onto me for half an hour.*

**lock out** *v adv*

**1** to prevent (someone, oneself, or something) from entering a room or building, with a lock and key: [X9 + OUT (*of*)] *If you come home as late at this again, you'll find yourself locked out of the house, and serve you right! I forgot my key and I've locked myself out by mistake.* → **lock in¹** (1)

*__2__ to prevent (workmen) from entering a place of work until a disagreement is settled as the employers want it: [T1] *Although the workers agreed to go on working while their pay claim was being considered, the employers locked them out in an attempt to force them to reduce their demands.* —**lockout** *n*

**lock together** *v adv*

to (cause to) connect or be fixed tightly together: [L9 + TOGETHER (*simple tenses*)] *His teeth locked together in anger.* [X9 + TOGETHER (*usu. pass.*)] *Several cars were locked together in the crash. The lovers were locked together in a long kiss.*

**lock up** *v adv*

**1** to keep (something) safe under lock and key; prevent (someone) from escaping; keep (oneself) under lock and key: [X9 + UP (*in*)] *Although the jewels were locked up in a strongbox, the thieves stole them without any difficulty. Jane has locked herself up in her room and refuses to speak to any member of the family. It's cruel to keep the dog locked up all day.* → **lock away** (1), **shut up** (3)

**2** to put (someone) in prison or a hospital for mad people and keep him there by force under lock and key: [X9 + UP] *Don't worry, the dangerous criminals have all been locked up. He ought to be locked up for behaving like that!* —**lockup** *n* → **lock away** (2), **put away** (6), **shut away, shut up** (2)

*__3__ to lock (a building) safely for the night: [T1] *I must go back, I forgot to lock up the garage* [IØ] *Don't forget to lock up before you leave.*

*__4__ to hide (something such as one's feelings) [T1 (*usu. simple tenses*)] *She locked her memories of him up in her heart. If you lock up your anger it will only cause trouble later.* → **lock away** (3)

*__5__ to place (one's money, esp. capital) where it cannot be easily moved: [T1 (*usu. pass.*)] *All his capital is locked up in foreign companies.* → **lock in¹** (4)

*__6__ (in printing) to fasten (a body of type) firmly: [T1] *This screw is for locking up the form.*

*__7__ esp. *AmE infml* to ensure the result of (something), often dishonestly: [T1 (*usu pass.*)] *It's not worth your writing for that job I'm pretty sure that it's been locked up.* → **sew up** (2)

*__8__ to prevent (something) from being used [T1 (*usu. pass.*)] *The harbour is locked up for two months every winter when the lake freezes*

**9 lock oneself up** to choose to be alone and private; not wish for the society of other people: [*usu. simple tenses*] *After the death of her husband, she locked herself up and hardly spoke to anyone.*

**lodge against** *v prep*

to place (something such as a complaint) officially against (someone or something) [T1 + *against*] *Several leading citizens have lodged complaints against the city councillor for their mishandling of public money.*

**lodge at** *v prep*

to be a paying guest at (a place such as a hotel or someone's house): [IØ + *at*] *I shall lodge at the inn for two nights. When the boy first went to university, he lodged at Mrs Page's.*

**lodge in** *v prep*

**1** to (cause to) stay as a paying guest in (a place such as someone's house); make (one's home or resting place) in (somewhere): [IØ + *in*] *Is there anywhere that I can lodge in the village tonight? Some of the students lodge in their college halls.* [T1 + *in*] *The army can lodge their tents in the fields.*

**2** to (cause to) become fixed in (something such as part of the body): [IØ + *in* (*usu. simple tenses*)] *The bullet lodged in the wall.*

*piece of metal has lodged in a sensitive part of the nervous system, making the man unable to move his arm.* [T1 + *in* (*usu. pass.*)] *A piece of bread got lodged in his throat.*

*__3__ *fml* to be found in; belong to (something or someone) by right or custom: [T1 (*no pass.*)] *Such rights lodge in his position.* [D1 (*usu. pass.*)] *"The power of the crown is always lodged in a single person."* (David Hume, *Essays: The Indian Parliament*)

**odge with** *v prep*

**1** to be a paying guest of (someone): [IØ + *with*] *You can lodge with your aunt when you go to college.* → **room with**

**2** to place (something such as a complaint) in the keeping of (an official or officials): [T1 + *with*] *The chief witness was allowed to leave the town only after lodging a sworn statement with the police.*

**og off** *v adv* → **log on**

(esp. concerning a large calculating machine) to finish work: [IØ] *It took two hours to complete the calculation, so we logged off at 4 o'clock.*

**og on** *v adv* → **log off**

(esp. concerning a large calculating machine) to start work: [IØ] *You must keep a record of the time that you used the machine; state when you logged on, and remember to write down the time you log off.*

**og out** *v adv*

to record one's leaving in a special book: [IØ] *They're no longer here; I'll see if they logged out this morning.*

**og up** *v adv*

**1** (usu. in a vehicle) to mark (a record, esp. of distance or time travelled): [T1 + UP] *The ship has now logged up voyages equal to a distance ten times round the world. A pilot in training has to log up a certain number of hours of flying alone before he is allowed to fly passengers.* → **clock up** (1)

**2** *not fml* to gain; record (something such as a victory): [T1] *Our team has logged up an unusual number of wins this season.* → **chalk up** (3), **clock up** (2), **notch up, score up**

**oiter about/around** *v adv; prep*

to stand or wander around (a place) as if waiting: [IØ + ABOUT/AROUND/*about/around*] *There's a nasty-looking man loitering around (your gate); shall I call the police?*

**oiter away** *v adv* → **idle away** (2), etc.

to waste (time) lazily: [T1] *I've another hour to loiter away before the train comes. "So have I loitered my life away, reading books, looking at pictures, going to plays, hearing, thinking, writing on what pleased me best."* (William Hazlitt, *Winterslow: My First Acquaintance with Poets*)

**oiter in** *v prep*

to stand around (a place) as if waiting: [IØ + *in*] *Please do not loiter in the streets.*

**oiter over** *v prep* → **linger over**

to spend a long time, lazily, on (something): [IØ + *over*] *You won't increase your earnings by loitering over your work.*

**loiter with** *v prep*

**loiter with intent** *BrE law* to stand or wander about a place, intending to perform a criminal act: [*often continuous tenses*] *The man was taken to the police station on a charge of loitering with intent.*

**loll about/around** *v adv* → **lounge about**

to wait, sit, or stand lazily, in a bent or careless position: [L9 + ABOUT/AROUND] *Do stand up straight, don't loll about like that!*

**loll back** *v adv*

to lean back lazily, in a careless position: [L9 + BACK] *He lolled back in his seat, enjoying the sunshine.*

**loll out** *v adv*

to (cause to) hang out lazily or at length: [L9 + OUT] *The dog's tongue was lolling out.* [T1 + OUT] *The dog lolled its tongue out in the heat.*

**long for** *v prep* → **itch for, sigh for** (2), **yearn for**

to wish very much for (someone or something): [L9 + *for*] *I'm longing for a cool drink, aren't you? Is this the house for which you longed so much? I hope Grace isn't going to spend the rest of her life longing for that red-haired boy. Price reductions are longed for, but unlikely. The crowd were longing for the performance to start. You seem to be longing for me to say something.* —**longed-for** *adj*

**look about/around**[1] *v adv* → **look round**[1]

**1** to look in several different directions: [IØ + ABOUT/AROUND] *Looking about, I could see no sign of life.*

*__2__ to make enquiries before choosing: [IØ] *We should look around carefully before deciding which house to buy. I'm not ready to choose yet, I'm still looking around.*

**look about/around**[2] *v prep* → **look round**[2]

**1** to see in various directions about (a place or one): [IØ + *about/around*] *I looked around the station but couldn't see my friend anywhere. Looking about the room, I could see no sign of life. The stranger looked about him at the wonderful new sights.*

*__2__ to search in (a place): [T1 (*for*) (*no pass.*)] *We've been looking about the country for a good place to camp. Although we've looked all around the city, we haven't found a house at a suitable price.*

***look about/around for** *v adv prep* → LOOK ROUND FOR

**look after** *v prep*

**1** to watch (someone or something), usu. from the back, as he/it moves away; follow the movement of (someone or something) with one's sight: [IØ + *after*] *Sadly we looked after the last bus as it disappeared round the corner. He turned and left her; but she looked after him with tears in her eyes.*

*__2__ to take care of; take the responsibility for (someone or something): [T1] *Who will look after the children while you go out to work?*

*Who's looking after the arrangements for the wedding? If you look after your new shoes, they will last longer. This house seems to have been well looked after. Mother was well looked after in hospital.*

*3 esp. *AmE infml* to kill; murder (someone): [T1 (*often simple tenses*)] *We can't let him live to tell stories about us to the police, leave him to me, I'll look after him.* → **bump off,** etc.

**4 look after oneself** to be independent, able to deal with life and one's business, including trouble: [*usu. simple tenses*] *Don't worry about me, I can look after myself.*

**look ahead** *v adv* → **see ahead**

**1** to try to see a long way in front of one: [IØ + AHEAD] *If you look ahead in the distance, you can just see the lights of the village.*

***2** to think about, prepare, or plan for the future: [IØ] *If you want to make a success of your life, you have to learn to look ahead. When choosing a profession, it is wise to look ahead and see what kind of a future each one offers. Looking ahead to the future, we can imagine a time when all cars will run on electricity. Planning officials are now looking ahead to the needs of the population in the year 2000.*

**look alike** *v adj*

(of two or more things or people) to have the same or nearly the same appearance: [L9 + **alike** (*simple tenses*)] *The two brothers look so much alike that even their own mother can hardly tell the difference between them. All the houses in this street look alike, it's very dull.* —**look-alike** *n* esp. *AmE*

***look alive/lively** *v adj* → **look sharp,** etc.

*not fml* to get busy; be quick: [IØ (*usu. imper.*)] *Look alive, everybody, the director's coming into the office! Now men, look lively! We need some action around here!*

**look around**[1] *v adv* → LOOK ABOUT[1]

**look around**[2] *v prep* → LOOK ABOUT[2]

***look around for** *v adv prep* → LOOK ABOUT FOR

**look aside** *v adv*

**1** to direct one's sight to one side: [IØ + ASIDE (*from*) (*usu. simple tenses*)] *The singer was afraid that if she looked aside, even for a moment, she would lose her place in the music.* → **look away**

***2** to turn one's attention away (from someone or something): [IØ (*from*) (*often simple tenses*)] *Once you're started in business, there's no looking aside from the work and responsibility.*

***look askance at** *v adv prep*

to regard (something or someone) with doubt or mistrust: [T1 (*no pass., usu. simple tenses*)] *Mother looked askance at the meal, hardly believing that her daughter could cook. Disbelieving his unlikely story, she looked askance at him.*

**look at** *v prep*

**1** to see; watch; direct one's eyes towards (something or someone): [IØ + *at*] *The children spend too much time looking at television. She looked at him in great surprise, wondering what he meant. My work hasn't been looked at for a week. Please don't wear that terrible suit; you'll get looked at. "'A cat may look at a king,' said Alice."* (Lewis Carroll, *Alice in Wonderland*) → **look on**[2] (1)

***2** to regard; judge; consider; take a point of view about (something or someone): [T1 (*usu. simple tenses*)] *Jim looks at his work in a different way now that he is in charge. Happiness depends on how you look at life. You have to look at these things as a scientist. The difficulty can now be looked at in a different light.* → **look on**[2] (2)

***3** to consider; examine (something): [T1] *I'll look at your report tomorrow. Would you look at this painting that I've found and tell me if it's valuable? That tooth wants looking at. You'd better have your ankle looked at* (*by the doctor*). → **take at** (7)

***4** to consider (something) as acceptable; be willing to touch or have to do with (something or someone): [T1 (*no pass., neg., usu. simple tenses*)] *I wouldn't look at such a poor offer. After that meal, I can't look at any more food! Such an unsuitable arrangement is not worth looking at. After the way he treated her, she wouldn't look at another man.*

**5 to look at** in appearance: *She's not much to look at but she is very nice. I want a building that's pleasant to look at.* → **look on**[2] (4)

**6 to look at** to judge by the appearance of (something or someone): *You wouldn't think, to look at him, that he was very rich, would you? To look at the house, you would never guess its age.*

**7 look daggers at** to look fiercely, angrily, or threateningly at (someone): *She looked daggers at me when I suggested that her cooking could be improved.*

**look away** *v adv* → **look aside** (1)

to turn one's eyes away (from something or someone): [IØ + AWAY (*from*)] *The singer was afraid that if she looked away, even for a moment, she would lose her place in the music. Look away dear, the sight is not fit for your eyes. I hate to see accidents, so I looked away as we passed the scene of the crash.*

**look back** *v adv*

**1** to direct one's eyes behind one: [IØ + BACK] *Looking back the way we had come, we could see the whole valley spread out behind us.*

***2** to remember; think about the past: [IØ (*at, on, to*)] *It's easy to make judgments looking back at the past. When we look back, we can now understand what caused the difficulty. Never look back, you can't relive the past. Looking back on the old days, I'm sure we were much happier then. 'Look Back in Anger.'* (title of play and film)

**3 not/never look back** to continue to advance: [*simple tenses*] *Since Jim got started in bus* *ness, he hasn't looked back. Once your first book is printed, you'll never look back.*

**look bad** *v adj*

**1** to appear to be of bad moral character: [L9 + **bad**] *I don't trust that man, he looks bad.* → **look good** (1)

**2** to appear unattractive, decaying, or ill: [L9 + **bad** (*usu. simple tenses*)] *I never wear yellow, it looks bad with my skin. I shan't buy that meat, it looks bad. You look bad, what's the matter? This cloth doesn't look too bad, does it?* → **look good** (2), **look well** (2)

***3** to seem hopeless or discouraging: [IØ (*for*)] *The weather looks bad for sailing today. The results of the vote look bad for you.* → **look good** (3)

***4** to seem improper: [IØ (*simple tenses*)] *It'll look bad if you're seen in a restaurant with another man's wife. Policemen are not allowed to drink on duty, partly because it might have an effect on their judgment, and partly because it would look bad.* → **look good** (4)

**look beyond** *v prep*

**1** to direct one's eyes past (something): [IØ + *beyond* (*usu. simple tenses*)] *If you look beyond the trees, you can just see the farm in the distance.* → **see beyond** (1)

***2** to consider, know, or imagine something further, after, or greater than (something, often in the future): [T1 (*no pass., usu. simple tenses*)] *Many young performers fail to look beyond the first stage of their training. It's a foolish businessman who won't look beyond the first year's profits. You have to look beyond these early difficulties to the hope of future success.* → **see beyond** (3)

**look black** *v adj*

**1** *not fml* to appear hopeless: [IØ] *Whenever the future looks black, remind yourself of other difficulties that you have conquered in the past.*

**2** *not fml* to seem angry: [IØ] *The director's looking very black this morning—who's been annoying him?*

**look blue** *v adj*

**1** to appear cold: [IØ] *Goodness, you look blue! Come in by the fire and get warm.*

**2** to seem sad: [IØ] *You're looking blue, what's the matter?* → **feel blue**

**look down[1]** *v adv*

**1** to direct one's eyes in a downward direction; watch someone or something below: [IØ + DOWN] *When you're on a high ladder, don't look down or you might fall. Mary looked down to hide the shame in her eyes. Looking down at my feet, I saw the ring that I had dropped.*

**2** to be placed on a higher level, overlooking something or someone: [IØ (*at, on*) (*usu. simple tenses*)] *The church stands on a hill, looking down on the village.*

**look down[2]** *v prep*

**1** to direct one's eyes down (something): [IØ + *down*] *Looking down the street, she could see the bus coming. Don't look down the barrel of a gun—you never know when it might be loaded.*

**2** **look down one's nose (at)** *not fml* to consider (something or someone) unworthy; disapprove of (something or someone): *There has always been a tendency in England for high-born people to look down their noses at the lower classes. I wouldn't advise you to look down your nose at the offer, even if it is less than you expected.* → **look down on** (2)

**look down on** *v adv prep*

**1** to be placed at a higher level than (something): [IØ + DOWN + *on* (*usu. simple tenses*)] *The church stands on a hill, looking down on the village.*

***2** to have a poor opinion of (someone), esp. as being below one's social level; disapprove of (someone or something): [T1 (*usu. simple tenses*)] *Women have grown tired of being looked down on by employers. She wouldn't let her daughter marry a boy from a poor family, as she looked down on him and thought he was not worthy of her daughter. The school looks down on such behaviour.* [V3] *At first, Mary's parents looked down on her marrying Jim.* → **look down[2]** (2)

**look for** *v prep*

**1** to try to find (something or someone, often that is lost): [IØ + *for*] *The police and the villagers are out in the woods, looking for the missing child. I spent hours looking for the ring that I had dropped. I'm looking for a suitable hotel; can you suggest one?* → **quest for, search for, seek for**

***2** to hope to get (something): [T1 (*often continuous tenses*)] *Many people who enjoy fast sports are looking for excitement. What results are you looking for? Some of the qualities that the employers are looking for in their workers are honesty, loyalty, and willingness to work hard. It's no good looking for help from that direction.* —**unlooked-for** *adj* → **search after, search for, seek after, seek for**

***3** esp. *old use* to expect (something or someone): [T1 (*often continuous tenses*)] *Are you looking for a parcel?*

***4** *infml* to behave in such a way as to cause or fail to avoid trouble, esp. in the phr. **look for trouble**: [T1 (*usu. continuous tenses*)] *If you drink and drive, you're looking for trouble. You're looking for a fight if you say things like that to me.* → **ask for** (3), **head for** (3)

***look forward to** *v adv prep*

to expect and usu. hope to enjoy (something or doing something): [T1] *I'm looking forward to some warmer weather after this bitter winter. The party, which had been greatly looked forward to, was ruined by the rude behaviour of an uninvited guest.* [T4] *We are all looking forward to seeing you again soon.* [V4] *Every year the children look forward to the holidays coming.*

**look good** *v adj*

**1** to appear to be of good moral character: [L9 + **good**] *I would never have believed such behaviour from such a sweet little girl, who looks so good.* → **look bad** (1)

**2** to look attractive or well: [L9 + **good**] *That cake looks good—can I have a piece? You do look good in black; why don't you wear it more often? You're looking particularly good today: have you had some pleasant news? It'll sell better if it looks good, even if it doesn't work.* → **look bad** (2), **look well** (2)

***3** to seem hopeful or encouraging: [IØ (*for*)] *The weather looks good for our garden party. How good does the voting look so far?* → **look bad** (3)

***4** to seem proper: [IØ (*simple tenses*)] *Whatever your excuse, make it look good. It doesn't look good if you drink too much. It doesn't matter if it isn't true so long as it looks good.* → **look bad** (4)

**look here** *v adv*

**1** to look in this direction: [IØ + HERE (*usu. imper.*)] *Look here, where I'm pointing, not over there.*

***2** to pay attention: [IØ (*imper.*)] *"Look here," the teacher called to the children who were talking.*

**look in**[1] *v adv*

**1** to direct one's eyes into something such as a building: [IØ + IN] *When I drew back the curtains, there outside the window stood a crowd of people looking in.*

***2** to watch television: [IØ] *I don't intend to look in tonight, there's nothing worth watching.* → **listen in** (1), **tune in** (1)

***3** to pay a short visit (to someone): [IØ (*on*) (*often simple tenses*)] *I'm glad to see you so much better; I'll look in again tomorrow. I thought I'd look in on you while I was passing. "Will 10 o'clock be too late to look in for half an hour?"* (Charles Dickens, *The Pickwick Papers*)

**look in**[2] *v prep*

**1** to direct one's eyes inside; try to see in (something): [IØ + *in*] *Look in the cupboard and see if we have any more coffee. If you don't know her telephone number, why don't you look in the book? It should be there. I got such a shock when I looked in the mirror.* → **look into** (1)

**2** to ask; try to find information in; turn one's attention to (something): [IØ + *in* (*usu. simple tenses*)] *"Fool!... look in thy heart, and write."* (Sir Philip Sidney, *Astrophel and Stella, Certain Sonnets*)

**3 look someone in the eye(s)/face** *not fml* to be able to face someone without shame or fear: [*usu. neg., simple tenses*] *I wonder you can look me in the face after the way you've behaved! She knew he was lying when he couldn't look her in the eyes.*

**4 look a gift horse in the mouth** *not fml* to look for faults or other things to complain about in something that is freely offered: [*usu. neg.*] *I shan't complain about the poor view since the ticket was free; after all, you don't look a gift horse in the mouth.*

**look into** *v prep*

**1** to direct one's eyes into; try to see in (something): [IØ + *into*] *I looked into the room but no one was there. She looked into my eyes for a long time without speaking. I got such a shock when I looked into the mirror and saw the colour of my hair.* → **look in**[2] (1)

***2** to try to find information in (something): [T1 (*often simple tenses*)] *"Not that I ever read them—no—I make it a rule never to look into a newspaper."* (R.B. Sheridan, *The Critic*)

***3** to examine (something) quickly or not deeply: [T1 (*often simple tenses*)] *I usually look into a book before deciding whether to read it.* → **dip into** (5)

***4** to examine (something); try to find the truth about (something); examine the meaning or causes of: [T1] *The police are looking into the disappearance of the jewellery. The committee must look into what hospital conditions exist for children.* [T6] *The government will look into how to reduce unemployment.* → **enquire into, see into** (4)

**look like** *v prep*

**1** to have an appearance the same or nearly the same as (someone or something else): [L9 + *like* (*simple tenses*)] *He looks so much like his brother that people often mistake them for each other. These houses look exactly like each other, which makes the street look very dull.*

***2** to be likely to result in (something or doing something): [T1 (*no pass.*)] *It looks like rain; do you see that big dark cloud?* [T4] *The party looks like being a success after all.*

**look lively** *v adj* → LOOK ALIVE

***look nippy** *v adj BrE* → LOOK SHARP

***look on**[1] *v adv*

**1** to watch instead of doing something: [IØ] *Two men stole the jewels while a large crowd looked on.* —**looker-on, onlooker** *n*

**2** to read over someone's shoulder; share a book, etc.: [IØ (*with*)] *There aren't enough books for one copy each; two of you will have to look on.*

**look on/upon**[2] *v prep*

**1** *old use* to see; direct one's eyes towards (something or someone): [IØ + *on/upon* (*usu. simple tenses*)] *"And Moses hid his face for he was afraid to look upon God."* (The Bible) → **look at** (1)

***2** to regard; consider; have a point of view about (someone or something): [X9 (*as/with*) (*usu. simple tenses*)] *I look upon you as my own son. She is looked upon as a very promising young singer. How do the voters look on the government's actions? Teachers look on such behaviour with disapproval. The old man looked kindly on the small boy.* → **look at** (2)

**3 look on the bright side** *not fml* to be cheerful and hopeful: *It's not been a complete failure; let's look on the bright side and count our gains.*

**4 to look on/upon** *old use* in appearance: *The woman was fair to look upon.* → **look at** (5)

*****look oneself** *v pron* → **feel oneself**

to seem in one's usual state of health of spirits: [IØ] *Is something the matter, Fred? You don't look yourself.*

**look onto** *v prep* → **look out** (4), **look over**[2] (2), **open on** (1), **open onto**

to have a view of (somewhere): [L9 + *onto* (*simple tenses*)] *My window looks onto the garden.*

**look out** *v adv*

**1** to direct one's eyes outside: [IØ + OUT (*of*)] *It wasn't raining when I last looked out. Look out of the car window, there's a deer crossing the road! A pair of bright eyes looked out from the darkness.*

***2** *not fml* to take care; be watchful: [IØ (*usu. imper.*)] *Look out! The roof is falling! You'll catch cold if you don't look out.* [I5 (*usu. imper.*)] *Look out (that) you don't catch cold.* —**lookout, outlook** *n* → **mind out** (1), **watch out** (1)

***3** to find (something) by choosing: [T1 (*for*)] *I must look out a special dress for the wedding. I'll look out a suitable train for you.* —**lookout** *n*

***4** to have a view (of something): [L9 (*across, into, on, over, upon*) (*simple tenses*)] *My hotel room looks out across the lake. The shop looks out into a busy street. My window looks out on the garden. The castle looked out over the distant forest.* —**outlook** *n* → **look onto, look over**[2] (2), **open on** (1), **open onto**

**look out for** *v adv prep*

**1** to try to find (someone or something) by searching: [T1] *Look out for your aunt at the station. The men in the tower are looking out for escaped prisoners.* —**lookout** *n* → **watch out** (2)

**2** to try to get (something): [T1] *I've been looking out for a new job for six months. The government is looking out for new methods of raising money without increasing taxes.* —**lookout, outlook** *n*

**look over**[1] *v adv*

**1** to direct one's eyes over something: [IØ + OVER] *The boy pulled himself to the top of the wall and looked over.*

***2** to examine (something or someone) carefully: [T1b] *We must look the school over before sending our son there. Give me time to look your suggestion over. After looking the new students over, I could see that there wasn't a first-class brain among the lot.* —**looking-over, look-over** *n*

**look over**[2] *v prep*

**1** to direct one's eyes over (something): [IØ + *over*] *The child was not tall enough to look over the wall. Our teacher had a way of looking over her glasses at us whenever we offered a silly answer.* → **see over** (1)

***2** to have a view of (something): [T1 (*no pass., simple tenses*)] *My window looks over the garden.* —**overlook** *v* → **look onto, look out** (4), **open on** (1), **open onto**

***3** to examine (something) carefully: [T1] *I wonder if you would be so kind as to look over my book before I send it to the printer's? The government sends officials to look over each factory, to see that it is keeping the safety rules. I always enjoy looking over country houses when I am on holiday.* —**look-over** *n* → **go over**[2] (3), **go through**[2] (9), **look round**[2] (2), etc.

***4** to excuse; choose not to notice or punish (a fault): [T1 (*usu. simple tenses*)] *I'll look over your carelessness this time, but be more careful in future.* —**overlook** *v*

***5** to study (something), as by repeating: [T1] *I've looked over these English exercises several times, but I still don't understand them.* → **go over**[2] (2), **go through**[2] (7), **run over**[2] (5), **run through**[2] (7), **take over**[2] (3), **take through**[2] (2)

***6** to consider (something): [T1] *I've looked over your suggestion, and have decided not to accept it.* → **go over**[2] (7)

**look round**[1] *v adv* → **look about**[1]

**1** to direct one's eyes in various directions, esp. behind oneself: [IØ + ROUND] *Don't look round now, but I think we're being followed. Out of habit, Mary looked round at the clock, but it was earlier than she thought.*

***2** to examine the possibilities of something before deciding: [IØ] *Can I help you? No, thanks, I'm just looking round. It's wise to look round for several days before choosing where to live.* —**look-round** *n*

***3** to visit; be shown round a place: [IØ] *You've expressed a great deal of interest in the new buildings; would you like to look round?* —**look-round** *n* → **show around**, etc.

**look round**[2] *v prep* → **look about**[2]

**1** to direct one's eyes round (something or one), as in various directions: [IØ + *round*] *I looked round the station but couldn't see my friend anywhere. Look round the corner of the building and see if there's a bus coming. I looked all round me, but could see no place to sit.*

***2** to examine (something such as a place): [T1] *When I'm in a strange city, I enjoy looking round the shops. We should look round all these houses before deciding which one to buy.* → **go round**[2] (5), **look over**[2] (3), **see around**[2] (2), **see over**[2] (2), **see round**[2] (2), **show around, show over, take over**[2] (4), **take round**[2] (2)

*****look round/about/around for** *v adv prep*

to try to find and get (something or someone) by searching: [T1 (*no pass., often continuous tenses*)] *I've been looking about for a better job since Christmas. How long have you been looking around for a suitable place to camp? Jim's father has been looking round for a new partner, one with some capital to put into the business.*

*__look sharp__ *v adj* also *BrE* **look nippy** → **look alive, look smart** (2), **look snappy, look spry** (2)
*infml* to hurry: [IØ (*usu. imper.*)] *Look sharp! We haven't all day to waste!*

*__look small__ *v adj* → **feel small**
to be made to appear unimportant or unworthy: [IØ (*simple tenses*)] *Changing his mind in public made the politician look (very) small.*

**look smart** *v adj*
**1** to have a neat, attractive, and fashionable appearance: [L9 + smart] *You do look smart in your new coat! The house will look smart when we've finished painting it.*
*__2__ *infml* to hurry: [IØ (*usu. imper.*)] *Look smart! We haven't all day to waste!* → **look sharp,** etc.

*__look snappy__ *v adj* → **look sharp,** etc.
*infml* to hurry: [IØ] *Look snappy, we haven't all day to waste!*

**look spry** *v adj*
**1** *not fml* to appear well and cheerful: [L9 + spry] *You're looking very spry this morning, what's cheered you up?*
*__2__ *infml* to hurry: [IØ (*usu. imper.*)] *Look spry! We haven't all day to waste!* → **look sharp,** etc.

*__look through[1]__ *v adv*
**1** to examine (something) carefully: [T1b] *I'll look your suggestion through before passing it to the committee.* —**look-through** *n*
**2** to look at without seeming to notice (someone), on purpose or because of deep thought: [T1b (*usu. simple tenses*)] *I said good morning but she looked me straight through and walked on.*

**look through[2]** *v prep*
**1** to direct one's eyes through (something): [IØ + *through*] *The boys watched the football match without paying, by looking through a hole in the fence. If you look through this special glass, you see things twice their actual size. I looked through the open door, but the room was empty.* → **see through[2]** (1)
*__2__ to look quickly in (something, often written or printed): [T1] *I'll look through my notes but I don't think I have a record of his name. Looking through a magazine in the doctor's waiting room, I found a photograph of my own daughter's wedding.*
*__3__ to examine or study carefully (something written or printed): [T1] *Look through your examination paper for any small mistakes, before you hand it in. I looked through the letter again but could find no sign of anxiety.*
*__4__ to look at without seeming to notice (someone), on purpose or because of deep thought: [T1 (*usu. simple tenses*)] *I said good morning but she looked straight through me and walked on.*
*__5__ to know the truth about; not be deceived by (something or someone): [T1 (*usu. simple tenses*)] *Every time I try to fool him, he looks through me/my tricks.* → **see through[2]** (3)

**look to** *v prep*
**1** to direct one's eyes towards (usu. something): [IØ + *to*] *We always look to the mountains to see what kind of weather we shall have next, as it always comes from that direction.* → **look towards** (1)
*__2__ to face (something): [T1 (*no pass., simple tenses*)] *The front of the house looks to the sea.* → **look towards** (2)
*__3__ *fml* to guard; be careful about; pay attention to; take care of (something or someone): [T1 (*often simple tenses*)] *The government will have to look to its position at the next election, since many of the voters are dissatisfied. We have to look to the future, for the good of our grandchildren. "Look to your health; and if you have it, praise God, and value it next to a good conscience."* (Izaak Walton, *The Compleat Angler*) → **look towards** (3), **see about** (3), **see to** (3)
*__4__ to depend on (someone) (to do something): [T1 (*as, for*)] *People whose homes have been flooded are looking to the government for help with the cost. The nation looks to its army as its chief means of defence.* [V3] *I look to you to give support to the movement.*
**5 look to it that** to make sure that . . . [*imper.*] *Look to it that all the arrangements are completed before next week. Look to it that you catch the train.* → **see to** (5)
**6 look to one's laurels** to guard against competition: [*usu. simple tenses*] *Jim has won the race every year for the past five years, but he will have to look to his laurels now that younger men are entering the competition.*

**look towards** *v prep*
**1** to direct one's eyes in the direction of (something or someone): [IØ + *towards*] *If you look towards the West, you can see the sky brightening. Look towards the front of the class, children!* → **look to** (1)
*__2__ to face (something): [T1 (*simple tenses*)] *The front of the house looks towards the sea.* → **look to** (2)
*__3__ to consider; think carefully about (the future): [T1 (*often simple tenses*)] *We have to look towards the future, for the good of our grandchildren. Looking towards next year, we can see a big rise in prices.* → **look to** (3), **see about** (3), **see to** (3)

**look up** *v adv*
**1** to direct one's eyes upwards: [IØ + UP] *I was buried in my book; when I looked up, he had gone.*
*__2__ *not fml* to improve: [IØ] *Trade usually looks up in the spring. Things are looking up now we've got that new contract.*
*__3__ to search for and usu. find (a word or other information) in a book of facts, usu. in alphabetical order: [T1] *If you don't know the meaning of a word, look it up in a good dictionary. You can look up her telephone*

*number in the book. Will you look up a train for me in the timetable?*

*4 to find and visit (someone) when in the same place: [T1 (*pass. rare, often simple tenses*)] *While you're in London, do look up our old teacher, he'll be pleased to see you. If I'm ever here on business again, I'll look you up.*

**5 look up and down** to search (someone) with the eyes; examine (someone) thoroughly, in an enquiring or sexual manner: [*often simple tenses*] *He looked her up and down and decided to ask her out. After looking me up and down for a few minutes, he decided that I was telling the truth.*

**look up to** *v adv prep*

**1** to direct one's eyes in an upward direction, towards (something or someone): [IØ + UP + *to* (*often simple tenses*)] *The boy was so short that he had to look up to his younger sister.*

*2 to respect; admire (someone): [T1 (*usu. simple tenses*)] *Every child needs someone to look up to and copy. It must be rewarding to be looked up to by so many people.*

**look upon** *v prep* → LOOK ON

**look well** *v adj*

**1** to seem healthy: [L9 + well] *You look well today: have you had good news? "My word! You do look well."* (song) → **get well**

*2 to have an attractive appearance: [IØ (*simple tenses*)] *That colour looks well on you, you should wear it more often. She looks well in black, doesn't she?* → **look bad** (2), **look good** (2)

**loom ahead** *v adv*

**1** to arise, often suddenly, in one's view in front of one: [L9 + AHEAD] *Out of the mist, another ship loomed ahead, and we had to take quick action to avoid striking her.*

*2 to exist threateningly in the future: [IØ] *An uncertain future looms ahead. Examinations are looming ahead again.*

**loom large** *v adj* → **bulk large**

*not fml* to seem important: [IØ (*usu. simple tenses*)] *The question of replacing the director looms large with the committee.*

**loom up** *v adv*

to appear suddenly, in a threatening manner: [L9 + UP] *A dark cloud loomed up over the horizon.*

**loose off** *v adv*

**1** to let (something such as a shot) loose: [T1 + OFF (*often simple tenses*)] *Loosing off his last arrow, the hunter prayed that the deer would fall.*

**2** to express (a loud sound): [T1 (*usu. simple tenses*)] *Playing war games, the child suddenly loosed off a terrible shout.*

**loosen up** *v adv*

**1** to (cause to) become less tight: [T1 + UP] *Loosen up his collar, he needs air. Singing loosens up the throat.* [IØ + UP] *The rope loosened up and the heavy box fell to the ground.* → **tighten up** (1)

*2 to exercise (oneself), esp. to be ready for action: [IØ] *The team spends half an hour loosening up before each game.* [T1] *It's dangerous to run a fast race without loosening yourself up first.* → **limber up**

*3 *not fml* to be less firm in demanding something such as the law: [IØ (*on*)] *Officials have been instructed to loosen up on the rules for admitting people into the country.* → **tighten up** (2)

*4 esp. *AmE infml* to talk freely: [IØ] *If you don't loosen up soon, I shall have to find other ways of making you talk.*

*5 esp. *AmE infml* to be generous with one's money: [IØ] *Do you think the old man will loosen up when we tell him our pitiful story?*

*6 *infml* to (cause to) take things easy; become less serious: [IØ] *Loosen up, this isn't a formal occasion.* [T1] *They're very nervous, but a few drinks should loosen them up.*

**lop off/away** *v adv*

to remove (something such as a branch) by cutting: [T1 + OFF/AWAY] *The villagers here have the ancient right to lop off the top branches of the trees in the forest for firewood. With a sharp knife, he lopped off the heads of the fish.*

**lord over** *v prep* → **queen over**

**lord it over** *not fml* to control (someone) by giving orders: *He may be the captain, but he has no right to lord it over the team in that offensive manner.*

**lose about** *v prep*

**not lose (any/much) sleep about** → LOSE OVER (2)

**lose at** *v prep*

to fail to be the winner at (a game, event, etc.); allow someone else to win (something such as money) at (a game, event, etc.): [IØ + *at*] *I always lose at cards, with my bad luck.* [T1 + *at*] *How much money did you lose at the races?*

***lose by** *v prep* → **gain by**

to suffer a disadvantage from (something or doing something): [T1 (*often neg. or in questions, simple tenses*)] *Put your money into our savings plan, and you can't lose by it.* [T4 (*often neg. or in questions, simple tenses*)] *What have you got to lose by trying?* [D1] *The government may lose seats by the reorganization of voting areas.*

**lose in** *v prep*

**1** to fail to know where (something or someone) is in (a place): [T1 + *in* (*often simple tenses*)] *I always get lost in a strange city. I've lost my ring in the garden. It's easy to lose one's way in this building. There you are! I'd lost you in the crowd! Your letter must have got lost in the post.*

*2 to busy (oneself) with (something): [D1 (*often simple tenses*)] *I can always lose myself in a good book. Mary was lost in the details of a new sewing pattern.*

*3 to become less or worse because of or during (something): [T1 (*no pass., simple tenses*)] *The effect of the story loses in translation.* [D1 (*simple tenses*)] *The song loses a great deal in repetition.*

**4 be lost in** (of a sound) to be drowned by (other sounds): *The chairman's remarks were lost in the public's shouts of disapproval.*

**5 be lost in** to be filled with (admiration, wonder, etc.): *I was lost in admiration for your performance under such difficult conditions. The child stood on the sand, lost in wonder at her first sight of the sea.*

**6 be lost in thought** to be filled with thought, so as not to notice someone or something: *I'm sorry, I didn't hear you, I was lost in thought.* → **sink in**[2] (4)

**7 lose belief/confidence/faith/trust in** to cease to trust or have faith in (something, someone, or oneself): *The one thing that might ruin your voice is if you lost confidence in your ability to sing. As they grow older, many children lose faith in their parents.*

**8 lose interest in** to cease to care about (something or someone): *Grace was heartbroken when her red-haired boy lost interest in her. I seem to have lost interest in my work recently; do you suppose that I need a holiday?*

**lose of** *v prep*

**1 lose control of** to cease to be able to control (something, someone, or oneself): *At last she lost control of her temper and shouted at him. This teacher has lost control of the class; he will have to be replaced.* → **keep of** (1)

**2 lose count of** to fail to continue counting, so that one no longer knows the number of (things or people); find that the number of (things or people) is too many to be counted: *Don't interrupt, you'll make me lose count of the pages. We have lost count of the number of people who have written expressing their admiration for our product.* → **keep of** (2)

**3 lose hold of: a** to cease to be able to seize or hold (something or someone): *The climber lost hold of the rope, and fell to his death.* **b** to forget or cease to keep (an ability, idea, etc.): *Never lose hold of your argument, or you're lost.* → **get of** (5), **keep of** (3), **keep on** (10), **lay of** (1), **take of** (10)

**4 lose sight of: a** to be no longer able to see (someone or something): *Don't lose sight of the car that you're chasing.* **b** to forget (an aim): *Never lose sight of your main purpose in life.* → **keep in** (16), etc.

**5 lose the thread of** to forget what (an argument or story) was about: *Once you lose the thread of the argument, you have no hope of defeating your opponent.*

**6 lose trace/track of: a** to no longer know where (someone or something) is: *All trace of the missing child has been lost. The police soon lose track of criminals if they don't catch them soon after the crime.* **b** to fail to follow (an idea): *I'm sorry, I've lost track of the events; would you start your story again?* → **keep of** (5), **keep on** (17)

**7 lose the use of** to cease to be able to use (usu. a part of the body): *The boy lost the use of his right eye in the shooting accident.*

**lose on** *v prep*

**1** to lose (money) in trying to gain more by spending it on (something): [IØ + *on*] *I think we may have lost on that contract.* [T1 + *on*] *Jim's father lost a fortune on one game of cards. I lost £5 on that horse!* → **make on** (2)

**2 be lost on** to be wasted on; not noticed by; fail to influence (someone): *Your remarks were lost on him, he simply doesn't care what you think. Jim's sympathy was not lost on the family of the dead man.*

**3 lose one's grasp/hold on** to lose control of (someone) or knowledge of (something): *Someone who is sick in the mind has lost his hold on reality. I seem to have lost my grasp on this subject and should take another course.* → **lose over** (1)

**lose oneself** *v pron*

**1** to lose one's way; become lost: [T1 + oneself (*usu. simple tenses*)] *It's easy to lose yourself in this building.*

***2** to give all one's attention (to something): [I7 (*in*) (*often simple tenses*)] *On a dull winter afternoon, I like to sit by the fire and lose myself in a good book.*

***3** to disappear: [IØ (*in*) (*usu. simple tenses*)] *The escaping prisoner was able to lose himsel in the crowd.*

***lose out** *v adv*

**1** to fail (in something): [IØ (*on, to*)] *Th firm lost out on the deal. Jim's father is afrai that he may lose out to larger firms.*

**2** to be defeated, esp. in an unlucky way: [I (*on, to*)] *Dicky came second again; he alway loses out. The theatre is losing out to television.*

**lose over** *v prep*

**1 lose one's hold over** to lose control o (someone): *This teacher has lost his hold ove the class, and must be replaced. After th general's death, the government lost its hol over the people, and all kinds of trouble be gan.* → **lose on** (3)

**2 not lose (any/much) sleep over** also **not los (any/much) sleep about** to fail to be worried b (something): *It's a pity that you didn't pass th examination, but I shan't lose any sleep ove it, there are more important things.*

**lose to** *v prep*

**1** to be defeated by (someone); pass (mone to (someone) by losing it in a game, etc.: [I + *to*] *The tennis player was ashamed to lose a much older opponent.* [T1 + *to*] *I lost a l of money to two men who were playing car on the train.*

**2 be lost to: a** to be no longer possessed b (someone): *The fortune was lost to the fami before the war.* **b** to fail to be concerned by o sensitive to (something): *He is lost to all sen* *of duty. When he is busy working, he is lost to the world.*

**3 lose ground to** to yield to; be defeated by (something such as competition); fail in competition with (someone): *The theatre is quickly losing ground to television.*

**4 lose one's heart to** to fall in love with (someone); like (something) very much: *Grace lost her heart to her red-haired boy two years ago. As soon as she saw the house, Mother lost her heart to it.*

**lose with** *v prep*

**1 lose contact/touch with** to be no longer able to send messages to (someone) by knowing where he/she is, etc.: *I was sorry to lose touch with my oldest friend after all these years.* →**get in² (3), keep in (6), put in² (12), remain in² (3), stay in (3)**

**2 lose favour with** to earn the low opinion of (someone): *This system has lost favour with the government. The government has lost favour with the voters.*

**lose without** *v prep*

**be lost without** to feel uncomfortable, helpless, etc., without (something or someone that one is used to): *I left my watch at home this morning, and was lost without it all day. Please don't leave the company, we shall be lost without you.*

**lounge about/around** *v adv; prep* → **loll about**

to stand around a place in a lazy position: [IØ + ABOUT/AROUND; *about/around*] *The young men stood at the street corners, lounging about, watching the girls walk past.*

**lounge away** *v adv* → **idle away** (2), etc.

to waste (time) lazily: [T1] *This warm sunshine encourages people to lounge away their working hours.*

**lour at/on/upon** *v prep* also esp. *AmE* **lower at/on/upon**

to look at (someone) threateningly or disapprovingly: [IØ + *at/on/upon*] *Why are you louring at me? What have I done?*

**louse up** *v adv* → **mess up** (2), etc.

esp. *AmE infml* to spoil (something) carelessly: [T1] *If John louses up his driving test again, I doubt if he'll ever pass it.*

**lower at/on/upon** *v prep* esp. *AmE* → **LOUR AT**

**lower away** *v adv*

*naut* to lower a boat or sail: [IØ (*usu. imper.*)] *We're ready for the lifeboats—lower away!*

**lower on** *v prep* esp. *AmE* → **LOWER AT**

**lower oneself** *v pron* → **descend to** (3), etc.

to behave unworthily: [I3 (*simple tenses*)] *I hope you wouldn't lower yourself to cheat in the examination.* [IØ (*by, to*) (*simple tenses*)] *I hope you wouldn't lower yourself by/to cheating in the examination.*

**lower upon** *v prep* esp. *AmE* → **LOUR AT**

**luck out** *v adv*

*AmE infml* to be lucky; have good luck: [IØ (*simple tenses*)] *At last I lucked out and found a good job.*

***luff up** *v adv*

*naut* to turn a boat towards the direction of the wind, so as to reduce the force of the wind on the sails: [IØ] *The wind is too strong, we shall have to luff up.*

**lull into** *v prep*

to persuade (someone) into (something or doing something) with calmness and peace: [X9 + *into*] *If you don't argue about it, you can easily lull the people into acceptance of new taxes. Anyone can be lulled into believing something that sounds so pleasant. When the bombing ceased for a time, the citizens were lulled into a false sense of safety.*

**lull to** *v prep*

**lull someone to sleep** to help someone to fall asleep by calm movements and sounds, etc.: *The movement of the train lulled me to sleep, and I went past my station. It took us all night to lull the baby to sleep, singing to him and walking up and down with him.*

**lumber with** *v prep*

**1** to fill (a space or someone's mind) with too much of (something or things): [T1 + *with* (*usu. pass*)] *The room was lumbered (up) with piles of furniture. His memory was lumbered with detailed facts and figures.*

***2** *infml* to force (someone) to accept (something or someone unwanted): [D1 (*often pass.*)] *I'm really lumbered now; I've been left with sixty cases of wine I can't sell. Why should we be lumbered with your aunt? Can't your brother take his share of looking after her? The director has lumbered me with the unpleasant job of dismissing perfectly good workers that the firm can no longer afford to employ.* → **land with,** etc.

***lump it** *v pron*

*infml* to accept unchangeable bad conditions without complaint: [IØ (*usu. inf.*)] *You have to like it or lump it!*

***lump together** *v adv* → **group together** (2)

to consider (things or people) as a unity; place (things or people) in the same class or division: [T1 (*often pass.*)] *All the students have been lumped together in one class although they have widely varying abilities. For our purposes, we can lump the separate costs together as they are all paid out of the same account. Which kinds of books can be lumped together to save space?*

**lunch in** *v adv*

to take one's midday meal in one's home, office, etc.: [IØ + IN] *Please bring me some cooked chicken, I shall have to lunch in today while I finish this work.*

**lunch off** *v prep*

to eat one's midday meal in the form of (certain food): [IØ + *off*] *I can lunch off this meat left over from yesterday.*

**lunch out** *v adv*

to take one's midday meal in a restaurant, out of doors, away from one's hotel, etc.: [IØ +

OUT] *I'm lunching out with a customer, and shall be back at 2 o'clock.*

**lunge at** *v prep*
to make a sudden forward movement towards (someone): [IØ + *at* (*often simple tenses*)] *The swordsman lunged at his opponent, wounding him.*

**lure away** *v adv*
to persuade (usu. someone) to leave (someone or something), often by deceit, promises, etc.: [X9 + AWAY (*from*)] *Don't you dare try to lure my new secretary away (from the firm), we value her work highly. No woman should allow herself to be lured away from her husband.*

**lure into** *v prep*
to deceive (someone or an animal) into entering (something) or (doing something): [X9 + *into*] *Cheese is very good for luring a mouse into a trap. How can you lure the owner into leaving the house unlocked so that we can steal the jewels?*

**lure on** *v adv*
to encourage; attract (someone or an animal): [X9 + ON] *The hunters lured the bears on to certain death. Her winning ways were always enough to lure any man on. The workers were lured on by false hopes of increased pay.*

**lurk about/around** *v adv; prep*
to wait around a place in an untrustworthy manner: [L9 + ABOUT/AROUND/*about*/*around*] *There are two men lurking about (my gate), making me nervous. Shall we call the police?*

**lust after/for** *v prep* → **lech after**
to have a violent, often improper and/or sexual desire for (someone or something): [L9 + *after*/*for*] *Some men lust for gold, but most lust for women.*

***luxuriate in** *v prep*
to enjoy (something) with great pleasure: [T1] *She sits here luxuriating in the sun, while her husband does all the work. People were out in the streets without coats, luxuriating in the unexpected warmth of the sun after such a bitter winter.*

# M

**madden with** *v prep*
to annoy; make (someone) angry or uncomfortable by means of (something): [T1 + *with* (*usu. pass.*)] *The travellers were maddened with thirst. Regular passengers are getting maddened with all these delays. The children madden me with their endless questions.*

**mail from** *v prep* → **post from** (1)
*AmE* to send (something such as a letter or parcel) by post from (somewhere): [T1 + *from*] *I see from the postmark that this postcard was mailed from Mary's holiday address.*

**mail to** *v prep* → **post to** (1)
*AmE* to send (something such as a letter or parcel) by post to (someone or an address): [T1 + *to*] *The cheque was mailed to you/to your home address yesterday.*

**maintain at** *v prep*
to keep (something) at (something such as a usual level): [T1 + *at*] *We must do our best to maintain sales at their usual rate in these times of poor trade.*

**maintain in** *v prep*
**1** to keep (something such as property or a machine) in (a state, usu. good): [T1 + *in*] *It's endless work maintaining the house in good repair.* → **keep in** (2)
**2** to support (someone such as a wife) in (a certain style): [T1 + *in*] *If you are going to marry my daughter, I must ask if you can afford to maintain her in the manner to which she has been accustomed?* → **keep in** (3)

***major in** *v prep*
esp. *AmE* to specialize in the study of (one's main subject), usu. at a university: [T1 (*pass. rare*)] *Are you majoring in English Literature?*

**make about** *v prep*
**1 make no bones about** to speak or act boldly and clearly, without pretence or hiding reality, about (something or doing something): *The chairman made no bones about the difficulties facing the committee, but warned them to be careful about their decision. The two newspaper reporters made no bones about holding the President responsible for the actions of his men.*
**2 make a fuss about** also **make over**[2] to express unreasonable anxiety or excitement about (someone, something, or doing something): *Do stop crying, you're making a fuss about nothing. Why do so many children make a fuss about going to school for the first time?* → **make of** (19)
**3 make a song and dance about** also **make over**[2] *not fml* to express unreasonable and sometimes foolish or childish concern about or opposition to (something or doing something): *Why are you making such a song and dance about the increase in your taxes? With your income, you can afford it better than most. There's no point in making a song and dance about missing the train; we can always catch the next one.*

***make after** *v prep*
esp. *old use* to chase (someone or an animal): [T1 (*usu. simple tenses*)] *The policeman made after the jewel thieves, but failed to catch them. Suddenly a cat walked in front of us, and th*

*dog made after it.* → **come after** (2), etc.

**make against** *v prep* → **provide against**
**make provision against** to take action to avoid or prevent (something bad) or to deal with (a danger or time of danger) in advance: *Steps can be taken to make provision against a severe winter. What can we do to make provision against a failure of the wheat crop?*

**make at** *v prep*
**1** to gain (an income) from (a profession or activity): [T1 + *at* (*usu. simple tenses*)] *Writing is fine as a way of using your free time, but can you make a living at it? How much does Jim make at his job?*
*__2__ to start or threaten to attack (someone): [T1 (*no pass., usu. simple tenses*)] *The prisoner made at the guard with a knife.* → **come after** (2), etc.
**3 make a dead set at** *infml* to make repeated and serious efforts to gain (someone, something, or doing something): *As soon as he saw the girl, he began to make a dead set at her. Jim intends to make a dead set at winning the tennis prize this year.*
**4 make (sheep's) eyes at** *infml* to try to attract (someone of the opposite sex) by the expression in one's eyes: *That boy over there is making eyes at me.* → **ogle at, roll at**
**5 make a face/faces at** to twist one's face into an ugly shape to shock or annoy (someone); give (someone) a message by the expression on one's face: *That nasty boy has been making faces at me in the street again! Mary made a face at Jim to show that she wanted to leave the party.*
**6 make a grab at** *not fml* to try to seize (something): *The climber made a grab at the rope, but missed and fell to his death.*
**7 make oneself at home** to feel welcome and comfortable; behave as informally as if in one's own home: *Sit where you like and help yourselves to coffee; make yourselves (completely) at home.*
**8 make a pass at** *not fml* to attempt to attract; make sexual suggestions to (someone of the opposite sex, often not free): *You'll get a bad name if you've been making a pass at other men's wives. "Men never make passes at girls who wear glasses."* (Dorothy Parker)

**make away** *v adv* → **make off**
to leave in haste, as to escape: [IØ] *I tried to speak to him, but he made away in a hurry.*

**make away with** *v adv prep*
**1** to steal and carry away (something): [T1] *The police gave chase, but the thieves made away with the jewels.* → **make off with** (1), etc.
**2** to murder; kill (esp. oneself): [T1 (*often simple tenses*)] *Our neighbour tried to make away with herself by drinking poison.* → **bump off**, etc.
**3** to destroy or waste (something): [T1] *He soon made away with the fortune which he had gained on his father's death. Those children have made away with the whole cake!* → **make off with** (2)

**make bold** *v adj*
**make so bold as** to have the courage (to do something): [*usu. simple tenses*] *May I make so bold as to say how much I admire your singing?*

**make certain** *v adj* → **make sure**
**1** to fix (something such as an idea) firmly: [T1 + **certain** (*usu. simple tenses*)] *I like to have a contract to make our agreement certain, so that I feel safe to continue with the work.*
*__2__ to be sure of the truth of something: [T5] *Make certain that this is the right road.* [T6] *Make certain where we are going/whether we are on the right road.*
*__3__ to ensure (that something happens): [T5] *I'm making certain that the hotel will keep a room for us, by paying in advance. I'll make certain that you get the job, I have influence with the director.*
*__4__ to feel sure: [T5 (*usu. simple tenses*)] *I made certain that I would get the job, but it was given to someone else.*

*__make certain of__ *v adj prep* → **make of** (8, 52), **make sure of**
**1** to be sure of the truth of (something): [T1 (*no pass.*)] *I hope the speaker has made certain of his facts. I made certain of his safe arrival.*
**2** to be sure of having (something): [T1] *To make certain of a table in the restaurant, it is wise to telephone earlier. Make certain of your position in the firm before you argue with the director. The best seats can only be made certain of by having a regular ticket to the theatre.*

**make clear** *v adj*
**1** to show; explain (something) clearly: [X9 + **clear**] *The workers' leader wants to talk to the directors, to make the union's position clear. The meaning of the story is made clear in the introduction.*
**2 make it clear that**... to declare firmly that ...: *The head teacher made it clear that he would not have such behaviour in his school.*
**3 make oneself clear** to express oneself clearly; speak in such a way as to be understood: *Do I make myself clear? This is your last chance!*

*__make down__ *v adv* → **cut down** (2)
to make (clothes) smaller, so as to fit someone of a smaller size: [T1] *Can you make the dress down for her younger sister?*

*__make fast__ *v adj*
to fasten (something) firmly: [T1b] *Tie the rope round the pole and then make it fast or the boat will float away.* —**makefast** *n*

**make for** *v prep*
**1** to produce; cause (something) to exist specially for (someone or something): [T1 + *for*] *He used to be so fat that he couldn't fit into any ready-made clothes, and had to have his suits made for him. It's time I made some new curtains for the living room.*

*__2__ to move, esp. quickly, in the direction of (something): [T1] *Though badly damaged by fire, the ship tried to make for her home port. After the concert, the crowd made for the nearest door.* → **make towards**

*__3__ to move towards (usu. someone) threateningly: [T1 (*no pass.*)] *When the thieves saw the big dog making for them, they ran away.* → **come after** (2), etc.

*__4__ to cause; lead to; result in; help; encourage; favour (something): [T1 (*no pass., simple tenses*)] *The large print makes for easier reading. Having different religions does not make for easy friendship. The plan might make for a good House of Lords.*

**5 be made for** to suit (someone or something) exactly: *These hills are made for winter sports. He seems made for politics. Jim and Mary seem to be made for one another.* → **mean for** (2)

**6 make allowance(s) for** to take (something) into consideration, as when making a judgment; consider (someone) sympathetically: *The music judges were instructed to make allowance for the singer's inexperience. We'd better make allowance for some delay. I shall make allowances for you and not punish you this time.* → **allow for** (2)

**7 make amends for** to repay someone for (harm done): *I will make amends for my lateness by working after hours. You must make amends (to your aunt) for the window that you broke.* → **make to** (2)

**8 make arrangements for** to organize (something): *Have you made arrangements for a photographer to attend the wedding? Who is making arrangements for the next meeting?*

**9 make a beeline for** *not fml* to go straight in the direction of (something), often eagerly: *As soon as they reached the park, the young people made a beeline for the swimming pool.*

**10 make a bid for: a** to offer a price for (goods), esp. at an auction: *Did you make a bid for the painting? Yes, but somebody else offered more.* **b** to attempt to win (something): *Will Jim make a bid for the big prize this year? The politician is making a bid for the women's vote. The prisoner made a bid for freedom, but was caught.*

**11 make a bolt/break for it** *not fml* to try to escape: *Two prisoners have made a bolt for it, and the guards are searching for them in the hills.*

**12 make a bolt/dash for** *not fml* to try to escape towards (something): *While the guard's back was turned, the prisoner made a bolt for the open door.*

**13 make a long arm for** *not fml* to try to reach (something) by stretching one's arm: *Why make a long arm for the salt? I would have passed it to you.*

**14 make a name for oneself** *not fml* to become famous or well-known: *It's difficult to make a name for yourself on the concert stage, where the competition is so strong.*

**15 make a play for** esp. *AmE infml* to try to get (something or someone): *It's often amusing at a party to see a young man making a play for a pretty girl, and failing. How many people are making a play for the director's job?*

**16 make provision for** to supply; fulfil the need of (someone or something): *I am sure, sir, that I shall be able to make provision for my wife and family. These people have saved during their whole lives to make provision for their old age. Politicians should learn to make provision for the opinions of the man in the street.* → **provide for** (2)

**17 make room for** to find space or time to be given to (something or someone): *Can you make room for another guest at the dinner table? I don't know how we can make room on the timetable for any more courses.*

**18 make tracks for** *not fml* to go in the direction of (a place, esp. home): *Well, we must leave now; it's time we were making tracks for home.*

**19 make way for** to move aside so as to allow room for (someone or something) to pass: [*usu. simple tenses*] *The crowd divided to make way for the police car. Make way for the king, there!*

*__make free of__ *v adj prep* → **make of** (16)
*fml* to give (someone) special rights in (something): [D1 (*usu. simple tenses*)] *I owe grateful thanks to my former university teacher who made me free of his library of rare books so that I could write this report.*

*__make free with__ *v adj prep* → **make with** (4)
to use (something that someone possesses) without permission: [T1] *You had no right to make free with my name in your report. I'm tired of your friends coming here and making free with my beer.*

**make from** *v prep* → **fashion from, form from, make of** (1), **make out of** (1), **produce from** (1)
to produce; shape; form; cause (something) to exist by using (an existing object as material): [T1 + *from*] *Can you make me (up) a suit from this length of cloth? Mother can make a wonderful meal from bits of food left over from the day before. The children's playhouse has been made from a pile of cardboard boxes. The natives make excellent boats from tree trunks.*

**make good** *v adj*

**1** to cause (something or someone) to become good in quality, condition, behaviour, etc: [X9 + good (*usu. simple tenses*)] *If you've got an excuse, make it good. You have to make the surface good before you can paint it. What kind of treatment will make this troublesome boy good?*

*__2__ to repay a debt of (money or time): [T1 (*usu. simple tenses*)] *You must make good th* *time that you have wasted this afternoon, by working late tonight. When the money was stolen, his father offered to make good the loss.* → **make up** (2)

*__3__ to live a more moral or successful life: [IØ (*simple tenses*)] *After spending a short time in prison, he made good and became a respected member of society. The youngest son was sent abroad, where he made good and soon earned a small fortune.*

*__4__ to fulfil (a promise or threat): [T1 (*usu. simple tenses*)] *When are you going to make good your promise to help with painting the house? He makes a lot of empty threats, but never makes them good.*

*__5__ to be successful in performing (something): [T1 (*simple tenses*)] *The committee likes your suggestion, but can you make it good? Running behind the bushes, the prisoner made good his escape.*

*__6__ to prove (something): [T1 (*usu. simple tenses*)] *He made good his argument by showing that it was based on reason.*

**make hot** *v adj*

**1** to cause (something or someone) to become heated or warm: [X9 + **hot**] *Do you like your coffee made hot? Please don't make the room so hot, it makes me uncomfortable. Exercise makes me hot.*

**2 make it hot for** to make (someone) feel uncomfortable or be in difficulties; punish (someone): *The opposing speaker made it hot for me by showing the faults in my argument. I'll make it hot for that boy the next time I catch him breaking my window!*

**make in** *v prep*

**1** to form; produce (something) in (something): [T1 + *in*] *The cake is made in a large bowl.*

**2 make a dent/hole in: a** to damage (something or part of the body) by causing it to have the mark of a blow or hole in it: *The crash was not serious, but it made a dent in the car door and a hole in the side window frame.* **b** *infml* to reduce (something) by a part: *Paying the increased taxes has made a dent in my income.* → **make into** (3)

**3 make one's way in the world** to become successful, as in business: *This young man has all the ability and character necessary to make his way in the world, whatever profession he chooses.*

**make into** *v prep*

**1** to shape (material) into (a finished object): [X9 + *into*] *Waste products from factories can be made into road-building material. All kinds of strange things can be made (up) into jewellery.*

*__2__ to change (something or someone) into (something else or a kind of person): [D1] *Can you make this dress into a skirt? It's a shame to see so many fine old houses being made into flats. If we buy the disused church, we could make it into an attractive home. School has made the boy into a coward.* → **change into** (2), etc.

**3 make inroads into** to take or use part of (something): *The fall in the value of the pound has made inroads into the amount of gold held by the Bank of England.* → **make in** (2)

***make it** *v pron*

**1** *not fml* to be successful; be able to do, reach, catch, or attend something, often as regards time or effort: [IØ (*usu. simple tenses*)] *I don't think this old car will make it to the top of the hill. We shall only make it if the train comes late. Quick, the doors are closing! You'll make it just in time! I'm sorry I missed your concert, but I was out of town and couldn't make it. It's a very difficult examination; are you sure you can make it?*

**2** *sl* to have sex (with someone of the opposite sex): [IØ (*with*)] *Did you make it with that girl we met?*

***make light of** *v adj prep* → **make of** (29)

to make (something) seem less serious than it really is; reduce the level or importance of (something bad), esp. when speaking about it: [T1] *No one will ever know how she made light of her suffering all those years. The climbers made light of the difficulties and dangers they had faced in reaching the top of the world's highest mountain. His crime was made light of by the other prisoners.*

***make like** *v prep*

*AmE infml* to copy; behave as if being (someone or something): [T1 (*no pass.*)] *Make like a helpless old lady and the police will let you go. The child was holding up his arms, making like a tree.*

***make merry** *v adj*

*old use* to have fun: [IØ] *On the first of May every year, the villagers would make merry in the village, dancing, singing, laughing, and drinking.* —**merrymaker, merrymaking** *n*

**make of** *v prep*

**1** to form; shape: produce (something) from (a material): [T1 + *of* (*usu. pass.*)] *The children like making houses of sticks and clay. I would rather make a house of stone. Are these shoes made of leather?* → **fashion from, form from, make from, make out of** (1), **produce from** (1)

*__2__ to understand (anything/little/much/nothing/something) by (something): [D1 (*simple tenses*)] *I don't know what to make of the boy's behaviour. Can you make anything of this strange letter? I could make nothing of the chairman's remark.*

*__3__ to train (someone) as; cause (someone) to develop into (a kind of person): [D1] *You'll never make a musician of that boy. Will Mary be able to make a faithful husband of Jim?*

**4 make the best of** to use (something) to the best of one's ability: *I'll help you to make the best of the voice that you do have, though it's*

*not good enough for professional singing.*
**5 make the best of it/of a bad job** *not fml* to accept something such as a disappointment, as cheerfully as possible: *The car's broken down again so we must make the best of it and catch the bus. I'm sorry you failed the examination; try to make the best of a bad job —you can always try again next year.*
**6 make the best of both worlds** to combine the advantages of two systems, ideas, etc.: *This house combines country surroundings with city convenience, so making the best of both worlds.* → **get of** (1)
**7 make capital (out) of** to use (something) to gain an advantage for oneself: *The opposition is trying to make capital of the Minister's unfortunate remark.* → **make out of** (2)
**8 make certain of** → MAKE CERTAIN OF
**9 make a clean breast of** to admit (a crime or doing something wrong): *After hours of questioning, the prisoner decided to make a clean breast of his part in the jewel robbery. He made a clean breast of helping to steal the jewels.*
**10 make a day/evening/night of it** *not fml* to spend the whole of a day/evening/night enjoying oneself: *Let's go out to dinner as well as to the play, and really make a night of it.*
**11 make demands of** to expect help or supplies from (usu. someone): *If the director keeps making demands of the office workers like that, some of them will leave. Too many demands have been made of the supply of wood.* → **make on** (7)
**12 make an example of** to show what happens to (someone) as a result of his behaviour, usu. bad: *We can't catch every drinking driver, but if we make an example of one or two and prevent them from driving for a year or longer, others may stop drinking for fear of the same punishment. Two of the prisoners have been made an example of.*
**13 make an exception of** to treat (someone) with greater favour: *I can't possibly make an exception of you, or every other student will want to hand his work in late.*
**14 make an exhibition/spectacle of oneself** to behave improperly in public: *Stop making me cry in the street, I hate making an exhibition of myself. When the old man got drunk he made a terrible exhibition of himself, shouting and swearing and breaking the furniture. I'm sorry I lost my temper and made such a spectacle of myself.*
**15 make a fool of** to make (someone or oneself) appear or feel foolish; deceive (someone): *The man who sold me this car really made a fool of me, it will never run properly. Those girls are always making fools of themselves at parties. Please stop correcting me in front of strangers, I don't like being made a fool of in public. What a fool you made of him, letting everyone read his letter!*
**16 make free of/with** → MAKE FREE OF, MAKE FREE WITH
**17 make a friend of** to purposely become friendly with; win the friendship of; treat (someone already known, or an animal) as a friend: *Our dog won't hurt you; you'll soon make a friend of him. Some of the teachers try to make a friend of their cleverest student, but it hardly ever works. Is it possible to make a friend of your own mother?* → **make with** (5)
**18 make fun/mock/sport of** also *BrE* **make game of** to cause people to laugh, often unkindly, at (someone or something); treat (someone or something) as a joke: *It's unkind to make fun of a foreign student's mistakes in English. Never make fun of a child.* → **laugh at** (2), etc.
**19 make a fuss of** to give a lot of attention to; treat (someone) very kindly and generously, as if he/she was important and special: *Mother always makes a fuss of visitors. What a fuss the family makes of every new baby!* → **make about** (2), **make over** (3)
**20 make a go of** *not fml* to attempt to succeed at (something such as a relationship): *After trying for several years to make a go of their marriage, Jim and Mary have now separated.*
**21 make a good/poor job of** *not fml* to do (something) well/badly; succeed/fail at (something or doing something): *This machine makes a good job of copying photographs. You make a poor job of washing the windows. The garage has made a terrible job of repairing the car. Mother has made an excellent job of the meal. What sort of a job did he make of the chairmanship? You haven't made much of a job of that skirt.*
**22 make good/effective use of** to use (something) well; put (something) to good use: *The writer has made effective use of the main character's dreams. Good use can be made of empty spaces in the city, as playgrounds for children. You could make better use of your time than wasting it in clubs and restaurants. The university should make the best possible use of the brains of its teachers.*
**23 make a habit of** to do (something or doing something) regularly: *Yes, you can borrow my car today, but don't make a habit of it. Do you make a habit of interrupting other people's conversations?*
**24 make a hash/mess/muddle of** *not fml* to spoil (something) carelessly: *If John makes a hash of his driving test again, I doubt if he'll ever pass it.* → **mess up** (2), etc.
**25 make hay of** *not fml* to destroy; ruin (something): *This weather has made hay of our holiday arrangements. The changing value of the pound makes hay of our calculations on the exchange rate.*
**26 make head (n)or tail of** *not fml* to understand (something or someone): [*simple tenses, with can, neg.*] *I can't make head or*

*tail of this map; how can we be expected to find our way? He's a strange character; I can't make head nor tail of him.*
**27 make heavy weather of** *not fml* to make (a job) seem more difficult than it is; struggle to perform (a job or doing something): *You seem to be making heavy weather of this piece of music; it's actually quite easy. Why is she making such heavy weather of telephoning her mother?*
**28 make an honest woman of** *not fml* to marry (a woman), esp. when she has had a sexual relationship with the man for some time: *We've been living together for six months; when are you going to make an honest woman of me?*
**29 make light of** → **MAKE LIGHT OF**
**30 make light work of** to consider (something or doing something) easy: *With their experience, the men made light work of moving the heavy furniture. It was a difficult job, but he made light work of it.*
**31 make a man of** to cause (a male) to grow up, behave like a man: *'The regular army will make a man of you!'* (advertisement)
**32 make a match of it** to be suited to each other in marriage: *"I had always supposed that you and Mrs Lupin would make a match of it."* (Charles Dickens, *Martin Chuzzlewit*)
**33 make a meal of: a** to eat (food); regard (food) as enough for a meal: *I can make a meal of a banana.* **b** *infml* to do (something) with unnecessarily great effort: *The chairman is certainly making a meal of his goodbye speech! Going to a different play every night is, I consider, making a meal of it.*
**34 make a mental note of** to try to remember (something): *I made a mental note of his name, so as to avoid him in future. Make a mental note of the position of the tree, so that we can find our way back.*
**35 make mention of** *fml* to mention (something or someone): [*usu. simple tenses*] *I must already have made mention of the people who were so kind to me on my travels. Mention has been made of the importance of considering the cost.*
**36 make mincemeat of** *not fml* to defeat or destroy (opposition) completely: *I'm afraid the other team made mincemeat of us; it was a terrible defeat. Our army made mincemeat of the enemy, and we won an important victory.*
**37 make a mockery/travesty of** to make a bad joke of; show a poor example of; destroy the idea of (something usu. good): *Buying votes makes a mockery of free elections. The judge's treatment of the prisoner made a mockery of justice.*
**38 make the most of** to enjoy or gain advantage from (something or doing something) while it lasts: *Make the most of the sunshine, we don't get much in the winter. Let's make the most of having the car for the day, and go for a long drive.*
**39 make much of: a** to understand (something): [*usu. neg., usu. simple tenses*] *I didn't make much of his speech, did you?* **b** to treat (something or someone) as important; be proud of (something): [*usu. simple tenses*] *Don't make too much of her rudeness, she's just a silly old woman. He likes to make much of the property he owns in different countries. Music has always been made much of in this school. Why is the government making so much of the foreign visitors?*
**40 make nonsense of** to show (something) to be worthless, untrue, etc.: *His wounded leg made nonsense of his claim to have run five miles. The examination system is made nonsense of if people cheat.*
**41 make a note of** to record (something that one wishes to remember), often in writing: *Make a note of that man's name, he'll be put on a charge. Will all members please make a note of the date of our next meeting. I made a careful note of where I had left the bag, so as to be sure to find it on my return.*
**42 make nothing of: a** to fail to understand something: [*usu. simple tenses*] *I can make nothing of his request.* **b** to do (something) very easily: [*usu. simple tenses*] *These experienced climbers make nothing of the difficulties of an ordinary climb. This is one of the most difficult pieces to play, yet this wonderful young pianist made nothing of it.*
**43 make a nuisance of oneself** to get in the way; annoy other people; be unwanted: *Go and play in the field where you won't be making nuisance of yourselves. "Am I making a nuisance of myself?" "No, no, please stay!"*
**44 make one of** *old use* to join (a group): [*usu. simple tenses*] *"It would be worth a journey . . . to see that sort of people together, and to make one of them."* (Charles Dickens, *David Copperfield*)
**45 make a pig of oneself** *infml* to eat too much and/or too fast: *Eat your dinner politely, children, don't make pigs of yourselves! I have such a weakness for nuts that I make a pig of myself every Christmas, eating too many at a time.*
**46 make a point of** to show clearly that one considers (something or doing something) to be important; take special care about (doing something): *The singer makes rather a point of her high notes, doesn't she? I make a point of always being early for a meeting. Why do you make such a point of rising early?*
**47 make a practice/business of** to do (something or doing something) regularly: *Do you make a practice of competing with international firms? Teachers make a practice of correcting the children's spoken English.*
**48 make a secret of** to refuse to tell (something): *Why do you make a secret of your feel-*

*ings? I make no secret of my fondness for nuts.*

**49 make sense of** to be able to understand (something): [*usu. simple tenses*] *Can you make sense of what he says? Will anyone ever make sense of the mysterious writing in the cave?*

**50 make a show of** to pretend to have (a feeling); pretend to be (doing something): *Father made a show of anger, but actually he was secretly amused by the boy's action. I think you're just making a show of agreeing with me, in order to get some peace.*

**51 make a success of** to succeed in (something such as a job or doing something): *We want someone who will make a success of the chairmanship. Gordon has made a success of translating the ancient poem into simple English.*

**52 make sure of** → **MAKE SURE OF**

**53 make a trade of** to exchange (a possession) for something else: [*usu. simple tenses*] *Will you make a trade of your blue ball for my green one?*

**54 make use of** to use (something): *Can you make use of some more help in the kitchen? I could make use of a new typewriter.*

**55 make a virtue of necessity** to declare or behave as if believing that something which one does naturally or from habit, etc., is good: *You always wake early in the morning, so you can't claim it as a moral advantage; I call that making a virtue of necessity.*

**56 make the worst of** to make (something) worse than it is by not trying to improve it: *She always makes the worst of any little disappointment.* → **get of** (13), **have of** (5)

**57 make the worst of both worlds** to combine the disadvantages of two systems, ideas, etc.: *Smoking as well as overeating is making the worst of both worlds, as far as your health is concerned.* → **get of** (14)

***make off** *v adv* → **make away**

to leave in haste, as to escape: [IØ] *I tried to speak to him, but he made off in a hurry.*

***make off with** *v adv prep* → **make away with**

**1** to steal and carry away (something): [T1] *The police chased them, but the thieves made off with the jewels.* → **fly off with, get away with** (2), **make away with** (1), **run away with** (4), **walk away with** (2), **walk off with** (2)

**2** to destroy or waste (something): [T1] *He soon made off with the fortune which he had gained when his father died. Those children have made off with the whole cake!* → **make away with** (3)

**make on** *v prep*

**1** to form; shape; produce (something) on top of (something): [T1 + *on*] *Those birds have made their nest on our chimney!*

***2** to make (a profit) by means of (something): [T1 (*no pass.*)] *With any luck, we might make on the deal.* [D1] *How much did you make on the house when you sold it? I made £500 on the old painting that I found in the house. You'll never make money on used furniture.* → **lose on** (1)

**3 make an attempt on** to try to reach or beat (something): *British climbers are making another attempt on the world's highest mountain. An attempt will be made on the long-distance swimming record by this brave young swimmer.*

**4 make an attempt on someone's life** to try to kill someone, usu. in an important position: *Terrorists have threatened to make an attempt on the life of a leading politician unless their demands are met. A further attempt has been made on the life of the ruler of a South American state.*

**5 make a beginning/start on** to start (something): *A beginning has been made on the building of the new library. When will Tom make a start on his next book?*

**6 make a claim on** to have the right to claim something such as money or loyalty from (something or someone): *You may make a claim on the firm for the costs of your journey. What claim can the company make on me after the way they have treated me?*

**7 make demands on** to expect help or supplies from (usu. someone): *If the director keeps making demands on the office workers like that, some of them will leave. Too many demands have been made on the supply of coffee so the price has risen.* → **make of** (11)

**8 make an impression on: a** to give (someone) an opinion about something, usu. that one does: *His behaviour made a bad impression on the class. The young singer has made a good impression on the public. What kind of impression did you make on the voters?* **b** to influence the judgment of (someone) in one's favour; cause (someone) to notice one: *The new secretary made an impression on the director on her first day. Are you trying to make an impression on me by wearing that hat?*

**9 make war on: a** to attack; fight; declare war against (usu. a nation): *In former times, kings of small states used to make war regularly on their neighbours.* → **declare against** (2), **declare on**[2] (1), **wage against** (1) **b** to oppose (something) violently: *All thinking people will join in making war on inequality. This group makes war on cruelty to animals.* → **declare against** (3), **declare on**[2] (2)

***make out** *v adv*

**1** to write; complete (something such as a paper): [T1] *When you make out the bill, please give me a copy. Cheques should be made out to Wise Brothers Limited. Have you made out your tax return yet? Be quiet, I'm trying to make out a shopping list.* (*AmE*) *Do you need help in making out the papers?* → **fill in** (2), **fill out** (1), **fill up** (2), **write out** (2)

**2** to see (something or someone) clearly: [T1 (*simple tenses*)] *You can just make out the farm in the distance. Can you make out the shape of the ship appearing over the horizon? Looking through the mist, I could make out the figure of a woman standing under the lamp.* [T5 (*simple tenses*)] *"She soon made out that she was in the pool of tears which she had wept when she was nine feet high."* (Lewis Carroll, *Alice in Wonderland*) [T6 (*simple tenses*)] *There's someone outside the window, but I can't make out who it is.*

**3** to understand (something or someone); discover (something): [L9 (*simple tenses*)] *As far as I can make out, there seem to be no bones broken.* [T1 (*simple tenses*)] *I can't make out the meaning of this poem. Can you make out what he is trying to say? I can't make her out, she's a mystery to me.* [T6 (*simple tenses*)] *No one can make out how the fire started. He could not make out whether he was in the right city.* → **figure out** (2), **puzzle out, work out** (5)

**4** to reach an answer: [T1 (*simple tenses*)] *How do you make that out?*

**5** to succeed; find a way to live: [IØ (*usu. simple tenses*)] *How did you make out with the committee? How did he make out while his wife was away? I'll make out with this old car for another year.* → **get on** (6), **go on**[1] **(12)**

**6** to have a friendly or sexual relationship (with someone): [L9 (*with*)] *"How did you make out with the pretty girl we met in the hotel?" "Oh, I made out all right!"*

**7** esp. *AmE not fml* to be successful: [L9] *Whatever profession this young man chooses, I'm sure he'll make out all right. The firm only offers a six-month contract to start with; when we see how you make out, we will talk about the possibility of more lasting employment.*

**8** to claim; describe (someone): [V3 (*usu. simple tenses*)] *You can't make yourself out to be younger than you are. He's not such a fool as he's made out to be.* [T5] *He made out that his car had been stolen.* → **give out** (4)

**9** to pretend; try to prove that . . .: [T5] *The lawyers tried to make out that Peter had not been present at the accident. Mary has always made out that her parents were rich, but it isn't true.*

**10** to fill; complete the quantity necessary for (something): [T1] *The article was included to make out a book.*

**11** esp. *AmE infml* to make love; have sex: [IØ (*usu. continuous tenses*)] *The park was full of lovers making out on the grass.*

**12 make out a case (against/for)** to show arguments or proof (against or in favour of something or someone): *The speaker made out an excellent case, but was defeated in the voting. The government can easily make out a good case for raising taxes again. A case can be made out against changing the gun laws. The lawyers made out their case that the prisoner was not guilty.*

**make out of** *v adv prep*

**1** to form; shape; produce (something) from (a material or existing object): [T1 + OUT + *of* (*often pass.*)] *This evening dress is made out of pure silk. The children enjoyed making a playhouse out of cardboard (boxes). The house was made out of stone in the last century. Scarlett O'Hara made the dress out of some old curtains.* → **fashion from, form from, make from, make of** (1), **produce from** (1)

**2 make capital out of** → **MAKE OF** (7)

**3 make a mountain out of a molehill** *not fml* to speak too much of the difficulty or seriousness of something: *It's really not all that important, you're making a mountain out of a molehill. She's always going to her doctor with the least little thing, I think she likes making mountains out of molehills.*

**4 be made out of whole cloth** *AmE not fml* to be completely untrue, invented: *It's quite clear that the prisoner's story is made out of whole cloth, and he will be found guilty.*

***make over**[1] *v adv*

**1** esp. *AmE* to remake (something): [T1b] *I'll have to make this dress over, it's all the wrong shape. Human nature can't be made over so easily.*

**2** to change (usu. something) (into something else): [T1 (*into*)] *The garage has been made over into a playroom. It'll cost a lot of money to make the room over.*

**3** to give possession of (something) formally (to someone): [T1 (*to*)] *Uncle has made over most of his land to his children. Has all his property been made over? He made over his house for use as a hospital in the war.* → **pay over**

**make over**[2] *v prep*

**1** to make more than a certain quantity of (things, money, etc.): [T1 + *over*] *The boys did well at the sale, making over £50 in an hour! The factory has made over 10,000 bicycles this year.*

***2** *AmE* to show fondness for (someone, usu. a child): [T1] *Aunt Mabel is making over the new baby again.*

**3 make a fuss over** → **MAKE ABOUT** (2)

**4 make a song and dance over** → **MAKE ABOUT** (3)

***make ready** *v adj*

to (cause to) be prepared (to do something): [IØ (*for*)] *Make the guestroom ready for your visitors. The Queen is coming! Make ready there! It's time to make ready for the performance. "Tomorrow you must die, go to your knees and make ready."* (Shakespeare, *Measure for Measure*) [I3] *Make ready to receive some bad news. His companions made ready to fight.*

**make round** *v prep* → **run round**[2] (2)

**make rings round** to defeat (someone) easily;

do something faster or better than (someone): *She can make rings round any competitor.*

***make sure** *v adj* → **make certain**

**1** to know the truth of something without doubt: [T5] *Make sure that this is the right road.* [T6] *Make sure where we are going/whether we are on the right road.*

**2** to ensure (that something happens): [T5] *I'm making sure that the hotel will have a room for us, by paying in advance. I'll make sure that you get the job, I have influence with the director.*

**3** to feel no doubt about something: [T5 (*usu. simple tenses*)] *I made sure that I would get the job, but it was given to someone else.*

***make sure of** *v adj prep* → **make certain of, make of** (8, 52)

**1** to know (something) without doubt: [T1 (*no pass.*)] *I hope the speaker has made sure of his facts. I made sure of his safe arrival.*

**2** to take action so as to succeed in having (something): [T1] *To make sure of a table in the restaurant, it is wise to telephone earlier. Make sure of your position in the firm before you argue with the director. The best seats can only be made sure of by having a regular ticket to the theatre.*

**make through** *v prep* → **thread through** (2)

**make one's way through** to pass with effort and care through (something such as a crowd or forest): *At busy times it's difficult to make your way through the crowds in the station. The early discoverers had to make their way through the thick forest with axes and knives.*

**make to** *v prep*

**1 make advances to: a** to make an offer, as in business, to (someone), so as to win something: *The international company has been making advances to our shareholders in the hope of gaining control of our small firm. The association asked me to make advances to the minister.* **b** to make an offer, as in love, to (someone), so as to win him/her: *This man has been making unwelcome advances to me; how can I get rid of him?*

**2 make amends to** to repay (someone) for harm done: *I will make amends to the firm for the time that I have wasted. You must make amends to your aunt for the window that you broke.* → **make for** (7)

**3 make application to** *fml* to make an official request to (someone or a group): *Application must be made to the correct division of government services for help with the cost.* → **apply to** (2)

**4 make approaches to** to ask (someone) humbly (for something): *The union leaders decided to make approaches to the employers for improvements in working conditions.*

**5 make a difference to** to have an effect on (something or someone), esp. in such a way as to cause a change: *It's made such a difference to my work, having my own room to work in. Does it make any difference to you whether you live in the city or the country? No difference has been made to the unemployment rate by the government's action.*

**6 make love to** to kiss and hold (someone) fondly; have sex with (someone): *Why don't you want to make love to me any more? "Make love to me," she whispered; he needed no persuasion.*

**7 make to measure** to make (an article of clothing) specially to fit someone: [*usu. pass.*] *He was so fat that all his clothes had to be made to measure. We have these suits to choose from, or I can make you one to measure.* —**made-to-measure** *adj*

**8 make something to order** to make something specially at someone's request: [*usu. pass.*] *We can make other styles to order. Wedding cakes can be made to order.* —**made-to-order** *adj*

**9 make overtures to** *not fml* to try to win the favour or agreement of (someone or a group), as by making an offer: *You won't persuade the owner of the house to reduce the price by making overtures to him. If you make overtures to enough firms you should be able to discover if any one has suitable work for you.* → **soften up** (3)

***make towards** *v prep* → **make for** (2)

*fml* to move in the direction of (something or someone): [T1 (*no pass.*)] *Traffic making towards the city is being delayed this morning. "I made steadily but slowly towards them."* (R.L. Stevenson, *Treasure Island*)

***make up** *v adv*

**1** to put a surface on (a road): [T1 (*usu. pass.*)] *When are the council going to make up this road? The road should be made up next year.* —**made-up** *adj*

**2** to repay a loss of (money or time): [T1] *You must make up the time that you have wasted this afternoon, by working late tonight. When the money was stolen, his father offered to make up the loss.* → **make good** (2)

**3** to invent (a story, poem, excuse, etc.): [T1] *I couldn't remember a fairy story to tell to the children, so I made one up as I went along.* → **dream up, think up**

**4** to change the appearance of one's face etc., with special paint and powder: [IØ] *Fewer women are making up these days, many prefer a more natural look.* [T1] *It took two hours every morning to make up the film actor for his character part. Wait a minute while I make up my face.* —**make-up** *n*

**5** to be part of; complete (a set, total, sum of money, etc.): [T1 (*usu. simple tenses*)] *Will you come, to make up the party? These three articles make up the whole book. The coat and trousers make up a suit. Can anyone make up a four at tennis? More men are needed to make up the police force to its full strength. She had to make up her income as a pianist b* *teaching piano students. He generously made up the necessary amount.*

**6** to arrange; put (something) together or in order: [T1] *Can you make up these papers into parcels of about twenty each? I'm making up a parcel of food to send to the children at camp. The train is made up but is not yet ready to start.*

**7** to fulfil (a written order), as by preparing something: [T1] *One of your jobs will be to make up the customers' orders. The chemist is still making up the doctor's order, and says it will be ready in half an hour.*

**8** to mix (a medicine): [T1] *My grandmother used to make up her own medicines.*

**9** to arrange (a page) for printing: [T1] *We need someone with experience of making up a page.* —**make-up** *n*

**10** to form (something) as a whole: [T1 (*often pass.*)] *Different qualities make up a person's character. The board of directors is made up of experienced men and women. The tea is made up from a mixture of several different types.* —**make-up** *n*

**11** to get ready (a new bed or hotel room): [T1] *We can make you up a bed on the floor, if you don't mind that. Many more wounded people are arriving at the hospital, but the beds are not made up for them yet. Leave this notice hanging on your door, asking the servant to make up your room.*

**12** to get (something such as food) ready: [T1] *Would you like me to make (you) up a packed meal for the journey?*

**13** to sew (cloth) into garments: [T1 (*often simple tenses*)] *This shop will make up a customer's own material.* [IØ (*into*) (*simple tenses*)] *This length of cloth should make up into three pairs of trousers.*

**14** to be friends again after (a quarrel): [T1 (*with*)] *Jim and Mary usually make up their quarrel the same day. Has Jim made it up with Mary yet?* [IØ (*usu. simple tenses*)] *Why don't you two kiss and make up?* → **patch up** (3), **stitch up** (2)

**15** to keep (a fire) burning by adding more wood, coal, etc.: [T1] *This wood burns so quickly that we have to make the fire up every hour.*

**16** *AmE* to take as an addition (an examination or course), often because of failure or lack of something such as a subject, regarded as necessary: [IØ] *I have three courses to make up before I can get my degree. Did you have to make up any of your examinations, or did you pass them all?* —**make-up** *adj*

**17 make up leeway** to reach a level where one should have been except for delay, etc.: *Since taking a short holiday, I have had to work more hours every day as I have such a lot of leeway to make up.*

**18 make up one's mind** to decide: *I can't make up my mind between these two dishes that the restaurant offers. First you say one thing and then another—make up your mind, can't you? My mind is made up; don't confuse me with facts.*

***make up for** *v adv prep*

**1** to repay someone for; provide a balance for (something lost or missed): [T1 (*pass. rare*)] *This beautiful autumn is making up for the wet summer. What he lacks in speed he makes up for in strength. You have a lot of faults to make up for.* → **compensate for, recompense for, recoup for, reimburse for, remunerate for, repay for** (1), (2), etc.

**2 make up for lost ground/time** to work hard or quickly, because of time, etc., lost earlier: *I had to work twice as hard to make up for lost time.*

**make up from** *v adv prep* → **MAKE FROM**

**make up into** *v adv prep* → **MAKE INTO** (1)

***make up on** *v adv prep*

to come nearer (someone ahead of one in a race): [T1] *Our horse was last, but now he is beginning to make up on the other runners.*

***make up to** *v adv prep*

**1** to add to, so as to complete (something): [D1] *If you give what you can, I'll make the money up to the full amount.*

**2** *not fml* to repay (someone) with good things in return for something good done or something bad experienced by him/her, esp. in the phr. **make it up to someone**: [D1] *What a pity you missed the concert through being ill; never mind, we'll make it up to you next year. There's nothing you can do that will make up to me for forgetting my birthday.*

**3** *not fml* to try to gain the favour of (someone), sometimes in a sexual sense: [T1] *It's no good making up to your brother, he won't help you. Some students make up to their teachers to get good marks. He tried to make up to her but she refused to have anything to do with him.* → **play up to** (2), **shine up to, suck up to**

**make useful** *v adj*

**make oneself useful** to perform helpful actions: *Why don't you make yourself useful instead of sitting around all day? There's plenty of work waiting in the garden.*

**make with** *v prep*

**1** to form; shape; produce (something) by using (something) or together with (someone): [T1 + *with*] *This cake is made with six eggs, which give it a rich taste.*

***2** esp. *AmE infml* to produce (something): [T1 (*no pass., often simple tenses*)] *When are you going to make with the music, man?*

**3 make a deal with** to have a business arrangement with (someone); agree to exchange favours with (someone): *The firm has made a deal with the government for six of its fighter planes. I'll make a deal with you: you cook the meal and I'll wash the dishes.*

**4 make free with** → **MAKE FREE WITH**

**5 make friends with** to form a friendly or pleasant relationship with (someone), often not formerly known: *Have you made friends with anyone in the new city yet?* → **make of** (17)
**6 make headway with** to gain an advanced position with (something) or in a relationship with (someone): *Are you making any headway with that pile of letters yet? We haven't made any headway with our new neighbours yet, they still seem afraid to meet us.*
**7 make a hit with** *infml* to have a successful effect on (someone); be favoured by or popular with (someone): *The young singer has made a hit with the public, and will soon be well-known.*
**8 make peace with** to end a war with (usu. a nation): *When the new ruler came to power, he made peace with all his country's former enemies.*
**9 make one's peace with** to end a quarrel with (someone); settle one's affairs with (God) at the end of one's life: [*often simple tenses*] *You'll have to make your peace with your neighbour if you are to go on living in the same village. Having made his peace with his Maker, he died calmly.*
**10 make play with** to handle or mention (something) in order to make an effect: [*usu. simple tenses*] *The speaker made great play with his opponent's weaknesses of argument. He made much play with the controls of his new car, so that his friends would have a high opinion of it.*
**11 make shift with** to be forced to use (something) for want of the correct or a better thing: [*often simple tenses*] *The shop had no more supplies of the best coffee, so we shall have to make shift with these poor quality beans.* —**makeshift** *n, adj*

**manage with** *v prep*
to use; succeed with (something, usu. not the best): [IØ + *with*] *We shall have to manage with these old pencils.*

***manage without**[1] *v adv* → **do without**[1], **go without**[1]
to continue to live in spite of lacking something: [IØ] *If we can't afford a new car, we shall have to manage without.*

***manage without**[2] *v prep* → **do without**[2] (1), **go without**[2] (2), **live without**
to live or continue in spite of the lack of (something, someone, or doing something): [T1] *I can't manage without a good night's sleep if I am to do a good day's work. The director should not have to manage without a secretary. Can you manage without help?* [T4] *Mr Sharp is not here, you will have to manage without speaking to him.*

**mangle up** *v adv*
to spoil (something such as part of the body or an idea) by wounding or treating it very badly: [T1 + UP (*often pass.*)] *I could hardly recognize the body of the driver, as it had been badly mangled up in the accident. I wrote a good speech for him, but he mangled it up and may have lost votes.*

**map out** *v adv*
**1** to show (something) in detail on a map: [T1 + OUT] *Some of the mountains in South America have not yet been mapped out.* → **lay down** (8), **set down** (6)
***2** to plan; organize (time, an event, etc., esp. in the future): [T1] *I like to map out the whole week in advance. Tom is already mapping out his next book.*

**mar up** *v adv*
to spoil the appearance of (something): [T1 + UP (*usu. pass.*)] *The surface of the table was badly marred up.*

***march past** *v adv*
to march in a ceremony past an officer: [IØ] *A division of soldiers who won honour for their bravery in the last war will march past during this afternoon's ceremony.* —**march-past** *n*

**mark down** *v adv*
**1** to record; write (something) down so as to remember it: [X9 + DOWN] *I marked down the address that she gave me over the telephone, and took care not to lose it.* → **write down** (1), etc.
***2** to choose; notice and remember (something or someone): [T1] *I marked down the spot as a suitable place for camping. The police have him marked down as a possible criminal.* → **mark out** (2)
***3** to reduce (goods) in price: [T1] *Some of the sale goods have been marked down by as much as 50%.* —**markdown** *n* → **mark up** (4) **write down** (4), **write up** (7)
***4** (of a teacher) to lower the marks given to (a student); regularly give low marks to (someone): [T1] *This teacher tends to mark students down even when they deserve a better result for their work.* → **mark up** (5)

**mark for** *v prep*
**1** (of a teacher) to mark (someone's work paying special attention to (a certain part) [T1 + *for*] *This time I shall not mark you English exercises for spelling and grammar but I shall be looking for pleasing expression.*
**2 be marked for** to seem to be chosen by fate for (a result): *All his life, this young man ha been marked for success.*
**3 mark someone for life** to make a lasting wound in the body or effect on the mind, etc. on someone: [*simple tenses*] *After the ca crash, the driver's face was marked for life Terrible grief can mark a mother for life.*

**mark in** *v adv*
to add (something) by marking it on paper [X9 + IN] *The local schools have bee marked in on this map so that parents ca choose a house in a suitable area. Mark in th changes you have made to the music.*

***mark off** *v adv*
to separate (something) by marking it with c

as with a line, etc.: [T1] *The builders have marked off a corner of the field ready for the new building. Life often seems to be marked off into different periods: schooldays, marriage, old age, for example.*

**mark out** *v adv*

**1** to mark (something such as a tennis court) with lines, often of paint: [X9 + OUT] *Now that it's spring, we must mark the tennis court out ready for play.*

*__2__ to make a note of (someone), usu. for advance in his work: [T1 (*as, for*) (*usu. pass.*)] *For some time, the directors have had you marked out as worthy of consideration for a better position in the firm.* → **mark down** (2)

**mark up** *v adv*

**1** to make a lot of usu. dirty marks on (something): [T1 + UP] *My floor is all marked up with their muddy boots!*

**2** to record; write (something) in public view: [X9 + UP] *A boy was kept busy marking up the runs on a board.* → **write up** (1)

*__3__ to charge (something such as alcohol) to someone's account: [T1 (*to*)] *I've no money to pay for the beer, will you mark it up (to me)?* → **chalk up** (2), etc.

*__4__ to fix the selling price of (goods); raise (goods) in price so as to make a profit: [T1] *Cigarettes will have to be marked up now that the tax on them has been increased. The shops often mark up the goods unfairly, so that the customer pays too much while the producer gets too little.* —**markup** *n, adj* → **mark down** (3), **write down, write up** (7)

*__5__ (of a teacher) to raise the marks of (a student); regularly give high marks to (someone): [T1] *Teachers have been given instructions to mark up the weaker students rather than run the risk of having half the class fail.* → **mark down** (4)

*__6__ to make notes on (written material) ready for printing: [T1] *You have to learn how to mark up your article for the printer.*

**mark with** *v prep*

**1** to make a mark on (something) by using or because of (something): [T1 + *with*] *Workmen are out marking the road with white lines. This skirt has got badly marked with engine oil.*

**2** (of a teacher) to make remarks and corrections on (someone's work) using (ink, pencil, etc.): [T1 + *with*] *Spelling mistakes have been marked with red ink.* [IØ + *with*] *I always mark with a red pencil so that the mistakes are easy to see.*

**3** to put a description on (something) of (something): [T1 + *with*] *All articles of clothing should be clearly marked with the owner's name.* → **label with**

**4 be marked with** to show clear signs of (something): *Her face is marked with years of suffering.*

**maroon on** *v prep* → **strand on**

to go away leaving (someone) on (usu. an island) without means of escape: [T1 + *on* (*usu. simple tenses*)] *The sailors took command of the ship from the cruel captain and marooned him on a desert island.*

**marry above** *v prep* → **marry beneath**

**marry above oneself/one's station** to marry someone of a higher social level: *The actress married above herself when a lord fell in love with her after seeing her performance at the theatre. No good can come of your marrying above your station!*

**marry beneath** *v prep* → **marry above**

**marry beneath one/oneself/one's station** to marry someone of a lower social level: *In former times, if a gentleman married beneath him, he would lose his share of the family fortune.*

**marry into** *v prep*

to gain (something) or join (a group) by marriage: [IØ + *into*] *What luck she had, marrying into money! Many parents want their daughters to marry into a good family.*

***marry off** *v adv*

(of a parent) to find a husband for (a daughter): [T1 (*usu. pass.*)] *I shall be glad when the last of my daughters is married off, then I might have some peace of mind.*

***marry up** *v adv* → **join up** (2), **link up**

to (cause to) join or fit together (with someone or something else): [IØ (*with*)] *Scattered groups of soldiers tried to marry up with each other after the army's defeat. We plan to marry up with the other party of climbers on the other side of the mountain.* [T1] *Can you marry up the two halves of the broken plate?*

**marry with** *v prep*

**1** *old use* to marry (someone): [T1] *"A bloody deed! almost as bad, good mother, As kill a king, and marry with his brother."* (Shakespeare, *Hamlet*)

**2 be married with** to be combined with: *Married with excellent taste is the writer's power of expressing the deep feelings of his characters.*

**marshal together** *v adv*

to gather (people or things such as qualities) together: [T1 + TOGETHER] *To write a good article, you need to marshal all the facts together and then judge and arrange them. All the soldiers were marshalled together in the yard, ready to march away.*

**marvel at** *v prep* → **wonder at**

to find (something or someone) surprising or wonderful: [IØ + *at*] *Even the cleverest people marvel at a child's ability to learn his native language in such a short time. I marvel at you sometimes, you behave so stupidly!*

**mash up** *v adv*

**1** to mix (potatoes) with milk and butter by beating them with a fork or other tool: [T1 + UP] *Yes, you can help, you can mash up the potatoes for me.*

*__2__ to damage or wound (something or someone) by pressing: [T1] *Two cars were mashed up in a bad crash on the main road.* → **smash up**, etc.

***mask out** *v adv*
(in photography) to cover (part of the picture) before printing it, so that it is removed from the finished photograph: [T1] *If we mask out those bushes in the bottom corner, the photograph will have a better balance.*

**mask with** *v prep*
**1** to cover (the eyes or other part of the face) with (a mask): [T1 + *with*] *Doctors and nurses working in an operating theatre have to mask their noses and mouths with a specially clean cloth.*
**2** to hide (something such as one's feelings or intentions) with (a pretence); hide (a taste) with (another taste): [T1 + *with*] *She masked her suffering with a cheerful smile, and no one doubted her pretended happiness. Most criminals mask their guilt with excuses. The cook masked the taste of the bad meat with onions.*

***masquerade as** *v prep* → **pose as**
to pretend to be (someone or something else): [T1 (*no pass.*)] *The thief got into the house by masquerading as a television repairman.*

**match against** *v prep*
**1** to equal; compare (something) with (something): [T1 + *against* (*usu. simple tenses*)] *How can we match our generosity against theirs?* → **match with** (2)
***2** to arrange a fight between (someone) and (an opponent): [D1 (*often pass.*)] *In his youth, he was matched against some of the most famous fighters of his day.* → **match with** (3)
***3** to oppose (something) to (something): [D1] *Are you willing to match your skill against that of our leading player? I'll match my strength against his any day.* → **match with** (4), **pit against**

**match up** *v adv*
to (cause to) fit; suit; balance: [T1 + UP] *It took hours to match up the torn pieces of the letter from the waste basket. How do you match up these opposing pieces of information from two different government departments?* [IØ + UP (*simple tenses*)] *The coat was not bought at the same time as the trousers, but they match up well enough to be considered a suit.*

***match up to** *v adv prep* → **measure up to**
to be equal to or the same as (something such as an idea): [T1 (*usu. simple tenses*)] *Can the boy match up to his father's hopes for him? The prisoner matches up to the description the police have of the wanted jewel thief.*

**match with** *v prep*
**1** to (cause to) suit; be the same kind as (something), as in colour or style: [IØ + *with* (*simple tenses*)] *It's hard to find words that match well with this music.* [T1 + *with* (*usu. simple tenses*)] *Take care to match the sewing thread with the cloth so that the stitches, being of the same colour, will not show. A good poet matches the movement of his lines with suitable words.* → **fit to** (2), **pair with** (1), **suit to** (1)
**2** to equal (something) with (something): [T1 + *with*] *We should match their generosity with our own. The government has promised to match the council's gift to the university with an equal payment. "Now God be thanked who has matched us with His hour, And caught our youth, and wakened us from sleeping."* (Rupert Brooke, *Peace*) → **match against** (1)
***3** to arrange a fight between (someone) and (an opponent): [D1 (*often pass.*)] *In his youth, he was matched with some of the most famous fighters of his day.* → **match against** (2)
***4** to oppose (something) to (something): [D1 (*usu. simple tenses*)] *I'll match my skill/strength with his any day.* → **match against** (3), **pit against**
***5** to join (someone) in marriage with (someone): [D1 (*simple tenses*)] *I should be pleased to match my daughter with your son, so that we could become even closer friends.*

**mate with** *v prep*
(esp. of animals) to (cause to) be joined in sexual union: [IØ + *with*] *Dogs do not mate with cats.* [T1 + *with*] *Farmers keep trying to produce better cattle by mating their strongest bulls with their healthiest cows.*

**matter to** *v prep*
to be important to (someone): [IØ + *to* (*simple tenses*)] *My health matters more to my doctor than to my family. Does it matter to you what people say?*

**maul about/around** *v adv*
to handle (someone or something) roughly, often causing damage or other harm: [T1 + ABOUT/AROUND] *Stop pulling my arm, you've no right to maul me about like this! The newspapers have mauled Tom's book about unmercifully. I can't wear that hat after it's been mauled about by the dog!*

**mean by** *v prep*
to intend (a meaning) through or by means of (something such as speech, action, or doing something): [IØ + *by* (*simple tenses*)] *What do you mean by that remark? Were you trying to be rude again? I meant nothing by it at all! I don't know what is meant by "equal pay for work of equal value." What do you mean by opening my letters without permission?*

***mean for** *v prep*
**1** to intend (something) to be received by (someone or something): [D1 (*simple tenses*)] *Some of the jokes in this play are not meant for children's ears. Wasn't that parcel meant for me? The praise seems to be meant for your performance, not mine.*
**2 be meant for** to be intended by or as if by fate for (a way of life): *He seems to have been meant for the Church from an early age.* → **make for** (5)

**mean to** *v prep*
**1** to express the idea of (something), as

understood by (someone): [T1 + *to* (*simple tenses*)] *The smell means dinner to the dog! Having my family around me means happiness to me. He spoke in a strange language that meant nothing to me.*

*__2__ to have (an amount of) importance for (someone), as in feeling: [D1 (*no pass., simple tenses*)] *It was a worthless toy, but it meant a lot to the child. Don't you know how much you mean to me? Money means everything to him. That red-haired boy broke Grace's heart by telling her that she meant nothing to him.*

**mean well** *v adv*

**1** to do or say what is intended to help, but often doesn't: [IØ (*by*) (*simple tenses*)] *He makes a lot of mistakes in his work, but he means well.*

**2 mean well by someone** to intend to do what is best for someone: *I wasn't hungry; I only ate that big meal because your mother meant well by us.*

**measure against** *v prep*

**measure swords/one's strength against** → MEASURE WITH

**measure off** *v adv*

to measure and usu. take (an amount) from a larger piece: [T1] *Please measure off enough cloth for three pairs of trousers. The salesman measured off three metres of the wood.*

**measure out** *v adv*

**1** to give (something) out little by little: [T1 (*often simple tenses*)] *This medicine must be measured out exactly. Life measures out its rewards in ways unrelated to how people deserve them.*

**2 measure out one's length** to fall flat: *Suddenly feeling faint, he measured out his length on the floor.*

**measure up** *v adv*

**1** to measure (something or someone): [T1 + UP (*often simple tenses*)] *I have to go to the shop to be measured up for my suit. Measure the wall up carefully, we don't want to buy too much wallpaper.* [IØ + UP (*usu. continuous tenses*)] *You'll find Father on top of the ladder, measuring up.*

*__2__ to guess at the size or quality of (something): [T1] *Take a little time to measure up your chances before deciding.*

*__3__ to prove one's worth: [IØ (*often simple tenses*)] *I always give new workers a short contract to begin with, as I want to see how they measure up before I employ them on a lasting basis.*

**measure up to** *v adv prep* → **match up to**

to be equal to or the same as (something): [T1 (*usu. simple tenses*)] *Each one of us has an imaginary perfect person inside us, that we try to measure up to. The prisoner measures up to the description the police have of the wanted jewel thief.*

**measure with/against** *v prep*

**measure swords/one's strength with/against** to test one's ability in opposing (someone): *I remember when I first measured swords with you and you defeated my argument in two minutes! I like to measure my strength against a worthy opponent.*

**meddle in** *v prep* → **interfere in**

to concern oneself and usu. take unwanted action about (something which is not one's concern): [IØ + *in*] *Don't meddle in matters that don't concern you; mind your own business.*

**meddle with** *v prep*

**1** to touch or cause damage to (something that is not one's concern): [IØ + *with*] *Somebody's been meddling with my papers again; I do wish everyone would leave them alone, I have them carefully organized.* → **be at** (5), **get at** (7), **interfere with** (1), **mess about with** (1), etc., **monkey with, tamper with**

*__2__ to have an improper relationship with (someone, usu. of the opposite sex): [T1] *I warned you not to meddle with married women, it always leads to trouble.* → **mess about with** (2), etc.

**mediate between** *v prep* → **liaise between**

*fml* to go between (two opposing parties) trying to arrange an agreement between them: [IØ + *between*] *A well-known local lawyer has been appointed to mediate between the employers and the union leaders, since they cannot reach agreement in direct talks.*

**meditate on** *v prep*

to think deeply and sincerely about (a subject): [IØ + *on*] *Thinking men have long meditated on the meaning of life.*

**meet halfway** *v adv*

**1** to join (usu. someone) at a midway point in a journey: [T1 + HALFWAY] *When my daughter was working in the North, we went to visit her; but she came south on a bus and met us halfway, at a little town where the two roads join.*

*__2__ to agree to some of the argument or demand by (someone) in order to gain part of a victory: [T1b] *The employers refused to give the workers the whole pay rise that they demanded, but offered to meet them halfway, paying some of the increase that they had asked for.*

**meet up** *v adv* → **meet with** (1)

*not fml* to meet (someone), esp. by chance: [IØ + UP (*with*)] *Many years were to pass before we met up again. I was so pleased to meet up with my old friend after all these years.*

**meet with** *v prep*

**1** esp. *AmE or lit* to meet (someone) or find (something), esp. by chance: [IØ + *with* (*simple tenses*)] *I met with an old friend in the town today!* → **happen on**, etc., **meet up**

*__2__ to have a formal meeting and talk with (someone or a group): [D1] *The politician will meet with his opposite number in the Foreign Ministry of the host country while he is on* *his official visit, to talk about matters of common concern. High school teachers are meeting with the Ministry of Education to talk about their demands for an increase in pay and a reduction in the size of classes.*

*3 to experience (something): [T1 (*no pass., simple tenses*)] *On my travels through the country, I met with kindness and consideration from ordinary people in the villages. Did your book meet with much success?*

*4 to receive (an opinion): [T1 (*pass. rare, simple tenses*)] *His suggestion met with a firm refusal. Did you meet with much opposition from the rest of the committee? The idea has met with approval but has proved too costly to perform.*

*5 to suffer (something such as misfortune): [T1 (*no pass., simple tenses*)] *I'm afraid your husband has met with a slight accident, but he isn't seriously hurt. Criminals who lead violent lives often meet with violent death.*

**melt away** *v adv*

**1** (of something solid, esp. frozen) to disappear by melting: [IØ + AWAY] *As the ice melted away, the river rose in dangerous floods.*

***2** to disappear gradually: [IØ] *His doubt soon melted away when he found that he could trust the other members. The crowd melted away as soon as the police arrived.*

***melt down** *v adv*

to change the shape of (a precious metal object) by heating it until it is liquid, for the value of its raw material: [T1] *Some of the stolen jewellery, such as the gold rings and silver candlesticks, can be melted down and sold for the value of the precious metal.*

**melt in** *v prep*

**1** to become part of (a liquid into which it is put) by melting: [IØ + *in*] *Salt melts in water.* → **dissolve in** (1), **dissolve into** (1), **melt into** (1)

**2 melt in one's mouth** (of food) to taste very pleasant and be easy to eat: *You need a light hand with pastry if it is to melt in the mouth as it should.*

**melt into** *v prep*

**1** to become (a liquid) by melting: [IØ + *into*] *I warmed the butter for too long, and it has melted into liquid. The tiger ran round and round the tree so fast that in the end he melted into a pool of butter.* (old story) → **melt in** (1), **dissolve into** (1)

***2** to disappear by becoming part of (something) gradually: [T1] *It is difficult to tell where the blue melts into the green.* → **dissolve in** (2), **dissolve into** (2)

**3 melt into tears** to begin to weep freely: *Mary melted into tears as Jim walked away without kissing her.* → **dissolve in** (3), **dissolve into** (3)

**mention in** *v prep*

**1** to speak or write about (someone or something) in (something written, printed, or spoken): [T1 + *in*] *In the introduction to his book, Tom mentioned his debt to his family for their help. The shameful affair was not mentioned in his speech to the House.*

**2 be mentioned in dispatches** *mil* (of a member of the armed forces) to receive an honourable mention of one's name in official papers, usu. as a reward for bravery, service, etc.: *The young motorcycle messenger was mentioned in dispatches during the war.*

**mention to** *v prep*

to speak about (something or someone) to (someone): [T1 + *to* (*often simple tenses*)] *Have I mentioned my holiday plans to you?* [T5 + *to* (*usu. simple tenses*)] *You didn't mention to me that you were only staying for a short time.* [T6 + *to* (*usu. simple tenses*)] *You didn't mention to me when you are leaving.*

**merge into** *v prep* → **merge with**

to (cause to) mix with, so as to become part of (something): [L9 + *into*] *The red sunset merged into darkness. The animal's colouring enabled it to merge into the forest.* [X9 + *into*] *The directors intend to merge the small firms into one large company.*

**merge together** *v adv* → **amalgamate with, combine with** (1), **merge with**

to (cause to) combine: [L9 + TOGETHER] *Don't paint the two colours next to each other, or they will merge together while the paint is wet.* [X9 + TOGETHER] *The directors have decided to merge the two small firms together.*

**merge with** *v prep* → **amalgamate with, combine with** (1), **merge into, merge together**

to combine (one thing) with (another, formerly separate): [X9 + *with*] *The members decided to merge the tennis club with the cricket club, forming one combined sports club.* *[T1 (*no pass.*)] *The company has decided to merge with the parent firm.*

**mesh with** *v prep*

**1** (of a wheel having teeth) to seize and lock onto (another wheel having teeth): [IØ + *with*] *There's something wrong with this machine; the wheels aren't meshing properly with each other.*

***2** to agree with; be the same as; fit (something): [T1 (*no pass., simple tenses*)] *I'm afraid that your ideas don't quite mesh with mine. This doesn't mesh with the idea that I was given of the work in this office.*

***mess about/around** *v adv*

**1** *infml* to spend time lazily, doing things slowly and with no particular plan: [IØ] *"What have you been doing today?" "Oh, nothing, just messing about."* → **arse about, bugger about** (1), **fool about, footle about, fuck about** (1), **fuck off** (1), **goof off, hack around, hell around, idle about, laze about, muck about** (1), **piss about** (1), **play about**[1]

**2** *infml* to act or speak stupidly: [IØ] *Come on, stop messing about and tell me clearly what happened.* → **fool about, footle about**

**3** *not fml* to cause disorder to (something); treat (something) carelessly: [T1b] *The bank* *has been messing my account around again; I think I shall move my money to another bank. Who's been messing my papers about?* → **bugger about** (3)

**4** *not fml* to treat (someone) carelessly or inconsiderately: [T1b] *I can't forgive him for messing me about. If you want to marry the girl, ask her; if you don't, then leave her alone —but at any rate, don't mess her about. Jim said the doctors has only messed him about in hospital; he felt worse when he came out than when he went in.* → **bugger about** (2), **fuck about** (2), **muck about** (2), **piss about** (2)

**mess about/around with** *v adv prep*

**1** to cause disorder to (something): [T1] *Who's been messing about with my papers? They're all out of order.* → **bugger about with, fool about with** (1), **fool with, fuck about with, meddle with** (1), etc., **mess with** (2), **muck about with, piss about with, play about with** (2)

**2** *not fml* to have an improper relationship with (someone, usu. of the opposite sex): [T1] *I warned you not to mess about with married women, it always leads to trouble.* → **fool about with** (2), **meddle with** (2), **mess with** (3)

**mess around** *v adv* → MESS ABOUT

**mess around with** *v adv prep* → MESS ABOUT WITH

**mess together** *v adv* → **mess with** (1)

*mil* to eat one's meals in the same place: [L9 + TOGETHER (*usu. simple tenses*)] *In this camp, only the officers mess together.*

**mess up** *v adv*

**1** to make (someone or something) dirty or untidy: [T1] *Try not to mess up your new dress before the party. May I wash my hands? I'm all messed up after working on the car. This wind will mess my hair up.* → **dirty up** (1), **foul up** (1), **muck up** (1)

**2** *not fml* to spoil (something) carelessly: [T1] *If John messes up his driving test again, I doubt if he'll ever pass it. Our travel arrangements have been messed up by the ticket office. Her late arrival messed up our plans.*

—**mess-up** *n* → **ball up** (2), **balls up, bitch up, botch up, bugger up, cock up** (2), **foul up** (2), **goof up, gum up** (2), **hash up** (2), **louse up, make of** (24), **muck up** (2), **prang up** (2), **screw up** (3)

**mess with** *v prep*

**1** *mil* to eat one's meals with (someone): [L9 + *with* (*usu. simple tenses*)] *In this camp, private soldiers do not mess with officers, but have a separate cookhouse.* → **mess together**

***2** to cause disorder to (something): [T1] *Somebody's been messing with my papers, they're all out of order.* → **mess about with** (1), etc.

***3** *not fml* to treat (someone) carelessly or inconsiderately, esp. in sexual matters; have to do with (someone) in an improper way: [T1] *I hear you've been messing with married women in spite of my advice. Don't mess with me, young man, tell me the truth. Who's been messing with my daughter?* → **mess about with** (2), etc.

***metamorphose into** *v prep* → **change into** (2), etc.

*rare* to change esp. the shape of (something or someone) into (something or someone different): [D1 (*usu. simple tenses*)] *The evil magician metamorphosed the prince into a beggar. In only a few years, this pleasant little town has been metamorphosed into a forest of ugly high office blocks, crowded streets, and poor housing.*

***mete out** *v adv* → **deal out** (2)

*fml* to give; make decisions about and see that people receive (something such as reward or punishment, esp. justice): [T1] *We need a judge who will mete out justice with a firm hand.*

**migrate between** *v prep*

(of animals and esp. birds) to travel for the winter and summer seasons between (different places, as northern and southern parts of the world): [IØ + *between*] *Birds are so sensible, migrating between the north and south, according to the weather; I wish we could do the same!*

**migrate from** *v prep*

(of animals and esp. birds) to travel regularly from (a place) when the weather becomes unsuitable: [IØ + *from*] *I wish we could migrate from here every winter, as the birds do!*

**migrate to** *v prep*

(esp. of fish and birds) to travel regularly to (another place) when the weather becomes unsuitable: [IØ + *to*] *These birds migrate to Europe in the summer season, returning to warmer places in the south for the winter. Wealthy people often migrate in winter to warmer sunnier countries.*

***mill about/around** *v adv*

*infml* (usu. of people or animals) to move without purpose, in large numbers: [IØ (*usu. continuous tenses*)] *There were crowds of people milling about in the streets. So many different ideas are milling about in my head, but I can't settle down to work on any one of them.*

***mind out** *v adv*

**1** *not fml* to take care; be watchful; move out of the way: [IØ (*often imper.*)] *Mind out! Somebody's trying to open the door! You'll catch cold if you don't mind out.* [I5 (*often imper.*)] *Mind out (that) you don't catch cold.* [I6 (*often imper.*)] *Mind out where you're walking, the ground is muddy.* → **look out** (2), **watch out** (1)

**2 mind out of the way** *not fml* to move to one side, as to let someone pass: [*often imper.*] *Can't you mind out of the way? You're standing right in the middle of the path!*

**mine as** *v prep*

to take (a mineral) from the ground in the form of (something): [T1 + *as* (*usu. pass.*)]

*Some of the world's supply of salt is mined as rock salt.*

***mine out** *v adv* → **farm out** (5), **fish out** (3), **lay in**[1] (4), **work out** (8)
to take all the minerals from (a mine): [T1 (*usu. pass.*)] *The whole area has been mined out, the miners have left and the town is empty, since it depended on the mining industry.*

**mingle in** *v prep*
to join together in (a combination or large object): [L9 + *in* (*often simple tenses*)] *Several streams mingle in this river on its way to the sea.*

**mingle with** *v prep*
**1** also *fml* **commingle with** to (cause to) mix with (something): [L9 + *with*] *Tears mingled with the blood from the cut on his face.* [X9 + *with*] *I think I'll mingle some of these blue flowers with the pink ones.* → **mix with** (1)
***2** to join (a group of people): [T1 (*no pass.*)] *One of the hostess's duties is to mingle with the guests.* → **mix with** (2)

***minister to** *v prep* also **administer to**
to serve; perform duties to help (someone or something): [T1] *The patient nurse ministered to the dying woman. The rich man had many servants to minister to his needs.*

***misconceive of** *v prep* → **mistake about**
*fml* to have a wrong idea about (something): [T1 (*no pass., often simple tenses*)] *Great dangers can result from misconceiving of the enemy's intentions.*

**misconduct with** *v prep*
**misconduct oneself with** *fml* to behave immorally or improperly with; perform immoral acts with (someone of the opposite sex): *The judge decided that the wife had misconducted herself with the husband's friend, and the marriage should therefore end.*

***miss out** *v adv*
**1** to fail to include (something or someone): [T1 (*of*)] *Please complete this cheque properly; you have missed out the date. When you were planning the meal, you missed out the cheese. The organizer has missed Jim out* (*of the team*). *I notice that the advertisement misses out the price of the product.* → **delete from, erase from** (1), **leave out**[1] (3), **omit from**
**2** to pay no attention to (someone): [T1 (*usu. pass.*)] *It's Mary's own fault if she feels missed out at the party; she makes no effort to be friendly to people.* → **be out of** (14), **feel out of** (1), **leave out**[1] (5)
**3** *not fml* to lose a chance to gain advantage or enjoyment, etc.: [IØ (*on*) (*often continuous tenses*)] *Will you feel as if you're missing out if you don't take part in the concert? Living in the country, I often feel that I am missing out on the activities of city life.*

***mist over/up** *v adv* → **cloud over** (2), **cloud up, steam over, steam up** (1)
(usu. of a glass surface) to (cause to) become less transparent, usu. with a film of liquid: [IØ] *Her eyes misted over with tears. The windows have misted up in the steam.* [T1] *The steam has misted the windows over. His breath misted up his glasses in the cold air.*

**mistake about** *v prep* → **misconceive of**
**be mistaken about** to have the wrong idea about (something or someone): *You were mistaken about the time of the train, it has left. I was mistaken about that student, he's not as clever as I thought.*

***mistake for** *v prep* → **confuse with** (2), **take for** (3)
to think wrongly that (someone or something) is (someone or something else): [D1] *I mistook you for your brother, you're so much alike. The traveller mistook the house for a hotel, and the owner's daughter for a servant. Kindness is easily mistaken for love.*

***mitigate against** *v prep*
*fml* to make (something or doing something) difficult: [T1 (*usu. simple tenses*)] *"And this state of the case . . . didn't seem to have mitigated against our becoming rather fond of each other."* (J.I.M. Stewart, *The Madonna of the Astrolabe*)

**mix in** *v adv*
**1** also **blend in** to combine (something or things) by mixing: [T1 + IN] *After you have beaten the eggs, mix in the flour gradually.*
***2** to be able to have a friendly social relationship with other people: [IØ (*with*) (*often simple tenses*)] *Mary has never liked parties as she doesn't mix in very easily. Even as a child, she found it difficult to mix in with other children.*

**mix up** *v adv*
**1** to combine (something or things): [T1 + UP] *The children enjoy mixing up the fruit and nuts in the cake before it is cooked. "The British Empire and the United States will have to be somewhat mixed up together in some of their affairs."* (Winston Churchill, *Speech House of Commons, 20 August 1940*)
***2** to confuse; mix; mistake; disorder (things or ideas): [T1 (*with*) (*often pass.*)] *My papers are all mixed up, and I was trying to keep them in alphabetical order. I'm sorry I mixed up your names, you're so much alike. I got him mixed up with his brother. I have a terrible headache, and my thoughts are all mixed up.* —**mix-up** *n infml* → **jumble up, muddle up** (1)
**3** **be mixed up** *not fml* to be confused, esp. in one's feelings: *Give Jane time to settle down in her new school, she's sure to feel mixed up at first. No wonder the boy turned criminal, he had been mixed up all through his childhood.* —**mixed-up** *adj*

**mix up in** *v adv prep*
**be mixed up in** to be concerned in (something such as an activity, usu. unfavourable): *How many more people were mixed up in the shameful harbour matter? Don't get mixed u*

*in dirty politics if you can help it.*

**mix up with** *v adv prep*

**be mixed up with** to have a relationship with (someone, often undesirable): *I don't want my son to be mixed up with criminal types like those new friends he has made.*

**mix with** *v prep*

**1** to (cause to) be combined with (something): [T1 + *with*] *You can mix this paint with water or oil. Mix the eggs with the flour.* [L9 + *with* (*usu. simple tenses*)] *Oil will not mix with water.* → **mingle with** (1)

* **2** to move among (people), speaking to many: [T1 (*no pass.*)] *One of the hostess's duties is to mix with her guests as much as possible.* → **mingle with** (2)

**moan about** *v prep*

*not fml* to complain about (something or doing something), sometimes without cause: [IØ + *about* (*often continuous tenses*)] *She's always moaning about not being treated properly. What are you moaning about this time?*

**mock at** *v prep* → **laugh at** (2), etc.

to make fun of; make unkind remarks about (someone or something): [T1] *It's rude and cruel to mock at a foreign student's mistakes in English. At first the public mocked at the modern painter's works, but later they proved to be highly regarded and valuable.*

**mock up** *v adv*

*not fml* to make a copy of (something), usu. the same size but not using the proper materials: [T1 (*often simple tenses*)] *As we can't have the hall till the night of the performance, we can mock up a model of the actual stage for the company to practise on. Have you had experience in mocking up a page?* —**mock-up** *n, adj*

**model after/on/upon** *v prep* → **fashion after, pattern after**

**1** to form (something) as a copy of (something): [D1 (*often pass.*)] *The railway system was modelled on the successful plan used in other countries.*

**2** to make (oneself) like (someone); [D1 (*often simple tenses*)] *Mary has always modelled herself on her mother.*

**modulate from** *v prep*

(in music) to pass by regular steps from (one key) to another: [IØ + *from* (*usu. simple tenses*)] *At the end of this phrase, the music modulates from C to G.*

**modulate to** *v prep*

(in music) to pass by regular steps to (a different key): [IØ + *to* (*usu. simple tenses*)] *Music students learn how to add other parts to a given tune, and how to modulate to a related key.*

**mold from/out of** *v prep; adv prep AmE* → **MOULD FROM**

**monkey about/around** *v adv*

*not fml* to play, often so as to cause damage or harm: [IØ] *I knew a window would soon get broken, with all those children monkeying around in the garden.*

* **monkey with** *v prep* → **meddle with** (1), etc.

*not fml* to touch (something not one's concern) so as to harm it: [T1] *Somebody's been monkeying (around/about) with my papers again; I wish everyone would leave them alone, I have them carefully organized.*

* **mooch about/around** *v adv; prep*

*infml* to wander without aim, activity, or interest (around a place): [IØ; T1 (*no pass.*)] *There's nothing to do in this town except mooch around (the streets); no wonder the young people get into trouble.*

* **moon about/around** *v adv; prep* → **mope about**

*infml* to seem or behave unhappily, often because of love: [IØ; T1 (*no pass.*)] *Grace must still be in love with her red-haired boy; all that she's done since he left her is moon about (the house)—it's pitiful, really.*

* **moon away** *v adv* → **mope away**

*infml* to pass (time) in unhappy thoughts, esp. of love: [T1] *It's no use dreaming about that boy, he won't come back—are you going to moon away the whole of your life?*

**mop down** *v adv*

to clean (something such as a large floor) with a mop: [T1 + DOWN] *It takes two women half the morning to mop down the hospital floors.*

**mop up** *v adv*

**1** to clean; remove (liquid) with a mop: [T1 + UP] *You'd better mop up that pool of water on the floor before Mother sees it.* → **clean up** (1), **soak up** (1), **sop up, take up** (4), **wipe up** (1)

* **2** *mil* to deal with; finish off (remaining members of a defeated enemy force), as by killing or seizing them: [T1] *After we have mopped up the last few groups of the enemy, we can advance to our next position.* —**mopping-up** *adj* —**mop-up** *n* → **clean up** (6), **wipe up** (3)

* **3** to finish (something such as work): [T1] *I shall be glad to mop up the last of the office work that was waiting for me on my return from holiday.* → **finish off** (1), **finish up** (1), **polish off** (1)

**mop with** *v prep*

**1** to clean (something) with (something used as a mop): [T1 + *with*] *Mop this floor with this old cloth.* → **wipe with** (1)

**2 mop the floor with** *not fml* to defeat (someone) completely: *A team as good as ours should be able to mop the floor with any competitor.* → **wipe with** (2)

**mope about/around** *v adv; prep* → **moon about**

to spend time unhappily, without aim or activity, in a dull manner: [IØ + ABOUT/AROUND/*about/around*] *It's sad to see Jane moping about (the house) like this: what's the matter with her?*

* **mope away** *v adv* → **moon away**

to spend (time) unhappily, in dull sadness:

[T1] *Poor Jane has been moping the whole week away, I'm getting quite worried about her.*

**moralize about/on/over** *v prep*
to write or speak about (something) in a manner dealing with moral questions; explain the rights and wrongs of (something): [IØ + *about/on/over*] *The speaker began moralizing on the right way for people to behave, and his listeners soon lost interest.*

***motion aside/away** *v adv*
to signal to (someone), usu. with the hands, to move to one side or to leave: [T1] *Motioning aside the other people in the room, the director signalled to me to come forward. There was a crowd of people outside the door demanding to see the Minister; when the doorman motioned them away, they took no notice, but stayed there, shouting.*

***motion to** *v prep* → **signal to**
to signal to (someone), usu. with the hands (to do something): [T1] *The director motioned to me to come forward.*

**mould from/out of** *v prep; adv prep* also *AmE* **mold from**
to shape (an object) from (a material): [T1 + *from*/OUT + *of*] *According to most native stories, the first man was moulded from clay by some kind of god.*

**mount on** *v prep*
**1** to (cause to) climb onto (an animal or bicycle): [IØ + *on*] *Mounting on my bicycle, I rode at full speed down the street.* [T1 + *on* (*usu. pass.*)] *The policemen were mounted on specially trained horses.*
**2** to place (something), for show or use, on top of (something): [T1 + *on*] *The gun was mounted on a strengthened gun carriage to stand the shock of its movements.*

**mount to** *v prep*
**1** to rise as far as (something higher): [IØ + *to*] *The old man mounted with difficulty to the top of the steps. The colour mounted to Mary's face as she saw Jim looking at her.*
**2** to reach (something such as a finish) by climbing, increasing, etc.: [IØ + *to*] *The music mounts to a climax at the end of the first movement.*

***mount up** *v adv*
to increase; form a large amount gradually: [IØ] *It's easy not to notice when you're putting on weight, but the pounds mount up uncomfortably fast. Our debts have been mounting up this past year.*

**mourn for/over** *v prep* → **grieve for, lament for**
to grieve for (usu. someone): [IØ + *for/over*] *Mrs Page is still mourning for her dead son, a year after he was killed in the accident.*

**move about/around/round** *v adv*
**1** to (cause to) move from place to place: [T1 + ABOUT/AROUND/ROUND] *Oh, you've moved the furniture around again!* [IØ + ABOUT/AROUND/ROUND] *Listen, you can hear a small animal moving about in the bushes.*
**2** to (cause to) move from place to place, as to work: [IØ + ABOUT/AROUND/ROUND] *You have to move around a lot in this job.* [T1 + ABOUT/AROUND/ROUND] *In my work I have been moved about from city to city.*

**move ahead** *v adv* → **be ahead, draw ahead, get ahead, keep ahead, pull ahead, remain ahead, stay ahead**
**1** to lead; go in front: [IØ + AHEAD (*of*)] *The horse that we were hoping would win began to move ahead halfway through the race.* [T1 + AHEAD (*of*)] *If you throw a six, you can move your man ahead three squares.*
***2** to advance; go in front, esp. in a competition: [IØ (*of*)] *Our team were at the bottom of the local competition, but now they are moving ahead. If you want to move ahead in your job, take advice from more experienced workers.*

**move along** *v adv* → **move on** (1)
to go away; not stand in a group; esp. said by a policeman to a crowd: [IØ + ALONG (*usu. imper.*)] *Move along there, please!*

**move around** *v adv* → **MOVE ABOUT**

**move away** *v adv*
**1** to leave: [IØ + AWAY] *Losing interest, the crowd moved slowly away. The taxi had moved away before I could signal to the driver.*
**2** to leave the town or neighbourhood, to live somewhere else: [IØ + AWAY (*from*)] *I don't know where you'll find your sister after all these years, she moved away* (*from the town*) *a long time ago.* → **move back** (2)
***3** to change one's opinion so as not to favour (an idea): [IØ (*from*)] *I came gradually to move away from the position that I had always held, and to see the value of opposing opinions.* → **move towards** (2)

**move back** *v adv*
**1** to (cause to) move in a backward direction [IØ + BACK] *Move back! The roof is falling* [T1 + BACK] *If we move the table back, there'll be room for another chair.* → **get back** (1), **go back** (1), **keep back** (1), **stand back** (1), **stay back, step back** (1)
**2** to return to live in a place that one had left [IØ + BACK (*into, to*)] *The family left town three years ago but moved back* (*into the neighbourhood*) *last week.* → **move away** (2)

**move down**[1] *v adv*
**1** to go to the other end of a bus, railway carriage, etc., furthest from the door: [IØ + DOWN] *Move* (*right*) *down inside, please* → **move forward** (1), **move up** (1), **pass along** (2), **pass down**[1] (3), **squash up** (2), **squeeze up**
**2** to place (someone) at a lower level or rank than before: [T1 + DOWN] *We had to move the student down into an easier class.* → **move up** (3)

**move down**[2] *v prep*
**1** to go along (a road, steps, etc.): [IØ + *down*] *The old man had difficulty in moving down the stairs.*
**2** to pass further along (a vehicle): [IØ +

*down] Move down the bus, please, make room for others!* → **pass along** (2), **pass down²** (2)

***move for** *v prep*
*fml* (in Parliament or law) to make a formal request for (something): [T1 (*usu. simple tenses*)] *The defence lawyer moved for a new trial because he had discovered some important new witnesses. An Opposition member moved for acceptance of the new law, which was passed by the whole House.*

**move forward** *v adv*
**1** to (cause to) go ahead or in front: [IØ + FORWARD] *At last the line of people waiting to go into the cinema began to move forward.* [T1 + FORWARD] *We shall have to move some more of our men forward if the enemy keeps attacking all night.* → **move down¹** (1), etc.
***2** to advance; improve: [IØ] *More and more newly independent nations are moving forward into civilized life.* —**move forward** *n*

**move in** *v adv*
**1** to (cause to) take possession of a new place to live: [IØ + IN (*to*)] *We've bought our new house, but we can't move in till the end of the month.* [T1 + IN (*to*)] *If the house stands empty for too long, the council will move a homeless family in.* —**moving-in** *n, adj* → **move into** (2), **move out** (1)
***2** esp. *mil* to (cause to) take control or attack: [IØ] *As they moved in closer, they could see the moon shining on the enemy guns. Our competitors have gone out of business, so now our firm can move in.* [T1] *When is the best time to move the next group in, to deal with the enemy?*

**move in on** *v adv prep*
**1** to share a place to live with (someone) without permission: [T1] *My brother's friend moved in on us without even as asking him.*
**2** to come closer to (something or someone): [T1] *The camera moved in on the table for a better view of the group. Even greater difficulties are moving in on the school system.*
**3** to surround and prepare to attack (someone): [T1] *The police are moving in on the criminals hiding in the house.* → **close in on**
**4** *not fml* to take control of (a business), often unlawfully: [T1] *Criminals have been moving in on the taxi business for some years. The government may move in on the steel industry.* → **take over¹** (2)

**move into** *v prep*
**1** to (cause to) move so as to take a position inside (a place): [IØ + *into*] *Let's move into the shade, it's cooler there. As the funeral cars moved into the town square, the drums began to roll.* [T1 + *into*] *We'd better move some more men into that poorly defended position.*
**2** to (cause to) begin to live in or take possession of (a building): [IØ + *into*] *What day do you plan to move into the new house?* [T1 + *into*] *The council will move a homeless family into your house if you leave it empty for too long.* → **move in** (1), **move out** (1)

**move off** *v adv* → **move out** (2)
to start a journey; leave: [IØ + OFF] *The bus moved off before all the passengers had got on board. The line of soldiers moved off at a quick march.*

**move on** *v adv*
**1** to (cause to) move to a different place; leave: [T1 + ON] *The police moved the crowd on when they threatened to damage the building.* [IØ + ON] *It's time we were moving on, we've a busy day ahead. "Come on, sir, move on," said the policeman.* → **move along**
**2** to place (something) ahead: [T1 + ON] *Let's trick Mother by moving the hands of the clock on, so that she thinks it's already dinner time!*
***3** to go further; continue; change (to something new): [IØ (*to*)] *Let's move on to the business of the meeting. I think we've talked enough about that subject; let's move on.* → **pass on¹** (3)
***4** to advance in one's way of life, work, etc.: [IØ (*to*)] *Having done many years of school teaching, I felt that it was time to move on into college or university work.*
**5 get a move on** *infml* to hurry: [*imper.*] *Get a move on, you two, we haven't all day to waste!*

**move out** *v adv*
**1** to (cause to) leave a place where one has lived: [IØ + OUT (*of*)] *No sooner had the family moved out (of the house) than the windows were broken and the paintwork damaged.* [T1 + OUT] *You'll be moved out by force if you don't pay the rent.* → **move in** (1), **move into** (2)
**2** to start a journey: [IØ + OUT] *Blowing its whistle, the train moved out, slowly at first.* → **move off**

**move over** *v adv* also *not fml* **shove over**
**1** to yield place; move to the far end of a shared piece of furniture: [IØ + OVER] *There's room for three if you move over.*
***2** to yield one's position: [IØ] *Uncle left his position on the board of directors as he felt that he should move over in favour of a younger man.* → **ease up** (3), **move up** (2)

**move round** *v adv* → MOVE ABOUT

**move to** *v prep*
**1** to (cause to) go and live in or take possession of (another place): [IØ + *to*] *When did your family move to the North?* [T1 + *to*] *When the new library was opened, all the books had to be moved to the new building.*
**2** to have an effect on the feelings of (someone) so as to produce (an effect): [T1 + *to*] *The sad song moved the crowd to tears of sympathy.*

**move towards** *v prep*
**1** to go in the direction of (something or someone): [IØ + *towards*] *A strange creature was moving steadily towards me.*
***2** to change one's opinion in the direction of; become closer to (an idea): [T1] *The talks*

*seem to be moving towards agreement at last.* → **move away** (3)

**move up** *v adv*

**1** to go forward or higher: [IØ + UP] *Move up, there's plenty of room at the front. The line of people waiting to go into the cinema began to move up a little.* → **move down**¹ (1), etc.

**2** also *not fml* **shove up** to yield place; move to the far end of a shared piece of furniture: [IØ + UP] *There's room for three if you move up. Move up, will you, you're taking up all the space!* → **ease up** (3), **move over** (2)

**3** to (cause to) rise in rank or level: [T1 + UP] *This student is finding the work too easy; she ought to be moved up into an more advanced class.* [IØ + UP] *It's possible to become a general by moving up through the ranks.* → **move down**¹ (2)

***4** *mil* to (cause to) come nearer to the front of the battle: [T1] *Move some more men up, we need help here! Another group of soldiers moved up to take the places of those who had been killed.*

***5** to rise in value: [IØ] *The pound moved up a little today on the world money market.*

***move upwards** *v adv*

to rise; improve: [IØ] *Sales moved upwards for the first time this year.*

**mow down** *v adv*

**1** to cut (grass or other plants): [T1 + DOWN] *We shall have to mow down the long grass in the big field.*

***2** to destroy; kill (people) in large numbers: [T1] *The front row of soldiers were mown down by machinegun fire.*

***muck about/around** *v adv*

**1** *infml* to spend time lazily: [IØ] *"What have you been doing today?" "Oh, nothing, just mucking around."* → **mess about** (1), etc.

**2** *infml* to treat (something or someone) carelessly or inconsiderately: [T1] *Give me a straight answer, don't muck me about! Who's been mucking the tools around? Some of them are damaged.* → **mess about** (4), etc.

***muck about /around with** *v adv prep* → **mess about with** (1), etc.

*infml* to cause disorder to (something): [T1] *Who's been mucking about with my papers? They're all out of order.*

***muck around** *v adv* → **MUCK ABOUT**

***muck around with** *v adv prep* → **MUCK ABOUT WITH**

***muck in** *v adv*

*infml* to share things; take part; work well together; have a friendly relationship (with someone): [IØ (TOGETHER, *with*)] *If we all muck in (together), we'll soon get the job done. Do you mind mucking in with the other boys?*

***muck out** *v adv* → **clean out** (1), **do out** (1)

to clean (a building where animals live): [T1] *Part of your job with the horses will be to muck out the stables every morning.* —**mucking-out** *n*

***muck up** *v adv*

**1** *infml* to make (someone or something) dirty or untidy: [T1] *I got my boots mucked up in the garden. Try not to muck up your new dress before the party.* → **dirty up** (1), **foul up** (1), **mess up** (1)

**2** *infml* to spoil (something) carelessly: [T1] *If John mucks up his driving test again, I doubt if he'll ever pass it. Our travel arrangements have been mucked up by the ticket office.* —**muck-up** *n* → **mess up** (2), etc.

**muddle about/around** *v adv*

*not fml* to (cause to) be confused: [T1 + ABOUT/AROUND] *Don't muddle me about like that, tell me exactly what you want.* [L9 + ABOUT/AROUND] *I've been muddling about all morning, and got nothing done.*

**muddle along/on** *v adv*

*not fml* to continue in a disorganized manner [L9 + ALONG/ON] *I don't know how he produces any results, the way he muddles along. The speaker was muddling on, and nobody could follow what he was trying to say.*

**muddle around** *v adv* → **MUDDLE ABOUT**

**muddle on** *v adv* → **MUDDLE ALONG**

***muddle through** *v adv* → **rub through**

*not fml* to reach some kind of success without proper organization: [IØ] *The British usually muddle through somehow.*

***muddle up** *v adv*

**1** *not fml* to confuse; mix; mistake; disorder (people, things, or ideas): [T1 (*with*) (*often pass.*)] *My papers are all muddled up, and I was trying to keep them in alphabetical order. I'm sorry I muddled up your names, they're so much alike. I got him muddled up with his brother. I have a terrible headache, and my thoughts are all muddled up.* —**muddle-up** *n* → **jumble up, mix up** (2)

**2 be muddled up** *not fml* to be confused, esp in one's feelings: *Give Jane time to settle down in her new school, she's sure to feel muddled up at first.* —**muddled-up** *adj*

**muddy up** *v adv*

esp. *AmE* to cover (something) with mud: [T1 + UP] *You'll get your good boots all muddied up in the garden.*

**muffle up** *v adv*

**1** to cover (part of the body) with cloth: [T1 + UP] *"And in his mantle muffling up his face . . . great Caeser fell."* (Shakespeare, *Julius Caesar*)

**2** to make (something) silent, with or as with cloth: [T1 + UP] *Can the noise of the engine be muffled up any better?*

***3** esp. *AmE infml* to be quiet: [IØ (*usu. imper.*)] *Muffle up at the back there! We need some quiet around here!* → **shut up** (4), etc.

***4** esp. *BrE not fml* to (cause to) wear warm clothing: [IØ] *Better muffle up, it's cold out* *side.* [T1] *Are the children muffled up against the cold?* → **bundle up** (2), **wrap up** (2)

***mug up** *v adv* → **bone up on, swot up**
*infml* to learn (something such as a subject) by hard study, usu. for a short time, as for an examination: [T1] *I must mug up some facts about Shakespeare's language if I am to take the examination next week. I'll mug up the laws on this subject before I advise my friends.*

**mull over** *v adv; prep* → **think about** (1), etc.
to consider (something) at length: [T1] *The committee have mulled over your suggestion but have decided not to accept it because of the cost. I haven't decided what to do; I'm still mulling it over.*

**multiply by** *v prep*
to combine two numbers by adding (one number) to itself (a certain number of times): [T1 + *by* (*usu. simple tenses*)] *3 multiplied by 4 makes 12.*

**multiply up** *v adv*
to increase the amount of (something): [T1 + UP (*usu. simple tenses*)] *The costs have been multiplied up many times.*

**murmur against/at** *v prep*
to complain about; express opposition to (something such as an injustice): [IØ + *against/at*] *The people are beginning to murmur against this additional rise in their taxes. Many people murmured at the lengthy imprisonment given to the young man.*

**muscle in** *v adv* → **horn in**
*sl* to use force to control or share control of (a group activity): [IØ (*on*)] *Our competitors have been trying to muscle in for some years. Other criminals have tried to muscle in on the criminal business.*

**muse on/over/upon** *v prep* → **think about** (1), etc.
to think dreamily about (something): [IØ + *on/over/upon*] *She sat musing for hours on her days in Africa. "And muse on Nature with a poet's eye."* (Thomas Campbell, *The Pleasures of Hope*)

***muss up** *v adv*
*not fml* to disorder (esp. someone's hair): [T1] *When you're helping me off with my coat, please take care not to muss up my hair.*

**muster up** *v adv*
**1** to gather together a group of (soldiers): [T1 + UP] *Where can we muster up more soldiers?*
**2 muster up courage** to defeat one's fears and show bravery: *The young soldier had to muster up all his courage to prevent himself from running away and being regarded as a coward.* → **pluck up, screw up** (6), **summon up** (3)
**3 muster up support** to gather people who give loyalty and attendance to (an activity, a person, a principle, etc.): *The politician spent years mustering up support for his views.*

**mutiny against** *v prep* → **rebel against, revolt against** (1), **rise against**
*mil* to refuse to obey the orders of (someone); take the control by force from (a commander); refuse to accept (treatment from an officer): [IØ + *against*] *At last the sailors mutinied against the captain's unjust use of his power; they seized the ship, and put him in an open boat to float at the mercy of the sea. If you mutiny against an officer, you can be shot.*

# N

**naff off** *v adv infml euph* → FUCK OFF (2)

**nag at** *v prep*
**1** to complain at; find fault with (someone) repeatedly, in an annoying manner: [IØ + *at*] *If she keeps on nagging at her husband like that, he'll leave her.* → **pick at** (4)
**2** to keep asking (someone) (to do something), in an annoying manner: [IØ + *at*] *How often do I have to nag at you to tidy your room?*

**nail back** *v adv*
to fasten (something) in a backward position with a nail or nails: [X9 + BACK] *If you want the cupboard door open all the time, why don't you nail it back?*

**nail down** *v adv*
**1** to fasten (something) down with a nail or nails: [X9 + DOWN] *The lid was nailed down, so we couldn't get it off.* → **peg down** (1), **pin down** (1)
***2** to force (someone) to make a decision, state his intentions, or take action, etc.: [T1 (*to*) (*usu. simple tenses*)] *See if you can nail the chairman down to an exact date. We shall have to nail him down to his promise.* → **peg down** (2), **pin down** (2), **tie down to** (2)
***3** to explain the exact nature of (something): [T1 (*usu. simple tenses*)] *At last we were able to nail the trouble down to a fault in the machine. This book is proving difficult to write, since I am trying to nail down the central idea of reasoning. It is difficult to nail down the exact meaning of this verb.* → **pin down** (3)
***4** to fix (something); be sure about; establish: [T1 (*usu. simple tenses*)] *Were you able to nail down an agreement?*

**nail on** *v adv*
to fasten (something) on with a nail or nails: [X9 + ON] *I can't get this lid off, it seems to be nailed on.*

**nail onto** *v prep* → **nail to** (1)
to fasten (something) onto (something) with a nail or nails: [T1 + *onto*] *Nail the boards onto the fence posts, they will make a good fence.*

**nail to** *v prep*
**1** to fasten (something) to (something) with a nail or nails: [T1 + *to*] *The message was nailed to the wall with an arrow.* → **nail onto**
**2 nail one's colours to the mast** to declare one's opinion and act according to it: [*often simple tenses*] *The young politician thought it was time that he nailed his colours to the mast; the risks he took by speaking plainly would be balanced by the votes he would gain for being so firm in his opinion.*
**3 nail a lie to the counter** to prove the falsehood of something: [*usu. simple tenses*] *Have you any proof that will enable you to nail his lie to the counter?*

**nail up** *v adv*
**1** to fasten (something) on high or in public view with a nail or nails: [X9 + UP] *A notice was nailed up on the church door.*
***2** to fasten (something) in a closed position with nails: [T1] *The windows had been boarded and nailed up to prevent thieves from entering the empty house.*

**name after** *v prep* also *AmE* **name for**
to give (someone or something) the name of (someone) as an honour: [T1 + *after*] *The child was named after her famous aunt. The machine is named after its inventor.*

**name as** *v prep*
to give the name of (someone) as being (something): [T1 + *as* (*usu. simple tenses*)] *Although Jim had come first, his competitor was named as the winner, as Jim started before he should have done.*

**name for** *v prep AmE* → NAME AFTER

***nark it** *v pron*
*BrE infml* to stop what one is doing; be quiet: [IØ (*imper.*)] *Nark it! The police are coming!*

***narrow down** *v adv*
to (cause to) be limited or reduced: [T1] *In the end the choice was narrowed down to three people who might be suitable for the job.* [IØ] *The search has narrowed down to a few streets where the gunman might be hiding.*

**negotiate about/for/over** *v prep*
to talk so as to try to reach agreement about (something): [IØ + *about/for/over*] *Are the unions and the employers still negotiating about working hours? The unions are negotiating for an improvement in working conditions. The director has been negotiating for a contract with the government. How long will the United Nations negotiate over this question?*

**negotiate with** *v prep*
to hold talks with (someone) in an attempt to reach agreement, as in business; try to arrange (an agreement) with (someone): [IØ + *with*] *The unions have been negotiating with the employers for an improvement in working conditions.* [T1 + *with*] *They hope to negotiate a successful agreement with the board of directors.*

***neighbour upon** *v prep*
*old use* (of land) to lie next to (another place): [T1 (*simple tenses*)] *The farm neighbours upon some of the richest land in the area.*

***neighbour with** *v prep*
*AmE* to have a friendly relationship with (someone): [T1 (*usu. simple tenses*)] *Why did she get so annoyed? I was only trying to neighbour with her!*

**nerve for** *v prep*
to prepare (oneself) for (something such as action) by gathering one's courage, strength etc.: [T1 + *for*] *I doubt if I would ever be able to nerve myself for public performance.*

**nest in** *v prep*
(of a bird or small animal) to build its nest in (a place): [IØ + *in*] *This wire frame is intended to prevent birds from nesting in our chimney.*

***nestle down** *v adv* → **snuggle down**
to (cause to) settle in comfort: [IØ] *The lost children nestled down under a pile of leaves.* [T1] *Are the children nestled down in bed yet?*

***nestle up** *v adv* → **snuggle up**
to settle close (to someone) in comfort: [IØ (TOGETHER, *against, to*)] *The baby animals nestled up together for warmth. The lost children nestled up to each other in their fear.*

**nibble at** *v prep*
**1** to take small bites at (usu. food): [IØ + *at*] *Try to eat your dinner, Jane, you've only nibbled at it. Mice have been nibbling (away) at the woodwork again.* → **peck at** (2), **pick at** (2)
***2** to take part of (something) little by little: [T1] *The rising cost of food has been nibbling (away) at our income.*
***3** to show interest in (an idea); accept (something) in part or principle without reaching firm agreement: [T1] *I think he's nibbling at your offer—give him another day and I think he'll bite!*

**nick up** *v adv*
to cut (something or someone) roughly: [T1 + UP (*usu. pass.*)] *His face was all nicked up with the dull edge of the blade.*

**niggle over** *v prep*
*not fml* to argue about unimportant or unnecessary details of (something or doing something): [IØ + *over*] *The lawyers can be expected to niggle over every little detail of the case. Many of the parents are niggling over paying the increase in school charges.*

***nip at** *v prep*
to be or follow next to (someone or something) and try to bite sharply: [T1] *The postman ran away with the dog nipping (away) at his heels. The cold wind nipped at her face.*

**nip in**[1] *v adv*
**1** *not fml* to enter; move inside quickly: [L

+ IN] *The cat nipped in just as I was closing the door. We saw a parking space free but another car nipped in ahead of us.*
*2 to make (clothing) narrower: [T1] *I'll nip the dress in at the waist for you, as you've lost so much weight.*

**nip in²** *v prep*
**1** to catch (usu. part of the body) in (something that hurts it): [T1 + *in*] *I've nipped my thumb in the fastener!*
**2 nip something in the bud** *not fml* to stop the development of something at the beginning: *Their new relationship was nipped in the bud when she discovered that he had been in prison. There is a tendency towards violence in the game, which the police are trying to nip in the bud before it gets serious.*

**nip off** *v adv*
**1** to remove (something, usu. part of a plant) with a quick movement and a sharp instrument or fingernail: [T1 + OFF] *Every time I pass the rose bushes, I nip off a dead flower head so as to improve the new roses.*
**2** also **nip out** *not fml* to leave in a hurry: [L9 + OFF] *Nip off to the shops before they close and fetch me some milk, will you?*

**nod off** *v adv* → **doze off**, etc.
*not fml* to fall asleep accidentally: [IØ] *I hope the Minister didn't notice that I nodded off in the middle of his speech—I should feel ashamed of being so rude!*

**noise abroad** *v adv* → **blaze abroad, bruit abroad, rumour abroad, spread abroad**
*not fml* to make (something) public; spread (news): [T1 (*usu. pass.*)] *Stories have been noised abroad about the government's intention to hold a quick election. It is being noised abroad that the Minister is to be dismissed from the government.*

**nominate for** *v prep*
to suggest the name of (someone or something) as being suitable for (a position, reward, etc.): [T1 + *for* (*often pass.*)] *Are you willing to be nominated for the chairmanship? This film has been nominated for the prize.*

**nominate to** *v prep*
to appoint (someone) without election to (a position or body;: [T1 + *to*] *It doesn't seem fair that some members are nominated to the committee while others have to be elected.*

**nose about/around/round** *v adv* → **poke about, pry about**
*infml* to search around (for something), often by examining other people's affairs: [IØ (*among, for, in*)] *That policeman should not be nosing around in our garage without a court order. Why was he nosing round among our things? What was he nosing about for? We have no stolen goods hidden in there.* —**nose-around** *n*

**nose into** *v prep* → **poke into** (2), **pry into**
*infml* to enquire into (other people's affairs): [T1] *I don't want our neighbour nosing into our affairs, so keep quiet about our plans.*

***nose out** *v adv*
**1** (of an animal) to find (something) by smell: [T1]. *Our dog will nose out a rabbit anywhere it hides.* → **smell out** (1), **sniff out** (1)
**2** *infml* to find (something) by searching: [T1] *Clever Jane has nosed out a perfect place for our camping holiday. It's part of a newspaper reporter's job to nose out unpleasant facts about people in the public eye.* → **smell out** (2), **sniff out** (2)

***nose round** *v adv* → NOSE ABOUT

***notch up** *v adv* → **chalk up** (3), **clock up** (2), **log up** (2), **score up**
to record (a victory or gain): [T1] *That's another win our team has notched up this year!*

***note down** *v adv* → **write down** (1), etc.
to record (something) in writing: [T1] *Note down her telephone number in case you forget it. I noted down every word he said.*

**note for** *v prep*
**be noted for** to be famous or well-known because of (something or doing something): *The cook was noted for his chocolate cake. The famous scientist is noted for his discovery of the drug that has helped cure the awful disease. Jim is noted for arriving late for work. The town is noted for its healthy air.*

**notify of** *v prep*
to inform (someone or a body) officially about (something): [T1 + *of* (*usu. pass.*)] *Have the police been notified of your father's death? The Health Ministry has to be notified of any infectious diseases in the area.*

**notify to** *v prep*
to give information officially about (something) to (someone or a body): [T1 + *to* (*usu. pass.*)] *Any infectious disease must be notified at once to the Health Ministry.*

**number among** *v prep*
to count (someone or something) as included in (a group): [X9 + *among* (*usu. simple tenses*)] *I am proud to number her among my friends. Numbered among the writer's successes is a useful book on making money in the property business.*

***number off** *v adv*
esp. *mil* to (cause to) call out one's number in a row, to declare one's presence: [IØ] *The soldiers numbered off from the right.* [T1] *The officer numbered the men off.*

**number with** *v prep*
to include (someone or something) among (a group): [X9 + *with* (*usu. pass.*)] *You shall be numbered with the great.*

***nurse along** *v adv*
**1** to sail (a boat) gently: [T1] *The wind is so light, you'll have to nurse the boat along.*
**2** *not fml* to cause (something) to advance steadily: [T1] *Just nurse the work along, don't rush it.*

**nurse through** *v prep*
**1** to care for (someone) during (an illness): [T1 + *through*] *It was a painful experience nursing Mother through her last illness.*

*2 *not fml* to give (someone) help in succeeding in (a difficulty): [D1] *Mary nursed her brother through the examination.*

***nuzzle up** *v adv*
(usu. of a horse or dog) to press the nose fondly (against someone): [IØ (*against, to*)] *My horse nuzzled up to me, pleased to welcome me home.*

# O

**object against** *v prep*
*fml* to express opposition to (someone): [IØ + *against* (*usu. simple tenses*)] *Why do you object against Mr Sharp for the chairmanship?*

**object to** *v prep* → **demur at, protest against, raise to** (6), **take to** (13)
to oppose; express opposition to (something or something being done): [IØ + *to*] *I object to being blamed for something that I haven't done. All the local farmers objected to the new airport. All the local farmers objected to the new airport being built on rich farmland. If it's objected to by all the people, the government can hardly refuse to take notice.*

**oblige by** *v prep*
to please; do (someone) a favour (by doing something); be so good as to help (someone) by (doing something); sometimes used when the speaker is being only falsely polite: [T1 + *by* (*simple tenses, usu.* + *could, would*)] *"Could you oblige me by opening the window?" "Thanks." You would oblige me by not parking your car in front of my gate. You could oblige the firm by arriving on time for work now and again.*

**oblige to** *v prep*
**be obliged to** to be grateful to (someone): *I'm much obliged to you for your help.*

***oblige with** *v prep* → **favour with**
*fml* to please (someone) with (something); do (someone) a kindness by giving or lending (something): [D1 (*often simple tenses*)] *Please oblige me with a reply as soon as possible. Mr Green will now oblige us with a song. Could you oblige me with some money? Can I oblige you with a cup of tea?*

***observe on/upon** *v prep*
to make a remark about (something): [T1 (*usu. simple tenses*)] *Did he observe on your unusual appearance?*

**obsess with/by** *v prep*
**be obsessed with/by** to have one's thoughts completely and unhealthily filled with, and often troubled by (something): *The writer was obsessed with thoughts of death. Some women are obsessed with/by the need to keep their home as clean as a hospital.*

**obtain for** *v prep* → **get for** (1), **procure for** (1)
to get; supply; put (something) in the possession of (someone or something): [T1 + *for*] *I think I know where I can obtain that rare book for you.*

**obtain from** *v prep* → **get from, get out of** (5), **procure from, produce from** (1), **take from** (4), **take out of** (6)
to come into the possession of (something) from (something or someone that supplies it): [T1 + *from*] *Some of the salt that we use is obtained from the sea.*

***obtrude on/upon** *v prep* → **intrude into, intrude on**
*fml* (of something or someone unwanted) to get in the way of; force (itself or oneself) into (something such as thoughts): [T1] *Unreasonable hopes keep obtruding upon my attempts to act realistically. The unwelcome question of cost is obtruding itself upon our plans. I wish he would stop obtruding himself and his opinions upon our peaceful gathering.*

**occupy in** *v prep*
to busy (oneself) in (doing something): [T1 + *in* (*usu. pass.*)] *How long has Tom been occupied in writing his new book?*

**occupy with** *v prep*
to busy (oneself) with (something): [T1 + *with* (*often pass.*)] *Don't interrupt Father when he's occupied with his newspaper. Can you occupy yourselves with something to do while I get the dinner ready?*

***occur to** *v prep*
to come to the mind of (someone): [T1 (*no pass., simple tenses*)] *Such a simple explanation never occurred to me!* [*It* + T1 (*no pass., simple tenses*)] *It occurred to me that I had seen her before somewhere.* [*It* + V3 (*simple tenses*)] *Didn't it occur to you to ask permission first?*

***offend against** *v prep*
to act in opposition to (law, custom, etc.) [T1 (*no pass.*)] *Why does he go on offending against the rules of the club?* [*It* + T1 (*no pass.*)] *It offends against my principles to tell a lie, even for my own advantage. You need not do military service if it offends against your religion.*

**offend with** *v prep*
to annoy (someone) with (something): [T1 + *with*] *She offended me with her rudeness.*

**offer for** *v prep*
to suggest that one gives (something, someone, or oneself) for (something): [T1 + *for*] *Did he offer a fair price for the house? Why are you offering yourself for additional work?*

**offer to** *v prep*
to suggest that one gives (something) to (someone): [T1 + *to*] *The universities are now offering a wider range of courses to students for them to choose from. Was the job offered to you?*

**offer up** *v adv*
to offer (something or someone) to a god: [T1] *The people offered up their prayers. We offer up our thanks to the Lord for his mercy and loving kindness.*

**officiate as** *v prep*
*fml* to fulfil the duties of (an official): [IØ + *as*] *Mr Sharp will officiate as chairman until a new one is appointed.*

**officiate at** *v prep*
*fml* to perform formal duties at (usu. a ceremony): [IØ + *at*] *Which priest would you like to officiate at your wedding?*

**ogle at** *v prep* → **make at** (4), **roll at**
to look at (usu. a woman) with a sexually suggestive expression: [IØ + *at*] *He'll get a bad name for himself if he ogles at every girl he meets. I don't enjoy parties because I hate being ogled at by all those rude men.*

**omit from** *v prep* → **delete from, erase from** (1), **leave out**[1] (3), **miss out** (1)
to fail to include (something or someone) in (something), either intentionally or unintentionally: [T1 + *from* (*often pass.*)] *You have omitted the date from this cheque; please complete it properly. Why has Jim been omitted from the team? No important person should be omitted from the guest list. The offending part has been omitted from the new printing of the book.*

**ooze away** *v adv*
**1** (of liquid) to flow away gradually: [L9 + AWAY] *No wonder the engine got too hot, all the oil had been oozing away during our journey.*
***2** (of a quality) to cease; be gradually lost: [IØ] *His courage oozed away when he faced the enemy in actual battle.*

**ooze out** *v adv*
(of a liquid) to flow out; escape slowly and with difficulty: [L9 + OUT] *Muddy flood water was oozing out through a hole in one of the sandbags.*

**open at** *v prep*
**open fire at** → **OPEN ON** (2)

**open into** *v prep*
(of a door, etc.) to open in an inward direction towards; give entry to (a place): [IØ + *into* (*simple tenses*)] *The door opened into a strange little room with no furniture.*

**open off** *v adv; prep*
to have a door leading from (something): [IØ + OFF/*off* (*simple tenses*)] *The house has a long narrow hall, with all the downstairs rooms opening off* (*it*).

**open on** *v prep*
**1** (usu. of a window) to give a view of (something): [IØ + *on* (*simple tenses*)] *The windows open on a beautiful view of the lake.* → **look onto, look out** (4), **look over**[2] (2), **open onto**
**2** **open fire on** also **open fire at** to begin shooting at (someone): *The officer was forced to give orders to open fire on the crowd.*

**open onto** *v prep* → **look onto, look out** (4), **look over**[2] (2), **open on** (1)
(usu. of a window) to give a view of (something): [IØ + *onto* (*simple tenses*)] *The window opens onto a beautiful view of the lake.*

**open out** *v adv*
**1** to (cause to) become wide open or spread: [T1 + OUT] *Open out the newspaper so that we can all see the photograph.* [IØ + OUT] *When we reached the top of the hill, a beautiful view opened out before us.*
***2** to exist more fully; increase; improve: [IØ] *Life opens out for a young man when he leaves school. Business has been opening out recently.*
***3** to speak more freely; be less nervous and more friendly: [IØ] *It's nice to see Mary opening out at a party for a change.* → **open up** (9)

**open to** *v prep*
**1** to cause (something) to be open so as to allow (something or someone) to enter, be seen, etc.: [T1 + *to*] *Don't open the door to strangers, it's not safe.*
**2** to allow (something) to be entered, visited, seen, etc., by (someone): [T1 + *to*] *Some members have expressed a wish to open Council meetings to the public. The gardens of the great house will be opened to visitors next week.*

**open up** *v adv*
**1** to open a door: [IØ + UP (*usu. imper.*)] *Open up! This is the police!*
**2** to open (something) completely, esp. if it has been closed for a long time: [T1 + UP] *The police had to get special permission to open up the grave. The children were allowed to open up their Christmas presents after breakfast.*
**3** to open (a shop) for business: [IØ + UP] *We don't open up till 9.30.* [T1 + UP] *The department store is opening up a new branch in one of the smaller towns.*
**4** to cut (something) open, as to provide a way through: [T1 + UP] *In some places there was no way through for the railway line, so new passages had to be opened up with explosives.*
**5** to cut (someone) open, as in a hospital: [T1 + UP] *We shall have to open you up and remove the diseased bone.*
***6** to make possible the development of; bring (something) within someone's reach: [T1] *The government is hoping to open up new areas of industry to provide employment. The building of the new road has really opened up the distant areas.*
***7** (esp. of a possibility) to (cause to) begin to

exist and grow: [T1] *That chance meeting opened up new possibilities for me.* [IØ] *The council are examining possibilities which are opening up in local affairs.*

***8** (of a gun) to begin firing: [IØ] *We knew that there was no hope left for the town when the big guns opened up.*

***9** to speak more freely: [IØ (*often simple tenses*)] *He was silent at first, but soon he opened up and told us about his terrible experiences.* → **open out** (3)

***10** (of a vehicle) to (cause to) go fast: [IØ (*often simple tenses*)] *Once we were on the main road, the car really opened up.* [T1 (*often simple tenses*)] *Can't you open up the engine a little more?*

***11** (esp. in sport) to become more active; play more actively: [IØ (*often simple tenses*)] *After a slow start, the team really opened up and hit 180 in two hours.*

**open with** *v prep*

**1** to make (something) come open by using (a tool): [T1 + *with*] *Try opening the packet with your thumbnail. You can only open a tin of food with a tin opener.*

**2** to (cause to) start with (something): [IØ + *with* (*usu. simple tenses*)] *The concert opened with a lively performance of a piece for two pianos. The famous play opens with the appearance of a spirit, and closes with the deaths of four people.* [T1 + *with* (*often simple tenses*)] *The priest opened the service with a prayer. The first artist opened the concert with a song.*

**operate against** *v prep*

**1** to work against (something or someone): [IØ + *against*] *His actions operated against the principles of freedom. His behaviour in the committee meeting operated against the chairman.*

**2** *mil* to fulfil planned actions against (the enemy): [IØ + *against*] *The Secret Service operated against the enemy during the war.*

**operate from** *v prep*

to do one's work using (a place) as a base: [IØ + *from*] *The company is presently operating from London, but is planning to move to the country. The general operated from a tent on the battlefield.*

**operate on** *v prep*

(of a doctor) to cut (someone or part of the body) in an attempt to heal him/her or it: [IØ + *on*] *This famous doctor has operated on many important people. I'm afraid that your leg will have to be operated on, there's no other way to stop the pain.*

**oppose to** *v prep*

**be opposed to** to dislike; refuse to accept (something or doing something): *The government is opposed to any further increase in taxes, and will try to raise money by some other means. The firm is not opposed to making changes where these are seen to be really necessary.*

***opt for** *v prep* also **opt in favour of**

*not fml* to choose (something such as a plan or course of study): [T1] *Weaker students often opt for the easier courses. The suggestion was opted for by most members of the committee.* [T4] *When the government opted for building the airport on rich farmland, there was much opposition, especially locally.*

***opt in**[1] *v adv* → **cop out** (2), **opt out**

*not fml* to choose to join something: [IØ] *When the firm offered a special insurance plan, many of the workers opted in.*

**opt in**[2] *v prep*

**opt in favour of** → **OPT FOR**

***opt out** *v adv* → **cop out** (2), **opt in**[1]

*not fml* to choose to leave (something): [IØ (*of*)] *If you don't like the firm's insurance plan, you may opt out. Many more students these days are opting out of the system.*

**order about/around** *v adv* → **kick about** (5), **push about**

to try to control (someone) by giving (too) many orders, esp. unpleasantly: [T1] *The workers are refusing to be ordered about by the employers; they will give a fair day's work for a fair day's pay, but they will not be treated like servants.*

**order from** *v prep*

to request a supply of (something such as goods) from (someone or somewhere): [T1 + *from* (*usu. pass.*)] *There will be a delay on your request as the parts have to be ordered from overseas. Further supplies of paper must be ordered from Head Office.*

**order in** *v adv*

**1** to order (someone) to enter: [X9 + IN] *The teacher ordered the children in (to the school).*

**2** to obtain (supplies) by ordering, usu. in quantity: [T1 + IN] *Have you ordered in enough envelopes this month?*

**order off** *v prep*

**order a player off the field** to send a player off the field of play for a fault such as bad behaviour or breaking the rules: *The other team won the football game easily because our most skilful player was ordered off the field for fighting.*

**order out** *v adv*

**1** to force (someone) to leave: [X9 + OUT] *Order those children out (of the building)—they're not allowed in school after hours.*

**2** to order (someone) to appear on duty: [X9 + OUT] *Additional police have been ordered out to control the expected crowds.*

**order up** *v adv*

*mil* to command (soldiers or vehicles) to come to a position in the front of the battle: [X9 + UP (*to*)] *More men will have to be ordered up (to the front) if we are to avoid a defeat.*

***orientate oneself** *v pron* also *AmE* **orient oneself**

to become familiar with one's surroundings; be conscious of what is happening and wha decisions to take, etc.: [IØ (*to*)] *It should only take you about a week to orientate yourself in your new job. Wait, I think we're lost; give me a minute to get myself orientated. I have very lifelike dreams, and every morning when I wake I have difficulty in orientating myself to the real world.*

**originate from** *v prep*
to come from; have its beginnings in (something, a place, or person): [L9 + *from* (*usu. simple tenses*)] *Her book originated from a short story. The disease originated from the Far East. The idea originates from the chairman.*

**originate in** *v prep*
to have its cause in (something): [L9 + *in* (*usu. simple tenses*)] *The trouble originated in a fault in the machinery.*

**originate with** *v prep*
to start from (someone): [L9 + *with* (*usu. simple tenses*)] *The idea originated with the chairman. This style of music originated with four popular young musicians in the 1950s.*

**ornament with** *v prep* → **decorate with** (1), etc.
to make (something) more attractive by adding (usu. pretty things): [T1 + *with*] *At Christmas time we ornament the tree with lights and coloured balls.*

**oscillate about/around** *v prep*
to swing backwards and forwards around (a position): [IØ + *about/around*] *The figures have been oscillating about an average.*

**oscillate between** *v prep*
to swing backwards and forwards between (two positions): [IØ + *between*] *The opinions of the voters have been oscillating between approval and opposition.*

**oust from** *v prep*
to force (someone) to leave (usu. a position): [T1 + *from* (*often pass.*)] *The Minister was ousted from his position of influence with the government, as a result of the shameful harbour affair.*

**overcrowd with** *v prep*
**be overcrowded with** to be filled too full with (things or people): *The room was overcrowded with furniture.*

**overflow with** *v prep*
**1** to be filled too full with (a liquid): [IØ + *with*] *The pan overflowed with boiling milk.*
**2** to be very full of (something such as a feeling): [T1 (*no pass.*)] *My heart is overflowing with gratitude.*

***overreach oneself** *v pron*
to fail by trying too hard: [IØ] *Jim's father has overreached himself this time, aiming for the contract with the international company; his firm is too small to handle such business, and he could have avoided wasting so much time and effort.*

**owe for** *v prep*
to have a duty to repay (money) (to someone) for the cost of (something): [L9 + *for* (*simple tenses*)] *Do I still owe for the concert tickets?* [X9 + *for* (*often simple tenses*)] *Don't let me forget that I owe you for the concert tickets.* [T1 + *for* (*usu. simple tenses*)] *I owe $30 for the concert tickets.* [D1 + *for* (*often simple tenses*)] *I owe you $30 for the concert tickets.*

**owe to** *v prep*
**1** to have a duty to repay (money) to (someone or a group): [T1 + *to* (*usu. simple tenses*)] *We still owe £19,000 to the building society for the interest on the house payments.*
***2** to feel or have (something) as a debt to (someone): [D1 (*simple tenses*)] *I owe my knowledge of music to my mother. I owe it to my family that I have been able to finish this book.*
***3** to believe (something) to be the result of (something): [D1 (*simple tenses*)] *I owe my good health to your care. Jim says that he owes his success to hard work. To what do you owe your long life?* → **attribute to** (1), etc.
**4 owe it to** to have as a duty to (someone or oneself) (to do something): [*simple tenses*] *You owe it to your family to repay them for the effort they have spent on you. You owe it to yourself to choose work which is best suited to your abilities.*

***own to** *v prep*
*fml* to admit (something such as a feeling, or feeling something): [T1] *I must own to a feeling of anxiety.* [T4] *I must own to feeling anxious.*

***own up** *v adv*
to admit a fault or crime, or doing something wrong: [IØ (*to*)] *It used to be a matter of honour among schoolboys that the guilty member of class would own up, and so save the others from punishment. Is no one prepared to own up to the theft of the clock? If no one will own up to misbehaving, all pupils will be kept in after school.*

# P

**pace about/around/round** *v adv; prep*
to move restlessly about (a place): [L9 + ABOUT/AROUND/ROUND] *I couldn't sleep, and paced about most of the night.* [L9 + *about/around/round*] *The tiger paced round its cage, swinging its tail.*

**pace along** *v prep*
to walk along (a path) or beside (a wall), restlessly or thoughtfully: [L9 + *along*] *I paced along the shore, deep in thought.*

**pace around** *v adv; prep* → **PACE ABOUT**

**pace off** *v adv*
to measure (part of a distance) by walking: [X9 + OFF] *You can get your fence posts evenly spaced by pacing off the distance between them. Pace off three metres, and then stop.*

**pace out** *v adv*
to measure the length of (a distance or place) by walking: [X9 + OUT] *Pace out the hall and see if it is as big as the stage that we shall use for the performance.*

**pace round** *v adv; prep* → **PACE ABOUT**

**pace up** *v adv*
**pace up and down** also **pace to and fro** to walk backwards and forwards within the same space, usu. with anxiety: *Many more fathers these days are staying with their wives during the birth of their babies, and most have said that it is much better than pacing up and down in the waiting room.*

**pack away** *v adv*
**1** to store (something), as in a box: [T1 + AWAY] *I'll try to find that old book, but it's been packed away for years. It's going to rain —we'd better pack away our things and go indoors.* → **put away** (1), **tuck away** (1)
***2** *not fml* to eat a lot of (food): [T1 (*often simple tenses*)] *You'd be surprised at the amount that boy can pack away in a single day.* → **put away** (2), **put down** (6), **tuck away** (2)

***pack down** *v adv*
**1** to make a solid mass: [IØ (*usu. simple tenses*)] *If the snow isn't cleared from the roads quickly, it packs down hard and makes driving difficult.*
**2** (of forwards in opposing teams playing rugby football) to lock together in a tight group: [IØ] *What are all those players doing in the middle of the field? Oh, they're packing down; the ball will be thrown in among them, and then one of them will seize it and run with it.*

**pack in** *v adv*
**1** to (cause to) be pressed together, as in a container or space: [T1 + IN (*to*)] *This case is full, I can't pack any more clothes in. No more supporters are allowed into the football ground: it's impossible to pack any more in.* [IØ + IN (*to*)] *"Have the crowds started to arrive yet?" "Yes, they're packing in!"* → **crowd in** (1), etc.
***2** *not fml* to attract (crowds, them) in large numbers: [T1] *The new music group is packing the crowds in.*
***3** also esp. *BrE* **jack in** *infml* to stop; be unwilling to continue (something, as work): [T1] *She didn't like her new job at all and was thinking of packing it in.* → **give up** (2), etc.
**4 pack it in!** *infml* stop what you are doing!: [*imper.*] *You're making too much noise—pack it in, will you!* → **chuck in** (7), **cut out** (14), **knock off** (13), **pack up** (4), **turn in** (9), **turn up** (11)

**pack into** *v prep*
**1** to (cause to) be pressed into (a container or space): [T1 + *into*] *I can't pack any more clothes into this suitcase, it's full. It's impossible to pack any more football supporters into the ground.* [IØ + *into*] *The buyers packed into the sale room, until there was no more space to stand.* → **crowd into** (1), etc.
***2** to crowd (activity) into (time): [D1] *It would be foolish for you to try to pack any more courses into your already busy timetable.* → **crowd into** (2)

**pack off** *v adv*
**1** to send (something) in a parcel: [T1 + OFF] *Could you pack these clothes off to my sister?* → **bundle off** (1)
***2** to send (someone) away hurriedly: [T1 (*to*)] *The children were packed off to bed as soon as the guests arrived. The family were so ashamed of the youngest son that they packed him off to the United States.*

**pack out** *v adv*
**1** to make (something) thicker or fuller: [T1 + OUT (*with*)] *You'll need to pack the chair out with some more cloth before re-covering it.* → **pad out** (1)
**2** to fill (a space such as a building) with people: [T1 + OUT (*often pass.*)] *The hall was packed out for the concert.* —**packed-out** *adj*

**pack together** *v adv*
to make (things) form a tight mass: [T1 + TOGETHER (*often pass.*)] *The cells of this substance are closely packed together.*

**pack up** *v adv*
**1** to place (things) in a container; pack all one's possessions: [T1 + UP] *We've packed up the books ready for the movers. I hear that her husband has packed up his things and moved out.*
***2** *not fml* to finish work; stop trying: [IØ

*When we've finished this pile of papers, let's pack up and go home. If I don't find a job soon, I might as well pack up.*
*3 *not fml* (of a machine) to stop working: [IØ] *Halfway up the hill, the engine packed up.* → **break down** (3), **conk out** (1), **cut out** (8), **give out** (6), **kick off** (6)
4 **pack it up!** *infml* stop what you are doing!: [*imper.*] *You're making too much noise—pack it up, will you?* → **chuck in** (7), **cut out** (14), **knock off** (13), **pack in** (4), **turn in** (9), **turn up** (11)

**pad out** *v adv*
**1** to make (something) thicker or fuller: [T1 + OUT] *You'll have to pad out the chair with some more cloth before re-covering it.* → **pack out** (1)
***2** to make (something written) unnecessarily longer: [T1 (*often pass.*)] *The book was padded out with uninteresting descriptions.* → **fatten out** (2), **fill out** (6), **flesh out** (2)

**pad up** *v adv*
(in cricket, of a batsman) to put protective clothing on the legs: [IØ (*often continuous tenses*)] *"Is your next man ready?" "No, he's still padding up."*

**page up** *v adv*
*AmE* to put (printed material) into numbered page order: [T1] *These papers are all out of order—will you page them up for me? When the book is ready for printing, someone has to page it up.*

**paint in** *v adv*
to add (something) with paint, often to a finished picture: [X9 + IN] *They painted the whole wall yellow, and then painted in a false door to balance the effect. The trees in the background were painted in later by a different artist.*

**paint on**[1] *v adv*
**1** to continue painting: [IØ + ON] *The artist painted on in spite of his family's opposition. Sometimes the only way I can get a picture finished is to paint on into the night.*
**2** to make (something) appear by using paint: [X9 + ON (*to*) (*usu. pass.*)] *That isn't a real drawer in the table, it's just painted on.*

**paint on/upon**[2] *v prep*
to put paint on (something); make (something) appear on (something) by using paint: [T1 + *on/upon*] *The painter is already painting the name of the new owner on the shop front.* [IØ + *on/upon*] *Would you rather paint on wood or paper?*

**paint out** *v adv*
to remove (something) by covering it with paint: [X9 + OUT (*usu. pass.*)] *The ship's name has been painted out and replaced with a new one.*

**paint over** *v prep* → **paper over** (1), **plaster over**[2] (1)
to put paint on top of (something): [IØ + *over*] *If you paint over the cracks in the wood-work, they won't show so badly.*

**paint upon** *v prep* → **PAINT ON**

***pair off** *v adv* → **partner off**
(of a group of people) to (cause to) form pairs, usu. male and female, for any purpose including marriage: [IØ] *The dancers paired off, each with her partner. Most of the friends we knew at school have now paired off and have families.* [T1 (*with*) (*usu. pass.*)] *I've been paired off for the evening with that unpleasant man from the tennis club.*

***pair up** *v adv*
to join in pairs, usu. for purposes of work or sport: [IØ (*with*) (*often simple tenses*)] *We each paired up with our opposite number from the other school, to exchange ideas.*

**pair with** *v prep*
**1** to match (something) with (something): [X9 + *with* (*often simple tenses*)] *Try to pair this card with one exactly the same from the other pack.* → **fit to** (2), **match with** (1), **suit to** (1)
***2** (in Parliament) to (cause to) form a pair with (a member of the other party) so as to balance the voting: [D1 (*often pass.*)] *For this vote, three of our Members were paired with three from the other party.* [T1 (*often simple tenses*)] *For this vote, three of our Members paired with three from the other party.*

***pal up** *v adv* → **chum up**
*not fml* to make friends (with someone): [IØ (*with*)] *It's good to see your children and mine palling up so well. Did the boys pal up with any other campers?*

**pale at** *v prep*
to become pale, as through fear or shock, because of (something bad): [IØ + *at* (*often simple tenses*)] *Mary paled at the sight of the terrible accident. The student paled at the thought of how near the examinations were.*

***pale beside/before** *v prep*
to seem unimportant in comparison with (usu. something): [T1 (*no pass., simple tenses*)] *The dangers that you mention pale beside the risks that these climbers are taking. These floods pale beside the ones we had last year when the whole river overflowed its banks.*

**pall on/upon** *v prep*
to cease to interest (someone) when he/she becomes accustomed to it: [IØ + *on/upon* (*usu. simple tenses*)] *When even beautiful scenery begins to pall on you, you will know that you are tired of travelling. Her voice is rather dull, and quickly palls on her listeners.*

***palm off** *v adv* → **pass off** (4)
*infml* to pass (something false) as real by deceit: [T1] *This law is intended to prevent dishonest people from palming off worthless goods.*

***palm off as** *v adv prep* → **pass off as**
*infml* to claim that (something) is (something different or better) so as to make someone

accept it: [D1] *He palmed the painting off as a Renoir.*

***palm off on** *v adv prep* → **fob off on, foist off on**
*infml* to force acceptance of (something such as worthless goods) on (someone) by deceit: [D1] *The salesman palmed off the faulty machine on the lady.*

***palm off with** *v adv prep* → **fob off with**
*infml* to deceive (someone) into accepting (something such as worthless goods or an excuse): [D1] *He palmed his brother off with some story or other. The salesman palmed the lady off with a faulty machine. I don't believe he means to do the job: he keeps palming me off with promises.*

***palter with** *v prep*
**1** *fml* to treat (something or someone) in a not very serious manner: [T1] *Don't palter with the question, answer it properly.*
**2** *fml* to speak about (something) so as to deceive: [T1] *Presidents should not palter with the truth.*

**pan for** *v prep*
to search for (gold) by washing sand, etc., from the bed of a stream in a special pan: [IØ + *for*] *Some old miners are still panning for gold in the streams where fortunes were found in the last century.*

**pan in** *v adv* → **pan out** (1)
(of a camera, esp. in film) to take a narrow-angled view, so that the subject seems nearer: [IØ + IN] *The camera then panned in for a close view of the actor's expression.*

***pan off** *v adv* → **pan out** (2)
(in goldmining) to wash (bits of rock and soil) from a pan which might contain gold dust: [T1] *You dip the pan into the bed of the stream, and then pan off the sand and dirt, hoping that some gold will be left.*

**pan out** *v adv*
**1** (of a camera, esp. in film) to take a wide-angled view, so that the subject seems further away: [IØ + OUT] *The camera then panned out to show us a view of the whole valley.* → **pan in**
***2** (in goldmining) to wash (bits of rock and soil) from a pan which might contain gold dust: [T1] *You dip the pan into the bed of the stream, and then pan out the sand and dirt, hoping that some gold will be left.* → **pan off**
***3** (in goldmining) to yield gold: [IØ (*usu. simple tenses*)] *Only one of the streams in this area ever panned out, and even then the yield of gold dust was very small. Those whose land panned out could become rich very quickly.*
***4** *not fml* to result; develop; succeed: [L9] *The book seems to be panning out quite well so far. How did your arrangements pan out? I thought it was a good idea, but now I don't think it will pan out.* → **work out** (7)

**pander to** *v prep*
**1** to act as a messenger for (a man), finding women for him; act as a messenger so as to aid (someone's sexual desires); provide for the needs of (someone or his sexual desire) by acting as a messenger: [IØ + *to*] *For many years he lived an evil life, pandering to men's sexual desires. He became well-known for pandering to any man who needed a woman.* → **pimp for**
***2** to yield to; serve; provide for; encourage (someone or a desire for something unfavourable): [T1] *Don't pander to the child, it's no good for him to have everything he wants. Many television plays pander to the public keenness for tasteless violence.*

**pant for** *v prep*
**1** to breathe quickly with a need for (something, esp. water or air): [IØ + *for* (*often continuous tenses*)] *After the long race, the runner was panting for breath. What a hot day! I'm panting for a cold drink, aren't you?* → **gasp for** (1)
***2** *not fml* to desire (something) strongly: [T1 (*no pass., usu. continuous tenses*)] *For a long time, she's been panting for a chance to show her acting ability, and now her chance has come!* → **gasp for** (2)

***pant out** *v adv* → **gasp out** (2)
to tell (something such as a story) while breathing quickly and with difficulty: [T1] *The runner panted out his message, then fell unconscious to the ground.*

**paper over** *v prep*
**1** to put wallpaper on top of (usu. a surface or a fault in a surface): [IØ + *over*] *Paint won't cover the mark on the wall, we shall have to paper over it. If we paper over the spaces between the wallboards, they won't show.* → **paint over, plaster over**[2] **(1)**
***2** *not fml* to hide or make a show of covering (something such as a fault or disagreement in an organization), esp. in the phr. **paper over the cracks**: [T1] *You can't hide a lack of unity in the party by papering over the cracks. We can try to paper over the disagreement in the union by printing a statement declaring our complete unity.* —**papered-over** *adj* → **plaster over**[2] (2)

***parcel out** *v adv*
to divide (something such as land) into smaller parts: [T1 (*often pass.*)] *More and more areas of countryside are being parcelled out into suitable pieces for housebuilding, as the population moves further from the city. After the farmer's death, his land was parcelled out among his children.*

**parcel up** *v adv* → **bundle up, wrap up**
to wrap (something or things) in a parcel: [T1 + UP] *Can you parcel up these urgent papers in time for the collection of the last post?*

**pardon for** *v prep*
**1** to forgive; not punish (someone) for (a crime): [T1 + *for* (*often simple tenses*)] *Your offence is so serious that I doubt whether you*

*can be pardoned for it. One of the first things that the young king did when he became king was to pardon his enemies for having opposed him.*
**2** to excuse (someone) for (a fault or doing something wrong): [T1 + *for* (*usu. simple tenses*)] *It is easy to pardon a child for forgetfulness, but not for rudeness. I hope you will pardon me for telephoning you at such an early hour. Pardon me for interrupting, but I have to correct something that you said.*

**pare down** *v adv*
**1** to reduce the size of (something) by cutting off thin pieces with a sharp tool: [T1 + DOWN] *This door has swollen in the wet weather and will have to be pared down with a sharp knife. To make this dish, pare the vegetables down into the fine pieces, as they are eaten raw.*
*2 to reduce (something such as a cost): [T1] *The universities and colleges have been asked to pare down their spending to the least possible, so they are employing no new teachers and are trying to save on paper and telephone calls.* —**pared-down** *adj*

**pare off** *v adv*
to remove (thin pieces of something), usu. with a sharp knife or other tool: [T1 + OFF] *Pare off the skin of this fruit very gently, as the flesh is delicate and damages easily. With great care, the artist pared off the top coat of paint, and discovered, as he had hoped, a valuable old painting underneath.*

**arley with** *v prep*
esp. *mil* to talk about a possible agreement, as for peace, with (an enemy): [IØ + *with* (*for*)] *We must send our most trusted officer to parley with their leaders for an exchange of prisoners.*

**art from** *v prep*
**1** to (cause to) leave (someone): [IØ + *from* (*often simple tenses*)] *It's hard to part from friends you love.* [T1 + *from* (*often pass.*)] *No child should be parted from its mother by force.*
**2** to make (someone) spend or give (money); separate (someone) from (something): [T1 + *from* (*often pass.*)] *A fool is soon parted from his money. The children refused to be parted from their dog, so he had to travel with us all the way to the new country.*

**rt over** *v prep*
to find cause for separation in (something): [IØ + *over*] *After years of marriage, the husband and wife parted over his relationships with other women.*

**rt with** *v prep*
**1** to lose, sell, or give (something such as money or goods): [IØ + *with*] *He was very unwilling to part with his money, even to buy a house. It was sad to have to part with Grandmother's lovely old furniture, but we needed the money.*
**2 part company with** to become separated from (someone), as at the end of a journey or a relationship: *Sadly, we parted company with our fellow travellers at the end of the voyage; they had been such good friends. The actor was forced to part company with his friends in the theatre, when he was offered a good part in another city.*
**3 part company with** to disagree with (someone): [*usu. simple tenses*] *I'm afraid that I must part company with the chairman on this question.*

**partake in** *v prep* → **participate in**
to take part in (something such as an activity): [L9 + *in*] *How many workers are partaking in the firm's insurance plan? Are you partaking in the music competition?*

**partake of** *v prep*
**1** *fml* to share (something such as a meal or success): [L9 + *of*] *You are welcome to partake of our simple food. I am delighted to have partaken of your success.*
*2 *fml* to be partly like; have some of the qualities of (something, often unfavourable): [T1 (*no pass., simple tenses*)] *Her so-called honesty partakes of rudeness.*

**participate in** *v prep* → **partake in**
to share; take part in (something such as an activity): [IØ + *in*] *Many more firms are participating in the growth of demand on the world markets. The people are demanding a chance to participate more in government. I like the whole school to participate in the sports.*

**participate with** *v prep*
to take part in something together with (someone else): [IØ + *with*] *It's good to see our runners participating with the best competitors from other countries.*

**partition off** *v adv*
to separate (usu. part of a room) with a thin dividing wall: [T1 + OFF (*from, into*) (*often pass.*)] *Several offices have been partitioned off from the original large room. The original large room has been partitioned off into separate offices.*

***partner off** *v adv* → **pair off**
to (cause to) form a pair, usu. male and female: [IØ (*usu. simple tenses*)] *The guests at the party quickly partnered off; luckily there were equal numbers of boys and girls.* [T1] *The lady of the house had no difficulty in partnering off her attractive daughter for the evening with a rich young man.*

**pass along** *v adv; prep*
**1** to send (something such as information) from person to person (in a row): [T1 + ALONG/*along*] *Pass this message along* (*the line of people*), *will you?* → **hand on (2), pass down[1,2] (1), pass on[1] (2)**
**2** to move further, esp. to the other end (of a vehicle): [IØ + ALONG/*along*] *Pass right along* (*the bus*), *please!* → **move down[1,2] (1),** etc., **(2), pass down[1] (3)**

**pass away** *v adv*
**1** to spend (time, esp. an evening) pleasantly:

[T1 + AWAY] *Conversation with friends soon passes an evening away.*

***2** to cease to exist: [IØ] *The storm should pass away before dark. The pain was severe to begin with, but soon passed away. "And I saw a new heaven and a new earth: for the first heaven and the first earth were passed away; and there was no more sea."* (The Bible) → **go away** (3), **go off**[1] (3), **pass off** (1), **take away** (3), **wear off** (3)

***3** *euph* to die: [IØ (*usu. simple tenses*)] *I'm sorry to hear that your uncle passed away last week.* → **conk out** (3), **kick off** (5), **pass on**[1] (4), **pass over**[1] (5), **peg out** (4), **pop off** (3), **snuff it, snuff out** (4)

**pass back** *v adv*

**1** to return (something): [T1 + BACK] *When you've read the letter, will you pass it back to me? I must reply to it at once.*

**2** to throw, send, or kick (something such as a ball) to a player behind one: [T1 + BACK] *One of the rules of the game is that the ball can only be passed back.* → **pass forward**

**3** to send (information) to someone further away: [T1 + BACK] *Your complaint has been passed back to the makers, who should be writing to you soon.*

**pass between** *v prep*

to be spoken by (two people): [IØ + *between*] *After the angry words that passed between us last Christmas, I doubt if we shall ever speak to each other again. Tell no one of the secret that has passed between us.*

**pass by**[1] *v adv*

**1** to move past someone or something, esp. without offering help: [IØ + BY] *So many people pass by and never notice the old lonely people who stay in their homes all day. "Is it nothing to you, all ye that pass by?"* (The Bible) —**bypass, passer-by** *n*

**2** (of time) to go; grow later: [IØ + BY] *A year passed by, and still she had not found a suitable job.* → **fly by**[1] (2), **go by**[1] (2), **go on**[1] (8), **go past**[1] (2), **run on**[1] (2), **wear on**[1], **wear out** (4)

***3** to disregard; pay no attention to; overlook (someone or something): [T1b] *The voters passed him by and elected his opponent. We'll pass that matter by for the moment.* → **pass over**[1] (2)

***4** (of life) to pass without pleasure or reward for (someone): [T1b] *Life has passed me by.*

**pass by**[2] *v prep*

**1** to move past (someone or something): [IØ + *by*] *When you have passed by the church, take the next turning on your left. She passed close by me without a sign of recognition.*

***2** to be known by (a name): [T1 (*no pass.*)] *He passed by the name of Baker for many years, so avoiding discovery by the police.* → **go by**[2] (7), etc.

**pass down**[1] *v adv*

**1** to send (something such as information) from person to person: [T1 + DOWN] *Pass the message down to the people at the end of the table.* → **hand on** (2), **pass along** (1), **pass on**[1] (2)

**2** to give (something) usu. with one's hand to someone on a lower level: [T1 + DOWN] *Pass the paint pots down to me before you come down the ladder.* → **hand down** (1), **hand up** (1), **pass up** (1)

**3** to move further, esp. to the far end of a vehicle: [IØ + DOWN] *Pass (right) down inside, please!* → **move down**[1] (1), etc.

***4** to give or leave to people who are younger or come later: [T1 (*often pass.*)] *This custom has been passed down since the 18th century. This ring has been passed down in my family.* → **hand down** (3), etc.

***5** to give (usu. clothes) to a younger or smaller member of the family: [T1 (*to*)] *We hoped that the next child would be a boy, so that we could pass his brother's clothes down to him.* → **hand down** (4), **hand on** (3), **pass on**[1] (6) **reach down**

**pass down**[2] *v prep*

**1** to send (something such as information) from person to person in (a line): [T1 + *down*] *Pass the message down the line, the general's coming!*

**2** to move further down (a vehicle), away from the door: [IØ + *down*] *Pass down the bus, please!* → **move down**[2] (2), **pass along** (2)

**pass for** *v prep*

**1** to pass examinations in order to become (a member of a profession): [IØ + *for* (*usu. simple tenses*)] *My son hopes to pass for a lawye at the end of his three years' study at the uni versity.*

***2** to gain (usu. false) recognition and accep tance as (something or someone): [T1 (*n pass., usu. simple tenses*)] *Do you think h will pass for a cook wearing that hat? Sh could pass for a much younger woman. "Go made him, and therefore let him pass for man."* (Shakespeare, *The Merchant of Venice*)

**pass forward** *v adv* → **pass back** (2)

to throw, send or kick (something such as ball) to a player ahead of one: [T1 + FORWARD] *One of the defence players passed th ball forward to another member of his team s that he could shoot.* [IØ; T1 + FORWARD] *rugby football, passing (the ball) forward against the rules.* —**forward pass** *n*

**pass from** *v prep*

**1** to change from (something): [IØ + *from*] *The weather should soon pass from this bitt cold to more springlike temperatures.* → **pa into** (2)

**2** to leave (someone): [IØ + *from*] *"If it possible, let this cup pass from me."* (The Bi ble)

**pass in**[1] *v adv*

**1** to (cause to) enter: [IØ + IN (*to*)] *Is the room for two people at a time to pass in?* [T1 + IN (*to*)] *The hole in the wall was big enou to pass a note in to the prisoner.*

*2 to send (something) to someone in charge, usu. handing it from person to person: [T1] *Pass your papers in when you have finished.* → **give in** (1), **give into** (1), **hand in** (2)

**pass in²** *v prep*

**1 pass in a crowd** to be unnoticed; be satisfactory: [*usu. simple tenses*] *She's not exactly beautiful, but she would pass in a crowd.*

**2 pass in review** to (cause to) be seen, mentioned, or considered one by one: *As we pass the school year in review, we can be proud of our many successes. When a man is drowning, it is said that his whole life passes in review.*

**pass into** *v prep*

**1** to enter (something): [IØ + *into*] *They passed into the house without my noticing them.*

**2** to change gradually into (something else): [IØ + *into*] *The sky was a deep pink, passing into gold. As we got higher up the mountain, the rain passed into snow.* → **pass from** (1)

*3 to gain entry to (something such as a college): [T1 (*often simple tenses*)] *It is not easy to pass into this medical school.*

*4 to become part of (something such as history): [T1 (*no pass., often simple tenses*)] *The deeds of these few brave men have passed into history.*

*5 to enter (a state such as sleep): [T1 (*no pass., often simple tenses*)] *The magician made the princess pass into a deep sleep for 100 years.* → **get into** (11), etc.

**pass off** *v adv*

**1** to cease to exist: [IØ] *The storm should pass off before dark. The pain was severe to begin with, but soon passed off.* → **go away** (3), **go off¹** (3), **pass away** (2), **take away** (3), **wear off** (3)

**2** to take place, usu. successfully: [L9 (*usu. simple tenses*)] *The meeting passed off well. How did your performance pass off?* → **bring off** (2), **carry off¹** (6), **come off¹** (6), **go off¹** (6), **pull off¹** (4)

**3** to direct attention away from (something): [T1 (*usu. simple tenses*)] *He passed off the difficult question. The remark was intended as rudeness, but he passed it off with a laugh.*

**4** to make someone accept (something) by deceit: [T1] *The police caught him for passing off false money.* → **palm off**

**pass off as** *v adv prep* → **palm off as**

to succeed in pretending that (someone or something) is (someone or something else): [D1] *She passed herself off as an experienced actress. He passed the idea off as his own.*

**pass on¹** *v adv*

**1** to move away or further: [IØ + ON] *He stopped for a moment, and then passed on.*

**2** to send (something such as information or work) from person to person: [T1 + ON (*to*)] *The secret word is "sugar": pass it on (to the next person). He tried to pass the job on to me, but I soon got rid of it.* → **hand on** (2), **pass along** (1), **pass down¹** (1)

*3 to go further; continue: [IØ (*to*)] *Let's pass on to the urgent business of the meeting.* → **move on** (3)

*4 *euph* to die: [IØ (*simple tenses*)] *I'm sorry to hear that your favourite uncle passed on last week.* → **pass away** (3), etc.

*5 to give or leave to people who are younger or come later: [T1] *This ring has been passed on in my family from mother to daughter. The possession of language enables man to pass on his wisdom and experience to his children and grandchildren.*

*6 to give (usu. clothes) to a younger or smaller member of the family: [T1] *The girl was ashamed of wearing clothes that had been passed on by her elder sister.* → **hand down** (4), **hand on** (3), **pass down¹** (5), **reach down**

*7 to give (esp. an advantage) to someone further down the line of trade, etc.: [T1 (*to*)] *The savings which have been made in the cost of the raw materials will be passed on to the customer.*

**pass on²** *v prep*

**1 pass judgment/an opinion on** to express an opinion about the worth of (something or someone): *I do not feel that I have the necessary knowledge to pass judgment on a work of modern art. Most people are too ready to pass an opinion on their neighbours.*

**2 pass sentence on** (of a judge) to tell the punishment being given to (a prisoner): *Before I pass sentence on you, have you anything to say for yourself?* → **pronounce on** (2)

***pass out** *v adv*

**1** to give (things) freely: [T1] *The theatre company are passing out free tickets for the opening night: do you want one?* → **dish out** (3), **give out** (3), **hand out** (2, 3)

**2** *not fml* to lose consciousness: [IØ] *When the young man heard the news, he passed out with the shock.* → **black out** (5)

**3** to gain success at a military college: [IØ] *How many of the young men passed out this year?* —**passing-out** *n, adj*

***pass out of** *v adv prep*

to leave (something): [T1 (*no pass.*)] *All joy passed out of my life when I heard the terrible news. When he left the city, he passed out of our group of friends.*

**pass over¹** *v adv*

**1** to move or travel overhead: [IØ + OVER] *As we were standing in the garden, three planes passed over, flying very low.*

*2 to disregard; pay no attention to; fail to deal with; not mention (something): [T1] *Don't pass any detail over. No chance to improve conditions should be passed over.* → **pass by¹** (3), **pass up**

*3 to overlook; disregard (something): [T1 (*often simple tenses*)] *We will pass over your unfortunate remarks. The committee has* generously decided to pass over the small faults in your report, as the general effect is very good. The chairman passed the interruption over in silence.*

*4 to fail to choose (someone), usu. for advancement: [T1a (*for*) (*usu. pass.*)] *He was passed over for the chairmanship, and another man was appointed instead.*

*5 *euph* to die: [IØ (*simple tenses*)] *I'm sorry to hear that your favourite uncle passed over last week.* → **pass away** (3), etc.

**pass over²** *v prep*

1 to move above (something); travel past without touching (something): [IØ + *over*] *As we were standing in the garden, three planes passed over the house, flying very low.*

2 (of a road, bridge, etc.) to cross (something such as a road or railway line): [IØ + *over* (*simple tenses*)] *The new road will pass over the dangerous railway crossing where nine people were killed in a bus last year.* —**overpass** *n* → **fly over²**

*3 to mention, read, or deal with (something) quickly: [T1 (*often simple tenses*)] *Let us pass quickly over these less urgent questions and attend to the important business of the meeting. It should not take long to pass over the answers to the first group of examination questions.*

4 **pass one's eye over** to look at (something) quickly: *I just passed my eye over the letter; I haven't studied it in detail yet.* → **cast over²** (2)

**pass round¹** *v adv*

1 to hand (something) round a group of people: [T1 + ROUND] *Pass the cake round so that everyone can take a piece.* → **hand round**

2 **pass round the hat** to collect money, usu. to help someone: *One of the secretaries left to get married, so the other office workers passed the hat round to buy her a wedding present.* → **take round¹** (5)

**pass round²** *v prep*

1 to make (something) go round (something or someone): [T1 + *round*] *If we can pass a rope round the sunken object, we might be able to raise it.*

2 to send (something) round (a group): [T1 + *round*] *The story was quickly passed round the office. Pass the rest of the notices round the table so that everyone can have a copy.*

**pass through¹** *v adv*

to travel through a place without stopping: [IØ + THROUGH] *We're not staying in the town, we're just passing through.*

**pass through²** *v prep*

1 to travel through (a place), usu. without stopping: [IØ + *through*] *I've passed through Bath on my way to Wales, but have never stayed there.*

2 to make (something) move through (something): [T1 + *through*] *You'd look neater if you passed a comb through your hair now and again. Passing his hand through the hole, he could feel a hard object.*

*3 to complete a course in (a college, universi-ty, etc.): [T1 (*usu. simple tenses*)] *He passec through three years of college without reall learning anything.*

*4 to experience; suffer (something): [T1 *The country is passing through troublesom times. The university is passing through a dif ficult period of change.* → **go through²** (6)

**pass under** *v prep*

1 to (cause to) move under; travel beneat (something): [IØ + *under* (*often simpl tenses*)] *Is there room for a person to pas under the floorboards to examine the wiring. The river passes under several famous Lon don streets, but few people know of its exis tence.* [T1 + *under*] *Pass the end of the rop under the wounded man's arms.* —**underpas** *n*

*2 to be known by (a name): [T1 (*no pass. usu. simple tenses*)] *For years, he passed unde the name of Baker, to avoid discovery by th police.* → **go by²** (7), etc.

3 **a lot of water has passed under the bridg** many changes have taken place (since then) *Since I first met him a lot of water has passe under the bridge and we are now good friends*

**pass up** *v adv*

1 to hand (something) to someone on a high er level: [T1 + UP] *When I get to the top the ladder, please pass up the hammer an nails.* → **hand down** (1), **hand up** (1), **pass dow** (2)

2 to rise: [IØ + UP] *This cover is to preve the smells from passing up into the air.*

*3 to miss; let slip; fail to make use of (som thing, as a chance): [T1a] *Never pass up chance to improve your English.* → **pass ov** (2)

*4 *AmE* to pass (someone) without recogni ing him: [T1 (*usu. simple tenses*)] *I saw Ji in the street but he passed me up.*

**paste up** *v adv*

1 to fix (something such as a notice), usu. a wall, with a sticky substance: [T1 + U *Help me to paste up these notices.*

2 to mend (something such as a crack) covering it with something fastened with sticky substance: [T1 + UP] *He was pasti up the holes in the glass with brown paper.*

*3 (in printing) to arrange (papers or oth material for printing) on a larger paper make a page: [T1] *One of my jobs in printing house was to paste up pictures a blocks of type ready for approval as a finish page.* [IØ] *We need someone in the newspap office who has experience of pasting u* —**paste-up** *n, adj*

**pat down** *v adv*

to make (something) lie flat by hitting it ge ly: [T1 + DOWN] *The cook patted down so lumps in the pastry.*

**pat on** *v prep*

1 to touch (usu. someone or an animal) lig ly and quickly on (usu. a part of the bod

[T1 + *on*] *Most children dislike being patted on the head. It's safe to pat the dog on his back but not on his nose.*

**2 pat someone/oneself on the back** to show pride in the ability or action of; encourage or praise someone or oneself: *All the members of the team gathered round him, patting him on the back. Her performance wasn't so wonderful—I don't know what cause she has to pat herself on the back.*

**patch up** *v adv*

**1** to mend (usu. clothing) with added pieces of cloth: [T1 + UP] *His trousers were patched up, and he was ashamed of them.*

***2** *not fml* to treat (someone or a part of the body) for wounds: [T1] *After the car crash, the driver was taken to the hospital to be patched up.*

***3** *not fml* to settle (a disagreement); become friends again after (a quarrel): [T1] *Have Jim and Mary patched up their quarrel yet? The new director and the chairman seem to have patched up their differences of opinion.* → **make up** (14), **stitch up** (2)

**patter about/around** *v adv*

to move about with light quick steps: [IØ + ABOUT/AROUND] *I'm sure I can hear a small animal pattering about in the bushes.*

**pattern after/on/upon** *v prep* → **fashion after, model after**

**1** to form (something) as a copy of (something): [D1 (*often pass.*)] *The railway system was patterned after the successful plan used in other countries.*

**2** to make (oneself) like (someone): [D1 (*usu. simple tenses*)] *Mary has always patterned herself on her mother.*

**pattern with** *v prep*

to ornament (something) with a pattern of (something): [T1 + *with* (*usu. pass.*)] *I want a wallpaper patterned with roses.*

**pause on/upon** *v prep* → **think about** (1), etc.

to think about (something) carefully: [T1] *Let me pause on these matters for a time before I make a decision.*

**pave with** *v prep*

**1** to provide (a road, path, etc.) with a surface of (a material such as stones): [T1 + *with* (*often pass.*)] *Old roads used to be paved with round stones to help the horses to walk easily. "O London is a fine town, A very famous city, Where all the streets are paved with gold."* (George Colman, *Heir-at-Law*) → **strew with** (1)

**2** to fill or cover (something) with or base (something) on (something): [D1 (*usu. pass.*)] *The way to misfortune is paved with good intentions.*

**paw about/around** *v adv*

to handle (someone or something) roughly and awkwardly: [T1 + ABOUT/AROUND] *Girls don't like being pawed about by strange men. Who's been pawing this cake around? It's covered with fingermarks.*

**pay away** *v adv*

**1** to spend (money): [T1 + AWAY] *I seem to pay away half my income on taxes of one kind or another.*

***2** to allow (something such as a rope) to be gradually lengthened: [T1] *Pay the rope away a little at a time.* → **pay out** (4), **play out** (7), **run out** (5)

**pay back** *v adv*

**1** to return (money owed) to (someone) (for something): [T1 + BACK (*for, to*)] *I must remember to pay you back for the concert tickets. We must pay the money back to the firm before they notice that it's missing.*

***2** to return punishment to (someone) for a wrong done to oneself: [T1 (*for*)] *We will pay them back for the trick they played on us.* → **get even**, etc.

**pay by** *v prep* → **pay with** (1)

to use (a means such as a cheque) to pay a bill: [IØ + *by*] *This shop does not allow its customers to pay by cheque.*

***pay down** *v adv*

**1** to pay money immediately (for something): [T1 (*for*)] *Are you able to pay down the whole cost? The buyer paid $6,000 down for the new car.*

**2** to pay part of the price for (something) with a promise to pay the rest, usu. over a period of time: [T1] *You can buy this house by paying 10% down and the rest over 25 years, at interest.* —**down payment** *n* → **put down** (9)

**pay for** *v prep*

**1** to pay (a sum of money) to obtain (something); provide the price of (something); give (someone) money in return for (goods or services) or as the cost of (something): [T1 + *for*] *To think that I paid £25 for that coat when I could have got the same one for £18! I'll pay you for the damage. The artist, like the baker, should be paid for his work.* [IØ + *for*] *How are you going to pay for your holiday?* → **get for** (2), **give for** (1), **go for** (3), **take for** (2)

***2** to receive punishment or suffering for (something); suffer the result of (something): [T1 (*with*)] *You'll have to pay (dearly/heavily) for your crime. We are paying for the fine summer with a wet winter.*

**3 pay for itself** to cover its cost in other savings, over a period of time: *This machine will pay for itself in five years, by saving labour costs.*

**pay in** *v adv*

to put (money, a cheque, etc.) into a bank or other account: [T1 + IN] *I have to pay in $20 to cover a cheque that I wrote. I want to stop in the bank to pay in these cheques.* [IØ + IN] *Use this special book for paying in.* —**paying-in** *adj*

**pay into** *v prep*

to put or add (money, a cheque, etc.) into (a bank or other account): [T1 + *into*] *I have to pay $20 into my account for a cheque that I* *wrote. I want to stop in the bank to pay these cheques into my account.* [I∅ + *into*] *Use this special book for paying into your account. You haven't paid into the insurance plan for some months.*

***pay off** *v adv*

**1** to pay the whole of (a debt); settle accounts with (someone): [T1] *It's a good feeling to pay off the house after all these years. Once we have paid off the store, we shall owe money to no one.* —**payoff** *n not fml*

**2** *not fml* to act so as to settle (an old quarrel, etc.); return punishment to (someone): [T1] *I'll pay him off for treating me like that. That's a neat way of paying off old scores.* —**payoff** *n* → **get even**, etc.

**3** to pay (someone) to leave one's employment: [T1] *100 workers will be paid off when the factory closes next week.*

**4** *not fml* to pay (someone) to be silent about a wrong act, or not to fulfil a threat, etc.: [T1] *Do you think you can pay the criminals off? We had to pay off the man who got us the contract, with 5% of the profit.* —**payoff** *n* → **kick back** (4), **rake off**

**5** *not fml* to be successful: [I∅ (*usu. simple tenses*)] *Did your daring plan pay off?*

**6** *naut* to allow a ship to swing away from the wind: [I∅] *If your course continues to call for paying off you will have to take suitable action.* → **fall away** (8), **fall off**[1] (6), **sag away**

**7** *naut* to take (a ship) out of use, for repair or at the end of her last voyage: [T1 (*usu. pass.*)] *When a ship is paid off, she flies a special flag when entering harbour for the last time.* —**paying-off** *adj*

**pay on** *v prep*

**pay on the nail** to pay a debt at once: *He's been a good customer for many years, always paying on the nail.*

***pay out** *v adv*

**1** *not fml* to spend (money) in small amounts or unwillingly: [T1] *I'm tired of paying out something more every week. The government is paying out more money than ever before to people out of work.*

**2** to pay (money saved) back to the people who paid the money in: [T1] *The bank pays out interest on its savings accounts every six months.* [I∅] *The savings club always pays out in time for Christmas.*

**3** to return punishment to (someone) for a wrong done to oneself: [T1] *We'll pay them out for the trick they played on us.* → **get even**, etc.

**4** to allow (something such as a rope) to be gradually lengthened: [T1] *Pay the rope out a little at a time.* → **pay away** (2), **play out** (7), **run out** (5)

***pay over** *v adv* → **make over**[1] (3)

*fml* to make formal payments of (money): [T1] *The lawyers will be able to pay over the money left to you by your uncle when it has been approved by the court. The agreed sum will be paid over on completion of the contract. The insurance claim cannot be paid over until the accident has been reported to the police.*

**pay through** *v prep* → **hold up** (4), **rip off** (3)

**pay through the nose** to be charged too high a price: *I shan't shop at that store again, they make you pay through the nose for perfectly ordinary goods.*

**pay to** *v prep*

**1** to give (something such as money) to (someone): [T1 + *to*] *Pay your entrance money to the man at the door. The prisoner has paid his debt to society with all those years in prison.*

**2 pay attention to** to listen carefully to (someone or usu. someone's words); take notice of (something or someone): *Pay attention to me, children, I shall not repeat these instructions. I wish now that I'd paid attention to his advice. Pay attention to your work! Stop talking! Attention must be paid even to the most unimportant details. Many criminals were not paid enough attention to as children.* → **attend to** (1, 2)

**3 pay court to** to show admiration for (someone), so as to win his favour or love: *It's no use paying court to the director, he treats all the workers equally on principle. Sir, I wish to have your permission to pay court to your daughter.*

**4 pay heed to** to pay attention to; take notice of (someone or something): *Pay no heed to her rudeness: she wants to hurt you, so pretend it doesn't matter, and then she'll have failed. Many more people are paying heed to the government's warnings about the dangers of cigarette smoking.* → **give to** (12), **take of** (9)

**5 pay homage to** to show one's respect for (someone), often in a formal manner: *Crowds of people gathered to pay homage to the king when he visited their city. The public walked slowly past the grave, paying homage to the dead general.* → **do to** (7)

**6 pay lip service to** *not fml* to support in words, but not in fact; give loyalty, interest etc., in speech, while thinking the opposite *Many governments pay lip service to the importance of education but refuse to allow enough money for its needs.*

**7 pay tribute to** *old use* to pay money to (usu a conqueror): *In the old days, a conquered people had to pay tribute to the victors, giving them all their gold and precious things; every year after that, a yearly tribute had to be paid to the rulers, of a large part of the people's wealth.*

**8 pay tribute to** to express thanks or admiration for (someone or his work): *In closing, should like to pay tribute to the hard work put in by the women's committee.*

***pay up** *v adv*

to pay (a debt) in full, often unwillingly: [T1 *Pay up what you owe before you leave town.*

*shall be glad when all these debts are paid up. Every club member must pay up his membership money before the end of the season.* [IØ] *Did the insurance company pay up after all that argument? If you pay up now, you will not be taken to court.* —**paid-up** *adj* → **cough out** (2), **cough up** (2), **stump up**

**pay with** *v prep*

**1** to pay (a debt or someone) by using (a supply): [T1 + *with*] *You can pay the bill with a cheque if you like. Insurance companies pay their claims with the money that they receive from other people.* → **pay by**

*__2__ to reward (someone or usu. an action) by giving (something) in return: [T1] *I have made it a rule always to pay respect with respect.* → **repay by, repay with, requite with**

**peach on** *v prep* → **inform against,** etc.

*not fml* to report (a guilty person) to people in charge: [IØ + *on*] *How did the police know where we were hiding? Someone must have peached on us!*

**peal out** *v adv*

(usu. of a bell or voice) to sound with a ringing note: [IØ + OUT] *The church bells pealed out at the end of the war, to declare victory. Mary's laughter pealed out across the room—for once, she was enjoying the party.*

**peck at** *v prep*

**1** (usu. of a bird) to use its beak to pick up, make holes in, or attack (something): [IØ (AWAY) + *at*] *That bird makes such a terrible noise, pecking at the tree in search of insects. The chickens fight by pecking at each other.*

*__2__ *not fml* to take only small amounts of (food): [T1] *Try to eat your dinner, Jane, you've only pecked at it.* → **nibble at** (1), **pick at** (2)

*__3__ *not fml* to deal with only the surface of (a subject): [T1] *Let's deal properly with the question, instead of just pecking at it.* → **pick at** (3)

*__4__ *not fml* to find fault repeatedly with (someone or something): [T1] *That new teacher is always pecking at our spelling mistakes.*

**peck up** *v adv*

(of a bird) to lift (something) from the ground with its beak: [T1 + UP] *The chickens will peck up all the grain that you throw on the ground for them.*

**peek at** *v prep* → **peep at**

to take a quick, often secret, look at (something): [IØ + *at*] *No peeking at your presents before Christmas morning!*

**peel away** *v adv*

**1** (usu. of a skin or covering, etc.) to (cause to) be removed in thin pieces: [T1 + AWAY] *As you peel away the onion skin, you find another skin underneath. Peeling away the wrapping paper, she got such a surprise when she saw what was inside!* [IØ + AWAY] *He has a terrible disease in which the skin on the hands peels away. The paint is peeling away already: you can't have prepared the surface properly.* → **peel off** (1)

*__2__ (of planes) to leave a group in flight by turning to one side: [IØ] *The leading pair of planes peeled away, one to the right and one to the left.* → **peel off** (2), **veer off**

**peel back** *v adv*

to turn back (something such as a skin or covering): [T1 + BACK] *Peeling back his trouser leg, he showed them the wound. If you peel a banana skin only halfway back, you still have some left for holding it.*

**peel off** *v adv*

**1** (usu. of a skin or covering, etc.) to (cause to) be removed in thin pieces: [T1 + OFF] *He neatly peeled off the thick skin of the orange. Peel the label off and send it to the makers, then they will send some of your money back.* [IØ + OFF] *He has a terrible disease in which the skin on the hands peels off. The paint is peeling off already: you can't have prepared the surface properly.* → **peel away** (1)

*__2__ (of planes) to leave a group in flight by turning to one side: [IØ] *The leading pair of planes peeled off, one to the right and one to the left.* → **peel away, veer off**

*__3__ to remove (all one's clothing); get undressed: [T1] *She peeled off her coat and jumped into the water.* [IØ] *The girls peeled off before swimming.*

**peep at** *v prep* → **peek at**

to look in a small and sometimes improper way at (someone or something): [IØ + *at*] *Would you like to peep at the room before renting it? She spends half her day peeping at her neighbours from behind her curtains.*

**peep into** *v prep*

to take a small look into (something): [IØ + *into*] *Which of the students would dare to peep into a teacher's desk to see if the examination papers were there?*

**peep out** *v adv*

**1** to take a small look out: [IØ + OUT] *The child peeped out from behind her fingers.*

**2** to appear, as through a narrow opening: [IØ + OUT] *Spring must have begun at last, the young leaves are just peeping out. The stars peeped out as the clouds hurried past.*

**peep over** *v adv; prep*

to take a small look over (something): [IØ + OVER/*over*] *He held the small child above the level of the wall so that he could peep over. I can see a little face peeping over the fence—who is it?*

**peep through** *v adv; prep*

to take a small look through (something); appear through (something) for a short time: [IØ + THROUGH/*through*] *She moved the curtains to one side and peeped through. The moon peeped through the clouds for a moment. You get quite a good view if you peep through this crack in the fence.*

**peer about/around** *v adv; prep*

to look with or as with difficulty in various directions: [IØ + ABOUT/AROUND/*about/*

*around*] *When you enter a cinema, you often have to peer about (you) for your seat until your eyes get used to the darkness.*

**peer at** *v prep*
to look closely at (something or someone): [IØ + *at*] *Even after peering at the letter, I still could not recognize the signature. Excuse me for peering at you, but you are so like someone I know; perhaps you're a relative of his?*

**peer into** *v prep*
to look with effort into (something): [IØ + *into*] *She stood on the shore for some time, peering into the distance, long after the ship had gone.*

**peer out** *v adv*
to look out with some difficulty: [L9 + OUT] *Opening the window, she peered out into the darkness, but could see nothing.*

**peer through** *v adv; prep*
to look closely through (something): [IØ + THROUGH/*through*] *There's a hole in the wall where/that you can peer through.*

**peg as** *v prep*
*AmE not fml* to regard (someone) as being (a kind of person): [T1 + *as* (*usu. pass.*)] *We soon had him pegged as a liar.*

***peg away at** *v adv prep* → **plod away, plug away at, slog at**
*not fml* to work hard and steadily at (something or doing something): [T1 (*no pass.*)] *If you peg away at cricket practice all your youth, there is some hope that you may be chosen for the team. If I peg away at painting the room I may get it finished tonight.*

**peg down** *v adv*
**1** to fasten (something) down with wooden nails: [T1 + DOWN] *Make sure the tent is safely pegged down in this high wind.* → **nail down** (1), **pin down** (1)
***2** *not fml* to limit (someone) by controlling his actions: [T1] *If he's not pegged down to a certain course of action, he gets lazy. Can you peg him down to a firm date?* → **nail down** (2), **pin down** (2), **tie down to** (2)
***3** to fix (prices) at a lower level: [T1] *The government is attempting to peg down the price of food.*

***peg out** *v adv*
**1** *BrE* to hang (washing) on a line with clothes pins: [T1] *It's a lovely windy day, help me to peg out the washing.* → **hang out** (2)
**2** to mark (a piece of ground) with wooden markers: [T1] *The builders have pegged out the land for the house. Have you pegged out your claim yet?*
**3** to stretch (something such as cloth or paper) with pins: [T1] *The map was pegged out on the ground.*
**4** *infml* (of animals or people) to lose consciousness; die; (of a machine) fail: [IØ (*often simple tenses*)] *Two of the climbers pegged out before they reached the top of the mountain. The poor old dog pegged out last week; he had lived to a ripe old age. The engine pegged out halfway up the hill.* → **pass away** (3), etc.

**pelt along** *v adv; prep*
*not fml* to move at great speed (along a road, etc.): [L9 + ALONG/*along*] *The rabbit pelted along, with the dog giving chase. He was last seen pelting along the road as if devils were after him.*

**pelt at** *v prep* → **pelt with** (1)
to throw (usu. things) at (someone): [T1 + *at*] *Stop those boys pelting stones at the poor cat!*

***pelt down** *v adv* → **pelt with** (2), **pour down**[1], **pour with, sheet down, teem with** (2)
*not fml* (of rain) to descend heavily and quickly: [IØ (*often continuous tenses*)] *The rain was pelting down, and I had gone out without a coat. It's pelting down outside, hadn't you better wait a few minutes before going out?*

**pelt out** *v adv*
*not fml* to run outside quickly: [L9 + OUT] *As soon as school was over, the children pelted out to play.*

**pelt with** *v prep*
**1** to attack (someone) by throwing (usu. things) at him or asking him a lot of (questions): [T1 + *with*] *Stop those boys pelting the poor cat with stones! The crowd pelted the speaker with questions until the chairman had to stop them, as there was no more time.* → **pelt at**
***2** *not fml* (of weather) to give a lot of (rain): [*It* + T1 (*no pass., often continuous tenses*)] *It's pelting with rain outside, hadn't you better wait a few minutes before going out?* → **pelt down, pour down**[1], **pour with, sheet down, teem with** (2)

***pen in** *v adv* → **pen up** (1)
to enclose or imprison (someone or an animal) in a small space: [T1 (*usu. pass.*)] *Work does not stop for the day until all the cattle are safely penned in. I can't help feeling penned in by this long winter.*

***pen up** *v adv*
**1** to enclose or imprison (someone or an animal) in a small space: [T1 (*usu. pass.*)] *When all the cattle are safely penned up, the farmer can stop work for the day. How long have you been penned up in the house by your illness?* → **pen in**
**2** to control (usu. one's feelings): [T1 (*usu. pass.*)] *His anger had been pent up for so long that at last he exploded.* —**pent-up** *adj*

**penalize for** *v prep*
*fml* to punish (someone or his work) for (a fault or doing something wrong): [T1 + *for*] *Your work will be penalized for spelling mistakes. Workers are penalized for arriving late for work.*

**penetrate into** *v prep*
to find a way to get inside (something): [IØ + *into*] *The water has penetrated into the bed*

*rooms, so there must be a hole in the roof. These new ideas are penetrating into the framework of society.*

**penetrate through** *v prep*
to find a way to pass through (something): [IØ + *through*] *We shall need a strong light to penetrate through this mist.*

**penetrate to** *v prep*
to reach (something) by passing through something in the way: [IØ + *to*] *The knife wound penetrated to the bone, and his life was in danger.*

**penetrate with** *v prep* → **imbue with; permeate with**
**be penetrated with** *fml* to be thoroughly filled with (something such as a quality): *All his poems seem to be penetrated with the idea of death and hopelessness.*

*__pension off__ *v adv*
**1** to dismiss (someone) from work but continue to pay him/her a reduced income: [T1 (*often pass.*)] *One way to deal with unemployment is to pension off the firm's older workers at an earlier age than usual.* —**pensioned-off** *adj*
**2** *not fml* to stop employing (a person, animal, machine, etc.) that is worn out, too old to be useful, etc.: [T1 (*often pass.*)] *It's time this old washing machine was pensioned off; it keeps breaking down.*

**people with** *v prep*
*fml* to fill (something such as a place) with (people or things): [D1 (*usu. pass.*)] *The city is becoming peopled with foreigners. The sky was peopled with stars.*

**pep up** *v adv*
*not fml* to make (something or someone) more active or cheerful: [T1] *This party is very dull; what can we do to pep it up? A holiday will pep you up.*

**pepper with** *v prep*
to attack (something or someone) with (things such as stones, shot, or questions): [D1 (*usu. pass.*)] *The deer fell wounded, peppered with shot. The speaker was peppered with questions by a crowd of eager students.*

**perch on** *v prep*
to (cause to) rest on (usu. something narrow): [IØ + *on*] *The bird perched on a branch of the tree above our heads and sang beautifully.* [T1 + *on* (*usu. pass.*)] *The little house was perched on an overhanging cliff in a most dangerous position.*

**percolate through**[1] *v adv* → **filter through**[1]
**1** to pass slowly through something which removes part: [L9 + THROUGH] *The liquid percolated through, and the solids were left behind.*
***2** to become gradually known: [IØ] *Slowly the idea percolated through, and at last he understood.*

**percolate through**[2] *v prep* → **filter through**[2]
**1** to (cause to) pass through (a material which removes part): [X9 + *through*] *You percolate the coffee through this special paper, and it takes out the bitterness.* [L9 + *through*] *The rain will percolate through the soil.*
**2** to pass in a reduced form through (something): [L9 + *through*] *Sunlight percolated through the thick leaves.*
***3** to become gradually known in (a place): [T1 (*no pass*)] *The news percolated through the village until everyone knew.*

**perform on** *v prep*
to do or play (something) on (something or someone): [T1 + *on* (*often simple tenses*)] *Have you ever performed a musical play on this stage? The doctor has performed this operation on many famous people. After the trick he performed on us, it is difficult to forgive him.* [IØ + *on*] *How well your daughter performs on the piano! The famous actor has performed on all the great stages of the world.*

**perish by** *v prep* → **perish from, perish with** (1)
*fml* to die by means of (something): [IØ + *by* (*often simple tenses*)] *Anyone who opposes the king shall perish by the sword.*

**perish from** *v prep* → **perish by, perish with** (1)
*fml* to die from (a cause): [IØ + *from* (*often simple tenses*)] *Many people in tropical countries perish from disease.*

**perish in** *v prep*
*fml* to die in (something such as a cause): [IØ + *in* (*often simple tenses*)] *More than 200 people perished in the great floods.*

**perish with** *v prep*
**1** *fml* to die by means of (something): [IØ + *with* (*often simple tenses*)] *"All they that take the sword shall perish with the sword."* (The Bible) → **perish by, perish from**
**2** to suffer because of (something such as cold or hunger): [IØ + *with*] *The children are always complaining that they are perishing with hunger; don't take them seriously. Let me in, I'm perishing with cold.*
**3** (of a material) to decay because of (a cause): [IØ + *with*] *Even the best quality rubber will perish with age.*

*__perjure oneself__ *v pron* → **forswear oneself**
*fml* to tell lies in a court of law; break one's solemn promise to tell the truth: [IØ] *If you perjure yourself you will be severely punished.*

*__perk up__ *v adv*
**1** (of an animal) to raise (usu. ears) usu. in expectation: [T1] *The dog perked up its ears at the sound of its master's return.* → **prick up** (1)
**2** *not fml* to (cause to) become more cheerful, show interest, etc.: [T1] *You need a holiday to perk you up. We need more young people to perk up this dull party.* [IØ] *Mary perked up as soon as Jim's name was mentioned.* → **cheer up,** etc.

**permeate among/through** *v prep*
*fml* to spread thoroughly into (something): [IØ + *among*] *New ways of thinking are permeating among the students.* [IØ + *through*]

*The rain will permeate through the soil and reach the roots. The heavy rain permeated right through my coat!*

**permeate with** *v prep* → **imbue with, penetrate with**

**be permeated with** to be thoroughly filled with (something such as a quality): *His public speeches were permeated with hatred of injustice.*

**permit in** *v adv; prep* → **allow in**

to allow (usu. someone) to enter (a place): [X9 + IN (*usu. pass.*)] *Children are not permitted in without their parents.* [X9 + *in* (*usu. simple tenses*)] *I don't permit cats in my kitchen!*

**permit into** *v prep* → **allow into**

to allow (usu. someone) to enter (something such as a place): [X9 + *into* (*usu. pass.*)] *Children are not permitted into the cinema without their parents.*

* **permit of** *v prep* → ALLOW OF

**permit out** *v adv* → **allow out**

to give (someone) permission to go out of doors, leave a room or building, etc.: [X9 + OUT (*usu. pass.*)] *The prisoners are permitted out for half an hour's exercise each day.*

**permit through** *v adv; prep* → **allow through**

to give (someone) permission to pass through (something): [X9 + THROUGH/*through* (*usu. simple tenses*)] *The soldiers had orders to permit no stranger through (the gates).*

**permit up** *v adv* → **allow up**

to give (someone who has been ill) permission to get out of bed: [X9 + UP (*usu. simple tenses*)] *The doctor will not permit Mother up until her leg is better.*

**persevere at/in** *v prep* → **persevere with**

to work hard and continuously at (something or doing something) patiently: [IØ + *at/in*] *If you persevere at/in your search for a job, you are sure to find something suitable in the end. If you persevere in looking for a job, you are sure to find something suitable in the end.*

**persevere with** *v prep* → **persevere at**

to work hard and continuously at (something) patiently: [IØ + *with*] *It's not easy to persevere with such dull work, but it has to be finished.*

**persist in** *v prep* → **persist with**

to keep on (doing (something)) with patience, often in spite of difficulties or opposition: [IØ + *in*] *Why does the boy persist in his troublesome behaviour? If this behaviour is persisted in it could lead to serious trouble. Why do you persist in interrupting me when I have repeatedly asked you to stop?*

**persist with** *v prep* → **persist in**

to keep on doing (something) with patience, often in spite of difficulties or opposition: [IØ + *with*] *The salesman is still persisting with his demands.*

**persuade into** *v prep* → **argue into,** etc.

to cause (someone) to follow (a course of action or doing something) by talking to him/her, encouraging him/her, etc.: [X9 + *into*] *Can you persuade your father into lending us the car? The boy claims that he was persuaded into the crime.*

**persuade of** *v prep*

to make (someone) understand the truth of (something): [T1 + *of*] *We were able to persuade the prisoner of the wisdom of telling the truth.*

**persuade out of** *v adv prep* → **argue out of**, etc.

to prevent (someone) from (a course of action, or doing something) by talking to him/her: [T1 + OUT + *of*] *Can't the boy be persuaded out of such behaviour? We persuaded him out of lending his money to that untrustworthy man.*

* **pertain to** *v prep*

**1** *fml* to belong to (usu. a place): [T1 (*no pass., usu. participle*)] *These are all the grounds pertaining to the castle.*

**2** *fml* to have a connection with (something): [T1 (*no pass., usu. participle*)] *What proofs do you have pertaining to the case?*

**3** *fml* to be suitable to (something): [T1 (*no pass., usu. participle*)] *This is not the kind of behaviour pertaining to a gentleman.*

* **pervade with** *v prep*

to fill (something) throughout with (something such as a quality): [D1 (*usu. pass.*)] *Everything he says seems to be pervaded with a mistrust of the human race.*

**pester out of** *v adv prep*

**pester the life out of** *not fml* to throughly annoy or trouble (someone), esp. in order to gain something: *She's been pestering the life out of me over the telephone, trying to get an invitation to the party, but she won't succeed.*

**pester with** *v prep*

to thoroughly annoy or trouble (someone) with (something such as questions): [T1 + *with*] *Stop pestering me with your advice, I don't want it!*

* **peter out** *v adv*

to come gradually to an end: [IØ] *His voice petered out as fear took away his power of speech. Don't let the supply of coffee peter out. The climbers' efforts to reach the top petered out, and they had to return home with the mountain unconquered.*

**petition for** *v prep*

*fml* to ask (someone) formally for (a favour): [T1 + *for*] *The local people have again petitioned the council for improved street lighting. The defence lawyers decided to petition for a new trial when they found an important new witness.*

* **phase in** *v adv* → **phase out, run down[1] (9)**

to introduce (something) in stages: [T1] *The government is planning to phase in its increases in payments to old people, so that they will be receiving the full amount by Christmas.*

—**phase-in** *n*

*__phase out__ *v adv* → **phase in, run down**[1] (9)
to stop or remove (something) in stages: [T1] *This course will be phased out as the students now taking it complete it, and will not be offered to new students. The makers have decided to phase out the production of this unsuccessful car, and change the machinery to make a better-selling type as soon as all the existing models are sold.* —**phase-out** *n*

*__phone in__ *v adv* → **telephone in**
to send (a message) to a certain place by telephone: [T1] *The newspaper reporter had to phone in his story before midnight. Listeners to this radio show can phone in their opinions.* —**phone-in** *n, adj*

**phone up** *v adv*
*BrE not fml* to telephone (someone): [T1 + UP] *Have you phoned up all your relatives to tell them the change of date yet?*

**pick apart** *v adv*
**1** to separate the pieces of (something) by pulling: [T1 + APART] *The small child sat happily on the grass, picking the flowers apart. I can't change the size of this dress without picking the whole thing apart.*
*__2__ *not fml* to find fault in (something): [T1] *It was very unkind of the newspapers to pick the young singer's performance apart as they did; there were many good things that they could have found to say about it, instead of destroying her hopes just because it wasn't perfect.*

**pick at** *v prep*
**1** to pull at; touch (something), esp. with the fingers: [IØ + *at*] *Don't pick at a sore place, you will only make it worse.*
*__2__ *not fml* to play with (one's food) instead of eating it; take only small amounts of (food): [T1] *Try to eat your dinner, Jane, you've just been picking at it.* → **nibble at** (1), **peck at** (2)
*__3__ *not fml* to deal with only the surface of (a subject): [T1] *Let's deal properly with the question, instead of just picking at it.* → **peck at** (3)
*__4__ *not fml* to complain at; find fault with (someone) repeatedly: [T1] *Stop picking at me! Why should I get the blame for everything?* → **nag at** (1)

**pick away** *v adv*
to remove (parts of something) in small pieces: [T1 + AWAY] *If you pick away the copper-coloured surface, you can see that the metal of the pipes is actually lead.*

**pick from** *v prep*
**1** to lift or remove (something) from (somewhere): [T1 + *from*] *You must not pick the apples from our neighbour's tree, only from our own.*
**2** to choose (something or someone) from (a group): [T1 + *from* (*usu. simple tenses*)] *Jim picked Mary from all the beautiful girls in the city, to be his wife. I have picked this poem from the book as my favourite.*

**pick in** *v prep*
**1** to make (usu. a hole or holes) in (something): [T1 + *in*] *Don't just sit there picking holes in your meat with your fork, get on with your dinner! This cloth is so thin that you can pick a hole in it with your finger.*
**2 pick flaws/holes in** to find fault in (something such as a product, argument, etc.): *Tom is angry that the newspapers have picked so many holes in his book. There are many flaws that can be picked in such a weak argument.*

**pick off** *v adv*
**1** to remove (something), esp. from a plant: [T1 + OFF] *These birds have picked off all the flower heads! All the best apples have been picked off by the children.* → **take off**[1] (1), etc.
*__2__ to shoot (people or animals) one by one, taking careful aim: [T1] *It is a common trick for an army which has just lost possession of a place to leave behind a few men with special skill in shooting, hidden on roofs or up trees, to pick off the leaders of the victorious army as they enter the town.*

*__pick on__ *v prep*
**1** to choose (something): [T1 (*usu. simple tenses*)] *We have picked on a perfect place for our holiday.* → **drop on** (2), **fasten on** (3), **pitch on** (1)
**2** to choose (someone) for a purpose, often unpleasant: [T1 (*for*)] *Why am I always picked on for the worst jobs?* [V3] *The examiners can pick on any student to answer questions.* → **drop on** (3), **fasten on** (4), **pitch on** (2)
**3** *not fml* to choose (someone) for punishment or blame; find fault with (something): [T1] *Why pick on me? Go pick on someone your own size! The weak points in his argument were eagerly picked on by his opponent.* → **drop on** (4), **fasten on** (3), **jump on** (2), **land on** (3), **pitch on** (3)

**pick out** *v adv*
**1** to remove (something), usu. with a sharp instrument or the fingers: [T1 + OUT (*of*)] *This special blade on the boy's knife is for picking stones out of horses' feet. The child refuses to eat this fruit without first picking out the stones.*
**2** to choose (something or someone), esp. from a group: [T1 + OUT (*from*) (*often simple tenses*)] *This fruit shop lets you pick out for yourself the apples that you want to buy. Pick out the dress that you like best and I'll buy it for your birthday. It's not easy to pick out the best actors for this play, they're all so good. She was picked out from the whole class to represent them at the other school.*
*__3__ to recognize; see (someone or something) clearly among others: [T1 (*usu. simple tenses*)] *The witness picked out the thief from a group of men. Can you pick out your sister in this crowd? Try to pick me out in this old school photograph.*
*__4__ to find (a tune) by ear on a musical instrument: [T1] *He can't read music, but he can pick out on the piano a tune that he's heard so that you can recognize it.*

*__5__ to understand (something) by careful study: [T1] *I had to pick out the meaning of this poem word by word.*

*__6__ to make (something) clear to see, esp. in a different colour: [T1] *The houses in the painting were picked out in blue. The pillars were painted white, with their ornamentation picked out in gold to enrich the appearance of the room.*

***pick over** *v adv*

to examine (a collection of things) carefully, usu. by hand, so as to choose from it: [T1] *Pick these apples over and choose the best. By the end of the day, all the vegetables had been picked over and only the bad ones left.*

***pick up** *v adv*

**1** to lift (something or someone), as from the floor or furniture: [T1] *Jim dropped his pen and bent to pick it up, causing a sharp pain in his back. If you drop a knife, don't pick it up, take a clean one. The telephone rang just as I was about to pick up the receiver. Pick up your feet there, men! Picking up her bag, she swept out of the room. The game of rugby was invented when a boy at the school, tired of kicking the ball, picked it up and ran with it. When the box of fireworks exploded, I picked a small child up under each arm and ran to the other end of the garden.* —**picker-up** *n* —**pick-up** *n, adj* → **gather up** (1), **get up** (3), **jerk up, lift up** (1), **pluck up** (1), **pull up** (1), **take up** (1), **tear up** (2), **yank up**

**2** to collect (someone or something); arrange to meet (someone), esp. for a journey: [T1] *Please will you pick up my parcel at the Post Office as you pass? They weren't able to deliver it today because I was out. I'll pick you up at your place at 8 o'clock. It should be reasonably easy to pick up a taxi outside the station. The ship calls at each port on this coast to pick up passengers and mail.* —**pick-up** *n, adj* → **call for** (1)

**3** to collect (someone) to save him/her from danger, esp. on the sea: [T1] *We picked up as many people from the burning ship as we could. The shipwrecked sailors were picked up by a passing boat.*

**4** to give (someone) a ride in a vehicle: [T1] *It's not safe to travel by standing at the roadside hoping to be picked up by passing motorists.* —**pick-up** *n*

**5** *not fml* to meet; become friendly with (someone), often for sexual purposes: [T1] *Some men go to dances just to see if they can pick up a girl for the night. The policeman took the woman to the police station for picking up men outside the hotel.* [IØ (*with*)] *In the theatre, you can pick up with all sorts of unlikely characters.* —**pick-up** *n*

**6** to catch (a criminal): [T1] *The escaped prisoners were picked up by the police only a short distance from the prison.*

**7** to bring (something such as a sound, smell, or sight) within the range of one's senses: [T1] *The trained dogs soon picked up the smell of the creature that they were hunting. His ears are so sensitive that they can pick up very faint sounds from a long way away. Our powerful lights soon picked up the enemy plane. The car headlights picked up a deer crossing the road.*

**8** to be able to receive (something such as electricity, sound waves, etc.) with a machine: [T1] *The searchers at last picked up a signal from the crashed plane. This powerful radio can pick up stations from halfway round the world. These new electric buses pick up their power from overhead wires. In a record player, a special instrument in the arm holding the needle picks up patterns of movement from the shape of the cuts in the surface of the record, and changes them into sound.* —**pick-up** *n*

**9** to tidy (a room): [T1] *Pick up your room before you go out, please.* [IØ (*after*)] *I refuse to pick up after children who are old enough to keep their own things in order.*

**10** *not fml* to earn (an income, usu. small): [T1] *She tried to pick up a humble living by selling baskets that she had made by hand. Car factory workers can pick up good wages, especially with overtime.*

**11** *not fml* to obtain (something), usu. cheaply: [T1] *Where did you pick up that book? I've been trying to get it for weeks! My friend knows where he can pick up a good used car for you at a very reasonable price.* —**pick-up** *adj AmE*

**12** *not fml* to learn; (something such as information), often informally or by chance: [T1] *I don't know where my children have picked up those rude words! He can only have picked up such excellent English by living in the country for some years. Wherever did you pick up that story? I don't want to pick up any bad habits from those people. You can always pick up new ideas if you keep your eyes open.*

**13** (usu. of weather or trade) to (cause to) improve: [IØ] *Trade has been picking up again since the winter. When is the weather going to pick up? It's been bad for weeks.* [T1] *The writer's personal appearance picked up the sales of the book considerably.* —**pick-up** *n*

**14** to make (someone) feel better; improve (in) health: [IØ] *Mother soon began picking up after her operation.* [T1] *This medicine will help to pick up your strength/health.* —**pick-me-up** *n infml*

**15** (of an engine) to start working; gain speed: [IØ] *The engine coughed for a few minutes, then picked up, and soon we were on our way.* —**pick-up** *n*

**16** to re-form (something such as a woven thread or a knitted stitch that has fallen off the needle): [T1] *It's very difficult to pick up dropped stitches in this pattern.* → **take up** (5)

**17** to restart or regain (something); begin

again: [T1] *We lost the animal's track for some time, but picked it up further ahead. It's difficult to pick up the thread of a conversation when it has been interrupted.* [IØ] *Let's pick up where we left off before our coffee break.* → **take up** (28)

**18** to be prepared to pay (a bill): [T1] *The government should pick up the bill for the damaged ship. It is the custom for the new wife's father to pick up the bill for the wedding.*

**19** to raise (oneself) after a fall, loss, defeat, or disappointment: [T1] *When the child fell off her bicycle, she picked herself up, got back on and rode away. After the failure of his business, he had to pick himself up and start all over again. It's hard to pick yourself up after such a terrible shock.*

**20** *not fml* to correct (someone or something); scold (someone): [T1] *I'm always having to pick up the children for rude behaviour. While reading this book, I have picked up twenty-five printing mistakes.*

**21** to break (hard soil) with a pickaxe: [T1] *The frozen ground will have to be picked up by hand before machine digging can begin.*

**22** **pick up a cue** (of an actor in the theatre) to speak one's lines in a suitable, often short, time after another actor has spoken: *The director complained that the actors were not picking up their cues fast enough.*

**23** **pick up the gauntlet** to accept an invitation to compete: *He's said you can't possibly finish in the time: are you going to pick up the gauntlet?* → **fling down** (3), **take up** (23), **throw down** (5)

**24** **pick up the pieces** *not fml* to save something after failure; do one's best to find or make some result: *We must pick up the pieces of our political defeat, and start working towards the next election. If you fail now, who will pick up the pieces?*

**25** **pick up speed** (of an engine or vehicle) to begin to go faster: *The train started slowly, but picked up speed as soon as it has left the station, and was soon travelling very fast.*

**26** **pick up the threads** to make a fresh start in something such as a relationship, work, etc.: *It's a pleasant surprise to be able to pick up the threads of a former friendship after such a long absence. When I had not studied for some years, it was difficult trying to pick up the threads again.* → **gather up** (4), **take up** (12)

**pick with** *v prep*

**1** **pick a bone with** *infml* to suggest a disagreement with or complaint about (someone): *I'm afraid I must pick a bone with you; you've not been doing your share of the household jobs. I've a bone to pick with you—you never returned that book that I lent you.*

**2** **pick a fight/quarrel with** to start an argument or fight with (someone): *Pick a fight with someone your own size instead of attacking the little boys. Never pick a fight with your wife: she's sure to win! I don't want to pick a quarrel with you, but I disagree violently with your opinion.*

**picture to** *v prep*

to imagine (something) to (oneself): [T1 + *to*] *We can only picture to ourselves the life of ancient man, without the tools and comforts of modern civilization. You know some of the story: the rest can be pictured to yourselves easily enough.*

* **piddle away** *v adv* → **idle away** (2), etc.

*sl* to waste (time) lazily: [T1] *Why don't you get on with some work instead of piddling away the whole afternoon doing nothing?*

* **piece out** *v adv* → **piece together**

to complete (something such as a story or income) by adding other parts: [T1] *The police had to piece out the prisoner's story with details obtained from other witnesses. She had to piece out her small regular income by writing occasional articles for the local newspaper.*

* **piece together** *v adv* → **fit together, piece out**

to join; add the separate parts of (something) into one whole: [T1] *The shipwrecked sailors were able to piece together a rough shelter from building materials that they found on the island. The police had to piece the story together from details given by different witnesses. When the dress is pieced together, you can sew it properly.*

* **piece up** *v adv*

*not fml* to mend or complete (something) by adding a piece: [T1] *The parts of the scenery have a space between them but we can piece it up with a new bit representing leaves.*

**pierce through** *v adv; prep*

to strike through; make a hole in (something) with a sharp point; drive a point through (something): [T1 + THROUGH] *The knife pierced his hand (right) through.* [IØ + *through*] *Our soldiers fought all day to pierce through the enemy's defences.*

* **pig it** *v pron*

*not fml* to live in uncomfortable conditions: [IØ] *You may have to pig it for a time while the repairs get finished.*

* **pig out** *v adv*

*AmE infml* to eat a lot of food: [IØ] *After trying to lose weight for so long I had a meal of bread and bananas and ice cream: did I pig out!*

* **pig together** *v adv*

*not fml* to live together in a crowd, often in discomfort: [IØ] *As a child, I always wanted a room of my own, but had to pig together with my sisters in one small bedroom.*

**pile in** *v adv* → **pile into**

**1** to (cause to) enter in a mass or crowd: [X9 + IN] *We'll never be able to pile any more furniture in.* *not fml* [L9 + IN] *As soon as the gates were opened, crowds of football supporters piled in.* → **crowd in** (1), etc.

* **2** *infml* to begin or join an activity such as an attack or meal: [IØ] *If everyone piles in, we'll*

*soon have the job finished. He could never pass a street fight without piling in. As soon as the food was put on the table, all the children piled in.* → **tuck in** (4), etc.

***pile in on** *v adv prep*
to surround (someone) as if to attack: [T1 (*no pass.*)] *Unpleasant memories have been piling in on me since that unfortunate meeting with my old enemy.*

**pile into** *v prep* → **pile in**
**1** to (cause to) enter (a place) in a mass or crowd: [X9 + *into*] *How many more plates do you think you can pile into that cupboard?* *not fml* [L9 + *into*] *As soon as the gates were opened, crowds of football supporters piled into the ground.* → **crowd into** (1), etc.
***2** *infml* to begin or join (an activity such as an attack or food): [T1 (*no pass.*)] *If everyone piles into the job, we'll soon get it finished. Why do you have to pile into every street fight that we happen to pass? Don't wait to be served, just pile into whatever food you want.* → **tuck into** (3), etc.

**pile off** *v adv; prep*
*not fml* to leave (something such as a vehicle) in a crowd: [L9 + OFF/*off*] *The train stopped, and crowds of passengers piled off* (*it*).

**pile on**[1] *v adv*
**1** to (cause to) be added in a mass or crowd: [X9 + ON] *Pile some more wood on, let's have a really big fire.* *not fml* [L9 + ON] *When the train arrived, all the schoolchildren piled on.*
**2 pile on the agony** *not fml* to enjoy making something seem worse than it actually is: *Is Mother telling the story of her operation again? She does love to pile on the agony and have everyone feel sorry for her.*
**3 pile it on** *infml* to stretch the truth: *Don't believe everything he says, he's probably piling it on as usual.*
**4 pile on the pressure** *not fml* to demand effort: *I know the play is to be performed next week, but if the director piles on any more pressure, the actors will become ill with overwork.*

**pile on/upon**[2] *v prep*
**1** to make a mass of (something or things) on top of (something): [X9 + *on/upon*] *Our host was very generous, piling food on our plates.* → **heap on**[2] (1), **heap with** (1), **pile onto** (1), **pile with** (1)
***2** to give a lot of (something such as honour) to (someone): [D1] *Praises were piled on him after the game. The crowd piled curses on the unpopular speaker.* → **heap on**[2] (2), **heap with** (2), **pile onto** (2), **pile with** (2)
**3 pile insult on insult** to continue to be rude to someone: *I was prepared to forgive one thoughtless remark, but she kept piling insult on insult, so I asked her to leave my house.* → **heap on**[2] (3)
**4 pile Pelion upon Ossa** to make something big even bigger: *Then, having won the national competiton, the team went on to win the international competition, piling Pelion upon Ossa. Asking me to run the department and teach a full load of courses is piling Pelion upon Ossa.*

**pile onto** *v prep*
**1** to (cause to) take a position on top of (something) in a mass or crowd: [X9 + *onto*] *Pile some more wood onto the fire, let's get really warm.* *not fml* [L9 + *onto*] *Crowds of schoolchildren piled onto the train as soon as it arrived.* → **heap on**[2] (1), **heap with** (1), **pile on**[2] (1), **pile with** (1)
***2** to give (a lot of something) to (something or someone): [T1] *If any more work is piled onto this office, I shall leave!* → **heap on** (2), **heap with** (2), **pile on** (2), **pile with** (2)

**pile out** *v adv*
*not fml* to leave in a crowd: [L9 + OUT (*of*)] *After the game, crowds of football supporters piled out* (*of the ground*).

***pile up** *v adv*
**1** to (cause to) form into a mass or large quantity: [T1] *The child piled up the bricks until they fell over.* [IØ] *The clouds are piling up, so it might rain after all. My mail has been piling up while I've been on holiday.* —**pileup** *n* → **heap up** (1)
**2** (of a number of vehicles) to crash: [IØ] *A bus and three cars piled up on the main road this morning.* — **pileup** *n*
**3** *not fml* to cause or encourage (something bad) to happen: [T1] *If you always give the children everything they want, you will be piling up trouble for yourself later!* → **heap up** (2)

**pile upon** *v prep* → PILE ON

**pile with** *v prep*
**1** to load (a container) with a mass of (something or things): [X9 + *with*] *Our very generous host piled our plates with food.* → **heap on**[2] (1), **heap with** (1), **pile on**[2] (1), **pile onto** (1)
***2** to give (someone or something) a lot of (something): [D1 (*usu. pass.*)] *The office has been piled with work ever since the new director arrived.* → **heap on**[2] (2), **heap with** (2), **pile on**[2] (2), **pile onto** (2)

**pillow on/upon** *v prep*
to allow (something) to rest comfortably on (something): [T1 + *on/upon* (*usu. simple tenses*)] *She pillowed his head on her shoulder to comfort him.*

**pilot in** *v adv*
to guide (something such as a ship) when entering usu. a harbour: [T1 + IN] *The ship stops outside the harbour so that a specially trained person may pilot her in.*

**pilot into** *v prep*
to guide (something such as a ship) into (a place): [T1 + *into*] *With great skill, he piloted the boat into the little harbour.*

**pilot out** *v prep*
to guide (something such as a ship) when

leaving a place: [T1 + OUT (*of*)] *A specially trained person has to pilot the ship out* (*of these dangerous waters*).

**pilot through** *v adv; prep*

**1** to guide (something such as a ship) through (something): [T1 + THROUGH/*through*] *With great skill, the captain piloted the big ship through* (*the narrow entrance to the harbour*).

*__2__ to be responsible for (something such as a new law) passing (a law-making body): [T1b] *The old politician was proud of having piloted the first rent control law through.* [D1] *I will personally pilot your suggestion through the committee.*

**pimp for** *v prep* → **pander to** (1)

to act as a messenger for (a man), finding women for him: [IØ + *for*] *He lived an immoral life, pimping for any man who needed a woman.*

**pin against** *v prep*

to trap; hold (something or someone) by force next to (something): [T1 + *against*] *The crash pinned the driver against the wheel, wounding his chest. Pinning his arms against his sides, the thieves searched his pockets.*

**pin back** *v adv*

**1** to fasten or hold (something) back with or as with pins: [T1 + BACK] *If the collar won't stay in place, I shall have to pin it back. Pinning his arms back against the wall, the thieves searched his pockets. The dog pinned its ears back to catch the faint sound.*

**2 pin back one's ears** esp. *BrE infml* to listen carefully: [*often imper.*] *Pin back your ears, people, this is quite a story!*

**3 pin someone's ears back** *AmE infml* to give someone a thorough scolding or beating: [*often simple tenses*] *The other team won a victory over us that really pinned our ears back. The teacher's severe words pinned the children's ears back.*

**pin down** *v adv*

**1** to fasten or hold (something or someone) down with or as with pins; trap; prevent (someone) from moving: [T1 + DOWN] *Don't try to move the map, it's pinned down to the table. The tree fell, pinning him down. Pinned down by enemy gunfire, our soldiers were unable to advance.* → **nail down** (1), **peg down** (1)

*__2__ to force (someone) to make a decision, state his intentions, or take action, etc.: [T1 (*to*)] *See if you can pin the chairman down to an exact date. We shall have to pin him down to his promise.* → **nail down** (2), **peg down** (2), **tie down to** (2)

*__3__ to explain the exact nature of (something); find or recognize (someone or something): [T1 (*to*)] *At last we were able to pin the trouble down to a fault in the machine. This book is proving difficult to write, since I am trying to pin down the central idea of reasoning. It is difficult to pin down the exact meaning of this verb. There was something in his manner which was impossible to pin down, but which made people obey him. There's a tune going round my head, but I can't pin it down. There was a lot of noise coming from the classroom, but I couldn't pin it down to any particular group of students.* → **nail down** (3)

**pin on[1]** *v adv*

to fasten (something) on with a pin or pins: [T1 + ON] *Be careful with that dress, it's only pinned on. When you go to the palace to receive your Military Cross, the Queen herself will pin it on.*

**pin on[2]** *v prep*

**1** to fasten (something) on (something) with a pin or pins: [T1 + *on*] *The Queen pinned the Military Cross on the brave soldier's chest. A list of winners will be pinned on the notice board tomorrow.*

*__2__ *not fml* to fix, place, or force (something such as a responsibility) on (someone): [D1] *Why are you trying to pin the blame on me? He tried to pin the crime on his companions.* → **fasten on[2]** (2), **lay on[2]** (2), **place on** (2), **put on[2]** (2), **throw on[2]** (4)

**3 pin one's faith on** to place one's trust in (something or someone): *The opposition party are pinning their faith on their newly chosen leader to bring them victory in the next election. It's unwise to pin your faith on any system of government.*

**4 pin one's hopes on** to have one's hopes depend on (someone, something, or doing something): *Many parents pin their hopes on their children for the future. Don't pin your hopes on this job, you may not get it. Jim has pinned all his hopes on winning this race.* → **lay on[2]** (13), **place in** (7), **place on** (6), **put in[2]** (11), **put on[2]** (22), **set on[2]** (14)

**pin to** *v prep*

to fix, hold, or trap (someone or something) to (something) with or as with a pin or pins: [T1 + *to*] *The warning was pinned to the door with an arrow. The tree fell, pinning him to the ground. Be careful with that collar, it's just pinned to the dress.*

**pin under** *v prep*

to trap (usu. someone) beneath (something): [T1 + *under* (*often pass.*)] *The driver was pinned under the wreck of his car, and had to be freed by firemen using special machinery.*

**pin up** *v adv*

**1** to fasten (something) with pins so that it stays up: [T1 + UP] *Will you help me to pin up my hair? I can't reach it at the back. Pin the skirt up before you sew it.*

**2** to fasten (something such as a picture) in public view: [T1 + UP] *The teachers usually pin up the best work on the board. Soldiers often pin up photographs of pretty girls above their beds.* —**pinup** *n, adj*

**pinch back/off/out** *v adv*

(in gardening) to remove (an unwanted part of a plant) with one's fingers: [T1 + BACK/

OFF/OUT] *If you regularly pinch back the dead flower heads, new ones will grow.*

**pine after** *v prep* → **PINE FOR**

**pine away** *v adv*
to waste away; grow thin and weak through unhappiness: [IØ + AWAY] *For a year after that red-haired boy left her, Grace missed him so badly that she almost pined away to nothing.*

**pine for/after** *v prep* → **languish for, languish over**
to grow weak and unhappy with a desire for (something or someone): [IØ + *for/after*] *We always have to take the dog with us on holiday, or he would pine for his master and become ill. Although the boy had lived in his new country for three years, he was still pining for his homeland.*

**pine over** *v prep* → **languish for, languish over**
to grow weak and unhappy on account of (usu. something): [IØ + *over*] *The boy has been pining over his dead dog for more than a week now.*

**pinion to** *v prep*
to fasten (a wing or arm) firmly to (something): [T1 + *to* (*usu. pass.*)] *The prisoner's arms were pinioned to his sides with ropes.*

**pinion together** *v adv*
to fasten (wings or arms) together: [T1 + TOGETHER (*usu. simple tenses*)] *The cruel owners used to pinion the birds' wings together to prevent them from flying.*

**pink out** *v adv*
to cut (something such as a pattern of specially shaped holes) from cloth with a special tool: [T1 + OUT (*often pass.*)] *An ornamental edge was pinked out with special scissors.*

**pipe aboard** *v adv*
to welcome (an important person) formally onto a ship by blowing a special whistle: [X9 + ABOARD] *The Queen was piped aboard, and all the sailors cheered.*

**pipe ashore** *v adv*
to say goodbye formally to (someone leaving a ship) by blowing a special whistle: [X9 + ASHORE] *When the captain left his ship for the last time at the end of his period of service, he was piped ashore.*

**pipe away** *v adv*
**1** to play a wind instrument continuously: [IØ + AWAY] *Haven't the band finished practising that music? They've been piping away all morning.*
**2** to remove; carry (something such as liquid) away through a pipe: [X9 + AWAY] *The waste water is piped away to a special place.*

***pipe down** *v adv* → **shut up** (4), etc.
*infml* to be quiet: [IØ (*usu. imper.*)] *Pipe down, you boys at the back there, we can hardly hear ourselves think.*

**pipe in** *v adv*
**1** to bring (something such as liquid or music) in through pipes or wires: [X9 + IN] *The water for the town has to be piped in from a great distance, as there is no river nearby. Pleasant music to listen to is piped in through the whole building.*
**2** to play music, usu. on a wind instrument, while (someone or something) enters or is carried in: [X9 + IN] *There are customs in certain parts of the country, in which a special dish is piped in on some ceremonial occasion.*

**pipe into** *v prep*
to bring (something such as liquid) into (a place) through pipes: [X9 + *into*] *Some of the older houses in this country area have their own wells, but town water is piped into the more modern buildings.*

***pipe up** *v adv*
**1** to begin to sing in a high voice or play a wind instrument: [IØ] *I love to hear the boys pipe up in church.* [T1] *Suddenly the band piped up a military tune.*
**2** to begin to speak, esp. in a high voice: [IØ] *Suddenly a child at the back of the room piped up, asking an awkward question.*

**pipe with** *v prep*
to ornament (something) with (something): [T1 + *with* (*usu. pass.*)] *The shoulders of his uniform were piped with signs of his rank. The top of the cake was piped with the words "Happy Birthday".*

**pique on** *v prep* → **plume on, preen on, pride on**
**pique oneself on** *old use* to be very proud of (something or doing something): [*usu. simple tenses*] *The hunter piqued himself on his skill with a bow and arrows. Do not pique yourself on defeating so weak an enemy.*

***piss about/around** *v adv*
**1** *taboo* to spend time lazily: [IØ] *"What have you been doing today?" "Oh, nothing, just pissing about."* → **mess about** (1), etc.
**2** *taboo* to treat (something or someone) carelessly or inconsiderately: [T1] *I can't forgive him for pissing me about. The bank has been pissing my account around again; I think I shall move my money to another bank. If you want to marry the girl, ask her; if you don't, then leave her alone—but at any rate don't piss her about. The doctors in that hospital only succeeded in pissing me about; I felt worse when I came out than when I went in.* → **mess about** (4), etc.

***piss about/around with** *v adv prep* → **mess about with** (1), etc.
*taboo* to cause disorder to (something): [T1] *Who's been pissing about with my papers? They're all out of order.*

***piss around** *v adv* → **PISS ABOUT**

***piss around with** *v adv prep* → **PISS ABOUT WITH**

***piss off** *v adv*
**1** *taboo* to go away: [IØ (*usu. imper.*)] *Piss off, can't you? You can see you're not wanted here!* → **push off** (3), etc.

**2** *taboo* to tire (someone); make (someone) lose interest: [T1b] *This same old music pisses me off. I get pissed off with hearing the same old tunes.* → **feed up** (2), etc.

***pit against** *v prep* → **match against** (3), **match with** (4)
to oppose (something) to (something): [D1] *The small island state has no hope of pitting its strength against its more powerful neighbours. Are you willing to pit your skill against that of our leading player?*

**pit with** *v prep* → **pock with**
**be pitted with** to be marked with (hollow places): *The surface of the wood was pitted with holes made by insects. His skin is pitted with the marks left by the disease.*

**pitch forward** *v adv*
to fall sharply in a forward direction: [L9 + FORWARD] *A shot rang out; the man pitched forward and fell dead.*

**pitch in** *v adv*
**1** to throw (something) in: [T1 + IN] *Please pitch your waste paper in here.* → **chuck in** (1), **fling in**[1] (1), **throw in**[1] (1), **toss in**[1] (1)
***2** *infml* to begin or join an activity such as an attack or meal: [IØ (*with*)] *If everyone pitches in, we'll soon have the job finished. He could never pass a street fight without pitching in. As soon as the food was put on the table, all the children pitched in without waiting to be invited. The theatre company was about to close when luckily the city council pitched in with an offer of money.* → **tuck in** (4), etc.

**pitch into** *v prep*
**1** to throw (something or someone) into (something such as a container): [T1 + *into*] *Watch me pitch this empty cigarette packet into the basket from across the room. The boat suddenly rocked and pitched him into the water.* → **fling into** (1, 2), **hurl into** (1), **throw into** (1), **toss into** (1)
***2** *not fml* to attack (someone), with blows or words: [T1] *Fearlessly Jim pitched into his attackers, who soon all lay unconscious on the ground. The opposition speaker made a lively speech, pitching into the government for its ineffective actions.* → **lay into,** etc.
***3** *infml* to begin or join (an activity such as an attack or food): [T1 (*no pass.*)] *If everyone pitches into the job, we'll soon get it finished. Don't wait to be served, just pitch into whatever food you want.* → **tuck into** (3), etc.
***4** *not fml* to force (someone) to take (a position): [D1 (*often pass.*)] *I didn't ask for the chairmanship, I was pitched into it.*

**pitch on/upon** *v prep*
**1** to choose (something): [T1 (*usu. simple tenses*)] *We have pitched on a perfect place for our holiday, by lucky chance.* → **drop on** (2), **fasten on** (3), **pick on** (1)
**2** to choose (someone) for a purpose, often unpleasant: [T1 (*for*)] *Why does he always pitch on me for the worst jobs?* [V3] *The examiners can pitch on any student to answer questions.* → **drop on** (3), **fasten on** (4), **pick on** (2)
**3** *not fml* to choose (someone) for punishment or blame: [T1] *Why pitch on me? I'm not to blame!* → **pick on** (3), etc.

**pitch out** *v adv*
**1** to (cause to) move, fall, or pass out of something: [T1 + OUT (*of*)] *The player pitched the ball out of the way it was expected to go.* [L9 + OUT (*usu. simple tenses*)] *He lost his balance, and pitched out of the window head first.* —**pitch-out** *n* → **throw out** (1), etc.
***2** to make (someone) leave because of a fault: [T1 (*of*)] *Two members were pitched out (of the club) for failing to pay the money they owed.* → **throw out** (4), etc.

**pitch up** *v adv*
**1** (in cricket) to throw (the ball) nearer to the batsman: [T1 + UP] *Snow decided to pitch the ball up to surprise his opponent into making a mistake.* —**well-pitched-up** *adj*
**2** to make (music) with higher notes: [X9 + UP (*often simple tenses*)] *Ask the singers to pitch the song up a little, they sound rather flat.*

**pitch upon** *v prep* → PITCH ON

**pivot on** *v prep*
**1** to turn with the centre of movement fixed on (something): [IØ + *on*] *The dancer pivoted on the point of one foot. This door pivots on a single screw.*
***2** to depend on; centre on (something): [T1 (*no pass., simple tenses*)] *The story pivots on the relationship between the two sisters.* → **depend on** (3), **hang on**[2] (2), **hing on, rely on** (2), **ride on**[2] (4), **turn on**[2] (3)

**place above** *v prep*
**1** to put (something) in a position higher than (something): [X9 + *above*] *The notice was placed above the door, and I didn't see it.* → **put above** (1), **set above** (1)
***2** to consider (something or someone) as being more important or worthy of attention than (something or someone else): [D1] *Mothers are well-known for placing the needs of the family above their own interests.* [V4a] *Getting out of debt must be placed above buying anything new. Above myself I place my God.* → **put before** (4), etc.

**place aside** *v adv*
**1** to put (something) on one side, esp. for a short time: [X9 + ASIDE] *She placed her sewing aside when the telephone rang.* → **lay aside** (1), etc.
***2** to discontinue (something such as work), esp. for a time: [T1] *Tom placed his new book aside for a year while he wrote some magazine articles and informative material.* → **lay aside** (2), etc.
***3** to cease (something such as a habit): [T1] *It's time to place our differences aside and*

*work together for a common purpose.* → **lay aside** (3), etc.

*__4__ to save (usu. money or time): [T1 (*for*)] *I have a little money placed aside for a rainy day. I've placed aside the whole weekend for househunting.* → **lay aside** (4), **lay away** (2), **lay by** (4), **put apart** (2), **put aside** (4), **put away** (3), **put by** (4), **set apart** (2), **set aside** (4), **set by** (4)

*__5__ to save (a supply of goods) for a customer: [T1] *Would you like us to place the rest of the wool aside for you? Then you'll be sure to match the colour.* → **lay aside** (5), **lay away** (3), **lay by** (5), **place on** (7), **put aside** (5), **put away** (4), **put by** (5), **put on**[2] (32), **set aside** (5), **set on** (17)

**place at** *v prep*

**1** to put (something) in position in front of (usu. a place): [X9 + *at*] *The worshippers placed their gifts at the feet of the god. The natives placed the food at the entrance to the cave.* → **put at** (1), etc.

*__2__ to guess (something) to be (an amount, number, etc.): [D1 (*usu. simple tenses*)] *I placed her age at 33. His income can probably be placed at £5000 a year.* → **put as, put at** (3), **set at** (4)

**3 place someone at his/her ease** to make someone feel comfortable, not nervous: *His behaviour did nothing to place me at my ease. Do your best to place new students at their ease; show them the classrooms and the library, introduce them to helpful people and warn them how to avoid trouble, so that they won't feel anxious on their first day of classes.* → **put at** (4), **set at** (7)

**4 place something at a premium** to put a high value on something such as a quality: [*often pass.*] *Hard work and honesty are placed at a premium in this school; brains without character and willingness are worthless.* → **place on** (8), **put at** (5), **put on**[2] (35), **set at** (12)

**place back** *v adv* → **put back** (2), etc.

to return (usu. something) to its former position: [X9 + BACK] *Place the book back where you found it when you have finished reading it. When I returned from the police station, the jewels had been placed back in their box; the thieves must have become nervous.*

**place before** *v prep*

**1** to put (something) in position in front of (something or someone): [X9 + *before*] *Entering the temple, the worshippers placed their gifts before the gods.* → **put at** (1), etc.

*__2__ to send (something such as an idea) for consideration or approval by (someone or a group in power); bring (something) to the notice or attention of (someone): [D1 (*often pass.*)] *Your suggestion will be placed before the board of directors at their next meeting.* → **put before** (2), etc.

*__3__ to consider (something or someone) more important or worthy of attention than (something or someone else): [D1] *Mothers are well-known for placing the needs of the family before their own interests.* [V4a] *Getting out of debt must be placed before buying anything new. A selfish person is one who places himself before his fellows.* → **put before** (4), etc.

**4 place one foot before/in front of the other** to be able to walk: [*simple tenses + can, could, usu. neg.*] *She was so tired that she could hardly place one foot before the other.* → **put before** (6), **set before** (5)

**place behind** *v prep*

**1** to put (something) in a position at the back of (something or someone): [X9 + *behind*] *I'll place the letter behind the clock and then I shan't forget it.* → **be behind**[2] (1), **keep behind** (1), **put behind**[2] (1)

**2** to give (usu. someone) a position as the result of competition: [X9 + *behind* (*usu. pass.*)] *Jim was placed behind two other runners in the race that he had hoped to win.* → **place in** (3), **put in**[2] (3), **put into** (5)

**3 place someone behind bars** *not fml* to imprison someone: *People like that should be placed behind bars for the rest of their lives.* → **be behind**[2] (4), **put behind**[2] (2)

**place down** *v adv* → **lay down** (1), **put down** (1), **set down** (1), **stick down** (2)

to put (something) in position on a floor or surface: [X9 + DOWN (*on*)] *He placed his heavy bag down on the ground and rested for a few minutes. Just as I placed the telephone receiver down, the doorbell rang.*

**place in** *v prep*

**1** to put (something) in position inside (something such as a container): [X9 + *in*] *Place the vegetables in the pan with very little water and heat quickly. I wish to place some money in this bank. Place the eggs gently in the basket.* → **fit into** (1), etc.

**2** also **place into** to give (someone or something) to (the care of someone): [T1 + *in*] *We must make sure to place the children in the right schools for their interests and abilities. Social workers try to place all their motherless children in good homes.* [X9 + *in*] *The boy was placed in the care of his aunt after his parents were killed in the accident. Can I place my precious paintings in your safe keeping while I'm away? I place myself in your hands, I am completely at your mercy.* → **put in**[2] (2), **put into** (4)

**3** to give (usu. someone) a position among (the competitors) as the result of competition [X9 + *in* (*often pass.*)] *After all his high hopes of winning the race, Jim wasn't even placed in the first three!* → **place behind** (2), **put in**[2] (3), **put into** (5)

*__4__ to cause (someone) to be in (a certain position), usu. morally, socially, or politically [D1 (*usu. simple tenses*)] *What an awkward position I'm now placed in! If I say yes, I'm too demanding; if I say no, I'm too proud—I can't win! You placed me in an impossible* *position with your behaviour at the party. The opposition member's request for an enquiry has placed the government in a difficult position, especially just before the election.* → **put in² (4), put into (6)**

***5** to appoint (someone) to (a position of responsibility): [D1] *The captain hopes to be placed in command of a bigger ship. Who has been placed in charge during the director's absence?* → **put in² (5)**

***6** to arrange (things or people) in (a certain order, position, etc.): [D1] *The teacher placed the children in order of height. These verbs are placed in alphabetical order. Let's place the chairs in a circle, it makes talking so much easier.* → **put in² (6)**

**7 place one's confidence/faith/hope//trust in** to trust; depend on (someone, something, or doing something): *It's not safe to place too much confidence in your ability to pass the examination without working hard. We all place our faith in the team to win this important game. Jim placed his hope in winning this race. Place your trust in the Lord, and all will be well.* → **pin on² (4)**, etc.

**8 place all one's eggs in one basket** *not fml* to place all one's money on one risk; risk everything on one chance: *Insurance firms generally spread a large risk among several companies, so that they don't place all their eggs in one basket.* → **have in² (1), put in² (13)**

**9 place something in jeopardy** to threaten the safety of something; cause something to be at risk: *Our chances of winning are being placed in jeopardy by frequent illnesses among the team. The miners' refusal to work has placed in jeopardy the nation's supply of coal.* → **put in² (17)**

**10 place oneself in someone else's position/shoes** *not fml* to imagine how someone feels; sympathize with someone: *You have to try to place yourself in the director's shoes before you can know how difficult his job is. Place yourself in my position, and then perhaps you'll stop complaining.* → **put in² (24), put into (19)**

**11 place words in inverted commas** esp. *BrE* to put speech marks round a certain word or words to show that it is spoken, or special in some other way: *In this sentence, "Fred" has been placed in inverted commas. Many public speakers are so nervous of using informal expressions that even when they are speaking, you can hear that they have placed them in inverted commas.* → **put in² (30), set in² (12)**

**place on** *v prep*

**1** to put (something or someone) into position on top of (something): [X9 + *on*] *Place the plates gently on the table, they are very delicate. He placed his hand on my shoulder comfortingly. Placing the child on his back, he continued the long walk home.* → **lay on² (1), lay with (1), put on² (1), set on² (1), stick on (3)**

***2** to fix; force acceptance of (something such as responsibility) on (someone or something): [D1] *Why are you trying to place the blame on me? Parents place heavy duties on their children. The government has placed another tax on cigarettes.* → **fasten on (2), impose on (1), lay on² (2), pin on² (2), put on² (2), throw on (4)**

**3 place one's cards on the table** to be completely honest, esp. about one's intentions or point of view: *I see that it's time to place my cards on the table; I am interested in this affair because the woman in the case is my sister.* → **lay on² (5), put on² (11), set on²** *(6)*

**4 place a construction on** to decide the meaning of (something): *Make sure that you don't place the wrong construction on his remark; I'm sure he didn't mean to be rude. A different construction was placed on the wording of the law by each of the judges.* → **put on² (12)**

**5 place someone on his/her honour/on oath** to make someone promise to tell the truth or behave correctly: *I place you all on your honour not to cheat while I am out of the room. All witnesses must remember that they have been placed on oath and must speak the exact truth.* → **put on² (21)**, etc.

**6 place one's hopes on** to have one's hopes depend on (someone, something, or doing something): *Many parents place their hopes on their children for the future. Don't place your hopes on this job, you may not get it. Jim has placed all his hopes on winning this race.* → **pin on² (4)**, etc.

**7 place something on one side: a** to put something down; stop holding something; move something to a different position next to one: *She placed her sewing on one side when the telephone rang.* → **lay aside (1)**, etc. **b** to discontinue something such as work, esp. for a time: *Tom placed his new book on one side for a year while he wrote some magazine articles and informative material.* → **lay aside (2)**, etc. **c** to disregard; cease something such as a habit: [*often simple tenses*] *It's time to place our differences on one side and work together for a common purpose.* → **lay aside (3)**, etc. **d** to save (a supply of goods) for a customer: *I'll place the goods on one side until you have made a decision about whether you want them.* → **lay aside (5)**, etc.

**8 place a premium on** to put a high value on (something such as a quality): [*usu. simple tenses*] *In this school we place a premium on hard work and honesty; brains without character and willingness are worthless.* → **place at (4), put at (5), put on² (35), set at (12)**

**9 place pressure on** to try to force (someone) (to do something) by argument, threats, etc.: *The unions have been placing pressure on the government to reduce its limits on wage increases.* → **put on² (36)**

**10 place a strain on** to make things hard for; test the strength of (someone or something):

*This rope will not break unless a strain of more than 250 pounds is placed on it. All this additional work, and my present worries, are placing an unbearable strain on me.* → **put on² (40)**

***place out** *v adv*
to find a home for (a child without parents): [T1 (*into*)] *The local social workers have been largely successful in placing out most of the children in their care (into suitable homes).*

**place to** *v prep*
**1** to lay (something) next to (something): [X9 + *to*] *She placed a finger to her lips to signal silence.* → **put to² (1), set to² (1), touch to (1)**
**2 place a call to** to telephone (someone or a place): *Ask my secretary to place a call to Head Office in London, will you?* → **put to² (10)**
**3 place a match to** to start (something) burning by striking a match next to it: *Placing a match to the letter, he made her watch it burn.* → **catch alight (1), put to² (17), set alight (1), set on² (10), set to² (5)**

**place under** *v prep*
**1** to put (something) in a position beneath (something): [X9 + *under*] *Placing his hand under his shirt, he could feel the blood flowing from the wound. I placed the envelope under the rest of the pile, so that it would be dealt with last.* → **put under² (1)**
**2 place someone under arrest/guard** to limit someone's freedom by guarding him/her before a trial: *The jewel thieves were placed under arrest, and will face their trial next month. Place those disobedient soldiers under guard; I will deal with them in the morning.* → **put under² (2)**
**3 place someone under oath** *law* to make someone swear a solemn promise, as in court: *Witnesses must remember that they have been placed under oath and must speak the exact truth.* → **put on² (21)**, etc.
**4 place someone under an obligation** to cause someone to owe a debt, as of service, to someone else: [*often simple tenses*] *Their frequent invitations place us under an obligation to invite them to our house for a change.* → **put under² (4)**
**5 place someone under observation** to watch someone closely, as a criminal or someone in hospital: *The police place most newly freed prisoners under observation to see if they will return to a life of crime. The doctors cannot decide what he is suffering from and have placed him under observation for a few days.* → **put under² (5)**

**place with** *v prep*
**1** to give (an order for goods) to (a supplier): [T1 + *with*] *I have had my order placed with this bookstore for three months, but there is still no sign of the books.*
**2** to find a home for (a child without parents) with (someone): [T1 + *with*] *Social workers are always delighted when they can place a child with a suitable family.*

***plague with** *v prep*
**1** to trouble (someone or something such as a place) with a lot of (something or things unpleasant): [D1 (*usu. pass.*)] *The farms have been plagued with disease-carrying insects in this warm wet summer. This bridge has been plagued with accidents ever since it was built. Why am I always plagued with bad luck?*
**2** *not fml* to annoy (someone) very much by giving a lot of (things): [D1] *Do stop plaguing me with all these questions—I'll answer them when I can. The employment office is being plagued with requests for jobs.*

**plan ahead** *v adv*
to make advance arrangements (for something): [L9 + AHEAD] *If you plan ahead far enough, you can save a lot of money on your plane tickets.* [T1 + AHEAD] *The wedding was planned weeks ahead.*

**plan for** *v prep*
to make plans concerning (someone or the future): [L9 + *for*] *Planning for their old age gives people an aim in life.* [T1 + *for*] *What wonderful futures we have planned for our children! What events have you got planned for next week?*

**plan on** *v prep*
to intend (doing something); expect; make allowances for (something): [L9 + *on*] *Do you plan on staying here another year? I had not planned on their early arrival, and the meal was not ready.*

**plan out** *v adv*
to make careful thorough arrangements for (something): [T1 + OUT] *I have the next three months' work all planned out. Do you plan out the whole story before you begin to write it, or do you make it up as you go along?*

**plane away/off** *v adv*
to reduce (a part of the surface of something such as wood) with a plane: [X9 + AWAY/OFF] *We had to plane nearly half an inch off before the door would fit.*

**plane down** *v adv*
**1** to make (something such as wood) thinner, smoother, or more level with a plane: [X9 + DOWN] *There are still a few rough places on the surface of the table that need to be planed down.*
**2** (of a plane) to move in a downward direction without engine power: [IØ + DOWN] *The aircraft planed down before landing.*

**plane off** *v adv* → **PLANE AWAY**

**plank down** *v adv*
**1** *not fml* to set (something) down heavily: [X9 + DOWN] *The workman planked down his heavy bag of tools.* → **plonk down (1), plump down (2), plunk down (1)**
***2** *not fml* to pay (money) readily or in a showy manner: [T1 (*usu. simple tenses*)] *He planked down the money and called for drinks for everyone. Few people can afford to plank*

*down the whole cost of a house.* → **plank out, plonk down** (2), **plump down** (3), **plunk down** (2)

**plank on** *v prep* → **plonk on**
*not fml* to put (something) heavily on (something): [X9 + *on*] *The workman planked his heavy bag of tools on the floor.*

***plank out** *v adv* → **plank down** (2), **plonk down** (2), **plump down** (3), **plunk down** (2)
*not fml* to pay (money) readily or in a showy manner: [T1] *It's typical of him to plank out the whole cost all at once.*

**plant in** *v prep*
**1** to place (usu. a seed or plant) in (soil, a garden, etc.): [T1 + *in*] *I'd like to plant vegetables in this half of the garden, and flowers in the rest.*
***2** also **plant into** to cause (something such as an idea) to enter (someone's mind): [D1] *Whatever planted that idea in/into your head? The writer has planted into his characters the right thoughts.*

**plant on** *v prep*
**1** to place (something) firmly on (something such as a surface): [X9 + *on*] *Planting his case on the table, he looked at us expectantly. Plant your feet firmly on the floor before you start to speak.*
**2** to make (a blow) hit (part of the body): [T1 + *on*] *After a few minutes, the young fighter planted a blow on his opponent's chin that seemed to hurt him.* → **land on** (2)
***3** *not fml* to hide (usu. stolen goods) so that they seem to be in the possession of (someone), so as to make him/her seem guilty: [D1] *I Didn't steal these jewels, they've been planted on me: I didn't even know they were in my house!*

**plant out** *v adv*
to place (young plants) in enough room for growth: [T1 + OUT (*in*)] *When the seeds have grown in their small box, plant them out in the garden, leaving plenty of space between them.*

**plant with** *v prep*
to fill (a place such as a garden) with (plants): [X9 + *with*] *Since I now have enough vegetables growing, I would like to plant the rest of the garden with flowers. Most of the land is planted with wheat.*

**plaster down** *v adv*
to fix (something such as hair) in a flat position with a sticky substance: [X9 + DOWN] *These days, boys seem to have stopped the fashion of plastering their hair down with smelly creams.*

**plaster on** *v adv; prep*
to spread (something) thickly on (usu. something): [X9 + ON/*on*] *Look at that boy, plastering butter on (his bread)! Don't plaster the paint on (the wall), spread it thinly. Outside the cinema, a man on a ladder was plastering an advertisement for a film on top of the old notice.*

**plaster over**[1] *v adv* → **plaster up**
to cover (something such as a wall or crack) with a thick kind of cement: [X9 + OVER] *The holes in the wall had been plastered over so that they didn't show.*

**plaster over**[2] *v prep*
**1** to put a kind of cement on top of (usu. a surface, or a fault in a surface): [L9 + *over*] *Paint won't cover the holes in the wall, we shall have to plaster over them.* → **paint over** (1), **paper over** (1)
***2** *not fml* to hide or make a show of covering (something such as a fault or disagreement in an organization): [T1] *We can try to plaster over the disagreement in the union by printing a statement declaring our complete unity. You can't hide lack of unity in the party by plastering over the cracks.* → **paper over** (2)

**plaster up** *v adv* → **plaster over**[1]
to cover (something such as a wall or crack) with a thick kind of cement: [X9 + UP] *The holes in the wall had been plastered up so that they didn't show.*

**plaster with** *v prep*
to cover (something) thickly with (something spread on it, or a lot of things): [X9 + *with*] *Your boots are plastered with mud; take them off before you come into my kitchen! You can plaster the outside of the house with coloured cement to protect it and avoid regular painting. His hair was plastered with smelly cream. The whole city was plastered with advertisements for the show.*

**plate with** *v prep*
to cover (an object) with a thin coat of (usu. precious metal): [T1 + *with* (*usu. pass.*)] *The knives and forks are not as valuable as they look; they've only been plated with silver.*

**play about/around**[1] *v adv* → **mess about** (1), etc.
to spend time having fun: [IØ + ABOUT] *The seashore was full of children, playing about in the sand.* [IØ + AROUND] *You're old enough now to stop playing around and start earning a living.*

**play about/around/round**[2] *v prep*
to have fun; spend time near (something): [IØ + *about/around/round*] *Tell the children not to play around the electricity station. Many an insect has met its death playing about a flame.*

**play about/around with** *v adv prep*
**1** to amuse oneself with; examine the possibilities of (something) in an unorganized manner: [IØ + ABOUT/AROUND + *with*] *Children learn a great deal by playing about with sand and water. Many important discoveries have been made by scientists playing around with unusual combinations of chemicals.*
***2** to cause disorder to (something): [T1] *Who's been playing about with my papers? They're all out of order.* → **mess about with** (1), etc.
***3** *not fml* to have an improper relationship with (someone, usu. of the opposite sex): [T1] *I warned you not to play around with*

*married women, it always leads to trouble.* → **mess about with** (2), etc.

**play against** *v prep*

**1** to oppose (someone or a team) in sport: [I∅ + *against*] *I see we're playing against my old school next month!* [T1 + *against*] *Don't play cards against your father, he always wins.* → **play at (1), play with (1)**

**2 play both ends against the middle** *not fml* to attempt to gain some advantage either way from the result of two chances or two opposing forces: *By playing both ends against the middle, and letting the Government and the Opposition parties attack each other, the smallest of the three parties was able to win votes and gain more seats in the House.* → **play off against** (2)

***play along**[1] *v adv*

**1** *not fml* to keep (someone) waiting for an answer or decision: [T1b] *Instead of writing a letter of acceptance at once, the committee decided to play her along for a time, hoping to obtain her services for lower pay.*

**2** *not fml* to pretend to agree (with someone or his ideas): [I∅ (*with*)] *I think the union leaders are just playing along and have no real intention of accepting the offer. Perhaps we should play along with his suggestion, although it's not exactly what we wanted.* → **go along with (3)**

**play along**[2] *v prep* → **play on**[2] **(3), play over**[2]

to (cause to) be directed along (something): [L9 + *along*] *The sunlight played along the water ahead of us, making it difficult to see where the boat was going.* [X9 + *along*] *The firemen played the water along the whole side of the burning building.*

**play around**[1] *v adv* → PLAY ABOUT[1]

**play around**[2] *v prep* → PLAY ABOUT[2]

**play around with** *v adv prep* → PLAY ABOUT WITH

**play as** *v prep*

**1** (of an actor) to perform (a part) so as to seem (a certain kind of person): [T1 + *as*] *Hamlet is usually played as a sorrowful person who cannot make decisions or take action. The director would like you to play the sister as a sympathetic character.*

**2** to play (music) so as to seem (something): [T1 + *as*] *Play the piece as music and not as a struggle between yourself and your instrument.*

**3** to (cause to) take (a certain position in a team game): [T1 + *as*] *The captain wants to play Mills as defence in our next game.* [I∅ + *as*] *But has he ever played as defence before?* → **play at** (3)

**play at** *v prep*

**1** to take part in (a game) (against someone): [I∅ + *at*] *Can we play at cards this evening, Dad?* [T1 + *at*] *Don't play Father at cards, he always wins* → **play against (1), play with (1)**

**2** to perform (music, a character, etc.) at (a place): [I∅ + *at*] *"The Mousetrap" played at the same London theatre for many years from 1952.* [T1 + *at*] *Who is playing Hamlet at Stratford this year? The band played excellent music at the children's show.*

**3** to (cause to) take (a certain position in a team game): [T1 + *at*] *The captain wants to play Brown at left half in the next game.* [I∅ + *at*] *But he's always played at centre forward.* → **play as** (3)

**4** (usu. of children) to pretend to be (something or doing something): [I∅ + *at*] *Small children love playing at bears. Later, they tend to play at mothers and fathers. What Victor likes best is playing at driving a train.*

***5** *not fml* to perform (something or doing something) in a not very serious manner: [T1] *It's no good playing at business, you have to take it seriously.* [T4] *The chairman should be dismissed, he's just playing at running this department.*

**6 play (music) at sight** to play music by reading the printed notes for the first time: *As your piano examinations get more and more advanced, you are expected to be able to play (music) at sight with increasing skill.*

**7 what are you playing at?** *infml* what do you think you're doing? *What are you playing at? You can't take that car; it isn't yours!*

**play back** *v adv*

**1** (in many sports) to return (a ball) to an opposing player: [T1 + BACK] *He played the ball back close to the net.*

**2** (in cricket) to take one step backwards before hitting the ball: [L9 + BACK (*to*)] *When a fast ball lands short of you, you have to play back (to it).* → **play forward**

***3** to control a recording machine so as to hear (a sound) again: [T1] *Can you play back the last piece again, I want to hear how my voice sounds. It's always a shock when you first hear your own voice played back.* [I∅] *To record, press these two buttons together; then rewind, and then press the red button to play back.* —**playback** *n*

**play by** *v prep*

**1 play (music) by ear** to play a tune which one has heard, remembered, or invented but not seen written in notes: *Mr grandfather had had no musical training and couldn't read music, but every time he went to see a musical show at the theatre, he would come home and sit down at the piano and play all the tunes from the show by ear. I wish I could play by ear like that.*

**2 play it by ear** to judge the correct way to deal with something as it happens, without fixed plans in advance: *I can't advise you how the meeting is likely to go, you'll have to play it by ear. I could make no preparations for talking to the firm about a possible job, so I had to play it by ear. I don't like making fixed plans for my travel; it's much more fun to wander as I please, playing it by ear.*

**play cool** *v adj*
**play it cool** *infml* to refuse to become excited: *When we made him the offer, he played it very cool so we thought he wasn't interested. There's no need to be nervous of meeting the Director; just play it cool and he'll probably appoint you because of your past successes.*

*__play down__ *v adv* → **play up** (2)
*not fml* to reduce the seeming importance of (something): [T1] *The doctors thought it kind to play down the serious nature of her illness.*

***play down to*** *v adv prep* → **talk down to**
to treat (someone) on his/her own level, so as to make him/her feel equally important, often to gain his/her support: [T1] *Politicians have to learn to play down to the voters, so that they seem to be ordinary worthy people and not someone too clever and untrustworthy.*

**play fair** *v adv*
**1** to obey the rules of a game: [IØ] *He's a hard opponent to beat, but at least he plays fair.*
**2** to behave honourably (towards someone): [IØ (*with*)] *The government is not playing fair with the taxpayers by refusing to declare details of public spending.*

**play false** *v adj*
to deceive (someone): [T1b] *I trusted my friend with my money, but he played me false and disappeared with it.*

**play for** *v prep*
**1** to perform (music or theatre) for (someone or an occasion): [T1 + *for*] *Would you play that again for me? I'm playing this scene for a special friend who is in the theatre tonight.* [IØ + *for*] *I'm still only a beginner on the instrument, it'll be years before I'm ready to play for the public. Jane was hurt that she wasn't asked to play for the wedding.*
**2** to perform (something such as music or a play) so as to gain (something such as a result): [T1 + *for*] *She dreams of the day when she will be playing the piano for a living.* [IØ + *for*] *I only play for my own amusement, I've no intention of becoming a professional.*
**3** to take part in (a game) to win (money): [T1 + *for*] *Never play cards for money.* [IØ + *for*] *Let's just play for pennies.*
**4** (in sport) to be an active member of (a team); represent (a group): [IØ + *for*] *What team do you play for? All promising young cricketers would like to play for England.*
**5** **play someone for a fool** esp. *AmE not fml* to treat someone as if he/she were stupid; take advantage of someone: *Stop this nonsense! Do you think you can play me for a fool?*
**6** **play for sympathy** to try to make people feel sorry for one: *The former Minister spoke only of his personal troubles, hoping that by playing for sympathy, he could draw the public's attention away from his mistakes, and be forgiven.*
**7** **play for time** to cause delays in order to have more time to think, win, etc.: *If we play for time on this contract, we may get a better price. Give me your decision now, stop playing for time!* → **stall for**

**play forward** *v adv* → **play back** (2)
(in cricket) to take one step forward before hitting the ball: [L9 + FORWARD (*to*)] *If the ball lands near you, you should play forward (to it)*

*__play in__[1] *v adv*
**1** to play music while (someone) enters: [T1 (*to*)] *The town band played the victorious team in to the dinner given in their honour.* → **play out** (4)
**2** to mark the coming of (the new year) with music: [T1] *In this part of the country, a ceremony used to be held, during which pipers played in the new year.* → **ring in** (2), etc.
**3** **play oneself in** (in sport, esp. cricket) to accustom oneself to playing; become ready through playing carefully at the beginning of the game or one's turn: *This player has always been known for taking about half an hour to play himself in.*

**play in**[2] *v prep*
**1** to amuse oneself (with a game) in (something such as a place): [IØ + *in*] *It's healthy for children to play in the fresh air. The local farmer used to let us play in his fields.* [T1 + *in*] *Why are children not allowed to play ball games in the park? On Wednesdays, all our neighbours play cards in the village hall.*
**2** to perform (music, an instrument, or a part) in (a band, play, place, etc.): [IØ + *in*] *A famous actress is to play in our next production. Many of the workers play in the factory's brass band.* [T1 + *in*] *He is perfectly suited to play Bottom in "A Midsummer Night's Dream". There is a part for every child to play in the school play. Jane is too nervous to play the piano in public. What an honour to play the drums in the town band! This piece is not suitable to be played in the open air.*
**3** to (cause to) fill (a position) in (a team game); take (a position): [IØ + *in*] *But I've never played in a defence position.* [T1 + *in*] *I think we should play one of the younger men in goal. That man will not be played in any more games this year after his violent behaviour.*
**4** **play a part/role in** to be partly responsible for (something or doing something): *The director claimed that he had played a large part in the successful agreement. An important role was played by the radio in forming my interest in music. Modern drugs have a new role/part to play in controlling diseases of the mind.* → **have in**[2] (4), **take in**[2] (9)

**play into** *v prep*
**play into someone's hands** *not fml* to do something that lets one's opponent gain an advantage over one: *By leading his men into a valley without another way out, the general play-*

*ed (right) into the enemy's hands. By admitting that he had not thoroughly studied the facts, the speaker played into his opponent's hands.*

**play like** *v prep*

**1** to perform (music, an instrument, a character, scene, etc.) in the manner of (someone or something): [IØ + *like*] *The pianist played like a man possessed by devils. All horn players wish they could play like Mr Brain.* [T1 + *like*] *He plays the instrument like a master. She played Queen Victoria like the old Queen herself. We should play this scene like professionals.*

**2 play someone like a fish** to control someone easily: *One of the secrets of the speaker's success is his ability to play his opponent like a fish.*

*__play off__ *v adv* → **run off**[1] (8)

(usu. in sport) to finish playing (a set of games); play (an additional game) to decide the winner; cause (two equal winners) to play again: [T1 (*against*)] *The top teams in each group play off seven games against each other. The two equal winners had to play off an additional game to decide the winner of the whole competition. There was no clear result, so the organizers of the competition had to play off the two winners.* [IØ] *If the two top teams reach the same result, they will have to play off next week.* —**play-off** *n*

*__play off against__ *v adv prep*

**1** to finish playing (equal games) against (the other winner): [T1 + *against*] *The top teams in each group play off seven games against each other.*

**2** *not fml* to oppose (someone) against (someone else) for one's own advantage: [D1] *By playing off the Government party against the Opposition party, the smallest of the three parties was able to win votes and gain more seats in the House.* → **play against** (2)

**play on**[1] *v adv*

**1** to continue playing, as in sport or music: [IØ + ON] *The cricket teams played on until it was almost dark. "Play on!" said the judge when the loose ball had been picked up. "If music be the food of love, play on."* (Shakespeare, *Twelfth Night*)

*__2__ (in cricket) to hit one's own wicket with the ball after it has struck the bat; hit (the ball) accidentally on to one's wicket: [IØ (*to*) (*often simple tenses*)] *A difficult ball came through; the batsman played on* (*to his wicket*) *and was out.* [T1 (*to*)] *Be careful not to play the ball on to your wicket.*

*__3__ (in football) to cause (a player) to be onside: [T1b (*often simple tenses*)] *Smith accidentally played Sanchez on, so the Spanish goal was allowed.*

**play on/upon**[2] *v prep*

**1** (usu. of children) to amuse oneself on (something, as an object or place): [IØ + *on/upon*] *My children love to play on the seashore.*

**2** to perform (something such as music or a play) on (an instrument, stage, etc.): [IØ + *on/upon*] *It's many years since I played on this stage. A man stood at the corner of the city street, playing on a drum.* [T1 + *on/upon*] *This piece of music can be played on almost any instrument. Have you ever played Hamlet on such a small stage?*

**3** to (cause to) pass over; be directed onto (something): [L9 + *on/upon*] *The sunlight played on the lake, brightening the whole area. When I saw a secret smile playing on his lips, I knew that he was telling a lie. The wind was playing on the wrong side, and the ship could not make any speed.* [X9 + *on/upon*] *The firemen played the water on the front of the burning building, but could not control the flames. The policeman played his light on the objects in the room, but the stolen jewellery was not there.* → **play along**[2], **play over**[2]

*__4__ to make use of; try to develop (something such as someone's feelings or a quality) so as to make use or advantage of it: [T1] *By playing on the old lady's fears, the criminals were able to persuade her to give them her money. Politicians often win votes by playing on the electors' distrust of the party in power. He made money by playing on the reading public's taste for violent stories. The plan can be defeated if you play on its weaknesses.*

**5 play a joke/jape/prank on** to deceive (someone) for fun: *I know you're really awake, you're just playing a joke on me. Teachers often wonder what pranks the children will play on them next.*

**6 play a trick on** to deceive (someone) for fun or profit: *The firm won the contract unfairly by playing a trick on its competitors and not showing its intentions.*

**7 play on words** to make a joke, as with two words of different meanings that sound alike: *Much English humour consists of playing on words.* —**play on words** *n*

**play out** *v adv*

**1** to play out of doors: [IØ + OUT] *It's too wet for the children to play out today, they'll have to amuse themselves indoors.*

*__2__ to finish performing (a play) or playing (a game): [T1] *The tennis game was played out although the light was bad.*

*__3__ to perform (something such as a struggle): [T1] *The battle for the leadership of the party was played out with much bitter personal hatred.*

*__4__ to play music while (someone) leaves: [T1] *The pianist played the happy pair out with the Wedding March.* → **play in**[1] (1)

*__5__ to mark the end of (the old year) with music: [T1] *Gather round the piano, let's play out the old year with a loud joyful tune.* → **ring in**[1] (2), etc.

*6 to give expression to (usu. a feeling) so as to be free of it: [T1] *When children pretend to be violent, they may well be playing out evil in a lawful setting, preventing trouble in later life.* → **act out** (2)
*7 to allow (something such as a rope) to be gradually lengthened: [T1] *Play out the rope a little at a time.* → **pay away** (2), **pay out** (4), **run out** (5)
**8 be played out** *not fml* to be tired, worn out, finished, used up, out of date, etc.: *Don't ask me to move, I'm played out. At the end of a busy year, the performers feel played out. That supply of money is played out, you'll have to try elsewhere. The idea that there is only one correct form of English is now played out.* —**played-out** *adj*
**9 play out time** (in sport) to finish a game without losing a point, etc.: *There's no hope of victory but at least we can play out time and perhaps not lose.*

**play over¹** *v adv*
to play (something such as music or a game) again: [T1 + OVER] *The tennis players refused to accept the linesman's decision, so the judge ordered them to play that point over.*

**play over²** *v prep* → **play along², play on²** (3)
to (cause to) pass over; be directed onto (something): [L9 + *over*] *When I saw a secret smile playing over his lips, I knew that he was telling a lie.* [X9 + *over*] *The watchers played a powerful light over the whole sky, searching for enemy planes.*

**play round** *v prep* → PLAY ABOUT²

**play safe** *v adj*
*not fml* to take care not to fail, by avoiding risks: [IØ] *I thought I should play safe by keeping the old machine until the new one actually arrived, in case there was any delay. Do you want to put your money into high-interest shares which vary according to the market, or would you rather play safe by lending it to the government?*

**play through** *v adv*
**1** to complete the playing of (something such as music or a game): [T1 + THROUGH] *Let's see if we can play the whole piece through without a mistake.*
**2** (in sport) to keep winning games: [IØ (*to*)] *Our team played through right up to the last game, and then lost, so they could not keep the prize.*
**3** (in golf) to continue playing while others in front of one wait for one to go past: [IØ] *We'll give you a few minutes to play through.*

**play to** *v prep*
**1** to perform (usu. music or theatre) to (someone listening or watching): [IØ + *to*] *The touring company was such a success that it played to full theatres wherever it went.* [T1 + *to*] *Jane will only play her piano pieces to a small group of friends. It's quite an experience playing Shakespeare to a crowd of children at a school performance.*
**2** (in cricket) to strike (the ball) in the direction of (a certain position): [T1 + *to*] *Underwood played the ball to the fielder's left, and took a quick run.*
**3 play to the gallery** *derog* to perform or behave so as to win the favour of those with least judgment: *This actor is not highly regarded by his fellow professionals, as he tends to play to the gallery to win public popularity. Some politicians think they can win the votes of unthinking members of the public by playing to the gallery.*

***play up** *v adv*
**1** to play a game actively: [IØ (*usu. simple tenses*)] *"Play up! Play up! and play the game!"* (Sir Henry Newbolt, *The Island Race*)
**2** to draw attention to; make (something) seem more important than it is: [T1] *In trying to get a job, you have to play up the better parts of your past. Advertisers always play up the good qualities of the house for sale and fail to mention its disadvantages.* → **play down**
**3** esp. *AmE not fml* to advertise (something): [T1] *This new film will attract the crowds, whatever its quality, provided that it gets played up in the right way.*
**4** also **act up** *not fml* to misbehave; perform badly: [IØ (*usu. continuous tenses*)] *The children have been playing up all morning. The washing machine is playing up again.*
**5** to cause suffering or annoyance to (someone): [T1b] *My bad leg has been playing me up again. Children often play their mothers up, just for fun.* → **act up** (2)

***play up to** *v adv prep*
**1** (of an actor) to act so as to support (another actor) in a performance: [T1] *Your job as a supporting actor is to play up to the leading character.*
**2** to try to gain the favour of (someone): [T1] *Some students play up to their teachers to get good marks.* → **make up to** (3), **shine up to, suck up to**

**play upon** *v prep* → PLAY ON²

**play with** *v prep*
**1** to amuse oneself (with a game) with (someone or something): [IØ + *with*] *Play with your own toys, don't take your brother's. All the time he was talking, he was playing with a pencil.* [T1 + *with*] *Don't play cards with your father, he always wins.* → **fiddle with** (1), etc., **play against** (1), **play along¹** (1)
*2 to treat (someone or someone's feelings) in a not very serious manner: [T1] *He's never mentioned marriage, and I'm beginning to think he's just playing with me, which is unkind.* → **flirt with** (1), etc.
*3 → TOY WITH (2)
**4 play ball with** *infml* to act so as to help or agree with (someone): *The other members of the committee refused to play ball with the*

*chairman, and defeated his suggestion in a vote.*

**5 play the devil/hell with: a** *sl* to cause harm to (something): *Salt on the roads melts the ice, but it plays hell with the car's paintwork. The delay on the track has played the (very) devil with the train timetable.* **b** *sl* to be very angry with (someone): *The teacher will play hell with you if you don't finish your work on time.*

**6 play with fire** *not fml* to take dangerous risks: *Any student who tries to cheat while the examiner is watching is playing with fire.*

**7 play games with** *not fml* to treat (someone or something) not seriously: *Don't play games with me, tell me what you really think. Some people consider that the government is playing games with the taxpayers' money.*

**8 play havoc with** *not fml* to cause trouble to; ruin (something): *The delay on the track has played havoc with the train timetable.*

**plead against** *v prep*
*law* to make a case in court against (the other party, what he/she says, a decision, etc.): [L9 + *against* (*usu. simple tenses*)] *Are you ready to plead against the case offered by the defendant? I advise you to plead against the decision.*

**plead for** *v prep*
**1** *fml* to request (something such as mercy or forgiveness) eagerly and seriously: [L9 + *for*] *She went down on her knees, pleading for mercy.*
**2** *law* to represent (someone) in court: [L9 + *for* (*usu. simple tenses*)] *Mr Jones will plead for you in this case.* → **act for, appear for**

**plead guilty** *v adj*
to admit one's guilt in a court of law: [L9 + guilty (*usu. simple tenses*)] *How do you plead —guilty or not guilty?*

**plead with** *v prep*
to ask (someone) eagerly and seriously (for something or to do something): [L9 + *with*] *The prisoner pleaded with the king for forgiveness. The prisoner pleaded with the king to set him free.*

***please oneself** *v pron*
to do as one chooses: [IØ (*usu. simple tenses, usu. imper.*)] *I don't mind which one you have, please yourself. Please yourselves what you do today.*

**pledge to** *v prep*
**1** *fml* to promise to give (something) to (usu. something): [T1 + *to*] *Each member of the club has pledged £10 to the collection.*
***2** *fml* to make (someone) give a promise concerning (something): [D1 (*usu. pass.*)] *I'm sorry, I can't tell you, I'm pledged to secrecy.*
**3 pledge allegiance to** *fml* to promise solemnly to be loyal to (usu. something): [*usu. simple tenses*] *We pledge allegiance to this flag.*

***plight oneself** *v pron*
*old use* to promise to marry someone: [IØ (*to*) (*usu. simple tenses*)] *Think carefully before you plight yourself to such a man.*

**plod along/on** *v adv; prep*
to move or walk heavily and steadily along (a road, etc.): [IØ + ALONG/ON/*along/on*] *All that we could hear were the footsteps of the local policeman plodding along (the path). If we plod on (our way), we shall reach the town before dark.*

**plod away** *v adv* → **peg away at, plug away at, slog at**
to continue working slowly but steadily (at something or doing something): [IØ + AWAY (*at*)] *He's a slow worker, but he gets the job finished by plodding away until it's done. Tom wrote his last book in such a short time by plodding away at the typewriter for hours on end. By plodding away at writing, Tom soon got the book finished.*

**plod on** *v adv; prep* → **PLOD ALONG**

**plonk down** *v adv*
**1** *not fml* to set (something) down heavily: [X9 + DOWN] *The workman plonked down his heavy bag of tools.* → **plank down** (1), **plump down** (2), **plunk down** (1)
***2** *not fml* to pay (money) readily or in a showy manner: [T1 (*usu. simple tenses*)] *He plonked down the money and called for drinks for everyone. Few people can afford to plonk down the whole cost of a house.* → **plank down** (2), **plank out, plump down** (3), **plunk down** (2)

**plonk on** *v prep* → **plank on**
*not fml* to put (something) heavily on (something): [X9 + *on*] *The workman plonked his heavy bag of tools on the floor.*

**plot against** *v prep* → **conspire against, intrigue against**
to make secret plans, usu. with other people against (someone or something): [IØ + *against*] *The men were imprisoned for plotting against the government.*

**plot on** *v prep*
to mark (something) in its correct place on (something such as a map): [T1 + *on*] *During the sea battle, the positions of the ships were plotted on a big wall map in the control centre. The firm plots its sales figures on the special squared paper.*

**plot out** *v adv*
**1** *naut* to decide and mark (a ship's course): [T1 + OUT] *The captain has the responsibility for plotting out the ship's course.*
***2** to decide (a plan of action): [T1] *All our activities for the next month are plotted out in advance.*
***3** to divide (land) into pieces suitable for building: [T1] *The builders have plotted out the area ready for the houses.*

**plot with** *v prep* → **connive with, conspire with, intrigue with** (1)
to make secret plans together with (someone) (to do something): [IØ + *with*] *Politicians plot with each other all the time (to get what they want).*

**plough back** *v adv* also *AmE* **plow back**
**1** to return (the remains of a crop) to th

earth with a plough: [X9 + BACK] *After the vegetable crop had been picked, there were a lot of loose leaves lying on the field, so the farmer ploughed them back to enrich the soil.* → **plough in**

*2 to return (money earned) into a business so as to increase it: [T1 (*into*)] *There's very little to show for the first year's work as we have ploughed back all the profits into methods of increasing trade next year.*

**plough in** *v adv* also *AmE* **plow in** → **plough back** (1)
to bury; mix (something such as the remains of a crop or chemical) with the earth with a plough: [X9 + IN (*to*)] *After the wheat crop has been gathered, many farmers burn the remains and plough the ash in, so as to enrich the soil.*

**plough into** *v prep* also *AmE* **plow into**
**1** to bury; mix (something such as the remains of a crop or chemical) with (the earth) with a plough: [T1 + *into*] *After the wheat crop has been gathered, many farmers burn the remains and plough the ash into the soil, so as to enrich it.*
***2** *not fml* to start (work) actively: [T1 (*no pass.*)] *If I really plough into my studies now, I should be ready for the examination.*
***3** *not fml* to strike against (something or someone) with force: [T1 (*no pass., usu. simple tenses*)] *The car turned over twice, left the road, and ploughed into a fence.*

**plough on** *v adv* also *AmE* **plow on**
**1** to continue to turn the earth with a plough: [IØ + ON] *If we plough on until it's dark, we should get this field finished.*
***2** *not fml* to continue or advance with determination: [IØ] *We must plough on somehow in spite of all the difficulties.* → **press forward** (3), **press on¹**, **push ahead** (2), **push forward** (3), **push on¹** (1)

**plough out** *v adv* also *AmE* **plow out** → **plough up** (2), **turn up** (8)
to uncover (something buried) with a plough: [X9 + OUT] *Halfway across the field, the farmer ploughed out some very large stones which nearly broke his machine.*

**plough through** *v prep* also *AmE* **plow through**
**1** to move slowly or with difficulty through; force (one's way) through (something such as water): [T1 (*no pass.*)] *It took over an hour to reach the farmhouse, ploughing through the deep snow in my high boots.* [D1] *The ship rolled as she ploughed her way through the stormy seas. The famous actress had to plough her way through the crowd to reach her car.*
**2** *not fml* to get slowly to the end of; make (one's way) with difficulty through (something such as work): [T1 (*no pass.*)] *I doubt if I shall be home for dinner; I've suddenly a lot of urgent work to plough through.* [D1] *She spent the weekend ploughing her way through the pile of letters that she owed to people.* → **wade through** (2)

**plough under** *v adv* also *AmE* **plow under**
**1** to bury (something) in the earth with a plough: [X9 + UNDER (*often pass.*)] *When the forest was cleared, a lot of small branches were ploughed under.*
***2** *AmE not fml* to destroy (something): [T1 (*usu. pass.*)] *All our hopes for winning the election were ploughed under when the votes were counted.*

**plough up** *v adv* also *AmE* **plow up**
**1** to turn over the earth in (an area such as a field) with or as with a plough: [T1 + UP] *All the fields are now ploughed up, ready for the seeds. The car's wheels only ploughed up the mud further, and we could not move.* → **turn over** (1), **turn up** (4)
**2** to uncover (something buried) with a plough: [X9 + UP] *There is a good chance in this area that you might plough up some valuable ancient coins.* → **plough out, turn up** (8)

**plow back** *v adv AmE* → PLOUGH BACK
**plow in** *v adv AmE* → PLOUGH IN
**plow into** *v prep AmE* → PLOUGH INTO
**plow on** *v adv AmE* → PLOUGH ON
**plow out** *v adv AmE* → PLOUGH OUT
***plow through** *v prep AmE* → PLOUGH THROUGH
**plow under** *v adv AmE* → PLOUGH UNDER
**plow up** *v adv AmE* → PLOUGH UP

***pluck at** *v prep* → **pull at** (1), **pull on** (1), **tug at** (1), **yank at, yank on**
to pull at (something) sharply with the fingers: [T1] *This stringed instrument is played by plucking at the wires. She sat nervously plucking at her hair while waiting for her turn. Do stop plucking at my skirt! I'm coming!*

**pluck from** *v prep*
to take; remove (something), often quickly from (something): [T1 + *from*] *Plucking a flower from the garden, he gave it to her with a smile.*

**pluck off** *v adv; prep* → **take off¹** (1), etc.
to remove (something) sharply, with or as with the fingers: [T1 + OFF/*off*] *Those birds have plucked all the flower heads off (the roses)! Let me pluck that piece of thread off (your skirt). When you get hungry, just pluck an apple off (the tree) and eat it.*

**pluck out** *v adv* → **take out** (2), etc.
to take; pull (something) out quickly, with or as with the fingers: [T1 + OUT (*of*)] *He plucked the arrow out of his arm with his other hand. This tool is for plucking hairs out of your nose.*

**pluck up** *v adv*
**1** to pull (something or someone) up sharply: [T1 + UP] *You'll find her in the garden, plucking up all the unwanted plants. As the boy sank for the third time, the swimmer plucked him up by the hair.* → **pull up** (1), etc.
**2 pluck up courage** to defeat one's fears and show bravery: *The young soldier had to pluck up all his courage to prevent himself from running away and being regarded as a coward.* → **muster up** (2), **screw up** (6), **summon up** (3)

**plug at** *v prep*
*AmE infml* to shoot at (something or someone): [IØ + *at*] *You can practise with your gun by plugging at the tree, not the chickens!*

***plug away at** *v adv prep* → **peg away at, plod away, slog at**
*not fml* to work hard and steadily at (something or doing something): [T1 (*no pass.*)] *If you plug away at cricket practice all your youth, there is some hope that you may be chosen for the team. If I plug away at painting the room, I may get it finished tonight.*

***plug in** *v adv*
**1** to connect (something) to a supply of electricity: [T1] *No wonder the lamp didn't come on, it's not plugged in!*
**2 be plugged in to** *infml* to be deeply concerned with (something such as an idea): *Are all the students really plugged in to these modern ideas about life?*

**plug up** *v adv*
to block (something such as a hole) with something solid: [T1 + UP] *The pipe seems to be plugged up and the water can't flow away. If you will play that loud music, I shall have to plug up my ears.*

**plume on** *v prep* → **pique on, preen on, pride on**
**plume oneself on** to be very proud of (something or doing something): *The director is pluming himself on his success in winning the contract. There's no need to plume yourself quite so much on winning the race.*

**plump against** *v prep*
*not fml* to fall heavily against (something): [L9 + *against* (*often simple tenses*)] *Losing his balance, he plumped against the doorpost.*

**plump down** *v adv*
**1** *not fml* to (cause to) sit down heavily: [L9 + DOWN (*often simple tenses*)] *Tired after her walk, she plumped down on a comfortable chair.* [X9 + DOWN (*often simple tenses*)] *Tired after her walk, she plumped herself down in a comfortable chair.*
**2** *not fml* to set (something) down heavily: [X9 + DOWN] *The workman plumped down his heavy bag of tools.* → **plank down** (1), **plonk down** (1), **plunk down** (1)
***3** *not fml* to pay (money) readily: [T1 (*usu. simple tenses*)] *He plumped down the money and called for drinks for everyone.* → **plank down** (2), **plank out, plonk down** (2), **plunk down** (2)

***plump for** *v prep* → **plunk for**
*not fml* to be keen to choose or vote for (someone or something, as an idea): [T1 (*usu. simple tenses*)] *Although we could vote for three people, many of us just plumped for one man as he was so well suited to the job. Every member of the committee plumped for the chairman's new suggestion. All the children plumped for a camping holiday.*

***plump out** *v adv* → **fatten out** (1), **fill out** (4), **flesh out** (1)
to (cause to) become fatter: [IØ] *Mother grew so thin during her illness, but she is beginning to plump out now.* [T1] *He plumped out his cheeks in an expression of annoyance.*

***plump up** *v adv* → **fluff up, shake up** (2)
to make (something, esp. a cushion or pillow) fat with air, by beating it with the hands: [T1] *Tidy the room and plump up the cushions ready for our guests.*

**plunge down** *v adv; prep*
**1** to descend (something) steeply: [L9 + DOWN/*down*] *Without stopping to think of his own safety, he plunged down (the river bank) to save the drowning child. The path plunges down (the cliff) to the sea.*
**2** to push (something) down (something): [X9 + DOWN/*down*] *As soon as the rabbit had disappeared into its hole, the dog plunged its nose down (it) to see if the rabbit was still there.*

**plunge in[1]** *v adv* → **press in[1]** (1), **push in[1]** (1), **thrust in[1]**
to (cause to) enter (something or someone) suddenly: [L9 + IN (*to*)] *He ran to the water's edge and plunged in.* [X9 + IN (*to*)] *He took the prisoner by the neck and plunged his sword in (to his body).*

**plunge in[2]** *v prep*
**1** to (cause to) enter (something) suddenly: [L9 + *in*] *He ran to the edge and plunged in the water.* [X9 + *in*] *He took the prisoner by the neck and plunged his sword in his body. You will only find the soap if you are prepare to plunge your hand in the hot water.* → **plunge into** (1), **thrust into** (1)
**2 be plunged in thought** to be thinking deeply *It's no good talking to your father when he' plunged in thought, he won't hear you.*

**plunge into** *v prep*
**1** to (cause to) enter (something) suddenly [L9 + *into*] *The children plunged into th cold water without complaining.* [X9 + *into She plunged the burning pan into water an put out the flames. Taking the prisoner by th neck, he plunged his sword into his body* → **plunge in[2]** (1), **thrust into** (1)
***2** to (cause to) rush into (a state of activity) [T1 (*no pass.*)] *Don't be too keen to plung into argument with him, he's an experience speaker. We do not readily plunge into battl with such powerful forces. We were powerles to help as the boy plunged deeper and deepe into debt.* [D1 (*often pass.*)] *Foolish mistake by the nation's leaders have plunged the coun try into a war that could have been avoided The company was plunged into ruin when th exchange rate dropped. The city was plunge into darkness when the electricity supply wa cut off in the storm.* → **precipitate into, thrus into** (3)
***3** to cause (someone) to feel (something

suddenly: [D1 (*often pass.*)] *The news of her mother's death plunged Mary into grief.*

**plunk down** *v adv*

**1** *not fml* to set (something) down heavily: [X9 + DOWN] *The workman plunked down his heavy bag of tools.* → **plank down** (1), **plonk down** (1), **plump down** (2)

*__2__ *not fml* to pay (money) readily: [T1 (*usu. simple tenses*)] *He plunked down the money and called for drinks for everyone.* → **plank down** (2), **plank out**, **plonk down** (2), **plump down** (3)

***plunk for** *v prep* → **plump for**

*AmE not fml* to be keen to vote for (one person from a wide choice): [T1 (*usu. simple tenses*)] *Although we could vote for three people, many of us just used one vote, plunking for the one man who seemed fit for the job.*

**ply across** *v prep*

(of a ship) to make regular voyages across (water): [L9 + *across*] *This shipping line plies across the ocean.*

**ply between** *v prep*

(of a ship) to make regular voyages between (two places): [L9 + *between*] *There are passenger ships plying between Liverpool and Ireland.*

***ply with** *v prep*

to provide (someone) with (supplies of food or drink, or frequent questions): [D1] *She keeps plying her guests with tea, when many of them would rather have coffee. The crowd kept the speaker late after his speech, plying him with questions.*

**poach for** *v prep*

to hunt and catch (animals or fish) unlawfully on someone else's land: [IØ + *for*] *The police caught the young man late one night poaching for rabbits on the lord's land.*

**poach on** *v prep*

**1** to hunt and catch animals or fish unlawfully on (someone else's land): [IØ + *on*] *The young man was taken to the police station on a charge of poaching on private property.*

**2 poach on someone's preserves** to try to take part in someone else's business: *Kindly remember that I give the orders around here: I don't want you poaching on my preserves, telling my workers what to do!*

**pock with** *v prep* → **pit with**

**be pocked with** to be marked with (hollow places): *Most of the buildings in the town were pocked with bullet holes after the battle.*

**point at** *v prep*

**1** to show the way to; draw attention to (something or someone), with or as with a finger: [IØ + *at*] *It's rude to point at people. The child was pointing at the animals, shouting with excitement.* → **point to** (1)

**2** to aim; direct (something) towards (something or someone): [T1 + *at*] *Never point a gun at someone, even in fun, as it might be loaded; always point it at the sky. He pointed his long bony finger at me in disapproval.*

*__3__ *AmE* to suggest (something) in an indirect way: [T1 (*no pass.*)] *The Minister's remarks seemed to be pointing at an early election.* → **hint at, point to** (4)

**point down** *v adv*

**1** to direct attention in a downward direction, as with a finger: [IØ + DOWN (*at, to*)] *Pointing down to the bottom of the cliff, he showed us the dangerous rocks. 'There's the coin you dropped!' she said, pointing down (at my feet).*

*__2__ *AmE* to make (a surface) smooth: [T1] *Do you use a special tool to point the wood down?* → **point up** (3)

***point off** *v adv*

to place a decimal point before (a number): [T1] *He pointed off the last two figures.*

***point out** *v adv*

to show; explain; draw attention to (something or someone): [T1 (*to*)] *Look at the photographs and see if you can point out the man who attacked you. Mistakes in the printing should be pointed out at once. The guide took us through the city, pointing interesting sights out (to us).* [T5] *I would like to point out that it is getting very late. It was pointed out to us that the office was closed.* [T6] *Please point out (to me) where I went wrong.*

**point to/towards** *v prep*

**1** to show the way to; show the direction or position of; draw attention to (something or someone), with or as with a finger: [IØ + *to/towards*] *Pointing to a man on the front row, the man on the stage asked to borrow his watch. Using a long stick, the teacher pointed to a place on the map and asked the children to name it. A compass needle always points to/towards the north. There is a sign pointing to the way out.* → **point at** (1)

*__2__ to direct (something or someone) towards (something or someone): [D1] *A loaded gun was pointed towards me. Education is a matter of pointing the children to/towards ways in which they can improve the world, and then leaving the job to them.*

*__3__ to offer (something) as proof or explanation: [T1 (*usu. simple tenses*)] *When asked to explain where all the housekeeping money had gone, Mary pointed to the rising prices. One need only point to the increase in violence as an example of the fall in moral values in our time.*

*__4__ to give signs of; suggest (something): [T1 (*no pass., simple tenses*)] *All the signs point to/towards an early election.* → **hint at, point at** (3)

**point up** *v adv*

**1** to draw attention in an upward direction, with or as with a finger: [IØ + UP (*to*)] *When asked where the director was, for answer he simply pointed up (to the floor above).*

*__2__ to add more force to; show clearly the qualities of (something): [T1] *The writer has pointed up his story with an effective use of local scenery. Recent world figures of average incomes point up the ever-widening distance between rich and poor nations.*

*3 *AmE* to roughen (a surface): [T1] *This wall should be pointed up before it is covered with the cement; it will help to make it stick.* → **point down** (2)

**poise on** *v prep*
to balance (something) on (something): [T1 + *on* (*usu. simple tenses*)] *A dancer has to learn how to poise her weight on one foot. Since part of the cliff broke away, the house is now poised on the very edge, ready to fall.*

**poise over** *v prep*
to make (something) hang over (something or someone): [T1 + *over* (*usu. pass.*)] *Danger seemed to be poised over our heads.*

**poison against** *v prep*
to give (someone or someone's mind) bad ideas about (someone or something); influence (someone) to have a low opinion of (someone): [T1 + *against*] *The unhappy mother had poisoned the children's minds against their father, and they no longer wanted to see him.*

**poison with** *v prep*
**1** to harm (something) or kill (someone) with (a dangerous substance): [T1 + *with*] *A certain ruler in the Middle Ages was famous for poisoning her guests with chemicals put into their drinks. The soil has been poisoned with chemical waste from the factory.*
**2** to influence (someone's mind) wrongly with (bad ideas): [T1 + *with*] *His character had been poisoned with evil suggestions from his criminal companions. Teachers are not allowed to poison the children's minds with their own political opinions. During the war, the minds of ordinary people on both sides were poisoned with false statements about the enemy.*

***poke about/around/round** *v adv* → **nose about, pry about**
*not fml* to search (in or for something) by examining other people's business: [IØ (*among, for, in*)] *That policeman had no business poking around in our garage without a court order. Why was he poking round among our things? What was he poking about for? We have no stolen goods hidden in there.* —**poke-round** *n*

**poke along** *v adv*
to move slowly and lazily: [L9 + ALONG] *The cows were poking along, holding up the traffic.*

***poke around** *v adv* → POKE ABOUT

**poke at** *v prep*
**1** to give a quick sharp push or blow to (something or someone): [L9 + *at*] *He poked at the meat with his fork, but it seemed undercooked. The fighter won not by a single blow, but by poking at his opponent so often that he weakened him. The women in the market were poking at the fruit to see if it was ripe.* [X9 + *at*] *Stop those boys poking their sticks at that poor dog!* → **jab at, prod at**
**2 poke fun at** *not fml* to make a joke against (something or someone), unkindly: *It's cruel, as well as rude, to poke fun at a foreigner's mistakes in English.* → **laugh at** (2), etc.

**poke forward** *v adv*
to (cause to) move forward or be held in a forward position, awkwardly: [L9 + FORWARD] *His head poked forward as he walked.* [X9 + FORWARD] *Why does he walk with his head poked forward?*

**poke in[1]** *v adv*
**1** to push (something) sharply into something: [X9 + IN] *He poked the stick in a long way, but no animal came out.* → **put in** (1), **stick in[1]** (1)
*__2__ *not fml* to enquire into other people's business: [IØ] *Has that policeman been poking in again? Stop poking in where you're not wanted!*
**3 poke one's nose in** *not fml* to enquire into something that is not one's own affair: [*usu. continuous tenses*] *Stop poking your nose in where you're not wanted!* → **stick in[1]** (5)

**poke in[2]** *v prep*
**1** to push (something) sharply in (something): [X9 + *in*] *He poked his stick in the hole, but no animal came out.* → **stick into** (2), etc.
**2** to make (a hole) by pushing sharply into (something): [X9 + *in*] *His sword did no more than poke a hole in his enemy's shield.* → **stick in[2]** (3)
**3 poke one's nose in** *not fml* to enquire into (something that is not one's own affair): *He's always poking his nose in other people's affairs; I wish he would mind his own business.* → **stick in[2]** (8)

**poke into** *v prep*
**1** to push (something) sharply into (something): [X9 + *into*] *Don't poke your finger into my stomach like that—it's rude as well as painful! Poke your stick into the hole and see if the rabbit is there.* → **jab into, stick into** (2)
*__2__ *not fml* to examine (something that is not one's own affair): [T1] *That policeman has been here again, poking into the drawers for some urgent papers.* → **nose into, pry into**
**3 poke one's nose into** *not fml* to enquire into (something that is not one's own affair): *I don't want anyone poking their nose into my affairs; what I choose to do with my life depends only on me.* → **stick into** (3)

**poke out** *v adv*
**1** to (cause to) be put or left outside: [L9 + OUT (*of*)] *We knew the animal was in there because it left its tail poking out.* [X9 + OUT (*of*)] *Poke your nose out (of the window) and see if it's still raining.* → **jut out, project from, protrude from, stand out** (2), **stick out** (1, 2)
**2** to push (something) out with a sharp blow:

[X9 + OUT] *Mind where you put your elbow, you nearly poked my eye out!* → **jab out**

**oke round** *v adv* → POKE ABOUT

**oke through** *v adv; prep*
to push (something) sharply through (something): [L9 + THROUGH/*through*] *The tops of his shoes had worn so thin that his toes were poking through (the leather).* [X9 + THROUGH/*through*] *Poke your hand through (the fence) and see if you can reach the piece of paper.*

**oke up** *v adv*
to push the materials of (a fire) so as to make it burn more brightly by providing more air: [T1 + UP] *The room is cold, poke the fire up a little.*

**olish off** *v adv*
**1** *infml* to finish (something such as food, work, etc.) completely: [T1] *I've a pile of letters to polish off before I can go home. Those children have polished off the whole cake!* → **end off, finish off** (1), **finish up** (1), **mop up** (3)
**2** *infml* to defeat (a competitor) thoroughly: [T1] *You have to polish off three experienced players before you can win the prize.* → **finish off** (3)
**3** *sl* to kill; murder (someone): [T1 (*usu. simple tenses*)] *Don't hit the old man too hard, you might polish him off by mistake.* → **bump off**, etc.

**olish up** *v adv*
**1** to make (something) shine by rubbing it with polish: [T1 + UP] *Polish up the silver ready for the important dinner.* → **rub up** (1)
**2** *not fml* to improve (something) by study or practice: [T1] *I must polish up my French before I go to Paris. Your performance is promising, but it needs polishing up a little before it 's ready for the public.* → **brush up** (2), **rub up** (2)

**llute with** *v prep*
o spoil; make (something) dirty or impure with (something nasty): [T1 + *with*] *Factories re no longer allowed to pollute the air with lack smoke. Parents are afraid that their childen's minds will be polluted with the violence hat they see on television.*

**nce about/around** *v adv*
*l* to act in a showy way, usu. unpleasantly: [Ø] *I'd like him better if he didn't ponce about o much.*

**nder on/over/upon** *v prep* → **think about** ), etc.
o consider (a matter) deeply: [IØ + *on/over/pon*] *The director is still pondering over the isdom of accepting the contract, and will give is decision tomorrow.*

**ny up** *v adv*
*mE not fml* to pay (money, usu. owed): T1] *After all the arguing, he was forced to ony up the $10 that he owed.* [IØ] *I suppose I hall have to pony up, whether I like it or not.*

**ny up for** *v adv prep*
*mE not fml* to make a request for (something): [T1] *Those children regularly pony up for a second helping of my cheesecake.* → **be in for** (3), **put in for** (4)

***poop out** *v adv* → **tire out,** etc.
*AmE infml* to (cause to) fail, become tired, worn out, etc.: [IØ (*usu. simple tenses*)] *Halfway up the hill, the engine pooped out.* [T1 (*usu. pass.*)] *Don't ask me to move, I'm pooped out.*

**pop across** *v adv; prep* → **pop down** (2), **pop in, pop over, pop round**[1]
*not fml* to move quickly across (something); pay a short visit: [L9 + ACROSS/*across* (*often simple tenses*)] *Pop across (the road) to the shop and bring me a packet of tea, will you? As we're neighbours now, why don't you pop across some afternoon for a talk?*

**pop along** *v adv*
*not fml* to move quickly; pay a short visit: [L9 + ALONG (*often simple tenses*)] *Pop along to bed now, it's getting late. The club are holding a special meeting tonight; I thought I might pop along for an hour or so.*

**pop back** *v adv*
*not fml* to (cause to) return quickly: [L9 + BACK (*often simple tenses*)] *I just popped back to give you the tickets; I forgot them earlier.* [X9 + BACK (*often simple tenses*)] *You'd better pop the ring back before your aunt misses it.*

**pop down** *v adv*
**1** *not fml* to descend quickly: [L9 + DOWN (*often simple tenses*)] *If air is needed, the oxygen mask in the plane will pop down by itself.*
**2** *not fml* to pay a short visit: [L9 + DOWN (*often simple tenses*)] *Do pop down to see us while you're so near.* → **pop across, pop in, pop over, pop round**[1]

**pop in** *v adv; prep* → **pop across, pop down** (2), **pop over, pop round**[1]
*not fml* to (cause to) enter (something) quickly; pay a short visit: [L9 + IN/*in* (*often simple tenses*)] *I thought I'd pop in and see how you are.* [X9 + IN/*in* (*often simple tenses*)] *One of the guests popped his head in (the room) to say goodbye and thank you. Pop this letter in (the postbox) as you pass, will you?*

**pop into** *v prep*
*not fml* to (cause to) enter (something) quickly or for a short time: [L9 + *into* (*often simple tenses*)] *Will you pop into the bank on your way home and order a new cheque book?* [X9 + *into* (*often simple tenses*)] *Don't forget to pop the letter into the post.*

**pop off** *v adv*
**1** *not fml* to leave quickly: [L9 + OFF (*often simple tenses*)] *Pop off home, now, children, before it gets dark.*
**2** *not fml* to (cause to) explode: [L9 + OFF (*often simple tenses*)] *Distant fireworks could be heard popping off.* [X9 + OFF (*often simple tenses*)] *Go and pop your guns off in the garden, not in the house.*

*3 *infml* to die: [IØ (*usu. simple tenses*)] *If you don't take care of your heart, you might pop off sooner than you think.* → **pass away** (3), etc.

*4 esp. *AmE infml* to speak or write without care, in anger, etc.: [IØ] *There he goes, popping off again!* —**pop-off** *n*

**pop on** *v adv*
*not fml* to put (something) on; start (something) cooking quickly: [X9 + ON (*often simple tenses*)] *You run ahead and pop the water on for the tea.*

**pop out** *v adv*
**1** *not fml* to (cause to) come or go out for a short time or suddenly: [L9 + OUT (*of*) (*often simple tenses*)] *The window opened and a head popped out. I had just popped out for a breath of fresh air, and missed your telephone call.* [X9 + OUT (*of*) (*often simple tenses*)] *Pop your head out (of the window) and see if it's still raining.*
**2** *not fml* to spring; esp. in the phrs. **his/her eyes almost popped out of his/her head**: [L9 + OUT (*of*)] *She looked so surprised, her eyes nearly popped out of her head.*

**pop over** *v adv* → **pop across, pop down** (2), **pop in, pop round**[1]
*not fml* to (cause to) arrive; pay a short visit: [L9 + OVER (*to*) (*often simple tenses*)] *Pop over to your grandmother's and see if she's all right. Why don't you pop over and see us one weekend?* [X9 + OVER (*to*) (*often simple tenses*)] *I'll pop your book over as soon as I've finished reading it.*

**pop round**[1] *v adv* → **pop across, pop down** (2), **pop in, pop over**
*not fml* to pay a short visit: [L9 + ROUND (*often simple tenses*)] *I'll just pop round to the library for a few minutes.*

**pop round**[2] *v prep*
*not fml* to (cause to) move or appear round (something) for a short time or suddenly: [L9 + *round* (*often simple tenses*)] *Pop round the corner and post this letter, will you?* [X9 + *round* (*often simple tenses*)] *The office boy popped his head round the door to ask permission to leave.*

**pop up** *v adv*
**1** *not fml* to move, jump, or stand up suddenly: [L9 + UP (*often simple tenses*)] *Put the pieces of bread in the machine, press the button, and when they're cooked they will pop up. The pictures in this book pop up when the pages are opened, to amuse children.* —**pop-up** *adj*
*2 *not fml* to arise; happen or arrive unexpectedly: [IØ (*often simple tenses*)] *Some difficulties have just popped up, so we must work late to deal with them. A wonderful idea has just popped up. He always pops up when he's least expected.* → **crop up** (2)
*3 *not fml* (in team ball games) to hit (the ball) high into the air rather than a long distance: [T1 (*often simple tenses*)] *He's popped the ball up—if you can catch it, he's out* —**pop-up** *n*

**pore on/upon** *v prep* → **think about** (1), etc.
to consider (something) deeply: [L9 + *on/upon*] *After poring upon the matter for some days, he was able to reach a decision.*

**pore over** *v prep*
to study; give close attention to (usu. something written or printed): [L9 + *over*] *The artist pored over every drawing, trying to guess who drew each one.*

**pore upon** *v prep* → PORE ON

**portion out** *v adv*
to share (something) (among several things, people or groups): [X9 + OUT (*among*) (*often simple tenses*)] *The world's riches are not portioned out fairly among the different nations. You will have to portion your time out more evenly among your different activities.*

**portion to** *v prep*
*fml* to give a share of (something such as property) to (someone): [X9 + *to* (*usu. pass.*)] *When the farmer died, how much of his land was portioned to his eldest son?*

**portray as** *v prep*
to give (usu. someone) the character of (a kind of person), as in a book, play, film, or picture: [X9 + *as*] *The old queen was portrayed as a selfish bitter woman in the writer's account of her last days. Most actors portray Hamlet as an unhappy young man, lacking the power of decision.*

**portray in** *v prep*
to describe or show the character of (someone) in (a book, play, film, or picture): [X9 + *in*] *It is still not considered proper to portray Christ in a play or film.*

***pose as** *v prep* → **masquerade as**
to pretend to be (someone or something else): [T1 (*no pass.*)] *The thief got into the house by posing as a television repairman. His ideas are worthless; they are half-truths posing as wisdom.*

**pose for** *v prep*
**1** to (cause to) take and hold a position necessary for (an artist) or for (a painting, photograph, etc.): [IØ + *for*] *In her youth she earned a reasonable living by posing for art students in the drawing class. Please sit still while you pose for your photograph.* [T1 + *for*] *He takes special care to pose people for their pictures in the best position to suit them.* → **sit for** (1), **sit to**
**2** to cause (something such as difficulties) for (someone or a group): [T1 + *for*] *The continuing increase in population numbers poses some awkward questions for the government.*

***posh up** *v adv*
*BrE infml* to make (oneself) appear well dressed, of high class, etc.: [T1 (*often pass.*)] *You wouldn't recognize her as the ordinary person she is, when she'll all poshed up to meet her gentleman. If you want to get that job, you should posh yourself up a bit.*

**possess by** *v prep*
**be possessed by**
**1** to be owned by (someone or a group): *Land that is possessed by the city should be turned into parks and playgrounds.*
**2** to have one's whole character powerfully influenced or controlled by (something): *People used to think that madmen were possessed by devils. Once he is possessed by a single idea, he has to express this in his painting.*

**possess of** *v prep*
**1 be possessed of** *fml* to have (a quality, etc.): *As a musician, she is possessed of unusual ability and sensitivity.*
**2 possess oneself of** *old use fml* to become the owner of; take possession of (something): [*usu. simple tenses*] *At what date do you intend to possess yourself of the house?*

**post away** *v adv*
to send (someone such as a soldier) to a different place: [X9 + AWAY (*usu. pass.*)] *One of the uncertainties of military duty is that you never know when you might suddenly get posted away.*

**post from** *v prep*
**1** esp. *BrE* to send (something such as a letter or parcel) by post from (somewhere): [T1 + *from*] *I see from the postmark that this card was posted from Mary's holiday address.* → **mail from**
**2** *old use* to travel quickly from (one place) (to another) by changing horses on the way: [L9 + *from*] *This carriage can post from London to Bath in only two days!* → **post to** (3)

**post on** *v prep*
**1** to fix (something such as a notice) on (a wall, etc.): [T1 + *on*] *Please post this important message on your notice board so that all the students can read it.*
**2 keep someone posted on** to give or send someone regular information about (a matter): *Keep me posted on the developments in our plan while I'm away, will you?*

**post to** *v prep*
**1** esp. *BrE* to send (something such as a letter or parcel) by post to (someone or an address): [T1 + *to*] *The cheque was posted to you/to your home address yesterday.* → **mail to**
**2** to send (someone) on government or military duty to (a job, group, or place): [X9 + *to* (*often pass.*)] *Many of the men will be pleased when their commanding officer is posted to another station.*
**3** *old use* to travel quickly to (a place) by changing horses on the way: [L9 + *to*] *How fast can you post to the port with this urgent message?* → **post from** (2)

**post up** *v adv*
**1** to fix (something such as a notice) in a position where it can easily be seen: [T1 + UP] *Please post up this advertisement for our concert in your shop window.*
**2** to make (someone or oneself) familiar with information: [T1 (*on*) (*often pass.*)] *Post me up on your activities in the committee. The writer shows himself to be thoroughly posted up on the facts of his subject.*
***3** (in bookkeeping) to write (something such as figures) in a record of accounts: [T1] *Have all the sales figures been posted up yet?*

**postpone to/till/until** *v prep* →**put off**[1] (4), etc.
to delay (usu. an event) until (a later date): [T1 + *to/till/until* (*often pass.*)] *The concert has had to be postponed to next week because of the singer's illness.*

***pot at** *v prep*
*not fml* to shoot at (usu. a small animal): [T1] *He's in the big field, potting at rabbits with his new gun.*

**pot up** *v adv*
to place (a plant) in a pot for growth: [T1 + UP] *Father is in the garden hut, potting up his favourite indoor plants.*

***potter about/around** *v adv; prep* → **putter about**
to spend time in activities that demand little effort: [IØ] *The old man liked nothing better than pottering about in his garden, doing a few odd jobs here and there.* [T1 (*no pass.*)] *The doctor says that you are still not fit for heavy work, but you can get up and potter around the house for a few days.*

***potter away** *v adv* → **idle away** (2), etc.
to spend (time) lazily: [T1] *I enjoy pottering away the afternoon in the shops in a strange city.*

**pounce on/upon** *v prep*
**1** also **pounce at** to jump suddenly on, usu. so as to attack (someone or something): [IØ + *on/upon* (*usu. simple tenses*)] *After waiting by the hole for hours, the dog pounced on the rabbit as it came out.*
***2** *not fml* to be eager to discover (a fault) or seize (a chance, etc.): [T1 (*often simple tenses*)] *This teacher pounces on spelling mistakes, so use your dictionary. Jane pounced on the offer to let her play the piano at the school concert.*

**pound along** *v adv; prep*
to move quickly and heavily along (something such as a road): [IØ + ALONG/*along*] *We could hear elephants pounding along (the forest path).*

**pound at** *v prep*
**1** to hit or knock heavily on (something such as a door); strike (the ears) continuously: [IØ + *at*] *Who's that pounding at the door in the middle of the night? The noise of the drums pounded at our ears till we thought we would lose our hearing.* → **knock at,** etc.
**2** (of guns) to fire steadily at (the same place): [IØ (AWAY) + *at*] *The citizens yielded after the big guns had been pounding (away) at the town for a week.*

**pound down/up** *v adv*
to reduce (a solid material) to powder: [T1 + DOWN/UP] *This machine will pound the rocks down/up into suitable road-building material.*

**pound in** *v adv*
**1** to force; drive (something) inwards: [T1 + IN] *As I hadn't a hammer, I had to pound the nail in with a stone.* → **drive in** (2), **hammer in** (1)
*__2__ *not fml* to try to teach (something) by force: [T1 (*to*)] *Instead of trying to pound the grammar in, why not let the children discover the rules as they write?* → **hammer in** (3), etc.

**pound into** *v prep*
**1** to beat (a material) so that it becomes (something else): [T1 + *into*] *This machine will pound the rocks into powder. The villagers used to pound the grain into flour by hand.* → **beat into** (2), **hammer into** (2)
**2** to force or drive (something) into (something else): [T1 + *into*] *I had to pound the heavy wooden stick into the ground with a stone.*
*__3__ *not fml* to teach (something) by force to (someone): [D1] *All morning I've been trying to pound the facts into these stupid children's heads.* → **hammer into** (3), etc.

**pound on** *v prep* → **knock at,** etc.
to hit or knock heavily on (something such as a door): [IØ + *on*] *Who's that pounding on the door in the middle of the night? I don't want those children pounding on my piano, it's a delicate instrument.*

**pound out** *v adv*
**1** to flatten (something such as metal) by beating it heavily and continuously: [T1 + OUT] *The car door was so badly damaged in the crash that the garage men had to pound it out to its proper shape again.*
*__2__ *not fml* to produce (something) by hitting something: [T1] *I hate to hear such an insensitive player pounding out a tune on the piano like that. All morning I've been pounding out letters on the typewriter.*

**pound up** *v adv* → POUND DOWN

**pour across** *v adv; prep*
**1** to flow freely across (something): [L9 + ACROSS/*across*] *When the pipes burst, water poured across (the street).*
**2** to move quickly, in a crowd, across (something): [L9 + ACROSS/*across*] *When the new bridge was built, cars poured across (the river).*

**pour along** *v adv; prep*
to move quickly, in a crowd, along (something): [L9 + ALONG/*along*] *When the lights failed, the police used hand signals to keep the traffic pouring along (the streets).*

**pour away** *v adv*
to get rid of (liquid) by making it flow away: [X9 + AWAY] *Pour the rest of the soup away, it won't keep fresh till tomorrow.*

**pour back** *v adv*
**1** to make (liquid or a loose solid) flow back freely: [X9 + BACK] *"I've poured too much milk out." "Well, pour some back then."*
**2** to return quickly in a crowd: [L9 + BACK] *As soon as the floods had gone down, the people poured back into the village.*

*__pour down__[1] *v adv* → **pelt down, pelt with** (2), **pour with, sheet down, teem with** (2)
to (cause to) descend heavily and continuously: [T1] *The sun poured down its merciless heat on the unsheltered men in the open boat.* [IØ] *The rain poured down all day. Don't go out yet, it's still pouring down.* —**downpour** *n*

**pour down**[2] *v prep*
**1** to (cause to) flow freely down (something): [L9 + *down*] *Flood water poured down the street.* [X9 + *down*] *Pour the dirty water down the pipe.*
**2** to move quickly in a crowd down (something such as a road): [L9 + *down*] *Children poured down the street to see the fire engine go by. The supporters got off the train and poured down the road towards the football ground.*

**pour forth** *v adv*
**1** *old use* (usu. of liquid or light) to (cause to) flow out freely: [L9 + FORTH] *Her tears poured forth as she watched the sad scene. He struck the rock with his stick, and fresh water poured forth from the living rock. Light poured forth from the many lamps.* [X9 + FORTH] *Pour forth the wine as an offering to the gods!* → **pour out** (1)
**2** *old use* to come out in a crowd; express a lot of (noise): [L9 + FORTH] *When the gates were opened, the townspeople poured forth to greet their victorious army.* [X9 + FORTH] *Many politicians, given a chance to make a speech, pour forth a stream of worthless nonsense.* → **pour out** (2)

**pour in**[1] *v adv*
**1** (usu. of liquid or light) to (cause to) flow in freely: [L9 + IN] *Rain has been pouring in through a hole in the roof. When I opened the curtains, bright sunshine poured in.* [X9 + IN] *When you make my coffee, please don't pour too much cream in.*
**2** to arrive or enter in a crowd: [L9 + IN] *When the gates were opened, crowds of football supporters poured in. Complaints about the washing machines have been pouring in all week.*
*__3__ *not fml* to put a lot of (money) into something such as a firm: [T1 (*to*)] *Unless the government pours more money in, the whole shipbuilding industry will fail.* → **pump in** (2)

**pour in**[2] *v prep* → **pour into** (1)
(usu. of liquid or light) to (cause to) flow in freely: [L9 + *in*] *Rain has been pouring in the house through that hole in the roof. When I opened the curtains, bright sunshine poured into the room.* [X9 + *in*] *Please don't pour too much cream in my coffee.*

**pour into** *v prep*
**1** (usu. of liquid or light) to (cause to) flow into (something such as a container): [L9 + *into*] *Rain is still pouring into the bedroom through the hole that you thought you*

*mended. When I opened the curtains, bright sunshine poured into the room.* [X9 + *into*] *You can't pour a litre of wine into a half-litre bottle.* → **pour in²**
**2** to (cause to) arrive in large numbers in (something): [L9 + *into*] *A crowd of football supporters poured into the ground as soon as the gates were opened. Letters have been pouring into the office complaining about the washing machines.*
***3** *not fml* to put a lot of (money) into (something or doing something): [D1] *The government has poured money into the production of these fast new planes.* [V4] *The government has poured money into building these fast new planes.* → **pump into** (2)
**pour off¹** *v adv*
to make (something such as liquid) flow away: [X9 + OFF] *Pour off the remaining liquid, and heat the solid to make a chemical action with the air. When you have poured off the fat left in the meat tin, add a little flour to thicken the meat juices.*
**pour off²** *v prep*
(usu. of liquid) to flow away from (something or someone): [L9. + *off*] *Water pours off a duck's back because of the oil on its feathers.*
**pour on¹** *v adv*
**pour it on**
**1** *AmE infml* to overpraise someone or something: *I know she was good, but was there any need to pour it on like that?*
**2** *AmE infml* to work hard; use a lot of effort: [*often simple tenses*] *Pour it on, boys, and we'll soon have the job done!*
**3** *AmE infml* to move quickly: [*often imper.*] *Better pour it on if you're to catch your plane!*
**pour on²** *v prep*
**1** to make (liquid) flow on (something): [X9 + *on*] *The priest poured the wine on the ground as an offering to the gods.*
**2 pour cold water on** *not fml* to try to prevent (something or someone) by discouragement: *The chairman was very keen on his plan, but the director poured cold water on it by explaining that it would cost too much.* → **throw on²** (5)
**3 pour contempt/ridicule/scorn on** to find serious fault with in an unkind way; express an opinion strongly against (something or someone); declare (something such as an idea) to be worthless: *Why do you always pour scorn on my ideas? They're not all as stupid as you say. After all the ridicule that has been poured on me in my attempt to start my own business, I am determined to prove you wrong.*
**4 pour oil on flames** *not fml* to make matters worse: *Don't remind him of the cause of his anger, that would be pouring oil on flames.*
**5 pour oil on troubled waters** *not fml* to try to stop trouble or violence by calming the people causing it: *The angry crowd is out of control; we need someone who can speak to them calmly, pouring oil on troubled waters. To pour oil on troubled waters, I pretended to agree with what Mother had said, so as to avoid a quarrel.*
**pour out** *v adv*
**1** (usu. of liquid or light) to (cause to) flow out freely; serve (a drink): [L9 + OUT] *When the pipe was unblocked, the dirty water poured out. Light pours out all night from every window in the office block: it's such a waste!* [X9 + OUT (*for*)] *Would you like me to pour out the tea? Yes, please pour me some out straight away, before it gets too strong.* **—outpour** *n* → **pour forth** (1)
**2** to come out in large numbers: [L9 + OUT] *The factory workers poured out when the whistle blew.* → **pour forth** (2)
***3** to tell; express (something such as words) quickly or eagerly: [T1] *After weeks of questioning, the prisoner decided to pour out his story. Weeping, she poured out her troubles to her closest friend.* **—outpouring** *n*
**pour over** *v prep*
**1** (usu. of liquid) to (cause to) flow freely over (something): [L9 + *over*] *The river poured over its banks, flooding the fields.* [X9 + *over*] *Pour the meat juices over the meat, they will give it a richer taste.*
**2** to move quickly in a crowd over (something): [L9 + *over*] *Enemy soldiers poured over the broken walls, and soon conquered the town.*
**pour through** *v adv; prep*
**1** (usu. of liquid or light) to pass freely through (something): [L9 + *through*] *When I woke, sunlight was already pouring through the windows.* [L9 + THROUGH] *There's a hole in the roof, and the rain is pouring through!* [X9 + THROUGH/*through*] *Pour the liquid through (this narrow pipe) here, and it will get rid of all the impurities.*
**2** to move quickly in a crowd through (something): [L9 + THROUGH/*through*] *When the gates were opened, crowds of football supporters poured through (them).*
**pour with** *v prep* → **pelt down, pelt with** (2), **pour down¹, sheet down, teem with** (2)
to give a lot of (rain): [*It* + IØ + *with*] *It's pouring with rain outside, hadn't you better wait a few minutes before going out?*
**power by/with** *v prep*
to give (something) power or driving force by means of (something such as an engine): [X9 + *by/with* (*often pass.*)] *This boat is powered with the latest improved model of our most famous engine.*
**practise on/upon** *v prep* also *AmE* **practice on**
**1** to perform (something) on (something or someone) in preparation for a real activity: [IØ + *on/upon*] *Jane was always unwilling to practise on the piano as regularly as she should have done. Medical students often practise on each other.* [T1 + *on/upon*] *She has been*

*practising the same piece on her instrument for weeks now.*

*****2** *old use* to take advantage of (someone's feeling); control (someone) by means of a trick: [T1] *By practising on her fears, the criminals made the old lady give them her money.*

***prance about/around** *v adv*

**1** (usu. of horses) to run about with the feet held high: [IØ + ABOUT/AROUND] *Young horses were prancing about in the field in the first warm days of spring.*

*****2** (usu. of children) to move about for fun, in a playful or silly way: [IØ] *Will you children stop prancing about in your night clothes and get back into bed!*

***prang up** *v adv*

**1** *BrE infml* to cause (a plane, car, etc.) to crash: [T1 (*often simple tenses*)] *He's pranged up the plane, but he's all right.* → **smash up**, etc.

**2** *BrE infml* to spoil (something): [T1 (*often simple tenses*)] *The pilots were supposed to drop supplies to the snowbound villages, but the organization was poor and they pranged up the whole operation.* → **mess up** (2), etc.

**3** *sl* to make (a woman) pregnant: [T1 (*often simple tenses*)] *One of the boys has been careless enough to prang up his girlfriend.* → **bang up** (3), **knock up** (10)

***prate about** *v prep*

to talk foolishly about (something): [T1 (*no pass.*)] *She's always prating about her wealthy relations, as if anybody cared.*

**prattle about** *v prep*

to speak quickly or in a childish manner about (usu. something): [IØ (ON) + *about*] *What's she prattling on about now?*

**prattle away** *v adv*

to continue talking quickly or in a childish manner: [IØ + AWAY] *She went on prattling away, but I had stopped listening.*

**pray for** *v prep*

**1** to request (something); ask for help for (someone); express a wish for (something or someone) (to do something) in a prayer: [IØ + *for*] *Let us pray for peace on earth. I'm praying for Mother to get better. It's no use praying for the weather to change.*

**2 be past praying for** to be beyond help or hope: *That man is so evil, he is past praying for. I think she must be dying; she's certainly past praying for.*

**pray over** *v prep*

to say a prayer near and about (someone): [IØ + *over*] *You needn't start praying over me yet, I'm still alive!*

**pray to** *v prep*

to say a prayer to (God, a god, or holy object of any faith): [IØ + *to*] *We pray to God to deliver us from evil.*

**preach against** *v prep*

(usu. of a priest or minister of religion) to declare one's solemn opposition to (something), esp. in a speech in church: [IØ + *against*] *All the great churchmen have preached against immorality.*

**preach at** *v prep* → **preach to** (1)

to speak to (someone) in the manner of a priest or minister of religion, esp. to give unwelcome advice on moral matters: [IØ + *at*] *I do wish the teacher would stop preaching at the class about how to behave. I don't mind listening to advice that I've asked for, but I refuse to be preached at.*

**preach to** *v prep*

**1** (of a priest or minister of religion) to address a speech on religious or moral matters; explain and try to spread the ideas of (holy writings); urge (a way of behaviour) to (people in church): [IØ + *to*] *Many ministers are becoming increasingly worried abou[t] preaching to empty churches.* [T1 + *to*] *You'l[l] find him in the village church, preaching the word of God to a small crowd of worshippers. Our minister often preaches honesty to the young people.* → **preach at**

**2 preach to the converted** to try to persuade someone of something that he/she already believes: *You can't win new votes by addressing your speech only to members of your own party, since you will simply be preaching to the converted. If women want to make their mark on the world, they must get out and make men understand their difficulties and rights; if they only talk to women who share their troubles they are preaching to the converted, which will have no result.*

***precipitate into** *v prep* → **plunge into** (2), **thrust into** (3)

*fml* to force (someone or something) suddenl[y] into (a state or activity, usu. bad): [D1 (*ofte[n] pass.*)] *The country was precipitated into wa[r] that could have been avoided, by foolish mistakes by its leaders. The company was precipitated into ruin when the exchange rate dropped.*

***preclude from** *v prep*

*fml* to prevent (someone) from (doing something), often by a rule: [D1 (*often pass.*)] *Any person having a family connection wi[th] the advertising firm is precluded from enterin[g] its competition.*

**predestine for/to** *v prep*

to give (someone) the fate of (something); in[tend] (someone) by fate for (something): [T[1] + *for/to* (*usu. pass.*)] *She always had a feelin[g] that she was predestined to an early death.*

***predispose to/towards** *v prep*

to cause (someone) to have a tendency towards (something): [D1 (*often pass.*)] *H[er] early training and natural ability predispose[d] her to musicianship as a profession. Born in a wealthy family, and always attended by se[r]vants, he was predisposed to laziness.*

**predominate over** *v prep*

to control; have greater numbers or pow[er] than (someone or something else): [IØ *over* (*usu. simple tenses*)] *Italians predominate over every other nationality in this city. Sensitivity predominates over all his other characteristics.*

**preen on** *v prep* → **pique on, plume on, pride on**
**preen oneself on** to be very proud of (something or doing something): *The young fighter preened himself on his number of victories. Do not preen yourself on defeating so weak an enemy.*

**preface by/with** *v prep*
to begin (a book, speech, etc.) with (words or actions): [D1 (*often simple tenses*)] *I should like to preface my speech with a few words of introduction to my subject. The book is prefaced with a statement of gratitude to the writer's husband.* [V4b (*often simple tenses*)] *I shall preface my remarks by thanking the chairman for her welcome.*

**prefer against** *v prep* → **bring against, lay against** (2), **level against**
to formally state (a charge or charges) against (someone) which he/she will have to answer in court: [T1 + *against*] *Will the police prefer charges against the boys, or just give them a warning?*

**prefer to** *v prep*
**1** to choose; like (one thing, person, or doing something) better than (another): [T1 + *to*] *At this time of day, I prefer tea to coffee. Do you prefer this new teacher to the old one?* [T4 + *to*] *For his favourite exercise, Jim prefers running to swimming.*
**2** *fml* to appoint (someone) to (a more important position): [D1] *The Queen has agreed to prefer the Minister to a seat in the House of Lords.*

**prefix to** *v prep*
to add (something) to the beginning of (something such as a word): [T1 + *to*] *A new introduction has been prefixed to the third printing of the book. At last, after years of study, she was allowed to prefix the title 'Doctor' to her name.*

**prejudice against** *v prep*
to cause (someone) to dislike (usu. a kind of thing or person, or doing something) without good reason: [T1 + *against* (*often pass.*)] *What has prejudiced you against modern music? Early in my life, I was prejudiced against living in the country by some unfortunate experiences with farm animals.*

**prepare for** *v prep*
to (cause to) become ready for (something or someone): [IØ + *for*] *You'd better prepare for Mother's arrival. When I'm preparing for my performance, I don't like to be interrupted.* [T1 + *for*] *Prepare yourselves for a surprise when you go into the room. I always have to be prepared for yet another move to a new city. I'm preparing a speech for the meeting on Thursday. I only send in students who are properly prepared for the examination. Be prepared for bad news. The doctor prepared Mother for her operation. I'll prepare a bed for you. Is the meal prepared for our guests?*

**prescribe for** *v prep*
to order (something such as medicine or books) specially for (someone or a purpose): [T1 + *for*] *Never take medicine which has been prescribed for somebody else. What treatment would you prescribe for the common cold? Here is a list of books which have been prescribed for this course.*

**present at** *v prep*
to point; aim (a weapon) towards (someone): [T1 + *at*] *Never present a gun at someone, even in fun; you never know when it might be loaded.*

**present to** *v prep*
**1** to give (something) to (someone or a group), often formally: [X9 + *to*] *I am happy to present this gift of money to the hospital. The prettiest little girl was chosen to present the flowers to the important visitor.* → **present with**
**2** to introduce (someone) to (someone else) in a formal manner: [T1 + *to* (*usu. simple tenses*)] *Allow me to present my husband to you. The daughters of wealthy families used to be presented to the Queen when they reached marrying age.*

**present with** *v prep* → **present to** (1)
to give (someone) (something); make (someone) accept (something): [X9 + *with* (*often pass.*)] *I am happy to present the hospital with this gift of money. When you're presented with a chance to improve your position, take advantage of it. Presented with a question like that, I need time to answer.*

**preserve for** *v prep*
to save (usu. something) for (something or someone), by taking care of it: [T1 + *for*] *These fine old houses should be preserved for the future. We must try to preserve the best of our moral values for our children and grandchildren.*

**preserve from** *v prep*
to save (something or someone) from (usu. a bad fate) by taking care: [T1 + *from*] *God preserve me from such a fate! These ancient trees must be preserved from destruction. What can we do to preserve the company from ruin?*

**preside at** *v prep* → **preside over** (1)
to lead; be president of (a ceremony or meeting, etc.): [IØ + *at*] *The Minister was asked to preside at the independence ceremonies of the small island state.*

**preside over** *v prep*
**1** to lead; be president of (a ceremony or meeting): [IØ + *over*] *Who will preside over the committee meeting while the chairman is away? At the moment it is being presided over by each member in turn.* → **preside at**
*__2__ to be present at; watch (usu. bad events) from a position of power in which one is

actually helpless: [T1] *It was his misfortune to preside over the failure of the firm.*

**press against** *v prep* → **push against, thrust against**
to (cause to) push with weight or force against (something or someone): [L9 + *against*] *I felt something hard, like a gun, pressing against my side.* [X9 + *against*] *Press your hand against the door as hard as you can, to make it shut.*

**press ahead** *v adv* → PUSH AHEAD (2)

**press down** *v adv* → **push down**[1]
to push (something) down with weight or force: [L9 + DOWN (*on*)] *Press down on the handle with all your strength.* [X9 + DOWN] *The grass had been pressed down in places where people had been lying.*

***press for** *v prep*
**1** to urge; demand; keep requesting (something) (from someone) or (to do something): [T1 (*no pass.*)] *The rent collector is pressing for payment again. We must press for a reduction in the number of students in a class.* [D1] *The newspaper reporters have been pressing the government for details.* [V3] *Many parents have been pressing for the local school to be reopened. The opposition keeps pressing for taxes to be reduced. The native people should not have to press for their rights to be recognized.* → **push for** (1)
**2 be pressed for** *not fml* to have hardly enough (money, time, etc.): *I can't see any one else today, I'm pressed for time as it is. The universities are becoming increasingly pressed for money, and cannot employ any new teachers.* → **press hard** (3), **push for** (2)

**press forward** *v adv*
**1** (usu. of people) to move forward by pushing heavily: [L9 + FORWARD] *The crowd, pressing forward to see the Queen, broke the fence that was supposed to keep them in place.* → **push forward** (1), **thrust forward** (1)
***2** esp. *mil* to continue (something) with force: [T1] *The officer ordered the soldiers to press their advance forward in spite of heavy enemy gunfire.* → **push forward** (2), **thrust forward** (2)
***3** *not fml* to continue (with something); move forward with haste or determination: [IØ (*with*)] *Whatever happens, we must press forward with our plans to increase production. If we press forward, we can get home before dark.* → **plough on** (2), **press on**[1], **push ahead** (2), **push forward** (3), **push on**[1] (1)

**press hard** *v adv*
**1** to push with a lot of strength (on something): [L9 + HARD (*on*)] *Press hard on the two surfaces, to make them stick together.* [X9 + HARD] *Children press wet snow hard to make snowballs.*
***2** *mil* to force an attack on (an enemy): [T1b] *After pressing the enemy hard for several days, our army won the victory. Although our soldiers were hard pressed, they kept up their spirits and ended by winning the battle.*
**3 be hard pressed** to be in difficulties, as with time, work, money, etc., or (to do something): *I can't see anyone else today, I'm hard pressed for time. If this train is delayed any further, we shall be hard pressed to reach the meeting in time to vote. I'll pay the rest of what I owe you when I'm not quite so hard pressed.* → **press for** (2), **push for** (2)

***press home** *v adv*
**1** to make someone such as an opponent feel the forceful effect of (something): [T1] *The speaker pressed home his point, and his opponent admitted that he had been wrong.* → **push home** (2), **thrust home** (1)
**2 press home an/one's advantage** to make good use of a chance that is offered: *The owner seemed to be weakening about his price, so, pressing home our advantage, we mentioned again the faults in the house and offered a lower price.* → **push home** (3), **thrust home** (2)

**press in**[1] *v adv*
**1** to force (something) inwards: [X9 + IN] *The lid of the box had been pressed in by the weight of the books on top. I had to press my way in through the crowd.* → **plunge in**[1], **push in**[1] (1), **thrust in**[1]
***2** to surround; advance steadily: [IØ (*on*)] *Night was already pressing in as we reached the village high in the mountains.*

**press in**[2] *v prep* → **fit into** (1), etc.
to push a lot of (things or people) hard into (something such as a container): [X9 + *in*] *He tried to press more clothes in the case, but there was not enough room. Too many people were pressed in the room.*

**press into** *v prep*
**1** to use force or weight to push (things or people) in a mass into (something such as a container): [X9 + *into*] *He tried to press more clothes into the case, but there was not enough room. Too many people were pressed into the room, and we could hardly breathe.* → **push into** (1), **thrust into** (1)
**2** to use force or weight to make (something) become (something else): [T1 + *into*] *This machine presses vegetables into juice.*
**3** *old use* to force (someone) to join (the armed forces, esp. the navy): [T1 + *into*] *In the old days, men were often pressed into the navy by groups of men who would seize them in the streets and force them towards the ship.*
**4 press something into service** to use something in a time of need: [*often pass.*] *The old typewriter had to be pressed into service while the usual one was under repair.*

***press on**[1] *v adv* → **plough on** (2), **press forward** (3), **push ahead** (2), **push forward** (3), **push on**[1] (1)
*not fml* to continue; advance with determination: [IØ (*with*)] *We must press on with the work if we are to finish it in time. If we press on, we shall reach the town before dark.*

**press on/upon²** *v prep*
**1** to push hard on (something or someone): [L9 + *on/upon*] *You have to press on the handle to turn it, it's very stiff. The weight of the sleeping child's body was pressing on me and making me uncomfortable.* → **push on² (1)**
*__2__ to cause worry to (someone): [T1 (*no pass.*)] *I can see that his new responsibilities are pressing (down) on the young father. Steadily rising prices press most heavily on the poor and on old people with fixed incomes.* → **prey on (3), weigh on**
*__3__ to force acceptance of (something) by (someone): [D1] *I do wish she wouldn't press more food on us when we've already refused politely. I was often ashamed as a child when visiting aunts and uncles would press money on me as they were leaving. Teachers are not allowed to press their political views on the children.*

**press out** *v adv* → **push out (1)**
to force (something) out by pushing or holding tightly: [X9 + OUT (*of*)] *Use your thumbs to press out the pourer on the side of the box of washing powder. This kitchen tool is for pressing juice out of fruit and vegetables.*

**press round** *v adv; prep* → **push round**
to form a tight crowd (near someone); surround (someone): [L9 + ROUND/*round*] *Newspaper reporters pressed round (the Minister), urging him to give them a statement.*

**press to** *v prep*
to hold (someone) tightly next to (one or a part of one's body), usu. with love: [X9 + *to*] *She pressed the child to her heart, thankful that he had been found. Jim pressed Mary to him and kissed her.*

**press together** *v adv*
to (cause to) be tightly held to each other: [L9 + TOGETHER] *The crowd pressed together so tightly that we could hardly breathe. His hands pressed together with the force of his feeling.* [X9 + TOGETHER] *She pressed her lips together in disapproval.*

**press towards** *v prep* → **push towards (3), thrust towards (2)**
to aim in a determined way towards (a result): [T1 (*no pass.*)] *All our efforts are pressing towards a reorganization of the prison system.*

**press up** *v adv* → **pull up (1)**
to raise (something) by force or strength: [X9 + UP] *A good exercise is to press your body up from the floor with your arms, and then lower it slowly.* —**press-up** *n*

**press upon** *v prep* → PRESS ON²

**presume on/upon** *v prep*
*fml* to take improper advantage of (someone's good nature or other quality): [T1] *I hope I'm not presuming on your kindness by staying to dinner. Take care that you don't presume on our short friendship. His good nature can be presumed upon once too often.*

***pretend to** *v prep*
*fml* to claim (something such as a quality) without good cause: [T1] *Poets rarely pretend to modesty. I don't pretend to a complete knowledge of the city, but I can find my way around with the help of a map. The popular young prince started a war by pretending to the crown.*

***pretty up** *v adv*
*not fml* to make (someone, oneself, or something) more beautiful or attractive, often in a false way: [T1] *I wish the family wouldn't pretty the children up in their best clothes for the photograph; I'd much rather that they looked natural. Since every town is always specially prettied up for a visit by the Queen, she must gain a false idea of what places are really like.*

**prevail against/over** *v prep* → **avail against, triumph over (2)**
*fml* to defeat; be successful in opposing; win a victory over (someone or usu. something): [I∅ + *against/over*] *Can all our efforts towards morality prevail over the forces of evil?*

***prevail on/upon** *v prep*
*fml* to persuade (someone) (to do something): [V3] *Can the government be prevailed upon to lower taxes?*

**prevail over** *v prep* → PREVAIL AGAINST

**prevail upon** *v prep* → PREVAIL ON

**prevent from** *v prep* → **hinder from, keep from (2), restrain from, stop from (1)**
to stop (someone or something) from (doing something): [T1 + *from*] *Nothing shall prevent us from reaching our aim! Only an act of God can prevent the wedding from taking place. I was prevented from arriving on time by a delay in the railway system.*

***prey on/upon** *v prep*
**1** to hunt and kill (an animal) for food: [T1 (*usu. simple tenses*)] *The lions in this area prey on deer and other wild animals.*
**2** to rob (someone); take advantage of (someone weaker): [T1] *Bands of robbers living in the hills would prey on any traveller foolish enough to wander into their land.*
**3 prey on someone's mind/thoughts** to be a cause of worry, anxiety, and sometimes guilt: *The thought of the coming examination is already preying on my mind. The failure of his company preyed on the businessman's mind so severely that he killed himself. His crime preyed on his mind until he gave himself up to the police.* → **press on² (2), weigh on**

***price out** *v adv*
to make (something or someone) cost too much (for something): [T1 (*of*)] *The goods are priced out of our reach. The photographer has priced himself out of business. One of the dangers of the Common Market is that it may price out British meat.*

***price up** *v adv*
*not fml* to raise the price of (goods) unreason-

ably: [T1] *Don't buy your camera at that shop, they price them up terribly.*

* **prick down** *v adv* → **call on** (2), **knock down** (10)
*not fml* to choose; make a demand on (someone) (for something or to do something): [T1 (*for*) (*usu. simple tenses*)] *We'll prick you down for £10, then, shall we? You've been pricked down for the next turn.* [V3 (*usu. simple tenses*)] *Who was pricked down to take our suggestion to the director?*

* **prick on** *v adv*
*not fml* to encourage; urge (someone) (to do something): [T1] *"Honour pricks me on."* (Shakespeare, *King Henry IV, Part 1*) [V3] *His conscience pricked him on to admit his crime to the police.*

* **prick out/off** *v adv*
to place (young plants) in holes specially made in the earth: [T1] *While the soil is nice and soft after the rain, let's prick out the onion plants that we have grown from seed.*

* **prick up** *v adv*
**1** (of an animal) to raise (its ears), as to listen or to express something: [T1] *The dog pricked up its ears at the sound of its master's return.* → **perk up** (1)
**2** **prick up one's ears** *not fml* to listen carefully; pay attention: *When the director mentioned holidays, all the office workers pricked up their ears, as most of them had already made their plans.*

**pride on** *v prep* → **pique on, plume on, preen on**
**pride oneself on** to be very proud of; satisfied with (something or doing something): [*usu. simple tenses*] *Mary prides herself on her ability to remain calm when trouble suddenly happens. I think you have a right to pride yourself on being accepted into the men's cricket team.*

**prime with** *v prep*
**1** to make (something) ready for use with (something): [T1 + *with*] *Are your guns primed with powder? Prime the pump with a little water to get it started. Sometimes you have to prime the engine with a drop of petrol. The wood has to be primed with a special undercoat to close the surface before it can be painted.*
**2** to prepare (someone) by supplying (usu. facts): [T1 + *with* (*usu. pass.*)] *As a reporter, you must be well primed with facts before you start to write your article.*
***3** to fill (someone) with (food or esp. drink): [D1] *He's too nervous to make a speech unless you first prime him with beer.*

* **primp/prink up** *v adv*
*not fml* (usu. of women) to make (oneself) look showy: [T1b] *If you're going to take my photograph, I must go and primp/prink myself up a bit first.*

**print in** *v adv*
to add (words or figures) in printing or careful writing: [T1 + IN] *Will you print in the missing names for me?*

**print off** *v adv*
to make (a copy of) a photograph or something written such as a book or an article in a magazine: [T1 + OFF] *How many copies do you want printed off?* —**offprint, print-off** *n*

**print out** *v adv* → **read out** (2)
(of a computer) to produce (a printed form of the results of an inquiry or calculation): [T1 + OUT] *The machine will print out the results of the calculation, and the names of suitable books on this subject.* —**printout** *n*

**prise from** *v prep* → **PRISE OUT OF**

**prise/prize off** *v adv* also *AmE* **pry off**
to lift (something such as a lid) by force: [X9 + OFF] *Use this long bar to prise the lid off.*

**prise/prize open** *v adj* also *AmE* **pry open**
to open (something such as a container) by force: [X9 + **open**] *The jewel boxes had been prised open, and their contents scattered about the room.*

**prise/prize out of/from** *v adv prep; prep* also *AmE* **pry out of**
to force (information) from (someone): [X9 + OUT + *of/from*] *The police had the greatest difficulty in prising the truth out of the prisoner. Newspaper reporters have been trying to prise the details from government speakers.*

**prise/prize up** *v adv* also *AmE* **pry up**
to lift (something) by force: [X9 + UP] *The police prised up the floorboards to look for the hidden jewels.*

**prize above** *v prep*
to value (something or someone) more than (something): [T1 + *above* (*simple tenses*)] *A good woman is prized above jewels. I prize my library above my kingdom. Freedom is to be prized above riches.*

**prize from** *v prep* → **PRISE OUT OF**

**prize off** *v adv* → **PRISE OFF**

**prize open** *v adj* → **PRISE OPEN**

**prize out of/from** *v adv prep; prep* → **PRISE OUT OF**

**prize up** *v adv* → **PRISE UP**

**probe into** *v prep*
**1** to search into (something hollow), often with something sharp: [IØ + *into*] *Probing into my bad tooth with my tongue, I could feel the enlarged hole.*
***2** to examine (an activity that appears wrong): [T1] *The police have been asked to probe into the council's spending of public money. It's a newspaper reporter's job to probe into any unpleasant facts that might make a story. The mystery of the missing woman has been probed into by police from all over the country, but without result.*

* **proceed against** *v prep*
*fml* to bring (someone) to trial: [T1 (*no pass.*)] *Are you sure that you want to proceed against your neigbour over such a small matter as a noisy dog?*

**proceed from** *v prep*
**1** to move forward; travel from (one place) (to another): [IØ + *from* (*simple tenses*)] *If we all proceed from the same point but move in different directions, we can soon cover the whole city with our advertisements. This flight is now proceeding from New York to London.* → **proceed to** (1), **progress to** (1)
**2** to continue from (a point in an argument): [IØ + *from*] *In this argument I am proceeding from first principles.*
***3** *fml* to arise from; have a cause or beginning in (something): [T1 (*no pass.*)] *Our opinions often proceed from lack of information. From such a small beginning have proceeded many important decisions.*

**proceed to** *v prep*
**1** to travel to (a place): [IØ + *to*] *This flight is now proceeding to London at a speed of 800 kilometres an hour.* → **proceed from** (1), **progress to** (1)
**2** *fml* to continue to (the next stage in something such as an argument or meeting): [IØ + *to*] *Proceeding to your next point, I think we may safely forget such a silly idea. Can we please proceed to the next question on our list?* → **progress to** (2)
***3** *fml* (in a university) to advance from a first degree to (a higher degree): [T1 (*no pass.*)] *If you wish to proceed to the MA, be sure to inform the university of your choice.* → **progress to** (3)

**proceed with** *v prep*
to continue with (something that one had been doing): [IØ + *with*] *Never mind the interruption, proceed with your story. The gardener rested for a moment on his spade, then proceeded with his work.*

**procure for** *v prep*
**1** *fml* to supply (something) for (someone or something), often with difficulty: [T1 + *for* (*usu. simple tenses*)] *I think I know where I can procure that rare book for you.* → **get for** (1), **obtain for**
**2** to supply (a woman) for the sexual needs of (someone): [T1 + *for*] *He made an immoral living procuring women for tourists arriving in the city.*

**procure from** *v prep* → **obtain from,** etc.
*fml* to obtain (something) from (something or someone that supplies it), often with difficulty: [T1 + *from* (*usu. simple tenses*)] *These valuable coins were procured from a famous collector, who was willing to consider your price.*

**prod at** *v prep* → **jab at, poke at** (1)
to give a quick sharp push or blow to (something or someone): [L9 + *at*] *He prodded at the meat with his knife, but it was too hard to cut. The fighter won not by a single blow, but by prodding at his opponent so effectively that he weakened him. The women in the market were prodding at the fruit to see if it was ripe.* [X9 + *at*] *Stop those boys prodding their sticks at that poor dog!*

**produce from** *v prep*
**1** to make (a material) from (a substance): [T1 + *from*] *Paper is produced from wood. Much of the salt that we use is produced from the sea.* → **form from, make from, make of** (1), **make out of** (1), **obtain from,** etc.
**2** to bring (something) out from (somewhere): [T1 + *from*] *Producing a handkerchief from his pocket, he held it to his eyes. What magician can't produce a rabbit from a top hat?*

***profit by/from** *v prep*
to learn or gain advantage from (something or doing something): [T1 (*no pass.*)] *I hope you have profited by your unfortunate experience, and will not make the same mistake again. A lucky group of students will profit by an exchange visit overseas. Do you suppose that anyone profits by remaining unmarried? You can even profit from your mistakes, if you take care not to repeat them. On holiday, even if the weather is bad, you still profit from a change of scene. She will never be a professional musician, but I'm sure that she has profited from her lessons.* [T4] *You could profit from listening to such a wise person.*

**progress in/with** *v prep*
to advance in relation to (an activity): [IØ + *in/with*] *How are you progressing in your studies? Tom progressed well with his book until he met a difficulty.*

**progress to** *v prep*
**1** *old use* to travel to (a place): [IØ + *to*] *The carriage progressed to Bath at a gentle speed.* → **proceed from** (1), **proceed to** (1)
**2** to continue to (the next stage in something such as an argument or meeting): [IØ + *to*] *Progressing to your next point, I think we may safely forget such a silly idea. Can we please progress to the next question on our list?* → **proceed to** (2)
***3** (in a university) to advance from a first degree to (a higher degree): [T1 (*no pass.*)] *If you wish to progress to the MA, be sure to inform the university of your choice.* → **proceed to** (3)

**progress with** *v prep* → PROGRESS IN

***prohibit from** *v prep*
to try to prevent (someone) from (doing something) by forbidding him/her: [D1 (*often pass.*)] *Why do park keepers always prohibit people from walking on the grass? Visitors are prohibited from feeding the animals.*

**project from** *v prep* → **jut out, poke out** (1), **protrude from, stand out** (2), **stick out** (1)
to stand out a little way in front of (something): [IØ + *from*] *I caught my coat on a loose brick projecting from the wall. The fireplace projects from the wall rather too far into the room, taking up a lot of space.*

**project onto** *v prep*
**1** to cause (a picture, etc.) to be seen on (a surface) by means of a light: [T1 + *onto*] *You don't need to spend money on special things; you can project the picture onto an empty white wall just as effectively.*
*__2__ to imagine (one's own feelings and thoughts) as being experienced by (someone else): [D1] *He projects his own guilt onto his parents.*

**promise to** *v prep*
**1** to declare that (something) will be given to (someone): [T1 + *to*] *I've promised the next dance to Jim. I promise you an answer tomorrow. I'm sorry, that house has been promised to some other young people.*
**2 be promised to** *old use* to be going to marry (someone): *You mustn't kiss me, I am promised to another.* → **betroth to, engage to**

**promise well** *v adv*
to show good signs of possible success: [IØ + WELL (*simple tenses*)] *From what little I've seen of your book so far, I would say that it promises well.*

**promote to** *v prep*
to raise (someone) to (a higher rank or position): [T1 + *to* (*usu. pass.*)] *I'm happy to inform you that you have been promoted to captain. What chance is there of ever being promoted to department head? All the children have been promoted to the next class.*

**pronounce against** *v prep* → **pronounce for**
*law* to give judgment against (someone): [L9 + *against* (*usu. simple tenses*)] *The judge pronounced against the prisoner, and he was led away by the policeman.* [T1 + *against*] *It is my solemn duty to pronounce judgment against you.*

**pronounce for** *v prep* → **pronounce against**
*law* to give judgment in favour of (someone): [L9 + *for* (*usu. simple tenses*)] *The judge pronounced for the defendant, and also said that his opponent should pay the court costs.*

**pronounce on/upon** *v prep*
**1** *fml* to give one's fixed opinion on (a matter): [L9 + *on/upon*] *That member annoys the committee by pronouncing on every question before it has been considered. We have asked the chief engineer to pronounce on the effect of widening the bridge.*
**2 pronounce judgment/sentence on** *fml* to state the judgment of the court, esp. the punishment decided for (someone): *It is my solemn duty to pronounce sentence on you. Judges used to wear a black cap to pronounce sentence of death on a guilty murderer.* → **pass on²** (2)

**prop against** *v prep*
to lean (something or someone) against (something such as a wall): [X9 + *against*] *He propped himself against the door and waited for it to open. When you prop a ladder against a wall, be sure that its feet are placed firmly in the ground.*

**prop open** *v adj*
to hold (something such as a door) open with something preventing it from shutting: [X9 + **open**] *Use these heavy books to prop the door open, we need some air in here.*

**prop up** *v adv*
**1** to support (something or someone) from falling: [X9 + UP] *Wooden beams were used to prop up the roof. Propping myself up on my elbow, I could talk more easily to my visitors.*
*__2__ *not fml* to support (someone or an idea): [IØ] *The shipbuilding industry had to be propped up with government money.* [T1] *The Bank of England took further action today to prop up the falling pound.*

**propose to** *v prep*
**1** to offer (marriage) to (someone): [IØ + *to*] *Do tell me about when Jim first proposed to you.* [T1 + *to*] *Do you think he'll propose marriage to you tonight?*
**2 propose a toast to** to offer to drink to the health of (someone or something): *I propose a toast to the Queen—everyone please rise! Shall we propose a toast to the future of the company?* → **drink to** (1), **raise to** (3)

**prospect for** *v prep*
to search, usu. underground, for (a valuable mineral or minerals): [IØ + *for*] *Some miners in the North are still prospecting for gold, although no fortune has been made since the beginning of the century. Oil companies spend much of their profit in prospecting for oil in fields where the rocks appear suitable.*

**prosper from** *v prep*
to gain advantage from (something): [IØ + *from*] *I hope you have prospered from your stay in this country. Prospering from a lucky chance, the player landed the ball square in the net.*

**prostrate before** *v prep* → **bow before** (1)
**prostrate oneself before** to lie down flat on the ground in a humble position before (someone important): *The natives prostrated themselves before the figure of the god.*

**protect against/from** *v prep* → **guard against, guard from, safeguard against, screen from, shade from** (1), **shelter from, shield from**
to shelter; defend (someone or something) from (something or doing something bad): [T1 + *against/from*] *Take this medicine regularly; it will protect you against a return of the illness. May God protect you from harm this night. The fence along the middle of the road is intended to protect vehicles against crashing into each other. Parents are demanding that the school put a gate at the entrance to the playground, to protect the children from running into the road. In the early days of summer you would be wise to protect your skin from the burning sun with this special cream. You can't protect your brother from blame in the accident. It is hopeless trying to protect your child from the harmful effects of*

*television until the material improves.*

**protest against** *v prep* → **demur at, object to, raise to** (6), **take to** (13)
to express, aloud or in actions, one's opposition to (something or something being done): [IØ + *against*] *I protest against being blamed for something that I haven't done. All the local farmers protested against the new airport. All the local farmers protested against the new airport being built on rich farmland. If it's protested against by all the people, the government can hardly refuse to take notice.*

**protrude from** *v prep* → **jut out, poke out** (1), **project from, stand out** (2), **stick out** (1)
to stand out a little way in front of (something): [IØ + *from*] *Don't stand there with your tongue protruding from your mouth, it looks so rude. The fireplace protrudes from the wall rather too far into the room, taking up a lot of space.*

***prove oneself** *v pron*
to show that one has ability and usu. character: [IØ (*to*)] *Some people do the strangest things just to prove themselves (to themselves), like facing unnecessary dangers.*

**prove to** *v prep*
to give proof of something to (someone); show something beyond doubt to (someone): [T1 + *to*] *Why should I have to prove my loyalty to you? I wonder what he's trying to prove to himself. What are you trying to prove to the public?* [T5 + *to*] *You will have to prove to the police that you were at home that night.* [T6 + *to*] *Can you prove where you were to the police?*

**provide against** *v prep* → **make against**
to take action to avoid or prevent (something bad) or to deal with (a danger or time of danger) in advance: [T1] *Steps can be taken to provide against a severe winter. What can we do to provide against a failure of the wheat crop?*

**provide for** *v prep*
**1** to supply (something or someone) for the needs of (someone or something): [T1 + *for*] *It is the duty of the government to provide homes for old people. Who is going to provide the money for the additional workers? There is no way that we can provide another teacher for that class. How can I be expected to provide food for so many people?*
***2** to supply necessary things such as food, clothing, and shelter for (someone, a time, or life): [T1] *I'm sure, sir, that I shall be well able to provide for my wife and family. These people have saved during their whole lives to provide for their old age, but are being defeated by rising prices. Has every member of the family been equally provided for?* —**unprovided for** *adj* → **make for** (16)
***3** to fulfil the needs of (someone or something): [T1] *All kinds of music are provided for by the various record companies. Politicians should learn to provide for the opinions of the man in the street.* → **cater for** (2, 4), **cater to**
***4** to make all necessary arrangements for (something): [T1] *Has the safety of the workers been properly provided for? How can anyone provide for unexpected events? Insurance helps to provide for a sudden loss of income. Accidental damage is not provided for.*
***5** (of a law) to ensure; demand the enforcement of (something): [T1] *The new law provides for equality of human rights. Rent control is now fully provided for.*

**provide under** *v prep*
to supply (something) according to (a law): [T1 + *under* (*often pass.*)] *A public health centre in every city is provided under the health laws.*

***provide with** *v prep*
to supply (someone or something) with (necessary things or people): [D1] *The ship is provided with enough food to last the whole voyage. The firm provides its workers with their uniforms, but they are expected to keep them regularly cleaned. Each child needing special help should be provided with a teacher to himself for at least part of each school day. Have you been provided with enough money for the journey?*

***provoke into** *v prep* → **goad into, sting into**
to urge, annoy, or drive (someone) into (an action or doing something): [D1] *The children's bad behaviour at last provoked their mother into anger.* [V4b] *The opposition is trying to provoke the government into calling an election. The students did their best to provoke the teacher into losing his temper.*

***prowl about/around/round** *v adv*
to move around carefully, as if waiting for a chance to hunt or steal: [IØ (*usu. continuous tenses*)] *Be careful here, there are lions prowling about in the bush. I'm sure I can hear somebody prowling around outside the windows; I'll go and have a look while you call the police.*

**prune away** *v adv*
**1** to remove (unwanted parts of a plant) by cutting: [T1 + AWAY] *If you prune the dead wood away, the tree has a better chance of growth.*
**2** to remove (unwanted parts of anything): [T1 + AWAY] *I think your writing would be improved if you pruned away some of those unnecessary adjectives.*

**prune down** *v adv*
**1** to shorten (a plant) by cutting: [T1 + DOWN] *Shall I prune this bush down? It's beginning to shut out some light from the house.*
**2** to reduce (something): [T1 + DOWN] *Is there any way we can prune the costs down still further?*

**prune from** *v prep*
**1** to remove (unwanted parts) from (a plant): [T1 + *from*] *I think some of the overhanging branches should be pruned from this tree.*

**2** to remove (unwanted parts) from (something): [T1 + *from*] *I think you should prune some of the adjectives from your writing, so as to improve it. The city council has been trying to prune unnecessary costs from its list.*

**prune of** *v prep*

**1** to reduce (a plant) by removing (unwanted parts): [T1 + *of*] *The bush should be pruned of any untidy growth so that it keeps its shape.*
**2** to reduce (something) by removing (unwanted parts): [T1 + *of*] *Your sentences would read better if they were pruned of some of those adjectives that you're so fond of. The builders have reduced the cost by pruning the house of all but the most necessary things.*

**pry about** *v adv* → **nose about, poke about**
to look around enquiringly, esp. into other people's affairs: [L9 + ABOUT (*among, for, in*) (*usu. continuous tenses*)] *That policeman had no business prying about in our garage without a court order. Why was he prying about among our things? What was he prying about for? We have no stolen goods hidden in there.*

**pry from** *v prep* → **PRY OUT OF**

**pry into** *v prep* → **nose into, poke into** (2)
to enquire into (other people's affairs): [L9 + *into* (*usu. continuous tenses*)] *I don't want our neighbours prying into our affairs, so keep quiet about our plans.*

**pry off** *v adv AmE* → **PRISE OFF**

**pry open** *v adj AmE* → **PRISE OPEN**

**pry out of/from** *v adv prep; prep AmE* → **PRISE OUT OF**

**pry up** *v adv AmE* → **PRISE UP**

***psych out** *v adv*

**1** esp. *AmE infml* to sympathize with (someone); understand the feelings of (someone): [T1] *One of the first things a teacher has to do is to psych the children out.*
**2** esp. *AmE infml* to cause (someone) to suffer or be uncomfortable in their feelings: [T1] *I don't enjoy talking to Mrs Wood at parties; I always feel that she's trying to psych me out all the time. "His attempt to psych out the other competitors seemed to work."* (Toronto *Globe and Mail,* 9 August 1976)
**3** *AmE infml* to become afraid, nervous, etc.: [IØ (*usu. simple tenses*)] *I psych out every time I enter an examination room.*
**4** *AmE infml* to pretend to be mad so as to avoid something unpleasant: [IØ] *Some men were able to get out of the army by psyching out.*

***psych up** *v adv* → **hop up** (2), **hype up**
esp. *AmE infml* to prepare (someone), esp. for action, by encouragement, excitement, etc.: [T1 (*usu. pass.*)] *If you can get the committee members (all) psyched up before the meeting, we might get some lively action and some meaningful voting.*

***pucker up** *v adv* → **purse up, wrinkle up**
(usu. of someone's face or mouth) to (cause to) tighten into folds: [T1] *She puckered up her lips for a kiss.* [IØ] *The child's face puckered up and he began to cry.*

**puff at/on** *v prep* → **drag at, drag on, draw at** (1), **pull at** (2), **pull on²** (2)
to suck at; draw smoke from (a pipe): [IØ (AWAY) + *at/on*] *Harold puffed (away) at his pipe.*

**puff away** *v adv*

**1** to take short breaths; make small clouds of smoke or steam, continuously: [IØ + AWAY] *The steam engine stood in the field, puffing away, turning the wheels of the farm machine. Harold puffed away (at his pipe).*
**2** to move away in clouds of smoke or steam: [L9 + AWAY] *The train puffed away, slowly at first, then gathered speed.*

**puff out** *v adv*

**1** to (cause to) swell with air: [IØ + OUT] *As the wind rose, the sails puffed out and the little boat moved faster.* [T1 + OUT] *In cold weather, birds puff out their feathers to keep warm. Jim puffed out his chest with pride.*
**2** to move out; leave in clouds of smoke or steam: [L9 + OUT (*of*)] *The train puffed out of the station.*
***3** to send out (breath, smoke, steam, etc.): [T1] *This chimney is puffing out too much smoke. The runner puffed out the news of the victory.*
**4 be puffed out** to be out of breath: *Wait a minute, I'm puffed out.*

**puff up** *v adv*

**1** to rise in small clouds: [IØ + UP] *Smoke puffed up from the forest fire.*
**2** to (cause to) swell: [T1 + UP (*usu. pass.*)] *His face was (all) puffed up with the infection in his tooth.*
***3** *infml* to overpraise; speak too highly of the good qualities of (usu. something): [T1] *I think the newspapers have puffed up her performance; she wasn't all that good.*
**4 be puffed up** *infml* to be too proud: *I don't like the new girl, she seems rather puffed up as if she thinks she's too important to talk to anybody.*

***pull about/around** *v adv*
to take hold of (someone or something) roughly; mishandle (someone or something), often violently: [T1b] *Stop pulling your little brother about, he doesn't deserve such rough treatment. The child's toys don't last very long as he pulls them about so.*

***pull ahead** *v adv* → **move ahead,** etc.

**1** to lead; go further in front (of someone or something): [IØ (*of*)] *The horse that we had chosen to win began to pull ahead halfway through the race. Let that fast car pull ahead; I'd rather have such a driver in front of me than behind me.*
**2** to advance; go in front, esp. in a competition: [IØ (*of*)] *Our team were bottom of the local competition, but now they are pulling ahead (of the nearest competitor).*

**pull along** *v adv; prep*
to make (something or someone) follow by pulling: [T1 + ALONG/*along*] *Why does she pull the child along like that? These toys are intended to be pulled along (the floor).* —**pull-along** *adj*

**pull alongside** *v adv; prep* → **draw alongside, lay alongside, lie alongside**
to come to rest or move at an equal speed next to (something such as a ship): [IØ] *A police car pulled alongside, and signalled to me to stop.* [T1 (*no pass.*)] *Pull alongside the ship and we will help you aboard.*

**pull apart** *v adv*
**1** to (cause to) separate, usu. with force, into pieces: [T1 + APART] *The dog has pulled the newspaper apart again!* [IØ + APART (*simple tenses*)] *This toy is made to pull apart. These pieces of ice don't pull apart easily.* —**pull-apart** *adj* → **pull to**[2] (2), **rend to** (1), **rip apart** (1), **rip to** (1), **take apart** (2), **take to** (7a), **tear apart** (1), **tear to** (1)
*__2__ *not fml* to find severe fault with (usu. someone's work): [T1b] *Tom's latest book has been pulled apart by the newspapers. Don't pull her performance apart as unkindly as you did last time even if it was bad; it could destroy her.* → **take apart** (4), etc.

**pull around** *v adv* → PULL ABOUT

**pull aside** *v adv*
**1** to make (something) move to one side: [T1 + ASIDE] *Pulling the curtain aside, he looked down into the street.* → **draw aside** (1)
*__2__ to take (someone) on one side for private conversation: [T1b] *Try to pull the chairman aside after the meeting and let him know our views.* → **draw aside** (2), **go aside, take apart** (1), **take aside, take on**[2] (11), **take to** (20)

**pull at** *v prep*
**1** to try to draw (something such as a rope) towards one by pulling; take hold of (something) tightly and move it nearer to one: [IØ + *at*] *Pull at that bell rope, and a servant will come. He pulled at the controls, but the horse refused to obey. Stop pulling at my skirt: I'm coming!* → **pluck at, pull on**[2] (1), **tug at** (1), **yank at, yank on**
**2** to suck at; draw smoke through (usu. a pipe): [IØ (AWAY) + *at*] *Harold pulled (away) at his pipe while he considered what decision to make.* → **drag at, drag on, draw at** (1), **puff at, pull on**[2] (2)
**3** to take a drink from (a bottle): [IØ + *at*] *Not stopping to fill a glass, he just pulled at the bottle until he was satisfied.*
**4 pull at one's pipe** *taboo* to masturbate. → **jerk off, play with** (9), **toss off** (5)

**pull away** *v adv*
**1** to remove (something, someone, or oneself) by pulling: [T1 + AWAY (*from*)] *Don't pull your hand away like that, it makes me think that you don't care for me. The mother pulled the child away from the fire just in time.* → **drag away** (1), **drag off, jerk away, take away** (1), **yank away**
**2** to row continuously: [IØ + AWAY] *Pull away, boys! A little more effort, and we'll soon reach the shore.*
*__3__ to move away; (of a horse or runner) to lead: [IØ (*from*) (*often continuous tenses*)] *Just as I was pulling away from the parking place, another car crashed into mine. The leader is pulling away now, and is sure to win.* → **go away** (5)
*__4__ to cause (someone or oneself) to leave (something or someone): [T1b (*from*) (*often simple tenses*)] *Do pull yourself away from the window, there can't be anything interesting out there. How can I pull myself away from you/your arms?* → **drag away** (2), **tear away** (3)

**pull back** *v adv*
**1** to move (something or someone) back by pulling: [T1 + BACK (*from*)] *He pulled the curtain back and looked down into the street. The mother pulled the child back from the flames just in time.* → **draw back** (1)
*__2__ to move backwards or away: [IØ (*often simple tenses*)] *The crowd pulled back to let the firemen through. The mouse pulled back in terror as the cat sprang.* → **draw back** (2)
*__3__ to be unwilling to fulfil a promise; pause; reduce one's demands: [IØ (*from*)] *The firm pulled back from its agreement and wanted to talk about a new contract. It may be already too late to pull back. We thought he had decided but then he pulled back.* → **draw back** (4)
*__4__ to take (soldiers) away; move (an army) back from a battle: [T1] *We decided to pull back our forces and try to advance again tomorrow.* —**pullback** *n* → **pull out** (6)
*__5__ to spend less money: [IØ] *With the reduction in the money allowed, we shall have to pull back on our spending.*
*__6__ (in music) to go slower: [IØ] *When you sing this song, try not to pull back as it makes it dull.*
*__7__ to make (usu. someone) return (to a former state): [T1b (*to*)] *The doctors are doing all that they can to pull Mother back to health.* → **bring back** (3)

**pull by** *v prep* → **take by** (1)
to seize (someone or an animal) by pulling (part of the body): [T1 + *by*] *That teacher had a nasty habit of pulling the children by the ears. Don't pull the cat by its tail, that's cruel.*

**pull down** *v adv*
**1** to lower (something) by pulling; make (someone) fall: [T1 + DOWN] *Pull down the window coverings, the light is too bright. He pulled his hat down firmly over his eyes. Try to pull your opponent down and get the ball from him.* → **draw down** (1)
**2** to move (something) downwards by pulling: [T1 + DOWN] *The box is too heavy to lift down the slope, we shall have to pull it down.* → **drag down** (1)

*3 to destroy (something such as a building): [T1] *It's such a pity that those fine old houses had to be pulled down to make way for the new road. The old London Bridge was pulled down stone by stone, and rebuilt in the middle of a desert in the United States.* → **come down** (3), **take down** (3)

*4 to weaken (someone) in health: [T1] *My recent cold has pulled me down. It's the fever that's been pulling him down.* → **drag down** (2)

*5 to reduce (someone) to a lower level, as socially, morally, or in a competition; make (someone) humble: [T1 (*often simple tenses*)] *If you marry that man, he will pull you down to his own level. He is too proud and should be pulled down. I was doing well until the last question, but that one proved too difficult and has probably pulled me/my marks down.* → **drag down** (3)

*6 esp. *AmE not fml* to earn (money): [T1] *You can pull down good wages at this factory. He's been pulling down $20,000 a year dealing in property.* → **bring in** (3), etc.

**pull for** *v prep*

**1** also **pull towards** to row in the direction of (a place): [IØ + *for*] *"Pull for the shore, sailor, pull for the shore."* (I.D. Sankey, *Sacred Songs: The Life Boat*)

*2 *not fml* to cheer for (usu. one's team): [T1 (*no pass.*)] *I'm sure we owe part of our victory to the number of supporters who were there, pulling for our side.* → **cheer for, cheer on, root for**

**pull in** *v adv*

**1** to gather; bring (something or someone) in by pulling: [T1 + IN] *The fishermen pulled in their nets full of fish. The Bank of England has had to pull in more gold. One of the men will climb through the window and pull the others in after him. Lower a rope, and pull me in!* → **draw in** (1), **haul in** (1)

**2** to hold (something such as a muscle) in tightly: [T1 + IN] *Stand straight and pull your stomachs in, men!* → **hold in**[1] (1), **keep in** (1), **tuck in** (2)

*3 to arrive: [IØ (*at, to*)] *The train pulled in and all the passengers got off.* → **draw in** (4)

*4 (of a vehicle or boat) to move to one side: [IØ (*to*)] *The bus pulled in to let the cars pass. Pull in, will you? We need room to get past where the water is deep enough!* → **draw in** (5), **pull off**[1] (3), **pull over**[1]

*5 to stop on a journey, esp. for a purpose: [IØ (*at, to*)] *We'd better pull in at the next garage for some petrol. Let's pull in here and have something to eat: it looks a good place.* —**pull-in** *n* → **draw up** (4), **pull up** (3)

*6 to control (an animal): [T1] *Your horse is trying to go too fast; you must pull him in.* → **hold in**[1] (2)

*7 to attract (the public): [T1] *The new singer is pulling the crowds in.* → **draw in** (6)

*8 *not fml* to persuade (someone) to join, esp. to help: [T1 (*usu. pass.*)] *Against my better judgment, I got pulled in to help with the school concert again!* → **rope in** (2)

*9 *not fml* to seize (a possible criminal): [T1] *The police have pulled him in for questioning.* → **bring in** (6), **take in**[1] (17), **yank in**

*10 *not fml* to earn (money): [T1] *You can pull in over £6,000 a year at that factory.* → **bring in** (3), etc.

*11 *not fml* to reduce (costs): [IØ (*often simple tenses*)] *Better pull in now, before the money's all gone.* [T1 (*often simple tenses*)] *You have to pull in your spending somehow.*

**12 pull in one's belt** *not fml* to spend less money, esp. on food: *In these hard times, we all have to pull in our belts.*

**13 pull in one's horns** *not fml* to be less keen or active, and more careful: *You've been using up your strength too much recently; hadn't you better pull in your horns a little? You'd better pull in your horns or the voters will know that you're trying to trick them.* → **draw in** (11), **haul in** (2)

**14 pull oneself in** to stand straight, with tight stomach muscles: [*often imper.*] *Pull yourselves in there, men, look like soldiers!*

**pull into** *v prep*

**1** to help or force (something or someone) to enter (something such as a place): [T1 + *into*] *We pulled the drowning man into the boat just in time to save his life. You'll have to pull the dog into the car, he doesn't want to go.*

*2 to arrive; stop one's journey at (a place): [T1 (*no pass.*)] *The train is just pulling into the station, so we shall be in time to meet her. Let's pull into this roadside restaurant for something to eat.*

*3 (of a vehicle or boat) to move to (one side): [T1 (*no pass.*)] *The bus pulled into the side of the road to let the cars pass. Pull into the side, will you? We need room to get past where the water is deep enough.*

*4 to persuade (someone) to join, esp. to help (something or doing something): [D1 (*usu. pass.*)] *Against my better judgment, I was pulled into the organization of the school concert again.* [V4a (*usu. pass.*)] *Against my better judgment, I was pulled into helping with the school concert again!*

**5 pull something into shape: a** to stretch something until it is the right shape: *When you have finished making the pieces of the garment, pull each one into shape and press firmly with a steam iron.* **b** *not fml* to make something correct, fit, in good order, etc.: *We have a lot of work to do to pull this show into shape before it is fit to perform to the public.*

**pull off**[1] *v adv*

**1** to remove (something): [T1 + OFF] *These birds have pulled off all the flower heads. There's a piece of thread on your skirt; let me pull it off. Some people can pull a tablecloth off without moving any of the dishes on top.* → **take off**[1] (1), etc.

**2** to remove (clothing): [T1 + OFF] *Help m*

*to pull off these muddy boots. Pulling off his coat, he jumped into the water to save the child.* → **take off**[1] (2), etc.

*__3__ to be driven or moved away or onto the side of the road: [IØ (*often simple tenses*)] *The boat pulled off from the shore. There is a place two kilometres ahead where we can pull off and have a rest on our journey.* —**pull-off** *n AmE* → **draw in** (5), **pull in** (4), **pull over**[1]

*__4__ *not fml* to succeed in (a difficult attempt): [T1 (*pass. rare, usu. simple tenses*)] *After failing his driving test eight times, John at last pulled it off. The trick looked impossible but the magician pulled it off. This is the most delicate deal that we've ever pulled off; we have reason to be proud of ourselves.* → **bring off** (2), **carry off**[1] (6), **come off**[1] (6), **go off**[1] (6), **pass off** (2)

**pull off**[2] *v prep*

**1** to remove (something or someone) from (something) by force: [T1 + *off*] *The cat has pulled the cloth off the table, and all the dishes are scattered all over the floor. Those birds have pulled all the flower heads off the roses! Let me pull that piece of thread off your skirt.* → **take off**[2] (1)

**2** to remove (clothing) from (a part of the body): [T1 + *off*] *I can't pull these boots off my feet, they're so tight. Entering the house, he pulled his hat quickly off his head to show his good manners.*

*__3__ (of a vehicle) to be driven to (the side of the road): [T1 (*no pass., often simple tenses*)] *We're not allowed to pull off the road for a rest until we reach a special place about two kilometres ahead.*

**pull on**[1] *v adv*

**1** to put on (clothing) by pulling: [T1 + ON] *Help me to pull on these boots, they're very tight.* → **put on**[1] (2), etc.

**2** to continue to row: [IØ + ON] *If we want to reach the shore, we shall have to pull on until our strength fails.*

**pull on**[2] *v prep*

**1** to try to draw (something such as a rope) towards one by pulling; take hold of (something) tightly and move it nearer to one; weigh heavily on (part of the body): [IØ + *on*] *Pull on that bell rope, and a servant will come. Stop pulling on my skirt: I'm coming! The weight of this parcel is pulling on my arms.* → **pull at** (1), **yank at, yank on**

**2** to suck at; draw smoke through (a pipe, cigarette, etc.): [IØ (AWAY) + *on*] *Harold pulled (away) on his pipe while he considered what decision to make. Most of the men who were waiting were pulling nervously on cigarettes.* → **drag at, drag on**[2], **draw at** (1), **puff at, pull at** (2)

**3 pull rank on** *not fml* to take unfair advantage of one's position in an organization to force (someone) in a lower position to act in a certain way: *I don't like to pull rank on you, but I think you ought to complete that work today.*

**pull out** *v adv*

**1** to produce; take (something) out: [T1 + OUT (*of*)] *Before I could see what he was doing, he had pulled out a gun. Putting his hand in his pocket, he pulled out a handkerchief.* → **bring out** (1), **draw out** (1), **get out** (5), **take out** (3), **take out of** (3)

**2** to (cause to) be removed, often by force: [T1 + OUT (*of*)] *I shall have to have this tooth pulled out. Can you pull this nail out? I can't move it. He pulled the arrow out of his arm with his other hand. This tool is for pulling hairs out of your nose. Swimming against the current, he was able to pull the child out (of the river). You can pull the middle pages out of this magazine, to keep separately.* [IØ + OUT (*simple tenses*)] *Will these pages pull out separately? This drawer is stiff and won't pull out.* —**pullout** *n, adj* → **take out** (2), etc.

*__3__ *not fml* to produce (something such as an idea): [T1 (*often simple tenses*)] *I hope you can pull out a better answer before the end of the meeting.*

*__4__ to stretch (something): [T1] *Pull out the wire until it is very thin. The wool from the sheep has to be pulled out until it forms a thread.* → **draw out** (2)

*__5__ to move away; (of a train) leave a station; (of a boat) leave the shore; (of a vehicle) move across the stream of traffic: [IØ (*of*)] *We reached the station too late, just as the train was pulling out. We should be able to pull out when the wind rises. Suddenly the car in front of us pulled out and nearly caused an accident.* → **draw out** (5, 6)

*__6__ *not fml* to (cause to) leave a place or time of trouble; escape: [IØ] *Jim saw that the firm was going to fail, so he pulled out before he got ruined. When will the soldiers have finished pulling out?* [T1 (*of*)] *British forces will be pulled out of the troubled area as quickly as possible.* —**pullout** *n* → **pull back** (4)

*__7__ (of a plane) to (cause to) change to a level flight after descending: [T1 (*of*)] *The plane was descending dangerously steeply but the pilot was able to pull it out just in time.* [IØ (*of*)] *From the ground, we could see the plane pull out of its steep descent.* —**pullout** *n*

*__8__ *not fml* to (cause to) regain cheerfulness or good health, etc.: [IØ (*of*) (*often simple tenses*)] *Jim loses his temper easily, but soon pulls out (of it).* [T1 (*of*) (*often simple tenses*)] *You're feeling low because you're overtired; a good holiday will pull you out (of that feeling).*

**9 pull one's finger out** *sl* to stop being lazy and start working hard: [*usu. simple tenses*] *The director wants that report by midnight tonight: tell the writers to pull their fingers out and get working!*

**10 pull out (all) the stops: a** (on an organ) to use all the possible controls for changing or increasing the sound: *You should hear this great instrument with all its stops pulled out.* **b**

*infml* to make all possible effort: *You'll have to pull out (all) the stops to persuade your mother to leave her old home.*

**pull out of** *v adv prep*

**1** to produce or remove (something or someone) from (something such as a place): [T1 + OUT + *of*] *He pulled a gun out of a secret drawer. Quickly she pulled some money out of her bag. Can you pull this nail out of my shoe? He pulled the arrow out of his arm with his other hand. Swimming against the current, he was able to pull the child out of the river.* → **go out of** (1), **take out of** (1)

*__2__ to produce (something such as an idea) from (something): [D1] *The director has the ability to pull success out of a seemingly impossible set of events.*

*__3__ to move away from (a station, shore, or stream of traffic): [IØ (*of*)] *The train was just pulling out of the station; we were too late. Suddenly the car in front of us pulled out of the main stream of traffic and nearly caused an accident.*

*__4__ to (cause to) leave (something such as a group, place, or time of trouble): [T1 (*of*)] *After many years of fighting, the soldiers were pulled out of the battle area.* [IØ (*of*)] *I shall have to pull out of the team because of my hurt ankle.*

*__5__ (of a plane) to (cause to) regain level flight after (descending): [T1 (*of*)] *Can the pilot pull the plane out of its steep descent?* [IØ (*of*)] *The plane pulled out of its dangerous downward path just in time.*

*__6__ *not fml* to (cause to) regain cheerfulness or good health after (a bad feeling or illness): [T1 (*often simple tenses*)] *Jim loses his temper easily, but just as quickly pulls out of it.* [D1] *A good holiday should pull you out of this feeling of sadness.*

**7 pull something/someone out of danger** to save something from defeat or someone from death: *We must decide what action to take to pull the firm out of danger. Modern drugs have helped to pull many seriously ill people out of danger.*

***pull over¹** *v adv* → **draw in** (5), **pull in** (4), **pull off¹** (3)

to drive to the side of the road, esp. in order to stop: [IØ (*to*)] *When the fire engines came rushing down the street, all the cars pulled over to the side to let them pass.*

**pull over²** *v prep*

**1** to move or force (something) into a position covering or passing over (something or someone): [T1 + *over*] *Pull the sheet over the dead body. This garment has no buttons and has to be pulled over your head.* —**pullover** *n* —**pull-over** *adj* → **draw over** (1), **lay over²**, **put across²** (1), **put over²** (1), **set across, set over** (1), **take across, throw on²** (1), **throw over²** (2)

**2 pull it/the wool over someone's eyes** *infml* to deceive someone: *It's no good trying to pull the wool over the director's eyes, he can't be fooled easily. Don't try to pull it over me, I've been caught by that trick before!*

**pull round** *v adv*

**1** to make (something or someone) face the opposite way: [T1 + ROUND] *A sudden shout pulled me round. The captain had to pull the ship's head round in heavy seas.* → **bring about** (2), etc.

*__2__ *not fml* to (cause to) live; regain consciousness or good health, etc.: [T1b] *Peter has fainted; try to pull him round. Mother was so ill after her operation that the doctors wondered if they would be able to pull her round.* [IØ] *It will be several weeks before she pulls round.* → **bring to** (1), etc., **pull through¹**

*__3__ *not fml* to (cause to) succeed completely: [T1b] *A gift of money from the government helped to pull the theatre company round, when it was in danger of failing.* [IØ] *The firm will soon pull round once the trade position improves.* → **pull through¹** (3)

*__4__ *not fml* to persuade (someone) to change his/her opinion: [T1b (*to*)] *What can we do to pull more voters round (to our party)?* → **bring round** (3), etc.

**pull through¹** *v adv*

**1** to make (something or someone) pass through something such as a space by pulling: [T1 + THROUGH] *The eye of the needle is too small and I can't pull the thread through. We're locked out! The window isn't wide enough for me to pull myself through; we shall have to ask the police to break down the door. The gun has to be cleaned regularly by pulling a piece of old cloth through.* —**pullthrough** *n*

*__2__ *not fml* to (cause to) live in spite of illness or wounds, etc.; regain health: [T1b] *Mother was so ill after her operation that the doctors wondered if they would be able to pull her through.* [IØ] *Only after several weeks were they certain that she would pull through.* → **bring through¹**, **carry through¹** (3), **come through¹** (7), **pull round** (2)

*__3__ *not fml* to (cause to) succeed, esp. in a particular difficulty: [T1b] *The theatre company were in great difficulties this year until a gift of money from the government pulled them through.* [IØ] *Unless you work hard for the examination, you haven't a hope of pulling through. Although the value of the pound has been falling recently, Britain can still pull through, with help from other countries.* → **pull round** (3)

**pull through²** *v prep*

**1** to make (something or someone) pass through (something such as a space) by pulling: [T1 + *through*] *I can't pull the thread through the eye of this needle, it's too small. If you can't pull yourself through the window, you'll have to break down the door. A gun is cleaned by pulling a piece of old cloth through its barrel.*

*__2__ *not fml* to (cause to) live or regain health after (illness, etc.): [D1] *The doctors pulled*

*Mother through a serious illness following her operation, using special care and modern drugs.* [T1 (*no pass.*)] *For some weeks we wondered if Mother would pull through her illness.* → **bring through²**

*3 *not fml* to (cause to) succeed in spite of (a difficulty): [D1] *Their courage pulled the people through the war. A gift of money from the government pulled the theatre company through their money troubles.* [T1 (*no pass.*)] *You'll never pull through the examination unless you work hard.* → **bring through², carry through² (2), come through² (3)**

**pull to¹** *v adv* → **draw to¹, push to, put to¹, shut to¹, slam to**
to close (something such as curtains or a door): [T1 + TO] *Pull the curtains to, the light is hurting my eyes. As you leave, will you please pull the door to gently.*

**pull to²** *v prep*
**1** to make (something or someone) move to (a place) by pulling: [T1 + *to*] *Fancy having to pull that load to the village in this heat! Horses used to be used to pull cartloads of crops to the market. Just as the car reached the spot where she was standing, I pulled the child to safety.*
**2 pull something to pieces** to separate (something) into parts, often with force: *The dog has pulled the newspaper to pieces again!* → **pull apart** (1), etc.
**3 pull something/someone to pieces** *not fml* to find severe fault with something such as someone's work or someone: *Tom's latest book has been pulled to pieces by the newspapers. There's no point in pulling her to pieces; she did the job to the best of her ability.* → **take apart** (4), etc.

**pull together** *v adv*
**1** to row in time with each other: [IØ + TOGETHER] *If we are to win the race, we must practise pulling together.*
*2 (of a group) to work together so as to help a common effort: [IØ] *We must all pull together if we are to win this election.*
*3 to improve (something such as a group) through proper organization: [T1b] *The directors called in an experienced man to pull the department together.*
**4 pull oneself together** to control oneself; be in command of one's feelings, etc.: *Pull yourself together, man, stop behaving like a baby.* → **gather together** (2), **get together** (8)

**pull towards** *v prep* → **PULL FOR** (1)

**pull under** *v adv; prep*
(of a current) to force (someone or something) beneath (water): [T1 + UNDER/*under*] *The current is so dangerous in this part of the river that even a strong swimmer can be pulled under. The current pulled the boy under the surface of the water, and he drowned.*

**pull up** *v adv*
**1** to lift; raise (something or someone) by pulling: [T1 + UP] *The climbers obtained their supplies by letting down a rope and pulling them up. You'll find my mother in the garden as usual, pulling up unwanted plants. The old tree will have to be pulled up by its roots. As the boy sank for the third time, the swimmer pulled him up by the hair. A good exercise is to hold a high bar and pull yourself up by your arms until your chin is level with the bar.* —**pull-up** *n* → **get up** (3), **jerk up, lift up** (1), **pick up** (1), **pluck up** (1), **press up, push up** (1), **take up** (1), **tear up¹** (2), **yank up**
*2 to (cause to) move forward: [T1 (*to*)] *Pull up a chair (to the table) and join the conversation. The boat was pulled up on the shore.* [IØ (*to*)] *Please pull up to the next car, so that we can park some more in this space.* → **drag up** (1), **draw up** (1)
*3 to (cause to) come to a stop: [T1] *The driver pulled the bus up only just in time to avoid hitting the child. You must learn how to pull up your horse when he is going too fast. The police pulled us up just inside city limits, and asked to see our papers.* [IØ (*usu. simple tenses*)] *The bus pulled up with a loud noise of its tyres. The car pulled up when the light turned red. Let's pull up at this restaurant.* —**pull-up** *n* → **draw up** (4), **pull in** (5)
*4 *not fml* to scold; find fault with; correct (someone): [T1] *The director pulled Jim up for being late again today. The police pulled the driver up for breaking the speed limit.* → **tell off** (1), etc.
*5 *not fml* to correct; improve (something such as one's knowledge of a subject): [T1] *You'll have to pull up your English to a higher standard if you want to pass the examination.*
*6 to make (oneself) stand straight, often proudly: [T1] *He pulled himself up to his full height.* → **draw up** (5)
*7 to come level (with another competitor): [IØ (*to, with*)] *Once he gets his breath, he'll soon pull up to the leading runner.*
**8 pull oneself up by one's (own) bootstraps/laces** *infml* to help oneself to improve without depending on other people; succeed by one's own efforts: *It's all very well the doctor telling me to pull myself up by my own bootstraps, but when one is really ill one needs help.*
**9 pull up one's roots** *not fml* to leave a place where one has lived for a long time, with difficulty: *I shall miss you if you go to live in another country, but don't expect me to pull up my roots and join you there, I've lived here too long to make a new start in life.* → **put down** (17)
**10 pull one's socks up** *infml* to make greater effort, esp. to control oneself or improve one's work: *I won't allow lazy students in this class; you'll all have to pull your socks up if you are to meet the expected standard.*
**11 pull up stakes** *AmE not fml* to leave a place where one has lived or worked: *He can't seem to settle in a steady job; every two years*

*or so he pulls up stakes, moves to another city and starts again.*

**pulse through** *v prep*

**1** (of the blood) to pass through (the body) by means of the regular beating of the heart: [IØ + *through*] *His blood pulsed through his blood vessels faster and faster as he ran up the stairs.*

***2** *not fml* to happen in an exciting way in; excite the people in (a place): [T1 (*no pass.*)] *You can feel the nervousness pulsing through the crowd as they wait for her arrival.*

**pump in** *v adv*

**1** to force (air or liquid) inside or into something with a pump: [T1 + IN (*to*)] *This tyre is flat; you didn't pump enough air in. The village is so far from the river that their water has to be pumped in from the nearest water supply.* → **pump into** (1)

***2** *not fml* to put a lot of (money) in something such as a firm: [T1 (*to*)] *Unless the government pumps more money in, the whole shipbuilding industry will fail.* → **pour in**[1] (3), **pour into** (2), **pump into** (2)

***3** *not fml* to try to teach (something) by force: [T1 (*to*)] *The advertising industry believes that if you can, by repetition, pump in enough attractive information, the public will buy anything.* → **hammer in** (3), etc.

**pump into** *v prep*

**1** to force (air or liquid) inside (something) with a pump: [T1 + *into*] *Pump some more air into this tyre, it's still flat. This machine pumps the oil directly into the barrels.* → **pump in** (1)

***2** *not fml* to put a lot of (money) into (something such as a firm or doing something): [D1] *The government has pumped a lot of money into the production of these fast new planes, and does not want to see it wasted.* [V4] *The government has pumped money into building these fast new planes.* → **pour into** (3), **pump in** (2)

***3** *not fml* to try to teach (something) to (someone) by force: [D1] *Education is not a matter of pumping facts into the children's heads, but of helping them to learn how to think and choose.* → **hammer into** (3), etc.

**pump out** *v adv*

**1** to remove (air or liquid) by using a pump; empty (something) with a pump: [T1 + OUT (*of*)] *If we can pump all this water out, we can save the ship from sinking. So far, we've been able to pump out most of the lower floors.*

***2** *not fml* to force (something such as information) (from someone): [T1 (*of*)] *At last the police were able to pump the truth out (of the prisoner).* [T6 (*of*)] *You'll never pump out of me where the plans are hidden.*

**pump through** *v prep*

to force (usu. air or liquid) through (something such as a pipe) with a pump: [T1 + *through*] *The hot water is pumped through these narrow pipes, so keeping the whole house warm.*

**pump up** *v adv*

**1** to raise (usu. liquid) with a pump: [T1 + UP] *The water for the house is pumped up from a deep well.*

***2** to fill (something such as a tyre) with air: [T1] *You can pump up the tyres by hand or with this special machine.* → **blow up** (4)

**punch down** *v adv* → **punch in**[1] (1)

to drive (something such as a nail) below the surface of the wood, often using a special tool: [T1 + DOWN] *Punch down any loose nails so that the floor is quite smooth.*

**punch in**[1] *v adv*

**1** to drive (something such as a nail) below the surface of the wood, often using a special tool; beat (something) inwards: [T1 + IN] *Make sure that all the nails are punched in so that the floor is smooth.* → **punch down**

***2** *AmE* to record the time of one's arrival at work by putting one's card into a machine with a clock: [IØ] *Have all the workers punched in yet? They're supposed to punch in by 8.30.* → **clock in,** etc.

**punch in**[2] *v prep*

**1** to drive (a hole or holes) in (something), often with a special tool: [T1 + *in*] *This school paper comes provided with holes already punched in it, to fit into the binders.*

**2** to give (someone) a blow with one's fist on (a certain part of the body such as nose, face, stomach, or eye): [T1 + *in*] *If you say that again, I'll punch you in the nose!*

**punch on** *v prep*

to give (someone) a blow on (a part of the body): [T1 + *on*] *Jim punched one of his attackers on the nose, and another on the chin, making them unconscious.*

**punch out** *v adv*

**1** to shape (a hole or metal or plastic object) with a special tool: [T1 + OUT] *The places where the holes are punched out mark the right answers. The railway official punched a hole out of my ticket to show that I had started my journey. A line of small holes is punched out to show you where to tear the card. This machine can punch out 20,000 coins a day* —**punch-out** *n* → **stamp out** (2)

**2** to remove (something such as a nail) with a special tool: [T1 + OUT] *If you can't pull the nails out by their heads, punch them out from the other side of the board.*

***3** *AmE* to record the time of finishing work [IØ] *What time do the workers punch out on Fridays?* → **clock out,** etc.

**punch up** *v adv*

**1** to record (usu. the amount of a sale) on money machine with keys: [T1 + UP] *I got a shock when the sales girl punched up the total of my shopping.*

***2** *BrE infml* to fight (someone) with bare hands: [T1] *I will have no one punching any* *one else up in my hotel.* [IØ] *I will not allow anyone to punch people up in my hotel* —**punch-up** *n*

**punctuate with** *v prep*
**1** to mark (writing) with (stops, question marks, etc.): [T1 + *with*] *Be sure to punctuate your sentences with the correct marks in the right places.*
*__2__ also **punctuate by** to interrupt (something such as a speech) with (actions, noise, etc.): [D1 (*often pass.*)] *The speaker punctuated his speech with movements of his hands, intended to help express his meaning. The Minister's speech was punctuated with laughter from the Opposition. The night silence was punctuated only by the occasional cry of a bird.*

**punish by** *v prep* → PUNISH WITH

**punish for** *v prep*
to give (someone or an animal) a punishment because of (something or doing something wrong): [T1 + *for*] *You can't punish me for something I didn't do. The dog will have to be punished for biting the postman.*

**punish with** *v prep* also **punish by**
to give (someone) a punishment consisting of (something): [T1 + *with* (*often pass.*)] *For your crime, the court will punish you with two years in prison. Any sailor who disobeys will be punished with six strokes of the whip. The schoolboys are generally punished with some loss of their free time.*

**purge away/off/out** *v adv*
to remove; get rid of (something bad) by cleaning or clearing: [T1 + AWAY/OFF/OUT (*often simple tenses*)] *This medicine will help to purge away the poison in your blood. When all the evil in the world is purged away, there will still be the poor to feed and the sorrowful to comfort.*

**purge from** *v prep*
to get rid of (something nasty or unwanted) from (something): [T1 + *from* (*often simple tenses*)] *This medicine will help to purge waste matter from the bowels. The factory has been ordered to purge the dangerous chemicals from the liquid that it pours into the river. How can I purge this shame from my heart? Several former leaders were purged from the Party when there was a change of power.*

**purge of** *v prep*
**1** to clean (the body) of (bad matter): [T1 + *of* (*often simple tenses*)] *In the old days, doctors used to draw blood from people, hoping to purge the body of bad matter causing the disease. Being sick will purge your stomach of the bad food.*
*__2__ *fml* to make (someone or a group) free of (a feeling such as guilt or shame, or an unwanted person): [D1 (*often simple tenses*)] *Only my father's death purged me of the guilt that I had felt in not loving him as much as my duty towards him demanded. The Party must be purged of disloyal members at once.*

**purge off** *v adv* → PURGE AWAY

**purge out** *v adv* → PURGE AWAY

**purify of** *v prep*
**1** to make (something) clean and pure, free of (dirt, impurity, etc.): [T1 + *of* (*usu. pass.*)] *All water in this area has been purified of undesirable chemicals.*
*__2__ *fml* to make (someone) pure and free of (immorality): [D1 (*usu. simple tenses*)] *This ceremony is held in the church to purify the worshippers of their wrongdoings. The death of our Lord purified mankind of evil.*

**purse up** *v adv* → **pucker up, wrinkle up**
to draw (the lips) tightly together: [T1 + UP] *She pursed up her lips in disapproval.* —**pursed-up** *adj*

***push about/around** *v adv* also *not fml* **shove about** → **kick about** (5), **order about**
*not fml* to try to control (someone) in an unpleasant way, as by giving orders: [T1b] *The workers are refusing to be pushed around by the employers; they will give a fair day's work for a fair day's pay, but demand to be treated as human beings. Stop pushing me around! I'm quite able to make my own decisions!*

**push against** *v prep* also *not fml* **shove against** → **press against, thrust against**
to (cause to) be forced against (something or someone): [IØ + *against*] *I felt something hard, like a gun, pushing against my side.* [T1 + *against*] *Push your hand against the door as hard as you can, to make it shut.*

**push ahead** *v adv*
**1** to make (something or someone) move in front of one: [T1 + AHEAD (*of*)] *The old man was walking along the street, pushing a small cart ahead of him. I didn't want to be first to speak, so I pushed the others ahead.*
*__2__ *not fml* to advance in spite of difficulties; continue (with something); move forward with haste or determination: [IØ (*with*)] *Whatever happens, we must push ahead with our plans to increase production. If we push ahead, we can get home before dark.* also **press ahead** → **press forward** (3), **press on**[1], **push forward** (3), **push on**[1] (1)

**push along** *v adv* also *not fml* **shove along**
**1** to make (something) move forward by pushing it: [T1 + ALONG] *Does the old man spend all day pushing that cart along?*
*__2__ *infml* to leave: [IØ] *Well, I must be pushing along now, it's getting late.* → **push off** (3), etc.

***push around** *v prep* → PUSH ABOUT

**push aside** *v adv* also *not fml* **shove aside** → **elbow aside, shoulder aside, thrust aside**
**1** to make (someone) move to one side, often by pushing him/her roughly: [T1 + ASIDE] *That rude man pushed me aside and got on the bus ahead of me!*
*__2__ to make (someone) yield place to someone else: [T1a (*usu. pass.*)] *When jobs are scarce, young people entering the work force tend to*

*get pushed aside in favour of experienced workers with more to offer the firm.*

**push at** *v prep* also *not fml* **shove at** → **push towards, thrust at** (2), **thrust towards** (1)
to try to push (something), usu. without success; push (something) towards (someone), as to attract his/her attention: [IØ + *at*] *I pushed and pushed at the heavy box but could not move it. You have to push at the window to make it open, it sometimes sticks.* [T1 + *at*] *He pushed the letter at me so that I could read the signature for myself.*

**push away** *v adv* also *not fml* **shove away**
**1** to continue pushing: [IØ + AWAY] *Push away, men, we'll soon move this rock.*
**2** to make (something or someone) move away by pushing: [T1 + AWAY] *Jane pushed her plate away, unable to face her dinner again; there must be something seriously wrong with the girl. She ran to him for a kiss, but he pushed her away unkindly.* → **thrust away**

**push back** *v adv* also *not fml* **shove back**
**1** to move (something or someone) further back; make (something or someone) return to a former position: [T1 + BACK] *The papers are falling out of the envelope; push them back. Pushing her hair back with her other hand, she picked up the telephone. Children tend to get pushed back in crowds.*
***2** *mil* to cause (an enemy) to move back, losing ground: [T1] *Our forces have succeeded in pushing the enemy back on all fronts.* → **thrust back**

**push by/past** *v adv; prep* also *not fml* **shove by**
to touch (usu. someone) roughly as one tries to pass (him): [IØ + BY/PAST/*by/past*] *It's rude to push by like that—wait your turn! He must have been in a hurry—he pushed past me without excusing himself.*

**push down¹** *v adv* also *not fml* **shove down** → **press down**
to force (something) in a downward direction, using weight or strength: [IØ + DOWN] *Push down on the handle with all your strength.* [T1 + DOWN] *The grass had been pushed down in places where people had been lying. It wasn't very kind of you to push your little brother's sandcastle down after he had spent so long building it.*

**push down²** *v prep* also *not fml* **shove down**
**1** to force (something) to pass down (something): [T1 + *down*] *You'll have to push the brush down the pipe to get it clear.* → **force down** (1), **ram down** (1), **stuff down** (1), **thrust down** (1)
**2 push something down someone's throat** *not fml* to force someone to accept something such as an idea: *The parents are complaining that some unpopular subjects are being pushed down the students' throats.* → **force down** (2), **ram down** (2), **stuff down** (2), **thrust down** (2)

***push for** *v prep*
**1** to urge; demand; repeatedly request (something) (from someone or to do something): [T1 (*no pass.*)] *The rent collector has been pushing for payment for three months now. We must push for a reduction in the size of our classes.* [D1] *The newspaper reporters have been pushing the government for details.* [V3] *Many parents have been pushing for the local school to be reopened. The opposition keeps pushing for taxes to be reduced. The native people should not have to push for their rights to be recognized.* → **press for** (1)
**2 be pushed for** *not fml* to have hardly enough (money, time, etc.): *I can't see anyone else today, I'm pushed for time as it is. The universities are becoming increasingly pushed for money, and cannot employ any new teachers.* → **press for** (2), **press hard** (3)

**push forward** *v adv*
**1** to (cause to) move forward by pushing heavily: [IØ + FORWARD] *The crowd, pushing forward to see the Queen, broke the fence that was supposed to keep them in place.* [T1 + FORWARD] *The weight of the bushes has been gradually pushing the wall forward, and it is now leaning at a dangerous angle.* → **press forward** (1), **thrust forward** (1)
***2** esp. *mil* to (cause to) advance, often with difficulty: [T1] *The officer ordered the soldiers to push their advance forward in spite of heavy enemy gunfire.* [IØ] *Our army has pushed forward to new positions.* → **press forward** (2), **thrust forward** (2)
***3** *not fml* to continue (with something); move forward with haste or determination: [IØ (*with*)] *Whatever happens, we must push forward with our plans to increase production. If we push forward, we can get home before dark.* → **plough on** (2), **press forward** (3), **press on¹**, **push ahead** (2), **push on¹** (1)
***4** also *not fml* **shove forward** to try to force people's attention on (something, someone, or oneself): [T1b] *I think the Minister's speech has pushed the case forward to the attention of the public. The newspaper report has certainly pushed the idea forward. I do dislike mothers who push their daughters forward as the best girls for any part. You have to push yourself forward rather, to succeed as a salesman. Mary has always hated parties, never being one to push herself forward.* → **push oneself** (1), **thrust forward** (3)
**5 push one's way forward** to force one's way ahead, esp. roughly, as in a crowd: *It's not fair, he got to the front by pushing his way forward; make him move to the back.* → **elbow forward, shoulder forward, thrust forward** (4)

**push from** *v prep* → **thrust from**
to make (someone or something) move away by pushing, often with dislike: [T1 + *from*] *Jane pushed her dinner from her; she didn't feel like eating again. Why do you push me from you? I thought you loved me?*

**push home** *v adv* also *not fml* **shove home**
**1** to make (usu. something) move in the direction of one's home by pushing it: [T1 + HOME] *Luckily the car was facing downhill when it stopped, and we were able to push it home.*
***2** to make someone such as an opponent feel the forceful effect of (something): [T1] *The speaker pushed home his point, and his opponent admitted that he had been wrong. The soldiers were ordered to push the attack home with all their remaining strength.* → **press home** (1), **thrust home** (1)
**3 push home an/one's advantage** to make good use of a chance that is offered: *The owner seemed to be weakening about his price, so, pushing home our advantage, we mentioned again the faults in the house and offered a lower price.* → **press home** (2), **thrust home** (2)

**push in¹** *v adv* also *not fml* **shove in¹**
**1** to force (something or someone) inwards or inside something: [T1 + IN (*to*)] *The lid of the box had been pushed in by the weight of the books on top. I had to push my way in through the crowd. We can't push any more people in, the bus is full!* → **plung in¹**, **press in¹** (1), **thrust in¹**
***2** *not fml* to force one's way into something such as a group, esp. out of turn: [IØ] *Don't push in, wait in line like everyone else.*
***3** *not fml* to interrupt rudely: [IØ] *We were just having a peaceful conversation when my neighbour pushed in without being asked.*

**push in²** *v prep* also *not fml* **shove in²** → **fit into** (1), etc.
to force (things or people) into (something such as a container): [T1 + *in*] *He tried to push more clothes in the case, but there was not enough room. It's impossible to push any more people in this bus.*

**push into** *v prep* also *not fml* **shove into**
**1** to force (things or people) to enter (something such as a container): [T1 + *into*] *He tried to push more clothes into the case, but there was not enough room. It's impossible to push any more people into this train!* → **fit into** (1), etc.
***2** to persuade, urge, or force (someone) into (an action or doing something): [D1] *She was unwilling to try, and had to be pushed into it.* [V4a] *Some of the students had to be pushed into working for the examination.* → **thrust into** (2)

**push off** *v adv* also *not fml* **shove off**
**1** to force (something or someone) to leave (a place, often high) by pushing it or him/her: [T1 + OFF] *Did she fall off the cliff by accident, or was she pushed off?*
***2** to set sail in a small boat: [IØ (*usu. simple tenses*)] *When I give the command, everybody push off together!* —**push-off** *n* → **push out** (2)
***3** *sl* to leave; go away: [IØ (*often imper.*)] *What are you doing in this garden? Push off at once! Well, I must be pushing off now; it's getting late.* → **be off** (3), **bog off, bugger off, buzz off, clean out** (5), **clear off** (4), **clear out** (5), **fuck off** (2), **get off¹** (19), **get off with** (5), **get out** (7), **get out of** (6), **hop off** (2), **piss off** (1), **push along** (2), **sod off**
***4** *infml* to (cause to) start: [T1] *The year has been pushed off to a successful start by winning the new contract.* [IØ] *The curtain will rise in two minutes; it's time to push off.*

***push off on** *v adv prep* also *not fml* **shove off on** → **push on²** (2)
*infml* to force (something unwanted) onto (someone): [D1 (*to*)] *They've been trying to push all the unpleasant jobs off on (to) me again.*

***push on¹** *v adv* also *not fml* **shove on¹**
**1** *not fml* to continue; advance with determination; hurry: [IØ (*to, with*)] *Can the army push on to the next town? We must push on with the work if we are to finish it in time. We really must push on if we're to reach home before dark.* → **plough on** (2), **press forward** (3), **press on¹**, **push ahead** (2), **push forward** (3)
**2** *not fml* to persuade, urge, or force (someone) (to do something): [V3] *All her life she had been pushed on by her family to be a success as a singer.*

**push on/upon²** *v prep* also *not fml* **shove on²**
**1** to use force or weight on (something or someone): [IØ + *on/upon*] *You have to push on the handle to turn it, it's very stiff. The weight of the sleeping child's body was pushing on my arm and making it uncomfortable.* → **press on²** (1)
***2** *infml* to force (something unwanted) onto (someone): [D1 (*to*)] *They've been trying to push all the unpleasant jobs on (to) me again.* → **push off on, thrust on**

***push oneself** *v pron*
**1** to try to make people notice one's efforts; sell one's abilities: [IØ] *Professional acting is highly competitive work, and you really have to push yourself if you want to be a success.* → **push forward** (4), **thrust forward** (3)
**2** to make an effort; force oneself (to do something): [I3] *I shall really have to push myself to finish this book before the contract date.* [IØ] *I'd like the work done by Thursday, but don't push yourself if you're busy or tired. If you push yourself too hard you will make yourself ill.*

**push out** *v adv* also *not fml* **shove out**
**1** to make (something or someone) move outwards by pushing it: [T1 + OUT] *Use your thumbs to push out the pourer on the side of the box of washing powder. The cat wouldn't leave my kitchen, so I had to push it out.* → **press out**
***2** also *not fml* **shove off** *naut* to set sail in a small boat: [IØ (*usu. simple tenses*)] *When I give the command, everybody push out together!* → **push off** (2)

*__3__ *not fml* to ask (someone) to leave (a place): [T1 (*of*)] *I arranged to have a private conversation in the office with the new teacher, so do you mind if I push you out for a few minutes?*

*__4__ *infml* to dismiss (someone), often unfairly: [T1] *One of our best workers was pushed out to make way for the director's son.* → **thrust out** (3)

**5 push the boat out** *infml* to have a cheerful, often noisy, party: *After the concert, all the performers and many of their guests came to my home and we really pushed the boat out; the next morning, one of my neighbours complained about the noise.*

**push over** *v adv* also *not fml* **shove over**
to make (someone or something) fall over by pushing: [T1 + OVER] *That boy, running round the corner, nearly pushed the old lady over. The wall is leaning at such a dangerous angle that it wouldn't take much effort to push it over.*

**push past** *v adv; prep* → **PUSH BY**

**push round** *v adv; prep* → **press round**
to form a tight crowd near (someone); force one's weight on (someone): [IØ + ROUND/*round*] *Newspaper reporters pushed round (the Minister), urging him to give them a statement. I could feel the cat pushing round my legs.*

**push through** *v adv; prep* also *not fml* **shove through**

**1** to (cause to) pass through (something such as a group, mass or space): [T1 + THROUGH/*through*] *The hole is too small; I can't push my arm through (it).* [IØ + THROUGH/*through*] *The crowd in the station was so thick that I had to push through (a mass of people) to reach my friend. The early spring flowers are just pushing through (the soil).*

*__2__ *not fml* to help (someone or something) to pass (something such as a test, stage, or approving group): [T1b; D1] *We shall need all the votes we can get to push the new law through (Parliament). His sister was a great help in pushing the student through (his examination).*

**3 push one's way through** to force one's way through (something such as a crowd) by pushing: *The man got to the front in a most rude manner, by pushing his way through (the people).* → **elbow through, shoulder through, thrust through**

**push to** *v adv* also *not fml* **shove to** → **pull to**[1] etc.
to close (usu. a door) firmly: [T1 + TO] *Will you please push the door to, it's not quite shut.*

**push towards** *v prep* also *not fml* **shove towards**

**1** to make (usu. something) move nearer to (something or someone) by pushing it: [T1 + *towards*] *He pushed the money towards me across the table, but I refused to take it. An old man pushed his way towards the front of the crowd. He pushed the letter towards me, forcing me to read the address. We seem to have been pushing our bicycles towards the next town for more than an hour.* → **push at, thrust at** (2), **thrust towards** (1)

*__2__ to try to reach (a place) in spite of opposition: [T1 (*no pass.*)] *Our army is still pushing towards the next village, under heavy enemy gunfire.* → **thrust towards** (2)

*__3__ to aim in a determined way towards (a result): [T1 (*no pass.*)] *All our efforts are pushing towards a reorganization of the prison system.* → **press towards, thrust towards** (2)

**push up** *v adv*

**1** to force (something) to rise: [T1 + UP] *The strength of the growing plants has pushed up the stones in the path. If you can't ride your bicycle to the top of the hill, you'll have to push it up.*

*__2__ to force (something such as prices) to become higher: [T1] *Shops are no longer allowed to push up their prices whenever they want. This latest murder has pushed up the average to one a week.*

*__3__ *not fml* to advance forcefully, esp. in competition: [IØ (*behind*)] *Competition is so fierce in the labour market that there is always someone pushing up behind you.*

**4 push up the daisies** *infml* to be dead and buried: *I look after my health; I don't intend to be pushing up the daisies for a long time yet!*

**push upon** *v prep* → **PUSH ON**[2]

***put about** *v adv*

**1** *naut* (of a ship) to (cause to) change course so as to face the opposite direction: [IØ (*often simple tenses*)] *The ship put about to pick up the man who had fallen overboard. To sail forward against the wind, we had to put about.* [T1b (*often simple tenses*)] *If the wind changes, you'll have to put her about.* → **bring about** (2), etc.

**2** to spread (news, often bad or false): [T1 (*often continuous tenses*)] *Who's been putting about these stories concerning the government's secret intentions? It has been put about that several workers are to be dismissed.* → **go about**[1] (3), etc.

**3** esp. *ScotE* to trouble; worry (someone or oneself): [T1 (*usu. pass.*)] *Jim was greatly put about by the message. I am much put about by your recent behaviour. I hope I'm not putting you about by arriving unexpectedly.* → **put out** (15), etc.

**put above** *v prep*

**1** to place (something) in a position higher than (something): [X9 + *above*] *The notice was put above the door, and I didn't see it.* → **place above** (1), **set above** (1)

*__2__ to consider (something or someone) as being more important or worthy of attention than (something or someone else): [D1] *Mothers are well-known for putting the needs* *of the family above their own interests.* [V4b] *Getting out of debt must be put above buying anything new.* → **place before** (4), etc.

**put across**[1] *v adv*

**1** to place (something) in a position lying across something: [X9 + ACROSS] *It will be easier to cross the river when the builders have finished putting the new bridge across.*

***2** *not fml* to make (something such as an idea, or oneself) understood and well received (by someone): [T1 (*to*) (*usu. simple tenses*)] *Advertisements are intended to put across the best qualities of the product (to the public). How can I put such an unpopular message across (to the crowd)? The politician was able to put himself across (to the voters) as a suitable leader.* → **come across**[1] (2), etc.

***3** *not fml* to fulfil (something as an arrangement) successfully: [T1] *The director put the business deal across in record time.* → **go through**[1] (3), **put through**[1] (1), **railroad through, ram through, take through**[1] (2)

**put across**[2] *v prep*

**1** to place or move (something or someone) in/to a position across (something): [X9 + *across*] *We must put a new bridge across the river to take the increased traffic. If you do that again, I'll put you across my knee and beat you! The bigger boats will be able to put more people across the river.* → **go across**[2], etc., **pull over**[2] (1), etc.

**2** *infml* to cause acceptance of or belief in (something) by (someone), by deceit, esp. in the phrs. **put it/one/that across someone**: [D1] *I put one across Father this morning: made him think it was my birthday, and he'd forgotten! The woman in the market put it across me by selling me some bad eggs. That class will never succeed in putting anything across the new teacher, he's too experienced.* → **put over**[2] (2)

**put ahead** *v adv*

**1** to make (something) advance: [T1 (*by*)] *The warm weather has put the crops ahead by a month.* → **bring on** (3), etc.

**2** to move; change (something such as an event) to an earlier time or date: [T1] *We shall have to put the meeting ahead because of the holiday next week; can you all be here this Friday?* → **put off**[1] (4), etc.

**3** to move the hands of (a clock or watch) to a later time: [T1] *In spring we usually put the clocks ahead one hour, to take advantage of the summer daylight.* → **go back** (7), **put back** (8), **put forward** (6), **put on**[1] (8), **set ahead** (3), **set back** (5), **set forward** (6)

**put among** *v prep*

**1** to place (something or someone) in the middle of (a group): [X9 + *among*] *Let's put some white flowers among the blue ones. If you put the boy among all those tall children, he looks even shorter.* → **set among** (1)

**2** **put the cat among the pigeons** also **put the cat among the canaries** *not fml* to cause trouble, esp. by saying or doing something wrong, often without thinking: *The boy who missed class yesterday was not sick, but taking a holiday; when one of the other children said this and the teacher heard it, it really put the cat among the pigeons!* → **set among** (2)

**put apart** *v adv*

**1** to place (something or someone) separately: [X9 + APART (*from*)] *One chair was put apart from the others. In former times, people suffering from an infectious disease were put apart until they were better, to save infecting the rest of the village.* → **set apart** (1)

***2** to save (something such as money): [T1] *I have a little money put apart for a rainy day* (= a time when money will be needed). *I've put the whole weekend apart for house-hunting.* → **lay aside** (4), etc.

**put as** *v prep* → **place at** (2), **put at** (3), **set at** (4)
to guess that (something) is (usu. a number): [X9 + *as* (*usu. simple tenses*)] *I would put her time of birth as around 8.30 p.m. The size of the crowd has been put as over 10,000.*

**put aside** *v adv*

**1** to place (something) on one side, esp. for a short time: [X9 + ASIDE] *She put her sewing aside when the telephone rang.* → **lay aside** (1), etc.

***2** to discontinue (something such as work) esp. for a short time: [T1] *Tom put his new book aside for a year while he wrote some magazine articles and informative material.* → **lay aside** (2), etc.

***3** to cease (something such as a habit or feeling): [T1] *It's time to put our differences aside and work together for a common purpose. Putting aside her disappointment, she smiled and praised the winner.* → **lay aside** (3), etc.

***4** to save (usu. money or time): [T1 (*for*)] *I have a little money put aside for a rainy day* (= a time when money will be needed). *I've put aside the whole weekend for house-hunting.* → **lay aside** (4), etc.

***5** to save (a supply of goods) for a customer: [T1] *Would you like us to put the rest of the wool aside for you? Then you'll be sure to match the colour.* → **lay aside** (5), etc.

***6** to choose not to notice or consider (something): [T1] *Putting aside the fact that the man has been in prison, he would seem to be a suitable worker for the job.* → **put by** (6), **set aside** (6)

**put at** *v prep*

**1** to place (something) in position in front of (usu. a place): [X9 + *at*] *The worshippers put their gifts at the feet of the god. The natives put the food at the entrance to the cave.* → **lay at** (1), **lay before** (1), **place at** (1), **place before** (1), **put before** (1), **set at** (1), **set before** (1)

**2** to make (usu. a horse) jump (something such as a fence): [X9 + *at* (*often simple tenses*)] *She put her horse at the first jump, but* *it refused, and threw her to the ground.* → **set at** (2)

**3** to guess (something) to be (an amount, number, etc.): [X9 + *at* (*simple tenses*)] *I put her age at 33. His income can probably be put at £8,000 a year.* → **place at** (2), **put as, set as** (4)

**4 put someone at his/her ease** to make someone feel comfortable, not nervous: *His behaviour did nothing to put me at my ease. Do your best.to put the new students at their ease; show them the classrooms and the library, introduce them to helpful people, and warn them how to avoid trouble, so that they won't feel anxious on their first day of classes.* → **place at** (3), **set at** (7).

**5 put something at a premium** to place a high value on something such as a quality: [*often pass.*] *Hard work and honesty are put at a premium in this school; brains without character and willingness are worthless.* → **place at** (4), **place on** (8), **put on² (35), set at (12)**

**put away** *v adv*

**1** to store (something), as in a box or space: [X9 + AWAY] *Please put your toys away before you go to bed. It's going to rain: we'd better put away our things and go indoors. Will you put the car away while I see to the cases?* → **pack away** (1), **tuck away** (1)

***2** *not fml* to eat a lot of (food); drink a lot of (drink): [T1] *You'd be surprised at the amount that boy can put away in a single day.* → **pack away** (2), **put down** (6), **tuck away** (2)

***3** to save (usu. money): [T1] *I have a little money put away for a rainy day* (= a time when money will be needed). → **lay aside** (4), etc.

***4** to save (a supply of goods) for a customer: [T1] *Would you like me to put the rest of the red wool away for you? Then you can buy it a little at a time and be sure to match the colour.* → **lay aside** (5), etc.

***5** to cease to consider (something): [T1] *It's time to put away those foolish ideas and become serious. The loss of our money caused us to put away our holiday plans until we had saved the cost again.* → **put off¹ (9)**

***6** *euph* to place (someone) in prison or a hospital for mad people: [T1] *The judge put the criminal away for ten years, where he could do no harm. You can get put away for saying things like that: people will think you're mad!* → **lock away** (2), **lock up** (2), **shut away, shut up** (2)

***7** *euph* to kill (an animal), usu. out of mercy: [T1 (*usu. simple tenses*)] *The dear old dog got so old and ill that it was kinder to put him away than to let him suffer.* → **put down** (11), **put out of** (6), **put to²** (27)

***8** *bibl* to end one's marriage with (one's wife or husband): [T1 (*usu. simple tenses*)] *"Then Joseph, her husband, being a just man, and not willing to make her a public example, was minded to put her away."* (The Bible)

**put back** *v adv*

**1** to move (something) in a backward direc tion: [X9 + BACK] *Put your collar back, it' sticking out. Putting back some loose hairs she put on her hat. Why don't you put you chair back a little to get a better view? Min that dog when he puts his ears back, it mean he's angry.* → **lay back, put forward** (1), **se back** (1), **set forward** (1)

**2** to return; replace (usu. something): [X9 BACK] *When I returned from the police statio the jewels had been put back in their box; th thieves must have become nervous. Put th book back where you found it when you hav finished reading it. I had just put the telepho receiver back when the bell rang again. Wh he returned to his former firm after the war, was put back in his old department, but at higher rank.* → **be back** (3), **bring back** (1), **g back** (5), **place back, put down** (1), **send bac take back** (1)

***3** to regain (weight or size): [T1] *You'll so put back all the weight that you lost if you sta eating cakes again. It didn't take long to p back all those unwanted inches.* → **put on¹ ( take off¹ (12)**

***4** (of a boat or ship) to return on its cours [IØ] *The storm became so fierce that we had put back into the harbour at the very beginni of our voyage.* → **turn back** (3)

***5** to cost (someone) (an amount): [D1 (*si ple tenses*)] *Our holiday put us back $1,0* → **knock back** (4), **set back** (6)

***6** to delay the advance of (something): [ (*by*) (*usu. simple tenses*)] *The cost of the w has put back national development by years. The fire in the factory put back prod tion by several weeks.* → **bring on** (3), etc.

***7** to delay (something such as an event) ti later time or date: [T1] *The election will put back to July to avoid the June holid The concert had to be put back to the foll ing week because one of the singers hurt throat.* → **put off¹** (4), etc.

***8** to move the hands of (a clock or watch an earlier time: [T1] *In the autumn we us ly put the clocks back one hour. My watch fast so I put it back three minutes.* → **go b** (7), **put ahead** (3), **put forward** (6), **put on¹** (8), **ahead** (3), **set back** (5), **set forward** (6)

***9** *AmE* to move (a student) to a lower c than would be expected: [T1 (*usu. pa Jane failed her examinations and was put b a whole year.*

**10 put the clock back** *not fml* to follow fashioned ideas; try to return to the p [*often simple tenses*] *Many employers w like to put the clock back to the good old when workers were under their control, they are too late—the world has chan* → **set back** (7), **turn back** (5)

**put before** *v prep*

**1** to place (something) in position in fro (something or someone): [X9 + *before*] *tering the temple, the worshippers put their gifts before the gods.* → **put at** (1), etc.

*2 to send (something such as an idea) for consideration or approval by (someone or a group in power); bring (something) to the notice or attention of (someone): [D1 (*often pass.*)] *Your suggestion will be put before the board of directors at their next meeting.* → **bring before** (2), **come before** (3), **go before**[2] (4), **lay before** (2), **place before** (2), **send before** (2), **set before** (2), **take before** (2)

*3 to offer (a choice or choices) to (someone): [D1] *The government party has put two choices before the voters: to control wages and prices, or to suffer further increases in the cost of living.* → **set before** (3)

*4 to consider (something or someone) more important or worthy of attention than (something or someone else): [D1] *Mothers are well-known for putting the needs of the family before their own interests. Putting yourself before anyone else is very selfish.* [V4a] *Getting out of debt must be put before buying anything new.* → **come before** (5), **lie before** (3), **place above** (2), **place before** (3), **put above** (2), **set above** (2), **set before** (4)

**5 put the cart before the horse** *not fml* to think or do things in the wrong order: *Building a railway line to a town that does not yet exist is putting the cart before the horse. You're putting the cart before the horse if you try to write a language before you have learned to speak it.*

**6 put one foot before/in front of the other** to be able to walk: [*simple tenses + can, could, usu. neg.*] *She was so tired that she could hardly put one foot before the other.* → **place before** (4), **set before** (5)

**put behind**[1] *v adv* → **bring on**[1] (3), etc.
to delay the advance of (something): [T1b (*by*)] *The cold weather has put the crops behind by a month.*

**put behind**[2] *v prep*
**1** to place (something or someone) in a position at the back of (something or someone): [X9 + *behind*] *I'll put the letter behind the clock, and then I shan't forget it. Put the taller children behind the shorter ones so that they can all be seen in the photograph.* → **be behind**[2] (1), **keep behind** (1), **place behind** (1)
**2 put someone behind bars** *not fml* to imprison someone: *People who kill others should be put behind bars for the rest of their lives.* → **be behind**[2] (4), **place behind** (3)
**3 put something behind one** *not fml* also *not fml* **shove behind** to regard something as being in the past, not important any more; be able to forget something, usu. bad: *It was disappointing to fail the examination, but you've put that behind you now and can make a fresh start. The arguments of the past must be put behind us.*

**put by** *v adv*
**1** to put (something) on one side, esp. for a short time: [X9 + BY] *She was reading a book, but put it by when the telephone rang.* → **lay aside** (1), etc.

*2 to discontinue (something such as work) for a time: [T1b] *Tom put his new book by for a year while he wrote some magazine articles and informative material.* → **lay aside** (2), etc.

*3 to cease (something such as a habit): [T1b] *It's time to put our differences by and work together for a common purpose.* → **lay aside** (3), etc.

*4 to save (usu. money): [T1b] *I have a little money put by for a rainy day* (= a time when money will be needed). → **lay aside** (4), etc.

*5 to save (a supply of goods) for a customer: [T1b] *The shop will put the wool by for you; then you can buy it a little at a time, to be sure to match the colour.* → **lay aside** (5), etc.

*6 to choose not to notice or consider; refuse to accept; avoid (something): [T1b] *I felt that his question was dangerous, so I put it by and began to speak of other things.* → **put aside** (6), **set aside** (6)

**put down** *v adv*
**1** to put (something) in position on a floor or surface: [X9 + DOWN (*on*)] *The dinner guest put down his knife and fork with a look of complete satisfaction. He put his heavy bag down on the ground and rested for a few minutes. Just as I put the telephone receiver down, the doorbell rang.* → **lay down** (1), **place down, put back** (2), **set down** (1), **stick down** (2)
**2** to lower (something such as part of the body): [X9 + DOWN] *The rest of you can put your hands down now, I can't answer any more questions. If you feel faint, it often helps to put your head down between your knees.*
**3** (of a plane, etc.) to (cause to) land: [X9 + DOWN] *The pilot was able to put the damaged plane down safely in a field.* [L9 + DOWN] *That looks like a good place to put down.* → **set down** (3)
**4** to allow (someone) to leave a vehicle: [X9 + DOWN] *Can you put me down at the next corner, please?* → **alight from**, etc., **set down** (4)
**5** to cease (something such as work); leave (someone): [X9 + DOWN] *Put down whatever you're doing and join the party! It's unkind to take someone up and then put him down whenever you wish, without considering his feelings.*

*6 *not fml* to eat a lot of (food); drink a lot of (drink): [T1] *You'd be surprised at the amount that boy can put down in a single day.* → **pack away** (2), **put away** (2), **tuck away** (2)

*7 to record (something) in writing: [T1] *Make sure that you put down every word she says.* → **write down** (1), etc.

*8 to charge (goods bought) (to an account): [T1 (*to*)] *I'll take three boxes please; would you deliver them and put them down (to my account)?* → **chalk up** (2), etc.

*9 to pay part of the price for (something), with a promise to pay the rest, usu. over a period of time: [T1] *You can buy this house* *by putting 10% down and paying the rest over twenty-five years, at interest.* → **pay down** (2)

*__10__ to store a supply of (usu. wine or eggs) for the future: [T1] *When his grandson was born, the old lord put down a case of best wine for the boy's twenty-first birthday. I have put down over 100 eggs this winter, so as to have plenty at the cheap price, for cooking.* —**put-down** *adj* → **lay down** (5)

*__11__ *BrE* to kill (an animal), usu. out of mercy: [T1 (*often pass.*)] *The dear old dog got so old and ill that it was kinder to have him put down than to let him go on suffering.* → **put away** (7), **put out of** (6), **put to²** (27)

*__12__ to control; defeat; stop (someone or something, esp. in opposition); make (someone) silent: [T1 (*often pass.*)] *The people's attempt to win power was quickly put down, and the government regained control. The police are attempting to put down violent crime in the city. We should be able to put the opposing team down in the first half of the game. Tired of being put down by cruel rulers, the citizens planned to defeat them by surprise. Any writer who opposes the government will be put down.*

*__13__ *not fml* to express disapproval or a poor opinion of (something or someone): [T1] *Tom's latest book has been severely put down in the newspaper reports. You shouldn't put anyone down for his religious views.*

*__14__ *infml* to make (someone) feel humble or hurt: [T1] *He made an unkind remark, intended to put her down; but she refused to allow her spirits to be defeated.* —**put-down** *n*

*__15__ to change the use of (land) (to another crop): [T1 (*in, to, under, with*)] *This year I intend to put the rose border down to vegetables.* → **lay down** (6), **lay off¹** (10)

**16 put one's foot down: a** *not fml* to press on the speed control in a car, so as to go faster: *If you really put your foot down we can get home before the shops close.* **b** *not fml* to make a strong decision; act firmly: *I shall have to put my foot down and stop this nonsense. The children were allowed to do as they liked until Father put his foot down and made them obey him.*

**17 put down (new) roots** *not fml* to settle in a (new) place: *It's good to put down roots at last; we don't intend to move from here. She has moved so often that she finds no difficulty in putting down new roots, making friends and finding a place in the society.* → **pull up** (9)

**18 put down one's tools** *not fml* to stop working because of disagreement: *The union leaders have asked workers in all the car factories to put down their tools, starting tomorrow, until an agreement is reached.* → **bring out** (7), etc.

*__put down as__ *v adv prep*

**1** to record (something or someone) as (being or doing something): [T1] *You can put the telephone bill down as a business cost. I see that you're put down as a former police officer; why do you want this job? I'm sorry, I'd put you down as belonging to the other group.* → **set down as** (1)

**2** to consider (usu. someone) to be (something such as a kind of person): [X1 (*usu. simple tenses*)] *As the man had rough hands, I put him down as a farm worker.* [X7 (*usu. simple tenses*)] *I put her rudeness down as accidental. Since she did not answer, I put her down as fearful and nervous.* → **be down as, put down for** (1), **set down as** (2), **set down for** (2), **write down as**

*__put down for__ *v adv prep*

**1** to regard (someone) as being (a certain kind of person): [X1 (*usu. simple tenses*)] *The man looked so uneasy that I put him down for a criminal. As the man had rough hands, I put him down for a farm worker.* → **put down as** (2), etc.

**2** to write the name of (someone) as willing to give (an amount of money): [D1] *I have put you down for £5, is that all right?*

**3** to put (someone's name) on a waiting list for (something such as a race or school): [D1] *Families have to put their sons down for this famous old school as soon as they are born. Will you put me down for a tennis court as soon as one is free? I've put my name down for a ticket, but I don't know if I'll get one.* [T1] *You have to put down for government housing well in advance.* → **enter for**, etc.

*__put down to__ *v adv prep*

**1** to charge (goods bought) to (someone's account): [T1] *I'll take three; will you please deliver them and put them down to my account?*

**2** to consider (something) to be the result of (something): [D1 (*usu. simple tenses*)] *I put his bad temper down to his recent illness. Jim puts his success down to hard work.* → **attribute to** (1), etc.

**put forth** *v adv*

**1** *old use* to stretch (something) out: [X9 + FORTH] *The soldier put forth his hand, asking for mercy, but his enemy cut it off.* → **put out** (1), etc.

*__2__ *old use* (of a plant) to send out (new growth): [T1] *The bush put forth new branches after being cut. In spring the trees put forth new leaves.* → **put out** (4), **send forth** (2), **send out** (4)

*__3__ *fml* to use; show; bring (something such as strength) into action: [T1] *Putting forth great effort, he uprooted the tree.* → **put out** (

*__4__ *old use* to begin a voyage: [IØ] *And when the storm had passed, three tall ships put forth to cross the whole ocean.* → **put off¹** (5), **put out** (5)

*__5__ *AmE fml* to state; offer (something such as a plan): [T1] *The heads of government of many countries have put forth a better system for preventing world war.* → **put forward** (3), **put out** (7), **set forward** (3)

*6 *old use* to bring out (something printed) onto public view and sale: [T1] *The printers put forth three numbers of the magazine in its first year.* → **put out** (9), **send forth** (2)

**put forward** *v adv*

1 to move (something) into a position further in front: [X9 + FORWARD] *Why don't you put your chair forward, to get a better view? If you put your hair forward, it would suit your face better.* → **lay back, put back** (1), **set back** (1), **set forward** (1)

*2 to offer; suggest (something such as an idea) for consideration: [T1 (*often pass.*)] *A suitable answer has already been put forward by the chairman. The heads of government of many countries have put forward a better system for preventing world war.* → **put forth** (5), **put out** (9), **set forth** (2), **set forward** (3), **set out** (8)

*3 to offer; suggest (someone or oneself), usu. for a position: [T1 (*often pass.*)] *Several people have been put forward for the chairmanship. I've put your name forward as the best man for the job.* → **go forward** (5), **send forward** (2)

*4 to make (something) advance: [T1 (*by*)] *The warm weather has put the crops forward by a month.* → **bring on** (3), etc.

*5 to move; change (something such as an event) to an earlier time or date: [T1] *We shall have to put the meeting forward because of the holiday next week; can you all be here this Friday?* → **put off** (4)

*6 to move the hands of (a clock or watch) to a later time: [T1] *In spring, we usually put the clocks forward one hour, to take advantage of the summer daylight. My watch was slow so I put it forward three minutes.* → **go back** (7), **put ahead** (3), **put back** (8), **put on**[1] (8), **set ahead** (3), **set back** (5), **set forward** (6)

7 **put one's best foot forward** *not fml* to make an effort to move or act quickly: *Put your best foot forward and you'll soon be home. If you put your best foot forward, you can finish the work on time.*

**ut in**[1] *v adv*

1 to place (something, things, or people) inside something: [X9 + IN] *Put your hand in and see what's in the box. The room is crowded already; I hope you're not going to try to put any more furniture in. We can't put any more people in, the bus is full. I'll just put my head in and see if there's anyone here that I know.* → **fit in**[1] (1), **get in**[1] (1), **go in**[1] (2), **poke in**[1] (1), **stick in**[1] (1)

2 to plant (a crop) in the ground: [X9 + IN] *You ought to put potatoes in there, they will help to break up the heavy soil.*

3 to include; add (something such as in writing): [X9 + IN] *At the last moment, Tom decided to put in a new character, to make the story seem more likely. Don't forget to put in your full name and address. In his letters, he always puts in some amusing remarks about his neighbours' activities. There is no room to put in a single additional word.* [T5 + IN] *Have you put in that you were away that day?* [T6 + IN] *I forgot to put in where I went.* → **throw in**[1] (6), **toss in**[1] (4), **write in** (1)

*4 to interrupt; add (words) to a conversation: [IØ (*simple tenses, usu. past*)] *"But wait," Jane put in, "I haven't finished my story."* [T1] May *I put in a word or two?* → **chuck in** (4), **chuck out** (6), **fling in**[1] (4), **fling off** (7), **fling out** (7), **throw in**[1] (4), **throw off**[1] (8), **throw out** (7), **toss in**[1] (3), **toss off** (2), **toss out** (6)

*5 (of a ship or boat) to arrive (at a port): [IØ (*at, to*)] *The ship has just put in (to the harbour) for repairs. This boat puts in at several different places along the river.* → **put in for** (1), **put into** (7)

*6 to add; offer one's share of (money), as to a collection: [T1 (*to*)] *Between them, the girls have put in £2, and only need another £1.* → **put into** (9)

*7 to perform (work); use (effort): [T1 (*on, to*)] *I have put in over three years' work on this book. It's worth putting in a lot of effort and study, in order to improve your English.* → **put into** (10)

*8 to spend (time): [T1] *I put in two hours on my English studies every day. How do you put in your time on holiday? We have an hour and a half to put in before the plane leaves.*

*9 to place (someone or something) in a building or room, for a purpose such as work: [T1] *The new owners put a man in to look after the building at night. We had a new water heater put in last week, and now we shall have to put in some new window glass. How much does it cost to put in central heating?*

*10 to offer (a request, claim, etc.): [T1 (*for*)] *I'll put in a claim for damages, if you will put in your special request.* → **put in for** (2)

*11 to offer; enter (oneself or someone) (for an examination, reward, etc.): [T1 (*for*) (*often simple tenses*)] *Have you put yourself in for the competition? How many of your runners are you putting in (for the race)? The examination is difficult, and I refuse to put in any student who is not ready.* → **enter for**, etc.

*12 to elect (someone or a party): [T1] *We only need three more votes to put our man in. Put our party in and we will make this country fit to live in.* → **get in**[1] (13), etc.

*13 *law* to offer; enter (a plea, defence, etc.): [T1] *I have been advised to put in a plea of guilty. What defence are your lawyers putting in?*

*14 to strike (a blow): [T1] *The experienced fighter put in a heavy blow which won the match.*

*15 (in cricket and other sports) **a** to send (a player) to take his/her turn on the field of play: [T1] *At this difficult stage of the game, the captain would be wise to put in his most experienced player.* **b** (of the captain of a cricket team who has won the right to say which team will play first) to make (the opposing team) take the first turn to hit the ball: [T1] *The captain decided to put the opposing team in first, so that his team would know how many runs to make to defeat them.* → **go in**[1] (5), etc.

**16 put in an appearance: a** *law* to appear in court, so as not to lose a case by not appearing: *If your opponent in this case does not put in an appearance, you will win.* **b** *not fml* to allow oneself to be seen at an occasion where one is expected: *I don't really want to go to the party, but I'd better put in an appearance, if only for a short time, or my students will be disappointed.*

**17 put the boot in: a** *sl* to kick (someone) roughly, as in a fight: *Someone's been putting the boot in: see those marks on his head and on his back?* **b** to treat someone badly or unkindly when he is already defeated: *You've won your argument, now leave him alone; there's no need to put the boot in when he's admitted defeat.*

**18 put one's oar in** *not fml* also *not fml* **shove in**[1] to offer unwanted help: *Oh dear, here comes Aunt Mabel to put her oar in as usual; let's go before she starts telling us what to do.*

**put in**[2] *v prep*

**1** to place (something or someone) in position inside (something such as a container): [X9 + *in*] *Put the vegetables in the pan with very little water and heat quickly. I wish to put some money in this bank account. We are having electricity put in the house. Put the eggs gently in the basket. The object of the game is to put the ball in the hole. Putting his hands in his pockets, he whistled a tune. Put your voting paper in the black box. Don't try to put any more furniture in this room. You've put too much milk in my tea. She put the baby in my arms and ran away. We ought to put the children in the back seat, it's safer.* → **fit into** (1), etc.

**2** to give (someone or something) to (the care of someone): [X9 + *in*] *Why has my daughter been put in this class? The boy was put in the care of his aunt after his parents were killed in the accident. Can I put my precious paintings in your safe keeping while I'm away? I put myself in your hands; I am completely at your mercy.* → **place in** (2), **put into** (4)

**3** to give (usu. someone) a position among (the competitors) as a result of competition: [X9 + *in* (*often pass.*)] *After all his high hopes of winning the photography competition, Jim wasn't even put in the first three!* → **place behind** (2), **place in** (3), **put into** (5).

*__4__ to cause (someone) to be in (a certain position, usu. bad), as morally, socially, or politically: [D1] *What an awkward position I'm now put in—if I say yes, I'm too demanding; if I say no, I'm too proud— I can't win! You put me in an impossible position with your behaviour at the party. The opposition member's request for an enquiry has put the government in a difficult position, especially just before the election.* → **place in** (4), **put into** (6)

*__5__ to appoint (someone) to (a position of responsibility): [D1] *The captain hopes to be put in command of a bigger ship. Who has been put in charge during the director's absence?* → **place in** (5)

*__6__ to arrange (things or people) in (a certain order, position, etc.): [D1] *The teacher put the children in order of height. These verbs are put in alphabetical order. Let's put the chairs in a circle, it makes talking so much easier.* → **place in** (6)

*__7__ to place (one's money) in (something such as a business) in the hope of gain: [D1] *People with small savings are advised not to put their money in companies where there is a high risk.* → **put into** (9)

*__8__ to express (a thought) in (language or a language): [D1 (*usu. simple tenses*)] *We put this idea differently in English. Try to put your ideas in simpler wording.* → **put into** (8)

*__9__ to give (effort) to (something): [D1] *If you put more effort in your work, you'd see better results. I've put a lot of work in this piece of music, so I'd like to hear you sing it well.* → **put into** (10)

**10 put someone in awe (of)** to make (someone) have deep respect or fear (of something or someone): *A service of worship should put you in awe of God's greatness.*

**11 put one's confidence/faith/trust in** to trust; depend on (someone, something, or doing something): *It's not safe to put too much confidence in your ability to pass the examination without working hard. We all put our faith in the team to win this important game. Put your trust in the Lord, and all will be well.* → **pin on**[2] (4), etc.

**12 put someone in contact/touch with** to enable someone to meet or send messages to (usu. someone): *I can put you in touch with a very good eye doctor, if you would like him to examine you. This lady claims to be able to put you in contact with your dead relatives.* → **get in**[2] (3), **keep in** (6), **lose with** (1), **remain in**[2] (3), **stay in**[2] (3)

**13 put all one's eggs in one basket** *not fml* to place all one's money on one risk; risk everything on a single chance: *Insurance firms generally spread a large risk among several companies, so that they don't put all their eggs in one basket.* → **have in**[2] (1), **place in** (8)

**14 put the fear of God in someone** *not fml* to make someone greatly afraid: *I will not have this nonsense from the workers; go out there and put the fear of God in them, so that they obey orders. The new teacher put the fear of God in the class on his very first day, and had no trouble with the children from then on.* → **put into** (13), **put up**[2] (2)

**15 put one's foot in it** *infml* to cause trouble

usu. accidentally, as by making a social mistake, being careless with words or actions: *Jane didn't know you were still in town at the time of her party: now you've put your foot in it! Every time she opens her mouth she puts her foot in it!*

**16 put one's (own) house in order** *not fml* to arrange one's affairs properly, especially before suggesting improvements to others: *The chairman has declared that the department must put its house in order before he will allow any additional money to be spent on machinery and paper.* → **set in² (8)**

**17 put something in jeopardy** to threaten the safety of something; cause something to be at risk: *Our chances of winning are being put in jeopardy by frequent illness among the team. The miners' refusal to work has put the nation's supply of coal in jeopardy.* → **place in** (9)

**18 put someone in mind of** to cause someone to remember (something or someone): [*usu. simple tenses*] *That tune always puts me in mind of a fine summer day. His voice put her in mind of her father.* → **set in² (9)**

**19 put something in motion** to start something: *It may be a long time before you hear the answer to your request, but at least we have put the machinery in motion, and it will go through all the usual stages.* → **set in² (10)**

**20 put something in a nutshell** *not fml* to express an idea very clearly and in a few words: [*usu. simple tenses*] *Interest rates are high, prices are still rising, there is widespread unemployment: to put it in a nutshell, the country is in a very bad state.*

**21 put something in order** to arrange something neatly: *Help me to put the dining room in order before our guests arrive. I hope you have all put your papers in order before we start the meeting. When the doctor gave him six months to live, the first thing he did was to put his affairs in order, so as not to cause trouble for his relatives.* → **be in² (25a)**, etc., **be out of (19a)**, **keep in** (11), **set in² (11)**

**22 put someone in the picture** *not fml* to give someone information about something or someone in particular; explain the facts to someone: [*often simple tenses*] *I don't understand what's going on; will someone please put me in the picture?* → **be in² (26)**, **be out of (20)**

**23 put someone in his/her (proper) place** to make someone remember, and behave according to, his/her humble position: [*often simple tenses*] *If the children behave badly while they're staying with you, don't be afraid to put them in their (proper) place.* → **keep in** (13)

**24 put oneself in someone else's place/position/shoes** *not fml* to imagine how someone feels; sympathize with someone: *You have to try to put yourself in the director's shoes before you can know how difficult his job is. Put yourself in my place, and then perhaps you'll stop complaining.* → **place in** (10), **put into** (19)

**25 put someone/something in the shade** *not fml* to perform very much better than someone or something else, making their results seem less worthy: *We thought the first singer was very good, but the second one put her in the shade. Tom's earlier books were very popular, but have been put in the shade by his latest story, which is so much better.*

**26 put a sock in it** *infml* to stop doing something, as being noisy or annoying: [*usu. imper.*] *I've heard enough of your silly jokes, put a sock in it!*

**27 put a spanner in the works** esp. *BrE infml* to spoil something: *Everything was going nicely with our plan, until my uncle refused to give us his money and put a spanner in the works.* → **throw in² (4)**, **throw into (9)**

**28 put a spoke in someone's wheel** *not fml* to make matters difficult for someone, often when doing something wrong: *The children were about to steal the paints when the arrival of the teacher put a spoke in their wheel.*

**29 put that in one's pipe and smoke it** *infml* to be forced to face unpleasant facts: [*usu. imper., or with can*] *We refuse to go, so you can put that in your pipe and smoke it.*

**30 put words in inverted commas** esp. *BrE* to place speech marks round a certain word or words to show that it is spoken, or special in some other way: [*often simple tenses*] *When you are writing your story, put all conversation in inverted commas. Many public speakers are so nervous of using informal expressions that even when they are speaking, you can hear that they have put them in inverted commas.* → **place in** (11), **set in² (12)**

**31 put someone/oneself in the wrong** to make someone or oneself seem to be wrong; give or take the blame for something: *Your mother put herself in the wrong with that unfortunate remark, and she should have the grace to say she's sorry. Why are you always trying to put me in the wrong? It's not my fault.* → **be in²** (30)

***put in for** *v adv prep*

**1** (of a ship or boat) to enter (a port) for (a purpose): [IØ (*for*)] *The ship has just put in for repairs.* → **put in¹** (5), **put into** (7)

**2** to offer (a request, claim, etc.) for (something): [T1 (*for*)] *I want to put in a claim for damages.* → **put in¹** (10)

**3** *not fml* to offer; enter (someone or oneself) for (an examination, reward, etc): [T1 (*for*)] *Have you put yourself in for the competition? I will not put any student in for the examination until he is ready.* → **enter for**, etc.

**4** to make a formal request for (something): [T1] *The workers are putting in for yet another pay rise. A surprising number of people have put in for the chairman's job.* → **be in for** (3), **pony up for**

**5 put a good word in for someone** *not fml* to speak in someone's favour or support: *You* *should get the job all right: I've put in a good word for you with the director.*

**put inside** *v adv*

**1** to place (usu. something) within something such as a container or building: [X9 + INSIDE] *It's raining, we'd better put the chairs inside. Put your hand inside and see if you can feel the rough place.*

***2** *infml* to put (someone) in prison: [T1b] *Criminals like that should be put inside for many years.*

**put into** *v prep*

**1** to place (something or someone) in position inside (something such as a container or room): [X9 + *into*] *Put the vegetables into the pan with very little water, and heat quickly. I wish to put some money into my account. The object of the game is to put the ball into the hole. Someone's put poison into my drink! He killed himself by putting a bullet into his brain. We are having electricity put into the house. I had just put my mother into the train when the whistle blew.* → **fit into** (1), etc.

**2** to add; give (something such as a quality) to (something or someone): [X9 + *into*] *I'm glad she's coming, she'll put life into this dull party. His first small success put new heart into him.*

**3** to clothe (someone such as a child) in (a type of clothing, bedding, etc.): [X9 + *into*] *Isn't it time that boy was put into long trousers? I'll help you to put the children into their night clothes. We'll soon put you into a nice warm bed.*

**4** to give (someone or something) to (the care of someone): [X9 + *into*] *Why has my daughter been put into this class? The boy was put into the care of his aunt after his parents were killed in the accident. Can I put my precious paintings into your safe keeping while I'm away? I put myself into your hands; I am completely at your mercy.* → **place in** (2), **put in**[2] (2)

**5** to give (usu. someone) a position among (the competitors) as a result of competition: [X9 + *into* (*often pass.*)] *After all his high hopes of winning the photography competition, Jim wasn't even put into the first three!* → **place behind** (2), **place in** (3), **put in**[2] (3)

***6** to cause (someone) to be in (a certain position, usu. bad), as morally, socially, or politically: [D1] *What an awkward position I'm now put into—if I say yes, I'm too demanding; if I say no, I'm too proud—either way I lose! You put me into an impossible position with your behaviour at the party. The opposition member's demand for an enquiry has put the government into a difficult position, especially just before the election.* → **place in** (4), **put in**[2] (4)

***7** *naut* (of a ship or boat) to arrive and stay at (a place such as a port): [T1 (*no pass.*)] *The ship has just put into the harbour for repairs.* → **put in**[1] (5), **put in for** (1)

***8** to express (a thought) in (words); translate (something) into (a language): [D1 (*usu. simple tenses*)] *Try to put your ideas into simpler sentences. This poem is difficult to put into English; its thoughts belong to the original language.* → **put in**[2] (8)

***9** to place (one's money) in (something such as a business): [D1] *People with small savings are advised to put their money into companies offering a low rate of interest but little risk. You need only put a few coins into the collection.* → **put in**[2] (7)

***10** to give (time or effort) to (something): [D1] *If you put more effort into your work, you'd see better results. I've put many hours of hard work and study into this piece of music, so I'd like to hear you sing it well.* → **put in**[2] (9)

**11 put something into action/effect/execution/practice** to perform; fulfil something planned or threatened: *It's time that I put my intentions of hard work into action. The new law will be put into effect next Monday. These old rules are rarely put into practice.*

**12 put one's back/oneself into** *not fml* to work hard at (something): *He made a success of the part by really putting himself into it. I shall have to put my back into finishing this writing on time.*

**13 put the fear of God into someone** *not fml* to make someone greatly afraid: *I will not have this nonsense from the workers; go out there and put the fear of God into them, so that they obey orders. The new teacher put the fear of God into the class on his very first day, and had no trouble with the children from then on.* → **put in**[2] (14), **put up**[2] (2)

**14 put something into force** to cause (something such as a law) to be active, have to be obeyed: *The new controls will be put into force next month.* → **be in**[2] (13), **bring into** (5), **come into** (7)

**15 put one's hand into one's pocket** *not fml* to pay for something: *I seem to have done nothing but put my hand into my pocket since the children went back to school.*

**16 put (one's) heart and soul into** *not fml* to enjoy (something such as an activity) so much that one works hard at it: *Every singer was putting her heart and soul into the music, and the effect was wonderful.*

**17 put an idea/notion/thought into someone's head** *not fml* to make someone think of something: *Whatever put that strange idea into your head? Reading the book put many new thoughts into my head.*

**18 put ideas into someone's head** *not fml* to give someone a falsely high opinion of himself/herself or his/her abilities: *Robert didn't become a serious painter until that fool of a teacher put ideas into his head.*

**19 put oneself into someone else's place/position/shoes** *not fml* to imagine how someo feels; sympathize with someone: [*often simple tenses*] *You have to try to put yourself into the director's shoes before you can know how difficult his job is. Put yourself into my position, and then perhaps you'll stop complaining.* → **place in** (10), **put in²** (24)

**20 put something into perspective** to gain a properly balanced view of something: [*often simple tenses*] *I know the weather seems bad, but do put it into perspective: we had an unusually fine summer. Putting our losses this year into perspective, I should say that they were more than balanced by our gains.*

**21 put someone/a party into power** to elect someone or a political party or otherwise give them control of a country: [*often simple tenses*] *The general was put into power by military force. I wonder which party will be put into power at the next election?* → **get in¹** (13), etc.

**22 put something into words** to express something such as a feeling using language: [*usu. simple tenses*] *My love for you is hard to put into words.*

**23 put words into someone's mouth** *not fml* to make statements that one claims are the opinions of someone else with whom one is speaking: *I never mentioned going away for a holiday: don't put words into my mouth!*

**put off¹** *v adv*

**1** *old use* to remove (clothing): [X9 + OFF] *Please put off your shoes before entering this holy building.* → **take off¹** (2), etc.

**2** to allow (someone) to leave a vehicle: [X9 + OFF (*at*)] *Would you please put me off at the railway station? I don't know which stop that is. If you boys don't behave yourselves, I'll have you put off.* → **alight from,** etc., **get off¹** (3), **get off with** (1), **get on¹** (3), **get out** (3), **get out of** (3), **let off¹** (1), **put down** (4), **set down** (4)

**3** esp. *BrE* to disconnect (electricity or other power); stop (an electric machine) working: [X9 + OFF] *Please put off all the lights as you leave the building.* → **be off¹** (1), **go off¹** (4), **put on¹** (3), etc., **put out** (13), **shut off** (1), **snap off** (2), **switch off** (1), **switch out, turn off¹** (3), **turn out** (1)

***4** to delay (something such as an event or doing something) till a later time or date: [T1 (*till, to, until*)] *Tonight's concert will be put off till next week, as one of the singers has hurt her throat. Never put off till tomorrow what you can do today.* [T4 (*till, to, until*)] *Don't put off making the arrangements until the last minute.* —**put-off** *n* → **bring forward** (4), **carry over** (2), **call off** (2), **hold over¹**, **lay over¹** (2), **leave over** (1), **lie over, postpone to, put ahead** (2), **put back** (7), **put over¹** (3), **set ahead** (2), **set back** (4), **set forward** (5), **stand over**

***5** (of a ship or boat) to begin a voyage: [IØ (*often simple tenses*)] *The ship at last put off, to the cheers of the waiting crowd.* → **put forth** (4), **put out** (7)

***6** to discourage; make excuses to (someone), as to avoid a duty, prevent something happening, etc.: [T1b] *Tom was to arrive this weekend, but I put him off because you were ill. I've been trying to see you, but your secretary keeps putting me off. The rent collector comes tomorrow, and I've no money; how can I put him off?* —**put-off** *n infml*

***7** *not fml* to discourage (someone), as from liking someone or something: [T1b (*usu. simple tenses*)] *Those smelly animals put me off. I quite like working for the director, but his bad temper puts me off. I was hungry, but the smell of the bad meat put me off, and I didn't want my food. Don't be put off by his appearance, he's actually quite a charming person.* —**off-putting** *adj* → **turn off¹** (7), etc.

***8** to discourage (someone) from something such as work or an activity: [T1 (*often simple tenses*)] *Don't laugh while I'm playing the piano, you put me off. The singer was put off by a sudden noise outside, and was unable to continue.*

***9** to get rid of; cease to have or consider (something such as a feeling or duty): [T1 (*usu. simple tenses*)] *It's good to have put off the responsibility of the chairmanship. It's time to put off those foolish ideas and become serious. How can I put off these fearful doubts?* → **put away** (5)

***10** *not fml* to make (someone) lose consciousness, as in sleep: [T1 (*to*) (*usu. simple tenses*)] *A cup of hot milk will put you off to sleep better than anything. I need calm thoughts to put me off.* → **doze off,** etc.

**put off²** *v prep*

**1** to allow or cause (someone) to leave (a vehicle): [X9 + *off*] *Please put me off the train at the station serving the airport. If you boys at the back don't behave yourselves, I'll have you put off the bus!* → **alight from,** etc.

***2** to discourage (someone) from liking (someone or something): [D1 (*usu. simple tenses*)] *The smell put me off my food. Don't be put off him by his appearance; he's actually quite a charming person.* → **be off** (4), **go off²** (2), **turn off** (3)

***3** to discourage (someone) from (something such as work or an activity, or doing something): [D1 (*often simple tenses*)] *Don't talk, it puts him off his game.* [V4b (*often simple tenses*)] *The smell of your cigarette puts me off finishing my meal.*

**4 put someone off the scent/track/trail** to prevent usu. someone from catching or discovering one, as by providing false information, suggestions, etc.: [*usu. simple tenses*] *The dogs were chasing me, so I crossed the river to put them off the scent. The thieves tried to put the police off the scent by leaving one of the jewels in a distant place, but they were still caught and brought to trial.* → **throw off²** (4b)

**5 put someone off his/her stride/stroke** *not fml* to interrupt someone and prevent him/her from finishing an action properly: [*usu. simple tenses*] *Don't laugh when I'm playing the piano, it puts me off my stroke.*

**put on**[1] *v adv*

**1** to place (usu. something) on top of something: [X9 + ON] *I can't put the lid on, the box is too full.* → **fit on**[1] **(1), get on**[1] **(1), go on**[1] **(3)**

**2** to dress oneself in (clothing): [X9 + ON] *He put his coat on hurriedly and ran out of the house.* → **draw off** (1), **draw on**[1] (1), **fit on**[1] (2), **get off**[1] (1), **get on**[1] (1), **go on**[1] (3), **have on**[1] (1), **pull off**[1] (2), **pull on**[1] (1), **put off**[1] (1), **slip off** (3), **slip out of** (3), **take off**[1] (2), etc.

*__3__ to cause (something electrical such as light) to begin working: [T1] *Please put the light on, it's getting dark. I'll go in and put the fire on while you put the car in the garage.* → **be on**[1] (2), **come on**[1] (3), **get on**[1] (2), **go on**[1] (10), **have on**[1] (2), **keep on** (2), **leave on**[1] (3), **put off**[1] (3), etc., **remain on**[1], **snap on** (2), **stay on**[1] (2), **stick on**[1] (3), **stop on** (2), **switch on** (1), **turn on**[1] (1)

*__4__ to start cooking (a meal): [T1] *Phone me as soon as you leave the office and I'll put the dinner on, so that it's ready when you get home.*

*__5__ to gain (weight or size): [T1] *How can I have put on a pound since yesterday? I've eaten nothing! If I put on another inch, I shan't be able to wear this dress.* → **put back** (3), **take off**[1] (12)

*__6__ to increase (speed): [T1 (*no pass.*)] *The train put on speed as soon as it reached the long straight stretch of track.*

*__7__ to add (something): [T1 (*usu. simple tenses*)] *After tea, the home team put on 50 runs. British Rail will put on an additional train to carry the expected crowd of football supporters. Every bill has an additional charge put on, to cover increased costs.* → **stick on**[1] (5)

*__8__ to move the hands of (a clock or watch) to a later time: [T1] *In spring we put the clocks on one hour, to take advantage of the summer daylight. I must put my watch on three minutes, it's running slow.* → **go back** (7), **put ahead** (3), **put back** (8), **put forward** (6), **set ahead** (3), **set back** (5), **set forward** (6)

*__9__ to cause (something such as a performance or show) to take place: [T1] *The school always puts on a concert and a show of the children's paintings in the week before Christmas. Which play is the Theatre Group putting on next?* → **be on**[1] (3), **have on**[1] (3)

*__10__ to ask (someone) to perform, on the stage or sports field: [T1] *I'm putting you on next; are you ready?*

*__11__ *infml* to pretend (something such as an opinion or quality); deceive by means of (something): [T1] *He put on a pretence of bravery, but we all knew that it was false. Don't listen to her, she's just putting on an act. Jane put on a show of cheerfulness to make her doctor think that she was well.* —**put-on** *n, adj*

*__12__ esp. *AmE infml* to deceive (someone) into believing something, for fun: [T1b (*continuous tenses*)] *I don't believe you, you're just putting me on!* —**put-on** *n* → **have on**[1] (4)

**13 put on airs** *not fml* to pretend to be very grand: *My neighbour is always putting on airs, pretending she knows important people and is invited to rich parties, and so on.*

**14 put one's best face on** *not fml* to pretend to be pleasant to someone: *I hated listening to the director, and always had to put my best face on so that he wouldn't know this.*

**15 put the brake(s) on: a** to try to stop a vehicle: *The driver put his brakes on hard as soon as he saw the bus, but he was too late to avoid a crash.* **b** *not fml* to slow down or stop some activity: *You can't go on spending at this rate, you really must put the brake on.*

**16 put on the gloves** *not fml* to box: *This famous fighter first put on the gloves professionally after he won an important fight at the age of twenty.*

**17 put on the heat/screws/squeeze** *infml* to persuade someone by force, as a threat, etc. to do something: *He threatened to put the screws on if we did not agree to his demands. "The effect was like that of a burning glass. It was an unfailing method of putting on the heat."* (John Wain, *The Smaller Sky*)

**18 put it on** *infml* **a** to overstate something: *When he talks about his success, I can tell that he's just putting it on.* **b** to charge too much: *I refuse to shop at that store any more, they are well known for putting it on.*

**19 put on a spurt** to increase speed, often quite suddenly: *Jim could see that he was losing the race, so he put on a spurt in the last few yards, and passed his opponents.*

**20 put one's thinking cap on** *not fml* to give a matter serious thought: *Your request is rather sudden; let me put my thinking cap on, and I will give you an answer tomorrow.*

**put on**[2] *v prep*

**1** also **put upon** to place (usu. something) in position on top of (something): [X9 + ON] *Put the plates gently on the table, they are very delicate. He put his hand on my shoulder comfortingly. Putting the child on his back, he continued the long walk home. She put a finger on her lips to signal silence. Our grandparents never seriously imagined that we would be able to put a man on the moon.* → **lay on**[2] (1), **place on** (1), **set on**[2] (1), **stick on**[2] (1)

*__2__ to fix; force acceptance of (something such as a responsibility) on (someone or something): [D1] *Why are you trying to put the blame on me? Parents put heavy duties on their children. The government has put yet another tax on cigarettes. We shall have to put a limit on government spending.* → **fasten on** (2), **impose on** (1), **lay on**[2] (2), **pin on**[2] (2), **throw on** (4)

*__3__ to add (a charge or amount) to (the price

something): [D1] *The restaurant puts an additional charge on the bill, to cover increased costs.* → **stick on²** (4)

*__4__ to gain (weight or size) on (a certain part of the body): [D1] *You seem to have put a little more flesh on your face since your illness. If I put another inch on my waist, I shan't be able to wear this dress.*

*__5__ to risk (usu. money) on the success of (something or someone): [D1] *Foolishly, he put all his possessions on the result of the card game. How much are you prepared to put on this horse?* → **bet on** (1), etc.

*__6__ *not fml* also **put upon** to cause trouble for (someone): [T1 (*often continuous tenses*)] *You're sure I shan't be putting on you if I stay for dinner?*

*__7__ to give (someone) (a duty or job): [D1] *Who are you putting on the special report? "Put none but Americans on guard tonight."* (George Washington)

**8 put the arm/bite on** *infml* to force (someone), esp. to give money: *We need another £1,000; can't you put the arm on your rich aunt?*

**9 put a bold/brave/good face on** to face (something which is discouraging) bravely; make the best of (something): *After the failure of his company, the businessman put a bold face on it and began all over again from the beginning.*

**10 put the brake on** *not fml* to stop or slow (some activity): *We shall have to put the brake on our spending, or we shall have no money left at this rate.*

**11 put one's cards on the table** to be completely honest, esp. about one's intentions or point of view: *I see that it's time to put my cards on the table: I am interested in this affair because the woman in the case is my sister.* → **lay on²** (5), **place on** (3), **set on²** (6)

**12 put a construction on** to decide the meaning of (something): [*usu. simple tenses*] *Make sure you don't put the wrong construction on his remark: I'm sure he didn't mean to be rude. A different construction was put on the wording of the law by each of the judges.* also **put upon** → **place on** (4)

**13 put emphasis/stress/weight on** also **put upon** to regard (something such as a fact) as important; make others know the importance of (something or doing something): [*often simple tenses*] *When giving orders, the captain put stress on the urgency of the work. In every sentence that she speaks, she puts heavy emphasis on all the important words. The director put stress on completing the contract on time.* → **lay on²** (6)

**14 put something on its feet** *not fml* to make something improve, esp. in making a good beginning: *This summer's good trade should put the new business on its feet. The workers must change their ways of thinking if we are to put the nation on its feet after all these struggles.* → **set on²** (8)

**15 not to put too fine a point on it** *not fml* to speak very plainly and honestly, esp. about something bad: *Your father is really very ill and his chances are slight; not to put too fine a point on it, he may not live long.*

**16 put one's finger on** *not fml* to be able to state (a fault or cause): [*usu. simple tenses + can, could*] *The doctor was able to treat the disease, although he could not put his finger on the exact cause.* → **lay on²** (9)

**17 put the finger on** *infml* to inform against (someone such as a criminal): *How did you know I was here? Who's been putting the finger on me?*

**18 put someone on his/her guard** *not fml* also **put upon** to give someone warning: *I was about to tell the enquirer the facts, when a look from my friend put me on my guard.* → **be on²** (12)

**19 put one's hands on: a** *not fml* to find (something): *I can't put my hands on the account book: have you seen it?* → **lay on²** (11) **b** *not fml* to gain possession of (something): *I'd like to know where I can put my hands on the special tobacco.* → **get on²** (8), **lay on²** (11), **set on²** (13) **c** *not fml* to seize (something or someone), esp. violently; harm (someone): *The police will soon put their hands on the jewel thieves. I'd like to put my hands on the man who attacked my daughter.* → **get on²** (9), **lay on²** (11), **set on²** (13)

**20 put a hex/jinx on** *not fml* also *AmE not fml* **put a whammy on** to cause (someone) to have bad luck, as if by magic: *It's as if some evil magician has put a hex on the team: they haven't won once this year, although they have played so well.*

**21 put someone on his/her honour/oath** to make someone promise to tell the truth or behave correctly: *I put you all on your honour not to cheat while I am out of the room. All witnesses must remember that they have been put on oath and must speak the exact truth.* → **be on²** (16, 21), **place on** (5), **place under** (3), **put under²** (3)

**22 put one's hopes on/upon** to have one's hopes depend on (someone, something, or doing something): *Many parents put their hopes on their children for the future. Don't put all your hopes on this job, you may not get it. Jim has put all his hopes on winning this race.* → **pin on²** (4), etc.

**23 put something on ice** *not fml* to save consideration of something for a later time: *The government's plans for the new airport have been put on ice until there is more money, and less opposition from the farmers.* → **be on²** (19)

**24 put the kibosh on** *infml* to spoil (something such as a plan), esp. to bring it to an end: *I'm afraid that the sudden rainfall has put the kibosh on our garden party.*

**25 put something on the map** *not fml* to make something such as a place seem more important or worthy of notice than it was: *The big popular music concert has succeeded in putting the small village on the map; everyone has now heard of it. With even greater efforts next year, we should be able to put the firm on the map.* → **be on² (20)**

**26 put something on the market** to begin to sell something such as a product or house: *I was very pleased when this new cleaning product was put on the market, as it helped me with a particular difficulty. Try not to put your house on the market in the winter, when sales are slow.* → **come onto**

**27 put someone on his/her mettle** to encourage someone to give his/her best effort: [*usu. simple tenses*] *The arrival of experienced competitors from other countries has put our sportsmen on their mettle.*

**28 put one's mind on** to think carefully about (usu. something): *I can't put my mind on my work with all this noise going on.*

**29 put (one's) money on** *not fml* to be certain of the success or result of (something or someone): *I think it will stay fine, but I wouldn't put money on it. Many people are putting their money on Jim to win the race.*

**30 put the mouth on** *BrE and AustrE sl* to make or seem to make (someone) fail by telling others that he/she is succeeding: *I'd have won if you hadn't put the mouth on me at the wrong moment; why did you have to say anything?*

**31 put a new face on** *not fml* to make (something) seem different: *These unexpected results put a new face on the matter.*

**32 put something on one side: a** to put something down; stop holding something; move something to a different position next to one: *She put her sewing on one side when the telephone rang.* → **lay aside** (1), etc. **b** to discontinue something such as work, esp. for a time: *Tom put his new book on one side for a year while he wrote some magazine articles and informative material.* → **lay aside** (2), etc. **c** to disregard; cease something such as a habit: *It's time to put our differences on one side and work together for a common purpose.* → **lay aside** (3), etc. **d** to save (a supply of goods) for a customer: *I'll put the goods on one side until you have made a decision about whether you want them.* → **lay aside** (5), etc.

**33 put someone/something on the pan** *AmE infml* to find fault with someone or something: *Don't let the director catch you making telephone calls from the office, or he'll put you on the pan!*

**34 put someone on a pedestal** *not fml* to admire someone too much; think someone is faultless: [*often simple tenses*] *It's unhealthy in marriage to put your wife on a pedestal; better to accept her as a human being, with faults and failings as well as good qualities.* → **knock off** (4), **set on² (18)**

**35 put a premium on** also **put upon** to place a high value on (something such as a quality): [*usu. simple tenses*] *In this school, we put a premium on hard work and honesty; brains without character and willingness are worthless.* → **place at** (4), **place on** (8), **put at** (5), **set at** (12)

**36 put pressure on** also **put upon** to try to force (someone) (to do something) by argument, threats, etc.: *The unions have been putting pressure on the government to reduce its limits on wage increases.* → **place on** (9)

**37 put a price/value on** to judge the worth in money of (something): [*usu. simple tenses*] *It's impossible to put a price on such a rare painting.*

**38 put the screws/squeeze on** *infml* to persuade (someone) by force, as a threat, to do something such as to give money: *We need another £1,000; can you put the squeeze on your rich aunt? He'll tell us where he's hidden the jewels if we put the screws on him.*

**39 put one's shirt on** *not fml* to risk all one's money on (usu. something): *The horse lost, and Jim had put his shirt on it!*

**40 put a strain on** to make things hard for; test the strength of (someone or something): *This rope will not break unless a strain of more than 250 pounds is put on it. All this additional work, and my present worries, are putting an unbearable strain on me.* → **place on** (10)

**41 put the tin lid on** *infml* to stop or ruin (something) in the end: *Costs have been rising, the men have been refusing to work, and now the loss of the contract has really put the tin lid on things!*

**42 put years on** to make (someone) feel older or less happy: *All these recent worries have put years on me in a few weeks.* → **take off² (15)**

**put onto** *v prep*

**1** to place (usu. something) on (something): [X9 + *onto*] *You need a bigger brush to put the paint onto the wall. When I put my hand onto the shelf, there was nothing there.*

***2** to put (someone) in touch with (someone), esp. by telephone: [D1 (*often simple tenses*)] *I'll put you onto the director; he may be able to help.* → **be onto** (1), **get onto** (6)

***3** to inform (someone) about (a secret or someone doing wrong): [D1] *Who put the police onto our plan? The thieves would have got away with the jewels if their companions had not put the police onto them.* → **be onto** (3), **get onto** (9)

***4** to give (someone) information about (something, usu. good): [D1 (*often simple tenses*)] *Don't go to that shop for your art supplies; I can put you onto a much cheaper one. Thank you for putting me onto a good thing.* → **be onto** (4)

**put out** *v adv*

**1** to stretch (something) out or forward: [X9 + OUT] *Put your hand out, I have a surprise for you. It's rude to put out your tongue at people.* → **hold forth** (3), **hold out** (1), **put forth** (1), **reach out** (1), **shoot out** (2), **shove out** (1), **spread out** (1), **stick out** (3), **stretch forth, stretch out** (2), **throw out** (3), **thrust out** (1)

**2** to place (something) out of doors: [X9 + OUT] *If it turns fine, I shall put the washing out. I put the garden chairs out when the sun shone, but I soon had to take them in again.* → **take out** (1)

**3** to prepare or spread (something such as clothes or food) ready for use: [X9 + OUT (*often simple tenses*)] *Shall I put out the best plates? I'll leave a meal put out for you in the kitchen. Please put out my best suit for the governors' meeting.* → **drag out** (1), **get out** (5), **lay out** (2), **set forth** (3), **set out** (5)

*__4__ (of a plant) to send out (new growth): [T1] *We thought the bush was dead, but it has already put out some new branches.* → **put forth** (2), **send forth** (2), **send out** (4)

*__5__ to force (someone or an animal) to leave, usu. a building: [T1] *Troublemakers will be put out. Two families who could not pay the rent were put out onto the street. Put the cat out before you go to bed.* → **throw out** (4), etc., (5), etc.

*__6__ to send (someone or an animal) elsewhere, usu. for a purpose: [T1 (*often pass.*)] *The baby was put out to the nurse when the mother had no milk. After many years of faithful service, the old horse was put out to grass* (= no longer had to work).

*__7__ (of a ship or boat) to begin a voyage: [IØ (*to*)] *The wind was calm when we first put out to sea.* → **put forth** (4), **put off¹** (5)

*__8__ to show; use; bring (something such as strength) into action; use effort: [T1] *Putting out all his strength, he uprooted the tree.* [IØ (*usu. simple tenses*)] *Everyone has to put out if we are to be ready on time.* —**output** *n* → **put forth** (3)

*__9__ to state; offer (something such as a plan): [T1 (*usu. simple tenses*)] *If you can put out a better system, please do so.* → **put forth** (5), **put forward** (2), **set forth** (2), **set forward** (3), **set out** (8)

*__10__ to produce (something such as goods or power): [T1] *The firm has put out an increased number of bicycles this month. This engine puts out more electric current than the other one.* —**output** *n*

*__11__ to make (something such as news) public, as in broadcasting or print: [T1] *A report has been put out from the government information office about the worsening unemployment figures. The police have put out a description of the jewel thieves, in an attempt to catch them with the help of the public. The sinking ship put out a call for help over its radio.*

*__12__ to print (material such as a book): [T1] *The printers put out three numbers of the magazine in its first year.* → **put forth** (6), **send forth** (2)

*__13__ to make (a light or fire) stop burning: [T1] *Put out all fires before leaving the camping ground. Please put the lights out as you leave the building.* → **be out** (3), **blow out** (4), **go out** (5), **keep in** (6), etc., **let out** (6), **put off¹** (3), etc., **snuff out** (1)

*__14__ to cause damage to (a part of the body such as a joint): [T1 (*usu. simple tenses*)] *I can't play tennis with you this week, I've put my shoulder out. Mind that sharp point, you nearly put my eye out!* → **throw out** (14)

*__15__ to cause (someone or oneself) to take trouble: [T1] *Are you sure it won't put you out if I stay to dinner? Say thank you to your aunt; she has put herself out to amuse you while you were ill. Please don't put yourself out, I can do it myself.* [V3] *Mother was always willing to put herself out to help people.* → **impose on** (3), **lay out** (8), **put about** (3), **put on** (6), **set out** (9), **throw out** (15)

*__16__ to cause (someone) to feel worried, annoyed, or uncomfortable: [T1 (*often pass.*)] *He seemed greatly put out by the arrival of the new workers. She never gets put out even by the most difficult matters.* → **throw out** (15)

*__17__ to make (someone) lose consciousness: [T1 (*usu. simple tenses*)] *It was a careless blow, I didn't mean to put him out. This gas will put you out during your operation, you won't feel a thing.* → **knock out** (3, etc., 4)

*__18__ *not fml* to spoil (something such as a calculation): [T1 (*usu. simple tenses*)] *I didn't know that cheque had been paid in, now that's put my calculations out.* → **throw out** (9), etc.

*__19__ to spend or risk (money): [T1 (*at, to*) (*usu. simple tenses*)] *Having put out his father's fortune into shares, he was able to live on the interest. Make sure you put out your savings at a high rate of interest.* → **lay out** (4)

*__20__ *not fml* to send (work) to be done in another place: [T1] *We had so many orders to complete that we had to put the work out to other factories, to fulfil the contract on time.*

*__21__ (in cricket and other team ball games) to cause (a player) to end his/her turn on the field: [T1 (*usu. simple tenses*)] *A skilful ball from Snow put out the opposing team's prize hope in the first five minutes.* —**put out** *n* → **be out** (7), etc.

*__22__ esp. *AmE sl* to produce; deliver the expected result, as money or sex, in return for what one owes: [IØ (*usu. simple tenses*)] *People who take our free flights to see the property development are expected to put out when they get there. What do you mean no? We've been to the theatre, you've had a good dinner, why don't you put out?*

**23 put something out (of action)** to stop something such as a machine or gun working: *The brave soldier was given the Military Cross for putting three large enemy guns out of action single-handed. Something's put this washing machine out of action again. I'm sending three of you in the night to put out the enemy position.* → **be out of** (5), **bring into** (3), **call into** (2), **come into** (5), **go into** (15), **go out of** (3), **put out of** (2)

**24 put someone/a firm out (of business)** to cause someone or a firm to fail: *This slow trade will soon put me out of business. Jim's father's firm was soon put out of business by big competitors. Watch that other firm, or they will put us out.* → **go out of** (4), **put out of** (3)

**25 put out feelers** *not fml* to test what people will think of an idea, before taking action: *The government party workers have been putting out feelers to see what changes in the tax law are necessary to encourage people to vote for them in the coming election.*

**26 put someone out to service** *becoming rare* to place someone, usu. one's child, in a home as a servant: *Rose was put out to service as a child, and never knew any other kind of life.*

***put out of** *v adv prep*

**1** to make (someone or something) leave (something such as a building): [D1] *Put that cat out of the house, I don't want it in my kitchen. When she was rude to me in my own home, I had her put out of my house. The cruel father put his children out of house and home, and made them earn their own living while they were very young.*

**2 put something out of action** → PUT OUT (23)

**3 put someone/a firm out of business** → PUT OUT (24)

**4 put someone out of countenance** *not fml* to cause someone to feel anxious or uncomfortable: [*often pass.*] *I was badly put out of countenance when I arrived for the meeting and found no one else there.*

**5 put something out of one's head/mind** to forget something intentionally: *You have to try to put your past suffering out of your head, and make a fresh start with better intentions.*

**6 put an animal out of its misery** *not fml* to kill an animal painlessly, out of mercy: *The dear old dog was suffering so much that we thought it kinder to put him out of his misery.* → **put away** (7), **put down** (11), **put to**[2] (27)

**7 put someone out of his/her misery** *not fml* to stop someone's anxiety: [*often simple tenses*] *At last the examination results have arrived, and the students will be put out of their misery: it's better to know the worst than be in uncertainty. Tell me the end of the story, put me out of my misery.*

**8 put someone's nose out of joint** *not fml* to annoy someone, as by taking action to spoil his/her plans; stop someone doing something annoying: *She expected always to receive royal treatment, and her nose was badly put out of joint when she found she was not at the head of the table. If that salesman comes round here again, I'll put his nose out of joint!*

**9 put someone out of work** to cause someone to lose his/her job: [*often simple tenses*] *The serious fire at the bicycle factory has put 2,000 men and women out of work.* → **throw out** (18)

**put over**[1] *v adv*

**1** to make (usu. something) pass over the top of something: [X9 + OVER] *At the third attempt, she put her horse over, and won the jumping competition. If you can't get your bag under the fence, you'll have to put it over.*

*__2__ *not fml* to make (something such as an idea, or oneself) understood and well received (by someone): [T1 (*to*)] *Advertisements are intended to put over the best qualities of the product (to the public). How can put such an unpopular message over (to th crowd)? The politician was able to put himsel over (to the voters) as a suitable leader.* → **come across**[1] (2), etc.

*__3__ *not fml* to delay (something such as an event) till a later time or date: [T1] *We shall have to put the garden party over until the weather is fine.* → **put off**[1] (4), etc.

*__4__ (of a ship or boat) to move to one side [IØ] *There's a sailing boat coming towards us you'd better put over to give her room.*

**put over**[2] *v prep*

**1** to place (something) in a position; cause (something) to pass above (something): [X9 + *over*] *The girl rider had great difficulty i putting her nervous horse over the fence. Put warm cover over the sleeping child.* → **pu over**[2] (1), etc.

*__2__ *infml* to cause acceptance or belief i (something) by (someone), by deceit, esp. i the phr. **put one over someone:** [D1] *I pu one over Father this morning: made him thin it was my birthday, and he'd forgotten! Th class will never succeed in putting anythin over the new teacher, he's too experience* → **put across**[2] (2)

***put over on** *v adv prep*

*infml* to deceive; trick; cheat (someone), es in the phr. **put one over on someone**: [D *The judge is very wise and experienced; don think that you will be able to put one over o him! Can you put it over on the teacher, s that he doesn't discover our secret plan?*

**put past** *v prep*

**would not (have) put it past someone** *not fml* consider it possible for someone (to do something, usu. bad): *I don't think he's the type person to do that, but I wouldn't put it pa him. I wouldn't put it past her to cheat in th examination.*

**put right** *v adj*

**1** to mend (something): [X9 + **right**] *T washing machine broke down again, so I ca ed the repairman to see if he could put it righ* → **set right** (1)

*__2__ to correct (something wrong): [T1b] *I glad that you've been able to put your re* *tionship with your mother right. There were some mistaken notes in that last passage; let's put them right now, before the performance.* → **put straight** (2), **set right** (2), **set straight** (2)

****3** to correct (someone who is misinformed): [T1b (*often simple tenses*)] *The firm sent me an incorrect bill, but I soon put them right. If I make a mistake when I read out the results, please put me right.* → **put straight (2), set right** (3), **set straight** (3)

****4** to make (someone) feel better: [T1b] *This medicine will quickly put you right after your illness.*

**put straight** *v adj*

**1** to tidy (something such as a room): [X9 + **straight**] *Please put your things straight before you leave the house. I must put the living room straight before the visitors arrive.* → **set straight** (1)

****2** to correct (someone who is misinformed or something): [T1b] *If I make a mistake when I read out the results, please put me straight. She said my name wrongly so I put her straight. I would like to put the record straight; this is our third successful year, not our second.* → **put right** (2), **set right** (2), **set straight** (2)

**put there** *v adv*

**1** to cause (something or someone) to be in a certain place: [X9 + THERE] *There's a parcel on the table, but I don't know who put it there.*

**2 put it there!** *infml* shake hands with me, esp. in agreement: [*imper.*] *Spoken like a true man—put it there!*

**put through¹** *v adv*

**1** to complete; fulfil (something such as an arrangement) successfully: [T1] *The director put the business deal through very quickly. We are trying to put through a complete reorganization of our accounting system, using modern machinery.* → **go through¹** (3), **put across¹** (3), **railroad through, ram through, take through¹** (2)

**2** to connect (someone) by telephone; obtain (a telephone connection): [T1 (*to*)] *Can you put me through to this number? I have several calls to put through, so I need a clear line. With this new machinery, we can put through more calls at a time than ever before.* → **be through** (2), **come through¹** (6), **get through¹** (6), **get through to** (1)

**3** to enable (someone) to pass an examination, standard, etc.: [T1b (*usu. simple tenses*)] *With additional classes, I was able to put all my students through, except three whose English was weakest.* → **get through¹** (3)

**4** to cause (a law) to be passed, as by Parliament or other law-making body: [T1b] *We should have no difficulty in putting the new law through, it has been demanded by the public for some time.* → **get through¹** (4), **go through¹** (2)

**put through²** *v prep*

**1** to make (something) pass through (something such as a space or object): [X9 + through] *It's difficult to put this thick thread through the narrow eye of this needle. I can stop him being entered by simply putting a pencil through his name on the list.*

****2** to cause (someone) to enter or pass (a test or standard or college): [D1 (*usu. simple tenses*)] *Do you intend to put all the students through the examination? It's costing us a lot of money to put our son through law school.* → **get through²** (2)

****3** to make (a law) be passed by (Parliament or other law-making body): [D1] *We should have no difficulty in putting the new law through Parliament, it has been demanded by the public for some time.* → **get through²** (3), **go through²** (2), **take through²** (3)

****4** to cause (someone) to undergo or suffer (something difficult): [D1 (*often simple tenses*)] *You have put him through a lot of pain with your thoughtless actions. All new young soldiers are put through some hard training before being sent into battle.*

****5** to cause (someone or an animal) to perform (action): [D1] *You can't put an old dog through new tricks.*

**6 put someone through the hoop** *not fml* to make (someone) undergo a test, often to show his/her ability: *All students are put through the hoop at the beginning of the year, to see if they have the right qualities.* → **go through²** (16)

**7 put someone through it** *not fml* to give someone a severe test of ability or courage: *The young soldiers' first taste of battle should really put them through it.*

**8 put someone through the mill** *not fml* to give someone a lot of hard practical tests, as making him/her learn from humble experience, etc.: *The newspaper owners put every new reporter through the mill so that they are certain that he understands the whole activity.* → **go through²** (17)

**9 put someone through his/her paces** *not fml* to make someone show his/her ability, as in performance: *Let's put all these hopeful young actors through their paces, and then we can choose the best for our production.*

**put to¹** *v adv* → **pull to¹** etc.

esp. *BrE* to close (something such as a door) firmly: [X9 + TO] *Please put the door to, it's come open a little.*

**put to²** *v prep*

**1** to place (something) next to (something); join (something) with (something): [X9 + *to*] *She put a finger to her lips to signal silence. You can't put an unwilling horse to a cart.* → **place to** (1), **set to²** (1), **touch to** (1)

**2** to add (something) to (something): [X9 + *to*] *Can you put words to this music?* → **set to²** (9)

****3** to cause (someone) to reach or be in (something such as a state): [D1] *Anyone who opposes the king will be put to death. This gas will put you to sleep during the opera-*

*tion. The whole enemy army was put to flight. I don't want to put you to any trouble. We put the whole family to work on building the boathouse.* → **go to** (8, 10)

*4 to offer (something such as an idea) to (someone): [D1] *Let me put a question to you. You may put your suggestion to the director at a suitable time, not now.*

*5 to decide (something) by using (a vote) or asking (a group): [D1] *Let's put the matter to a vote. We must put the difficulty to the whole committee.*

*6 to aim the effort of (someone or oneself) towards (doing something): [V4b (*often simple tenses*)] *If you really put yourself to winning, instead of hoping for good luck, you might have a better chance. Will you put the men to clearing the road so that there is room for our vehicles to get through?*

**7 put someone to bed** to help someone to lie down in bed, as when ill or to prepare for the night: *It's time to put the children to bed. Night after night he came home drunk and she had to put him to bed.* → **go to** (15), **retire to** (4), **send to** (2)

**8 put (a newspaper) to bed** to finish preparing (a newspaper) for printing: *Has the paper been put to bed yet? There is some fresh news to include if it's not too late.*

**9 put someone to the blush** to shame someone: *Her kindness, after my lack of consideration, quite put me to the blush.*

**10 put a call to** to telephone (someone or a place): *Ask my secretary to put a call to Head Office in London, will you?* → **place to** (2)

**11 put something to effective/good use** to use something well; make the best use of something; gain advantage from something: *Our neighbour seems to have put the ladder to good use while he was borrowing it: he has repaired the whole roof and painted the upper windows.*

**12 put an end/a stop to** to cause (something) to cease: *The police are trying to put an end to the wave of violent crime. It's time this rise in the cost of living was put a stop to.* → **be at** (12), **bring to**$^{2}$ **(8)**

**13 put someone to (great) expense** to make someone pay (a lot): *I've been put to great expense to get the business started, and I don't intend to waste the time and effort by stopping now.*

**14 put the final/finishing touches to** to complete (something) in detail: *We need a professional to put the finishing touches to the paintwork. It took longer than we expected to put the final touches to the contract.*

**15 be (hard) put to it** *not fml* to find something difficult (to do): *I should be hard put to it to find a more suitable name for the boat.*

**16 put it to someone (that)** to suggest; invite someone to consider (that): *I put it to you that you have not been telling the complete truth. I spoke to the minister earlier and I put it to him that the government were not being fair to the unions.*

**17 put a match to** to start (something) burning by striking a match next to it: *Putting a match to the letter, he made her watch it burn.* → **catch alight** (1), **place to** (3), **set alight** (1), **set on**$^{2}$ (10), **set to**$^{2}$ (5)

**18 put one's mind to** to work hard at; use one's brains together with (something): *If you put your mind to your work instead of being lazy, you might see some results.* → **set to**$^{2}$ (8)

**19 put a name to** to remember the name of (something or someone): [*usu. simple tenses*] *I do know that flower, but I can't put a name to it. I would find it difficult to put a name to everyone in this room.*

**20 put one's nose to the grindstone** *not fml* to work very hard: *I needed a holiday after putting my nose to the grindstone for so many months. If you put your nose to the grindstone, you can get all those facts learned in time for the examination.*

**21 put paid to** *BrE* to destroy (something such as an idea): [*usu. simple tenses*] *I'm afraid this sudden wet weather has put paid to our garden party.*

**22 put pen to paper** to write something: *I am often unwilling to put pen to paper, but when I do begin, I write really long letters.*

**23 put someone to the question** *old use* to torture someone: *If he does not admit his guilt, we can always put him to the question.*

**24 put something to rights** to correct something wrong; make something proper, esp. in a moral sense: *Our native people have often been treated as unworthy people; this is a state of affairs that must quickly be put to rights.* → **set to**$^{2}$ (10)

**25 put someone/something to shame** to compare something or someone unfavourably; show someone or something as unworthy by comparison: *We thought that our entry was very praiseworthy, but the entry from the neighbouring school put us to shame.*

**26 put one's shoulder to the wheel** *not fml* to put effort into one's activity: *If we all put our shoulders to the wheel we can bring the nation out of its present troubles.* → **set to**$^{2}$ (12)

**27 put (an animal) to sleep: a** to make an animal unconscious: *Don't worry, your dog will be put to sleep for the operation.* **b** *euph* to kill an animal out of mercy: *The dear old dog was so old and ill that we thought it kinder to have him put to sleep.* → **put away** (7), **put down** (11), **put out of** (6)

**28 put someone/something to the test/to trial** to test someone or something: *Her first public performance will certainly put the young singer to the test. We can't tell if the product will be successful until we have put it to trial.*

**29 put someone to a trade** *old use* to train someone, as one's son, for a skilled job: *The* *boy is wasting his time in school; it's time he was put to a useful trade.*

**put together** *v adv*

**1** to join (two or more things): [X9 + TOGETHER] *Can you put the pieces of the broken plate together? Put your hands together and close your eyes, ready to pray.* → **lay together** (1)

**2* to form (something such as a unity) from different things or people: [T1] *It will be difficult to put a team together with many of our best players away. Mother is skilled at putting a meal together out of bits of food left over. You still have to learn how to put a sentence together properly.*

***3** to gather (scattered things): [T1] *First, I have to put my thoughts together before preparing the actual speech.*

**4 put together** combined: *His share was more than all the others' put together.*

**5 put our/your/their heads together** *not fml* to combine several people's ideas; make a plan by considering it with others: *We shall come to a decision sooner if we all put our heads together; it's too difficult for one person to decide.* → **lay together** (2)

**6 put two and two together** *not fml* to make sense of what one hears or sees; understand the meaning of something: *He didn't exactly say what he thought, but I put two and two together and knew that he intended to leave.*

**put under**[1] *v adv* → **knock out** (3), etc.

to make (someone or an animal) unconscious: [T1b] *This gas will put you under so that you don't feel the pain of the operation.*

**put under**[2] *v prep*

**1** to place (something) in a position beneath (something): [X9 + *under*] *Putting his hand under his shirt, he could feel the blood flowing from the wound. I put the envelope under the rest of the pile, so that it would be dealt with last.* → **place under** (1)

**2 put someone under arrest/guard** to limit someone's freedom by seizing and guarding him, often before a trial: *The jewel thieves were put under arrest, and will face their trial next month. Put those disobedient soldiers under guard; I will deal with them in the morning.* → **place under** (2)

**3 put someone under oath** *law* to make someone swear a solemn promise, as in court: *Witnesses must remember that they have been put under oath and must speak the exact truth.* → **put on**[2] (21), etc.

**4 put someone under an obligation** to cause someone to owe a debt, as of service, to someone else: *Their frequent invitations put us under an obligation to invite them to our house for a change.* → **place under** (4)

**5 put someone under observation** to watch someone closely, as a criminal or someone in hospital: *The police put most newly freed prisoners under observation to see if they will return to a life of crime. The doctors cannot decide what he is sufffering from, and have put him under observation for a few days.* → **place under** (5)

**put up**[1] *v adv*

**1** to raise (something) to a higher position, as in the air: [X9 + UP] *Put up your hand if you know the answer. Girls used to put their hair up on their seventeenth birthdays. Would you please help me to put the shelf up: I can't do it by myself. Scientists have put up a new machine into space, to improve telephone connections.* → **stick up** (1)

**2** to build; raise (something) into a fixed position: [X9 + UP] *Do you know how to put up a tent? Has the machinery been put up ready for the broadcast? I want to put up a fence between our property and our neighbour's. The original college buildings were put up in the 16th century.* → **go up**[1] (6), **set up** (1)

**3** to show (something such as a notice) in a public place: [X9 + UP] *You are not allowed to put up advertisements on this wall without special permission. The examination results will be put up on this board tomorrow.* → **stick up** (2)

***4** to increase; raise (a cost): [T1] *Rents are fixed and cannot be put up. Many people think that Britain's entry into the Common Market has put food prices up. The government has promised that taxes will not be put up again this year.* → **go down**[1] (6), etc.

***5** to pack (goods such as food or a parcel): [T1a] *Mother will put up a packed meal for us to take on our walk. The farmers put up the apples in barrels. She put up a parcel for her daughter, who was away at college. The medicine is put up in small bottles.*

***6** to provide (money needed for something), usu. in advance: [T1a] *If you put up your share, Father will put up the rest.* [IØ] *That's the rule of the game, so put up or shut up!*

***7** to offer (opposition): [T1a] *Don't be defeated without at least putting up a fight. She didn't put up much of a struggle, so I thought she was willing.*

***8** to state (a position in an argument, etc.): [T1a] *What argument do you have to put up against that? You have put up a good case, but I still have to decide against you. What excuse can you put up for your actions?*

***9** to offer (something) for sale: [T1] *After grandmother's death, the furniture was put up for sale. The next lot I shall put up is a fine set of old pictures.*

***10** to find food and lodging; provide food and lodging for (someone): [L9 (*at, for, with*)] *Where can we put up tonight? We can put up at the hotel, or with friends.* [T1] *Can you put us up for the weekend? I can put up two adults, but no children. Yes, I can put up one more person on this seat which folds down into a bed.* —**put-you-up** *n, adj*

*__11__ to provide shelter for (something): [T1a] *Is there anywhere for me to put up my horse? You can put up your car in our garage, as it's empty at the moment.*

*__12__ to offer (oneself) for election; ask to be elected: [T1b (*for*)] *Do you intend to put yourself up (for the empty seat in the House)?* [L9 (*for*)] *Do you really intend to put up for that seat?* → **be up for** (1), **come up for** (3)

*__13__ to suggest (someone) for a job or position: [T1 (*as, for*)] *I know an excellent man whom I would like to put up as the best person for the chairmanship.*

*__14__ to preserve (food such as fruit) in a special bottle or tin: [T1a] *Every summer, Mother puts up a large quantity of ripe fruit for us to eat during the winter.* → **do up** (6)

*__15__ to call (a prisoner) to be examined in court: [T1a] *Put up the prisoners! The jewel thieves will be put up for trial next month.*

*__16__ to make (an animal, or bird) leave its hiding place: [T1a] *These dogs are often used for putting up birds, for shooting.*

*__17__ *infml* to arrange (something) as a secret plan: [T1a (*usu. pass.*)] *All the office workers believe that the appointment of the new chairman was put up.* —**put-up** *adj*

*__18__ *old use* to put (something) away in a safe place: [T1a] *Put up your sword; we are enemies no longer. All this valuable jewellery should be put up somewhere safe so that it isn't stolen.*

*__19__ to take (something) out of use, esp. for a time: [T1] *We had to put the car up for the winter, it was not fit to drive in snow.* → **lay up** (3), **lie up** (2)

**20 put someone's back/hackles up** *not fml* to annoy or offend someone: *It puts people's hackles up, the way she is so unfair to the girls who work for her. Your mother puts my back up with her endless complaints.* → **get up** (17)

**21 put up the banns** to give formal notice of a coming wedding: *The banns are usually put up in church for three weeks, to give anyone the chance to state reasons why the man and woman should not be married.*

**22 put one's feet up** *not fml* to rest: *You've been working too hard; why don't you put your feet up for a change?*

**23 put up one's fists/guard** to raise one's hands, made like tight balls, ready to fight: *Put up your fists and fight like a man! He hit me before I had chance to put my guard up.*

**24 put your hands up!** *not fml* to yield, as to a gunman: [*usu. imper.*] *Put your hands up, all of you; I've got a gun.* → **stick up** (4)

**25 put someone's monkey up** *not fml* to make someone angry: *One little remark put her monkey up, and a terrible quarrel resulted.*

**26 put up a (good) show** *not fml* to perform well; act bravely; make a good effect: *What sort of a show did he put up when he heard the news? It doesn't matter that you lost—at least you put up a good show. I intended to put up a very good show, but in the face of severe pain, I didn't have the courage.*

**27 put up the shutters: a** to close a shop for the night by closing fastenings over the windows: *Put up the shutters before you lock up the shop and go home.* **b** to cease trading: *The old bookseller has at last put up the shutters and gone to live in the country.*

**put up**[2] *v prep*

**1** to place (something) higher, often inside (something): [X9 + *up*] *Put your hand up the pipe and see if you can feel what is blocking it. It's very offensive to put your hand up a woman's skirt. He had a rude habit of putting a pencil up his nose.*

**2 put the fear of God up someone** *not fml* to make someone greatly afraid: *I will not have this nonsense from the workers; go out there and put the fear of God up them, so that they obey orders. The new teacher put the fear of God up the class on his very first day, and had no trouble with the children from then on.* → **put in**[2] (14), **put into** (13)

**3 put the wind up** *not fml* to put fear into (someone): *I didn't intend to put the wind up you, I thought you had heard me coming. Real battle conditions will put the wind up the bravest of soldiers.* → **get up** (22), **have up** (5)

***put up to** *v adv prep*

**1** to encourage; give (someone) the idea of (something or doing something, usu. wrong): [D1] *Who put you up to a silly trick like that?* [V4b] *I think I know who put him up to cheating. "The Little Theatre have put me up to asking you if you'd let them do the play here."* (Robertson Davies, *Tempest-Tost*)

**2** to suggest; offer (something) to (someone): [D1] *Your idea is good; I'll put it up to the director tomorrow. What other means can we put up to him to show that we demand proof of his ability?*

**3** to make (someone) familiar with (something): [D1 (*often simple tenses*)] *Please put me up to the system of keeping records in this office.*

**4** to leave (a decision) to (someone): [D1 (*often simple tenses*)] *I put the decision up to you.* [D6 (*often simple tenses*)] *I put it up to you whether we should accept or not.*

**5** to warn (someone) about (something): [D1 (*often pass.*)] *Don't worry, I've been put up to all the tricks I can expect from this class.*

**put up with** *v adv prep*

**1** to raise (something) to a higher level or position by means of (something): [X9 + UP + *with*] *You can put the shelf up with a hammer and nails.*

*__2__ to stay with (someone), as overnight: [L9 (*with*)] *During the holidays, I put up with my grandmother, as I am not allowed to stay in the college rooms.*

*__3__ *not fml* to bear or suffer (something or someone bad) without complaining: [T1] *I cannot put up with your behaviour any longer.*

*Why should we put up with such terrible working conditions? I can't put up with her another day, she never stops complaining.* → **bear with** (2), **contend with** (2), **stand for** (5)

**put upon** *v prep* → **PUT ON** (1, 6, 12, 13, 18, 22, 35, 36)

***put wise** *v adj*
esp. *AmE infml* to inform (someone) of the correct information: [T1b (*to*)] *I thought I was in the right room until the other people put me wise. Isn't it time you put him wise to the real facts of the matter? He might make a terrible mistake.*

***putter about/around** *v adv; prep* → **potter about**
*AmE* to spend time in activities that demand little effort: [IØ] *The old man liked nothing better than puttering about in his garden, doing a few odd jobs here and there.* [T1 (*no pass.*)] *The doctor says that you are still not fit for heavy work, but you can get up and putter around the house for a few days.*

***putter along** *v adv; prep*
*not fml* (often of a machine) to move in a slow uneven manner: [IØ] *The old car can't get up steep hills, but it can putter along on the flat all right.* [T1 (*no pass.*)] *His motorcycle was puttering gently along the road when it struck a rock and threw him off.*

***putter around** *v adv; prep* → **PUTTER ABOUT**

***putter out** *v adv* → **flicker out** (1)
(of a flame or engine) to stop burning little by little, unevenly: [IØ (*often simple tenses*)] *When the candle was only half an inch high, it puttered out and the room became dark. The way the engine puttered out, I imagine that we are out of petrol.*

***puzzle out** *v adv* → **figure out** (2), **make out** (3), **work out** (5)
to understand (something or someone); find the answer to (something difficult) by thinking hard: [T1a] *A clever person should be able to puzzle out a way out of our difficulty. It's good for the students to puzzle things out for themselves. New students spend hours in the library, trying to puzzle out the system of arranging the books. I still can't puzzle out what he meant. I've never been able to puzzle her out, and still can't.* [T6] *Can you puzzle out what to do next? I've been trying to puzzle out which piece of work is most urgent.*

***puzzle over** *v prep*
to think hard about (something confusing): [T1] *After hours of puzzling over the book, at last it suddenly made sense. Why waste effort puzzling over his intentions? If you don't like his idea, don't accept it.*

# Q

**quail at/before** *v prep*
to lose courage; feel afraid because of an unpleasant (thought, possibility, or prospect) about to happen: [IØ + *at/before* (*simple tenses*)] *I quail at the prospect of waiting another weekend for some fine weather. The politician quailed at the possibility of losing so many votes by his careless remark. Having refused to take out fire insurance, the businessman quailed before the thought of ruin through fire.*

**quake with** *v prep* → **quiver with, shake with** (1), **shiver with, tremble with**
to shake the body strongly because of (cold or a strong feeling): [IØ + *with* (*often continuous tenses*)] *The children stood outside the school, quaking with cold. The prisoner was quaking with fear as he was about to be shot.*

**qualify as** *v prep*
to win recognition, usu. official, as by passing examinations, as being (usu. a professional person): [IØ + *as*] *At the end of three years, our son hopes to qualify as a lawyer.* [T1 + *as* (*usu. pass.*)] *Have you been qualified as a teacher yet? What makes you think you're qualified as a judge of painting?*

**qualify for** *v prep*
to (cause to) be fitted for; deserve; reach the condition recognized as enabling one to receive (something): [IØ + *for* (*usu. simple tenses*)] *Certain factories in areas of high unemployment may qualify for government money. If that boy goes on behaving like that, he'll qualify for severe punishment.* [T1 + *for* (*usu. simple tenses*)] *This degree will qualify you for teaching. Your action in helping the police to catch the jewel thieves could qualify you for a reward. Our recent victory has qualified the team for the first-class competition.*

**quarrel about/over** *v prep* → **argue about, bicker about, squabble about, wrangle about**
to disagree, often violently or unpleasantly, on the subject of (something or someone): [IØ + *about/over*] *Let us not quarrel about such unimportant matters. Let us not quarrel over going out tonight. Let us not quarrel over whether (it is safe) to sail in this weather.*

**quarrel with** *v prep*
**1** to disagree, often violently or unpleasantly, with (someone): [IØ + *with*] *Father always quarrels with his brother whenever they meet; they cannot seem to be friendly.* → **argue against, argue with** (1), **row with, squabble with**
***2** to disagree with (an idea); refuse to believe or accept (something): [T1] *I do not quarrel with the facts, only with the meaning that you give them.* → **argue with** (2), **disagree with** (2)
**3 quarrel with one's bread and butter** *not fml* to

take risks concerning one's job: [*usu. neg.*] *I know you don't agree with the director, but you'd better not say anything; after all, you don't want to quarrel with your bread and butter, do you?*

**queen over** *v prep* → **lord over**

**queen it over** *not fml* to control (someone) by giving orders: *She may be the leading singer, but that does not give her the right to queen it over the other performers in that offensive manner.*

**query with** *v prep*

to ask advice about the correctness, truth, or fitness of (something such as an idea) from (someone or a group), often when one does not approve of it oneself: [T1 + *with*] *I must query your suggestion with the director, it doesn't seem completely suitable at a first look. I wish to query my recent bill with your accounts department, I think there has been a mistake and I have been charged for goods that I did not buy.*

***quest for** *v prep* → **look for** (1), **search for, seek for**

*old use fml* to try very hard to find (something precious): [T1] *For over 100 years, men have been questing for gold in the hills. Noble men of old used to quest for the holy cup used by Christ at His last meal.*

**queue up** *v adv* → **line up** (1)

esp. *BrE* to wait in order of arrival: [IØ + UP] *I hate queueing up in the cold to get into a cinema.*

**quibble about/over** *v prep*

to ask unnecessary questions about the details of (something); express doubt about (something unimportant): [IØ + *about/over*] *If you're satisfied with the contract, why are you quibbling about the exact hours of work? The disagreement between the employers and the union could have been settled weeks ago if both sides had not wasted effort quibbling about pennies.*

**quicken up** *v adv* → **speed up**

to (cause to) move faster: [IØ + UP] *The rise in the cost of living has been quickening up in recent years.* [T1 + UP] *You'll have to quicken up your rate of work if you want to finish by the agreed date.* —**quickening-up** *n*

**quicken with** *v prep*

*old use* to suddenly begin very small movements because of (something such as a feeling): [IØ + *with* (*often simple tenses*)] *To everyone's surprise, Sarah quickened with new life (became pregnant), in her later years. Her heart quickened with fear as the lights went out.*

**quiet/quieten down** *v adv*

to (cause to) become quieter or calmer: [IØ + DOWN] *At last the wind quietened down, and the storm was over.* [T1 + DOWN] *See if you can quiet the dog down, he's annoying the neighbours with his noise.*

***quirk up** *v adv*

(usu. of part of the face) to (cause to) rise quickly, as in surprise, esp. with a curling or twisting movement: [IØ (*often simple tenses*)] *His eyebrows quirked up when he heard the name of his visitor.* [T1 (*often simple tenses*)] *Quirking up his forehead at the sudden noise, he looked out of the window to see what it was. He quirked up the corners of his mouth with amusement.*

***quit of** *v prep*

to rid (oneself) of (something unwanted): [D1 (*often pass., simple tenses*)] *I'd like to quit myself of any blame in this affair. I'm glad to be quit of that unsuitable job.*

**quiver with** *v prep* → **quake with, shake with** (1), **shiver with, tremble with**

to move the body in very quick waves caused by (cold or a strong feeling): [IØ + *with*] *The children waited outside the school, quivering with cold. The prisoner was quivering with fear as he faced the court.*

**quote from** *v prep*

to use the exact words of (someone or printed matter): [IØ + *from*] *Many people quote from the Bible without knowing that they are doing so. Here, I am quoting from my former teacher, who always gave good advice.* [T1 + *from*] *It's easy to quote phrases from any of Shakespeare's plays.*

# R

***rabbit on** *v adv*
*infml* to talk continuously and rather foolishly: [IØ (*about*)] *I suppose her mother is still rabbiting on as usual; let's go in the other door so that she doesn't see us.*

**race against** *v prep*
**1** also **race with** to try to move faster than (usu. someone): [IØ + *against*] *Jim was a little worried about racing against the best runners from other countries; he feared that he could not stand up to the competition.*
**2 race against the clock/time** to have to do something quickly; be forced to hurry: *I don't like racing against time; I would rather do my work carefully and well. If you got up earlier you wouldn't spend half the morning racing against the clock.*

**race around/round** *v adv; prep*
to move or act quickly (in a place), esp. going to several different places quickly: [IØ + AROUND/ROUND/*around/round*] *By racing round, we were able to get all the horses out safely before the fire reached their hut. I had to race round (the house) tidying before the visitors arrived.*

**race through** *v prep*
to (cause to) hurry to complete (something): [L9 + *through*] *Don't race through the list like that, read each name carefully.* [X9 + *through*] *The government raced the new law through all its stages, so as to complete it before the election.*

**race up** *v adv* also **shoot up**
to rise very quickly; hurry to the top: [IØ + UP (*into, to*)] *The cost of living has been racing up in the past year. We had just settled into autumn when the temperature raced up to summer conditions again.*

**race with** *v prep* → **RACE AGAINST** (1)

***rack up** *v adv*
**1** *infml* (usu. in sport) to gain; win (a measure of victory): [T1 (*often simple tenses*)] *With a skilful game, he racked up ten more very useful points for his team.*
**2** *AmE infml* to cause (someone) to fall, as with a blow: [T1 (*often simple tenses*)] *He racked up his opponent with a well-placed blow.*
**3** *AmE infml* to defeat (someone) completely: [T1 (*often simple tenses*)] *By clever planning, we were able to rack up the other team in the first half of the game.*

**rack with** *v prep*
**be racked with pain** to suffer severely from (pain or sorrow): *It was a mercy that she died, for she had been racked with pain through her last long illness.*

**radiate from** *v prep*
**1** (of lines or something like lines) to show or take a direction outwards from (a centre): [IØ + *from*] *Many of the railway lines in England radiate from London. This pattern shows lines of different colours radiating from a middle point.*
**2** to come or spread outwards from (something): [IØ + *from*] *When the mist cleared, welcome warmth radiated from the sun. Wisdom and goodness radiated from his face.*

**rage against/at** *v prep*
to express great anger directed towards (usu. something): [IØ + *against/at*] *It's no use raging at unjust laws; there's nothing you can do to change them.*

**rage out** *v adv* → **blow out** (5)
**rage itself out** (of a storm) to cease, by using all its violence: *Once the storm has raged itself out, we shall be able to set sail again.*

**rage through** *v prep*
to move violently through (something such as a place): [IØ + *through*] *The storm that raged through the western islands last night has now died down. Bands of law breakers used to rage through the town, shooting and robbing.*

**rail against/at/on** *v prep*
to express opposition to (something), usu. in bitter words; scold (someone) bitterly: [L9 + *against/at/on*] *It's no good railing against fate; better learn to live with what you have.*

**rail in** *v adv* → **fence in** (1), **hedge in, hem in, wall in** (1)
to enclose (an area or animal) with a wooden fence: [X9 + IN] *The cattle owners let their animals wander across open country, but the farmers railed in their cattle and their land, and this is what caused many bitter fights in the old West.* —**railed-in** *adj*

**rail off** *v adv* → **divide off, fence off** (1), **separate off, wall off**
to separate (part of something such as land) with a wooden fence: [X9 + OFF] *This part of the field has been railed off to keep the cattle out.* —**railed-off** *adj*

**rail on** *v prep* → **RAIL AGAINST**

**railroad into** *v prep* → **coerce into**
*infml* to persuade (someone) into (doing something), by using force or other improper influence: [V4a (*usu. pass.*)] *No voter may be railroaded into giving his vote for any particular person; he must be free to choose which one he wants to elect. I will no longer allow myself to be railroaded into serving on the same committee again.*

***railroad through** *v adv; prep* → **go through**[1] (3), **put across**[1] (3), **put through**[1] (1), **ram through, take through**[1] (2)
*not fml* to force (a law) to pass (a law-making body), usu. wrongly: [T1b (*usu. pass.*)] *Changes in the tax laws were railroaded*

*through to suit richer people, in spite of the opposition of members sympathetic to the poor.* [D1 (*usu. pass.*)] *Changes in the law were railroaded through Parliament by unprincipled politicians.*

**rain down** *v adv*

**1** (of water) to fall in large amounts: [L9 + DOWN (*on*)] *Long after the storm, water still rained down from the roofs where it had collected.*

***2** to (cause to) descend quickly and in quantity (on someone or something): [T1a (*on*)] *The old woman rained down curses on our heads.* [IØ (*on*)] *Pieces of broken glass were still raining down long after the explosion. Troubles rained down on the city during the war.* → **hail down on**

**rain in** *v adv*

(of rain) to enter a building: [IØ + IN] *There must be a hole in the roof, it's raining in.*

**rain off** *v adv* also esp. *AmE* **rain out** → **snow off**

**be rained off** (of an outdoor event) to be prevented from taking place because of rain: *Two cricket matches were rained off this weekend, and will have to be played next week.*

**rain on/upon** *v prep*

**1** (of rain) to fall on (someone or something): [IØ + *on/upon*] *It's raining on one side of the street and not on the other; we must be under the edge of a cloud. I shall take a hat as I don't like being rained on.*

***2** to (cause to) descend quickly or in quantity on (someone or something): [T1 (*no pass.*)] *I lay still as the blows continued to rain on my head.* [D1] *The crowd rained kisses on the popular actor. Angrily, he rained blows on the door, but no one came.* → **shower on**

**rain out** *v adv* esp. *AmE* → **RAIN OFF**

**rain upon** *v prep* → **RAIN ON**

**raise against** *v prep*

**raise one's voice against** to express opposition to (something such as an action): *I feel I must raise my voice against suggested changes in the law.*

**raise from** *v prep*

**1** to educate (someone) from the time when he was (a child); cause (something) to grow from (a small beginning): [T1 + *from*] *I should know my own son, I've raised him from a baby. I'm very proud of having raised these bushes from seed.*

**2 raise someone from the dead** to bring a dead person back to life: *Jesus was able to raise many sick people from the dead.* → **call up** (6), **raise up** (2), **rise from** (4), **summon up** (4)

**raise to** *v prep*

**1** to lift (something or someone) towards (something): [T1 + *to*] *He raised his hand to his forehead in a way that expressed worry. He reached high to raise the child to the top branch. We should be able to raise the sunken ship to the surface.*

***2** to cause (someone) to reach (a higher position): [D1 (*often simple tenses*)] *The King raised the brave general to great heights as a reward for his victory. Any worker who makes a useful suggestion to the firm will be raised to a higher position.*

**3 raise a glass to** to drink the health of (someone): *I raise my glass to the happy pair, wishing them a long life together and many children.* → **drink to** (1), **propose to** (2)

**4 raise a hand to** to hit (someone): *Don't you dare raise a hand to my son!*

**5 raise one's hat to: a** to lift the hat from one's head in polite greeting: *I knew that my father regarded me as a woman instead of a girl, the first time he raised his hat to me when we met.* **b** *not fml* to express admiration for (someone): [*usu. first person, present simple tenses*] *You've done a remarkably fine job—I raise my hat to you!* → **take off**[1] (21)

**6 raise an objection to** to express particular opposition to (something such as an idea): *I wish to raise an objection to the chairman's last remark. If too many objections are raised to the building of the new airport, we shall have to delay the plan.* → **demur at, object to, protest against, take to** (13)

**7 raise someone to the peerage** *fml* to make someone a lord or lady: [*often simple tenses*] *The Queen has chosen to honour Mr Brown for his services to British industry by raising him to the peerage.*

**8 raise a man to the purple** (in the Roman Catholic Church) to make a priest into a cardinal: [*often pass.*] *Towards the end of the well-loved priest's honourable life in the Church, he was raised to the purple.*

**raise up** *v adv*

**1** to lift (something or someone) higher: [T1 + UP] *Raise me up higher, I can't see. Raise your hands up straight so that I can count them.*

***2** to bring (someone) back to life; call (a spirit) into being: [T1 (*often simple tenses*)] *This woman claims to be able to raise up spirits.* → **call up** (6), **raise from** (2), **rise from** (4), **summon up** (4)

**raise with** *v prep* → **bring up** (3), **come up** (8)

to introduce (something such as a matter) in talk with (someone): [T1 + *with* (*often simple tenses*)] *I should like to raise another question with this committee. May I raise a delicate subject with you?*

***rake about/around/round** *v adv; prep*

*not fml* to search thoroughly in many places (in somewhere) (for something such as a sign): [IØ (*for*); T1 (*for*)] *I spent the day raking around (the house) (for proof)*, but found *nothing. I've raked about in my memory, but cannot remember the name.* **—rake-around** *n*

**rake in** *v adv*

**1** to gather (money or something representing it) from a table where people are risking money on games: [T1 + IN] *The man in charge of the game has a long-handled tool for raking in the money that the players lose. At last her number came up, and she raked in her winnings.*

***2** *infml* to earn, gain, or share (money): [T1 (*often continuous tenses*)] *Too many people are raking in large profits from the housing market.* → **shovel in** (3)

**3 rake it in** *infml* to earn or gain a lot of money: *He must be raking it in!*

**rake off** *v adv; prep* → **kick back** (4), **pay off** (4)
*infml* to take a share of (money earned or won), sometimes wrongly: [T1] *How much did your lawyer rake off this time?* [D1] *The tax man rakes a third off everything I earn.* —**rake-off** *n*

**rake out** *v adv*
**1** to clear (a fireplace), usu. by shaking and pulling a tool inside it: [T1 + OUT] *The boiler should be thoroughly raked out once a month, to prevent blocking by old ashes.*

**2** to remove (something blocking a space) with a tool: [T1 + OUT] *I shall have to rake these dead leaves out before water will flow through the pipe again.*

***3** *not fml* to find (something) by thorough searching: [T1 (*often simple tenses*)] *At last I raked out a worn old coat to give to the man at the door.* → **dredge up** (2), **rake up** (3), **root out** (3), **root up** (3), **rout out** (1), **rout up** (1)

**rake over**[1] *v adv*
**1** to work (soil) with a rake: [T1 + OVER] *The vegetable garden must be throughly raked over before you plant the seeds for next year's crop.*

***2** *not fml* to remember (something) in talk: [T1a] *Let's not rake over things that we would rather forget.* → **rake up** (2)

**3 rake over old ashes** *not fml* to talk about unhappy times in the past: *Rather than rake over old ashes, let us look ahead to the future.*

**rake over**[2] *v prep*
**1** *not fml* to search among (something or things): [T1] *I spent the morning in the library, raking over the newspapers, looking for the article that I wanted.* → **rake through**

**2 rake someone over the coals** *infml* to scold someone for a fault: *I daren't be late for work again or the director will rake me over the coals.* → **call over**[2], **haul over**

**rake round** *v adv; prep* → RAKE ABOUT

**rake through** *v prep* → **rake over**[2] (1)
*not fml* to search among (something or things): [T1] *I spent the morning in the library, raking through the newspapers, looking for the article that I wanted.* —**rake-through** *n*

**rake up** *v adv*
**1** to make a pile of (dried grass) with a rake: [T1 + UP] *In the summer, we used to help the farmer to rake up the dried grass into piles for the cattle to eat during the winter.*

***2** *not fml* to remind someone of (something in the past which is best forgotten); produce; discover (unpleasant facts in the past): [T1] *Please don't rake up that old quarrel.* → **rake over**[1] (2)

***3** *not fml* to find (something or someone) with difficulty: [T1 (*often simple tenses*)] *Can't you rake up some other players for the team? At last I raked up an old coat to give to the man at the door. Let's see what excuse you can rake up this time.* → **dredge up** (2), **rake out** (3), **root out** (3), **root up** (3), **rout out** (1), **rout up** (1)

***rally from** *v prep*
to begin to show signs of better health after the worst of (an illness): [IØ + *from*] *Has the child rallied from her fever yet?*

***rally round**[1] *v adv*
to unite to give help when needed: [IØ] *If the whole family rallies round, we can get Jim out of debt.*

***rally round**[2] *v prep*
to gather to support (someone or something such as an idea): [T1] *The nation must rally round its chosen leaders to fight our present troubles. Rally round the flag, boys, rally round the flag.*

**rally to** *v prep*
**rally to the support of** to gather to support (someone or something): *If powerful countries will rally to the support of small independent nations, the danger of their being conquered will pass.*

**ram down**[1] *v adv*
to push (something) firmly in place, as with a heavy tool: [X9 + DOWN] *You have to put the metal ball in the big gun and then ram it down. The men are using a heavy machine to ram down the surface of the newly mended road.*

**ram down**[2] *v prep*
**1** to force (something) to pass down (a space) by pushing: [X9 + *down*] *We had to ram the pipe down a narrow hole to get it through.* → **force down** (1), **push down**[2] (1), **stuff down** (1), **thrust down** (1)

**2 ram something down someone's throat** *not fml* to force someone to remember, believe, or accept something unpleasant: *I do not like having our lack of money rammed down my throat every time I want some new clothes.* → **force down** (2), **push down**[2] (2), **stuff down** (2), **thrust down** (2)

**ram home** *v adv*
**1** to force (something) into position by pushing: [X9 + HOME] *He put the point of the knife on the surface, and then rammed it home.* → **drive home** (2)

***2** to make (something) clearly understood, as by force: [T1 (*to*)] *Advertisers keep repeating the name of the product in order to ram the message home (to the public). The harm that I had done was rammed home to me when my husband told me his terrible dream.* → **drive home** (3)

**ram into** *v prep*
to (cause to) hit (something); be pushed against (an object) or into (a space): [L9 + *into*] *I see from the condition of the front of the car that you've rammed into the garage door again. I didn't cause the damage; I was rammed into from behind.* [X9 + *into*] *The only way that I could stop the car sliding on the ice was to ram the wheels into the edge of the road. I had to ram my clothes into the suitcase, there was so little room.*

***ram through** *v adv; prep* → **go through**¹ (3), **put across**¹ (3), **put through**¹ (1), **railroad through, take through**¹ (2)
*not fml* to force (a law) to pass (a law-making body), usu. wrongly: [T1a (*usu. pass.*)] *Changes in the tax laws were rammed through to suit richer people, in spite of the opposition of members sympathetic to the poor.* [D1 (*usu. pass.*)] *Changes in the law were rammed through Parliament by unprincipled politicians.*

**ramble on** *v adv*
*not fml* to talk or write continuously without saying much, in a disconnected style: [IØ + ON] *I try to avoid getting into conversation with him, as he always rambles on so, and I can't get away. Her letter doesn't contain any news, but it rambles on for pages.*

***ramp about/around** *v adv* → **horse about, lark about, romp about**
*not fml* to play roughly: [IØ] *The children love ramping about in the wild garden.*

**rampage about/around** *v adv*
to behave wildly in a place: [IØ + ABOUT/AROUND] *Groups of lawbreakers have been rampaging about all night, putting fear into the villagers.*

**rampage along** *v adv*
(of a boat) to move quickly: [IØ + ALONG] *The wind blew stronger, and the little boat rampaged along effortlessly.*

**rampage around** *v adv* → RAMPAGE ABOUT

**range against** *v prep*
to place; direct (something, someone, or oneself) in opposition to (someone or something): [X9 + *against* (*often pass.*)] *All the enemy's guns were ranged against us from both sides. It's unwise to range yourself against opponents who are certain to defeat you. The opposition's attack was ranged against the government's attempt to control rising prices.*

**range from/to** *v prep* → **run from** (4), **run to** (4), **vary from**
to vary from (something smaller or less) to (something bigger or more): [L9 + *from/to* (*simple tenses*)] *Temperatures here range from the low 30's to the upper 80's Fahrenheit. His feelings on the matter have ranged from bitterness to hope.*

***range in** *v adv* → **home in on, zero in on**
*mil* to fix the range between one's guns and the object aimed at: [IØ (*on*) (*usu. simple tenses*)] *Wait until the men have ranged in on the enemy positions before you open fire.* [T1 (*usu. pass.*)] *We've got all the ships ranged in now; shall we start the guns?*

**range over/through** *v prep*
to spread; move among (a large area or areas): [L9 + *over/through*] *The cattle range over many miles in search of food. There are many wild animals ranging through these woods. His speech ranged over a wide field of interest.*

**range to** *v prep* → RANGE FROM

**range with** *v prep*
**range oneself with** to support (someone or an opinion): *I'm surprised to hear that he has ranged himself with the workers, I thought he was always loyal to the employers' ideas.*

**rank among/with** *v prep* → **rate among, rate with** (1)
to (cause to) be regarded as equal to; be fit to share a position with (things or people of a certain level, usu. best or worst): [L9 + *among/with* (*simple tenses*)] *Tom's book ranks among the most important to be printed this year. Jim ranks with the best runners of any country.* [X9 + *among/with* (*simple tenses*)] *Would you rank this car among the fastest?*

**rank as** *v prep* → **rate as** (1)
to (cause to) be considered as having the quality of (someone or something, usu. good): [L9 + *as* (*simple tenses*)] *She ranks as the finest teacher we have. This student ranks as the most promising in the college.* [X9 + *as* (*simple tenses*)] *Would you rank this politician as the greatest leader of our time? I would rank this wine as the finest I have ever tasted.*

**rank with** *v prep* → RANK AMONG

**ransack for** *v prep*
to search (something such as a place) thoroughly, as by moving things, trying to find (something or someone): [T1 + *for*] *I've ransacked the house for that piece of paper with the telephone number, but I can't find it. The forest has been ransacked unsuccessfully for the missing child.*

**rap at** *v prep* → **knock at,** etc.
to beat on; give blows on; make a noise on (something such as a door), often with something hard: [IØ + *at*] *There's someone rapping at the door; see who it is, will you? It's only a branch rapping at the window, that's all.*

**rap on** *v prep*
**1** to beat on (something such as a surface) with something hard: [IØ + *on*] *Rap on the wall with the heel of your shoe, someone will surely hear and let us out. The king rapped on the table with his heavy metal ring, and the company fell silent.* → **knock at,** etc.
**2 rap someone on the knuckles** also **rap over** *not fml* to scold someone for a fault: *You'll get rapped on the knuckles if you're late for work again.*

**rap out** *v adv*
**1** to knock repeatedly to send (a message):

[T1 + OUT] *Keep silent, and the spirits will rap out a message for you.* → **tap out** (1)

*__2__ to say (something) suddenly and sharply: [T1a (*often simple tenses*)] *The officer rapped out an order, and all the soldiers raised their guns.* → **snap out**

**rap over** *v prep* → **RAP ON** (2)

**rap with** *v prep*

**1** to knock using (something): [I∅ + *with*] *Rap with the heel of your shoe on the door, someone is sure to hear and let us out of here.* → **tap with**

**2** *infml* to talk with (someone) informally, as to exchange opinions: [I∅ + *with*] *You can learn a lot by rapping with people you think might be your enemies.*

***rasp out** *v adv*

to say (something) in a rough voice: [T1a (*often simple tenses*)] *"Help me, I'm dying of thirst," he rasped out. The officer rasped out an order.*

***rat on** *v prep*

**1** *infml* to tell someone in charge such as the police, about the wrongful activities of (someone one knows): [T1] *The rules of honour among the students state that you don't rat on a fellow student who cheats in an examination. Never rat on a friend.* → **inform against,** etc.

**2** *infml* to fail to fulfil (something such as a duty or agreement): [T1] *Never rat on your debts.*

**rate above** *v prep*

to consider the worth of someone to be higher than (a certain position, job, etc.): [X9 + *above* (*simple tenses*)] *Why should you rate yourself above this job? We all have to take our turn at unpleasant work. He has always rated himself above ordinary musicians.*

**rate among** *v prep* → **rank among, rate with** (1)

to (cause to) be regarded as equal to; be fit to share a position with (things or people of a certain level, usu. best or worst): [L9 + *among* (*simple tenses*)] *Tom's book rates among the most important to be printed this year.* [X9 + *among* (*simple tenses*)] *Would you rate this car among the fastest?*

**rate as** *v prep*

**1** to (cause to) be considered as having the quality of (someone or something, usu. good): [L9 + *as* (*simple tenses*)] *She rates as the finest teacher we have. This student rates as the most promising in the college.* [X9 + *as* (*simple tenses*)] *Would you rate this politician as the greatest leader of our time? I would rate this wine as the finest I have ever tasted.* → **rank as**

**2** *mil* to place; class (someone) as belonging to (a certain rank): [X9 + *as* (*usu. pass.*)] *The sailor was rated as an ordinary seaman.*

**rate at** *v prep*

**1** to consider (usu. something) to have a value, power, etc., of (a certain amount): [X9 + *at* (*simple tenses*)] *I would rate our monthly sales at about $45,000.* → **value at**

**2** *BrE* to consider (property) to have a value of (an amount) for tax purposes: [X9 + *at* (*usu. pass.*)] *The house has been rated at £500 a year.*

***rate up** *v adv*

esp. *AmE* to increase (usu. a payment) by an equal share: [T1 (*usu. pass.*)] *The insurance payments have to be rated up for people with poor health.*

**rate with** *v prep*

**1** to (cause to) be regarded as equal to; be fit to share a position with (things or people of a certain level, usu. best or worst): [L9 + *with* (*simple tenses*)] *Tom's book rates with the most important to be printed this year.* [X9 + *with* (*simple tenses*)] *Would you rate this car with the fastest?* → **rank among, rate among**

*__2__ *not fml* to be favoured by (someone): [T1 (*no pass., simple tenses*)] *The new secretary really rates with the director, doesn't she? How does our new method rate with the workers?*

**ration out** *v adv*

to give a share of (something) equally among several people, things, or places: [T1 + OUT] *The shipwrecked sailors rationed out their precious water supply over several days, hoping that they would soon meet a ship. We must ration the food out among the members of the climbing party; each climber will look after his own share.*

**rattle along** *v adv*

*not fml* (usu. of a vehicle) to move noisily and not very quickly: [L9 + ALONG] *Is your old car still rattling along?*

***rattle around in** *v adv prep*

*not fml* to live or work in (a place too big for one's needs): [T1] *When the children left home, we found that we were just rattling around in that big house, so we sold it and bought a smaller place.*

**rattle away** *v adv*

*not fml* to work noisily: [L9 + AWAY (*at, on*)] *The printing machines were rattling away so loudly that we could hardly hear each other speak. The children must learn not to rattle away at the piano, but treat it like the delicate instrument it is.*

***rattle down** *v adv*

*naut* to make ratlines (short ropes for a rope ladder on a ship): [I∅ (*usu. continuous tenses*)] *The sailors finished rattling down before going ashore.*

***rattle off** *v adv* → **reel off, roll off** (3), **run off**[1] (7), **spiel off**

*not fml* to repeat (words) quickly and too easily from memory; perform (an action) with ease and speed: [T1] *What is the point of teaching the children to rattle off the names of the kings and queens of England if they know nothing about history? Our local tennis star can rattle off any stroke in the book.*

**rattle on**[1] *v adv*

**1** *not fml* (of a vehicle) to move noisily, con-

tinuously: [L9 + ON] *I believe that old car would rattle on even if the engine fell out.*
*2 *not fml* to talk continuously and uninterestingly: [IØ] *At every meeting of the women's club, Mrs White rattles on for hours.*

**rattle on[2]** *v prep*
to hit (something) with sharp repeated noises: [IØ + *on*] *Small stones rattled on the underside of the car as we drove along the rough road.*

**rattle over** *v prep*
*not fml* to move noisily across (something): [L9 + *over*] *The car rattled over the stony street.*

***rattle through** *v prep*
*not fml* to perform (something) quickly: [T1] *After a rest, I was able to rattle through my work without feeling tired. The politician rattled through his speech, failing to keep the interest of the crowd.*

**rave about** *v prep*
**1** also **rave over** *not fml* to praise (something or someone) with great keenness: [L9 + *about*] *The newspaper reporters are all raving about the young singer's performance, which has given the whole city such pleasure.*
**2** to speak angrily about (something): [IØ + *about*] *In court, the prisoner raved about the unjust decision made by the judge regarding his guilt.* → **rave against**

**rave against/at** *v prep* → **rave about** (2)
to oppose (something or someone) violently in words: [IØ + *against/at*] *The prisoner refused to accept the judge's decision that he was guilty, but shouted in court, raving against injustice. The old man stood on a street corner, raving at his wife for her bad treatment of him, as he imagined it.*

**rave over** *v prep* → **RAVE ABOUT** (1)

**ravel out** *v adv*
to (cause to) separate into single threads: [IØ + OUT] *The end of the rope has ravelled out and the knot will not hold the climbers safely.* [T1 + OUT] *Can you ravel out this piece of string: it's all in knots. If you ravel out the end of the wool, you can count the threads in it and make sure that you buy the same thickness next time.*

**raze to** *v prep*
**raze a building/town to the ground** to destroy a building or town completely, as by burning: *The castle was razed to the ground by the conquering army.*

***reach after** *v prep*
to try to obtain (something such as an idea): [T1] *For years he studied many forms of religion, reaching after the truth.*

**reach back** *v adv*
**1** to lean in a backward direction so as to touch something with the hand: [L9 + BACK] *If you reach back carefully, you can pass me the book from the shelf behind you.*
*2 to return in memory: [IØ (*to*) (*usu. simple tenses*)] *If you reach back in your mind, you should be able to recall the name. The old woman's memory reaches back to the last century.*

**reach down** *v adv* → **hand down** (4), **pass down[1]** (5), **pass on[1]** (6)
to (cause to) move in a downward direction, usu. by stretching one's body: [L9 + DOWN] *Reaching down, he pulled the cat from the well.* [T1 + DOWN] *Can you reach down the big dish for me from the top shelf? I can touch it, but it's too high to reach down. Please reach me down that book on the high shelf.*

**reach for** *v prep*
**1** to stretch (usu. one's hand) so as to touch or hold (usu. something): [L9 + *for*] *Sinking in the sand, he reached for his friend's hand, but it was too far away. There was no time for me to reach for my gun.* [X9 + *for*] *Don't you dare reach your thieving hand for that cake!*
**2 reach for the moon** *not fml* to try to do something impossible: *Why can't she learn to live within the limits of her ability? She's always reaching for the moon and getting disappointed.*
**3 reach for the sky** *infml* to raise one's hands, at a gunman's command: [*usu. imper.*] *Reach for the sky, I've got a gun!*

**reach forward** *v adv*
**1** to stretch (the hand) in a forward direction: [L9 + FORWARD] *Reaching forward, I touched him on the back.* [X9 + FORWARD] *Reach your hand forward and see what you get.*
*2 to try; make an effort towards something such as an aim: [IØ (*to*)] *In middle age, many people begin to reach forward to higher matters of the spirit.*

**reach into** *v prep*
**1** to (cause to) stretch so as to enter (something): [L9 + *into*] *I can't reach into the pipe, it's too narrow.* [X9 + *into*] *I saw you reaching your hand into the cake tin!*
*2 to stretch as far as the beginning of (something such as an amount, space, or time): [T1 (*no pass., usu. simple tenses*)] *The cold weather has reached well into the spring. The tax bill reaches into thousands of dollars.* → **run into** (10), **run to** (7), **run up to** (2)

**reach out** *v adv*
**1** to (cause to) stretch forward: [L9 + OUT] *Reaching out, he took a firm hold of the rope.* [X9 + OUT] *You can feel the rain if you reach out your hand. He reached out a hand for the money.* → **put out** (1), etc.
*2 to try; make an effort to persuade or inform someone or understand something: [IØ (*to, towards*)] *The churches are trying to reach out in an effort to attract young people to services. Modern politicians try to reach out to ordinary people in their broadcast speeches.*
—**outreach** *n*

**reach to/towards** *v prep*
**1** to stretch (a hand, arm, or finger) as far as (something): [IØ + *to/towards* (*simple*

*tenses*)] *The rope won't reach to the ground so you'll have to jump the last few feet. My voice doesn't reach to those very high notes. I like curtains that reach to the floor.* [T1 + *to*/*towards* (*usu. simple tenses*)] *Can you reach a hand to that dish on the top shelf?* → **go to** (2), **lead to** (2)

*__2__ to make an effort to understand or accept (someone or an idea): [T1 (*no pass., often simple tenses*)] *The churches are trying to reach towards young people and persuade them to attend services. His ideas are difficult to reach to.*

**reach up** *v adv*

**1** to (cause to) stretch high: [L9 + UP] *I can get that apple on the high branch if I reach up.* [X9 + UP] *Can you reach up your arm to that book on the top shelf?*

*__2__ to have hopes and expectations for one's future; attempt to win: [IØ (*to*) (*often simple tenses*)] *You'll never get anywhere in your job unless you reach up to the highest position in the firm and take steps to fullfil your aim.*

**react against** *v prep*

to feel and usu. express opposition as a result of meeting (something such as an idea): [IØ + *against*] *The unions have reacted strongly against the government's wage and price controls.*

***react on/upon** *v prep*

to have an effect on (something); influence (someone): [T1 (*usu. simple tenses*)] *Certain acids react on metals to cause chemical changes. It will take a strong politician to react on this angry crowd.*

**react to** *v prep* → **respond to** (2)

to feel and express the effect of; judge (something or someone): [IØ + *to*] *She reacted to the news by bursting into tears. How do you react to this modern artist's paintings? The children reacted to the new teacher by showing their worst behaviour.*

***react upon** *v prep* → **REACT ON**

**read about/of** *v prep*

to receive information concerning (something) through printed material: [IØ + *about*/*of*] *It was sad to read of the death of the famous old actress in this morning's newspaper. It must be true, I read about it in the newspaper! "Read all about it!"* (newspaper seller's cry)

**read around/round** *v prep*

**1** to study material as background to (something such as a subject): [IØ + *around*/*round*] *I've read around the subject of law and understand it quite well now.*

**2** to read in turn, aloud, among different people in (a class or room): [IØ + *around*/*round*] *It's uninteresting reading the play round the class, can't we try to act it?*

**read as** *v prep*

to judge or mistake (something such as a word) to be (something else): [T1 + *as* (*usu. simple tenses*)] *I read the word 'has' as 'as'. Silence cannot always be read as agreement.*

**read back** *v adv*

to read (something) in return, to someone who has read it to one: [T1 + BACK] *Take down the names as I read them to you, and then read your list back to me, to see if you have got them all right.*

**read between** *v prep*

**read between the lines** to find a meaning that is not expressed: *His letter sounds friendly enough, but if you read between the lines, you will see that he doesn't really welcome us to his home.*

**read for** *v prep*

to study so as to obtain (a degree) or become a member of (the bar, the profession of lawyers who have the right to speak in higher courts of law): [IØ + *for*] *He was reading for his degree when his studies were interrupted by the war. My son is reading for the bar, and hopes to become a lawyer at the end of next year.*

**read from/out of** *v prep; adv prep*

to read (something) aloud using words printed in (a book, newspaper, etc.) or written in (notes): [IØ + *from*/OUT + *of*] *Are you inventing this story or are you reading from the newspaper?* [T1 + *from*/OUT + *of*] *The speaker quite spoiled the effect by reading his speech from notes, so that he seemed insincere, and failed to excite the crowd.*

**read in** *v prep*

**1** to read (words) printed in (a book, newspaper, etc.): [T1 + *in*] *The story must be true, I read it in the newspaper.*

**2** to study (a subject) by reading: [IØ + *in*] *I like to read deeply in any subject that I choose to study.*

**3** to understand (something) by reading or studying (something): [T1 + *in* (*simple tenses*)] *I could read the answer in her face, before she spoke.*

**4 be (well) read in** to have deep knowledge of (a subject), usu. gained by reading: *Few students these days are well read in ancient writers.*

***read into** *v prep*

to understand (something more than it contains) from (something): [D1] *Don't read more into her letter than she intended. Try not to read evil intentions into the ordinary actions of people around you.*

**read of** *v prep* → **READ ABOUT**

**read off** *v adv*

to read (something such as words) thoroughly, often aloud: [T1 + OFF] *Reading off the names on the list, he found two members of his family missing. Read off the figures to me, and I will see if they are correct.*

**read on** *v adv*

to continue reading: [IØ + ON (*often imper.*)] *Our story finished at this point last week; now read on. I'm sorry I interrupted; please read on.*

**read out** *v adv*
**1** to read (words) aloud: [T1 + OUT] *Read out the names as the people come in, so that we can all hear.*
***2** (of a computer) to produce (a printed form of the results of an enquiry or calculation): [T1 (*usu. simple tenses*)] *The machine will read out the results of the calculation, and the names of suitable books on the subject.* —**readout** *n* → **print out**
***3** *AmE* to make (someone) leave an organization, usu. for a fault: [T1 (*of*) (*usu. pass.*)] *The former leader was read out of the Party after his guilt was proved.*

**read out of** *v adv prep* → **READ FROM**

**read over** *v adv*
**1** to read (something) again: [T1 + OVER] *Let me read that over, I must have mistaken the name. Although I read the instructions over several times, I still could not follow them.*
***2** to study (printed or written matter) thoroughly: [T1] *I'll give you my opinion when I've had time to read the book through.* → **read over** (2)

**read round** *v prep* → **READ AROUND**

***read through** *v adv*
**1** to study (printed or written matter) thoroughly: [T1] *I'll give you my opinion when I've had time to read the book through.* → **read over** (2)
**2** (in theatre) to practise the words of a play only, without the movements, usu. by reading: [T1] *Let's read the play through at the first practice, and put in the moves later.* —**read-through** *n*

**read to** *v prep*
**1** to read (something) aloud to (someone); read (something) silently to (oneself): [I∅ + *to*] *Shall I read to the children before they go to sleep?* [T1 + *to*] *I shall now read your favourite story to you: "The Three Bears!"*
**2 read oneself to sleep** to read in bed until one falls asleep: *When I'm alone I like to read myself to sleep, rather than lie there awake, waiting for sleep to come and worrying about it.*

***read up** *v adv*
to study (something): [T1] *I must read up the notes I made for my class. Read up the rules and you will see that I am right.*

***read up on** *v adv prep*
to study (something such as a subject) thoroughly, as by reading: [T1] *I shall have to read up on this subject if I am to give a talk about it.*

**realize from/on** *v prep*
to gain (money as profit) by the sale of (goods): [T1 + *from/on* (*simple tenses*)] *How much did you realize on the house? We hope to realize over $1000 for the children's hospital from the paintings which people have given.*

**reap from** *v prep*
**1** to gather (a crop) as the product of (seeds, plants, etc.): [T1 + *from*] *We reaped a fine crop of fruit from the bushes that we planted last year.*
**2** to gain (something in return) as the result of (something such as an activity): [T1 + *from*] *We have reaped an excellent profit from the efforts we have made over the years to improve the house. Only unhappiness can be reaped from selfish actions.*

**rear up** *v adv*
**1** (usu. of a horse or other four-legged animal) to stand on its back legs, lifting the front feet high: [I∅ + UP] *The horse reared up in fear, throwing its rider off.*
***2** to rise suddenly, as in anger: [I∅] *The crowd reared up and attacked the speaker.*

**reason against** *v prep*
to oppose (something), usu. by thoughtful argument: [I∅ + *against* (*usu. simple tenses*)] *The lawyer reasoned against any changes being made in the law.*

**reason from** *v prep*
to make a judgment based on (something such as an idea): [I∅ + *from* (*usu. simple tenses*)] *The employer reasoned from his opinion of the workers and decided to increase their pay.*

**reason into** *v prep* → **argue into,** etc.
to persuade (someone) by thoughtful argument to believe (something) or start (doing something): [X9 + *into*] *See if you can reason the members into agreement with each other. You can easily reason yourself into even greater fear if you always think about the worst possibilities. See if you can reason the members into agreeing with the plan. No one can be reasoned into accepting an idea that his feelings oppose.*

***reason out** *v adv*
to find an answer to (something) by thinking of all possible arguments: [T1 (*often simple tenses*)] *Let's reason the matter out instead of quarrelling.* [T5 (*usu. simple tenses*)] *The workers have reasoned out that the real power is in their own hands.* [T6 (*usu. simple tenses*)] *We could not reason out where we were, because of the mist.*

**reason out of** *v adv prep* → **argue out of,** etc.
to persuade (someone) against (something or doing something) by thoughtful argument: [X9 + OUT + *of*] *How can you reason her out of fears that she has had all her life? Can't you reason the boy out of such stupid behaviour? Father must be reasoned out of driving home in such dangerous conditions.*

***reason with** *v prep*
to try to persuade (usu. someone), by fair argument: [T1] *The teacher tried to reason with the boy but he refused to listen; people like that can often not be reasoned with.*

**rebel against** *v prep* → **mutiny against, revolt against** (1), **rise against**
to oppose; fight against; refuse to obey (someone in power or something with which

one disagrees); try to take power from (someone) by force: [IØ + *against*] *The citizens at last rebelled against their cruel rulers, drove them from the country, and took power themselves. Children naturally rebel against their parents; the difficulty is to find a balance between allowing them some expression of this feeling, and keeping some control, for the child's good. The workers are rebelling against conditions in the old factories.*

**rebel at** *v prep* → **revolt against** (2)
to feel angry and unwilling because of (something or doing something): [IØ + *at*] *I know I have to get up every morning, but my mind rebels at the thought. Rebelling at waiting any longer for the meal, they left the restaurant.*

**rebound from** *v prep*
(of something, as a ball, bullet, etc.) to return in a quick movement in the opposite direction after striking (something such as a surface): [IØ + *from* (*often simple tenses*)] *The bullet rebounded from the stone wall and hit him in the chest. Light and heat will rebound from any surface that is shiny or white.*

**rebound on/upon** *v prep* → **recoil on, redound on**
(usu. of a bad action) to return so as to have an effect on (usu. someone): [T1 (*no pass., usu. simple tenses*)] *Take care that your selfish behaviour doesn't rebound on you; if you are inconsiderate of others, they will be inconsiderate of you.*

**rebuke for** *v prep* → **tell off** (1), etc.
to scold (someone) severely because of (something or doing something wrong): [T1 + *for*] *That boy will have to be rebuked for his bad behaviour. I could hear the director rebuking Jim for being late for work again.*

**recall from** *v prep*
to order the return of (someone, usu. a political or military representative), usu. to the home base, from (a place or duty): [T1 + *from*] *Our representative will have to be recalled from the small island state if the danger of war becomes real. We demand that you recall your army from our border.*

**recall to** *v prep*
**1** to order the return of (someone, usu. a political or military representative) to (a duty or home base): [T1 + *to*] *Our representative to the small island state will have to be recalled to the capital if the danger of war becomes real. Additional soldiers must be recalled to active duty in the face of this military threat.*
**2** to force the consciousness of (someone) to return to (a sense of duty or correct behaviour): [D1 (*simple tenses*)] *The shame which he suffered as a result of his inaction recalled him to a sense of duty, and he made sure to fulfil his promises in the future.*
**3 recall something/someone to mind** to remember something or someone: [*usu. simple tenses*] *I know him well, but I can't recall his name to mind. I can't recall to mind where I have seen her before.* → **bring to²** (19), **call to** (5), **come to²** (30)

**recast in** *v prep* → **cast in** (2)
to rewrite (an expression) in (another form of words): [T1 + *in*] *I would advise you to recast that last sentence in more formal wording.*

**recede from** *v prep*
**1** to go back or away from (something), usu. by flowing: [IØ + *from*] *As the sea receded from the shore, many beautiful shells were left behind. The waves receded from the ship, only to return to beat with renewed force upon its weakening boards.*
***2** *fml* to take away; fail to fulfil (something such as a promise): [T1] *The government has receded from its promise to control prices.*

**receive as** *v prep*
**1** to be given (something) in the form of (something): [T1 + *as* (*usu. simple tenses*)] *I didn't buy the book, I received it as a gift.*
**2** to accept (someone) as being (a certain kind of person): [T1 + *as* (*usu. pass.*)] *How soon can I be received as a member of the Church?*

**receive back** *v adv*
**receive someone back into the fold** to welcome the return of someone into a group which he/she had left: *When she wanted to return to the Church after a long absence, she was received back into the fold most warmly, with no questions asked.*

**receive from** *v prep*
to obtain (usu. something) from (someone); be given (something) by (someone): [T1 + *from*] *No, I didn't buy the book, I received it from the writer as a gift. I have received nothing but excuses from you for weeks.*

**receive into** *v prep*
to admit (someone) as a member of (an organization such as the Church): [T1 + *into* (*usu. pass.*)] *You can be received into the Church after instruction into our beliefs.*

***reck of** *v prep*
*old use lit* to consider; take care about (something such as danger): [T1 (*usu. neg., simple tenses*)] *The flier recked little of the suffering that she would face, but began her long flight alone with calm courage.*

**reckon among** *v prep* → **count among**
*not fml* to consider (something or someone) as belonging to (a group): [X9 + *among* (*simple tenses*)] *I am proud to reckon you among my friends. Her poetry is reckoned among the best-known this century.*

**reckon as** *v prep* → **count as, regard as**
*not fml* to consider (someone or something) to be (something): [X9 + *as* (*simple tenses*)] *They reckoned him as their enemy. The city council reckons its library as an important part of public service. She has always been reckoned as clever. Any member of the committee is reckoned as fit to take the chairmanship. A member of the tennis club is reckoned as belonging to the combined sports club.* [L1 +

*as*] *In cricket, a no ball reckons as one run. A student over sixteen reckons as two under eleven in the calculation of school building costs.* [L4 + *as*] *Any unemployed person reckons as deserving government help.* [L7 + *as*] *A person's birth in a country which was formerly part of the British Empire reckons as equal to British citizenship.*

***reckon for** *v prep* → **bargain for** (2), **calculate for** (2)
*not fml* to plan for (something, often unexpected): [T1 (*simple tenses*)] *He got more than he reckoned for when he chose to play against such an opponent.* [T4 (*simple tenses*)] *We didn't reckon for having such bad weather when we planned the garden party.* [V4a[ *We didn't reckon for the weather turning bad so suddenly.*

**reckon from** *v prep* → **date back to, go back** (6), **go back to** (5)
to count or date the beginning of (something) starting with (a point in time): [X9 + *from* (*usu. pass.*)] *The Christian age is usually reckoned from the birth of Christ.*

***reckon in** *v adv* → **count in** (1), **count out** (2)
*not fml* to include (people, or things such as figures) in a calculation of a group, cost, etc.: [T1] *When the city declares its population numbers, does it reckon in the farmers in outer areas? Have you reckoned in the members who are absent?*

***reckon on/upon** *v prep* → **depend on** (1), etc.
*not fml* to trust in; depend on (someone, something, or doing something): [T1] *You can always reckon on Jim, he'll never fail you. I'd like to come with you but that's not a promise, don't reckon on it.* [T4] *Don't reckon going abroad this summer, we may not be able to afford it.* [V3] *Don't reckon on your relatives to help you out of trouble.* [V4a] *Don't reckon on the weather being fine for your garden party.*

**reckon to** *v prep* → **count from, count to** (1)
to count, usu. from zero, as far as (a number): [L9 + *to*] *You reckon* (*up*) *to 100 while we hide. If you start counting at 0, how far can you reckon* (*up*) *to in an hour?*

**reckon up** *v adv*
**1** esp. *BrE not fml* to find the total of (something, things, or people): [X9 + UP] *Reckon up all your money and see if you have enough. Have you reckoned up the books to see if we have enough for the children to have one each? It's difficult to reckon the members up when so many are absent. The great poets still living can be reckoned up on the fingers of one hand.* → **count up**
***2** esp. *BrE infml* to understand the nature of (someone): [T1] *Sometimes he gives one opinion and sometimes another; I can't reckon him up. The new teacher soon had the class reckoned up and was able to control them.*

***reckon upon** *v prep* → RECKON ON

**reckon with** *v prep*
**1** to count by means of (something): [L9 + *with*] *We reckon your pay with our adding machine.*
***2** to settle an account owing to (someone): [T1] *Before deciding how much money we have for our holiday, we must reckon with the shopkeepers and anyone else we are in debt to.*
***3** to face; deal with (someone): [T1] *I wouldn't like to have to reckon with the director when he's in a bad temper. Women have become a force to be reckoned with in the affairs of the world.* → **deal with** (4)
***4** to consider (something such as a matter) carefully: [T1 (*simple tenses*)] *We must reckon with all possible difficulties when we are considering the cost of the contract. Anyone thinking of becoming a professional actor must reckon with the hard facts of unemployment.* [T4 (*simple tenses*)] *I didn't reckon with having to cook dinner for twenty unexpected guests.* → **reckon without** (2)
***5** to face; deal with; defeat (something such as danger): [T1] *After all the suffering that you have had to reckon with in the past, your present struggle will seem easy.*
***6** *not fml* to punish (someone): [T1] *I'll reckon with that boy when he gets home! All those who opposed us have now been reckoned with.* → **deal with** (5)

***reckon without** *v prep*
**1** *not fml* to fail to expect or include (something or someone): [T1 (*simple tenses*)] *We had hoped to hold the garden party this weekend, but we reckoned without the weather!* [V4a (*simple tenses*)] *When we planned to make this particular connection, we reckoned without our train being late.*
**2** *not fml* to calculate on not having (something): [T1 (*simple tenses*)] *We shall have to reckon without your competitors.* [V4a (*simple tenses*)] *You will have to reckon without receiving money from the council for the future, as they have stopped paying for such plans.* → **reckon with** (4)
**3 reckon without one's host** *not fml* to act or plan without asking the person most concerned: *In making plans regardless of the opinion of the person providing the money you are guilty of reckoning without your host.*

**reclaim from** *v prep*
**1** to save; bring (land) back to use after having been made unsuitable for crops because of (water or lack of water): [T1 + *from*] *Many square miles of land in this low-lying country have been reclaimed from the sea. The new nation is hoping to reclaim much of its land from the desert.*
**2** to save (someone) from (a bad way of life): [T1 + *from*] *The Church has reclaimed many men from a life of crime. Many sufferers have been reclaimed from a dependence on alcohol*

**recognize as** *v prep*
**1** to accept; admit (someone or something) formally as having the right to claim (a position, rank, etc.) or possess (a quality): [T1 + *as* (*usu. simple tenses*)] *Have the whole Council recognized the boy as the rightful Prince? The new island state has been recognized as a nation by most of the leading countries of the world. The operation is not recognized as legal in many states.*
***2** to regard (someone or something) as being (something such as a quality, usu. good): [X1 (*usu. pass.*)] *It did not take long for him to be recognized as the natural leader of his society.* [X7 (*usu. pass.*)] *Tom's first book was soon recognized as the most informative on the subject.*

**recognize by/from** *v prep*
to be able to know who or what someone or something is, by means of (something such as a part): [T1 + *by/from* (*usu. simple tenses*)] *This bird is easily recognized from its size and the unusual shape of its tail. Your face was turned away, but I recognized you by your hair.*

**recoil from** *v prep*
to draw back in fear or dislike from (something or doing something): [IØ + *from*] *Most people will recoil from a poisonous snake if they suddenly meet one. You have to learn not to recoil from touching the insects.*

***recoil on/upon** *v prep* → **rebound on, redound on**
(usu. of a bad action) to return so as to have an effect on (usu. someone): [T1 (*no pass., usu. simple tenses*)] *Take care that your selfish action doesn't recoil on you; if you are inconsiderate of others, they will be inconsiderate of you.*

**recommend as** *v prep*
to praise (someone or something) and suggest that he/she or it is good as being (something): [T1 + *as* (*often simple tenses*)] *My neighbour recommended her own daughter as an excellent secretary! I can recommend these poems as some of the most moving that I have read this year.*

**recommend for** *v prep*
**1** to praise (someone or something) for (a good quality or action): [T1 + *for (often pass.)*] *These members deserve to be recommended for their regular attendance at the meetings.* → **commend for**
**2** to suggest the name of (someone or something) as being suitable for (a reward, position, purpose, etc.): [T1 + *for* (*often simple tenses*)] *This girl should be recommended for a reward for her bravery in saving the drowning child. I can recommend this piece of music for a group of your size and experience. Who would you recommend for the chairmanship? She's a clever student who often gets recommended for prizes.*

**recommend to** *v prep*
**1** to praise (something or someone) when speaking to (someone), suggesting it or him/her as being worthy of attention: [T1 + *to* (*often simple tenses*)] *I can recommend this play to all lovers of good theatre. This book was recommended to me by my teacher.* → **commend to** (2)
**2** to praise (someone), suggesting that he/she is suitable for employment by or service to (someone): [T1 + *to* (*often pass.*)] *You have been recommended to me for the position of chairman; have you any remarks to add? I've come to you, doctor, because you were recommended to me by a friend.*
***3** *fml* to entrust (someone or something) to (someone or something): [D1 (*usu. simple tenses*)] *The dying man recommended his spirit to God. Being forced to leave, the woman recommended her child to my care.* → **commend to** (1)

**recommit to** *v prep*
to send (a matter for consideration) back to (a group): [T1 + *to* (*usu. simple tenses*)] *This is a difficult question, which we should perhaps recommit to the whole meeting.*

**recompense for** *v prep* → **repay for** (1), etc.
to reward; repay (someone) for (an action, usu. good, or money lost): [T1 + *for* (*often simple tenses*)] *People wounded by criminals are now fully recompensed for their suffering by the government. The firm will recompense you for any travelling costs which you may have paid while on your business trip.*

***reconcile to** *v prep* → **resign to** (2)
to accustom (oneself) to and be prepared to accept (something, usu. bad): [D1 (*often pass.*)] *After years of suffering, she had become reconciled to her fate. The people must reconcile themselves to a reduced standard of living.* [D4 (*often pass.*)] *How can I become reconciled to suffering any more pain?*

***reconcile with** *v prep*
**1** to cause (someone) to become friendly again with (someone) after a quarrel: [D1 (*usu. pass.*)] *After many years she was reconciled with her husband's mother, who at last said that she was sorry.*
**2** to find or cause agreement between (something) and (something else): [D1 (*simple tenses*)] *How do you reconcile your principles with your behaviour, which is exactly opposite? The call for a better society must be reconciled with the demands of ordinary people.* → **square with** (3)

**reconstruct from** *v prep*
to make a copy or likeness of (something) by putting together (things such as parts): [T1 + *from*] *The police are trying to reconstruct the crime from all the separate pieces of information. At last they were able to reconstruct the story from accounts by several different witnesses.*

**record from** *v prep*
to use a machine such as a tape recorder to make a lasting record of (a sound or picture) produced in the course of (a performance) or taken from (an earlier recording): [T1 + *from*] *These songs were recorded from a concert during last year's season. The electricians have done wonderful work in recording performances by famous artists of the past, from their early and very imperfect recordings. Firms are now selling packages of favourite performances recorded from films.*

**record on** *v prep*
to use a machine such as a tape recorder to make a lasting record of (a sound or picture) using (certain materials as means of reproducing the sound or picture); mark (an effect) on (something): [T1 + *on*] *In the early days, performances used to be recorded on wax. Nowadays, one's voice, appearance or movement can be recorded on tape or film. Her sufferings are recorded on her face for the rest of her life.*

**record onto** *v prep*
to move (a reproduction of a sound or picture) from one type or material onto (another): [T1 + *onto*] *The electricians have performed wonders in recording these long dead voices from old wax recordings onto modern plastic surfaces.*

**recount to** *v prep* → **tell to** (1)
to tell (a story) to (someone): [T1 + *to*] *He thoroughly enjoyed recounting his adventures to the newspaper reporters.*

***recoup for** *v prep* → **repay for** (1), etc.
*fml* to repay (someone) on account of (something such as a loss): [D1 (*usu. pass.*)] *Will you be recouped for your travelling costs while on the firm's business?*

**recover from** *v prep*
**1** to regain; get (something) back from (someone): [T1 + *from*] *Don't lend books to your friends; it's difficult to recover them from them when you want them.*
**2** to regain health or success after (illness, failure, etc.): [IØ + *from*] *A healthy child quickly recovers from a fever. It always takes some time to recover from the shock of someone's death. How long will it be before the nation recovers from its present troubles? She recovered from her surprise, and answered calmly.* → **get over**[2] (4), **recuperate from**

**recriminate against** *v prep*
*fml* to blame (someone) in return, for a fault such as blaming one: [IØ + *against*] *It's natural to want to recriminate against someone who has tried to put the blame on you.*

**recruit from** *v prep*
to obtain the services of (someone such as a soldier or worker) by choosing among (a group or class of people): [T1 + *from*] *Most private soldiers are recruited from the working classes, but the army tries to recruit its officers from well-born and well-educated men. Help was recruited from neighbouring farmers to put out the crop fire. The firm recruits its brightest young men from the ranks of students who have recently obtained their degrees.*

**recruit into** *v prep*
to persuade (someone) to join (usu. a group or doing something): [T1 + *into*] *It is easy to recruit English boys into the Navy, as so many of them are keen on the sea. The priest tried every Sunday to recruit all the worshippers into the service of the Lord. Do you think the neighbours can be recruited into helping us to put out the fire?*

**recuperate from** *v prep* → **get over**[2] (4), **recover from** (2)
to be in a good state again after (usu. an illness): [IØ + *from*] *How long did it take you to recuperate completely from your operation?*

***recur to** *v prep*
**1** to return in thought or consideration to (an earlier point): [T1 (*no pass., usu. simple tenses*)] *Let us recur to what was said in this morning's meeting.*
**2** (of a memory) to return to (someone or someone's mind): [T1 (*no pass., often simple tenses*)] *Pleasant thoughts of my childhood recurred to me as I listened to the gentle music. At last her name recurred to me, when I had stopped trying to remember it!*
**3** *fml* to make use of (something helpful): [T1 (*no pass., usu. simple tenses*)] *The nation may have to recur to unusual methods of controlling rising prices.* → **resort to** (2)

**redeem from** *v prep*
**1** to regain (something given in exchange for money) from (pawn): [T1 + *from*] *How much will it cost to redeem my watch from pawn?*
**2** to gain the freedom of (someone), esp. (in the Christian religion) from (evil): [T1 + *from*] *Christ redeems us from evil ways.*
**3** to save (something such as an event) from (something such as failure or doing something bad): [T1 + *from* (*often pass.*)] *Only the young singer's performance redeemed the concert from complete failure. The family gathering was redeemed from turning into a quarrel by the presence of the youngest children.*

***redound on** *v prep* → **rebound on, recoil on**
*fml* (usu. of a bad action) to return having a[n] effect on (someone) as a result: [T1 (*no pass., usu. simple tenses*)] *His dishonesty wi[ll] redound on him, and he will be cheated just a[s] he cheats.*

***redound to** *v prep*
*fml* to help; add to; result in (a good condition such as fame): [T1 (*no pass., simple tenses*)] *The children's excellent behaviour redounds to the honour of the school.*

**reduce by** *v prep*
to make (something such as an amount o[r] price) less, to the amount of (something): [T1 + *by*] *We have been able to reduce o[ur] tax bill by 10%.*

**reduce from** *v prep*
to make (something such as a price) less than (a former level): [T1 + *from* (*often pass.*)] *I bought the coat as it was considerably reduced from its original price.*

**reduce in** *v prep*
to bring (something or someone) down with regard to (a level, price, etc.): [T1 + *in* (*often pass.*)] *Have these goods really been reduced in price? The officer was reduced in rank, for dishonourable action.*

**reduce to** *v prep*
**1** to make (something) smaller or less; bring (something such as a price, size, or amount) (down to a lower level or smaller size): [T1 + *to* (*often pass., often simple tenses*)] *I bought the coat as it was reduced to only $29.99. Your speed must be reduced to the city speed limit as soon as you cross the border. Taxes for poorer people should be reduced to an amount that they can afford to pay. The book will have to be reduced to 200 pages, as printing costs have risen so much. If you are to give a talk, try to reduce your ideas to a few points in note form, so that you can speak freely from your notes rather than read out the whole speech. The great fire reduced the forest to a few trees. The whole town was reduced to ashes in the bombing. This crushing machine reduces big rocks to powder. Use your drawing instruments to reduce this three-sided figure to an exact copy a quarter the size. This machine can reduce copies of the original page to half size.*
**2** to limit; keep (something or someone) within (the stated limits): [T1 + *to* (*usu. pass.*)] *The conquered people were reduced to a small corner of their once large country. Business was reduced to local buying and selling when international trading ceased.*
**3** to change; separate (something such as a mixture or combination) into (its parts): [T1 + *to* (*often simple tenses*)] *This substance can be reduced to a single chemical and oxygen, by passing an electrical charge through it.*
**4** to express (a number) as (its lowest parts): [T1 + *to* (*often simple tenses*)] *To calculate the cost, reduce the prices to pence from pounds and pence. To multiply these measurements, reduce the feet and inches to inches.*
**5** to consider (separate things) together as (a unity); simplify (something made up of many parts) as (a single thing or idea): [T1 + *to* (*often pass.*)] *We can reduce his remarks to a single statement of fact. Every action of the enemy nation can be reduced to a threat to our national safety. His life's work can be reduced to a search for truth. We are trying to reduce our difficult relationship to a simple form of shared love and common interests.*
**6** to cause (something) to be expressed in (a particular form): [T1 + *to* (*often pass.*)] *Most natural events can be reduced to a set of laws: what happens on one occasion will be repeated on other occasions where the conditions are the same. The agreement between you should be reduced to writing, thus forming a lawful contract.*
**7** to cause (something or someone) to reach (a certain condition): [T1 + *to* (*often simple tenses*)] *Try to reduce your tax affairs to order before the examiner arrives to look at your account books. The new teacher was quickly able to reduce the noisy class to silence. If a man is prevented from expressing his anger, he may be reduced to violence. I think that long rest will now succeed in reducing the broken bone to its usual state of health and strength.*
**8** to weaken (something) so as to become (something else): [T1 + *to* (*often simple tenses*)] *Use this special oil to reduce the thick paint to a liquid thin enough to spread easily. Most English vowel sounds which are not given weight in speech become reduced to a rather formless central vowel.*
***9** to bring (someone or an animal) to (a weakened state): [D1] *Hunger had reduced the poor dog to skin and bone. Worry will reduce anyone to a nervous wreck.*
***10** to weaken; lower the importance or value of (an argument) by showing (its parts or true nature): [D1 (*often simple tenses*)] *His opponent's clever speech reduced the speaker's argument to nonsense.*
***11** to move (someone) to (a lower level of importance), usu. as a punishment: [D1 (*usu. pass.*)] *The captain was reduced to the ranks for his dishonourable action. For frequent absences from committee meetings, the chairman was reduced to ordinary membership.*
***12** to force (someone) into (a lower social state or doing something humble, unpleasant, or dishonourable): [D1 (*usu. pass.*)] *I was sorry to hear that the family had been reduced to such a humble standard of living, after the father's sudden death.* [V4b (*usu. pass.*)] *Alone and unsupported, she was reduced to begging for her living.* → **come down to** (6), **come to**[2] (11)
**13** **reduce someone to tears** to make someone weep: *You may choose to scold the child, but there's no need to reduce him to tears.*

**reef in** *v adv*
to fold part of (a sail) so as to face the wind with a smaller area: [T1 + IN] *Reef in the main sail, there's a storm coming!*

***reek of** *v prep* → **reek with**
**1** to smell strongly of (something nasty): [T1 (*no pass.*)] *The whole room reeked of tobacco smoke.*
**2** to suggest (something bad) strongly: [T1 (*simple tenses*)] *His story reeks of dishonesty; I don't believe a word of it.*

***reek with** *v prep* → **reek of**
**1** to be covered in (something, usu. something that smells nasty): [T1 (*no pass.*)] *The murderess's hands seemed to be reeking with blood long after they had been washed clean.*

**2** to be full of (something bad): [T1 (*no pass., simple tenses*)] *The government's action reeks with injustice.*

**reel back** *v adv*
to move unsteadily backwards, losing one's balance or control: [IØ + BACK] *The fighter reeled back when the heavy blow landed unexpectedly on his chin.*

**reel from** *v prep*
to move back unsteadily, losing one's balance or control, as a result of (something such as a blow): [IØ + *from*] *The fighter reeled from the blow which had landed unexpectedly on his chin. She read the letter and almost fell backwards, reeling from the shock.*

**reel in** *v adv*
**1** to enter unsteadily: [IØ + IN] *He spent the evening drinking, and reeled in at midnight.* → **reel out** (1)
**2** also **reel up** to pull (a fishing line or fish) closer to oneself: [X9 + IN] *Reel in your line steadily, or the fish might break it. Help me to reel in this powerful fish.* [L9 + IN] *When you're sure that you have hooked the fish, reel in at once.*

***reel off** *v adv* → **rattle off, roll off** (3), **run off**[1] (7), **spiel off**
*not fml* to repeat (words) from memory quickly and without thinking; perform (an action) with ease and speed; produce (something, usu. written) quickly and effortlessly: [T1] *What is the point of teaching children to reel off the names of the kings and queens of England if they know nothing of history? Our local tennis star can reel off any stroke in the book. Tom can always reel off a poem or two if the magazine asks for one.*

**reel out** *v adv*
**1** to leave a place unsteadily: [IØ + OUT] *You can tell which of the men have had too much to drink, by the way they reel out at closing time.* → **reel in** (1)
**2** to unwind (rope or line) from a roller: [X9 + OUT] *Reel out more line, the fish is getting away and may break it!*

**reel up** *v adv* → **REEL IN** (2)

***refer back** *v adv*
to send (a matter for consideration) back (to someone or a group that has considered it earlier): [T1 (*to*)] *The decision must be referred back (to the committee), as there is now fresh information to be considered.*

***refer back to** *v adv prep*
**1** to send (a matter for consideration) back to (someone or a group, that has considered it earlier): [D1] *The decision must be referred back to the committee, as there is now fresh information to be considered.*
**2** to mention (something) again; remind (someone) of (something already seen, spoken, or known): [T1 (*often simple tenses*)] *In requesting an answer, it is wise to refer back to earlier letters on the subject.* [D1 (*often simple tenses*)] *If the committee members are uncertain, refer them back to the rules originally agreed upon. May I refer you back to my earlier remarks on this subject?*

***refer to** *v prep*
**1** to mention; speak or write about (something or someone): [T1] *It was unwise in your speech to refer to rising unemployment. Too many teachers talk at length about educational principles without once referring to a real child.* → **talk about** (1), etc.
**2** to (cause to) look at (something) for information: [T1] *By referring to his notes, the speaker was able to give the exact details required. Refer to the dictionary when you don't know how to spell a word.* [D1] *The reader's attention is referred to page 27, last sentence.*
**3** to concern; be directed towards (something or someone): [T1 (*no pass., simple tenses*)] *Does your remark refer to all of us? The new law does not refer to land used for farming.* → **apply to** (3), **relate to** (3)
**4** to send (someone or something) to (usu. someone else) for action: [D1] *The members referred the question to the committee, as they were unable to reach a decision. Your illness is so mysterious that I need to refer you to a specialist.*
**5** to (cause to) ask (someone) for information or opinions concerning the ability or character of someone else: [T1 (*usu. simple tenses*)] *For remarks on my recent teaching experience, please refer to Mrs Grey at Lowland School.* [D1 (*usu. simple tenses*)] *I refer you to my former employer, who will support my request.*
**6** *fml* to place or class (something) as belonging to (a time, place, class, etc.): [D1 (*usu. pass.*)] *This style of music is generally referred to the 18th century.*
**7** *fml* to believe (something) to be the result of (something): [D1 (*simple tenses*)] *Many successful businessmen refer their success to hard work and good judgment.* → **attribute** (1), etc.

***refine on/upon** *v prep*
to improve (something such as a method) esp. in details: [T1] *We shall have to refine on our methods of advertising if we are to reach a wider public.*

**reflect back** *v adv*
**1** (usu. of a shiny surface such as a mirror) throw back (something such as light or an appearance): [T1 + BACK] *The sea reflected back the bright sunlight.*
**2** to show a true or exact copy of (something such as an idea): [T1 + BACK] *The election results do not always reflect back the views of the voters.*

**reflect in** *v prep*
**be reflected in: a** (of an image) to be thrown back from (a shiny surface such as a mirror): *On a still day, you can see your face reflected in the water.* **b** (of an idea or feeling) to be clearly shown in (a result): *The low level*

*interest in the election has been reflected in the unwillingness of the citizens to vote.*

**reflect on/upon** *v prep*

**1** to consider (something) carefully and at length: [IØ + *on/upon*] *As you get older you begin to reflect on the uncertainty of life.* → **ruminate about**

*__2__ to bring (something) into disfavour or question: [T1 (*no pass., simple tenses*)] *Your behaviour reflects on the good name of the school. He made remarks which reflected unfavourably/badly on the workers' trustworthiness.*

**3 reflect favourably/well on/upon** to bring honour on (something such as a quality); show (something) to be good: [*simple tenses*] *Your sales figures reflect favourably on your ability as a salesman. The decision you have made reflects well on your judgment.*

**4 reflect credit/honour or discredit/dishonour on/upon** to bring favourable or unfavourable notice to (someone, a group, or something): [*simple tenses*] *Do nothing which will reflect discredit on the firm. The examination results reflect credit on our teaching methods. Your decision reflects little honour on your good sense. His action reflected dishonour on the family.*

**refrain from** *v prep*

**1** to hold oneself back from (doing something); prevent (something): [IØ + *from*] *How shall I refrain from tears when we part? It is difficult to refrain from interrupting someone with whom one disagrees.* → **forbear from** (1), **withhold from** (2)

*__2__ to prevent oneself from (doing something that one wished to do): avoid (something) intentionally, but often with an effort: [T1] *The people were asked to refrain from baths while water was scarce. His family have always refrained from drink, on principle. After his heart attack, uncle was advised to refrain from sex for several weeks.* [T4] *Jim finds it difficult to refrain from smoking.* → **abstain from, forbear from** (2)

**refresh with** *v prep*

**1** to make (someone or oneself) feel cooler, better in health and spirits, etc., by having (something usu. to eat or drink): [T1 + *with*] *I think I'll just refresh myself with a cup of tea before I go to meet the children.*

**2** to make (something) newer, more lively or active, etc., by means of (something): [T1 + *with*] *As the play has been showing for so long, it now needs to be refreshed with some new details in the style of production or a change of actors.*

**refund to** *v prep* → **reimburse to**

to pay back (money already given) to (the person who paid it), usu. because he/she did not receive the goods or services paid for or because they are unsatisfactory: [T1 + *to*] *The price of your ticket will be refunded to you if you cannot make your journey as planned.*

**refuse to** *v prep* → **deny to** (2)

to not allow or give (something) to (someone): [T1 + *to*] *The cinema owners have the right to refuse admission to anyone under eighteen years of age.*

**regain from** *v prep*

to get possession again of (something that one had lost) by taking it back from (someone, something, or a group): [T1 + *from*] *The small island state at last regained its independence from the conquerors who had ruled it for two centuries.*

***regale with** *v prep* also **regale on**

to give enjoyment to (someone or oneself) by means of (something such as food or amusement); force (someone) to accept (something pleasant): [D1] *The children regaled the visitors with the story of their imaginary adventures in the secret cave. She was lying in the bath, regaling herself with an amusing book. The generous host regaled his guests with wine and cheese.*

***regard as** *v prep* → **count as, reckon as**

to consider (someone or something) to be (something or doing something): [X1 (*often pass., simple tenses*)] *They regarded him as their enemy. The city council regards its library as an important part of public service.* [V4b (*often pass., simple tenses*)] *A member of the tennis club is regarded as belonging to the combined sports club.* [X7 (*often pass., simple tenses*)] *She has always been regarded as clever. Any member of the committee is regarded as fit to take the chairmanship.*

**regard with** *v prep*

to have an opinion about (someone or something) showing (a way of feeling about him/her or it): [X9 + *with* (*often pass., simple tenses*)] *Mary's father regarded Jim with disapproval even after they were married. Your request has been regarded with favour by the committee.*

**register as** *v prep*

to enter one's name, as on a list, and sometimes pay money, so as to become (a certain kind of person): [IØ + *as*] *How many of you have already registered as students?* [T1 + *as*] *In fomer times, only property owners could be registered as voters.*

**register for** *v prep*

to enter one's name, as on a list, and sometimes pay money, so as to become (a certhing such as a course): [IØ + *for*] *An increasing number of students are registering for degree courses each year.*

**register in** *v prep*

to enter one's name, as on a list, and sometimes pay money, so as to join (an organization); take the name of (a member): [IØ + *in*] *How many members have officially registered in the club?* [T1 + *in*] *How many members are officially registered in the club?*

**register on** *v prep*

to be easily seen on (something such as someone's face): [IØ + *on* (*often simple tenses*)] *A surprise that he was unable to hide registered on his face.*

**register with** *v prep*
to leave one's name as a record with (someone in charge): [IØ + *with*] *All foreign visitors must register with the state officials on entering the country.*

**regress to** *v prep* → **return to** (5), **revert to** (3)
to return, as in form or behaviour, to (a simpler type or earlier time of life): [IØ + *to*] *Many men, when very angry, regress to their childhood and show their bad temper by shouting and stamping their feet.*

**reign over** *v prep* → **rule over**
(usu. of a royal person) to rule (people or a nation): [IØ + *over*] *May the Queen reign over us a long time.*

**reimburse for** *v prep* → **repay for** (1), etc.
to repay (someone) for (money spent): [T1 + *for*] *The firm will reimburse you for any travelling costs which you may have paid while on your business trip.*

**reimburse to** *v prep* → **refund to**
to repay (costs) to (someone): [T1 + *to*] *The cost of your journey will be reimbursed to you, when you send in the proper claim.*

**rein back/in** *v adv*
**1** to control the speed of (a horse) by pulling on leather bands: [X9 + BACK/IN] *The rider had to rein his horse back suddenly when the child ran across his path.*
*__2__ to control (one's feelings): [T1] *Jim had great difficulty in reining in his anger when Mary's father expressed his disapproval of the marriage.*

**rein up** *v adv*
to make (a horse) come to a stop, by pulling on leather bands: [X9 + UP] *Be prepared to rein up your horse at the word of command.*

**reinforce with** *v prep*
**1** to strengthen (something or a group) by adding (materials, men, ships, etc.): [T1 + *with*] *This cement building is reinforced with bands of steel. The army was reinforced with a fresh group of soldiers.*
**2** to support (an idea) by means of (something): [T1 + *with*] *Any good speaker should be able to reinforce his argument with facts.*
**3** to reward, and so increase the likelihood of repetition of (correct behaviour) by giving (something): [T1 + *with*] *It is easy to direct a child's pattern of behaviour by reinforcing good behaviour with some kind of reward.*

**reinstate in** *v prep*
to place (someone) again in (a position, usu. of power, which he had lost): [T1 + *in*] *His supporters failed in their attempt to reinstate the President in the White House.*

**rejoice at** *v prep* → **delight in, glory in** (1), **rejoice in** (1), **rejoice over, take in²** (7)
to take pride and pleasure in; be glad about (something): [IØ + *at*] *The whole family are rejoicing at their unexpected good fortune.*

**rejoice in** *v prep*
**1** to take great pride and pleasure in; find joy in; be glad about (someone, something, or doing something): [IØ + *in*] *The young singer rejoiced in her unexpected success. "Rejoice in the Lord always; and again I will say, Rejoice."* (The Bible) *That teacher rejoices in making his students feel uncomfortable.* → **delight in, glory in** (1), **rejoice at, rejoice over, take in²** (7)
*__2__ to be lucky enough to have; possess (something good such as a quality): [T1 (*simple tenses*)] *His family have always rejoiced in great wealth. I have rejoiced in good health most of my life.* → **glory in** (2)
**3 rejoice in the name of** to be called (something amusing): [*no pass., simple tenses*] *There is an English village which rejoices in the name of Cold Christmas. I know an old unmarried man who rejoices in the name of Young-husband.*

**rejoice over** *v prep* → **delight in, glory in** (1), **rejoice at, rejoice in** (1), **take in²** (7)
to take great pride and pleasure in; be glad about (something or someone); [IØ + *over*] *The team are still in their dressing room, rejoicing over their victory.*

**relapse into** *v prep* → **lapse into** (1)
to return or fall back into (a bad former state or action): [IØ + *into*] *After showing much improvement in health, she suddenly relapsed into weakness. It is easy to relapse into lazy habits when you have been away from work for a while.*

**relate to** *v prep*
**1** *fml* to tell (a story) to (someone): [T1 + *to*] *The children enjoyed relating their imagin ary adventures to the visitors.*
*__2__ also **relate with** to show a connection be tween (something such as an event) an (something else): [D1 (*often pass.*)] *The un employment figures are not necessarily relate to the rise in prices. It is difficult to relate hi argument to the facts.*
*__3__ to concern; be directed towards (somethin or someone): [T1 (*no pass., simple tenses*) *The new tax law does not relate to land use for farming. Many changes in the national pa tern of life have recently taken place, especiall those relating to housing and jobs. Peopl especially children, only understand statemen which relate to their private view of the worl* → **apply to** (3), **refer to** (3)
*__4__ to understand and like (something): [T (*simple tenses*)] *I can't relate to loud mode music.*
*__5__ to have a friendly, understanding, and syr pathetic relationship with (someone): [T (*usu. simple tenses*)] *A good teacher is o who can relate to the students, not one w has a lot of information.*
**6 be related to** to be a member of the sar family or type as (someone or somethin *Jim is related to Jack: Jack is his uncle. S*

*claims to be distantly related to a noble family, by marriage. Wheat is related to grass.*

**relax in/into** *v prep*

**1** to sit comfortably in; let the weight of the body sink into (furniture such as a chair): [IØ + *in/into*] *When I'm tired, I like to relax in/ into a deep armchair.*

*__2__ to show less stiffness and anxiety by having or changing into (something such as an expression or feeling): [T1 (*no pass.*)] *His worried face relaxed into a smile of greeting when he recognized us. The crowd relaxed into laughter at the speaker's excellent joke.*

**relax on** *v prep*

**1** to sit or lie comfortably on; let the weight of the body sink loosely and without effort on (usu. something such as a surface): [IØ + *on*] *Relax on this bed, and tell me your worries.*

**2 relax one's grip/hold on: a** to stop holding (something or someone) tightly: *Please relax your grip on my arm, you're hurting me.* **b** to cease having or using power over (someone or something); loosen one's control of (someone or something): *The climber dared not relax his hold on his nerves until he was safely at the top. After a few weeks of firm control, the teacher was able to relax his grip on the class, who continued to obey him out of habit.*

**relay out** *v adv*

to send out; pass on (something such as a message received from elsewhere), as by radio, to a distant place or additional people: [T1 + OUT (*to*)] *The church was crowded, so electrical machinery was used to relay the service out to the people.*

**relay to** *v prep*

to send out; pass on (a message received from elsewhere) to (someone else or a distant place), as by radio: [T1 + *to*] *This metal tower is used to relay television signals to distant villages which were formerly unable to receive them.*

**release from** *v prep*

to set (someone or something) free from (something, usu. bad or unpleasant): [T1 + *from*] *You can be released from prison early, for good behaviour. I wish to be released from my contract. Death at last released her from her pain.*

**release to** *v prep*

to allow (news) to be given to (someone): [T1 + *to*] *When is the best moment to release the date of the election to the newspapers?*

**relegate to** *v prep*

**1** *old use* to send (someone) away from his own country, as a punishment, to (another place): [T1 + *to*] *Anyone who offended against the king used to be relegated to a distant lonely island.*

**2** to treat or class (usu. someone) as belonging to (a lower level or humble rank): [T1 + *to* (*usu. pass.*)] *If they don't win more games, the football team may be relegated to a lower group. His new wife, a famous actress, refused to be relegated to the position of servant in his household.*

**relieve from** *v prep*

**1** to take from (someone) the worst or greatest part of (something unpleasant): [T1 + *from*] *This medicine will help to relieve you from your pain. More help in the office would relieve me from some of this responsibility.* → **ease of** (1), **relieve of** (1)

*__2__ *euph* to dismiss (someone) from (a position, often responsible): [D1 (*often pass.*)] *The captain was relieved from his post when his guilt was proved.* → **relieve of** (2), **remove from** (4)

***relieve of** *v prep*

**1** to take from (someone) (something heavy to carry or hard to do): [D1] *Let me relieve you of that heavy parcel. I could use another secretary to relieve me of some of this work. You will not be relieved of the care of your children for twenty years.* → **ease of** (1), **relieve from** (1)

**2** *euph* to dismiss (someone) from (a position, often responsible): [D1 (*often pass.*)] *The captain was relieved of his post when his guilt was proved.* → **relieve from** (2), **remove from** (1)

**3** *humor* to rob (someone) of (something): [D1] *It did not take the thieves long to relieve the passengers of all their money.* → **deliver of** (1), **ease of** (2)

***relieve oneself** *v pron*

*fml euph* to pass water or empty the bowels: [IØ] *People who live in houses without bathrooms have to relieve themselves in the garden.*

**relinquish of/over** *v prep*

**relinquish one's hold of/over** to stop controlling (someone), often cruelly: *The mother had such power over her son that her hold over him was only relinquished on her death.*

**relinquish to** *v prep*

to yield; give up (something or someone) to (usu. someone) often unwillingly or after a struggle: [T1 + *to*] *The farmers at last agreed to relinquish their land rights to the government for the new airport. The father was forced by law to relinquish the children to their mother.*

**relocate in** *v prep*

to move to (another place) in order to work: [IØ + *in*] *If we want to consider you seriously for the job, would you be willing to relocate in New England?* [T1 + *in*] *I'm looking for work here because my wife was relocated in this city, and so I had to give up my former job.*

***rely on** *v prep*

**1** to depend on; trust in (someone, something, or doing something): [T1] *You can always rely on Jim, he won't fail you. I relied on the map but it was wrong. I'd like to come with you but that's not a promise, don't rely on it.* [T4] *Don't rely on going abroad for our*

*holiday, we may not be able to afford it.* [V3] *You can't rely on workmen these days to do a proper job.* [V4a] *You can't rely on the weather being fine for anything you plan in England.* → **depend on** (1), etc.
**2** to be dependent on (something): [T1] *"The town relies on the seasonal tourist industry for jobs."* (Toronto *Sun*, 11 April 1976) → **depend on** (3), **hang on** (2), **hinge on, pivot on** (2), **ride on²** (4), **turn on²** (3)

**remain abreast of** *v adv prep*
**1** to stay at the same level as (someone or something ahead): [L9 + ABREAST + *of* (*no pass.*)] *You will have to run fast to remain abreast of our best runner and prevent him from winning.* → **keep abreast of** (1), etc.
*****2** to remain fully informed about (new facts and information): [T1 (*no pass.*)] *Scientists have to work hard to remain abreast of new discoveries and developments.* → **keep abreast of** (2), etc.

**remain ahead** *v adv* → **move ahead,** etc.
**1** to stay in a forward or leading position, in front of others: [L9 + AHEAD (*of*)] *If I can only remain ahead for a few more yards, I can win this race.*
**2** to keep an advanced position, as in competition: [L9 + AHEAD] *Jane used to have difficulty with her school work, but she has improved a lot recently, and now finds it easier to remain ahead. Getting a good position is only half the story; once you've got ahead you have to work twice as hard to remain ahead.*

**remain ahead of** *v adv prep* → **keep ahead of,** etc.
**1** to be able to keep a position in front of, beyond or past (someone or something), esp. in a competition, race, etc.: [L9 + AHEAD + *of*] *If I can only remain ahead of the other runners, now that I am first I can win this race!*
**2** to keep a position in advance of (something or someone such as a competitor): [L9 + AHEAD + *of*] *You have to work hard to remain ahead of your competitors in business, or you can easily lose your leading position. Jane was able to bring her work up to a higher standard than that of the others in her class; then she had to work hard to remain ahead of her fellow students.*
**3 remain one step ahead of** *not fml* to stay in a position only a little way in advance of (someone or something): *Jim's father often said that one secret of his success in business was that he always remained one step ahead of public demand.*

**remain at** *v prep*
**1** to stay behind at (a place): [L9 + *at*] *The women remained at home while the men went to war.* → **stay at** (1), **stop at** (2)
**2 remain at one's post** to stay on duty in the proper place: *The guard had orders to remain at his post whatever happened.* → **stand to²** (4), **stay at** (4), **stick to** (12), **stop at** (6)

**remain away** *v adv* → **keep away,** etc.
to stay at a distance; be absent: [L9 + AWAY (*from*) (*usu. simple tenses*)] *Many of his former supporters disapproved of his latest opinions, and remained away (from the meeting) when he came to give a speech.*

**remain behind¹** *v adv*
**1** to stay at a distance behind someone or something: [L9 + BEHIND] *It's safest to remain a good distance behind, in case the car in front suddenly stops.* → **keep behind** (1), **stay behind¹** (1)
*****2** to stay in a place after others have left: [IØ] *If you remain behind after class, I will repeat the instructions to you.* → **keep in** (5), etc.

**remain behind²** *v prep*
to stay at a distance behind (something or someone): [L9 + *behind*] *It's safest to remain well behind the car in front, in case it suddenly stops. After remaining behind the leading runner for most of the race, Jim suddenly passed him and won.*

*****remain clear of** *v adv prep* → **keep clear of, stay clear of, steer clear of** (2)
*not fml* to continue to avoid (something or someone): [T1 (*no pass., usu. simple tenses*)] *At busy times, it's best to avoid the main roads, and remain clear of them until the worst of the traffic is over.*

**remain cool** *v adj* → **keep cool, stay cool**
**1** to prevent oneself from becoming too hot: [L9 + cool] *How do you remain so cool in such hot weather? If you begin the day with a cold bath, it's easier to remain cool than to get cool if you once allow yourself to become overheated.*
**2** to continue to be calm; refuse to become excited, anxious, etc.: [L9 + cool (*usu. simple tenses*)] *The soldier owed his courage to his ability to remain cool in the face of danger.*

**remain down** *v adv*
**1** to continue to be in a lower position: [L9 + DOWN] *If there's shooting going on, get down, and remain down where it's safe until I call you.* → **keep down** (1), **stay down** (1), **stop down** (1)
**2** to stay at a lower level; continue to be less; not increase: [L9 + DOWN] *I hope the wind remains down now that it's calmer, so that we can risk putting up the sails.* → **hold down** (2), **keep down** (2), **stay down** (2), **stop down** (2)

**remain in¹** *v adv*
**1** to stay indoors, as because of illness or as punishment: [L9 + IN] *If your cold's no better, you should remain in tomorrow, and not go out till the weather improves or you are feeling better. This class will remain in for half an hour after school!* → **keep in** (5)
**2** (of a fire) to continue burning: [L9 + IN (*usu. simple tenses*)] *Will the fire remain in until we get back?* → **keep in** (6)

**remain in²** *v prep*
**1** to continue to be present in (a place): [IØ + *in*] *It's very difficult to remain in one spot without moving at all. My parents remained in England when I moved to Australia.* → **be in²** (1), etc.
**2** to continue to be in (a state, usu. good): [L9 + *in*] *How has the car remained in such good condition after all those miles of travelling?* → **get into** (11)
**3 remain in contact/touch (with)** to continue to be able to meet or send messages (to someone): *It's easier to remain in touch with an old friend than to try to reach her again after many years' absence.* → **get in²** (3), **keep in** (6), **lose with** (1), **put in²** (12), **stay in²** (3)
**4 remain in office/power** to continue to have control, usu. political: *The people will not allow the President to remain in office once his guilt is known.* → **stay in²** (4)
**5 remain in sight (of)** to stay in a position where one can be seen: *The children were told to remain in sight (of the house) when they went outside to play.* → **keep in** (16), etc.

**remain indoors** *v adv* → **keep in** (5), etc.
to stay inside a building, as at home: [L9 + INDOORS] *Mother was advised to remain indoors for a week after her cough seemed better.*

**remain of** *v prep*
to be left from (something bigger or more complete): [IØ + *of* (*simple tenses*)] *Nothing remained of the body but bones and ashes. What will remain of the old city if the new road is built through the centre?*

**remain off** *v prep* → **stay off** (3), etc.
to continue not to attend (school, work, etc.): [L9 + *off*] *The doctor says that Jane should remain off school until her stomach trouble is completely better.*

**remain on¹** *v adv* → **put on¹** (3), etc.
(of something electrical such as a light) to continue burning: [L9 + ON (*usu. simple tenses*)] *When the lights remained on in his room long after his usual bedtime, I knew that something was wrong.*

**remain on²** *v prep*
**1** to continue travelling in (a certain direction): [L9 + *on*] *Remain on the way you're going, and you'll soon come to the town. How long should we remain on this course?* → **be on²** (2), **keep on** (2), **stay on²** (2)
**2** → STAY ON² (3)
**3 remain on one's feet** to continue to stand: *The old fighter remained on his feet in spite of powerful blows from his strong young opponent.* → **get to** (11), etc.
**4 remain on the right side of** *not fml* to continue to be friendly with; not annoy (someone): *It would be sensible for you to remain on the right side of the director, at least until the sales figures arrive.* → **get in with** (2), etc.
**5 remain on the right side of the law** to continue to behave lawfully: *Few former prisoners remain on the right side of the law for very long after they have been freed.* → **keep on** (16), **stay on²** (7)
**6 remain on top (of)** → STAY ON² (8)

**remain open** *v adj*
**1** to continue to be wide open, apart, etc.: [L9 + open (*usu. simple tenses*)] *He closed his eyes but his mouth remained open. Our door remains open at all times for our friends.* → **leave open** (1), etc.
**2** to continue to do business: [L9 + open] *In the week before Christmas, the shops remain open until late every evening.* → **stay open** (2), etc.

**remain together** *v adv* → **keep together** (1), **stay together** (1)
(of two or more things or people) to continue to be in the same time or place: [L9 + TOGETHER] *The horses remained together for most of the race, until a leader at last came to the front. You singers must remain together or you will spoil the music. When the mist comes down, we must remain together or we'll get lost.*

**remain under¹** *v adv* → **hold under** (1), **keep under** (1), **stay under, stop under**
to continue to be beneath (something such as the surface of water): [L9 + UNDER (*usu. simple tenses*)] *If the swimmer remains under for more than a minute, pull him out, he may be drowning.*

**remain under²** *v prep* → **stay under, stop under**
to continue to be beneath (something such as a surface): [L9 + *under* (*usu. simple tenses*)] *The child remained under the table in a temper until his father came home. How long can you remain under water?*

**remain up** *v adv*
**1** to continue to be raised or in the proper position: [L9 + UP] *My trousers won't remain up, I've lost so much weight.* → **hold up** (1), etc.
**2** to continue to be high: [L9 + UP] *Prices of meat have remained up even though the farmers are receiving less money for their cattle. It is difficult to make sure that the quality remains up without increasing the price. Her spirits remained up in spite of her disappointment.* → **be up** (6, 7), **go down** (6), etc.
**3** to stay out of bed, as at night: [L9 + UP] *To see the best films on television, you often have to remain up late.* → **stay up** (3), etc.

**remain within** *v prep*
**1** to continue to keep within or be limited by (something): [L9 + *within*] *The police are watching to see that all motorists remain within the new lower speed limit.* → **keep within** (1), **stay within** (1), **stick within, stop within**
**2 remain within bounds** to continue to obey or not go beyond a limit: *Make sure your spending on this contract remains within bounds, or the firm could be in trouble.* → **stay within** (2)

**remand in** *v prep*
**remand someone in custody** to keep someone in prison before his trial: [*often pass.*] *The prisoner was charged with murder, and remanded in custody while further enquiries were made, and witnesses found.*

**remand for** *v prep*
to send (someone) to prison before his trial, for (a certain time): [T1 + *for*] *The prisoner had to be remanded for a week while the missing witness was found.*

**remand to** *v prep*
to send (someone) to (a particular kind of prison) to wait for his trial: [T1 + *to*] *The judge has the power to remand young offenders to the special home until their case can be heard.*

***remark on/upon** *v prep*
to mention (something) particularly; express an opinion about (something that one has noticed): [T1 (*often simple tenses*)] *The examiners, while failing the student because his answers lacked the necessary facts, remarked on his ability to express his thoughts in a natural and interesting manner. The variety of styles of building in our city is often remarked upon by visitors.* —**remarked-upon** *adj*

**remember as** *v prep*
to think of (someone or something) as (being what they were in the past): [X1] *Is she really a film star now? I remember her as a fat little girl.* [V4b] *I didn't realise the town had grown so much; I remember it as being just a small place.*

**remember in** *v prep*
**1** to have a memory of (something or someone) during (something): [T1 + *in* (*often simple tenses*)] *I remembered our old dog in my dreams last night.*
**2 remember someone in one's will** to leave something such as money to someone after one's death, often as a reward: [*usu. simple tenses*] *Although she hated the old man, she continued to serve him faithfully, hoping to be remembered in his will. I intend to remember each of the servants in my will.*

***remember to** *v prep*
to send good wishes from (oneself) as a greeting to (someone) by means of someone else: [D1 (*usu. imper. or pass.*)] *Remember me to your mother when you get home. Mother asked to be remembered to you.*

**remind of** *v prep*
**1** also **remind about** to make sure that (someone) does not forget (something): [T1 + *of*] *Thank you for reminding me of the meeting I have to attend. Please remind me of the time when I should be finishing my speech.*
***2** to cause (someone) to have a memory of (something or someone): [D1 (*simple tenses*)] *That tune reminds me of the production of the same play that we did many years ago.*
***3** to give (someone) the idea that one is like (someone or something else): [D1 (*simple tenses*)] *You remind me so much of your father, especially when you smile. This hotel reminds me of the one we stayed in last year.*

**reminisce about** *v prep*
(usu. of two or more people) to talk about (something in the past), usu. happily: [IØ + *about*] *The old men gathered regularly in the park, to smoke their pipes and reminisce about the good old days.*

**reminisce with** *v prep*
to share happy memories with (someone else): [IØ + *with*] *Grandfather liked nothing better than sitting in the park, reminiscing with the other old men.*

**remit to** *v prep*
**1** to send (money) to (someone in a distant place): [T1 + *to* (*often simple tenses*)] *Please remit the full cost to the company when sending your order. He lived on money remitted to him by his family back at home.*
**2** *fml* to send (a matter) to (someone in a higher position) for consideration: [T1 + *to* (*usu. simple tenses*)] *All questions of cost will be remitted to the officer in charge of the accounts.*

**remonstrate about** *v prep*
to have an argument or deliver a scolding on the subject of (something): [IØ + *about*] *I could often hear the teacher's voice in the next room, remonstrating about some unimportant matter.*

**remonstrate with** *v prep*
to argue with, complain to, or scold (someone): [IØ + *with*] *I could hear Father remonstrating with the children about the noise they were making, but it didn't make much difference.*

**remove from** *v prep*
**1** to take (something) away from (something or someone): [T1 + *from*] *Remove that dangerous weapon from the child! Kindly remove your hands from my knee. Please remove your belongings from my office.*
**2** to take out; get rid of (something unwanted) from (something): [T1 + *from*] *Grass marks can be removed from a cricketer's trousers with a special chemical. How do you remove burns from woodwork?*
**3** *fml* to move one's home from (a place): [IØ + *from*] *I'm sorry, they don't live here any more; I think they removed from the city last spring.*
**4** to dismiss (someone) from (a position, usu. of responsibility): [T1 + *from* (*often pass.*)] *When he was proved guilty of cheating on the accounts, Mr Green was removed from the chairmanship of the club.* → **relieve from** (2) **relieve of** (2)
**5 be (far) removed from** to be very distant or different from (something): *Our present system is far removed from the original idea.*

**remunerate for** *v prep* → **repay for** (1), etc.
*fml* to repay (someone) for (work done or money spent or lost): [T1 + *for* (*often simple*

*tenses)] All the musicians will be remunerated for their services at the concert. The firm will remunerate you for your travelling costs.*

**rend from** *v prep* → **rip away** (1), **rip from, rip out** (1), **tear away** (1), **tear from**
*lit* to seize; take away (something or someone) roughly or by force from (something): [T1 + *from* (*often simple tenses*)] *The soldiers had orders to rend the children from their mothers' arms, if necessary, by force.*

**rend in** *v prep* → **rip in, tear in, tear into** (1)
to tear or break (something) so as to be in (usu. a number of parts): [T1 + *in* (*often pass.*)] *The tree was rent in two by the stroke of lightning.*

**rend to** *v prep*
**1** to destroy; tear (something) into (smaller parts such as pieces): [T1 + *to* (*often simple tenses*)] *The sudden high wind rent the sail to pieces.* → **pull apart** (1), etc.
**2 rend to pieces** to find severe fault with (usu. someone's work): *This newspaper reporter has a way of rending to pieces any new book by a foreign writer.* → **take apart** (4), etc.

***render down** *v adv*
**1** to melt (fat) to make it clear and pure: [T1] *These lumps of fat from the meat can be rendered down and used for cooking.* → **try out** (1)
**2** to reduce (something); express (something made up of different parts) as something simple: [T1 (*often pass.*)] *Most of his ideas can be rendered down to a system of thinking based on outdated facts.*

**render for** *v prep*
*fml* to return (something), as in exchange for (something else): [T1 + *for*] *Christ taught us to render good for evil. The villagers were expected to render part of their crops for the lord's protection.*

**render into** *v prep* → **do into, translate from** (1), **translate into** (1), **turn into** (3), **turn to** (7)
*fml* to translate (words or writing) into (another language): [D1] *The translator has done a good job of rendering this difficult poem into his native language. Certain expressions in other languages cannot be properly rendered into English.*

**render to** *v prep*
**1** *fml* to give (something) formally to (someone, usu. in a position of power, to whom it is owed): [D1] *Every year, the people gathered on the mountain to render up their prayers to the gods. "Render therefore to Caesar the things that are Caesar's; and to God the things that are God's."* (The Bible)
**2 render help/(a) service to** *fml* to give help willingly, and usu. without payment, to (someone): *We all have a duty to render what service we can to our suffering fellow creatures.*

**ender up** *v adv* → **give up** (7), etc.
to yield (something such as a possession) to an enemy: [T1 (*to*)] *At last the citizens were forced to render up their town to the conqueror.*

***renege on** *v prep* also *AmE* **renig on**
to break (a promise): [T1] *The government has been charged with reneging on the promises that it made to the voters during the election.*

**rent at** *v prep*
to (cause to) cost (a certain amount) to rent: [T1 + *at*] *This car is rented at $18 a day.* [L9 + *at*] *This flat rents at £100 a month.*

**rent out** *v adv* → **hire out, let out** (10)
*AmE* to offer (something such as a place to live) for rent: [T1 + OUT] *I'm thinking of renting out my house for the summer while I'm away.*

**rent to** *v prep*
to allow the use of (something) to (someone) for a payment of rent: [T1 + *to*] *You have to be particular what kind of people you rent your own home to, during your absence.*

***repair to** *v prep* → **resort to** (1)
*fml* to go to (a place) often or in large numbers: [T1 (*no pass., often simple tenses*)] *It was our custom after the play, to repair to the local coffee house to argue about the quality of the performance.*

**repatriate to** *v prep*
to bring (someone or something) back to (the country of origin): [T1 + *to*] *Prisoners of war may be exchanged and repatriated to their homeland.*

**repay by** *v prep* → **pay with** (2), **repay with, requite with**
to reward (someone or an action) by (doing something) in return: [T1 + *by*] *It was unjust of your mother to repay my kindness to her by making offensive remarks to me in my own home.*

**repay for** *v prep*
**1** to pay (someone) in return for (money lent, lost, spent, etc.): [T1 + *for*] *The firm will repay you for your travelling costs.* → **compensate for** (1), **make up for** (1), **recompense for, recoup for, reimburse for, remunerate for**
**2** to reward (someone) for (something or doing something): [T1 + *for* (*usu. simple tenses*)] *How can I repay you for your trouble? You will be repaid in another life for your suffering in this one. I can never repay you for coming to my help as you did.* → **compensate for** (2)

**repay with** *v prep* → **pay with** (2), **repay by, requite with**
to reward (someone or an action) by giving (something) in return: [T1 + *with* (*usu. simple tenses*)] *It was unjust of your mother to repay my kindness with rudeness.*

**repeat by** *v prep*
**repeat something by heart** to speak something from memory: *All Christian children learn to repeat the Lord's Prayer by heart when they are very young even if they do not always understand it.*

***repeat itself** *v pron*
(usu. of history or an event) to happen again in the same way: [IØ] *It pays to study the events of the past, since history has a habit of repeating itself. Will the bad weather of last winter repeat itself this year?*

***repeat oneself** *v pron*
to say the same thing twice: [IØ] *At the risk of repeating myself, I must state the facts again as no one seems to be paying attention to the dangers. You just said that; you're repeating yourself.*

**repel from** *v prep* → **repulse from**
*fml* to drive (someone such as an enemy) back or away from (a place), usu. by force; keep (something) away: [T1 + *from* (*often simple tenses*)] *Only after a long hard struggle were we able to repel the enemy from our shores. The oil in a duck's feathers repels the water from its body.*

***repent of** *v prep*
**1** *fml* to be sincerely sorry for (something bad that one has done, or doing something wrong): [T1 (*pass. rare*)] *The priest urged the people to repent of their wickedness, for the kingdom of heaven was near. Repenting of his crime, the thief returned the jewels and confessed to the police.* [T4] *I deeply repent of having deceived my husband.*
**2** *fml* to change one's mind about; wish that one had not thought or done (a former intention, thought, or deed): [T1 (*pass. rare, usu. simple tenses*)] *I repent of my kindness to her, since she was so rude to me in return.*

***repine against/at** *v prep*
*fml* to be discontented with; complain about (something): [T1 (*pass. rare, often simple tenses*)] *The selfish young woman repined against the duties that she had to perform in the household.*

**replace by/with** *v prep*
to change (something or someone) for (something or someone else): [T1 + *by/with* (*often pass.*)] *We have replaced slave labour with machines. The old gas lighting has been replaced by electricity. We suggest replacing the present chairman with a younger more active person.*

**replenish with** *v prep*
to provide (something) with (a new supply of something): [T1 + *with*] *It's time to replenish the shop with the new year's goods. Allow me to replenish your glass with some more wine.*

**reply for** *v prep*
(of one of a group) to give an answer on behalf of (the whole group): [T1 (*no pass.*)] *Shall I reply for us all?*

**reply to** *v prep*
**1** to speak to (someone) in answer; answer (something) by speaking: [IØ + *to*] *She replied to me in a very rude manner. Reply to the question at once, or you will seem guilty.*
**2** to give an answer to (something such as a letter) usu. in writing: [IØ + *to*] *The director hasn't replied to my note yet. All these invitations must be replied to.*
***3** to return; give back something similar or suitable as a way of returning (something such as gunfire, an attack, or an argument) in answer: [T1] *Don't reply to the enemy fire until I give the order. Do you intend to reply to this attack on your character? The next speaker will reply to the argument that you have just heard.*
***4** to give one's ideas; defend oneself in answer to (a charge): [T1] *How shall I reply to the charge? You will soon get your turn to reply to these charges.*

**report back** *v adv*
to bring back an account of something; give (information) in return: [IØ + BACK (*to*)] *Your job is to attend all the meetings and report back to the committee.* [T1 + BACK] *Teams of enquirers were sent out with orders to report their findings back to the group.*

**report for** *v prep*
**1** to inform against (someone) because of (a fault): [T1 + *for*] *I shall have to report you for repeated lateness.*
***2** to declare one's presence and readiness for (duty, work, etc.): [T1 (*no pass.*] *How many men have reported for duty this morning?*

**report on/upon** *v prep*
to give an account or news of (something such as an event): [IØ + *on/upon*] *What do you have to report on the development of the talks with the government? I was told to witness the ceremony and report on it later.*

***report out** *v adv*
*AmE* to return (a matter sent for further study or decision) to people who can put it into action: [T1] *When did the committee report the bill out?*

***report sick** *v adj* → **fall ill, fall sick, go sick, take ill[1], take sick**
to declare one's inability to work because of illness: [IØ] *The workers showed their opposition by reporting sick in large numbers.*

**report to** *v prep*
**1** to give information about (something) to (someone in charge): [T1 + *to*] *Report any changes in his temperature to the head nurse.*
**2** to give the name of (someone) in a complaint to (someone in charge): [T1 + *to*] *I'll report you to the police if you don't stop annoying me.*
**3** to declare one's arrival to (someone or place): [IØ + *to*] *All visitors to the hospital must report to the main desk. Anyone entering the military camp must report to the guardhouse.*
***4** to owe duty to; be responsible to; be under the command of (someone in a position of power): [T1 (*no pass., usu. simple tenses*)] *In this new job you will report to the director on all matters.*

**report upon** *v prep* → **REPORT ON**

**repose in** *v prep*
**1** *fml* to (cause to) lie at rest, in sleep or death, in (something such as furniture or a place): [IØ + *in*] *He was asleep, reposing in an armchair. The body of the dead leader reposed in the cathedral for the people to pay their respects.* [T1 + *in*] *He was asleep, having reposed his body in a soft armchair.* → **rest in** (1)
*__2__ *fml* to exist because of; be due to (something): [T1 (*no pass., simple tenses*)] *The chief attractions of this holiday town repose in its peace and fresh air.* → **embody in, lie in²** (3), **reside in** (2), **rest in** (2)
*__3__ *fml* to give (something such as power) to (someone): [D1 (*usu. simple tenses*)] *The nation reposes too much power in the President.* → **reside in** (3), **rest in** (3), **vest in** (3)
*__4__ *fml* to place (trust, faith, etc.) in (someone): [D1 (*usu. simple tenses*)] *I have always reposed complete faith in your ability to deal with matters of sudden urgency.* → **rest in** (4)

**repose on** *v prep*
**1** *fml* to lie at rest, in sleep or death, on (something such as furniture or a surface); be supported by (something): [IØ + *on*] *In sunny weather you can see many of these large sea creatures reposing on the sand. This band of precious mineral rock reposes on a layer of clay.* → **rest on** (1)
*__2__ *fml* to depend on; be decided or fixed by (something): [T1 (*no pass., simple tenses*)] *The committee's decision reposes on the chairman's vote. Ideas should not repose on unsupported facts. The truth of my argument reposes on my honesty.* → **rest on** (3)

**represent as** *v prep*
**1** to give a picture or idea of (something or someone) as being (something or someone): [T1 + *as* (*often pass.*)] *In this picture, Love is represented as a child with a flower.*
**2** to describe; state; suggest that (someone or something) is (something): [X9 + *as* (*often simple tenses*)] *The teacher has been falsely represented as one who knows everything.* [X7 + *as*] *Never represent yourself as perfect.*

**represent to** *v prep*
**1** to give a picture or idea of (something or someone) to (someone): [T1 + *to* (*simple tenses*)] *This photograph represents my childhood to me.*
**2** to explain; make (something) clear to (someone): [T1 + *to* (*simple tenses*)] *The play represents to those watching it, the inner struggle in a man's mind between duty and doubt. How do you intend to represent your ideas to the committee?*
*__3__ *fml* to express (an idea) to (someone): [D1] *You must represent your complaints to Head Office.* [D5] *I represented to him that it would be dangerous to do what he suggested.*

**reprimand for** *v prep* → **tell off** (1), etc.
to scold (someone) officially for (something or doing something wrong or against the rules): [T1 + *for* (*often pass.*)] *The military court reprimanded the captain for his failure to perform his duty. The officer will have to be severely reprimanded for striking a private soldier.*

**reprint from** *v prep* → **reproduce from**
to print a copy of (written material) taking it from (the original): [T1 + *from*] *You have to have special permission to reprint any article from this magazine.*

**reprint in** *v prep* → **reproduce in**
to print a copy of (something written) in (something such as a book): [T1 + *in*] *Your article will be reprinted in the next copy of the magazine.*

**reproach for** *v prep* → **tell off** (1), etc.
to scold (someone) gently; express disappointment in (someone) because of (a fault or doing something wrong): [T1 + *for*] *The boy should be reproached for his accidental rudeness. Don't reproach the child for forgetting, he couldn't help it.*

**reproach with** *v prep* → **tell off** (1), etc.
to find fault with (someone); charge (someone) with (a fault); blame (someone) for (something or doing something wrong): [T1 + *with*] *The city council was reproached with injustice in its treatment of new citizens. The parents have reproached the school with failing to teach the child how to read.*

**reproduce from** *v prep* → **reprint from**
to make a copy of (something), taking it from (an original); cause the growth of (something new) from (something already in existence): [T1 + *from*] *New bushes can be reproduced from roots taken from the parent plant. The map has been reproduced from an original drawing by the famous map-maker.*

**reproduce in** *v prep* → **reprint in**
to show a copy of (something) in (something such as a book): [T1 + *in*] *We obtained special permission to reproduce the famous old map in our magazine. The photograph can be reproduced in colour.*

**reprove for** *v prep* → **tell off** (1), etc.
to scold (someone) rather severely for (something or doing something wrong): [T1 + *for*] *The children must be reproved for their wild behaviour. I have to reprove you for repeating the same mistakes over and over again.*

**repulse from** *v prep* → **repel from**
to drive (someone such as an enemy) back or away from (a place) by force: [T1 + *from*] *Only after a long hard struggle were we able to repulse the enemy from our shores.*

**repute as** *v prep*
**be reputed as** to be considered by most people to be (something): *This teacher is reputed as the best we have ever had. She is reputed as the most famous singer in Europe.*

**request from/of** *v prep* → **ask of**, etc.
to ask for (something), usu. politely, from (someone): [T1 + *from/of* (*usu. simple tenses*)] *May I request a favour of you? It's not*

*too much to request of you to clean your own shoes.*

***require of** *v prep* → **ask of**, etc.
to demand; claim (something), as by right, from (someone): [D1 (*usu. simple tenses*)] *Hard work will be required of students in this course. "What does the Lord require of you but to do justice, and to love kindness, and to walk humbly with your God?"* (The Bible) [D5 (*usu. simple tenses*)] *The teacher required of the students that they should know all about the battles of their nation's history.*

**requisition as/for** *v prep*
to seize (something) officially for (a purpose): [T1 + *as/for*] *During the war, many schools were requisitioned for hospitals.*

**requisition from** *v prep*
to seize; demand (something), as by right, from (usu. someone): [T1 + *from*] *The soldiers requisitioned food from the citizens.*

**requite with** *v prep* → **pay with** (2), **repay by, repay with**
*fml* to repay (something such as an action) by means of (something in return): [T1 + *with*] *Why does he requite my love with complete lack of interest? We shall requite these wrongs with fire and destruction.*

**rescue from** *v prep*
**1** to save (someone or something) from (danger): [T1 + *from*] *The three children were rescued from the burning house by their uncle.* → **save from** (1)
**2** to save (something) from (an unpleasant or undesirable state): [T1 + *from* (*usu. simple tenses*)] *Only the young singer's excellent performance rescued the concert from complete failure. The writer's study of his characters is just able to rescue the book from dullness.* → **salvage from** (2), **save from** (2)

**research into** *v prep*
to study (something such as a subject or area of difficulty) carefully and thoroughly, in order to gain information about it: [IØ + *into*] *Scientists have spent years researching into the effects of certain chemicals on the human brain, and still have left many questions unanswered.*

**resemble in** *v prep*
to be like (someone or something) with regard to (some part): [T1 + *in (simple tenses)*] *Mary resembles her mother in looks but not in character. This part of the country resembles England in its scenery.*

**reserve for** *v prep*
**1** to keep a supply of (something); keep (something) back so as to use it for (a purpose) or at (a later time): [T1 + *for*] *Don't forget to reserve some of your money for your holidays. The shipwrecked sailors tried to reserve some of their precious water for days without rain. Runners learn to reserve their strength for the last few yards.* → **hold for** (1), **keep for** (1), **save for** (1)
**2** to save; keep; put aside (something) for (someone): [T1 + *for*] *I have reserved a table for us at the best restaurant in town. The library will keep the book reserved for you till Wednesday.* → **hold for** (1), **keep for** (2), **save for** (2)
**3 be reserved for** to be intended, as by fate, for (someone): *Fame and honour are reserved for very special people. I feel sure that a promising future is reserved for this young singer.*

**reside in** *v prep*
**1** also **reside at** to live; have one's home in (a place): [L9 + *in*] *When you have resided in the country for five years, you may become a citizen.* → **live at, live in**[2] (1), **live on**[2] (1)
***2** to exist in the form of (something such as a quality): [T1 (*no pass., simple tenses*)] *His chief attraction resides in his character, not his looks. As a singer, her strength resides in her musical expression.* → **embody in, lie in**[2] (3), **repose in** (2), **rest in** (2)
***3** to be present in; be the property or power of (something or someone): [T1 (*no pass., simple tenses*)] *The power to change the law resides in Parliament. The responsibility for decision-making resides in the director.* → **repose in** (3), **rest in** (3), **vest in** (3)

**resign from** *v prep* → **give up** (2), etc.
to give formal notice that one will cease working at (a job or doing something) or belonging to (a group): [IØ + *from*] *Many young teachers resign from teaching when they discover how tiring it is. Is he going to resign from the chairmanship? Many angry members resigned from the club, to show their opposition to the committee's decision.*

***resign to** *v prep*
**1** to entrust (something or someone) to (usu. someone): [D1] *The mother was unwilling to resign the child to the care of her relatives. On his deathbed, he resigned his spirit to his Maker.*
**2** to accustom (oneself) to, and be prepared to accept (something or doing something, often unpleasant): [D1 (*often pass.*)] *You must resign yourself to your fate.* [V4b (*often pass.*)] *Is the firm resigned to losing the contract? Students can quickly become resigned to failing examinations.* → **reconcile to**

***resolve into** *v prep*
**1** to separate (something) into (its parts): [D1 (*simple tenses*)] *We can resolve this difficulty into two areas of misunderstanding. This specially shaped glass resolves light into its different colours. This chemical substance can be resolved into an acid and oxygen.*
**2** to change (itself) into (something else): [D1 (*usu. simple tenses*)] *Any misunderstanding can resolve itself into a quarrel. The council resolved itself into a special committee to examine the question.*

***resolve on** *v prep*
to decide firmly on; intend (something or doing something): [T1 (*often simple tenses*)] *The director has resolved on a plan to save the*

*firm.* [T4 (*often simple tenses*)] *Success is gained by resolving on winning.* [D1 (*usu. pass.*)] *Don't try to change my mind; I am resolved on it.* [V4b (*usu. pass.*)] I am resolved *on leaving this country.*

***resort to** *v prep*

**1** *old use fml* to visit (a pleasant place), esp. often, usu. for a purpose: [T1] *Following the example of the Prince, wealthy people used to resort to Bath to drink the waters for their health. We resorted to the hotel for some coffee.* → **repair to**

**2** to make use of (something or doing something, often something bad) to gain an advantage, often when everything else has failed: [T1] *Unhappy people often resort to violence as a means of expressing their suffering. Poets sometimes resort to strange uses of the language. If persuasion won't work, we may have to resort to force.* [T4] *I'm sorry to hear that you resorted to cheating.* → **recur to** (3)

**resound in/through** *v prep*

**1** to sound in a loud and hollow manner in (a space): [L9 + *in/through*] *The sea continued to resound in my ears long after it was out of sight. Church bells resounded through the town to declare victory.* → **reverberate in** (1), **ring in**[2] (1)

***2** to be famous throughout (a time): [T1 (*no pass., simple tenses*)] *Her brave decision resounds through history as an example to us all.* → **reverberate in** (2)

**resound with** *v prep* → **echo with, reverberate with, ring with** (1)

(of a space) to be filled with the sound of (something): [L9 + *with*] *The air resounded with the noise of the planes. The great actor could make the whole theatre resound with his voice. The woods and hills must resound with his grief.*

**respect for** *v prep*

to admire; give (someone) honour because of (something such as a quality or action): [T1 + *for* (*usu. simple tenses*)] *Jim's father was respected for his fairness by all his customers. I respect you for keeping silent about his secret.*

**respect oneself** *v pron*

to have regard for one's own worth; show self-respect: [IØ (*usu. simple tenses*)] *No one who truly respected himself could act as you have done.*

**respond to** *v prep*

**1** to speak or write an answer to (something spoken or written): [IØ + *to*] *I should like to respond to my opponent's remarks about the government's actions. Would anyone care to respond to the last question? How did you respond to the invitation? The worshippers responded to each line of the prayer with the words, "Have mercy on us."*

***2** to feel and express the result or effect of (something): [T1 (*simple tenses*)] *She responded to the news by bursting into tears. How do you respond to this modern artist's paintings?* → **react to**

***3** to act well or change for the better, as a result of (something): [T1] *Is Mother's leg responding to treatment? Children will respond to kindness but not to cruelty.*

***4** to obey (a control): [T1] *The horse responded well to his control. The sails are not responding to our pull on the ropes; the fastenings must have got twisted somehow.* → **answer to** (5)

**rest against** *v prep*

to lean against; be supported by (something): [L9 + *against*] *The wood's not safe, it's only resting against the wall.* [X9 + *against*] *Here, rest your head against the back of the chair.*

**rest from** *v prep*

to stop working after (work); change one's activity to something different or less tiring than (something): [IØ + *from*] *You need to rest from your labours: you look very tired.*

**rest in** *v prep*

**1** to (cause to) lie in comfort, sleep, or death in (something such as furniture, the ground, or a state): [IØ + *in*] *It was so comfortable resting in his arms. My father is dead; may he rest in peace.* [T1 + *in*] *Let us rest his body in his family grave. Resting his chin in his hands, he looked steadily at her.* → **repose in** (1)

***2** to exist because of; be due to (something): [T1 (*no pass., simple tenses*)] *The trouble rests in the people's dissatisfaction with the government's performance.* → **embody in, lie in**[2] (3), **repose in** (2), **reside in** (2)

***3** to give (something such as power) to (someone): [D1 (*usu. simple tenses*)] *The nation rests too much power in the President.* → **repose in** (3), **reside in** (3), **vest in** (3)

***4** to place (faith, trust, etc.) in (someone): [D1 (*usu. simple tenses*)] *I have always rested complete faith in your ability to deal with matters of sudden urgency.* → **repose in** (4)

**rest on/upon** *v prep*

**1** to (cause to) lie safely, comfortably, or in sleep or death on top of (something); be supported by (something): [IØ + *on/upon*] *In sunny weather you can see many of these large sea creatures resting on the sand. This band of precious mineral rocks rests on a bed of clay.* [T1 + *on/upon*] *The dog rested his wet nose on my hand in greeting. Rest the bottom of the ladder firmly on the ground.* → **repose on** (1)

***2** to (cause to) touch; reach; descend on; be directed towards (someone or something): [T1 (*no pass., usu. simple tenses*)] *His eyes rested on the peaceful valley below. "And the spirit of the Lord shall rest upon him, the spirit of wisdom and understanding."* (The Bible) [D1 (*usu. simple tenses*)] *It's good to rest one's eyes on such a beautiful view.*

***3** to depend on; be decided or fixed by (something): [D1 (*usu. simple tenses*)] *The committee's decision rests on the chairman's vote.* → **repose on** (2)

*__4__ to (cause to) be based on (something): [T1 (*simple tenses*)] *His fame rests upon one action that caught the public's attention years ago.* [D1 (*simple tenses*)] *It's not enough to rest your argument on unsupported facts.*

**5 rest on one's laurels** to be satisfied with one's success: *With these excellent examination results, you have earned the right to rest on your laurels for a time; take a holiday, enjoy yourself for a change.*

**6 rest on one's oars: a** (of a boatman) to stop rowing: *At the end of the race, the team could be seen sitting in the boat looking very tired, resting on their oars.* **b** to stop working after effort or success: *There's no resting on your oars here; once one job is finished, we start on the next!*

**rest up** *v adv*
to have a complete rest, as from illness or weakness: [IØ + UP] *I think I'll just rest up for an hour or two before starting work again.*

**rest upon** *v prep* → **REST ON**

***rest with** *v prep* → **lie with** (1)
to be the responsibility of (someone): [T1 (*no pass., simple tenses*)] *The decision rests with you.* [*It* + V3 (*simple tenses*)] *It rests with the court to prove the prisoner's guilt.*

**restitute to** *v prep*
*fml* to give (something) formally back to (someone): [T1 + *to*] *The court ordered the people living in the house to restitute it to its rightful owners.*

**restore in** *v prep*
**restore belief/confidence/faith in** to renew a usu. general or public belief in the worth of (something such as a quality or a group): *The city council has done its best to restore our belief in their honesty, but many people still have their doubts. The tax reductions were intended to restore confidence in the government. His recent success has helped to restore his faith in his own ability.*

**restore to** *v prep*
**1** to give or send back (something or someone that was lost or taken away) to (usu. someone): [T1 + *to*] *The court will make every effort to restore the child to his mother. The thieves decided to restore the valuable musical instrument to its owner, with a warning.* → **return to** (2)

**2** to bring (something or someone) back to (a former condition): [T1 + *to*] *The city council has voted money to help restore some older buildings to their former glory. A good rest will restore you to health.*

**3** to cause (a state such as peace or order) to return to (something such as a place, group, or event): [T1 + *to*] *A more experienced teacher was sent in to restore order to the class. After the shooting, it was some hours before the police could restore calm to the neighbourhood.*

*__4__ to give (a rank) back to (someone); cause (someone) to return to (a former position): [D1 (*often pass.*)] *After his trial, the captain's command was restored to him. The government hopes to be restored to power at the next election.* → **return to** (3)

**restrain from** *v prep* → **prevent from,** etc.
to prevent (usu. someone or an animal) by force or effort from (something or doing something, usu. wrong): [T1 + *from*] *The man lost his temper, and had to be restrained from violence by neighbours who held his arms. They built a fence to restrain local children from falling into the swimming pool. It's difficult to restrain oneself from eating too much.*

**restrict to** *v prep* → **limit to**
to reduce; control; keep (something or someone) down to (a place, level, etc.); limit (someone) to (something); save (something) for (certain people): [T1 + *to* (*often pass.*)] *In severe weather, traffic is restricted to certain roads that have been cleared of snow. The reports are restricted to descriptions, and give no opinions about the facts. It is unlawful for the club to restrict membership to people of certain races. The sale of alcohol is restricted to people over eighteen years of age. Certain information is restricted to government officials.*

**result from** *v prep* → **arise from,** etc.
to be caused by (something): [IØ + *from* (*usu. simple tenses*)] *The nation's troubles result from the government's stupidity. Let us hope that peace will result from our talks.*

***result in** *v prep*
to cause; have (something) as a result; end in (something): [T1 (*no pass., usu. simple tenses*)] *The game resulted in another victory for our team. Isn't it time that the talks resulted in a decision?* [V4a (*usu. simple tenses*)] *All our efforts only resulted in the knot becoming tighter. The quarrel resulted in his mother leaving the house.*

**retail at/for** *v prep*
to (cause to) be sold to the public for (a stated price): [L9 + *at/for* (*usu. simple tenses*)] *This book retails at £10 overseas. Do you think that the shoes could retail for $30?* [X9 + *at/for* (*to*) (*often simple tenses*)] *We can't afford to retail the jewellery at less than the price we paid for it, even to our most valued customers.*

**retail to** *v prep*
**1** to sell (goods) to (a customer): [X9 + *to* (*often simple tenses*)] *We should be able to retail most of these products to overseas customers.*

**2** *fml* to tell (amusing or interesting news) again to (a listener): [T1 + *to*] *Come and retail the story of Jack's relationship with Mary to my friend here: he'll want to hear every detail.*

**retain on/over/upon** *v prep*
to keep (something such as influence) over (someone or something): [T1 + *on/over*

*upon*] *The Bank of England has taken further steps to retain control over the value of the pound. How does an aging politician retain his hold on the loyalty of the voters?*

**retaliate against/on/upon** *v prep*
to return punishment to (someone who has done wrong to oneself); return (an attack): [IØ + *against/on/upon*] *You have to learn means of retaliating against your opponent's skilful play. Any healthy-minded person will retaliate on someone who is rude to him, usually with equal rudeness.*

**retire from** *v prep*
**1** to stop working at (a job or activity) or for (an employer), usu. at the end of one's life's work: [IØ + *from*] *When Jim's uncle retired from the railway company, he was given a gold watch. Keen swimmers retire from competitive sport at an age when most people are only just starting work.*
**2** esp. *mil* to move back from (a position): [IØ + *from*] *The soldiers received orders to retire from the positions that they had just won.* → **retreat from** (1)
**3 retire from the world** to enter a religious order, or live alone from principle, seeing no one: *After a busy life teaching, he retired from the world and considered his own inner development.*

**retire into** *v prep* → **withdraw into**
**retire into oneself** to become very quiet and unwilling to talk to people: *It's no use taking Mary to a party, she just retires into herself and makes everyone uncomfortable.*

**retire on** *v prep*
to have as (income) at the end of one's working life: [IØ + *on*] *People who retire on fixed incomes have the greatest difficulty with rising prices.*

**retire to** *v prep*
**1** to go away to (a quiet or private place: [IØ + *to*] *At the end of the meal, we all retired to the garden.*
**2** to move to (a place) at the end of one's life's work: [IØ + *to*] *Many people retire to the country, where they can enjoy peace and fresh air.*
**3** *mil* to move back to (a position): [IØ + *to*] *The soldiers received orders to retire to safer positions behind the lines.* → **retreat to**
**4 retire to bed** to go to bed: *Every time her husband won an argument, she would retire to bed and refuse to speak to him until the next day.* → **go to** (15), **put to²** (7), **send to** (2)

**retreat from** *v prep*
**1** esp. *mil* to yield place; move back from (a position or danger): [IØ + *from*] *Even the bravest army has been known to retreat from danger and certain defeat. At last we forced the enemy to retreat from the town. The crowd retreated from the soldiers' horses as they charged.* → **retire from** (2)
**2** to move away from or try to get rid of (something or someone), as in fear: [IØ + *from* (*often simple tenses*)] *You cannot retreat from your responsibility in this affair.* → **back away, back off** (1)

**retreat to** *v prep* → **retire to** (3)
esp. *mil* to yield place; move back to (another place or position): [IØ + *to*] *The soldiers were ordered to retreat to safer positions behind the lines.*

**retrieve from** *v prep*
to save; regain or bring back (something lost or in danger) from (a place or condition): [T1 + *from* (*often simple tenses*)] *Only just in time, I retrieved my paper from the waste paper basket, where it was about to be destroyed. These dogs are trained to retrieve birds from the places where they fall when they are shot. Only great efforts can retrieve the firm from ruin.*

**return for** *v prep*
to use (something) as a means of repaying (something else): [T1 + *for* (*usu. simple tenses*)] *We must return good for evil.*

**return from** *v prep*
to go or come back from (a place, or doing something): [IØ + *from*] *When I return from the coast, I shall bring good news. We were tired out when we returned from taking the dog for a walk.*

**return to** *v prep*
**1** to go back to (a place): [IØ + *to*] *Returning to a city where one used to live can be a saddening experience.*
**2** to give or send (something) back to (someone): [T1 + *to*] *Please return the book to its exact place on the shelf. Parcels which cannot be delivered will be returned to the sender.* → **restore to** (1)
**3** to cause (someone or a group) to have (power, office) again: [T1 + *to*] *The government hopes to be returned to power at the next election.* → **restore to** (4)
**4** to talk or write again about (a subject): [IØ + *to* (*often simple tenses*)] *Let us return to the question we were first considering.* → **revert to** (2)
**5** to take up again; use; make use of (something such as a former method or habit) again: [IØ + *to* (*often simple tenses*)] *The only answer to rising prices is to return to wage and price controls. It's difficult not to return to old ways of thinking. Many prisoners, on being freed, return to a life of crime.* → **regress to, revert to** (3)
**6** to go back to (a former state): [IØ + *to*] *Without endless watering, these fields will quickly return to desert.* → **revert to** (4)

**return with** *v prep*
**1** to come back with (someone or a thing): [T1 + *with*] *Calling at my uncle's on our way home, we returned with his two children. After two weeks' hot weather in Spain we returned with very brown skins.*

**2** to elect (someone or a party) with (a number of votes): [T1 + *with* (*usu. pass.*)] *The Member of Parliament was returned with an increased number of votes.* → **elect with**

**reunite with** *v prep* → **unite with**
to bring (someone) together with (a group) again: [T1 + *with*] *The Red Cross was successful in reuniting the prisoner with his family.*

***rev up** *v adv*
**1** *not fml* (of an engine) to (cause to) be increased in the speed of the motor: [IØ (*often continuous tenses*)] *I could hear the motorcycles revving up in preparation for leaving.* [T1] *If you rev up your engine too fast, you may damage it.*
**2** *infml* to (cause to) be increased in speed or activity: [T1] *The factory will have to rev up production to stay level with demand.* [IØ (*often continuous tenses*)] *The crime rate is revving up in most big cities.*

**reveal to** *v prep*
to show (something or someone that has been hidden) clearly to (someone); make known (something secret) to (someone): [T1 + *to* (*often simple tenses*)] *Drawing back the curtain, she revealed the sleeping criminal to the police. Why don't you reveal your thoughts to me?*

***revel in** *v prep* → **riot in**
to enjoy (something) greatly; take great pleasure in (someone, something, or doing something): [T1] *The dogs ran round the garden, revelling in their new-found freedom. The young singer revelled in the public's admiration.* [T4] *Why do children revel in making trouble?*

**revenge on/upon** *v prep*
**1** to repay (a crime) by punishing (the criminal): [T1 + *on/upon* (*usu. simple tenses*)] *Hamlet revenged his father's death on his uncle.* → **avenge on**
*__2__ to satisfy (oneself) by punishing (someone who has done wrong to oneself): [D1 (*often pass.*)] *Hamlet revenged himself on his uncle. Hamlet was revenged on his uncle.* → **get even,** etc.

**reverberate in/through** *v prep*
**1** (of a sound) to be repeated again and again loudly in (a space): [IØ + *in/through*] *The noise of the plane engines is still reverberating in my ears.* → **resound in** (1), **ring in**[2] (1)
*__2__ to be famous throughout (a time): [T1 (*no pass., often simple tenses*)] *Her brave decision reverberates through history as an example to us all.* → **resound in** (2)

**reverberate with** *v prep* → **echo with, resound with, ring with** (1)
(of a space) to be filled with the loud repeated sound of (something): [IØ + *with*] *The cave reverberated with the cries of the crowds of birds that lived there.*

***revert to** *v prep*
**1** (of property) to return to the possession of; be taken back by (usu. someone) formally: [T1 (*no pass., usu. simple tenses*)] *After his death, his lands will revert to the government. Possession of the house reverts to the original landowner when the contract comes to an end.*
**2** to talk or write about (a subject) again: [T1] *Reverting to the earlier question, we didn't actually reach a decision.* → **return to** (4)
**3** to take up; use; make use of (something such as a former method or habit) again: [T1] *Many prisoners, on being freed, revert to a life of crime. The schools will not improve education by reverting to the old system. Reverting to her former manner for a moment, she forgot her good intentions.* [T4] *Many prisoners, on being freed, revert to stealing.* → **regress to, return to** (5)
**4** to go back to (a former state): [T1 (*no pass.*)] *Without endless watering, these fields will quickly revert to desert. The state of the nation has reverted to a condition of hopelessness.* → **return to** (6)

***revile against/at** *v prep*
to swear at; oppose (someone or something) with bitter anger: [T1] *The angry crowd reviled at the police who were trying to control them. A man stood on a wooden box in the park, reviling against civilization.*

**revolt against** *v prep*
**1** to oppose; fight against; refuse to obey (someone in power, or something with which one disagrees); try to take power from (someone) by force: [IØ + *against*] *The citizens at last revolted against their cruel rulers, drove them from the country, and took power themselves. The prisoners are revolting against living conditions in the prisons by refusing to eat.* → **mutiny against, rebel against, rise against**
*__2__ to feel angry and unwilling in relation to (something or doing something); feel a strong dislike of (something); refuse to consider (something or doing something): [T1 (*often simple tenses*)] *I know I have to get up every morning, but my mind revolts against the thought.* [T4 (*often simple tenses*)] *I eat vegetables because my conscience revolts against killing animals.* → **rebel at**

**revolve about/around** *v prep*
**1** to have (something) as the middle point of its movement: [IØ + *about/around*] *The earth revolves around the sun. Traffic is kept revolving about an island in the middle of the area where the four roads meet.*
*__2__ to be chiefly concerned with (something); have as a centre or main subject: [T1 (*no pass., simple tenses*)] *The action of the play revolves around the struggle between two women. A baby's life revolves around its mother.* → **centre on** (2), **focus on** (4)

**reward for** *v prep*
to give (someone) something valuable or something that he desires, on account of (something or doing something good): [T1 + *for*] *In our society, children are rewarded for good behaviour and punished for disobedi-*

*ence. We rewarded him for finding our lost cat.*

**rhapsodize about/over** *v prep*
to praise; express great keenness and delight in (something or someone): [IØ + *about/over*] *The newspapers all rhapsodized over the young singer's performance.*

**rhyme with** *v prep*
(of a word or line of poetry) to have the same ending sound as (another word or line); use (a word or words) with the same ending sound as (another word): [IØ + *with* (*simple tenses*)] *"Mine" rhymes with "wine." "Brother" rhymes with "another". At the end of a scene in Shakespeare's plays, the closing line often rhymes with the one before it.* [T1 + *with* (*usu. simple tenses*)] *You can't rhyme "sleep" with "feet"!*

*__rid of__ *v prep* → **be of** (4), **get of** (10)
to make (someone, oneself, or something) free of (something or someone unwanted): [D1 (*often pass.*)] *You must learn to rid yourself of such troublesome thoughts. I doubt if London will ever be rid of its terrible housing shortage. Who will rid the country of this particular evil?*

*__riddle with__ *v prep*
**1** to make (someone or something) full of (holes); fill (someone or something) with holes made by (bullets, etc.): [D1 (*usu. pass.*)] *The enemy have riddled the walls of the town with bullet holes. His body lay on the battlefield, riddled with bullets. I can't carry water in this pot, it's riddled with holes.*
**2 be riddled with** *not fml* to be very full of; have a lot of (things such as faults): *The politician's speech was riddled with lies. This article is riddled with printing mistakes.*

**ride at** *v prep* → **lie at** (3)
**ride at anchor** (of a ship) to be still; stop moving; be fixed to the sea bottom by its anchor, usu. out of a harbour: *Will the ship be safe riding at anchor in this storm?*

**ride away/off** *v adv*
to leave on horseback, a bicycle, etc.: [IØ + AWAY/OFF] *Without saying a word, she got on her bicycle and rode off.*

**ride down** *v adv*
**1** to chase and catch (someone) by means of a horse: [T1] *Police on horseback tried to ride the criminal down.*
**2** to knock (someone) down with a horse: [T1] *Help this poor boy; he's been ridden down by huntsmen crossing the fields.*
**3** to tire (a horse) by riding too hard or long: [T1] *Don't ride the horse down, he's not as young as he was.*

**ide for** *v prep*
**ride for a fall: a** to ride a horse or bicycle in a dangerous manner: [*often continuous tenses*] *Don't make your horse go so fast on this rough ground, you're riding for a fall.* **b** to act so as to bring trouble on oneself: [*often continuous tenses*] *I dare not put my money into such a risky plan—that would really be riding for a fall.*

*__ride high__ *v adv*
*not fml* to enjoy a feeling of success and well-being: [IØ (*usu. continuous tenses*)] *Our team are really riding high after all their victories.*

**ride off** *v adv* → RIDE AWAY

**ride on**[1] *v adv*
to continue to ride: [IØ + ON] *"Ride on, ride on in majesty".* (Henry Hart Milman, religious song)

**ride on/upon**[2] *v prep*
**1** to (cause to) sit and be carried on (something such as an animal or vehicle): [IØ + *on/upon*] *The children loved to ride on Father's back. Passengers are not allowed to ride on the roof of the train. The boy caused quite a scene by arriving at school riding on a horse.* [T1 + *on/upon*] *Will you ride the baby on your knee for a minute?*
***2** to be supported by (opinion in one's favour): [T1] *As a politician, he rode on great popularity for some years, but then lost favour with the public.*
***3** *not fml* (of money) to be placed on (usu. a horse) as a bet: [T1 (*no pass.*)] *How much money was riding on the winning horse?*
***4** to be dependent on (something): [T1 (*no pass., simple tenses, usu. present*)] *The committee's decision often rides on the chairman's vote.* → **depend on** (3), **hang on**[2] (2), **hinge on, pivot on** (2), **rely on** (2), **turn on**[2] (3)
**5 ride herd on** *not fml* to watch (a group) so as to control them; keep a check on: *How many teachers have we ready to ride herd on such a large number of children?*
**6 ride someone on a rail** *AmE not fml* to tie someone to a fence post and carry him out of town as a punishment: *It's not so many years since anyone who offended against the moral standard of the village would be ridden on a rail.*

**ride out** *v adv*
**1** to ride a long distance, as out of town: [IØ + OUT] *Let's ride out to the mountains while the weather is good.*
***2** *naut* to come safely through (something such as a storm): [T1a] *The ship should be strong enough to ride out the storm.*
***3** *not fml* to come safely through (any kind of trouble): [T1a] *It is difficult to be certain whether the government will be able to ride out its present troubles with the unions.*

**ride over** *v prep*
**1** to (cause to) pass across (something such as land) on horseback or bicycle: [IØ + *over*] *Huntsmen have no right to ride over other people's land without permission.* [T1 + *over*] *Who said you could ride your bicycle over my garden?*
**2 ride roughshod over** *not fml* to treat (someone) unkindly or without consideration for his feelings or wishes: *It's no wonder that some children grow up troublesome when their pa-*

*rents have treated them as less than human, allowing them no rights and riding roughshod over them from an early age.*

**ride to** *v prep*
**1** to (cause to) travel as far as (a place) on horseback or bicycle: [IØ + *to*] *It's too far to ride to your grandmother's, you'd better take the bus.* [T1 + *to*] *I rode my bicycle to school every day for ten years.*
**2 ride to hounds** *BrE* to hunt small animals such as foxes on horseback for sport: *It used to be the custom for most wealthy families to ride to hounds, but nowadays hunting is often considered to be cruelty to animals.*

***ride up** *v adv*
(usu. of clothing) to move out of place in an upward direction: [IØ] *Wait a minute while I pin this shirt to stop it riding up.*

**ride upon** *v prep* → RIDE ON[2]

***riffle through** *v prep*
to turn over the edges of (cards, papers, etc.) quickly with one's fingers: [T1] *The magician riffled through the cards with skilful fingers that moved like lightning. It only took him a few moment riffling through the records to find the right name.*

***rifle through** *v prep* → **go into** (5)
to search quickly through (papers, a container, etc.); examine with one's hands, usu. with dishonest intentions: [T1] *I've rifled through these papers, but I still can't find the one I'm looking for. Someone's been rifling through my drawers, there's some money missing. All the cupboards in the house had been rifled through by the thieves, looking for the jewels.*

***rig out** *v adv*
**1** *not fml* to provide (someone) with clothes and other equipment: [T1] *As winter gets near, we have to rig the whole family out with warm clothing and winter sports things.* —**rig-out** *n*
**2** *infml* to dress (someone) in unusual clothes: [T1 (*usu. pass.*)] *People came to the party rigged out as sailors, policemen, characters from stories, fairies, animals, and other strange creatures.* —**rig-out** *n* → **dress up** (2), etc.

***rig up** *v adv*
**1** to put together the parts, esp. ropes, of (a boat or ship); put together the parts of (a plane): [T1] *Has the boat been properly rigged up with suitable ropes and sails? Make sure you rig up the wires correctly.*
**2** *not fml* to make (something) for a short time out of materials easily found: [T1] *The first thing to do when you're shipwrecked is to rig up some kind of a shelter, and only afterwards look for food.*
**3** *infml* to think of (a plan, often dishonest): [T1] *He's sure to have rigged up some method of beating the other firm to the contract. Any clever politician can usually rig up a way to make the voters believe what he says.*

**ring about/around** *v adv* → **ring round[1]** (2), **ring with** (3)
to surround (something or someone), as with a circle: [T1 + ABOUT/AROUND (*with*) (*usu. pass.*)] *The city is ringed about with hills. Our efforts are ringed around with difficulties.*

***ring around** *v prep* → **ring round[2]** (1)
to make telephone calls to (several different places such as shops): [T1] *I found the cheapest price for enlarging the photograph by ringing around all the photographic dealers.*

**ring back** *v adv* → **call back** (5)
esp. *BrE* to return a telephone call to (someone); make a telephone call again: [T1 + BACK] *I'll find out the address, and ring you back.* [IØ + BACK] *He's not in; why don't you ring back after 6 o'clock?*

**ring down** *v adv* → **ring up** (3)
**ring down the curtain (on): a** to lower the curtain, as on a signal or at the end of a play or part of a play; end a play, as by lowering the curtain: *I'll give you a signal to ring down the curtain when the scene is over. The curtain has been rung down; the theatre company are leaving town tomorrow.* **b** to signal the end of something; end something: *The death of King Richard III in 1485 rang down the curtain on the Middle Ages. I'm sorry to hear that they have decided to ring down the curtain on their marriage.*

**ring for** *v prep*
to sound a bell or press a button to demand or cause the appearance of (something or someone) or to ask for (something to be done): [IØ + *for*] *You'd better ring for the housekeeper to bring more soap. How do you ring for room service in this hotel? You have to ring for the dirty dishes to be taken away.*

***ring hollow** *v adj* → **ring true** (2)
(of someone's words or voice) to sound false or insincere: [IØ (*simple tenses*)] *He declared that he was telling the truth, but his words rang hollow.*

***ring in[1]** *v adv*
**1** *AmE* to mark the time of one's arrival at work: [IØ] *Most of the workers had already rung in by the time I arrived.* → **clock in**, etc.
**2 ring in the new year** to mark the beginning of a year with bells, etc.: *We ring in the new year with the church bells.* → **bring in** (7), **play in[1]** (2), **play out** (5), **ring out** (5), **see in[1]** (4), **see out** (6)

**ring in/through[2]** *v prep*
**1** to sound like a bell in (a space): [IØ + *in/through*] *The children's laughter was still ringing in my ears as I left the playground. Church bells rang through the whole country to declare victory.* → **resound in** (1), **reverberate in** (1)
***2** to be repeated in (someone's ears, mind etc.): [T1] *My former teacher's words of wisdom still ring in my memory as a guide to my actions.*

***ring off** *v adv* → **hang up** (2)
esp. *BrE* to end a telephone conversation by putting the receiver down: [IØ] *Don't ring off, I haven't finished my story.*

**ring on** *v prep*
**ring the changes on: a** to make different tunes using (a small number of bells): [*often simple tenses*] *It is possible to ring the changes on five bells for over two hours.* **b** to try to find variety in (a limited set of things): [*often simple tenses*] *Having separate pieces of clothing enables you to ring the changes on the garments by wearing them in various combinations.*

***ring out** *v adv*
**1** (of a voice, bell, or other sound) to sound loudly and suddenly: [IØ (*usu. simple tenses*)] *A shot rang out, and then there was silence. A voice rang out from the back of the church, interrupting the wedding.*
**2** (of a telephone bell) to be heard at the receiving end of a call: [IØ] *I could hear the telephone at the other end ringing out, but no one answered.*
**3** esp. *BrE* to make an outgoing telephone call: [IØ] *"With all these incoming calls, it was some time before Judith could ring out."* (Margaret Forster, *The Park*)
**4** *AmE* to mark the time of leaving work: [IØ] *What time do you ring out on a Friday?* → **clock out,** etc.
**5 ring out the old year** to mark the end of a year with bells, etc.: *Can you hear the church bells ringing out the old year?* → **ring in[1]** (2) etc.

***ring round[1]** *v adv*
**1** to make telephone calls to several different places such as shops: [IØ] *It is a good thing to ring round to find the best price.*
**2** to surround (something), as with a circle: [T1 (*with*) (*usu. pass.*)] *The city is ringed round with hills.* → **ring about, ring with** (3)

***ring round[2]** *v prep*
**1** to make telephone calls to (several different places such as shops): [T1] *I found the cheapest price for enlarging the photograph by ringing round all the photographic dealers.* → **ring around**
**2** to draw a circle round (something such as a word): [T1] *Ring round the words which you think mean the same in this sentence.*

**ring through** *v prep* → **RING IN[2]**

***ring true** *v adj*
**1** (of a coin) to make the sound, as when thrown on the ground, of a coin of real value: [IØ (*simple tenses*)] *People used to test coins that were offered in payment, to see if they rang true or were made of false metal.*
**2** (of someone's words or voice) to sound believable; seem sincere: [IØ (*simple tenses*)] *When a judge has to decide between two people arguing about facts, he will pay attention to the one whose story rings true.* → **ring hollow**

**ring up** *v adv*
**1** esp. *BrE* to call (someone) on the telephone; make a telephone call: [T1 + UP] *Have you rung up your mother recently?* [IØ + UP] *How many people have rung up while I've been out?* → **call up** (3)
***2** to record (money paid) on a machine, especially one with a bell: [T1] *The bill came to £3.25, but the sales person rang up £3.75 by mistake. In a single busy day, the little shop had rung up more than $300.*
**3 ring up the curtain (on): a** to start a play, as by signalling for the theatre curtain to be raised: *It's time to ring up the curtain on the opening scene. The international theatre company rings up the curtain on its new production this week.* **b** to make a start on (something new): *The government intends to ring up the curtain on a whole new range of plans to bring down the unemployment rate.* → **ring down**

**ring with** *v prep*
**1** (of a space) to be filled with the sound of (something such as a bell): [IØ + *with*] *My ears are still ringing with the noise of the plane. The football ground rang with the cheers of the crowd.* → **echo with, resound with, reverberate with**
***2** to be filled with (something such as fame): [T1 (*no pass.*)] *The whole sports world is ringing with the wonderful performance by the young girl.*
***3** to surround (something) with (something), as in a circle: [D1 (*usu. pass.*)] *The country is ringed with mountains.* → **ring about, ring round[1]** (2)

***rinse down** *v adv* → **rinse with** (2)
to cause (something solid) to be easily swallowed by drinking something afterwards: [T1 (*with*)] *What shall I drink to rinse the medicine down?*

**rinse out** *v adv*
**1** to clean (something such as a container) thoroughly with a lot of water: [T1 + OUT] *Make sure that the bottle is completely rinsed out before you refill it. Rinse your mouth out now.*
***2** (of dirt, etc.) to (cause to) be removed, usu. by the action of water: [T1 (*of*)] *It took hours to rinse the heavy black oil out of the poor bird's feathers. If the poisonous chemical gets into your eyes, rinse it out well.* [IØ] *The mark of the blood should rinse out in time.*

**rinse with** *v prep*
**1** to remove usu. soapy water from (something being washed) with clear water: [T1 + *with*] *After you've washed your hair, rinse it twice with clean warm water.*
***2** to follow the eating of (something) by drinking (something such as alcohol): [D1 (*often pass.*)] *You can get stomachache from eating worthless food rinsed with beer.* → **rinse down**

***riot in** *v prep* → **revel in**
to delight in; take great pleasure in (something or doing something, usu. something bad or

active): [T1 (*usu. simple tenses*)] *Some politicians riot in fierce argument. There must be something wrong with people who riot in cruelty to animals.* [T4 (*usu. simple tenses*)] *The horses kicked up their heels, rioting in being let loose at last. Some unsatisfied youths riot in driving fast and taking risks.*

**rip across** *v adv* → **tear across[1]**
to tear (something) in two parts: [T1 + ACROSS] *Offended at being offered payment, he ripped the cheque across and sent it back.*

**rip apart** *v adv*
**1** to separate; divide (something) with violence; cause disorder in (something), as when searching: [T1 + APART] *"A large number of travellers had a narrow escape this morning when a bomb ripped apart the train in which they had been travelling."* (CBS radio news, 4 March 1976) *The thieves ripped the house apart but could find nothing.* → **pull apart** (1), etc.
*__2__ to hurt; cause (someone) severe grief or pain: [T1b (*usu. pass.*)] *"In this film, a family is ripped apart by a young mother's death, and the policeman has to break the news that the 'accident' was planned."* (*Toronto Star Week*, 24 January 1976) → **tear apart** (2)

**rip away** *v adv*
**1** to remove (something) with a violent movement: [X9 + AWAY (*from*)] *The telephone wires have been ripped away by the criminals. Last night's high wind has ripped all the leaves away from the trees.* → **rend from, rip from, rip off** (1), **rip out, tear away** (1), **tear from, tear off[1]** (1), **tear out** (1)
*__2__ to remove (something acting as a covering); show the falsity of (a pretence): [T1 (*from*) (*often simple tenses*)] *His political opponents were able to rip away the show of sincerity covering his deceitful intentions.* → **rip off** (4), **tear away** (4), **tear off[1]** (3)

**rip down** *v adv* → **tear down[1]** (1)
to remove; pull down; lower (something) with a violent movement: [X9 + DOWN] *The photographs of the unpopular leader had been ripped down in the night by his enemies.*

**rip from** *v prep* → **rend from, rip away** (1), **rip off** (1), **rip out, tear away[1]** (1), **tear from, tear off**(1), **tear out** (1)
to pull; remove (something or someone) from (usu. something) with a violent movement: [X9 + *from*] *Jim ripped the cover from the book.*

**rip in** *v prep* → **rend in, tear in, tear into** (1)
to tear, pull, or break (something) so as to be in (usu. a number of parts): [T1 + *in*] *The sails were ripped in two by the high wind. I have accidentally ripped this pound note in half; can I still spend it?*

***rip into** *v prep*
**1** to enter or cut (something) with a violent movement, as of teeth: [T1] *See those lions ripping into the bodies of the animals that they have killed for food.* → **tear into** (2)
**2** to attack (something or someone), esp. so as to destroy it or him: [T1] *This successful politician never fails to rip into his opponents, showing the weakness of their arguments.* → **lay into**, etc.

**rip off** *v adv*
**1** to remove (something) violently from the top or front of something: [X9 + OFF] *"The explosion ripped off the whole front of the restaurant."* (CBC radio news 29 October 1975) → **rip away** (1), **rip from, rip out, tear away[1]** (1), **tear off** (1)
*__2__ *sl* to steal (goods); steal from (someone or a shop, etc.): [T1 (*often simple tenses*)] *He tried to sell me some jewellery, but I thought it had been ripped off so I wouldn't buy it. I wouldn't dare to rip off a bank, would you?* —**rip-off** *n* —**ripped off** *adj* → **knock off** (6), **knock over** (5)
*__3__ *infml* to charge (someone) too much: [T1] *Look at the price I've been charged, I've been ripped off again! I don't shop at that store any more, they're known for ripping off the customers whenever they get a chance.* —**rip-off** *n* → **hold up** (4), **pay through**
*__4__ *old use not fml* to express (angry words): [T1 (*usu. simple tenses*)] *Seeing his enemy, he ripped off a curse.* → **rip away** (2), **tear away** (4), **tear off[1]** (3)

**rip out** *v adv*
to remove (something) with a violent movement: [X9 + OUT (*of*)] *The criminals have ripped the telephone wires out, so we can't call the police. A single blow ripped out two of his opponent's teeth. The builders decided to rip out the whole inside of the house and rebuild within the outer walls.* → **rip away** (1), etc.

**rip to** *v prep*
**1** to tear (something) into (smaller parts, as pieces): [T1 + *to*] *The sudden high wind ripped the sail to pieces.* → **pull apart** (1), etc.
**2 rip someone/something to pieces/shreds** to attack someone or something without mercy: *The next speaker ripped his opponent's argument to shreds in a few minutes. It is not the job of the examiners to rip your argument to pieces, only to set a value on your style.* → **take apart** (4), etc.

**rip up** *v adv*
**1** to lift (something) upwards with a violent movement; destroy (something) by pulling: [X9 + UP] *During the night, workmen ripped up the middle of the road so as to lay new pipes. That dog has ripped this morning's newspaper up again!* → **tear up[1]** (1)
*__2__ to break or completely disregard (an agreement): [T1] *He can't be trusted; he's been known to rip up a contract as soon as it's signed.* → **tear up[1]** (3)

**rise above** *v prep*
**1** to move or float to a higher level than (something): [IØ + *above*] *Smoke could be*

*seen rising above the trees.*

***2** to have a higher standard of behaviour than (something or doing something): [T1 (*often simple tenses*)] *It is difficult to rise above ordinary desires. The children have been taught to rise above selfish considerations.* [T4 (*often simple tenses*)] *I thought you had risen above lying to your mother.*

***3** to conquer (difficulties): [T1] *The company has risen above its early problems, and is now doing well.*

**rise against** *v prep* → **mutiny against, rebel against, revolt against** (1)
to begin to oppose (someone or something such as unjust rule): [IØ + *against*] *At last the citizens rose against their cruel rulers and took power themselves. Any self-respecting person will rise against unjust treatment.*

**rise from** *v prep*
**1** to get up from (something such as a position); move to a higher level out of or away from (something); reach a higher social level than (something): [IØ + *from*] *Smoke could be seen rising from the chimney. All the guests rose from the table to drink the health of the happy pair. The greatest leader of the nation rose from humble origins.*

***2** to have its origin in; be caused by (something): [T1 (*no pass., usu. simple tenses*)] *This uncomfortable feeling probably rises from your guilt about your action.* → **arise from,** etc.

**3 rise from the ashes** to be rebuilt after destruction, esp. by fire: *After many years of collecting money and planning its style, the people saw the great church rise from the ashes of the original which had been destroyed by enemy bombs.*

**4 rise from the dead/grave** to come back to life: [*usu. simple tenses*] *Jesus rose from the dead.* → **call up** (6), **raise from** (2), **raise up** (2), **summon up** (4)

**5 rise from the ranks** to become an officer after having served as an ordinary soldier: [*usu. simple tenses*] *The best professional military man is often the one who has risen from the ranks, rather than the one who entered the army as an officer through military school or social connections.*

**rise in** *v prep*
**1 rise in someone's estimation/opinion** to be better thought of; be more highly valued or considered more worthy than formerly: *Your mother has risen in my estimation since she said how sincerely sorry she was for having offended me. This restaurant has risen in my opinion since they've employed their new cook.*

**2 rise in the world** to reach a higher social position, as through wealth: *Since she rose in the world by marrying a nobleman, she has not even spoken to her own relatives. I hope that if I ever rise in the world, I shall still regard my former friends as worthy of consideration.*

**rise to** *v prep*
**1** to move; float upwards towards (something): [IØ + *to*] *If you let the liquid stand till it cools, the fat will rise to the top. You can test eggs by putting them in water; a good egg will sink but a bad egg will rise to the surface.*

**2** to reach (a high level, position, etc.): [IØ + *to*] *This young man should do well, and may even rise to great fame. After many years of faithful service, the politician deserved to rise to the leadership of his party.*

**3 rise to the bait: a** (of fish) to take food offered on a hook, and so get caught: *There are plenty of fish in the river, and good flies on my line, but the fish are getting clever and refuse to rise to the bait today.* **b** *not fml* to accept something intended to attract one; be trapped in something prepared for one: *Shopkeepers know that if they offer one product at a cheap price, customers will rise to the bait, come into the shop, and then buy other goods.*

**4 rise to the challenge/occasion** to be equal to; be able to deal with a difficulty or test, usu. unexpected, with courage and inventiveness: *When the invited speaker did not arrive, the chairman rose to the occasion and gave an excellent unprepared speech.*

**5 rise to one's feet** to stand up, as to speak in public: *At the end of the game, the whole crowd rose to their feet, cheering wildly. If two people rise to their feet at the same time, which one should the chairman hear first?* → **get to** (11), etc.

**6 rise to the surface** to become seen or known: *The facts of the matter are only now beginning to rise to the surface; the politicians kept them successfully hidden for many years.*

**rise up** *v adv*
**1** to raise oneself; be lifted; get up; move or float upwards: [IØ + UP] *"And the people sat down to eat and to drink and rose up to play."* (The Bible)

**2** to refuse to obey those in power: [IØ + UP] *At last the citizens rose up and defeated their cruel rulers.*

**3** (of a feeling) to develop: [IØ + UP] *Fear rose up in their hearts as the enemy came near.*

**risk on** *v prep*
to take a chance with (something such as money) by placing it to win or be lost in (something such as a game): [T1 + *on*] *He risked £5 on the horse race and lost it all.*

**rivet on** *v prep*
to fix (the attention or eyes) steadily on (something or someone): [T1 + *on* (*often pass.*)] *The animal's eyes were riveted on the creature that it intended to kill. Only by riveting his attention on his work could he forget his worries.*

**rivet to** *v prep* → **root to**
**rivet someone to the ground/spot** to make

someone or an animal stay in one place, completely still: [*often pass.*] *The shock of seeing the bear riveted him to the spot, although the danger should have made him run. The animal stood, riveted to the ground with fear.*

**roam about/around** *v adv; prep*
to wander around (a place): [IØ + ABOUT/AROUND/*about/around*] *The children love roaming about in the fields and woods. Let's just roam around the town this afternoon, looking in the shop windows.*

**roar at** *v prep* → **shout at**
to shout at (usu. someone) loudly: [IØ + *at*] *It's a poor teacher who can only control the class by roaring at the children.*

***roar down** *v adv* → **shout down** (2)
to drown the voice of (a speaker) with loud noise, as by shouting: [T1] *The next speaker tried to make himself heard, but the crowd roared him down.*

**roar out** *v adv*
1 to express something loudly; make a loud noise: [IØ + OUT] *The wounded animal roared out in pain.* → **call out** (1), **shout out** (1), **yell out**
**2** to express (something) loudly: [T1 + OUT] *The baby was roaring out its hunger. The officer roared out a command, and all the soldiers stood to attention.* → **call out** (1), **cry out** (1), **shout out** (2), **thunder out, yell out**

**rob of** *v prep*
**1** to take; steal from (usu. someone) (his property or rights): [T1 + *of*] *The thieves robbed the passengers of all their money and jewels.*
***2** to stop (someone or something) from having (something deserved, expected, or usual): [D1] *Just as Jim neared the winning post, another runner appeared from behind and robbed him of the prize. Television has robbed the cinema of its former popularity.*

**rock about/around** *v adv*
to (cause to) move up and down or from side to side: [IØ + ABOUT/AROUND (*often continuous tenses*)] *Several boats were rocking about on the rough water.* [T1 + ABOUT/AROUND] *The waves were rocking the little boat about, rather uncomfortably.*

**rock to** *v prep*
**rock someone to sleep** to cause someone to fall asleep by a regular up-and-down or side-to-side movement: *Take the baby in your arms and see if you can rock him to sleep. The movement of the train was rocking me to sleep, and I nearly missed my station.*

**roll about** *v adv*
**1** also **roll around** (of something round) to (cause to) move around loosely: [IØ + ABOUT] *I can hear some dried beans rolling about in this box.* [T1 + ABOUT] *Don't roll your eyes about like that, it looks nasty.*
***2** *not fml* to laugh uncontrollably; be amused: [IØ (*often continuous tenses*)] *The public were difficult to amuse tonight, but this new performer soon had them rolling about.*

***roll along** *v adv*
*not fml* to keep going; continue without stopping; travel; move: [IØ (*usu. continuous tenses*)] *How's the old car? Oh, still rolling along. "For my own part, looking out upon the future . . . I could not stop it if I wished; no one can stop it. Like the Mississippi, it just keeps rolling along."* (Winston Churchill, *Speech, House of Commons*, 20 August 1940)

**roll around** *v adv* → **ROLL ABOUT** (1), **ROLL ROUND**

**roll at** *v prep* → **make at** (4), **ogle at**
**roll one's eyes at** *not fml* to try to attract (someone of the opposite sex) by moving one's eyes round and round: *Don't you roll your eyes at me, young man!*

**roll away** *v adv*
to (cause to) move away by rolling: [IØ + AWAY] *Quick, catch the wheel—it's rolling away!* [T1 + AWAY] *The sun soon rolled the mist away, and the view became clear.* —**roll-away** *adj*

**roll back** *v adv*
**1** to (cause to) move backwards or away by rolling: [IØ + BACK] *As the waves roll back, more and more sand can be seen. The lid of the desk rolls back to show the writing surface.* [T1 + BACK] *I think it would look better if you rolled the hair back from your face. Can you roll back the edge of the mat? It's too big.*
***2** (of time) to disappear; seem to go back into the past: [IØ] *Standing in the castle yard, we could feel the centuries roll back, and imagine ourselves there in the days of its glory.*
***3** to force (opposition) to move back; (cause to) yield: [T1] *Enemy forces are being rolled back on all fronts.* [IØ] *Opposition to our plan seems to be rolling back, after all our efforts at persuasion.*
***4** esp. *AmE* to reduce (something such as a price): [T1] *The firm is on trial for refusing to roll back its pay increases to the level allowed by law.* —**rollback** *n*

***roll by** *v adv*
**1** to pass, esp. smoothly or steadily: [IØ] *Many vehicles rolled by, but no one offered us a ride.*
**2** (of time) to pass, esp. quickly: [IØ] *My, how the summer has simply rolled by! The years rolled by and still there was no improvement in his health.* → **roll on** (4)

**roll down** *v adv; prep*
**1** to cause to fall steadily down (something such as a slope or face): [IØ + DOWN/*down*] *Put a block under the back wheels to stop the car rolling down (the slope). Alice's tears rolled down (her face), forming a pool at her feet.* [T1 + DOWN/*down*] *The easiest way to get the big cheeses to the village in the valley was to roll them down (the hill).*
***2** to travel easily a long way down (something such as a river): [T1 (*no pass.*)] *The little boa*

*rolled down the river without effort, with the wind behind her.*

**roll in¹** *v adv*

**1** to (cause to) enter or arrive with a rolling movement: [IØ + IN] *As the waves rolled in, the sand was gradually covered.* [T1 + IN] *If you hold the door open, we can roll the packet in.*

*__2__ *not fml* to arrive in large numbers: [IØ (*often continuous tenses*)] *Letters of enquiry have been rolling in ever since the broadcast. We must find some new attraction to keep the crowds rolling in.*

***roll in²** *v prep*

**1** *infml* to have plenty of (money or good living): [T1 (*no pass., continuous tenses*)] *Thieves always aim for houses where the people are known to be rolling in money.* → **wallow in** (3)

**2 roll in the aisles** *infml* to be helpless with laughter, as in a theatre: [*usu. continuous tenses*] *"Is this new man funny?" "I'll say he is: he keeps them rolling in the aisles!"* → **knock in**

**roll off** *v adv; prep*

**1** to fall off by rolling: [IØ + OFF/*off*] *Put the ball carefully on the table, so that it won't roll off. Mind that the baby doesn't roll off the bed.*

*__2__ to produce (copies) quickly from (a machine): [T1] *This machine can roll off two prints a second. How many copies do you want rolled off?* [D1] *Books roll off the printing machine at the rate of two a week.*

*__3__ to speak (something such as words) quickly and easily from memory: [T1] *Children delight in being able to roll off long lists of difficult words.* [D1] *Some long words are easy to roll off your tongue.* → **rattle off, reel off, run off¹** (7), **spiel off**

*__4__ (of a goods vehicle) to (cause to) leave (a boat) already loaded: [T1] *The boat is made so that the vehicles can easily be rolled off. In this system, the vehicles roll off the boat, already loaded.* [IØ] *It saves so much time and money if the loaded vehicles can roll off and go straight to the shops.* [D1] *The men can roll the vehicles straight off the boat and drive the goods directly to the shops.* → **roll on** (6)

**roll on** *v adv*

**1** to continue rolling or moving: [IØ + ON] *The great river rolled on.*

**2** to put (clothing) on by rolling: [T1 + ON] *Roll your stockings on, to avoid damaging them.* —**roll-on** *n*

**3** to put (paint) onto a surface with a roller: [T1 + ON] *The paint will go much further if you roll it on instead of using a brush.*

*__4__ (of time) to pass: [IØ] *The years rolled on, but there was still no improvement in his health.* → **roll by** (2)

*__5__ (of a future time or event) to come soon; used to express a wish: [IØ (*imper.*)] *Roll on spring—this winter's been long enough! Roll on the weekend!*

*__6__ (of a goods vehicle) to (cause to) be driven onto a boat, already loaded: [T1] *The ship is made so that the vehicles can be rolled on at one end of the journey, and rolled off the other, without having to be unloaded each time.* [IØ] *It saves so much time and money if the vehicles can just roll on with their load already in place.* —**roll-on-roll-off** *n, adj* → **roll off** (4)

**roll out** *v adv*

**1** to leave a place such as a bed by rolling: [IØ + OUT] *Roll out, you men, the day's already started! A pot fell over and some stones rolled out.*

**2** to bring (something) out by rolling or pushing: [T1 + OUT] *If the old car won't start in the garage, you'll just have to roll it out. "Roll out the barrel! We'll have a barrel of fun!"* (song)

**3** to spread (something) by unrolling: [T1 + OUT] *Roll out the map so that we can all see it.*

*__4__ to speak, express, or sound (something) loudly and clearly: [T1] *The actor rolled out his words so that everyone in the theatre could hear. The village drums rolled out a threatening message.*

*__5__ to flatten and widen (something) by pressing with a roller: [T1] *Roll out the pastry very thin and cut it into squares. The metal is rolled out by heavy machinery.*

*__6__ to produce (goods) in large quantities: [T1] *This factory rolls out 200 boxes of its products every day.*

**roll over** *v adv* → **turn over** (1), **turn up** (2)

to (cause to) turn over, as moving to another place in bed: [IØ + OVER] *The car hit a lamppost and rolled over twice before coming to a stop. Every time I rolled over, I woke up because I put my weight on my wounded knee.* [T1 + OVER] *The policeman rolled the body over to look for the missing gun.* —**rollover** *n, adj*

**roll round** *v adv* also **roll around**

**1** to (cause to) move in a circle: [IØ + ROUND] *How can we stop these balls from rolling round?* [T1 + ROUND] *Can you roll the balls round?*

*__2__ *not fml* to arrive, often unexpectedly: [IØ] *One of my neighbours had a habit of rolling round just when I was getting tea ready.*

*__3__ *not fml* (of time or an event) to happen regularly: [IØ] *Christmas seems to roll round faster every year.* → **come round** (4)

**roll up** *v adv*

**1** to (cause to) form into a ball or roll; fold (something) back; wrap (something or someone): [IØ + UP] *This animal protects itself by rolling up into a ball, with sharp hairs pointing outwards.* [T1 + UP] *The sails should be rolled up and put away for the winter. I kept myself warm by rolling myself up in all the clothes.*

**2** (usu. of smoke) to rise in rolling masses: [IØ + UP] *Smoke was rolling up from the burning oil tanks.*

*__3__ *not fml* to arrive, esp. in a group or in a way that is unacceptable: [IØ (*often simple tenses*)] *He didn't care about being late, and rolled up when it suited him. A big car rolled up to the hotel, and a famous musician got out. Roll up, roll up! See the great magician perform his famous tricks!*

*__4__ *not fml* to (cause to) increase by gradual additions: [T1] *Our man seems to be rolling up a good share of the votes.* [IØ (*often continuous tenses*)] *Club membership has been rolling up for the past few months.*

*__5__ *mil* to force (an enemy) to move away and towards the centre: [T1] *A clever move on our part rolled up the enemy's weak side and we soon surrounded his whole army.*

**6 roll one's sleeves up** *not fml* to prepare to work hard: *It's time to roll your sleeves up now that the examinations are near.*

**roll with** *v prep*

**roll with a/the punch** *not fml* to move or act so as to avoid the worst of something such as a blow or trouble by accepting some of it: [*no pass.*] *If you are struck by sudden grief, it is better to roll with the punch rather than try to fight it. The young fighter was able to roll with the punches that landed, and so not get seriously hurt.*

**romp about** *v adv* → **horse about, lark about, ramp about**

to play roughly: [IØ + ABOUT] *The children love romping about in the wild garden.*

*__romp home__ *v adv*

*not fml* to gain an easy victory in a race: [IØ] *Jim romped home well ahead of all the other runners.*

*__romp through__ *v adv; prep* → **breeze through,** etc.

to pass (something such as an examination) easily: [IØ] *John was afraid that he would fail his driving test again, but this time, to his own surprise, he romped through.* [T1] *Why are you so anxious? You should romp through the test, it's an easy one for you.*

*__roof in/over__ *v adv* → **cover in**[1], **cover over, fill in** (1)

to cover (a space, area, etc.) with a roof: [T1 (*often pass.*)] *When the swimming pool is roofed over, we shall be able to swim all through the winter.*

**room together** *v adv*

to share lodgings: [L9 + TOGETHER] *Of course I know him well, we roomed together for a year when we first went to college.*

**room with** *v prep* → **lodge with** (1)

to take or share lodgings with (someone): [L9 + *with*] *John had to room with a friend when he first went to college, until he could find a place for himself.*

*__root about__ *v adv*

**1** (of pigs) to search (for food) by digging with the nose: [IØ (*for, in*)] *People believe that pigs are dirty animals because they root about in the mud for their food.* → **rootle about**

**2** to search (for something): [IØ (*for, in*) (*often continous tenses*)] *I found the lost key by rooting about in all my drawers.*

*__root for__ *v prep* → **cheer for, cheer on, pull for** (2)

*not fml* to cheer for (usu. one's team): [T1] *Half the school came to the sports meeting to root for their team. It helps that winning feeling when you can hear your supporters rooting for you.*

**root in** *v prep*

**1** (of a plant) to (cause to) grow roots in (earth): [IØ + *in*] *Once the bush has rooted in this rich soil, it should grow well.* [T1 + *in* (*usu. pass.*)] *I can't pull this bush up, it's firmly rooted in the ground.*

**2 be rooted in** to be firmly based on (something such as a cause): *His opinion is rooted in experience.*

*__root out__ *v adv*

**1** to pull out (a plant) by the roots: [T1] *We must root out all the dead plants and replace them with healthy ones.* → **root up** (1)

**2** to get rid of; destroy (something unwanted): [T1] *The government must make efforts to root out ineffective parts of the system. Outdated ideas must be rooted out.*

**3** to find (something) for (someone) by searching: [T1] *I'll see if I can root out some old clothes to give to the man at the door. Can you root out some good players for the team?* [D1] *I'll try and root you out something dry to wear.* → **dredge up** (2), **rake out** (3), **rake up** (3), **root up** (3), **rout out** (1), **rout up** (1)

**root to** *v prep* → **rivet to**

**root someone to the ground/spot** to make someone or an animal stay in one place, completely still: [*often pass.*] *The shock of seeing the bear rooted him to the spot, although the danger should have made him run. The animal stood rooted to the ground with fear.*

*__root up__ *v adv*

**1** to pull up (a plant) by the roots: [T1] *Make sure that you root up the whole bush, otherwise it will grow again from any remaining roots.* —**uproot** *v* → **root out** (1)

**2** (of pigs) to turn (earth) with the nose: [T1] *The pigs have rooted up the muddy ground, looking for food.*

**3** to find (something) by searching: [T1] *I'll see if I can root up some old clothes to give to the man at the door.* → **rake out** (3), **rake up** (3), **root out** (3), **rout out** (1), **rout up** (1)

*__rootle about__ *v adv* → **root about** (1)

(of pigs) to search (for food) by digging with the nose: [IØ (*for, in*)] *People believe that pigs are dirty animals because they rootle about in the mud for their food.*

**rope in** *v adv*
**1** to enclose (a space or animals) with ropes: [X9 + IN] *The cattle are all roped in now.*
*__2__ *not fml* to persuade (someone) to help or join an activity: [T1 (*to*)] *Who else can we rope in to organize the tour?* → **pull in** (8)

***rope into** *v prep*
*not fml* to persuade (someone) to help or join (something such as an activity or doing something): [T1 (*often pass.*)] *I don't want to get roped into any more of your activities.* [V4b (*often pass.*)] *I've been roped into organizing the tour; I wish I hadn't said yes.*

**rope off** *v adv*
to separate (land or animals) with ropes: [X9 + OFF] *The farmer has roped off the field where the new crop is growing, to keep the animals out.*

**rope together** *v adv* → **lash together**
to fasten (usu. people) together with ropes: [X9 + TOGETHER (*often pass.*)] *"Three climbers have been found dead, roped together on the mountain."* (CBC radio news, 9 May 1976)

**rope up** *v adv*
**1** to fasten (things or something) with ropes: [X9 + UP] *Is the load properly roped up?*
*__2__ (of mountain climbers) to be fastened to the same rope: [IØ] *When the whole party has roped up, we shall be ready to start.*

**rot away** *v adv*
**1** to decay slowly and steadily: [IØ + AWAY (*continuous tenses*)] *The soil in the forest is rich with dead leaves and branches that have been rotting away for centuries.*
**2** to decay and fall away: [IØ + AWAY] *The wood of the stairs has rotted away in places; be careful where you tread. His teeth had rotted away, and were black at the edges.* → **rot off, rot out**

**rot off** *v adv* → **rot away** (2), **rot out**
to fall off through decay: [IØ + OFF] *We knew that the bush had a disease when its lower branches began to rot off.*

**rot out** *v adv* → **rot away** (2), **rot off**
to form holes through decay: [IØ + OUT] *The middle of the floor had rotted out, and was unsafe.*

**rough in** *v adv* → **rough out**
to draw (something) in an incomplete way, as to give a general but not detailed picture: [T1] *The artist has roughed in some trees to give an idea of the general look of the place when it's built. I've roughed in the general shape of the pattern in pencil, and will fill in the details with paint.* —**roughed-in** *adj*

**rough it** *v pron* → **live rough, sleep rough**
*not fml* to live in a simple usu. uncomfortable manner: [IØ] *If I lose this job, I shall have to be prepared to rough it for a time until I find something really suitable.*

**rough out** *v adv* → **rough in**
to make a general plan of (something such as an idea): [T1] *I've roughed out the direction that we should take, but I'll leave it to you to choose the details and the exact roads.*

***rough up** *v adv*
**1** also **roughen up** to make (something) untidy, rough, etc.: [T1] *The wind will rough up my hair, and I've just had it done! If you rough up the surface a bit, the paint will stick better.* → **ruffle up** (1)
**2** *not fml* to treat (someone) roughly; attack and beat (someone) slightly: [T1] *Rough him up a little to make it seem as if he fought us, but don't really hurt him.*

***round down** *v adv* → **round off** (2), **round up** (1)
to change (an exact figure) into the nearest whole number below it: [T1] *The shop is trying to encourage people to buy its goods by rounding the price down to the nearest pound.*

***round in** *v adv* → **flatten in, harden in**
to pull in (ropes controlling certain sails): [T1] *You can control the speed by letting go one small sail and rounding in the other.*

***round into** *v prep*
to develop into (something): [T1 (*no pass., often simple tenses*)] *Our talk gradually rounded into a plan for improving the organization of the club.*

***round off** *v adv*
**1** to make (something sharp) more smooth: [T1] *Round off the edges of the table so that it feels smooth to the touch, and will not damage people's clothing.*
**2** to change (an exact figure) into the nearest whole number, either less or more: [T1] *Your answer should be rounded off to three decimal places.* → **round down, round up** (1)
**3** to bring (something) to a suitable finish: [T1 (*with*)] *We rounded off the party by singing well-known songs. Let us have a drink to round the evening off. It would be better to round off your story with a surprise ending.*

***round on/upon** *v prep*
**1** to turn and attack (someone or an animal): [T1 (*often simple tenses*)] *Forced into a corner when its hole was blocked with earth, the fox rounded on the hunting dogs and fought to the death.*
**2** to scold or blame (someone) suddenly; attack (someone) with words: [T1 (*often simple tenses*)] *It was quite a shock when she rounded on me and charged me with telling lies about her.*

***round out** *v adv*
**1** to (cause to) swell; grow fatter: [IØ] *She was very thin after her illness, but is rounding out nicely now.* [T1] *The wind rounded out the sails as the little boat rushed along.*
**2** to complete (something) by making it fuller: [T1] *The best way to round out your education is by travelling.*

***round up** *v adv*
**1** to change (an exact figure) to the nearest whole number above it: [T1] *I'll round the cheque up to $10, and you can keep the change.* → **round down, round off** (2)
**2** to gather together (animals, people, or

things) which have been scattered: [T1] *In the autumn, the cattle have to be rounded up and counted. See if you can round up the rest of the class, it's time to go back to the school.* —**roundup** *n*

**3** to catch (criminals): [T1] *The police are trying to round up the jewel thieves and bring them to justice.* —**roundup** *n*

**4** esp. *AmE not fml* to give a short account of (something such as news): [T1] *And now here's Jim Brown to round up the main stories in today's news.* —**roundup** *n*

**5** to stop (a boat) by turning it to face the wind: [T1] *We stopped to pick up the drowning man by rounding up the boat.*

***round upon** *v prep* → **ROUND ON**

**rouse from** *v prep*

to wake (someone) from (inactivity such as sleep): [T1 + *from*] *I had to shake him several times to rouse him from his sleep. Who can rouse the people from their lack of care?*

**rouse to** *v prep*

to urge; encourage (someone) towards (something such as action); make (someone) feel or do (something): [T1 + *to*] *The speaker tried to rouse the crowd to excitement, but his words only roused them to opposition. He is not easily roused to anger.*

***roust out** *v adv* → **tell off** (1), etc.

*not fml* to scold (someone) for a fault: [T1] *I would advise you to keep out of the way when the teacher is rousting out the bad boys in the class.*

***rout out** *v adv*

**1** to find (something) by searching: [T1] *I'll see if I can rout out some old clothes to give to the man at the door.* → **dredge up** (2), **rake out** (3), **rake up** (3), **root out** (3), **root up** (3), **rout out** (1)

**2** to get (someone) out of bed or hiding: [T1 (*of*)] *We must rout the last enemy soldier out of the town. Night after night we were routed out of bed by the firebell, only to find that it was a false warning.*

***rout up** *v adv*

**1** to find (something) by searching: [T1] *I'll see if I can rout up some old clothes to give to the man at the door.* → **dredge up** (2), **rake out** (3), **rake up** (3), **root out** (3), **root up** (3), **rout out** (1)

**2** to make (someone) get out of bed: [T1] *I hated that camp; they always routed us up at daybreak.*

**row with** *v prep* → **argue with** (1), etc. (1), **quarrel with** (1), **squabble with**

to have an unpleasant, often noisy, disagreement with (someone): [IØ + *with*] *Children hate to hear their parents rowing with each other; it has a bad effect on their nerves.*

**rub against** *v prep* → **brush up against** (1), **rub up against** (1)

to (cause to) touch (something or someone) closely and often repeatedly: [L9 + *against*] *I could feel the cat rubbing against my leg.* [T1 + *against*] *Try not to rub your coat against the wet paint.*

***rub along** *v adv*

**1** *not fml* to find a way to live with some difficulty; continue to do what is necessary, but with difficulty: [IØ (*on*)] *"How are you doing with your work?" "Oh, just rubbing along, thank you." He's not a good student; he can only just rub along in class. We haven't much money but we rub along all right. I can rub along on a reduced income for a short time, but not for ever.* → **get by**[1] (2), etc.

**2** *not fml* to have a reasonably good relationship (with someone): [IØ (TOGETHER, *with*)] *Jim and Mary may not be the world's most happily married pair, but they rub along (together) all right. The workers seem to be rubbing along with the new director, although he's far from perfect.*

**rub away** *v adv*

**1** to continue rubbing: [IØ + AWAY (*at*) (*usu. continuous tenses*)] *This modern polish saves the effort of rubbing away for hours trying to get the silver clean.*

**2** to (cause to) be removed by repeated rubbing: [L9 + AWAY] *The middle of each step has rubbed away with passing feet.* [T1 + AWAY] *The lettering has been rubbed away by the hands of countless worshippers over the centuries, and the whole wall has had to be replaced.* → **rub down** (1), **rub off**[1] (1), **rub out** (1)

**rub down** *v adv*

**1** to wear (a surface) by rubbing: [T1 + DOWN] *The steps have been rubbed down by the passing of so many feet.* → **rub away** (2), **rub off**[1] (1), **rub out** (1)

**2** to make (a surface) smooth by rubbing it with sandpaper: [T1 + DOWN] *The quality of the finished paintwork depends on how well the wood was rubbed down in the preparation stage.* → **sand down**

***3** to dry (oneself or an animal) by thorough rubbing: [T1] *The children used to rub each other down after their bath. That dog has been in the water again; you'd better rub him down with this old cloth, or he'll catch cold.* —**rubdown** *n* → **towel down**

**rub in**[1] *v adv*

**1** to cause (something such as a liquid) to enter a surface by rubbing: [T1 + IN] *Leave the mud to dry; if you try to clean it now, you'll only rub it in.*

***2** *not fml* to teach (something) by forceful repetition: [T1 (*often simple tenses*)] *A skilled teacher can make any class learn any set of facts by simply rubbing the information in. The lesson of this sad story should be well rubbed in.* → **hammer in** (3), etc.

**3 rub it in** *not fml* to keep reminding someone of a fault, failure, etc.: *I know I ruined the performance, there's no need to rub it in.*

**rub in²** *v prep*

**1** to force (something such as a liquid) to enter (usu. a surface) by rubbing: [T1 + *in*] *Rub this oil in the wood to protect it. "Rubbing salt in a wound" is a way of expressing the idea of making something bad even worse.* → **rub into** (1)

**2 rub someone's nose in it** *not fml* to keep on reminding someone, esp. in an unkind manner, about something he has done wrong: *Don't keep talking about that letter. I know I shouldn't have written it, but there's no need to rub my nose in it.*

**rub into** *v prep*

**1** to force (something such as a liquid) to enter (usu. a surface) by rubbing: [T1 + *into*] *Rubbing this special cream into the insect bite will help to take away the worst of the pain.* → **rub in²** (1)

***2** *not fml* to teach (something) to (someone) by forceful repetition: [D1 (*often simple tenses*)] *Living as we did near the sea, we had the danger of drowning rubbed into us from an early age.* [D5 (*often simple tenses*)] *I thought that by now I had been able to rub into you that you must ask permission first.* [D6 (*often simple tenses*)] *Parents often try to rub into their children how much they owe to them.* → **hammer into** (3), etc.

**rub off¹** *v adv*

**1** to (cause to) be removed by rubbing: [L9 + OFF] *This isn't solid gold; look, it rubs off. If you don't prepare the surface properly, the paint will rub off.* [T1 + OFF] *This rough clothing has nearly rubbed my skin off. Who wrote these rude words on the board? Rub them off at once!* → **rub away** (2), **rub down** (1), **rub out** (1), **wear off** (1)

***2** *not fml* (of success) to become less effective; lose its first. joy: [IØ (*often simple tenses*)] *It did not take long for the glory of our election victory to rub off.*

**rub off²** *v prep*

**1** to (cause to) be removed from (something) by rubbing: [T1 + *off*] *These new boots are so stiff that they rub the skin off my ankles. When the mud is dry, you can easily rub it off your shoes.* [L9 + *off*] *The chalk marks are so heavy that they won't rub off the board.*

**2 rub the shine off** *not fml* to reduce or remove the effect or pleasure of: [*often simple tenses*] *Our team's recent losses have rubbed some of the shine off their earlier victories.*

**rub off on/onto** *v adv prep*

**1** to be moved from one thing to (another) by close touching: [L9 + OFF + *on/onto*] *The car has been parked too near the wall, and some of the paint has rubbed off on the brick.*

***2** *not fml* (of an effect quality, etc.) to spread to (usu. someone) as a result of close contact: [T1 (*no pass.*)] *I like your new friend, and hope that some of her fine qualities of character will rub off onto you. We have encouraged the children to hear good music, in the hope that its calming power would rub off onto them.*

**rub on** *v adv; prep*

to spread (something) on (a surface) by rubbing: [T1 + ON/*on*] *She has kept her skin smooth all these years by rubbing cream on (her face) every night of her life.*

**rub out** *v adv*

**1** to (cause to) be removed by rubbing, as with a piece of rubber: [L9 + OUT (*usu. simple tenses*)] *I don't think that dirty mark will rub out: your coat will have to go to the cleaners.* [T1 + OUT] (esp. *BrE*) *Write your answer in pencil so that you can rub it out if you change your mind. Will this rubber rub out ink marks?* → **rub away** (2), **rub down** (1), **rub off¹** (1)

***2** *AmE infml* to murder (someone): [T1 (*usu. simple tenses*)] *Anyone who opposes our organization will get rubbed out.* → **bump off,** etc.

***rub through** *v adv* → **get by¹** (2), etc., **muddle through**

*not fml* to reach some kind of success without proper methods: [IØ] *There's a difficult time ahead, and I don't know what to suggest, but we'll rub through somehow.*

**rub together** *v adv*

to make two things touch each other repeatedly: [T1 + TOGETHER] *The boys claim to be able to light a fire by rubbing two sticks together. This insect makes its strange noise by rubbing its back legs together.*

**rub up** *v adv*

**1** to make (something) shine by rubbing: [T1 + UP] *When you have put the polish on the silver, rub it up with a clean dry cloth.* **—rub-up** *n* → **polish up** (1)

***2** *not fml* to improve (something) by study or practice: [T1a] *I must rub up my French before I go to Paris.* **—rubbing-up** *n* → **brush up** (2), **polish up** (2)

**3 rub someone up the wrong/right way** esp. *BrE not fml* to treat someone in a way that offends/pleases him: *When Father is in a bad temper, it's very easy to rub him up the wrong way and make him really angry. If you rub the teacher up the right way, he might give you better marks.* → **ruffle up** (3)

**rub up against** *v adv prep*

**1** to keep touching (something): [L9 + UP + *against*] *I could feel the cat rubbing up against my leg. I got this mark on my coat by rubbing up against some wet paint.* → **rub against, brush up against** (1)

***2** to meet (someone) or be close to (something), often by chance: [T1 (*no pass., usu. simple tenses*)] *The people you rub up against in your early years at work will make a lot of difference to your future. You rub up against a lot of famous people at Robert's parties.* → **brush up against** (2)

**rub with** *v prep*
**1** to touch (something) repeatedly and firmly with (something): [T1 + *with*] *Rub the inside of the bowl with an onion before putting in the vegetables.*
**2 rub elbows/shoulders with** *not fml* to meet; live or work closely with (someone, esp. someone rich or famous): *In this club, any member can rub shoulders with the great players of the past.*

**ruck/ruckle up** *v adv*
to (cause to) become unevenly folded: [IØ + UP] *If the tablecloth ruckles up, pull it straight.* [T1 + UP] *Help me to smooth out the sheets, they're all rucked up. Don't pack your clothes too tightly in the case or it will ruckle them up.*

**ruffle up** *v adv*
**1** to make (something) untidy, rough, or uneven, esp. by raising and spreading it: [T1 + UP] *This wind will ruffle up my hair, and I've only just had it done! Birds keep warm by ruffling up their feathers.* → **rough up** (1)
**2** to excite; destroy the calmness of (someone or something): [T1 + UP (*often pass.*)] *Mother is all ruffled up about the coming wedding.*
**3 ruffle someone up the wrong way** *not fml* to treat someone in a way that offends him: *When Father is in a bad temper, it's very easy to ruffle him up the wrong way and make him really angry.* → **rub up** (3)

**rule against** *v prep*
to make a formal decision not in favour of (someone, something, or doing something): [IØ + *against* (*usu. simple tenses*)] *I'm afraid that the judge might rule against you. The government has ruled against any increase in taxes this year. The governors have ruled against allowing girls into the school.*

***rule off** *v adv*
to separate (part of a page or piece of work) by drawing a straight line at the end of it, using a ruler; draw a straight line with a ruler below a piece of work: [T1 (*often simple tenses*)] *Rule off each exercise as you finish it.* [IØ (*often simple tenses*)] *When you have finished an exercise, rule off.*

**rule on** *v prep*
to make a formal decision about (something): [IØ + *on* (*usu. simple tenses*)] *The judges have been asked to rule on the question of the lawfulness of the drug in medical use.*

***rule out** *v adv*
**1** to cover (something written) with a straight line so that it cannot be read: [T1 (*often simple tenses*)] *Rule out neatly any words which you do not wish the examiner to read.*
**2** to declare the impossibility of (something): [T1 (*often simple tenses*)] *The police have stated that they cannot rule out murder in the case of the girl's death. His guilt is ruled out by his absence from the scene at the time of the crime. The government has ruled out any further support for the industry because of the cost.* [T4 (*often simple tenses*)] *The government has now ruled out nationalizing the shipbuilding industry.*
**3** to prevent (something): [T1 (*usu. simple tenses*)] *A sudden storm ruled out the boat race.*

**rule over** *v prep* → **reign over**
to act as the king, queen, or other governor of (usu. a nation): [IØ + *over*] *Queen Victoria ruled over the British Empire for more than 60 years.*

**ruminate about/on/over/upon** *v prep* → **reflect on** (1)
to consider (something) carefully and at length: [IØ + *about/on/over/upon*] *As people grow older, they begin to ruminate on the uncertainty of life. Many valuable ideas have come through ruminating over various possibilities.*

**rummage about/around** *v adv*
to search among an untidy heap: [IØ + ABOUT/AROUND (*for*)] *By rummaging about among the pile of old clothes, I found the old coat in which I had left the key.*

***rummage out/up** *v adv*
to find (something) by searching in an untidy heap: [T1] *Were you able to rummage out some old clothes to give to the man at the door?*

**rumour abroad** *v adv* also *AmE* **rumor abroad** → **blaze abroad, bruit abroad, noise abroad, spread abroad**
to spread news, not necessarily true, about (something) widely: [T1 + ABROAD (*usu. pass.*)] *Stories have been rumoured abroad about the government's intention to hold an early election. It is being rumoured abroad that the Minister is to be dismissed from the government.*

**run about** *v adv; prep*
**1** to run without direction, for fun; play freely; move in (a place): [IØ + ABOUT/*about*] *Children love to run about (in) the open fields. You'll catch cold running about with no coat on.* → **run around**[1] (1)
**2** to use something such as a vehicle for pleasure in (a place): [IØ + ABOUT/*about* (*often continuous tenses*)] *Jim bought Mary an old car, just for running about (town) in.* —**run about** *n, adj* → **knock about** (7), **run around**[1] (2)

**run across**[1] *v adv*
**1** to cross a space such as a road, by running or moving quickly: [IØ + ACROSS (*to*)] *Tell the children to walk calmly across the road, not run across.* → **run over**[1] (1)
**2** esp. *BrE* to give a ride to (someone): [X + ACROSS (*to*)] *Don't wait for the bus in this cold weather; I'll get the car and run you across to your mother's.* → **run over**[1] (2)

**run across**[2] *v prep*
**1** to pass over (a space such as a road) b

running or moving quickly: [IØ + *across*] *Tell the children not to run across the road, but to wait until it's clear and then walk calmly across.*

**2** (of a liquid) to flow across (a space): [IØ + *across*] *The river has overflowed its banks, and the water is running across the fields.*

**3** esp. *BrE* to give (someone) a ride across (something): [X9 + *across*] *Jim has a car and will run you across town to your mother's.*

***4** to find (something) or meet (someone) by chance: [T1 (*simple tenses*)] *I ran across my former teacher in the High Street this afternoon. I ran across an excellent book on the subject, in the public library.* → **happen on,** etc.

**run afoul of** *v adv prep* → **RUN FOUL OF**

**run after** *v prep*

**1** to chase (something or someone), as by running: [IØ + *after*] *Run after your father, he's forgotten his hat. We ran after the bus as it was leaving, and caught it just in time.*

***2** to make efforts to gain the company or attention of (someone of the opposite sex): [T1 (*often continuous tenses*)] *All the girls are running after the attractive new student.* → **trot after** (2)

***3** to be keen to get (something such as knowledge): [T1 (*often continuous tenses*)] *He's always running after the latest ideas in his field.*

***4** *not fml* to perform the duties of a servant for (someone): [T1] *Don't expect me to run after you all your life!* → **run round[1]** (4)

**run against** *v prep*

**1** to (cause to) hit (something) with a quick movement: [IØ + *against*] *The horse hurt its knee by running against the fence.* [X9 + *against*] *If you run your head against a brick wall, of course it will hurt!* → **knock against** (1), etc.

**2** to (cause to) take part in a running race, competing with (someone): [IØ + *against*] *Jim is prepared to run against the world's best runners.* [T1 + *against*] *I'll run my best horse against any horse you name.* → **run with** (2)

**3** esp. *AmE* to compete with (someone) in an election: [IØ + *against*] *At least you are running against some worthy opponents, so that even if you lose, you needn't feel ashamed.*

**4 run one's head against a brick wall** *not fml* to keep trying something impossible: [*usu. continuous tenses*] *Trying to persuade the director to change his plans is like running your head against a brick wall.* → **bang against** (2), **run into** (12)

**run aground** *v adv*

**1** (of a ship or boat) to (cause to) become stuck or trapped in water not deep enough: [IØ (*on*) (*often simple tenses*)] *We were winning the boat race until our boat ran aground on a sandbank.* [T1 (*often simple tenses*)] *The captain's own carelessness ran the boat aground.* → **go aground**

**2** *not fml* (of something such as a plan) to meet impossible difficulties: [IØ (*often simple tenses*)] *Our plans for rebuilding have run aground, as the council have refused to allow the necessary money.*

**run along** *v adv*

**1** to move quickly forward, as by running: [IØ + ALONG] *The dog used to love running along beside the car.*

**2** esp. *BrE* to give (someone) a ride to a place: [X9 + ALONG] *There's no hurry to get there; I can run you along in the car.*

***3** to leave; go away; often used to children: [IØ (*often imper.*)] *Run along now, I'm busy, I'll talk to you later.*

***run amok/amuck** *v adv* also **go amok** → **drive crazy** (2), **drive mad** (2), **drive out** (3), **go berserk, send berserk**

(usu. of an animal) to behave wildly and violently, out of control: [IØ] *One of the big male elephants is running amok in the village, tearing up the trees by their roots.*

**run around[1]** *v adv*

**1** to run without direction for fun; play freely; move aimlessly: [IØ + AROUND] *Children love to run around in the open fields. You'll catch cold running around without a coat.* → **run about** (1)

**2** to use something such as a vehicle, for short journeys or pleasure: [IØ + AROUND (*often continuous tenses*)] *Mary bought herself an old car, just for running around in.* → **knock about** (7), **run about** (2)

***3** *not fml* to keep company (with someone usu. undesirable); change lovers frequently: [IØ (*with*) (*often continuous tenses*)] *He was sorry that he had wasted his youth running around with criminal types. Don't trust him; he's too well-known for running around (with other men's wives).*

**run around[2]** *v prep* → **RUN ROUND**

***run ashore** *v adv*

*naut* to be forced to aim for shelter near land: [IØ] *A storm suddenly arose and we had to run ashore.*

**run at** *v prep*

**1** to move quickly towards (something or someone) on foot, in order to take action: [IØ + *at*] *If you run at the fence fast enough, you should be able to jump it. The dog ran at the visitor and bit him. The brave woman ran at her attacker with a pair of scissors.*

***2** (usu. of trade, a debt, etc.) to be presently existing at (a rate of something): [IØ (*usu. continuous tenses*)] *Our mail orders are now running at £1,000 a week. The national debt was running at an impossible amount until we received international support in lending us money.*

**run away** *v adv*

**1** to go away, as by running; leave; escape: [IØ + AWAY] *Run away, I'm busy. Don't run away, I want to talk to you.* → **run off[1]** (1)

**2** (usu. of liquid) to flow away: [IØ + AWAY] *There's a hole in my bucket, and the water is running away.* → **run off¹** (2)

***3** to escape, as from home, duty, etc.; take flight: [IØ (*from*)] *He was so unhappy that he tried to run away from school. Our dog was very fond of the family, but had an unfortunate habit of running away, so we had to spend a lot of money on fences to keep him safe. Jim and Mary threatened to run away to get married if Mary's father continued to refuse his permission for the wedding.* → **run off¹** (3)

**run away from** *v adv prep*

**1** to leave (something or someone) by running: [IØ + AWAY + *from*] *I saw two children running away from the house.*

**2** (of liquid) to flow away from (something): [IØ + AWAY + *from*] *These pipes are provided to allow rain water to run away from the house.*

***3** to escape from (something or someone): [T1] *He was so unhappy that he tried to run away from school. Most healthy children reach a stage in their development when they have a desire to run away from home.*

***4** to avoid facing (something unpleasant): [T1 (*usu. simple tenses*)] *We can't run away from the facts: the firm is in serious trouble. Responsibilities like yours are not such as can be run away from.*

**run away with** *v adv prep* also **run off with**

**1** to leave together with (something or someone) by running: [IØ + AWAY + *with*] *I saw two children running away with your brother.*

***2** (of a horse or sometimes a car) to go too fast for (the rider or driver) to control: [T1 (*no pass.*)] *He was an inexperienced rider, and the horse soon ran away with him.* —**runaway** *n, adj*

***3** to get out of the control of (someone): [T1 (*no pass.*)] *His temper ran away with him and he hit the man. When you're writing the story, don't let your imagination run away with you. I'm sorry I let my tongue run away with me; please forgive me for my accidental rudeness.*

***4** to steal (something): [T1] *Someone has run away with the jewels while we were out. We thought he was a faithful servant, but he has run away with the silver.* → **make off with** (1), etc.

***5** to take (someone of the opposite sex, esp. one who is married to someone else) away: [T1] *The writer has run away with his teacher's wife.* → **abscond with**, etc.

***6** to win (something such as a game or prize) easily: [T1 (*often simple tenses*)] *Our team should run away with the cricket competition, they're easily the best.* → **walk away with** (3), **walk off with** (3), **waltz off with** (1)

***7** to use; spend (something such as money or time) freely: [T1 (*usu. simple tenses*)] *Your education runs away with most of my money.*

**8 run away with the idea/impression/notion** to believe something too readily: [*usu. simple tenses*] *Don't run away with the idea that you can be lazy in this job. People tend to run away with the impression that all young people take drugs and are selfish.* → **get away with** (3), **go away with** (3)

**run back** *v adv*

**1** to return quickly, as by running or driving: [IØ + BACK] *I must run back to the shop, I left my bag there.*

**2** to flow in return: [IØ + BACK] *If you unblock the pipe, the water will run back into the house.*

**3** esp. *BrE* to take (someone) back in a vehicle: [X9 + BACK] *Don't worry about getting home so late, Jim will run you back.*

***4** to wind back (esp. a film) so as to repeat it: [T1 (*to*)] *Would you please run the film back, I'd like to see the early part again. If we run the story back to its origin, we might understand the cause.* → **run to** (10), **wind back, wind on** (2)

***run back over** *v adv prep*

to remember or repeat (something); consider (something) again: [T1 (*pass. rare, usu. simple tenses*)] *Let's run back over what has just been said.*

**run before** *v adv; prep* → **sail before** (1)

to go fast in front (of) or earlier than (something or someone): [IØ + BEFORE/*before*] *The boat is running well before the wind.*

**run behind** *v adv; prep*

**1** to move fast at the back of (something o someone) usu. by running: [IØ + BEHIND/*behind*] *Jim is in front and the rest of the competitors are running well behind. The fighte increased his strength by running behind a ca for an hour every morning.*

***2** to be delayed beyond (the intende time): [IØ (*continuous tenses*)] *It will be a fev minutes before the doctor can see you, as he' running behind this morning.* [T1 (*no pass.*) *Can we please start the next committee meetin on time, so that we're not running behind tim as usual?*

***run close** *v adv* → **run hard** (2)

to be nearly equal to (a competitor): [T1 *Our team did win the cricket cup, but ou nearest competitors ran us close.* —**close-ru** *adj*

**run cold** *v adj*

**1** (of a liquid) to become less warm as th warm water is used up: [IØ + **cold**] *Som body's been using all the hot water, and m bath water ran cold before I'd filled the bath*

**2 one's blood run cold** to be greatly afrai [*usu. simple tenses*] *My blood ran cold as saw the terrible sight. I can tell you ghost st ries that will make your blood run cold.*

***run counter to** *v adj prep* → **conflict with** ( etc.

to oppose; be opposite to (something): [ (*no pass., simple tenses*)] *The governmen actions run counter to their election promise*

**run deep** *v adj*
**still waters run deep** people who say little often have strong characters or deep feelings.

**run down[1]** *v adv*
**1** to move quickly downhill or to a distance, as by running: [IØ + DOWN] *Run down to the shop and bring some milk, will you? Walk down the stairs, don't run down.*
**2** (of liquid) to flow in a downward direction: [IØ + DOWN] *There's a hidden valley where the river runs down to the sea.*
**3** esp. *BrE* to give (someone) a ride, as in a car, to a place down a slope or at a distance: [X9 + DOWN] *Don't worry about getting to the station, Jim will run you down in the car.*
***4** to knock down and damage (something) or wound (someone) with a vehicle or ship: [T1 (*usu. simple tenses*)] *The poor boy has been run down by a bus. The box is crushed; did something run it down? The big ship had to take urgent action to avoid running down the little boat.* → **knock down** (2), **knock over** (2), **run into** (6), **run over[1]** (5), **strike down** (1)
***5** to find (something) after searching: [T1 (*usu. simple tenses*)] *At last I ran down the article that I had been looking for.*
***6** to chase and catch (someone or an animal): [T1 (*often simple tenses*)] *The police were able to run the jewel thieves down after a long search.*
***7** to express a poor opinion of; speak badly of (something or someone): [T1] *There's no need to run my ideas down all the time. She's always running down her son's wife to her face!* → **crack up** (4), **cry down** (3), **cry up, do down** (2)
***8** (esp. of a clock or an electric battery to gradually stop working; lose power: [IØ] *I think the clock must have run down, it's slow. When the motor runs down it can be replaced.*
***9** to (cause or allow to) stop working, slow down, or cease to be used: [IØ (*often continuous tenses*)] *The coal industry is running down as coal supplies are used up.* [T1 (*often pass.*)] *The teacher-training system is being run down as fewer teachers are needed.* → **phase in, phase out**
***10** to tire; use the strength of: [T1 (*usu. pass.*)] *In spite of my holiday in the sun, I've been run down recently.* —**run-down** *adj*

**run down[2]** *v prep*
**1** to pass or move quickly down (something), as by running: [IØ + *down*] *The two thieves were last seen running down the road away from the police.*
**2** (of liquid) to flow down (something): [IØ + *down*] *Tears were running down her face. Water was running down the walls, and there were rats in the furniture.*
**3** to make (something such as part of the body) pass down (something): [X9 + *down*] *Running her eye down the page, she caught sight of another mistake. Just run your finger down the list and see if all the names are there, will you?* [L9 + *down*] *A whisper ran down the line of people waiting to get tickets.*

**run down to** *v adv prep*
**1** to reach (a place downhill or at a distance) by moving quickly, as by running: [IØ + DOWN + *to*] *Run down to the bottom of the garden and pick some fruit for our dinner, will you?*
**2** (of liquid) to flow down or away as far as (a place): [IØ + DOWN + *to* (*often simple tenses*)] *All the rivers on this side of the mountains run down to the east coast, while the rivers on the other side run down to the western ocean.*
**3** esp. *BrE* to give a ride to (someone) as far as (a place): [X9 + DOWN + *to*] *Jim will run you down to the station after dinner.*
***4** (usu. of land) to reach as far as (somewhere): [T1 (*no pass., simple tenses*)] *The land belonging to the castle runs (all the way) down to the sea.* → **run to** (5)
***5** to declare that (something) belongs to or is caused by (something or someone): [T1 (*often simple tenses*)] *A wide range of opinions can be run down to the people who write in the Sunday newspapers.*

***run dry** *v adj*
(usu. of a river or other body of water) to have no more water; stop flowing: [IØ] *The valley was formed ages ago when an ancient river ran dry.*

**run for** *v prep*
**1** to run so as to get (something or someone): [IØ + *for*] *I'm getting a little old to run for the bus as I used to. Run for help, the man is bleeding to death!*
**2** (usu. of a performance or arrangement) to continue for (a time): [IØ + *for*] *The play has now been running for twenty-five years. Our account with this bank has now run for two years.*
***3** esp. *AmE* to offer oneself for election to (a group) or for (a position): [T1 (*no pass.*)] *More people than ever before are running for the city council. Who will run for President next year?* → **sit for** (3), **stand as, stand for** (2)
**4 run for it** *not fml* to escape, as by running: [*often imper.*] *Run for it, the police are coming!* → **swim for** (2)
**5 run for dear life/one's life** *not fml* to run very fast, usu. to escape something or someone: [*often imper.*] *He's got a gun: run for your lives! Everyone in the crowd ran for dear life when the bomb warning was given.*

***run foul of** *v adv prep* also **run afoul of** → **fall foul of**
**1** to hit (another ship): [T1] *The sailing boat ran foul of a motor speedboat.*
**2** to become caught in (something) in a disorderly way: [T1] *The chain has run foul of some plants in the water.*
**3** to meet difficulty in (something): [T1 (*no pass.*)] *The chairman's plans have run foul of unexpected opposition.*

**run from** *v prep*
**1** to leave (a place or someone) by running: [IØ + *from*] *I saw two men running from the house; they might have been the thieves. Why didn't you run from the bear?*
**2** (of liquid) to flow away from (something): [IØ + *from*] *The water runs from the tap all day, I can't turn it off.*
**3** (of a performance, arrangement, etc.) to continue, starting at (a date): [IØ + *from* (*to*) (*often simple tenses*)] *Your payments will run from the first of next month. The play ran from 1951 to 1976. The sale will run from next Monday.* → **run to** (4)
***4** to range from (something) (to something): [T1 (*no pass., simple tenses*)] *The colours of this flower run from pink to blue. The music that the group can play runs from large-scale works to smaller pieces suitable for private performance.* → **range from, run to** (4), **vary from**
**5 run a mile from** *not fml* to make an effort to avoid (something or someone): [*simple tenses, usu. + would*] *I'd run a mile from any attempt to make me the chairman.*

**run hard** *v adv*
**1** to run fast, with effort: [IØ + HARD] *If you run hard you might just catch the bus, it's leaving now.*
***2** to be nearly equal to (a competitor): [T1b] *We won the election narrowly; the other party ran us hard.* → **run close**

***run high** *v adv*
**1** (of the sea) to be rough, with big waves: [IØ (*continuous tenses*)] *The sea is running high; is it safe to set sail?*
**2** (of prices) to continue to be at a high level: [IØ (*continuous tenses*)] *Egg prices have been running high this month, but should be lower in the spring. Drug companies' profits are running too high, and should be controlled by the government.*
**3** (of feelings) to be excited, powerful, etc.: [IØ (*usu. continuous tenses*)] *Interest in the game has been running high this year. Opposition to the government's action is running high among the voters; it would not seem wise to call an election now. Feelings ran high among the students when they learned of the teacher's dismissal.*

**run in¹** *v adv*
**1** to enter a place quickly, as by running: [IØ + IN] *Run in and bring my other coat, would you, dear? I opened the door and the cat ran in.*
**2** (of liquid) to flow into a place: [IØ + IN] *There's water still running in; you can't have mended the roof properly.*
**3** esp. *BrE* to give (someone) a ride into a place; pay a short visit, as by car: [X9 + IN] *If the trains aren't going into town in the morning because of the snow, Jim will run you in.* [L9 + IN] *Let's run in and see your relatives this afternoon.*
**4** to cause (something) to pass into something: [X9 + IN (*often simple tenses*)] *You run the wire in through this little hole in the top. He ran his sword in with a fearless hand.*
***5** to add (something such as words) to existing material: [T1] *We can run in a sentence about the politician's recent death.* —**run-in** *n, adj*
***6** *infml* (of the police) to seize (someone) and take him to the police station: [T1b] *You've no cause to run me in, I've done nothing!*
***7** to drive (a new car or other motor vehicle) slowly when it is new: [T1 (*usu. continuous tenses*)] *I'm running in my new car, and cannot go fast.* → **break in** (5)
***8** *AmE* → **RUN ON** (3)

**run in²** *v prep*
**1** to enter (a place) by moving quickly, as by running: [IØ + *in*] *Run in the house and bring my other coat, will you, dear?* → **run into** (1)
**2** to (cause to) compete in (a race or election): [IØ + *in*] *How many people are running in this election?* [T1 + *in*] *I intend to run my best horse in this race.*
**3 run in the/one's family** to be characteristic of family members: [*simple tenses, usu. present*] *Red hair runs in our family, so it was no surprise when the new baby was red-headed. I was certain that he would go on the stage, as acting runs in the family.* → **run to** (9)

***run in for** *v adv prep* → **let in for**
*rare not fml* to cause (someone or oneself) to have (something such as trouble): [D1] *Does the director understand what his action is running the firm in for? The boy's careless treatment of the car has run me in for a large repair bill. The government's plans will run the country in for a lot of spending.*

**run into** *v prep*
**1** to enter (a place) by moving quickly, as by running: [IØ + *into*] *It's raining, run into the house! The ship had to run into the harbour for shelter when the sudden storm arose.* → **run in²** (1)
**2** (of liquid) to flow into (something): [IØ + *into*] *The rivers on the other side of the mountains run into the western ocean.*
**3** esp. *BrE* to give (someone) a ride into (a place); pay a short visit to (somewhere), as by car: [X9 + *into*] *Jim will run us into town to see the play.* [L9 + *into*] *Let's run into the country this afternoon; the trees should be very pretty in the forest.*
**4** to cause (something) to pass into (something): [X9 + *into* (*often simple tenses*)] *He ran his sword into his enemy's body. Mind you don't run the needle into your finger by mistake.*
**5** to (cause to) hit (someone or something) by running: [IØ + *into*] *I ran into the gatepost and hurt my knee.* [X9 + *into*] *I ran my head into the glass door; it hurts badly.* → **knock against** (1), etc.
***6** to (cause to) hit (usu. something) with a

vehicle: [T1] *This lamppost looks as if it's been run into by a bus.* [D1] *I'm afraid I have run the car into the garage door again.* → **run down**[1] (4)

**7* to meet (someone) by chance: [T1 (*usu. simple tenses*)] *Guess who I ran into in the High Street this afternoon?* → **bump into** (2), **happen on,** etc.

**8* to meet (weather, usu. bad): [T1 (*no pass.*)] *We were sailing along nicely until we ran into a patch of mist just off the shore. I hope that the climbers don't run into a snowstorm halfway up.*

**9* to (cause to) meet (difficulties, debt, etc.): [T1] *Our plan ran into unexpected opposition.* [D1] *Taking risks like that might run the firm into debt.*

**10* to add up to; amount to; reach (an amount, quantity, etc.): [T1 (*no pass., often simple tenses*)] *The national debt runs into eight figures. The book is now running into six printings. Months ran into years and still the book was not finished.* → **reach into** (2), **run to** (7), **run up to** (2)

**11 run someone/oneself into the ground** *not fml* to tire someone or oneself with too much work: *I wish you would take a rest in your long hours of work; you'll run yourself into the ground.*

**12 run one's head into a brick wall** *not fml* to keep trying something impossible: [*usu. continuous tenses*] *Trying to persuade the director to change his plans is like running your head into a brick wall.* → **bang against** (2), **run against** (4)

**un low** *v adj* → **run short**
to be in short supply: [IØ] *World supplies of coffee have been running low, causing a sudden rise in the price.*

**un off**[1] *v adv*

**1** to (cause to) go away, as by running; leave: [IØ + OFF] *Don't run off just yet, I want to talk to you. Off you run now; come back to see me tomorrow.* [X9 + OFF] *Any people found on my land will be run off without further warning.* → **run away** (1)

**2** (of liquid) to (cause to) flow away: [IØ + OFF] *The pipes on the roof are to allow the rainwater to run off. Every spring, the ice and snow on the mountains melt, and the water runs off, flooding the rivers.* [X9 + OFF] *Please don't run off all the hot water, save some for my bath!* —**run-off** *n* esp. *AmE* → **run away** (2)

**3** to escape, as from home or duty: [IØ] *Jim and Mary threatened to run off to get married, if Mary's father continued to refuse his permission for the wedding. Our dog was very fond of the family, but had an unfortunate habit of running off, so we had to spend a lot of money on fences to keep him safe.* → **run away** (3)

**4** to steal (animals such as cattle) by driving them away: [T1] *Someone ran the cattle off during the night; there are only twenty-five left.*

**5* to produce (something such as writing) quickly: [T1] *I can run off the article that you want in a few days. I'll just run off this letter and then I'll be ready.*

**6* to make or print (copies): [T1] *Can you run off 200 copies of this notice before the post goes? This machine can run off two copies a second.*

**7* to speak (words) quickly and easily from memory: [T1] *He ran off the poem like a machinegun, showing no understanding or sensitivity.* → **rattle off, reel off, roll off** (3), **spiel off**

**8* to decide the result of (part of a competition such as a race): [T1] *All the early races have been run off, so the next competition will be for the main prize.* —**run-off** *n* → **play off**

**9 run one's feet/legs off** *not fml* to become tired through too much activity: *I've no intention of running my feet off doing your job as well as mine.*

**run off**[2] *v prep*

**1** to (cause to) leave (a place) quickly, as by running: [IØ + *off*] *The winning team ran off the field before the crowd ran on.* [X9 + *off*] *I'll run you off my land if I have to call the police!*

**2** (of liquid) to flow away from (something): [IØ + *off*] *The rainwater can run off the roof through these pipes. Melted ice and snow runs off the mountain every spring, flooding the rivers.*

**3** to (cause to) move quickly beyond the edge of (something), usu. by accident: [IØ + *off* (*often simple tenses*)] *I fell asleep while writing, and my pen ran off the edge of the page. The car ran off the road and turned upside down.* [T1 + *off* (*often simple tenses*)] *The driver had run the car off the road while under the influence of alcohol.*

**4* to have no effect on (someone): [T1 (*no pass., often simple tenses*)] *All your arguments just run off her: she never changes her point of view.*

**5 run someone off his feet/legs** *not fml* to make someone work too hard, esp. actively: *I love looking after the children, but they do run me off my feet. She says she's run off her feet in her new job.* → **rush off**[2]

**6 run off the rails** *not fml* to behave improperly, as by being unfaithful in marriage, or by immoral or unlawful actions: *Who would have thought that Mary, of all people, would run off the rails? She seemed to be the perfect faithful wife. Many young people run off the rails without an older person to guide them.* → **go off**[2] (8), **keep on** (14), **stay on**[2] (5)

**run off with** *v adv prep* → RUN AWAY WITH

***run on**[1] *v adv*

**1** to talk continuously: [IØ] *How she does run on! The teacher ran on and on about good behaviour, as usual.* → **be off** (9), **be on about, go on**[1] (7), **keep on** (8)

**2** (of time) to pass: [IØ] *Months ran on, and*

*still there was no letter. Life was running on much as usual when the shock happened. The fever may run on for a few days, and then get better.* → **fly by**[1] (2), **go by**[1] (2), **go on**[1] (8), **go past**[1] (2), **pass by**[1] (2), **wear on**[1]

**3** also *AmE* **run in** (usu. of words) to (cause to) be joined or added: [T1] *Instead of making a break here, I want you to run the next sentence on. The children are learning to run their letters on instead of making each one separately. I would rather have the entries in this dictionary set out in lines, not run on. You have run on two sentences here, with no connection between them.* [IØ (*simple tenses*)] *In Shakespeare's later poetry, the sense runs on from one line to the next.* —**run-on** *n, adj*

**4** to keep a boat's direction and speed, with the wind behind: [IØ] *With the wind behind her, the little boat ran on easily.*

**run on/upon**[2] *v prep*

**1** to run on top of (something): [IØ + *on/upon*] *The only exercise that we got at school was running on the spot. Do you like running on grass or on a sandy track best?*

**2** to (cause to) move or work by means of (something such as power): [L9 + *on/upon* (*often simple tenses*)] *The width of the railway lines was soon standardized so that the different companies' trains could run on the same lines. I sent the baby a toy mouse that ran on little wheels. This washing machine runs on very little electricity.* [X9 + *on/upon* (*often simple tenses*)] *The whole city is run on electric power made from falling water. You can run this car on a very small quantity of petrol.* → **go by**[2] (2), **work by**

**3** to print (something such as a book) on (certain paper): [X9 + *on/upon* (*often simple tenses*)] *The book is now so long that it will have to be run on very thin paper.*

***4** to hit (something); force (something) onto (something), as by running: [T1] *The boat ran on the rocks. Brutus killed himself by running on his sword.* [D1] *Take care not to run the boat on the rocks.*

***5** (of one's mind, thoughts, talk, etc.) to be concerned with (a subject): [T1 (*no pass.*)] *My thoughts have recently been running on the future more and more. His thoughts ran upon the happy times that he had spent there. My husband's ideas and mine usually run on the same lines. Our talk with the governor ran upon various matters of public importance.*

**run out** *v adv*

**1** to go outside by running: [IØ + OUT (*of*)] *When the loud bang was heard, lots of people ran out (of their houses) to see what had caused the noise.*

**2** (of liquid) to flow out: [IØ + OUT (*of*)] *The water runs in at this end and runs out at the other.*

**3** esp. *BrE* to (cause to) be driven to a place, as for a short visit: [X9 + OUT] *Can anyone run me out to the village? The last bus has gone.* [L9 + OUT] *Let's run out into the country this afternoon, while the weather is so good.*

**4** to (cause to) stretch out; reach: [L9 + OUT (*simple tenses*)] *The wall runs out into the field beyond this gate.* [X9 + OUT (*usu. simple tenses*)] *Run this row of scenery out past the edge of the stage.*

***5** to lengthen (something such as rope) gradually: [T1] *Run the rope out a little at a time.* [IØ] *Let the rope run out a little at a time.* → **pay away** (2), **pay out** (4), **play out** (7)

***6** to come to an end: [IØ] *The contract runs out next week. Time is running out.*

***7** to be no longer of value: [IØ] *Your library ticket runs out at the end of the year, when you can renew it.*

***8** to be no longer in supply; no longer have a supply (of something): [IØ (*of*)] *What shall we use for power when all the oil in the world has run out? The hot water has run out again, just when I wanted a bath. Sell the goods at a cheap price until they run out. I can't give you coffee, we've run out (of it); will you have tea? I went to the shop for some milk but they had run out.* → **be out of** (3), **give out** (5), **run out of** (4)

***9** (in cricket) to cause (a player) to leave the field of play when he fails to reach his wicket in time: [T1 (*usu. simple tenses*)] *We had nearly won the game, when our best player was unexpectedly run out.* → **be out** (7), etc.

***10** to tire (oneself) completely by running; complete (something) by running: [T1 (*usu. simple tenses*)] *I've run myself out, I can't go any further.*

***11** esp. *AmE not fml* to force (someone) to leave: [T1 (*of*) (*often simple tenses*)] *If he refuses to leave town of his own free will, the boys will run him out.*

**12** **run out the clock** esp. *AmE* (in certain ba[illegible] and other team games) to keep control of the ball in defensive play until the end of the game: [*often continuous tenses*] *The Flyers, with a 3–0 lead, are simply running out the clock—there are only ten minutes to go.*

***run out at** *v adv prep* → **come out at, work out at**

(of a calculation) to amount to; reach (a sum): [T1 (*no pass., usu. simple tenses*)] *The actual cost may run out at rather more than we originally expected. The total area runs out at 25,000 square miles.*

**run out of** *v adv prep*

**1** to leave (a place such as a building) by running: [IØ + OUT + *of*] *All the people ran out of the burning building.*

**2** (of liquid) to flow out of (something): [IØ + OUT + *of*] *Many rivers run out of the mountains. A strange dark strong-smelling liquid ran out of the pipe when it was unblocked.*

***3** esp. *AmE not fml* to force (someone) to leave (a place): [T1 (*often simple tenses*)] *you refuse to leave of your own free will, the boys will run you out of town.*

*4 to have no further supply of; lack (something): [T1] *I've run out of coffee; will you have tea? What will the world use for power when it has run out of oil? Do you, too, run out of money long before the next payday?* → **be out of** (3), **give out** (5), **run out** (8)

**5 run out of steam** *not fml* to be unable to make further effort; lose excitement and interest; slowly cease: *The performing group began well, but seemed to run out of steam halfway through the year. The schoolchildren's collection for the hospital, after a good start, ran out of steam and did not reach the sum that they were aiming for.*

***run out on** *v adv prep*

**1** to leave or desert (someone): [T1] *You can't run out on your family at a time like this. His wife ran out on him, and was later seen in a neighbouring city with another man.* → **walk out on** (1)

**2** *not fml* to leave (one's responsibility for something); fail to fulfil (an agreement): [T1] *The government has been charged with running out on its election promises. You can't run out on the contract, or you could be taken to court.* → **walk out on** (2)

**run over**[1] *v adv*

**1** to visit a place for a short time, as by running: [IØ + OVER (*to*)] *Will you run over to the shop and get some butter?* → **run across**[1] (1), **run round**[1] (2)

**2** esp. *BrE* to (cause to) be driven (to a place): [X9 + OVER (*to*)] *Don't get a bus, I'll run you over to the theatre.* [L9 + OVER (*to*)] *Let's run over to the Browns' this evening.* → **run across**[1] (2)

*3 (of liquid or a container) to overflow: [IØ] *You left the tap running, and the bathwater is running over! You can't pour any more tea into that cup, it will run over.* —**overrun** *v*

*4 to go beyond the edge; pass a limit: [IØ] *I can't get all the words on this page, they're running over. We've tried to keep the cost of the repairs to the original sum, but we may run over by a few pounds.* —**run-over** *n, adj*

*5 to knock down and wound (someone) or damage (something) with a vehicle: [T1b (*often pass., often simple tenses*)] *The neighbours are complaining about the road crossing where three children were run over last month. This box looks as if it's been run over by a bus. Wear something light-coloured at night so that the drivers can see you and are less likely to run you over. Drunk drivers run more people over than drivers who have not been drinking. Slow down, you might run someone over.* → **knock down** (2), **knock over** (2), **run down**[1] (4), **run over**[2] (4), **strike down** (1)

**run over**[2] *v prep*

**1** to pass over (something) by running: [IØ + *over*] *The horse was running over the fields as if it could never stop.*

**2** (of liquid) to flow over (something): [IØ + *over*] *The river is running over its banks and we shall be flooded.*

**3** to (cause to) pass over (something): [L9 + *over*] *His eye ran quickly over the letter to see who it was from.* [X9 + *over*] *The blind man ran his fingers lightly over my face to see if he knew me.*

*4 to knock down and wound (someone) or damage (something) with a vehicle: [T1a (*often simple tenses*)] *Go slower, you might run over those children playing in the road. The train ran over the bus, killing nine people.* → **knock down** (2), **knock over** (2), **run down**[1] (4), **run over**[1] (5)

*5 to practise or learn (something) by repetition: [T1] *Let's run over the second act again. Just run over your notes before the examination.* → **go over**[2] (2), **go through**[2] (7), **look over**[2] (5), **run through**[2] (7), **take over**[2] (3), **take through**[2] (2)

***run over with** *v adv prep*

to have a great deal, perhaps too much, of (something such as a feeling or idea): [T1 (*no pass., often simple tenses*)] *Students tend to run over with inventiveness, and show too little concern for the practical reality of their ideas. I love the dogs, but they do run over with excitement, and I think we should separate them.*

***run ragged** *v adj*

*not fml* to tire (someone) very much: [T1b] *I always loved teaching, but the children were so active that they ran me ragged.*

***run rife** *v adj*

*not fml* to be actively in existence; be common or frequent: [IØ (*often continuous tenses*)] *Stories about an early election are running rife in government circles.*

***run riot** *v n* → **run wild**

**1** (of plants) to grow fast, out of control: [IØ] *In this wet weather, grass runs riot in the vegetable beds.*

**2** to behave wildly: [IØ] *Where's the teacher? The children are running riot with no one in charge.*

**run round**[1] *v adv*

**1** to move around a space, as by running: [IØ + ROUND] *This cage is too small, and the animals have nothing to do all day but run round and round, these conditions must be improved.*

**2** to visit a place, usu. for a short time: [IØ + ROUND] *Will you run round to the shop and get some butter?* → **run over**[1] (1)

**3** esp. *BrE* to (cause to) be driven to a place: [X9 + ROUND] *Don't wait for a bus, I'll run you round there.* [L9 + ROUND] *Would you like to run round to the Millers' for an hour or so?*

*4 *not fml* to perform the duties of a servant for (someone): [T1b] *Don't expect me to run you round for the rest of your life!* → **run after** (4)

**run round**[2] *v prep* also **run around**

**1** to move round (a space), as by running:

[IØ + *round*] *Those poor animals have nothing to do all day but run round their cage!*
**2 run rings round** *not fml* to defeat (someone) easily: *Jim can run rings round any other tennis player in this town.* → **make round**

***run scared** *v adj*
*AmE infml* to behave as if expecting failure: [IØ (*often continuous tenses*)] *I think the election is ours; the other party are running scared.*

***run short** *v adj* → **run low**
to be in short supply; no longer be enough or have enough (of something): [IØ (*of*)] *The supply ran short long before the demand was satisfied. The world is gradually running short of oil.*

**run through**[1] *v adv*
**1** to (cause to) flow through something: [IØ + THROUGH] *Unblock the pipe to let the dirty water run through.* [X9 + THROUGH] *Run some clean water through, and then you'll see its true colour.*
**2** to make (something such as a film) pass through something such as a machine: [X9 + THROUGH] *You'll see what I mean when you run the film through.*
***3** to make a hole through (something or someone), as with a sword: [T1b (*with*) (*often simple tenses*)] *At last, with a cry of victory, he ran his opponent through (with his sword). I've run my finger through with the needle; it's bleeding.*

**run through**[2] *v prep*
**1** to move through (something), as by running: [IØ + *through*] *Running through the forest in the dark, the lost children were greatly afraid.*
**2** (of liquid) to (cause to) flow through (something): [IØ + *through*] *The rainwater is supposed to run through this pipe. The river runs through several underground caves which store the water for the city's use.* [T1 + *through*] *Run lots of soapy water through the pipe to clean it.*
**3** to (cause to) pass through (something or a group of people): [L9 + *through*] *The news ran through the village, as they waited to hear about the future of their land. I've had this tune running through my head all day. This line of chalky soil runs through all the gardens in the neighbourhood.* [X9 + *through*] *He ran his pencil through the offending word. You'll see what I mean when you run the film through the machine. He ran his fingers through his hair nervously, unable to think clearly in his anxiety.*
***4** to be part of; spread through (something): [T1 (*no pass., simple tenses*)] *A feeling of sadness runs through his poetry.*
***5** to spend (money) fast: [T1] *How can you have run through so much money so quickly?*
***6** to read (something) quickly: [T1] *Let me just run through this letter and then I'll come.*
***7** to repeat; practise (something such as words or music): [T1] *Let's run through the whole play from the beginning. The school band will have to stay late to run through the pieces for the concert. Run through your notes the night before the examination, and otherwise do nothing special. Would you please run through your suggestion again? I missed some of the details.* – **run-through** *n* → **go over**[2] (2), **go through**[2] (7); **look over**[2] (5), **run over**[2] (5), **take over**[2] (3), **take through**[2] (2)
**8 run a comb through one's hair** *not fml* to comb one's hair quickly: *I'll look better in this photograph if you give me a moment to run a comb through my hair.*

**run to** *v prep*
**1** to move towards (something or someone), as by running: [IØ + *to*] *Run to the shop and get some butter, would you? The child ran to its mother in fear.*
**2** (of liquid) to flow towards (somewhere): [IØ + *to*] *All rivers run to the sea. These pipes are intended to let the rainwater run to the ground.*
**3** esp. *BrE* to (cause to) be driven to (a place): [X9 + *to*] *Jim will run you to the station, so there's no hurry to catch your train.* [L9 + *to*] *Would you like to run to the harbour to look at the ships?*
**4** (of a performance or arrangement) to continue until (a time): [IØ + *to* (*often simple tenses*)] *The sale will run to the end of the month. Do you think the play will run to Christmas? Your house payments run to 1999.* → **run from** (3, 4)
**5** to (cause to) reach towards (something): [L9 + *to* (*simple tenses*)] *The wall runs to the end of the park. Prices run (from £3) to £10 for tickets.* [X9 + *to* (*often simple tenses*)] *We should run the fence to the bottom of the garden, to keep the rabbits out.* → **run down to** (4)
***6** to complain to; ask for help, advice, or action from (someone in charge): [T1 (*no pass.*)] *It's no use running to the teacher every time the other children behave badly, she won't listen to you. Don't run to me with your troubles! She runs to the doctor with every little pain. I am not in the habit of running to the Council with any suggestion for improving the town, but this is one that I feel you should consider.*
***7** to amount to; reach as far as (a size, quantity, etc.): [T1 (*no pass., simple tenses*)] *Tom's latest book runs to 300 pages. The national debt runs to millions of pounds.* → **reach into** (2), **run into** (10), **run up to** (2)
***8** to afford; (of money) be enough to provide (something): [T1 (*no pass., simple tenses*)] *I'm afraid we can't run to a holiday abroad this year. My income won't run to a second car.*
***9** to have (something) as a characteristic; have a tendency towards (something): [T1 (*no pass., simple tenses, usu. present*)] *Our family runs to red hair. His taste runs to t*

*popular. The writer runs to descriptive details.* → **run in²** (3)

*10 to follow (something) to its beginning; find the cause of (something): [D1 (*often simple tenses*)] *Can you run the story to its origin?* → **run back** (4), **wind back, wind on** (2)

**11 run oneself to death** *not fml* to kill oneself through overwork: *You'll run yourself to death, working every day of the week!*

**12 run something/someone to earth/ground: a** to chase an animal as far as its home: *Has the fox been run to earth yet?* **b** to find something or someone after much effort: *I searched in the library for weeks before I ran the article to earth. At last the police ran the criminals to earth.* → **go to** (19)

**13 run to fat** to become unhealthily overweight: *I was annoyed that I had let myself run to fat, so I made efforts to lose weight.*

**14 run to ruin** to become ruined by not being cared for: [*often pass.*] *The castle is old, and will cost a lot of public money if it is not to run to ruin.*

**15 run to seed: a** (of a plant) to grow too fast and reach the seeding stage too early: *The beans have run to seed because of the heavy rain, and there will be very few worth eating.* **b** *not fml* to become worse; lower one's standard: *She used to be active but has let herself run to seed since the children left home.* → **go to** (36)

**16 run to waste** to be allowed to be wasted: *Water is precious in a dry season, and must not run to waste. Without proper farming, all that rich land will run to waste.*

**run together** *v adv*

**1** to (cause to) move quickly, as by running with someone: [IØ + TOGETHER] *The children were last seen running together along the sand.* [T1 + TOGETHER] *I'm going to run two of my horses together in the next race, to double my chances of winning.*

**2** to (cause to) become joined together: [X9 + TOGETHER] *If you run all your words together, foreigners will not understand you. Run the wires together to make a tight connection.* [IØ + TOGETHER] *The paint got wet, and the colours have run together.*

**un up¹** *v adv*

**1** to move in an upward direction such as upstairs, as by running: [IØ + UP] *Would you run up and get my glasses? I've left them beside the bed.*

*2 (in cricket and other sports) to gather speed by running before delivering the ball, jumping, etc.; prepare to take action: [IØ] *Botham runs up and delivers the ball perfectly.* —**run-up** *n*

*3 to raise (something such as a flag): [T1] *The ship has run up the yellow flag, to signal that there is infectious disease on board.*

**4** to allow (something such as a debt) to increase: [T1] *Have you been running up bills at the dress shop again?*

*5 to increase quickly: [IØ] *The price of coffee is running up all over the world. House sales generally run up during the summer months.*

*6 to make (something) quickly: [T1] *I can run up a dress in a day, but it won't look properly made. The shipwrecked sailors ran up a rough shelter and then searched for food and water.*

*7 to add up (figures) quickly: [T1] *Can you run up this list of figures for me?*

*8 (of a ship or boat) to move quickly forward: [IØ (*often continuous tenses*)] *Take down those two sails, to stop her running up into the wind.*

*9 to run (an aircraft engine) quickly, as to test it: [T1 (*often continuous tenses*)] *That noise is because the engineers are running up the engine to see if the plane is ready to fly.*

**run up²** *v prep*

**1** to move quickly up (something such as a slope or stairs), as by running: [IØ + *up*] *I got out of breath running up the hill from the station.*

**2** to move quickly along (something such as part of the body): [L9 + UP] *A sudden pain ran up her leg.*

**run up against** *v adv prep*

**1** to hit (something) by running: [IØ + UP + *against*] *I ran up against a glass door and hurt my head.* → **knock against** (1), etc.

*2 *infml* to meet (someone or something such as trouble): [T1 (*usu. simple tenses*)] *I ran up against my former teacher in the shop. The firm ran up against strong competition.* → **happen on**, etc.

**run up to** *v adv prep*

**1** to come near to (someone or something), as by running: [IØ + UP + *to*] *The child ran up to the teacher to show her his drawing.*

*2 to amount to; reach (a size or figure, etc.): [T1] *The bill for the repairs might run up to £300.* → **reach into** (2), **run into** (10), **run to** (7)

**run upon** *v prep* → RUN ON²

***run wild** *v adj* → **run riot**

**1** (of plants) to grow out of control: [IØ] *The vegetable garden has run wild while I've been away.*

**2** to behave wildly: [IØ] *Why does she let the children run wild like that? They should be trained to behave properly.*

**run with** *v prep*

**1** to move together with (someone or something), as by running: [IØ + *with*] *I last saw the dog running with the children along the sand.*

**2** to compete against (someone) in a running race: [IØ + *with*] *Jim is prepared to run with anyone you want to name.* → **run against** (2)

**3** to keep company with (someone): [IØ + *with*] *In his younger days he ran with some very undesirable types.*

**4** to be covered with a flow of (liquid): [IØ + *with*] *The floors are unsafe, there are rats in* *the furniture, and the walls are running with water.*

**5 run with the hare and hunt with the hounds** *not fml* to take both sides in a disagreement: *Is it good politics to state your opinion or play for safety, running with the hare and hunting with the hounds?*

**rush at** *v prep*

**1** to run towards (someone) in order to attack him: [IØ + *at*] *He rushed at his enemy with drawn sword.*

*__2__ to work at (something or doing something) hastily: [T1] *Don't rush at your work or you'll spoil it.* [T4] *There's no need to rush at finishing the job, it can wait till tomorrow. Painting is something that can't be rushed at.*

**rush for** *v prep*

**1** to hurry in order to get (something or someone): [IØ + *for*] *So many people rushed for the bus that people could hardly get off.*

*__2__ *not fml* to charge (someone) too much for (goods): [D1 (*usu. simple tenses*)] *How much did they rush you for that coat?*

**3 be rushed for** to be short of (time): *I'll read it tomorrow, I'm rather rushed for time today.*

**rush in** *v adv*

to enter hastily: [IØ + IN] *Why did you have to rush in when I was talking to my wife? You could have knocked. "For fools rush in where angels fear to tread."* (Alexander Pope, *An Essay on Criticism*)

**rush into** *v prep*

**1** to enter (a space) hastily: [IØ + *into*] *Firemen rushed into the burning building to save the child.*

**2** to come into (one's mind) quickly: [IØ + *into*] *Suddenly an idea rushed into my head.*

*__3__ to be hasty about entering ( a state, agreement, etc.) or about (doing something): [T1 (*often simple tenses*)] *Think before you rush into a contract with that firm. People who rush into marriage rarely stay together.* [T4 (*often simple tenses*)] *Never rush into signing anything.*

**4 rush into print** to be eager to have one's writing printed: *The former politician is well-known for rushing into print with every idea that he has.*

**rush off**[1] *v adv*

**1** to (cause to) hurry away: [IØ + OFF] *The children rushed off as soon as the teacher gave them permission.* [X9 + OFF (*to*)] *As soon as the doctor had examined her, he rushed her off to hospital.*

*__2__ to produce or print (something) hastily: [T1] *Can you rush off another twenty copies?*

**rush off**[2] *v prep*

**rush someone off his feet** *not fml* to demand haste from someone; make him hurry: [*usu. pass.*] *We were so busy in the office today, I was rushed off my feet!* → **run off**[2] (5)

**rush out** *v adv*

**1** to hurry outside: [IØ + OUT] *The children rushed out when they saw the snow.*

*__2__ to produce (goods) hastily: [T1] *These bicycles have been rushed out and are not up to our usual standard.*

***rush through** *v adv*

to complete the stages of (something such as a law) hastily: [T1b] *Government members are trying to rush the tax cuts through before the next election.*

**rush to** *v prep*

**1** to (cause to) hurry towards (someone or something): [IØ + *to*] *The children rushed to the door when the postman arrived.* [X9 + *to*] *Mother had to be rushed to hospital when the snake bit her. Please rush these goods to our customer.*

**2 rush to conclusions** *not fml* to be too quick to make a judgment based on too few facts: *Wait till you have all the proofs, don't rush to conclusions.* → **jump to** (3)

**rust away** *v adv*

to (cause to) disappear through the action of rust: [IØ + AWAY] *The old lock had almost rusted away, so the door opened easily.*

**rust in** *v adv*

to become fixed in place by rust: [IØ + IN (*usu. pass.*)] *I can't get these screws out, they've rusted in.*

***rustle up** *v adv* → **scare up, scrape together** (2) **scrape up** (2)

*infml* to find a supply of (something, things or people): [T1a] *Can you rustle up some more players—two of the team are sick. My secretary can usually rustle up some envelopes if you have none.* [D1] *I'll try and rustle you up something to eat.*

# S

*__sack out__ *v adv* also **sack in**
*AmE infml* to go to sleep: [IØ (*often simple tenses*)] *The children were so tired that they sacked out as soon as they reached home.*

*__sack up__ *v adv*
*AmE infml* to gain (a profit): [T1 (*often simple tenses*)] *How much did we sack up this time?*

**sacrifice to** *v prep*
**1** to make a sacred gift of (something or someone) to (a god): [T1 + *to*] *The people here used to sacrifice lambs to their gods, by killing them and burning their bodies, sending up prayers with the smoke.*
**2** to give up; yield (something or oneself) in favour of (something or someone else): [T1 + *to*] *Many mothers sacrifice themselves to their families. I've sacrificed my own professional needs to your interests.*
***3** to lose (something) in order to have (something else): [D1 (*often simple tenses*)] *Are you prepared to sacrifice the pleasures of nature to the convenience of city life?*

*__saddle on/upon__ *v prep* → **land with,** etc.
*not fml* to force acceptance of (something or someone unwanted) on (someone): [D1] *Don't try to saddle your dirty work on me! I had three of the neighbours' children saddled on me for the whole afternoon!*

**saddle up** *v adv*
to put a saddle on (a horse); be ready to ride: [T1 + UP] *Have all the horses been saddled up yet?* [IØ + UP] *When all the riders have saddled up, we can set off.*

**saddle upon** *v prep* → **SADDLE ON**

**saddle with** *v prep* → **land with,** etc.
*not fml* to force (someone or oneself) to accept (something or someone unwanted); give (someone or oneself) the responsibility for (something or someone): [D1 (*often pass.*)] *The director tried to saddle me with the unpleasant job of telling the workers that they were dismissed. I got saddled with three of the neighbours' children for the whole afternoon. Was it wise to saddle yourself with such a big debt before you were sure of your professional success?* [V4b (*often pass.*)] *How did I let myself get saddled with making all the cakes for the office party?*

**safeguard against** *v prep* → **protect against**
to take care to prevent or avoid (something or doing something harmful); protect (someone) from (something or doing something harmful): [T1 + *against* (*often simple tenses*)] *Take this medicine regularly; it will safeguard you against a return of the disease.* *[L9 + *against* (*often simple tenses*)] *If you are conscious of your own weaknesses of character, you have a better chance of safeguarding against them. Warm clothing helps to safeguard against catching cold.*

**sag (away) to** *v (adv) prep* → **fall away** (8), **fall off**[1] (6), **pay off** (6)
(of a boat or ship) to swing or float away from the wind, towards (a certain direction): [IØ (+ AWAY) + *to*] *When the wind dropped, the boat sagged away to leeward.*

**sag down** *v adv*
to sink: [IØ + DOWN] *The chair sagged down under the fat man's weight.*

**sail against** *v prep*
**1** (of a sailing boat or ship) to follow a course in opposition to, or different from, the direction of (the wind): [IØ + *against*] *You have to fix the sails in a special way if you want to sail against the wind.*
**2 sail against the wind** *not fml* to meet opposition or difficulty, as in one's work: *We succeeded in winning the contract, but for a long time we were sailing against the wind, and were doubtful of our success.*

**sail before** *v prep*
**1** to sail with the wind behind one: [IØ + *before*] *Sailing before the wind was easy, and we moved along at a good speed.* → **run before**
**2 sail before the mast** *old use* to serve as an ordinary seaman: *The writer spent two years sailing before the mast, and wrote a famous book about his experiences.*

**sail for** *v prep* also **sail to**
to sail in the direction of; make a voyage to (a place): [IØ + *for*] *There's a boat sailing for England in the morning, if you're anxious to leave at once.*

**sail in** *v adv*
**1** to enter a place by sailing: [IØ + IN] *We had almost given up hope of the ship's safe return when she sailed in, late but victorious.* → **sail into** (1)
***2** *not fml* to enter a room, a conversation, etc., in a proud or active manner: [IØ (*often simple tenses*)] *The director sailed in, demanding to know who had disobeyed his orders. We were enjoying a pleasant conversation, until she sailed in with her unpleasant remarks.* → **sail into** (2)

**sail into** *v prep*
**1** to (cause to) enter (a place) by sailing: [IØ + *into*] *We stopped worrying about the ship's safe arrival when she sailed into the harbour with all her flags flying.* [T1 + *into*] *There's a storm coming; we'd better sail the boat into port.* → **sail in** (1)
***2** *not fml* to enter or begin (something) in a proud or active manner: [T1 (*no pass., often simple tenses*)] *The director sailed into the*

*room, demanding to know who had disobeyed his orders. Then the band sailed into the familiar tune.* → **sail in** (2)

*__3__ *not fml* to attack (something) actively: [T1 (*no pass.*)] *You should see the way that those children sailed into the food that we offered them!*

*__4__ *not fml* to attack (someone) with words: [T1 (*no pass., often simple tenses*)] *The speaker sailed into his opponent showing the weaknesses of his argument in an unmistakable way.*

*__5__ *not fml* to scold (someone) for a fault: [T1 (*no pass.*)] *I could hear Mother sailing into the children for bringing mud into the house.* → **tell off** (1), etc.

**sail through** *v adv; prep*

**1** to pass through (a place) by sailing: [IØ + THROUGH/*through*] *The harbour entrance was narrow, but we sailed through (it) without much difficulty.* [T1 + THROUGH/*through*] *It takes a lot of skill to sail such a big ship through such a narrow passage between the rocks.*

*__2__ *not fml* to pass (something such as an examination) easily: [IØ (*often simple tenses*)] *John thought that he would fail his driving test again, but this time, to his own surprise, he sailed through.* [T1 (*pass. rare*)] *Of course, you'll sail through English as usual, you seem to find it easy.* → **breeze through,** etc.

*__3__ *not fml* to deal successfully with (something such as a difficulty): [T1] *Once you're used to the organization, you should sail through the necessary preparations for the class. I've had a good day, sailing through my work with unexpected ease.* [IØ] *Why worry about the difficulties ahead? I know you'll just sail through!*

**sail to** *v prep* → **SAIL FOR**

***sally forth/out** *v adv*

*old use or humor* to go out, esp. to begin a journey or attack: [IØ (*often simple tenses*)] *The soldiers sallied forth to the battle. The king sallied out with all his servants. Mother has sallied forth to the sales again.*

**salt away** *v adv*

**1** to preserve (food) from decaying by covering it with salt: [X9 + AWAY] *The rest of the meat can be salted away for the winter.* → **salt down**

*__2__ *not fml* to save (money): [T1] *Don't worry about the hospital bill, I have a little money salted away for just such an occasion.*

**salt down** *v adv* → **salt away** (1)

to preserve (food) from decaying by covering it with salt: [X9 + DOWN] *If the beans are salted down they will keep all winter.*

***salt out** *v adv*

(in chemistry) to (cause to) be separated from a liquid by the addition of a salt: [T1 (*usu. pass.*)] *The chemical must then be salted out and allowed to dry.* [IØ] *How long will the substance take to salt out?*

**salt with** *v prep*

**1** to make (food) more tasty by adding (salt): [T1 + *with*] *If you salt the vegetables with a little onion salt, they will taste better.*

**2** to cover (something) with a scattering of (something): [T1 + *with*] *Scientists have learned to make rain by salting clouds with certain chemicals. The hills were salted with a light fall of snow.*

*__3__ *not fml* to make (something) more lively by adding (something): [D1] *The book is a little dull, and needs salting with some interesting examples. People who print modern magazines often consider that the public will not read articles unless they are salted with sex and violence.*

**salute with** *v prep*

*fml* to greet, welcome, or honour (someone or something) by (making a special sign or movement): [T1+ *with*] *He saluted his new wife with a gentle kiss. It is the custom to salute the Queen's birthday with twenty-one guns. Soldiers are taught to salute their officers with a special hand movement.* [IØ + *with*] *All soldiers must salute with the right hand.*

**salvage from** *v prep* also **salve from**

**1** to save (something in danger of being lost or ruined) from (destruction or a place): [T1 + *from*] *Is it possible to salvage the sunken ship from the bottom of the ocean? Luckily, our precious records were salvaged from the fire.* → **save from** (1)

**2** to save (something or someone) from (a bad state): [T1 + *from*] *How can we salvage the firm from complete failure? This organization has succeeded in salvaging many people from a dependence on alcohol. There is not much now that can be salvaged from the wreck of our political hopes.* → **rescue from** (2), **save from** (2)

**sand down** *v adv* → **rub down** (2)

to make (a surface) smooth by rubbing with sandpaper: [T1 + DOWN] *The quality of the finished paintwork depends on how well you sanded the wood down in the preparation stage.*

***sandwich (in) between** *v* (*adv*) *prep*

to crush or fit (someone or something) tightly between (two things or people): [D1] *We'll have to sandwich the meeting (in) between lunch and the opening ceremony. I couldn't get out of the bus, as I was sandwiched (in) between an old lady with stiff legs, and a kicking schoolchild.*

**satiate with** *v prep* also **sate with**

**be satiated with** to be completely satisfied or filled with (something desired): *After the excellent meal, we were satiated with food and drink. She stayed in the library for hours on end until she was satiated with knowledge of the subject. It's an unusual feeling to be satiated with joy.*

***satisfy of** *v prep*

to make (someone or oneself) completely

sure about (something such as a quality): [D1 (*often pass.*)] *What else can I do to satisfy the police of my honesty? I like to examine all the goods that I intend to buy, to satisfy myself of their quality. Are you satisfied of the truth of his story?*

**satisfy with** *v prep*

**be satisfied with** to be completely pleased with (usu. something): [*usu. pass.*] *I am not satisfied with your work; you must improve it. Your money will be returned if you are not satisfied with the goods.*

**saturate with** *v prep*

**1** to fill (something) with a lot of (liquid): [T1 + *with* (*usu. pass.*)] *Our clothes were saturated with the sudden heavy rain.* → **drench in, soak with**

**2** to fill (a liquid) with as much of (a substance) as will melt in it at the same temperature: [T1 + *with* (*usu. pass.*)] *The liquid in this holder has been saturated with a special chemical.*

**3** to supply for (sale to the public) as much of (a certain kind of goods) as can possibly be bought: [T1 + *with* (*usu. pass.*)] *After a particularly good apple crop, the market was saturated with the fruit, and the price began to fall.* → **glut with** (2)

***4** to fill (something or someone) with a great deal of (something): [D1 (*usu. pass.*)] *The music filled the room until we were saturated with it. The room was saturated with smoke.*

**save for** *v prep*

**1** to preserve or keep back (something or someone) to wait for (usu. someone); keep (something) free for (someone): [T1 + *for*] *I've been saving myself for you. The shopkeeper saved a pound of my special cheese for me, as I'm a regular customer. Please save my place for me while I make a telephone call.* → **hold for** (1), **keep for** (1), **reserve for** (1)

**2** to put (something such as money or a supply) away until (a certain time or occasion) or for (someone or a purpose): [T1 + *for*] *Are you saving the best wine for the party? I'm trying to save as much of my income as I can for my old age. We must save the rest of the milk for tomorrow.* [IØ + *for*] *I'm saving for a new car. "Everyone has someone worth saving for."* (Advertisement for government savings plan). → **hold for** (1), **keep for** (2), **reserve for** (2)

**3 save (something) for a rainy day** *not fml* to save usu. money for a time of need: *I have a few pounds left, but I'm saving them for a rainy day. My parents told me always to save for a rainy day, as you never knew when you may need a little additional money.*

**save from** *v prep*

**1** to preserve (something or someone) from (danger, ruin, etc.): [T1 + *from*] *How can the city save these fine old buildings from destruction? Luckily our precious records were saved from the fire.* → **rescue from** (1), **salvage from** (1)

**2** to prevent (someone or something) from (having or doing something bad): [T1 + *from* (*often simple tenses*)] *What can we do to save him from the results of his own foolishness? A lot can be done to save their marriage from failure. Thank you; you saved me from making a fool of myself.* → **rescue from** (2), **salvage from** (2)

**save till/until** *v prep* → **keep till** (1)

to preserve (something) until (a point in time): [T1 + *till/until*] *Let's save this bottle of wine till Christmas.*

**save up** *v adv*

to save money gradually over a period of time (to buy something): [IØ + UP (*for*)] *How long did it take you to save up for a new car? We're saving up to buy the plane tickets for our holiday abroad.*

***savour of** *v prep* also *AmE* **savor of** → **smack of, smell of** (2), **stink of** (2)

(usu. of words) to contain a suggestion of (a quality, usu. bad): [T1 (*no pass., simple tenses*)] *Your last remark savoured of rudeness.*

**saw down** *v adv*

to cause (a tree) to fall by using a sharp-toothed cutting tool: [X9 + DOWN] *We shall have to saw the old tree down, it's not safe.*

**saw into** *v prep*

to cut (something such as wood) into (pieces) with a sharp-toothed tool: [T1 + *into*] *If you can saw the branches into equal lengths of wood, we shall make a bigger profit.*

**saw off** *v adv; prep*

to remove part of (something) with or as with a sharp-toothed tool: [X9 + OFF/*off*] *Half his leg below the knee had been sawn off by the teeth of the terrible fish. Have you ever tried sawing an equal amount off each leg of a table?* —**sawn-off** *adj BrE* —**sawed-off** *adj AmE*

**saw through** *v adv; prep*

to cut through or divide (something such as wood) with a sharp-toothed tool: [X9 + THROUGH; IØ + *through*] *The bars had been sawn (clean) through, and the prisoner had escaped. The animal's teeth had sawed (right) through the tree trunk.*

**saw up** *v adv*

to cut (usu. wood) into pieces, using a sharp-toothed tool: [T1 + UP (*into*)] *First you have to cut down the tree and saw it up into logs, before you can build your shelter.*

**say about** *v prep*

to express (something) in words as explanation or opinion about (something or someone), esp. in the phrs. **say something/anything/much about**: [T1 + *about* (*often simple tenses*)] *Did your parents have much to say about your being so late home last night? Can't you say anything about the meal? Please say something about my new dress! What does the newspaper say about our concert last night? The window is broken, and you were seen* *picking up a stone; what do you have to say about that?*

**say after** *v prep*
to repeat (words) spoken by (someone): [T1 + *after* (*often simple tenses*)] *At the wedding ceremony, the priest said, "Say after me, 'I, Jim, take you, Mary, to be my lawful wedded wife.'"*

**say against** *v prep*
to express (something) in opposition to (usu. something), esp. in the phrs. **say something/anything/much against**: [T1 + *against* (*often simple tenses*)] *What did the police say against your story? The villagers had plenty to say against the building of the new airport on their land. Did the director say anything against your suggestion? Mother is sure to have something to say against your desire to leave home.*

**say for** *v prep*
**1** to express (something) in support of (oneself, someone, or something), as in argument or defence, esp. in the phrs. **say much/little/something for**: [T1 + *for* (*often pass., simple tenses*)] *There is much to be said for both sides of this question. What has she to say for herself? She seems a nice person, but has little to say for herself. Have you anything to say for yourself before I pass judgment? "There's a lot to be said for not being known to the readers of the 'Daily Mirror.'"* (Anthony Burgess, *Inside Mr Enderby*)
**2 say a (good) word for** to speak in support or praise of (someone): [*often simple tenses*] *It might help you to get the job if I say a good word for you to the director. Don't you have one good word to say for her?* → **speak for** (2)
**3 not say much for** to show (something such as an ability) in an unfavourable way: [*often simple tenses*] *Losing that contract doesn't say much for the director's skill in business.*

**say of** *v prep*
**1** to express an opinion about (someone or something): [T5 + *of* (*often pass., often simple tenses*)] *People say of her that she uses black magic. It is often said of our island that it is like a jewel set in the sea.*
**2 to say nothing of** not to mention; not including (something or someone): *I have sales figures to calculate, letters to answer, and papers to sign before lunch, to say nothing of urgent meetings with three people; I don't know how I can get it all into the time.*

**say on** *v adv*
*not fml* to continue to speak: [IØ + ON (*imper.*)] *Say on, we're still listening.*

**say out** *v adv*
to express (something); finish speaking (something) fully or honestly: [T1 + OUT (*often simple tenses*)] *Say your piece out and pay no attention to our feelings; it's important that we know exactly what you think.*

**say over** *v adv*
to repeat (words): [T1 + OVER] *Do you say your prayers over every night? The actor would say over his lines until he knew them perfectly.*

**say to** *v prep*
**1** to tell (something) to (someone): [T1 + *to*] *What did you say to your mother?* [T5 + *to*] *I say to you that I did not take your money.* [T6 + *to*] *Say to the teacher where you've been.*
**2** to express (something) to (someone), esp. in the phrs. **say much/something/nothing to**: [T1 + *to* (*often simple tenses*)] *I've so much to say to you, it will cost too much over the telephone! Sit down; I've a lot to say to you and I want to be sure that you're listening. Be quiet, I've something to say to you. I've nothing to say to you until you say sincerely that you are sorry for your rudeness. Have you anything to say to the court before judgment is passed?*
*3 to have an opinion about (something or doing something): [D1 (*simple tenses, often as a question*)] *What would you say to a party next week?* [V4b (*simple tenses*)] *What do you say to going to a cinema tonight?*

***scale down** *v adv* → **scale up**
to reduce (usu. a figure) by a certain rate: [T1] *The nurses have offered to scale down their pay demands to a lower figure. The students' marks were scaled down because the examination was too easy.* —**scale-down** *n*

***scale to** *v prep*
to fix (something) at a rate varying with (something): [D1 (*usu. pass.*)] *Tax demands are scaled to the income earner's ability to pay.*

***scale up** *v adv* → **scale down**
to increase (usu. a figure) by a certain rate: [T1] *If all the students' marks are low, they will be scaled up to give a more usual average.* —**scale-up** *n*

**scar over** *v adv*
(of something such as a wound) to close healthily but leaving a mark of thickened skin: [IØ + OVER] *The doctor will put some stitches in that cut to prevent it from scarring over.*

**scare away/off** *v adv* → **frighten away**
*not fml* to discourage (someone) by fear; make (someone or an animal) leave through fear: [X9 + AWAY/OFF] *Higher coffee prices are scaring away the customers; many are drinking tea instead. If Grace pays too much attention to that red-haired boy, she could easily scare him off.*

**scare into** *v prep* → **frighten into, intimidate into, terrify into**
*not fml* to persuade (someone) through fear into (doing something): [X9 + *into*] *The salesman scared the old lady into signing the paper by threatening to take away the goods*

**scare off** *v adv* → SCARE AWAY

**scare out of** *v adv prep* → **frighten out of (, terrify out of**
**scare someone out of his mind/wits** *not fml* make someone greatly afraid, esp. throu

shock: *You scared me out of my wits, coming up behind me suddenly like that. I was scared out of my mind, giving my first public performance.*

**scare stiff** *v adj*
*not fml* to make (someone) very anxious or afraid: [T1 + stiff (*usu. pass.*)] *I was scared stiff of meeting the director until I discovered what a pleasant woman she was!*

***scare up** *v adv* → **rustle up, scrape together** (2), **scrape up** (2)
*AmE infml* to find and produce a supply of (something, things, or people): [T1] *Can you scare up another player for the team—one of our players is sick. Where can I scare up some more paper? I don't want to have to buy some.*

**scatter about/around/round** *v adv; prep* → **dot about**
to place (things or people) in various parts of (an area) or irregularly round (something): [T1 + ABOUT/AROUND/ROUND/*about/around/round*] *Why do you have to scatter your clothes about the house? Pick them up and keep them in one place! You can tell which is my office by all the books and papers scattered around. Scatter some of this powder round the roots to help the plant grow.*

**scent out** *v adv*
*not fml* to find (something or someone) by or as by smell, or by noticing signs: [T1a (*often simple tenses*)] *The police were able in the end to scent out the criminals' hiding place.*

**scheme for** *v prep*
to make a plan, often deceitful, in order to obtain (something), [IØ + *for*] *Many politicians are less concerned with working for the good of the citizens, than with scheming for personal power. Companies can be prevented by law from scheming for higher profits by agreeing between them on a fixed price.*

**school in** *v prep*
to train or enable (someone) to learn the idea of (something), often informally: [X9 + *in* (*usu. pass.*)] *Every soldier has to be schooled in the care of his weapons. This politician has shown that he has been well schooled in the art of decieving the public.*

**school to** *v prep*
*fml* to control; train (someone or oneself) to have (a quality): [X9 + *to* (*often pass.*)] *All the soldiers are well schooled to obedience. It is difficult for someone with my character to school myself to patience.*

**scoff at** *v prep*
**1** to make fun of (someone or something) unkindly; not treat (something or someone) seriously: [IØ + *at*] *Teachers and parents should never scoff at small children's attempts to draw.* → **laugh at** (2), etc.
***2** to regard (something) as unworthy: [T1 (*usu. simple tenses*)] *People who are out of work cannot afford to scoff at any job.*

**scold for** *v prep* → **tell off** (1), etc.
to blame; be angry with; find fault with (someone or an animal), usu. in noisy words, for (something or doing something wrong): [T1 + *for*] *It's no use scolding the child for his behaviour without showing him a good example. I could hear Mother scolding the dog for bringing mud into the house.*

**scoop out** *v adv*
**1** to lift; remove (loose material such as soil) with or as with a curved tool: [X9 + OUT] *This machine can scoop out the soil in preparation for the new building, at a very fast rate.* → **scoop up**
**2** to make (a hollow space) in earth with or as with a curved tool: [X9 + OUT] *This animal scoops out a nesting place in the sand with its tail and then lays its eggs in it.*

**scoop up** *v adv* → **scoop out** (1)
to lift or gather (something such as soil) with or as with a curved tool or container: [X9 + UP] *Use buckets to scoop up the water. It took a long time to scoop up the sugar that had fallen. She scooped the baby up in her arms and ran from the flames.*

***scorch out** *v adv*
to destroy (something such as an area) by burning: [T1 (*often pass.*)] *The whole village was scorched out by enemy gunfire.*

***score for** *v prep*
to arrange (music) to be performed on (certain instruments) or by (certain voices): [D1] *The piece is scored for piano, strings, and drums. The music students are learning how to score tunes for various combinations of instruments, according to the desired effect.*

**score off** *v prep*
**1** (in cricket) to make (runs) from (a bowler or his bowling): [T1 + *off*] *Richards scored a century off Willis and Botham. It's possible to score six runs off a single ball, if you hit it far and high enough. These fast balls are difficult to score off.*
***2** to defeat (someone); make (someone) appear stupid, usu. by making a clever point in an argument: [T1 (*no pass.*)] *It's not difficult to score off Jim in an argument, because he can never think of the right thing to say.*

***score out** *v adv* → **cross out**, etc.
to draw a line through (writing) so that it cannot be read: [T1] *Score out that last name, I no longer intend to invite her.* —**scored-out** *adj*

***score over** *v prep*
to gain an advantage over (someone): [T1] *One of the faults of the other writers is their failure to separate the different kinds of animals in this area, so this is certainly where we can score over them.*

**score up** *v adv* → **chalk up** (3), etc.
to record (something): [T1 + UP] *The youngest player scored up an unexpected fifty runs. Now we can score up another victory for our team.*

***score up against** *v adv prep*
to record (something bad) to show the unworthiness of (someone): [D1 (*often pass.*)]

*Every time a piece of work is badly done, it will be scored up against you.*

***scour about/around** *v adv* → **SCOUT ABOUT**

**scour away/off** *v adv* → **scrub away** (2)
to remove (usu. dirt) with rough action and a heavy cleaning tool: [X9 + AWAY/OFF] *This new cooker has a special way of cleaning itself, so it saves all the trouble of scouring off the dirt.*

***scour for** *v prep*
to search (a place) thoroughly looking for (someone or something): [D1 (*often continuous tenses*)] *The police are scouring the woods for the missing child. I have been scouring the city for some good boots with flat heels. The famous film-maker spent weeks scouring the country for the right actress for the part.*

**scour out** *v adv* → **scrub out** (1)
to clean (a container) thoroughly with rough action and a heavy tool: [X9 + OUT] *Milk bottles should be scoured out before being returned to the milkman for refilling.*

***scout about/around** *v adv* also **scour about/around**
*not fml* to search thoroughly by moving around looking (for something or someone): [IØ (*for*)] *Scout about and see if you can find some fruit growing that we could eat. Scouting around all over the town, I at last found the boots that I was looking for.* —**scout-around** *n*

***scout out** *v adv*
**1** to examine (an area) thoroughly by moving around it: [T1a] *Scout out the land and see which is the best place for our battle lines.*
**2** to find (someone or something) by moving around searching: [T1a] *Trust you to scout out the best restaurant in town. It took weeks to scout out the boots I wanted.*

**scowl at** *v prep* → **frown at** (1), **glower at**
to look at (someone) in a threatening or angry manner: [IØ + *at*] *Why are you scowling at me? I've done nothing. The teacher kept the class under control by scowling at the children, making them afraid of him.*

***scrabble about** *v adv*
to feel about in an awkward manner, usu. with the hands or feet (to try to get something): [IØ (*for*)] *The climber scrabbled about wildly for a handhold, but missed and fell to his death. The pigs are scrabbling about (for food) among the roots.*

***scramble for** *v prep*
to compete in an active, hurried, or disorganized way to get (something): [T1] *Too many firms are scrambling for a share of profits in the new industry. If all your players scramble for the ball together, we might lose it to the other team; organize the defence players to seize it. Not everyone in this city is wealthy; some people are just scrambling for a living.*

***scrape along/by** *v adv* also **scratch along** → **get by**[1] (2), etc.
*not fml* to be just able to live (with little money): [IØ (*on*)] *I can scrape along on a reduced income for a short time, but not for ever. I scraped by until my next cheque arrived, by borrowing from my relations.*

**scrape away** *v adv*
**1** to rub continuously with something sharp: [IØ + AWAY] *Scraping away patiently in the soil with their fingers, the team of scientists discovered the ruins of an ancient civilization.*
**2** to remove (a covering) by rubbing with something sharp: [X9 + AWAY] *Scraping the snow away, they found a car buried underneath!* → **scrape off**

***scrape by** *v adv* → **SCRAPE ALONG**

**scrape in** *v adv*
**1** to be only just able to enter a place: [L9 + IN (*often simple tenses*)] *The train was crowded, but I scraped in just before the door closed.* → **squeeze in** (1)
***2** *not fml* to be only just able to enter or be admitted (to something such as a school with competitive entrance): [IØ (*to*) (*often simple tenses*)] *Jane thought that she had failed the entrance examination, but then learned that she had scraped in by a few marks. Many men who only scrape in to the army college make the best officers.* → **squash in, squeeze in** (3)

**scrape off** *v adv; prep* → **scrape away** (2)
to remove (something such as a mark) from (a surface) by rubbing with something sharp or rough: [X9 + OFF/*off*] *Carefully scraping the paint off (the wall), they discovered a valuable old painting underneath. Let the mud dry, so that it will be easier to scrape off (your shoes). My new boots rub my ankles so hard that they have scraped some of the skin off.*

**scrape out** *v adv*
**1** to empty or clean (a container) by rubbing it, as with something sharp: [T1 + OUT] *The children always loved scraping out the bowl in which we had mixed the cake.*
**2** to remove (something); make (a hole) in something by rubbing with something sharp: [X9 + OUT] *First scrape out the seeds, then cut the fruit into pieces. This animal scrapes out a hole in the sand to lay its eggs in.*

**scrape through** *v adv; prep*
**1** to be only just able to pass through (a narrow space): [L9 + THROUGH/*through*] *Our dog used to escape by scraping through the bars of his fence; they were so close together that I don't know how he was able to scrape through. The walls of the cave come to a narrow point just ahead, but I think we can scrape through.* → **skin through** (1), **squeak through** (1), **squeeze through** (1)
***2** *not fml* to be only just able to pass (an examination, etc.): [IØ (*often simple tenses*)] *Some of you deserved to succeed, and others only scraped through.* [T1 (*often simple tenses*)] *Jane got into the music school by scraping through the examination.* → **skin through** (2), **squeak through** (2), **squeeze through** (2)

**scrape together** *v adv*
**1** to gather (scattered things) by pushing with something sharp: [X9 + TOGETHER] *Scrape the dead leaves together into a pile, and then we can burn them.*
*__2__ also **scratch together** *not fml* to collect or obtain (something such as money or a group) with effort: [T1] *By working hard, the villagers scraped together enough money to send the boy to hospital. Many of the players were delayed by the snow storm, but we were able to scrape a team together.* → **rustle up, scare up, scrape together** (2), **scrape up** (2)

**scrape up** *v adv*
**1** to lift (something) by using a tool with a sharp edge: [X9 + UP] *When it has dried, you'll be able to scrape up most of the mud from the mat with a knife.*
*__2__ also **scratch up** *not fml* to save or collect (something such as money or a group) with effort: [T1] *I'm not sure if I can scrape up the price of the plane ticket.* → **rustle up, scare up, scrape together** (2)
*__3__ *not fml* to invent (a story): [T1] *What kind of excuse can you scrape up this time?*
**4 scrape up an acquaintance (with)** *not fml* to make friends (with someone) to a slight degree: [*often simple tenses*] *Those two? Oh, they're some people we scraped up an acquaintance with on holiday; I can't claim to know them well. After years of living in the same street, my neighbour and I had done no more than scrape up an acquaintance.*

**scratch about** *v adv*
to dig with quick light movements, as with nails (looking for something): [IØ + ABOUT (*for*)] *The farmyard was quiet, with just a few chickens scratching about (for food).*

*__scratch along__ *v adv* → SCRAPE ALONG

**scratch away** *v adv*
**1** to make very small movements, as with finger nails, continuously: [IØ + AWAY] *If you keep scratching away at that spot, you'll break the skin.*
**2** to remove (something such as a surface) little by little, as with finger nails: [T1 + AWAY] *Most of the paint has been scratched away by heavy wear.*

**scratch from** *v prep*
to (cause to) be removed from (a competition or list of competitors): [IØ + *from* (*often simple tenses*)] *Jim should have an easy victory, as two of the best runners have scratched from the race.* [T1 + *from*] *We had to scratch two players from the team because of damaged knee joints.*

**scratch out** *v prep*
**1** to draw a deep line through (something such as writing) with a sharp pen, pencil, or knife, so that it cannot be read: [X9 + OUT] *Names had been cut on the wall, but had then been scratched out.* —**scratching-out** *n* —**scratched-out** *adj* → **cross out**, etc.
*__2__ to be only just able to make (a living): [T1a] *It wasn't easy scratching out a living in those hard times.* → **eke out**
**3 scratch someone's eyes out** *not fml* to attack someone violently, esp. about the face; often said as a jealous threat: *If I meet that woman you've been sleeping with, I'll scratch her eyes out!*

*__scratch together__ *v adv* → SCRAPE TOGETHER (2)

**scratch up** *v adv*
**1** to spoil (a surface) thoroughly by making marks with something sharp: [T1 + UP (*usu. pass.*)] *The surface of the table has been all scratched up by years of heavy use.*
**2** to produce (something) by digging lightly with something sharp, as finger nails: [X9 + UP] *That cat has scratched up all my young plants again!*
**3** → SCRAPE UP (2)

**scream down** *v adv*
**1** to descend, making a loud high noise: [IØ + DOWN] *As the bombs came screaming down, the villagers tried to take shelter.*
**2 scream the place down** *not fml* to fill a place with a loud high noise, as from pain, anger, fear, or laughter: *We all knew when our neighbours had a terrible quarrel, because we could hear the wife screaming the place down, crying with helpless anger. What's the matter? You've been screaming the place down! Did you have a bad dream?*

**scream for** *v prep*
to try to get (something, esp. help) by crying with a loud high voice: [IØ + *for*] *Listen! Isn't that a faint voice screaming for help from that deep snow over there?*

**scream off** *v adv*
**scream one's head off** to cry with a loud high voice, as with pain, anger, or fear, for a long time or violently: *I can't bear to hear that child screaming his head off with temper. In this hospital you can scream your head off all night and still the nurse won't come to give you drugs for the pain.*

**scream out** *v adv* → **shriek out**
to give a high loud cry; express (something) in a high loud voice: [IØ + OUT] *He screamed out in pain as the flames reached his leg.* [T5 + OUT] *She screamed out that there was a mouse in the room.* [T1 +OUT] *If she hadn't screamed out the warning, there would have been a nasty accident.*

**scream with** *v prep* → **shriek with**
to express (pain or laughter) in a loud high voice: [IØ + *with*] *The rest of the people in the cinema were screaming with laughter, but I didn't see what was so funny. How can you take no notice of an animal that is screaming with pain, with its leg caught in a trap?*

**screen from** *v prep* also **screen against**
**1** to cover (something) or hide (someone) so as to protect it or him from (something harmful): [T1 + *from* (*often simple tenses*)] *In the early days of summer you would be wise to*

*screen your skin from the burning sun with this special cream. These special coverings screen the windows from the bright light.* → **protect against**, etc.

*2 to protect; shelter (someone) from (something or doing something harmful): [D1] *It is hopeless trying to screen your child from the harmful effects of television, as he can always watch it at a friend's house. You can't screen your brother from blame in the accident.* [V4b] *He tried to screen his friend from knowing of his father's death, but it was no use, as the news had already reached him.* → **protect against, shelter from** (2), **shield from** (2)

**screen off** *v adv*
to separate (usu. part of a room) with movable walls: [X9 + OFF (*often simple tenses*)] *The nurse screened off the corner around the hospital bed, so that the doctor could make his examination in private.*

***screen out** *v adv*
**1** to remove part of (something) by placing a covering in the way: [T1 (*often simple tenses*)] *The sunlight was screened out by the curtains. These window coverings screen out the heat of the sun, but allow enough light through to work by.* → **filter out** (2)
**2** to choose to take no notice of or be unconscious of (something unwanted): [T1] *The child was able to screen out the noises surrounding him as he was so busy in his play.* → **filter out** (3)
**3** to separate (unwanted things or usu. people), by testing or other means: [T1] *So far we have screened out four people who wanted the job but were unsuitable, so that leaves three good people to choose from.*

**screw down** *v adv*
to fasten (something such as a lid) down in place with screws: [X9 + DOWN] *He has screwed the lid down so tightly that I can't get it off!*

**screw on** *v adv*
**1** to (cause to) be fastened onto something with screws or a turning movement: [X9 + ON (*to*)] *Next time please screw the handle on (to the door) so that it won't fall off again.* [IØ + ON] *This lid won't screw on properly.*
**2 have one's head screwed on (properly/the right way)** *not fml* to be sensible, able to make decisions: *I'm not worried about that boy even though he is so young to be in business; he's always had his head screwed on the right way and no one will be able to fool or cheat him.*

**screw out of** *v adv prep*
**1** to remove (usu. liquid) from (something) with a twisting movement: [X9 + OUT + *of*] *Screw the soapy water out of the cloth before you dip it in the clean water.*
*2 *infml* to get (money) from (someone) by force or other unfair means: [D1] *By threatening to give his wife the photograph, the criminal was able to screw every last penny out of the poor man.*

**screw to** *v prep*
**1** to fasten (something) to (something) with screws: [X9 + *to*] *In old-fashioned schools, the desks were screwed to the floor.*
**2 screw one's courage to the sticking-place** to be brave and daring: *"We fail! But screw your courage to the sticking-place, And we'll not fail."* (Shakespeare, *Macbeth*)

**screw up** *v adv*
**1** to fix (something) firmly in place by screwing: [T1 + UP] *Can you screw up this handle for me? It's falling off again. Screw the board up firmly to the window frame until we can replace the broken glass.*
**2** to (cause to) twist, fold, or tighten: [T1 + UP] *He screwed up the letter into a ball and threw it out of the window. She screwed up her face at the nasty smell. You will need to screw the strings up to get them in tune.* [L9 + UP (usu. simple tenses)] *Her face screwed up as her tongue touched the bitter fruit.*
*3 *infml* to spoil; ruin (something): [T1] *Don't tell me that John has screwed up his driving test yet again! That last operation on the famous player's knee has screwed up his chances of staying in the team.* [IØ] *When I'd finished the exam, I thought I'd screwed up, but I found out later that I'd passed.* → **mess up** (2), etc.
*4 *sl* to cause harm to (someone): [T1] *You have to know who to trust with your personal difficulties, as an insensitive adviser can screw you up and make matters worse. If you think your marriage is screwing you up, why don't you leave him?*
*5 *infml* to make (someone) nervous: [T1 (*usu. pass.*)] *There's no need to get all screwed up about your first class, the students won't eat you. Starting a new job always screws me up for the first few days. Waiting for an operation tends to screw most people up.* → **tense up**
**6 screw up one's courage/oneself** to conquer one's fears and show bravery: *The young soldier had to screw up all his courage to prevent himself from running away and being regarded as a coward. I really had to screw myself up to face the director when I knew that I was to blame.* → **muster up** (2), **pluck up** (2), **summon up** (3)

**scribble away** *v adv*
**1** to write continuously in a hasty untidy manner: [IØ + AWAY (*often continuous tenses*)] *The family were always amused that she spent so many hours scribbling away, and were surprised when she became a writer.*
*2 to waste (time) by writing hastily: [T1] *Here you've been scribbling half your life away, and nothing that you've written has ever been printed!*

***scribble down** *v adv* → **write down** (1), etc.
to record (something) by writing hastily: [T

*I scribbled down the telephone number, and now I can't read the figures!*

**scrub away** *v adv*

**1** to rub continuously with or as with a brush: [IØ + AWAY] *After scrubbing away for half an hour, I still couldn't get the mark off.*

**2** to remove (something such as a mark) with or as with a brush: [X9 + AWAY] *Don't rub too hard with your cleaning brush or you could scrub the paint away!* → **scour away**

**scrub down** *v adv*

to clean (a surface) thoroughly by rubbing hard with or as with a brush: [T1 + DOWN] *Would you like me to scrub your back down? Scrub the walls down well before painting them.* —**scrub-down** *n*

**scrub out** *v adv*

**1** to clean (a room or container) thoroughly with or as with a brush: [T1 + OUT] *I didn't hear the telephone, I was scrubbing out the bathroom. Always scrub the tins out before using them again.* → **scour out**

**2** to (cause to) be removed by rubbing with or as with a brush: [X9 + OUT] *Can you scrub out that dirty mark on the wall?* [L9 + OUT] *That oil mark has been on the cloth for so long that I doubt if it will scrub out.*

***3** *not fml* to cause (an event) not to take place: [T1] *The football game had to be scrubbed out because of the snowstorm.* → **call off** (2), **scrub round** (1)

***4** to draw a line through (writing); remove (something) so that it cannot be read and no notice will be taken of it: [T1 (*usu. pass.*)] *Scrub out that last part of the message, the wording is not very polite.* → **cross out,** etc.

**scrub round** *v prep*

**1** *not fml* to decide not to continue with (an attempt, activity, etc.): [T1 (*often simple tenses*)] *So few people came that we decided to scrub round the meeting and try again next week.* → **call off** (2), **scrub out** (3)

**2** *not fml* to disobey (a rule): [T1 (*often simple tenses*)] *There's no way we can scrub round the entrance rules, you'll have to take the examination after all.* → **get round²** (2), **skate round** (3), **slide round** (2)

**scrub up** *v adv*

(of doctors and nurses) to wash oneself thoroughly, esp. before an operation, to prevent infection: [IØ] *The doctor instructed the nurses to scrub up before the operation. Haven't you scrubbed up yet? We're nearly ready!* —**scrubbing-up** *n, adj*

**scuff up** *v adv*

*not fml* to make rough marks on the surface of (shoes), as by rubbing: [T1 + UP (*usu. pass.*)] *How ever did you get your new shoes scuffed up so soon?*

**scuffle with** *v prep*

to struggle in a fight against (someone) in a disorderly way: [IØ + *with*] *Many of the marchers were seen by television cameras scuffling with the police as they were being forced into police vehicles.*

**scurry for** *v prep*

to move quickly in the direction of (something such as a place), usu. out of fear, anxiety, etc.: [L9 + *for*] *When the forest caught fire, many of the animals could be seen scurrying for safety across the lake.*

**scuttle across** *v prep*

to cross (a space) in a quick nervous manner: [L9 + *across*] *I'm sure that was a mouse I saw scuttling across the mat.*

**scuttle away/off** *v adv*

to leave in a hurry, often secretly or guiltily, as from danger, trouble, etc.: [L9 + AWAY/OFF] *The terrorist placed the bomb on the doorstep and then scuttled off.*

**seal off** *v adv* → **block off**

to prevent (something such as an opening) from having its usual use by closing it: [X9 + OFF] *The gas pipe has been sealed off to prevent escapes. Police have sealed off the street where the gunman is hiding.*

**seal up** *v adv* → **block up** (1), **bung up** (1), **stop up** (1), **stuff up** (1)

to close (something) tightly: [X9 + UP] *Let me add a few words to the letter before you seal the envelope up. You'd better seal up that hole in the wall, it's letting the cold in.*

**seal with** *v prep*

to close (something) by means of (something): [T1 + *with* (*often pass.*)] *Messages from the king used to be sealed with wax and stamped with a ring bearing his mark. The letters S.W.A.L.K. on a letter mean "sealed with a loving kiss."*

**seam with** *v prep*

**1** to join (cloth) by sewing with (something such as thread): [T1 + *with*] *His garment was seamed with silk thread.*

**2** **be seamed with** to have many lines caused by (something): *Her face was seamed with age and sorrow.*

**search after** *v prep* → **look for** (2), **quest for, search for, seek after, seek for**

to try to gain (something that one desires such as a quality), as by inner enquiry: [IØ + *after*] *Many people spend years searching after peace of mind, often with little success.*

**search for** *v prep* → **look for** (1, 2), **quest for, search after, seek after, seek for**

to try very hard to find (something or someone), as by looking or by inner enquiry in (something): [IØ + *for*] *For over 100 years, men have been searching for gold in the hills. Many people spend years searching for peace of mind, often with little success.* [T1 + *for*] *The villagers are helping to search the woods for the missing child. I have searched my mind for a reason, but can find none.*

***search out** *v adv* → **seek out**

to find (something or someone) by looking

hard: [T1] *It took me several weeks to search out the boots that I wanted. How can we search out the right man for the job? The lawyer serached out the weaknesses in the witness's statement.*

**search through** *v prep*
to look in (a space) or among (things) trying to find something or someone: [IØ + *through* (*for*)] *I spent ten minutes searching through the drawer for the key, and it was in my bag all the time! We've searched through the records, but there is no sign of the information that you requested. Police with dogs are searching through the woods for the missing child.*

**season with** *v prep*
**1** to give (food) the taste of (something strong such as salt): [T1 + *with*] *Is this meat seasoned with onion salt? It tastes strange.*
*__2__ to make (something) more lively by adding (something): [D1] *Tom's latest book is seasoned with some amusing examples. I think he has been seasoning his story with a few inventions.*

**secede from** *v prep*
*fml* (usu. of part of a country) to stop belonging to (the nation or larger group); cease being loyal to (an organization): [IØ + *from* (*often simple tenses*)] *There are fears that Quebec may secede from Canada and become an independent nation.*

**seclude from** *v prep*
*fml* to keep (someone or oneself) apart from (a group or state): [T1 + *from* (*often pass.*)] *In many eastern countries, women are still secluded from public view. He secluded himself from civilization, to live and think among the mountains.*

***second to** *v prep*
*fml* to allow (someone) to leave his usual job and work in (another place), often for a limited time: [D1 (*usu. pass.*)] *After many years of teaching, she was seconded to the Ministry of Education to advise them on school planning. The officer was seconded to another branch of the army to lead special training courses.*

**secure against** *v prep* also **secure from**
to make (something) safe from (a danger): [T1 + *against* (*often pass.*)] *How can the town best be secured against attack? You need property to secure the money against loss.*

**seduce from** *v prep* → **entice from, tempt from**
to persuade or attract (someone) away from (something such as a duty): [X9 + *from*] *It doesn't take much to seduce me from my work: an interesting conversation, a good television show, or simply the need for rest.*

**seduce into** *v prep* → **entice into, tempt into**
to persuade or attract (someone) into (doing something wrong or foolish) by exciting his desires: [X9 + *into*] *The thief claimed that he had been seduced into a life of crime by friends who promised easy wealth. The advertisements try to seduce shoppers into buying more goods than they need.*

**see about** *v prep*
**1** to talk to (someone) about (someone, something, or doing something), as to ask advice, make an enquiry, etc.: [T1 + *about*] *You'll have to see the director about your complaint. See me about your work after class. Which nurse do I see about my sick daughter?*
*__2__ to enquire about or make arrangements about (something or someone): [T1] *I haven't had time to see about a hotel for the night yet. When are you going to see about a suitable music teacher for Jane?* [T4] *Did you see about renting a car for the weekend?* [T6] *When the snow has stopped, we'll see about how to get home. We must see about where we change trains.*
*__3__ to deal with or attend to (someone, something, or doing something): [T1 (*no pass.*)] *Excuse me, I must go and see about dinner. When are you going to see about your tax return? I'll see about that boy as soon as I get back.* [T4] *Excuse me, I must see about getting the dinner. I really will see about painting the bathroom next week.* → **look to** (3), **look towards** (3), **see to** (3)

**see across** *v adv; prep*
to take (someone) safely across (a road, etc.): [X9 + ACROSS/*across*] *The old man was employed to see the children across the busy street into the school yard. As you're not used to heavy traffic, let Jim see you across to the Post Office.*

***see after** *v prep* → **care for** (4), **look after** (2), **take of** (3)
to take care of or take the responsibility for (someone or something): [T1 (*often simple tenses*)] *Who's going to see after the visitors when they arrive? I'll see after the details of the contract, don't worry.*

**see against** *v prep*
**1** to have sight of or look at (something or someone) in front of (a background): [T1 + *against* (*usu. pass.*)] *Jewels look best seen against a dark background. Seen against the night sky, the buildings looked even taller.*
**2** to consider (usu. something) in relation to (something): [X9 + *against* (*usu. pass.*)] *Public opinion must be seen against the continuing low number of votes in local elections. The chairman's decision must be seen against the need for long talks and much enquiry.*

**see ahead** *v adv* → **look ahead**
**1** to have sight (of something) in the distance: [IØ + AHEAD] *The mist was so thick that we couldn't see ahead more than a few yards.* [T1 + AHEAD] *At last the sailors saw land ahead; their terrible voyage was nearly over.*
*__2__ to think ahead; prepare; plan for or have knowledge of the future: [IØ (*to*)] *It's difficult to make decisions about one's professional life when things change so fast and one cannot see*

*ahead very far. Imagine that you can see ahead to the year 2000; what sort of world do you think we shall be living in?*

**see around**[1] *v adv*
*not fml* to see or meet (someone) regularly; know that (someone) is usually in a particular place: [T1 + AROUND (*usu. simple tenses*)] *I don't know his name, but I've seen him around quite a lot. "I expect we shall meet again." "Yes, see you around!"*

**see around**[2] *v prep*
**1** to have sight (of something) beyond (something usu. round or angled) or in various parts of (an area): [IØ + *around* (*simple tenses*)] *These mirrors enable you to see around corners.* [T1 + *around* (*simple tenses*)] *We didn't see the car around the next building until it crashed into us. I've seen him around the neighbourhood, but I don't know his name.* → **see round**[2] (1)
**2** to take (someone) on a tour of (a place); make a tour of (a place): [X9 + *around*] *Mr Freeman will see the visitors around the factory.* [L9 + *around* (*no pass.*)] *May we see around the house? I understand that it's for sale.* → **go round**[2] (5), **look over**[2] (3), **look round**[2] (2), **see over**[2] (2), **see round**[2] (2), **show around, show over, take over**[2] (4), **take round** (2)

**see as** *v prep*
**1** to consider (something or someone) to be (something): [X9 + *as* (*often pass., simple tenses*)] *Do you see the new leader as the hope of the party? I see it as my duty to punish you. Most people see his action as possibly dangerous. Why are deaf children so often seen as stupid? Her questions were seen as interrupting the class.*
**2** to imagine or accept the possibility of (someone or something being or becoming) (something): [X9 + *as* (*simple tenses*)] *Can you really see Jackson as the new company director?*

**see back** *v adv* → **see home**
to take (someone) home; act as a companion to (someone) on a return journey: [X9 + BACK] *It's getting dark, I'll see you back to your house. Jim will see you back as far as the bus stop.*

**see beyond** *v prep*
**1** to have sight (of something or someone) further away than (something): [IØ + *beyond* (*simple tenses*)] *We couldn't see beyond the next line of hills, as they blocked the view.* [T1 + *beyond* (*simple tenses*)] *Do you see the church beyond those trees? That's the village.*
***2** to have knowledge or firm ideas about a time beyond (a certain point): [T1 (*no pass., simple tenses*)] *Sales figures are improving, but it's impossible just yet to see beyond the end of the year.* [D6] *The weathermen are unable to see beyond a few days what the weather will be like.*
***3** to understand and care about (something usu. in the near future): [T1 (*no pass., simple tenses*)] *Are you making plans for the future, or can't you see beyond your next pay packet?* [T6 (*simple tenses*)] *Some people are unable to see beyond how to get enough food for the day.* → **look beyond** (2)
**4 not be able to see beyond (the end of) one's nose** *not fml* to be blind to even the clear and simple truth: *You'll never get him to understand the risks he's running, he can't see beyond the end of his nose!*

***see fit** *v adj* → **think fit**
to decide that it is suitable (to do something): [T3 (*simple tenses*)] *The director did not see fit to call another committee meeting so soon. Didn't you see fit to close the door behind you as you came in?* [IØ (*simple tenses*)] *Feel free to make any necessary changes as you see fit.*

**see home** *v adv* → **see back**
to take (someone) back to his house; be a companion to (someone) on his journey home: [X9 + HOME] *I really should see you home, it's not safe to be out alone in this city after dark.*

**see for** *v prep*
**see for oneself** to use one's own judgment in forming an opinion, by experiencing or examining the facts directly: *I know you've warned me about taking the job, but I want to see for myself what it's like. Telling children something is useless until they can see for themselves. At last he saw for himself how to improve his performance.*

**see in**[1] *v adv*
**1** to have sight of someone or something indoors: [IØ + IN (*usu. simple tenses*)] *Close the curtains, so that no one can see in while I dress.* → **see out** (1)
**2** to show (someone) into a room or building; be with (someone) as he enters: [X9 + IN (*often simple tenses*)] *When my visitor arrives, see him in, will you?* → **see into** (2), **see out** (2), **show in**
**3** to guide (a driver) into a space: [X9 + IN (*often simple tenses*)] *The garage doors are rather narrow, you'd better let me see you in.* → **see into** (3), **see out** (3)
***4** to welcome the beginning of (the new year): [T1] *Are you going to stay up till midnight to see the new year in? I'm not sure that I want to see in another year like the last one!* → **ring in**[1] (2), etc.

**see in**[2] *v prep*
**1** to have sight (of something or someone) in (something): [T1 + *in* (*often simple tenses*)] *The face that you see in the mirror every day is not the same face that other people see on you. I could see you in the water, standing behind me. At last I saw the right kind of boots in a shop window.*
***2** *infml* to have (something) as a reason for liking (someone or something): [D1 (*no pass., often neg., simple tenses*)] *Some modern popular music is so noisy and tuneless that I wonder what the young people see in it. I won-*

*der why Mary fell in love with him: I'll never know what she sees in him.*

**3 see something/someone in a better/different/new light** to change one's opinion about something or someone, usu. for the better, often because of fresh information: *I saw her behaviour in a different light when I learned how ill she was at the time. Having gained new hope, I am trying to see life in a better light. Talks between teachers and parents are aimed at getting both to see the children in a new light.*

**see into** *v prep*

**1** to be able to have sight of something or someone within (something such as a space): [IØ + *into* (*often simple tenses*)] *I couldn't see into the room because of all the smoke. With a light to help him to see into the cave, he found wonderful treasures there, buried with the ancient king.*

**2** to bring (someone) into (a building or room): [X9 + *into*] *My secretary will see you into my office, and I'll be with you in a few minutes.* → **see in**[1] (2), **see out** (2)

**3** to guide (a driver) into (a space): [X9 + *into*] *Would you like me to see you into the garage?* → **see in**[1] (3), **see out** (3)

***4** to examine or enquire into (something): [T1] *When are you going to see into the customers' complaints? The police have promised to see into the disappearance of the jewellery.* → **enquire into, look into** (4)

***5** to understand or have knowledge of (someone, or something such as the future): [T1 (*no pass., simple tenses*)] *The old woman claims to be able to see into the future. He began to return to health when he was able to see into the causes of his trouble. I wish I had the gift of seeing into people's hearts as you do.*

***see of** *v prep*

**1** to be in (the company) of (someone), esp. in the phrs. **see much/something/a lot of**: [D1] *We don't see much of you these days, when can we get together again? They've been seeing such a lot of each other recently, do you suppose they're in love? Have you seen anything of Jim lately?*

**2 see an end of** to be present at the finish of (something, usu. unpleasant): *I can't see an end of this winter, it seems to be going on for ever. Shall we see an end of fighting in the world in our lifetime?* → **see to** (4)

**3 see the back/last of** to have no more dealings with (someone or something unpleasant or difficult): *This class has been a difficult one to teach, and I'll be glad to see the back of them.*

***see off**[1] *v adv*

**1** to be with (someone) as he begins a journey; be present to say goodbye to (someone) as he leaves: [T1b] *All the parents were at the railway station, seeing the children off to school.* → **send off** (3)

**2** to make sure that (someone) leaves a place such as one's property: [T1b] *If those boys get onto my land again, I'll see them off with a gun!*

**3** to remain unharmed until (something or someone dangerous) has ceased to be active: [T1] *They saw off three enemy attacks within three days.*

***see off**[2] *v prep*

**1** to make sure that (someone) leaves (a place such as one's property): [D1] *The farmer threatened to see the boys off his land with a gun.*

**2 see someone off the premises** to make sure that someone leaves property; get rid of someone: *See him off the premises, and make sure he never returns!*

**see out** *v adv*

**1** to have sight (of something or someone) out of doors or outside: [IØ + OUT (*of*) (*often simple tenses*)] *The window is so dirty that I can't see out.* [T1 + OUT (*often simple tenses*)] *I saw your mother out yesterday; does that mean her leg is better? You mustn't be seen out while the police are still looking for you.* → **see in**[1] (1)

**2** to take (someone) to the door as he leaves: [X9 + OUT (*of*)] *Don't trouble to see me out, I know the way. See the visitor out, would you, Mary?* → **see in**[1] (2), **see into** (2), **show out**

**3** to guide (a driver) out of a place or space: [X9 + OUT (*of*)] *The space between the gates is very narrow, could you please see me out?* → **see in**[1] (3), **see into** (3)

***4** to last until the end of (a period of time); last for (someone) until the end of a period of time: [T1 (*simple tenses*)] *Will our supplies see the winter out? Will our supplies see us out for the whole winter? I don't think Grandfather will see out another month. Let's see the rest of the year out here and then move to a new job.* → **last out** (2)

***5** to finish doing or seeing the whole of (something such as an activity or performance): [T1] *I'll see this film out now that I've started watching it, but it isn't as good as I thought it would be. The course is terrible, but I'll see it out now that I've paid for it.*

***6** to mark the end of (the old year): [T1] *At midnight we see out the old year and see in the new. I shall be glad to see this year out and make a fresh start.* → **ring in**[1] (2), etc.

**see over**[1] *v adv*

to have sight of something above the top of something: [IØ + OVER (*often simple tenses*)] *The little ones can't see over; will you lift them up?*

**see over**[2] *v prep*

**1** to have sight of something above the top of (something): [IØ + *over* (*often simple tenses*)] *The little ones can't see over the fence; please lift them up.* → **look over**[2] (1)

***2** to visit and examine (a place): [T1] *May we see over the house? I understand that it's* *for sale. Government officials must be allowed to see over the factory.* → **look round²** (2), etc.

***see red** *v adj*
*not fml* to become very angry: [IØ (*simple tenses*)] *Cruel treatment of children always makes me see red.*

***see right** *v adj*
*not fml* to provide enough for (someone): [T1b (*simple tenses*)] *This money should see you right for a week or so.*

***see round¹** *v adv* → **show around, etc.**
to visit or tour or be shown a place: [IØ] *You've expressed a great deal of interest in the new buildings; would you like to see round?*

**see round²** *v prep*
**1** to have sight (of something or someone) beyond (something usu. round or angled), or in various places within (an area): [IØ + *round* (*simple tenses*)] *The mirror enables you to see round corners.* [T1 + *round* (*simple tenses*)] *We didn't see the car round the building until it crashed into us. I've seen him round the neighbourhood but I don't know his name.* → **see around²** (1)
**2** to (cause to) visit; tour; be shown (a place): [X9 + *round*] *Mr Freeman will see the visitors round the factory.* [L9 + *round*] *May we see round the house? I understand it's for sale.* → **look round²** (2), etc.

**see through¹** *v adv*
**1** to have sight of something or someone on the other side of something such as material: [IØ + THROUGH (*simple tenses*)] *This window is so dirty that I can't see through.*
**2** to witness the whole of (a performance): [T1 + THROUGH (*usu. simple tenses*)] *I'd much rather see the film through from the beginning, so let's go to the second showing.* → **hear through, sit out** (3), **sit through** (2)
***3** *not fml* to work until (something) is finished, esp. in the phr. **see it through**: [T1b] *If you undertake to help the group with their plan, it's your responsibility to see it through however difficult it is for you. We must see this thing through now that we've started it.*
***4** *not fml* to support or help (someone), as in difficulty or for a time: [T1b (*simple tenses*)] *This money should see you through till the end of the month.*

**see through²** *v prep*
**1** to have sight of (something or someone) showing on the other side of (something such as material): [IØ + *through* (*simple tenses*)] *This window is so dirty that I can't see through it. The boys watched the football game without paying, as they could see through a hole in the fence.* [T1 + *through* (*simple tenses*)] *I know you're there, I can see you through the keyhole! We could just see the moon through the clouds. People can see your body through that thin cloth.* —**see-through** *adj* → **look through²** (1)
***2** to help (someone) to last to the end of (something such as a time or event): [D1 (*simple tenses*)] *This money should see you through the week. Where can I find enough courage to see me through this struggle?*
***3** *not fml* to understand or not be deceived by (someone or something such as a trick): [T1 (*to*) (*usu. simple tenses*)] *He's a poor liar; anyone can see through him. Children are quick to see through a teacher's manner to his true character. It's hard work to see through the words to what the statements really mean. You don't fool me: I can see through your tricks!* → **look through²** (5)

**see to** *v prep*
**1** to take (someone) to; show (someone) the way to (a place): [X9 + *to*] *Don't trouble to see me to the door, I know my way out.*
***2** to be enough to supply (usu. someone) as far as (a time or place): [D1 (*simple tenses*)] *Have we enough coffee to see us to the end of the week? There are enough oil supplies to see the world to the end of the century, but no further. The petrol already in the car should see us to the coast.*
***3** to deal with or attend to (someone, something, or doing something); care for (someone); mend (something): [T1] *Excuse me, I must go and see to the dinner. Who is seeing to the arrangements for the wedding? That knee ought to be seen to, it could get much worse. I'll see to the visitors when they arrive. The man has come to see to the television set. You must see to your spelling, it's really not good enough.* [T4] *I really will see to painting the bathroom next week.* → **look to** (3), **look towards** (3), **see about** (3)
**4 see an end to** to be present at the finish of (something, usu. unpleasant); believe that (something) will really end: *I can't see an end to this winter, it seems to be going on for ever. Shall we see an end to fighting in the world in our lifetime?* → **see of** (2)
**5 see to that/it (that...)** to make sure of something: [*usu. simple tenses*] *Don't worry about using up the rest of the food: the children will see to that! Of course the garden party was ruined, the weather saw to that! Would you see to it that the children get a hot meal after their swim? See to it that you're not late for work again!* → **look to** (5)

**see up** *v adv; prep*
**1** to have sight of (something or someone) high in (something): [IØ + UP (*simple tenses*)] *If there's light at the top you should be able to see up.* [T1 + *up* (*simple tenses*)] *I can see a bird up the chimney; how can we get it out?*
**2** to take (someone) upstairs; show (someone) the way to a place on a higher level: [X9 + UP (*to*)] *I'll see you up to the director's office on the top floor, you'll never find it on your own.*

**see with** *v prep*
**1** to use (something) for seeing (something or someone): [IØ + *with* (*simple tenses*)] *I see so much better with my new glasses!* [T1 + *with*

(*simple tenses*)] *You can see distant objects with this special instrument.*

**2 see eye to eye with** to agree with (someone); have the same opinion as (someone) about a matter: *Not all the members of the committee see eye to eye with the director about his recent decision.*

**3 see something with one's own eyes** to have direct experience of something: *It's not that I don't trust your judgment, but I do like to see the proof with my own eyes.*

**seek after** *v prep* → **look for** (2), **search after, search for, seek for**

*usu. fml, old use, or lit* to try to gain (something that one desires such as a quality), as by inner enquiry: [L9 + *after*] *Many people spend years seeking after peace of mind, often with little success. His wisdom and guidance were much sought after.*—**sought-after** *adj*

**seek for** *v prep* → **look for** (1, 2), **quest for, search after, search for, seek after**

*usu. fml, old use, or lit* to try very hard to find (something or someone), as by looking or by inner enquiry; go to (a place) hoping to find (something such as a quality): [L9 + *for*] *For over 100 years, men have sought for gold in the hills. Many people spend years seeking for peace of mind, often with little success.* [T1 + *for* (*simple tenses*)] *Other people seek the mountains for renewal of their inner lives.* —**long-sought-for, unsought-for** *adj*

**seek from** *v prep*

**1** *usu. fml, old use, or lit* to look for (something such as protection) to help against (something): [T1 + *from*] *When the snowstorm grew worse, we had to seek shelter from the cold in a hut that we found.*

**2** *usu. fml, old use, or lit* to try to get (something) from (something or someone): [T1 + *from*] *What advantages are you seeking from this change of job? What are you seeking from me? I doubt if I can help you.*

**seek into** *v prep*

*usu. fml, old use, or lit* to examine (something) in detail: [L9 + *into*] *The police have no right to seek into the lives of ordinary citizens without just cause.*

***seek out** *v adv* → **search out**

*usu. fml, old use, or lit* to find (something or someone) by looking hard: [T1] *It took me several weeks to seek out the boots that I wanted. How can we seek out a really good person for the job?*

**seep away** *v adv*

**1** (of liquid) to escape gradually, as through holes or thin material: [L9 + AWAY] *The level of the piles of snow has sunk a little since some of it has melted and seeped away into the ground.*

***2** to be gradually lost: [IØ (*often continuous tenses*)] *The international power of Britain has been seeping away ever since the loss of the Empire. Faith in the government is seeping away, and they are unlikely to win the next election.*

**seep in/through** *v adv*

**1** (of liquid) to pass through; enter something gradually: [L9 + IN/THROUGH (*often continuous tenses*)] *The roof must need mending again, the rain has been seeping in recently. Cover the surface with oil to prevent the water from seeping through.*

***2** to become gradually known or understood: [IØ] *The chairman stopped speaking to allow time for the meaning of his remark to seep through.*

***seethe with** *v prep*

**1** to be full of a crowd of (things or people): [T1 (*no pass.*)] *The town seethed with holiday visitors in bright clothes.*

**2** to be excited by (a strong usu. unpleasant feeling): [T1 (*no pass., usu. continuous tenses*)] *His face was red and he was seething with anger. Many countries in the world seethe with political unrest.*

***seize on/onto/upon** *v prep* → **fasten on** (6), **fasten onto** (2), **hook onto** (2), **latch onto** (3)

to be eager to take and use (something such as an idea): [T1 (*usu. simple tenses*)] *The children seized on the idea of camping in the mountains, and began making plans at once. You have to seize on every chance of success as it is not likely to be repeated. Jim seized on the possibility of winning the race now that two of the best runners were no longer taking part.*

***seize up** *v adv*

*not fml* (of something with working action, as machinery) to stop working suddenly, as because of a fault, a failure, or becoming stuck [IØ] *If you fail to oil the engine regularly, it could seize up without warning. His heart seized up and he dropped dead on the spot.*

***seize upon** *v prep* → SEIZE ON

**seize with** *v prep*

**1 be seized with** to have an attack of or be overcome by (something such as a feeling or illness): *She was seized with a sudden desire to laugh, at a most unsuitable moment in the performance. He has had to go to bed, seized with an attack of fever.* → **take with** (3)

**2 seize something with both hands** to take every possible advantage of (something such as a chance or offer): *If the government offers a new means of saving tax, we should seize it with both hands. Once he was given a chance to improve his position in the firm, he seized it with both hands and is now on his way to the top.*

**select as** *v prep* → **choose as, choose for, select for**

to choose (someone or something) to be (someone or something): [T1 + *as* (*usu. simple tenses*)] *The teacher selected the cleverest child as the leader of the class. Which place in the world would you select as your perfect home?*

**select for** *v prep* → **choose as, choose for, select as**
to choose (someone or something) to be part of (a group) or as being suitable for (something, esp. in the future): [T1 + *for* (*usu. simple tenses*)] *At last, after many tests, John was selected for the team. Come and help me select a good place for our camp.*

**select from** *v prep* → **choose from**
to choose (someone or something) from among (a group): [T1 + *from* (*usu. simple tenses*)] *Jane was selected from the whole class to go on the trip. This paint shop offers a wide range of colours for you to select from.*

**sell at** *v prep* → **sell for**
to be offered on sale in return for (a price); offer (goods) for sale in return for (a price) or so as to make (a profit or loss): [L9 + *at*] *These leather coats should sell at $100.* [T1 + *at*] *I don't want to sell the house at a loss. The shop is selling those boots at a 20% reduction.*

**sell down** *v prep* → **sell out** (3)
**sell someone down the river** *not fml* to treat someone in a manner unworthy of his trust in one; give someone away to the enemy; treat someone deceitfully or shamefully: *If the government is considered to have sold the voters down the river in relation to their election promises, they could easily be defeated at the next election.*

**sell for** *v prep* → **sell at**
to (cause to) be offered on sale in return for (a price, money, etc.): [L9 + *for*] *These leather coats should sell for $100.* [T1 + *for*] *The shop is selling those boots for only £10.*

***sell off** *v adv*
to sell (goods) cheaply, as to raise money quickly or at need, or to get rid of something: [T1] *The store is selling off their old television sets to make room for the latest models. When the old farmer died, his son had to sell off most of the best cattle to pay taxes on the property.*

***sell on** *v prep*
*not fml* to persuade (someone) completely of the value of (something such as an idea); give (someone) complete faith in (something): [D1 (*often pass.*)] *If you can sell the chairman on your plan, the rest of the committee will quickly agree. Is the director completely sold on the idea of combining the two firms?*

**sell oneself** *v pron*
**1** *not fml* to persuade others of one's ability: [IØ (*to*) (*usu. simple tenses*)] *If you really want to advance in the world of business, you have to know how to sell yourself (to the customers).*
**2** *not fml* to act in a dishonourable way, as for money: [IØ (*for*)] *If you agree to the plan to cheat your competitors, you will be selling yourself for a few pence. She became so poor that she was forced to sell herself for a living.*

**sell out** *v adv*
**1** to sell the whole supply (of something); make (someone) no longer able to supply goods; (of a supply) be all sold: [T1a (*of*) (*often pass.*)] *I'm sorry, all the coffee is sold out. Have you sold out all the tickets yet?* [IØ (*simple tenses*)] *I'm sorry, we have sold out of coffee. All the tickets for the last performance have sold out already!* —**sell-out** *n not fml*
**2** to sell one's whole share of a business: [IØ] *Green's in the High Street are selling out; there should be some very good prices there.* → **sell up** (1)
**3** *not fml* to give (someone) away (to an enemy); treat (someone) in a manner unworthy of his trust; take advantage of (someone); fail to keep (a promise, principle, etc.); yield deceitfully (to an enemy): [T1a] *He can't be trusted not to sell out his friends if he is in a position to make a profit. The country has sold out its principles in yielding to the demands of a small but powerful group.* [IØ (*to*)] *The officer was charged with selling out to the enemy.* —**sell-out** *n not fml* → **sell down**
**4** *AmE* to force (someone) to sell everything to pay a debt: [T1 (*often pass.*)] *Many businessmen, losing everything on the Wall Street crash, had to be sold out, and only a few were able to make a fresh start.* → **sell up** (2)

***sell short** *v adj*
**1** (in business) to sell goods, etc., that one does not yet have, hoping to obtain them cheaply in time to deliver them: [IØ] *Selling short is a risky practice in these days of rising prices and difficulties in obtaining supplies.*
**2** *not fml* to cheat (someone): [T1b (*often continuous tenses*)] *Many parents have an uneasy feeling that they are selling their children short in being unable to provide them with space to play and air fit to breathe.*
**3** *AmE not fml* to undervalue (usu. something): [T1b (*often simple tenses*)] *Take care that you don't sell his suggestion short, it could save the firm a lot of money.*

**sell to** *v prep*
to make an offer of (goods) in return for money, to (someone): [T1 + *to*] *We are thinking of selling the house to a building firm.* [L9 + *to*] *Children are easy to sell to.*

***sell up** *v adv*
**1** to sell the whole of one's share in a business; sell all one's goods or property: [IØ] *Green's in the High Street are selling up, as trade has been so bad recently. I'm thinking of selling up and leaving the country; it's impossible to make a living here.* → **sell out** (2)
**2** *BrE* to force (someone) to sell everything to pay a debt: [T1 (*often pass.*)] *In the hard times before the last war, Jim's father was sold up because he owed so much money.*
→ **sell out** (4)

**send about** *v prep* → **be about** (3), **go about²** (5), **send packing**
**send someone about his business** *not fml* to tell someone to mind his own affairs and stop annoying one; dismiss someone firmly: *If that*

*man comes here again asking for money, I'll soon send him about his business!*

**send across** *v adv; prep* → **come over**[1] (3), etc., **go across**[2], etc.
to cause (usu. someone) to pass or move across (something): [T1 + ACROSS/*across*] *I wish you hadn't sent Billy across to the Post Office on his own, that road is dangerous for a small child. During the war, our relatives in America sent food parcels across the ocean, for which we were most grateful.*

**send after** *v prep*
**1** to cause (someone or something) to follow (usu. someone): [T1 + *after*] *I'll send your clothes after you when you've found somewhere to live.*
*__2__ to send a message to (someone): [T1 (pass. rare)] *He had not been gone more than a week when his mother sent after him to ask how he was.*

**send ahead** *v adv*
**1** to send (someone or something) in advance (of someone or something): [T1 + AHEAD (*of*)] *It's best to send the heavy cases ahead so that they'll be there already when we arrive. A small party of soldiers was sent ahead of the main group to examine the enemy's positions.* → **send on**[1] (1)
*__2__ to send a message in advance of one: [IØ (to)] *Don't worry about a bed for tonight: I've sent ahead to the hotel to ask them to keep a room for us.* → **send forward** (1), **send on**[1] (2)

**send along** *v adv* → **come along** (2), etc.
*not fml* to cause (someone or something) to move to a place or towards one: [T1 + ALONG] *Send the letters along to my office when they're ready to sign, will you? When the visitors arrive, send them along straight away. I'll send the book along to you in a few days, I'd like you to read it. If you think she has such gifts as a singer, why don't you send her along, and we'll have a look at her?*

**send around** *v adv; prep* → **go round**[2] (7), **send round**[1] (1), **take round**[1] (1)
to cause (something such as a message) to be passed among different people in (a place): [X9 + AROUND/*around*] *Have you sent around the notice about the Christmas party yet? A message concerning details of the pay agreement has been sent around the factory.*

**send away** *v adv*
**1** to cause (someone) to leave: [X9 + AWAY] *I soon sent the salesman away, as I wasn't interested in what he was selling. I think it's best to send the boy away to school, he's getting no proper education here.* → **go away** (1), etc.
*__2__ to dismiss (someone such as a servant or lover): [T1] *We had to send the girl away for stealing the silver. News spread round the school that the teacher had been sent away on account of immoral behaviour. Please don't send me away, I want to be near you!* → **get away** (4), **take away** (2)

**send away with** *v adv prep*
**1** to cause (someone) to leave having (something such as a memory): [X9 + AWAY + *with*] *We like to send all our guests away with pleasant memories of their holiday.* → **bring away, come away with** (2), **go away with** (4)
**2** **send someone away with a flea in his ear** *not fml* to dismiss someone with a scolding: *I only went to ask the director's advice, but he was in a temper and sent me away with a flea in my ear!* → **send off** (6)

**send back** *v adv* → **go back** (2), etc.
to cause (something or someone) to return: [X9 + BACK (*to*)] *She went to live with her mother, but her mother sent her back to her husband. Will you send the book back to me when you've finished reading it? If you're not satisfied with the meal in this restaurant, you should send it back. For years after their quarrel, she sent his letters back unopened.*

**send back for** *v adv prep*
**1** to cause (someone) to return to get (something or someone): [X9 + BACK + *for*] *I left my bag on the table, so I sent the child back for it.*
*__2__ to request (something or someone) to be sent from the place where one started: [T1 (*to*)] *I've sent back for more supplies, we didn't bring enough. The attack was heavier than we expected, so we had to send back for some more soldiers.*

***send before** *v prep*
**1** to force (someone) to appear before (a court of law): [D1 (*often pass.*)] *Peter was sent before the court last week on a charge of drunken driving.* → **bring before** (1), etc.
**2** to offer (something such as an idea) for approval by (someone or a group in power): [D1] *Your suggestion will be sent before the board of directors at their next meeting.* → **put before** (2), etc.

**send below** *v adv* → **be below**[1] (2), **go below, take below**
to cause (someone) to go downstairs on a ship: [X9 + BELOW] *Anyone who makes too much noise will be sent below.*

***send berserk** *v adj* → **drive crazy** (2), **drive mad** (2), **drive out** (3), **go berserk, run amok**
to annoy (someone) very much: [T1b] *That continuous loud music is sending me berserk! Can't you put a stop to it?*

**send down** *v adv*
**1** to cause (someone or something) to move to a lower place: [X9 + DOWN (*to*)] *This special machine is for sending the dirty plates down to the kitchen, by pulling on a rope. The director sent me down with a message for you.* → **bring down** (1), **get down** (1), **take down** (1)
*__2__ to cause (something measurable such as a price or temperature) to fall, become lower: [T1] *Bad weather has sent the ticket sales down. This recent good crop should send the price of apples down.* → **go down**[1] (6), etc., **send up**[1] (2)

*3 *BrE* to dismiss (a student) from university, as for bad behaviour: [T1 (*from*)] *He led a wild youth and was sent down (from his university) for taking drugs.* → **go down¹** (14), etc.

*4 to cause (something) to fall: [T1] *Two of the enemy planes were sent down in flames.* → **bring down** (2), **come down** (2, 3), **get down** (4, 5), **go down¹** (5), **shoot down** (1)

***send down for** *v adv prep*
to request (something) to be sent (from a lower place): [T1 (*to*)] *We need some more envelopes from the store; would you send down for some? Perhaps we should send down to the kitchen for some more coffee.*

***send flying** *v adj*
to cause (something or someone) to fall violently; knock (someone or something) over; cause (people or things) to scatter: [T1b (*often simple tenses*)] *Running round the corner, the boy crashed into the old lady and sent her flying. On my last plane trip, the air currents were so rough that all the instruments in the little kitchen were sent flying, and the passengers had to keep their seat belts fastened for most of the journey. The enemy were sent flying by our sudden well-planned attack.*

***send for** *v prep*
**1** to ask (someone) to attend: [T1] *Send for a doctor, a man has been hurt. You sent for me, sir? Have the proper officials been sent for? Leave this house now, or I will send for the police.* → **go for** (2)

**2** to order (something such as goods) to be sent by post: [T1 (+ AWAY/OFF)] *You can send (away) for these seeds at a very cheap price. Have you sent (off) for the booklist yet?*

**send forth** *v adv*
**1** *old use* to cause (someone) to travel, as to perform a duty: [X9 + FORTH] *Men were sent forth to take Christianity to all parts of the world.* → **come over¹** (3), etc.

*2 *old use* to produce; give out (something such as leaves or light): [T1] *And the tree sent forth leaves and fruit in its season. The sun has sent forth its heat since the beginning of time.* → **bring forth** (1), **come forth, go forth** (1), **put forth** (2, 6), **put out** (4, 12), **send out** (4)

*3 *old use* to cause (an order) to reach others: [T1] *A command was sent forth that all the people should be numbered.* → **go forth** (2)

**send forward** *v adv*
**1** to cause (something such as a message or goods) to go to a place in advance: [X9 + FORWARD] *I'll have your bags sent forward to the hotel. Have any letters been sent forward yet?* → **send ahead** (2), **send on¹** (2)

*2 to send (someone's name) to be considered by people in power: [T1] *Your name has been sent forward to the committee, who will consider everyone wanting the job.* → **go forward** (5), **put forward** (3)

**send from** *v prep*
to cause (something or someone) to come from (someone, something or a place): [T1 + *from* (*usu. pass.*)] *The letter must have been sent from his home address, that's why it took so long to get here. "There was a man sent from God, whose name was John."* (The Bible)

**send in** *v adv*
**1** to cause (someone or something) to go into a place such as indoors or into a room: [X9 + IN] *Send in the next person waiting, please, nurse. If you can't play nicely out here, you'll be sent in. I thought I'd finished signing the letters when some more were sent in. A gentleman has just sent in his name, but he is not known to the family.* → **bring in** (1), **come in** (1), **get in** (2), **go in¹** (1), **take in¹** (1), **wheel in** (1)

*2 (esp. in cricket) to cause (a player) to take his turn on the field of play: [T1] *The captain decided to send in Murray to see what he could do to save the game.* → **go in¹** (5), etc. **put in** (15), **stay in¹** (4)

*3 to offer (someone or a piece of work) for competition: [T1 (*for*)] *The examination is very difficult; I don't send students in (for it) until they're fully prepared. Entries have been sent in from all over the country.*

*4 to offer (something) for consideration by people in charge: [T1 (*to*)] *All reports must be sent in by the end of the week. Have you sent your article in to the magazine yet? Be sure to send in your request in plenty of time.*

*5 to cause (soldiers) to move into a battle: [T1] *The attack is not succeeding well; we shall have to send in more men.* → **go in¹** (6)

***send in for** *v adv prep* → **enter for,** etc.
to offer (someone or a piece of work) for (competition): [D1] *The examination is very difficult; I don't send students in for it until they're fully prepared. Why don't you send your poem in for the competition?*

**send into** *v prep*
**1** to cause (someone or something) to move into (something such as an area or activity): [X9 + *into*] *I sent Jane into the town to buy the right colour of thread. With one stroke, he sent the ball into the long grass at the edge of the field. Many of our younger soldiers were sent into battle without proper preparation.*

*2 to cause (someone) to reach (a state): [D1 (*often simple tenses*)] *Jane's school report sent Father into a terrible temper.*

***send off** *v adv*
*1 to post; have delivered (mail, goods, etc.): [T1] *I'd like to send the parcel off by early post. Have you sent the boxes off yet?* → **get off¹** (8)

**2** to cause (someone) to leave; start (someone) on a journey: [T1 (*to*)] *Mary complained about getting up early in the morning to send her husband off to work, as he was a grown man who should be able to do this for himself. The best way to get rid of a troublesome politician is to send him off to a foreign country.* → **go away** (1), etc.

**3** to be with (someone) as he begins a journey; be present to say goodbye to (someone) as he leaves: [T1] *Let's all go to the airport to send Jim off!* – **send-off** *n not fml* → **see off**[1] (1)
**4** also **send someone off the field** to dismiss (a player) from the field of play, for a fault: [T1] *If you continue to break the rules you will be sent off. Two players were sent off for intentional violence against members of the opposing team.*
**5** to make (someone) lose consciousness, as in sleep: [T1 (*to*) (*often simple tenses*)] *A cup of hot milk will send you off to sleep better than anything. I need calm thoughts to send me off.* → **doze off**, etc.
**6 send someone off with a flea in his ear** *not fml* to dismiss someone with a scolding: *I only went to ask the director's advice, but he was in a bad temper, and sent me off with a flea in my ear.* → **send away with** (2)

***send on**[1] *v adv*
**1** to cause (possessions or someone) to travel in advance of oneself: [T1] *I've sent the heavy cases on so that they'll be there when we arrive. The more experienced climbers were sent on to make an advance camp ahead of the main party.* → **send ahead** (1)
**2** to send (a letter) to the receiver's next address: [T1] *If any letters come after you've left, I'll send them on.* → **send ahead** (2), **send forward** (1)
**3** to make (someone) take his place on the stage or sports field: [T1] *Who can we send on to save the game? The crowd are getting angry; send on the next act.* → **come on**[1] (4), etc.
**4** to make (someone) travel or enquire further: [T1 (*to*)] *We couldn't help him, so we had to send him on to the next town. I asked at the desk, and they sent me on to you.*

**send on**[2] *v prep* → **go on**[2] (1), **take on**[2] (2)
to cause (someone) to take part in (an activity), often elsewhere: [X9 + *on*] *If you refuse to take time off work, I must send you on holiday to make sure that you get a rest. Some of the students have been sent on a field trip to gain direct experience of the work. The company sends its best workers on courses to improve their ability and general knowledge. The easiest way to get rid of the child is to send him on a message to a neighbour's house.*

**send out** *v adv*
**1** to cause (someone) to go outside: [X9 + OUT (*of*)] *If you children don't behave properly, I will send you out (of the classroom). Why did you send the children out to play in this wet weather? The youngest child was sent out every morning to collect the bread.*
**2** to cause (someone or something) to move (to a distant place): [T1 + OUT (*to*)] *I'll send out some more money as soon as I have some. The youngest son was sent out to Canada to make his fortune. We should send some more soldiers out to help the small force under attack.* → **come over**[1] (3), etc.
***3** to cause (something such as a message or goods) to reach other people: [T1] *Have the wedding invitations been sent out yet? Head Office sends out a report of the accounts every year. You can send out a call for help over the radio. Orders are taken by mail, and the goods are sent out from a central point where they are stored.*
***4** to produce; give out (something such as leaves or light): [T1] *Look, the plant that I thought was dying is sending out new leaves! This hole in the cave wall sends out a strange noise when the wind blows in a certain direction. The fire sent out a lot of smoke but little damage was caused.* → **bring forth** (1), **come forth, go forth** (1), **put forth** (2), **put out** (4), **send forth** (2)

***send out for** *v adv prep* → **take away** (5), **take out** (7)
to order (goods such as food) to be delivered, as to one's home: [T1] *If you want a change from home cooking, we can always send out for some tasty foreign food, without having to go outside in the rain.*

**send over** *v adv* → **come over**[1] (3), etc., **send round**[1] (2), **take round**[1] (1)
to cause (someone or something) to move to a different place: [X9 + OVER (*to*)] *When the visitors arrive at your office, would you send them over (to mine)? He's not here; I just sent him over to your place, didn't you meet him? I would have gone, but they sent a message over to say that there was a delay. When are they sending the goods over?*

***send packing** *v adj* → **send about**, etc.
to dismiss (someone) roughly: [T1b] *When his mother was so rude to me in my own home, I sent her packing.*

**send round**[1] *v adv*
**1** to cause (something such as a message) to be passed among different people: [T1 + ROUND] *Have you sent round the notice about the Christmas party yet?* → **go round**[1] (7), **send around, take round**[1] (1)
**2** to cause (someone or something) to move to a different place: [X9 + ROUND (*to*)] *When the visitors arrive at your office, would you send them round (to mine)? When are they sending the goods round? They promised them last week! I'll send the boy round to collect the book.* → **send over**

**send round**[2] *v prep* → **get about**[2], etc.
to cause (something such as a message) to be passed among different people in (a place): [T1 + *round*] *Details of the pay agreement are being sent round the factory for all the workers to approve.*

**send to** *v prep*
**1** to cause (someone or something) to move to (a place or person): [T1 + *to*] *I sent a letter to my wife. Send the money to this address, and the goods will be sent to your home.* [X9 + *to*] *The shock sent the blood to his face. The boy was sent to relatives in the country for his*

*health. Sending a heavy blow to his stomach, he put his opponent on the floor.* → **come to** (1), **get to** (1), **go to** (1), **take to** (1)

**2** to cause (someone) to reach or be in (a place): [X9 + *to*] *The jewel thieves were sent to prison for two years. It's a struggle finding enough money to send the boy to college. If you don't behave properly, you'll be sent to bed without any dinner!* → **get to** (4), **go to** (15), **put to²** (7), **retire to** (4), **take to** (1)

*__3__ to cause (someone) to reach (a state): [D1] *By not telling the climber of the danger, you may have sent him to his death. This warm sun sends me to sleep.*

*__4__ to send a message to (someone or a place) (requesting usu. something): [T1 (*for*) (*no pass.*)] *When you get a place of your own, you can send to Mother for your clothes. I've sent to Head Office for a copy of the report.*

**5 send someone to Coventry** *BrE not fml* to refuse to speak to someone, as a punishment: *His fellow workers disapproved of his action, and sent him to Coventry for a week; it was very lonely with no one to talk to.*

***send under** *v adv* → **go under¹** (3)

to defeat (someone) in a competition, business, etc.: [T1b (*usu. simple tenses*)] *It was the tennis star's skill with ground strokes that sent his opponents under. Many small firms have been sent under by the poor trade resulting from the unusually severe winter conditions.*

**send up¹** *v adv*

**1** to cause (something or someone) to rise, move upwards, upstairs, etc.: [X9 + UP (*to*)] *He cleans the chimney by sending up a big brush. When the doctor arrives, send him up, will you? The people on the island are sending up smoke signals. While the main party of climbers remained at base camp, two men were sent up to the top of the mountain. Yet another spaceship has been sent up recently. This dishes are sent up to the restaurant from a kitchen on a lower floor.* → **bring up** (1), **come up** (2), **get up** (1), **go down¹** (1), **go up¹** (1), **go up to** (1), **take up** (3)

*__2__ to cause (something measurable such as a price or temperature) to rise: [T1] *The unusually severe winter in the south is sure to send up the price of oranges. That piece of cake will send your weight up. The increase in oil prices is sending up the cost of all other goods.* → **be down** (2), **be up** (7), **bring down** (4), **come down** (5), **go down¹** (6), **go up¹** (3), **go up to** (2), **put up¹** (4), **send down** (2)

*__3__ to offer (something such as a suggestion) (to people in charge): [T1 (*to*)] *We have sent your name up to Head Office, and you should hear about the job within a week. The marks have to be sent up to the office by the end of the month.*

*__4__ to destroy (something), as by fire, explosion, etc.: [T1 (*usu. simple tenses*)] *An enemy bomb has sent up the oil stores. The whole building was sent up in flames when the petrol exploded.* → **blow up** (6), **go up¹** (7)

*__5__ *infml* to send (someone) to prison: [T1 (*often simple tenses*)] *"I'm the one who sent him up."* (Gary Cooper in *High Noon*)

*__6__ *BrE infml* to make fun of (usu. a person or style): [T1] *The students used to enjoy themselves by sending up the teacher's manner of speaking. Much British humour consists in sending up the customs and leading figures of the country.* —**send-up** *n*

**send up²** *v prep*

**1** to cause (someone or something) to move up (something): [X9 + *up*] *He cleans the chimney by sending a big brush up it. When the doctor arrives, send him up the stairs, will you? Two men were sent up the mountain while the main party of climbers remained at base camp.*

**2 send someone up the wall** *infml* to annoy someone very much: *That continuous loud music sends me up the wall; turn it off, will you?* → **drive up²** (2), **go up²** (2)

**sentence to** *v prep*

**1** *law* to declare that (someone) must suffer (something) as a punishment: [T1 + *to*] *The judge sentenced the jewel thieves to two years in prison. Murderers are still sentenced to death in some parts of the world.*

*__2__ to force (someone or something) to suffer (something or doing something unpleasant): [D1 (*usu. simple tenses*)] *Many fine old houses in the city are being sentenced to destruction by the council's rebuilding plans. The old law could sentence a woman to an unbearable marriage for life, but this is now all changing. There's no need to think that you are sentenced to a lifetime of unhappiness; you can choose what kind of life you have.* [V4b (*usu. simple tenses*)] *There's no need to think you are sentenced to spending the rest of your life in a job you hate; why don't you change your work?* → **doom to**

**separate from** *v prep*

**1** to place (something or someone) apart from (someone or something else): [T1 + *from* (*usu. simple tenses*)] *No child should ever be separated from his mother by force. The action of heat will separate the salts from the solids. The garage is separated from the house by a path and a flower garden. "Nor height, nor depth, nor any other creature, shall be able to separate us from the love of God."* (The Bible) → **divide from**

*__2__ to prevent; stand between (usu. someone) and (something or doing something): [D1 (*simple tenses*)] *Only one game separates us from total victory.* [V4b (*simple tenses*)] *Only one game separates us from winning the prize.*

*__3__ to understand the difference between (something) and (something else): [D1 (*simple tenses*)] *To understand an argument, you have to be able to separate fact from opinion.*

*__4__ to leave (a group or person with whom one

has been connected): [T1 (*no pass.*)] *After twelve years, he decided to separate from the firm. To keep their slaves, the southern States had to separate from the Union. When did you separate from your husband?*

**separate into** *v prep* → **cut in, cut into** (1), **divide into**
to (cause to) split into (different parts): [IØ + *into*] *The class separated into several smaller groups to talk about the subject.* [T1 + *into* (*usu. simple tenses*)] *The action of heat will separate the chemical into a substance and oxygen.*

**separate off** *v adv* → **divide off, fence off** (1), **rail off, wall off**
to keep (something such as an area) apart: [T1 + OFF] *Separate off the top of the cream and use it to make butter. This part of the garden should be separated off for vegetable growing.*

***separate out** *v adv* → **sift out, sort out** (1)
to (cause to) become its different parts: [IØ] *The oil and water will separate out if the mixture is left standing.* [T1] *The two scientists spent a lifetime separating out the precious chemical from the substance in which it was found.*

**separate up** *v adv*
to divide (something) into shares: [T1 + UP] *The profit can be separated up between us.*

**serve as** *v prep*
**1** to perform military duties for (a time) while holding (a particular rank): [L9 + *as*] *The general had served as a private soldier in the earlier war.* [T1 + *as*] *He then served three years as an officer. When you have served your time as cook, you can be given other duties.*
***2** to fulfil the purpose of (something): [L1 + *as* (*often simple tenses*)] *His words serve as a reminder of our responsibility. Her illness certainly served as a means of getting attention. The children used an old sheet to serve as a curtain. The frozen river serves as a road throughout the bitter winters.* → **do for** (1), **serve for** (2), **use for, utilize for**

**serve for** *v prep*
**1** to perform military duties for (a time): [L9 + *for*] *He served for ten years before leaving the army.*
**2** to be suitable as a replacement for (something): [IØ + *for* (*often simple tenses*)] *This box will have to serve for a table until the furniture arrives.* → **do for** (1), **serve as** (2), **use for, utilize for**
***3** to be enough for (someone or something): [T1 (*often simple tenses*)] *This house will serve for my simple needs, but will it serve for the whole family?*

**serve in** *v prep*
to perform military or official duties as a member of (a group): [L9 + *in*] *My uncle served in the 8th Army during World War II. It will indeed be an honour to serve in your government.*

**serve on** *v prep*
**1** to be a member of; perform duties on (a group such as a committee): [L9 + *on*] *I've been asked to serve on yet another committee, and I really don't have the time.* → **sit on** (5)
**2 serve a summons/writ on** to give (someone) formal notice to appear in court or answer charges: [*often simple tenses*] *The first step is to serve a writ on him for nonpayment of debt, then he is forced to go to law.* → **serve with** (3)

**serve out** *v adv*
**1** to give a share of (something such as food) to each of several people: [T1 + OUT] *You can help to serve out the vegetables, while I cut the meat.*
***2** to return punishment to (someone) for a wrong done to oneself: [T1b (*often simple tenses*)] *We will serve them out for the trick that they played on us.* → **get even,** etc.
***3** to work or remain until one has finished (a period fixed for a duty or punishment): [T1a] *The president will serve out his full period of office and then leave owing to bad health. When the jewel thieves had served out their two years in prison, they returned to a life of crime.*

***serve right** *v adj*
to be what (someone) deserves as a result of action: [*It* + T1b (*for*) (*simple tenses, often present*)] *I'm not sorry he hit you—it serves you right for starting the fight!*

**serve round** *v adv; prep*
to give or provide shares of (something) to each of several people: [T1 + ROUND/*round*] *Would you be so kind as to help serve the drinks round (our guests)?*

**serve to** *v prep*
**1** to give or provide (something such as food) to (someone): [T1 + *to*] *When I was working in the hotel, I had to serve dinner to twenty-five people at a time.*
**2** to deliver (a tennis ball) to (one's opponent) at the start of a game: [T1 + *to*] *That was a tricky ball he served to me, there was no hope of returning it.* [IØ + *to*] *I find it awkward to serve to a left-handed player.*

**serve under** *v prep*
to follow the leadership of or be commanded by (a military or official leader): [L9 + *under*] *It was an honour for my uncle to serve under the famous general in the desert battle. He had no wish to serve under a Minister with whom he disagreed so deeply, so he left the service of the government.*

**serve up** *v adv*
**1** to provide (usu. a meal): [T1 + UP] *It's time to serve up the main course. To gain a shock effect, he served up the head of his enemy on a plate.* [IØ + UP] *Are you ready to serve up? Everyone's at table.*

*2 to provide (something): [T1] *Year after year, he served up the same old uninteresting facts, and soon he had no students left.*

**serve with** *v prep*

1 to provide (someone) with (something such as food): [T1 + *with*] *Shall I serve you with vegetables, or would you rather help yourself? Always serve the customers with whatever they want.*

2 to perform military duties together with (someone or a group): [L9 + *with*] *My uncle served with the 8th Army in the desert battle during World War II.*

3 **serve someone with a summons/writ** to give someone formal notice to appear in court or answer charges: [*often simple tenses*] *Your first step is to serve him with a writ for nonpayment of debt, and then he is forced to go to law.* → **serve on** (2)

***set about**[1] *v adv* → **go about**[1] (3), etc.

to spread (news, often bad or false): [T1] *Someone is always setting stories about that the Prince is to be married.*

***set about**[2] *v prep*

1 to start or deal with (something or doing something): [T1 (*pass. rare, often simple tenses*)] *I wanted to make a dress but I didn't know how to set about it.* [T4 (*often simple tenses*)] *How do you set about building a boat?* → **go about**[2] (2)

2 *not fml* to hit around (oneself) (with a weapon): [T1 (*no pass., often simple tenses*)] *The farmer set about him with a stick until he had driven the animals off.* → **lay about**[2] (1)

3 *not fml* to attack (someone): [T1 (*no pass., often simple tenses*)] *The three men set about him with their hands and boots.* → **lay about**[2] (2), etc., **lay into**[2], etc.

**set above** *v prep*

1 to place (something) in a position higher than (something): [X9 + *above* (*often pass.*)] *The notice was set above the door, and I didn't see it.* → **place about** (1), **put above** (1)

*2 to consider (something or someone) as being more important or worthy of attention than (something or someone else): [D1] *Mothers are well-known for setting the needs of the family above their own interests.* [V4b] *Getting out of debt must be set above buying anything new.* → **put before** (4), etc.

**set across** *v prep* → **go across**[2], etc., **pull over**[2] (1), etc.

to place or move (something or someone) into a position across (something): [X9 + *across* (*often simple tenses*)] *If you do that again, I'll set you across my knee and beat you.*

**set adrift** *v adv* → **turn adrift** (1)

to leave (someone or a boat) to float on the water, without direction: [X9 + ADRIFT] *The sailors, after quarrelling with their captain, set him adrift on the ocean in an open boat.*

**set against** *v prep*

1 to place (something or someone) next to (something or someone): [X9 + *against* (*often simple tenses*)] *I set the basket against the door, hoping that the housekeeper would find it. Set the sleeping child against his brother.* → **lay against** (1)

2 to show (something) in front of (a background): [X9 + *against* (*usu. pass.*)] *Diamonds look best when they are set against black cloth. The trees looked bare and threatening, set against the darkening sky.*

*3 to compare (something) with (something else): [D1 (*often simple tenses*)] *Setting the results against those of the last election, we can see a clear improvement.*

*4 to balance (something) against (something opposite): [D1 (*usu. simple tenses*)] *We must set the cost against the advantages of the new invention. But there is a disadvantage to be set against this fact.* → **set off** (9)

*5 to make (someone) an enemy of (someone else): [D1] *What have I ever done to set her against me? This terrible war has set neighbour against neighbour.*

6 **be set against** to oppose (something) firmly: *Mary's father was set against the marriage from the beginning.*

7 **set one's face against** to oppose (something) firmly: *Why did Mary's father set his face against her marriage? Jim seemed the perfect husband for her.*

***set ahead** *v adv*

1 to make (something) advance: [T1 (*by*)] *The warm weather has set the crops ahead by a month.* → **bring on** (3), etc.

2 to move or change (something such as an event) to an earlier time or date: [T1] *We were able to set the meeting ahead because the report was prepared earlier than we expected.* → **put off**[1] (4), etc.

3 to move the hands of (a clock or watch) to a later time: [T1] *In spring we usually set the clocks ahead one hour, to take advantage of the summer daylight.* → **go back** (7), **put ahead** (3), **put back** (8), **put forward** (6), **put on**[1] (8), **set back** (5), **set forward** (6)

**set alight** *v adj*

1 to make (something) start burning; set (something) on fire: [X9 + alight] *The insurance people think that the owner himself set the building alight, to get the money. One careless cigarette can set a whole forest alight.* → **catch alight** (1), **place to** (3), **put to**[2] (17), **set on**[2] (10), **set to**[2] (5)

*2 to cause great excitement among (a group): [T1b] *The leader's unusually cheerful speech has set the whole nation alight with hope.* → **catch alight** (2)

**set among** *v prep*

1 to place (something or someone) in the middle of (a group): [X9 + *among* (*often simple tenses*)] *Let's set some white flowers*

*among the blue ones. If you set the boy among all those tall children, he looks even shorter.* → **put among** (1)

**2 set the cat among the pigeons** *not fml* also **set the cat among the canaries** to cause trouble, esp. by saying or doing something wrong, often without thinking: *That boy who missed class yesterday was not sick, but taking a holiday; when one of the other children said this in the teacher's hearing, that really set the cat among the pigeons!* → **put among** (2)

**set apart** *v adv*

**1** to place (something or someone) separately: [X9 + APART (*from*)] *The chair was set apart from the others for the special guest. In former times, people suffering from an infectious disease were set apart until they were better, to save infecting the rest of the village.* → **put apart** (1)

***2** to save (something such as money or time): [T1] *I have a little money set apart for our holidays. We have set apart a special sum of money to help young people become professional singers. I have to set some hours apart specially for writing my paper.* → **lay aside** (4), etc.

***3** to make (someone) be or feel different (from other people): [T1 (*often pass., simple tenses*)] *Her special gifts set her apart from her fellow students. We are a people set apart from the common run of humanity. Why do I always feel set apart from any group that I'm in?*

**set aside** *v adv*

**1** to put (something) on one side, esp. for a short time: [X9 + ASIDE] *Setting the chair aside, he sat on the floor.* → **lay aside** (1), etc.

***2** to discontinue (something such as work) esp. for a time: [T1] *Tom set his new book aside for a year while he wrote some magazine articles to make a bit of money.* → **lay aside** (2), etc.

***3** to cease paying attention to (something such as a habit or feeling): [T1] *It's time to set our differences aside and work together for a common purpose. Setting aside her disappointment, she smiled and praised the winner.* → **lay aside** (3), etc.

***4** to save (usu. money or time): [T1] *I have a little money set aside for our holidays. I've set aside the whole weekend for househunting.* → **lay aside** (4), etc.

***5** to save (a supply of goods) for a customer: [T1] *Would you like me to set aside the rest of the wool for you? Then you'll be sure to match the colour.* → **lay aside** (5), etc.

***6** to choose not to notice or consider (something): [T1] *Setting aside the fact that the man has been in prison, he seems to be a suitable worker for the job. We set all other offers aside in favour of yours.* → **put aside** (6), **put by** (6)

***7** *law* to refuse to accept; declare (an agreement or decision) to be worthless: [T1 (*often simple tenses*)] *Three judges have set aside the lower court's decision on the case. He tried to have the contract set aside because conditions had changed.*

**set at** *v prep*

**1** to place (something or someone) in position next to or in front of (something): [X9 + *at*] *The worshippers set their gifts at the feet of the god. In view of the danger, we have set additional guards at the entrance to the palace.* → **put at** (1), etc.

**2** to make (usu. a horse) jump (something such as a fence): [X9 + *at* (*often simple tenses*)] *She set her horse at the first jump, but it refused, and threw her to the ground.*

**3** to fix (something measurable such as a price or temperature) at (a certain figure): [X9 + *at*] *The rate of interest is set at 11½%. The government has asked people to save power by setting their heating controls at 15° Centigrade.*

**4** to guess (something) to be (an amount, number, etc.): [X9 + *at* (*usu. pass., simple tenses*)] *His income can be set at £9000 a year.* → **place at** (2), **put as, put at** (3)

**5 set one's cap at** *not fml* to try to attract (someone of the opposite sex): *It's no use that new secretary setting her cap at the director, he's not interested in women.*

**6 set something at defiance** *fml* to refuse to obey something such as a law: *The prisoner's refusal to answer has set the court at defiance, and he must be punished.*

**7 set someone at his ease** to make someone feel comfortable, not nervous: *His behaviour did nothing to set me at my ease. Do your best to set the new students at their ease; show them the classrooms and the library, and introduce them to helpful people, so that they won't feel anxious on their first day of classes.* → **place at** (3), **put at** (4)

**8 set someone/an animal at liberty** to give someone or an animal his or its freedom: *Someone set the prisoners at liberty by cutting through the bars.* → **get free** (1), etc.

**9 set people at loggerheads/variance** *not fml* to make people quarrel: *Disagreement over the best methods of reducing prices has set the government and the trade unions at loggerheads.*

**10 set someone's/one's mind at ease/rest** to stop someone or oneself from feeling worried: *It would set my mind at rest if I knew whether we were moving south or not.*

**11 set something at naught** *fml* to consider something to be of little value: [*often pass*] *Most election promises can be set at naught. All our victories are set at naught if we lose sight of our principles.*

**12 set something at a premium** to place a high value on something such as a quality: [*often pass., simple tenses*] *Hard work and honesty are set at a premium in this school; brains without character and willingness are worthless.* → **place at** (4), **place on** (8), **put at** (5), **p[ut] on²** (35)

**set back** *v adv*
**1** to move (something) in a backward direction: [X9 + BACK] *Why don't you set your chair back a little to get a better view? Mind that dog when he sets his ears back, it's a sign that he's angry.* → **lay back, put back** (1), **put forward** (1), **set forward** (1)
**2** to place (something such as a building) in a position to the back, as away from a road: [X9 + BACK (*from*) (*usu. pass., simple tenses*)] *The house was set back (from the road) behind some trees.* → **sit back** (2), **stand back** (2)
*__3__ to delay the advance of (something); delay (someone) from advancing by (an amount of time): [T1 (*by*) (*usu. simple tenses*)] *The cost of the war has set back national development by ten years. The fire in the factory set back production by several weeks.* [D1] *The recent poor trade has set us back three months in our plans for sales development.* **—setback** *n* → **bring on** (3), etc.
*__4__ to delay (something such as an event) till a later time or date: [T1 (*usu. pass.*)] *The election will be set back to July to avoid the June holiday. The date of the wedding had to be set back a month when Jim broke his leg.* → **put off**[1] (4), etc.
*__5__ to move the hands of (a clock or watch) to show an earlier time, as standard time, or by a certain amount of time: [X9] *In the autumn we usually set the clocks back (one hour). My watch was fast so I set it back three minutes.* → **go back** (7), **put ahead** (3), **put back** (8), **put forward** (6), **put on**[1] (8), **set ahead** (3), **set forward** (6)
*__6__ *not fml* to cost (someone) (an amount): [D1 (*usu. simple tenses*)] *The boy's education has set me back more than $3000. This house will set us back a fair sum.* → **knock back** (4), **put back** (5)
**7 set the clock back** *not fml* to follow old-fashioned ideas; try to return to the past, esp. to its undesirable qualities: [*usu. simple tenses*] *Many employers would like to set the clock back to the good old days when workers were under their control, but they are too late: the world has changed.* → **put back** (10), **turn back** (5)

**set before** *v prep*
**1** to place (usu. something) in position in front of (something): [X9 + *before*] *Entering the temple, the worshippers set their gifts before the gods.* → **put at** (1), etc.
*__2__ to offer (something such as an idea) for consideration or approval by (someone or a group in power); bring (something) to the notice or attention of (someone): [D1 (*often pass.*)] *Your suggestion will be set before the board of directors at their next meeting.* → **put before** (2), etc.
*__3__ to offer (a choice or choices) to (someone): [D1] *The government has set two choices before the voter: to control wages and prices, or to suffer further increases in the cost of living.* → **put before** (3)
*__4__ to consider (something or someone) more important or worthy of attention than (something or someone else): [D1] *Mothers are well-known for setting the needs of the family before their own interests.* [V4b] *Getting out of debt must be set before buying anything new.* → **put before** (4), etc.
**5 be able to set one foot before/in front of the other** to be able to walk: [*usu. neg.*] *She was so tired that she could hardly set one foot before the other.* → **place before** (4), **put before** (6)

**set beside** *v prep*
**1** to place (something or someone) next to (something or someone): [X9 + *beside*] *Set the baby beside his mother. The bread mixture was set beside the fire to rise.*
*__2__ to compare (something or someone) with (something or someone else): [D1 (*usu. pass.*)] *Set beside the attractions of a place with continuous sunshine, living in this city seems very dull. Money seems unimportant when set beside the joys of family life. There is no one to set beside him as an actor.*

**set by**[1] *v adv*
**1** to put (something) on one side, esp. for a short time: [X9 + BY] *She was reading a book, but set it by when the telephone rang.* → **lay aside** (1), etc.
*__2__ to discontinue (something such as work) for a time: [T1b] *Tom set his new book by for a year while he wrote some magazine articles to make a bit of money.* → **lay aside** (2), etc.
*__3__ to cease paying attention to (something such as a habit or feeling): [T1b] *It's time to set our differences by and work together for a common purpose.* → **lay aside** (3), etc.
*__4__ to save (usu. money or time): [T1b] *I have a little money set by for our holidays. I set the whole afternoon by for work on the book.* → **lay aside** (4), etc.

**set by**[2] *v prep*
**1** to place (usu. something) beside (something or someone): [X9 + *by* (*often simple tenses*)] *The mother set the toy gently by the side of the sleeping child.* → **lay by**[2] (1)
**2 set great/much/little store by** to value (something) very much/little: [*usu. simple tenses*] *My grandfather set great store by his moral principles.* → **lay by**[2] (2), **lay on**[2] (10), **set on**[2] (23)
**3 set people by the ears** to start people quarrelling: *A careless mention of religious differences set the crowd by the ears.*

**set down** *v adv*
**1** to place (something, someone, or oneself) down, as on the ground, furniture, etc.: [X9 + DOWN] *The dinner guest set down his knife and fork with a look of complete satisfaction. Set the wounded soldier down carefully so as not to hurt him. Set yourself down in this comfortable chair and tell me your news.* → **lay**

**down** (1), **place down, put down** (1), **stick down** (2)

*__2__ to make (a rule); fix (something such as an arrangement): [T1 (*often simple tenses*)] *We had to set down rules for the behaviour of the members. Both firms may set down conditions for the contract. These price limits are set down by the government.* [T5 (*simple tenses*)] *The law sets down that speed limits must be obeyed.* [T6 (*often simple tenses*)] *The university sets down who shall be admitted as students.* [D5 (*simple tenses*)] *The law sets it down that speed limits must be obeyed.* → **lay down** (2)

*__3__ to land (a plane): [T1] *The pilot was able to set the damaged plane down safely in a field.* → **put down** (3)

*__4__ to allow (someone) to leave a vehicle: [T1] *The bus driver set the two men down on a lonely part of the road miles from the farm where they were to work. The second passenger asked to be set down at the church.* → **alight from,** etc., **put down**[1] (4)

*__5__ to record (something) in writing: [T1] *I have the details set down here in my notes. I have set down everything that happened, as I remember it.* → **write down** (1)

*__6__ to mark (something) on a plan, map, etc.: [T1 (*often pass.*)] *The areas of future redevelopment are set down clearly on the map.* → **lay down** (8), **map out** (1)

***set down as** *v adv prep*

**1** to record (something or someone) as (being or doing something): [T1] *You can set the telephone bill down as a business cost. I see that you're set down as a former police officer; why do you want this job? I have set myself down as a self-employed writer on the official papers. I'm sorry, I'd set you down as belonging to the other group.* → **put down as** (1)

**2** to judge (usu. someone) to be (something such as a kind of person): [X1 (*simple tenses*)] *As the man had rough hands, I set him down as a farm worker.* [X7 (*simple tenses*)] *Since she did not answer, I set her down as fearful and nervous. I am prepared to set her rudeness down as accidental if she sincerely says that she is sorry.* → **put down as** (2), etc.

***set down for** *v adv prep*

**1** to fix (a date) for (an event such as a trial); decide to hold (an event such as a trial) on (a certain day): [D1 (*usu. pass.*)] *The trial has been set down for 13 April. Monday has been set down for the next meeting.*

**2** to judge (someone) to be (a certain kind of person): [X1 (*simple tenses*)] *As the man had rough hands, I set him down for a farm worker.* → **put down as** (2), etc.

***set down to** *v adv prep* → **attribute to** (1), etc. to consider (something) to be the result of (something): [D1 (*simple tenses*)] *I set his bad temper down to his recent illness. Jim sets his success down to hard work.*

**set fair** *v adj*

**be set fair** (of the weather) to be likely to stay fine for some time: *The weatherman says it's set fair for several days, and there isn't a cloud in the sky, so we should be able to hold the garden party.*

**set for** *v prep*

**1** to decide on (something such as books or questions) to be used in (an examination) or for (students): [T1 + *for*] *Who is setting the questions for the examination? It seems foolish to set that book for such young students.*

**2** to arrange the controls of (a machine) so that it works at (a certain time): [T1 + *for*] *I've set the clock for 6.30 so that we can be up early to swim before breakfast.*

**3** to prepare (a table) for (a meal, a number of people, etc.): [T1 + *for*] *Shall I set the table for dinner? Yes, please, set it for six people.* → **lay for** (1)

**4 be (all) set for** to be completely prepared for (something): *Are you set for your new classes this year? We were all set for the journey when we heard that the plane was delayed.*

**5 set sail for** to begin a voyage to (a place): *Columbus set sail for the Far East, but discovered America instead.* → **set to**[2] (11)

**6 set the stage for** to make the necessary preparations for (something): *The government's action has unintentionally set the stage for a new election.*

**7 set a trap for: a** to make an instrument to catch (an animal): *I don't want to set a trap for that mouse in the bedroom, but it could be carrying disease so I suppose we have to get rid of it.* **b** to try to catch (someone) by a trick: *The next questioner tried to set a trap for the lady who was giving the talk, but she was too clever for him. It's useless trying to set a trap for that lawyer, he's too experienced.* → **lay for** (4)

***set forth** *v adv*

**1** *old use* to start a journey: [IØ (*on*)] *The king set forth with all his servants to visit the neighbouring ruler. Setting forth on a journey meant a great deal of preparation.* → **go away** (1), etc.

**2** *fml* to explain fully; give details of; show (something) clearly: [T1 (*in*) (*usu. pass.*)] *The details of the agreement are set forth in the contract.* → **put forward** (2), **put out** (9), **set forward** (3), **set out** (8)

**3** *old use* to show an arrangement of (something or things): [T1 (*usu. pass.*)] *The wedding gifts were set forth on a table for all the guests to admire.* → **drag out** (1), **get out** (5), **lay out** (2), **put out** (3), **set out** (5)

**set forward** *v adv*

**1** to move (something) into a position further in front: [X9 + FORWARD] *Why don't you set your chair forward, to get a better view?* → **lay back, put back** (1), **put forward** (1), **set back** (1)

*__2__ *old use* to start a journey: [IØ] *The climbers set forward towards the mountain in* *bright weather.* → **go away** (1), etc.

*__3__ to offer, suggest, or explain (an idea): [T1] *The heads of government of many countries have set forward a better system for preventing world war. The committee's plans are set forward in the report.* → **put forth** (5), **put forward** (2), **put out**[1] (9), **set forth** (2), **set out** (8)

*__4__ to make (something) advance: [T1 (*by*)] *This warm weather has set the crops forward by a month.*

*__5__ to move or change (something such as an event) to an earlier time or date: [T1] *We shall have to set the meeting forward because of the holiday next week; can you all be here on Friday?* → **put off**[1] (4), etc.

*__6__ to move the hands of (a clock or watch) to a later time: [X9] *In spring, we usually set the clocks forward one hour, to take advantage of the summer daylight. My watch was slow so I set it forward three minutes. On my journey east, I had to set my watch forward to London time.* → **go back** (7), **put ahead** (3), **put back** (8), **put forward** (6), **put on** (8), **set ahead** (3), **set back** (5)

*__set free__ *v adj* → **get free** (1), etc.

to give (someone or an animal) freedom; free (a nation): [T1b] *Someone has cut through the bars and set the prisoners free. Who will set the people free from these cruel rulers? The slaves were set free a century ago, but the black people are still not given their full human rights.*

**set in**[1] *v adv*

**1** to fix (something) by placing it carefully inside something: [X9 + IN] *Set the glass in carefully so that it fits the window frame exactly.*

*__2__ (usu. of bad weather or conditions) to begin and seem likely to continue: [IØ] *I'd like to get home before darkness sets in. An infection has set in, and his leg will have to be removed. You'd better paint the woodwork before decay sets in.* [*It* + I3] *It set in to snow at daybreak, and soon a severe storm covered the whole lakeshore area.* → **settle in**[1] (2)

*__3__ to add (something) to existing material: [T1] *The builders can set a cupboard in here, in the angles of the corner. This additional page must be set in at the correct point in the article.* —**inset, set-in** *n*

*__4__ (in sewing) to fit and sew (a sleeve) properly into the armhole of a garment: [T1] *Can you help me to set in the sleeves? I've never found that particular sewing job easy.* —**set-in** *adj*

*__5__ (in theatre) to add (scenery), usu. at an angle: [T1] *The scenery does not fill the space properly, we should set in an additional piece here. The set for the second act is smaller so we can set it in.* —**inset** *n, adj* → **jog in**

*__6__ (in printing) to place (type) in a position away from the edge of the page: [T1] *The next three sentences should be set in, as they are someone else's words.*

*__7__ (of the wind or sea) to begin to blow or flow inwards towards the shore: [IØ] *Don't leave your things on the sand, the sea is setting in and they could get wet. The wind set in strongly and we were unable to leave the shore.*

*__8__ to cause (a ship) to move towards the shore: [T1] *It's time to set the ship in, we're expected in the harbour in an hour.*

**9 the rot set in** *not fml* to worsen; become lower in standards: *This used to be a peaceful city, but the rot set in when criminals came here escaping the law in their own country, and now it is not safe to live here. Since the ablest politicians left the party, the rot has set in and the public no longer have faith in their elected representatives.*

**set in**[2] *v prep*

**1** to place (something or someone) in position in (something such as a frame): [X9 + *in*] *Be sure that the glass is set firmly in the window frame. Set the eggs gently in the basket. She set the baby in my arms and ran away.* → **fit into** (1), etc.

**2** to fix (hair) when wet into (a certain style): [T1 + *in*] *Why do you always set your hair in large waves, when it suits your face to wear it in a straight style?*

**3** to fix (something such as a jewel) in (a setting): [X9 + *in* (*often pass.*)] *The diamonds were set in gold, making the ring very dear. The delicate model was set in plastic to protect it.* → **set with**

**4** to print (words or written material) by using (a certain kind of type): [T1 + *in* (*often pass.*)] *This book is set in 10 point Times.*

**5** to provide (a scene in a story, play, etc.) with a setting in (a particular place): [X9 + *in* (*usu. pass.*)] *The scene is set in a forest surrounding a mysterious castle.* → **lay in**[2] (2)

**6 set foot in** to enter (a place): [*often simple tenses*] *The moment he sets foot in the United States he will be seized by the police.* → **set on**[2] (12)

**7 be set in one's habits/ways** to have fixed opinions: *Grandmother is getting set in her ways now that she is over 70.*

**8 set one's (own) house in order** *not fml* to arrange one's affairs properly, esp. before suggesting improvements to others: *The chairman has declared that the department must set its own house in order before he will allow any additional money to be spent on machinery and paper.* → **put in**[2] (16)

**9 set someone in mind of** to cause someone to remember (something or someone): [*simple tenses*] *That tune always sets me in mind of a fine summer day. Her voice set me in mind of her mother.* → **put in**[2] (18)

**10 set something in motion** to start something: *It may be a long time before you start feeling better, but at least we have set things in motion, and you can be sure of improvement in the long run.* → **put in**[2] (19)

**11 set something in order** to arrange something neatly: *Help me to set the dining room in order before our guests arrive. When the doctor gave him six months to live, the first thing he did was to set his affairs in order, so as not to cause trouble for his relatives.* → **be in²** (25a), **be out of** (19a), **keep in** (11), **put in²** (21)

**12 set (words) in inverted commas** esp. *BrE* to place speech marks round (a certain word or words) to show that it is spoken or special in some other way: *Why do you set the name of the shop in inverted commas whenever you write it?* → **place in** (11), **put in²** (30)

*__set loose__ *v adj* → **get free** (1), etc.
to free (someone, an animal, etc.): [T1b] *Someone has set the tigers loose from their cages and they are terrorizing the town. When we escape, shall we set the other prisoners loose?*

*__set off__ *v adv*

**1** to begin a journey: [IØ (*for, on*)] *He set off for work an hour ago, hasn't he arrived? The children were always excited to set off on a camping trip.* [I4] *Having missed the last bus, we had to set off walking.* → **go away** (1), etc.

**2** to intend (to do something): [I3 (*usu. simple tenses*)] *I set off to make the dress by myself, but in the end I had to ask for help.* → **set out** (3), **start off** (3), **start out** (3)

**3** to cause (something) to explode: [T1] *Terrorists have been setting off bombs in Underground trains. The children gathered in the garden to set the fireworks off.* → **go off¹** (5), etc.

**4** to start (something such as chemical or mechanical action) working: [T1] *This instrument sets off an effect in the atoms of this substance, which causes it to produce power that can be made into electricity. The owner accidentally set off the fire bell, and two fire engines arrived.*

**5** to start (something such as an action) happening, esp. unintentionally: [T1 (*usu. simple tenses*)] *The politician's speech set off violence in the crowd. Careless handling of international relations can set off a war.* → **spark off** (2), **touch off** (2), **trigger off** (2)

**6** *not fml* to (cause to) begin (something such as talk or laughter, or doing something): [T1 (*on*)] *If you set Father off on his favourite subject, he'll talk for hours. One amusing remark was enough to set the crowd off.* [V4b] *Don't set her off crying again, whatever you do.* [T4] *Once he sets off talking he never stops.* → **start off** (5), **start out** (4)

**7** to show (something) to advantage, as by providing a different or suitable background: [T1 (*simple tenses*)] *The black cloth sets off the jewels nicely. The blue dress sets off the colour of Mary's eyes. The fine old house was set off by its formal gardens.* → **show off** (1)

**8** to separate (something) to make it more easily seen or recognized: [T1 (*in, by*) (*usu. pass.*)] *The headwords are set off in black ink. Spoken words are set off from the rest of the sentence by speech marks.*

**9** to balance (something) (against something else): [T1 (*against*) (*simple tenses*)] *Some of your debts can be set off by other money owing to you. At least there are good restaurants in this city to set off the disadvantages of the weather. We can set off the cost of the car against the saving in taxi rides.* —**set-off** *n* —**offset** *v* → **set against** (4)

*__set on¹__ *v adv*

**1** *old use fml* to move ahead or advance, as to an attack: [IØ (*imper.*)] *The enemy is near us; now, set on!*

**2** *not fml* to encourage (someone) (to do something wrong): [T1] *I refuse to have that child to the party, he always sets the others on (to misbehave).*

**3** *BrE* to begin employing (someone): [T1] *Trade was so good that the firm was able to set on more workers.*

**set on²** *v prep*

**1** to put (usu. something) in position on top of (something): [X9 + *on* (*often simple tenses*)] *Set the plates gently on the table, they are very delicate. He set his hand on my shoulder comfortingly. She set a finger on her lips to signal silence. Setting the child on his back, he continued the long walk home.* → **lay on²** (1), **lay with** (1), **place on** (1), **put on²** (1), **stick on²** (3)

**2** to put (something) in position on (its side, end, etc.): [X9 + *on* (*often simple tenses*)] *We had to set the piano on end to get it through the doorway. A title should be printed from top to bottom so that when the book is set on its side, it can be read easily.*

*__3__ also **set onto** to cause (an animal) to attack (someone): [D1] *I'll set my dog on you if you don't leave at once!* → **sick on**

*__4__ to attack (someone): [T1 (*often simple tenses*)] *The youths set on the old man and robbed him. "She was set on by a thief in the park."* (*BBC radio news*, 9 September 1974)

**5 be set on** also **be set upon** to be determined on (something or doing something): *He seemed to be set on his aims. John is set on playing cricket for England.*

**6 set one's cards on the table** to be completely honest, esp. about one's intentions or point of view: *I see that it's time to set my cards on the table; I am interested in this affair because the woman in the case is my sister.* → **lay on²** (5), **place on** (3), **put on²** (11)

**7 set eyes on** *not fml* to see (someone or something): [*often neg., simple tenses*] *Don't ask me where Jim is, I haven't set eyes on him for weeks.* → **clap on²** (4), **lay on²** (7)

**8 set someone/something on his/its feet** to help someone or something to improve, esp. in making a good beginning: *This medicine will help to set you on your feet after your illness. This summer's good trade should set the new business on its feet.* → **put on²** (14)

**9 set a finger/hand on** *not fml* to touch or

harm (someone): [*often simple tenses*] *Don't you dare set a finger on my son! If you set a hand on me I shall send for the police!* → **lay on²** (8)

**10 set something on fire** to start something burning: *The insurance people think that the owner himself set the building on fire, to get the money. One careless cigarette can set a whole forest on fire.* → **catch alight** (1), **place to** (3), **put to²** (17), **set alight** (1), **set to²** (5)

**11 set something on foot** *not fml* to start something such as an activity: *The director wants to set changes on foot to improve the sales.*

**12 set foot on** to enter (a place): [*often simple tenses*] *The moment he sets foot on American soil he will be seized by the police.* → **set in²** (6)

**13 set one's hands on** *not fml* **a** to gain possession of (something): [*often simple tenses*] *I'd like to know where I can set my hands on the special cloth.* → **get on²** (8), **lay on²** (11), **put on²** (19b); **b** to seize (something or someone, esp. violently; harm someone): [*often simple tenses*] *The police will soon set their hands on the jewel thieves. I'd like to set my hands on the man who attacked my daughter.* → **lay on²** (11), **put on²** (19c), **get on²** (9)

**14 set one's heart/hopes on/upon** *not fml* to desire or have one's hopes depend on (someone, something, or doing something): *Many parents set their hopes on their children for the future. Don't set all your hopes on this job, you may not get it. Jim has set his heart on winning the race.* → **pin on²** (4), etc.

**15 set one's/its mark on** to make a noticeable difference to (something): [*often simple tenses*] *Years of suffering have set their mark on her face. He has set his mark on the field of scientific enquiry with this recent study.*

**16 set one's mind on** to be determined about (something or doing something): [*usu. simple tenses*] *If you set your mind on the directorship, you can get there in the end. The way to succeed in anything is to set your mind on winning.*

**17 set something on one side: a** to put something down; stop holding something; move something to a different position next to one: *She set her sewing on one side when the telephone bell rang.* → **lay aside** (1), etc.; **b** to discontinue (something such as work), esp. for a time: *Tom set his new book on one side for a year while he wrote some magazine articles and informative material.* → **lay aside** (2), etc.; **c** to disregard or cease (something such as a habit): *It's time to set our differences on one side and work together for a common purpose.* → **lay aside** (3), etc.; **d** to save (a supply of goods) for a customer: *I'll set the goods on one side until you have made a decision about whether you want them.* → **lay aside** (5), etc.

**18 set someone on a pedestal** *not fml* to admire someone too much; think someone is faultless: *It's unhealthy in marriage to set your wife on a pedestal; it is better to accept her as a human being, with faults and failings as well as good qualities.* → **knock off** (4), **put on²** (34)

**19 set a price on** to state the cost of (something): [*often simple tenses*] *What price shall we set on this painting?*

**20 set a price on someone's head** to offer a reward for seizing someone, as a criminal: [*often simple tenses*] *A price of $300 was set on the train robber's head.*

**21 set the seal on** to formalize; complete (something such as a plan): *The politician formally opened the new theatre building, so setting the seal on the group's effort to be recognized.*

**22 set one's sights on** *not fml* to want; decide to aim for (something or doing something): [*often simple tenses*] *You can tell that the new committee member has set his sights on the chairmanship. Once he has set his sights on winning, there's no stopping him.*

**23 set great/much/little store on** to value (something) very much/little, etc.: [*simple tenses*] *My grandfather set great store on his moral principles.* → **lay by²** (2), **lay on²** (10), **set by²** (2)

**24 set someone's teeth on edge** to give someone a nervous, unpleasant feeling, as with a sudden sharp noise or taste: [*often simple tenses*] *The noise of that chalk on the blackboard sets my teeth on edge.*

**25 set the Thames on fire** *BrE not fml* to do something unusual and wonderful; have an important effect: [*usu. neg.*] *Tom's new book won't set the Thames on fire, but it should influence thinking people in important positions.*

**26 set someone on his way** to go with someone as he leaves, esp. to make sure that he is on the right road: *You're not familiar with this part of the town, I'd better set you on your way until you reach streets that you know.*

***set onto** *v prep* → **SET ON** (3)

***set out** *v adv*

**1** to begin a journey: [I∅ (*for, on*)] *He set out for work an hour ago, hasn't he arrived? The children were always excited to set out on a camping trip.* [T4] *All the villagers have set out looking for the missing child.* → **go away** (1), etc.

**2** to begin any activity such as a profession: [L9 (*as, in, on*) (*often simple tenses*)] *Her uncle helped her to set out as a professional singer. Setting out in business is no easy job. It's twenty years since the scientist set out on his life's work of discovering the valuable chemical.* —**outset, set-out** *n* → **start out** (5)

**3** to intend (to do something): [I3 (*usu. simple tenses*)] *I set out to make the dress by myself, but in the end I had to ask for help. This is not what I set out to learn when I took this course.* → **set off** (2), **start off** (3), **start out** (3)

**4** to spread (something), as to view: [T1

(*often pass.*)] *The scenery was set out before the travellers when they reached the top of the hill. The goods for sale were set out attractively. The wedding gifts are set out in the next room for guests to admire.* → **lay out** (1)

**5** to spread (clothes, food, etc.) for use: [T1 (*often simple tenses*)] *I'll leave a meal set out in the kitchen. Please set out my best suit for the governors' meeting.* → **drag out** (1), **get out** (5), **lay out** (2), **put out** (3), **set forth** (3)

**6** to arrange the plan or appearance of (something): [T1] *If you set your answers out neatly, the examiners will be influenced in your favour. The garden was set out in formal style.* —**set-out** *adj* → **lay out** (3)

**7** to put (young plants) into the ground separately for growing outside: [T1] *The young plants should be set out three inches apart.*

**8** to make (reasons, ideas, etc.) known or clear: [T1] *The committee's plans are set out in the report. Be sure to set out the points of your argument carefully. Set out your reasons for wanting a rise in pay.* → **put forward** (2), **put out** (9), **set forth** (2), **set forward** (3)

**9** to put (oneself) to some trouble; give (oneself) an aim (to do something): [V3 (*often simple tenses*)] *Mother was always willing to set herself out to help people.* → **put out** (15), etc.

**10** to ornament (oneself): [X9] *She set herself out in her best dress for the party.*

**11 set out one's stall** *BrE not fml* to show one's abilities: *What matters when you're asking for a job is not so much what you know as how well you can set out your stall.*

**set over** *v prep*

**1** to place (someone or something) in a position across or on top of (something or someone): [X9 + *over* (*often simple tenses*)] *If you do that again, I'll set you over my knee and beat you.* → **pull over**[2] (1), etc.

*__2__ to give (someone) command over (usu. someone): [D1] *I've not been happy in the company since a new director was set over me.*

***set right** *v adj*

**1** to mend (something): [T1b] *The washing machine broke down again, so I called the repairman to see if he could set it right.* → **put right** (1)

**2** to correct (something wrong): [T1b] *There were some mistaken notes in that last passage; let's set them right now, before the performance.* → **put right** (2), **put straight** (2), **set straight** (2)

**3** to correct (someone who is misinformed): [T1b] *The firm sent me an incorrect bill, but I soon set them right. If I make a mistake when I read out the results, please set me right.* → **put right** (3), **put straight** (3), **set straight** (3)

**4** to make (someone) feel better: [T1b] *This medicine will quickly set you right after your illness.*

***set straight** *v adj*

**1** to tidy (something such as a room): [T1b] *I must set the living room straight before the visitors arrive.* → **put straight** (1)

**2** to correct (something wrong): [T1b] *There were some mistaken notes in that last passage; let's set them straight now, before the performance. We must set the facts straight so that he isn't charged unfairly.* → **put right** (2), **put straight** (2), **set right** (3)

**3** to correct (someone who is misinformed): [T1b] *She said my name wrongly so I set her straight. The firm sent me an incorrect bill, but I soon set them straight.* → **put right** (3), **put straight** (3), **set right** (3)

***set to**[1] *v adv* → **fall to**[1] (2)

**1** *not fml* to begin working hard: [IØ (*often simple tenses*)] *Find a spade and set to, there's a lot of work to do in the garden.*

**2** *not fml* to begin eating eagerly: [IØ (*often simple tenses*)] *When the children saw the table full of party food, they set to with a will and soon ate it all.*

**3** *not fml* (of two people) to begin fighting or quarrelling: [IØ (*often simple tenses*)] *The two brothers set to and fought bitterly.* —**set-to** *n*

**set to**[2] *v prep*

**1** to place (something) next to (something); join or touch (something) with (something): [X9 + *to* (*often simple tenses*)] *She set a finger to her lips to signal silence. He set the whip to his horse to make it go faster.* → **place to** (1), **put to**[2] (1), **touch to** (1)

*__2__ to turn to face (someone) in a square dance: [T1 (*no pass., usu. simple tenses*)] *Se to your partners, set to your corners.*

**3 set the axe to: a** to cut down (a tree): *We ha better set the axe to that old apple tree, it's get ting dangerous.* **b** to put an end to (somethin such as a plan): *The opposition has set the ax to the government's plans for increasing taxes.*

**4 set a (good/bad) example to** to show (some one) the (right/wrong) way to do something *His brave action set an example to the whol army. I expect you to set a good example t the younger children.*

**5 set fire/light/a match to** to start (something burning: *Setting light to the letter, he made he watch it burn.* → **catch alight** (1), **place to** (3 **put to**[2] (17), **set alight** (1), **set on**[2] (10)

**6 set one's hand to** to begin to use effort o or start working at (something): [*often simpl tenses*] *I thought it was time to set my hand t some serious study.*

**7 set measures to** to limit (something): *W have to set measures to our spending if we a to save for our old age.*

**8 set one's mind to** to work hard at; give s rious attention to (something): *If you set yo mind to your work instead of being lazy, yc might see some results.* → **put to**[2] (18)

**9 set to music** to write a tune to fit (certa words): *This poem has been set to music many different musicians.* → **put to**[2] (2)

**10 set something to rights** to correct something wrong; make something proper, esp. in a moral sense: *Our native people have often been treated as second-class citizens; this is a state of affairs that must clearly be set to rights. The only way to set this injustice to rights is to free them from prison.* → **put to²** (24)
**11 set sail to** to begin a voyage to (a place): *The ship sets sail to London tomorrow morning.* → **set for** (5)
**12 set one's shoulder to the wheel** *not fml* to put effort into one's activity: *If we all set our shoulders to the wheel, we can bring the nation out of its present troubles.* → **put to²** (26)
**13 set to work on** to start (something) with keenness or effort: *As soon as one performance is over, we set to work on the next. It didn't take the children long to set to work on all that party food.* → **get to** (16), **go to** (41)
**14 set someone to work** to make someone start working: *The men were set to work building a bridge.*

**set up** *v adv*
**1** to build; raise (something) into a fixed position: [T1] *Do you know how to set up a tent? The machinery has been set up ready for the broadcast.* → **go up¹** (6), **put up¹** (2)
**2** to start (something such as an organization): [T1] *They needed the money to set up a special school for gifted children. That new doctor has set up his practice in the office next door. A special committee has been set up to examine the details of the suggestion.* —**set-up** *n*
**3** to prepare or organize (something): [T1] *All the arrangements have been set up for the newspapermen to meet the Queen.* —**set-up** *n*
**4** (usu. in sport) to reach or establish (a new record): [T1a] *The young swimmer has set up a new fast time for the backstroke.*
**5** (in printing) to arrange (something such as type or a book) in order: [T1] *You can set up the type by hand or by machine. We can't change any wording once the article is set up.*
**6** to place (drinks or glasses) ready: [T1 (*for*)] *Will you set up the drinks while I look after the party food?*
**7** to cause (pain or infection): [T1a] *This wet weather sets up the ache in my old wound.*
**8** to express (a loud noise): [T1a] *The crowd set up a shout as the winner neared the post.*
**9** *not fml* to make (someone) feel better: [T1b (*often simple tenses*)] *You need a holiday to set you up again after all that hard work.*
**10** to (cause to) start in business or in some other activity, as by giving money or other help; provide (someone or a group) with something needed: [T1 (*as, in, with*)] *He gave his son some capital to set him up. His father set him up in the furniture trade. We had to set him up with a large sum of money before the firm would take him. It will take a lot of work by the party to set up the young politician.* [L9 (*as, in*)] *It takes money to set up as a lawyer.*
**11** to claim (oneself) to be (a certain kind of person): [X1 (*simple tenses*)] *He doesn't set himself up to be an experienced painter, but his work is pleasing to the eye.*
**12** *not fml* to cause (someone) to receive (something such as blame): [T1b (*for*) (*usu. simple tenses*)] *The thief tried to set his companion up for punishment, but he too was caught and tried. I'm not to blame; I've been set up.*
**13** (in theatre) to put (scenery) into position:
[T1] *We shall need help in setting up the scenery for the second act.* [IØ] *Have the stage workers set up yet?*
**14** *naut* to tighten (ropes): [T1] *Set up those ropes there, the sail is too loose!*
**15 be well set up: a** to have a strong body: *He was not a tall man, but seemed well set up.* —**well-set-up** *adj*; **b** to be well supplied with money: *You're set up for life once you've written a book like that.*
**16 set up home/house** to start one's own home: *Some people have the ability to set up home wherever they happen to find themselves. It's time I left home and set up house for myself. Jim and Mary threatened to set up house together if Mary's father continued to refuse his permission for their marriage.*
**17 set up shop** to start any kind of business: *It takes years to get a law degree, and even after you've set up shop it is a long time before you are making a good income.* → **shut up** (5)

***set up against** *v adv prep*
**1** to raise (opposition) against (someone or something): [D1] *Too much opposition was set up against the government's plan to control wages and prices, so that they had to cease it.*
**2 set oneself up against** to decide to go into competition against (someone or something): *If you set yourself up against an international company of that size, you can expect failure.*

***set up as** *v adv prep*
**1** to (cause to) start in business as (a kind of professional worker): [D1] *His father lent him some money to set him up as a shoemaker.* [T1] *It takes money to set up as a lawyer.*
**2** also **set up for** to claim (oneself) to be (a certain kind of person): [D1 (*usu. simple tenses*)] *He doesn't set himself up as an experienced painter, but his work is pleasing to the eye.* [T1 (*no pass., usu. simple tenses*)] *He sets up as a leader in the scientific field, but many other scientists disagree with him.*

***set up in** *v adv prep*
to (cause to) start in (a trade): [D1] *His father set him up in the furniture trade, by providing enough capital to buy the goods to sell.* [T1] *How much money does it take to set up in business on one's own?*

**set up with** *v adv prep*
to provide (someone or a group) with (something needed): [D1] *The new library can set*

*me up with enough reading matter for a month at a time. The government usually sets a new school up with supplies of books and paper.*

**set upon** *v prep* → **SET ON** (5, 14)

**set with** *v prep* → **set in** (3)

to ornament (something) with (things such as jewels): [X9 + *with* (*usu. pass.*)] *Her crown is set with precious jewels, each telling part of the history of the kings and queens of England. The sky was set with countless stars.*

**settle down** *v adv*

**1** (of a loose substance) to (cause to) fall to the bottom of a container or onto a surface: [IØ + DOWN] *The contents of the packet may settle down in travelling.* [T1 + DOWN] *Shaking will settle the powder down.* → **shake down** (1)

**2** to (cause to) sit or lie comfortably, as on a soft surface: [IØ + DOWN] *I love to settle down in a deep armchair with a good book.* [T1 + DOWN] *Settling himself down in his favourite chair, he lit his pipe.*

**3** (of a bird) to land and take a firm position: [IØ + DOWN] *The bird landed on the branch then settled down and folded its wings.*

**4** (of a ship) to sink: [IØ + DOWN] *The damaged ship leaned over and slowly settled down on the ocean floor.*

***5** to (cause to) become used to living (in a place); make a home: [IØ (*in*)] *How long did it take you to settle down in this country?* [T1 (*in*)] *The organization aims to settle newcomers down in the city.* → **settle in**[1] (1), **shake down** (2)

***6** to (cause to) live in a regular way, as in marriage or work; behave in a responsible manner: [IØ] *Isn't it time that Jim got married and settled down? You'll soon settle down after a few days on the job.* [T1b] *Having a baby often settles a young man and woman down.*

***7** to (cause to) become calm: [IØ] *The marriage began in a stormy fashion, but soon settled down. I can't seem to settle down today; something must be worrying me. Has that noisy class settled down yet?* [T1] *Please go upstairs and settle the children down for me, they're restless again and won't sleep. That class needs a strong teacher to settle them down.*

***8** to cease to be active: [IØ] *When all the excitement had settled down, it was clear that there had been no real cause for anxiety. Wait till the police hunt has settled down and then make your escape. The long struggle between the unions and the government may settle down into an uneasy peace.* → **die down** (2)

***9** to begin giving one's whole attention, as to work: [IØ] *I must settle down this morning and do the cleaning.*

***settle down to** *v adv prep*

to give one's whole attention to (something such as work, or doing something): [T1] *You can't interrupt the committee once they've settled down to their meeting. The guests have already settled down to dinner.* [T4] *I really must settle down to finishing the book, it's now urgent.*

***settle for** *v prep*

to accept (something or doing something less than one had hoped): [T1 (*usu. simple tenses*)] *Although he was jumping so well, he failed to win the first prize and had to settle for the second.* [T4 (*usu. simple tenses*)] *The politician's wife has found it difficult to settle for playing a supporting part instead of living her own life. Many women refuse to settle for staying at home. If you can't gain happiness, you may have to settle for just existing.*

***settle in**[1] *v adv*

**1** to (cause to) become used to a new home or job: [IØ (*to*)] *When we've settled in properly, we'll invite all our friends to a housewarming party.* [T1] *Experienced workers were asked to settle their new girls in, so that they would be working well quite soon after starting.* → **settle down** (5), **shake down** (2)

**2** (usu. of bad weather or conditions) to begin and seem likely to continue: [IØ] *Rain settled in shortly before midday and lasted all afternoon.* [*It* + I3] *It settled in to snow soon after daybreak, and a severe storm covered the whole lakeshore area.* → **set in**[1] (2)

**settle in**[2] *v prep*

**1** to place (something, someone, or oneself) firmly in (something): [T1 + *in*] *Once he settled his body in the comfortable bed, he was soon asleep. It's so nice to sit here and settle my feet in the sand. Settling himself in the chair, he began to address the meeting.*

**2** to (cause to) start living in (a place): [IØ + *in*] *My family settled in this city over a century ago.* [T1 + *in*] *The people who had escaped from the war were settled in a special camp.*

**3** to (cause to) become used to a new home job etc.: [IØ + *in*] *How long did it take you to settle in your new home?* [T1 + *in*] *Let me get the children settled in their new school first and then I'll look for a job.*

**settle on/upon** *v prep*

**1** to land on (a surface) and take a firm position there: [IØ + *on/upon*] *The bird settled on the branch and folded its wings. Look at the dust that has settled on the furniture while we've been away!*

***2** to decide on (something or doing something): [T1 (*often simple tenses*)] *At last Mar settled on blue paint for the bedroom.* [T (*often simple tenses*)] *Have you settled on spending your holiday at home?* [T6 (*often simple tenses*)] *The children could not settle o where to put the tent.* → **agree on** (2), **decid against** (1), **decide on, determine on**

***3** to give (money or property) formally (someone): [D1] *The old lady settled a sma* *fortune on the young man who had helped her.*

**settle to** *v prep*

**1** (of small bits of solid matter such as powder) to fall after a time to (the bottom of a container): [IØ + *to*] *The heavier parts of the grain will settle to the bottom.*

*__2__ to begin working hard at (work): [T1 (*no pass.*)] *Isn't it time you settled to work on your paper? It will have to be finished by next week.* → **settle down to**

***settle up** *v adv* → **square up** (2)

to pay a debt such as a bill (to someone): [IØ (*with*)] *Give me a minute to settle up, and I'll meet you outside the hotel. I'd like to settle up with all the tradesmen before we leave town.*

**settle upon** *v prep* → SETTLE ON

**settle with** *v prep*

**1** to finish (a matter such as a quarrel) with (someone): [T1 + *with*] *I have an old quarrel to settle with her before we can ever be friends again.*

*__2__ to finish paying (someone): [T1] *I would feel better if I settled with all the people we owe money to. I should be able to settle with you at the end of the month.* → **square with** (1)

*__3__ to deal with (someone) by fighting: [T1] *I'd like to settle with the man who attacked my daughter!*

**sew up** *v adv*

**1** to close (a space in cloth) with needle and thread: [T1 + UP] *Can you sew up this tear in my coat?*

*__2__ *infml* to complete (an arrangement) successfully; make sure of (something): [T1 (*usu. pass.*)] *The contract was all sewn up before the offer was even advertised. I want to sew up as many votes in the election as possible.* → **lock up** (7)

**shack up** *v adv*

*infml* to live together with someone, usu. of the opposite sex: [IØ (TOGETHER, *with*)] *They don't intend to get married, but they've been shacking up together for a year now. I'll shack up with my boyfriend whether my parents like it or not—it's my own life!*

**shackle with** *v prep*

**1** to limit the movement of (someone or an animal) by means of (something such as a chain): [T1 + *with*] *In the old days, the slaves used to be shackled with heavy metal chains to prevent them from running away.*

*__2__ *not fml* to give (someone or oneself) a heavy load of (something such as responsibility); limit (someone) by means of (something): [D1 (*often pass.*)] *Don't shackle yourself with property until you are sure where you're going to live. How can the state of the nation improve if firms are shackled with stupid rules that prevent them from increasing trade?*

**shade from** *v prep*

**1** to provide shelter for (something or someone) from (usu. heat or light): [T1 + *from* (*often pass.*)] *The house is shaded from the midday heat by those tall trees.* → **protect against,** etc.

**2** to change gradually from (something such as a colour) (to something else): [L9 + *from*] *As the sun set, the sky shaded from blue to pink.*

***shade in** *v adv*

to make lines with a pencil in (a shape) on (a surface): [IØ] *Now that you've drawn the shape completely, start shading in carefully.* [T1] *If you shade in one side of your drawing, the shape will look solid.*

**shade into** *v prep*

to change gradually into (something else such as another colour): [L9 + *into*] *As the autumn passed, the leaves shaded into gold and red. The colour of the sky shaded off into wonderful pinks and greens.*

**shade with** *v prep*

to provide (something or someone) with shelter from heat or light by means of (something): [T1 + *with*] *Shading his eyes with his hand, he looked far out to sea. If we build the house facing south, we ought to shade it with some tall trees.*

**shaft into** *v prep* → **trick into,** etc.

*AmE sl* to persuade (someone) into (usu. doing something) by a deceitful trick: [X9 + *into*] *I've been shafted into signing for something I don't want!*

**shag out** *v adv* → **tire out,** etc.

**be shagged out** *sl* to be very tired: *I'm shagged out after all that work.*

**shake by** *v prep* → **shake with** (2)

**shake someone by the hand** to greet or agree with someone by shaking his hand: *I'm honoured to shake you by the hand.*

**shake down** *v adv*

**1** to (cause to) fall, as to the ground or the bottom of a container, by shaking: [L9 + DOWN (*often simple tenses*)] *The contents of the packet may shake down in travelling.* [X9 + DOWN] *You don't have to climb the tree; it may be possible to shake the apples down.* → **settle down** (1)

*__2__ *BrE not fml* to become accustomed to new conditions of life or work: [IØ] *You'll soon shake down in your new job.* —**shakedown** *adj* → **settle down** (5), **settle in**[1] (1)

*__3__ *not fml* to make a rough bed for the night: [IØ] *Don't worry about me, I can shake down anywhere.* —**shakedown** *n*

*__4__ *AmE infml* to obtain money from (someone) by force, threat, etc.: [T1] *This looks like a good neighbourhood; we can shake down every small shopkeepeer in the street for at least $100.* —**shakedown** *n*

*__5__ *not fml* to test (something such as a ship) under real conditions: [T1] *Next week we should be able to shake down the new ship.* —**shakedown** *n, adj*

*6 esp. *AmE infml* to search (something) thoroughly: [T1] *The police had to shake down every building in the street before they found the gunman.* —**shakedown** *n*

**shake from** *v prep* → **SHAKE OUT OF** (1)

**shake off¹** *v adv*

**1** to remove (something) by shaking: [X9 + OFF] *The horse moved its tail to shake off the flies. Angrily, she shook off his hand. He stamped his feet to shake off the snow from his boots.* → **cast off** (1), **chuck off** (1), **fling off** (1), **throw off¹** (1), **toss off** (1)

*2 to escape from (someone who is chasing one): [T1] *After a three-mile chase through the woods, he was able to shake off the police.* → **chuck off** (2), **fling off** (2), **throw off¹** (3)

*3 to get rid of or free oneself from (trouble, illness, etc.): [T1 (*often simple tenses*)] *I can't seem to shake off this fever, I've had it all winter. How am I to shake off a way of thinking that I have had for thirty years?* → **fling off** (3), etc.

**shake off²** *v prep*

**1** to remove (something or someone) from (usu. something) by shaking: [X9 + *off*] *He stamped his feet to shake the snow off his boots. With a violent movement, he shook his attacker off his back.* → **throw off²** (1)

**2 shake the dust of a place off one's feet** *not fml* to leave an unpleasant place thankfully: [*often simple tenses*] *As the boy left school for the last time, he said how glad he was to shake the dust of that place off his feet.*

**shake out** *v adv*

**1** to remove (something) by shaking: [X9 + OUT (*of*)] *Turning his trousers upside down, she shook out a lot of coins. "What are you doing with that coat?" "I'm trying to shake the dust out (of it)."*

*2 to empty (something) by shaking: [T1] *Don't forget to shake the pockets out before you take your coat to the cleaner's.*

*3 to spread (something) by shaking or holding it to the wind: [T1] *It's time to shake out the flag. If you shake the sheets out, they will lie flatter.*

*4 *mil* to spread out so as to be less easy to hit: [IØ (*often simple tenses*)] *Tell the men to shake out as they cross the field.*

*5 *not fml* to reorganize (something) thoroughly: [T1 (*often pass.*)] *The committee needs to be shaken out to get rid of some of the older members.* —**shake-out** *n* → **shake up** (5)

**shake out of** *v adv prep*

**1** also **shake from** to remove (something) from (a container) by shaking: [X9 + OUT + *of*] *Wait a minute, I want to shake some of this water out of my boots.*

*2 to change (someone) from (a way of thinking) with a shock: [D1 (*often simple tenses*)] *Violent exercise might help to shake him out of his feelings of self-pity. She needs a strong adviser to shake her out of her usual way of thinking.*

**shake up** *v adv*

**1** to mix (something such as liquid) by shaking; shake (a bottle) to mix its contents: [T1 + UP] *Shake up the medicine before drinking it. Shake up the bottle well before drinking the medicine.*

**2** to make (a cushion or pillow) fat and comfortable by shaking: [T1 + UP] *Mother ran round the room shaking up all the cushions when the doorbell rang.* → **fluff up, plump up**

**3** to give (someone) a bad shock: [T1 + UP (*usu. simple tenses*)] *The bad news shook me up. No one was hurt, but many of the passengers were severely shaken up by the accident.* —**shake-up** *n* —**shook-up** *adj not fml*

*4 *not fml* to shock (someone) into activity: [T1] *That lazy boy needs shaking up and being made to think for himself.* —**shake-up** *n*

*5 *not fml* to reorganize (something) thoroughly: [T1] *That government department needs shaking up, it has not been doing its job properly.* —**shake-up, shaking-up** *n* → **shake out** (5)

**shake with** *v prep*

**1** to move the body in very quick waves caused by (cold or a strong feeling): [IØ + *with*] *The children waited outside the school, shaking with cold. The prisoner shook with fear as he faced the court. Her hands were shaking with nervousness as she admitted her fault to the group.* → **quake with, quiver with, shiver with, tremble with**

**2 shake (hands) with** to greet or agree with (someone) by shaking hands: *Children quickly learn to shake hands with someone to whom they are introduced. "First, Marcus Brutus, will I shake with you."* (Shakespeare, *Julius Caesar*) → **shake by**

**shame into** *v prep*

to force (someone) into (an action or doing something) by making him feel guilty: [X9 + *into*] *It did not take long to shame the boy into a change of behaviour. It did not take long to shame the boy into changing his behaviour.*

**shame out of** *v adv prep*

to prevent (someone) from (an action or doing something) by making him feel guilty: [X9 + OUT + *of*] *How can we shame the boy out of such unacceptable behaviour? How can we shame the boy out of beating his little sister?*

**shape into** *v prep*

to form (material or ideas) into (a particular shape or form): [T1 + *into*] *The children enjoyed shaping the snow into figures of people and animals. It's difficult to know how best to shape these ideas into an article.*

**shape to** *v prep*

**1** to fit (clothing, covering, etc.) closely to (something such as part of the body): [T1 + *to* (*often pass.*)] *The fashion at the time was for garments to be shaped to the upper part of*

*the body. The style that suits her best is to have her hair shaped to her head.*
**2** to make (something) fit (something) closely: [T1 + *to* (*usu. pass.*)] *The educational system should be shaped to the needs of the children, not to politicians' ideas.*

*** shape up** *v adv*
*not fml* to show effort to improve or advance; prove one's ability: [L9 (*usu. continuous tenses*)] *The young soldiers who arrived last month are shaping up nicely now. How is the new director shaping up? You'd better shape up, young man, or expect to be punished!*

*** shape up to** *v adv prep* → **face up to, square up to**
*not fml* to face (something difficult) with courage and determination: [T1] *It will not be easy for you to change your whole way of thinking, but I believe that you have the strength to shape up to it.*

**share among** *v prep* → **divide among**
to give a part of (something) to each of (several people): [X9 + *among*] *Share the cake equally among all the children. The different responsibilities are shared among the committee members.*

**share between** *v prep* → **divide between** (1)
to give an equal part of (something) to each of (a number of people): [X9 + *between*] *Share the money equally between your two brothers. The class duties are shared between all the teachers.*

*** share in** *v prep*
**1** to have part of or take part in (something): [T1] *How many people are to share in the profits? All the members of the department share in the use of the copying machine. Newspapers help us to share in the events of the outside world.*
**2** to sympathize with (a feeling): [T1 (*simple tenses*)] *All your neighbours share in your sorrow at the loss of your son.*

**share out** *v adv* → **divide out**
to give part of (something) to each of an unstated number of people: [X9 + OUT (*among*)] *How shall we share out the money that we have collected?* —**share-out** *n*

**share with** *v prep*
**1** to give a part of (something) to (someone else): [X9 + *with*] *I'll share my apple with you, if you'll give me half of your cake. It was generous of the eldest son to share the property with his brothers.* [T1 + *with*] *I was lucky not to have to share my office with another teacher.* → **divide with**
**2** to tell (something such as one's feelings) to (someone else): [T1 + *with*] *Have you any experiences that you would like to share with the group? It helps to share your sorrow with someone else.*

**shave off** *v adv* also **shave away**
to remove (a thin covering, esp. hair) with something sharp: [T1 + OFF] *Please don't shave off your beard without warning me, I'm so used to your face with it. Some people entering religious groups have to shave their hair off as proof of their sincerity. I was just able to get the car into the garage, but I'm afraid I shaved off some of the paint from the door.*

**shear away** *v adv* → **SHEAR OFF**

**shear of** *v prep*
**be shorn of** to have nothing left of (something); have (something) taken away: *Shorn of his costly clothes and jewels, the king looked like any ordinary person. The system must be shorn of unnecessary details if it is to work without costing too much. The native people have been unjustly shorn of their rights to their ancient lands.*

**shear off** *v adv* also **shear away**
to cut (something) off with or as with scissors; to come off, as if cut by a blade: [T1 + OFF] *Every spring the sheep farmers shear off the sheep's wool and sell it. When all the wool has been shorn off it can be sold. If I make a mistake at the bottom of a page, I can shear off the edge of the paper.* [L9 + OFF] *The handle has sheared off and will have to be mended.*

**shed on/upon** *v prep*
**1** to let (something such as tears or hair) fall on (something such as a surface): [T1 + *on/upon*] *Look, you're sheddding tears on my best coat! In the spring the dog used to shed its fur on the furniture, so it had to stay outside.*
**2 shed light on/upon** to make (a matter) clear or understood: *Can you shed any light on the mysterious disappearance of the precious papers? The police hope that the new witness will be able to shed some light on the case of the stolen jewels.* → **throw on²** (7)

**shed over** *v prep*
**shed tears over** to weep or be sorry because of (someone, something, or doing something): [*often neg.*] *Grace decided that the red-haired boy was not worth shedding tears over. It's no use shedding tears over one little failure. Don't expect me to shed any tears over her absence since she offended me so deeply. I hope you won't shed tears over leaving this city.*

**shed upon** *v prep* → **SHED ON**

*** sheer off** *v adv* also **sheer away**
**1** esp. *naut* to go away; leave in a different direction; take avoiding action: [IØ (*often simple tenses*)] *The boat was able to sheer off in time to avoid an accident. I saw her in the High Street, but she sheered off so as not to meet me!*
**2** to avoid something unpleasant such as an idea: [IØ (*from*) (*often simple tenses*)] *Every time that delicate subject was mentioned, he would sheer off (from it).*

*** sheet down** *v adv* → **pelt down, pelt with** (2), **pour down¹, pour with, teem with** (2)
(of rain) to fall continuously and heavily: [IØ (*usu. continuous tenses*)] *We can't possibly hold the garden party, it's been sheeting down all morning.*

*** sheet home** *v adv*
**1** to open (a square sail) wide by pulling on the ropes holding it: [T1 (*usu. simple tenses*)] *Sheet the sail home, we need all the wind we can get!*
**2** *AmE not fml* to cause (something) to be clearly understood: [T1 (*usu. simple tenses*)] *The failure of the firm's efforts at last sheeted home the need for proper preparation of business conditions.*
*** sheet in** *v adv*
to take in (a sail): [T1 (*usu. simple tenses*)] *Sheet in the main sail, there's a storm coming!*
*** shell out** *v adv*
**1** *fml* to pay (money), usu. in quantity and unwillingly: [T1] *I'm tired of having to shell out payments for such worthless property.* [IØ (*for*)] *How long do I have to go on shelling out for the boy's education?*
**2** *AmE not fml* to give (small presents such as sweets) freely to children visiting homes on Halloween (the night of October 31): [T1] *I think I'll buy fruit this year to shell out when the children come round, as too many sweets are bad for their teeth.* —**shell-out** *n*
**shelter from** *v prep*
**1** to (cause to) be covered from (something such as weather): [IØ + *from*] *The climbers had to shelter from the snowstorm in a mountain hut.* [T1 + *from*] *This woollen hat is to shelter your face from the bitter cold.* → **protect against,** etc.
**2** to protect (someone) from (something or doing something harmful): [T1 + *from*] *You can't shelter your brother from blame in the accident. It is impossible to shelter your children from the harmful effects of television, until the broadcasters improve the material. He tried to shelter his friend from knowing of his father's death, but he was too late.* → **protect against, screen from** (2), **shield from** (2)
*** shelve down to** *v adv prep* → **slope down**
(of land) to slope gradually downwards in the direction of (something): [T1 (*simple tenses*)] *The rocky land at the end of the garden is quite high nearer the house, but then shelves down to the shore.*
**shield from** *v prep*
**1** also **shade from** to provide shelter for (something or someone) from (something harmful): [T1 + *from*] *Shielding his eyes from the bright light, he looked far out to sea to watch for the ship's arrival. He threw himself across the room shielding the child's body from the bullets.* → **protect against**, etc.
**2** to save (someone) from the harmful effect of (something or doing something): [T1 + *from*] *He tried to shield his friend from discovery by the police. You can't shield your brother from blame in the accident. He tried to shield his friend from knowing of her father's death, but was too late as the news had already reached her.* → **protect against, screen from** (2), **shelter from** (2)

**shift for** *v prep* → **fend for**
**shift for oneself** *not fml* to take the responsibility for one's own life: *You'll have to shift for yourself without help from me if you're determined to take that job.*
**shift from** *v prep*
to (cause to) move from (somewhere): [T1 + *from*] *I was glad to shift the weight from my back.* [IØ + *from*] *When at last he decided to shift from the position he had been sitting in, he found his legs very stiff.*
**shift onto** *v prep*
**1** to move (something) to be carried by (something): [T1 + *onto*] *Shifting the load onto my other arm from time to time helped me to carry it.* → **shift to**
**2 shift the blame/responsibility onto** *not fml* to make (someone) take the responsibility for something: *Don't try to shift the blame onto anyone else; it's your fault and you know it!*
**shift to** *v prep* → **shift onto**
to (cause to) move or change direction to (something): [T1 + *to*] *I was glad to shift the load to my other arm.* [IØ + *to*] *At last the wind shifted to the west, and the rain stopped.*
**shin down** *v adv; prep* also *AmE* **skin down** → **shin up, skid up, swarm up**
*not fml* to climb quickly and easily down (something): [L9 + DOWN/*down*] *The jewel thief got away by shinning down a pipe. Take hold of the rope at the top and then just shin down.*
**shin up** *v adv; prep* also *AmE* **skin up** → **shin down, skid up, swarm up**
*not fml* to climb quickly and easily up (something): [L9 + UP/*up*] *The children are so skilled at climbing trees that they shin up (them) like little monkeys.*
*** shine at** *v prep* also **shine in**
*not fml* to be clever or skilled at (a subject, sport, etc.); be noticeably good at (something): [T1 (*no pass., simple tenses*)] *None of my family shine at maths.* [T4 (*simple tenses*)] *The child who found that she shone at swimming soon improved in other work.*
**shine on/upon** *v prep* also **shine over**
(of the sun, moon, or light) to (cause to) give light on (something or someone): [IØ + *on/upon*] *If the sun shines on your wedding you are supposed to be lucky.* [T1 + *on/upon*] *She shone her light on the sleeping child to see that all was well.*
**shine out** *v adv*
**1** (of a light) to shine brightly: [IØ + OUT (*usu. simple tenses*)] *A lonely star shone out against the black sky.*
*** 2** to be noticeably good: [IØ (*simple tenses*)] *His abilities shine out when compared to his companions. Her courage continued to shine out in the middle of her misfortunes.* —**outshine** *v*
**shine over** *v prep* → SHINE ON
**shine through** *v adv; prep*
**1** (of a light) to (cause to) be able to be seen

through (something in the way): [IØ + THROUGH/*through*] *The curtains are so thin that the light shines through and keeps me awake.* [T1 + THROUGH/*through*] *It's difficult to shine a light through this thick mist.*

*2 to be clearly seen or understood (in something): [IØ (*simple tenses*)] *She could not find the right words, but her meaning shone through without doubt.* [T1 (*no pass., simple tenses*)] *Her continuing courage shines through all her actions.*

***shine up to** *v adv prep* → **make up to** (3), **play up to** (2), **suck up to**
esp. *AmE infml* to try to win the favour of (someone) by insincere praise: [T1 (*often simple tenses*)] *It won't do the student any good to shine up to the teacher like that, he will only get the marks he deserves.*

**shine upon** *v prep* → **SHINE ON**

**shine with** *v prep* → **glow with** (2), **kindle with** (3)
to appear bright because of (something): [IØ + *with*] *The sky shone with the lights from the fireworks. Her eyes shone with excitement as she opened the parcel.*

***ship off** *v adv*
*not fml* to send (someone or something) away, as to another place: [T1 (*to*) (*often pass.*)] *The best thing to do with that boy is to ship him off to a good school. Have you shipped those books off at last?*

***ship out** *v adv*
**1** to send (something or someone) to a distant place, esp. across water: [T1] *I've asked Mother to ship out my good boots, I'm going to need them in this country. The price is high because the goods have to be shipped out.*
**2** to work as a sailor: [IØ (*simple tenses*)] *I first shipped out when I was a very young man.*

***shit on** *v prep* → **inform against,** etc.
*taboo sl* to report (someone) to the police: [T1] *If you shit on your criminal friends, they'll turn against you and could be violent.*

**shiver with** *v prep* → **quake with, quiver with, shake with** (1), **tremble with**
to move the body in very quick waves caused by (cold or a strong feeling): [IØ + *with*] *The children waited outside the school, shivering with cold. The women shivered with fear as they faced the gunman.*

**shock into** *v prep*
to force (someone) into (something or doing something) by means of a shock: [T1 + *into*] *Jane's last school report shocked her parents into action. It would do her good to be shocked into changing her opinion.*

**shoe with** *v prep*
to give (someone or an animal) a shoe made of (a material): [T1 + *with* (*usu. pass.*)] *It's best for children's feet to be shod with real leather. All the horses must be shod with new horseshoes for the show.*

***shoo away/off** *v adv*
*not fml* to drive (someone or an animal) away with a cry: [T1] *Shoo those chickens away, they're eating my garden seeds!*

**shoot at** *v prep*
**1** to fire (a gun) directed at (something or someone); direct (something) with a gun at (usu. someone): [IØ + *at*] *Don't shoot at me please! He shot at a bird but missed it.* [T1 *at*] *I only shot a pea at him, he's not hurt! This gun can shoot small stones at rabbits.* → **aim at** (1), **take at** (2)
*2 also **shoot for** esp. *AmE not fml* to aim at or try to gain (something): [T1] *There's no harm in shooting at the directorship, but I think you're too inexperienced for the job.* → **aim at** (2), **drive at** (2), **drive for** (2), **go after** (2), **go for** (6), **take at** (2)
**3 shoot a glance/look at** to look at (someone) very quickly for a moment, and at once look away: [*usu. simple tenses*] *While the others were talking, Jim shot an enquiring glance at Mary to see if she agreed with them. Shoot a quick look at the child when he's not watching, and see if you think he looks guilty.* → **dart at, flash at, throw at** (2)
**4 shoot at the mouth** *AmE infml* → **SHOOT OFF** (5)
**5 shoot questions at** *not fml* to ask (someone) a lot of questions quickly: *The crowd were eager to shoot questions at the speaker, and the chairman had to make sure that everyone had a chance.*

**shoot away** *v adv*
**1** to fire a gun continuously: [IØ + AWAY (*often continuous tenses*)] *We've been shooting away for three hours, and haven't hit anything yet!*
**2** to remove (something) with gunfire: [X9 + AWAY (*usu. pass.*)] *The castle tower has been shot away. The lower part of his face was all shot away.* → **shoot off** (1)
**3** to move away quickly: [L9 + AWAY (*usu. simple tenses*)] *As soon as I let the boy go, he shot away and disappeared round a corner. The rabbit shot away as soon as it smelt the dog coming near.* → **shoot off** (2)

***shoot down** *v adv*
**1** to destroy (a plane) in the air; kill (a pilot) or make him leave a burning plane in flight: [T1 (*often simple tenses*)] *Today our fighters have shot down twenty enemy planes. He was shot down over England and was almost killed.* → **bring down** (2), **come down** (2), **get down** (5), **go down** (5), **send down** (4)
**2** also **shoot down in flames** *infml* to destroy (someone's ideas) by argument; defeat (someone) severely in argument: [T1 (*usu. simple tenses*)] *The others soon shot down his supposedly bright ideas. I tried to give my opinion, but was soon shot down in flames.* → **bring down** (2), **come down** (3), **get down** (4), **go down**[1] (5), **send down** (4)

***shoot for** *v prep* → **SHOOT AT** (2)

**shoot from** *v prep*
**1** to fire (something such as a bullet) from (a gun): [T1 + *from* (*usu. pass.*)] *Was the murder bullet shot from this gun?*
**2 shoot from the hip** *AmE infml* to speak or behave carelessly or foolishly: *Don't take any notice of what he says, he's always shooting from the hip without thinking first.*

**shoot in** *v adv*
**1** to fire a gun indoors or in an inward direction: [IØ + IN] *If you hide behind the door, you won't get hit when they shoot in.*
**2** to enter a place very quickly: [L9 + IN] *I opened the door and the cat shot in, with the dog after it.*
***3** to protect (soldiers) while attacking, by firing: [T1] *We'll give your men covering fire by shooting them in while they attack the enemy positions.*

**shoot into** *v prep*
to fire (a gun) into (a space); direct (something such as a bullet) into (a space): [IØ + *into*] *It will take a lot of skill to shoot into that narrow opening where the enemy are hiding.* [T1 + *into*] *"I shot an arrow into the air, It fell to earth, I know not where."* (H.W. Longfellow, *The Arrow and the Song*)

**shoot off** *v adv*
**1** to remove (something) with gunfire: [X9 + OFF] *The top of the castle tower has been shot off. The soldier avoided military duty by shooting off one of his toes.* → **shoot away** (2)
**2** to leave quickly: [L9 + OFF (*usu. simple tenses*)] *As soon as I let go of the boy, he shot off and disappeared round a corner. The rabbit shot off as soon as it smelt the dog coming near.* → **shoot away** (3)
***3** to complete a shooting competition: [IØ (*for*)] *Our two best men are shooting off for the prize.*
***4** to fire (a weapon or fireworks) into the air without aiming: [T1] *The soldiers shot off their weapons as a sign of victory.*
**5 shoot one's mouth off** *infml* also **shoot at the mouth** *AmE infml* to talk too freely, without care: [*often continuous tenses*] *Don't you go shooting your mouth off about the secret I've told you; remember, I trust you.*

**shoot out** *v adv*
**1** to fire a gun out of doors or in an outward direction: [IØ + OUT] *Break the window so that you can shoot out.*
**2** to (cause to) move quickly outwards: [L9 + OUT (*usu. simple tenses*)] *As we got near to the hole, a rabbit shot out and ran towards the woods.* [X9 + OUT (*usu. simple tenses*)] *As the teacher turned his back, the child shot out his tongue. All the children shot out their hands for the money. The rider was shot out of his seat by the sudden shock.* → **put out** (1), etc.
**3** to put (a light) out by shooting at it: [X9 + OUT] *The gunman showed his skill by shooting out all the lights above the door.*
***4** to express (words) quickly or forcefully: [T1 (*often simple tenses*)] *He shot out a stream of curses when he learned what his enemy had done.*
***5** *not fml* to dismiss or get rid of (someone) quickly: [T1 (*usu. pass.*)] *If the party leaders are not careful, they could be shot out at the next election.*
**6 shoot it out** *infml* to bring a quarrel to an end with a gun battle: *The families have been quarrelling bitterly for many years, and now the boys have decided to shoot it out; one of them will be killed.* —**shoot-out** *n*

***shoot through** *v adv*
*infml* to leave; go away: [IØ] *It's getting late — I think I'll shoot through.*

**shoot through with** *v adv prep* → **shoot with** (2)
**be shot through with** *not fml* to have a lot of (something such as a quality): *His stories are shot through with moral examples and good humour.*

**shoot to** *v adv*
**1** to close (a lock) firmly: [X9 + TO] *Make sure that you shoot the lock to as you close the door.*
***2** to bring (a ship) to a stop: [T1b] *We shall have to shoot her to, there's no room in the harbour.*

**shoot up** *v adv*
**1** to fire a gun in an upward direction: [IØ + UP] *Is the chimney straight enough for you to shoot up?*
**2** to move quickly upwards: [L9 + UP (*usu. simple tenses*)] *The boy shot up out of the chair as soon as he heard the doorbell ring. He ran towards the stairs and shot up in half a minute.* → **jump up** (2), **leap up** (2), **spring up** (1), **start up** (2)
***3** to rise quickly or suddenly: [IØ] *Prices have been shooting up even more quickly this year. I thought the fire was out until flames shot up and burned my face.* → **race up**
***4** *not fml* to grow quickly: [IØ] *The boy has shot up this summer, I hardly recognized him.* → **spring up** (2), **sprout up** (1)
***5** to damage (something such as a building) or wound (someone) with bullets or shells: [T1 (*usu. pass.*)] *The castle was badly shot up during the war. He hasn't been the same since he was shot up by the gunman.*
***6** *infml* to cause terror in (a place) by wild shooting: [T1] *The robbers decided to shoot up the town to stop the people from chasing them.* —**shoot-up** *n*
***7** *sl* to inject (a drug); inject oneself with a drug: [IØ] *More than half the students in this school are shooting up regularly.* [T1] *Some take the drug by mouth, others shoot it up.* —**shoot-up** *n*

**shoot with** *v prep*
**1** to fire on (someone) using (a gun): [IØ + *with*] *Soldiers have to learn to shoot with all kinds of guns.* [T1 + *with*] *The murdered man was shot with a small handgun.*

**2 be shot with: a** to be varied with (unclear lines of something different such as another colour): *The sky was a deep blue shot with pink from the setting sun.* **b** *not fml* to have a lot of (something such as a quality): *His stories are shot with moral examples. His life was shot with excitement.* → **shoot through with**

***shop around/round** *v adv*

**1** to compare prices or values of goods in different shops: [IØ (*for*)] *Don't buy the first television set that you see advertised; spend a little time shopping round for the best price.*

**2** *not fml* to examine various possibilities before deciding: [IØ (*for*)] *I won't take the first job that's offered as I need to shop around a little and see what other chances there are. Voters should shop around among the different politicians to see who will truly represent their interests best, rather than be guided simply by party loyalty.*

***shop on** *v prep* → **inform against,** etc.

*infml* to report (someone) to the police: [T1] *Never shop on your friends unless you want them to turn violent against you when they come out of prison.*

***shop round** *v adv* → SHOP AROUND

***shore up** *v adv*

**1** to support (something such as a building in danger of falling) with something solid: [T1 (*often pass.*)] *The house was so old that it was leaning over the street and had to be shored up with blocks of wood.*

**2** *not fml* to support (something in danger of failing): [T1 (*often pass.*)] *The government has had to shore up the National Health Service, which was in danger of ruin.*

**shorn of** → SHEAR OF

**shoulder aside** *v adv* → **elbow aside, push aside, thrust aside**

**1** to make (someone) move to one side, by or as by pushing with the shoulder: [T1b] *That rude man shouldered me aside and got on the bus ahead of me!*

**2** *not fml* to make (someone) yield place to someone else: [T1b] *When jobs are scarce, young people entering the work force tend to get shouldered aside in favour of experienced workers with more to offer the firm.*

**shoulder forward** *v adv* → **elbow forward, push forward** (5), **thrust forward** (4)

**shoulder one's way forward** to force one's way ahead, as by pushing with the shoulders, usu. in a crowd: *It's not fair, he got to the front by shouldering his way forward; make him move to the back!*

**shoulder through** *v adv; prep* → **elbow through, push through** (3), **thrust through**

**shoulder one's way through** to force one's way through (something such as a crowd) by pushing with the shoulders: *The man got to the front in a most rude manner, by shouldering his way through (the crowd).*

**shout about** *v prep*

**1** to raise one's voice loudly when speaking about (something or someone): [IØ + *about*] *What's that boy shouting about now?*

**2 be nothing to shout about** to be unworthy of much praise; not be especially good: *Tom's new book is not bad, but it's nothing to shout about.*

**shout at** *v prep* → **roar at**

to raise one's voice to a loud level when speaking to (someone): [IØ + *at*] *It's a poor teacher who can only control the class by shouting at the children. You'll have to shout at her, she can't hear very well.*

**shout down** *v adv*

**1** to speak loudly in a downward direction: [IØ + DOWN] *You might be able to make the trapped miners hear if you shout down loudly enough.*

***2** to make it impossible for (a speaker or his words) to be heard, by shouting: [T1] *His questions were shouted down, and the suggestion was passed. Please let me speak, don't shout me down without giving me a fair chance to express my opinion.* → **roar down**

**shout for** *v prep*

**1** to raise one's voice because of (a strong feeling): [IØ + *for*] *Joe shouted for joy when he heard he'd passed the exam.*

**2** to raise one's voice in support of (someone): [IØ + *for*] *All our supporters were shouting for the home team.*

**shout out** *v adv*

**1** to express something loudly; make a loud noise: [IØ + OUT] *When I call your name, shout out so that we know you're here.* → **call out** (1), **roar out** (1), **yell out**

**2** to express (something) loudly: [T1 + OUT] *You'll have to shout out the names to make yourself heard above all this noise. The officer shouted out an order, and all the soldiers stood to attention.* [T5 + OUT] *Just then, one of the villagers shouted out that he had found the missing child.* → **call out** (1), **cry out** (1), **roar out** (2), **thunder out, yell out**

***shove about/around** *v adv not fml* → PUSH ABOUT

**shove against** *v prep not fml* → PUSH AGAINST

**shove along** *v adv not fml* → PUSH ALONG

***shove around** *v adv* → SHOVE ABOUT

**shove aside** *v adv not fml* → PUSH ASIDE

**shove at** *v prep*

**1** *not fml* → PUSH AT

***2** *not fml* to force acceptance of (something) by (someone): [D1] *I don't like having the sorrowful state of the world shoved at me in every news broadcast.*

**shove away** *v adv not fml* → PUSH AWAY

**shove back** *v adv not fml* → PUSH BACK

**shove behind** *v adv not fml* → PUT BEHIND (3)

**shove by/past** *v adv; prep not fml* → PUSH BY

**shove down**[1] *v adv not fml* → PUSH DOWN[1], WRITE DOWN (1)

**shove down**[2] *v prep not fml* → PUSH DOWN[2]

***shove forward** *v adv not fml* → PUSH FORWARD (4)

**shove home** *v adv not fml* → **PUSH HOME**
**shove in¹** *v adv*
**1** *not fml* → **PUSH IN¹**
**2 shove one's oar in** *not fml* → **PUT IN** (18)
**shove in²** *v prep not fml* → **PUSH IN²**
**shove into** *v prep not fml* → **PUSH INTO**
**shove off** *v adv not fml* → **PUSH OFF, PUSH OUT** (2)
***shove off on** *v adv prep not fml* → **PUSH OFF ON**
***shove on¹** *v adv not fml* → **PUSH ON¹**
**shove on²** *v prep not fml* → **PUSH ON²**
**shove out** *v adv not fml* → **PUSH OUT**
**shove over** *v adv not fml* → **MOVE OVER, PUSH OVER**
**shove past** *v adv; prep* → **SHOVE BY**
**shove through** *v adv; prep not fml* → **PUSH THROUGH**
**shove to** *v adv not fml* → **PUSH TO**
**shove towards** *v prep not fml* → **PUSH TOWARDS**
**shove up** *v adv not fml* → **MOVE UP** (2)
**shovel down** *v adv* → **shovel in** (2)
*not fml* to eat (food) hastily and in large quantities: [X9 + DOWN] *It's rude to shovel your food down like that—try to eat more slowly and less noisily.*
**shovel in** *v adv*
**1** to lift (something) in with a tool like a spade: [X9 + IN] *The engineer shovelled the coal in as fast as he could, but the steam engine would go no faster.*
**2** *not fml* to eat (food) hastily and in large quantities: [X9 + IN] *Don't shovel your food in like that, it's rude to eat so quickly; take a little at a time on your fork.* → **shovel down**
***3** *not fml* to gain (money) quickly: [T1] *All you have to do once you've got the business started is sit in your office shovelling in the profits.* → **rake in** (2)
**shovel into** *v prep*
**1** to lift (something) into (something such as a container or hole) with a tool like a spade: [X9 + *into*]. *The engineer shovelled the coal into the firehole as fast as he could, but the steam engine could go no faster.*
**2** *not fml* to push (food) into (one's mouth) hastily and in large quantities: [X9 + *into*] *That boy has developed a nasty habit of shovelling his food into his mouth as if he hadn't eaten for a week.*
**3** to push (something) so as to form (a shape) with or as with a tool like a spade: [T1 + *into*] *This machine goes along the road, shovelling the snow into great piles at the sides.*
***show around/round** *v adv; prep* → **go round** (5), **look round²** (2), etc., (3), **see round¹**, **show over, take round¹** (4), **take round²** (2)
to take (someone) on a tour of (a place) to visit or examine it: [T1b] *My husband will show you round while I get the tea.* [D1] *The director will show the party of students around the factory himself.*

***show down** *v adv*
(in card games) to show the face of (the cards): [T1] *At the end of the game, the players show their cards down and count the points won or lost.*
**show for** *v prep*
**have nothing to show for** to have no result from (something or doing something): *After all these months, it's disappointing to have nothing to show for all my efforts. I'm afraid he'll have nothing to show for waiting so long.*
**show in** *v adv* → **see in¹** (2), **usher in** (1)
to show (someone) the way to enter; take (someone) politely in: [X9 + IN (*to*)] *Show the visitors in, will you, please? Part of the nurse's job is to show people in to the doctor's office.*
***show itself** *v pron*
to be clearly known: [IØ (*in*) (*usu. simple tenses*)] *Jim's jealousy of the winning runner showed itself in his manner of speech. Her anxiety showed itself in a nervous restlessness of the hands.*
***show off** *v adv*
**1** to allow (something) to be seen to advantage: [T1 (*simple tenses*)] *A plain black background shows the diamonds off best.* → **set off** (7)
**2** *not fml* to show pride in, trying to draw attention to (someone or something that is one's own such as possessions or abilities): [T1] *It's unwise to show off your greater knowledge in front of the director. I think he visited us just to show off his new car. It's nice to have a beautiful grandchild to show off.*
**3** *not fml* to behave with offensive pride and false self-importance, trying to attract admiration: [IØ] *Don't take any notice of the children's behaviour, they're just showing off. He hasn't much acting ability, but uses the stage as a chance to show off.* —**show-off** *n*
***show oneself** *v pron*
**1** to allow oneself to be seen: [IØ (*usu. simple tenses*)] *I suppose we ought to show ourselves at the office party, if only for a short time.*
**2** to prove (to be something): [L3 (*simple tenses, usu. perfect*)] *Has he always shown himself to be trustworthy?* [L7 (*simple tenses, usu. perfect*)] *Yes, he has always shown himself completely trustworthy.*
**show out** *v adv* → **see out** (2), **usher out**
to show (someone) the way out; take (someone) politely to the door: [X9 + OUT (*of*)] *Thank you for coming to see me; my secretary will now show you out. Don't trouble to show me out (of the building); I know my way.*
***show over** *v prep* → **look round²** (2), etc., **show around,** etc.
to take (someone) on a tour of (a place) to visit or examine it: [D1] *The director shows parties of students over the newspaper building himself. My husband will show you over the house if you are interested in buying it.*

***show round** *v adv; prep* → SHOW AROUND

**show through** *v adv; prep*

**1** to be able to be seen through (something such as a covering): [IØ + *through*] *The old dog was so thin that his bones showed through his skin.* [IØ + THROUGH] *The new colour is lighter, and the old paint shows through.*

***2** (of a feeling or quality) to be clear in spite of (something hiding it): [IØ (*usu. simple tenses*)] *Whatever part he is playing his own character still shows through.* [T1 (*no pass., usu. simple tenses*)] *Her delight in life shows through the formal manner which she has to use on official occasions.* → **come through**[1] (4)

**show to** *v prep*

**1** to give sight or knowledge of (something or someone) to (someone): [T1 + *to*] *How dare you show my letter to your friends? Filled with pride, she showed the new baby to her neighbours.*

**2** to take (someone) to (a place), showing him the way or being polite: [X9 + *to*] *I'll show you to the office where you can wait for the director. Let me show you to your room.*

**show up** *v adv*

**1** to show (someone) the way upstairs; take (someone) politely to a higher place: [X9 + UP (*often imper.*)] *Show the doctor up when he comes.*

***2** *not fml* to arrive: [IØ (*usu. simple tenses*)] *Only thirty members showed up for the yearly General Meeting.* → **turn up** (9)

***3** to (cause to) be easily seen: [T1 (*often simple tenses*)] *The bright sunlight shows up the cracks in the walls.* [IØ (*often simple tenses*)] *The lines on her face show up in the pale spring light.*

***4** (of a fault) to (cause to) be uncovered or made clear: [IØ (*simple tenses*)] *The faults in the recording will show up on this expensive record-player.* [T1 (*simple tenses*)] *A struggle of this nature shows up any weaknesses of character.*

***5** to make clear the truth, usu. unfavourable, about (someone): [T1b (*as, for*) (*usu. simple tenses*)] *Performing by herself showed her up as a rather poor singer. His thoughtless treatment of people below him in the firm shows him up for what he really is.*

***6** esp. *BrE* to make (someone) feel shame or look foolish in public: [T1b] *Please don't argue with me in front of our guests, it shows me up. Why won't you take me with you to your meeting? Are you afraid that I'll make some silly remark and show you up in front of all those important people? When you visit the school be sure to wear sensible clothes, to avoid showing the boy up.*

***7** → BRING OUT (4)

**shower on/upon** *v prep* → **rain on** (2)

to (cause to) descend quickly or in quantity on (someone or something); give a lot of (something or things) to (someone): [T1 (*no pass.*)] *Invitations showered on her as soon as her presence in the city was known.* [D1] *He showered gifts on her, but still she refused to marry him. Honours were showered upon the victorious team.*

***shower with** *v prep*

**1** to cover (someone or something) with a lot of (something falling such as water): [D1] *A passing car showered us with water from a pool in the road. Buildings nearby were showered with broken glass after the explosion.*

**2** to give (someone) a lot of (something or things): [D1 (*often pass.*)] *He showered her with gifts, but still she refused to marry him. Our victorious team was showered with honours. The best way to help a troubled child is to shower him with love.*

**shriek out** *v adv* → **scream out**

to give a sharp loud cry; express (something) in a sharp loud voice: [IØ + OUT] *He shrieked out in pain as the flames reached his leg.* [T5 + OUT] *She shrieked out that there was a mouse in the room.* [T1a] *She shrieked out a warning just in time to avoid a nasty accident.*

**shriek with** *v prep* → **scream with**

to express (pain or laughter) in a sharp loud voice: [IØ + *with*] *The rest of the public were shrieking with laughter, but I didn't see what was supposed to be so funny. How can you take no notice of an animal that is shrieking with pain, with its leg caught in a trap?*

**shrink back** *v adv*

**1** to move backwards (away from something or someone), usu. out of fear: [L9 + BACK (*from*)] *The crowd shrank back from the sight of the body covered with blood.*

***2** to fail to have courage (to accept something such as a duty): [IØ (*from*) (*often simple tenses*)] *When the call to action comes, don't shrink back, but face your fate. Why do you always shrink back from the possibility of change?*

***shrink from** *v prep*

to avoid (something or doing something), esp. because of fear: [T1 (*often simple tenses*)] *He shrank from the thought of having to kill anyone. It's no wonder that he shrank from such a responsibility.* [T4 (*often simple tenses*)] *At first I shrank from meeting the director face to face, but soon learned that he was actually a charming person. You shouldn't shrink from taking your proper share of the blame.*

***shrink up** *v adv* → **shrivel up** (2)

*not fml* to try to become unnoticeable, because of fear or nervousness: [IØ (*often simple tenses*)] *Whenever Mary goes to a party, she shrinks up and hopes that no one will talk to her.*

**shrivel up** *v adv*

**1** (of a leaf, skin, etc.) to curl and die through dryness or old age: [IØ + UP] *It's late in the year and the leaves have all shrivelled up now. The dead skin around the wound will shrivel up and fall off.* → **curl up** (1)

***2** *not fml* to try to become unnoticeable, because of fear or nervousness: [IØ (*often simple tenses*)] *Why do you always seem to shrivel up when we meet new people at parties? You can't always avoid them.* → **shrink up**

***shrug off** *v adv*

**1** to remove (clothes) by twisting the body: [T1 (*often simple tenses*)] *He shrugged off his coat carelessly and let it fall to the floor.*

**2** to get rid of (something such as a feeling): [T1 (*often simple tenses*)] *It takes me a long time in the morning to shrug off sleep. How can you simply shrug off a feeling of helplessness?*

**3** *not fml* also **shrug away** to treat or regard (something or someone) as unimportant, not worthy of attention: [T1 (*often simple tenses*)] *It's unwise to shrug off the voters' complaints, as they can show their displeasure at the next election. He was even able to shrug off the reporters who had been following him everywhere.*

***shuck off** *v adv AmE* → **SHUFFLE OFF** (3)

**shudder at** *v prep*

**1** to shake with or as with fear or dislike because of (something terrible): [IØ + *at*] *The children shuddered at the sight of the dead pig with its throat cut.*

***2** to have fear of (something such as a thought): [T1 (*simple tenses*)] *I shudder at the thought of fire in this building. She shuddered at the idea of facing further struggle.*

**shuffle off** *v adv*

**1** also **shuffle away** to move away awkwardly, without lifting the feet: [L9 + OFF] *The old man shuffled off in his worn shoes.*

***2** (usu. of an animal) to remove (its old skin): [T1] *Every spring this snake shuffles off its old skin, as it has grown too big for it.* → **cast off** (5), **slough off** (1)

***3** *not fml* also *AmE* **shuck off** to get rid of (someone or something such as a responsibility) (and pass it onto someone else): [T1 (*onto*) (*often simple tenses*)] *He was glad to shuffle off the load of responsibility for the firm onto a younger man. It's difficult to shuffle off old habits of thought. When he grew rich, he shuffled off his former companions.* → **fling off** (3), etc.

**shuffle out of** *v adv prep*

**1** to remove (clothes) awkwardly: [L9 + OUT + *of*] *With his wounded arm bound up, he had to shuffle out of his coat as best he could.*

**2** to leave (a room) awkwardly, without lifting the feet: [L9 + OUT + *of*] *The old man shuffled out of the room, complaining about the way he had been treated.*

***3** *not fml* to escape from (something bad such as trouble) in a tricky manner: [T1 (*often simple tenses*)] *He's always been able to shuffle out of any difficulty; how will he do it this time?* → **get out of** (13), etc.

**shunt onto** *v prep*

**1** to move (a train) by pushing it with another train, onto (a different track): [T1 + *onto* (*often pass.*)] *The damaged goods train will have to be shunted onto a side line to make way for the passenger train.*

***2** *not fml* to pass (something) onto (something or someone else): [D1 (*often simple tenses*)] *How can we shunt the talks onto more productive subjects? She tried to shunt the blame onto her mother.*

**shut away** *v adv* → **lock away** (2), **lock up** (2), **put away** (6), **shut up** (2)

to place (someone, oneself, or an animal) in a private place: [X9 + AWAY] *Tom had to shut himself away from his family for a month to finish the book. Mad people used to be shut away in special buildings; now they can be treated in hospitals.*

**shut down** *v adv*

**1** to close (something) firmly: [T1 + DOWN] *He shut the lid down with a loud noise.*

***2** (of a business or factory) to (cause to) close or stop production: [IØ] *The factory may shut down if supplies cease. The whole company shuts down for three weeks' holiday every year.* [T1] *The severe winter shut many factories down this year.* —**shutdown** *n* → **close down** (1), **close up** (4), **shut up** (3)

***3** to stop (a supply such as electricity): [T1] *On Monday, the power supply will be shut down for the whole building.* —**shutdown** *n, adj*

**shut in**[1] *v adv*

**1** to force (someone or an animal) to stay indoors: [X9 + IN (*often pass.*)] *Is it kind to shut the dog in all day while you're at work? Old Mrs Price has been shut in for many years now because of her bad leg.* —**shut-in** *n, adj*

***2** to surround (something) closely: [T1 (*usu. pass.*)] *The farmhouse was shut in by tall trees. The valley is shut in between the hills.* —**shut-in** *adj*

***3** to refuse to allow (something) to escape: [T1 (*often simple tenses*)] *With an effort, he was able to shut in whatever words he had been about to say.*

**shut in**[2] *v prep*

**1** to imprison (someone or an animal) in (a place): [X9 + *in*] *Is it kind to shut the dog in the house all day?*

***2** to trap (part of the body or clothing) in (usu. a door): [D1 (*often simple tenses*)] *I shut my finger in the door and made it bleed.* → **close on** (3), **shut on** (1)

**shut of** *v prep*

**be shut of** *not fml* to have got rid of or escaped from (something unpleasant): *I was glad to be shut of that terrible school. How can I get shut of such an unwelcome duty?*

***shut off** *v adv*

**1** (of a machine or switch) to (cause to) stop working: [T1] *Do please shut off that terrible loud music! Shut off the motor, and you should be able to hear the birds singing.* [IØ] *The machine shuts off by itself at the end of the recording.* → **turn off** (3), **put off**[1] (3), etc.

**2** to keep (something or oneself) away (from people or things): [T1 (*from*)] *On his wife's death, he shut himself off from his old friends to deal with his grief. This is a beautiful valley, shut off by mountains from the rest of the world. It's nice to be shut off from the pressures of work while on holiday.*

**shut on/upon** *v prep*

**1** to close (a door or window) so that it traps (part of the body or clothing): [T1 + *on/upon* (*often simple tenses*)] *I shut the door on my finger by mistake, and made it bleed.* → **close on** (3), **shut in²** (2)

**2 shut a/the door on/upon: a** to refuse to admit (someone): *I shut the door on the stranger so that he could not come in.* **b** *not fml* to refuse or fail to take advantage of (a chance, offer, etc.); declare that there is no hope for (someone or something): *Why don't you at least have a look at the firm? It seems a pity to shut the door on what could be an exciting opportunity. The country's military leaders have shut the door on any further peace talks.* → **close on** (4)

**shut out** *v adv*

**1** to refuse to allow (someone) to enter: [X9 + OUT (*of*)] *Any member of the public who arrives late will find himself shut out of the performance.*

*__2__ to refuse to allow (something) to enter, be heard, felt, etc.: [T1 (*of*)] *He stopped his ears with his hands to shut out the terrible noise. The trees are very beautiful, but they do shut out the light. How can I shut out such harmful thoughts?*

*__3__ esp. *AmE* (in a game) to prevent (one's opponent) from gaining a point; defeat (usu. an opposing team): [T1] *There are ways of shutting out the other players by playing certain cards. The Flyers shut out the Leaps 3–2 in last night's game.* —**shut-out** *n*

**shut to¹** *v adv* → **pull to¹**, etc.

to fasten (a door) firmly: [T1 + TO] *Make sure that you shut the door to as you leave, will you?*

**shut to²** *v prep* → **turn to²** (16)

**shut one's eyes to** *not fml* to pretend not to notice (something, usu. wrong): *If everyone shut their eyes to the injustices in the world, no laws would ever be changed.*

**shut up** *v adv*

**1** to close (a container) firmly: [T1 + UP] *Shut up the box, the game is over.*

**2** to imprison (someone or an animal); keep (oneself) private: [X9 + UP] *That poor dog has been shut up in the house all day while the owners were out. The only way Father can get any peace is to shut himself up in his study.* → **lock away** (2), **lock up** (2), **put away** (6), **shut away**

*__3__ to make (something such as a building or goods) safe, usu. by locking: [T1] *We're going to shut the house up for the summer while we're away. The bookseller was just shutting up his shop for the night. Those jewels ought to be shut up in a safe.* → **close down** (1), **close up** (4), **lock away** (1), **lock up** (1), **shut down** (2)

*__4__ *infml* to (cause to) be silent, in speaking or writing: [IØ (*usu. imper.*)] *Shut up, can't you! I'm trying to think.* [T1] *Can you do something to shut those children up, I can hardly hear myself think. The government was unable to shut the writer up, as he had the support of the rest of the world. Tell him it's his own fault; that should shut him up.* → **belt up** (3), **clam up, dry up** (4), **hush up** (1), **muffle up** (3), **pipe down, wrap up** (5)

**5 shut up shop** *not fml* to stop any kind of work: *It's time to shut up shop and go home now. I think I'll shut up shop, I can't do any more letters tonight.* → **set up** (17)

**shut upon** *v prep* → SHUT ON

**shy at¹** *v prep*

(usu. of a horse) to take sudden action to avoid (something), as out of fear: [IØ + *at* (*often simple tenses*)] *At the last moment the horse shied at the fence and threw its rider.*

**shy at²** *v prep* → **chuck at** (1), **fling at** (1), **hurl at** (1), **sling at** (1), **throw at** (1), **toss at**

*not fml* to throw (something) hard at (something or someone): [T1 + *at*] *You have to stop those boys shying rocks at passing cars, they could cause an accident.*

*__shy away from__ *v adv prep*

*not fml* to avoid (something such as a subject or doing something): [T1 (*often simple tenses*)] *Why does she shy away from the idea of taking a leading part?* [T4 (*often simple tenses*)] *Insurance firms tend to shy away from advertising.*

*__sic(k) on/onto__ *v prep* → **set on²** (3)

(*old use*) to cause (usu. a dog) to attack (someone or an animal): [D1] *Go away, or I'll sick my dog on you!*

*__sick up__ *v adv* → **bring up** (4), etc.

to be sick; vomit (one's food or drink): [IØ] *Jane can't come, she's been sicking up all morning.* [T1] *"No drink, thank you, I'd sick it up at once."* (Anthony Burgess, *A Tremor of Intent*)

*__sicken at__ *v prep*

to dislike (something) so much that it makes one feel ill: [T1 (*usu. simple tenses*)] *Don't show me your wound, I sicken at the sight of blood.*

*__sicken for__ *v prep*

to begin to show signs of (a disease): [T1 (*usu. continuous tenses*)] *She's not usually in such low spirits; perhaps she's sickening for a fever.*

*__sicken of__ *v prep*

to become thoroughly tired of (something or doing something): [T1 (*simple tenses*)] *At last I sickened of her rudeness and asked her to leave my house.* [T4 (*simple tenses*)] *I long since sickened of hearing her complaints.*

*__side against__ *v prep* → **side with, take against** (3), **take with** (7)
to oppose (someone), as in argument: [T1 (*usu. simple tenses*)] *Why do you always side against me? There's no reason to suppose that I'm at fault.*

*__side with__ *v prep* → **side against, take against** (3), **take with** (7)
to sympathize with or support (someone or a principle), as in argument or decision: [T1 (*often simple tenses*)] *Why do you side with your mother? She was at fault, not me.*

**sidle away** *v adv*
to move smoothly, often secretively, away, by or as by turning sideways: [L9 + AWAY (*from*)] *She sidled away from me while I was talking to a neighbour, and I didn't notice that she had left.*

**sidle in** *v adv*
to enter in a smooth or secretive manner, as sideways: [L9 + IN] *As I opened the door a little way, the cat sidled in.*

**sidle out** *v adv*
to leave a room or building in a smooth or secretive manner, as sideways: [L9 + OUT] *If you sit at the back you can sidle out without anyone seeing you leave.*

**sidle up** *v adv*
**1** to move (a boat) sideways (towards something): [X9 + UP (*to*)] *The captain sidled the little boat up to the place where the passengers could get out.*
**2** to come near (someone) in a smooth or secretive manner, as sideways: [L9 + UP (*to*)] *Just then a man sidled up (to me) and offered to sell me some jewels cheaply, so I called the police.*

**sift out** *v adv* → **separate out, sort out** (1)
to separate (someone or something) from a group or mass: [T1 + OUT] *Sift out the most important names from this list of possible speakers. She sifted out the stones from the soil.*

*__sift through__ *v prep*
to look through (a collection) looking for something: [T1] *I had to sift through a pile of papers looking for the missing article.*

**sigh about** *v prep* → **sigh for** (1), **sigh over**
to breathe loudly, expressing a feeling, usu. sad, on account of (something or someone): [IØ + *about* (*usu. simple tenses*)] *What are you sighing about? Is something wrong? It's no good sighing about your failure, it is better to start again.*

**sigh away** *v adv*
**1** to continuously breathe loudly expressing a feeling, usu. sad: [IØ + AWAY (*often continuous tenses*)] *By sighing away for hours, she hoped to attract her family's attention to her suffering.*
*__2__ to spend or waste (time) in expressing sad feelings by loud breathing: [T1] *You can sigh away half your youth if you choose to allow failed relationships to sadden you.*

**sigh for** *v prep*
**1** to make loud breathing noises to express a feeling, usu. sad, on account of (something or someone): [IØ + *for*] *Sighing for sorrow can be harmful.* → **sigh about, sigh over**
*__2__ to desire (something, someone, or to do something) very much: [T1] *Many a woman sighs for a house of her own. Surely Grace is not still sighing for that red-haired boy?* [V3] *We're all sighing for the weather to change, after this bitter winter.* → **itch for, long for, yearn for**

**sigh over** *v prep* → **sigh about, sigh for** (1)
to express a feeling, usu. sad, by breathing loudly, on account of (something or someone): [IØ + *over* (*usu. continuous tenses*)] *It's no good sighing over a failure, it is better to start again. I hope Grace is not still sighing over that red-haired boy. All the women around here are sighing over the beautiful new baby.*

*__sign away__ *v adv* → **sign over**
to yield (one's rights to something such as property) by signing a paper, sometimes without considering the results: [T1] *Do you understand that you have just signed away your freedom for the next twenty years? The British government is not about to sign away its control of the island without proper arrangements for its political future.*

**sign for** *v prep*
to sign one's name as an agreement that one has received (something): [IØ + *for*] *Has every key been signed for? Would you please sign for this parcel?*

*__sign in__ *v adv*
to sign one's name or that of (someone else) so as to declare one's arrival or admittance: [IØ] *Every morning when we go swimming, we have to sign in at the Health Club.* [T1] *Members must sign in any guests that they bring to the club.*

*__sign off__ *v adv*
**1** to cease employment with a company, etc.: [IØ] *After ten years, I at last decided to sign off and go into business by myself.* → **join up** (3), **sign on[1]** (1), **sign up** (1)
**2** to end a letter: [IØ] *I'd better sign off now or I shall miss the collection of the post.*
**3** (of a radio or television station) to cease broadcasting, esp. for the day: [IØ] *It's time to sign off for the day; listen again tomorrow.* —**sign-off** *n*—**signing-off** *adj* → **sign on[1]** (3)
**4** *AmE not fml* to stop talking: [IØ (*often simple tenses*)] *I hope this speaker signs off soon, I'm tired of the sound of his voice.*

*__sign on[1]__ *v adv*
**1** to begin work, as with a company, ship, or army, by or as by signing an agreement: [IØ] *How many men have signed on so far? If you join the army you have to sign on for at least three years.* → **join up** (3), **sign off** (1), **sign up** (1)
**2** to begin to employ (someone): [T1] *We*

*have been lucky to sign on so many experienced workers since we won the government contract.* → **sign up** (2)

**3** (of a radio or television station) to start broadcasting for the day: [IØ] *Let's use a nice cheerful tune to sign on in the morning.* —**sign-on** *n* —**signing-on** *adj* → **sign off** (3)

**4** *BrE* to declare that one is available for work, when unemployed, by signing a paper; be unemployed: [IØ] *Have you signed on this week? How long have you been signing on?*

***sign on²** *v prep*

**sign on the dotted line** *not fml* to put one's signature in the correct place on a paper: *Just sign on the dotted line, and the contract is complete.*

***sign out** *v adv*

**1** to sign one's name on a paper or in a book to show that one is leaving: [IØ] *Students are asked to sign out as they leave, so that a count can be made of people in case of fire.*

**2** to sign one's name to show that one has taken (something): [T1 (*often simple tenses*)] *All books must be signed out when they are borrowed from my office.*

***sign over** *v adv* → **sign away**

to pass (something) formally (to someone else) by signing a paper: [T1 (*to*)] *If you sign over the property to your children during your lifetime, they may be able to escape paying death taxes. The building will be signed over to its new owners on Monday.*

***sign up** *v adv*

**1** to (cause to) sign one's name when joining an organization, a group, or a course of study: [IØ (*for*)] *Many men sign up for the army because they can't get ordinary jobs. How many students have signed up for this course?* [T1 (*for*)] *There was an attempt to sign up more men for the police, but not many wanted to.* [I3] *I've signed up to take a course at the local college.* [V3] *Can we sign up any more students to come to our college?* → **join up, sign off** (1), **sign on¹** (1)

**2** to cause (someone such as a performer) to sign a contract agreeing to do something: [T1] *The director was pleased to have been able to sign up the popular music group for the next concert. Arsenal have just signed up two new players. Have you actually signed up all the speakers for our meetings, or have they just promised? You have to sign up a certain number of customers each day, to earn your pay as a salesman.* → **sign on¹** (2)

**signal to** *v prep* → **motion to**

to make a sign, as with the hands, expressing (something) to (someone); send a message to (someone or a group) (to do something); send (a message) to (someone): [IØ + *to*] *The director signalled to me to come forward. Can you signal to base camp for some more supplies? This is how you signal to other drivers that you are going to turn right.* [T1 + *to*] *Jim signalled his helplessness to Mary with his eyes when he was unable to leave the party.*

**silhouette against** *v prep*

**be silhouetted against** (of a dark shape) to be seen only in outline in front of (a background): *The trees look like threatening figures, silhouetted against the evening sky.*

***silt up** *v adv*

to (cause to) become blocked, as with mud: [IØ] *The river silted up long ago, so that no boats can sail up it.* [T1 (*usu. pass.*)] *The council is meeting to decide on further efforts to prevent the harbour from becoming silted up again.*

**simmer down** *v adv*

**1** (of liquid) to become reduced by slow boiling: [IØ + DOWN] *The soup has simmered down after all this time, so that there is hardly any left.*

***2** *not fml* to become calmer: [IØ] *You know how careful you have to be with your father when he's in a temper; don't try to ask him a favour until he's simmered down.* → **cool down** (2), **cool off¹** (2)

***simmer with** *v prep*

to be hardly able to control (a strong feeling such as anger or laughter): [T1 (*no pass., usu. continuous tenses*)] *Still simmering with anger, I was forced to be polite to that rude woman.*

**sin against** *v prep*

to do something morally wrong to offend (someone or a law): [IØ + *against*] *But to cheat him would be sinning against your own principles. We all sin against God and His laws.*

**sing away** *v adv*

**1** to make music with the voice, continuously: [IØ + AWAY (*usu. continuous tenses*)] *I knew she was happy again when I heard her singing away in the kitchen.*

***2** to get rid of (a bad feeling) by singing: [T1] *You can sing your cares away!*

***sing low** *v adv*

*not fml* to express one's opinion humbly after a defeat: [IØ] *He thought his team was the best until they were thoroughly beaten; that made him sing low, for a change.*

**sing of** *v prep*

*old use* to praise or express joy in (someone or something), as in poetry or music: [IØ + *of* (*simple tenses*)] *I sing of the daring deeds of the young prince.*

**sing out** *v adv*

**1** to be daring in making music with the voice: [IØ + OUT (*often imper.*)] *Don't be afraid, sing out!*

***2** to shout or call (a message): [IØ (*often simple tenses*)] *When you're ready to leave, just sing out.* [T1 (*often simple tenses*)] *If you hadn't sung out a warning in time, there might have been a nasty accident. "I'm ready!" she sang out.* [T5 (*often simple tenses*)] *A voice at the back sang out that there were not enough members present for a vote.*

**3 sing one's heart out** to sing loudly and with feeling: [*often continuous tenses*] *Can't you hear the birds singing their hearts out? The children were singing their hearts out on the stage.*

**sing small** *v adj*

**1** to make music with the voice quietly: [IØ + **small** (*usu. simple tenses*)] *I want you to sing small in this part of the performance, it's about a quiet moment in the man's thoughts.*

***2** *not fml* to behave humbly, as after being scolded; have little to say: [IØ (*usu. simple tenses*)] *After what the director said to me, I could only sing small.*

**sing to** *v prep*

**1** to make music with the voice with the help of (an instrument): [IØ + *to*] *Singing to the piano at home is not the same as facing the public.*

**2** to make music with the voice directed at (someone): [IØ + *to* (*usu. simple tenses*)] *I like to sing to many people.* [T1 + *to*] *I like to sing Christmas songs to my family at home.*

**3 sing someone to sleep** to make music with the voice until someone or oneself falls asleep with the sound: *My father used to take me in his arms and sing me to sleep when I was troubled as a child.*

**sing together** *v adv*

to make music with the voice at the same time: [IØ + TOGETHER] *It's so pleasant hearing the different voices singing together.*

**sing up** *v adv*

to make music with the voice more loudly: [IØ + UP (*usu. imper.*)] *We are short of men in the group today, so you'll have to sing up so as to be heard above the women.*

***single out** *v adv* → **center out**

to choose (someone or something) from a group (for special treatment): [T1 (*for*)] *Why single him out for punishment? His book has been singled out for special praise.* [V3 (*often pass.*)] *You have been singled out to represent the school.*

**sink back** *v adv*

**1** to let oneself fall back: [L9 + BACK (*into*)] *Thankfully, he sank back into his comfortable chair; someone else would do the job.*

***2** to fall back out of fear or guilt: [IØ (*often simple tenses*)] *She sank back, unwilling to face her father's anger.*

**sink down** *v adv*

to become lowered: [L9 + DOWN] *She sank down on the floor in a dead faint. His head sank down as he fell asleep.* [IØ + DOWN] *'The broad sun is sinking down in its tranquillity.'* (William Wordsworth, *It is a Beauteous Evening*)

**sink in[1]** *v adv*

**1** (of liquid) to enter a material: [L9 + IN] *Wait till the first coat of paint has sunk in, and then give the wood another coat. Has the oil sunk in yet? The screw should be looser soon.* → **soak in[1]** (1)

**2** to pass into something by becoming lower: [L9 + IN] *The snow had almost melted, and my boots sank in up to the ankle.*

**3** to become hollow; form lower parts of the surface: [IØ + IN] *You could see how his cheeks had sunk in during the fever. Parts of the road have sunk in; it's dangerous to drive.*

***4** *not fml* to become gradually and clearly understood: [IØ (*to*)] *The chairman waited until his suggestion had had time to sink in before inviting the committee's opinions. I heard what she said, but it didn't sink in till some time later.* → **soak in[1]** (2)

**sink in[2]** *v prep*

**1** (usu. of a boat or ship) to (cause to) be lowered below the surface of (water): [IØ + *in*] *My grandfather's boat sank in the same river three times, and was pulled up each time.* [T1 + *in*] *The bridge is made by sinking barrels in the harbour and then placing boards of wood across them.* → **sink into** (1)

**2** (usu. of the sun) to go down in (a certain direction): [IØ + *in* (*simple tenses*)] *The sun rises in the east, and sinks in the west.*

***3** to place (money) to earn interest or profit in (a business): [D1 (*usu. simple tenses*)] *Although we sank all our money in the firm, it still failed to make a profit.*

**4 be sunk in thought** to be deeply thinking: *Father was sunk in thought, and didn't hear a word I said to him.* → **lose in** (6)

**sink into** *v prep*

**1** to (cause to) be lowered into (something such as water): [IØ + *into*] *My foot sank into the mud. As the ship sank into the muddy waters, the sailors jumped clear. Tired out from his efforts, he sank into his comfortable chair.* [T1 + *into*] *You can sink your hand into the pile of feathers and feel how soft it is. He sank his fork into the meat to see if it was well cooked. Sink the fence posts carefully into the soil.* → **sink in[2]** (1)

**2** (of liquid) to enter (something such as material): [IØ + *into*] *It will take a little time for the rain to sink into the dried earth.* → **soak into** (1)

***3** to reach (a state, usu. less conscious or less desirable): [T1 (*no pass., often simple tenses*)] *At last I sank into a deep sleep. Don't allow yourself to sink into grief, it can do no good. These fine principles have sunk into disuse this century. I'm afraid that he may sink into evil.*

***4** *not fml* to be gradually understood and accepted by (one's mind): [T1 (*no pass., often simple tenses*)] *I heard what she said, but it didn't sink into my mind until much later.* → **soak into** (2)

**5 one's courage/heart sink into one's boots** *not fml* to begin to be of low spirits; lose courage: [*usu. simple tenses*] *When he understood the harm that he had unintentionally done, his heart sank into his boots.*

**6 sink one's teeth into: a** to bite (something

hard: *I like sinking my teeth into a good apple.* **b** *not fml* to deal with (something such as a difficulty) firmly; delight in working at (something hard): [*usu. simple tenses*] *I like a demanding job, something to sink my teeth into.* → **get into** (28)

**sink to** *v prep*
**1** to (cause to) go below the surface of something such as water or ground as far as (somewhere such as the bottom): [IØ + *to*] *The boat sank gently to the bottom of the harbour.*
**2** (of ground) to slope downwards towards (something): [L9 + *to* (*simple tenses*)] *The bottom of the garden sinks to the shore.*
**3** to be lowered towards (something): [L9 + *to*] *She sank to the ground in a dead faint.*
**4** to be reduced to (a lesser part): [L9 + *to*] *The storm at last sank to a gentle wind. The price of gold has sunk to a new low level. His voice sank to a whisper, and I could hardly hear him.*
*__5__ to become morally lower so as to reach (a state) or start (doing something): [T1 (*no pass., usu. simple tenses*)] *I am ashamed to learn that you would sink to such depths of behaviour. I fear that he may sink to a life of crime.* [T4] *I did not imagine that you would sink to cheating.* → **descend to** (3), etc.
**6 one's courage/heart sink to one's boots** *not fml* to begin to be of low spirits; lose courage: [*usu. simple tenses*] *When she really understood what was actually expected of her, her courage sank to her boots.* → **sink into** (5)
**7 sink to rest** to die; (of the sun) set: *Many sank to rest when the disease attacked the city. As the sun sank to rest behind the hills, the sky became pink and green.*

**sink together** *v adv*
**1** to go below the surface of the water at the same time: [IØ + TOGETHER] *The two boats sank together.*
*__2__ *not fml* to be defeated together; be joined in defeat: [IØ (*simple tenses*)] *The government and the unions should never fight; they may both sink together.*

***siphon off** *v adv*
**1** also **siphon out** to remove (liquid) through a bent pipe: [T1 (*from, into*)] *Someone has siphoned off all the petrol from my car!*
**2** *not fml* to take (something such as money) and use it for a purpose other than that for which it was intended: [T1 (*from, into*)] *He was charged with siphoning off most of the club's money into his personal account.*

**sit about/around** *v adv; prep*
to sit lazily (in a place) doing nothing: [IØ + ABOUT/AROUND/*about/around*] *I got tired of sitting about (the airport) waiting, so I went home. It's lucky for some people, who can sit around (the house) with nothing to do, while I do all the work.*

**sit at** *v prep*
**1** to (cause to) take one's place at (a table, meal, etc.): [IØ + *at*] *Are the children sitting at the dinner table yet?* [X9 + *at* (*simple tenses*)] *We can sit twelve guests at our large dinner table.*
**2 sit at someone's feet** *not fml* to admire someone very much; be eager to learn from someone: *This teacher is very popular; all the students sit at his feet, listening to every word. He expects us to sit at the feet of the master, not questioning any of his opinions.*

**sit back** *v adv*
**1** to (cause to) take a sitting position leaning backwards or deep in a chair: [IØ + BACK] *Sit back, there's no need to be nervous.* [X9 + BACK (*usu. simple tenses*)] *Let me sit you further back, you'll be more comfortable.*
**2** to be in a position away from a road: [L9 + BACK (*simple tenses*)] *The church sits well back from the main street, behind the graveyard.* → **set back** (2), **stand back** (2)
*__3__ *not fml* to take no active part while others are busy or concerned: [IØ] *He's the sort of person who never helps, just sits back and lets others work. Many people just sit back and do not get concerned about the world's difficulties.* → **sit by, stand aside** (2), **stand back** (4), **stand by**[1] (2), **step back** (3)

**sit by** *v adv*
to fail to take proper or needed action; be inactive: [IØ] *Many people just sit by and let the politicians try to deal with the country's problems; they do nothing themselves* → **sit back** (3), etc.

**sit down** *v adv*
**1** to (cause to) rest the weight of one's body in a sitting position; take or be in a sitting position: [IØ + DOWN (*on*)] *You may not sit down in the presence of the Queen until she gives you permission. Have you counted the people who are sitting down?* [X9 + DOWN (*often simple tenses*)] *Why don't you sit yourself down beside me and talk to me? I tried to sit the child down on the floor, but he wouldn't stay there.*
*__2__ *mil* to settle in position (before a town) to wait for its people to yield: [IØ (*before*)] *The whole army sat down before the town for several months.*
*__3__ to sit on the ground to express opposition to something, or refusal to work, etc.: [IØ] *All the students sat down and refused to leave the building.* —**sit-down** *n, adj*

***sit down on** *v adv prep*
*not fml* to oppose (something such as an idea): [T1 (*usu. simple tenses*)] *The whole committee sat down on the suggestion as being completely unsuitable.*

**sit down to** *v adv prep*
**1** to take a seat ready for (something such as a meal): [IØ + DOWN + *to*] *We sat down to a wonderful meal prepared by my uncle.*
*__2__ to start being busy with (something such as a talk): [T1 (*no pass.*)] *Both sides in the disagreement are prepared to sit down to long talks if necessary.*

***sit down under** *v adv prep* → **lie down under**
*not fml* to suffer (something bad) without complaint or attempt at opposition: [T1 (*no pass., usu. simple tenses*)] *The men will not sit down under such treatment. Why should I sit down under her continued offensive remarks?*

**sit for** *v prep*
**1** to take and hold a position necessary for (an artist) or for (a painting, photograph, etc.): [IØ + *for*] *In her youth, she earned a reasonable living by sitting for art students in the life class. Please keep still while you sit for your photograph.* → **pose for** (1), **sit to**
***2** to enter (an examination): [T1] *More students than ever before have sat for their law examinations this year.*
***3** *BrE* to represent (a place) in Parliament: [T1 (*often simple tenses*)] *Members of his family have sat for the town for over a century.* → **run for** (3), **stand as, stand for** (2)

***sit in¹** *v adv*
**1** esp. *BrE* to take care of a child during the parent's absence: [IØ] *Have you found anyone suitable to sit in this evening?* —**sitter-in** *n*
**2** to remain in a place to show opposition to people in charge: [IØ] *The students entered the president's office and sat in all night.* —**sit-in** *n*
**3** to be allowed to attend (something such as a meeting) as a visitor: [IØ (*on*)] *I'm not sure if I want to take this class; may I sit in for the first week to see if I like it? Friends of the band who give their support may sit in on practices. The public may sit in on all council meetings.*

**sit in²** *v prep*
**1** to (cause to) be seated in (a piece of furniture): [IØ + *in*] *Why don't you sit in this chair? It's more comfortable.* [X9 + *in* (*usu. simple tenses*)] *It's unsafe to sit the child in such a high chair.*
**2** to remain out of action in (a place): [L9 + *in*] *What's the use of the car sitting in the garage all winter?* → **stand in** (3)
**3 sit in judgment (on/over)** to consider that one has the right to judge (usu. someone else): *Why do you think that you should sit in judgment over the rest of the family?*

***sit in for** *v adv prep* → **stand in for,** etc.
to take the place of (someone): [T1] *Have you found anyone to sit in for you while you're away?*

**sit on/upon** *v prep*
**1** to (cause to) be seated on top of (something such as furniture or a surface): [IØ + *on/upon*] *Why are you sitting on wet ground? The mother bird has been sitting on the nest for days now, she must have eggs in there.* [X9 + *on/upon* (*usu. simple tenses*)] *She sat the baby on her knee and played a game with him.*
**2** to be placed on top of (something such as a surface): [L9 + *on/upon*] *The newspapers have been sitting on the table for days now.* → **stand on²** (2)
**3** (of clothing) to rest on (part of the body): [L9 + *on/upon* (*simple tenses*)] *The coat doesn't sit too well on the shoulders, we may have to recut it.*
***4** (of food) to rest on (the stomach): [T1 (*no pass.*)] *That meal we just had is sitting heavily on my stomach.*
***5** to be a member of (a group such as a committee): [T1] *Please don't ask me to sit on any more committees this year, I already have my share of meetings.* → **serve on** (1)
***6** *not fml* to keep (something) for a time: [T1 (*no pass.*)] *We'd better sit on the jewels for several months, until it's safe to try to sell them.*
***7** *not fml* to keep (something such as a request) without dealing with it; delay action on (something): [T1] *The shop has been sitting on my complaint for more than a month. Are those people still sitting on your letter? It's time you had a reply!*
***8** *not fml* to control (someone) severely; force rudely into silence or inactivity: [T1 (*often pass.*)] *That boy will have to be sat on hard; he simply can't be allowed to go on behaving like that. She was always sat on by her elder brothers.* → **tell off** (1), etc.
***9** to examine (something such as a case): [T1 (*often continuous tenses*)] *Which judge is sitting on this case? The police are still sitting on the mystery of the stolen jewels.*
***10** to have an effect on (someone): [T1 (*no pass., simple tenses*)] *His troubles sit lightly on him.*
**11 sit on the fence** *not fml* to take neither side in an argument: *You can't sit on the fence for ever, you'll have to make a decision or the voters will no longer trust you.*
**12 sit on one's hands** *not fml* **a** to refuse to praise a performance: *The crowd seemed to enjoy the piece, but I thought it was poorly played; I sat on my hands, and left early.* **b** to refuse to do what is expected of one: *But it's your job to answer these complaints, you can't sit on your hands!*
**13 sit well on** to suit (usu. someone): [*simple tenses*] *The chairmanship sits well on Mr Price, doesn't it?* → **sit with** (3)

**sit out** *v adv*
**1** to sit out of doors: [IØ + OUT] *Isn't it nice when the sun is warm enough for us to sit out?*
***2** to take no part in (an activity, esp. a dance): [T1] *I think I'll sit out the next dance, I'm tired. The general sat out the war in a nice safe office in the home base.* [IØ] *No thanks, I won't dance this time, I'm sitting out for a few minutes.*
***3** to stay till the end of (a performance): [T1 (*often simple tenses*)] *I decided to sit out the rest of the film although I wasn't especially enjoying it, but my friends were.* → **hear through, see through¹** (2), **sit through** (2)

*4 to stay longer than (someone): [T1 (*often simple tenses*)] *It was her turn to leave, but she was determined to sit the other woman out.* —**outsit** *v*

*5 to balance a sailing boat with one's weight by sitting or standing on the side which faces the wind: [IØ (*often simple tenses*)] *Two of you will have to sit out, or the boat will be blown over.*

**sit pretty** *v adj*

**be sitting pretty** *not fml* to be at an advantage or in a favourable position: *Once you've had the contract signed, you'll be sitting pretty. Wait a few years till house prices have risen again, and then when you sell the house you'll be sitting pretty.*

**sit through** *v prep*

**1** to remain seated until the end of (an activity): [IØ + *through*] *Were you able to sit through the meeting, or did you have to stand?*

*2 to stay till the end of (a performance), esp. without interest: [T1 (*often simple tenses*)] *Jane's parents sat through the first part of the school concert, waiting to hear their daughter sing.* → **hear through, see through**[1] (2), **sit out** (3)

***sit tight** *v adj*

**1** *not fml* to stay in the same place, as on a horse, in hiding, etc.: [IØ (*often simple tenses*)] *You must learn to sit tight so that you don't fall off! We'd better sit tight for a few weeks until the police have stopped looking for us.*

**2** *not fml* to refuse to change one's decision: [IØ (*often simple tenses*)] *Everyone disagreed, but the chairman sat tight until all the members accepted the plan.*

**sit to** *v prep* → **pose for** (1), **sit for** (1)

to hold a position for (an artist) while he paints one: [IØ + *to* (*often simple tenses*)] *One of the most beautiful women of her day, she sat to many famous painters.*

***sit under** *v prep*

esp. *AmE* to attend classes or religious services given by (a teacher): [T1 (*often simple tenses*)] *In my youth I had the great honour to sit under a very famous teacher.*

**sit up** *v adv*

**1** to (cause to) take a sitting position after lying down: [IØ + UP] *I sat up in bed, wondering what the time was.* [X9 + UP (*usu. simple tenses*)] *Here, let me sit you up, you'll be more comfortable.*

**2** to pull oneself into a position with the back straight: [IØ + UP] *Sit up* (*straight*), *children! Don't lean over the table! I sat up as an idea suddenly came to me.* —**sit-up** *n, adj*

*3 (of an animal such as a dog) to sit on the back legs with the front legs raised: [IØ] *How long did it take you to teach the dog to sit up and beg?*

*4 *not fml* to become suddenly interested and active: [IØ (*simple tenses*)] *The unexpected news made him sit up. This will make you sit up: Jane is going to have a baby!*

*5 to stay out of bed late: [IØ] *Mother, please don't sit up for me, I don't like to think that you're worrying about me. Grandfather sits up till all hours reading, he hardly seems to need any sleep now.* → **stay up** (3), etc.

**6 sit up and take notice** *not fml* to become surprised, excited, or afraid; become more conscious of something: *The government will have to sit up and take notice now that the unions are becoming so much more powerful. The only way to make the teacher sit up and take notice is to do something really shocking. The man's invention made the whole world sit up and take notice.*

**sit upon** *v prep* → SIT ON

**sit with** *v prep*

**1** to be seated together with (someone): [IØ + *with*] *I refuse to sit with that rude woman at your table.*

**2** to stay with (someone who is ill or very young or old) to be a companion to him/her: [IØ + *with*] *Would you be so kind as to sit with my mother tonight? I have to go out, but she does need company. I spent the afternoon sitting with my aunt in the hospital.*

**3 sit well with** to suit or be agreeable to (something or someone): [*simple tenses*] *The decision did not sit well with the rest of the committee, who had voted against it. The painting sits well with the rest of the room, doesn't it?* → **sit on** (13)

***size up** *v adv*

**1** to guess the size of (something): [T1] *Sizing up the wall, we decided that we should need three tins of paint.*

**2** *not fml* to judge or form an opinion about (someone or something) quite quickly: [T1] *I can't quite size him up, he's a bit of a mystery to me. The director has the ability to size up the firm's chances of winning the contract and take action straight away.*

**skate around** *v prep* → SKATE ROUND

**skate on** *v prep*

**1** to move on top of (ice) on blades fixed to boots: [IØ + *on*] *Lots of people skate on the river when it freezes every winter.*

**2 skate on thin ice** *not fml* also **skate over thin ice** to take risks, esp. in speaking: *You were skating on thin ice, weren't you, mentioning that delicate subject!*

**skate over** *v prep*

**1** to cross (ice) on blades fixed to boots: [IØ + *over*] *How long does it take to skate over the frozen lake to the other side?*

*2 *not fml* to avoid dealing with (something such as a difficulty) by making only passing mention of it: [T1] *Don't try to skate over the question by changing the subject. Every time we come to that particular matter, the chairman skates over it.* → **skate round** (2), **slide over** (2), **slide round** (2)

**3 skate over thin ice** → SKATE ON (2)

**skate round** *v prep* also **skate around** I

**1** to move round (ice) on blades fixed to

boots: [IØ + *round*] *Round and round the frozen lake the children skated.*

*2 *not fml* to avoid dealing with (something such as a difficulty) by making only passing mention of it: [T1] *Don't try to skate round the question by changing the subject.* → **skate over** (2), **slide over** (2), **slide round** (2)

*3 *not fml* to find a way to deal with (something such as a difficulty) to one's advantage: [T1] *If you are clever you can sometimes skate round the tax laws. We could skate round the lack of players by removing the last piece from the concert list.* → **get round²** (2), **scrub round** (2), **slide round** (2)

**sketch in** *v adv* also **etch in**

**1** to add (something) by drawing: [T1 + IN] *The artist has sketched in a few trees to show what the new building will look like in its natural surroundings.* —**sketched-in** *adj*

*2 to explain or describe more fully by adding (detail): [T1 (*often simple tenses*)] *I don't quite understand; can you sketch in a few details of what you're suggesting?*

**sketch out** *v adv*

**1** to make a rough drawing of (something): [T1 + OUT] *The new buildings have only been sketched out so far; we'll send a more complete drawing when all the facts have been considered.* —**sketched-out** *adj*

*2 to make a rough plan of (something); suggest the general nature of (an idea): [T1 (*often simple tenses*)] *The general sketched out his battle plan to a special group of officers, leaving them to organize the details.*

***skid up** *v adv; prep* → **shin down, shin up, swarm up**

*not fml* to climb quickly and easily up (something such as a tree): [IØ;T1] *"You can go where you please, you can skid up the trees, but you can't get away from the guns!"* (Rudyard Kipling, *Screw-Guns*)

**skim off** *v adv*

**1** to remove (floating fat) from (liquid): [T1 + OFF] *Remember to skim off the fat from the soup before you give it to our guests.* → **cream off** (1)

*2 *not fml* to remove (the best) by choosing: [T1 (*often pass.*)] *The country's best scientists have been skimmed off for military purposes.* → **cream off** (2)

**skim over** *v prep*

**1** to move very quickly and lightly over the surface of (something such as water): [L9 + *over*] *Look at the way those insects skim over the water!*

*2 *not fml* to look at (something) very quickly without paying much attention: [T1] *I've only had time to skim over the plans for the new buildings, but they look good so far.* → **skim through, skip through**

***skim through** *v prep* → **skim over** (2), **skip through**

*not fml* to read (something) very quickly, simply to get the main ideas: [T1] *I only had time to skim through your article, but it seemed very interesting.*

**skin down** *v adv; prep AmE* → **SHIN DOWN**

***skin over** *v adv*

**1** to become covered with a new growth of skin: [IØ] *The wound should skin over quite quickly now, it's clean and healthy.*

**2** to form a skin: [IØ] *You didn't put the lid on the paint tin, and the paint has skinned over; we can't use it now.*

**skin through** *v adv; prep*

**1** *AmE* to be only just able to pass through (something narrow): [L9 + THROUGH/*through* (*often simple tenses*)] *The cave is very narrow ahead, but we should be able to skin through (it)* → **scrape through** (1), **squeak through** (1), **squeeze through** (1)

*2 *AmE* to be only just able to pass (something such as an examination): [IØ;T1 (*usu. simple tenses*)] *Some of you passed well, but most of you only skinned through (the examination).* → **scrape through** (2), **squeak through** (2), **squeeze through** (2)

**skin up** *v adv; prep AmE* → **SHIN UP**

***skip it** *v pron*

*not fml* it doesn't matter; forget it: [IØ (*usu. imper.*)] *"But I don't understand your joke!" "Oh, well, skip it, it's of no importance."*

***skip off/out** *v adv*

*not fml* to leave, usu. without permission: [IØ (*usu. simple tenses*)] *Every time I ask that boy to do a job for me, he skips off and plays with his friends!*

**skip over** *v prep*

**1** to pass over (an area) by jumping with a rope: [IØ + *over*] *'She skipped over water, she danced over sea, And all the birds in the air couldn't catch me!'* (children's song)

*2 *not fml* to pass quickly over (a matter): [T1 (*usu. simple tenses*)] *I'm prepared to skip over one or two mistakes, but not this repeated carelessness. Let's skip over the first few things on the list, and get to the really important matters.*

***skip through** *v prep* → **skim over** (2), **skim through**

*not fml* to read (something) very quickly, simply to get the main idea: [T1] *I skipped through the first part of the book, eager to get to the exciting bits.*

***skirt around/round** *v prep*

*not fml* to find a way to deal with (a difficulty) indirectly: [T1] *You can't skirt round the matter, you'll have to give the workers a satisfactory answer.*

***skittle out** *v adv*

(in cricket) to dismiss (a whole team) for a low score: [T1 (*usu. simple tenses*)] *The village team were skittled out for only fifty runs by the experienced visiting players.*

***skive off** *v adv*

*sl* to avoid work, esp. by staying out of the way: [IØ] *No skiving off now, everyone must stay till the job is finished.*

***slacken off** *v adv* also **slack off**

**1** also **slack away, slacken away** to loosen (something such as a rope): [T1] *Slacken off those ropes there, there's a storm coming!*

**2** to become more lazy or inactive: [IØ] *House sales in this city usually slacken off during our severe winters. The students tend to slacken off after the first few weeks when their interest is new.* → **ease off** (3), **ease up** (2)

**3** → EASE OFF (2)

***slacken up** *v adv* also **slack up**

to (cause to) reduce speed or effort: [IØ] *The doctor advised Jim to slacken up for a few months, as his lifestyle was having a bad effect on his heart.* [T1] *Please slacken up your speed, I can't run as fast as you!*

***slam down** *v adv* → **slap down** (1)

to put (something) down with a loud noise: [T1 (*usu. simple tenses*)] *She slammed down the letter and walked angrily out of the office.*

**slam in** *v prep*

**slam the door in someone's face**

**1** *not fml* to close the door while someone outside is still speaking or waiting: *Looking for somewhere to live when I was expecting our first baby, I grew very tired of having the door slammed repeatedly in my face.*

**2** *not fml* to refuse to see or talk to someone, esp. in a disagreement that needs to be settled: *The workers only asked for a small increase in pay, but the employers just slammed the door in their faces.*

***slam on** *v adv*

**1** to put on (clothes) hurriedly: [T1 (*usu. simple tenses*)] *He slammed on his hat and ran out of the house.* → **clap on**[1] (1), **jam on** (1), **slap on**[1] (1)

**2** to use (something) hurriedly, as by pressing: [T1 (*usu. simple tenses*)] *The driver slammed on the brakes but failed to stop in time.* → **clap on**[1] (2), **jam on** (2)

***slam to** *v adv* → **pull to**[1], etc.

(of a door or window) to (cause to) close with a loud noise: [T1 (*often simple tenses*)] *Every time that boy leaves the house he slams the door to, it's quite unnecessary.* [IØ (*often simple tenses*)] *The door slammed to in the high wind, locking her out.*

***slant against** *v prep* → **weight against**

*not fml* to express (something written) in a way that is unfavourable to (an idea or a particular group of people): [D1 (*usu. pass.*)] *The article seems to be slanted against the present popularity of Eastern religions.*

**slant towards** *v prep*

**1** to be in a position at an angle in the direction of (something): [IØ + *towards* (*often simple tenses*)] *The old house slants towards the street, because its beams are cracked with age.* → **slope towards**, etc.

***2** *not fml* to express (something such as a story) from the point of view of (a particular group of people) so as to interest them: [D1 (*usu. pass.*)] *The article seems to be slanted towards modern young women in search of equality.* → **angle towards**

**slap down** *v adv*

**1** to place (something) down with a loud noise: [T1 + DOWN (*usu. simple tenses*)] *She slapped her letter down on the office table and walked out in a bad temper.* → **slam down**

***2** *not fml* to control or scold (someone): [T1 (*usu. simple tenses*)] *It's time somebody slapped that boy down; he can't be allowed to go on behaving like that.* → **tell off** (1), etc.

**slap on**[1] *v adv*

**1** to put (clothing) on carelessly: [T1 + ON (*to*) (*usu. simple tenses*)] *He slapped his hat on and ran out of the house.* → **clap on**[1] (1), **jam on** (1), **slam on** (1)

**2** to put (something such as paint or clay) on hastily and thickly: [T1 + ON (*to*)] *I thought I asked you to do this carefully? The paint has just been slapped on!*

**slap on**[2] *v prep*

**1** to put (clothing) on (part of the body) hastily and thickly: [T1 + ON *(to)] He slapped his hat on his head and ran out of the house.* → **clap on**[2] (1)

**2** to hit (someone) with the open hand on (part of the body): [T1 + *on*] *All his friends slapped him on the back to praise him for his good shot.* → **clap on**[2] (3)

***3** *not fml* to add (an amount or rate) to increase the cost of (something): [D1] *When the new tax laws were passed, the taxpayers found that the government had slapped another 5% on cigarettes.* → **clap on**[2] (3)

***slap up** *v adv*

to prepare (a meal) hastily: [T1 (*usu. simple tenses*)] *Can you slap up a quick meal for my friends before we rush to the game?*

**slave at** *v prep*

*not fml* to work too hard and unwillingly at (something or doing something): [IØ + *at*] *I get so tired of slaving at this work day after day. By slaving at finishing the book, I might have only a few more months of hard work.*

**slave away** *v adv*

to work very hard and unwillingly for a long time: [IØ + AWAY (*at*) (*often continuous tenses*)] *Travelling round the world is better than slaving away at some dull job for poor pay. By slaving away for two hours, I at last got the cooker clean.*

**slave over** *v prep*

to work very hard and unwillingly at (something such as a machine): [IØ + *over*] *Here I've been, slaving over a hot cooker while you have been out enjoying yourselves, and what thanks do I get?*

***sleep around** *v adv*

*not fml* (esp. of a woman) to have sexual relations with several different people: [IØ] *Many of today's young people think it's a good idea to sleep around before they decide which partner to marry. Her friends don't approve of her since she started sleeping around.*

**sleep away** *v adv*
**1** to sleep continuously: [IØ + AWAY (*often continuous tenses*)] *When I last looked in the bedroom, he was still sleeping away.*
***2** to pass (time) in sleep: [T1] *Are you going to sleep the whole morning away?*
***3** to get rid of (something such as trouble) by sleeping: [T1] *Go and have a good rest, you might be able to sleep your troubles away.* → **sleep off**

***sleep in** *v adv*
**1** to sleep late in the morning: [IØ] *Don't wake me in the morning, I'd like to sleep in for a time. I'm sorry I'm late, I slept in by mistake.* —**sleep-in** *n* → **lie in** (1)
**2** to sleep at one's place of work: [IØ (*usu. simple tenses*)] *My mother used to have a female servant who slept in.* —**sleep-in** *adj* → **live in**[1], **live out, sleep out** (2)

***sleep off** *v adv* → **sleep away** (3)
to get rid of (something bad such as a feeling, effect, or trouble) during one's sleep: [T1] *She should be able to sleep off the effects of the drug within a few hours. I hope Father will sleep off his bad temper.*

**sleep on** *v prep*
**1** also **sleep upon** to take one's nightly rest, or lose consciousness while lying on top of (furniture or a surface); rest on (something): [IØ + *on*] *I like to sleep on a nice soft bed. Look at those sea animals sleeping on the sand.*
**2 sleep on it** to consider and usu. make a decision about something, overnight or by resting: *Don't worry about making a decision now; sleep on it, and let us know in the morning what you want to do.*

**sleep out** *v adv*
**1** to sleep out of doors: [IØ + OUT] *It's so hot tonight, can't we sleep out in the garden? The children love sleeping out in tents when we go camping.*
***2** to sleep away from one's place of work: [IØ (*usu. simple tenses*)] *There are two other servants who sleep out.* → **live in**[1], **live out** (1), **sleep in** (2)
***3** to spend the night away from home: [IØ] *Their children are always going to parties and seem to sleep out nearly every night.*
***4** to pass (time) or consider (an idea) in sleep: [T1 (*often simple tenses*)] *Sometimes he feels that he would like to sleep out the rest of his days without having to work or think any more.*

***sleep over** *v adv*
esp. *AmE* to stay overnight at someone else's home: [IØ (*at*)] *You must get permission from your mother to sleep over at your friend's house.*

***sleep rough** *v adv* → **live rough, rough it**
to sleep without a proper bed: [IØ] *Jobless and penniless, he had to sleep rough in the fields for several months.*

**sleep round** *v adv; prep*
**sleep the clock round/sleep round the clock** to sleep for twenty-four hours: *The climbers, when they returned, were so tired with their efforts that they fell into bed and slept the clock round.*

**sleep through** *v prep*
to fail to be woken by (a noise, clock, etc.): [IØ + *through*] *I was a small child at the beginning of the war, and soon learned to sleep through heavy bombing. I'm sorry I'm late, I slept through the clock this morning.*

**sleep together** *v adv*
**1** (of two or more people) to share a bed: [IØ + TOGETHER] *When they were younger, the sisters had to sleep together in a narrow bed, as the house was so crowded.* → **sleep with** (1)
***2** *not fml* (of two people, usu. a man and woman) to have sexual relations: [IØ] *Did Jim and Mary sleep together before they were married?* → **couple with** (1), **lie with** (2), **sleep with** (2)

**sleep upon** *v prep* → SLEEP ON (1)

**sleep with** *v prep*
**1** to share one's bed with (someone or something): [IØ + *with*] *Are you seriously telling me that at his age, your son still sleeps with his toy bear?* → **sleep together** (1)
***2** *not fml* also *sl* **bed with** to have sexual relations with (someone, usu. of the opposite sex): [T1] *Did Jim sleep with Mary before they were married? "Never sleep with anyone whose troubles are worse than your own."* (Nelson Algren, in H.E.F. Donohue, *Conversations with Nelson Algren, Foreword*) → **couple with** (1), **lie with** (2), **sleep together** (2)

***slew around/round** *v adv* also *AmE* **slue around**
(of a heavy object) to (cause to) turn in a different direction, usu. awkwardly: [IØ (*usu. simple tenses*)] *The car slewed round on the icy road.* [T1 (*usu. simple tenses*)] *The captain could not slew the ship round in time to avoid an accident. The wind slewed the notice board round so that it pointed in the wrong direction.*

***slice into** *v prep* → **cut into** (2)
to begin to cut (something) by putting a sharp blade into it: [T1] *It's best to slice into a rich cake from the middle. Mind you don't slice into your hand with that sharp sword.*

***slice off** *v adv* → **cut off** (1), **snip off, strike off** (1), **swish off**
to remove (a piece of something) by cutting with a sharp blade: [T1] *Just slice off enough meat for your dinner, and put the rest back. He put his hand too near the machine and it sliced his finger off. Show the child how to slice the top off before he eats his boiled egg.*

***slice through** *v prep*
to pass through (something) with or as with a sharp blade: [T1] *The train, unable to stop in time, sliced through the bus, killing nine passengers.*

**slice up** *v adv* → **cut up** (1)
to divide or cut (something) in thin pieces:

[T1 + UP] *I have to slice up the meat, ready to put it between bread. First slice all the fruit up, then add the ice cream.*

*__slick down__ *v adv*
to control (hair), making it smooth with oil: [T1] *I don't like that fashion the men used to have of slicking their hair down.*

*__slick up__ *v adv* → **smarten up, spiff up, spruce up**
*not fml* to make (oneself or something) neat and attractive: [T1] *I can see you're going to the dance, you're all slicked up. I suppose we'd better slick up the house a bit if we want to sell it.*

**slide around** *v prep* → **SLIDE ROUND**

**slide into** *v prep*
**1** to (cause to) enter (something) by sliding: [I∅ + *into*] *The car turned on the wet road and slid into the fence.* [T1 + *into*] *You slide your coin into the machine here, and that is supposed to start it working.* → **slip into** (1)
**2** to enter (a place) silently: [L9 + *into*] *She had the ability to slide into a room without anyone noticing.* → **slip into** (2)
*__3__ to pass (something) into (something such as a hand or pocket) secretly: [D1] *She slid a note into my hand when the teacher wasn't looking.* → **slip into** (3)
*__4__ to begin to enter (a state, often bad) gradually or unintentionally: [T1] *It's sad to see one's own son sliding into evil ways. You have slid into a bad habit of repeating yourself. It's too easy to slide into crime again when you get out of prison.* → **get into** (11), etc.

**slide out of** *v adv prep*
**1** to leave (a place) silently: [L9 + OUT + *of*] *Can you slide out of the room without the chairman seeing you?*
*__2__ *not fml* to become free of or escape from (something unwanted or bad): [T1] *It's no good trying to slide out of the punishment you deserve; this time you've been well and truly caught. You can't slide out of your responsibility in this matter.* → **get out of** (13), etc.

**slide over** *v prep*
**1** to (cause to) move smoothly on top of (a surface): [I∅ + *over*] *The dancers appeared to slide over the floor, their feet hardly touching it.* [T1 + *over*] *Slide your hand over the door to see if you can feel the crack.*
*__2__ *not fml* to avoid dealing with (something) by making only passing mention of it: [T1] *The politician tried to slide over the delicate subject, but the crowd would not let him forget it.*

**slide round** *v prep* also **slide around**
**1** to move smoothly around (an area): [I∅ + *round*] *The children loved sliding round the newly polished floor.*
*__2__ *not fml* to avoid dealing with (something such as a difficulty) by making only passing mention of it: [T1] *Don't allow the chairman to slide round that urgent matter; it must be dealt with at once.* → **get round**[2] (2), **scrub round** (2), **skate over** (2), **skate round** (2, 3), **slide over** (2)

**slim down** *v adv*
to (cause to) become thinner or less: [I∅ + DOWN] *You've slimmed down such a lot since we last met!* [T1 + DOWN] *We've had to slim down our holiday plans since costs have risen so much. The railway system in our country is being slimmed down.*

**sling at** *v prep*
**1** *not fml* to throw (something) at (someone or something): [T1 + *at*] *Stop those boys slinging rocks at the cars, they'll cause an accident!* → **throw at** (1), etc.
**2** **sling mud at** *infml* to speak rudely or offensively about (someone): *No politician will win the votes of serious-minded people if all he does is sling mud at his opponent.* → **fling at** (3), **throw at** (4)

*__sling out__ *v adv*
**1** *not fml* to get rid of (something): [T1] *Do sling out those old newspapers, they've been here for weeks.* → **throw out** (2), etc.
**2** *not fml* to make (someone) leave: [T1 (*of*)] *The family down the road have been slung out of the house for not paying their rent.* → **throw out** (4), etc., (5), etc.

**sling up** *v adv*
**1** to hang (something) high in a support, as of rope or cloth: [T1 + UP (*often pass.*)] *His broken leg was slung up above the hospital bed.*
*__2__ *not fml* to remind someone of (something unpleasant): [T1] *Every time she wanted to make him feel uncomfortable, she would sling up his past in his face.* → **bring up** (3), **cast up** (4), **fling up** (6), **throw up** (7)

**slink out** *v adv*
*not fml* to leave in a secretive manner: [L9 + OUT (*of*)] *We were still deciding his punishment when we found that the boy had slunk out of the room while we weren't looking.*

**slip away** *v adv*
**1** to leave quietly: [L9 + AWAY] *I'd like to slip away before the end of the meeting, so I'll sit at the back. Mary could not enjoy the party, and slipped away after an hour, with a quick word of thanks to her hostess.* → **slip off** (2), **slip out** (2), **sneak away, sneak out**
*__2__ (of time) to pass quickly: [I∅] *This summer has simply slipped away, we've had such fun!* → **slip by**[1] (2)

**slip back** *v adv*
**1** to slide in a backward direction, unintentionally: [I∅ + BACK] *Be careful, the car is slipping back on this steep hill.*
*__2__ *not fml* to fail to improve; become worse; return to a lower standard: [I∅ (*often continuous tenses*)] *Your work has been slipping back recently, you must make more effort. Try as I might, I keep slipping back and am quickly losing hope.*

**slip by/past**[1] *v adv*
**1** to pass quietly: [L9 + BY/PAST] *The enemy*

*guns were facing inland, so our ship slipped by without being seen.*
*__2__ (of time) to pass quickly: [I∅] *All these weeks have slipped by, and I've hardly any work to show for it!* → **slip away** (2)
*__3__ (of something such as a chance) to pass without being used: [I∅ (*often simple tenses*)] *Never let a chance to improve your English slip by!*

**slip by/past[2]** *v prep*
**1** to move quietly past (something or someone): [L9 + *by/past*] *You should be able to slip past the open door without the teacher seeing you.*
*__2__ (of time) to pass (someone): [T1 (*no pass.*)] *Sometimes I feel that life is slipping by me, and I've done nothing!*
*__3__ to (cause to) be passed by (someone); (cause to) be unnoticed by (someone): [T1 (*no pass., usu. simple tenses*)] *How did a mistake like that slip by the printers?* [D1 (*usu. simple tenses*)] *You'll never slip an idea like that past the examiners.*

**slip down** *v adv*
**1** to fall over accidentally by sliding: [I∅ + DOWN] *My aunt has slipped down in the High Street and hurt her ankle, so I have to take her to the doctor.*
**2** to fall easily down something: [L9 + DOWN] *The coin has slipped down behind the books, and I can't reach it.*
*__3__ (usu. of a liquid) to be easily swallowed: [I∅] *The medicine slipped down well enough, but tasted terrible.*

**slip from** *v prep*
**1** to fall accidentally from (something): [I∅ + *from* (*often simple tenses*)] *The wheel slipped from my frozen hand, and the car went right across the road.*
**2** to fall below (a former standard); get worse: [I∅ + *from*] *Your work has been slipping from the standard that we expect of you.*
*__3__ to be forgotten by (usu. one's mind): [T1 (*no pass., simple tenses*)] *I knew her face, but her name had completely slipped from my mind.*

**slip in** *v adv*
**1** to (cause to) enter a place or group quietly: [L9 + IN] *You can slip in after the first piece of music is played.* [X9 + IN] *I'll see if I can slip you in, though I think the course is filled.* → **sneak in** (1)
*__2__ to be able to add (something, usu. spoken or written): [T1 (*usu. simple tenses*)] *I wasn't able to slip in a single remark! Every time he appears on television, he slips in a mention of his latest book.* → **sneak in** (2)

**slip into** *v prep*
**1** to (cause to) enter (something) by sliding: [I∅ + *into*] *The car turned on the wet road and slipped into the fence.* [T1 + *into* (*usu. simple tenses*)] *You slip the envelope into the hole in the top of the box, so that its contents are kept secret.* → **slide into** (1)
**2** to (cause to) enter (a place) silently or secretly: [L9 + *into*] *I have to come late, so I'll slip into the room at the back, if you'll save me a place.* [X9 + *into*] *How can you slip me into the concert without a ticket?* → **slide into** (2)
*__3__ to pass (something) into (something such as a hand or pocket) secretly: [D1] *She slipped a note into my hand when the teacher wasn't looking.* → **slide into** (3)
*__4__ to begin to enter (a state, often bad): [T1] *It's sad to see one's own son slipping into evil ways. You have slipped into a bad habit of repeating yourself.* → **get into** (11), etc.
*__5__ to (cause to) be added to (something, usu. spoken or written): [T1 (*no pass.*)] *Some careless mistakes have slipped into the printing. Bad habits are slipping into your speech.* [D1 (*usu. simple tenses*)] *Can you slip a mention of my new film into your broadcast talk?*
*__6__ to put on (clothes) quickly: [T1 (*no pass.*)] *Wait here while I slip into something cooler.*

**slip off** *v adv*
**1** to fall off by sliding unintentionally: [I∅ + OFF] *I thought I was safe on the branch, until my foot slipped off and I fell to the ground.*
**2** to leave quietly: [L9 + OFF] *Mary couldn't bear the party, so she slipped off while no one was looking.* → **slip away** (1), **slip out** (2), **sneak away, sneak out**
*__3__ to remove (clothes) quickly: [T1 (*usu. simple tenses*)] *He slipped his coat off and jumped into the river to save the drowning child.* → **take off[1]** (2), etc.

***slip on** *v adv*
to put on (clothes) quickly: [T1 (*usu. simple tenses*)] *He stopped only long enough to slip a coat on, and then ran out into the rain.* —**slip-on** *n, adj*

**slip out** *v adv*
**1** to fall out by sliding unintentionally: [I∅ + OUT (*of*)] *Where's my key? It must have slipped out when I opened my bag to get the money!*
**2** to leave quietly without being noticed: [L9 + OUT] *Where's that boy? He must have slipped out when my back was turned?* → **slip away** (1), **slip off** (2), **sneak away, sneak out**
*__3__ *not fml* (of a secret) to be said without intention: [I∅ (*usu. simple tenses*)] *I didn't mean to tell you his name, it just slipped out.*

**slip out of** *v adv prep*
**1** to fall out of (something) by sliding unintentionally: [I∅ + OUT + *of*] *The key must have slipped out of my bag when I opened it to get the money.*
**2** to (cause to) leave (a place or group) quietly and without being noticed: [L9 + OUT + *of*] *I'll slip out of the meeting as quietly as I can—I have a train to catch so I can't stay to the end.* [X9 + OUT + *of*] *How can we slip the escaped prisoner out of the country?* → **sneak out of** (1)
*__3__ to take off (clothes) quickly: [T1] *Just give*

*me a minute to slip out of these wet things, and I'll join you.* → **take off**[1] (2), etc.

*4 *not fml* to become free of or escape from (something bad or unwanted): [T1] *It's no good trying to slip out of the punishment you deserve; this time you've been well and truly caught. You can't slip out of your responsibility in this matter.* → **get out of** (13), etc.

**slip over** *v prep*

**1** to (cause to) be pulled easily over (something such as the head or body): [L9 + *over* (*simple tenses*)] *The cover is made to slip over the chair and be removed for washing. Will this woollen garment slip over your head all right?* [X9 + *over*] *I'll just slip a coat over my shoulders, it's cool outside.* —**slipover** *n, adj*

*2 *AmE infml* to use (a trick) in order to deceive (someone): [D1 (*usu. simple tenses*)] *You'll never slip that old trick over our chairman, he knows too much.*

**3 slip one over** *AmE infml* to deceive (someone) by means of a trick: *He took great delight in slipping one over the guards.*

**slip past**[1] *v adv* → SLIP BY[1]

**slip past**[2] *v prep* → SLIP BY[2]

**slip through**[1] *v adv*

**1** to pass quietly: [L9 + THROUGH] *The ship slipped through while the enemy guns were pointed in the opposite direction.*

*2 to (cause to) be allowed to pass, often secretly or illegally: [IØ] *How did that new law slip through? I hope my request slips through.* [T1] *Some tourists are still slipping goods through without paying taxes.*

**slip through**[2] *v prep*

**1** to (cause to) pass quickly, quietly, or secretly through (something): [L9 + *through*] *How many fish have slipped through the net? The ship slipped through the water with great ease.* [X9 + *through*] *We have been able to slip three men through the enemy defences.*

**2 slip through one's fingers/the net** *not fml* to be allowed to escape: *We thought we had caught the thieves, but they slipped through our fingers and got free.*

**slip up** *v adv*

**1** to rise accidentally by sliding: [L9 + UP] *Your collar has slipped up again; let me put it in place.*

*2 *not fml* to make a careless mistake: [IØ] *Someone must have slipped up—the note should have left the office for approval two weeks ago.* —**slip-up** *n*

**slit up** *v adv*

**1** to make a long cut in (cloth, a garment, or stitches): [T1 + UP (*often simple tenses*)] *The coat was too narrow, so I had to slit it up and add another piece, to make it bigger.*

*2 *infml* to wound (someone) intentionally: [T1 (*usu. simple tenses*)] *Threaten to slit him up if he won't give the money, that should make him do it!* → **carve up** (4), **cut up** (7)

**slobber over** *v prep*

**1** to allow liquid to fall from the mouth at the sight of (usu. food): [IØ + *over*] *I don't like watching animals eat, they always slobber over the food so much.* → **drool over** (1)

*2 *not fml* to show too much love for (someone such as a child or an animal): [T1] *Every time a new baby arrives in the neighbourhood, the old woman has to go and slobber over it. I do dislike the way she slobbers over those cats as if they're so wonderful.* → **drool over**[2] (2), **slop over**[2] (2)

***slog at** *v prep* → **peg away at, plod away, plug away at**

*not fml* to work hard and continuously at (a difficulty or job): [T1 (*pass. rare*)] *Jane at last passed the examination by slogging (away) at her studies for months on end.*

**slog out** *v adv*

**slog it out** *not fml* **a** to work hard at something difficult until it is finished: *There's no way I can get any help with this big job; I just have to slog it out on my own.* **b** → SLUG OUT

**slop about/around** *v adv; prep*

**1** (of liquid) to move loosely in (a container): [IØ + ABOUT/AROUND/*about/around*] *There must be a hole somewhere, I can hear the water slopping about in the bottom of the boat.* → **slosh about**

*2 *not fml* to be lazily inactive in (a place): [IØ] *You'll never have a future if all you do is slop around all day.* [T1] *He just slops around the house all day.* → **slouch about**

***slop out** *v adv*

to empty (a container); remove the contents of (a bucket): [T1] *When you've slopped out the waste bucket, clean it thoroughly.* [IØ] *Have all the prisoners finished slopping out?*

***slop over**[1] *v adv* → **spill over** (1)

(of liquid) to overflow a container, usu. with movement: [IØ] *If you fill the cup too full, the coffee might slop over when you carry it to the table.*

**slop over**[2] *v prep*

**1** to cause (liquid) to fall on top of (something or someone): [X9 + *over*] *As she fell, she slopped the wine all over his shirt.*

*2 esp. *AmE not fml* to show too much love for (someone such as a child, or an animal): [T1] *Every time a new baby arrives in the neighbourhood, she has to go and slop (all) over it.* → **drool over** (2), **slobber over** (2)

**slope down** *v adv* → **shelve down to**

(usu. of land) to descend gradually (in the direction of something): [IØ + DOWN (*to*) (*simple tenses*)] *The garden slopes down so steeply that it's difficult to grow anything.*

***slope off** *v adv*

*not fml* to go away, esp. secretly so as to avoid work: [IØ] *Where's that boy? Every time I want him for a little job, he's sloped off somewhere!*

**slope towards** *v prep* → **incline towards** (1), **lean towards** (1), **slant towards** (1)

to descend at an angle in the direction of (something): [IØ + *towards* (*simple tenses*)]

*The roof slopes towards the back of the house. The garden slopes towards the road, so that we have a clear view.*

**slope up** *v adv*
to rise at an angle: [IØ + UP (*simple tenses*)] *The garden slopes up so steeply at the back that we can see nothing out of the windows.*

**slosh about/around** *v adv* → **slop about** (1)
(of liquid) to (cause to) move noisily in a container: [IØ + ABOUT/AROUND] *There must be a hole somewhere, I can hear water sloshing about in the bottom of the boat.*

**slosh on** *v adv; prep*
to put (something such as paint) thickly and carelessly on (something): [T1 + ON/*on*] *Don't slosh the paint on so thickly, we want a nice smooth surface. Who's been sloshing mud on the walls?*

***slot in** *v adv*
**1** to fit, add, or include (something or someone) in the right place: [T1 (*to*)] *We can slot in the new entry in aplhabetical order. It's not easy to slot all the young school-leavers in to suitable jobs.*
**2** *infml* (in football) to kick (the ball) neatly into the goal: [T1] *Brown slotted the ball in during the last few minutes of the game, and victory was certain.*

**slouch about/around** *v adv; prep* → **slop about** (2)
to behave lazily, esp. moving inactively in (a place): [IØ + ABOUT/AROUND/*about/around*] *Ever since he lost his job, he's done nothing but slouch unhappily around (the house).*

**slough off** *v adv*
**1** (usu. of an animal) to remove (its old skin): [T1 + OFF] *Every spring this snake sloughs off its old skin, as it has grown too big for it.* → **cast off** (5), **shuffle off** (2)
***2** *not fml* to get rid of (something such as a responsibility): [T1] *It's difficult to slough off old habits even when you want to.* → **fling off** (3), etc.

***slough over** *v prep* → **gloss over, slur over, smooth over**[2]
esp. *AmE not fml* to deal quickly with (something, usu. wrong) so as to reduce its importance: [T1 (*often simple tenses*)] *The chairman tried to slough over the problems in the contract because he was keen to get it signed.*

**slow down/up** *v adv*
**1** to (cause to) move at a slower rate: [T1 + DOWN/UP] *The severe snowstorm has slowed the traffic up. Can't you slow this machine down? It's ruining the cloth. She's quite fit, but her bad leg slows her down when we're out for a walk.* [IØ + DOWN/UP] *Slow down, will you, there's a police car ahead. The bus slowed up to allow the passenger to get on board.*
***2** to live at a slower rate, in a quieter less active manner: [IØ] *The doctor advised Jim to slow up for a time, to give his heart a chance.* → **go easy** (1), **go slow** (2), **take easy**
***3** to reduce (production): [T1] *The factory has had to slow down production since the workers refused to do their best.* —**slowdown** *n*

***slue around/round** *v adv AmE* → SLEW AROUND

**slug out** *v adv* also **slog out** → **fight out** (1, 2), **fight through**[1] (1)
**slug it out** to fight or argue to the end: *The two evenly-matched fighters had to slug it out over all twelve rounds until a decision could be made as to who was the winner. When I left, the politicians were still slugging it out, but I had lost interest in their argument.*

**sluice down** *v adv*
to wash (a surface) thoroughly with a lot of freely flowing water: [T1 + DOWN] *The sailors had to sluice the ship's floors down every day to get rid of the salt.*

**sluice out** *v adv*
to clean (something such as a pipe, container, or building) with a lot of freely flowing water: [T1 + OUT] *The pipe is blocked again; you'd better sluice it out so that we don't have any more trouble with it.*

**slump down** *v adv*
to sit down heavily: [IØ + DOWN (*often simple tenses*)] *I was so tired that I slumped down in the chair and fell asleep.*

**slump over** *v adv; prep*
to fall or place (oneself) with the back bent, in a heavy manner: [IØ + OVER/*over* (*often simple tenses*)] *When I touched him, he slumped over and I saw that he was dead.* [X9 + OVER/*over* (*usu. pass.*)] *After a day at work slumped over a desk, it's good to get some exercise.*

***slur over** *v prep* → **gloss over, slough over, smooth over**[2]
to deal with (a mistake or difficulty) quickly so as to reduce its importance: [T1 (*often simple tenses*)] *The Minister tried to slur over his department's mistake although it had cost the taxpayers a lot of money.*

***smack down** *v adv* → **tell off** (1), etc.
*AmE infml* to scold (someone) for a fault: [T1 (*often pass.*)] *That boy deserves to be thoroughly smacked down, offering work like that!*

***smack of** *v prep* → **savour of, smell of** (2), **stink of**
to contain a taste or suggestion of (a quality): [T1 (*no pass., simple tenses*)] *Your last remark smacked of rudeness. This arrangement smacks of dishonest dealing. That wine seems to smack of sunny hillsides.*

**smart for** *v prep*
*not fml* to suffer the results of (usu. wrong action): [IØ + *for*] *I hope you smart for your carelessness! When the police catch the men who stole the jewels, they'll make them smart for it!*

**smarten up** *v adv* → **slick up, spiff up, spruce up**
to (cause to) become more neat and attractive; work harder; behave better: [T1 + UP

*We shall have to spend some time smartening up the house if we want to get a good price for it. Don't you want to smarten yourself up a bit before you meet your girlfriend? This new officer should smarten the soldiers up a bit.* [IØ + UP] *That boy has begun to smarten up recently, since we complained about his work. The young people have stopped dressing untidily, and are smartening up since it has become so difficult to get jobs.*

**smash in** *v adv*
**1** to break (something) in an inward direction: [T1 + IN] *The firemen had to smash the door in to get into the house. The side of the car was all smashed in when it hit the bus.*
**2 smash someone's face in** *infml* to beat someone severely (often said as a threat): *Give me the money, or I'll smash your face in!*

**smash up** *v adv* → **bang up** (1), **bash up** (1), **batter up, mash up** (2), **prang up** (1)
to destroy or damage (something) or wound (someone) seriously as in an accident: [T1 + UP] *The thieves not only stole the jewels, but smashed up most of the valuable furniture in the room. The wreck of the plane lay smashed up on the ground. I daren't let the children drive in case they smash up the car. He was a promising student until he got smashed up in a road accident.*

**smear on** *v prep*
to spread (something liquid or nearly liquid) on (a surface) to mark it: [X9 + *on*] *The murderess smeared blood on the faces of the two men so that they would seem guilty.*

**smear with** *v prep* → **bedaub with, besmear with**
to cover (a surface) with a mark or marks made by (something liquid or nearly liquid): [X9 + *with*] *Her clothes were soon smeared with mud from passing cars.*

**smell at** *v prep* → **sniff at** (1)
to put the nose to (something or someone) so as to smell it or him/her, usu. in order to find something out: [IØ + *at*] *Will you smell at this meat and tell me if it's gone bad? The dog smelt at the stranger for a minute but did not recognize him.*

**smell of** *v prep*
**1** to have a smell like that of (something causing the smell): [T1 + *of* (*no pass.*)] *The whole room smelt of roses. I keep this pan separate so that other pans won't smell of fish.* → **stink of** (1), **stink with** (1)
*__2__ to contain the suggestion of (something, usu. bad): [T1 (*no pass.*)] *This arrangement smells of dishonest dealing. His offer smelt of a trap, so I didn't accept it.* → **savour of, smack of, stink of** (2)
**3 smell of the lamp** *lit old use* (esp. of books or other written work) to appear to have been done, written, etc., with much study rather than with natural original power: *His best poems were written when he was young, and most of his later books smell too much of the lamp.*

***smell out** *v adv*
**1** to find (something or someone) by smelling: [T1] *The police used dogs to smell out the criminals in their hiding place. Other dogs are used to smell out unlawful drugs which travellers are carrying.* → **nose out** (1), **sniff out** (1)
**2** to discover (something, often bad) by guessing: [T1] *He has a strange ability for smelling out a mystery.* → **nose out** (2), **sniff out** (2)
**3** to fill (a place) with a smell, usu. bad: [T1] *Those terrible cigarettes smell the whole room out, I wish you'd get rid of them.* → **smell up, stink out** (2), **stink up**

**smell to** *v prep* → **stink to**
**smell to (high) heaven: a** to smell very bad: [*usu. simple tenses*] *Throw that meat away, it smells to high heaven!* **b** to strongly suggest wrongful dealings; be offensive or improper: *We all think he has stolen all the money and the whole affair smells to high heaven.*

***smell up** *v adv* → **smell out** (3), **stink out** (2), **stink up**
*AmE* to fill (a place) with a smell, usu. bad: [T1] *Please don't smoke, your cigarettes smell up the car and some of us can hardly breathe.*

**smile at** *v prep*
**1** to direct a smile towards (someone): [IØ + *at*] *It often prevents an argument if you smile at people who are rude to you.* → **smile on** (1)
*__2__ to be amused by (something or someone); not be saddened by (something): [T1] *He smiled at the thought of hearing his friend's jokes again. Not many of us can smile at grief. The teacher smiled at my answer.*

**smile on/upon** *v prep*
**1** to direct a smile towards (someone or something): [IØ + *on/upon*] *I smiled on the happy scene* → **smile at** (1)
*__2__ to approve of or favour (someone or something): [T1 (*no pass.*)] *The weather smiled on us: it was a fine day. Heaven seemed to be smiling on our efforts, as we all passed the exam. Fortune has rarely smiled on me.*

**smite on/upon** *v prep*
**1** *old use* to hit (someone) on (part of the body): [T1 + *on/upon*] *The soldiers smote one another on their legs.*
*__2__ *fml* to strike or beat heavily on (something): [T1] *The noise of the guns smote on our ears with unbearable force. I smote on the door more loudly to see if anyone was there.* → **knock at,** etc.

**smite with** *v prep*
**1** *old use* to hit (something or someone) hard with (something): [T1 + *with*] *And he smote them with his strong right arm, and they fell to the ground.*
**2 be smitten with: a** also **be smitten by** to feel the sudden effect of (something): *Half the school has been smitten with fever. Then he was smitten with an attack of conscience, and*

*returned the money.* **b** to be greatly attracted to (usu. someone or his qualities): *The music teacher is much smitten with Jane. All the girls are smitten with the new young performer. The public were soon smitten with her charms.*

***smoke out** *v adv*
to force (someone or an animal) to leave, by using smoke: [T1] *We'll have to call a man in to smoke the insects out. The few remaining enemy soldiers can easily be smoked out of their hiding place.*

***smoke up** *v adv*
**1** *AmE not fml* to fill (a place) with smoke: [T1] *Open the window, the committee have smoked the whole room up!*
**2** esp. *AmE infml* to smoke drugged tobacco: [IØ] *How many high school students in this city regularly smoke up?*

**smooth away** *v adv*
**1** to make (something) go away by flattening it: [T1 + AWAY] *I can't smooth these folds away, they keep coming back.*
***2** to get rid of (trouble): [T1] *The chairman has made efforts to smooth away any difficulties that might prevent our plan from being followed.*

**smooth back** *v adv*
to push (something) in a backward direction so that it lies flat: [T1 + BACK] *She smoothed back her hair with a movement of which she was unconscious. Let me smooth your collar back, it's sticking out again.*

**smooth down** *v adv*
**1** to make (something) lie flat or smooth: [T1 + DOWN] *She smoothed her dress down over her knees as her father entered the room. This wood has not been smoothed down well enough.*
***2** to make (something or someone) calmer: [T1] *See if you can smooth the chairman down, he's still very angry about the decision. What can we do to smooth his hurt feelings down?*

**smooth in/on** *v adv; prep*
to spread (something such as a liquid) in or on (a surface): [T1 + IN/ON/*in/on*] *If you smooth this special cream on (your face) every night, your skin will stay young-looking. Put the cream on with your fingers and then gently smooth it in.*

**smooth out** *v adv* → **iron out**
**1** to flatten (something): [T1 + OUT] *The bed will be more comfortable if you smooth out the sheets. Smooth out any unevenness in the cloth before you cut it.*
***2** to make (something) free of trouble: [T1] *They need a friend to smooth the matter out between them. His advice helped to smooth out their relationship.*

***smooth over**[1] *v adv*
to make (an affair) calmer: [T1 (*often simple tenses*)] *Perhaps a gift of flowers will help to smooth your quarrel over.*

***smooth over**[2] *v prep* → **gloss over, slough over, slur over**
to deal with (something, usu. wrong) quickly so as to lessen its importance: [T1 (*often simple tenses*)] *We could see that he was trying to smooth over his own responsibility for the delay, instead of accepting his fault.*

**smother in/with** *v prep*
**1** to cover (someone or something) with a heavy cover of (something): [T1 + *in/with*] *The miners were soon smothered in coal dust as the roof fell. Smother the fire with earth to make sure it stops burning.*
***2** to give (someone) a lot of (something or things): [D1] *As soon as we arrived in the city, we were smothered with invitations. She smothered the child in kisses as soon as they met.*

***smother up** *v adv* → **cover up** (2), **hush up** (2)
*not fml* to try to hide (wrongdoing): [T1] *They tried to smother up the murder by pretending that his death was accidental. Any politician will want to smother up such a dishonourable affair.*

**smother with** *v prep* → **SMOTHER IN**

**smoulder in** *v prep*
(of a feeling) to remain unexpressed but active in (someone): [IØ + *in*] *Her anger smouldered in her heart long after the quarrel was finished.*

**smoulder out** *v adv*
(of a fire) to stop burning very gradually: [IØ + OUT] *The fire was still red all night, but by morning it had at last smouldered out.*

**smoulder with** *v prep*
to feel strongly (a powerful, usu. bad feeling): [IØ + *with*] *He greeted the other man politely enough, but inside he was smouldering with jealousy.*

**smuggle in** *v adv*
to bring (goods or someone) unlawfully into a country or prison: [T1 + IN (*to*)] *Some of these jewels have been smuggled in; we have no record of the taxes payable on them. It's difficult to smuggle tools in to this prison.*

**smuggle out** *v adv*
to take (goods or someone) unlawfully out of a country or prison: [T1 + OUT (*of*)] *Now how are we going to smuggle the stolen jewels out (of the country) to a place where they can safely be sold? It should be possible to smuggle two more prisoners out (of the prison camp) and send them across the water.*

**smuggle past** *v prep*
to take (goods or someone) unlawfully, unnoticed by (officials): [T1 + *past*] *How can we smuggle the precious packet past the guards?*

**smuggle through** *v adv; prep*
to take (goods or someone) unlawfully (past a customs post), as when entering a country: [T1 + THROUGH/*through*] *Don't worry, we'*

*smuggle you through somehow. For years he has been smuggling watches through customs.*

**snap at** *v prep*

**1** to make a biting movement directed towards (usu. someone or an animal): [IØ + *at*] *You'll have to find a way to stop your dog from snapping at the postman or he'll be in trouble. As the fish snaps at the fly, he gets caught on the hook.*

**2** to speak suddenly and angrily to (someone): [IØ + *at* (*often simple tenses*)] *"I'm tired of hearing your complaints," she snapped at me. It's not good for a teacher to keep order by snapping at the children all day.*

*3 *not fml* to be eager to accept or take advantage of (something): [T1 (*usu. simple tenses*)] *He snapped at an invitation to the palace. Of course I snapped at the price, it was so low. The chairman snapped at the committee member's suggestion to break for coffee.* → **catch at** (2), **clutch at** (2), **grab at** (2), **snap up, scratch at** (2)

**4 snap one's fingers at** *not fml* to treat (someone or something) without respect: *The boy took delight in causing trouble, snapping his fingers at the school rules. If you continue to snap your fingers at your teachers, you'll be severely punished!*

**snap back** *v adv*

**1** to return with a sharp movement: [L9 + BACK (*usu. simple tenses*)] *Be careful, the wire might snap back and cut your hand.*

**2** to reply sharply: [IØ + BACK (*usu. simple tenses*)] *Don't try to be friendly to him: he'll only snap back.*

*3 *not fml* to improve or return to a former standard, suddenly: [IØ] *Share prices snapped back when the good news reached possible buyers.* —**snapback** *n*

**snap into** *v prep* → **snap to** (2)

**snap into it** *not fml* to hurry, as to start work: [*usu. imper.*] *Snap into it, you men, we haven't got time to waste!*

***snap off** *v adv*

**1** to (cause to) break off sharply: [IØ (*usu. simple tenses*)] *The branch snapped off under the weight of the snow.* [T1 (*usu. simple tenses*)] *The weight snapped the branch off.*

**2** to turn off (a light) suddenly: [T1 (*usu. simple tenses*)] *Suddenly the light was snapped off and no one could see the murderer escape.* → **put off**[1] (3), etc.

**3 snap someone's head off** → BITE OFF (2)

***snap on** *v adv*

**1** to fasten (something) on firmly by pressing: [IØ + ON (*simple tenses*)] *These earrings snap on with a special fastener.* [T1 + ON (*usu. simple tenses*)] *He snapped the lid on to keep the contents dry.* —**snap-on** *adj* → **put on**[1], etc.

*2 to put (a light) on suddenly: [T1 (*usu. simple tenses*)] *The policeman snapped the light on and caught the thief stealing the jewels.* → **put on**[1] (3), etc.

***snap out** *v adv* → **rap out** (2)

to express (something such as an order or warning) sharply: [T1 (*usu. simple tenses*)] *The passenger snapped out a warning, and the driver was able to stop just in time to avoid killing the dog.*

***snap out of** *v adv prep*

*infml* to bring oneself out of (a bad feeling such as low spirits) suddenly, by an effort of will, esp. in the phr. **snap out of it**: [T1 (*no pass.*)] *"I feel so sad again, today." "Oh, do snap out of it—you're all right really." If I could snap out of this sadness, don't you think I would?*

**snap to** *v prep*

**1 snap to attention** *mil* to bring oneself sharply to a stiff standing position: [*usu. simple tenses*] *The officer gave an order, and the whole country snapped to attention.* → **be at** (7), **bring to** (4a), **come to** (16a), **jump to** (2), **spring to** (2), **stand at** (3), **stand to**[2] (2)

**2 snap to it** *not fml* to hurry, as to start work: [*usu. imper.*] *Snap to it, men, we haven't got time to waste!* → **snap into**

***snap up** *v adv* → **clutch at** (2), **grab at** (2), **snap at** (3), **snatch at** (2)

*not fml* to buy or obtain (something); marry (someone) eagerly: [T1] *Of course I snapped up the coat at that cheap price! Such a beautiful daughter is going to be snapped up as soon as she is old enough.*

**snarl at** *v prep*

**1** (usu. of a dog or other animal) to make a threatening noise, showing the teeth, directed towards (usu. someone or another animal): [IØ + *at*] *What's the matter with the dog? He's usually so friendly, but today he snarled at me as I arrived.*

**2** to speak roughly to (someone): [IØ + *at*] *The director has a bad habit of snarling at people who disagree with him.*

***snarl up** *v adv*

**1** to mix, confuse, block, or prevent (something) from free movement: [T1 (*often pass.*)] *The wool has got all snarled up; I shall have to cut it. The traffic was snarled up in the town today.* —**snarl-up** *n*

**2** *not fml* to confuse (someone) so as to defeat him; cause confusion in (something such as an arrangement): [T1] *There are various means of snarling up the opposition in this election. Bad weather has snarled up the efforts of people trying to repair the oil well. As there is no post, everyone is trying to use the telephones, which has snarled up the whole system.* —**snarl-up** *n*

**snatch at** *v prep*

**1** to try to seize (something or someone): [IØ + *at* (*often simple tenses*)] *The climber snatched at the rope, but missed and fell to his death.* → **grab at** (1), etc.

*2 to make every effort to gain or take advantage of (something): [T1] *You should snatch* *at every chance to improve your English.* → **catch at** (2), **clutch at** (2), **grab at** (2), **snap at** (3), **snap up**

**3 snatch at a straw** *not fml* to try to save oneself by any means, however hopeless: *They say that a drowning man will snatch at a straw.* → **grab at** (3), etc.

**snatch away** *v adv*

**1** to remove (something) sharply or suddenly: [T1 + AWAY (*from*) (*often simple tenses*)] *He snatched his hand away* (*from the hot pan*) *with a cry of pain.*

***2** to take (something) away from someone suddenly: [T1 (*often simple tenses*)] *All hope of improvement has been snatched away by the sudden worsening of her condition.*

**snatch from** *v prep* → **snatch out of**

to take (something or someone) sharply or suddenly away from (someone or something): [T1 + *from* (*often simple tenses*)] *He snatched the baby from its mother's arms. The child was snatched from the burning building. The thief snatched the jewels from the woman.*

**snatch out of** *v adv prep* → **snatch from**

to take (someone or something) sharply or suddenly from inside (something): [T1 + OUT + *of* (*often simple tenses*)] *He snatched the baby out of its mother's arms. The child was snatched out of the flames.*

**snatch up** *v adv*

to seize (something or someone) and lift it or him/her suddenly: [T1 + UP (*often simple tenses*)] *When the powder exploded, she snatched up the nearest child and ran as fast as she could. Snatching up a knife, he chased the thief out of the house. In a fire, you are supposed to take whatever is most precious to you; I found that I had snatched up my keys.*

**sneak away/off** *v adv* → **slip away** (1), **slip off** (2), **slip out** (2), **sneak out**

to leave secretly: [L9 + AWAY/OFF] *How did he sneak away in the middle of the meeting without being noticed?*

**sneak in** *v adv*

**1** to (cause to) enter a place secretly: [L9 + IN (*to*)] *The boys used to sneak in without paying.* [X9 + IN (*to*)] *I'll see if I can sneak you in after dark.* → **slip in** (1)

***2** to be able to add (something, usu. spoken or written) in a slightly dishonest manner: [T1] *Every time he appears on television, he finds a way to sneak in a mention of his latest book.* → **slip in** (2)

**sneak off** *v adv* → SNEAK AWAY

**sneak on** *v prep* → **inform against,** etc.

*not fml* (esp. among schoolchildren) to give information about (a guilty person) (to someone in charge): [IØ + *on* (*to*)] *The class had an agreement not to sneak on each other to the teacher.*

**sneak out** *v adv* → **slip away** (1), **slip off** (2), **slip out** (2), **sneak away**

to (cause to) leave in a secretive manner: [L9 + OUT (*of*)] *We were still deciding his punishment when we found that the boy had sneaked out of the room while we weren't looking.* [X9 + OUT (*of*)] *The soldier was charged with sneaking army food out of the camp. We have to invent a new method for sneaking prisoners out without the guards noticing.*

**sneak out of** *v adv prep*

**1** to (cause to) leave a place secretly: [L9 + OUT + *of*] *How did you find a way to sneak out of the meeting? "Unfortunately, this world is full of people who are ready to believe the worst when they see a man sneaking out of the wrong bedroom in the middle of the night."* (Will Cuppy, *The Decline and Fall of Practically Everybody: Catherine the Great*) [X9 + OUT + *of*] *How can we sneak the escaped prisoners out of the country?* → **slip out of**

***2** *not fml* to escape improperly from (something unwanted): [T1] *And don't try to sneak out of your duties like you did last time!* → **get out of** (13), etc.

***sneak up on** *v adv prep* → **creep up on, steal up on**

**1** *not fml* to come near (someone or something) gradually and secretively: [T1] *The jewel thief sneaked up on the house without being seen. Don't sneak up on me like that, you gave me a shock!*

**2** *not fml* to happen to or reach (someone) gradually: [T1] *Darkness was sneaking up on the travellers as they entered the forest.*

**sneer at** *v prep*

**1** to smile unpleasantly, curling the lip, at (someone): [IØ + *at*] *The fighter sneered at his opponent, trying to make him feel threatened.*

***2** to express a low opinion of (something or someone) in strong words: [T1] *Don't sneer at the child's efforts, however weak they may seem. The opposition sneered at the government's plan but were unable to defeat it.*

**sneeze at** *v prep* → **sniff at** (2)

**not sneeze at** *not fml* to consider (something) as valuable or worthy of consideration: *You wouldn't sneeze at a fortune if you won it in a game, would you? Your father's offer may not be what you desire, but it's not to be sneezed at.*

**sniff at** *v prep*

**1** to put the nose to (something or someone) and take short breaths so as to smell it or him/her: [IØ + *at*] *The baby sat on the grass sniffing at the flowers. The dog sniffed at the stranger for a minute but did not recognize him.* → **smell at**

**2 not sniff at** *not fml* to consider (something) as valuable or worthy of consideration: *[illegible] wouldn't sniff at any pay rise in these difficult times. Your father's offer may not be what you desire, but it's not to be sniffed at.* → **sneeze at**

***sniff out** *v adv*

**1** to find (something or someone) by using the nose with short breaths: [T1] *The police used dogs to sniff out the criminals in their* *hiding place. Other dogs are used to sniff out unlawful drugs which travellers are carrying.* → **nose out** (1), **smell out** (1)

**2** to discover (something, often bad) by guessing: [T1] *He has a strange ability for sniffing out the cause of the trouble.* → **nose out** (2), **smell out** (2)

* **sniff up** *v adv*

to take (something such as liquid or steam) into the nose with short breaths: [T1] *If you sniff up this special drug, it will clear your head.*

**snip off** *v adv* → **cut off** (1), **slice off, strike off** (1), **swish off**

to remove (something) by cutting with a small quick movement: [T1 + OFF] *Mother is in the garden, snipping off the dead roses.*

**snipe at** *v prep*

**1** to shoot at (people) one at a time from a hidden position: [IØ + *at*] *There's an enemy soldier on the roof, sniping at our men.*

***2** *not fml* to attack (someone or his work) unkindly or in a dishonest way: [T1] *One of the newspapers has been sniping at Tom's latest book, although the others have liked it. The opposition party put people in the crowd to snipe at the speaker.*

**snitch on** *v prep* → **inform against**, etc.

*sl* to give information about (a guilty person) (to someone in charge): [IØ + *on*] *The children considered it a crime to snitch on one of their own group (to the teacher).*

**snoop around** *v adv; prep*

to pay improper attention to other people's business in (a place): [IØ + AROUND/*around* (*often continuous tenses*)] *There's a man been snooping around outside, shall I call the police? A woman has been snooping around the neighbourhood asking questions.*

**snoop into** *v prep*

to enquire into (someone else's affairs): [IØ + *into*] *The policeman has special permission to snoop into the office records.*

**snort at** *v prep*

to make a loud disapproving noise through the nose, directed at (someone) or concerning (something considered wrong): [IØ + *at* (*often simple tenses*)] *The director rather rudely snorted at his visitor's suggestion for improving the organization. Grandfather snorted at the children for interrupting his rest.*

**snow in** *v adv* → **snow up**

**be snowed in** to be kept indoors or in one place by snow: *All the villages on the east coast are snowed in this morning after last night's snowstorm. Many office workers were forced to stay home as they were snowed in.*

**snow off** *v adv* → **rain off**

to prevent (an event) from taking place because of snow: [T1 (*usu. pass.*)] *The opening game of the year was snowed off.*

**snow under** *v adv*

**be snowed under: a** to be covered with snow: *All the fields are snowed under; the animals will have to feed indoors.* **b** *not fml* to be very busy with or have too much (of something or things): [*with*] *I shan't finish work till midnight, I'm snowed under. We were snowed under with complaints about the washing machines.* **c** *AmE not fml* to be completely defeated: *The opposing team were snowed under by our well-planned attack.*

* **snow up** *v adv* → **snow in**

to cover (someone or a place) with snow so that movement is impossible: [T1 (*usu. pass.*)] *In the winter the farm is often snowed up for several weeks.*

* **snuff it** *v pron* → **pass away** (3), etc.

*infml* to die: [IØ (*simple tenses*)] *Did you hear old Charlie snuffed it last week?*

**snuff out** *v adv*

**1** to stop (a candle) burning: [T1 + OUT] *Snuff out the candles, it's time to go to bed.* → **put out** (13), etc.

***2** *not fml* to put a stop to (something such as opposition): [T1] *The citizens' plan was quickly snuffed out by the military rulers. There came a time when the learning of the ancient world had been snuffed out.*

***3** *not fml* to kill (someone or something): [T1 (*usu. simple tenses*)] *The soldiers had orders to snuff out any enemy guards.*

***4** *infml* to die: [Ø (*simple tenses*)] *Did you hear old Charlie snuffed out last week?* → **pass away** (3), etc.

* **snug down** *v adv*

*naut* to make everything safe on board a ship; tie (things) down firmly, as to prepare for rough weather: [IØ] *I don't like the look of that black cloud advancing so fast; we'd better snug down just in case.* [T1] *Is everything snugged down? There's a storm coming.*

* **snuggle down** *v adv* → **nestle down**

to (cause to) settle in comfort: [IØ] *The lost children snuggled down under a pile of leaves.* [T1] *Are the children snuggled down in bed yet?*

* **snuggle up** *v adv* → **nestle up**

to settle close (to someone) in comfort: [IØ (TOGETHER, *against, to*)] *The baby animals snuggled up together for warmth. The lost children snuggled up to each other in their fear.*

* **soak in**[1] *v adv*

**1** (of liquid) to enter a material by passing through the surface: [IØ (*to*)] *When the melted snow has all soaked in, the fields will be ready for the seeds* → **sink in**[1] (1)

**2** esp. *AmE not fml* to become gradually and clearly understood: [IØ] *The chairman waited until his suggestion had had time to soak in before inviting the committee's opinions.* → **sink in**[1] (4)

**soak in**[2] *v prep*

**1** to place and leave (something) in (liquid or a container of liquid); lie for a long time in (liquid or a container of liquid): [T1 + *in*] *If the clothes are very dirty, soak them in soapy water overnight. Soaking the rice in fruit juice* *instead of water makes a tasty change.* [IØ + *in*] *The clothes have been soaking in the bowl all night and should be really clean by now.* → **immerse in** (1), **steep in** (1), **submerge in** (1)

*__2__ to make (oneself) give one's whole attention to; fill (oneself) with (something such as knowledge): [D1] *I have a talk to give on the famous writer next month, so first I must soak myself in his books. Only by soaking yourself in the details can you gain a thorough understanding of the subject.* → **absorb in,** etc.

***soak into** *v prep*

**1** (of liquid) to enter (something such as material): [T1 (*no pass.*)] *It will not take long for the melted snow to soak into the soil.* → **sink into** (2)

**2** esp. *AmE not fml* to be gradually understood and accepted by (one's mind): [T1 (*no pass.*)] *You need a rest from studying to allow the facts to soak into your mind.* → **sink into** (4)

***soak off** *v adv*

to remove (something) by leaving it for a time in liquid: [T1] *I didn't want Mother to know what I had paid for the bottle of wine, so I soaked the price ticket off overnight.*

***soak out** *v adv*

to (cause to) be removed by being left in liquid: [IØ] *Do you think the dirt will soak out, or should I take the coat to the cleaners?* [T1] *You can soak out most marks in this special cleaning liquid if you leave the clothes in it long enough.*

***soak through**[1] *v adv*

**1** (of liquid) to pass through a material or garment: [IØ] *This coat was supposed to keep rain out, but the water has soaked (right) through.*

**2 be soaked through** to be very wet, as through all one's clothing: *The children came in soaked through, so we put them in a hot bath.*

***soak through**[2] *v prep*

(of liquid) to pass completely through (a material or garment): [T1 (*no pass.*)] *The wet snow has soaked through my new boots, so I shall complain to the shop.*

***soak up** *v adv*

**1** to take in (something such as liquid); be filled with (something): [T1] *We had to use such a lot of cloths to soak up the pool on the floor! On these hot days you can see all the young people lying on the sand, soaking up the sunshine. This thirsty plant soaks up all the water I give it every day!* → **mop up** (1), **sop up, take up** (4), **wipe up** (1)

**2** to take in or learn (something) easily, quickly, and in quantity: [T1] *He was such an eager student that he soaked up knowledge as fast as his teachers could supply it. She went from doctor to doctor, soaking up advice.*

**soak with** *v prep* → **drench in, saturate with** (1)

to fill (something) with a lot of (usu. liquid): [T1 + *with*] *Don't soak the brush with paint, just put a little on. Our clothes were soaked with the sudden heavy rain.*

**soap down** *v adv*

to cover (someone or oneself) with soap: [T1 + DOWN] *She soaped herself down and then got into the hot bath.*

***sob out** *v adv*

*__1__ to tell (something) while weeping noisily: [T1]. *As she sobbed out her story, it became clear why she had not dared to go to the police before.*

**2 sob one's heart out** *not fml* to weep bitterly and noisily: *How long has this child been sobbing her heart out, with no one comforting her?*

**sob to** *v prep*

**sob oneself to sleep** to fall asleep as a result of weeping noisily: *In her grief, she sobbed herself to sleep night after night.*

***sober down** *v adv*

to (cause to) become less excited: [IØ] *The crowd sobered down when the speaker turned to more serious matters.* [T1] *You must find a way to sober the children down, they can't visit their grandparents in that state!*

***sober up** *v adv*

to (cause to) cease being drunk: [IØ] *He'll soon sober up when he gets into the cold air outside.* [T1] *"I've been drunk about a week now, and I thought it might sober me up to sit in a library."* (F. Scott Fitzgerald, *The Great Gatsby*)

***sock away** *v adv*

*AmE not fml* to save (money) by putting it aside: [T1] *When the debt has been paid, we should start socking away an equal amount each month into our bank account.*

**sock in** *v adv*

**be socked in** *AmE not fml* (of a plane) to be prevented from flying; (of an airfield) be closed for flying, as by bad weather: *The mist got so thick that all the planes were socked in for the day. Is there an airport near here that hasn't been socked in yet, where we can land?*

**sock to** *v prep*

**sock it to** esp. *AmE infml* to hit (someone) hard; express oneself forcefully: *The old fighter won't win this fight until he socks it to his opponent the way he used to. It was a great performance: you really socked it to them!*

***sod off** *v adv* → **push off** (3), etc.

*taboo sl* to go away: [IØ (*imper.*)] *Sod off, I tell you! Get out of here!*

**soften up** *v adv*

**1** to (cause to) become softer: [IØ + UP] *The ground has softened up a little after last night's rain.* [T1 + UP] *The special cream will help to soften up your skin.*

*__2__ to weaken (an enemy), as by bombing: [T1] *Once the enemy positions have been softened up, we can move the foot soldiers in.* —**softening-up** *n, adj*

*__3__ *not fml* to prepare (someone) to listen to persuasion: [T1] *You go in and soften Fathe* *up, and then I'll ask him for the money.* → **make to** (9)

***soldier on** *v adv*
*not fml* to continue (with work, effort, etc.) with determination, in spite of difficulties: [IØ] *Mother soldiered on for several years with her bad leg before she was forced to have the operation. It's not easy to soldier on when all you seem to meet is failure and defeat.*

**solicit for** *v prep*
*becoming rare* to ask (customers) for (trade): [T1 + *for*] *When someone new arrived in the town, all the shopkeepers would go and solicit the family for their trade.*

***sop up** *v adv* → **mop up** (1), **soak up** (1), **take up** (4), **wipe up** (1)
to take (a liquid) into a solid material so as to leave a dry surface: [T1] *We need some thick cloths to sop up the pool of milk on the kitchen floor.*

**sorrow over** *v prep* → **grieve over, lament over**
esp. *lit* to express grief concerning (something or someone): [IØ + *over*] *Two years later, she was still sorrowing over her dead son. It's no use sorrowing over the bad times of the past; better to look forward to the future.*

**sort out** *v adv*
**1** to put (things or ideas) into order; choose (a certain kind); divide (things or people) into classes: [T1 + OUT] *Mind you keep the papers in alphabetical order, or it takes such a long time to sort them out. I'm just sorting out some suitable clothes to take on holiday. Sort out the washing into white and coloured materials. It takes me a long time to sort out my thoughts before I can start writing.* —**sort-out** *n* → **separate out, sift out**
***2** to set (a matter) straight; make (something) clear: [T1] *It's up to the director to sort out difficulties like this one. Jim and Mary must be left to sort out their own affairs—it does not concern anyone else.* → **straighten out** (2)
***3** to make order among (people) with proper organization: [T1] *The new director was asked to sort the workers out so as to get the best work out of them.*
***4** *infml* to punish (someone), as by attacking him: [T1] *Wait till I get you outside, and I'll sort you out!*
**5** to cause (itself or oneself) to return to a usual or proper state: [T1b (*often pass.*)] *Don't worry, things will sort themselves out in the end. It's time that boy got himself sorted out—I think he should see a doctor.* → **strraighten out** (3)

**ort with** *v prep*
*fml* to suit or agree (badly or well) with (something or someone): [T1 (*simple tenses*)] *His actions sort ill with his family's wishes. The present conditions sort well with the workers.*

**ound off** *v adv*
**1 a** *mil* to play a signal or musical instrument: [IØ] *Ask the musician to sound off, and then we can start.* **b** *mil* to count while marching: [IØ] *The men must not make any mistakes while sounding off.*
**2** *not fml* to express an opinion freely, with force, or at length: [IØ (*about, on, to*)] *I could hear Father sounding off to his class on his favourite subject again.*

***sound out** *v adv* → **feel out**
to try to discover the opinion or intention of (someone): [T1 (*on, about*)] *Could you sound the director out on the question of the new appointments?*

***soup up** *v adv* → **hop up** (3)
*infml* to increase the power and speed of (an engine): [T1 (*often pass.*)] *Members are not allowed to race any cars which have been souped up.* —**souped-up** *adj*

**souse in** *v prep*
to place and leave (something such as food) for a long time in (salt water): [T1 + *in* (*often pass.*)] *These fish have been soused in sea water for weeks.*

**space out** *v adv*
**1** to (cause to) be placed apart, in positions separated by space: [T1] *Please don't space the flowers out too evenly when you plant them, they look so much nicer in a natural-looking mass.* [IØ] *Tell the men to space out as they cross the field, so that they won't be so easily hit. Space out, children, so that you have plenty of room to move.* → **fan out, spread out** (3)
**2** to spread (something or things) out in time, leaving spaces in between: [T1 (*over*)] *The bank should allow you to space out your payments over several months. We should space out our visits sensibly, so that she doesn't miss us for too long at a time. The hospital offers advice on how to space out your family.* → **spread out** (4), **stretch out** (5)
**3 be spaced out** *sl* to be influenced by drugs or otherwise out of touch with reality: *It's no good trying to have a conversation with him, he's spaced out and nothing he says will make sense. How is it that some people seem to get spaced out more easily than others?*

**spade up** *v adv*
esp. *AmE not fml* to dig (soil or a garden) with or as with a spade: [T1 + UP] *The garden needs spading up well before we can plant the seeds.*

***spank along** *v adv*
*not fml* to move along at a good rate: [IØ (*usu. continuous tenses*)] *We were spanking along nicely when suddenly a tyre burst. The horses are spanking along; it's impossible to tell which one will win the race.*

**spar with** *v prep*
**1** to practise fighting with (someone): [IØ + *with*] *This promising young fighter needs a tough opponent to spar with, to prepare him for the big fight.*
**2** *not fml* to argue with (someone): [IØ +

*with* (*often continuous tenses*)] *Have you been sparring with the neighbours again?*

**spare for** *v prep*
to be willing to give up (money, time, or thought) to (someone or something): [T1 + *for* (*simple tenses*)] *I can't spare the time for a dinner party this week. Can you spare a few pennies for a cup of coffee? Spare a thought for those less fortunate than yourself.*

***spark off** *v adv*
**1** to cause (something) to explode or burst into flames, usu. accidentally: [T1 (*often simple tenses*)] *Some hot ash fell into the box of matches, and sparked off the whole lot.* → **go off**[1] (5), etc.
**2** *not fml* to cause; start (something, often violent): [T1] *Stories about the fall of the government sparked off much of the selling of shares. It would not take more than one careless remark to spark off violence in this angry crowd.* → **set off** (5), **touch off** (2), **trigger off** (2)

**sparkle with** *v prep*
**1** to shine in flashes because of (something very bright or a strong feeling): [IØ + *with*] *Many of the ladies present were sparkling with diamonds. At night the whole city sparkles with coloured lights. Her eyes sparkled with anger.*
**2** (of writing or a speech) to be interesting and amusing with light touches of (usu. a form of humour): [IØ + *with* (*usu. simple tenses*)] *Every story he writes sparkles with amusing moments.*

**spatter on/onto/over** *v prep* → **spatter with, splash on, splash over** (1), **splash with**
to scatter drops of (usu. liquid) onto (something or someone); fall in drops on (something or someone): [X9 + *on/onto/over*] *Be careful with that brush, you're spattering paint* (*all*) *over the floor.* [L9 *on/onto/over*] *There was a hole in the roof, and rainwater was spattering on our heads.*

**spatter up** *v adv* → **splash up**
esp. *AmE* to spoil (something) with drops (of usu. liquid): [T1 + UP (*with*)] *Passing traffic has spattered the wall up with mud.*

**spatter with** *v prep* also **bespatter with** → **spatter on, splash on, splash over** (1) **splash with**
to cover (something or someone) with drops of (usu. liquid): [T1 + *with*] *This poor bird is all spattered with oil. Mind that brush, you're spattering the floor with paint.*

**speak about** *v prep* → **talk about** (1), etc.
to mention or talk openly about (something or someone): [IØ + *about* (*usu. simple tenses*)] *We don't speak about that unfortunate period in our family history. Nice people don't speak about such unpleasant matters.*

**speak against** *v prep* → **speak for** (2)
to oppose (something such as an argument or doing something); say bad things about (someone): [IØ + *against*] *Only a few of the committee members spoke against the plan. The chairman spoke against accepting the suggestion in its present form.*

**speak for** *v prep*
**1** to go on talking for (a certain length of time): [IØ + *for*] *Each speaker is allowed to speak for five minutes, and then a vote will be taken.* → **talk for**
**2** to support (someone, something, or doing something); say (something) in favour of (someone or something): [IØ + *for* (*often simple tenses*)] *How many members spoke for the plan? Mr Price spoke for accepting the suggestion, with some changes. I should like to speak for the boy before you punish him.* [T1 + *for*] *May I speak a few words for the boy before you punish him?* → **say for** (2), **speak against**
***3** to act as representative for (someone), so as to give his views: [T1 (*no pass.*)] *I speak for my wife as well as myself when I thank you all for your great kindness. You must choose one person to speak for the whole group.* → **answer for** (1)
***4** to represent (someone) in a court of law: [T1 (*no pass., simple tenses*)] *Who speaks for the prisoner?*
**5 be spoken for** to be promised to someone: *Sir, if your daughter is not spoken for, I should like to ask for her hand in marriage. The model that you want is spoken for, but I'll see if I can get another. I'm afraid you can't have these seats—they're already spoken for.* → **answer for** (5)
**6 speak for itself** to need no further explanation; provide all the information one needs: [*usu. simple present tense*] *The sales figures speak for themselves; you can see what a successful year this has been. She said that she was willing to help, but her absence speaks for itself.*
**7 speak for oneself** to express one's own opinions: *Speaking for myself, I find the housing quite satisfactory. He is old enough; ask him he can speak for himself.*
**8 speak for yourself!** *not fml* don't make decisions for me!; don't suppose that other people necessarily agree with you!: [*imper.*] *"Of course, we all want to hear about Mary's new baby." "Speak for yourself—I'm not interested at all."*
**9 speak volumes for** *not fml* to tell a great deal about (something such as a quality), usu. in its favour: [*usu. simple tenses*] *Her continued efforts in the face of defeat speak volumes for her courage and strength of character.*
**10 speak well for** to give proof in favour of (usu. something): [*usu. simple tenses*] *His generous gift speaks well for his willingness to help others.*

**speak from** *v prep*
**1** to use (something such as notes) to help one make a speech: [IØ + *from*] *Will yo*

*speak from notes or can you remember everything you want to say?*

**2 speak from the heart** to say something most sincerely: *I speak from the heart when I offer you our deepest thanks.*

**3 speak (something) from memory** to speak without a written reminder; remember (one's words) exactly: *Speaking from memory, I would say it was about ten years ago. At the next practice I want you all to try speaking your parts from memory.*

**speak of** *v prep*

**1** to mention; talk about (something or someone): [IØ + *of* (*often simple tenses*)] *She spoke of the government's plans for the unemployed.* → **talk about** (1), etc.

*__2__ to suggest the idea of (somthing): [T1 (*simple tenses*)] *This gift of money speaks of your generosity.*

**3 speaking of** since we are mentioning (something such as a subject or someone); on the subject of (something or someone): *Speaking of books, have you read "Gone With the Wind"?* → **talk of** (3)

**4 speak of the devil** *not fml* here comes the person we were just talking about: *Speak of the devil—here she is!* → **talk of** (4)

**5 speak ill/well of** to express a bad/good opinion of (someone or something): [*usu. simple tenses*] *Do not speak ill of the dead.*

**6 no/nothing to speak of** so little as to be not worth mentioning: *It's been a pleasant winter, with no snow to speak of. There's no news, at least nothing to speak of.*

**speak on/upon** *v prep* → **talk on**[2]

to deliver a speech or talk about (a subject): [IØ + *on/upon*] *I've been asked to speak on the future of education for very young children.*

**speak out** *v adv* → **answer up**

**1** to speak loudly: [IØ (*often imper.*)] *Speak out, we can't hear you.* → **speak up** (1), **talk up** (1)

**2** to speak boldly and freely: [IØ (*against*)] *Nothing will be done until more women have the courage to speak out. No one dared to speak out against the new law.* —**outspoken** *adj* → **speak up** (2), **talk up** (2)

**speak small** *v adv*

to speak in a low, quiet voice: [IØ (*usu. simple tenses*)] "*She has brown hair, and speaks small like a woman.*" (Shakespeare, *The Merry Wives of Windsor*)

**speak to** *v prep*

**1** to talk to; have conversation with (someone): [IØ + *to*] *The councillor was asked to speak to the crowd, to beg them to remain calm. I've asked you not to speak to that rough boy. I shall never speak to her again if she refuses to say she's sorry.* → **speak with** (1), **talk at, talk to** (1), **talk with** (1)

*__2__ to ask (someone) to do something: [T1] *I'll speak to the director about a pay rise for you.*

*__3__ *not fml* to scold (someone): [T1] *I'll speak to that boy the minute he gets in.* —**speaking-to** *n* → **tell off** (1), etc.

*__4__ *fml* to express one's opinion, or make a statement, about (a matter being talked about, as in a meeting): [T1 (*often simple tenses*)] *Would any committee member care to speak to the question? I'm not prepared to speak to a title like that.*

*__5__ to support (someone's idea): [T1 (*often simple tenses*)] *Many members spoke to their friend's suggestion.*

***speak up** *v adv* → **answer up**

**1** to speak loudly: [IØ (*often imper.*)] *Speak up, we can't hear you.* → **speak out** (1), **talk up** (1)

**2** to express one's opinion fearlessly: [IØ] *If you thought that wasn't fair, why didn't you speak up?* → **speak out** (2), **talk up** (2)

* **speak up for** *v adv prep*

to support (usu. someone) with words: [T1] *The poor child has no one to speak up for him; why don't you offer your help?*

**speak upon** *v prep* → **SPEAK ON**

**speak with** *v prep*

**1** to have conversation with (someone): [IØ + *with* (*often continuous tenses*)] *I saw you speaking with our neighbour; what did he have to say? I will not have you speaking with that rough boy.* → **speak to** (1), **talk to** (1), **talk with** (1)

*__2__ *not fml* to scold (someone): [T1] *I shall ask your father to speak with you when he comes home.* → **tell off** (1), etc.

**spear up** *v adv*

*not fml* (in ice hockey) to wound (a player on the opposing team) by bringing one's stick up at an angle into the body or face: [T1 + UP (*often pass.*)] *One of our best players got speared up at the beginning of the game, and had to go off the ice.* [IØ + UP] *Spearing up is against the rules, and any player who does it will be punished.*

**specialize in** *v prep*

to study (a small part of a subject) in detail; work, study, or be very knowledgeable in (a particular kind of work or subject, etc.): [IØ + *in*] *After he had worked as a doctor for some years, he decided to specialize in children's diseases. Are you going to specialize in arts or sciences?*

**speculate about/on** *v prep* → **theorize about**

to guess about (something, usu. in the future): [IØ + *about/on*] *There's little point in speculating about the result of the election when any victory will be very narrow. We can only speculate on whether there will be enough oil for the world's needs by the end of this century.*

**speculate in** *v prep*

to buy (something such as shares) in the hope of selling at a profit; risk one's money on (something): [IØ + *in*] *People who speculated in oil shares years ago are now enjoying big profits. Speculating in gold is risky, as the price goes up and down so quickly.*

**speculate on** *v prep* → **SPECULATE ABOUT**

* **speed up** *v adv* → **quicken up**
to (cause to) move or develop faster: [T1] *You'll have to speed up your rate of work if you want to finish by the agreed date. The workers have been asked to speed up production without an increase in pay. The government is speeding up plans to reduce the number of teachers being trained.* [IØ (*often continuous tenses*)] *The rise in the cost of living has been speeding up in recent years.* —**speeding-up, speed-up** *n*

* **spell down** *v adv*
esp. *AmE* to defeat (someone) in a spelling competition: [T1] *See if you can spell all the other students down by knowing all the difficult words.* —**spelldown** *n*

**spell for** *v prep*
**1** to tell the letters of (a word) in the right order for (someone): [T1 + *for*] *Will you please spell your name for me, it's one I'm not familiar with.*
**2** to mean (something, often bad) for (someone or a group): [T1 + *for* (*simple tenses*)] *The results of the local election spell trouble for the government. That last blow spelt defeat for his opponent.*

* **spell out** *v adv*
**1** to read (something) word by word or letter by letter: [T1 (*often simple tenses*)] *His handwriting was so bad that I had to spell out what he had written with great difficulty.*
**2** *not fml* to make clear the details or meaning of (something): [T1] *Get a lawyer to spell out the contract for you, so that you understand your responsibilities if you sign it. Please spell out what you mean, I don't quite understand.* [T6] *You must spell out for the examiners how you have reached this unusual answer. The director makes all the young people spell out why they want to work for this particular firm.*

**spend for** *v prep* → **expend on, spend on**
*AmE* to use (an amount of money) to pay for (something): [T1 + *for*] *How much did you spend for that book?*

**spend in** *v prep* → **expend in**
to use (usu. time) for (doing something): [T1 + *in*] *You've spent the whole afternoon in digging one small flower garden!*

**spend on** *v prep* → **expend on, spend for**
to use (usu. money, time, or effort) for (something or someone): [T1 + *on*] *The city council has been charged with spending too much of the taxpayers' money on sports buildings. You may have to spend more than a year on your book. This student seems to have spent too much effort on this piece of writing.*

**spend up** *v adv*
**be spent up** *not fml* to have no money left: *I can't afford a ticket, I'm spent up.* —**spend-up** *n*

* **spew out** *v adv* also **spue out**
**1** to send out a lot of (something bad): [T1] *The child was saved from drowning, but spewed out dirty water for several minutes. Factories are no longer allowed to spew out black smoke from their chimneys.*
**2** *not fml* to express a lot of (something unpleasant): [T1] *The dying man spewed out curses against his murderer.*

* **spew up** *v adv* also **spue up**
**1** to bring a lot of (usu. food) up from the stomach; vomit (something) in quantity; be violently sick: [T1] *The poor child has spewed up everything I tried to give her, she can't even keep liquid down.* [IØ] *Jane has been spewing up all morning and will not be at school today.* → **bring up** (4), etc.
**2** *not fml* to produce a lot of (something bad): [T1] *"Sure the poet . . . spewed up a good lump of . . . nonsense at once."* (John Dryden, *On Settle*)

**spice up** *v adv*
**1** to make (food) more tasty: [T1 + UP] *What can I use to spice up this dull meal?*
***2** *not fml* to make (something such as an activity, writing, or film) more interesting or improper: [T1] *It will spice up the party if we bring in some unlawful drugs.*

**spice with** *v prep*
**1** to make (food) more tasty by adding (something): [T1 + *with*] *You've spiced the soup with too much pepper, I can't drink it!*
***2** *not fml* to make (something such as an activity, writing, or film) more interesting or improper by adding (something): [D1] *The makers believe that the public will not watch television films unless they are spiced with sex and violence, which is completely false. What I like about Tom's latest book is the way he has been able to spice such dull material with flashes of humour.*

* **spiel off** *v adv* → **rattle off, reel off, roll off** (3), **run off**[1] (7)
esp. *AmE infml* to speak (words) quickly and easily from memory: [T1] *The child can spiel off the names of all the Presidents, but does he really understand his country's history?*

* **spiff up** *v adv* → **slick up, smarten up, spruce up**
*infml* to make (something, someone, or oneself) more neat and attractive: [T1] *Why are you all spiffed up? Are you going to a party? She spends hours in front of the mirror, spiffing herself up, and all for this worthless boy. I've simply got to spiff this room up somehow, my parents are coming!*

**spill out** *v adv*
**1** to (cause to) overflow or leave a container accidentally: [IØ + OUT (*of*)] *The top has come off the bottle, and the wine is spilling out! Blood was spilling out all over the floor.* [T1 + OUT (*of*)] *The car turned over, spilling*

*out the passengers into the road. Try not to spill the beans out of the bowl, although it's very full.*

***2** to leave quickly in a disorganized crowd: [IØ (*of*)] *As soon as the train stopped, the crowd spilled out into the station.*

***3** *not fml* to tell (a story) freely: [T1] *At last he felt able to go to the police station and spill out the story of his part in the crime.*

**spill over** *v adv*

**1** to overflow: [IØ + OVER] *Carry the coffee carefully to the table; it's so full that it might spill over.* → **slop over**[1]

***2** to be too great to be contained by something: [IØ] *The cities have grown so crowded that the population is spilling over into new towns.* —**overspill, spillover** *n, adj*

***3** to develop (into something else): [IØ (*into*)] *His keenness to get the job done spilled over into lack of consideration for the workers.*

**spin along** *v adv* → **bowl along** (1)

to move forward easily and quite quickly with a rolling movement: [L9 + ALONG (*usu. continuous tenses*)] *The car was spinning along nicely when suddenly the engine made a peculiar noise and stopped.*

**spin off** *v adv*

**1** to leave its position, with a rolling movement: [L9 + OFF] *Luckily we were not going very fast when the wheel spun off and the car crashed into the fence.*

***2** *not fml* to happen as a general result of some particular development; produce (something) unexpectedly from another invention: [T1] *The invention of new materials for space travel has spun off a great many useful products for home and industry.* [IØ (*from*)] *Many new things found useful in the home have spun off from the machinery of space travel.* —**spin-off** *n*

**spin out** *v adv*

**1** to lengthen (thread) by spinning: [T1 + OUT] *Her skilful fingers spun the wool out to a fine thread.*

***2** *not fml* to make (something) last longer than necessary or expected: [T1] *The broadcaster will have to spin out his talk to make it last the full half hour. How can I spin my money out till the end of the month? We would all like to spin out happy times and shorten bad days.*

***3** *infml* to confuse (someone): [T1] *All these new ideas have really spun me out; I must have time to think.*

***4** *AmE* (of a vehicle) to leave a road by turning accidentally, as on a slippery surface: [IØ (*usu. simple tenses*)] *Suddenly the car spun out and crashed into the fence.* —**spinout** *n*

**spin round** *v adv*

to turn round very fast: [L9 + ROUND] *He spun round at the sound of his name, ready to defend himself. The car spun round on the oily road, and the driver was helpless to control it.*

**spiral down** *v adv*

to descend with a twisting curling movement: [L9 + DOWN] *The dead bird spiralled down into the field, where the hunting dogs picked it up.*

**spiral up** *v adv*

**1** to rise with a twisting curling movement: [L9 + UP] *Black smoke was spiralling up from the burning ship.*

***2** *not fml* to rise to a higher position, often rather quickly: [IØ] *As costs have risen, prices have spiralled up to match them. Such a promising young man may well spiral up to the directorship before very long.*

***spirit away/off** *v adv*

to remove (someone or something) as if by magic: [T1 (*often pass.*)] *I can't find my glasses—they must have been spirited away. The princess was spirited off to a desert island by the evil magician.*

**spit at** *v prep*

**1** to send liquid from the mouth, usu. rudely, towards (someone): [IØ + *at*] *It's very rude to spit at someone. The cat spat at me!* → **spit on**[2] (1)

***2** *not fml* to treat (something such as an offer or suggestion) with disapproval, hatred, etc.: [T1 (*usu. simple tenses*)] *You wouldn't dare to spit at the director's offer, would you?* → **spit on**[1] (2)

**spit in** *v prep*

**1** to send liquid from the mouth into (something): [IØ + *in*] *If you must spit at all, please spit in the bucket provided.*

**2 spit in someone's eye/face** to show a complete lack of respect for someone: [*usu. simple tenses*] *That boy is so badly behaved that he cares nothing for manners, and spits in the eye of all the teachers.*

**spit on/upon**[1] *v prep*

**1** to send liquid from the mouth onto (something or someone): [IØ + *on/upon*] *Please do not spit on the floor.*

***2** *not fml* to treat (something) with disrespect, hatred, etc.: [T1 (*simple tenses*)] *Sir, I spit on your army; it is not fit to waste bullets on.* → **spit at** (2)

**spit on/upon**[2] *v prep*

to fix (something such as meat) on (a pointed stick or metal pole) for cooking: [T1 + *on/upon*] *Spit the meat on this stick and turn it over the fire.*

**spit out** *v adv*

**1** to send (something) from the mouth: [X9 + OUT] *The child spat out the nasty-tasting medicine.*

***2** *not fml* to say (something) with effort, force, or anger: [T1 (*usu. simple tenses*)] *The dying man spat out a curse upon his murderer.*

**3 spit it out!** *infml* tell your story quickly, without fear: [*imper.*] *Come on, let's hear the whole story—spit it out!*

**spit up** *v adv*

**1** to bring (something) up from the mouth or

throat with effort: [X9 + UP] *You'd better call the doctor, the child has been spitting up blood all morning.* → **cough out** (1), **cough up** (1)

**2* to bring up (usu. food) from the stomach; vomit (something): [T1] *Jane can't keep anything down this morning, she's spat up her breakfast and everything since.* → **bring up** (4), etc.

**spit upon**[1] *v prep* → SPIT ON[1]

**spit upon**[2] *v prep* → SPIT ON[2]

**splash about/around** *v adv* also **splosh about**

**1** to play in water: [IØ + ABOUT/AROUND (*in*)] *The children love splashing about in pools of rainwater. He's not really swimming, he's just splashing around.*

**2 splash one's money about/around** *not fml* to make a show of one's wealth; spend freely: *My only worry about having a rich friend is that it makes me uncomfortable to see him splashing his money around.*

**splash down** *v adv*

**1** also **splosh down** (of liquid) to fall in large or many drops: [IØ + DOWN] *Water was splashing down from a large hole in the roof.*

***2** (of a spacecraft) to land in the sea: [IØ (*often simple tenses*)] *The spacecraft is expected to splash down at about 3 o'clock Eastern Standard Time.* —**splashdown** *n*

**splash on** *v adv; prep* → **spatter on, spatter with, splash over, splash with**

to scatter drops of (usu. liquid) on (something or someone); (of liquid) fall with a scattering of drops on (something or someone): [X9 + ON/*on* (*to*)] *Don't splash the paint on, you'll waste it! A passing car splashed mud on my best coat!* [L9 + *on*] *There was a hole in the roof, and rainwater was splashing on our heads.*

**splash over** *v prep*

**1** (of liquid) to (cause to) flow quickly onto or across (something): [L9 + *over*] *The little stream splashed noisily over the rocks.* [X9 + *over*] *Splash water over her face, it'll help to wake her.* → **spatter on, spatter with, splash on, splash with**

***2** *not fml* to print (news) across (part of a newspaper) usu. in large type, so as to gain eager attention: [D1 (*usu. pass.*)] *The story of their failing marriage was splashed (all) over the front page.*

**splash up** *v adv* also **splatter up** → **spatter up**

to spoil (something) with many or large drops (usu. of liquid): [T1 + UP (*with*)] *Passing traffic has splashed the wall up with mud.*

***splash with** *v prep* → **spatter on, spatter with, splash on, splash over** (1)

to cover (something or someone) with large or many drops of (a liquid): [T1 + *with*] *This poor bird is splashed with oil. Mind that brush, you're splashing the floor with paint. A passing car splashed us with mud from head to foot!*

**splatter up** *v adv* → SPLASH UP

**splay out** *v adv*

to (cause to) spread wide, with the parts or edges facing away from each other: [IØ + OUT (*usu. simple tenses*)] *The ends of the pipe have splayed out, and no longer fit well together.* [T1 + OUT (*usu. pass.*)] *In this style of furniture, the feet of the chair legs are splayed out to provide balance.*

**splice together** *v adv*

to join (usu. ropes) by weaving: [T1 + TOGETHER] *Sailors have to learn how to splice together the broken ends of ropes, by weaving the threads.*

**splinter off** *v adv*

**1** to break off with a long uneven break: [IØ + OFF] *Look at the mark made where that thin branch has splintered off.* → **split off** (1)

***2** *not fml* to separate from a larger group; form a different group: [IØ] *A small group of party members, who no longer agreed with the party thought, splintered off and formed a new political movement.* → **split off** (2)

**split in** *v prep*

**split in two: a** to (cause to) be divided into halves: *The ship split in two under the force of the stormy waves.* **b** *not fml* to divide (someone) in opinion or feeling: [*usu. pass.*] *A mother who also has a demanding job often feels split in two by the demands of both work and home.*

**split into** *v prep*

to (cause to) separate into (smaller parts): [IØ + *into*] *At this point in the music, the singers split into three groups.* [T1 + *into*] *With a single blow of his axe, he split the log into two equal halves. The action of heat will split this substance into a chemical and oxygen.*

**split off** *v adv*

**1** to break off; remove (something) by breaking or other means: [IØ + OFF (*from*)] *Look at the mark made where that branch split off from the trunk.* [T1 + OFF] *The box is made so that you can split off the handle. There must be some way of splitting off the new combination formed by the chemical action.* → **splinter off** (1)

***2** *not fml* to separate; form a different group: [IØ (*from*)] *A small group who no longer agreed with the party's ideas split off and formed a new political movement.* → **splinter off** (2)

**split on** *v prep* → **inform against,** etc.

*not fml* (esp. among schoolchildren) to report the guilty activities of (someone) to people in charge: [IØ + *on*] *It was against the children's sense of honour to split on their friends to the teacher.*

**split up** *v adv*

**1** to cut or divide (something); (cause to) fall apart: [T1 + UP] *Can you split up this piece of wood? I'll split up the apples so that we can each have one.* [IØ + UP] *After days battling the rough sea, the ship at last split up.*

**2** to (cause to) separate into smaller parts: [IØ + UP (*into*)] *The committee can split up into small groups to talk about each of these matters in greater detail.* [T1 + UP] *A good teacher splits up a large class for practice in skills such as reading.*

***3** *not fml* to divide (something such as profit): [T1] *The jewel thieves agreed to split up the profit from the robbery equally between them.*

***4** *not fml* (of two or more people) to (cause to) cease having a relationship: [IØ] *Jim and Mary have been quarrelling so much recently that their friends are afraid they might split up. The two firms which were combined some years ago are going to split up again.* [T1] *What was it that split them up?* —**split-up** *n* → **break up** (6), **bust up** (3)

**splosh about/around** *v adv* → SPLASH ABOUT

**splosh down** *v adv* → SPLASH DOWN (1)

**splurge on** *v prep*
*not fml* to spend money freely on (something or someone): [IØ + *on*] *I decided to give myself a present, and really splurge on some new clothes.*

**splutter out** *v adv*
**1** (of an engine) to cease working gradually, making little noises: [IØ + OUT] *After several miles, the engine coughed and then spluttered out and the car stopped.* → **sputter out** (1)

***2** to say (something) in a hasty and confused manner, esp. from fear or shock: [T1] *She was so anxious that she could only splutter out her story of the crime that she had witnessed.*

**spoil for** *v prep*
**1** to be so pleasant as to make it difficult for (someone) to face (worse conditions): [T1 + *for*] *Some people think that enjoying school might spoil children for the real world, so they do their best to make it unpleasant.*

**2 be spoiling for** *not fml* to desire (usu. a fight) eagerly: *Those two boys have been spoiling for a fight for some time, you'd better keep an eye on them or they'll be in trouble.*

**sponge away/off/out** *v adv*
to (cause to) be removed with a sponge: [X9 + AWAY/OFF/OUT] *Sponge the blood away before you cover the wound. Can you sponge off this oil mark? It will be difficult to sponge out a mark that has been on the cloth for so long.* [L9 + AWAY/OFF/OUT (*usu. simple tenses*)] *Will this mark sponge off? This oil will never sponge out, it's been on the cloth so long.*

**sponge down** *v adv*
to wash (someone or something) with a sponge: [X9 + DOWN] *It's so nice to sponge myself down in a hot bath, it makes me feel so much cleaner.* —**sponge-down** *n*

**sponge from** *v prep*
*infml* to obtain (something) from (someone) by asking, without paying, giving, or doing anything in return: [D1] *Do you think we can sponge a meal from your parents?*

**sponge off** *v adv* → SPONGE AWAY

***sponge on** *v prep*
*infml* to live at the cost of (someone else) without invitation: [T1] *I didn't mind giving the boy an occasional meal, but before I knew what had happened, he had moved in, and sponged on us for over two weeks!*

**sponge out** *v adv* → SPONGE AWAY

**sponge up** *v adv*
to take up (liquid) with or as with a sponge: [X9 + UP] *It'll take a long time to sponge up all that pool of water.*

**spook at** *v prep*
esp. *AmE not fml* to become suddenly afraid because of (something): [IØ + *at*] *The cattle are so nervous at this time of year that they will spook at a bush, and run wild for no reason.*

***spoon out** *v adv*
to serve (food) with or as with a spoon: [T1] *I spooned out some soup to each of the guests.*

***spoon up** *v adv*
to lift (food) to the mouth with or as with a spoon: [T1] *Mouthful after mouthful the boy spooned up, before he had time to swallow each bite.*

**sport with** *v prep*
**1** *old use or fml* to play with (someone or something): [IØ + *with*] *You can see the big sea animals in the water, sporting with their young ones.*

***2** *fml* to make fun or a joke of (someone or something); treat (someone) not seriously: [T1] *It's unkind to sport with a young girl's feelings like that.* → **flirt with** (1), etc.

**spout from** *v prep*
(of liquid) to (cause to) come out in a strong stream from (something): [L9 + *from*] *Water was spouting from a hole in the pipe.* [T1 + *from*] *These big sea animals spout water from holes in the top of their heads.*

***spout off** *v adv*
esp. *AmE not fml* to speak in a careless irresponsible way: [IØ] *He's not fit to be chairman, he has a bad habit of spouting off about things that concern him, without thinking of the results of what he says.*

**spot with** *v prep*
**1** to mark (something) with scattered dots of (something): [T1 + *with*] *A dog ran past, spotting my coat with mud. Her face was spotted with fever.*

**2** to rain in small drops of (rain): [*It* + IØ + *with*] *It began to spot with rain an hour ago, but I don't think it will last.*

**sprawl about** *v adv*
to lie stretched out in a comfortable and lazy position: [IØ + ABOUT] *If you sprawl about on the seat like that, there won't be room for anyone else.*

**sprawl out** *v adv*
**1** to take a comfortable position with the arms and legs stretched out loosely; spread (the arms and/or legs) out loosely and lazily: [IØ + OUT] *It's nice to be able to sprawl out when there's plenty of room in this big bed.*

[T1 + OUT *usu. pass.*)] *When I came home I found Father drunk, sprawled out on the bed.* —**sprawled-out** *adj*

**2** to spread in a disorganized way: [IØ + OUT] *As the city grew, housing developments sprawled out for miles either side of the river.*

**spray on** *v adv; prep*

to scatter (liquid) on (something) in fine drops produced under pressure: [T1 + ON/*on* (*to*)] *If you spray the paint on, instead of using a brush, you get a nice even surface. A passing car sprayed mud on our clothes.* —**spray-on** *adj*

**spray with** *v prep*

to cover (something or someone) with a fine scattering of (a liquid) produced under pressure: [T1 + *with*] *The front of the house had been sprayed with white paint. A passing car sprayed us with mud.*

**spread about/around** *v adv; prep*

**1** to scatter (something or things) around (an area): [T1 + ABOUT/AROUND/*about*/*around*)] *If you spread salt around* (*the path*), it helps to melt the snow. All those crowds who come to the shore spread bits of paper and food about (*the sand*).

**2** to cause (news) to be generally known in (a place): [T1 + ABOUT/AROUND/*about*/*around*] *Who's been spreading around that story about trouble in our marriage? The news was quickly spread around informed circles that there was to be an election soon.*

**spread abroad** *v adv* → **blaze abroad, bruit abroad, noise abroad, rumour abroad**

to make (something) widely and publicly known: [T1 + ABROAD] *Stories are being spread abroad about the government's intention to hold a quick election.*

**spread around** *v adv; prep* → **SPREAD ABOUT**

**spread on**[1] *v adv*

**1** to put a coat of (something thick) on top of something: [T1 + ON] *If you spread the butter on as thickly as that, there won't be enough for all the bread.*

**2 spread it on thick(ly)** *not fml* to try to persuade people to believe something unlikely; make too much of a story, beyond the truth: *You're spreading it on rather thick, aren't you? It can't have been as bad as that!* → **lay on**[1] (7)

**spread on**[2] *v prep*

**1** to put (something such as a thick liquid) evenly on (a surface): [T1 + *on*] *Spread the paint thinly on the prepared wood and allow it to dry. This cream is best spread on the face at night. Spread the butter on the bread as thinly as you can, to make it last.* → **apply to** (1), **spread over** (2), **spread with** (1)

**2** to place (something wide) on top of (a surface): [T1 + *on*] *Spread the cloth on the table and get the knives and forks.* → **spread over** (1), **spread with** (2)

**spread oneself** *v pron*

**1** to lie at full length, taking up a lot of room: [T1 + **oneself** (*usu. simple tenses*)] *Tired with running, he spread himself* (*out*) *on the ground. If you spread yourself on the seat like that, there'll be no room for anyone else.*

***2** *not fml* to express one's opinion at length, often so as to influence others to think well of oneself: [IØ (*usu. simple tenses*)] *You'll get a chance to spread yourself when it's your turn to speak.*

***3** *not fml* to spend or otherwise behave freely: [IØ] *He's really spread himself this time, providing all this food! If you spread yourself too much you could offend other people.*

**4 spread oneself (too) thin(ly)** *not fml* to try to do too many different things, so that one cannot give one's full attention to anything: *Your trouble is that you tend to spread yourself too thin, so that nothing gets done properly.*

**spread out** *v adv*

**1** to lay (something) to cover a wide area; unfold or unroll (something): [T1 + OUT] *Spread out the map so that we can all see it. He spread his arms out as if to hold the whole world. The big bird spread out its wings, throwing a large shadow over the ground.* —**outspread** *adj* → **put out** (1), etc.

**2** to (cause to) stretch in space or time: [IØ + OUT (*simple tenses*)] *The branches spread out far across the clearing. A hopeless future seemed to spread out before him.* [T1 + OUT (*usu. pass.*)] *The whole valley was spread out before his eyes.* → **stretch out** (4)

***3** to (cause to) scatter into positions separated by space: [T1] *The plants should be spread out well to allow room for growth.* [IØ] *Tell the men to spread out as they cross the field, so that they won't be so easily hit. Spread out, children, there's more space at the back.* → **fan out, space out** (1)

***4** to place (something or things) at different times, leaving spaces in between: [T1 (*over*)] *The bank should allow you to spread out your payments over several months. We should spread out our visits sensibly, so that she doesn't miss us for too long at a time.* → **space out** (2), **stretch out** (5)

***5** (of a business) to increase: [IØ] *After some difficult early years, the firm is now spreading out, and promises to do well.*

***spread over**[1] *v adv*

to (cause to) be delayed or take a longer time: [IØ (*into*)] *Some of the work spread over into the following year.* [T1] *We may have to spread some decisions over till our next meeting.*

**spread over**[2] *v prep*

**1** to place (something wide) so as to cover (something such as a surface): [T1 + *over*] *Let me spread this cloth over the grass for the family to sit on.* → **spread on**[2] (2), **spread with** (2)

**2** to put (something such as a thick liquid) as to cover the surface of (something): [T1 *over*] *Spreading paint over the dirty marks* *no way to make a lasting improvement.* → **apply to** (1), **spread on²** (1), **spread with** (1)

*3 to give time for (something) during (a stated period): [D1] *The bank should allow you to spread the payments over several months. You may spread your hours of work over any period containing the necessary time.* —**spread-over** *n*

**spread to** *v prep*

to (cause to) reach (someone or something else), as by touching or other means of passing: [IØ + *to*] *You must keep the child at home, or the disease could spread to all the other children in the school. Firemen succeeded in preventing the fire from spreading to other office buildings in the business area of the city.* [T1 + *to*] *We have been asked to spread the news to all our friends. If you allow the child to attend school he could spread the fever to all the other children.*

**spread under** *v prep*

to place (something wide) beneath (something or someone): [T1 + *under*] *Shall I spread the cloths under your feet?*

**spread with** *v prep*

**1** to cover (something such as a surface) with (something such as a thick liquid) laid on it: [D1] *I spread the bread thickly with the cream cheese, and it was very tasty. I spread my face with cream every night.* → **apply to** (1), **spread on²** (1), **spread over²** (2)

**2** to cover (a surface) with (something usu. wide, or a lot of things): [D1] *Spread the table with this cloth, and get the knives and forks. If you spread the floor with newspapers, you can deal more easily with the mud that is brought in. I like to spread the bed with a pretty cover.* → **spread on²** (2), **spread over²** (1)

**spring at** *v prep* → **spring on** (1)

(usu. of an animal) to attack (someone or an animal) by jumping suddenly: [IØ + *at* (*usu. simple tenses*)] *Fire at the tiger's eyes the moment before he springs at you.*

**spring back** *v adv*

**1** to jump in a backward direction: [IØ + BACK (*usu. simple tenses*)] *The cat sprang back after touching the hot stone.*

**2** to return suddenly to its former position: [IØ + BACK (*often simple tenses*)] *Mind that the window frame doesn't spring back and trap your hand.* —**spring-back** *adj*

**spring from** *v prep*

**1** to appear suddenly from (somewhere): [T1 (*no pass., simple tenses*)] *Where did you spring from? I didn't hear you coming.*

**2** to have its or one's origin in (usu. something): [T1 (*no pass., simple tenses*)] *Her doubts spring from too much experience of failure.* → **arise from**, etc.

**spring on/upon** *v prep*

**1** (usu. of an animal) to attack (someone or an animal) by jumping suddenly: [IØ + *on/upon* (*usu. simple tenses*)] *Fire at the tiger's eyes the moment before he springs on you.* → **spring at**

*2 *not fml* to suddenly make known (something unexpected) so as to surprise (someone): [D1] *Please don't spring decisions like that on me without warning me. The government is hoping to keep the date of the election secret so that they can spring it on the voters. Don't tell Father about our wedding yet, I want to spring the news on him tomorrow.*

**spring out** *v adv*

to jump suddenly from a hiding place: [IØ + OUT (*usu. simple tenses*)] *We were taking a peaceful walk in the country, when two men sprang out from behind a bush and attacked us.*

**spring to** *v prep*

**1** to jump suddenly towards (usu. something): [IØ + *to* (*usu. simple tenses*)] *I sprang to the door, but I was too late; he had locked me in.*

**2 spring to attention** *mil* to be quick to move into a formal standing position: [*usu. simple tenses*] *Spring to attention when the captain enters.* → **come to** (16a), **jump to** (2), **snap to** (1), **stand to²** (2)

**3 spring to the defence of** to be eager to support (someone or something): [*usu. simple tenses*] *Why didn't you spring to my defence when you heard your mother being so rude to me?*

**4 spring to one's feet** to rise quickly, as from a sitting position: [*usu. simple tenses*] *The whole crowd sprang to their feet and cheered the victorious team.* → **get to** (11), etc.

**5 spring to life** to start moving or acting quickly or unexpectedly: [*usu. simple tenses*] *After the curtain was lowered, the "dead" actor sprang to life and walked off the stage.*

**6 spring to one's lips** (of a word or words) to be suddenly expressed, often without conscious control: [*usu. simple tenses*] *A rude remark sprang to my lips, but I prevented myself from saying it just in time!*

**spring up** *v adv*

**1** to move quickly upwards: [IØ + UP (*usu. simple tenses*)] *The boy sprang up out of the chair as soon as he heard the doorbell ring.* → **jump up** (2), **leap up** (2), **shoot up** (2), **start up** (2)

*2 to grow quickly: [IØ] *The boy has really sprung up this summer, I hardly recognized him. How that plant has sprung up since I last saw it!* → **shoot up** (4), **sprout up** (1)

*3 *not fml* to begin suddenly; increase quickly: [IØ] *A strong wind sprang up soon after we left the harbour. Opposition to the plan has sprung up in some political groups. What caused this doubt to spring up in your mind? New towns are springing up to house the increasing population.* → **sprout up** (2), **start up** (3)

**spring upon** *v prep* → SPRING ON

**sprinkle on/onto/over/upon** *v prep* → **sprinkle with**
to scatter (things, powder, or fine drops of liquid) on (something or someone): [X9 + *on/onto/over/upon*] *Should you sprinkle salt over your food, or put a pile on the side of your plate? If you sprinkle this chemical on your grass it will help to keep it in good condition.*

**sprinkle with** *v prep* → **sprinkle on**
to cover (something such as a surface or someone) with a scattering of (things, powder, or fine drops of liquid): [X9 + *with*] *The priest sprinkled the baby with holy water when giving him his name.*

**sprout up** *v adv*
**1** (usu. of a plant) to grow, esp. in early stages: [IØ + UP] *The plant you gave me for my birthday is sprouting up nicely.* → **shoot up** (4), **spring up** (2)
***2** *not fml* to come into existence and increase: [IØ] *New towns are sprouting up all over the country as part of the government's plan to find homes for the increasing population.* → **spring up** (3), **start up** (3)

***spruce up** *v adv* → **slick up, smarten up, spiff up**
*not fml* to make (something, someone, or oneself) more neat and attractive: [T1] *Would you like me to help you get all spruced up for the party? In spring, one's thoughts turn to sprucing up the home inside and out.*

***spue out** *v adv* → SPEW OUT

***spue up** *v adv* → SPEW UP

***spunk up** *v adv* → **cheer up,** etc.
*AmE infml* to (cause to) become more cheerful: [IØ] *Spunk up, there's nothing to worry about!* [T1] *Perhaps you need a holiday to spunk you up.*

**spur on** *v adv*
**1** to cause (a horse) to go faster by pricking: [T1 + ON] *The horse was tired, but the rider spurred him on and reached the post first.*
***2** to encourage or urge (someone) (to do something): [T1b (*to*)] *Even a small success would spur me on to greater effort.* [V3] *The threat of unemployment has spurred students on to work harder at their studies.*

**spurt out** *v adv*
(of liquid or gas) to pour out in a sudden, forceful, or uneven stream: [IØ + OUT] *If the blood starts spurting out instead of flowing evenly, it's dangerous and you should call a doctor. The workman's tool burst the water main, and water spurted our all over the street.*

***sputter out** *v adv*
**1** (esp. of a candle) to cease burning unevenly, making little noises: [IØ] *At last the candle sputtered out, the wax getting in the flame and making noises.* → **splutter out** (1)
**2** *not fml* to come to an end unevenly: [IØ] *The wave of violence that has been causing so much trouble is sputtering out bit by bit.*

**spy into** *v prep*
to enquire secretly into (something): [IØ + *into*] *What right have you to spy into my affairs? It is not the business of government to spy into the bedrooms of the nation.*

**spy on/upon** *v prep*
to watch (someone) secretly: [IØ + *on/upon*] *How much did you pay the man to spy on your husband?*

***spy out** *v adv*
**1** to discover or study (something) secretly; find information secretly about (something): [T1] *Men were trained to spy out the opposing party's methods.*
**2 spy out the land: a** to see what the country is like: *Some soldiers were sent ahead to spy out the land and see if the enemy positions were open to attack. "And Moses sent them to spy out the land of Canaan."* (The Bible) **b** *not fml* to see what state matters are in; examine conditions: *It's best to spy out the land before accepting the job.*

**spy upon** *v prep* → SPY ON

**squabble about/over** *v prep* → **argue about, bicker about, quarrel about, wrangle about**
to quarrel about (something or someone); quarrel about who is to have (usu. something unimportant), often in a childish manner: [IØ + *about/over*] *It's just like those two brothers to keep squabbling over one small toy!*

**squabble with** *v prep* → **argue against, argue with** (1), **quarrel with** (1), **row with**
to quarrel with (someone), often in a childish manner or over something unimportant: [IØ + *with*] *I'm sick of hearing you squabbling with your little brother: can't you play in peace?*

***squander away** *v adv*
to waste (something) in foolish spending or by failing to take advantage: [T1] *It doesn't take long to squander a fortune away if you're not careful. Every chance is precious; don't squander any away!*

**squander on/upon** *v prep*
to waste (usu. money or time) by spending it on (something or doing something not worth the cost): [T1 + *on/upon*] *Isn't it foolish to squander so much money on educating such a stupid boy? I wouldn't squander a fine afternoon on cleaning the garage, I'd rather be out of doors. The children squander all their pocket-money on sweets.*

***square away** *v adv*
**1** to place (sails) at right angles to the ship's direction: [T1] *We want to make the best of the wind behind us, so square her away!* [IØ] *We want to make the best of the wind behind us, so square away!*
**2** *not fml* to put (things) in order; get (something) ready: [T1] *Square those papers away, the director's coming.* [IØ] *We must square away before the examiners come into the office.* → **square off** (4)
**3** esp. *AmE not fml* (of two people) to prepare to fight or defend themselves, as by standing face to face: [IØ (*often simp*

*tenses)] The two brothers squared away, this time seriously determined to fight.* → **square off** (3), **square up** (3)

***square off** *v adv*

**1** to divide (an area) into squares: [T1] *The board is squared off ready for the game.*

**2** to make (something) square, with straight sides or edges: [T1] *If you can square the parcel off somehow, it will be easier to wrap. The ends of the shelves must be squared off to fit the wall.*

**3** esp. *AmE not fml* (of two people) to prepare to fight or defend themselves, as by standing face to face: [IØ] *The two brothers are squaring off; I think they're really determined to fight this time!* → **square away** (3), **square up** (3)

**4** *not fml* to put (things) in order; get (something) ready: [T1] *Square those papers off, the director's coming.* [IØ] *We must square off before the examiners come into the office.* → **square away** (2)

***square round** *v adv*

*naut* to make sure that all right angles are correct: [IØ] *When you've tightened the ropes, square round just to make sure.*

***square up** *v adv*

**1** to set (something or things) at right angles: [T1 (*with*)] *Square up the books to make them look neat. You have to square the wallpaper up with the corners of the room.*

**2** *not fml* to pay a debt such as a bill; pay for (something) fairly: [IØ (*with*)] *Give me a minute to square up, and I'll meet you outside the hotel. I'd like to square up with the tradesmen before we leave town.* [T1] *Let's pay the bill and square up the difference between our meals later. Don't worry about the damage, I promise to square it up.* → **settle up**

**3** *not fml* (of two people) to prepare to fight or defend themselves, as by standing face to face: [IØ] *When I saw the two brothers squaring up, I ran home to warn Mother that their threats to fight each other were real.* → **square away** (3), **square off** (3)

***square up to** *v adv prep*

**1** *not fml* to prepare to fight or defend oneself against (someone): [T1] *It was brave of you to square up to that big man who threatened to attack us.*

**2** *not fml* to show courage in accepting, bearing, or dealing with (something difficult or painful): [T1] *Young fathers have heavy responsibilities that they must square up to. The only way is to square up to your difficulties and not try to escape them.* → **face up to, shape up to**

**square with** *v prep*

**1** *not fml* to finish paying (someone): [T1 (*no pass., usu. simple tenses*)] *I should be able to square with you at the end of the month.* → **settle with** (2)

**2** *not fml* to put (a matter or matters) right with (someone); arrange (things) with (someone) in a satisfactory way: [D1] *Can you square things with the director so that the worker won't be punished for his accidental damage?*

**3** to find or cause agreement between (something) and (something else): [T1 (*simple tenses*)] *His actions do not square with his principles. The reason I'm disappointed is that the results do not square with the promises I was given.* [D1 (*simple tenses*)] *How can you square your decision with your stated political views?* **reconcile with** (2)

**squash in** *v adv; prep* → **scrape in** (1), **squeeze in** (1)

to press (something, things, or people) tightly in (something); crowd together in (something): [T1 + IN (*to*)/*in*] *I can't squash any more clothes in (the case), there's no more room. How many people can you squash in (the football ground)?*

**squash up** *v adv*

**1** to press (something) into a mass, usu. accidentally: [T1 + UP (*usu. pass.*)] *The fruit has got all squashed up in the box, we can't eat it.*

***2** *not fml* to (cause to) crowd together, as on a seat: [IØ] *If you two squash up, there'll be room for another one.* [T1] *I don't like being squashed up with all these children.* → **move down**[1] (1), etc.

**squat down** *v adv*

to rest with the knees bent, close to the ground: [IØ + DOWN] *The children squatted down to draw on the sand.*

***squeak by** *v adv* → **get by**[1] (2), etc.

*not fml* to be only just able to succeed or live: [IØ (*usu. simple tenses*)] *We have hardly any money, but we can squeak by till the end of the month. Don't worry about how I'm to live while I'm away at college, I'll squeak by somehow.*

***squeak out** *v adv*

to express (something) in a high voice: [T1 (*usu. simple tenses*)] *She squeaked out a cry of fear as the mouse ran across the floor.*

***squeak through** *v adv; prep*

**1** to be only just able to pass through (a narrow space): [IØ (*usu. simple tenses*)] *The walls of the cave come to a narrow point just ahead, but I think we can squeak through.* [T1 (*usu. simple tenses*)] *I don't know how our dog was able to squeak through the bars of all the fences that we built for him, but he did!* → **scrape through** (1), **skin through** (1), **squeeze through** (1)

**2** *not fml* to be only just able to pass (something such as an examination): [IØ (*usu. simple tenses*)] *Some of you deserved to succeed, and others only squeaked through.* [T1 (*usu. simple tenses*)] *Jane got into the music school by squeaking through the examination.* → **scrape through** (2), **skin through** (2), **squeeze through** (2)

**squeeze by** *v adv*
**1** to pass with difficulty: [L9 + BY] *Could you please move a little? I can hardly squeeze by.*
*__2__ *not fml* to be only just able to succeed or live: [IØ] *We have hardly any money, but we can squeeze by till the end of the month.* → **get by**[1] (2), etc.

**squeeze from** *v prep*
**1** to obtain (liquid) from (something) by pressing: [T1 + *from*] *This machine helps you to squeeze more juice from the oranges.* → **squeeze out** (1)
*__2__ *not fml* to obtain (something) from (someone) with difficulty: [D1] *Can you squeeze any more money from your father?* → **squeeze out** (2)

**squeeze in** *v adv*
**1** to press (something, things, or people) tightly in something; crowd together in a place: [T1 + IN (*to*)] *The case is full—I can't squeeze any more clothes in.* [IØ + IN] *The train was full but we were able to squeeze in.* → **scrape in** (1), **squash in**
*__2__ *not fml* to find time, with difficulty, to see (someone) or do (something): [T1] *The doctor is busy, but I'll see if he can squeeze you in between two other people, as your case is urgent. If you try to squeeze any more activities in, you'll make yourself ill.* → **crowd in** (2), **fit in**[1] (3)
*__3__ *not fml* to be only just able to enter something such as a school by passing an examination: [IØ] *Jane was worried about her examination for the music school, but she heard that she had just squeezed in.* → **scrape in** (2)

**squeeze out** *v adv*
**1** to remove (liquid) (from something) by pressing: [T1 + OUT (*of*)] *This machine helps you to squeeze more juice out (of the oranges).* → **squeeze from** (1)
*__2__ *not fml* to obtain (something) (from someone) with difficulty: [T1 (*of*)] *Your father has already paid so much, I doubt if you can squeeze any more money out (of him).* → **squeeze from** (2)
**3 be squeezed out (of)** *not fml* to be forced to leave (a place) for lack of room: *We stayed at home until the family grew so large that we were squeezed out (of the house). Competition is now so fierce that all but the best salesmen are being squeezed out (of the firm).* → **crowd out** (2), **crush out** (2)

**squeeze through** *v adv; prep*
**1** to be only just able to pass through (a narrow space): [L9 + THROUGH/*through* (*usu. simple tenses*)] *The walls of the cave come to a narrow point just ahead, but I think we can squeeze through (it).* → **scrape through** (1), **skin through** (1), **squeak through** (1)
*__2__ *not fml* to be only just able to pass (something such as an examination): [IØ (*usu. simple tenses*)] *Some of you deserved to pass, but others only squeezed through.* [T1 (*usu. simple tenses*)] *Jane got into the music school by squeezing through the examination.* → **scrape through** (2), **skin through** (2), **squeak through** (2)

***squeeze up** *v adv* → **move down**[1] (1), etc.
*not fml* to (cause to) move closer to others, as on a seat: [IØ] *If you two squeeze up, there'll be room for one more.* [T1] *I don't like being squeezed up with all these children.*

**squint at** *v prep*
to look at (something or someone) with the eyes crossed or half-closed; see through half-closed eyes because of (bright light): [IØ + *at* (*usu. continuous tenses*)] *When the teacher saw the boy squinting at the page, she suggested to his parents that he might need glasses. We came out of the cinema, squinting at the bright sunshine.*

***squirm out of** *v adv prep* → **get out of** (13), etc.
*not fml* to escape or avoid (something such as a responsibility): [T1 (*no pass.*)] *Now you promised to dig the garden for me—don't try to squirm out of it!*

**squirm with** *v prep*
to twist the body as an expression of (an uncomfortable feeling): [IØ + *with*] *The child squirmed with anxiety as she waited for the results. I knew he was guilty when I saw him squirming with shame.*

***squirrel away** *v adv*
esp. *AmE not fml* to store (something such as money): [T1] *If we squirrel away most of the profit, we won't get into difficulties next year when we want to order supplies. By squirrelling away his pocket money for several months, the boy was able to buy his own radio.*

**squirt out** *v adv*
(of a liquid) to (cause to) come out (of a container) in a sudden stream: [X9 + OUT (*of*)] *You can squirt the paint out of the tube instead of using a brush.* [L9 + OUT (*of*)] *As his tool hit the pipe, water squirted out all over him.*

***stab at** *v prep*
to attempt to wound (someone) or make a hole in (something) with a sharp point such as a knife: [T1 (*often simple tenses*)] *The woman stabbed at her attacker with a pair of scissors that she was carrying in her bag. It's rude to stab at the meat with your knife to see if it is well cooked.*

**stab in** *v prep*
**1** to wound (someone) in (a part of the body) with a sharp point such as a knife: [T1 + *in* (*often simple tenses*)] *The thief stabbed me in the arm with a knife as he seized my bag.*
**2 stab someone in the back** *not fml* to attack or fail to support someone in a disloyal way: *The chairman expected his friends to vote for him, but they stabbed him in the back by electing his opponent.* —**stab in the back** *n*

**stab to** *v prep*
**stab someone to the heart** *not fml* to hurt someone's feelings severely; cause someone so

row: [*usu. simple tenses*] *It stabs me to the heart when I remember how happy we were then. His disloyalty stabbed me to the heart.*

**stack against** *v prep*

**stack the cards/chances/chips/odds against** *not fml* to prevent (someone) from succeeding; put (someone) in a position of disadvantage: [*usu. pass.*] *Your lack of education really stacks the cards against you when it comes to finding a good job. Do you ever get the feeling that the odds are stacked against you, and nothing can ever go right?*

**stack up** *v adv*

**1** to make a pile of (things) one on top of another: [T1 + UP] *The bricks are stacked up over there, all ready to be used for the new wall. Please help to stack up the plates at the end of the meal.*

**2** to make (a plane) wait its turn to land: [T1 + UP (*often pass.*)] *Twenty-five planes were stacked up, circling round the airport.* **—stack-up** *n*

***3** *not fml* to gain (money); amount (to a sum): [T1] *We should be able to stack up a reasonable profit if we sell now.* [L9 (*to*)] *What did our sales stack up to last month?*

***4** esp. *AmE not fml* to be in a certain state: [L9] *This is how things stack up today. The firm is stacking up pretty well these days.*

***5** to measure, esp. in relation to an opponent; be worth something: [L9 (*against, with*)] *How does our product stack up against those of our competitors?*

**stagger about/around** *v adv; prep*

to move in an unsteady manner and an uncertain direction around (a place): [IØ + ABOUT/AROUND/*about/around*] *Why is that man staggering about (the room) like that? Is he drunk?*

**stain with** *v prep*

**1** to mark (something such as cloth) with (something dirty, dark, or oily) so that the mark cannot be removed easily: [T1 + *with* (*often pass.*)] *The murderess felt that her hands were stained with blood long after the marks had been removed. You can stain the wood with this special liquid, to give it a pleasing colour.*

**2** to spoil (something) with (something bad): [T1 + *with*] *He has strained the good honour of his family with the guilt of his crime.*

**stake off** *v adv* → **stake out** (1)

to separate (an area) with wooden posts: [T1 (*usu. pass.*)] *This corner of the wheat field has been staked off for the cattle.*

**stake on/upon** *v prep*

**1** to risk (usu. money) on the success of (something or someone): [T1 + *on/upon*] *Foolishly, he staked all his possessions on the result of the card game. You can make a fortune by staking a small amount on a promising singing group.* → **be on** (5), **bet on** (1), **gamble on, put on** (5), **wager on** (1)

***2** to be prepared to give up (something highly valued) as a promise that (something such as an idea) is good: [D1 (*usu. simple tenses*)] *I would stake my life on that boy's honesty. The firm stakes its honour on every product that it sells.*

***stake out** *v adv*

**1** to mark usu. the borders of (an area) with wooden posts: [T1] *The builders have staked out the land where the houses are to be built.* → **stake off**

**2** *sl* to place police or other guards to watch (someone or a place where there is a possibility of criminal activity): [T1] *Additional police were called in to stake out the hotel where the gunman was thought to be hiding. It's wise to stake out each prisoner for the first months after he gets out of prison.* **—stake out** *n*

**3 stake out a claim (to): a** to declare formally that one owns or has rights to certain land where precious minerals may be found: *You'd better stake out your claim (to that land) before others hear that there is gold there.* **b** *not fml* to feel or state that one has a right to claim (something or someone): *He seems to have staked out a claim to the rich man's daughter.*

**stalk away/off** *v adv*

**1** to move away: [IØ + AWAY/OFF] *What did I say to make her bang the door and stalk off like that?*

**2** to leave in an offended manner: [L9 + AWAY/OFF] *What did I say to make her stalk off with her nose in the air?*

**stall for** *v prep* → **play for** (7)

**stall for time** to cause delays in order to have more time to think, win, collect money, etc.: *If we stall for time on this contract, we may get a better price. Can you stall for time till the end of the month, when we shall have enough money to pay them?*

**stall off** *v adv*

to cause (someone to whom one owes money) to wait: [T1 + OFF] *How can we stall off the angry tradesmen till the end of the month?*

***stammer out** *v adv*

to say (something) in an unsteady uncertain manner: [T1] *At last the child stammered out his guilt. Filled with shame, he stammered out a few words to say how sorry he was for his thoughtless action.*

***stamp as** *v prep*

to cause (someone) to be recognized as being (a certain kind of person): [X1 (*simple tenses*)] *Such generous actions stamps him as a man of honour.*

**stamp on/upon** *v prep*

**1** to put the feet heavily on top of (usu. something): [IØ + *on/upon*] *I'm sorry I stamped on your foot. Please stamp on that insect for me!* → **step on** (1), **trample on** (1), **tread on** (1)

**2** to mark the shape of (something such as a word) on (a surface) by pressing or printing:

[T1 + *on/upon* (*often simple tenses*)] *This machine stamps the date on the paper. His name was stamped on the case.* → **stamp with** (1)

***3** *not fml* to discourage (something such as an idea) firmly and actively; try to prevent (something): [T1 (*usu. simple tenses*)] *The students' suggestion must be stamped on before it becomes a threat. No teacher should stamp on a child's idea without considering it fairly.* → **stamp out** (4)

**stamp out** *v adv*

**1** to produce (a regular musical beat) with the feet: [T1 + OUT] *The whole crowd at the game were stamping out the rhythm of the song, and the noise was terrible.*

**2** to shape (something, usu. metal or plastic) by pressing: [T1 + OUT] *This machine can stamp out 20,000 coins a day.* → **punch out** (1)

***3** to put out (a fire) by treading with the feet: [T1] *Be sure to stamp the fire out, and then cover it with earth just in case.* → **trample out** (2), **tread out** (2)

***4** *not fml* to put a stop to (something) by forceful or violent means: [T1 (*usu. simple tenses*)] *Any attempt to overthrow the king must be stamped out. The government is determined to stamp out crime in the big cities.* → **stamp on** (3)

**stamp upon** *v prep* → STAND ON

**stamp with** *v prep*

**1** to mark (something) with (something such as a word) by pressing or printing: [T1 + *with*] *The library book is stamped with the date by which it must be returned.* → **stamp on** (2)

**2** to place postage stamps on (an envelope, parcel, etc.) to (an amount): [T1 + *with*] *All letters must be stamped with the correct postage.*

**3** **be stamped with** to bear the signs of (something such as an ability or quality): *His speech was stamped with the qualities of greatness.*

***stampede into** *v prep*

to persuade (someone) into (something or doing something) hurriedly, through fear or anger: [V4b] *Many people were stampeded into selling gold when the price began to fall.* [D1 (*often pass.*)] *It was the seeming injustice that stampeded the students into action.*

**stand about/around** *v adv; prep*

to stand lazily or inactively near or around (something): [IØ + ABOUT/AROUND/*about/around*] *People were standing around (the bus stop) waiting for the bus. Why are you standing about doing nothing?*

**stand above** *v prep*

**stand head and shoulders above** *not fml* to have much greater ability than (someone else): [*simple tenses*] *This new young singer stands head and shoulders above all the other performers in the concert. Give him the job—he stands head and shoulders above the other people who asked to be considered for it.*

**stand against** *v prep*

**1** to (cause to) lean or take a position against (something such as a wall): [IØ + *against*] *The ladder stood against the wall, making it easy for the thieves to enter the house.* [X9 + *against*] *The prisoner was stood against the wall and shot.*

***2** to be seen clearly in front of (a background): [T1 (*no pass., usu. simple tenses*)] *The church tower stood against the sky like a finger pointing towards heaven.* → **stand out against** (1)

***3** to oppose (something): [T1 (*often simple tenses*)] *I stand against all forms of cruelty, especially to children.* → **stand up to** (1)

***stand aloof** *v adv* → **hang back,** etc.

to remain at a distance (from other people) in an unfriendly manner: [IØ (*from*) (*often simple tenses*)] *Mary doesn't enjoy parties, and tends to stand aloof (from everyone else).*

**stand apart** *v adv* → **hang back,** etc., **stand aside** (1), **stand out** (3), **step aside** (1)

to keep oneself separate (from others): [IØ + APART (*from*)] *There was one boy rather noticeably standing apart from the other children. No thank you, I won't sit, I'll stand apart over here where the smoke isn't so thick.*

**stand around** *v adv; prep* → STAND ABOUT

**stand as** *v prep* → **run for** (3), **sit for** (3), **stand for** (2)

*BrE* to offer oneself as a representative of (a particular party or point of view) in an election: [IØ + *as*] *If he cannot agree with the party, he may choose to stand as an Independent, and still hope to be elected.*

**stand aside** *v adv*

**1** to move to one side, out of the way: [IØ + ASIDE (*often imper.*)] *Stand aside, please, the firemen can't get through!* → **stand apart, stand out** (3), **step aside** (1)

***2** to take no action; remain inactive, esp. while something bad is happening. [IØ (*often simple tenses*)] *How can you stand aside and see the child badly treated?* → **sit back** (3), **sit by, stand back** (4), **stand by**[1] (2), **step back** (3)

***3** to take no further part in a competition, as for a position: [IØ] *I feel that when there are so many better people for the chairmanship, I should stand aside.* → **stand down, step aside** (2), **stand down** (2)

**stand at** *v prep*

**1** to wait in a standing position at or near (something): [IØ + *at*] *We stood at the bus stop waiting for the bus. They kept me standing at the door for ten minutes!*

***2** (of a measure or level) to reach or remain at (a certain amount): [L1 (*no pass., simple tenses*)] *The collection of money to save the ancient church now stands at £35,000. The flood level stood at three feet above usual for several weeks.*

**3** **stand at attention** *mil* to be standing in a formal position, stiffly upright: *You can't expect the men to stand at attention for the whole* *afternoon in this hot weather.* → **be at** (7), **bring to** (4a), **come to²** (16a), **jump to** (2), **snap to** (1), **spring to** (2), **stand to²** (2)

**4 stand at ease** *mil* to stand with the feet apart and the hands behind the back: [*usu. imper.*] *Company, stand at ease!* → **be at** (10), **stand easy**

***stand away** *v adv*
to take or have a position at a distance from something: [IØ (*simple tenses*)] *In those days, skirts were made to stand away from the body.* —**standaway** *adj*

**stand back** *v adv*
**1** to stand further away (from something or someone): [IØ + BACK (*from*)] *The firemen asked the crowd to stand back (from the burning building) as there was a danger of falling beams. Stand back! This is a very powerful explosive!* → **move back** (1), etc.
**2** to be in a position behind or further away, as from a road: [L9 + BACK (*from*) (*simple tenses*)] *The church stands (well) back from the road, behind the graveyard.* → **set back** (2), **sit back** (2)
***3** to consider something as if from a distance: [IØ (*from*) (*usu. simple tenses*)] *This meeting gives us a chance to stand back (from the everyday activities of the department) and view its workings as a stranger might do, so as to value it correctly. It's difficult to know what you're doing unless you can stand back to look at it from another point of view.* → **step back** (2)
***4** to refuse to take part in or influence something such as an event: [IØ (*usu. simple tenses*)] *From time to time, the teachers should stand back and let the children run things their own way. There's no way you can stand back and allow such injustice to take place.* → **sit back** (3), **sit by, stand aside** (2), **stand by¹** (2), **step back** (3)

**stand behind** *v prep*
**1** to be or get on one's feet at the back of (something or someone): [IØ + *behind*] *Stand behind a person who is taller than you are. A man was standing behind the pillar, half-hidden from sight.*
**2** to be situated or kept in a position at the back of (something): [L9 + *behind* (*simple tenses*)] *Behind the new shopping centre stood an old church. "Where does the teapot go?" "It stands behind the cups."*
***3** to support (someone): [T1 (*no pass., simple tenses*)] *The whole family stood behind him in his struggle. Behind every successful man stands a strong woman.*
***4** to be the guiding principle of (something): [T1 (*no pass., simple tenses*)] *A sense of the importance of national unity stands behind the party's thinking.*

**stand between** *v prep*
**1** to be or get on one's feet between (two things or people): [IØ + *between*] *Stand between your sisters, to balance the photograph.*
**2** to be in a position between (usu. two things): [L9 + *between* (*simple tenses*)] *The little shops stands between the railway station and the Post Office.*
***3** to try to prevent (someone) from having or doing (something): [T1 (*no pass., usu. simple tenses*)] *He will let no opposition stand between himself and his future.* → **come between** (3), **get between** (3)

**stand by¹** *v adv*
**1** to be present, as standing, near something or someone: [IØ + BY] *The police took accounts of the accident from two witnesses who happened to be standing by at the time of the crash.* —**bystander** *n*
***2** to watch without taking action: [IØ (*simple tenses*)] *How can a crowd stand by while a woman is attacked and robbed? Unable to swim, she stood by helplessly while the child drowned.* → **sit back** (3), **sit by, stand aside** (2), **stand back** (4), **step back** (3)
***3** to be ready for action, flight, duty, etc., at a moment's notice: [IØ] *Stand by for firing! Stand by to receive the radio message. The city firemen had the flames under control, but additional firemen were kept standing by in case of need. The plane is full, and we have ten hopeful passengers standing by in addition. The hospital has an additional electricity supply standing by in case of a power failure.* —**stand-by** *n, adj*

**stand by²** *v prep*
**1** to be or get on one's feet next to (someone or something): [IØ + *by*] *Go and stand by the wall, it's more sheltered there. Would you stand by your mother so that I can take your photograph?*
**2** to be in a position next to (usu. something): [L9 + *by* (*simple tenses*)] *The house stands by a river, and gets flooded every spring.* → **stick by** (1), **stick to** (7)
***3** to be loyal to (someone or a promise); support (someone) loyally: [T1 (*no pass.*)] *I stand by my word at all times. Can the government stand by its promise to reduce taxes? His family can be trusted to stand by him through his struggle.* → **adhere to** (2), etc., **stay with** (3), **stick with** (4)

**stand clear** *v adv*
to stand to one side (so as to leave room for someone, or avoid something): [IØ + CLEAR (*of*)] *The firemen asked the crowd to stand clear so that they could get the fire engine through. Stand clear of the doors!*

***stand down** *v adv*
**1** to leave a witness box in a court of law: [IØ (*often simple tenses*)] *Thank you, you may now stand down.*
**2** to yield one's position or chance of election: [IØ] *I've spent so many years as chairman that I feel it's time I stood down.* → **stand aside** (3), **step aside** (2), **step down** (2)
**3** *mil* to (cause to) be no longer ready as a group organized for action: [IØ (*often simple*

*tenses*)] *"Stand down, men," said the captain.* [T1 (*often simple tenses*)] *The captain stood the men down.* → **stand to**

***stand easy** *v adj* → **be at** (10), **stand at** (4)
*mil* to stand comfortably, in an informal position: [IØ (*often imper.*)] *The officer gave the order to stand easy.*

***stand fast** *v adv* → **hold firm, stand firm, stand pat** (2), **stick fast** (2)
to be firm in keeping to one's opinions or actions: [IØ (*often simple tenses*)] *All the family tried to persuade Jim to change his mind, but he stood fast and refused to be influenced.* —**standfast** *n*

***stand firm** *v adj* → **hold firm, stand fast, stand pat, stick fast** (2)
to keep one's position, in place or argument, in spite of attack or disagreement: [IØ] *The enemy attacked fiercely, but our men stood firm. In spite of the unions' efforts to defeat the new wage and price controls, the government is standing firm.*

**stand for** *v prep*
**1** to rise to one's feet as a mark of respect for (someone or something): [IØ + *for*] *Will all present in court stand for the judge. At the opening ceremony, the whole crowd stood for the national song.*
**2** *BrE* to offer oneself for election to Parliament to represent (a place): [IØ + *for*] *Do you intend to stand for this town in the next election? Three women with the same name are standing for this seat.* → **run for** (3), **sit for** (3), **stand as**
***3** (of single letters, as in the name of an organization to represent (words, usu. which begin with these letters): [T1 (*no pass., simple tenses, usu. present*)] *The letters NSPCC stand for National Society for the Prevention of Cruelty to Children.*
***4** to hold (an opinion); mean or believe (something such as a principle): [T1 (*no pass., simple tenses*)] *This decision goes against everything I stand for. The party stands for equality in employment, and fair trading.*
***5** *not fml* to accept or bear (something bad): [T1 (*usu. neg., simple tenses*)] *I won't stand for any more of her rudeness, I shall ask her to leave my house. Why do you stand for such bad working conditiions? I've now stood for this treatment as long as I can!* [T4 (*simple tenses*)] *I won't stand for hearing any more of your complaints!* → **bear with** (2), **contend with** (2), **put up with** (3)
***6** *naut* to move or aim in the direction of (somewhere): [T1] *"Still bent to make some port he knows not where, Still standing for some false impossible shore."* (Matthew Arnold, *A Summer Night*)

**stand in** *v prep*
**1** to (cause to) be or get on one's feet in (something): [IØ + *in*] *The fisherman was standing in water over his knees.* [X9 + *in*] *Stand the baby in the seat while I fasten the belt. Bad children will be stood in the corner in shame.*
**2** to be in position in (a place): [L9 + *in* (*simple tenses*)] *The church stands in a quiet corner of the village. The shop stood in the main street to catch the busy trade.*
**3** to remain present or inactive in (a place): [L9 + *in*] *The car has stood in the garage all winter. Tears were standing in her eyes as she spoke.* → **sit in**[2] (2)
**4 stand in awe (of)** to feel fear mixed with respect (for someone or something): *There's no need to stand in awe of the director because of his position, he's just an ordinary person.*
**5 stand in someone's/one's own light: a** to throw one's shadow over someone's or one's own work: *If you do your painting at this side of the room, you'll be standing in your own light. Excuse me, would you mind moving away from the window? You're standing in my light.* **b** *not fml* to prevent someone's or one's own work or activity: *I haven't finished the job because my brother kept standing in my light.*
**6 stand in (the) need of** to be in a state in which one needs (something): *That boy stands in need of correction, the way he behaves all the time. "It's me, it's me, it's me, O Lord, standing in the need of prayer."* (song)
**7 stand someone in better/good stead** to be (more) useful to someone in a time of need: [*often simple tenses*] *Your education will stand you in good stead in later years, even though at the moment it must seem as if training for a job would stand you in better stead.*
**8 stand in someone's way: a** to prevent someone from moving: *The man stood in my way and I was afraid that he would attack me.* **b** to prevent someone from doing something; oppose someone's wishes: *If you really want to leave home, I won't stand in your way, but I think it's a foolish idea at your age.*
**9 stand in the way of** to prevent (something or someone doing something): *There's nothing standing in the way of our marriage. Does anything stand in the way of the firm accepting this contract?*

***stand in for** *v adv prep* → **cover for** (1), **deputize for, double for, fill in** (6), **fill in for, sit in for, step in for, substitute for** (2)
to take the place of (someone); act as a replacement for (someone): [T1 (*no pass.*)] *Can you stand in for me at the meeting? I can't go, but I must send a representative. The actor might get wounded in this dangerous action, so someone who looks like him should stand in for him in this scene.* —**stand-in** *n*

***stand in to/towards** *v adv prep*
to sail in the direction of (a place on or near the shore): [T1 (*no pass.*)] *The ship is still a long way out to sea, but she seems to be standing in towards the harbour.*

***stand in with** *v adv prep*
**1** esp. *AmE not fml* to have a friendly relationship with (someone): [T1 (*no pass.*)] *O*

*course if you stood in with the chairman there'd be no difficulty in having your plan accepted.*

**2** *not fml* to share a cost with (someone): [T1 (*no pass.*)] *All the members agreed to stand in with the secretary, who had bought the club supplies with his own money.*

***stand off**[1] *v adv*

**1** *naut* to remain at a distance from the shore: [IØ] *Three battleships were kept standing off as a silent threat to the island people.*

**2** *not fml* to keep away from people: [IØ (*from*) (*often simple tenses*)] *Mary dislikes parties, and tends to stand off (from everyone else) if she does attend one.* —**standoffish** *adj* → **hang back,** etc.

**3** to keep (someone such as an enemy) at a distance: [T1] *We stood off 500 of the enemy forces for nine days.*

**4** to stop employing (someone) often for a short time, as because of conditions preventing work: [T1] *300 workers at the car factory were stood off when there was a lack of steel.* → **lay off**[1] (3), **lie off** (2)

***stand off**[2] *v prep*

*naut* to keep at a distance from (a shore): [T1 (*no pass.*)] *Three battleships were kept standing off the island as a silent threat to the people.*

***stand on**[1] *v adv*

to keep a boat's direction and speed: [IØ] *We stood on for the next hour while the wind was in our favour.*

**stand on/upon**[2] *v prep*

**1** to rest one's weight on (usu. a leg, foot, etc.) or have one's feet resting on (a surface): [IØ + *on/upon*] *How long can you stand on one leg? I have to stand on a chair to reach the top of the window to clean it. The children were standing on the desks, shouting. Don't stand on the cold floor with bare feet, you'll catch cold.*

**2** to (cause to) be placed on top of (a surface): [L9 + *on/upon* (*usu. simple tenses*)] *The photograph of my daughter as a small child has stood on the piano for many years.* [X9 + *on/upon* (*simple tenses*)] *We had to stand the lamp on the floor as it was too big to stand on the table.* → **sit on** (2)

**3** to take a position in (a direction or place): [IØ + *on/upon* (*often simple tenses*)] *Please stand on one side, we need a lot of room to get by.* → **stand to**[2] (1)

***4** to act firmly according to (one's principles, rights, etc.): [T1 (*no pass., simple tenses*)] *I stand on my rights in this matter, and will take the matter to court if necessary. Always stand on your principles and let no one persuade you otherwise.*

***5** *old use* to wait for (something): [T1 (*no pass., usu. simple tenses*)] *"Stand not upon the order of your going, But go at once."* (Shakespeare, *Macbeth*)

***6** to continue to declare the truth of (something): [T1 (*no pass., usu. simple tenses*)] *Do you still stand on your original story?*

**7 stand on ceremony** to be formally polite: *Do please make yourself at home here and be comfortable, we don't stand on ceremony in this house!*

**8 stand on one's dignity** to demand respectful treatment: [*usu. simple tenses*] *It's no longer possible for a teacher to stand on his dignity with students these days, those times have changed.*

**9 stand on end: a** to (cause to) be turned on one side: *Why is the chair standing on end? Turn it the right way up! The books were all stood on end, which would damage them.* **b** (of hair) to rise, as with shock or fear: *I thought I was alone in the house until I heard the mysterious noise again, and my hair stood on end.*

**10 stand on one's own (two) feet** to be independent: [*often simple tenses*] *No, I won't lend you any money, it's time you stood on your own two feet and earned your own living.*

**11 stand something on its head** to turn (an idea) upside down; see or suggest the opposite of something: [*usu. simple tenses*] *The chairman stood the decision on its head by showing that far from saving money, it would cost more.*

**12 standing on one's head** *not fml* very easily, without effort: *Why are you worrying about the examination? You can pass that standing on your head.*

**stand out** *v adv*

**1** *mil* to take a step forward, out of line: [IØ + OUT] *Stand out that man in the back row, the one with the dirty boots!*

***2** to be in a position further forward from something: [IØ (*from*) (*usu. simple tenses*)] *The pot has two handles standing out. The house stands out from the rest of the row as it had another room added on the front.* → **jut out, poke out** (1), **project from, protrude from, stick out** (1)

***3** to leave a group: [IØ] *The children were all in the middle of the room except one boy standing out. We only need three people for this game, so anyone else will have to stand out.* → **stand apart, stand aside** (1), **step aside** (1)

***4** to continue to show opposition, disagreement, etc., as by refusing to work: [IØ] *The miners are determined to stand out until they get what they are demanding. Some of the workers still stood out even after the rest had agreed to accept the pay offer.* → **hang out for, hold out for, stand out for, stick out** (6), **stick out for**

***5** to be noticeable: [IØ (*usu. simple tenses*)] *To make the figures stand out, paint them in a lighter colour. Red always stands out among other colours. The house stood out because of its unusual shape. I don't like to stand out in a crowd. No one in this singing group* *should stand out as a separate voice.* → **stick out** (4)

*6 to be noticeably of better quality: [IØ (*from*) (*simple tenses*)] *The two girls stood out from the whole class, and were always winning prizes for school work. Only three paintings stood out as deserving special praise.* —**standout** *n* —**outstanding** *adj*

**7 stand out a mile** *not fml* to be very noticeable: [*simple tenses*] *In an uninteresting school concert, Jane's performance stood out a mile. It stands out a mile that the government has no intention of calling an election this year.* → **stick out (8)**

***stand out against** *v adv prep*

**1** to be clearly seen against a background of (something): [T1 (*no pass., often simple tenses*)] *The bare shapes of the winter trees stood out against the pale sky.* → **stand against**

**2** to oppose (something) in a determined way: [T1 (*no pass.*)] *The trade unions have continued to stand out against the government's wage and price controls.* → **stick out against**

***stand out for** *v adv prep* → **hang out for, hold out for, stand out** (4), **stick out** (6), **stick out for, strike against** (1), **strike for**

to demand (something such as money) firmly and wait in order to get it: [T1 (*no pass.*)] *You may have to stand out for your pay rise longer than your expect.*

**stand out of** *v adv prep*

**1** to take a step out of (a line, row, etc.): [IØ + OUT + *of*] *The teacher asked the boy to stand out of line so that she could speak to him later.*

**2 one's eyes stand out of one's head** *not fml* to express or feel surprise, shock, etc.: *The country boy's eyes stood out of his head when he visited the big city for the first time.*

**stand outside** *v adv; prep*

**1** to take a position, as standing, out of doors or otherwise not in (a place): [IØ + OUTSIDE/*outside*] *There's someone standing outside (the door), but I didn't hear the bell ring. A stone lion stood outside the building.*

***2** → FALL OUTSIDE

***stand over**[1] *v adv* → **put off**[1] (4), etc.

to wait or be delayed till a later time: [IØ] *We still have some small debts standing over. We'll have to let the rest of the questions stand over till the next meeting.*

***stand over**[2] *v prep*

to watch (someone at work), as if examining their work: [T1] *Mother, please don't stand over me while I'm cooking, you make me nervous.*

***stand pat** *v adj*

**1** (in a card game) to play the given cards without taking any additional ones: [IØ] *No thanks, I'll stand pat with the cards I already have.*

**2** *not fml* to refuse to change, esp. in opinion: [IØ] *I've always had the bedroom blue, and I'll stand pat on that choice. Stand pat, don't let them persuade you that you're wrong.* —**stand patter** *n* —**stand pat** *adj* → **hold firm, stand fast, stand firm, stick fast** (2)

**stand still** *v adj*

**1** to stand or remain without moving: [IØ + **still**] *Why is it that children can never stand still for more than a minute? Stand still while I pin your dress, or I might prick you.* → **stop still** (1)

***2** to stay at the same level or rate, without advancing; be inactive: [IØ] *Production has stood still at the factory since the men began demanding higher wages. Time seemed to stand still at this moment of such beauty.* —**standstill** *n* → **stop still** (2)

***stand to**[1] *v adv* → **stand down** (3)

*mil* to (cause to) be ready for action: [IØ] *How many men do you have standing to?* [T1 (*often simple tenses*)] *I thought I ordered you to stand the men to: where are they?* —**stand-to** *n*

**stand to**[2] *v prep*

**1** to take a standing position in (a direction or place): [IØ + *to*] *Please stand to one side, we need a lot of room to get by. Will those people standing to the left please move closer?* → **stand on**[2] (3)

**2 stand to attention** *mil* to take up or bring oneself to a formal position, standing stiffly upright: *Every private soldier must stand to attention when an officer enters the room.* → **be at** (7), **bring to** (4a), **come to** (16a), **jump to** (2), **snap to** (1), **spring to** (2), **stand at**[2] (3)

**3 stand to one's guns/principles** *not fml* to keep firmly to what one believes or is arguing, as in an argument: *It should be an interesting argument, as both politicians are well-known for standing to their guns. If you stand to your principles, the director will have to take notice of you.* → **stick to** (9)

**4 stand to one's post** *mil* to stay at one's place of duty: *A soldier is expected to stand to his post whatever danger threatens him.* → **remain at** (2), **stay at** (4), **stick to** (12), **stop at** (6)

**5 it stands to reason** it must follow as a matter of course; it is naturally true (that): *If he supports the trade unions, then it stands to reason that he will vote Labour. Jane's knowledge of history is very poor, so it stands to reason that she will fail the history examination. Of course the weather will improve, it stands to reason.*

**stand together** *v adv*

**1** to stand in position side by side: [IØ + TOGETHER] *I'd like mother and daughter to stand together in this photograph.*

***2** to remain united, often in the face of opposition: [IØ] *The workers have to stand together if they are not to be treated as slaves without human rights. Women must stand together against the injustice which they have suffered throughout history.* → **stick together** (2), etc.

**stand up** *v adv*
**1** to (cause to) rise to or be on one's feet: [IØ + UP] *Stand up when the judge enters the court. I don't like standing up for very long, it makes my back ache. Let's sing the next piece standing up.* [X9 + UP] *He mustn't lie in the road drunk: can't you help me to stand him up?* —**stand-up, upstanding** *adj*
**2** to remain upright; point upwards; be raised: [IØ + UP] *What keeps that old house standing up? The church tower stands up very tall. The fashion was to have one's collar standing up.* —**stand-up** *adj*
*__3__ to last or remain in working condition, as in spite of wear, use, etc.: [L9 (*simple tenses*)] *How long do you think the engine will stand up? This little machine has stood up well for many years.* → **stand up to** (3)
*__4__ to be seen to be true; be believed: [IØ (*simple tenses*)] *Will his story stand up in court?*
*__5__ *not fml* to fail to meet (someone, usu. of the opposite sex) as arranged: [T1 (*usu. simple tenses*)] *Jim said he'd be at the station, but he stood me up!*
**6 stand up and be counted** to be unafraid to express one's opinion in the face of threats or opposition: [*usu. infinitive*] *It takes courage to stand up and be counted when most people are against you, but that's better than pretending to believe something that you know to be false.*
*__stand up against__ *v adv prep* → **STAND UP TO** (1)
*__stand up for__ *v adv prep*
**1** to support (someone or something): [T1] *I stood up for him and said I had always found him to be honest. You need a lawyer to stand up for you in court. More people are beginning to stand up for children's rights.* → **stick up for** (1)
**2** to demand and make sure that one gets (one's rights): [T1] *If you don't stand up for your rights, no one is going to fight your battles for you.* → **stick up for** (2)
*__3__ → **STAND UP WITH**
**4 stand up for oneself** to be independent; refuse to be controlled by others: *Living on your own for the first time is useful experience in standing up for yourself. I don't worry about that boy: he's able to stand up for himself in any affair.*
*__stand up to__ *v adv prep*
**1** also **stand up against** to oppose (usu. someone) without fear: [T1] *Mary found it difficult to stand up to Jim's father when he disapproved of their marriage.* → **stand against** (3)
**2** to continue to live in spite of (suffering, hardship, etc., or doing something difficult): [T1 (*simple tenses*)] *I don't know how you stand up to the severe winters in your part of the world. Will she stand up to the operation all right?* [T4 (*simple tenses*)] *Can you stand up to living with my mother?*
**3** to last in spite of (wear, use, damage, etc., or doing something harmful): [T1 (*simple tenses*)] *The paint won't stand up to bad weather, it's too cheap. These cars are made to stand up to hard wear and rough treatment. "The British soldier can stand up to anything except the British War Office."* (Bernard Shaw, *The Devil's Disciple*) [T4 (*simple tenses*)] *Will the car stand up to being kept outside all winter? It's not easy for the piano to stand up to moving around so often.* → **stand up** (3)
**4** to match (something) in quality: [T1 (*usu. simple tenses*)] *This doesn't stand up to the other firm's product, we shall have to improve it or lose business.*
**5** to pass (a test): [T1 (*usu. simple tenses*)] *We must make a product that will stand up to any comparison. Will your tax statement stand up to detailed examination? It's questionable whether she can stand up to such a severe test of her courage.*
*__stand up with__ *v adv prep* also **stand up for** to be an attendant at the wedding of (someone): [T1 (*no pass.*)] *I was honoured when Jim asked me to stand up with him at his wedding to Mary.*
**stand upon** *v prep* → **STAND ON**[2]
**stand with** *v prep*
**1** to take a position on one's feet next to (someone): [IØ + *with*] *Will you stand with your mother for the photograph?*
*__2__ to be in the favour of (someone); be regarded by (someone) in a particular way: [X9 (*no pass., simple tenses*)] *I like to know where I stand with people. That depends on how well you stand with the director.*
**star in** *v prep*
to take a leading part in (a play, film, of a play, film, etc.); to have as (a leading actor): [IØ + *in*] *Who is starring in the film at the local cinema?* [T1 + *in*] *The film stars a famous actor in the part of the mad scientist.*
**starch up** *v adv*
**1** to make (a lot of cloth or clothes) stiff by dipping in a special substance which is then allowed to dry: [T1 + UP] *I spend all morning starching up a month's supply of collars.*
**2 be starched up** *AmE not fml* to be dressed showily: *The children were all starched up in their new dresses for the wedding ceremony.*
**stare after** *v prep*
to follow the movements of (usu. someone) with fixed eyes: [IØ + *after*] *She stared after him as he left her, tears blinding her eyes.*
**stare at** *v prep* → **gape at, gawk at, goggle at**
to look at (someone or something) with fixed eyes, usu. from interest, surprise, disapproval, or other heightened feeling: [IØ + *at*] *When the country boy visited the big city for the first time, all he could do was to stare at the tall buildings in wonder. Why are you staring at me? Are my clothes not fastened properly? Mary stared at her father in disbelief when he*

*refused to give his approval to her marriage with Jim.*

***stare down** *v adv* → **stare out** (2)
to defeat (someone) by looking at him steadily with fixed eyes until he lowers his eyes: [T1] *Children enjoy a silly competition in which they try to stare each other down.*

**stare in** *v prep*
**stare someone in the face**
**1** to look directly at someone, with fixed eyes: *I stared her in the face to see if she was lying, but she seemed to be telling the truth.*
**2** *not fml* to be very easy to see: [*usu. continuous tenses*] *I was looking for the Post Office and there it was in front of me all the time, staring me in the face!*
**3** *not fml* to be very easy to understand, by being unmistakably true: [*usu. continuous tenses*] *The policeman woke in the night with the answer to the mystery, which had been staring him in the face, but he had missed it! How can you go on pretending that all is well, when the sad truth about your relationship is staring you in the face?*

**stare out** *v adv*
**1** to look steadily outside or into the distance with fixed eyes or for a long time: [IØ + OUT (*of*)] *She stood on the steps of the great house, staring out over the valley. Why is the dog staring out of the window? Something must have caught his attention.*
***2** to make (someone) feel nervous, or defeat (someone), by looking at him steadily, with fixed eyes, often until he lowers his eyes: [T1] *The time and place were unsuitable for an argument, but at least I could express my opposition to the woman by staring her out.* → **stare down**
**3 stare someone out of countenance** *not fml* to make someone feel very nervous or defeated, with a steady look: [*often simple tenses*] *The director tries to stare out of countenance every person who comes to ask him about the job, as a kind of test of the strength of their character.*

**start as** *v prep* → **begin as**
to begin one's life at work by being (a worker in a certain trade or position): [L1 + *as* (*often simple tenses*)] *Many important businessmen started as workers on the factory floor.* [X1] *We're prepared to start you as a secretary and encourage you to work up to a higher position later.*

**start away** *v adv* → START OFF (1)

**start back** *v adv*
**1** to jump backwards, as in surprise: [L9 + BACK (*simple tenses*)] *There was a sudden noise in front of me which made me start back.*
**2** to begin a return journey: [IØ + BACK] *I think we should start back fairly soon if we want to get home before dark.*

***start for** *v prep*
to begin a journey to (a place): [T1 (*no pass.*)] *When do you start for London?*

**start from** *v prep*
**1** (usu. of an animal) to (cause to) leave a place suddenly; jump out of (somewhere): [L9 + *from* (*usu. simple tenses*)] *As the dogs got nearer, two rabbits started from a hole in the ground.* [T1 + *from*] *Going through the wood, I started several small animals from the bushes.*
***2** to come out of (somewhere) quickly or forcefully: [T1 (*no pass.*)] *Blood started from the wound. His eyes nearly started from his head when he saw the strange sight.* → **start out of** (1)
***3** to begin a journey from (a place): [T1 (*no pass.*)] *The climbers started from the village at daybreak. The train starts from this station, so there is usually one waiting. We should start from the house early to get to the camping ground before dinner.*
**4 starting from** beginning with: *Starting from the idea that all people should be equal, the laws are made to be as fair as possible.*
**5 start from scratch** *not fml* to begin (again) at the beginning: *When the factory was destroyed in the fire, the firm had to start from scratch in building up a business.*

***start in** *v adv* → **start on** (1)
to begin (work, activity, or doing something): [IØ (*on*)] *If we start in at once, we can get the job finished early. The children started in on the food without waiting for an invitation. I'd like to start in on this pile of work as soon as possible.* [I3] *It's about time we started in to reorganize the department.*

***start in on** *v adv prep*
*infml* to attack (someone) with words: [T1] *Don't start in on me, it's not my fault.*

**start off** *v adv*
**1** also **start away** (usu. of an animal) to move away quickly, as in fear, shock, etc.: [L9 + OFF (*simple tenses*)] *The rabbit started off as soon as it smelt the dogs.*
***2** to begin a journey: [IØ (*for, on*) (*usu. simple tenses*)] *He started off for work an hour ago, hasn't he arrived yet? The children were always excited to start off on a camping trip.* [I4 (*usu. simple tenses*)] *Having missed the last bus, we had to start off walking.* → **go away** (1), etc.
***3** to begin with the intention (to do something): [I3] *I started off to make the dress by myself, but in the end I had to ask for help.* → **set off** (2), **set out** (3), **start out** (3)
***4** to (cause to) make a start (on something); begin (something): [T1 (*on*)] *I'll give you £5 to start off your bank account. Jane had private lessons to start her off (on her study of music). What does it cost to start a young man off as a lawyer?* [IØ (*on*)] *Whatever made you start off on househunting at this time of year?*
***5** *not fml* to (cause to) begin doing something such as speaking at length: [IØ (*usu. simple tenses*)] *The chairman started off by attacking*

*the first speaker.* [T1 (*on*) (*usu. simple tenses*)] *Don't start Father off on his favourite subject, or he'll never stop.* [I4 (*usu. simple tenses*)] *Whatever you do, don't start off crying again.* [V4b (*usu. simple tenses*)] *Once you start him off telling about his adventures, he goes on all night.* → **set off** (6), **start out** (4)

**6 start off on the right/wrong foot (with)** *not fml* to begin something such as work or a relationship, in a good/bad way: *The director is a tricky person to work for, and it's a good idea to try to start off on the right foot with him. Once you've started off on the wrong foot, it's difficult to relearn new ways of thinking.* → **get off**[1] (20), **step off** (4)

* **start on** *v prep* → **begin on**

**1** to begin work on or start dealing with (something): [T1] *He's a very busy lawyer and has already started on another case. Tom and his drinking companions have started on their third bottle in an hour.* → **start in**

**2** *not fml* to attack (someone) with words: [T1 (*no pass.*)] *Don't start on me! It's not my fault!*

**start out** *v adv*

**1** (usu. of an animal) to leave a place suddenly: [L9 + OUT (*simple tenses*)] *As we pushed our way through the bushes, a rabbit started out.*

***2** to begin a journey: [IØ (*for, on*)] *He started out for work an hour ago, hasn't he arrived yet? The children were always excited to start out on a camping trip.* [I4] *Having missed the last bus, we had to start out walking.* → **go away** (1), etc.

***3** to begin with the intention (to do something): [I3 (*usu. simple tenses*)] *I started out to make the dress by myself, but in the end I had to ask for help.* → **set off** (2), **set out** (3), **start off** (3)

***4** to begin speaking: [IØ (*usu. simple tenses*)] *The chairman started out by attacking the first speaker.* → **set off** (6), **start off** (5)

***5** to (cause to) begin one's business or professional life: [IØ (*as, in*)] *When did you start out as a lawyer? The money from my uncle helped me to start out in business on my own.* [T1b (*as, in*)] *My uncle gave me some money to start me out in trade.* → **set out** (2)

* **start out of** *v adv prep*

**1** to leave (somewhere) suddenly; come quickly or forcefully from (something): [T1 (*no pass.*)] *Blood started out of the wound. His eyes nearly started out of his head when he saw the terrible sight.* → **start from** (2)

**2** to shock (someone) into consciousness from (sleep or another state): [D1 (*simple tenses*)] *The explosion started the whole population of the town out of their sleep. The unions are doing their best to start the workers out of their lazy acceptance of the conditions.* → **startle out of** (1)

**start over** *v adv*

*AmE not fml* to begin again: [IØ + OVER] *After the fire, we had to start over and build the business again from the beginning. That scene didn't go well; let's start over and see if we can get it right this time. In the end she returned to her husband and asked if they could try to start over.*

**start up** *v adv*

**1** (usu. of an animal, esp. a bird) to (cause to) jump up quickly, as from a hiding place: [L9 + UP (*simple tenses*)] *A bird started up out of the lower branches.* [T1 + UP] *We use the dogs to start the birds up for the men to shoot.*

**2** to jump up suddenly, as with a shock: [L9 + UP (*simple tenses*)] *The boy started up out of his chair as soon as he heard the doorbell ring. The sudden ringing of the telephone made me start up. The young lovers started up when the girl's mother entered the room.* → **jump up** (2), **leap up** (2), **shoot up** (2), **spring up** (1)

***3** to arise; begin; come into existence: [IØ] *When did your troubles first start up? A strong wind started up soon after we left the harbour. Opposition to the plan has started up in some political circles. What caused this doubt to start up in your mind? New fashions started up when the bicycle was invented.* → **spring up** (3), **sprout up** (2)

***4** to make (something such as an engine) start working; (of an engine) to begin working: [T1] *How do you start up this motorcycle?* [IØ] *I can hear the bus starting up, let's run to catch it!* —**start-up**

***5** to begin (something such as a business); begin working (in a trade, profession, etc.): [T1] *It was a brave move to start up one's own business in wartime.* [IØ (*in*)] *How much would it cost to start up in the insurance business?* —**start-up** *n*

**start with** *v prep*

**1** to make a quick nervous movement, because of (shock or a strong feeling): [L9 + *with* (*simple tenses*)] *The girl started with fear as the shadow of a man fell across her arm.*

**2** to have (something) at the beginning; cause (something) to begin by having or doing (something): [IØ + *with*] *The day started with bad news, and looks like getting worse.* [T1 + *with*] *It's very worrying to start the day with bad news.* → **begin with** (1)

**3 starting with** continuing from (a beginning point): *We need the figures for the twelve months starting with April. We will now hear the students read their poems, starting with Tom.* → **begin with** (2)

**4 to start with: a** at first: *It was fine to start with, and then it began to rain.* **b** as a first consideration or statement: *Our difficulties are many; to start with, we can't get the workers.* → **begin with** (3)

**startle out of** *v adv prep* → **start out of** (2)

**1** to cause (someone) to leave (a state such as sleep) by a shock: [T1 + OUT + *of* (*usu. simple tenses*)] *The whole population of the town* *were startled out of their sleep by the noise of the explosion.*

**2 startle someone out of his mind/wits** *not fml* to shock someone very much: [*usu. simple tenses*] *Please don't come up behind me quietly like that: you startled me out of my wits!*

**starve for** *v prep*

**1** to need (food) very much; be hungry for (food): [IØ + *for* (*often continuous tenses*)] *The poor children in the streets are starving for bread.* → **hunger for** (1), **thirst for** (1)

***2** to need (something) very much: [T1 (*no pass., usu. continuous tenses*)] *Here inland I am starving for a sight of the sea. The children are starving for love.* → **hunger for** (2), **thirst for** (2)

**3 be starved for** also **be starved of** to lack (something needed): *If a child is starved for love he could easily die.*

***starve into** *v prep*

to force (someone) into (the stated position) through hunger: [D1] *If the enemy completely surround the town, it will not be long before they starve the townspeople into submission.*

***starve out** *v adv*

to defeat (people or animals); cause (someone) to move by making him go hungry: [T1] *If you can't force the criminals out of their hiding place by any other means, you can always starve them out.*

***stash away** *v adv*

*infml* to save or hide (money or goods): [T1] *He has some bottles of beer stashed away where his wife won't discover them. Do you know where the thieves have stashed the money away?*

**station at/in/on** *v prep*

to place (someone) for duty, as military or political, in (a place): [X9 + *at/in/on* (*usu. pass.*)] *Were you ever stationed at Cambridge? No, I was stationed in Hong Kong when I was a soldier. We must station some additional men on the island in case of trouble.*

***stave in** *v adv* → **bash in** (1), **beat in** (2), **crush in** (1)

to break (something) inwards; make a hole or hollow in (something); break inwards: [T1 (*often pass.*)] *The crash staved in the sides of the barrel. The whole side of the car was staved in during the accident.* [IØ (*usu. simple tenses*)] *The ship staved/stove in as she hit the rocks.* —**stove-in** *adj*

***stave off** *v adv*

**1** to delay or prevent (something unwanted): [T1a] *This piece of bread will stave off hunger for another hour. We need another highly skilled player to stave off defeat for our team.* → **fend off** (2), **ward off** (1)

**2** to keep (someone unwanted) at a distance: [T1] *I'll stave off the police while you leave by the back door. She was so beautiful that she had difficulty staving off all the men who wanted to marry her.* → **fend off** (3), **ward off** (2)

**stave up** *v adv*

**be stove up** *AmE infml* to be tired, worn out: *Don't ask me to move, I'm stove up.* —**stove-up** *adj*

**stay abreast of** *v adv prep*

**1** to remain at the same level as (someone or something): [L9 + ABREAST + *of*] *You will have to run fast to stay abreast of our best runner and prevent him from winning.* → **keep abreast of** (1), etc.

***2** to remain fully informed about (new developments): [T1 (*no pass.*)] *Scientists have to work hard to stay abreast of new discoveries.* → **keep abreast of** (2), etc.

**stay ahead** *v adv* → **move ahead,** etc.

**1** to remain in a forward or leading position, in front of others, as in a race: [L9 + AHEAD (*of*)] *If I can only stay ahead for a few more yards, I can win this race.*

***2** to keep an advanced position, as in a competition: [IØ (*of*)] *Jane used to have difficulty with her school work, but since she showed great improvement recently, she has been able to stay ahead and not get behind the others again. Getting a good position is only half the story; once you've got ahead you have to work twice as hard to say ahead.*

**stay ahead of** *v adv prep*

**1** to be able to keep a position in front of, beyond, or past (someone or something), as in a race: [L9 + AHEAD + *of*] *If I can only stay ahead of the other runners, now that I am in the lead, I can win this race!* → **keep ahead of** (1), etc.

***2** to keep a position in advance of (something or someone such as a competitor): [T1 (*no pass.*)] *You have to work hard to stay ahead of your competitors in business, or you can easily lose your leading position. Jane was able to bring her work up to the standard of the others in her class; then she had to work hard to stay ahead of her fellow students.* → **keep ahead of** (2), etc.

**3 stay one step ahead of** *not fml* to keep a position only a little way in advance of (someone or something): *Jim's father often said that one secret of his success in business was that he always stayed one step ahead of public demand.* → **keep ahead of** (3), etc.

**stay at** *v prep*

**1** to remain behind at (a place): [L9 + *at*] *The woman stayed at home while the men went to war. I'll stay at the bus stop while you go to see if there's a bus coming.* → **remain at, stop at** (2)

**2** to be a guest at (a place such as a home or hotel): [L9 + *at*] *Which hotel are you staying at? I'll be able to stay at my aunt's house while I'm in the town.* → **stop at** (3)

**3 stay at home** to be contented with an unadventurous life; be inactive in the world: [*often simple tenses*] *Don't you want to do something better with your life than just stay at* *home doing nothing?* —**stay-at-home** *n, adj* → **stick at** (4), **stop at** (4)

**4 stay at one's post** to remain on duty in the proper place: *The guard had orders to stay at his post whatever happened.* → **remain at** (2), **stand to²** (4), **stick to** (12), **stop at** (6)

**stay away** *v adv* → **be away** (2), **keep away, remain away, stop away**
to be absent; remain at a distance (from something or someone): [L9 + AWAY (*from*) (*often simple tenses*)] *Many of his former supporters disapproved of his latest opinions, and stayed away (from the meeting) when he came to give a speech. I've asked you to stay away from those rough boys. Stay away from dangerous electrical things. Although her stomach trouble was much better, Jane stayed away (from school) as it was Friday.*

**stay away from** *v adv prep* → **keep away from**
**1** to remain at a distance from (someone or something): [L9 + AWAY + *from* (*often simple tenses*)] *Stay away from me, I've got a bad cold. I asked you to stay away from those rough boys. Stay away from dangerous electrical things. Why is Jane still staying away from school?* → **be off** (2), **keep off** (2), **remain off, stay off** (2), **stop away, stop off**
*__2__ to avoid (something harmful): [T1 (*pass. rare*)] *The doctor advised Jim to stay away from fattening foods.* → **keep off** (4), **stay off** (3)

**stay back** *v adv*
to remain in a position away from something: [L9 + BACK (*from*) (*often simple tenses*)] *The firemen asked the crowd to stay back, as there was danger from falling beams.*

**stay behind¹** *v adv*
**1** to remain at a distance behind something or someone: [L9 + BEHIND (*often simple tenses*)] *Stay close behind, then you won't get lost. It's safest to stay a good distance behind, in case the car in front suddenly stops.* → **keep behind** (1), **remain behind¹** (1)
*__2__ to remain in a place when others leave: [IØ] *If you stay behind after class, I will repeat the instructions.* → **keep in** (5), etc.

**stay behind²** *v prep* → **keep behind** (2)
to remain at a distance at the back of (usu. something): [L9 + *behind* (*often simple tenses*)] *It's safest to stay well behind the car in front, in case it suddenly stops. After staying behind the leading runner for most of the race, Jim suddenly passed him and won.*

**stay by** *v prep* → **cling onto** (1), **cling to** (2), **keep by** (2), **stick to** (2), **stick with** (2)
to remain in a position near (something or someone): [L9 + *by* (*often simple tenses*)] *Stay close by the leader and then you won't lose your way. The child was so ill that I had to stay by his bedside all night.*

*__stay clear of__ *v adv prep* → **keep clear of, remain clear of, steer clear of** (2)
*not fml* to (continue to) avoid (something or someone): [T1 (*no pass., often simple tenses*)] *When you're in a tropical country, stay clear of insects which may be carrying dangerous diseases. At busy times, it's best to avoid the main roads, and stay clear of them until the worst of the traffic is over.*

**stay cool** *v adj* → **keep cool, remain cool**
**1** to continue to be cold; prevent oneself from becoming too hot: [L9 + **cool** (*often simple tenses*)] *How do you stay so cool in such hot weather? This building material stays cool even in the hottest weather.*
**2** to continue to be calm; refuse to become excited, anxious, etc.: [L9 + **cool** (*usu. simple tenses*)] *The soldier's courage was partly owing to his ability to stay cool in the face of danger.*

**stay down** *v adv*
**1** to continue to be in a lower position: [L9 + DOWN (*often simple tenses*)] *If there's shooting going on, get down and stay down until I tell you the danger is over.* → **keep down** (1), **remain down** (1), **stop down** (1)
**2** to remain at a lower level; not increase: [L9 + DOWN] *I hope the wind stays down now that it's calmer, so that we can risk putting up the sails. Egg prices go down in the spring, when eggs are plentiful, but unfortunately they don't stay down. If Jane's temperature stays down all day, she can go back to school tomorrow.* → **hold down** (2), **keep down** (2), **remain down** (2), **stop down** (2)
*__3__ (of food) to remain in the stomach after being eaten: [IØ] *Jane is sick again; nothing she eats will stay down.* → **hold down** (3), **keep down** (3), **stop down** (3)
*__4__ (of miners) to stop work and remain down a mine as a form of protest: [IØ] *The miners are determined to stay down until their pay demands are met, in spite of the discomfort.*
*__5__ *BrE* to be made to stay in the same class for a second year, instead of moving to a higher class, as is usual: [IØ] *Jane was afraid that if she failed her examinations again she would have to stay down, repeat the work, and miss her friends.* → **go up¹** (11), **go up to** (5), **keep down** (7)

**stay for** *v prep*
**1** to be a guest for (a length of time): [L9 + *for*] *I didn't think the boy would stay for two whole weeks without an invitation.* → **stop for** (2)
*__2__ to remain and share (a meal) as a guest: [T1 (*no pass.*)] *Please stay for dinner, we'd love to have you.* → **stay to, stop for** (3), **stop to**

**stay in¹** *v adv*
**1** to remain in position: [L9 + IN] *I've put the screw in the wood as tightly as I can, but it won't stay in, it keeps slipping out.* → **stop in¹** (1)
*__2__ to remain indoors, or be kept in school as a punishment: [IØ] *I'll stay in to wait for his telephone call. Who wants to stay in on such a beautiful day? This class will stay in for half an hour after school!* → **keep in** (5), etc.
*__3__ (of a fire) to continue burning: [IØ (*simple*

*tenses*)] *Will the fire stay in until we get back?* → **keep in** (6), etc.

*__4__ (esp. in cricket) to keep one's place on the field of play without being dismissed: [IØ (*often simple tenses*)] *Don't try to get any runs, just stay in for half an hour and we shall have won!* → **be in¹** (7), **be out** (7), **come in** (6), **go in¹** (5), **put in¹** (15), **send in** (2)

*__5__ to remain in one's place of work as a form of strike: [IØ] *The factory workers have declared their intention of staying in until their demands are met.* —**stay-in** *adj*

**stay in²** *v prep*

**1** to continue to be present in (a place): [L9 + *in* (*often simple tenses*)] *It's very difficult to stay in one spot without moving at all. My parents stayed in my home country when we moved overseas.* → **be in²** (1), **keep in** (1), **remain in²** (1), **stick in²** (6), **stop in²** (1)

**2** to continue to be in (a state, usu. good): [L9 + *in* (*often simple tenses*)] *How has the car stayed in such good condition after all those miles of travelling?* → **get into** (11), etc.

**3 stay in contact/touch (with)** to continue to be able to meet or send messages (to someone): [*often simple tenses*] *It's easier to stay in touch with an old friend than to try to reach her again after years of absence.* → **keep in** (6), **remain in²** (3), **put in²** (12)

**4 stay in office/power** to continue to have control, usu. political: *The present government is unlikely to stay in power after the next election.* → **remain in²** (4)

**5 stay in sight (of)** to remain in a position where one can be seen (from a place): [*often simple tenses*] *The children were told to stay in sight (of the house) when they went outside to play.* → **keep in** (16), etc.

**stay indoors** *v adv* → **keep in** (5), etc.

to remain inside a building, as at home: [L9 + INDOORS] *Mother was advised to stay indoors for a week even after her cough seemed better.*

**stay off** *v prep*

**1** to continue to be at a distance from (something): [L9 + *off* (*often simple tenses*)] *Tell the children to stay off the road, the traffic is dangerous.* → **get off²** (2), **keep off** (1)

*__2__ to avoid or cease having (food, a habit, etc.): [T1 (*no pass., often simple tenses*)] *The doctor advised Jim to stay off fattening foods.* → **keep away from, stay away from**

*__3__ to continue not to attend (something such as school): [T1 (*no pass.*)] *Jane should stay off school until her stomach trouble is really better.* → **be off** (2), **remain off, stay away from** (1), **stop off²**

**stay on¹** *v adv*

**1** to remain fixed or in position on top of something or someone: [L9 + ON] *I put the lid on the pot, but the water is boiling so fiercely that it won't stay on. When you first learn to ride a horse, you fall off several times until you find out how to stay on. How does your hat stay on in this high wind?* → **stick on²** (2), **stop on** (1)

**2** (of something electrical such as a light) to remain in operation: [L9 + ON (*usu. simple tenses*)] *When the lights stayed on in his room long after his usual bedtime, I knew that something was wrong. Something's wrong with the switch, I turned the light off but it stayed on!* → **put on¹** (3), etc.

*__3__ to remain in a place, as at work: [IØ (*at*)] *You're supposed to stop work here when you're 65, but many people are allowed to stay on. The promising young doctor was asked to stay on at the hospital after his period of training. Please stay on as our chairman, there's no one else suitable to do the job as well as you.* → **keep on** (6), **stick on¹** (4), **stop on** (3)

**stay on²** *v prep*

**1** to continue to be in position on top of (something or someone): [L9 + *on*] *How do you learn to stay on a horse? Her hat stayed on her head in the high wind because of a long pin that she used* → **be on²** (1), **keep on** (1)

**2** to continue travelling in (a certain direction): [L9 + *on* (*usu. simple tenses*)] *Stay on the way you're going, and you'll soon come to the town. How long should the ship stay on this course?* → **be on²** (2), **keep on** (2), **remain on²** (1)

**3** also **remain on** to continue taking (medicine) or following (a course): [L9 + *on*] *The doctor would like Jane to stay on the special medicine for another month to see if her stomach trouble improves. Will you stay on this course or exercises until you are thinner?* → **be on²** (4), **keep on** (3)

**4 stay on one's feet** to remain standing: *The old fighter stayed on his feet in spite of punishing blows from his strong young opponent. How do you stay on your feet so long? I would have needed a rest hours ago.* → **get to** (11), etc.

**5 stay on the rails** *not fml* to continue to behave correctly and lawfully: *It's hard for a former prisoner to stay on the rails.* → **go off²** (8), **keep on** (14), **run off** (6)

**6 stay on the right side of** *not fml* to continue to be friendly with; not annoy (someone): *It will pay you to stay on the right side of the director, as if you annoy him it could cost you your job.* → **be in with** (1), **get in with** (2), **keep in with, keep on** (15), **remain on²** (4)

**7 stay on the right side of the law** to continue to behave lawfully: *The courts will punish less severely someone who has formerly stayed on the right side of the law.* → **keep on** (16), **remain on²** (5)

**8 stay on top (of)** *not fml* also **be/keep/remain on top (of)** to continue to have power, control, or leadership (of something): *Whatever the competition, Jim's father has always found a way to stay on top. It's very hard to stay on top of my work at busy times.*

**stay open** *v adj*

**1** to continue to be wide apart, open, etc.: [L9 + open (*usu. simple tenses*)] *He closed his mouth, but his eyes stayed open. How do you make this door stay open? I want to get some air into the house?* → **leave open** (1), etc.

***2** to remain open for business: [IØ] *The shops in central London stay open late on Thursday evenings.* → **be open, keep open** (2), **remain open** (2), **stop open** (2)

**stay out** *v adv*

**1** to remain outside a building or room, or away from home: [L9 + OUT (*of*) (*often simple tenses*)] *Who gave you permission to stay out all night? No thanks, I think I'll stay out here in the sun while it's nice and warm. The garden chair doesn't seem to have suffered from staying out all night. There's no garage so the car will have to stay out all winter. Tell the children to stay out of the farmer's fields while the crops are growing.* → **keep out, stop out** (1)

***2** to remain in a place until (a time) has passed: [T1] *Can't I persuade you to stay the week out?*

***3** to continue to refuse to work; remain on strike: [IØ] *All the workers are staying out until their demands are met.* → **bring out** (7), etc.

**stay out of** *v adv prep*

**1** to remain outside; not enter (something): [L9 + OUT + *of* (*often simple tenses*)] *Tell the children to stay out of the farmer's fields while the crops are growing.* → **keep out of** (1), **stop out of** (2)

***2** to remain at a distance from or have nothing to do with (something such as trouble or other people's affairs): [T1 (*no pass., often simple tenses*)] *I always try to stay out of other people's affairs that don't concern me. I hope you'll stay out of trouble while I'm away. It's not easy to stay out of debt while prices are rising so fast.* → **get into** (11), etc.

**3 stay out of harm's way** to remain in a safe place or activity: [*often simple tenses*] *The children don't do much at their youth club, but at least they stay out of harm's way.* → **be out of** (12), **keep out of** (3)

**4 stay out of one's/the way** to remain or move to a position not annoying someone: [*often simple tenses*] *The director is in a bad temper, I would stay out of his way, if I were you.* → **be out of** (32a), **get out of** (37), **keep out of** (5)

***stay over** *v adv* → **stop off**[1] (2), **stop over** (1)

to spend the night away from home: [IØ (*at, in*)] *We need two days for the journey, staying over at a small town on the way. Because of the severe snowstorm, we couldn't get home that night, and had to stay over in a hotel.*

***stay put** *v adj*

*not fml* to remain in one place: [IØ (*often simple tenses*)] *There, I've fixed the handle, it should stay put now. Isn't it time we stayed put in a city for more than three years at a time?*

***stay to** *v prep* → **stay for** (2), **stop for** (3), **stop to**

to remain and share (a meal): [T1 (*no pass.*)] *Won't you stay to dinner? We'd love to have you as our guest.*

**stay together** *v adv*

**1** (of two or more things or people) to continue to be in the same place or at the same point: [L9 + TOGETHER (*often simple tenses*)] *The horses stayed together for most of the race, until a leader at last came to the front. You singers must stay together or you will spoil the music. When the mist comes down, we must stay together or we'll be lost.* → **keep together** (1), **remain together**

**2** (of two people in a relationship such as marriage) to continue to live together or have a good relationship: [L9 + TOGETHER] *Do you think Jim and Mary will stay together in spite of their frequent quarrels?*

***3** to remain united: [IØ] *The family that prays together stays together. The party must stay together in spite of differing opinions.* → **stick together** (2), etc.

**stay under** *v adv; prep* → **hold under** (1), **keep under** (1), **remain under, stop under**

to continue to be beneath (something such as the surface of water): [L9 + UNDER/*under* (*often simple tenses*)] *If the swimmer stays under (water) for more than a minute, pull him out, he may be drowning. The child stayed under the table in a bad temper until his father came home.*

**stay up** *v adv*

**1** to (cause to) be or remain raised: [L9 + UP (*usu. simple tenses*)] *How does the tower stay up? My husband has lost so much weight that he has to wear a belt to make his trousers stay up. The picture won't stay up long if you use one of those weak hooks.* [T1 + UP (*often simple tenses*)] *Pull the ropes tight to stay the tent up.* → **be up** (1), **hold up** (1), **keep up** (1), **remain up** (1), **stop up** (2)

**2** to continue to be high: [L9 + UP] *Prices of meat have stayed up even though the farmers are receiving less money for their cattle. Is it difficult to make sure that the quality stays up without increasing the price? If June's temperature stays up all day, call the doctor.* → **be up** (6), **go up** (3), **keep up** (2), **put up** (4), **remain up** (2)

***3** to remain late out of bed, as at night: [IØ] *Please don't stay up for me, I may be in late.* → **be up** (5), **keep up** (6), **remain up** (3), **sit up** (5), **stop up** (3), **wait up** (2)

**stay with** *v prep*

**1** to be a guest of (someone); continue to work for (someone): [L9 + *with*] *I hope you'll stay with me on your next visit, too. How long do you intend to stay with the firm?* → **stop with** (2)

***2** to remain level with (a competitor): [T1 (*no pass.*)] *Jim was able to stay with the leading runner for most of the race until he* *weakened and had to drop back.* → **stick with** (4)

*__3__ to continue to use (something): [T1 (*no pass.*)] *Let's stay with the present arrangements until a better plan is thought of. How long have you stayed with this method?* → **stand by**² (3), **stick by** (2), **stick to** (6), **stick with** (4)

*__4__ *not fml* to continue to pay attention to (someone): [T1 (*no pass., often imper.*)] *Stay with me for a few more minutes and you'll see the point of the story.* → **stick with** (6)

**stay within** *v prep*

**1** to continue to obey or be limited by (something): [L9 + *within*] *The police are watching to see that all motorists stay within the new speed limit.* → **keep within** (1), **remain within** (1), **stick within, stop within**

**2 stay within bounds** to continue to obey a limit: *Make sure that your spending on this contract stays within bounds, or the firm could be in trouble.* → **remain within** (2)

**steady down** *v adv*

to (cause to) behave in a more settled way: [T1 + DOWN (*often simple tenses*)] *Having a baby often steadies young parents down.* [IØ (*often simple tenses*)] *Don't worry, he'll steady down after a few years, and cause no more trouble.*

**steal at** *v prep*

**steal a glance at** to look at (usu. someone) quickly and secretly: *Jim stole a glance at Mary to see if she approved of what he was suggesting.*

**steal away** *v adv*

**1** to leave silently and secretly: [L9 + AWAY] *Jim stole away without anyone seeing him. "Then steal away, give little warning."* (Anna L. Barbauld, *Ode To Life*)

**2** to take (something) without permission: [T1 + AWAY] *"I come not, friends, to steal away your hearts."* (Shakespeare, *Julius Caesar*)

**steal from** *v prep*

**1** to take (something such as property) from (someone or a place) without permission: [T1 + *from*] *How much jewellery did the thieves steal from the house?* [IØ + *from*] *Robin Hood stole from the rich to give to the poor. Would you steal from your own family?*

**2** to obtain (something such as an action) from (someone), as by deceit: [T1 + *from*] *How do you steal a kiss from a girl like that?*

**3** to leave (a place) silently and secretly: [L9 + *from*] *The boy stole from the room while they were talking about his punishment.*

**steal on** *v prep*

**steal a march on** *not fml* to gain an advantage over (someone) by doing something before he does: *By advertising our sale a week ahead of the other firm, we stole a march on them.*

**steal over** *v prep*

to pass over or have a gradual effect on (someone): [L9 + *over* (*often simple tenses*)] *A sense of mystery stole over him as he looked out on the wide sea.*

*__steal up on__ *v adv prep* → **creep up on, sneak up on**

**1** to come near (someone or something) gradually, noiselessly, and secretly: [T1] *The jewel thief stole up on the house without being seen. Watch that cat stealing up on the mouse.*

**2** to begin to happen to, reach, or have an effect on (someone) gradually: [T1] *Doubt stole up on me about his truthfulness.*

**steam into** *v prep*

to arrive in (a place) by a vehicle using steam power such as a boat or train: [L9 + *into*] *As the royal train steamed into the station, the crowd cheered.*

**steam off** *v adv*

**1** to leave under steam power: [L9 + OFF] *The train slowly steamed off, making a lot of noise.*

**2** to remove (something stuck on something) with steam: [X9 + OFF] *Be careful how you steam the stamp off, it's a valuable one.*

**steam out** *v adv*

to leave under steam power: [L9 + OUT] *The ship steamed out, all her flags flying.*

*__steam over__ *v adv* → **cloud over** (2), **cloud up, mist over, steam up** (1)

to (cause to) become less transparent because of steam: [IØ (*simple tenses*)] *The windows have steamed over, and I can't see out.* [T1 (*usu. pass.*)] *The windows are steamed over, and I can't see out.*

*__steam up__ *v adv*

**1** to (cause to) become less transparent by covering with steam: [IØ] *The windows have steamed up, I can't see out.* [T1] *The warm air steamed up my glasses as I entered the room.* → **cloud over** (2), **cloud up, mist over, steam over**

**2 be steamed up (about)** *not fml* to be very angry, excited, or annoyed (about something or someone): *There's no need to get steamed up about such a little remark.* —**steamed-up** *adj*

**steel against** *v prep*

to prepare, as by hardening (oneself, one's heart, etc.) to oppose or face (something): [T1 + *against* (*often simple tenses*)] *He steeled himself against the blow that he could see coming. It helps if you can steel yourself against failure. He had to steel his heart against her pitiful cries.*

**steel for** *v prep*

to prepare (usu. oneself) mentally to deal with (something expected) or to do (something): [T1 + *for* (*often simple tenses*)] *Our men must steel themselves for further attack. Can you steel yourself for yet more effort?*

**steep in** *v prep*

**1** to place and leave (something) in (liquid) for a long time: [T1 + *in*] *If the clothes are very dirty, steep them in soapy water overnight. Steep the wood in the special chemcial* *and let it dry before you paint it, then it will be protected against decay.* → **immerse in** (1), **soak in²** (1), **submerge in** (1)

*2 to make (oneself) give one's whole attention to and esp. learn about (something); fill (something) with (a quality): [D1] *I have a talk to give on the famous writer next month, so first I must steep myself in his books. This whole area is steeped in history.* → **absorb in,** etc.

**steer clear of** *v adv prep*

1 to guide (a ship) so as to avoid (something): [IØ + CLEAR + *of*] *Steer clear of those rocks, they're dangerous!* [T1 + CLEAR + *of*] *Can you steer the ship clear of those rocks?*

*2 *not fml* to avoid (something or someone): [T1 (*no pass.*)] *He likes to steer clear of trouble if he can.* → **keep clear of, remain clear of, stay clear of**

**steer for** *v prep* → **steer towards** (1)

to direct (a ship) towards (something): [IØ + *for*] *Steer for the shore, boys!* [T1 + *for*] *Try to steer the boat for the harbour.*

**steer into** *v prep*

1 to direct (a boat or vehicle) into (usu. a space): [T1 + *into*] *The fool steered the boat into the harbour wall and broke the beams!* [IØ + *into*] *It took Mary weeks learning how to steer into the garage.*

2 to guide (someone) into (a space such as a room): [X9 + *into*] *He tried to steer her into the bedroom, but she understood his intentions and refused to move.*

*3 to persuade (someone) into (action or doing something): [D1] *It's no use trying to steer the boy into a course of action that suits you, he'll do whatever he pleases.* [V4b] *Father tried to steer Jim into becoming a musician.* → **steer towards** (1)

**steer through** *v adv; prep*

1 to direct (a boat) through (something such as an opening): [T1 + THROUGH/*through*] *It takes a skilled pilot to steer the ship through (the narrow entrance to the harbour).*

*2 to guide (someone) so as to pass (something such as an examination) or find his way through (difficulties): [T1b] *Don't worry about the difficulties of selling the house, our lawyer will steer you through.* [D1] *Students need someone to steer them through the mass of courses offered to them, to choose the best ones for their needs.*

**steer towards** *v prep*

1 to guide (a ship) in the direction of (something): [IØ + *towards*] *Steer towards the light, and we may reach the harbour.* [T1 + *towards*] *Try to steer the little boat towards the big ship so that we can be picked up.* → **steer for**

*2 to guide (someone) in the direction of (action or doing something): [D1] *The chairman was able to steer the committee towards a decision.* [V4b] *Father tried to steer Jim towards becoming a musician.* → **steer into** (3)

***stem from** *v prep* → **emanate from**

to originate in (something or doing something): [T1 (*no pass., often simple present tense*)] *Dependence on alcohol often stems from unhappiness in the home.* [T4] *Nervous illness can stem from being treated inconsiderately in childhood.*

**step aside** *v adv*

1 to move to one side, as out of the way: [L9 + ASIDE (*often imper.*)] *Step aside, please, the firemen can't get through.* → **stand apart, stand out** (3), **stand aside** (1)

*2 to cease to take part in a competition, as for a position: [IØ] *I feel that when there are so many better people for the chairmanship, I should step aside.* → **stand aside** (3), **stand down** (2), **step down** (2)

**step back** *v adv*

1 to take a step backwards: [L9 + BACK (*often simple tenses*)] *If you step back, you could fall down the cliff. He stepped back to have a better view of the house.* → **move back** (1), etc.

*2 to consider something from a distance: [IØ (*from*) (*usu. simple tenses*)] *This meeting gives us a chance to step back (from the everyday activities of the department) and have a good look at our problems.* → **stand back** (3)

*3 to refuse to take part in or influence something such as an event or activity: [IØ] *From time to time, the teachers should step back and let the children run things their own way.* → **sit back** (3), **sit by, stand aside** (2), **stand back** (4), **stand by¹** (2)

**step down** *v adv*

1 to move to a lower level, as by taking a step: [L9 + DOWN (*from*)] *Stepping down from the stage, he took a member of the crowd by the hand and led him up the steps.*

*2 to yield one's position or chance of election: [IØ] *I've spent so many years as chairman that I feel it's time I stepped down.* → **stand aside** (3), **stand down** (2), **step aside** (2)

*3 to yield an argument: [IØ (*often simple tenses*)] *His forceful argument soon made the opposing speaker step down.*

*4 to reduce (something such as an amount or electric current): [T1 (*often pass.*)] *The quantity of medicine to be taken can be stepped down gradually after the first week.* —**step-down** *n, adj* → **step up** (3)

**step forward** *v adv*

1 to take a step so as to move forward from one's present position: [L9 + FORWARD] *Just then, the crowd divided and three men stepped forward to hand the citizens' request to the king.* → **come forward** (1), **go forward** (1)

*2 to offer oneself, as to help: [IØ (*usu. simple tenses*)] *The police have asked for witnesses of the accident to step forward to help with enquiries.* → **come forward** (3)

**step in¹** *v adv*

1 to enter a building or room, often for a

short time: [L9 + IN (*to*)] *Won't you step in and have a cup of tea with us?*

*2 to interrupt so as to give one's help or take necessary action: [IØ (*usu. simple tenses*)] *The government may have to step in to settle the disagreement between the union and the employers.*

**step in²** *v prep*

**1** to take a step into (something such as a material): [L9 + *in*] *We had to step in mud over our ankles.*

**2** to put one's foot into (something): [L9 + *in* (*usu. simple tenses*)] *It's convenient to be able to step in these shoes without having to fasten them.* —**step-in** *n, adj*

***step in for** *v adv prep* → **stand in for,** etc.

to fill the place of (someone), as on duty: [T1 (*no pass.*)] *Can you step in for me at the meeting? I can't go, so I must send a replacement.*

**step inside** *v adv; prep*

to enter (usu. a building or room), usu. for a short time: [L9 + INSIDE/*inside*] *If you care to step inside (my office) for a minute, we can sign the contract straight away.*

**step off¹** *v adv*

**1** to leave something such as a high level or vehicle, by moving the feet: [L9 + OFF (*often simple tenses*)] *Be careful how you step off, it's a long way from the ground.* —**stepping-off** *adj*

*2 to mark or measure (a length) by walking: [T1] *Step off ten feet and then place a marker in the ground.* → **step out** (2)

*3 *mil* to start marching: [IØ] *The men stepped off in good spirits.*

**4 step off on the right/wrong foot (with)** *not fml* to begin something such as work or a relationship, in a good/bad way: *The director is a tricky person to work for, and it's a good idea to try to step off on the right foot with him. Once you've stepped off on the wrong foot, it's difficult to make a fresh start.* → **get off¹** (20), **start off** (6)

**step off²** *v prep*

to leave (a high level such as a vehicle) by moving the feet: [L9 + *off* (*often simple tenses*)] *As the Queen stepped off the royal train, the crowd cheered.*

**step on/upon** *v prep*

**1** to move with the feet on top of (usu. something): [L9 + *on/upon*] *Mind where you put your feet, you could step on some broken glass.* → **stamp on** (1), **trample on** (1), **tread on** (1)

*2 *not fml* to hurt (someone's feelings): [T1] *It's difficult to avoid stepping on her sensitive feelings.* → **trample on** (2), **tread on** (2), **walk on²** (2), **walk over** (1)

*3 *not fml* to scold (someone): [T1] *I shall step on her very firmly if she interrupts me again.* → **tell off** (1), etc.

**4 step on it/the gas** *infml* to hurry: [*usu. imper.*] *Step on it, we haven't all day to waste. Step on the gas, the plane leaves in half an hour.*

**5 step on someone's corns/toes** *not fml* to hurt someone's feelings; annoy someone, usu. accidentally; offend someone's sensitivity: *The director is in a bad temper this morning; take more than the usual care not to step on his corns.* → **tread on** (5)

**step out** *v adv*

**1** to walk outside, esp. for a short time: [L9 + OUT] *He's not in the office, he's just stepped out for a breath of fresh air.* → **step outside** (1)

*2 to measure (a distance) by walking: [T1] *Step out ten feet and then put a marker in the ground.* → **step off²** (2)

*3 to walk fast: [IØ (*usu. simple tenses*)] *She steps out so actively that I have difficulty keeping up with her. When I go for a walk in cold weather, I like to step out to keep warm.*

*4 *not fml* to have fun; enjoy one's life: [IØ (*usu. continuous tenses*)] *She's really stepping out these days, isn't she? Parties every week, trips all over the place, it's all a life of enjoyment.*

***step out on** *v adv prep*

*not fml* to be unfaithful to (someone such as one's wife or husband): [T1 (*often continuous tenses*)] *No one told him that she had been stepping out on him for over a year.*

**step outside** *v adv*

**1** to walk out of doors, esp. for a short time: [L9 + OUTSIDE] *He's not in the office, he's just stepped outside for a breath of fresh air.* → **step out** (1)

*2 *not fml* to have a fight, as to settle an argument; usu. said as an invitation: [IØ] *If you care to step outside we can soon settle this.*

**step over¹** *v adv*

to move to a place nearer to someone: [L9 + OVER (*to*)] *Would you like to step over to my office? I have a suggestion that may be to your advantage.*

**step over²** *v prep*

to lift the feet so as to pass above (something or someone): [L9 + *over*] *We had to step over piles of broken bricks when we went to see our new house being built.*

**step up** *v adv*

**1** to walk forward or to a higher level: [L9 + UP (*to*) (*often simple tenses*)] *The child had to step up as high as he could reach, to get to the next stair. Would Mr Fisher please step up to receive his prize? Would you step up to my office for a moment? It's on the floor above.*

*2 to fix (a tall pole or mast) so as to stand firmly: [T1] *Has the mast been properly stepped up?*

*3 *not fml* to (cause to) increase or move faster: [T1] *The firm will have to step up production if it is to defeat its competitors. If the medicine has little effect after a week, step up the quantity. This machine works by stepping* *up the electric current.* [I∅] *Trade has been stepping up recently, since the weather turned warmer.* —**step-up** *n, adj* —**stepped-up** *adj* → **step down** (4)

**step upon** *v prep* → STEP ON

**stew in** *v prep*

**1** to boil (food) slowly in (liquid); (of food) to boil slowly in (liquid): [T1 + *in*] *Stew the vegetables in the meat juice to make them tasty.* [I∅ + *in*] *The fruit has been stewing in sugar water for three hours.*

**2 stew in one's own juice** *not fml* to suffer the deserved results of one's own action: *There's no need to punish him; just leave him to stew in his own juice for a few days, and his conscience will do the work!*

***stick about/around** *v adv*

*not fml* to wait, or remain in the same place or with the same people: [I∅ (*often simple tenses*)] *Stick around, we might need you later. I wasn't prepared to stick around at the airport for more than an hour, so I left when my friend's plane did not come in.*

***stick at** *v prep*

**1** to continue to work hard at (a job or doing something) in spite of difficulties: [T1 (*no pass.*)] *Learning any skill is largely a matter of sticking at it until you can do it better.* [T4] *If you can stick at practising for long enough, you could play the piano quite well.* → **be at** (3, 14), **keep at** (3), **stick to** (5), **stick with** (3)

**2** to be discouraged by (something): [T1 (*no pass., usu. simple tenses*)] *Don't stick at small difficulties, but keep going.*

**3** to stop at; refuse to go as far as or beyond (something or doing something bad): [T1 (*no pass., usu. nonassertive*)] *Would you stick at dishonesty if you could gain by it?* [T4 (*usu. nonassertive*)] *He wouldn't stick at cheating to get what he wanted.*

**4 stick at home** *not fml* to be contented with an unadventurous life; be inactive in the world: [*often simple tenses*] *I'm tired of sticking at home with the children while you go out and meet people.* → **stay at** (3), **stop at** (4)

**5 stick at nothing** to be prepared to use any means (to do something): [*simple tenses*] *He would stick at nothing to gain his own desires.* → **stop at** (5)

***stick by** *v prep*

**1** to be loyal to (someone): [T1 (*no pass.*)] *His family can be trusted to stick by him whatever happens.* → **stand by²** (2), **stick to** (7)

**2** to act according to (something such as an idea): [T1 (*no pass.*)] *Throughout the struggle he stuck by his principles. Do you always stick by your promises?* → **adhere to** (2), etc., **stay with** (3), **stick with** (4)

**stick down** *v adv*

**1** to fix (something), as to a surface with a sticky substance: [X9 + DOWN] *Stick the mat down at the edges to stop it curling. Don't stick the envelope down till it's ready to post. I can't remove this photograph, it's been stuck down.* → **glue down, gum down, stick on¹** (1)

**2** *infml* to place (something) carelessly down in position; lower (something such as part of the body): [X9 + DOWN] *Stick the boxes down anywhere, we'll sort them out later. If you stick your head down between your knees, it helps to stop you fainting.* → **lay down** (1), **place down, put down** (1), **set down** (1)

***3** *infml* to write (something) down: [T1] *Stick down the first idea you have, and develop the article from there. I've stuck his name down in my little book. You can stick the telephone bill down as a business cost.* → **write down** (1), etc.

**stick fast** *v adv*

**1** to (cause to) remain fixed in one place, be unable to move: [I∅ + FAST] *Help me to pull the car, it's sticking fast in the mud.* [T1 + FAST (*usu. pass.*)] *Help me to pull the car, it's stuck fast in the mud.*

***2** to be firm in keeping to one's opinions or actions: [I∅ (*usu. simple tenses*)] *All the family tried to persuade Jim to change his mind, but he stuck fast and refused to be influenced.* → **hold firm, stand fast, stand firm, stand pat** (2)

**stick for** *v prep*

**be stuck for** *not fml* to lack (something): *I can't afford it yet, I'm stuck for money. The factory is stuck for raw material, and has had to cease production. The speaker stopped for a moment, stuck for the right word.*

**stick in¹** *v adv*

**1** to place or push (usu. something) inside something such as a space: [X9 + IN] *Stick your hand in and see what's in the box. I'll just stick my head in and see if there's anyone here that I know. You have to stick the fence posts in deep to make sure they stand upright.* → **fit in¹** (1), **get in¹** (1), **go in¹** (2), **poke in¹** (1), **put in¹** (1)

**2** *not fml* to remain indoors, as unwillingly or from necessity: [L9 + IN] *What a pity to have to stick in on a lovely day like this!* → **keep in** (5), etc.

***3** *not fml* to (cause to) work hard: [I∅] *Stick in, and we'll soon have the job done!* [T1 (*to*) (*usu. pass.*)] *Once you've got stuck in (to the work), it doesn't seem so bad.*

**4 stick one's heels in** *not fml* to act firmly; refuse to change one's mind: *The committee wanted the chairman to allow more time for decisions, but he stuck his heels in and refused to listen.* → **dig in¹** (6)

**5 stick one's nose in** *not fml* to enquire into something that is not one's own affair: *Stop sticking your nose in where you're not wanted!* → **poke in¹** (3)

**stick in²** *v prep*

**1** to fasten (something) inside (something) with a sticky substance: [X9 + *in*] *Have you stuck all the family photographs in the book yet?*

**2** *infml* to place (something) in position inside (something such as a container), esp. carelessly: [X9 + *in*] *He stuck his hand in his pocket and leaned back. The child stuck a finger in his mouth. Just stick the letter in the box, we'll deal with it later.* → **lay in² (1), place in (1), poke in² (1), put in² (1), put into (1), set in² (1), stick into (1)**

**3** to make (a hole) by pushing sharply into (something): [X9 + *in*] *His sword did no more than stick a hole in his enemy's shield.* → **poke in² (2)**

**4** to push (something sharp) into (something or someone); (of something sharp) to be fixed in (something): [X9 + *in*] *I've stuck a needle in my finger! Stick your fork in the meat to see if it's cooked.* [L9 + *in*] *I think that fishbone is still sticking in my throat.*

**5** to (cause to) remain fixed in (a place), unable to move: [IØ + *in*] *The wheels are still sticking in the mud.* [T1 + *in* (*usu. pass.*)] *The poor cat has been stuck in the top branches all morning.*

**6** *not fml* to (cause to) remain in (a place), as unwillingly or through necessity: [L9 + *in* (*often simple tenses*)] *I didn't see why I should stick in the kitchen all morning while the rest of the family were off enjoying themselves.* [X9 + *in* (*often pass.*)] *What's the use of keeping the car stuck in the garage all winter?* → **be in² (1), be out of (1), come into (1), get into (1), go into (1), keep in (1), remain in² (1), stay in² (1), stop in² (1)**

**7 stick in someone's mind** to (cause to) stay in the memory; be difficult to forget: [*often simple tenses*] *The tune seems to be stuck in my mind, I can't forget it. Why do some facts of history stick in the mind, and others get forgotten so quickly?*

**8 stick one's nose in** *not fml* to enquire into (something that is not one's affair): *He's always sticking his nose in other people's affairs; I wish he would mind his own business.* → **poke in² (3)**

**9 stick in one's throat: a** to be difficult to express: [*usu. simple tenses*] *When I went on stage for the first time, the words stuck in my throat and I stood there silent, covered in shame.* **b** *not fml* also **stick in one's craw/gizzard** to be difficult to accept: [*simple tenses*] *Giving those students a fail mark stuck in my throat when I knew they had tried their best. It sticks in my throat to pay taxes for things that I don't approve of.*

***stick in with** *v adv prep*
*infml* to join (someone) as a companion, to share living, etc.: [T1] *"My mother wants me to stick in with my uncle, who has no children of his own."* (Muriel Spark, *The Public Image*)

**stick indoors** *v adv* → **keep in** (5), etc.
*not fml* to remain inside a building, esp. unwillingly or from necessity: [L9 + INDOORS] *Children should not have to stick indoors doing school work when the weather is so good for playing games.*

**stick into** *v prep*
**1** *infml* to place (something) in position inside (something such as a container): [X9 + *into*] *He stuck his hand into his pocket and looked at her threateningly. Stick the vegetables into the pan, I'll cook them later.* → **fit into (1), get in (1), get into (1), go in (3), go into (4), lay in (1), place in (1), poke in² (1), put in (1), put into (1), set in² (1), stick in² (2)**

**2** to push (something sharp) into (something such as material): [X9 + *into*] *With a shout, he stuck his sword into his enemy's body. Stick your fork into the meat to see if it's properly cooked.* → **jab into, poke into (1)**

**3 stick one's nose into** *not fml* to enquire into (something that is not one's affair): *I don't want anyone sticking their nose into my affairs; what I choose to do with my life is my own affair.* → **poke into (3)**

**stick on¹** *v adv*
**1** to fix (something), usu. to a surface, with a sticky substance: [X9 + ON] *I can't get this photograph off the page, it's stuck on. Please don't stick the stamps on, I like to collect them.* —**stick-on** adj → **glue down, gum down, stick down (1)**

**2** *not fml* to remain fixed or in position on top of something or someone: [L9 + ON] *I put the lid on the pot, but the water is boiling so fiercely that it won't stick on. When you first learn to ride a horse, one of the biggest difficulties is simply sticking on! How does your hat stick on in this high wind?* → **stay on¹ (1), stop on (1)**

***3** *infml* to cause (something electrical such as a light) to start working: [T1 (*usu. simple tenses*)] *Stick the radio on, will you, I want to hear the news.* → **put on¹ (3), etc.**

***4** *not fml* to remain in a place, as at work: [IØ (*at*)] *I don't want to stick on here for the rest of my life!* → **keep on (6), stay on¹ (3), stop on (3)**

***5** *not fml* to add (something): [T1] *British Rail might stick on an additional train to carry the football supporters. Every bill has an additional charge stuck on, to cover increased costs. The government has promised not to stick on any further tax.* → **put on¹ (7)**

**stick on²** *v prep*
**1** to have doubts about or refuse to be persuaded concerning (something such as a subject): [IØ + *on* (*usu. continuous tenses*)] *The workers are still sticking on the question of holiday pay.*

**2** to fasten (something) onto (something such as a surface) with a sticky substance: [X9 + *on*] *If you stick the wallpaper on the wall, it is difficult to remove. Stick enough stamps on the letter to pay for the postage.* —**stick-on** *adj*

**3** *infml* to place (something) esp. carelessly in position on top of (something): [X9 + *on* (*often simple tenses*)] *Just stick your bags on the floor, we can unpack later.* → **put on²** (1), etc.

*__4__ *infml* to add (a charge or amount) to the price of (something): [D1] *The restaurant sticks an additional charge on the bill, to cover increased costs. The government has promised not to stick any further tax on cigarettes.* → **put on²** (3)

**5 be stuck on** *not fml* to be very fond of, keen about, unable to leave (something or someone): *Grace was really stuck on that red-haired boy, wasn't she, until she learned sense!*

***stick out** *v adv*

**1** to be in a position further forward than or away from something: [IØ (*from*)] *The pot has two handles sticking out. I hurt my arm on the stone that sticks out from the wall. One branch stuck out and caught the rider by the hair.* → **jut out, poke out** (1), **project from, protrude from, stand out** (2)

**2** to (cause to) be put or left outside something: [IØ] *We knew the animal was in there because it left its tail sticking out.* [T1] *Why have our neighbours stuck a flag out?* → **poke out** (1)

**3** *not fml* to stretch (something) out or forward: [T1] *Stick your hand out, I have a surprise for you! It's rude to stick your tongue out at people. Stick your nose out of the window and see if it's still raining.* → **put out** (1), etc.

**4** *infml* to be noticeable: [IØ (*usu. simple tenses*)] *To make the figures stick out, paint them in a darker colour. The house stuck out because of its unusual shape. I don't like to stick out in a crowd. No one in this singing group should stick out as a separate voice.* → **stand out** (5)

*__5__ *not fml* to continue to show opposition, disagreement, etc.: [IØ] *The miners are determined to stick out until they get their demands.* → **hang out for, hold out for, stand out** (4), **stand out for, stick out for**

*__6__ *not fml* to continue to declare the truth (that something): [T5 (*often simple tenses*)] *The prisoner stuck out that he had not been present at the scene of the crime, in accordance with his original statement.*

**7 stick it out** *not fml* to continue in spite of difficulties; refuse to yield: *Painting the house is tiring, but if you stick it out, the results are worth the effort. Can our team stick it out until the end of the competition?* → **hang on¹** (3), etc.

**8 stick out a mile** *not fml* to be very noticeable: [*simple tenses*] *The teacher's favouritism sticks out a mile. It sticks out a mile that the government will call an early election.* → **stand out** (7)

**9 stick one's neck out** *not fml* to invite trouble by one's actions; take risks: *Aren't you rather sticking your neck out, telling the director what you think of him? I'm prepared to stick my neck out and oppose the opinions of the leader of our party.*

***stick out against** *v adv prep* → **stand out against** (2)

*not fml* to oppose (something) in a determined way: [T1 (*no pass.*)] *The trade unions are continuing to stick out against the government's wage and price controls.*

***stick out for** *v adv prep* → **hang out for, hold out for, stand out for, stick out** (6), **strike against** (2), **strike for**

*not fml* to demand (something) and wait in order to get it: [T1 (*no pass.*)] *You may have to stick out for your pay rise longer than you expected.*

**stick to** *v prep*

**1** to (cause to) be fixed to or closely touching (usu. something) with or as with a sticky substance: [IØ + *to*] *Wet clothes stick to the skin. This stamp won't stick to the envelope!* [X9 + *to*] *The mat seems to be stuck to the floor, I can't move it. Please don't stick pictures to the wall.* → **adhere to** (1), **cleave to** (1), **cling to**

*__2__ to stay near (something or someone); closely follow (a course or direction): [T1 (*pass. rare, often simple tenses*)] *Stick (close) to me and you won't get lost. You'll be all right if you stick to the main roads, they're kept clear of snow. The ship had to stick to the shore because of the heavy mist. "Stick close to your desks and never go to sea, And you may all be Rulers of the Queen's Navy!"* (W.S. Gilbert, *H.M.S. Pinafore*) → **cling onto** (1), **cling to** (2), **hold to** (2), **keep by** (2), **keep to** (1), **stay by, stick with** (2)

*__3__ to limit oneself to (something) without wandering or changing the subject: [T1] *Please stick to the facts, don't guess. Stick to the point! That's not what we were talking about! When writing an article, stick to one style throughout.* → **keep to** (2)

*__4__ to try to keep (something): [T1] *He made every effort to stick to the job that he had. It's no use trying to stick to the old ways, times have changed. The old ladies were determined to stick to their home in spite of the new road going through.* → **cling onto** (2), **cling to** (3), **hang onto** (3), **hold onto** (2)

*__5__ to continue to work hard at (a job or doing something): [T1 (*no pass.*)] *Learning any skill is largely a matter of sticking to it until you can do it better.* [T4] *If you stick to practising the piano every day, you could become quite a good musician.* → **be at** (3, 14), **keep at** (3), **stick at** (1), **stick with** (3)

*__6__ to follow or be faithful to (something such as an idea): [T1] *Loyal party members stick to their party's political principles. Whatever your argument, I shall stick to my decision. Is the prisoner still sticking to his original story? If you make a good plan to win the game, you should stick to it. Do you always stick to your promises?* → **adhere to** (2), etc., **stand by** (3), **stay with** (3), **stick with** (4)

*__7__ to be loyal to (someone): [T1] *His family can be trusted to stick to him always.* → **stand by** (2), **stick by**[2] (1)
**8** **stick to someone's fingers** *not fml* (of money) to be stolen by someone: *She was a good worker, but if she found any money lying around, it had a way of sticking to her fingers.*
**9** **stick to one's guns** *not fml* to keep firmly to what one believes or is arguing, as in an argument: *It should be an interesting argument, as both politicians are known for sticking to their guns, and neither is likely to give way to the other.* → **stand to**[2] (3)
**10** **stick to it!** *not fml* keep going: [*imper.*] *Stick to it! There's not long to go before the end!*
**11** **stick to one's last** *not fml* to do whatever one is good at or fitted for: *Leave the director to organize the firm; you stick to your last, keeping the workers happy, as no one can do that as well as you.*
**12** **stick to one's post** *not fml* to stay at one's place of duty: *A soldier is expected to stick to his post whatever the danger.* → **remain at** (2), **stand to**[2] (4), **stay at** (4), **stop at** (6)
**13** **stick to one's ribs** *not fml* (of food) to be satisfying: *That was a good meal, it's really sticking to my ribs.*

**stick together** *v adv*
**1** (of two or more things) to (cause to) be fixed together, with or as with a sticky substance: [IØ + TOGETHER] *The pages are sticking together, I can't get them apart.* [X9 + TOGETHER] *Can you stick the parts of the broken plate together?* → **cling together** (1)
*__2__ *not fml* to remain united: [IØ] *Members of a family should stick together in times of trouble.* → **cling together** (2), **hold together** (2), **keep together** (2), **stand together** (2), **stay together** (3)

***stick up** *v adv*
**1** *not fml* to (cause to) be raised or kept upright: [T1] *Stick up your hand if you know the answer.* [IØ] *The garden fork was left sticking up out of the hard soil. His feet stuck up in the air as he fell over backwards.* → **put up**[1] (1)
**2** *not fml* to show (something such as a notice) in a public place: [T1] *The examination results will be stuck up on this board tomorrow.* → **put up**[1] (3)
**3** *infml* to rob (someone or a place), usu. by threatening with a gun: [T1] *Someone has stuck up the bank! The thieves stuck up all the passengers on the train and demanded their money.* —**stick-up** *n* → **hold up** (3)
**4** **stick 'em up/stick up your hands** *infml* raise your hands in the air; I am pointing a gun at you: [*imper.*] *Stick your hands up and turn to face the wall, we've got a gun!* → **put up**[1] (24)
**5** **be stuck up** *not fml* to have too high an opinion of oneself; be unpleasantly proud: *I don't like the new girl—she seems very stuck up!* —**stuck-up** *adj*

***stick up for** *v adv prep*
**1** *not fml* to support (someone or something): [T1] *I stuck up for him and said I had always found him to be honest. More people are beginning to stick up for children's rights.* → **stand up for** (1)
**2** *not fml* to demand and make sure one gets (one's rights): [T1] *If you don't stick up for your rights, no one else is going to fight your battles for you.* → **stand up for** (2)

**stick with** *v prep*
**1** to make holes in (something) with (usu. sharp things left sticking in it): [X9 + *with* (*usu. pass.*)] *The body was stuck with arrows. Stick the meat all over with pieces of the flavouring. His hat was stuck with feathers.*
*__2__ to stay close by (someone): [T1 (*no pass.*)] *Stick with me and you won't get lost.* → **cling onto** (1), **cling to** (2), **keep by** (2), **stay by, stick to** (2)
*__3__ to continue to work hard at (something): [T1 (*no pass.*)] *I know it's not easy at first, but stick with it and it will soon seem easier.* → **be at** (3, 14), **keep at** (3), **stick at** (1), **stick to** (5)
*__4__ *not fml* to continue to deal with or act according to (something): [T1 (*no pass.*)] *Let's stick with the present arrangements until a better plan is thought of. I'll stick with my decision, thank you.* → **stand by**[2] (3), **stay with** (2, 3), **stick by** (2), **stick to** (6)
*__5__ *not fml* to remain level with (a competitor): [T1 (*no pass.*)] *Jim was able to stick with the leading runner for most of the race until he weakened and had to drop back.*
*__6__ *not fml* to continue to pay attention to (someone): [T1 (*no pass., often imper.*)] *Stick with me for a few more minutes and you'll see the point of the story.* → **stay with** (4)
*__7__ to remain loyal to (someone): [T1 (*no pass.*)] *Thank you for sticking with me when all the others deserted me.*
**8** **be stuck with** *not fml* to have no choice about dealing with (someone, something, or doing something unwanted or unpleasant): *Why am I always stuck with the dirty work? Shall we be stuck with your mother until the end of the holiday? Jim always got stuck with cleaning the garage.*

***stick within** *v prep* → **keep within** (1), **remain within** (1), **stay within** (1), **stop within**
*not fml* to continue to be limited by (something): [T1 (*no pass.*)] *It won't be easy to stick within the cost limits of the contract.*

***stickle at** *v prep*
*AmE* to oppose (an idea) because of one's conscience: [T1] *One of the committee members is stickling at the plan because it offends him morally.*

**stimulate into/to** *v prep*
to urge (someone) towards (something); give (someone) cause for (action): [T1 + *into/to*] *The workers must be stimulated to greater effort by an offer to share in the firm's profits.*

**stiffen up** *v adv*
to (cause to) become stiffer or more severe: [IØ + UP] *My leg has stiffened up again, just when I thought it was getting better.* [T1 + UP] *Laws against child cruelty should be stiffened up. You can stiffen up the collars by dipping them in this special liquid.*

**sting for** *v prep*
*sl* to charge (someone) too much as the price of (goods): [D1 + *for* (*usu. simple tenses*)] *How much did they sting you for that pair of boots?*

***sting into** *v prep* → **goad into, provoke into**
to urge, annoy, or drive (someone) into (an action or doing something): [D1 (*often simple tenses*)] *The children's bad behaviour at last stung their patient mother into anger.* [V4b (*often simple tenses*)] *The students did their best to sting the teacher into losing his temper.*

**stink of** *v prep*
**1** to have a bad smell as if coming from (something causing the smell): [IØ + *of*] *The whole factory stank of decaying fish. The lake stinks of waste products from the chemical factories along the shore.* → **smell of** (1), **stink with** (1)
***2** *not fml* to contain the suggestion of (something bad): [T1 (*no pass., simple tenses*)] *This whole arrangement between the parties stinks of dishonest dealing.* → **savour of, smack of, smell of** (2)

***stink out** *v adv*
**1** *infml* to force (usu. an animal) to leave a hiding place by means of a bad smell: [T1] *If the rats won't eat the poison or get caught in the traps, we may have to stink them out with this special chemical that animals hate.*
**2** *infml* to fill (a place) with a bad smell: [T1] *Those terrible cigarettes stink the whole room out, I wish you'd get rid of them. Those bad fish are stinking out the restaurant: what will happen to our trade?* → **smell out** (3), **smell up, stink up**

**stink to** *v prep* → **smell to**
**stink to high heaven** *not fml* to smell very bad indeed: *Throw that decayed fish away, it stinks to high heaven!*

**stink up** *v adv* → **smell out** (3), **smell up, stink out** (2)
*AmE not fml* to fill (a place) with a bad smell: [T1] *"Preparing a good meal for an airline needs much more planning than goes into the average restaurant. In one day the kitchen may produce 3,000 meals. We have to bear in mind that they have to serve the meal in 45 minutes. There is that time to consider, and then, you can't have food that will stink up the plane either."* (*Toronto Sun*, 25 January 1976)

**stink with** *v prep*
**1** to have the bad smell of (something): [IØ + *with*] *The whole street was soon stinking with the decayed fish in the restaurant.* → **smell of** (1), **stink of** (1)
**2 be stinking with** *infml* to have a lot of (usu. money), causing offence to others: *He's simply stinking with money and yet he won't give it away.*

**stint of** *v prep*
to make (someone or oneself) not have enough of (something or things): [T1 + *of* (*usu. simple tenses*)] *When the children were young, we had to stint ourselves of necessities in order to feed and clothe them.*

***stipulate for** *v prep*
*fml* to demand (something particular) firmly, as in a formal agreement: [T1] *The other firm are stipulating for an early exchange of information regarding the contract. The workers have stipulated for the use of only union labour in their new agreement with the employers.*

**stir about/around** *v adv*
to move (a mixture) with a tool such as a spoon, in various directions: [T1 + ABOUT/AROUND] *The children liked to stir the cake mixture about, making a wish.* —**stirabout** *n*

**stir in** *v adv*
to add (something) to a mixture by moving it with a tool such as a spoon: [T1 + IN (*to*)] *Next, stir in the beaten eggs.*

**stir to** *v prep*
**1** to urge (someone) to (action or doing something): [T1 + *to*] *It doesn't take much to stir the students to violence. How can we stir the government to improving prison conditions?*
**2 stir someone to the depths** to move someone's feelings deeply: [(*often pass.*)] *I was stirred to the depths by the news of so many people's deaths in the terrible fire.*

**stir up** *v adv*
**1** to mix (something or things) by moving it or them with a tool such as a spoon or the hand: [T1 + UP] *Next, stir up the eggs with the milk. His hand, leaning over the edge of the boat, stirred up the muddy waters.*
***2** to cause or encourage (trouble, excitement, etc.) to arise, by one's actions: [T1 (*among*)] *The opposition are trying to stir up feelings of dissatisfaction among the voters. The soldiers were sent into the foreign country to stir up violence among the natives.* → **stoke up** (3)
***3** to excite or annoy (someone); make (something) more active: [T1] *"Good friends, sweet friends, let me not stir you up to such a sudden flood of mutiny."* (Shakespeare, *Julius Caesar*) *"Stir up, O Lord, the wills of thy faithful people."* (*Book of Common Prayer*)
**4 stir up mud** *not fml* to make unpleasant facts known: *Stirring up mud is the politician's favourite method of destroying his opponent.*
**5 stir up a hornet's nest** *not fml* to cause trouble: *You've fairly stirred up a hornets' nest. haven't you, telling the workers what the director earns!*

**stitch up** *v adv*
**1** to mend (something such as a hole) by

drawing the edges together with thread: [T1 + UP] *Take your coat off, and I'll stitch up that tear. If the wound is stitched up skilfully, it will hardly leave a mark.*

*2 *not fml* to mend (a quarrel): [T1] *Have Jim and Mary stitched up their disagreement yet?* → **make up** (14), **patch up** (3)

**stock up** *v adv*
to obtain a supply (of goods); fill (a shop) (with goods): [T1 + UP (*for, on, with*)] *Is the shop well stocked up with camping supplies?* [IØ + (*for, on, with*)] *All the toyshops are now stocking up for Christmas. We must stock up on pencils, we seem to have very few left.* —**stocking-up** *n*

**stock with** *v prep*
to supply (a shop or body of water) with (goods or fish): [T1 + *with*] *Yes, the shop is well stocked with camping supplies. The city council have suggested stocking the lake with fish to provide food and fun for the citizens.*

***stoke up** *v adv*
**1** to supply (a fire) with more material to burn: [T1] *The fire needs stoking up—there's some wood in the yard.*
**2** *not fml* to eat well: [IØ] *We'd better stoke up at the inn, as we've a long way to go and don't know when we shall next eat.*
**3** *not fml* to cause to encourage (trouble, excitement, etc.) to arise or develop, by one's actions: [T1] *The enemy have sent men into the villages to stoke up opposition to our help. Who has been stoking up all this discontent among the voters?* → **stir up** (2)

***stooge about/around** *v adv*
**1** *BrE sl* (of a pilot) to fly to and fro over quite a small area: [IØ] *For the last hour we've been stooging around at 25,000 feet, waiting for the enemy planes.*
**2** *BrE sl* to walk or go to and fro without any fixed purpose: [IØ] *'What have you been doing?' 'Oh, nothing, just stooging about most of the morning.'*

**stoop down** *v adv* → **bend down**, etc.
to bend the back, leaning forwards towards the ground: [IØ + DOWN] *Stooping down to pick up the pen, Jim felt a sharp pain in his back.*

**stoop to** *v prep*
**1** to bend the back towards (something or someone): [IØ + *to*] *I had to stoop to the child's height to hear what he was saying. Stooping to the ground, I picked up the pin.*
*2 to lower oneself morally to (something or doing something bad): [T1 (*no pass., simple tenses*)] *I'm surprised that you would stoop to such behaviour!* [T4 (*simple tenses*)] *I'm disappointed that any student of mine would stoop to cheating.* → **descend to** (3), etc.

**stop at** *v prep*
**1** to (cause to) cease moving on reaching (something): [IØ + *at*] *The motorist was charged with failing to stop at a red light.* [T1 + *at*] *The driver has to stop the bus at the railway lines.*
**2** to remain behind at (a place): [L9 + *at*] *The women stopped at home while the men went to war. I'll stop at the desk while you go to make your telephone call.* → **remain at** (1), **stay at** (1)
**3** to be a guest at (a place such as a home or hotel): [L9 + *at*] *Which hotel are you stopping at? I'll be able to stop at my aunt's house while I'm in the town.* → **stay at** (2)
**4 stop at home** to be contented with an unadventurous life; be inactive in the world: [*often simple tenses*] *Don't you want to do something better with your life than just stop at home doing nothing?* → **stay at** (3), **stick at** (4)
**5 stop at nothing** to use every means (to do something): [(*simple tenses*)] *He would stop at nothing to gain his own desires.* → **stick at** (5)
**6 stop at one's post** to remain on duty in the proper place: *The guard had orders to stop at his post whatever happened.* → **remain at** (2), **stand to**[2] (4), **stay at** (4), **stick to** (12)

***stop away** *v adv* → **keep away**, etc.
to be absent; remain at a distance (from something or someone): [IØ (*from*) (*often simple tenses*)] *Many of his former supporters disapproved of his latest opinions, and stopped away (from the meeting) when he came to give a speech. Although her stomach trouble was much better, Jane stopped away (from school) as it was Friday. I've asked you to stop away from those rough boys.*

***stop behind** *v adv* → **keep in** (5), etc.
to remain in a place when others leave: [IØ] *If you stop behind after class, I will repeat the instructions.*

***stop by** *v adv; prep* → **stop in**[1] (2), **stop off**[1] (1)
esp. *AmE* to pay a short visit during a journey elsewhere: [IØ (*often simple tenses*)] *Can you stop by for a moment on your way home from the shops? We could have a cup of tea together.* [T1 (*no pass., often simple tenses*)] *Please stop by the cleaner's on your way home and collect my coat.*

**stop dead** *v adj*
to (cause to) cease moving suddenly; come to a sharp stop: [IØ + dead (*simple tenses*)] *I stopped dead when I discovered that I had left my bag behind.* [T1 + dead (*simple tenses*)] *The policeman stepped into the road and with one upraised hand stopped the traffic dead.*

**stop down** *v adv*
**1** to continue to be in a lower position: [L9 + DOWN (*often simple tenses*)] *If there's shooting going on, get down and stop down until I tell you it's safe to move.* → **keep down** (1), **remain down** (1), **stay down** (1)
**2** to remain at a lower level; continue to be less; not increase: [L9 + DOWN] *I hope the wind stops down now that it's calmer, so that we can risk putting up the sails. If Jane's*

*temperature stops down all day, she can go back to school tomorrow.* → **hold down** (2), **keep down** (2), **remain down** (2), **stay down** (2)

*__3__ (of food) to remain in the stomach: [IØ] *Jane is sick again; nothing she eats will stop down.* → **hold down** (3), **keep down** (3), **stay down** (3)

*__4__ (in photography) to make the opening narrower so that less light reaches the film: [IØ (*often simple tenses*)] *The light's too bright for the setting you have on the camera; you should stop down.*

**stop for** *v prep*

**1** to (cause to) cease moving because of or to yield to (something or someone): [IØ + *for* (*often simple tenses*)] *You have to stop for horses in this town, they have the right of way.* [T1 + *for* (*often simple tenses*)] *These gates are to stop the traffic for passing trains.*

**2** to be a guest for (a length of time): [L9 + *for*] *I didn't think the boy would stop for two whole weeks without an invitation.* → **stay for** (1)

*__3__ to remain in order to share (a meal): [T1 (*no pass.*)] *Please stop for dinner, we'd love to have you.* → **stay for** (2), **stay to, stop to**

**stop from** *v prep*

**1** to prevent (someone or something) from (something or doing something): [T1 + *from*] *How do you stop children from playing with matches? Don't let me stop you from your work. No one's stopping you from doing what you want.* → **prevent from,** etc.

**2** to take (part of the money) out of (someone's pay) before he receives it: [T1 + *from* (*often pass.*)] *The amount that you have to pay to the National Health Insurance is usually stopped from your wages.* → **stop out of** (1), **take out of** (8)

**stop in[1]** *v adv*

**1** to remain in position inside something: [L9 + IN (*often simple tenses*)] *I've put the screws in the wood as tightly as I can, but they won't stop in, they keep slipping out.* → **stay in[1]** (1)

*__2__ to pay a short informal visit, in passing: [IØ (*at*)] *I stopped in at the music teacher's house on my way home from school to give her a copy of the music.* → **stop by, stop off[1]** (1)

*__3__ to remain indoors, esp. after school as a punishment: [IØ] *Who wants to stop in on such a beautiful day? I had to stop in all day waiting for the gasman to call. This class will stop in for half an hour after school!* → **keep in** (5), etc.

*__4__ (of a fire) to continue burning: [IØ (*simple tenses*)] *Will the fire stop in until we get back?* → **keep in** (6), etc.

**stop in[2]** *v prep*

**1** to continue to be present in (a place): [L9 + *in* (*often simple tenses*)] *It's very difficult to stop in one spot without moving at all. How long are you stopping in the town?* → **be in[2]** (1), etc.

**2 stop in one's tracks** *not fml* to (cause to) cease moving suddenly, as from shock: [(*usu. simple tenses*)] *I stopped in my tracks when I discovered that I had lost my bag. Firing a gun over their heads should stop them in their tracks.*

***stop indoors** *v adv* → **keep in** (5), etc.
to remain inside a building, as at home: [IØ] *Mother was advised to stop indoors until he cough was properly better.*

***stop off[1]** *v adv*

**1** to pay a short informal visit, usu. in passing: [IØ] *Do stop off on your way home and have a cup of tea with me.* → **stop by, stop in[1]** (2)

**2** to interrupt a journey: [IØ] *I'd like to stop off for a few days while I'm in the North, to see something of the country.* → **stay over, stop over** (1)

***stop off[2]** *v prep* → **stay off** (3), etc.
to fail to attend (something such as school): [T1 (*no pass.*)] *Jane should stop off school until her stomach trouble is really better.*

**stop on** *v adv*

**1** to remain fixed or in position on top of something or someone: [L9 + ON] *When you first learn to ride a horse, one of the chief difficulties is simply stopping on and not falling off. How does your hat stop on in this high wind?* → **stay on[1]** (1), **stick on[1]** (2)

**2** (of something electrical such as a light) to continue working: [L9 + ON (*usu. simple tenses*)] *Something's wrong, I switched the radio off but it stopped on!* → **put on[1]** (3), etc.

*__3__ to remain in a place or position, as at work: [IØ (*at*)] *I've been asked to stop on at the firm after the usual age. Can you persuade the chairman to stop on? No one else is suitable.* → **keep on** (6), **stay on[1]** (3), **stick on[1]** (4)

**stop open** *v adj*

**1** to continue to be wide apart, open, etc.: [L9 + **open** (*simple tenses*)] *How can we make the door stop open? We need some air in the house.* → **leave open** (1), etc.

*__2__ to remain open for business: [IØ] *Do the shops stop open late here on Fridays?* → **stay open** (2), etc.

**stop out** *v adv*

**1** to remain outside a building or room, or away from home: [L9 + OUT (*of*)] *Who gave you permission to stop out all night? There's no garage so the car will have to stop out all winter. I think I'll stop out here in the sun while it's nice and warm.* —**stop-out** *n* → **keep out, stay out** (1)

*__2__ to remain on strike: [IØ] *All the workers are stopping out until their demands are met.* → **bring out** (7), etc.

**stop out of** *v adv prep*

**1** to take (part of the money) from (someone's pay) before he receives it: [T1 + OUT + *of* (*often pass.*)] *Income tax is usually stopped*

*out of your wages, so you never get the whole amount.* → **stop from, take out of** (8)
**2** to remain outside, not enter (something): [L9 + OUT + *of* (*often simple tenses*)] *Tell the children to stop out of the farmer's fields while the crops are growing.* → **keep out of** (1), **stay out of** (1)

***stop over** *v adv*
**1** to spend the night away from home: [IØ (*at, in*)] *We need two days for the journey, stopping over at a small town on the way. Because of the severe snowstorm, we couldn't get home that night, and had to stop over in a hotel.* → **stay over, stop off**[1] (2)
**2** to interrupt a plane journey: [IØ] *Are you allowed to stop over without additional cost? The plane stops over at Grand Falls on its way to Newtown.*—**stopover** *n, adj* → **lay over**[1] (1)

***stop short at/of** *v adj prep*
to refuse to act so as to reach (something or doing something): [T1 (*no pass., usu. simple tenses*)] *The city council will use every means to raise money, but stops short at an increase in taxes.* [T4 (*usu. simple tenses*)] *Will they actually stop short of increasing taxes?*

***stop still** *v adj*
**1** to remain without moving: [IØ (*simple tenses*)] *Can't you children stop still for a moment? Stop still for a minute and listen carefully.* → **stand still** (1)
**2** to stay at the same level or rate, without advancing; be inactive: [IØ (*simple tenses*)] *Production has stopped still at the factory since the men began demanding higher wages. Time seemed to stop still during her first kiss.* → **stand still** (2)

***stop to** *v prep* → **stay for** (2), **stay to, stop for** (3)
to remain in order to share (a meal): [T1 (*no pass.*)] *How many of these people are stopping to dinner?*

**stop under** *v adv; prep* → **hold under** (1), **keep under** (1), **remain under, stay under**
to continue to be beneath (something such as the surface of water): [L9 + UNDER/*under* (*usu. simple tenses*)] *If the swimmer stops under (water) for more than a minute, pull him out, he may be drowning.*

**stop up** *v adv*
**1** to block (a hole) with something solid: [T1 + UP] *My ears frequently get stopped up with wax. What can we use to stop up the hole in the wall?* → **block up** (1), **bung up** (1), **seal up, stuff up** (1)
**2** to remain raised, high, etc.: [L9 + UP (*simple tenses*)] *How does that narrow building stop up? The picture won't stop up long if you use one of those weak hooks.* → **hold up** (1), etc.
***3** to remain late out of bed, as at night: [IØ] *Please don't stop up for me, I may be in very late.* → **stay up** (3), etc.

**stop with** *v prep*
**1** to block (something such as an opening) with (something): [T1 + *with*] *You could stop the hole in the wall with some of this clay.*
**2** to be a guest of (someone); continue to work for (someone): [L9 + *with*] *I hope you'll stop with me on your return visit. How long do you intend to stop with the firm?* → **stay with** (1)

***stop within** *v prep* → **keep within** (1), **remain within** (1), **stay within** (1), **stick within**
to continue to be limited by (something): [T1 (*no pass.*)] *Are motorists in general stopping within the new speed limits? As long as you stop within the law, I'll agree to your plan.*

**store away** *v adv*
**1** to keep (something or things) packed; save (something or things) for the future: [T1 + AWAY] *Now it's time to store away your fur coats for the summer. This is where the animals store their nuts away.*
**2** to keep (something such as information) in the mind: [T1 + AWAY] *Thank you, I'll store that piece of news away for a time when I might need it.*

**store in** *v prep*
to pack or save (something or things) for the future, in (a place or container): [T1 + *in*] *Furs can be stored in special cold rooms during the summer. These little animals often store their nuts in holes in trees.*

**store up** *v adv*
**1** to save a supply of (something or things) for the future: [T1 + UP] *These little tree animals store up nuts for the winter.* → **lay up** (1)
***2** to keep (a strong feeling such as anger) in the mind, often with a later result: [T1 (*often pass.*)] *The bitterness which she had been storing up against her husband's mother at last broke out into a violent quarrel.* —**stored-up** *adj*

**storm at** *v prep*
**1** to become very angry because of (something): [L9 + *at* (*often continuous tenses*)] *It's no use storming at such injustices, the thing to do is to try to correct them.*
**2** to be very angry with (someone): [L9 + *at* (*often continuous tenses*)] *I could hear Mother storming at the children for bringing mud into the house.*

**storm in** *v adv*
to enter in a very angry manner: [L9 + IN (*to*)] *The door flew open, and Father stormed in, in a very bad temper. The teacher came storming in to the classroom, determined this time to make the children obey him.*

**storm out** *v adv*
to leave in a very angry manner: [L9 + OUT (*of*)] *Several members, refusing to accept the decision of the vote, got up and stormed out (of the meeting).*

**stove up** *v adv* → STAVE UP

**stow away** *v adv*
**1** to pack or store (something or things, often large), as for a long time: [X9 + AWAY] *Th*

*other mats can be stowed away until we move to a bigger house. We stow the sails away in this space at the front of the boat.*

*__2__ to eat a lot of (food): [T1] *Have you seen the amount of food those children can stow away at one meal?*

*__3__ to hide on a ship until after she has sailed, so as to obtain a free passage: [IØ] *Having no money for the voyage, he succeeded in the end in stowing away on a passenger ship heading for England.* —**stowaway** *n*

**stow into** *v prep*
to pack (something or things) into (a container, usu. large): [X9 + *into*] *Supplies for the whole voyage were stowed into lockers on board the big ship.*

***stow it** *v pron*
*infml* stop doing that!: [IØ (*imper.*)] *I can't sleep if you are talking so stow it!*

***stow with** *v prep*
to fill (a large container) with (something or things): [D1 (*often pass.*)] *The boxes beside the road are stowed with sand and salt for putting on icy roads to make them safer.*

**straighten out** *v adv*
**1** to (cause to) become more straight: [T1 + OUT] *Why does she spend so much time and money trying to straighten out the waves in her hair? The curls look pretty.* [IØ + OUT] *After twisting for several miles, the road straightens out here and driving is easier.*

*__2__ to make (something) clear; remove confusions in (something); set (something) right: [T1] *I hope the misunderstanding will soon be straightened out. Jim and Mary must be left to straighten out their own affairs, it's no one else's responsibility. Can the struggle between the two countries straighten itself out in time?* → **sort out** (2)

*__3__ to guide (someone) into right behaviour or thinking; remove difficulties, esp. bad behaviour or worries in the life of (someone): [T1] *A warning from the judge should help to straighten him out. It's time that boy got himself straightened out, even if that means getting professional help.* → **sort out** (5)

***straighten up** *v adv*
**1** to rise to a standing position with the back straight: [IØ] *As Jim straightened up, the ache in his back grew worse.*
**2** to tidy (something, someone, or oneself): [T1] *I must straighten up this room, my parents are coming! He took a few moments to straighten himself up before entering the meeting.*

**strain after** *v prep* → **strive after** (2)
**strain after an effect/effects** to make too great an effort to seem important or of high quality: *The writer has spoiled an otherwise good story by putting in too much detail and straining after the effect that he wanted to make.*

**strain at** *v prep*
**1** to pull hard on (something) so that it costs effort or pain: [L9 + *at*] *Although several sailors were straining at the rope, they could not control the sail in the high wind.* also **strain on**

*__2__ to have difficulty in accepting (something, usu. unimportant or not difficult); trouble oneself about an unimportant matter, esp in the phr. **strain at a gnat**: [T1 (*often simple tenses*)] *Why do you strain at such a small request? He's very slow at his work because he's always straining at a gnat.*

**3 strain at the leash** *not fml* to be eager for freedom: *Children are rarely ready to leave home when they want to, so they spend several years straining at the leash, making life difficult for themselves and their parents.*

***strain away/off** *v adv*
to remove (part of something, usu. liquid) by passing through something such as a cloth: [T1] *Strain the fat away before you serve the soup.*

**strain on** *v prep* → **STRAIN AT** (1)

**strain through** *v prep*
to pass (liquid) through (something such as a cloth) so as to separate the parts: [T1 + *through*] *If you strain the sour cream through this thin cloth overnight, it makes excellent cheese.*

**strain to** *v prep*
**strain someone to one's bosom/heart** *old use* to hold someone fondly: *She strained her long-lost sister to her heart, weeping for joy.*

**strand on** *v prep* → **maroon on**
to leave (someone) on (usu. an island) without means of leaving: [T1 + *on* (*often simple tenses*)] *The sailors took command of the ship by force from the captain, and stranded him on a desert island.*

**strap down** *v adv*
to fasten (something or someone) down with leather or cloth bands: [X9 + DOWN (*often pass.*)] *Are the boxes safely strapped down? He was wild with anger, and had to be strapped down.*

***strap in** *v adv* → **belt up** (4), **buckle up** (3)
to fasten (by means of) one's seat belt, as on a plane: [IØ] *Experienced travellers strap in without waiting to be asked.* [T1] *Experienced travellers often stay strapped in for the whole flight, in case of unexpected rough air.*

**strap on** *v adv; prep*
to fasten (usu. something) on with leather or cloth bands: [X9 + ON/*on*] *Climbers can strap sharp points on (their boots) to help get a foothold on a slippery slope.*

**strap up** *v adv*
to bind (something) with leather or cloth bands: [T1 + UP] *Are the boxes safely strapped up? You'll have to keep your leg strapped up until the wound is completely better, to keeep out infection.*

**stray from** *v prep*
**1** to wander accidentally away from (a place): [IØ + *from*] *The sheep have strayed from our*

*fields, and are on the neighbouring farmer's land.* → **wander from** (1), **wander off**[1]

*2 to leave (a subject, right behaviour, etc.), often unintentionally: [T1] *You're straying from the subject again, do please keep to the point. "We have erred, and strayed from thy ways like lost sheep."* (*Book of Common Prayer: General Confession*) → **wander from** (2), **wander off**[2]

**stream along** *v adv; prep*
to pass quickly and evenly along (something such as a road), as in a crowd: [L9 + ALONG/*along*] *The people were streaming along (the street) as if eager to get out of the rain.*

**stream down** *v adv; prep*
to flow down (something): [L9 + DOWN/*down*] *Water was streaming down, and the windows were impossible to see out of. Tears of joy streamed down her face as she greeted her long-lost sister.*

**stream with** *v prep*
to be covered with a flow of (usu. liquid): [IØ + *with* (*often continuous tenses*)] *All the streets in the village were streaming with flood water.*

**stretch away** *v adv*
(usu. of time) to reach into the distance: [L9 + AWAY (*usu. simple tenses*)] *The future seemed to stretch away as far as he could imagine.*

**stretch forth** *v adv* → **put out** (1), etc.
*old use* to (cause to) reach forward, as with the hands: [T1 + FORTH] *He stretched forth his hand, begging for mercy.* [IØ + FORTH] *His hand stretched forth, begging for mercy.*

**stretch out** *v adv*
**1** to lengthen (something) by pulling: [T1 + OUT] *You can stretch this rubber out to twice its length.*
**2** to (cause to) reach forward, as with the hands: [T1 + OUT] *You can feel the rain if you stretch out your hand. It's nice to have room to stretch my legs out.* [IØ + OUT] *Stretching out, he took a firm hold of the rope.* —**outstretched** *adj* → **put out** (1), etc.
**3** to make (something) last longer: [T1 + OUT] *We shall have to stretch the food out till the end of the week.*
*__4__ to lie at full length; place (oneself) at full length: [IØ] *It's so pleasant to stretch out in the sun.* [T1] *It's so pleasant to stretch myself out in the sun.* → **spread out** (2)
*__5__ to (cause to) lengthen in time: [IØ (*usu. simple tenses*)] *The years ahead seemed to stretch out for ever.* [T1 (*often simple tenses*)] *Some of the members tried to stretch the meeting out.* → **space out** (2), **spread out** (4)

**strew on/over** *v prep*
to scatter or spread (something or things) on top of (something or someone): [T1 + *on/over*] *There were papers strewn all over the floor.*

**strew with** *v prep*
**1** to cover (something) freely with (something or things, often scattered): [T1 + *with* (*often pass.*)] *His desk is always strewn with papers. The floor of the building was strewn with bodies.* → **pave with** (1)
*__2__ to fill (something such as writing or an idea) with (something or things): [D1 (*usu. pass.*)] *His poetry is strewn with images of death.*

**stricken with** → STRIKE WITH (2)

**strike against** *v prep*
**1** to refuse to work to express opposition to (something): [IØ + *against*] *The women have threatened to strike against unequal pay.* → **hang out for, hold out for, stand out for, stick out for, strike for**
**2** to (cause to) land with a blow against (usu. a hard object): [T1 + *against* (*usu. simple tenses*)] *He struck his head against the doorpost and fell to the ground in a faint. How did the ship strike against the rocks? My arm accidentally struck against the table.* → **knock against** (1), etc.

**strike as** *v prep*
to seem to (someone) to be (something or doing something): [X9 + *as* (*simple tenses*)] *He has always struck me as an honest worker. This activity strikes me as wasting our time. The idea at first struck me as stupid, but now I think it is a good one.*

**strike at** *v prep*
**1** to try to hit or aim a blow at (someone or something): [L9 + *at* (*usu. simple tenses*)] *The fighter struck at his opponent but missed.* → **hit at** (1)
*__2__ to attack (someone or something) with words: [T1 (*usu. simple tenses*)] *Many of the newspapers struck at the government's latest plan.* → **hit at** (2)
*__3__ to attempt to destroy (something such as an idea): [T1 (*simple tenses*)] *This new law strikes at the rights of every citizen.*

**strike back** *v adv* → **hit back**
**1** to return a blow (to someone): [T1 + BACK] *Waiting only for him to strike me, I struck him back with all my strength.* [L9 + BACK (*at*)] *In reply to last night's bombing attack, our planes this morning have struck back at the enemy port.*
*__2__ to return an attack, as in words (to someone): [IØ (*at*)] *In a letter to the newspaper, Tom had a chance to strike back at those who had found fault with his latest book. The only way the taxpayers can strike back at an unjust government is to vote against them at the next election.*

**strike down** *v adv*
**1** to make (someone) fall by hitting him as with a blow or vehicle: [T1 + DOWN (*usu simple tenses*)] *Jim was struck down by a bus in the middle of the main street. At last he struck his attacker down, just as the police arrived.* → **knock down** (2), **knock over** (2), **run down**[1] (4), **run over**[1] (5)
*__2__ to make (someone) very ill or dead: [T

(*usu. pass.*)] *The businessman was struck down with a heart attack in the middle of the meeting. So many young men have been struck down in their youth in this terrible war. Half the population was stricken down with the fever.* → **lay low** (2)

**strike dumb** *v adj*

**1** to make (someone) unable to speak: [X9 + **dumb** (*simple tenses*)] *The evil magician's curse struck him dumb.*

**2 be struck dumb** *not fml* to be very surprised: *I was struck dumb by the unexpected news.*

**strike for** *v prep* → **hang out for, hold out for, stand out for, stick out for, strike against** (1)

to refuse to work in order to gain (something): [IØ + *for*] *The women have threatened to strike for equal pay.*

**strike from** *v prep* → **strike off** (4)

to remove (a word or words such as a name) from (a list): [X9 + *from*] *I shall have to strike three more names from the guest list, we simply haven't room. He was struck from the official list of doctors for immoral behaviour.*

***strike home** *v adv*

**1** (of a blow) to reach its aim: [IØ (*simple tenses*)] *Just as the old fighter was tiring, his blow struck home and the young fighter fell unconscious to the floor.*

**2** to have the desired effect on someone; be deeply understood: [IØ (*simple tenses*)] *The news struck home as he suddenly saw the effect that it would have on his own life. At first he didn't recognize the name, but then it suddenly struck home.*

***strike in** *v adv*

to interrupt suddenly: [IØ (*usu. simple tenses*)] *'I know where she was!' Jane struck in.*

**strike into** *v prep*

***1** to interrupt (a conversation, argument, etc.): [T1 (*no pass.*)] *It's unwise to strike into someone else's quarrel without being invited.*

***2** to push (roots) into (soil): [D1] *That strong little bush soon struck its roots into the rich earth.*

**3 strike alarm/dread/fear/terror into** to fill (someone) with fear: [(*usu. simple tenses*)] *The appearance of the ghost struck terror into the soldiers guarding the castle.* also **strike in**

**strike of** *v prep*

**be struck all of a heap** to be overcome by surprise, shock, etc.: *He was struck all of a heap when he heard of their generosity to him.*

**strike off** *v adv*

**1** to remove (a part of something), as by cutting: [X9 + OFF] *The boy was striking off all the flower heads with his stick. The king's head was struck off while the crowd cheered.*

→ **cut off** (1), **slice off, snip off, swish off**

**2** to move away, esp. by changing direction: [L9 + OFF (*usu. simple tenses*)] *The boys struck off through the woods.*

**3** to remove (something in writing): [T1] *Strike off her name, I refuse to have her as a guest!* → **cross out,** etc.

***4** to remove the name of (someone, esp. a doctor or lawyer) from a list of people allowed to practise their profession: [T1 (*usu. pass.*)] *He used to be our doctor until he was struck off for immoral behaviour.* → **strike from**

***5** *not fml* to print (copies): [T1 (*usu. simple tenses*)] *How many copies of this article do you want struck off?*

***6** *not fml* to write (something) clearly and easily: [T1 (*usu. simple tenses*)] *This reporter has the ability to strike off a good description of the scene he is covering.*

**strike on/upon** *v prep*

**1** to (cause to) land, as with a blow, on (something): [L9 + *on/upon*] *The sun was striking on the sea, making it shine. The ship might strike on the rocks.* [T1 + *on/upon*] *I've never been able to avoid striking my head on the low doorway.* → **knock against** (1), etc.

**2** to hit (someone) on (a part of the body): [T1 + *on/upon* (*usu. simple tenses*)] *He struck me on the face!* → **hit on** (2)

***3** *not fml* to discover (something) by lucky chance: [T1 (*simple tenses*)] *I hope that after all these talks, someone will strike on a way out of our difficulty. If we can only strike on the best combination of people, we should have a good team. At last the miners struck on an undiscovered gold mine.* → **hit it, hit on** (3)

**strike out** *v adv*

**1** to deal strong blows, often without direction: [IØ + OUT (*at*)] *Surrounded by three men who were threatening him, Jim struck out in all directions and soon had them all lying unconscious on the ground.* → **hit out** (1), **kick out** (2), **lam out, lash out** (1)

***2** to remove (something written): [T1] *Strike out the witness's last remark, it has no place in the court record.* → **cross out,** etc.

***3** to move, esp. swim, actively (towards somewhere): [IØ (*for, towards*)] *The swimmer struck out bravely for the shore. Striking out across the fields, the boys made for home. The climbers struck out at daybreak, hoping to reach the mountain before dark.*

***4** *not fml* to make an independent effort, esp. in the phr. **strike out on one's own**: [IØ] *Martin decided to leave the company to strike out on his own as a writer.*

***5** (in baseball) to (cause to) leave the field of play at the end of one's turn, by missing or faultily hitting a delivered ball after three attempts: [IØ (*simple tenses*)] *When our best player struck out, we knew that the game was lost.* [T1 (*usu. simple tenses*)] *After striking out half the opposing team, the player took a rest.*

***6** esp. *AmE not fml* to miss a chance; fail: [IØ (*usu. simple tenses*)] *You really struck out that time, didn't you! I tried to find a hotel room in the popular tourist town, but struck* *out twice before finding a hotel that could take us.*

***strike over** *v adv*
to cover (a mistaken letter or letters) on a typewriter by typing over the top: [T1a] *Use this special paint to remove the mark, and then strike over the letters that you got wrong.* —**strikeover** *n*

**strike rich** *v adj*
**strike it rich** *not fml* to find wealth, often suddenly, as by discovering a valuable mineral: [(*usu. simple tenses*)] *The farmer struck it rich when oil was found on his land. With this unusual product, and good advertising, any businessman can strike it rich!*

***strike through** *v adv* → **cross out,** etc.
to remove (something written): [T1b] *Strike that last word through, I've changed my mind.*

***strike up** *v adv*
**1** to (cause to) begin playing (music): [IØ (*simple tenses*)] *The band struck up as soon as the Queen stepped ashore.* [T1a (*simple tenses*)] *The musicians struck up the wedding march. Strike up the band!*
**2** to begin (a relationship or conversation, usu. informal): [T1a (*simple tenses*)] *It's easy to strike up a friendship with people you meet on holiday. I struck up a conversation with this other woman in the shop.*

**strike upon** *v prep* → STRIKE ON

**strike with** *v prep*
**1** to hit (someone or something) by using (something): [T1 + *with*] *It's not easy to strike the ball with this narrow piece of wood. He struck me with his open hand!*
**2 be stricken with** to begin to suffer from (something such as a disease), often suddenly: *She was stricken with fever in her youth. Many businessmen are stricken with heart disease at a comparatively young age.*
**3 be struck with: a** to feel the effect of (a strong feeling): *I was struck with wonder as I saw the great ship for the first time.* **b** to be attracted to (someone or a quality): *No one can fail to be struck with his charm. I was greatly struck with the new young singer.*

***string along** *v adv*
**1** *infml* to follow or go with someone: [IØ (*with*) (*usu. simple tenses*)] *I'll string along with someone who's driving into the next town.*
**2** *infml* to pretend to agree (with someone), usu. for one's own advantage: [IØ (*with*) (*often continuous tenses*)] *Don't believe his loyalty, he's just stringing along. I decided to string along with him for a time to see if I could gain by it.*
**3** *infml* to deceive (someone) by encouraging hopes: [T1b (*usu. continuous tenses*)] *He has no intention of marrying her, he's just stringing her along.*

***string out** *v adv*
**1** to (cause to) spread in a line: [IØ] *We'd better string out along this narrow path.* [T1 (*often pass.*)] *The pack horses were strung out along the mountain road. She strung out twelve pairs of socks along the washing line.*
**2 be strung out** *infml* to be under the influence of a hard drug: *What's he been taking? He's strung out.*

**string together** *v adv*
**1** to fasten (things) together with string: [X9 + TOGETHER] *The jewels are strung together on a fine silver chain.*
***2** to join or combine (words): [T1] *She has difficulty in stringing together a single sentence of good English. English words are sometimes strung together in the strangest way.*

**string up** *v adv*
**1** to hang (something or things) up with or on string: [X9 + UP] *Help me to string the little lights up on the Christmas tree.*
***2** *infml* to hang (someone): [T1] *People like that should be strung up from the nearest tree. 'String him up!' shouted the crowd.*
**3 be strung up** *not fml* to be nervous: *Try not to get too strung up before the examination, it doesn't help. Jane is a nice child with lots of musical ability, but she always seems so strung up, and that may be what causes her frequent stomach trouble.*

**string with** *v prep*
**1** to put strings on (something such as a musical instrument or object used to hit a ball in a sport, etc.) with (a material): [T1 + *with* (*usu. pass.*)] *These instruments are now strung with nylon, which makes them much easier to play than the old wire strings.*
**2** *AmE infml* to make fun of (someone) by tricking into believing (something): [T1 + *with*] *The older workers always enjoy stringing the new boys with stories about the director's fierce temper.*

**strip away** *v adv*
**1** to remove a thin covering of (a material little by little: [T1 + AWAY] *Carefully stripping away centuries of paint, the scientists uncovered a valuable old wall painting.* → **strip o**[ff] (1)
***2** *not fml* to uncover (a pretence): [T1 (*ofte*[n] *simple tenses*)] *Once his show of power ha*[s] *been stripped away, you can see that he's* [a] *very ordinary human being. If you can stri*[p] *away that false manner she has, you will qui*[te] *like her.* → **strip off** (2)

***strip down** *v adv*
**1** to remove all clothing (from oneself [or] someone): [IØ (*to*)] *The climbers had to str*[ip] *down to their underwear to get out of w*[et] *clothing.* [T1] *Strip the children down, g*[et] *them out of those wet clothes.* → **strip off** (3)
**2** to take (something such as an engine) [to] pieces, usu. for repair: [T1] *Your car will* [be] *in the garage for a few days as we have to str*[ip] *the whole engine down to discover the fau*[lt.] → **take down** (2), **tear down**[1] (3)

**3** *not fml* to scold (someone): [T1] *Jim got stripped down for being late for work again.* → **tell off** (1), etc.

**strip from** *v prep*
to remove a thin covering of (something) from (something): [X9 + *from*] *Stripping the shirt from his back, he bound the wound. The birds have stripped all the fruit from the bushes!*

***strip of** *v prep*
to rob (someone) of (something); make (someone or something) be without (something): [D1 (*often pass.*)] *The thieves stripped the house of its valuables. The birds have stripped the bushes of all the fruit! The king was stripped of his power.*

**strip off** *v adv*
**1** to remove a thin covering of (a material) little by little: [X9 + OFF] *These fruit knives are very good for stripping apple skins off.* → **strip away** (1)
***2** *not fml* to uncover (a pretence): [T1 (*often simple tenses*)] *If you can strip off that false manner she has, you will quite like her.* → **strip away** (2)
***3** to remove all one's clothing; remove (clothes): [IØ] *Quickly stripping off, he jumped into the river to save the drowning child.* [T1] *Strip off those wet clothes as fast as you can!* → **strip down** (1)
***4** *not fml* to scold (someone): [T1] *Jim got stripped off for being late for work again.* → **tell off** (1), etc.

**strive after** *v prep*
**1** *fml* to make an effort to reach or gain (something): [L9 + *after*] *Most people continually strive after perfection, even though they know it's impossible to reach.* → **strive for, strive towards**
**2 strive after effects/an effect** to make too great an effort to seem important or of high quality: *The writer has spoiled an otherwise good story by striving after effects.* → **strain after**

**strive against** *v prep* → **strive with**
*fml* to oppose (someone or something) forcefully: [L9 + *against*] *The minister begged the worshippers to strive against evil.*

**strive for** *v prep* → **strive after** (1), **strive towards**
*fml* to make efforts to support or gain (something): [L9 + *for*] *The councillors are striving for improvements in public housing.*

**strive over** *v prep*
*fml* to disagree or fight about (something): [L9 + *over*] *The neighbouring farmers have been striving over that piece of land for many years.*

**strive towards** *v prep* → **strive after** (1), **strive for**
*fml* to make efforts to reach or gain (something): [L9 + *towards*] *The world leaders must continue to strive towards peace.*

**strive with** *v prep* → **strive against**
*fml* to oppose (someone) forcefully: [L9 + *with*] *We all have to strive with evil men.*

***stroke down** *v adv*
*not fml* to make (someone) feel calmer: [T1] *See if you can stroke him down, he's still very angry.*

**struck dumb** → STRIKE DUMB (2)

**struck with** → STRIKE WITH (3)

**struggle against** *v prep*
to oppose (usu. something) with difficulty: [L9 + *against*] *The workers have been struggling against bad conditions for too long. What is the use of trying to struggle against the system?*

**struggle along** *v adv*
**1** to move forward with difficulty: [L9 + ALONG] *The poor old man was only just able to struggle along with the help of a stick.*
***2** to be able to live, with difficulty: [IØ] *We struggled along for many years until things got better.*

**struggle for** *v prep*
**1** to try to obtain (something) from someone, with difficulty, as by fighting: [IØ + *for*] *The two men were struggling for the gun for several minutes.*
**2** to try to gain (something) with difficulty: [L9 + *for*] *The two men have been struggling for the leadership of the party since last year. Most animals have to struggle for existence in a dangerous world.*

**struggle in** *v prep*
**1** to fight or make awkward movements in (something such as a place or material): [IØ + *in*] *Still fighting, the two brothers struggled in the water. I struggled in the snow, trying to make my way forward.*
**2** to have difficulty in (something): [L9 + *in*] *We all have to struggle in life.*

**struggle on** *v adv*
to continue to live although with difficulty: [L9 + ON] *Whatever the trouble, we have to struggle on with our lives, we have no choice.*

**struggle out** *v adv*
to leave a place, with difficulty: [L9 + OUT (*of*)] *One by one, the insects struggled out of the smoke-filled hole.*

**struggle through** *v adv; prep*
**1** to make one's way through (something), with difficulty: [L9 + THROUGH/*through*] *The forest ahead is thick, but we should be able to struggle through (it) somehow.*
***2** to succeed, with difficulty (in something): [IØ] *The examination is difficult, but most of my students should be able to struggle through if they work hard.* [T1 (*no pass.*)] *I don't know how I'm going to struggle through the next month without any money.*

**struggle with** *v prep*
**1** to fight with (someone): [IØ + *with*] *Don't struggle with a man who attacks you, you've*

*no hope of winning and it will only make matters worse.* → **tussle with** (1)

*2 to have an inner battle with (oneself, one's conscience, etc.): [T1] *After struggling with myself for some days, I decided to accept his offer. You could almost see him struggling with his conscience before he chose to tell the truth.* → **battle with** (2), **do with** (12b), **tussle with** (2), **wrestle with** (3)

**strum on** *v prep* → **thrum on**
to play (a tune) rather carelessly on (a musical instrument): [T1 + *on*] *Jane can come home from any musical show and strum every tune on the piano.* [IØ + *on*] *She often likes strumming on the piano for hours at a time.*

**strung up** → STRING UP (3)

**strut about/around** *v adv; prep*
to walk about (a place) in a falsely proud manner, often with the head or heels held high: [IØ + ABOUT/AROUND/*about/around*] *Who does he think he is, strutting about (the theatre) as if he owns the place?*

***stub out** *v adv*
to stop (something such as a cigarette) burning by pressing: [T1] *Please stub out your cigarettes in the objects provided and not on the table top.*

**stuck for** → STICK FOR

**stuck up** → STICK UP (5)

**stuck with** → STICK WITH (8)

**stud with** *v prep*
**be studded with** to have (many smaller things) set in or scattered on the surface: *The sky was studded with stars. The Queen's crown is studded with precious jewels, each one rich in history.*

**study for** *v prep*
to work hard at learning (from something such as a book) in preparation for (something such as an examination): [IØ + *for*] *It's difficult to study for a law degree in evening classes while working during the day.* [T1 + *for*] *Please be quiet, I have to study this book for a test tomorrow.*

**study under** *v prep*
to have (someone) as one's teacher, usu. at a high level: [IØ + *under*] *Jane will be lucky to study under such a famous singer.*

**stuff down** *v prep*
**1** to force (something such as material) to pass down (a space) by pushing: [X9 + *down*] *He stuffed some old newspapers down the legs of the trousers to keep warm in the bitter wind.* → **force down** (1), **push down**[2] (1), **ram down**[2] (1), **thrust down** (1)
**2 stuff something down someone's throat** *not fml* to force someone to remember, believe, or accept something unpleasant or against his will: *There are complaints that the study of English is being stuffed down some students' throats.* → **force down** (2), **push down**[2] (2), **ram down**[2] (2), **thrust down** (2)

**stuff into** *v prep*
to pack (something such as material or things) tightly in (something); force (food) on (someone): [X9 + *into*] *I simply can't stuff any more clothes into this case. Please don't stuff worthless food into my children, I like to control what they eat.*

***stuff it** *v pron*
*sl* to be prepared to bear something unpleasant: [IØ (*usu. inf. or imper.*)] *You may not like it, but you're going to have to stuff it anyway.*

**stuff up** *v adv*
**1** to block (something): [T1 + UP] *You could stuff the hole in the window up with newspaper until the man can put some new glass in. He stuffed his ears up with his hands to shut out the terrible noise.* → **block up** (1), **bung up** (1), **seal up, stop up** (1)
**2 be stuffed up** (usu. of a nose) to be filled, as with a cold: *I can't possibly speak in public tonight, I've got a bad cold and my nose is all stuffed up.* → **bung up** (2)

**stuff with** *v prep*
**1** to pack (something) tightly with (something or things): [T1 + *with*] *Every case he had was already stuffed with clothes. You could stuff the chair with this torn material. For Christmas, we stuff the chicken with a mixture of bread and flavourings.*
**2** to fill (someone) very full with (food and drink): [T1 + *with*] *Please don't stuff my children with worthless food, I like to control what they eat.*
**3 stuff someone's head with** *not fml* to give someone ideas about (something); teach someone (usu. something useless or wrong): *Who's been stuffing these children's heads with this nonsense?*

***stumble across/on/onto/upon** *v prep* → **happen on**, etc.
to find (usu. something) by lucky chance: [T1 (*simple tenses*)] *I stumbled across this old photograph in the back of the drawer.*

**stumble over** *v prep*
**1** to move awkwardly because of (something) in the way; almost fall over (something in one's path): [IØ + *over*] *Mind you don't stumble over these roots, they're difficult to see under these leaves.* → **fall over**[2] (2), **trip over** (1)
*2 to say (words) awkwardly, as missing one or two: [T1] *After stumbling over the introduction because of his nervousness, he delivered the rest of the speech smoothly.* → **fall over**[2] (3), **trip over** (2)

***stumble through** *v prep*
to give (a performance) in an awkward and unsure manner: [T1] *The chairman stumbled through his opening speech as if he were afraid of making a mistake. At least Jane never stumbles through a performance, she can always be trusted to sing well.*

***stumble upon** *v prep* → STUMBLE ACROSS

***stump up** *v adv* → **cough out** (2), **cough up** (2) **pay up**
*BrE not fml* to pay (money requested), usu

unwillingly: [IØ (*for*) (*usu. simple tenses*)] *Shall I have to stump up for the wedding?* [T1 (*for*) (*usu. simple tenses*)] *I had to stump up £25 for a suitable present.*

***sub for** *v prep infml* → **SUBSTITUTE FOR** (2)

***subject to** *v prep*

**1** to make (something) have (treatment, a test, etc.): [D1 (*often pass.*)] *This metal should not be subjected to too high temperatures. Every winter subjects these cars to a severe test. Has the book been subjected to a detailed examination?*

**2** to bring (someone) under the control of (someone or something): [D1 (*usu. pass.*)] *The people were subjected to the conqueror's rule.*

**3** *fml* to allow (oneself) to receive and accept (something): [D1 (*usu. simple tenses*)] *Will you subject yourself to the judgment of the court?*

**4** to make (oneself) have (something usu. bad): [D1 (*usu. simple tenses*)] *Why should you subject yourself to such inconvenience? Women have been subjected to unjust treatment for too long.*

**submerge in** *v prep*

**1** to put (something) under the surface of (a liquid): [T1 + *in*] *The ship has been submerged in the ocean for many years; will it be possible to raise her? Try not to submerge your hands in the soapy water, it will harm the skin.* → **immerse in** (1), **soak in²** (1), **steep in** (1)

***2** to make (oneself) give all one's attention to (something): [D1 (*often pass.*)] *It's no use trying to talk to Father when he's submerged in his work.* [V4a (*usu. pass.*)] *I was submerged in reading an exciting book, and didn't hear the doorbell ring.* → **absorb in,** etc.

**submit to** *v prep*

**1** to offer (an idea, something written, etc.) for consideration, to (someone or a group): [T1 + *to*] *Tom submitted 35 articles to the magazine before one was accepted. Have you submitted your entry to the judges yet?*

***2** to yield to (something): [T1] *Never submit to a threat. The boy submitted to the punishment without a sound. Are you prepared to submit to my decision?* → **defer to**

***3** to make (oneself) obey (someone or something): [D1] *The people had to submit to the new rulers when they lost the war.*

**subordinate to** *v prep*

*fml* to make (something) less important than (something else): [D1 (*often pass.*)] *All other considerations had to be subordinated to the needs of the family.*

**subscribe for** *v prep*

**1** to pay money in advance so as to receive (something): [T1] *Over 5,000 shares have already been subscribed for. How many people have subscribed for the book when it is printed?*

**2** to give (money): [T1] *Most people are subscribing for £3 or so.*

***subscribe to** *v prep*

**1** to pay (money) to (a collection): [T1] *I regularly subscribe to the Red Cross.* [D1] *Some people subscribe a tenth of their income to the Church.*

**2** to pay money regularly so as to receive (something such as a newspaper or a service): [T1] *Do you subscribe to the Daily News? More people than ever before are subscribing to the theatre ticket service and will have their tickets sent through the post.*

**3** *fml* to sign (one's name) as an agreement to (something): [T1 (*usu. simple tenses*)] *I was unwilling to subscribe to the contract, but it seemed that I had no choice.* [D1 (*usu. simple tenses*)] *I refuse to subscribe my name to this paper!*

**4** *fml* to agree with (something such as an opinion): [T1 (*often simple tenses*)] *Only mad people would subscribe to such views. More and more members are refusing to subscribe to the party leader's point of view.*

***subsist in** *v prep* → **consist in, consist of, inhere in**

*fml* to have its existence in (something): [T1 (*no pass., simple tenses*)] *The special nature of life in any country subsists in its customs and beliefs rather than in its language or weather.*

**subsist on** *v prep*

to be only just able to live on a little of (usu. money or food): [IØ + *on*] *How can the poor woman subsist on such a small income, with such a large family to feed? The old man subsisted on pieces of bread, and weak tea.*

**substitute for** *v prep*

**1** to use (something) to replace (something else): [T1 + *for*] *In this cake mixture, you can substitute oil for butter. If you substitute the writer's work for your own, you could be in serious trouble.*

***2** to (cause to) take the place of (someone): [T1] *Can you substitute for the singer who is ill? I need someone to substitute for me at the meeting.* [D1] *Another actor has been substituted for the famous player, who was refused permission to work in this country.* also *infml* **sub for** → **stand in for,** etc.

***subsume under** *v prep*

*fml* to include (a particular example) within (a general class); place (a word) under (a heading): [D1] *We could subsume that entry under General Methods. Many verbs in this book starting with 'shove' have been subsumed under 'push.'*

**subtract from** *v prep* → **take away** (4), **take away from** (3), **take from** (2)

to take (a smaller number) away from (a larger number): [T1 + *from*] *If you subtract 2 from 7, the answer is 5.*

**succeed at/in** *v prep*

**1** to have success; do well in (something such as a business): [IØ + *at/in*] *Without experience, do you think such a young man can suc-*

*ceed in this skilled trade? What makes Jim think he could succeed at music?*
*2 to be successful at (something or doing something): [T1] *The day the Queen was crowned, the climbers succeeded in their attempt on the world's highest mountain. I'm glad to hear that you're succeeding at English.* [T4] *At last the climbers succeeded in conquering the difficult mountain.*

**succeed to** *v prep* → **accede to** (1)
to obtain (property, a position, or title) on the death of the person coming before one: [IØ + *to*] *With no direct descendents, who will succeed to the title?*

***succumb to** *v prep*
**1** to yield to (something such as persuasion): [T1] *How could I fail to succumb to such gentle urging? It's difficult not to succumb to such an attractive offer.*
**2** to fall ill with (a disease): [T1] *In spite of her efforts, she at last succumbed to the terrible fever and died in the hospital.*

**suck down** *v adv* → **suck under**
to pull (something or someone) downwards, as under water, with a sucking power: [T1 + DOWN] *I felt myself being sucked down in the water, until I lost hope of breathing.*

**suck from** *v prep*
to draw (usu. liquid or gas) from (a container or room) by sucking or pulling with or as wiith the breath: [T1 + *from*] *The baby should not be left to suck milk from the bottle by himself. This machine is intended to suck the smoke and steam from the kitchen.*

**suck in** *v adv*
**1** to draw in (usu. air) with the mouth: [T1 + IN] *It's good to suck in such clean fresh air for a change.*
*2 to make (part of the face or body) hollow, as with the breath or muscles: [T1] *He sucked in his cheeks whenever he was thinking hard. He had to suck in his stomach to pass between the chairs.*
*3 *infml* to deceive (someone), as by attraction: [T1 (*usu. pass.*)] *You were properly sucked in that time, weren't you!*

**suck under** *v adv* → **suck down**
to pull (someone or something) beneath the surface of water: [T1 + UNDER] *There are dangerous currents in this part of the river, which can easily suck an inexperienced swimmer under.*

**suck up** *v adv*
**1** to draw (something such as liquid or gas) upward, as by sucking: [T1 + UP] *As the sun got hotter, it sucked up the mist from the sea. The firemen's pump is intended to suck up the pools of water from the burned-out building.*
*2 *not fml* to be eager to learn (something such as knowledge): [T1] *The cleverest students can suck up as much information as you can give them.*

***suck up to** *v adv prep* → **make up to** (3), **play up to** (2), **shine up to**
*infml* (esp. among children) to try to gain the favour of (someone in power), as by attentive and obedient behaviour: [T1] *Sucking up to the teacher won't get her any higher marks, and will only make her unpopular with the other children.*

**sue for** *v prep*
**1** to bring (someone) to a court of law to demand (a claim): [T1 + *for*] *After the accident, the workmen successfully sued the firm for damages.*
*2 *fml* to ask formally for (something): [T1] *Messengers were sent to the enemy to sue for peace.* → **arbitrate for**

***sue to** *v prep*
*fml* to ask (someone) formally for something, as a favour: [T1 (*for*] *Why don't you sue to the court for more time to prepare your case?*

**suffer from** *v prep*
**1** to have pain or bad health because of (a disease): [IØ + *from*] *How long has the child been suffering from repeated stomach trouble?* also **suffer with** → **complain of** (2)
*2 to be worse because of (something): [T1 (*no pass., usu. simple tenses*)] *The firm suffers from overorganization. Your writing suffers from lack of attention to detail.*

**suffice for** *v prep*
*fml* to be enough for (something such as one's needs): [IØ + *for* (*simple tenses*)] *Will this money suffice for your present needs?*

**suffuse with** *v prep*
**be suffused with** to be slowly spread or filled with (colour, liquid, etc.): *As the sun set, the sky became suffused with a bright pink.*

***sugar off** *v adv*
*EAmE or* esp. *CanE* to take sugar from the maple tree: [IØ] *Which is the right season for sugaring off?* —**sugaring-off** *n, adj*

**suggest to** *v prep*
**1** to mention or offer (an idea) to (someone): [T1 + *to*] *I have a better plan to suggest to the committee.* [T5 + *to*] *I would like to suggest to you that this is not a suitable time.*
**2 suggest itself to** (of an idea) to come to the mind of (someone): [(*usu. simple tenses*)] *An answer to the difficulty usually suggests itself to me if I go to bed thinking about it.*

**suit for** *v prep*
**be suited for** → SUIT TO (2)

***suit oneself** *v pron*
to do as one likes: [IØ (*often imper.*)] *It doesn't matter to me where you sit: suit yourself!*

**suit to** *v prep*
*1 to make (something) fit or match (something): [D1] *You have to suit your spending to your income. You must suit the garment to the cloth.* → **fit to** (2), **match with** (1), **pair with** (1)
**2 be suited to** to have the right qualities to be

come (something such as a position) or to please (someone): *Do you think David is suited to teaching? Jim and Mary seem suited to each other, in spite of their quarrels. Some people are simply not suited to the competitive world.* also **be suited for**

**3 suit someone (down) to the ground** *not fml* to be very acceptable to someone: [(*simple tenses*)] *At last I've found a house that suits us down to the ground.*

***suit up** *v adv*
esp. *AmE* to put on special clothing, as for work: [IØ] *When you've suited up, come into the machine room.*

***suit with** *v prep*
to match (something) well: [T1 (*no pass., usu. simple tenses*)] *Does the job suit with his experience? The hours of work don't suit with his lifestyle.*

***sum up** *v adv*
**1** to make a total (of an amount): [T1 (*simple tenses*)] *These ten books sum up this year's production.* [IØ (*simple tenses*)] *Your marks sum up to 87.*

**2** to give a short account of (something); give the main ideas of (something written or spoken); repeat the chief facts: [IØ] *It is the chairman's duty to sum up at the end of the meeting.* [T1] *You have only 100 words in which to sum up his speech. I can best sum up the advantages of the system by describing some recent encouraging results.* —**summing-up, sum-up** *n*

**3** (of a judge in a court of law) to give the main facts of the case to the jury: [IØ] *When both sides have presented their case, the judge will sum up.* [T1] *The judge has a responsibility to sum up the case as clearly and fairly as possible.* —**summing-up** *n*

**4** to judge (someone or something) quickly: [T1] *It didn't take the class long to sum up the teacher's level of control. I can't sum him up, first he seems one kind of person and then another.*

**summon to** *v prep*
*fml* to demand the presence of (someone) in or at (a place or event): [T1 + *to*] *All the officers were summoned to the general's tent before the battle.*

**summon up** *v adv*
**1** *fml* to demand the presence of (someone) upstairs: [T1 + UP (*to*)] *Get on the telephone, and summon all the directors up to my office at once.*

***2** to make an efffort to bring to mind (something such as a memory): [T1 (*often simple tenses*)] *I couldn't summon up a single good idea.* → **bring back** (2), **call up** (5), **come back** (4), **come back to** (2)

***3** to gather (a quality such as courage): [T1] *He had to summon up all his goodwill and honest feeling to avoid becoming very angry. The young soldier had to summon up all his courage to prevent himself from running away.* → **muster up** (2), **pluck up** (2), **screw up** (6)

***4** to cause (someone or something) to appear: [T1] *A message was sent summoning additional soldiers up to the front. The magician claims to be able to summon up the spirits of the dead.* → **call up** (6), **raise from** (2), **raise up** (2), **rise from** (4)

**sup off/on** *v prep*
*old use* to have (food and drink) as a meal, often late: [IØ + *off/on*] *Supping on cold meat was never very satisfying.*

**sup with** *v prep*
**1** *old use* to take a meal, often late, with (someone): [IØ + *with*] *Don't keep dinner for me, I shall be supping with my uncle.*

**2 he who sups with the devil must have a long spoon** *not fml* be careful when dealing with someone untrustworthy.

***superimpose on** *v prep*
**1** to place (something) on top of (something else) so as to mix or make a new whole: [D1] *The outline of the old prison was superimposed on the plan of the square, so that people could see where it had once stood. We can superimpose another image on the television picture, to make it appear that the speaker was at the scene.*

**2** to force acceptance of (an idea) in addition to (existing ideas): [D1] *The conquerors tried to superimpose their way of life on the customs of the town, but did not succeed.*

**supply from** *v prep*
**1** to provide (something) out of (a place or store): [T1 + *from*] *We can supply the goods from our main store.*

**2** to provide (something) by using (a quality, as of mind): [T1 + *from*] *I should be able to supply all the names from memory. His answer was supplied from experience.*

**supply to** *v prep*
to provide (something) for (someone or something): [T1 + *to*] *The army supplies two pairs of boots to each soldier. When is power going to be supplied to the distant farms?*

***supply with** *v prep*
to provide (someone or something) with (something): [D1] *Each soldier is supplied with two pairs of boots. The government has promised to supply the farms with power next year.*

**surge in** *v adv*
**1** (of liquid) to arrive in a flood: [L9 + IN] *As soon as the pipe was opened, the water surged in.*

**2** to arrive in a crowd, quickly: [L9 + IN (*to*)] *As soon as the gates were opened, the football supporters surged in (to the ground).*

**surge out** *v adv*
**1** (of liquid) to flow out quickly in a flood: [L9 + OUT] *When the block was removed from the pipe, dirty water surged out.*

**2** to leave quickly, in large numbers: [L9 +

OUT] *As soon as the train reached the station, crowds of passengers surged out on their way to work.*

*__surge up__ *v adv*
(of a feeling) to arise strongly: [IØ (*usu. simple tenses*)] *Uncontrollable anger surged up when he saw what had been done.*

**surmount with** *v prep*
**be surmounted with** *fml* to have (something) on top: *The tower was surmounted with a flagpole.* also **be surmounted by**

**surpass in** *v prep*
to do better than (usu. someone) with regard to (something such as a subject): [T1 + *in* (*often simple tenses*)] *Jane is not the best student in ordinary school subjects, but she surpasses all the others in music.*

**surprise into** *v prep*
to force (someone) into (action or doing something) by surprising: [T1 + *into* (*often simple tenses*)] *With an unexpected question, the clever lawyer surprised the prisoner into an admission of his guilt. The prisoner was surprised into admitting his guilt.*

**surprise with** *v prep*
to give (someone) a surprise of (something unexpected): [T1 + *with*] *Let's surprise Father with a birthday party! You have surprised me with your good behaviour.*

**surrender to** *v prep*
**1** to yield (a possession) to (someone such as an enemy): [T1 + *to* (*often simple tenses*)] *At last the citizens were forced to surrender the town to the enemy.* [IØ + *to* (*often simple tenses*)] *We shall never surrender to a conqueror.* → **yield to** (2)
*__2__ to yield (oneself) to (a feeling, usu. unfortunate): [T1] *It's best to surrender to your grief for a time, then you will be able to deal with your feeling.* [D1] *Surrendering himself to his feelings of worthlessness, he killed himself.* → **give in to** (3), **give over to** (4), **give to** (23), **give up** (4), **yield to** (3)

**surround with** *v prep*
to encircle (something or someone) with (something or things): [T1 + *with* (*often pass.*)] *The original builders surrounded the city with a wall.*

**suspect of** *v prep*
to consider that (someone) may be guilty of (something or doing something wrong): [T1 + *of* (*often simple tenses*)] *Which of these people do you suspect of the murder? The police suspect him of having a part in the jewel robbery.*

**suspend from** *v prep*
**1** to (cause to) hang from (something high): [T1 + *from*] *Paper lamps for the party were suspended from the roof on strings.* [IØ + *from*] *These monkeys can suspend from the branches by their tails.*
**2** to remove from (someone) the right to have (a duty) or be a member of (a group): [T1 + *from*] *The officer was suspended from duty while his case was examined. The only way to deal with that boy is to suspend him from school for a week. Our best player has been suspended from the team for breaking too many rules.*

**suss out** *v adv*
esp. *BrE infml* to discover; get to know (someone or something): [T1 + OUT] *John and Walter sussed out the party before deciding to stay. "The scouts sussed him out, ready and eager to be sussed."* (*The Guardian*, 5 September 1975) *"Youth susses things out for itself."* (Anthony Burgess, *1985*) [T5 + OUT (*often simple tenses*)] *The army soon sussed out that he had the ability to mend electrical machinery.*

**sustain in** *v prep*
*fml* to support (someone) in (something such as a belief or claim): [T1 + *in*] *His comforting words helped to sustain me in my faith during those dark days.*

**swab down** *v adv* also *AmE* **swob down**
to wash (usu. a floor) thoroughly with a lot of water and a heavy mass of cloth or string: [T1 + DOWN] *Every morning, the sailors had to swab down the floor of the ship.* —**swab-down** *n*

*__swab out__ *v adv* also *AmE* **swob out**
to clean (a room or wound) thoroughly with a lot of water and a thick cloth: [T1] *Every hospital room has to be swabbed out to prevent infection. Has the nurse swabbed the wound out properly?* —**swab-out** *n*

**swallow down** *v adv*
**1** to cause (something) to pass down the throat: [T1 + DOWN] *Nasty medicine is difficult to swallow down.*
**2** to control (a feeling): [T1 + DOWN] *Swallowing down his pride, he accepted the humble position offered him.*

**swallow up** *v adv*
**1** to cause (usu. something) to pass down the throat, often in a large piece: [T1 + UP] *The great fish opened its mouth and swallowed him up whole.*
*__2__ to take in, causing (something) to disappear: [T1] *The cloud swallowed up the small plane. His income was swallowed up by rising costs.*
*__3__ to make (someone) disappear: [T1 (*often simple tenses*)] *Filled with shame, she wished the earth would open and swallow her up.*

**swamp with** *v prep* → **deluge with, flood with, inundate with**
**1** to flood (a place) with (usu. water): [T1 + *with*] *Last night's storm has swamped the wheat fields with rain.*
*__2__ to crowd or overwhelm (someone or a place) with (a lot of things or something): [D1 (*usu. pass.*)] *I've been swamped with work this week, I simply can't afford the time to go to the concert with you. The office has*

*been swamped with complaints about the washing machines.*

**swap around/over/round** *v adv* also **swop around**
*not fml* to change places: [IØ] *After a few minutes, we'll swap round so that you can have a good view.*

**swap for** *v prep* also **swop for → exchange for, trade for**
esp. *BrE not fml* to exchange (something or someone) for (something or someone else): [T1 + *for*] *Will you swap your knife for my stamp collection? We could offer to swap the prisoner for our officer.* [D1 + *for*] *I'll swap you my pen for your ball.*

**swap over** *v adv* → **SWAP AROUND**

**swap round** *v adv* → **SWAP AROUND**

**swap with** *v prep* also **swop with**
*not fml* to exchange (things or people) with (someone in possession of the other one): [IØ + *with*] *Will you swap with me? I don't like this one.* [T1 + *with*] *I wouldn't swap places with anyone on earth. We have arranged to swap prisoners with the enemy.*

**swarm over/through** *v prep*
to pass in a crowd over or through (a place): [L9 + *over/through*] *Police were swarming over the fields and through the woods looking for the criminals' hiding place.*

**swarm round** *v prep*
to gather in a crowd round (someone), usu. in admiration: [L9 + *round*] *After the performance, the public swarmed round her, asking her to sign their books.*

**swarm through** *v prep* → **SWARM OVER**

**swarm up** *v adv; prep* → **shin down, shin up, skid up**
to climb quickly and easily up (something): [L9 + UP/*up*] *At a signal, the sailors swarmed up (the ropes).*

***swarm with** *v prep* → **abound in** (2), **abound with, teem with** (1)
to be crowded with (large numbers of people or things): [T1 (*no pass., often continuous tenses*)] *The streets were swarming with hotel guests trying to escape the flames. I shan't go there again, the whole place was swarming with flies.*

***swathe in** *v prep*
**1** to wrap (someone or something) in a lot of (covering): [D1 (*often pass.*)] *If you swathe the baby in too many wool covers, he will get overheated. The hills were swathed in mist.*
**2** to hide (something) in (something such as secrecy): [D1 (*usu. pass.*)] *Relations between governments are often swathed in secrecy.*

***sway up** *v adv*
to raise (a mast): [T1] *We shall need at least three men to sway the mast up.*

**swear at** *v prep*
**1** to speak curses to (someone): [IØ + *at*] *Mind your language! Don't swear at me, if you please!*
**2** to curse (something or doing something): [IØ + *at*] *He was marching up and down, swearing at the delay which was costing him so much money every minute. Why did you swear at missing the bus? There'll be another soon.*

**swear by** *v prep*
**1** to call (someone or something holy) as witness to the truth of what one says or the trustworthiness of one's promise: [IØ + *by*] *I swear by the name of God that what I say is true.* → **swear on**
***2** *not fml* to have trust in, and tell others of, the value of (a product): [T1 (*simple tenses*)] *Mothers swears by Brown's silver polish; she has used it for years with excellent results. She swears by hand washing and won't have a machine.*

***swear for** *v prep*
*AmE* to promise that (something or someone) is trustworthy: [T1 (*usu. simple tenses*)] *I will swear for his appearance in court next Monday. I could call many people prepared to swear for this method.*

***swear in** *v adv*
to cause (someone) to take a solemn promise to perform duties responsibly at the beginning of a period of office: [T1 (*often pass.*)] *The newly elected President was sworn in today.*
—**swearing-in** *n, adj*

***swear off** *v prep*
to state one's intention to stop (something or doing something): [T1 (*often simple tenses*)] *No thanks, I've sworn off drugs.* [T4 (*often simple tenses*)] *No thanks, I've sworn off smoking.*

**swear on/upon** *v prep* → **swear by** (1)
to make a solemn promise using (something holy) as a sign of one's trustworthiness: [IØ + *on/upon*] *I swear on the head of my son here that I made no threat to the king. The witness is asked to swear on the Bible that he will tell the truth, the whole truth, and nothing but the truth.*

**swear out** *v adv*
**swear out a warrant** to obtain a paper enabling one to seize a criminal, by making a solemn declaration of his likely guilt: *How many warrants have been sworn out today?*

**swear to** *v prep*
**1** to declare firmly the truth of (something or having done something): [IØ + *to* (*usu. simple tenses*)] *The prisoner swore to the truth of his statement. He swore to having been elsewhere at the time of the crime. Will you swear to it that you were not present?*
**2 swear allegiance to** to promise loyalty to (someone or something): *In schools in the United States, children swear allegiance to the flag every morning.*
**3 swear someone to secrecy/silence** to make someone promise to keep silent: *I'm sorry, I can't tell you his name, I'm sworn to secrecy.*

*If you allow him to join the group, you must swear him to silence.*

**swear upon** *v prep* → **SWEAR ON**

***sweat for** *v prep*
*not fml* to gain (something) by great effort: [T1 (*often simple tenses*)] *Well, the other team won the prize, but we made them sweat for it!*

***sweat off** *v adv*
to lose (weight) by losing liquid from the body: [T1] *In the steam bath, he sweated off two pounds in an hour.*

***sweat out** *v adv*
**1** to remove or get rid of (something) by getting hot and losing liquid from the body: [T1] *Sometimes it's possible to sweat out a cold by staying in a warm bed and drinking hot liquids.*
**2 sweat one's guts out** *infml* to work very hard indeed: *Here I've been sweating my guts out all afternoon, and hardly anything to show for it!*
**3 sweat it out** *infml* to wait for the end or arrival of something, in discomfort; suffer something unpleasant till it ends: *You'll just have to sweat it out now until the examination results are ready. It was a terrible performance, but I felt I had to sweat it out, waiting for my daughter to sing.*

**sweep along** *v adv*
**1** to (cause to) move forward easily, as driven by the wind: [L9 + ALONG] *With all the sails up, the little boat swept along in the pleasant wind.* [X9 + ALONG] *The wind swept us along towards the shore.*
***2** to persuade (someone, usu. a crowd) of the truth of one's speech: [T1] *The speaker had the ability to sweep his listeners along with him. Almost against their will, the crowd were swept along by the speaker's important-sounding words.*

**sweep aside** *v adv*
**1** to push (someone, something, or things) to one side with a brush or one's hand: [X9 + ASIDE] *He swept aside the papers on his desk to make room for the large book. Sweeping all others aside, she pushed her way to the front.* → **brush aside** (1)
***2** to refuse to pay attention to (something): [T1] *Sweeping aside all opposition, he put the matter to a vote. You can't sweep your difficulties aside in that easy manner.* → **brush aside** (3)

**sweep away** *v adv*
**1** to push (something) away with or as with a brush: [T1 + AWAY] *Sweep that dirt away before the director arrives.*
**2** to drive (something or someone) away by the action of wind or water: [X9 + AWAY] *A high wind soon swept the clouds away, and the sun shone once more. The bridge has been swept away in the floods. Even a strong swimmer can be swept away by these dangerous currents.*
***3** to destroy (something such as an idea): [T1 (*often pass.*)] *Will the new government sweep away many of the old laws? Old-fashioned values are being swept away by changing customs.*

**sweep back** *v adv*
to (cause to) lie at an angle away from something to which it is attached: [L9 + BACK (*simple tenses*)] *The other part of the house sweeps back towards the gardens.* [X9 + BACK] *She swept her hair back with her free hand. If the wings are swept back, the plane will be faster.* —**sweep-back** *n* —**swept-back** *adj*

**sweep before** *v prep*
**sweep all before one** *not fml* to be continuously successful: *Jim won every race that afternoon, sweeping all before him.*

**sweep in** *v adv*
**1** to (cause to) enter by the action of wind or water: [L9 + IN] *These leaves must have swept in when the door was opened.* [X9 + IN] *A sudden wind swept a pile of leaves in.*
**2** to enter a place in a grand manner: [L9 + IN (*to*)] *Just then the door opened and a tall figure swept in, commanding the attention of everyone in the room.*
***3** to win an election easily: [IØ (*to*)] *The party in power expected to sweep in this time, but in fact they lost votes.*
***4** *not fml* to collect (one's winnings): [T1] *Did you see the amount of money that player swept in after the last game?*

***sweep in on** *v adv prep* → **sweep over**
(of a feeling) to reach (someone): [T1 (*no pass., usu. simple tenses*)] *Uncontrollable anger swept in on Jim when he learned how Mary had been treated.*

**sweep into** *v prep*
**1** to push (something) with or as with a brush, into (a place or pile): [T1 + *into*] *Sweep the leaves into the corner where they won't be noticed.*
**2** to enter (a place) in a grand manner: [L9 + *into*] *The director swept into the meeting, demanding to know why he hadn't been sent the message about it.*
**3 sweep into office/power** (of a political party) to (cause to) win an election easily: [(*often simple tenses*)] *It was the women's vote that swept the party into power. They hoped to sweep into office, but in fact they lost votes.*

**sweep off** *v prep*
**1** to push (something) with or as with a brush or the hand off (something): [T1 + *off*] *With an angry shout, she swept the papers off the table.*
**2** to drive (something or someone) off (something) by the action of wind or water: [X9 + *off* (*often simple tenses*)] *Three cars were swept off the bridge in the high wind. You'll be swept off your feet if you go out in this storm. The rising flood swept the travellers off their*

*feet as they struggled to hold onto the branches.*
**3 sweep someone off his feet** *not fml* to fill someone with keenness, excitement, love, or other strong favourable feeling: *Mary agreed to marry Jim after he had swept her off her feet at their first meeting. Swept off their feet with admiration, the crowd stood and cheered the young singer.* → **carry off²** (2)

**sweep out** *v adv*
**1** to clean (a room or building) with a brush: [T1 + OUT] *Have you swept out the garage as you promised?*
**2** to remove (dirt) with or as with a brush: [T1 + OUT] *It's going to take me hours to sweep all this dust out, it must have been here for months.*
**3** to leave a place in a grand manner: [L9 + OUT (*of*) (*often simple tenses*)] *She hit him on the face and swept out of the room.*

***sweep over** *v prep* → **sweep in on**
(of a feeling) to reach and sometimes conquer (someone) by greater strength: [T1 (*no pass., usu. simple tenses*)] *Uncontrollable anger swept over Jim when he learned how Mary had been treated.*

***sweep through¹** *v adv* → **breeze through,** etc.
*not fml* to pass something, as an examination easily: [IØ (*often simple tenses*)] *John thought that he would fail his driving test again, but this time, to his own surprise, he swept through.*

**sweep through²** *v prep*
**1** to (cause to) pass smoothly through (something): [L9 + *through*] *Can you hear the wind sweeping through the branches?* [X9 + *through*] *She swept her free hand through her hair with a movement of impatience.*
***2** (of a fashion, disease, story, etc.) to be passed quickly among (large numbers of people); pass quickly through (a place): [T1 (*no pass.*)] *Tropical fevers can sweep through whole populations in a remarkably short time. The news swept through the village like fire. The fire swept through the business area of the city.*
***3** *not fml* to pass (something such as an examination) easily: [T1 (*pass. rare, often simple tenses*)] *To his own surprise, John swept through his driving test on his most recent attempt.* → **breeze through,** etc.

**sweep under** *v prep*
**1** to clean (dirt) with a brush beneath (something): [IØ + *under*] *Don't forget to sweep under the beds.* [T1 + *under*] *The servant had a lazy habit of sweeping the dust under the edge of the mat.*
**2 sweep something under the carpet/mat** *not fml* to try to hide something wrong: *The government is trying to sweep its failure to keep its election promises under the carpet, but the voters will not let them forget. We have made a serious mistake, and have no intention of sweeping it under the mat; we shall inform all our customers.*

**sweep up** *v adv*
**1** to clean (a room), as with a brush: [IØ + UP] *The poor women of the area were employed to sweep up after office hours.* [T1 + UP] *This room needs sweeping up every night!* —**sweeping-up, sweep-up** *n*
**2** to remove (dirt) with or as with a brush: [T1 + UP] *Help me to sweep up the broken glass, someone might cut their feet.*

**swell out** *v adv* → **swell up** (1)
to (cause to) become bigger, as with air, liquid, etc.: [IØ + OUT] *This disease of childhood makes the cheeks swell out.* [T1 + OUT] *The bird swelled out its chest to attract the attention of the female.*

**swell up** *v adv*
**1** to become bigger, as with air, liquid, etc.: [IØ + UP] *That ankle has swelled up rather nastily, hadn't you better wrap it in cold wet cloths?* → **swell out**
**2** to become filled with pride: [IØ + UP] *His heart swelled up when he learned that he had won the prize.* —**swelled-up** *adj*

**swell with** *v prep*
**1** to (cause to) become enlarged because of (usu. air or liquid): [IØ + *with*] *Your feet often swell with the heat in the afternoon.* [T1 + *with*] *Birds swell their feathers with air in order to keep warm.*
**2** to become filled with (a feeling such as pride): [IØ + *with* (*often simple tenses*)] *Mary swelled with pride as she watched Jim receive his prize.*
**3** to make (a collection of money) bigger by giving (money): [T1 + *with* (*often simple tenses*)] *Our neighbour has most generously swelled the collection with a gift of £25.*

**swerve from** *v prep*
**1** to move suddenly away from (a direction): [IØ + *from*] *Did you see that dangerous driver, swerving from his course just when the other drivers least expected it?*
***2** to leave (a course of action, decision, etc.), as by a failure of willpower: [T1] *It's difficult not to swerve from your determination to do better. A strong man does not swerve from the right decisions.*

**swig at** *v prep*
*not fml* to take a drink from (usu. a bottle): [IØ (AWAY) + *at* (*often continuous tenses*)] *Are they still swigging (away) at that bottle? They'll soon be drunk!*

***swill down** *v adv*
**1** to drink a lot of (liquid): [T1] *Peter is in the kitchen, swilling down the beer as usual.*
**2** to wash (a surface) with a lot of water: [T1] *Father has asked me to swill down the garage floor, but I wanted to play in the sports team today.* → **flush off**

***swill out** *v adv*
to clean (a room, building, or container) thor-

oughly with a lot of water: [T1] *Don't forget to swill out the bottle before returning it to the milkman. If we clear everything off the floor, we can swill out the whole garage and get it clean in one day.* —**swill-out** *n*

**swim about/around** *v adv*

**1** to move the arms and legs so as to keep floating or advance in water, without any particular direction: [IØ + ABOUT/AROUND] *The children like swimming about in the pool, not racing or exercising hard, just enjoying themselves.*

**2** to float in liquid: [L9 + ABOUT/AROUND (*usu. continuous tenses*)] *What's this strange object swimming about in my soup?*

**swim before** *v prep*

**swim before one's eyes/sight** to be seen unclearly; appear to be unsteady; seem to turn round: *The room swam before his eyes before he fell fainting on the floor.*

**swim for** *v prep*

**1** to make one's way towards (something) by swimming: [IØ + *for*] *Swim for the shore, there's a dangerous fish coming!*

**2 swim for it** to escape or save one's life by swimming: *With the boat gone, we had no choice but to swim for it.* → **run for** (4)

**swim in** *v prep*

**1** to move by using the arms and legs to keep afloat in (liquid or a container of liquid): [IØ + *in*] *Would your children like to come and swim in my pool? I only like swimming in water that is comfortably warm.*

**2** to float in (a lot of liquid): [L9 + *in* (*usu. continuous tenses*)] *She always serves the meat swimming in its own juice.*

***3** *not fml* to be crowded with (something or things): [T1 (*no pass., continuous tenses*)] *The office is swimming in papers after the meeting last night.*

***4** *not fml* to enjoy (a feeling, usu. sad): [T1 (*no pass., continuous tenses*)] *Is your aunt still swimming in her sorrows?*

***swim into** *v prep*

to enter (something such as someone's consciousness, memory, etc.): [T1 (*no pass.*)] *Good ideas swim into my mind from time to time.*

***swim with** *v prep*

**1** to be full of or flooded with (a liquid): [T1 (*no pass., usu. continuous tenses*)] *Her eyes were swimming with tears as she watched the plane leave.*

**2 swim with the tide** *not fml* to follow the easiest, most popular, and successful course of action: *A politician soon learns to swim with the tide and offer the voters things that they want, so as to gain their votes.*

**swindle out of** *v adv prep* → **cheat out of,** etc.

**1** to deceive (someone) in order to gain (something he possesses): [X9 + OUT + *of*] *The clever salesman swindled the old lady out of all her money, by pretending that the goods cost less than they actually did.*

**2** to prevent (someone) unfairly from having or using (something such as a right): [X9 + OUT + *of*] *Many children are swindled out of their chance for a good education, simply by living in the wrong place.*

***swing at** *v prep*

to aim a heavy blow at (someone or something): [T1 (*pass. rare, usu. simple tenses*)] *He swung at the man, but missed, and fell. Don't swing at the ball, take careful aim.*

***swing for** *v prep*

**1** *not fml* to be hanged for (a crime): [T1 (*no pass., usu. simple tenses*)] *He deserves to swing for that cruel murder.*

**2** *not fml* to be punished for (a wrong action): [T1 (*no pass., usu. simple tenses*)] *When your father comes home, you'll swing for it!*

***swing round** *v adv*

**1** to turn suddenly; change direction quickly: [IØ] *If the wind swings round, we will have to change the sails. He swung round at the mention of his name.*

**2** *not fml* to make (someone) change opinion: [T1b] *Can you swing him round to our point of view?*

**swing to** *v adv*

(of a door) to close by itself, by its own weight: [L9 + TO] *When I heard the door swing to behind me, I knew that I was locked out.*

***swipe at** *v prep*

to try to hit (someone or something) with a wide movement: [T1] *Don't swipe at the ball carelessly, take more careful aim. Jim tried to swipe at his attackers, but they got out of the way.*

**swirl about/around** *v adv*

(usu. of liquid) to move in circles, quite quickly: [IØ + ABOUT/AROUND] *Where the water is swirling around, there are dangerous currents.*

***swish off** *v adv* → **cut off** (1), etc.

to remove (something) with a cutting movement of something not sharp: [T1] *Ask the boy to stop swishing the flower heads off with his stick.*

**switch around** *v adv* → SWITCH ROUND

**switch back** *v adv*

*not fml* to change one's plans so as to return (to something such as a method): [L9 + BACK] *This system doesn't work too well, so we may have to switch back (to our old style).*

**switch from** *v prep* → **switch to**

*not fml* to (cause to) move or change from (someone or something) (to someone or something else): [L9 + *from*] *In his new book, the writer has switched from his usual poetic style to a plainer manner.* [X9 + *from*] *The government will switch the money from London to other parts of the world. Never switch your loyalty from old friends.*

**switch off** *v adv*

**1** to cause (something electrical) to stop

working: [X9 + OFF] *Why did you switch off the radio? I was enjoying the music. Please switch off all lights as you leave the room, to save electricity.* → **put off**[1] (3), etc.

*__2__ *not fml* to stop (someone) talking: [T1] *Once he starts telling his favourite adventures, it's impossible to switch him off.*

*__3__ *infml* to stop (someone) being interested or keen; lose interest: [T1] *Dull subjects like this are enough to switch any student off.* [IØ] *Halfway through his speech, I switched off and began to plan the dinner in my head.* → **put off** (7), **turn out** (2), **turn off**[1] (7), **turn on**[1] (3)

**switch on** *v adv*

**1** to cause (something electrical) to start working; start working: [X9 + ON] *Please switch the light on, it's getting dark.* [L9 + ON] *With this special instrument, you can set the cooker to switch on by itself while you're out.* → **put on**[1] (3), etc.

*__2__ *infml* to (cause to) become interested or excited: [IØ] *Many young people these days are using drugs to switch on.* [T1] *It takes a very special teacher to switch the students on.* —**switched-on** *adj* → **trip out, tune in** (2), **turn on**[1] (3)

**switch out** *v adv* → **put off**[1] (3), etc

to cause (an electric light) to stop burning: [X9 + OUT] *Please switch out all lights as you leave the building.*

**switch over** *v adv*

**1** to change the current in (an electrical machine): [X9 + OVER (*usu. pass.*)] *The power machine will be switched over at midnight.*

*__2__ *not fml* to (cause to) exchange places: [IØ] *Can we switch over? I'd like to sit in the sun, too.* [T1] *If you switch the words over, the sentence sounds better.* → **change over** (1), **change round** (1), **switch round**

*__3__ to (cause to) make a complete change (to something else): [IØ (*to*)] *In 1971 Britain switched over to decimal money. Many factories are switching over to a shorter working week.* [T1 (*to*)] *The chairman decided to switch the factory over to bicycle production.* —**switchover** *n* → **change over** (2)

***switch round** *v adv* also **switch round** → **change over** (1), **change round** (1), **switch over** (2)

*not fml* to (cause to) exchange places: [IØ] *Can we switch round? I'd like to sit in the sun, too.* [T1] *If you switch the words round, the sentence sounds better.*

**switch to** *v prep* → **switch from**

*not fml* to (cause to) move or change (from someone or something) to (someone or something else): [L9 + *to*] *The firm has decided to switch to another line of products, as these are not selling well.* [X9 + *to*] *It's time to switch the talks to a different subject.*

**swivel round** *v adv*

to (cause to) turn round, usu. several times, as by twisting: [L9 + ROUND] *If you swivel round, you should be able to reach the bookshelf. This special piano seat swivels round on a large screw so that you can put it at the right height.* [T1 + ROUND] *You have to swivel the handle round before you can open the lock, it's rather loose.*

**swob down** *v adv AmE* → **SWAB DOWN**

***swob out** *v adv AmE* → **SWAB OUT**

**swoon with** *v prep*

*fml* to feel or become faint because of (a strong feeling, usu. good): [IØ + *with*] *Hearing the news, the ladies of the court swooned with joy.*

**swoop on/upon** *v prep* → **descend on**

**1** (usu. of a bird) to descend quickly to attack or seize (something such as an animal): [IØ (DOWN) + *on/upon*] *Having seen the mouse from a great height with its sharp eyes, the big bird swooped (down) on it and carried it off for its meal.*

*__2__ to arrive unexpectedly to seize (usu. someone): [T1] *The police swooped (down) on the criminals in their hiding place.*

*__3__ *infml* to attack (food) eagerly: [T1] *Just look at those children swooping on the cake in that rude manner!*

**swop around/over/round** *v adv* → **SWAP AROUND**

**swop for** *v prep* → **SWAP FOR**

**swop over** *v adv* → **SWOP AROUND**

**swop round** *v adv* → **SWOP AROUND**

**swop with** *v prep* → **SWAP WITH**

**swot for** *v prep* → **cram for**

*BrE not fml* to study hard for (something such as an examination): [IØ + *for*] *Did you have to swot for your examinations, or did the work come easily?*

***swot up** *v adv* → **bone up on, mug up**

*BrE not fml* to learn (something) by hard and detailed study: [T1] *I must swot up some facts about Shakespeare's language if I am to take the class next week.*

**sympathize with** *v prep* → **commiserate with, condole with**

to share the sad feeling of (someone); feel sorry for (someone or his trouble): [IØ + *with* (*usu. simple tenses*)] *We all sympathize with the Brown family about the loss of their son. I do sympathize with your difficulties, but there's nothing I can do to help.*

# T

*__tack about__ *v adv*
*naut* to keep changing the direction of a boat, as by moving the sails from one side to the other: [IØ] *By tacking about, we were able to avoid the enemy guns.*

**tack down** *v adv*
**1** to fasten (something) down with small nails: [T1 + DOWN] *The edges of the mat should be tacked down to prevent them from curling.*
**2** to fasten (cloth) down with loose stitches: [T1 + DOWN] *Tack the folds down before you sew them firmly into place.*

**tack on** *v adv*
**1** to fasten (cloth or part of a garment) on with loose stitches: [T1 + ON (*to*)] *The collar should be tacked on to the shirt to hold it in place before you sew it properly.*
*__2__ to add (something new or different) (at the end of something): [T1 (*to*) (*often pass.*)] *The speaker amused the crowd with some jokes tacked on to his speech.*
*__3__ to (cause to) join (something): [IØ (*to*)] *Let's tack on to the end of this line, it must lead somewhere interesting.* [T1 (*to*)] *The young woman tacked herself on to the group at the beginning of the evening.*

**tackle about/on/over** *v prep*
to speak to (someone) firmly concerning (a subject): [T1 + *about/on/over*] *Are you going to tackle the boy about his school report? The committee determined to tackle the director on the matter which he had refused to talk about at the last meeting.*

*__tag along/on__ *v adv*
*not fml* to go with someone without invitation, often in a dependent way: [IØ (BEHIND) (*usu. continuous tenses*)] *I've got quite enough to do looking after this group without having any more children tagging along (behind me).*

*__tag out__ *v adv*
esp. *AmE* (in baseball) to cause (a player) to leave the field when he fails to reach base in time: [T1] *"I am tagged out a good ten feet down the line."* (J. Searle, *Speech Acts*)

*__tag together__ *v adv*
to join or combine (two or more things), often carelessly: [T1] *We could tag the two ends together, it should hold for a short time. This book consists of articles already printed, just tagged together.*

**tail after** *v prep*
to follow (someone): [L9 + *after*] *You can't tail after me all day, find something of your own to do!*

*__tail away__ *v adv* → TAIL OFF

**tail back** *v adv*
to stretch or reach behind, usu. for a long way: [L9 + BACK] *"Traffic tailed back for 25 miles when the road was blocked by an accident."* (BBC radio news, 12 September 1975)
—**tailback** *n*

*__tail in__ *v adv*
to fix (a board or brick) into a wall by one end: [T1 (*often pass.*)] *The wood can be tailed in, ready to continue on the other angle.*

*__tail off__ *v adv* also **tail away** → **taper off** (2), **trail off** (2)
to lessen in quantity, quality, or strength: [IØ] *Your work has been tailing off this year; we expect you to keep up your former standard. Membership has tailed off recently, but should improve at the beginning of the new year. His voice tailed off as he lost courage.*

*__tailor to__ *v prep*
to form (something) so as to fit (something) exactly: [D1 (*often pass.*)] *You have to tailor your spending to your income. The school system should be tailored to the needs of the children, and not the other way round.*

**taint with** *v prep*
to spoil (something) by adding (something bad): [T1 + *with* (*usu. pass.*)] *The lake water is tainted with chemicals from the factory, and the fish are not fit to eat. Their relationship was tainted with jealousy on both sides.*

*__take aback__ *v adv* also rare **take about**
to greatly surprise and confuse (someone): [T1a (*usu. pass., simple tenses*)] *His sudden change of opinion took us all aback. They were taken aback by his unexpected appearance.*

**take aboard** *v adv* → **come aboard, go aboard, go ashore, take ashore, take on**[1] (1)
to carry (something) or go with (someone) onto a ship or boat: [X9 + ABOARD] *No dangerous explosives may be taken aboard. The children were so excited to be taken aboard for the first time.*

**take about**[1] *v adv*
**1** to show (someone) round a place, as on a visit: [X9 + ABOUT] *When I come to stay, there's no need to take me about seeing the sights, I'll be quite happy just to share your ordinary family life.* → **get about**[1] (1), **get round**[1] (1), **go about**[1] (1)
*__2__ → TAKE ABACK

**take about**[2] *v prep*
**1 take action about** to do something about (something or someone): *The government has been asked to take action about the continuing rise in unemployment.*
**2 take one's time about: a** to work at (something or usu. doing something) slowly and carefully: *I like to take my time about preparing a meal for important visitors.* **b** *not fml* to

be too slow about (something or usu. doing something): *You've taken your time about getting here, haven't you?* → **take over**² (8)

**3 take umbrage about** to be offended by (something): *I'm afraid she took umbrage about your remark, which I know was not intended to be rude.* → **take at** (10)

**take abroad** *v adv* → **get abroad** (1), **go abroad**
to allow (someone) to go with one to a foreign country; carry (something) overseas: [X9 + ABROAD (*with*)] *Shall we be able to afford to take the whole family abroad for our holiday this year? You have to have special permission to take your car abroad.*

**take across** *v adv; prep* → **come over** (3), etc., **go across**², etc., **pull over**² (1), etc.
to help or cause (someone) to cross (water, a road, etc.); move (something) across (a space or object): [X9 + ACROSS (*to*)/*across*] *These bigger boats take more people across (to the island) in half the time, and can also take cars across. Thank you, young man, for taking me across that busy road.*

**take after** *v prep*
**1** to swallow (something) after (a point in time): [T1 + *after*] *Take this medicine after meals.*
*__2__ to look or behave like (an older relative): [T1 (*no pass., simple tenses*)] *The boy takes after his father, he has the same red hair, big feet, and quick temper.*
*__3__ to begin to chase (someone): [T1 (*no pass., simple tenses*)] *The policeman dropped his load and took after the criminal, but failed to catch him.*

***take against** *v prep*
**1** to dislike (someone), esp. at the beginning of a relationship: [T1 (*no pass., simple tenses*)] *I've never done anything to offend her, but she just took against me from the start.* → **take kindly** (2), **take to** (3)
**2 take action against** to begin to work or do something against (something or someone) so as to prevent or stop it or him/her: *It's time someone took action against the rising crime rate in this city. Action will be taken against anyone who breaks the law.*
**3 take sides against** to oppose (someone), as in argument or fight: *Why do you always take sides against me in a family argument? I'm not necessarily at fault. The two elder boys always took sides against their younger brothers, and so got the best of any quarrel.* → **side against, side with, take with** (7)

**take along** *v adv* → **come along** (2), etc.
to cause (someone or something) to go with one; take (something or someone) in the same direction (as oneself): [X9 + ALONG (*to, with*)] *I took my music along (with me), but no one asked me to sing. Why don't you take your mother along (to the concert)? I'm sure she would enjoy it.*

***take amiss** *v adv*
**1** *fml* to misunderstand (something): [T1b (*simple tenses*)] *I think you have taken my words amiss, that was not my meaning.*
**2 take it amiss** to be hurt or offended by (something), esp. by mistaking its intention: [(*simple tenses*)] *I shall take it amiss if you don't come to my party. Please don't take it amiss that I treated your article so severely in my report; it was a mark of respect for its worth.* → **take ill**²

**take apart** *v adv*
**1** to take (someone) on one side, as for private conversation: [X9 + APART] *I saw that he was taking members of his family apart and giving them instructions.* → **draw aside** (2), **go aside, pull aside** (2), **take aside, take on**² (11), **take to** (20)
*__2__ to (cause to) separate into its parts: [T1b] *We had to take the whole engine apart to discover the cause of the trouble.* [IØ (*simple tenses*)] *Does this toy take apart so that the child can find out how it works?* —**take-apart** *adj* → **pull apart** (1), etc.
*__3__ *not fml* to punish or defeat (someone) severely: [T1b] *An experienced fighter like that should be able to take his young opponent apart in a few rounds.*
*__4__ to find severe fault with (something such as someone's work): [T1a] *Tom's latest book has been taken apart by the newspapers. Don't take her performance apart as unkindly as you did last time, even if it is bad; it could destroy her.* → **pull apart** (2), **pull to**² (3), **rend to** (2), **rip to** (2), **take to** (7b), **tear apart** (3), **tear to** (2)
*__5__ *not fml* to scold (someone): [T1b] *I'll take that boy apart when he gets back: look what he's done now!* → **tell off** (1), etc.

**take around**¹ *v adv* → **TAKE ROUND**¹

**take around**² *v prep* → **TAKE ROUND**²

***take as** *v prep*
**1** to understand or suppose (something) to be (something): [X1 (*usu. simple tenses*)] *Am I to take this excuse as a reason for your behaviour? These first six books can be taken as the pattern of the whole work.* [X7 (*usu. simple tenses*)] *Can we take it as agreed that we accept the plan?*
**2 take something as read: a** to accept something such as a report of an earlier meeting, supposing that all members present have read it: [*simple tenses*] *Can we take the report as read and go on to the first new business?* **b** to suppose acceptance or the likelihood of anything: [*simple tenses*] *I think we can take it as read that the government will call an election this autumn.*

**take ashore** *v adv* → **come aboard, go aboard, go ashore, take aboard, take on** (1)
to take (someone or something) off a ship and onto land: [X9 + ASHORE] *Make sure that you take all your possessions ashore with you and leave nothing on the ship, as she will sail to another country tomorrow. Take the young man ashore with you, and make sure he never sets foot on my ship again!*

**take aside** *v adv* → **draw aside** (2), **go aside, pull aside** (2), **take apart** (1), **take on²** (11), **take to** (20)
to lead (someone) away from someone else or a group, usu. for private conversation: [X9 + ASIDE] *Try to take the chairman aside after the meeting and discover his real opinion.*

***take at** *v prep*
**1** to aim (an action or a movement of force or speed) in the direction of (something or someone): [D1] *I took a shot at the passing bird, but missed. You might clear the jump if you take a run at it. If we all take a push at the car, we might get it out of the mud.*
**2 take aim at: a** to point something such as a gun, towards (something or someone): *Taking careful aim at the top branch, I shot it in two pieces.* → **aim at** (1), **shoot at** (1) **b** to make an effort towards (something or doing something); decide to reach (something): *You have to take aim at what you want and then be determined to get it. Last year we took aim at saving more money, and succeeded.* → **aim at** (2), etc.
**3 take someone at a disadvantage** to be in a favourable position relative to someone else: *Quick to take his opponent at a disadvantage, and rarely making mistakes of his own, the tennis player won the prize in an excellent game.*
**4 take something at its face value** to believe the worth of something as stated, without enquiry: *Can the chairman's offer be taken at its face value, or is he trying to gain some political advantage for himself?*
**5 take fright at** to become suddenly afraid of (something): *This horse is so nervous he will take fright at his own shadow, so be careful.*
**6 take a hand at: a** to join a group in (a card game): *Please take a hand at cards, we're one player short.* **b** to help or join someone (in doing something): *If we all take a hand at digging the garden, it'll soon be done.*
**7 take a look at** to examine (something or someone): *Take a look at this strange object hidden behind the fireplace! Jane has been sick again this morning, so I've asked the doctor to take a look at her.* → **look at** (3)
**8 take offence at** to be offended by (something): *Please don't take offence at her manner, she doesn't mean to be rude. She's so sensitive that she will take offence at the most harmless remark.*
**9 take a running jump at: a** to run towards (something) in order to jump over it: *You could jump over the gate if you took a running jump at it.* **b** *not fml* to be too eager to start (something or doing something), often with the possibility of failing: *I wish the boy wouldn't take a running jump at every job he does, he never finishes one of them properly. The firm took a running jump at producing these fashionable objects, but they soon fell out of favour and the company lost a lot of money.*
**10 take umbrage at** to be offended by (something): *I'm afraid she took umbrage at your remark, which I know was not intended to be rude.* → **take about²** (3)
**11 take someone at his word** to believe exactly what someone says: *I'll take you at your word, but make sure that you have a better excuse next time. Can any politician be taken at his word?*

***take away** *v adv*
**1** to remove (something): [T1] *I've just come in to take the dirty dishes away. Please don't take your hand away, it makes me think that you don't like me. If you can move up behind the gunman you may be able to take his gun away without a fight. These books are for reading in the library, and may not be taken away.* → **drag away** (1), **drag off, jerk away, pull away** (1), **take away from** (1), **yank away**
**2** to lead (someone) to another place; remove (someone): [T1 (*to*)] *I'd like to take you away for a holiday, but I don't know when we shall be able to afford it. That school is terrible; I shall take the child away at once. The prisoner was taken away by an armed guard. You have no business taking another man's wife away with you.* → **go away** (1), etc.
**3** to cause (something such as a feeling or attention) to cease: [T1] *This drug should help to take the pain away. I'm sorry, my attention was taken away for a moment.* → **go away** (3), **go off¹** (3), **pass away** (2), **pass off** (1), **wear off** (3)
**4** to lessen a larger number by removing (a smaller number): [T1 (*simple tenses*)] *27 take away 3 leaves 24.* → **subtract from, take away from** (3), **take from** (2)
**5** to take (food) home or outside from a restaurant: [T1 (*usu. simple tenses*)] *I'd like three pieces of chicken to take away, please.* —**take-away** *n, adj* → **send out for, take out** (7)
**6** to cause someone to lack (something); be in the habit of seizing something from people: [T1 (*from*)] *No government shall take away the rights of the native people. Don't let him take away your freedom to think for yourself.* [IØ] *Under the present tax system, the government gives with one hand and takes away with the other.*
**7 take someone's breath away** *not fml* to surprise someone very much, often in a favourable sense: [(*simple tenses*)] *The shock of the news quite took my breath away. The view from the top of the hill will take your breath away.*

***take away from** *v adv prep*
**1** to remove (something) from (usu. someone or a place): [T1] *Take that box of matches away from the baby! The police over-powered the gunman and took his gun away from him. When he took his finger away from the knot, it*

*all came undone. I saw him taking the car away from the house.* → **get away from** (1), **take away** (1), **take from** (1)

**2** to lead or carry (someone) away from (usu. someone or a place): [T1] *I shall take the children away from that school at once! I shall not forgive the man who took my wife away from me. Can't you take me away from this cold and dirty city? Sadly, I watched the train taking my loved ones away from me.* → **get away from** (1)

**3** to remove (a smaller number) from (a larger number): [T1 (*usu. simple tenses*)] *If you take 3 away from 27 it leaves 24.* → **subtract from, take away** (4), **take from** (2)

**4** to remove (something such as a quality) from (someone who had it): [T1 (*often simple tenses*)] *No government should take their rights away from the native people. No one shall take my life away from me!* → **take from** (3)

**5** to lessen the effective value of (something): [T1 (*no pass., simple tenses*)] *The fact that you had help does not take away from your success. His refusal to accept the prize does not take away from his success in winning it.* → **detract from, take from** (10)

**take back** *v adv*

**1** to return (something), as to a place or owner: [X9 + BACK (*to*)] *I have to take these books back to the library; do you want any more? I shall take these goods back to the shop, I'm not satisfied with them.* → **put back** (2), etc.

**2** to lead or carry (someone) on a return journey: [X9 + BACK (*to*)] *Will you take the children back to school this afternoon, or shall I? Don't worry, I'll take you back to your room without anyone seeing you. This bus will take you back to the city.* → **go back** (2), etc.

***3** to accept (something) in return: [T1] *The shop has promised to take back any unsatisfactory goods.*

***4** to allow (usu. a wife or husband) to return to a marriage: [T1] *It's very sad; after a year's separation, Mary decided to return to Jim, but he refused to take her back.* → **have back** (2)

***5** to repeat (something being practised): [T1 (*to*)] *Let's take that scene back to the beginning and get it right this time.*

***6** to admit that one was wrong in (something one said): [T1 (*simple tenses*)] *I take back my unkind remarks, I see that they were not justified.*

***7** to remind (someone, usu. oneself) (of an earlier time): [T1 (*to*) (*simple tenses*)] *The smell of new bread takes me back to my childhood. My! How that tune takes me back!* → **carry back** (2), **go back** (5), **go back to** (4)

***8** esp. *AmE* to lend (money for buying one's own house): [T1 (*usu. simple tenses*)] *The seller will take back the mortgage.* —**take-back** *n, adj*

**take before** *v prep*

**1** to make (someone) appear on a charge in (a court of law) or to face (a judge): [X9 + *before*] *You will be taken before the judge on Thursday morning.* → **bring before** (1), etc.

***2** to send (something such as an idea) for approval by (someone or a group in power): [D1] *The director intends to take your suggestion before the rest of the Board at their next meeting.* → **put before** (2), etc.

**take below** *v adv* → **be below**[1] (2), **go below, send below**

to lead (someone) or carry (something) downstairs on a ship or boat: [X9 + BELOW] *Take her below if she's feeling sick. Take these lifebelts below, we shan't be needing all these.*

**take between** *v prep*

**1** to seize (something) in the middle space dividing (two things): [X9 + *between*] *Take the wool between your first and third fingers, and then put it over the hook. Taking the rope between his teeth, he hung high over the ring in the big tent.*

**2 take the bit between one's teeth** to start a job eagerly and actively, with keenness and determination: *Once he takes the bit between his teeth, he won't stop until the job is finished, no matter what it costs him.* → **get between** (4)

**take by** *v prep*

**1** to seize (something or someone) by holding (a part): [X9 + *by*] *He took me by the hand and led me to his room. Make sure that you take the hot pan by its handle, or you'll burn yourself. Taking the elephant by its ear, he guided it through the woods.* → **pull by**

**2 take the bull by the horns** to face danger or threat boldly: *Called to the director's office, I decided that the best way was to take the bull by the horns and admit it was all my mistake.*

**3 take something/someone by storm: a** to conquer (a place) by force of arms, often suddenly: *The town was taken by storm last night; we had too few soldiers to defend it.* **b** *not fml* to have a marked effect on something or someone; conquer something or someone easily, as by making them keen; be very successful with something or someone: *Her wonderful performance has taken the public by storm. A product as good as this should take the shops by storm!*

**4 take someone by surprise** to catch someone off guard; surprise someone: [(*usu. simple tenses*)] *Your good examination results have taken all the teachers by surprise; they didn't expect you to do so well! Every year, winter takes the English by surprise, as if there had never been one before!* → **take unawares**

**take down** *v adv*

**1** to move (something) to a lower level; remove (something) from a higher position: [X9 + DOWN] *When do we take the Christmas lights down? Please take these envelopes down to the office on the floor below. The librarian* *took the book down from its shelf and handed it to the reader. We must take the curtains down for cleaning next week.* → **bring down** (1), **get down** (1), **send down** (1)

*__2__ to take (something such as a machine) to pieces, often for repair or cleaning; be made so as to take apart: [T1] *I shall have to take the engine down completely, so it will be a long job.* [IØ (*simple tenses*)] *Does this gun take down easily?* —**takedown** *n, adj* → **strip down** (2), **tear down**[1] (3)

*__3__ to pull (something such as a building) to pieces, usu. to destroy or remove it: [T1] *It's sad to see the old theatre being taken down to make way for a new shopping centre. When the building is complete, its supports can be taken down. Don't take the framework down, it's holding up the wall! The famous old bridge was taken down the rebuilt in the desert.* → **come down** (3), **pull down** (3)

*__4__ to record (something) in writing: [T1] *Go to the meeting and take down everything that the chairman says. I must warn you that anything you say may be taken down and repeated in court.* → **write down** (1), etc.

**5 take someone down (a peg or two)** *not fml* to make someone humble, show someone in an unfavourable light: [*usu. simple tenses*] *She has too high an opinion of herself: it's time someone took her down a peg or two!* → **bring down** (14)

***take easy** *v adj* → **go easy** (1), **go slow** (2), **slow down** (2)

*not fml* to refuse to be worried by (usu. life) esp. in the phrs. **take it/things easy:** [T1b] *Take it easy, there's no need to be nervous. It's nice to take things easy for a change! You'll be much happier if you learn to take life easy.*

**take for** *v prep*

**1** to lead (someone or an animal) out on (a walk, drive, etc.): [X9 + *for*] *Which of us is going to take the dog for a walk? May I take your sister for a ride in my new car? It'll do Mother good to be taken for a drive in the country.* → **go for** (1)

**2** to accept (a price) in exchange for (goods): [T1 + *for* (*simple tenses*)] *How much will you take for the painting?* → **pay for** (1), etc.

*__3__ to suppose (someone or something) wrongly to be (someone or something else): [D1 (*simple tenses*)] *I'm sorry, I took you for your brother, you're so much alike. The traveller took the house for a hotel, and the owner's daughter for a servant. Do you take me for a fool? I've often been taken for my daughter, to my delight.* → **confuse with** (2), **mistake for**

*__4__ *not fml* to rob or cheat (someone) of (usu. a sum of money): [D1] *The old lady was taken for all her money. We should be able to take the old man for $1,000.*

**5 take credit for** to receive the honour resulting from (something or doing something); state that one is responsible for (something usu. good): *You have no right to take credit for inventing the excellent system now in use, when it was someone else's work. Many countries try to take credit for the invention of the telephone. The terrorist group are taking credit for the murder of their enemy.* → **credit with** (2), **give for** (5), **give to** (8)

**6 take something/someone for granted** to treat something or someone as unimportant; expect the presence or activity of something or someone without reward: *Mothers sometimes get tired of being taken for granted by their children. You can't take fine weather for granted in this country. Why do you take it for granted that you will fail?*

**7 take revenge for** to punish someone for (a wrong done to oneself): [*usu. simple tenses*] *The villagers have sworn to take revenge for the murder of the child. The Prince felt it his duty to take revenge for the murder of his father.* → **get even,** etc.

**8 take someone for a ride: a** *not fml* to fool or cheat someone: *She'll believe anything, she's too easy to take for a ride!* **b** *not fml* to murder someone: *The criminals intend to take you for a ride unless you get out of town tonight.*

**9 take thought for** to consider (something such as a matter) seriously: [*usu. simple tenses*] *He took no thought for the future, and ended up penniless.*

**10 what do you take me for?** *not fml* what kind of (silly or bad) person do you think I am? *I didn't take that money. What do you take me for?*

**11 take someone's word for it/that** to believe what someone says: [*usu. simple tenses, often future*] *I've not seen the proof myself, but I'll take your word for that. Are you prepared to take his word for it without examining the papers?*

**take from** *v prep*

**1** to remove (something) from (usu. someone or a place): [X9 + *from*] *Take that box of matches from the baby! The police overpowered the gunman and took his gun from him. I saw him taking the car from the house.* → **get away from** (1), **take away from** (1)

**2** to remove (a smaller number) from (a larger number): [X9 + *from* (*usu. simple tenses*)] *If you take 3 from 27 it leaves 24.* → **subtract from, take away from** (3)

**3** to remove (something such as quality) from (someone who had it): [X9 + *from* (*often simple tenses*)] *No government should be allowed to take their rights from the native people. No one shall take my life from me!* → **take away from** (4)

**4** to choose or translate (words) from (a book, language, etc.): [X9 + *from* (*often simple tenses*)] *Our reading today is taken from the Bible. His story isn't original, he took it from a book. "Not a translation—only taken from the French."* (R.B. Sheridan, *The Critic*) → **obtain from,** etc.

**5** to accept suffering as a result of (something

such as treatment) by (someone): [T1 + *from*] *I will not take any more rudeness from your mother, she can leave my house!*

*__6__ to repeat or practise (something) starting from (a place): [D1 (*usu. simple tenses*)] *No, that piece needs to be sung faster; let's take it from the beginning again. We'll take that scene from page 27. Take the poem* (*again*) *from the beginning.* → **go from** (3)

*__7__ to receive (a name, title, etc.) copying (something or someone): [D1 (*simple tenses*)] *The ship took its name from a famous rock near the harbour. The book 'David Copperfield' takes its title from the name of the young man whose life story it tells.*

*__8__ to receive (something such as a blow) from (usu. someone): [D1 (*often simple tenses*)] *I took a nasty knock from the thief as he ran away.*

*__9__ to accept (something such as a suggestion) from (someone): [D1] *I don't have to take advice from you.*

*__10__ to lessen the effect of (something usu. good): [T1 (*no pass., simple tenses*)] *His refusal to accept the prize does not take from his success in winning it. There are a few disadvantages that take from the perfection of the house.* → **detract from, take away from** (5)

*__11__ to understand (usu. that something...) from (something or someone): [D5 + *it* (*simple tenses*)] *I take it from your silence that you agree. I take it from the director that you are leaving the firm.*

**12 be taken from** (of a relative) to die, leaving (someone): *I'm sorry to hear that your mother has been taken from you at such an early age.*

**13 take one's cue from: a** (in theatre or music) to know when to have one's turn, as to speak, move, play, or sing, by seeing or hearing (someone or something): *Take your cue from the lighting change; when it begins to get darker on stage, move across to the window and begin your long speech. We don't have all the music here, and will have to take our cue from the drum beat. We can all rise together if we take our cue from the leader in the front row.* **b** to regard (something) as a signal to begin: *Taking his cue from the silence of the crowd, the speaker began to attack his opponent.*

**14 take heart from** to feel encouraged by (something): *In spite of a bad start to the year, the company can take heart from the improved sales figures of the last quarter.*

**15 take it from here** *not fml* to continue something already begun, usu. by someone else: *I've got the job started, now you can take it from here!*

**16 take it from me** believe me, I know what I am saying: [*usu. imper.*] *Take it from me, this product will be a success.*

**17 take one's pick from** to have a free choice among (many good things, people, or a group): *Take your pick from the whole collection. I will give you any piece you choose. Of course that team always wins, they can take their pick from the best players in the country.* → **take of** (17)

***take hard** *v adj*

to suffer severely because of (something): [T1b] *'How has Mrs Hill been since her son's death?' 'Oh, I'm afraid she's taking it* (*very*) *hard and is still sunk in grief even after all these months.' The villagers took the news hard when they learnt that the missing child had been given up as lost.*

**take home** *v adv*

**1** to lead (someone) or carry (something) to one's home: [X9 + HOME] *Are we allowed to take the books home, or do we have to read them in the library? Have you taken your boyfriend home yet to meet your parents?* → **bring home** (1), **get back** (2), **get home** (1), **go home** (1)

*__2__ to receive (actual money) out of one's pay after taxes, etc.: [T1] *After taxes and unemployment and health insurance, these workers take home less than £60 a week each.* —**take-home** *adj*

***take ill[1]** *v adj* → **fall ill, fall sick, go sick, report sick, take sick**

to (cause to) become unwell, often suddenly: [T1 (*usu. pass.*)] *The director was taken ill in the middle of the meeting, and had to go to hospital.* [IØ (*simple tenses*)] *not fml Jane took ill again yesterday, and won't be at school for a few days.*

***take ill[2]** *v adv* → **take amiss** (2)

*to hurt or be offended by (something): [T1b (*often simple tenses*)] *When he heard of his dismissal, he took the news ill. I take it ill of you to have told my secret.*

**take in[1]** *v adv*

**1** to lead (someone) or carry (something) indoors or into a room: [X9 + IN] *Take the washing in, it's raining! When the letters have all been opened, take them in to the director. Please take the children in, it's getting too cold out here. 'May I take you in to dinner?' he said, offering the lady his arm.* → **bring in** (1), **come in** (1), **get in[1]** (2), **go in[1]** (1), **send in** (1), **wheel in** (1)

*__2__ to receive (something such as water or air) inside: [T1a] *It's good to stand on top of the hill and take in deep breaths of fresh air. The boat is taking in water!*

*__3__ to receive (someone) in one's home with welcome, as a guest: [T1] *Now that his parents are dead, who will take the boy in?* → **take into** (2)

*__4__ to receive (someone) in one's home as a paying guest: [T1] *Some of the local people take in students to add to their income.*

*__5__ to accept (someone) as a worker in the same business: [T1 (*to*)] *The firm may take you in just to please your uncle.* → **take into** (3)

*__6__ to receive (work) to be done in the home: [T1] *Mrs Gardener has taken in washing for many years now.*

***7** to collect (something such as money): [T1] *If this warm weather continues, the farmers will be able to take the crops in a week earlier than usual. It costs almost as much to take in the new taxes as they will produce in income for the government. The shop takes in twice as much money every day as it used to.* → **be in**[1] (9), **bring in** (2), (3), etc., **come in** (3), **get in**[1] (5)

***8** to receive (a newspaper) delivered regularly: [T1] *Which newspaper do you take in?*

***9** to notice (something): [T1 (*usu. simple tenses*)] *It was amusing to see his surprise as he took in the scene.*

***10** to fully understand (something, esp. spoken words): [T1 (*simple tenses, nonassertive*)] *I listened to the speech carefully, but still I couldn't take it all in. Tell me your wonderful news again, I can't take it in! Could you take in what he was saying?* → **go in**[1] (7)

***11** to believe (something false): [T1] *The poor man takes in all the lies she tells him.*

***12** to deceive (someone): [T1 (*often pass.*)] *The salesman finds it easy to take in old ladies and persuade them to give him their money. Were you really taken in by an old trick like that?* —**take-in** *n*

***13** to make (clothing) narrower: [T1] *I've lost so much weight that I've had to take in all my clothes.* → **let out** (8)

***14** *naut* to lessen the total size of (a sail) presented to the wind: [T1] *When the wind blows hard, we have to take in sail.* → **take up** (27)

***15** to include (usu. a place or places): [T1a (*usu. simple tenses*)] *The British Empire once took in a quarter of the world. While in Italy, the tour takes in the famous old ruins.*

***16** *AmE not fml* to visit (a place of amusement): [T1a] *What shall we do while we're here on holiday? Shall we take in a show?*

***17** to seize (a possible criminal) and take him to a police station: [T1] *Are you taking me in?* → **bring in** (6), **pull in** (9), **yank in**

**take in**[2] *v prep*

**1** to lead (someone) or carry (something) into (a space) or through (an opening): [X9 + *in*] *Would you take these cups in the kitchen as you're going that way? Let me take you in the back door so that the others won't see you.* → **go in**[2] (2), **take into** (1)

**2** to give (someone) a ride in (a vehicle); carry (something) in (a vehicle): [T1 + *in*] *I can take two of you in my car, if Jim will take the food in his car.* → **go in**[2] (1)

**3** to like to have (something added) in (food or drink): [T1 + *in*] *Do you take cream in your coffee?*

**4** to seize or hold (something or someone) in (usu. one's arms): [X9 + *in*] *Taking Mary in his arms, he kissed her fondly.*

**5** to catch (an animal) in (something such as a trap): [T1 + *in*] *Do you take many small animals in these traps?*

**6** to hit (someone) in (part of the body): [X9 + *in* (*usu. simple tenses*)] *The blow took him in the face.* → **take on**[2] (3)

**7 take delight/pleasure in** to enjoy (usu. something or doing something): *Old people take pleasure in warm sunshine even more than younger people. I don't see what pleasure the young people take in such loud music. I take such pleasure in watching the children grow up.* → **delight in, rejoice at, rejoice in** (1), **rejoice over**

**8 take something in good part** to enjoy something such as a joke against oneself, with good humour: *The children played a silly trick on my visitor, but luckily he took it in good part and wasn't annoyed.*

**9 take a hand in** to be partly the cause of or have an effect on (something): *The weather takes a hand in most of our plans.* → **be in**[2] (16), **have in**[2] (4), **play in**[2] (4)

**10 take something in hand** to begin to control something: *The plans for the development of the city must be taken in hand by the council before too much building takes place without proper controls.* → **have in**[2] (5), **be in**[2] (16)

**11 take someone in hand** to control someone, as to show him how to behave or act: *That boy will have to be taken in hand by the school if the parents can't control him. We ask each of you to take one new student in hand and show him how the library system works.*

**12 take (an) interest in** to show that one is interested in (something or someone); work actively for (something); be attracted to (someone): *How long have you been taking an interest in children's rights? Jim took an interest in Mary from the first time he saw her. Jane takes no interest in her school work, only in her music. "Decent people do not take interest in politics, or elderly people in sport."* (Ford Madox Ford, *The Good Soldier*)

**13 take one's life in one's hands** to do something risky, often foolishly: *Those climbers are taking their lives in their hands, climbing the north face of the mountain in this weather. If you try complaining to the director while he's in a temper, you could be taking your life in your hands!*

**14 take someone's name in vain** to mention someone without respect: *Who's been taking my name in vain? I do not hold such an opinion. "You shall not take the name of the Lord your God in vain."* (The Bible)

**15 take part in** to join or act in (an activity): *The whole school will take part in the concert.*

**16 take pride in** to be proud of (someone, something, or doing something): [*usu. simple tenses*] *You can take pride in your success, you earned it. The parents took such pride in the boy when he improved his behaviour. I take pride in always being on time for work.*

**17 take refuge in** to find shelter or protection

in (a place, activity, or doing something): *It's beginning to rain; look, we can take refuge in the hut. I sometimes think that perhaps she takes refuge in her illness to avoid her responsibilities. When I am sad, I take refuge in remembering happier times. He took refuge in telling lies.*

**take into** *v prep*

**1** to lead (someone) or carry (something) into (a space): [X9 + *into*] *Would you take these cups into the kitchen as you pass? Tomorrow I'll take you into town and we'll look at the shops.* → **go into** (1), **take in**[2] (1)

***2** to accept (someone) into (one's home): [D1] *Many of the townspeople took the foreign visitors into their homes, and made them feel welcome.* → **take in**[1] (3)

***3** to admit (someone) into (a business) as a worker: [D1] *It's easy for you to find a job when you know that your uncle will take you into the family firm.* → **take in**[1] (5)

**4 take something into account/consideration** to consider something seriously; make allowance for something: *When you're planning a garden party you'll have to take the weather into account. The prisoner's good behaviour will be taken into consideration when the length of his imprisonment is being decided.* → **take of** (1)

**5 take a child into care** to make arrangements for a child to live in an official home, not with his family: *Since the parents' sudden death in the accident, we have no choice but to take the children into care.*

**6 take someone into one's confidence** to trust someone, as with one's secrets: *I'll take you into my confidence as I know you can be trusted not to tell anyone else.* → **confide in**

**7 take it into one's head that** *not fml* to get a fixed idea that (something); start to believe that (something), often mistakenly: [*usu. simple tenses*] *Why did she take it into her head that I was to blame? I wasn't even there at the time!* → **get into** (20)

**8 take it into one's head to do something** *not fml* to decide to do something, often because of a sudden idea: [*usu. simple tenses*] *Why would she take it into her head to blame me? It wasn't my fault. Jim took it into his head to give up his good job and go off for a holiday by himself.*

**9 take the law into one's own hands** *not fml* to act as an unofficial judge, making decisions, giving punishments, etc.: *You can't take the law into your own hands; you must tell the police who you think the murderer is, and let them punish him. Tired of waiting for justice from the courts, the townspeople decided to take the law into their own hands and catch the bank robber themselves.*

**take kindly** *v adv*

**1 take it kindly (of)** to consider (someone) to be doing a favour: [*simple tenses, usu.* + *would*] *I would take it kindly of you to move your car from in front of my house. I would take it kindly if you would send my letters on to my new address for me.*

**2 take kindly to** to begin to like (someone, something, or an activity); accept easily or willingly: *He didn't take kindly to his new responsibilities.* → **take against** (1), **take to** (3)

**take of** *v prep*

**1 take account of** to consider or pay attention to (something or someone): *Did you take account of the number of guests when you were planning the seating for the party? I took account of the time as we left the house.* → **take into** (4)

**2 take advantage of** to make use of (something or someone) for one's own gain: *Such a skilled tennis player knows how to take advantage of his opponent's chief weakness. It's unfair to take advantage of your father's good nature. I think she's taking advantage of me, using me for her own gains.*

**3 take care of: a** to look after (something, someone, or oneself); attend to the needs of (something or someone); see that (something or someone) receives proper treatment: *Don't worry, I'll take care of you. The wood will last longer if you take (proper) care of it.* → **care for** (4, 5), **look after** (2), **see after: b** to be careful about (something dangerous); watch out for (something dangerous): [*usu. simple tenses*] *The children must be warned to take (more) care of the trains as they cross the tracks on their way to school.* **c** *not fml* to pay for (something): [*usu. simple tenses*] *Here's a £5 note—that should take care of the drinks. Have the tickets been taken care of?* **d** to deal with (something such as a difficulty): [*often simple tenses*] *This new law should take care of the trouble we have been having with men who beat their wives. Each factory has to have special machinery to take care of dangerous chemical wastes.* **e** esp. *AmE not fml* to give money to (someone) to persuade him to do something wrong, as keep out of a criminal's way: [*often simple tenses*] *Have the police in this area been taken care of yet?* **f** *not fml* to murder or kill (someone or an animal): [*often simple tenses*] *You take care of the guard, and I'll warn the other prisoners to be ready. It's all right, the policeman who's been watching us has been taken care of. The dogs are easily taken care of with poison.*

**4 take charge of: a** to begin to act as the leader of (a group): *The general was asked to take charge of the whole army. Who is to take charge of this class while I'm out?* **b** to begin to control (something or someone): *Someone ought to take charge of that boy and make him behave properly. The young pilot took charge of the plane when his captain became ill during the flight.*

**5 take command of** *often mil* to start performing the duties of leader or controller of (usu. something): *Every officer should be trained to take command of the ship in case of accident.*

**6 take control of** to begin to have power over (something or someone such as a group): *At last the day came when he took (complete) control of the company, by buying all the shares. Take control of yourself, aren't you ashamed? The new government must take control of the country as soon as the election results are clear.* → **have of**[2] (2), **have over** (1)

**7 take a dim/poor view of** *not fml* to regard (something) unfavourably: [*often simple tenses*] *I take a dim view of your action in sending the boy home with no parent present.*

**8 take a fancy to** to attract the attention or liking of (someone): [*usu. simple tenses*] *The public seems to have taken a fancy to the play, it's very popular and has had to be repeated.* → **take to** (14)

**9 take heed of** to pay attention to (someone or something); be guided by (something or someone): [*usu. simple tenses*] *I do not intend to take heed of your school report as I know that it is a poor guide to your actual improvement. You would be wise to take heed of his advice.* → **give to** (12), **pay to** (4)

**10 take hold of** to seize (something or someone): *Take hold of your end of the rope, and we'll pull you up. The child took hold of my hand when he became nervous.* → **catch of, get of** (5), **keep of** (3a), **keep on** (10), **lay of** (1), **lay on**[2] (12), **lose of** (3)

**11 take (one's) leave of** to say goodbye to (someone): *Now I must take my leave of you, I'm already late.*

**12 take leave of one's senses** *not fml* to behave foolishly, as if mad: [*usu. perfect tense*] *Have you taken leave of your senses? Do you know what harm that would do to the firm?*

**13 take the liberty of** to feel free in (doing something) without first asking permission: *I took the liberty of borrowing your pen, I hope you don't mind.*

**14 take note of** to notice and remember (something): *Did you take note of the time as we left the house?*

**15 take notice of: a** to pay attention to (someone or something): *The children always behave wildly when we have visitors, hoping to be taken notice of.* **b** to listen to (someone or his words) with the intention of obeying: *You speak to the boy, he takes more notice of you. You havent't taken notice of my last warning, I see!*

**16 take the opportunity of** to use the chance of (something or doing something): *You should take the opportunity of every job that's offered to you. May I as chairman take the opportunity of thanking you for your interesting talk on cricket. Did you take the opportunity of seeing your aunt while you were in the town?*

**17 take one's pick of** to choose from (a group of things or people): [(*usu. simple tenses*)] *Take your pick of these excellent records at specially reduced prices!* → **take from** (17)

**18 take the place of** to replace (something or someone): [*often simple tenses*] *I know that no one can take the place of your own mother, but I'll do my best to give you a good home. What can take the place of lost happiness?*

**19 take the risk of** to risk (doing something): *If you buy these shares, you take the risk of losing your whole fortune.*

**20 take stock of** to examine the value of (one's affairs, possibilities, etc.): *Many people in middle age begin to take stock of their lives and to search for new meaning in life. Isn't it time to take stock of your position in the firm and see whether it's worth staying with them?*

**21 take a/its toll of** to reduce (something), as in size or strength; harm or weaken something) in a lasting way: *Her last long fever must have taken its toll of her failing health. Last month's severe storm has taken a toll of the value of the fruit crop.*

**take off**[1] *v adv*

**1** to remove (something): [X9 + OFF] *I can't take the lid off, it's stuck! Help me to take this handle off. I asked you not to put hot cups on the piano: take them off at once, please! Last night's strong wind nearly took the roof off! "Some women can't see a telephone without taking the receiver off."* (W. Somerset Maugham, *The Constant Wife*) [L9 + OFF (*simple tenses*)] *The lid takes off to show the contents.* → **come away** (2), **come off**[1] (1), **draw off** (1), **get off**[1] (1), **have off** (1), **pick off** (1), **pluck off, pull off**[1] (1), **yank off** (1)

***2** to remove (clothing or anything on the body): [T1] *I can't take my boots off, they're so tight! I shall never take off this ring which you gave me until I die. Taking off his coat, he jumped into the river to save the drowning child. A gentleman takes his hat off when greeting a lady.* → **draw off** (1), **get off**[1] (1), **pull off**[1] (2), **put off**[1] (1), **put on**[1] (2), **slip off** (3), **slip out of** (3)

***3** to cut off (part of the body such as an arm or leg): [T1] *I'm afraid the disease can't be stopped, so we shall have to take your leg off.*

***4** to save (someone) from a ship and take him to safety: [T1] *Before the ship sank, all the passengers were safely taken off.* → **bring off** (1)

***5** to (cause to) leave or go away: [IØ (*for, to*)] *I'd like to take off for the country as soon as I've finished work tomorrow. I'll take off now, and see you later.* [T1 (*for, to*)] *The director has taken the visitors off to his office. Take yourself off, you're not wanted here. I think I'll take myself off now.* → **go away** (1), etc.

***6** to begin a jump or flight: [IØ (*from*)] *The tiger took off from the ground with a powerful spring. Watch that bird taking off from the branch!*

*7 (of a plane) to rise from the ground: [I0] *It's exciting to feel the plane taking off. We took off so smoothly that the passengers could hardly feel it.* —**takeoff** *n*

*8 to have a starting point: [I0 (*from*)] *The attack will take off from our position near the harbour.* —**take off, taking-off** *adj*

*9 to remove (a train, bus, plane, etc.) from regular operation: [T1] *The early morning train is being taken off for the summer.* → **take out of** (7)

*10 to remove (a play or film) from public performance: [T1] *The play was taken off after only three performances.* → **come off**[1] (8)

*11 to remove (a dish) from a list of food in a restaurant: [T1 (*usu. simple tenses*)] *We have taken the fish off, as it was not good.* → **be off**[1] (6)

*12 to reduce (weight): [T1] *I'm so pleased that I've been able to take off all that weight and get into my good clothes again!* → **put back** (3), **put on**[1] (5)

*13 to reduce a price by (a certain amount or rate): [T1] *Our prices are very good this week; everything has 10% taken off. The government has promised to take off the new tax as soon as possible.*

*14 to take (time) as a holiday from work: [T1] *I'd like to take next Monday off to visit my sister in hospital.* → **get off**[1] (14), **have off** (4)

*15 *not fml* to copy (someone), esp. his speech or manner, as a joke: [T1] *The children do like to take off the new teacher, who has a noticeable manner of walking.* —**takeoff** *n* → **have off** (5), **hit off** (1)

*16 (esp. in cricket) to remove (a player of one's own team) from action on the sports field: [T1] *The captain decided to take Snow off and try a slower bowler.* → **come on**[1] (4), **etc.**

*17 (of an idea) to begin to be successful: [I0 (*often simple tenses*)] *After a slow start, the plan soon took off and was accepted by all the directors. The circle of supply and demand should soon take off as the country's trade position improves.*

*18 *not fml* to become excited or keen: [I0 (*on*)] *We must provide some really interesting new courses where the students can really take off. Many young people take off on loud music.* → **get off**[1] (17)

*19 *AmE* to kill (someone): [T1 (*often pass.*)] *She was taken off by a rare tropical fever some years ago.*

**20 take off the gloves to** to fight or argue with (someone) seriously: *Watch out for trouble when the director takes off the gloves to his Board!*

**21 take off one's hat to: a** to lift the hat from one's head in polite greeting or respect: *I knew that my father regarded me as a woman instead of a girl, the first time he took off his hat to me when we met.* **b** *not fml* to express admiration for (someone): [*usu. first person, present simple tense*] *You've done a remarkably fine job—I take off my hat to you!* → **raise to** (5)

**take off**[2] *v prep*

**1** to remove (something or someone) from (something): [X9 + *off*] *Take your elbows off the table, children! Let me take that piece of thread off your skirt. I'll take the books off the table so that we have room to eat.* [L9 + *off* (*simple tenses*)] *The lid takes off the container to show the contents.* → **come off**[2] (1), **get off**[2] (1), **pull off**[2]

*2 to remove (something such as clothing) from (the body): [D1] *I can't take my boots off my feet, they're too tight! The wind took his hat off his head. I shall never take my ring off my finger.*

*3 to save (someone) from (usu. a ship): [D1] *All the passengers were safely taken off the burning ship.*

*4 to cause (someone or something) to leave (something such as an activity): [D1] *Shall I take your name off the list? The policeman has been taken off the case.* → **come off**[2] (4), **go off**[2] (1)

*5 to remove (a bus, train, plane, etc.) from a regular line of travel: [D1] *The early morning bus will be taken off this route during the summer months.*

*6 to remove (part) of (a price): [D1] *The shop is taking 10% off all dresses this week.*

**7 take the edge off** to soften the effect of (an uncomfortable feeling): *If you don't expect too much, it takes the edge off your disappointment. A piece of cheese will take the edge off your hunger. This small fire only takes the edge off the cold, it doesn't make the room really warm.*

**8 take one's eyes off** to stop looking at or watching (someone or something): [*often simple tenses*] *If you take your eyes off the children, they go wild! Can't you take your eyes off any pretty girl that passes? If I take my eyes off the music for even a moment, I lose my place.*

**9 take the gilt off the gingerbread** *not fml* to spoil the effect of something good: [*often simple tenses*] *Many wives enjoy the early years of marriage and then find that the hard work of caring for the children takes the gilt off the gingerbread.*

**10 take something/someone off someone's hands** to free someone from the care of or responsibility for something or someone: *We shall have to reduce the price if we want this buyer to take the house off our hands. I'd be grateful for someone to take the children off my hands for an afternoon.* → **have on**[2] (12)

**11 take a load/weight off someone's mind/shoulders** to free someone from worrying about something such as a responsibility: [*often simple tenses*] *Thank you for offering to organize the food, that takes (quite) a weight off my mind. A (great) load was taken* *off my shoulders when the children went away to school.*

**12 take one's mind/thoughts off** to stop one worrying or thinking about (someone or something); take one's attention away from (something causing concern): [*often simple tenses*] *Go for a walk or do something active, that should help to take your mind off your troubles. There seemed to be little that Grace could do to take her thoughts off that red-haired boy.* → **have on**[2] (13)

**13 take the smile off one's face** *not fml* to stop one being amused by or feeling good about something, usu. that one should not be laughing at: [*usu. simple tenses*] *It'll take the smile off your face when you hear the results of the competition that you were so certain of winning!*

**14 take the weight off one's feet/legs** *not fml* to sit down and rest: *After a whole day standing at work, it's good to take the weight off my feet when I get home.* → **get off**[2] (14)

**15 take years off** *not fml* to make (someone) feel younger, fitter, or happier: [*often simple tenses*] *The doctor is so pleased about Jim's loss of weight, and says it will take years off him. Just seeing you again takes years off me.* → **put on**[2] (42)

**take on**[1] *v adv*

**1** to lead (someone) or carry (something) on board a ship, plane, etc.: [X9 + ON] *Each passenger is allowed to take on one small suitcase to fit under the plane seat. Can we take the children on, or are they too young?* → **take aboard**[1]

**2** to carry (someone) further on a journey: [X9 + ON (*to*)] *When you get to the town, another bus will take you on (to where you want to go). This is as far as we go; you have to get someone to meet you and take you on.* → **go on to** (1)

***3** (usu. of a vehicle) to obtain a supply of (something or people): [T1a] *The train stops here to take on water. We can't take on any more passengers, the bus is full.* → **take up** (11)

***4** to accept (work, responsibility, etc.): [T1] *I think you've taken on as much as you can do this year, please don't start any other activity. The doctor says that Jim should take on much less heavy work.*

***5** to rent (a home): [T1] *We've taken on a house in the country for the summer.*

***6** to employ (a worker); accept (a pupil): [T1] *The factory has to take on 1,000 additional workers in order to complete the contract on time. Jane showed such promise as a singer that the famous teacher agreed to take her on, although she was so young.*

***7** to accept (someone) as an opponent in a competition or fight: [T1 (*at*)] *It was brave of you to take on a man twice your size. Would you take her on at tennis? Now that the government has defeated the employers, it can take on the unions.*

***8** to seem or begin to have (a quality, form, or appearance): [T1a (*usu. simple tenses*)] *His face took on the look of a hunted animal. These insects can take on the colour of their background, so that their enemies can't see them. His dreams took on the quality of reality. As the word was repeated over and over again, it began to take on a different meaning.*

***9** *not fml* to become fashionable or popular: [IØ (*simple tenses*)] *The new style didn't take on, so it was quickly dropped.* → **catch on**[1] (1)

***10** *not fml* to become excited; express anxiety, anger, or grief, as shouting, weeping, etc.: [IØ (SO) (*simple tenses*)] *Mother did take on when she heard the terrible news. Don't take on so, he'll soon come back.* → **carry on** (6)

**take on/upon**[2] *v prep*

**1** to lead (someone) or carry (something) on or onto (something such as a vehicle): [X9 + *on/upon*] *Each passenger is allowed to take one case on the plane, if it is small enough to fit under the seat. I shall have to take Jane on the bus, it's too far to walk to the music teacher's place. Taking the load on his back, he struggled forward.*

**2** to lead (someone) or carry (something) with one on a journey for (a purpose): [X9 + *on/upon*] *The theatre company has decided to take three plays on tour. Do we have to take the children on holiday with us, or can we make some other arrangement for them?* → **go on**[2] (1), **send on**[2]

**3** to hit (someone) on (part of the body): [X9 + *on/upon* (*usu. simple tenses*)] *The blow took him on the nose.* → **take in**[2] (6)

**4 take action on** to perform whatever is necessary to fulfil (something such as an idea): *Now that the committee has made its decision, how soon can the directors take action on it?*

**5 take a chance/gamble on** to risk usu. a hope of (something, doing something, or someone or something doing something): *I don't know whether we have enough money to last the whole holiday as we have planned, but I'm prepared to take a chance on it. You can put your money in a safe savings plan, or take a gamble on getting a higher rate of interest by putting it into high-risk shares. The train should have left by now, but I'll take a chance on its being late, and run to the station in the hope of catching it.*

**6 take something (right) on the chin** *not fml* to accept a blow or disappointment bravely: *He had not expected to fail the examination, but he took it (right) on the chin like the man he is. It takes many years to learn to take life's blows on the chin.*

**7 take a (firm) grip/hold on oneself** to control oneself, esp. the expression of one's feelings such as sadness or anxiety: *Take a firm grip on yourself, there's really not much to be afraid of. I had to take a hold on myself when facing the director for the first time.* → **get on**[2] (7)

**8 take it upon one(self) to do something** to

accept the responsibility for doing something: *You shouldn't take it upon yourself to judge all men. Don't blame me for your difficulties; you took it upon yourself to attempt this, no one forced you. If you have a child, you take it upon yourself to provide for his future.*

**9 take pity on** to sympathize with (someone or his suffering), often so as to take action to help: *How can anyone fail to take pity on those children dying of hunger in distant lands? She prayed that God would take pity on her suffering and end her life.*

**10 take revenge on** to repay (someone) for a wrong done to oneself: [*usu. simple tenses*] *The Prince felt it his duty to take revenge on his uncle for the murder of his father.* → **get even,** etc.

**11 take someone on one side** to lead someone away from a group, as for private conversation: *Try to find a chance to take the director on one side after the meeting, and discover his real opinion.* → **draw aside** (2), **go aside, pull aside** (2), **take apart** (1), **take aside, take to** (20)

**12 take a (firm) stand on** to act firmly on one's judgment about (a matter or doing something): *The government decided to take a firm stand on admitting more foreigners to the country. The United States is now taking a stand on human rights.* → **take over²** (7)

**13 take something on trust** to believe something without proof: *I can't show you anything to prove my story, you'll just have to take it on trust.*

**take out** *v adv*

**1** to lead (someone or an animal) or carry (something) outside a room, building, etc.: [X9 + OUT (*of*)] *The building is burning—take the horses out, quickly! Will you take the dog out for a walk, or shall I? Please take the children out (of this room), their noise is making my head ache. When the weather gets warmer, we'll take the chairs out and have tea in the garden.* → **carry out** (1), **go out** (1), etc., **put out** (2)

*__2__ to remove (something), as from material in which it is fixed: [T1 (*of*)] *I shall have to have this tooth taken out, it's aching unbearably. Please help me to take this nail out (of my shoe).* → **be in¹** (1), **be out** (1), **be out of** (2), **come out** (2), **draw out** (12), **get out** (2), **get out of** (2), **have out** (1), **pluck out, pull out** (2), **take out of** (2), **yank out**

*__3__ to produce (something), as from a container: [T1 (*from, of*)] *He took out a handkerchief and blew his nose. The thief took out a gun and forced the owner to give him the jewels.* → **draw out** (1), **get out** (5), **pull out** (1), **take out of** (3)

*__4__ to take (something such as money or a book) from a place where it is kept: [T1 (*of*)] *The library allows you to take out three books at a time. I shall have to go to the bank again and take some more money out (of our account).* → **draw out** (11), **get out** (6), **get out of** (4), **take out of** (4)

*__5__ to clean or remove (a mark, dirt, etc.): [T1 (*of*)] *There's a nasty mark on the tablecloth, and I don't think the usual washing powder will take it out.* → **come off** (3), **come out** (3), **get off¹** (4), **get out** (4), **take out of** (5), **wash off, wash out** (1)

*__6__ to lead (someone) to a distant place such as overseas: [T1 (*to*)] *If you go overseas, will you take the family out with you?* → **come over¹** (3), etc.

*__7__ to take (food) home or outside from a restaurant: [T1 (*usu. simple tenses*)] *I'd like three pieces of chicken to take out, please.* —**take-out** *n, adj* → **send out for, take away** (5)

*__8__ to obtain (a piece of paper giving one the right to something): [T1] *Did we remember to take out insurance on the contents of the house? Any person over the age of seventeen can take out a driving licence. The court may take out a summons against you.*

*__9__ to invite (someone) socially, as to a meal in a restaurant, a show, etc.: [T1 (*for, to*)] *How long did Jim take Mary out before they were married? I'd like to take you out to a meal on your birthday to give you a holiday from cooking.* → **ask out,** etc.

*__10__ to prevent (an opponent in a card game or sport) from reaching his aim: [T1] *That was a clever move with your cards, to take out your opponent. It's your job to take out the other player so that members of your team can get control of the play.*

**11 take the easy way out: a** to find an easy way to do something: *I think I'll take the easy way out and give money instead of time.* → **take out of** (10) **b** to kill oneself: *Most people would be ashamed to take the easy way out, however bad their sufferings.*

***take out in** *v adv prep*

esp. *AmE* to pay (a debt) with (something other than money): [D1] *I owe you $5—can I take it out in beer and cigarettes? When the boy broke the window, the owner let him take it out in garden work.*

**take out of** *v adv prep*

**1** to lead (someone or an animal) or carry (something) out of (a room, building, etc.); cause (someone) to leave (a place): [X9 + OUT + *of*] *Take the horses out of the burning building! Please take the children out of this room, their noise is making my head ache. I shall take the children out of that school if what they say about their treatment is true. All the furniture was taken out of the house and left in the road.* → **be out of** (1), etc., **pull out of** (1)

**2** to remove (something), as from material in which it is fixed: [T1 + OUT + *of*] *Please help me to take this nail out of my shoe.* → **take out** (2), etc.

**3** to produce (something) from (a container): [T1 + OUT + *of*] *He took a handkerchief out* *of his pocket and blew his nose. The owner took a gun out of a drawer and pointed it at the thief.* → **draw out** (1), **get out** (5), **pull out** (1), **take out** (3)

**4** to take (something such as money or a book) from a place where it is kept: [T1 + OUT + *of*] *Only three books may be taken out of the library at a time. I shall have to go to the bank again and take some more money out of our account.* → **draw out** (11), **get out of** (4), **take out** (4)

**5** to clean or remove (a mark, dirt, etc.) from (something): [T1 + OUT + *of*] *Will the usual washing powder take this nasty mark out of the tablecloth?* → **wash off**, etc.

**6** to copy (something) from (something such as a book): [X9 + OUT + *of*] *His story isn't original, he took it out of a book.* → **obtain from**, etc.

***7** to remove (a regular train, bus, etc.) from (operation): [D1] *The early morning train will be taken out of operation during the summer months.* → **come into** (4), **take off[1]** (9)

***8** to take (part of the amount) from (someone's pay) before he receives it: [D1 (*often pass.*)] *Unemployment insurance and income tax are taken out of your pay before you get it.* → **stop from** (2), **stop out of** (1)

***9** *not fml* to express (usu. one's anger) by making (someone else) suffer for it: [D1] *If you've had a bad day at work, there's no need to take it out of the children when you get home.* → **take out on, vent on, work off on**

**10 take the easy way out of** to find an easy answer to (a difficulty): *You can take the easy way out of this difficulty by leaving the town, and no one will know.* → **take out** (11)

**11 take something out of someone's hands** to take the responsibility for something from someone, often against his will: [*often pass.*] *The decision has been taken out of my hands so I can't help you.*

**12 take someone out of himself** to amuse or interest someone so that he forgets his worries: [*often simple tenses*] *Why don't you join the club? It would help to take you out of yourself since you're now alone in the world.*

**13 take it/a lot out of** *not fml* to weaken (someone): [*simple tenses*] *Looking after three active children all day really takes it out of me.*

**14 take a leaf out of someone's book** *not fml* to copy someone's idea: *I think I'll take a leaf out of your book and ask all the students to arrive early, so that we can finish sooner.*

**15 take the mickey out of** *infml* to make fun of (someone) in order to annoy him: *Will you stop taking the mickey out of me! It's not fun any more.* also *sl* **take the piss out of**

**16 take a/the rise out of** *not fml* to make fun of (someone) by pretending something: *I didn't mean it, I was only trying to take a rise out of you!* → **get out of** (33)

**17 take the sting out of** *not fml* to reduce the worst effect of (something): [*usu. simple tenses*] *All the sting was taken out of her remark by the gentle manner in which she made it. Additional personal allowances will help to take the sting out of the latest tax increases.*

**18 take the wind out of someone's sails** *not fml* to destroy the effect of what someone is saying or doing: *He came in very excited to give us the news, but Jim took the wind out of his sails by telling him that we already knew.*

**19 take the words of someone's mouth** *not fml* to say what someone was just thinking: [*often simple tenses*] *You've taken the words out of my mouth—I just had the very same thought!*

***take out on** *v adv prep* → **take out of** (9), **vent on, work off on**

to express (usu. one's anger) by making (someone else) suffer for it: [D1] *If you've had an annoying day at the office, there's no need to take it out of your wife when you get home!*

**take over[1]** *v adv*

**1** to lead (someone) or carry (something) to another place, usu. a short distance: [X9 + OVER (*to*)] *These bigger boats can take people over (to the island) in half the time. He took the letter over to the window to read it in a good light. Why don't you take the children over to your mother's more often?* → **come over[1]** (13), etc.

***2** to win control of (usu. something): [T1a (*from*)] *Military leaders have taken over the country. The young prince was allowed to take over the controls of the plane for a few minutes, to his delight. Our soldiers have succeeded in taking over some important enemy positions. Larger companies are taking over smaller firms by buying their shares.* —**takeover** *n, adj* → **move in on** (4)

***3** to accept (something or duty, responsibility, etc.) (from someone else): [T1a (*from*)] *The government has promised to take over the responsibility for paying people hurt by criminals. I shall be glad when my daughter is old enough to take over some of the cooking. Who will take over the leadership of the party next time? If you rent this house, you can take over the furniture from the former owner.*

***4** to become the person or group in charge: [IØ (*from*) (*often simple tenses*)] *The night nurse takes over at midnight. Thank you for your introduction; now I'll ask the next speaker to take over. Prices seem to go on rising whichever political party takes over. When do you take over from the former chairman?*

**take over[2]** *v prep*

**1** to enable (someone or something) to cross (something such as water or a road): [X9 + *over*] *Run and take that old lady over this busy road, she might get hurt without help. Will this boat take all our possessions over the water?* → **go across[2]**, etc.

**2** to spend (time) on (an activity such as work): [T1 + *over*] *How long are you going to take over that simple little job? I have taken nearly three years over this book already.* → **be over**[2] (3)

*****3** to help (someone) to learn, repeat, or practise (something): [D1] *Will you take me over my lines? I have to learn them before tomorrow. The teacher will take the class over the answers to the test.* → **go over**[2] (2), **go through**[2] (7), **look over**[2] (5), **run over**[2] (5), **run through**[2] (7), **take through**[2] (2)

*****4** to show (someone) round (a place): [D1] *The director himself will take the visitors over the factory.* → **look round**[2] (2), etc.

**5 take pains/trouble over** to be thorough in dealing with (something or doing something): *I can see that you've taken pains over your article, but it is still too long. Don't take too much trouble over finding the exact right word.* —**painstaking** *adj*

**6 take precedence over** to come first before (someone or something) in importance, esp. on a formal occasion: [*simple tenses*] *Does the wife of the chairman of the city council take precedence over the important lady visitor? The needs of my family take precedence over my own interests.*

**7 take a (firm) stand on/over** to act firmly on one's judgment about (a matter or doing something): *The government has decided to take a firm stand over admitting more foreigners to this country. The United States is taking a stand on human rights.* → **take on**[2] (12)

**8 take one's time over: a** to work at (something or usu. doing something) slowly and carefully: *I like to take my time over preparing a meal for important visitors.* **b** *not fml* to be too slow about (something or usu. doing something): *You've taken your time over getting here, haven't you?* → **take about**[2] (2)

**take round**[1] *v adv* also **take around**

**1** to lead (someone) or carry (something) a short distance: [X9 + ROUND] *Why did you take us round the long way? Please take these letters round to the chairman.* → **get about**[1] (1), **get round**[1] (1), **go about**[1] (1), **go round**[1] (7), **send around, send over, send round**[1] (1)

**2** to have (someone or an animal) with one as one moves about; help (someone) to move about a place: [X9 + ROUND (*with*)] *When I come to stay, there's no need to take me round showing me the sights, I shall be quite happy just to share your ordinary family life. Our milkman takes his dog round with him when he delivers the milk. You don't need a car here with such a good bus service to take you round.* → **bring over** (1), etc.

*****3** to have (someone of the opposite sex) as a social or sexual companion: [T1b] *How long has Jim been taking Mary round? Do they intend to get married?* → **ask out,** etc.

*****4** to show (someone) round a place on a visit or examination: [T1a] *Parties of students may visit our factory, and will be taken round by an experienced worker who will explain our methods.* → **show around,** etc.

**5 take the hat round** *not fml* to collect money, usu. to help someone: *One of the secretaries left to get married, so the other office workers took the hat round to buy her a wedding present.* → **pass round**[1] (2)

**take round**[2] *v prep* also **take around**

**1** to lead (someone) or carry (something) round (a place): [X9 + *round*] *Do let me take you round the city, there's so much to see. Have you taken the message round all the offices in the building?* → **get about**[2], etc.

*****2** to show (someone) round (a place), as on a visit or examination: [D1] *The director likes to take visitors round the factory personally.* → **look round**[2] (2), etc.

**take short** *v adj* → **catch short**

**be taken short** *not fml* to have a sudden urgent need to empty one's bowels: *It was kind of the taxi driver to wait for the lady who was taken short in the middle of London.*

*****take sick** *v adj* → **fall ill, fall sick, go sick, report sick, take ill**[1]

to (cause to) become unwell, often suddenly: [T1 (*usu. pass.*)] *Mother has been taken sick again, and we ought to call the doctor.* [IØ (*simple tenses*)] *Jane took sick again yesterday, and won't be at school for a few days.*

**take through**[1] *v adv*

**1** to cause (someone or something) to pass through something: [X9 + THROUGH (*often simple tenses*)] *The gate is very narrow, but if you drive the car very slowly, you should be able to take it through.*

*****2** to enable (something such as an idea) to reach completion: [T1 (*to*) (*often simple tenses*)] *Only an experienced politician like Hill has the ability to take such a daring suggestion through to completion.* → **go through**[1] (3), **put across**[1] (3), **put through**[1] (1), **railroad through, ram through**

**take through**[2] *v prep*

**1** to lead (someone) or carry (something) through (a space): [X9 + *through*] *The cattle don't need the boy to take them through the gateway, they know their way home at milking time.* → **get through**[2] (1), **go through**[2] (1)

*****2** to watch and help (someone) as he repeats, learns, or practises (something): [D1] *Will you take me through this scene? We are going to practise it tomorrow. The teacher will take us through likely examination questions.* → **go over**[2] (2), **go through**[2] (7), **look over**[2] (5), **run over**[2] (5), **run through**[2] (7), **take over**[2] (3)

*****3** to enable (a law) to pass (a law-making body: [D1] *Were you able to take the new law through Parliament?* → **get through**[2] (3), **go through**[2] (2), **put through**[2] (3)

**take to** *v prep*

**1** to lead (someone) or carry (something) in

the direction of (something or someone): [X9 + *to*] *Take me to your leader! I must go now, I have to take a cheque to the bank. I'd like to take you to a show on your birthday. Please take this message to the director. Mother is out taking the younger children to school.* → **come to**[2] (1), **get to** (1, 2), **go to, send to** (1, 2)

*__2__ to escape to or hide in (a place such as hills or woods): [T1 (*no pass., often perfect tenses*)] *The robbers have taken to the hills, where it will be difficult to catch them.*

*__3__ to begin to like (someone or something such as an activity): [T1 (*no pass., simple tenses*)] *I took to her at once, she seemed such a charming person. Jane took to music as soon as she learned about it, as if it was intended for her.* → **take against** (1), **take kindly** (2)

*__4__ to begin (an activity or doing something): [T1 (*no pass., simple tenses, often perfect*)] *I'm sorry to hear that he has taken to drink.* [T4] *Recently I have taken to getting up earlier in the morning.*

*__5__ to use (a tool) to attack (something): [D1] *I shall have to take an axe to that tree.*

**6 take to one's bed** to be forced, as by illness, to stay in bed: [*simple tenses*] *Mother took to her bed at the beginning of last winter, and may never get up again.*

**7 take something to bits/pieces: a** to separate something into its parts: *We had to take the whole engine to bits to discover the cause of the trouble.* → **pull apart** (1), etc. **b** *not fml* to find fault with (something): *Tom's latest book has been taken to pieces by the newspapers.* → **take apart** (4), etc.

**8 take to the boats/water** to go in a boat or ship; start to float; set sail: *The whole population of the village took to the boats to defend their island against attackers arriving by sea. The formal gathering will take to the water and sail down the river, watched by large crowds.*

**9 take someone to one's bosom** *lit or humor* to seize or regard someone fondly: *The crowd took the young prince to their bosom and cheered him wherever he went.*

**10 take someone to the cleaners** *infml* to get a lot of money from someone, as to settle a court case: *He had hoped to be made to pay a reasonable amount for the damage that he had caused, but the other person took him to the cleaners!*

**11 take someone to court** to force someone to answer charges in a court of law: *If our neighbour continues to refuse to keep his dog under control, we may have to take him to court.*

**12 take a dislike to** to begin to dislike (usu. someone), as at first meeting: [*usu. simple tenses*] *She must have taken a dislike to me from the beginning, to treat me so unkindly.*

**13 take exception to** to disagree with or be offended by (something): [*usu. simple tenses*] *I take exception to your last remark; it is not true that we were to blame.* → **demur at, object to, protest against, raise to** (6)

**14 take a fancy to** *not fml* to be attracted by (someone or something): [*usu. simple tenses*] *Tell me which of these rings you take a fancy to, and I'll buy it for you. The director seems to have taken a fancy to the new secretary, doesn't he!* → **take of** (8)

**15 take something to heart: a** to treat something such as words seriously: *I'm glad to see that you have taken my advice to heart and done as I suggested.* **b** to suffer because of something such as a misfortune: *Don't take your loss to heart, you can always start again.*

**16 take someone to one's heart** to receive someone such as a performer, warmly and keenly: *The public have really taken this new young singer to their hearts, so her success is certain.*

**17 take to one's heels** to escape on foot: [*usu simple past tense*] *The criminal took to his heels but was soon caught by the police.*

**18 take kindly to** to welcome (an idea): [*often neg.*] *I'm afraid the children may not take kindly to the thought of moving to yet another new school.*

**19 take a liking to** to like (usu. someone), often at once: [*simple tenses*] *I took a liking to our new neighbour as soon as we met.*

**20 take someone to one side** to lead someone away from someone else or a group, as for private conversation: *Try to take the chairman to one side after the meeting and discover his real opinion.* → **draw aside** (2), **go aside, pull aside** (2), **take apart** (1), **take aside, take on**[2] (11)

**21 take to the road** (of a person, often in an unfavourable sense, or a group such as a theatre company) to travel from place to place; go on tour: *I had a relative who gave up his usual work and took to the road, earning a living at odd jobs and sleeping in the open. The theatre company plans to take to the road for the summer, performing in various small towns outside the city.*

**22 take a shine to** *not fml* to like or be attracted to (someone), often at first meeting: [*usu. perfect tenses*] *Jane seems to have taken a shine to her new music teacher, doesn't she?*

**23 take someone to task** to scold someone: *I could hear Father taking the children to task for interrupting his midday sleep.* → **tell off** (1), etc.

**24 take someone to wife** *old use* to marry (a woman): *"I am a woman, but... a woman that Lord Brutus took to wife."* (Shakespeare, *Julius Caesar*)

**take together** *v adv*

**be taken together** to be seen in relation to each other: *When all the facts are taken together, the reason for the trouble becomes clear.*

***take unawares** *v adv* → **take by** (4)

to catch (someone) by surprise or off guard [T1b (*usu. simple tenses*)] *Every year, winter takes the English unawares, as if there had never been one before! You took me unawares, coming up behind me so silently! The only way to get his gun is to take him unawares and seize it without warning.*

**take under** *v prep*

**1 take something under advisement** *fml* to consider something carefully: *The committee is taking your suggestion under advisement, and will give you a decision shortly.*

**2 take someone under one's wing** *not fml* to help, advise, and protect someone: *Please take this new student under your wing; show him where the library is, and where he can buy some books.*

**take up** *v adv*

**1** to lift or raise (something or someone): [X9 + UP] *Take care not to take up the hot coals with your bare hands. This old tree will have to be taken up by its roots. Taking up a child under each arm, she ran from the fire.* → **pull up** (1), etc.

**2** to remove (something) from a place where it is fixed: [X9 + UP] *The men are coming tomorrow to take the stair mat up, ready for our move. Half the road surface is being taken up, to lay new electric wires.*

**3** to lead (someone) or carry (something) upstairs or to a higher level: [X9 + UP (*to*)] *Who will take breakfast up to your mother? Please take these letters up to the main office.* → **bring up** (1), **come up** (2), **get up** (1), **go down**[1] (1), **go up**[1] (1), **go up to** (1), **send up**[1] (1)

*__4__ to remove (liquid) by drawing inside itself: [T1 (*usu. simple tenses*)] *This kind of paper claims to be able to take up more liquid than any other kind.* → **mop up** (1), **soak up** (1), **sop up** (1), **wipe up** (1)

*__5__ to reform (something such as a woven thread, or knitted stitch that has fallen off the needle): [T1] *It's very difficult to take up a dropped stitch in this pattern.* → **pick up** (16)

*__6__ to raise or shorten (a garment): [T1] *Now the fashion tells us all to take our skirts up again!* → **let down** (2), **turn up** (3)

*__7__ to fill or use (time, space, or attention): [T1a] *It can take up the whole afternoon to prepare a meal. That big clock will have to go, it takes up too much space in the small hall. Writing in another language demands so much effort that it takes up all my attention.*

*__8__ to begin (new duties, work, etc.): [T1] *When does the Minister take up his office? I hope to take up my new duties as your chairman at the next meeting.*

*__9__ to begin to take an interest in (a subject, habit, or profession): [T1a] *When did Jane first take up music?* [T4] *I wish I'd never taken up smoking. When did Jim first take up running in competitions?* → **go in for** (3)

*__10__ to help and encourage (someone, usu. young) in his work or life: [T1 (*often pass.*)] *Jane will be lucky if she is taken up by the famous singer. Beckett was taken up by Joyce before becoming a famous writer.*

*__11__ (usu. of a vehicle) to obtain a supply of (something or people): [T1] *The train stops here to take up any further passengers, and then goes fast all the way to London.* → **take on**[1] (3)

*__12__ to continue (something such as an activity or speech) after an interruption: [T1a (*often simple tenses*)] *Jane took up the story when her sister forgot the next detail. I put the telephone down and took up my work again.* [IØ (*often simple tenses*)] *Let's take up where we left off before our coffee break.* → **pick up** (26)

*__13__ to join in (something such as voice sounds): [T1a] *All the other children in the bus took up the song. The whole crowd took up the shout.*

*__14__ to raise consideration of (a matter): [T1 (*with*)] *I'd like to take the boy's case up with a good lawyer. The question of public housing should be taken up with the Minister whose responsibility it is. I'll ask the next speaker to take up your suggestion.*

*__15__ to accept (an offer): [T1] *I'd like to take up your offer of a ride into town.*

*__16__ to interrupt (someone), usu. so as to correct him or disagree with what he says: [T1 (*usu. simple tenses*)] *I must take you up here, I cannot agree. You won't get far with your statement before the chairman takes you up short! I took him up sharply when he mentioned the wrong date.*

*__17__ to collect (money): [T1a] *The girls will take up a collection at the end of the concert.*

*__18__ to pay money for (something written): [T1a] *When can we take up the new shares? He kindly offered to take up the note of my debt.*

*__19__ to (cause to) tighten: [T1 (*often simple tenses*)] *These wires must be taken up or the machine will not work. Take up those loose ropes, your tent will fall down! This part of the machine is for taking up the film.* [IØ (*often simple tenses*)] (*naut*) *The boat has been in the water a long time, and the boards have taken up.* —**take-up** *n, adj*

**20 take up arms (against)** to begin a war (against an enemy): *All the young men of the village offered to take up arms against the neighbouring people who kept attacking them and stealing their cattle.*

**21 take up an attitude** to state or show one's opinion or frame of mind: *Once he's taken up a defensive attitude, it's difficult to persuade him that there's nothing to be afraid of.*

**22 take up a cause** to defend and support a purpose in which people believe: *More people are beginning to take up the cause of children's rights.*

**23 take up a challenge/the gauntlet** to accept an invitation to compete: *He said you can't possibly finish in time: are you going to take up his challenge?* → **fling down** (3), **pick up** (23), **throw down**[1] (5)

**24 take up the cudgels (for)** to support someone, an idea, or argument powerfully: *Someone has to take up the cudgels for children's rights, as the children are helpless to do it themselves.*
**25 take up a position** to state or show one's opinion: *I wonder if he really means that, or if he's just taking up a position on the matter? What position is the chairman taking up on that delicate question?*
**26 take up residence** *fml* to begin to live in an official home: *When will the new representative from the United States take up residence in this country?*
**27 take up the slack: a** *naut* to pull a rope to its full length: *Take up the slack there, the sails are too loose!* → **take in** (14) **b** *not fml* to make full use of something, leaving no waste: *There's some money left over in the department; what's the most important use for it, to take up the slack?*
**28 take up the thread(s)** to make a fresh start in something: *It's good to take up the threads of our old friendship after such a long absence.* → **pick up** (17)

***take up on** *v adv prep*
**1** to be willing to accept (a promise or offer) made by (someone) if made again in the future: [D1 (*usu. simple tenses*)] *I'll take you up on your invitation some other time, if I may.*
**2** to offer opposition or question to (someone) about (something he has said or written): [D1 (*usu. simple tenses*)] *I'd like to take you up on your last remark, which seems a doubtful statement of the facts.*

***take up to** *v adv prep* → **get to** (3), **get up to** (2), **go up to** (7)
to enable (someone) to reach (a place or time such as in something written): [D1 (*simple tenses*)] *This book only takes the reader up to 1930.*

**take up with** *v adv prep*
**1** to raise consideration of (a matter) with (someone or a group): [T1 + UP + *with*] *I'd like to take up the boy's case with a good lawyer. The question of public housing should be taken up with the Minister concerned.*
***2** to become friendly with (someone, often undesirable): [T1 (*no pass., usu. simple tenses*)] *I'm afraid that your son has taken up with some very rough boys.*
**3 be taken up with** to be greatly interested in or attracted to (usu. someone): *The young man seems to be much taken up with that pretty girl who came to the party uninvited.* → **take with** (2)

**take upon** *v prep* → TAKE ON[2]

**take with** *v prep*
**1** to lead (someone) or carry (something) together with (one): [X9 + *with*] *I think she must have taken the wrong coat with her! Please take the dog with you, he's been begging for a walk. Spend your money while you live, you can't take it with you!* → **go together** (1), **go with** (1)
**2 be taken with** to be pleased with or attracted to (someone or something): *The young man seems to be greatly taken with that pretty girl. Mother was quite taken with her unexpected birthday present.* → **take up with** (3)
**3 be taken with** to have an attack of (usu. a movement of the body): *She was taken with a fit of laughing at a most unsuitable moment in the performance.* → **seize with** (1)
**4 take issue with** *fml* to disagree with (someone or an idea): *Two of the committee members chose to take issue with the chairman on the question of voting rights.*
**5 take liberties with** to behave too freely or familiarly towards (someone); treat (something) informally or without respect: *I allow no man to take liberties with my wife! Who's been taking liberties with my private papers?*
**6 take the rough with the smooth** *not fml* to accept both good and bad: [(*often simple tenses*)] *In life, few things always go right; you have to learn to take the rough with the smooth.*
**7 take sides with** to sympathize with or support (someone): *Why do you always take sides with your mother! She's often in the wrong.* → **join with** (5), **side against, side with, take against** (3)
**8 take turns with** to share (work) one at a time: *Would you like me to take turns with the cooking? I can do it one day and you the next.*

**talk about** *v prep*
**1** to mention or have a conversation about (a subject); speak concerning (someone, something, or doing something): [IØ + *about*] *Whatever did you two find to talk about all morning? We were talking about our children, and how well they're doing in school.* —**talked-about** *adj* → **advert to, refer to** (1), **speak about, speak of** (1), **talk of** (1)
***2** to mention (someone) in an unfavourable sense; tell shocking stories about (someone): [T1 (*often pass.*)] *If your daughter goes on behaving like that, she could get herself talked about in the town. "There is only one thing in the world worse than being talked about, and that is not being talked about."* (Oscar Wilde, *The Picture of Dorian Gray*)
***3** to consider the idea of (something or usu. doing something): [T1 (*continuous when present tense*)] *If he starts talking about another job, that means he wants a rise in pay. The most suitable punishment for the boy has been talked about for long enough now, hadn't we better get on with the job?* [T4 (*continuous when present tense*)] *Are you still talking about moving to another city, or have you still not made up your minds?* → **talk of** (2), **think about** (4), **think of** (6)
**4 talk about...!** *not fml* look at this as an example of (something such as an action or quality, or its opposite): *Talk about rising*

*prices! Have you seen what coffee is costing these days? Talk about a wonderful holiday! All our money was stolen!*

**talk above** *v prep* → **talk over**[2]

**talk above someone's head** to speak in words or a manner which someone cannot understand: [*no pass.*] *The next time you invite a visiting speaker, please make sure you get someone who won't talk above the members' heads: no one was in the least interested in his talk.*

**talk around**[1] *v adv* → **TALK ROUND**[1]

**talk around**[2] *v prep* → **TALK ROUND**[2]

**talk at** *v prep* → **speak to** (1), **talk to** (1), **talk with** (1)

to address words to (someone, usu. a group) in an unfeeling way, not expecting a reply: [IØ + *at*] *I wish this new teacher could feel able to talk to the class in a more interesting way, instead of just talking at them as if they were not human.*

**talk away** *v adv*

**1** to speak continuously: [IØ + AWAY (*often continuous tenses*)] *He's been talking away for over an hour; when is he going to give the other speakers a turn?* → **talk on**[1]

***2** to spend (time) in talking: [T1] *The young lovers talked the night away.*

***3** to get rid of (a feeling) with words: [T1] *Stay with the child as he goes into hospital; you may be able to talk his fears away.*

***talk back** *v adv*

to reply, often rudely or to express one's opinion: [IØ (*to*)] *Don't talk back to your grandmother when she is giving you advice, you should be polite to your elders. This telephone show gives radio listeners a chance to talk back.* —**backtalk, talkback** *n*

***talk big** *v adj*

*not fml* to speak with too much pride in oneself, one's actions, or possessions; make one's actions seem more important than they are: [IØ] *I don't believe he really met all those famous people at one party; he's so fond of talking big that only half of what he says might be the truth.*

***talk down** *v adv*

**1** to defeat (someone) in a competition such as an election, by more powerful speech: [T1] *Don't worry, our next speaker is very experienced and will easily talk their man down.*

**2** to guide (the pilot of a plane) in bringing the plane safely to the ground, by giving instructions by radio: [T1] *His flying instruments have all been destroyed by enemy gunfire, so the air traffic controllers will have to talk him down.*

**3** *not fml* to help (someone) to deal with the bad effects of a drug, by talking to him until he becomes calm: [T1] *That drug has made him terribly nervous and overexcited; see what you can do to talk him down.*

***talk down to** *v adv prep* → **play down to**

to speak to (someone or a group) as if he/she is/they are less important or clever than oneself, so as to place oneself at a seemingly higher level: [T1] *Be careful not to talk down to the students, they're very sensitive about being treated as stupid. Children can always tell when they're being talked down to, and they hate it.*

**talk for** *v prep* → **speak for** (1)

to give a speech or hold a conversation, for (a certain length of time): [IØ + *for*] *Each committee member may talk for not more than five minutes, and then we will put the question to a vote. The children went on talking for an hour after being put to bed.*

**talk into** *v prep*

**1** to direct the voice into (an instrument): [IØ + *into*] *When you talk into the telephone receiver, don't have your mouth too near the mouthpiece as it makes the words difficult to hear.*

***2** to persuade (someone) into (action or doing something) by talking: [D1] *I don't think Father is willing to lend us the car, but I'll see if I can talk him into it.* [V4b] *See if you can talk Father into lending us the car tomorrow.* → **argue into,** etc.

**talk of** *v prep*

**1** to mention or have a conversation about (a subject); speak concerning (someone, something, or doing something): [IØ + *of*] *We were just talking of the most exciting books that we have read recently. Who's talking of failing? This is a success! "And a few men talked of freedom, while England talked of ale."* (G.K. Chesterton, *The Secret People*) *"No healthy male ever really thinks or talks of anything save himself."* (H.L. Mencken, *Prejudices*) → **talk about** (1), etc.

***2** to consider the idea of (something or usu. doing something): [T1 (*continuous when present tense*)] *If he starts talking of another job, that means he wants a rise in pay.* [T4 (*continuous when present tense*)] *Are you still talking of moving to another city, or are you still making up your minds?* → **talk about** (3), **think about** (4), **think of** (6)

**3 talking of** since we are mentioning (something such as a subject or someone); on the subject of (something or someone): *Talking of books, have you read 'Gone With the Wind?'* → **speak of** (3)

**4 talk of the devil!** *not fml* here comes the person we were just mentioning: *Talk of the devil —here she is!* → **speak of** (4)

**talk off** *v adv*

**talk one's head/a donkey's hind leg off** *not fml* to speak at great length: *Here I've been talking my head off, and not giving you a chance to tell your news! Once our neighbour starts talking, she will talk a donkey's hind leg off, so it's as well not to let her get started.*

**talk on**[1] *v adv* → **talk away** (1)

to continue talking: [IØ + ON] *My mother just talks on when I want her to stop. "He* [Coleridge] *talked on for ever; and you wished him to talk on for ever.*" (William Hazlitt, *Lectures on English Poets*)

**talk on/upon²** *v prep* → **speak on**

to deliver a speech or talk about (a subject): [IØ + *on/upon*] *I've been asked to talk on the importance of the arts in education.*

***talk out** *v adv*

**1** to consider (something) thoroughly until nothing further of use can be said about it: [T1 (*usu. pass.*)] *I think the whole question has now been talked out.* → **talk over¹** (1), **talk through**

**2** *BrE* to prevent (a law) from being passed by Parliament by talking until no time is left: [T1 (*often pass.*)] *The new law will not take effect as planned, as it was talked out in the last meeting of the House.*

**3** to settle (something such as a quarrel) by talking: [T1] *Unions and employers should try to talk out their differences before taking action against each other.*

**4 be talked out** to be tired by talking: *Well, you now know all my opinions on the subject; my throat is dry, I'm talked out.*

***talk out of** *v adv prep* → **argue out of,** etc.

to persuade (someone) against (an action or doing something): [D1] *Jim wants to give up his job—can't you talk him out of such a foolish idea?* [V4b] *Just in time, we talked Mother out of selling the house.*

***talk over¹** *v adv*

**1** to consider (a matter) at length (with someone else): [T1 (*with*)] *Come and see me in my office and we'll talk it over. I'd like to talk over that article you wrote about the firm. I'd like to talk your offer over with my family before deciding.* → **talk out** (1), **talk through¹**

**2** to persuade (someone) to change his opinion: [T1b] *In the end I was able to talk the other committee members over, and they agreed to vote in favour of the plan.* → **talk round¹**

**talk over²** *v prep* → **talk above**

**talk over someone's head** to speak in words or a manner which someone cannot understand: [(*no pass.*)] *The next time you invite a visiting speaker, please make sure you get someone who won't talk over the members' heads: no one was in the least interested in his talk.*

***talk round¹** *v adv* also **talk around** → **talk over¹** (2)

to persuade (someone) to change his opinion: [T1b] *In the end I was able to talk the other committee members round, and they agreed to vote in favour of the plan.*

**talk round²** *v prep* also **talk around**

to avoid speaking directly about (a subject): [IØ + *round*] *He never came to the point, but talked round the subject throughout the meeting.*

***talk through¹** *v adv* → **talk out¹** (1), **talk over¹** (1)

to finish considering (a matter) thoroughly: [T1 (*often pass.*)] *After three long meetings, the question seemed to be talked through.*

**talk through²** *v prep*

**talk through one's hat** *not fml* to speak foolishly; not make sense: [(*usu. continuous tenses*)] *What did he mean, there would be no money? He's talking through his hat, we all know there's a special allowance for this plan!*

**talk to** *v prep*

**1** to have conversation with or speak to (someone): [IØ + *to*] *I've asked you not to talk to that rough boy! "A good newspaper, I suppose, is a nation talking to itself."* (Arthur Miller, in *Observer, Sayings of the Week*, 26 November 1961) → **speak to** (1), **speak with** (1), **talk at, talk with** (1)

***2** *not fml* to scold (someone): [T1] *I'll talk to that boy when he gets in!* —**talking-to** *n* → **tell off** (1), etc.

**3 talk nineteen/forty to the dozen** *infml* to speak very fast: *She was talking nineteen to the dozen, so that I couldn't hear one word from another: I wish she'd slow down and speak clearly!*

***talk up** *v adv*

**1** to speak louder: [IØ] *You'll have to talk up a bit, we can't hear you above the noise of the traffic.* → **answer up, speak out** (1), **speak up** (1)

**2** to express one's opinion boldly: [IØ (*usu. simple tenses*)] *If you thought that wasn't fair, why didn't you talk up?* → **answer up, speak out** (2), **speak up** (2)

**3** esp. *AmE not fml* to praise or try to encourage support of (something): [T1] *I suppose Tom will use the chance of appearing on television to talk up his latest book. People who support children's rights are beginning to talk the idea up among groups wherever they go.*

**talk upon** *v prep* → TALK ON

**talk with** *v prep*

**1** to have conversation with (someone), esp. in order to reach a decision: [IØ + *with*] *I saw you talking with our neighbour: what did he have to say? "Did not our heart burn within us, while he talked with us by the way?"* (The Bible) → **speak to** (1), **speak with** (1), **talk at, talk to** (1)

***2** *not fml* to scold (someone): [T1] *I shall ask your father to talk with you when he comes home.* → **tell off** (1), etc.

***tally with** *v prep* → **correspond to,** etc.

to match (something that should be the same): [T1 (*no pass., simple tenses*)] *Does the prisoner's story tally with his friend's? The numbers of students present should tally with the class list that you have been provided with.*

***tamp down** *v adv*

to press or flatten (material such as tobacco) with light blows: [T1] *To give himself time to think, he tamped down the tobacco in his pipe and then lit it slowly.*

***tamper with** *v prep* → **meddle with** (1), etc.
to touch or change (something) so as to damage or make false: [T1] *Someone has been tampering with this machine; it won't work, and I can see marks on the paint. I'm very much afraid that the course of justice appears to have been tampered with.*

**tangle up** *v adv*
to cause (something such as loose material) to become mixed, knotted, and difficult to separate: [T1 + UP (*usu. pass.*)] *The string has got all tangled up, I don't know if I shall be able to unfasten it. The wind tangled up my hair, making it painful to comb.*

***tangle with** *v prep*
**1** *not fml* to oppose (someone) in argument or fight: [T1] *I wouldn't advise you to tangle with my brother, he's the strongest man in the village. I wish I hadn't tangled with such an experienced politician, he twisted my words to make me look stupid.*
**2 be tangled with** *not fml* to have a close relationship with (someone), often in an unfavourable sense: *I'm sorry to hear that you've been tangled with such unsuitable people, and glad that you are now making new friends.*

***tank up** *v adv*
**1** *not fml* to supply a vehicle with petrol: [IØ (*with*)] *We can stop here and tank up (with best quality petrol) at a good price.* → **gas up**
**2** *infml* to drink (alcohol) so as to become drunk: [IØ (*on*)] *I saw your brother in the hotel, tanking up on beer with two of his friends.* [T1 (*pass.*)] *If he gets tanked up again, who will drive us home?* → **light up** (5), **load up** (3)

**tap at** *v prep* → **knock at,** etc.
to beat with quick light blows on (something): [IØ + *at*] *It's only a branch tapping at the window, nothing to worry about.*

**tap down** *v adv*
to fasten (something) down with quick light blows: [X9 + DOWN] *Tap the lid down carefully so as not to break the contents.*

***tap for** *v prep*
*not fml* to ask (someone) for (something such as money or information): [D1] *Do you think you can tap your father for another $10?*

**tap in** *v adv*
to drive (something) inwards with quick light blows: [X9 + IN] *If you tap the nail in gently you won't risk bending it.*

**tap off** *v adv*
to draw (liquid) (from a container) by means of a control: [T1 + OFF (*from*)] *Someone has been tapping off most of the beer from this barrel. At the right season, the natives go into the forest to tap off the rubber (from the trees).*

**tap on** *v prep*
**1** to (cause to) beat lightly on (a surface): [IØ + *on*] *It's no use tapping on the door, we don't hear you in the back room; you have to knock quite loudly. All the people who were not dancing were tapping on the floor with their feet to the music.* [T1 + *on*] *All those not dancing were tapping their feet on the floor.* → **knock at**, etc.
**2** to hit (someone or something) lightly on (a part): [T1 + *on*] *Suddenly I felt someone tapping me on the shoulder. If you tap a glass on its side, it gives off a nice ringing sound.*

**tap out** *v adv*
**1** to knock repeatedly with quick light blows to send (a message): [T1 + OUT] *In the Signals Branch, the men learn to tap out messages at twelve words a minute.* → **rap out** (1)
***2** to empty (usu. a pipe) by knocking against something hard, so as to shake out the ash: [T1] *Please tap your pipe out into the fireplace, not onto the floor.* → **knock out** (2)
**3 be tapped out** *infml* to have no money: *Can you lend me some money? I'm tapped out.*

**tap with** *v prep* → **rap with** (1)
to beat quick light blows (on something) using (something): [IØ + *with*] *Tap with the heel of your shoe on the window, and he will let us in.* [T1 + *with*] *All those not dancing were tapping the floor with their feet in time to the music.*

***taper off** *v adv*
**1** to (cause to) come gradually to a point; narrow: [IØ (*simple tenses*)] *The end of the pipe tapers off so that it can fit into the narrow hole.* [T1] *Make sure that you taper off the wood at exactly the right angle.*
**2** to (cause to) come gradually to an end; lessen in quantity or strength: [IØ] *Membership has tapered off recently, but should improve at the beginning of the new year. His voice tapered off as he lost courage.* [T1 (*often pass.*)] *House building is being tapered off as the demand for renting property is falling.* → **tail off, trail off** (2)

**tar with** *v prep*
**be tarred with the same brush** *not fml* (of a group of people or things or each member in such a group) to have the same character, esp. faults: *His father was lazy, his grandfather was lazy, and this boy seems to be tarred with the same brush.*

***tart up** *v adv*
*BrE sl* to dress (someone such as a woman) showily, often improperly, or ornament (something) to appear better than in fact: [T1 (*usu. pass.*)] *Where's she going, all tarted up like that? To meet her latest boyfriend, I'd say! Do what you can to tart up the house before the buyers come to look at it; cover up the bad marks on the walls with some paint, and polish the floors.*

***taste of** *v prep*
to have a taste like that of (something): [T1 (*no pass., simple tenses*)] *This root vegetable tastes slightly of lemon, isn't it nice! The soup tasted of old boots. "Why does the tea generally*

*taste of boiled boots?"* (W.M. Thackeray, *The Kicklebury's on the Rhine*)

**taunt with** *v prep*
to make (someone) feel uncomfortable by mentioning (something unpleasant, as in the past or something he has done): [T1 + *with*] *It's too cruel to taunt the child with his failure in the examination. Why do the other children taunt him with having red hair?*

***tax with** *v prep*
**1** to charge (someone) with (something or doing something, usu. wrong); make (someone) face (something unpleasant): [D1 (*often simple tenses*)] *Are you going to tax the boy with the proof of his part in the theft of that money?* [V4a (*often simple tenses*)] *Each of the children in turn was taxed with breaking the window.*
**2** to give (someone) a heavy responsibility of (something): [D1 (*often pass.*)] *The chairman is taxed with the job of finding a suitable person to replace the director in case of sudden illness.*

***team up** *v adv*
**1** to (cause to) work together as a group: [IØ (*with*)] *It's a pleasure to team up with such excellent workers.* [T1 (*often pass.*)] *It's a long time since we've been teamed up: I hope everything goes as well as last time.*
**2** (of colours, etc.) to match or suit: [IØ (*simple tenses*)] *The coat and skirt team up very well, don't they, although they weren't bought as a set.*

**tear about/around** *v adv*
*not fml* to move around quickly or wildly: [L9 + ABOUT/AROUND] *All the boy does is tear around on his motorcycle with the other rough boys.*

**tear across**[1] *v adv* → **rip across**
to pull (something such as paper) into two pieces: [T1 + ACROSS] *Offended at being offered payment, he tore the cheque across and sent it back.*

**tear across**[2] *v prep*
*not fml* to move quickly across (something such as a road): [L9 + *across*] *I was very afraid as I watched the child tearing across that busy road.*

**tear along** *v adv; prep*
*not fml* to move quickly along (something such as a road): [L9 + ALONG/*along*] *The little boat was simply tearing along in the high wind. It's dangerous the way cars tear along these narrow winding streets.*

**tear apart** *v adv*
**1** to divide (something or things) by pulling; cause disorder to (something), as when searching: [T1 + APART] *He tore the curtains apart, but there was no one hiding there. The thieves had torn the house apart, but found no jewels. We had to tear the whole engine apart to discover the cause of the trouble.* → **pull apart** (1), etc.
*__2__ to hurt or cause (someone) severe grief or pain; cause trouble in (a nation) by dividing its people: [T1a (*usu. pass.*)] *She was torn apart by the struggle within her between her desires and her conscience. We do not want this country to be torn apart by the language question.* → **rip apart** (2)
*__3__ *not fml* to find severe fault with (something such as someone's work): [T1b] *Don't tear her performance apart as unkindly as you did last time, even if it is bad; it could destroy her.* → **take apart** (4), etc.
*__4__ *not fml* to scold (someone): [T1] *I'll tear that boy apart when he comes home: look what he's done now!* → **tell off** (1), etc.

**tear around** *v adv* → TEAR ABOUT

**tear at** *v prep*
**1** to pull at (something), as trying to open or divide: [IØ + *at*] *The child tore at the parcel, eager to find his birthday present. Look at those tigers tearing at the meat.*
**2 tear at someone's heart** to make someone feel sad or sympathetic: [*usu. simple tenses*] *The sad story of the dead baby tore at my heart.* → **tear out** (4)

**tear away** *v adv*
**1** to remove (something) with a quick or violent pulling movement; come away roughly: [T1 + AWAY (*from*)] *Tearing the cover away, the child reached into the box to see what his birthday present was. The ship was torn away (from its mooring) in the high wind. Last night's storm has torn all the leaves away from the trees.* [IØ + AWAY] *The cover of the book has torn away, but it's still readable.* → **rend from, rip away** (1), **rip from, rip off** (1), **rip out, tear from, tear off**[1] (1), **tear out** (1)
*__2__ *not fml* to leave quickly: [IØ (*usu. simple tenses*)] *As the policeman came round the corner, the thief tore away in full flight.* → **dash away** (1), **dash off** (1), **dash out** (1), **tear off**[1] (2), **tear out** (2)
*__3__ to remove or cause (someone or oneself) to leave (something or someone): [T1b (*from*)] *I was enjoying the film so much that when the time came to leave, I could hardly tear myself away. Have you ever tried tearing a child away from a television set? How can I tear myself away from you/your arms?* → **drag away** (2), **pull away** (4)
*__4__ to remove or show the falsity of (a pretence): [T1] *His political opponents were able to tear away the show of sincerity covering his deceitful intention.* → **rip away** (2), **rip off** (4), **rip out** (2), **tear off**[1] (3)

**tear between** *v prep*
**be torn between** to find it painful to choose between (two things, people, or actions) both greatly desired: *I'm torn between the cake and the fruit: which are you having? You can't remain long in the position of being torn between two men: you must choose between them. I'm so torn between buying a new car*

*and having a good holiday, I can't decide!*

**tear down[1]** *v adv*

**1** to remove or pull (something) down roughly: [T1 + DOWN] *The photograph of the unpopular leader had been torn down in the night by his enemies.* → **rip down**

**2* to destroy (a building): [T1] *The old theatre is to be torn down and replaced by offices.*

**3* to take (something such as a machine) to pieces, often for repair or cleaning: [T1] *We shall have to tear the engine down completely and oil every part.* → **strip down** (2), **take down** (2)

**4* to destroy (something such as an idea): [T1] *It shouldn't be difficult to tear down such a weak argument. But these people want to tear down our whole system of government! They can't be allowed to do that!*

**tear down[2]** *v prep*

*not fml* to move quickly down (something such as a road): [L9 + *down*] *I just saw Jim tearing down the street: what was all the hurry about?*

**tear from** *v prep* → **rend from, rip away** (1), **rip from, rip out, tear away** (1)

to pull or seize (someone or something) roughly from (something or someone): [X9 + *from*] *The soldiers had orders to tear the children from their mothers' arms if they refused to give them up.*

**tear in** *v prep* → **rend in, rip in, tear into** (1)

to pull (something) roughly so that it divides in (usu. a division or number of parts): [T1 + *in*] *This man is so strong that he can tear a thick telephone book in four. The sail was torn in two by the high wind. This pound note got accidentally torn in half; can I claim its value and get a new one?*

**tear into** *v prep*

**1** to pull (something) roughly into (a number of parts): [T1 + *into*] *If you tear the paper into four pieces, we can each have something to write on.* → **rend in, rip in, tear in**

**2* to cut (something) roughly: [T1] *Don't use that knife, it's not sharp enough and tears into the meat. See those lions tearing into the bodies of the animals that they have killed for food. This electric tool tears into the wood like a knife going through butter.* → **rip into** (1)

**3* to eat (food) eagerly: [T1] *Trust those children to tear into their dinner as usual, not having the patience to eat it properly and calmly.* → **tuck into** (3), etc.

**4* to attack (something or someone): [T1] *This successful politician never fails to tear into his opponents, showing the weakness of their arguments. Jim tore into the men who had attacked him, and soon had all three lying unconscious on the ground.* → **lay into,** etc.

**5* to scold (someone): [T1] *I could hear the teacher tearing into that class for their bad behaviour.* → **tell off** (1), etc.

**tear off[1]** *v adv*

**1** to remove (something) by pulling roughly: [T1 + OFF] *The child tore the wrapping off in his eagerness to find his birthday present. The explosion tore off the whole front of the restaurant.* —**tear-off** *n, adj* → **rip away** (1), **rip from, rip off** (1), **rip out, tear away** (1)

**2* *not fml* to leave hurriedly: [IØ (*usu. simple tenses*)] *Suddenly he tore off down the road as if a wild animal was chasing him!* → **dash away** (1), **dash off** (1), **dash out** (1), **tear away** (2)

**3* to remove or show the falsity of (a pretence): [T1] *His political opponents were able to tear off the show of sincerity that had been covering his deceitful intentions.* → **rip away** (2), **rip off** (4), **tear away** (4)

**4* to write (something) quickly: [T1] *I'm afraid this article reads as if you tore it off in half an hour.* → **dash off** (2), etc.

**5 tear someone off a strip** *not fml* to scold someone: *If you're late for work again, the director is sure to tear you off a strip, and might even reduce your pay until you improve.* → **tell off** (1), etc.

**tear off[2]** *v prep*

**1** to remove (something such as a covering) from (something): [T1 + *off*] *The child tore the wrapping off his birthday present, to see what he had received.*

**2 tear a strip off** *not fml* to scold (someone): *The head teacher called the new teacher into his office and tore a strip off him for using such unsuitable methods of controlling the class.* → **tell off** (1), etc.

**tear out** *v adv*

**1** to remove (something) roughly by pulling: [T1 + OUT (*of*)] *The telephone wires have been torn out, so we can't call the police. Look at this picture which I tore out of the newspaper. In former times, a man who told lies had his tongue torn out.* → **rip away** (1), **rip from, rip out, tear away** (1)

**2** *not fml* to leave a place hastily: [L9 + OUT (*usu. simple tenses*)] *The cat tore out, with the dog close behind, as soon as I opened the door.* → **dash off** (1), **dash out** (1), **tear away** (2), **tear off** (2)

**3 tear one's hair out** *not fml* to be very excited and anxious; worry: [*often continuous tenses*] *I was tearing my hair out waiting for you: where were you?*

**4 tear one's/someone's heart out** *not fml* to fill someone with usu. sadness; move someone to tears or other strong feeling; feel strongly: [*usu. simple tenses*] *The story of the dead baby tore my heart out.* → **tear at** (2)

**tear to** *v prep*

**tear something to bits/pieces/shreds**

**1** to separate something into its parts by pulling it roughly: *The sudden high wind tore the sail to pieces. The animal's body had been torn to bits by wild tigers.* → **pull apart** (1), etc.

**2** *not fml* to attack usu. something without

mercy: *The next speaker tore his opponent's argument to shreds in a few minutes. Tom's latest book has been torn to pieces by the newspapers.* → **take apart** (4), etc.

**tear up**[1] *v adv*

**1** to destroy (something) by pulling roughly: [T1 + UP] *That dog has torn up my newspaper again, it's not fit to read! Heavy vehicles like that will tear up the road surface. The workmen are tearing up the road to lay new electric wires.* → **rip up** (1)

***2** to pull (something) up roughly: [T1] *We shall have to tear the old tree up by its roots. It's a hard job tearing up all these unwanted plants in the garden.* → **pull up** (1), etc.

***3** to break (an agreement): [T1 (*often simple tenses*)] *He can't be trusted; he's been known to tear up a contract before the ink was dry where it had been signed.* → **rip up** (2)

**tear up**[2] *v prep*

*not fml* to move quickly up (a road): [L9 + *up* (*usu. simple tenses*)] *The policeman tore up the road after the criminals, but they ran too fast for him to catch them.*

***tease out** *v adv*

**1** to separate the threads of (a material) by combing: [T1] *You will have to tease out the wool before you can use it for weaving.*

**2** to separate (something) (from among something else): [T1 (*from*)] *It will take much hard study to tease out the really important facts from this mass of detail.*

***tee off** *v adv*

**1** (in golf to make the first stroke; begin playing: [IØ (*usu. simple tenses*)] *Which of us should tee off first?*

**2** *not fml* to begin something such as an activity: [IØ (*usu. simple tenses*)] *If everybody's ready, let's tee off at once.*

**3** esp. *AmE not fml* to express anger (about something): [IØ (*on*)] *I could hear the director teeing off on his favourite complaint, as usual.*

**4 be teed off** *AmE infml* to be annoyed: *I got really teed off when she kept on being so rude to me.*

***tee up** *v adv*

**1** (in golf to place (the ball) in a position ready to begin playing: [IØ (*usu. simple tenses*)] *It's important at the start of a game to tee up very carefully.* [T1 (*usu. simple tenses*)] *First you tee the ball up, then you can tee off.*

**2** *not fml* to arrange (something): [T1 (*often pass.*)] *Have all our travel arrangements been properly teed up?*

**teem down** *v adv*

(usu. of rain) to fall in quantity: [IØ + DOWN (*usu. continuous tenses*)] *The rain is still teeming down, but I can't wait any longer to go out.*

***teem in** *v prep* → **abound in** (1)

to exist in quantity in (a place): [T1 (*no pass., simple tenses*)] *Good fish teem in the North Sea.*

***teem with** *v prep*

**1** to be full of (something or things): [T1 (*no pass.*)] *The North Sea teems with good fish. I shan't go there again, the whole place was teeming with flies. I couldn't sleep, as my head was teeming with new ideas. "Some word that teems with hidden meaning—like Basingstoke."* (W.S. Gilbert, *Ruddigore*) → **abound in** (2), **abound with, swarm with**

**2** to give a lot of (rain): [*It* + T1 (*no pass., usu. continuous tenses*)] *I shan't go out to the shops yet, it's still teeming with rain.* → **pelt down, pelt with, pour down**[1]**, pour with, sheet down**

**telephone in** *v adv* → **phone in**

to send (a message) into a place by telephone: [T1 + IN (*to*)] *The reporter stopped for only a few minutes to telephone his story in before rushing home.*

**telescope into** *v prep*

to shorten (something) by making it into (something shorter) or fitting it into (a shorter time): [T1 + *into*] *How are you going to telescope all those articles into one short book? You will have to reduce the length of each one, or remove some altogether. The usual year's course can be telescoped into six weeks if the classes are held daily.*

**tell about** *v prep*

**1** to give (someone) information such as a story, concerning (something or someone): [T1 + *about*] *Tell me about what you've been doing at school today.* [IØ + *about* (*usu. simple tenses*)] *I don't want to tell about my failure.* → **tell of** (1)

**2** *not fml* to tell (a secret), as to someone in charge: [IØ + *about*] *I'll tell about you stealing the cakes. Don't you dare tell about the hiding place.*

***tell against** *v prep* → **hold against,** etc.

to be recorded as unfavourable to (someone): [T1 (*no pass., simple tenses*)] *His frequent lateness will tell against him when the new appointments are being decided.*

***tell apart** *v adv* → **tell from** (2), etc.

to be able to recognize the difference between (two or more things or people): [T1b (*usu. simple tenses*)] *The two brothers are so much alike that their own mother can hardly tell them apart.*

**tell between** *v prep* → **distinguish between,** etc.

**be able to tell the difference between** to be able to know which is which of (two or more things or people): *Can you tell the difference between these two colours? Some of these performers can't tell the difference between sincerity and pretence.*

**tell by** *v prep*

**1** to know (the correct time) by looking at (a clock or watch): [T1 + *by*] *How old is a child usually when he can learn to tell the time by the clock?*

**2** to know (or recognize something or that

someone ... judging by (something): [T1 + *by* (*usu. simple tenses*)] *In England, it is easy to tell a person's class by his speech.* [T5 + *by* (*usu. simple tenses*)] *I could tell by your face that you were lying.* → **tell from** (1)

**tell from** *v prep*

**1** to know or recognize (something or that something) judging by (something): [T1 + *from* (*usu. simple tenses*)] *In England, it is easy to tell what part of the country someone was born in, from his speech.* [T5 + *from* (*usu. simple tenses*)] *I could tell that you were lying from the look on your face.* → **tell by** (2)

***2** to be able to see the difference between (something or someone) and (something or someone else): [D1 (*usu. simple tenses*)] *The two brothers are so much alike that it is almost impossible to tell one from the other. Some people can't tell red from green, as there is a fault in their eyes.* → **differentiate from** (2), **discriminate from** (2), **distinguish from** (2), **know apart, know from** (1), **tell apart**

**tell of** *v prep*

**1** to give (someone) information such as a story, concerning (someone, something, or doing something): [T1 + *of*] *Have you told your mother of your intentions? He told us of having found a perfect place for the camp. Are you telling me of your own father or someone else's?* [IØ + *of* (*usu. simple tenses*)] *I don't like telling of my failures. The poem tells of the poet's love for his lady. He told of having seen a strange creature in the lake.* → **tell about** (1)

***2** *infml* (esp. among schoolchildren) to inform against (someone): [T1 (*no pass.*)] *I'll tell of you if you don't stop hurting my arm!* → **inform against**, etc.

**3 hear tell of** to be familiar with the idea of (usu. something): [*simple tenses*] *Did you ever hear tell of such nonsense? I've heard tell of strange creatures like that in the sea.*

***tell off** *v adv*

**1** *not fml* to scold (someone), as for a fault; find fault with (someone): [T1] *The director told Jim off for being late for work again.* —**telling-off** *n* → **bawl out** (2), **be down on** (1), **blow up** (10), **bring up** (9), **brush down** (2), **burn up** (4), **call down** (4), **chew out, chew up** (3), **choke off** (3), **come down on** (3), **dress down** (2), **dust down** (2), **hop on** (2), **jack up** (5), **jump on** (2), **land on** (4), **lay out** (9), **pull up** (4), **rebuke for, reprimand for, reproach for, reproach with, reprove for, roust out, sail into** (5), **scold for, sit on** (8), **slap down** (2), **smack down, speak to** (3), **speak with** (2), **step on** (3), **strip down** (3), **strip off** (4), **take apart** (5), **take to** (23), **talk to** (2), **talk with** (2), **tear apart** (4), **tear into** (5), **tear off**[1] (5), **tear off**[2] (2), **tick off** (2), **walk into** (8), **wipe with** (3)

**2** *old use* to count (things or people): [T1a] *The farmers used a special system of counting to tell off their sheep. His job was to sit in the box and tell off the buses as they came by. The secretary told off the members as they came in, to see how many were attending the meeting.*

**3** *usu. mil* to order (a group usu. of soldiers) for a special duty, or to do a special job: [T1 (*for*) (*often pass.*)] *A small party of men were told off for burial duty.* [V3 (*often pass.*)] *The officer told off a small group, and put them to clearing the road. Some of the soldiers were told off to dig ditches.* → **detail off**

***tell on** *v prep*

**1** to have a usu. bad effect on (someone or something): [T1 (*no pass.*)] *All those late nights are beginning to tell on Jim's health.*

**2** *infml* (usu. among schoolchildren) to inform against (someone): [T1 (*no pass.*)] *I'll tell on you when the teacher gets back!* → **inform against**, etc.

**tell over** *v adv*

to count (something or things) repeatedly; repeat (a story): [T1 + OVER] *The old man sat in his study, telling over his money. Is he telling his adventures over again?*

**tell to** *v prep*

**1** to say (something) to (someone); make (something) known to (someone): [T1 + *to*] *Are you willing to tell your story to the police?* → **recount to**

**2 tell something to someone's face/teeth** *not fml* to say something directly to someone, as to hurt him, make him feel guilty, etc.: *I told him to his face that I thought he was a fool.*

**tell with** *v prep*

to know the truth about (someone); know what to expect from (someone): [IØ + *with* (*often neg., simple tenses*)] *You can't tell with Jane whether she's really sick or just pretending. I don't promise that the director will approve; after all, you can never tell with him, he has some strange ideas. There's no telling with that boy what he'll do next.*

***temper with** *v prep*

to make (something) less cruel or strong by adding (something usu. gentler): [D1] *The courts try to temper justice with mercy. "To learn true patience, and to temper joy with fear."* (John Milton, *Paradise Lost*)

**tempt from** *v prep* → **entice from, seduce from**

to persuade or attract (someone) away from (something or someone that he should stay with) by offering some kind of reward: [T1 + *from* (*with*)] *It's easy enough to tempt me from my work with a good television film or something else that I enjoy.*

**tempt into** *v prep* → **entice into, seduce into**

to persuade or attract (someone) into (something or doing something, usu. wrong) by offering some kind of reward: [T1 + *into* (*with*)] *Young children are easily tempted into a life of crime. The boy claimed that he had been tempted into stealing the jewels with a promise of a good share of the profit. Can I tempt you into trying another piece of cake?*

**tempt to** *v prep* → **entice to**
to persuade (someone) to have (something offered): [T1 + *to*] *Can I tempt you to another piece of cake?*

***tend to** *v prep* → **incline to** (2), **lean to** (2)
to be likely to have, do, or think (something such as a quality): [T1 (*no pass., simple tenses*)] *His family have always tended to overweight. Tom's books tend to dullness.*

***tend towards** *v prep* → **lean towards** (2), etc.
to move one's opinion more in favour of (something such as a belief): [T1 (*no pass.*)] *More and more countries in Europe are now tending towards some form of Socialism.*

**tender for** *v prep*
**1** to offer (money in a certain form) in exchange for (usu. goods): [T1 + *for*] *£10 and £20 notes should not be tendered for bus fares.*
***2** to make a formal offer to do or supply (something) at a certain price: [T1] *Many firms have tendered for the building of the new bridge, and the government will probably accept the lowest offer.*

**tense for** *v prep*
to (cause to) become tight in preparation for (usu. an action): [IØ + *for*] *All his muscles were tensing for a fight.* [T1 + *for*] *The tiger tensed its muscles for the spring. Try not to tense your voice for the effort of reaching the high notes, it only makes the difficulty worse.*

**tense up** *v adv* → **screw up** (5)
to (cause to) become tight or nervous: [IØ + UP (*usu. simple tenses*)] *Jane is sick so often because her stomach tenses up when she is worried about something at school.* [T1 + UP (*usu. simple tenses*)] *There's no need to get all tensed up about your first class, the students won't eat you. Waiting for an operation tends to tense most people up.*

**terrify into** *v prep* → **frighten into, intimidate into, scare into**
to persuade (someone) through great fear into (doing something): [T1 + *into*] *The robbers terrified the old man into giving them all his money, by threatening him in the street.*

**terrify out of** *v adv prep* → **frighten out of** (2), **scare out of**
**terrify someone out of his mind/wits** to make someone greatly afraid: *You terrified me out of my wits, threatening to kill yourself! I was terrified out of my mind, giving my first public performance.*

**test for** *v prep*
to examine (something) or make an examination looking for (something such as a quality or part): [T1 + *for*] *Has this plastic been tested for safety in great heat? We can test your blood for signs of the disease.* [IØ + *for*] *The scientists are testing for poisonous chemicals in the lake where so many people have fallen ill. The radio engineers want to test for sound.*

**test out** *v adv*
to examine (something or an idea) thoroughly: [T1 + OUT] *The model must be tested out before we put the product on sale. Working in the new school gave him a chance to test out some of the latest ideas in education.*

**testify against** *v prep*
to be a witness, usu. in court, proving the guilt of (someone): [IØ + *against*] *When so many people have testified against the prisoner, he stands little chance of going free.*

**testify for** *v prep*
to be a witness, usu. in court, in favour of (someone): [IØ + *for*] *Only members of his family have testified for him.*

**testify to** *v prep*
**1** to be a witness, usu. in court, declaring (something): [IØ + *to* (*usu. simple tenses*)] *How many people have testified to the truth of the prisoner's statement?* → **witness to** (1)
***2** to prove (something) by showing clearly: [T1 (*simple tenses*)] *His actions testify to his good character. His handwriting testifies to a certain amount of impatience.* → **witness to** (2)

**thank for** *v prep*
**1** to express that one is grateful to (someone) for (something that one has received or an action done in one's favour): [T1 + *for*] *"Thank you for the world so sweet."* (child's prayer) *Thank you, young man, for seeing me across that busy street.*
**2 have someone to thank for** to have to blame someone for (something, usu. bad): *Who do we have to thank for the broken window? I have no one to thank for all my suffering except myself.*

**thaw out** *v adv*
**1** to (cause to) melt or become warmer: [T1 + OUT] *Leave the chicken out overnight to thaw it out.* [IØ + OUT] *Use the ice quickly before it thaws out.*
***2** *not fml* to become comfortably warm: [IØ] *Let me get by the fire to thaw out: it's bitterly cold outside!*
***3** *not fml* to (cause to) become more informal, friendly, and without anxiety in company: [T1] *The children's cheerful talk will help to thaw our guest out.* [IØ] *After a good meal, he began to thaw out and tell us more about himself.*

**theorize about** *v prep* → **speculate about**
to suggest an idea about (something): [IØ + *about*] *It's no good theorizing about the results of the election—we shall have to wait and see what the voters decide. Too many people are theorizing about the best system of education, and not enough people are actually doing it!*

**thicken up** *v adv*
to (cause to) become thicker: [IØ + UP] *The mist has thickened up since this morning, I don't think it's safe to go out now.* [T1 + UP] *This soup needs to be thickened up with some flour: it's so watery.*

**thin down** *v adv* → **thin out** (2, 3)
to (cause to) become less in thickness, num-

ber, or weight: [T1 + DOWN] *Can you thin the paint down so that it spreads more easily?* [I∅ + DOWN] *The population of the villages is thinning down now that so many people are going to the cities. Mary has thinned down a lot since last year.*

***thin out** *v adv*
**1** to remove (some young plants) to leave room for others to grow: [T1] *Mother is in the garden thinning out the onion plants; she should have a good crop this year.*
**2** to become less in quantity: [I∅] *The crowd thinned out when all the excitement was over.* → **thin down**
**3** to lose weight: [I∅] *Mary has thinned out a lot since last year.* → **thin down**

**think about** *v prep*
**1** to have thoughts concerning (something or someone); have (something or someone) in the mind: [I∅ + *about*] *Grace still thinks about her red-haired boy every day. I'm sorry, I wasn't listening, I was thinking about something else. You ought to spend more time thinking about your work. "We never do anything well till we cease to think about the manner of doing it."* (William Hazlitt, *Sketches and Essays: On Prejudice*) → **brood about, dwell on** (2), **linger on**[2], **mull over, muse on, pause on, ponder on, pore on, think of** (1), **think on**[2]
***2** to consider (something or someone): [T1] *We must think about Mother's health when choosing a home. Think about what you're saying! I have my family to think about, so I must find the best job that I can. I'm only thinking about your best interests!* [T6] *Do you think about whether anyone would be hurt by your action?* → **think of** (2)
***3** to have an opinion about (something or someone): [T1 (*no pass., simple tenses*)] *What do you think about the government's latest decision? I don't know what to think about the new chairman, he's a mystery to me.* → **think of** (7), **think to**
***4** to consider the idea of (something or usu. doing something): [T1 (*continuous when present tense*)] *His offer isn't the best possible, but it's the only one you've had so far, so it's worth thinking about.* [T4 (*continuous when present tense*)] *Are you still thinking about moving to the south, or have you not yet decided?* → **talk about** (3), **talk of** (2), **think of** (6)
**5 think twice about** → THINK TWICE

***think again** *v adv*
to reconsider; change one's mind: [I∅ (*usu. simple tenses*)] *The sudden drop in house prices has made me think again about selling the house.*

***think ahead** *v adv*
to consider the future: [I∅ (*to*)] *Thinking ahead, we might be wise to build the new factory now before prices rise again. We've taken the first step, but haven't yet thought ahead to our next move. It's difficult to think ahead a whole year and make plans according to future products.*

***think aloud** *v adv* also **think out loud**
to speak one's thoughts without addressing anyone: [I∅ (*usu. continuous tenses*)] *Sorry, no, I wasn't talking to you, I was just thinking aloud.*

***think back** *v adv*
to remember: [I∅ (*on, to*)] *That tune makes me think back to my childhood. If you think back on the past year, you can see what great changes you have made. Thinking back, it must have been before the war.*

**think before** *v prep*
**1** to have careful thoughts in advance of (doing something): [I∅ + *before* (*often simple tenses*)] *I wish Jane would learn to think before speaking, then she wouldn't offend so many people with careless remarks.*
**2 think twice before** → THINK TWICE

***think fit** *v adj* → **see fit**
*not fml* to decide it is suitable (to do something): [I∅ (*simple tenses*)] *It's not my place to advise you: do as you think fit.* [I3 (*simple tenses*)] *The chairman didn't think fit to close the meeting with the usual prayer, as he is not a Christian.*

**think for** *v prep*
**1** to have thoughts; use one's brain for (a certain length of time): [I∅ + *for*] *Please think for a moment before answering. "I could never find any man who could think for two minutes together."* (Sydney Smith, *Sketches of Moral Philosophy*)
***2** *old use* to imagine; suppose; guess; expect: [T1 (*no pass., simple tenses*)] *"She really is sorry to lose poor Miss Taylor, and I am sure she will miss her more than she thinks for."* (Jane Austen, *Emma*)
**3 think for oneself** to make one's own decisions; be independent in thought and opinion: *Not every politician seems able to think for himself: they seem to follow their leaders. "The average man's opinions are much less foolish than they would be if he thought for himself."* (Bertrand Russell)

**think of** *v prep*
**1** to have thoughts concerning (something or someone); have (something or someone) in one's mind: [I∅ + *of*] *You're very quiet; what are you thinking of? You're quite wrong: I was thinking of something completely different. Don't tell me Grace is still thinking of that red-haired boy!* → **think about** (1), etc.
***2** to consider (someone or something): [T1] *When I said that, I was not thinking of her feelings. I have so many things to think of that sometimes I forget my own needs. I was thinking particularly of the children when I chose the house. I can't go tonight, I have my mother to think of.* → **think about** (2)
***3** to imagine (something or doing something): [T1 (*usu. simple tenses*)] *I'd like to go, but think of the cost! If you think of the possi-*

*ble results before you act, you won't do anything so foolish.* [T4 (*usu. simple tenses*)] *I can't think of living in a place which has no seasons, it seems so strange.* [T6 (*usu. simple tenses*)] *I can't think of where I've put my glasses; have you seen them? Can you think of why she should do such a thing? I can't think of how to get out of this difficulty.* [V4a (*usu. simple tenses*)] *To think of Jim winning the prize year after year!* —**unthought-of** *adj*

***4** to remember (something or someone): [T1 (*usu. simple tenses*)] *Will you think of me after I've left? That tune makes me think of my childhood. I'm glad you thought of this hotel, where you stayed last year. I can't think of the title of the book, but it's a fat red one on the top shelf near the left.*

***5** to suggest, invent, or have the idea of (something or doing something): [T1 (*usu. simple tenses*)] *Can you think of a good person to become the next chairman? Children can always think of something interesting to pass the time. How did you think of such a wonderful idea? Don't worry, I'll think of a way out of our difficulty.* [T4 (*usu. simple tenses*)] *Did anyone think of bringing a rope? I would never have thought of asking him directly.* → **dream up, make up** (3), **think up**

***6** to consider the idea of (something or usu. doing something) before deciding: [T1 (*continuous when present tense*)] *Now I'm thinking of a smaller house; the big ones cost too much and take a lot of work.* [T4 (*continuous when present tense*)] *Are you still thinking of moving south? The winters here are terrible. I've been thinking of sending the children to another school.* → **talk about** (3), **talk of** (2), **think about** (4)

***7** to have an opinion about (something or someone): [X9 (*simple tenses*)] *What do you think of the government's latest action? I know that the director thinks highly of your work. Mary doesn't think much of Jane's new boyfriend.* —**well-thought-of** *adj* → **think about** (3), **think to**

***8** to regard (someone or something) (as or for something): [X9 (*as, for*) (*usu. simple tenses*)] *How do you think of your mother now that she is dead? I think of her as a sad person with little success in her life. So many people have thought of Mr Brown for the chairmanship.*

***9** to consider or be capable of (something or doing something): [T1 (*neg., simple tenses, usu. with would*)] *You needn't tell me not to sell the piano, I wouldn't think of such a thing. Such dishonest action is not to be thought of.* [T4 (*neg., simple tenses, usu. with would*)] *I wouldn't think of hurting a child.* —**unthought-of** *adj* → **dream of** (3)

**10 think better of: a** to have an improved opinion of (someone or something): [*usu. simple tenses*] *I think better of her now that she has said she's sorry she offended me; that takes moral courage.* **b** to decide not to follow (a plan originally intended): [*usu. simple tenses*] *I was going to sell the piano but then I thought better of it when you said that its value could increase if I waited.*

**11 think nothing of** to consider (doing something) as being not very special or difficult; regard (doing something) as easy: [*simple tenses*] *Jane thinks nothing of practising on the piano for two hours before breakfast.*

**12 think nothing of it** it doesn't matter: [*simple tenses*] *"I'm very grateful for your help." "Oh, think nothing of it."*

***think on**[1] *v adv*
esp. *NBrE not fml* to remember: [IØ (*simple tenses*)] *I'll get that letter written now, while I think on; I've been meaning to do it for a week.*

**think on/upon**[2] *v prep* → **think about** (1), etc.
esp. *old use* to direct one's mind towards thoughts of (something or someone): [IØ + *on/upon* (*often simple tenses*)] *We should think more on moral matters than we do.*

***think out** *v adv*
**1** to consider (something) in detail, with care, so as to arrive at an answer: [T1] *All possible ways out of our difficulty have now been thought out. Have you thought out the best method?* —**well-thought-out** *adj* → **think over** (1), **think through**
**2 think out loud** → THINK ALOUD

***think over** *v adv*
**1** to consider (something) seriously, at length, often alone: [T1b] *Think it over and let me have your decision tomorrow. Father likes to go into his study by himself to think things over.* → **think out** (1), **think through**
**2** to reconsider (something), often with a change of opinion: [T1b] *I've thought the plan over and decided not to join it after all.*

***think through** *v adv* → **think out** (1), **think over** (1)
to spend time considering (a matter): [T1b] *Now that we've thought the matter through, can we come to a decision?*

**think to** *v prep* → **think about** (3), **think of** (7)
*not fml* to have an opinion about (something or someone): [IØ + *to*] *I don't think much to the latest change in the tax laws. What do you think to this new musical group?*

***think twice** *v adv*
*not fml* to reconsider; have more careful thought: [IØ (*about, before*) (*usu. simple tenses*)] *I'd like to think twice about the contract before signing it. Always think twice before paying out large sums of money.*

***think up** *v adv* → **dream up, make up** (3), **think of** (5)
to invent (usu. an idea): [T1] *How did you think up such a clever way out of our difficulty? You can earn good money thinking up new ways to improve production in the firm?*

**think upon** *v prep* → THINK ON[2]

**thirst for** *v prep* → **hunger for, starve for**

**1** to desire or need (a drink): [IØ + *for*] *On these dry days, you soon thirst for a cool drink.*

*__2__ to desire (something) eagerly: [T1] *Young children thirst for knowledge; only later do the schools dull the edge of their keenness. The enemy soldiers were thirsting for blood. The villagers are thirsting for news; is there nothing to tell them?*

**thrash about/around** *v adv*

**1** to move about restlessly, as in discomfort: [L9 + ABOUT/AROUND (*often continuous tenses*)] *The poor child has been thrashing about in bed for hours, unable to get to sleep because of the fever. Look at all those fishes thrashing around in the net!* → **toss about** (2)

*__2__ to behave in an anxious fashion; act wildly but often in an undirected manner, (looking for something): [IØ (*for*) (*often continuous tenses*)] *I've been thrashing about for an answer to the difficulty, but without success. After all these weeks of thrashing around, I'm no nearer the answer.*

**thrash out** *v adv*

**1** to beat (something) out (of someone): [T1 + OUT (*of*)] *If the boy won't tell, we shall have to thrash the truth out (of him).*

*__2__ *not fml* to find an answer to (a difficulty) by talking with effort: [T1] *We must thrash out the question of Mr Brown's appointment, to which there is a good deal of opposition. The committee have already spent many hours thrashing out the best answer.* → **hash out**

**thread through** *v prep*

**1** to pass (something such as a thread) through (a hole): [T1 + *through*] *This wool is too thick for me to thread it through the eye of this fine needle.*

**2 thread one's way through** to find a way to pass carefully through (something such as a crowd) or deal satisfactorily with (something such as a difficulty): *Threading my way through the crowd, I soon reached the front. If I take things slowly, I should be able to thread my way through the difficulties facing me in my new job.* → **make through**

**threaten with** *v prep*

to promise harm to (someone) by means of or in the form of (something): [T1 + *with*] *The robber threatened the owner of the jewels with a gun. If you threaten the prisoner with severe pain he might admit his guilt.*

**thrill at/to** *v prep*

to feel excitement and pleasure because of (usu. something): [L9 + *at/to* (*usu. simple tenses*)] *She thrilled to the sound of his voice. All the villagers thrilled at the good news.*

**thrill with** *v prep*

to excite and please (someone) by means of (something): [T1 + *with*] *This young singer has thrilled crowds all over the world with her fine and sensitive singing.*

**thrive on/upon** *v prep*

to grow strong by eating (certain food); enjoy (an activity or lifestyle): [IØ + *on/upon* (*usu. simple tenses*)] *These animals thrive on the leaves of certain trees. My children thrived on this product. He's the sort of person who thrives on hard work.*

**throb away** *v adv*

to beat or ache continuously: [IØ + AWAY] *My tooth has been throbbing away all morning: I might have to have it out.*

**throng in** *v adv* → **crowd in** (1), etc.

to enter a building or enclosed space in a crowd: [L9 + IN] *When the gates of the ground were opened, all the football supporters thronged in.*

**throng into** *v prep* → **crowd into** (1), etc.

to enter (a building or enclosed space) in a crowd: [L9 + *into*] *The buyers thronged into the sale room where the prices promised to be so good.*

**throng out** *v adv* → **crowd out** (1)

to leave in a crowd: [L9 + OUT (*of*)] *When the performance was over, the public thronged out (of the theatre).*

*__throttle back/down__ *v adv*

**1** (of an engine) to (cause to) go slower by changing the controls: [IØ] *Remember to throttle back before you go round a sharp corner.* [T1] *Failing to throttle the engine down in time, he crashed the motorcycle into the fence.*

**2** *not fml* to make (something) advance more slowly: [T1] *While business is so unsure, it might be wise to throttle down the development of the firm until trade seems to be improving.*

**throw about/around[1]** *v adv*

**1** to scatter (something or things): [X9 + ABOUT/AROUND] *I wish the children would stop throwing stones about, it's quite dangerous for the little ones.* → **chuck about** (1), **fling about** (1), **hurl about** (1), **toss about** (1)

**2** to wave (one's arms and/or legs) without direction: [X9 + ABOUT/AROUND] *You'll never keep afloat if you keep throwing your arms and legs about like that; you have to make the proper swimming strokes.* → **chuck about** (2), **fling about** (2), **hurl about** (2)

**3 throw one's money about/around** *not fml* to spend money foolishly, often so as to show one's wealth: *Our new neighbour is always throwing his money around, paying for local parties, supporting groups, and anything to make us notice how rich he is.* → **chuck about** (3), **fling about** (3), **hurl about** (3), **toss about** (4)

**4 throw one's weight about/around** *not fml* to give unnecessary orders; try to use one's power over other people: *Ever since he was put in charge of a bigger group of workers, he's been throwing his weight about in the factory, and* *losing a lot of old friends.* → **chuck about** (4), **fling about** (4), **hurl about** (4), **toss about** (5)

**throw about/around²** *v prep*
to place (something, things, or people) so as to cover or surround (something): [X9 + *about/around*] *She threw a thin coat about her shoulders to keep off the wind. A ring of police has been thrown around the building where the gunman is hiding.*

**throw around¹** *v adv* → THROW ABOUT¹

**throw around²** *v prep* → THROW ABOUT²

**throw aside** *v adv*
**1** to throw (something or someone) to one side: [X9 + ASIDE] *Throwing his school work aside, he ran to join the other children.* → **cast off** (1), etc., **lay aside** (1), etc.
*__2__ to disregard, give up, or have nothing more to do with (someone or something): [T1 (*often simple tenses*)] *Once he became rich, he threw aside his old friends. Henry joined the opposing political party, throwing aside his former loyalties. Throwing aside all his usual care, he risked all his money on a wild plan. These rules are not made to be thrown aside lightly.* → **cast aside** (2), etc.

**throw at** *v prep*
**1** to lift (something) and direct it towards (someone or something), esp. so as to harm: [T1 + *at*] *Those boys have been throwing stones at passing cars. The speaker did not care to have eggs thrown at him during his speech.* → **chuck at** (1), **fling at** (1), **hurl at** (1), **shy at²**, **sling at** (1), **throw to** (1), **toss at**
*__2__ to direct (a look) towards (someone): [D1] *He threw a fierce look at me, so I wondered what I had done wrong.* → **dart at, shoot at** (3)
**3 throw the book (of rules) at** to charge (someone) with having broken a rule; threaten (someone) with punishment: [*often simple tenses*] *Make sure that you behave very correctly towards the officer, or he's likely to throw the book at you for disobedience.*
**4 throw mud at** *not fml* to speak rudely or offensively about (someone) in public: *No politician will win the votes of serious-minded people if all he does is throw mud at his opponent.* → **sling at** (2)
**5 throw oneself at someone** to force one's attention on someone so as to win his or her love: *If you throw yourself at that boy, he's likely to run away.* → **chuck at** (2), **fling at** (4), **hurl at** (2)

**throw away** *v adv*
**1** to get rid of (something): [X9 + AWAY] *Let's throw the old television set away, it's been giving more and more trouble; we should get a new one.* —**throwaway** *n, adj* → **throw out** (2), etc.
*__2__ to waste or fail to take advantage of (something): [T1] *Never throw away a chance to improve your English. If you leave now, you will be throwing away your education. You have a good lead in the tennis game; don't throw it away by being careless. I'm surprised that he would consider throwing away his life-long principles to behave like that.* → **chuck away** (2), **chuck up** (5), **fling away** (2), **fling up** (2), **give away** (6), **hurl away** (2), **throw up** (2), **toss away** (2), **toss up** (3)
*__3__ to speak (words) carelessly, as by lowering the voice: [T1] *You threw away that last line, no one could hear you.* —**throwaway** *n, adj* → **chuck away** (3), **fling away** (3)

***throw away on/upon** *v adv prep*
**1** to waste (something) by using it for (a purpose) or giving it to (someone): [D1 (*often pass.*)] *Why did you throw your money away on such a risky way to get interest? I'm afraid that your good advice is thrown away on that boy.* → **chuck away on** (1), **fling away on** (1), **hurl away on** (1)
**2** to waste the worth of (someone or oneself) in a bad relationship such as marriage with (someone): [D1] *Mary's father did not want to throw his daughter away on a man he disapproved of. Why are you throwing yourself away on a woman like that, who can wreck your life?* → **chuck away on** (2), **fling away on** (2), **hurl away on** (2)

**throw back** *v adv*
**1** to return (something directed at one): [T1 + BACK (*at, to*)] *All day balls come over our fence from children playing in the park: I seem to spend half my life throwing them back!* → **fling back** (2)
**2** to move (part of the body) backwards: [X9 + BACK] *Throwing his head back, the dog gave a terrible cry. Throw your shoulders back: stand up straight!* → **fling back** (1), **toss back** (1)
**3** to fold (cloth) back, as to uncover something: [X9 + BACK] *Throwing back the curtains, he let the sunlight into the room again. I threw the bedclothes back and jumped out of bed. She threw her fur coat back to show her lovely shoulders.*
*__4__ to delay the advance of (something): [T1 (*often simple tenses*)] *The recent fire has thrown back production badly. A week's illness throws me back in my work badly.* → **bring on** (3), etc.
*__5__ to be or look like a relative in the distant past: [IØ (*to*) (*simple tenses*)] *The boy throws back to his great-great-grandfather, who had that unusually red hair.* —**throwback** *n* → **cast back** (2)
**6 throw one's mind back (to)** to remember (usu. something): [*usu. simple tenses*] *If you throw your mind back a few years, you will understand how much the city has changed. Hearing that tune again threw my mind back to my childhood.* → **cast back** (1)

***throw back at** *v adv prep*
to use a memory of (something bad in the past) against (someone): [D1 (*often pass.*)] *Time after time when he tried to get a job, his*

*time in prison was thrown back at him.*

***throw back on/upon** *v adv prep*

to force or reduce (someone) to depend on (something): [D1 (*usu. pass.*)] *The father's unemployment had the effect of throwing the family back on their savings. When the electric power failed, people were thrown back on conversation for amusement. Lost in the desert, we were thrown back on our own natural abilities.*

**throw down**[1] *v adv*

**1** to direct (something or someone) with force onto the ground or furniture, or in a downward direction: [X9 + DOWN] *The child threw his schoolbooks down on the ground and ran to join the other children at play. He threw down some money and left. The baby was thrown down by the explosion with such force that his legs broke.* → **chuck down** (1), **fling down** (1), **hurl down** (1), **toss down**

***2** to place (oneself) quickly at full length on the ground or floor: [T1 (*usu. simple tenses*)] *He threw himself down as the bullet flew overhead.* → **chuck down** (2), **fling down** (2), **hurl down** (2), **throw to** (4)

***3** to defeat (someone) or destroy (something): [T1 (*often simple tenses*)] *The people need a strong leader to help them to throw down their unjust rulers. True believers must throw down the temples of the false gods.* → **cast down** (2)

**4 throw down one's arms** to yield to the enemy: *You have lost the battle, and your general has admitted defeat; throw down your arms, and we will show mercy!*

**5 throw down the gauntlet** to offer an invitation to compete: *By calling the election at this time, the government has thrown down the gauntlet to the opposing parties.* → **fling down** (3), **take up** (23)

**6 throw down one's tools** to refuse to work because of disagreement: *The mine workers have thrown down their tools again, demanding shorter hours and higher pay.* → **chuck down** (3), **fling down** (4)

**throw down**[2] *v prep*

to direct (something or someone) with force to the bottom of (something): [X9 + *down*] *The murderer threw the body down the cliff, hoping that it would never be discovered.*

**throw for** *v prep* → **knock for** (2)

**throw someone for a loop** *AmE infml* **a** to defeat someone in a fight: [*usu. simple tenses*] *The young man was proud of his strength and ability, but the experienced old fighter soon threw him for a loop.* **b** to confuse someone; make someone helpless in argument: [*usu. simple tenses*] *The listener's next question threw the speaker for a loop; he had not expected such informed opinion.*

**throw in**[1] *v adv*

**1** to direct (something) with some force into something such as a place, space, or container: [X9 + IN] *Please throw your waste paper in here. A bomb has been thrown in, but it hasn't yet exploded. Will you children hang up your clothes properly, instead of just opening the cupboard door and throwing them in!* → **chuck in** (1), **fling in**[1] (1), **pitch in** (1), **toss in**[1] (1)

***2** (in many ball games) to throw (the ball) into the main area of play from an outlying part of the field or court: [T1] *Which player should throw the ball in when it has gone out of play?* —**throw-in** *n*

***3** to add (something), often as a gift: [T1 (*often simple tenses*)] *If you buy the furniture, the store will throw in a small television set. All these troubles, and bad weather thrown in!* → **chuck in** (3), **fling in**[1] (3), **toss in**[1] (2)

***4** to add (words), often as an interruption: [T1 (*usu. simple tenses*)] *There was no need for you to throw in that unnecessary remark. 'But I did go!' she threw in. Although the argument was fierce, I was able to throw a word in from time to time.* → **put in**[1] (4), etc.

***5** *not fml* to stop attempting (something): [T1] *Jim has thrown in his studies. Why did you throw in such a good job when they're so hard to find? I've had enough of this competition, I'm going to throw it in.* → **give up** (2), etc.

***6** to include or add (something, as in speech or writing): [T1 (*usu. simple tenses*)] *In his letters, he always throws in some amusing remark about his neighbour's activities. Don't forget to throw in a mention of the chairman when you give the vote of thanks.* → **put in**[1] (3), **toss in**[1] (4), **write in** (1)

**7 throw in one's cards/hand: a** to stop playing cards: *I've had enough of this game; I'll throw my cards in and go to bed.* **b** *not fml* to give up any attempt: *I'm tired of trying to write a successful book, I think I'll throw my hand in.* → **chuck in** (5), **fling in**[1] (5)

**8 throw in the towel/sponge: a** *not fml* (in boxing) to admit defeat; yield a fight: *Isn't it time the old fighter threw in the towel?* **b** to give up any attempt; admit defeat: *If you leave the competition now, everyone will think you're throwing in the towel, unless you give your real reasons.* → **chuck in** (6), **chuck up** (6), **fling in**[1] (6), **fling up** (10)

**throw in**[2] *v prep*

**1** to direct (something) with some force into (a space): [X9 + *in*] *Don't throw your shoes in the cupboard, put them in neatly. It's so easy these days to do the washing, you just throw the clothes in the washing machine!* → **fling in**[2] (1), **toss in**[2]

**2 throw dust in someone's eyes** *not fml* to deceive someone: *The director is a tricky woman to do a business deal with; she has a way of throwing dust in the customer's eyes, so that he thinks he is getting a better offer than he really is.*

**3 throw something in someone's face/teeth** *not fml* to blame someone for something: *There's no need to throw his recent failure in his teeth in that unkind way.* → **cast in** (4), **fling in²** (2)
**4 throw a spanner in the works** *not fml* to spoil something, usu. on purpose: *Everything was going nicely with our plans, until my uncle refused his money and threw a spanner in the works.* also *AmE not fml* **throw a monkey wrench in the works** → **put in²** (27), **throw into** (9)

**throw in with** *v adv prep* → **cast in with, fling in with**
**throw in one's lot with** to join (someone), esp. in a plan or attempt, often wrong: *It's sad to see that he's thrown in his lot with criminals.* also *AmE* **throw in with**

**throw into** *v prep*
**1** to direct (something) with some force, as with the hand, inside (something); cause (someone) to fall into (something): [X9 + *into*] *I just throw the clothes into the washing machine and switch it on. The boat rocked wildly, throwing him into the water.* → **fling into** (1, 2), **hurl into** (1), **pitch into** (1), **toss into** (1)
*__2__ to force (someone) to go to (prison): [D1 (*often pass.*)] *The criminal was thrown into prison as soon as he was found guilty.* → **fling into** (3), **hurl into** (2), **toss into** (2)
*__3__ to cause (someone or something) to reach (a state): [D1 (*usu. simple tenses*)] *Your remarks have thrown her into a temper. His speech threw the meeting into confusion.* → **get into** (11), etc.
*__4__ to add (words) to (something such as a conversation): [D1 (*usu. simple tenses*)] *I wasn't able to throw a word into the argument the whole time I was there. She sat silently, throwing the odd word into the conversation from time to time.* → **fling into** (4)
*__5__ to add or give (something such as help) towards (a purpose, event, or doing something): [D1] *We threw all the men we had into the battle. She tries to throw too much influence into the group's decision.* [V4b] *The villagers threw all possible effort into rebuilding the bombed houses.* → **fling into** (6)
**6 throw one's hat into the ring** *not fml* to declare one's intention of taking part in a competition, esp. an election: *Now that the election of the President is about to take place, how many people have thrown their hats into the ring?* → **fling into** (8), **toss into** (4)
**7 throw oneself into** to put much effort, time, and keenness into (something such as an activity, or doing something): [*often simple tenses*] *The best cure for unhappiness is to throw yourself into your work. After school, John always threw himself into cricket. Jane really throws herself into learning any new song, doesn't she?* → **fling into** (7), **hurl into** (4)
**8 throw something into relief** to make something clearly seen, as against a different background: [*usu. simple tenses*] *The reddening sky threw into relief a line of trees on the horizon.*
**9 throw a spanner into the works** *not fml* to spoil something usu. on purpose: *The jewel thieves thought they had the robbery perfectly planned, until the day before, when the owner unexpectedly took the jewels to the bank, so throwing a spanner into the works. Government talks with the trade union were going well until the chief union leader threw a spanner into the works by declaring that his group were not prepared to yield on any matter in the talks.* also *AmE not fml* **throw a monkey wrench into the works** → **put in²** (27), **throw in²** (4)

**throw off¹** *v adv*
**1** to remove (something), as with some force: [X9 + OFF] *Look how the duck shakes its back to throw the water off! He put his hand on her shoulder, but she threw it off.* → **cast off** (1), **chuck off** (1), **fling off** (1), **shake off¹** (1), **toss off** (1)
**2** to remove (clothing) quickly: [X9 + OFF] *Throwing off his coat, he jumped into the river to save the drowning child. It's good to throw off heavy clothes now that summer's here.* → **cast off** (1), etc.
*__3__ to escape from (someone, esp. someone chasing one): [T1] *If we run fast we might be able to throw the police off. I wish I could throw off these newspaper reporters who are following me everywhere. Jane is having considerable difficulty in throwing off her former boyfriend.* → **chuck off** (2), **fling off** (2), **shake off¹** (2)
*__4__ to get free from (something unwanted): [T1 (*usu. simple tenses*)] *Will Jane be able to throw off her cold in time for the concert? It's very difficult to throw off old habits of thought. He was pleased to be able to throw off such an unwelcome responsibility.* → **fling off** (3)
*__5__ to defeat (an opponent): [T1] *This young tennis player will have a hard time throwing off the more experienced competitors.* → **fling off** (4)
*__6__ to give out (heat, smell, etc.): [T1 (*usu. simple tenses*)] *When this material burns, it throws off a nasty smell and a lot of smoke.* → **fling off** (5), **give forth, give off, give out** (1), **throw out** (12)
*__7__ to write (something) easily: [T1] *I can throw off a poem in half an hour. It shouldn't take me more than an afternoon to throw this article off.* → **dash off** (2), etc.
*__8__ to speak (something) carelessly: [T1 (*often simple tenses*)] *He threw off a list of things he wanted done, too fast for me to write them down. Be careful what remarks you throw off in front of her, she's very sensitive* → **put in¹** (4), etc.
*__9__ esp. *AmE* to confuse (someone or an animal); cause (someone) to make a mistake (in something); cause mistakes in (something): [T1 (*in*) (*usu. simple tenses*)] *Let's go through*

*the river, it might throw the dogs off. Any small interruption is likely to throw off my calculations. Any small interruption is likely to throw me off in my calculations.* → **throw out** (9), etc.

**throw off²** *v prep*

**1** to remove (something) with some force from (something): [X9 + *off*] *The dog shakes all over to throw the water off his back. Angrily, she threw his hand off her shoulder.* → **shake off²** (1)

**2 throw someone off (his/her) balance: a** to make someone lose his balance, as to fall: [*usu. simple tenses*] *A sudden noise from the crowd threw him off balance for a moment and he fell to his death.* **b** to confuse, shock, or surprise (someone): [*usu. simple tenses*] *The unexpected question threw the speaker off balance for a moment while he collected his thoughts.*

**3 throw someone off guard** to surprise someone, often into showing his true thoughts: [*often simple tenses*] *If you can throw the chairman off guard with a carefully worded question, he may tell us of the company's plans. The prisoner was thrown off guard by a remark from the lawyer, and made a mistake which showed his guilt.* → **catch off**

**4 throw someone off the scent/track/trail: a** to lead someone or an animal the wrong way: [*often simple tenses*] *Let's go through the river, it might throw the dogs off the scent. Walking backwards in our own footsteps will help to throw the police off the track.* **b** to give someone a false idea, often so as to prevent the discovery of one's actions, guilt, etc.: [*often simple tenses*] *These unrelated events tend to throw the reader off the track (of the story). If the police believe our story, it should throw them off the trail for a time.* → **put off²** (4)

**throw on¹** *v adv*

**1** to add (something), as to a pile, by directing it with the hand: [X9 + ON] *The fire's getting low, throw some more wood on, will you?*

**2** to put (clothes) on hurriedly: [X9 + ON] *We haven't time to dress, just throw a coat on, over your nightclothes, before the fire gets worse. Throw a dress on and let's go to the party at once.* → **fling on¹**

**throw on/upon²** *v prep*

**1** to direct (something) onto (something), as with the hand: [X9 + *on/upon*] *Throw some more wood on the fire, will you, it's getting low. Throwing some money on the table, he walked out angrily. The ship has been thrown on the rocks and is sinking!* → **cast on²** (1), **fling on²** (1), **pull over²** (1), etc.

**2** to cause (light or shade) to fall on (something or someone): [X9 + *on/upon* (*often simple tenses*)] *Please throw some light on this corner to see if the lost ring is there. After dinner, the office block to the west throws its shadow on our windows, so we don't see the setting sun.* → **cast on²** (5), **cast over²** (3), **throw over²** (3)

*__3__ to make (oneself) depend on (something): [D1] *I throw myself on your support to help me win this election.*

*__4__ to place (something such as blame) on (someone): [D1] *I'm tired of having the blame thrown on me for everything that goes wrong. The jewel thief tried to throw the responsibility on his companion so that he could go free.* → **pin on²** (2), **put on²** (2)

**5 throw cold water on** *not fml* to discourage (a plan): *The children planned to go sailing alone, but Father threw cold water on the idea because he thought it was too dangerous.* → **pour on²** (2)

**6 throw doubt on** *not fml* to make people wonder about the truth of (something): *Everyone was prepared to accept the statement until the chairman threw doubt on it.* → **cast on²** (3)

**7 throw light on** *not fml* to make (something) clear: [*usu. simple tenses*] *Have the police been able to throw any light on the mystery of the stolen jewels yet? "It all came about in a way which is worth recalling if only for the light it throws on our Captain's character."* (Laurens van der Post, *The Hunter and the Whale*) → **shed on** (2)

**8 throw oneself on someone's mercy** to place one's trust in someone's kindness; ask for a light punishment or sense of justice: *If the judge finds you guilty, you can only throw yourself on the mercy of the court.* → **cast on²** (4), **fling on²** (2)

**throw open** *v adv*

**1** to open (something such as a door) violently: [X9 + OPEN] *The angry father threw the door open and marched into his daughter's room.*

*__2__ to declare (something such as a place or competition) free for anyone to enter: [T1 (*to*) (*usu. pass., simple tenses*)] *The gardens of the great house are being thrown open to the public. Since the tennis competition was thrown open to professionals, the standard of play has improved.*

**throw out** *v adv*

**1** to direct (something or someone) outside a place, as with the hand, usu. with some force: [X9 + OUT (*of*)] *Climb into the hole and throw the ball out, will you? When the fire reached the bedroom, they had to throw the baby out of the window, where she was safely caught by the firemen. In the crash, passengers were thrown out onto the tracks.* → **chuck out** (1), **fling out** (1), **pitch out** (1), **toss out** (1)

*__2__ to get rid of (something): [T1] *I really must throw out those old newspapers.* —**throw-out** *n* → **cast away** (1), **chuck away** (1), **chuck out** (2), **fling away** (1), **fling out** (2), **hurl away** (1), **sling out** (1), **throw away** (1), **toss away** (1), **toss out** (2), **turn out** (4)

*3 to push or stretch (part of the body) forward: [T1] *She threw out a leg and made him fall. Throw out your chests, men! Look like soldiers! He threw out his arms to welcome her.* → **put out** (1), etc.

*4 to make (someone) leave because of a fault: [T1 (*of*) (*usu. simple tenses*)] *Two members were thrown out (of the club) for failing to pay the money they owed.* → **be out** (14), **boot out, bounce out** (2), **cast out** (2), **chuck out** (3), **eject from** (2), **fling out** (4), **hurl out** (1), **kick out** (4), **pitch out** (2), **put out** (5), **shove out** (6), **sling out** (2), **toss out** (3), **turf out, turn out** (2)

*5 to make (someone) leave a home: [T1 (*of*) (*often pass.*)] *The old lady was thrown out of the house because the owner wanted to pull it down.* → **chuck out** (4), **eject from** (2), **fling out** (5), **kick out** (5), **put out** (5), **sling out** (2), **toss out** (4), **turf out, turn out** (3)

*6 to refuse to accept (a suggestion, law, etc.): [T1 (*usu. simple tenses*)] *The new law was thrown out when it reached the last stage in Parliament. Why did the committee throw my entry out? I'm old enough to compete.* → **chuck out** (5), **fling out** (6), **hurl out** (2), **toss out** (5), **turn down** (4)

*7 to say (something) carelessly: [T1 (*often simple tenses*)] *Throwing out an instruction as he left, he rushed from the office.* → **put in**[1] (4), etc.

*8 to offer or produce (something such as a suggestion): [T1 (*often simple tenses*)] *If none of these ideas are good enough let's hear you throw a better one out yourself! After talking together, the group threw out several good ideas.* → **fling out** (8), **toss out** (7)

*9 to confuse (someone); make (someone) make a mistake (in something); cause mistakes in (something): [T1 (*usu. simple tenses*)] *The unexpected answer threw the speaker out for a moment. You interrupted me, and threw me out in my calculations. Any small interruption is likely to throw out my calculations.* → **be out** (9), **be out in** (1), **put out** (18), **throw off**[1] (9)

*10 to spoil (something): [T1 (*often pass.*)] *Our plans were thrown out by bad weather.* → **chuck out** (7)

*11 *mil* to strengthen a line of defence by placing (additional men) in front or at the sides: [T1] *We shall have to throw out a line of experienced soldiers to protect our weak front.*

*12 to give out (heat, light, etc.): [T1] *The dying fire was throwing out a dull red light.* → **fling off** (5), **give forth, give off, give out** (1), **throw off**[1] (6)

*13 (in cricket) to cause (a player) to end his turn by throwing the ball to touch his wicket before he reaches it: [T1 (*often simple tenses*)] *A fielder has the ball: can he throw him out?* → **be out** (7), etc.

*14 to cause damage to (part of the body): [T1 (*usu. simple tenses*)] *I can't play tennis with you this week, I've thrown my elbow out.* → **put out** (14)

*15 to cause (someone) to feel worried, annoyed, or uncomfortable: [T1 (*usu. simple tenses*)] *He seemed grealty thrown out by the arrival of the new workers. Nothing ever throws her out, she always stays calm and cool.* → **put out** (15), etc., (16)

*16 to build (an additional part of a building): [T1] *With the gift of money, the college intends to throw out a new wing for science studies.*

**17 throw out the baby with the bathwater** *not fml* to lose something valuable when getting rid of something worthless: *There are some good points to the system; let's not destroy the method for a few faults, or we shall be throwing out the baby with the bathwater.*

**18 throw someone out of work** to cause someone to lose his job: *The serious fire at the bicycle factory has thrown 2,000 men and women out of work.* → **put out of** (9)

**throw over**[1] *v adv*

**1** to cause (something) to pass over something, by directing it with some force, usu. with the hand: [T1 + OVER] *Our ball's on your side of the fence: would you please throw it over?*

*2 *not fml* to end a relationship with (someone) (usu. sexual): [T1a (*usu. simple tenses*)] *Helen was the girl that Jim threw over in order to marry Mary.*

*3 *not fml* to end (something such as a habit): [T1 (*often simple tenses*)] *I've decided to throw over the lifestyle I've been used to in my parents' home, and go my own way.*

**throw over**[2] *v prep*

**1** to direct (something) to pass above (something), usu. with the hand, with some force: [T1 + *over*] *Will you throw our ball over your fence, please?*

**2** to cause (something or someone) to cover or cross (something): [X9 + *over*] *Throw a warm cover over the sleeping child. If you do that again, I'll throw you over my knee and beat you. The soldiers can throw a bridge over the river in a few hours. Throw the rope over the hook and fasten it tight.* → **pull over**[2] (1), etc.

**3** to cause (light or shade) to fall on (something or someone): [X9 + *over*] *Please stand to one side, you're throwing your shadow over my work.* → **cast on**[2] (5), **cast over**[2] (3), **throw on**[2] (2)

**throw overboard** *v adv*

**1** to cause (something or someone) to fall off a ship into the water: [X9 + OVERBOARD] *Do you mean to tell me that you just throw the kitchen waste overboard into the clean lake? The murderer knocked the man unconscious and threw him overboard, so that it would seem as if he simply drowned.*

*2 to give up or fail to fulfil (something such as an idea): [T1b] *The chairman seems to* *have thrown all his principles overboard, acting like that.*

**throw to** *v prep*

**1** to direct (something) towards (someone or something) with some force, as with the hand, for him to catch it: [X9 + *to*] *Don't throw the ball to me, throw it to the man over there. The animal was up the tree, throwing the nuts to the ground.* → **fling to** (1), **throw at** (1)

**2 throw caution/discretion to the winds** to be bold; take risks: *The only thing to do is to throw caution to the winds and make a decision, right or wrong; anything is better than uncertainty.* → **fling to** (2)

**3 throw something to the dogs** *not fml* **a** to waste something: [*usu. pass.*] *If you leave now, all that education will be thrown to the dogs.* **b** to yield something in order to save oneself: [*usu. pass.*] *Something will have to be thrown to the dogs; why don't you offer him one of the small contracts, so that we can keep the bigger one?*

**4 throw someone/oneself to the floor/ground** to (cause to) lie down quickly: [*usu. simple tenses*] *Throwing the children to the floor, he saved their lives from the gunman. He threw himself to the ground as the shells flew overhead.* → **fling to** (3), **throw down**[1] (2)

**5 throw someone to the wolves** *not fml* to let someone suffer, for one's own gain: *Are you actually prepared to throw your brother to the wolves so that you can take over his job?*

**throw together** *v adv*

**1** to gather (things) in a hurry: [X9 + TOGETHER] *Give me a minute to throw my clothes together, and I'll join you. Throwing together a few books and possessions, he ran out of the house.* → **chuck together** (1), **fling together** (1), **toss together** (1)

*__2__ to build, make, or write (something) hastily: [T1 (*often pass.*)] *This poem reads as if it was thrown together in half an hour. The hut isn't safe; it was thrown together some years ago. Can you throw a meal together in a few minutes?* → **chuck together** (2), **chuck up** (4), **fling together** (3), **fling up** (5), **knock together** (2), **knock up** (3), **throw up** (6), **toss together** (2)

*__3__ to cause (usu. two people) to meet: [T1b (*usu. pass.*)] *Jim and Mary were thrown together by the war.* → **bring together** (2), etc.

**throw up** *v adv*

**1** to cause (something or someone) to rise, as into the air, by directing with some force, as with the hands: [X9 + UP] *For hours the boy would stand throwing a ball up and catching it again. The machine threw up great heaps of earth. Come to the bottom of the ladder and throw up the other brush, will you? She threw the window up and shouted to her friend in the street. All the crowd cheered and threw their hats up in the air. The baby used to love being thrown up into the air and safely caught again.* → **cast up** (1), **chuck up** (1), **fling up**[1] (1), **toss up** (1)

*__2__ to waste (something): [T1] *You shouldn't throw up a chance like that! Don't throw up your education by leaving now.* → **throw away** (2), etc.

*__3__ to stop attempting; give up (something): [T1] *Jim has thrown up his studies. Why did you throw up such a good job, when they're so hard to get?* → **give up** (2), etc.

*__4__ *sl* to be sick; vomit (something such as food): [IØ] *Jane can't come, she's been throwing up all morning.* [T1] *The child has thrown up her dinner again!* → **bring up** (4), etc.

*__5__ to produce (something or someone): [T1 (*usu. simple tenses*)] *His long search threw up one old letter. When did Britain last throw up a great musician?* → **fling up** (4)

*__6__ to build (usu. a building) hastily: [T1] *Let's use this wood to throw up a shelter for the night.* → **throw together** (2), etc.

*__7__ to bring (something usu. bad) to people's attention; mention (something harmful to someone): [T1 (*often pass.*)] *I don't want his past thrown up in court.* → **fling up** (6), **sling up** (2)

**8 throw up one's hands (in despair)** to lose all hope; admit defeat: [*usu. simple tenses*] *His mother threw up her hands in despair when the boy failed yet another examination. That's the last time I'm trying: I throw up my hands!* → **fling up** (7)

**9 throw up one's hands in horror** to express violent fear: [*usu. simple tenses*] *She entered the room, then threw up her hands in horror at the terrible sight that met her eyes.* → **fling up** (8)

**throw upon** *v prep* → THROW ON[2]

**thrum on** *v prep* → **strum on**

to play rather carelessly on (a musical instrument): [IØ + *on*] *Jane often likes thrumming on the piano instead of doing her formal practice.*

**thrust against** *v prep* → **press against, push against**

to push (something) with force against (something or someone): [X9 + *against* (*usu. simple tenses*)] *He thrust the gun against my side, urging me to move over to the wall.* [L9 + *against*] *I could feel the people behind me in the crowd thrusting against me, pushing me forward.*

**thrust aside** *v adv* → **elbow aside, push aside, shoulder aside**

**1** to push (someone) on one side with sudden rough force: [X9 + ASIDE (*usu. simple tenses*)] *That rude man thrust me aside and got on the bus ahead of me!*

*__2__ to make (someone) yield place to someone else: [T1a (*usu. pass.*)] *When jobs are scarce, young people entering the work force tend to get thrust aside in favour of experienced workers with more to offer the firm.*

**thrust at** *v prep*

**1** to aim to strike (someone), usu. with a sharp instrument: [IØ + *at* (*usu. simple*

*tenses)] He thrust at his opponent with his sword, but the man was too quick for him.*
**2** to push (something) suddenly or with force towards (someone), as to attract his attention: [X9 + *at*] *He thrust the letter at me so that I could see the signature for myself.* → **push at, push towards** (1), **thrust towards** (1)

**thrust away** *v adv* → **push away** (2)
to make (something or someone) move away by pushing violently: [X9 + AWAY (*usu. simple tenses*)] *Jane thrust her plate away in a bad temper, refusing to eat. She ran to him for a kiss, but he thrust her away unkindly.*

***thrust back** *v adv* → **push back** (2)
*mil* to cause (an enemy) to move back, losing ground: [T1] *The enemy are being thrust back on all fronts.*

**thrust down** *v prep*
**1** to push (something) roughly down (something): [X9 + *down* (*usu. simple tenses*)] *Quickly, she thrust the money down her stocking so that he wouldn't find it. Thrust your hand down the hole to see if the rabbit is still there.* → **force down** (1), **push down²** (1), **ram down²** (1), **stuff down** (1)
**2 thrust something down someone's throat** *not fml* to force someone to accept something such as an idea: *The parents are complaining that some unpopular subjects are being thrust down the students' throats.* → **force down** (2), **push down²** (2), **ram down** (2), **stuff down** (2)

**thrust forward** *v adv*
**1** to (cause to) move forward by pushing heavily: [L9 + FORWARD] *The crowd, thrusting forward to see the Queen, broke the fence that was supposed to keep them in place.* [X9 + FORWARD (*usu. simple tenses*)] *Eager hands thrust Oliver forward to ask for more.* → **press forward** (1), **push forward** (1)
***2** esp. *mil* to advance, often with difficulty: [IØ] *Our army succeeded in thrusting forward to new positions formerly held by the enemy.* → **press forward** (2), **push forward** (2)
***3** to try to force people's attention on (something, someone, or oneself): [T1b (*often simple tenses*)] *I think the Minister's speech has thrust the case forward into the public eye. I do dislike mothers who thrust their daughters forward as the best girls for any part. Mary has always hated parties, never being one to thrust herself forward.* → **push forward** (4), **push oneself** (1)
**4 thrust one's way forward** to force one's way ahead, esp. violently: *It's not fair, he got to the front by thrusting his way forward; make him move to the back and wait his turn!* → **elbow forward, push forward** (5), **shoulder forward**

**thrust from** *v prep* → **push from**
to make (something or someone) move away by pushing violently: [X9 + *from* (*usu. simple tenses*)] *Jane thrust her dinner from her in a bad temper, refusing to eat. Why do you thrust me from you so unkindly? I thought you loved me!*

***thrust home** *v adv*
**1** to make someone such as an opponent feel the forceful effect of (something): [T1 (*usu. simple tenses*)] *The speaker thrust home his point, and the argument was won. The soldiers were ordered to thrust the attack home with all their remaining force.* → **press home** (1), **push home** (2)
**2 thrust home an/one's advantage** to make good use of a chance that is offered: *The owner seemed to be weakening about his price, so, thrusting home our advantage, we mentioned again the faults in the house and offered a lower price.* → **push home** (3)

**thrust in¹** *v adv* → **plunge in¹, press in¹** (1), **push in¹** (1)
to force (something or someone) inwards or inside something: [X9 + IN (*to*) (*usu. simple tenses*)] *I had to thrust my way in through the crowd. The door opened, and the guards thrust the prisoner in with rough force. He took the prisoner by the neck and thrust his sword in.*

**thrust in²** *v prep* → **fit into** (1), etc.
to force (things or people) into (something): [X9 + *in* (*usu. simple tenses*)] *He tried to thrust some more clothes in the case, but there was no room. The door opened, and the guards thrust another prisoner in the room. He took the prisoner by the neck and thrust his sword in his body.*

**thrust into** *v prep*
**1** to push (something or someone) forcefully into (something such as a space or container): [X9 + *into* (*usu. simple tenses*)] *With a shout of victory, he thrust his sword into his enemy's body. The guard thrust another prisoner into the room.* → **fit into** (1), etc., **plunge in²** (1), **plunge into** (1)
***2** to persuade, urge, or force (someone) into (something): [D1 (*usu. simple tenses*)] *Unwillingly, he found himself thrust into a position of power.* → **push into** (2)
***3** to force (usu. something) into (a state): [D1 (*usu. simple tenses*)] *Foolish mistakes by the nation's leaders have thrust it into a war that could have been avoided. The city was thrust into darkness when lightning struck the electricity supply station.* → **plunge into** (2)

***thrust on/upon** *v prep* → **land with,** etc., **push on²** (2)
to force acceptance of (something or someone) on (someone): [D1 (*usu. pass.*)] *I've had three of the neighbours' children thrust on me for the afternoon! I didn't want this job, it was thrust on me. "But be not afraid of greatness: some men are born great, some achieve greatness, and some have greatness thrust upon them."* (Shakespeare, *Twelfth Night*)

**thrust out** *v adv*
**1** to move or push (part of the body) sudden-

ly forward: [X9 + OUT (*usu. simple tenses*)] *She thrust out a leg and made him fall. Thrust out your chests, men! Look like soldiers! As people passed, he thrust out a hand for money.* → **put out** (1), etc.

**2** to push (something) forwards, as with force: [X9 + OUT (*usu. simple tenses*)] *He thrust out the letter to me as if it contained a threat. Thrusting out the burning stick as far as he could reach, he ran to light the next fire.*

***3** *not fml* to dismiss (someone), often unfairly: [T1] *One of our best workers has been thrust out to make way for the director's son.* → **push out** (4)

**thrust through** *v adv; prep* → **elbow through, push through** (3), **shoulder through**

**thrust one's way through** to force one's way through (something such as a crowd) by pushing roughly: *That man has got to the front in the most rude manner, thrusting his way through (the people).*

**thrust towards** *v prep*

**1** to push (something) suddenly in the direction of (someone): [X9 + *towards* (*usu. simple tenses*)] *He thrust the money towards me across the table, but I refused to take it. He thrust the letter towards me, forcing me to read the address.* → **push at, push towards** (1), **thrust at** (2)

***2** to try to reach (a place) in spite of heavy opposition: [T1 (*no pass.*)] *Our army is still thrusting towards the next town, under heavy gunfire.* → **press towards, push towards** (2, 3)

***thrust up** *v adv*

(of plants) to grow quickly and strongly: [IØ] *It's good to see the flowers thrusting up through the last of the snow.*

***thrust upon** *v prep* → **THRUST ON**

***thud against/into** *v prep*

to hit (something) with a loud dull sound: [T1 (*simple tenses*)] *The car went out of control and thudded against the wall. The bullet thudded into the metal shield, but did no harm.*

**thumb at** *v prep*

**thumb one's nose at: a** to point the thumb to the nose in a rude manner towards (someone), intending to offend: *Don't you dare thumb your nose at me like that!* **b** to refuse to obey (something); show no respect for (a principle): *Sometimes the students behave wildly just for a chance to thumb their noses at the sillier college rules.*

***thumb through** *v prep*

to turn the pages of (a book) quickly, as looking for something: [T1] *If you thumb through any dictionary you can find many strange words.* —**thumb-through** *n*

**thump on** *v prep* → **knock at**, etc.

to beat on (something such as a door) heavily and loudly: [IØ + *on*] *You'll have to thump on the door or she'll never hear you in the back room. The rabbit got its name, Thumper, from its habit of thumping on the ground with its back foot.*

**thump out** *v adv*

to play (a tune) heavily (on an instrument such as a piano): [T1 + OUT (*on*)] *It hurts Jane's sensitive musical ears to hear other people thumping out a tune on her precious piano.*

***thunder against** *v prep*

to oppose (something or someone) in violent words: [T1 (*no pass.*)] *The speaker had a marked effect on the crowd, thundering against the injustices shown to certain people.*

***thunder out** *v adv* → **call out** (1), **cry out** (1), **roar out** (2)

to express (an opinion) very loudly, usu. in a group: [T1] *The crowd thundered out its support of the speaker's opinion.*

**thunder overhead/past** *v adv*

(usu. of a plane or heavy vehicle) to pass with a loud noise: [L9 + OVERHEAD/PAST] *All night the heavy bombers thundered overhead. The traffic thunders past all day long.*

**tick away** *v adv*

**1** (of a machine, esp. a clock) to beat time with a quiet noise, continuously: [IØ + AWAY (*often continuous tenses*)] *That bomb has been ticking away for over an hour now, and we are all getting nervous about when it will explode.*

***2** (usu. of a clock or watch) to mark the passing of (time): [T1] *The railway station clock ticked away the hours of waiting.*

***tick off** *v adv*

**1** esp. *BrE* to mark (something) on a list, so as to record that it has been examined, passed, counted, etc.: [T1] *Tick off the names of the members as they vote.* → **check off** (1)

**2** esp. *BrE not fml* to scold (someone): [T1] *You'll get ticked off for being late for work again.* —**ticking-off** *n* → **tell off** (1), etc.

**3** *AmE not fml* to make (someone) angry: [T1 (*simple tenses*)] *Her rudeness really ticked me off.*

***tick over** *v adv*

**1** (of an engine) to continue working at the lowest possible speed, without producing any result, esp. movement: [IØ (*continuous tenses*)] *If you stay in the car with the engine ticking over, the police cannot charge you with unlawful parking.* → **turn over** (5)

**2** (of an activity, such as work) to continue at a usual or slow speed, fairly successfully but without excitement: [IØ (*continuous tenses*)] *After a good start, the organization to help get our member re-elected is just ticking over and is in need of fresh ideas.* → **turn over** (6)

**tickle to** *v prep*

**tickle someone to death** *not fml* to amuse someone very much: [*usu. pass.*] *I was tickled to death to hear how Mary had at last won a victory over her rude neighbour.*

***tide over** *v adv; prep* → **bridge over** (2)

*not fml* to help (someone in difficulty) to keep going (for a short time): [T1b (*simple tenses*)]

*This money should tide you over until your cheque arrives.* [D1 (*no pass., simple tenses*)] *I'll lend you $20 to tide you over the rest of this week.*

***tidy away** *v adv*
to put (things) away neatly in their proper places: [T1] *How many times have I asked you children to tidy your toys away at the end of a day?* [I∅] *Please tidy away before you leave.*

**tidy out** *v adv*
to clear (a room or container), leaving it neat: [T1 + OUT] *It has taken us the whole day to tidy out the garage, and it still needs cleaning.* **—tidy-out** *n*

**tidy up** *v adv*
**1** to make (a room) neat; bring neatness out of confusion: [T1 + UP] *Help me to tidy this room up before my parents arrive!* [I∅ + UP] *I wasn't doing anything special, just tidying up generally.* **—tidying-up, tidy-up** *n*
***2** to make (oneself) neater; freshen one's appearance: [T1] *I must have a few minutes to tidy myself up before we go in.* [I∅] *There's a bathroom on this floor where you can tidy up if you wish.* **—tidy-up** *n*

**tie back** *v adv*
to fasten (something) back, as with rope, string, etc.: [T1 + BACK] *I must tie my hair back, it keeps getting in my eyes. The curtains are tied back in a pretty fashion.* **—tie-back** *n*

**tie down** *v adv*
**1** to fasten (something or someone) down, as with rope, string, etc.: [T1 + DOWN] *The traveller awoke to find himself tied down with long ropes to the ground. Help me to tie this lid down, it keeps coming off.* → **bind down** (1), **fasten down** (1)
***2** to take the time of or limit the freedom of (someone): [T1 (*simple tenses*)] *The worst of having a dog is that it ties you down. I don't want to tie you down; feel free to use your own ideas.* → **bind down** (2), **chain down** (2)
***3** esp. *mil* to keep (usu. an enemy) in one place: [T1 (*often pass.*)] *We've not been able to advance any further, but at least we've got them tied down for a time.*

**tie down to** *v adv prep*
**1** to fasten (something or someone) down to (usu. something), as with rope: [T1 + DOWN + *to*] *The traveller awoke to find himself tied down to the ground with long ropes.*
***2** to make (someone or oneself) keep (a promise or agreement) or be limited by (something): [D1 (*simple tenses*)] *If he tries to cheat, we must tie him down to his contract. You shouldn't tie yourself down to your job so much.* → **fasten down** (2), **nail down** (2)

**tie in[1]** *v adv*
**1** to (cause to) be fastened to something existing, as with rope: [T1 + IN] *Tie the other thread in here, so that all the holes are joined.* [I∅ + IN] *Do all the wires tie in together?*
***2** to join (something) to an existing part: [T1] *When the machine is ready, we will tie in the new system of accounting.*
***3** to have a connection or agree (with something else): [I∅ (*with*) (*simple tenses*)] *The different stories all tie in, so I think the prisoners are telling the truth. Does this tie in with what he said yesterday?* **—tie-in** *n* → **tie up** (9)

**tie in[2]** *v prep*
**tie oneself in knots** *not fml* to become greatly confused: *Worried by the question, the speaker tied himself in knots trying to give a satisfactory answer, causing great amusement in the crowd.*

***tie in with** *v adv prep* → **bind up with, tie up with**
to (cause to) have a connection with (something else): [I∅ (*simple tenses*)] *Does this tie in with what he said yesterday?* [D1 (*usu. pass., simple tenses*)] *Decisions about trade agreements are often tied in with political considerations. The future of the island is tied in with the fortunes of the ruling power.*

***tie into** *v prep*
*AmE not fml* to attack (someone) forcefully: [T1 (*simple tenses*)] *You should have seen how our Jim tied into that man!*

**tie off** *v adv*
to fasten the ends of (rope, string, etc.) as with a knot, to keep in place: [T1 + OFF] *When you've fastened the boards, tie the ropes off so that they don't slip.*

**tie on** *v adv*
**1** to fasten (something) on oneself or an object: [T1 + ON] *The woman in front of me was wearing a dress with the price ticket still tied on.* **—tie-on** *adj*
**2 tie one on** *AmE infml* to get drunk: [*simple tenses*] *The boys really tied one on last night, didn't they?*

**tie to** *v prep*
**1** to fasten (something or someone) to (usu. something), as with rope, string, etc.: [T1 + *to*] *Don't worry about the dog, he's tied to the gate. There's a proper way to tie your boat to the post so that it doesn't slip away. The prisoner was tied to a post and shot. "I am tied to a stake, and I must stand the course."* (Shakespeare, *King Lear*) → **bind to** (1)
***2** to fix (someone) to (something or doing something): [D1 (*usu. pass., simple tenses*)] *It's so inconvenient being tied to the house with the child so ill.* [V4a (*usu. pass., simple tenses*)] *I'm sorry, I'm tied to working in the office tonight.*
**3 be tied to someone's apron strings** *not fml* to be helplessly dependent on one's mother, wife, etc.: *No, you must make your own decision; you can't stay tied to your mother's apron strings all your life, you're a grown man now.*

**tie together** *v adv*
**1** to fasten (things or people) together, as

with rope, string, etc.: [T1 + TOGETHER] *If you tie the firewood together in bunches, it's easier to carry.* → **bind together** (1)

*__2__ to (cause to) match or make sense: [T1 (*simple tenses*)] *When writing a story, you have to tie the different events together so that your readers can follow it.* [IØ (*simple tenses*)] *Do the two prisoners' stories tie together?*

**tie up** *v adv*

**1** to fasten (something or someone) with rope, string, etc.; wrap (something) firmly; tie the arms and legs of (someone) so as to prevent movement: [T1 + UP] *The thieves left the owner of the jewels tied up in the bedroom. Tie up your horse and come in for a drink. Has the parcel been properly tied up?* → **bind up** (1)

*__2__ to wrap (a wound, or wounded part of the body) in a bandage: [T1] *Here, let me tie up that arm for you.* → **bind up** (2)

*__3__ to fasten (a boat) to a post on land: [T1] *There's a proper way to tie up your boat so that it doesn't float away.* [IØ] *Is this where we tie up?* —**tie-up** *n*

*__4__ to combine: [IØ] *When are the two firms going to tie up?* —**tie-up** *n*

*__5__ to arrange (something): [T1] *Is the organization of the wedding completely tied up yet?*

*__6__ *not fml* to make (someone) very busy: [T1 (*in*) (*usu. pass., simple tenses*)] *Writing this article should not tie me up for more than a week or two. I'm afraid I can't possibly attend, I'm tied up in meetings all that day. The director is tied up just now, but could see you later.* → **bind up in**

*__7__ to prevent (someone or something) from working, as by keeping him or it busy: [T1 (*usu. pass.*)] *The telephone has been tied up all morning with unnecessary calls. The firm is tied up for lack of supplies.* —**tie-up** *n*

*__8__ to limit the free movement of (usu. money or property): [T1 (*in*) (*usu. pass.*)] *My aunt's money is all tied up in shares. His fortune should be tied up till his 21st birthday.*

*__9__ to agree: [IØ (*simple tenses*)] *The different stories all tie up, so perhaps they are telling the truth.* → **tie in**[1] (3)

**10 get tied up** *not fml* to get married: *When are Jim and Mary getting tied up? Soon, I hope.*

**11 tie up the loose ends** *not fml* to finish doing the things still to be dealt with: *Yes, the contract is almost ready for signing; there are just one or two loose ends to be tied up.*

*__tie up with__ *v adv prep* → **bind up with, tie in with**

to connect (something or someone) with (something or someone else); agree with (something): [D1 (*often pass., simple tenses*)] *The police are trying to tie up the murder with the recent escape from prison. The future of the island is tied up with the fortunes of the ruling power. My uncle's firm is tied up with the larger company.* [T1 (*no pass., simple tenses*)] *Does this tie up with what the other prisoner said?*

*__tie with__ *v prep*

(of a competitor) to reach the same number of points, etc., as (another competitor): [T1 (*no pass., usu. simple tenses*)] *Our village team has tied with the visitors, so they will have to play an additional game to decide the winner.*

**tighten up** *v adv*

**1** to (cause to) become tighter: [T1 + UP] *Have you tightened all the screws up properly? Try not to tighten up your throat, or you will sing badly.* [IØ + UP] *The knot has tightened up in the water, and I can't unfasten it.* → **loosen up** (1)

*__2__ to (cause to) become more firm or severely controlled: [T1] *The government's rules for drawing unemployment pay are to be tightened up.* [IØ (*on*)] *The police are tightening up on safety for the Queen's visit.*

**tilt at** *v prep*

**1** *old use* to charge at (an opponent) with a long spearlike weapon: [IØ + *at*] *Noblemen used to tilt at each other on horseback for sport.*

*__2__ to attack (an idea) with words: [T1 (*pass. rare*)] *Wherever he spoke, he made a point of tilting at the injustices which he had noticed in the system.*

**3 tilt at windmills** *not fml* to attack wrongs which do not really exist: *Many opponents of the system enjoy tilting at windmills when there is nothing really to complain about.*

**tilt back** *v adv*

to cause (something) to lean backwards: [T1 + BACK] *Tilt your head back so that I can look down your throat to see if there's anything wrong with it. Don't tilt your chair back so far, it might fall over.*

**tilt up** *v adv*

to cause (something) to lean upwards: [T1 + UP] *Can you tilt the lid up a little further?*

*__tinge with__ *v prep*

**1** to give (something) a little (colour) mixed in: [D1 (*usu. pass.*)] *The colour of the mat is blue tinged with brown.* → **touch with** (2b)

**2 be tinged with** to have a little (quality): *Our joy at having finished was tinged with sadness at leaving.* → **touch with** (2c)

**tingle with** *v prep*

**1** (of part of the body, esp. the skin) to have slight prickly feelings because of (a condition such as cold): [IØ + *with* (*often continuous tenses*)] *His hands began tingling with the warm blood running back into his cold fingers.*

*__2__ to have slight prickly feelings because of (a feeling): [T1 (*no pass., often continuous tenses*)] *Every nerve was tingling with excitement as she waited for her lover to return.*

*__tinker about/around__ *v adv*

to play aimlessly, esp. with machines: [IØ

(*with*)] *Ever since he was very young, he has enjoyed tinkering about, making radios, mending engines, and so on.*

***tinker with** *v prep* → **fiddle with** (2)
to play with or move the parts of (a machine) without direction, as to discover a fault: [T1] *He always had the ability to tinker with an engine and set it going again, even when he didn't know what was wrong.*

**tip at** *v prep*
**tip the scale(s) at** to weigh (a certain amount): [*simple tenses*] *Luckily, my suitcase tipped the scale at exactly 20 kilos, so it could travel on the plane without additional charge.*

**tip in** *v adv*
**1** to cause (something) to enter by raising a container at an angle: [X9 + IN] *The delivery man used to take the lid off our coal hole and simply tip the coal in.*
***2** (in basketball) to place (the ball) in the net with the ends of the fingers, as it comes through the air: [T1] *At the last moment, our best player tipped the ball in and so we won the game.* —**tip-in** *n*
***3** (in bookbinding) to add (a page such as a picture or map) by fastening it along one edge with a sticky substance: [T1 (*often pass.*)] *All the pictures in the book were tipped in carelessly and are beginning to come loose.*

**tip into** *v prep*
to cause (something or someone) to enter (something) by raising a container at an angle: [X9 + *into*] *Just tip the wood into this box, will you? Her hand slipped and she tipped some of the tea into her plate by mistake. The boat rocked, tipping some of the passengers into the river.*

**tip off** *v adv*
**1** to cause (something or someone) to fall off something, by raising a level at an angle: [X9 + OFF] *The cart stopped suddenly, tipping its load off in the middle of the road. Suddenly the horse jumped up and tipped its rider off.*
***2** *not fml* to give (someone) helpful advice: [T1 (*often simple tenses*)] *A man in Newmarket tipped me off about the big horse race today.* —**tip-off** *n*
***3** *not fml* to give (someone, esp. the police) information, as a warning: [T1 (*often simple tenses*)] *The police caught the murderer because they were tipped off by someone unknown.* —**tip-off** *n*

**tip out** *v adv*
to cause (something or someone) to fall out (of something) by raising it at an angle: [X9 + OUT (*of*)] *Several passengers were tipped out (of the boat) when the waves got very rough.*

**tip over** *v adv* → **fall over**[1] (1), **topple over, tumble over**
to (cause to) overturn: [X9 + OVER] *The ladder fell, tipping the tin of paint over so that the paint ran all over the floor.* [IØ + OVER] *The boat tipped over, throwing the passengers into the river.*

**tip up** *v adv*
**1** to (cause to) lean upwards at an angle; overbalance; turn upwards around a hinge: [X9 + UP] *You can make the table bigger for a family dinner by tipping up this end.* [IØ + UP (*usu. simple tenses*)] *The bucket tipped up, pouring water all over the floor. The seats in this cinema tip up so that you can get past the other people in the row.* —**tip-up** *adj*
***2** esp. *AmE not fml* to pay, esp. for drinks: [IØ (*for*)] *He generously offered to tip up for the drinks.*

**tip with** *v prep*
**1** to give (a waiter, waitress, etc.) a small gift of money as a reward for service, in the form of (a coin or note): [T1 + *with*] *Did you see him tip the taxi driver with a pound note?*
**2** to put a finishing end on (something often pointed) made of (something): [T1 + *with* (*usu. simple tenses*)] *"That thin red line tipped with steel."* (William Howard Russell, *The British Expedition to the Crimea*)

***tire of** *v prep*
**1** to lose interest in or patience with (someone, something, or doing something): [T1 (*no pass.*)] *One can quickly tire of a city view, but never of a beautiful country scene. She soon tired of him and found another lover.* [T4] *It's a story that children never tire of hearing.* → **weary of**
**2 be tired of** to have had enough of, or begin to be annoyed by (someone, something, or doing something): *When you're tired of one dress, change to another. "No, sir, when a man is tired of London he is tired of life; for there is in London all that life can afford."* (Boswell's *Life of Johnson*) → **feed up** (2)

**tire out** *v adv* → **do in** (3), **do up** (9), **fag out, knock out** (6), **knock up** (7), **lay flat** (3), **lay out** (6), **poop out, shag out, tucker out, wash out** (7), **wash up** (5)
to tire (someone) completely: [T1 + OUT (*often pass.*)] *Going to school all day soon tires little children out. I must sit down and rest, I'm tired out!*

**toady to** *v prep* → **fawn on**
to try to gain the favour of (someone) by overpraising and being insincerely attentive: [IØ + *to*] *He toadies to his uncle, hoping to gain some of his money. The former servant made his way into power by toadying to the king.*

**toddle along/away/off** *v adv*
**1** (of a small child) to move further or away with uncertain steps: [IØ + ALONG/AWAY/OFF] *The child toddled along quite nicely until he fell over the mat. He was last seen toddling off in the direction of the sea.*
***2** *not fml* to leave: [IØ] *Well, I really must be toddling along now, I promised my wife that I wouldn't be late again. Toddle off.*

*will you, you know I don't want you in my kitchen!*

*__tog up__ *v adv* also **tog out** → **dress up** (2), etc.
*not fml* to dress (someone or oneself) well or showily: [T1 (*usu. pass.*)] *Where can she be going, all togged up like that? All the children were carefully togged up for the party.*

*__toil at/over__ *v prep* → **labour at, work at** (2)
to work hard or put much effort into (an action or doing something): [T1] *After toiling at the article for weeks, he suddenly found the right way to organize it.* [T4] *If you toil over perfecting your style, make sure it doesn't sound false and stiff.*

**toil up** *v prep*
to climb (something) with great effort: [L9 + *up*] *After toiling up the steep slope for many hours, the climbers had no strength left.*

**toll for** *v prep*
(of a bell, usu. in a church) to ring to signal the death of (someone): [IØ + *for*] *"And therefore never send to know for whom the bell tolls; it tolls for thee."* (John Donne, *Devotions*)

*__tone down__ *v adv*
**1** to (cause to) become less loud or bright: [T1] *How can we tone down these bright colours? Please tone the radio down, it's too loud.* [IØ] *Over the years, her voice has toned down quite a lot. The bright blue will tone down with the effect of sunlight.*
**2** to make (something) less exciting, violent, etc.: [T1] *I must ask you to tone down your remarks; they are giving offence to some of our visitors. You had better tone down some of the opinions in your article.*

*__tone in__ *v adv*
(usu. of colours) to match or suit: [IØ (*with*) (*simple tenses*)] *I like the way the artist makes his greens tone in so well. Does the furniture tone in with the curtains?*

*__tone up__ *v adv*
to (cause to) become stronger or more effective: [T1] *Swimming is the best way to tone up your muscles.* [IØ] *My legs seem to have toned up with all that walking.*

*__tool up__ *v adv*
(usu. of a factory) to prepare the machinery (for new work): [IØ (*for*)] *The contract is signed, and we only need about a week to tool up (for the production of these models).*

*__top off__ *v adv*
**1** to put a top on (something): [T1] *The builders have topped off the outside wall with broken glass to discourage thieves.*
**2** *not fml* to complete (something), esp. successfully or satisfactorily: [T1 (*often simple tenses*)] *Let's top off this delightful evening with a drink.*
**3** to reach the highest level: [IØ] *The rise in prices seems to have topped off, so goods should cost the same for a longer time now.* → **top out** (2)
**4** *AmE* to hold a ceremony to mark the completion of the highest part of (a tall building): [T1] *Has the tower been topped off yet?* —**topping-off** *n, adj* → **top out** (1)
**5** *AmE* to supply (something) again, as with petrol: [T1] *Does the car need topping off?* → **top up** (2)

*__top out__ *v adv*
**1** to hold a ceremony to mark the completion of the highest part of (a tall building): [T1] *When is the tower going to be topped out?* —**topping-out** *n, adj* → **top off** (4)
**2** esp. *AmE* to reach the highest level: [IØ] *The rise in prices seems to have topped out, so goods should cost the same for a longer time now.* → **top off** (3)

*__top up__ *v adv*
**1** esp. *BrE not fml* to fill (a partly empty container) to the top; fill a drink for (someone): [T1] *Let me top up your drink, it's half gone. Do let me top you up.* —**top-up** *n*
**2** esp. *BrE* to supply (something) again, as with petrol: [T1] *Does the car need topping up?* → **top off** (5)
**3** to raise (a level of liquid) to the top of the container: [T1] *Make sure to top up the water level so that it always remains the same.*

**topple down** *v adv*
**1** to fall unsteadily: [IØ + DOWN] *I tried to build a house of cards but it soon toppled down. The child, taking his first steps, toppled down time after time.* → **fall down** (1), **fall over[1]** (1), **topple over, tumble down** (1)
*__2__ *not fml* to fail or cease: [IØ] *His ideas of winning power quickly toppled down when he learned who his opponent was. The organization toppled down when its leader died.* → **fall down** (3), **fall through[1]** (2), **tumble down** (2)

**topple from** *v prep*
**1** to (cause to) fall from (a position): [IØ + *from*] *The baby bird toppled from the nest, unable to fly yet.* [T1 + *from*] *The monkeys shake the trees, trying to topple the nuts from the branches.* → **fall from** (1)
**2** to (cause to) cease to have (a position of power): [IØ + *from*] *At the election, a surprising number of popular politicians toppled from their places as Members of Parliament.* [T1 + *from*] *How can we topple the chief from his position of trust?* → **fall from** (4), **fall out of** (2)

**topple over** *v adv* → **fall over[1]** (1), **tip over, topple down** (1), **tumble over**
to overturn or overbalance, unsteadily: [IØ + OVER] *I saw the small child topple over and hit her head. The boat toppled over, throwing the passengers into the water. As the earth shook, great buildings toppled over into the street.*

**torn between** → TEAR BETWEEN

**toss about/around** *v adv*
**1** to throw (something or things) carelessly in various directions: [X9 + ABOUT/AROUND] *I*

*wish the children would stop tossing those stones about, it's quite dangerous for the little ones.* → **chuck about** (1), **fling about** (1), **hurl about** (1), **throw about**[1] (1)

*****2** to move restlessly; be shaken by a vehicle or boat: [IØ] *Poor Jane has been tossing around all night with that fever. When you cross the sea, you often toss about in your bed at night.* → **thrash about** (1)

*****3** *not fml* to consider (an idea), esp. from different points of view: [T1b] *After tossing the suggestion around for over an hour, the committee were still no nearer a decision.* → **blow about** (2)

**4 toss one's money about/around** *not fml* to spend money foolishly, as to show one's wealth: *Our new neighbour is always tossing his money about, paying for local parties, supporting groups, and other things to draw attention to how rich he is.* → **chuck about** (3), **fling about** (3), **hurl about** (3), **throw about**[1] (3)

**5 toss one's weight about/around** *not fml* to give unnecessary orders; try to use one's power over other people: *Ever since he was put in charge of a bigger group of workers, he's been tossing his weight around in the factory, and getting himself disliked.* → **chuck about** (4), **fling about** (4), **hurl about** (4), **throw about**[1] (4)

**toss aside** *v adv*

**1** to throw (something) carelessly to one side: [X9 + ASIDE] *Tossing his school work aside, he ran to join the other children at play.* → **cast off** (1), etc., **lay aside** (1), etc.

*****2** to disregard, give up, or have nothing more to do with (usu. something): [T1 (*often simple tenses*)] *Henry joined the opposing political party, tossing aside his former loyalties. Tossing aside all his usual care, he risked all his money on a wild plan. These rules are not made to be tossed aside lightly.* → **cast aside** (2), etc.

**toss at** *v prep* → **throw at** (1), etc.

to throw (something) carelessly towards (someone or something): [T1 + *at*] *Those stupid boys used to amuse themselves by tossing rocks at passing cars. The speaker did not care to have eggs tossed at him during his speech.*

**toss away** *v adv*

**1** to throw (something) away from oneself; get rid of (something): [X9 + AWAY] *He picked up his sister's ball and with an unpleasant smile tossed it away into the middle of the long grass. Isn't it time we tossed away all those old newspapers?* → **throw out** (2), etc.

*****2** to waste or fail to take advantage of (something): [T1] *Never toss away a chance to improve your English. If you leave now, you'll be tossing away your education. You have a good lead in the tennis game; don't toss it away by being careless.* → **throw away** (2), etc.

**toss back** *v adv*

**1** to move (part of the body) quickly backwards: [X9 + BACK] *She tossed her head back in a temper and left the room. Tossing her long hair back, she dived into the water.* → **throw back** (2)

*****2** *not fml* to drink a lot of (liquid, usu. alcohol): [T1] *You should see the amount of beer those boys have been tossing back this evening!* → **knock back** (3), **toss off** (4)

**toss down** *v adv* → **chuck down** (1), **fling down** (1), **hurl down** (1), **throw down**[1] (1)

to throw (something) carelessly and forcefully onto the ground: [X9 + DOWN] *The child tossed his schoolbooks down and ran to join the other children at play. Tossing some money down as he left, he showed how little he cared for the meal.*

*****toss for** *v prep*

to compete (with someone), as for first choice, by means of a coin: [T1 (*no pass., usu. simple tenses*)] *Let's toss for the prize, as we both gained the same points.* [T6 (*usu. simple tenses*)] *The captains usually toss for which team will play first.* [D1 (*no pass., usu. simple tenses*)] *I don't know whose turn it is to pay, so I'll toss you for it.*

**toss in**[1] *v adv*

**1** to throw (something) carelessly into a container: [X9 + IN] *Some men ran past the door, tossing a bomb in as they passed. There's a ball in our garden: those children playing in the park must have tossed it in.* → **chuck in** (1), **fling in**[1] (1), **pitch in** (1), **throw in**[1] (1)

*****2** to add (something), often as a gift: [T1 (*often simple tenses*)] *If you buy the furniture, the store will toss in a television set.* → **chuck in** (3), **fling in**[1] (3), **throw in**[1] (3)

*****3** to add (words), often as an interruption: [T1 (*usu. simple tenses*)] *There was no need for her to toss in her opinion where it wasn't wanted. Although the argument was fierce, I succeeded in tossing in the odd word from time to time.* → **put in**[1] (4), etc.

*****4** to include or add (something such as in speech or writing): [T1 (*usu. simple tenses*)] *Don't forget to toss in a mention of the chairman when you give the vote of thanks.* → **put in**[1] (3), **throw in**[1] (6), **write in** (1)

**toss in**[2] *v prep* → **throw in**[2] (1)

to throw (something) carelessly into (a space): [X9 + *in*] *It's so easy these days to do the washing, you just toss the clothes in the washing machine!*

**toss into** *v prep*

**1** to throw (something) carelessly into (something such as a space); cause (someone) to fall into (something): [X9 + *into*] *The office workers compete to see who can best toss a ball of waste paper into the basket. The boat rocked wildly, tossing the passengers into the water.* → **fling into** (1), **hurl into** (1), **pitch into** (1), **throw into** (1)

*****2** to force (someone) to go to (prison): [D1 (*often pass.*)] *The criminal was tossed into* *prison without ceremony or trial.* → **fling into** (3), **hurl into** (2), **throw into** (2)

*3 to add (words) to (something such as a conversation): [D1 (*usu. simple tenses*)] *She sat silently, tossing the odd word into the conversation from time to time.* → **fling into** (4), **throw into** (4)

**4 toss one's hat into the ring** *not fml* to declare one's intention of taking part in a competition such as an election: *No one dreamed that he wanted to be President until he tossed his hat into the ring at the last possible moment.* → **fling into** (8), **throw into** (6)

**toss off** *v adv*

**1** to remove (something) by shaking or throwing it off one's person: [X9 + OFF] *He put his hand on her shoulder, but she tossed it off angrily.* → **cast off** (1), **chuck off** (1), **fling off** (1), **shake off**[1] (1), **throw off**[1] (1)

*2 to speak (something) carelessly: [T1] *He tossed off a list of things he wanted done, too fast for me to write them down. He does enjoy tossing off the names of important people he's met in his travels.* → **put in**[1] (4), etc.

*3 to write (something) easily: [T1] *I can toss off a poem in half an hour. It shouldn't take more than an afternoon to toss this article off.* → **dash off** (2), etc.

*4 *not fml* to drink (liquid such as alcohol) quickly: [T1] *I think he's still in there, tossing off the rest of the beer.* → **knock back** (3), **toss back** (2)

*5 esp. *BrE taboo sl* (of males) to (cause to) give pleasure by rubbing the sexual organ; masturbate: [IØ] *A few of the boys who had escaped from the school were found tossing off in the bushes.* [T1b] *They had been taking turns to toss each other off.* → **jerk off, play with** (9), **pull at** (4)

**toss out** *v adv*

**1** to throw (usu. something) outside a place, carelessly: [X9 + OUT (*of*)] *Climb into the hole and toss the ball out, will you?* → **chuck out** (1), **fling out** (1), **throw out** (1)

*2 to get rid of (something): [T1] *It really is time we tossed out all those old newspapers.* → **throw out** (2), etc.

*3 to make (someone) leave because of a fault: [T1 (*of*) (*usu. simple tenses*)] *Two members were tossed out (of the club) for failing to pay the money they owed.* → **throw out** (4), etc.

*4 to make (someone) leave a home: [T1 (*of*) (*often pass.*)] *The old lady was tossed out of the house because the owner wanted to pull it down.* → **throw out** (5), etc.

*5 to refuse to accept (a suggestion, law, etc.): [T1 (*usu. simple tenses*)] *The new law was tossed out when it reached the last stage in Parliament. Why did the committee toss my entry out? I'm old enough to compete.* → **chuck out** (5), **fling out** (6), **hurl out** (2), **throw out** (6), **turn down** (4)

*6 to say (something) carelessly: [T1 (*often simple tenses*)] *Tossing out an instruction as he left, he hurried from the office, already late for his meeting.* → **put in**[1] (4), etc.

*7 to offer or produce (something such as a suggestion): [T1 (*often simple tenses*)] *After talking together, the group tossed out several bright ideas fit for further consideration.* → **fling out** (8), **throw out** (8)

**toss together** *v adv*

**1** to gather (things) in a hurry: [X9 + TOGETHER] *Tossing together a few books and possessions, he ran out of the house.* → **chuck together** (1), **fling together** (1), **throw together** (1)

*2 to build, make, or write (something) hastily: [T1a (*often pass.*)] *This poem reads as if it was tossed together in half an hour. Can you toss a meal together in a few minutes?* → **throw together** (2), etc.

*3 to cause (usu. two people) to meet: [T1a (*usu. pass.*)] *Many unlikely pairs of people were tossed together by the war.* → **bring together** (2), etc.

**toss up** *v adv*

**1** to throw (something or someone) into the air: [X9 + UP] *For hours the boy would stand tossing a ball up into the air and catching it again. The baby loves being tossed up and safely caught. The cheering crowd were tossing their hats up into the air.* → **cast up** (1), **chuck up** (1), **fling up** (1), **throw up** (1)

**2** to throw (a coin) into the air to decide a choice: [T1 + UP] *Let's toss up a penny for the chance to go first. The captains usually toss up to see which team shall play first.* —**toss-up** *n* → **toss for**

*3 to waste (something): [T1] *If you leave now, you'll be tossing up a good education. Why toss up such a good chance?* → **throw away** (2), etc.

***tot up** *v adv* also **total up, tote up**

**1** *not fml* to add (figures): [T1] *Working in this office has taught me to tot up a row of figures very quickly. If you tot up what I owe you, you will see that it comes even with what you owe me.*

**2** to make a total (of an amount): [IØ (*to*) (*simple tenses*)] *How much did the bill tot up to?*

***total up** *v adv* → TOT UP

***tote up** *v adv* → TOT UP

***touch at** *v prep* → **call at**

(usu. of a ship) to call for a short time at (a port or ports) while on a voyage: [T1 (*no pass., usu. simple tenses*)] *Before crossing the ocean, the ship will touch at two small ports on the opposite shore to pick up passengers.*

**touch bottom** *v n*

**1** to reach the lowest place: [X9 + bottom] *The water was not as deep as we thought, and the boat touched bottom and could not move.*

*2 *not fml* to reach the lowest level: [IØ] *After so many misfortunes, his spirits touched bottom; soon afterwards he began to feel better.*

*The market for used cars will soon touch bottom.*

*__touch down__ *v adv*

**1** (of a plane or boat) to land: [IØ] *In spite of the damaged wheel, the plane touched down safely in the hands of her skilled pilot.* —**touchdown** *n*

**2** (in rugby or American football) to place (the ball), as with the hands, behind the opposing team's line: [IØ] *Running the length of the field, he was able to touch down just as the opposing players were about to reach him.* [T1] *Running the length of the field, he was able to touch the ball down just in time.* —**touchdown** *n*

*__touch for__ *v prep*

*not fml* to beg (someone) to give or lend (money): [D1 (*usu. simple tenses*)] *An old man on the street touched me for $1 this morning. Do you think you can touch your father for the ticket money?*

*__touch in__[1] *v adv*

to finish (part of a picture), as with detail, colour, etc.: [T1] *The front of the house on this drawing has been touched in to show people what it will look like when it's built.*

**touch in**[2] *v prep*

**be touched in the head** *not fml* to be slightly mad: *He gets some silly ideas; sometimes I wonder if he isn't touched in the head.*

*__touch off__ *v adv*

**1** to start (a large gun) firing: [T1a] *In the old days, soldiers used a flaming piece of wood to touch off the big gun.* → **go off**[1] (5), etc.

**2** to cause (something violent) to begin: [T1a (*often simple tenses*)] *Careless political action can easily touch off a war. His stupid remarks touched off a fight.* → **set off** (5), **spark off** (2), **trigger off** (2)

**3** *AmE* to describe (usu. something) exactly or suitably: [T1 (*usu. simple tenses*)] *The newspaper reports have really touched off the causes of the difficulty this time.*

**touch on/upon** *v prep*

**1** to feel (someone) on (a part of the body): [T1 + *on/upon*] *Suddenly I felt someone touching me on the arm to attract my attention.*

***2** to mention (something such as a subject) for a short time or in passing: [T1 (*usu. simple tenses*)] *The book only touches on the causes of the war and does not do justice to the influence of the slave trade.*

***3** to relate to or show some connection with (a subject): [T1 (*no pass., simple tenses*)] *How does your story touch on this case?* → **bear on** (1), **have on**[2] (4)

***4** to come very near, or be much like (something): [X1 (*simple tenses*)] *His manner was very inconsiderate, touching on rudeness.* [X7 (*simple tenses*)] *His remarks were more than slightly unsuitable; they touched on the offensive.* → **border on** (2), **verge on** (2)

**5 touch someone on the raw** *not fml* to make someone suffer by mentioning a delicate subject about which he is sensitive: *Your mention of his time in prison touched him on the raw, so no wonder he took offence.*

**touch to** *v prep*

**1** to place (something) next to (something): [T1 + *to*] *All you have to do is touch a match to this firelighter and your fire will start. You should not need to touch your whip to this horse.* → **place to** (1), **put to**[2] (1), **set to**[2] (1)

**2 touch someone to the quick** to hurt someone's feelings in a sensitive area: [*often pass.*] *She was touched to the quick when charged with an action so much against her principles.*

*__touch up__ *v adv*

**1** to improve (paint, a painting, photograph, or writing) by removing small faults or adding details: [T1] *This is the original photograph, without being touched up in any way; it is a true record of the event. Your painting needs touching up a little before you enter it for the competition. I want to spend a few days touching up the article before I send it to the printer.* —**touch-up** *n*

**2** *AmE* to urge (usu. a horse) to go faster, with or as with a light touch of a whip; waken (someone) with a light blow: [T1] *By just touching the horse up a little as they neared the winning post, the rider drew ahead of his nearest competitor. You can make the men hurry by touching them up as you pass.*

**3** *sl* to touch (usu. a girl or woman) sexually, without permission: [T1] *The girl complained to the police that the man had been touching her up on the train.* → **feel up**

**touch upon** *v prep* → TOUCH ON

**touch with** *v prep*

**1** to feel (something or someone) by using (something such as part of the body or a tool): [T1 + *with*] *Don't touch that very cold metal with bare hands, or your skin will stick to it. He touched the body with a stick to see if it would move.*

**2 be touched with: a** to show the effect of (something such as sunlight): *Her face was a little touched with the sun, brown on the forehead but red on the nose.* **b** to have a little (colour) mixed in: *The sky was a deep blue touched with gold at the edges of the clouds.* → **tinge with** (1) **c** to have a little (quality): *Some of his ideas are touched with madness. Our delight at leaving was touched with sorrow for the friends we had made here.* → **tinge with** (2)

**3 not touch something with a bargepole** *infml* to have nothing to do with something: [*usu. with would*] *I wonder who has the unpleasant job of dismissing the older workers? I wouldn't touch it with a bargepole. I wouldn't touch the food in that restaurant with a bargepole.*

**touch wood** *v n* → **knock on** (3)

**touch wood** to put one's hand on something wooden, in the belief that this will prevent bad luck: *We should have the job finished by Thursday, touch wood!*

**tough out** *v adv*

**tough it out** *AmE infml* to bear or live through a difficult time or event; suffer a difficulty until it is past: *It looks like this snow will stop the supplies getting through and we shall be hungry for a time, but we've no choice but to tough it out.*

**toughen up** *v adv*

**1** to (cause to) become stronger: [T1 + UP] *All this mountain climbing will toughen the boys up.* [IØ + UP] *She seems to have toughened up a lot since last year.*

***2** to make (something such as a rule or effort) tighter or more severe: [T1] *The city council is determined to toughen up the fight against crime.*

**tout about/around** *v adv; prep*

*not fml* to try to sell or praise (something or someone) by repeated efforts (in many places), often in an unfavourable sense: [T1 + ABOUT/AROUND/*about/around*] *You might be able to get rid of that old bicycle if you tout it around (the streets) for a week or so. It does not give a very good idea of a product if it has to be touted around (the market) in that offensive way.*

**tout as** *v prep*

to suggest that (something or someone) is (something good) by describing it with praise: [T1 + *as* (*often pass.*)] *This new hotel is being touted as the best in town. Which new singing group is being touted as the worthy followers of the leading band of last year?*

**tout for** *v prep*

to try to win (trade, votes, etc.) by praising something or someone aloud; try to gain trade for (a business), esp. in public places: [IØ + *for*] *We think he won the election by sending his supporters into all the villages, touting for votes. Several men stood outside the ground, touting for the various sideshows.*

**tow away** *v adv*

to remove (a vehicle) by pulling it, as with another vehicle: [T1 + AWAY] *Any cars parked on this side of the street will be towed away at the owner's cost.* **—tow-away** *adj*

***towel down/off** *v adv* → **rub down** (3)

to dry (someone or oneself) on a rough cloth: [T1] *Do towel the children down very thoroughly, they're wet to the skin and might catch cold!* [IØ] *I like to towel off by rubbing hard after a bath or swim.*

***tower above/over** *v prep*

**1** to stand much taller than (someone or something): [T1 (*no pass., usu. simple tenses*)] *How maddening to have your younger brother tower over you, at his age, too! The mountains tower above the town, reducing the effect of its importance.*

**2** to be much greater than (others or a standard) in ability, quality, or character: [T1 (*no pass., usu. simple tenses*)] *I hope Mr Green will be the new chairman, he towers above any of the other members who have been suggested. The general may not have been the perfect leader for his country, but at the time he towered over anyone else.*

***toy with** *v prep*

**1** to handle (something) in a playful manner, as to amuse oneself or express nervousness: [T1] *All the time he was talking, he was toying with a pencil.* → **fiddle with** (1), etc.

**2** to consider (an idea) not very seriously: [T1] *Father often toys with the thought of going to live on a tropical island.* also **dally with, play with, trifle with**

**3** to treat (someone or someone's feelings) inconsiderately, not seriously: [T1] *He's never mentioned marriage, and I'm beginning to think he's just toying with me, which is unkind. Never toy with a woman's feelings, or it could be the worse for you!* → **flirt with** (1), etc.

**trace back** *v adv*

**1** to find the origin of (one's family) (in an earlier time): [T1 + BACK (*to*)] *His father claims to be able to trace the family back many centuries, to the time of the Conqueror.*

**2** to find the origin of (something) (in a cause): [T1 + BACK (*to*) (*often simple tenses*)] *I think we can trace the fever back to that long cold swim that she took against our advice.*

**trace out** *v adv*

**1** to mark (something) lightly or roughly: [T1 + OUT] *With his finger, he traced out the shape of the buildings in the sand.*

***2** to suggest (an idea): [T1] *So far, he has only been able to trace out the outline of the plan, without any details.*

**trace over** *v adv; prep*

to draw on top of (a drawing), as through a transparent paper or over lines made with dots: [T1 + OVER/*over*] *Even the youngest child can trace over the shapes of the letters with a pencil.*

**trace to** *v prep*

to find (something or someone) as being in or caused by (something): [T1 + *to* (*often simple tenses*)] *At last the noise was traced to a fault in the pipes. Will the police be able to trace us to our hiding place?*

***track down** *v adv*

to find (someone or something) by or as by hunting: [T1] *Were the doctors able to track down the cause of the infection? All citizens should help the police in tracking the criminals down. After many days, the hunters were able to track down the dangerous bear.*

***track in** *v adv*

to bring (usu. mud) indoors by walking: [T1] *Look at all that mud that you've tracked in on your feet!*

***track up** *v adv*

esp. *AmE not fml* to make (usu. a floor) dirty with one's shoes: [T1] *Get out of my kitchen I don't want you children tracking up my nice clean floor!*

**trade at** *v prep* → **deal at, deal with** (1), **trade with**
to do one's shopping regularly at (a certain shop): [L9 + *at*] *My family has traded at Mr Green's vegetable store for over twenty years.*

***trade down** *v adv* → **trade in**[1]
esp. *AmE* to exchange (goods) for something of a lower value: [T1] *It's unusual to trade your existing car down; most people want a bigger or newer vehicle.*

**trade for** *v prep* → **exchange for, swap for**
to exchange (something) for (something else): [T1 + *for*] *I'd like to trade this knife for your book.* [D1 + *for*] *I'll trade you my pen for your ball.*

***trade in**[1] *v adv* also esp. *AmE* **trade up** → **trade down**
to exchange (goods) for part of the value (of a newer object): [T1 (*for*)] *Will the dealer allow us to trade in the car for the latest model?* —**trade-in** *n, adj*

**trade in**[2] *v prep* → **deal in**[2]
to sell (a certain kind of goods): [L9 + *in*] *My uncle made a small fortune trading in precious shells which he found on the tropical island. It's difficult to make a living by trading in original works of art.*

***trade off** *v adv*
*not fml* to exchange (something) (for something else): [T1 (*for*)] *The government has offered to trade off a reduction in taxes for a period without wage demands. The two armies agreed to trade off their prisoners.* —**trade-off** *n*

***trade on/upon** *v prep*
to take advantage of (usu. someone's good nature, etc.): [T1 (*no pass., often simple tenses*)] *It wasn't very fair of you to trade on your mother's well-known generosity like that, accepting her offer of a meal.*

***trade up** *v adv esp. AmE* → **TRADE IN**[1]

***trade upon** *v prep* → **TRADE ON**

**trade with** *v prep* → **deal at, deal with** (1), **do with** (13), **trade at**
to shop at (a store) regularly; buy goods regularly from (someone); have dealings with (someone): [L9 + *with*] *My family have been trading with Mr Green for over twenty years. I refuse to trade with that store ever again, they keep cheating us on the bills!*

***traffic in** *v prep*
to buy and sell (goods, esp. of an unlawful or improper kind) (from and to people): [T1 (*no pass.*) (*with*)] *The old hunters used to traffic in furs with the local natives. He was charged with trafficking in drugs.*

**trail away** *v adv* → **TRAIL OFF**

**trail behind** *v adv; prep* → **lag behind** (1), etc., **fall behind**[2] (3), etc.
**1** to fail to remain level (with someone); follow (someone) slowly: [L9 + BEHIND/*behind*] *Everywhere the old man went, he always had a crowd of children trailing behind* (*him*).
***2** to fail to remain level (with something or someone): [IØ] *Compared with other nations, we seem to be trailing behind in our efforts to improve conditions for prisoners.* [T1 (*no pass.*)] *Production is trailing behind last year's total.*

**trail by** *v prep*
to lose a game by having (a number of points, runs, etc.) less than the other team: [IØ + *by* (*often continuous tenses*)] *At half time, our team were trailing by twelve points, but were able to win in the end.*

**trail off** *v adv* also **trail away**
**1** to move away in an aimless way: [L9 + OFF] *The crowd began to trail off when the speaker continued for over an hour.*
***2** (usu. of a voice) to lose strength gradually: [IØ] *When he saw who had entered the room, his voice trailed off in fear.* → **tail off, taper off** (2)

**trail on** *v adv*
to continue moving slowly: [L9 + ON] *The long line of climbers trailed on and on over the mountain pass to the gold mines.*

**trail over** *v prep*
to lie stretching across (something): [L9 + *over*] *Her long hair trailed over her shoulders. These plants have roots that trail over the ground, ready to reroot and form a new plant.*

**train as** *v prep*
to (cause to) learn to be (a kind of person): [L9 + *as*] *Her son is training as an engineer.* [T1 + *as*] *Were you trained as a teacher of young children?*

**train for** *v prep*
to (cause to) learn in order to be able to do (a job) or enter (a competition): [L9 + *for*] *Jim has been training for the big race for weeks now.* [T1 + *for*] *Is it the business of the universities to train students for suitable jobs?*

***train on/upon** *v prep*
to aim (a gun or sighting instrument) at (an object): [D1] *The enemy will not dare to move, with all our big guns trained on his harbour. Can you train your field glasses on the distant church tower?*

**train up** *v adv*
to teach (someone or something) for a purpose: [T1 + UP (*to*)] *Can such young children be trained up to the standard of the best international musicians? "Train up a child in the way he should go: and when he is old, he will not depart from it."* (The Bible) *"Train up a fig tree in the way it should go, and when you are old sit under the shade of it."* (Charles Dickens, *Dombey and Son*)

***train upon** *v prep* → **TRAIN ON**

**traipse round** *v adv; prep* also **traipse around**
to walk a long and tiring way round (a place): [L9 + ROUND/*round*] *The new department in the hospital is very large, so I get lots of exercise traipsing round* (*it*).

**trample down** *v adv* → **tread down** (1)
to flatten (something) heavily, usu. with the feet: [T1 + DOWN] *The cows have got into the*

*field and trampled the wheat down just as it was ripening!*

**trample in** *v adv* → **tread in**

to press (something) heavily into the ground, usu. with the feet: [T1 + IN] *Spread the powder over the earth and let the cattle trample it in as they walk over it.*

**trample on/upon** *v prep*

**1** to press heavily with the feet on top of (something or someone): [L9 + *on/upon*] *Many people in the crowd were trampled on when the fire began. Mind you don't trample on my flowers when you play in the garden!* → **stamp on** (1), **step on** (1), **tread on** (1)

***2** *not fml* to hurt (someone's feelings): [T1] *It's difficult to avoid trampling on her sensitivity, which is so much finer than other people's.* → **step on** (2), **tread on** (2), **walk on²** (2), **walk over²** (1)

**trample out** *v adv*

**1** to make (a path) by pressing heavily with the feet: [T1 + OUT] *See where the animals have trampled out a narrow path over the years.* → **tread out** (1)

***2** to put out (a fire) by treading: [T1] *Be sure to trample the fire out before you leave, and cover it with earth just in case there is a flame left.* → **stamp out** (3), **tread out** (2)

***3** to press (usu. grapes), as with the feet; cause (juice) to flow from fruit by pressing, as with the feet: [T1] *Help me to trample out the grapes for the wine. "Mine eyes have seen the glory of the coming of the Lord: He is trampling out the vintage where the grapes of wrath are stored."* (Julia Ward Howe, *Battle Hymn of the American Republic*) → **tread out** (3)

**trample to** *v prep*

**trample someone/an animal to death** to kill someone or an animal by pressing heavily, as with many feet: [*usu. pass.*] *The thunder made the animals afraid; they started running wildly, and many young cows were trampled to death in the rush. More people were trampled to death than were actually killed by the fire.*

**trample under** *v prep*

**trample someone/something under foot: a** to press someone or something heavily with the feet, usu. so as to cause hurt or harm: *Those cattle have trampled the crops under foot again! Many people were trampled under foot in the rush to get to the outside door.* **b** *not fml* to rule (someone) severely: *The new teacher mistakenly thought that the best way to control the class was to trample them under foot.*

**trample upon** *v prep* → TRAMPLE ON

**transact with** *v prep*

*fml* to do (usu. business) with (someone): [T1 + *with*] *Please leave us for a minute or so, I have some private business to transact with your father.*

**transfer from** *v prep* → **transfer to**

to (cause to) move or change from (someone, a place, or vehicle): [IØ + *from* (*to*)] *At this point, passengers will transfer from the train to a special bus.* [T1 + *from* (*to*)] *I'm looking for work in this city because my husband has been transferred from the West Coast. The rights in the property will be transferred from the present owner to your family. There's no fear that he might transfer his loyalty from the party.*

**transfer to** *v prep* → **transfer from**

to (cause to) move or change to (someone, a different place, or vehicle): [IØ + *to*] *At this point, passengers will transfer to a special bus.* [T1 + *to* (*from*)] *My husband has been transferred to this city, so I am also looking for a job. The rights in the property will be transferred to your family from the present owner. There's no fear that he might transfer his loyalty to the other party. I would like to transfer my money to a different account. The material of the walls helps to transfer the heat to the inside of the house.*

**transform into** *v prep* → **change into** (2), etc.

to change (something or someone) into (something or someone else), esp. by changing the shape or appearance: [T1 + *into*] *The prince was transformed by magic into an ugly animal. A poet is one who can transform ordinary words into a meaningful and effective piece of writing. What else can we do to transform the room into a fairyland for the children's party? In only a few years, this pleasant little town has been transformed into a forest of ugly high office buildings, crowded streets, and poor housing.*

**translate from** *v prep*

**1** to change (words) from (usu. another language): [T1 + *from*] *This poem has been translated from Old English.* → **translate into**

**2** *fml* to move (someone) from (another place): [T1 + *from* (*to*) (*often pass.*)] *The priest has been translated from his old church to this area.* → **translate to**

**translate into** *v prep*

**1** to change (words) into (usu. another language): [T1 + *into*] *Please translate this passage into good English. Give me a moment to translate my words into what I really mean.* → **do into, render into, translate from** (1), **turn into** (3)

***2** to change (something) into (another form); express (a thought) in (action): [D1] *When shall we get a chance to translate these good ideas into action? This school offers the possibility of translating the latest educational principles into practice.*

**translate to** *v prep* → **translate from** (2)

*fml* to move (someone) to (a different place): [T1 + *to* (*often pass.*)] *The priest has recently been translated to another area. Are all brave soldiers translated to the skies?*

**transliterate into** *v prep*

to rewrite (words) in the letters of (another alphabet): [T1 + *into* (*often pass.*)] *The ancient writings will first have to be transliterated into a known alphabet before they can be translated. Do we transliterate the Russian 'X' into English as 'kh'?*

**transmit to** *v prep*

**1** to signal (a message) to (someone), usu. by radio: [T1 + *to*] *The election results will be transmitted directly to the newsroom.*

**2** to pass (something such as a disease or quality) to (someone else): [T1 + *to*] *Can this fever be transmitted to other members of the family? Luckily the mother was able to transmit some of her own fine qualities of character to her children.*

**transmute into** *v prep*

*fml or old use* to change the nature of (something) by making it become (something else): [T1 + *into*] *Chemists in former times spent whole lifetimes trying to transmute lead into gold, without success.*

**transport to** *v prep*

**1** to move (goods or people) to (another place): [T1 + *to*] *Heavy vehicles are used to transport the coal to distant parts of the country.*

**2** *old use* to send (a prisoner) to (a distant country) as a punishment: [T1 + *to* (*usu. pass.*)] *In the early 19th century, a man could be transported to Australia for life, for stealing a sheep.*

**transport with** *v prep*

**be transported with** *fml* to be seized by (a strong feeling, usu. good): *Upon seeing her long-lost son again, the mother was transported with joy.*

**transpose into** *v prep*

to copy or play (music) or rewrite (words) in (another key or form of words): [T1 + *into*] *This song's too high for my voice; could you please transpose it down into E flat?*

**trap in** *v prep*

to seize (usu. an animal) or cause (someone) to be unable to move by holding him in (something): [T1 + *in*] *How many rabbits have you trapped in your special trap this week? Thirty miners are still trapped in the mine following yesterday's explosion.*

***trap into** *v prep* also **entrap into** → **trick into,** etc.

to persuade (someone) by deceit into (action or doing something): [D1] *His lawyer may trap the witness into an admission that he did not actually see the crime. It's no longer possible to trap a sensible man into marriage.* [V4a] *I got trapped into agreeing to speak to the school about my adventures.*

**travel by** *v prep* → **travel on**

to make a journey using (a vehicle, ship, or plane): [IØ + *by*] *I would rather travel by train than by plane. Some of the guests travelled by bicycle, others by bus.*

**travel from** *v prep* → **travel to**

to make a journey leaving (a place): [IØ + *from*] *We're very tired, having travelled from London in a day.*

**travel in** *v prep*

**1** to make a journey or journeys through (a large place): [IØ + *in*] *Have you travelled much in Europe?*

***2** to go from place to place selling (certain goods): [T1 (*no pass.*) (*for*)] *For many years, he travelled in brushes for the Better Brush Company.*

**travel on** *v prep* → **travel by**

to make a journey on (horseback or foot): [IØ + *on*] *Not many of the children travel on horseback to school even in these country areas. Travelling on foot takes such a long time compared with modern ways of getting about.*

**travel over**[1] *v adv*

to cross (a large area) when making a journey or journeys: [T1 + OVER] *"Though we travel the world over to find the beautiful we must carry it with us or we find it not."* (Ralph Waldo Emerson, *Essays, 12: Art*)

**travel over**[2] *v prep*

**1** to pass over (a large area) when making a journey: [IØ + *over*] *He travelled over land and water before he found what he was looking for.*

***2** to pass over (something): [T1 (*no pass.*)] *His eyes travelled over her face but could find no sign of guilt. He let his mind travel over all that he had seen, hoping to discover the secret of the place.*

**travel to** *v prep* → **travel from**

to make a journey in the direction of (usu. a place): [IØ + *to*] *Are you travelling to Liverpool as well? We can go together.*

**travel with** *v prep*

**1** to have (someone) as a companion on a journey; go together with (something): [IØ + *with*] *I'd rather you travelled with the group than alone, it's much safer. Some of our people are travelling with the show on its tour.*

***2** to share the activities or ideas of (someone): [T1 (*no pass.*)] *I was so sorry to hear that your son had been travelling with those criminal types.*

**tread down** *v adv*

**1** to press (something), as with the feet: [T1 + DOWN] *You could see where the grass had been trodden down by all the people passing across the field.* —**trodden-down** *adj* → **trample down**

***2** to rule (people) severely and cruelly: [T1 (*usu. pass.*)] *The people have been trodden down for too long, and soon will rise to overthrow their unjust rulers.* —**downtrodden** *adj*

**tread in** *v adv* → **trample in**

to press (something) into the ground, as with the feet: [T1 + IN] *Spread the chemical over the soil and let the cattle tread it in as they walk over it.*

**tread into** *v prep*

to press (something) into (a surface), as with

the feet: [T1 + *into*] *You've been treading mud into the best mat!*

**tread on/upon** *v prep*

**1** to move with the feet on top of (usu. something): [L9 + *on/upon*] *Mind where you put your feet, you could tread on some broken glass. I'm sorry I trod on your foot!* → **stamp on** (1), **step on** (1), **trample on** (1)

***2** to hurt (someone's feelings); offend or harm (something): [T1] *It's difficult to avoid treading on her sensitivity, which is so much finer than other people's.* → **step on** (2), **trample on** (2), **walk on²** (2), **walk over²** (1)

**3 tread on air** *not fml* to be very happy: [*often continuous tenses*] *Ever since Jane heard that she's been admitted to the music school, she's been treading on air.*

**4 tread on someone's heels** to follow someone very closely: [*often continuous tenses*] *If you must walk behind me, please keep a little further back; you're treading on my heels.*

**5 tread on someone's toes/corns** *not fml* to annoy someone by treating him insensitively; offend someone: *Mind you don't go treading on Father's toes again by mentioning his trouble at work. I hope I'm not treading on any teacher's toes by complaining about our educational system.* → **step on** (5)

**tread out** *v adv*

**1** to make (a path) by pressing with the feet: [T1 + OUT] *See where the animals have trodden out a narrow path over the years.* → **trample out** (1)

***2** to put out (a fire) with the feet: [T1] *Be sure to tread the fire out before you leave, and cover it with earth to make sure the flames won't start burning again. "A little fire is quickly trodden out."* (Shakespeare, *King Henry VI, Part III*) → **stamp out** (3), **trample out** (2)

***3** to press (usu. grapes) with the feet; cause (juice) to flow from fruit by pressing, as with the feet: [T1] *Help me to tread out the grapes for this year's wine. Has all the juice been trodden out?* → **trample out** (3)

**tread upon** *v prep* → TREAD ON

**treasure up** *v adv*

to store (something precious such as a memory) for the future: [T1 + UP] *I am treasuring up my thoughts of this happy time to give me joy in the future.*

**treat as** *v prep*

to behave towards (someone) as if he were (something): [X7 + *as* (*often simple tenses*)] *The best way to deal with someone who is drinking too much is to treat him as sick.*

**treat for** *v prep*

**1** to give (someone) medicine, advice, etc., to cure (an illness or condition): [T1 + *for*] *What is the doctor giving Jane to treat her for her frequent stomach trouble?*

***2** *fml* to try to gain (something) by talking formally with someone else: [T1] *How long have the two parties been treating for a settlement?*

***treat of** *v prep* → **deal with** (3)

*fml* (of writing, usu. formal) to have (something) as its subject: [T1 (*no pass., simple tenses*)] *This article treats of the dangers facing certain groups of wild animals.*

**treat like** *v prep*

**treat someone like dirt** *not fml* to treat someone very badly; be rude to someone: *Mother left that office; she said she wasn't going to be treated like dirt, and wanted a job where people would pay her proper respect.*

**treat to** *v prep*

to provide (someone or oneself) with (something, often food) as a gift, favour, or special pleasure: [T1 + *to*] *Let me treat you to a good meal. I think I'll treat myself to a holiday in Spain next year.*

**treat with** *v prep*

**1** to behave towards (someone) by showing (a quality): [X9 + *with*] *But the family have always treated me with great kindness and consideration!*

**2** to give (someone or a disease) (certain medicine): [T1 + *with*] *The doctor is treating Jane with some special medicine. This fever can be successfully treated with the new drug.*

***3** *fml* to have formal talks with (someone, usu. the enemy) so as to reach an agreement: [T1 (*no pass.*)] *Our best man was sent to treat with the native leaders.*

**trek to** *v prep*

to make a very long and tiring journey to (a place): [IØ + *to*] *It took the climbers a month to trek to the foot of the mountain before they even started their climb.*

**tremble at** *v prep*

to show fear of (something), as by shaking: [IØ + *at*] *I'm trembling at the thought of tomorrow's examination.*

***tremble for** *v prep*

to be very worried about (something or someone: [T1 (*no pass., simple tenses, usu. present*)] *"Indeed I tremble for my country when I reflect that God is just."* (Thomas Jefferson, *Notes on Virginia, Query 18: Manners*)

**tremble from** *v prep* → TREMBLE WITH

**tremble in** *v prep*

**tremble in the balance** to be not yet decided: *The fate of the nations trembled in the balance while the two armies fought a bitter battle.*

**tremble with** *v prep* also **tremble from** → **quake with, quiver with, shake with** (1), **shiver with**

to shake; move the body in small waves because of (fear, cold, etc.): [IØ + *with*] *The children waited outside the school, trembling with cold. The prisoner trembled with fear as he faced the court. Her voice trembled with nervousness as she began her song.*

***trench on/upon** *v prep* → **encroach on** (2), **impinge on** (2), **infringe on**

*fml* to make unreasonable demands on

(something); take part of (something) unjustly: [T1] *He has no right to trench upon my time like this.*

*__trend towards__ *v prep* → **lean towards** (2), etc.
to move one's opinion more in favour of (something such as a belief): [T1 (*no pass.*)] *More and more countries in Europe are now trending towards some form of Socialism.*

**trespass against** *v prep*
*old use fml* to offend (someone or something) by opposing a right: [IØ + *against* (*usu. simple tenses*)] *"And forgive us our trespasses, as we forgive them that trepass against us."* (The Lord's Prayer)

**trespass on/upon** *v prep*
**1** to enter (someone's land or property) without permission: [IØ + *on/upon*] *Anyone caught trespassing on my land will be taken to court.*
*__2__ to use or offend against (something) without right; take more of (something) than what is right, proper, or usual: [T1 (*no pass.*)] *By making this decision, you are trespassing upon the rights of the native people. It would be trespassing upon their generosity to accept any more from them.*

*__trice up__ *v adv*
*naut* to fix and support (a sail) in position with many ropes: [T1] *The big sail won't stay in position unless you trice it up.*

**trick into** *v prep* → **beguile into, cheat into, con into, cozen into, deceive into, delude into** (1), **gull into, shaft into, trap into, trick out of**
to persuade (someone) into (action or doing something) by deceit: [T1 + *into*] *A clever lawyer should be able to trick the prisoner into an admission of guilt. I was tricked into giving the old man some money.*

*__trick out__ *v adv* also **trick up** → **dress up** (2), etc.
*not fml* to dress and ornament (someone or something) showily: [T1 (*usu. pass.*)] *Look at the way she has tricked her daughter out for the wedding! Where are you going, all tricked out like that?*

**trick out of** *v adv prep* → **cheat out of,** etc., **trick into**
to rob (someone) of (something) by a trick: [T1 + OUT + *of*] *The clever salesman was able to trick the old lady out of her money, with his charm.*

*__trick up__ *v adv* → TRICK OUT

**trickle away** *v adv*
**1** (of liquid) to flow away slowly in small quantities: [L9 + AWAY] *There must be a small hole in the pipe, look at the water trickling away!*
**2** (of a crowd) to leave gradually: [L9 + AWAY] *As the speaker went on speaking, the crowd gradually trickled away until only a few were left.*

**trickle in** *v adv*
**1** (of liquid) to flow in slowly in small quantities: [L9 + IN] *You didn't mend that hole in the roof very well, there's still a little rain trickling in.*
**2** to arrive one or a few at a time: [L9 + IN (*to*)] *Some early theatregoers began to trickle in an hour before the show. At last the replies began to trickle in (to the office).*

**trickle out** *v adv*
**1** (of liquid) to flow out slowly in small quantities: [L9 + OUT (*of*)] *Even after the lid was put on, some water still trickled out.*
**2** (usu. of people) to leave gradually; (of news) reach the public slowly: [L9 + OUT (*of*)] *At first the hall was full, but people began to trickle out soon after the beginning of his speech, and soon there were very few left to hear the speaker. News has begun to trickle out of the flooded area about the number of dead.*

*__trifle away__ *v adv* → **idle away** (2), etc.
to waste (usu. time or money) foolishly: [T1] *He got a large fortune when his father died, but trifled it away in only a few years of needless spending.*

*__trifle with__ *v prep*
**1** → TOY WITH (2)
**2** to treat (someone or someone's feelings) inconsiderately, not seriously: [T1] *He's never mentioned marriage, and I'm beginning to think he's just trifling with me, which is unkind. Don't play games with the director; he's a powerful man, and not to be trifled with.* → **flirt with** (1), etc.

*__trig out/up__ *v adv*
esp. *BrE infml* to make (something) neat: [T1 (*usu. pass.*)] *Is his office all trigged out ready for the new director?*

*__trigger off__ *v adv*
**1** to start (an explosion): [T1 (*usu. simple tenses*)] *The explosion in the mine was triggered off by a careless miner who lit a match looking for gas.* → **go off**[1] (5), etc.
**2** to cause (something violent) to begin: [T1a (*usu. simple tenses*)] *Careless political action can trigger off a war. His stupid remarks triggered off a fight.* → **set off** (5), **spark off** (2), **touch off** (2)

**trim away/off** *v adv*
**1** to remove (unwanted fat or other substance) by cutting: [T1 + AWAY/OFF] *Ask the meat man to trim away the fat edges of the meat.*
*__2__ to remove (something unwanted): [T1] *We shall have to trim off the unnecessary parts of our spending.* → **trim down** (2)

**trim down** *v adv*
**1** to make (something or someone) thinner: [T1 + DOWN] *Weeks of exercise succeeded in trimming down her waistline.*
*__2__ to reduce (something): [T1] *We shall have to trim our spending down to fit our income.* → **trim away** (2)

**trim off** *v adv* → TRIM AWAY

*****trip out** *v adv* → **tune in** (2), **turn on¹** (3)
*infml* to experience the bad effects of a mind-changing drug: [IØ (*often simple tenses*)] *Have you ever tripped out?*

**trip over** *v prep*
**1** to fall over (something in one's way), as by catching the foot: [IØ + *over*] *Mind you don't trip over these roots, they're difficult to see under all these leaves.* → **fall over²** (2), **stumble over** (1)
*****2** to make an awkward mistake in (something such as words): [T1] *Can you read the whole of the news without tripping over some of those difficult foreign names? The speaker answered most questions well, except one that he tripped over because he didn't have the necessary facts.* → **fall over²** (3), **stumble over** (2)

**trip up** *v adv*
**1** to fall awkwardly, as by catching the foot: [IØ + UP] *Jim was running well until he tripped up and fell, losing the race.*
*****2** to catch (someone) in a mistake; make a mistake or misjudgment: [T1] *The opposing lawyer tripped the prisoner up when he lied about where he had been on the night of the crime, and so made him admit his guilt.* [IØ (*on*)] *The leading politician was greatly admired until he began tripping up on his own standards.*

*****triumph over** *v prep*
**1** to defeat (an enemy): [T1 (*often simple tenses*)] *The victorious general had triumphed over enemies far more powerful than this.*
**2** to conquer (something bad): [T1 (*often simple tenses*)] *Ill for many years, she became a successful writer and so triumphed over her misfortune.* → **avail against, prevail against**

**trot after** *v prep*
**1** to move on horseback or with a child's movement at a steady speed following (someone or something); (of an animal such as a horse) follow (someone or something) at a steady speed, with quick light steps: [IØ + *after*] *We trotted after the leading horse for some minutes. The dog always trotted after his master wherever he went.*
*****2** to make efforts to gain the company or attention of (someone, often of the opposite sex): [T1] *All the girls are trotting after the attractive new student. I don't want you trotting after me with your demands!* → **run after** (2)

*****trot out** *v adv*
**1** to show (a horse moving at a steady speed) to someone: [T1] *Trot out the horses for the buyers to watch.*
**2** *not fml* to produce (something such as words or figures) with ease: [T1] *He keeps on trotting out the same old arguments.*

*****trouble about/over** *v prep* → **worry about**
to concern oneself about (something or someone): [T1 (*no pass., often simple tenses*)] *She can look after herself, and she's not worth troubling over. Please don't trouble about that one little mistake, you're forgiven.*

*****trouble for** *v prep*
to ask (someone) politely to give one (something): [D1 (*often simple tenses*)] *May I trouble you for a match?*

*****trouble over** *v prep* → TROUBLE ABOUT

**trouble with** *v prep*
to worry (someone or oneself) because of (something often in the mind): [T1 + *with* (*often pass., often simple tenses*)] *I don't want to trouble you with all my little difficulties, but I wonder if you could help me just once more? Jane has been troubled with bad dreams recently.*

*****truckle to** *v prep*
to yield to (someone) out of weakness: [T1] *Why do you truckle to your mother like that? She has no right to give you orders, you're a grown woman now!*

*****true up** *v adv*
to change (something) to make it fit well, esp. in line with something else: [T1] *Has the wheel been properly trued up? First you must true up the pieces of wood to make a straight edge.*

*****trump up** *v adv*
to invent (usu. a false charge): [T1a (*often pass.*)] *I'm not guilty; someone has trumped up a charge against me.* —**trumped-up** *adj*

**truss up** *v adv*
to bind (someone or something) tightly: [T1 + UP (*usu. pass.*)] *The prisoners were left trussed up on the floor. Do you know how to truss up a chicken?*

**trust for** *v prep*
**1** *not fml* to believe that (someone) would usually do (something): [T1 + *for* (*usu. imper.*)] *You mean he took the money? Well, trust him for that!*
*****2** to allow (someone) to have (money or goods) and to return or pay for them at a later date: [T1 + *for*] *Can you trust me for a packet of cigarettes until Friday?*

*****trust in** *v prep* → **depend on** (1), etc.
to believe in or have faith in (someone or something): [T1] *Soon you will learn to trust in your own good judgment. Trust in God.*

*****trust to** *v prep*
**1** to depend on (something such as chance): [T1] *I don't know if it will work, but I'll just trust to luck. I'm trusting to memory and cannot swear it is the right name.* → **depend on** (1), etc.
**2** to give the charge of (something or someone) to (someone): [D1] *I trusted the child to your care, and look what's happened! He trusted the job to me, not you; I'll finish it myself.* → **entrust to**

**trust with** *v prep* → **entrust with**
to give (someone) the care of (something or someone), with complete faith: [T1 + *with*] *Do you think it's wise to trust the boy with all that money? I have no intention of trusting her with any secret of mine.*

**try at** *v prep*
**try one's hand at** to attempt (something or doing something): *Well, I've never played this instrument, but I'm always willing to try my hand at (learning) anything new.*

**try for** *v prep*
**1** to attempt to prove the guilt of (someone) in a court of law, for (a possible crime): [T1 + *for* (*usu. pass.*)] *The prisoner is being tried for robbery with violence.*
***2** to attempt to win (something such as a prize): [T1] *Will Jim try for the first prize, or will he wait till next year when his chances will be better?*

***try on** *v adv*
**1** to put on (clothes) to test the fit, examine the appearance, etc.: [T1] *Never buy shoes without trying them on first.*
**2** *infml* to attempt (something such as a trick) to see if it will be accepted, esp. in the phr. **try it on**: [T1] *It's no use trying on that old trick with me! Has he been trying it on again? I hope you took no notice.* —**try-on** *n*

***try out** *v adv*
**1** to remove (oil) from the fat of an animal such as a whale: [T1] *The best time to try out the oil is soon after the creature is killed, on board the ship.* → **render down** (1)
**2** to test (something or someone): [T1 (*on*)] *Have the advertisers tried out the new soap on real people yet? The new engine must be thoroughly tried out before being out on the market. I want to try out several of the new singers for the part.* —**try-out** *n*
**3** to offer oneself to be tested, as for a team: [IØ (*for*)] *Are you going to try out for the team?* —**try-out** *n*

***try over** *v adv*
to retest or practise (something): [T1] *I could hear her trying her voice over before the curtain went up.*

**tuck away** *v adv*
**1** to put (something) away tidily: [X9 + AWAY] *The papers were all tucked away behind the books.* → **put away** (1)
***2** *not fml* to eat a lot of (food): [T1] *You should see the amount of food that boy can tuck away in one meal!* → **pack away** (2), **put away** (2), **put down** (6)
***3** *not fml* to hide (something or someone): [T1 (*usu. pass.*)] *The house was tucked away behind the trees. I'm sure you have a lady friend tucked away somewhere. I keep some money tucked away where no one can find it.* → **tuck in** (5)

**tuck down** *v adv; prep*
to push (something) firmly down (something): [X9 + DOWN/*down* (*usu. pass.*)] *I found this handkerchief tucked down (the back of the chair). Have the sheets been tucked down properly?*

**tuck in** *v adv*
**1** to push (something) neatly into place: [X9 + IN (*to*)] *Tuck your handkerchief in, dear, it looks silly sticking out.* → **tuck into** (1)
***2** to pull (part of the body) in stiffly: [T1] *Tuck in your stomach and stand up straight! You'll never be able to sing if you tuck your chin in like that.* → **hold in**[1] (1), **keep in** (1), **pull in** (2)
***3** to make (someone such as a child or sick person) comfortable in bed: [T1 (*to*)] *I shan't be long, I must just tuck the children in for the night.* → **tuck into** (2), **tuck up** (3)
***4** *not fml* to eat eagerly: [IØ (*to*)] *Those climbers must be really hungry: did you see how they tucked in (to the food)?* —**tuck-in** *n* → **dig in**[1] (5), **dive in** (2), **pile in** (2), **pitch in** (2), **tuck into** (3), **wade in** (2)
**5 be tucked in** to be placed so as to be seen with difficulty: *I couldn't find the house, it was tucked in behind the trees.* → **tuck away**

**tuck into** *v prep*
**1** to push (something such as clothing) neatly into place, as into (other clothing): [X9 + *into*] *Do tuck your shirt into your trousers, dear, it looks so silly hanging out.* → **tuck in** (1)
***2** to make (someone such as a child or sick person) comfortable in (bed): [D1] *Let me tuck you into your bed, you'll get a better night.* → **tuck in** (3), **tuck up** (3)
***3** *not fml* to eat (food) eagerly: [T1] *I do enjoy seeing the children really tuck into a meal that I've prepared for them.* → **dig into** (3), **dive into** (2), **pile into** (2), **pitch into** (3), **tear into** (3), **tuck in** (4), **wade into** (3), **walk into** (7)

**tuck up** *v adv*
**1** to pull or gather (clothing) upwards: [X9 + UP] *Tucking up her long skirt, she walked into the water to save the child.*
***2** to fold (usu. one's legs) underneath one: [T1 (*usu. pass.*)] *She sat with her legs tucked up beneath her, looking quite comfortable.*
***3** to make (someone such as a child or sick person) comfortable in bed: [T1] *Here, I'll tuck you up and then you'll sleep well.* → **tuck in** (3), **tuck into** (2)

**tucker out** *v adv* → **tire out,** etc.
**be tuckered out** *AmE infml* to be very tired: *I can't go any further, I'm tuckered out. Let me rest here.*

**tug at** *v prep*
**1** to pull hard at (something such as a rope or part of the body): [IØ + *at*] *I'll tug at the rope once as a signal to pull me up. Suddenly I felt someone tugging at my arm.* → **pluck at, pull at** (1), **pull on** (1), **yank at, yank on**
**2 tug at someone's heartstrings** *not fml* to move someone's feelings deeply: [*usu. simple tenses*] *The way the child sang her song*

*really tugged at my heartstrings.*

**tumble down** *v adv*

**1** (usu. of a building) to fall down in ruin, usu. through decay: [IØ + DOWN] *That old building could tumble down any day now.* —**tumbledown** *adj* → **fall down** (1, 2), **topple down** (1)

***2** *not fml* to fail (in something): [IØ (*on*) (*usu. simple tenses*)] *His plan tumbled down when it proved too costly. Don't tumble down on this easy test.* → **fall down** (3), **fall through**[1] (2), **topple down** (2)

***tumble for** *v prep*

**1** *not fml* to fall in love with (someone); like (something) very much: [T1 (*simple tenses*)] *Jim tumbled for Mary the first time he met her. The whole family tumbled for the new house, although it badly needed painting.* → **fall for** (1)

**2** *not fml* to be attracted to, be tricked by, or believe (something, often deceitful): [T1 (*usu. simple tenses*)] *Don't tumble for that old trick, he's just trying to get you to buy his goods. Did the committee tumble for the chairman's clever plan?* → **fall for** (2)

**tumble into** *v prep*

**1** to fall awkwardly into (something): [IØ + *into*] *The child tumbled into the lake and had to be pulled out.* → **fall into** (1)

***2** to allow oneself to get carelessly or helplessly into (bed): [T1 (*no pass., often simple tenses*)] *She was so tired after the concert that she just tumbled into bed.*

**3 tumble into one's lap** *not fml* to be found by chance; be gained without effort: "*Fortunes . . . come tumbling into some men's laps.*" (Francis Bacon, *Advancement of Learning*)

**tumble off** *v adv; prep* → **fall off**[1] (1)

to come off (something) by falling carelessly, heavily, or helplessly: [IØ + OFF/*off*] *When you are learning to ride a bicycle, you often tumble off, but this teaches you how to keep your balance.*

***tumble on/upon** *v prep* → **happen on,** etc.

*not fml* to find or discover (something) by chance: [T1 (*simple tenses*)] *Quite accidentally, the police tumbled on the answer to the mystery.*

**tumble out** *v adv* → **fall out** (1)

to fall carelessly, heavily, or helplessly out (of something): [IØ + OUT (*of*)] *The wind blew so strongly that the nest turned upside down and three baby birds tumbled out. As she opened the cupboard door, a pile of old books tumbled out.*

**tumble over** *v adv; prep* → **fall over**[1] (1), **tip over, topple over**

to lose one's balance; fall accidentally, often carelessly, heavily, or helplessly over (something): [IØ + OVER/*over*] *I saw the little girl tumble over and hit her head. He tried to build a house of cards but it soon tumbled over. The hunter fired and the deer tumbled over, quite dead.*

***tumble to** *v prep*

*not fml* to understand or become conscious of (something such as a joke, a secret, or deceit) often suddenly: [T1 (*usu. simple tenses*)] *Have the opposition tumbled to our plan yet, or are they more stupid that I thought? All the general's supporters knew what was about to be suggested, but I didn't tumble to it even then.*

***tumble upon** *v prep* → TUMBLE ON

***tune in** *v adv*

**1** to listen (to a radio station); move the switch of (a radio) to choose a certain station: [IØ (*to*)] *Tune in again tomorrow to hear the continuation of our exciting story.* [T1 (*to*) (*often pass.*)] *You don't seem to have the radio tuned in to the station properly, the sound isn't clear. I always keep the radio tuned in to the same station, my favourite.* → **listen in** (1), **look in**[1] (1)

**2** *infml* to (cause to) be conscious (of others or ideas) in a modern way: [IØ (*to*)] *He has a way of tuning in to what people are meaning even when they don't know how to say it. Many young people are using drugs to tune in.* [T1 (*usu. pass.*)] *He's right up to date, completely tuned in.* → **switch on** (2), **trip out, turn on**[1] (3)

***tune out** *v adv*

**1** to switch off (a radio); stop listening to (a radio station): [T1] *Do please tune out that terrible music, I can't bear the noise.*

**2** esp. *AmE infml* to show no interest; allow one's attention to wander: [IØ] *All the students tuned out when the speaker began on a long list of uninteresting facts.* → **switch off** (3), **turn off**[1] (7)

***tune up** *v adv*

**1** to play a few notes to see if an instrument is in tune; change (an instrument) to make the notes correct: [IØ] *We got to the concert late, but not too late; the band were just tuning up ready to play the first piece.* [T1] *Have all the instruments been properly tuned up?* —**tuning-up** *n*

**2** to make (an engine) be in good condition so as to turn smoothly and fast: [T1] *I have to take the car to a garage as it needs tuning up.* —**tune-up** *n*

***turf out** *v adv* → **throw out** (4), etc., (5), etc.

esp. *BrE not fml* to (cause to) leave a place such as a home or because of a fault: [T1] *The old lady has been turfed out of her home, and I demand to know why. Two of our members have been turfed out for breaking the rules.* [IØ] *We were very comfortable in the club chairs, but we had to turf out when the members arrived.*

***turn about** *v adv*

**1** *mil* to (cause to) face in the opposite direction: [IØ (*imper.*)] *'About turn!' shouted the captain to his men.* [T1 (*usu pass.*)] *The whole army had to be turned about to face the* *new enemy coming from behind.* → **face about** (1), **turn around** (1)

**2** to change one's opinion or argument: [IØ (*usu. simple tenses*)] *The chairman seems to have turned completely about.* —**turnabout** *n* → **turn around** (4)

**turn adrift** *v adv*

**1** to set (someone or a boat) to float on the water without direction: [X9 + ADRIFT (*usu. simple tenses*)] *The sailors refused to obey their captain, and after a fight, turned him adrift on the ocean in an open boat. The boat full of prisoners was turned adrift by order of the guard.* → **set adrift**

*__2__ to send (someone) away without help or support: [T1b (*usu. simple tenses*)] *In the end he was forced to turn his son adrift, as he was becoming too dependent on the family wealth.*

***turn against** *v prep* → **turn on²** (2)

**1** to (cause to) attack (someone or an animal): [T1 (*usu. simple tenses*)] *The rat, driven to a corner, turned against the dogs and bit three before it was killed.* [D1] *I wonder what turned the dog against his own master?*

**2** to (cause to) oppose (someone or something), often after earlier support: [T1] *Why did you turn against the party which had given you your first chance in politics?* [D1] *Mary's father did his best to turn her against Jim, but without success. The speaker's words were turned against himself.*

**turn around/round** *v adv*

**1** to (cause to) move so as to face the other way: [IØ + AROUND/ROUND] *I thought I heard a voice I knew; turning round, I saw my long-lost brother.* [T1 + AROUND/ROUND] *Please help me to turn the car around, it's stuck in the mud. When we came home, she had spent the day turning all the furniture around.* → **face round, turn about** (1)

*__2__ (of trade or business) to improve after failure; change for the better: [IØ] *Do you think our housing sales will turn round during this year?* —**turn-(a)round** *n*

*__3__ to make (an idea or opinion) completely different: [T1] *He was clever enough to turn my question around so that it sounded foolish.* → **twist around** (2)

*__4__ to change one's opinion or argument: [IØ (*usu. simple tenses*)] *The chairman seems to have quite turned round.* → **turn about** (2)

*__5__ *not fml* to make an effort: [IØ (*usu. simple tenses*)] *Well, after all that, I'd better turn round and get some work done!*

*__6__ (usu. of a ship or plane) to (cause to) finish one journey and prepare to return: [IØ] *These big ships need half a day to turn round.* [T1] *I'll send some more men to help you turn the plane around.* —**turnround** *n*

**turn aside** *v adv*

**1** to (cause to) move or move the head to one side: [L9 + ASIDE] *"And some that came to scoff at him now turned aside and wept."* (William Aytoun, *The Execution of Montrose*) [X9 + ASIDE] *She turned her head aside when he tried to kiss her.* → **turn away** (1)

*__2__ to deal with (something such as an attack) so as to make ineffective: [T1 (*usu. simple tenses*)] *She was successful in turning aside all opposition. Quickly turning the blow aside, he got in a good blow himself. "The President has so far turned aside questions on the subject."* (CBC radio news, 19 September 1977) → **turn away** (2)

*__3__ to refuse one's sympathy or support (for someone): [IØ (*from*) (*usu. simple tenses*)] *How can you turn aside from suffering humanity?* → **turn away** (5)

**turn away** *v adv*

**1** to (cause to) move in a direction away from something or someone: [L9 + AWAY (*from*)] *"And then you suddenly cried, and turned away."* (Rupert Brooke, *The Hill*) [X9 + AWAY (*from*)] *Please don't turn your head away when I'm trying to kiss you.* → **turn aside** (1)

*__2__ to deal with (something such as an attack) so as to make ineffective: [T1 (*usu. simple tenses*)] *"For all this his anger is not turned away, but his hand is stretched out still."* (The Bible) → **turn aside** (2)

*__3__ to refuse to allow (someone) to enter: [T1 (*from*)] *When the famous singer appeared at the theatre, crowds of people were turned away, for lack of room.*

*__4__ to refuse to accept (something): [T1] *I'm afraid your request for a pay rise has been turned away.* → **turn down** (4)

*__5__ to refuse one's sympathy or support (for someone): [IØ (*from*) (*usu. simple tenses*)] *How can you turn away from a child that is being cruelly treated?* → **turn aside** (3)

**turn back** *v adv*

**1** to (cause to) bend backwards: [L9 + BACK (*simple tenses*)] *The collar turns back in the latest fashion. The top of the box turns back to show the goods.* [X9 + BACK] *Please don't turn the corners of the pages back. Turning back the cover, she found a pool of blood on the top.* → **bend down** (1), **fold back**, etc., **turn in** (1)

**2** to turn to an earlier page in reading: [L9 + BACK] *I had to turn back to page 10 to find where I had met the character before. Please turn back to the Table of Contents and find another poem on the same subject.*

*__3__ to (cause to) return or stop moving forward: [IØ] *If you don't think we can reach the town before dark, we'd better turn back now while there's still time.* [T1] *We had intended to escape from the country, but we were turned back at the border.* → **put back** (4)

*__4__ to change one's course of action, esp. to its opposite: [IØ] *Remember, once you've signed the contract, there's no turning back.*

**5 turn back the clock:** to follow old-fashioned ideas; try to return to the past: *Many employers would like to turn the clock back to the* *good old days when workers were under their control, but they are too late: the world has changed.* → **put back** (10), **set back** (7)

**turn down** *v adv*

**1** to fold (something) in a downward or backward direction: [X9 + DOWN] *Please don't turn down the corners of the pages. I've just come in to turn the bedclothes down.* → **bend down**, etc.

**2** to turn (something) upside down; place (a flat object) on its face: [X9 + DOWN] *We start this game with all the cards on the table, turned down so that we don't know what they are.*

**3** to reduce (flame, a sound, etc.), usu. by moving a switch or other control: [X9 + DOWN] *Can't you turn the flame down on your cigarette lighter? It looks very dangerous. Please turn the radio down, I'm trying to sleep.*

***4** to refuse to accept (something or someone): [T1] *Why was I turned down for the job? Is it because I'm a woman? I'm afraid your request for a pay rise was turned down again.* → **throw out** (16), **toss out** (5), **turn away** (4)

***5** (of a money market or system) to become weaker: [IØ] *The housing sales have been turning down since the summer.* —**downturn, turndown** *n*

**turn from** *v prep*

**1** to (cause to) move away from (someone or something): [L9 + *from*] *At last he turned from me and walked away.* [X9 + *from*] *Please don't turn your head from me when you're speaking, I can't hear you.*

***2** to (cause to) leave or cease (something such as a subject or a way of life): [T1 (*no pass. usu. simple tenses*)] *I was glad to turn from those old ways of thought which had made me so unhappy. Turning from such an unpleasant subject, let us consider better things like this year's holiday.* [D1] *No one could turn him from his purpose once he had made up his mind.*

**turn in**[1] *v adv*

**1** to (cause to) bend, fold, or point inwards: [L9 + IN (*simple tenses*)] *Why do your toes turn in?* [X9 + IN] *The edges of the cloth should be turned in and sewn firmly. Turn your feet in more as you walk, they point outwards too much.* → **bend down**, etc., **turn back** (1), **turn down** (1)

**2** to make a turning into a side road or private drive, as when driving a car: [L9 + IN] *When you pass the church, remember to turn in at the next street. There's a car turning in: who can it be coming here?*

***3** *naut* to fasten (a rope) round an object: [T1] *Fix the rope around the post by turning it in.*

***4** to give back (something no longer needed such as an unwanted ticket, goods, or official clothing): [T1] *Don't forget to turn in your gun when you leave the police force. Tickets may be turned in at the box office, or exchanged for ones for the new show.* → **give in** (4), **give into** (4), **give up** (7), etc., **hand in** (3)

***5** to give (something, someone, or oneself) to the police: [T1 (*usu. simple tenses*)] *You'd better turn in the money that you found. The escaped criminal decided to turn himself in. You'd turn in your own brother, wouldn't you, if he broke the law?* → **give up** (8), etc.

***6** to offer (something such as written work or a performance): [T1] *This is a poor piece of work you've turned in. In spite of the difficulties, she turned in the best performance of her life.*

***7** *not fml* to stop working at (something): [T1] *Jim decided to turn in his job and look for a new life.* → **give up** (2), etc.

***8** *not fml* to go to bed: [IØ] *I think it's time I turned in; goodnight, everybody.*

**9 turn it in!** *infml* stop that!: [*imper.*] → **knock off** (13), **pack in** (4), **pack up** (4), **turn up** (11)

**turn in**[2] *v prep*

**1** to drive a car into (a side road or private drive); make a turn in (a space): [L9 + *in*] *The driver had difficulty turning in such a narrow drive.*

**2 turn in one's grave** *not fml* to disapprove of something or someone after one's death: *If your grandmother heard you swearing like that, I'm sure she would turn in her grave!*

**turn in on** *v adv prep*

**turn in on oneself** to have as little as possible to do with others: *Please try to encourage Mary to enjoy parties more; I'm afraid that she may turn in on herself completely and never be able to have a social life.*

**turn inside out** *v adv*

**1** to turn (something, esp. clothing) to the other side; be able to be turned or turn to the other side: [X9 + INSIDE OUT] *I turned my pockets inside out to shake the dust out.* [L9 + INSIDE OUT (*simple tenses*)] *This useful coat turns inside out so that you can wear it on wet days, too.* → **turn out** (6), **turn topsy-turvy, turn upside down** (1)

***2** to search (a place) thoroughly, causing disorder: [T1b] *Some robbers had broken into the house while we were away, and had turned the place inside out looking for the jewels.*

***3** to confuse (something such as an idea): [T1a (*usu. simple tenses*)] *His whole idea of justice has been turned inside out by his experience in prison.*

**turn into** *v prep*

**1** to drive a car into (a side street or private drive): [L9 + *into*] *When I was turning into your drive, I hit the gatepost. There's a strange vehicle turning into our street: what can it be?*

***2** to (cause to) become (something or someone) by changing: [T1] *Jane is turning into quite a skilled musician. He's turned into a nice boy after all. The funny dry little stick turned into a beautiful bush. The city is turn-*

*ing into a meeting place for criminals.* [D1] *Her bitter experience has turned her into a stronger person. Is it possible for such a person to turn himself into a good writer? The mice were turned into horses by a magic spell. I'm thinking of turning the flower garden into a vegetable field. Why don't we turn the empty bedroom into a guest bathroom? Every time she is rude to you, try turning her hard words into a joke against herself.* → **change into** (2), etc.

*****3** to translate (words) into (another language): [D1] *Shakespeare's plays are difficult to turn into any other language.* → **do into, render into, translate into** (1), **turn to**[2] (7)

**turn left/right** *v adv* → **bear left, keep left**

to change one's direction towards the left/right: [L9 + LEFT/RIGHT] *When you've passed the church, turn left and you will see our road leading off.*

**turn loose** *v adj*

**1** to free (someone or an animal): [X9 + **loose**] *Someone turned the lion loose from its cage, and it has been wandering all over the town, terrifying people.* → **get free** (1), etc.

*****2** to give (someone) freedom to act as he wishes: [T1b] *Who turned those children loose in my kitchen with my cooking things?* [V3] *Many of the students would rather be turned loose to discover things of interest to themselves, than have to study subjects decided for them.* → **let loose** (2)

*****3** *AmE mil* to start using (guns) freely: [T1] *The general gave orders to turn loose all the big guns.*

**turn off**[1] *v adv*

**1** to drive in a different direction; take a new road: [L9 + OFF] *Let's turn off and find a quieter road.*

**2** (of a road) to take a new direction: [L9 + OFF (*simple tenses*)] *The road turns off to the station a little further ahead.* —**turn-off** *n* → **branch off**

**3** (of a supply of water, gas, electricity, etc.) to (cause to) stop working by a switch control: [L9 + OFF (*simple tenses*)] *The tap won't turn off, and there's water all over the floor.* [X9 + OFF] *I can't turn the tap off, and there's water all over the floor. Please turn all the lights off as you leave the building, we can't afford to waste power.* → **put off**[1] (3), etc

*****4** to stop having (a characteristic or an expression on one's face): [T1] *Suddenly he turned off his false smile and showed his true nature. She can turn off the charm as quickly as she can turn it on.* → **turn on**[1] (2)

*****5** *BrE* to stop employing (someone): [T1] *His faithful servant was turned off without a penny after twenty years' service.*

*****6** *not fml* to produce (something): [T1 (*often simple tenses*)] *I turned off a good piece of work this morning.*

*****7** *infml* to (cause to) stop paying attention or taking interest: [IØ] *Half the crowd turned off when the speaker began talking about national unity.* [T1] *Such poor teaching always turns students off.* → **put off**[1] (7), **switch off** (3), **tune out** (2), **turn on**[1] (3)

**turn off**[2] *v prep*

**1** (of a road or vehicle) to leave a main road: [L9 + *off*] *Let's turn off this busy road and find a quieter way.*

*****2** to make (someone or an animal) leave (something): [D1] *Turn that cat off my chair! Unwanted visitors will be turned off my land.*

*****3** to cease to like (someone or something): [T1 (*no pass.*)] *I turned right off that subject when we got the new teacher.* [D1] *Her unfortunate manner of speech really turns me off her.* → **be off**[2] (4), **go off**[2] (2), **put off**[2] (2)

**turn on**[1] *v adv*

**1** (of a supply of water, gas, electricity, etc.) to (cause to) begin working by a switch control: [L9 + ON (*simple tenses*)] *This tap is stiff, it won't turn on.* [X9 + ON] *Please turn the light on for me, it's getting dark.* → **put on**[1] (3), etc.

*****2** to begin to use (a characteristic or expression of the face): [T1] *She turned on a bright smile to fool her family. You should see him turning on the charm when he wants something from his grandmother!* → **turn off**[1] (4)

*****3** *infml* to (cause to) become interested or excited, as under the influence of a person or drug: [IØ (*to*)] *Many young people are using drugs to turn on. Some of the students really turned on to these different classes.* [T1 (*to*)] *Loud modern music really turns some of the young people on. It takes a really special kind of teacher to turn on these disappointed students.* —**turned-on** *adj* → **switch on** (2), **trip out, tune in** (2), **turn off**[1] (7)

**turn on/upon**[2] *v prep*

**1** to direct (something) onto (something or someone): [X9 + *on/upon*] *Please turn your light on this pile of old clothes; I think it's a person, still breathing. The firemen were called to turn the water on the crowd to make them leave.*

*****2** to attack (someone or something): [T1 (*usu. simple tenses*)] *The dog went mad and turned on his own master. Why did she turn on me like that? Have I said something to offend her?* → **turn against**

*****3** to depend on (something): [T1 (*no pass., simple tenses*)] *The case turns on the judge's opinion of the prisoner's character.* → **depend on** (3), **hang on**[2] (2), **hinge on, pivot on** (2), **rely on** (2), **ride on**[2] (4)

**4 turn one's back on: a** to turn rudely away from (someone): *Never turn your back on a violent group of students.* **b** *not fml* to refuse to take any notice of or give support to (a person, organization, etc.): *The unions have turned their back on the employer's latest offer of talks and the arguments over pay continue.*

**5 turn on one's heel** to leave suddenly, often rudely: [*usu. simple tenses*] *Suddenly he turned on his heel and walked away without an explanation.*
**6 turn the key on** to lock (someone) out: *If you come home after midnight, you'll find the key turned on you!*
**7 turn the tables on** to make (someone) receive the results of his own action: *After he had been so unkind to us, we turned the tables on him by refusing to invite him to the party.*

**turn out** *v adv*
**1** to stop (something usu. electrical such as light) working by turning a switch: [X9 + OUT] *Will the last person to leave the office please turn out all the lights?* → **put off**[1] (3), etc.
***2** to make (someone) leave because of a fault: [T1 (*of*) (*often simple tenses*)] *Two members were turned out for failing to pay the money that they owed.* → **throw out** (4), etc.
***3** to make (someone) leave a home: [T1 (*of*)] *The old lady was turned out after twenty years because the owner wanted to pull the building down.* → **throw out** (5), etc.
***4** to get rid of (something unwanted): [T1] *Isn't it time we turned out all those old newspapers?* → **throw out** (2), etc.
***5** to empty (a container or room) for cleaning: [T1] *Help me to turn out the bedroom drawers ready for our guest. I'd like to turn the playroom out before painting the walls.* —**turn out** *n*
***6** to turn (a pocket) inside out: [T1] *Turn out all your pockets; I know one of you boys has the stolen money!* → **turn inside out** (1)
***7** to produce (something or a kind of person): [T1] *When was the last time this school turned out a really able musician? The factory turns out 20,000 bicycles a month.* —**turnout** *n*
***8** to get out of bed, as in the morning: [IØ] *I never feel like turning out on cold mornings.*
***9** to (cause to) gather out of doors, esp. in large numbers: [IØ] *A large crowd turned out to cheer the wedding party.* —**turnout** *n*
***10** to dress (someone or oneself) well, or keep a good (carriage): [T1 (*usu. simple tenses*)] *Mrs Greenwood turns her girls out well, doesn't she? Yes, they always look well turned out.* —**turnout** *n* —**turned-out** *adj*
***11** to result, develop, or end: [*It* + IØ (*simple tenses*)] *As it has turned out, there was no need to worry.* [L7] *The boy turned out successful after all.* [L9] *Did your play turn out well?* [L9] *The accident has turned out to be a good thing after all.* [*It* + 15 (*simple tenses*)] *It turned out that the jewels had been in the bank all the time!* → **fall out** (5)
**12 turn out the guard** to cause a body of men to begin guard duty: *Turn out the guard! Some prisoners have escaped!*

**turn out of** *v adv prep*
to make (someone or an animal) leave (something): [T1 + OUT + *of*] *Turn that dog out of my chair! The old lady was turned out of her home after twenty years. Why should I be turned out of my job, when I have always given a fair day's work for a fair day's pay?*

**turn over** *v adv*
**1** to (cause to) face the other way up: [L9 + OVER] *Turn over, please dear, your elbows are digging into me. I heard the clock, but then I turned over and went back to sleep. The car turned over three times after the crash.* [X9 + OVER] *Turn over two of the cards at a time and see if they match. Be careful how you turn the body over. You must turn your collar over to be in the latest fashion. Fill the pastry with cooked apple and turn it over. The soil must be thoroughly turned over before planting.* —**turnover** *n, adj* —**overturn** *v* → **plough up** (1), **roll over, turn up** (2, 4)
***2** to turn to a new page; turn (a page): [IØ (*to*)] *Please turn over, and read the directions on the back. When the children turn over, they will be surprised at the picture on the next page.* [T1] *I wasn't really reading, just turning over the pages. Turn the page over very carefully; there is a surprise on the next page!*
***3** to search in (something): [T1] *"A man will turn over half a library to make one book."* (Boswell's *Life of Johnson*)
***4** to start (an engine): [T1] *How do you turn this engine over? I can't get it to start!*
***5** (of an engine) to continue working at the lowest possible speed, without producing movement: [IØ (*continuous tenses*)] *If you stay in the car with the engine just turning over, the police cannot charge you with unlawful parking.* → **tick over** (1)
***6** (of an activity such as work) to continue at a usual or slow speed, fairly successfully but without excitement: [IØ (*continuous tenses*)] *After a good start, the organization to help get our member re-elected is now just turning over, and is in need of fresh ideas.* → **tick over** (2)
***7** (of a business) to trade (a sum of money) every week, month, or year: [T1] *The shop is doing quite well, turning over more than $1,000 a week.* —**turnover** *n*
***8** to spend (money) in order to gain more: [T1 (*often pass.*)] *The faster your money is turned over, the more profit you make.* —**turnover** *n*
***9** (of a group of workers) to leave a firm; change jobs: [IØ (*usu. simple tenses*)] *Only a third of our workers turn over every 10 years or so.*
***10** *not fml* to make (someone) feel sick: [T1b (*simple tenses*)] *The sight of all that blood quite turns me over.* → **turn up** (7)
***11** (of the stomach or heart) to feel moved, as by fear or other excitement: [IØ] *My stomach was turning over and over as I waited for my turn on the stage. Mary's heart turned over when Jim entered the room.*

*12 to think about; consider (something), esp. in the phr. **turn something over in one's mind**: [T1] *I turned the idea over for a week before replying.*

**13 turn over a new leaf** to begin again with good intentions: *I know the boy behaved very badly on his last visit, but I promise you that he's turned over a new leaf and will be good from now on.*

***turn over to** *v adv prep*

**1** to give the control of (something) to (usu. someone): [D1] *This difficulty is not something we can deal with, so we had better turn it over to the director.*

**2** to yield (someone) to (someone such as the police): [D1] *I turned the thief over to the guards at the building.*

**3** to change one's methods to (a different system): [D1] *The factory has turned over to machine production of the boxes. The firm has decided to turn over to the making of plastics.*

**turn professional** *v adj* also *not fml* **turn pro**

to start earning one's living at work formerly done without pay, as sport or music: [L7 + professional] *After winning the tennis competition, Rose decided to turn professional, and was soon winning a lot of money in international competitions.*

**turn right** *v adv* → TURN LEFT

**turn round** *v adv* → TURN AROUND

**turn to[1]** *v adv*

*not fml* to start working hard, as to help: [IØ (*often simple tenses*)] *Let's all turn to, and get the job finished before dark. Many husbands have to turn to and help with the dishes when their wives are out at work.*

**turn to[2]** *v prep*

**1** to move one's body or head so as to face (someone): [IØ + *to* (*often simple tenses*)] *Turn to me a little more, I can't see your eyes in the shadow. Please turn to me when you're speaking, so that I can hear what you're saying.* → **turn towards** (1)

**2** to move (part of the body) so as to face (someone or something): [X9 + *to*] *I love turning my face to the sun in the early spring. Rudely, he turned his back to me and refused to say anything further.* → **turn towards** (1)

**3** to change or move (something) to make it reach (a level or direction): [X9 + *to*] *You will have to turn the cooker to a higher temperature than the cake mix packet says. Turn the handle to the right a bit more.* → **turn towards** (1)

**4** to turn the pages of a book, magazine, etc., so as to reach (a certain page number, picture, etc.); look at (papers): [L9 + *to*] *Please turn to page 33 for the continuation of this story. Turning to the picture on the next page, we see that the criminal was not at all the person we had expected. Let me turn to my notes to refresh my memory of the figures.*

**5** to lead in (a certain direction) by changing direction: [IØ + *to* (*simple tenses*)] *Be careful here, the road turns to the right without warning.* → **veer to**

*6 to (cause to) become (usu. the same thing in a different form): [T1 (*no pass.*)] *The funny dry little stick turned to a beautiful bush after only a season's growth. The snow turned to rain as we got further down the mountain. Water turns to ice at 0° Centigrade.* [D1] *Is it the low temperature that turns the water to ice? Where can I turn these pounds to dollars?* → **change into** (2), etc.

*7 to change (words) into (a different meaning): [D1] *Every time she is rude to you, try to turn her hard words to a joke against herself.* → **turn into** (3)

*8 to go to (someone or something) for help, advice, comfort, etc.: [T1] *When he's in trouble, he always turns to his sister. One can always turn to music for comfort.*

*9 to begin (a way of life): [T1] *Why did he turn to crime in the first place? "All we like sheep have gone astray; we have turned, every one, to his own way."* (The Bible)

*10 to begin (something or doing something different): [T1] *In a time of grief, it often helps to turn to some new activity.* [T4] *Refused permission to work in the country, he was able to turn to writing to earn a living.*

*11 to direct (something such as an ability) towards (a purpose): [D1] *He was determined to turn his hard-won skill to the service of his fellow human beings.*

*12 to direct (one's attention) to (something such as a new subject): [T1] *Turning to the next question, we must ask our chairman for his opinion.* [D1] *We are all turning our thoughts to the matter.*

**13 turn something to (good) account/use** to make good use of something: *Even painful experience can always be turned to good account in this cruel world. I don't know what this object is intended for, but I'm sure I can turn it to good use.*

**14 turn something to one's advantage** to gain from something not intended to do one good: *A really clever politician is even able to turn an election loss to his (own) advantage, by claiming that the time was not right for him to come to power.*

**15 turn a deaf ear to** to pretend not to hear (something or someone that one does not wish to hear): *Can't you find a way of turning a deaf ear to her endless complaints?*

**16 turn a blind eye to** to pretend not to notice (something, usu. bad): *The police have been instructed to turn a blind eye to unimportant breakages of the law so that they can use their time and power to fight real crime.* → **shut to[2]**

**17 turn one's hand to** to be able to work at (something or doing something): [*usu. simple tenses* + *can*] *She's a most useful person to have in the office, she can turn her hand to anything. Can you turn your hand to repairing an engine if necessary?*

**18 turn a cold shoulder to** pretend not to notice (someone) in a rude, offensive, or unkind manner: *Why are all the people in the village turning a cold shoulder to me? What have I done to offend them?*

**turn topsy-turvy** *v adv* → **turn inside out** (1), **turn turtle, turn upside down** (1)

**1** *not fml* to turn (something or someone) the other way up: [X9 + TOPSY-TURVY] *The child used to love being turned topsy-turvy so that her hair brushed the floor. Don't turn the box topsy-turvy, the dish might fall out.*

***2** *not fml* to cause disorder in (a room), as when searching it: [T1b] *The thieves turned the whole room topsy-turvy, but they didn't find the jewels!*

***3** *not fml* to cause disorder and confusion in (something): [T1b] *The refusal of some of the actors to sign the contract is turning all our arrangements for the performance topsy-turvy.*

**turn towards** *v prep*

**1** to (cause to) turn so as to face (someone, something, or a direction): [L9 + *towards*] *Please turn towards me when you're speaking, so that I can hear what you're saying. If you turn towards the right and look in the mirror, you will be able to see the mark.* [X9 + *towards*] *Rudely, he turned his back towards me and refused to say anything further. This garden hut is set on wheels so that you can turn it towards the sun at any time of day. Turn the handle towards the left a bit more.* → **turn to²** (1, 2, 3)

***2** to change one's opinion more in the direction of (an idea); (of an opinion) to change in the direction of (an idea): [T1 (*no pass.*)] *The chairman seems to be turning towards our point of view at last. Is his opinion turning towards the party's?*

**3 turn one's face towards** to make a journey or begin travelling in the direction of (a place): *At last I was able to turn my face towards home.*

***turn turtle** *v adv* → **turn topsy-turvy, turn upside down** (1)

(of a boat or ship) to turn upside down, usu. before sinking: [IØ] *Get all the passengers off quickly; these ships have a nasty habit of turning turtle before they sink, and we could all be drowned!*

**turn under** *v adv*

**1** to fold (something) beneath part of itself: [T1 + UNDER] *This is how you turn the sheet under so that it's comfortable.*

***2** (in printing) to print (the rest of a line of poetry) near the end of a second line: [T1] *The lines in this poem are very long and may take more than one line, so you'll have to turn them under.* —**turnunder** *n*

**turn up** *v adv*

**1** to (cause to) fold or point in an upward direction: [L9 + UP (*simple tenses*)] *Collars in the latest fashion all turn up. I can't help it if my nose turns up, I was born that way.* [X9 + UP] *Turn your collar up, it will at least keep the rain off the back of your neck. Trouser legs are not turned up any more at the bottom.* —**turn-up** *n BrE* —**turned-up** *adj*

**2** to turn (something flat) so as to show the other side: [X9 + UP] *Turn up two of the cards at a time and see if they match.* → **turn over** (1)

***3** to shorten (clothing such as a skirt or trousers) by folding or cutting the bottom edge: [T1] *Can you turn my skirt up for me? They're being worn shorter this year. One leg of the trousers is longer than the other; get the shop people to turn it up for you.* → **take up** (6)

***4** to separate (soil) into small bits by digging, as before planting: [T1] *This new farm machinery turns the soil up very thoroughly, doesn't it?* → **plough up** (1), **turn over** (1)

***5** to increase (a flame, sound, etc.): [T1] *Please turn the radio up, I'd like to hear the news.*

***6** (of trade or a money system) to improve: [IØ] *The pound seems to be turning up at last.* —**upturn** *n*

***7** *infml* to make (someone) feel sick: [T1b (*simple tenses*)] *The sight of all that blood quite turns me up.* → **turn over** (10)

***8** to find (something) by chance, as by digging or searching: [T1] *You never know when you may turn up an ancient coin in this part of the country, which is so rich in history. Just how do you intend to turn up the necessary proof?* → **plough up** (2)

***9** *not fml* to arrive or be found, often unexpectedly: [IØ (*usu. simple tenses*)] *Guess who turned up at Mary's wedding? The long-lost watch turned up down the back of the old chair.* → **show up** (2)

***10** to happen without effort on one's part: [IØ (*usu. simple tenses*)] *It's no good waiting for something to turn up, you have to take action. "'In case anything turned up,' which was his [Mr Micawber's] favourite expression."* (Charles Dickens, *David Copperfield*) → **come along** (3)

**11 turn it up!** *infml* stop that!: [*imper.*] → **knock off** (13), **pack in** (4), **pack up** (4), **turn in** (9)

**12 turn up one's nose at something** *not fml* to dislike something; consider something to be beneath one's standard; refuse something with distaste: *There's no need for you to turn up your nose at my cooking, just because you're used to eating in grand restaurants. These days, you can't afford to turn up your nose at any reasonable job.*

**13 turn up trumps** *not fml* to be surprisingly successful, helpful, or lucky: *I didn't expect Father to turn up trumps and pay for our holiday, did you? It was a risky idea, but it turned up trumps after all, and the firm made a lot of money.* → **come up** (21)

**turn upon** *v prep* → **TURN ON²**

**turn upside down** *v adv*
**1** to turn (something or someone) the other way up: [X9 + UPSIDE DOWN] *The child used to love being turned upside down so that her hair brushed the floor. If you turn the envelope upside down, the key will fall out.* → **turn inside out, turn topsy-turvy**
*__2__ *not fml* to cause disorder in (a room), as when searching it: [T1b] *The thieves turned the whole room upside down, but they didn't find the jewels!*
*__3__ *not fml* to cause disorder and confusion in (something): [T1b] *Did you have to turn our arrangements upside down by being late for your own wedding? "These that have turned the world upside down."* (The Bible)

**tussle with** *v prep*
**1** to fight with (someone): [IØ + *with*] *After tussling with my attackers for a few minutes, I succeeded in breaking free, and ran for help.* → **struggle with** (1)
*__2__ to have an inner battle with (oneself, one's conscience, etc.): [T1] *After tussling with myself for some days, I decided to accept his offer. You could almost see him tussling with his conscience before he chose to tell the truth.* → **battle with, struggle with** (1), **wrestle with** (3)

**tweak off** *v adv* → TWIST OFF

***twiddle with** *v prep* → **fiddle with** (1), etc.
to play with (something) aimlessly, with small, often twisting movements: [T1] *She has a most annoying habit of twiddling with her hair all the time she's talking. Perhaps if you twiddle with the controls for a few minutes you could make the television work better.*

**twine around/round¹** *v adv* → TWIST AROUND¹
**twine around/round²** *v prep* → TWIST AROUND²
**twine round¹** *v adv* → TWIST AROUND¹
**twine round²** *v prep* → TWIST AROUND²

**twinkle with** *v prep*
**1** to be brightly lit by (many small shining things): [IØ + *with*] *The night was so clear that the whole sky was twinkling with stars. The towns twinkle with fairy lights all through Christmas.*
**2** to shine brightly because of (a feeling, usu. happy or excited): [IØ + *with*] *Her eyes twinkled with amusement as she told the story against herself.*

**twist around/round¹** *v adv* also **twine around**
**1** to (cause to) turn round in a curling movement, like a screw: [IØ + AROUND/ROUND] *Our dog used to twist round in the air to catch the ball.* [T1 + AROUND/ROUND] *Pull the wire tight and then twist the ends round.*
**2** to make (words) seem to mean the opposite of their intended meaning: [T1 + AROUND/ROUND] *I didn't say that! You're twisting my words around!* → **turn around** (3)

**twist around/round²** *v prep* also **turn around**
**1** to fasten (something or itself) around (something) with a turn, like a screw; surround (something) by turning like a screw: [T1 + *around/round*] *Twist the ends of the wire round the neck of the plastic bag, so that the air can't get out. The rope had twisted itself around the wheel, stopping the motor.* [IØ + *around/round*] *The rope must be packed very carefully so that there's no danger of it twisting around someone's neck.* → **wind around** (1), **wreathe around**
**2 twist someone around/round one's little finger** *not fml* to control someone easily: *Jim worships his daughter and will do anything she wants; she can twist him round her little finger.* → **wind around** (2)

**twist into** *v prep*
**1** to (cause to) turn tighly around so as to become (something with many folds or screw-like turns): [IØ + *into*] *Her face twisted into a picture of pain.* [T1 + *into*] *Twist the newspaper into a screw and use it to light the fire.*
**2** to change the meaning of (words) so as to become (something other than was intended): [T1 + *into*] *A very clever lawyer might be able to twist the prisoner's story into an admission of guilt.*

**twist off** *v adv* also **tweak off**
to remove (something) with a sharp turning movement; come off by unscrewing: [T1 + OFF] *You have to twist the lid off, not pull it. Those children have been twisting the flower heads off again.* [IØ + OFF (*usu. simple tenses*)] *The wheel twisted off in the middle of the car race.*

**twist up** *v adv*
**1** to move upwards in a curving manner, like a screw: [IØ + UP (*simple tenses*)] *The mountain road began to twist up, steeper and steeper.*
**2** to become screwed tightly, as with pain: [IØ + UP (*often simple tenses*)] *Her face twisted up with pain as her leg lay bent beneath her.*
**3** to turn (something) tightly into a screw shape: [T1 + UP (*often simple tenses*)] *He twisted the letter up into a ball and threw it into the fire, swearing softly.*

**type as** *v prep*
**1** to write (a letter, word, or figure) on the typewriter mistakenly in the form of (another letter, figure, or word): [T1 + *as*] *Look, you've typed 'do' as 'so,' and made nonsense of the whole sentence.*
*__2__ to regard (someone) as being always (the same kind of person), as when acting: [D1 (*usu. pass.*)] *I'm tired of being always typed as the bad man in the plays!*

**type in** *v adv*
to add (letters, words, or figures) to writing already typed: [T1 + IN (*to*)] *Can you type the additional figures in at the bottom of the page?*

**type out** *v adv*
to make a typewritten copy of (words or figures): [T1 + OUT] *When you type out the*

*letter, it will take less space than this pencil copy.*

**type up** *v adv*
to make a last typewritten copy of (matter, often long): [T1 + UP] *"Do I have to type up the whole play?" "Yes, I want it typed up properly and neatly."*

***tyrannize over** *v prep*
to control (someone or something) cruelly and with great power: [T1] *The new king tyrannized over the natives. "It is better that a man should tyrannize over his bank balance than over his fellow citizens."* (John Maynard Keynes, *General Theory of Employment*)

# U

***unbosom oneself** *v pron*
*old use* to tell one's secret troubles (to someone): [IØ (*to*)] *At last she decided to unbosom herself to her mother, and share her secret sorrow.*

***unburden oneself** *v pron*
*fml* to free (oneself, one's conscience, etc.) of (a load of guilt, secrets, etc.): [IØ (*of, to*)] *I feel I want to unburden myself of the guilt for what I did so many years ago. Unburden yourself to me, dear; what is troubling you?*

***understand by** *v prep* → **gather from** (3)
to regard (a meaning) as belonging to (usu. a word or words): [D1 (*simple tenses*)] *What do you understand by justice?* [T5 (*simple tenses*)] *I understand by your remark that you intend leaving the firm.*

***unfit for** *v prep*
to make (someone or something) unsuitable, usu. through bad health for (something or doing something): [D1 (*usu. simple tenses*)] *My bad leg has unfitted me for heavy work.* [V4a (*often pass.*)] *She was unfitted for riding a bicycle by her heart condition.*

***unfold before** *v prep*
to appear gradually to (someone, someone's eyes, etc.): [T1 (*no pass.*)] *As the mist cleared, a most beautiful view unfolded before their eyes.*

**unfold to** *v prep*
*fml* to tell (something formerly secret) to (someone): [T1 + *to*] *At a special meeting, the scientist unfolded his plan to the government committee.*

**unify into** *v prep* also **unite into**
to put (parts) together into (a whole): [T1 + *into*] *How can we unify such scattered islands into a nation?*

**unify with** *v prep*
to make (something) match (something else in the same whole): [T1 + *with*] *Someone in charge of quality control should unify the printing with the rest of the book.*

**unite in** *v prep*
to (cause to) come together in (something or doing something): [IØ + *in*] *The voters united in support of the aging politician. Mary's whole family united in disapproving of Jim.* [T1 + *in* (*often pass.*)] *The committee were united in their praise of the boy's behaviour, and gave him a reward. We must unite the workers in fighting inhuman conditions.*

**unite into** *v prep* → **UNIFY INTO**

**unite with** *v prep* → **reunite with**
to bring (someone or something) together with (a group): [T1 + *with* (*often pass.*)] *How glad he was to be united with his family after all those years! The ceremony marked the uniting of the last island with the others forming the new nation.*

**unleash on/upon** *v prep*
**1** to set (usu. a dog or dogs) loose to attack (someone or an animal): [T1 + *on/upon*] *Go at once, or I will unleash my dog on you! Don't unleash the dogs on the rats until they are in a corner.*
***2** to start to use (a quality such as power) against (someone): [D1] *The speaker replied by unleashing the full force of his argument upon his opponent.*

***unload on/upon** *v prep*
to give the weight and worry of (something bad) to (someone else): [D1] *You can always unload your troubles on the priest, he's there to listen.*

**upbraid for** *v prep* → **upbraid with**
*fml* to scold (someone) for (a fault or doing something wrong): [T1 + *for*] *I could hear the chairman upbraiding the committee member for his absence from all the earlier meetings. Jim was being upbraided for being late again.*

**upbraid with** *v prep* → **upbraid for**
*fml* to charge (someone) with having done (a wrong action): [T1 + *with*] *The director was upbraiding the chief of delivery with the delay in the shipment of the goods to a valued customer.*

**upgrade to** *v prep*
to raise the standard of (something) to (a higher level): [T1 + *to*] *The farmers have been trying to upgrade their cattle to the required standard of meat.*

**urge along/forward/on** *v adv*
**1** to encourage (someone or an animal) to move ahead: [X9 + ALONG/FORWARD/ON] *The man was urging the cows along with a stick. You must urge the children forward or we'll never get home. Can you urge the horse on any faster?*

**2** to encourage (usu. someone) to greater effort: [X9 + ALONG/FORWARD/ON] *The speaker tried to urge the crowd on to show their opposition to the new law. I did have to urge the students along in the last few weeks before their examination.*

***urge on/upon** *v prep*
to try to force (something such as an idea) on (someone) by encouragement: [D1] *The teacher urged on her students the importance of passing the examination.*

**urge to** *v prep*
to encourage (someone) in the direction of (action): [X9 + *to*] *What can we do to urge these lazy workers to greater production?*

***urge upon** *v prep* → **URGE ON**

**use as** *v prep* → **use for, utilize for**
to employ (someone or something) to serve the purpose of (something): [T1 + *as*] *I'm tired of being used as a servant around this place! Here, you can use this box as a table to rest the papers on.*

**use before/by** *v prep*
to finish with (usu. a product that can decay) before (a date): [T1 + *before/by* (*simple tenses*)] *This milk should be used before 5 October. Any medicine not used by the end of the year should be thrown away.*

**use for** *v prep* → **use as, utilize for**
to employ (usu. something) for (a purpose or doing something): [T1 + *for*] *Please don't use my best plates for your party! He had been using my good handkerchief for a dust cloth! Don't use the silver spoon for opening a tin.*

**use to** *v prep* → **accustom to, habituate to be/get used to** to be/become in the habit of (something or doing something): *You won't mind the long hours once you get used to them. It doesn't matter, I'm quite used to waiting.*

***use up** *v adv*
to use (something) till none is left: [T1] *Who's used up all the milk? There's none to put in my coffee! When you have used up the polish, let's try this new kind.*

**use with** *v prep*
to make use of (something) in connection with, or having (something such as a correct match, quality, etc): [T1 + *with*] *Use this iron with alternating current only. This instrument should be used with great care.*

**usher in** *v adv*
**1** to show (someone) into a room or building: [X9 + IN (*to*)] *When my secretary ushered the visitor in, I received a great shock.* → **show in**
***2** to give warning or notice of (something about to come); come, bringing or causing to enter: [T1a (*usu. simple tenses*)] *The first snowfall ushers in the winter. When was the atomic age ushered in?*

**usher out** *v adv* → **show out**
to show (someone) out of a room or building: [X9 + OUT (*of*)] *I will ask the servant to usher you out.*

**utilize for** *v prep* → **use as, use for**
*fml* to make use of (something) for (a purpose): [T1 + *for* (*usu. pass.*)] *The empty building can be utilized for city storage.*

# V

**vaccinate against** *v prep* → **immunize against, inoculate against**
to protect (someone) against catching (a certain disease), as by giving him a little of the substance which causes it: [T1 + *against* (*usu. pass.*)] *If you are travelling to a tropical country, you should be vaccinated against yellow fever.*

**vaccinate with** *v prep* → **inoculate with**
to give (someone) a small amount of (something causing a certain disease) so as to prevent him from catching it: [T1 + *with*] *All the men in the camp have been vaccinated with the smallpox virus.*

**vacillate between** *v prep* → **hover between, waver between**
*fml* to be unable to decide between (two things or doing two things): [IØ + *between*] *For weeks she vacillated between a home in the city and one in the country. Many voters are still vacillating between the two parties. Why you do vacillate so long between staying and going? Make up your mind!*

**value above** *v prep*
to regard (something or someone) more highly than (usu. something): [T1 + *above* (*simple tenses*)] *I value my honour above my life!*

**value as** *v prep*
to think highly of (someone or something) because he or it is (something): [T1 + *as* (*simple tenses*)] *He is greatly valued as a good worker. I value this car only as a means of getting to work; it has no other importance for me.*

**value at** *v prep* → **rate at** (1)
to place a price on (something) of (an amount): [T1 + *at* (*simple tenses*)] *The house has recently been valued at £31,750.*

**value for** *v prep*
to love or have a high opinion of (someone or something) because of (a quality): [T1 + *for* (*simple tenses*)] *Children should be valued for who they are, not for what their parents would like them to be. I value this old book for its content, not its looks.*

*__vamp up__ *v adv*
**1** *not fml* to invent (something) from little material: [T1] *Will you be able to vamp up an excuse that sounds true?*
**2** to repair (something) with pieces of material: [T1] *I can vamp up the wall, but it won't look good.*

**vanish away** *v adv*
to disappear: [IØ + AWAY (*usu. simple tenses*)] *When morning came, the mist had vanished away. No one saw who stole the jewels: they just vanished away! All your troubles will vanish away when he returns safely.*

**vanish from** *v prep*
to disappear and be seen no longer in (something): [IØ + *from*] *Many kinds of fish are vanishing from the oceans of the world. I can't find the key anywhere—it seems to have vanished from the room! They waved and waved until the ship vanished from sight.*

**vary between** *v prep*
to change, turn, or move from (one thing) to another, and back again; be different with regard to (one kind or another): [IØ + *between* (*simple tenses*)] *Her feelings varied between joy and fear as she watched him fight. The buildings in this city vary between very old and very new.*

**vary from/to** *v prep* → **range from, run from** (4), **run to** (4)
to change, turn, or move from (one thing) to (another); be different with regard to (one kind) or (another): [IØ + *from/to* (*simple tenses*)] *Opinions in the committee vary from approval to complete opposition. The weather has varied from beautiful to terrible this month.*

**vary in** *v prep*
to be different concerning (a quality): [IØ + *in* (*simple tenses*)] *The two chairmen vary in their manner of dealing with a question. The hotels vary in size and comfort.*

**vary to** *v prep* → **VARY FROM**

**vary with** *v prep*
to be different because of the influence of (something): [IØ + *with* (*simple tenses*)] *Every person's usual temperature varies with the time of day, so it should always be taken at the same time each day.*

**vault into** *v prep*
**vault into the saddle** to get on a horse quickly: *Vaulting into the saddle, he rode away as fast as he could.*

**vault over** *v adv; prep*
to jump over (something), usu. pushing with the hands: [IØ + OVER/*over*] *He took a running jump at the fence and vaulted over (it).*

**veer from** *v prep*
**1** (of the wind) to change direction slightly from (a former course), usu. in a clockwise direction; (of a boat) turn a little from (a course), usu. into the wind: [L9 + *from*] *Don't worry, the wind is veering from its course and we shall soon be able to reach home. It was hard to keep the little boat from veering from the course that we wanted to take.*
*__2__ to change one's behaviour slightly from (a course of action): [T1 (*no pass.*)] *There's no danger, is there, that she might veer from her brave new intentions?*

**veer off** *v adv* → **peel away** (2), **peel off** (2)
(of planes) to leave a group in flight by turning to one side: [IØ + OFF] *The leading pair of planes veered off, one to the right and one to the left.*

**veer round** *v adv*
**1** (of the wind) to change or turn in a clockwise direction: [IØ + ROUND] *When the wind veers round, we shall have to change the sails.*
**2** (of a boat) to (cause to) change direction, usu. into the wind: [IØ + ROUND] *At the end of the race, the boats veered round and headed for home.* [T1 + ROUND] *Help me to veer her round, the ropes are stiff!*

**veer to** *v prep* → **turn to²** (5)
to lead in (a certain direction) by changing direction slightly: [IØ + *to* (*usu. simple tenses*)] *Be careful here, the road veers to the left without warning.*

*__vent on/upon__ *v prep* → **take out of** (9), **take out on, work off on**
to express (a strong feeling, usu. bad) at the cost of (someone): [D1] *It's wrong to vent your anger on the children, they were not at fault.*

**venture forth** *v adv*
*old use* to set out bravely: [L9 + FORTH] *In the fairy stories, the youngest son usually ventures forth to try to find his fortune.*

*__venture on/upon__ *v prep*
*fml* to risk (something) on (something uncertain): [D1] *Don't venture your whole fortune on these shares, but spread it among various profit-making ideas. I wouldn't dare to venture my hopes on his success.*

**venture out** *v adv*
to go outside in unsuitable weather: [L9 + OUT] *No thanks, I'd rather not venture out in pouring rain if I don't have to!*

*__venture upon__ *v prep* → **VENTURE ON**

*__verge into__ *v prep* → **merge into**
to change slowly so as to become part of (something else): [T1 (*no pass.*)] *We looked at the sky, where the last of the sunlight was verging into darkness.*

*__verge on/upon__ *v prep*
**1** to touch or be next to (something): [T1 (*simple tenses*)] *The bottom of our garden verges on the park.* → **abut on, border on** (1)
**2** to be very much like (something): [L1 (*simple tenses*)] *Your remarks verge on rudeness.* [L7 (*simple tenses*)] *His words were so inconsiderate as to verge on the offensive.* → **border on** (2), **touch on** (4)

**vest in** *v prep*
**1** *fml* to dress (someone or oneself) in (formal clothing): [T1 + *in*] *It took several hours to vest the priest in all the ceremonial garments of his high office.*
***2** to belong by right to (someone or a group): [T1 (*no pass., simple tenses*)] *This power has always vested in the Church.*
**3 be vested in** to be given to (someone or a group) as a right: *The greatest power in the Middle Ages was vested in the Church.* → **repose in** (3), **reside in** (3), **rest in** (3)

***vest with** *v prep*
to give (someone or a group) the right to (something): [D1 (*usu. pass.*)] *The Church in the Middle Ages was vested with the greatest power.*

**vex at** *v prep*
**be vexed at** to be annoyed by (something or doing something): *Mother was so vexed at the failure of the old car to start on the very day of her holiday. He was so vexed at missing the train that he jumped up and down.*

**vex with** *v prep*
to cause (someone) annoyance directed at (something or someone): [T1 + *with* (*often pass.*)] *Please don't vex me with your ceaseless complaints, I've heard enough! I'm so vexed with the boy, forgetting to write like this. There's no point in getting vexed with the machine, it doesn't care how you feel.*

**vie for** *v prep*
to compete for (something): [L9 + *for*] *The best teams in the country are vying for the prize.*

**vie in** *v prep*
to compete in (a competition or doing something): [L9 + *in*] *How many runners are vying in this race? Jim and his brother have always vied in getting first to the top of their profession.*

**vie with** *v prep*
to compete with (someone): [L9 + *with*] *Jim will have to run his best, as he will be vying with some of the best runners in the country.*

**vindicate for** *v prep*
*fml or old use* to claim (property) for (someone or oneself): [T1 + *for* (*usu. simple tenses*)] *Has anyone vindicated the land for the dead man's daughter?*

**vindicate to** *v prep*
*fml* to prove (something) as right to (someone): [T1 + *to* (*usu. simple tenses*)] *How can you vindicate your behaviour to the judge?*

***visit on/upon** *v prep*
esp. *bibl* to give punishment for (something) to (someone): [D1 (*usu. pass.*)] *Be sure that your most evil deeds will be visited upon you. God has visited his anger on us.*

**visit with** *v prep*
**1** *AmE* to talk socially with (someone) on a short visit: [IØ + *with*] *Let's go and visit with your grandmother this afternoon.*
***2** to punish (someone) with (punishment): [D1 (*often pass.*)] *Take care, or you will be visited with punishment from heaven!*

**volunteer for** *v prep*
to (cause to) offer oneself or one's name for (a duty, job, or doing something) without being forced: [IØ + *for*] *How many young men in the World War I volunteered for the army? Did I hear you volunteer for additional guard duty? No one volunteered for cleaning the henhouse.* [T1 + *for*] *I volunteered your name for the parents' game. I will volunteer my daughters for helping with the church sale.*

**vomit out** *v adv*
**1** to cause (liquid, esp. waste) to rush out: [T1 + OUT] *These pipes vomit out bad-smelling liquid into the sea.*
**2** to express (something bad): [T1 + OUT] *There he stands, vomiting out lie after lie.*

**vote against** *v prep*
to oppose (someone or something) in an election or vote: [IØ + *against*] *The committee were equally divided, so the chairman voted against the suggestion to prevent it being passed. The politician was deeply hurt when many of his former supporters voted against him, and he lost his place in Parliament.*

***vote down** *v adv*
to defeat (someone or something) by a vote: [T1] *In spite of the chairman's support, the suggestion was voted down by the rest of the committee.*

***vote in** *v adv*
to elect (someone): [T1 (*usu. pass.*)] *Many new young members have been voted in this time, which should give the House a fresh start. The President has been voted in for the third time running.*

**vote on/upon** *v prep*
to express one's opinion about (a matter) by one's vote: [IØ + *on/upon*] *How many members voted on the housing question? Have all the matters before us now been voted on?*

***vote onto** *v prep*
to elect (someone) to serve on (a group) by voting: [D1 (*usu. pass.*)] *Jim has been voted onto the Membership Committee of the club.*

***vote out** *v adv*
to defeat (someone or something) by voting; make (someone) leave by one's vote: [T1 (*usu. pass.*)] *After so many years' service, it was a shock when the chairman was voted out. Your suggestion has been voted out; try again next year.*

***vote through** *v adv*
to pass (something such as an idea) by voting: [T1a (*usu. pass.*)] *You don't just send your suggestion to the Board; it has to be voted through in every stage of its passage.*

**vote upon** *v prep* → **VOTE ON**

**vote with** *v prep*
**1** to give one's vote to the same party as (someone else): [IØ + *with*] *Do you always vote with your husband, or do you have different political opinions?*

**2 vote with one's feet** to leave a place where one does not like the political system: *You can tell what the villagers think of the new rulers; they've been leaving in crowds, voting with their feet.*

***vouch for** *v prep* also *rare* **avouch for**
to declare one's belief in (someone or his honesty, etc.); take the responsibility for (someone's behaviour, trustworthiness, etc.): [T1 (*usu. simple tenses*)] *I'll vouch for that boy; he has promised to be good. Let him in, I'll vouch for this man. Have all those present been vouched for?*

# W

**wade in** *v adv*
**1** to enter water above the level of one's feet: [IØ + IN] *The toy boat is stuck in the middle of the lake; someone will have to wade in and fetch it.*
***2** *not fml* to join a fight or argument: [IØ (*to*)] *There were already five people fighting when your brother decided to wade in and join them.* → **tuck in** (4), etc.

**wade into** *v prep*
**1** to enter (water above the level of one's feet): [IØ + *into*] *Father had to wade into the little lake to save the toy boat when it got stuck.*
***2** *not fml* to attack (someone or something): [T1] *Quite fearless, he was prepared to wade into the whole crowd! The speaker really waded into the government's lack of action on housing, didn't he!*
***3** *not fml* to eat (food) eagerly: [T1] *You should see the way those boys waded into the meal, as if they hadn't eaten for a week!* → **tuck into** (3), etc.

**wade through** *v prep*
**1** to walk usu. with difficulty so as to pass through (water, snow, etc.): [IØ + *through*] *We had to wade through thick mud to reach the crashed plane.*
***2** *not fml* to get slowly to the end of (something); make one's way with difficulty through (something such as work): [T1] *I shan't be home for dinner, I'm still wading through all those urgent letters.* → **plough through** (2)

**waffle about** *v prep*
*not fml* to talk endlessly and meaninglessly about (a subject): [IØ + *about*] *What's he waffling on about now? He never seems to make any sense.*

**wage against** *v prep*
**1 wage war against** to fight (an enemy, usu. an enemy nation): *In the past, the great powers would wage war against helpless little countries so as to gain their land.* also **wage on** → **declare against** (2), **declare on** [2] (1)
**2 wage a campaign/war against** to oppose (something or someone) violently: *The chairman has promised to wage a campaign against waste in the company. The students have stopped waging war against the system and are working hard for good marks. The government seems to be waging a war of nerves against the trade unions in its fight to keep wages under control.*

**wager on** *v prep* → **bet on, gamble on**
**1** to risk (money) on the result of (something such as a horse race) or the performance of (a competitor): [T1 + *on* (*usu. simple tenses*)] *I've wagered all my money on the third race. Would you wager much money on Jim? I wouldn't wager a penny on Jim winning this race.* [IØ + *on* (*usu. simple tenses*)] *Are you going to wager on the fight?*
***2** to take a chance on or be too sure of (something, or something or someone doing something): [T1 (*usu. simple tenses*)] *You simply can't wager on the weather in England. I'm prepared to wager on the possibility of finding empty seats at the theatre. I think I'll come, but don't wager on it.* [T4 (*usu. simple tenses*)] *Don't wager on getting the job, there are plenty of people wanting it.* [V4a (*usu. simple tenses*)] *It's not safe to wager on the train arriving on time.* [D1 (*usu. simple tenses*)] *Don't wager too much on the results of the examination.* → **depend on** (1), etc.

**wail for** *v prep* → **weep for** (1)
to make a loud noise expressing sorrow on account of (something or someone): [IØ + *for*] *The child was wailing for her mother.*

**wail over** *v prep*
to express sorrow noisily because of (something or someone): [IØ + *over* (*often continuous tenses*)] *The boy was wailing over his dead dog. The other team are still wailing over their defeat.*

**wait about/around** *v adv*
to wait for some time without activity: [IØ + ABOUT/AROUND (*for*) (*often continuous tenses*)] *Where have you been? I've been waiting around for you for more than an hour! I couldn't see the girls anywhere, there were just a few old men waiting about doing nothing.*

**wait at** *v prep*
**1** to stay in (a place) expecting something or someone: [IØ + *at*] *Six people were waiting at the bus stop. "There was I, waiting at the church."* (song)
**2 wait at table** *BrE* to serve people in a restaurant: [*often continuous tenses*] *She couldn't get any other job except waiting at table, so she had to do that although it was poorly paid and hard on her feet.* → **wait on** [2] (7)

**wait behind** *v adv* → **keep in** (5), etc.
to stay in a place when others have left: [IØ + BEHIND] *If you wait behind after class, I will give you some help with that difficult exercise.*

**wait for** *v prep*
**1** to stay in a place expecting (someone or something); expect (someone or something) or (someone or something to do something): [IØ + *for*] *I've been waiting for the bus for half an hour. I'll wait for you for ever. You must wait for permission to enter. I can't wait for this week to end. "When a man says he's willing," said Mr Barkis, "it's as much as to say, that a man's waiting for an answer."* (Charles Dickens, *David Copperfield*) *"It's odd how people waiting for you stand out far less clearly than people you are waiting for."* (Jean Giraudoux, *Tiger at the Gates*) *"The average man finds life very uninteresting as it is. And I think that the reason why . . . is that he is always waiting for something to happen to him instead of setting to work to make things happen."* (A.A. Milne, *If I May: The Future*) → **wait on²** (1)
**2** *not fml* to delay (a meal) until (someone) arrives: [T1 + *for*] *Don't wait dinner for me, I may be late.*
**3 wait for a dead man's shoes** to wait to take someone else's job after his death: *The only way you'll get to the top in this firm is by waiting for dead men's shoes.*
**4 wait for it!** *not fml* to be careful; the right moment has yet to come: [*imper.*] *'But what happened to the girl?' 'Wait for it, I'm coming to that part.' Ready, aim, wait for it! Fire!*

**wait in** *v adv*
to stay at home expecting someone to call: [IØ + IN] *I've been waiting in all day for your television repair man to collect the set, but he didn't come as he promised.*

**wait on¹** *v adv*
**1** to continue waiting: [IØ + ON (*simple tenses*)] *We waited on for another hour, but still she didn't come.*
***2** *NEngE not fml* wait for me; wait a minute: [IØ (*usu. imper.*)] *Wait on, will you, I'm just coming!* → **wait up** (1)

**wait on/upon²** *v prep*
**1** *old use* to delay action until (something or someone) happens or arrives: [IØ + *on/upon* (*simple tenses*)] *We wait on your reply to our letter.* → **wait for** (1)
***2** to attend (someone) as a servant, helper, follower, etc.: [T1 (*usu. simple tenses*)] *They all wait on the king.*
***3** *old use fml* to visit (someone) formally: [T1 (*usu. simple tenses*)] *Our representative will wait on you in the morning.* → **call on** (1)
***4** to serve (someone) with food and drink in a restaurant: [T1] *Is there anyone here to wait on us?*
***5** to result from (something): [T1 (*simple tenses*)] *His whole future waits on the results of the examinations. Success waits on effort.*
**6 wait on someone hand and foot** *not fml* to do humble actions for someone: *That woman has no idea how to bring up her children to be independent and self-respecting; she waits on them hand and foot.*
**7 wait on table** *AmE* to serve people in a restaurant: [(*often continuous tenses*)] *The only job he could get was waiting on table, but it was better than nothing.* → **wait at** (2)

***wait out** *v adv*
to defeat or deal successfully with (someone or something) by waiting: [T1] *We waited out the storm all night, and made our way into the harbour in the morning. The enemy are still advancing, but we can wait them out in this valley.*

***wait up** *v adv*
**1** *not fml* to delay one's movement so as to wait for others: [IØ (*for*) (*simple tenses*)] *Wait up, I shan't be long. Hadn't we better wait up for the slower ones?* → **wait on¹** (2)
**2** to stay late out of bed (until someone arrives): [IØ (*for*)] *I may be late, but please don't wait up for me.* → **stay up** (3), etc.

**wait upon** *v prep* → WAIT ON²

**wake from** *v prep* → **arouse from** (1), **awake from, awaken from** (1), **waken from** (1)
to (cause to) become conscious again after (sleep): [IØ + *from*] *It takes me a long time to wake from my night's sleep.* [T1 + *from*] *Why did you wake me from such a beautiful dream?*

**wake to** *v prep*
**1** to become conscious again after sleep, hearing or seeing (something): [IØ + *to* (*often simple tenses*)] *I woke to bright sunlight filling my room; it was already midday. Do you like waking to the sound of a radio?* → **awake to** (1)
**2** to (cause to) begin to understand or become watchful about (something such as a threat): [IØ + *to* (*often simple tenses*)] *We must wake to the dangers facing our country.* [T1 + *to* (*often simple tenses*)] *We must wake the people to the dangers facing our country.* → **awaken to**, etc.

**wake up** *v adv*
**1** to (cause to) come awake, stop sleeping: [IØ + UP] *What time did you wake up this morning?* [T1 + UP] *Be quiet, your father's asleep; don't wake him up.*
***2** to (cause to) begin to understand true reality or become watchful (about something): [IØ (*to*) (*often simple tenses*)] *We must wake up to the dangers facing our country.*

**waken from** *v prep*
**1** to make (someone) conscious again after (sleep): [T1 + *from* (*often simple tenses*)] *I hate being wakened from a deep sleep by a loud bell.* → **awake from, awaken from** (1), **wake from**

**2** to make (someone) conscious of reality instead of (false ideas): [T1 + *from* (*often simple tenses*)] *Do you think that this price list will waken Mother from her dreams of owning a large house in the country?* → **arouse from** (2), **awaken from** (2)

**waken to** *v prep* → **awaken to**, etc.
to warn (someone) (about something); make (someone) watchful (about something such as a threat): [T1 + *to* (*often simple tenses*)] *We must waken the people to the dangers facing our country.*

**walk about/around** *v adv*
**1** to (cause to) walk in a place without direction: [IØ + ABOUT/AROUND] *There were just a few people walking about in the town square, but no traffic in the streets.* [T1 + ABOUT/AROUND] *After the race, walk the horse around for a time to cool him off.*
**2** to move freely among crowds: [IØ + ABOUT/AROUND] *Is it safe for the President to walk about without a guard?* —**walkabout** *n*

**walk abroad** *v adv*
**1** *lit* to be seen in public or in the open: [IØ + ABROAD] *"And then, they say, no spirit can walk abroad."* (Shakespeare, *Hamlet*)
****2** *lit* to be common and uncontrolled: [IØ (*often simple tenses*)] *Violence walks abroad in our great cities.*

**walk ahead** *v adv*
to walk in front (of someone or something): [IØ + AHEAD (*of*)] *When the first trains ran, a man would walk ahead carrying a red flag. Why do you always walk ahead of me when we walk together?*

**walk around** *v adv* → **WALK ABOUT**

**walk away** *v adv* → **walk off**[1] (1)
to (cause to) leave on foot: [IØ + AWAY (*from*)] *I didn't approve of what she was saying, so I walked away.* [T1 + AWAY (*from*)] *Please walk your dog away from my garden.*

**walk away from** *prep*
**1** to leave (something or someone) on foot: [IØ + AWAY + *from*] *Why did you walk away from me like that? Have I said something to offend you? As I was walking away from the shop, I remembered that I had left my bag inside.*
***2** to leave (an accident) unhurt: [T1 (*no pass., usu. simple tenses*)] *How could he walk away from a crash like that without a mark on him?*
***3** *infml* to defeat (a competitor) without difficulty; run faster than: [T1 (*no pass.*)] *My horse had no trouble in simply walking away from all the others in that race. Before half time, I knew we were going to walk away from the other team.*

**walk away with** *v adv prep*
**1** to leave on foot together with (someone or something): [IØ + AWAY + *with*] *Why didn't you walk away with your father when he left? You didn't have to stay.* → **walk off with** (1)
***2** *infml* to steal (something): [T1] *Someone got in and walked away with the jewels while we were out.* → **make off with** (1), etc.
***3** *infml* to win (something such as a competition or a prize) easily: [T1] *Our team should walk away with the cricket competition, they're easily the best.* → **run away with** (6), **walk off with** (3), **waltz off with** (1)
***4** *not fml* to take attention from the rest of (a performance): [T1] *The new young singer has simply walked away with the show.* → **walk off with** (4)

**walk back** *v adv* also **walk home**
**1** to return on foot: [IØ + BACK] *I missed the last bus home, and had to walk back.*
**2** to take (someone) home on foot: [X9 + BACK] *Don't worry about going home in the dark, Jim will walk you back.*

**walk in** *v adv*
**1** to enter on foot: [IØ + IN (*to*)] *I had just put the dinner on when Jim walked in unexpectedly. You won't need a ticket, just walk in. The clothes cupboard is big enough for you to walk in.* —**walk-in** *adj*
***2** to enter without permission: [IØ (*to*)] *While we were out, somebody walked in and stole the jewels!*
***3** esp. *AmE not fml* to obtain a job easily, often in spite of competition: [IØ (*to*) (*simple tenses*)] *With your background, you should walk in (to that job).* —**walk-in** *n*

**walk into** *v prep*
**1** to enter (a place) on foot: [IØ + *into*] *He was last seen walking into the Town Hall. I walked into a pool of water and got my feet wet.*
***2** to enter (a place) without permission: [T1] *While we were out, somebody just walked into the house and stole the jewels!*
***3** to hit (something) by accident, on foot: [T1] *I got this lump on my head by walking into a glass door that I hadn't seen.*
***4** to meet (trouble) through carelessness: [T1] *It was his own fault, he just walked into the blow. Mind you don't walk into a trap!*
***5** *not fml* to attack (someone) fearlessly: [T1] *Bravely, Jim walked into his attackers.*
***6** *not fml* to obtain (a job) easily, often in spite of competition: [T1 (*simple tenses*)] *No one was surprised when she walked into the top position.*
***7** *not fml* to eat (food) eagerly: [T1 (*simple tenses*)] *That boy walked into the meal as if he hadn't seen food for a week.* → **tuck into** (3), etc.
***8** *not fml* to scold (someone), often loudly: [T1] *I could hear the director walking into Jim for being late again.* → **tell off** (1), etc.

**walk off**[1] *v adv*
**1** to leave on foot, esp. suddenly: [IØ + OFF] *We said goodbye; then he turned and walked off without another word.* → **walk away**
***2** to reduce (something) by walking: [T1] *He*

*tried to walk off the effect of the drink. I have to walk off this ache in my knee. You might be able to walk off the odd pound or two if you go out regularly.*

**walk off²** *v prep*

**walk someone off his feet** to tire someone very much with long walking; be better able to walk for a long time: *My mother, in spite of her age, is so healthy that she can still walk me off my feet.*

**walk off with** *v adv prep*

**1** to leave on foot in the company of (someone): [IØ + OFF + *with*] *If he walks off, I'm walking off with him, do you hear?* → **walk away with** (1)

*__2__ *infml* to steal (something): [T1] *Someone got in and walked off with the jewels while we were out.* → **make off with** (1)

*__3__ *infml* to win (something such as a competition or prize) easily: [T1] *Jim walks off with the top prize every year, it hardly seems fair to the others.* → **run away with** (6), **walk away with** (3), **waltz off with** (1)

*__4__ *not fml* to take attention from the rest of (a performance): [T1] *The new young singer just walked off with the show; the crowd weren't interested in anyone else.* → **walk away with** (4)

**walk on¹** *v adv*

**1** to continue walking: [IØ + ON] *Let's walk on a bit further before we stop to eat.*

*__2__ to take a small, usu. silent, part in a play or film: [IØ] *I didn't have much to do in the play, I just walked on in the second act.* —**walk-on** *n, adj*

**walk on²** *v prep*

**1** to move on foot on top of (a surface): [IØ + *on*] *I like walking on grass rather than paths, it's so much softer.*

*__2__ to treat (someone) inconsiderately; be inconsiderate of (someone's feelings): [T1 (*often simple tenses*)] *Why do you let him walk on you like that all the time? It's difficult not to walk on her feelings, as her sensitivity is so much finer than other people's.* → **step on** (2), **trample on** (2), **tread on** (2), **walk over** (1)

**3 walk on eggshells** *not fml* to behave very carefully: *Why are you walking on eggshells? I'm not sensitive about that matter any more.*

**walk out** *v adv*

**1** to go outside on foot: [IØ + OUT] *I think I'll walk out for a little while, to get a breath of fresh air.*

*__2__ to leave so as to show one's opposition: [IØ (*of, on*) (*often simple tenses*)] *Several people walked out (on the film) as they disapproved of its morals. Representatives of six nations walked out (of the United Nations meeting) to show their opposition to the vote.* —**walkout** *n*

*__3__ to refuse to work because of disagreement: [IØ] *The electricians have walked out, and will stay out until their demands are met.* —**walkout** *n* → **bring out** (7), etc.

*__4__ *old use* (of a man and woman) to be seen together in public, as before marriage; (of a woman) to be taken out socially (by a man): [IØ (*with*)] *The footman and the cook have been walking out for several months now. "On Sunday I walk out with a soldier."* (A. Wimperis, *Song: On Sunday*)

***walk out on** *v adv prep*

**1** *infml* to desert (someone): [T1 (*usu. simple tenses*)] *You can't walk out on your family at a time like this. His wife walked out on him, and was later seen in a neighbouring city with another man.* → **run out on** (1)

**2** *not fml* to leave (one's responsibility for something); fail to fulfil (an agreement): [T1 (*usu. simple tenses*)] *The government has been charged with walking out on its election promises. You can't walk out on the contract, or you could be taken to court.* → **run out on** (2)

**3** to leave so as to show one's opposition to (someone or something): [T1 (*often simple tenses*)] *Half the committee walked out on the chairman while he was still speaking.*

**walk over¹** *v adv*

**1** to move (to another place) on foot: [IØ + OVER (*to*)] *He walked over to the window to read the letter more easily. Let's not take the car, we can easily walk over.* → **walk round** (1)

**2** to take (something) or lead (someone) on foot (to another place): [X9 + OVER (*to*)] *I'll walk you over to your place, you shouldn't go alone on such a dark night. The cheque should have reached your account by now, as it was walked over to the bank this morning; we always walk the cheques over so that they don't get lost in the post.* → **walk round** (2)

*__3__ to win easily, as by being the only competitor: [IØ (*usu. simple tenses*)] *The horse walked over in the third race.*—**walkover** *n*

***walk over²** *v prep*

**1** to disobey (someone); treat (someone) inconsiderately: [T1] *She lets those children walk (all) over her.* → **trample on** (2), **tread on** (2), **walk on²** (2)

**2 walk over the course** (of a racehorse or runner) to be the only runner, so win easily: *None of the other runners arrived, so all he had to do was walk over the course to claim the prize.* → **knock over** (4)

**walk round** *v adv*

**1** to move (to another place) on foot: [IØ + ROUND (*to*)] *Shall we walk round to your aunt's house, or take the car?* → **walk over¹** (1)

**2** to take (something) or lead (someone) on foot (to another place): [X9 + ROUND (*to*)] *Why don't you walk the dog round for half an hour or so? It'll give you some exercise, and probably calm you.* → **walk over¹** (2)

**walk through** *v prep*

**1** to pass through (a place or substance) on foot: [IØ + *through*] *Walking through the forest one day, we found a strange little hut that no one had ever seen before. I'm sorry*

*I'm late, it took me so long to walk through the deep snow. People are allowed to walk through the big house at weekends, admiring the old paintings and furniture.*

*__2__ to practise the movements of (a play) in the early stages, before learning the words: [T1] *Shall we walk through Act One, so that you get used to the movements?* —**walk-through** *n*

*__3__ *not fml* to pass (something such as an examination) easily: [T1 (*simple tenses*)] *John thought that he would fail his driving test, as usual, but this time, to his own surprise, he walked through it.* → **breeze through,** etc.

**walk together** *v adv*

**1** to go on foot in a group or pair: [IØ + TOGETHER] *The path is too narrow for two people to walk together.*

*__2__ to keep pleasant company; be in agreement: [IØ (*usu. simple tenses*)] *It's unusual for people of such different political opinions to be able to walk together. "Can two walk together, except they be agreed?"* (The Bible)

**walk up** *v adv*

**1** to go upstairs or uphill on foot: [IØ + UP] *There's a little train to take you to the top of the hill, but I'd rather walk up. We're on the fourth floor and there's no lift, you have to walk up.* —**walk-up** *n, adj AmE infml*

*__2__ *not fml* to enter or come near to see the performance; esp. outdoors, such as a circus: [IØ (*imper.*)] *Walk up, walk up! See the strongest man on earth!*

**walk with** *v prep*

**1** to go, usu. on foot, in the company of (someone): [IØ + *with*] *I'll walk with you as far as the bus stop.*

**2 walk with God** to live a truly religious, pure, good life: *"What doth the Lord require of thee, but to do justly and to love mercy, and to walk humbly with thy God?"* (The Bible)

**wall in** *v adv*

**1** to enclose (an area, person, or animal) with a wall: [X9 + IN (*often pass., simple tenses*)] *The garden was walled in during the 18th century. Don't worry, the prisoners are safely walled in and can't escape. Dry stone walls were built across the field long ago to wall the cattle in.* —**walled-in** *adj* → **fence in** (1), **hedge in, rail in**

*__2__ to close off or prevent (something such as consciousness) from meeting or touching others: [T1 (*usu. pass., simple tenses*)] *She spent years in the hospital with her mind walled in by needless fears.*

**wall off** *v adv* → **divide off, fence off** (1), **rail off, separate off**

to separate (usu. an area) with a wall: [X9 + OFF (*from*) (*simple tenses*)] *The conquering nation has now walled off its part of the city so that people cannot move freely from side to side. I think I might wall off the living room so that we have a separate place to eat.* —**walled-off** *adj*

**wall round** *v adv*

to surround (something) with or as with a wall: [X9 + ROUND (*simple tenses*)] *The castle was walled round with rocks.*

**wall up** *v adv*

**1** to close (something such as a space) with or as with a wall: [X9 + UP (*simple tenses*)] *I think we should wall up the fireplace, it lets too much wind into the house. In the 17th century, many windows of large houses were walled up to avoid a window tax. The man's eye was walled up as if he had had a terrible accident.* —**walled-up** *adj*

*__2__ to imprison (someone) within a wall of bricks or stones, as a former punishment by slow death: [T1 (*simple tenses*)] *In the old house they found the bones of three prisoners who had been walled up many years ago.* —**walled-up** *adj*

**wallow in** *v prep*

**1** to roll about in (something such as mud): [IØ + *in*] *These big river creatures like to wallow in the mud to cool their skins. The pigs were wallowing in the dirt as usual.* → **grovel in** (1), **welter in** (1)

*__2__ to delight in (something, usu. bad): [T1 (*often continuous tenses*)] *Leave her alone, she just loves wallowing in her sorrow. Why are you always wallowing in self-pity? It does no good.* → **grovel in** (2), **welter in** (2)

*__3__ *not fml* to have plenty of (usu. money): [T1 (*no pass., continuous tenses*)] *He came to this country without a penny, but after only a few years, he's already wallowing in money and property!* → **roll in**[2] (1)

**waltz in** *v adv*

*not fml* to enter in a light-hearted manner: [L9 + IN] *Just then the door opened and that silly woman from next door waltzed in.*

***waltz off with** *v adv prep*

**1** *infml* to win (a prize) easily: [T1] *Don't tell me Jim has waltzed off with the top prize as usual!* → **walk away with** (3), **walk off with** (3)

**2** *infml* to take (someone) away without permission: [T1] *And then do you know what he did? Waltzed off with his teacher's wife!* → **abscond with,** etc.

**waltz round** *v adv; prep*

to (cause to) move quickly round (somewhere), as by dancing: [IØ + ROUND/*round*] *When I left her, she was still waltzing round (the room) alone, to music on a record.* [X9 + ROUND/*round*] *He waltzed me round so delicately, I felt as if I was floating on air.*

***waltz through** *v prep* → **breeze through,** etc.

*not fml* to pass (something such as an examination) easily: [T1 (*simple tenses*)] *To his own surprise, John simply waltzed through his driving test this time; it seemed very easy.*

**wander about/around** *v adv; prep*

to move around (an area or place) without direction or haste: [IØ + ABOUT/AROUND/*about/around*] *This man was found wandering about with no money or papers. When the children left home, she used to wander around the house as if she'd lost something.*

**wander from** *v prep*

**1** to move accidentally away from (a place): [IØ + *from*] *The dog loved us dearly, but he had a habit of wandering from home.* → **stray from** (1), **wander off**[1]

*__2__ to leave (a subject, right behaviour, etc.), often unintentionally: [T1] *You're wandering from the point again, so please keep to the subject. We have wandered from the paths of truth.* → **stray from** (2), **wander off**[2]

**wander off**[1] *v adv* → **stray from** (1), **wander from** (1)

to leave a place unintentionally: [IØ + OFF] *When she forgot what she was supposed to be doing, she used to wander off, and would often be found quite a long way from home.*

***wander off**[2] *v prep* → **stray from** (2), **wander from** (2)

to leave (a subject, right behaviour, etc.) unintentionally: [T1] *You're wandering off the point again, do please try to keep to the subject.*

**wangle out of** *v adv prep*

*sl* to obtain (something) from (someone) by cleverness or trickery: [X9 + OUT + *of*] *Do you think you can wangle another $20 out of your father? She's always wangling invitations out of important people.*

**want back** *v adv*

to desire the return of (something or someone): [T1 + BACK (*often simple tenses*)] *Don't forget, I want my ladder back the moment you have finished with it! Are you sure you want me back?*

**want for** *v prep*

**1** to need or desire (something or someone) for (a purpose, job, etc.) or to be (a kind of person): [T1 + *for* (*simple tenses*)] *What do you want more money for? You're earning good pay as it is! Two men are wanted for special duties. I want you for my wife: will you marry me?*

**2** to wish to seize (someone) to punish him for (a crime): [T1 + *for* (*usu. pass., simple tenses*)] *Doesn't he look like that man who's wanted for the jewel robbery? "It's better to be wanted for murder than not to be wanted at all."* (Marty Winch, *Psychology in the Wry*)

*__3__ *fml* to have need of (something): [T1 (*no pass., usu. neg., simple tenses*)] *You shall never want for money while I am alive. I'll see that you want for nothing while you attend college.* → **lack for**

**want in**[1] *v adv*

**1** *AmE* to wish to enter: [L9 + IN (*to*) (*simple tenses*)] *Open the door, will you, the cat wants in.*

**2** to wish to have (someone) arrive, usu. for a purpose: [T1 + IN (*often simple tenses*)] *Mother wants the doctor in, but I don't think it's as serious as that.*

**want in**[2] *v prep*

**be wanting in** to lack (something necessary such as a quality): *His book, while truthful, is wanting in excitement.*

**want off** *v adv*

*AmE* to wish to leave a vehicle: [L9 + OFF (*simple tenses*)] *I must ring the bell, I want off at the next stop.*

**want out** *v adv*

**1** *AmE* to wish to leave a building: [L9 + OUT (*of*) (*simple tenses*)] *I could hear knocking, as if someone wanted out.*

*__2__ *not fml* to wish not to be present or be suffering present events; wish not to take part in whatever is happening; wish to leave a marriage or business arrangement; wish to die, etc.: [IØ (*simple tenses*)] *I can't stand this job a minute longer, I want out! I thought you were happy, it was such a shock when you said you wanted out. Life is too unbearable, I want out!*

**want up** *v adv*

*AmE* to wish to get out of bed: [L9 + UP] *The boy must be feeling better, he's been wanting up all day.*

**war against** *v prep*

**1** to fight (an enemy nation): [IØ + *against*] *For years they have warred against the people from the neighbouring islands.*

*__2__ to oppose (an idea): [T1] *The farmers have been warring against the building of the new airport ever since it was suggested.*

**war over** *v prep*

to fight or argue about which side should possess (something or someone): [IØ + *over*] *The natives have been warring over this small piece of land without either side winning. The saddest part about a broken marriage is the way the parents so often war over the children.*

**war with** *v prep*

to fight or oppose (something or someone): [IØ + *with*] *The natives have been warring with each other for centuries.*

***ward off** *v adv*

**1** to stop, prevent, delay, or deal with (something unwanted): [T1] *The fighter had to ward off a dangerous blow. This soup will help you to ward off hunger for a time. Warm clothing and good food helps to ward off a cold.* → **fend off** (2), **stave off** (1)

**2** to keep (someone unwanted) at a distance: [T1] *She was so beautiful that she had difficulty in warding off all the men who wanted to marry her.* → **fend off** (3), **stave off** (2)

**warm over** *v adv*

**1** esp. *AmE* to reheat (food): [T1 + OVER] *It won't take a minute to warm the soup over for you.* —**warmed-over** *adj* → **heat up** (1), **warm up** (1)

*__2__ esp. *AmE* to repeat (an idea): [T1] *He's just warming over ideas he's heard from other people.* —**warmed-over** *adj* → **warm up** (7)

***warm to/towards** *v prep*

**1** to begin to like (someone): [T1] *At first he*

*seemed a little strange, but recently I've been warming to him more.*
**2** to begin to talk about (a subject) eagerly and in an interesting manner: [T1] *As he warmed towards his subject, he infected his listeners with his own excitement.*

**warm up** *v adv*
**1** to cause (a thing) to become warm; reheat (food): [T1 + UP] *The sun warmed up the seat nicely. Let me warm up the soup for you, it won't take a minute.* —**warmed-up** *adj* → **heat up** (1), **hot up** (1), **warm over** (1)
***2** to become warmer: [IØ] *The day began cold, but warmed up a little in the afternoon. This room takes a long time to warm up in the winter. You'll soon warm up when you've walked for a little way.*
***3** (of a machine, radio, etc.) to (cause to) become fully ready to work: [IØ] *This radio has always taken a long time to warm up. How long should the engine warm up before we start?* [T1] *Don't forget to warm the car up for a few minutes before you start.*
***4** to (cause to) prepare for action such as sport, music, etc., with warming exercises: [IØ] *Let's sing a few exercises first to warm up. All the players spend some minutes warming up before the game.* [T1] *Have you all warmed up your instruments? This is a good exercise for warming you up.* —**warm-up** *n, adj*
***5** to (cause to) become more excited or interesting: [IØ] *He warmed up the more he got into his speech.* [T1] *Let's warm up this party with a little action!* → **heat up** (2), **hot up** (2)
***6** *not fml* to prepare (a crowd) to accept a performance: [T1] *Before the show starts, we have a man who tells jokes to warm up the crowd so that they will seem to enjoy the performance.* —**warm-up** *n*
***7** to repeat (an idea): [T1] *There's nothing new in this method, it's just the same old system warmed up a bit. They think that by warming up the old plan, everyone will think it's a new idea.* —**warmed-up** *adj* → **warm over** (2)

**warn about/of** *v prep*
to give (someone) warning or advice concerning (something such as a danger): [IØ + *about/of*] *The motoring organization is warning of thick mist and blowing snow on high ground.* [T1 + *about/of*] *I warned you about that thin ice! Why didn't you warn me about his quick temper?*

**warn against** *v prep*
to advise (someone) to avoid (someone, something, or doing something): [T1 + *against*] *No one ever warned me about that type of man, and so I believed everything he told me. I've been warned against that company, so I'll take a job somewhere else. Didn't I warn you against putting your money into that foolish plan?* [IØ + *against*] *I've warned against that woman time and time again. Gardeners have warned against that plant, which can spread and destroy everything else in the garden. The weathermen are warning against travelling north in these conditions.*

**warn of** *v prep* → WARN ABOUT

***warn off** *v adv; prep*
**1** to order (someone) to leave and stay away (from a place): [T1 (*often pass.*)] *The children used to be allowed on the farm, but they've been warned off since one of them let the cows out.* [D1] *I'm warning you off my land; don't dare be found here again!*
**2** (in sport such as horseracing) to prevent (someone) from taking further part, as a punishment: [T1 (*usu. pass.*)] *The rider was found guilty of giving the horse drugs, and was warned off for a year.*

**wash away** *v adv*
**1** to destroy (something such as a road or bridge) by the action of a lot of water: [X9 + AWAY] *The river banks have been washed away by the flood; the villagers must be warned of the danger!* [L9 + AWAY] *Part of the cliff face washed away in the heavy rain; the council must put a fence round it to prevent people from getting hurt.* → **wash out** (3)
***2** to remove the effect of (guilt), esp. in the phr. **wash away your sins**: [T1 (*usu. simple tenses*)] *Nothing can ever wash away my feeling of responsibility for his death. Prayer can wash away your sins.*

**wash down** *v adv*
**1** to clean (something large) with a lot of water: [T1 + DOWN] *I need some help to wash the walls down before painting. The children are earning money washing people's cars down.*
**2** (of soil) to (cause to) move downwards with the action of water: [X9 + DOWN] *The floods have washed most of the soil down from the river banks.* [L9 + DOWN] *Most of the soil in the river bed has washed down over the years from the mountains.*
***3** to swallow (food or medicine) with the help of liquid: [T1 (*with*)] *The meal was so bad that we had to wash it down with cheap wine. Have you some tea to wash this dry cake down?*

**wash of** *v prep*
**wash one's hands of** to refuse to take any responsibility for (something): [*simple tenses, usu. present*] *That's your affair—I wash my hands of the whole business!*

**wash off** *v adv* → **come off**[1] (3), **come out** (3), **get off**[1] (4), **get out** (4), **take out** (5), **take out of** (5), **wash out** (1)
to (cause to) be removed by cleaning, as with water: [X9 + OFF] *I let some ink fall on the tablecloth, and I'm not sure if I can wash it off.* [L9 + OFF (*usu. simple tenses*)] *No, thick black ink like that won't wash off easily.*

**wash out** *v adv*
**1** to (cause to) be removed by cleaning, as with water: [X9 + OUT] *I can't seem to wash out that ink that got onto the tablecloth.* [L9 + OUT (*usu. simple tenses*)] *No, thick black ink*

*like that doesn't usually wash out. The colour has washed out and looks faded.* —**washed-out** *adj* → **wash off,** etc.

**2** to clean (a container) thoroughly, as with water: [T1 + OUT] *Remember to wash the bottle out properly before returning it to the milkman.*

**3** to destroy or make (something such as a bridge, road) impossible to use by the action of a lot of water: [X9 + OUT (*usu. simple tenses*)] *You can't use the bridge any more, it's been washed out in the floods. Heavy rain washed out three important roads overnight.* —**washout** *n* → **wash away** (1)

*__4__ to prevent or spoil (an outdoor event) by rain: [T1 (*usu. simple tenses*)] *I'm afraid this rain will wash out our garden party again. Two cricket matches were washed out this afternoon.* —**washout** *n*

*__5__ to spoil (something): [T1 (*usu. pass.*)] *Our plans were completely washed out by the unexpected opposition.*

*__6__ *AmE* to (cause to) fail a course, as for military training: [T1 (*simple tenses*)] *How many pilots in training were washed out in the last examination?* [I∅ (*simple tenses*)] *Only three washed out, I'm glad to say.* —**washout** *n*

**7 be/feel/look/seem washed out** *not fml* to be, feel, or look tired and pale, possibly ill: *You seem all washed out, what's the matter? I feel completely washed out after an ordinary day at the office.* → **tire out,** etc.

**wash over** *v prep*

**1** (of water) to flow across or on top of (something): [L9 + *over*] *The waves washed over the sea wall with a loud crashing noise.*

*__2__ to pass into the mind of (someone): [T1 (*no pass., usu. simple tenses*)] *The thought washed over me that I might never see them again.*

*__3__ → **FLOW OVER**

**wash overboard** *v adv*

to cause (someone or something) to fall from a ship or boat: [X9 + OVERBOARD (*usu. pass.*)] *Stop the ship! A man has been washed overboard!*

**wash up** *v adv*

**1** *BrE* to clean (dishes, etc.) with water; wash the dishes and pans, etc., after a meal: [X9 + UP] *How many plates are there to wash up? I'll wash up after dinner, you take a rest, you've done all the cooking.* —**washing-up** *n*

**2** *AmE* to wash one's face, hands, etc.: [I∅ + UP] *There's a bathroom on this floor if you would like to wash up before dinner.*

*__3__ to carry (something) onto the shore with the waves: [T1 (*usu. pass.*)] *Big logs are washed up every day on the west coast. The body was washed up the following morning.* → **cast up** (2)

**4 be washed up** *not fml* to be ruined: no longer happily married: *After only a few years of marriage, it seems that their relationship is completely washed up. Someone told me that Jim and Mary are washed up, but I don't believe it.* —**washed-up** *adj*

**5 be/feel/look/seem washed up** *not fml* to be, feel, or look tired and pale, possibly ill: *You look all washed up, what's the matter? After an ordinary day at the office I feel completely washed up.* → **tire out,** etc.

***waste away** *v adv*

to weaken; become thin and ill: [I∅] *Since my aunt's operation, she has simply been wasting away and may not last long.*

**waste on** *v prep*

to spend (money or time) foolishly on (someone, something, or doing something): [T1 + *on*] *Don't waste your money on that new soap powder, it's no good. I won't waste another minute on you unless you're going to help!*

**watch for** *v prep*

to look for or expect (something or someone) (in a place): [I∅ + *for*] *Will you watch for the bus while I go into the shop for a moment? Watch for our new improved product, which will be on the market next week! I'm just watching for a chance to punish him in return!* [T1 + *for*] *Watch this space for notice of our next sale. Have you been watching the papers for news of changing exchange rates?*

***watch out** *v adv*

**1** to take care: [I∅ (*usu. simple tenses*)] *Watch out! The roof is falling! You'll catch cold if you don't watch out: you need a warmer coat than that.* [I5 (*usu. imper.*)] *Watch out that you don't catch cold, going out in the pouring rain.* [I6 (*usu. imper.*)] *Watch out where you're walking, the ground is muddy.* → **look out** (2), **mind out** (1)

**2** to be ready to notice (something or someone): [I∅ (*for*)] *Are you all watching out? The Queen will come this way in a few minutes! Watch out for a chance to improve your position in the firm, they don't come very often. I'm always watching out for mistakes that I may have missed before.* —**watch-out** *n* → **look out for** (1)

***watch over** *v prep* → **have on**[2] (10), **keep on** (5)

to guard or take care of (someone or something): [T1] *I've watched over passengers on this line for nearly forty years. Is anyone watching over the jewels while we're out? The committee's responsibility is to watch over the safety of the workers.*

**water down** *v adv*

**1** to weaken (a liquid) by adding water: [T1 + DOWN] *This beer has been watered down!* —**watered-down** *adj*

*__2__ to weaken the effect of (something): [T1 (*usu. pass.*)] *His political statement has been so watered down to avoid offending certain groups, that it hardly has any meaning left.* —**watered-down** *adj*

**wave about/around** *v adv*

to move (something) from side to side, without direction: [T1 + ABOUT/AROUND] *She stood in the passage waving her arms about, I couldn't imagine why! He's been waving a notice around—something to do with an increase in pay.*

***wave aside** *v adv*

**1** to signal to (someone) to move to one side or be quiet, etc.; signal to have (something) removed: [T1] *I tried to speak, but she waved me aside and called on my neighbour to speak. Waving the next person aside, he pointed to me as I waited in line. The policeman waved the other cars aside; they were not the one which the criminal had stolen. He refused to eat the dish, waving it aside when it was offered to him again.* → **wave away** (1)

**2** to refuse to accept (something such as opposition): [T1 (*often simple tenses*)] *Waving aside all opposition to the plan, the Minister spoke about the government's intentions to go ahead with it.*

**wave at/to** *v prep*

to move the hand and arm as a greeting to (someone); signal (a greeting) to (someone) by moving the hand and arm: [IØ + *at/to*] *Is that woman waving at me? I don't know her! The baby is waving to you—please wave back.* [T1 + *at/to*] *Wave goodbye to your grandfather.*

***wave away** *v adv*

**1** to refuse to accept (something offered): [T1 (*often simple tenses*)] *The restaurant owner offered another dish instead of the bad fish, but this, too, was waved away by the angry man.* → **wave aside** (1)

**2** to signal goodbye to (someone) by moving the hand and arm; signal to (someone) to leave by waving: [T1] *We waved them away until the ship was out of sight. I went over to interrupt their conversation, but he waved me away; it was clear that I wasn't wanted just then.* also **wave off**

***wave on** *v adv*

to signal to (someone) to continue moving: [T1] *There were policemen at the scene of the accident, but they waved us on so as to keep the traffic moving.*

**wave to** *v prep* → WAVE AT

**waver between** *v prep* → **hover between, vacillate between**

to be unable to decide between (two things or doing two things): [IØ + *between* (*often continuous tenses*)] *I'm wavering between the concert and the play tonight; they're both very attractive events. Many voters are still wavering between the two parties. After years of wavering between buying and renting a house, we at last decided that it was better to own property.*

**wean from** *v prep*

**1** to train (a young animal) to stop depending on the milk of (its mother): [T1 + *from* (*often pass.*)] *The lamb is too young to be weaned from its mother yet.*

***2** to turn (someone) gradually away from (an idea, habit, bad companions, etc.): [D1] *I don't know how I'm going to be able to wean that boy from the influence of those bad boys down the street. It took months to wean him from his dependence on alcohol, but the attempt was successful in the end. You'll never wean me away from my usual escape into a good book.* [V4b] *She tried to wean him from playing football.*

**wear away** *v adv*

**1** to (cause to) be reduced gradually, as through rubbing: [T1 + AWAY] *Water can wear away rock after a long time, even though the rock is harder.* [IØ + AWAY] *The letters on this gravestone have worn away with time.* → **wear down** (1), **wear off** (1)

***2** to reduce (opposition) gradually: [T1] *All those years spent in prison have worn away the prisoner's resistance.* → **wear down** (2)

***3** to (cause to) lessen: [T1] *My patience is almost worn away by her endless complaints.* [IØ] *Even my patience will wear away in the end.*

***4** to (cause to) weaken: [T1 (*usu. pass.*)] *My aunt has been worn away to a shadow by her recent illness.* [IØ] *After the operation, she just seemed to wear away until she died.* → **wear down** (4)

***5** (of time) to (cause to) pass slowly: [IØ (*often simple tenses, usu. past*)] *As the afternoon wore away, I found it more and more difficult to stay awake. Winter wore away slowly as she waited for his return.* [T1 (*often simple tenses*)] *I can't bear to think of him wearing away his youth in prison.* → **go past**[1] (2), **wear on**[1], **wear out** (4)

**wear down** *v adv*

**1** to (cause to) be reduced gradually, as through rubbing: [T1 + DOWN] *The steps have been worn down over the years by all those passing feet.* [IØ + DOWN (*often simple tenses*)] *My shoes have worn down a lot since I started walking so much.* → **wear away** (1), **wear off** (1)

***2** to reduce (opposition) gradually; (of opposition) to weaken: [T1] *It should not take us long, with our methods, to wear down the prisoner's resistance.* [IØ] *His defences will wear down after a few weeks in prison.* → **wear away** (2)

***3** to defeat (an enemy) gradually: [T1] *Our endless gunfire will soon wear the enemy down, so that he will yield.*

***4** to tire or weaken (someone): [T1 (*often pass.*)] *I don't wonder that so many mothers look worn down with hard work, looking after children.* → **wear away** (4)

***5** to defeat (someone or an argument) in speaking: [T1] *Our speaker will soon wear the other speaker down, never fear. He's so clever, he will soon wear down the other man's argument.*

**wear off** *v adv*

**1** (usu. of a pattern on a surface) to (cause

to) be reduced, as by rubbing: [X9 + OFF] *All these years of hard driving on those once-new tyres has soon worn the tread off.* [L9 + OFF] *I bought those new plates cheaply, and the pretty rose pattern has worn off already!* → **rub off**[1] (1), **wear away** (1), **wear down** (1)

***2** to cease gradually: [IØ] *The smell of the new paint will wear off in about a week.*

***3** (of a feeling) to pass away gradually: [IØ] *If this pain doesn't wear off soon, I shall go mad. The effect of the drug will wear off after three hours or so. I can tell that the charm of working outside the home is already wearing off. The feeling of strangeness began wearing off.* → **go off**[1] (3), **pass away** (2), **pass off** (1)

***wear on**[1] *v adv* → **go by**[1] (2), **go on**[1] (8), **go past**[1] (2), **pass by**[1] (2), **run on**[1] (2), **wear away** (5), **wear out** (4)
(of time) to seem to pass slowly; (of an event) last long in an uninteresting manner; become later: [IØ (*simple tenses*)] *As the afternoon wore on, I found it more and more difficult to keep awake. Winter wore on slowly as she waited for his return. The meeting wore on all afternoon. Time wears on more slowly when you are not interested.*

**wear on/upon**[2] *v prep*
**1** to have (something such as a garment or ornament) placed on or fixed to (usu. part of the body or clothing): [T1 + *on/upon*] *Why do you wear all those gold things on your arms? She wore a tall hat on her head. He was wearing a nameplate on his left breast.*
**2 wear one's heart on/upon one's sleeve** to be open about one's feelings, esp. to show that one is in love with a certain person: [*simple tenses, often present*] *"But I will wear my heart upon my sleeve . . . I am not what I am."* (Shakespeare, *Othello*)
**3 wear on/upon someone's nerves/patience** to annoy someone; be hard for someone to bear: *The child's endless crying has been wearing on my nerves all day.*

**wear out** *v adv*
**1** to pass away with wearing: [L9 + OUT] *The folds in the material will soon wear out.*

***2** to use (something) until it is finished; (cause to) become unfit for further use: [T1 (*often pass.*)] *The machinery is worn out and will have to be replaced. This is the third pair of shoes that you've worn out this year.* [IØ] *This cheap leather wears out so quickly.* —**worn-out** *adj*

***3** to tire (someone or oneself) greatly: [T1 (*often pass.*)] *Looking after the children wears me out in a short time. Why do I feel worn out after an ordinary day's work at the office? She keeps wearing herself out for other people.* [IØ] *"It is better to wear out than rust out."* (Bishop R. Cumberland)

***4** (of time) to pass slowly or without interest; spend (time), usu. unpleasantly: [IØ (*usu. simple tenses*)] *The meeting wore out all afternoon. Winter wears out more slowly every year.* [T1 (*usu. simple tenses*)] *How can we wear out this dull afternoon? I hate to think of him wearing out his youth in prison.* → **go past**[1] (2), **pass by**[1] (2), **wear away** (5), **wear on**[1]

***5** (of a quality) to (cause to be) used up: [IØ] *After about an hour, my patience began to wear out.* [T1] *Why doesn't she learn that she has already worn out her welcome?* —**outworn** *adj*

***6** *AmE not fml* to wear (a garment) so as to get full use from it and finish its use quickly, in order to change to something new: [T1] *I'm just wearing this old coat out so that I can have a new one sooner.* → **wear up**

***7** *AmE infml* to beat (someone): [T1 (*usu. simple tenses*)] *Let me get at him, I'll soon wear him out!*

***8** to use (an expression) until it is no longer original or interesting: [T1 (*usu. pass.*)] *This writer uses phrases that were worn out fifty years ago.* —**outworn** *adj*

**wear thin** *v adj*
**1** to (cause to) become thin through much wearing: [X9 + thin] *I've worn the seat of this skirt thin.* [L9 + thin] *The knees of these trousers have worn thin; can you mend them?*

***2** *not fml* to become less, weaker, etc., as through use: [IØ] *My courage began to wear thin as the hour drew near. That excuse is wearing thin; you've used it three times this week already!*

**wear through** *v adv; prep* → **go through**[1] (4)
to wear a hole in (something); wear into a hole: [X9 + THROUGH (*often pass.*)] *The knees of these trousers have been completely worn through!* [L9 + THROUGH/*through* (*often simple tenses*)] *I've worn through the elbow of this old coat at last. The knees of these trousers have completely worn through! The bottom of the bucket has worn through after all this time.*

***wear up** *v adv* → **wear out** (6)
esp. *BrE not fml* to wear (a garment) so as to get full use from it, save better garments and have a reason for buying new ones: [T1] *I do have other coats, but I'm wearing this one up so that I can finish with it and get a new one.*

**wear upon** *v prep* → WEAR ON

***weary of** *v prep* → **tire of** (1)
to lose interest in or patience with (someone, something, or doing something): [T1 (*no pass., simple tenses*)] *One can quickly weary of a city view, but never of a beautiful country scene, as it is always changing. She soon wearied of him and found another lover.* [T4 (*simple tenses*)] *Don't you weary of hearing the same complaints over and over again?*

**weary with** *v prep*
to tire (someone) with (annoying behaviour): [T1 + *with*] *How she wearies me with her endless complaints!*

***weather through** *v adv; prep*
to pass through (troubles) successfully: [IØ

(*usu. simple tenses*)] *You're strong enough; whatever happens, you'll weather through somehow.* [T1 (*no pass.*)] *After weathering through troubles like that, you're strong enough for anything.*

**weave from** *v prep*
**1** to make (cloth) from (threads): [T1 + *from* (*often pass.*)] *His coat was woven from wool of many colours.* → **weave into** (1)
**2** to invent (a story or other writing) using (material): [T1 + *from* (*often simple tenses*)] *He wove the book from his own experiences.* → **weave into** (3)

**weave into** *v prep*
**1** to make (threads) into (cloth): [T1 + *into*] *She wove the silk thread into a beautiful shirt.* → **weave from** (1)
**2** to mix (a thread) into (cloth) by weaving: [T1 + *into* (*often pass.*)] *Threads of real gold were woven into the cloth for the royal garments.*
**3** to make (material) into (a story or other writing): [T1 + *into*] *He has a way of weaving dull material (up) into an interesting article.* → **weave from** (2)
**4** to work (details) by mixing them into (a story): [T1 + *into* (*often simple tenses*)] *He has woven some invented facts into his account of the battle.*

**weave through** *v prep*
to drive in and out of other vehicles to make one's way through (traffic): [IØ + *through*] *The advantage of a little car is that it can weave through the traffic and often get there faster than the big cars.* [X9 + *through*] *A motorcycle can weave its way through the cars and get to the front of a waiting line quickly.*

**wed to** *v prep*
**1** *old use or lit* to cause (someone) to marry (someone of the opposite sex): [T1 + *to* (*usu. pass.*)] *He has been wedded to his wife for nearly twenty-five years. Why did you wed your daughter to that terrible man?*
**2 be wedded to** to be strongly fixed to or keen on (an idea, opinion, etc.): *This firm is still wedded to old-fashioned methods, and is sure to fail.*

***weed out** *v adv*
**1** to remove (unwanted plants) from a crop: [T1] *Please help me to weed out those yellow flowers that keep growing among the onions.*
**2** *not fml* to remove (unwanted parts or people) from a whole or group: [T1] *It's the committee's job to weed out at this stage those students who are not likely to succeed. Tom ought to have weeded out the duller articles from his book.* → **comb out** (5)

**weep about/over** *v prep*
to express grief concerning (something or someone); cry (tears) because of (something or someone): [IØ + *about/over*] *What ever is that child weeping about now? Is he still weeping over his lost dog?* [T1 + *about/over*] *She wept bitter tears over the loss of her lover.*

**weep away** *v adv*
**1** to cry continuously: [IØ + AWAY (*often continuous tenses*)] *Is she still weeping away? She's been crying all day!*
***2** to pass (time) in crying: [T1] *I could weep the whole afternoon away, I'm so sad.*

**weep for** *v prep*
**1** to cry hoping to gain (something or someone): [IØ + *for*] *It's no use you weeping for a new bicycle, you won't get one that way! She wept for her mother, but no one came all night.* → **wail for**
**2** to cry to express (joy or sorrow): [IØ + *for*] *"I weep for joy to stand upon my kingdom once again."* (Shakespeare, *King Richard II*)
**3** to cry to express sympathy with (someone); express sympathy with (someone or something): [IØ + *for* (*usu. simple tenses*)] *I weep for the future of the human race. I weep for the loss of your husband.*
**4** to express grief because of (a fault): [IØ + *for*] *Evil men should weep for their evil deeds.*

**weep over** *v prep* → WEEP ABOUT

***weigh against** *v prep*
**1** to balance (something such as an idea) with (another): [D1] *We must weigh one fact against the next to arrive at an answer. The quality of the product must be weighed against its cost.* → **weigh with** (2)
**2** to be recorded as unfavourable to (someone): [T1 (*no pass., simple tenses*)] *His frequent lateness will weigh against him when the new appointments are being decided.* → **hold against**, etc.

***weigh down** *v adv*
**1** to press on (something or someone) with heavy weight: [T1] *The branches of the fruit trees were weighed down with the crop. We need someone else to weigh down the boat on the other side.* → **load down** (1), etc.
**2** to make (someone) very sad: [T1 (*usu. pass.*)] *For months after her husband's sudden death, my aunt was weighed down with grief.* → **bow down** (2), **lade with** (2), **load down** (2)

**weigh in¹** *v adv*
**1** to (cause to) be weighed, as at the beginning of a journey or esp. a fight: [T1 + IN (*usu. pass.*)] *Have all the suitcases been weighed in? The plane leaves in half an hour. Who is responsible for weighing the two men in? When they weighed in before the fight, Brown was six pounds heavier than Clay. Clay weighed in at 235 pounds.* —**weigh-in, weighing-in** *n* → **weigh out** (2)
***2** *not fml* to add an opinion, as to help decide an argument: [IØ (*with*) (*usu. simple tenses*)] *"Jones weighs in to save the social contract."* (*The Guardian,* 2 September 1974) *We would have won if you hadn't tried to weigh in with your silly ideas.*

**weigh in²** *v prep*
**1 be weighed in the balance(s)** to be judged:

*"Thou art weighed in the balances, and art found wanting."* (The Bible)
**2 weigh in someone's favour** to cause others to have a better opinion of someone: [*usu. simple tenses*] *His improved behaviour should weigh in his favour when the school board are considering his fate.*

*__weigh on/upon__ *v prep* → **press on²** (2), **prey on** (3)
to cause worry to (someone or someone's mind): [T1 (*no pass.*)] *I can see that his new responsibilities are weighing heavily on the young father. The thought of the coming examination is already weighing on the students' minds.*

**weigh out** *v adv*
**1** to weigh a measured quantity of (something) exactly: [T1 + OUT] *The cook weighed out the flour and fat for the pastry.*
***2** to be weighed, as at the end of a fight, race, etc.: [IØ (*at*) (*usu. simple tenses*)] *After the fight, the young fighter weighed out at two pounds lighter.* → **weigh in¹** (1)

*__weigh up__ *v adv*
**1** *not fml* to judge or form an opinion about (someone or something): [T1] *She's a strange person, I can't quite weigh her up. The firm must have time to weigh up the new system.*
**2** to consider (something) before deciding: [T1] *When I've had a chance to weigh up our chances of winning, I'll tell you whether we should enter the competition.* [T6] *We haven't quite weighed up yet whether to enter.*

*__weigh upon__ *v prep* → WEIGH ON

*__weigh with__ *v prep*
**1** (of advice, opinion, etc.) to influence (someone): [T1 (*no pass., simple tenses*)] *He is greatly respected in the town, which should weigh (heavily) with the council when they are making their decision. His political opinions weigh little with her.*
**2** to balance (something such as an idea) against (another): [D1] *We must weigh one fact with the next to arrive at an answer.* → **weigh against** (1)

*__weight against__ *v prep* → **slant against**
to direct (writing) so as to oppose (an idea or a particular group of people): [D1 (*usu. pass.*)] *The article seems to be weighted against the present popularity of Eastern religions.*

*__weight down__ *v adv* → **load down** (1), etc.
to press on (someone or something) with a heavy weight: [D1 (*usu. pass.*)] *The boat is weighted down with too many passengers; someone should go ashore. She was weighted down with a heavy load of shopping.*

*__welch on__ *v prep* also **welsh on**
to fail to pay (a debt) intentionally: [T1] *We heard, too late, that he had left town in order to welch on all his debts. I've never welched on a debt in my life and don't intend to start now!*

**welcome back** *v adv*
to be glad to see the return of (someone or something); greet (someone) on return with pleasure: [T1 + BACK] *If you decide to return to me, I will welcome you back. All the relatives gathered at the airport to welcome back the people who had been freed from the terrorists. Many parents are welcoming back the old standards of grammar instruction.*

**welcome in** *v adv*
to be pleased to have (someone) enter a building, group, etc.: [T1 + IN (*to*)] *I like to stand at the door to welcome the children in when they come home from school. We are pleased to welcome in several new members this year.*

**welcome to** *v prep*
to take pleasure in admitting (usu. someone) to a place, group, etc.: [T1 + *to*] *I am so pleased to have the chance at last to welcome you both to my home. I would like you to welcome six new members to the club.*

**welcome with** *v prep*
to greet (someone) with pleasure by giving (something) or showing (a quality), esp. in the phrs. **welcome someone/something with open arms**: [T1 + *with*] *Newcomers to the town are welcomed with baskets of fruit by the local shopkeepers. Any reduction in income tax will be welcomed with open arms. The whole population of the city welcomed the Queen with great warmth and loyalty.*

**weld together** *v adv*
**1** to join (metal parts) with great heat: [T1 + TOGETHER (*often pass.*)] *The parts of the crashed car had to be welded together in the garage.*
***2** to cause (a group or parts) to combine or be united firmly: [T1 (*usu. simple tenses*)] *It often takes trouble from outside to weld a family together and cause them to forget their quarrels. Only firm action by the government can weld the nation together to face the troubles ahead.*

**well out** *v adv*
(of a lot of liquid) to flow freely: [L9 + OUT (*from, of*)] *Blood welled out from the wound, and no one could stop the flow.*

**well over** *v adv; prep*
(of a lot of liquid) to overflow (the edge of a container): [L9 + OVER/*over*] *She poured too much milk in the glass, and it welled over (the lip).*

**well up** *v adv*
**1** (of a lot of liquid) to rise: [L9 + UP (*in*)] *Tears welled up in his eyes as he said goodbye to her.*
***2** (of a feeling) to rise, increase, or be felt more powerfully: [IØ (*in*)] *Pity welled up in her heart as she watched the poor child.*

*__welsh on__ *v prep* → WELCH ON

*__welter in__ *v prep*
**1** *fml* to swim, float, or be covered in (a lot of liquid): [T1 (*no pass., usu. continuous tenses*)] *After the battle, the whole field was weltering in blood.* → **grovel in** (1), **wallow in** (1)

**2** *fml* to delight in (something bad): [T1 (*no pass., usu. continuous tenses*)] *The chiefs of all the villages were weltering in evil.* → **grovel in** (2), **wallow in** (2)

**wet down** *v adv* → **damp down** (1)
to make (a surface) wet all over: [T1 + DOWN] *If you wet the walls down first, the surface will take the water-based paint more smoothly.*

***wet off** *v adv*
to remove or break off (blown glass) by wetting: [T1] *When you have blown the glass to the shape you want, wet the end off; you can make it smooth when it has cooled.*

***wet out** *v adv*
to make (cloth) thoroughly wet before dipping it in a chemical to change its colour: [T1] *The colour will not be evenly fixed unless the cloth is first properly wetted out.*

**whack off** *v adv*
*not fml* to remove (usu. the top of something) by hitting it violently: [T1 + OFF] *Do try to stop that boy whacking all the flower heads off with his stick.*

***whack up** *v adv*
**1** *AmE infml* to share (usu. money): [T1] *Have we decided how to whack up the profits from the robbery?*
**2** *infml* to cause (something) to increase: [T1] *I see the government has whacked up the taxes again!*

**wheedle into** *v prep*
to persuade (someone) into (doing something) by being insincerely pleasant: [X9 + *into*] *Do you think you can wheedle Father into paying for our flight?*

**wheedle out** *v adv*
to get (something such as money or information) from (someone) by insincerely pleasant persuasion: [X9 + OUT (*of*)] *I think we should be able to wheedle the price of the plane tickets out of Father. She'll wheedle out your secret if you're not careful.*

**wheel about/around/round** *v adv*
**1** to push (someone) from place to place in a wheelchair or baby carriage: [X9 + ABOUT/AROUND/ROUND] *The young people took turns to wheel the wounded girl around in the fresh air.*
**2** to turn round rather sharply: [L9 + ABOUT/AROUND/ROUND (*usu. simple tenses*)] *He wheeled round at the sound of his name.* → **whip round** (2), **whirl round**
***3** to change one's opinion to the opposite view, rather suddenly: [IØ (*usu. simple tenses*)] *Whatever made the chairman wheel about like that?*

**wheel away** *v adv*
to push (someone or something on wheels) away from a place: [X9 + AWAY] *My bicycle has been stolen! Someone just wheeled it away from the front of the house! I shall be glad when she wheels the old man away, I've had enough of his complaints.*

**wheel in** *v adv*
**1** to push (something or someone on wheels) into a place: [X9 + IN (*to*)] *We'll find someone to wheel you in when the doors are opened. Please don't ride your bicycle into the yard, wheel it in.* → **send in** (1), **take in**[1] (1)
***2** *infml humor* to lead (someone) as he enters: [T1] *If he's arrived at last, do wheel him in!*

**wheel out** *v adv*
to push (something or someone on wheels) outside: [X9 + OUT] *I'd like to wheel the baby out for a few minutes in the fresh air.*

**wheel round** *v adv* → WHEEL ABOUT

***wheeze out** *v adv*
to say (words) or sing or play (a tune) in a dry cracked voice: [T1] *This old instrument can only wheeze out a tune now. The old man wheezed out a greeting, then began to cough.*

***while away** *v adv*
to find a way to pass (time) lazily: [T1] *Lying here in the sun is a very pleasant way to while away the afternoon! I'm just whiling away my time, waiting for the train to come in.*

**whip away** *v adv*
**1** to remove (something) suddenly: [X9 + AWAY (*simple tenses*)] *He can whip the tablecloth away while leaving all the dishes still standing on the table. She whipped her hand away, unwilling to let him touch it.* → **whip off** (1), **whisk away** (1)
**2** to take (someone) away quickly: [X9 + AWAY (*simple tenses*)] *Why did you whip me away when I was just beginning to enjoy the party?* → **whip off** (2), **whirl away, whisk away** (2)

**whip in** *v adv*
**1** to drive (dogs) together into a group with or as with a whip: [T1 + IN] *His job in the hunt is to whip the dogs in when they scatter.* —**whipper-in** *n*
**2** to enter or move quickly: [L9 + IN (*to*) (*simple tenses*)] *That was a dangerous thing to do, whipping in like that just as the train doors were closing.*
***3** (in Parliament) to gather (party members), as for a vote: [T1] *His job is to whip the members in if the vote looks like being close.* —**whipper-in** *n*

**whip into** *v prep*
**1** to beat (something) fast until it becomes (a form): [T1 + *into*] *Whip the eggs and sugar into a stiff cream.*
***2** to urge (someone) into (a state), usu. with words: [D1] *The speaker soon whipped the crowd into a fever of excitement.*
**3 whip something/someone into shape** *not fml* to make something or someone reach a fit condition, for a purpose: *With a lot of training, we might be able to whip the team into shape in time for next year's games. With some more practice, we'll soon whip this piece of music into shape ready for the concert.* → **lick into**

**whip off** *v adv*
**1** to remove (a covering) suddenly: [X9 + OFF (*simple tenses*)] *Seeing that he was in the presence of ladies, he whipped off his hat. The storm just whipped the roof off during the night!* → **whip away** (1), **whisk away** (1)
**2** to take (someone) away quickly: [X9 + OFF (*simple tenses*)] *She whipped the child off to the doctor before I had time to look at him.* → **whip away** (2), **whirl away, whisk away** (2)
**3** to leave quickly: [L9 + OFF (*simple tenses*)] *When I turned round, I found that she had whipped off to avoid awkward questions.*

**whip on** *v adv* → **whip up** (2)
to urge (a horse) to move forward, with or as with a whip: [T1 + ON] *Whipping his horse on, he reached the finishing post just ahead of the other riders.*

**whip out** *v adv*
**1** to produce (something) suddenly: [X9 + OUT (*simple tenses*] *But then the robber whipped out a gun, and everyone stopped moving. He has a way of whipping out a reply just when you least expect it.*
**2** to leave a room or building quickly: [L9 + OUT (*simple tenses*)] *Just then the door opened and the cat whipped out, with the dog chasing it.*

**whip over** *v prep*
to travel very fast across (an area): [L9 + *over* (*simple tenses*)] *The train simply whips over the country.*

**whip round** *v adv*
**1** to visit someone or a place for a very short time: [L9 + ROUND (*to*) (*simple tenses*)] *I can whip round (to your place) after work and collect the papers that I need for tomorrow.*
**2** to turn round suddenly: [L9 + ROUND (*simple tenses*)] *He whipped round at the mention of his name.* → **wheel about** (2), **whirl round**
***3** to collect money from each of a group of people, often to help a fellow member: [IØ (*for*) (*usu. simple tenses*)] *All the girls in the office whipped round to give Mary a wedding present.* —**whip-round** *n*

**whip through** *v prep*
to finish (work) quickly: [L9 + *through*] *If I whip through the work this afternoon, I'll be able to go home early.*

**whip up** *v adv*
**1** to beat (something such as food) fast: [T1 + UP] *Whip up the eggs with the cream and pour into the mixture.*
**2** to make (a horse) go faster, with or as with a whip: [T1 + UP] *Can't you whip up the horses? We must get there quickly!* → **whip on**
**3** to seize (something or someone) suddenly: [X9 + UP (*simple tenses*)] *She whipped up a knife and faced the man bravely. Whipping up the baby, she ran from the burning house.*
***4** to excite (someone), usu. with words: [T1] *The speaker soon whipped the crowd up until they were ready to march.*
***5** to gather or increase (something such as a quality): [T1] *We haven't been able to whip up any further interest in our product in the trade. You'd better whip up some keenness if you're to win the game!*
***6** to make (something) quickly: [T1 (*simple tenses*)] *Can your cook whip up a meal for us in half an hour? She can whip up a dress in an afternoon.*

**whirl away** *v adv* → **whip away** (2), **whip off** (2), **whisk away** (2)
to take (someone) away quickly, esp. on a social occasion: [X9 + AWAY (*usu. simple tenses*)] *Just then, our host whirled me away to meet some of the other guests.*

**whirl round** *v adv* → **wheel about** (2), **whip round** (2)
to (cause to) turn round fast: [L9 + ROUND (*simple tenses*)] *He whirled round at the sound of his name.* [X9 + ROUND] *This little stand is on wheels, so you can whirl it round and choose the cup you want. Please stop whirling me round, it makes me feel sick.*

**whisk away/off** *v adv*
**1** to remove (something) with light movements of a brush, tail, etc.: [X9 + AWAY/OFF] *The cow stood contentedly in the field, whisking flies away with her tail. Let me just whisk off those little pieces of dirt that have got on your coat.* → **whip away** (1), **whip off** (1)
**2** to remove (something or someone) suddenly: [X9 + AWAY/OFF (*simple tenses*)] *Can he really whisk away the tablecloth without breaking any of the dishes? Before I knew what was happening, I was being whisked off to the other side of the room.* → **whip away** (2), **whip off** (2), **whirl away**

***whisper about/around** *v adv; prep*
to spread (a story) quietly (round a place): [T1; D5 (*usu. pass.*)] *It's being whispered about (the town) that Jim and Mary are to separate.*

***whistle for** *v prep*
*not fml* to want (something) without getting it: [T1 (*simple tenses*)] *I'm not prepared to use any of the firm's money to pay this man: let him whistle for his money!*

**whistle in** *v prep*
**whistle in the dark** *not fml* to pretend fearlessness in the face of danger, threat, etc.: [(*usu. continuous tenses*)] *She says that she's not afraid of losing her job because of what she did, but I think she's just whistling in the dark.*

**whistle up** *v adv*
**1** to call (a dog, horse, etc.) by whistling: [T1 + UP] *If we're all ready, I'll just whistle up the dogs and then we can go.*
***2** *not fml* to make (something) from poor or scarce materials: [T1 (*often simple tenses*)] *Life's not easy for a good teacher, having to whistle up new ideas for lessons every day.*

***white out** *v adv*
**1** to cover (writing) with white paint so as to

remove it: [T1] *Can you white out those letters at the edge of the page?*

**2** esp. *CanE* to make (a road) impossible to see because of ice, mist, and blowing snow: [T1] *If this winter storm gets any worse, it could white out the highway from here to King City.* —**white-out** *n*

**whittle away** *v adv* → **whittle down**

**1** to remove (small piece of wood) with a sharp knife: [T1 + AWAY] *If you whittle away the end of the stick, you could have a nice sharp point. He made the figure by whittling away the wood around the shape that he wanted.*

*__2__ to reduce or weaken (something) gradually: [T1] *The recent election results have whittled away the government's power.*

**whittle down** *v adv* → **whittle away**

**1** to reduce (a piece of wood) by removing small pieces: [T1 + DOWN] *Don't whittle the stick down too much or it won't be long enough.*

*__2__ to reduce or weaken (something) gradually: [T1] *It didn't take him long to whittle down his opponent's argument.*

**whizz through** *v prep*

**1** *not fml* to pass very quickly through (something such as a place): [L9 + *through*] *The children liked to watch the fast trains whizzing through the station on their way to London.*

*__2__ to finish (something such as work) quickly: [T1] *The examination was easy, I whizzed through it in half the time allowed.*

*__whomp up__ *v adv*

**1** esp. *AmE not fml* to excite (someone): [T1] *The girls do this special dance to whomp up the crowd before the football game.*

**2** esp. *AmE* to prepare (something) hastily: [T1] *Get your wife to whomp up a meal for us: we have to leave in half an hour.*

**whoop up** *v adv*

**whoop it up** *infml* to have a wildly enjoyable time, usu. with drink: *Let's go to the party and whoop it up together!* —**whoop-up** *n*

*__whore after__ *v prep*

esp. *AmE* to desire or try to obtain (something immoral): [T1 (*no pass., usu. continuous tenses*)] *The last we heard of him, he was still whoring after the pleasures of evil living.*

**widen out** *v adv*

**1** to (cause to) become wider: [IØ + OUT (*often simple tenses*)] *The river widens out here as the land gets flatter.* [T1 + OUT (*often simple tenses*)] *We shall have to widen out the river bed to avoid flooding.*

*__2__ to enlarge (something): [T1] *The system needs widening out if it is to include all the modern developments.*

*__wig out__ *v adv*

*AmE infml* to (cause to) become madly excited: [IØ (*usu. simple tenses*)] *He'll wig out when he reads the letter!* [T1 (*usu. simple tenses*)] *Your letter should wig him out, all right!*

*__will away__ *v adv*

**1** to get rid of (possessions) after one's death, by means of a formal paper: [T1 (*to*) (*often simple tenses*)] *That foolish old man has willed away his whole fortune, in stupid gifts to people who don't deserve it!*

**2** to make (something such as a feeling) disappear by using one's willpower: [T1] *The old man claims to be able to will away any form of pain, just by thinking about it.*

*__will to__ *v prep*

to leave (possessions) to (someone else) after one's death, by means of a formal paper: [D1 (*often simple tenses*)] *The stupid old man willed half his fortune to the cats' home!*

*__win around/round__ *v adv* → WIN OVER

**win at** *v prep* → **lose at**

to gain a victory in (a game, event, etc.); gain (something such as money, a prize, etc.) in (a game, event, etc.): [IØ + *at*] *John is so lucky, he always wins at cards.* [T1 + *at*] *Did you win any money at the races today? Jim won most of the prizes at the Games.*

*__win away__ *v adv*

to cause (someone) to change his loyalty (from someone or something): [T1 (*from*)] *His action might encourage the party to try to win more members away (from the opposition party).*

*__win back__ *v adv*

to regain (something or someone): [T1] *It took all day to win back a few hundred metres from the enemy. What can I do to win my wife back? The team are determined to win the prize back next year!*

*__win free__ *v adj* also **win clear**

to become free or successful: [IØ (*of*) (*usu. simple tenses*)] *After many long arguments, the under-director won free and was allowed to run the system his own way. It took a long battle in the courts for the prisoner to win free although he knew that he was not guilty. The young man was glad to win free of his mother's control at last.*

*__win out__ *v adv*

**1** to be successful in the end: [IØ (*simple tenses*)] *I know that whatever you try, you're sure to win out in spite of early difficulties.* → **win through**

**2** esp. *AmE not fml* to gain a victory (over someone or something): [IØ (*over*)] *Our product is sure to win out (over those of our competitors).*

*__win over__ *v adv* also **win around/round** → **gain over**

to gain the support of (someone), often by persuasion: [T1] *She didn't like me at first, but I was soon able to win her over by being especially considerate. Can you win the director over? We need his vote. The thought of being alone in the winter won him over to the idea of staying with his daughter.*

*__win through__ *v adv* → **win out** (1)
to be successful in the end: [IØ (*simple tenses*)] *I know that whatever you try, you're sure to win through in spite of early difficulties.*

*__win to__ *v prep*
to persuade (someone) to join (a group) or accept (an idea): [D1] *His forceful speeches have won many young people to the Party. He speaks so well that he should be able to win most of the committee to his opinion.*

**wince at** *v prep*
to make a small sharp movement, as of the face, to express pain or fear because of (something): [IØ + *at* (*simple tenses*)] *She winced at the cold wind hitting her face. He winced at the mention of his enemy's name.*

**wind around/round** *v prep*
**1** to fasten (something or itself) around (something) by turning several times; surround (something) by turning: [X9 + *around/round*] *Wind the end of the string round your finger, so that the toy plane can't get loose. The belt had wound itself around the wheel, stopping the motor.* [L9 + *around/round*] *Keep the plants well separated so that there's no danger of that green climbing plant winding around the roses.* → **coil around, twist around**[2] **(1), wreathe around**
**2 wind someone around/round one's little finger** *not fml* to control someone easily: *Jim worships his daughter and will do anything she wants; she can wind him round her little finger.* → **twist around**[2] (2)

**wind back** *v adv* → **run back** (4), **wind on** (2)
to turn (a film) back to an earlier part; rewind: [X9 + BACK] *Would you please wind the film back to the part where the child comes in, I'd like to see that again.* [L9 + BACK] *Wait a minute, it won't take me long to wind back to the beginning, and then I can put the film away.*

**wind down** *v adv*
**1** to lower (something) by turning a handle; be able to be lowered with a handle: [X9 + DOWN] *I had to wind the car window down to hear what she was saying.* [L9 + DOWN (*simple tenses*)] *The windows don't wind down very easily.*
***2** (of clockwork) to run more and more slowly until it stops: [IØ] *My watch had been winding down, and I didn't know it was slow, that's why I'm late.*
***3** *not fml* to rest until calmer, after work or excitement: [IØ] *Television is very useful for winding down before going to bed. The football crowd don't wind down after a good game until they're nearly home.*
***4** to cause to be no longer in operation, esp. gradually: [T1] *The company is winding down its business in Hong Kong.*
***5** to come to a gradual rest: [IØ] *At school, things start winding down a few weeks before the summer holidays begin.*

**wind in** *v adv*
to gather (something such as a line) by turning it, as round a wheel: [X9 + IN] *Wind your line in very carefully or the fish might get away.*

**wind into** *v prep*
**1** to wrap, twist, or roll (something) into (a shape, usu. round): [X9 + *into*] *Would you help me to wind this wool into a ball?*
**2 wind one's way into someone's affections** to make someone gradually become fond of one, often for a purpose: *I suppose she got that money from your father by winding her way into his affections over the years.*

**wind off** *v adv*
to remove (something) by turning it round and round: [X9 + OFF] *It may take some time to wind off all the thread.*

**wind on** *v adv*
**1** to fix (something) onto a holder or pole by turning or twisting it: [X9 + ON] *There are special hooks at the sides of the frame for winding the wool on. How long will it take you to wind on a further 100 metres of line?*
**2** to move (film) to a later point: [X9 + ON] *Let's not see this uninteresting part, I'll wind the film on to the exciting bit near the end.* [L9 + ON (*to*)] *Please wait while I wind on to the end.* → **wind back**

**wind round** *v prep* → WIND AROUND

**wind through** *v prep*
**1** to pass through (a place) in a twisting direction: [IØ + *through* (*simple tenses*)] *The path winds through the forest for quite a long way.*
**2** to (cause to) be introduced throughout (something such as writing): [L9 + *through* (*simple tenses*)] *A thread of sorrow winds through her poetry.* [X9 + *through* (*simple tenses*)] *He has wound his opinions through each of his statements.*

**wind up** *v adv*
**1** to raise (something) by turning a handle; be able to be raised by turning a handle: [X9 + UP] *Would you please wind the car windows up? It's cold.* [L9 + UP (*simple tenses*)] *The car windows don't wind up very quickly.*
**2** to tighten the spring of (clockwork), usu. by turning a key: [T1 + UP] *I forgot to wind my watch up, so of course it stopped.* —**wind-up** *adj*
***3** to roll (something such as a line) into a ball: [T1] *Sailors know how to wind up a long rope neatly.*
***4** to bring (something) to an orderly end; end (something): [T1] *The lawyers are still winding up your father's business. I hope to be able to wind up my affairs without too much trouble before leaving the country. Can you think of a good joke I can use to wind up my speech? I think it's time to wind up this meeting.*
***5** to cause (someone) to take part in or be very concerned with (something or doing something): [D1 (*in*) (*usu. pass.*)] *He got so*

*wound up in the play that his family hardly saw him.*

**6** *not fml* to finish by becoming (something): [L1 (*simple tenses*)] *In spite of people's opinions, she wound up the winner. The general began his army life as a private soldier and wound up as ruler of his country.* [L7 (*simple tenses*)] *After gaining and losing two fortunes, he wound up poor at the end of his life.* → **end up** (1), **fetch up** (4), **finish up** (2), **land up** (3)

*__7__ *not fml* to finish by (doing something): [L4 (*simple tenses*)] *I never dreamed that I would wind up owning such a lot of property! Be careful, you could wind up by getting hurt.* → **end up** (2), **fetch up** (5), **finish up** (3), **land up** (4)

*__8__ *not fml* to arrive at or in (a place), esp. after time or events: [L9 (*at, in, on*) (*simple tenses*)] *With Jim driving, you never know where you're going to wind up. The traveller took the wrong train and wound up at a country village. He'll wind up in prison if he goes on taking risks like that. The boy's ball wound up on the garage roof.* → **end up** (3), **fetch up** (6), **finish up** (4), **land up** (5)

*__9__ *not fml* to (cause to) reach (an unfavourable end): [L9 (*in*) (*simple tenses*)] *The business might wind up in failure unless more care is taken with the accounts.* [X9 (*in*) (*simple tenses*)] *Stop spending so fast, or goodness knows where you'll wind us up!* → **end up** (4), **fetch up** (7), **finish up** (5), **land up** (6)

*__10__ *not fml* to receive (something) in the end: [L9 (*with*) (*simple tenses*)] *After much effort, the writer wound up with a contract. Jim entered the competition without much hope, not thinking he would wind up with first prize!* → **end up** (5), **fetch up** (8), **finish up** (6), **land up** (7)

*__11__ *not fml* to cause (someone) to become excited: [T1 (*often pass.*)] *This man is specially employed to wind up the crowd ready to be influenced by our speaker. Don't get so wound up, there's nothing to get excited or nervous about!*

*__12__ (in baseball) to swing the arm in preparation for throwing the ball: [IØ] *This man is an excellent player, but he takes so long to wind up!* —**wind-up** *n*

**13 wind up nowhere** *not fml* to gain no success: [*often simple tenses*] *If you don't work hard you'll wind up nowhere. What's the use of taking exams, when so many people with higher degrees wind up nowhere when they can't get a job.* → **end up** (6), **fetch up** (9), **finish up** (7)

**wink at** *v prep*

**1** to close one eye quickly as a signal or greeting to (someone): [IØ + *at*] *Jim, that man over there is winking at me: ask him to stop annoying me! Mary winked at Jim to show how much she agreed with what he was saying.*

*__2__ *fml* to pretend not to know about (something wrong) in order to allow it to take place; give one's silent approval to (something wrong): [T1 (*usu. simple tenses*)] *The thieves paid the servants to wink at their entrance into the house. Many of the teachers wink at the boys' secret smoking.* → **connive at**

**wink away** *v adv*

**1** to continue closing and opening one eye quickly: [IØ + AWAY] *He has something wrong with his left eye, which makes him wink away all day.*

*__2__ to try to remove (usu. tears) by closing and opening the eyes quickly: [T1] *Mary tried hard to wink her tears away, but Jim could see that she had been crying.* → **blink away, wink back** (2)

**wink back** *v adv*

**1** to return a signal or greeting by closing one eye quickly: [IØ + BACK (*often simple tenses*)] *If he winks at you, why don't you wink back if you like him?*

*__2__ to try to remove (usu. tears) by closing and opening the eyes quickly: [T1] *Mary tried hard to wink back her tears, but Jim could see that she had been crying.* → **blink away, wink away** (2)

*__winkle out__ *v adv*

*not fml* to find and produce (something or someone) with difficulty: [T1 (*of*) (*often simple tenses*)] *After much searching, I was able to winkle out a real old suit of armour for the play. Can you try your best to winkle the secret list out of the director?*

*__winter over__ *v adv*

to spend the whole winter in a place, usu. without being able to leave: [IØ] *Once the ice comes, the ship will have to winter over; do we have enough supplies?* —**overwinter** *v*

**wipe away** *v adv*

to remove (something) by rubbing, as with a hand or cloth: [X9 + AWAY] *We tried to wipe away all signs of our presence. "And God shall wipe away all tears from their eyes; and there shall be no more death, neither sorrow, nor crying, neither shall there be any more pain: and the former things are passed away."* (The Bible)

**wipe off**[1] *v adv*

**1** to remove (something such as a mark) by rubbing, usu. with a cloth: [X9 + OFF] *Here's a brush to wipe off the mud before you come into the house.*

**2** *AmE* to clean (something) after use, as with a cloth: [T1 + OFF] *Don't forget to wipe off the sink when you've finished the dishes.* → **wipe out** (1)

*__3__ to put an end to (something such as a debt): [T1 (*often simple tenses*)] *Generously, he agreed to wipe off their small debt to him as a mark of respect for their dead father.* → **wipe out** (3)

**4 wipe off old scores** to settle a long-standing argument and be friends again; pay someone back for a wrong: [*usu. simple tenses*] *After* *years of family fighting, the uncles agreed to wipe off old scores so that their children could marry. I shan't rest till I've wiped off all the old scores against me.* → **wipe out** (6)

**wipe off²** *v prep*

**1** to remove (something such as a mark) from (a surface): [X9 + *off*] *I'm sorry, I wiped those words off the chalkboard before I remembered that you wanted them left on.*

**2 wipe someone/something off the face of the earth** to make someone or something disappear completely and be forgotten: [*usu. pass.*] *People who treat other people like that deserve to be wiped off the face of the earth. This evil practice should be wiped off the face of the earth.*

**3 wipe something off the map** to destroy the existence of something: [*often simple tenses*] *The enemy were determined to wipe the town off the map as if it had never been.*

**4 wipe something off the slate** to pay for something owed; pay a debt, as of service: *"He's out on active service, wiping something off a slate."* (Rudyard Kipling, *The Absent-Minded Beggar*)

**wipe out** *v adv*

**1** to clean (something such as a container) after use, as with a cloth: [T1 + OUT] *Don't forget to wipe out the sink when you've finished the dishes. We always wipe the bottles out before returning them to the milkman.* → **wipe off¹** (2)

***2** to destroy (something) or kill (someone, usu. a group): [T1] *The arms factory has been wiped out by our bombs. These tropical diseases can wipe out the populations of whole villages.* —**wipe-out** *n*

***3** to put an end to (something): [T1 (*often simple tenses*)] *This last payment will wipe out your debt to me. We must make every effort to wipe out injustice in the system. Your generous gift has helped to wipe out our loss.* → **wipe off¹** (3)

***4** esp. *AmE* (in surfing) to be thrown from one's board by a wave: [IØ (*usu. simple tenses*)] *Yes, it was fun, but I wiped out twice.* —**wipe-out** *n*

**5 be wiped out** *not fml* to be drunk: *It's no use trying to talk sense to him, he's wiped out.*

**6 wipe out old scores** to settle a long-standing argument and be friends again; pay someone back for a wrong: [*usu. simple tenses*] *After years of family fighting, the uncles agreed to wipe out the old scores so that their children could marry. I shan't rest until I've wiped out all the old scores against me.* →**wipe off¹** (4)

**wipe over** *v adv; prep*

to clean (a surface), as with a cloth; pass (a cloth) over (a surface) to clean it: [T1 + OVER] *Make sure the table top is properly wiped over before you put the cloth on.* [L9 + *over*] *Have you wiped over the table properly?* [X9 + *over*] *By wiping the dirty cloth over the window, you've left more marks than bef* —**wipe-over** *n*

**wipe up** *v adv*

**1** to remove (liquid) from a surface, as with cloth: [X9 + UP] *You'd better wipe up th milk on the floor before someone slips in it.* → **mop up** (1)

**2** *BrE* to dry (dishes) after washing; dry dishes: [T1 + UP] *Will you wipe these plates up? I've no more room here.* [IØ + UP] *You wash up, and I'll wipe up.*

***3** to deal with or destroy (a defeated enemy): [T1] *It's a small enemy force; we should be able to wipe it up in no time.* → **mop up** (2)

**wipe with** *v prep*

**1** to clean (something such as a surface) by rubbing with (a cloth); use (a cloth) for cleaning: [T1 + *with*] *I like to wipe the windows with a very soft cloth.* [IØ + *with*] *Use this old cloth to wipe with.* → **mop with** (1)

**2 wipe the floor/ground with** *not fml* to defeat (someone) completely: *A team as good as ours should be able to wipe the floor with any competitor.* → **mop with** (2)

**3 wipe the floor with** *not fml* to scold someone severely: *I could hear the director wiping the floor with Jim for being late every morning this week.* → **tell off** (1), etc.

**wire for** *v prep*

to provide (a building or room) with wires to provide (something such as electricity): [T1 + *for* (*usu. pass.*)] *Has this meeting room been properly wired for sound?*

**wire in** *v adv*

**1** to fix wires to join (electrical machinery) (to a main supply); join (wires): [T1 + IN (*to*) (*usu. pass.*)] *Are both ends wired in yet? The cooker is not yet wired in to the main supply.*

***2** *old use not fml* to begin to work actively: [IØ (*usu. simple tenses*)] *All the family wired in and soon the job was finished.*

**wire off** *v adv*

to send (a message or money) by telegraph; send a telegraph message: [T1 + OFF (*often simple tenses*)] *I wired the money off at once as soon as I got your request.* [IØ + OFF (*for*)] *I shall have to wire off for some more money.*

**wire up** *v adv*

to provide (a building) with an electrical supply: [T1 + UP (*usu. pass.*)] *The house has recently been wired up, so we can cook by electricity now.*

***wise up** *v adv*

esp. *AmE not fml* to (cause to) learn or use common sense: [IØ (*often imper.*)] *Wise up! Don't you understand what he's trying to do to you?* [T1 (*usu. simple tenses*)] *I think you'd better wise that young man up, he's helpless!*

**wish away** *v adv*

**1** to continue to express one's wishes: [IØ + AWAY (*often continuous tenses*)] *It's no use just wishing away for week after week, you have to take some action!*

*2 to desire (something or someone) to leave; try to make (someone or something) disappear by wishing: [T1 (*usu. simple tenses*)] *It would be nice, wouldn't it, if we could wish this terrible weather away and make the sun shine! With all her heart, she wished him away, but he refused to go. She kissed the child's knee and said that she would wish the pain away.*

**wish for** *v prep*
to desire (usu. something): [IØ + *for*] *The fisherman wished for a new house, but he was soon sorry. This city has everything that one could wish for, except good weather.*

***wish ill** *v adv* → **wish well**
to hope that (someone) will have bad luck or bad health: [T1b (*usu. simple tenses*)] *Why don't you forgive her? It only does you harm as well to wish her ill for so long.* [IØ (*to*) (*usu. simple tenses*)] *I wish ill to no one except those who intentionally offend me.* —**illwisher** *n*

**wish on/upon** *v prep*
**1** to use (something) as a means or hope of obtaining a wish: [IØ + *on/upon*] *'When you wish upon a star.'* (song)
*2 to cause (something bad or someone unwanted) to trouble (someone): [D1 (*usu. simple tenses*)] *I wouldn't wish such an illness on my worst enemy. I had my old aunt wished on me for a whole week!* also **wish onto**

***wish well** *v adv* → **wish ill**
to hope that (someone) will have good luck, health, etc.; express support for (someone): [T1b (*usu. simple tenses*)] *I wish you well in your future with the other firm. She has a pleasant nature and seems to wish everyone well.* —**wellwisher** *n*

**withdraw from** *v prep*
**1** to (cause to) leave (something such as a position formerly held): [IØ + *from*] *Why is Jim withdrawing from the race? The speaker agreed to withdraw from the position that he had just stated. Tell the men to withdraw from their new position.* [T1 + *from*] *I wish to withdraw my name from the guest list. She withdrew her eyes from the terrible sight. We must withdraw the children from that unsuitable school. Our forces have been withdrawn from the danger area.*
**2** to take (money) out of (a bank account, etc.): [T1 + *from*] *I would like to withdraw $30 from my savings account and put it in my cheque account.*

**withdraw into** *v prep* → **retire into**
to try to leave reality and find peace in (a quality or oneself): [IØ + *into*] *Mary hates parties and always looks for a chance to withdraw into herself and not speak to people.*

**wither away** *v adv*
to cease gradually to exist or be worthwhile: [IØ + AWAY] *Older people are complaining that the old values are withering away in this free society.*

**wither up** *v adv*
**1** (usu. of an arm, hand, etc.) to cease to have life and become lined and dry: [IØ + UP] *After the accident, his left arm withered up and became useless.*
*2 (of a feeling) to cease; become less warm: [IØ] *All her former pity had withered up through bitter experience.*

**withhold from** *v prep*
**1** to keep (something) back from (usu. someone): [T1 + *from*] *I think you are withholding the truth from me; please tell me, however painful it is. The employers have to withhold the tax from your pay before you receive it.*
*2 *fml* to prevent oneself, as with patience, from (something or doing something): [T1 (*no pass., simple tenses*)] *How shall I withhold from tears when we part?* [T4 (*simple tenses*)] *It is often difficult to withhold from expressing one's opinion.* → **forbear from** (1), **refrain from** (1)

**witness for** *v prep*
**witness for Christ** to declare one's faith in Christ: *More people at our meeting today came forward to witness for Christ.*

***witness to** *v prep*
**1** to declare the truth of (something), as in court: [T1 (*often continuous tenses*)] *How many people have witnessed to the prisoner's good character?* → **testify to** (1).
**2** to prove (something) by showing it clearly: [T1 (*simple tenses*)] *His actions witness to his trustworthiness. The material she writes witnesses to her abilities.* also **bear to** → **testify to** (2)

**wobble about/around** *v adv*
to move unsteadily: [IØ + ABOUT/AROUND] *You can tell he's never ridden a bicycle before by the way he's wobbling about on it. After a week in the hospital bed, I was only able to wobble around a bit.*

**wolf down** *v adv*
*not fml* to eat (food) eagerly: [T1 + DOWN] *That boy wolfed down the whole cake, while my back was turned!*

**wonder about** *v prep*
to think about what (something or someone) might be; think about the possibility of (something or doing something); think about (something or someone) that one wishes to know: [IØ + *about*] *Do you often wonder about the future of the world? I sometimes wonder about my old friend, where she is now and what she's doing. I'm still wondering about taking a further degree. I often wonder about why she treated me like that.*

***wonder at** *v prep* → **marvel at**
to be surprised by (something): [T1 (*usu. simple tenses*)] *I wonder at your rudeness, when I have always been so kind to you. A severe winter like this is not to be wondered at, in view of the summer we've had. I don't won-*

*der at your shock! I wonder at your nerve in asking him directly!* [V4a (*usu. simple tenses*)] *I don't wonder at her falling asleep in the middle of the play, it was a very uninteresting performance.* [D5 (*usu. simple tenses*)] *Can you wonder at it that he should be so angry? That the criminal was caught so quickly is not to be wondered at.*

***woo away** *v adv*
to persuade (someone) to leave (someone or a group): [T1 (*from*)] *You had no business wooing her away from her husband. This product will help to woo our customers away from our competitors.*

**work against** *v prep*
**1** to put effort into opposing (something): [IØ + *against*] *Some members of the other party are working against suggested changes in the law.*
***2** to cause or increase the chance of failure of (someone or something): [T1 (*no pass.*)] *Time is working against you. His appearance works against his chance of success as a politician.*

**work among** *v prep*
to do social work with (a group or type of people): [IØ + *among*] *For the first year of his training, he had to work among the poor in his home town.*

***work around to** *v adv prep* → **WORK ROUND TO**

**work as** *v prep*
to perform the duties of (a kind of worker): [IØ + *as*] *It must be a hard life, working as a nurse in the far North. Before making a success of his writing, he worked as a taxidriver, a newspaper seller, a miner, and a railwayman.*

**work at** *v prep*
**1** to have one's job in (a place): [IØ + *at*] *How long have you been working at the bank?*
**2** to put effort into (something or doing something): [IØ + *at*] *You will have to work at the weak points in your English if you want to pass the examination. Is Tom still working at the new book that he promised? I want to work at perfecting my style before trying anything new.* → **toil at, work on²** (2)
**3 work at it** *not fml* to continue with an attempt, as to change something: *I haven't yet persuaded the director to accept my suggestions, but don't worry, I'm still working at it!* → **work on²** (5)

**work away** *v adv*
**1** to work continuously: [IØ + AWAY (*at, on*) (*often continuous tenses*)] *Is Tom still working away on that new book? You've been working away since the early hours of this morning, and I think you should stop for the good of your health.*
**2** (usu. of part of the face such as the mouth) to keep making small movements: [IØ + AWAY (*usu. continuous tenses*)] *Her mouth was working away all the time he was speaking: I think she was trying not to laugh!*

**work by** *v prep* → **go by²** (2), **run on²** (2)
(of a machine) to use (something) as its power for working: [IØ + *by* (*simple tenses*)] *The chid thought the toy car worked by magic, but in fact it worked by electricity.*

**work down** *v adv*
**1** to reduce (something) gradually: [T1 + DOWN (*usu. pass.*)] *The metal has become worked down over the years.*
**2** to become gradually lower: [IØ + DOWN] *If you can get onto the branch below you, you could work down from there.*
***3** to descend socially or professionally: [IØ] *Most of us have to start at the bottom and work up; but some people use their time and money badly and start at the top only to work down to the proper level of their poor abilities.* → **work up** (6)

**work for** *v prep*
**1** to be employed by (someone such as a company): [IØ + *for*] *How long have you been working for this firm?* → **labour for** (1)
**2** to do one's job so as to gain (money or a purpose): [IØ + *for*] *The girls in the match factories used to work for a few pennies a day. The politician declared his willingness to work for the good of the people. Leaders of many nations are still working for peace.* → **labour for** (2)

**work in¹** *v adv*
**1** to (cause to) be able to enter gradually or with effort: [L9 + IN (*to*)] *The dust still works in however we try to cover the furniture.* [X9 + IN (*to*)] *You may have to work the needle in, the cloth is very stiff.*
***2** to be able to include (something), as in writing or speaking, by a clever arrangement of words: [T1 (*to*) (*usu. simple tenses*)] *Were you able to work in a mention of your latest book? Try to work in a few jokes when you are preparing your speech.*
**3 work oneself in** to get used to a job: *Don't worry, you'll do quite well once you've worked yourself in.*

**work in²** *v prep*
**1** to have one's job in (a place or type of work): [IØ + *in*] *Many people no longer wish to work in London. How long have you been working in marketing?*
**2** to make (something) from (a material); do one's work using (a material): [T1 + *in*] *These little jewel boxes are worked in fine leather.* [IØ + *in*] *I only work in the best wood.*

***work in with** *v adv prep*
to (cause to) be able to join in work with (other people or ideas): [T1 (*no pass.*)] *But will he be able to work in with our existing team?* [D1] *I'll try to work my timetable in with yours.*

**work into** *v prep*
**1** to (cause to) enter (something such as material) or fit (a space) by gradual move-

ment: [L9 + *into*] *The mark will have worked right into the wood, we shall never get it out.* [X9 + *into*] *I really had to work the needle into the cloth, it was so stiff. I shall need someone to help me work this board into place, it's a tight fit.*

*__2__ to make (someone or oneself) reach (a state of mind, usu. violent): [D1] *Have you ever seen him work himself into a temper? The speaker worked the crowd into a fever of excitement.*

*__3__ to be able to include (something) in (something usu. written or spoken), by a clever arrangement of words: [D1 (*usu. simple tenses*)] *Were you able to work a mention of your latest book into your broadcast? I hope you can work a few jokes into your speech to make it more interesting.*

***work it** *v pron*
*not fml* to make an effort, often unlawful, to be sure of a result: [IØ (*simple tenses*)] *Leave it to me, I'll see if I can work it.* [I5 (*simple tenses*)] *I think I can work it so that you won't have to leave.*

***work loose** *v adj*
to (cause to) become gradually unfixed: [IØ] *The board had been working loose for several months, and in the end it slid to one side, showing a hole underneath.* [T1] *If you can work the nail loose, I could pull it out.*

**work nights** *v adv*
*not fml* to have a job in which one works regularly at night: [IØ + NIGHTS] *He's working nights this month, so he needs to rest during the day.*

**work off** *v adv*
**1** to (cause to) become loose and fall off by gradual movement: [L9 + OFF] *The handle has worked off, it's useless now.* [X9 + OFF] *Can you work this lid off, it seems to be stuck?*

*__2__ to (cause to) cease through working or movement: [T1] *You can work off the stiffness with some exercise. I was trying to work off a few pounds.* [IØ] *The pain worked off when I started walking.*

*__3__ to finish (something) by working: [T1] *I hope to work off most of the urgent letters by tomorrow. How long does it take to work off the requirements for the degree?*

*__4__ to put an end to (something) by working: [T1] *Heavy work with your hands will help to work off your anger.*

*__5__ to pay (a debt) with work instead of money: [T1] *He offered to work off the debt, but I needed the money more.* → **work out** (11)

**6 work one's head off** *not fml* to work very hard: *How can you say I'm lazy? I've been working my head off to get this book finished!*

**7 work off steam** to get rid of feelings, usu. bad, by activity: *I go out for a long walk when I feel anxious, it helps me to work off steam.*

***work off on** *v adv prep* → **take out of** (9), **take out on, vent on**
to express (usu. one's anger) by making (someone else) suffer for it: [D1] *There's no need to work your bad temper off on your children, they're not to blame for the way you feel!*

**work on¹** *v adv*
to work continuously: [IØ + ON] *I'll just have to stay in the office and work on until the report is ready, it's urgently required for tomorrow's meeting.*

**work on/upon²** *v prep*
**1** to make (something such as a pattern) appear on (a surface) by working, as with a needle, knife, etc: [T1 + *on/upon*] *What a pretty rose pattern you've worked on the tablecloth!*

**2** to have (something) as the subject of thought or effort: [IØ + *on/upon*] *You will have to work on the weak points in your English if you want to pass the examination. Is Tom still working on the new book that he promised? I want to work on perfecting my style before trying anything new. The scientists are still working on inventing new methods of reaching outer space.* → **work at** (2)

*__3__ to have an effect on (someone or someone's feelings, etc.): [T1 (*no pass., usu. simple tenses*)] *The added struggle worked on his already weakened heart. The sight of so much suffering worked on our hearts so that we were filled with pity.*

*__4__ *not fml* to attempt to influence (someone): [T1 (*no pass.*)] *Can you work on the director? He might accept our suggestion if someone works on him properly.*

**5 work on it** *not fml* to continue with an attempt, as to change something: *I haven't yet persuaded the director to change his mind, but don't worry, I'm still working on it.* → **work at** (3)

**6 work one's will on** *old use* to persuade (someone), often forcefully, to do what one wants: *The Prince would work his will on the people without mercy.*

**work out** *v adv*
**1** to (cause to) come out of something by gradual movement: [L9 + OUT (*of*)] *There's a piece of dust in your eye but it should work out by itself.* [X9 + OUT] *The coin has fallen through a hole in the pocket; I'll see if I can work it out.*

*__2__ to calculate (something): [T1] *Father is still trying to work out his tax.* [T5] *It didn't take her long to work out that she would soon have no money left.* [T6] *Can you work out how much it costs to feed the average family? I'll work out when the last payment will be and let you know.* → **figure out** (1)

*__3__ to invent, develop, or produce (something such as an idea) by thinking: [T1] *We must work out a better method of saving paper.*

*We'll leave it to the committee to work out the details of the plan.* [T6] *Did you work out how to cheat in the examination?*

***4** to (cause to) reach an answer, as by working: [T1] *I can't work out this sum.* [IØ] *This sum won't work out.* → **come out** (10), **get out** (15)

***5** to understand (usu. something), as by working: [T1 (*often simple tenses*)] *I can't work out the meaning of this poem. The government employs men with special abilities to work out the enemy's secret messages. New students spend hours in the library, trying to work out the system of arranging the books.* [T5 (*usu. simple tenses*)] *This map is wrong, I can't work out where we are. When did you work out that he had been lying to you?* [T6 (*usu. simple tenses*)] *He could not work out whether he was in the right city. No one can work out how the fire started.* → **figure out** (2), **make out** (3), **puzzle out**

***6** to decide or find an answer to (something such as a difficulty): [T1] *At your age, you should be able to work out your own future. We do have trouble in our relationship, but I feel that we can work it out between us without professional help. Don't worry, I'll work things out. These forces are working themselves out in the Labour Party.*

***7** to result; develop; succeed: [IØ] *Did your plan work out? I'm sure things will work out for the best in the end. The book seems to be working out quite well so far.* → **pan out** (4)

***8** to finish all possible use of (something such as a supply): [T1 (*usu. pass.*)] *This old mine was worked out long ago.* → **farm out** (5), **fish out** (3), **lay in¹** (4), **mine out**

***9** to exercise: [IØ] *The famous actor keeps fit by working out for an hour every morning.* —**workout** *n*

***10** to pass (time) in work: [T1] *Most of the men would rather work out their time in prison than sit around doing nothing. The boys are encouraged to work out part of their period of training on the job.*

***11** *AmE* to pay (a debt) with work instead of money: [T1] *He offered to work out the debt, but I needed the money more.* → **work off** (5)

**12 work out one's own salvation** to be responsible for saving oneself, esp. in a moral or religious sense; finish something with effort: *The Bible tells Christians to work out their own salvation.*

***work out as/to** *v adv prep* → **come out at, run out at**

(of a calculation) to amount to or reach (a sum): [L1 (*simple tenses*)] *The actual cost may work out at rather more than we now expect. The total area works out to 25,000 square miles.*

**work over** *v adv*

**1** esp. *AmE* to redo (something such as work): [T1 + OVER] *Every time I work the sum over, I get a different answer. I shall have to work the report over if it's not satisfactory.*

***2** *infml* to attack and wound (someone): [T1b] *When they had worked him over for some minutes, they left him for dead, and escaped.* —**working-over** *n* → **beat up** (2), etc.

***work round¹** *v adv*

**1** (usu. of the wind) to change direction: [IØ] *We can't get the boat into the harbour tonight unless the wind works round.*

**2** to change one's opinion (to another point of view): [IØ (*to*)] *I think the chairman is working round to our point of view after all.*

**work round²** *v prep*

**work round the clock** to work all day and all night: *With this sudden rush of orders, we can only get the goods ready if the factory works round the clock.*

***work round to** *v adv prep* also **work around to**

**1** to reach (something or doing something) gradually: [T1 (*no pass.*)] *I haven't had time to start the new article yet, but I'm working round to it.* [T4] *Don't hurry me, I shall work round to finishing the letters all in good time.*

**2** to prepare to say (something); gradually get near (saying something): [T1] *What is she working round to? The speaker took far too long working round to his main point.* [T4] *It takes a long time to work round to mentioning a possible increase in pay.* → **lead up to** (5), **work up to** (3)

**work through** *v prep*

**1** to (cause to) pass through (something) by gradual movement: [L9 + *through*] *The rain is still working through the roof.* [X9 + *through*] *It was difficult to work the needle through the stiff cloth.*

***2** to finish working at (something): [T1] *I'm still working through this pile of papers. We must work through the difficulties until we find an answer.*

**3 work one's way through** to advance through (something): *It takes years to work your way through the examination system until you gain a degree. She paid for her own education by working her way through college.*

**work to** *v prep*

**1** to work while usu. hearing (something): [IØ + *to*] *Do you like working to music?*

**2** to plan one's work so as to obey or fit (a plan or limit, as of time or length): [IØ + *to*] *Some writers are at their best when working to a plan. Working quickly does not improve the quality of the work.* → **write to** (4)

**3 work someone/an animal to death** to force someone or an animal to work too hard and become very tired: *The company expects hard work, but refuses to work its employees to death.*

**4 work something to death** *not fml* to overuse something such as an idea: *Don't copy that writer's ideas, the story he uses has been worked to death many times and is no longer interesting.*

**5 work one's fingers to the bone** *not fml* to

work very hard: *Why should you sit around being lazy all day while I'm stuck in here, working my fingers to the bone?*

**6 work to rule** esp. *BrE* to refuse to work harder or longer than the rules allow; work intentionally slowly as a form of strike: *Our flight may be delayed in landing, as the air-traffic controllers are working to rule again in support of their demand for better working conditions and shorter hours.* —**work-to-rule** *n* → **go slow** (3)

**work together** *v adv*

**1** to work in the same place: [IØ + TOGETHER] *Some people think that husband and wife should never work together.*

*__2__ to unite; join in an effort; support each other; agree when working: [IØ (*usu. simple tenses*)] *If two people can't work together in this department, one of them will have to leave the firm. "All things work together for good to them that love God."* (The Bible)

**work towards** *v prep*

to direct one's work in order to reach (an aim or doing something): [IØ + *towards*] *Representatives of many nations at the peace talks are working towards agreement. They are working towards having all countries sign a peace agreement.*

**work under** *v prep*

**1** to have one's job beneath (something): [IØ + *under*] *The worst of being a miner is working under the ground, and not seeing the sun or feeling fresh air.* → **labour under** (1)

**2** to have (someone) as one's director in one's job: [IØ + *under*] *Many men still don't like working under a woman, and would rather have a male director.*

**work up** *v adv*

**1** to (cause to) rise by gradual movement: [L9 + UP] *That nail in my shoe has been working up and hurting my foot; I must hammer it down.* [X9 + UP] *If you screw the frame too tightly, it will work the metal up and make a mark on the paper.* —**work-up** *n*

*__2__ to (cause to) develop or increase: [T1] *He has worked this business up from small beginnings. It took years to work up a successful act in this form of theatre.* [IØ] *His law practice is beginning to work up at last. Support from party members has been working up recently. The wind is working up for a storm.*

*__3__ to excite (the feelings of oneself or others): [T1 (*into, to*)] *Don't let the child work up his anger, turn his attention to something else. A really powerful speaker can work up the feelings of the crowd to a fever of excitement. Don't mention the letter to her, I don't want her to work up any false hopes.* —**worked-up** *adj* → **get up** (8)

*__4__ to make (someone or oneself) excited, nervous, or anxious: [T1 (*often pass.*)] *I have to work myself up to face the examiners. Don't get all worked up over nothing.* —**worked-up, wrought-up** *adj* → **steam up** (2)

*__5__ to gain skill or information about (something such as a subject); complete: [T1] *It takes experience to work up a knowledge of sailing. I have to work up the history of music for my broadcast. I must go and work up my notes ready for the test.* → **get up** (9)

*__6__ to advance (one's way), as in business: [IØ (*to*)] *With her ability, it shouldn't take her long to work up to the directorship.* [T1] *Most young men have to start at the bottom and work their way up.* → **work down** (3)

**7 work up an appetite** to act so as to make oneself feel hungry: *I think I'll go for a walk to work up an appetite for the meal that you've promised.* → **get up** (15)

**8 work up an appetite for** *not fml* to begin to want (something or doing something): *I have to make an effort to work up an appetite for teaching every day.* → **get up** (16)

**9 work up steam** *not fml* to become more active; make an effort: *Can't you work up enough steam to get out of bed in the morning?* → **get up** (21)

***work up into** *v adv prep*

**1** to excite (someone) so as to reach (a state): [T1 (*into*)] *Our speaker can easily work any crowd up into a fever of excitement.*

**2** to develop (written material) into (a full form): [T1 (*into*)] *Can you work up your notes into an article for our magazine?*

**3** to form (material) into (a shape): [D1] *His skilled hands soon worked the clay up into a pot.*

**work up to** *v adv prep*

**1** to excite (someone) so as to reach (a state): [T1 + UP + *to*] *Our speaker can easily work any crowd up to a fever of excitement.*

*__2__ to begin to reach (a high point): [T1 (*no pass.*)] *Soon the engine was working up to its top speed. By working up to our greatest effort, we can get the job finished on time.*

*__3__ to prepare to say (something); gradually get near (saying something): [T1] *What is she working up to? The speaker took far too long working up to his main point.* [T4] *It takes a long time to work up to mentioning more pay.* → **lead up to** (5), **work round to** (2)

**work upon** *v prep* → **WORK ON**[2]

**work with** *v prep*

**1** to have the company and help of (someone) in one's job: [IØ + *with*] *I find it so refreshing to work with young people in this department.*

**2** to be able to work in agreement with (someone): [IØ + *with* (*usu. simple tenses*)] *If you can't work with the other women, you will have to leave.*

**3** to have (someone, usu. a group) as the object of one's work: [IØ + *with*] *One of the advantages of teaching is that it's so rewarding to work with children.*

**4** to use (something) as an object or tool in one's work or thinking: [IØ + *with*] *He has always liked working with machinery. Plants* *seem to know if you like working with them. Do you like working with your head or your hands? I would rather work with the bigger brush, it's faster.*

**5** to dig (soil), sew (needlework), or act on (a material) by working, using (something) as a tool or means: [T1 + *with*] *It's hard, working this soil with such an old spade. You can't work a fine pattern with a thick needle and wool, you need silk and a sharp point. He likes working the clay with his hands.*

***work wonders** *v n*

to be remarkably successful: [IØ (*usu. simple tenses*)] *This new drug works wonders on formerly incurable diseases, the doctors are saying.*

**worm in** *v adv*

**1** to enter a narrow space by twisting slowly: [L9 + IN (*to*)] *The thieves must have wormed in through the narrow space between the boards in the hall cupboard.*

***2** *not fml* to enter by indirect, often dishonest, means: [IØ (*to*)] *Don't let any nonmembers worm in.*

**3 worm one's way in(to): a** to enter by twisting or effort: *How did the thieves worm their way in?* **b** *not fml* to make oneself accepted (in something) by degrees or through one's effort; become part (of something) indirectly: *Some of these people are not members and must have wormed their way in (to the meeting). Over the years, he wormed his way into the director's favour.*

**worm out of** *v adv prep*

**1** to leave a narrow space by twisting slowly: [L9 + OUT + *of*] *How did the prisoner worm out of the hole where we trapped him?* [X9 + OUT + *of*] *The rabbits must have wormed their way out of the cage by bending the wire.* → **get out of** (7)

***2** to obtain (information) from (someone), usu. by indirect means: [D1] *Her sister was very clever at worming her secrets out of her.* → **get out of** (8)

***3** to avoid or escape from (one's responsibilities, etc., or doing something): [T1 (*no pass.*)] *How is she going to worm out of the charge? That boy is always trying to worm out of the jobs I give him to do in the house.* [T4] *How can I worm out of giving that report?* → **get out of** (13), etc.

**worry about/over** *v prep* → **trouble about**

**1** to have (something or someone) as the cause or object of deep concern: [IØ + *about/over*] *Why worry about the future? There's nothing you can do about it! She's always worrying over stupid little things that don't really matter. Are you at all worried about your health? There's no sense in worrying about the boy, he'll be all right.*

**2 worry oneself sick/silly about/over** to be greatly anxious about (something or someone): *Some students worry themselves sick over the coming examinations, and so don't do as well as they should. All parents worry themselves silly over their children.*

***worry along/through** *v adv* → **get by**[1] (2), etc.

*not fml* to live in spite of difficulties: [IØ (*usu. simple tenses*)] *Don't be nervous about me, I'll worry along somehow. In spite of her fears, she always worried through.*

***worry at** *v prep*

to pull and twist at (something), as nervously or playfully: [T1 (*no pass.*)] *You can tell how nervous she is by the way her fingers worry at the edge of the tablecloth. I could see the dog in the garden, worrying at a bone.*

***worry out** *v adv*

**1** to get (something such as an answer) by worrying or thinking: [T1 (*often simple tenses*)] *I've been trying to worry out an answer to our difficulty, but I've no more ideas —can you help?*

**2** to get (something) by patiently repeated questioning (from someone): [T1 (*of*) (*often simple tenses*)] *The children worried the necessary permission out of their father.*

**worry over** *v prep* → WORRY ABOUT

**worry through** *v adv* → WORRY ALONG

**wrangle about/over** *v prep* → **quarrel about**, etc.

to disagree, often violently or unpleasantly, on the subject of (usu. something): [IØ + *about/over*] *Let us not wrangle about such unimportant matters. When she died, her family spent months wrangling over the property.*

**wrap around/round** *v prep*

to fold (something or itself) so as to surround (something or someone): [T1 + *around/round*] *You'd better wrap a clean cloth around your arm till the wound closes. I like to feel you wrapping your arms around me. This skirt is made so that you can wrap it around your waist, so it will fit any size.* [IØ + *around/round* (*simple tenses*)] *These sunglasses wrap around your eyes to protect them on all sides.* —**wraparound** *n, adj*

**wrap in** *v prep*

**1** to enfold (something or someone) in (usu. paper or cloth): [T1 + *in*] *Have you wrapped Father's present in pretty paper? The baby was wrapped in wool clothes and was far too hot on such a sunny day.* → **envelop in** (1), **swathe in** (1)

***2** to surround (something) with (something such as clouds or mist): [D1 (*usu. pass.*)] *You could not see the tops of the mountains, as they were always wrapped in clouds.* → **envelop in** (2), **swathe in** (2)

***3** to surround (something) with (a quality): [D1 (*usu. pass.*)] *The whole business is wrapped in mystery.* → **envelop in** (3), **swathe in** (3)

**wrap round** *v prep* → WRAP AROUND

**wrap up** *v adv*

**1** to enfold (something), as in a parcel: [T1

+ UP (*in*)] *If you wrap the books up for me, I'll take them to the post office.* → **bundle up** (1), **parcel up**

*2 to (cause to) wear warm clothing: [T1] *Be sure the children are well wrapped up in this sudden cold weather.* [IØ] *In this cold wind, you'd be wise to wrap up well.* → **bundle up** (2), **muffle up** (4)

*3 *not fml* to close (a business); complete (an agreement); bring (an event) to an end: [T1] *Well, that just about wraps it up for another Saturday afternoon's popular music broadcast.* —**wrap-up** *n, adj*

*4 *not fml* to produce a report at the close of (something): [T1] *I can't wrap up the peace talks in less than fifty pages.* —**wrap-up** *n*

*5 *infml* to be quiet, esp. in the phr. **wrap it up**: [IØ (*simple tenses, usu. imper.*)] *Wrap up, you boys, I can't hear myself think!* [T1 (*simple tenses, usu. imper.*)] *Wrap it up, you lot, we've heard enough of your complaints.* → **shut up** (4), etc.

**wrap up in** *v adv prep*

1 to enfold (something such as goods) in (usu. paper or cloth): [T1 + UP + *in*] *If you wrap up the cooking pot in hot cloths, you can keep it warm on the journey.*

*2 to (cause to) dress warmly in (warm clothing): [T1 (*in*)] *Be sure to wrap up the children in lots of wool.* [IØ (*in*)] *If you wrap up in several garments, you will keep warm.*

3 **be wrapped up in** to give one's whole attention to (something): *It's no use trying to talk to Father when he's wrapped up in his work.* → **absorb in**, etc.

**wreak on/upon** *v prep* → **get even**, etc.

**wreak vengeance on/upon** *fml* to return a wrong to (someone) who has wronged oneself: [*usu. simple tenses*] *Hamlet was determined to wreak vengeance on his uncle, by killing him in return for his father's murder.*

**wreathe around/round** *v prep* → **twist around**[2] (1), **wind around** (1)

*fml* to (cause to) surround (something) by twisting: [L9 + *around/round*] *Look at that snake wreathing around the pole.* [X9 + *around/round*] *Let us wreathe the flowers around a wire frame.*

**wreathe in** *v prep*

1 *fml* to surround (something) with (something in a circle): [X9 + *in* (*often pass.*)] *The people used to wreathe the conqueror's head in leaves. The tops of the mountains were always wreathed in mist.*

2 **be wreathed in** to be covered with an expression of (something): *Her face was wreathed in smiles as she ran to greet him.*

**wreathe into** *v prep*

*fml* to form (usu. flowers or leaves) into (a shape): [X9 + *into*] *It was part of her job at the flower shop to wreathe flowers into ornaments for people's doors at Christmas time.*

**wreathe round** *v prep* → WREATHE AROUND

**wrench from** *v prep* → **wrench off, wrest off**

to seize (something or someone) by force from (someone or something): [X9 + *from* (*usu. simple tenses*)] *Pulling hard, she unintentionally wrenched the handle from the door. With an effort, she wrenched herself from his hold and ran off. All the noblemen tried to wrench the sword from the stone, but only the true king was able to do so because of the magic in it.*

**wrench off** *v adv; prep* → **wrench from, wrest off**

to pull (something) off (something) by force: [X9 + OFF/*off* (*usu. simple tenses*)] *I pulled hard on the handle to open the door, and accidentally wrenched it off! I had to wrench the lid off the barrel, it was stuck tight.*

***wrest from** *v prep*

1 to seize (something or someone) from (someone) with a struggle: [D1 (*usu. simple tenses*)] *How brave of you to wrest the knife from the murderer! You will need a court order to wrest the child from his mother.*

2 to remove (something such as a quality) from (usu. someone): [D1 (*usu. simple tenses*)] *Knowledgeable people can easily wrest advantage from the law. The people had to fight to wrest power from their rulers. It took a clever lawyer to wrest an admission of guilt from the prisoner.*

3 to gain (something such as a reward) with difficulty from (usu. something): [D1] *Farmers have always had a struggle to wrest a living from the soil.*

**wrest off** *v adv; prep* → **wrench from, wrench off**

to pull (something) violently off (something): [X9 + OFF/*off* (*usu. simple tenses*)] *He had to use all his strength to wrest the lid off* (*the barrel*).

**wrestle into** *v prep*

to struggle to move (something) into (usu. a position): [X9 + *into*] *It took four men to wrestle the heavy rock into place.*

**wrestle with** *v prep*

1 to fight (someone) by holding him, trying to throw him to the ground using esp. one's arms: [IØ + *with*] *Is it wise for the boy to offer to wrestle with such an experienced opponent, however much money he is offered?*

*2 to have difficulty in carrying or dealing with (something, esp. heavy or awkward); oppose (someone): [T1] *Can't you help that woman wrestling with that heavy parcel? "But God, . . . wrestled with him, and . . . marked him; marked him for his own."* (Izaak Walton, *Life of Donne*)

*3 to have an inner battle with (oneself, one's conscience, or feelings): [T1] *After wrestling with myself for some days, I decided to accept her offer. For years she bravely wrestled with her fears until at last she conquered them. You* *could almost see him still wrestling with doubt.* → **struggle with** (2), etc.

**wriggle out of** *v adv prep*

**1** to be able to leave (a place) by twisting one's body; make (one's way) from (somewhere) with difficulty: [IØ + OUT + *of*] *That dog has wriggled out of the garden gate again!* [X9 + OUT + *of*] *How did the prisoners wriggle their way out of the prison camp?* → **get out of** (7)

***2** *not fml* to avoid or escape (something such as a duty or doing something): [T1] *You promised me you would finish the painting, and you're not going to wriggle out of it now! He always finds a way to wriggle out of punishment.* [T4] *How did you wriggle out of washing the car?* → **get out of** (13), etc.

**wring from** *v prep*

**1** to get (liquid) out of (something such as cloth) by twisting it: [T1 + *from*] *Make sure you wring all the dirty water from the cloth before washing it.*

***2** to get (something) by force or with difficulty from (usu. someone): [D1 (*usu. simple tenses*)] *The clever lawyer at last wrung the truth from the prisoner. Were you able to wring any more information from the guard? I expect I can wring a little more money from my aunt.* → **wring out** (2)

**wring out** *v adv*

**1** to twist (a cloth or garment) so as to remove liquid: [T1 + OUT] *Remember to wring your swimsuit out after your swim.*

***2** to force (something) out (of someone): [T1 (*of*) (*usu. simple tenses*)] *Be careful, he is clever enough to wring your secret out (of you). The police at last wrung the truth out (of the prisoner). How did you wring out a promise after talking to the girl for only half an hour?* → **wring from** (2)

**3 be wrung out** *not fml* to be very tired, anxious, etc.: *Oh, I must sit down, I'm quite wrung out. After waiting so long she felt completely wrung out with worry.*

**wrinkle up** *v adv* → **pucker up, purse up**

to (cause to) tighten into folds: [T1 + UP] *She wrinkled up her nose at the nasty smell.* [IØ + UP (*simple tenses*)] *This material wrinkles up rather easily, so be careful when you pack it.*

**write about** *v prep* → **write of, write on²** (1)

to have (something or someone) as the subject of writing; write (a quantity or form) on the subject of (something or someone): [IØ + *about*] *If you don't know what to say to your aunt, write about the school play, she'll be interested in that. The castle has been written about in books for tourists.* [T1 + *about*] *I must write a letter about the nasty smell coming from the water pipes. Tom has written a great many articles about the effect of treeplanting on city air. I could write a book about you! Whole books have been written about these ancient castles.*

**write against** *v prep*

to oppose (something or someone) in writing; write (a quantity or form) opposing (something or someone): [IØ + *against*] *You can be imprisoned for writing against the government.* [T1 + *against*] *Tom has written another article against waste.*

**write away** *v adv* → **write on¹**

to write continuously: [IØ + AWAY (*often continuous tenses*)] *Don't interrupt him; he's been writing away all morning and likes to have a long period free of other considerations.*

**write back** *v adv*

to reply in writing; send a letter in return: [IØ + BACK (*to*)] *Have you written back (to your aunt) yet, thanking her for her invitation?*

***write down** *v adv*

**1** to record (something) in writing: [T1] *Make sure that you write down every word the speaker says.* also *not fml* **shove down** → **be down** (4), **get down** (8), **go down** (13), **mark down** (1), **note down, put down** (7), **scribble down, stick down** (3), **take down** (4)

**2** to write (something) in a plain way so as to reduce its effect: [T1 (*often pass.*)] *At the request of the police, the details of the murder were written down in the newspapers. The reporter wrote the play down, as he had not liked it.* → **write up** (5)

**3** to write (something) in a simple way so as to try to please the readers: [T1 (*to*) (*simple tenses*)] *Writers of children's stories soon learn never to write their books down (to the children).* → **write down to**

**4** to reduce the written or formal value of (something): [T1 (*usu. pass.*)] *These shares should be written down, as we want to attract more buying at present. "The aircraft, which originally cost about $6,000,000 each, were fully covered by . . . insurance, although they had been written down over the years to the point where only their residual value was carried on the carrier's books."* (*Toronto Globe and Mail*, 8 October 1976) —**write-down** *n* → **mark down** (3), **write up** (7)

**5** *old use* to attack or defeat (someone or oneself) in writing: [T1 (*usu. simple tenses*)] *"He writes as fast as they can read, and he does not write himself down."* (William Hazlitt, *English Literature*, on Sir Walter Scott)

***write down as** *v adv prep* → **put down as** (2), etc.

to classify or regard (usu. someone) as being (a certain kind of person): [X1 (*usu. simple tenses*)] *I thought he was being uncommonly stupid, and wrote him down as a fool.*

***write down to** *v adv prep* → **write down** (3)

to write in a simple way so as to try to please (a certain group of readers): [T1 (*simple tenses*)] *Children do not like being written down to, and writers of children's stories soon discover this fact.*

**write for** *v prep*

**1** to be employed as a writer (of pieces) for (a company, newspaper, etc.); write (pieces) so as to please (someone): [IØ + *for*] *This famous writer wrote for a newspaper for many years, learning his skills. Do you like writing for children?* [T1 + *for*] *Part of the secretary's job is to write short reports for the director. The great musician wrote simple pieces for his young wife, when she was learning to play.*

**2** to write (pieces) in order to gain (money or other reward): [IØ + *for*] *She wrote for fun for many years before starting to write seriously for a living.* [T1 + *for*] *Tom refuses to write another magazine article for less than $100. Have you ever tried writing music for money?*

**3** to write (words or music) as part of (a work) or intended for (performance): [T1 + *for*] *What music have you been writing for the play? [IØ + for] After writing for the theatre for many years, he turned to the art of film.*

*__4__ to order (something such as goods, information, etc.) by post: [T1 (*to*)] *Have you written for the booklist yet?* → **send for** (2), etc.

**write home** *v adv*

**1** to write (letters) to one's relatives, esp. parents, wife, or husband: [IØ + HOME] *The children at this school are made to write home once a week.* [T1 + HOME] *Writing letters home was the only thing the soldiers had to do when they were not on duty.*

**2 nothing to write home about** nothing especially remarkable: *The play was quite good, but nothing (much) to write home about.*

***write in** *v adv*

**1** to add (something) in writing: [T1 (*to*)] *It would be a good idea to write in another example, to make the meaning of this passage quite clear.*—**written-in** *adj* → **put in**[1] (3), **throw in**[1] (6), **toss in**[1] (4)

**2** to write to a given address: [IØ (*to*)] *Many listeners have written in (to the radio station) to express their opinion.* → **write up** (6)

**3** *AmE* to add (a name) to an official list in an election; vote for (someone) by writing his or her name on the voting paper: [T1] *His name was written in by over 10,000 voters.* —**write-in** *n, adj*

***write into** *v prep*

**1** to write to (a given address): [T1] *How many people have written into the television station to complain about the moral level of the show?*

**2** to add (something) in writing to (something written): [D1] *Did Tom have the right to write his own ideas into the article that he was correcting for the printer?*

**3** to make (an agreement) part of (a formal paper): [D1 (*usu. pass.*)] *Make sure that the film rights for your book are written into your contract. Three weeks' holiday every year is written into the agreement with the union.* —**written-in** *adj*

**4** to make (someone or oneself) reach (a state) by means of one's writing: [D1 (*usu. simple tenses*)] *Tom never guessed that with his latest book he would write himself into sudden fame.*

**write large** *v adj*

**writ large** *old use or fml* the same thing but in a wider sense: *"New Presbyter is but old Priest writ large."* (John Milton, Sonnet: *On the New Forces of Conscience under the Long Parliament*)

**write of** *v prep* → **write about, write on**[2] (1)

to have (something) as the subject of one's writing: [IØ + *of*] *Harry wrote of his adventures in the war every week.*

**write off** *v adv*

**1** to write immediately: [IØ + OFF] *Thank you for giving me the address, I'll write off at once.* → **dash off** (2), etc.

**2** to write (something) quickly and easily: [T1 + OFF (*often simple tenses*)] *He can write off a poem in half an hour.*

*__3__ to enter (something) in the account books as having no value: [T1 (*usu. simple tenses*)] *After the crash, the insurance company agreed to write off the car as a total loss. The library writes off a certain quantity of books each year.* —**write-off** *n*

*__4__ *not fml* to regard (something or someone) as a failure: [T1 (*as*) (*usu. simple tenses*)] *They wrote their marriage off years ago, I don't know why they still stay together. The climbers had to write off their attempt on the mountain because of bad weather. All the newspaper reporters wrote the play off as useless. The school tries not to write off any boy, however badly behaved. Some young soldiers have to be written off as unsuitable for army life.* —**write-off** *n* → **write off as**

*__5__ to end (something such as a debt) formally: [T1 (*usu. simple tenses*)] *He generously agreed to write off the debt in return for certain services. It will be a great day when we can at last write off the payments on the house.* → **charge off** (1)

***write off as** *v adv prep* → **write off** (4)

**1** *not fml* to regard (someone or something) as unsuitable to be (something): [T1 (*as*) (*usu. simple tenses*)] *You can write him off as a possible President, he can't be trusted. Surely this old building shouldn't be written off as a suitable theatre for young people?*

**2** *not fml* to regard (someone or something) as (something such as a failure): [T1 (*as*) (*usu. simple tenses*)] *Some of our soldiers had been written off as dead. People wrote the king off as a madman. We shall have to write your suggestion off as a useless idea.*

**write on**[1] *v adv* → **write away**

to continue writing: [IØ + ON] *She wrote on all day, filling page after page.*

**write on/upon**[2] *v prep*

**1** to have (usu. something) as the subject of writing, often formal; write (a quantity or form) on the subject of (usu. something): [T1 + *on/upon*] *Write 1500 words on your view of the advance of civilization in this century.* [IØ + *on/upon*] *What is Tom writing on now?* → **write about, write of**

**2 be written on someone's face** to be clearly seen: *Sympathy for the prisoner was written on the judge's face.*

**write out** *v adv*

**1** to write (something) in full: [T1 + OUT] *Write out the small numbers, don't use figures. The boy was kept in school, writing out lines for the teacher.*

**2** to write (something formal): [T1 + OUT] *I can write out a cheque for you if you will accept it. The director has asked me to write out a report of the decisions taken at the last committee meeting.* → **make out** (1)

***3** *not fml* to remove (a character) from a radio or television play in many parts, by writing a reason into the story: [T1 (*of*) (*usu. pass.*)] *The actress found another part that she wanted to play, so she asked to be written out (of the television play). They've written me out! The character I was playing dies in the third part!*

***4** to use up the ability of (oneself) as a writer: [T1 (*simple tenses*)] *The poet had written himself out before he was 30, and produced no other good poems for the rest of his long life.*

**write to** *v prep*

**1** to address (usu. a letter or postcard) to (someone); address something in writing to (someone or a place): [T1 + *to*] *You haven't written one letter to me since the summer!* [IØ + *to*] *I intend to write to the shop asking for an explanation of this bill. When did you last write to your mother?*

**2** to invent (words) to fit (something): [T1 + *to*] *Words have now been written to that well-known piece of music.*

**3** to write (something such as a poem) in praise of or intended for (someone or something): [T1 + *to*] *He wrote poem after poem to her beauty. The book was written to his children.*

**4** to plan one's writing (of something) so as to fit or obey (a plan or limit, as of time or length): [T1 + *to*] *The article should be written to a careful plan. Writing to a contract date is the only way some writers would ever finish a book.* [IØ + *to*] *It is good practice to write to a certain length.* → **work to** (2)

**write up** *v adv*

**1** to write (something) in a public place: [T1 + UP] *I saw your name written up on the wall.* → **mark up** (2)

***2** to write (something) in a more complete form: [T1] *I must go now, I have to spend several hours writing up my notes into a proper article.*

***3** to bring (something) up to date in writing: [T1] *Every night he would write up his account of the day's events, hoping that this record would be of some use in the future.*

***4** to write one's opinion of (something such as a performance) in a newspaper, magazine, etc.: [T1] *Has anyone written up last night's concert? "It's very pleasant to be written up, even by a writer."* (Joyce Cary, *The Horse's Mouth*) —**write-up** *n*

***5** to write about (something) in an exciting way so as to increase its effect: [T1 (*often pass.*)] *The account of the murder was written up to attract more readers.* → **write down** (2)

***6** to write to a given address: [IØ (*to*)] *Lots of people have written up to the radio station, asking for gardening advice.* → **write in** (2)

***7** to increase the formal or written value of (something such as goods): [T1 (*usu. pass.*)] *The shares have been written up to £3.50 each.* —**write-up** *n* → **mark up** (4), **write down** (4)

**write upon** *v prep* → WRITE ON

**writhe at** *v prep*

to twist one's body, as in pain or anxiety, because of (something such as a feeling): [IØ + *at*] *"But were there ever any writhed not at passing joy?"* (John Keats, *Stanzas: In a Drear-nighted December*)

**writhe under** *v prep*

**1** to twist the body, as in pain, when beaten with (something): [IØ + *under*] *Even from this distance, you could see the slaves writhing under their master's whip.*

***2** to be made very uncomfortable by (something): [T1 (*no pass.*)] *Of course students will writhe under such unjust treatment.*

**wrought up** → WORK UP (4)

**wrung out** → WRING OUT (3)

# Y

*__yammer for__ *v prep* → **clamour for**
to demand (something) loudly: [T1 (*no pass.*)] *The crowd gathered outside the gates, yammering for the appearance of their favourite singer.*

**yank at** *v prep* → **pluck at, pull at** (1), **pull on²** (1), **tug at** (1), **yank on**
*not fml* to take hold of (usu. something) tightly and pull sharply on it: [L9 + *at*] *Stop yanking at my skirt, I've nearly finished! After yanking at the bellrope for some minutes, he heard a low distant sound of the bell.*

**yank away** *v adv* → **jerk away, pull away** (1), **take away** (1)
*not fml* to remove (something) by pulling it away with a sharp movement: [X9 + AWAY (*usu. simple tenses*)] *By accident he touched the hot metal, and yanked his hand away with a cry of pain.*

*__yank in__ *v adv* → **bring in** (6), **pull in** (9), **take in¹** (17)
*not fml* to seize (a possible criminal) roughly: [T1] *If you're not careful, the police could yank you in on a small charge and then find out about the jewel robbery.*

**yank off** *v adv*
**1** *not fml* to remove (something): [X9 + OFF] *She has a nervous habit of yanking off the leaves of a plant on her desk.* → **take off** (1), etc.
*__2__ *not fml* to take (someone) away roughly: [T1 (*usu. simple tenses*)] *Some men came into the house and yanked him off, I don't know where.*

**yank on** *v prep* → **pull at** (1), **pull on²** (1), **yank at**
*not fml* to pull on (something) sharply: [L9 + *on*] *You just yank twice on the rope as a signal to be pulled up.*

**yank out** *v adv* → **take out** (2), etc.
*not fml* to remove (something) sharply or roughly: [X9 + OUT (*usu. simple tenses*)] *He had to use force to yank the tooth out, and my mouth still hurts. This tool is for yanking out old nails from the boards.*

**yank up** *v adv* → **pull up** (1), etc.
*not fml* to pull (usu. something) up sharply or roughly: [X9 + UP] *Be careful not to yank the box up, but raise it gently.*

**yap away** *v adv*
**1** (of a dog) to make a continuous noise: [IØ + AWAY] *The little dog of hers yaps away all day while she's out.*
**2** *not fml* to talk without stopping, usu. in a meaningless fashion: [IØ + AWAY] *I don't want to stop to talk with that woman, she'll yap away for hours about nothing.*

*__yearn for__ *v prep* also **yearn after, yen for** → **itch for, long for, sigh for** (2)
to desire (something or someone) very much: [T1] *After such a long winter, she yearned for warm sunshine. The world is yearning for peace, but does not seem to know how to win it.* [V3] *Everyone is yearning for the weather to change, after this bitter winter.*

**yell off** *v adv*
**yell one's head off** *not fml* to shout loudly: *Will you boys stop yelling your heads off just outside my window!*

**yell out** *v adv* → **roar out, shout out, thunder out**
to shout (something): [IØ + OUT] *She yelled out for help, but no one came.* [T1 + OUT (*usu. simple tenses*)] *Just in time, he yelled out a warning.*

*__yen for__ *v prep* → YEARN FOR

**yield to** *v prep*
**1** to let (someone or something) have the victory: [IØ + *to*] *The chairman spoke so forcefully that the rest of the committee yielded to his opinion. Jane must stop yielding to her desire for chocolate. I yield to your better judgment. He will soon be forced to yield to his more experienced opponent. We shall never yield to a conqueror.* → **give in to** (5), **give to** (24), **give up** (7), etc., (8), etc.
**2** to let (something such as a possession) be taken by (someone): [T1 + *to*] *At last the citizens were forced to yield the town to the enemy.* → **surrender to** (1)
*__3__ to allow (oneself) to be overcome by (a feeling, usu. unpleasant): [T1] *It's best to yield to your grief for a time, then you will be able to deal with your feelings.* [D1] *Yielding himself to his feelings of worthlessness, he tried to kill himself.* → **give in to** (3), **give over to** (4), **give to** (23), **give up to** (4), **surrender to** (2)
*__4__ to be followed or replaced by (someone or something): [T1] *The long cruel winter came to an end at last, yielding to a gentle warm spring. I'm leaving the firm after all these years as I feel that I should yield to a younger man.* [D1] *Her keenness for sport soon yielded place to an interest in music.* → **give to** (17)
*__5__ to be able to be moved by (something): [T1] *At last the stiff door began to yield to our efforts to push it open.*
*__6__ to allow oneself to be influenced or persuaded by (usu. an idea): [T1] *Yielding to demands from the public, the Minister made a statement. Don't yield to pity, or you will lose your independence in the family. You will meet much evil in life; try not to yield to temptation.*
**7 yield to none** to be best, strongest, etc.: [(*simple tenses*)] *Our products yield to none in today's world.*

**yield up** *v adv*
**1** to give possession of (usu. something) (to

someone): [T1 + UP (*often simple tenses*)] *Are the citizens still refusing to yield up the town?* → **give up** (7), etc.

**2** to give (something) (to someone): [T1 + UP (*usu. simple tenses*)] *The sea will never yield up its secrets. It's still polite to yield up your seat on the bus to an old lady.* → **give up** (8), etc.

**3 yield up the ghost** to die: [(*simple tenses*)] *"Jesus, when he had cried again with a loud voice, yielded up the ghost."* (The Bible) → **give up** (12)

**yoke together** *v adv*

**1** to fasten (animals) together with a wooden pole: [T1 + TOGETHER] *The boy soon learned how to yoke the oxen together.*

*__2__ to join (usu. people): [T1 (*usu. pass.*)] *Jim and Bill have been yoked together in the business for many years.*

# Z

***zero in** *v adv*

**1** to fix the sighting instrument of (a gun) without allowing for wind: [T1 (*often pass.*)] *Have all these guns been properly zeroed in?*

**2** to aim (a gun or set of guns) (towards an object): [T1 (*at, on*) (*often simple tenses*)] *Now, men, zero in your guns (at that ship).*

***zero in on** *v adv prep* → **home in on, range on**

**1** to aim (a gun or set of guns) towards (an object): [T1 (*on*) (*often simple tenses*)] *When we had all zeroed in our guns on the enemy post, we opened fire.*

**2** to aim exactly towards (a place): [T1] *The plane zeroed in on the arms factory and destroyed it with one bomb.*

**3** to direct one's attention towards (something): [T1] *With his usual skill, the chairman zeroed in on the most delicate subject of our meeting.*

**zip along** *v adv*

*not fml* to move forward quickly: [L9 + ALONG] *The little car zipped along so pleasantly that we decided to buy it.*

**zip on/up** *v adv*

to (cause to) fasten with a special fastener: [X9 + ON/UP] *Please help me to zip my dress on, the fastener's at the back and I can't reach.* [IØ + ON/UP (*simple tenses*)] *This dress zips on easily. Help me, it won't zip up.* —**zip-up** *adj*

***zone for** *v prep*

esp. *AmE* to give official permission for (usu. part of a town or city) to be used for (a certain kind of building): [D1 (*usu. pass.*)] *Has this area been zoned for office buildings?*

***zone off** *v adv*

to separate (an area) by dividing from the rest: [T1 (*usu. pass.*)] *The whole hospital area has been zoned off until the infection is under control.*

**zonk out** *v adv*

**be zonked out** *infml* to be unconscious, drunk, or under the influence of a drug: *What's the matter with that man? He looks as if he's zonked out!*

**zoom across/along** *v adv; prep*

to pass across or along (an area) quickly: [L9 + ACROSS/ALONG/*across/along*] *The little boat zoomed across (the lake) as if without effort. The boy went zooming along (the road) in his new car.*

***zoom in** *v adv*

(of a camera or photographer) to change an instrument so as to appear to take a picture (of an object) from a nearer position: [IØ (*on*)] *I'll try to zoom in and get a good picture of the baby ducks. If you zoom in on the top window, you might be able to see inside.*

***zoom out** *v adv*

(of a camera or photographer) to change an instrument so as to appear to take a picture (on an object) from a distance: [IØ] *If you zoom out at this point, we shall get a view of the whole farm.*

**zoom over/past** *v adv; prep*

(usu. of a plane) to fly overhead (above or past a place) quickly: [L9 + OVER/PAST/*over/past*] *Just then, a whole flight of bombers zoomed over (the house).*

**zoom up** *v adv*

**1** (of a plane) to rise quickly: [L9 + UP] *With the skilled pilot at its controls, the plane zoomed up into the sky, and was soon out of sight.*

*__2__ *not fml* to rise or increase quickly: [IØ] *Prices, which zoomed up in the first part of this year, are now steady and should not increase again for several months.*